NIGHTWALKER

presented to

_____

by

_____

on

_____

Your word is a lamp to my feet and a light for my path.

Psalm 119:105

today's
DEVOTIONAL / BIBLE

ZONDERVAN®

GRAND RAPIDS, MICHIGAN 49530 USA

WWW.ZONDERVAN.COM

TABLE OF CONTENTS

OLD TESTAMENT

NEW TESTAMENT

BOOKS OF THE BIBLE
IN ALPHABETICAL ORDER

Books of the New Testament are in *italics*.

WELCOME

Welcome to *Today's Devotional Bible*. This Bible was created to be your companion in your walk with God. Through the use of a combination of devotional readings tied to Scripture and mediations on Scripture, *Today's Devotional Bible* will encourage your growth and draw you more deeply into God's Word.

This Bible contains devotional readings for each day of the week and a reading for every weekend. In the weekday readings you will find two Bible passages to choose from: a longer passage that provides greater context and depth, and a shorter passage for those days when your time must be kept short. You'll want to be sure to begin each devotional time by reading and reflecting on the words that come directly from God himself through his Word.

After spending time with the day's Scripture passage, you'll find devotional thoughts in the form of two quotations that both reflect on a similar theme found within the Bible reading. One quote will come from a classic Christian author and the other will come from a contemporary Christian author. While the authors of each quote often lived generations apart, you'll be surprised and encouraged at how much they had in common as they contemplated the truths of Scripture, how the issues that people have wrestled with throughout the ages have remained a constant, and how the quotations each give insight in their own way. The reflection questions at the end of each reading will help you examine and explore these common threads for yourself.

As you read, we hope your faith will be strengthened. You'll discover that for 2000 years, Christianity has remained unchanged in its core beliefs. Christians throughout the ages have faced similar challenges regarding their faith and the Christian life. The common themes in these readings illustrate the truth of Hebrews 13:8, "Jesus Christ is the same yesterday and today and forever."

In the course of these weekday readings, you'll encounter the words of over 200 authors who are all members of the family of God. As with any family, you'll relate well to certain members, while others won't be as familiar to you. While Christianity is a big family, our identifying and unifying trait is faith in Jesus Christ as the only means of salvation for sinful people. While all the writers whose quotes we've included in the daily readings share this view of Christ and salvation, we have not lim-

ited ourselves to one style, time period or denomination. We've intentionally included a wide variety of contributors. Since the Christian family is a diverse group, you'll find readings from Catholics, Charismatics, Presbyterians, Baptists and everything in between. Our hope is that fresh voices and new perspectives—from both the past and the present—will encourage and challenge you as you walk with the God who is the father of us all.

In addition to the weekday readings, this Bible includes several other features that we hope will help you along the way:

Weekend Readings. We encourage you to find a few minutes on Saturday or Sunday to reflect on God's Word. These special readings will lead you through a few quiet moments of reflective Bible reading and prayer. At the close of each reading you'll find a couple of quotes from some well-known voices. Some of these quotes come from Christians while others come from cultural or historical icons. Each of these quotes offers further insight, reflection or thoughts on the weekend's theme.

Additional Reading Plans. These can be found in the back of the Bible. In addition to the primary, year-long reading plan found within the text of the Scripture, you may wish to explore what the Bible says on specific topics. For example, you'll find reading plans that take you through 30 days in the Psalms, or 30 days on what the Bible says on leadership. Turn to page 1469 to see the other available reading plans.

Contributor biographies. These provide a very short overview of each author quoted in the weekday readings. Turn here to learn more about each contributor or to discover where their comments are located within the readings in this Bible.

It's our prayer that this edition of the Bible will prove useful in encouraging your reading of God's word and in growing your relationship with him.

Zondervan and the
Today's Devotional Bible editorial team

WHAT IS THE BIBLE?

The Bible is made up of 66 individual books written by different authors. Each of these authors used different writing styles and lived in different eras of history. Each had their own purpose and occasion in mind as they wrote. What separates the Bible from other anthologies is the fact that God himself guided the writing of Scripture. The result is one amazingly cohesive book made up of wildly disparate parts. Here's a quick look at the different genres you'll find as you explore the books of Scripture.

OLD TESTAMENT

Books of the Law
Genesis through Deuteronomy

The first five books of the Bible (the Pentateuch) detail God's interaction with his human creation. They offer vivid descriptions of God making himself known to individuals, including Noah, Abraham and Sarah, Joseph and Moses. Specifically these books catalog God's dealings with the Israelites, his chosen people. They give us snapshots of his love, mercy, justice and holiness—the way he rewards faithfulness and punishes disobedience. In these books, God establishes the rules for living that he expects to govern the lives of his people.

Books of History
Joshua through Esther

These books record the history of the Israelites and the lives of such notables as Joshua, Samson, Deborah, David and Esther. They also establish an unfortunate pattern in the relationship between God and his people. The pattern goes like this: God gives instructions on how to live in such a way that we can enjoy his blessings and fellowship; humans ignore his instructions and disobey him, putting an obstacle in our relationship with him; God punishes the disobedience and withholds his blessings; humans recognize their error and repent; God forgives and restores his blessings. That pattern of disobedience-rejection-repentance-acceptance is repeated time and again throughout the books of history.

Books of Poetry
Job through Song of Songs

These books record the thoughts, personal struggles and hard-earned wisdom of God's people. They address timeless topics such as why people suffer, what kind of worship pleases the Lord and how God's wisdom can be applied to everyday life.

Books of the Prophets
Isaiah through Malachi

You've heard the expression "God works in mysterious ways." The fact is, God often gives his people advance notice of his intentions and plans. That notice can be found in the books of prophecy. Not only do the prophets offer warnings to the people of Israel, they also point to the long-awaited Messiah, the One who would ultimately restore the relationship between God and humans.

NEW TESTAMENT

Books of History
Matthew through Acts

The first four books of the New Testament— the Gospels—present four different yet ultimately complementary accounts of the life of Christ. The accounts are culled from personal recollections and eyewitness testimony.

Before Jesus returned to heaven, he instructed his followers to spread his Good News across the globe. The Book of Acts details the efforts of the early believers to do just that. In its pages you'll find the beginning of the church, the body of Christ on earth.

Letters
Romans through Revelation

God commissioned men such as Paul, Peter and John to write letters to various early churches and church leaders, encouraging them in their faith and addressing problems they faced. In the process, the Lord outlined the basic doctrines of the Christian life and spelled out the responsibilities of believers throughout history.

A WORD TO THE READER

Today's New International Version (TNIV) is a revision of the New International Version (NIV). Among the many English versions of the Bible that appeared in the twentieth century, the NIV (1973, 1978, 1984) has gained the widest readership in all parts of the English-speaking world. It was a completely new translation made by over a hundred scholars working directly from the best available Hebrew, Aramaic and Greek texts. The fact that participants from the United States, Great Britain, Canada, Australia and New Zealand worked together gave the project its international scope. That they were from many denominations—including Anglican, Assemblies of God, Baptist, Brethren, Christian Reformed, Church of Christ, Evangelical Covenant, Evangelical Free, Lutheran, Mennonite, Methodist, Nazarene, Presbyterian, Wesleyan and other churches—helped to safeguard the translation from sectarian bias. Responsibility for the NIV text, and now also for the text of the TNIV, is held by a self-governing body, the Committee on Bible Translation (CBT), composed of biblical scholars from colleges, universities and seminaries. During the revision process, many of the original members of CBT have been replaced by other scholars owing to retirement and other causes, but a similar geographical and denominational mix has been maintained.

From the beginning the translators have been united in their commitment to the authority and infallibility of the Bible as God's Word in written form. For them, the Bible contains the divine answer to the deepest needs of humanity, sheds unique light on our path in a dark world and sets forth the way to our eternal well-being. Out of this deep conviction, the Committee has held to certain goals for the NIV and for the present revision: that it would be an accurate translation and one that would have clarity and literary quality and so prove suitable for public and private reading, teaching, preaching, memorizing and liturgical use. The Committee has also sought to preserve a measure of continuity with the long tradition of translating the Scriptures into English.

There is a sense in which the work of translating the Bible is never finished. This very fact has prompted the Committee to engage in an ongoing review of the text of the NIV with the assistance of many other scholars. The chief goal of this review has always been to bring the text of the NIV abreast of contemporary biblical scholarship and of shifts in English idiom and usage. Already in 1978 and again in 1984 various corrections and revisions to the NIV text were made. In the TNIV the Committee offers to the reading public the latest fruits of its review.

The first concern of the translators has continued to be the accuracy of the translation and its faithfulness to the intended meaning of the biblical writers. This has moved the translators to go beyond a formal word-for-word rendering of the original texts. Because thought patterns and syntax differ from language to language, accurate communication of the meaning of the biblical authors demands constant regard for varied contextual uses of words and idioms and for frequent modifications in sentence structures.

To achieve clarity the translators have sometimes supplied words not in the original texts but required by the context. In a few instances, where some uncertainty about such material remained, it is enclosed in corner brackets. As an aid to the reader, italicized sectional headings have been inserted. They are not to be regarded as part of the biblical text and are not intended for oral reading. It is the Committee's hope that these headings may prove more helpful to the reader than the traditional chapter divisions (which were introduced in the thirteenth century).

For the Old Testament the standard Hebrew text, the Masoretic Text as published in the latest editions of *Biblia Hebraica*, has been used throughout. The Masoretic Text tradition contains marginal notations that offer variant readings. These have sometimes been followed instead of the text itself. Because such instances involve variants within the Masoretic tradition, they have not been indicated in the textual notes. In a few cases, words in the basic consonantal text have been divided differently than in the Masoretic Text. Such cases are usually indicated in the textual footnotes. The Dead Sea Scrolls contain biblical texts that represent an earlier stage of the transmission of the Hebrew text. They have been consulted, as have been the Samaritan Pentateuch and the ancient scribal traditions concerning deliberate textual changes. The translators also consulted the more important early versions—the Greek Septuagint, Aquila, Symmachus and Theodotion, the Latin Vulgate, the Syriac Peshitta, the Aramaic Targums, and for the Psalms the *Juxta Hebraica* of Jerome. Readings from the Dead Sea Scrolls, the scribal traditions and these versions were occasionally followed where the Masoretic Text seemed doubtful and where accepted principles of textual criticism showed that one or more of these textual witnesses appeared to provide the correct reading. In rare cases, the translators have emended the Hebrew text where it appears to have become corrupted at an even earlier stage of its transmission. These departures from the Masoretic Text are also indicated in the textual footnotes. Sometimes the vowel indicators (which are later additions to the basic consonantal text) found in the Masoretic Text did not, in the judgment of the translators, represent the correct vowels for the original text. Accordingly, some words have been read with a different set of vowels. These instances are usually not indicated in the footnotes.

The Greek text used in translating the New Testament has been an eclectic one, based on the latest editions of the Nestle-Aland / United Bible Societies' Greek New Testament. The translators have made their choices among the variant readings in accordance with widely accepted principles of New Testament textual criticism. Footnotes call attention to places where uncertainty remains.

The New Testament authors, writing in Greek, often quote the Old Testament from its ancient Greek version, the Septuagint. This is one reason why some of the Old Testament quotations in the TNIV New Testament are not identical to the corresponding passages in the TNIV Old Testament. Such quotations in the New Testament are indicated with the footnote "(see Septuagint)."

Other footnotes in this version are of several kinds, most of which need no explanation. Those giving alternative translations begin with "Or" and generally introduce the alternative with the last word preceding it in the text, except when it is a single-word alternative. In poetry quoted in a footnote a slash mark indicates a line division.

It should be noted that references to diseases, minerals, flora and fauna, architectural details, clothing, jewelry, musical instruments and other articles cannot always be identified with precision. Also, linear measurements and measures of capacity can only be approximated (see Appendix I). The manner in which Hebrew proper names are to be represented in English has not become fully standardized. In the TNIV the spelling of many names has been revised to conform more closely to current scholarly practice and to the phonetics of the Hebrew originals. A list of such changes can be found in Appendix II, following the biblical text. A parallel list provides the spelling of these names in the NIV. Although *Selah*, used mainly in the Psalms, is probably a musical term, its meaning is uncertain. Since it may interrupt reading and distract the reader, this word has not been kept in the English text, but every occurrence has been signaled by a footnote.

Three changes of special note in the TNIV are the frequent substitution of "Messiah" for the more traditional "Christ," the replacement of "saints" in most cases with alternative renderings, and a greater sensitivity to shifts in English idiom. A word about each is in order.

While "Messiah" (from the Hebrew) and "Christ" (from the Greek) both mean "Anointed One," what began as a title full of meaning to the early Jewish hearers of the gospel tended in the later Greek-speaking churches to become just another name for Jesus. So where the term is clearly used to designate the God-sent deliverer of Jewish expectations (primarily in the Gospels and Acts), it was judged more appropriate to use "Messiah." However, where this sense seems less prominent (primarily in the Epistles), the transliteration of the Greek word ("Christ") has been retained.

Concerning "saints," current usage (as reflected in major dictionaries of the English language) burdens it with meanings that lie outside the sense of the original-language words. The main Old Testament term that has traditionally been rendered "saints" refers to those who are faithful to God. The New Testament term primarily designates those who have become followers of the Christian Way as people consecrated to God and thus belonging to the Lord in a special sense.

Although a basic core of the English language remains relatively stable, many diverse and complex cultural forces continue to bring about subtle shifts in the meanings and/or connotations of even old, well-established words and phrases. Among the more programmatic changes in the TNIV are the removal of nearly all vocative "O"s and the elimination of most instances of the generic use of masculine nouns and pronouns. Relative to the second of these, the so-called singular "they/their/them," which has been gaining acceptance among careful writers and which actually has a venerable place in English idiom, has been employed to fill in the vocabulary gap in generic nouns and pronouns referring to human beings. Where an individual emphasis is deemed to be present, "anyone" or "everyone" or some other equivalent is generally used as the antecedent of such pronouns.

Sometimes the chapter and/or verse numbering in English translations of the Old Testament differs from that found in published Hebrew texts. This is particularly the case in the Psalms, where the traditional titles are included in the Hebrew verse numbering. Such differences are marked by asterisks (*) in the text and informative footnotes set off in a separate line (or lines) at the bottom of the page. In the New Testament, verse numbers that marked off portions of the traditional English text not supported by the best Greek manuscripts are now set alongside the immediately preceding verse numbers and placed in brackets (see, for example, Matthew 17:20[21]).

Mark 16:9–20 and John 7:53—8: 11, although long accorded virtually equal status with the rest of the Gospels in which they stand, have a very questionable—and confused—standing in the textual history of the New Testament, as noted in the bracketed annotations with which they are set off. A different typeface has now been chosen for these passages to indicate even more clearly their uncertain status.

Basic formatting of the text, such as lining the poetry, paragraphing (both prose and poetry), setting up of (administrative-like) lists, indenting letters and lengthy prayers within narratives and the insertion of sectional headings, has been the work of the Committee. However, the choice between single-column and double-column formats has been left to the publishers. Also the issuing of "red-letter" editions is a publisher's choice—one that the Committee does not endorse.

The Committee has again been reminded that every human effort is flawed—including this revision of the NIV. We trust, however, that many will find in it an improved representation of the Word of God, through which they hear his call to faith in our Lord Jesus Christ and to service in his kingdom. We offer this version of the Bible to him in whose name and for whose glory it has been made.

The Committee on Bible Translation
August 2003

The Old Testament

The Books of Moses

Genesis

Exodus

Leviticus

Numbers

Deuteronomy

genesis

AUTHOR: Moses

DATE: During the 1400s B.C., while the Israelites were traveling in the desert

THEME: God interacts with us in all we experience—love, loss, broken relationships, real life.

The Beginning

1 In the beginning God created the heavens and the earth. ²Now the earth was formless and empty, darkness was over the surface of the deep, and the Spirit of God was hovering over the waters.

³And God said, "Let there be light," and there was light. ⁴God saw that the light was good, and he separated the light from the darkness. ⁵God called the light "day," and the darkness he called "night." And there was evening, and there was morning—the first day.

⁶And God said, "Let there be a vault between the waters to separate water from water." ⁷So God made the vault and separated the water under the vault from the water above it. And it was so. ⁸God called the vault "sky." And there was evening, and there was morning—the second day.

⁹And God said, "Let the water under the sky be gathered to one place, and let dry ground appear." And it was so. ¹⁰God called the dry ground "land," and the gathered waters he called "seas." And God saw that it was good.

¹¹Then God said, "Let the land produce vegetation: seed-bearing plants and trees on the land that bear fruit with seed in it, according to their various kinds." And it was so. ¹²The land produced vegetation: plants bearing seed according to their kinds and trees bearing fruit with seed in it according to their kinds. And God saw that it was good. ¹³And there was evening, and there was morning—the third day.

¹⁴And God said, "Let there be lights in the vault of the sky to separate the day from the night, and let them serve as signs to mark seasons and days and years, ¹⁵and let them be lights in the vault of the sky to give light on the earth." And it was so. ¹⁶God made two great lights—the greater light to govern the day and the lesser light to govern the night. He also made the stars. ¹⁷God set them in the vault of the sky to give light on the earth, ¹⁸to govern the day and the night, and to separate light from darkness. And God saw that it was good. ¹⁹And there was evening, and there was morning—the fourth day.

²⁰And God said, "Let the water teem with living creatures, and let birds fly above the earth across the vault of the sky." ²¹So God created the great creatures of the sea and every living and moving thing with which the water teems, according to their kinds, and every winged bird according to its kind. And God saw that it was good. ²²God blessed them and said, "Be fruitful and increase in number and fill the water in the seas, and let the birds increase on the earth." ²³And there was evening, and there was morning—the fifth day.

²⁴And God said, "Let the land produce living creatures according to their kinds: livestock, creatures that move along the ground, and wild animals, each according to its kind." And it was so. ²⁵God made the wild animals according to their kinds, the livestock according to their kinds, and all the creatures that move along the ground according to their kinds. And God saw that it was good.

²⁶Then God said, "Let us make hu-

MONDAY

KNOWING GOD

Genesis 1:1–31 *or* 1:1–5,31

Billy Graham

If I thought the Bible was only "a bunch of myths and legends," then I wouldn't want to base my life on it. But that's not what it is—not at all.

This is why I invite you to discover the Bible for yourself, and not simply go on what you've heard others say about it. You see, the Bible tells us about real events and real people—people who faced the same challenges we do, and had the same hopes and dreams we have. But many of them had another dimension to their lives also: a spiritual dimension. The reason wasn't just because they believed in God, but because they knew God in a personal way. We can, too.

Most of all, the Bible tells us about Jesus Christ. It tells us who He was and what He did; most of all it tells us He was God in human flesh, sent from heaven to save us from sin and death and judgment. Do you honestly want to know what God is like? Look at Jesus Christ, for in Him "all the fullness of the Deity lives in bodily form" (Colossians 2:9). He proved it by doing something no one else has ever done: He rose from the dead.

Don't let pride, or fear, or anything else keep you from the Bible, and from the One who is its center: Jesus Christ. When you honestly examine it, you'll discover the greatest truth anyone can ever know: God loves you, and He will change your life as you open your heart to Christ.

D. L. MOODY {AD 1837–1899}

Some look upon the Bible as a garden of spices, in which you may walk and at your leisure pluck the flowers and gather the fruits of the Eden of God. But this does not accord with my experience. I have found it more like a mine, in which you must dig and labor, the wealth of which is not to be obtained without labor—a mine rich in gold and precious things, but it must be mined day and night in order to produce them.

reflection

1. Why are you reading the Bible?

2. In what ways are you open to having this Book change your life?

3. Many people believe that God lacks "relevance." Do you believe this? Why or why not?

For your next devotional reading, go to page 6.

|| 4 ||

man beings in our image, in our like-ness, so that they may rule over the fish in the sea and the birds in the sky, over the livestock and all the wild animals,ᵃ and over all the creatures that move along the ground."

²⁷So God created human beings in his
own image,
in the image of God he created them;
male and female he created them.

²⁸God blessed them and said to them, "Be fruitful and increase in number; fill the earth and subdue it. Rule over the fish in the sea and the birds in the sky and over every living creature that moves on the ground." ²⁹Then God said, "I give you every seed-bearing plant on the face of the whole earth and every tree that has fruit with seed in it. They will be yours for food. ³⁰And to all the beasts of the earth and all the birds in the sky and all the creatures that move on the ground— everything that has the breath of life in it—I give every green plant for food." And it was so.

³¹God saw all that he had made, and it was very good. And there was eve-ning, and there was morning—the sixth day.

2 Thus the heavens and the earth were completed in all their vast array. ²By the seventh day God had finished the work he had been doing; so on the sev-enth day he rested from all his work. ³Then God blessed the seventh day and made it holy, because on it he rested from all the work of creating that he had done.

Adam and Eve

⁴This is the account of the heavens and the earth when they were created, when the LORD God made the earth and the heavens.

⁵Now no shrub had yet appeared on the earthᵇ and no plant had yet sprung up, for the LORD God had not sent rain on the earth

and there was no one to work the ground, ⁶but streamsᶜ came up from the earth and watered the whole surface of the ground. ⁷Then the LORD God formed a manᵈ from the dust of the ground and breathed into his nostrils the breath of life, and the man be-came a living being.

⁸Now the LORD God had planted a garden in the east, in Eden; and there he put the man he had formed. ⁹The LORD God made all kinds of trees grow out of the ground— trees that were pleasing to the eye and good for food. In the middle of the garden were the tree of life and the tree of the knowledge of good and evil.

¹⁰A river watering the garden flowed from Eden; from there it was separated into four headwaters. ¹¹The name of the first is the Pi-shon; it winds through the entire land of Havilah, where there is gold. ¹²(The gold of that land is good; aromatic resinᵉ and onyx are also there.) ¹³The name of the second riv-er is the Gihon; it winds through the entire land of Cush.ᶠ ¹⁴The name of the third river is the Tigris; it runs along the east side of Ash-ur. And the fourth river is the Euphrates.

¹⁵The LORD God took the man and put him in the Garden of Eden to work it and take care of it. ¹⁶And the LORD God commanded the man, "You are free to eat from any tree in the garden; ¹⁷but you must not eat from the tree of the knowledge of good and evil, for when you eat of it you will certainly die."

¹⁸The LORD God said, "It is not good for the man to be alone. I will make a helper suitable for him."

¹⁹Now the LORD God had formed out of the ground all the wild animals and all the birds in the sky. He brought them to the man to see what he would name them; and whatever the man called each living crea-ture, that was its name. ²⁰So the man gave names to all the livestock, the birds in the sky and all the wild animals.

But for Adamᵍ no suitable helper was found. ²¹So the LORD God caused the man to fall into a deep sleep; and while he was sleeping, he took one of the man's ribsʰ and then closed up the place with flesh. ²²Then the LORD God made a woman from the ribⁱ

ᵃ 26 Probable reading of the original Hebrew text (see Syriac); Masoretic Text *the earth*   ᵇ 5 Or *land*; also in verse 6   ᶜ 6 Or *mist*   ᵈ 7 The Hebrew for *man (adam)* sounds like and may be related to the Hebrew for *ground (adamah)*; it is also the name *Adam* (see Gen. 2:20).   ᵉ 12 Or *good; pearls* ᶠ 13 Possibly southeast Mesopotamia   ᵍ 20 Or *the man*   ʰ 21 Or *took part of the man's side* ⁱ 22 Or *part*

TUESDAY

GOD OF AGES

Genesis 2:1–25 *or* 2:4–9

GEORGE FOX {AD 1624–1691}

He is the living God, that clothes the earth with grass and herbs, causes the trees to grow and bring forth food for you, and makes the fishes of the sea to breathe and live. He makes the fowls of the air to breed and causes the buck and the doe, the creatures, and all the beasts to bring forth whereby they may be food for you. He is the living God, that causes the sun to give warmth to you, to nourish you when you are cold. He is the living God, that causes the snow and frost to melt and causes the rain to water the plants. He is the living God, that made heaven and earth, the clouds, causes the springs to break out of the rocks, and divided the great sea from the earth. He divides the light from the darkness, by which it is called day and the darkness night, and divided the great waters from the earth, together, which great waters he called sea and the dry land earth. He is to be worshiped that does this. He is the living God that gives you breath, life and strength and gives you beasts and cattle whereby you may be fed and clothed. He is the living God, and he is to be worshiped. This is the King of kings and Lord of lords, in whose hand is the breath of all mankind.

Ann Spangler

A mighty God could have created a world quite different from the one we know. It could have had perpetually dark skies, grass that hurt to walk on, dogs that couldn't be housebroken and people incapable of love. Have you ever wondered why the world you take for granted is often so stunningly beautiful? So pleasant to live in? Why the people around you are capable of so much kindness?

So often we miss life's beauty because we are preoccupied by its flaws. Instead of taking off our shoes to feel the feathery soft grass beneath our feet, we complain that it's growing so fast that we don't have time to mow it. Rather than enjoying the gregarious woman behind the supermarket counter, we blame her friendly chatter for delaying the checkout line. And what about us? Who stares back from the mirror each morning? A child of God who is growing daily in his image or someone whose nose is too big or too small, whose hair is in a state of perpetual rebellion or whose skin is aged and worn?

Today, ask the God who made you to remake your sense of wonder at his creative power.

reflection

1. What does the vastness of creation teach you about God?

2. How could the fact that God is the creator of all things affect your perception of yourself and the world around you?

3. How does your understanding of God's sovereignty affect your view of him?

For your next devotional reading, go to page 10.

he had taken out of the man, and he brought her to the man.

²³The man said,

"This is now bone of my bones
and flesh of my flesh;
she shall be called 'woman,'
for she was taken out of man."

²⁴For this reason a man will leave his father and mother and be united to his wife, and they will become one flesh.

²⁵The man and his wife were both naked, and they felt no shame.

The Fall

3 Now the serpent was more crafty than any of the wild animals the Lord God had made. He said to the woman, "Did God really say, 'You must not eat from any tree in the garden'?"

²The woman said to the serpent, "We may eat fruit from the trees in the garden, ³but God did say, 'You must not eat fruit from the tree that is in the middle of the garden, and you must not touch it, or you will die.' "

⁴"You will not certainly die," the serpent said to the woman. ⁵"For God knows that when you eat of it your eyes will be opened, and you will be like God, knowing good and evil."

⁶When the woman saw that the fruit of the tree was good for food and pleasing to the eye, and also desirable for gaining wisdom, she took some and ate it. She also gave some to her husband, who was with her, and he ate it. ⁷Then the eyes of both of them were opened, and they realized they were naked; so they sewed fig leaves together and made coverings for themselves.

⁸Then the man and his wife heard the sound of the Lord God as he was walking in the garden in the cool of the day, and they hid from the Lord God among the trees of the garden. ⁹But the Lord God called to the man, "Where are you?"

¹⁰He answered, "I heard you in the garden, and I was afraid because I was naked; so I hid."

¹¹And he said, "Who told you that you were naked? Have you eaten from the tree that I commanded you not to eat from?"

¹²The man said, "The woman you put here with me—she gave me some fruit from the tree, and I ate it."

¹³Then the Lord God said to the woman, "What is this you have done?"

The woman said, "The serpent deceived me, and I ate."

¹⁴So the Lord God said to the serpent, "Because you have done this,

"Cursed are you above all livestock
and all wild animals!
You will crawl on your belly
and you will eat dust
all the days of your life.
¹⁵And I will put enmity
between you and the woman,
and between your offspring*a* and hers;
he will crush*b* your head,
and you will strike his heel."

¹⁶To the woman he said,

"I will make your pains in childbearing
very severe;
with pain you will give birth to
children.
Your desire will be for your husband,
and he will rule over you."

¹⁷To Adam he said, "Because you listened to your wife and ate from the tree about which I commanded you, 'You must not eat of it,'

"Cursed is the ground because of you;
through painful toil you will eat of it
all the days of your life.
¹⁸It will produce thorns and thistles for
you,
and you will eat the plants of the
field.
¹⁹By the sweat of your brow
you will eat your food
until you return to the ground,
since from it you were taken;
for dust you are
and to dust you will return."

²⁰Adam*c* named his wife Eve,*d* because she would become the mother of all the living.

²¹The Lord God made garments of skin for Adam and his wife and clothed them. ²²And the Lord God said, "The man has now become like one of us, knowing good and evil. He must not be allowed to reach out his

---

a 15 Or *seed*   *b 15* Or *strike*   *c 20* Or *The man*   *d 20* *Eve* probably means *living.*

hand and take also from the tree of life and eat, and live forever." 23So the LORD God banished him from the Garden of Eden to work the ground from which he had been taken. 24After he drove them out, he placed on the east side*a* of the Garden of Eden cherubim and a flaming sword flashing back and forth to guard the way to the tree of life.

Cain and Abel

4 Adam*b* made love to his wife Eve, and she became pregnant and gave birth to Cain.*c* She said, "With the help of the LORD I have brought forth*d* a man." 2Later she gave birth to his brother Abel.

Now Abel kept flocks, and Cain worked the soil. 3In the course of time Cain brought some of the fruits of the soil as an offering to the LORD. 4And Abel also brought an offering—fat portions from some of the firstborn of his flock. The LORD looked with favor on Abel and his offering, 5but on Cain and his offering he did not look with favor. So Cain was very angry, and his face was downcast.

6Then the LORD said to Cain, "Why are you angry? Why is your face downcast? 7If you do what is right, will you not be accepted? But if you do not do what is right, sin is crouching at your door; it desires to have you, but you must rule over it."

8Now Cain said to his brother Abel, "Let's go out to the field."*e* While they were in the field, Cain attacked his brother Abel and killed him.

9Then the LORD said to Cain, "Where is your brother Abel?"

"I don't know," he replied. "Am I my brother's keeper?"

10The LORD said, "What have you done? Listen! Your brother's blood cries out to me from the ground. 11Now you are under a curse and driven from the ground, which opened its mouth to receive your brother's blood from your hand. 12When you work the ground, it will no longer yield its crops for you. You will be a restless wanderer on the earth."

13Cain said to the LORD, "My punishment is more than I can bear. 14Today you are driving me from the land, and I will be hidden from your presence; I will be a restless wanderer on the earth, and whoever finds me will kill me."

15But the LORD said to him, "Not so*f*; anyone who kills Cain will suffer vengeance seven times over." Then the LORD put a mark on Cain so that no one who found him would kill him. 16So Cain went out from the LORD's presence and lived in the land of Nod,*g* east of Eden.

17Cain made love to his wife, and she became pregnant and gave birth to Enoch. Cain was then building a city, and he named it after his son Enoch. 18To Enoch was born Irad, and Irad was the father of Mehujael, and Mehujael was the father of Methushael, and Methushael was the father of Lamech.

19Lamech married two women, one named Adah and the other Zillah. 20Adah gave birth to Jabal; he was the father of those who live in tents and raise livestock. 21His brother's name was Jubal; he was the father of all who play stringed instruments and pipes. 22Zillah also had a son, Tubal-Cain, who forged all kinds of tools out of*h* bronze and iron. Tubal-Cain's sister was Naamah.

23Lamech said to his wives,

"Adah and Zillah, listen to me;
    wives of Lamech, hear my words.
I have killed a man for wounding me,
    a young man for injuring me.
24 If Cain is avenged seven times,
    then Lamech seventy-seven times."

25Adam made love to his wife again, and she gave birth to a son and named him Seth,*i* saying, "God has granted me another child in place of Abel, since Cain killed him." 26Seth also had a son, and he named him Enosh.

At that time people began to call on*j* the name of the LORD.

From Adam to Noah

5 This is the written account of Adam's family line.

When God created human beings, he

---

a 24 Or *placed in front*   *b* 1 Or *The man*   *c* 1 *Cain* sounds like the Hebrew for *brought forth* or *acquired.*   *d* 1 Or *have acquired*   *e* 8 Samaritan Pentateuch, Septuagint, Vulgate and Syriac; Masoretic Text does not have *"Let's go out to the field."*   *f* 15 Septuagint, Vulgate and Syriac; Hebrew *Very well*   *g* 16 *Nod* means *wandering* (see verses 12 and 14).   *h* 22 Or *who instructed all who work in*   *i* 25 *Seth* probably means *granted.*   *j* 26 Or *to proclaim* made them in the likeness of God. ²He created them male and female and blessed them. And when they were created, he called them "human beings."

³When Adam had lived 130 years, he had a son in his own likeness, in his own image; and he named him Seth. ⁴After Seth was born, Adam lived 800 years and had other sons and daughters. ⁵Altogether, Adam lived a total of 930 years, and then he died.

⁶When Seth had lived 105 years, he became the father*ᵃ* of Enosh. ⁷After he became the father of Enosh, Seth lived 807 years and had other sons and daughters. ⁸Altogether, Seth lived a total of 912 years, and then he died.

⁹When Enosh had lived 90 years, he became the father of Kenan. ¹⁰After he became the father of Kenan, Enosh lived 815 years and had other sons and daughters. ¹¹Altogether, Enosh lived a total of 905 years, and then he died.

¹²When Kenan had lived 70 years, he became the father of Mahalalel. ¹³After he became the father of Mahalalel, Kenan lived 840 years and had other sons and daughters. ¹⁴Altogether, Kenan lived a total of 910 years, and then he died.

¹⁵When Mahalalel had lived 65 years, he became the father of Jared. ¹⁶After he became the father of Jared, Mahalalel lived 830 years and had other sons and daughters. ¹⁷Altogether, Mahalalel lived a total of 895 years, and then he died.

¹⁸When Jared had lived 162 years, he became the father of Enoch. ¹⁹After he became the father of Enoch, Jared lived 800 years and had other sons and daughters. ²⁰Altogether, Jared lived a total of 962 years, and then he died.

²¹When Enoch had lived 65 years, he became the father of Methuselah. ²²After he became the father of Methuselah, Enoch walked faithfully with God 300 years and had other sons and daughters. ²³Altogether, Enoch lived a total of 365 years. ²⁴Enoch walked faithfully with God; then he was no more, because God took him away.

²⁵When Methuselah had lived 187 years, he became the father of Lamech. ²⁶After he became the father of Lamech, Methuselah lived 782 years and had other sons and daughters. ²⁷Altogether, Methuselah lived a total of 969 years, and then he died.

²⁸When Lamech had lived 182 years, he had a son. ²⁹He named him Noah*ᵇ* and said, "He will comfort us in the labor and painful toil of our hands caused by the ground the Lᴏʀᴅ has cursed." ³⁰After Noah was born, Lamech lived 595 years and had other sons and daughters. ³¹Altogether, Lamech lived a total of 777 years, and then he died.

³²After Noah was 500 years old, he became the father of Shem, Ham and Japheth.

Wickedness in the World

6 When human beings began to increase in number on the earth and daughters were born to them, ²the sons of God saw that these daughters were beautiful, and they married any of them they chose. ³Then the Lᴏʀᴅ said, "My Spirit will not contend with*ᶜ* human beings forever, for they are mortal*ᵈ*; their days will be a hundred and twenty years."

⁴The Nephilim were on the earth in those days—and also afterward—when the sons of God went to the daughters of the human beings and had children by them. They were the heroes of old, men of renown.

⁵The Lᴏʀᴅ saw how great the wickedness of the human race had become on the earth, and that every inclination of the thoughts of the human heart was only evil all the time. ⁶The Lᴏʀᴅ regretted that he had made human beings on the earth, and his heart was deeply troubled. ⁷So the Lᴏʀᴅ said, "I will wipe from the face of the earth the human race I have created—and with them the animals, the birds and the creatures that move along the ground—for I regret that I have made them." ⁸But Noah found favor in the eyes of the Lᴏʀᴅ.

Noah and the Flood

⁹This is the account of Noah and his family.

Noah was a righteous man, blameless among the people of his time, and he walked faithfully with God. ¹⁰Noah had three sons: Shem, Ham and Japheth.

¹¹Now the earth was corrupt in God's sight and was full of violence. ¹²God saw how corrupt the earth had become, for all

---

ᵃ 6 Father *may mean* ancestor; *also in verses 7-26.*   *ᵇ 29* Noah *sounds like the Hebrew for* comfort.
ᶜ 3 Or My spirit will not remain in   *ᵈ 3 Or* corrupt

WEDNESDAY

THE MAIN POINT

Genesis 6:1–22 *or* 6:9–10

John Walton

When the text identifies Noah as "righteous," it does not imply that he deserves to be spared or that he has earned God's grace. It indicates rather that God takes careful note of righteousness. Blamelessness matters to God. It is an accolade to be called righteous in one's generation, but undoubtedly Noah was considered by many in his generation simply as an oddball. Chesterton straightens us out on that account:

"A man with a definite belief always appears bizarre, because he does not change with the world; he has climbed into a fixed star and the earth whizzes below him like a zoetrope. Millions of mild black coated men call themselves sane and sensible merely because they always catch the fashionable insanity, because they are hurried into madness after madness by the maelstrom of the world."

We can all learn from Noah's refusal to conform to this world, but in the end we are not supposed to be impressed with Noah but with God. The text is in fact oddly silent about Noah on a number of serious counts; more to the point, Noah is silent—he never speaks through the whole flood account. He has no response to God's announcement, no questions about the ark or the animals, no plea on the behalf of anyone else, no cries for mercy, no bursts of joyful gratitude at the prospect of being saved, no grief for a world destroyed, no impatience in the ark, no prayers of thanksgiving accompanying sacrifice. The narrator leaves Noah a "flat" character. The only personality he has is found in the characteristics attributed to him by God. The text could not be clearer that Noah is a bit player and that the star of the account is God. Whatever we might learn from Noah is totally eclipsed by what we learn about God.

MARK GUY PEARSE {AD 1842–1932}

All eyes see God's benefits, but few see God.

reflection

1. In what ways do these readings shed new light on the way you read the familiar story of Noah?
2. Why do you suppose we're not given more "character development" details on Noah?
3. Who is the main character in your life story?

For your next devotional reading, go to page 14.

the people on earth had corrupted their ways. [13]So God said to Noah, "I am going to put an end to all people, for the earth is filled with violence because of them. I am surely going to destroy both them and the earth. [14]So make yourself an ark of cypress[a] wood; make rooms in it and coat it with pitch inside and out. [15]This is how you are to build it: The ark is to be three hundred cubits long, fifty cubits wide and thirty cubits high.[b] [16]Make a roof for it, leaving below the roof an opening one cubit[c] high all around.[d] Put a door in the side of the ark and make lower, middle and upper decks. [17]I am going to bring floodwaters on the earth to destroy all life under the heavens, every creature that has the breath of life in it. Everything on earth will perish. [18]But I will establish my covenant with you, and you will enter the ark—you and your sons and your wife and your sons' wives with you. [19]You are to bring into the ark two of all living creatures, male and female, to keep them alive with you. [20]Two of every kind of bird, of every kind of animal and of every kind of creature that moves along the ground will come to you to be kept alive. [21]You are to take every kind of food that is to be eaten and store it away as food for you and for them."

[22]Noah did everything just as God commanded him.

7 The LORD then said to Noah, "Go into the ark, you and your whole family, because I have found you righteous in this generation. [2]Take with you seven pairs of every kind of clean animal, a male and its mate, and one pair of every kind of unclean animal, a male and its mate, [3]and also seven pairs of every kind of bird, male and female, to keep their various kinds alive throughout the earth. [4]Seven days from now I will send rain on the earth for forty days and forty nights, and I will wipe from the face of the earth every living creature I have made."

[5]And Noah did all that the LORD commanded him.

[6]Noah was six hundred years old when the floodwaters came on the earth. [7]And Noah and his sons and his wife and his sons'

wives entered the ark to escape the waters of the flood. [8]Pairs of clean and unclean animals, of birds and of all creatures that move along the ground, [9]male and female, came to Noah and entered the ark, as God had commanded Noah. [10]And after the seven days the floodwaters came on the earth.

[11]In the six hundredth year of Noah's life, on the seventeenth day of the second month—on that day all the springs of the great deep burst forth, and the floodgates of the heavens were opened. [12]And rain fell on the earth forty days and forty nights.

[13]On that very day Noah and his sons, Shem, Ham and Japheth, together with his wife and the wives of his three sons, entered the ark. [14]They had with them every wild animal according to its kind, all livestock according to their kinds, every creature that moves along the ground according to its kind and every bird according to its kind, everything with wings. [15]Pairs of all creatures that have the breath of life in them came to Noah and entered the ark. [16]The animals going in were male and female of every living thing, as God had commanded Noah. Then the LORD shut him in.

[17]For forty days the flood kept coming on the earth, and as the waters increased they lifted the ark high above the earth. [18]The waters rose and increased greatly on the earth, and the ark floated on the surface of the water. [19]They rose greatly on the earth, and all the high mountains under the entire heavens were covered. [20]The waters rose and covered the mountains to a depth of more than fifteen cubits.[e,f] [21]Every living thing that moved on the earth perished—birds, livestock, wild animals, all the creatures that swarm over the earth, and the entire human race. [22]Everything on dry land that had the breath of life in its nostrils died. [23]Every living thing on the face of the earth was wiped out; human beings and animals and the creatures that move along the ground and the birds were wiped from the earth. Only Noah was left, and those with him in the ark.

[24]The waters flooded the earth for a hundred and fifty days.

---

a 14 The meaning of the Hebrew for this word is uncertain.   b 15 That is, about 450 feet long, 75 feet wide and 45 feet high or about 135 meters long, 22.5 meters wide and 13.5 meters high   c 16 That is, about 18 inches or about 45 centimeters   d 16 The meaning of the Hebrew for this clause is uncertain. e 20 That is, about 22 feet or about 6.8 meters   f 20 Or rose more than fifteen cubits, and the mountains were covered

8 But God remembered Noah and all the wild animals and the livestock that were with him in the ark, and he sent a wind over the earth, and the waters receded. ²Now the springs of the deep and the floodgates of the heavens had been closed, and the rain had stopped falling from the sky. ³The water receded steadily from the earth. At the end of the hundred and fifty days the water had gone down, ⁴and on the seventeenth day of the seventh month the ark came to rest on the mountains of Ararat. ⁵The waters continued to recede until the tenth month, and on the first day of the tenth month the tops of the mountains became visible.

⁶After forty days Noah opened a window he had made in the ark ⁷and sent out a raven, and it kept flying back and forth until the water had dried up from the earth. ⁸Then he sent out a dove to see if the water had receded from the surface of the ground. ⁹But the dove could find nowhere to perch because there was water over all the surface of the earth; so it returned to Noah in the ark. He reached out his hand and took the dove and brought it back to himself in the ark. ¹⁰He waited seven more days and again sent out the dove from the ark. ¹¹When the dove returned to him in the evening, there in its beak was a freshly plucked olive leaf! Then Noah knew that the water had receded from the earth. ¹²He waited seven more days and sent the dove out again, but this time it did not return to him.

¹³By the first day of the first month of Noah's six hundred and first year, the water had dried up from the earth. Noah then removed the covering from the ark and saw that the surface of the ground was dry. ¹⁴By the twenty-seventh day of the second month the earth was completely dry.

¹⁵Then God said to Noah, ¹⁶"Come out of the ark, you and your wife and your sons and their wives. ¹⁷Bring out every kind of living creature that is with you—the birds, the animals, and all the creatures that move along the ground—so they can multiply on the earth and be fruitful and increase in number on it."

¹⁸So Noah came out, together with his sons and his wife and his sons' wives. ¹⁹All the animals and all the creatures that move along the ground and all the birds—everything that moves on the earth—came out of the ark, one kind after another.

²⁰Then Noah built an altar to the LORD and, taking some of all the clean animals and clean birds, he sacrificed burnt offerings on it. ²¹The LORD smelled the pleasing aroma and said in his heart: "Never again will I curse the ground because of human beings, even though*a* every inclination of the human heart is evil from childhood. And never again will I destroy all living creatures, as I have done.

²²"As long as the earth endures,
   seedtime and harvest,
   cold and heat,
   summer and winter,
   day and night
   will never cease."

God's Covenant With Noah

9 Then God blessed Noah and his sons, saying to them, "Be fruitful and increase in number and fill the earth. ²The fear and dread of you will fall on all the beasts of the earth and all the birds in the sky, on every creature that moves along the ground, and on all the fish in the sea; they are given into your hands. ³Everything that lives and moves will be food for you. Just as I gave you the green plants, I now give you everything.

⁴"But you must not eat meat that has its lifeblood still in it. ⁵And for your lifeblood I will surely demand an accounting. I will demand an accounting from every animal. And from each human being, too, I will demand an accounting for the life of another human being.

⁶"Whoever sheds human blood,
   by human beings shall their blood be shed;
for in the image of God
   has God made humankind.

⁷As for you, be fruitful and increase in number; multiply on the earth and increase upon it."

⁸Then God said to Noah and to his sons with him: ⁹"I now establish my covenant with you and with your descendants after you ¹⁰and with every living creature that was with you—the birds, the livestock and all

a 21 Or *human beings, for*

the wild animals, all those that came out of the ark with you—every living creature on earth. ¹¹I establish my covenant with you: Never again will all life be destroyed by the waters of a flood; never again will there be a flood to destroy the earth."

¹²And God said, "This is the sign of the covenant I am making between me and you and every living creature with you, a covenant for all generations to come: ¹³I have set my rainbow in the clouds, and it will be the sign of the covenant between me and the earth. ¹⁴Whenever I bring clouds over the earth and the rainbow appears in the clouds, ¹⁵I will remember my covenant between me and you and all living creatures of every kind. Never again will the waters become a flood to destroy all life. ¹⁶Whenever the rainbow appears in the clouds, I will see it and remember the everlasting covenant between God and all living creatures of every kind on the earth."

¹⁷So God said to Noah, "This is the sign of the covenant I have established between me and all life on the earth."

The Sons of Noah

¹⁸The sons of Noah who came out of the ark were Shem, Ham and Japheth. (Ham was the father of Canaan.) ¹⁹These were the three sons of Noah, and from them came the people who were scattered over the whole earth.

²⁰Noah, a man of the soil, proceeded*ᵃ* to plant a vineyard. ²¹When he drank some of its wine, he became drunk and lay uncovered inside his tent. ²²Ham, the father of Canaan, saw his father's nakedness and told his two brothers outside. ²³But Shem and Japheth took a garment and laid it across their shoulders; then they walked in backward and covered their father's nakedness. Their faces were turned the other way so that they would not see their father's nakedness.

²⁴When Noah awoke from his wine and found out what his youngest son had done to him, ²⁵he said,

"Cursed be Canaan!
    The lowest of slaves
    will he be to his brothers."

²⁶He also said,

"Praise be to the LORD, the God of Shem!
    May Canaan be the slave of Shem.
²⁷May God extend Japheth's*ᵇ* territory;
    may Japheth live in the tents of
    Shem,
and may Canaan be the slave of
    Japheth."

²⁸After the flood Noah lived 350 years. ²⁹Noah lived a total of 950 years, and then he died.

The Table of Nations

10 This is the account of Shem, Ham and Japheth, Noah's sons, who themselves had sons after the flood.

The Japhethites

²The sons*ᶜ* of Japheth:
    Gomer, Magog, Madai, Javan, Tubal,
    Meshek and Tiras.
³The sons of Gomer:
    Ashkenaz, Riphath and Togarmah.
⁴The sons of Javan:
    Elishah, Tarshish, the Kittites and the
    Rodanites.*ᵈ* ⁵(From these the maritime peoples spread out into their territories by their clans within their nations, each with its own language.)

The Hamites

⁶The sons of Ham:
    Cush, Egypt, Put and Canaan.
⁷The sons of Cush:
    Seba, Havilah, Sabtah, Raamah and
    Sabteka.
The sons of Raamah:
    Sheba and Dedan.

⁸Cush was the father*ᵉ* of Nimrod, who became a mighty warrior on the earth. ⁹He was a mighty hunter before the LORD; that is why it is said, "Like Nimrod, a mighty hunter before the LORD." ¹⁰The first centers of his kingdom were Babylon, Uruk, Akkad and Kalneh, in*ᶠ* Shinar.*ᵍ* ¹¹From that land he went to Assyria, where he built Nineveh, Rehoboth Ir,*ʰ* Calah ¹²and Resen, which is be-

---

ᵃ 20 Or *soil, was the first*   *ᵇ 27 Japheth* sounds like the Hebrew for *extend.*   *ᶜ 2 Sons* may mean *descendants* or *successors* or *nations*; also in verses 3, 4, 6, 7, 20-23, 29 and 31.   *ᵈ 4* Some manuscripts of the Masoretic Text and Samaritan Pentateuch (see also Septuagint and 1 Chron. 1:7); most manuscripts of the Masoretic Text *Dodanites*   *ᵉ 8* Father may mean *ancestor* or *predecessor* or *founder*; also in verses 13, 15, 24 and 26.   *ᶠ 10* Or *Uruk and Akkad—all of them in*   *ᵍ 10* That is, Babylonia   *ʰ 11* Or *Nineveh with its city squares*

THURSDAY

BIBLE GENEALOGIES

Genesis 10:1–32 *or* 10:1–4

Ruth Tucker

When Jo Shelter began working as a Wycliffe Bible translator among the remote Balangao people of the Philippines in 1962, she found them entirely puzzled as to why she would want to translate God's Word into . . . their own lowly language.

They were discouraging times for Jo as she worked in the Balangao valley. During her first six years of missionary service, only two Balangaos became Christians. Most people simply were not interested in her concept of God. One such individual was Canao, who had become a father of sorts to her. "When Juami arrived, I was shocked," he later recalled. "Didn't she know it wasn't safe for girls in our area? Didn't she realize we were headhunters? So I had to become her 'father' and take care of her. I had to be sure people saw her eating at our house so they would know I was protecting her with my life, as is our custom here in Balangao."

But, Canao was not interested in her God. "Juami always talked about God, but I didn't like to always talk about Him," he confessed. "Juami kept telling me about God and how to believe. I already believed there was a god, so I just tried to be polite."

Then one day Jo showed him some of the translation work she had done and asked him to help her with it. Canao was amazed to find that God's Word could actually be written in a book and be read in a language he could understand. Most astonishingly of all was that it was true. How did he know that? "It actually had a genealogy—absolute proof to a Balangao that it's true. This one went back to the beginning of time. Through the impact of the genealogy, I really began to understand and believe the truth about Jesus Christ."

JOHN M'EWAN {ca. AD 1880}

In the diamond fields of South Africa a diamond was found, celebrated lately under the title of flystone; placed under a magnifying glass, you see enclosed in all its brilliancy a little fly, with body, wings and eyes in a most perfect state of preservation. How it came there no one knows, but no human skill can take it out. So in Holy Scripture the Spirit of God is found in a place from which no human power can remove it.

— *reflection* —

1. When have you experienced God's presence while reading the Bible?

2. Why would God consider it important to include genealogies in the Bible?

3. How has today's Bible reading given you new insight into the workings of the Spirit of God?

For your next devotional reading, go to page 19.

tween Nineveh and Calah—which is the great city.

¹³Egypt was the father of
the Ludites, Anamites, Lehabites, Naphtuhites, ¹⁴Pathrusites, Kasluhites (from whom the Philistines came) and Caphtorites.
¹⁵Canaan was the father of
Sidon his firstborn,ᵃ and of the Hittites, ¹⁶Jebusites, Amorites, Girgashites, ¹⁷Hivites, Arkites, Sinites, ¹⁸Arvadites, Zemarites and Hamathites.

Later the Canaanite clans scattered ¹⁹and the borders of Canaan reached from Sidon toward Gerar as far as Gaza, and then toward Sodom, Gomorrah, Admah and Zeboyim, as far as Lasha.

²⁰These are the sons of Ham by their clans and languages, in their territories and nations.

The Semites

²¹Sons were also born to Shem, whose older brother wasᵇ Japheth; Shem was the ancestor of all the sons of Eber.

²²The sons of Shem:
Elam, Ashur, Arphaxad, Lud and Aram.
²³The sons of Aram:
Uz, Hul, Gether and Meshek.ᶜ
²⁴Arphaxad was the father ofᵈ Shelah, and Shelah the father of Eber.
²⁵Two sons were born to Eber:
One was named Peleg,ᵉ because in his time the earth was divided; his brother was named Joktan.
²⁶Joktan was the father of
Almodad, Sheleph, Hazarmaveth, Jerah, ²⁷Hadoram, Uzal, Diklah, ²⁸Obal, Abimael, Sheba, ²⁹Ophir, Havilah and Jobab. All these were sons of Joktan.

³⁰The region where they lived stretched from Mesha toward Sephar, in the eastern hill country.

³¹These are the sons of Shem by their clans and languages, in their territories and nations.

³²These are the clans of Noah's sons, according to their lines of descent, within their nations. From these the nations spread out over the earth after the flood.

The Tower of Babel

11 Now the whole world had one language and a common speech. ²As people moved eastward,ᶠ they found a plain in Shinarᵍ and settled there. ³They said to each other, "Come, let's make bricks and bake them thoroughly." They used brick instead of stone, and tar for mortar. ⁴Then they said, "Come, let us build ourselves a city, with a tower that reaches to the heavens, so that we may make a name for ourselves and not be scattered over the face of the whole earth."

⁵But the LORD came down to see the city and the tower they were building. ⁶The LORD said, "If as one people speaking the same language they have begun to do this, then nothing they plan to do will be impossible for them. ⁷Come, let us go down and confuse their language so they will not understand each other."

⁸So the LORD scattered them from there over all the earth, and they stopped building the city. ⁹That is why it was called Babelʰ— because there the LORD confused the language of the whole world. From there the LORD scattered them over the face of the whole earth.

From Shem to Abram

¹⁰This is the account of Shem's family line.

Two years after the flood, when Shem was 100 years old, he became the fatherⁱ of Arphaxad. ¹¹And after he became the father of Arphaxad, Shem lived 500 years and had other sons and daughters.

¹²When Arphaxad had lived 35 years, he became the father of Shelah. ¹³And after he became the father of Shelah, Arphaxad lived 403 years and had other sons and daughters.ʲ

ᵃ 15 Or of the Sidonians, the foremost   ᵇ 21 Or Shem, the older brother of   ᶜ 23 See Septuagint and 1 Chron. 1:17; Hebrew Mash.   ᵈ 24 Hebrew; Septuagint father of Cainan, and Cainan was the father of ᵉ 25 Peleg means division.   ᶠ 2 Or from the east; or in the east   ᵍ 2 That is, Babylonia   ʰ 9 That is, Babylon; Babel sounds like the Hebrew for confused.   ⁱ 10 Father may mean ancestor; also in verses 11-25.   ʲ 12,13 Hebrew; Septuagint (see also Luke 3:35, 36 and note at Gen. 10:24) 35 years, he became the father of Cainan. ¹³And after he became the father of Cainan, Arphaxad lived 430 years and had other sons and daughters, and then he died. When Cainan had lived 130 years, he became the father of Shelah. And after he became the father of Shelah, Cainan lived 330 years and had other sons and daughters

¹⁴When Shelah had lived 30 years, he became the father of Eber. ¹⁵And after he became the father of Eber, Shelah lived 403 years and had other sons and daughters.

¹⁶When Eber had lived 34 years, he became the father of Peleg. ¹⁷And after he became the father of Peleg, Eber lived 430 years and had other sons and daughters.

¹⁸When Peleg had lived 30 years, he became the father of Reu. ¹⁹And after he became the father of Reu, Peleg lived 209 years and had other sons and daughters.

²⁰When Reu had lived 32 years, he became the father of Serug. ²¹And after he became the father of Serug, Reu lived 207 years and had other sons and daughters.

²²When Serug had lived 30 years, he became the father of Nahor. ²³And after he became the father of Nahor, Serug lived 200 years and had other sons and daughters.

²⁴When Nahor had lived 29 years, he became the father of Terah. ²⁵And after he became the father of Terah, Nahor lived 119 years and had other sons and daughters.

²⁶After Terah had lived 70 years, he became the father of Abram, Nahor and Haran.

Abram's Family

²⁷This is the account of Terah's family line.

Terah became the father of Abram, Nahor and Haran. And Haran became the father of Lot. ²⁸While his father Terah was still alive, Haran died in Ur of the Chaldeans, in the land of his birth. ²⁹Abram and Nahor both married. The name of Abram's wife was Sarai, and the name of Nahor's wife was Milkah; she was the daughter of Haran, the father of both Milkah and Iskah. ³⁰Now Sarai was childless because she was not able to conceive.

³¹Terah took his son Abram, his grandson Lot son of Haran, and his daughter-in-law Sarai, the wife of his son Abram, and together they set out from Ur of the Chaldeans to go to Canaan. But when they came to Harran, they settled there.

³²Terah lived 205 years, and he died in Harran.

The Call of Abram

12 The LORD had said to Abram, "Go from your country, your people and your father's household to the land I will show you.

²"I will make you into a great nation,
    and I will bless you;
I will make your name great,
    and you will be a blessing.ᵃ
³I will bless those who bless you,
    and whoever curses you I will curse;
and all peoples on earth
    will be blessed through you."ᵇ

⁴So Abram went, as the LORD had told him; and Lot went with him. Abram was seventy-five years old when he set out from Harran. ⁵He took his wife Sarai, his nephew Lot, all the possessions they had accumulated and the people they had acquired in Harran, and they set out for the land of Canaan, and they arrived there.

⁶Abram traveled through the land as far as the site of the great tree of Moreh at Shechem. At that time the Canaanites were in the land. ⁷The LORD appeared to Abram and said, "To your offspringᶜ I will give this land." So he built an altar there to the LORD, who had appeared to him.

⁸From there he went on toward the hills east of Bethel and pitched his tent, with Bethel on the west and Ai on the east. There he built an altar to the LORD and called on the name of the LORD.

⁹Then Abram set out and continued toward the Negev.

Abram in Egypt

¹⁰Now there was a famine in the land, and Abram went down to Egypt to live there for a while because the famine was severe. ¹¹As he was about to enter Egypt, he said to his wife Sarai, "I know what a beautiful woman you are. ¹²When the Egyptians see you, they will say, 'This is his wife.' Then they will kill me but will let you live. ¹³Say you are my sister, so that I will be treated well for your sake and my life will be spared because of you."

¹⁴When Abram came to Egypt, the Egyptians saw that Sarai was a very beautiful woman. ¹⁵And when Pharaoh's officials saw

---

ᵃ 2 Or great, / and you will be seen as blessed   ᵇ 3 Or earth / will use your name in blessings (see Gen. 48:20)   ᶜ 7 Or seed her, they praised her to Pharaoh, and she was taken into his palace. ¹⁶He treated Abram well for her sake, and Abram acquired sheep and cattle, male and female donkeys, male and female servants, and camels.

¹⁷But the LORD inflicted serious diseases on Pharaoh and his household because of Abram's wife Sarai. ¹⁸So Pharaoh summoned Abram. "What have you done to me?" he said. "Why didn't you tell me she was your wife? ¹⁹Why did you say, 'She is my sister,' so that I took her to be my wife? Now then, here is your wife. Take her and go!" ²⁰Then Pharaoh gave orders about Abram to his men, and they sent him on his way, with his wife and everything he had.

Abram and Lot Separate

13 So Abram went up from Egypt to the Negev, with his wife and everything he had, and Lot went with him. ²Abram had become very wealthy in livestock and in silver and gold.

³From the Negev he went from place to place until he came to Bethel, to the place between Bethel and Ai where his tent had been earlier ⁴and where he had first built an altar. There Abram called on the name of the LORD.

⁵Now Lot, who was moving about with Abram, also had flocks and herds and tents. ⁶But the land could not support them while they stayed together, for their possessions were so great that they were not able to stay together. ⁷And quarreling arose between Abram's herders and the herders of Lot. The Canaanites and Perizzites were also living in the land at that time.

⁸So Abram said to Lot, "Let's not have any quarreling between you and me, or between your herders and mine, for we are close relatives. ⁹Is not the whole land before you? Let's part company. If you go to the left, I'll go to the right; if you go to the right, I'll go to the left."

¹⁰Lot looked around and saw that the whole plain of the Jordan was well watered, like the garden of the LORD, like the land of Egypt, toward Zoar. (This was before the LORD destroyed Sodom and Gomorrah.) ¹¹So Lot chose for himself the whole plain of the Jordan and set out toward the east. The two men parted company: ¹²Abram lived in the land of Canaan, while Lot lived among the cities of the plain and pitched his tents near Sodom. ¹³Now the people of Sodom were wicked and were sinning greatly against the LORD.

¹⁴The LORD said to Abram after Lot had parted from him, "Look around from where you are, to the north and south, to the east and west. ¹⁵All the land that you see I will give to you and your offspring*a* forever. ¹⁶I will make your offspring like the dust of the earth, so that if anyone could count the dust, then your offspring could be counted. ¹⁷Go, walk through the length and breadth of the land, for I am giving it to you."

¹⁸So Abram went to live near the great trees of Mamre at Hebron, where he pitched his tents. There he built an altar to the LORD.

Abram Rescues Lot

14 At the time when Amraphel was king of Shinar,*b* Arioch king of Ellasar, Kedorlaomer king of Elam and Tidal king of Goyim, ²these kings went to war against Bera king of Sodom, Birsha king of Gomorrah, Shinab king of Admah, Shemeber king of Zeboyim, and the king of Bela (that is, Zoar). ³All these latter kings joined forces in the Valley of Siddim (that is, the Dead Sea Valley). ⁴For twelve years they had been subject to Kedorlaomer, but in the thirteenth year they rebelled.

⁵In the fourteenth year, Kedorlaomer and the kings allied with him went out and defeated the Rephaites in Ashteroth Karnaim, the Zuzites in Ham, the Emites in Shaveh Kiriathaim ⁶and the Horites in the hill country of Seir, as far as El Paran near the desert. ⁷Then they turned back and went to En Mishpat (that is, Kadesh), and they conquered the whole territory of the Amalekites, as well as the Amorites who were living in Hazezon Tamar.

⁸Then the king of Sodom, the king of Gomorrah, the king of Admah, the king of Zeboyim and the king of Bela (that is, Zoar) marched out and drew up their battle lines in the Valley of Siddim ⁹against Kedorlaomer king of Elam, Tidal king of Goyim, Amraphel king of Shinar and Arioch king of Ellasar—four kings against five. ¹⁰Now the Valley of Siddim was full of tar pits, and

a 15 Or *seed*; also in verse 16   *b 1* That is, Babylonia; also in verse 9 when the kings of Sodom and Gomorrah fled, some of the men fell into them and the rest fled to the hills. ¹¹The four kings seized all the goods of Sodom and Gomorrah and all their food; then they went away. ¹²They also carried off Abram's nephew Lot and his possessions, since he was living in Sodom.

¹³A man who had escaped came and reported this to Abram the Hebrew. Now Abram was living near the great trees of Mamre the Amorite, a brother*a* of Eshkol and Aner, all of whom were allied with Abram. ¹⁴When Abram heard that his relative had been taken captive, he called out the 318 trained men born in his household and went in pursuit as far as Dan. ¹⁵During the night Abram divided his men to attack them and he routed them, pursuing them as far as Hobah, north of Damascus. ¹⁶He recovered all the goods and brought back his relative Lot and his possessions, together with the women and the other people.

¹⁷After Abram returned from defeating Kedorlaomer and the kings allied with him, the king of Sodom came out to meet him in the Valley of Shaveh (that is, the King's Valley).

¹⁸Then Melchizedek king of Salem brought out bread and wine. He was priest of God Most High, ¹⁹and he blessed Abram, saying,

"Blessed be Abram by God Most High,
    Creator of heaven and earth.
²⁰And praise be to God Most High,
    who delivered your enemies into your hand."

Then Abram gave him a tenth of everything.

²¹The king of Sodom said to Abram, "Give me the people and keep the goods for yourself."

²²But Abram said to the king of Sodom, "With raised hand I have sworn an oath to the LORD, God Most High, Creator of heaven and earth, ²³that I will accept nothing belonging to you, not even a thread or the thong of a sandal, so that you will never be able to say, 'I made Abram rich.' ²⁴I will accept nothing but what my men have eaten and the share that belongs to the men who went with me—to Aner, Eshkol and Mamre. Let them have their share."

God's Covenant With Abram

15 After this, the word of the LORD came to Abram in a vision:

"Do not be afraid, Abram.
    I am your shield,*b*
    your very great reward.*c*"

²But Abram said, "Sovereign LORD, what can you give me since I remain childless and the one who will inherit*d* my estate is Eliezer of Damascus?" ³And Abram said, "You have given me no children; so a servant in my household will be my heir."

⁴Then the word of the LORD came to him: "This man will not be your heir, but a son coming from your own body will be your heir." ⁵He took him outside and said, "Look up at the heavens and count the stars—if indeed you can count them." Then he said to him, "So shall your offspring*e* be."

⁶Abram believed the LORD, and he credited it to him as righteousness.

⁷He also said to him, "I am the LORD, who brought you out of Ur of the Chaldeans to give you this land to take possession of it."

⁸But Abram said, "Sovereign LORD, how can I know that I will gain possession of it?"

⁹So the LORD said to him, "Bring me a heifer, a goat and a ram, each three years old, along with a dove and a young pigeon."

¹⁰Abram brought all these to him, cut them in two and arranged the halves opposite each other; the birds, however, he did not cut in half. ¹¹Then birds of prey came down on the carcasses, but Abram drove them away.

¹²As the sun was setting, Abram fell into a deep sleep, and a thick and dreadful darkness came over him. ¹³Then the LORD said to him, "Know for certain that for four hundred years your descendants will be strangers in a country not their own and that they will be enslaved and mistreated there. ¹⁴But I will punish the nation they serve as slaves, and afterward they will come out with great possessions. ¹⁵You, however, will go to your ancestors in peace and be buried at a good old age. ¹⁶In the fourth generation your descendants will come back here, for the sin of the Amorites has not yet reached its full measure."

¹⁷When the sun had set and darkness had

---

a 13 Or *a relative;* or *an ally*   *b 1* Or *sovereign*   *c 1* Or *shield; / your reward will be very great*
d 2 The meaning of the Hebrew for this phrase is uncertain.   *e 5* Or *seed*

WHY GOD MADE A COVENANT WITH US

Genesis 15:1–21 *or* 15:6

THOMAS WATSON {AD 1620–1686}

Why should God make a covenant with us?

It is out of indulgence, favor and respect to us. A tyrant will not enter into a covenant with slaves. He will not show them that kind of respect. God's entering into a covenant with us, to be our God, is a dignity he bestows upon us. A covenant is *insigne honouris* (a sign of honor), that is to say, it is a way of proclaiming the difference between God's people and those who are not his people … When the Lord told Abraham that he would enter into a covenant with him, Abraham fell upon his face because he was amazed that the God of glory should bestow such a favor upon him (see Genesis 17:1–3).

Dallas Willard

What did Abraham believe that led God to declare or "[credit]" him righteous [Genesis 15:6]? Was it that God had arranged payment for his sins? Not at all. The story makes it very clear that Abraham believed God was going to give him a male baby, an heir, and through that baby a multitude of descendants who would possess the land promised to him. He trusted God, of course, but it was for things involved in his current existence.

He believed that God would interact with him now—just as those who later gathered around Jesus did. He even dared to ask God how he could know that the promise of a male heir would be fulfilled …

In the face of such faith, God declared Abraham to be righteous. Does that mean he declared he would go to heaven when he died? Not precisely that, but certainly that Abraham's sins and failures would not cut him off from God in the present moment and in their ongoing relationship in life together.

But would he go to heaven when he died? Of course! What else would God do with such a person? They were friends, a fact made much of in Scripture (2 Chronicles 20:7; Isaiah 41:8; James 2:23), as we are to be friends of Jesus by immersing ourselves in his work (John 15:15). No friend of God will be in hell.

reflection

1. What did God's covenant with Abraham reveal about the kind of relationship he wanted to have with Abraham?

2. Jesus died on the cross so that God could establish an everlasting covenant with you. What does this reveal about the kind of relationship he wants to have with you?

3. What does God require from you in order to enter into this covenant with him?

For your next devotional reading, go to page 21.

fallen, a smoking firepot with a blazing torch appeared and passed between the pieces. ¹⁸On that day the LORD made a covenant with Abram and said, "To your descendants I give this land, from the Wadi ᵃ of Egypt to the great river, the Euphrates— ¹⁹the land of the Kenites, Kenizzites, Kadmonites, ²⁰Hittites, Perizzites, Rephaites, ²¹Amorites, Canaanites, Girgashites and Jebusites."

Hagar and Ishmael

16 Now Sarai, Abram's wife, had borne him no children. But she had an Egyptian servant named Hagar; ²so she said to Abram, "The LORD has kept me from having children. Go, sleep with my servant; perhaps I can build a family through her."

Abram agreed to what Sarai said. ³So after Abram had been living in Canaan ten years, Sarai his wife took her Egyptian servant Hagar and gave her to her husband to be his wife. ⁴He slept with Hagar, and she conceived.

When she knew she was pregnant, she began to despise her mistress. ⁵Then Sarai said to Abram, "You are responsible for the wrong I am suffering. I put my servant in your arms, and now that she knows she is pregnant, she despises me. May the LORD judge between you and me."

⁶"Your servant is in your hands," Abram said. "Do with her whatever you think best." Then Sarai mistreated Hagar; so she fled from her.

⁷The angel of the LORD found Hagar near a spring in the desert; it was the spring that is beside the road to Shur. ⁸And he said, "Hagar, servant of Sarai, where have you come from, and where are you going?"

"I'm running away from my mistress Sarai," she answered.

⁹Then the angel of the LORD told her, "Go back to your mistress and submit to her." ¹⁰The angel added, "I will increase your descendants so much that they will be too numerous to count."

¹¹The angel of the LORD also said to her:

"You are now pregnant
and you will give birth to a son.

You shall name him Ishmael,ᵇ
for the LORD has heard of your misery.
¹²He will be a wild donkey of a man;
his hand will be against everyone
and everyone's hand against him,
and he will live in hostility
towardᶜ all his brothers."

¹³She gave this name to the LORD who spoke to her: "You are the God who sees me," for she said, "I have now seenᵈ the One who sees me." ¹⁴That is why the well was called Beer Lahai Roiᵉ; it is still there, between Kadesh and Bered.

¹⁵So Hagar bore Abram a son, and Abram gave the name Ishmael to the son she had borne. ¹⁶Abram was eighty-six years old when Hagar bore him Ishmael.

The Covenant of Circumcision

17 When Abram was ninety-nine years old, the LORD appeared to him and said, "I am God Almightyᶠ; walk before me faithfully and be blameless. ²Then I will make my covenant between me and you and will greatly increase your numbers."

³Abram fell facedown, and God said to him, ⁴"As for me, this is my covenant with you: You will be the father of many nations. ⁵No longer will you be called Abramᵍ; your name will be Abraham,ʰ for I have made you a father of many nations. ⁶I will make you very fruitful; I will make nations of you, and kings will come from you. ⁷I will establish my covenant as an everlasting covenant between me and you and your descendants after you for the generations to come, to be your God and the God of your descendants after you. ⁸The whole land of Canaan, where you now reside as a foreigner, I will give as an everlasting possession to you and your descendants after you; and I will be their God."

⁹Then God said to Abraham, "As for you, you must keep my covenant, you and your descendants after you for the generations to come. ¹⁰This is my covenant with you and your descendants after you, the covenant you are to keep: Every male among you shall be circumcised. ¹¹You are to undergo circumcision, and it will be the sign of the cov-

---

ᵃ 18 Or river   ᵇ 11 Ishmael means God hears.   ᶜ 12 Or live to the east / of   ᵈ 13 Or seen the back of
ᵉ 14 Beer Lahai Roi means well of the Living One who sees me.   ᶠ 1 Hebrew El-Shaddai   ᵍ 5 Abram
means exalted father.   ʰ 5 Abraham probably means father of many.

Running Away

Genesis 16:1-9

read/meditate

Read Hagar's story. Consider her solitude as she sat by the spring. Consider that she lived in a culture in which a single, pregnant woman had nowhere to turn. Now read Hagar's story again, and think about God meeting her in that lonely, desperate place. Do you imagine she heard him more clearly because of her desperation? Or do you think it was a miracle she heard him at all?

pray

Imagine yourself beside your own spring. You have many mistakes behind you, much baggage to carry with you, and many unknowns ahead. Imagine God meeting you in that place. What do you want to say to him? What do you need from him? What can you thank him for? Be honest before him, as Hagar was.

contemplate

Think about God's question to Hagar: "Where have you come from, and where are you going?" Consider your own answer to God's question. Is there anything you are running from? Anything you're running toward? Does God have direction for you today—whether it's easy to hear or not?

additional reflection

The wind of God is always blowing . . . but you must hoist your sail.

—François Fénelon

Man does not recognize the place he should fill. He has obviously gone astray. He has fallen from the true status, and he cannot find it again. So he searches everywhere anxiously but in vain, in the midst of great darkness.

—Blaise Pascal

For your next devotional reading, go to page 23.

enant between me and you. ¹²For the generations to come every male among you who is eight days old must be circumcised, including those born in your household or bought with money from a foreigner—those who are not your offspring. ¹³Whether born in your household or bought with your money, they must be circumcised. My covenant in your flesh is to be an everlasting covenant. ¹⁴Any uncircumcised male, who has not been circumcised in the flesh, will be cut off from his people; he has broken my covenant."

¹⁵God also said to Abraham, "As for Sarai your wife, you are no longer to call her Sarai; her name will be Sarah. ¹⁶I will bless her and will surely give you a son by her. I will bless her so that she will be the mother of nations; kings of peoples will come from her."

¹⁷Abraham fell facedown; he laughed and said to himself, "Will a son be born to a man a hundred years old? Will Sarah bear a child at the age of ninety?" ¹⁸And Abraham said to God, "If only Ishmael might live under your blessing!"

¹⁹Then God said, "Yes, but your wife Sarah will bear you a son, and you will call him Isaac.ᵃ I will establish my covenant with him as an everlasting covenant for his descendants after him. ²⁰And as for Ishmael, I have heard you: I will surely bless him; I will make him fruitful and will greatly increase his numbers. He will be the father of twelve rulers, and I will make him into a great nation. ²¹But my covenant I will establish with Isaac, whom Sarah will bear to you by this time next year." ²²When he had finished speaking with Abraham, God went up from him.

²³On that very day Abraham took his son Ishmael and all those born in his household or bought with his money, every male in his household, and circumcised them, as God told him. ²⁴Abraham was ninety-nine years old when he was circumcised, ²⁵and his son Ishmael was thirteen; ²⁶Abraham and his son Ishmael were both circumcised on that same day. ²⁷And every male in Abraham's household, including those born in his household or bought from a foreigner, was circumcised with him.

The Three Visitors

18

The LORD appeared to Abraham near the great trees of Mamre while he was sitting at the entrance to his tent in the heat of the day. ²Abraham looked up and saw three men standing nearby. When he saw them, he hurried from the entrance of his tent to meet them and bowed low to the ground.

³He said, "If I have found favor in your eyes, my lord,ᵇ do not pass your servant by. ⁴Let a little water be brought, and then you may all wash your feet and rest under this tree. ⁵Let me get you something to eat, so you can be refreshed and then go on your way—now that you have come to your servant."

"Very well," they answered, "do as you say."

⁶So Abraham hurried into the tent to Sarah. "Quick," he said, "get three seahsᶜ of the finest flour and knead it and bake some bread."

⁷Then he ran to the herd and selected a choice, tender calf and gave it to a servant, who hurried to prepare it. ⁸He then brought some curds and milk and the calf that had been prepared, and set these before them. While they ate, he stood near them under a tree.

⁹"Where is your wife Sarah?" they asked him.

"There, in the tent," he said.

¹⁰Then the LORDᵈ said, "I will surely return to you about this time next year, and Sarah your wife will have a son."

Now Sarah was listening at the entrance to the tent, which was behind him. ¹¹Abraham and Sarah were already very old, and Sarah was past the age of childbearing. ¹²So Sarah laughed to herself as she thought, "After I am worn out and my lord is old, will I now have this pleasure?"

¹³Then the LORD said to Abraham, "Why did Sarah laugh and say, 'Will I really have a child, now that I am old?' ¹⁴Is anything too hard for the LORD? I will return to you at the appointed time next year and Sarah will have a son."

¹⁵Sarah was afraid, so she lied and said, "I did not laugh."

But he said, "Yes, you did laugh."

ᵃ 19 *Isaac* means *he laughs.*   ᵇ 3 Or *eyes, Lord*   ᶜ 6 That is, probably about 36 pounds or about 16 kilograms   ᵈ 10 Hebrew *Then he*

MONDAY

BIGGER THAN YOU THINK

Genesis 18:1–33 or 18:13–14

ARTHUR W. PINK {AD 1885–1952}

The sovereignty of God. What do we mean by this expression? We mean the supremacy of God, the kingship of God, the godhood of God. To say that God is sovereign is to declare that God is God. To say that God is sovereign is to declare that he is the Most High. It means that he acts according to his will both in the army of heaven and among the inhabitants of the earth. "No one can hold back his hand or say to him: 'What have you done?'" (Daniel 4:35). To say that God is sovereign is to declare that he is the Almighty, the possessor of all power in heaven and earth. It means that no one can defeat his plans, thwart his purpose or resist his will (Psalm 115:3). To say that God is sovereign is to declare that he "rules over the nations" (Psalm 22:28). It means he sets up kingdoms, overthrows empires and determines the course of dynasties just as he pleases. To say that God is sovereign is to declare that he is the "blessed and only Ruler, the King of kings and Lord of lords" (1 Timothy 6:15). Such is the God of the Bible.

Carolyn Custis James

The questions about God that seem to surface most often in conversations I have ... center on God's sovereignty and character. Is God really in control, or does sovereignty change hands from moment to moment, shifting between God, the devil, and pure chance? Does God care only about the major events and choices of my life, or does he also rule over the details? What kind of God would allow such painful things to happen to us? Do I really matter to God, or am I less important than others who seem more entitled to his attentions? These questions about God (which weighed heavily on my own heart) send us back to read the Scriptures again, this time with theological eyes, searching for God. It can be a mind-expanding experience, for theology inevitably enlarges our vision of God. As one startled woman admitted, "God is a lot bigger than I thought." When God is big, everything begins to look different.

reflection

1. When have you had your "small" view of God blown away and expanded?

2. How can knowing that God is big—bigger than you think—make a difference in your life?

3. How does the sovereignty of God affect your faith?

For your next devotional reading, go to page 27.

Abraham Pleads for Sodom

¹⁶When the men got up to leave, they looked down toward Sodom, and Abraham walked along with them to see them on their way. ¹⁷Then the LORD said, "Shall I hide from Abraham what I am about to do? ¹⁸Abraham will surely become a great and powerful nation, and all nations on earth will be blessed through him.ᵃ ¹⁹For I have chosen him, so that he will direct his children and his household after him to keep the way of the LORD by doing what is right and just, so that the LORD will bring about for Abraham what he has promised him."

²⁰Then the LORD said, "The outcry against Sodom and Gomorrah is so great and their sin so grievous ²¹that I will go down and see if what they have done is as bad as the outcry that has reached me. If not, I will know."

²²The men turned away and went toward Sodom, but Abraham remained standing before the LORD.ᵇ ²³Then Abraham approached him and said: "Will you sweep away the righteous with the wicked? ²⁴What if there are fifty righteous people in the city? Will you really sweep it away and not spareᶜ the place for the sake of the fifty righteous people in it? ²⁵Far be it from you to do such a thing—to kill the righteous with the wicked, treating the righteous and the wicked alike. Far be it from you! Will not the Judge of all the earth do right?"

²⁶The LORD said, "If I find fifty righteous people in the city of Sodom, I will spare the whole place for their sake."

²⁷Then Abraham spoke up again: "Now that I have been so bold as to speak to the Lord, though I am nothing but dust and ashes, ²⁸what if the number of the righteous is five less than fifty? Will you destroy the whole city for lack of five people?"

"If I find forty-five there," he said, "I will not destroy it."

²⁹Once again he spoke to him, "What if only forty are found there?"

He said, "For the sake of forty, I will not do it."

³⁰Then he said, "May the Lord not be angry, but let me speak. What if only thirty can be found there?"

He answered, "I will not do it if I find thirty there."

³¹Abraham said, "Now that I have been so bold as to speak to the Lord, what if only twenty can be found there?"

He said, "For the sake of twenty, I will not destroy it."

³²Then he said, "May the Lord not be angry, but let me speak just once more. What if only ten can be found there?"

He answered, "For the sake of ten, I will not destroy it."

³³When the LORD had finished speaking with Abraham, he left, and Abraham returned home.

Sodom and Gomorrah Destroyed

19 The two angels arrived at Sodom in the evening, and Lot was sitting in the gateway of the city. When he saw them, he got up to meet them and bowed down with his face to the ground. ²"My lords," he said, "please turn aside to your servant's house. You can wash your feet and spend the night and then go on your way early in the morning."

"No," they answered, "we will spend the night in the square."

³But he insisted so strongly that they did go with him and entered his house. He prepared a meal for them, baking bread without yeast, and they ate. ⁴Before they had gone to bed, all the men from every part of the city of Sodom—both young and old—surrounded the house. ⁵They called to Lot, "Where are the men who came to you tonight? Bring them out to us so that we can have sex with them."

⁶Lot went outside to meet them and shut the door behind him ⁷and said, "No, my friends. Don't do this wicked thing. ⁸Look, I have two daughters who have never slept with a man. Let me bring them out to you, and you can do what you like with them. But don't do anything to these men, for they have come under the protection of my roof."

⁹"Get out of our way," they replied. "This fellow came here as a foreigner, and now he wants to play the judge! We'll treat you worse than them." They kept bringing pressure on Lot and moved forward to break down the door.

¹⁰But the men inside reached out and pulled Lot back into the house and shut the

---

ᵃ 18 Or will use his name in blessings (see Gen. 48:20)   ᵇ 22 Masoretic Text; an ancient Hebrew scribal tradition but the LORD remained standing before Abraham   ᶜ 24 Or forgive; also in verse 26 door. ¹¹Then they struck the men who were at the door of the house, young and old, with blindness so that they could not find the door.

¹²The two men said to Lot, "Do you have anyone else here—sons-in-law, sons or daughters, or anyone else in the city who belongs to you? Get them out of here, ¹³because we are going to destroy this place. The outcry to the LORD against its people is so great that he has sent us to destroy it."

¹⁴So Lot went out and spoke to his sons-in-law, who were pledged to marry^a his daughters. He said, "Hurry and get out of this place, because the LORD is about to destroy the city!" But his sons-in-law thought he was joking.

¹⁵With the coming of dawn, the angels urged Lot, saying, "Hurry! Take your wife and your two daughters who are here, or you will be swept away when the city is punished."

¹⁶When he hesitated, the men grasped his hand and the hands of his wife and of his two daughters and led them safely out of the city, for the LORD was merciful to them. ¹⁷As soon as they had brought them out, one of them said, "Flee for your lives! Don't look back, and don't stop anywhere in the plain! Flee to the mountains or you will be swept away!"

¹⁸But Lot said to them, "No, my lords,^b please! ¹⁹Your^c servant has found favor in your^c eyes, and you^c have shown great kindness to me in sparing my life. But I can't flee to the mountains; this disaster will overtake me, and I'll die. ²⁰Look, here is a town near enough to run to, and it is small. Let me flee to it—it is very small, isn't it? Then my life will be spared."

²¹He said to him, "Very well, I will grant this request too; I will not overthrow the town you speak of. ²²But flee there quickly, because I cannot do anything until you reach it." (That is why the town was called Zoar.^d)

²³By the time Lot reached Zoar, the sun had risen over the land. ²⁴Then the LORD rained down burning sulfur on Sodom and Gomorrah—from the LORD out of the heavens. ²⁵Thus he overthrew those cities and the entire plain, destroying all those living in the cities—and also the vegetation in the land. ²⁶But Lot's wife looked back, and she became a pillar of salt.

²⁷Early the next morning Abraham got up and returned to the place where he had stood before the LORD. ²⁸He looked down toward Sodom and Gomorrah, toward all the land of the plain, and he saw dense smoke rising from the land, like smoke from a furnace.

²⁹So when God destroyed the cities of the plain, he remembered Abraham, and he brought Lot out of the catastrophe that overthrew the cities where Lot had lived.

Lot and His Daughters

³⁰Lot and his two daughters left Zoar and settled in the mountains, for he was afraid to stay in Zoar. He and his two daughters lived in a cave. ³¹One day the older daughter said to the younger, "Our father is old, and there is no man around here to give us children—as is the custom all over the earth. ³²Let's get our father to drink wine and then sleep with him and preserve our family line through our father."

³³That night they got their father to drink wine, and the older daughter went in and slept with him. He was not aware of it when she lay down or when she got up.

³⁴The next day the older daughter said to the younger, "Last night I slept with my father. Let's get him to drink wine again tonight, and you go in and sleep with him so we can preserve our family line through our father." ³⁵So they got their father to drink wine that night also, and the younger daughter went in and slept with him. Again he was not aware of it when she lay down or when she got up.

³⁶So both of Lot's daughters became pregnant by their father. ³⁷The older daughter had a son, and she named him Moab^e; he is the father of the Moabites of today. ³⁸The younger daughter also had a son, and she named him Ben-Ammi^f; he is the father of the Ammonites^g of today.

Abraham and Abimelek

20 Now Abraham moved on from there into the region of the Negev and lived between Kadesh

^a 14 Or were married to ^b 18 Or No, Lord; or No, my lord ^c 19 The Hebrew is singular. ^d 22 Zoar means small. ^e 37 Moab sounds like the Hebrew for from father. ^f 38 Ben-Ammi means son of my father's people. ^g 38 Hebrew Bene-Ammon

and Shur. For a while he stayed in Gerar, ²and there Abraham said of his wife Sarah, "She is my sister." Then Abimelek king of Gerar sent for Sarah and took her.

³But God came to Abimelek in a dream one night and said to him, "You are as good as dead because of the woman you have taken; she is a married woman."

⁴Now Abimelek had not gone near her, so he said, "Lord, will you destroy an innocent nation? ⁵Did he not say to me, 'She is my sister,' and didn't she also say, 'He is my brother'? I have done this with a clear conscience and clean hands."

⁶Then God said to him in the dream, "Yes, I know you did this with a clear conscience, and so I have kept you from sinning against me. That is why I did not let you touch her. ⁷Now return the man's wife, for he is a prophet, and he will pray for you and you will live. But if you do not return her, you may be sure that you and all who belong to you will die."

⁸Early the next morning Abimelek summoned all his officials, and when he told them all that had happened, they were very much afraid. ⁹Then Abimelek called Abraham in and said, "What have you done to us? How have I wronged you that you have brought such great guilt upon me and my kingdom? You have done things to me that should never be done." ¹⁰And Abimelek asked Abraham, "What was your reason for doing this?"

¹¹Abraham replied, "I said to myself, 'There is surely no fear of God in this place, and they will kill me because of my wife.' ¹²Besides, she really is my sister, the daughter of my father though not of my mother; and she became my wife. ¹³And when God had me wander from my father's household, I said to her, 'This is how you can show your love to me: Everywhere we go, say of me, "He is my brother."'"

¹⁴Then Abimelek brought sheep and cattle and male and female slaves and gave them to Abraham, and he returned Sarah his wife to him. ¹⁵And Abimelek said, "My land is before you; live wherever you like."

¹⁶To Sarah he said, "I am giving your brother a thousand shekels ᵃ of silver. This is to cover the offense against you before all

who are with you; you are completely vindicated."

¹⁷Then Abraham prayed to God, and God healed Abimelek, his wife and his female slaves so they could have children again, ¹⁸for the LORD had kept all the women in Abimelek's household from conceiving because of Abraham's wife Sarah.

The Birth of Isaac

21 Now the LORD was gracious to Sarah as he had said, and the LORD did for Sarah what he had promised. ²Sarah became pregnant and bore a son to Abraham in his old age, at the very time God had promised him. ³Abraham gave the name Isaac ᵇ to the son Sarah bore him. ⁴When his son Isaac was eight days old, Abraham circumcised him, as God commanded him. ⁵Abraham was a hundred years old when his son Isaac was born to him.

⁶Sarah said, "God has brought me laughter, and everyone who hears about this will laugh with me." ⁷And she added, "Who would have said to Abraham that Sarah would nurse children? Yet I have borne him a son in his old age."

Hagar and Ishmael Sent Away

⁸The child grew and was weaned, and on the day Isaac was weaned Abraham held a great feast. ⁹But Sarah saw that the son whom Hagar the Egyptian had borne to Abraham was mocking, ¹⁰and she said to Abraham, "Get rid of that slave woman and her son, for that slave woman's son will never share in the inheritance with my son Isaac."

¹¹The matter distressed Abraham greatly because it concerned his son. ¹²But God said to him, "Do not be so distressed about the boy and your servant. Listen to whatever Sarah tells you, because it is through Isaac that your offspring ᶜ will be reckoned. ¹³I will make the son of the servant into a nation also, because he is your offspring."

¹⁴Early the next morning Abraham took some food and a skin of water and gave them to Hagar. He set them on her shoulders and then sent her off with the boy. She went on her way and wandered in the Desert of Beersheba.

ᵃ 16 That is, about 25 pounds or about 11.5 kilograms   ᵇ 3 *Isaac* means *he laughs.*   ᶜ 12 Or *seed*

TUESDAY

BE REAL

Genesis 20:1–18 *or* 20:8–13

Adrian Plass

Most of us, whether we like it or not, are works in progress. God certainly knows that. We know it, if we're honest. What point is there in trying to persuade others or ourselves that this is not the case? Folks will always see through religious or moral posing in the end. People have quite often seen through some nonsense of mine. I wonder how many of God's lost and beloved children have turned disappointedly away from the idea of following Jesus because of the hypocrisy they detected in Christians, people who managed to impress them greatly on a personal level in the initial stages of their relationship and subsequently simply couldn't keep it up.

FYODOR DOSTOYEVSKY {AD 1821–1881}

The important thing is to stop lying to yourself. A man who lies to himself, and believes his own lies, becomes unable to recognize truth, either in himself or in anyone else, and he ends up losing respect for himself as well as for others. When he has no respect for anyone, he can no longer love and, in order to divert himself, having no love in him he yields to his impulses, indulges in the lowest forms of pleasure, and behaves in the end like an animal, in satisfying his vices. And it all comes from lying—lying to others and to yourself.

reflection

1. Why did Abraham choose to trust in his own power to deceive rather than in God's power to protect?

2. What did God do to protect Abraham, Sarah and Abimelek from the consequences of Abraham's deception?

3. Have you ever been caught in a lie like Abraham was? What was the result in your own life and in those who witnessed it?

For your next devotional reading, go to page 36.

¹⁵When the water in the skin was gone, she put the boy under one of the bushes. ¹⁶Then she went off and sat down about a bowshot away, for she thought, "I cannot watch the boy die." And as she sat there, sheᵃ began to sob.

¹⁷God heard the boy crying, and the angel of God called to Hagar from heaven and said to her, "What is the matter, Hagar? Do not be afraid; God has heard the boy crying as he lies there. ¹⁸Lift the boy up and take him by the hand, for I will make him into a great nation."

¹⁹Then God opened her eyes and she saw a well of water. So she went and filled the skin with water and gave the boy a drink.

²⁰God was with the boy as he grew up. He lived in the desert and became an archer. ²¹While he was living in the Desert of Paran, his mother got a wife for him from Egypt.

The Treaty at Beersheba

²²At that time Abimelek and Phicol the commander of his forces said to Abraham, "God is with you in everything you do. ²³Now swear to me here before God that you will not deal falsely with me or my children or my descendants. Show to me and the country where you now reside as a foreigner the same kindness I have shown to you."

²⁴Abraham said, "I swear it."

²⁵Then Abraham complained to Abimelek about a well of water that Abimelek's servants had seized. ²⁶But Abimelek said, "I don't know who has done this. You did not tell me, and I heard about it only today."

²⁷So Abraham brought sheep and cattle and gave them to Abimelek, and the two men made a treaty. ²⁸Abraham set apart seven ewe lambs from the flock, ²⁹and Abimelek asked Abraham, "What is the meaning of these seven ewe lambs you have set apart by themselves?"

³⁰He replied, "Accept these seven lambs from my hand as a witness that I dug this well."

³¹So that place was called Beersheba,ᵇ because the two men swore an oath there.

³²After the treaty had been made at Beersheba, Abimelek and Phicol the commander of his forces returned to the land of the Philistines. ³³Abraham planted a tamarisk tree in Beersheba, and there he called on the name of the LORD, the Eternal God. ³⁴And Abraham stayed in the land of the Philistines for a long time.

Abraham Tested

22 Some time later God tested Abraham. He said to him, "Abraham!"

"Here I am," he replied.

²Then God said, "Take your son, your only son, whom you love—Isaac—and go to the region of Moriah. Sacrifice him there as a burnt offering on a mountain I will show you."

³Early the next morning Abraham got up and loaded his donkey. He took with him two of his servants and his son Isaac. When he had cut enough wood for the burnt offering, he set out for the place God had told him about. ⁴On the third day Abraham looked up and saw the place in the distance. ⁵He said to his servants, "Stay here with the donkey while I and the boy go over there. We will worship and then we will come back to you."

⁶Abraham took the wood for the burnt offering and placed it on his son Isaac, and he himself carried the fire and the knife. As the two of them went on together, ⁷Isaac spoke up and said to his father Abraham, "Father?"

"Yes, my son?" Abraham replied.

"The fire and wood are here," Isaac said, "but where is the lamb for the burnt offering?"

⁸Abraham answered, "God himself will provide the lamb for the burnt offering, my son." And the two of them went on together.

⁹When they reached the place God had told him about, Abraham built an altar there and arranged the wood on it. He bound his son Isaac and laid him on the altar, on top of the wood. ¹⁰Then he reached out his hand and took the knife to slay his son. ¹¹But the angel of the LORD called out to him from heaven, "Abraham! Abraham!"

"Here I am," he replied.

¹²"Do not lay a hand on the boy," he said. "Do not do anything to him. Now I know that you fear God, because you have not withheld from me your son, your only son."

¹³Abraham looked up and there in a thicket he saw a ramᶜ caught by its horns. He

---

ᵃ 16 Hebrew; Septuagint *the child*   ᵇ 31 *Beersheba* can mean *well of seven* and *well of the oath*.
ᶜ 13 Many manuscripts of the Masoretic Text, Samaritan Pentateuch, Septuagint and Syriac; most manuscripts of the Masoretic Text *a ram behind him*

went over and took the ram and sacrificed it as a burnt offering instead of his son. ¹⁴So Abraham called that place The LORD Will Provide. And to this day it is said, "On the mountain of the LORD it will be provided."

¹⁵The angel of the LORD called to Abraham from heaven a second time ¹⁶and said, "I swear by myself, declares the LORD, that because you have done this and have not withheld your son, your only son, ¹⁷I will surely bless you and make your descendants as numerous as the stars in the sky and as the sand on the seashore. Your descendants will take possession of the cities of their enemies, ¹⁸and through your offspringᵃ all nations on earth will be blessed,ᵇ because you have obeyed me."

¹⁹Then Abraham returned to his servants, and they set off together for Beersheba. And Abraham stayed in Beersheba.

Nahor's Sons

²⁰Some time later Abraham was told, "Milkah is also a mother; she has borne sons to your brother Nahor: ²¹Uz the firstborn, Buz his brother, Kemuel (the father of Aram), ²²Kesed, Hazo, Pildash, Jidlaph and Bethuel." ²³Bethuel became the father of Rebekah. Milkah bore these eight sons to Abraham's brother Nahor. ²⁴His concubine, whose name was Reumah, also had sons: Tebah, Gaham, Tahash and Maakah.

The Death of Sarah

23 Sarah lived to be a hundred and twenty-seven years old. ²She died at Kiriath Arba (that is, Hebron) in the land of Canaan, and Abraham went to mourn for Sarah and to weep over her.

³Then Abraham rose from beside his dead wife and spoke to the Hittites.ᶜ He said, ⁴"I am a foreigner and stranger among you. Sell me some property for a burial site here so I can bury my dead."

⁵The Hittites replied to Abraham, ⁶"Sir, listen to us. You are a mighty prince among us. Bury your dead in the choicest of our tombs. None of us will refuse you his tomb for burying your dead."

⁷Then Abraham rose and bowed down before the people of the land, the Hittites.

⁸He said to them, "If you are willing to let me bury my dead, then listen to me and intercede with Ephron son of Zohar on my behalf ⁹so he will sell me the cave of Machpelah, which belongs to him and is at the end of his field. Ask him to sell it to me for the full price as a burial site among you."

¹⁰Ephron the Hittite was sitting among his people and he replied to Abraham in the hearing of all the Hittites who had come to the gate of his city. ¹¹"No, my lord," he said. "Listen to me; I giveᵈ you the field, and I giveᵈ you the cave that is in it. I giveᵈ it to you in the presence of my people. Bury your dead."

¹²Again Abraham bowed down before the people of the land ¹³and he said to Ephron in their hearing, "Listen to me, if you will. I will pay the price of the field. Accept it from me so I can bury my dead there."

¹⁴Ephron answered Abraham, ¹⁵"Listen to me, my lord; the land is worth four hundred shekelsᵉ of silver, but what is that between me and you? Bury your dead."

¹⁶Abraham agreed to Ephron's terms and weighed out for him the price he had named in the hearing of the Hittites: four hundred shekels of silver, according to the weight current among the merchants.

¹⁷So Ephron's field in Machpelah near Mamre—both the field and the cave in it, and all the trees within the borders of the field—was deeded ¹⁸to Abraham as his property in the presence of all the Hittites who had come to the gate of the city. ¹⁹Afterward Abraham buried his wife Sarah in the cave in the field of Machpelah near Mamre (which is at Hebron) in the land of Canaan. ²⁰So the field and the cave in it were deeded to Abraham by the Hittites as a burial site.

Isaac and Rebekah

24 Abraham was now very old, and the LORD had blessed him in every way. ²He said to the senior servant in his household, the one in charge of all that he had, "Put your hand under my thigh. ³I want you to swear by the LORD, the God of heaven and the God of earth, that you will not get a wife for my son from the daughters of the Canaanites, among whom I am living, ⁴but will go to my country and my

---

ᵃ 18 Or seed   ᵇ 18 Or and all nations on earth will use the name of your offspring in blessings (see Gen. 48:20)   ᶜ 3 Or the descendants of Heth; also in verses 5, 7, 10, 16, 18 and 20   ᵈ 11 Or sell
ᵉ 15 That is, about 10 pounds or about 4.6 kilograms

own relatives and get a wife for my son Isaac."

⁵The servant asked him, "What if the woman is unwilling to come back with me to this land? Shall I then take your son back to the country you came from?"

⁶"Make sure that you do not take my son back there," Abraham said. ⁷"The LORD, the God of heaven, who brought me out of my father's household and my native land and who spoke to me and promised me on oath, saying, 'To your offspring*a* I will give this land'—he will send his angel before you so that you can get a wife for my son from there. ⁸If the woman is unwilling to come back with you, then you will be released from this oath of mine. Only do not take my son back there." ⁹So the servant put his hand under the thigh of his master Abraham and swore an oath to him concerning this matter.

¹⁰Then the servant left, taking with him ten of his master's camels loaded with all kinds of good things from his master. He set out for Aram Naharaim*b* and made his way to the town of Nahor. ¹¹He had the camels kneel down near the well outside the town; it was toward evening, the time the women go out to draw water.

¹²Then he prayed, "LORD, God of my master Abraham, make me successful today, and show kindness to my master Abraham. ¹³See, I am standing beside this spring, and the daughters of the townspeople are coming out to draw water. ¹⁴May it be that when I say to a girl, 'Please let down your jar that I may have a drink,' and she says, 'Drink, and I'll water your camels too'—let her be the one you have chosen for your servant Isaac. By this I will know that you have shown kindness to my master."

¹⁵Before he had finished praying, Rebekah came out with her jar on her shoulder. She was the daughter of Bethuel son of Milkah, who was the wife of Abraham's brother Nahor. ¹⁶The girl was very beautiful, a virgin; no man had ever slept with her. She went down to the spring, filled her jar and came up again.

¹⁷The servant hurried to meet her and said, "Please give me a little water from your jar."

¹⁸"Drink, my lord," she said, and quickly lowered the jar to her hands and gave him a drink.

¹⁹After she had given him a drink, she said, "I'll draw water for your camels too, until they have had enough to drink." ²⁰So she quickly emptied her jar into the trough, ran back to the well to draw more water, and drew enough for all his camels. ²¹Without saying a word, the man watched her closely to learn whether or not the LORD had made his journey successful.

²²When the camels had finished drinking, the man took out a gold nose ring weighing a beka*c* and two gold bracelets weighing ten shekels.*d* ²³Then he asked, "Whose daughter are you? Please tell me, is there room in your father's house for us to spend the night?"

²⁴She answered him, "I am the daughter of Bethuel, the son that Milkah bore to Nahor." ²⁵And she added, "We have plenty of straw and fodder, as well as room for you to spend the night."

²⁶Then the man bowed down and worshiped the LORD, ²⁷saying, "Praise be to the LORD, the God of my master Abraham, who has not abandoned his kindness and faithfulness to my master. As for me, the LORD has led me on the journey to the house of my master's relatives."

²⁸The girl ran and told her mother's household about these things. ²⁹Now Rebekah had a brother named Laban, and he hurried out to the man at the spring. ³⁰As soon as he had seen the nose ring, and the bracelets on his sister's arms, and had heard Rebekah tell what the man said to her, he went out to the man and found him standing by the camels near the spring. ³¹"Come, you who are blessed by the LORD," he said. "Why are you standing out here? I have prepared the house and a place for the camels."

³²So the man went to the house, and the camels were unloaded. Straw and fodder were brought for the camels, and water for him and his men to wash their feet. ³³Then food was set before him, but he said, "I will not eat until I have told you what I have to say."

"Then tell us," Laban said.

³⁴So he said, "I am Abraham's servant.

---

a 7 Or *seed*   *b 10* That is, Northwest Mesopotamia   *c 22* That is, about 1/5 ounce or about 5.7 grams
d 22 That is, about 4 ounces or about 115 grams

³⁵The LORD has blessed my master abundantly, and he has become wealthy. He has given him sheep and cattle, silver and gold, male and female servants, and camels and donkeys. ³⁶My master's wife Sarah has borne him a son in her old age, and he has given him everything he owns. ³⁷And my master made me swear an oath, and said, 'You must not get a wife for my son from the daughters of the Canaanites, in whose land I live, ³⁸but go to my father's family and to my own clan, and get a wife for my son.'

³⁹"Then I asked my master, 'What if the woman will not come back with me?'

⁴⁰"He replied, 'The LORD, before whom I have walked faithfully, will send his angel with you and make your journey a success, so that you can get a wife for my son from my own clan and from my father's family. ⁴¹Then, when you go to my clan, you will be released from my oath even if they refuse to give her to you—you will be released from my oath.'

⁴²"When I came to the spring today, I said, 'LORD, God of my master Abraham, if you will, please grant success to the journey on which I have come. ⁴³See, I am standing beside this spring. If a young woman comes out to draw water and I say to her, "Please let me drink a little water from your jar," ⁴⁴and if she says to me, "Drink, and I'll draw water for your camels too," let her be the one the LORD has chosen for my master's son.'

⁴⁵"Before I finished praying in my heart, Rebekah came out, with her jar on her shoulder. She went down to the spring and drew water, and I said to her, 'Please give me a drink.'

⁴⁶"She quickly lowered her jar from her shoulder and said, 'Drink, and I'll water your camels too.' So I drank, and she watered the camels also.

⁴⁷"I asked her, 'Whose daughter are you?'

"She said, 'The daughter of Bethuel son of Nahor, whom Milkah bore to him.'

"Then I put the ring in her nose and the bracelets on her arms, ⁴⁸and I bowed down and worshiped the LORD. I praised the LORD, the God of my master Abraham, who had led me on the right road to get the granddaughter of my master's brother for his son. ⁴⁹Now if you will show kindness and faithfulness to

my master, tell me; and if not, tell me, so I may know which way to turn."

⁵⁰Laban and Bethuel answered, "This is from the LORD; we can say nothing to you one way or the other. ⁵¹Here is Rebekah; take her and go, and let her become the wife of your master's son, as the LORD has directed."

⁵²When Abraham's servant heard what they said, he bowed down to the ground before the LORD. ⁵³Then the servant brought out gold and silver jewelry and articles of clothing and gave them to Rebekah; he also gave costly gifts to her brother and to her mother. ⁵⁴Then he and the men who were with him ate and drank and spent the night there.

When they got up the next morning, he said, "Send me on my way to my master."

⁵⁵But her brother and her mother replied, "Let the girl remain with us ten days or so; then youᵃ may go."

⁵⁶But he said to them, "Do not detain me, now that the LORD has granted success to my journey. Send me on my way so I may go to my master."

⁵⁷Then they said, "Let's call the girl and ask her about it." ⁵⁸So they called Rebekah and asked her, "Will you go with this man?"

"I will go," she said.

⁵⁹So they sent their sister Rebekah on her way, along with her nurse and Abraham's servant and his men. ⁶⁰And they blessed Rebekah and said to her,

"Our sister, may you increase
    to thousands upon thousands;
may your offspring possess
    the cities of their enemies."

⁶¹Then Rebekah and her attendants got ready and mounted their camels and went back with the man. So the servant took Rebekah and left.

⁶²Now Isaac had come from Beer Lahai Roi, for he was living in the Negev. ⁶³He went out to the field one evening to meditate,ᵇ and as he looked up, he saw camels approaching. ⁶⁴Rebekah also looked up and saw Isaac. She got down from her camel ⁶⁵and asked the servant, "Who is that man in the field coming to meet us?"

"He is my master," the servant answered. So she took her veil and covered herself.

ᵃ 55 Or she   ᵇ 63 The meaning of the Hebrew for this word is uncertain.

⁶⁶Then the servant told Isaac all he had done. ⁶⁷Isaac brought her into the tent of his mother Sarah, and he married Rebekah. So she became his wife, and he loved her; and Isaac was comforted after his mother's death.

The Death of Abraham

25 Abraham had taken another wife, whose name was Keturah. ²She bore him Zimran, Jokshan, Medan, Midian, Ishbak and Shuah. ³Jokshan was the father of Sheba and Dedan; the descendants of Dedan were the Ashurites, the Letushites and the Leummites. ⁴The sons of Midian were Ephah, Epher, Hanok, Abida and Eldaah. All these were descendants of Keturah.

⁵Abraham left everything he owned to Isaac. ⁶But while he was still living, he gave gifts to the sons of his concubines and sent them away from his son Isaac to the land of the east.

⁷Abraham lived a hundred and seventy-five years. ⁸Then Abraham breathed his last and died at a good old age, an old man and full of years; and he was gathered to his people. ⁹His sons Isaac and Ishmael buried him in the cave of Machpelah near Mamre, in the field of Ephron son of Zohar the Hittite, ¹⁰the field Abraham had bought from the Hittites.ᵃ There Abraham was buried with his wife Sarah. ¹¹After Abraham's death, God blessed his son Isaac, who then lived near Beer Lahai Roi.

Ishmael's Sons

¹²This is the account of the family line of Abraham's son Ishmael, whom Sarah's servant, Hagar the Egyptian, bore to Abraham.

¹³These are the names of the sons of Ishmael, listed in the order of their birth: Nebaioth the firstborn of Ishmael, Kedar, Adbeel, Mibsam, ¹⁴Mishma, Dumah, Massa, ¹⁵Hadad, Tema, Jetur, Naphish and Kedemah. ¹⁶These were the sons of Ishmael, and these are the names of the twelve tribal rulers according to their settlements and camps. ¹⁷Ishmael lived a hundred and thirty-seven years. He breathed his last and died, and he was gathered to his people. ¹⁸His descendants settled in the area from Havilah to Shur, near the eastern border of Egypt, as you go toward Ashur. And they lived in hostility towardᵇ all the tribes related to them.

Jacob and Esau

¹⁹This is the account of the family line of Abraham's son Isaac.

Abraham became the father of Isaac, ²⁰and Isaac was forty years old when he married Rebekah daughter of Bethuel the Aramean from Paddan Aramᶜ and sister of Laban the Aramean.

²¹Isaac prayed to the LORD on behalf of his wife, because she was childless. The LORD answered his prayer, and his wife Rebekah became pregnant. ²²The babies jostled each other within her, and she said, "Why is this happening to me?" So she went to inquire of the LORD.

²³The LORD said to her,

"Two nations are in your womb,
  and two peoples from within you will
    be separated;
one people will be stronger than the
    other,
  and the older will serve the younger."

²⁴When the time came for her to give birth, there were twin boys in her womb. ²⁵The first to come out was red, and his whole body was like a hairy garment; so they named him Esau.ᵈ ²⁶After this, his brother came out, with his hand grasping Esau's heel; so he was named Jacob.ᵉ Isaac was sixty years old when Rebekah gave birth to them.

²⁷The boys grew up, and Esau became a skillful hunter, a man of the open country, while Jacob was content to stay at home among the tents. ²⁸Isaac, who had a taste for wild game, loved Esau, but Rebekah loved Jacob.

²⁹Once when Jacob was cooking some stew, Esau came in from the open country, famished. ³⁰He said to Jacob, "Quick, let me have some of that red stew! I'm famished!" (That is why he was also called Edom.ᶠ)

³¹Jacob replied, "First sell me your birthright."

ᵃ 10 Or *the descendants of Heth*   ᵇ 18 Or *lived to the east of*   ᶜ 20 That is, Northwest Mesopotamia
ᵈ 25 *Esau* may mean *hairy*.   ᵉ 26 *Jacob* means *he grasps the heel*, a Hebrew idiom for *he deceives*.
ᶠ 30 *Edom* means *red*.

³²"Look, I am about to die," Esau said. "What good is the birthright to me?"

³³But Jacob said, "Swear to me first." So he swore an oath to him, selling his birthright to Jacob.

³⁴Then Jacob gave Esau some bread and some lentil stew. He ate and drank, and then got up and left.

So Esau despised his birthright.

Isaac and Abimelek

26 Now there was a famine in the land—besides the previous famine in Abraham's time—and Isaac went to Abimelek king of the Philistines in Gerar. ²The LORD appeared to Isaac and said, "Do not go down to Egypt; live in the land where I tell you to live. ³Stay in this land for a while, and I will be with you and will bless you. For to you and your descendants I will give all these lands and will confirm the oath I swore to your father Abraham. ⁴I will make your descendants as numerous as the stars in the sky and will give them all these lands, and through your offspring[a] all nations on earth will be blessed,[b] ⁵because Abraham obeyed me and did everything I required of him, keeping my commands, my decrees and my instructions." ⁶So Isaac stayed in Gerar.

⁷When the men of that place asked him about his wife, he said, "She is my sister," because he was afraid to say, "She is my wife." He thought, "The men of this place might kill me on account of Rebekah, because she is beautiful."

⁸When Isaac had been there a long time, Abimelek king of the Philistines looked down from a window and saw Isaac caressing his wife Rebekah. ⁹So Abimelek summoned Isaac and said, "She is really your wife! Why did you say, 'She is my sister'?"

Isaac answered him, "Because I thought I might lose my life on account of her."

¹⁰Then Abimelek said, "What is this you have done to us? One of the men might well have slept with your wife, and you would have brought guilt upon us."

¹¹So Abimelek gave orders to all the people: "Anyone who harms this man or his wife shall surely be put to death."

¹²Isaac planted crops in that land and the same year reaped a hundredfold, because the LORD blessed him. ¹³The man became rich, and his wealth continued to grow until he became very wealthy. ¹⁴He had so many flocks and herds and servants that the Philistines envied him. ¹⁵So all the wells that his father's servants had dug in the time of his father Abraham, the Philistines stopped up, filling them with earth.

¹⁶Then Abimelek said to Isaac, "Move away from us; you have become too powerful for us."

¹⁷So Isaac moved away from there and encamped in the Valley of Gerar, where he settled. ¹⁸Isaac reopened the wells that had been dug in the time of his father Abraham, which the Philistines had stopped up after Abraham died, and he gave them the same names his father had given them.

¹⁹Isaac's servants dug in the valley and discovered a well of fresh water there. ²⁰But the herders of Gerar quarreled with those of Isaac and said, "The water is ours!" So he named the well Esek,[c] because they disputed with him. ²¹Then they dug another well, but they quarreled over that one also; so he named it Sitnah.[d] ²²He moved on from there and dug another well, and no one quarreled over it. He named it Rehoboth,[e] saying, "Now the LORD has given us room and we will flourish in the land."

²³From there he went up to Beersheba. ²⁴That night the LORD appeared to him and said, "I am the God of your father Abraham. Do not be afraid, for I am with you; I will bless you and will increase the number of your descendants for the sake of my servant Abraham."

²⁵Isaac built an altar there and called on the name of the LORD. There he pitched his tent, and there his servants dug a well.

²⁶Meanwhile, Abimelek had come to him from Gerar, with Ahuzzath his personal adviser and Phicol the commander of his forces. ²⁷Isaac asked them, "Why have you come to me, since you were hostile to me and sent me away?"

²⁸They answered, "We saw clearly that the LORD was with you; so we said, 'There ought to be a sworn agreement between us'—between us and you. Let us make a treaty with you ²⁹that you will do us no

---

a 4 Or *seed*   *b 4* Or *and all nations on earth will use the name of your offspring in blessings* (see Gen. 48:20)   *c 20* *Esek* means *dispute.*   *d 21* *Sitnah* means *opposition.*   *e 22* *Rehoboth* means *room.*

harm, just as we did not harm you but always treated you well and sent you away peacefully. And now you are blessed by the LORD."

³⁰Isaac then made a feast for them, and they ate and drank. ³¹Early the next morning the men swore an oath to each other. Then Isaac sent them on their way, and they went away peacefully.

³²That day Isaac's servants came and told him about the well they had dug. They said, "We've found water!" ³³He called it Shibah,ᵃ and to this day the name of the town has been Beersheba.ᵇ

Jacob Takes Esau's Blessing

³⁴When Esau was forty years old, he married Judith daughter of Beeri the Hittite, and also Basemath daughter of Elon the Hittite. ³⁵They were a source of grief to Isaac and Rebekah.

27 When Isaac was old and his eyes were so weak that he could no longer see, he called for Esau his older son and said to him, "My son."

"Here I am," he answered.

²Isaac said, "I am now an old man and don't know the day of my death. ³Now then, get your equipment—your quiver and bow—and go out to the open country to hunt some wild game for me. ⁴Prepare me the kind of tasty food I like and bring it to me to eat, so that I may give you my blessing before I die."

⁵Now Rebekah was listening as Isaac spoke to his son Esau. When Esau left for the open country to hunt game and bring it back, ⁶Rebekah said to her son Jacob, "Look, I overheard your father say to your brother Esau, ⁷'Bring me some game and prepare me some tasty food to eat, so that I may give you my blessing in the presence of the LORD before I die.' ⁸Now, my son, listen carefully and do what I tell you: ⁹Go out to the flock and bring me two choice young goats, so I can prepare some tasty food for your father, just the way he likes it. ¹⁰Then take it to your father to eat, so that he may give you his blessing before he dies."

¹¹Jacob said to Rebekah his mother, "But my brother Esau is a hairy man while I have smooth skin. ¹²What if my father touches me? I would appear to be tricking him and

would bring down a curse on myself rather than a blessing."

¹³His mother said to him, "My son, let the curse fall on me. Just do what I say; go and get them for me."

¹⁴So he went and got them and brought them to his mother, and she prepared some tasty food, just the way his father liked it. ¹⁵Then Rebekah took the best clothes of Esau her older son, which she had in the house, and put them on her younger son Jacob. ¹⁶She also covered his hands and the smooth part of his neck with the goatskins. ¹⁷Then she handed to her son Jacob the tasty food and the bread she had made.

¹⁸He went to his father and said, "My father."

"Yes, my son," he answered. "Who is it?"

¹⁹Jacob said to his father, "I am Esau your firstborn. I have done as you told me. Please sit up and eat some of my game, so that you may give me your blessing."

²⁰Isaac asked his son, "How did you find it so quickly, my son?"

"The LORD your God gave me success," he replied.

²¹Then Isaac said to Jacob, "Come near so I can touch you, my son, to know whether you really are my son Esau or not."

²²Jacob went close to his father Isaac, who touched him and said, "The voice is the voice of Jacob, but the hands are the hands of Esau." ²³He did not recognize him, for his hands were hairy like those of his brother Esau; so he proceeded to bless him. ²⁴"Are you really my son Esau?" he asked.

"I am," he replied.

²⁵Then he said, "My son, bring me some of your game to eat, so that I may give you my blessing."

Jacob brought it to him and he ate; and he brought some wine and he drank. ²⁶Then his father Isaac said to him, "Come here, my son, and kiss me."

²⁷So he went to him and kissed him. When Isaac caught the smell of his clothes, he blessed him and said,

"Ah, the smell of my son
    is like the smell of a field
    that the LORD has blessed.
²⁸May God give you of heaven's dew
    and of earth's richness—
    an abundance of grain and new wine.

[29] May nations serve you
and peoples bow down to you.
Be lord over your brothers,
and may the sons of your mother bow
down to you.
May those who curse you be cursed
and those who bless you be blessed."

[30]After Isaac finished blessing him, and Jacob had scarcely left his father's presence, his brother Esau came in from hunting. [31]He too prepared some tasty food and brought it to his father. Then he said to him, "My father, please sit up and eat some of my game, so that you may give me your blessing."

[32]His father Isaac asked him, "Who are you?"

"I am your son," he answered, "your firstborn, Esau."

[33]Isaac trembled violently and said, "Who was it, then, that hunted game and brought it to me? I ate it just before you came and I blessed him—and indeed he will be blessed!"

[34]When Esau heard his father's words, he burst out with a loud and bitter cry and said to his father, "Bless me—me too, my father!"

[35]But he said, "Your brother came deceitfully and took your blessing."

[36]Esau said, "Isn't he rightly named Jacob[a]? This is the second time he has taken advantage of me: He took my birthright, and now he's taken my blessing!" Then he asked, "Haven't you reserved any blessing for me?"

[37]Isaac answered Esau, "I have made him lord over you and have made all his relatives his servants, and I have sustained him with grain and new wine. So what can I possibly do for you, my son?"

[38]Esau said to his father, "Do you have only one blessing, my father? Bless me too, my father!" Then Esau wept aloud.

[39]His father Isaac answered him,

"Your dwelling will be
away from the earth's richness,
away from the dew of heaven above.
[40] You will live by the sword
and you will serve your brother.
But when you grow restless,
you will throw his yoke
from off your neck."

[41]Esau held a grudge against Jacob because of the blessing his father had given him. He said to himself, "The days of mourning for my father are near; then I will kill my brother Jacob."

[42]When Rebekah was told what her older son Esau had said, she sent for her younger son Jacob and said to him, "Your brother Esau is planning to avenge himself by killing you. [43]Now then, my son, do what I say: Flee at once to my brother Laban in Harran. [44]Stay with him for a while until your brother's fury subsides. [45]When your brother is no longer angry with you and forgets what you did to him, I'll send word for you to come back from there. Why should I lose both of you in one day?"

[46]Then Rebekah said to Isaac, "I'm disgusted with living because of these Hittite women. If Jacob takes a wife from among the women of this land, from Hittite women like these, my life will not be worth living."

28

So Isaac called for Jacob and blessed him. Then he commanded him: "Do not marry a Canaanite woman. [2]Go at once to Paddan Aram,[b] to the house of your mother's father Bethuel. Take a wife for yourself there, from among the daughters of Laban, your mother's brother. [3]May God Almighty[c] bless you and make you fruitful and increase your numbers until you become a community of peoples. [4]May he give you and your descendants the blessing given to Abraham, so that you may take possession of the land where you now reside as a foreigner, the land God gave to Abraham." [5]Then Isaac sent Jacob on his way, and he went to Paddan Aram, to Laban son of Bethuel the Aramean, the brother of Rebekah, who was the mother of Jacob and Esau.

[6]Now Esau learned that Isaac had blessed Jacob and had sent him to Paddan Aram to take a wife from there, and that when he blessed him he commanded him, "Do not marry a Canaanite woman," [7]and that Jacob had obeyed his father and mother and had gone to Paddan Aram. [8]Esau then realized how displeasing the Canaanite women were to his father Isaac; [9]so he went to Ishmael and married Mahalath, the sister of Nebaioth and daughter of Ishmael son of Abra-

---

a 36 Jacob means he grasps the heel, a Hebrew idiom for he takes advantage of or he deceives.   b 2 That is, Northwest Mesopotamia; also in verses 5, 6 and 7   c 3 Hebrew El-Shaddai

WEDNESDAY

RIGHT GOAL—WRONG WAY

Genesis 27:1–45 *or* 27:32–37

HERBERT C. LEUPOLD {AD 1892–1972}

Jacob was really a spiritually minded man with an appreciation of spiritual values. He had distinct spiritual ambitions, especially in the matter of continuing the line of promise from which the Savior would come. His aspirations were not his own idea; they were birthed by the divine word of promise. The Lord had destined Jacob to this place of honor. Jacob gladly accepted the choice and aspired to reach the promised treasure. His eagerness was commendable. His choice of means in arriving at the desired end was not always as commendable. He felt he had to help the good Lord along occasionally. He was not fully confident of God's methods for arriving at the goal. Thus, he felt the need to occasionally insert a bit of assistance of his own. Such an attitude was one of mistrust. Jacob had confidence in human ingenuity rather than in divine dependability, an attitude described in one word—unbelief.

Marva J. Dawn

When we can rest enough to trust with our times the One who is trustable, then we don't have to ask the "how long?" questions. We will be able to see that however long God allows certain processes to continue is partly the gift of his perfect wisdom . . .

We are all challenged by the need to grow in our ability to trust. We will sometimes fail to depend on God, because we will always be human—yet in those times the character of YHWH is all the more precious to us, because we perpetually learn afresh that he is a forgiving and affirming God, our Comforter. Just when we trust him least, he is the most trustable, continuing to love us with perfect mercy. Therefore, we are set free to go on, feebly trusting, but learning to trust him more.

reflection

1. In what scenarios are you most likely to ask God, "How long"?

2. When have you been guilty of taking matters into your own hands?

3. Have you found that those times drew you closer to God or did they overwhelm you so much that you forget about him?

For your next devotional reading, go to page 43.

ham, in addition to the wives he already had.

Jacob's Dream at Bethel

¹⁰Jacob left Beersheba and set out for Harran. ¹¹When he reached a certain place, he stopped for the night because the sun had set. Taking one of the stones there, he put it under his head and lay down to sleep. ¹²He had a dream in which he saw a stairway*a* resting on the earth, with its top reaching to heaven, and the angels of God were ascending and descending on it. ¹³There above it*b* stood the LORD, and he said: "I am the LORD, the God of your father Abraham and the God of Isaac. I will give you and your descendants the land on which you are lying. ¹⁴Your descendants will be like the dust of the earth, and you will spread out to the west and to the east, to the north and to the south. All peoples on earth will be blessed through you and your offspring.*c* ¹⁵I am with you and will watch over you wherever you go, and I will bring you back to this land. I will not leave you until I have done what I have promised you."

¹⁶When Jacob awoke from his sleep, he thought, "Surely the LORD is in this place, and I was not aware of it." ¹⁷He was afraid and said, "How awesome is this place! This is none other than the house of God; this is the gate of heaven."

¹⁸Early the next morning Jacob took the stone he had placed under his head and set it up as a pillar and poured oil on top of it. ¹⁹He called that place Bethel,*d* though the city used to be called Luz.

²⁰Then Jacob made a vow, saying, "If God will be with me and will watch over me on this journey I am taking and will give me food to eat and clothes to wear ²¹so that I return safely to my father's household, then the LORD*e* will be my God ²²and*f* this stone that I have set up as a pillar will be God's house, and of all that you give me I will give you a tenth."

Jacob Arrives in Paddan Aram

29 Then Jacob continued on his journey and came to the land of the eastern peoples. ²There he saw a well in the open country, with three

flocks of sheep lying near it because the flocks were watered from that well. The stone over the mouth of the well was large. ³When all the flocks were gathered there, the shepherds would roll the stone away from the well's mouth and water the sheep. Then they would return the stone to its place over the mouth of the well.

⁴Jacob asked the shepherds, "My brothers, where are you from?"

"We're from Harran," they replied.

⁵He said to them, "Do you know Laban, Nahor's grandson?"

"Yes, we know him," they answered.

⁶Then Jacob asked them, "Is he well?"

"Yes, he is," they said, "and here comes his daughter Rachel with the sheep."

⁷"Look," he said, "the sun is still high; it is not time for the flocks to be gathered. Water the sheep and take them back to pasture."

⁸"We can't," they replied, "until all the flocks are gathered and the stone has been rolled away from the mouth of the well. Then we will water the sheep."

⁹While he was still talking with them, Rachel came with her father's sheep, for she was their shepherd. ¹⁰When Jacob saw Rachel daughter of Laban, his mother's brother, and Laban's sheep, he went over and rolled the stone away from the mouth of the well and watered his uncle's sheep. ¹¹Then Jacob kissed Rachel and began to weep aloud. ¹²He had told Rachel that he was a relative of her father and a son of Rebekah. So she ran and told her father.

¹³As soon as Laban heard the news about Jacob, his sister's son, he hurried to meet him. He embraced him and kissed him and brought him to his home, and there Jacob told him all these things. ¹⁴Then Laban said to him, "You are my own flesh and blood."

Jacob Marries Leah and Rachel

After Jacob had stayed with him for a whole month, ¹⁵Laban said to him, "Just because you are a relative of mine, should you work for me for nothing? Tell me what your wages should be."

¹⁶Now Laban had two daughters; the name of the older was Leah, and the name of the younger was Rachel. ¹⁷Leah had

---

a 12 Or *ladder*   *b 13* Or *There beside him*   *c 14* Or *will use your name and the name of your offspring in blessings* (see Gen. 48:20)   *d 19* Bethel *means* house of God.   *e 20,21* Or *Since God . . . father's household, the* LORD   *f 21,22* Or *household, and the* LORD *will be my God,* ²²then weak^a eyes, but Rachel had a lovely figure and was beautiful. ¹⁸Jacob was in love with Rachel and said, "I'll work for you seven years in return for your younger daughter Rachel."

¹⁹Laban said, "It's better that I give her to you than to some other man. Stay here with me." ²⁰So Jacob served seven years to get Rachel, but they seemed like only a few days to him because of his love for her.

²¹Then Jacob said to Laban, "Give me my wife. My time is completed, and I want to make love to her."

²²So Laban brought together all the people of the place and gave a feast. ²³But when evening came, he took his daughter Leah and brought her to Jacob, and Jacob made love to her. ²⁴And Laban gave his servant Zilpah to his daughter as her attendant.

²⁵When morning came, there was Leah! So Jacob said to Laban, "What is this you have done to me? I served you for Rachel, didn't I? Why have you deceived me?"

²⁶Laban replied, "It is not our custom here to give the younger daughter in marriage before the older one. ²⁷Finish this daughter's bridal week; then we will give you the younger one also, in return for another seven years of work."

²⁸And Jacob did so. He finished the week with Leah, and then Laban gave him his daughter Rachel to be his wife. ²⁹Laban gave his servant Bilhah to his daughter Rachel as her attendant. ³⁰Jacob made love to Rachel also, and his love for Rachel was greater than his love for Leah. And he worked for Laban another seven years.

Jacob's Children

³¹When the LORD saw that Leah was not loved, he enabled her to conceive, but Rachel remained childless. ³²Leah became pregnant and gave birth to a son. She named him Reuben,^b for she said, "It is because the LORD has seen my misery. Surely my husband will love me now."

³³She conceived again, and when she gave birth to a son she said, "Because the LORD heard that I am not loved, he gave me this one too." So she named him Simeon.^c

³⁴Again she conceived, and when she gave birth to a son she said, "Now at last my husband will become attached to me, because I have borne him three sons." So he was named Levi.^d

³⁵She conceived again, and when she gave birth to a son she said, "This time I will praise the LORD." So she named him Judah.^e Then she stopped having children.

30

When Rachel saw that she was not bearing Jacob any children, she became jealous of her sister. So she said to Jacob, "Give me children, or I'll die!"

²Jacob became angry with her and said, "Am I in the place of God, who has kept you from having children?"

³Then she said, "Here is Bilhah, my servant. Sleep with her so that she can bear children for me and I too can build a family through her."

⁴So she gave him her servant Bilhah as a wife. Jacob slept with her, ⁵and she became pregnant and bore him a son. ⁶Then Rachel said, "God has vindicated me; he has listened to my plea and given me a son." Because of this she named him Dan.^f

⁷Rachel's servant Bilhah conceived again and bore Jacob a second son. ⁸Then Rachel said, "I have had a great struggle with my sister, and I have won." So she named him Naphtali.^g

⁹When Leah saw that she had stopped having children, she took her servant Zilpah and gave her to Jacob as a wife. ¹⁰Leah's servant Zilpah bore Jacob a son. ¹¹Then Leah said, "What good fortune!"^h So she named him Gad.ⁱ

¹²Leah's servant Zilpah bore Jacob a second son. ¹³Then Leah said, "How happy I am! The women will call me happy." So she named him Asher.^j

¹⁴During wheat harvest, Reuben went out into the fields and found some mandrake plants, which he brought to his mother Leah. Rachel said to Leah, "Please give me some of your son's mandrakes."

¹⁵But she said to her, "Wasn't it enough that you took away my husband? Will you take my son's mandrakes too?"

---

^a 17 Or *delicate*   ^b 32 *Reuben* sounds like the Hebrew for *he has seen my misery*; the name means *see, a son.*   ^c 33 *Simeon* probably means *one who hears.*   ^d 34 *Levi* sounds like and may be derived from the Hebrew for *attached.*   ^e 35 *Judah* sounds like and may be derived from the Hebrew for *praise.*   ^f 6 *Dan* here means *he has vindicated.*   ^g 8 *Naphtali* means *my struggle.*   ^h 11 Or *"A troop is coming!"*   ⁱ 11 *Gad* can mean *good fortune* or *a troop.*   ^j 13 *Asher* means *happy.*

"Very well," Rachel said, "he can sleep with you tonight in return for your son's mandrakes."

¹⁶So when Jacob came in from the fields that evening, Leah went out to meet him. "You must sleep with me," she said. "I have hired you with my son's mandrakes." So he slept with her that night.

¹⁷God listened to Leah, and she became pregnant and bore Jacob a fifth son. ¹⁸Then Leah said, "God has rewarded me for giving my servant to my husband." So she named him Issachar.ª

¹⁹Leah conceived again and bore Jacob a sixth son. ²⁰Then Leah said, "God has presented me with a precious gift. This time my husband will treat me with honor, because I have borne him six sons." So she named him Zebulun.ᵇ

²¹Some time later she gave birth to a daughter and named her Dinah.

²²Then God remembered Rachel; he listened to her and enabled her to conceive. ²³She became pregnant and gave birth to a son and said, "God has taken away my disgrace." ²⁴She named him Joseph,ᶜ and said, "May the Lᴏʀᴅ add to me another son."

Jacob's Flocks Increase

²⁵After Rachel gave birth to Joseph, Jacob said to Laban, "Send me on my way so I can go back to my own homeland. ²⁶Give me my wives and children, for whom I have served you, and I will be on my way. You know how much work I've done for you."

²⁷But Laban said to him, "If I have found favor in your eyes, please stay. I have learned by divination that the Lᴏʀᴅ has blessed me because of you." ²⁸He added, "Name your wages, and I will pay them."

²⁹Jacob said to him, "You know how I have worked for you and how your livestock has fared under my care. ³⁰The little you had before I came has increased greatly, and the Lᴏʀᴅ has blessed you wherever I have been. But now, when may I do something for my own household?"

³¹"What shall I give you?" he asked.

"Don't give me anything," Jacob replied. "But if you will do this one thing for me, I will go on tending your flocks and watching over them: ³²Let me go through all your flocks today and remove from them every speckled or spotted sheep, every dark-colored lamb and every spotted or speckled goat. They will be my wages. ³³And my honesty will testify for me in the future, whenever you check on the wages you have paid me. Any goat in my possession that is not speckled or spotted, or any lamb that is not dark-colored, will be considered stolen."

³⁴"Agreed," said Laban. "Let it be as you have said." ³⁵That same day he removed all the male goats that were streaked or spotted, and all the speckled or spotted female goats (all that had white on them) and all the dark-colored lambs, and he placed them in the care of his sons. ³⁶Then he put a three-day journey between himself and Jacob, while Jacob continued to tend the rest of Laban's flocks.

³⁷Jacob, however, took fresh-cut branches from poplar, almond and plane trees and made white stripes on them by peeling the bark and exposing the white inner wood of the branches. ³⁸Then he placed the peeled branches in all the watering troughs, so that they would be directly in front of the flocks when they came to drink. When the flocks were in heat and came to drink, ³⁹they mated in front of the branches. And they bore young that were streaked or speckled or spotted. ⁴⁰Jacob set apart the young of the flock by themselves, but made the rest face the streaked and dark-colored animals that belonged to Laban. Thus he made separate flocks for himself and did not put them with Laban's animals. ⁴¹Whenever the stronger females were in heat, Jacob would place the branches in the troughs in front of the animals so they would mate near the branches, ⁴²but if the animals were weak, he would not place them there. So the weak animals went to Laban and the strong ones to Jacob. ⁴³In this way the man grew exceedingly prosperous and came to own large flocks, and female and male servants, and camels and donkeys.

Jacob Flees From Laban

31 Jacob heard that Laban's sons were saying, "Jacob has taken everything our father owned and has gained all this wealth from what belonged

---

ª 18 *Issachar* sounds like the Hebrew for *reward.*   ᵇ 20 *Zebulun* probably means *honor.*   ᶜ 24 *Joseph* means *may he add.*

to our father." ²And Jacob noticed that Laban's attitude toward him was not what it had been.

³Then the LORD said to Jacob, "Go back to the land of your fathers and to your relatives, and I will be with you."

⁴So Jacob sent word to Rachel and Leah to come out to the fields where his flocks were. ⁵He said to them, "I see that your father's attitude toward me is not what it was before, but the God of my father has been with me. ⁶You know that I've worked for your father with all my strength, ⁷yet your father has cheated me by changing my wages ten times. However, God has not allowed him to harm me. ⁸If he said, 'The speckled ones will be your wages,' then all the flocks gave birth to speckled young; and if he said, 'The streaked ones will be your wages,' then all the flocks bore streaked young. ⁹So God has taken away your father's livestock and has given them to me.

¹⁰"In breeding season I once had a dream in which I looked up and saw that the male goats mating with the flock were streaked, speckled or spotted. ¹¹The angel of God said to me in the dream, 'Jacob.' I answered, 'Here I am.' ¹²And he said, 'Look up and see that all the male goats mating with the flock are streaked, speckled or spotted, for I have seen all that Laban has been doing to you. ¹³I am the God of Bethel, where you anointed a pillar and where you made a vow to me. Now leave this land at once and go back to your native land.' "

¹⁴Then Rachel and Leah replied, "Do we still have any share in the inheritance of our father's estate? ¹⁵Does he not regard us as foreigners? Not only has he sold us, but he has used up what was paid for us. ¹⁶Surely all the wealth that God took away from our father belongs to us and our children. So do whatever God has told you."

¹⁷Then Jacob put his children and his wives on camels, ¹⁸and he drove all his livestock ahead of him, along with all the goods he had accumulated in Paddan Aram,ᵃ to go to his father Isaac in the land of Canaan.

¹⁹When Laban had gone to shear his sheep, Rachel stole her father's household gods. ²⁰Moreover, Jacob deceived Laban the Aramean by not telling him he was running away. ²¹So he fled with all he had, crossed

the Euphrates River, and headed for the hill country of Gilead.

Laban Pursues Jacob

²²On the third day Laban was told that Jacob had fled. ²³Taking his relatives with him, he pursued Jacob for seven days and caught up with him in the hill country of Gilead. ²⁴Then God came to Laban the Aramean in a dream at night and said to him, "Be careful not to say anything to Jacob, either good or bad."

²⁵Jacob had pitched his tent in the hill country of Gilead when Laban overtook him, and Laban and his relatives camped there too. ²⁶Then Laban said to Jacob, "What have you done? You've deceived me, and you've carried off my daughters like captives in war. ²⁷Why did you run off secretly and deceive me? Why didn't you tell me, so I could send you away with joy and singing to the music of timbrels and harps? ²⁸You didn't even let me kiss my grandchildren and my daughters good-by. You have done a foolish thing. ²⁹I have the power to harm you; but last night the God of your father said to me, 'Be careful not to say anything to Jacob, either good or bad.' ³⁰Now you have gone off because you longed to return to your father's household. But why did you steal my gods?"

³¹Jacob answered Laban, "I was afraid, because I thought you would take your daughters away from me by force. ³²But if you find anyone who has your gods, that one shall not live. In the presence of our relatives, see for yourself whether there is anything of yours here with me; and if so, take it." Now Jacob did not know that Rachel had stolen the gods.

³³So Laban went into Jacob's tent and into Leah's tent and into the tent of the two female servants, but he found nothing. After he came out of Leah's tent, he entered Rachel's tent. ³⁴Now Rachel had taken the household gods and put them inside her camel's saddle and was sitting on them. Laban searched through everything in the tent but found nothing.

³⁵Rachel said to her father, "Don't be angry, my lord, that I cannot stand up in your presence; I'm having my period." So he

ᵃ 18 That is, Northwest Mesopotamia

searched but could not find the household gods.

³⁶Jacob was angry and took Laban to task. "What is my crime?" he asked Laban. "How have I wronged you that you hunt me down? ³⁷Now that you have searched through all my goods, what have you found that belongs to your household? Put it here in front of your relatives and mine, and let them judge between the two of us.

³⁸"I have been with you for twenty years now. Your sheep and goats have not miscarried, nor have I eaten rams from your flocks. ³⁹I did not bring you animals torn by wild beasts; I bore the loss myself. And you demanded payment from me for whatever was stolen by day or night. ⁴⁰This was my situation: The heat consumed me in the daytime and the cold at night, and sleep fled from my eyes. ⁴¹It was like this for the twenty years I was in your household. I worked for you fourteen years for your two daughters and six years for your flocks, and you changed my wages ten times. ⁴²If the God of my father, the God of Abraham and the Fear of Isaac, had not been with me, you would surely have sent me away empty-handed. But God has seen my hardship and the toil of my hands, and last night he rebuked you."

⁴³Laban answered Jacob, "The women are my daughters, the children are my children, and the flocks are my flocks. All you see is mine. Yet what can I do today about these daughters of mine, or about the children they have borne? ⁴⁴Come now, let's make a covenant, you and I, and let it serve as a witness between us."

⁴⁵So Jacob took a stone and set it up as a pillar. ⁴⁶He said to his relatives, "Gather some stones." So they took stones and piled them in a heap, and they ate there by the heap. ⁴⁷Laban called it Jegar Sahadutha, and Jacob called it Galeed.ᵃ

⁴⁸Laban said, "This heap is a witness between you and me today." That is why it was called Galeed. ⁴⁹It was also called Mizpah,ᵇ because he said, "May the LORD keep watch between you and me when we are away from each other. ⁵⁰If you mistreat my daughters or if you take any wives besides my daughters, even though no one is with

us, remember that God is a witness between you and me."

⁵¹Laban also said to Jacob, "Here is this heap, and here is this pillar I have set up between you and me. ⁵²This heap is a witness, and this pillar is a witness, that I will not go past this heap to your side to harm you and that you will not go past this heap and pillar to my side to harm me. ⁵³May the God of Abraham and the God of Nahor, the God of their father, judge between us."

So Jacob took an oath in the name of the Fear of his father Isaac. ⁵⁴He offered a sacrifice there in the hill country and invited his relatives to a meal. After they had eaten, they spent the night there.

*⁵⁵Early the next morning Laban kissed his grandchildren and his daughters and blessed them. Then he left and returned home.

Jacob Prepares to Meet Esau

32 *¹Jacob also went on his way, and the angels of God met him. ²When Jacob saw them, he said, "This is the camp of God!" So he named that place Mahanaim.ᶜ

³Jacob sent messengers ahead of him to his brother Esau in the land of Seir, the country of Edom. ⁴He instructed them: "This is what you are to say to my lord Esau: 'Your servant Jacob says, I have been staying with Laban and have remained there till now. ⁵I have cattle and donkeys, sheep and goats, male and female servants. Now I am sending this message to my lord, that I may find favor in your eyes.'"

⁶When the messengers returned to Jacob, they said, "We went to your brother Esau, and now he is coming to meet you, and four hundred men are with him."

⁷In great fear and distress Jacob divided the people who were with him into two groups,ᵈ and the flocks and herds and camels as well. ⁸He thought, "If Esau comes and attacks one group,ᵉ the groupᵉ that is left may escape."

⁹Then Jacob prayed, "O God of my father Abraham, God of my father Isaac, LORD, you who said to me, 'Go back to your country and your relatives, and I will make you pros-

---

ᵃ 47 The Aramaic *Jegar Sahadutha* and the Hebrew *Galeed* both mean *witness heap.*   ᵇ 49 *Mizpah* means *watchtower.*   ᶜ 2 *Mahanaim* means *two camps.*   ᵈ 7 Or *camps*   ᵉ 8 Or *camp*

* 31:55 is numbered 32:1 in Hebrew texts.   * 32:1-32 is numbered 32:2-33 in Hebrew texts.

per,' ¹⁰I am unworthy of all the kindness and faithfulness you have shown your servant. I had only my staff when I crossed this Jordan, but now I have become two camps. ¹¹Save me, I pray, from the hand of my brother Esau, for I am afraid he will come and attack me, and also the mothers with their children. ¹²But you have said, 'I will surely make you prosper and will make your descendants like the sand of the sea, which cannot be counted.' "

¹³He spent the night there, and from what he had with him he selected a gift for his brother Esau: ¹⁴two hundred female goats and twenty male goats, two hundred ewes and twenty rams, ¹⁵thirty female camels with their young, forty cows and ten bulls, and twenty female donkeys and ten male donkeys. ¹⁶He put them in the care of his servants, each herd by itself, and said to his servants, "Go ahead of me, and keep some space between the herds."

¹⁷He instructed the one in the lead: "When my brother Esau meets you and asks, 'Who do you belong to, and where are you going, and who owns all these animals in front of you?' ¹⁸then you are to say, 'They belong to your servant Jacob. They are a gift sent to my lord Esau, and he is coming behind us.' "

¹⁹He also instructed the second, the third and all the others who followed the herds: "You are to say the same thing to Esau when you meet him. ²⁰And be sure to say, 'Your servant Jacob is coming behind us.' " For he thought, "I will pacify him with these gifts I am sending on ahead; later, when I see him, perhaps he will receive me." ²¹So Jacob's gifts went on ahead of him, but he himself spent the night in the camp.

Jacob Wrestles With God

²²That night Jacob got up and took his two wives, his two female servants and his eleven sons and crossed the ford of the Jabbok. ²³After he had sent them across the stream, he sent over all his possessions. ²⁴So Jacob was left alone, and a man wrestled with him till daybreak. ²⁵When the man saw that he could not overpower him, he touched the socket of Jacob's hip so that his hip was wrenched as he wrestled with the

man. ²⁶Then the man said, "Let me go, for it is daybreak."

But Jacob replied, "I will not let you go unless you bless me."

²⁷The man asked him, "What is your name?"

"Jacob," he answered.

²⁸Then the man said, "Your name will no longer be Jacob, but Israel,ᵃ because you have struggled with God and with human beings and have overcome."

²⁹Jacob said, "Please tell me your name."

But he replied, "Why do you ask my name?" Then he blessed him there.

³⁰So Jacob called the place Peniel,ᵇ saying, "It is because I saw God face to face, and yet my life was spared."

³¹The sun rose above him as he passed Peniel,ᶜ and he was limping because of his hip. ³²Therefore to this day the Israelites do not eat the tendon attached to the socket of the hip, because the socket of Jacob's hip was touched near the tendon.

Jacob Meets Esau

33 Jacob looked up and there was Esau, coming with his four hundred men; so he divided the children among Leah, Rachel and the two female servants. ²He put the female servants and their children in front, Leah and her children next, and Rachel and Joseph in the rear. ³He himself went on ahead and bowed down to the ground seven times as he approached his brother.

⁴But Esau ran to meet Jacob and embraced him; he threw his arms around his neck and kissed him. And they wept. ⁵Then Esau looked up and saw the women and children. "Who are these with you?" he asked.

Jacob answered, "They are the children God has graciously given your servant."

⁶Then the female servants and their children approached and bowed down. ⁷Next, Leah and her children came and bowed down. Last of all came Joseph and Rachel, and they too bowed down.

⁸Esau asked, "What do you mean by all these flocks and herds I met?"

"To find favor in your eyes, my lord," he said.

ᵃ 28 *Israel* probably means *he struggles with God.*   ᵇ 30 *Peniel* means *face of God.*   ᶜ 31 Hebrew
Penuel, a variant of *Peniel*

THURSDAY

WRESTLING WITH GOD

Genesis 32:1–32 *or* 32:22–32

CHARLES HADDON SPURGEON {AD 1834–1892}

In ancient times, a smack on the ear given by a master to a slave meant liberty: little would the newly freed slave care how hard the blow was. By a stroke from the sword the warrior was knighted by his monarch: small matter was it to the newly made knight if the hand was heavy. When the Lord intends to lift his servants into the higher stage of spiritual life, he frequently sends them a severe trial; he makes his Jacobs to be prevailing princes, but he confers the honor after a night of wrestling and accompanies it with a lasting wound. Be it so: Who among us would wish to be deprived of the trials, if they are the necessary attendants of spiritual advancement?

Michael Marshall

At the outset of his long journey of faith, Augustine had declared that it was the very nature of the human condition that our hearts would always be restless until we had come to rest totally in God. Much later in his pilgrimage, when he was a bishop, he wrote these reassuring words: "Even while we are being tossed about by the waves of the sea, we have the anchor of hope already fixed upon the land." Augustine lived in this world in the sure and confident hope that the day would come when faith would become sight, when desire would be swallowed up in delight, when the things that could be shaken off would be shaken off for ever, and when all that remained would be the One who remains for ever. Nothing less, he now knew, was worth living for, and nothing less constituted a life worth living.

We might say that in middle life Augustine became "homesick for heaven" and experienced the deep desire and yearning which overtook his earlier, more negative restlessness. He had discovered, if you like, "the point of it all"—sometimes summed up in the words, "In the end, God."

reflection

1. When was the last time you wrestled with God?

2. What lasting wounds have helped you grow closer to God?

3. When are you most likely to resonate with the phrase, "In the end, God"?

For your next devotional reading, go to page 49.

⁹But Esau said, "I already have plenty, my brother. Keep what you have for yourself."

¹⁰"No, please!" said Jacob. "If I have found favor in your eyes, accept this gift from me. For to see your face is like seeing the face of God, now that you have received me favorably. ¹¹Please accept the present that was brought to you, for God has been gracious to me and I have all I need." And because Jacob insisted, Esau accepted it.

¹²Then Esau said, "Let us be on our way; I'll accompany you."

¹³But Jacob said to him, "My lord knows that the children are tender and that I must care for the ewes and cows that are nursing their young. If they are driven hard just one day, all the animals will die. ¹⁴So let my lord go on ahead of his servant, while I move along slowly at the pace of the flocks and herds before me and the pace of the children, until I come to my lord in Seir."

¹⁵Esau said, "Then let me leave some of my men with you."

"But why do that?" Jacob asked. "Just let me find favor in the eyes of my lord."

¹⁶So that day Esau started on his way back to Seir. ¹⁷Jacob, however, went to Sukkoth, where he built a place for himself and made shelters for his livestock. That is why the place is called Sukkoth. ᵃ

¹⁸After Jacob came from Paddan Aram, ᵇ he arrived safely at the ᶜ city of Shechem in Canaan and camped within sight of the city. ¹⁹For a hundred pieces of silver, ᵈ he bought from the sons of Hamor, the father of Shechem, the plot of ground where he pitched his tent. ²⁰There he set up an altar and called it El Elohe Israel. ᵉ

Dinah and the Shechemites

34 Now Dinah, the daughter Leah had borne to Jacob, went out to visit the women of the land. ²When Shechem son of Hamor the Hivite, the ruler of that area, saw her, he took her and raped her. ³His heart was drawn to Dinah daughter of Jacob; he loved the young woman and spoke tenderly to her. ⁴And Shechem said to his father Hamor, "Get me this young woman as my wife."

⁵When Jacob heard that his daughter Dinah had been defiled, his sons were in the fields with his livestock; so he did nothing about it until they came home.

⁶Then Shechem's father Hamor went out to talk with Jacob. ⁷Meanwhile, Jacob's sons had come in from the fields as soon as they heard what had happened. They were shocked and furious, because Shechem had done an outrageous thing inᶠ Israel by sleeping with Jacob's daughter—a thing that should not be done.

⁸But Hamor said to them, "My son Shechem has his heart set on your daughter. Please give her to him as his wife. ⁹Intermarry with us; give us your daughters and take our daughters for yourselves. ¹⁰You can settle among us; the land is open to you. Live in it, tradeᵍ in it, and acquire property in it."

¹¹Then Shechem said to Dinah's father and brothers, "Let me find favor in your eyes, and I will give you whatever you ask. ¹²Make the price for the bride and the gift I am to bring as great as you like, and I'll pay whatever you ask me. Only give me the young woman as my wife."

¹³Because their sister Dinah had been defiled, Jacob's sons replied deceitfully as they spoke to Shechem and his father Hamor. ¹⁴They said to them, "We can't do such a thing; we can't give our sister to a man who is not circumcised. That would be a disgrace to us. ¹⁵We will enter into an agreement with you on one condition only: that you become like us by circumcising all your males. ¹⁶Then we will give you our daughters and take your daughters for ourselves. We'll settle among you and become one people with you. ¹⁷But if you will not agree to be circumcised, we'll take our sister and go."

¹⁸Their proposal seemed good to Hamor and his son Shechem. ¹⁹The young man, who was the most honored of all his father's family, lost no time in doing what they said, because he was delighted with Jacob's daughter. ²⁰So Hamor and his son Shechem went to the gate of their city to speak to the men of their city. ²¹"These men are friendly toward us," they said. "Let them live in our land and trade in it; the land has plenty of room for them. We can marry their daugh-

---

ᵃ 17 *Sukkoth* means *shelters.*   ᵇ 18 That is, Northwest Mesopotamia   ᶜ 18 Or *arrived at Shalem, a*
ᵈ 19 Hebrew *hundred kesitahs*; a kesitah was a unit of money of unknown weight and value.   ᵉ 20 *El Elohe Israel* can mean *El is the God of Israel* or *mighty is the God of Israel.*   ᶠ 7 Or *against*
ᵍ 10 Or *move about freely*; also in verse 21

ters and they can marry ours. ²²But the men will agree to live with us as one people only on the condition that our males be circumcised, as they themselves are. ²³Won't their livestock, their property and all their other animals become ours? So let us agree to their terms, and they will settle among us."

²⁴All the men who went out of the city gate agreed with Hamor and his son Shechem, and every male in the city was circumcised.

²⁵Three days later, while all of them were still in pain, two of Jacob's sons, Simeon and Levi, Dinah's brothers, took their swords and attacked the unsuspecting city, killing every male. ²⁶They put Hamor and his son Shechem to the sword and took Dinah from Shechem's house and left. ²⁷The sons of Jacob came upon the dead bodies and looted the city where[a] their sister had been defiled. ²⁸They seized their flocks and herds and donkeys and everything else of theirs in the city and out in the fields. ²⁹They carried off all their wealth and all their women and children, taking as plunder everything in the houses.

³⁰Then Jacob said to Simeon and Levi, "You have brought trouble on me by making me obnoxious to the Canaanites and Perizzites, the people living in this land. We are few in number, and if they join forces against me and attack me, I and my household will be destroyed."

³¹But they replied, "Should he have treated our sister like a prostitute?"

Jacob Returns to Bethel

35 Then God said to Jacob, "Go up to Bethel and settle there, and build an altar there to God, who appeared to you when you were fleeing from your brother Esau."

²So Jacob said to his household and to all who were with him, "Get rid of the foreign gods you have with you, and purify yourselves and change your clothes. ³Then come, let us go up to Bethel, where I will build an altar to God, who answered me in the day of my distress and who has been with me wherever I have gone." ⁴So they

gave Jacob all the foreign gods they had and the rings in their ears, and Jacob buried them under the oak at Shechem. ⁵Then they set out, and the terror of God fell on the towns all around them so that no one pursued them.

⁶Jacob and all the people with him came to Luz (that is, Bethel) in the land of Canaan. ⁷There he built an altar, and he called the place El Bethel,[b] because it was there that God revealed himself to him when he was fleeing from his brother.

⁸Now Deborah, Rebekah's nurse, died and was buried under the oak below Bethel. So it was named Allon Bakuth.[c]

⁹After Jacob returned from Paddan Aram,[d] God appeared to him again and blessed him. ¹⁰God said to him, "Your name is Jacob,[e] but you will no longer be called Jacob; your name will be Israel.[f]" So he named him Israel.

¹¹And God said to him, "I am God Almighty[g]; be fruitful and increase in number. A nation and a community of nations will come from you, and kings will come from your body. ¹²The land I gave to Abraham and Isaac I also give to you, and I will give this land to your descendants after you." ¹³Then God went up from him at the place where he had talked with him.

¹⁴Jacob set up a stone pillar at the place where God had talked with him, and he poured out a drink offering on it; he also poured oil on it. ¹⁵Jacob called the place where God had talked with him Bethel.[h]

The Deaths of Rachel and Isaac

¹⁶Then they moved on from Bethel. While they were still some distance from Ephrath, Rachel began to give birth and had great difficulty. ¹⁷And as she was having great difficulty in childbirth, the midwife said to her, "Don't despair, for you have another son." ¹⁸As she breathed her last—for she was dying—she named her son Ben-Oni.[i] But his father named him Benjamin.[j]

¹⁹So Rachel died and was buried on the way to Ephrath (that is, Bethlehem). ²⁰Over her tomb Jacob set up a pillar, and to this day that pillar marks Rachel's tomb.

---

a 27 Or because   b 7 El Bethel means God of Bethel.   c 8 Allon Bakuth means oak of weeping.
d 9 That is, Northwest Mesopotamia; also in verse 26   e 10 Jacob means he grasps the heel, a Hebrew idiom for he deceives.   f 10 Israel probably means he struggles with God.   g 11 Hebrew El-Shaddai
h 15 Bethel means house of God.   i 18 Ben-Oni means son of my trouble.   j 18 Benjamin means son of my right hand.

²¹Israel moved on again and pitched his tent beyond Migdal Eder. ²²While Israel was living in that region, Reuben went in and slept with his father's concubine Bilhah, and Israel heard of it.

Jacob had twelve sons:

²³ The sons of Leah:
Reuben the firstborn of Jacob,
Simeon, Levi, Judah, Issachar and
Zebulun.
²⁴ The sons of Rachel:
Joseph and Benjamin.
²⁵ The sons of Rachel's servant Bilhah:
Dan and Naphtali.
²⁶ The sons of Leah's servant Zilpah:
Gad and Asher.
These were the sons of Jacob, who were born to him in Paddan Aram.

²⁷Jacob came home to his father Isaac in Mamre, near Kiriath Arba (that is, Hebron), where Abraham and Isaac had stayed. ²⁸Isaac lived a hundred and eighty years. ²⁹Then he breathed his last and died and was gathered to his people, old and full of years. And his sons Esau and Jacob buried him.

Esau's Descendants

36 This is the account of the family line of Esau (that is, Edom).

²Esau took his wives from the women of Canaan: Adah daughter of Elon the Hittite, and Oholibamah daughter of Anah and granddaughter of Zibeon the Hivite— ³also Basemath daughter of Ishmael and sister of Nebaioth.

⁴Adah bore Eliphaz to Esau, Basemath bore Reuel, ⁵and Oholibamah bore Jeush, Jalam and Korah. These were the sons of Esau, who were born to him in Canaan.

⁶Esau took his wives and sons and daughters and all the members of his household, as well as his livestock and all his other animals and all the goods he had acquired in Canaan, and moved to a land some distance from his brother Jacob. ⁷Their possessions were too great for them to remain together; the land where they were staying could not support them both because of their livestock. ⁸So Esau (that is, Edom) settled in the hill country of Seir.

⁹This is the account of the family line of Esau the father of the Edomites in the hill country of Seir.

¹⁰ These are the names of Esau's sons:
Eliphaz, the son of Esau's wife Adah, and Reuel, the son of Esau's wife Basemath.
¹¹ The sons of Eliphaz:
Teman, Omar, Zepho, Gatam and Kenaz.
¹² Esau's son Eliphaz also had a concubine named Timna, who bore him Amalek. These were grandsons of Esau's wife Adah.
¹³ The sons of Reuel:
Nahath, Zerah, Shammah and Mizzah. These were grandsons of Esau's wife Basemath.
¹⁴ The sons of Esau's wife Oholibamah daughter of Anah and granddaughter of Zibeon, whom she bore to Esau:
Jeush, Jalam and Korah.

¹⁵These were the chiefs among Esau's descendants:
The sons of Eliphaz the firstborn of Esau:
Chiefs Teman, Omar, Zepho, Kenaz, ¹⁶Korah,ᵃ Gatam and Amalek. These were the chiefs descended from Eliphaz in Edom; they were grandsons of Adah.
¹⁷ The sons of Esau's son Reuel:
Chiefs Nahath, Zerah, Shammah and Mizzah. These were the chiefs descended from Reuel in Edom; they were grandsons of Esau's wife Basemath.
¹⁸ The sons of Esau's wife Oholibamah:
Chiefs Jeush, Jalam and Korah. These were the chiefs descended from Esau's wife Oholibamah daughter of Anah.
¹⁹These were the sons of Esau (that is, Edom), and these were their chiefs.

²⁰These were the sons of Seir the Horite, who were living in the region:
Lotan, Shobal, Zibeon, Anah, ²¹Dishon, Ezer and Dishan. These sons of Seir in Edom were Horite chiefs.

ᵃ 16 Masoretic Text; Samaritan Pentateuch (see also Gen. 36:11 and 1 Chron. 1:36) does not have *Korah*.

²²The sons of Lotan:

    Hori and Homam.ª Timna was Lotan's sister.

²³The sons of Shobal:

    Alvan, Manahath, Ebal, Shepho and Onam.

²⁴The sons of Zibeon:

    Aiah and Anah. This is the Anah who discovered the hot springs*b* in the desert while he was grazing the donkeys of his father Zibeon.

²⁵The children of Anah:

    Dishon and Oholibamah daughter of Anah.

²⁶The sons of Dishon*c*:

    Hemdan, Eshban, Ithran and Keran.

²⁷The sons of Ezer:

    Bilhan, Zaavan and Akan.

²⁸The sons of Dishan:

    Uz and Aran.

²⁹These were the Horite chiefs:

    Lotan, Shobal, Zibeon, Anah, ³⁰Dishon, Ezer and Dishan. These were the Horite chiefs, according to their divisions, in the land of Seir.

The Rulers of Edom

³¹These were the kings who reigned in Edom before any Israelite king reigned:

³²Bela son of Beor became king of Edom. His city was named Dinhabah.

³³When Bela died, Jobab son of Zerah from Bozrah succeeded him as king.

³⁴When Jobab died, Husham from the land of the Temanites succeeded him as king.

³⁵When Husham died, Hadad son of Bedad, who defeated Midian in the country of Moab, succeeded him as king. His city was named Avith.

³⁶When Hadad died, Samlah from Masrekah succeeded him as king.

³⁷When Samlah died, Shaul from Rehoboth on the river succeeded him as king.

³⁸When Shaul died, Baal-Hanan son of Akbor succeeded him as king.

³⁹When Baal-Hanan son of Akbor died, Hadad*d* succeeded him as king. His city was named Pau, and his wife's name was Mehetabel daughter of Matred, the daughter of Me-Zahab.

⁴⁰These were the chiefs descended from Esau, by name, according to their clans and regions:

    Timna, Alvah, Jetheth, ⁴¹Oholibamah, Elah, Pinon, ⁴²Kenaz, Teman, Mibzar, ⁴³Magdiel and Iram. These were the chiefs of Edom, according to their settlements in the land they occupied.

This was Esau the father of the Edomites.

Joseph's Dreams

37 Jacob lived in the land where his father had stayed, the land of Canaan.

²This is the account of Jacob's family line.

Joseph, a young man of seventeen, was tending the flocks with his brothers, the sons of Bilhah and the sons of Zilpah, his father's wives, and he brought their father a bad report about them.

³Now Israel loved Joseph more than any of his other sons, because he had been born to him in his old age; and he made a richly ornamented*e* robe for him. ⁴When his brothers saw that their father loved him more than any of them, they hated him and could not speak a kind word to him.

⁵Joseph had a dream, and when he told it to his brothers, they hated him all the more. ⁶He said to them, "Listen to this dream I had: ⁷We were binding sheaves of grain out in the field when suddenly my sheaf rose and stood upright, while your sheaves gathered around mine and bowed down to it."

⁸His brothers said to him, "Do you intend to reign over us? Will you actually rule us?" And they hated him all the more because of his dream and what he had said.

⁹Then he had another dream, and he told it to his brothers. "Listen," he said, "I had another dream, and this time the sun and moon and eleven stars were bowing down to me."

¹⁰When he told his father as well as his brothers, his father rebuked him and said,

---

a 22 Hebrew *Hemam*, a variant of *Homam* (see 1 Chron. 1:39)   *b 24* Vulgate; Syriac *discovered water*; the meaning of the Hebrew for this word is uncertain.   *c 26* Hebrew *Dishan*, a variant of *Dishon* *d 39* Many manuscripts of the Masoretic Text, Samaritan Pentateuch and Syriac (see also 1 Chron. 1:50); most manuscripts of the Masoretic Text *Hadar*   *e 3* The meaning of the Hebrew for *richly ornamented* is uncertain; also in verses 23 and 32.

"What is this dream you had? Will your mother and I and your brothers actually come and bow down to the ground before you?" ¹¹His brothers were jealous of him, but his father kept the matter in mind.

Joseph Sold by His Brothers

¹²Now his brothers had gone to graze their father's flocks near Shechem, ¹³and Israel said to Joseph, "As you know, your brothers are grazing the flocks near Shechem. Come, I am going to send you to them."

"Very well," he replied.

¹⁴So he said to him, "Go and see if all is well with your brothers and with the flocks, and bring word back to me." Then he sent him off from the Valley of Hebron.

When Joseph arrived at Shechem, ¹⁵a man found him wandering around in the fields and asked him, "What are you looking for?"

¹⁶He replied, "I'm looking for my brothers. Can you tell me where they are grazing their flocks?"

¹⁷"They have moved on from here," the man answered. "I heard them say, 'Let's go to Dothan.'"

So Joseph went after his brothers and found them near Dothan. ¹⁸But they saw him in the distance, and before he reached them, they plotted to kill him.

¹⁹"Here comes that dreamer!" they said to each other. ²⁰"Come now, let's kill him and throw him into one of these cisterns and say that a ferocious animal devoured him. Then we'll see what comes of his dreams."

²¹When Reuben heard this, he tried to rescue him from their hands. "Let's not take his life," he said. ²²"Don't shed any blood. Throw him into this cistern here in the wilderness, but don't lay a hand on him." Reuben said this to rescue him from them and take him back to his father.

²³So when Joseph came to his brothers, they stripped him of his robe—the richly ornamented robe he was wearing— ²⁴and they took him and threw him into the cistern. The cistern was empty; there was no water in it.

²⁵As they sat down to eat their meal, they looked up and saw a caravan of Ishmaelites coming from Gilead. Their camels were loaded with spices, balm and myrrh, and they were on their way to take them down to Egypt.

²⁶Judah said to his brothers, "What will we gain if we kill our brother and cover up his blood? ²⁷Come, let's sell him to the Ishmaelites and not lay our hands on him; after all, he is our brother, our own flesh and blood." His brothers agreed.

²⁸So when the Midianite merchants came by, his brothers pulled Joseph up out of the cistern and sold him for twenty shekels[a] of silver to the Ishmaelites, who took him to Egypt.

²⁹When Reuben returned to the cistern and saw that Joseph was not there, he tore his clothes. ³⁰He went back to his brothers and said, "The boy isn't there! Where can I turn now?"

³¹Then they got Joseph's robe, slaughtered a goat and dipped the robe in the blood. ³²They took the ornamented robe back to their father and said, "We found this. Examine it to see whether it is your son's robe."

³³He recognized it and said, "It is my son's robe! Some ferocious animal has devoured him. Joseph has surely been torn to pieces."

³⁴Then Jacob tore his clothes, put on sackcloth and mourned for his son many days. ³⁵All his sons and daughters came to comfort him, but he refused to be comforted. "No," he said, "in mourning will I go down to the grave to my son." So his father wept for him.

³⁶Meanwhile, the Midianites[b] sold Joseph in Egypt to Potiphar, one of Pharaoh's officials, the captain of the guard.

Judah and Tamar

38 At that time, Judah left his brothers and went down to stay with a man of Adullam named Hirah. ²There Judah met the daughter of a Canaanite man named Shua. He married her and made love to her; ³she became pregnant and gave birth to a son, who was named Er. ⁴She conceived again and gave birth to a son and named him Onan. ⁵She gave birth to still another son and named

---

a 28 That is, about 8 ounces or about 230 grams Syriac (see also verse 28); Masoretic Text *Medanites*   b 36 Samaritan Pentateuch, Septuagint, Vulgate and

FRIDAY

DON'T EXPECT RESPECT
Genesis 37:1–36 *or* 37:23–28

ROBERT JAMIESON {AD 1802–1880}

Imagine Joseph approaching his brothers in all the unsuspecting openness of brotherly affection. How astonished and terrified must he have been at their cold reception, their ferocious facial expressions and the rough treatment by his perverse assailants! . . . Their common share in this conspiracy is not the only dismal feature in the story. The rapidity, the almost instantaneous manner in which the proposal of attacking Joseph was followed by their joint agreement to do so, is astonishing. And the cool indifference that followed, or rather the fiendish satisfaction, with which his brothers sat down to feast themselves, is equally astonishing. It is impossible that mere envy at his dreams, his colorful coat or the doting partiality of their common father could have goaded them on to such a pitch of frenzied resentment or solidified their decision to commit such complete wickedness. Their hatred of Joseph must have had a far deeper source . . . His brothers' envy must have been produced by their dislike of his piety and other excellencies, which made his character and conduct a constant and unspoken condemnation of theirs. On account of this, they found that they could never be at ease until they had rid themselves of Joseph's hated presence. This was the true explanation for the mystery of Joseph's brothers' hostility, just as it was in the case of Cain.

Derek Kidner

It was God's intention, already revealed to Abraham (Genesis 15:13–16), to bring the chosen family under foreign domination until "the [sin] of the Amorites" should be full and Canaan ripe for possession. So the train of events to lead Israel into Egypt is set in motion through the rivalries and predicaments of the 12 brothers, under the hand of God . . . [It also exhibits] a human pattern that runs through the Old Testament to culminate at Calvary: the rejection of God's chosen deliverers, through the envy and unbelief of their kith and kin— yet a rejection which is finally made to play its own part in bringing about the deliverance.

reflection

1. Why did Joseph's goodness inspire his brothers' hostility?

2. In what ways can you relate to Joseph? How have you been on the receiving end of another's hostility—all because of your desire to follow God and do what's right?

3. Do you expect that your life will go well because of your faith in Christ? What does this passage say about such an expectation?

For your next devotional reading, go to page 52.

him Shelah. It was at Kezib that she gave birth to him.

⁶Judah got a wife for Er, his firstborn, and her name was Tamar. ⁷But Er, Judah's firstborn, was wicked in the LORD's sight; so the LORD put him to death.

⁸Then Judah said to Onan, "Sleep with your brother's wife and fulfill your duty to her as a brother-in-law to raise up offspring for your brother." ⁹But Onan knew that the child would not be his; so whenever he slept with his brother's wife, he spilled his semen on the ground to keep from providing offspring for his brother. ¹⁰What he did was wicked in the LORD's sight; so he put him to death also.

¹¹Judah then said to his daughter-in-law Tamar, "Live as a widow in your father's household until my son Shelah grows up." For he thought, "He may die too, just like his brothers." So Tamar went to live in her father's household.

¹²After a long time Judah's wife, the daughter of Shua, died. When Judah had recovered from his grief, he went up to Timnah, to the men who were shearing his sheep, and his friend Hirah the Adullamite went with him.

¹³When Tamar was told, "Your father-in-law is on his way to Timnah to shear his sheep," ¹⁴she took off her widow's clothes, covered herself with a veil to disguise herself, and then sat down at the entrance to Enaim, which is on the road to Timnah. For she saw that, though Shelah had now grown up, she had not been given to him as his wife.

¹⁵When Judah saw her, he thought she was a prostitute, for she had covered her face. ¹⁶Not realizing that she was his daughter-in-law, he went over to her by the roadside and said, "Come now, let me sleep with you."

"And what will you give me to sleep with you?" she asked.

¹⁷"I'll send you a young goat from my flock," he said.

"Will you give me something as a pledge until you send it?" she asked.

¹⁸He said, "What pledge should I give you?"

"Your seal and its cord, and the staff in your hand," she answered. So he gave them

to her and slept with her, and she became pregnant by him. ¹⁹After she left, she took off her veil and put on her widow's clothes again.

²⁰Meanwhile Judah sent the young goat by his friend the Adullamite in order to get his pledge back from the woman, but he did not find her. ²¹He asked the men who lived there, "Where is the shrine prostitute who was beside the road at Enaim?"

"There hasn't been any shrine prostitute here," they said.

²²So he went back to Judah and said, "I didn't find her. Besides, the men who lived there said, 'There hasn't been any shrine prostitute here.' "

²³Then Judah said, "Let her keep what she has, or we will become a laughingstock. After all, I did send her this young goat, but you didn't find her."

²⁴About three months later Judah was told, "Your daughter-in-law Tamar is guilty of prostitution, and as a result she is now pregnant."

Judah said, "Bring her out and have her burned to death!"

²⁵As she was being brought out, she sent a message to her father-in-law. "I am pregnant by the man who owns these," she said. And she added, "See if you recognize whose seal and cord and staff these are."

²⁶Judah recognized them and said, "She is more righteous than I, since I wouldn't give her to my son Shelah." And he did not sleep with her again.

²⁷When the time came for her to give birth, there were twin boys in her womb. ²⁸As she was giving birth, one of them put out his hand; so the midwife took a scarlet thread and tied it on his wrist and said, "This one came out first." ²⁹But when he drew back his hand, his brother came out, and she said, "So this is how you have broken out!" And he was named Perez.ᵃ ³⁰Then his brother, who had the scarlet thread on his wrist, came out and he was given the name Zerah.ᵇ

Joseph and Potiphar's Wife

39 Now Joseph had been taken down to Egypt. Potiphar, an Egyptian who was one of Pharaoh's officials, the captain of the guard,

---

ᵃ 29 *Perez* means *breaking out.*   ᵇ 30 *Zerah* can mean *scarlet* or *brightness.*

bought him from the Ishmaelites who had taken him there.

[2]The LORD was with Joseph so that he prospered, and he lived in the house of his Egyptian master. [3]When his master saw that the LORD was with him and that the LORD gave him success in everything he did, [4]Joseph found favor in his eyes and became his attendant. Potiphar put him in charge of his household, and he entrusted to his care everything he owned. [5]From the time he put him in charge of his household and of all that he owned, the LORD blessed the household of the Egyptian because of Joseph. The blessing of the LORD was on everything Potiphar had, both in the house and in the field. [6]So Potiphar left everything he had in Joseph's care; with Joseph in charge, he did not concern himself with anything except the food he ate.

Now Joseph was well-built and handsome, [7]and after a while his master's wife took notice of Joseph and said, "Come to bed with me!"

[8]But he refused. "With me in charge," he told her, "my master does not concern himself with anything in the house; everything he owns he has entrusted to my care. [9]No one is greater in this house than I am. My master has withheld nothing from me except you, because you are his wife. How then could I do such a wicked thing and sin against God?" [10]And though she spoke to Joseph day after day, he refused to go to bed with her or even be with her.

[11]One day he went into the house to attend to his duties, and none of the household servants was inside. [12]She caught him by his cloak and said, "Come to bed with me!" But he left his cloak in her hand and ran out of the house.

[13]When she saw that he had left his cloak in her hand and had run out of the house, [14]she called her household servants. "Look," she said to them, "this Hebrew has been brought to us to make sport of us! He came in here to sleep with me, but I screamed. [15]When he heard me scream for help, he left his cloak beside me and ran out of the house."

[16]She kept his cloak beside her until his master came home. [17]Then she told him this story: "That Hebrew slave you brought us came to me to make sport of me. [18]But as soon as I screamed for help, he left his cloak beside me and ran out of the house."

[19]When his master heard the story his wife told him, saying, "This is how your slave treated me," he burned with anger. [20]Joseph's master took him and put him in prison, the place where the king's prisoners were confined.

But while Joseph was there in the prison, [21]the LORD was with him; he showed him kindness and granted him favor in the eyes of the prison warden. [22]So the warden put Joseph in charge of all those held in the prison, and he was made responsible for all that was done there. [23]The warden paid no attention to anything under Joseph's care, because the LORD was with Joseph and gave him success in whatever he did.

The Cupbearer and the Baker

40 Some time later, the cupbearer and the baker of the king of Egypt offended their master, the king of Egypt. [2]Pharaoh was angry with his two officials, the chief cupbearer and the chief baker, [3]and put them in custody in the house of the captain of the guard, in the same prison where Joseph was confined. [4]The captain of the guard assigned them to Joseph, and he attended them.

After they had been in custody for some time, [5]each of the two men—the cupbearer and the baker of the king of Egypt, who were being held in prison—had a dream the same night, and each dream had a meaning of its own.

[6]When Joseph came to them the next morning, he saw that they were dejected. [7]So he asked Pharaoh's officials who were in custody with him in his master's house, "Why do you look so sad today?"

[8]"We both had dreams," they answered, "but there is no one to interpret them."

Then Joseph said to them, "Do not interpretations belong to God? Tell me your dreams."

[9]So the chief cupbearer told Joseph his dream. He said to him, "In my dream I saw a vine in front of me, [10]and on the vine were three branches. As soon as it budded, it blossomed, and its clusters ripened into grapes. [11]Pharaoh's cup was in my hand, and I took the grapes, squeezed them into Pharaoh's cup and put the cup in his hand."

[12]"This is what it means," Joseph said to

God's Providence

Genesis 39:1–23

read/meditate

Read this story aloud, as you would a dramatic reading. Focus on Joseph as a real person, just like you. Watch his choices and opportunities. Imagine his ponderings as someone who is living the story, not simply reading it as you are.

pray

Be honest with God about the way you would like to be used by him. Admit any fears or misgivings you have. Be bold about your passions and gifts (which he has given you). Give him time to adjust your hopes and dreams to his.

contemplate

Close your eyes and scroll through the different areas of your life. Could there be places where God has specifically placed you—at just the right place and just the right time—to be a part of his plan? Whether he reveals that to you or not, surrender your heart to his process. Let Joseph's story remind you that it's God's hand that makes the difference.

additional reflection

When we are obedient, God guides our steps and our stops.
—Corrie ten Boom

The world has yet to see what God will do with and for and through and in and by the man who is fully consecrated to Him.
—Henry Varley

Trust the past to God's mercy, the present to God's love and the future to God's providence.
—Saint Augustine

For your next devotional reading, go to page 59.

him. "The three branches are three days. [13]Within three days Pharaoh will lift up your head and restore you to your position, and you will put Pharaoh's cup in his hand, just as you used to do when you were his cupbearer. [14]But when all goes well with you, remember me and show me kindness; mention me to Pharaoh and get me out of this prison. [15]I was forcibly carried off from the land of the Hebrews, and even here I have done nothing to deserve being put in a dungeon."

[16]When the chief baker saw that Joseph had given a favorable interpretation, he said to Joseph, "I too had a dream: On my head were three baskets of bread.[a] [17]In the top basket were all kinds of baked goods for Pharaoh, but the birds were eating them out of the basket on my head."

[18]"This is what it means," Joseph said. "The three baskets are three days. [19]Within three days Pharaoh will lift off your head and impale your body on a pole. And the birds will eat away your flesh."

[20]Now the third day was Pharaoh's birthday, and he gave a feast for all his officials. He lifted up the heads of the chief cupbearer and the chief baker in the presence of his officials: [21]He restored the chief cupbearer to his position, so that he once again put the cup into Pharaoh's hand— [22]but he impaled the chief baker, just as Joseph had said to them in his interpretation.

[23]The chief cupbearer, however, did not remember Joseph; he forgot him.

Pharaoh's Dreams

41 When two full years had passed, Pharaoh had a dream: He was standing by the Nile, [2]when out of the river there came up seven cows, sleek and fat, and they grazed among the reeds. [3]After them, seven other cows, ugly and gaunt, came up out of the Nile and stood beside those on the riverbank. [4]And the cows that were ugly and gaunt ate up the seven sleek, fat cows. Then Pharaoh woke up.

[5]He fell asleep again and had a second dream: Seven heads of grain, healthy and good, were growing on a single stalk. [6]After them, seven other heads of grain sprouted— thin and scorched by the east wind. [7]The thin heads of grain swallowed up the seven healthy, full heads. Then Pharaoh woke up; it had been a dream.

[8]In the morning his mind was troubled, so he sent for all the magicians and wise men of Egypt. Pharaoh told them his dreams, but no one could interpret them for him.

[9]Then the chief cupbearer said to Pharaoh, "Today I am reminded of my shortcomings. [10]Pharaoh was once angry with his servants, and he imprisoned me and the chief baker in the house of the captain of the guard. [11]Each of us had a dream the same night, and each dream had a meaning of its own. [12]Now a young Hebrew was there with us, a servant of the captain of the guard. We told him our dreams, and he interpreted them for us, giving each man the interpretation of his dream. [13]And things turned out exactly as he interpreted them to us: I was restored to my position, and the other man was impaled."

[14]So Pharaoh sent for Joseph, and he was quickly brought from the dungeon. When he had shaved and changed his clothes, he came before Pharaoh.

[15]Pharaoh said to Joseph, "I had a dream, and no one can interpret it. But I have heard it said of you that when you hear a dream you can interpret it."

[16]"I cannot do it," Joseph replied to Pharaoh, "but God will give Pharaoh the answer he desires."

[17]Then Pharaoh said to Joseph, "In my dream I was standing on the bank of the Nile, [18]when out of the river there came up seven cows, fat and sleek, and they grazed among the reeds. [19]After them, seven other cows came up—scrawny and very ugly and lean. I had never seen such ugly cows in all the land of Egypt. [20]The lean, ugly cows ate up the seven fat cows that came up first. [21]But even after they ate them, no one could tell that they had done so; they looked just as ugly as before. Then I woke up.

[22]"In my dream I saw seven heads of grain, full and good, growing on a single stalk. [23]After them, seven other heads sprouted—withered and thin and scorched by the east wind. [24]The thin heads of grain swallowed up the seven good heads. I told this to the magicians, but none of them could explain it to me."

a 16 Or *three wicker baskets*

25Then Joseph said to Pharaoh, "The dreams of Pharaoh are one and the same. God has revealed to Pharaoh what he is about to do. 26The seven good cows are seven years, and the seven good heads of grain are seven years; it is one and the same dream. 27The seven lean, ugly cows that came up afterward are seven years, and so are the seven worthless heads of grain scorched by the east wind: They are seven years of famine.

28"It is just as I said to Pharaoh: God has shown Pharaoh what he is about to do. 29Seven years of great abundance are coming throughout the land of Egypt, 30but seven years of famine will follow them. Then all the abundance in Egypt will be forgotten, and the famine will ravage the land. 31The abundance in the land will not be remembered, because the famine that follows it will be so severe. 32The reason the dream was given to Pharaoh in two forms is that the matter has been firmly decided by God, and God will do it soon.

33"And now let Pharaoh look for a discerning and wise man and put him in charge of the land of Egypt. 34Let Pharaoh appoint commissioners over the land to take a fifth of the harvest of Egypt during the seven years of abundance. 35They should collect all the food of these good years that are coming and store up the grain under the authority of Pharaoh, to be kept in the cities for food. 36This food should be held in reserve for the country, to be used during the seven years of famine that will come upon Egypt, so that the country may not be ruined by the famine."

37The plan seemed good to Pharaoh and to all his officials. 38So Pharaoh asked them, "Can we find anyone like this man, one in whom is the spirit of God*a*?"

39Then Pharaoh said to Joseph, "Since God has made all this known to you, there is no one so discerning and wise as you. 40You shall be in charge of my palace, and all my people are to submit to your orders. Only with respect to the throne will I be greater than you."

Joseph in Charge of Egypt

41So Pharaoh said to Joseph, "I hereby put you in charge of the whole land of Egypt." 42Then Pharaoh took his signet ring from his finger and put it on Joseph's finger. He dressed him in robes of fine linen and put a gold chain around his neck. 43He had him ride in a chariot as his second-in-command,*b* and people shouted before him, "Make way*c*!" Thus he put him in charge of the whole land of Egypt.

44Then Pharaoh said to Joseph, "I am Pharaoh, but without your word no one will lift hand or foot in all Egypt." 45Pharaoh gave Joseph the name Zaphenath-Paneah and gave him Asenath daughter of Potiphera, priest of On,*d* to be his wife. And Joseph went throughout the land of Egypt.

46Joseph was thirty years old when he entered the service of Pharaoh king of Egypt. And Joseph went out from Pharaoh's presence and traveled throughout Egypt. 47During the seven years of abundance the land produced plentifully. 48Joseph collected all the food produced in those seven years of abundance in Egypt and stored it in the cities. In each city he put the food grown in the fields surrounding it. 49Joseph stored up huge quantities of grain, like the sand of the sea; it was so much that he stopped keeping records because it was beyond measure.

50Before the years of famine came, two sons were born to Joseph by Asenath daughter of Potiphera, priest of On. 51Joseph named his firstborn Manasseh*e* and said, "It is because God has made me forget all my trouble and all my father's household." 52The second son he named Ephraim*f* and said, "It is because God has made me fruitful in the land of my suffering."

53The seven years of abundance in Egypt came to an end, 54and the seven years of famine began, just as Joseph had said. There was famine in all the other lands, but in the whole land of Egypt there was food. 55When all Egypt began to feel the famine, the people cried to Pharaoh for food. Then Pharaoh told all the Egyptians, "Go to Joseph and do what he tells you."

56When the famine had spread over the whole country, Joseph opened all the storehouses and sold grain to the Egyptians, for the famine was severe throughout Egypt. 57And all the world came to Egypt to buy

---

a 38 Or of the gods   b 43 Or in the chariot of his second-in-command; or in his second chariot   c 43 Or Bow down   d 45 That is, Heliopolis; also in verse 50   e 51 Manasseh sounds like and may be derived from the Hebrew for forget.   f 52 Ephraim sounds like the Hebrew for twice fruitful.

grain from Joseph, because the famine was severe everywhere.

Joseph's Brothers Go to Egypt

42 When Jacob learned that there was grain in Egypt, he said to his sons, "Why do you just keep looking at each other?" [2]He continued, "I have heard that there is grain in Egypt. Go down there and buy some for us, so that we may live and not die."

[3]Then ten of Joseph's brothers went down to buy grain from Egypt. [4]But Jacob did not send Benjamin, Joseph's brother, with the others, because he was afraid that harm might come to him. [5]So Israel's sons were among those who went to buy grain, for the famine was in the land of Canaan also.

[6]Now Joseph was the governor of the land, the person who sold grain to all its people. So when Joseph's brothers arrived, they bowed down to him with their faces to the ground. [7]As soon as Joseph saw his brothers, he recognized them, but he pretended to be a stranger and spoke harshly to them. "Where do you come from?" he asked.

"From the land of Canaan," they replied, "to buy food."

[8]Although Joseph recognized his brothers, they did not recognize him. [9]Then he remembered his dreams about them and said to them, "You are spies! You have come to see where our land is unprotected."

[10]"No, my lord," they answered. "Your servants have come to buy food. [11]We are all the sons of one man. Your servants are honest men, not spies."

[12]"No!" he said to them. "You have come to see where our land is unprotected."

[13]But they replied, "Your servants were twelve brothers, the sons of one man, who lives in the land of Canaan. The youngest is now with our father, and one is no more."

[14]Joseph said to them, "It is just as I told you: You are spies! [15]And this is how you will be tested: As surely as Pharaoh lives, you will not leave this place unless your youngest brother comes here. [16]Send one of your number to get your brother; the rest of you will be kept in prison, so that your words may be tested to see if you are telling the truth. If you are not, then as surely as Pharaoh lives, you are spies!" [17]And he put them all in custody for three days.

[18]On the third day, Joseph said to them, "Do this and you will live, for I fear God: [19]If you are honest men, let one of your brothers stay here in prison, while the rest of you go and take grain back for your starving households, [20]But you must bring your youngest brother to me, so that your words may be verified and that you may not die." This they proceeded to do.

[21]They said to one another, "Surely we are being punished because of our brother. We saw how distressed he was when he pleaded with us for his life, but we would not listen; that's why this distress has come on us."

[22]Reuben replied, "Didn't I tell you not to sin against the boy? But you wouldn't listen! Now we must give an accounting for his blood." [23]They did not realize that Joseph could understand them, since he was using an interpreter.

[24]He turned away from them and began to weep, but then came back and spoke to them again. He had Simeon taken from them and bound before their eyes.

[25]Joseph gave orders to fill their bags with grain, to put each man's silver back in his sack, and to give them provisions for their journey. After this was done for them, [26]they loaded their grain on their donkeys and left.

[27]At the place where they stopped for the night one of them opened his sack to get feed for his donkey, and he saw his silver in the mouth of his sack. [28]"My silver has been returned," he said to his brothers. "Here it is in my sack."

Their hearts sank and they turned to each other trembling and said, "What is this that God has done to us?"

[29]When they came to their father Jacob in the land of Canaan, they told him all that had happened to them. They said, [30]"The man who is lord over the land spoke harshly to us and treated us as though we were spying on the land. [31]But we said to him, 'We are honest men; we are not spies. [32]We were twelve brothers, sons of one father. One is no more, and the youngest is now with our father in Canaan.'

[33]"Then the man who is lord over the land said to us, 'This is how I will know whether you are honest men: Leave one of your brothers here with me, and take food for your starving households and go. [34]But bring your youngest brother to me so I will know that you are not spies but honest men. Then

I will give your brother back to you, and you can trade[a] in the land.' "

³⁵As they were emptying their sacks, there in each man's sack was his pouch of silver! When they and their father saw the money pouches, they were frightened. ³⁶Their father Jacob said to them, "You have deprived me of my children. Joseph is no more and Simeon is no more, and now you want to take Benjamin. Everything is against me!"

³⁷Then Reuben said to his father, "You may put both of my sons to death if I do not bring him back to you. Entrust him to my care, and I will bring him back."

³⁸But Jacob said, "My son will not go down there with you; his brother is dead and he is the only one left. If harm comes to him on the journey you are taking, you will bring my gray head down to the grave in sorrow."

The Second Journey to Egypt

43 Now the famine was still severe in the land. ²So when they had eaten all the grain they had brought from Egypt, their father said to them, "Go back and buy us a little more food."

³But Judah said to him, "The man warned us solemnly, 'You will not see my face again unless your brother is with you.' ⁴If you will send our brother along with us, we will go down and buy food for you. ⁵But if you will not send him, we will not go down, because the man said to us, 'You will not see my face again unless your brother is with you.' "

⁶Israel asked, "Why did you bring this trouble on me by telling the man you had another brother?"

⁷They replied, "The man questioned us closely about ourselves and our family. 'Is your father still living?' he asked us. 'Do you have another brother?' We simply answered his questions. How were we to know he would say, 'Bring your brother down here'?"

⁸Then Judah said to Israel his father, "Send the boy along with me and we will go at once, so that we and you and our children may live and not die. ⁹I myself will guarantee his safety; you can hold me personally responsible for him. If I do not bring him back to you and set him here before you, I will bear the blame before you all my life.

¹⁰As it is, if we had not delayed, we could have gone and returned twice."

¹¹Then their father Israel said to them, "If it must be, then do this: Put some of the best products of the land in your bags and take them down to the man as a gift—a little balm and a little honey, some spices and myrrh, some pistachio nuts and almonds. ¹²Take double the amount of silver with you, for you must return the silver that was put back into the mouths of your sacks. Perhaps it was a mistake. ¹³Take your brother also and go back to the man at once. ¹⁴And may God Almighty[b] grant you mercy before the man so that he will let your other brother and Benjamin come back with you. As for me, if I am bereaved, I am bereaved."

¹⁵So the men took the gifts and double the amount of silver, and Benjamin also. They hurried down to Egypt and presented themselves to Joseph. ¹⁶When Joseph saw Benjamin with them, he said to the steward of his house, "Take these men to my house, slaughter an animal and prepare a meal; they are to eat with me at noon."

¹⁷The man did as Joseph told him and took the men to Joseph's house. ¹⁸Now the men were frightened when they were taken to his house. They thought, "We were brought here because of the silver that was put back into our sacks the first time. He wants to attack us and overpower us and seize us as slaves and take our donkeys."

¹⁹So they went up to Joseph's steward and spoke to him at the entrance to the house. ²⁰"We beg your pardon, our lord," they said, "we came down here the first time to buy food. ²¹But at the place where we stopped for the night we opened our sacks and each of us found his silver—the exact weight—in the mouth of his sack. So we have brought it back with us. ²²We have also brought additional silver with us to buy food. We don't know who put our silver in our sacks."

²³"It's all right," he said. "Don't be afraid. Your God, the God of your father, has given you treasure in your sacks; I received your silver." Then he brought Simeon out to them.

²⁴The steward took the men into Joseph's house, gave them water to wash their feet and provided fodder for their donkeys. ²⁵They prepared their gifts for Joseph's arriv-

al at noon, because they had heard that they were to eat there.

²⁶When Joseph came home, they presented to him the gifts they had brought into the house, and they bowed down before him to the ground. ²⁷He asked them how they were, and then he said, "How is your aged father you told me about? Is he still living?"

²⁸They replied, "Your servant our father is still alive and well." And they bowed down, prostrating themselves before him.

²⁹As he looked about and saw his brother Benjamin, his own mother's son, he asked, "Is this your youngest brother, the one you told me about?" And he said, "God be gracious to you, my son." ³⁰Deeply moved at the sight of his brother, Joseph hurried out and looked for a place to weep. He went into his private room and wept there.

³¹After he had washed his face, he came out and, controlling himself, said, "Serve the food."

³²They served him by himself, the brothers by themselves, and the Egyptians who ate with him by themselves, because Egyptians could not eat with Hebrews, for that is detestable to Egyptians. ³³The men had been seated before him in the order of their ages, from the firstborn to the youngest; and they looked at each other in astonishment. ³⁴When portions were served to them from Joseph's table, Benjamin's portion was five times as much as anyone else's. So they feasted and drank freely with him.

A Silver Cup in a Sack

44 Now Joseph gave these instructions to the steward of his house: "Fill the men's sacks with as much food as they can carry, and put each man's silver in the mouth of his sack. ²Then put my cup, the silver one, in the mouth of the youngest one's sack, along with the silver for his grain." And he did as Joseph said.

³As morning dawned, the men were sent on their way with their donkeys. ⁴They had not gone far from the city when Joseph said to his steward, "Go after those men at once, and when you catch up with them, say to them, 'Why have you repaid good with evil? ⁵Isn't this the cup my master drinks from and also uses for divination? This is a wicked thing you have done.'"

⁶When he caught up with them, he re-

peated these words to them. ⁷But they said to him, "Why does my lord say such things? Far be it from your servants to do anything like that! ⁸We even brought back to you from the land of Canaan the silver we found inside the mouths of our sacks. So why would we steal silver or gold from your master's house? ⁹If any of your servants is found to have it, he will die; and the rest of us will become my lord's slaves."

¹⁰"Very well, then," he said, "let it be as you say. Whoever is found to have it will become my slave; the rest of you will be free from blame."

¹¹Each of them quickly lowered his sack to the ground and opened it. ¹²Then the steward proceeded to search, beginning with the oldest and ending with the youngest. And the cup was found in Benjamin's sack. ¹³At this, they tore their clothes. Then they all loaded their donkeys and returned to the city.

¹⁴Joseph was still in the house when Judah and his brothers came in, and they threw themselves to the ground before him. ¹⁵Joseph said to them, "What is this you have done? Don't you know that a man like me can find things out by divination?"

¹⁶"What can we say to my lord?" Judah replied. "What can we say? How can we prove our innocence? God has uncovered your servants' guilt. We are now my lord's slaves—we ourselves and the one who was found to have the cup."

¹⁷But Joseph said, "Far be it from me to do such a thing! Only the man who was found to have the cup will become my slave. The rest of you, go back to your father in peace."

¹⁸Then Judah went up to him and said: "Pardon your servant, my lord, let me speak a word to my lord. Do not be angry with your servant, though you are equal to Pharaoh himself. ¹⁹My lord asked his servants, 'Do you have a father or a brother?' ²⁰And we answered, 'We have an aged father, and there is a young son born to him in his old age. His brother is dead, and he is the only one of his mother's sons left, and his father loves him.'

²¹"Then you said to your servants, 'Bring him down to me so I can see him for myself.' ²²And we said to my lord, 'The boy cannot leave his father; if he leaves his father, his father will die.' ²³But you told your servants, 'Unless your youngest brother comes down with

you, you will not see my face again.' ²⁴When we went back to your servant my father, we told him what my lord had said.

²⁵"Then our father said, 'Go back and buy a little more food.' ²⁶But we said, 'We cannot go down. Only if our youngest brother is with us will we go. We cannot see the man's face unless our youngest brother is with us.'

²⁷"Your servant my father said to us, 'You know that my wife bore me two sons. ²⁸One of them went away from me, and I said, "He has surely been torn to pieces." And I have not seen him since. ²⁹If you take this one from me too and harm comes to him, you will bring my gray head down to the grave in misery.'

³⁰"So now, if the boy is not with us when I go back to your servant my father, and if my father, whose life is closely bound up with the boy's life, ³¹sees that the boy isn't there, he will die. Your servants will bring the gray head of our father down to the grave in sorrow. ³²Your servant guaranteed the boy's safety to my father. I said, 'If I do not bring him back to you, I will bear the blame before you, my father, all my life!'

³³"Now then, please let your servant remain here as my lord's slave in place of the boy, and let the boy return with his brothers. ³⁴How can I go back to my father if the boy is not with me? No! Do not let me see the misery that would come on my father."

Joseph Makes Himself Known

45 Then Joseph could no longer control himself before all his attendants, and he cried out, "Have everyone leave my presence!" So there was no one with Joseph when he made himself known to his brothers. ²And he wept so loudly that the Egyptians heard him, and Pharaoh's household heard about it.

³Joseph said to his brothers, "I am Joseph! Is my father still living?" But his brothers were not able to answer him, because they were terrified at his presence.

⁴Then Joseph said to his brothers, "Come close to me." When they had done so, he said, "I am your brother Joseph, the one you sold into Egypt! ⁵And now, do not be distressed and do not be angry with yourselves for selling me here, because it was to save lives that God sent me ahead of you. ⁶For

two years now there has been famine in the land, and for the next five years there will be no plowing and reaping. ⁷But God sent me ahead of you to preserve for you a remnant on earth and to save your lives by a great deliverance.ᵃ

⁸"So then, it was not you who sent me here, but God. He made me father to Pharaoh, lord of his entire household and ruler of all Egypt. ⁹Now hurry back to my father and say to him, 'This is what your son Joseph says: God has made me lord of all Egypt. Come down to me; don't delay. ¹⁰You shall live in the region of Goshen and be near me—you, your children and grandchildren, your flocks and herds, and all you have. ¹¹I will provide for you there, because five years of famine are still to come. Otherwise you and your household and all who belong to you will become destitute.'

¹²"You can see for yourselves, and so can my brother Benjamin, that it is really I who am speaking to you. ¹³Tell my father about all the honor accorded me in Egypt and about everything you have seen. And bring my father down here quickly."

¹⁴Then he threw his arms around his brother Benjamin and wept, and Benjamin embraced him, weeping. ¹⁵And he kissed all his brothers and wept over them. Afterward his brothers talked with him.

¹⁶When the news reached Pharaoh's palace that Joseph's brothers had come, Pharaoh and all his officials were pleased. ¹⁷Pharaoh said to Joseph, "Tell your brothers, 'Do this: Load your animals and return to the land of Canaan, ¹⁸and bring your father and your families back to me. I will give you the best of the land of Egypt and you can enjoy the fat of the land.'

¹⁹"You are also directed to tell them, 'Do this: Take some carts from Egypt for your children and your wives, and get your father and come. ²⁰Never mind about your belongings, because the best of all Egypt will be yours.' "

²¹So the sons of Israel did this. Joseph gave them carts, as Pharaoh had commanded, and he also gave them provisions for their journey. ²²To each of them he gave new clothing, but to Benjamin he gave three hundred shekelsᵇ of silver and five sets of clothes. ²³And this is what he sent to his fa-

---

ᵃ 7 Or *save you as a great band of survivors*   ᵇ 22 That is, about 7 1/2 pounds or about 3.5 kilograms

MONDAY

BEING OF SPIRITUAL USE TO GOD

Genesis 45:1–28 *or* 45:7

Mike Pilavachi

When we see that the God we worship is the creator of the entire universe, even when things don't go so well for us, then problems and disappointments no longer seem quite so bad. After all, since He is the ultimate boss, who are we to argue when He seems to take things in a slightly different direction from the one we had in mind?

For example, when something bad happened to Joseph—like being sold into slavery by his brothers—he decided not to get bitter. He told his brothers years later that what they meant for harm, God meant for good. "God sent me ahead of you . . . to save your lives by a great deliverance," Joseph said to his brothers (Genesis 45:7). If Joseph had refused to forgive his brothers, then all his claims about God's greatness, all his worship and devotion, would have meant nothing. If we are to have integrity, if our worship is to have integrity, then it must spill over to the attitudes of our lives.

We Christians have often been on the receiving end of the criticism that we can be too focused on heaven to be of any earthly use. I think the same can be said the other way around: that we can also be too focused on the things of Earth to be any heavenly use. When we are focused on heaven in the best way, then we are fit for a life on Earth. It helps when we see things the right way around, get things in the right order and realize our place in the universe.

C. S. LEWIS {AD 1898–1963}

If you read history, you will find that the Christians who did most for the present world were just those who thought most of the next. The apostles themselves, who set on foot the conversion of the Roman Empire, the great men who built up the Middle Ages, the English evangelicals who abolished the slave trade, all left their mark on earth, precisely because their minds were occupied with heaven. It is since Christians have largely ceased to think of the other world that they have become so ineffective in this.

reflection

1. How have you responded when God took your life in a different direction than the one you'd planned?

2. What did you learn through that time?

3. How does focusing your heart on heaven affect the way you live on earth?

For your next devotional reading, go to page 65.

ther: ten donkeys loaded with the best things of Egypt, and ten female donkeys loaded with grain and bread and other provisions for his journey. ²⁴Then he sent his brothers away, and as they were leaving he said to them, "Don't quarrel on the way!"

²⁵So they went up out of Egypt and came to their father Jacob in the land of Canaan. ²⁶They told him, "Joseph is still alive! In fact, he is ruler of all Egypt." Jacob was stunned; he did not believe them. ²⁷But when they told him everything Joseph had said to them, and when he saw the carts Joseph had sent to carry him back, the spirit of their father Jacob revived. ²⁸And Israel said, "I'm convinced! My son Joseph is still alive. I will go and see him before I die."

Jacob Goes to Egypt

46 So Israel set out with all that was his, and when he reached Beersheba, he offered sacrifices to the God of his father Isaac.

²And God spoke to Israel in a vision at night and said, "Jacob! Jacob!"

"Here I am," he replied.

³"I am God, the God of your father," he said. "Do not be afraid to go down to Egypt, for I will make you into a great nation there. ⁴I will go down to Egypt with you, and I will surely bring you back again. And Joseph's own hand will close your eyes."

⁵Then Jacob left Beersheba, and Israel's sons took their father Jacob and their children and their wives in the carts that Pharaoh had sent to transport him. ⁶So Jacob and all his offspring went to Egypt, taking with them their livestock and the possessions they had acquired in Canaan. ⁷Jacob brought with him to Egypt his sons and grandsons and his daughters and granddaughters—all his offspring.

⁸These are the names of the sons of Israel (Jacob and his descendants) who went to Egypt:

Reuben the firstborn of Jacob.
⁹The sons of Reuben:
  Hanok, Pallu, Hezron and Karmi.
¹⁰The sons of Simeon:
  Jemuel, Jamin, Ohad, Jakin, Zohar

and Shaul the son of a Canaanite woman.
¹¹The sons of Levi:
  Gershon, Kohath and Merari.
¹²The sons of Judah:
  Er, Onan, Shelah, Perez and Zerah (but Er and Onan had died in the land of Canaan).
  The sons of Perez:
    Hezron and Hamul.
¹³The sons of Issachar:
  Tola, Puah,ᵃ Jashubᵇ and Shimron.
¹⁴The sons of Zebulun:
  Sered, Elon and Jahleel.
¹⁵These were the sons Leah bore to Jacob in Paddan Aram,ᶜ besides his daughter Dinah. These sons and daughters of his were thirty-three in all.

¹⁶The sons of Gad:
  Zephon,ᵈ Haggi, Shuni, Ezbon, Eri, Arodi and Areli.
¹⁷The sons of Asher:
  Imnah, Ishvah, Ishvi and Beriah.
  Their sister was Serah.
  The sons of Beriah:
    Heber and Malkiel.
¹⁸These were the children born to Jacob by Zilpah, whom Laban had given to his daughter Leah—sixteen in all.

¹⁹The sons of Jacob's wife Rachel:
  Joseph and Benjamin. ²⁰In Egypt, Manasseh and Ephraim were born to Joseph by Asenath daughter of Potiphera, priest of On.ᵉ
²¹The sons of Benjamin:
  Bela, Beker, Ashbel, Gera, Naaman, Ehi, Rosh, Muppim, Huppim and Ard.
²²These were the sons of Rachel who were born to Jacob—fourteen in all.

²³The son of Dan:
  Hushim.
²⁴The sons of Naphtali:
  Jahziel, Guni, Jezer and Shillem.
²⁵These were the sons born to Jacob by Bilhah, whom Laban had given to his daughter Rachel—seven in all.

²⁶All those who went to Egypt with Jacob—those who were his direct descen-

---

ᵃ 13 Samaritan Pentateuch and Syriac (see also 1 Chron. 7:1); Masoretic Text *Puvah*   ᵇ 13 Samaritan Pentateuch and some Septuagint manuscripts (see also Num. 26:24 and 1 Chron. 7:1); Masoretic Text *Iob*   ᶜ 15 That is, Northwest Mesopotamia   ᵈ 16 Samaritan Pentateuch and Septuagint (see also Num. 26:15); Masoretic Text *Ziphion*   ᵉ 20 That is, Heliopolis dants, not counting his sons' wives—numbered sixty-six persons. ²⁷With the two sons^a who had been born to Joseph in Egypt, the members of Jacob's family, which went to Egypt, were seventy^b in all.

²⁸Now Jacob sent Judah ahead of him to Joseph to get directions to Goshen. When they arrived in the region of Goshen, ²⁹Joseph had his chariot made ready and went to Goshen to meet his father Israel. As soon as Joseph appeared before him, he threw his arms around his father^c and wept for a long time.

³⁰Israel said to Joseph, "Now I am ready to die, since I have seen for myself that you are still alive."

³¹Then Joseph said to his brothers and to his father's household, "I will go up and speak to Pharaoh and will say to him, 'My brothers and my father's household, who were living in the land of Canaan, have come to me. ³²The men are shepherds; they tend livestock, and they have brought along their flocks and herds and everything they own.' ³³When Pharaoh calls you in and asks, 'What is your occupation?' ³⁴you should answer, 'Your servants have tended livestock from our boyhood on, just as our fathers did.' Then you will be allowed to settle in the region of Goshen, for all shepherds are detestable to the Egyptians."

47 Joseph went and told Pharaoh, "My father and brothers, with their flocks and herds and everything they own, have come from the land of Canaan and are now in Goshen." ²He chose five of his brothers and presented them before Pharaoh.

³Pharaoh asked the brothers, "What is your occupation?"

"Your servants are shepherds," they replied to Pharaoh, "just as our fathers were." ⁴They also said to him, "We have come to live here for a while, because the famine is severe in Canaan and your servants' flocks have no pasture. So now, please let your servants settle in Goshen."

⁵Pharaoh said to Joseph, "Your father and your brothers have come to you, ⁶and the land of Egypt is before you; settle your father and your brothers in the best part of

the land. Let them live in Goshen. And if you know of any among them with special ability, put them in charge of my own livestock."

⁷Then Joseph brought his father Jacob in and presented him before Pharaoh. After Jacob blessed^d Pharaoh, ⁸Pharaoh asked him, "How old are you?"

⁹And Jacob said to Pharaoh, "The years of my pilgrimage are a hundred and thirty. My years have been few and difficult, and they do not equal the years of the pilgrimage of my fathers." ¹⁰Then Jacob blessed^e Pharaoh and went out from his presence.

¹¹So Joseph settled his father and his brothers in Egypt and gave them property in the best part of the land, the district of Rameses, as Pharaoh directed. ¹²Joseph also provided his father and his brothers and all his father's household with food, according to the number of their children.

Joseph and the Famine

¹³There was no food, however, in the whole region because the famine was severe; both Egypt and Canaan wasted away because of the famine. ¹⁴Joseph collected all the money that was to be found in Egypt and Canaan in payment for the grain they were buying, and he brought it to Pharaoh's palace. ¹⁵When the money of the people of Egypt and Canaan was gone, all Egypt came to Joseph and said, "Give us food. Why should we die before your eyes? Our money is all gone."

¹⁶"Then bring your livestock," said Joseph. "I will sell you food in exchange for your livestock, since your money is gone." ¹⁷So they brought their livestock to Joseph, and he gave them food in exchange for their horses, their sheep and goats, their cattle and donkeys. And he brought them through that year with food in exchange for all their livestock.

¹⁸When that year was over, they came to him the following year and said, "We cannot hide from our lord the fact that since our money is gone and our livestock belongs to you, there is nothing left for our lord except our bodies and our land. ¹⁹Why should we perish before your eyes—we and our land as well? Buy us and our land in exchange for

^a 27 Hebrew; Septuagint *the nine children*   ^b 27 Hebrew (see also Exodus 1:5 and footnote); Septuagint (see also Acts 7:14) *seventy-five*   ^c 29 Hebrew *around him*   ^d 7 Or *greeted*   ^e 10 Or *said farewell to*

food, and we with our land will be in bondage to Pharaoh. Give us seed so that we may live and not die, and that the land may not become desolate."

²⁰So Joseph bought all the land in Egypt for Pharaoh. The Egyptians, one and all, sold their fields, because the famine was too severe for them. The land became Pharaoh's, ²¹and Joseph reduced the people to servitude,ᵃ from one end of Egypt to the other. ²²However, he did not buy the land of the priests, because they received a regular allotment from Pharaoh and had food enough from the allotment Pharaoh gave them. That is why they did not sell their land.

²³Joseph said to the people, "Now that I have bought you and your land today for Pharaoh, here is seed for you so you can plant the ground. ²⁴But when the crop comes in, give a fifth of it to Pharaoh. The other four-fifths you may keep as seed for the fields and as food for yourselves and your households and your children."

²⁵"You have saved our lives," they said. "May we find favor in the eyes of our lord; we will be in bondage to Pharaoh."

²⁶So Joseph established it as a law concerning land in Egypt—still in force today—that a fifth of the produce belongs to Pharaoh. It was only the land of the priests that did not become Pharaoh's.

²⁷Now the Israelites settled in Egypt in the region of Goshen. They acquired property there and were fruitful and increased greatly in number.

²⁸Jacob lived in Egypt seventeen years, and the years of his life were a hundred and forty-seven. ²⁹When the time drew near for Israel to die, he called for his son Joseph and said to him, "If I have found favor in your eyes, put your hand under my thigh and promise that you will show me kindness and faithfulness. Do not bury me in Egypt, ³⁰but when I rest with my fathers, carry me out of Egypt and bury me where they are buried."

"I will do as you say," he said.

³¹"Swear to me," he said. Then Joseph swore to him, and Israel worshiped as he leaned on the top of his staff.ᵇ

Manasseh and Ephraim

48 Some time later Joseph was told, "Your father is ill." So he took his two sons Manasseh and Ephraim along with him. ²When Jacob was told, "Your son Joseph has come to you," Israel rallied his strength and sat up on the bed.

³Jacob said to Joseph, "God Almightyᶜ appeared to me at Luz in the land of Canaan, and there he blessed me ⁴and said to me, 'I am going to make you fruitful and increase your numbers. I will make you a community of peoples, and I will give this land as an everlasting possession to your descendants after you.'

⁵"Now then, your two sons born to you in Egypt before I came to you here will be reckoned as mine; Ephraim and Manasseh will be mine, just as Reuben and Simeon are mine. ⁶Any children born to you after them will be yours; in the territory they inherit they will be reckoned under the names of their brothers. ⁷As I was returning from Paddan,ᵈ to my sorrow Rachel died in the land of Canaan while we were still on the way, a little distance from Ephrath. So I buried her there beside the road to Ephrath" (that is, Bethlehem).

⁸When Israel saw the sons of Joseph, he asked, "Who are these?"

⁹"They are the sons God has given me here," Joseph said to his father.

Then Israel said, "Bring them to me so I may bless them."

¹⁰Now Israel's eyes were failing because of old age, and he could hardly see. So Joseph brought his sons close to him, and his father kissed them and embraced them.

¹¹Israel said to Joseph, "I never expected to see your face again, and now God has allowed me to see your children too."

¹²Then Joseph removed them from Israel's knees and bowed down with his face to the ground. ¹³And Joseph took both of them, Ephraim on his right toward Israel's left hand and Manasseh on his left toward Israel's right hand, and brought them close to him. ¹⁴But Israel reached out his right hand and put it on Ephraim's head, though he was the younger, and crossing his arms, he put

---

ᵃ 21 Samaritan Pentateuch and Septuagint (see also Vulgate); Masoretic Text *and he moved the people into the cities*   ᵇ 31 Or *Israel bowed down at the head of his bed*   ᶜ 3 Hebrew *El-Shaddai*   ᵈ 7 That is, Northwest Mesopotamia his left hand on Manasseh's head, even though Manasseh was the firstborn. [15]Then he blessed Joseph and said,

"May the God before whom my fathers
Abraham and Isaac walked faithfully,
the God who has been my shepherd
all my life to this day,
[16]the Angel who has delivered me from all harm
—may he bless these boys.
May they be called by my name
and the names of my fathers
Abraham and Isaac,
and may they increase greatly
on the earth."

[17]When Joseph saw his father placing his right hand on Ephraim's head he was displeased; so he took hold of his father's hand to move it from Ephraim's head to Manasseh's head. [18]Joseph said to him, "No, my father, this one is the firstborn; put your right hand on his head."

[19]But his father refused and said, "I know, my son, I know. He too will become a people, and he too will become great. Nevertheless, his younger brother will be greater than he, and his descendants will become a group of nations." [20]He blessed them that day and said,

"In your[a] name will Israel pronounce
this blessing:
'May God make you like Ephraim and
Manasseh.' "

So he put Ephraim ahead of Manasseh.

[21]Then Israel said to Joseph, "I am about to die, but God will be with you[b] and take you[b] back to the land of your[b] fathers. [22]And to you I give one more ridge of land[c] than to your brothers, the ridge I took from the Amorites with my sword and my bow."

Jacob Blesses His Sons

49 Then Jacob called for his sons and said: "Gather around so I can tell you what will happen to you in days to come.

[2]"Assemble and listen, sons of Jacob;
listen to your father Israel.

[3]"Reuben, you are my firstborn,
my might, the first sign of my
strength,
excelling in honor, excelling in power.
[4]Turbulent as the waters, you will no
longer excel,
for you went up onto your father's bed,
onto my couch and defiled it.

[5]"Simeon and Levi are brothers—
their swords[d] are weapons of
violence.
[6]Let me not enter their council,
let me not join their assembly,
for they have killed men in their anger
and hamstrung oxen as they pleased.
[7]Cursed be their anger, so fierce,
and their fury, so cruel!
I will scatter them in Jacob
and disperse them in Israel.

[8]"Judah,[e] your brothers will praise you;
your hand will be on the neck of your
enemies;
your father's sons will bow down to
you.
[9]You are a lion's cub, Judah;
you return from the prey, my son.
Like a lion he crouches and lies down,
like a lioness—who dares to rouse
him?
[10]The scepter will not depart from Judah,
nor the ruler's staff from between his
feet,[f]
until he to whom it belongs[g] shall come
and the obedience of the nations be
his.
[11]He will tether his donkey to a vine,
his colt to the choicest branch;
he will wash his garments in wine,
his robes in the blood of grapes.
[12]His eyes will be darker than wine,
his teeth whiter than milk.[h]

[13]"Zebulun will live by the seashore
and become a haven for ships;
his border will extend toward Sidon.

[14]"Issachar is a rawboned[i] donkey
lying down among the sheep pens.[j]
[15]When he sees how good is his resting
place

---

[a] 20 The Hebrew is singular.   [b] 21 The Hebrew is plural.   [c] 22 The Hebrew for *ridge of land* is identical with the place name Shechem.   [d] 5 The meaning of the Hebrew for this word is uncertain.
[e] 8 *Judah* sounds like and may be derived from the Hebrew for *praise*.   [f] 10 Or *from his descendants*
[g] 10 Or *to whom tribute belongs*; the meaning of the Hebrew for this phrase is uncertain.   [h] 12 Or *will be dull from wine, / his teeth white from milk*   [i] 14 Or *strong*   [j] 14 Or *the campfires*; or *the saddlebags*

and how pleasant is his land,
he will bend his shoulder to the burden
and submit to forced labor.

¹⁶ "Dan^a will provide justice for his people
as one of the tribes of Israel.
¹⁷ Dan will be a snake by the roadside,
a viper along the path,
that bites the horse's heels
so that its rider tumbles backward.

¹⁸ "I look for your deliverance, LORD.

¹⁹ "Gad^b will be attacked by a band of
raiders,
but he will attack them at their heels.

²⁰ "Asher's food will be rich;
he will provide delicacies fit for a
king.

²¹ "Naphtali is a doe set free
that bears beautiful fawns.^c

²² "Joseph is a fruitful vine,
a fruitful vine near a spring,
whose branches climb over a wall.^d
²³ With bitterness archers attacked him;
they shot at him with hostility.
²⁴ But his bow remained steady,
his strong arms stayed^e limber,
because of the hand of the Mighty One
of Jacob,
because of the Shepherd, the Rock of
Israel,
²⁵ because of your father's God, who helps
you,
because of the Almighty,^f who blesses
you
with blessings of the heavens above,
blessings of the deep that lies below,
blessings of the breast and womb.
²⁶ Your father's blessings are greater
than the blessings of the ancient
mountains,
than^g the bounty of the age-old hills.
Let all these rest on the head of Joseph,
on the brow of the prince among^h his
brothers.

²⁷ "Benjamin is a ravenous wolf;
in the morning he devours the prey,
in the evening he divides the
plunder."

²⁸ All these are the twelve tribes of Israel, and this is what their father said to them when he blessed them, giving each the blessing appropriate to him.

The Death of Jacob

²⁹ Then he gave them these instructions: "I am about to be gathered to my people. Bury me with my fathers in the cave in the field of Ephron the Hittite, ³⁰the cave in the field of Machpelah, near Mamre in Canaan, which Abraham bought along with the field as a burial place from Ephron the Hittite. ³¹There Abraham and his wife Sarah were buried, there Isaac and his wife Rebekah were buried, and there I buried Leah. ³²The field and the cave in it were bought from the Hittites.ⁱ"

³³When Jacob had finished giving instructions to his sons, he drew his feet up into the bed, breathed his last and was gathered to his people.

50 Joseph threw himself on his father and wept over him and kissed him. ²Then Joseph directed the physicians in his service to embalm his father Israel. So the physicians embalmed him, ³taking a full forty days, for that was the time required for embalming. And the Egyptians mourned for him seventy days.

⁴When the days of mourning had passed, Joseph said to Pharaoh's court, "If I have found favor in your eyes, speak to Pharaoh for me. Tell him, ⁵'My father made me swear an oath and said, "I am about to die; bury me in the tomb I dug for myself in the land of Canaan." Now let me go up and bury my father; then I will return.' "

⁶Pharaoh said, "Go up and bury your father, as he made you swear to do."

⁷So Joseph went up to bury his father. All Pharaoh's officials accompanied him—the dignitaries of his court and all the dignitaries of Egypt— ⁸besides all the members of Joseph's household and his brothers and those belonging to his father's household. Only their children and their flocks and herds were left in Goshen. ⁹Chariots and

---

^a 16 Dan here means he provides justice.   ^b 19 Gad sounds like the Hebrew for attack and also for band of raiders.   ^c 21 Or free; / he utters beautiful words   ^d 22 Or Joseph is a wild colt, / a wild colt near a spring, / a wild donkey on a terraced hill   ^e 23,24 Or archers will attack . . . will shoot . . . will remain . . . will stay   ^f 25 Hebrew Shaddai   ^g 26 Or of my progenitors, / as great as   ^h 26 Or of the one separated from   ⁱ 32 Or the descendants of Heth

TUESDAY

JOSEPH'S FORGIVENESS

Genesis 50:1–21 or 50:19–21

Joyce G. Baldwin

In his exalted office Joseph could have become an overbearing tyrant, getting his own back in full measure. This is what his brothers expected him to do, and presumably what they themselves would have done in the same circumstances. Joseph's "[Don't be afraid]" was intended to reassure them that nothing of the sort was in his mind. He freely forgave them, so setting an example of forgiveness unsurpassed in the Old Testament.

By what process of thought did Joseph overcome his natural resentment of the cruel treatment he received at the hand of his brothers? "[You intended to harm me]," he said. Joseph did not minimize the wrong they had done him, nor pretend that it could be overlooked. On the contrary, he stated it plainly, for they needed to be faced with their crime. Joseph's approach had nothing in common with the permissiveness that indulges the wrongdoer and minimizes the need for a change of heart and life. The truth that had gripped him gave him the conviction that "[God intended it for good]." Despite all the injustice he had suffered, and the years of imprisonment, Joseph could see God's hand at work in the outcome of events. He himself had been vindicated by his promotion to the highest office in the land. His reputation was such that under his regime fair distribution of the emergency food supplies was never in doubt. Everyone trusted him. But more than that, God had used the evil "[to accomplish . . . the saving of many lives]." Thousands lived who otherwise would have starved to death, and not least Joseph's would-be assassins, the chosen family.

MATTHEW HENRY {AD 1662–1714}

Notice what an excellent spirit Joseph had, and learn from him to return good for evil. He did not tell his brothers that they must be on their best behavior. He did not say he would be kind to them only if he saw they conducted themselves well. No, he would not hold them in suspense this way, nor seem jealous of them, though they had been suspicious of him. "He reassured them," and to banish all their fears, he "spoke kindly to them." Note that broken spirits must be bandaged up and encouraged. We must not only do well for those we love and forgive, but we must also speak kindly to them.

reflection

1. When have you seen God use the mistreatment of someone for a greater purpose?
2. When was the last time you were harmed by a family member, neighbor or coworker?
3. How can the lessons of Joseph affect your prayers about that situation?

For your next devotional reading, go to page 69.

horsemen[a] also went up with him. It was a very large company.

[10]When they reached the threshing floor of Atad, near the Jordan, they lamented loudly and bitterly; and there Joseph observed a seven-day period of mourning for his father. [11]When the Canaanites who lived there saw the mourning at the threshing floor of Atad, they said, "The Egyptians are holding a solemn ceremony of mourning." That is why that place near the Jordan is called Abel Mizraim.[b]

[12]So Jacob's sons did as he had commanded them: [13]They carried him to the land of Canaan and buried him in the cave in the field of Machpelah, near Mamre, which Abraham had bought along with the field as a burial place from Ephron the Hittite. [14]After burying his father, Joseph returned to Egypt, together with his brothers and all the others who had gone with him to bury his father.

Joseph Reassures His Brothers

[15]When Joseph's brothers saw that their father was dead, they said, "What if Joseph holds a grudge against us and pays us back for all the wrongs we did to him?" [16]So they sent word to Joseph, saying, "Your father left these instructions before he died: [17]'This is what you are to say to Joseph: I ask you to forgive your brothers the sins and the wrongs they committed in treating you so badly.' Now please forgive the sins of the servants of the God of your father." When their message came to him, Joseph wept.

[18]His brothers then came and threw themselves down before him. "We are your slaves," they said.

[19]But Joseph said to them, "Don't be afraid. Am I in the place of God? [20]You intended to harm me, but God intended it for good to accomplish what is now being done, the saving of many lives. [21]So then, don't be afraid. I will provide for you and your children." And he reassured them and spoke kindly to them.

The Death of Joseph

[22]Joseph stayed in Egypt, along with all his father's family. He lived a hundred and ten years [23]and saw the third generation of Ephraim's children. Also the children of Makir son of Manasseh were placed at birth on Joseph's knees.[c]

[24]Then Joseph said to his brother Israelites, "I am about to die. But God will surely come to your aid and take you up out of this land to the land he promised on oath to Abraham, Isaac and Jacob." [25]And Joseph made the Israelites swear an oath and said, "God will surely come to your aid, and then you must carry my bones up from this place."

[26]So Joseph died at the age of a hundred and ten. And after they embalmed him, he was placed in a coffin in Egypt.

---

[a] 9 Or charioteers   [b] 11 Abel Mizraim means mourning of the Egyptians.   [c] 23 That is, were counted as his

exodus

AUTHOR: Moses

DATE: During the 1400s B.C., while the Israelites were traveling in the desert

THEME: God shows us who he is and how he provides for his people.

The Israelites Oppressed

1 These are the names of the sons of Israel who went to Egypt with Jacob, each with his family: ²Reuben, Simeon, Levi and Judah; ³Issachar, Zebulun and Benjamin; ⁴Dan and Naphtali; Gad and Asher. ⁵The descendants of Jacob numbered seventy*a* in all; Joseph was already in Egypt.

⁶Now Joseph and all his brothers and all that generation died, ⁷but the Israelites were exceedingly fruitful; they multiplied greatly, increased in numbers and became so numerous that the land was filled with them.

⁸Then a new king, to whom Joseph meant nothing, came to power in Egypt. ⁹"Look," he said to his people, "the Israelites have become far too numerous for us. ¹⁰Come, we must deal shrewdly with them or they will become even more numerous and, if war breaks out, will join our enemies, fight against us and leave the country."

¹¹So they put slave masters over them to oppress them with forced labor, and they built Pithom and Rameses as store cities for Pharaoh. ¹²But the more they were oppressed, the more they multiplied and spread; so the Egyptians came to dread the Israelites ¹³and worked them ruthlessly. ¹⁴They made their lives bitter with harsh labor in brick and mortar and with all kinds of work in the fields; in all their harsh labor the Egyptians used them ruthlessly.

¹⁵The king of Egypt said to the Hebrew midwives, whose names were Shiphrah and Puah, ¹⁶"When you help the Hebrew women in childbirth and observe them on the delivery stool, if it is a boy, kill him; but if it is a girl, let her live." ¹⁷The midwives, however, feared God and did not do what the king of Egypt had told them to do; they let the boys live. ¹⁸Then the king of Egypt summoned the midwives and asked them, "Why have you done this? Why have you let the boys live?"

¹⁹The midwives answered Pharaoh, "Hebrew women are not like Egyptian women; they are vigorous and give birth before the midwives arrive."

²⁰So God was kind to the midwives and the people increased and became even more numerous. ²¹And because the midwives feared God, he gave them families of their own.

²²Then Pharaoh gave this order to all his people: "Every Hebrew boy that is born you must throw into the Nile, but let every girl live."

The Birth of Moses

2 Now a man of the house of Levi married a Levite woman, ²and she became pregnant and gave birth to a son. When she saw that he was a fine child, she hid him for three months. ³But when she could hide him no longer, she got a papyrus basket*b* for him and coated it with tar and pitch. Then she placed the child in it and put it among the reeds along the bank of the Nile. ⁴His sister stood at a distance to see what would happen to him.

⁵Then Pharaoh's daughter went down to the Nile to bathe, and her attendants were walking along the riverbank. She saw the basket among the reeds and sent her female slave to get it. ⁶She opened it and saw the baby. He was crying, and she felt sorry for

a 5 Masoretic Text (see also Gen. 46:27); Dead Sea Scrolls and Septuagint (see also Acts 7:14 and note at Gen. 46:27) *seventy-five*   *b 3* The Hebrew can also mean *ark*, as in Gen. 6:14.

him. "This is one of the Hebrew babies," she said.

⁷Then his sister asked Pharaoh's daughter, "Shall I go and get one of the Hebrew women to nurse the baby for you?"

⁸"Yes, go," she answered. And the girl went and got the baby's mother. ⁹Pharaoh's daughter said to her, "Take this baby and nurse him for me, and I will pay you." So the woman took the baby and nursed him. ¹⁰When the child grew older, she took him to Pharaoh's daughter and he became her son. She named him Moses,ᵃ saying, "I drew him out of the water."

Moses Flees to Midian

¹¹One day, after Moses had grown up, he went out to where his own people were and watched them at their hard labor. He saw an Egyptian beating a Hebrew, one of his own people. ¹²Glancing this way and that and seeing no one, he killed the Egyptian and hid him in the sand. ¹³The next day he went out and saw two Hebrews fighting. He asked the one in the wrong, "Why are you hitting your fellow Hebrew?"

¹⁴The man said, "Who made you ruler and judge over us? Are you thinking of killing me as you killed the Egyptian?" Then Moses was afraid and thought, "What I did must have become known."

¹⁵When Pharaoh heard of this, he tried to kill Moses, but Moses fled from Pharaoh and went to live in Midian, where he sat down by a well. ¹⁶Now a priest of Midian had seven daughters, and they came to draw water and fill the troughs to water their father's flock. ¹⁷Some shepherds came along and drove them away, but Moses got up and came to their rescue and watered their flock.

¹⁸When the girls returned to Reuel their father, he asked them, "Why have you returned so early today?"

¹⁹They answered, "An Egyptian rescued us from the shepherds. He even drew water for us and watered the flock."

²⁰"And where is he?" he asked his daughters. "Why did you leave him? Invite him to have something to eat."

²¹Moses agreed to stay with the man, who gave his daughter Zipporah to Moses in marriage. ²²Zipporah gave birth to a son, and Moses named him Gershom,ᵇ saying, "I have become a foreigner in a foreign land."

²³During that long period, the king of Egypt died. The Israelites groaned in their slavery and cried out, and their cry for help because of their slavery went up to God. ²⁴God heard their groaning and he remembered his covenant with Abraham, with Isaac and with Jacob. ²⁵So God looked on the Israelites and was concerned about them.

Moses and the Burning Bush

3 Now Moses was tending the flock of Jethro his father-in-law, the priest of Midian, and he led the flock to the far side of the wilderness and came to Horeb, the mountain of God. ²There the angel of the LORD appeared to him in flames of fire from within a bush. Moses saw that though the bush was on fire it did not burn up. ³So Moses thought, "I will go over and see this strange sight—why the bush does not burn up."

⁴When the LORD saw that he had gone over to look, God called to him from within the bush, "Moses! Moses!"

And Moses said, "Here I am."

⁵"Do not come any closer," God said. "Take off your sandals, for the place where you are standing is holy ground." ⁶Then he said, "I am the God of your father,ᶜ the God of Abraham, the God of Isaac and the God of Jacob." At this, Moses hid his face, because he was afraid to look at God.

⁷The LORD said, "I have indeed seen the misery of my people in Egypt. I have heard them crying out because of their slave drivers, and I am concerned about their suffering. ⁸So I have come down to rescue them from the hand of the Egyptians and to bring them up out of that land into a good and spacious land, a land flowing with milk and honey—the home of the Canaanites, Hittites, Amorites, Perizzites, Hivites and Jebusites. ⁹And now the cry of the Israelites has reached me, and I have seen the way the Egyptians are oppressing them. ¹⁰So now, go. I am sending you to Pharaoh to bring my people the Israelites out of Egypt."

¹¹But Moses said to God, "Who am I that I should go to Pharaoh and bring the Israelites out of Egypt?"

ᵃ 10 Moses sounds like the Hebrew for draw out.   ᵇ 22 Gershom sounds like the Hebrew for a foreigner there.   ᶜ 6 Masoretic Text; Samaritan Pentateuch (see Acts 7:32) fathers

WEDNESDAY

"I Am" He—"He" Is God

Exodus 3:1–20 or 3:14

John Cassian {ca. AD 360–433}

When addressing the Jews, Jesus said, "Before Abraham was born, I am!" (John 8:58). But to Moses he said, "I AM WHO I AM." He certainly announced the eternity of his divine nature with marvelous grandeur of language, for nothing can be spoken so worthily of God, as that he should be said ever to be. For "to be" leaves no room for a beginning in the past or an end in the future. And so this very clearly speaks of the nature of the eternal God, as it exactly describes his eternity. When he was speaking of Abraham, the Lord Jesus Christ himself showed this by the difference of terms used, saying, "Before Abraham was born, I am!" Of Abraham he said, "before he was born." Of himself he said, "I am." For it belongs to things temporal to be born. But to *be* belongs to eternity. And so "was born" he assigns to human transitoriness; but "to be" to his own nature. And all this was found in Christ who, by virtue of the mystery of the manhood and divinity joined together in him who ever "was," could say that he already "was."

Lee Strobel

Think of the story of Jesus walking on the water, found in Matthew 14:22–33 and Mark 6:45–52. Most English translations hide the Greek by quoting Jesus as saying, "Fear not, it is I." Actually, [the] Greek literally says, "Fear not, I am." Those last two words are identical to what Jesus said in John 8:58, when he took upon himself the divine name "I AM," which is the way God revealed himself to Moses in the burning bush in Exodus 3:14. So Jesus is revealing himself as the one who has the same divine power over nature as Yahweh, the God of the Old Testament.

reflection

1. What do you learn about God from the name he gives himself: "I AM"?
2. How does the eternality of God separate him from all other beings?
3. Why is it significant that Jesus also referred to himself several times as "I am"?

For your next devotional reading, go to page 71.

¹²And God said, "I will be with you. And this will be the sign to you that it is I who have sent you: When you have brought the people out of Egypt, you*ᵃ* will worship God on this mountain."

¹³Moses said to God, "Suppose I go to the Israelites and say to them, 'The God of your fathers has sent me to you,' and they ask me, 'What is his name?' Then what shall I tell them?"

¹⁴God said to Moses, "I AM WHO I AM.ᵇ This is what you are to say to the Israelites: 'I AM has sent me to you.' "

¹⁵God also said to Moses, "Say to the Israelites, 'The LORD,ᶜ the God of your fathers—the God of Abraham, the God of Isaac and the God of Jacob—has sent me to you.'

"This is my name forever,
    the name you shall call me
    from generation to generation.

¹⁶"Go, assemble the elders of Israel and say to them, 'The LORD, the God of your fathers—the God of Abraham, Isaac and Jacob—appeared to me and said: I have watched over you and have seen what has been done to you in Egypt. ¹⁷And I have promised to bring you up out of your misery in Egypt into the land of the Canaanites, Hittites, Amorites, Perizzites, Hivites and Jebusites—a land flowing with milk and honey.'

¹⁸"The elders of Israel will listen to you. Then you and the elders are to go to the king of Egypt and say to him, 'The LORD, the God of the Hebrews, has met with us. Let us take a three-day journey into the wilderness to offer sacrifices to the LORD our God.' ¹⁹But I know that the king of Egypt will not let you go unless a mighty hand compels him. ²⁰So I will stretch out my hand and strike the Egyptians with all the wonders that I will perform among them. After that, he will let you go.

²¹"And I will make the Egyptians favorably disposed toward this people, so that when you leave you will not go empty-handed. ²²Every woman is to ask her neighbor and any woman living in her house for articles of silver and gold and for clothing, which you will put on your sons and daughters. And so you will plunder the Egyptians."

Signs for Moses

4 Moses answered, "What if they do not believe me or listen to me and say, 'The LORD did not appear to you'?"

²Then the LORD said to him, "What is that in your hand?"

"A staff," he replied.

³The LORD said, "Throw it on the ground." Moses threw it on the ground and it became a snake, and he ran from it. ⁴Then the LORD said to him, "Reach out your hand and take it by the tail." So Moses reached out and took hold of the snake and it turned back into a staff in his hand. ⁵"This," said the LORD, "is so that they may believe that the LORD, the God of their fathers—the God of Abraham, the God of Isaac and the God of Jacob—has appeared to you."

⁶Then the LORD said, "Put your hand inside your cloak." So Moses put his hand into his cloak, and when he took it out, the skin was leprousᵈ—it had become as white as snow.

⁷"Now put it back into your cloak," he said. So Moses put his hand back into his cloak, and when he took it out, it was restored, like the rest of his flesh.

⁸Then the LORD said, "If they do not believe you or pay attention to the first sign, they may believe the second. ⁹But if they do not believe these two signs or listen to you, take some water from the Nile and pour it on the dry ground. The water you take from the river will become blood on the ground."

¹⁰Moses said to the LORD, "Pardon your servant, Lord. I have never been eloquent, neither in the past nor since you have spoken to your servant. I am slow of speech and tongue."

¹¹The LORD said to him, "Who gave human beings their mouths? Who makes them deaf or mute? Who gives them sight or makes them blind? Is it not I, the LORD? ¹²Now go; I will help you speak and will teach you what to say."

¹³But Moses said, "Pardon your servant, Lord. Please send someone else."

¹⁴Then the LORD's anger burned against Moses and he said, "What about your brother, Aaron the Levite? I know he can speak well. He is already on his way to meet you,

---

ᵃ 12 The Hebrew is plural.   ᵇ 14 Or I WILL BE WHAT I WILL BE   ᶜ 15 The Hebrew for LORD sounds like and may be related to the Hebrew for I AM in verse 14.   ᵈ 6 The Hebrew word for leprous was used for various diseases affecting the skin.

THURSDAY

GOD GOES WITH THE WEAK

Exodus 4:1–31 *or* 4:10–13

Louie Giglio

God is always looking for ordinary people to play significant roles in His unfolding story. And, given that He is God and supremely confident in Himself, He is free to choose the least among us—the slowest, the lesser-known, the last, the smallest, the poorest—to accomplish amazing, God-sized stuff. While as humans we try to partner with the brightest and most powerful, God is simply looking for people who are willing to take Him at His word—those confident that with Him in the equation everything is possible.

So try to put yourself in God's shoes for a minute. Your people are enslaved in Egypt, toiling day and night building monuments to the fame and greatness of the pharaohs. Yet you have a redemption plan, a deliverance mission, and you're looking for a spokesman to take your agenda to the most powerful man in the most powerful empire on the planet, demanding that he let your people go free. Who are you going to choose to lead Israel out of bondage? What criteria are you going to use to narrow the field of candidates? How will you train the person you choose to lead? How will you ensure the success of the mission?

Well, you probably wouldn't choose a stuttering shepherd with wilting self-esteem—an aging man on the downslope of life who for years had been on the run from the mighty Pharaoh after killing one of his slave drivers back in Egypt. Would you? But that's exactly who God chose; just the guy He invited to take the helm in this chapter of His unfolding story.

CARDINAL JOHN HENRY NEWMAN {AD 1801–1890}

O wisdom of the world and strength of the world! What are you when matched beside the foolishness and the weakness of the Christian? You are great in resources, manifold in methods, hopeful in prospects; but one thing you have not—and that is peace. You are always tumultuous, restless, apprehensive. You have nothing you can rely upon. You have no rock under your feet. The humblest, feeblest Christian has that which is impossible to you.

reflection

1. Why does God choose to use the weak and the foolish to accomplish his plans?

2. We often hold back from stepping out boldly for God because we don't trust our own abilities. What's wrong with this mind-set?

3. God uses ordinary people to do extraordinary things—if they're willing. How willing are you to be used by God just as you are?

For your next devotional reading, go to page 77.

and his heart will be glad when he sees you. [15]You shall speak to him and put words in his mouth; I will help both of you speak and will teach you what to do. [16]He will speak to the people for you, and it will be as if he were your mouth and as if you were God to him. [17]But take this staff in your hand so you can perform the signs with it."

Moses Returns to Egypt

[18]Then Moses went back to Jethro his father-in-law and said to him, "Let me return to my own people in Egypt to see if any of them are still alive."

Jethro said, "Go, and I wish you well."

[19]Now the LORD had said to Moses in Midian, "Go back to Egypt, for all those who wanted to kill you are dead." [20]So Moses took his wife and sons, put them on a donkey and started back to Egypt. And he took the staff of God in his hand.

[21]The LORD said to Moses, "When you return to Egypt, see that you perform before Pharaoh all the wonders I have given you the power to do. But I will harden his heart so that he will not let the people go. [22]Then say to Pharaoh, 'This is what the LORD says: Israel is my firstborn son, [23]and I told you, "Let my son go, so he may worship me." But you refused to let him go; so I will kill your firstborn son.' "

[24]At a lodging place on the way, the LORD met Moses[a] and was about to kill him. [25]But Zipporah took a flint knife, cut off her son's foreskin and touched Moses' feet with it.[b] "Surely you are a bridegroom of blood to me," she said. [26]So the LORD let him alone. (At that time she said "bridegroom of blood," referring to circumcision.)

[27]The LORD said to Aaron, "Go into the wilderness to meet Moses." So he met Moses at the mountain of God and kissed him. [28]Then Moses told Aaron everything the LORD had sent him to say, and also about all the signs he had commanded him to perform.

[29]Moses and Aaron brought together all the elders of the Israelites, [30]and Aaron told them everything the LORD had said to Moses. He also performed the signs before the people, [31]and they believed. And when they heard that the LORD was concerned about

them and had seen their misery, they bowed down and worshiped.

Bricks Without Straw

5 Afterward Moses and Aaron went to Pharaoh and said, "This is what the LORD, the God of Israel, says: 'Let my people go, so that they may hold a festival to me in the wilderness.' "

[2]Pharaoh said, "Who is the LORD, that I should obey him and let Israel go? I do not know the LORD and I will not let Israel go."

[3]Then they said, "The God of the Hebrews has met with us. Now let us take a three-day journey into the wilderness to offer sacrifices to the LORD our God, or he may strike us with plagues or with the sword."

[4]But the king of Egypt said, "Moses and Aaron, why are you taking the people away from their labor? Get back to your work!" [5]Then Pharaoh said, "Look, the people of the land are now numerous, and you are stopping them from working."

[6]That same day Pharaoh gave this order to the slave drivers and overseers in charge of the people: [7]"You are no longer to supply the people with straw for making bricks; let them go and gather their own straw. [8]But require them to make the same number of bricks as before; don't reduce the quota. They are lazy; that is why they are crying out, 'Let us go and sacrifice to our God.' [9]Make the work harder for them so that they keep working and pay no attention to lies."

[10]Then the slave drivers and the overseers went out and said to the people, "This is what Pharaoh says: 'I will not give you any more straw. [11]Go and get your own straw wherever you can find it, but your work will not be reduced at all.' " [12]So the people scattered all over Egypt to gather stubble to use for straw. [13]The slave drivers kept pressing them, saying, "Complete the work required of you for each day, just as when you had straw." [14]And Pharaoh's slave drivers beat the Israelite overseers they had appointed, demanding, "Why haven't you met your quota of bricks yesterday or today, as before?"

[15]Then the Israelite overseers went and appealed to Pharaoh: "Why have you treated your servants this way? [16]Your servants are given no straw, yet we are told, 'Make

---

a 24 Hebrew *him*   *b 25* The meaning of the Hebrew for this clause is uncertain.

bricks!' Your servants are being beaten, but the fault is with your own people."

[17]Pharaoh said, "Lazy, that's what you are—lazy! That is why you keep saying, 'Let us go and sacrifice to the LORD.' [18]Now get to work. You will not be given any straw, yet you must produce your full quota of bricks."

[19]The Israelite overseers realized they were in trouble when they were told, "You are not to reduce the number of bricks required of you for each day." [20]When they left Pharaoh, they found Moses and Aaron waiting to meet them, [21]and they said, "May the LORD look on you and judge you! You have made us obnoxious to Pharaoh and his officials and have put a sword in their hand to kill us."

God Promises Deliverance

[22]Moses returned to the LORD and said, "Why, Lord, why have you brought trouble on this people? Is this why you sent me? [23]Ever since I went to Pharaoh to speak in your name, he has brought trouble on this people, and you have not rescued your people at all."

6 Then the LORD said to Moses, "Now you will see what I will do to Pharaoh: Because of my mighty hand he will let them go; because of my mighty hand he will drive them out of his country."

[2]God also said to Moses, "I am the LORD. [3]I appeared to Abraham, to Isaac and to Jacob as God Almighty,[a] but by my name the LORD[b] I did not make myself known to them.[c] [4]I also established my covenant with them to give them the land of Canaan, where they resided as foreigners. [5]Moreover, I have heard the groaning of the Israelites, whom the Egyptians are enslaving, and I have remembered my covenant.

[6]"Therefore, say to the Israelites: 'I am the LORD, and I will bring you out from under the yoke of the Egyptians. I will free you from being slaves to them, and I will redeem you with an outstretched arm and with mighty acts of judgment. [7]I will take you as my own people, and I will be your God. Then you will know that I am the LORD your God, who brought you out from under the yoke of the Egyptians. [8]And I will bring you to the land I swore with uplifted hand to give to

Abraham, to Isaac and to Jacob. I will give it to you as a possession. I am the LORD.' "

[9]Moses reported this to the Israelites, but they did not listen to him because of their discouragement and harsh labor.

[10]Then the LORD said to Moses, [11]"Go, tell Pharaoh king of Egypt to let the Israelites go out of his country."

[12]But Moses said to the LORD, "If the Israelites will not listen to me, why would Pharaoh listen to me, since I speak with faltering lips[d]?"

Family Record of Moses and Aaron

[13]Now the LORD spoke to Moses and Aaron about the Israelites and Pharaoh king of Egypt, and he commanded them to bring the Israelites out of Egypt.

[14]These were the heads of their families[e]:

The sons of Reuben the firstborn son of Israel were Hanok and Pallu, Hezron and Karmi. These were the clans of Reuben.

[15]The sons of Simeon were Jemuel, Jamin, Ohad, Jakin, Zohar and Shaul the son of a Canaanite woman. These were the clans of Simeon.

[16]These were the names of the sons of Levi according to their records: Gershon, Kohath and Merari. Levi lived 137 years.

[17]The sons of Gershon, by clans, were Libni and Shimei.

[18]The sons of Kohath were Amram, Izhar, Hebron and Uzziel. Kohath lived 133 years.

[19]The sons of Merari were Mahli and Mushi.

These were the clans of Levi according to their records.

[20]Amram married his father's sister Jochebed, who bore him Aaron and Moses. Amram lived 137 years.

[21]The sons of Izhar were Korah, Nepheg and Zikri.

[22]The sons of Uzziel were Mishael, Elzaphan and Sithri.

[23]Aaron married Elisheba, daughter of Amminadab and sister of Nahshon,

---

a 3 Hebrew *El-Shaddai*   b 3 See note at Exodus 3:15.   c 3 Or *Almighty, and by my name the LORD did I not let myself be known to them?*   d 12 Hebrew *I am uncircumcised of lips*; also in verse 30   e 14 The Hebrew for *families* here and in verse 25 refers to units larger than clans.

and she bore him Nadab and Abihu, Eleazar and Ithamar.

24The sons of Korah were Assir, Elkanah and Abiasaph. These were the Korahite clans.

25Eleazar son of Aaron married one of the daughters of Putiel, and she bore him Phinehas.

These were the heads of the Levite families, clan by clan.

26It was this Aaron and Moses to whom the LORD said, "Bring the Israelites out of Egypt by their divisions." 27They were the ones who spoke to Pharaoh king of Egypt about bringing the Israelites out of Egypt—this same Moses and Aaron.

Aaron to Speak for Moses

28Now when the LORD spoke to Moses in Egypt, 29he said to him, "I am the LORD. Tell Pharaoh king of Egypt everything I tell you."

30But Moses said to the LORD, "Since I speak with faltering lips, why would Pharaoh listen to me?"

7 Then the LORD said to Moses, "See, I have made you like God to Pharaoh, and your brother Aaron will be your prophet. 2You are to say everything I command you, and your brother Aaron is to tell Pharaoh to let the Israelites go out of his country. 3But I will harden Pharaoh's heart, and though I multiply my signs and wonders in Egypt, 4he will not listen to you. Then I will lay my hand on Egypt and with mighty acts of judgment I will bring out my divisions, my people the Israelites. 5And the Egyptians will know that I am the LORD when I stretch out my hand against Egypt and bring the Israelites out of it."

6Moses and Aaron did just as the LORD commanded them. 7Moses was eighty years old and Aaron eighty-three when they spoke to Pharaoh.

Aaron's Staff Becomes a Snake

8The LORD said to Moses and Aaron, 9"When Pharaoh says to you, 'Perform a miracle,' then say to Aaron, 'Take your staff and throw it down before Pharaoh,' and it will become a snake."

10So Moses and Aaron went to Pharaoh and did just as the LORD commanded. Aaron threw his staff down in front of Pharaoh and his officials, and it became a snake. 11Phar-

aoh then summoned wise men and sorcerers, and the Egyptian magicians also did the same things by their secret arts: 12Each one threw down his staff and it became a snake. But Aaron's staff swallowed up their staffs. 13Yet Pharaoh's heart became hard and he would not listen to them, just as the LORD had said.

The Plague of Blood

14Then the LORD said to Moses, "Pharaoh's heart is unyielding; he refuses to let the people go. 15Go to Pharaoh in the morning as he goes out to the river. Wait on the bank of the Nile to meet him, and take in your hand the staff that was changed into a snake. 16Then say to him, 'The LORD, the God of the Hebrews, has sent me to say to you: Let my people go, so that they may worship me in the wilderness. But until now you have not listened. 17This is what the LORD says: By this you will know that I am the LORD: With the staff that is in my hand I will strike the water of the Nile, and it will be changed into blood. 18The fish in the Nile will die, and the river will stink; the Egyptians will not be able to drink its water.'"

19The LORD said to Moses, "Tell Aaron, 'Take your staff and stretch out your hand over the waters of Egypt—over the streams and canals, over the ponds and all the reservoirs—and they will turn to blood.' Blood will be everywhere in Egypt, even in the wooden buckets and stone jars."

20Moses and Aaron did just as the LORD had commanded. He raised his staff in the presence of Pharaoh and his officials and struck the water of the Nile, and all the water was changed into blood. 21The fish in the Nile died, and the river smelled so bad that the Egyptians could not drink its water. Blood was everywhere in Egypt.

22But the Egyptian magicians did the same things by their secret arts, and Pharaoh's heart became hard; he would not listen to Moses and Aaron, just as the LORD had said. 23Instead, he turned and went into his palace, and did not take even this to heart. 24And all the Egyptians dug along the Nile to get drinking water, because they could not drink the water of the river.

The Plague of Frogs

25Seven days passed after the LORD struck

8 the Nile. *[1]Then the LORD said to Moses, "Go to Pharaoh and say to him, 'This is what the LORD says: Let my people go, so that they may worship me. [2]If you refuse to let them go, I will send a plague of frogs on your whole country. [3]The Nile will teem with frogs. They will come up into your palace and your bedroom and onto your bed, into the houses of your officials and on your people, and into your ovens and kneading troughs. [4]The frogs will come up on you and your people and all your officials.' "

*[5]Then the LORD said to Moses, "Tell Aaron, 'Stretch out your hand with your staff over the streams and canals and ponds, and make frogs come up on the land of Egypt.' "

[6]So Aaron stretched out his hand over the waters of Egypt, and the frogs came up and covered the land. [7]But the magicians did the same things by their secret arts; they also made frogs come up on the land of Egypt.

[8]Pharaoh summoned Moses and Aaron and said, "Pray to the LORD to take the frogs away from me and my people, and I will let your people go to offer sacrifices to the LORD."

[9]Moses said to Pharaoh, "I leave to you the honor of setting the time for me to pray for you and your officials and your people that you and your houses may be rid of the frogs, except for those that remain in the Nile."

[10]"Tomorrow," Pharaoh said.

Moses replied, "It will be as you say, so that you may know there is no one like the LORD our God. [11]The frogs will leave you and your houses, your officials and your people; they will remain only in the Nile."

[12]After Moses and Aaron left Pharaoh, Moses cried out to the LORD about the frogs he had brought on Pharaoh. [13]And the LORD did what Moses asked. The frogs died in the houses, in the courtyards and in the fields. [14]They were piled into heaps, and the land reeked of them. [15]But when Pharaoh saw that there was relief, he hardened his heart and would not listen to Moses and Aaron, just as the LORD had said.

The Plague of Gnats

[16]Then the LORD said to Moses, "Tell Aaron, 'Stretch out your staff and strike the dust of the ground,' and throughout the land of Egypt the dust will become gnats." [17]They did this, and when Aaron stretched out his hand with the staff and struck the dust of the ground, gnats came on people and animals. All the dust throughout the land of Egypt became gnats. [18]But when the magicians tried to produce gnats by their secret arts, they could not.

Since the gnats were on people and animals everywhere, [19]the magicians said to Pharaoh, "This is the finger of God." But Pharaoh's heart was hard and he would not listen, just as the LORD had said.

The Plague of Flies

[20]Then the LORD said to Moses, "Get up early in the morning and confront Pharaoh as he goes to the river and say to him, 'This is what the LORD says: Let my people go, so that they may worship me. [21]If you do not let my people go, I will send swarms of flies on you and your officials, on your people and into your houses. The houses of the Egyptians will be full of flies; even the ground will be covered with them.

[22]" 'But on that day I will deal differently with the land of Goshen, where my people live; no swarms of flies will be there, so that you will know that I, the LORD, am in this land. [23]I will make a distinction[a] between my people and your people. This sign will occur tomorrow.' "

[24]And the LORD did this. Dense swarms of flies poured into Pharaoh's palace and into the houses of his officials; throughout Egypt the land was ruined by the flies.

[25]Then Pharaoh summoned Moses and Aaron and said, "Go, sacrifice to your God here in the land."

[26]But Moses said, "That would not be right. The sacrifices we offer the LORD our God would be detestable to the Egyptians. And if we offer sacrifices that are detestable in their eyes, will they not stone us? [27]We must take a three-day journey into the wilderness to offer sacrifices to the LORD our God, as he commands us."

[28]Pharaoh said, "I will let you go to offer sacrifices to the LORD your God in the wil-

a 23 Septuagint and Vulgate; Hebrew will put a deliverance

* 8:1-4 is numbered 7:26-29 in Hebrew texts.   * 8:5-32 is numbered 8:1-28 in Hebrew texts.

derness, but you must not go very far. Now pray for me."

²⁹Moses answered, "As soon as I leave you, I will pray to the LORD, and tomorrow the flies will leave Pharaoh and his officials and his people. Only let Pharaoh be sure that he does not act deceitfully again by not letting the people go to offer sacrifices to the LORD."

³⁰Then Moses left Pharaoh and prayed to the LORD, ³¹and the LORD did what Moses asked. The flies left Pharaoh and his officials and his people; not a fly remained. ³²But this time also Pharaoh hardened his heart and would not let the people go.

The Plague on Livestock

9 Then the LORD said to Moses, "Go to Pharaoh and say to him, 'This is what the LORD, the God of the Hebrews, says: "Let my people go, so that they may worship me." ²If you refuse to let them go and continue to hold them back, ³the hand of the LORD will bring a terrible plague on your livestock in the field—on your horses, donkeys and camels and on your cattle, sheep and goats. ⁴But the LORD will make a distinction between the livestock of Israel and that of Egypt, so that no animal belonging to the Israelites will die.' "

⁵The LORD set a time and said, "Tomorrow the LORD will do this in the land." ⁶And the next day the LORD did it: All the livestock of the Egyptians died, but not one animal belonging to the Israelites died. ⁷Pharaoh investigated and found that not even one of the animals of the Israelites had died. Yet his heart was unyielding and he would not let the people go.

The Plague of Boils

⁸Then the LORD said to Moses and Aaron, "Take handfuls of soot from a furnace and have Moses toss it into the air in the presence of Pharaoh. ⁹It will become fine dust over the whole land of Egypt, and festering boils will break out on people and animals throughout the land."

¹⁰So they took soot from a furnace and stood before Pharaoh. Moses tossed it into the air, and festering boils broke out on people and animals. ¹¹The magicians could not stand before Moses because of the boils that were on them and on all the Egyptians. ¹²But the LORD hardened Pharaoh's heart and he would not listen to Moses and Aaron, just as the LORD had said to Moses.

The Plague of Hail

¹³Then the LORD said to Moses, "Get up early in the morning, confront Pharaoh and say to him, 'This is what the LORD, the God of the Hebrews, says: Let my people go, so that they may worship me, ¹⁴or this time I will send the full force of my plagues against you and against your officials and your people, so you may know that there is no one like me in all the earth. ¹⁵For by now I could have stretched out my hand and struck you and your people with a plague that would have wiped you off the earth. ¹⁶But I have raised you upᵃ for this very purpose, that I might show you my power and that my name might be proclaimed in all the earth. ¹⁷You still set yourself against my people and will not let them go. ¹⁸Therefore, at this time tomorrow I will send the worst hailstorm that has ever fallen on Egypt, from the day it was founded till now. ¹⁹Give an order now to bring your livestock and everything you have in the field to a place of shelter, because the hail will fall on every person and animal that has not been brought in and is still out in the field, and they will die.' "

²⁰Those officials of Pharaoh who feared the word of the LORD hurried to bring their slaves and their livestock inside. ²¹But those who ignored the word of the LORD left their slaves and livestock in the field.

²²Then the LORD said to Moses, "Stretch out your hand toward the sky so that hail will fall all over Egypt—on people and animals and on everything growing in the fields of Egypt." ²³When Moses stretched out his staff toward the sky, the LORD sent thunder and hail, and lightning flashed down to the ground. So the LORD rained hail on the land of Egypt; ²⁴hail fell and lightning flashed back and forth. It was the worst storm in all the land of Egypt since it had become a nation. ²⁵Throughout Egypt hail struck everything in the fields—both people and animals; it beat down everything growing in the fields and stripped every tree. ²⁶The only place it did not hail was the land of Goshen, where the Israelites were.

ᵃ 16 Or *have spared you*

FRIDAY

SMALL VISION, GREAT PRIDE

Exodus 9:1–35 or 9:27–35

FREDERICK W. ROBERTSON {AD 1816–1853}

Pharaoh is presented in Scripture as a type of pride. His pride arose from ignorance of God. "[Who is the LORD, that I should obey him and let Israel go? I do not know the LORD and I will not let Israel go]" (Exodus 5:2). This was not intellectual pride; it was pride in a matter of duty.

Pharaoh had been immersing his whole heart in the narrow politics of Egypt. The great problem of his day was to aggrandize his own people and prevent an insurrection of the Israelites. That small kingdom of Egypt had been his universe.

Pharaoh shut his heart to the voice of justice and the voice of humanity. In other words, he was great in [the] pride of human majesty but small in the sight of the high and lofty One. He shut himself out from the knowledge of God.

Les Parrott

When the Israelites were slaves of the Egyptians, God sent numerous plagues to convince Pharaoh of his power and to force him to let the Israelites go. Time after time, Pharaoh promised to release the people if God would stop the plague, and time after time, Pharaoh reneged on his promise. Pharaoh cared more about taking away the pain of the plagues than he cared about his relationship with the one true God. His "confessions" and "repentance" were more manipulative than genuine.

Some of us act like Pharaoh. We change our behavior simply to get rid of the plague of guilt and to feel better about ourselves—not to be better people. We confess our sins but never question our motives. And as T. S. Eliot said in his play *Murder in the Cathedral*, "The greatest sin is to do all the right things for all the wrong reasons."

reflection

1. What small kingdom of yours do you find yourself consumed with each day?

2. In what way does your concern with your own interests block out thoughts about God and his greater kingdom?

3. When are you most tempted to shut your heart to the voice of justice and humanity?

For your next devotional reading, go to page 79.

27Then Pharaoh summoned Moses and Aaron. "This time I have sinned," he said to them. "The LORD is in the right, and I and my people are in the wrong. 28Pray to the LORD, for we have had enough thunder and hail. I will let you go; you don't have to stay any longer."

29Moses replied, "When I have gone out of the city, I will spread out my hands in prayer to the LORD. The thunder will stop and there will be no more hail, so you may know that the earth is the LORD's. 30But I know that you and your officials still do not fear the LORD God."

31(The flax and barley were destroyed, since the barley had headed and the flax was in bloom. 32The wheat and spelt, however, were not destroyed, because they ripen later.)

33Then Moses left Pharaoh and went out of the city. He spread out his hands toward the LORD; the thunder and hail stopped, and the rain no longer poured down on the land. 34When Pharaoh saw that the rain and hail and thunder had stopped, he sinned again: He and his officials hardened their hearts. 35So Pharaoh's heart was hard and he would not let the Israelites go, just as the LORD had said through Moses.

The Plague of Locusts

10 Then the LORD said to Moses, "Go to Pharaoh, for I have hardened his heart and the hearts of his officials so that I may perform these signs of mine among them 2that you may tell your children and grandchildren how I dealt harshly with the Egyptians and how I performed my signs among them, and that you may know that I am the LORD."

3So Moses and Aaron went to Pharaoh and said to him, "This is what the LORD, the God of the Hebrews, says: 'How long will you refuse to humble yourself before me? Let my people go, so that they may worship me. 4If you refuse to let them go, I will bring locusts into your country tomorrow. 5They will cover the face of the ground so that it cannot be seen. They will devour what little you have left after the hail, including every tree that is growing in your fields. 6They will fill your houses and those of all your officials and all the Egyptians—something neither your par-ents nor your ancestors have ever seen from the day they settled in this land till now.' " Then Moses turned and left Pharaoh.

7Pharaoh's officials said to him, "How long will this man be a snare to us? Let the people go, so that they may worship the LORD their God. Do you not yet realize that Egypt is ruined?"

8Then Moses and Aaron were brought back to Pharaoh. "Go, worship the LORD your God," he said. "But tell me who will be going."

9Moses answered, "We will go with our young and our old, with our sons and our daughters, and with our flocks and herds, because we are to celebrate a festival to the LORD."

10Pharaoh said, "The LORD be with you— if I let you go, along with your women and children! Clearly you are bent on evil.a 11No! Have only the men go and worship the LORD, since that's what you have been asking for." Then Moses and Aaron were driven out of Pharaoh's presence.

12And the LORD said to Moses, "Stretch out your hand over Egypt so that locusts swarm over the land and devour everything growing in the fields, everything left by the hail."

13So Moses stretched out his staff over Egypt, and the LORD made an east wind blow across the land all that day and all that night. By morning the wind had brought the locusts; 14they invaded all Egypt and settled down in every area of the country in great numbers. Never before had there been such a plague of locusts, nor will there ever be again. 15They covered all the ground until it was black. They devoured all that was left after the hail—everything growing in the fields and the fruit on the trees. Nothing green remained on tree or plant in all the land of Egypt.

16Pharaoh quickly summoned Moses and Aaron and said, "I have sinned against the LORD your God and against you. 17Now forgive my sin once more and pray to the LORD your God to take this deadly plague away from me."

18Moses then left Pharaoh and prayed to the LORD. 19And the LORD changed the wind to a very strong west wind, which caught up the locusts and carried them into the Red Sea.b Not a locust was left anywhere in

a 10 Or Be careful, trouble is in store for you!   b 19 Or the Sea of Reeds

Obedient Choices

Exodus 10:16–20

read/meditate

In this passage, Pharaoh swings like a pendulum. When a bad circumstance befalls his kingdom, he tells Moses to take the people and run. Then when tragedy has passed . . . he swings back to his original, hard-nosed position. Read through Pharaoh's indecision a couple of times.

pray

Ask God to reveal any fickleness in your heart. Be still before him, allowing him to bring to mind any circumstances in your life that have created a false obedience like Pharaoh's—a deal-striking that appears to be integrity, but really is an attempt to escape the current difficulty.

contemplate

Think back through the difficult seasons of your life. How did you perceive God differently in those times? Did he seem closer? Farther away? Inaccessible? Did you make choices differently? Let a moment pass as you consider how much of your faith-walk is affected by the circumstances around you.

additional reflection

The power of choosing good and evil is within the reach of all.

—Origen

We are not necessarily doubting that God will do the best for us; we are wondering how painful the best will turn out to be.

—C. S. Lewis

For your next devotional reading, go to page 83.

Egypt. ²⁰But the Lᴏʀᴅ hardened Pharaoh's heart, and he would not let the Israelites go.

The Plague of Darkness

²¹Then the Lᴏʀᴅ said to Moses, "Stretch out your hand toward the sky so that darkness spreads over Egypt—darkness that can be felt." ²²So Moses stretched out his hand toward the sky, and total darkness covered all Egypt for three days. ²³No one could see anyone else or move about for three days. Yet all the Israelites had light in the places where they lived.

²⁴Then Pharaoh summoned Moses and said, "Go, worship the Lᴏʀᴅ. Even your women and children may go with you; only leave your flocks and herds behind."

²⁵But Moses said, "You must allow us to have sacrifices and burnt offerings to present to the Lᴏʀᴅ our God. ²⁶Our livestock too must go with us; not a hoof is to be left behind. We have to use some of them in worshiping the Lᴏʀᴅ our God, and until we get there we will not know what we are to use to worship the Lᴏʀᴅ."

²⁷But the Lᴏʀᴅ hardened Pharaoh's heart, and he was not willing to let them go. ²⁸Pharaoh said to Moses, "Get out of my sight! Make sure you do not appear before me again! The day you see my face you will die."

²⁹"Just as you say," Moses replied. "I will never appear before you again."

The Plague on the Firstborn

11 Now the Lᴏʀᴅ had said to Moses, "I will bring one more plague on Pharaoh and on Egypt. After that, he will let you go from here, and when he does, he will drive you out completely. ²Tell the people that men and women alike are to ask their neighbors for articles of silver and gold." ³(The Lᴏʀᴅ made the Egyptians favorably disposed toward the people, and Moses himself was highly regarded in Egypt by Pharaoh's officials and by the people.)

⁴So Moses said, "This is what the Lᴏʀᴅ says: 'About midnight I will go throughout Egypt. ⁵Every firstborn son in Egypt will die, from the firstborn son of Pharaoh, who sits on the throne, to the firstborn son of the female slave, who is at her hand mill, and all the firstborn of the cattle as well. ⁶There will

be loud wailing throughout Egypt—worse than there has ever been or ever will be again. ⁷But among the Israelites not a dog will bark at any person or animal.' Then you will know that the Lᴏʀᴅ makes a distinction between Egypt and Israel. ⁸All these officials of yours will come to me, bowing down before me and saying, 'Go, you and all the people who follow you!' After that I will leave." Then Moses, hot with anger, left Pharaoh.

⁹The Lᴏʀᴅ had said to Moses, "Pharaoh will refuse to listen to you—so that my wonders may be multiplied in Egypt." ¹⁰Moses and Aaron performed all these wonders before Pharaoh, but the Lᴏʀᴅ hardened Pharaoh's heart, and he would not let the Israelites go out of his country.

The Passover and the Festival of Unleavened Bread

12 The Lᴏʀᴅ said to Moses and Aaron in Egypt, ²"This month is to be for you the first month, the first month of your year. ³Tell the whole community of Israel that on the tenth day of this month each man is to take a lambᵃ for his family, one for each household. ⁴If any household is too small for a whole lamb, they must share one with their nearest neighbor, having taken into account the number of people there are. You are to determine the amount of lamb needed in accordance with what each person will eat. ⁵The animals you choose must be year-old males without defect, and you may take them from the sheep or the goats. ⁶Take care of them until the fourteenth day of the month, when all the members of the community of Israel must slaughter them at twilight. ⁷Then they are to take some of the blood and put it on the sides and tops of the doorframes of the houses where they eat the lambs. ⁸That same night they are to eat the meat roasted over the fire, along with bitter herbs, and bread made without yeast. ⁹Do not eat the meat raw or boiled in water, but roast it over a fire—with the head, legs and internal organs. ¹⁰Do not leave any of it till morning; if some is left till morning, you must burn it. ¹¹This is how you are to eat it: with your cloak tucked into your belt, your sandals on your feet and your staff in your hand. Eat it in haste; it is the Lᴏʀᴅ's Passover.

ᵃ 3 The Hebrew word can mean *lamb* or *kid*; also in verse 4.

12"On that same night I will pass through Egypt and strike down every firstborn of both people and animals, and I will bring judgment on all the gods of Egypt. I am the LORD. 13The blood will be a sign for you on the houses where you are, and when I see the blood, I will pass over you. No destructive plague will touch you when I strike Egypt.

14"This is a day you are to commemorate; for the generations to come you shall celebrate it as a festival to the LORD—a lasting ordinance. 15For seven days you are to eat bread made without yeast. On the first day remove the yeast from your houses, for whoever eats anything with yeast in it from the first day through the seventh must be cut off from Israel. 16On the first day hold a sacred assembly, and another one on the seventh day. Do no work at all on these days, except to prepare food for everyone to eat; that is all you may do.

17"Celebrate the Festival of Unleavened Bread, because it was on this very day that I brought your divisions out of Egypt. Celebrate this day as a lasting ordinance for the generations to come. 18In the first month you are to eat bread made without yeast, from the evening of the fourteenth day until the evening of the twenty-first day. 19For seven days no yeast is to be found in your houses. And anyone, whether foreigner or native-born, who eats anything with yeast in it must be cut off from the community of Israel. 20Eat nothing made with yeast. Wherever you live, you must eat unleavened bread."

21Then Moses summoned all the elders of Israel and said to them, "Go at once and select the animals for your families and slaughter the Passover lamb. 22Take a bunch of hyssop, dip it into the blood in the basin and put some of the blood on the top and on both sides of the doorframe. None of you shall go out of the door of your house until morning. 23When the LORD goes through the land to strike down the Egyptians, he will see the blood on the top and sides of the doorframe and will pass over that doorway, and he will not permit the destroyer to enter your houses and strike you down.

24"Obey these instructions as a lasting ordinance for you and your descendants. 25When you enter the land that the LORD will give you as he promised, observe this ceremony. 26And when your children ask you, 'What does this ceremony mean to you?' 27then tell them, 'It is the Passover sacrifice to the LORD, who passed over the houses of the Israelites in Egypt and spared our homes when he struck down the Egyptians.' " Then the people bowed down and worshiped. 28The Israelites did just what the LORD commanded Moses and Aaron.

29At midnight the LORD struck down all the firstborn in Egypt, from the firstborn of Pharaoh, who sat on the throne, to the firstborn of the prisoner, who was in the dungeon, and the firstborn of all the livestock as well. 30Pharaoh and all his officials and all the Egyptians got up during the night, and there was loud wailing in Egypt, for there was not a house without someone dead.

The Exodus

31During the night Pharaoh summoned Moses and Aaron and said, "Up! Leave my people, you and the Israelites! Go, worship the LORD as you have requested. 32Take your flocks and herds, as you have said, and go. And also bless me."

33The Egyptians urged the people to hurry and leave the country. "For otherwise," they said, "we will all die!" 34So the people took their dough before the yeast was added, and carried it on their shoulders in kneading troughs wrapped in clothing. 35The Israelites did as Moses instructed and asked the Egyptians for articles of silver and gold and for clothing. 36The LORD had made the Egyptians favorably disposed toward the people, and they gave them what they asked for; so they plundered the Egyptians.

37The Israelites journeyed from Rameses to Sukkoth. There were about six hundred thousand men on foot, besides women and children. 38Many other people went up with them, and also large droves of livestock, both flocks and herds. 39With the dough the Israelites had brought from Egypt, they baked loaves of unleavened bread. The dough was without yeast because they had been driven out of Egypt and did not have time to prepare food for themselves.

40Now the length of time the Israelite people lived in Egypt[a] was 430 years. 41At

---

a 40 Masoretic Text; Samaritan Pentateuch and Septuagint *Egypt and Canaan* the end of the 430 years, to the very day, all the LORD's divisions left Egypt. ⁴²Because the LORD kept vigil that night to bring them out of Egypt, on this night all the Israelites are to keep vigil to honor the LORD for the generations to come.

Passover Restrictions

⁴³The LORD said to Moses and Aaron, "These are the regulations for the Passover:

"No foreigner is to eat of it. ⁴⁴Any slave you have bought may eat of it after you have circumcised him, ⁴⁵but a temporary resident or a hired worker may not eat of it.

⁴⁶"It must be eaten inside one house; take none of the meat outside the house. Do not break any of the bones. ⁴⁷The whole community of Israel must celebrate it.

⁴⁸"A foreigner residing among you who wants to celebrate the LORD's Passover must have all the males in his household circumcised; then he may take part like one born in the land. No uncircumcised male may eat of it. ⁴⁹The same law applies both to the native-born and to the foreigner residing among you."

⁵⁰All the Israelites did just what the LORD had commanded Moses and Aaron. ⁵¹And on that very day the LORD brought the Israelites out of Egypt by their divisions.

Consecration of the Firstborn

13 The LORD said to Moses, ²"Consecrate to me every firstborn male. The first offspring of every womb among the Israelites belongs to me, whether human or animal."

³Then Moses said to the people, "Commemorate this day, the day you came out of Egypt, out of the land of slavery, because the LORD brought you out of it with a mighty hand. Eat nothing containing yeast. ⁴Today, in the month of Aviv, you are leaving. ⁵When the LORD brings you into the land of the Canaanites, Hittites, Amorites, Hivites and Jebusites—the land he swore to your ancestors to give you, a land flowing with milk and honey—you are to observe this ceremony in this month: ⁶For seven days eat bread made without yeast and on the seventh day hold a festival to the LORD. ⁷Eat unleavened bread during those seven days; nothing with yeast in it is to be seen among you, nor shall any yeast be seen anywhere within your borders. ⁸On that day tell your children, 'I do this because of what the LORD did for me when I came out of Egypt.' ⁹This observance will be for you like a sign on your hand and a reminder on your forehead that this law of the LORD is to be on your lips. For the LORD brought you out of Egypt with his mighty hand. ¹⁰You must keep this ordinance at the appointed time year after year.

¹¹"After the LORD brings you into the land of the Canaanites and gives it to you, as he promised on oath to you and your ancestors, ¹²you are to give over to the LORD the first offspring of every womb. All the firstborn males of your livestock belong to the LORD. ¹³Redeem with a lamb every firstborn donkey, but if you do not redeem it, break its neck. Redeem every firstborn among your sons.

¹⁴"In days to come, when your children ask you, 'What does this mean?' say to them, 'With a mighty hand the LORD brought us out of Egypt, out of the land of slavery. ¹⁵When Pharaoh stubbornly refused to let us go, the LORD killed the firstborn of both people and animals in Egypt. This is why I sacrifice to the LORD the first male offspring of every womb and redeem each of my firstborn sons.' ¹⁶And it will be like a sign on your hand and a symbol on your forehead that the LORD brought us out of Egypt with his mighty hand."

Crossing the Sea

¹⁷When Pharaoh let the people go, God did not lead them on the road through the Philistine country, though that was shorter. For God said, "If they face war, they might change their minds and return to Egypt." ¹⁸So God led the people around by the desert road toward the Red Sea.ᵃ The Israelites went up out of Egypt ready for battle.

¹⁹Moses took the bones of Joseph with him because Joseph had made the Israelites swear an oath. He had said, "God will surely come to your aid, and then you must carry my bones up with you from this place."ᵇ

²⁰After leaving Sukkoth they camped at Etham on the edge of the desert. ²¹By day the LORD went ahead of them in a pillar of cloud to guide them on their way and by night in a pillar of fire to give them light, so

---

ᵃ 18 Or *the Sea of Reeds*   ᵇ 19 See Gen. 50:25.

MONDAY

TAKING THE LONG WAY

Exodus 13:1–22 *or* 13:17–22

Carol L. Fitzpatrick

Finally the Israelites were on their way. They had lived in Egypt for 430 years. Can we even fathom the logistical nightmare of moving millions of people? And don't forget, they took the sheep, all the livestock and even the silver, gold and clothing they managed to wrangle from the Egyptians.

Now talk about fanfare! As they leave, their mighty God positions Himself before them, leading them in a pillar of cloud.

God did not lead them through the land of the Philistines, even though it was a more direct route, because He didn't want them to be involved in a battle and long for Egypt again. So instead, He led them around the wilderness to the Red Sea.

Following a few quiet days of reflection and recovery from all the plagues, old Pharaoh has a change of heart. Six hundred chariots and drivers were made ready, and the chase was on for the Israelites. But God was prepared. He's prepared today to move mountains for you.

WILLIAM WILLIAMS {AD 1717–1791}

Guide me, O thou great Jehovah,
Pilgrim through this barren land;
I am weak, but thou art mighty,
Hold me with thy powerful hand;
Bread of heaven,
Feed me now and evermore.

reflection

1. When have you felt that God has taken you the long way to reach your destination?

2. What lesson can you learn from the Israelites about God's leading and direction in your life?

3. What obstacles do you face that only God's miraculous hand can remove?

For your next devotional reading, go to page 91.

that they could travel by day or night. ²²Neither the pillar of cloud by day nor the pillar of fire by night left its place in front of the people.

¹⁴ Then the LORD said to Moses, ²"Tell the Israelites to turn back and encamp near Pi Hahiroth, between Migdol and the sea. They are to encamp by the sea, directly opposite Baal Zephon. ³Pharaoh will think, 'The Israelites are wandering around the land in confusion, hemmed in by the desert.' ⁴And I will harden Pharaoh's heart, and he will pursue them. But I will gain glory for myself through Pharaoh and all his army, and the Egyptians will know that I am the LORD." So the Israelites did this.

⁵When the king of Egypt was told that the people had fled, Pharaoh and his officials changed their minds about them and said, "What have we done? We have let the Israelites go and have lost their services!" ⁶So he had his chariot made ready and took his army with him. ⁷He took six hundred of the best chariots, along with all the other chariots of Egypt, with officers over all of them. ⁸The LORD hardened the heart of Pharaoh king of Egypt, so that he pursued the Israelites, who were marching out boldly. ⁹The Egyptians—all Pharaoh's horses and chariots, horsemen^a and troops—pursued the Israelites and overtook them as they camped by the sea near Pi Hahiroth, opposite Baal Zephon.

¹⁰As Pharaoh approached, the Israelites looked up, and there were the Egyptians, marching after them. They were terrified and cried out to the LORD. ¹¹They said to Moses, "Was it because there were no graves in Egypt that you brought us to the desert to die? What have you done to us by bringing us out of Egypt? ¹²Didn't we say to you in Egypt, 'Leave us alone; let us serve the Egyptians'? It would have been better for us to serve the Egyptians than to die in the desert!"

¹³Moses answered the people, "Do not be afraid. Stand firm and you will see the deliverance the LORD will bring you today. The Egyptians you see today you will never see again. ¹⁴The LORD will fight for you; you need only to be still."

¹⁵Then the LORD said to Moses, "Why are you crying out to me? Tell the Israelites to move on. ¹⁶Raise your staff and stretch out your hand over the sea to divide the water so that the Israelites can go through the sea on dry ground. ¹⁷I will harden the hearts of the Egyptians so that they will go in after them. And I will gain glory through Pharaoh and all his army, through his chariots and his horsemen. ¹⁸The Egyptians will know that I am the LORD when I gain glory through Pharaoh, his chariots and his horsemen."

¹⁹Then the angel of God, who had been traveling in front of Israel's army, withdrew and went behind them. The pillar of cloud also moved from in front and stood behind them, ²⁰coming between the armies of Egypt and Israel. Throughout the night the cloud brought darkness to the one side and light to the other side; so neither went near the other all night long.

²¹Then Moses stretched out his hand over the sea, and all that night the LORD drove the sea back with a strong east wind and turned it into dry land. The waters were divided, ²²and the Israelites went through the sea on dry ground, with a wall of water on their right and on their left.

²³The Egyptians pursued them, and all Pharaoh's horses and chariots and horsemen followed them into the sea. ²⁴During the last watch of the night the LORD looked down from the pillar of fire and cloud at the Egyptian army and threw it into confusion. ²⁵He jammed^b the wheels of their chariots so that they had difficulty driving. And the Egyptians said, "Let's get away from the Israelites! The LORD is fighting for them against Egypt."

²⁶Then the LORD said to Moses, "Stretch out your hand over the sea so that the waters may flow back over the Egyptians and their chariots and horsemen." ²⁷Moses stretched out his hand over the sea, and at daybreak the sea went back to its place. The Egyptians were fleeing toward^c it, and the LORD swept them into the sea. ²⁸The water flowed back and covered the chariots and horsemen—the entire army of Pharaoh that had followed the Israelites into the sea. Not one of them survived.

²⁹But the Israelites went through the sea on dry ground, with a wall of water on their

^a 9 Or charioteers; also in verses 17, 18, 23, 26 and 28 Syriac; Masoretic Text removed   ^c 27 Or from   ^b 25 See Samaritan Pentateuch, Septuagint and

right and on their left. ³⁰That day the Lord saved Israel from the hands of the Egyptians, and Israel saw the Egyptians lying dead on the shore. ³¹And when the Israelites saw the great power the Lord displayed against the Egyptians, the people feared the Lord and put their trust in him and in Moses his servant.

The Song of Moses and Miriam

15 Then Moses and the Israelites sang this song to the Lord:

"I will sing to the Lord,
    for he is highly exalted.
Both horse and driver
    he has hurled into the sea.

² "The Lord is my strength and my
       defense^a;
    he has become my salvation.
He is my God, and I will praise him,
    my father's God, and I will exalt him.
³ The Lord is a warrior;
    the Lord is his name.
⁴ Pharaoh's chariots and his army
    he has hurled into the sea.
The best of Pharaoh's officers
    are drowned in the Red Sea.^b
⁵ The deep waters have covered them;
    they sank to the depths like a stone.
⁶ Your right hand, Lord,
    was majestic in power.
Your right hand, Lord,
    shattered the enemy.

⁷ "In the greatness of your majesty
    you threw down those who opposed
       you.
You unleashed your burning anger;
    it consumed them like stubble.
⁸ By the blast of your nostrils
    the waters piled up.
The surging waters stood up like a wall;
    the deep waters congealed in the
       heart of the sea.
⁹ The enemy boasted,
    'I will pursue, I will overtake them.
I will divide the spoils;
    I will gorge myself on them.
I will draw my sword
    and my hand will destroy them.'
¹⁰ But you blew with your breath,

    and the sea covered them.
They sank like lead
    in the mighty waters.
¹¹ Who among the gods
    is like you, Lord?
Who is like you—
    majestic in holiness,
awesome in glory,
    working wonders?

¹² "You stretch out your right hand,
    and the earth swallows your enemies.
¹³ In your unfailing love you will lead
    the people you have redeemed.
In your strength you will guide them
    to your holy dwelling.
¹⁴ The nations will hear and tremble;
    anguish will grip the people of
       Philistia.
¹⁵ The chiefs of Edom will be terrified,
    the leaders of Moab will be seized
       with trembling,
the people^c of Canaan will melt away;
¹⁶   terror and dread will fall on them.
By the power of your arm
    they will be as still as a stone—
until your people pass by, Lord,
    until the people you bought^d pass by.
¹⁷ You will bring them in and plant them
    on the mountain of your
       inheritance—
the place, Lord, you made for your
       dwelling,
the sanctuary, Lord, your hands
       established.

¹⁸ "The Lord reigns
    for ever and ever."

¹⁹When Pharaoh's horses, chariots and horsemen^e went into the sea, the Lord brought the waters of the sea back over them, but the Israelites walked through the sea on dry ground. ²⁰Then Miriam the prophet, Aaron's sister, took a timbrel in her hand, and all the women followed her, with timbrels and dancing. ²¹Miriam sang to them:

"Sing to the Lord,
    for he is highly exalted.
Both horse and driver
    he has hurled into the sea."

---

^a 2 Or song   ^b 4 Or the Sea of Reeds; also in verse 22   ^c 15 Or rulers   ^d 16 Or created
^e 19 Or charioteers

The Waters of Marah and Elim

²²Then Moses led Israel from the Red Sea and they went into the Desert of Shur. For three days they traveled in the desert without finding water. ²³When they came to Marah, they could not drink its water because it was bitter. (That is why the place is called Marah.ᵃ) ²⁴So the people grumbled against Moses, saying, "What are we to drink?"

²⁵Then Moses cried out to the LORD, and the LORD showed him a piece of wood. He threw it into the water, and the water became sweet.

There the LORD issued a ruling and instruction for them and put them to the test. ²⁶He said, "If you listen carefully to the LORD your God and do what is right in his eyes, if you pay attention to his commands and keep all his decrees, I will not bring on you any of the diseases I brought on the Egyptians, for I am the LORD, who heals you."

²⁷Then they came to Elim, where there were twelve springs and seventy palm trees, and they camped there near the water.

Manna and Quail

16 The whole Israelite community set out from Elim and came to the Desert of Sin, which is between Elim and Sinai, on the fifteenth day of the second month after they had come out of Egypt. ²In the desert the whole community grumbled against Moses and Aaron. ³The Israelites said to them, "If only we had died by the LORD's hand in Egypt! There we sat around pots of meat and ate all the food we wanted, but you have brought us out into this desert to starve this entire assembly to death."

⁴Then the LORD said to Moses, "I will rain down bread from heaven for you. The people are to go out each day and gather enough for that day. In this way I will test them and see whether they will follow my instructions. ⁵On the sixth day they are to prepare what they bring in, and that is to be twice as much as they gather on the other days."

⁶So Moses and Aaron said to all the Israelites, "In the evening you will know that it was the LORD who brought you out of Egypt, ⁷and in the morning you will see the glory of the LORD, because he has heard your grumbling against him. Who are we, that you should grumble against us?" ⁸Moses also said, "You will know that it was the LORD when he gives you meat to eat in the evening and all the bread you want in the morning, because he has heard your grumbling against him. Who are we? You are not grumbling against us, but against the LORD."

⁹Then Moses told Aaron, "Say to the entire Israelite community, 'Come before the LORD, for he has heard your grumbling.' "

¹⁰While Aaron was speaking to the whole Israelite community, they looked toward the desert, and there was the glory of the LORD appearing in the cloud.

¹¹The LORD said to Moses, ¹²"I have heard the grumbling of the Israelites. Tell them, 'At twilight you will eat meat, and in the morning you will be filled with bread. Then you will know that I am the LORD your God.' "

¹³That evening quail came and covered the camp, and in the morning there was a layer of dew around the camp. ¹⁴When the dew was gone, thin flakes like frost on the ground appeared on the desert floor. ¹⁵When the Israelites saw it, they said to each other, "What is it?" For they did not know what it was.

Moses said to them, "It is the bread the LORD has given you to eat. ¹⁶This is what the LORD has commanded: 'Each one is to gather as much as they need. Take an omerᵇ for each person you have in your tent.' "

¹⁷The Israelites did as they were told; some gathered much, some little. ¹⁸And when they measured it by the omer, the one who gathered much did not have too much, and the one who gathered little did not have too little. Each one had gathered just as much as they needed.

¹⁹Then Moses said to them, "No one is to keep any of it until morning."

²⁰However, some of them paid no attention to Moses; they kept part of it until morning, but it was full of maggots and began to smell. So Moses was angry with them.

²¹Each morning everyone gathered as much as they needed, and when the sun grew hot, it melted away. ²²On the sixth day,

---

ᵃ 23 *Marah* means *bitter.*   ᵇ 16 That is, possibly about 3 pounds or about 1.4 kilograms; also in verses 18, 32, 33 and 36 they gathered twice as much—two omers*a* for each person—and the leaders of the community came and reported this to Moses. 23He said to them, "This is what the LORD commanded: 'Tomorrow is to be a day of sabbath rest, a holy sabbath to the LORD. So bake what you want to bake and boil what you want to boil. Save whatever is left and keep it until morning.' "

24So they saved it until morning, as Moses commanded, and it did not stink or get maggots in it. 25"Eat it today," Moses said, "because today is a sabbath to the LORD. You will not find any of it on the ground today. 26Six days you are to gather it, but on the seventh day, the Sabbath, there will not be any."

27Nevertheless, some of the people went out on the seventh day to gather it, but they found none. 28Then the LORD said to Moses, "How long will you*b* refuse to keep my commands and my instructions? 29Bear in mind that the LORD has given you the Sabbath; that is why on the sixth day he gives you bread for two days. Everyone is to stay where they are on the seventh day; no one is to go out." 30So the people rested on the seventh day.

31The people of Israel called the bread manna.*c* It was white like coriander seed and tasted like wafers made with honey. 32Moses said, "This is what the LORD has commanded: 'Take an omer of manna and keep it for the generations to come, so they can see the bread I gave you to eat in the wilderness when I brought you out of Egypt.' "

33So Moses said to Aaron, "Take a jar and put an omer of manna in it. Then place it before the LORD to be kept for the generations to come."

34As the LORD commanded Moses, Aaron put the manna with the tablets of the covenant law, so that it might be preserved. 35The Israelites ate manna forty years, until they came to a land that was settled; they ate manna until they reached the border of Canaan.

36(An omer is one-tenth of an ephah.)

Water From the Rock

17 The whole Israelite community set out from the Desert of Sin, traveling from place to place as the LORD commanded. They camped at Rephidim, but there was no water for the people to drink. 2So they quarreled with Moses and said, "Give us water to drink."

Moses replied, "Why do you quarrel with me? Why do you put the LORD to the test?"

3But the people were thirsty for water there, and they grumbled against Moses. They said, "Why did you bring us up out of Egypt to make us and our children and livestock die of thirst?"

4Then Moses cried out to the LORD, "What am I to do with these people? They are almost ready to stone me."

5The LORD answered Moses, "Go out in front of the people. Take with you some of the elders of Israel and take in your hand the staff with which you struck the Nile, and go. 6I will stand there before you by the rock at Horeb. Strike the rock, and water will come out of it for the people to drink." So Moses did this in the sight of the elders of Israel. 7And he called the place Massah*d* and Meribah*e* because the Israelites quarreled and because they tested the LORD saying, "Is the LORD among us or not?"

The Amalekites Defeated

8The Amalekites came and attacked the Israelites at Rephidim. 9Moses said to Joshua, "Choose some of our men and go out to fight the Amalekites. Tomorrow I will stand on top of the hill with the staff of God in my hands."

10So Joshua fought the Amalekites as Moses had ordered, and Moses, Aaron and Hur went to the top of the hill. 11As long as Moses held up his hands, the Israelites were winning, but whenever he lowered his hands, the Amalekites were winning. 12When Moses' hands grew tired, they took a stone and put it under him and he sat on it. Aaron and Hur held his hands up—one on one side, one on the other—so that his hands remained steady till sunset. 13So Joshua overcame the Amalekite army with the sword.

14Then the LORD said to Moses, "Write

---

a 22 That is, possibly about 6 pounds or about 2.8 kilograms   *b 28* The Hebrew is plural.
c 31 *Manna* means *What is it?* (see verse 15).   *d 7* *Massah* means *testing.*   *e 7* *Meribah* means *quarreling.*

this on a scroll as something to be remembered and make sure that Joshua hears it, because I will completely blot out the name of Amalek from under heaven."

¹⁵Moses built an altar and called it The Lord is my Banner. ¹⁶He said, "Because hands were lifted up against[a] the throne of the Lord,[b] the Lord will be at war against the Amalekites from generation to generation."

Jethro Visits Moses

18 Now Jethro, the priest of Midian and father-in-law of Moses, heard of everything God had done for Moses and for his people Israel, and how the Lord had brought Israel out of Egypt. ²After Moses had sent away his wife Zipporah, his father-in-law Jethro received her ³and her two sons. One son was named Gershom,[c] for Moses said, "I have become a foreigner in a foreign land"; ⁴and the other was named Eliezer,[d] for he said, "My father's God was my helper; he saved me from the sword of Pharaoh."

⁵Jethro, Moses' father-in-law, together with Moses' sons and wife, came to him in the wilderness, where he was camped near the mountain of God. ⁶Jethro had sent word to him, "I, your father-in-law Jethro, am coming to you with your wife and her two sons."

⁷So Moses went out to meet his father-in-law and bowed down and kissed him. They greeted each other and then went into the tent. ⁸Moses told his father-in-law about everything the Lord had done to Pharaoh and the Egyptians for Israel's sake and about all the hardships they had met along the way and how the Lord had saved them.

⁹Jethro was delighted to hear about all the good things the Lord had done for Israel in rescuing them from the hand of the Egyptians. ¹⁰He said, "Praise be to the Lord, who rescued you from the hand of the Egyptians and of Pharaoh, and who rescued the people from the hand of the Egyptians. ¹¹Now I know that the Lord is greater than all other gods, for he did this to those who had treated Israel arrogantly." ¹²Then Jethro, Moses' father-in-law, brought a burnt offering and other sacrifices to God, and Aaron

came with all the elders of Israel to eat bread with Moses' father-in-law in the presence of God.

¹³The next day Moses took his seat to serve as judge for the people, and they stood around him from morning till evening. ¹⁴When his father-in-law saw all that Moses was doing for the people, he said, "What is this you are doing for the people? Why do you alone sit as judge, while all these people stand around you from morning till evening?"

¹⁵Moses answered him, "Because the people come to me to seek God's will. ¹⁶Whenever they have a dispute, it is brought to me, and I decide between the parties and inform them of God's decrees and instructions."

¹⁷Moses' father-in-law replied, "What you are doing is not good. ¹⁸You and these people who come to you will only wear yourselves out. The work is too heavy for you; you cannot handle it alone. ¹⁹Listen now to me and I will give you some advice, and may God be with you. You must be the people's representative before God and bring their disputes to him. ²⁰Teach them his decrees and instructions, and show them the way they are to live and how they are to behave. ²¹But select capable men from all the people—men who fear God, trustworthy men who hate dishonest gain—and appoint them as officials over thousands, hundreds, fifties and tens. ²²Have them serve as judges for the people at all times, but have them bring every difficult case to you; the simple cases they can decide themselves. That will make your load lighter, because they will share it with you. ²³If you do this and God so commands, you will be able to stand the strain, and all these people will go home satisfied."

²⁴Moses listened to his father-in-law and did everything he said. ²⁵He chose capable men from all Israel and made them leaders of the people, officials over thousands, hundreds, fifties and tens. ²⁶They served as judges for the people at all times. The difficult cases they brought to Moses, but the simple ones they decided themselves.

²⁷Then Moses sent his father-in-law on his way, and Jethro returned to his own country.

---

a 16 Or to   *b* 16 The meaning of the Hebrew for this clause is uncertain.   *c* 3 *Gershom* sounds like the Hebrew for *a foreigner there*.   *d* 4 *Eliezer* means *my God is helper*.

At Mount Sinai

19 On the first day of the third month after the Israelites left Egypt—on that very day—they came to the Desert of Sinai. ²After they set out from Rephidim, they entered the Desert of Sinai, and Israel camped there in the desert in front of the mountain.

³Then Moses went up to God, and the LORD called to him from the mountain and said, "This is what you are to say to the house of Jacob and what you are to tell the people of Israel: ⁴'You yourselves have seen what I did to Egypt, and how I carried you on eagles' wings and brought you to myself. ⁵Now if you obey me fully and keep my covenant, then out of all nations you will be my treasured possession. Although the whole earth is mine, ⁶you*ᵃ* will be for me a kingdom of priests and a holy nation.' These are the words you are to speak to the Israelites."

⁷So Moses went back and summoned the elders of the people and set before them all the words the LORD had commanded him to speak. ⁸The people all responded together, "We will do everything the LORD has said." So Moses brought their answer back to the LORD.

⁹The LORD said to Moses, "I am going to come to you in a dense cloud, so that the people will hear me speaking with you and will always put their trust in you." Then Moses told the LORD what the people had said.

¹⁰And the LORD said to Moses, "Go to the people and consecrate them today and tomorrow. Have them wash their clothes ¹¹and be ready by the third day, because on that day the LORD will come down on Mount Sinai in the sight of all the people. ¹²Put limits for the people around the mountain and tell them, 'Be careful that you do not approach the mountain or touch the foot of it. Whoever touches the mountain is to be put to death. ¹³They are to be stoned or shot with arrows; not a hand is to be laid on them. Whether people or animals, they shall not be permitted to live.' Only when the ram's horn sounds a long blast may they approach the mountain."

¹⁴After Moses had gone down the mountain to the people, he consecrated them, and they washed their clothes. ¹⁵Then he said to the people, "Prepare yourselves for the third day. Abstain from sexual relations."

¹⁶On the morning of the third day there was thunder and lightning, with a thick cloud over the mountain, and a very loud trumpet blast. Everyone in the camp trembled. ¹⁷Then Moses led the people out of the camp to meet with God, and they stood at the foot of the mountain. ¹⁸Mount Sinai was covered with smoke, because the LORD descended on it in fire. The smoke billowed up from it like smoke from a furnace, and the whole mountain*ᵇ* trembled violently. ¹⁹As the sound of the trumpet grew louder and louder, Moses spoke and the voice of God answered him.*ᶜ*

²⁰The LORD descended to the top of Mount Sinai and called Moses to the top of the mountain. So Moses went up ²¹and the LORD said to him, "Go down and warn the people so they do not force their way through to see the LORD and many of them perish. ²²Even the priests, who approach the LORD, must consecrate themselves, or the LORD will break out against them."

²³Moses said to the LORD, "The people cannot come up Mount Sinai, because you yourself warned us, 'Put limits around the mountain and set it apart as holy.' "

²⁴The LORD replied, "Go down and bring Aaron up with you. But the priests and the people must not force their way through to come up to the LORD, or he will break out against them."

²⁵So Moses went down to the people and told them.

The Ten Commandments

20 And God spoke all these words:

²"I am the LORD your God, who brought you out of Egypt, out of the land of slavery.

³"You shall have no other gods before*ᵈ* me.

⁴"You shall not make for yourself an image in the form of anything in heaven above or on the earth beneath or in the waters below. ⁵You shall not bow down to them or worship them; for I, the LORD your God, am a jealous God, punishing

---

ᵃ 5,6 Or *possession, for the whole earth is mine.* ⁶*You* manuscripts and Septuagint *and all the people*   *ᶜ 19* Or *and God answered him with thunder*   *ᵇ 18* Most Hebrew manuscripts; a few Hebrew   *ᵈ 3* Or *besides* the children for the sin of the parents to the third and fourth generation of those who hate me, ⁶but showing love to a thousand generations of those who love me and keep my commandments.

⁷"You shall not misuse the name of the LORD your God, for the LORD will not hold anyone guiltless who misuses his name.

⁸"Remember the Sabbath day by keeping it holy. ⁹Six days you shall labor and do all your work, ¹⁰but the seventh day is a sabbath to the LORD your God. On it you shall not do any work, neither you, nor your son or daughter, nor your male or female servant, nor your animals, nor any foreigner residing in your towns. ¹¹For in six days the LORD made the heavens and the earth, the sea, and all that is in them, but he rested on the seventh day. Therefore the LORD blessed the Sabbath day and made it holy.

¹²"Honor your father and your mother, so that you may live long in the land the LORD your God is giving you.

¹³"You shall not murder.

¹⁴"You shall not commit adultery.

¹⁵"You shall not steal.

¹⁶"You shall not give false testimony against your neighbor.

¹⁷"You shall not covet your neighbor's house. You shall not covet your neighbor's wife, or his male or female servant, his ox or donkey, or anything that belongs to your neighbor."

¹⁸When the people saw the thunder and lightning and heard the trumpet and saw the mountain in smoke, they trembled with fear. They stayed at a distance ¹⁹and said to Moses, "Speak to us yourself and we will listen. But do not have God speak to us or we will die."

²⁰Moses said to the people, "Do not be afraid. God has come to test you, so that the fear of God will be with you to keep you from sinning."

²¹The people remained at a distance, while Moses approached the thick darkness where God was.

Idols and Altars

²²Then the LORD said to Moses, "Tell the Israelites this: 'You have seen for yourselves that I have spoken to you from heaven: ²³Do not make any gods to be alongside me; do not make for yourselves gods of silver or gods of gold.

²⁴" 'Make an altar of earth for me and sacrifice on it your burnt offerings and fellowship offerings, your sheep and goats and your cattle. Wherever I cause my name to be honored, I will come to you and bless you. ²⁵If you make an altar of stones for me, do not build it with dressed stones, for you will defile it if you use a tool on it. ²⁶And do not go up to my altar on steps, lest your nakedness be exposed on it.'

21

"These are the laws you are to set before them:

Hebrew Servants

²"If you buy a Hebrew servant, he is to serve you for six years. But in the seventh year, he shall go free, without paying anything. ³If he comes alone, he is to go free alone; but if he has a wife when he comes, she is to go with him. ⁴If his master gives him a wife and she bears him sons or daughters, the woman and her children shall belong to her master, and only the man shall go free.

⁵"But if the servant declares, 'I love my master and my wife and children and do not want to go free,' ⁶then his master must take him before the judges.ᵃ He shall take him to the door or the doorpost and pierce his ear with an awl. Then he will be his servant for life.

⁷"If a man sells his daughter as a servant, she is not to go free as male servants do. ⁸If she does not please the master who has selected her for himself,ᵇ he must let her be redeemed. He has no right to sell her to foreigners, because he has broken faith with her. ⁹If he selects her for his son, he must grant her the rights of a daughter. ¹⁰If he marries another woman, he must not deprive the first one of her food, clothing and marital rights. ¹¹If he does not provide her with these three things, she is to go free, without any payment of money.

ᵃ 6 Or *before God*   ᵇ 8 Or *master so that he does not choose her*

TUESDAY

PUTTING GOD FIRST

Exodus 20:1–26 *or* 20:1–11

Andrea Johnson

We have to make sure that we do not reverence that which has been created over the Creator. We go to work every day, watch TV, go to the movies, see the stars and plan our lives without recognizing who reigns. God is Sovereign, Omnipotent and Omnipresent, yet He sometimes ends up last on the list of things to which we give our time, attention and energy. The Word of God is clear on what we should do. We are the created, and we must reverence Him in everything we do. The first commandment found in Exodus 20:3 is, "[You shall have no other gods before me.]" So let us remember this when we want to put so much of our time, talent and investment into something that is not of Him. Think about it when we try to reverence something by seeking out its pleasures over the wisdom of God, when they [in] no way compare to Him. For Habakkuk 2:19–20 says, " '[Woe to him who says to wood, "Come to life!" Or to lifeless stone, "Wake up!" Can it give guidance? It is covered with gold and silver; there is no breath in it.' The LORD is in his holy temple; let all the earth be silent before him.]" We need to reverence Him, be still before Him and glorify and honor the One who created us, not what has been created.

OSCAR ROMERO {AD 1917–1980}

We could cite truly shameful situations of people who should be giving us an example of honesty in their government posts, in their business, with their wealth. And why do they take advantage of these posts, these situations? Nothing is done now for the common good. It is done out of selfishness. Ah, yes, there is reckoning to be made! We ask for accountability in public works! The law of God has not been respected by the very ones who should be models—the legislators, those who command. Naturally, the example of these higher-ups creates doubt and uncertainty in the people and also a desire to take advantage. Then, we have a corrupt nation from top to bottom, because all of them have forgotten the law of God. We have forgotten the law of God.

reflection

1. Into what have you invested the bulk of your time, energy, and emotions in the last 24 hours? What does that reveal about what is most important to you?

2. Think of at least three examples of how the law of God has been disregarded in our society. How would your community be different if God's law was respected in these areas?

3. What actions will you take in the next few days that will differ from the actions of those who don't remember to put God and his Word first?

For your next devotional reading, go to page 94.

Personal Injuries

¹²"Anyone who strikes someone a fatal blow is to be put to death. ¹³However, if it is not done intentionally, but God lets it happen, they are to flee to a place I will designate. ¹⁴But if anyone schemes and kills someone deliberately, that person is to be taken from my altar and put to death.

¹⁵"Anyone who attacks*a* their father or mother is to be put to death.

¹⁶"Anyone who kidnaps someone is to be put to death, whether the victim has been sold or is still in the kidnapper's possession.

¹⁷"Anyone who curses their father or mother is to be put to death.

¹⁸"If two people quarrel and one hits the other with a stone or with a fist*b* and the victim does not die but is confined to bed, ¹⁹the one who struck the blow will not be held liable if the other can get up and walk around outside with a staff; however, the guilty party must pay the injured person for any loss of time and see that the victim is completely healed.

²⁰"Anyone who beats their male or female slave with a rod must be punished if the slave dies as a direct result, ²¹but they are not to be punished if the slave recovers after a day or two, since the slave is their property.

²²"If people are fighting and a pregnant woman is hit and gives birth prematurely*c* but there is no serious injury, the offender must be fined whatever the woman's husband demands and the court allows. ²³But if there is serious injury, you are to take life for life, ²⁴eye for eye, tooth for tooth, hand for hand, foot for foot, ²⁵burn for burn, wound for wound, bruise for bruise.

²⁶"An owner who hits a male or female slave in the eye and destroys it must let the slave go free to compensate for the eye. ²⁷And an owner who knocks out the tooth of a male or female slave must let the slave go free to compensate for the tooth.

²⁸"If a bull gores a man or a woman to death, the bull is to be stoned to death, and its meat must not be eaten. But the owner of the bull will not be held responsible. ²⁹If, however, the bull has had the habit of goring and the owner has been warned but has not kept it penned up and it kills a man or woman, the bull is to be stoned and its owner also is to be put to death. ³⁰However, if payment is demanded, the owner's life may be redeemed by the payment of whatever is demanded. ³¹This law also applies if the bull gores a son or daughter. ³²If the bull gores a male or female slave, the owner must pay thirty shekels*d* of silver to the master of the slave, and the bull is to be stoned to death.

³³"If anyone uncovers a pit or digs one and fails to cover it and an ox or a donkey falls into it, ³⁴the one who opened the pit must pay the owner for the loss and take the dead animal in exchange.

³⁵"If anyone's bull injures the bull of another and it dies, the two parties are to sell the live one and divide both the money and the dead animal equally. ³⁶However, if it was known that the bull had the habit of goring, yet the owner did not keep it penned up, the owner must pay, animal for animal, and take the dead animal in exchange.

Protection of Property

22 *"Whoever steals an ox or a sheep and slaughters it or sells it must pay back five head of cattle for the ox and four sheep for the sheep.

*²"If a thief is caught breaking in and is struck a fatal blow, the defender is not guilty of bloodshed; ³but if it happens*e* after sunrise, the defender is guilty of bloodshed.

"Anyone who steals must certainly make restitution, but if they have nothing, they must be sold to pay for their theft. ⁴If the stolen animal is found alive in their possession—whether ox or donkey or sheep—they must pay back double.

⁵"If anyone grazes their livestock in a field or vineyard and lets them stray and they graze in another person's field, restitution must be made from the best of the livestock owner's field or vineyard.

⁶"If a fire breaks out and spreads into thornbushes so that it burns shocks of grain or standing grain or the whole field, the one who started the fire must make restitution.

⁷"If anyone gives a neighbor silver or goods for safekeeping and they are stolen

---

a 15 Or *kills*   *b* 18 Or *with a tool*   *c* 22 Or *and has a miscarriage*   *d* 32 That is, about 12 ounces or about 345 grams   *e* 3 Or *if the defender kills the thief*

* 22:1 is numbered 21:37 in Hebrew texts.   * 22:2-31 is numbered 22:1-30 in Hebrew texts.

from the neighbor's house, the thief, if caught, must pay back double. ⁸But if the thief is not found, the owner of the house must appear before the judges, and they must*a* determine whether the owner of the house has laid hands on the other person's property. ⁹In all cases of illegal possession of an ox, a donkey, a sheep, a garment, or any other lost property about which somebody says, 'This is mine,' both parties are to bring their cases before the judges.*b* The one whom the judges declare*c* guilty must pay back double to the other.

¹⁰"If anyone gives a donkey, an ox, a sheep or any other animal to a neighbor for safekeeping and it dies or is injured or is taken away while no one is looking, ¹¹the issue between them will be settled by the taking of an oath before the LORD that the neighbor did not lay hands on the other person's property. The owner is to accept this, and no restitution is required. ¹²But if the animal was stolen from the neighbor, restitution must be made to the owner. ¹³If it was torn to pieces by a wild animal, the neighbor shall bring in the remains as evidence and shall not be required to pay for the torn animal.

¹⁴"If anyone borrows an animal from a neighbor and it is injured or dies while the owner is not present, restitution must be made. ¹⁵But if the owner is with the animal, the borrower will not have to pay. If the animal was hired, the money paid for the hire covers the loss.

Social Responsibility

¹⁶"If a man seduces a virgin who is not pledged to be married and sleeps with her, he must pay the bride-price, and she shall be his wife. ¹⁷If her father absolutely refuses to give her to him, he must still pay the bride-price for virgins.

¹⁸"Do not allow a sorceress to live.

¹⁹"Anyone who has sexual relations with an animal is to be put to death.

²⁰"Whoever sacrifices to any god other than the LORD must be destroyed.*d*

²¹"Do not mistreat or oppress a foreigner, for you were foreigners in Egypt.

²²"Do not take advantage of a widow or an orphan. ²³If you do and they cry out to me, I will certainly hear their cry. ²⁴My anger will be aroused, and I will kill you with the sword; your wives will become widows and your children fatherless.

²⁵"If you lend money to one of my people among you who is needy, do not treat it like a business deal; charge no interest. ²⁶If you take your neighbor's cloak as a pledge, return it by sunset, ²⁷because that cloak is the only covering your neighbor has. What else can your neighbor sleep in? When he cries out to me, I will hear, for I am compassionate.

²⁸"Do not blaspheme God*e* or curse the ruler of your people.

²⁹"Do not hold back offerings from your granaries or your vats.*f*

"You must give me the firstborn of your sons. ³⁰Do the same with your cattle and your sheep. Let them stay with their mothers for seven days, but give them to me on the eighth day.

³¹"You are to be my holy people. So do not eat the meat of an animal torn by wild beasts; throw it to the dogs.

Laws of Justice and Mercy

23 "Do not spread false reports. Do not help a guilty person by being a malicious witness.

²"Do not follow the crowd in doing wrong. When you give testimony in a lawsuit, do not pervert justice by siding with the crowd, ³and do not show favoritism to the poor in a lawsuit.

⁴"If you come across your enemy's ox or donkey wandering off, be sure to return it. ⁵If you see the donkey of someone who hates you fallen down under its load, do not leave it there; be sure you help your enemy with it.

⁶"Do not deny justice to your poor people in their lawsuits. ⁷Have nothing to do with a false charge and do not put an innocent or honest person to death, for I will not acquit the guilty.

⁸"Do not accept a bribe, for a bribe blinds those who see and twists the words of the righteous.

⁹"Do not oppress a foreigner; you yourselves know how it feels to be foreigners, because you were foreigners in Egypt.

---

a 8 Or *before God, and he will*   *b* 9 Or *before God*   *c* 9 Or *whom God declares*   *d* 20 The Hebrew term refers to the irrevocable giving over of things or persons to the LORD, often by totally destroying them.   *e* 28 Or *Do not revile the judges*   *f* 29 The meaning of the Hebrew for this phrase is uncertain.

WEDNESDAY

GOD'S LAW MAKES US PERFECT AND COMPLETE

Exodus 23:1–33 *or* 23:1–9

CHARLES G. FINNEY {AD 1792–1875}

Let the law be exalted. Let it be magnified and given honor. Let it be shown to be as strict and pure, and as perfect, as its Author. Spread its claims over the whole field of human and angelic accountability. Carry it like a blaze of fire to the deepest recess of every human heart. Exalt it as high as heaven, and thunder its authority and claims to the depths of hell ...

Yet let it be remembered forever, that the grace of the gospel extends the same distance as the claims of the law ... Let no one make the mistake of proclaiming the unholy idea that the glorious gospel of the blessed God is insufficient to fulfill in us "the righteous requirement of the law" (Romans 8:4) or that it is unable to cause us to "stand firm in all the will of God, mature and fully assured" (Colossian 4:12). For this gospel was sent to live in our hearts and is made powerful by the strong, effective application of the Holy Spirit.

J. A. Motyer

We could well pause at any and every prescription of the Book of the Covenant to underline the truth that the Lord desires his people to be distinct. What he wants in us, however, is the distinctiveness which arises as a by-product of obeying his Word. He wants us to live in the courts of earth according to the rules of the courts of heaven. Christians of older generations will still recall today the reactive distinctiveness which passed for "separation from the world" when they were young. If it was customary in the world around, it was forbidden to Christians—and for no other reason! Generations of Christians were deprived of the pleasures and benefits of the arts, for example, because they were considered the province of "the world." But this sort of isolationist difference is not what the Bible looks for. We are called, rather, to ransack Scripture to discover the distinctive features of a godly lifestyle and to follow through with a discipline of obedience to the Word of God. This is what the Lord sought in his redeemed at Sinai, and it is still the calling of the Israel of God (Galatians 6:16).

reflection

1. What was God's purpose in giving his people the law?

2. How can you discover what it means to be "distinct" as you live in this world?

3. How does minimizing the importance of God's law minimize the greatness of his grace?

For your next devotional reading, go to page 105.

Sabbath Laws

¹⁰"For six years you are to sow your fields and harvest the crops, ¹¹but during the seventh year let the land lie unplowed and unused. Then the poor among your people may get food from it, and the wild animals may eat what they leave. Do the same with your vineyard and your olive grove.

¹²"Six days do your work, but on the seventh day do not work, so that your ox and your donkey may rest, and so that the slave born in your household and the foreigner living among you may be refreshed.

¹³"Be careful to do everything I have said to you. Do not invoke the names of other gods; do not let them be heard on your lips.

The Three Annual Festivals

¹⁴"Three times a year you are to celebrate a festival to me.

¹⁵"Celebrate the Festival of Unleavened Bread; for seven days eat bread made without yeast, as I commanded you. Do this at the appointed time in the month of Aviv, for in that month you came out of Egypt.

"No one is to appear before me empty-handed.

¹⁶"Celebrate the Festival of Harvest with the firstfruits of the crops you sow in your field.

"Celebrate the Festival of Ingathering at the end of the year, when you gather in your crops from the field.

¹⁷"Three times a year all the men are to appear before the Sovereign Lord.

¹⁸"Do not offer the blood of a sacrifice to me along with anything containing yeast.

"The fat of my festival offerings must not be kept until morning.

¹⁹"Bring the best of the firstfruits of your soil to the house of the Lord your God.

"Do not cook a young goat in its mother's milk.

God's Angel to Prepare the Way

²⁰"See, I am sending an angel ahead of you to guard you along the way and to bring you to the place I have prepared. ²¹Pay attention to him and listen to what he says. Do not rebel against him; he will not forgive your rebellion, since my Name is in him. ²²If you listen carefully to what he says and do all that I say, I will be an enemy to your en-

emies and will oppose those who oppose you. ²³My angel will go ahead of you and bring you into the land of the Amorites, Hittites, Perizzites, Canaanites, Hivites and Jebusites, and I will wipe them out. ²⁴Do not bow down before their gods or worship them or follow their practices. You must demolish them and break their sacred stones to pieces. ²⁵Worship the Lord your God, and his blessing will be on your food and water. I will take away sickness from among you, ²⁶and none will miscarry or be barren in your land. I will give you a full life span.

²⁷"I will send my terror ahead of you and throw into confusion every nation you encounter. I will make all your enemies turn their backs and run. ²⁸I will send the hornet ahead of you to drive the Hivites, Canaanites and Hittites out of your way. ²⁹But I will not drive them out in a single year, because the land would become desolate and the wild animals too numerous for you. ³⁰Little by little I will drive them out before you, until you have increased enough to take possession of the land.

³¹"I will establish your borders from the Red Sea *a* to the Mediterranean Sea, *b* and from the desert to the Euphrates River. I will give into your hands the people who live in the land, and you will drive them out before you. ³²Do not make a covenant with them or with their gods. ³³Do not let them live in your land or they will cause you to sin against me, because the worship of their gods will certainly be a snare to you."

The Covenant Confirmed

24

Then he said to Moses, "Come up to the Lord, you and Aaron, Nadab and Abihu, and seventy of the elders of Israel. You are to worship at a distance, ²but Moses alone is to approach the Lord; the others must not come near. And the people may not come up with him."

³When Moses went and told the people all the Lord's words and laws, they responded with one voice, "Everything the Lord has said we will do." ⁴Moses then wrote down everything the Lord had said.

He got up early the next morning and built an altar at the foot of the mountain and set up twelve stone pillars representing the twelve tribes of Israel. ⁵Then he sent young

a 31 Or *the Sea of Reeds*   *b 31* Hebrew *to the Sea of the Philistines*

Israelite men, and they offered burnt offerings and sacrificed young bulls as fellowship offerings to the LORD. ⁶Moses took half of the blood and put it in bowls, and the other half he splashed against the altar. ⁷Then he took the Book of the Covenant and read it to the people. They responded, "We will do everything the LORD has said; we will obey."

⁸Moses then took the blood, sprinkled it on the people and said, "This is the blood of the covenant that the LORD has made with you in accordance with all these words."

⁹Moses and Aaron, Nadab and Abihu, and the seventy elders of Israel went up ¹⁰and saw the God of Israel. Under his feet was something like a pavement made of lapis lazuli, as bright blue as the sky. ¹¹But God did not raise his hand against these leaders of the Israelites; they saw God, and they ate and drank.

¹²The LORD said to Moses, "Come up to me on the mountain and stay here, and I will give you the tablets of stone with the law and commandments I have written for their instruction."

¹³Then Moses set out with Joshua his aide, and Moses went up on the mountain of God. ¹⁴He said to the elders, "Wait here for us until we come back to you. Aaron and Hur are with you, and anyone involved in a dispute can go to them."

¹⁵When Moses went up on the mountain, the cloud covered it, ¹⁶and the glory of the LORD settled on Mount Sinai. For six days the cloud covered the mountain, and on the seventh day the LORD called to Moses from within the cloud. ¹⁷To the Israelites the glory of the LORD looked like a consuming fire on top of the mountain. ¹⁸Then Moses entered the cloud as he went on up the mountain. And he stayed on the mountain forty days and forty nights.

Offerings for the Tabernacle

25 The LORD said to Moses, ²"Tell the Israelites to bring me an offering. You are to receive the offering for me from everyone whose heart prompts them to give. ³These are the offerings you are to receive from them: gold, silver and bronze; ⁴blue, purple and scarlet yarn and fine linen; goat hair; ⁵ram skins dyed red and another durable leather*ᵃ*; acacia wood; ⁶olive oil for the light; spices for the anointing oil and for the fragrant incense; ⁷and onyx stones and other gems to be mounted on the ephod and breastpiece.

⁸"Then have them make a sanctuary for me, and I will dwell among them. ⁹Make this tabernacle and all its furnishings exactly like the pattern I will show you.

The Ark

¹⁰"Have them make an ark*ᵇ* of acacia wood—two and a half cubits long, a cubit and a half wide, and a cubit and a half high.*ᶜ* ¹¹Overlay it with pure gold, both inside and out, and make a gold molding around it. ¹²Cast four gold rings for it and fasten them to its four feet, with two rings on one side and two rings on the other. ¹³Then make poles of acacia wood and overlay them with gold. ¹⁴Insert the poles into the rings on the sides of the ark to carry it. ¹⁵The poles are to remain in the rings of this ark; they are not to be removed. ¹⁶Then put in the ark the tablets of the covenant law, which I will give you.

¹⁷"Make an atonement cover of pure gold—two and a half cubits long and a cubit and a half wide. ¹⁸And make two cherubim out of hammered gold at the ends of the cover. ¹⁹Make one cherub on one end and the second cherub on the other; make the cherubim of one piece with the cover, at the two ends. ²⁰The cherubim are to have their wings spread upward, overshadowing the cover with them. The cherubim are to face each other, looking toward the cover. ²¹Place the cover on top of the ark and put in the ark the tablets of the covenant law that I will give you. ²²There, above the cover between the two cherubim that are over the ark of the covenant law, I will meet with you and give you all my commands for the Israelites.

The Table

²³"Make a table of acacia wood—two cubits long, a cubit wide and a cubit and a half high.*ᵈ* ²⁴Overlay it with pure gold and make a gold molding around it. ²⁵Also make around it a rim a handbreadth*ᵉ* wide and put

a 5 Possibly the hides of dugongs   *b 10* That is, a chest   *c 10* That is, about 3 3/4 feet long and 2 1/4 feet wide and high or about 1.1 meters long and 67 centimeters wide and high; also in verse 17   *d 23* That is, about 3 feet long, 1 1/2 feet wide and 2 1/4 feet high or about 90 centimeters long, 45 centimeters wide and 67 centimeters high   *e 25* That is, about 3 inches or about 7.5 centimeters a gold molding on the rim. ²⁶Make four gold rings for the table and fasten them to the four corners, where the four legs are. ²⁷The rings are to be close to the rim to hold the poles used in carrying the table. ²⁸Make the poles of acacia wood, overlay them with gold and carry the table with them. ²⁹And make its plates and dishes of pure gold, as well as its pitchers and bowls for the pouring out of offerings. ³⁰Put the bread of the Presence on this table to be before me at all times.

The Lampstand

³¹"Make a lampstand of pure gold. Hammer out its base and shaft, and make its flowerlike cups, buds and blossoms of one piece with them. ³²Six branches are to extend from the sides of the lampstand—three on one side and three on the other. ³³Three cups shaped like almond flowers with buds and blossoms are to be on one branch, three on the next branch, and the same for all six branches extending from the lampstand. ³⁴And on the lampstand there are to be four cups shaped like almond flowers with buds and blossoms. ³⁵One bud shall be under the first pair of branches extending from the lampstand, a second bud under the second pair, and a third bud under the third pair— six branches in all. ³⁶The buds and branches shall all be of one piece with the lampstand, hammered out of pure gold.

³⁷"Then make its seven lamps and set them up on it so that they light the space in front of it. ³⁸Its wick trimmers and trays are to be of pure gold. ³⁹A talent ᵃ of pure gold is to be used for the lampstand and all these accessories. ⁴⁰See that you make them according to the pattern shown you on the mountain.

The Tabernacle

26

"Make the tabernacle with ten curtains of finely twisted linen and blue, purple and scarlet yarn, with cherubim worked into them by skilled hands. ²All the curtains are to be the same size—twenty-eight cubits long and four cubits wide.ᵇ ³Join five of the curtains together, and do the same with the other five. ⁴Make loops of blue material along the edge of the end curtain in one set, and do the same with the end curtain in the other set. ⁵Make fifty loops on one curtain and fifty loops on the end curtain of the other set, with the loops opposite each other. ⁶Then make fifty gold clasps and use them to fasten the curtains together so that the tabernacle is a unit.

⁷"Make curtains of goat hair for the tent over the tabernacle—eleven altogether. ⁸All eleven curtains are to be the same size— thirty cubits long and four cubits wide.ᶜ ⁹Join five of the curtains together into one set and the other six into another set. Fold the sixth curtain double at the front of the tent. ¹⁰Make fifty loops along the edge of the end curtain in one set and also along the edge of the end curtain in the other set. ¹¹Then make fifty bronze clasps and put them in the loops to fasten the tent together as a unit. ¹²As for the additional length of the tent curtains, the half curtain that is left over is to hang down at the rear of the tabernacle. ¹³The tent curtains will be a cubitᵈ longer on both sides; what is left will hang over the sides of the tabernacle so as to cover it. ¹⁴Make for the tent a covering of ram skins dyed red, and over that a covering of the other durable leather.ᵉ

¹⁵"Make upright frames of acacia wood for the tabernacle. ¹⁶Each frame is to be ten cubits long and a cubit and a half wide,ᶠ ¹⁷with two projections set parallel to each other. Make all the frames of the tabernacle in this way. ¹⁸Make twenty frames for the south side of the tabernacle ¹⁹and make forty silver bases to go under them—two bases for each frame, one under each projection. ²⁰For the other side, the north side of the tabernacle, make twenty frames ²¹and forty silver bases—two under each frame. ²²Make six frames for the far end, that is, the west end of the tabernacle, ²³and make two frames for the corners at the far end. ²⁴At these two corners they must be double from the bottom all the way to the top and fitted into a single ring; both shall be like that.

ᵃ 39 That is, about 75 pounds or about 34 kilograms or about 13 meters long and 1.8 meters wide   ᶜ 8 That is, about 45 feet long and 6 feet wide or about 13.5 meters long and 1.8 meters wide   ᵈ 13 That is, about 18 inches or about 45 centimeters ᵉ 14 Possibly the hides of dugongs   ᶠ 16 That is, about 15 feet long and 2 1/4 feet wide or about 4.5 meters long and 67 centimeters wide

ᵇ 2 That is, about 42 feet long and 6 feet wide or

²⁵So there will be eight frames and sixteen silver bases—two under each frame.

²⁶"Also make crossbars of acacia wood: five for the frames on one side of the tabernacle, ²⁷five for those on the other side, and five for the frames on the west, at the far end of the tabernacle. ²⁸The center crossbar is to extend from end to end at the middle of the frames. ²⁹Overlay the frames with gold and make gold rings to hold the crossbars. Also overlay the crossbars with gold.

³⁰"Set up the tabernacle according to the plan shown you on the mountain.

³¹"Make a curtain of blue, purple and scarlet yarn and finely twisted linen, with cherubim worked into it by skilled hands. ³²Hang it with gold hooks on four posts of acacia wood overlaid with gold and standing on four silver bases. ³³Hang the curtain from the clasps and place the ark of the covenant law behind the curtain. The curtain will separate the Holy Place from the Most Holy Place. ³⁴Put the atonement cover on the ark of the covenant law in the Most Holy Place. ³⁵Place the table outside the curtain on the north side of the tabernacle and put the lampstand opposite it on the south side.

³⁶"For the entrance to the tent make a curtain of blue, purple and scarlet yarn and finely twisted linen—the work of an embroiderer. ³⁷Make gold hooks for this curtain and five posts of acacia wood overlaid with gold. And cast five bronze bases for them.

The Altar of Burnt Offering

27 "Build an altar of acacia wood, three cubits[a] high; it is to be square, five cubits long and five cubits wide.[b] ²Make a horn at each of the four corners, so that the horns and the altar are of one piece, and overlay the altar with bronze. ³Make all its utensils of bronze—its pots to remove the ashes, and its shovels, sprinkling bowls, meat forks and firepans. ⁴Make a grating for it, a bronze network, and make a bronze ring at each of the four corners of the network. ⁵Put it under the ledge of the altar so that it is halfway up the altar. ⁶Make poles of acacia wood for the altar and overlay them with bronze. ⁷The poles are to

be inserted into the rings so they will be on two sides of the altar when it is carried. ⁸Make the altar hollow, out of boards. It is to be made just as you were shown on the mountain.

The Courtyard

⁹"Make a courtyard for the tabernacle. The south side shall be a hundred cubits[c] long and is to have curtains of finely twisted linen, ¹⁰with twenty posts and twenty bronze bases and with silver hooks and bands on the posts. ¹¹The north side shall also be a hundred cubits long and is to have curtains, with twenty posts and twenty bronze bases and with silver hooks and bands on the posts.

¹²"The west end of the courtyard shall be fifty cubits[d] wide and have curtains, with ten posts and ten bases. ¹³On the east end, toward the sunrise, the courtyard shall also be fifty cubits wide. ¹⁴Curtains fifteen cubits[e] long are to be on one side of the entrance, with three posts and three bases, ¹⁵and curtains fifteen cubits long are to be on the other side, with three posts and three bases.

¹⁶"For the entrance to the courtyard, provide a curtain twenty cubits[f] long, of blue, purple and scarlet yarn and finely twisted linen—the work of an embroiderer—with four posts and four bases. ¹⁷All the posts around the courtyard are to have silver bands and hooks, and bronze bases. ¹⁸The courtyard shall be a hundred cubits long and fifty cubits wide,[g] with curtains of finely twisted linen five cubits[h] high, and with bronze bases. ¹⁹All the other articles used in the service of the tabernacle, whatever their function, including all the tent pegs for it and those for the courtyard, are to be of bronze.

Oil for the Lampstand

²⁰"Command the Israelites to bring you clear oil of pressed olives for the light so that the lamps may be kept burning. ²¹In the tent of meeting, outside the curtain that shields the ark of the covenant law, Aaron and his sons are to keep the lamps burning before

---

a 1 That is, about 4 1/2 feet or about 1.4 meters   b 1 That is, about 7 1/2 feet or about 2.3 meters long and wide   c 9 That is, about 150 feet or about 45 meters; also in verse 11   d 12 That is, about 75 feet or about 22.5 meters; also in verse 13   e 14 That is, about 22 feet or about 6.8 meters; also in verse 15   f 16 That is, about 30 feet or about 9 meters   g 18 That is, about 150 feet long and 75 feet wide or about 45 meters long and 22.5 meters wide   h 18 That is, about 7 1/2 feet or about 2.3 meters the LORD from evening till morning. This is to be a lasting ordinance among the Israelites for the generations to come.

The Priestly Garments

28 "Have Aaron your brother brought to you from among the Israelites, along with his sons Nadab and Abihu, Eleazar and Ithamar, so they may serve me as priests. ²Make sacred garments for your brother Aaron to give him dignity and honor. ³Tell all the skilled workers to whom I have given wisdom in such matters that they are to make garments for Aaron, for his consecration, so he may serve me as priest. ⁴These are the garments they are to make: a breastpiece, an ephod, a robe, a woven tunic, a turban and a sash. They are to make these sacred garments for your brother Aaron and his sons, so they may serve me as priests. ⁵Have them use gold, and blue, purple and scarlet yarn, and fine linen.

The Ephod

⁶"Make the ephod of gold, and of blue, purple and scarlet yarn, and of finely twisted linen—the work of skilled hands. ⁷It is to have two shoulder pieces attached to two of its corners, so it can be fastened. ⁸Its skillfully woven waistband is to be like it—of one piece with the ephod and made with gold, and with blue, purple and scarlet yarn, and with finely twisted linen.

⁹"Take two onyx stones and engrave on them the names of the sons of Israel ¹⁰in the order of their birth—six names on one stone and the remaining six on the other. ¹¹Engrave the names of the sons of Israel on the two stones the way a gem cutter engraves a seal. Then mount the stones in gold filigree settings ¹²and fasten them on the shoulder pieces of the ephod as memorial stones for the sons of Israel. Aaron is to bear the names on his shoulders as a memorial before the LORD. ¹³Make gold filigree settings ¹⁴and two braided chains of pure gold, like a rope, and attach the chains to the settings.

The Breastpiece

¹⁵"Fashion a breastpiece for making decisions—the work of skilled hands. Make it like the ephod: of gold, and of blue, purple and scarlet yarn, and of finely twisted linen. ¹⁶It is to be square—a span*ᵃ* long and a span wide—and folded double. ¹⁷Then mount four rows of precious stones on it. The first row shall be carnelian, chrysolite and beryl; ¹⁸the second row shall be turquoise, lapis lazuli and emerald; ¹⁹the third row shall be jacinth, agate and amethyst; ²⁰the fourth row shall be topaz, onyx and jasper.*ᵇ* Mount them in gold filigree settings. ²¹There are to be twelve stones, one for each of the names of the sons of Israel, each engraved like a seal with the name of one of the twelve tribes.

²²"For the breastpiece make braided chains of pure gold, like a rope. ²³Make two gold rings for it and fasten them to two corners of the breastpiece. ²⁴Fasten the two gold chains to the rings at the corners of the breastpiece, ²⁵and the other ends of the chains to the two settings, attaching them to the shoulder pieces of the ephod at the front. ²⁶Make two gold rings and attach them to the other two corners of the breastpiece on the inside edge next to the ephod. ²⁷Make two more gold rings and attach them to the bottom of the shoulder pieces on the front of the ephod, close to the seam just above the waistband of the ephod. ²⁸The rings of the breastpiece are to be tied to the rings of the ephod with blue cord, connecting it to the waistband, so that the breastpiece will not swing out from the ephod.

²⁹"Whenever Aaron enters the Holy Place, he will bear the names of the sons of Israel over his heart on the breastpiece of decision as a continuing memorial before the LORD. ³⁰Also put the Urim and the Thummim in the breastpiece, so they may be over Aaron's heart whenever he enters the presence of the LORD. Thus Aaron will always bear the means of making decisions for the Israelites over his heart before the LORD.

Other Priestly Garments

³¹"Make the robe of the ephod entirely of blue cloth, ³²with an opening for the head in its center. There shall be a woven edge like a collar*ᶜ* around this opening, so that it will not tear. ³³Make pomegranates of blue, pur-

---

ᵃ 16 That is, about 9 inches or about 22.5 centimeters   *ᵇ 20* The precise identification of some of these precious stones is uncertain.   *ᶜ 32* The meaning of the Hebrew for this word is uncertain.

ple and scarlet yarn around the hem of the robe, with gold bells between them. ³⁴The gold bells and the pomegranates are to alternate around the hem of the robe. ³⁵Aaron must wear it when he ministers. The sound of the bells will be heard when he enters the Holy Place before the LORD and when he comes out, so that he will not die.

³⁶"Make a plate of pure gold and engrave on it as on a seal: HOLY TO THE LORD. ³⁷Fasten a blue cord to it to attach it to the turban; it is to be on the front of the turban. ³⁸It will be on Aaron's forehead, and he will bear the guilt involved in the sacred gifts the Israelites consecrate, whatever their gifts may be. It will be on Aaron's forehead continually so that they will be acceptable to the LORD.

³⁹"Weave the tunic of fine linen and make the turban of fine linen. The sash is to be the work of an embroiderer. ⁴⁰Make tunics, sashes and caps for Aaron's sons to give them dignity and honor. ⁴¹After you put these clothes on your brother Aaron and his sons, anoint and ordain them. Consecrate them so they may serve me as priests.

⁴²"Make linen undergarments as a covering for the body, reaching from the waist to the thigh. ⁴³Aaron and his sons must wear them whenever they enter the tent of meeting or approach the altar to minister in the Holy Place, so that they will not incur guilt and die.

"This is to be a lasting ordinance for Aaron and his descendants.

Consecration of the Priests

29 "This is what you are to do to consecrate them, so they may serve me as priests: Take a young bull and two rams without defect. ²And from the finest wheat flour make round loaves without yeast, thick loaves without yeast and with olive oil mixed in, and thin loaves without yeast and brushed with olive oil. ³Put them in a basket and present them along with the bull and the two rams. ⁴Then bring Aaron and his sons to the entrance to the tent of meeting and wash them with water. ⁵Take the garments and dress Aaron with the tunic, the robe of the ephod, the ephod itself and the breastpiece. Fasten the ephod on him by its skillfully woven waistband. ⁶Put the turban on his head

and attach the sacred emblem to the turban. ⁷Take the anointing oil and anoint him by pouring it on his head. ⁸Bring his sons and dress them in tunics ⁹and fasten caps on them. Then tie sashes on Aaron and his sons.ᵃ The priesthood is theirs by a lasting ordinance. Then you shall ordain Aaron and his sons.

¹⁰"Bring the bull to the front of the tent of meeting, and Aaron and his sons shall lay their hands on its head. ¹¹Slaughter it in the LORD's presence at the entrance to the tent of meeting. ¹²Take some of the bull's blood and put it on the horns of the altar with your finger, and pour out the rest of it at the base of the altar. ¹³Then take all the fat on the internal organs, the long lobe of the liver, and both kidneys with the fat on them, and burn them on the altar. ¹⁴But burn the bull's flesh and its hide and its intestines outside the camp. It is a sin offering.ᵇ

¹⁵"Take one of the rams, and Aaron and his sons shall lay their hands on its head. ¹⁶Slaughter it and take the blood and splash it against the sides of the altar. ¹⁷Cut the ram into pieces and wash the internal organs and the legs, putting them with the head and the other pieces. ¹⁸Then burn the entire ram on the altar. It is a burnt offering to the LORD, a pleasing aroma, a food offering presented to the LORD.

¹⁹"Take the other ram, and Aaron and his sons shall lay their hands on its head. ²⁰Slaughter it, take some of its blood and put it on the lobes of the right ears of Aaron and his sons, on the thumbs of their right hands, and on the big toes of their right feet. Then splash blood against the sides of the altar. ²¹And take some blood from the altar and some of the anointing oil and sprinkle it on Aaron and his garments and on his sons and their garments. Then he and his sons and their garments will be consecrated.

²²"Take from this ram the fat, the fat tail, the fat on the internal organs, the long lobe of the liver, both kidneys with the fat on them, and the right thigh. (This is the ram for the ordination.) ²³From the basket of bread made without yeast, which is before the LORD, take one round loaf, one thick loaf with olive oil mixed in, and one thin loaf. ²⁴Put all these in the hands of Aaron and his sons and have them wave them before the

a 9 Hebrew; Septuagint on them   b 14 Or purification offering; also in verse 36

LORD as a wave offering. 25Then take them from their hands and burn them on the altar along with the burnt offering for a pleasing aroma to the LORD, a food offering presented to the LORD. 26After you take the breast of the ram for Aaron's ordination, wave it before the LORD as a wave offering, and it will be your share.

27"Consecrate those parts of the ordination ram that belong to Aaron and his sons: the breast that was waved and the thigh that was presented. 28This is always to be the perpetual share from the Israelites for Aaron and his sons. It is the contribution the Israelites are to make to the LORD from their fellowship offerings.

29"Aaron's sacred garments will belong to his descendants so that they can be anointed and ordained in them. 30The son who succeeds him as priest and comes to the tent of meeting to minister in the Holy Place is to wear them seven days.

31"Take the ram for the ordination and cook the meat in a sacred place. 32At the entrance to the tent of meeting, Aaron and his sons are to eat the meat of the ram and the bread that is in the basket. 33They are to eat these offerings by which atonement was made for their ordination and consecration. But no one else may eat them, because they are sacred. 34And if any of the meat of the ordination ram or any bread is left over till morning, burn it up. It must not be eaten, because it is sacred.

35"Do for Aaron and his sons everything I have commanded you, taking seven days to ordain them. 36Sacrifice a bull each day as a sin offering to make atonement. Purify the altar by making atonement for it, and anoint it to consecrate it. 37For seven days make atonement for the altar and consecrate it. Then the altar will be most holy, and whatever touches it will be holy.

38"This is what you are to offer on the altar regularly each day: two lambs a year old. 39Offer one in the morning and the other at twilight. 40With the first lamb offer a tenth of an ephah a of the finest flour mixed with a quarter of a hin b of oil from pressed olives, and a quarter of a hin of wine as a drink offering. 41Sacrifice the other lamb at twilight with the same grain offering and its drink

offering as in the morning—a pleasing aroma, a food offering presented to the LORD.

42"For the generations to come this burnt offering is to be made regularly at the entrance to the tent of meeting before the LORD. There I will meet you and speak to you; 43there also I will meet with the Israelites, and the place will be consecrated by my glory.

44"So I will consecrate the tent of meeting and the altar and will consecrate Aaron and his sons to serve me as priests. 45Then I will dwell among the Israelites and be their God. 46They will know that I am the LORD their God, who brought them out of Egypt so that I might dwell among them. I am the LORD their God.

The Altar of Incense

30 "Make an altar of acacia wood for burning incense. 2It is to be square, a cubit long and a cubit wide, and two cubits high c—its horns of one piece with it. 3Overlay the top and all the sides and the horns with pure gold, and make a gold molding around it. 4Make two gold rings for the altar below the molding—two on each of the opposite sides—to hold the poles used to carry it. 5Make the poles of acacia wood and overlay them with gold. 6Put the altar in front of the curtain that shields the ark of the covenant law—before the atonement cover that is over the tablets of the covenant law—where I will meet with you.

7"Aaron must burn fragrant incense on the altar every morning when he tends the lamps. 8He must burn incense again when he lights the lamps at twilight so incense will burn regularly before the LORD for the generations to come. 9Do not offer on this altar any other incense or any burnt offering or grain offering, and do not pour a drink offering on it. 10Once a year Aaron shall make atonement on its horns. This annual atonement must be made with the blood of the atoning sin offering d for the generations to come. It is most holy to the LORD."

Atonement Money

11Then the LORD said to Moses, 12"When you take a census of the Israelites to count

---

a 40 That is, probably about 3 1/2 pounds or about 1.6 kilograms   b 40 That is, probably about 1 quart or about 0.9 liter   c 2 That is, about 1 1/2 feet long and wide and 3 feet high or about 45 centimeters long and wide and 90 centimeters high   d 10 Or purification offering them, each one must pay the LORD a ransom for his life at the time he is counted. Then no plague will come on them when you number them. ¹³Each one who crosses over to those already counted is to give a half shekel,ᵃ according to the sanctuary shekel, which weighs twenty gerahs. This half shekel is an offering to the LORD. ¹⁴All who cross over, those twenty years old or more, are to give an offering to the LORD. ¹⁵The rich are not to give more than a half shekel and the poor are not to give less when you make the offering to the LORD to atone for your lives. ¹⁶Receive the atonement money from the Israelites and use it for the service of the tent of meeting. It will be a memorial for the Israelites before the LORD, making atonement for your lives."

Basin for Washing

¹⁷Then the LORD said to Moses, ¹⁸"Make a bronze basin, with its bronze stand, for washing. Place it between the tent of meeting and the altar, and put water in it. ¹⁹Aaron and his sons are to wash their hands and feet with water from it. ²⁰Whenever they enter the tent of meeting, they shall wash with water so that they will not die. Also, when they approach the altar to minister by presenting a food offering to the LORD, ²¹they shall wash their hands and feet so that they will not die. This is to be a lasting ordinance for Aaron and his descendants for the generations to come."

Anointing Oil

²²Then the LORD said to Moses, ²³"Take the following fine spices: 500 shekelsᵇ of liquid myrrh, half as much (that is, 250 shekels) of fragrant cinnamon, 250 shekelsᶜ of fragrant calamus, ²⁴500 shekels of cassia—all according to the sanctuary shekel—and a hinᵈ of olive oil. ²⁵Make these into a sacred anointing oil, a fragrant blend, the work of a perfumer. It will be the sacred anointing oil. ²⁶Then use it to anoint the tent of meeting, the ark of the covenant law, ²⁷the table and all its articles, the lampstand and its accessories, the altar of incense, ²⁸the altar of burnt offering and all its utensils, and the basin with its stand. ²⁹You shall

consecrate them so they will be most holy, and whatever touches them will be holy.

³⁰"Anoint Aaron and his sons and consecrate them so they may serve me as priests. ³¹Say to the Israelites, 'This is to be my sacred anointing oil for the generations to come. ³²Do not pour it on anyone else's body and do not make any other oil using the same formula. It is sacred, and you are to consider it sacred. ³³Whoever makes perfume like it and puts it on anyone other than a priest must be cut off from their people.' "

Incense

³⁴Then the LORD said to Moses, "Take fragrant spices—gum resin, onycha and galbanum—and pure frankincense, all in equal amounts, ³⁵and make a fragrant blend of incense, the work of a perfumer. It is to be salted and pure and sacred. ³⁶Grind some of it to powder and place it in front of the ark of the covenant law in the tent of meeting, where I will meet with you. It shall be most holy to you. ³⁷Do not make any incense with this formula for yourselves; consider it holy to the LORD. ³⁸Whoever makes incense like it to enjoy its fragrance must be cut off from their people."

Bezalel and Oholiab

31 Then the LORD said to Moses, ²"See, I have chosen Bezalel son of Uri, the son of Hur, of the tribe of Judah, ³and I have filled him with the Spirit of God, with wisdom, with understanding, with knowledge and with all kinds of skills— ⁴to make artistic designs for work in gold, silver and bronze, ⁵to cut and set stones, to work in wood, and to engage in all kinds of crafts. ⁶Moreover, I have appointed Oholiab son of Ahisamak, of the tribe of Dan, to help him. Also I have given ability to all the skilled workers to make everything I have commanded you: ⁷the tent of meeting, the ark of the covenant law with the atonement cover on it, and all the other furnishings of the tent— ⁸the table and its articles, the pure gold lampstand and all its accessories, the altar of incense, ⁹the altar of burnt offering and all its utensils, the basin with its stand— ¹⁰and also the woven garments, both the sacred garments for Aaron the

---

ᵃ 13 That is, about 1/5 ounce or about 5.7 grams; also in verse 15   ᵇ 23 That is, about 12 1/2 pounds or about 5.8 kilograms; also in verse 24   ᶜ 23 That is, about 6 1/4 pounds or about 2.9 kilograms
ᵈ 24 That is, probably about 1 gallon or about 3.6 liters

priest and the garments for his sons when they serve as priests, [11]and the anointing oil and fragrant incense for the Holy Place. They are to make them just as I commanded you."

The Sabbath

[12]Then the LORD said to Moses, [13]"Say to the Israelites, 'You must observe my Sabbaths. This will be a sign between me and you for the generations to come, so you may know that I am the LORD, who makes you holy.

[14] 'Observe the Sabbath, because it is holy to you. Anyone who desecrates it is to be put to death; those who do any work on that day must be cut off from their people. [15]For six days work is to be done, but the seventh day is a day of sabbath rest, holy to the LORD. Whoever does any work on the Sabbath day is to be put to death. [16]The Israelites are to observe the Sabbath, celebrating it for the generations to come as a lasting covenant. [17]It will be a sign between me and the Israelites forever, for in six days the LORD made the heavens and the earth, and on the seventh day he abstained from work and rested.' "

[18]When the LORD finished speaking to Moses on Mount Sinai, he gave him the two tablets of the covenant law, the tablets of stone inscribed by the finger of God.

The Golden Calf

32 When the people saw that Moses was so long in coming down from the mountain, they gathered around Aaron and said, "Come, make us gods[a] who will go before us. As for this fellow Moses who brought us up out of Egypt, we don't know what has happened to him."

[2]Aaron answered them, "Take off the gold earrings that your wives, your sons and your daughters are wearing, and bring them to me." [3]So all the people took off their earrings and brought them to Aaron. [4]He took what they handed him and made it into an idol cast in the shape of a calf, fashioning it with a tool. Then they said, "These are your gods,[b] Israel, who brought you up out of Egypt."

[5]When Aaron saw this, he built an altar in front of the calf and announced, "Tomorrow there will be a festival to the LORD." [6]So the next day the people rose early and sacrificed burnt offerings and presented fellowship offerings. Afterward they sat down to eat and drink and got up to indulge in revelry.

[7]Then the LORD said to Moses, "Go down, because your people, whom you brought up out of Egypt, have become corrupt. [8]They have been quick to turn away from what I commanded them and have made themselves an idol cast in the shape of a calf. They have bowed down to it and sacrificed to it and have said, 'These are your gods, Israel, who brought you up out of Egypt.'

[9]"I have seen these people," the LORD said to Moses, "and they are a stiff-necked people. [10]Now leave me alone so that my anger may burn against them and that I may destroy them. Then I will make you into a great nation."

[11]But Moses sought the favor of the LORD his God. "LORD," he said, "why should your anger burn against your people, whom you brought out of Egypt with great power and a mighty hand? [12]Why should the Egyptians say, 'It was with evil intent that he brought them out, to kill them in the mountains and to wipe them off the face of the earth'? Turn from your fierce anger; relent and do not bring disaster on your people. [13]Remember your servants Abraham, Isaac and Israel, to whom you swore by your own self: 'I will make your descendants as numerous as the stars in the sky and I will give your descendants all this land I promised them, and it will be their inheritance forever.' " [14]Then the LORD relented and did not bring on his people the disaster he had threatened.

[15]Moses turned and went down the mountain with the two tablets of the covenant law in his hands. They were inscribed on both sides, front and back. [16]The tablets were the work of God; the writing was the writing of God, engraved on the tablets.

[17]When Joshua heard the noise of the people shouting, he said to Moses, "There is the sound of war in the camp."

[18]Moses replied:

"It is not the sound of victory,
    it is not the sound of defeat;
    it is the sound of singing that I hear."

a 1 Or *a god*; also in verses 23 and 31   *b 4* Or *This is your god*; also in verse 8

¹⁹When Moses approached the camp and saw the calf and the dancing, his anger burned and he threw the tablets out of his hands, breaking them to pieces at the foot of the mountain. ²⁰And he took the calf they had made and burned it in the fire; then he ground it to powder, scattered it on the water and made the Israelites drink it.

²¹He said to Aaron, "What did these people do to you, that you led them into such great sin?"

²²"Do not be angry, my lord," Aaron answered. "You know how prone these people are to evil. ²³They said to me, 'Make us gods who will go before us. As for this fellow Moses who brought us up out of Egypt, we don't know what has happened to him.' ²⁴So I told them, 'Whoever has any gold jewelry, take it off.' Then they gave me the gold, and I threw it into the fire, and out came this calf!"

²⁵Moses saw that the people were running wild and that Aaron had let them get out of control and so become a laughingstock to their enemies. ²⁶So he stood at the entrance to the camp and said, "Whoever is for the LORD, come to me." And all the Levites rallied to him.

²⁷Then he said to them, "This is what the LORD, the God of Israel, says: 'Each man strap a sword to his side. Go back and forth through the camp from one end to the other, each killing his brother and friend and neighbor.' " ²⁸The Levites did as Moses commanded, and that day about three thousand of the people died. ²⁹Then Moses said, "You have been set apart to the LORD today, for you were against your own sons and brothers, and he has blessed you this day."

³⁰The next day Moses said to the people, "You have committed a great sin. But now I will go up to the LORD; perhaps I can make atonement for your sin."

³¹So Moses went back to the LORD and said, "Oh, what a great sin these people have committed! They have made themselves gods of gold. ³²But now, please forgive their sin—but if not, then blot me out of the book you have written."

³³The LORD replied to Moses, "Whoever has sinned against me I will blot out of my book. ³⁴Now go, lead the people to the place I spoke of, and my angel will go before you. However, when the time comes for me to punish, I will punish them for their sin."

³⁵And the LORD struck the people with a plague because of what they did with the calf Aaron had made.

33 Then the LORD said to Moses, "Leave this place, you and the people you brought up out of Egypt, and go up to the land I promised on oath to Abraham, Isaac and Jacob, saying, 'I will give it to your descendants.' ²I will send an angel before you and drive out the Canaanites, Amorites, Hittites, Perizzites, Hivites and Jebusites. ³Go up to the land flowing with milk and honey. But I will not go with you, because you are a stiff-necked people and I might destroy you on the way."

⁴When the people heard these distressing words, they began to mourn and no one put on any ornaments. ⁵For the LORD had said to Moses, "Tell the Israelites, 'You are a stiff-necked people. If I were to go with you even for a moment, I might destroy you. Now take off your ornaments and I will decide what to do with you.' " ⁶So the Israelites stripped off their ornaments at Mount Horeb.

The Tent of Meeting

⁷Now Moses used to take a tent and pitch it outside the camp some distance away, calling it the "tent of meeting." Anyone inquiring of the LORD would go to the tent of meeting outside the camp. ⁸And whenever Moses went out to the tent, all the people rose and stood at the entrances to their tents, watching Moses until he entered the tent. ⁹As Moses went into the tent, the pillar of cloud would come down and stay at the entrance, while the LORD spoke with Moses. ¹⁰Whenever the people saw the pillar of cloud standing at the entrance to the tent, they all stood and worshiped at the entrances to their tents. ¹¹The LORD would speak to Moses face to face, as one speaks to a friend. Then Moses would return to the camp, but his young aide Joshua son of Nun did not leave the tent.

Moses and the Glory of the LORD

¹²Moses said to the LORD, "You have been telling me, 'Lead these people,' but you have not let me know whom you will send with me. You have said, 'I know you by name and you have found favor with me.' ¹³If you are pleased with me, teach me your ways so I may know you and continue to find favor with you. Remember that this nation is your people."

BECOMING GOD'S FRIEND

Exodus 33:1–23 *or* 33:11

Rick Warren

Friendship with God is possible only because of the grace of God and the sacrifice of Jesus. "[All this is from God, who reconciled us to himself through Christ]" (2 Corinthians 5:18). The old hymn says, "What a friend we have in Jesus," but actually, God invites us to enjoy friendship and fellowship with all three persons of the Trinity: our Father, the Son and the Holy Spirit.

Jesus said, "I no longer call you servants, because [servants do] not know [their] master's business. Instead, I have called you friends, for everything that I learned from my Father I have made known to you" (John 15:15). The word for *friend* in this verse does not mean a casual acquaintance but a close, trusted relationship . . .

God deeply desires that we know him intimately. In fact, he planned the universe and orchestrated history, including the details of our lives, so that we could become his friends. The Bible says, "[From one man he made all the nations, that they should inhabit the whole earth; and he marked out their appointed times in history and the boundaries of their lands. God did this so that they would seek him and perhaps reach out for him and find him, though he is not far from any one of us]" (Acts 17:26–27).

Knowing and loving God is our greatest privilege, and being known and loved is God's greatest pleasure.

GREGORY OF NYSSA {ca. AD 335–394}

Since the goal of the virtuous way of life is the very thing we have been seeking, it is time for you, noble friend, to be known by God and to become his friend.

This is true perfection: not to avoid a wicked life because like slaves we severely fear punishment, nor to do good because we hope for rewards, as if cashing in on the virtuous life by some business-like arrangement. On the contrary, disregarding all those things for which we hope and which have been reserved by promise, we regard falling from God's friendship as the only thing dreadful, and we consider becoming God's friend the only thing worthy of honor and desire. This, as I have said, is the perfection of life.

reflection

1. What qualities do you value most in your friends? What makes them good friends?

2. How does the relationship God wants to have with you fulfill—even go beyond—the qualities you find in human friendship?

3. Why would God create us to enjoy a friendship with him?

For your next devotional reading, go to page 115.

¹⁴The LORD replied, "My Presence will go with you, and I will give you rest."

¹⁵Then Moses said to him, "If your Presence does not go with us, do not send us up from here. ¹⁶How will anyone know that you are pleased with me and with your people unless you go with us? What else will distinguish me and your people from all the other people on the face of the earth?"

¹⁷And the LORD said to Moses, "I will do the very thing you have asked, because I am pleased with you and I know you by name."

¹⁸Then Moses said, "Now show me your glory."

¹⁹And the LORD said, "I will cause all my goodness to pass in front of you, and I will proclaim my name, the LORD, in your presence. I will have mercy on whom I will have mercy, and I will have compassion on whom I will have compassion. ²⁰But," he said, "you cannot see my face, for no one may see me and live."

²¹Then the LORD said, "There is a place near me where you may stand on a rock. ²²When my glory passes by, I will put you in a cleft in the rock and cover you with my hand until I have passed by. ²³Then I will remove my hand and you will see my back; but my face must not be seen."

The New Stone Tablets

34 The LORD said to Moses, "Chisel out two stone tablets like the first ones, and I will write on them the words that were on the first tablets, which you broke. ²Be ready in the morning, and then come up on Mount Sinai. Present yourself to me there on top of the mountain. ³No one is to come with you or be seen anywhere on the mountain; not even the flocks and herds may graze in front of the mountain."

⁴So Moses chiseled out two stone tablets like the first ones and went up Mount Sinai early in the morning, as the LORD had commanded him; and he carried the two stone tablets in his hands. ⁵Then the LORD came down in the cloud and stood there with him and proclaimed his name, the LORD. ⁶And he passed in front of Moses, proclaiming, "The LORD, the LORD, the compassionate and gracious God, slow to anger, abounding in love and faithfulness, ⁷maintaining love to thousands, and forgiving wickedness, rebellion and sin. Yet he does not leave the guilty unpunished; he punishes the children and their children for the sin of the parents to the third and fourth generation."

⁸Moses bowed to the ground at once and worshiped. ⁹"Lord," he said, "if I have found favor in your eyes, then let the Lord go with us. Although this is a stiff-necked people, forgive our wickedness and our sin, and take us as your inheritance."

¹⁰Then the LORD said: "I am making a covenant with you. Before all your people I will do wonders never before done in any nation in all the world. The people you live among will see how awesome is the work that I, the LORD, will do for you. ¹¹Obey what I command you today. I will drive out before you the Amorites, Canaanites, Hittites, Perizzites, Hivites and Jebusites. ¹²Be careful not to make a treaty with those who live in the land where you are going, or they will be a snare among you. ¹³Break down their altars, smash their sacred stones and cut down their Asherah poles. *a* ¹⁴Do not worship any other god, for the LORD, whose name is Jealous, is a jealous God.

¹⁵"Be careful not to make a treaty with those who live in the land; for when they prostitute themselves to their gods and sacrifice to them, they will invite you and you will eat their sacrifices. ¹⁶And when you choose some of their daughters as wives for your sons and those daughters prostitute themselves to their gods, they will lead your sons to do the same.

¹⁷"Do not make any idols.

¹⁸"Celebrate the Festival of Unleavened Bread. For seven days eat bread made without yeast, as I commanded you. Do this at the appointed time in the month of Aviv, for in that month you came out of Egypt.

¹⁹"The first offspring of every womb belongs to me, including all the firstborn males of your livestock, whether from herd or flock. ²⁰Redeem the firstborn donkey with a lamb, but if you do not redeem it, break its neck. Redeem all your firstborn sons.

"No one is to appear before me empty-handed.

²¹"Six days you shall labor, but on the

a 13 That is, wooden symbols of the goddess Asherah

seventh day you shall rest; even during the plowing season and harvest you must rest.

²²"Celebrate the Festival of Weeks with the firstfruits of the wheat harvest, and the Festival of Ingathering at the turn of the year.ᵃ ²³Three times a year all your men are to appear before the Sovereign LORD, the God of Israel. ²⁴I will drive out nations before you and enlarge your territory, and no one will covet your land when you go up three times each year to appear before the LORD your God.

²⁵"Do not offer the blood of a sacrifice to me along with anything containing yeast, and do not let any of the sacrifice from the Passover Festival remain until morning.

²⁶"Bring the best of the firstfruits of your soil to the house of the LORD your God.

"Do not cook a young goat in its mother's milk."

²⁷Then the LORD said to Moses, "Write down these words, for in accordance with these words I have made a covenant with you and with Israel." ²⁸Moses was there with the LORD forty days and forty nights without eating bread or drinking water. And he wrote on the tablets the words of the covenant—the Ten Commandments.

The Radiant Face of Moses

²⁹When Moses came down from Mount Sinai with the two tablets of the covenant law in his hands, he was not aware that his face was radiant because he had spoken with the LORD. ³⁰When Aaron and all the Israelites saw Moses, his face was radiant, and they were afraid to come near him. ³¹But Moses called to them; so Aaron and all the leaders of the community came back to him, and he spoke to them. ³²Afterward all the Israelites came near him, and he gave them all the commands the LORD had given him on Mount Sinai.

³³When Moses finished speaking to them, he put a veil over his face. ³⁴But whenever he entered the LORD's presence to speak with him, he removed the veil until he came out. And when he came out and told the Israelites what he had been commanded, ³⁵they saw that his face was radiant. Then Moses would put the veil back over his face until he went in to speak with the LORD.

Sabbath Regulations

35 Moses assembled the whole Israelite community and said to them, "These are the things the LORD has commanded you to do: ²For six days, work is to be done, but the seventh day shall be your holy day, a day of sabbath rest to the LORD. Whoever does any work on it is to be put to death. ³Do not light a fire in any of your dwellings on the Sabbath day."

Materials for the Tabernacle

⁴Moses said to the whole Israelite community, "This is what the LORD has commanded: ⁵From what you have, take an offering for the LORD. Everyone who is willing is to bring to the LORD an offering of gold, silver and bronze; ⁶blue, purple and scarlet yarn and fine linen; goat hair; ⁷ram skins dyed red and another durable leatherᵇ; acacia wood; ⁸olive oil for the light; spices for the anointing oil and for the fragrant incense; ⁹and onyx stones and other gems to be mounted on the ephod and breastpiece.

¹⁰"All who are skilled among you are to come and make everything the LORD has commanded: ¹¹the tabernacle with its tent and its covering, clasps, frames, crossbars, posts and bases; ¹²the ark with its poles and the atonement cover and the curtain that shields it; ¹³the table with its poles and all its articles and the bread of the Presence; ¹⁴the lampstand that is for light with its accessories, lamps and oil for the light; ¹⁵the altar of incense with its poles, the anointing oil and the fragrant incense; the curtain for the doorway at the entrance to the tabernacle; ¹⁶the altar of burnt offering with its bronze grating, its poles and all its utensils; the bronze basin with its stand; ¹⁷the curtains of the courtyard with its posts and bases, and the curtain for the entrance to the courtyard; ¹⁸the tent pegs for the tabernacle and for the courtyard, and their ropes; ¹⁹the woven garments worn for ministering in the sanctuary—both the sacred garments for Aaron the priest and the garments for his sons when they serve as priests."

²⁰Then the whole Israelite community withdrew from Moses' presence, ²¹and everyone who was willing and whose heart moved them came and brought an offering to the LORD for the work on the tent of meet-

---

ᵃ 22 That is, in the autumn   ᵇ 7 Possibly the hides of dugongs; also in verse 23 ing, for all its service, and for the sacred garments. ²²All who were willing, men and women alike, came and brought gold jewelry of all kinds: brooches, earrings, rings and ornaments. They all presented their gold as a wave offering to the Lord. ²³Everyone who had blue, purple or scarlet yarn or fine linen, or goat hair, ram skins dyed red or the other durable leather brought them. ²⁴Those presenting an offering of silver or bronze brought it as an offering to the Lord, and everyone who had acacia wood for any part of the work brought it. ²⁵Every skilled woman spun with her hands and brought what she had spun—blue, purple or scarlet yarn or fine linen. ²⁶And all the women who were willing and had the skill spun the goat hair. ²⁷The leaders brought onyx stones and other gems to be mounted on the ephod and breastpiece. ²⁸They also brought spices and olive oil for the light and for the anointing oil and for the fragrant incense. ²⁹All the Israelite men and women who were willing brought to the Lord freewill offerings for all the work the Lord through Moses had commanded them to do.

Bezalel and Oholiab

³⁰Then Moses said to the Israelites, "See, the Lord has chosen Bezalel son of Uri, the son of Hur, of the tribe of Judah, ³¹and he has filled him with the Spirit of God, with wisdom, with understanding, with knowledge and with all kinds of skills— ³²to make artistic designs for work in gold, silver and bronze, ³³to cut and set stones, to work in wood and to engage in all kinds of artistic crafts. ³⁴And he has given both him and Oholiab son of Ahisamak, of the tribe of Dan, the ability to teach others. ³⁵He has filled them with skill to do all kinds of work as engravers, designers, embroiderers in blue, purple and scarlet yarn and fine linen, and weavers—all of them skilled workers and designers. **36** ¹So Bezalel, Oholiab and every skilled person to whom the Lord has given skill and ability to know how to carry out all the work of constructing the sanctuary are to do the work just as the Lord has commanded."

²Then Moses summoned Bezalel and Oholiab and every skilled person to whom the Lord had given ability and who was willing to come and do the work. ³They received from Moses all the offerings the Israelites had brought to carry out the work of constructing the sanctuary. And the people continued to bring freewill offerings morning after morning. ⁴So all the skilled workers who were doing all the work on the sanctuary left what they were doing ⁵and said to Moses, "The people are bringing more than enough for doing the work the Lord commanded to be done."

⁶Then Moses gave an order and they sent this word throughout the camp: "No man or woman is to make anything else as an offering for the sanctuary." And so the people were restrained from bringing more, ⁷because what they already had was more than enough to do all the work.

The Tabernacle

⁸All those who were skilled among the workers made the tabernacle with ten curtains of finely twisted linen and blue, purple and scarlet yarn, with cherubim worked into them by expert hands. ⁹All the curtains were the same size—twenty-eight cubits long and four cubits wide.ᵃ ¹⁰They joined five of the curtains together and did the same with the other five. ¹¹Then they made loops of blue material along the edge of the end curtain in one set, and the same was done with the end curtain in the other set. ¹²They also made fifty loops on one curtain and fifty loops on the end curtain of the other set, with the loops opposite each other. ¹³Then they made fifty gold clasps and used them to fasten the two sets of curtains together so that the tabernacle was a unit.

¹⁴They made curtains of goat hair for the tent over the tabernacle—eleven altogether. ¹⁵All eleven curtains were the same size— thirty cubits long and four cubits wide.ᵇ ¹⁶They joined five of the curtains into one set and the other six into another set. ¹⁷Then they made fifty loops along the edge of the end curtain in one set and also along the edge of the end curtain in the other set. ¹⁸They made fifty bronze clasps to fasten the tent together as a unit. ¹⁹Then they made for

---

ᵃ 9 That is, about 42 feet long and 6 feet wide or about 13 meters long and 1.8 meters wide   ᵇ 15 That is, about 45 feet long and 6 feet wide or about 13.5 meters long and 1.8 meters wide the tent a covering of ram skins dyed red, and over that a covering of the other durable leather.ᵃ

²⁰They made upright frames of acacia wood for the tabernacle. ²¹Each frame was ten cubits long and a cubit and a half wide,ᵇ ²²with two projections set parallel to each other. They made all the frames of the tabernacle in this way. ²³They made twenty frames for the south side of the tabernacle ²⁴and made forty silver bases to go under them—two bases for each frame, one under each projection. ²⁵For the other side, the north side of the tabernacle, they made twenty frames ²⁶and forty silver bases—two under each frame. ²⁷They made six frames for the far end, that is, the west end of the tabernacle, ²⁸and two frames were made for the corners of the tabernacle at the far end. ²⁹At these two corners the frames were double from the bottom all the way to the top and fitted into a single ring; both were made alike. ³⁰So there were eight frames and sixteen silver bases—two under each frame.

³¹They also made crossbars of acacia wood: five for the frames on one side of the tabernacle, ³²five for those on the other side, and five for the frames on the west, at the far end of the tabernacle. ³³They made the center crossbar so that it extended from end to end at the middle of the frames. ³⁴They overlaid the frames with gold and made gold rings to hold the crossbars. They also overlaid the crossbars with gold.

³⁵They made the curtain of blue, purple and scarlet yarn and finely twisted linen, with cherubim worked into it by expert hands. ³⁶They made four posts of acacia wood for it and overlaid them with gold. They made gold hooks for them and cast their four silver bases. ³⁷For the entrance to the tent they made a curtain of blue, purple and scarlet yarn and finely twisted linen— the work of an embroiderer; ³⁸and they made five posts with hooks for them. They overlaid the tops of the posts and their bands with gold and made their five bases of bronze.

The Ark

37 Bezalel made the ark of acacia wood—two and a half cubits long, a cubit and a half wide, and a cubit and a half high.ᶜ ²He overlaid it with pure gold, both inside and out, and made a gold molding around it. ³He cast four gold rings for it and fastened them to its four feet, with two rings on one side and two rings on the other. ⁴Then he made poles of acacia wood and overlaid them with gold. ⁵And he inserted the poles into the rings on the sides of the ark to carry it.

⁶He made the atonement cover of pure gold—two and a half cubits long and a cubit and a half wide. ⁷Then he made two cherubim out of hammered gold at the ends of the cover. ⁸He made one cherub on one end and the second cherub on the other; at the two ends he made them of one piece with the cover. ⁹The cherubim had their wings spread upward, overshadowing the cover with them. The cherubim faced each other, looking toward the cover.

The Table

¹⁰Theyᵈ made the table of acacia wood— two cubits long, a cubit wide and a cubit and a half high.ᵉ ¹¹Then they overlaid it with pure gold and made a gold molding around it. ¹²They also made around it a rim a handbreadthᶠ wide and put a gold molding on the rim. ¹³They cast four gold rings for the table and fastened them to the four corners, where the four legs were. ¹⁴The rings were put close to the rim to hold the poles used in carrying the table. ¹⁵The poles for carrying the table were made of acacia wood and were overlaid with gold. ¹⁶And they made from pure gold the articles for the table—its plates and dishes and bowls and its pitchers for the pouring out of drink offerings.

The Lampstand

¹⁷They made the lampstand of pure gold. They hammered out its base and shaft, and made its flowerlike cups, buds and blossoms of one piece with them. ¹⁸Six branches extended from the sides of the lampstand— three on one side and three on the other.

ᵃ 19 Possibly the hides of dugongs   ᵇ 21 That is, about 15 feet long and 2 1/4 feet wide or about 4.5 meters long and 67 centimeters wide   ᶜ 1 That is, about 3 1/4 feet long and 2 1/4 feet wide and high or about 1.1 meters long and 67 centimeters wide and high; also in verse 6   ᵈ 10 Or He; also in verses 11-29   ᵉ 10 That is, about 3 feet long, 1 1/2 feet wide and 2 1/4 feet high or about 90 centimeters long, 45 centimeters wide and 67 centimeters high   ᶠ 12 That is, about 3 inches or about 7.5 centimeters

¹⁹Three cups shaped like almond flowers with buds and blossoms were on one branch, three on the next branch and the same for all six branches extending from the lampstand. ²⁰And on the lampstand were four cups shaped like almond flowers with buds and blossoms. ²¹One bud was under the first pair of branches extending from the lampstand, a second bud under the second pair, and a third bud under the third pair—six branches in all. ²²The buds and the branches were all of one piece with the lampstand, hammered out of pure gold.

²³They made its seven lamps, as well as its wick trimmers and trays, of pure gold. ²⁴They made the lampstand and all its accessories from one talentᵃ of pure gold.

The Altar of Incense

²⁵They made the altar of incense out of acacia wood. It was square, a cubit long and a cubit wide and two cubits highᵇ—its horns of one piece with it. ²⁶They overlaid the top and all the sides and the horns with pure gold, and made a gold molding around it. ²⁷They made two gold rings below the molding—two on each of the opposite sides—to hold the poles used to carry it. ²⁸They made the poles of acacia wood and overlaid them with gold.

²⁹They also made the sacred anointing oil and the pure, fragrant incense—the work of a perfumer.

The Altar of Burnt Offering

38 Theyᶜ built the altar of burnt offering of acacia wood, three cubitsᵈ high; it was square, five cubits long and five cubits wide.ᵉ ²They made a horn at each of the four corners, so that the horns and the altar were of one piece, and they overlaid the altar with bronze. ³They made all its utensils of bronze—its pots, shovels, sprinkling bowls, meat forks and firepans. ⁴They made a grating for the altar, a bronze network, to be under its ledge, halfway up the altar. ⁵They cast bronze rings to hold the poles for the four corners of the bronze grating. ⁶They

made the poles of acacia wood and overlaid them with bronze. ⁷They inserted the poles into the rings so they would be on the sides of the altar for carrying it. They made it hollow, out of boards.

The Basin for Washing

⁸They made the bronze basin and its bronze stand from the mirrors of the women who served at the entrance to the tent of meeting.

The Courtyard

⁹Next they made the courtyard. The south side was a hundred cubitsᶠ long and had curtains of finely twisted linen, ¹⁰with twenty posts and twenty bronze bases, and with silver hooks and bands on the posts. ¹¹The north side was also a hundred cubits long and had twenty posts and twenty bronze bases, with silver hooks and bands on the posts.

¹²The west end was fifty cubitsᵍ wide and had curtains, with ten posts and ten bases, with silver hooks and bands on the posts. ¹³The east end, toward the sunrise, was also fifty cubits wide. ¹⁴Curtains fifteen cubitsʰ long were on one side of the entrance, with three posts and three bases, ¹⁵and curtains fifteen cubits long were on the other side of the entrance to the courtyard, with three posts and three bases. ¹⁶All the curtains around the courtyard were of finely twisted linen. ¹⁷The bases for the posts were bronze. The hooks and bands on the posts were silver, and their tops were overlaid with silver; so all the posts of the courtyard had silver bands.

¹⁸The curtain for the entrance to the courtyard was of blue, purple and scarlet yarn and finely twisted linen—the work of an embroiderer. It was twenty cubitsⁱ long and, like the curtains of the courtyard, five cubitsʲ high, ¹⁹with four posts and four bronze bases. Their hooks and bands were silver, and their tops were overlaid with silver. ²⁰All the tent pegs of the tabernacle and of the surrounding courtyard were bronze.

ᵃ 24 That is, about 75 pounds or about 34 kilograms   ᵇ 25 That is, about 1 1/2 feet long and wide and 3 feet high or about 45 centimeters long and wide and 90 centimeters high   ᶜ 1 Or He; also in verses 2–9   ᵈ 1 That is, about 4 1/2 feet or about 1.4 meters   ᵉ 1 That is, about 7 1/2 feet or about 2.3 meters long and wide   ᶠ 9 That is, about 150 feet or about 45 meters   ᵍ 12 That is, about 75 feet or about 22.5 meters   ʰ 14 That is, about 22 feet or about 6.8 meters   ⁱ 18 That is, about 30 feet or about 9 meters   ʲ 18 That is, about 7 1/2 feet or about 2.3 meters

The Materials Used

²¹These are the amounts of the materials used for the tabernacle, the tabernacle of the covenant law, which were recorded at Moses' command by the Levites under the direction of Ithamar son of Aaron, the priest. ²²(Bezalel son of Uri, the son of Hur, of the tribe of Judah, made everything the LORD commanded Moses; ²³with him was Oholiab son of Ahisamak, of the tribe of Dan—an engraver and designer, and an embroiderer in blue, purple and scarlet yarn and fine linen.) ²⁴The total amount of the gold from the wave offering used for all the work on the sanctuary was 29 talents and 730 shekels,ᵃ according to the sanctuary shekel.

²⁵The silver obtained from those of the community who were counted in the census was 100 talentsᵇ and 1,775 shekels,ᶜ according to the sanctuary shekel— ²⁶one beka per person, that is, half a shekel,ᵈ according to the sanctuary shekel, from everyone who had crossed over to those counted, twenty years old or more, a total of 603,550 men. ²⁷The 100 talents of silver were used to cast the bases for the sanctuary and for the curtain—100 bases from the 100 talents, one talent for each base. ²⁸They used the 1,775 shekels to make the hooks for the posts, to overlay the tops of the posts, and to make their bands.

²⁹The bronze from the wave offering was 70 talents and 2,400 shekels.ᵉ ³⁰They used it to make the bases for the entrance to the tent of meeting, the bronze altar with its bronze grating and all its utensils, ³¹the bases for the surrounding courtyard and those for its entrance and all the tent pegs for the tabernacle and those for the surrounding courtyard.

The Priestly Garments

39 From the blue, purple and scarlet yarn they made woven garments for ministering in the sanctuary. They also made sacred garments for Aaron, as the LORD commanded Moses.

The Ephod

²Theyᶠ made the ephod of gold, and of blue, purple and scarlet yarn, and of finely twisted linen. ³They hammered out thin sheets of gold and cut strands to be worked into the blue, purple and scarlet yarn and fine linen—the work of skilled hands. ⁴They made shoulder pieces for the ephod, which were attached to two of its corners, so it could be fastened. ⁵Its skillfully woven waistband was like it—of one piece with the ephod and made with gold, and with blue, purple and scarlet yarn, and with finely twisted linen, as the LORD commanded Moses.

⁶They mounted the onyx stones in gold filigree settings and engraved them like a seal with the names of the sons of Israel. ⁷Then they fastened them on the shoulder pieces of the ephod as memorial stones for the sons of Israel, as the LORD commanded Moses.

The Breastpiece

⁸They fashioned the breastpiece—the work of a skilled craftsman. They made it like the ephod: of gold, and of blue, purple and scarlet yarn, and of finely twisted linen. ⁹It was square—a spanᵍ long and a span wide—and folded double. ¹⁰Then they mounted four rows of precious stones on it. The first row was carnelian, chrysolite and beryl; ¹¹the second row was turquoise, lapis lazuli and emerald; ¹²the third row was jacinth, agate and amethyst; ¹³the fourth row was topaz, onyx and jasper.ʰ They were mounted in gold filigree settings. ¹⁴There were twelve stones, one for each of the names of the sons of Israel, each engraved like a seal with the name of one of the twelve tribes.

¹⁵For the breastpiece they made braided chains of pure gold, like a rope. ¹⁶They made two gold filigree settings and two gold rings, and fastened the rings to two of the corners of the breastpiece. ¹⁷They fastened the two gold chains to the rings at the corners of the breastpiece, ¹⁸and the other ends of the chains to the two settings, attaching them to the shoulder pieces of the ephod at the front. ¹⁹They made two gold rings and attached them to the other two corners of the breastpiece on the inside edge next to the ephod. ²⁰Then they made

---

ᵃ 24 The weight of the gold was a little over a ton or about 1 metric ton.   ᵇ 25 That is, about 3 3/4 tons or about 3.4 metric tons; also in verse 27   ᶜ 25 That is, about 45 pounds or about 20 kilograms; also in verse 28   ᵈ 26 That is, about 1/5 ounce or about 5.7 grams   ᵉ 29 The weight of the bronze was about 2 1/2 tons or about 2.4 metric tons.   ᶠ 2 Or He; also in verses 7, 8 and 22   ᵍ 9 That is, about 9 inches or about 22.5 centimeters   ʰ 13 The precise identification of some of these precious stones is uncertain.

two more gold rings and attached them to the bottom of the shoulder pieces on the front of the ephod, close to the seam just above the waistband of the ephod. ²¹They tied the rings of the breastpiece to the rings of the ephod with blue cord, connecting it to the waistband so that the breastpiece would not swing out from the ephod—as the Lord commanded Moses.

Other Priestly Garments

²²They made the robe of the ephod entirely of blue cloth—the work of a weaver— ²³with an opening in the center of the robe like the opening of a collar,ᵃ and a band around this opening, so that it would not tear. ²⁴They made pomegranates of blue, purple and scarlet yarn and finely twisted linen around the hem of the robe. ²⁵And they made bells of pure gold and attached them around the hem between the pomegranates. ²⁶The bells and pomegranates alternated around the hem of the robe to be worn for ministering, as the Lord commanded Moses.

²⁷For Aaron and his sons, they made tunics of fine linen—the work of a weaver— ²⁸and the turban of fine linen, the linen caps and the undergarments of finely twisted linen. ²⁹The sash was of finely twisted linen and blue, purple and scarlet yarn—the work of an embroiderer—as the Lord commanded Moses.

³⁰They made the plate, the sacred emblem, out of pure gold and engraved on it, like an inscription on a seal: HOLY TO THE LORD. ³¹Then they fastened a blue cord to it to attach it to the turban, as the Lord commanded Moses.

Moses Inspects the Tabernacle

³²So all the work on the tabernacle, the tent of meeting, was completed. The Israelites did everything just as the Lord commanded Moses. ³³Then they brought the tabernacle to Moses: the tent and all its furnishings, its clasps, frames, crossbars, posts and bases; ³⁴the covering of ram skins dyed red and the covering of another durable leatherᵇ and the shielding curtain; ³⁵the ark of the covenant law with its poles and the atonement cover; ³⁶the table with all its articles and the bread of the Presence; ³⁷the pure gold lampstand with its row of lamps and all its accessories, and the oil for the light; ³⁸the gold altar, the anointing oil, the fragrant incense, and the curtain for the entrance to the tent; ³⁹the bronze altar with its bronze grating, its poles and all its utensils; the basin with its stand; ⁴⁰the curtains of the courtyard with its posts and bases, and the curtain for the entrance to the courtyard; the ropes and tent pegs for the courtyard; all the furnishings for the tabernacle, the tent of meeting; ⁴¹and the woven garments worn for ministering in the sanctuary, both the sacred garments for Aaron the priest and the garments for his sons when serving as priests.

⁴²The Israelites had done all the work just as the Lord had commanded Moses. ⁴³Moses inspected the work and saw that they had done it just as the Lord had commanded. So Moses blessed them.

Setting Up the Tabernacle

40 Then the Lord said to Moses: ²"Set up the tabernacle, the tent of meeting, on the first day of the first month. ³Place the ark of the covenant law in it and shield the ark with the curtain. ⁴Bring in the table and set out what belongs on it. Then bring in the lampstand and set up its lamps. ⁵Place the gold altar of incense in front of the ark of the covenant law and put the curtain at the entrance to the tabernacle.

⁶"Place the altar of burnt offering in front of the entrance to the tabernacle, the tent of meeting; ⁷place the basin between the tent of meeting and the altar and put water in it. ⁸Set up the courtyard around it and put the curtain at the entrance to the courtyard.

⁹"Take the anointing oil and anoint the tabernacle and everything in it; consecrate it and all its furnishings, and it will be holy. ¹⁰Then anoint the altar of burnt offering and all its utensils; consecrate the altar, and it will be most holy. ¹¹Anoint the basin and its stand and consecrate them.

¹²"Bring Aaron and his sons to the entrance to the tent of meeting and wash them with water. ¹³Then dress Aaron in the sacred garments, anoint him and consecrate him so he may serve me as priest. ¹⁴Bring his sons and dress them in tunics. ¹⁵Anoint them just

---

ᵃ 23 The meaning of the Hebrew for this word is uncertain.   ᵇ 34 Possibly the hides of dugongs as you anointed their father, so they may serve me as priests. Their anointing will be to a priesthood that will continue throughout their generations." 16Moses did everything just as the LORD commanded him.

17So the tabernacle was set up on the first day of the first month in the second year. 18When Moses set up the tabernacle, he put the bases in place, erected the frames, inserted the crossbars and set up the posts. 19Then he spread the tent over the tabernacle and put the covering over the tent, as the LORD commanded him.

20He took the tablets of the covenant law and placed them in the ark, attached the poles to the ark and put the atonement cover over it. 21Then he brought the ark into the tabernacle and hung the shielding curtain and shielded the ark of the covenant law, as the LORD commanded him.

22Moses placed the table in the tent of meeting on the north side of the tabernacle outside the curtain 23and set out the bread on it before the LORD, as the LORD commanded him.

24He placed the lampstand in the tent of meeting opposite the table on the south side of the tabernacle 25and set up the lamps before the LORD, as the LORD commanded him.

26Moses placed the gold altar in the tent of meeting in front of the curtain 27and burned fragrant incense on it, as the LORD commanded him.

28Then he put up the curtain at the entrance to the tabernacle. 29He set the altar of burnt offering near the entrance to the tabernacle, the tent of meeting, and offered on it burnt offerings and grain offerings, as the LORD commanded him.

30He placed the basin between the tent of meeting and the altar and put water in it for washing, 31and Moses and Aaron and his sons used it to wash their hands and feet. 32They washed whenever they entered the tent of meeting or approached the altar, as the LORD commanded Moses.

33Then Moses set up the courtyard around the tabernacle and altar and put up the curtain at the entrance to the courtyard. And so Moses finished the work.

The Glory of the LORD

34Then the cloud covered the tent of meeting, and the glory of the LORD filled the tabernacle. 35Moses could not enter the tent of meeting because the cloud had settled on it, and the glory of the LORD filled the tabernacle.

36In all the travels of the Israelites, whenever the cloud lifted from above the tabernacle, they would set out; 37but if the cloud did not lift, they did not set out—until the day it lifted. 38So the cloud of the LORD was over the tabernacle by day, and fire was in the cloud by night, in the sight of all the house of Israel during all their travels.

leviticus

AUTHOR: Moses

DATE: During the 1400s B.C., while the Israelites were traveling in the desert

THEME: God reveals his holiness and what he expects of his holy people.

The Burnt Offering

1 The LORD called to Moses and spoke to him from the tent of meeting. He said, ²"Speak to the Israelites and say to them: 'When you bring an offering to the LORD, bring as your offering an animal from either the herd or the flock.

³" 'If the offering is a burnt offering from the herd, you are to offer a male without defect. You must present it at the entrance to the tent of meeting so that you may be acceptable to the LORD. ⁴You are to lay your hand on the head of the burnt offering, and it will be accepted on your behalf to make atonement for you. ⁵You are to slaughter the young bull before the LORD, and then Aaron's sons the priests shall bring the blood and splash it against the sides of the altar at the entrance to the tent of meeting. ⁶You are to skin the burnt offering and cut it into pieces. ⁷The sons of Aaron the priest are to put fire on the altar and arrange wood on the fire. ⁸Then Aaron's sons the priests shall arrange the pieces, including the head and the fat, on the wood that is burning on the altar. ⁹You are to wash the internal organs and the legs with water, and the priest is to burn all of it on the altar. It is a burnt offering, a food offering, an aroma pleasing to the LORD.

¹⁰" 'If the offering is a burnt offering from the flock, from either the sheep or the goats, you are to offer a male without defect. ¹¹You are to slaughter it at the north side of the altar before the LORD, and Aaron's sons the priests shall splash its blood against the sides of the altar. ¹²You are to cut it into pieces, and the priest shall arrange them, including the head and the fat, on the wood that is burning on the altar. ¹³You are to wash the internal organs and the legs with water, and the priest is to bring all of them and burn them on the altar. It is a burnt offering, a food offering, an aroma pleasing to the LORD.

¹⁴" 'If the offering to the LORD is a burnt offering of birds, you are to offer a dove or a young pigeon. ¹⁵The priest shall bring it to the altar, wring off the head and burn it on the altar; its blood shall be drained out on the side of the altar. ¹⁶He is to remove the crop and the feathers[a] and throw them down east of the altar where the ashes are. ¹⁷He shall tear it open by the wings, not dividing it completely, and then the priest shall burn it on the wood that is burning on the altar. It is a burnt offering, a food offering, an aroma pleasing to the LORD.

The Grain Offering

2 " 'When anyone brings a grain offering to the LORD, your offering is to be of the finest flour. You are to pour olive oil on it, put incense on it ²and take it to Aaron's sons the priests. The priest shall take a handful of the flour and oil, together with all the incense, and burn this as a memorial[b] portion on the altar, a food offering, an aroma pleasing to the LORD. ³The rest of the grain offering belongs to Aaron and his sons; it is a most holy part of the food offering presented to the LORD.

⁴" 'If you bring a grain offering baked in an oven, it is to consist of the finest flour: either thick loaves made without yeast and with olive oil mixed in or thin loaves made without yeast and brushed with olive oil. ⁵If

---

a 16 Or crop with its contents; the meaning of the Hebrew for this word is uncertain.
b 2 Or representative; also in verses 9 and 16

FRIDAY

THE NEW SACRIFICE

Leviticus 1:1–17 *or* 1:1–5

Carol L. Fitzpatrick

God communicated His Word and His desire for proper worship through His chosen leaders. These spokesmen then communicated His message to His chosen people. Before the coming of the Holy Spirit, at Pentecost, this chain of command was vital so that God's flock was not misled.

God required proper and orderly worship. Only an unblemished male animal could be used as the burnt offering. Down through the ages men and women were to make a connection between this sacrifice and the one Christ would willingly make at Calvary's cross.

The priests carried out God's specific requirements for slaughtering the animal, sprinkling its blood against the altar and cutting and arranging these pieces in a certain order. Finally, the sacrifice was burned upon the wood. And when these instructions were carried out, they made a "pleasing aroma" to the Lord.

There have not been any animal sacrifices since the temple in Jerusalem was destroyed in AD 70. Since Christ made His atoning sacrifice on the cross, our sins are forgiven based on His shed blood.

ISAAC WATTS {AD 1674–1748}

Not all the blood of beasts,
On Jewish altars slain,
Could give the guilty conscience peace,
Or wash away the stain.

But Christ, the heavenly lamb,
Takes all our sin away;
A sacrifice of nobler name,
And richer blood than they.

reflection

1. Put yourself in the place of an Israelite in Old Testament times. How would it feel to give up one of your few precious lambs as a sacrifice to atone for your sins?

2. Try to envision the sacrificial process. Why do you think God required such a messy task to pay for sin?

3. How does the sacrifice of Christ on the cross compare to the sacrifices made by the priests in the tent of meeting?

For your next devotional reading, go to page 117.

your grain offering is prepared on a griddle, it is to be made of the finest flour mixed with oil, and without yeast. ⁶Crumble it and pour oil on it; it is a grain offering. ⁷If your grain offering is cooked in a pan, it is to be made of the finest flour and some olive oil. ⁸Bring the grain offering made of these things to the LORD; present it to the priest, who shall take it to the altar. ⁹He shall take out the memorial portion from the grain offering and burn it on the altar as a food offering, an aroma pleasing to the LORD. ¹⁰The rest of the grain offering belongs to Aaron and his sons; it is a most holy part of the food offerings presented to the LORD.

¹¹" 'Every grain offering you bring to the LORD must be made without yeast, for you are not to burn any yeast or honey in a food offering presented to the LORD. ¹²You may bring them to the LORD as an offering of the firstfruits, but they are not to be offered on the altar as a pleasing aroma. ¹³Season all your grain offerings with salt. Do not leave the salt of the covenant of your God out of your grain offerings; add salt to all your offerings.

¹⁴" 'If you bring a grain offering of firstfruits to the LORD, offer crushed heads of new grain roasted in the fire. ¹⁵Put oil and incense on it; it is a grain offering. ¹⁶The priest shall burn the memorial portion of the crushed grain and the oil, together with all the incense, as a food offering presented to the LORD.

The Fellowship Offering

3 " 'If your offering is a fellowship offering, and you offer an animal from the herd, whether male or female, you are to present before the LORD an animal without defect. ²You are to lay your hand on the head of your offering and slaughter it at the entrance to the tent of meeting. Then Aaron's sons the priests shall splash the blood against the sides of the altar. ³From the fellowship offering you are to bring a food offering to the LORD: the internal organs and all the fat that is connected to them, ⁴both kidneys with the fat on them near the loins, and the long lobe of the liver, which you will remove with the kidneys. ⁵Then Aaron's sons are to burn it on the altar on top of the burnt offering that is lying

on the burning wood; it is a food offering, an aroma pleasing to the LORD.

⁶" 'If you offer an animal from the flock as a fellowship offering to the LORD, you are to offer a male or female without defect. ⁷If you offer a lamb, you are to present it before the LORD, ⁸lay your hand on its head and slaughter it in front of the tent of meeting. Then Aaron's sons shall splash its blood against the sides of the altar. ⁹From the fellowship offering you are to bring a food offering to the LORD: its fat, the entire fat tail cut off close to the backbone, the internal organs and all the fat that is connected to them, ¹⁰both kidneys with the fat on them near the loins, and the long lobe of the liver, which you will remove with the kidneys. ¹¹The priest shall burn them on the altar as a food offering presented to the LORD.

¹²" 'If your offering is a goat, you are to present it before the LORD, ¹³lay your hand on its head and slaughter it in front of the tent of meeting. Then Aaron's sons shall splash its blood against the sides of the altar. ¹⁴From what you offer you are to present this food offering to the LORD: the internal organs and all the fat that is connected to them, ¹⁵both kidneys with the fat on them near the loins, and the long lobe of the liver, which you will remove with the kidneys. ¹⁶The priest shall burn them on the altar as a food offering, a pleasing aroma. All the fat is the LORD's.

¹⁷" 'This is a lasting ordinance for the generations to come, wherever you live: You must not eat any fat or any blood.' "

The Sin Offering

4 The LORD said to Moses, ²"Say to the Israelites: 'When anyone sins unintentionally and does what is forbidden in any of the LORD's commands—

³" 'If the anointed priest sins, bringing guilt on the people, he must bring to the LORD a young bull without defect as a sin offeringᵃ for the sin he has committed. ⁴He is to present the bull at the entrance to the tent of meeting before the LORD. He is to lay his hand on its head and slaughter it there before the LORD. ⁵Then the anointed priest shall take some of the bull's blood and carry it into the tent of meeting. ⁶He is to dip his finger into the blood and sprinkle some of it

---

ᵃ 3 Or purification offering; here and throughout this chapter

Giving the Best

Leviticus 3:1–5

read/meditate

Continue to read through the description of this offering until you feel like you are familiar with the requirements and description. Let it bring to mind the spiritual rituals that have meant something in your life.

pray

Offer up a prayer as an offering. Tell God how much your relationship with him is worth to you. Then be still before him.

contemplate

Think back over the specifics of the offering. Do any phrases or particular parts of the sacrifice stand out to you? What personal offerings might God be calling you to make?

additional reflection

Mere outward correctness and attention to forms and ceremonies will not do. God must have reality.

—H. A. Ironside

Worship is giving to God the best he has given us.

—Oswald Chambers

For your next devotional reading, go to page 132.

seven times before the Lᴏʀᴅ, in front of the curtain of the sanctuary. ⁷The priest shall then put some of the blood on the horns of the altar of fragrant incense that is before the Lᴏʀᴅ in the tent of meeting. The rest of the bull's blood he shall pour out at the base of the altar of burnt offering at the entrance to the tent of meeting. ⁸He shall remove all the fat from the bull of the sin offering—all the fat that is connected to the internal organs, ⁹both kidneys with the fat on them near the loins, and the long lobe of the liver, which he will remove with the kidneys— ¹⁰just as the fat is removed from the oxᵃ sacrificed as a fellowship offering. Then the priest shall burn them on the altar of burnt offering. ¹¹But the hide of the bull and all its flesh, as well as the head and legs, the internal organs and the intestines— ¹²that is, all the rest of the bull—he must take outside the camp to a place ceremonially clean, where the ashes are thrown, and burn it there in a wood fire on the ash heap.

¹³" 'If the whole Israelite community sins unintentionally and does what is forbidden in any of the Lᴏʀᴅ's commands, even though the community is unaware of the matter, when they realize their guilt ¹⁴and the sin they committed becomes known, the assembly must bring a young bull as a sin offering and present it before the tent of meeting. ¹⁵The elders of the community are to lay their hands on the bull's head before the Lᴏʀᴅ, and the bull shall be slaughtered before the Lᴏʀᴅ. ¹⁶Then the anointed priest is to take some of the bull's blood into the tent of meeting. ¹⁷He shall dip his finger into the blood and sprinkle it before the Lᴏʀᴅ seven times in front of the curtain. ¹⁸He is to put some of the blood on the horns of the altar that is before the Lᴏʀᴅ in the tent of meeting. The rest of the blood he shall pour out at the base of the altar of burnt offering at the entrance to the tent of meeting. ¹⁹He shall remove all the fat from it and burn it on the altar, ²⁰and do with this bull just as he did with the bull for the sin offering. In this way the priest will make atonement for them, and they will be forgiven. ²¹Then he shall take the bull outside the camp and burn it as he burned the first bull. This is the sin offering for the community.

²²" 'When a leader sins unintentionally and does what is forbidden in any of the commands of the Lᴏʀᴅ his God, when he realizes his guilt ²³and the sin he has committed becomes known, he must bring as his offering a male goat without defect. ²⁴He is to lay his hand on the goat's head and slaughter it at the place where the burnt offering is slaughtered before the Lᴏʀᴅ. It is a sin offering. ²⁵Then the priest shall take some of the blood of the sin offering with his finger and put it on the horns of the altar of burnt offering and pour out the rest of the blood at the base of the altar. ²⁶He shall burn all the fat on the altar as he burned the fat of the fellowship offering. In this way the priest will make atonement for the leader's sin, and he will be forgiven.

²⁷" 'If any member of the community sins unintentionally and does what is forbidden in any of the Lᴏʀᴅ's commands, when they realize their guilt ²⁸and the sin they have committed becomes known, they must bring as their offering for the sin they committed a female goat without defect. ²⁹They are to lay their hand on the head of the sin offering and slaughter it at the place of the burnt offering. ³⁰Then the priest is to take some of the blood with his finger and put it on the horns of the altar of burnt offering and pour out the rest of the blood at the base of the altar. ³¹They shall remove all the fat, just as the fat is removed from the fellowship offering, and the priest shall burn it on the altar as an aroma pleasing to the Lᴏʀᴅ. In this way the priest will make atonement for them, and they will be forgiven.

³²" 'If they bring a lamb as their sin offering, they are to bring a female without defect. ³³They are to lay their hand on its head and slaughter it for a sin offering at the place where the burnt offering is slaughtered. ³⁴Then the priest shall take some of the blood of the sin offering with his finger and put it on the horns of the altar of burnt offering and pour out the rest of the blood at the base of the altar. ³⁵They shall remove all the fat, just as the fat is removed from the lamb of the fellowship offering, and the priest shall burn it on the altar on top of the food offerings presented to the Lᴏʀᴅ. In this way the priest will make atonement for

ᵃ 10 The Hebrew word can refer to either male or female.

them for the sin they have committed, and they will be forgiven.

5 " 'If anyone sins because they do not speak up when they hear a public charge to testify regarding something they have seen or learned about, they will be held responsible. ²Or if anyone unwittingly touches anything ceremonially unclean—whether the carcass of an unclean animal, wild or domestic, or of any unclean creature that moves along the ground—and they are unaware that they have become unclean, but then they come to realize their guilt; ³or if they touch human uncleanness—anything that would make them unclean—even though they are unaware of it, but then they learn of it and realize their guilt; ⁴or if anyone thoughtlessly takes an oath to do anything, whether good or evil—in any matter one might carelessly swear about—even though they are unaware of it, but then they learn of it and realize their guilt— ⁵when anyone realizes their guilt in any of these matters, they must confess in what way they have sinned ⁶and, as a penalty for the sin they have committed, they must bring to the LORD a female lamb or goat from the flock as a sin offering*ᵃ*; and the priest shall make atonement for them for their sin.

⁷" 'Anyone who cannot afford a lamb is to bring two doves or two young pigeons to the LORD as a penalty for their sin—one for a sin offering and the other for a burnt offering. ⁸They are to bring them to the priest, who shall first offer the one for the sin offering. He is to wring its head from its neck, not dividing it completely, ⁹and is to splash some of the blood of the sin offering against the side of the altar; the rest of the blood must be drained out at the base of the altar. It is a sin offering. ¹⁰The priest shall then offer the other as a burnt offering in the prescribed way and make atonement for them for the sin they have committed, and they will be forgiven.

¹¹" 'If, however, they cannot afford two doves or two young pigeons, they are to bring as an offering for their sin a tenth of an ephah*ᵇ* of the finest flour for a sin offering. They must not put oil or incense on it, be-

cause it is a sin offering. ¹²They are to bring it to the priest, who shall take a handful of it as a memorial*ᶜ* portion and burn it on the altar on top of the food offerings presented to the LORD. It is a sin offering. ¹³In this way the priest will make atonement for them for any of these sins they have committed, and they will be forgiven. The rest of the offering will belong to the priest, as in the case of the grain offering.' "

The Guilt Offering

¹⁴The LORD said to Moses: ¹⁵"When anyone is unfaithful to the LORD by sinning unintentionally in regard to any of the LORD's holy things, they are to bring to the LORD as a penalty a ram from the flock, one without defect and of the proper value in silver, according to the sanctuary shekel.*ᵈ* It is a guilt offering. ¹⁶They must make restitution for what they have failed to do in regard to the holy things, pay an additional penalty of a fifth of its value and give it all to the priest. The priest will make atonement for them with the ram as a guilt offering, and they will be forgiven.

¹⁷"If anyone sins and does what is forbidden in any of the LORD's commands, even though they do not know it, they are guilty and will be held responsible. ¹⁸They are to bring to the priest as a guilt offering a ram from the flock, one without defect and of the proper value. In this way the priest will make atonement for them for the wrong they have committed unintentionally, and they will be forgiven. ¹⁹It is a guilt offering; they have been guilty of*ᵉ* wrongdoing against the LORD."

6 *The LORD said to Moses: ²"If anyone sins and is unfaithful to the LORD by deceiving a neighbor about something entrusted to them or left in their care or about something stolen, or if they cheat a neighbor, ³or if they find lost property and lie about it, or if they swear falsely about any such sin that people may commit— ⁴when they thus sin and realize their guilt, they must return what they have stolen or taken by extortion, or what was entrusted to them, or the lost property they found, ⁵or whatever it was they swore falsely about.

ᵃ 6 Or *purification offering*; here and throughout this chapter   *ᵇ* 11 That is, probably about 3 1/2 pounds or about 1.6 kilograms   *ᶜ* 12 Or *representative*   *ᵈ* 15 That is, about 2/5 ounce or about 11.5 grams   *ᵉ* 19 Or *have made full expiation for their*

* 6:1-7 is numbered 5:20-26 in Hebrew texts.

They must make restitution in full, add a fifth of the value to it and give it all to the owner on the day they present their guilt offering. ⁶And as a penalty they must bring to the priest, that is, to the LORD, their guilt offering, a ram from the flock, one without defect and of the proper value. ⁷In this way the priest will make atonement for them before the LORD, and they will be forgiven for any of the things they did that made them guilty."

The Burnt Offering

*⁸The LORD said to Moses: ⁹"Give Aaron and his sons this command: 'These are the regulations for the burnt offering: The burnt offering is to remain on the altar hearth throughout the night, till morning, and the fire must be kept burning on the altar. ¹⁰The priest shall then put on his linen clothes, with linen undergarments next to his body, and shall remove the ashes of the burnt offering that the fire has consumed on the altar and place them beside the altar. ¹¹Then he is to take off these clothes and put on others, and carry the ashes outside the camp to a place that is ceremonially clean. ¹²The fire on the altar must be kept burning; it must not go out. Every morning the priest is to add firewood and arrange the burnt offering on the fire and burn the fat of the fellowship offerings on it. ¹³The fire must be kept burning on the altar continuously; it must not go out.

The Grain Offering

¹⁴" 'These are the regulations for the grain offering: Aaron's sons are to bring it before the LORD, in front of the altar. ¹⁵The priest is to take a handful of the finest flour and some olive oil, together with all the incense on the grain offering, and burn the memorialᵃ portion on the altar as an aroma pleasing to the LORD. ¹⁶Aaron and his sons shall eat the rest of it, but it is to be eaten without yeast in the sanctuary area; they are to eat it in the courtyard of the tent of meeting. ¹⁷It must not be baked with yeast; I have given it as their share of the food offerings presented to me. Like the sin offeringᵇ and the guilt offering, it is most holy. ¹⁸Any male

descendant of Aaron may eat it. For all generations to come it is his perpetual share of the food offerings presented to the LORD. Whatever touches them will become holy.ᶜ' "

¹⁹The LORD also said to Moses, ²⁰"This is the offering Aaron and his sons are to bring to the LORD on the day heᵈ is anointed: a tenth of an ephahᵉ of the finest flour as a regular grain offering, half of it in the morning and half in the evening. ²¹It must be prepared with oil on a griddle; bring it well-mixed and present the grain offering brokenᶠ in pieces as an aroma pleasing to the LORD. ²²The son who is to succeed him as anointed priest shall prepare it. It is the LORD's perpetual share and is to be burned completely. ²³Every grain offering of a priest shall be burned completely; it must not be eaten."

The Sin Offering

²⁴The LORD said to Moses, ²⁵"Say to Aaron and his sons: 'These are the regulations for the sin offering: The sin offering is to be slaughtered before the LORD in the place the burnt offering is slaughtered; it is most holy. ²⁶The priest who offers it shall eat it; it is to be eaten in the sanctuary area, in the courtyard of the tent of meeting. ²⁷Whatever touches any of the flesh will become holy, and if any of the blood is spattered on a garment, you must wash it in the sanctuary area. ²⁸The clay pot the meat is cooked in must be broken; but if it is cooked in a bronze pot, the pot is to be scoured and rinsed with water. ²⁹Any male in a priest's family may eat it; it is most holy. ³⁰But any sin offering whose blood is brought into the tent of meeting to make atonement in the Holy Place must not be eaten; it must be burned up.

The Guilt Offering

7 " 'These are the regulations for the guilt offering, which is most holy: ²The guilt offering is to be slaughtered in the place where the burnt offering is slaughtered, and its blood is to be splashed against the sides of the altar. ³All its fat shall be offered: the fat tail and the fat that cov-

---

ᵃ 15 Or *representative*   *ᵇ 17* Or *purification offering*; also in verses 25 and 30   *ᶜ 18* Or *Whoever touches them must be holy*; similarly in verse 27   *ᵈ 20* Or *each*   *ᵉ 20* That is, probably about 3 1/2 pounds or about 1.6 kilograms   *ᶠ 21* The meaning of the Hebrew for this word is uncertain.

* 6:8-30 is numbered 6:1-23 in Hebrew texts.

ers the internal organs, [4]both kidneys with the fat on them near the loins, and the long lobe of the liver, which is to be removed with the kidneys. [5]The priest shall burn them on the altar as a food offering presented to the LORD. It is a guilt offering. [6]Any male in a priest's family may eat it, but it must be eaten in the sanctuary area; it is most holy.

[7]" 'The same law applies to both the sin offering[a] and the guilt offering: They belong to the priest who makes atonement with them. [8]The priest who offers a burnt offering for anyone may keep its hide for himself. [9]Every grain offering baked in an oven or cooked in a pan or on a griddle belongs to the priest who offers it, [10]and every grain offering, whether mixed with oil or dry, belongs equally to all the sons of Aaron.

The Fellowship Offering

[11]" 'These are the regulations for the fellowship offering anyone may present to the LORD:

[12]" 'If they offer it as an expression of thankfulness, then along with this thank offering they are to offer thick loaves made without yeast and with olive oil mixed in, thin loaves made without yeast and brushed with olive oil, and thick loaves of the finest flour well-kneaded and with olive oil mixed in. [13]Along with their fellowship offering of thanksgiving they are to present an offering with thick loaves of bread made with yeast. [14]They are to bring one of each kind as an offering, a contribution to the LORD; it belongs to the priest who splashes the blood of the fellowship offering against the altar. [15]The meat of their fellowship offering of thanksgiving must be eaten on the day it is offered; they must leave none of it till morning.

[16]" 'If, however, their offering is the result of a vow or is a freewill offering, the sacrifice shall be eaten on the day they offer it, but anything left over may be eaten on the next day. [17]Any meat of the sacrifice left over till the third day must be burned up. [18]If any meat of the fellowship offering is eaten on the third day, the one who offered it will not be accepted. It will not be reckoned to their

credit, for it has become impure; the person who eats any of it will be held responsible. [19]" 'Meat that touches anything ceremonially unclean must not be eaten; it must be burned up. As for other meat, anyone ceremonially clean may eat it. [20]But if anyone who is unclean eats any meat of the fellowship offering belonging to the LORD, they must be cut off from their people. [21]Anyone who touches something unclean—whether human uncleanness or an unclean animal or any unclean creature that moves along the ground[b]—and then eats any of the meat of the fellowship offering belonging to the LORD must be cut off from their people.' "

Eating Fat and Blood Forbidden

[22]The LORD said to Moses, [23]"Say to the Israelites: 'Do not eat any of the fat of cattle, sheep or goats. [24]The fat of an animal found dead or torn by wild animals may be used for any other purpose, but you must not eat it. [25]Anyone who eats the fat of an animal from which a food offering may be[c] presented to the LORD must be cut off from their people. [26]And wherever you live, you must not eat the blood of any bird or animal. [27]Anyone who eats blood must be cut off from their people.' "

The Priests' Share

[28]The LORD said to Moses, [29]"Say to the Israelites: 'Anyone who brings a fellowship offering to the LORD is to bring part of it as their sacrifice to the LORD. [30]With their own hands they are to present the food offering to the LORD; they are to bring the fat, together with the breast, and wave the breast before the LORD as a wave offering. [31]The priest shall burn the fat on the altar, but the breast belongs to Aaron and his sons. [32]You are to give the right thigh of your fellowship offerings to the priest as a contribution. [33]The son of Aaron who offers the blood and the fat of the fellowship offering shall have the right thigh as his share. [34]From the fellowship offerings of the Israelites, I have taken the breast that is waved and the thigh that is presented and have given them to Aaron the priest and his sons as their perpetual share from the Israelites.' "

[35]This is the portion of the food offerings

---

[a] 7 Or *purification offering*; also in verse 37   [b] 21 A few Hebrew manuscripts, Samaritan Pentateuch, Syriac and Targum (see Lev. 5:2); most Hebrew manuscripts *unclean, detestable thing*   [c] 25 Or *offering is*

presented to the LORD that were allotted to Aaron and his sons on the day they were presented to serve the LORD as priests. ³⁶On the day they were anointed, the LORD commanded that the Israelites give this to them as their perpetual share for the generations to come.

³⁷These, then, are the regulations for the burnt offering, the grain offering, the sin offering, the guilt offering, the ordination offering and the fellowship offering, ³⁸which the LORD gave Moses on Mount Sinai in the Desert of Sinai on the day he commanded the Israelites to bring their offerings to the LORD.

The Ordination of Aaron and His Sons

8 The LORD said to Moses, ²"Bring Aaron and his sons, their garments, the anointing oil, the bull for the sin offering,ᵃ the two rams and the basket containing bread made without yeast, ³and gather the entire assembly at the entrance to the tent of meeting." ⁴Moses did as the LORD commanded him, and the assembly gathered at the entrance to the tent of meeting.

⁵Moses said to the assembly, "This is what the LORD has commanded to be done." ⁶Then Moses brought Aaron and his sons forward and washed them with water. ⁷He put the tunic on Aaron, tied the sash around him, clothed him with the robe and put the ephod on him. He also fastened the ephod with a decorative waistband, which he tied around him. ⁸He placed the breastpiece on him and put the Urim and Thummim in the breastpiece. ⁹Then he placed the turban on Aaron's head and set the gold plate, the sacred emblem, on the front of it, as the LORD commanded Moses.

¹⁰Then Moses took the anointing oil and anointed the tabernacle and everything in it, and so consecrated them. ¹¹He sprinkled some of the oil on the altar seven times, anointing the altar and all its utensils and the basin with its stand, to consecrate them. ¹²He poured some of the anointing oil on Aaron's head and anointed him to consecrate him. ¹³Then he brought Aaron's sons forward, put tunics on them, tied sashes around them and fastened caps on them, as the LORD commanded Moses.

¹⁴He then presented the bull for the sin offering, and Aaron and his sons laid their hands on its head. ¹⁵Moses slaughtered the bull and took some of the blood, and with his finger he put it on all the horns of the altar to purify the altar. He poured out the rest of the blood at the base of the altar. So he consecrated it to make atonement for it. ¹⁶Moses also took all the fat around the internal organs, the long lobe of the liver, and both kidneys and their fat, and burned it on the altar. ¹⁷But the bull with its hide and its flesh and its intestines he burned up outside the camp, as the LORD commanded Moses.

¹⁸He then presented the ram for the burnt offering, and Aaron and his sons laid their hands on its head. ¹⁹Then Moses slaughtered the ram and splashed the blood against the sides of the altar. ²⁰He cut the ram into pieces and burned the head, the pieces and the fat. ²¹He washed the internal organs and the legs with water and burned the whole ram on the altar. It was a burnt offering, a pleasing aroma, a food offering presented to the LORD, as the LORD commanded Moses.

²²He then presented the other ram, the ram for the ordination, and Aaron and his sons laid their hands on its head. ²³Moses slaughtered the ram and took some of its blood and put it on the lobe of Aaron's right ear, on the thumb of his right hand and on the big toe of his right foot. ²⁴Moses also brought Aaron's sons forward and put some of the blood on the lobes of their right ears, on the thumbs of their right hands and on the big toes of their right feet. Then he splashed blood against the sides of the altar. ²⁵After that, he took the fat, the fat tail, all the fat around the internal organs, the long lobe of the liver, both kidneys and their fat and the right thigh. ²⁶And from the basket of bread made without yeast, which was before the LORD, he took one thick loaf, one thick loaf with olive oil mixed in, and one thin loaf, and he put these on the fat portions and on the right thigh. ²⁷He put all these in the hands of Aaron and his sons, and they waved them before the LORD as a wave offering. ²⁸Then Moses took them from their hands and burned them on the altar on top of the burnt offering as an ordination offering, a pleasing aroma, a food offering pre-

ᵃ 2 Or *purification offering*; also in verse 14

sented to the LORD. 29Moses also took the breast, which was his share of the ordination ram, and waved it before the LORD as a wave offering, as the LORD commanded Moses.

30Then Moses took some of the anointing oil and some of the blood from the altar and sprinkled them on Aaron and his garments and on his sons and their garments. So he consecrated Aaron and his garments and his sons and their garments.

31Moses then said to Aaron and his sons, "Cook the meat at the entrance to the tent of meeting and eat it there with the bread from the basket of ordination offerings, as I was commanded: 'Aaron and his sons are to eat it.' 32Then burn up the rest of the meat and the bread. 33Do not leave the entrance to the tent of meeting for seven days, until the days of your ordination are completed, for your ordination will last seven days. 34What has been done today was commanded by the LORD to make atonement for you. 35You must stay at the entrance to the tent of meeting day and night for seven days and do what the LORD requires, so you will not die; for that is what I have been commanded." 36So Aaron and his sons did everything the LORD commanded through Moses.

The Priests Begin Their Ministry

9 On the eighth day Moses summoned Aaron and his sons and the elders of Israel. 2He said to Aaron, "Take a bull calf for your sin offering[a] and a ram for your burnt offering, both without defect, and present them before the LORD. 3Then say to the Israelites: 'Take a male goat for a sin offering, a calf and a lamb—both a year old and without defect—for a burnt offering, 4and an ox[b] and a ram for a fellowship offering to sacrifice before the LORD, together with a grain offering mixed with olive oil. For today the LORD will appear to you.'"

5They took the things Moses commanded to the front of the tent of meeting, and the entire assembly came near and stood before the LORD. 6Then Moses said, "This is what the LORD has commanded you to do, so that the glory of the LORD may appear to you."

7Moses said to Aaron, "Come to the altar and sacrifice your sin offering and your burnt offering and make atonement for yourself and the people; sacrifice the offering that is for the people and make atonement for them, as the LORD has commanded."

8So Aaron came to the altar and slaughtered the calf as a sin offering for himself. 9His sons brought the blood to him, and he dipped his finger into the blood and put it on the horns of the altar; the rest of the blood he poured out at the base of the altar. 10On the altar he burned the fat, the kidneys and the long lobe of the liver from the sin offering, as the LORD commanded Moses; 11the flesh and the hide he burned up outside the camp.

12Then he slaughtered the burnt offering. His sons handed him the blood, and he splashed it against the sides of the altar. 13They handed him the burnt offering piece by piece, including the head, and he burned them on the altar. 14He washed the internal organs and the legs and burned them on top of the burnt offering on the altar.

15Aaron then brought the offering that was for the people. He took the goat for the people's sin offering and slaughtered it and offered it for a sin offering as he did with the first one.

16He brought the burnt offering and offered it in the prescribed way. 17He also brought the grain offering, took a handful of it and burned it on the altar in addition to the morning's burnt offering.

18He slaughtered the ox and the ram as the fellowship offering for the people. His sons handed him the blood, and he splashed it against the sides of the altar. 19But the fat portions of the ox and the ram—the fat tail, the layer of fat, the kidneys and the long lobe of the liver— 20these they laid on the breasts, and then Aaron burned the fat on the altar. 21Aaron waved the breasts and the right thigh before the LORD as a wave offering, as Moses commanded.

22Then Aaron lifted his hands toward the people and blessed them. And having sacrificed the sin offering, the burnt offering and the fellowship offering, he stepped down.

23Moses and Aaron then went into the tent of meeting. When they came out, they blessed the people; and the glory of the LORD appeared to all the people. 24Fire came out

---

a 2 Or purification offering; here and throughout this chapter   b 4 The Hebrew word can refer to either male or female; also in verses 18 and 19.

from the presence of the LORD and consumed the burnt offering and the fat portions on the altar. And when all the people saw it, they shouted for joy and fell facedown.

The Death of Nadab and Abihu

10 Aaron's sons Nadab and Abihu took their censers, put fire in them and added incense; and they offered unauthorized fire before the LORD, contrary to his command. ²So fire came out from the presence of the LORD and consumed them, and they died before the LORD. ³Moses then said to Aaron, "This is what the LORD spoke of when he said:

" 'Among those who approach me
I will be proved holy;
in the sight of all the people
I will be honored.' "

Aaron remained silent.

⁴Moses summoned Mishael and Elzaphan, sons of Aaron's uncle Uzziel, and said to them, "Come here; carry your cousins outside the camp, away from the front of the sanctuary." ⁵So they came and carried them, still in their tunics, outside the camp, as Moses ordered.

⁶Then Moses said to Aaron and his sons Eleazar and Ithamar, "Do not let your hair become unkempt[a] and do not tear your clothes, or you will die and the LORD will be angry with the whole community. But your relatives, all the house of Israel, may mourn for those the LORD has destroyed by fire. ⁷Do not leave the entrance to the tent of meeting or you will die, because the LORD's anointing oil is on you." So they did as Moses said.

⁸Then the LORD said to Aaron, ⁹"You and your sons are not to drink wine or other fermented drink whenever you go into the tent of meeting, or you will die. This is a lasting ordinance for the generations to come, ¹⁰so that you can distinguish between the holy and the common, between the unclean and the clean, ¹¹and so you can teach the Israelites all the decrees the LORD has given them through Moses."

¹²Moses said to Aaron and his remaining sons, Eleazar and Ithamar, "Take the grain offering left over from the food offerings prepared without yeast and presented to the LORD and eat it beside the altar, for it is most holy. ¹³Eat it in the sanctuary area, because it is your share and your sons' share of the food offerings presented to the LORD; for so I have been commanded. ¹⁴But you and your sons and your daughters may eat the breast that was waved and the thigh that was presented. Eat them in a ceremonially clean place; they have been given to you and your children as your share of the Israelites' fellowship offerings. ¹⁵The thigh that was presented and the breast that was waved must be brought up with the fat portions of the food offerings, to be waved before the LORD as a wave offering. This will be the perpetual share for you and your children, as the LORD has commanded."

¹⁶When Moses inquired about the goat of the sin offering[b] and found that it had been burned up, he was angry with Eleazar and Ithamar, Aaron's remaining sons, and asked, ¹⁷"Why didn't you eat the sin offering in the sanctuary area? It is most holy; it was given to you to take away the guilt of the community by making atonement for them before the LORD. ¹⁸Since its blood was not taken into the Holy Place, you should have eaten the goat in the sanctuary area, as I commanded."

¹⁹Aaron replied to Moses, "Today they sacrificed their sin offering and their burnt offering before the LORD, but such things as this have happened to me. Would the LORD have been pleased if I had eaten the sin offering today?" ²⁰When Moses heard this, he was satisfied.

Clean and Unclean Food

11 The LORD said to Moses and Aaron, ²"Say to the Israelites: 'Of all the animals that live on land, these are the ones you may eat: ³You may eat any animal that has a divided hoof and that chews the cud.

⁴" 'There are some that only chew the cud or only have a divided hoof, but you must not eat them. The camel, though it chews the cud, does not have a divided hoof; it is ceremonially unclean for you. ⁵The hyrax, though it chews the cud, does not have a divided hoof; it is unclean for you. ⁶The rabbit, though it chews the cud, does not

a 6 Or Do not uncover your heads   _b 16 Or purification offering; also in verses 17 and 19_ have a divided hoof; it is unclean for you. 7And the pig, though it has a divided hoof, does not chew the cud; it is unclean for you. 8You must not eat their meat or touch their carcasses; they are unclean for you.

9" 'Of all the creatures living in the water of the seas and the streams you may eat any that have fins and scales. 10But all creatures in the seas or streams that do not have fins and scales—whether among all the swarming things or among all the other living creatures in the water—you are to regard as unclean. 11And since you are to regard them as unclean, you must not eat their meat; you must regard their carcasses as unclean. 12Anything living in the water that does not have fins and scales is to be regarded as unclean by you.

13" 'These are the birds you are to regard as unclean and not eat because they are unclean: the eagle,a the vulture, the black vulture, 14the red kite, any kind of black kite, 15any kind of raven, 16the horned owl, the screech owl, the gull, any kind of hawk, 17the little owl, the cormorant, the great owl, 18the white owl, the desert owl, the osprey, 19the stork, any kind of heron, the hoopoe and the bat.

20" 'All flying insects that walk on all fours are to be regarded as unclean by you. 21There are, however, some flying insects that walk on all fours that you may eat: those that have jointed legs for hopping on the ground. 22Of these you may eat any kind of locust, katydid, cricket or grasshopper. 23But all other flying insects that have four legs you are to regard as unclean.

24" 'You will make yourselves unclean by these; whoever touches their carcasses will be unclean till evening. 25Whoever picks up one of their carcasses must wash their clothes, and they will be unclean till evening.

26" 'Every animal that does not have a divided hoof or that does not chew the cud is unclean for you; whoever touches the carcass of any of them will be unclean. 27Of all the animals that walk on all fours, those that walk on their paws are unclean for you; whoever touches their carcasses will be unclean till evening. 28Anyone who picks up their carcasses must wash their clothes, and

they will be unclean till evening. These animals are unclean for you.

29" 'Of the animals that move about on the ground, these are unclean for you: the weasel, the rat, any kind of great lizard, 30the gecko, the monitor lizard, the wall lizard, the skink and the chameleon. 31Of all those that move along the ground, these are unclean for you. Whoever touches them when they are dead will be unclean till evening. 32When one of them dies and falls on something, that article, whatever its use, will be unclean, whether it is made of wood, cloth, hide or sackcloth. Put it in water; it will be unclean till evening, and then it will be clean. 33If one of them falls into a clay pot, everything in it will be unclean, and you must break the pot. 34Any food you are allowed to eat that has come into contact with water from any such pot is unclean, and any liquid that is drunk from such a pot is unclean. 35Anything that one of their carcasses falls on becomes unclean; an oven or cooking pot must be broken up. They are unclean, and you are to regard them as unclean. 36A spring, however, or a cistern for collecting water remains clean, but anyone who touches one of these carcasses is unclean. 37If a carcass falls on any seeds that are to be planted, they remain clean. 38But if water has been put on the seed and a carcass falls on it, it is unclean for you.

39" 'If an animal that you are allowed to eat dies, anyone who touches its carcass will be unclean till evening. 40Anyone who eats some of its carcass must wash their clothes, and they will be unclean till evening. Anyone who picks up the carcass must wash their clothes, and they will be unclean till evening.

41" 'Every creature that moves about on the ground is to be regarded as unclean; it is not to be eaten. 42You are not to eat any creature that moves about on the ground, whether it moves on its belly or walks on all fours or on many feet; it is unclean. 43Do not defile yourselves by any of these creatures. Do not make yourselves unclean by means of them or be made unclean by them. 44I am the LORD your God; consecrate yourselves and be holy, because I am holy. Do not make yourselves unclean by any creature that moves about on the ground. 45I am the LORD,

---

a 13 The precise identification of some of the birds, insects and animals in this chapter is uncertain.

who brought you up out of Egypt to be your God; therefore be holy, because I am holy. 46" 'These are the regulations concerning animals, birds, every living thing that moves in the water and every creature that moves about on the ground. 47You must distinguish between the unclean and the clean, between living creatures that may be eaten and those that may not be eaten.' "

Purification After Childbirth

12 The LORD said to Moses, 2"Say to the Israelites: 'A woman who becomes pregnant and gives birth to a son will be ceremonially unclean for seven days, just as she is unclean during her monthly period. 3On the eighth day the boy is to be circumcised. 4Then the woman must wait thirty-three days to be purified from her bleeding. She must not touch anything sacred or go to the sanctuary until the days of her purification are over. 5If she gives birth to a daughter, for two weeks the woman will be unclean, as during her period. Then she must wait sixty-six days to be purified from her bleeding.

6" 'When the days of her purification for a son or daughter are over, she is to bring to the priest at the entrance to the tent of meeting a year-old lamb for a burnt offering and a young pigeon or a dove for a sin offering.a 7He shall offer them before the LORD to make atonement for her, and then she will be ceremonially clean from her flow of blood.

" 'These are the regulations for the woman who gives birth to a boy or a girl. 8If she cannot afford a lamb, she is to bring two doves or two young pigeons, one for a burnt offering and the other for a sin offering. In this way the priest will make atonement for her, and she will be clean.' "

Regulations About Defiling Skin Diseases

13 The LORD said to Moses and Aaron, 2"When anyone has a swelling or a rash or a shiny spot on their skin that may be a defiling skin disease,b they must be brought to Aaron the priest or to one of his sonsc who is a priest. 3The priest is to examine the sore on the skin, and if the hair in the sore has turned

white and the sore appears to be more than skin deep, it is a defiling skin disease. When the priest examines them, he shall pronounce them ceremonially unclean. 4If the shiny spot on the skin is white but does not appear to be more than skin deep and the hair in it has not turned white, the priest is to isolate the affected person for seven days. 5On the seventh day the priest is to examine them, and if he sees that the sore is unchanged and has not spread in the skin, he is to isolate them for another seven days. 6On the seventh day the priest is to examine them again, and if the sore has faded and has not spread in the skin, the priest shall pronounce them clean; it is only a rash. They must wash their clothes, and they will be clean. 7But if the rash does spread in their skin after they have shown themselves to the priest to be pronounced clean, they must appear before the priest again. 8The priest is to examine them, and if the rash has spread in the skin, he shall pronounce them unclean; it is a defiling skin disease.

9"When anyone has a defiling skin disease, they must be brought to the priest. 10The priest is to examine them, and if there is a white swelling in the skin that has turned the hair white and if there is raw flesh in the swelling, 11it is a chronic skin disease and the priest shall pronounce them unclean. He is not to isolate them, because they are already unclean.

12"If the disease breaks out all over their skin and, so far as the priest can see, it covers all the skin of the affected person from head to foot, 13the priest is to examine them, and if the disease has covered their whole body, he shall pronounce them clean. Since it has all turned white, they are clean. 14But whenever raw flesh appears on them, they will be unclean. 15When the priest sees the raw flesh, he shall pronounce them unclean. The raw flesh is unclean; they have a defiling disease. 16If the raw flesh changes and turns white, they must go to the priest. 17The priest is to examine them, and if the sores have turned white, the priest shall pronounce the affected person clean; then they will be clean.

18"When someone has a boil on their skin and it heals, 19and in the place where the

---

a 6 Or purification offering; also in verse 8   b 2 The Hebrew word for defiling skin disease, traditionally translated "leprosy," was used for various diseases affecting the skin; here and throughout verses 3-46.   c 2 Or descendants boil was, a white swelling or reddish-white spot appears, they must present themselves to the priest. ²⁰The priest is to examine it, and if it appears to be more than skin deep and the hair in it has turned white, the priest shall pronounce them unclean. It is a defiling skin disease that has broken out where the boil was. ²¹But if, when the priest examines it, there is no white hair in it and it is not more than skin deep and has faded, then the priest is to isolate them for seven days. ²²If it is spreading in the skin, the priest shall pronounce them unclean; it is a defiling disease. ²³But if the spot is unchanged and has not spread, it is only a scar from the boil, and the priest shall pronounce them clean.

²⁴"When someone has a burn on their skin and a reddish-white or white spot appears in the raw flesh of the burn, ²⁵the priest is to examine the spot, and if the hair in it has turned white, and it appears to be more than skin deep, it is a defiling disease that has broken out in the burn. The priest shall pronounce them unclean; it is a defiling skin disease. ²⁶But if the priest examines it and there is no white hair in the spot and if it is not more than skin deep and has faded, then the priest is to isolate them for seven days. ²⁷On the seventh day the priest is to examine them, and if it is spreading in the skin, the priest shall pronounce them unclean; it is a defiling skin disease. ²⁸If, however, the spot is unchanged and has not spread in the skin but has faded, it is a swelling from the burn, and the priest shall pronounce them clean; it is only a scar from the burn.

²⁹"If a man or woman has a sore on their head or chin, ³⁰the priest is to examine the sore, and if it appears to be more than skin deep and the hair in it is yellow and thin, the priest shall pronounce them unclean; it is a defiling skin disease on the head or chin. ³¹But if, when the priest examines the sore, it does not seem to be more than skin deep and there is no black hair in it, then the priest is to isolate the affected person for seven days. ³²On the seventh day the priest is to examine the sore, and if it has not spread and there is no yellow hair in it and it does not appear to be more than skin deep, ³³then the man or woman must shave themselves, except for the affected area, and the

priest is to keep them isolated another seven days. ³⁴On the seventh day the priest is to examine the sore, and if it has not spread in the skin and appears to be no more than skin deep, the priest shall pronounce the man or woman clean. They must wash their clothes, and they will be clean. ³⁵But if the sore does spread in the skin after they are pronounced clean, ³⁶the priest is to examine them, and if he finds that the sore has spread in the skin, he does not need to look for yellow hair; they are unclean. ³⁷If, however, the sore is unchanged so far as the priest can see, and if black hair has grown in it, the affected person is healed. They are clean, and the priest shall pronounce them clean.

³⁸"When a man or woman has white spots on the skin, ³⁹the priest is to examine them, and if the spots are dull white, it is a harmless rash that has broken out on the skin; they are clean.

⁴⁰"A man who has lost his hair and is bald is clean. ⁴¹If he has lost his hair from the front of his scalp and has a bald forehead, he is clean. ⁴²But if he has a reddish-white sore on his bald head or forehead, it is a defiling disease breaking out on his head or forehead. ⁴³The priest is to examine him, and if the swollen sore on his head or forehead is reddish-white like a defiling skin disease, ⁴⁴the man is diseased and is unclean. The priest shall pronounce him unclean because of the sore on his head.

⁴⁵"Anyone with such a defiling disease must wear torn clothes, let their hair be unkempt,ᵃ cover the lower part of their face and cry out, 'Unclean! Unclean!' ⁴⁶As long as they have the disease they remain unclean. They must live alone; they must live outside the camp.

Regulations About Defiling Molds

⁴⁷"As for any fabric that is spoiled with a defiling mold—any woolen or linen clothing, ⁴⁸any woven or knitted material of linen or wool, any leather or anything made of leather— ⁴⁹if the affected area in the fabric, the leather, the woven or knitted material, or any leather article, is greenish or reddish, it is a defiling mold and must be shown to the priest. ⁵⁰The priest is to examine the affected area and isolate the article for seven

a 45 Or clothes, uncover their head

days. ⁵¹On the seventh day he is to examine it, and if the mold has spread in the fabric, the woven or knitted material, or the leather, whatever its use, it is a persistent defiling mold; the article is unclean. ⁵²He must burn the fabric, the woven or knitted material of wool or linen, or any leather article that has been spoiled; because the defiling mold is persistent, the article must be burned.

⁵³"But if, when the priest examines it, the mold has not spread in the fabric, the woven or knitted material, or the leather article, ⁵⁴he shall order that the spoiled article be washed. Then he is to isolate it for another seven days. ⁵⁵After the article has been washed, the priest is to examine it again, and if the mold has not changed its appearance, even though it has not spread, it is unclean. Burn it, no matter which side of the fabric has been spoiled. ⁵⁶If, when the priest examines it, the mold has faded after the article has been washed, he is to tear the spoiled part out of the fabric, the leather, or the woven or knitted material. ⁵⁷But if it reappears in the fabric, in the woven or knitted material, or in the leather article, it is a spreading mold; whatever has the mold must be burned. ⁵⁸Any fabric, woven or knitted material, or any leather article that has been washed and is rid of the mold, must be washed again. Then it will be clean."

⁵⁹These are the regulations concerning defiling molds in woolen or linen clothing, woven or knitted material, or any leather article, for pronouncing them clean or unclean.

Cleansing From Defiling Skin Diseases

14 The Lord said to Moses, ²"These are the regulations for any diseased person at the time of their ceremonial cleansing, when they are brought to the priest: ³The priest is to go outside the camp and examine them. If they have been healed of their defiling skin disease,ᵃ ⁴the priest shall order that two live clean birds and some cedar wood, scarlet yarn and hyssop be brought for the person to be cleansed. ⁵Then the priest shall order that one of the birds be killed over fresh water in a clay pot. ⁶He is then to take the live

bird and dip it, together with the cedar wood, the scarlet yarn and the hyssop, into the blood of the bird that was killed over the fresh water. ⁷Seven times he shall sprinkle the one to be cleansed of the defiling disease, and then pronounce them clean. After that, he is to release the live bird in the open fields.

⁸"The person to be cleansed must wash their clothes, shave off all their hair and bathe with water; then they will be ceremonially clean. After this they may come into the camp, but they must stay outside their tent for seven days. ⁹On the seventh day they must shave off all their hair; they must shave their head, their beard, their eyebrows and the rest of their hair. They must wash their clothes and bathe themselves with water, and they will be clean.

¹⁰"On the eighth day they must bring two male lambs and one ewe lamb a year old, each without defect, along with three-tenths of an ephahᵇ of the finest flour mixed with olive oil for a grain offering, and one logᶜ of oil. ¹¹The priest who pronounces them clean shall present both the one to be cleansed and their offerings before the Lord at the entrance to the tent of meeting.

¹²"Then the priest is to take one of the male lambs and offer it as a guilt offering, along with the log of oil; he shall wave them before the Lord as a wave offering. ¹³He is to slaughter the lamb in the sanctuary area where the sin offeringᵈ and the burnt offering are slaughtered. Like the sin offering, the guilt offering belongs to the priest; it is most holy. ¹⁴The priest is to take some of the blood of the guilt offering and put it on the lobe of the right ear of the one to be cleansed, on the thumb of their right hand and on the big toe of their right foot. ¹⁵The priest shall then take some of the log of oil, pour it in the palm of his own left hand, ¹⁶dip his right forefinger into the oil in his palm, and with his finger sprinkle some of it before the Lord seven times. ¹⁷The priest is to put some of the oil remaining in his palm on the lobe of the right ear of the one to be cleansed, on the thumb of their right hand and on the big toe of their right foot, on top of the blood of the guilt offering. ¹⁸The rest

ᵃ 3 The Hebrew word for *defiling skin disease*, traditionally translated "leprosy," was used for various diseases affecting the skin; also in verses 7 and 32.   ᵇ 10 That is, probably about 11 pounds or about 5 kilograms   ᶜ 10 That is, about 1/2 pint or about 0.3 liter; also in verses 12, 15, 21 and 24   ᵈ 13 Or *purification offering*; also in verses 19, 22 and 31 of the oil in his palm the priest shall put on the head of the one to be cleansed and make atonement for them before the LORD.

¹⁹"Then the priest is to sacrifice the sin offering and make atonement for the one to be cleansed from their uncleanness. After that, the priest shall slaughter the burnt offering ²⁰and offer it on the altar, together with the grain offering, and make atonement for them, and they will be clean.

²¹"If, however, they are poor and cannot afford these, they must take one male lamb as a guilt offering to be waved to make atonement for them, together with a tenth of an ephah*a* of the finest flour mixed with olive oil for a grain offering, a log of oil, ²²and two doves or two young pigeons, such as they can afford, one for a sin offering and the other for a burnt offering.

²³"On the eighth day they must bring them for their cleansing to the priest at the entrance to the tent of meeting, before the LORD. ²⁴The priest is to take the lamb for the guilt offering, together with the log of oil, and wave them before the LORD as a wave offering. ²⁵He shall slaughter the lamb for the guilt offering and take some of its blood and put it on the lobe of the right ear of the one to be cleansed, on the thumb of their right hand and on the big toe of their right foot. ²⁶The priest is to pour some of the oil into the palm of his own left hand, ²⁷and with his right forefinger sprinkle some of the oil from his palm seven times before the LORD. ²⁸Some of the oil in his palm he is to put on the same places he put the blood of the guilt offering—on the lobe of the right ear of the one to be cleansed, on the thumb of their right hand and on the big toe of their right foot. ²⁹The rest of the oil in his palm the priest shall put on the head of the one to be cleansed, to make atonement for them before the LORD. ³⁰Then he shall sacrifice the doves or the young pigeons, such as the person can afford, ³¹one as a sin offering and the other as a burnt offering, together with the grain offering. In this way the priest will make atonement before the LORD on behalf of the one to be cleansed."

³²These are the regulations for anyone who has a defiling skin disease and who cannot afford the regular offerings for their cleansing.

Cleansing From Defiling Molds

³³The LORD said to Moses and Aaron, ³⁴"When you enter the land of Canaan, which I am giving you as your possession, and I put a spreading mold in a house in that land, ³⁵the owner of the house must go and tell the priest, 'I have seen something that looks like a defiling mold in my house.' ³⁶The priest is to order the house to be emptied before he goes in to examine the mold, so that nothing in the house will be pronounced unclean. After this the priest is to go in and inspect the house. ³⁷He is to examine the mold on the walls, and if it has greenish or reddish depressions that appear to be deeper than the surface of the wall, ³⁸the priest shall go out the doorway of the house and close it up for seven days. ³⁹On the seventh day the priest shall return to inspect the house. If the mold has spread on the walls, ⁴⁰he is to order that the contaminated stones be torn out and thrown into an unclean place outside the town. ⁴¹He must have all the inside walls of the house scraped and the material that is scraped off dumped into an unclean place outside the town. ⁴²Then they are to take other stones to replace these and take new clay and plaster the house.

⁴³"If the defiling mold reappears in the house after the stones have been torn out and the house scraped and plastered, ⁴⁴the priest is to go and examine it and, if the mold has spread in the house, it is a persistent defiling mold; the house is unclean. ⁴⁵It must be torn down—its stones, timbers and all the plaster—and taken out of the town to an unclean place.

⁴⁶"Anyone who goes into the house while it is closed up will be unclean till evening. ⁴⁷Anyone who sleeps or eats in the house must wash their clothes.

⁴⁸"But if the priest comes to examine it and the mold has not spread after the house has been plastered, he shall pronounce the house clean, because the defiling mold is gone. ⁴⁹To purify the house he is to take two birds and some cedar wood, scarlet yarn and hyssop. ⁵⁰He shall kill one of the birds over fresh water in a clay pot. ⁵¹Then he is to take the cedar wood, the hyssop, the scarlet yarn and the live bird, dip them into the blood of the dead bird and the fresh water, and sprin-

a 21 That is, probably about 3 1/2 pounds or about 1.6 kilograms kle the house seven times. ⁵²He shall purify the house with the bird's blood, the fresh water, the live bird, the cedar wood, the hyssop and the scarlet yarn. ⁵³Then he is to release the live bird in the open fields outside the town. In this way he will make atonement for the house, and it will be clean."

⁵⁴These are the regulations for any defiling skin disease, for a sore, ⁵⁵for defiling molds in fabric or in a house, ⁵⁶and for a swelling, a rash or a shiny spot, ⁵⁷to determine when something is clean or unclean.

These are the regulations for defiling skin diseases and defiling molds.

Discharges Causing Uncleanness

15 The LORD said to Moses and Aaron, ²"Speak to the Israelites and say to them: 'When any man has an unusual bodily discharge, such a discharge is unclean. ³Whether it continues flowing from his body or is blocked, it will make him unclean. This is how his discharge will bring about uncleanness:

⁴" 'Any bed the man with a discharge lies on will be unclean, and anything he sits on will be unclean. ⁵Anyone who touches his bed must wash their clothes and bathe with water, and they will be unclean till evening. ⁶Whoever sits on anything that the man with a discharge sat on must wash their clothes and bathe with water, and they will be unclean till evening.

⁷" 'Whoever touches the man who has a discharge must wash their clothes and bathe with water, and they will be unclean till evening.

⁸" 'If the man with the discharge spits on anyone who is clean, they must wash their clothes and bathe with water, and they will be unclean till evening.

⁹" 'Everything the man sits on when riding will be unclean, ¹⁰and whoever touches any of the things that were under him will be unclean till evening; whoever picks up those things must wash their clothes and bathe with water, and they will be unclean till evening.

¹¹" 'Anyone the man with a discharge touches without rinsing his hands with water must wash their clothes and bathe with water, and they will be unclean till evening.

¹²" 'A clay pot that the man touches must

be broken, and any wooden article is to be rinsed with water.

¹³" 'When a man is cleansed from his discharge, he is to count off seven days for his ceremonial cleansing; he must wash his clothes and bathe himself with fresh water, and he will be clean. ¹⁴On the eighth day he must take two doves or two young pigeons and come before the LORD to the entrance to the tent of meeting and give them to the priest. ¹⁵The priest is to sacrifice them, the one for a sin offering*a* and the other for a burnt offering. In this way he will make atonement before the LORD for the man because of his discharge.

¹⁶" 'When a man has an emission of semen, he must bathe his whole body with water, and he will be unclean till evening. ¹⁷Any clothing or leather that has semen on it must be washed with water, and it will be unclean till evening. ¹⁸When a man has sexual relations with a woman and there is an emission of semen, both of them must bathe with water, and they will be unclean till evening.

¹⁹" 'When a woman has her regular flow of blood, the impurity of her monthly period will last seven days, and anyone who touches her will be unclean till evening.

²⁰" 'Anything she lies on during her period will be unclean, and anything she sits on will be unclean. ²¹Anyone who touches her bed will be unclean; they must wash their clothes and bathe with water, and they will be unclean till evening. ²²Anyone who touches anything she sits on will be unclean; they must wash their clothes and bathe with water, and they will be unclean till evening. ²³Whether it is the bed or anything she was sitting on, anyone who touches it will be unclean till evening.

²⁴" 'If a man has sexual relations with her and her monthly flow touches him, he will be unclean for seven days; any bed he lies on will be unclean.

²⁵" 'When a woman has a discharge of blood for many days at a time other than her monthly period or has a discharge that continues beyond her period, she will be unclean as long as she has the discharge, just as in the days of her period. ²⁶Any bed she lies on while her discharge continues will be unclean, as is her bed during her monthly

period, and anything she sits on will be unclean, as during her period. ²⁷Anyone who touches them will be unclean; they must wash their clothes and bathe with water, and they will be unclean till evening.

²⁸ 'When she is cleansed from her discharge, she must count off seven days, and after that she will be ceremonially clean. ²⁹On the eighth day she must take two doves or two young pigeons and bring them to the priest at the entrance to the tent of meeting. ³⁰The priest is to sacrifice one for a sin offering and the other for a burnt offering. In this way he will make atonement for her before the LORD for the uncleanness of her discharge.

³¹ 'You must keep the Israelites separate from things that make them unclean, so they will not die in their uncleanness for defiling my dwelling place,ᵃ which is among them.' "

³²These are the regulations for a man with a discharge, for anyone made unclean by an emission of semen, ³³for a woman in her monthly period, for a man or a woman with a discharge, and for a man who has sexual relations with a woman who is ceremonially unclean.

The Day of Atonement

16 The LORD spoke to Moses after the death of the two sons of Aaron who died when they approached the LORD. ²The LORD said to Moses: "Tell your brother Aaron that he is not to come whenever he chooses into the Most Holy Place behind the curtain in front of the atonement cover on the ark, or else he will die. For I will appear in the cloud over the atonement cover.

³"This is how Aaron is to enter the Most Holy Place: He must first bring a young bull for a sin offeringᵇ and a ram for a burnt offering. ⁴He is to put on the sacred linen tunic, with linen undergarments next to his body; he is to tie the linen sash around him and put on the linen turban. These are sacred garments; so he must bathe himself with water before he puts them on. ⁵From the Israelite community he is to take two male goats for a sin offering and a ram for a burnt offering.

⁶"Aaron is to offer the bull for his own sin offering to make atonement for himself and his household. ⁷Then he is to take the two goats and present them before the LORD at the entrance to the tent of meeting. ⁸He is to cast lots for the two goats—one lot for the LORD and the other for the scapegoat.ᶜ ⁹Aaron shall bring the goat whose lot falls to the LORD and sacrifice it for a sin offering. ¹⁰But the goat chosen by lot as the scapegoat shall be presented alive before the LORD to be used for making atonement by sending it into the wilderness as a scapegoat.

¹¹"Aaron shall bring the bull for his own sin offering to make atonement for himself and his household, and he is to slaughter the bull for his own sin offering. ¹²He is to take a censer full of burning coals from the altar before the LORD and two handfuls of finely ground fragrant incense and take them behind the curtain. ¹³He is to put the incense on the fire before the LORD, and the smoke of the incense will conceal the atonement cover above the tablets of the covenant law, so that he will not die. ¹⁴He is to take some of the bull's blood and with his finger sprinkle it on the front of the atonement cover; then he shall sprinkle some of it with his finger seven times before the atonement cover.

¹⁵"He shall then slaughter the goat for the sin offering for the people and take its blood behind the curtain and do with it as he did with the bull's blood: He shall sprinkle it on the atonement cover and in front of it. ¹⁶In this way he will make atonement for the Most Holy Place because of the uncleanness and rebellion of the Israelites, whatever their sins have been. He is to do the same for the tent of meeting, which is among them in the midst of their uncleanness. ¹⁷No one is to be in the tent of meeting from the time Aaron goes in to make atonement in the Most Holy Place until he comes out, having made atonement for himself, his household and the whole community of Israel.

¹⁸"Then he shall come out to the altar that is before the LORD and make atonement for it. He shall take some of the bull's blood and some of the goat's blood and put it on all the horns of the altar. ¹⁹He shall sprinkle

ᵃ 31 Or my tabernacle   ᵇ 3 Or purification offering; here and throughout this chapter   ᶜ 8 The meaning of the Hebrew for this word is uncertain; also in verses 10 and 26.

MONDAY

THE DAY OF ATONEMENT
Leviticus 16:1–34 *or* 16:6–10

THE EPISTLE OF BARNABAS {ca. AD 130}

[Rabbinic teachings gave further instructions, in addition to the Biblical text, regarding the scapegoat.] "Take a couple of goats, unblemished and well-matched; bring them for an offering and let the priest take one of them for a burnt offering." And what are they to do with the other? The other is to be declared accursed. "Spit on it, all of you; thrust your sticks into it, wreathe its head with scarlet wool, and so let it be driven out into the desert."

Once this is done, the animal is led into the desert, and the wool is taken off and left on the bush we call a bramble. Now what does that signify?

Notice that the first goat is for the altar, and the other is accursed; and that it is the accursed one that wears the wreath of scarlet wool. That is so the Israelites would one day see Jesus clad to the ankles in his red woolen robe, and say, "Is not this he whom we crucified, and mocked and pierced and spat upon? Yes, this is the man who told us that he was the Son of God."

Nick Harrison

What is forgiveness? . . .

Forgiveness is becoming aware of our anger toward someone, then choosing not to hold the offense against the person. It is deciding not to call up the memory of the offense, not to dwell on it, not to look for opportunities to take revenge.

In effect, this principle is illustrated in an event which took place annually in the life of Israel in the Old Testament. It was the tradition in those days to offer a ceremonial sacrifice by investing a "scapegoat" with all the wrongs done by the Israelites and then leading the animal into the wilderness. The scapegoat was taken to such a remote location that it would be impossible for it ever to rejoin the Israelite camp. This explains why the biblical word for forgiveness, used in both the Old and New Testaments, translates as "sending the offense away." In the New Testament this same principle is dramatically illustrated when Christ assumes the burden of human sin and makes the ultimate sacrifice of dying for our sin on the cross. He assures our forgiveness by taking our offenses away.

reflection

1. Why do you suppose sin matters so much to God?
2. How do you think it would feel to wait until the Day of Atonement (once a year) to find relief from your burden of sin?
3. What sins can Jesus, your scapegoat, relieve you of today?

For your next devotional reading, go to page 136.

some of the blood on it with his finger seven times to cleanse it and to consecrate it from the uncleanness of the Israelites.

²⁰"When Aaron has finished making atonement for the Most Holy Place, the tent of meeting and the altar, he shall bring forward the live goat. ²¹He is to lay both hands on the head of the live goat and confess over it all the wickedness and rebellion of the Israelites—all their sins—and put them on the goat's head. He shall send the goat away into the wilderness in the care of someone appointed for the task. ²²The goat will carry on itself all their sins to a remote place; and the man shall release it in the wilderness.

²³"Then Aaron is to go into the tent of meeting and take off the linen garments he put on before he entered the Most Holy Place, and he is to leave them there. ²⁴He shall bathe himself with water in the sanctuary area and put on his regular garments. Then he shall come out and sacrifice the burnt offering for himself and the burnt offering for the people, to make atonement for himself and for the people. ²⁵He shall also burn the fat of the sin offering on the altar.

²⁶"The one who releases the goat as a scapegoat must wash his clothes and bathe himself with water; afterward he may come into the camp. ²⁷The bull and the goat for the sin offerings, whose blood was brought into the Most Holy Place to make atonement, must be taken outside the camp; their hides, flesh and intestines are to be burned up. ²⁸The man who burns them must wash his clothes and bathe himself with water; afterward he may come into the camp.

²⁹"This is to be a lasting ordinance for you: On the tenth day of the seventh month you must deny yourselvesᵃ and not do any work—whether native-born or a foreigner residing among you— ³⁰because on this day atonement will be made for you, to cleanse you. Then, before the LORD, you will be clean from all your sins. ³¹It is a day of sabbath rest, and you must deny yourselves; it is a lasting ordinance. ³²The priest who is anointed and ordained to succeed his father as high priest is to make atonement. He is to put on the sacred linen garments ³³and make atonement for the Most Holy Place, for the tent of meeting and the altar, and for

the priests and all the members of the community. ³⁴"This is to be a lasting ordinance for you: Atonement is to be made once a year for all the sins of the Israelites."

And it was done, as the LORD commanded Moses.

Eating Blood Forbidden

17 The LORD said to Moses, ²"Speak to Aaron and his sons and to all the Israelites and say to them: 'This is what the LORD has commanded: ³Any Israelite who sacrifices an ox,ᵇ a lamb or a goat in the camp or outside of it ⁴instead of bringing it to the entrance to the tent of meeting to present it as an offering to the LORD in front of the tabernacle of the LORD—such persons shall be considered guilty of bloodshed; they have shed blood and must be cut off from their people. ⁵This is so the Israelites will bring to the LORD the sacrifices they are now making in the open fields. They must bring them to the priest, that is, to the LORD, at the entrance to the tent of meeting and sacrifice them as fellowship offerings. ⁶The priest is to splash the blood against the altar of the LORD at the entrance to the tent of meeting and burn the fat as an aroma pleasing to the LORD. ⁷They must no longer offer any of their sacrifices to the goat idolsᶜ to whom they prostitute themselves. This is to be a lasting ordinance for them and for the generations to come.'

⁸"Say to them: 'Any Israelite or any foreigner residing among them who offers a burnt offering or sacrifice ⁹and does not bring it to the entrance to the tent of meeting to sacrifice it to the LORD must be cut off from their people.

¹⁰" 'I will set my face against any Israelite or any foreigner residing among them who eats blood, and I will cut them off from their people. ¹¹For the life of a creature is in the blood, and I have given it to you to make atonement for yourselves on the altar; it is the blood that makes atonement for one's life.ᵈ ¹²Therefore I say to the Israelites, "None of you may eat blood, nor may any foreigner residing among you eat blood."

¹³" 'Any Israelite or any foreigner residing among you who hunts any animal or bird

---

ᵃ 29 Or must fast; also in verse 31   ᵇ 3 The Hebrew word can refer to either male or female.
ᶜ 7 Or the demons   ᵈ 11 Or atonement by the life in the blood

that may be eaten must drain out the blood and cover it with earth, ¹⁴because the life of every creature is its blood. That is why I have said to the Israelites, "You must not eat the blood of any creature, because the life of every creature is its blood; anyone who eats it must be cut off."

¹⁵" 'Anyone, whether native-born or foreigner, who eats anything found dead or torn by wild animals must wash their clothes and bathe with water, and they will be ceremonially unclean till evening; then they will be clean. ¹⁶But if they do not wash their clothes and bathe themselves, they will be held responsible.' "

Unlawful Sexual Relations

18 The LORD said to Moses, ²"Speak to the Israelites and say to them: 'I am the LORD your God. ³You must not do as they do in Egypt, where you used to live, and you must not do as they do in the land of Canaan, where I am bringing you. Do not follow their practices. ⁴You must obey my laws and be careful to follow my decrees. I am the LORD your God. ⁵Keep my decrees and laws, for whoever obeys them will live by them. I am the LORD.

⁶" 'No one is to approach any close relative to have sexual relations. I am the LORD.

⁷" 'Do not dishonor your father by having sexual relations with your mother. She is your mother; do not have relations with her.

⁸" 'Do not have sexual relations with your father's wife; that would dishonor your father.

⁹" 'Do not have sexual relations with your sister, either your father's daughter or your mother's daughter, whether she was born in the same home or elsewhere.

¹⁰" 'Do not have sexual relations with your son's daughter or your daughter's daughter; that would dishonor you.

¹¹" 'Do not have sexual relations with the daughter of your father's wife, born to your father; she is your sister.

¹²" 'Do not have sexual relations with your father's sister; she is your father's close relative.

¹³" 'Do not have sexual relations with your mother's sister, because she is your mother's close relative.

¹⁴" 'Do not dishonor your father's brother by approaching his wife to have sexual relations; she is your aunt.

¹⁵" 'Do not have sexual relations with your daughter-in-law. She is your son's wife; do not have relations with her.

¹⁶" 'Do not have sexual relations with your brother's wife; that would dishonor your brother.

¹⁷" 'Do not have sexual relations with both a woman and her daughter. Do not have sexual relations with either her son's daughter or her daughter's daughter; they are her close relatives. That is wickedness.

¹⁸" 'Do not take your wife's sister as a rival wife and have sexual relations with her while your wife is living.

¹⁹" 'Do not approach a woman to have sexual relations during the uncleanness of her monthly period.

²⁰" 'Do not have sexual relations with your neighbor's wife and defile yourself with her.

²¹" 'Do not give any of your children to be sacrificed to Molek, for you must not profane the name of your God. I am the LORD.

²²" 'Do not have sexual relations with a man as one does with a woman; that is detestable.

²³" 'Do not have sexual relations with an animal and defile yourself with it. A woman must not present herself to an animal to have sexual relations with it; that is a perversion.

²⁴" 'Do not defile yourselves in any of these ways, because this is how the nations that I am going to drive out before you became defiled. ²⁵Even the land was defiled; so I punished it for its sin, and the land vomited out its inhabitants. ²⁶But you must keep my decrees and my laws. The native-born and the foreigners residing among you must not do any of these detestable things, ²⁷for all these things were done by the people who lived in the land before you, and the land became defiled. ²⁸And if you defile the land, it will vomit you out as it vomited out the nations that were before you.

²⁹" 'Everyone who does any of these detestable things—such persons must be cut off from their people. ³⁰Keep my requirements and do not follow any of the detestable customs that were practiced before you came and do not defile yourselves with them. I am the LORD your God.' "

Various Laws

19 The LORD said to Moses, ²"Speak to the entire assembly of Israel and say to them: 'Be holy because I, the LORD your God, am holy.

³" 'Each of you must respect your mother and father, and you must observe my Sabbaths. I am the LORD your God.

⁴" 'Do not turn to idols or make metal gods for yourselves. I am the LORD your God.

⁵" 'When you sacrifice a fellowship offering to the LORD, sacrifice it in such a way that it will be accepted on your behalf. ⁶It shall be eaten on the day you sacrifice it or on the next day; anything left over until the third day must be burned up. ⁷If any of it is eaten on the third day, it is impure and will not be accepted. ⁸Whoever eats it will be held responsible because they have desecrated what is holy to the LORD; they must be cut off from their people.

⁹" 'When you reap the harvest of your land, do not reap to the very edges of your field or gather the gleanings of your harvest. ¹⁰Do not go over your vineyard a second time or pick up the grapes that have fallen. Leave them for the poor and the foreigner. I am the LORD your God.

¹¹" 'Do not steal.

" 'Do not lie.

" 'Do not deceive one another.

¹²" 'Do not swear falsely by my name and so profane the name of your God. I am the LORD.

¹³" 'Do not defraud your neighbors or rob them.

" 'Do not hold back the wages of a hired worker overnight.

¹⁴" 'Do not curse the deaf or put a stumbling block in front of the blind, but fear your God. I am the LORD.

¹⁵" 'Do not pervert justice; do not show partiality to the poor or favoritism to the great, but judge your neighbor fairly.

¹⁶" 'Do not go about spreading slander among your people.

" 'Do not do anything that endangers your neighbor's life. I am the LORD.

¹⁷" 'Do not hate a fellow Israelite in your heart. Rebuke your neighbor frankly so you will not share in their guilt.

¹⁸" 'Do not seek revenge or bear a grudge against anyone among your people, but love your neighbor as yourself. I am the LORD.

¹⁹" 'Keep my decrees.

" 'Do not mate different kinds of animals.

" 'Do not plant your field with two kinds of seed.

" 'Do not wear clothing woven of two kinds of material.

²⁰" 'If a man sleeps with a female slave who is promised to another man but who has not been ransomed or given her freedom, there must be due punishment.ᵃ Yet they are not to be put to death, because she had not been freed. ²¹The man, however, must bring a ram to the entrance to the tent of meeting for a guilt offering to the LORD. ²²With the ram of the guilt offering the priest is to make atonement for him before the LORD for the sin he has committed, and his sin will be forgiven.

²³" 'When you enter the land and plant any kind of fruit tree, regard its fruit as forbidden.ᵇ For three years you are to consider it forbiddenᵇ; it must not be eaten. ²⁴In the fourth year all its fruit will be holy, an offering of praise to the LORD. ²⁵But in the fifth year you may eat its fruit. In this way your harvest will be increased. I am the LORD your God.

²⁶" 'Do not eat any meat with the blood still in it.

" 'Do not practice divination or seek omens.

²⁷" 'Do not cut the hair at the sides of your head or clip off the edges of your beard.

²⁸" 'Do not cut your bodies for the dead or put tattoo marks on yourselves. I am the LORD.

²⁹" 'Do not degrade your daughter by making her a prostitute, or the land will turn to prostitution and be filled with wickedness.

³⁰" 'Observe my Sabbaths and have reverence for my sanctuary. I am the LORD.

³¹" 'Do not turn to mediums or seek out spiritists, for you will be defiled by them. I am the LORD your God.

³²" 'Stand up in the presence of the aged, show respect for the elderly and revere your God. I am the LORD.

³³" 'When foreigners reside among you in your land, do not mistreat them. ³⁴The foreigners residing among you must be treated

ᵃ 20 Or be an inquiry   ᵇ 23 Hebrew uncircumcised

TUESDAY

People Prejudice

Leviticus 19:1–37 *or* 19:33–34

Matthew Henry {AD 1662–1714}

People of all nations and races are welcome to God's grace. Therefore we should do what we can to invite them to it, and to help them form a good opinion of Christianity. When you are kind to foreigners (those of different nations and races), it indicates a generous character and a devoted respect for God as a common Father—for those of different countries, customs and languages are all made of one blood.

Jill Briscoe

Few of us would admit to being prejudiced. A dictionary defines prejudice as suspicion, intolerance or hatred of other races or creeds. This type of unfair judging goes against God's law in the Old Testament (Leviticus 19:15). It is also forbidden to the followers of Jesus (Matthew 7:1–2).

Consider the New Testament story of a man called Cornelius, who was a high-ranking Roman officer. Cornelius was "[devout and God-fearing]" (Acts 10:2). Honoring Cornelius's religious sincerity, God sent Peter to show him the way of salvation. But first God needed to deal with Peter's prejudice. You see, Peter, like all Jews in his time, would refuse to fellowship in the home or at table with a Gentile (that is, a non-Jew). So God used a Gentile soldier— the very type of person that Peter was prejudiced against—to teach Peter some important lessons! First, God calls no human being common or unclean and offers salvation to all (Acts 10:15,34–35). Second, if God isn't prejudiced, we certainly must not be. Peter was a man of principle, but his religious traditions were in danger of overshadowing the truth that is in Jesus.

Do you have "people prejudices"—even subtle ones? Prejudice can be a big barrier to our willingness to share the gospel with people who need it. Many, like Cornelius, have not rejected Jesus; they just haven't had an opportunity to receive him. Beware of prejudice!

reflection

1. It's time for some gut-level honesty: What "people prejudices" do *you* harbor?
2. With whom do you shy away from sharing the gospel?
3. In what ways do you isolate yourself from people who are different from you— either racially, economically, socially, intellectually, etc.?

For your next devotional reading, go to page 138.

as your native-born. Love them as yourself, for you were foreigners in Egypt. I am the LORD your God.

35" 'Do not use dishonest standards when measuring length, weight or quantity. 36Use honest scales and honest weights, an honest ephah*a* and an honest hin.*b* I am the LORD your God, who brought you out of Egypt.

37" 'Keep all my decrees and all my laws and follow them. I am the LORD.' "

Punishments for Sin

20 The LORD said to Moses, 2"Say to the Israelites: 'Any Israelite or any foreigner residing in Israel who sacrifices any of his children to Molek is to be put to death. The members of the community are to stone him. 3I myself will set my face against him and will cut him off from his people; for by sacrificing his children to Molek, he has defiled my sanctuary and profaned my holy name. 4If the members of the community close their eyes when that man sacrifices one of his children to Molek and if they fail to put him to death, 5I myself will set my face against him and his family and will cut them off from their people together with all who follow him in prostituting themselves to Molek.

6" 'I will set my face against anyone who turns to mediums and spiritists to prostitute themselves by following them, and I will cut them off from their people.

7" 'Consecrate yourselves and be holy, because I am the LORD your God. 8Keep my decrees and follow them. I am the LORD, who makes you holy.

9" 'Anyone who curses their father or mother is to be put to death. Because they have cursed their father or mother, their blood will be on their own head.

10" 'If a man commits adultery with another man's wife—with the wife of his neighbor—both the adulterer and the adulteress are to be put to death.

11" 'If a man has sexual relations with his father's wife, he has dishonored his father. Both the man and the woman are to be put to death; their blood will be on their own heads.

12" 'If a man has sexual relations with his daughter-in-law, both of them are to be put to death. What they have done is a perversion; their blood will be on their own heads.

13" 'If a man has sexual relations with a man as one does with a woman, both of them have done what is detestable. They are to be put to death; their blood will be on their own heads.

14" 'If a man marries both a woman and her mother, it is wicked. Both he and they must be burned in the fire, so that no wickedness will be among you.

15" 'If a man has sexual relations with an animal, he is to be put to death, and you must kill the animal.

16" 'If a woman approaches an animal to have sexual relations with it, kill both the woman and the animal. They are to be put to death; their blood will be on their own heads.

17" 'If a man marries his sister, the daughter of either his father or his mother, and they have sexual relations, it is a disgrace. They are to be publicly removed from their people. He has dishonored his sister and will be held responsible.

18" 'If a man has sexual relations with a woman during her monthly period, he has exposed the source of her flow, and she has also uncovered it. Both of them are to be cut off from their people.

19" 'Do not have sexual relations with the sister of either your mother or your father, for that would dishonor a close relative; both of you would be held responsible.

20" 'If a man has sexual relations with his aunt, he has dishonored his uncle. They will be held responsible; they will die childless.

21" 'If a man marries his brother's wife, it is an act of impurity; he has dishonored his brother. They will be childless.

22" 'Keep all my decrees and laws and follow them, so that the land where I am bringing you to live may not vomit you out. 23You must not live according to the customs of the nations I am going to drive out before you. Because they did all these things, I abhorred them. 24But I said to you, "You will possess their land; I will give it to you as an inheritance, a land flowing with milk and honey." I am the LORD your God, who has set you apart from the nations.

25" 'You must therefore make a distinction between clean and unclean animals

a 36 An ephah was a dry measure having the capacity of about 3/5 of a bushel or about 22 liters.
b 36 A hin was a liquid measure having the capacity of about 1 gallon or about 3.6 liters.

WEDNESDAY

TRUE HOLINESS

Leviticus 20:1–27 *or* 1:7,26

WILLIAM LONGSTAFF {AD 1822–1894}

Take time to be holy.
Speak oft with the Lord.
Abide in him always,
And feed on his Word.

Paul Enns

If you were to ask a man on the street, "What does it mean to be holy?" he would probably answer something like this: "A holy man is someone from India who wears white robes and a turban and sits cross-legged meditating all day." That, of course, is not what it means to be holy.

The Lord revealed Himself to Israel as a God who is holy, and as a holy God He demands holiness from His people. But what does it mean to be holy? Holy means "to set apart." His people are to be set apart from the world and set apart to God. When God called the Israelites as His people and established them as a nation, He commanded Moses, "Go to the people and consecrate them today and tomorrow. [Have them wash their clothes]" (Exodus 19:10). Washing clothes was a symbol of consecration and holiness . . . God also appointed a special priesthood to serve Him; even their garments were holy—they were set apart in service for Him ([Exodus] 28:2–5).

What does all that teach us? That God is a holy God. He is entirely set apart from His creation, and He demands that His people be set apart for fellowship with Him and separate from the world. Christians are called to be holy (1 Peter 1:16). What does that mean? It means that we are to guard our minds from impure thoughts; we should abandon our former lifestyle through which once flowed fleshly desires. It means that we are to love one another and declare God's excellencies in an unholy world.

Living a holy life [is] not an option. In a day when distinctions between Christians and non-Christians have become increasingly blurred, there is greater need than ever for Christians to take seriously our Lord's injunction: You shall be holy, for I am holy.

reflection

1. What are some behaviors Christians accept today that previous generations wouldn't have accepted?

2. What distinctions do you believe should exist between Christians and non-Christians?

3. Be honest: when you consider the enjoyable temptations in our world, how strongly do you want to be set apart from those things?

For your next devotional reading, go to page 144.

and between unclean and clean birds. Do not defile yourselves by any animal or bird or anything that moves along the ground—those which I have set apart as unclean for you. ²⁶You are to be holy to me because I, the LORD, am holy, and I have set you apart from the nations to be my own.

²⁷" 'A man or woman who is a medium or spiritist among you must be put to death. You are to stone them; their blood will be on their own heads.' "

Rules for Priests

21 The LORD said to Moses, "Speak to the priests, the sons of Aaron, and say to them: 'A priest must not make himself ceremonially unclean for any of his people who die, ²except for a close relative, such as his mother or father, his son or daughter, his brother, ³or an unmarried sister who is dependent on him since she has no husband—for her he may make himself unclean. ⁴He must not make himself unclean for people related to him by marriage,ᵃ and so defile himself.

⁵" 'Priests must not shave their heads or shave off the edges of their beards or cut their bodies. ⁶They must be holy to their God and must not profane the name of their God. Because they present the food offerings to the LORD, the food of their God, they are to be holy.

⁷" 'They must not marry women defiled by prostitution or divorced from their husbands, because priests are holy to their God. ⁸Regard them as holy, because they offer up the food of your God. Consider them holy, because I the LORD am holy—I who make you holy.

⁹" 'If a priest's daughter defiles herself by becoming a prostitute, she disgraces her father; she must be burned in the fire.

¹⁰" 'The high priest, the one among his brothers who has had the anointing oil poured on his head and who has been ordained to wear the priestly garments, must not let his hair become unkemptᵇ or tear his clothes. ¹¹He must not enter a place where there is a dead body. He must not make himself unclean, even for his father or mother, ¹²nor leave the sanctuary of his God or desecrate it, because he has been dedi-

cated by the anointing oil of his God. I am the LORD.

¹³" 'The woman he marries must be a virgin. ¹⁴He must not marry a widow, a divorced woman, or a woman defiled by prostitution, but only a virgin from his own people, ¹⁵so that he will not defile his offspring among his people. I am the LORD, who makes him holy.' "

¹⁶The LORD said to Moses, ¹⁷"Say to Aaron: 'For the generations to come none of your descendants who has a defect may come near to offer the food of his God. ¹⁸No man who has any defect may come near: no man who is blind or lame, disfigured or deformed; ¹⁹no man with a crippled foot or hand, ²⁰or who is a hunchback or a dwarf, or who has any eye defect, or who has festering or running sores or damaged testicles. ²¹No descendant of Aaron the priest who has any defect is to come near to present the food offerings to the LORD. He has a defect; he must not come near to offer the food of his God. ²²He may eat the most holy food of his God, as well as the holy food; ²³yet because of his defect, he must not go near the curtain or approach the altar, and so desecrate my sanctuary. I am the LORD, who makes them holy.' "

²⁴So Moses told this to Aaron and his sons and to all the Israelites.

22 The LORD said to Moses, ²"Tell Aaron and his sons to treat with respect the sacred offerings the Israelites consecrate to me, so they will not profane my holy name. I am the LORD.

³"Say to them: 'For the generations to come, if any of your descendants is ceremonially unclean and yet comes near the sacred offerings that the Israelites consecrate to the LORD, that person must be cut off from my presence. I am the LORD.

⁴" 'If a descendant of Aaron has a defiling skin diseaseᶜ or a bodily discharge, he may not eat the sacred offerings until he is cleansed. He will also be unclean if he touches something defiled by a corpse or by anyone who has an emission of semen, ⁵or if he touches any crawling thing that makes him unclean, or any person who makes him unclean, whatever the uncleanness may be. ⁶The one who touches any such thing will be

---

ᵃ 4 Or *unclean as a leader among his people*   ᵇ 10 Or *not uncover his head*   ᶜ 4 The Hebrew word for *defiling skin disease*, traditionally translated "leprosy," was used for various diseases affecting the skin.

unclean till evening. He must not eat any of the sacred offerings unless he has bathed himself with water. ⁷When the sun goes down, he will be clean, and after that he may eat the sacred offerings, for they are his food. ⁸He must not eat anything found dead or torn by wild animals, and so become unclean through it. I am the LORD.

⁹ 'The priests are to perform my service in such a way that they do not become guilty and die for treating it with contempt. I am the LORD, who makes them holy.

¹⁰ 'No one outside a priest's family may eat the sacred offering, nor may the guest of a priest or his hired worker eat it. ¹¹But if a priest buys a slave with money, or if slaves are born in his household, they may eat his food. ¹²If a priest's daughter marries anyone other than a priest, she may not eat any of the sacred contributions. ¹³But if a priest's daughter becomes a widow or is divorced, yet has no children, and she returns to live in her father's household as in her youth, she may eat of her father's food. No unauthorized person, however, may eat any of it.

¹⁴ 'Anyone who eats a sacred offering by mistake must make restitution to the priest for the offering and add a fifth of the value to it. ¹⁵The priests must not desecrate the sacred offerings the Israelites present to the LORD ¹⁶by allowing them to eat the sacred offerings and so bring upon them guilt requiring payment. I am the LORD, who makes them holy.' "

Unacceptable Sacrifices

¹⁷The LORD said to Moses, ¹⁸"Speak to Aaron and his sons and to all the Israelites and say to them: 'If any of you—whether an Israelite or a foreigner residing in Israel—presents a gift for a burnt offering to the LORD, either to fulfill a vow or as a freewill offering, ¹⁹you must present a male without defect from the cattle, sheep or goats in order that it may be accepted on your behalf. ²⁰Do not bring anything with a defect, because it will not be accepted on your behalf. ²¹When anyone brings from the herd or flock a fellowship offering to the LORD to fulfill a special vow or as a freewill offering, it must be without defect or blemish to be acceptable. ²²Do not offer to the LORD the blind, the injured or the maimed, or anything with

warts or festering or running sores. Do not place any of these on the altar as a food offering presented to the LORD. ²³You may, however, present as a freewill offering an oxᵃ or a sheep that is deformed or stunted, but it will not be accepted in fulfillment of a vow. ²⁴You must not offer to the LORD an animal whose testicles are bruised, crushed, torn or cut. You must not do this in your own land, ²⁵and you must not accept such animals from the hand of a foreigner and offer them as the food of your God. They will not be accepted on your behalf, because they are deformed and have defects.' "

²⁶The LORD said to Moses, ²⁷"When a calf, a lamb or a goat is born, it is to remain with its mother for seven days. From the eighth day on, it will be acceptable as a food offering presented to the LORD. ²⁸Do not slaughter a cow or a sheep and its young on the same day.

²⁹"When you sacrifice a thank offering to the LORD, sacrifice it in such a way that it will be accepted on your behalf. ³⁰It must be eaten that same day; leave none of it till morning. I am the LORD.

³¹"Keep my commands and follow them. I am the LORD. ³²Do not profane my holy name, for I must be acknowledged as holy by the Israelites. I am the LORD, who made you holy ³³and who brought you out of Egypt to be your God. I am the LORD."

23

The LORD said to Moses, ²"Speak to the Israelites and say to them: 'These are my appointed festivals, the appointed festivals of the LORD, which you are to proclaim as sacred assemblies.

The Sabbath

³" 'There are six days when you may work, but the seventh day is a day of sabbath rest, a day of sacred assembly. You are not to do any work; wherever you live, it is a sabbath to the LORD.

The Passover and the Festival of Unleavened Bread

⁴" 'These are the LORD's appointed festivals, the sacred assemblies you are to proclaim at their appointed times: ⁵The LORD's Passover begins at twilight on the fourteenth day of the first month. ⁶On the fif-

teenth day of that month the LORD's Festival of Unleavened Bread begins; for seven days you must eat bread made without yeast. ⁷On the first day hold a sacred assembly and do no regular work. ⁸For seven days present a food offering to the LORD. And on the seventh day hold a sacred assembly and do no regular work.' "

Offering the Firstfruits

⁹The LORD said to Moses, ¹⁰"Speak to the Israelites and say to them: 'When you enter the land I am going to give you and you reap its harvest, bring to the priest a sheaf of the first grain you harvest. ¹¹He is to wave the sheaf before the LORD so it will be accepted on your behalf; the priest is to wave it on the day after the Sabbath. ¹²On the day you wave the sheaf, you must sacrifice as a burnt offering to the LORD a lamb a year old without defect, ¹³together with its grain offering of two-tenths of an ephahᵃ of the finest flour mixed with olive oil—a food offering presented to the LORD, a pleasing aroma—and its drink offering of a quarter of a hinᵇ of wine. ¹⁴You must not eat any bread, or roasted or new grain, until the very day you bring this offering to your God. This is to be a lasting ordinance for the generations to come, wherever you live.

The Festival of Weeks

¹⁵" 'From the day after the Sabbath, the day you brought the sheaf of the wave offering, count off seven full weeks. ¹⁶Count off fifty days up to the day after the seventh Sabbath, and then present an offering of new grain to the LORD. ¹⁷From wherever you live, bring two loaves made of two-tenths of an ephah of the finest flour, baked with yeast, as a wave offering of firstfruits to the LORD. ¹⁸Present with this bread seven male lambs, each a year old and without defect, one young bull and two rams. They will be a burnt offering to the LORD, together with their grain offerings and drink offerings—a food offering, an aroma pleasing to the LORD. ¹⁹Then sacrifice one male goat for a sin offeringᶜ and two lambs, each a year old, for a fellowship offering. ²⁰The priest is to wave the two lambs before the LORD as a wave offering, together with the bread of the

firstfruits. They are a sacred offering to the LORD for the priest. ²¹On that same day you are to proclaim a sacred assembly and do no regular work. This is to be a lasting ordinance for the generations to come, wherever you live.

²²" 'When you reap the harvest of your land, do not reap to the very edges of your field or gather the gleanings of your harvest. Leave them for the poor and for the foreigner residing among you. I am the LORD your God.' "

The Festival of Trumpets

²³The LORD said to Moses, ²⁴"Say to the Israelites: 'On the first day of the seventh month you are to have a day of sabbath rest, a sacred assembly commemorated with trumpet blasts. ²⁵Do no regular work, but present a food offering to the LORD.' "

The Day of Atonement

²⁶The LORD said to Moses, ²⁷"The tenth day of this seventh month is the Day of Atonement. Hold a sacred assembly and deny yourselves,ᵈ and present a food offering to the LORD. ²⁸Do not do any work on that day, because it is the Day of Atonement, when atonement is made for you before the LORD your God. ²⁹Those who do not deny themselves on that day must be cut off from their people. ³⁰I will destroy from among their people anyone who does any work on that day. ³¹You shall do no work at all. This is to be a lasting ordinance for the generations to come, wherever you live. ³²It is a day of sabbath rest for you, and you must deny yourselves. From the evening of the ninth day of the month until the following evening you are to observe your sabbath."

The Festival of Tabernacles

³³The LORD said to Moses, ³⁴"Say to the Israelites: 'On the fifteenth day of the seventh month the LORD's Festival of Tabernacles begins, and it lasts for seven days. ³⁵The first day is a sacred assembly; do no regular work. ³⁶For seven days present food offerings to the LORD, and on the eighth day hold a sacred assembly and present a food offer-

---

ᵃ 13 That is, probably about 7 pounds or about 3.2 kilograms; also in verse 17   ᵇ 13 That is, about 1 quart or about 0.9 liter   ᶜ 19 Or purification offering   ᵈ 27 Or and fast; also in verses 29 and 32 ing to the LORD. It is the closing special assembly; do no regular work.

37("'These are the LORD's appointed festivals, which you are to proclaim as sacred assemblies for bringing food offerings to the LORD—the burnt offerings and grain offerings, sacrifices and drink offerings required for each day. 38These offerings are in addition to those for the LORD's Sabbaths and*a* in addition to your gifts and whatever you have vowed and all the freewill offerings you give to the LORD.)

39" 'So beginning with the fifteenth day of the seventh month, after you have gathered the crops of the land, celebrate the festival to the LORD for seven days; the first day is a day of sabbath rest, and the eighth day also is a day of sabbath rest. 40On the first day you are to take branches from luxuriant trees—from palms, willows and other leafy trees—and rejoice before the LORD your God for seven days. 41Celebrate this as a festival to the LORD for seven days each year. This is to be a lasting ordinance for the generations to come; celebrate it in the seventh month. 42Live in temporary shelters for seven days: All native-born Israelites are to live in such shelters 43so your descendants will know that I had the Israelites live in temporary shelters when I brought them out of Egypt. I am the LORD your God.' "

44So Moses announced to the Israelites the appointed festivals of the LORD.

Oil and Bread Set Before the LORD

24 The LORD said to Moses, 2"Command the Israelites to bring you clear oil of pressed olives for the light so that the lamps may be kept burning continually. 3Outside the curtain that shields the ark of the covenant law in the tent of meeting, Aaron is to tend the lamps before the LORD from evening till morning, continually. This is to be a lasting ordinance for the generations to come. 4The lamps on the pure gold lampstand before the LORD must be tended continually.

5"Take the finest flour and bake twelve loaves of bread, using two-tenths of an ephah*b* for each loaf. 6Arrange them in two stacks, six in each stack, on the table of pure gold before the LORD. 7By each stack put some pure incense as a memorial*c* portion to represent the bread and to be a food offering presented to the LORD. 8This bread is to be set out before the LORD regularly, Sabbath after Sabbath, on behalf of the Israelites, as a lasting covenant. 9It belongs to Aaron and his sons, who are to eat it in the sanctuary area, because it is a most holy part of their perpetual share of the food offerings presented to the LORD."

A Blasphemer Stoned

10Now the son of an Israelite mother and an Egyptian father went out among the Israelites, and a fight broke out in the camp between him and an Israelite. 11The son of the Israelite woman blasphemed the Name with a curse; so they brought him to Moses. (His mother's name was Shelomith, the daughter of Dibri the Danite.) 12They put him in custody until the will of the LORD should be made clear to them.

13Then the LORD said to Moses: 14"Take the blasphemer outside the camp. All those who heard him are to lay their hands on his head, and the entire assembly is to stone him. 15Say to the Israelites: 'Anyone who curses their God will be held responsible; 16anyone who blasphemes the name of the LORD is to be put to death. The entire assembly must stone them. Whether foreigner or native-born, when they blaspheme the Name they are to be put to death.

17" 'Anyone who takes the life of a human being is to be put to death. 18Anyone who takes the life of someone's animal must make restitution—life for life. 19Anyone who injures a neighbor is to be injured in the same manner: 20fracture for fracture, eye for eye, tooth for tooth. The one who has inflicted the injury must suffer the same injury. 21Whoever kills an animal must make restitution, but whoever kills a human being is to be put to death. 22You are to have the same law for the foreigner and the native-born. I am the LORD your God.' "

23Then Moses spoke to the Israelites, and they took the blasphemer outside the camp and stoned him. The Israelites did as the LORD commanded Moses.

---

a 38 Or *These festivals are in addition to the LORD's Sabbaths, and these offerings are*   *b 5* That is, probably about 7 pounds or about 3.2 kilograms   *c 7* Or *representative*

The Sabbath Year

25 The Lord said to Moses on Mount Sinai, ²"Speak to the Israelites and say to them: 'When you enter the land I am going to give you, the land itself must observe a sabbath to the Lord. ³For six years sow your fields, and for six years prune your vineyards and gather their crops. ⁴But in the seventh year the land is to have a year of sabbath rest, a sabbath to the Lord. Do not sow your fields or prune your vineyards. ⁵Do not reap what grows of itself or harvest the grapes of your untended vines. The land is to have a year of rest. ⁶Whatever the land yields during the sabbath year will be food for you—for yourself, your male and female servants, and the hired worker and temporary resident who live among you, ⁷as well as for your livestock and the wild animals in your land. Whatever the land produces may be eaten.

The Year of Jubilee

⁸" 'Count off seven sabbath years—seven times seven years—so that the seven sabbath years amount to a period of forty-nine years. ⁹Then have the trumpet sounded everywhere on the tenth day of the seventh month; on the Day of Atonement sound the trumpet throughout your land. ¹⁰Consecrate the fiftieth year and proclaim liberty throughout the land to all its inhabitants. It shall be a jubilee for you; each of you is to return to your family property and to your own clan. ¹¹The fiftieth year shall be a jubilee for you; do not sow and do not reap what grows of itself or harvest the untended vines. ¹²For it is a jubilee and is to be holy for you; eat only what is taken directly from the fields.

¹³" 'In this Year of Jubilee everyone is to return to their own property.

¹⁴" 'If you sell land to any of your own people or buy land from them, do not take advantage of each other. ¹⁵You are to buy from your own people on the basis of the number of years since the Jubilee. And they are to sell to you on the basis of the number of years left for harvesting crops. ¹⁶When the years are many, you are to increase the price, and when the years are few, you are to decrease the price, because what is really being sold to you is the number of crops. ¹⁷Do not take advantage of each other, but fear your God. I am the Lord your God.

¹⁸" 'Follow my decrees and be careful to obey my laws, and you will live safely in the land. ¹⁹Then the land will yield its fruit, and you will eat your fill and live there in safety. ²⁰You may ask, "What will we eat in the seventh year if we do not plant or harvest our crops?" ²¹I will send you such a blessing in the sixth year that the land will yield enough for three years. ²²While you plant during the eighth year, you will eat from the old crop and will continue to eat from it until the harvest of the ninth year comes in.

²³" 'The land must not be sold permanently, because the land is mine and you reside in my land as foreigners and strangers. ²⁴Throughout the land that you hold as a possession, you must provide for the redemption of the land.

²⁵" 'If anyone among you becomes poor and sells some of their property, their nearest relative is to come and redeem what they have sold. ²⁶If, however, there is no one to redeem it for them but later on they prosper and acquire sufficient means to redeem it themselves, ²⁷they are to determine the value for the years since they sold it and refund the balance to the one to whom they sold it; they can then go back to their own property. ²⁸But if they do not acquire the means to repay, what was sold will remain in the possession of the buyer until the Year of Jubilee. It will be returned in the Jubilee, and they can then go back to their property.

²⁹" 'Anyone who sells a house in a walled city retains the right of redemption a full year after its sale. During that time the seller may redeem it. ³⁰If it is not redeemed before a full year has passed, the house in the walled city shall belong permanently to the buyer and the buyer's descendants. It is not to be returned in the Jubilee. ³¹But houses in villages without walls around them are to be considered as belonging to the open country. They can be redeemed, and they are to be returned in the Jubilee.

³²" 'The Levites always have the right to redeem their houses in the Levitical towns, which they possess. ³³So the property of the Levites is redeemable—that is, a house sold in any town they hold—and is to be returned in the Jubilee, because the houses in the towns of the Levites are their property among the Israelites. ³⁴But the pastureland belonging to their towns must not be sold; it is their permanent possession.

THURSDAY

THE JUBILEE

Leviticus 25:8–55 *or* 25:8–17

Gary Henry

In Israel, the priestly trumpets were to be blown on several important occasions. One of these was the onset of war . . . In this instance, the joyful sound would be that of *victory*.

Also, the trumpets were to be blown at various times of sacrifice . . . at these times, the people would rejoice to hear the sound of *worship*.

But there was another occasion also, and that was the Day of Jubilee, that great day every 50 years when slaves were released and debts were canceled . . . This trumpet-sounding might have been the most joyous of all. It was the welcome sound of *freedom*.

CHARLES WESLEY {AD 1707–1788}

Blow, blow the trumpet, blow!
The gladly solemn sound
Let all the nations know,
To earth's remotest bound:
The Year of Jubilee is come!
The Year of Jubilee is come!
Return, you ransomed sinners, home.

You slaves of sin and hell,
Your liberty receive,
And safe in Jesus dwell,
And blessed in Jesus live:
The Year of Jubilee is come!
The Year of Jubilee is come!
Return, you ransomed sinners, home.

Jesus, our great high priest,
Has full atonement made;
You weary spirits, rest;
You mournful souls, be glad:
The Year of Jubilee is come!
The Year of Jubilee is come!
Return, you ransomed sinners, home.

The gospel trumpet hear,
The news of heavenly grace;
And saved from earth, appear
Before your Savior's face:
The Year of Jubilee is come!
The Year of Jubilee is come!
Return, you ransomed sinners, home.

reflection

1. What made the Year of Jubilee special? What do you learn about God from this celebration?

2. What parallels can you draw between the Year of Jubilee and your future home in heaven?

3. How can you bring the spirit of Jubilee to someone you know who needs the freedom that Jesus brings?

For your next devotional reading, go to page 154.

³⁵" 'If any of your own people become poor and are unable to support themselves among you, help them as you would a foreigner and stranger, so they can continue to live among you. ³⁶Do not take interest or any profit from them, but fear your God, so that your poor neighbors may continue to live among you. ³⁷You must not lend them money at interest or sell them food at a profit. ³⁸I am the LORD your God, who brought you out of Egypt to give you the land of Canaan and to be your God.

³⁹" 'If any of your own people become poor and sell themselves to you, do not make them work as slaves. ⁴⁰They are to be treated as hired workers or temporary residents among you; they are to work for you until the Year of Jubilee. ⁴¹Then they and their children are to be released, and they will go back to their own clans and to the property of their ancestors. ⁴²Because the Israelites are my servants, whom I brought out of Egypt, they must not be sold as slaves. ⁴³Do not rule over them ruthlessly, but fear your God.

⁴⁴" 'Your male and female slaves are to come from the nations around you; from them you may buy slaves. ⁴⁵You may also buy some of the temporary residents living among you and members of their clans born in your country, and they will become your property. ⁴⁶You can bequeath them to your children as inherited property and can make them slaves for life, but you must not rule over your fellow Israelites ruthlessly.

⁴⁷" 'If a foreigner residing among you becomes rich and any of your own people become poor and sell themselves to the foreigner or to a member of the foreigner's clan, ⁴⁸they retain the right of redemption after they have sold themselves. One of their relatives may redeem them: ⁴⁹An uncle or a cousin or any blood relative in their clan may redeem them. Or if any of them prosper, they may redeem themselves. ⁵⁰They and their buyer are to count the time from the year they sold themselves up to the Year of Jubilee. The price for their release is to be based on the rate paid to a hired worker for that number of years. ⁵¹If many years remain, they must pay for their redemption a larger share of the price paid for them. ⁵²If only a few years remain until the Year of Ju-

bilee, they are to compute that and pay for their redemption accordingly. ⁵³They are to be treated as hired workers from year to year; you must see to it that those to whom they owe service do not rule over them ruthlessly.

⁵⁴" 'Even if they are not redeemed in any of these ways, they and their children are to be released in the Year of Jubilee, ⁵⁵for the Israelites belong to me as servants. They are my servants, whom I brought out of Egypt. I am the LORD your God.

Reward for Obedience

26 " 'Do not make idols or set up an image or a sacred stone for yourselves, and do not place a carved stone in your land to bow down before it. I am the LORD your God.

²" 'Observe my Sabbaths and have reverence for my sanctuary. I am the LORD.

³" 'If you follow my decrees and are careful to obey my commands, ⁴I will send you rain in its season, and the ground will yield its crops and the trees their fruit. ⁵Your threshing will continue until grape harvest and the grape harvest will continue until planting, and you will eat all the food you want and live in safety in your land.

⁶" 'I will grant peace in the land, and you will lie down and no one will make you afraid. I will remove wild beasts from the land, and the sword will not pass through your country. ⁷You will pursue your enemies, and they will fall by the sword before you. ⁸Five of you will chase a hundred, and a hundred of you will chase ten thousand, and your enemies will fall by the sword before you.

⁹" 'I will look on you with favor and make you fruitful and increase your numbers, and I will keep my covenant with you. ¹⁰You will still be eating last year's harvest when you will have to move it out to make room for the new. ¹¹I will put my dwelling place*ᵃ* among you, and I will not abhor you. ¹²I will walk among you and be your God, and you will be my people. ¹³I am the LORD your God, who brought you out of Egypt so that you would no longer be slaves to the Egyptians; I broke the bars of your yoke and enabled you to walk with heads held high.

a 11 Or my tabernacle

Punishment for Disobedience

¹⁴" 'But if you will not listen to me and carry out all these commands, ¹⁵and if you reject my decrees and abhor my laws and fail to carry out all my commands and so violate my covenant, ¹⁶then I will do this to you: I will bring on you sudden terror, wasting diseases and fever that will destroy your sight and sap your strength. You will plant seed in vain, because your enemies will eat it. ¹⁷I will set my face against you so that you will be defeated by your enemies; those who hate you will rule over you, and you will flee even when no one is pursuing you.

¹⁸" 'If after all this you will not listen to me, I will punish you for your sins seven times over. ¹⁹I will break down your stubborn pride and make the sky above you like iron and the ground beneath you like bronze. ²⁰Your strength will be spent in vain, because your soil will not yield its crops, nor will the trees of your land yield their fruit.

²¹" 'If you remain hostile toward me and refuse to listen to me, I will multiply your afflictions seven times over, as your sins deserve. ²²I will send wild animals against you, and they will rob you of your children, destroy your cattle and make you so few in number that your roads will be deserted.

²³" 'If in spite of these things you do not accept my correction but continue to be hostile toward me, ²⁴I myself will be hostile toward you and will afflict you for your sins seven times over. ²⁵And I will bring the sword on you to avenge the breaking of the covenant. When you withdraw into your cities, I will send a plague among you, and you will be given into enemy hands. ²⁶When I cut off your supply of bread, ten women will be able to bake your bread in one oven, and they will dole out the bread by weight. You will eat, but you will not be satisfied.

²⁷" 'If in spite of this you still do not listen to me but continue to be hostile toward me, ²⁸then in my anger I will be hostile toward you, and I myself will punish you for your sins seven times over. ²⁹You will eat the flesh of your sons and the flesh of your daughters. ³⁰I will destroy your high places, cut down your incense altars and pile your dead bodiesᵃ on the lifeless forms of your idols, and I will abhor you. ³¹I will turn your cities into ruins and lay waste your sanctu-

aries, and I will take no delight in the pleasing aroma of your offerings. ³²I myself will lay waste the land, so that your enemies who live there will be appalled. ³³I will scatter you among the nations and will draw out my sword and pursue you. Your land will be laid waste, and your cities will lie in ruins. ³⁴Then the land will enjoy its sabbath years all the time that it lies desolate and you are in the country of your enemies; then the land will rest and enjoy its sabbaths. ³⁵All the time that it lies desolate, the land will have the rest it did not have during the sabbaths you lived in it.

³⁶" 'As for those of you who are left, I will make their hearts so fearful in the lands of their enemies that the sound of a wind-blown leaf will put them to flight. They will run as though fleeing from the sword, and they will fall, even though no one is pursuing them. ³⁷They will stumble over one another as though fleeing from the sword, even though no one is pursuing them. So you will not be able to stand before your enemies. ³⁸You will perish among the nations; the land of your enemies will devour you. ³⁹Those of you who are left will waste away in the lands of their enemies because of their sins; also because of their ancestors' sins they will waste away.

⁴⁰" 'But if they will confess their sins and the sins of their ancestors—their unfaithfulness and their hostility toward me, ⁴¹which made me hostile toward them so that I sent them into the land of their enemies—then when their uncircumcised hearts are humbled and they pay for their sin, ⁴²I will remember my covenant with Jacob and my covenant with Isaac and my covenant with Abraham, and I will remember the land. ⁴³For the land will be deserted by them and will enjoy its sabbaths while it lies desolate without them. They will pay for their sins because they rejected my laws and abhorred my decrees. ⁴⁴Yet in spite of this, when they are in the land of their enemies, I will not reject them or abhor them so as to destroy them completely, breaking my covenant with them. I am the LORD their God. ⁴⁵But for their sake I will remember the covenant with their ancestors whom I brought out of Egypt in the sight of the nations to be their God. I am the LORD.' "

ᵃ 30 Or your funeral offerings

⁴⁶These are the decrees, the laws and the regulations that the LORD established on Mount Sinai between himself and the Israelites through Moses.

Redeeming What Is the LORD's

27 The LORD said to Moses, ²"Speak to the Israelites and say to them: 'If anyone makes a special vow to dedicate a person to the LORD by giving the equivalent value, ³set the value of a male between the ages of twenty and sixty at fifty shekels*ᵃ* of silver, according to the sanctuary shekel*ᵇ*; ⁴for a female, set her value at thirty shekels*ᶜ*; ⁵for a person between the ages of five and twenty, set the value of a male at twenty shekels*ᵈ* and of a female at ten shekels*ᵉ*; ⁶for a person between one month and five years, set the value of a male at five shekels*ᶠ* of silver and that of a female at three shekels*ᵍ* of silver; ⁷for a person sixty years old or more, set the value of a male at fifteen shekels*ʰ* and of a female at ten shekels. ⁸If anyone making the vow is too poor to pay the specified amount, the person being dedicated is to be presented to the priest, who will set the value according to what the one making the vow can afford.

⁹" 'If what anyone vowed is an animal that is acceptable as an offering to the LORD, such an animal given to the LORD becomes holy. ¹⁰They must not exchange it or substitute a good one for a bad one, or a bad one for a good one; if they should substitute one animal for another, both it and the substitute become holy. ¹¹If what they vowed is a ceremonially unclean animal—one that is not acceptable as an offering to the LORD—the animal must be presented to the priest, ¹²who will judge its quality as good or bad. Whatever value the priest then sets, that is what it will be. ¹³If the owner wishes to redeem the animal, a fifth must be added to its value.

¹⁴" 'If anyone dedicates their house as something holy to the LORD, the priest will judge its quality as good or bad. Whatever value the priest then sets, so it will remain.

¹⁵If the one who dedicates their house wishes to redeem it, they must add a fifth to its value, and the house will again become theirs.

¹⁶" 'If anyone dedicates to the LORD part of their family land, its value is to be set according to the amount of seed required for it—fifty shekels of silver to a homer*ⁱ* of barley seed. ¹⁷If they dedicate a field during the Year of Jubilee, the value that has been set remains. ¹⁸But if they dedicate a field after the Jubilee, the priest will determine the value according to the number of years that remain until the next Year of Jubilee, and its set value will be reduced. ¹⁹If the one who dedicates the field wishes to redeem it, they must add a fifth to its value, and the field will again become theirs. ²⁰If, however, they do not redeem the field, or if they have sold it to someone else, it can never be redeemed. ²¹When the field is released in the Jubilee, it will become holy, like a field devoted to the LORD; it will become priestly property.

²²" 'If anyone dedicates to the LORD a field they have bought, which is not part of their family land, ²³the priest will determine its value up to the Year of Jubilee, and that person must pay its value on that day as something holy to the LORD. ²⁴In the Year of Jubilee the field will revert to the person from whom it was bought, the one whose land it was. ²⁵Every value is to be set according to the sanctuary shekel, twenty gerahs to the shekel.

²⁶" 'No one, however, may dedicate the firstborn of an animal, since the firstborn already belongs to the LORD; whether an ox*ʲ* or a sheep, it is the LORD's. ²⁷If it is one of the unclean animals, it may be bought back at its set value, adding a fifth of the value to it. If it is not redeemed, it is to be sold at its set value.

²⁸" 'But nothing that a person owns and devotes*ᵏ* to the LORD—whether a human being or an animal or family land—may be sold or redeemed; everything so devoted is most holy to the LORD.

---

a 3 That is, about 1 1/4 pounds or about 575 grams; also in verse 16   *b 3* That is, about 2/5 ounce or about 11.5 grams; also in verse 25   *c 4* That is, about 12 ounces or about 345 grams   *d 5* That is, about 8 ounces or about 230 grams   *e 5* That is, about 4 ounces or about 115 grams; also in verse 7   *f 6* That is, about 2 ounces or about 55 grams   *g 6* That is, about 1 1/4 ounces or about 35 grams   *h 7* That is, about 6 ounces or about 170 grams   *i 16* That is, probably about 300 pounds or about 135 kilograms   *j 26* The Hebrew word can refer to either male or female.   *k 28* The Hebrew term refers to the irrevocable giving over of things or persons to the LORD.

²⁹" 'No persons devoted to destruction[a] may be ransomed; they are to be put to death.

³⁰" 'A tithe of everything from the land, whether grain from the soil or fruit from the trees, belongs to the LORD; it is holy to the LORD. ³¹Whoever would redeem any of their tithe must add a fifth of the value to it. ³²Every tithe of the herd and flock—every tenth animal that passes under the shepherd's rod—will be holy to the LORD. ³³No one may pick out the good from the bad or make any substitution. If anyone does make a substitution, both the animal and its substitute become holy and cannot be redeemed.' "

³⁴These are the commands the LORD gave Moses on Mount Sinai for the Israelites.

---

a 29 The Hebrew term refers to the irrevocable giving over of things or persons to the LORD, often by totally destroying them.

numbers

AUTHOR: Moses

DATE: During the 1400s B.C., while the Israelites were traveling in the desert

THEME: God has a plan. When we don't follow that plan, we lose our way.

The Census

1 The LORD spoke to Moses in the tent of meeting in the Desert of Sinai on the first day of the second month of the second year after the Israelites came out of Egypt. He said: 2"Take a census of the whole Israelite community by their clans and families, listing every man by name, one by one. 3You and Aaron are to count according to their divisions all the men in Israel who are twenty years old or more and able to serve in the army. 4One man from each tribe, each of them the head of his family, is to help you. 5These are the names of the men who are to assist you:

from Reuben, Elizur son of Shedeur;
6from Simeon, Shelumiel son of Zurishaddai;
7from Judah, Nahshon son of Amminadab;
8from Issachar, Nethanel son of Zuar;
9from Zebulun, Eliab son of Helon;
10from the sons of Joseph:
from Ephraim, Elishama son of Ammihud;
from Manasseh, Gamaliel son of Pedahzur;
11from Benjamin, Abidan son of Gideoni;
12from Dan, Ahiezer son of Ammishaddai;
13from Asher, Pagiel son of Okran;
14from Gad, Eliasaph son of Deuel;
15from Naphtali, Ahira son of Enan."

16These were the men appointed from the community, the leaders of their ancestral tribes. They were the heads of the clans of Israel.

17Moses and Aaron took these men whose names had been specified, 18and they called the whole community together on the first day of the second month. The people registered their ancestry by their clans and families, and the men twenty years old or more were listed by name, one by one, 19as the LORD commanded Moses. And so he counted them in the Desert of Sinai:

20From the descendants of Reuben the firstborn son of Israel:
All the men twenty years old or more who were able to serve in the army were listed by name, one by one, according to the records of their clans and families. 21The number from the tribe of Reuben was 46,500.

22From the descendants of Simeon:
All the men twenty years old or more who were able to serve in the army were counted and listed by name, one by one, according to the records of their clans and families. 23The number from the tribe of Simeon was 59,300.

24From the descendants of Gad:
All the men twenty years old or more who were able to serve in the army were listed by name, according to the records of their clans and families. 25The number from the tribe of Gad was 45,650.

26From the descendants of Judah:
All the men twenty years old or more who were able to serve in the army were listed by name, according to the records of their clans and families. 27The number from the tribe of Judah was 74,600.

28From the descendants of Issachar:
All the men twenty years old or more

who were able to serve in the army were listed by name, according to the records of their clans and families. ²⁹The number from the tribe of Issachar was 54,400.

³⁰From the descendants of Zebulun:
All the men twenty years old or more who were able to serve in the army were listed by name, according to the records of their clans and families. ³¹The number from the tribe of Zebulun was 57,400.

³²From the sons of Joseph:
From the descendants of Ephraim:
All the men twenty years old or more who were able to serve in the army were listed by name, according to the records of their clans and families. ³³The number from the tribe of Ephraim was 40,500.

³⁴From the descendants of Manasseh:
All the men twenty years old or more who were able to serve in the army were listed by name, according to the records of their clans and families. ³⁵The number from the tribe of Manasseh was 32,200.

³⁶From the descendants of Benjamin:
All the men twenty years old or more who were able to serve in the army were listed by name, according to the records of their clans and families. ³⁷The number from the tribe of Benjamin was 35,400.

³⁸From the descendants of Dan:
All the men twenty years old or more who were able to serve in the army were listed by name, according to the records of their clans and families. ³⁹The number from the tribe of Dan was 62,700.

⁴⁰From the descendants of Asher:
All the men twenty years old or more who were able to serve in the army were listed by name, according to the records of their clans and families. ⁴¹The number from the tribe of Asher was 41,500.

⁴²From the descendants of Naphtali:
All the men twenty years old or more who were able to serve in the army were listed by name, according to

the records of their clans and families. ⁴³The number from the tribe of Naphtali was 53,400.

⁴⁴These were the men counted by Moses and Aaron and the twelve leaders of Israel, each one representing his family. ⁴⁵All the Israelites twenty years old or more who were able to serve in Israel's army were counted according to their families. ⁴⁶The total number was 603,550.

⁴⁷The ancestral tribe of the Levites, however, was not counted along with the others. ⁴⁸The LORD had said to Moses: ⁴⁹"You must not count the tribe of Levi or include them in the census of the other Israelites. ⁵⁰Instead, appoint the Levites to be in charge of the tabernacle of the covenant law—over all its furnishings and everything belonging to it. They are to carry the tabernacle and all its furnishings; they are to take care of it and encamp around it. ⁵¹Whenever the tabernacle is to move, the Levites are to take it down, and whenever the tabernacle is to be set up, the Levites shall do it. Anyone else who approaches it is to be put to death. ⁵²The Israelites are to set up their tents by divisions, each of them in their own camp under their standard. ⁵³The Levites, however, are to set up their tents around the tabernacle of the covenant law so that my wrath will not fall on the Israelite community. The Levites are to be responsible for the care of the tabernacle of the covenant law."

⁵⁴The Israelites did all this just as the LORD commanded Moses.

The Arrangement of the Tribal Camps

2 The LORD said to Moses and Aaron: ²"The Israelites are to camp around the tent of meeting some distance from it, each of them under their standard and holding the banners of their family."

³On the east, toward the sunrise, the divisions of the camp of Judah are to encamp under their standard. The leader of the people of Judah is Nahshon son of Amminadab. ⁴His division numbers 74,600.

⁵The tribe of Issachar will camp next to them. The leader of the people of Issachar is Nethanel son of Zuar. ⁶His division numbers 54,400.

⁷The tribe of Zebulun will be next. The leader of the people of Zebulun is

Eliab son of Helon. ⁸His division numbers 57,400.

⁹All the men assigned to the camp of Judah, according to their divisions, number 186,400. They will set out first.

¹⁰On the south will be the divisions of the camp of Reuben under their standard. The leader of the people of Reuben is Elizur son of Shedeur. ¹¹His division numbers 46,500.

¹²The tribe of Simeon will camp next to them. The leader of the people of Simeon is Shelumiel son of Zurishaddai. ¹³His division numbers 59,300.

¹⁴The tribe of Gad will be next. The leader of the people of Gad is Eliasaph son of Deuel.ᵃ ¹⁵His division numbers 45,650.

¹⁶All the men assigned to the camp of Reuben, according to their divisions, number 151,450. They will set out second.

¹⁷Then the tent of meeting and the camp of the Levites will set out in the middle of the camps. They will set out in the same order as they encamp, each in their own place under their standard.

¹⁸On the west will be the divisions of the camp of Ephraim under their standard. The leader of the people of Ephraim is Elishama son of Ammihud. ¹⁹His division numbers 40,500.

²⁰The tribe of Manasseh will be next to them. The leader of the people of Manasseh is Gamaliel son of Pedahzur. ²¹His division numbers 32,200.

²²The tribe of Benjamin will be next. The leader of the people of Benjamin is Abidan son of Gideoni. ²³His division numbers 35,400.

²⁴All the men assigned to the camp of Ephraim, according to their divisions, number 108,100. They will set out third.

²⁵On the north will be the divisions of the camp of Dan under their standard. The leader of the people of Dan is Ahiezer son of Ammishaddai. ²⁶His division numbers 62,700.

²⁷The tribe of Asher will camp next to them. The leader of the people of Asher is Pagiel son of Okran. ²⁸His division numbers 41,500.

²⁹The tribe of Naphtali will be next. The leader of the people of Naphtali is Ahira son of Enan. ³⁰His division numbers 53,400.

³¹All the men assigned to the camp of Dan number 157,600. They will set out last, under their standards.

³²These are the Israelites, counted according to their families. All the men in the camps, by their divisions, number 603,550. ³³The Levites, however, were not counted along with the other Israelites, as the LORD commanded Moses.

³⁴So the Israelites did everything the LORD commanded Moses; that is the way they encamped under their standards, and that is the way they set out, each of them with their clan and family.

The Levites

3 This is the account of the family of Aaron and Moses at the time the LORD spoke to Moses on Mount Sinai.

²The names of the sons of Aaron were Nadab the firstborn and Abihu, Eleazar and Ithamar. ³Those were the names of Aaron's sons, the anointed priests, who were ordained to serve as priests. ⁴Nadab and Abihu, however, died before the LORD when they made an offering with unauthorized fire before him in the Desert of Sinai. They had no sons, so Eleazar and Ithamar served as priests during the lifetime of their father Aaron.

⁵The LORD said to Moses, ⁶"Bring the tribe of Levi and present them to Aaron the priest to assist him. ⁷They are to perform duties for him and for the whole community at the tent of meeting by doing the work of the tabernacle. ⁸They are to take care of all the furnishings of the tent of meeting, fulfilling the obligations of the Israelites by doing the work of the tabernacle. ⁹Give the Levites to Aaron and his sons; they are the Israelites who are to be given wholly to him.ᵇ ¹⁰Appoint Aaron and his sons to serve as priests;

---

a 14 Many manuscripts of the Masoretic Text, Samaritan Pentateuch and Vulgate (see also Num. 1:14); most manuscripts of the Masoretic Text *Reuel*   *b 9* Most manuscripts of the Masoretic Text; some manuscripts of the Masoretic Text, Samaritan Pentateuch and Septuagint (see also Num. 8:16) *to me* anyone else who approaches the sanctuary is to be put to death."

[11] The LORD also said to Moses, [12] "I have taken the Levites from among the Israelites in place of the first male offspring of every Israelite woman. The Levites are mine, [13] for all the firstborn are mine. When I struck down all the firstborn in Egypt, I set apart for myself every firstborn in Israel, whether human or animal. They are to be mine. I am the LORD."

[14] The LORD said to Moses in the Desert of Sinai, [15] "Count the Levites by their families and clans. Count every male a month old or more." [16] So Moses counted them, as he was commanded by the word of the LORD.

[17] These were the names of the sons of Levi:

Gershon, Kohath and Merari.

[18] These were the names of the Gershonite clans:

Libni and Shimei.

[19] The Kohathite clans:

Amram, Izhar, Hebron and Uzziel.

[20] The Merarite clans:

Mahli and Mushi.

These were the Levite clans, according to their families.

[21] To Gershon belonged the clans of the Libnites and Shimeites; these were the Gershonite clans. [22] The number of all the males a month old or more who were counted was 7,500. [23] The Gershonite clans were to camp on the west, behind the tabernacle. [24] The leader of the families of the Gershonites was Eliasaph son of Lael. [25] At the tent of meeting the Gershonites were responsible for the care of the tabernacle and tent, its coverings, the curtain at the entrance to the tent of meeting, [26] the curtains of the courtyard, the curtain at the entrance to the courtyard surrounding the tabernacle and altar, and the ropes—and everything related to their use.

[27] To Kohath belonged the clans of the Amramites, Izharites, Hebronites and Uzzielites; these were the Kohathite clans. [28] The number of all the males a month old or more was 8,600.[a] The Kohathites were responsible for the care of the sanctuary. [29] The Kohathite clans were to camp on the

south side of the tabernacle. [30] The leader of the families of the Kohathite clans was Elizaphan son of Uzziel. [31] They were responsible for the care of the ark, the table, the lampstand, the altars, the articles of the sanctuary used in ministering, the curtain, and everything related to their use. [32] The chief leader of the Levites was Eleazar son of Aaron, the priest. He was appointed over those who were responsible for the care of the sanctuary.

[33] To Merari belonged the clans of the Mahlites and the Mushites; these were the Merarite clans. [34] The number of all the males a month old or more who were counted was 6,200. [35] The leader of the families of the Merarite clans was Zuriel son of Abihail; they were to camp on the north side of the tabernacle. [36] The Merarites were appointed to take care of the frames of the tabernacle, its crossbars, posts, bases, all its equipment, and everything related to their use, [37] as well as the posts of the surrounding courtyard with their bases, tent pegs and ropes.

[38] Moses and Aaron and his sons were to camp to the east of the tabernacle, toward the sunrise, in front of the tent of meeting. They were responsible for the care of the sanctuary on behalf of the Israelites. Anyone else who approached the sanctuary was to be put to death.

[39] The total number of Levites counted at the LORD's command by Moses and Aaron according to their clans, including every male a month old or more, was 22,000.

[40] The LORD said to Moses, "Count all the firstborn Israelite males who are a month old or more and make a list of their names. [41] Take the Levites for me in place of all the firstborn of the Israelites, and the livestock of the Levites in place of all the firstborn of the livestock of the Israelites. I am the LORD."

[42] So Moses counted all the firstborn of the Israelites, as the LORD commanded him. [43] The total number of firstborn males a month old or more, listed by name, was 22,273.

[44] The LORD also said to Moses, [45] "Take

a 28 Hebrew; some Septuagint manuscripts 8,300

the Levites in place of all the firstborn of Israel, and the livestock of the Levites in place of their livestock. The Levites are to be mine. I am the LORD. ⁴⁶To redeem the 273 firstborn Israelites who exceed the number of the Levites, ⁴⁷collect five shekels[a] for each one, according to the sanctuary shekel, which weighs twenty gerahs. ⁴⁸Give the money for the redemption of the additional Israelites to Aaron and his sons."

⁴⁹So Moses collected the redemption money from those who exceeded the number redeemed by the Levites. ⁵⁰From the firstborn of the Israelites he collected silver weighing 1,365 shekels,[b] according to the sanctuary shekel. ⁵¹Moses gave the redemption money to Aaron and his sons, as he was commanded by the word of the LORD.

The Kohathites

4 The LORD said to Moses and Aaron: ²"Take a census of the Kohathite branch of the Levites by their clans and families. ³Count all the men from thirty to fifty years of age who come to serve in the work at the tent of meeting.

⁴"This is the work of the Kohathites at the tent of meeting: the care of the most holy things. ⁵When the camp is to move, Aaron and his sons are to go in and take down the shielding curtain and put it over the ark of the covenant law. ⁶Then they are to cover the curtain with a durable leather,[c] spread a cloth of solid blue over that and put the poles in place.

⁷"Over the table of the Presence they are to spread a blue cloth and put on it the plates, dishes and bowls, and the jars for drink offerings; the bread that is continually there is to remain on it. ⁸They are to spread a scarlet cloth over them, cover that with the durable leather and put the poles in place.

⁹"They are to take a blue cloth and cover the lampstand that is for light, together with its lamps, its wick trimmers and trays, and all its jars for the olive oil used to supply it. ¹⁰Then they are to wrap it and all its accessories in a covering of the durable leather and put it on a carrying frame.

¹¹"Over the gold altar they are to spread a blue cloth and cover that with the durable leather and put the poles in place.

¹²"They are to take all the articles used for ministering in the sanctuary, wrap them in a blue cloth, cover that with the durable leather and put them on a carrying frame.

¹³"They are to remove the ashes from the bronze altar and spread a purple cloth over it. ¹⁴Then they are to place on it all the utensils used for ministering at the altar, including the firepans, meat forks, shovels and sprinkling bowls. Over it they are to spread a covering of the durable leather and put the poles in place.

¹⁵"After Aaron and his sons have finished covering the holy furnishings and all the holy articles, and when the camp is ready to move, only then are the Kohathites to come and do the carrying. But they must not touch the holy things or they will die. The Kohathites are to carry those things that are in the tent of meeting.

¹⁶"Eleazar son of Aaron, the priest, is to have charge of the oil for the light, the fragrant incense, the regular grain offering and the anointing oil. He is to be in charge of the entire tabernacle and everything in it, including its holy furnishings and articles."

¹⁷The LORD said to Moses and Aaron, ¹⁸"See that the Kohathite tribal clans are not destroyed from among the Levites. ¹⁹So that they may live and not die when they come near the most holy things, do this for them: Aaron and his sons are to go into the sanctuary and assign to each man his work and what he is to carry. ²⁰But the Kohathites must not go in to look at the holy things, even for a moment, or they will die."

The Gershonites

²¹The LORD said to Moses, ²²"Take a census also of the Gershonites by their families and clans. ²³Count all the men from thirty to fifty years of age who come to serve in the work at the tent of meeting.

²⁴"This is the service of the Gershonite clans in their carrying and their other work: ²⁵They are to carry the curtains of the tabernacle, that is, the tent of meeting, its covering and its outer covering of durable leather, the curtains for the entrance to the tent of meeting, ²⁶the curtains of the courtyard sur-

---

a 47 That is, about 2 ounces or about 55 grams   b 50 That is, about 35 pounds or about 16 kilograms
c 6 Possibly the hides of dugongs; also in verses 8, 10, 11, 12, 14 and 25

FRIDAY

ACCEPTING GOD'S ASSIGNMENT

Numbers 4:1–20 *or* 4:4–5,15

Jill Briscoe

How many people does it take to run a large church? It took 8,580 Levites (Numbers 4:47–48) to care for and carry the tabernacle under the direction of Aaron and his sons, whom God had put in charge. Aaron and his sons prepared the holy things to be moved when God said so, and then the Kohathites came to do the carrying.

Two generations later, Korah, Kohath's grandson (Numbers 16:1), and others of his peers became insolent and incited a rebellion along with 250 community leaders. They wanted to be in charge, to be the leaders, the priests, not the grunt workers (Numbers 16:1–10). Being in charge looked like so much more fun than being called to carry! Moses reminded them, "[Isn't it enough for you that the God of Israel has separated you from the rest of the Israelite community and brought you near himself to do the work at the LORD's tabernacle?]" (Numbers 16:9). But they wanted more. God punished their insolence and rebellion with death (Numbers 16:16–35).

There is great joy in accepting the place God has assigned us among his people. Paul tells us in the New Testament that confusion and divisions come when we write our own job descriptions (1 Corinthians 12:4–31). A sense of contentment and belonging comes when we discover our niche. No ministry should be seen as a small thing, for God has given a special ministry only to you. Have you been "called to carry"? Then carry with joy and pride. For God chose you for that special task.

BROTHER LAWRENCE {AD 1605–1691}

We can do little things for God: I turn the cake that is frying on the pan, for love of him; and that done, if there is nothing else to call me, I prostrate myself in worship before him who has given me grace to work; afterwards I rise happier than a king.

reflection

1. Why do we want to do "big" things for God instead of the "small" things?

2. What happens in the church—in God's kingdom—if no one is willing to do the little things?

3. In what ways are the little things we do as valuable as the big things?

For your next devotional reading, go to page 157.

rounding the tabernacle and altar, the curtain for the entrance to the courtyard, the ropes and all the equipment used in the service of the tent. The Gershonites are to do all that needs to be done with these things. ²⁷All their service, whether carrying or doing other work, is to be done under the direction of Aaron and his sons. You shall assign to them as their responsibility all they are to carry. ²⁸This is the service of the Gershonite clans at the tent of meeting. Their duties are to be under the direction of Ithamar son of Aaron, the priest.

The Merarites

²⁹"Count the Merarites by their clans and families. ³⁰Count all the men from thirty to fifty years of age who come to serve in the work at the tent of meeting. ³¹As part of all their service at the tent, they are to carry the frames of the tabernacle, its crossbars, posts and bases, ³²as well as the posts of the surrounding courtyard with their bases, tent pegs, ropes, all their equipment and everything related to their use. Assign to each man the specific things he is to carry. ³³This is the service of the Merarite clans as they work at the tent of meeting under the direction of Ithamar son of Aaron, the priest."

The Numbering of the Levite Clans

³⁴Moses, Aaron and the leaders of the community counted the Kohathites by their clans and families. ³⁵All the men from thirty to fifty years of age who came to serve in the work at the tent of meeting, ³⁶counted by clans, were 2,750. ³⁷This was the total of all those in the Kohathite clans who served at the tent of meeting. Moses and Aaron counted them according to the LORD's command through Moses.

³⁸The Gershonites were counted by their clans and families. ³⁹All the men from thirty to fifty years of age who came to serve in the work at the tent of meeting, ⁴⁰counted by their clans and families, were 2,630. ⁴¹This was the total of those in the Gershonite clans who served at the tent of meeting. Moses and Aaron counted them according to the LORD's command.

⁴²The Merarites were counted by their clans and families. ⁴³All the men from thirty

to fifty years of age who came to serve in the work at the tent of meeting, ⁴⁴counted by their clans, were 3,200. ⁴⁵This was the total of those in the Merarite clans. Moses and Aaron counted them according to the LORD's command through Moses.

⁴⁶So Moses, Aaron and the leaders of Israel counted all the Levites by their clans and families. ⁴⁷All the men from thirty to fifty years of age who came to do the work of serving and carrying the tent of meeting ⁴⁸numbered 8,580. ⁴⁹At the LORD's command through Moses, each was assigned his work and told what to carry.

Thus they were counted, as the LORD commanded Moses.

The Purity of the Camp

5 The LORD said to Moses, ²"Command the Israelites to send away from the camp anyone who has a defiling skin diseaseᵃ or a discharge of any kind, or who is ceremonially unclean because of a dead body. ³Send away male and female alike; send them outside the camp so they will not defile their camp, where I dwell among them." ⁴The Israelites did so; they sent them outside the camp. They did just as the LORD had instructed Moses.

Restitution for Wrongs

⁵The LORD said to Moses, ⁶"Say to the Israelites: 'Any man or woman who wrongs another in any wayᵇ and so is unfaithful to the LORD is guilty ⁷and must confess the sin they have committed. They must make full restitution for the wrong they have done, add a fifth of the value to it and give it all to the person they have wronged. ⁸But if that person has no close relative to whom restitution can be made for the wrong, the restitution belongs to the LORD and must be given to the priest, along with the ram with which atonement is made for the wrongdoer. ⁹All the sacred contributions the Israelites bring to a priest will belong to him. ¹⁰All sacred gifts belong to the donors, but what they give to the priest will belong to the priest.' "

The Test for an Unfaithful Wife

¹¹Then the LORD said to Moses, ¹²"Speak

ᵃ 2 The Hebrew word for *defiling skin disease*, traditionally translated "leprosy," was used for various diseases affecting the skin.   ᵇ 6 Or *woman who commits any wrong common to humankind* to the Israelites and say to them: 'If a man's wife goes astray and is unfaithful to him ¹³so that another man has sexual relations with her, and this is hidden from her husband and her impurity is undetected (since there is no witness against her and she has not been caught in the act), ¹⁴and if feelings of jealousy come over her husband and he suspects his wife and she is impure—or if he is jealous and suspects her even though she is not impure— ¹⁵then he is to take his wife to the priest. He must also take an offering of a tenth of an ephah*a* of barley flour on her behalf. He must not pour oil on it or put incense on it, because it is a grain offering for jealousy, a reminder-offering to draw attention to wrongdoing.

¹⁶" 'The priest shall bring her and have her stand before the Lord. ¹⁷Then he shall take some holy water in a clay jar and put some dust from the tabernacle floor into the water. ¹⁸After the priest has had the woman stand before the Lord, he shall loosen her hair and place in her hands the reminder-offering, the grain offering for jealousy, while he himself holds the bitter water that brings a curse. ¹⁹Then the priest shall put the woman under oath and say to her, "If no other man has had sexual relations with you and you have not gone astray and become impure while married to your husband, may this bitter water that brings a curse not harm you. ²⁰But if you have gone astray while married to your husband and you have made yourself impure by having sexual relations with a man other than your husband"— ²¹here the priest is to put the woman under this curse—"may the Lord cause you to become a curse*b* among your people when he makes your womb miscarry and your abdomen swell. ²²May this water that brings a curse enter your body so that your abdomen swells or your womb miscarries."

" 'Then the woman is to say, "Amen. So be it."

²³" 'The priest is to write these curses on a scroll and then wash them off into the bitter water. ²⁴He shall make the woman drink the bitter water that brings a curse, and this water that brings a curse and causes bitter suffering will enter her. ²⁵The priest is to take from her hands the grain offering for jealousy, wave it before the Lord and bring it to the altar. ²⁶The priest is then to take a handful of the grain offering as a memorial*c* offering and burn it on the altar; after that, he is to have the woman drink the water. ²⁷If she has made herself impure and been unfaithful to her husband, this will be the result: When she is made to drink the water that brings a curse and causes bitter suffering, it will enter her, her abdomen will swell and her womb will miscarry, and she will become a curse. ²⁸If, however, the woman has not made herself impure, but is clean, she will be cleared of guilt and will be able to have children.

²⁹" 'This, then, is the law of jealousy when a woman goes astray and makes herself impure while married to her husband, ³⁰or when feelings of jealousy come over a man because he suspects his wife. The priest is to have her stand before the Lord and is to apply this entire law to her. ³¹The husband will be innocent of any wrongdoing, but the woman will bear the consequences of her sin.' "

The Nazirite

6 The Lord said to Moses, ²"Speak to the Israelites and say to them: 'If a man or woman wants to make a special vow, a vow of dedication to the Lord as a Nazirite, ³they must abstain from wine and other fermented drink and must not drink vinegar made from wine or other fermented drink. They must not drink grape juice or eat grapes or raisins. ⁴As long as they remain under their Nazirite vow, they must not eat anything that comes from the grapevine, not even the seeds or skins.

⁵" 'During the entire period of the Nazirite's vow, no razor may be used on their head. They must be holy until the period of their dedication to the Lord is over; they must let their hair grow long.

⁶" 'Throughout the period of their dedication to the Lord, the Nazirite must not go near a dead body. ⁷Even if their own father or mother or brother or sister dies, they must not make themselves ceremonially unclean on account of them, because the symbol of their dedication to God is on their

---

a 15 That is, probably about 3 1/2 pounds or about 1.6 kilograms   *b 21* That is, may he cause your name to be used in cursing (see Jer. 29:22); or, may others see that you are cursed; similarly in verse 27.
c 26 Or *representative*

Secret's Out

Numbers 5:23-28

read/meditate

Read through Numbers 5:23–28 a first time just to observe the elements of a ritual that is quite foreign to the modern mind. Then try to put yourself in the place of those people who believed they could divine the truth through this ritual. Read it again, imagining you are an unfaithful woman, guilty as charged, who is about to drink the dirty water she believes could leave her infertile. Read it through a final time, from the perspective of a woman who is innocent of the charges.

pray

The point of the ritual was to impress upon people that we can be found out; nothing is completely hidden, even the secrets of the soul. Whether we engage in a ritual or not, the truth is still the truth. We stand before God with all of our secrets revealed. Given that God knows every secret act and emotion you try to hide, confess to him your gut-level concerns, fears, failings and disappointments. Approach him unhidden, humble and honest.

contemplate

Imagine that your inner "demons," the things you struggle with in your own soul, were going to be revealed to the community around you a few days from now. What would you do with your secrets? How would you walk through life differently tomorrow?

additional reflection

All of our goodness is a loan; God is the owner.
—John of the Cross

It is not when we are conscious of our faults that we are the most wicked; on the contrary, we are less so.
—François Fénelon

For your next devotional reading, go to page 158.

MONDAY

WHEN GOD SMILES

Numbers 6:1–27 *or* 6:22–26

Kenneth Ulmer

When God [turns His face toward you], it means He's smiling. I want to make God smile. I want to live my life in such a way that when He looks into my life, He smiles. His smile indicates His pleasure and His acceptance. Have you ever considered just how much is communicated by a smile? Parents who are really wired to their children don't have to use a lot of words. Sometimes a parent at the bedside of a suffering child will muster up all the strength he or she has and smile, and that baby knows that everything will be all right. There's something about mommy's or daddy's smile that chases fear away. There's something about the smile you get from your children. There's something about my wife's smile. And there's really something about God's smile!

ALEXANDER MACLAREN {AD 1826–1910}

There are no outcasts in the eyes of Christ. He dismisses no people out of his hospital as incurable, because anybody and everybody—even the blackest, the most rooted in evil, those who have longest indulged in any given form of transgression—may come to him. They can do this with the certainty that if they will cling to him, he will read all their character and all its weaknesses, and then with a glad smile of welcome and assured confidence on his face, will ensure to them a new nature and new dignities.

reflection

1. What does it take to make God smile?
2. Which do you picture more often: God smiling at you or God frowning at you?
3. Why would God bless you?

For your next devotional reading, go to page 166.

head. ⁸Throughout the period of their dedication, they are consecrated to the LORD.

⁹" 'If someone dies suddenly in the Nazirite's presence, thus defiling the hair that symbolizes their dedication, they must shave their head on the seventh day—the day of their cleansing. ¹⁰Then on the eighth day they must bring two doves or two young pigeons to the priest at the entrance to the tent of meeting. ¹¹The priest is to offer one as a sin offering*a* and the other as a burnt offering to make atonement for the Nazirite because they sinned by being in the presence of the dead body. That same day they are to consecrate their head again. ¹²They must rededicate themselves to the LORD for the same period of dedication and must bring a year-old male lamb as a guilt offering. The previous days do not count, because they became defiled during their period of dedication.

¹³" 'Now this is the law for the Nazirite when the period of their dedication is over. The Nazirite is to be brought to the entrance to the tent of meeting. ¹⁴There they are to present their offerings to the LORD: a year-old male lamb without defect for a burnt offering, a year-old ewe lamb without defect for a sin offering, a ram without defect for a fellowship offering, ¹⁵together with their grain offerings and drink offerings, and a basket of bread made with the finest flour and without yeast—thick loaves with olive oil mixed in, and thin loaves brushed with olive oil.

¹⁶" 'The priest is to present the Nazirite before the LORD and make the sin offering and the burnt offering. ¹⁷He is to present the basket of unleavened bread and is to sacrifice the ram as a fellowship offering to the LORD, together with its grain offering and drink offering.

¹⁸" 'Then at the entrance to the tent of meeting, the Nazirite must shave off the hair that symbolizes their dedication. They are to take the hair and put it in the fire that is under the sacrifice of the fellowship offering.

¹⁹" 'After the Nazirite has shaved off the hair that symbolizes their dedication, the priest is to place in their hands a boiled shoulder of the ram, and one thick loaf and one thin loaf from the basket, both made without yeast. ²⁰The priest shall then wave these before the LORD as a wave offering; they are holy and belong to the priest, together with the breast that was waved and the thigh that was presented. After that, the Nazirite may drink wine.

²¹" 'This is the law of the Nazirite who vows offerings to the LORD in accordance with their dedication, in addition to whatever else they can afford. They must fulfill the vows they have made, according to the law of the Nazirite.' "

The Priestly Blessing

²²The LORD said to Moses, ²³"Tell Aaron and his sons, 'This is how you are to bless the Israelites. Say to them:

²⁴" ' "The LORD bless you
 and keep you;
²⁵the LORD make his face shine on you
 and be gracious to you;
²⁶the LORD turn his face toward you
 and give you peace." '

²⁷"So they will put my name on the Israelites, and I will bless them."

Offerings at the Dedication of the Tabernacle

7 When Moses finished setting up the tabernacle, he anointed and consecrated it and all its furnishings. He also anointed and consecrated the altar and all its utensils. ²Then the leaders of Israel, the heads of families who were the tribal leaders in charge of those who were counted, made offerings. ³They brought as their gifts before the LORD six covered carts and twelve oxen—an ox from each leader and a cart from every two. These they presented before the tabernacle.

⁴The LORD said to Moses, ⁵"Accept these from them, that they may be used in the work at the tent of meeting. Give them to the Levites as each man's work requires."

⁶So Moses took the carts and oxen and gave them to the Levites. ⁷He gave two carts and four oxen to the Gershonites, as their work required, ⁸and he gave four carts and eight oxen to the Merarites, as their work required. They were all under the direction of Ithamar son of Aaron, the priest. ⁹But Moses did not give any to the Kohathites, because

a 11 Or *purification offering*; also in verses 14 and 16

they were to carry on their shoulders the holy things, for which they were responsible.

¹⁰When the altar was anointed, the leaders brought their offerings for its dedication and presented them before the altar. ¹¹For the LORD had said to Moses, "Each day one leader is to bring his offering for the dedication of the altar."

¹²The one who brought his offering on the first day was Nahshon son of Amminadab of the tribe of Judah.

¹³His offering was one silver plate weighing a hundred and thirty shekels ᵃ and one silver sprinkling bowl weighing seventy shekels, ᵇ both according to the sanctuary shekel, each filled with the finest flour mixed with olive oil as a grain offering; ¹⁴one gold dish weighing ten shekels, ᶜ filled with incense; ¹⁵one young bull, one ram and one male lamb a year old for a burnt offering; ¹⁶one male goat for a sin offering ᵈ; ¹⁷and two oxen, five rams, five male goats and five male lambs a year old to be sacrificed as a fellowship offering. This was the offering of Nahshon son of Amminadab.

¹⁸On the second day Nethanel son of Zuar, the leader of Issachar, brought his offering.

¹⁹The offering he brought was one silver plate weighing a hundred and thirty shekels and one silver sprinkling bowl weighing seventy shekels, both according to the sanctuary shekel, each filled with the finest flour mixed with olive oil as a grain offering; ²⁰one gold dish weighing ten shekels, filled with incense; ²¹one young bull, one ram and one male lamb a year old for a burnt offering; ²²one male goat for a sin offering; ²³and two oxen, five rams, five male goats and five male lambs a year old to be sacrificed as a fellowship offering. This was the offering of Nethanel son of Zuar.

²⁴On the third day, Eliab son of Helon, the leader of the people of Zebulun, brought his offering.

²⁵His offering was one silver plate weighing a hundred and thirty shekels and one silver sprinkling bowl weighing seventy shekels, both according to the sanctuary shekel, each filled with the finest flour mixed with olive oil as a grain offering; ²⁶one gold dish weighing ten shekels, filled with incense; ²⁷one young bull, one ram and one male lamb a year old for a burnt offering; ²⁸one male goat for a sin offering; ²⁹and two oxen, five rams, five male goats and five male lambs a year old to be sacrificed as a fellowship offering. This was the offering of Eliab son of Helon.

³⁰On the fourth day Elizur son of Shedeur, the leader of the people of Reuben, brought his offering.

³¹His offering was one silver plate weighing a hundred and thirty shekels and one silver sprinkling bowl weighing seventy shekels, both according to the sanctuary shekel, each filled with the finest flour mixed with olive oil as a grain offering; ³²one gold dish weighing ten shekels, filled with incense; ³³one young bull, one ram and one male lamb a year old for a burnt offering; ³⁴one male goat for a sin offering; ³⁵and two oxen, five rams, five male goats and five male lambs a year old to be sacrificed as a fellowship offering. This was the offering of Elizur son of Shedeur.

³⁶On the fifth day Shelumiel son of Zurishaddai, the leader of the people of Simeon, brought his offering.

³⁷His offering was one silver plate weighing a hundred and thirty shekels and one silver sprinkling bowl weighing seventy shekels, both according to the sanctuary shekel, each filled with the finest flour mixed with olive oil as a grain offering; ³⁸one gold dish weighing ten shekels, filled with incense; ³⁹one young bull, one ram and one male lamb a year old for a burnt offering; ⁴⁰one male goat for a sin offering; ⁴¹and two oxen, five rams, five male goats and five male lambs a year old to be sacrificed as a fellowship offering. This

ᵃ 13 That is, about 3 1/4 pounds or about 1.5 kilograms; also elsewhere in this chapter   ᵇ 13 That is, about 1 3/4 pounds or about 800 grams; also elsewhere in this chapter   ᶜ 14 That is, about 4 ounces or about 115 grams; also elsewhere in this chapter   ᵈ 16 Or *purification offering*; also elsewhere in this chapter was the offering of Shelumiel son of Zurishaddai.

⁴²On the sixth day Eliasaph son of Deuel, the leader of the people of Gad, brought his offering.

⁴³His offering was one silver plate weighing a hundred and thirty shekels and one silver sprinkling bowl weighing seventy shekels, both according to the sanctuary shekel, each filled with the finest flour mixed with olive oil as a grain offering; ⁴⁴one gold dish weighing ten shekels, filled with incense; ⁴⁵one young bull, one ram and one male lamb a year old for a burnt offering; ⁴⁶one male goat for a sin offering; ⁴⁷and two oxen, five rams, five male goats and five male lambs a year old to be sacrificed as a fellowship offering. This was the offering of Eliasaph son of Deuel.

⁴⁸On the seventh day Elishama son of Ammihud, the leader of the people of Ephraim, brought his offering.

⁴⁹His offering was one silver plate weighing a hundred and thirty shekels and one silver sprinkling bowl weighing seventy shekels, both according to the sanctuary shekel, each filled with the finest flour mixed with olive oil as a grain offering; ⁵⁰one gold dish weighing ten shekels, filled with incense; ⁵¹one young bull, one ram and one male lamb a year old for a burnt offering; ⁵²one male goat for a sin offering; ⁵³and two oxen, five rams, five male goats and five male lambs a year old to be sacrificed as a fellowship offering. This was the offering of Elishama son of Ammihud.

⁵⁴On the eighth day Gamaliel son of Pedahzur, the leader of the people of Manasseh, brought his offering.

⁵⁵His offering was one silver plate weighing a hundred and thirty shekels and one silver sprinkling bowl weighing seventy shekels, both according to the sanctuary shekel, each filled with the finest flour mixed with olive oil as a grain offering; ⁵⁶one gold dish weighing ten shekels, filled with incense; ⁵⁷one young bull, one ram and one male lamb a year old for a burnt offering; ⁵⁸one male goat for a sin offering; ⁵⁹and

two oxen, five rams, five male goats and five male lambs a year old to be sacrificed as a fellowship offering. This was the offering of Gamaliel son of Pedahzur.

⁶⁰On the ninth day Abidan son of Gideoni, the leader of the people of Benjamin, brought his offering.

⁶¹His offering was one silver plate weighing a hundred and thirty shekels and one silver sprinkling bowl weighing seventy shekels, both according to the sanctuary shekel, each filled with the finest flour mixed with olive oil as a grain offering; ⁶²one gold dish weighing ten shekels, filled with incense; ⁶³one young bull, one ram and one male lamb a year old for a burnt offering; ⁶⁴one male goat for a sin offering; ⁶⁵and two oxen, five rams, five male goats and five male lambs a year old to be sacrificed as a fellowship offering. This was the offering of Abidan son of Gideoni.

⁶⁶On the tenth day Ahiezer son of Ammishaddai, the leader of the people of Dan, brought his offering.

⁶⁷His offering was one silver plate weighing a hundred and thirty shekels and one silver sprinkling bowl weighing seventy shekels, both according to the sanctuary shekel, each filled with the finest flour mixed with olive oil as a grain offering; ⁶⁸one gold dish weighing ten shekels, filled with incense; ⁶⁹one young bull, one ram and one male lamb a year old for a burnt offering; ⁷⁰one male goat for a sin offering; ⁷¹and two oxen, five rams, five male goats and five male lambs a year old to be sacrificed as a fellowship offering. This was the offering of Ahiezer son of Ammishaddai.

⁷²On the eleventh day Pagiel son of Okran, the leader of the people of Asher, brought his offering.

⁷³His offering was one silver plate weighing a hundred and thirty shekels and one silver sprinkling bowl weighing seventy shekels, both according to the sanctuary shekel, each filled with the finest flour mixed with olive oil as a grain offering; ⁷⁴one gold dish weighing ten shekels, filled with incense; ⁷⁵one young bull, one ram and one male

lamb a year old for a burnt offering; [76]one male goat for a sin offering; [77]and two oxen, five rams, five male goats and five male lambs a year old to be sacrificed as a fellowship offering. This was the offering of Pagiel son of Okran.

[78]On the twelfth day Ahira son of Enan, the leader of the people of Naphtali, brought his offering.

[79]His offering was one silver plate weighing a hundred and thirty shekels and one silver sprinkling bowl weighing seventy shekels, both according to the sanctuary shekel, each filled with the finest flour mixed with olive oil as a grain offering; [80]one gold dish weighing ten shekels, filled with incense; [81]one young bull, one ram and one male lamb a year old for a burnt offering; [82]one male goat for a sin offering; [83]and two oxen, five rams, five male goats and five male lambs a year old to be sacrificed as a fellowship offering. This was the offering of Ahira son of Enan.

[84]These were the offerings of the Israelite leaders for the dedication of the altar when it was anointed: twelve silver plates, twelve silver sprinkling bowls and twelve gold dishes. [85]Each silver plate weighed a hundred and thirty shekels, and each sprinkling bowl seventy shekels. Altogether, the silver dishes weighed two thousand four hundred shekels,[a] according to the sanctuary shekel. [86]The twelve gold dishes filled with incense weighed ten shekels each, according to the sanctuary shekel. Altogether, the gold dishes weighed a hundred and twenty shekels.[b] [87]The total number of animals for the burnt offering came to twelve young bulls, twelve rams and twelve male lambs a year old, together with their grain offering. Twelve male goats were used for the sin offering. [88]The total number of animals for the sacrifice of the fellowship offering came to twenty-four oxen, sixty rams, sixty male goats and sixty male lambs a year old. These were the offerings for the dedication of the altar after it was anointed.

[89]When Moses entered the tent of meeting to speak with the LORD, he heard the voice speaking to him from between the two cherubim above the atonement cover on the ark of the covenant law. In this way the LORD spoke to him.

Setting Up the Lamps

8 The LORD said to Moses, [2]"Speak to Aaron and say to him, 'When you set up the lamps, see that all seven light up the area in front of the lampstand.' "

[3]Aaron did so; he set up the lamps so that they faced forward on the lampstand, just as the LORD commanded Moses. [4]This is how the lampstand was made: It was made of hammered gold—from its base to its blossoms. The lampstand was made exactly like the pattern the LORD had shown Moses.

The Setting Apart of the Levites

[5]The LORD said to Moses: [6]"Take the Levites from among all the Israelites and make them ceremonially clean. [7]To purify them, do this: Sprinkle the water of cleansing on them; then have them shave their whole bodies and wash their clothes. And so they will purify themselves. [8]Have them take a young bull with its grain offering of the finest flour mixed with olive oil; then you are to take a second young bull for a sin offering.[c] [9]Bring the Levites to the front of the tent of meeting and assemble the whole Israelite community. [10]You are to bring the Levites before the LORD, and the Israelites are to lay their hands on them. [11]Aaron is to present the Levites before the LORD as a wave offering from the Israelites, so that they may be ready to do the work of the LORD.

[12]"Then the Levites are to lay their hands on the heads of the bulls, using one for a sin offering to the LORD and the other for a burnt offering, to make atonement for the Levites. [13]Have the Levites stand in front of Aaron and his sons and then present them as a wave offering to the LORD. [14]In this way you are to set the Levites apart from the other Israelites, and the Levites will be mine.

[15]"After you have purified the Levites and presented them as a wave offering, they are to come to do their work at the tent of meeting. [16]They are the Israelites who are to be given wholly to me. I have taken them as my own in place of the firstborn, the first male offspring from every Israelite woman. [17]Ev-

---

a 85 That is, about 61 pounds or about 28 kilograms   *b 86* That is, about 3 pounds or about 1.4 kilograms   *c 8* Or *purification offering*; also in verse 12 ery firstborn male in Israel, whether human or animal, is mine. When I struck down all the firstborn in Egypt, I set them apart for myself. ¹⁸And I have taken the Levites in place of all the firstborn sons in Israel. ¹⁹From among all the Israelites, I have given the Levites as gifts to Aaron and his sons to do the work at the tent of meeting on behalf of the Israelites and to make atonement for them so that no plague will strike the Israelites when they go near the sanctuary."

²⁰Moses, Aaron and the whole Israelite community did with the Levites just as the LORD commanded Moses. ²¹The Levites purified themselves and washed their clothes. Then Aaron presented them as a wave offering before the LORD and made atonement for them to purify them. ²²After that, the Levites came to do their work at the tent of meeting under the supervision of Aaron and his sons. They did with the Levites just as the LORD commanded Moses.

²³The LORD said to Moses, ²⁴"This applies to the Levites: Men twenty-five years old or more shall come to take part in the work at the tent of meeting, ²⁵but at the age of fifty, they must retire from their regular service and work no longer. ²⁶They may assist their brothers in performing their duties at the tent of meeting, but they themselves must not do the work. This, then, is how you are to assign the responsibilities of the Levites."

The Passover

9 The LORD spoke to Moses in the Desert of Sinai in the first month of the second year after they came out of Egypt. He said, ²"Have the Israelites celebrate the Passover at the appointed time. ³Celebrate it at the appointed time, at twilight on the fourteenth day of this month, in accordance with all its rules and regulations."

⁴So Moses told the Israelites to celebrate the Passover, ⁵and they did so in the Desert of Sinai at twilight on the fourteenth day of the first month. The Israelites did everything just as the LORD commanded Moses.

⁶But some of them could not celebrate the Passover on that day because they were ceremonially unclean on account of a dead body. So they came to Moses and Aaron that same day ⁷and said to Moses, "We have become unclean because of a dead body, but why should we be kept from presenting the

LORD's offering with the other Israelites at the appointed time?"

⁸Moses answered them, "Wait until I find out what the LORD commands concerning you."

⁹Then the LORD said to Moses, ¹⁰"Tell the Israelites: 'When any of you or your descendants are unclean because of a dead body or are away on a journey, they are still to celebrate the LORD's Passover, ¹¹but they are to do it on the fourteenth day of the second month at twilight. They are to eat the lamb, together with unleavened bread and bitter herbs. ¹²They must not leave any of it till morning or break any of its bones. When they celebrate the Passover, they must follow all the regulations. ¹³But if anyone who is ceremonially clean and not on a journey fails to celebrate the Passover, they must be cut off from their people for not presenting the LORD's offering at the appointed time. They will bear the consequences of their sin.

¹⁴" 'A foreigner residing among you is also to celebrate the LORD's Passover in accordance with its rules and regulations. You must have the same regulations for both the foreigner and the native-born.' "

The Cloud Above the Tabernacle

¹⁵On the day the tabernacle, the tent of the covenant law, was set up, the cloud covered it. From evening till morning the cloud above the tabernacle looked like fire. ¹⁶That is how it continued to be; the cloud covered it, and at night it looked like fire. ¹⁷Whenever the cloud lifted from above the tent, the Israelites set out; wherever the cloud settled, the Israelites encamped. ¹⁸At the LORD's command the Israelites set out, and at his command they encamped. As long as the cloud stayed over the tabernacle, they remained in camp. ¹⁹When the cloud remained over the tabernacle a long time, the Israelites obeyed the LORD's order and did not set out. ²⁰Sometimes the cloud was over the tabernacle only a few days; at the LORD's command they would encamp, and then at his command they would set out. ²¹Sometimes the cloud stayed only from evening till morning, and when it lifted in the morning, they set out. Whether by day or by night, whenever the cloud lifted, they set out. ²²Whether the cloud stayed over the tabernacle for two days or a month or a year, the Israelites would remain in camp and not set

out; but when it lifted, they would set out. ²³At the LORD's command they encamped, and at the LORD's command they set out. They obeyed the LORD's order, in accordance with his command through Moses.

The Silver Trumpets

10 The LORD said to Moses: ²"Make two trumpets of hammered silver, and use them for calling the community together and for having the camps set out. ³When both are sounded, the whole community is to assemble before you at the entrance to the tent of meeting. ⁴If only one is sounded, the leaders—the heads of the clans of Israel—are to assemble before you. ⁵When a trumpet blast is sounded, the tribes camping on the east are to set out. ⁶At the sounding of a second blast, the camps on the south are to set out. The blast will be the signal for setting out. ⁷To gather the assembly, blow the trumpets, but not with the signal for setting out.

⁸"The sons of Aaron, the priests, are to blow the trumpets. This is to be a lasting ordinance for you and the generations to come. ⁹When you go into battle in your own land against an enemy who is oppressing you, sound a blast on the trumpets. Then you will be remembered by the LORD your God and rescued from your enemies. ¹⁰Also at your times of rejoicing—your appointed festivals and New Moon feasts—you are to sound the trumpets over your burnt offerings and fellowship offerings, and they will be a memorial for you before your God. I am the LORD your God."

The Israelites Leave Sinai

¹¹On the twentieth day of the second month of the second year, the cloud lifted from above the tabernacle of the covenant law. ¹²Then the Israelites set out from the Desert of Sinai and traveled from place to place until the cloud came to rest in the Desert of Paran. ¹³They set out, this first time, at the LORD's command through Moses.

¹⁴The divisions of the camp of Judah went first, under their standard. Nahshon son of Amminadab was in command. ¹⁵Nethanel son of Zuar was over the division of the tribe of Issachar, ¹⁶and Eliab son of Helon was over the division of the tribe of Zebulun. ¹⁷Then the tabernacle was taken down, and the Gershonites and Merarites, who carried it, set out.

¹⁸The divisions of the camp of Reuben went next, under their standard. Elizur son of Shedeur was in command. ¹⁹Shelumiel son of Zurishaddai was over the division of the tribe of Simeon, ²⁰and Eliasaph son of Deuel was over the division of the tribe of Gad. ²¹Then the Kohathites set out, carrying the holy things. The tabernacle was to be set up before they arrived.

²²The divisions of the camp of Ephraim went next, under their standard. Elishama son of Ammihud was in command. ²³Gamaliel son of Pedahzur was over the division of the tribe of Manasseh, ²⁴and Abidan son of Gideoni was over the division of the tribe of Benjamin.

²⁵Finally, as the rear guard for all the units, the divisions of the camp of Dan set out under their standard. Ahiezer son of Ammishaddai was in command. ²⁶Pagiel son of Okran was over the division of the tribe of Asher, ²⁷and Ahira son of Enan was over the division of the tribe of Naphtali. ²⁸This was the order of march for the Israelite divisions as they set out.

²⁹Now Moses said to Hobab son of Reuel the Midianite, Moses' father-in-law, "We are setting out for the place about which the LORD said, 'I will give it to you.' Come with us and we will treat you well, for the LORD has promised good things to Israel."

³⁰He answered, "No, I will not go; I am going back to my own land and my own people."

³¹But Moses said, "Please do not leave us. You know where we should camp in the wilderness, and you can be our eyes. ³²If you come with us, we will share with you whatever good things the LORD gives us."

³³So they set out from the mountain of the LORD and traveled for three days. The ark of the covenant of the LORD went before them during those three days to find them a place to rest. ³⁴The cloud of the LORD was over them by day when they set out from the camp.

³⁵Whenever the ark set out, Moses said,

"Rise up, LORD!
    May your enemies be scattered;
    may your foes flee before you."

³⁶Whenever it came to rest, he said,

"Return, LORD,
    to the countless thousands of Israel."

Fire From the LORD

11

Now the people complained about their hardships in the hearing of the LORD, and when he heard them his anger was aroused. Then fire from the LORD burned among them and consumed some of the outskirts of the camp. ²When the people cried out to Moses, he prayed to the LORD and the fire died down. ³So that place was called Taberah,^a because fire from the LORD had burned among them.

Quail From the LORD

⁴The rabble with them began to crave other food, and again the Israelites started wailing and said, "If only we had meat to eat! ⁵We remember the fish we ate in Egypt at no cost—also the cucumbers, melons, leeks, onions and garlic. ⁶But now we have lost our appetite; we never see anything but this manna!"

⁷The manna was like coriander seed and looked like resin. ⁸The people went around gathering it, and then ground it in a hand mill or crushed it in a mortar. They cooked it in a pot or made it into loaves. And it tasted like something made with olive oil. ⁹When the dew settled on the camp at night, the manna also came down.

¹⁰Moses heard the people of every family wailing at the entrance to their tents. The LORD became exceedingly angry, and Moses was troubled. ¹¹He asked the LORD, "Why have you brought this trouble on your servant? What have I done to displease you that you put the burden of all these people on me? ¹²Did I conceive all these people? Did I give them birth? Why do you tell me to carry them in my arms, as a nurse carries an infant, to the land you promised on oath to their ancestors? ¹³Where can I get meat for all these people? They keep wailing to me, 'Give us meat to eat!' ¹⁴I cannot carry all these people by myself; the burden is too heavy for me. ¹⁵If this is how you are going to treat me, please go ahead and kill me—if I have found favor in your eyes—and do not let me face my own ruin."

¹⁶The LORD said to Moses: "Bring me seventy of Israel's elders who are known to you as leaders and officials among the people. Have them come to the tent of meeting, that they may stand there with you. ¹⁷I will come down and speak with you there, and I will take some of the power of the Spirit that is on you and put it on them. They will share the burden of the people with you so that you will not have to carry it alone.

¹⁸"Tell the people: 'Consecrate yourselves in preparation for tomorrow, when you will eat meat. The LORD heard you when you wailed, "If only we had meat to eat! We were better off in Egypt!" Now the LORD will give you meat, and you will eat it. ¹⁹You will not eat it for just one day, or two days, or five, ten or twenty days, ²⁰but for a whole month—until it comes out of your nostrils and you loathe it—because you have rejected the LORD, who is among you, and have wailed before him, saying, "Why did we ever leave Egypt?" ' "

²¹But Moses said, "Here I am among six hundred thousand men on foot, and you say, 'I will give them meat to eat for a whole month!' ²²Would they have enough if flocks and herds were slaughtered for them? Would they have enough if all the fish in the sea were caught for them?"

²³The LORD answered Moses, "Is the LORD's arm too short? Now you will see whether or not what I say will come true for you."

²⁴So Moses went out and told the people what the LORD had said. He brought together seventy of their elders and had them stand around the tent. ²⁵Then the LORD came down in the cloud and spoke with him, and he took some of the power of the Spirit that was on him and put it on the seventy elders. When the Spirit rested on them, they prophesied—but did not do so again.

²⁶However, two men, whose names were Eldad and Medad, had remained in the camp. They were listed among the elders, but did not go out to the tent. Yet the Spirit also rested on them, and they prophesied in the camp. ²⁷A young man ran and told Moses, "Eldad and Medad are prophesying in the camp."

²⁸Joshua son of Nun, who had been Moses' aide since youth, spoke up and said, "Moses, my lord, stop them!"

²⁹But Moses replied, "Are you jealous for my sake? I wish that all the LORD's people were prophets and that the LORD would put his Spirit on them!" ³⁰Then Moses and the elders of Israel returned to the camp.

---

a 3 Taberah means burning.

TUESDAY

COMPLAINING IS CONTAGIOUS

Numbers 11:1–35 or 11:1–3

Jill Briscoe

Moses was the pastor of the "First Church of the Wilderness." This popular church had thousands of members, but many of them were chronic complainers who displeased the Lord. The mixed multitudes, or the rabble who were with them, started it all. "[The rabble with them began to crave other food, and again the Israelites started wailing and said, 'If only we had meat to eat!']" (Numbers 11:4). What did the members of Moses' church have to complain about? They complained about the manna they were eating. Soon they began to pine for the good old days! They didn't like anything about the church—the location or the preacher—and they said so.

Every church has to contend with the rabble-rousers. The problem is, their grumbling grows, and before you know it, the members have begun to grumble, too!

It's hard for a pastor to cope with that sort of talk . . . Complaining, grumbler's gripe, is caught like measles. Once started, it spreads like wildfire. It can become very discouraging.

Moses fell into the trap that many pastors fall into. He caught the disease and began griping too. The Lord is displeased with such behavior; he gripes about gripers, and that should be enough to stop it!

JOHN BAILLIE {AD 1886–1960}

Teach me, O God, to use all the circumstances of my life today that they may bring forth in me the fruits of holiness rather than the fruits of sin.

Let me use disappointment as material for patience: . . .

Let me use reproach as material for longsuffering:

Let me use praise as material for humility:

Let me use pleasures as material for temperance:

Let me use pains as material for endurance.

reflection

1. Would you generally describe yourself as a "the glass is half empty" or "the glass is half full" type of person?

2. Complaining is contagious. Have you seen this disease spread through your own church?

3. In what ways have you either contributed to an attitude of grumbling or attempted to stop it?

For your next devotional reading, go to page 169.

³¹Now a wind went out from the Lord and drove quail in from the sea. It scattered them up to two cubits^a deep all around the camp, as far as a day's walk in any direction. ³²All that day and night and all the next day the people went out and gathered quail. No one gathered less than ten homers.^b Then they spread them out all around the camp. ³³But while the meat was still between their teeth and before it could be consumed, the anger of the Lord burned against the people, and he struck them with a severe plague. ³⁴Therefore the place was named Kibroth Hattaavah,^c because there they buried the people who had craved other food.

³⁵From Kibroth Hattaavah the people traveled to Hazeroth and stayed there.

Miriam and Aaron Oppose Moses

12 Miriam and Aaron began to talk against Moses because of his Cushite wife, for he had married a Cushite. ²"Has the Lord spoken only through Moses?" they asked. "Hasn't he also spoken through us?" And the Lord heard this.

³(Now Moses was a very humble man, more humble than anyone else on the face of the earth.)

⁴At once the Lord said to Moses, Aaron and Miriam, "Come out to the tent of meeting, all three of you." So the three of them went out. ⁵Then the Lord came down in a pillar of cloud; he stood at the entrance to the tent and summoned Aaron and Miriam. When the two of them stepped forward, ⁶he said, "Listen to my words:

"When there are prophets of the Lord
    among you,
  I reveal myself to them in visions,
  I speak to them in dreams.
⁷But this is not true of my servant Moses;
    he is faithful in all my house.
⁸With him I speak face to face,
    clearly and not in riddles;
  he sees the form of the Lord.
Why then were you not afraid
    to speak against my servant Moses?"

⁹The anger of the Lord burned against them, and he left them.

¹⁰When the cloud lifted from above the tent, Miriam's skin was leprous^d—it became as white as snow. Aaron turned toward her and saw that she had a defiling skin disease, ¹¹and he said to Moses, "Please, my lord, I ask you not to hold against us the sin we have so foolishly committed. ¹²Do not let her be like a stillborn infant coming from its mother's womb with its flesh half eaten away."

¹³So Moses cried out to the Lord, "Please, God, heal her!"

¹⁴The Lord replied to Moses, "If her father had spit in her face, would she not have been in disgrace for seven days? Confine her outside the camp for seven days; after that she can be brought back." ¹⁵So Miriam was confined outside the camp for seven days, and the people did not move on till she was brought back.

¹⁶After that, the people left Hazeroth and encamped in the Desert of Paran.

Exploring Canaan

13 The Lord said to Moses, ²"Send some men to explore the land of Canaan, which I am giving to the Israelites. From each ancestral tribe send one of its leaders."

³So at the Lord's command Moses sent them out from the Desert of Paran. All of them were leaders of the Israelites. ⁴These are their names:

from the tribe of Reuben, Shammua son of Zakkur;
⁵from the tribe of Simeon, Shaphat son of Hori;
⁶from the tribe of Judah, Caleb son of Jephunneh;
⁷from the tribe of Issachar, Igal son of Joseph;
⁸from the tribe of Ephraim, Hoshea son of Nun;
⁹from the tribe of Benjamin, Palti son of Raphu;
¹⁰from the tribe of Zebulun, Gaddiel son of Sodi;
¹¹from the tribe of Manasseh (a tribe of Joseph), Gaddi son of Susi;
¹²from the tribe of Dan, Ammiel son of Gemalli;

¹³from the tribe of Asher, Sethur son of Michael;
¹⁴from the tribe of Naphtali, Nahbi son of Vophsi;
¹⁵from the tribe of Gad, Geuel son of Maki.

¹⁶These are the names of the men Moses sent to explore the land. (Moses gave Hoshea son of Nun the name Joshua.)

¹⁷When Moses sent them to explore Canaan, he said, "Go up through the Negev and on into the hill country. ¹⁸See what the land is like and whether the people who live there are strong or weak, few or many. ¹⁹What kind of land do they live in? Is it good or bad? What kind of towns do they live in? Are they unwalled or fortified? ²⁰How is the soil? Is it fertile or poor? Are there trees in it or not? Do your best to bring back some of the fruit of the land." (It was the season for the first ripe grapes.)

²¹So they went up and explored the land from the Desert of Zin as far as Rehob, toward Lebo Hamath. ²²They went up through the Negev and came to Hebron, where Ahiman, Sheshai and Talmai, the descendants of Anak, lived. (Hebron had been built seven years before Zoan in Egypt.) ²³When they reached the Valley of Eshkol,ᵃ they cut off a branch bearing a single cluster of grapes. Two of them carried it on a pole between them, along with some pomegranates and figs. ²⁴That place was called the Valley of Eshkol because of the cluster of grapes the Israelites cut off there. ²⁵At the end of forty days they returned from exploring the land.

Report on the Exploration

²⁶They came back to Moses and Aaron and the whole Israelite community at Kadesh in the Desert of Paran. There they reported to them and to the whole assembly and showed them the fruit of the land. ²⁷They gave Moses this account: "We went into the land to which you sent us, and it does flow with milk and honey! Here is its fruit. ²⁸But the people who live there are powerful, and the cities are fortified and very large. We even saw descendants of Anak there. ²⁹The Amalekites live in the Negev; the Hittites, Jebusites and Amorites live in the hill country; and the Canaanites live near the sea and along the Jordan."

³⁰Then Caleb silenced the people before Moses and said, "We should go up and take possession of the land, for we can certainly do it."

³¹But the men who had gone up with him said, "We can't attack those people; they are stronger than we are." ³²And they spread among the Israelites a bad report about the land they had explored. They said, "The land we explored devours those living in it. All the people we saw there are of great size. ³³We saw the Nephilim there (the descendants of Anak come from the Nephilim). We seemed like grasshoppers in our own eyes, and we looked the same to them."

The People Rebel

14 That night all the members of the community raised their voices and wept aloud. ²All the Israelites grumbled against Moses and Aaron, and the whole assembly said to them, "If only we had died in Egypt! Or in this wilderness! ³Why is the LORD bringing us to this land only to let us fall by the sword? Our wives and children will be taken as plunder. Wouldn't it be better for us to go back to Egypt?" ⁴And they said to each other, "We should choose a leader and go back to Egypt."

⁵Then Moses and Aaron fell facedown in front of the whole Israelite assembly gathered there. ⁶Joshua son of Nun and Caleb son of Jephunneh, who were among those who had explored the land, tore their clothes ⁷and said to the entire Israelite assembly, "The land we passed through and explored is exceedingly good. ⁸If the LORD is pleased with us, he will lead us into that land, a land flowing with milk and honey, and will give it to us. ⁹Only do not rebel against the LORD. And do not be afraid of the people of the land, because we will devour them. Their protection is gone, but the LORD is with us. Do not be afraid of them."

¹⁰But the whole assembly talked about stoning them. Then the glory of the LORD appeared at the tent of meeting to all the Israelites. ¹¹The LORD said to Moses, "How long will these people treat me with contempt? How long will they refuse to believe in me, in spite of all the signs I have performed among them? ¹²I will strike them

---

ᵃ 23 *Eshkol* means *cluster*; also in verse 24.

WEDNESDAY

UNDERSTANDING GOD'S POWER

Numbers 14:1–38 *or* 14:2,26–31

JOSEPH PARKER {AD 1830–1902}

It is a fearful thing to fall into the hands of the living God. It is better to fall into the hands of men. Our God is a consuming fire—God is love. These are great, yet contradicting truths about our God.

The combination of great power and great restraint—indeed, the combination of opposite qualities and uses generally—is well-known in civilized life and in the laws of nature. The fire that warms the room when properly regulated will, if abused, reduce the proudest palaces to ashes. The river, which softens and refreshes the landscape, if allowed to escape its banks, can devastate the most fruitful fields . . .

The mighty God is the everlasting father; the terrible One is more gentle than the gentlest friend . . .

In pointing out the terribleness of God, I do not appeal to fear. I do so to support and encourage the most loving confidence in His government. We do not say, "Be good, or God will crush you." That is not virtue, that is not liberty—it is vice put on its good behavior . . .

The great truth to be learned is that all the terribleness of God is the good man's security. When the good man sees God wasting the mountains and the hills, and drying up the rivers, he does not say, "I must worship Him or He will destroy me." He says, "The beneficent side of that power is all mine. Because of that power I am safe."

Leonidas A. Johnson

God is still on the throne! The great liberating power of the one and only living God—the same God who was with the Word in the beginning, the same God of Abraham, Isaac, and Jacob, the same God who delivered the Israelites . . . the same God who delivered Daniel from the lion's Den, the same God who delivered three Hebrew boys out of a burning fire, the same God who sent his son to set captives free—is still available to us. God's liberating power can set anyone free!

reflection

1. How did God's power validate his word in this Bible passage?

2. What other Biblical events illustrate both the power of God's judgment on sinners and his freeing love for those who follow him?

3. In what ways is God's power your security?

For your next devotional reading, go to page 178.

down with a plague and destroy them, but I will make you into a nation greater and stronger than they.'"

[13] Moses said to the LORD, "Then the Egyptians will hear about it! By your power you brought these people up from among them. [14] And they will tell the inhabitants of this land about it. They have already heard that you, LORD, are with these people and that you, LORD, have been seen face to face, that your cloud stays over them, and that you go before them in a pillar of cloud by day and a pillar of fire by night. [15] If you put these people to death all at one time, the nations who have heard this report about you will say, [16] 'The LORD was not able to bring these people into the land he promised them on oath, so he slaughtered them in the wilderness.'

[17] "Now may the Lord's strength be displayed, just as you have declared: [18] 'The LORD is slow to anger, abounding in love and forgiving sin and rebellion. Yet he does not leave the guilty unpunished; he punishes the children for the sin of the parents to the third and fourth generation.' [19] In accordance with your great love, forgive the sin of these people, just as you have pardoned them from the time they left Egypt until now."

[20] The LORD replied, "I have forgiven them, as you asked. [21] Nevertheless, as surely as I live and as surely as the glory of the LORD fills the whole earth, [22] not one of those who saw my glory and the signs I performed in Egypt and in the wilderness but who disobeyed me and tested me ten times— [23] not one of them will ever see the land I promised on oath to their ancestors. No one who has treated me with contempt will ever see it. [24] But because my servant Caleb has a different spirit and follows me wholeheartedly, I will bring him into the land he went to, and his descendants will inherit it. [25] Since the Amalekites and Canaanites are living in the valleys, turn back tomorrow and set out toward the desert along the route to the Red Sea.[a]"

[26] The LORD said to Moses and Aaron: [27] "How long will this wicked community grumble against me? I have heard the complaints of these grumbling Israelites. [28] So tell them, 'As surely as I live, declares the LORD, I will do to you the very thing I heard you say: [29] In this wilderness your bodies will fall—every one of you twenty years old or more who was counted in the census and who has grumbled against me. [30] Not one of you will enter the land I swore with uplifted hand to make your home, except Caleb son of Jephunneh and Joshua son of Nun. [31] As for your children that you said would be taken as plunder, I will bring them in to enjoy the land you have rejected. [32] But as for you, your bodies will fall in this wilderness. [33] Your children will be shepherds here for forty years, suffering for your unfaithfulness, until the last of your bodies lies in the wilderness. [34] For forty years—one year for each of the forty days you explored the land—you will suffer for your sins and know what it is like to have me against you.' [35] I, the LORD, have spoken, and I will surely do these things to this whole wicked community, which has banded together against me. They will meet their end in this wilderness; here they will die."

[36] So the men Moses had sent to explore the land, who returned and made the whole community grumble against him by spreading a bad report about it— [37] these men who were responsible for spreading the bad report about the land were struck down and died of a plague before the LORD. [38] Of the men who went to explore the land, only Joshua son of Nun and Caleb son of Jephunneh survived.

[39] When Moses reported this to all the Israelites, they mourned bitterly. [40] Early the next morning they set out for the highest point in the hill country, saying, "Now we are ready to go up to the land the LORD promised. Surely we have sinned!"

[41] But Moses said, "Why are you disobeying the LORD's command? This will not succeed! [42] Do not go up, because the LORD is not with you. You will be defeated by your enemies, [43] for the Amalekites and Canaanites will face you there. Because you have turned away from the LORD, he will not be with you and you will fall by the sword."

[44] Nevertheless, in their presumption they went up toward the highest point in the hill country, though neither Moses nor the ark of the LORD's covenant moved from the camp. [45] Then the Amalekites and Canaanites who lived in that hill country came down and at-

a 25 Or the Sea of Reeds

tacked them and beat them down all the way to Hormah.

Supplementary Offerings

15 The Lord said to Moses, ²"Speak to the Israelites and say to them: 'After you enter the land I am giving you as a home ³and you present to the Lord food offerings from the herd or the flock, as an aroma pleasing to the Lord— whether burnt offerings or sacrifices, for special vows or freewill offerings or festival offerings— ⁴then the person who brings an offering shall present to the Lord a grain offering of a tenth of an ephah*ª* of the finest flour mixed with a quarter of a hin*ᵇ* of olive oil. ⁵With each lamb for the burnt offering or the sacrifice, prepare a quarter of a hin of wine as a drink offering.

⁶" 'With a ram prepare a grain offering of two-tenths of an ephah*ᶜ* of the finest flour mixed with a third of a hin*ᵈ* of olive oil, ⁷and a third of a hin of wine as a drink offering. Offer it as an aroma pleasing to the Lord.

⁸" 'When you prepare a young bull as a burnt offering or sacrifice, for a special vow or a fellowship offering to the Lord, ⁹bring with the bull a grain offering of three-tenths of an ephah*ᵉ* of the finest flour mixed with half a hin*ᶠ* of olive oil, ¹⁰and also bring half a hin of wine as a drink offering. This will be a food offering, an aroma pleasing to the Lord. ¹¹Each bull or ram, each lamb or young goat, is to be prepared in this manner. ¹²Do this for each one, for as many as you prepare.

¹³" 'Everyone who is native-born must do these things in this way when they present a food offering as an aroma pleasing to the Lord. ¹⁴For the generations to come, whenever a foreigner or anyone else living among you presents a food offering as an aroma pleasing to the Lord, they must do exactly as you do. ¹⁵The community is to have the same rules for you and for the foreigner residing among you; this is a lasting ordinance for the generations to come. You and the foreigner shall be the same before the Lord: ¹⁶The same laws and regulations will apply both to you and to the foreigner residing among you.' "

¹⁷The Lord said to Moses, ¹⁸"Speak to the Israelites and say to them: 'When you enter the land to which I am taking you ¹⁹and you eat the food of the land, present a portion as an offering to the Lord. ²⁰Present a loaf from the first of your ground meal and present it as an offering from the threshing floor. ²¹Throughout the generations to come you are to give this offering to the Lord from the first of your ground meal.

Offerings for Unintentional Sins

²²" 'Now if you as a community unintentionally fail to keep any of these commands the Lord gave Moses— ²³any of the Lord's commands to you through him, from the day the Lord gave them and continuing through the generations to come— ²⁴and if this is done unintentionally without the community being aware of it, then the whole community is to offer a young bull for a burnt offering as an aroma pleasing to the Lord, along with its prescribed grain offering and drink offering, and a male goat for a sin offering.*ᵍ* ²⁵The priest is to make atonement for the whole Israelite community, and they will be forgiven, for it was not intentional and they have presented to the Lord for their wrong a food offering and a sin offering. ²⁶The whole Israelite community and the foreigners residing among them will be forgiven, because all the people were involved in the unintentional wrong.

²⁷" 'But if just one person sins unintentionally, that person must bring a year-old female goat for a sin offering. ²⁸The priest is to make atonement before the Lord for the one who erred by sinning unintentionally, and when atonement has been made for them, they will be forgiven. ²⁹One and the same law applies to everyone who sins unintentionally, whether a native-born Israelite or a foreigner residing among you.

³⁰" 'But anyone who sins defiantly, whether native-born or foreigner, blasphemes the Lord and must be cut off from their people. ³¹Because they have despised the Lord's word and broken his commands,

---

a 4 That is, probably about 3 1/2 pounds or about 1.6 kilograms   *b 4* That is, about 1 quart or about 0.9 liter; also in verse 5   *c 6* That is, probably about 7 pounds or about 3.2 kilograms   *d 6* That is, about 2 2/3 pints or about 1.2 liters; also in verse 7   *e 9* That is, probably about 11 pounds or about 5 kilograms   *f 9* That is, about 1/2 gallon or about 1.8 liters; also in verse 10   *g 24* Or *purification offering*; also in verses 25 and 27 they must surely be cut off; their guilt remains on them.' "

The Sabbath-Breaker Put to Death

³²While the Israelites were in the wilderness, a man was found gathering wood on the Sabbath day. ³³Those who found him gathering wood brought him to Moses and Aaron and the whole assembly, ³⁴and they kept him in custody, because it was not clear what should be done to him. ³⁵Then the LORD said to Moses, "The man must die. The whole assembly must stone him outside the camp." ³⁶So the assembly took him outside the camp and stoned him to death, as the LORD commanded Moses.

Tassels on Garments

³⁷The LORD said to Moses, ³⁸"Speak to the Israelites and say to them: 'Throughout the generations to come you are to make tassels on the corners of your garments, with a blue cord on each tassel. ³⁹You will have these tassels to look at and so you will remember all the commands of the LORD, that you may obey them and not prostitute yourselves by chasing after the lusts of your own hearts and eyes. ⁴⁰Then you will remember to obey all my commands and will be consecrated to your God. ⁴¹I am the LORD your God, who brought you out of Egypt to be your God. I am the LORD your God.' "

Korah, Dathan and Abiram

16 Korah son of Izhar, the son of Kohath, the son of Levi, and certain Reubenites—Dathan and Abiram, sons of Eliab, and On son of Peleth—became insolentᵃ ²and rose up against Moses. With them were 250 Israelite men, well-known community leaders who had been appointed members of the council. ³They came as a group to oppose Moses and Aaron and said to them, "You have gone too far! The whole community is holy, every one of them, and the LORD is with them. Why then do you set yourselves above the LORD's assembly?"

⁴When Moses heard this, he fell facedown. ⁵Then he said to Korah and all his followers: "In the morning the LORD will show who belongs to him and who is holy, and he will have that person come near him. The one he chooses he will cause to come near him. ⁶You, Korah, and all your followers are to do this: Take censers ⁷and tomorrow put burning coals and incense in them before the LORD. The man the LORD chooses will be the one who is holy. You Levites have gone too far!"

⁸Moses also said to Korah, "Now listen, you Levites! ⁹Isn't it enough for you that the God of Israel has separated you from the rest of the Israelite community and brought you near himself to do the work at the LORD's tabernacle and to stand before the community and minister to them? ¹⁰He has brought you and all your fellow Levites near himself, but now you are trying to get the priesthood too. ¹¹It is against the LORD that you and all your followers have banded together. Who is Aaron that you should grumble against him?"

¹²Then Moses summoned Dathan and Abiram, the sons of Eliab. But they said, "We will not come! ¹³Isn't it enough that you have brought us up out of a land flowing with milk and honey to kill us in the wilderness? And now you also want to lord it over us! ¹⁴Moreover, you haven't brought us into a land flowing with milk and honey or given us an inheritance of fields and vineyards. Do you want to treat these men like slavesᵇ? No, we will not come!"

¹⁵Then Moses became very angry and said to the LORD, "Do not accept their offering. I have not taken so much as a donkey from them, nor have I wronged any of them."

¹⁶Moses said to Korah, "You and all your followers are to appear before the LORD tomorrow—you and they and Aaron. ¹⁷Each one is to take his censer and put incense in it—250 censers in all—and present it before the LORD. You and Aaron are to present your censers also." ¹⁸So each one took his censer, put burning coals and incense in it, and stood with Moses and Aaron at the entrance to the tent of meeting. ¹⁹When Korah had gathered all his followers in opposition to them at the entrance to the tent of meeting, the glory of the LORD appeared to the entire assembly. ²⁰The LORD said to Moses and Aaron, ²¹"Separate yourselves from this assembly so I can put an end to them at once."

²²But Moses and Aaron fell facedown and cried out, "O God, God of every human spir-

---

ᵃ 1 Or Peleth—took men   ᵇ 14 Or to deceive these men; Hebrew Will you gouge out the eyes of these men it, will you be angry with the entire assembly when only one man sins?"

²³Then the LORD said to Moses, ²⁴"Say to the assembly, 'Move away from the tents of Korah, Dathan and Abiram.' "

²⁵Moses got up and went to Dathan and Abiram, and the elders of Israel followed him. ²⁶He warned the assembly, "Move back from the tents of these wicked men! Do not touch anything belonging to them, or you will be swept away because of all their sins." ²⁷So they moved away from the tents of Korah, Dathan and Abiram. Dathan and Abiram had come out and were standing with their wives, children and little ones at the entrances to their tents.

²⁸Then Moses said, "This is how you will know that the LORD has sent me to do all these things and that it was not my idea: ²⁹If these men die a natural death and suffer the common fate of all human beings, then the LORD has not sent me. ³⁰But if the LORD brings about something totally new, and the earth opens its mouth and swallows them, with everything that belongs to them, and they go down alive into the realm of the dead, then you will know that these men have treated the LORD with contempt."

³¹As soon as he finished saying all this, the ground under them split apart ³²and the earth opened its mouth and swallowed them and their households, and all those associated with Korah, together with their possessions. ³³They went down alive into the realm of the dead, with everything they owned; the earth closed over them, and they perished and were gone from the community. ³⁴At their cries, all the Israelites around them fled, shouting, "The earth is going to swallow us too!"

³⁵And fire came out from the LORD and consumed the 250 men who were offering the incense.

*³⁶The LORD said to Moses, ³⁷"Tell Eleazar son of Aaron, the priest, to remove the censers from the charred remains and scatter the coals some distance away, for the censers are holy— ³⁸the censers of the men who sinned at the cost of their lives. Hammer the censers into sheets to overlay the altar, for they were presented before the LORD and have become holy. Let them be a sign to the Israelites."

³⁹So Eleazar the priest collected the bronze censers brought by those who had been burned to death, and he had them hammered out to overlay the altar, ⁴⁰as the LORD directed him through Moses. This was to remind the Israelites that no one except a descendant of Aaron should come to burn incense before the LORD, or he would become like Korah and his followers.

⁴¹The next day the whole Israelite community grumbled against Moses and Aaron. "You have killed the LORD's people," they said.

⁴²But when the assembly gathered in opposition to Moses and Aaron and turned toward the tent of meeting, suddenly the cloud covered it and the glory of the LORD appeared. ⁴³Then Moses and Aaron went to the front of the tent of meeting, ⁴⁴and the LORD said to Moses, ⁴⁵"Get away from this assembly so I can put an end to them at once." And they fell facedown.

⁴⁶Then Moses said to Aaron, "Take your censer and put incense in it, along with burning coals from the altar, and hurry to the assembly to make atonement for them. Wrath has come out from the LORD; the plague has started." ⁴⁷So Aaron did as Moses said, and ran into the midst of the assembly. The plague had already started among the people, but Aaron offered the incense and made atonement for them. ⁴⁸He stood between the living and the dead, and the plague stopped. ⁴⁹But 14,700 people died from the plague, in addition to those who had died because of Korah. ⁵⁰Then Aaron returned to Moses at the entrance to the tent of meeting, for the plague had stopped.

The Budding of Aaron's Staff

17 *¹The LORD said to Moses, ²"Speak to the Israelites and get twelve staffs from them, one from the leader of each of their ancestral tribes. Write the name of each man on his staff. ³On the staff of Levi write Aaron's name, for there must be one staff for the head of each ancestral tribe. ⁴Place them in the tent of meeting in front of the ark of the covenant law, where I meet with you. ⁵The staff belonging to the man I choose will sprout, and I will rid myself of this constant grumbling against you by the Israelites."

---

* 16:36-50 is numbered 17:1-15 in Hebrew texts.   * 17:1-13 is numbered 17:16-28 in Hebrew texts.

[6]So Moses spoke to the Israelites, and their leaders gave him twelve staffs, one for the leader of each of their ancestral tribes, and Aaron's staff was among them. [7]Moses placed the staffs before the LORD in the tent of the covenant law.

[8]The next day Moses entered the tent and saw that Aaron's staff, which represented the house of Levi, had not only sprouted but had budded, blossomed and produced almonds. [9]Then Moses brought out all the staffs from the LORD's presence to all the Israelites. They looked at them, and each of the leaders took his own staff.

[10]The LORD said to Moses, "Put back Aaron's staff in front of the ark of the covenant law, to be kept as a sign to the rebellious. This will put an end to their grumbling against me, so that they will not die." [11]Moses did just as the LORD commanded him.

[12]The Israelites said to Moses, "We will die! We are lost, we are all lost! [13]Anyone who even comes near the tabernacle of the LORD will die. Are we all going to die?"

Duties of Priests and Levites

18 The LORD said to Aaron, "You, your sons and your ancestral family are to bear the responsibility for offenses connected with the sanctuary, and you and your sons alone are to bear the responsibility for offenses connected with the priesthood. [2]Bring your fellow Levites from your ancestral tribe to join you and assist you when you and your sons minister before the tent of the covenant law. [3]They are to be responsible to you and are to perform all the duties of the tent, but they must not go near the furnishings of the sanctuary or the altar. Otherwise both they and you will die. [4]They are to join you and be responsible for the care of the tent of meeting—all the work at the tent—and no one else may come near where you are.

[5]"You are to be responsible for the care of the sanctuary and the altar, so that my wrath will not fall on the Israelites again. [6]I myself have selected your fellow Levites from among the Israelites as a gift to you, dedicated to the LORD to do the work at the tent of meeting. [7]But only you and your sons may serve as priests in connection with everything at the altar and inside the curtain. I am giving you the service of the priesthood as a gift. Anyone else who comes near the sanctuary is to be put to death."

Offerings for Priests and Levites

[8]Then the LORD said to Aaron, "I myself have put you in charge of the offerings presented to me; all the holy offerings the Israelites give me I give to you and your sons as your portion, your perpetual share. [9]You are to have the part of the most holy offerings that is kept from the fire. From all the gifts they bring me as most holy offerings, whether grain or sin[a] or guilt offerings, that part belongs to you and your sons. [10]Eat it as something most holy; every male shall eat it. You must regard it as holy.

[11]"This also is yours: whatever is set aside from the gifts of all the wave offerings of the Israelites. I give this to you and your sons and daughters as your perpetual share. Everyone in your household who is ceremonially clean may eat it.

[12]"I give you all the finest olive oil and all the finest new wine and grain they give the LORD as the firstfruits of their harvest. [13]All the land's firstfruits that they bring to the LORD will be yours. Everyone in your household who is ceremonially clean may eat it.

[14]"Everything in Israel that is devoted[b] to the LORD is yours. [15]The first offspring of every womb, both human and animal, that is offered to the LORD is yours. But you must redeem every firstborn son and every firstborn male of unclean animals. [16]When they are a month old, you must redeem them at the redemption price set at five shekels[c] of silver, according to the sanctuary shekel, which weighs twenty gerahs.

[17]"But you must not redeem the firstborn of a cow, a sheep or a goat; they are holy. Splash their blood against the altar and burn their fat as a food offering, an aroma pleasing to the LORD. [18]Their meat is to be yours, just as the breast of the wave offering and the right thigh are yours. [19]Whatever is set aside from the holy offerings the Israelites present to the LORD I give to you and your sons and daughters as your perpetual share. It is an everlasting covenant of salt before the LORD for both you and your offspring."

---

a 9 Or *purification*   b 14 The Hebrew term refers to the irrevocable giving over of things or persons to the LORD.   c 16 That is, about 2 ounces or about 55 grams

20The LORD said to Aaron, "You will have no inheritance in their land, nor will you have any share among them; I am your share and your inheritance among the Israelites.

21"I give to the Levites all the tithes in Israel as their inheritance in return for the work they do while serving at the tent of meeting. 22From now on the Israelites must not go near the tent of meeting, or they will bear the consequences of their sin and will die. 23It is the Levites who are to do the work at the tent of meeting and bear the responsibility for any offenses they commit against it. This is a lasting ordinance for the generations to come. They will receive no inheritance among the Israelites. 24Instead, I give to the Levites as their inheritance the tithes that the Israelites present as an offering to the LORD. That is why I said concerning them: 'They will have no inheritance among the Israelites.' "

25The LORD said to Moses, 26"Speak to the Levites and say to them: 'When you receive from the Israelites the tithe I give you as your inheritance, you must present a tenth of that tithe as the LORD's offering. 27Your offering will be reckoned to you as grain from the threshing floor or juice from the winepress. 28In this way you also will present an offering to the LORD from all the tithes you receive from the Israelites. From these tithes you must give the LORD's portion to Aaron the priest. 29You must present as the LORD's portion the best and holiest part of everything given to you.'

30"Say to the Levites: 'When you present the best part, it will be reckoned to you as the product of the threshing floor or the winepress. 31You and your households may eat the rest of it anywhere, for it is your wages for your work at the tent of meeting. 32By presenting the best part of it you will not be guilty in this matter; then you will not defile the holy offerings of the Israelites, and you will not die.' "

The Water of Cleansing

19 The LORD said to Moses and Aaron: 2"This is a requirement of the law that the LORD has commanded: Tell the Israelites to bring you a red heifer without defect or blemish and that has never been under a yoke. 3Give it to Eleazar the priest; it is to be taken outside the camp and slaughtered in his presence. 4Then Eleazar the priest is to take some of its blood on his finger and sprinkle it seven times toward the front of the tent of meeting. 5While he watches, the heifer is to be burned—its hide, flesh, blood and intestines. 6The priest is to take some cedar wood, hyssop and scarlet wool and throw them onto the burning heifer. 7After that, the priest must wash his clothes and bathe himself with water. He may then come into the camp, but he will be ceremonially unclean till evening. 8The man who burns it must also wash his clothes and bathe with water, and he too will be unclean till evening.

9"A man who is clean shall gather up the ashes of the heifer and put them in a ceremonially clean place outside the camp. They are to be kept by the Israelite community for use in the water of cleansing; it is for purification from sin. 10The man who gathers up the ashes of the heifer must also wash his clothes, and he too will be unclean till evening. This will be a lasting ordinance both for the Israelites and for the foreigners residing among them.

11"Whoever touches a human corpse will be unclean for seven days. 12They must purify themselves with the water on the third day and on the seventh day; then they will be clean. But if they do not purify themselves on the third and seventh days, they will not be clean. 13If they fail to purify themselves after touching a human corpse, they defile the LORD's tabernacle. They must be cut off from Israel. Because the water of cleansing has not been sprinkled on them, they are unclean; their uncleanness remains on them.

14"This is the law that applies when a person dies in a tent: Anyone who enters the tent and anyone who is in it will be unclean for seven days, 15and every open container without a lid fastened on it will be unclean.

16"Anyone out in the open who touches someone who has been killed with a sword or someone who has died a natural death, or anyone who touches a human bone or a grave, will be unclean for seven days.

17"For the unclean person, put some ashes from the burned purification offering into a jar and pour fresh water over them. 18Then a man who is ceremonially clean is to take some hyssop, dip it in the water and sprinkle the tent and all the furnishings and the people who were there. He must also sprinkle anyone who has touched a human bone or a grave or anyone who has been killed or anyone who has died a natural death. ¹⁹The man who is clean is to sprinkle those who are unclean on the third and seventh days, and on the seventh day he is to purify them. Those who are being cleansed must wash their clothes and bathe with water, and that evening they will be clean. ²⁰But if those who are unclean do not purify themselves, they must be cut off from the community, because they have defiled the sanctuary of the LORD. The water of cleansing has not been sprinkled on them, and they are unclean. ²¹This is a lasting ordinance for them.

"The man who sprinkles the water of cleansing must also wash his clothes, and anyone who touches the water of cleansing will be unclean till evening. ²²Anything that an unclean person touches becomes unclean, and anyone who touches it becomes unclean till evening."

Water From the Rock

20 In the first month the whole Israelite community arrived at the Desert of Zin, and they stayed at Kadesh. There Miriam died and was buried.

²Now there was no water for the community, and the people gathered in opposition to Moses and Aaron. ³They quarreled with Moses and said, "If only we had died when our brothers fell dead before the LORD! ⁴Why did you bring the LORD's community into this wilderness, that we and our livestock should die here? ⁵Why did you bring us up out of Egypt to this terrible place? It has no grain or figs, grapevines or pomegranates. And there is no water to drink!"

⁶Moses and Aaron went from the assembly to the entrance to the tent of meeting and fell facedown, and the glory of the LORD appeared to them. ⁷The LORD said to Moses, ⁸"Take the staff, and you and your brother Aaron gather the assembly together. Speak to that rock before their eyes and it will pour out its water. You will bring water out of the rock for the community so they and their livestock can drink."

⁹So Moses took the staff from the LORD's presence, just as he commanded him. ¹⁰He and Aaron gathered the assembly together

in front of the rock and Moses said to them, "Listen, you rebels, must we bring you water out of this rock?" ¹¹Then Moses raised his arm and struck the rock twice with his staff. Water gushed out, and the community and their livestock drank.

¹²But the LORD said to Moses and Aaron, "Because you did not trust in me enough to honor me as holy in the sight of the Israelites, you will not bring this community into the land I give them."

¹³These were the waters of Meribah,ᵃ where the Israelites quarreled with the LORD and where he was proved holy among them.

Edom Denies Israel Passage

¹⁴Moses sent messengers from Kadesh to the king of Edom, saying:

"This is what your brother Israel says: You know about all the hardships that have come on us. ¹⁵Our ancestors went down into Egypt, and we lived there many years. The Egyptians mistreated us and our ancestors, ¹⁶but when we cried out to the LORD, he heard our cry and sent an angel and brought us out of Egypt.

"Now we are here at Kadesh, a town on the edge of your territory. ¹⁷Please let us pass through your country. We will not go through any field or vineyard, or drink water from any well. We will travel along the King's Highway and not turn to the right or to the left until we have passed through your territory."

¹⁸But Edom answered:

"You may not pass through here; if you try, we will march out and attack you with the sword."

¹⁹The Israelites replied:

"We will go along the main road, and if we or our livestock drink any of your water, we will pay for it. We only want to pass through on foot—nothing else."

²⁰Again they answered:

"You may not pass through."

Then Edom came out against them with a large and powerful army. ²¹Since Edom re-

---

ᵃ 13 Meribah means quarreling.

fused to let them go through their territory, Israel turned away from them.

The Death of Aaron

22The whole Israelite community set out from Kadesh and came to Mount Hor. 23At Mount Hor, near the border of Edom, the LORD said to Moses and Aaron, 24"Aaron will be gathered to his people. He will not enter the land I give the Israelites, because both of you rebelled against my command at the waters of Meribah. 25Get Aaron and his son Eleazar and take them up Mount Hor. 26Remove Aaron's garments and put them on his son Eleazar, for Aaron will be gathered to his people; he will die there."

27Moses did as the LORD commanded: They went up Mount Hor in the sight of the whole community. 28Moses removed Aaron's garments and put them on his son Eleazar. And Aaron died there on top of the mountain. Then Moses and Eleazar came down from the mountain, 29and when the whole community learned that Aaron had died, the entire house of Israel mourned for him thirty days.

Arad Destroyed

21 When the Canaanite king of Arad, who lived in the Negev, heard that Israel was coming along the road to Atharim, he attacked the Israelites and captured some of them. 2Then Israel made this vow to the LORD: "If you will deliver these people into our hands, we will totally destroy*a* their cities." 3The LORD listened to Israel's plea and gave the Canaanites over to them. They completely destroyed them and their towns; so the place was named Hormah.*b*

The Bronze Snake

4They traveled from Mount Hor along the route to the Red Sea,*c* to go around Edom. But the people grew impatient on the way; 5they spoke against God and against Moses, and said, "Why have you brought us up out of Egypt to die in the wilderness? There is no bread! There is no water! And we detest this miserable food!"

6Then the LORD sent venomous snakes

among them; they bit the people and many Israelites died. 7The people came to Moses and said, "We sinned when we spoke against the LORD and against you. Pray that the LORD will take the snakes away from us." So Moses prayed for the people.

8The LORD said to Moses, "Make a snake and put it up on a pole; anyone who is bitten can look at it and live." 9So Moses made a bronze snake and put it up on a pole. Then when anyone was bitten by a snake and looked at the bronze snake, they lived.

The Journey to Moab

10The Israelites moved on and camped at Oboth. 11Then they set out from Oboth and camped in Iye Abarim, in the wilderness that faces Moab toward the sunrise. 12From there they moved on and camped in the Zered Valley. 13They set out from there and camped alongside the Arnon, which is in the wilderness extending into Amorite territory. The Arnon is the border of Moab, between Moab and the Amorites. 14That is why the Book of the Wars of the LORD says:

". . . Zahab*d* in Suphah and the ravines,
    the Arnon 15and*e* the slopes of the
        ravines
that lead to the settlement of Ar
    and lie along the border of Moab."

16From there they continued on to Beer, the well where the LORD said to Moses, "Gather the people together and I will give them water."

17Then Israel sang this song:

"Spring up, O well!
    Sing about it,
18about the well that the princes dug,
    that the nobles of the people sank—
        the nobles with scepters and staffs."

Then they went from the wilderness to Mattanah, 19from Mattanah to Nahaliel, from Nahaliel to Bamoth, 20and from Bamoth to the valley in Moab where the top of Pisgah overlooks the wasteland.

Defeat of Sihon and Og

21Israel sent messengers to say to Sihon king of the Amorites:

---

a 2 The Hebrew term refers to the irrevocable giving over of things or persons to the LORD, often by totally destroying them; also in verse 3.   *b 3* Hormah means *destruction.*   *c 4* Or *the Sea of Reeds*   *d 14* Septuagint; Hebrew *Waheb*   *e 14,15* Or *"I have been given from Suphah and the ravines / of the Arnon* 15*to*

THURSDAY

LIFTED UP TO SEEK AND TO SAVE

Numbers 21:1–35 or 21:8–9

Raymond Brown

[The Israelites] had been thundering at God with their incessant complaints, and [they] had to be represented at his throne by someone who could approach God for them. The grossly maligned leader became the urgently needed intercessor. Adversity sifts our priorities; they were no longer interested in more refined culinary provisions. They knew that Moses was a friend of God, and [they] pleaded earnestly for something that now mattered more than food or drink. Trouble had changed their values and reshaped their ambitions. P. T. Forsyth made the point that God's "final purpose in all trouble" is to drive us closer to himself: "The joiner, when he glues together two boards, keeps them tightly clamped till the cement sets . . . So with calamities, depressions and disappointments that crush us into closer contact with God. The pressure on us is kept up till the soul's union with God is set." Nobody could deny that these threatened and dying Israelites were "tightly clamped." They urged Moses to plead with God: "Pray that the LORD will take the snakes away from us" (Numbers 21:7).

CHARLES G. FINNEY {AD 1792–1875}

"Just as Moses lifted up the snake in the wilderness, so the Son of Man must be lifted up, that everyone who believes may have eternal life in him" (John 3:14–15). "And I, when I am lifted up from the earth, will draw all people to myself.' He said this to show the kind of death he was going to die" (John 12:32–33).

The object in both cases—with Moses and Jesus—was to save people from the bite of the serpent. Its influence, if left unchecked, is the death of the body; likewise, the effects of sin, unpardoned and uncleansed from the heart, are the ruin of the soul. Christ is lifted up so that sinners, believing in him, "shall not perish but have eternal life" (John 3:16).

reflection

1. How was the serpent on Moses' staff symbolic of Jesus?

2. How has the "bite of the serpent" in your life caused you to look to Jesus to save you?

3. When you find yourself in trouble—in a difficult or painful place in your life—where do you turn first?

For your next devotional reading, go to page 202.

22"Let us pass through your country. We will not turn aside into any field or vineyard, or drink water from any well. We will travel along the King's Highway until we have passed through your territory."

23But Sihon would not let Israel pass through his territory. He mustered his entire army and marched out into the wilderness against Israel. When he reached Jahaz, he fought with Israel. 24Israel, however, put him to the sword and took over his land from the Arnon to the Jabbok, but only as far as the Ammonites, because their border was fortified. 25Israel captured all the cities of the Amorites and occupied them, including Heshbon and all its surrounding settlements. 26Heshbon was the city of Sihon king of the Amorites, who had fought against the former king of Moab and had taken from him all his land as far as the Arnon.

27That is why the poets say:

"Come to Heshbon and let it be rebuilt;
    let Sihon's city be restored.

28"Fire went out from Heshbon,
    a blaze from the city of Sihon.
It consumed Ar of Moab,
    the citizens of Arnon's heights.
29Woe to you, Moab!
    You are destroyed, people of
        Chemosh!
He has given up his sons as fugitives
    and his daughters as captives
to Sihon king of the Amorites.

30"But we have overthrown them;
    Heshbon's dominion has been
        destroyed all the way to Dibon.
We have demolished them as far as
        Nophah,
    which extends to Medeba."

31So Israel settled in the land of the Amorites.

32After Moses had sent spies to Jazer, the Israelites captured its surrounding settlements and drove out the Amorites who were there. 33Then they turned and went up along the road toward Bashan, and Og king of Bashan and his whole army marched out to meet them in battle at Edrei.

34The LORD said to Moses, "Do not be afraid of him, for I have delivered him into your hands, along with his whole army and his land. Do to him what you did to Sihon king of the Amorites, who reigned in Heshbon."

35So they struck him down, together with his sons and his whole army, leaving them no survivors. And they took possession of his land.

Balak Summons Balaam

22 Then the Israelites traveled to the plains of Moab and camped along the Jordan across from Jericho.

2Now Balak son of Zippor saw all that Israel had done to the Amorites, 3and Moab was terrified because there were so many people. Indeed, Moab was filled with dread because of the Israelites.

4The Moabites said to the elders of Midian, "This horde is going to lick up everything around us, as an ox licks up the grass of the field."

So Balak son of Zippor, who was king of Moab at that time, 5sent messengers to summon Balaam son of Beor, who was at Pethor, near the Euphrates River, in his native land. Balak said:

"A people has come out of Egypt; they cover the face of the land and have settled next to me. 6Now come and put a curse on these people, because they are too powerful for me. Perhaps then I will be able to defeat them and drive them out of the land. For I know that whoever you bless is blessed, and whoever you curse is cursed."

7The elders of Moab and Midian left, taking with them the fee for divination. When they came to Balaam, they told him what Balak had said.

8"Spend the night here," Balaam said to them, "and I will report back to you with the answer the LORD gives me." So the Moabite officials stayed with him.

9God came to Balaam and asked, "Who are these men with you?"

10Balaam said to God, "Balak son of Zippor, king of Moab, sent me this message: 11'A people that has come out of Egypt covers the face of the land. Now come and put a curse on them for me. Perhaps then I will be able to fight them and drive them away.'"

12But God said to Balaam, "Do not go with them. You must not put a curse on those people, because they are blessed."

¹³The next morning Balaam got up and said to Balak's officials, "Go back to your own country, for the LORD has refused to let me go with you."

¹⁴So the Moabite officials returned to Balak and said, "Balaam refused to come with us."

¹⁵Then Balak sent other officials, more numerous and more distinguished than the first. ¹⁶They came to Balaam and said:

"This is what Balak son of Zippor says: Do not let anything keep you from coming to me, ¹⁷because I will reward you handsomely and do whatever you say. Come and put a curse on these people for me."

¹⁸But Balaam answered them, "Even if Balak gave me all the silver and gold in his palace, I could not do anything great or small to go beyond the command of the LORD my God. ¹⁹Now spend the night here so that I can find out what else the LORD will tell me."

²⁰That night God came to Balaam and said, "Since these men have come to summon you, go with them, but do only what I tell you."

Balaam's Donkey

²¹Balaam got up in the morning, saddled his donkey and went with the Moabite officials. ²²But God was very angry when he went, and the angel of the LORD stood in the road to oppose him. Balaam was riding on his donkey, and his two servants were with him. ²³When the donkey saw the angel of the LORD standing in the road with a drawn sword in his hand, it turned off the road into a field. Balaam beat it to get it back on the road.

²⁴Then the angel of the LORD stood in a narrow path through the vineyards, with walls on both sides. ²⁵When the donkey saw the angel of the LORD, it pressed close to the wall, crushing Balaam's foot against it. So he beat the donkey again.

²⁶Then the angel of the LORD moved on ahead and stood in a narrow place where there was no room to turn, either to the right or to the left. ²⁷When the donkey saw the angel of the LORD, it lay down under Balaam, and he was angry and beat it with his staff.

²⁸Then the LORD opened the donkey's mouth, and it said to Balaam, "What have I done to you to make you beat me these three times?"

²⁹Balaam answered the donkey, "You have made a fool of me! If only I had a sword in my hand, I would kill you right now."

³⁰The donkey said to Balaam, "Am I not your own donkey, which you have always ridden, to this day? Have I been in the habit of doing this to you?"

"No," he said.

³¹Then the LORD opened Balaam's eyes, and he saw the angel of the LORD standing in the road with his sword drawn. So he bowed low and fell facedown.

³²The angel of the LORD asked him, "Why have you beaten your donkey these three times? I have come here to oppose you because your path is a reckless one before me.ᵃ ³³The donkey saw me and turned away from me these three times. If it had not turned away, I would certainly have killed you by now, but I would have spared it."

³⁴Balaam said to the angel of the LORD, "I have sinned. I did not realize you were standing in the road to oppose me. Now if you are displeased, I will go back."

³⁵The angel of the LORD said to Balaam, "Go with the men, but speak only what I tell you." So Balaam went with Balak's officials.

³⁶When Balak heard that Balaam was coming, he went out to meet him at the Moabite town on the Arnon border, at the edge of his territory. ³⁷Balak said to Balaam, "Did I not send you an urgent summons? Why didn't you come to me? Am I really not able to reward you?"

³⁸"Well, I have come to you now," Balaam replied. "But I can't say whatever I please. I must speak only what God puts in my mouth."

³⁹Then Balaam went with Balak to Kiriath Huzoth. ⁴⁰Balak sacrificed cattle and sheep, and gave some to Balaam and the officials who were with him. ⁴¹The next morning Balak took Balaam up to Bamoth Baal, and from there he could see the outskirts of the Israelite camp.

ᵃ 32 The meaning of the Hebrew for this clause is uncertain.

Balaam's First Message

23 Balaam said, "Build me seven altars here, and prepare seven bulls and seven rams for me." ²Balak did as Balaam said, and the two of them offered a bull and a ram on each altar.

³Then Balaam said to Balak, "Stay here beside your offering while I go aside. Perhaps the LORD will come to meet with me. Whatever he reveals to me I will tell you." Then he went off to a barren height.

⁴God met with him, and Balaam said, "I have prepared seven altars, and on each altar I have offered a bull and a ram."

⁵The LORD put a word in Balaam's mouth and said, "Go back to Balak and give him this word."

⁶So he went back to him and found him standing beside his offering, with all the Moabite officials. ⁷Then Balaam spoke his message:

"Balak brought me from Aram,
    the king of Moab from the eastern
        mountains.
'Come,' he said, 'curse Jacob for me;
    come, denounce Israel.'
⁸How can I curse
    those whom God has not cursed?
How can I denounce
    those whom the LORD has not
        denounced?
⁹From the rocky peaks I see them,
    from the heights I view them.
I see a people who live apart
    and do not consider themselves one
        of the nations.
¹⁰Who can count the dust of Jacob
    or number the fourth part of Israel?
Let me die the death of the righteous,
    and may my final end be like theirs!"

¹¹Balak said to Balaam, "What have you done to me? I brought you to curse my enemies, but you have done nothing but bless them!"

¹²He answered, "Must I not speak what the LORD puts in my mouth?"

Balaam's Second Message

¹³Then Balak said to him, "Come with me to another place where you can see them; you will not see them all but only the outskirts of their camp. And from there, curse them for me." ¹⁴So he took him to the field of Zophim on the top of Pisgah, and there he built seven altars and offered a bull and a ram on each altar.

¹⁵Balaam said to Balak, "Stay here beside your offering while I meet with him over there."

¹⁶The LORD met with Balaam and put a word in his mouth and said, "Go back to Balak and give him this word."

¹⁷So he went to him and found him standing beside his offering, with the Moabite officials. Balak asked him, "What did the LORD say?"

¹⁸Then he spoke his message:

"Arise, Balak, and listen;
    hear me, son of Zippor.
¹⁹God is not a human, that he should lie,
    not a human being, that he should
        change his mind.
Does he speak and then not act?
    Does he promise and not fulfill?
²⁰I have received a command to bless;
    he has blessed, and I cannot change
        it.

²¹"No misfortune is seen in Jacob,
    no misery observed*a* in Israel.
The LORD their God is with them;
    the shout of the King is among them.
²²God brought them out of Egypt;
    they have the strength of a wild ox.
²³There is no divination against*b* Jacob,
    no evil omens against*b* Israel.
It will now be said of Jacob
    and of Israel, 'See what God has
        done!'
²⁴The people rise like a lioness;
    they rouse themselves like a lion
that does not rest till it devours its prey
    and drinks the blood of its victims."

²⁵Then Balak said to Balaam, "Neither curse them at all nor bless them at all!"

²⁶Balaam answered, "Did I not tell you I must do whatever the LORD says?"

Balaam's Third Message

²⁷Then Balak said to Balaam, "Come, let me take you to another place. Perhaps it will please God to let you curse them for me from there." ²⁸And Balak took Balaam to the top of Peor, overlooking the wasteland.

²⁹Balaam said, "Build me seven altars

---

a 21 Or *He has not looked on Jacob's offenses / or on the wrongs found*   *b 23* Or *in* here, and prepare seven bulls and seven rams for me." ³⁰Balak did as Balaam had said, and offered a bull and a ram on each altar.

24 Now when Balaam saw that it pleased the LORD to bless Israel, he did not resort to divination as at other times, but turned his face toward the wilderness. ²When Balaam looked out and saw Israel encamped tribe by tribe, the Spirit of God came on him ³and he spoke his message:

"The prophecy of Balaam son of Beor,
    the prophecy of one whose eye sees
        clearly,
⁴the prophecy of one who hears the
        words of God,
    who sees a vision from the Almighty,ᵃ
    who falls prostrate, and whose eyes
        are opened:

⁵"How beautiful are your tents, Jacob,
    your dwelling places, Israel!

⁶"Like valleys they spread out,
    like gardens beside a river,
    like aloes planted by the LORD,
    like cedars beside the waters.
⁷Water will flow from their buckets;
    their seed will have abundant water.

"Their king will be greater than Agag;
    their kingdom will be exalted.

⁸"God brought them out of Egypt;
    they have the strength of a wild ox.
They devour hostile nations
    and break their bones in pieces;
    with their arrows they pierce them.
⁹Like a lion they crouch and lie down,
    like a lioness—who dares to rouse
        them?

"May those who bless you be blessed
    and those who curse you be cursed!"

¹⁰Then Balak's anger burned against Balaam. He struck his hands together and said to him, "I summoned you to curse my enemies, but you have blessed them these three times. ¹¹Now leave at once and go home! I said I would reward you handsomely, but the LORD has kept you from being rewarded."

¹²Balaam answered Balak, "Did I not tell the messengers you sent me, ¹³'Even if Balak gave me all the silver and gold in his palace, I could not do anything of my own accord, good or bad, to go beyond the command of the LORD—and I must say only what the LORD says'? ¹⁴Now I am going back to my people, but come, let me warn you of what this people will do to your people in days to come."

Balaam's Fourth Message
¹⁵Then he spoke his message:

"The prophecy of Balaam son of Beor,
    the prophecy of one whose eye sees
        clearly,
¹⁶the prophecy of one who hears the
        words of God,
    who has knowledge from the Most
        High,
    who sees a vision from the Almighty,
    who falls prostrate, and whose eyes
        are opened:

¹⁷"I see him, but not now;
    I behold him, but not near.
A star will come out of Jacob;
    a scepter will rise out of Israel.
He will crush the foreheads of Moab,
    the skullsᵇ ofᶜ all the people of
        Sheth.ᵈ
¹⁸Edom will be conquered;
    Seir, his enemy, will be conquered,
    but Israel will grow strong.
¹⁹A ruler will come out of Jacob
    and destroy the survivors of the city."

Balaam's Fifth Message
²⁰Then Balaam saw Amalek and spoke his message:

"Amalek was first among the nations,
    but they will come to ruin at last."

Balaam's Sixth Message
²¹Then he saw the Kenites and spoke his message:

"Your dwelling place is secure,
    your nest is set in a rock;
²²yet you Kenites will be destroyed
    when Ashur takes you captive."

ᵃ 4 Hebrew *Shaddai*; also in verse 16   ᵇ 17 Samaritan Pentateuch (see also Jer. 48:45); the meaning of the word in the Masoretic Text is uncertain.   ᶜ 17 Or possibly *Moab, / batter*   ᵈ 17 Or *all the noisy boasters*

Balaam's Seventh Message

23Then he spoke his message:

"Ah, who can live when God does this?a

24   Ships will come from the shores of
          Cyprus;
     they will subdue Ashur and Eber,
          but they too will come to ruin."

25Then Balaam got up and returned home, and Balak went his own way.

Moab Seduces Israel

25 While Israel was staying in Shittim, the men began to indulge in sexual immorality with Moabite women, 2who invited them to the sacrifices to their gods. The people ate the sacrificial meal and bowed down before these gods. 3So Israel yoked themselves to the Baal of Peor. And the LORD's anger burned against them.

4The LORD said to Moses, "Take all the leaders of these people, kill them and expose them in broad daylight before the LORD, so that the LORD's fierce anger may turn away from Israel."

5So Moses said to Israel's judges, "Each of you must put to death those of your people who have yoked themselves to the Baal of Peor."

6Then an Israelite man brought into the camp a Midianite woman right before the eyes of Moses and the whole assembly of Israel while they were weeping at the entrance to the tent of meeting. 7When Phinehas son of Eleazar, the son of Aaron, the priest, saw this, he left the assembly, took a spear in his hand 8and followed the Israelite into the tent. He drove the spear into both of them, right through the Israelite man and into the woman's stomach. Then the plague against the Israelites was stopped; 9but those who died in the plague numbered 24,000.

10The LORD said to Moses, 11"Phinehas son of Eleazar, the son of Aaron, the priest, has turned my anger away from the Israelites. Since he was as zealous for my honor among them as I am, I did not put an end to them in my zeal. 12Therefore tell him I am making my covenant of peace with him. 13He and his descendants will have a cov-enant of a lasting priesthood, because he was zealous for the honor of his God and made atonement for the Israelites."

14The name of the Israelite who was killed with the Midianite woman was Zimri son of Salu, the leader of a Simeonite family. 15And the name of the Midianite woman who was put to death was Kozbi daughter of Zur, a tribal chief of a Midianite family.

16The LORD said to Moses, 17"Treat the Midianites as enemies and kill them. 18They treated you as enemies when they deceived you in the Peor incident involving their sister Kozbi, the daughter of a Midianite leader, the woman who was killed when the plague came as a result of that incident."

The Second Census

26 After the plague the LORD said to Moses and Eleazar son of Aaron, the priest, 2"Take a census of the whole Israelite community by families—all those twenty years old or more who are able to serve in the army of Israel." 3So on the plains of Moab by the Jordan across from Jericho, Moses and Eleazar the priest spoke with them and said, 4"Take a census of the men twenty years old or more, as the LORD commanded Moses."

These were the Israelites who came out of Egypt:

5The descendants of Reuben, the firstborn son of Israel, were:
     through Hanok, the Hanokite clan;
     through Pallu, the Palluite clan;
     6through Hezron, the Hezronite clan;
     through Karmi, the Karmite clan.
7These were the clans of Reuben; those numbered were 43,730.

8The son of Pallu was Eliab, 9and the sons of Eliab were Nemuel, Dathan and Abiram. The same Dathan and Abiram were the community officials who rebelled against Moses and Aaron and were among Korah's followers when they rebelled against the LORD. 10The earth opened its mouth and swallowed them along with Korah, whose followers died when the fire devoured the 250 men. And they served as a warning sign. 11The line of Korah, however, did not die out.

---

a 23 Masoretic Text; with a different word division of the Hebrew *The people from the islands will gather from the north.*

¹²The descendants of Simeon by their clans were:

through Nemuel, the Nemuelite clan;
through Jamin, the Jaminite clan;
through Jakin, the Jakinite clan;
¹³through Zerah, the Zerahite clan;
through Shaul, the Shaulite clan.

¹⁴These were the clans of Simeon; those numbered were 22,200.

¹⁵The descendants of Gad by their clans were:

through Zephon, the Zephonite clan;
through Haggi, the Haggite clan;
through Shuni, the Shunite clan;
¹⁶through Ozni, the Oznite clan;
through Eri, the Erite clan;
¹⁷through Arodi,ᵃ the Arodite clan;
through Areli, the Arelite clan.

¹⁸These were the clans of Gad; those numbered were 40,500.

¹⁹Er and Onan were sons of Judah, but they died in Canaan.
²⁰The descendants of Judah by their clans were:

through Shelah, the Shelanite clan;
through Perez, the Perezite clan;
through Zerah, the Zerahite clan.
²¹The descendants of Perez were:
through Hezron, the Hezronite clan;
through Hamul, the Hamulite clan.

²²These were the clans of Judah; those numbered were 76,500.

²³The descendants of Issachar by their clans were:

through Tola, the Tolaite clan;
through Puah, the Puiteᵇ clan;
²⁴through Jashub, the Jashubite clan;
through Shimron, the Shimronite clan.

²⁵These were the clans of Issachar; those numbered were 64,300.

²⁶The descendants of Zebulun by their clans were:

through Sered, the Seredite clan;
through Elon, the Elonite clan;
through Jahleel, the Jahleelite clan.

²⁷These were the clans of Zebulun; those numbered were 60,500.

²⁸The descendants of Joseph by their clans through Manasseh and Ephraim were:

²⁹The descendants of Manasseh:
through Makir, the Makirite clan (Makir was the father of Gilead);
through Gilead, the Gileadite clan.
³⁰These were the descendants of Gilead:
through Iezer, the Iezerite clan;
through Helek, the Helekite clan;
³¹through Asriel, the Asrielite clan;
through Shechem, the Shechemite clan;
³²through Shemida, the Shemidaite clan;
through Hepher, the Hepherite clan.
³³(Zelophehad son of Hepher had no sons; he had only daughters, whose names were Mahlah, Noah, Hoglah, Milkah and Tirzah.)

³⁴These were the clans of Manasseh; those numbered were 52,700.

³⁵These were the descendants of Ephraim by their clans:

through Shuthelah, the Shuthelahite clan;
through Beker, the Bekerite clan;
through Tahan, the Tahanite clan.
³⁶These were the descendants of Shuthelah:
through Eran, the Eranite clan.

³⁷These were the clans of Ephraim; those numbered were 32,500.

These were the descendants of Joseph by their clans.

³⁸The descendants of Benjamin by their clans were:

through Bela, the Belaite clan;
through Ashbel, the Ashbelite clan;
through Ahiram, the Ahiramite clan;
³⁹through Shupham,ᶜ the Shuphamite clan;
through Hupham, the Huphamite clan.
⁴⁰The descendants of Bela through Ard and Naaman were:
through Ard,ᵈ the Ardite clan;
through Naaman, the Naamite clan.

⁴¹These were the clans of Benjamin; those numbered were 45,600.

ᵃ 17 Samaritan Pentateuch and Syriac (see also Gen. 46:16); Masoretic Text *Arod*   ᵇ 23 Samaritan Pentateuch, Septuagint, Vulgate and Syriac (see also 1 Chron. 7:1); Masoretic Text *through Puvah, the Punite*   ᶜ 39 A few manuscripts of the Masoretic Text, Samaritan Pentateuch, Vulgate and Syriac (see also Septuagint); most manuscripts of the Masoretic Text *Shephupham*   ᵈ 40 Samaritan Pentateuch and Vulgate (see also Septuagint); Masoretic Text does not have *through Ard.*

⁴²These were the descendants of Dan by their clans:

through Shuham, the Shuhamite clan. These were the clans of Dan: ⁴³All of them were Shuhamite clans; and those numbered were 64,400.

⁴⁴The descendants of Asher by their clans were:

through Imnah, the Imnite clan;
through Ishvi, the Ishvite clan;
through Beriah, the Beriite clan;
⁴⁵and through the descendants of Beriah:
through Heber, the Heberite clan;
through Malkiel, the Malkielite clan.

⁴⁶(Asher had a daughter named Serah.)

⁴⁷These were the clans of Asher; those numbered were 53,400.

⁴⁸The descendants of Naphtali by their clans were:

through Jahzeel, the Jahzeelite clan;
through Guni, the Gunite clan;
⁴⁹through Jezer, the Jezerite clan;
through Shillem, the Shillemite clan.

⁵⁰These were the clans of Naphtali; those numbered were 45,400.

⁵¹The total number of the men of Israel was 601,730.

⁵²The LORD said to Moses, ⁵³"The land is to be allotted to them as an inheritance based on the number of names. ⁵⁴To a larger group give a larger inheritance, and to a smaller group a smaller one; each is to receive its inheritance according to the number of those listed. ⁵⁵Be sure that the land is distributed by lot. What each group inherits will be according to the names for its ancestral tribe. ⁵⁶Each inheritance is to be distributed by lot among the larger and smaller groups."

⁵⁷These were the Levites who were counted by their clans:

through Gershon, the Gershonite clan;
through Kohath, the Kohathite clan;
through Merari, the Merarite clan.

⁵⁸These also were Levite clans:

the Libnite clan,
the Hebronite clan,
the Mahlite clan,
the Mushite clan,
the Korahite clan.

(Kohath was the forefather of Amram; ⁵⁹the name of Amram's wife was Jochebed, a descendant of Levi, who was born to the Levites[a] in Egypt. To Amram she bore Aaron, Moses and their sister Miriam. ⁶⁰Aaron was the father of Nadab and Abihu, Eleazar and Ithamar. ⁶¹But Nadab and Abihu died when they made an offering before the LORD with unauthorized fire.)

⁶²All the male Levites a month old or more numbered 23,000. They were not counted along with the other Israelites because they received no inheritance among them.

⁶³These are the men counted by Moses and Eleazar the priest when they counted the Israelites on the plains of Moab by the Jordan across from Jericho. ⁶⁴Not one of them was among those counted by Moses and Aaron the priest when they counted the Israelites in the Desert of Sinai. ⁶⁵For the LORD had told those Israelites they would surely die in the wilderness, and not one of them was left except Caleb son of Jephunneh and Joshua son of Nun.

Zelophehad's Daughters

27 The daughters of Zelophehad son of Hepher, the son of Gilead, the son of Makir, the son of Manasseh, belonged to the clans of Manasseh son of Joseph. The names of the daughters were Mahlah, Noah, Hoglah, Milkah and Tirzah. They came forward ²and stood before Moses, Eleazar the priest, the leaders and the whole assembly at the entrance to the tent of meeting and said, ³"Our father died in the wilderness. He was not among Korah's followers, who banded together against the LORD, but he died for his own sin and left no sons. ⁴Why should our father's name disappear from his clan because he had no son? Give us property among our father's relatives."

⁵So Moses brought their case before the LORD, ⁶and the LORD said to him, ⁷"What Zelophehad's daughters are saying is right. You must certainly give them property as an inheritance among their father's relatives and give their father's inheritance to them.

⁸"Say to the Israelites, 'If a man dies and leaves no son, give his inheritance to his

---

a 59 Or *Jochebed, a daughter of Levi, who was born to Levi* daughter. ⁹If he has no daughter, give his inheritance to his brothers. ¹⁰If he has no brothers, give his inheritance to his father's brothers. ¹¹If his father had no brothers, give his inheritance to the nearest relative in his clan, that he may possess it. This is to have the force of law for the Israelites, as the LORD commanded Moses.' "

Joshua to Succeed Moses

¹²Then the LORD said to Moses, "Go up this mountain in the Abarim Range and see the land I have given the Israelites. ¹³After you have seen it, you too will be gathered to your people, as your brother Aaron was, ¹⁴for when the community rebelled at the waters in the Desert of Zin, both of you disobeyed my command to honor me as holy before their eyes." (These were the waters of Meribah Kadesh, in the Desert of Zin.)

¹⁵Moses said to the LORD, ¹⁶"May the LORD, the God of every human spirit, appoint someone over this community ¹⁷to go out and come in before them, one who will lead them out and bring them in, so the LORD's people will not be like sheep without a shepherd."

¹⁸So the LORD said to Moses, "Take Joshua son of Nun, a man in whom is the spirit of leadership,ᵃ and lay your hand on him. ¹⁹Have him stand before Eleazar the priest and the entire assembly and commission him in their presence. ²⁰Give him some of your authority so the whole Israelite community will obey him. ²¹He is to stand before Eleazar the priest, who will obtain decisions for him by inquiring of the Urim before the LORD. At his command he and the entire community of the Israelites will go out, and at his command they will come in."

²²Moses did as the LORD commanded him. He took Joshua and had him stand before Eleazar the priest and the whole assembly. ²³Then he laid his hands on him and commissioned him, as the LORD instructed through Moses.

Daily Offerings

28

The LORD said to Moses, ²"Give this command to the Israelites and say to them: 'Make sure that you present to me at the appointed time my food offerings, as an aroma pleasing to me.' ³Say to them: 'This is the food offering you are to present to the LORD: two lambs a year old without defect, as a regular burnt offering each day. ⁴Offer one lamb in the morning and the other at twilight, ⁵together with a grain offering of a tenth of an ephahᵇ of the finest flour mixed with a quarter of a hinᶜ of oil from pressed olives. ⁶This is the regular burnt offering instituted at Mount Sinai as a pleasing aroma, a food offering presented to the LORD. ⁷The accompanying drink offering is to be a quarter of a hin of fermented drink with each lamb. Pour out the drink offering to the LORD at the sanctuary. ⁸Offer the second lamb at twilight, along with the same kind of grain offering and drink offering that you offer in the morning. This is a food offering, an aroma pleasing to the LORD.

Sabbath Offerings

⁹" 'On the Sabbath day, make an offering of two lambs a year old without defect, together with its drink offering and a grain offering of two-tenths of an ephahᵈ of the finest flour mixed with olive oil. ¹⁰This is the burnt offering for every Sabbath, in addition to the regular burnt offering and its drink offering.

Monthly Offerings

¹¹" 'On the first of every month, present to the LORD a burnt offering of two young bulls, one ram and seven male lambs a year old, all without defect. ¹²With each bull there is to be a grain offering of three-tenths of an ephahᵉ of the finest flour mixed with oil; with the ram, a grain offering of two-tenths of an ephah of the finest flour mixed with oil; ¹³and with each lamb, a grain offering of a tenth of an ephah of the finest flour mixed with oil. This is for a burnt offering, a pleasing aroma, a food offering presented to the LORD. ¹⁴With each bull there is to be a drink offering of half a hinᶠ of wine; with the ram, a third of a hinᵍ; and with each lamb, a quarter of a hin. This is the monthly burnt offering to be made at each new moon during the year.

ᵃ 18 Or the Spirit   ᵇ 5 That is, probably about 3 1/2 pounds or about 1.6 kilograms; also in verses 13, 21 and 29   ᶜ 5 That is, about 1 quart or about 0.9 liter; also in verses 7 and 14   ᵈ 9 That is, probably about 7 pounds or about 3.2 kilograms; also in verses 12, 20 and 28   ᵉ 12 That is, probably about 11 pounds or about 5 kilograms; also in verses 20 and 28   ᶠ 14 That is, about 1/2 gallon or about 1.8 liters   ᵍ 14 That is, about 2 2/3 pints or about 1.2 liters

15Besides the regular burnt offering with its drink offering, one male goat is to be presented to the LORD as a sin offering.*a*

The Passover

16" 'On the fourteenth day of the first month the LORD's Passover is to be held. 17On the fifteenth day of this month there is to be a festival; for seven days eat bread made without yeast. 18On the first day hold a sacred assembly and do no regular work. 19Present to the LORD a food offering consisting of a burnt offering of two young bulls, one ram and seven male lambs a year old, all without defect. 20With each bull offer a grain offering of three-tenths of an ephah of the finest flour mixed with oil; with the ram, two-tenths; 21and with each of the seven lambs, one-tenth. 22Include one male goat as a sin offering to make atonement for you. 23Offer these in addition to the regular morning burnt offering. 24In this way present the food offering every day for seven days as an aroma pleasing to the LORD; it is to be offered in addition to the regular burnt offering and its drink offering. 25On the seventh day hold a sacred assembly and do no regular work.

The Festival of Weeks

26" 'On the day of firstfruits, when you present to the LORD an offering of new grain during the Festival of Weeks, hold a sacred assembly and do no regular work. 27Present a burnt offering of two young bulls, one ram and seven male lambs a year old as an aroma pleasing to the LORD. 28With each bull there is to be a grain offering of three-tenths of an ephah of the finest flour mixed with oil; with the ram, two-tenths; 29and with each of the seven lambs, one-tenth. 30Include one male goat to make atonement for you. 31Offer these together with their drink offerings, in addition to the regular burnt offering and its grain offering. Be sure the animals are without defect.

The Festival of Trumpets

29 " 'On the first day of the seventh month hold a sacred assembly and do no regular work.

It is a day for you to sound the trumpets. 2As an aroma pleasing to the LORD, offer a burnt offering of one young bull, one ram and seven male lambs a year old, all without defect. 3With the bull offer a grain offering of three-tenths of an ephah*b* of the finest flour mixed with olive oil; with the ram, two-tenths*c*; 4and with each of the seven lambs, one-tenth.*d* 5Include one male goat as a sin offering*e* to make atonement for you. 6These are in addition to the monthly and daily burnt offerings with their grain offerings and drink offerings as specified. They are food offerings presented to the LORD, a pleasing aroma.

The Day of Atonement

7" 'On the tenth day of this seventh month hold a sacred assembly. You must deny yourselves*f* and do no work. 8Present as an aroma pleasing to the LORD a burnt offering of one young bull, one ram and seven male lambs a year old, all without defect. 9With the bull offer a grain offering of three-tenths of an ephah of the finest flour mixed with olive oil; with the ram, two-tenths; 10and with each of the seven lambs, one-tenth. 11Include one male goat as a sin offering, in addition to the sin offering for atonement and the regular burnt offering with its grain offering, and their drink offerings.

The Festival of Tabernacles

12" 'On the fifteenth day of the seventh month, hold a sacred assembly and do no regular work. Celebrate a festival to the LORD for seven days. 13Present as an aroma pleasing to the LORD a food offering consisting of a burnt offering of thirteen young bulls, two rams and fourteen male lambs a year old, all without defect. 14With each of the thirteen bulls offer a grain offering of three-tenths of an ephah of the finest flour mixed with olive oil; with each of the two rams, two-tenths; 15and with each of the fourteen lambs, one-tenth. 16Include one male goat as a sin offering, in addition to the regular burnt offering with its grain offering and drink offering.

17" 'On the second day offer twelve young bulls, two rams and fourteen male lambs a

---

a 15 Or *purification offering*; also in verse 22   *b 3* That is, probably about 11 pounds or about 5 kilograms; also in verses 9 and 14   *c 3* That is, probably about 7 pounds or about 3.2 kilograms; also in verses 9 and 14   *d 4* That is, probably about 3 1/2 pounds or about 1.6 kilograms; also in verses 10 and 15   *e 5* Or *purification offering*; also elsewhere in this chapter   *f 7* Or *must fast* year old, all without defect. ¹⁸With the bulls, rams and lambs, offer their grain offerings and drink offerings according to the number specified. ¹⁹Include one male goat as a sin offering, in addition to the regular burnt offering with its grain offering, and their drink offerings.

²⁰" 'On the third day offer eleven bulls, two rams and fourteen male lambs a year old, all without defect. ²¹With the bulls, rams and lambs, offer their grain offerings and drink offerings according to the number specified. ²²Include one male goat as a sin offering, in addition to the regular burnt offering with its grain offering and drink offering.

²³" 'On the fourth day offer ten bulls, two rams and fourteen male lambs a year old, all without defect. ²⁴With the bulls, rams and lambs, offer their grain offerings and drink offerings according to the number specified. ²⁵Include one male goat as a sin offering, in addition to the regular burnt offering with its grain offering and drink offering.

²⁶" 'On the fifth day offer nine bulls, two rams and fourteen male lambs a year old, all without defect. ²⁷With the bulls, rams and lambs, offer their grain offerings and drink offerings according to the number specified. ²⁸Include one male goat as a sin offering, in addition to the regular burnt offering with its grain offering and drink offering.

²⁹" 'On the sixth day offer eight bulls, two rams and fourteen male lambs a year old, all without defect. ³⁰With the bulls, rams and lambs, offer their grain offerings and drink offerings according to the number specified. ³¹Include one male goat as a sin offering, in addition to the regular burnt offering with its grain offering and drink offering.

³²" 'On the seventh day offer seven bulls, two rams and fourteen male lambs a year old, all without defect. ³³With the bulls, rams and lambs, offer their grain offerings and drink offerings according to the number specified. ³⁴Include one male goat as a sin offering, in addition to the regular burnt offering with its grain offering and drink offering.

³⁵" 'On the eighth day hold a closing special assembly and do no regular work. ³⁶Present as an aroma pleasing to the Lord a food offering consisting of a burnt offering of one bull, one ram and seven male lambs a year old, all without defect. ³⁷With the bull, the

ram and the lambs, offer their grain offerings and drink offerings according to the number specified. ³⁸Include one male goat as a sin offering, in addition to the regular burnt offering with its grain offering and drink offering.

³⁹" 'In addition to what you vow and your freewill offerings, offer these to the Lord at your appointed festivals: your burnt offerings, grain offerings, drink offerings and fellowship offerings.' "

*⁴⁰Moses told the Israelites all that the Lord commanded him.

Vows

30 *Moses said to the heads of the tribes of Israel: "This is what the Lord commands: ²When a man makes a vow to the Lord or takes an oath to obligate himself by a pledge, he must not break his word but must do everything he said.

³"When a young woman still living in her father's household makes a vow to the Lord or obligates herself by a pledge ⁴and her father hears about her vow or pledge but says nothing to her, then all her vows and every pledge by which she obligated herself will stand. ⁵But if her father forbids her when he hears about it, none of her vows or the pledges by which she obligated herself will stand; the Lord will release her because her father has forbidden her.

⁶"If she marries after she makes a vow or after her lips utter a rash promise by which she obligates herself ⁷and her husband hears about it but says nothing to her, then her vows or the pledges by which she obligated herself will stand. ⁸But if her husband forbids her when he hears about it, he nullifies the vow that obligates her or the rash promise by which she obligates herself, and the Lord will release her.

⁹"Any vow or obligation taken by a widow or divorced woman will be binding on her.

¹⁰"If a woman living with her husband makes a vow or obligates herself by a pledge under oath ¹¹and her husband hears about it but says nothing to her and does not forbid her, then all her vows or the pledges by which she obligated herself will stand. ¹²But if her husband nullifies them when he hears about them, then none of the vows or pledg-

---

* 29:40 is numbered 30:1 in Hebrew texts.   * 30:1-16 is numbered 30:2-17 in Hebrew texts.

es that came from her lips will stand. Her husband has nullified them, and the LORD will release her. [13]Her husband may confirm or nullify any vow she makes or any sworn pledge to deny herself.[a] [14]But if her husband says nothing to her about it from day to day, then he confirms all her vows or the pledges binding on her. He confirms them by saying nothing to her when he hears about them. [15]If, however, he nullifies them some time after he hears about them, then he must bear the consequences of her wrongdoing."

[16]These are the regulations the LORD gave Moses concerning relationships between a man and his wife, and between a father and his young daughter still living at home.

Vengeance on the Midianites

31 The LORD said to Moses, [2]"Take vengeance on the Midianites for the Israelites. After that, you will be gathered to your people."

[3]So Moses said to the people, "Arm some of your men to go to war against the Midianites so that they may carry out the LORD's vengeance on them. [4]Send into battle a thousand men from each of the tribes of Israel." [5]So twelve thousand men armed for battle, a thousand from each tribe, were supplied from the clans of Israel. [6]Moses sent them into battle, a thousand from each tribe, along with Phinehas son of Eleazar, the priest, who took with him articles from the sanctuary and the trumpets for signaling.

[7]They fought against Midian, as the LORD commanded Moses, and killed every man. [8]Among their victims were Evi, Rekem, Zur, Hur and Reba—the five kings of Midian. They also killed Balaam son of Beor with the sword. [9]The Israelites captured the Midianite women and children and took all the Midianite herds, flocks and goods as plunder. [10]They burned all the towns where the Midianites had settled, as well as all their camps. [11]They took all the plunder and spoils, including the people and animals, [12]and brought the captives, spoils and plunder to Moses and Eleazar the priest and the Israelite assembly at their camp on the plains of Moab, by the Jordan across from Jericho.

[13]Moses, Eleazar the priest and all the leaders of the community went to meet them outside the camp. [14]Moses was angry with the officers of the army—the commanders of thousands and commanders of hundreds—who returned from the battle.

[15]"Have you allowed all the women to live?" he asked them. [16]"They were the ones who followed Balaam's advice and enticed the Israelites to be unfaithful to the LORD in the Peor incident, so that a plague struck the LORD's people. [17]Now kill all the boys. And kill every woman who has slept with a man, [18]but save for yourselves every girl who has never slept with a man.

[19]"Anyone who has killed someone or touched someone who was killed must stay outside the camp seven days. On the third and seventh days you must purify yourselves and your captives. [20]Purify every garment as well as everything made of leather, goat hair or wood."

[21]Then Eleazar the priest said to the soldiers who had gone into battle, "This is what is required by the law that the LORD gave Moses: [22]Gold, silver, bronze, iron, tin, lead [23]and anything else that can withstand fire must be put through the fire, and then it will be clean. But it must also be purified with the water of cleansing. And whatever cannot withstand fire must be put through that water. [24]On the seventh day wash your clothes and you will be clean. Then you may come into the camp."

Dividing the Spoils

[25]The LORD said to Moses, [26]"You and Eleazar the priest and the family heads of the community are to count all the women and animals that were captured. [27]Divide the spoils equally between the soldiers who took part in the battle and the rest of the community. [28]From the soldiers who fought in the battle, set apart as tribute for the LORD one out of every five hundred, whether women, cattle, donkeys or sheep. [29]Take this tribute from their half share and give it to Eleazar the priest as the LORD's part. [30]From the Israelites' half, select one out of every fifty, whether women, cattle, donkeys, sheep or other animals. Give them to the Levites, who are responsible for the care of the LORD's tabernacle." [31]So Moses and Ele-

a 13 Or to fast

azar the priest did as the LORD commanded Moses.

³²The plunder remaining from the spoils that the soldiers took was 675,000 sheep, ³³72,000 cattle, ³⁴61,000 donkeys ³⁵and 32,000 women who had never slept with a man.

³⁶The half share of those who fought in the battle was:

337,500 sheep, ³⁷of which the tribute for the LORD was 675;
³⁸36,000 cattle, of which the tribute for the LORD was 72;
³⁹30,500 donkeys, of which the tribute for the LORD was 61;
⁴⁰16,000 women, of whom the tribute for the LORD was 32.

⁴¹Moses gave the tribute to Eleazar the priest as the LORD's part, as the LORD commanded Moses.

⁴²The half belonging to the Israelites, which Moses set apart from that of the fighting men— ⁴³the community's half— was 337,500 sheep, ⁴⁴36,000 cattle, ⁴⁵30,500 donkeys ⁴⁶and 16,000 women. ⁴⁷From the Israelites' half, Moses selected one out of every fifty women and animals, as the LORD commanded him, and gave them to the Levites, who were responsible for the care of the LORD's tabernacle.

⁴⁸Then the officers who were over the units of the army—the commanders of thousands and commanders of hundreds— went to Moses ⁴⁹and said to him, "Your servants have counted the soldiers under our command, and not one is missing. ⁵⁰So we have brought as an offering to the LORD the gold articles each of us acquired—armlets, bracelets, signet rings, earrings and necklaces—to make atonement for ourselves before the LORD."

⁵¹Moses and Eleazar the priest accepted from them the gold—all the crafted articles. ⁵²All the gold from the commanders of thousands and commanders of hundreds that Moses and Eleazar presented as a gift to the LORD weighed 16,750 shekels.ᵃ ⁵³Each soldier had taken plunder for himself. ⁵⁴Moses and Eleazar the priest accepted the gold from the commanders of thousands and commanders of hundreds and brought it

into the tent of meeting as a memorial for the Israelites before the LORD.

The Transjordan Tribes

32 The Reubenites and Gadites, who had very large herds and flocks, saw that the lands of Jazer and Gilead were suitable for livestock. ²So they came to Moses and Eleazar the priest and to the leaders of the community, and said, ³"Ataroth, Dibon, Jazer, Nimrah, Heshbon, Elealeh, Sebam, Nebo and Beon— ⁴the land the LORD subdued before the people of Israel—are suitable for livestock, and your servants have livestock. ⁵If we have found favor in your eyes," they said, "let this land be given to your servants as our possession. Do not make us cross the Jordan."

⁶Moses said to the Gadites and Reubenites, "Should your own people go to war while you sit here? ⁷Why do you discourage the Israelites from crossing over into the land the LORD has given them? ⁸This is what your fathers did when I sent them from Kadesh Barnea to look over the land. ⁹After they went up to the Valley of Eshkol and viewed the land, they discouraged the Israelites from entering the land the LORD had given them. ¹⁰The LORD's anger was aroused that day and he swore this oath: ¹¹'Because they have not followed me wholeheartedly, not one of those who were twenty years old or more when they came up out of Egypt will see the land I promised on oath to Abraham, Isaac and Jacob— ¹²not one except Caleb son of Jephunneh the Kenizzite and Joshua son of Nun, for they followed the LORD wholeheartedly.' ¹³The LORD's anger burned against Israel and he made them wander in the wilderness forty years, until the whole generation of those who had done evil in his sight was gone.

¹⁴"And here you are, a brood of sinners, standing in the place of your fathers and making the LORD even more angry with Israel. ¹⁵If you turn away from following him, he will again leave all this people in the wilderness, and you will be the cause of their destruction."

¹⁶Then they came up to him and said, "We would like to build pens here for our livestock and cities for our women and children. ¹⁷But we will arm ourselves for battleᵇ

ᵃ 52 That is, about 420 pounds or about 190 kilograms   ᵇ 17 Septuagint; Hebrew *will be quick to arm ourselves* and go ahead of the Israelites until we have brought them to their place. Meanwhile our women and children will live in fortified cities, for protection from the inhabitants of the land. ¹⁸We will not return to our homes until all the Israelites have received their inheritance. ¹⁹We will not receive any inheritance with them on the other side of the Jordan, because our inheritance has come to us on the east side of the Jordan."

²⁰Then Moses said to them, "If you will do this—if you will arm yourselves before the LORD for battle ²¹and if all of you who are armed cross over the Jordan before the LORD until he has driven his enemies out before him— ²²then when the land is subdued before the LORD, you may return and be free from your obligation to the LORD and to Israel. And this land will be your possession before the LORD.

²³"But if you fail to do this, you will be sinning against the LORD; and you may be sure that your sin will find you out. ²⁴Build cities for your women and children, and pens for your flocks, but do what you have promised."

²⁵The Gadites and Reubenites said to Moses, "We your servants will do as our lord commands. ²⁶Our children and wives, our flocks and herds will remain here in the cities of Gilead. ²⁷But your servants, every man who is armed for battle, will cross over to fight before the LORD, just as our lord says."

²⁸Then Moses gave orders about them to Eleazar the priest and Joshua son of Nun and to the family heads of the Israelite tribes. ²⁹He said to them, "If the Gadites and Reubenites, all those armed for battle, cross over the Jordan with you before the LORD, then when the land is subdued before you, you must give them the land of Gilead as their possession. ³⁰But if they do not cross over with you armed, they must accept their possession with you in Canaan."

³¹The Gadites and Reubenites answered, "Your servants will do what the LORD has said. ³²We will cross over before the LORD into Canaan armed, but the property we inherit will be on this side of the Jordan."

³³Then Moses gave to the Gadites, the Reubenites and the half-tribe of Manasseh son of Joseph the kingdom of Sihon king of the Amorites and the kingdom of Og king of Bashan—the whole land with its cities and the territory around them.

³⁴The Gadites built up Dibon, Ataroth, Aroer, ³⁵Atroth Shophan, Jazer, Jogbehah, ³⁶Beth Nimrah and Beth Haran as fortified cities, and built pens for their flocks. ³⁷And the Reubenites rebuilt Heshbon, Elealeh and Kiriathaim, ³⁸as well as Nebo and Baal Meon (these names were changed) and Sibmah. They gave names to the cities they rebuilt.

³⁹The descendants of Makir son of Manasseh went to Gilead, captured it and drove out the Amorites who were there. ⁴⁰So Moses gave Gilead to the Makirites, the descendants of Manasseh, and they settled there. ⁴¹Jair, a descendant of Manasseh, captured their settlements and called them Havvoth Jair.ᵃ ⁴²And Nobah captured Kenath and its surrounding settlements and called it Nobah after himself.

Stages in Israel's Journey

33 Here are the stages in the journey of the Israelites when they came out of Egypt by divisions under the leadership of Moses and Aaron. ²At the LORD's command Moses recorded the stages in their journey. This is their journey by stages:

³The Israelites set out from Rameses on the fifteenth day of the first month, the day after the Passover. They marched out defiantly in full view of all the Egyptians, ⁴who were burying all their firstborn, whom the LORD had struck down among them; for the LORD had brought judgment on their gods.

⁵The Israelites left Rameses and camped at Sukkoth.

⁶They left Sukkoth and camped at Etham, on the edge of the desert.

⁷They left Etham, turned back to Pi Hahiroth, to the east of Baal Zephon, and camped near Migdol.

⁸They left Pi Hahirothᵇ and passed through the sea into the desert, and when they had traveled for three days in the Desert of Etham, they camped at Marah.

⁹They left Marah and went to Elim,

where there were twelve springs and seventy palm trees, and they camped there.

¹⁰They left Elim and camped by the Red Sea.ᵃ

¹¹They left the Red Sea and camped in the Desert of Sin.

¹²They left the Desert of Sin and camped at Dophkah.

¹³They left Dophkah and camped at Alush.

¹⁴They left Alush and camped at Rephidim, where there was no water for the people to drink.

¹⁵They left Rephidim and camped in the Desert of Sinai.

¹⁶They left the Desert of Sinai and camped at Kibroth Hattaavah.

¹⁷They left Kibroth Hattaavah and camped at Hazeroth.

¹⁸They left Hazeroth and camped at Rithmah.

¹⁹They left Rithmah and camped at Rimmon Perez.

²⁰They left Rimmon Perez and camped at Libnah.

²¹They left Libnah and camped at Rissah.

²²They left Rissah and camped at Kehelathah.

²³They left Kehelathah and camped at Mount Shepher.

²⁴They left Mount Shepher and camped at Haradah.

²⁵They left Haradah and camped at Makheloth.

²⁶They left Makheloth and camped at Tahath.

²⁷They left Tahath and camped at Terah.

²⁸They left Terah and camped at Mithkah.

²⁹They left Mithkah and camped at Hashmonah.

³⁰They left Hashmonah and camped at Moseroth.

³¹They left Moseroth and camped at Bene Jaakan.

³²They left Bene Jaakan and camped at Hor Haggidgad.

³³They left Hor Haggidgad and camped at Jotbathah.

³⁴They left Jotbathah and camped at Abronah.

³⁵They left Abronah and camped at Ezion Geber.

³⁶They left Ezion Geber and camped at Kadesh, in the Desert of Zin.

³⁷They left Kadesh and camped at Mount Hor, on the border of Edom. ³⁸At the LORD's command Aaron the priest went up Mount Hor, where he died on the first day of the fifth month of the fortieth year after the Israelites came out of Egypt. ³⁹Aaron was a hundred and twenty-three years old when he died on Mount Hor.

⁴⁰The Canaanite king of Arad, who lived in the Negev of Canaan, heard that the Israelites were coming.

⁴¹They left Mount Hor and camped at Zalmonah.

⁴²They left Zalmonah and camped at Punon.

⁴³They left Punon and camped at Oboth.

⁴⁴They left Oboth and camped at Iye Abarim, on the border of Moab.

⁴⁵They left Iye Abarim and camped at Dibon Gad.

⁴⁶They left Dibon Gad and camped at Almon Diblathaim.

⁴⁷They left Almon Diblathaim and camped in the mountains of Abarim, near Nebo.

⁴⁸They left the mountains of Abarim and camped on the plains of Moab by the Jordan across from Jericho. ⁴⁹There on the plains of Moab they camped along the Jordan from Beth Jeshimoth to Abel Shittim.

⁵⁰On the plains of Moab by the Jordan across from Jericho the LORD said to Moses, ⁵¹"Speak to the Israelites and say to them: 'When you cross the Jordan into Canaan, ⁵²drive out all the inhabitants of the land before you. Destroy all their carved images and their cast idols, and demolish all their high places. ⁵³Take possession of the land and settle in it, for I have given you the land to possess. ⁵⁴Distribute the land by lot, according to your clans. To a larger group give a larger inheritance, and to a smaller group a smaller one. Whatever falls to them by lot

will be theirs. Distribute it according to your ancestral tribes.

55 " 'But if you do not drive out the inhabitants of the land, those you allow to remain will become barbs in your eyes and thorns in your sides. They will give you trouble in the land where you will live. 56And then I will do to you what I plan to do to them.' "

Boundaries of Canaan

34 The LORD said to Moses, 2"Command the Israelites and say to them: 'When you enter Canaan, the land that will be allotted to you as an inheritance is to have these boundaries:

3 " 'Your southern side will include some of the Desert of Zin along the border of Edom. Your southern boundary will start in the east from the southern end of the Dead Sea, 4cross south of Scorpion Pass, continue on to Zin and go south of Kadesh Barnea. Then it will go to Hazar Addar and over to Azmon, 5where it will turn, join the Wadi of Egypt and end at the Mediterranean Sea.

6 " 'Your western boundary will be the coast of the Mediterranean Sea. This will be your boundary on the west.

7 " 'For your northern boundary, run a line from the Mediterranean Sea to Mount Hor 8and from Mount Hor to Lebo Hamath. Then the boundary will go to Zedad, 9continue to Ziphron and end at Hazar Enan. This will be your boundary on the north.

10 " 'For your eastern boundary, run a line from Hazar Enan to Shepham. 11The boundary will go down from Shepham to Riblah on the east side of Ain and continue along the slopes east of the Sea of Galilee.a 12Then the boundary will go down along the Jordan and end at the Dead Sea.

" 'This will be your land, with its boundaries on every side.' "

13Moses commanded the Israelites: "Assign this land by lot as an inheritance. The LORD has ordered that it be given to the nine and a half tribes, 14because the families of the tribe of Reuben, the tribe of Gad and the half-tribe of Manasseh have received their inheritance. 15These two and a half tribes have received their inheritance east of the Jordan across from Jericho, toward the sunrise."

16The LORD said to Moses, 17"These are the names of the men who are to assign the land for you as an inheritance: Eleazar the priest and Joshua son of Nun. 18And appoint one leader from each tribe to help assign the land. 19These are their names:

Caleb son of Jephunneh,
    from the tribe of Judah;
20Shemuel son of Ammihud,
    from the tribe of Simeon;
21Elidad son of Kislon,
    from the tribe of Benjamin;
22Bukki son of Jogli,
    the leader from the tribe of Dan;
23Hanniel son of Ephod,
    the leader from the tribe of Manasseh son of Joseph;
24Kemuel son of Shiphtan,
    the leader from the tribe of Ephraim son of Joseph;
25Elizaphan son of Parnak,
    the leader from the tribe of Zebulun;
26Paltiel son of Azzan,
    the leader from the tribe of Issachar;
27Ahihud son of Shelomi,
    the leader from the tribe of Asher;
28Pedahel son of Ammihud,
    the leader from the tribe of Naphtali."

29These are the men the LORD commanded to assign the inheritance to the Israelites in the land of Canaan.

Towns for the Levites

35 On the plains of Moab by the Jordan across from Jericho, the LORD said to Moses, 2"Command the Israelites to give the Levites towns to live in from the inheritance the Israelites will possess. And give them pasturelands around the towns. 3Then they will have towns to live in and pasturelands for the cattle they own and all their other animals.

4"The pasturelands around the towns that you give the Levites will extend a thousand cubitsb from the town wall. 5Outside the town, measure two thousand cubitsc on the east side, two thousand on the south side, two thousand on the west and two thousand on the north, with the town in the center. They will have this area as pastureland for the towns.

a 11 Hebrew Kinnereth   b 4 That is, about 1,500 feet or about 450 meters   c 5 That is, about 3,000 feet or about 900 meters

Cities of Refuge

6"Six of the towns you give the Levites will be cities of refuge, to which a person who has killed someone may flee. In addition, give them forty-two other towns. 7In all you must give the Levites forty-eight towns, together with their pasturelands. 8The towns you give the Levites from the land the Israelites possess are to be given in proportion to the inheritance of each tribe: Take many towns from a tribe that has many, but few from one that has few."

9Then the LORD said to Moses: 10"Speak to the Israelites and say to them: 'When you cross the Jordan into Canaan, 11select some towns to be your cities of refuge, to which a person who has killed someone accidentally may flee. 12They will be places of refuge from the avenger, so that anyone accused of murder may not die before standing trial before the assembly. 13These six towns you give will be your cities of refuge. 14Give three on this side of the Jordan and three in Canaan as cities of refuge. 15These six towns will be a place of refuge for Israelites and for foreigners residing among them, so that anyone who has killed another accidentally can flee there.

16"'If anyone strikes someone a fatal blow with an iron object, that person is a murderer; the murderer is to be put to death. 17Or if anyone is holding a stone and strikes someone a fatal blow with it, that person is a murderer; the murderer is to be put to death. 18Or if anyone is holding a wooden object and strikes someone a fatal blow with it, that person is a murderer; the murderer is to be put to death. 19The avenger of blood shall put the murderer to death; when the avenger comes upon the murderer, the avenger shall put the murderer to death. 20If anyone with malice aforethought shoves another or throws something at them intentionally so that they die 21or if out of enmity one person hits another with their fist so that the other dies, that person is to be put to death; that person is a murderer. The avenger of blood shall put the murderer to death when they meet.

22"'But if without enmity someone suddenly pushes another or throws something at them unintentionally 23or, without seeing them, drops on them a stone heavy enough to kill them, and they die, then since that other person was not an enemy and no harm

was intended, 24the assembly must judge between the accused and the avenger of blood according to these regulations. 25The assembly must protect the one accused of murder from the avenger of blood and send the accused back to the city of refuge to which they fled. The accused must stay there until the death of the high priest, who was anointed with the holy oil.

26"'But if the accused ever goes outside the limits of the city of refuge in which refuge was taken 27and the avenger of blood finds that person outside the city, the avenger of blood may kill the accused without being guilty of murder. 28The accused must stay in the city of refuge until the death of the high priest; only after the death of the high priest may an accused person return home.

29"'This is to have the force of law for you throughout the generations to come, wherever you live.

30"'Anyone who kills a person is to be put to death as a murderer only on the testimony of witnesses. But no one is to be put to death on the testimony of only one witness.

31"'Do not accept a ransom for the life of a murderer, who deserves to die. A murderer is to be put to death.

32"'Do not accept a ransom for anyone who has fled to a city of refuge and so allow them to go back and live on their own land before the death of the high priest.

33"'Do not pollute the land where you are. Bloodshed pollutes the land, and atonement cannot be made for the land on which blood has been shed, except by the blood of the one who shed it. 34Do not defile the land where you live and where I dwell, for I, the LORD, dwell among the Israelites.'"

Inheritance of Zelophehad's Daughters

36 The family heads of the clan of Gilead son of Makir, the son of Manasseh, who were from the clans of the descendants of Joseph, came and spoke before Moses and the leaders, the heads of the Israelite families. 2They said, "When the LORD commanded my lord to give the land as an inheritance to the Israelites by lot, he ordered you to give the inheritance of our brother Zelophehad to his daughters. 3Now suppose they marry men from other Israelite tribes; then their inheritance will be taken from our ancestral inheritance and

added to that of the tribe they marry into. And so part of the inheritance allotted to us will be taken away. ⁴When the Year of Jubilee for the Israelites comes, their inheritance will be added to that of the tribe into which they marry, and their property will be taken from the tribal inheritance of our ancestors."

⁵Then at the LORD's command Moses gave this order to the Israelites: "What the tribe of the descendants of Joseph is saying is right. ⁶This is what the LORD commands for Zelophehad's daughters: They may marry anyone they please as long as they marry within their father's tribal clan. ⁷No inheritance in Israel is to pass from one tribe to another, for each of the Israelites shall keep the tribal inheritance of their ancestors. ⁸Every daughter who inherits land in any Israel-

ite tribe must marry someone in her father's tribal clan, so that all Israelites will possess the inheritance of their ancestors. ⁹No inheritance may pass from one tribe to another, for each Israelite tribe is to keep the land it inherits.

¹⁰So Zelophehad's daughters did as the LORD commanded Moses. ¹¹Zelophehad's daughters—Mahlah, Tirzah, Hoglah, Milkah and Noah—married their cousins on their father's side. ¹²They married within the clans of the descendants of Manasseh son of Joseph, and their inheritance remained in their father's tribe and clan.

¹³These are the commands and regulations the LORD gave through Moses to the Israelites on the plains of Moab by the Jordan across from Jericho.

deuteronomy

> AUTHOR: Moses
>
> DATE: During the 1400s B.C., while the Israelites were traveling in the desert
>
> THEME: God has committed himself to a covenant relationship with his children.

The Command to Leave Horeb

1 These are the words Moses spoke to all Israel in the wilderness east of the Jordan—that is, in the Arabah—opposite Suph, between Paran and Tophel, Laban, Hazeroth and Dizahab. ²(It takes eleven days to go from Horeb to Kadesh Barnea by the Mount Seir road.)

³In the fortieth year, on the first day of the eleventh month, Moses proclaimed to the Israelites all that the LORD had commanded him concerning them. ⁴This was after he had defeated Sihon king of the Amorites, who reigned in Heshbon, and at Edrei had defeated Og king of Bashan, who reigned in Ashtaroth.

⁵East of the Jordan in the territory of Moab, Moses began to expound this law, saying:

⁶The LORD our God said to us at Horeb, "You have stayed long enough at this mountain. ⁷Break camp and advance into the hill country of the Amorites; go to all the neighboring peoples in the Arabah, in the mountains, in the western foothills, in the Negev and along the coast, to the land of the Canaanites and to Lebanon, as far as the great river, the Euphrates. ⁸See, I have given you this land. Go in and take possession of the land the LORD swore he would give to your fathers—to Abraham, Isaac and Jacob—and to their descendants after them."

The Appointment of Leaders

⁹At that time I said to you, "You are too heavy a burden for me to carry alone. ¹⁰The LORD your God has increased your numbers so that today you are as many as the stars in the sky. ¹¹May the LORD, the God of your ancestors, increase you a thousand times and bless you as he has promised! ¹²But how can I bear your problems and your burdens and your disputes all by myself? ¹³Choose some wise, understanding and respected men from each of your tribes, and I will set them over you."

¹⁴You answered me, "What you propose to do is good."

¹⁵So I took the leading men of your tribes, wise and respected men, and appointed them to have authority over you—as commanders of thousands, of hundreds, of fifties and of tens and as tribal officials. ¹⁶And I charged your judges at that time: Hear the disputes between your people and judge fairly, whether the case is between two Israelites or between an Israelite and a foreigner residing among you. ¹⁷Do not show partiality in judging; hear both small and great alike. Do not be afraid of anyone, for judgment belongs to God. Bring me any case too hard for you, and I will hear it. ¹⁸And at that time I told you everything you were to do.

Spies Sent Out

¹⁹Then, as the LORD our God commanded us, we set out from Horeb and went toward the hill country of the Amorites through all that vast and dreadful wilderness that you have seen, and so we reached Kadesh Barnea. ²⁰Then I said to you, "You have reached the hill country of the Amorites, which the LORD our God is giving us. ²¹See, the LORD your God has given you the land. Go up and take possession of it as the LORD, the God of your ancestors, told you. Do not be afraid; do not be discouraged."

²²Then all of you came to me and said, "Let us send men ahead to spy out the land for us and bring back a report about the

route we are to take and the towns we will come to."

²³The idea seemed good to me; so I selected twelve of you, one man from each tribe. ²⁴They left and went up into the hill country, and came to the Valley of Eshkol and explored it. ²⁵Taking with them some of the fruit of the land, they brought it down to us and reported, "It is a good land that the LORD our God is giving us."

Rebellion Against the LORD

²⁶But you were unwilling to go up; you rebelled against the command of the LORD your God. ²⁷You grumbled in your tents and said, "The LORD hates us; so he brought us out of Egypt to deliver us into the hands of the Amorites to destroy us. ²⁸Where can we go? Our brothers have made our hearts melt in fear. They say, 'The people are stronger and taller than we are; the cities are large, with walls up to the sky. We even saw the Anakites there.' "

²⁹Then I said to you, "Do not be terrified; do not be afraid of them. ³⁰The LORD your God, who is going before you, will fight for you, as he did for you in Egypt, before your very eyes, ³¹and in the wilderness. There you saw how the LORD your God carried you, as a father carries his son, all the way you went until you reached this place."

³²In spite of this, you did not trust in the LORD your God, ³³who went ahead of you on your journey, in fire by night and in a cloud by day, to search out places for you to camp and to show you the way you should go.

³⁴When the LORD heard what you said, he was angry and solemnly swore: ³⁵"No one from this evil generation shall see the good land I swore to give your ancestors, ³⁶except Caleb son of Jephunneh. He will see it, and I will give him and his descendants the land he set his feet on, because he followed the LORD wholeheartedly."

³⁷Because of you the LORD became angry with me also and said, "You shall not enter it, either. ³⁸But your assistant, Joshua son of Nun, will enter it. Encourage him, because he will lead Israel to inherit it. ³⁹And the little ones that you said would be taken captive, your children who do not yet know good from bad—they will enter the land. I will give it to them and they will take pos-

session of it. ⁴⁰But as for you, turn around and set out toward the desert along the route to the Red Sea.ᵃ

⁴¹Then you replied, "We have sinned against the LORD. We will go up and fight, as the LORD our God commanded us." So every one of you put on his weapons, thinking it easy to go up into the hill country.

⁴²But the LORD said to me, "Tell them, 'Do not go up and fight, because I will not be with you. You will be defeated by your enemies.' "

⁴³So I told you, but you would not listen. You rebelled against the LORD's command and in your arrogance you marched up into the hill country. ⁴⁴The Amorites who lived in those hills came out against you; they chased you like a swarm of bees and beat you down from Seir all the way to Hormah. ⁴⁵You came back and wept before the LORD, but he paid no attention to your weeping and turned a deaf ear to you. ⁴⁶And so you stayed in Kadesh many days—all the time you spent there.

Wanderings in the Wilderness

2 Then we turned back and set out toward the wilderness along the route to the Red Sea,ᵃ as the LORD had directed me. For a long time we made our way around the hill country of Seir.

²Then the LORD said to me, ³"You have made your way around this hill country long enough; now turn north. ⁴Give the people these orders: 'You are about to pass through the territory of your relatives the descendants of Esau, who live in Seir. They will be afraid of you, but be very careful. ⁵Do not provoke them to war, for I will not give you any of their land, not even enough to put your foot on. I have given Esau the hill country of Seir as his own. ⁶You are to pay them in silver for the food you eat and the water you drink.' "

⁷The LORD your God has blessed you in all the work of your hands. He has watched over your journey through this vast wilderness. These forty years the LORD your God has been with you, and you have not lacked anything.

⁸So we went on past our relatives the descendants of Esau, who live in Seir. We turned from the Arabah road, which comes

ᵃ 40,1 Or the Sea of Reeds

up from Elath and Ezion Geber, and traveled along the desert road of Moab.

⁹Then the LORD said to me, "Do not harass the Moabites or provoke them to war, for I will not give you any part of their land. I have given Ar to the descendants of Lot as a possession."

¹⁰(The Emites used to live there—a people strong and numerous, and as tall as the Anakites. ¹¹Like the Anakites, they too were considered Rephaites, but the Moabites called them Emites. ¹²Horites used to live in Seir, but the descendants of Esau drove them out. They destroyed the Horites from before them and settled in their place, just as Israel did in the land the LORD gave them as their possession.)

¹³And the LORD said, "Now get up and cross the Zered Valley." So we crossed the valley.

¹⁴Thirty-eight years passed from the time we left Kadesh Barnea until we crossed the Zered Valley. By then, that entire generation of fighting men had perished from the camp, as the LORD had sworn to them. ¹⁵The LORD's hand was against them until he had completely eliminated them from the camp.

¹⁶Now when the last of these fighting men among the people had died, ¹⁷the LORD said to me, ¹⁸"Today you are to pass by the region of Moab at Ar. ¹⁹When you come to the Ammonites, do not harass them or provoke them to war, for I will not give you possession of any land belonging to the Ammonites. I have given it as a possession to the descendants of Lot."

²⁰(That too was considered a land of the Rephaites, who used to live there; but the Ammonites called them Zamzummites. ²¹They were a people strong and numerous, and as tall as the Anakites. The LORD destroyed them from before the Ammonites, who drove them out and settled in their place. ²²The LORD had done the same for the descendants of Esau, who lived in Seir, when he destroyed the Horites from before them. They drove them out and have lived in their place to this day. ²³And as for the Avvites who lived in villages as far as Gaza, the Caphtorites coming out from Caphtorᵃ destroyed them and settled in their place.)

Defeat of Sihon King of Heshbon

²⁴"Set out now and cross the Arnon Gorge. See, I have given into your hand Sihon the Amorite, king of Heshbon, and his country. Begin to take possession of it and engage him in battle. ²⁵This very day I will begin to put the terror and fear of you on all the nations under heaven. They will hear reports of you and will tremble and be in anguish because of you."

²⁶From the Desert of Kedemoth I sent messengers to Sihon king of Heshbon offering peace and saying, ²⁷"Let us pass through your country. We will stay on the main road; we will not turn aside to the right or to the left. ²⁸Sell us food to eat and water to drink for their price in silver. Only let us pass through on foot— ²⁹as the descendants of Esau, who live in Seir, and the Moabites, who live in Ar, did for us—until we cross the Jordan into the land the LORD our God is giving us." ³⁰But Sihon king of Heshbon refused to let us pass through. For the LORD your God had made his spirit stubborn and his heart obstinate in order to give him into your hands, as he has now done.

³¹The LORD said to me, "See, I have begun to deliver Sihon and his country over to you. Now begin to conquer and possess his land."

³²When Sihon and all his army came out to meet us in battle at Jahaz, ³³the LORD our God delivered him over to us and we struck him down, together with his sons and his whole army. ³⁴At that time we took all his towns and completely destroyedᵇ them— men, women and children. We left no survivors. ³⁵But the livestock and the plunder from the towns we had captured we carried off for ourselves. ³⁶From Aroer on the rim of the Arnon Gorge, and from the town in the gorge, even as far as Gilead, not one town was too strong for us. The LORD our God gave us all of them. ³⁷But in accordance with the command of the LORD our God, you did not encroach on any of the land of the Ammonites, neither the land along the course of the Jabbok nor that around the towns in the hills.

ᵃ 23 That is, Crete   ᵇ 34 The Hebrew term refers to the irrevocable giving over of things or persons to the LORD, often by totally destroying them.

Defeat of Og King of Bashan

3 Next we turned and went up along the road toward Bashan, and Og king of Bashan with his whole army marched out to meet us in battle at Edrei. ²The LORD said to me, "Do not be afraid of him, for I have delivered him into your hands, along with his whole army and his land. Do to him what you did to Sihon king of the Amorites, who reigned in Heshbon."

³So the LORD our God also gave into our hands Og king of Bashan and all his army. We struck them down, leaving no survivors. ⁴At that time we took all his cities. There was not one of the sixty cities that we did not take from them—the whole region of Argob, Og's kingdom in Bashan. ⁵All these cities were fortified with high walls and with gates and bars, and there were also a great many unwalled villages. ⁶We completely destroyed*a* them, as we had done with Sihon king of Heshbon, destroying*a* every city— men, women and children. ⁷But all the livestock and the plunder from their cities we carried off for ourselves.

⁸So at that time we took from these two kings of the Amorites the territory east of the Jordan, from the Arnon Gorge as far as Mount Hermon. ⁹(Hermon is called Sirion by the Sidonians; the Amorites call it Senir.) ¹⁰We took all the towns on the plateau, and all Gilead, and all Bashan as far as Salekah and Edrei, towns of Og's kingdom in Bashan. ¹¹(Og king of Bashan was the last of the Rephaites. His bed was decorated with iron and was more than nine cubits long and four cubits wide.*b* It is still in Rabbah of the Ammonites.)

Division of the Land

¹²Of the land that we took over at that time, I gave the Reubenites and the Gadites the territory north of Aroer by the Arnon Gorge, including half the hill country of Gilead, together with its towns. ¹³The rest of Gilead and also all of Bashan, the kingdom of Og, I gave to the half-tribe of Manasseh. (The whole region of Argob in Bashan used to be known as a land of the Rephaites. ¹⁴Jair, a descendant of Manasseh, took the whole region of Argob as far as the border of the Geshurites and the Maakathites; it was

named after him, so that to this day Bashan is called Havvoth Jair.*c*) ¹⁵And I gave Gilead to Makir. ¹⁶But to the Reubenites and the Gadites I gave the territory extending from Gilead down to the Arnon Gorge (the middle of the gorge being the border) and out to the Jabbok River, which is the border of the Ammonites. ¹⁷Its western border was the Jordan in the Arabah, from Kinnereth to the Sea of the Arabah (that is, the Dead Sea), below the slopes of Pisgah.

¹⁸I commanded you at that time: "The LORD your God has given you this land to take possession of it. But all your able-bodied men, armed for battle, must cross over ahead of the other Israelites. ¹⁹However, your wives, your children and your livestock (I know you have much livestock) may stay in the towns I have given you, ²⁰until the LORD gives rest to all your people as he has to you, and they too have taken over the land that the LORD your God is giving them across the Jordan. After that, each of you may go back to the possession I have given you."

Moses Forbidden to Cross the Jordan

²¹At that time I commanded Joshua: "You have seen with your own eyes all that the LORD your God has done to these two kings. The LORD will do the same to all the kingdoms over there where you are going. ²²Do not be afraid of them; the LORD your God himself will fight for you."

²³At that time I pleaded with the LORD: ²⁴"Sovereign LORD, you have begun to show to your servant your greatness and your strong hand. For what god is there in heaven or on earth who can do the deeds and mighty works you do? ²⁵Let me go over and see the good land beyond the Jordan—that fine hill country and Lebanon."

²⁶But because of you the LORD was angry with me and would not listen to me. "That is enough," the LORD said. "Do not speak to me anymore about this matter. ²⁷Go up to the top of Pisgah and look west and north and south and east. Look at the land with your own eyes, since you are not going to cross this Jordan. ²⁸But commission Joshua, and encourage and strengthen him, for he will lead this people across and will cause them

a 6 The Hebrew term refers to the irrevocable giving over of things or persons to the LORD, often by totally destroying them. *b 11* That is, about 13 feet long and 6 feet wide or about 4 meters long and 1.8 meters wide *c 14* Or *called the settlements of Jair* to inherit the land that you will see." ²⁹So we stayed in the valley near Beth Peor.

Obedience Commanded

4 Now, Israel, hear the decrees and laws I am about to teach you. Follow them so that you may live and may go in and take possession of the land the LORD, the God of your ancestors, is giving you. ²Do not add to what I command you and do not subtract from it, but keep the commands of the LORD your God that I give you.

³You saw with your own eyes what the LORD did at Baal Peor. The LORD your God destroyed from among you everyone who followed the Baal of Peor, ⁴but all of you who held fast to the LORD your God are still alive today.

⁵See, I have taught you decrees and laws as the LORD my God commanded me, so that you may follow them in the land you are entering to take possession of it. ⁶Observe them carefully, for this will show your wisdom and understanding to the nations, who will hear about all these decrees and say, "Surely this great nation is a wise and understanding people." ⁷What other nation is so great as to have their gods near them the way the LORD our God is near us whenever we pray to him? ⁸And what other nation is so great as to have such righteous decrees and laws as this body of laws I am setting before you today?

⁹Only be careful, and watch yourselves closely so that you do not forget the things your eyes have seen or let them slip from your heart as long as you live. Teach them to your children and to their children after them. ¹⁰Remember the day you stood before the LORD your God at Horeb, when he said to me, "Assemble the people before me to hear my words so that they may learn to revere me as long as they live in the land and may teach them to their children." ¹¹You came near and stood at the foot of the mountain while it blazed with fire to the very heavens, with black clouds and deep darkness. ¹²Then the LORD spoke to you out of the fire. You heard the sound of words but saw no form; there was only a voice. ¹³He declared to you his covenant, the Ten Commandments, which he commanded you to follow and then wrote them on two stone tablets. ¹⁴And the LORD directed me at that time to teach you the decrees and laws you are to follow in the land that you are crossing the Jordan to possess.

Idolatry Forbidden

¹⁵You saw no form of any kind the day the LORD spoke to you at Horeb out of the fire. Therefore watch yourselves very carefully, ¹⁶so that you do not become corrupt and make for yourselves an idol, an image of any shape, whether formed like a man or a woman, ¹⁷or like any animal on earth or any bird that flies in the air, ¹⁸or like any creature that moves along the ground or any fish in the waters below. ¹⁹And when you look up to the sky and see the sun, the moon and the stars—all the heavenly array—do not be enticed into bowing down to them and worshiping things the LORD your God has apportioned to all the nations under heaven. ²⁰But as for you, the LORD took you and brought you out of the iron-smelting furnace, out of Egypt, to be the people of his inheritance, as you now are.

²¹The LORD was angry with me because of you, and he solemnly swore that I would not cross the Jordan and enter the good land the LORD your God is giving you as your inheritance. ²²I will die in this land; I will not cross the Jordan; but you are about to cross over and take possession of that good land. ²³Be careful not to forget the covenant of the LORD your God that he made with you; do not make for yourselves an idol in the form of anything the LORD your God has forbidden. ²⁴For the LORD your God is a consuming fire, a jealous God.

²⁵After you have had children and grandchildren and have lived in the land a long time—if you then become corrupt and make any kind of idol, doing evil in the eyes of the LORD your God and arousing his anger, ²⁶I call the heavens and the earth as witnesses against you this day that you will quickly perish from the land that you are crossing the Jordan to possess. You will not live there long but will certainly be destroyed. ²⁷The LORD will scatter you among the peoples, and only a few of you will survive among the nations to which the LORD will drive you. ²⁸There you will worship gods of wood and stone made by human hands, which cannot see or hear or eat or smell. ²⁹But if from there you seek the LORD your God, you will find him if you seek him with all your heart and with all your soul. ³⁰When you are in

distress and all these things have happened to you, then in later days you will return to the LORD your God and obey him. ³¹For the LORD your God is a merciful God; he will not abandon or destroy you or forget the covenant with your ancestors, which he confirmed to them by oath.

The LORD Is God

³²Ask now about the former days, long before your time, from the day God created human beings on the earth; ask from one end of the heavens to the other. Has anything so great as this ever happened, or has anything like it ever been heard of? ³³Has any other people heard the voice of God*a* speaking out of fire, as you have, and lived? ³⁴Has any god ever tried to take for himself one nation out of another nation, by testings, by signs and wonders, by war, by a mighty hand and an outstretched arm, or by great and awesome deeds, like all the things the LORD your God did for you in Egypt before your very eyes?

³⁵You were shown these things so that you might know that the LORD is God; besides him there is no other. ³⁶From heaven he made you hear his voice to discipline you. On earth he showed you his great fire, and you heard his words from out of the fire. ³⁷Because he loved your ancestors and chose their descendants after them, he brought you out of Egypt by his Presence and his great strength, ³⁸to drive out before you nations greater and stronger than you and to bring you into their land to give it to you for your inheritance, as it is today.

³⁹Acknowledge and take to heart this day that the LORD is God in heaven above and on the earth below. There is no other. ⁴⁰Keep his decrees and commands, which I am giving you today, so that it may go well with you and your children after you and that you may live long in the land the LORD your God gives you for all time.

Cities of Refuge

⁴¹Then Moses set aside three cities east of the Jordan, ⁴²to which anyone who had killed a person could flee if they had unintentionally killed a neighbor without malice aforethought. They could flee into one of these cities and save their life. ⁴³The cities were these: Bezer in the wilderness plateau, for the Reubenites; Ramoth in Gilead, for the Gadites; and Golan in Bashan, for the Manassites.

Introduction to the Law

⁴⁴This is the law Moses set before the Israelites. ⁴⁵These are the stipulations, decrees and laws Moses gave them when they came out of Egypt ⁴⁶and were in the valley near Beth Peor east of the Jordan, in the land of Sihon king of the Amorites, who reigned in Heshbon and was defeated by Moses and the Israelites as they came out of Egypt. ⁴⁷They took possession of his land and the land of Og king of Bashan, the two Amorite kings east of the Jordan. ⁴⁸This land extended from Aroer on the rim of the Arnon Gorge to Mount Sirion*b* (that is, Hermon), ⁴⁹and included all the Arabah east of the Jordan, as far as the Dead Sea,*c* below the slopes of Pisgah.

The Ten Commandments

5 Moses summoned all Israel and said: Hear, Israel, the decrees and laws I declare in your hearing today. Learn them and be sure to follow them. ²The LORD our God made a covenant with us at Horeb. ³It was not with our ancestors*d* that the LORD made this covenant, but with us, with all of us who are alive here today. ⁴The LORD spoke to you face to face out of the fire on the mountain. ⁵(At that time I stood between the LORD and you to declare to you the word of the LORD, because you were afraid of the fire and did not go up the mountain.) And he said:

> ⁶"I am the LORD your God, who brought you out of Egypt, out of the land of slavery.
> ⁷"You shall have no other gods before*e* me.
> ⁸"You shall not make for yourself an image in the form of anything in heaven above or on the earth beneath or in the waters below. ⁹You shall not bow down to them or worship them; for I, the LORD your God, am a jealous God, punishing the children for the sin of the par-

a 33 Or of a god   *b* 48 Syriac (see also Deut. 3:9); Hebrew *Siyon*   *c* 49 Hebrew *the Sea of the Arabah*
d 3 Or *not only with our parents*   *e* 7 Or *besides*

FRIDAY

TAKE A BREAK

Deuteronomy 5:1–33 *or* 5:12–15

Marva J. Dawn

When we know the spiritual rest of Sabbath keeping, we are thoroughly set free to rest physically. My Sabbath days often include sleeping later in the morning or taking naps or going to bed earlier at night . . .

The emphasis upon physical rest as the meaning of the Sabbath is especially strong in the account of the commandment recorded in Deuteronomy 5, in contrast to the account in Exodus 20, which celebrates the Sabbath as an imitation of God's ceasing from his creative activity on the seventh day . . . The commandment is quite clear: each person is to cease from work—not only the masters, but also all the servants and the foreigners and the animals . . .

We might have trouble putting this idea into modern terms . . . however, we can look for a similar contrast between our weekday and Sabbath activity. If we are primarily engaged in physical exertion during the week, the Sabbath offers a physical respite. For those of us involved in the opposite rhythm of sedentary labor, the Sabbath offers us a contrasting change of gentle physical enjoyment . . .

We must often take extra care to make it possible to rest from our labors on the Sabbath. Sometimes it means doing extra work the day before or spreading our work throughout the week a bit better so that the Sabbath can truly be restful. If I'm going to teach on Monday, I need to do the final review of my plans on Saturday—which usually means double duty, since I'm generally teaching on Sunday, too . . . but in the freedom I experience through the complete day of Sabbath rest I continually find that the extra effort to get everything done before Sunday is worth it.

JOHN CALVIN {AD 1509–1564}

Believers should be intentional about the worship of God since we know how easily we tend to fall into indifference. By being intentional about our worship, however, we can maintain our care and zeal for our faith.

reflection

1. How difficult is it for you to take a break from your schedule?
2. Based on your typical work week, what would be your ideal Sabbath?
3. What keeps you from enjoying that Sabbath rest?

For your next devotional reading, go to page 204.

ents to the third and fourth generation of those who hate me, [10]but showing love to a thousand generations of those who love me and keep my commandments.

[11] "You shall not misuse the name of the LORD your God, for the LORD will not hold anyone guiltless who misuses his name.

[12] "Observe the Sabbath day by keeping it holy, as the LORD your God has commanded you. [13]Six days you shall labor and do all your work, [14]but the seventh day is a sabbath to the LORD your God. On it you shall not do any work, neither you, nor your son or daughter, nor your male or female servant, nor your ox, your donkey or any of your animals, nor any foreigner residing in your towns, so that your male and female servants may rest, as you do. [15]Remember that you were slaves in Egypt and that the LORD your God brought you out of there with a mighty hand and an outstretched arm. Therefore the LORD your God has commanded you to observe the Sabbath day.

[16] "Honor your father and your mother, as the LORD your God has commanded you, so that you may live long and that it may go well with you in the land the LORD your God is giving you.

[17] "You shall not murder.

[18] "You shall not commit adultery.

[19] "You shall not steal.

[20] "You shall not give false testimony against your neighbor.

[21] "You shall not covet your neighbor's wife. You shall not set your desire on your neighbor's house or land, his male or female servant, his ox or donkey, or anything that belongs to your neighbor."

[22]These are the commandments the LORD proclaimed in a loud voice to your whole assembly there on the mountain from out of the fire, the cloud and the deep darkness; and he added nothing more. Then he wrote them on two stone tablets and gave them to me.

[23]When you heard the voice out of the darkness, while the mountain was ablaze with fire, all the leaders of your tribes and your elders came to me. [24]And you said, "The LORD our God has shown us his glory and his majesty, and we have heard his voice from the fire. Today we have seen that people can live even if God speaks with them. [25]But now, why should we die? This great fire will consume us, and we will die if we hear the voice of the LORD our God any longer. [26]For what mortal has ever heard the voice of the living God speaking out of fire, as we have, and survived? [27]Go near and listen to all that the LORD our God says. Then tell us whatever the LORD our God tells you. We will listen and obey."

[28]The LORD heard you when you spoke to me, and the LORD said to me, "I have heard what this people said to you. Everything they said was good. [29]Oh, that their hearts would be inclined to fear me and keep all my commands always, so that it might go well with them and their children forever!

[30]"Go, tell them to return to their tents. [31]But you stay here with me so that I may give you all the commands, decrees and laws you are to teach them to follow in the land I am giving them to possess."

[32]So be careful to do what the LORD your God has commanded you; do not turn aside to the right or to the left. [33]Walk in obedience to all that the LORD your God has commanded you, so that you may live and prosper and prolong your days in the land that you will possess.

Love the LORD Your God

6 These are the commands, decrees and laws the LORD your God directed me to teach you to observe in the land that you are crossing the Jordan to possess, [2]so that you, your children and their children after them may fear the LORD your God as long as you live by keeping all his decrees and commands that I give you, and so that you may enjoy long life. [3]Hear, Israel, and be careful to obey so that it may go well with you and that you may increase greatly in a land flowing with milk and honey, just as the LORD, the God of your ancestors, promised you.

[4]Hear, O Israel: The LORD our God, the LORD is one.[a] [5]Love the LORD your God with

a 4 Or The LORD our God is one LORD; or The LORD is our God, the LORD is one; or The LORD is our God, the LORD alone

In the Presence of God

Deuteronomy 5:22–32

read/meditate

Read the words that were spoken by the Israelites in this passage. Here were a people who had always believed that if they came into contact with God, they would die. But Moses didn't die. Yet the people were so sure that humanity could not bear to exist in the presence of deity that they begged Moses to mediate. Read their words several times as you wrap your mind around their perspective on God's "dreadful" presence.

pray

Examine your own attitude toward God's presence. What words would you use to describe your attitude? Fear? Dread? Awe? Indifference? Tell God how you would like to honor him. Then be still until you can sense him around you; let him mold your attitude toward him.

contemplate

Where do your perspectives toward God come from? Your upbringing? Your life experiences? Your subculture? Your media exposure? Think about why you approach God the way you do . . . or why you do or don't approach him at all.

additional reflection

We trust, not because *a* God exists, but because *this* God exists.

—C. S. Lewis

Nothing can make a man truly great but being truly good and partaking of God's holiness.

—Matthew Henry

For your next devotional reading, go to page 206.

all your heart and with all your soul and with all your strength. ⁶These commandments that I give you today are to be on your hearts. ⁷Impress them on your children. Talk about them when you sit at home and when you walk along the road, when you lie down and when you get up. ⁸Tie them as symbols on your hands and bind them on your foreheads. ⁹Write them on the doorframes of your houses and on your gates.

¹⁰When the LORD your God brings you into the land he swore to your fathers, to Abraham, Isaac and Jacob, to give you—a land with large, flourishing cities you did not build, ¹¹houses filled with all kinds of good things you did not provide, wells you did not dig, and vineyards and olive groves you did not plant—then when you eat and are satisfied, ¹²be careful that you do not forget the LORD, who brought you out of Egypt, out of the land of slavery.

¹³Fear the LORD your God, serve him only and take your oaths in his name. ¹⁴Do not follow other gods, the gods of the peoples around you; ¹⁵for the LORD your God, who is among you, is a jealous God and his anger will burn against you, and he will destroy you from the face of the land. ¹⁶Do not put the LORD your God to the test as you did at Massah. ¹⁷Be sure to keep the commands of the LORD your God and the stipulations and decrees he has given you. ¹⁸Do what is right and good in the LORD's sight, so that it may go well with you and you may go in and take over the good land the LORD promised on oath to your ancestors, ¹⁹thrusting out all your enemies before you, as the LORD said.

²⁰In the future, when your children ask you, "What is the meaning of the stipulations, decrees and laws the LORD our God has commanded you?" ²¹tell them: "We were slaves of Pharaoh in Egypt, but the LORD brought us out of Egypt with a mighty hand. ²²Before our eyes the LORD sent signs and wonders—great and terrible—on Egypt and Pharaoh and his whole household. ²³But he brought us out from there to bring us in and give us the land he promised on oath to our ancestors. ²⁴The LORD commanded us to obey all these decrees and to fear the LORD our God, so that we might always prosper and be kept alive, as is the

case today. ²⁵And if we are careful to obey all this law before the LORD our God, as he has commanded us, that will be our righteousness."

Driving Out the Nations

7 When the LORD your God brings you into the land you are entering to possess and drives out before you many nations—the Hittites, Girgashites, Amorites, Canaanites, Perizzites, Hivites and Jebusites, seven nations larger and stronger than you— ²and when the LORD your God has delivered them over to you and you have defeated them, then you must destroy them totally.ᵃ Make no treaty with them, and show them no mercy. ³Do not intermarry with them. Do not give your daughters to their sons or take their daughters for your sons, ⁴for they will turn your children away from following me to serve other gods, and the LORD's anger will burn against you and will quickly destroy you. ⁵This is what you are to do to them: Break down their altars, smash their sacred stones, cut down their Asherah polesᵇ and burn their idols in the fire. ⁶For you are a people holy to the LORD your God. The LORD your God has chosen you out of all the peoples on the face of the earth to be his people, his treasured possession.

⁷The LORD did not set his affection on you and choose you because you were more numerous than other peoples, for you were the fewest of all peoples. ⁸But it was because the LORD loved you and kept the oath he swore to your ancestors that he brought you out with a mighty hand and redeemed you from the land of slavery, from the power of Pharaoh king of Egypt. ⁹Know therefore that the LORD your God is God; he is the faithful God, keeping his covenant of love to a thousand generations of those who love him and keep his commandments. ¹⁰But

those who hate him he will repay to
their face by destruction;
he will not be slow to repay to their
face those who hate him.

¹¹Therefore, take care to follow the commands, decrees and laws I give you today. ¹²If you pay attention to these laws and

---

ᵃ 2 The Hebrew term refers to the irrevocable giving over of things or persons to the LORD, often by totally destroying them; also in verse 26.   ᵇ 5 That is, wooden symbols of the goddess Asherah; here and elsewhere in Deuteronomy

MONDAY

A PARENT'S BEST GIFT

Deuteronomy 6:1–25 *or* 6:4–9

FYODOR DOSTOYEVSKY {AD 1821–1881}

Let parents, then, bequeath to their children not riches, but the spirit of reverence.

D. A. Carson

We have come across other passages dealing with the importance of passing on the heritage of Biblical truth to the next generation. That theme lies at the heart of Deuteronomy 6 . . .

1. The ancient Israelites were to teach the next generation *to fear* the God of the covenant. Moses teaches the people "so that you, your children and their children after them may fear the LORD your God as long as you live" (6:2) . . . We might well ask ourselves what steps we take to teach our children to fear the Lord our God, not with the cringing terror that is frightened of whimsical malice but with the profound conviction that this God is perfectly just and does not play around with sin.

2. Moses underscores *the constancy* with which the next generation is to be taught . . . Out of this abundance, the next words follow "Impress them on your children. Talk about [them] when you sit at home and when you walk along the road, when you lie down and when you get up" (6:7) . . . In ancient Israel children usually learned their vocational skills from their parents, spending countless hours with them, which provided many opportunities to pass on the blessings of the covenant. Our more fragmented culture means we must make opportunities.

3. Above all, the older generation was *to model* utter loyalty to God (6:13–19). This consistent modeling was to include an utter repudiation of idolatry, obedience to the demands of the covenant, revering the name of the Lord God, doing "what is right and good in the LORD's sight" (6:18). How faithfully have we, by our own living, commended serious God-centeredness to our children?

4. There must be a sensitive awareness of the opportunities *to answer questions* our children raise (6:20–25). Never bluff. If you do not know the answer, find out, or find someone who does. We must ask ourselves if we make maximum use of the questions our children raise.

reflection

1. How natural is it for you to talk about God with others?

2. Would the children in your life say that you live a God-centered life? What would your friends say? Or your coworkers?

3. How well do you demonstrate the fear of the Lord to the children in your life?

For your next devotional reading, go to page 208.

are careful to follow them, then the LORD your God will keep his covenant of love with you, as he swore to your ancestors. ¹³He will love you and bless you and increase your numbers. He will bless the fruit of your womb, the crops of your land—your grain, new wine and olive oil—the calves of your herds and the lambs of your flocks in the land he swore to your ancestors to give you. ¹⁴You will be blessed more than any other people; none of your men or women will be childless, nor will any of your livestock be without young. ¹⁵The LORD will keep you free from every disease. He will not inflict on you the horrible diseases you knew in Egypt, but he will inflict them on all who hate you. ¹⁶You must destroy all the peoples the LORD your God gives over to you. Do not look on them with pity and do not serve their gods, for that will be a snare to you.

¹⁷You may say to yourselves, "These nations are stronger than we are. How can we drive them out?" ¹⁸But do not be afraid of them; remember well what the LORD your God did to Pharaoh and to all Egypt. ¹⁹You saw with your own eyes the great trials, the signs and wonders, the mighty hand and outstretched arm, with which the LORD your God brought you out. The LORD your God will do the same to all the peoples you now fear. ²⁰Moreover, the LORD your God will send the hornet among them until even the survivors who hide from you have perished. ²¹Do not be terrified by them, for the LORD your God, who is among you, is a great and awesome God. ²²The LORD your God will drive out those nations before you, little by little. You will not be allowed to eliminate them all at once, or the wild animals will multiply around you. ²³But the LORD your God will deliver them over to you, throwing them into great confusion until they are destroyed. ²⁴He will give their kings into your hand, and you will wipe out their names from under heaven. No one will be able to stand up against you; you will destroy them. ²⁵The images of their gods you are to burn in the fire. Do not covet the silver and gold on them, and do not take it for yourselves, or you will be ensnared by it, for it is detestable to the LORD your God. ²⁶Do not bring a detestable thing into your house or you, like it, will be set apart for destruction. Regard it as vile and utterly detest it, for it is set apart for destruction.

Do Not Forget the LORD

8 Be careful to follow every command I am giving you today, so that you may live and increase and may enter and possess the land the LORD promised on oath to your ancestors. ²Remember how the LORD your God led you all the way in the wilderness these forty years, to humble and test you in order to know what was in your heart, whether or not you would keep his commands. ³He humbled you, causing you to hunger and then feeding you with manna, which neither you nor your ancestors had known, to teach you that people do not live on bread alone but on every word that comes from the mouth of the LORD. ⁴Your clothes did not wear out and your feet did not swell during these forty years. ⁵Know then in your heart that as a man disciplines his son, so the LORD your God disciplines you.

⁶Observe the commands of the LORD your God, walking in obedience to him and revering him. ⁷For the LORD your God is bringing you into a good land—a land with streams and pools of water, with springs flowing in the valleys and hills; ⁸a land with wheat and barley, vines and fig trees, pomegranates, olive oil and honey; ⁹a land where bread will not be scarce and you will lack nothing; a land where the rocks are iron and you can dig copper out of the hills.

¹⁰When you have eaten and are satisfied, praise the LORD your God for the good land he has given you. ¹¹Be careful that you do not forget the LORD your God, failing to observe his commands, his laws and his decrees that I am giving you this day. ¹²Otherwise, when you eat and are satisfied, when you build fine houses and settle down, ¹³and when your herds and flocks grow large and your silver and gold increase and all you have is multiplied, ¹⁴then your heart will become proud and you will forget the LORD your God, who brought you out of Egypt, out of the land of slavery. ¹⁵He led you through the vast and dreadful wilderness, that thirsty and waterless land, with its venomous snakes and scorpions. He brought you water out of hard rock. ¹⁶He gave you manna to eat in the wilderness, something your ancestors had never known, to humble and test you so that in the end it might go well with you. ¹⁷You may say to yourself, "My power and the strength of my hands have produced this wealth for me." ¹⁸But remember the LORD

TUESDAY

PROMISES KEPT

Deuteronomy 7:1–26 *or* 7:6–9

JOHN BUNYAN {AD 1628–1688}

"He has raised up a horn of salvation for us . . . as he said through his holy prophets of long ago . . . Indeed, beginning with Samuel, all the prophets who have spoken have foretold these days" (Luke 1:69–70; Acts 3:24). From these texts it is evident that in every period or generation of the world God gave his people a promise: that he would one day send a Savior. This promise provides the grounds for a "believing remembrance"; God's people can not only remember this promise but also believe it. Because God is truth, and he cannot lie and will not change his mind (Numbers 23:19), what he says is sufficient grounds for faith. But that is not the only basis for our "believing remembrance," for all God's heart was involved in the promise of sending us a Savior . . . For just as soon as humankind had sinned, God came to him with a heart full of promise—and continued to renew that promise again and again—until the time for the promised Messiah to be revealed had finally come . . . Therefore it's no wonder when he speaks in the Scriptures of the new covenant—in which the Lord Jesus is wrapped and presented in a word of promise to the world—that he says, "I will rejoice in doing them good . . . with all my heart and soul" (Jeremiah 32:41).

Tony Evans

Don't fix your eyes on how you feel inside or what is happening around you, but fix them on Jesus. Keep your eyes on faith set on God and His promises, and remember that the issue is whom you are going to believe. Faith is no mystical concept. It is simply taking God at His Word and acting in light of that.

When you do this, you will begin to see the invisible world of the Spirit controlling your visible world, and not the other way around.

reflection

1. Deep down, in your heart of hearts, how fully do you really believe that God saved you because of his love for you and not because of how good you are?

2. How would you live differently if you truly believed that God loves you and you do not have to earn his salvation?

3. How difficult (or easy) do you find it to both remember and believe God's promises of love for you? Why?

For your next devotional reading, go to page 210.

your God, for it is he who gives you the ability to produce wealth, and so confirms his covenant, which he swore to your ancestors, as it is today.

¹⁹If you ever forget the LORD your God and follow other gods and worship and bow down to them, I testify against you today that you will surely be destroyed. ²⁰Like the nations the LORD destroyed before you, so you will be destroyed for not obeying the LORD your God.

Not Because of Israel's Righteousness

9 Hear, Israel: You are now about to cross the Jordan to go in and dispossess nations greater and stronger than you, with large cities that have walls up to the sky. ²The people are strong and tall—Anakites! You know about them and have heard it said: "Who can stand up against the Anakites?" ³But be assured today that the LORD your God is the one who goes across ahead of you like a devouring fire. He will destroy them; he will subdue them before you. And you will drive them out and annihilate them quickly, as the LORD has promised you.

⁴After the LORD your God has driven them out before you, do not say to yourself, "The LORD has brought me here to take possession of this land because of my righteousness." No, it is on account of the wickedness of these nations that the LORD is going to drive them out before you. ⁵It is not because of your righteousness or your integrity that you are going in to take possession of their land; but on account of the wickedness of these nations, the LORD your God will drive them out before you, to accomplish what he swore to your fathers, to Abraham, Isaac and Jacob. ⁶Understand, then, that it is not because of your righteousness that the LORD your God is giving you this good land to possess, for you are a stiff-necked people.

The Golden Calf

⁷Remember this and never forget how you aroused the anger of the LORD your God in the wilderness. From the day you left Egypt until you arrived here, you have been rebellious against the LORD. ⁸At Horeb you aroused the LORD's wrath so that he was angry enough to destroy you. ⁹When I went up on the mountain to receive the tablets of stone, the tablets of the covenant that the LORD had made with you, I stayed on the mountain forty days and forty nights; I ate no bread and drank no water. ¹⁰The LORD gave me two stone tablets inscribed by the finger of God. On them were all the commandments the LORD proclaimed to you on the mountain out of the fire, on the day of the assembly.

¹¹At the end of the forty days and forty nights, the LORD gave me the two stone tablets, the tablets of the covenant. ¹²Then the LORD told me, "Go down from here at once, because your people whom you brought out of Egypt have become corrupt. They have turned away quickly from what I commanded them and have made an idol for themselves."

¹³And the LORD said to me, "I have seen this people, and they are a stiff-necked people indeed! ¹⁴Let me alone, so that I may destroy them and blot out their name from under heaven. And I will make you into a nation stronger and more numerous than they."

¹⁵So I turned and went down from the mountain while it was ablaze with fire. And the two tablets of the covenant were in my hands. ¹⁶When I looked, I saw that you had sinned against the LORD your God; you had made for yourselves an idol cast in the shape of a calf. You had turned aside quickly from the way that the LORD had commanded you. ¹⁷So I took the two tablets and threw them out of my hands, breaking them to pieces before your eyes.

¹⁸Then once again I fell prostrate before the LORD for forty days and forty nights; I ate no bread and drank no water, because of all the sin you had committed, doing what was evil in the LORD's sight and so arousing his anger. ¹⁹I feared the anger and wrath of the LORD, for he was angry enough with you to destroy you. But again the LORD listened to me. ²⁰And the LORD was angry enough with Aaron to destroy him, but at that time I prayed for Aaron too. ²¹Also I took that sinful thing of yours, the calf you had made, and burned it in the fire. Then I crushed it and ground it to powder as fine as dust and threw the dust into a stream that flowed down the mountain.

²²You also made the LORD angry at Taberah, at Massah and at Kibroth Hattaavah.

²³And when the LORD sent you out from Kadesh Barnea, he said, "Go up and take

WEDNESDAY

DON'T FORGET GOD

Deuteronomy 8:1–20 *or* 8:10–11

Philip Yancey

Nothing, apparently, bothers God more than the simple act of being forgotten. During the years of wilderness wanderings, forced to depend on God daily, the Hebrews did not have the luxury of forgetting. God fed the Israelites, clothed them, planned their daily itinerary and fought their battles. No Hebrew questioned the existence of God in those days, for he hovered before them in a thick cloud and a pillar of fire.

Soon, however, God would withdraw from that smothering parental role. On the first day they ate produce from the promised land, the manna would stop. From then on they must cultivate their own land and plant their own crops. They would build cities, fight wars, appoint a king. They would prosper and grow plump. They would trust their armies and chariots instead of their God, forgetting the lesson inflicted on almighty Egypt. They would discriminate against the poor and the aliens, forgetting they were once both. In a word, they would forget God . . .

Success, not failure, is the greatest danger facing any follower of God.

MADAME GUYON {AD 1648–1717}

Relying on the many good works they imagine they have performed, self-righteous people seem to hold salvation in their own hands, and they consider heaven as a just reward of their merits. In the bitterness of their zeal they vehemently cry out against all sinners— representing the gates of mercy as barred against them and heaven as a place to which they have no claim. What need do such self-righteous persons have for a Savior? They are burdened with the flattering load of their own merits. Meanwhile, those who recognize themselves as sinners are free of any such burden and fly rapidly on the wings of faith and love into their Savior's arms, who freely bestows on them that which he has so freely promised!

reflection

1. Why do people tend to rely more on themselves—rather than God—when things are going well?

2. At what points in your life have you been the most dependent on God?

3. What things can you do to ensure that you remember God—in both the good times and the bad?

For your next devotional reading, go to page 212.

possession of the land I have given you." But you rebelled against the command of the LORD your God. You did not trust him or obey him. ²⁴You have been rebellious against the LORD ever since I have known you.

²⁵I lay prostrate before the LORD those forty days and forty nights because the LORD had said he would destroy you. ²⁶I prayed to the LORD and said, "Sovereign LORD, do not destroy your people, your own inheritance that you redeemed by your great power and brought out of Egypt with a mighty hand. ²⁷Remember your servants Abraham, Isaac and Jacob. Overlook the stubbornness of this people, their wickedness and their sin. ²⁸Otherwise, the country from which you brought us will say, 'Because the LORD was not able to take them into the land he had promised them, and because he hated them, he brought them out to put them to death in the wilderness.' ²⁹But they are your people, your inheritance that you brought out by your great power and your outstretched arm."

Tablets Like the First Ones

10 At that time the LORD said to me, "Chisel out two stone tablets like the first ones and come up to me on the mountain. Also make a wooden ark.ᵃ ²I will write on the tablets the words that were on the first tablets, which you broke. Then you are to put them in the ark."

³So I made the ark out of acacia wood and chiseled out two stone tablets like the first ones, and I went up on the mountain with the two tablets in my hands. ⁴The LORD wrote on these tablets what he had written before, the Ten Commandments he had proclaimed to you on the mountain, out of the fire, on the day of the assembly. And the LORD gave them to me. ⁵Then I came back down the mountain and put the tablets in the ark I had made, as the LORD commanded me, and they are there now.

⁶(The Israelites traveled from the wells of Bene Jaakan to Moserah. There Aaron died and was buried, and Eleazar his son succeeded him as priest. ⁷From there they traveled to Gudgodah and on to Jotbathah, a land with streams of water. ⁸At that time the LORD set apart the tribe of Levi to carry the ark of the covenant of the LORD, to stand before the LORD to minister and to pronounce blessings in his name, as they still do today. ⁹That is why the Levites have no share or inheritance among their fellow Israelites; the LORD is their inheritance, as the LORD your God told them.)

¹⁰Now I had stayed on the mountain forty days and nights, as I did the first time, and the LORD listened to me at this time also. It was not his will to destroy you. ¹¹"Go," the LORD said to me, "and lead the people on their way, so that they may enter and possess the land I swore to their ancestors to give them."

Fear the LORD

¹²And now, Israel, what does the LORD your God ask of you but to fear the LORD your God, to walk in obedience to him, to love him, to serve the LORD your God with all your heart and with all your soul, ¹³and to observe the LORD's commands and decrees that I am giving you today for your own good?

¹⁴To the LORD your God belong the heavens, even the highest heavens, the earth and everything in it. ¹⁵Yet the LORD set his affection on your ancestors and loved them, and he chose you, their descendants, above all the nations—as it is today. ¹⁶Circumcise your hearts, therefore, and do not be stiff-necked any longer. ¹⁷For the LORD your God is God of gods and Lord of lords, the great God, mighty and awesome, who shows no partiality and accepts no bribes. ¹⁸He defends the cause of the fatherless and the widow, and loves the foreigners residing among you, giving them food and clothing. ¹⁹And you are to love those who are foreigners, for you yourselves were foreigners in Egypt. ²⁰Fear the LORD your God and serve him. Hold fast to him and take your oaths in his name. ²¹He is the one you praise; he is your God, who performed for you those great and awesome wonders you saw with your own eyes. ²²Your ancestors who went down into Egypt were seventy in all, and now the LORD your God has made you as numerous as the stars in the sky.

Love and Obey the LORD

11 Love the LORD your God and keep his requirements, his decrees, his laws and his commands always.

ᵃ 1 That is, a chest

THURSDAY

DO THE STUFF!

Deuteronomy 10:1–20 *or* 10:12–13

Dave Roberts

Are you waiting for spiritual insight to simply arrive in your mind? Are you waiting for that moment when you feel adequate to the task of serving God or taking responsibility within your church or Christian community?

Stop. And then start.

Stop waiting to be perfect or enlightened or mature. Start "doing the stuff," as the preacher John Wimber used to say. You'll learn by doing the small and commonplace. Ask a friend over for a relaxed night and help them feel at home in your community. Say a 30-second prayer for someone facing a challenge in the coming days. Offer to sell sweets at the youth club night or be an extra helper in the Sunday school.

I've been told so many times that many leading figures in church were children's ministry volunteers in their young adult years. They became immersed in the foundations of their faith because they had to be ready to pass it on to the children in their care. They learned by doing.

Spirituality isn't usually expressed in the heroic, although it can be. Its whisper is heard in the word of encouragement, the warm greeting, the tone of forgiveness.

Doing takes us from being spectators to whole person involvement. It tests our faith and expands our knowledge.

Do the Stuff. Follow Jesus.

JONATHAN EDWARDS {AD 1703–1758}

Those who are genuine Christians need to be engaged in the service of God with great earnestness and diligence. They must devote themselves to this work and make it the main business of their lives ... God's true servants will give themselves up to his service, and make it their whole work—something which involves their whole hearts, and the most important part of their strength ... When God calls Christians to himself, he does not call them to idleness. He calls them to labor in his vineyard, to spend their day in doing a great and laborious service.

reflection

1. How much of your heart, soul and strength have you given up to God for the purpose of serving him? All? Most? Some? A little? Not much?

2. What keeps you from serving God with all that you are? What holds you back?

3. What are three small things—new things—you can do to serve God tomorrow?

For your next devotional reading, go to page 219.

²Remember today that your children were not the ones who saw and experienced the discipline of the Lord your God: his majesty, his mighty hand, his outstretched arm; ³the signs he performed and the things he did in the heart of Egypt, both to Pharaoh king of Egypt and to his whole country; ⁴what he did to the Egyptian army, to its horses and chariots, how he overwhelmed them with the waters of the Red Sea*a* as they were pursuing you, and how the Lord brought lasting ruin on them. ⁵It was not your children who saw what he did for you in the wilderness until you arrived at this place, ⁶and what he did to Dathan and Abiram, sons of Eliab the Reubenite, when the earth opened its mouth right in the middle of all Israel and swallowed them up with their households, their tents and every living thing that belonged to them. ⁷But it was your own eyes that saw all these great things the Lord has done.

⁸Observe therefore all the commands I am giving you today, so that you may have the strength to go in and take over the land that you are crossing the Jordan to possess, ⁹and so that you may live long in the land the Lord swore to your ancestors to give to them and their descendants, a land flowing with milk and honey. ¹⁰The land you are entering to take over is not like the land of Egypt, from which you have come, where you planted your seed and irrigated it by foot as in a vegetable garden. ¹¹But the land you are crossing the Jordan to take possession of is a land of mountains and valleys that drinks rain from heaven. ¹²It is a land the Lord your God cares for; the eyes of the Lord your God are continually on it from the beginning of the year to its end.

¹³So if you faithfully obey the commands I am giving you today—to love the Lord your God and to serve him with all your heart and with all your soul— ¹⁴then I will send rain on your land in its season, both autumn and spring rains, so that you may gather in your grain, new wine and olive oil. ¹⁵I will provide grass in the fields for your cattle, and you will eat and be satisfied.

¹⁶Be careful, or you will be enticed to turn away and worship other gods and bow down to them. ¹⁷Then the Lord's anger will burn against you, and he will shut the heavens so that it will not rain and the ground will yield no produce, and you will soon perish from the good land the Lord is giving you. ¹⁸Fix these words of mine in your hearts and minds; tie them as symbols on your hands and bind them on your foreheads. ¹⁹Teach them to your children, talking about them when you sit at home and when you walk along the road, when you lie down and when you get up. ²⁰Write them on the doorframes of your houses and on your gates, ²¹so that your days and the days of your children may be many in the land the Lord swore to give your ancestors, as many as the days that the heavens are above the earth.

²²If you carefully observe all these commands I am giving you to follow—to love the Lord your God, to walk in obedience to him and to hold fast to him— ²³then the Lord will drive out all these nations before you, and you will dispossess nations larger and stronger than you. ²⁴Every place where you set your foot will be yours: Your territory will extend from the desert to Lebanon, and from the Euphrates River to the Mediterranean Sea. ²⁵No one will be able to stand against you. The Lord your God, as he promised you, will put the terror and fear of you on the whole land, wherever you go.

²⁶See, I am setting before you today a blessing and a curse— ²⁷the blessing if you obey the commands of the Lord your God that I am giving you today; ²⁸the curse if you disobey the commands of the Lord your God and turn from the way that I command you today by following other gods, which you have not known. ²⁹When the Lord your God has brought you into the land you are entering to possess, you are to proclaim on Mount Gerizim the blessings, and on Mount Ebal the curses. ³⁰As you know, these mountains are across the Jordan, westward, toward the setting sun, near the great trees of Moreh, in the territory of those Canaanites living in the Arabah in the vicinity of Gilgal. ³¹You are about to cross the Jordan to enter and take possession of the land the Lord your God is giving you. When you have taken it over and are living there, ³²be sure that you obey all the decrees and laws I am setting before you today.

a 4 Or the Sea of Reeds

The One Place of Worship

12

These are the decrees and laws you must be careful to follow in the land that the LORD, the God of your ancestors, has given you to possess—as long as you live in the land. ²Destroy completely all the places on the high mountains, on the hills and under every spreading tree, where the nations you are dispossessing worship their gods. ³Break down their altars, smash their sacred stones and burn their Asherah poles in the fire; cut down the idols of their gods and wipe out their names from those places.

⁴You must not worship the LORD your God in their way. ⁵But you are to seek the place the LORD your God will choose from among all your tribes to put his Name there for his dwelling. To that place you must go; ⁶there bring your burnt offerings and sacrifices, your tithes and special gifts, what you have vowed to give and your freewill offerings, and the firstborn of your herds and flocks. ⁷There, in the presence of the LORD your God, you and your families shall eat and shall rejoice in everything you have put your hand to, because the LORD your God has blessed you.

⁸You are not to do as we do here today, everyone doing as they see fit, ⁹since you have not yet reached the resting place and the inheritance the LORD your God is giving you. ¹⁰But you will cross the Jordan and settle in the land the LORD your God is giving you as an inheritance, and he will give you rest from all your enemies around you so that you will live in safety. ¹¹Then to the place the LORD your God will choose as a dwelling for his Name—there you are to bring everything I command you: your burnt offerings and sacrifices, your tithes and special gifts, and all the choice possessions you have vowed to the LORD. ¹²And there rejoice before the LORD your God—you, your sons and daughters, your male and female servants, and the Levites from your towns who have no allotment or inheritance of their own. ¹³Be careful not to sacrifice your burnt offerings anywhere you please. ¹⁴Offer them only at the place the LORD will choose in one of your tribes, and there observe everything I command you.

¹⁵Nevertheless, you may slaughter your animals in any of your towns and eat as much of the meat as you want, as if it were gazelle or deer, according to the blessing the LORD your God gives you. Both the ceremonially unclean and the clean may eat it. ¹⁶But you must not eat the blood; pour it out on the ground like water. ¹⁷You must not eat in your own towns the tithe of your grain and new wine and olive oil, or the firstborn of your herds and flocks, or whatever you have vowed to give, or your freewill offerings or special gifts. ¹⁸Instead, you are to eat them in the presence of the LORD your God at the place the LORD your God will choose—you, your sons and daughters, your male and female servants, and the Levites from your towns—and you are to rejoice before the LORD your God in everything you put your hand to. ¹⁹Be careful not to neglect the Levites as long as you live in your land.

²⁰When the LORD your God has enlarged your territory as he promised you, and you crave meat and say, "I would like some meat," then you may eat as much of it as you want. ²¹If the place where the LORD your God chooses to put his Name is too far away from you, you may slaughter animals from the herds and flocks the LORD has given you, as I have commanded you, and in your own towns you may eat as much of them as you want. ²²Eat them as you would gazelle or deer. Both the ceremonially unclean and the clean may eat. ²³But be sure you do not eat the blood, because the blood is the life, and you must not eat the life with the meat. ²⁴You must not eat the blood; pour it out on the ground like water. ²⁵Do not eat it, so that it may go well with you and your children after you, because you will be doing what is right in the eyes of the LORD.

²⁶But take your consecrated things and whatever you have vowed to give, and go to the place the LORD will choose. ²⁷Present your burnt offerings on the altar of the LORD your God, both the meat and the blood. The blood of your sacrifices must be poured beside the altar of the LORD your God, but you may eat the meat. ²⁸Be careful to obey all these regulations I am giving you, so that it may always go well with you and your children after you, because you will be doing what is good and right in the eyes of the LORD your God.

²⁹The LORD your God will cut off before you the nations you are about to invade and dispossess. But when you have driven them out and settled in their land, ³⁰and after they

have been destroyed before you, be careful not to be ensnared by inquiring about their gods, saying, "How do these nations serve their gods? We will do the same." ³¹You must not worship the LORD your God in their way, because in worshiping their gods, they do all kinds of detestable things the LORD hates. They even burn their sons and daughters in the fire as sacrifices to their gods.

*³²See that you do all I command you; do not add to it or take away from it.

Worshiping Other Gods

13 *If a prophet, or one who foretells by dreams, appears among you and announces to you a sign or wonder, ²and if the sign or wonder spoken of takes place, and the prophet says, "Let us follow other gods" (gods you have not known) "and let us worship them," ³you must not listen to the words of that prophet or dreamer. The LORD your God is testing you to find out whether you love him with all your heart and with all your soul. ⁴It is the LORD your God you must follow, and him you must revere. Keep his commands and obey him; serve him and hold fast to him. ⁵That prophet or dreamer must be put to death for inciting rebellion against the LORD your God, who brought you out of Egypt and redeemed you from the land of slavery. That prophet or dreamer tried to turn you from the way the LORD your God commanded you to follow. You must purge the evil from among you.

⁶If your very own brother, or your son or daughter, or the wife you love, or your closest friend secretly entices you, saying, "Let us go and worship other gods" (gods that neither you nor your ancestors have known, ⁷gods of the peoples around you, whether near or far, from one end of the land to the other), ⁸do not yield to them or listen to them. Show them no pity. Do not spare them or shield them. ⁹You must certainly put them to death. Your hand must be the first in putting them to death, and then the hands of all the people. ¹⁰Stone them to death, because they tried to turn you away from the LORD your God, who brought you

out of Egypt, out of the land of slavery. ¹¹Then all Israel will hear and be afraid, and no one among you will do such an evil thing again.

¹²If you hear it said about one of the towns the LORD your God is giving you to live in ¹³that wicked persons have arisen among you and have led the people of their town astray, saying, "Let us go and worship other gods" (gods you have not known), ¹⁴then you must inquire, probe and investigate thoroughly. And if it is true and it has been proved that this detestable thing has been done among you, ¹⁵you must certainly put to the sword all who live in that town. Destroy it completely,ᵃ both its people and its livestock. ¹⁶Gather all the plunder of the town into the middle of the public square and completely burn the town and all its plunder as a whole burnt offering to the LORD your God. It is to remain a ruin forever, never to be rebuilt. ¹⁷None of those condemned thingsᵃ shall be found in your hands, so that the LORD will turn from his fierce anger; he will show you mercy, have compassion on you, and increase your numbers, as he promised on oath to your ancestors, ¹⁸because you obey the LORD your God, keeping all his commands that I am giving you today and doing what is right in his eyes.

Clean and Unclean Food

14 You are the children of the LORD your God. Do not cut yourselves or shave the front of your heads for the dead, ²for you are a people holy to the LORD your God. Out of all the peoples on the face of the earth, the LORD has chosen you to be his treasured possession.

³Do not eat any detestable thing. ⁴These are the animals you may eat: the ox, the sheep, the goat, ⁵the deer, the gazelle, the roe deer, the wild goat, the ibex, the antelope and the mountain sheep.ᵇ ⁶You may eat any animal that has a divided hoof and that chews the cud. ⁷However, of those that chew the cud or that have a divided hoof you may not eat the camel, the rabbit or the hyrax. Although they chew the cud, they do not have a divided hoof; they are ceremonially

---

ᵃ 15,17 The Hebrew term refers to the irrevocable giving over of things or persons to the LORD, often by totally destroying them.   ᵇ 5 The precise identification of some of the birds and animals in this chapter is uncertain.

* 12:32 is numbered 13:1 in Hebrew texts.   * 13:1-18 is numbered 13:2-19 in Hebrew texts.

unclean for you. 8The pig is also unclean; although it has a divided hoof, it does not chew the cud. You are not to eat their meat or touch their carcasses.

9Of all the creatures living in the water, you may eat any that has fins and scales. 10But anything that does not have fins and scales you may not eat; for you it is unclean.

11You may eat any clean bird. 12But these you may not eat: the eagle, the vulture, the black vulture, 13the red kite, the black kite, any kind of falcon, 14any kind of raven, 15the horned owl, the screech owl, the gull, any kind of hawk, 16the little owl, the great owl, the white owl, 17the desert owl, the osprey, the cormorant, 18the stork, any kind of heron, the hoopoe and the bat.

19All flying insects that swarm are unclean to you; do not eat them. 20But any winged creature that is clean you may eat.

21Do not eat anything you find already dead. You may give it to the foreigners residing in any of your towns, and they may eat it, or you may sell it to any other foreigner. But you are a people holy to the LORD your God.

Do not cook a young goat in its mother's milk.

Tithes

22Be sure to set aside a tenth of all that your fields produce each year. 23Eat the tithe of your grain, new wine and olive oil, and the firstborn of your herds and flocks in the presence of the LORD your God at the place he will choose as a dwelling for his Name, so that you may learn to revere the LORD your God always. 24But if that place is too distant and you have been blessed by the LORD your God and cannot carry your tithe (because the place where the LORD will choose to put his Name is so far away), 25then exchange your tithe for silver, and take the silver with you and go to the place the LORD your God will choose. 26Use the silver to buy whatever you like: cattle, sheep, wine or other fermented drink, or anything you wish. Then you and your household shall eat there in the presence of the LORD your God and rejoice. 27And do not neglect the Levites living in your towns, for they have no allotment or inheritance of their own.

28At the end of every three years, bring all the tithes of that year's produce and store it in your towns, 29so that the Levites (who have no allotment or inheritance of their own) and the foreigners, the fatherless and the widows who live in your towns may come and eat and be satisfied, and so that the LORD your God may bless you in all the work of your hands.

The Year for Canceling Debts

15 At the end of every seven years you must cancel debts. 2This is how it is to be done: Every creditor shall cancel any loan they have made to another Israelite. They shall not require payment from anyone among their own people, because the LORD's time for canceling debts has been proclaimed. 3You may require payment from a foreigner, but you must cancel any debt one of your people owes you. 4However, there need be no poor people among you, for in the land the LORD your God is giving you to possess as your inheritance, he will richly bless you, 5if only you fully obey the LORD your God and are careful to follow all these commands I am giving you today. 6For the LORD your God will bless you as he has promised, and you will lend to many nations but will borrow from none. You will rule over many nations but none will rule over you.

7If anyone is poor among your people in any of the towns of the land the LORD your God is giving you, do not be hardhearted or tightfisted toward them. 8Rather, be openhanded and freely lend them whatever they need. 9Be careful not to harbor this wicked thought: "The seventh year, the year for canceling debts, is near," so that you do not show ill will toward the needy among your people and give them nothing. They may then appeal to the LORD against you, and you will be found guilty of sin. 10Give generously to them and do so without a grudging heart; then because of this the LORD your God will bless you in all your work and in everything you put your hand to. 11There will always be poor people in the land. Therefore I command you to be openhanded toward those of your people who are poor and needy in your land.

Freeing Servants

12If any of your people, men or women, sell themselves to you and serve you six years, in the seventh year you must let them go free. 13And when you release them, do not send them away empty-handed. ¹⁴Supply them liberally from your flock, your threshing floor and your winepress. Give to them as the LORD your God has blessed you. ¹⁵Remember that you were slaves in Egypt and the LORD your God redeemed you. That is why I give you this command today.

¹⁶But if your servant says to you, "I do not want to leave you," because he loves you and your family and is well off with you, ¹⁷then take an awl and push it through his ear lobe into the door, and he will become your servant for life. Do the same for your female servant.

¹⁸Do not consider it a hardship to set your servants free, because their service to you these six years has been worth twice as much as that of a hired hand. And the LORD your God will bless you in everything you do.

The Firstborn Animals

¹⁹Set apart for the LORD your God every firstborn male of your herds and flocks. Do not put the firstborn of your cows to work, and do not shear the firstborn of your sheep. ²⁰Each year you and your family are to eat them in the presence of the LORD your God at the place he will choose. ²¹If an animal has a defect, is lame or blind, or has any serious flaw, you must not sacrifice it to the LORD your God. ²²You are to eat it in your own towns. Both the ceremonially unclean and the clean may eat it, as if it were gazelle or deer. ²³But you must not eat the blood; pour it out on the ground like water.

The Passover

16 Observe the month of Aviv and celebrate the Passover of the LORD your God, because in the month of Aviv he brought you out of Egypt by night. ²Sacrifice as the Passover to the LORD your God an animal from your flock or herd at the place the LORD will choose as a dwelling for his Name. ³Do not eat it with bread made with yeast, but for seven days eat unleavened bread, the bread of affliction, because you left Egypt in haste—so that all the days of your life you may remember the time of your departure from Egypt. ⁴Let no yeast be found in your possession in all your land for seven days. Do not let any of the meat you sacrifice on the

evening of the first day remain until morning.

⁵You must not sacrifice the Passover in any town the LORD your God gives you ⁶except in the place he will choose as a dwelling for his Name. There you must sacrifice the Passover in the evening, when the sun goes down, on the anniversaryᵃ of your departure from Egypt. ⁷Roast it and eat it at the place the LORD your God will choose. Then in the morning return to your tents. ⁸For six days eat unleavened bread and on the seventh day hold an assembly to the LORD your God and do no work.

The Festival of Weeks

⁹Count off seven weeks from the time you begin to put the sickle to the standing grain. ¹⁰Then celebrate the Festival of Weeks to the LORD your God by giving a freewill offering in proportion to the blessings the LORD your God has given you. ¹¹And rejoice before the LORD your God at the place he will choose as a dwelling for his Name—you, your sons and daughters, your male and female servants, the Levites in your towns, and the foreigners, the fatherless and the widows living among you. ¹²Remember that you were slaves in Egypt, and follow carefully these decrees.

The Festival of Tabernacles

¹³Celebrate the Festival of Tabernacles for seven days after you have gathered the produce of your threshing floor and your winepress. ¹⁴Be joyful at your festival—you, your sons and daughters, your male and female servants, and the Levites, the foreigners, the fatherless and the widows who live in your towns. ¹⁵For seven days celebrate the festival to the LORD your God at the place the LORD will choose. For the LORD your God will bless you in all your harvest and in all the work of your hands, and your joy will be complete.

¹⁶Three times a year all your men must appear before the LORD your God at the place he will choose: at the Festival of Unleavened Bread, the Festival of Weeks and the Festival of Tabernacles. No one should appear before the LORD empty-handed: ¹⁷Each of you must bring a gift in proportion to the way the LORD your God has blessed you.

ᵃ 6 Or *down, at the time of day*

Judges

[18]Appoint judges and officials for each of your tribes in every town the LORD your God is giving you, and they shall judge the people fairly. [19]Do not pervert justice or show partiality. Do not accept a bribe, for a bribe blinds the eyes of the wise and twists the words of the righteous. [20]Follow justice and justice alone, so that you may live and possess the land the LORD your God is giving you.

Worshiping Other Gods

[21]Do not set up any wooden Asherah pole beside the altar you build to the LORD your God, [22]and do not erect a sacred stone, for these the LORD your God hates.

17 Do not sacrifice to the LORD your God an ox or a sheep that has any defect or flaw in it, for that would be detestable to him.

[2]If a man or woman living among you in one of the towns the LORD gives you is found doing evil in the eyes of the LORD your God in violation of his covenant, [3]and contrary to my command has worshiped other gods, bowing down to them or to the sun or the moon or the stars in the sky, [4]and this has been brought to your attention, then you must investigate it thoroughly. If it is true and it has been proved that this detestable thing has been done in Israel, [5]take the man or woman who has done this evil deed to your city gate and stone that person to death. [6]On the testimony of two or three witnesses a person is to be put to death, but no one is to be put to death on the testimony of only one witness. [7]The hands of the witnesses must be the first in putting that person to death, and then the hands of all the people. You must purge the evil from among you.

Law Courts

[8]If cases come before your courts that are too difficult for you to judge—whether bloodshed, lawsuits or assaults—take them to the place the LORD your God will choose. [9]Go to the Levitical priests and to the judge who is in office at that time. Inquire of them and they will give you the verdict. [10]You must act according to the decisions they give you at the place the LORD will choose. Be careful to do everything they instruct you to do. [11]Act according to whatever they teach you and the decisions they give you. Do not turn aside from what they tell you, to the right or to the left. [12]Anyone who shows contempt for the judge or for the priest who stands ministering there to the LORD your God is to be put to death. You must purge the evil from Israel. [13]All the people will hear and be afraid, and will not be contemptuous again.

The King

[14]When you enter the land the LORD your God is giving you and have taken possession of it and settled in it, and you say, "Let us set a king over us like all the nations around us," [15]be sure to appoint over you the king the LORD your God chooses. He must be from among your own people. Do not place a foreigner over you, one who is not an Israelite. [16]The king, moreover, must not acquire great numbers of horses for himself or make the people return to Egypt to get more of them, for the LORD has told you, "You are not to go back that way again." [17]He must not take many wives, or his heart will be led astray. He must not accumulate large amounts of silver and gold.

[18]When he takes the throne of his kingdom, he is to write for himself on a scroll a copy of this law, taken from that of the Levitical priests. [19]It is to be with him, and he is to read it all the days of his life so that he may learn to revere the LORD his God and follow carefully all the words of this law and these decrees [20]and not consider himself better than his fellow Israelites and turn from the law to the right or to the left. Then he and his descendants will reign a long time over his kingdom in Israel.

Offerings for Priests and Levites

18 The Levitical priests—indeed, the whole tribe of Levi—are to have no allotment or inheritance with Israel. They shall live on the food offerings presented to the LORD, for that is their inheritance. [2]They shall have no inheritance among their fellow Israelites; the LORD is their inheritance, as he promised them.

[3]This is the share due the priests from the people who sacrifice a bull or a sheep: the shoulder, the jowls and the internal organs. [4]You are to give them the firstfruits of your grain, new wine and olive oil, and the first wool from the shearing of your sheep, [5]for the LORD your God has chosen them and

FRIDAY

LEADERSHIP REQUIREMENT

Deuteronomy 17:1–20 *or* 17:14–20

Michael Green

The first requirement in any leader is total loyalty and commitment to Jesus Christ. Any Christian leader is only an under-shepherd to the one whom St. Peter calls the Chief Shepherd. That requires personal surrender to Christ . . .

It is also obvious that, if Christian leadership is based on Jesus Christ, we must be loyal to the Scriptures which Jesus studied and obeyed for his own life and inspired for his followers. Although he was the Lord, Jesus based his ministry and teaching on the Old Testament revelation. Indeed, that is one of the reasons why I regard the Bible as normative for Christian belief and behaviour: Jesus clearly did. My second reason is empirical: it works. A Christianity which detracts from Scripture, denies its authority, or adds significantly to it is headed for the decline that the liberal churches of the world are almost without exception experiencing, while the Bible-based churches are generally growing. I have therefore tried in my leadership to follow the teaching of the Bible.

ARTHUR W. PINK {AD 1885–1952}

Christianity is the religion of a Book. Christianity is based upon the impregnable rock of Holy Scripture. The starting point of all doctrinal discussion must be the Bible. Upon the foundation of the divine inspiration of the Bible stands or falls the entire edifice of Christian truth. "When the foundations are being destroyed, what can the righteous do?" (Psalm 11:3). Surrender the dogma of verbal inspiration and you are left like a rudderless ship on a stormy sea—at the mercy of every wind that blows. Deny that the Bible is, without any qualifications, the very Word of God, and you are left without any ultimate standard of measurement and without any supreme authority. It is useless to discuss any doctrine taught by the Bible until you are prepared to acknowledge, unreservedly, that the Bible is the final court of appeal. Grant that the Bible is a divine revelation and communication of God's own mind and will to people, and you have a fixed starting point from which advance can be made into the domain of truth.

reflection

1. Why do you believe it's important for Christian leaders to build their lives and ministry on the words of the Bible?

2. To what degree do the leaders you know demonstrate a high regard and respect for the Scriptures?

3. When have you seen a leader of a church or ministry build on a foundation other than the Word of God?

For your next devotional reading, go to page 221.

their descendants out of all your tribes to stand and minister in the LORD's name always.

⁶If a Levite moves from one of your towns anywhere in Israel where he is living, and comes in all earnestness to the place the LORD will choose, ⁷he may minister in the name of the LORD his God like all other Levites who serve there in the presence of the LORD. ⁸He is to share equally in their benefits, even though he has received money from the sale of family possessions.

Occult Practices

⁹When you enter the land the LORD your God is giving you, do not learn to imitate the detestable ways of the nations there. ¹⁰Let no one be found among you who sacrifices their son or daughter in the fire, who practices divination or sorcery, interprets omens, engages in witchcraft, ¹¹or casts spells, or who is a medium or spiritist or who consults the dead. ¹²Anyone who does these things is detestable to the LORD, and because of these detestable practices the LORD your God will drive out those nations before you. ¹³You must be blameless before the LORD your God.

The Prophet

¹⁴The nations you will dispossess listen to those who practice sorcery or divination. But as for you, the LORD your God has not permitted you to do so. ¹⁵The LORD your God will raise up for you a prophet like me from among you, from your own people. You must listen to him. ¹⁶For this is what you asked of the LORD your God at Horeb on the day of the assembly when you said, "Let us not hear the voice of the LORD our God nor see this great fire anymore, or we will die."

¹⁷The LORD said to me: "What they say is good. ¹⁸I will raise up for them a prophet like you from among their people, and I will put my words in his mouth. He will tell them everything I command him. ¹⁹I myself will call to account anyone who does not listen to my words that the prophet speaks in my name. ²⁰But a prophet who presumes to speak in my name anything I have not commanded, or a prophet who speaks in the name of other gods, is to be put to death."

²¹You may say to yourselves, "How can we know when a message has not been spoken by the LORD?" ²²If what a prophet proclaims in the name of the LORD does not take place or come true, that is a message the LORD has not spoken. That prophet has spoken presumptuously. No one should be alarmed.

Cities of Refuge

19 When the LORD your God has destroyed the nations whose land he is giving you, and when you have driven them out and settled in their towns and houses, ²then set aside for yourselves three cities in the land the LORD your God is giving you to possess. ³Build roads to them and divide into three parts the land the LORD your God is giving you as an inheritance, so that anyone who kills someone else may flee there.

⁴This is the rule concerning anyone who kills a person and flees there for safety—anyone who kills a neighbor unintentionally, without malice aforethought. ⁵For instance, a man may go into the forest with his neighbor to cut wood, and as he swings his ax to fell a tree, the head may fly off and hit his neighbor and kill him. That man may flee to one of these cities and save his life. ⁶Otherwise, the avenger of blood might pursue him in a rage, overtake him if the distance is too great, and kill him even though he is not deserving of death, since he did it to his neighbor without malice aforethought. ⁷This is why I command you to set aside for yourselves three cities.

⁸If the LORD your God enlarges your territory, as he promised on oath to your ancestors, and gives you the whole land he promised them, ⁹because you carefully follow all these laws I command you today—to love the LORD your God and to walk always in obedience to him—then you are to set aside three more cities. ¹⁰Do this so that innocent blood will not be shed in your land, which the LORD your God is giving you as your inheritance, and so that you will not be guilty of bloodshed.

¹¹But if out of hate someone lies in wait, assaults and kills a neighbor, and then flees to one of these cities, ¹²the killer shall be sent for by the town elders, be brought back from the city, and be handed over to the avenger of blood to die. ¹³Show no pity. You must purge from Israel the guilt of shedding innocent blood, so that it may go well with you.

¹⁴Do not move your neighbor's boundary stone set up by your predecessors in the in-

God's Holiness

Deuteronomy 18:9–13

read/meditate

Walk through this passage on holiness several times. Each time you do, read it from a different perspective—from God's perspective, from the writer's perspective, from the original readers' perspective. Finally, focus on it from your own perspective as you sort through the ramifications of God's holiness in your life.

pray

Share with God your thoughts and questions (and struggles, if you have them) about his holiness and your own.

contemplate

Spend a quiet moment surrendering to God's ideas of holiness, even if you don't feel completely clear on them. Ask for willingness to live a holy life as he reveals to you the specifics of what that means. Revisit your commitment to the Christian walk.

additional reflection

The greatness of a man's power is the measure of his surrender.
—William Booth

However holy or Christlike a Christian may become, he is still in the condition of "being changed."

—John R. W. Stott

For your next devotional reading, go to page 225.

heritance you receive in the land the LORD your God is giving you to possess.

Witnesses

¹⁵One witness is not enough to convict anyone accused of any crime or offense they may have committed. A matter must be established by the testimony of two or three witnesses.

¹⁶If a malicious witness takes the stand to accuse someone of a crime, ¹⁷the two involved in the dispute must stand in the presence of the LORD before the priests and the judges who are in office at the time. ¹⁸The judges must make a thorough investigation, and if the witness proves to be a liar, giving false testimony, ¹⁹then do to the false witness as that witness intended to do to the other party. You must purge the evil from among you. ²⁰The rest of the people will hear of this and be afraid, and never again will such an evil thing be done among you. ²¹Show no pity: life for life, eye for eye, tooth for tooth, hand for hand, foot for foot.

Going to War

20 When you go to war against your enemies and see horses and chariots and an army greater than yours, do not be afraid of them, because the LORD your God, who brought you up out of Egypt, will be with you. ²When you are about to go into battle, the priest shall come forward and address the army. ³He shall say: "Hear, Israel: Today you are going into battle against your enemies. Do not be fainthearted or afraid; do not be terrified or give way to panic before them. ⁴For the LORD your God is the one who goes with you to fight for you against your enemies to give you victory."

⁵The officers shall say to the army: "Has anyone built a new house and not yet begun to live in it? Let him go home, or he may die in battle and someone else may begin to live in it. ⁶Has anyone planted a vineyard and not begun to enjoy it? Let him go home, or he may die in battle and someone else enjoy it. ⁷Has anyone become pledged to a woman and not married her? Let him go home, or he may die in battle and someone else marry her." ⁸Then the officers shall add, "Is anyone afraid or fainthearted? Let him go home so that the others will not become disheartened too." ⁹When the officers have finished speaking to the army, they shall appoint commanders over it.

¹⁰When you march up to attack a city, make its people an offer of peace. ¹¹If they accept and open their gates, all the people in it shall be subject to forced labor and shall work for you. ¹²If they refuse to make peace and they engage you in battle, lay siege to that city. ¹³When the LORD your God delivers it into your hand, put to the sword all the men in it. ¹⁴As for the women, the children, the livestock and everything else in the city, you may take these as plunder for yourselves. And you may use the plunder the LORD your God gives you from your enemies. ¹⁵This is how you are to treat all the cities that are at a distance from you and do not belong to the nations nearby.

¹⁶However, in the cities of the nations the LORD your God is giving you as an inheritance, do not leave alive anything that breathes. ¹⁷Completely destroyᵃ them—the Hittites, Amorites, Canaanites, Perizzites, Hivites and Jebusites—as the LORD your God has commanded you. ¹⁸Otherwise, they will teach you to follow all the detestable things they do in worshiping their gods, and you will sin against the LORD your God.

¹⁹When you lay siege to a city for a long time, fighting against it to capture it, do not destroy its trees by putting an ax to them, because you can eat their fruit. Do not cut them down. Are the trees people, that you should besiege them?ᵇ ²⁰However, you may cut down trees that you know are not fruit trees and use them to build siege works until the city at war with you falls.

Atonement for an Unsolved Murder

21 If someone is found slain, lying in a field in the land the LORD your God is giving you to possess, and it is not known who the killer was, ²your elders and judges shall go out and measure the distance from the body to the neighboring towns. ³Then the elders of the town nearest the body shall take a heifer that has never been worked and has never worn a yoke ⁴and lead it down to a valley that has

---

ᵃ 17 The Hebrew term refers to the irrevocable giving over of things or persons to the LORD, often by totally destroying them.   ᵇ 19 Or *down to use in the siege, for the fruit trees are for the benefit of people.*

not been plowed or planted and where there is a flowing stream. There in the valley they are to break the heifer's neck. ⁵The priests, the sons of Levi, shall step forward, for the LORD your God has chosen them to minister and to pronounce blessings in the name of the LORD and to decide all cases of dispute and assault. ⁶Then all the elders of the town nearest the body shall wash their hands over the heifer whose neck was broken in the valley, ⁷and they shall declare: "Our hands did not shed this blood, nor did our eyes see it done. ⁸Accept this atonement for your people Israel, whom you have redeemed, LORD, and do not hold your people guilty of the blood of an innocent person." And the bloodshed will be atoned for. ⁹So you will purge from yourselves the guilt of shedding innocent blood, since you have done what is right in the eyes of the LORD.

Marrying a Captive Woman

¹⁰When you go to war against your enemies and the LORD your God delivers them into your hands and you take captives, ¹¹if you notice among the captives a beautiful woman and are attracted to her, you may take her as your wife. ¹²Bring her into your home and have her shave her head, trim her nails ¹³and put aside the clothes she was wearing when captured. After she has lived in your house and mourned her father and mother for a full month, then you may go to her and be her husband and she shall be your wife. ¹⁴If you are not pleased with her, let her go wherever she wishes. You must not sell her or treat her as a slave, since you have dishonored her.

The Right of the Firstborn

¹⁵If someone has two wives, and he loves one but not the other, and both bear him sons but the firstborn is the son of the wife he does not love, ¹⁶when he wills his property to his sons, he must not give the rights of the firstborn to the son of the wife he loves in preference to his actual firstborn, the son of the wife he does not love. ¹⁷He must acknowledge the son of his unloved wife as the firstborn by giving him a double share of all he has. That son is the first sign of his father's strength. The right of the firstborn belongs to him.

A Rebellious Son

¹⁸If someone has a stubborn and rebellious son who does not obey his father and mother and will not listen to them when they discipline him, ¹⁹his father and mother shall take hold of him and bring him to the elders at the gate of his town. ²⁰They shall say to the elders, "This son of ours is stubborn and rebellious. He will not obey us. He is a profligate and a drunkard." ²¹Then all the men of his town are to stone him to death. You must purge the evil from among you. All Israel will hear of it and be afraid.

Various Laws

²²If anyone guilty of a capital offense is put to death and their body is exposed on a pole, ²³you must not leave the body hanging on the pole overnight. Be sure to bury it that same day, because anyone who is hung on a pole is under God's curse. You must not desecrate the land the LORD your God is giving you as an inheritance.

22

If you see someone else's ox or sheep straying, do not ignore it but be sure to take it back to its owner. ²If the owner does not live near you or if you do not know who owns it, take it home with you and keep it until the owner comes looking for it. Then give it back. ³Do the same if you find someone's donkey or cloak or anything else they have lost. Do not ignore it.

⁴If you see someone's donkey or ox fallen on the road, do not ignore it. Help the owner get it to its feet.

⁵A woman must not wear men's clothing, nor a man wear women's clothing, for the LORD your God detests anyone who does this.

⁶If you come across a bird's nest beside the road, either in a tree or on the ground, and the mother is sitting on the young or on the eggs, do not take the mother with the young. ⁷You may take the young, but be sure to let the mother go, so that it may go well with you and you may have a long life.

⁸When you build a new house, make a parapet around your roof so that you may not bring the guilt of bloodshed on your house if someone falls from the roof.

⁹Do not plant two kinds of seed in your vineyard; if you do, not only the crops you plant but also the fruit of the vineyard will be defiled. ᵃ

a 9 Or *be forfeited to the sanctuary*

¹⁰Do not plow with an ox and a donkey yoked together.

¹¹Do not wear clothes of wool and linen woven together.

¹²Make tassels on the four corners of the cloak you wear.

Marriage Violations

¹³If a man takes a wife and, after sleeping with her, dislikes her ¹⁴and slanders her and gives her a bad name, saying, "I married this woman, but when I approached her, I did not find proof of her virginity," ¹⁵then the young woman's father and mother shall bring to the town elders at the gate proof that she was a virgin. ¹⁶Her father will say to the elders, "I gave my daughter in marriage to this man, but he dislikes her. ¹⁷Now he has slandered her and said, 'I did not find your daughter to be a virgin.' But here is the proof of my daughter's virginity." Then her parents shall display the cloth before the elders of the town, ¹⁸and the elders shall take the man and punish him. ¹⁹They shall fine him a hundred shekels^a of silver and give them to the young woman's father, because this man has given an Israelite virgin a bad name. She shall continue to be his wife; he must not divorce her as long as he lives.

²⁰If, however, the charge is true and no proof of the young woman's virginity can be found, ²¹she shall be brought to the door of her father's house and there the men of her town shall stone her to death. She has done an outrageous thing in Israel by being promiscuous while still in her father's house. You must purge the evil from among you.

²²If a man is found sleeping with another man's wife, both the man who slept with her and the woman must die. You must purge the evil from Israel.

²³If a man happens to meet in a town a virgin pledged to be married and he sleeps with her, ²⁴you shall take both of them to the gate of that town and stone them to death— the young woman because she was in a town and did not scream for help, and the man because he violated another man's wife. You must purge the evil from among you.

²⁵But if out in the country a man happens to meet a young woman pledged to be mar- ried and rapes her, only the man who has done this shall die. ²⁶Do nothing to the woman; she has committed no sin deserving death. This case is like that of someone who attacks and murders a neighbor, ²⁷for the man found the young woman out in the country, and though the betrothed woman screamed, there was no one to rescue her.

²⁸If a man happens to meet a virgin who is not pledged to be married and rapes her and they are discovered, ²⁹he shall pay her father fifty shekels^b of silver. He must mar- ry the young woman, for he has violated her. He can never divorce her as long as he lives.

*³⁰A man is not to marry his father's wife; he must not dishonor his father's bed.

Exclusion From the Assembly

23 *No one who has been emascu- lated by crushing or cutting may enter the assembly of the LORD.
²No one born of a forbidden marriage^c nor any offspring from such a marriage may enter the assembly of the LORD, not even in the tenth generation.

³No Ammonite or Moabite or any of their descendants may enter the assembly of the LORD, not even in the tenth generation. ⁴For they did not come to meet you with bread and water on your way when you came out of Egypt, and they hired Balaam son of Beor from Pethor in Aram Naharaim^d to pro- nounce a curse on you. ⁵However, the LORD your God would not listen to Balaam but turned the curse into a blessing for you, be- cause the LORD your God loves you. ⁶Do not seek a treaty of friendship with them as long as you live.

⁷Do not despise an Edomite, for the Edomites are related to you. Do not despise an Egyptian, because you resided as foreign- ers in their country. ⁸The third generation of children born to them may enter the assem- bly of the LORD.

Uncleanness in the Camp

⁹When you are encamped against your enemies, keep away from everything im- pure. ¹⁰If one of your men is unclean be- cause of a nocturnal emission, he is to go outside the camp and stay there. ¹¹But as

---

^a 19 That is, about 2 1/2 pounds or about 1.2 kilograms   ^b 29 That is, about 1 1/4 pounds or about 575 grams   ^c 2 Or one of illegitimate birth   ^d 4 That is, Northwest Mesopotamia

* 22:30 is numbered 23:1 in Hebrew texts.   * 23:1-25 is numbered 23:2-26 in Hebrew texts.

MONDAY

MARRIAGE: A MIRROR

Deuteronomy 22:13–30 *or* 22:22

Raymond Brown

These laws [in Deuteronomy 22] were specifically designed to preserve the sanctity of marriage and maintain the general well-being of Hebrew family life. In our own time, whilst not wishing to adopt the punishments which are prescribed, we need to expose the transgression ... A recent issue of an international news magazine carried a comment by a Belgian legislator, Jean-Pierre Detremmerie, on European reaction to allegations of marital infidelity on the part of American politicians: "In Europe, extramarital affairs are considered a sign of good health, a feat." It is astonishing that, in today's world, anyone could equate sexual permissiveness with healthy behaviour when contemporary society is confronted with the serious increase on a world scale of a fatal sexually-transmitted disease ... Commenting on this passage, J. A. Thompson reminds us ... "Great nations in centuries past lost their nationhood in considerable measure because of their unrestrained licence in sexual matters."

CHARLES HODGE {AD 1797–1878}

The strongest proof of the sanctity of the marriage relationship in the sight of God is to be found in the fact that, both in the Old and New Testaments, marriage is made the symbol of the relationship between God and his people. "Your Maker is your husband," are the words of God, and [they] contain a world of truth, of grace and of love (Isaiah 54:5). The departure of the people from God is illustrated by a reference to a wife forsaking her husband; while God's forbearance, tenderness and love are compared to those of a faithful husband to his wife. "As a bridegroom rejoices over his bride, so will your God rejoice over you" (Isaiah 62:5). In the New Testament, this reference to the marriage relationship, to illustrate the union between Christ and the church, is frequent and instructive. The church is called "the bride, the wife of the Lamb" (Revelation 21:9). And the consummation of the work of salvation is set forth as the marriage, or the [wedding supper] of the Lamb (Revelation 19:7,9). In Ephesians 5:22–33, the union between husbands and wives and the duties resulting from marriage are presented as so similar to the union between Christ and his church that it is hard to determine to which union the Apostle refers in some cases.

reflection

1. How were the laws God gave the Hebrews designed to protect the sanctity of marriage?

2. Why does God consider marriage such a holy, sacred relationship?

3. How does the world's view of marriage compare with God's view?

For your next devotional reading, go to page 227.

evening approaches he is to wash himself, and at sunset he may return to the camp.

¹²Designate a place outside the camp where you can go to relieve yourself. ¹³As part of your equipment have something to dig with, and when you relieve yourself, dig a hole and cover up your excrement. ¹⁴For the LORD your God moves about in your camp to protect you and to deliver your enemies to you. Your camp must be holy, so that he will not see among you anything indecent and turn away from you.

Miscellaneous Laws

¹⁵If a slave has taken refuge with you, do not hand them over to their master. ¹⁶Let them live among you wherever they like and in whatever town they choose. Do not oppress them.

¹⁷No Israelite man or woman is to become a shrine prostitute. ¹⁸You must not bring the earnings of a female prostitute or of a male prostitute[a] into the house of the LORD your God to pay any vow, because the LORD your God detests them both.

¹⁹Do not charge an Israelite interest, whether on money or food or anything else that may earn interest. ²⁰You may charge a foreigner interest, but not another Israelite, so that the LORD your God may bless you in everything you put your hand to in the land you are entering to possess.

²¹If you make a vow to the LORD your God, do not be slow to pay it, for the LORD your God will certainly demand it of you and you will be guilty of sin. ²²But if you refrain from making a vow, you will not be guilty. ²³Whatever your lips utter you must be sure to do, because you made your vow freely to the LORD your God with your own mouth.

²⁴If you enter your neighbor's vineyard, you may eat all the grapes you want, but do not put any in your basket. ²⁵If you enter your neighbor's grainfield, you may pick kernels with your hands, but you must not put a sickle to the standing grain.

24 If a man marries a woman who becomes displeasing to him because he finds something indecent about her, and he writes her a certificate of divorce, gives it to her and sends her from his house, ²and if after she leaves his house she becomes the wife of another man, ³and her second husband dislikes her and writes her a certificate of divorce, gives it to her and sends her from his house, or if he dies, ⁴then her first husband, who divorced her, is not allowed to marry her again after she has been defiled. That would be detestable in the eyes of the LORD. Do not bring sin upon the land the LORD your God is giving you as an inheritance.

⁵If a man has recently married, he must not be sent to war or have any other duty laid on him. For one year he is to be free to stay at home and bring happiness to the wife he has married.

⁶Do not take a pair of millstones—not even the upper one—as security for a debt, because that would be taking a person's livelihood as security.

⁷If someone is caught kidnapping another Israelite and treating or selling that Israelite as a slave, the kidnapper must die. You must purge the evil from among you.

⁸In cases of defiling skin diseases,[b] be very careful to do exactly as the Levitical priests instruct you. You must follow carefully what I have commanded them. ⁹Remember what the LORD your God did to Miriam along the way after you came out of Egypt.

¹⁰When you make a loan of any kind to a neighbor, do not go into the neighbor's house to get what is offered to you as a pledge. ¹¹Stay outside and let the neighbor to whom you are making the loan bring the pledge out to you. ¹²If the neighbor is poor, do not go to sleep with that pledge in your possession. ¹³Return the cloak by sunset so that your neighbor may sleep in it. Then you will be thanked, and it will be regarded as a righteous act in the sight of the LORD your God.

¹⁴Do not take advantage of a hired worker who is poor and needy, whether that worker is an Israelite or is a foreigner residing in one of your towns. ¹⁵Pay them their wages each day before sunset, because they are poor and are counting on it. Otherwise they may cry to the LORD against you, and you will be guilty of sin.

¹⁶Parents are not to be put to death for their children, nor children put to death for

---

a 18 Hebrew *of a dog*   b 8 The Hebrew word for *defiling skin diseases*, traditionally translated "leprosy," was used for various diseases affecting the skin.

TUESDAY

CLOSENESS IN MARRIAGE

Deuteronomy 24:1–22 *or* 24:5

Emerson Eggerichs

It is no coincidence that early on in the Bible—in describing the first marriage in human history—there is a living definition of the meaning of closeness. "[For this reason a man will leave his father and mother and be united to his wife, and they will become one flesh]" (Genesis 2:24).

When Scripture speaks of "[being united]," the idea in the Hebrew is to cling, hold or keep close. Two are joined together face-to-face, becoming one flesh. Did you know that in all of God's creation only human beings are sexually intimate face-to-face? [Being united], however, is more than sexual. [It] also means spiritual and emotional closeness. This is a salient passage for husbands—full of insight. Your wife will feel loved when you move toward her and let her know you want to be close with a look, a touch or a smile.

In the book of Deuteronomy we find still more about what it means to be close. "[If a man has recently married, he must not be sent to war or have any other duty laid on him. For one year he is to be free to stay at home and bring happiness to the wife he has married]" (Deuteronomy 24:5). This is a fascinating passage because it shows how well the Israelites understood marriage. Why the whole first year? They knew that the first year of marriage is fundamental. It is important to set the tone for the closeness of the relationship, before the wear and tear of life takes the husband away for periods of time, before they face other problems.

JEREMY TAYLOR {AD 1613–1667}

Marriage has in it less of beauty, but more of safety, than the single life; it has more care, but less danger; it is more merry, and more sad; it is fuller of sorrows, and fuller of joys; it lies under more burdens, but it is supported by all the strengths of love, and charity, and those burdens are delightful.

reflection

1. Do you know a couple that really exemplifies the kind of closeness God calls for in marriage? What can you learn from them?

2. What does it take to have this kind of close relationship?

3. How can you pray for the married people you know?

For your next devotional reading, go to page 234.

their parents; each of you will die for your own sin.

¹⁷Do not deprive the foreigner or the fatherless of justice, or take the cloak of the widow as a pledge. ¹⁸Remember that you were slaves in Egypt and the LORD your God redeemed you from there. That is why I command you to do this.

¹⁹When you are harvesting in your field and you overlook a sheaf, do not go back to get it. Leave it for the foreigner, the fatherless and the widow, so that the LORD your God may bless you in all the work of your hands. ²⁰When you beat the olives from your trees, do not go over the branches a second time. Leave what remains for the foreigner, the fatherless and the widow. ²¹When you harvest the grapes in your vineyard, do not go over the vines again. Leave what remains for the foreigner, the fatherless and the widow. ²²Remember that you were slaves in Egypt. That is why I command you to do this.

25 When people have a dispute, they are to take it to court and the judges will decide the case, acquitting the innocent and condemning the guilty. ²If the one who is guilty deserves to be beaten, the judge shall make them lie down and have them flogged in his presence with the number of lashes the crime deserves, ³but the judge must not impose more than forty lashes. If the guilty party is flogged more than that, your Israelite neighbor will be degraded in your eyes.

⁴Do not muzzle an ox while it is treading out the grain.

⁵If brothers are living together and one of them dies without a son, his widow must not marry outside the family. Her husband's brother shall take her and marry her and fulfill the duty of a brother-in-law to her. ⁶The first son she bears shall carry on the name of the dead brother so that his name will not be blotted out from Israel.

⁷However, if a man does not want to marry his brother's wife, she shall go to the elders at the town gate and say, "My husband's brother refuses to carry on his brother's name in Israel. He will not fulfill the duty of a brother-in-law to me." ⁸Then the elders of his town shall summon him and talk to him. If he persists in saying, "I do not want to marry her," ⁹his brother's widow shall go up to him in the presence of the elders, take off one of his sandals, spit in his face and say, "This is what is done to the man who will not build up his brother's family line." ¹⁰That man's line shall be known in Israel as The Family of the Unsandaled.

¹¹If two men are fighting and the wife of one of them comes to rescue her husband from his assailant, and she reaches out and seizes him by his private parts, ¹²you shall cut off her hand. Show her no pity.

¹³Do not have two differing weights in your bag—one heavy, one light. ¹⁴Do not have two differing measures in your house—one large, one small. ¹⁵You must have accurate and honest weights and measures, so that you may live long in the land the LORD your God is giving you. ¹⁶For the LORD your God detests anyone who does these things, anyone who deals dishonestly.

¹⁷Remember what the Amalekites did to you along the way when you came out of Egypt. ¹⁸When you were weary and worn out, they met you on your journey and attacked all who were lagging behind; they had no fear of God. ¹⁹When the LORD your God gives you rest from all the enemies around you in the land he is giving you to possess as an inheritance, you shall blot out the name of Amalek from under heaven. Do not forget!

Firstfruits and Tithes

26 When you have entered the land the LORD your God is giving you as an inheritance and have taken possession of it and settled in it, ²take some of the firstfruits of all that you produce from the soil of the land the LORD your God is giving you and put them in a basket. Then go to the place the LORD your God will choose as a dwelling for his Name ³and say to the priest in office at the time, "I declare today to the LORD your God that I have come to the land the LORD swore to our ancestors to give us." ⁴The priest shall take the basket from your hands and set it down in front of the altar of the LORD your God. ⁵Then you shall declare before the LORD your God: "My father was a wandering Aramean, and he went down into Egypt with a few people and lived there and became a great nation, powerful and numerous. ⁶But the Egyptians mistreated us and made us suffer, subjecting us to harsh labor. ⁷Then we cried out to

the Lord, the God of our ancestors, and the Lord heard our voice and saw our misery, toil and oppression. ⁸So the Lord brought us out of Egypt with a mighty hand and an outstretched arm, with great terror and with signs and wonders. ⁹He brought us to this place and gave us this land, a land flowing with milk and honey; ¹⁰and now I bring the firstfruits of the soil that you, Lord, have given me." Place the basket before the Lord your God and bow down before him. ¹¹Then you and the Levites and the foreigners residing among you shall rejoice in all the good things the Lord your God has given to you and your household.

¹²When you have finished setting aside a tenth of all your produce in the third year, the year of the tithe, you shall give it to the Levite, the foreigner, the fatherless and the widow, so that they may eat in your towns and be satisfied. ¹³Then say to the Lord your God: "I have removed from my house the sacred portion and have given it to the Levite, the foreigner, the fatherless and the widow, according to all you commanded. I have not turned aside from your commands nor have I forgotten any of them. ¹⁴I have not eaten any of the sacred portion while I was in mourning, nor have I removed any of it while I was unclean, nor have I offered any of it to the dead. I have obeyed the Lord my God; I have done everything you commanded me. ¹⁵Look down from heaven, your holy dwelling place, and bless your people Israel and the land you have given us as you promised on oath to our ancestors, a land flowing with milk and honey."

Follow the Lord's Commands

¹⁶The Lord your God commands you this day to follow these decrees and laws; carefully observe them with all your heart and with all your soul. ¹⁷You have declared this day that the Lord is your God and that you will walk in obedience to him, that you will keep his decrees, commands and laws—that you will listen to him. ¹⁸And the Lord has declared this day that you are his people, his treasured possession as he promised, and that you are to keep all his commands. ¹⁹He has declared that he will set you in praise, fame and honor high above all the nations he has made and that you will be a people holy to the Lord your God, as he promised.

The Altar on Mount Ebal

27 Moses and the elders of Israel commanded the people: "Keep all these commands that I give you today. ²When you have crossed the Jordan into the land the Lord your God is giving you, set up some large stones and coat them with plaster. ³Write on them all the words of this law when you have crossed over to enter the land the Lord your God is giving you, a land flowing with milk and honey, just as the Lord, the God of your ancestors, promised you. ⁴And when you have crossed the Jordan, set up these stones on Mount Ebal, as I command you today, and coat them with plaster. ⁵Build there an altar to the Lord your God, an altar of stones. Do not use any iron tool on them. ⁶Build the altar of the Lord your God with fieldstones and offer burnt offerings on it to the Lord your God. ⁷Sacrifice fellowship offerings there, eating them and rejoicing in the presence of the Lord your God. ⁸And you shall write very clearly all the words of this law on these stones you have set up."

Curses From Mount Ebal

⁹Then Moses and the Levitical priests said to all Israel, "Be silent, Israel, and listen! You have now become the people of the Lord your God. ¹⁰Obey the Lord your God and follow his commands and decrees that I give you today."

¹¹On the same day Moses commanded the people:

¹²When you have crossed the Jordan, these tribes shall stand on Mount Gerizim to bless the people: Simeon, Levi, Judah, Issachar, Joseph and Benjamin. ¹³And these tribes shall stand on Mount Ebal to pronounce curses: Reuben, Gad, Asher, Zebulun, Dan and Naphtali.

¹⁴The Levites shall recite to all the people of Israel in a loud voice:

¹⁵"Cursed is anyone who makes an idol—a thing detestable to the Lord, the work of skilled hands—and sets it up in secret."

Then all the people shall say,
"Amen!"

¹⁶"Cursed is anyone who dishonors their father or mother."

Then all the people shall say,
"Amen!"

¹⁷"Cursed is anyone who moves their neighbor's boundary stone."

Then all the people shall say, "Amen!"

¹⁸"Cursed is anyone who leads the blind astray on the road."

Then all the people shall say, "Amen!"

¹⁹"Cursed is anyone who withholds justice from the foreigner, the fatherless or the widow."

Then all the people shall say, "Amen!"

²⁰"Cursed is anyone who sleeps with his father's wife, for he dishonors his father's bed."

Then all the people shall say, "Amen!"

²¹"Cursed is anyone who has sexual relations with any animal."

Then all the people shall say, "Amen!"

²²"Cursed is anyone who sleeps with his sister, the daughter of his father or the daughter of his mother."

Then all the people shall say, "Amen!"

²³"Cursed is anyone who sleeps with his mother-in-law."

Then all the people shall say, "Amen!"

²⁴"Cursed is anyone who kills their neighbor secretly."

Then all the people shall say, "Amen!"

²⁵"Cursed is anyone who accepts a bribe to kill an innocent person."

Then all the people shall say, "Amen!"

²⁶"Cursed is anyone who does not uphold the words of this law by carrying them out."

Then all the people shall say, "Amen!"

Blessings for Obedience

28 If you fully obey the LORD your God and carefully follow all his commands I give you today, the LORD your God will set you high above all the nations on earth. ²All these blessings will come on you and accompany you if you obey the LORD your God:

³You will be blessed in the city and blessed in the country.

⁴The fruit of your womb will be blessed, and the crops of your land and the young of your livestock—the calves of your herds and the lambs of your flocks.

⁵Your basket and your kneading trough will be blessed.

⁶You will be blessed when you come in and blessed when you go out.

⁷The LORD will grant that the enemies who rise up against you will be defeated before you. They will come at you from one direction but flee from you in seven.

⁸The LORD will send a blessing on your barns and on everything you put your hand to. The LORD your God will bless you in the land he is giving you.

⁹The LORD will establish you as his holy people, as he promised you on oath, if you keep the commands of the LORD your God and walk in obedience to him. ¹⁰Then all the peoples on earth will see that you are called by the name of the LORD, and they will fear you. ¹¹The LORD will grant you abundant prosperity—in the fruit of your womb, the young of your livestock and the crops of your ground—in the land he swore to your ancestors to give you.

¹²The LORD will open the heavens, the storehouse of his bounty, to send rain on your land in season and to bless all the work of your hands. You will lend to many nations but will borrow from none. ¹³The LORD will make you the head, not the tail. If you pay attention to the commands of the LORD your God that I give you this day and carefully follow them, you will always be at the top, never at the bottom. ¹⁴Do not turn aside from any of the commands I give you today, to the right or to the left, following other gods and serving them.

Curses for Disobedience

¹⁵However, if you do not obey the LORD your God and do not carefully follow all his commands and decrees I am giving you today, all these curses will come on you and overtake you:

¹⁶You will be cursed in the city and cursed in the country.

¹⁷Your basket and your kneading trough will be cursed.

¹⁸The fruit of your womb will be cursed, and the crops of your land, and

the calves of your herds and the lambs of your flocks.

¹⁹You will be cursed when you come in and cursed when you go out.

²⁰The LORD will send on you curses, confusion and rebuke in everything you put your hand to, until you are destroyed and come to sudden ruin because of the evil you have done in forsaking him. ᵃ ²¹The LORD will plague you with diseases until he has destroyed you from the land you are entering to possess. ²²The LORD will strike you with wasting disease, with fever and inflammation, with scorching heat and drought, with blight and mildew, which will plague you until you perish. ²³The sky over your head will be bronze, the ground beneath you iron. ²⁴The LORD will turn the rain of your country into dust and powder; it will come down from the skies until you are destroyed.

²⁵The LORD will cause you to be defeated before your enemies. You will come at them from one direction but flee from them in seven, and you will become a thing of horror to all the kingdoms on earth. ²⁶Your carcasses will be food for all the birds and the wild animals, and there will be no one to frighten them away. ²⁷The LORD will afflict you with the boils of Egypt and with tumors, festering sores and the itch, from which you cannot be cured. ²⁸The LORD will afflict you with madness, blindness and confusion of mind. ²⁹At midday you will grope about like a blind person in the dark. You will be unsuccessful in everything you do; day after day you will be oppressed and robbed, with no one to rescue you.

³⁰You will be pledged to be married to a woman, but another will take her and ravish her. You will build a house, but you will not live in it. You will plant a vineyard, but you will not even begin to enjoy its fruit. ³¹Your ox will be slaughtered before your eyes, but you will eat none of it. Your donkey will be forcibly taken from you and will not be returned. Your sheep will be given to your enemies, and no one will rescue them. ³²Your sons and daughters will be given to another nation, and you will wear out your eyes watching for them day after day, powerless to lift a hand. ³³A people that you do not know will eat what your land and labor produce, and you will have nothing but cruel oppression all your days. ³⁴The sights you see will drive you mad. ³⁵The LORD will afflict your knees and legs with painful boils that cannot be cured, spreading from the soles of your feet to the top of your head.

³⁶The LORD will drive you and the king you set over you to a nation unknown to you or your ancestors. There you will worship other gods, gods of wood and stone. ³⁷You will become a thing of horror, a byword and an object of ridicule among all the peoples where the LORD will drive you.

³⁸You will sow much seed in the field but you will harvest little, because locusts will devour it. ³⁹You will plant vineyards and cultivate them but you will not drink the wine or gather the grapes, because worms will eat them. ⁴⁰You will have olive trees throughout your country but you will not use the oil, because the olives will drop off. ⁴¹You will have sons and daughters but you will not keep them, because they will go into captivity. ⁴²Swarms of locusts will take over all your trees and the crops of your land.

⁴³The foreigners who reside among you will rise above you higher and higher, but you will sink lower and lower. ⁴⁴They will lend to you, but you will not lend to them. They will be the head, but you will be the tail.

⁴⁵All these curses will come on you. They will pursue you and overtake you until you are destroyed, because you did not obey the LORD your God and observe the commands and decrees he gave you. ⁴⁶They will be a sign and a wonder to you and your descendants forever. ⁴⁷Because you did not serve the LORD your God joyfully and gladly in the time of prosperity, ⁴⁸therefore in hunger and thirst, in nakedness and dire poverty, you will serve the enemies the LORD sends against you. He will put an iron yoke on your neck until he has destroyed you.

⁴⁹The LORD will bring a nation against you from far away, from the ends of the earth, like an eagle swooping down, a nation whose language you will not understand, ⁵⁰a fierce-looking nation without respect for the old or pity for the young. ⁵¹They will devour the young of your livestock and the crops of your land until you are destroyed. They will leave you no grain, new wine or olive oil, nor any calves of your herds or lambs of your

ᵃ 20 Hebrew *me*

flocks until you are ruined. 52They will lay siege to all the cities throughout your land until the high fortified walls in which you trust fall down. They will besiege all the cities throughout the land the LORD your God is giving you.

53Because of the suffering that your enemy will inflict on you during the siege, you will eat the fruit of the womb, the flesh of the sons and daughters the LORD your God has given you. 54Even the most gentle and sensitive man among you will have no compassion on his own brother or the wife he loves or his surviving children, 55and he will not give to one of them any of the flesh of his children that he is eating. It will be all he has left because of the suffering your enemy will inflict on you during the siege of all your cities. 56The most gentle and sensitive woman among you—so sensitive and gentle that she would not venture to touch the ground with the sole of her foot—will begrudge the husband she loves and her own son or daughter 57the afterbirth from her womb and the children she bears. For in her dire need she intends to eat them secretly because of the suffering your enemy will inflict on you during the siege of your cities.

58If you do not carefully follow all the words of this law, which are written in this book, and do not revere this glorious and awesome name—the LORD your God— 59the LORD will send fearful plagues on you and your descendants, harsh and prolonged disasters, and severe and lingering illnesses. 60He will bring on you all the diseases of Egypt that you dreaded, and they will cling to you. 61The LORD will also bring on you every kind of sickness and disaster not recorded in this Book of the Law, until you are destroyed. 62You who were as numerous as the stars in the sky will be left but few in number, because you did not obey the LORD your God. 63Just as it pleased the LORD to make you prosper and increase in number, so it will please him to ruin and destroy you. You will be uprooted from the land you are entering to possess.

64Then the LORD will scatter you among all nations, from one end of the earth to the other. There you will worship other gods—gods of wood and stone, which neither you nor your ancestors have known. 65Among those nations you will find no repose, no resting place for the sole of your foot. There the LORD will give you an anxious mind, eyes weary with longing, and a despairing heart. 66You will live in constant suspense, filled with dread both night and day, never sure of your life. 67In the morning you will say, "If only it were evening!" and in the evening, "If only it were morning!"—because of the terror that will fill your hearts and the sights that your eyes will see. 68The LORD will send you back in ships to Egypt on a journey I said you should never make again. There you will offer yourselves for sale to your enemies as male and female slaves, but no one will buy you.

Renewal of the Covenant

29 *These are the terms of the covenant the LORD commanded Moses to make with the Israelites in Moab, in addition to the covenant he had made with them at Horeb.

*2Moses summoned all the Israelites and said to them:

Your eyes have seen all that the LORD did in Egypt to Pharaoh, to all his officials and to all his land. 3With your own eyes you saw those great trials, those signs and great wonders. 4But to this day the LORD has not given you a mind that understands or eyes that see or ears that hear. 5During the forty years that I led you through the wilderness, your clothes did not wear out, nor did the sandals on your feet. 6You ate no bread and drank no wine or other fermented drink. I did this so that you might know that I am the LORD your God.

7When you reached this place, Sihon king of Heshbon and Og king of Bashan came out to fight against us, but we defeated them. 8We took their land and gave it as an inheritance to the Reubenites, the Gadites and the half-tribe of Manasseh.

9Carefully follow the terms of this covenant, so that you may prosper in everything you do. 10All of you are standing today in the presence of the LORD your God—your leaders and chief men, your elders and officials, and all the other men of Israel, 11together with your children and your wives, and the foreigners living in your camps who chop your wood and carry your water. 12You are

---

* 29:1 is numbered 28:69 in Hebrew texts.   * 29:2-29 is numbered 29:1-28 in Hebrew texts.

standing here in order to enter into a covenant with the LORD your God, a covenant the LORD is making with you this day and sealing with an oath, [13]to confirm you this day as his people, that he may be your God as he promised you and as he swore to your fathers, Abraham, Isaac and Jacob. [14]I am making this covenant, with its oath, not only with you [15]who are standing here with us today in the presence of the LORD our God but also with those who are not here today.

[16]You yourselves know how we lived in Egypt and how we passed through the countries on the way here. [17]You saw among them their detestable images and idols of wood and stone, of silver and gold. [18]Make sure there is no man or woman, clan or tribe among you today whose heart turns away from the LORD our God to go and worship the gods of those nations; make sure there is no root among you that produces such bitter poison.

[19]When such persons hear the words of this oath and invoke a blessing on themselves, thinking, "I will be safe, even though I persist in going my own way," they will bring disaster on the watered land as well as the dry. [20]The LORD will never be willing to forgive them; his wrath and zeal will burn against them. All the curses written in this book will fall on them, and the LORD will blot out their names from under heaven. [21]The LORD will single them out from all the tribes of Israel for disaster, according to all the curses of the covenant written in this Book of the Law.

[22]Your children who follow you in later generations and foreigners who come from distant lands will see the calamities that have fallen on the land and the diseases with which the LORD has afflicted it. [23]The whole land will be a burning waste of salt and sulfur—nothing planted, nothing sprouting, no vegetation growing on it. It will be like the destruction of Sodom and Gomorrah, Admah and Zeboyim, which the LORD overthrew in fierce anger. [24]All the nations will ask: "Why has the LORD done this to this land? Why this fierce, burning anger?"

[25]And the answer will be: "It is because this people abandoned the covenant of the LORD, the God of their ancestors, the covenant he made with them when he brought them out of Egypt. [26]They went off and worshiped other gods and bowed down to them, gods they did not know, gods he had not given them. [27]Therefore the LORD's anger burned against this land, so that he brought on it all the curses written in this book. [28]In furious anger and in great wrath the LORD uprooted them from their land and thrust them into another land, as it is now."

[29]The secret things belong to the LORD our God, but the things revealed belong to us and to our children forever, that we may follow all the words of this law.

Prosperity After Turning to the LORD

30 When all these blessings and curses I have set before you come on you and you take them to heart wherever the LORD your God disperses you among the nations, [2]and when you and your children return to the LORD your God and obey him with all your heart and with all your soul according to everything I command you today, [3]then the LORD your God will restore your fortunes[a] and have compassion on you and gather you again from all the nations where he scattered you. [4]Even if you have been banished to the most distant land under the heavens, from there the LORD your God will gather you and bring you back. [5]He will bring you to the land that belonged to your ancestors, and you will take possession of it. He will make you more prosperous and numerous than your ancestors. [6]The LORD your God will circumcise your hearts and the hearts of your descendants, so that you may love him with all your heart and with all your soul, and live. [7]The LORD your God will put all these curses on your enemies who hate and persecute you. [8]You will again obey the LORD and follow all his commands I am giving you today. [9]Then the LORD your God will make you most prosperous in all the work of your hands and in the fruit of your womb, the young of your livestock and the crops of your land. The LORD will again delight in you and make you prosperous, just as he delighted in your ancestors, [10]if you obey the LORD your God and keep his commands and decrees that are written in this Book of the

a 3 Or *will bring you back from captivity*

WEDNESDAY

THE KINDNESS OF GOD

Deuteronomy 30:1–20 *or* 30:1–5

S. J. Hill

If we recognize that God's heart is filled with passion for us even in our weakness, we will be catapulted into personal wholeness and spiritual maturity.

When my two sons left home and ventured out on their own, I realized even more how much I loved them. I would think about them all the time. I would call them on the phone just to hear their voices. I would picture in my mind what they looked like. More than once I heard the Lord speak so gently to me, "If you feel this way about your sons, how do you think I feel about you?"

I was often reminded of the words of Jesus in Matthew 7:9-11: "[Which of you, if your son asks for bread, will give him a stone? Or if he asks for a fish, will give him a snake? If you, then, though you are evil, know how to give good gifts to your children, how much more will your Father in heaven give good gifts to those who ask him!]"

Today as I was thinking about my sons and reflecting on those experiences, I was so overcome by the love of the Father that I broke down and wept. I realized again that when we, as His children, catch a glimpse of the beauty of His heart, it will ignite such deep passions within us that we will gladly abandon ourselves to Him.

MOTHER TERESA {AD 1910–1997}

Be the living expression of God's kindness:
> kindness in your face,
> kindness in your eyes,
> kindness in your smile,
> kindness in your warm greeting.

reflection

1. What do you learn about God by hearing his promise to restore Israel?

2. Think of someone in your life who is going through a trial. What can you do to encourage them right now?

3. How might your outlook about life change if you were to remember God's promise to be kind to his people?

For your next devotional reading, go to page 244.

Law and turn to the LORD your God with all your heart and with all your soul.

The Offer of Life or Death

¹¹Now what I am commanding you today is not too difficult for you or beyond your reach. ¹²It is not up in heaven, so that you have to ask, "Who will ascend into heaven to get it and proclaim it to us so we may obey it?" ¹³Nor is it beyond the sea, so that you have to ask, "Who will cross the sea to get it and proclaim it to us so we may obey it?" ¹⁴No, the word is very near you; it is in your mouth and in your heart so you may obey it.

¹⁵See, I set before you today life and prosperity, death and destruction. ¹⁶For I command you today to love the LORD your God, to walk in obedience to him, and to keep his commands, decrees and laws; then you will live and increase, and the LORD your God will bless you in the land you are entering to possess.

¹⁷But if your heart turns away and you are not obedient, and if you are drawn away to bow down to other gods and worship them, ¹⁸I declare to you this day that you will certainly be destroyed. You will not live long in the land you are crossing the Jordan to enter and possess.

¹⁹This day I call the heavens and the earth as witnesses against you that I have set before you life and death, blessings and curses. Now choose life, so that you and your children may live ²⁰and that you may love the LORD your God, listen to his voice, and hold fast to him. For the LORD is your life, and he will give you many years in the land he swore to give to your fathers, Abraham, Isaac and Jacob.

Joshua to Succeed Moses

31

Then Moses went out and spoke these words to all Israel: ²"I am now a hundred and twenty years old and I am no longer able to lead you. The LORD has said to me, 'You shall not cross the Jordan.' ³The LORD your God himself will cross over ahead of you. He will destroy these nations before you, and you will take possession of their land. Joshua also will cross over ahead of you, as the LORD said. ⁴And the LORD will do to them what he did to Sihon and Og, the kings of the Amorites, whom he destroyed along with their land. ⁵The LORD will deliver them to you, and you must do to them all that I have commanded you. ⁶Be strong and courageous. Do not be afraid or terrified because of them, for the LORD your God goes with you; he will never leave you nor forsake you."

⁷Then Moses summoned Joshua and said to him in the presence of all Israel, "Be strong and courageous, for you must go with this people into the land that the LORD swore to their ancestors to give them, and you must divide it among them as their inheritance. ⁸The LORD himself goes before you and will be with you; he will never leave you nor forsake you. Do not be afraid; do not be discouraged."

Public Reading of the Law

⁹So Moses wrote down this law and gave it to the priests, the sons of Levi, who carried the ark of the covenant of the LORD, and to all the elders of Israel. ¹⁰Then Moses commanded them: "At the end of every seven years, in the year for canceling debts, during the Festival of Tabernacles, ¹¹when all Israel comes to appear before the LORD your God at the place he will choose, you shall read this law before them in their hearing. ¹²Assemble the people—men, women and children, and the foreigners residing in your towns—so they can listen and learn to fear the LORD your God and follow carefully all the words of this law. ¹³Their children, who do not know this law, must hear it and learn to fear the LORD your God as long as you live in the land you are crossing the Jordan to possess."

Israel's Rebellion Predicted

¹⁴The LORD said to Moses, "Now the day of your death is near. Call Joshua and present yourselves at the tent of meeting, where I will commission him." So Moses and Joshua came and presented themselves at the tent of meeting.

¹⁵Then the LORD appeared at the tent in a pillar of cloud, and the cloud stood over the entrance to the tent. ¹⁶And the LORD said to Moses: "You are going to rest with your ancestors, and these people will soon prostitute themselves to the foreign gods of the land they are entering. They will forsake me and break the covenant I made with them. ¹⁷And in that day I will become angry with them and forsake them; I will hide my face from them, and they will be destroyed.

Many disasters and calamities will come on them, and in that day they will ask, 'Have not these disasters come on us because our God is not with us?' ¹⁸And I will certainly hide my face in that day because of all their wickedness in turning to other gods.

¹⁹"Now write down this song and teach it to the Israelites and have them sing it, so that it may be a witness for me against them. ²⁰When I have brought them into the land flowing with milk and honey, the land I promised on oath to their ancestors, and when they eat their fill and thrive, they will turn to other gods and worship them, rejecting me and breaking my covenant. ²¹And when many disasters and calamities come on them, this song will testify against them, because it will not be forgotten by their descendants. I know what they are disposed to do, even before I bring them into the land I promised them on oath." ²²So Moses wrote down this song that day and taught it to the Israelites.

²³The LORD gave this command to Joshua son of Nun: "Be strong and courageous, for you will bring the Israelites into the land I promised them on oath, and I myself will be with you."

²⁴After Moses finished writing in a book the words of this law from beginning to end, ²⁵he gave this command to the Levites who carried the ark of the covenant of the LORD: ²⁶"Take this Book of the Law and place it beside the ark of the covenant of the LORD your God. There it will remain as a witness against you. ²⁷For I know how rebellious and stiff-necked you are. If you have been rebellious against the LORD while I am still alive and with you, how much more will you rebel after I die! ²⁸Assemble before me all the elders of your tribes and all your officials, so that I can speak these words in their hearing and call the heavens and the earth to testify against them. ²⁹For I know that after my death you are sure to become utterly corrupt and to turn from the way I have commanded you. In days to come, disaster will fall on you because you will do evil in the sight of the LORD and arouse his anger by what your hands have made."

The Song of Moses

³⁰And Moses recited the words of this song from beginning to end in the hearing of the whole assembly of Israel:

32

Listen, you heavens, and I will
    speak;
  hear, you earth, the words of my
    mouth.
²Let my teaching fall like rain
  and my words descend like dew,
like showers on new grass,
  like abundant rain on tender plants.

³I will proclaim the name of the LORD.
  Oh, praise the greatness of our God!
⁴He is the Rock, his works are perfect,
  and all his ways are just.
A faithful God who does no wrong,
  upright and just is he.

⁵They are corrupt and not his children;
  to their shame they are a warped and
    crooked generation.
⁶Is this the way you repay the LORD,
  you foolish and unwise people?
Is he not your Father, your Creator,^a
  who made you and formed you?

⁷Remember the days of old;
  consider the generations long past.
Ask your father and he will tell you,
  your elders, and they will explain to
    you.
⁸When the Most High gave the nations
    their inheritance,
  when he divided all the human race,
he set up boundaries for the peoples
  according to the number of the sons
    of Israel.^b
⁹For the LORD's portion is his people,
  Jacob his allotted inheritance.

¹⁰In a desert land he found him,
  in a barren and howling waste.
He shielded him and cared for him;
  he guarded him as the apple of his eye,
¹¹like an eagle that stirs up its nest
  and hovers over its young,
that spreads its wings to catch them
  and carries them aloft.
¹²The LORD alone led him;
  no foreign god was with him.

¹³He made him ride on the heights of the
    land
  and fed him with the fruit of the
    fields.

---

^a 6 Or *Father, who bought you*   ^b 8 Masoretic Text; Dead Sea Scrolls (see also Septuagint) *sons of God*

He nourished him with honey from the
rock,
and with oil from the flinty crag,
¹⁴with curds and milk from herd and flock
and with fattened lambs and goats,
with choice rams of Bashan
and the finest kernels of wheat.
You drank the foaming blood of the
grape.

¹⁵Jeshurunᵃ grew fat and kicked;
filled with food, he became heavy and
sleek.
He abandoned the God who made him
and rejected the Rock his Savior.
¹⁶They made him jealous with their
foreign gods
and angered him with their detestable
idols.
¹⁷They sacrificed to demons, which are
not God—
gods they had not known,
gods that recently appeared,
gods your ancestors did not fear.
¹⁸You deserted the Rock, who bore you;
you forgot the God who gave you
birth.

¹⁹The LORD saw this and rejected them
because he was angered by his sons
and daughters.
²⁰"I will hide my face from them," he said,
"and see what their end will be;
for they are a perverse generation,
children who are unfaithful.
²¹They made me jealous by what is no god
and angered me with their worthless
idols.
I will make them envious by those who
are not a people;
I will make them angry by a nation
that has no understanding.
²²For a fire will be kindled by my wrath,
one that burns down to the realm of
the dead below.
It will devour the earth and its harvests
and set afire the foundations of the
mountains.

²³"I will heap calamities on them
and spend my arrows against them.
²⁴I will send wasting famine against them,
consuming pestilence and deadly
plague;

I will send against them the fangs of
wild beasts,
the venom of vipers that glide in the
dust.
²⁵In the street the sword will make them
childless;
in their homes terror will reign.
The young men and young women will
perish,
the infants and those with gray hair.
²⁶I said I would scatter them
and erase their name from human
memory,
²⁷but I dreaded the taunt of the enemy,
lest the adversary misunderstand
and say, 'Our hand has triumphed;
the LORD has not done all this.' "

²⁸They are a nation without sense,
there is no discernment in them.
²⁹If only they were wise and would
understand this
and discern what their end will be!
³⁰How could one man chase a thousand,
or two put ten thousand to flight,
unless their Rock had sold them,
unless the LORD had given them up?
³¹For their rock is not like our Rock,
as even our enemies concede.
³²Their vine comes from the vine of
Sodom
and from the fields of Gomorrah.
Their grapes are filled with poison,
and their clusters with bitterness.
³³Their wine is the venom of serpents,
the deadly poison of cobras.

³⁴"Have I not kept this in reserve
and sealed it in my vaults?
³⁵It is mine to avenge; I will repay.
In due time their foot will slip;
their day of disaster is near
and their doom rushes upon them."

³⁶The LORD will vindicate his people
and relent concerning his servants
when he sees their strength is gone
and no one is left, slave or free.ᵇ
³⁷He will say: "Now where are their gods,
the rock they took refuge in,
³⁸the gods who ate the fat of their
sacrifices
and drank the wine of their drink
offerings?
Let them rise up to help you!

ᵃ 15 *Jeshurun* means *the upright one,* that is, Israel.   ᵇ 36 Or *and they are without a ruler or leader*

Let them give you shelter!

[39] "See now that I myself am He!
There is no god besides me.
I put to death and I bring to life,
I have wounded and I will heal,
and no one can deliver out of my
hand.
[40] I lift my hand to heaven and declare:
As surely as I live forever,
[41] when I sharpen my flashing sword
and my hand grasps it in judgment,
I will take vengeance on my adversaries
and repay those who hate me.
[42] I will make my arrows drunk with blood,
while my sword devours flesh:
the blood of the slain and the captives,
the heads of the enemy leaders."

[43] Rejoice, you nations, with his people,[a, b]
for he will avenge the blood of his
servants;
he will take vengeance on his enemies
and make atonement for his land and
people.

[44] Moses came with Joshua[c] son of Nun
and spoke all the words of this song in the
hearing of the people. [45] When Moses finished reciting all these words to all Israel,
[46] he said to them, "Take to heart all the
words I have solemnly declared to you this
day, so that you may command your children to obey carefully all the words of this
law. [47] They are not just idle words for you—
they are your life. By them you will live long
in the land you are crossing the Jordan to
possess."

Moses to Die on Mount Nebo

[48] On that same day the LORD told Moses,
[49] "Go up into the Abarim Range to Mount
Nebo in Moab, across from Jericho, and view
Canaan, the land I am giving the Israelites
as their own possession. [50] There on the
mountain that you have climbed you will die
and be gathered to your people, just as your
brother Aaron died on Mount Hor and was
gathered to his people. [51] This is because
both of you broke faith with me in the presence of the Israelites at the waters of Meribah Kadesh in the Desert of Zin and because

you did not uphold my holiness among the
Israelites. [52] Therefore, you will see the land
only from a distance; you will not enter the
land I am giving to the people of Israel."

Moses Blesses the Tribes

33 This is the blessing that Moses
the man of God pronounced on
the Israelites before his death.
[2] He said:

"The LORD came from Sinai
and dawned over them from Seir;
he shone forth from Mount Paran.
He came with[d] myriads of holy ones
from the south, from his mountain
slopes.[e]
[3] Surely it is you who love the people;
all the holy ones are in your hand.
At your feet they all bow down,
and from you receive instruction,
[4] the law that Moses gave us,
the possession of the assembly of
Jacob.
[5] He was king over Jeshurun[f]
when the leaders of the people
assembled,
along with the tribes of Israel.

[6] "Let Reuben live and not die,
nor[g] his people be few."

[7] And this he said about Judah:

"Hear, LORD, the cry of Judah;
bring him to his people.
With his own hands he defends his
cause.
Oh, be his help against his foes!"

[8] About Levi he said:

"Your Thummim and Urim belong
to your faithful servant.
You tested him at Massah;
you contended with him at the waters
of Meribah.
[9] He said of his father and mother,
'I have no regard for them.'
He did not recognize his brothers
or acknowledge his own children,
but he watched over your word
and guarded your covenant.
[10] He teaches your precepts to Jacob

---

[a] 43 Or Make his people rejoice, you nations   [b] 43 Masoretic Text; Dead Sea Scrolls (see also
Septuagint) people, / and let all the angels worship him /   [c] 44 Hebrew Hoshea, a variant of Joshua
[d] 2 Or from   [e] 2 The meaning of the Hebrew for this phrase is uncertain.   [f] 5 Jeshurun means the
upright one, that is, Israel; also in verse 26.   [g] 6 Or but let

and your law to Israel.
He offers incense before you
and whole burnt offerings on your
altar.
¹¹Bless all his skills, LORD,
and be pleased with the work of his
hands.
Strike down those who rise against him,
his foes till they rise no more."

¹²About Benjamin he said:

"Let the beloved of the LORD rest secure
in him,
for he shields him all day long,
and the one the LORD loves rests
between his shoulders."

¹³About Joseph he said:

"May the LORD bless his land
with the precious dew from heaven
above
and with the deep waters that lie
below;
¹⁴with the best the sun brings forth
and the finest the moon can yield;
¹⁵with the choicest gifts of the ancient
mountains
and the fruitfulness of the everlasting
hills;
¹⁶with the best gifts of the earth and its
fullness
and the favor of him who dwelt in the
burning bush.
Let all these rest on the head of Joseph,
on the brow of the prince among[a] his
brothers.
¹⁷In majesty he is like a firstborn bull;
his horns are the horns of a wild ox.
With them he will gore the nations,
even those at the ends of the earth.
Such are the ten thousands of Ephraim;
such are the thousands of Manasseh."

¹⁸About Zebulun he said:

"Rejoice, Zebulun, in your going out,
and you, Issachar, in your tents.
¹⁹They will summon peoples to the
mountain
and there offer the sacrifices of the
righteous;
they will feast on the abundance of the
seas,
on the treasures hidden in the sand."

²⁰About Gad he said:

"Blessed is he who enlarges Gad's
domain!
Gad lives there like a lion,
tearing at arm or head.
²¹He chose the best land for himself;
the leader's portion was kept for him.
When the heads of the people
assembled,
he carried out the LORD's righteous
will,
and his judgments concerning Israel."

²²About Dan he said:

"Dan is a lion's cub,
springing out of Bashan."

²³About Naphtali he said:

"Naphtali is abounding with the favor of
the LORD
and is full of his blessing;
he will inherit southward to the lake."

²⁴About Asher he said:

"Most blessed of sons is Asher;
let him be favored by his brothers,
and let him bathe his feet in oil.
²⁵The bolts of your gates will be iron and
bronze,
and your strength will equal your
days.

²⁶"There is no one like the God of
Jeshurun,
who rides on the heavens to help you
and on the clouds in his majesty.
²⁷The eternal God is your refuge,
and underneath are the everlasting
arms.
He will drive out your enemies before
you,
saying, 'Destroy them!'
²⁸So Israel will live in safety;
Jacob will dwell[b] secure
in a land of grain and new wine,
where the heavens drop dew.
²⁹Blessed are you, Israel!
Who is like you,
a people saved by the LORD?
He is your shield and helper
and your glorious sword.
Your enemies will cower before you,
and you will tread on their heights."

---

[a] 16 Or *of the one separated from*   [b] 28 Septuagint; Hebrew *Jacob's spring is*

The Death of Moses

34

Then Moses climbed Mount Nebo from the plains of Moab to the top of Pisgah, across from Jericho. There the LORD showed him the whole land—from Gilead to Dan, ²all of Naphtali, the territory of Ephraim and Manasseh, all the land of Judah as far as the Mediterranean Sea, ³the Negev and the whole region from the Valley of Jericho, the City of Palms, as far as Zoar. ⁴Then the LORD said to him, "This is the land I promised on oath to Abraham, Isaac and Jacob when I said, 'I will give it to your descendants.' I have let you see it with your eyes, but you will not cross over into it."

⁵And Moses the servant of the LORD died there in Moab, as the LORD had said. ⁶He buried him*ᵃ* in Moab, in the valley opposite Beth Peor, but to this day no one knows where his grave is. ⁷Moses was a hundred and twenty years old when he died, yet his eyes were not weak nor his strength gone. ⁸The Israelites grieved for Moses in the plains of Moab thirty days, until the time of weeping and mourning was over.

⁹Now Joshua son of Nun was filled with the spirit*ᵇ* of wisdom because Moses had laid his hands on him. So the Israelites listened to him and did what the LORD had commanded Moses.

¹⁰Since then, no prophet has risen in Israel like Moses, whom the LORD knew face to face, ¹¹who did all those signs and wonders the LORD sent him to do in Egypt—to Pharaoh and to all his officials and to his whole land. ¹²For no one has ever shown the mighty power or performed the awesome deeds that Moses did in the sight of all Israel.

ᵃ 6 Or *He was buried*   *ᵇ 9* Or *Spirit*

The History of Israel

Joshua	2 Kings
Judges	1 Chronicles
Ruth	2 Chronicles
1 Samuel	Ezra
2 Samuel	Nehemiah
1 Kings	Esther

joshua

AUTHOR: Joshua

DATE: Around 1390 B.C.

THEME: God's promises can be trusted.

The LORD Commands Joshua

1 After the death of Moses the servant of the LORD, the LORD said to Joshua son of Nun, Moses' aide: ²"Moses my servant is dead. Now then, you and all these people, get ready to cross the Jordan River into the land I am about to give to them—to the Israelites. ³I will give you every place where you set your foot, as I promised Moses. ⁴Your territory will extend from the desert to Lebanon, and from the great river, the Euphrates—all the Hittite country—to the Mediterranean Sea in the west. ⁵No one will be able to stand against you all the days of your life. As I was with Moses, so I will be with you; I will never leave you nor forsake you. ⁶Be strong and courageous, because you will lead these people to inherit the land I swore to their ancestors to give them.

⁷"Be strong and very courageous. Be careful to obey all the law my servant Moses gave you; do not turn from it to the right or to the left, that you may be successful wherever you go. ⁸Keep this Book of the Law always on your lips; meditate on it day and night, so that you may be careful to do everything written in it. Then you will be prosperous and successful. ⁹Have I not commanded you? Be strong and courageous. Do not be afraid; do not be discouraged, for the LORD your God will be with you wherever you go."

¹⁰So Joshua ordered the officers of the people: ¹¹"Go through the camp and tell the people, 'Get your provisions ready. Three days from now you will cross the Jordan here to go in and take possession of the land the LORD your God is giving you for your own.'"

¹²But to the Reubenites, the Gadites and the half-tribe of Manasseh, Joshua said,

¹³"Remember the command that Moses the servant of the LORD gave you after he said, 'The LORD your God will give you rest by giving you this land.' ¹⁴Your wives, your children and your livestock may stay in the land that Moses gave you east of the Jordan, but all your fighting men, ready for battle, must cross over ahead of the other Israelites. You are to help them ¹⁵until the LORD gives them rest, as he has done for you, and until they too have taken possession of the land the LORD your God is giving them. After that, you may go back and occupy your own land, which Moses the servant of the LORD gave you east of the Jordan toward the sunrise."

¹⁶Then they answered Joshua, "Whatever you have commanded us we will do, and wherever you send us we will go. ¹⁷Just as we fully obeyed Moses, so we will obey you. Only may the LORD your God be with you as he was with Moses. ¹⁸Whoever rebels against your word and does not obey it, whatever you may command them, is to be put to death. Only be strong and courageous!"

Rahab and the Spies

2 Then Joshua son of Nun secretly sent two spies from Shittim. "Go, look over the land," he said, "especially Jericho." So they went and entered the house of a prostitute named Rahab and stayed there.

²The king of Jericho was told, "Look! Some of the Israelites have come here tonight to spy out the land." ³So the king of Jericho sent this message to Rahab: "Bring out the men who came to you and entered your house, because they have come to spy out the whole land."

⁴But the woman had taken the two men and hidden them. She said, "Yes, the men

A CHRISTIAN MIND

Joshua 1:1–18 *or* 1:7–8

SAINT DAVID OF WALES {ca. AD 542–601}

When we have doubts or are facing difficulties, when others suggest courses of action that are conflicting, when caution dictates one approach but faith another, we should be still. We should quiet each intruding person, calm ourselves in the sacred stillness of God's presence, study his Word for guidance, and with true devotion focus our attention on him. We should lift our nature into the pure light radiating from his face, having an eagerness to know only what God our Lord will determine for us. Soon he will reveal by his secret counsel a distinct and unmistakable sense of his direction.

Kent Hughes

You must remember this: You can never have a Christian mind without reading the Scriptures regularly because you cannot be profoundly influenced by that which you do not know. If you are filled with God's Word, your life can then be informed and directed by God—your domestic relationships, your child-rearing, your career, your ethical decisions, your interior moral life. The way to a Christian mind is through God's Word!

Again, we must be careful not to create a Bible-reading legalism—"good Christians read the Bible through once a year." The Bible nowhere demands this . . . Most people, however, will find that reading the Scripture through once a year is the best way because it requires only five pages a day and offers a reachable annual goal. Believers, whatever your ability, you must regularly read and study God's Word. If you refuse, you are in effect "editing God" and will never have a fully Christian mind.

reflection

1. Why is it important for a Christian to have a thorough knowledge of the Bible?
2. When do you find you need God's Word?
3. In what ways does the Word of God impact your life?

For your next devotional reading, go to page 249.

came to me, but I did not know where they had come from. ⁵At dusk, when it was time to close the city gate, they left. I don't know which way they went. Go after them quickly. You may catch up with them." ⁶(But she had taken them up to the roof and hidden them under the stalks of flax she had laid out on the roof.) ⁷So the men set out in pursuit of the spies on the road that leads to the fords of the Jordan, and as soon as the pursuers had gone out, the gate was shut.

⁸Before the spies lay down for the night, she went up on the roof ⁹and said to them, "I know that the LORD has given you this land and that a great fear of you has fallen on us, so that all who live in this country are melting in fear because of you. ¹⁰We have heard how the LORD dried up the water of the Red Sea ᵃ for you when you came out of Egypt, and what you did to Sihon and Og, the two kings of the Amorites east of the Jordan, whom you completely destroyed. ᵇ ¹¹When we heard of it, our hearts melted in fear and everyone's courage failed because of you, for the LORD your God is God in heaven above and on the earth below.

¹²"Now then, please swear to me by the LORD that you will show kindness to my family, because I have shown kindness to you. Give me a sure sign ¹³that you will spare the lives of my father and mother, my brothers and sisters, and all who belong to them—and that you will save us from death."

¹⁴"Our lives for your lives!" the men assured her. "If you don't tell what we are doing, we will treat you kindly and faithfully when the LORD gives us the land."

¹⁵So she let them down by a rope through the window, for the house she lived in was part of the city wall. ¹⁶She said to them, "Go to the hills so the pursuers will not find you. Hide yourselves there three days until they return, and then go on your way."

¹⁷Now the men had said to her, "This oath you made us swear will not be binding on us ¹⁸unless, when we enter the land, you have tied this scarlet cord in the window through which you let us down, and unless you have brought your father and mother, your brothers and all your family into your house. ¹⁹If any of them go outside your house into the

street, their blood will be on their own heads; we will not be responsible. As for those who are in the house with you, their blood will be on our head if a hand is laid on them. ²⁰But if you tell what we are doing, we will be released from the oath you made us swear."

²¹"Agreed," she replied. "Let it be as you say." So she sent them away, and they departed. And she tied the scarlet cord in the window.

²²When they left, they went into the hills and stayed there three days, until the pursuers had searched all along the road and returned without finding them. ²³Then the two men started back. They went down out of the hills, forded the river and came to Joshua son of Nun and told him everything that had happened to them. ²⁴They said to Joshua, "The LORD has surely given the whole land into our hands; all the people are melting in fear because of us."

Crossing the Jordan

3 Early in the morning Joshua and all the Israelites set out from Shittim and went to the Jordan, where they camped before crossing over. ²After three days the officers went throughout the camp, ³giving orders to the people: "When you see the ark of the covenant of the LORD your God, and the Levitical priests carrying it, you are to move out from your positions and follow it. ⁴Then you will know which way to go, since you have never been this way before. But keep a distance of about two thousand cubits ᶜ between you and the ark; do not go near it."

⁵Joshua told the people, "Consecrate yourselves, for tomorrow the LORD will do amazing things among you."

⁶Joshua said to the priests, "Take up the ark of the covenant and pass on ahead of the people." So they took it up and went ahead of them.

⁷And the LORD said to Joshua, "Today I will begin to exalt you in the eyes of all Israel, so they may know that I am with you as I was with Moses. ⁸Tell the priests who carry the ark of the covenant: 'When you reach the edge of the Jordan's waters, go and stand in the river.' "

ᵃ 10 Or *the Sea of Reeds*   ᵇ 10 The Hebrew term refers to the irrevocable giving over of things or persons to the LORD, often by totally destroying them.   ᶜ 4 That is, about 3,000 feet or about 900 meters

⁹Joshua said to the Israelites, "Come here and listen to the words of the LORD your God. ¹⁰This is how you will know that the living God is among you and that he will certainly drive out before you the Canaanites, Hittites, Hivites, Perizzites, Girgashites, Amorites and Jebusites. ¹¹See, the ark of the covenant of the Lord of all the earth will go into the Jordan ahead of you. ¹²Now then, choose twelve men from the tribes of Israel, one from each tribe. ¹³And as soon as the priests who carry the ark of the LORD—the Lord of all the earth—set foot in the Jordan, its waters flowing downstream will be cut off and stand up in a heap."

¹⁴So when the people broke camp to cross the Jordan, the priests carrying the ark of the covenant went ahead of them. ¹⁵Now the Jordan is at flood stage all during harvest. Yet as soon as the priests who carried the ark reached the Jordan and their feet touched the water's edge, ¹⁶the water from upstream stopped flowing. It piled up in a heap a great distance away, at a town called Adam in the vicinity of Zarethan, while the water flowing down to the Sea of the Arabah (that is, the Dead Sea) was completely cut off. So the people crossed over opposite Jericho. ¹⁷The priests who carried the ark of the covenant of the LORD stopped in the middle of the Jordan and stood on dry ground, while all Israel passed by until the whole nation had completed the crossing on dry ground.

4 When the whole nation had finished crossing the Jordan, the LORD said to Joshua, ²"Choose twelve men from among the people, one from each tribe, ³and tell them to take up twelve stones from the middle of the Jordan, from right where the priests are standing, and carry them over with you and put them down at the place where you stay tonight."

⁴So Joshua called together the twelve men he had appointed from the Israelites, one from each tribe, ⁵and said to them, "Go over before the ark of the LORD your God into the middle of the Jordan. Each of you is to take up a stone on his shoulder, according to the number of the tribes of the Israelites, ⁶to serve as a sign among you. In the future, when your children ask you, 'What do these stones mean?' ⁷tell them that the flow of the Jordan was cut off before the ark of the cov-

enant of the LORD. When it crossed the Jordan, the waters of the Jordan were cut off. These stones are to be a memorial to the people of Israel forever."

⁸So the Israelites did as Joshua commanded them. They took twelve stones from the middle of the Jordan, according to the number of the tribes of the Israelites, as the LORD had told Joshua; and they carried them over with them to their camp, where they put them down. ⁹Joshua set up the twelve stones that had been ᵃ in the middle of the Jordan at the spot where the priests who carried the ark of the covenant had stood. And they are there to this day.

¹⁰Now the priests who carried the ark remained standing in the middle of the Jordan until everything the LORD had commanded Joshua was done by the people, just as Moses had directed Joshua. The people hurried over, ¹¹and as soon as all of them had crossed, the ark of the LORD and the priests came to the other side while the people watched. ¹²The men of Reuben, Gad and the half-tribe of Manasseh crossed over, ready for battle, in front of the Israelites, as Moses had directed them. ¹³About forty thousand armed for battle crossed over before the LORD to the plains of Jericho for war.

¹⁴That day the LORD exalted Joshua in the sight of all Israel; and they stood in awe of him all the days of his life, just as they had stood in awe of Moses.

¹⁵Then the LORD said to Joshua, ¹⁶"Command the priests carrying the ark of the covenant law to come up out of the Jordan."

¹⁷So Joshua commanded the priests, "Come up out of the Jordan."

¹⁸And the priests came up out of the river carrying the ark of the covenant of the LORD. No sooner had they set their feet on the dry ground than the waters of the Jordan returned to their place and ran at flood stage as before.

¹⁹On the tenth day of the first month the people went up from the Jordan and camped at Gilgal on the eastern border of Jericho. ²⁰And Joshua set up at Gilgal the twelve stones they had taken out of the Jordan. ²¹He said to the Israelites, "In the future when your descendants ask their parents, 'What do these stones mean?' ²²tell them, 'Israel crossed the Jordan on dry ground.' ²³For the

ᵃ 9 Or *Joshua also set up twelve stones*

LORD your God dried up the Jordan before you until you had crossed over. The LORD your God did to the Jordan what he had done to the Red Sea^a when he dried it up before us until we had crossed over. ²⁴He did this so that all the peoples of the earth might know that the hand of the LORD is powerful and so that you might always fear the LORD your God."

5 Now when all the Amorite kings west of the Jordan and all the Canaanite kings along the coast heard how the LORD had dried up the Jordan before the Israelites until they^b had crossed over, their hearts melted in fear and they no longer had the courage to face the Israelites.

Circumcision and Passover at Gilgal

²At that time the LORD said to Joshua, "Make flint knives and circumcise the Israelites again." ³So Joshua made flint knives and circumcised the Israelites at Gibeath Haaraloth.^c

⁴Now this is why he did so: All those who came out of Egypt—all the men of military age—died in the wilderness on the way after leaving Egypt. ⁵All the people that came out had been circumcised, but all the people born in the wilderness during the journey from Egypt had not. ⁶The Israelites had moved about in the wilderness forty years until all the men who were of military age when they left Egypt had died, since they had not obeyed the LORD. For the LORD had sworn to them that they would not see the land that he had solemnly promised their ancestors to give us, a land flowing with milk and honey. ⁷So he raised up their sons in their place, and these were the ones Joshua circumcised. They were still uncircumcised because they had not been circumcised on the way. ⁸And after the whole nation had been circumcised, they remained where they were in camp until they were healed.

⁹Then the LORD said to Joshua, "Today I have rolled away the reproach of Egypt from you." So the place has been called Gilgal^d to this day.

¹⁰On the evening of the fourteenth day of the month, while camped at Gilgal on the plains of Jericho, the Israelites celebrated the Passover. ¹¹The day after the Passover, that very day, they ate some of the produce of the land: unleavened bread and roasted grain. ¹²The manna stopped the day after^e they ate this food from the land; there was no longer any manna for the Israelites, but that year they ate of the produce of Canaan.

The Fall of Jericho

¹³Now when Joshua was near Jericho, he looked up and saw a man standing in front of him with a drawn sword in his hand. Joshua went up to him and asked, "Are you for us or for our enemies?"

¹⁴"Neither," he replied, "but as commander of the army of the LORD I have now come." Then Joshua fell facedown to the ground in reverence, and asked him, "What message does my Lord^f have for his servant?"

¹⁵The commander of the LORD's army replied, "Take off your sandals, for the place where you are standing is holy." And Joshua did so.

6 Now the gates of Jericho were securely barred because of the Israelites. No one went out and no one came in.

²Then the LORD said to Joshua, "See, I have delivered Jericho into your hands, along with its king and its fighting men. ³March around the city once with all the armed men. Do this for six days. ⁴Have seven priests carry trumpets of rams' horns in front of the ark. On the seventh day, march around the city seven times, with the priests blowing the trumpets. ⁵When you hear them sound a long blast on the trumpets, have the whole army give a loud shout; then the wall of the city will collapse and the army will go up, everyone straight in."

⁶So Joshua son of Nun called the priests and said to them, "Take up the ark of the covenant of the LORD and have seven priests carry trumpets in front of it." ⁷And he ordered the army, "Advance! March around the city, with an armed guard going ahead of the ark of the LORD."

⁸When Joshua had spoken to the people, the seven priests carrying the seven trumpets before the LORD went forward, blowing their trumpets, and the ark of the LORD's covenant followed them. ⁹The armed guard

---

^a 23 Or *the Sea of Reeds*   ^b 1 Another textual tradition *we*   ^c 3 *Gibeath Haaraloth* means *the hill of foreskins.*   ^d 9 *Gilgal* sounds like the Hebrew for *roll.*   ^e 12 Or *the day*   ^f 14 Or *lord*

marched ahead of the priests who blew the trumpets, and the rear guard followed the ark. All this time the trumpets were sounding. ¹⁰But Joshua had commanded the army, "Do not give a war cry, do not raise your voices, do not say a word until the day I tell you to shout. Then shout!" ¹¹So he had the ark of the LORD carried around the city, circling it once. Then the army returned to camp and spent the night there.

¹²Joshua got up early the next morning and the priests took up the ark of the LORD. ¹³The seven priests carrying the seven trumpets went forward, marching before the ark of the LORD and blowing the trumpets. The armed men went ahead of them and the rear guard followed the ark of the LORD, while the trumpets kept sounding. ¹⁴So on the second day they marched around the city once and returned to the camp. They did this for six days.

¹⁵On the seventh day, they got up at daybreak and marched around the city seven times in the same manner, except that on that day they circled the city seven times. ¹⁶The seventh time around, when the priests sounded the trumpet blast, Joshua commanded the army, "Shout! For the LORD has given you the city! ¹⁷The city and all that is in it are to be devoted[a] to the LORD. Only Rahab the prostitute and all who are with her in her house shall be spared, because she hid the spies we sent. ¹⁸But keep away from the devoted things, so that you will not bring about your own destruction by taking any of them. Otherwise you will make the camp of Israel liable to destruction and bring trouble on it. ¹⁹All the silver and gold and the articles of bronze and iron are sacred to the LORD and must go into his treasury."

²⁰When the trumpets sounded, the army shouted, and at the sound of the trumpet, when the men gave a loud shout, the wall collapsed; so everyone charged straight in, and they took the city. ²¹They devoted the city to the LORD and destroyed with the sword every living thing in it—men and women, young and old, cattle, sheep and donkeys.

²²Joshua said to the two men who had spied out the land, "Go into the prostitute's house and bring her out and all who belong to her, in accordance with your oath to her." ²³So the young men who had done the spying went in and brought out Rahab, her father and mother, her brothers and sisters and all who belonged to her. They brought out her entire family and put them in a place outside the camp of Israel.

²⁴Then they burned the whole city and everything in it, but they put the silver and gold and the articles of bronze and iron into the treasury of the LORD's house. ²⁵But Joshua spared Rahab the prostitute, with her family and all who belonged to her, because she hid the men Joshua had sent as spies to Jericho—and she lives among the Israelites to this day.

²⁶At that time Joshua pronounced this solemn oath: "Cursed before the LORD is anyone who undertakes to rebuild this city, Jericho:

"At the cost of his firstborn son
    he will lay its foundations;
at the cost of his youngest
    he will set up its gates."

²⁷So the LORD was with Joshua, and his fame spread throughout the land.

Achan's Sin

7 But the Israelites were unfaithful in regard to the devoted things[b]; Achan son of Karmi, the son of Zimri,[c] the son of Zerah, of the tribe of Judah, took some of them. So the LORD's anger burned against Israel.

²Now Joshua sent men from Jericho to Ai,[d] which is near Beth Aven to the east of Bethel, and told them, "Go up and spy out the region." So the men went up and spied out Ai.

³When they returned to Joshua, they said, "Not all the army will have to go up against Ai. Send two or three thousand men to take it and do not weary the whole army, for only a few people live there." ⁴So about three thousand went up; but they were routed by the men of Ai, ⁵who killed about thirty-six of them. They chased the Israelites from the city gate as far as the stone quarries and struck them down on the slopes. At this the

---

a 17 The Hebrew term refers to the irrevocable giving over of things or persons to the LORD, often by totally destroying them; also in verses 18 and 21.   b 1 The Hebrew term refers to the irrevocable giving over of things or persons to the LORD, often by totally destroying them; also in verses 11, 12, 13 and 15.   c 1 See Septuagint and 1 Chron. 2:6; Hebrew *Zabdi*; also in verses 17 and 18.   d 2 Ai means *the ruin.*

FRIDAY

FREE TO RESIST ALL SIN
Joshua 7:1–26 *or* 7:1,20–21

Donald Drew

Temptation seems to have four stages: a thought, a look or a second thought, a fascination, a fall. If that surging advance is to be stopped, it must be at the first stage. The reformer Martin Luther records that on one occasion when he was undergoing prolonged temptation, in imagination he saw a black dog (which represented the devil) lying on his bed which he at once seized and threw out of the window. Is not the first stage, *"at once,"* the vital decision? "Thanks be to God! [He gives] us the victory through our Lord Jesus Christ" [1 Corinthians 15:57].

This "at once" applies in other ways. For example, I have a friend who, addicted to pornography, hoarded porn magazines. When he became a believer, he burned them all. I know of a man, addicted to alcohol, who on his way home each evening after work would generously imbibe at his local pub. After becoming a follower of Jesus Christ, he permanently changed his route home. Both these people wanted to be free from sin so they put their faith to work, acted at once and have continued—as did temptation—to witness to God's rescuing power through Christ. They were gripped by the truth that Christ has given us a life of freedom. Of course, that does not mean that believers have freedom to sin. Rather does it mean the freedom *not* to sin. When we call for help, we can be freed to do the will of God.

HANNAH WHITALL SMITH {ca. AD 1832–1911}

The secret lies in this: We must meet sin, not as a foe that has yet to be conquered, but as one that has already been conquered. When Rahab helped the spies who had been sent by Joshua to escape from the king of Jericho, she made this confession: "I know that the LORD has given this land to you and that a great fear of you has fallen on us, so that all who live in this country are melting in fear because of you" (Joshua 2:9). If we were gifted with eyes that could see the unseen kingdom of evil, I believe we also should find that a terror and faintness has fallen upon all the forces of that unknown region, and that they see in every man and woman of faith a sure and triumphant conqueror.

reflection

1. Why do you think Achan gave in to temptation?
2. When faced with temptation, you have a choice in whether or not you give in to it. Explain why this is true.
3. Think of a sin that you particularly struggle with. How can you immediately resist its temptation the next time you encounter it?

For your next devotional reading, go to page 264.

hearts of the people melted in fear and became like water.

⁶Then Joshua tore his clothes and fell facedown to the ground before the ark of the LORD, remaining there till evening. The elders of Israel did the same, and sprinkled dust on their heads. ⁷And Joshua said, "Ah, Sovereign LORD, why did you ever bring this people across the Jordan to deliver us into the hands of the Amorites to destroy us? If only we had been content to stay on the other side of the Jordan! ⁸Pardon your servant, Lord. What can I say, now that Israel has been routed by its enemies? ⁹The Canaanites and the other people of the country will hear about this and they will surround us and wipe out our name from the earth. What then will you do for your own great name?"

¹⁰The LORD said to Joshua, "Stand up! What are you doing down on your face? ¹¹Israel has sinned; they have violated my covenant, which I commanded them to keep. They have taken some of the devoted things; they have stolen, they have lied, they have put them with their own possessions. ¹²That is why the Israelites cannot stand against their enemies; they turn their backs and run because they have been made liable to destruction. I will not be with you anymore unless you destroy whatever among you is devoted to destruction.

¹³"Go, consecrate the people. Tell them, 'Consecrate yourselves in preparation for tomorrow; for this is what the LORD, the God of Israel, says: There are devoted things among you, Israel. You cannot stand against your enemies until you remove them.

¹⁴" 'In the morning, present yourselves tribe by tribe. The tribe the LORD chooses shall come forward clan by clan; the clan the LORD chooses shall come forward family by family; and the family the LORD chooses shall come forward man by man. ¹⁵Whoever is caught with the devoted things shall be destroyed by fire, along with all that belongs to him. He has violated the covenant of the LORD and has done an outrageous thing in Israel!' "

¹⁶Early the next morning Joshua had Israel come forward by tribes, and Judah was chosen. ¹⁷The clans of Judah came forward, and the Zerahites were chosen. He had the clan of the Zerahites come forward by families, and Zimri was chosen. ¹⁸Joshua had his family come forward man by man, and Achan son of Karmi, the son of Zimri, the son of Zerah, of the tribe of Judah, was chosen.

¹⁹Then Joshua said to Achan, "My son, give glory to the LORD, the God of Israel, and honor him. Tell me what you have done; do not hide it from me."

²⁰Achan replied, "It is true! I have sinned against the LORD, the God of Israel. This is what I have done: ²¹When I saw in the plunder a beautiful robe from Babylonia,ᵃ two hundred shekelsᵇ of silver and a bar of gold weighing fifty shekels,ᶜ I coveted them and took them. They are hidden in the ground inside my tent, with the silver underneath."

²²So Joshua sent messengers, and they ran to the tent, and there it was, hidden in his tent, with the silver underneath. ²³They took the things from the tent, brought them to Joshua and all the Israelites and spread them out before the LORD.

²⁴Then Joshua, together with all Israel, took Achan son of Zerah, the silver, the robe, the gold bar, his sons and daughters, his cattle, donkeys and sheep, his tent and all that he had, to the Valley of Achor. ²⁵Joshua said, "Why have you brought this trouble on us? The LORD will bring trouble on you today."

Then all Israel stoned him, and after they had stoned the rest, they burned them. ²⁶Over Achan they heaped up a large pile of rocks, which remains to this day. Then the LORD turned from his fierce anger. Therefore that place has been called the Valley of Achorᵈ ever since.

Ai Destroyed

8 Then the LORD said to Joshua, "Do not be afraid; do not be discouraged. Take the whole army with you, and go up and attack Ai. For I have delivered into your hands the king of Ai, his people, his city and his land. ²You shall do to Ai and its king as you did to Jericho and its king, except that you may carry off their plunder and livestock for yourselves. Set an ambush behind the city."

³So Joshua and the whole army moved out to attack Ai. He chose thirty thousand of

---

ᵃ 21 Hebrew *Shinar*   ᵇ 21 That is, about 5 pounds or about 2.3 kilograms   ᶜ 21 That is, about 1 1/4 pounds or about 575 grams   ᵈ 26 *Achor* means *trouble.*

his best fighting men and sent them out at night ⁴with these orders: "Listen carefully. You are to set an ambush behind the city. Don't go very far from it. All of you be on the alert. ⁵I and all those with me will advance on the city, and when the men come out against us, as they did before, we will flee from them. ⁶They will pursue us until we have lured them away from the city, for they will say, 'They are running away from us as they did before.' So when we flee from them, ⁷you are to rise up from ambush and take the city. The LORD your God will give it into your hand. ⁸When you have taken the city, set it on fire. Do what the LORD has commanded. See to it; you have my orders."

⁹Then Joshua sent them off, and they went to the place of ambush and lay in wait between Bethel and Ai, to the west of Ai—but Joshua spent that night with the people. ¹⁰Early the next morning Joshua mustered his army, and he and the leaders of Israel marched before them to Ai. ¹¹The entire force that was with him marched up and approached the city and arrived in front of it. They set up camp north of Ai, with the valley between them and the city. ¹²Joshua had taken about five thousand men and set them in ambush between Bethel and Ai, to the west of the city. ¹³So the soldiers took up their positions—with the main camp to the north of the city and the ambush to the west of it. That night Joshua went into the valley.

¹⁴When the king of Ai saw this, he and all the men of the city hurried out early in the morning to meet Israel in battle at a certain place overlooking the Arabah. But he did not know that an ambush had been set against him behind the city. ¹⁵Joshua and all Israel let themselves be driven back before them, and they fled toward the wilderness. ¹⁶All the men of Ai were called to pursue them, and they pursued Joshua and were lured away from the city. ¹⁷Not a man remained in Ai or Bethel who did not go after Israel. They left the city open and went in pursuit of Israel.

¹⁸Then the LORD said to Joshua, "Hold out toward Ai the javelin that is in your hand, for into your hand I will deliver the city." So Joshua held out toward the city the javelin that was in his hand. ¹⁹As soon as he did

this, the men in the ambush rose quickly from their position and rushed forward. They entered the city and captured it and quickly set it on fire.

²⁰The men of Ai looked back and saw the smoke of the city rising against the sky, but they had no chance to escape in any direction; the Israelites who had been fleeing toward the wilderness had turned back against their pursuers. ²¹For when Joshua and all Israel saw that the ambush had taken the city and that smoke was going up from it, they turned around and attacked the men of Ai. ²²Those in the ambush also came out of the city against them, so that they were caught in the middle, with Israelites on both sides. Israel cut them down, leaving them neither survivors nor fugitives. ²³But they took the king of Ai alive and brought him to Joshua.

²⁴When Israel had finished killing all the men of Ai in the fields and in the wilderness where they had chased them, and when every one of them had been put to the sword, all the Israelites returned to Ai and killed those who were in it. ²⁵Twelve thousand men and women fell that day—all the people of Ai. ²⁶For Joshua did not draw back the hand that held out his javelin until he had destroyed*ᵃ* all who lived in Ai. ²⁷But Israel did carry off for themselves the livestock and plunder of this city, as the LORD had instructed Joshua.

²⁸So Joshua burned Ai*ᵇ* and made it a permanent heap of ruins, a desolate place to this day. ²⁹He impaled the body of the king of Ai on a pole and left it there until evening. At sunset, Joshua ordered them to take the body from the pole and throw it down at the entrance of the city gate. And they raised a large pile of rocks over it, which remains to this day.

The Covenant Renewed at Mount Ebal

³⁰Then Joshua built on Mount Ebal an altar to the LORD, the God of Israel, ³¹as Moses the servant of the LORD had commanded the Israelites. He built it according to what is written in the Book of the Law of Moses—an altar of uncut stones, on which no iron tool had been used. On it they offered to the LORD burnt offerings and sacrificed fellow-

---

a 26 The Hebrew term refers to the irrevocable giving over of things or persons to the LORD, often by totally destroying them.   *b 28* Ai means *the ruin.*

ship offerings. [32]There, in the presence of the Israelites, Joshua copied on stones the law of Moses, which he had written. [33]All the Israelites, with their elders, officials and judges, were standing on both sides of the ark of the covenant of the LORD, facing the Levitical priests who carried it. Both the foreigners living among them and the native-born were there. Half of the people stood in front of Mount Gerizim and half of them in front of Mount Ebal, as Moses the servant of the LORD had formerly commanded when he gave instructions to bless the people of Israel.

[34]Afterward, Joshua read all the words of the law—the blessings and the curses—just as it is written in the Book of the Law. [35]There was not a word of all that Moses had commanded that Joshua did not read to the whole assembly of Israel, including the women and children, and the foreigners who lived among them.

The Gibeonite Deception

9 Now when all the kings west of the Jordan heard about these things—those in the hill country, in the western foothills, and along the entire coast of the Mediterranean Sea as far as Lebanon (the kings of the Hittites, Amorites, Canaanites, Perizzites, Hivites and Jebusites)— [2]they came together to make war against Joshua and Israel.

[3]However, when the people of Gibeon heard what Joshua had done to Jericho and Ai, [4]they resorted to a ruse: They went as a delegation whose donkeys were loaded[a] with worn-out sacks and old wineskins, cracked and mended. [5]They put worn and patched sandals on their feet and wore old clothes. All the bread of their food supply was dry and moldy. [6]Then they went to Joshua in the camp at Gilgal and said to him and the Israelites, "We have come from a distant country; make a treaty with us."

[7]The Israelites said to the Hivites, "But perhaps you live near us, so how can we make a treaty with you?"

[8]"We are your servants," they said to Joshua.

But Joshua asked, "Who are you and where do you come from?"

[9]They answered: "Your servants have come from a very distant country because of the fame of the LORD your God. For we have heard reports of him: all that he did in Egypt, [10]and all that he did to the two kings of the Amorites east of the Jordan—Sihon king of Heshbon, and Og king of Bashan, who reigned in Ashtaroth. [11]And our elders and all those living in our country said to us, 'Take provisions for your journey; go and meet them and say to them, "We are your servants; make a treaty with us." ' [12]This bread of ours was warm when we packed it at home on the day we left to come to you. But now see how dry and moldy it is. [13]And these wineskins that we filled were new, but see how cracked they are. And our clothes and sandals are worn out by the very long journey."

[14]The Israelites sampled their provisions but did not inquire of the LORD. [15]Then Joshua made a treaty of peace with them to let them live, and the leaders of the assembly ratified it by oath.

[16]Three days after they made the treaty with the Gibeonites, the Israelites heard that they were neighbors, living near them. [17]So the Israelites set out and on the third day came to their cities: Gibeon, Kephirah, Beeroth and Kiriath Jearim. [18]But the Israelites did not attack them, because the leaders of the assembly had sworn an oath to them by the LORD, the God of Israel.

The whole assembly grumbled against the leaders, [19]but all the leaders answered, "We have given them our oath by the LORD, the God of Israel, and we cannot touch them now. [20]This is what we will do to them: We will let them live, so that God's wrath will not fall on us for breaking the oath we swore to them." [21]They continued, "Let them live, but let them be woodcutters and water carriers for the entire community." So the leaders' promise to them was kept.

[22]Then Joshua summoned the Gibeonites and said, "Why did you deceive us by saying, 'We live a long way from you,' while actually you live near us? [23]You are now under a curse: You will never cease to serve as woodcutters and water carriers for the house of my God."

[24]They answered Joshua, "Your servants

---

a 4 Most Hebrew manuscripts; some Hebrew manuscripts, Vulgate and Syriac (see also Septuagint) *They prepared provisions and loaded their donkeys* were clearly told how the LORD your God had commanded his servant Moses to give you the whole land and to wipe out all its inhabitants from before you. So we feared for our lives because of you, and that is why we did this. ²⁵We are now in your hands. Do to us whatever seems good and right to you."

²⁶So Joshua saved them from the Israelites, and they did not kill them. ²⁷That day he made the Gibeonites woodcutters and water carriers for the community and for the altar of the LORD at the place the LORD would choose. And that is what they are to this day.

The Sun Stands Still

10 Now Adoni-Zedek king of Jerusalem heard that Joshua had taken Ai and totally destroyed*a* it, doing to Ai and its king as he had done to Jericho and its king, and that the people of Gibeon had made a treaty of peace with Israel and had become their allies. ²He and his people were very much alarmed at this, because Gibeon was an important city, like one of the royal cities; it was larger than Ai, and all its men were good fighters. ³So Adoni-Zedek king of Jerusalem appealed to Hoham king of Hebron, Piram king of Jarmuth, Japhia king of Lachish and Debir king of Eglon. ⁴"Come up and help me attack Gibeon," he said, "because it has made peace with Joshua and the Israelites."

⁵Then the five kings of the Amorites—the kings of Jerusalem, Hebron, Jarmuth, Lachish and Eglon—joined forces. They moved up with all their troops and took up positions against Gibeon and attacked it.

⁶The Gibeonites then sent word to Joshua in the camp at Gilgal: "Do not abandon your servants. Come up to us quickly and save us! Help us, because all the Amorite kings from the hill country have joined forces against us."

⁷So Joshua marched up from Gilgal with his entire army, including all the best fighting men. ⁸The LORD said to Joshua, "Do not be afraid of them; I have given them into your hand. Not one of them will be able to withstand you."

⁹After an all-night march from Gilgal, Joshua took them by surprise. ¹⁰The LORD threw them into confusion before Israel, so

Joshua and the Israelites defeated them completely at Gibeon. Israel pursued them along the road going up to Beth Horon and cut them down all the way to Azekah and Makkedah. ¹¹As they fled before Israel on the road down from Beth Horon to Azekah, the LORD hurled large hailstones down on them, and more of them died from the hail than were killed by the swords of the Israelites.

¹²On the day the LORD gave the Amorites over to Israel, Joshua said to the LORD in the presence of Israel:

"Sun, stand still over Gibeon,
  and you, moon, over the Valley of
    Aijalon."
¹³So the sun stood still,
  and the moon stopped,
    till the nation avenged itself on*b* its
      enemies,

as it is written in the Book of Jashar.

The sun stopped in the middle of the sky and delayed going down about a full day. ¹⁴There has never been a day like it before or since, a day when the LORD listened to a human being. Surely the LORD was fighting for Israel!

¹⁵Then Joshua returned with all Israel to the camp at Gilgal.

Five Amorite Kings Killed

¹⁶Now the five kings had fled and hidden in the cave at Makkedah. ¹⁷When Joshua was told that the five kings had been found hiding in the cave at Makkedah, ¹⁸he said, "Roll large rocks up to the mouth of the cave, and post some guards there. ¹⁹But don't stop; pursue your enemies! Attack them from the rear and don't let them reach their cities, for the LORD your God has given them into your hand."

²⁰So Joshua and the Israelites defeated them completely, but a few survivors managed to reach their fortified cities. ²¹The whole army then returned safely to Joshua in the camp at Makkedah, and no one uttered a word against the Israelites.

²²Joshua said, "Open the mouth of the cave and bring those five kings out to me." ²³So they brought the five kings out of the cave—the kings of Jerusalem, Hebron, Jarmuth, Lachish and Eglon. ²⁴When they had

---

a 1 The Hebrew term refers to the irrevocable giving over of things or persons to the LORD, often by totally destroying them; also in verses 28, 35, 37, 39 and 40.   *b 13* Or *nation triumphed over* brought these kings to Joshua, he summoned all the men of Israel and said to the army commanders who had come with him, "Come here and put your feet on the necks of these kings." So they came forward and placed their feet on their necks.

²⁵Joshua said to them, "Do not be afraid; do not be discouraged. Be strong and courageous. This is what the LORD will do to all the enemies you are going to fight." ²⁶Then Joshua put the kings to death and exposed their bodies on five poles, and they were left hanging on the poles until evening.

²⁷At sunset Joshua gave the order and they took them down from the poles and threw them into the cave where they had been hiding. At the mouth of the cave they placed large rocks, which are there to this day.

Southern Cities Conquered

²⁸That day Joshua took Makkedah. He put the city and its king to the sword and totally destroyed everyone in it. He left no survivors. And he did to the king of Makkedah as he had done to the king of Jericho.

²⁹Then Joshua and all Israel with him moved on from Makkedah to Libnah and attacked it. ³⁰The LORD also gave that city and its king into Israel's hand. The city and everyone in it Joshua put to the sword. He left no survivors there. And he did to its king as he had done to the king of Jericho.

³¹Then Joshua and all Israel with him moved on from Libnah to Lachish; he took up positions against it and attacked it. ³²The LORD gave Lachish into Israel's hands, and Joshua took it on the second day. The city and everyone in it he put to the sword, just as he had done to Libnah. ³³Meanwhile, Horam king of Gezer had come up to help Lachish, but Joshua defeated him and his army—until no survivors were left.

³⁴Then Joshua and all Israel with him moved on from Lachish to Eglon; they took up positions against it and attacked it. ³⁵They captured it that same day and put it to the sword and totally destroyed everyone in it, just as they had done to Lachish.

³⁶Then Joshua and all Israel with him went up from Eglon to Hebron and attacked it. ³⁷They took the city and put it to the sword, together with its king, its villages and everyone in it. They left no survivors. Just as at Eglon, they totally destroyed it and everyone in it.

³⁸Then Joshua and all Israel with him turned around and attacked Debir. ³⁹They took the city, its king and its villages, and put them to the sword. Everyone in it they totally destroyed. They left no survivors. They did to Debir and its king as they had done to Libnah and its king and to Hebron.

⁴⁰So Joshua subdued the whole region, including the hill country, the Negev, the western foothills and the mountain slopes, together with all their kings. He left no survivors. He totally destroyed all who breathed, just as the LORD, the God of Israel, had commanded. ⁴¹Joshua subdued them from Kadesh Barnea to Gaza and from the whole region of Goshen to Gibeon. ⁴²All these kings and their lands Joshua conquered in one campaign, because the LORD, the God of Israel, fought for Israel.

⁴³Then Joshua returned with all Israel to the camp at Gilgal.

Northern Kings Defeated

11 When Jabin king of Hazor heard of this, he sent word to Jobab king of Madon, to the kings of Shimron and Akshaph, ²and to the northern kings who were in the mountains, in the Arabah south of Kinnereth, in the western foothills and in Naphoth Dor on the west; ³to the Canaanites in the east and west; to the Amorites, Hittites, Perizzites and Jebusites in the hill country; and to the Hivites below Hermon in the region of Mizpah. ⁴They came out with all their troops and a large number of horses and chariots—a huge army, as numerous as the sand on the seashore. ⁵All these kings joined forces and made camp together at the Waters of Merom to fight against Israel.

⁶The LORD said to Joshua, "Do not be afraid of them, because by this time tomorrow I will hand all of them, slain, over to Israel. You are to hamstring their horses and burn their chariots."

⁷So Joshua and his whole army came against them suddenly at the Waters of Merom and attacked them, ⁸and the LORD gave them into the hand of Israel. They defeated them and pursued them all the way to Greater Sidon, to Misrephoth Maim, and to the Valley of Mizpah on the east, until no survivors were left. ⁹Joshua did to them as the LORD had directed: He hamstrung their horses and burned their chariots.

¹⁰At that time Joshua turned back and captured Hazor and put its king to the sword. (Hazor had been the head of all these kingdoms.) ¹¹Everyone in it they put to the sword. They totally destroyed*a* them, not sparing anyone that breathed, and he burned Hazor itself.

¹²Joshua took all these royal cities and their kings and put them to the sword. He totally destroyed them, as Moses the servant of the Lord had commanded. ¹³Yet Israel did not burn any of the cities built on their mounds—except Hazor, which Joshua burned. ¹⁴The Israelites carried off for themselves all the plunder and livestock of these cities, but all the people they put to the sword until they completely destroyed them, not sparing anyone that breathed. ¹⁵As the Lord commanded his servant Moses, so Moses commanded Joshua, and Joshua did it; he left nothing undone of all that the Lord commanded Moses.

¹⁶So Joshua took this entire land: the hill country, all the Negev, the whole region of Goshen, the western foothills, the Arabah and the mountains of Israel with their foothills, ¹⁷from Mount Halak, which rises toward Seir, to Baal Gad in the Valley of Lebanon below Mount Hermon. He captured all their kings and put them to death. ¹⁸Joshua waged war against all these kings for a long time. ¹⁹Except for the Hivites living in Gibeon, not one city made a treaty of peace with the Israelites, who took them all in battle. ²⁰For it was the Lord himself who hardened their hearts to wage war against Israel, so that he might destroy them totally, exterminating them without mercy, as the Lord had commanded Moses.

²¹At that time Joshua went and destroyed the Anakites from the hill country: from Hebron, Debir and Anab, from all the hill country of Judah, and from all the hill country of Israel. Joshua totally destroyed them and their towns. ²²No Anakites were left in Israelite territory; only in Gaza, Gath and Ashdod did any survive.

²³So Joshua took the entire land, just as the Lord had directed Moses, and he gave it as an inheritance to Israel according to their tribal divisions. Then the land had rest from war.

List of Defeated Kings

12 These are the kings of the land whom the Israelites had defeated and whose territory they took over east of the Jordan, from the Arnon Gorge to Mount Hermon, including all the eastern side of the Arabah:

²Sihon king of the Amorites, who reigned in Heshbon.

He ruled from Aroer on the rim of the Arnon Gorge—from the middle of the gorge—to the Jabbok River, which is the border of the Ammonites. This included half of Gilead. ³He also ruled over the eastern Arabah from the Sea of Galilee*b* to the Sea of the Arabah (that is, the Dead Sea), to Beth Jeshimoth, and then southward below the slopes of Pisgah.

⁴And the territory of Og king of Bashan, one of the last of the Rephaites, who reigned in Ashtaroth and Edrei.

⁵He ruled over Mount Hermon, Salekah, all of Bashan to the border of the people of Geshur and Maakah, and half of Gilead to the border of Sihon king of Heshbon.

⁶Moses, the servant of the Lord, and the Israelites conquered them. And Moses the servant of the Lord gave their land to the Reubenites, the Gadites and the half-tribe of Manasseh to be their possession.

⁷These are the kings of the land that Joshua and the Israelites conquered on the west side of the Jordan, from Baal Gad in the Valley of Lebanon to Mount Halak, which rises toward Seir (their lands Joshua gave as an inheritance to the tribes of Israel according to their tribal divisions— ⁸the hill country, the western foothills, the Arabah, the mountain slopes, the wilderness and the Negev—the lands of the Hittites, Amorites, Canaanites, Perizzites, Hivites and Jebusites):

⁹the king of Jericho	one
the king of Ai (near Bethel)	one
¹⁰the king of Jerusalem	one
the king of Hebron	one
¹¹the king of Jarmuth	one
the king of Lachish	one

---

a 11 The Hebrew term refers to the irrevocable giving over of things or persons to the Lord, often by totally destroying them; also in verses 12, 20 and 21.   *b 3* Hebrew *Kinnereth*

¹²the king of Eglon | one
the king of Gezer | one
¹³the king of Debir | one
the king of Geder | one
¹⁴the king of Hormah | one
the king of Arad | one
¹⁵the king of Libnah | one
the king of Adullam | one
¹⁶the king of Makkedah | one
the king of Bethel | one
¹⁷the king of Tappuah | one
the king of Hepher | one
¹⁸the king of Aphek | one
the king of Lasharon | one
¹⁹the king of Madon | one
the king of Hazor | one
²⁰the king of Shimron Meron | one
the king of Akshaph | one
²¹the king of Taanach | one
the king of Megiddo | one
²²the king of Kedesh | one
the king of Jokneam in Carmel | one
²³the king of Dor (in Naphoth Dor) | one
the king of Goyim in Gilgal | one
²⁴the king of Tirzah | one
thirty-one kings in all.

Land Still to Be Taken

13 When Joshua had grown old, the LORD said to him, "You are now very old, and there are still very large areas of land to be taken over.

²"This is the land that remains: all the regions of the Philistines and Geshurites, ³from the Shihor River on the east of Egypt to the territory of Ekron on the north, all of it counted as Canaanite though held by the five Philistine rulers in Gaza, Ashdod, Ashkelon, Gath and Ekron; the territory of the Avvites ⁴on the south; all the land of the Canaanites, from Arah of the Sidonians as far as Aphek and the border of the Amorites; ⁵the area of Byblos; and all Lebanon to the east, from Baal Gad below Mount Hermon to Lebo Hamath.

⁶"As for all the inhabitants of the mountain regions from Lebanon to Misrephoth Maim, that is, all the Sidonians, I myself will drive them out before the Israelites. Be sure to allocate this land to Israel for an inheri-

tance, as I have instructed you, ⁷and divide it as an inheritance among the nine tribes and half of the tribe of Manasseh."

Division of the Land East of the Jordan

⁸The other half of Manasseh,^a the Reubenites and the Gadites had received the inheritance that Moses had given them east of the Jordan, as he, the servant of the LORD, had assigned it to them.

⁹It extended from Aroer on the rim of the Arnon Gorge, and from the town in the middle of the gorge, and included the whole plateau of Medeba as far as Dibon, ¹⁰and all the towns of Sihon king of the Amorites, who ruled in Heshbon, out to the border of the Ammonites. ¹¹It also included Gilead, the territory of the people of Geshur and Maakah, all of Mount Hermon and all Bashan as far as Salekah— ¹²that is, the whole kingdom of Og in Bashan, who had reigned in Ashtaroth and Edrei. (He was the last of the Rephaites.) Moses had defeated them and taken over their land. ¹³But the Israelites did not drive out the people of Geshur and Maakah, so they continue to live among the Israelites to this day.

¹⁴But to the tribe of Levi he gave no inheritance, since the food offerings presented to the LORD, the God of Israel, are their inheritance, as he promised them.

¹⁵This is what Moses had given to the tribe of Reuben, according to its clans:

¹⁶The territory from Aroer on the rim of the Arnon Gorge, and from the town in the middle of the gorge, and the whole plateau past Medeba ¹⁷to Heshbon and all its towns on the plateau, including Dibon, Bamoth Baal, Beth Baal Meon, ¹⁸Jahaz, Kedemoth, Mephaath, ¹⁹Kiriathaim, Sibmah, Zereth Shahar on the hill in the valley, ²⁰Beth Peor, the slopes of Pisgah, and Beth Jeshimoth— ²¹all the towns on the plateau and the entire realm of Sihon king of the Amorites, who ruled at Heshbon. Moses had defeated him and the Midianite chiefs, Evi, Rekem, Zur, Hur and Reba—princes allied with Sihon—who lived in that

^a 8 Hebrew *With it* (that is, with the other half of Manasseh)

country. 22In addition to those slain in battle, the Israelites had put to the sword Balaam son of Beor, who practiced divination. 23The boundary of the Reubenites was the bank of the Jordan. These towns and their villages were the inheritance of the Reubenites, according to their clans.

24This is what Moses had given to the tribe of Gad, according to its clans:

25The territory of Jazer, all the towns of Gilead and half the Ammonite country as far as Aroer, near Rabbah; 26and from Heshbon to Ramath Mizpah and Betonim, and from Mahanaim to the territory of Debir; 27and in the valley, Beth Haram, Beth Nimrah, Sukkoth and Zaphon with the rest of the realm of Sihon king of Heshbon (the east side of the Jordan, the territory up to the end of the Sea of Galilee*a*). 28These towns and their villages were the inheritance of the Gadites, according to their clans.

29This is what Moses had given to the half-tribe of Manasseh, that is, to half the family of the descendants of Manasseh, according to its clans:

30The territory extending from Mahanaim and including all of Bashan, the entire realm of Og king of Bashan—all the settlements of Jair in Bashan, sixty towns, 31half of Gilead, and Ashtaroth and Edrei (the royal cities of Og in Bashan). This was for the descendants of Makir son of Manasseh—for half of the sons of Makir, according to their clans.

32This is the inheritance Moses had given when he was in the plains of Moab across the Jordan east of Jericho. 33But to the tribe of Levi, Moses had given no inheritance; the LORD, the God of Israel, is their inheritance, as he promised them.

Division of the Land West of the Jordan

14 Now these are the areas the Israelites received as an inheritance in the land of Canaan, which Eleazar the priest, Joshua son of Nun and the heads of the tribal clans of Israel allotted to them. 2Their inheritances were assigned by lot to the nine-and-a-half tribes, as the LORD had commanded through Moses. 3Moses had granted the two-and-a-half tribes their inheritance east of the Jordan but had not granted the Levites an inheritance among the rest, 4for the sons of Joseph had become two tribes—Manasseh and Ephraim. The Levites received no share of the land but only towns to live in, with pasturelands for their flocks and herds. 5So the Israelites divided the land, just as the LORD had commanded Moses.

Allotment for Caleb

6Now the people of Judah approached Joshua at Gilgal, and Caleb son of Jephunneh the Kenizzite said to him, "You know what the LORD said to Moses the man of God at Kadesh Barnea about you and me. 7I was forty years old when Moses the servant of the LORD sent me from Kadesh Barnea to explore the land. And I brought him back a report according to my convictions, 8but the others who went up with me made the hearts of the people melt in fear. I, however, followed the LORD my God wholeheartedly. 9So on that day Moses swore to me, 'The land on which your feet have walked will be your inheritance and that of your children forever, because you have followed the LORD my God wholeheartedly.'*b*

10"Now then, just as the LORD promised, he has kept me alive for forty-five years since the time he said this to Moses, while Israel moved about in the wilderness. So here I am today, eighty-five years old! 11I am still as strong today as the day Moses sent me out; I'm just as vigorous to go out to battle now as I was then. 12Now give me this hill country that the LORD promised me that day. You yourself heard then that the Anakites were there and their cities were large and fortified, but, the LORD helping me, I will drive them out just as he said."

13Then Joshua blessed Caleb son of Jephunneh and gave him Hebron as his inheritance. 14So Hebron has belonged to Caleb son of Jephunneh the Kenizzite ever since, because he followed the LORD, the God of Israel, wholeheartedly. 15(Hebron used to be called Kiriath Arba after Arba, who was the greatest man among the Anakites.)

Then the land had rest from war.

a 27 Hebrew *Kinnereth*   *b 9* Deut. 1:36

Allotment for Judah

15 The allotment for the tribe of Judah, according to its clans, extended down to the territory of Edom, to the Desert of Zin in the extreme south.

²Their southern boundary started from the bay at the southern end of the Dead Sea, ³crossed south of Scorpion Pass, continued on to Zin and went over to the south of Kadesh Barnea. Then it ran past Hezron up to Addar and curved around to Karka. ⁴It then passed along to Azmon and joined the Wadi of Egypt, ending at the Mediterranean Sea. This is their*ᵃ* southern boundary.

⁵The eastern boundary is the Dead Sea as far as the mouth of the Jordan.

The northern boundary started from the bay of the sea at the mouth of the Jordan, ⁶went up to Beth Hoglah and continued north of Beth Arabah to the Stone of Bohan son of Reuben. ⁷The boundary then went up to Debir from the Valley of Achor and turned north to Gilgal, which faces the Pass of Adummim south of the gorge. It continued along to the waters of En Shemesh and came out at En Rogel. ⁸Then it ran up the Valley of Ben Hinnom along the southern slope of the Jebusite city (that is, Jerusalem). From there it climbed to the top of the hill west of the Hinnom Valley at the northern end of the Valley of Rephaim. ⁹From the hilltop the boundary headed toward the spring of the waters of Nephtoah, came out at the towns of Mount Ephron and went down toward Baalah (that is, Kiriath Jearim). ¹⁰Then it curved westward from Baalah to Mount Seir, ran along the northern slope of Mount Jearim (that is, Kesalon), continued down to Beth Shemesh and crossed to Timnah. ¹¹It went to the northern slope of Ekron, turned toward Shikkeron, passed along to Mount Baalah and reached Jabneel. The boundary ended at the sea.

¹²The western boundary is the coastline of the Mediterranean Sea.

These are the boundaries around the people of Judah by their clans.

¹³In accordance with the LORD's command to him, Joshua gave to Caleb son of Jephunneh a portion in Judah—Kiriath Arba, that is, Hebron. (Arba was the ancestor of Anak.) ¹⁴From Hebron Caleb drove out the three Anakites—Sheshai, Ahiman and Talmai, the sons of Anak. ¹⁵From there he marched against the people living in Debir (formerly called Kiriath Sepher). ¹⁶And Caleb said, "I will give my daughter Aksah in marriage to the man who attacks and captures Kiriath Sepher." ¹⁷Othniel son of Kenaz, Caleb's brother, took it; so Caleb gave his daughter Aksah to him in marriage.

¹⁸One day when she came to Othniel, she urged him*ᵇ* to ask her father for a field. When she got off her donkey, Caleb asked her, "What can I do for you?"

¹⁹She replied, "Do me a special favor. Since you have given me land in the Negev, give me also springs of water." So Caleb gave her the upper and lower springs.

²⁰This is the inheritance of the tribe of Judah, according to its clans:

²¹The southernmost towns of the tribe of Judah in the Negev toward the boundary of Edom were:

Kabzeel, Eder, Jagur, ²²Kinah, Dimonah, Adadah, ²³Kedesh, Hazor, Ithnan, ²⁴Ziph, Telem, Bealoth, ²⁵Hazor Hadattah, Kerioth Hezron (that is, Hazor), ²⁶Amam, Shema, Moladah, ²⁷Hazar Gaddah, Heshmon, Beth Pelet, ²⁸Hazar Shual, Beersheba, Biziothiah, ²⁹Baalah, Iyim, Ezem, ³⁰Eltolad, Kesil, Hormah, ³¹Ziklag, Madmannah, Sansannah, ³²Lebaoth, Shilhim, Ain and Rimmon— a total of twenty-nine towns and their villages.

³³In the western foothills:

Eshtaol, Zorah, Ashnah, ³⁴Zanoah, En Gannim, Tappuah, Enam, ³⁵Jarmuth, Adullam, Sokoh, Azekah, ³⁶Shaaraim, Adithaim and Gederah (or Gederothaim)*ᶜ*—fourteen towns and their villages.

³⁷Zenan, Hadashah, Migdal Gad, ³⁸Dilean, Mizpah, Joktheel, ³⁹Lachish,

ᵃ 4 Septuagint; Hebrew *your*   ᵇ 18 Hebrew and some Septuagint manuscripts; other Septuagint manuscripts (see also note at Judges 1:14) *Othniel, he urged her*   ᶜ 36 Or *Gederah and Gederothaim*

Bozkath, Eglon, ⁴⁰Kabbon, Lahmas, Kitlish, ⁴¹Gederoth, Beth Dagon, Naamah and Makkedah—sixteen towns and their villages.

⁴²Libnah, Ether, Ashan, ⁴³Iphtah, Ashnah, Nezib, ⁴⁴Keilah, Akzib and Mareshah—nine towns and their villages.

⁴⁵Ekron, with its surrounding settlements and villages; ⁴⁶west of Ekron, all that were in the vicinity of Ashdod, together with their villages; ⁴⁷Ashdod, its surrounding settlements and villages; and Gaza, its settlements and villages, as far as the Wadi of Egypt and the coastline of the Mediterranean Sea.

⁴⁸In the hill country:

Shamir, Jattir, Sokoh, ⁴⁹Dannah, Kiriath Sannah (that is, Debir), ⁵⁰Anab, Eshtemoh, Anim, ⁵¹Goshen, Holon and Giloh—eleven towns and their villages.

⁵²Arab, Dumah, Eshan, ⁵³Janim, Beth Tappuah, Aphekah, ⁵⁴Humtah, Kiriath Arba (that is, Hebron) and Zior—nine towns and their villages.

⁵⁵Maon, Carmel, Ziph, Juttah, ⁵⁶Jezreel, Jokdeam, Zanoah, ⁵⁷Kain, Gibeah and Timnah—ten towns and their villages.

⁵⁸Halhul, Beth Zur, Gedor, ⁵⁹Maarath, Beth Anoth and Eltekon—six towns and their villages.ᵃ

⁶⁰Kiriath Baal (that is, Kiriath Jearim) and Rabbah—two towns and their villages.

⁶¹In the wilderness:

Beth Arabah, Middin, Sekakah, ⁶²Nibshan, the City of Salt and En Gedi—six towns and their villages.

⁶³Judah could not dislodge the Jebusites, who were living in Jerusalem; to this day the Jebusites live there with the people of Judah.

Allotment for Ephraim and Manasseh

16 The allotment for Joseph began at the Jordan, east of the springs of Jericho, and went up from there through the desert into the hill country of Bethel. ²It went on from Bethel (that is, Luz),ᵇ crossed over to the territory of the Arkites in At-

aroth, ³descended westward to the territory of the Japhletites as far as the region of Lower Beth Horon and on to Gezer, ending at the Mediterranean Sea.

⁴So Manasseh and Ephraim, the descendants of Joseph, received their inheritance.

⁵This was the territory of Ephraim, according to its clans:

The boundary of their inheritance went from Ataroth Addar in the east to Upper Beth Horon ⁶and continued to the Mediterranean Sea. From Mikmethath on the north it curved eastward to Taanath Shiloh, passing by it to Janoah on the east. ⁷Then it went down from Janoah to Ataroth and Naarah, touched Jericho and came out at the Jordan. ⁸From Tappuah the border went west to the Kanah Ravine and ended at the Mediterranean Sea. This was the inheritance of the tribe of the Ephraimites, according to its clans. ⁹It also included all the towns and their villages that were set aside for the Ephraimites within the inheritance of the Manassites.

¹⁰They did not dislodge the Canaanites living in Gezer; to this day the Canaanites live among the people of Ephraim but are required to do forced labor.

17 This was the allotment for the tribe of Manasseh as Joseph's firstborn, that is, for Makir, Manasseh's firstborn. Makir was the ancestor of the Gileadites, who had received Gilead and Bashan because the Makirites were great soldiers. ²So this allotment was for the rest of the people of Manasseh—the clans of Abiezer, Helek, Asriel, Shechem, Hepher and Shemida. These are the other male descendants of Manasseh son of Joseph by their clans.

³Now Zelophehad son of Hepher, the son of Gilead, the son of Makir, the son of Manasseh, had no sons but only daughters, whose names were Mahlah, Noah, Hoglah, Milkah and Tirzah. ⁴They went to Eleazar the priest, Joshua son of Nun, and the leaders and said, "The LORD commanded Moses to give us an inheritance among our rela-

---

ᵃ 59 The Septuagint adds another district of eleven towns, including Tekoa and Ephrathah (Bethlehem).
ᵇ 2 Septuagint; Hebrew *Bethel to Luz*

tives." So Joshua gave them an inheritance along with the brothers of their father, according to the LORD's command. [5]Manasseh's share consisted of ten tracts of land besides Gilead and Bashan east of the Jordan, [6]because the daughters of the tribe of Manasseh received an inheritance among the sons. The land of Gilead belonged to the rest of the descendants of Manasseh.

[7]The territory of Manasseh extended from Asher to Mikmethath east of Shechem. The boundary ran southward from there to include the people living at En Tappuah. [8](Manasseh had the land of Tappuah, but Tappuah itself, on the boundary of Manasseh, belonged to the Ephraimites.) [9]Then the boundary continued south to the Kanah Ravine. There were towns belonging to Ephraim lying among the towns of Manasseh, but the boundary of Manasseh was the northern side of the ravine and ended at the Mediterranean Sea. [10]On the south the land belonged to Ephraim, on the north to Manasseh. The territory of Manasseh reached the Mediterranean Sea and bordered Asher on the north and Issachar on the east.

[11]Within Issachar and Asher, Manasseh also had Beth Shan, Ibleam and the people of Dor, Endor, Taanach and Megiddo, together with their surrounding settlements (the third in the list is Naphoth[a]).

[12]Yet the Manassites were not able to occupy these towns, for the Canaanites were determined to live in that region. [13]However, when the Israelites grew stronger, they subjected the Canaanites to forced labor but did not drive them out completely.

[14]The people of Joseph said to Joshua, "Why have you given us only one allotment and one portion for an inheritance? We are a numerous people, and the LORD has blessed us abundantly."

[15]"If you are so numerous," Joshua answered, "and if the hill country of Ephraim is too small for you, go up into the forest and clear land for yourselves there in the land of the Perizzites and Rephaites."

[16]The people of Joseph replied, "The hill country is not enough for us, and all the Canaanites who live in the plain have chariots fitted with iron, both those in Beth Shan and its settlements and those in the Valley of Jezreel."

[17]But Joshua said to the house of Joseph—to Ephraim and Manasseh—"You are numerous and very powerful. You will have not only one allotment [18]but the forested hill country as well. Clear it, and its farthest limits will be yours; though the Canaanites have chariots fitted with iron and though they are strong, you can drive them out."

Division of the Rest of the Land

18 The whole assembly of the Israelites gathered at Shiloh and set up the tent of meeting there. The country was brought under their control, [2]but there were still seven Israelite tribes who had not yet received their inheritance.

[3]So Joshua said to the Israelites: "How long will you wait before you begin to take possession of the land that the LORD, the God of your ancestors, has given you? [4]Appoint three men from each tribe. I will send them out to make a survey of the land and to write a description of it, according to the inheritance of each. Then they will return to me. [5]You are to divide the land into seven parts. Judah is to remain in its territory on the south and the house of Joseph in its territory on the north. [6]After you have written descriptions of the seven parts of the land, bring them here to me and I will cast lots for you in the presence of the LORD our God. [7]The Levites, however, do not get a portion among you, because the priestly service of the LORD is their inheritance. And Gad, Reuben and the half-tribe of Manasseh have already received their inheritance on the east side of the Jordan. Moses the servant of the LORD gave it to them."

[8]As the men started on their way to map out the land, Joshua instructed them, "Go and make a survey of the land and write a description of it. Then return to me, and I will cast lots for you here at Shiloh in the presence of the LORD." [9]So they left and went through the land. They wrote its description on a scroll, town by town, in seven parts, and returned to Joshua in the camp at Shiloh. [10]Joshua then cast lots for them in Shiloh in the presence of the LORD, and

a 11 That is, Naphoth Dor

there he distributed the land to the Israelites according to their tribal divisions.

Allotment for Benjamin

[11] The first lot came up for the tribe of Benjamin according to its clans. Their allotted territory lay between the tribes of Judah and Joseph:

[12] On the north side their boundary began at the Jordan, passed the northern slope of Jericho and headed west into the hill country, coming out at the wilderness of Beth Aven. [13] From there it crossed to the south slope of Luz (that is, Bethel) and went down to Ataroth Addar on the hill south of Lower Beth Horon.

[14] From the hill facing Beth Horon on the south the boundary turned south along the western side and came out at Kiriath Baal (that is, Kiriath Jearim), a town of the people of Judah. This was the western side.

[15] The southern side began at the outskirts of Kiriath Jearim on the west, and the boundary came out at the spring of the waters of Nephtoah. [16] The boundary went down to the foot of the hill facing the Valley of Ben Hinnom, north of the Valley of Rephaim. It continued down the Hinnom Valley along the southern slope of the Jebusite city and so to En Rogel. [17] It then curved north, went to En Shemesh, continued to Geliloth, which faces the Pass of Adummim, and ran down to the Stone of Bohan son of Reuben. [18] It continued to the northern slope of Beth Arabah[a] and on down into the Arabah. [19] It then went to the northern slope of Beth Hoglah and came out at the northern bay of the Dead Sea, at the mouth of the Jordan in the south. This was the southern boundary.

[20] The Jordan formed the boundary on the eastern side.

These were the boundaries that marked out the inheritance of the clans of Benjamin on all sides.

[21] The tribe of Benjamin, according to its clans, had the following towns:

Jericho, Beth Hoglah, Emek Keziz, [22] Beth Arabah, Zemaraim, Bethel, [23] Avvim, Parah, Ophrah, [24] Kephar Ammoni, Ophni and Geba—twelve towns and their villages.

[25] Gibeon, Ramah, Beeroth, [26] Mizpah, Kephirah, Mozah, [27] Rekem, Irpeel, Taralah, [28] Zelah, Haeleph, the Jebusite city (that is, Jerusalem), Gibeah and Kiriath—fourteen towns and their villages.

This was the inheritance of Benjamin for its clans.

Allotment for Simeon

19

The second lot came out for the tribe of Simeon according to its clans. Their inheritance lay within the territory of Judah. [2] It included:

Beersheba (or Sheba),[b] Moladah, [3] Hazar Shual, Balah, Ezem, [4] Eltolad, Bethul, Hormah, [5] Ziklag, Beth Markaboth, Hazar Susah, [6] Beth Lebaoth and Sharuhen—thirteen towns and their villages;

[7] Ain, Rimmon, Ether and Ashan—four towns and their villages— [8] and all the villages around these towns as far as Baalath Beer (Ramah in the Negev).

This was the inheritance of the tribe of the Simeonites, according to its clans. [9] The inheritance of the Simeonites was taken from the share of Judah, because Judah's portion was more than they needed. So the Simeonites received their inheritance within the territory of Judah.

Allotment for Zebulun

[10] The third lot came up for Zebulun according to its clans:

The boundary of their inheritance went as far as Sarid. [11] Going west it ran to Maralah, touched Dabbesheth, and extended to the ravine near Jokneam. [12] It turned east from Sarid toward the sunrise to the territory of Kisloth Tabor and went on to Daberath and up to Japhia. [13] Then it continued eastward to Gath Hepher and Eth Kazin; it came out at Rimmon and turned toward Neah. [14] There the boundary went around on the north to Hannathon and ended at the Valley of Iphtah El. [15] In-

---

a 18 Septuagint; Hebrew *slope facing the Arabah Sheba.*   b 2 Or *Beersheba, Sheba*; 1 Chron. 4:28 does not have cluded were Kattath, Nahalal, Shimron, Idalah and Bethlehem. There were twelve towns and their villages. [16]These towns and their villages were the inheritance of Zebulun, according to its clans.

Allotment for Issachar

[17]The fourth lot came out for Issachar according to its clans. [18]Their territory included:

Jezreel, Kesulloth, Shunem, [19]Hapharaim, Shion, Anaharath, [20]Rabbith, Kishion, Ebez, [21]Remeth, En Gannim, En Haddah and Beth Pazzez. [22]The boundary touched Tabor, Shahazumah and Beth Shemesh, and ended at the Jordan. There were sixteen towns and their villages.

[23]These towns and their villages were the inheritance of the tribe of Issachar, according to its clans.

Allotment for Asher

[24]The fifth lot came out for the tribe of Asher according to its clans. [25]Their territory included:

Helkath, Hali, Beten, Akshaph, [26]Allammelek, Amad and Mishal. On the west the boundary touched Carmel and Shihor Libnath. [27]It then turned east toward Beth Dagon, touched Zebulun and the Valley of Iphtah El, and went north to Beth Emek and Neiel, passing Kabul on the left. [28]It went to Abdon,[a] Rehob, Hammon and Kanah, as far as Greater Sidon. [29]The boundary then turned back toward Ramah and went to the fortified city of Tyre, turned toward Hosah and came out at the Mediterranean Sea in the region of Akzib, [30]Ummah, Aphek and Rehob. There were twenty-two towns and their villages.

[31]These towns and their villages were the inheritance of the tribe of Asher, according to its clans.

Allotment for Naphtali

[32]The sixth lot came out for Naphtali according to its clans:

[33]Their boundary went from Heleph and the large tree in Zaanannim, passing Adami Nekeb and Jabneel to Lak-

kum and ending at the Jordan. [34]The boundary ran west through Aznoth Tabor and came out at Hukkok. It touched Zebulun on the south, Asher on the west and the Jordan[b] on the east. [35]The fortified towns were Ziddim, Zer, Hammath, Rakkath, Kinnereth, [36]Adamah, Ramah, Hazor, [37]Kedesh, Edrei, En Hazor, [38]Iron, Migdal El, Horem, Beth Anath and Beth Shemesh. There were nineteen towns and their villages.

[39]These towns and their villages were the inheritance of the tribe of Naphtali, according to its clans.

Allotment for Dan

[40]The seventh lot came out for the tribe of Dan according to its clans. [41]The territory of their inheritance included:

Zorah, Eshtaol, Ir Shemesh, [42]Shaalabbin, Aijalon, Ithlah, [43]Elon, Timnah, Ekron, [44]Eltekeh, Gibbethon, Baalath, [45]Jehud, Bene Berak, Gath Rimmon, [46]Me Jarkon and Rakkon, with the area facing Joppa.

[47](When the territory of the Danites was lost to them, they went up and attacked Leshem, took it, put it to the sword and occupied it. They settled in Leshem and named it Dan after their ancestor.)

[48]These towns and their villages were the inheritance of the tribe of Dan, according to its clans.

Allotment for Joshua

[49]When they had finished dividing the land into its allotted portions, the Israelites gave Joshua son of Nun an inheritance among them, [50]as the LORD had commanded. They gave him the town he asked for—Timnath Serah[c] in the hill country of Ephraim. And he built up the town and settled there.

[51]These are the territories that Eleazar the priest, Joshua son of Nun and the heads of the tribal clans of Israel assigned by lot at Shiloh in the presence of the LORD at the entrance to the tent of meeting. And so they finished dividing the land.

---

[a] 28 Some Hebrew manuscripts (see also Joshua 21:30); most Hebrew manuscripts *Ebron*
[b] 34 Septuagint; Hebrew *west, and Judah, the Jordan,* (Judges 2:9)
[c] 50 Also known as *Timnath Heres* (see

Cities of Refuge

20 Then the LORD said to Joshua: ²"Tell the Israelites to designate the cities of refuge, as I instructed you through Moses, ³so that anyone who kills a person accidentally and unintentionally may flee there and find protection from the avenger of blood. ⁴When they flee to one of these cities, they are to stand in the entrance of the city gate and state their case before the elders of that city. Then the elders are to admit them into their city and give them a place to live with them. ⁵If the avenger of blood pursues them, the elders must not surrender the accused, because they killed their neighbor unintentionally and without malice aforethought. ⁶They are to stay in that city until they have stood trial before the assembly and until the death of the high priest who is serving at that time. Then they may go back to their own home in the town from which they fled."

⁷So they set apart Kedesh in Galilee in the hill country of Naphtali, Shechem in the hill country of Ephraim, and Kiriath Arba (that is, Hebron) in the hill country of Judah. ⁸East of the Jordan (on the other side from Jericho) they designated Bezer in the wilderness on the plateau in the tribe of Reuben, Ramoth in Gilead in the tribe of Gad, and Golan in Bashan in the tribe of Manasseh. ⁹Any of the Israelites or any foreigner residing among them who killed someone accidentally could flee to these designated cities and not be killed by the avenger of blood prior to standing trial before the assembly.

Towns for the Levites

21 Now the family heads of the Levites approached Eleazar the priest, Joshua son of Nun, and the heads of the other tribal families of Israel ²at Shiloh in Canaan and said to them, "The LORD commanded through Moses that you give us towns to live in, with pasturelands for our livestock." ³So, as the LORD had commanded, the Israelites gave the Levites the following towns and pasturelands out of their own inheritance:

⁴The first lot came out for the Kohathites, according to their clans. The Levites who were descendants of Aaron the priest were allotted thirteen towns from the tribes of Judah, Simeon and Benjamin. ⁵The rest of Kohath's descendants were allotted ten towns from the clans of the tribes of Ephraim, Dan and half of Manasseh.

⁶The descendants of Gershon were allotted thirteen towns from the clans of the tribes of Issachar, Asher, Naphtali and the half-tribe of Manasseh in Bashan.

⁷The descendants of Merari, according to their clans, received twelve towns from the tribes of Reuben, Gad and Zebulun.

⁸So the Israelites allotted to the Levites these towns and their pasturelands, as the LORD had commanded through Moses.

⁹From the tribes of Judah and Simeon they allotted the following towns by name ¹⁰(these towns were assigned to the descendants of Aaron who were from the Kohathite clans of the Levites, because the first lot fell to them):

¹¹They gave them Kiriath Arba (that is, Hebron), with its surrounding pastureland, in the hill country of Judah. (Arba was the ancestor of Anak.) ¹²But the fields and villages around the city they had given to Caleb son of Jephunneh as his possession.

¹³So to the descendants of Aaron the priest they gave Hebron (a city of refuge for one accused of murder), Libnah, ¹⁴Jattir, Eshtemoa, ¹⁵Holon, Debir, ¹⁶Ain, Juttah and Beth Shemesh, together with their pasturelands—nine towns from these two tribes.

¹⁷And from the tribe of Benjamin they gave them Gibeon, Geba, ¹⁸Anathoth and Almon, together with their pasturelands—four towns.

¹⁹The total number of towns for the priests, the descendants of Aaron, came to thirteen, together with their pasturelands.

²⁰The rest of the Kohathite clans of the Levites were allotted towns from the tribe of Ephraim:

²¹In the hill country of Ephraim they were given Shechem (a city of refuge for one accused of murder) and Gezer, ²²Kibzaim and Beth Horon, together with their pasturelands—four towns.

²³Also from the tribe of Dan they received Eltekeh, Gibbethon, ²⁴Aijalon and Gath Rimmon, together with their pasturelands—four towns.

²⁵From half the tribe of Manasseh they received Taanach and Gath Rim-

A Place to Hide

Joshua 20:2–6

read/meditate

Joshua 20:2–6 gives instructions regarding the cities of refuge. Read the verses until you clearly understand under what circumstances a person could find sanctuary in these cities. The cities of refuge were about the "gray areas." If a person was killed, it mattered to God that the killer's intentions were taken into account. In your culture, how much attention is given to an offender's intentions when they are tried for a crime?

pray

Consider both your own intentions and the way you deal with the intentions of others. Ask God which area needs more adjustment in your life. Give him some time and space to give you direction.

contemplate

Think about the role of a city of refuge. Imagine the gates. Imagine a fearful soul arriving at those gates after being on the run for days, with an angry and bereaved family close on his heels. Do you have enough cities of refuge in your life? What happens when you foul things up—unintentionally? On the other hand, do you provide enough cities of refuge for those around you?

additional reflection

Good and evil both increase at compound interest. That is why the little decisions you and I make every day are of such infinite importance.

—C. S. Lewis

Ah, downcast soul, who are writing hard things of thyself, it may be that thy merciful Lord is viewing thy life more accurately and estimating it more lovingly than thou knowest!

—F. B. Meyer

For your next devotional reading, go to page 267.

mon, together with their pasturelands—two towns.
26All these ten towns and their pasturelands
were given to the rest of the Kohathite clans.

27The Levite clans of the Gershonites were
given:
from the half-tribe of Manasseh,
Golan in Bashan (a city of refuge for
one accused of murder) and Be Eshte-
rah, together with their pasturelands—
two towns;
28from the tribe of Issachar,
Kishion, Daberath, 29Jarmuth and En
Gannim, together with their pasturelands—four towns;
30from the tribe of Asher,
Mishal, Abdon, 31Helkath and Rehob,
together with their pasturelands—four
towns;
32from the tribe of Naphtali,
Kedesh in Galilee (a city of refuge for
one accused of murder), Hammoth
Dor and Kartan, together with their
pasturelands—three towns.
33The total number of towns of the Gershonite clans came to thirteen, together with
their pasturelands.

34The Merarite clans (the rest of the Levites)
were given:
from the tribe of Zebulun,
Jokneam, Kartah, 35Dimnah and Nahalal, together with their pasturelands—
four towns;
36from the tribe of Reuben,
Bezer, Jahaz, 37Kedemoth and Mephaath, together with their pasturelands—
four towns;
38from the tribe of Gad,
Ramoth in Gilead (a city of refuge for
one accused of murder), Mahanaim,
39Heshbon and Jazer, together with
their pasturelands—four towns in all.
40The total number of towns allotted to the
Merarite clans, who were the rest of the Levites, came to twelve.

41The towns of the Levites in the territory
held by the Israelites were forty-eight in all,
together with their pasturelands. 42Each of
these towns had pasturelands surrounding
it; this was true for all these towns.

43So the LORD gave Israel all the land he
had sworn to give their ancestors, and they
took possession of it and settled there. 44The
LORD gave them rest on every side, just as he
had sworn to their ancestors. Not one of
their enemies withstood them; the LORD
gave all their enemies into their hands.
45Not one of all the LORD's good promises to
the house of Israel failed; every one was fulfilled.

Eastern Tribes Return Home

22 Then Joshua summoned the
Reubenites, the Gadites and the
half-tribe of Manasseh 2and
said to them, "You have done all that Moses
the servant of the LORD commanded, and
you have obeyed me in everything I commanded. 3For a long time now—to this very
day—you have not deserted the other Israelites but have carried out the mission the
LORD your God gave you. 4Now that the LORD
your God has given them rest as he promised, return to your homes in the land that
Moses the servant of the LORD gave you on
the other side of the Jordan. 5But be very
careful to keep the commandment and the
law that Moses the servant of the LORD gave
you: to love the LORD your God, to walk in
obedience to him, to keep his commands, to
hold fast to him and to serve him with all
your heart and with all your soul."

6Then Joshua blessed them and sent
them away, and they went to their homes.
7(To the half-tribe of Manasseh Moses had
given land in Bashan, and to the other half
of the tribe Joshua gave land on the west
side of the Jordan along with the other Israelites.) When Joshua sent them home, he
blessed them, 8saying, "Return to your
homes with your great wealth—with large
herds of livestock, with silver, gold, bronze
and iron, and a great quantity of clothing—
and divide the plunder from your enemies
with the other members of your tribes."

9So the Reubenites, the Gadites and the
half-tribe of Manasseh left the Israelites at
Shiloh in Canaan to return to Gilead, their
own land, which they had acquired in accordance with the command of the LORD
through Moses.

10When they came to Geliloth near the
Jordan in the land of Canaan, the Reubenites, the Gadites and the half-tribe of Manasseh built an imposing altar there by the
Jordan. 11And when the Israelites heard that
they had built the altar on the border of Canaan at Geliloth near the Jordan on the Israelite side, 12the whole assembly of Israel

gathered at Shiloh to go to war against them.

¹³So the Israelites sent Phinehas son of Eleazar, the priest, to the land of Gilead—to Reuben, Gad and the half-tribe of Manasseh. ¹⁴With him they sent ten of the chief men, one from each of the tribes of Israel, each the head of a family division among the Israelite clans.

¹⁵When they went to Gilead—to Reuben, Gad and the half-tribe of Manasseh—they said to them: ¹⁶"The whole assembly of the LORD says: 'How could you break faith with the God of Israel like this? How could you turn away from the LORD and build yourselves an altar in rebellion against him now? ¹⁷Was not the sin of Peor enough for us? Up to this very day we have not cleansed ourselves from that sin, even though a plague fell on the community of the LORD! ¹⁸And are you now turning away from the LORD?

" 'If you rebel against the LORD today, tomorrow he will be angry with the whole community of Israel. ¹⁹If the land you possess is defiled, come over to the LORD's land, where the LORD's tabernacle stands, and share the land with us. But do not rebel against the LORD or against us by building an altar for yourselves, other than the altar of the LORD our God. ²⁰When Achan son of Zerah was unfaithful in regard to the devoted things,ᵃ did not wrath come on the whole community of Israel? He was not the only one who died for his sin.' "

²¹Then Reuben, Gad and the half-tribe of Manasseh replied to the heads of the clans of Israel: ²²"The Mighty One, God, the LORD! The Mighty One, God, the LORD! He knows! And let Israel know! If this has been in rebellion or disobedience to the LORD, do not spare us this day. ²³If we have built our own altar to turn away from the LORD and to offer burnt offerings and grain offerings, or to sacrifice fellowship offerings on it, may the LORD himself call us to account.

²⁴"No! We did it for fear that some day your descendants might say to ours, 'What do you have to do with the LORD, the God of Israel? ²⁵The LORD has made the Jordan a boundary between us and you—you Reubenites and Gadites! You have no share in

the LORD.' So your descendants might cause ours to stop fearing the LORD.

²⁶"That is why we said, 'Let us get ready and build an altar—but not for burnt offerings or sacrifices.' ²⁷On the contrary, it is to be a witness between us and you and the generations that follow, that we will worship the LORD at his sanctuary with our burnt offerings, sacrifices and fellowship offerings. Then in the future your descendants will not be able to say to ours, 'You have no share in the LORD.'

²⁸"And we said, 'If they ever say this to us, or to our descendants, we will answer: Look at the replica of the LORD's altar, which our people built, not for burnt offerings and sacrifices, but as a witness between us and you.'

²⁹"Far be it from us to rebel against the LORD and turn away from him today by building an altar for burnt offerings, grain offerings and sacrifices, other than the altar of the LORD our God that stands before his tabernacle."

³⁰When Phinehas the priest and the leaders of the community—the heads of the clans of the Israelites—heard what Reuben, Gad and Manasseh had to say, they were pleased. ³¹And Phinehas son of Eleazar, the priest, said to Reuben, Gad and Manasseh, "Today we know that the LORD is with us, because you have not been unfaithful to the LORD in this matter. Now you have rescued the Israelites from the LORD's hand."

³²Then Phinehas son of Eleazar, the priest, and the leaders returned to Canaan from their meeting with the Reubenites and Gadites in Gilead and reported to the Israelites. ³³They were glad to hear the report and praised God. And they talked no more about going to war against them to devastate the country where the Reubenites and the Gadites lived.

³⁴And the Reubenites and the Gadites gave the altar this name: A Witness Between Us—that the LORD is God.

Joshua's Farewell to the Leaders

23 After a long time had passed and the LORD had given Israel rest from all their enemies around them, Joshua, by then a very old man, ²summoned all Israel—their elders, leaders, judg-

---

ᵃ 20 The Hebrew term refers to the irrevocable giving over of things or persons to the LORD, often by totally destroying them.

MONDAY

OUR DUTY: OBEY GOD'S WORD

Joshua 23:1–16 or 23:6–8

Donald Drew

Ruthlessly and relentlessly, Satan tries to squeeze us into the world's way of thinking and living. Some Christians' lifestyle seems to be little different from unbelievers for they appear to have become so well-adjusted to the culture that they fit into it without even thinking. Such lifestyle has lovingly to be reproved and, if necessary, lovingly condemned. They watch the same TV programmes, read the same magazines, follow the same fashions. God's standards are often obliterated by such choices. In the political world, it is said that it's time to bring an ambassador home when he's learned the language and adopted the customs of the country to which he's been assigned.

The difference lies between those of us who believe that God is there and has truthfully spoken to all and those who do not. Today, to assert the validity and authority of the Bible as speaking truth about God, the cosmos, history and the human condition is probably met with incredulity or with the ultimate dismissal: "So what? Who cares?" Tragically, the iron has entered into so many peoples' souls. When the Bible is disregarded, its ethics are also disregarded. When Christian truth has been bulldozed, Christian morality can find no foothold. In the West for 14 centuries, the Bible's teaching about behaviour has been a tested and reliable foundation for individual and social behaviour. It is a blue-print for a healthy society.

CATHERINE WINKWORTH {AD 1827–1878}

Whoever doesn't keep God's word, yet says,
   "I know the Lord," is wrong;
In him is not that blessed faith
   Through which the truth is strong;
But he who hears and keeps the word,
Is not of this world, but of God.

For he does please the Father well
   Who simply can obey;
In him the love of God does dwell
   Who steadfast keeps His way;
A daily active life of love,
Such fruits a living faith must prove.

reflection

1. Can the people around you tell just by your lifestyle that you follow God?
2. How do you decide in what ways you'll be different?
3. How can a follower of Christ live in the world as a witness and ambassador for God without being squeezed by the world into its mold?

For your next devotional reading, go to page 274.

es and officials—and said to them: "I am very old. ³You yourselves have seen everything the LORD your God has done to all these nations for your sake; it was the LORD your God who fought for you. ⁴Remember how I have allotted as an inheritance for your tribes all the land of the nations that remain—the nations I conquered—between the Jordan and the Mediterranean Sea in the west. ⁵The LORD your God himself will push them out for your sake. He will drive them out before you, and you will take possession of their land, as the LORD your God promised you.

⁶"Be very strong; be careful to obey all that is written in the Book of the Law of Moses, without turning aside to the right or to the left. ⁷Do not associate with these nations that remain among you; do not invoke the names of their gods or swear by them. You must not serve them or bow down to them. ⁸But you are to hold fast to the LORD your God, as you have until now.

⁹"The LORD has driven out before you great and powerful nations; to this day no one has been able to withstand you. ¹⁰One of you routs a thousand, because the LORD your God fights for you, just as he promised. ¹¹So be very careful to love the LORD your God.

¹²"But if you turn away and ally yourselves with the survivors of these nations that remain among you and if you intermarry with them and associate with them, ¹³then you may be sure that the LORD your God will no longer drive out these nations before you. Instead, they will become snares and traps for you, whips on your backs and thorns in your eyes, until you perish from this good land, which the LORD your God has given you.

¹⁴"Now I am about to go the way of all the earth. You know with all your heart and soul that not one of all the good promises the LORD your God gave you has failed. Every promise has been fulfilled; not one has failed. ¹⁵But just as all the good things the LORD your God has promised you have come to you, so he will bring on you all the evil things he has threatened, until the LORD your God has destroyed you from this good land he has given you. ¹⁶If you violate the covenant of the LORD your God, which he commanded you, and go and serve other gods and bow down to them, the LORD's an-

ger will burn against you, and you will quickly perish from the good land he has given you."

The Covenant Renewed at Shechem

24 Then Joshua assembled all the tribes of Israel at Shechem. He summoned the elders, leaders, judges and officials of Israel, and they presented themselves before God.

²Joshua said to all the people, "This is what the LORD, the God of Israel, says: 'Long ago your ancestors, including Terah the father of Abraham and Nahor, lived beyond the Euphrates River and worshiped other gods. ³But I took your father Abraham from the land beyond the Euphrates and led him throughout Canaan and gave him many descendants. I gave him Isaac, ⁴and to Isaac I gave Jacob and Esau. I assigned the hill country of Seir to Esau, but Jacob and his family went down to Egypt.

⁵" 'Then I sent Moses and Aaron, and I afflicted the Egyptians by what I did there, and I brought you out. ⁶When I brought your people out of Egypt, you came to the sea, and the Egyptians pursued them with chariots and horsemen*a* as far as the Red Sea.*b* ⁷But they cried to the LORD for help, and he put darkness between you and the Egyptians; he brought the sea over them and covered them. You saw with your own eyes what I did to the Egyptians. Then you lived in the wilderness for a long time.

⁸" 'I brought you to the land of the Amorites who lived east of the Jordan. They fought against you, but I gave them into your hands. I destroyed them from before you, and you took possession of their land. ⁹When Balak son of Zippor, the king of Moab, prepared to fight against Israel, he sent for Balaam son of Beor to put a curse on you. ¹⁰But I would not listen to Balaam, so he blessed you again and again, and I delivered you out of his hand.

¹¹" 'Then you crossed the Jordan and came to Jericho. The citizens of Jericho fought against you, as did also the Amorites, Perizzites, Canaanites, Hittites, Girgashites, Hivites and Jebusites, but I gave them into your hands. ¹²I sent the hornet ahead of you, which drove them out before you—also the two Amorite kings. You did not do it with

---

a 6 Or *charioteers*   *b* 6 Or *the Sea of Reeds*

your own sword and bow. ¹³So I gave you a land on which you did not toil and cities you did not build; and you live in them and eat from vineyards and olive groves that you did not plant.'

¹⁴"Now fear the Lord and serve him with all faithfulness. Throw away the gods your ancestors worshiped beyond the Euphrates River and in Egypt, and serve the Lord. ¹⁵But if serving the Lord seems undesirable to you, then choose for yourselves this day whom you will serve, whether the gods your ancestors served beyond the Euphrates, or the gods of the Amorites, in whose land you are living. But as for me and my household, we will serve the Lord."

¹⁶Then the people answered, "Far be it from us to forsake the Lord to serve other gods! ¹⁷It was the Lord our God himself who brought us and our parents up out of Egypt, from that land of slavery, and performed those great signs before our eyes. He protected us on our entire journey and among all the nations through which we traveled. ¹⁸And the Lord drove out before us all the nations, including the Amorites, who lived in the land. We too will serve the Lord, because he is our God."

¹⁹Joshua said to the people, "You are not able to serve the Lord. He is a holy God; he is a jealous God. He will not forgive your rebellion and your sins. ²⁰If you forsake the Lord and serve foreign gods, he will turn and bring disaster on you and make an end of you, after he has been good to you."

²¹But the people said to Joshua, "No! We will serve the Lord."

²²Then Joshua said, "You are witnesses against yourselves that you have chosen to serve the Lord."

"Yes, we are witnesses," they replied.

²³"Now then," said Joshua, "throw away the foreign gods that are among you and yield your hearts to the Lord, the God of Israel."

²⁴And the people said to Joshua, "We will serve the Lord our God and obey him."

²⁵On that day Joshua made a covenant for the people, and there at Shechem he reaffirmed for them decrees and laws. ²⁶And Joshua recorded these things in the Book of the Law of God. Then he took a large stone and set it up there under the oak near the holy place of the Lord.

²⁷"See!" he said to all the people. "This stone will be a witness against us. It has heard all the words the Lord has said to us. It will be a witness against you if you are untrue to your God."

²⁸Then Joshua dismissed the people, each to their own inheritance.

Buried in the Promised Land

²⁹After these things, Joshua son of Nun, the servant of the Lord, died at the age of a hundred and ten. ³⁰And they buried him in the land of his inheritance, at Timnath Serah[a] in the hill country of Ephraim, north of Mount Gaash.

³¹Israel served the Lord throughout the lifetime of Joshua and of the elders who outlived him and who had experienced everything the Lord had done for Israel.

³²And Joseph's bones, which the Israelites had brought up from Egypt, were buried at Shechem in the tract of land that Jacob bought for a hundred pieces of silver[b] from the sons of Hamor, the father of Shechem. This became the inheritance of Joseph's descendants.

³³And Eleazar son of Aaron died and was buried at Gibeah, which had been allotted to his son Phinehas in the hill country of Ephraim.

a 30 Also known as *Timnath Heres* (see Judges 2:9)   b 32 Hebrew *hundred kesitahs*; a kesitah was a unit of money of unknown weight and value.

judges

AUTHOR: Unknown (possibly Samuel)

DATE: Around 1000 B.C.

THEME: God delivers his people from the consequences of doing things their own way.

Israel Fights the Remaining Canaanites

1 After the death of Joshua, the Israelites asked the LORD, "Who of us is to go up first to fight against the Canaanites?"

²The LORD answered, "Judah shall go up; I have given the land into their hands."

³The men of Judah then said to the Simeonites their fellow Israelites, "Come up with us into the territory allotted to us, to fight against the Canaanites. We in turn will go with you into yours." So the Simeonites went with them.

⁴When Judah attacked, the LORD gave the Canaanites and Perizzites into their hands, and they struck down ten thousand men at Bezek. ⁵It was there that they found Adoni-Bezek and fought against him, putting to rout the Canaanites and Perizzites. ⁶Adoni-Bezek fled, but they chased him and caught him, and cut off his thumbs and big toes.

⁷Then Adoni-Bezek said, "Seventy kings with their thumbs and big toes cut off have picked up scraps under my table. Now God has paid me back for what I did to them." They brought him to Jerusalem, and he died there.

⁸The men of Judah attacked Jerusalem also and took it. They put the city to the sword and set it on fire.

⁹After that, Judah went down to fight against the Canaanites living in the hill country, the Negev and the western foothills. ¹⁰They advanced against the Canaanites living in Hebron (formerly called Kiriath Arba) and defeated Sheshai, Ahiman and Talmai.

¹¹From there they advanced against the people living in Debir (formerly called Kiriath Sepher). ¹²And Caleb said, "I will give my daughter Aksah in marriage to the man who attacks and captures Kiriath Sepher." ¹³Othniel son of Kenaz, Caleb's younger brother, took it; so Caleb gave his daughter Aksah to him in marriage.

¹⁴One day when she came to Othniel, she urged him[a] to ask her father for a field. When she got off her donkey, Caleb asked her, "What can I do for you?"

¹⁵She replied, "Do me a special favor. Since you have given me land in the Negev, give me also springs of water." So Caleb gave her the upper and lower springs.

¹⁶The descendants of Moses' father-in-law, the Kenite, went up from the City of Palms[b] with the people of Judah to live among the inhabitants of the Desert of Judah in the Negev near Arad.

¹⁷Then the men of Judah went with the Simeonites their fellow Israelites and attacked the Canaanites living in Zephath, and they totally destroyed[c] the city. Therefore it was called Hormah.[d] ¹⁸Judah also took[e] Gaza, Ashkelon and Ekron—each city with its territory.

¹⁹The LORD was with the men of Judah. They took possession of the hill country, but they were unable to drive the people from the plains, because they had chariots fitted with iron. ²⁰As Moses had promised, Hebron was given to Caleb, who drove from it the three sons of Anak. ²¹The Benjamites, however, did not drive out the Jebusites, who were living in Jerusalem; to this day the Jebusites live there with the Benjamites.

---

a 14 Hebrew; Septuagint and Vulgate *Othniel, he urged her*   b 16 That is, Jericho   c 17 The Hebrew term refers to the irrevocable giving over of things or persons to the LORD, often by totally destroying them.   d 17 *Hormah* means *destruction*.   e 18 Hebrew; Septuagint *Judah did not take*

²²Now the house of Joseph attacked Bethel, and the LORD was with them. ²³When they sent men to spy out Bethel (formerly called Luz), ²⁴the spies saw a man coming out of the city and they said to him, "Show us how to get into the city and we will see that you are treated well." ²⁵So he showed them, and they put the city to the sword but spared the man and his whole family. ²⁶He then went to the land of the Hittites, where he built a city and called it Luz, which is its name to this day.

²⁷But Manasseh did not drive out the people of Beth Shan or Taanach or Dor or Ibleam or Megiddo and their surrounding settlements, for the Canaanites were determined to live in that land. ²⁸When Israel became strong, they pressed the Canaanites into forced labor but never drove them out completely. ²⁹Nor did Ephraim drive out the Canaanites living in Gezer, but the Canaanites continued to live there among them. ³⁰Neither did Zebulun drive out the Canaanites living in Kitron or Nahalol, so these Canaanites lived among them, but Zebulun did subject them to forced labor. ³¹Nor did Asher drive out those living in Akko or Sidon or Ahlab or Akzib or Helbah or Aphek or Rehob. ³²The Asherites lived among the Canaanite inhabitants of the land because they did not drive them out. ³³Neither did Naphtali drive out those living in Beth Shemesh or Beth Anath; but the Naphtalites too lived among the Canaanite inhabitants of the land, and those living in Beth Shemesh and Beth Anath became forced laborers for them. ³⁴The Amorites confined the Danites to the hill country, not allowing them to come down into the plain. ³⁵And the Amorites were determined also to hold out in Mount Heres, Aijalon and Shaalbim, but when the power of the house of Joseph increased, they too were pressed into forced labor. ³⁶The boundary of the Amorites was from Scorpion Pass to Sela and beyond.

The Angel of the LORD at Bokim

2 The angel of the LORD went up from Gilgal to Bokim and said, "I brought you up out of Egypt and led you into the land I swore to give to your ancestors. I said, 'I will never break my covenant with you, ²and you shall not make a covenant with the people of this land, but you shall break down their altars.' Yet you have disobeyed me. Why have you done this? ³And I have also said, 'I will not drive them out before you; they will become traps for you, and their gods will become snares to you.' "

⁴When the angel of the LORD had spoken these things to all the Israelites, the people wept aloud, ⁵and they called that place Bokim.ᵃ There they offered sacrifices to the LORD.

Disobedience and Defeat

⁶After Joshua had dismissed the Israelites, they went to take possession of the land, each to their own inheritance. ⁷The people served the LORD throughout the lifetime of Joshua and of the elders who outlived him and who had seen all the great things the LORD had done for Israel.

⁸Joshua son of Nun, the servant of the LORD, died at the age of a hundred and ten. ⁹And they buried him in the land of his inheritance, at Timnath Heresᵇ in the hill country of Ephraim, north of Mount Gaash.

¹⁰After that whole generation had been gathered to their ancestors, another generation grew up who knew neither the LORD nor what he had done for Israel. ¹¹Then the Israelites did evil in the eyes of the LORD and served the Baals. ¹²They forsook the LORD, the God of their ancestors, who had brought them out of Egypt. They followed and worshiped various gods of the peoples around them. They aroused the LORD's anger ¹³because they forsook him and served Baal and the Ashtoreths. ¹⁴In his anger against Israel the LORD gave them into the hands of raiders who plundered them. He sold them into the hands of their enemies all around, whom they were no longer able to resist. ¹⁵Whenever Israel went out to fight, the hand of the LORD was against them to defeat them, just as he had sworn to them. They were in great distress.

¹⁶Then the LORD raised up judges,ᶜ who saved them out of the hands of these raiders. ¹⁷Yet they would not listen to their judges but prostituted themselves to other gods and worshiped them. Unlike their ancestors,

---

ᵃ 5 Bokim means *weepers*.   ᵇ 9 Also known as *Timnath Serah* (see Joshua 19:50 and 24:30)
ᶜ 16 Or *leaders*; similarly in verses 17-19

they quickly turned from following the way of their ancestors, the way of obedience to the Lord's commands. [18]Whenever the Lord raised up a judge for them, he was with the judge and saved them out of the hands of their enemies as long as the judge lived; for the Lord relented because of their groaning under those who oppressed and afflicted them. [19]But when the judge died, the people returned to ways even more corrupt than those of their ancestors, following other gods and serving and worshiping them. They refused to give up their evil practices and stubborn ways.

[20]Therefore the Lord was very angry with Israel and said, "Because this nation has violated the covenant I ordained for their ancestors and has not listened to me, [21]I will no longer drive out before them any of the nations Joshua left when he died. [22]I will use them to test Israel and see whether they will keep the way of the Lord and walk in it as their ancestors did." [23]The Lord had allowed those nations to remain; he did not drive them out at once by giving them into the hands of Joshua.

3 These are the nations the Lord left to test all those Israelites who had not experienced any of the wars in Canaan [2](he did this only to teach warfare to the descendants of the Israelites who had not had previous battle experience): [3]the five rulers of the Philistines, all the Canaanites, the Sidonians, and the Hivites living in the Lebanon mountains from Mount Baal Hermon to Lebo Hamath. [4]They were left to test the Israelites to see whether they would obey the Lord's commands, which he had given their ancestors through Moses. [5]The Israelites lived among the Canaanites, Hittites, Amorites, Perizzites, Hivites and Jebusites. [6]They took their daughters in marriage and gave their own daughters to their sons, and served their gods.

Othniel

[7]The Israelites did evil in the eyes of the Lord; they forgot the Lord their God and served the Baals and the Asherahs. [8]The anger of the Lord burned against Israel so that he sold them into the hands of Cushan-Rishathaim king of Aram Naharaim,[a] to

whom the Israelites were subject for eight years. [9]But when they cried out to the Lord, he raised up for them a deliverer, Othniel son of Kenaz, Caleb's younger brother, who saved them. [10]The Spirit of the Lord came on him, so that he became Israel's judge[b] and went to war. The Lord gave Cushan-Rishathaim king of Aram into the hands of Othniel, who overpowered him. [11]So the land had peace for forty years, until Othniel son of Kenaz died.

Ehud

[12]Again the Israelites did evil in the eyes of the Lord, and because they did this evil the Lord gave Eglon king of Moab power over Israel. [13]Getting the Ammonites and Amalekites to join him, Eglon came and attacked Israel, and they took possession of the City of Palms.[c] [14]The Israelites were subject to Eglon king of Moab for eighteen years.

[15]Again the Israelites cried out to the Lord, and he gave them a deliverer—Ehud, a left-handed man, the son of Gera the Benjamite. The Israelites sent him with tribute to Eglon king of Moab. [16]Now Ehud had made a double-edged sword about a cubit[d] long, which he strapped to his right thigh under his clothing. [17]He presented the tribute to Eglon king of Moab, who was a very fat man. [18]After Ehud had presented the tribute, he dismissed those who had carried it. [19]But on reaching the stone images near Gilgal he himself went back to Eglon and said, "Your Majesty, I have a secret message for you."

The king said to his attendants, "Leave us!" And they all left.

[20]Ehud then approached him while he was sitting alone in the upper room of his palace[e] and said, "I have a message from God for you." As the king rose from his seat, [21]Ehud reached with his left hand, drew the sword from his right thigh and plunged it into the king's belly. [22]Even the handle sank in after the blade, and his bowels discharged. Ehud did not pull the sword out, and the fat closed in over it. [23]Then Ehud went out to the porch[f]; he shut the doors of the upper room behind him and locked them.

---

[a] 8 That is, Northwest Mesopotamia   [b] 10 Or leader   [c] 13 That is, Jericho   [d] 16 That is, about 18 inches or about 45 centimeters   [e] 20 The meaning of the Hebrew for this word is uncertain; also in verse 24.   [f] 23 The meaning of the Hebrew for this word is uncertain.

²⁴After he had gone, the servants came and found the doors of the upper room locked. They said, "He must be relieving himself in the inner room of the palace." ²⁵They waited to the point of embarrassment, but when he did not open the doors of the room, they took a key and unlocked them. There they saw their lord fallen to the floor, dead.

²⁶While they waited, Ehud got away. He passed by the stone images and escaped to Seirah. ²⁷When he arrived there, he blew a trumpet in the hill country of Ephraim, and the Israelites went down with him from the hills, with him leading them.

²⁸"Follow me," he ordered, "for the LORD has given Moab, your enemy, into your hands." So they followed him down and took possession of the fords of the Jordan that led to Moab; they allowed no one to cross over. ²⁹At that time they struck down about ten thousand Moabites, all vigorous and strong; not one escaped. ³⁰That day Moab was made subject to Israel, and the land had peace for eighty years.

Shamgar

³¹After Ehud came Shamgar son of Anath, who struck down six hundred Philistines with an oxgoad. He too saved Israel.

Deborah

4 Again the Israelites did evil in the eyes of the LORD, now that Ehud was dead. ²So the LORD sold them into the hands of Jabin king of Canaan, who reigned in Hazor. Sisera, the commander of his army, was based in Harosheth Haggoyim. ³Because he had nine hundred chariots fitted with iron and had cruelly oppressed the Israelites for twenty years, they cried to the LORD for help.

⁴Now Deborah, a prophet, the wife of Lappidoth, was leading*ᵃ* Israel at that time. ⁵She held court under the Palm of Deborah between Ramah and Bethel in the hill country of Ephraim, and the Israelites went up to her to have their disputes decided. ⁶She sent for Barak son of Abinoam from Kedesh in Naphtali and said to him, "The LORD, the God of Israel, commands you: 'Go, take with you ten thousand men of Naphtali and Zebulun and lead them up to Mount Tabor. ⁷I

will lead Sisera, the commander of Jabin's army, with his chariots and his troops to the Kishon River and give him into your hands.' "

⁸Barak said to her, "If you go with me, I will go; but if you don't go with me, I won't go."

⁹"Certainly I will go with you," said Deborah. "But because of the course you are taking, the honor will not be yours, for the LORD will deliver Sisera into the hands of a woman." So Deborah went with Barak to Kedesh. ¹⁰There Barak summoned Zebulun and Naphtali, and ten thousand men went up under his command. Deborah also went up with him.

¹¹Now Heber the Kenite had left the other Kenites, the descendants of Hobab, Moses' brother-in-law,*ᵇ* and pitched his tent by the great tree in Zaanannim near Kedesh.

¹²When they told Sisera that Barak son of Abinoam had gone up to Mount Tabor, ¹³Sisera summoned from Harosheth Haggoyim to the Kishon River all his men and his nine hundred chariots fitted with iron.

¹⁴Then Deborah said to Barak, "Go! This is the day the LORD has given Sisera into your hands. Has not the LORD gone ahead of you?" So Barak went down Mount Tabor, with ten thousand men following him. ¹⁵At Barak's advance, the LORD routed Sisera and all his chariots and army by the sword, and Sisera got down from his chariot and fled on foot.

¹⁶Barak pursued the chariots and army as far as Harosheth Haggoyim, and all Sisera's troops fell by the sword; not a man was left. ¹⁷Sisera, meanwhile, fled on foot to the tent of Jael, the wife of Heber the Kenite, because there was an alliance between Jabin king of Hazor and the family of Heber the Kenite.

¹⁸Jael went out to meet Sisera and said to him, "Come, my lord, come right in. Don't be afraid." So he entered her tent, and she covered him with a blanket.

¹⁹"I'm thirsty," he said. "Please give me some water." She opened a skin of milk, gave him a drink, and covered him up.

²⁰"Stand in the doorway of the tent," he told her. "If anyone comes by and asks you, 'Is there a man in here?' say 'No.' "

²¹But Jael, Heber's wife, picked up a tent

TUESDAY

GOD'S IMPARTIALITY

Judges 4:1–24 or 4:1–7

G. CAMPBELL MORGAN {AD 1863–1945}

In the light of subsequent Jewish prejudice against women as leaders, the story of Deborah is full of interest, as it reveals the fact that there never was any such prejudice in the mind of God. Whereas motherhood in all the sanctity and beauty of that great word, is the special function and glory of womanhood, yet when a woman is specially gifted for the exercise of prophetic and administrative work, she is not barred by any Divine law from such work. Deborah was a prophetess in the full sense of that word; that is, she was the inspired mouthpiece of the Word of God to her people. She also judged Israel, and whatever that meant in the case of the men who exercised that office, it also meant in her case. She was a savior, a deliver; she administered the affairs of the people, and led them out of the circumstances of difficulty into which their sin had brought them … The one great message of the story seems to be that it warns us to take heed that we do not imagine ourselves to be wiser than God. When he calls and equips a woman to high service, let us beware lest we dishonor him by refusing to recognize her, or cooperate with her.

Carolyn Custis James

Women in the Bible were quite familiar with roadblocks, disappointments, and feeling lost. They knew what it was like to hit bottom when their lives veered off in unexpected directions or when they didn't seem to count for much in the eyes of others … Many were thrown into circumstances that took them completely out of their comfort zone and compelled them to take a stand or fight a battle they undoubtedly expected someone else (presumably a man) to handle for them …

    Time after time, they put God to the test, and he displayed the greatness of his heart for women in powerful ways … I learned God has a larger vision for women than I realized, a vision that encompasses the vast diversity of all of our lives and that calls us to be more. It was clear … that the Bible strongly affirms [the] significance [of] wives and mothers, but I was stunned to learn God values [women] just as much when [their] lives follow other paths.

reflection

1.   When are you tempted to minimize a woman's ministry or gifts when comparing her to a man who serves in a similar role?

2.   What difference do you believe there should be between the ministry of men and the ministry of women?

3.   In what ways are you most likely to dishonor God by disrespecting the gifts he has given to either a man or woman in ministry?

For your next devotional reading, go to page 277.

peg and a hammer and went quietly to him while he lay fast asleep, exhausted. She drove the peg through his temple into the ground, and he died.

²²Just then Barak came by in pursuit of Sisera, and Jael went out to meet him. "Come," she said, "I will show you the man you're looking for." So he went in with her, and there lay Sisera with the tent peg through his temple—dead.

²³On that day God subdued Jabin king of Canaan before the Israelites. ²⁴And the hand of the Israelites pressed harder and harder against Jabin king of Canaan until they destroyed him.

The Song of Deborah

5 On that day Deborah and Barak son of Abinoam sang this song:

²"When the princes in Israel take the
    lead,
  when the people willingly offer
    themselves—
  praise the LORD!

³"Hear this, you kings! Listen, you rulers!
  I, even I, will sing to*ᵃ* the LORD;
  I will praise the LORD, the God of
    Israel, in song.

⁴"When you, LORD, went out from Seir,
  when you marched from the land of
    Edom,
  the earth shook, the heavens poured,
  the clouds poured down water.
⁵The mountains quaked before the LORD,
    the One of Sinai,
  before the LORD, the God of Israel.

⁶"In the days of Shamgar son of Anath,
  in the days of Jael, the highways were
    abandoned;
  travelers took to winding paths.
⁷Villagers in Israel would not fight;
  they held back until I, Deborah, arose,
  until I arose, a mother in Israel.
⁸God chose new leaders
  when war came to the city gates,
  but not a shield or spear was seen
  among forty thousand in Israel.
⁹My heart is with Israel's princes,

with the willing volunteers among the
  people.
Praise the LORD!

¹⁰"You who ride on white donkeys,
  sitting on your saddle blankets,
  and you who walk along the road,
consider ¹¹the voice of the singersᵇ at the
    watering places.
  They recite the victories of the LORD,
  the victories of his villagers in Israel.

"Then the people of the LORD
  went down to the city gates.
¹²'Wake up, wake up, Deborah!
  Wake up, wake up, break out in song!
Arise, Barak!
  Take captive your captives, son of
    Abinoam.'

¹³"The remnant of the nobles came down;
  the people of the LORD came down to
    me against the mighty.
¹⁴Some came from Ephraim, whose roots
    were in Amalek;
  Benjamin was with the people who
    followed you.
From Makir captains came down,
  from Zebulun those who bear a
    commander'sᵇ staff.
¹⁵The princes of Issachar were with
    Deborah;
  yes, Issachar was with Barak,
  sent under his command into the
    valley.
In the districts of Reuben
  there was much searching of heart.
¹⁶Why did you stay among the sheep pensᶜ
  to hear the whistling for the flocks?
In the districts of Reuben
  there was much searching of heart.
¹⁷Gilead stayed beyond the Jordan.
  And Dan, why did he linger by the
    ships?
Asher remained on the coast
  and stayed in his coves.
¹⁸The people of Zebulun risked their very
    lives;
  so did Naphtali on the terraced fields.

¹⁹"Kings came, they fought,
  the kings of Canaan fought.
At Taanach, by the waters of Megiddo,
  they took no plunder of silver.

ᵃ 3 Or *of*   *ᵇ 11,14* The meaning of the Hebrew for this word is uncertain.   *ᶜ 16* Or *the campfires*; or *the saddlebags*

²⁰ From the heavens the stars fought,
   from their courses they fought against
      Sisera.
²¹ The river Kishon swept them away,
   the age-old river, the river Kishon.
   March on, my soul; be strong!
²² Then thundered the horses' hooves—
   galloping, galloping go his mighty
      steeds.
²³ 'Curse Meroz,' said the angel of the Lord.
   'Curse its people bitterly,
   because they did not come to help the
      Lord,
      to help the Lord against the mighty.'

²⁴ "Most blessed of women be Jael,
   the wife of Heber the Kenite,
   most blessed of tent-dwelling
      women.
²⁵ He asked for water, and she gave him
      milk;
   in a bowl fit for nobles she brought
      him curdled milk.
²⁶ Her hand reached for the tent peg,
   her right hand for the laborer's
      hammer.
   She struck Sisera, she crushed his head,
   she shattered and pierced his temple.
²⁷ At her feet he sank,
   he fell; there he lay.
   At her feet he sank, he fell;
   where he sank, there he fell—dead.

²⁸ "Through the window peered Sisera's
      mother;
   behind the lattice she cried out,
   'Why is his chariot so long in coming?
   Why is the clatter of his chariots
      delayed?'
²⁹ The wisest of her ladies answer her;
   indeed, she keeps saying to herself,
³⁰ 'Are they not finding and dividing the
      spoils:
   a woman or two for each man,
   colorful garments as plunder for Sisera,
   colorful garments embroidered,
   highly embroidered garments for my
      neck—
   all this as plunder?'

³¹ "So may all your enemies perish, Lord!
   But may all who love you be like the
      sun
   when it rises in its strength."

Then the land had peace forty years.

Gideon

6 The Israelites did evil in the eyes of the Lord, and for seven years he gave them into the hands of the Midianites. ²Because the power of Midian was so oppressive, the Israelites prepared shelters for themselves in mountain clefts, caves and strongholds. ³Whenever the Israelites planted their crops, the Midianites, Amalekites and other eastern peoples invaded the country. ⁴They camped on the land and ruined the crops all the way to Gaza and did not spare a living thing for Israel, neither sheep nor cattle nor donkeys. ⁵They came up with their livestock and their tents like swarms of locusts. It was impossible to count them or their camels; they invaded the land to ravage it. ⁶Midian so impoverished the Israelites that they cried out to the Lord for help.

⁷When the Israelites cried out to the Lord because of Midian, ⁸he sent them a prophet, who said, "This is what the Lord, the God of Israel, says: I brought you up out of Egypt, out of the land of slavery. ⁹I rescued you from the hand of the Egyptians. And I delivered you from the hand of all your oppressors; I drove them out before you and gave you their land. ¹⁰I said to you, 'I am the Lord your God; do not worship the gods of the Amorites, in whose land you live.' But you have not listened to me."

¹¹The angel of the Lord came and sat down under the oak in Ophrah that belonged to Joash the Abiezrite, where his son Gideon was threshing wheat in a winepress to keep it from the Midianites. ¹²When the angel of the Lord appeared to Gideon, he said, "The Lord is with you, mighty warrior."

¹³"Pardon me, my lord," Gideon replied, "but if the Lord is with us, why has all this happened to us? Where are all his wonders that our ancestors told us about when they said, 'Did not the Lord bring us up out of Egypt?' But now the Lord has abandoned us and given us into the hand of Midian."

¹⁴The Lord turned to him and said, "Go in the strength you have and save Israel out of Midian's hand. Am I not sending you?"

¹⁵"Pardon me, my lord," Gideon replied, "but how can I save Israel? My clan is the weakest in Manasseh, and I am the least in my family."

¹⁶The Lord answered, "I will be with you,

Success From the Inside

Judges 6:1–24 or 6:11–16

Adrian Plass

I suppose angels get used to carrying out daft-sounding orders without question. This one must have been amazed when he was told to go and address Gideon, of all people, as "Mighty Warrior." Gideon was singularly unimpressed, wasn't he? So would I have been, if I was the least important member of the least important family in the whole community, and some stranger with an advanced case of religious mania had solemnly announced that I was going to defeat the entire opposing army as if they were one man. I'd have been on the phone to the local psychiatric facility insisting that they check numbers. And even if this was a messenger from the Lord, there was little recent evidence to suggest that God had either the power or the inclination to intervene as he had done in the past.

Gideon was going to take a lot of convincing, and I don't blame him. I know how it feels to be inwardly programmed for failure. I have felt small and useless. I've experienced the gnawing fear that when some awful crunch situation comes along I shall betray the people who rely on me most. Sometimes, usually in the middle of the night, I'm gripped by panic as my imagination pumps out grisly scenes in which members of my family die dreadful deaths while I stand uselessly aside, paralyzed by fear and inadequacy . . .

I suspect that we would be well-advised to concentrate on developing our closeness to Jesus, rather than dwelling gloomily on the probability that we will let him down, because it will be the reality or otherwise of that relationship that makes the difference when the crunch comes.

Alexander MacLaren {ad 1826–1910}

Just as a little child nestling on its mother's bosom, with its mother's arm around it, looks out with peaceful eye and a bright smile upon everything beyond the safe nest, so they who are near to God can bear to look at difficulties and perplexities, and the mysteries of their own sorrows and of the world's miseries, and say, "All things work together for good."

reflection

1. Have you ever felt like God asked you to do something that there was "no way" you could possibly do?

2. In what ways do you identify with Gideon and his insecurities?

3. How has God worked good from your weaknesses?

For your next devotional reading, go to page 284.

and you will strike down all the Midianites together."

¹⁷Gideon replied, "If now I have found favor in your eyes, give me a sign that it is really you talking to me. ¹⁸Please do not go away until I come back and bring my offering and set it before you."

And the Lord said, "I will wait until you return."

¹⁹Gideon went in, prepared a young goat, and from an ephah^a of flour he made bread without yeast. Putting the meat in a basket and its broth in a pot, he brought them out and offered them to him under the oak.

²⁰The angel of God said to him, "Take the meat and the unleavened bread, place them on this rock, and pour out the broth." And Gideon did so. ²¹With the tip of the staff that was in his hand, the angel of the Lord touched the meat and the unleavened bread. Fire flared from the rock, consuming the meat and the bread. And the angel of the Lord disappeared. ²²When Gideon realized that it was the angel of the Lord, he exclaimed, "Ah, Sovereign Lord! I have seen the angel of the Lord face to face!"

²³But the Lord said to him, "Peace! Do not be afraid. You are not going to die."

²⁴So Gideon built an altar to the Lord there and called it The Lord Is Peace. To this day it stands in Ophrah of the Abiezrites.

²⁵That same night the Lord said to him, "Take the second bull from your father's herd, the one seven years old.^b Tear down your father's altar to Baal and cut down the Asherah pole^c beside it. ²⁶Then build a proper kind of^d altar to the Lord your God on the top of this height. Using the wood of the Asherah pole that you cut down, offer the second^e bull as a burnt offering."

²⁷So Gideon took ten of his servants and did as the Lord told him. But because he was afraid of his family and the townspeople, he did it at night rather than in the daytime.

²⁸In the morning when the people of the town got up, there was Baal's altar, demolished, with the Asherah pole beside it cut down and the second bull sacrificed on the newly built altar!

²⁹They asked each other, "Who did this?"

When they carefully investigated, they were told, "Gideon son of Joash did it."

³⁰The people of the town demanded of Joash, "Bring out your son. He must die, because he has broken down Baal's altar and cut down the Asherah pole beside it."

³¹But Joash replied to the hostile crowd around him, "Are you going to plead Baal's cause? Are you trying to save him? Whoever fights for him shall be put to death by morning! If Baal really is a god, he can defend himself when someone breaks down his altar." ³²So that day they gave Gideon the name Jerub-Baal,^f saying, "Let Baal contend with him," because he broke down Baal's altar.

³³Now all the Midianites, Amalekites and other eastern peoples joined forces and crossed over the Jordan and camped in the Valley of Jezreel. ³⁴Then the Spirit of the Lord came on Gideon, and he blew a trumpet, summoning the Abiezrites to follow him. ³⁵He sent messengers throughout Manasseh, calling them to arms, and also into Asher, Zebulun and Naphtali, so that they too went up to meet them.

³⁶Gideon said to God, "If you will save Israel by my hand as you have promised— ³⁷look, I will place a wool fleece on the threshing floor. If there is dew only on the fleece and all the ground is dry, then I will know that you will save Israel by my hand, as you said." ³⁸And that is what happened. Gideon rose early the next day; he squeezed the fleece and wrung out the dew—a bowlful of water.

³⁹Then Gideon said to God, "Do not be angry with me. Let me make just one more request. Allow me one more test with the fleece, but this time make the fleece dry and let the ground be covered with dew." ⁴⁰That night God did so. Only the fleece was dry; all the ground was covered with dew.

Gideon Defeats the Midianites

7 Early in the morning, Jerub-Baal (that is, Gideon) and all his men camped at the spring of Harod. The camp of Midian was north of them in the valley near the hill of Moreh. ²The Lord said to Gideon, "You have too many men. I cannot deliver

---

^a 19 That is, probably about 36 pounds or about 16 kilograms   ^b 25 Or Take a full-grown, mature bull from your father's herd   ^c 25 That is, a wooden symbol of the goddess Asherah; also in verses 26, 28 and 30   ^d 26 Or build with layers of stone an   ^e 26 Or full-grown; also in verse 28   ^f 32 Jerub-Baal probably means let Baal contend.

Midian into their hands, or Israel would boast against me, 'My own strength has saved me.' ³Now announce to the army, 'Anyone who trembles with fear may turn back and leave Mount Gilead.' " So twenty-two thousand men left, while ten thousand remained.

⁴But the LORD said to Gideon, "There are still too many men. Take them down to the water, and I will sift them for you there. If I say, 'This one shall go with you,' he shall go; but if I say, 'This one shall not go with you,' he shall not go."

⁵So Gideon took the men down to the water. There the LORD told him, "Separate those who lap the water with their tongues like a dog from those who kneel down to drink." ⁶Three hundred of them lapped with their hands to their mouths. All the rest got down on their knees to drink.

⁷The LORD said to Gideon, "With the three hundred men that lapped I will save you and give the Midianites into your hands. Let all the others go, each to his own place." ⁸So Gideon sent the rest of the Israelites to their tents but kept the three hundred, who took over the provisions and trumpets of the others.

Now the camp of Midian lay below him in the valley. ⁹During that night the LORD said to Gideon, "Get up, go down against the camp, because I am going to give it into your hands. ¹⁰If you are afraid to attack, go down to the camp with your servant Purah ¹¹and listen to what they are saying. Afterward, you will be encouraged to attack the camp." So he and Purah his servant went down to the outposts of the camp. ¹²The Midianites, the Amalekites and all the other eastern peoples had settled in the valley, thick as locusts. Their camels could no more be counted than the sand on the seashore.

¹³Gideon arrived just as a man was telling a friend his dream. "I had a dream," he was saying. "A round loaf of barley bread came tumbling into the Midianite camp. It struck the tent with such force that the tent over-turned and collapsed."

¹⁴His friend responded, "This can be nothing other than the sword of Gideon son of Joash, the Israelite. God has given the Midianites and the whole camp into his hands."

¹⁵When Gideon heard the dream and its interpretation, he bowed down and wor-shiped. He returned to the camp of Israel and called out, "Get up! The LORD has given the Midianite camp into your hands." ¹⁶Dividing the three hundred men into three companies, he placed trumpets and empty jars in the hands of all of them, with torch-es inside.

¹⁷"Watch me," he told them. "Follow my lead. When I get to the edge of the camp, do exactly as I do. ¹⁸When I and all who are with me blow our trumpets, then from all around the camp blow yours and shout, 'For the LORD and for Gideon.' "

¹⁹Gideon and the hundred men with him reached the edge of the camp at the begin-ning of the middle watch, just after they had changed the guard. They blew their trum-pets and broke the jars that were in their hands. ²⁰The three companies blew the trumpets and smashed the jars. Grasping the torches in their left hands and holding in their right hands the trumpets they were to blow, they shouted, "A sword for the LORD and for Gideon!" ²¹While each man held his position around the camp, all the Midianites ran, crying out as they fled.

²²When the three hundred trumpets sounded, the LORD caused the men through-out the camp to turn on each other with their swords. The army fled to Beth Shittah toward Zererah as far as the border of Abel Meholah near Tabbath. ²³Israelites from Naphtali, Asher and all Manasseh were called out, and they pursued the Midianites. ²⁴Gideon sent messengers throughout the hill country of Ephraim, saying, "Come down against the Midianites and seize the waters of the Jordan ahead of them as far as Beth Barah."

So all the men of Ephraim were called out and they seized the waters of the Jordan as far as Beth Barah. ²⁵They also captured two of the Midianite leaders, Oreb and Zeeb. They killed Oreb at the rock of Oreb, and Zeeb at the winepress of Zeeb. They pursued the Midianites and brought the heads of Oreb and Zeeb to Gideon, who was by the Jordan.

Zebah and Zalmunna

8 Now the Ephraimites asked Gideon, "Why have you treated us like this? Why didn't you call us when you went to fight Midian?" And they challenged him vigorously.

²But he answered them, "What have I ac-

complished compared to you? Aren't the gleanings of Ephraim's grapes better than the full grape harvest of Abiezer? ³God gave Oreb and Zeeb, the Midianite leaders, into your hands. What was I able to do compared to you?" At this, their resentment against him subsided.

⁴Gideon and his three hundred men, exhausted yet keeping up the pursuit, came to the Jordan and crossed it. ⁵He said to the men of Sukkoth, "Give my troops some bread; they are worn out, and I am still pursuing Zebah and Zalmunna, the kings of Midian."

⁶But the officials of Sukkoth said, "Do you already have the hands of Zebah and Zalmunna in your possession? Why should we give bread to your troops?"

⁷Then Gideon replied, "Just for that, when the LORD has given Zebah and Zalmunna into my hand, I will tear your flesh with desert thorns and briers."

⁸From there he went up to Peniel*ᵃ* and made the same request of them, but they answered as the men of Sukkoth had. ⁹So he said to the men of Peniel, "When I return in triumph, I will tear down this tower."

¹⁰Now Zebah and Zalmunna were in Karkor with a force of about fifteen thousand men, all that were left of the armies of the eastern peoples; a hundred and twenty thousand swordsmen had fallen. ¹¹Gideon went up by the route of the nomads east of Nobah and Jogbehah and attacked the unsuspecting army. ¹²Zebah and Zalmunna, the two kings of Midian, fled, but he pursued them and captured them, routing their entire army.

¹³Gideon son of Joash then returned from the battle by the Pass of Heres. ¹⁴He caught a young man of Sukkoth and questioned him, and the young man wrote down for him the names of the seventy-seven officials of Sukkoth, the elders of the town. ¹⁵Then Gideon came and said to the men of Sukkoth, "Here are Zebah and Zalmunna, about whom you taunted me by saying, 'Do you already have the hands of Zebah and Zalmunna in your possession? Why should we give bread to your exhausted troops?'" ¹⁶He took the elders of the town and taught the men of Sukkoth a lesson by punishing

them with desert thorns and briers. ¹⁷He also pulled down the tower of Peniel and killed the men of the town.

¹⁸Then he asked Zebah and Zalmunna, "What kind of men did you kill at Tabor?"

"Men like you," they answered, "each one with the bearing of a prince."

¹⁹Gideon replied, "Those were my brothers, the sons of my own mother. As surely as the LORD lives, if you had spared their lives, I would not kill you." ²⁰Turning to Jether, his oldest son, he said, "Kill them!" But Jether did not draw his sword, because he was only a boy and was afraid.

²¹Zebah and Zalmunna said, "Come, do it yourself. 'As is the man, so is his strength.'" So Gideon stepped forward and killed them, and took the ornaments off their camels' necks.

Gideon's Ephod

²²The Israelites said to Gideon, "Rule over us—you, your son and your grandson—because you have saved us from the hand of Midian."

²³But Gideon told them, "I will not rule over you, nor will my son rule over you. The LORD will rule over you." ²⁴And he said, "I do have one request, that each of you give me an earring from your share of the plunder." (It was the custom of the Ishmaelites to wear gold earrings.)

²⁵They answered, "We'll be glad to give them." So they spread out a garment, and each of them threw a ring from his plunder onto it. ²⁶The weight of the gold rings he asked for came to seventeen hundred shekels,*ᵇ* not counting the ornaments, the pendants and the purple garments worn by the kings of Midian or the chains that were on their camels' necks. ²⁷Gideon made the gold into an ephod, which he placed in Ophrah, his town. All Israel prostituted themselves by worshiping it there, and it became a snare to Gideon and his family.

Gideon's Death

²⁸Thus Midian was subdued before the Israelites and did not raise its head again. During Gideon's lifetime, the land had peace forty years.

²⁹Jerub-Baal son of Joash went back

ᵃ 8 Hebrew *Penuel*, a variant of *Peniel*; also in verses 9 and 17   *ᵇ* 26 That is, about 43 pounds or about 20 kilograms home to live. ³⁰He had seventy sons of his own, for he had many wives. ³¹His concubine, who lived in Shechem, also bore him a son, whom he named Abimelek. ³²Gideon son of Joash died at a good old age and was buried in the tomb of his father Joash in Ophrah of the Abiezrites.

³³No sooner had Gideon died than the Israelites again prostituted themselves to the Baals. They set up Baal-Berith as their god ³⁴and did not remember the LORD their God, who had rescued them from the hands of all their enemies on every side. ³⁵They also failed to show any loyalty to the family of Jerub-Baal (that is, Gideon) in spite of all the good things he had done for them.

Abimelek

9 Abimelek son of Jerub-Baal went to his mother's brothers in Shechem and said to them and to all his mother's clan, ²"Ask all the citizens of Shechem, 'Which is better for you: to have all seventy of Jerub-Baal's sons rule over you, or just one man?' Remember, I am your flesh and blood."

³When the brothers repeated all this to the citizens of Shechem, they were inclined to follow Abimelek, for they said, "He is related to us." ⁴They gave him seventy shekels^a of silver from the temple of Baal-Berith, and Abimelek used it to hire reckless scoundrels, who became his followers. ⁵He went to his father's home in Ophrah and on one stone murdered his seventy brothers, the sons of Jerub-Baal. But Jotham, the youngest son of Jerub-Baal, escaped by hiding. ⁶Then all the citizens of Shechem and Beth Millo gathered beside the great tree at the pillar in Shechem to crown Abimelek king.

⁷When Jotham was told about this, he climbed up on the top of Mount Gerizim and shouted to them, "Listen to me, citizens of Shechem, so that God may listen to you. ⁸One day the trees went out to anoint a king for themselves. They said to the olive tree, 'Be our king.'

⁹"But the olive tree answered, 'Should I give up my oil, by which both gods and human beings are honored, to hold sway over the trees?'

¹⁰"Next, the trees said to the fig tree, 'Come and be our king.'

¹¹"But the fig tree replied, 'Should I give up my fruit, so good and sweet, to hold sway over the trees?'

¹²"Then the trees said to the vine, 'Come and be our king.'

¹³"But the vine answered, 'Should I give up my wine, which cheers both gods and human beings, to hold sway over the trees?'

¹⁴"Finally all the trees said to the thornbush, 'Come and be our king.'

¹⁵"The thornbush said to the trees, 'If you really want to anoint me king over you, come and take refuge in my shade; but if not, then let fire come out of the thornbush and consume the cedars of Lebanon!'

¹⁶"Have you acted honorably and in good faith by making Abimelek king? Have you been fair to Jerub-Baal and his family? Have you treated him as he deserves? ¹⁷Remember that my father fought for you and risked his life to rescue you from the hand of Midian. ¹⁸But today you have revolted against my father's family. You have murdered his seventy sons on a single stone and have made Abimelek, the son of his female slave, king over the citizens of Shechem because he is related to you. ¹⁹So have you acted honorably and in good faith toward Jerub-Baal and his family today? If you have, may Abimelek be your joy, and may you be his, too! ²⁰But if you have not, let fire come out from Abimelek and consume you, the citizens of Shechem and Beth Millo, and let fire come out from you, the citizens of Shechem and Beth Millo, and consume Abimelek!"

²¹Then Jotham fled, escaping to Beer, and he lived there because he was afraid of his brother Abimelek.

²²After Abimelek had governed Israel three years, ²³God stirred up animosity between Abimelek and the citizens of Shechem so that they acted treacherously against Abimelek. ²⁴God did this in order that the crime against Jerub-Baal's seventy sons, the shedding of their blood, might be avenged on their brother Abimelek and on the citizens of Shechem, who had helped him murder his brothers. ²⁵In opposition to him these citizens of Shechem set an ambush on the hilltops to rob everyone who passed by, and this was reported to Abimelek.

²⁶Now Gaal son of Ebed moved with his

a 4 That is, about 1 3/4 pounds or about 800 grams

brothers into Shechem, and its citizens put their confidence in him. ²⁷After they had gone out into the fields and gathered the grapes and trodden them, they held a festival in the temple of their god. While they were eating and drinking, they cursed Abimelek. ²⁸Then Gaal son of Ebed said, "Who is Abimelek, and who is Shechem, that we should be subject to him? Isn't he Jerub-Baal's son, and isn't Zebul his deputy? Serve the people of Hamor, Shechem's father! Why should we serve Abimelek? ²⁹If only this people were under my command! Then I would get rid of him. I would say to Abimelek, 'Call out your whole army!' "ᵃ

³⁰When Zebul the governor of the city heard what Gaal son of Ebed said, he was very angry. ³¹Under cover he sent messengers to Abimelek, saying, "Gaal son of Ebed and his relatives have come to Shechem and are stirring up the city against you. ³²Now then, during the night you and your men should come and lie in wait in the fields. ³³In the morning at sunrise, advance against the city. When Gaal and his men come out against you, do whatever your hand finds to do."

³⁴So Abimelek and all his troops set out by night and took up concealed positions near Shechem in four companies. ³⁵Now Gaal son of Ebed had gone out and was standing at the entrance of the city gate just as Abimelek and his troops came out from their hiding place.

³⁶When Gaal saw them, he said to Zebul, "Look, people are coming down from the tops of the mountains!"

Zebul replied, "You mistake the shadows of the mountains for men."

³⁷But Gaal spoke up again: "Look, people are coming down from the central hill,ᵇ and a company is coming from the direction of the diviners' tree."

³⁸Then Zebul said to him, "Where is your big talk now, you who said, 'Who is Abimelek that we should be subject to him?' Aren't these the men you ridiculed? Go out and fight them!"

³⁹So Gaal led outᶜ the citizens of Shechem and fought Abimelek. ⁴⁰Abimelek chased him all the way to the entrance of the gate, and many fell slain as they fled.

⁴¹Abimelek stayed in Arumah, and Zebul drove Gaal and his relatives out of Shechem.

⁴²The next day the people of Shechem went out to the fields, and this was reported to Abimelek. ⁴³So he took his troops, divided them into three companies and set an ambush in the fields. When he saw the people coming out of the city, he rose to attack them. ⁴⁴Abimelek and the companies with him rushed forward to a position at the entrance of the city gate. Then two companies attacked those in the fields and struck them down. ⁴⁵All that day Abimelek pressed his attack against the city until he had captured it and killed its people. Then he destroyed the city and scattered salt over it.

⁴⁶On hearing this, the citizens in the tower of Shechem went into the stronghold of the temple of El-Berith. ⁴⁷When Abimelek heard that they had assembled there, ⁴⁸he and all his men went up Mount Zalmon. He took an ax and cut off some branches, which he lifted to his shoulders. He ordered the men with him, "Quick! Do what you have seen me do!" ⁴⁹So all the men cut branches and followed Abimelek. They piled them against the stronghold and set it on fire with the people still inside. So all the people in the tower of Shechem, about a thousand men and women, also died.

⁵⁰Next Abimelek went to Thebez and besieged it and captured it. ⁵¹Inside the city, however, was a strong tower, to which all the men and women—all the people of the city—had fled. They had locked themselves in and climbed up on the tower roof. ⁵²Abimelek went to the tower and attacked it. But as he approached the entrance to the tower to set it on fire, ⁵³a woman dropped an upper millstone on his head and cracked his skull.

⁵⁴Hurriedly he called to his armor-bearer, "Draw your sword and kill me, so that they can't say, 'A woman killed him.' " So his servant ran him through, and he died. ⁵⁵When the Israelites saw that Abimelek was dead, they went home.

⁵⁶Thus God repaid the wickedness that Abimelek had done to his father by murdering his seventy brothers. ⁵⁷God also made the people of Shechem pay for all their

---

a 29 Septuagint; Hebrew *him." Then he said to Abimelek, "Call out your whole army!"*   *b 37* The Hebrew for this phrase means *the navel of the earth.*   *c 39* Or *Gaal went out in the sight of* wickedness. The curse of Jotham son of Jer-ub-Baal came on them.

Tola

10 After the time of Abimelek, a man of Issachar named Tola son of Puah, the son of Dodo, rose to save Israel. He lived in Shamir, in the hill country of Ephraim. ²He led*a* Israel twenty-three years; then he died, and was buried in Shamir.

Jair

³He was followed by Jair of Gilead, who led Israel twenty-two years. ⁴He had thirty sons, who rode thirty donkeys. They controlled thirty towns in Gilead, which to this day are called Havvoth Jair.*b* ⁵When Jair died, he was buried in Kamon.

Jephthah

⁶Again the Israelites did evil in the eyes of the LORD. They served the Baals and the Ashtoreths, and the gods of Aram, the gods of Sidon, the gods of Moab, the gods of the Ammonites and the gods of the Philistines. And because the Israelites forsook the LORD and no longer served him, ⁷he became angry with them. He sold them into the hands of the Philistines and the Ammonites, ⁸who that year shattered and crushed them. For eighteen years they oppressed all the Israelites on the east side of the Jordan in Gilead, the land of the Amorites. ⁹The Ammonites also crossed the Jordan to fight against Judah, Benjamin and the house of Ephraim; and Israel was in great distress. ¹⁰Then the Israelites cried out to the LORD, "We have sinned against you, forsaking our God and serving the Baals."

¹¹The LORD replied, "When the Egyptians, the Amorites, the Ammonites, the Philistines, ¹²the Sidonians, the Amalekites and the Maonites*c* oppressed you and you cried to me for help, did I not save you from their hands? ¹³But you have forsaken me and served other gods, so I will no longer save you. ¹⁴Go and cry out to the gods you have chosen. Let them save you when you are in trouble!"

¹⁵But the Israelites said to the LORD, "We have sinned. Do with us whatever you think best, but please rescue us now." ¹⁶Then they got rid of the foreign gods among them and served the LORD. And he could bear Israel's misery no longer.

¹⁷When the Ammonites were called to arms and camped in Gilead, the Israelites assembled and camped at Mizpah. ¹⁸The leaders of the people of Gilead said to each other, "Whoever will take the lead in attacking the Ammonites will be head over all who live in Gilead."

11 Jephthah the Gileadite was a mighty warrior. His father was Gilead; his mother was a prostitute. ²Gilead's wife also bore him sons, and when they were grown up, they drove Jephthah away. "You are not going to get any inheritance in our family," they said, "because you are the son of another woman." ³So Jephthah fled from his brothers and settled in the land of Tob, where a gang of scoundrels gathered around him and followed him.

⁴Some time later, when the Ammonites were fighting against Israel, ⁵the elders of Gilead went to get Jephthah from the land of Tob. ⁶"Come," they said, "be our commander, so we can fight the Ammonites."

⁷Jephthah said to them, "Didn't you hate me and drive me from my father's house? Why do you come to me now, when you're in trouble?"

⁸The elders of Gilead said to him, "Nevertheless, we are turning to you now; come with us to fight the Ammonites, and you will be head over all of us who live in Gilead."

⁹Jephthah answered, "Suppose you take me back to fight the Ammonites and the LORD gives them to me—will I really be your head?"

¹⁰The elders of Gilead replied, "The LORD is our witness; we will certainly do as you say." ¹¹So Jephthah went with the elders of Gilead, and the people made him head and commander over them. And he repeated all his words before the LORD in Mizpah.

¹²Then Jephthah sent messengers to the Ammonite king with the question: "What do you have against me that you have attacked my country?"

¹³The king of the Ammonites answered Jephthah's messengers, "When Israel came up out of Egypt, they took away my land

THE MYSTERY OF EVIL

Judges 10:6–14 *or* Judges 10:6

JAMES STEWART {AD 1896–1990}

God has created his world in such a way that sin and suffering are possibilities. But to hold, as some good people do, that God is the direct and immediate cause of everything that happens and, therefore, the cause of all the evil things that happen—that kind of rigid determinism, that almost mechanical predestination—affronts our moral sense and makes nonsense of the fact of human freedom.

Justo Gonzalez

The question of the origin of evil has puzzled and perturbed philosophical minds for centuries. The problem is in the difficulty in affirming three points that seem to be mutually contradictory: (1) God is good; (2) God is all powerful; (3) evil is real. Every solution that has been proposed throughout history simply ignores or minimizes one of these three points. Atheists use the existence of evil in order to deny the existence of a good and powerful God. Christian Science denies the existence of evil, attributing it to our imagination ... Some limit God's power claiming that God had to create free human beings, and that this required the possibility of sin.

Even though it would be very pleasant and edifying to claim the opposite, the truth is that the Bible does not offer a solution to this problem. If we say that the explanation lies in the human being, who introduced sin into creation, there still remains the question of the serpent and its origin. If we claim, as has sometimes been said by Christian tradition, that the serpent is Lucifer, who is a fallen angel, all that we have done is postpone the question, for one must still ask why God did not simply make angels who could not fall. Thus, what the Bible offers is not an explanation of the origin of evil so as to satisfy our intellectual curiosity, but rather an affirmation that evil is real, and that it draws us as well as all of creation away from the divine purposes.

reflection

1. Though we don't understand the beginning of evil, we do hold on to the promise that God will overcome evil. How did Jesus' death and resurrection gain the victory over evil?

2. How would you respond to someone who believed there's no such thing as evil, that "good" and "evil" are arbitrary standards?

3. How do you determine whether or not something's "evil"?

For your next devotional reading, go to page 290.

from the Arnon to the Jabbok, all the way to the Jordan. Now give it back peaceably."

[14]Jephthah sent back messengers to the Ammonite king, [15]saying:

"This is what Jephthah says: Israel did not take the land of Moab or the land of the Ammonites. [16]But when they came up out of Egypt, Israel went through the wilderness to the Red Sea[a] and on to Kadesh. [17]Then Israel sent messengers to the king of Edom, saying, 'Give us permission to go through your country,' but the king of Edom would not listen. They sent also to the king of Moab, and he refused. So Israel stayed at Kadesh.

[18]"Next they traveled through the wilderness, skirted the lands of Edom and Moab, passed along the eastern side of the country of Moab, and camped on the other side of the Arnon. They did not enter the territory of Moab, for the Arnon was its border.

[19]"Then Israel sent messengers to Sihon king of the Amorites, who ruled in Heshbon, and said to him, 'Let us pass through your country to our own place.' [20]Sihon, however, did not trust Israel[b] to pass through his territory. He mustered all his army and encamped at Jahaz and fought with Israel.

[21]"Then the LORD, the God of Israel, gave Sihon and his whole army into Israel's hands, and they defeated them. Israel took over all the land of the Amorites who lived in that country, [22]capturing all of it from the Arnon to the Jabbok and from the desert to the Jordan.

[23]"Now since the LORD, the God of Israel, has driven the Amorites out before his people Israel, what right have you to take it over? [24]Will you not take what your god Chemosh gives you? Likewise, whatever the LORD our God has given us, we will possess. [25]Are you any better than Balak son of Zippor, king of Moab? Did he ever quarrel with Israel or fight with them? [26]For three hundred years Israel occupied Heshbon, Aroer, the surrounding settlements and all the towns along the Arnon. Why didn't you retake them

during that time? [27]I have not wronged you, but you are doing me wrong by waging war against me. Let the LORD, the Judge,[c] decide the dispute this day between the Israelites and the Ammonites."

[28]The king of Ammon, however, paid no attention to the message Jephthah sent him.

[29]Then the Spirit of the LORD came on Jephthah. He crossed Gilead and Manasseh, passed through Mizpah of Gilead, and from there he advanced against the Ammonites. [30]And Jephthah made a vow to the LORD: "If you give the Ammonites into my hands, [31]whatever comes out of the door of my house to meet me when I return in triumph from the Ammonites will be the LORD's, and I will sacrifice it as a burnt offering."

[32]Then Jephthah went over to fight the Ammonites, and the LORD gave them into his hands. [33]He devastated twenty towns from Aroer to the vicinity of Minnith, as far as Abel Keramim. Thus Israel subdued Ammon.

[34]When Jephthah returned to his home in Mizpah, who should come out to meet him but his daughter, dancing to the sound of timbrels! She was an only child. Except for her he had neither son nor daughter. [35]When he saw her, he tore his clothes and cried, "Oh! My daughter! You have brought me down and I am devastated. I have made a vow to the LORD that I cannot break."

[36]"My father," she replied, "you have given your word to the LORD. Do to me just as you promised, now that the LORD has avenged you of your enemies, the Ammonites. [37]But grant me this one request," she said. "Give me two months to roam the hills and weep with my friends, because I will never marry."

[38]"You may go," he said. And he let her go for two months. She and her friends went into the hills and wept because she would never marry. [39]After the two months, she returned to her father, and he did to her as he had vowed. And she was a virgin.

From this comes the Israelite tradition [40]that each year the young women of Israel go out for four days to commemorate the daughter of Jephthah the Gileadite.

Jephthah and Ephraim

12 The Ephraimite forces were called out, and they crossed over to Zaphon and said to Jephthah, "Why did you go to fight the Ammonites without calling us to go with you? We're going to burn down your house over your head."

²Jephthah answered, "I and my people were engaged in a great struggle with the Ammonites, and although I called, you didn't save me out of their hands. ³When I saw that you wouldn't help, I took my life in my hands and crossed over to fight the Ammonites, and the LORD gave me the victory over them. Now why have you come up today to fight me?"

⁴Jephthah then called together the men of Gilead and fought against Ephraim. The Gileadites struck them down because the Ephraimites had said, "You Gileadites are renegades from Ephraim and Manasseh." ⁵The Gileadites captured the fords of the Jordan leading to Ephraim, and whenever a survivor of Ephraim said, "Let me cross over," the Gileadites asked him, "Are you an Ephraimite?" If he replied, "No," ⁶they said, "All right, say 'Shibboleth.'" If he said, "Sibboleth," because he could not pronounce the word correctly, they seized him and killed him at the fords of the Jordan. Forty-two thousand Ephraimites were killed at that time.

⁷Jephthah led*ᵃ* Israel six years. Then Jephthah the Gileadite died and was buried in a town in Gilead.

Ibzan, Elon and Abdon

⁸After him, Ibzan of Bethlehem led Israel. ⁹He had thirty sons and thirty daughters. He gave his daughters away in marriage to those outside his clan, and for his sons he brought in thirty young women as wives from outside his clan. Ibzan led Israel seven years. ¹⁰Then Ibzan died and was buried in Bethlehem.

¹¹After him, Elon the Zebulunite led Israel ten years. ¹²Then Elon died and was buried in Aijalon in the land of Zebulun.

¹³After him, Abdon son of Hillel, from Pirathon, led Israel. ¹⁴He had forty sons and thirty grandsons, who rode on seventy donkeys. He led Israel eight years. ¹⁵Then Abdon son of Hillel died and was buried at Pirathon

in Ephraim, in the hill country of the Amalekites.

The Birth of Samson

13 Again the Israelites did evil in the eyes of the LORD, so the LORD delivered them into the hands of the Philistines for forty years.

²A certain man of Zorah, named Manoah, from the clan of the Danites, had a wife who was childless, unable to give birth. ³The angel of the LORD appeared to her and said, "You are barren and childless, but you are going to become pregnant and give birth to a son. ⁴Now see to it that you drink no wine or other fermented drink and that you do not eat anything unclean. ⁵You will become pregnant and have a son whose head is never to be touched by a razor because the boy is to be a Nazirite, dedicated to God from the womb. He will begin to deliver Israel from the hands of the Philistines."

⁶Then the woman went to her husband and told him, "A man of God came to me. He looked like an angel of God, very awesome. I didn't ask him where he came from, and he didn't tell me his name. ⁷But he said to me, 'You will become pregnant and have a son. Now then, drink no wine or other fermented drink and do not eat anything unclean, because the boy will be a Nazirite of God from the womb until the day of his death.'"

⁸Then Manoah prayed to the LORD: "Pardon your servant, Lord. I beg you to let the man of God you sent to us come again to teach us how to bring up the boy who is to be born."

⁹God heard Manoah, and the angel of God came again to the woman while she was out in the field; but her husband Manoah was not with her. ¹⁰The woman hurried to tell her husband, "He's here! The man who appeared to me the other day!"

¹¹Manoah got up and followed his wife. When he came to the man, he said, "Are you the man who talked to my wife?"

"I am," he said.

¹²So Manoah asked him, "When your words are fulfilled, what is to be the rule that governs the boy's life and work?"

¹³The angel of the LORD answered, "Your wife must do all that I have told her. ¹⁴She must not eat anything that comes from the

---

ᵃ 7 Traditionally judged; also in verses 8-14

grapevine, nor drink any wine or other fermented drink nor eat anything unclean. She must do everything I have commanded her."

¹⁵Manoah said to the angel of the LORD, "We would like you to stay until we prepare a young goat for you."

¹⁶The angel of the LORD replied, "Even though you detain me, I will not eat any of your food. But if you prepare a burnt offering, offer it to the LORD." (Manoah did not realize that it was the angel of the LORD.)

¹⁷Then Manoah inquired of the angel of the LORD, "What is your name, so that we may honor you when your word comes true?"

¹⁸He replied, "Why do you ask my name? It is beyond understanding.ᵃ" ¹⁹Then Manoah took a young goat, together with the grain offering, and sacrificed it on a rock to the LORD. And the LORD did an amazing thing while Manoah and his wife watched: ²⁰As the flame blazed up from the altar toward heaven, the angel of the LORD ascended in the flame. Seeing this, Manoah and his wife fell with their faces to the ground. ²¹When the angel of the LORD did not show himself again to Manoah and his wife, Manoah realized that it was the angel of the LORD.

²²"We are doomed to die!" he said to his wife. "We have seen God!"

²³But his wife answered, "If the LORD had meant to kill us, he would not have accepted a burnt offering and grain offering from our hands, nor shown us all these things or now told us this."

²⁴The woman gave birth to a boy and named him Samson. He grew and the LORD blessed him, ²⁵and the Spirit of the LORD began to stir him while he was in Mahaneh Dan, between Zorah and Eshtaol.

Samson's Marriage

14 Samson went down to Timnah and saw there a young Philistine woman. ²When he returned, he said to his father and mother, "I have seen a Philistine woman in Timnah; now get her for me as my wife."

³His father and mother replied, "Isn't there an acceptable woman among your relatives or among all our people? Must you go to the uncircumcised Philistines to get a wife?"

But Samson said to his father, "Get her for me. She's the right one for me." ⁴(His parents did not know that this was from the LORD, who was seeking an occasion to confront the Philistines; for at that time they were ruling over Israel.)

⁵Samson went down to Timnah together with his father and mother. As they approached the vineyards of Timnah, suddenly a young lion came roaring toward him. ⁶The Spirit of the LORD came on him in power so that he tore the lion apart with his bare hands as he might have torn a young goat. But he told neither his father nor his mother what he had done. ⁷Then he went down and talked with the woman, and he liked her.

⁸Some time later, when he went back to marry her, he turned aside to look at the lion's carcass, and in it he saw a swarm of bees and some honey. ⁹He scooped out the honey with his hands and ate as he went along. When he rejoined his parents, he gave them some, and they too ate it. But he did not tell them that he had taken the honey from the lion's carcass.

¹⁰Now his father went down to see the woman. And there Samson held a feast, as was customary for young men. ¹¹When the people saw him, they chose thirty men to be his companions.

¹²"Let me tell you a riddle," Samson said to them. "If you can give me the answer within the seven days of the feast, I will give you thirty linen garments and thirty sets of clothes. ¹³If you can't tell me the answer, you must give me thirty linen garments and thirty sets of clothes."

"Tell us your riddle," they said. "Let's hear it."

¹⁴He replied,

"Out of the eater, something to eat;
    out of the strong, something sweet."

For three days they could not give the answer.

¹⁵On the fourthᵇ day, they said to Samson's wife, "Coax your husband into explaining the riddle for us, or we will burn you and your father's household to death. Did you invite us here to steal our property?"

¹⁶Then Samson's wife threw herself on him, sobbing, "You hate me! You don't real-

---

ᵃ 18 Or *is wonderful*   ᵇ 15 Some Septuagint manuscripts and Syriac; Hebrew *seventh* ly love me. You've given my people a riddle, but you haven't told me the answer."

"I haven't even explained it to my father or mother," he replied, "so why should I explain it to you?" [17]She cried the whole seven days of the feast. So on the seventh day he finally told her, because she continued to press him. She in turn explained the riddle to her people.

[18]Before sunset on the seventh day the men of the town said to him,

"What is sweeter than honey?
What is stronger than a lion?"

Samson said to them,

"If you had not plowed with my heifer,
you would not have solved my riddle."

[19]Then the Spirit of the LORD came on him in power. He went down to Ashkelon, struck down thirty of their men, stripped them of everything and gave their clothes to those who had explained the riddle. Burning with anger, he returned to his father's home. [20]And Samson's wife was given to one of his companions who had attended him at the feast.

Samson's Vengeance on the Philistines

15 Later on, at the time of wheat harvest, Samson took a young goat and went to visit his wife. He said, "I'm going to my wife's room." But her father would not let him go in.

[2]"I was so sure you hated her," he said, "that I gave her to your companion. Isn't her younger sister more attractive? Take her instead."

[3]Samson said to them, "This time I have a right to get even with the Philistines; I will really harm them." [4]So he went out and caught three hundred foxes and tied them tail to tail in pairs. He then fastened a torch to every pair of tails, [5]lit the torches and let the foxes loose in the standing grain of the Philistines. He burned up the shocks and standing grain, together with the vineyards and olive groves.

[6]When the Philistines asked, "Who did this?" they were told, "Samson, the Timnite's son-in-law, because his wife was given to his companion."

So the Philistines went up and burned her and her father to death. [7]Samson said to them, "Since you've acted like this, I swear that I won't stop until I get my revenge on you." [8]He attacked them viciously and slaughtered many of them. Then he went down and stayed in a cave in the rock of Etam.

[9]The Philistines went up and camped in Judah, spreading out near Lehi. [10]The people of Judah asked, "Why have you come to fight us?"

"We have come to take Samson prisoner," they answered, "to do to him as he did to us."

[11]Then three thousand men from Judah went down to the cave in the rock of Etam and said to Samson, "Don't you realize that the Philistines are rulers over us? What have you done to us?"

He answered, "I merely did to them what they did to me."

[12]They said to him, "We've come to tie you up and hand you over to the Philistines."

Samson said, "Swear to me that you won't kill me yourselves."

[13]"Agreed," they answered. "We will only tie you up and hand you over to them. We will not kill you." So they bound him with two new ropes and led him up from the rock. [14]As he approached Lehi, the Philistines came toward him shouting. The Spirit of the LORD came on him in power. The ropes on his arms became like charred flax, and the bindings dropped from his hands. [15]Finding a fresh jawbone of a donkey, he grabbed it and struck down a thousand men.

[16]Then Samson said,

"With a donkey's jawbone
I have made donkeys of them. *a*
With a donkey's jawbone
I have killed a thousand men."

[17]When he finished speaking, he threw away the jawbone; and the place was called Ramath Lehi. *b*

[18]Because he was very thirsty, he cried out to the LORD, "You have given your servant this great victory. Must I now die of thirst and fall into the hands of the uncircumcised?" [19]Then God opened up the hol-

---

a 16 Or *made a heap or two*; the Hebrew for *donkey* sounds like the Hebrew for *heap*.   *b 17* *Ramath Lehi* means *jawbone hill*.

low place in Lehi, and water came out of it. When Samson drank, his strength returned and he revived. So the spring was called En Hakkore,[a] and it is still there in Lehi.

²⁰Samson led[b] Israel for twenty years in the days of the Philistines.

Samson and Delilah

16 One day Samson went to Gaza, where he saw a prostitute. He went in to spend the night with her. ²The people of Gaza were told, "Samson is here!" So they surrounded the place and lay in wait for him all night at the city gate. They made no move during the night, saying, "At dawn we'll kill him."

³But Samson lay there only until the middle of the night. Then he got up and took hold of the doors of the city gate, together with the two posts, and tore them loose, bar and all. He lifted them to his shoulders and carried them to the top of the hill that faces Hebron.

⁴Some time later, he fell in love with a woman in the Valley of Sorek whose name was Delilah. ⁵The rulers of the Philistines went to her and said, "See if you can lure him into showing you the secret of his great strength and how we can overpower him so we may tie him up and subdue him. Each one of us will give you eleven hundred shekels[c] of silver."

⁶So Delilah said to Samson, "Tell me the secret of your great strength and how you can be tied up and subdued."

⁷Samson answered her, "If anyone ties me with seven fresh thongs[d] that have not been dried, I'll become as weak as any other man."

⁸Then the rulers of the Philistines brought her seven fresh thongs that had not been dried, and she tied him with them. ⁹With men hidden in the room, she called to him, "Samson, the Philistines are upon you!" But he snapped the thongs as easily as a piece of string snaps when it comes close to a flame. So the secret of his strength was not discovered.

¹⁰Then Delilah said to Samson, "You have made a fool of me; you lied to me. Come now, tell me how you can be tied."

¹¹He said, "If anyone ties me securely with new ropes that have never been used, I'll become as weak as any other man."

¹²So Delilah took new ropes and tied him with them. Then, with men hidden in the room, she called to him, "Samson, the Philistines are upon you!" But he snapped the ropes off his arms as if they were threads.

¹³Delilah then said to Samson, "Until now, you have been making a fool of me and lying to me. Tell me how you can be tied."

He replied, "If you weave the seven braids of my head into the fabric ₍on the loom₎ and tighten it with the pin, I'll become as weak as any other man." So while he was sleeping, Delilah took the seven braids of his head, wove them into the fabric ¹⁴and[e] tightened it with the pin.

Again she called to him, "Samson, the Philistines are upon you!" He awoke from his sleep and pulled up the pin and the loom, with the fabric.

¹⁵Then she said to him, "How can you say, 'I love you,' when you won't confide in me? This is the third time you have made a fool of me and haven't told me the secret of your great strength." ¹⁶With such nagging she prodded him day after day until he was tired to death.

¹⁷So he told her everything. "No razor has ever been used on my head," he said, "because I have been a Nazirite dedicated to God from my mother's womb. If my head were shaved, my strength would leave me, and I would become as weak as any other man."

¹⁸When Delilah saw that he had told her everything, she sent word to the rulers of the Philistines, "Come back once more; he has told me everything." So the rulers of the Philistines returned with the silver in their hands. ¹⁹Having put him to sleep on her lap, she called for someone to shave off the seven braids of his hair, and so began to subdue him.[f] And his strength left him.

²⁰Then she called, "Samson, the Philistines are upon you!"

He awoke from his sleep and thought, "I'll go out as before and shake myself free." But he did not know that the LORD had left him.

---

a 19 En Hakkore means *caller's spring.*   *b 20* Traditionally *judged*   *c 5* That is, about 28 pounds or about 13 kilograms   *d 7* Or *bowstrings;* also in verses 8 and 9   *e 13,14* Some Septuagint manuscripts; Hebrew *"₍I can₎, if you weave the seven braids of my head into the fabric ₍on the loom₎." ¹⁴So she*   *f 19* Hebrew; some Septuagint manuscripts *and he began to weaken*

FRIDAY

THE PRIVILEGE OF DEVOTION

Judges 16:1–31 *or* 16:23–31

Bryce Morgan

A theological question probably posed more often in Sunday School than seminary is this: "Was Samson's strength really in his hair?" But while this question may seem juvenile on the surface, it speaks to a bigger and deeper issue, an issue worthy of academic debate. The story of Samson, like other stories in the Bible, includes elements that might appropriately be described as magical. In Judges 16 the Israelite Samson is seduced by the woman Delilah into revealing the secret of his great strength: his hair. Moments later, after Delilah had shaved his head, Israel's enemies the Philistines use this knowledge to capture Samson. After we learn that Samson's eyes have been gouged out, the author of Judges, in verse 22, mentions an incidental, but interesting development. We learn that Samson's hair had begun to grow again. Now if we were to understand that Samson's hair truly possessed magical properties, then this verse might be a subtle affirmation that Samson would ultimately avenge himself. And the conclusion of the story seems to confirm this interpretation. But to assume such an interpretation would be to miss the broader context of Judges 13 through 16. Samson never told Delilah that his strength came from his hair. What he revealed to her is that his hair was a token of his consecration to God. Subsequently, his loss of power came not from his lack of hair, but from his failure to guard his privileged devotion to God's service. As the last judge mentioned in the book of Judges, Samson represents all that is wrong about Israel in this period of their history. A man of great promise and power, Samson wasted his heavenly calling on pleasure and personal gain.

JOHN BRIGHT {AD 1908–1995}

The good times that we desire are times of freedom from disturbing bother—in which a man can read his paper without worrying, and get on with his business, can have gas for his car and the pleasures and luxuries which we all enjoy. Those, we would say, are good times. But perhaps from the divine point of view they are not. For the purpose of God for us is not the comfort of our bodies or the preservation of our interests, but the discipline of our spirits that we may become truly his people.

reflection

1. What physical comforts are most likely to distract you from your devotion to God?

2. Which distractions are so great that you find yourself helpless to resist their temptation?

3. What will help you decide when drastic action may be required to avoid those temptations?

For your next devotional reading, go to page 292.

²¹Then the Philistines seized him, gouged out his eyes and took him down to Gaza. Binding him with bronze shackles, they set him to grinding grain in the prison. ²²But the hair on his head began to grow again after it had been shaved.

The Death of Samson

²³Now the rulers of the Philistines assembled to offer a great sacrifice to Dagon their god and to celebrate, saying, "Our god has delivered Samson, our enemy, into our hands."

²⁴When the people saw him, they praised their god, saying,

"Our god has delivered our enemy
    into our hands,
the one who laid waste our land
    and multiplied our slain."

²⁵While they were in high spirits, they shouted, "Bring out Samson to entertain us." So they called Samson out of the prison, and he performed for them.

When they stood him among the pillars, ²⁶Samson said to the servant who held his hand, "Put me where I can feel the pillars that support the temple, so that I may lean against them." ²⁷Now the temple was crowded with men and women; all the rulers of the Philistines were there, and on the roof were about three thousand men and women watching Samson perform. ²⁸Then Samson prayed to the LORD, "Sovereign LORD, remember me. Please, God, strengthen me just once more, and let me with one blow get revenge on the Philistines for my two eyes." ²⁹Then Samson reached toward the two central pillars on which the temple stood. Bracing himself against them, his right hand on the one and his left hand on the other, ³⁰Samson said, "Let me die with the Philistines!" Then he pushed with all his might, and down came the temple on the rulers and all the people in it. Thus he killed many more when he died than while he lived.

³¹Then his brothers and his father's whole family went down to get him. They brought him back and buried him between Zorah and Eshtaol in the tomb of Manoah his father. He had led *a* Israel twenty years.

Micah's Idols

17 Now a man named Micah from the hill country of Ephraim ²said to his mother, "The eleven hundred shekels *b* of silver that were taken from you and about which I heard you utter a curse—I have that silver with me; I took it."

Then his mother said, "The LORD bless you, my son!"

³When he returned the eleven hundred shekels of silver to his mother, she said, "I solemnly consecrate my silver to the LORD for my son to make an image overlaid with silver. I will give it back to you."

⁴So after he returned the silver to his mother, she took two hundred shekels *c* of silver and gave them to a silversmith, who used them to make the idol. And it was put in Micah's house.

⁵Now this man Micah had a shrine, and he made an ephod and some household gods and installed one of his sons as his priest. ⁶In those days Israel had no king; everyone did as they saw fit.

⁷A young Levite from Bethlehem in Judah, who had been living within the clan of Judah, ⁸left that town in search of some other place to stay. On his way *d* he came to Micah's house in the hill country of Ephraim.

⁹Micah asked him, "Where are you from?"

"I'm a Levite from Bethlehem in Judah," he said, "and I'm looking for a place to stay."

¹⁰Then Micah said to him, "Live with me and be my father and priest, and I'll give you ten shekels *e* of silver a year, your clothes and your food." ¹¹So the Levite agreed to live with him, and the young man became like one of his sons to him. ¹²Then Micah installed the Levite, and the young man became his priest and lived in his house. ¹³And Micah said, "Now I know that the LORD will be good to me, since this Levite has become my priest."

The Danites Settle in Laish

18 In those days Israel had no king. And in those days the tribe of the Danites was seeking a place of their own where they might settle, because they had not yet come into an inheritance among the tribes of Israel. ²So the Danites

---

a 31 Traditionally *judged*   *b 2* That is, about 28 pounds or about 13 kilograms   *c 4* That is, about 5 pounds or about 2.3 kilograms   *d 8* Or *To carry on his profession*   *e 10* That is, about 4 ounces or about 115 grams

As You See Fit

Judges 17:1-6

read/meditate

Be still for several minutes before you read this passage. Read it slowly, watching every word for the truth God has placed there for your life.

pray

Reflect on and then confess to God the times when you've done as you saw fit rather than as he instructed. Instead of simply regretting the consequences, celebrate the good that he can bring out of the lessons you've learned.

contemplate

Read the passage once more. Then look ahead to the opportunities you'll have to lay aside whatever drags you down, so that you can do what you feel called to do. In humility, allow your heavenly Father to give you a vision for that future.

additional reflection

A world of nice people, content in their own niceness, looking no further, turned away from God, would be just as desperately in need of salvation as a miserable world—and might even be more difficult to save.

—C. S. Lewis

For your next devotional reading, go to page 299.

sent five of their leading men from Zorah and Eshtaol to spy out the land and explore it. These men represented all the Danites. They told them, "Go, explore the land."

So they entered the hill country of Ephraim and came to the house of Micah, where they spent the night. ³When they were near Micah's house, they recognized the voice of the young Levite; so they turned in there and asked him, "Who brought you here? What are you doing in this place? Why are you here?"

⁴He told them what Micah had done for him, and said, "He has hired me and I am his priest."

⁵Then they said to him, "Please inquire of God to learn whether our journey will be successful."

⁶The priest answered them, "Go in peace. Your journey has the LORD's approval."

⁷So the five men left and came to Laish, where they saw that the people were living in safety, like the Sidonians, unsuspecting and secure. And since their land lacked nothing, they were prosperous.ᵃ Also, they lived a long way from the Sidonians and had no relationship with anyone else.ᵇ

⁸When they returned to Zorah and Eshtaol, the Danites asked them, "How did you find things?"

⁹They answered, "Come on, let's attack them! We have seen the land, and it is very good. Aren't you going to do something? Don't hesitate to go there and take it over. ¹⁰When you get there, you will find an unsuspecting people and a spacious land that God has put into your hands, a land that lacks nothing whatever."

¹¹Then six hundred men of the Danites, armed for battle, set out from Zorah and Eshtaol. ¹²On their way they set up camp near Kiriath Jearim in Judah. This is why the place west of Kiriath Jearim is called Mahaneh Danᶜ to this day. ¹³From there they went on to the hill country of Ephraim and came to Micah's house.

¹⁴Then the five men who had spied out the land of Laish said to their fellow Danites, "Do you know that one of these houses has an ephod, some household gods and an image overlaid with silver? Now you know what to do." ¹⁵So they turned in there and went to the house of the young Levite at Micah's place and greeted him. ¹⁶The six hundred Danites, armed for battle, stood at the entrance of the gate. ¹⁷The five men who had spied out the land went inside and took the idol, the ephod and the household gods while the priest and the six hundred armed men stood at the entrance of the gate.

¹⁸When the five went into Micah's house and took the idol, the ephod and the household gods, the priest said to them, "What are you doing?"

¹⁹They answered him, "Be quiet! Don't say a word. Come with us, and be our father and priest. Isn't it better that you serve a tribe and clan in Israel as priest rather than just one man's household?" ²⁰The priest was very pleased. He took the ephod, the household gods and the idol and went along with the people. ²¹Putting their little children, their livestock and their possessions in front of them, they turned away and left.

²²When they had gone some distance from Micah's house, the men who lived near Micah were called together and overtook the Danites. ²³As they shouted after them, the Danites turned and said to Micah, "What's the matter with you that you called out your men to fight?"

²⁴He replied, "You took the gods I made, and my priest, and went away. What else do I have? How can you ask, 'What's the matter with you?' "

²⁵The Danites answered, "Don't argue with us, or some of the men may get angry and attack you, and you and your family will lose your lives." ²⁶So the Danites went their way, and Micah, seeing that they were too strong for him, turned around and went back home.

²⁷Then they took what Micah had made, and his priest, and went on to Laish, against a peaceful and unsuspecting people. They attacked them with the sword and burned down their city. ²⁸There was no one to rescue them because they lived a long way from Sidon and had no relationship with anyone else. The city was in a valley near Beth Rehob.

The Danites rebuilt the city and settled there. ²⁹They named it Dan after their ancestor Dan, who was born to Israel—though

ᵃ 7 The meaning of the Hebrew for this clause is uncertain.   ᵇ 7 Hebrew; some Septuagint manuscripts *with the Arameans*   ᶜ 12 *Mahaneh Dan* means *Dan's camp.*

the city used to be called Laish. ³⁰There the Danites set up for themselves the idol, and Jonathan son of Gershom, the son of Moses,ᵃ and his sons were priests for the tribe of Dan until the time of the captivity of the land. ³¹They continued to use the idol Micah had made, all the time the house of God was in Shiloh.

A Levite and His Concubine

19 In those days Israel had no king. Now a Levite who lived in a remote area in the hill country of Ephraim took a concubine from Bethlehem in Judah. ²But she was unfaithful to him. She left him and went back to her parents' home in Bethlehem, Judah. After she had been there four months, ³her husband went to her to persuade her to return. He had with him his servant and two donkeys. She took him into her parents' home, and when her father saw him, he gladly welcomed him. ⁴His father-in-law, the woman's father, prevailed on him to stay; so he remained with him three days, eating and drinking, and sleeping there.

⁵On the fourth day they got up early and he prepared to leave, but the woman's father said to his son-in-law, "Refresh yourself with something to eat; then you can go." ⁶So the two of them sat down to eat and drink together. Afterward the woman's father said, "Please stay tonight and enjoy yourself." ⁷And when the man got up to go, his father-in-law persuaded him, so he stayed there that night. ⁸On the morning of the fifth day, when he rose to go, the woman's father said, "Refresh yourself. Wait till afternoon!" So the two of them ate together.

⁹Then when the man, with his concubine and his servant, got up to leave, his father-in-law, the woman's father, said, "Now look, it's almost evening. Spend the night here; the day is nearly over. Stay and enjoy yourself. Early tomorrow morning you can get up and be on your way home." ¹⁰But, unwilling to stay another night, the man left and went toward Jebus (that is, Jerusalem), with his two saddled donkeys and his concubine. ¹¹When they were near Jebus and the day was almost gone, the servant said to his master, "Come, let's stop at this city of the Jebusites and spend the night."

¹²His master replied, "No. We won't go into any city whose people are not Israelites. We will go on to Gibeah." ¹³He added, "Come, let's try to reach Gibeah or Ramah and spend the night in one of those places." ¹⁴So they went on, and the sun set as they neared Gibeah in Benjamin. ¹⁵There they stopped to spend the night. They went and sat in the city square, but no one took them in for the night.

¹⁶That evening an old man from the hill country of Ephraim, who was living in Gibeah (the inhabitants of the place were Benjamites), came in from his work in the fields. ¹⁷When he looked and saw the traveler in the city square, the old man asked, "Where are you going? Where did you come from?"

¹⁸He answered, "We are on our way from Bethlehem in Judah to a remote area in the hill country of Ephraim where I live. I have been to Bethlehem in Judah and now I am going to the house of the Lord.ᵇ No one has taken me in for the night. ¹⁹We have both straw and fodder for our donkeys and bread and wine for ourselves your servants—me, the woman and the young man with us. We don't need anything."

²⁰"You are welcome at my house," the old man said. "Let me supply whatever you need. Only don't spend the night in the square." ²¹So he took him into his house and fed his donkeys. After they had washed their feet, they had something to eat and drink.

²²While they were enjoying themselves, some of the wicked men of the city surrounded the house. Pounding on the door, they shouted to the old man who owned the house, "Bring out the man who came to your house so we can have sex with him."

²³The owner of the house went outside and said to them, "No, my friends, don't be so vile. Since this man is my guest, don't do this outrageous thing. ²⁴Look, here is my virgin daughter, and his concubine. I will bring them out to you now, and you can use them and do to them whatever you wish. But as for this man, don't do such an outrageous thing."

²⁵But the men would not listen to him. So the man took his concubine and sent her

ᵃ 30 Many Hebrew manuscripts, some Septuagint manuscripts and Vulgate; many other Hebrew manuscripts and some other Septuagint manuscripts *Manasseh*   ᵇ 18 Hebrew, Vulgate, Syriac and Targum; Septuagint *going home* outside to them, and they raped her and abused her throughout the night, and at dawn they let her go. ²⁶At daybreak the woman went back to the house where her master was staying, fell down at the door and lay there until daylight.

²⁷When her master got up in the morning and opened the door of the house and stepped out to continue on his way, there lay his concubine, fallen in the doorway of the house, with her hands on the threshold. ²⁸He said to her, "Get up; let's go." But there was no answer. Then he put her on his donkey and set out for home.

²⁹When he reached home, he took a knife and cut up his concubine, limb by limb, into twelve parts and sent them into all the areas of Israel. ³⁰Everyone who saw it said, "Such a thing has never been seen or done, not since the day the Israelites came up out of Egypt. Think about it! Consider it! Tell us what to do!"

The Israelites Punish the Benjamites

20 Then all the Israelites from Dan to Beersheba and from the land of Gilead came out with one accord and assembled before the LORD in Mizpah. ²The leaders of all the people of the tribes of Israel took their places in the assembly of the people of God, four hundred thousand soldiers armed with swords. ³(The Benjamites heard that the Israelites had gone up to Mizpah.) Then the Israelites said, "Tell us how this awful thing happened."

⁴So the Levite, the husband of the murdered woman, said, "I and my concubine came to Gibeah in Benjamin to spend the night. ⁵During the night the men of Gibeah came after me and surrounded the house, intending to kill me. They raped my concubine, and she died. ⁶I took my concubine, cut her into pieces and sent one piece to each region of Israel's inheritance, because they committed this lewd and outrageous act in Israel. ⁷Now, all you Israelites, speak up and give your verdict."

⁸All the people rose with one accord, saying, "None of us will go home. No, not one of us will return to his house. ⁹But now this is what we'll do to Gibeah: We'll go up against it as the lot directs. ¹⁰We'll take ten men out of every hundred from all the tribes of Israel, and a hundred from a thousand, and a thousand from ten thousand, to get provisions for the army. Then, when the army arrives at Gibeah*ᵃ* in Benjamin, it can give them what they deserve for this outrageous act done in Israel." ¹¹So all the Israelites got together and united against the city with one accord.

¹²The tribes of Israel sent messengers throughout the tribe of Benjamin, saying, "What about this awful crime that was committed among you? ¹³Now turn those wicked men of Gibeah over to us so that we may put them to death and purge the evil from Israel."

But the Benjamites would not listen to their fellow Israelites. ¹⁴From their towns they came together at Gibeah to fight against the Israelites. ¹⁵At once the Benjamites mobilized twenty-six thousand swordsmen from their towns, in addition to seven hundred able young men from those living in Gibeah. ¹⁶Among all these soldiers there were seven hundred who were left-handed, each of whom could sling a stone at a hair and not miss.

¹⁷Israel, apart from Benjamin, mustered four hundred thousand swordsmen, all of them fighting men.

¹⁸The Israelites went up to Bethel*ᵇ* and inquired of God. They said, "Who of us is to go up first to fight against the Benjamites?"

The LORD replied, "Judah shall go first."

¹⁹The next morning the Israelites got up and pitched camp near Gibeah. ²⁰The Israelites went out to fight the Benjamites and took up battle positions against them at Gibeah. ²¹The Benjamites came out of Gibeah and cut down twenty-two thousand Israelites on the battlefield that day. ²²But the Israelites encouraged one another and again took up their positions where they had stationed themselves the first day. ²³The Israelites went up and wept before the LORD until evening, and they inquired of the LORD. They said, "Shall we go up again to fight against the Benjamites, our fellow Israelites?"

The LORD answered, "Go up against them."

²⁴Then the Israelites drew near to Benjamin the second day. ²⁵This time, when the

ᵃ 10 One Hebrew manuscript; most Hebrew manuscripts *Geba,* a variant of *Gibeah*   *ᵇ 18* Or *to the house of God;* also in verse 26

Benjamites came out from Gibeah to oppose them, they cut down another eighteen thousand Israelites, all of them armed with swords.

²⁶Then all the Israelites, the whole army, went up to Bethel, and there they sat weeping before the LORD. They fasted that day until evening and presented burnt offerings and fellowship offerings to the LORD. ²⁷And the Israelites inquired of the LORD. (In those days the ark of the covenant of God was there, ²⁸with Phinehas son of Eleazar, the son of Aaron, ministering before it.) They asked, "Shall we go up again to fight against the Benjamites, our fellow Israelites, or not?"

The LORD responded, "Go, for tomorrow I will give them into your hands."

²⁹Then Israel set an ambush around Gibeah. ³⁰They went up against the Benjamites on the third day and took up positions against Gibeah as they had done before. ³¹The Benjamites came out to meet them and were drawn away from the city. They began to inflict casualties on the Israelites as before, so that about thirty of them fell in the open field and on the roads—the one leading to Bethel and the other to Gibeah.

³²While the Benjamites were saying, "We are defeating them as before," the Israelites were saying, "Let's retreat and draw them away from the city to the roads."

³³All the men of Israel moved from their places and took up positions at Baal Tamar, and the Israelite ambush charged out of its place on the westᵃ of Gibeah.ᵇ ³⁴Then ten thousand of Israel's able young men made a frontal attack on Gibeah. The fighting was so heavy that the Benjamites did not realize how near disaster was. ³⁵The LORD defeated Benjamin before Israel, and on that day the Israelites struck down 25,100 Benjamites, all armed with swords. ³⁶Then the Benjamites saw that they were beaten.

Now the men of Israel had given way before Benjamin, because they relied on the ambush they had set near Gibeah. ³⁷Those who had been in ambush made a sudden dash into Gibeah, spread out and put the whole city to the sword. ³⁸The Israelites had arranged with the ambush that they should send up a great cloud of smoke from the city, ³⁹and then the Israelites would turn in the battle.

The Benjamites had begun to inflict casualties on the Israelites (about thirty), and they said, "We are defeating them as in the first battle." ⁴⁰But when the column of smoke began to rise from the city, the Benjamites turned and saw the smoke of the whole city going up into the sky. ⁴¹Then the Israelites turned on them, and the Benjamites were terrified, because they realized that disaster had come on them. ⁴²So they fled before the Israelites in the direction of the wilderness, but they could not escape the battle. And the Israelites who came out of the towns cut them down there. ⁴³They surrounded the Benjamites, chased them and easilyᶜ overran them in the vicinity of Gibeah on the east. ⁴⁴Eighteen thousand Benjamites fell, all of them valiant fighters. ⁴⁵As they turned and fled toward the wilderness to the rock of Rimmon, the Israelites cut down five thousand men along the roads. They kept pressing after the Benjamites as far as Gidom and struck down two thousand more.

⁴⁶On that day twenty-five thousand Benjamite swordsmen fell, all of them valiant fighters. ⁴⁷But six hundred men turned and fled into the wilderness to the rock of Rimmon, where they stayed four months. ⁴⁸The men of Israel went back to Benjamin and put all the towns to the sword, including the animals and everything else they found. All the towns they came across they set on fire.

Wives for the Benjamites

21 The men of Israel had taken an oath at Mizpah: "Not one of us will give his daughter in marriage to a Benjamite."

²The people went to Bethel,ᵈ where they sat before God until evening, raising their voices and weeping bitterly. ³"LORD, God of Israel," they cried, "why has this happened to Israel? Why should one tribe be missing from Israel today?"

⁴Early the next day the people built an altar and presented burnt offerings and fellowship offerings.

⁵Then the Israelites asked, "Who from all the tribes of Israel has failed to assemble before the LORD?" For they had taken a sol-

---

ᵃ 33 Some Septuagint manuscripts and Vulgate; the meaning of the Hebrew for this word is uncertain.
ᵇ 33 Hebrew *Geba*, a variant of *Gibeah*   ᶜ 43 The meaning of the Hebrew for this word is uncertain.
ᵈ 2 Or *to the house of God*

emn oath that anyone who failed to assemble before the LORD at Mizpah was to be put to death.

⁶Now the Israelites grieved for Benjamin, one of their tribes. "Today one tribe is cut off from Israel," they said. ⁷"How can we provide wives for those who are left, since we have taken an oath by the LORD not to give them any of our daughters in marriage?" ⁸Then they asked, "Which one of the tribes of Israel failed to assemble before the LORD at Mizpah?" They discovered that no one from Jabesh Gilead had come to the camp for the assembly. ⁹For when they counted the people, they found that none of the people of Jabesh Gilead were there.

¹⁰So the assembly sent twelve thousand fighting men with instructions to go to Jabesh Gilead and put to the sword those living there, including the women and children. ¹¹"This is what you are to do," they said. "Kill every male and every woman who is not a virgin." ¹²They found among the people living in Jabesh Gilead four hundred young women who had never slept with a man, and they took them to the camp at Shiloh in Canaan.

¹³Then the whole assembly sent an offer of peace to the Benjamites at the rock of Rimmon. ¹⁴So the Benjamites returned at that time and were given the women of Jabesh Gilead who had been spared. But there were not enough for all of them.

¹⁵The people grieved for Benjamin, because the LORD had made a gap in the tribes of Israel. ¹⁶And the elders of the assembly said, "With the women of Benjamin destroyed, how shall we provide wives for the men who are left? ¹⁷The Benjamite survivors must have heirs," they said, "so that a tribe of Israel will not be wiped out. ¹⁸We can't give them our daughters as wives, since we Israelites have taken this oath: 'Cursed be anyone who gives a wife to a Benjamite.' ¹⁹But look, there is the annual festival of the LORD in Shiloh, to the north of Bethel, and east of the road that goes from Bethel to Shechem, and to the south of Lebonah."

²⁰So they instructed the Benjamites, saying, "Go and hide in the vineyards ²¹and watch. When the young women of Shiloh come out to join in the dancing, then rush from the vineyards and each of you seize a wife from the young women of Shiloh and go to the land of Benjamin. ²²When their fathers or brothers complain to us, we will say to them, 'Do us a kindness by helping them, because we did not get wives for them during the war, and you are innocent, since you did not give your daughters to them.' "

²³So that is what the Benjamites did. While the young women were dancing, each man caught one and carried her off to be his wife. Then they returned to their inheritance and rebuilt the towns and settled in them.

²⁴At that time the Israelites left that place and went home to their tribes and clans, each to his own inheritance.

²⁵In those days Israel had no king; everyone did as they saw fit.

ruth

AUTHOR: Unknown

DATE: Around 1000 B.C.

THEME: God can bring his glory and our good out of any situation—no matter how hopeless things may seem.

Naomi Loses Her Husband and Sons

1 In the days when the judges ruled,[a] there was a famine in the land. So a man from Bethlehem in Judah, together with his wife and two sons, went to live for a while in the country of Moab. ²The man's name was Elimelek, his wife's name was Naomi, and the names of his two sons were Mahlon and Kilion. They were Ephrathites from Bethlehem, Judah. And they went to Moab and lived there.

³Now Elimelek, Naomi's husband, died, and she was left with her two sons. ⁴They married Moabite women, one named Orpah and the other Ruth. After they had lived there about ten years, ⁵both Mahlon and Kilion also died, and Naomi was left without her two sons and her husband.

Naomi and Ruth Return to Bethlehem

⁶When Naomi heard in Moab that the LORD had come to the aid of his people by providing food for them, she and her daughters-in-law prepared to return home from there. ⁷With her two daughters-in-law she left the place where she had been living and set out on the road that would take them back to the land of Judah.

⁸Then Naomi said to her two daughters-in-law, "Go back, each of you, to your mother's home. May the LORD show you kindness, as you have shown kindness to your dead and to me. ⁹May the LORD grant that each of you will find rest in the home of another husband."

Then she kissed them good-by and they wept aloud ¹⁰and said to her, "We will go back with you to your people."

¹¹But Naomi said, "Return home, my daughters. Why would you come with me? Am I going to have any more sons, who could become your husbands? ¹²Return home, my daughters; I am too old to have another husband. Even if I thought there was still hope for me—even if I had a husband tonight and then gave birth to sons— ¹³would you wait until they grew up? Would you remain unmarried for them? No, my daughters. It is more bitter for me than for you, because the LORD's hand has turned against me!"

¹⁴At this they wept aloud again. Then Orpah kissed her mother-in-law good-by, but Ruth clung to her.

¹⁵"Look," said Naomi, "your sister-in-law is going back to her people and her gods. Go back with her."

¹⁶But Ruth replied, "Don't urge me to leave you or to turn back from you. Where you go I will go, and where you stay I will stay. Your people will be my people and your God my God. ¹⁷Where you die I will die, and there I will be buried. May the LORD deal with me, be it ever so severely, if even death separates you and me." ¹⁸When Naomi realized that Ruth was determined to go with her, she stopped urging her.

¹⁹So the two women went on until they came to Bethlehem. When they arrived in Bethlehem, the whole town was stirred because of them, and the women exclaimed, "Can this be Naomi?"

²⁰"Don't call me Naomi,[b]" she told them. "Call me Mara,[c] because the Almighty[d] has made my life very bitter. ²¹I went away full, but the LORD has brought me back empty. Why call me Naomi? The LORD has afflicted[e]

---

a 1 Traditionally *judged*   b 20 *Naomi* means *pleasant*; also in verse 21.   c 20 *Mara* means *bitter*.
d 20 Hebrew *Shaddai*; also in verse 21   e 21 Or *has testified against*

MONDAY

18 INCHES

Ruth 1:1–22 *or* 1:16–18

Anne Graham Lotz

For years, Tom Landry was an American icon. With the brim of his hat pulled down over a stoic face, he paced the sidelines of football fields where he presided as head coach over one of the greatest teams of all time, the Dallas Cowboys . . . He became a legend in his own time.

On more than one occasion, I have heard Coach Landry state that during his career he came across many good athletes—but very few great ones. He said the difference between a good athlete and a great one is 18 inches—the distance from the head to the heart. From his observation, based on a lifetime of involvement in sports, he explained that good athletes have exceptional ability and a thorough understanding of the game, but great athletes have heart—a passion to play that drives them to selfless sacrifice, brutally long hours of practice, undivided focus and ultimately, to achieve extraordinary accomplishments.

In almost 30 years of ministry, I have observed many good Christians, like Coach Landry's athletes, but *very* few great ones. And the difference is the same 18 inches—the distance from the head to the heart. While there are many good Christians who have a head knowledge of Scripture, attend church regularly, are familiar with church traditions and rituals and are comfortable with prayer, group Bible study and outreach ministries, there are very few who are great.

There are relatively few Christians who are in love with Jesus, who put Him first in their lives when doing so demands that they sacrifice their own time, money and desires. There are very few Christians who want what He wants more than what they want—and are willing to lay everything on the line to pursue it. There are very few Christians who are willing to risk their job, reputation, status, friendships, financial security and even their life for the sake of sharing the gospel and pleasing God. We just seem to lack a clear knowledge of God and a passionate heart for God that, combined, are the hub around which everything in our life should revolve.

C. S. LEWIS {AD 1898–1963}

We may think God wants actions of a certain kind, but God wants people of a certain kind.

— *reflection* —

1. Have you known any "great" Christians?
2. What was it that made them stand out?
3. What made Ruth so extraordinary? What did she give up in order to follow God? Why do you think she made such a sacrifice?

For your next devotional reading, go to page 305.

me; the Almighty has brought misfortune upon me."

²²So Naomi returned from Moab accompanied by Ruth the Moabite, her daughter-in-law, arriving in Bethlehem as the barley harvest was beginning.

Ruth Meets Boaz in the Grain Field

2 Now Naomi had a relative on her husband's side, a man of standing from the clan of Elimelek, whose name was Boaz.

²And Ruth the Moabite said to Naomi, "Let me go to the fields and pick up the left-over grain behind anyone in whose eyes I find favor."

Naomi said to her, "Go ahead, my daughter." ³So she went out, entered a field and began to glean behind the harvesters. As it turned out, she found herself working in a field belonging to Boaz, who was from the clan of Elimelek.

⁴Just then Boaz arrived from Bethlehem and greeted the harvesters, "The LORD be with you!"

"The LORD bless you!" they answered.

⁵Boaz asked the overseer of his harvesters, "Who does that young woman belong to?"

⁶The overseer replied, "She is the Moabite who came back from Moab with Naomi. ⁷She said, 'Please let me glean and gather among the sheaves behind the harvesters.' She came into the field and has remained here from morning till now, except for a short rest in the shelter."

⁸So Boaz said to Ruth, "My daughter, listen to me. Don't go and glean in another field and don't go away from here. Stay here with the women who work for me. ⁹Watch the field where the harvesters are working, and follow along after the women. I have told the men not to lay a hand on you. And whenever you are thirsty, go and get a drink from the water jars the men have filled."

¹⁰At this, she bowed down with her face to the ground. She asked him, "Why have I found such favor in your eyes that you notice me—a foreigner?"

¹¹Boaz replied, "I've been told all about what you have done for your mother-in-law since the death of your husband—how you left your father and mother and your homeland and came to live with a people you did not know before. ¹²May the LORD repay you for what you have done. May you be richly rewarded by the LORD, the God of Israel, under whose wings you have come to take refuge."

¹³"May I continue to find favor in your eyes, my lord," she said. "You have reassured me and have spoken kindly to your servant—though I do not have the standing of one of your servants."

¹⁴At mealtime Boaz said to her, "Come over here. Have some bread and dip it in the wine vinegar."

When she sat down with the harvesters, he offered her some roasted grain. She ate all she wanted and had some left over. ¹⁵As she got up to glean, Boaz gave orders to his men, "Let her gather among the sheaves and don't reprimand her. ¹⁶Even pull out some stalks for her from the bundles and leave them for her to pick up, and don't rebuke her."

¹⁷So Ruth gleaned in the field until evening. Then she threshed the barley she had gathered, and it amounted to about an ephah.ᵃ ¹⁸She carried it back to town, and her mother-in-law saw how much she had gathered. Ruth also brought out and gave her what she had left over after she had eaten enough.

¹⁹Her mother-in-law asked her, "Where did you glean today? Where did you work? Blessed be the man who took notice of you!"

Then Ruth told her mother-in-law about the one at whose place she had been working. "The name of the man I worked with today is Boaz," she said.

²⁰"The LORD bless him!" Naomi said to her daughter-in-law. "He has not stopped showing his kindness to the living and the dead." She added, "That man is our close relative; he is one of our family guardians.ᵇ"

²¹Then Ruth the Moabite said, "He even said to me, 'Stay with my workers until they finish harvesting all my grain.' "

²²Naomi said to Ruth her daughter-in-law, "It will be good for you, my daughter, to go with the women who work for him, because in someone else's field you might be harmed."

²³So Ruth stayed close to the women of

ᵃ 17 That is, probably about 30 pounds or about 13 kilograms   ᵇ 20 The Hebrew word for *family guardian* is a legal term for one who has the obligation to redeem a relative in serious difficulty (see Lev. 25:25-55).

Boaz to glean until the barley and wheat harvests were finished. And she lived with her mother-in-law.

Ruth and Boaz at the Threshing Floor

3 One day Naomi her mother-in-law said to her, "My daughter, I must find a home[a] for you, where you will be well provided for. 2Now Boaz, with whose women you have worked, is a relative of ours. Tonight he will be winnowing barley on the threshing floor. 3Wash and perfume yourself, and put on your best clothes. Then go down to the threshing floor, but don't let him know you are there until he has finished eating and drinking. 4When he lies down, note the place where he is lying. Then go and uncover his feet and lie down. He will tell you what to do."

5"I will do whatever you say," Ruth answered. 6So she went down to the threshing floor and did everything her mother-in-law told her to do.

7When Boaz had finished eating and drinking and was in good spirits, he went over to lie down at the far end of the grain pile. Ruth approached quietly, uncovered his feet and lay down. 8In the middle of the night something startled the man; he turned—and there was a woman lying at his feet!

9"Who are you?" he asked.

"I am your servant Ruth," she said. "Spread the corner of your garment over me, since you are a family guardian."

10"The LORD bless you, my daughter," he replied. "This kindness is greater than that which you showed earlier: You have not run after the younger men, whether rich or poor. 11And now, my daughter, don't be afraid. I will do for you all you ask. All the people of my town know that you are a woman of noble character. 12Although it is true that I am a family guardian, there is another who is more closely related than I. 13Stay here for the night, and in the morning if he wants to do his duty as your family guardian, good; let him redeem you. But if he is not willing, as surely as the LORD lives I will do it. Lie here until morning."

14So she lay at his feet until morning, but got up before anyone could be recognized;

and he said, "No one must know that a woman came to the threshing floor."

15He also said, "Bring me the shawl you are wearing and hold it out." When she did so, he poured into it six measures of barley and put it on her. Then he[b] went back to town.

16When Ruth came to her mother-in-law, Naomi asked, "How did it go, my daughter?"

Then she told her everything Boaz had done for her 17and added, "He gave me these six measures of barley, saying, 'Don't go back to your mother-in-law empty-handed.'"

18Then Naomi said, "Wait, my daughter, until you find out what happens. For the man will not rest until the matter is settled today."

Boaz Marries Ruth

4 Meanwhile Boaz went up to the town gate and sat down there just as the family guardian he had mentioned came along. Boaz said, "Come over here, my friend, and sit down." So he went over and sat down.

2Boaz took ten of the elders of the town and said, "Sit here," and they did so. 3Then he said to the family guardian, "Naomi, who has come back from Moab, is selling the piece of land that belonged to our relative Elimelek. 4I thought I should bring the matter to your attention and suggest that you buy it in the presence of these seated here and in the presence of the elders of my people. If you will redeem it, do so. But if you[c] will not, tell me, so I will know. For no one has the right to do it except you, and I am next in line."

"I will redeem it," he said.

5Then Boaz said, "On the day you buy the land from Naomi, you also acquire Ruth the Moabite, the[d] dead man's widow, in order to maintain the name of the dead with his property."

6At this, the family guardian said, "Then I cannot redeem it because I might endanger my own estate. You redeem it yourself. I cannot do it."

7(Now in earlier times in Israel, for the redemption and transfer of property to become final, one party took off his sandal and

---

a 1 Hebrew *find rest* (see Ruth 1:9)   b 15 Most Hebrew manuscripts; many Hebrew manuscripts, Vulgate and Syriac *she*   c 4 Many Hebrew manuscripts, Septuagint, Vulgate and Syriac; most Hebrew manuscripts *he*   d 5 Vulgate and Syriac; Hebrew (see also Septuagint) *Naomi and from Ruth the Moabite, you acquire the* gave it to the other. This was the method of legalizing transactions in Israel.)

⁸So the family guardian said to Boaz, "Buy it yourself." And he removed his sandal.

⁹Then Boaz announced to the elders and all the people, "Today you are witnesses that I have bought from Naomi all the property of Elimelek, Kilion and Mahlon. ¹⁰I have also acquired Ruth the Moabite, Mahlon's widow, as my wife, in order to maintain the name of the dead with his property, so that his name will not disappear from among his family or from his hometown. Today you are witnesses!"

¹¹Then the elders and all the people at the gate said, "We are witnesses. May the LORD make the woman who is coming into your home like Rachel and Leah, who together built up the house of Israel. May you have standing in Ephrathah and be famous in Bethlehem. ¹²Through the offspring the LORD gives you by this young woman, may your family be like that of Perez, whom Tamar bore to Judah."

Naomi Gains a Son

¹³So Boaz took Ruth and she became his wife. When he made love to her, the LORD enabled her to conceive, and she gave birth to a son. ¹⁴The women said to Naomi: "Praise be to the LORD, who this day has not left you without a family guardian. May he become famous throughout Israel! ¹⁵He will renew your life and sustain you in your old age. For your daughter-in-law, who loves you and who is better to you than seven sons, has given him birth."

¹⁶Then Naomi took the child in her arms and cared for him. ¹⁷The women living there said, "Naomi has a son!" And they named him Obed. He was the father of Jesse, the father of David.

The Genealogy of David

¹⁸This, then, is the family line of Perez:

Perez was the father of Hezron,
¹⁹Hezron the father of Ram,
  Ram the father of Amminadab,
²⁰Amminadab the father of Nahshon,
  Nahshon the father of Salmon,ᵃ
²¹Salmon the father of Boaz,
  Boaz the father of Obed,
²²Obed the father of Jesse,
  and Jesse the father of David.

ᵃ 20 A few Hebrew manuscripts, some Septuagint manuscripts and Vulgate (see also verse 21 and Septuagint of 1 Chron. 2:11); most Hebrew manuscripts Salma

1 samuel

AUTHOR: Unknown

DATE: Around 930 B.C.

THEME: What God wants most from a leader is a devoted heart.

The Birth of Samuel

1 There was a certain man from Ramathaim, a Zuphite^a from the hill country of Ephraim, whose name was Elkanah son of Jeroham, the son of Elihu, the son of Tohu, the son of Zuph, an Ephraimite. ²He had two wives; one was called Hannah and the other Peninnah. Peninnah had children, but Hannah had none.

³Year after year this man went up from his town to worship and sacrifice to the LORD Almighty at Shiloh, where Hophni and Phinehas, the two sons of Eli, were priests of the LORD. ⁴Whenever the day came for Elkanah to sacrifice, he would give portions of the meat to his wife Peninnah and to all her sons and daughters. ⁵But to Hannah he gave a double portion because he loved her, and the LORD had closed her womb. ⁶Because the LORD had closed Hannah's womb, her rival kept provoking her in order to irritate her. ⁷This went on year after year. Whenever Hannah went up to the house of the LORD, her rival provoked her till she wept and would not eat. ⁸Her husband Elkanah would say to her, "Hannah, why are you weeping? Why don't you eat? Why are you downhearted? Don't I mean more to you than ten sons?"

⁹Once when they had finished eating and drinking in Shiloh, Hannah stood up. Now Eli the priest was sitting on his chair by the doorpost of the LORD's house. ¹⁰In her deep anguish Hannah prayed to the LORD, weeping bitterly. ¹¹And she made a vow, saying, "LORD Almighty, if you will only look on your servant's misery and remember me, and not forget your servant but give her a son, then I

will give him to the LORD for all the days of his life, and no razor will ever be used on his head."

¹²As she kept on praying to the LORD, Eli observed her mouth. ¹³Hannah was praying in her heart, and her lips were moving but her voice was not heard. Eli thought she was drunk ¹⁴and said to her, "How long are you going to stay drunk? Put away your wine."

¹⁵"Not so, my lord," Hannah replied, "I am a woman who is deeply troubled. I have not been drinking wine or beer; I was pouring out my soul to the LORD. ¹⁶Do not take your servant for a wicked woman; I have been praying here out of my great anguish and grief."

¹⁷Eli answered, "Go in peace, and may the God of Israel grant you what you have asked of him."

¹⁸She said, "May your servant find favor in your eyes." Then she went her way and ate something, and her face was no longer downcast.

¹⁹Early the next morning they arose and worshiped before the LORD and then went back to their home at Ramah. Elkanah made love to his wife Hannah, and the LORD remembered her. ²⁰So in the course of time Hannah became pregnant and gave birth to a son. She named him Samuel,^b saying, "Because I asked the LORD for him."

Hannah Dedicates Samuel

²¹When Elkanah went up with all his family to offer the annual sacrifice to the LORD and to fulfill his vow, ²²Hannah did not go. She said to her husband, "After the boy is weaned, I will take him and present him be-

---

^a 1 See Septuagint and 1 Chron. 6:26-27,33-35; or *from Ramathaim Zuphim*.   ^b 20 *Samuel* sounds like the Hebrew for *heard by God*.

fore the LORD, and he will live there always."[a]

²³"Do what seems best to you," her husband Elkanah told her. "Stay here until you have weaned him; only may the LORD make good his[b] word." So the woman stayed at home and nursed her son until she had weaned him.

²⁴After he was weaned, she took the boy with her, young as he was, along with a three-year-old bull,[c] an ephah[d] of flour and a skin of wine, and brought him to the house of the LORD at Shiloh. ²⁵When the bull had been sacrificed, they brought the boy to Eli, ²⁶and she said to him, "Pardon me, my lord. As surely as you live, I am the woman who stood here beside you praying to the LORD. ²⁷I prayed for this child, and the LORD has granted me what I asked of him. ²⁸So now I give him to the LORD. For his whole life he will be given over to the LORD." And he worshiped the LORD there.

Hannah's Prayer

2 Then Hannah prayed and said:

"My heart rejoices in the LORD;
    in the LORD my horn[e] is lifted high.
My mouth boasts over my enemies,
    for I delight in your deliverance.

² "There is no one holy like the LORD;
    there is no one besides you;
    there is no Rock like our God.

³ "Do not keep talking so proudly
    or let your mouth speak such
        arrogance,
for the LORD is a God who knows,
    and by him deeds are weighed.

⁴ "The bows of the warriors are broken,
    but those who stumbled are armed
        with strength.
⁵ Those who were full hire themselves out
        for food,
    but those who were hungry are
        hungry no more.
She who was barren has borne seven
        children,
    but she who has had many sons pines
        away.

⁶ "The LORD brings death and makes alive;
    he brings down to the grave and
        raises up.
⁷ The LORD sends poverty and wealth;
    he humbles and he exalts.
⁸ He raises the poor from the dust
    and lifts the needy from the ash heap;
he seats them with princes
    and has them inherit a throne of
        honor.

"For the foundations of the earth are the
        LORD's;
    on them he has set the world.
⁹ He will guard the feet of his faithful
        servants,
    but the wicked will be silenced in the
        place of darkness.

"It is not by strength that one prevails;
¹⁰   those who oppose the LORD will be
        broken.
The Most High will thunder from
        heaven;
    the LORD will judge the ends of the
        earth.

"He will give strength to his king
    and exalt the horn of his anointed."

¹¹Then Elkanah went home to Ramah, but the boy ministered before the LORD under Eli the priest.

Eli's Wicked Sons

¹²Eli's sons were scoundrels; they had no regard for the LORD. ¹³Now it was the practice of the priests that, whenever any of the people offered a sacrifice, the priest's servant would come with a three-pronged fork in his hand while the meat was being boiled ¹⁴and would plunge the fork into the pan or kettle or caldron or pot. Whatever the fork brought up the priest would take for himself. This is how they treated all the Israelites who came to Shiloh. ¹⁵But even before the fat was burned, the priest's servant would come and say to the person who was sacrificing, "Give the priest some meat to roast; he won't accept boiled meat from you, but only raw."

¹⁶If the person said to him, "Let the fat be burned first, and then take whatever you

---

a 22 Masoretic Text; Dead Sea Scrolls *always. I have dedicated him as a Nazirite—all the days of his life."* b 23 Masoretic Text; Dead Sea Scrolls, Septuagint and Syriac *your*   c 24 Dead Sea Scrolls, Septuagint and Syriac; Masoretic Text *with three bulls*   d 24 That is, probably about 36 pounds or about 16 kilograms   e 1 *Horn* here symbolizes strength; also in verse 10.

TUESDAY

RAISE DISCERNING CHILDREN

1 Samuel 2:12–36 *or* 2:22–26

Judy Salisbury

We want to raise discerning children, and we cannot if we do not carefully examine what they are exposed to, whether through movies or books. I'm not suggesting that we shelter them to the point that we create an unreal environment, but we must help them become so familiar with the pure and good that they can readily spot what is impure or erroneous. The woman at the well knew exactly what Jesus was talking about with regard to her immoral lifestyle, yet Jesus did not give graphic details; he simply defined her relationships. She then said to the men of the city, "Come, see a man who told me everything *I ever did*" (John 4:29, emphasis added).

We can teach our children that, while the Christian life is often difficult (for we are being set apart for God's use and glory), they can be encouraged that God is faithful to give them what they need to handle the trials they will face. We can encourage them that the Christian walk is challenging and exciting as we have an opportunity to live out the book of Acts. And we can show them in creative ways how to do so. Christian bookstores, for example, sell representations of the full armor of God as outlined in Ephesians 6. What a great opportunity a mom or dad has during playtime, as they put a piece of the armor on their small child, to teach the child in a dramatic way why each piece is necessary. Their small child, then, will be actively participating in the learning experience instead of sitting idly by.

J. W. ALEXANDER {AD 1804-1859}

The daily, regular and solemn reading of God's holy word, by a parent before his children, is one of the most powerful activities of a Christian life. We are prone to undervalue this exercise. It is a constant dropping, but it wears its mark into the rock. A family thus trained cannot be ignorant of the Word. The whole Scriptures come repeatedly before the mind. The most heedless child will observe and retain some portion of the sacred oracles. The most forgetful will treasure up some passages for life. No part of a child's education is more important.

reflection

1. Why is it important to teach children about God?
2. How should children be taught differently than adults?
3. What role do you have to play in developing a child's relationship with God?

For your next devotional reading, go to page 313.

want," the servant would answer, "No, hand it over now; if you don't, I'll take it by force."

¹⁷This sin of the young men was very great in the LORD's sight, for they[a] were treating the LORD's offering with contempt.

¹⁸But Samuel was ministering before the LORD—a boy wearing a linen ephod. ¹⁹Each year his mother made him a little robe and took it to him when she went up with her husband to offer the annual sacrifice. ²⁰Eli would bless Elkanah and his wife, saying, "May the LORD give you children by this woman to take the place of the one she prayed for and gave to[b] the LORD." Then they would go home. ²¹And the LORD was gracious to Hannah; she gave birth to three sons and two daughters. Meanwhile, the boy Samuel grew up in the presence of the LORD.

²²Now Eli, who was very old, heard about everything his sons were doing to all Israel and how they slept with the women who served at the entrance to the tent of meeting. ²³So he said to them, "Why do you do such things? I hear from all the people about these wicked deeds of yours. ²⁴No, my sons; the report I hear spreading among the LORD's people is not good. ²⁵If anyone sins against another human being, God[c] may mediate for the offender; but if anyone sins against the LORD, who will intercede for them?" His sons, however, did not listen to their father's rebuke, for it was the LORD's will to put them to death.

²⁶And the boy Samuel continued to grow in stature and in favor with the LORD and with people.

Prophecy Against the House of Eli

²⁷Now a man of God came to Eli and said to him, "This is what the LORD says: 'Did I not clearly reveal myself to the family of your ancestor when they were in Egypt under Pharaoh? ²⁸I chose your ancestor out of all the tribes of Israel to be my priest, to go up to my altar, to burn incense, and to wear an ephod in my presence. I also gave your ancestor's family all the food offerings presented by the Israelites. ²⁹Why do you[d] scorn my sacrifice and offering that I prescribed for my dwelling? Why do you honor your sons more than me by fattening your-

selves on the choice parts of every offering made by my people Israel?'

³⁰"Therefore the LORD, the God of Israel, declares: 'I promised that the members of your family would minister before me forever.' But now the LORD declares: 'Far be it from me! Those who honor me I will honor, but those who despise me will be disdained. ³¹The time is coming when I will cut short your strength and the strength of the members of your family, so that no one in it will reach old age, ³²and you will see distress in my dwelling. Although good will be done to Israel, no one in your family line will ever reach old age. ³³Every one of you that I do not cut off from serving at my altar I will spare only to destroy your sight and sap your strength, and all your descendants will die in the prime of life.

³⁴"'And what happens to your two sons, Hophni and Phinehas, will be a sign to you—they will both die on the same day. ³⁵I will raise up for myself a faithful priest, who will do according to what is in my heart and mind. I will firmly establish his family line, and he will minister before my anointed one always. ³⁶Then everyone left in your family line will come and bow down before him for a piece of silver and a loaf of bread and plead, "Appoint me to some priestly office so I can have food to eat." ' "

The LORD Calls Samuel

3 The boy Samuel ministered before the LORD under Eli. In those days the word of the LORD was rare; there were not many visions.

²One night Eli, whose eyes were becoming so weak that he could barely see, was lying down in his usual place. ³The lamp of God had not yet gone out, and Samuel was lying down in the house of the LORD, where the ark of God was. ⁴Then the LORD called Samuel.

Samuel answered, "Here I am." ⁵And he ran to Eli and said, "Here I am; you called me."

But Eli said, "I did not call; go back and lie down." So he went and lay down.

⁶Again the LORD called, "Samuel!" And Samuel got up and went to Eli and said, "Here I am; you called me."

---

a 17 Dead Sea Scrolls and Septuagint; Masoretic Text *people*   *b 20* Dead Sea Scrolls; Masoretic Text *and asked from*   *c 25* Or *the judges*   *d 29* The Hebrew is plural.

"My son," Eli said, "I did not call; go back and lie down."

⁷Now Samuel did not yet know the LORD: The word of the LORD had not yet been revealed to him.

⁸A third time the LORD called, "Samuel!" And Samuel got up and went to Eli and said, "Here I am; you called me."

Then Eli realized that the LORD was calling the boy. ⁹So Eli told Samuel, "Go and lie down, and if he calls you, say, 'Speak, LORD, for your servant is listening.'" So Samuel went and lay down in his place.

¹⁰The LORD came and stood there, calling as at the other times, "Samuel! Samuel!"

Then Samuel said, "Speak, for your servant is listening."

¹¹And the LORD said to Samuel: "See, I am about to do something in Israel that will make the ears of everyone who hears about it tingle. ¹²At that time I will carry out against Eli everything I spoke against his family—from beginning to end. ¹³For I told him that I would judge his family forever because of the sin he knew about; his sons blasphemed God,ᵃ and he failed to restrain them. ¹⁴Therefore I swore to the house of Eli, 'The guilt of Eli's house will never be atoned for by sacrifice or offering.'"

¹⁵Samuel lay down until morning and then opened the doors of the house of the LORD. He was afraid to tell Eli the vision, ¹⁶but Eli called him and said, "Samuel, my son."

Samuel answered, "Here I am."

¹⁷"What was it he said to you?" Eli asked. "Do not hide it from me. May God deal with you, be it ever so severely, if you hide from me anything he told you." ¹⁸So Samuel told him everything, hiding nothing from him. Then Eli said, "He is the LORD; let him do what is good in his eyes."

¹⁹The LORD was with Samuel as he grew up, and he let none of Samuel's words fall to the ground. ²⁰And all Israel from Dan to Beersheba recognized that Samuel was attested as a prophet of the LORD. ²¹The LORD continued to appear at Shiloh, and there he revealed himself to Samuel through his word.

4

And Samuel's word came to all Israel.

The Philistines Capture the Ark

Now the Israelites went out to fight against the Philistines. The Israelites camped at Ebenezer, and the Philistines at Aphek. ²The Philistines deployed their forces to meet Israel, and as the battle spread, Israel was defeated by the Philistines, who killed about four thousand of them on the battlefield. ³When the soldiers returned to camp, the elders of Israel asked, "Why did the LORD bring defeat on us today before the Philistines? Let us bring the ark of the LORD's covenant from Shiloh, so that he may go with us and save us from the hand of our enemies."

⁴So the people sent men to Shiloh, and they brought back the ark of the covenant of the LORD Almighty, who is enthroned between the cherubim. And Eli's two sons, Hophni and Phinehas, were there with the ark of the covenant of God.

⁵When the ark of the LORD's covenant came into the camp, all Israel raised such a great shout that the ground shook. ⁶Hearing the uproar, the Philistines asked, "What's all this shouting in the Hebrew camp?"

When they learned that the ark of the LORD had come into the camp, ⁷the Philistines were afraid. "A god hasᵇ come into the camp," they said. "We're in trouble! Nothing like this has happened before. ⁸Woe to us! Who will deliver us from the hand of these mighty gods? They are the gods who struck the Egyptians with all kinds of plagues in the wilderness. ⁹Be strong, Philistines! Be men, or you will be subject to the Hebrews, as they have been to you. Be men, and fight!"

¹⁰So the Philistines fought, and the Israelites were defeated and every man fled to his tent. The slaughter was very great; Israel lost thirty thousand foot soldiers. ¹¹The ark of God was captured, and Eli's two sons, Hophni and Phinehas, died.

Death of Eli

¹²That same day a Benjamite ran from the battle line and went to Shiloh with his clothes torn and dust on his head. ¹³When

---

ᵃ 13 An ancient Hebrew scribal tradition (see also Septuagint); Masoretic Text *sons made themselves contemptible*   ᵇ 7 Or *"Gods have* (see Septuagint) he arrived, there was Eli sitting on his chair by the side of the road, watching, because his heart feared for the ark of God. When the man entered the town and told what had happened, the whole town sent up a cry.

¹⁴Eli heard the outcry and asked, "What is the meaning of this uproar?"

The man hurried over to Eli, ¹⁵who was ninety-eight years old and whose eyes had failed so that he could not see. ¹⁶He told Eli, "I have just come from the battle line; I fled from it this very day."

Eli asked, "What happened, my son?"

¹⁷The one who brought the news replied, "Israel fled before the Philistines, and the army has suffered heavy losses. Also your two sons, Hophni and Phinehas, are dead, and the ark of God has been captured."

¹⁸When he mentioned the ark of God, Eli fell backward off his chair by the side of the gate. His neck was broken and he died, for he was an old man, and he was heavy. He had led*a* Israel forty years.

¹⁹His daughter-in-law, the wife of Phinehas, was pregnant and near the time of delivery. When she heard the news that the ark of God had been captured and that her father-in-law and her husband were dead, she went into labor and gave birth, but was overcome by her labor pains. ²⁰As she was dying, the women attending her said, "Don't despair; you have given birth to a son." But she did not respond or pay any attention.

²¹She named the boy Ichabod,*b* saying, "The Glory has departed from Israel"—because of the capture of the ark of God and the deaths of her father-in-law and her husband. ²²She said, "The Glory has departed from Israel, for the ark of God has been captured."

The Ark in Ashdod and Ekron

5 After the Philistines had captured the ark of God, they took it from Ebenezer to Ashdod. ²Then they carried the ark into Dagon's temple and set it beside Dagon. ³When the people of Ashdod rose early the next day, there was Dagon, fallen on his face on the ground before the ark of the Lord! They took Dagon and put him back in his place. ⁴But the following morning when they rose, there was Dagon, fallen

on his face on the ground before the ark of the Lord! His head and hands had been broken off and were lying on the threshold; only his body remained. ⁵That is why to this day neither the priests of Dagon nor any others who enter Dagon's temple at Ashdod step on the threshold.

⁶The Lord's hand was heavy on the people of Ashdod and its vicinity; he brought devastation on them and afflicted them with tumors.*c* ⁷When the people of Ashdod saw what was happening, they said, "The ark of the god of Israel must not stay here with us, because his hand is heavy on us and on Dagon our god." ⁸So they called together all the rulers of the Philistines and asked them, "What shall we do with the ark of the god of Israel?"

They answered, "Have the ark of the god of Israel moved to Gath." So they moved the ark of the God of Israel.

⁹But after they had moved it, the Lord's hand was against that city, throwing it into a great panic. He afflicted the people of the city, both young and old, with an outbreak of tumors.*d* ¹⁰So they sent the ark of God to Ekron.

As the ark of God was entering Ekron, the people of Ekron cried out, "They have brought the ark of the god of Israel around to us to kill us and our people." ¹¹So they called together all the rulers of the Philistines and said, "Send the ark of the god of Israel away; let it go back to its own place, or it*e* will kill us and our people." For death had filled the city with panic; God's hand was very heavy on it. ¹²Those who did not die were afflicted with tumors, and the outcry of the city went up to heaven.

The Ark Returned to Israel

6 When the ark of the Lord had been in Philistine territory seven months, ²the Philistines called for the priests and the diviners and said, "What shall we do with the ark of the Lord? Tell us how we should send it back to its place."

³They answered, "If you return the ark of the god of Israel, do not send it back to him without a gift; by all means send a guilt offering to him. Then you will be healed, and you will know why his hand has not been lifted from you."

---

a 18 Traditionally *judged*   *b 21 Ichabod* means *no glory.*   *c 6* Hebrew; Septuagint and Vulgate *tumors. And rats appeared in their land, and there was death and destruction throughout the city*   *d 9* Or *with tumors in the groin* (see Septuagint)   *e 11* Or *he*

⁴The Philistines asked, "What guilt offering should we send to him?"

They replied, "Five gold tumors and five gold rats, according to the number of the Philistine rulers, because the same plague has struck both you and your rulers. ⁵Make models of the tumors and of the rats that are destroying the country, and give glory to Israel's god. Perhaps he will lift his hand from you and your gods and your land. ⁶Why do you harden your hearts as the Egyptians and Pharaoh did? When Israel's god dealt harshly with them, did they not send the Israelites out so they could go on their way?

⁷"Now then, get a new cart ready, with two cows that have calved and have never been yoked. Hitch the cows to the cart, but take their calves away and pen them up. ⁸Take the ark of the LORD and put it on the cart, and in a chest beside it put the gold objects you are sending back to him as a guilt offering. Send it on its way, ⁹but keep watching it. If it goes up to its own territory, toward Beth Shemesh, then the LORD has brought this great disaster on us. But if it does not, then we will know that it was not his hand that struck us but that it happened to us by chance."

¹⁰So they did this. They took two such cows and hitched them to the cart and penned up their calves. ¹¹They placed the ark of the LORD on the cart and along with it the chest containing the gold rats and the models of the tumors. ¹²Then the cows went straight toward Beth Shemesh, keeping on the road and lowing all the way; they did not turn to the right or to the left. The rulers of the Philistines followed them as far as the border of Beth Shemesh.

¹³Now the people of Beth Shemesh were harvesting their wheat in the valley, and when they looked up and saw the ark, they rejoiced at the sight. ¹⁴The cart came to the field of Joshua of Beth Shemesh, and there it stopped beside a large rock. The people chopped up the wood of the cart and sacrificed the cows as a burnt offering to the LORD. ¹⁵The Levites took down the ark of the LORD, together with the chest containing the gold objects, and placed them on the large rock. On that day the people of Beth Shemesh offered burnt offerings and made sacrifices to the LORD. ¹⁶The five rulers of the Philistines saw all this and then returned that same day to Ekron.

¹⁷These are the gold tumors the Philistines sent as a guilt offering to the LORD—one each for Ashdod, Gaza, Ashkelon, Gath and Ekron. ¹⁸And the number of the gold rats was according to the number of Philistine towns belonging to the five rulers—the fortified towns with their country villages. The large rock on which the Levites set the ark of the LORD is a witness to this day in the field of Joshua of Beth Shemesh.

¹⁹But God struck down some of the inhabitants of Beth Shemesh, putting seventy[a] of them to death because they looked into the ark of the LORD. The people mourned because of the heavy blow the LORD had dealt them. ²⁰And the people of Beth Shemesh asked, "Who can stand in the presence of the LORD, this holy God? To whom will the ark go up from here?"

²¹Then they sent messengers to the people of Kiriath Jearim, saying, "The Philistines have returned the ark of the LORD. Come down and take it up to your town."

7 ¹So the men of Kiriath Jearim came and took up the ark of the LORD. They brought it to Abinadab's house on the hill and consecrated Eleazar his son to guard the ark of the LORD. ²The ark remained at Kiriath Jearim a long time—twenty years in all.

Samuel Subdues the Philistines at Mizpah

Then all the people of Israel turned back to the LORD. ³So Samuel said to the whole house of Israel, "If you are returning to the LORD with all your hearts, then rid yourselves of the foreign gods and the Ashtoreths and commit yourselves to the LORD and serve him only, and he will deliver you out of the hand of the Philistines." ⁴So the Israelites put away their Baals and Ashtoreths, and served the LORD only.

⁵Then Samuel said, "Assemble all Israel at Mizpah, and I will intercede with the LORD for you." ⁶When they had assembled at Mizpah, they drew water and poured it out before the LORD. On that day they fasted and there they confessed, "We have sinned against the LORD." Now Samuel was serving as leader[b] of Israel at Mizpah.

---

a 19 A few Hebrew manuscripts; most Hebrew manuscripts and Septuagint 50,070   b 6 Traditionally judge; also in verse 15

⁷When the Philistines heard that Israel had assembled at Mizpah, the rulers of the Philistines came up to attack them. When the Israelites heard of it, they were afraid because of the Philistines. ⁸They said to Samuel, "Do not stop crying out to the LORD our God for us, that he may rescue us from the hand of the Philistines." ⁹Then Samuel took a suckling lamb and sacrificed it as a whole burnt offering to the LORD. He cried out to the LORD on Israel's behalf, and the LORD answered him.

¹⁰While Samuel was sacrificing the burnt offering, the Philistines drew near to engage Israel in battle. But that day the LORD thundered with loud thunder against the Philistines and threw them into such a panic that they were routed before the Israelites. ¹¹The men of Israel rushed out of Mizpah and pursued the Philistines, slaughtering them along the way to a point below Beth Kar.

¹²Then Samuel took a stone and set it up between Mizpah and Shen. He named it Ebenezer,ᵃ saying, "Thus far the LORD has helped us."

¹³So the Philistines were subdued and they stopped invading Israel's territory. Throughout Samuel's lifetime, the hand of the LORD was against the Philistines. ¹⁴The towns from Ekron to Gath that the Philistines had captured from Israel were restored, and Israel delivered the neighboring territory from the hands of the Philistines. And there was peace between Israel and the Amorites.

¹⁵Samuel continued as Israel's leader all the days of his life. ¹⁶From year to year he went on a circuit from Bethel to Gilgal to Mizpah, judging Israel in all those places. ¹⁷But he always went back to Ramah, where his home was, and there he also held court for Israel. And he built an altar there to the LORD.

Israel Asks for a King

8 When Samuel grew old, he appointed his sons as Israel's leaders.ᵇ ²The name of his firstborn was Joel and the name of his second was Abijah, and they served at Beersheba. ³But his sons did not follow his ways. They turned aside after dishonest gain and accepted bribes and perverted justice.

⁴So all the elders of Israel gathered together and came to Samuel at Ramah. ⁵They said to him, "You are old, and your sons do not follow your ways; now appoint a king to leadᶜ us, such as all the other nations have."

⁶But when they said, "Give us a king to lead us," this displeased Samuel; so he prayed to the LORD. ⁷And the LORD told him: "Listen to all that the people are saying to you; it is not you they have rejected, but they have rejected me as their king. ⁸As they have done from the day I brought them up out of Egypt until this day, forsaking me and serving other gods, so they are doing to you. ⁹Now listen to them; but warn them solemnly and let them know what the king who will reign over them will claim as his rights."

¹⁰Samuel told all the words of the LORD to the people who were asking him for a king. ¹¹He said, "This is what the king who will reign over you will claim as his rights: He will take your sons and make them serve with his chariots and horses, and they will run in front of his chariots. ¹²Some he will assign to be commanders of thousands and commanders of fifties, and others to plow his ground and reap his harvest, and still others to make weapons of war and equipment for his chariots. ¹³He will take your daughters to be perfumers and cooks and bakers. ¹⁴He will take the best of your fields and vineyards and olive groves and give them to his attendants. ¹⁵He will take a tenth of your grain and of your vintage and give it to his officials and attendants. ¹⁶Your male and female servants and the best of your cattleᵈ and donkeys he will take for his own use. ¹⁷He will take a tenth of your flocks, and you yourselves will become his slaves. ¹⁸When that day comes, you will cry out for relief from the king you have chosen, but the LORD will not answer you in that day."

¹⁹But the people refused to listen to Samuel. "No!" they said. "We want a king over us. ²⁰Then we will be like all the other nations, with a king to lead us and to go out before us and fight our battles."

²¹When Samuel heard all that the people said, he repeated it before the LORD. ²²The

---

ᵃ 12 Ebenezer means stone of help.   ᵇ 1 Traditionally judges   ᶜ 5 Traditionally judge; also in verses 6 and 20   ᵈ 16 Septuagint; Hebrew young men

LORD answered, "Listen to them and give them a king."

Then Samuel said to the Israelites, "Everyone go back to your own town."

Samuel Anoints Saul

9 There was a Benjamite, a man of standing, whose name was Kish son of Abiel, the son of Zeror, the son of Bekorath, the son of Aphiah of Benjamin. ²Kish had a son named Saul, as handsome a young man as could be found anywhere in Israel, and he was a head taller than anyone else.

³Now the donkeys belonging to Saul's father Kish were lost, and Kish said to his son Saul, "Take one of the servants with you and go and look for the donkeys." ⁴So he passed through the hill country of Ephraim and through the area around Shalisha, but they did not find them. They went on into the district of Shaalim, but the donkeys were not there. Then he passed through the territory of Benjamin, but they did not find them.

⁵When they reached the district of Zuph, Saul said to the servant who was with him, "Come, let's go back, or my father will stop thinking about the donkeys and start worrying about us."

⁶But the servant replied, "Look, in this town there is a man of God; he is highly respected, and everything he says comes true. Let's go there now. Perhaps he will tell us what way to take."

⁷Saul said to his servant, "If we go, what can we give the man? The food in our sacks is gone. We have no gift to take to the man of God. What do we have?"

⁸The servant answered him again. "Look," he said, "I have a quarter of a shekel*a* of silver. I will give it to the man of God so that he will tell us what way to take." ⁹(Formerly in Israel, if people went to inquire of God, they would say, "Come, let us go to the seer," because the prophet of today used to be called a seer.)

¹⁰"Good," Saul said to his servant. "Come, let's go." So they set out for the town where the man of God was.

¹¹As they were going up the hill to the town, they met some young women coming out to draw water, and they asked them, "Is the seer here?"

¹²"He is," they answered. "He's ahead of you. Hurry now; he has just come to our town today, for the people have a sacrifice at the high place. ¹³As soon as you enter the town, you will find him before he goes up to the high place to eat. The people will not begin eating until he comes, because he must bless the sacrifice; afterward, those who are invited will eat. Go up now; you should find him about this time."

¹⁴They went up to the town, and as they were entering it, there was Samuel, coming toward them on his way up to the high place.

¹⁵Now the day before Saul came, the LORD had revealed this to Samuel: ¹⁶"About this time tomorrow I will send you a man from the land of Benjamin. Anoint him ruler over my people Israel; he will deliver them from the hand of the Philistines. I have looked on my people, for their cry has reached me."

¹⁷When Samuel caught sight of Saul, the LORD said to him, "This is the man I spoke to you about; he will govern my people."

¹⁸Saul approached Samuel in the gateway and asked, "Would you please tell me where the seer's house is?"

¹⁹"I am the seer," Samuel replied. "Go up ahead of me to the high place, for today you are to eat with me, and in the morning I will send you on your way and will tell you all that is in your heart. ²⁰As for the donkeys you lost three days ago, do not worry about them; they have been found. And to whom is all the desire of Israel turned, if not to you and your whole family line?"

²¹Saul answered, "But am I not a Benjamite, from the smallest tribe of Israel, and is not my clan the least of all the clans of the tribe of Benjamin? Why do you say such a thing to me?"

²²Then Samuel brought Saul and his servant into the hall and seated them at the head of those who were invited—about thirty in number. ²³Samuel said to the cook, "Bring the piece of meat I gave you, the one I told you to lay aside."

²⁴So the cook took up the thigh with what was on it and set it in front of Saul. Samuel said, "Here is what has been kept for you. Eat, because it was set aside for you for this

a 8 That is, about 1/10 ounce or about 3 grams

occasion from the time I said, 'I have invited guests.'" And Saul dined with Samuel that day.

25After they came down from the high place to the town, Samuel talked with Saul on the roof of his house. 26They rose about daybreak, and Samuel called to Saul on the roof, "Get ready, and I will send you on your way." When Saul got ready, he and Samuel went outside together. 27As they were going down to the edge of the town, Samuel said to Saul, "Tell the servant to go on ahead of us"—and the servant did so—"but you stay here for a while, so that I may give you a message from God."

10 Then Samuel took a bottle of olive oil and poured it on Saul's head and kissed him, saying, "Has not the LORD anointed you ruler over his inheritance?*a* 2When you leave me today, you will meet two men near Rachel's tomb, at Zelzah on the border of Benjamin. They will say to you, 'The donkeys you set out to look for have been found. And now your father has stopped thinking about them and is worried about you. He is asking, "What shall I do about my son?"'

3"Then you will go on from there until you reach the great tree of Tabor. Three men going up to God at Bethel will meet you there. One will be carrying three young goats, another three loaves of bread, and another a skin of wine. 4They will greet you and offer you two loaves of bread, which you will accept from them.

5"After that you will go to Gibeah of God, where there is a Philistine outpost. As you approach the town, you will meet a procession of prophets coming down from the high place with lyres, timbrels, pipes and harps being played before them, and they will be prophesying. 6The Spirit of the LORD will come on you in power, and you will prophesy with them; and you will be changed into a different person. 7Once these signs are fulfilled, do whatever your hand finds to do, for God is with you.

8"Go down ahead of me to Gilgal. I will surely come down to you to sacrifice burnt offerings and fellowship offerings, but you must wait seven days until I come to you and tell you what you are to do."

Saul Made King

9As Saul turned to leave Samuel, God changed Saul's heart, and all these signs were fulfilled that day. 10When he and his servant arrived at Gibeah, a procession of prophets met him; the Spirit of God came on him in power, and he joined in their prophesying. 11When all those who had formerly known him saw him prophesying with the prophets, they asked each other, "What is this that has happened to the son of Kish? Is Saul also among the prophets?"

12A man who lived there answered, "And who is their father?" So it became a saying: "Is Saul also among the prophets?" 13After Saul stopped prophesying, he went to the high place.

14Now Saul's uncle asked him and his servant, "Where have you been?"

"Looking for the donkeys," he said. "But when we saw they were not to be found, we went to Samuel."

15Saul's uncle said, "Tell me what Samuel said to you."

16Saul replied, "He assured us that the donkeys had been found." But he did not tell his uncle what Samuel had said about the kingship.

17Samuel summoned the people of Israel to the LORD at Mizpah 18and said to them, "This is what the LORD, the God of Israel, says: 'I brought Israel up out of Egypt, and I delivered you from the power of Egypt and all the kingdoms that oppressed you.' 19But you have now rejected your God, who saves you out of all your disasters and calamities. And you have said, 'No, appoint a king over us.' So now present yourselves before the LORD by your tribes and clans."

20When Samuel had all Israel come forward by tribes, the tribe of Benjamin was taken by lot. 21Then he brought forward the tribe of Benjamin, clan by clan, and Matri's clan was taken. Finally Saul son of Kish was taken. But when they looked for him, he was not to be found. 22So they inquired further of the LORD, "Has the man come here yet?"

And the LORD said, "Yes, he has hidden himself among the supplies."

23They ran and brought him out, and as he stood among the people he was a head taller than any of the others. 24Samuel said

---

a 1 Hebrew; Septuagint and Vulgate over his people Israel? You will reign over the LORD's people and save them from the power of their enemies round about. And this will be a sign to you that the LORD has anointed you ruler over his inheritance:

WEDNESDAY

HANDLING REJECTION

1 Samuel 10:1–27 or 10:27

Mary Evans

In the new era that began once this ceremony was over, nobody was quite sure what ought to happen next. So Saul followed Samuel's general instruction to all the people and went home himself ... Those who opposed Saul here are described as [scoundrels]. In this new situation those who refused to accept Saul because they doubted his ability to save them, presumably from Philistine oppression, were in effect seen as rejecting God, of doubting his ability to save through Saul. That they brought no gifts emphasizes the fact that the majority had paid tribute to Saul. If Saul was to be able to do anything, he needed resources and the only way they could be provided was through the gifts of God's people. It must have been an encouragement to Saul that so many were willing to give financial support in this way even though no system of compulsory taxation had yet been installed. His silence in the face of the troublemakers' mockery reflects a wise realization that actions speak louder than words. Sometimes it is appropriate to refute the arguments and criticisms of those who oppose us, but it is rarely best to respond to mockery and doubt with anything other than silence. Time will prove the mockers to be right or wrong. By keeping silent and making his first action as king an inaction, Saul provides an excellent example to other leaders who might face the same kind of doubt of their abilities.

ROBERT JAMIESON {AD 1802–1880}

"Some scoundrels said, 'How can this fellow save us?' They despised him and brought him no gifts" (1 Samuel 10:27). In Eastern countries, the honor of the sovereign and the splendor of the royal household are upheld, not by a fixed rate of taxation, but by presents brought at certain seasons by officials and men of wealth from all parts of the kingdom. These gifts were to be chosen according to the means of the individual, and of a customary and proper value. Such was the tribute which Saul's opponents withheld. Lacking those, he was unable to set up a kingly establishment for a while. But "biding his time," he bore the insult with a prudence and magnanimity which were of great use in the beginning of his government.

reflection

1. God had anointed Saul and established him as king. How did those who rejected Saul as king also reject God?

2. How did Saul's silence in the face of their mockery reveal wisdom and insight?

3. What authority figures in your life do you find it difficult to honor and respect?

For your next devotional reading, go to page 319.

to all the people, "Do you see the man the LORD has chosen? There is no one like him among all the people."

Then the people shouted, "Long live the king!"

25Samuel explained to the people the rights and duties of kingship. He wrote them down on a scroll and deposited it before the LORD. Then Samuel dismissed the people to go to their own homes.

26Saul also went to his home in Gibeah, accompanied by valiant men whose hearts God had touched. 27But some scoundrels said, "How can this fellow save us?" They despised him and brought him no gifts. But Saul kept silent.

Saul Rescues the City of Jabesh

11 Nahash[a] the Ammonite went up and besieged Jabesh Gilead. And all the men of Jabesh said to him, "Make a treaty with us, and we will be subject to you."

2But Nahash the Ammonite replied, "I will make a treaty with you only on the condition that I gouge out the right eye of every one of you and so bring disgrace on all Israel."

3The elders of Jabesh said to him, "Give us seven days so we can send messengers throughout Israel; if no one comes to rescue us, we will surrender to you."

4When the messengers came to Gibeah of Saul and reported these terms to the people, they all wept aloud. 5Just then Saul was returning from the fields, behind his oxen, and he asked, "What is wrong with everyone? Why are they weeping?" Then they repeated to him what the men of Jabesh had said.

6When Saul heard their words, the Spirit of God came on him in power, and he burned with anger. 7He took a pair of oxen, cut them into pieces, and sent the pieces by messengers throughout Israel, proclaiming, "This is what will be done to the oxen of anyone who does not follow Saul and Samuel." Then the terror of the LORD fell on the people, and they turned out with one accord. 8When Saul mustered them at Bezek,

the men of Israel numbered three hundred thousand and those of Judah thirty thousand.

9They told the messengers who had come, "Say to the men of Jabesh Gilead, 'By the time the sun is hot tomorrow, you will be rescued.' " When the messengers went and reported this to the men of Jabesh, they were elated. 10They said to the Ammonites, "Tomorrow we will surrender to you, and you can do to us whatever you like."

11The next day Saul separated his men into three divisions; during the last watch of the night they broke into the camp of the Ammonites and slaughtered them until the heat of the day. Those who survived were scattered, so that no two of them were left together.

Saul Confirmed as King

12The people then said to Samuel, "Who was it that asked, 'Shall Saul reign over us?' Turn these men over to us so that we may put them to death."

13But Saul said, "No one will be put to death today, for this day the LORD has rescued Israel."

14Then Samuel said to the people, "Come, let us go to Gilgal and there renew the kingship." 15So all the people went to Gilgal and made Saul king in the presence of the LORD. There they sacrificed fellowship offerings before the LORD, and Saul and all the Israelites held a great celebration.

Samuel's Farewell Speech

12 Samuel said to all Israel, "I have listened to everything you said to me and have set a king over you. 2Now you have a king as your leader. As for me, I am old and gray, and my sons are here with you. I have been your leader from my youth until this day. 3Here I stand. Testify against me in the presence of the LORD and his anointed. Whose ox have I taken? Whose donkey have I taken? Whom have I cheated? Whom have I oppressed? From whose hand have I accepted a bribe to make me shut my eyes? If I have done any of these things, I will make it right."

---

a 1 Masoretic Text; Dead Sea Scrolls gifts. Now Nahash king of the Ammonites oppressed the Gadites and Reubenites severely. He gouged out all their right eyes and struck terror and dread in Israel. Not a man remained among the Israelites beyond the Jordan whose right eye was not gouged out by Nahash king of the Ammonites, except that seven thousand men fled from the Ammonites and entered Jabesh Gilead. About a month later, 1Nahash

⁴"You have not cheated or oppressed us," they replied. "You have not taken anything from anyone's hand."

⁵Samuel said to them, "The LORD is witness against you, and also his anointed is witness this day, that you have not found anything in my hand."

"We agree," they said.

⁶Then Samuel said to the people, "It is the LORD who appointed Moses and Aaron and brought your ancestors up out of Egypt. ⁷Now then, stand here, because I am going to confront you with evidence before the LORD as to all the righteous acts performed by the LORD for you and your ancestors.

⁸"After Jacob entered Egypt, they cried to the LORD for help, and the LORD sent Moses and Aaron, who brought your ancestors out of Egypt and settled them in this place.

⁹"But they forgot the LORD their God; so he sold them into the hand of Sisera, the commander of the army of Hazor, and into the hands of the Philistines and the king of Moab, who fought against them. ¹⁰They cried out to the LORD and said, 'We have sinned; we have forsaken the LORD and served the Baals and the Ashtoreths. But now deliver us from the hands of our enemies, and we will serve you.' ¹¹Then the LORD sent Jerub-Baal,ᵃ Barak,ᵇ Jephthah and Samuel,ᶜ and he delivered you from the hands of your enemies all around you, so that you lived in safety.

¹²"But when you saw that Nahash king of the Ammonites was moving against you, you said to me, 'No, we want a king to rule over us'—even though the LORD your God was your king. ¹³Now here is the king you have chosen, the one you asked for; see, the LORD has set a king over you. ¹⁴If you fear the LORD and serve and obey him and do not rebel against his commands, and if both you and the king who reigns over you follow the LORD your God—good! ¹⁵But if you do not obey the LORD, and if you rebel against his commands, his hand will be against you, as it was against your ancestors.

¹⁶"Now then, stand still and see this great thing the LORD is about to do before your eyes! ¹⁷Is it not wheat harvest now? I will call on the LORD to send thunder and rain.

And you will realize what an evil thing you did in the eyes of the LORD when you asked for a king."

¹⁸Then Samuel called on the LORD, and that same day the LORD sent thunder and rain. So all the people stood in awe of the LORD and of Samuel.

¹⁹The people all said to Samuel, "Pray to the LORD your God for your servants so that we will not die, for we have added to all our other sins the evil of asking for a king."

²⁰"Do not be afraid," Samuel replied. "You have done all this evil; yet do not turn away from the LORD, but serve the LORD with all your heart. ²¹Do not turn away after useless idols. They can do you no good, nor can they rescue you, because they are useless. ²²For the sake of his great name the LORD will not reject his people, because the LORD was pleased to make you his own. ²³As for me, far be it from me that I should sin against the LORD by failing to pray for you. And I will teach you the way that is good and right. ²⁴But be sure to fear the LORD and serve him faithfully with all your heart; consider what great things he has done for you. ²⁵Yet if you persist in doing evil, both you and your king will perish."

Samuel Rebukes Saul

13 Saul was thirtyᵈ years old when he became king, and he reigned over Israel forty-ᵉ two years.

²Saul chose three thousand men from Israel; two thousand were with him at Mikmash and in the hill country of Bethel, and a thousand were with Jonathan at Gibeah in Benjamin. The rest he sent back to their homes.

³Jonathan attacked the Philistine outpost at Geba, and the Philistines heard about it. Then Saul had the trumpet blown throughout the land and said, "Let the Hebrews hear!" ⁴So all Israel heard the news: "Saul has attacked the Philistine outpost, and now Israel has become obnoxious to the Philistines." And the people were summoned to join Saul at Gilgal.

⁵The Philistines assembled to fight Israel, with three thousandᶠ chariots, six thousand charioteers, and soldiers as numerous as the

---

ᵃ 11 Also called *Gideon*   ᵇ 11 Some Septuagint manuscripts and Syriac; Hebrew *Bedan*   ᶜ 11 Hebrew; some Septuagint manuscripts and Syriac *Samson*   ᵈ 1 A few late manuscripts of the Septuagint; Hebrew does not have *thirty*.   ᵉ 1 Probable reading of the original Hebrew text (see Acts 13:21); Masoretic Text does not have *forty-*.   ᶠ 5 Some Septuagint manuscripts and Syriac; Hebrew *thirty thousand*

sand on the seashore. They went up and camped at Mikmash, east of Beth Aven. [6]When the Israelites saw that their situation was critical and that their army was hard pressed, they hid in caves and thickets, among the rocks, and in pits and cisterns. [7]Some Hebrews even crossed the Jordan to the land of Gad and Gilead.

Saul remained at Gilgal, and all the troops with him were quaking with fear. [8]He waited seven days, the time set by Samuel; but Samuel did not come to Gilgal, and Saul's men began to scatter. [9]So he said, "Bring me the burnt offering and the fellowship offerings." And Saul offered up the burnt offering. [10]Just as he finished making the offering, Samuel arrived, and Saul went out to greet him.

[11]"What have you done?" asked Samuel.

Saul replied, "When I saw that the men were scattering, and that you did not come at the set time, and that the Philistines were assembling at Mikmash, [12]I thought, 'Now the Philistines will come down against me at Gilgal, and I have not sought the LORD's favor.' So I felt compelled to offer the burnt offering."

[13]"You have done a foolish thing," Samuel said. "You have not kept the command the LORD your God gave you; if you had, he would have established your kingdom over Israel for all time. [14]But now your kingdom will not endure; the LORD has sought out a man after his own heart and appointed him ruler of his people, because you have not kept the LORD's command."

[15]Then Samuel left Gilgal[a] and went up to Gibeah in Benjamin, and Saul counted the men who were with him. They numbered about six hundred.

Israel Without Weapons

[16]Saul and his son Jonathan and the men with them were staying in Gibeah[b] in Benjamin, while the Philistines camped at Mikmash. [17]Raiding parties went out from the Philistine camp in three detachments. One turned toward Ophrah in the vicinity of Shual, [18]another toward Beth Horon, and the third toward the borderland overlooking the Valley of Zeboyim facing the wilderness.

[19]Not a blacksmith could be found in the whole land of Israel, because the Philistines had said, "Otherwise the Hebrews will make swords or spears!" [20]So all Israel went down to the Philistines to have their plowpoints, mattocks, axes and sickles[c] sharpened. [21]The price was two-thirds of a shekel[d] for sharpening plowpoints and mattocks, and a third of a shekel[e] for sharpening forks and axes and for repointing goads.

[22]So on the day of the battle not a soldier with Saul and Jonathan had a sword or spear in his hand; only Saul and his son Jonathan had them.

Jonathan Attacks the Philistines

[23]Now a detachment of Philistines had gone out to the pass at Mikmash.

14

[1]One day Jonathan son of Saul said to his young armor-bearer, "Come, let's go over to the Philistine outpost on the other side." But he did not tell his father.

[2]Saul was staying on the outskirts of Gibeah under a pomegranate tree in Migron. With him were about six hundred men, [3]among whom was Ahijah, who was wearing an ephod. He was a son of Ichabod's brother Ahitub son of Phinehas, the son of Eli, the LORD's priest in Shiloh. No one was aware that Jonathan had left.

[4]On each side of the pass that Jonathan intended to cross to reach the Philistine outpost was a cliff; one was called Bozez and the other Seneh. [5]One cliff stood to the north toward Mikmash, the other to the south toward Geba.

[6]Jonathan said to his young armor-bearer, "Come, let's go over to the outpost of those uncircumcised fellows. Perhaps the LORD will act in our behalf. Nothing can hinder the LORD from saving, whether by many or by few."

[7]"Do all that you have in mind," his armor-bearer said. "Go ahead; I am with you heart and soul."

[8]Jonathan said, "Come on, then; we will cross over toward them and let them see us. [9]If they say to us, 'Wait there until we come to you,' we will stay where we are and not go up to them. [10]But if they say, 'Come up to

---

[a] 15 Hebrew; Septuagint *Gilgal and went his way; the rest of the people went after Saul to meet the army, and they went out of Gilgal*   [b] 16 Two Hebrew manuscripts; most Hebrew manuscripts *Geba*, a variant of *Gibeah*   [c] 20 Septuagint; Hebrew *plowpoints*   [d] 21 That is, about 1/4 ounce or about 8 grams   [e] 21 That is, about 1/8 ounce or about 4 grams

us,' we will climb up, because that will be our sign that the LORD has given them into our hands."

¹¹So both of them showed themselves to the Philistine outpost. "Look!" said the Philistines. "The Hebrews are crawling out of the holes they were hiding in." ¹²The men of the outpost shouted to Jonathan and his armor-bearer, "Come up to us and we'll teach you a lesson."

So Jonathan said to his armor-bearer, "Climb up after me; the LORD has given them into the hand of Israel."

¹³Jonathan climbed up, using his hands and feet, with his armor-bearer right behind him. The Philistines fell before Jonathan, and his armor-bearer followed and killed behind him. ¹⁴In that first attack Jonathan and his armor-bearer killed some twenty men in an area of about half an acre.

Israel Routs the Philistines

¹⁵Then panic struck the whole army—those in the camp and field, and those in the outposts and raiding parties—and the ground shook. It was a panic sent by God.ᵃ

¹⁶Saul's lookouts at Gibeah in Benjamin saw the army melting away in all directions. ¹⁷Then Saul said to the men who were with him, "Muster the forces and see who has left us." When they did, it was Jonathan and his armor-bearer who were not there.

¹⁸Saul said to Ahijah, "Bring the ark of God." (At that time it was with the Israelites.)ᵇ ¹⁹While Saul was talking to the priest, the tumult in the Philistine camp increased more and more. So Saul said to the priest, "Withdraw your hand."

²⁰Then Saul and all his men assembled and went to the battle. They found the Philistines in total confusion, striking each other with their swords. ²¹Those Hebrews who had previously been with the Philistines and had gone up with them to their camp went over to the Israelites who were with Saul and Jonathan. ²²When all the Israelites who had hidden in the hill country of Ephraim heard that the Philistines were on the run, they joined the battle in hot pursuit. ²³So on that day the LORD saved Israel, and the battle moved on beyond Beth Aven.

Jonathan Eats Honey

²⁴Now the Israelites were in distress that day, because Saul had bound the people under an oath, saying, "Cursed be anyone who eats food before evening comes, before I have avenged myself on my enemies!" So none of the troops tasted food.

²⁵The entire army entered the woods, and there was honey on the ground. ²⁶When they went into the woods, they saw the honey oozing out; yet no one put his hand to his mouth, because they feared the oath. ²⁷But Jonathan had not heard that his father had bound the people with the oath, so he reached out the end of the staff that was in his hand and dipped it into the honeycomb. He raised his hand to his mouth, and his eyes brightened.ᶜ ²⁸Then one of the soldiers told him, "Your father bound the army under a strict oath, saying, 'Cursed be anyone who eats food today!' That is why the men are faint."

²⁹Jonathan said, "My father has made trouble for the country. See how my eyes brightenedᵈ when I tasted a little of this honey. ³⁰How much better it would have been if the men had eaten today some of the plunder they took from their enemies. Would not the slaughter of the Philistines have been even greater?"

³¹That day, after the Israelites had struck down the Philistines from Mikmash to Aijalon, they were exhausted. ³²They pounced on the plunder and, taking sheep, cattle and calves, they butchered them on the ground and ate them, together with the blood. ³³Then someone said to Saul, "Look, the men are sinning against the LORD by eating meat that has blood in it."

"You have broken faith," he said. "Roll a large stone over here at once." ³⁴Then he said, "Go out among the men and tell them, 'Each of you bring me your cattle and sheep, and slaughter them here and eat them. Do not sin against the LORD by eating meat with blood still in it.' "

So everyone brought his ox that night and slaughtered it there. ³⁵Then Saul built an altar to the LORD; it was the first time he had done this.

³⁶Saul said, "Let us go down and pursue the Philistines by night and plunder them

---

ᵃ 15 Or a terrible panic   ᵇ 18 Hebrew; Septuagint "Bring the ephod." (At that time he wore the ephod before the Israelites.)   ᶜ 27 Or his strength was renewed   ᵈ 29 Or my strength was renewed till dawn, and let us not leave one of them alive."

"Do whatever seems best to you," they replied.

But the priest said, "Let us inquire of God here."

[37]So Saul asked God, "Shall I go down and pursue the Philistines? Will you give them into Israel's hand?" But God did not answer him that day.

[38]Saul therefore said, "Come here, all you who are leaders of the army, and let us find out what sin has been committed today. [39]As surely as the LORD who rescues Israel lives, even if it lies with my son Jonathan, he must die." But not one of them said a word.

[40]Saul then said to all the Israelites, "You stand over there; I and Jonathan my son will stand over here."

"Do what seems best to you," they replied.

[41]Then Saul prayed to the LORD, the God of Israel, "Why have you not answered your servant today? If the fault is in me or my son Jonathan, respond with Urim, but if the men of Israel are at fault,[a] respond with Thummim." Jonathan and Saul were taken by lot, and the men were cleared. [42]Saul said, "Cast the lot between me and Jonathan my son." And Jonathan was taken.

[43]Then Saul said to Jonathan, "Tell me what you have done."

So Jonathan told him, "I tasted a little honey with the end of my staff. And now I must die!"

[44]Saul said, "May God deal with me, be it ever so severely, if you do not die, Jonathan."

[45]But the men said to Saul, "Should Jonathan die—he who has brought about this great deliverance in Israel? Never! As surely as the LORD lives, not a hair of his head will fall to the ground, for he did this today with God's help." So the men rescued Jonathan, and he was not put to death.

[46]Then Saul stopped pursuing the Philistines, and they withdrew to their own land.

[47]After Saul had assumed rule over Israel, he fought against their enemies on every side: Moab, the Ammonites, Edom, the kings[b] of Zobah, and the Philistines. Wher-

ever he turned, he inflicted punishment on them.[c] [48]He fought valiantly and defeated the Amalekites, delivering Israel from the hands of those who had plundered them.

Saul's Family

[49]Saul's sons were Jonathan, Ishvi and Malki-Shua. The name of his older daughter was Merab, and that of the younger was Michal. [50]His wife's name was Ahinoam daughter of Ahimaaz. The name of the commander of Saul's army was Abner son of Ner, and Ner was Saul's uncle. [51]Saul's father Kish and Abner's father Ner were sons of Abiel.

[52]All the days of Saul there was bitter war with the Philistines, and whenever Saul saw a mighty or brave man, he took him into his service.

The LORD Rejects Saul as King

15 Samuel said to Saul, "I am the one the LORD sent to anoint you king over his people Israel; so listen now to the message from the LORD. [2]This is what the LORD Almighty says: 'I will punish the Amalekites for what they did to Israel when they waylaid them as they came up from Egypt. [3]Now go, attack the Amalekites and totally destroy[d] all that belongs to them. Do not spare them; put to death men and women, children and infants, cattle and sheep, camels and donkeys.'"

[4]So Saul summoned the men and mustered them at Telaim—two hundred thousand foot soldiers and ten thousand from Judah. [5]Saul went to the city of Amalek and set an ambush in the ravine. [6]Then he said to the Kenites, "Go away, leave the Amalekites so that I do not destroy you along with them; for you showed kindness to all the Israelites when they came up out of Egypt." So the Kenites moved away from the Amalekites.

[7]Then Saul attacked the Amalekites all the way from Havilah to Shur, near the eastern border of Egypt. [8]He took Agag king of the Amalekites alive, and all his people he totally destroyed with the sword. [9]But Saul and the army spared Agag and the best of the sheep and cattle, the fat calves[e] and

a 41 Septuagint; Hebrew does not have "Why . . . at fault.   b 47 Masoretic Text; Dead Sea Scrolls and Septuagint king   c 47 Hebrew; Septuagint he was victorious   d 3 The Hebrew term refers to the irrevocable giving over of things or persons to the LORD, often by totally destroying them; also in verses 8, 9, 15, 18, 20 and 21.   e 9 Or the grown bulls; the meaning of the Hebrew for this phrase is uncertain.

THURSDAY

CHANGE FROM THE INSIDE

1 Samuel 15:1–35 or 15:22–23

C. S. LEWIS {AD 1898–1963}

When I was a child I often had a toothache, which I knew that if I went to my mother she would give me something which would deaden the pain for that night and let me get to sleep. But I did not go to my mother—at least, not till the pain became very bad. And the reason I did not go was this: I did not doubt she would give me the aspirin, but I knew she would also do something else. I knew she would take me to the dentist next morning. I could not get what I wanted out of her without getting something more, which I did not want. I wanted immediate relief from pain, but I could not get it without having my teeth set permanently right. And I knew those dentists; I knew they started fiddling about with all sorts of other teeth which had not yet begun to ache. They would not let sleeping dogs lie; if you gave them an inch they took a mile.

Now, if I may put it that way, our Lord is like the dentists ... Dozens of people go to Him to be cured of some one particular sin which they are ashamed of (like masturbation or physical cowardice) or which is obviously spoiling daily life (like bad temper or drunkenness). Well, He will cure it all right; but He will not stop there. That may be all you asked; but if once you call Him in, He will give you the full treatment.

That is why He warned people to "count the cost" before becoming Christians. "Make no mistake," He says, "if you let me, I will make you perfect. The moment you put yourself in My hands, that is what you are in for. Nothing less, or other, than that."

Kenneth Osbeck

Saving faith is much more than a commitment to a creed, church or doctrinal system. It must be a commitment to a person—Jesus Christ. Doctrinal statements and creeds are important in defining and delineating truth, but they must never replace a personal relationship with "The Truth" ... Again and again we must take inventory of ourselves and determine what is the real foundation of our spiritual lives and the source of our resting place—Christ or merely a creed?

reflection

1. God doesn't want your "religious duty"; he wants your whole heart. What's the difference?

2. Why is it easier to obey God outwardly than it is to truly submit to him in your heart?

3. Instead of surrendering himself completely to God's commands, Saul tried to rewrite them. In what ways do you fall into this same trap? What happened to Saul as a result? What may happen to you as a result?

For your next devotional reading, go to page 322.

lambs—everything that was good. These they were unwilling to destroy completely, but everything that was despised and weak they totally destroyed.

¹⁰Then the word of the LORD came to Samuel: ¹¹"I regret that I have made Saul king, because he has turned away from me and has not carried out my instructions." Samuel was angry, and he cried out to the LORD all that night.

¹²Early in the morning Samuel got up and went to meet Saul, but he was told, "Saul has gone to Carmel. There he has set up a monument in his own honor and has turned and gone on down to Gilgal."

¹³When Samuel reached him, Saul said, "The LORD bless you! I have carried out the LORD's instructions."

¹⁴But Samuel said, "What then is this bleating of sheep in my ears? What is this lowing of cattle that I hear?"

¹⁵Saul answered, "The soldiers brought them from the Amalekites; they spared the best of the sheep and cattle to sacrifice to the LORD your God, but we totally destroyed the rest."

¹⁶"Enough!" Samuel said to Saul. "Let me tell you what the LORD said to me last night."

"Tell me," Saul replied.

¹⁷Samuel said, "Although you were once small in your own eyes, did you not become the head of the tribes of Israel? The LORD anointed you king over Israel. ¹⁸And he sent you on a mission, saying, 'Go and complete-ly destroy those wicked people, the Amalek-ites; make war on them until you have wiped them out.' ¹⁹Why did you not obey the LORD? Why did you pounce on the plunder and do evil in the eyes of the LORD?"

²⁰"But I did obey the LORD," Saul said. "I went on the mission the LORD assigned me. I completely destroyed the Amalekites and brought back Agag their king. ²¹The soldiers took sheep and cattle from the plunder, the best of what was devoted to God, in order to sacrifice them to the LORD your God at Gilgal."

²²But Samuel replied:

"Does the LORD delight in burnt offerings
     and sacrifices
   as much as in obeying the LORD?
To obey is better than sacrifice,
   and to heed is better than the fat of
     rams.

²³For rebellion is like the sin of
     divination,
   and arrogance like the evil of
     idolatry.
Because you have rejected the word of
     the LORD,
   he has rejected you as king."

²⁴Then Saul said to Samuel, "I have sinned. I violated the LORD's command and your instructions. I was afraid of the men and so I gave in to them. ²⁵Now I beg you, forgive my sin and come back with me, so that I may worship the LORD."

²⁶But Samuel said to him, "I will not go back with you. You have rejected the word of the LORD, and the LORD has rejected you as king over Israel!"

²⁷As Samuel turned to leave, Saul caught hold of the hem of his robe, and it tore. ²⁸Samuel said to him, "The LORD has torn the kingdom of Israel from you today and has given it to one of your neighbors—to one better than you. ²⁹He who is the Glory of Israel does not lie or change his mind; for he is not a human being, that he should change his mind."

³⁰Saul replied, "I have sinned. But please honor me before the elders of my people and before Israel; come back with me, so that I may worship the LORD your God." ³¹So Samuel went back with Saul, and Saul wor-shiped the LORD.

³²Then Samuel said, "Bring me Agag king of the Amalekites."

Agag came to him in chains.ᵃ And he thought, "Surely the bitterness of death is past."

³³But Samuel said,

"As your sword has made women
     childless,
   so will your mother be childless
     among women."

And Samuel put Agag to death before the LORD at Gilgal.

³⁴Then Samuel left for Ramah, but Saul went up to his home in Gibeah of Saul. ³⁵Until the day Samuel died, he did not go to see Saul again, though Samuel mourned for him. And the LORD regretted that he had made Saul king over Israel.

ᵃ 32 The meaning of the Hebrew for this phrase is uncertain.

Samuel Anoints David

16

The LORD said to Samuel, "How long will you mourn for Saul, since I have rejected him as king over Israel? Fill your horn with oil and be on your way; I am sending you to Jesse of Bethlehem. I have chosen one of his sons to be king."

²But Samuel said, "How can I go? If Saul hears about it, he will kill me."

The LORD said, "Take a heifer with you and say, 'I have come to sacrifice to the LORD.' ³Invite Jesse to the sacrifice, and I will show you what to do. You are to anoint for me the one I indicate."

⁴Samuel did what the LORD said. When he arrived at Bethlehem, the elders of the town trembled when they met him. They asked, "Do you come in peace?"

⁵Samuel replied, "Yes, in peace; I have come to sacrifice to the LORD. Consecrate yourselves and come to the sacrifice with me." Then he consecrated Jesse and his sons and invited them to the sacrifice.

⁶When they arrived, Samuel saw Eliab and thought, "Surely the LORD's anointed stands here before the LORD."

⁷But the LORD said to Samuel, "Do not consider his appearance or his height, for I have rejected him. The LORD does not look at the things human beings look at. People look at the outward appearance, but the LORD looks at the heart."

⁸Then Jesse called Abinadab and had him pass in front of Samuel. But Samuel said, "The LORD has not chosen this one either." ⁹Jesse then had Shammah pass by, but Samuel said, "Nor has the LORD chosen this one." ¹⁰Jesse had seven of his sons pass before Samuel, but Samuel said to him, "The LORD has not chosen these." ¹¹So he asked Jesse, "Are these all the sons you have?"

"There is still the youngest," Jesse answered. "He is tending the sheep."

Samuel said, "Send for him; we will not sit down until he arrives."

¹²So he sent and had him brought in. He was glowing with health and had a fine appearance and handsome features.

Then the LORD said, "Rise and anoint him; this is the one."

¹³So Samuel took the horn of oil and anointed him in the presence of his brothers, and from that day on the Spirit of the LORD came on David in power. Samuel then went to Ramah.

David in Saul's Service

¹⁴Now the Spirit of the LORD had departed from Saul, and an evil*ᵃ* spirit from the LORD tormented him.

¹⁵Saul's attendants said to him, "See, an evil spirit from God is tormenting you. ¹⁶Let our lord command his servants here to search for someone who can play the lyre. He will play when the evil spirit from God comes on you, and you will feel better."

¹⁷So Saul said to his attendants, "Find someone who plays well and bring him to me."

¹⁸One of the servants answered, "I have seen a son of Jesse of Bethlehem who knows how to play the lyre. He is a brave man and a warrior. He speaks well and is a fine-looking man. And the LORD is with him."

¹⁹Then Saul sent messengers to Jesse and said, "Send me your son David, who is with the sheep." ²⁰So Jesse took a donkey loaded with bread, a skin of wine and a young goat and sent them with his son David to Saul.

²¹David came to Saul and entered his service. Saul liked him very much, and David became one of his armor-bearers. ²²Then Saul sent word to Jesse, saying, "Allow David to remain in my service, for I am pleased with him."

²³Whenever the spirit from God came on Saul, David would take up his lyre and play. Then relief would come to Saul; he would feel better, and the evil spirit would leave him.

David and Goliath

17

Now the Philistines gathered their forces for war and assembled at Sokoh in Judah. They pitched camp at Ephes Dammim, between Sokoh and Azekah. ²Saul and the Israelites assembled and camped in the Valley of Elah and drew up their battle line to meet the Philistines. ³The Philistines occupied one hill and the Israelites another, with the valley between them.

⁴A champion named Goliath, who was from Gath, came out of the Philistine camp. His height was six cubits and a span.*ᵇ* ⁵He had a bronze helmet on his head and wore a

---

a 14 Or *harmful*; also in verses 15, 16 and 23   *b* 4 That is, about 9 1/2 feet or about 2.9 meters

FRIDAY

CHARACTER ABOVE ALL ELSE

1 Samuel 16:1–13 *or* 16:7

Craig Borlase

Surprising as it may seem, I don't think God is all that fussed about our physique. Whether the six-pack is spiritual or physical, I think the reaction would be far more "that's nice, dear" than "wow!" God's idea of success is something else altogether.

A quick glance through the Bible will turn up some common themes. Look at Samuel, Abraham and Sarah, David, Joseph, Elisha, Mary and Jesus—to name but a few—and you'll see that each of them went through long periods of what looked like inactivity before they finally kicked into the big time of carrying out God's public purpose for their lives. Why? It's all about the character. God doesn't need a selection of the most talented individuals to run things for Him while He's out of town for a few millennia; instead, He's after character to follow through with the calling even when things don't look so great.

PHILIP SCHAFF {AD 1819–1893}

One of the strongest proofs of the supernatural origin of Christianity is its elevation above the natural culture and moral standard of those who first professed it. The most perfect doctrine and life was described by unschooled fishermen from Galilee, who never before had been outside of Palestine and were scarcely able to read and to write! And the profoundest mysteries of the kingdom of heaven, the incarnation, redemption, regeneration and resurrection were taught by the apostles to congregations of poor and illiterate peasants, slaves and freedmen! For "Not many of you were wise by human standards; not many were influential; not many were of noble birth" when you were called. "But God chose the foolish things of the world to shame the wise; God chose the weak things of the world to shame the strong. God chose the lowly things of this world and the despised things—and the things that are not—to nullify the things that are, so that no one may boast before him" (1 Corinthians 1:26–29).

reflection

1. If outward appearance and external markers of status mean nothing to God, what *is* important to him?

2. What "case studies" from the Bible can you provide to prove that what matters most to God is the character of our hearts?

3. If we know that God values character above appearance, why do so many people, including Christians, place so much value on appearances?

For your next devotional reading, go to page 328.

coat of scale armor of bronze weighing five thousand shekels[a]; [6]on his legs he wore bronze greaves, and a bronze javelin was slung on his back. [7]His spear shaft was like a weaver's rod, and its iron point weighed six hundred shekels.[b] His shield bearer went ahead of him.

[8]Goliath stood and shouted to the ranks of Israel, "Why do you come out and line up for battle? Am I not a Philistine, and are you not the servants of Saul? Choose a man and have him come down to me. [9]If he is able to fight and kill me, we will become your subjects; but if I overcome him and kill him, you will become our subjects and serve us." [10]Then the Philistine said, "This day I defy the armies of Israel! Give me a man and let us fight each other." [11]On hearing the Philistine's words, Saul and all the Israelites were dismayed and terrified.

[12]Now David was the son of an Ephrathite named Jesse, who was from Bethlehem in Judah. Jesse had eight sons, and in Saul's time he was very old. [13]Jesse's three oldest sons had followed Saul to the war: The first-born was Eliab; the second, Abinadab; and the third, Shammah. [14]David was the youngest. The three oldest followed Saul, [15]but David went back and forth from Saul to tend his father's sheep at Bethlehem.

[16]For forty days the Philistine came forward every morning and evening and took his stand.

[17]Now Jesse said to his son David, "Take this ephah[c] of roasted grain and these ten loaves of bread for your brothers and hurry to their camp. [18]Take along these ten cheeses to the commander of their unit. See how your brothers are and bring back some assurance[d] from them. [19]They are with Saul and all the men of Israel in the Valley of Elah, fighting against the Philistines."

[20]Early in the morning David left the flock in the care of a shepherd, loaded up and set out, as Jesse had directed. He reached the camp as the army was going out to its battle positions, shouting the war cry. [21]Israel and the Philistines were drawing up their lines facing each other. [22]David left his things with the keeper of supplies, ran to the battle lines and asked his brothers how they were. [23]As he was talking with them, Goliath, the Philistine champion from Gath, stepped out from his lines and shouted his usual defiance, and David heard it. [24]Whenever the Israelites saw the man, they all fled from him in great fear.

[25]Now the Israelites had been saying, "Do you see how this man keeps coming out? He comes out to defy Israel. The king will give great wealth to the man who kills him. He will also give him his daughter in marriage and will exempt his family line from taxes in Israel."

[26]David asked those standing near him, "What will be done for the man who kills this Philistine and removes this disgrace from Israel? Who is this uncircumcised Philistine that he should defy the armies of the living God?"

[27]They repeated to him what they had been saying and told him, "This is what will be done for the man who kills him."

[28]When Eliab, David's oldest brother, heard him speaking with the men, he burned with anger at him and asked, "Why have you come down here? And with whom did you leave those few sheep in the wilderness? I know how conceited you are and how wicked your heart is; you came down only to watch the battle."

[29]"Now what have I done?" said David. "Can't I even speak?" [30]He then turned away to someone else and brought up the same matter, and the men answered him as before. [31]What David said was overheard and reported to Saul, and Saul sent for him.

[32]David said to Saul, "Let no one lose heart on account of this Philistine; your servant will go and fight him."

[33]Saul replied, "You are not able to go out against this Philistine and fight him; you are little more than a boy, and he has been a warrior from his youth."

[34]But David said to Saul, "Your servant has been keeping his father's sheep. When a lion or a bear came and carried off a sheep from the flock, [35]I went after it, struck it and rescued the sheep from its mouth. When it turned on me, I seized it by its hair, struck it and killed it. [36]Your servant has killed both the lion and the bear; this uncircumcised Philistine will be like one of them, because he has defied the armies of the living God.

a 5 That is, about 125 pounds or about 57 kilograms   b 7 That is, about 15 pounds or about 6.9 kilograms   c 17 That is, probably about 36 pounds or about 16 kilograms   d 18 Or some token; or some pledge of spoils

[37]The LORD who rescued me from the paw of the lion and the paw of the bear will rescue me from the hand of this Philistine."

Saul said to David, "Go, and the LORD be with you."

[38]Then Saul dressed David in his own tunic. He put a coat of armor on him and a bronze helmet on his head. [39]David fastened on his sword over the tunic and tried walking around, because he was not used to them.

"I cannot go in these," he said to Saul, "because I am not used to them." So he took them off. [40]Then he took his staff in his hand, chose five smooth stones from the stream, put them in the pouch of his shepherd's bag and, with his sling in his hand, approached the Philistine.

[41]Meanwhile, the Philistine, with his shield bearer in front of him, kept coming closer to David. [42]He looked David over and saw that he was little more than a boy, glowing with health and handsome, and he despised him. [43]He said to David, "Am I a dog, that you come at me with sticks?" And the Philistine cursed David by his gods. [44]"Come here," he said, "and I'll give your flesh to the birds and the wild animals!"

[45]David said to the Philistine, "You come against me with sword and spear and javelin, but I come against you in the name of the LORD Almighty, the God of the armies of Israel, whom you have defied. [46]This day the LORD will deliver you into my hands, and I'll strike you down and cut off your head. This very day I will give the carcasses of the Philistine army to the birds and the wild animals, and the whole world will know that there is a God in Israel. [47]All those gathered here will know that it is not by sword or spear that the LORD saves; for the battle is the LORD's, and he will give all of you into our hands."

[48]As the Philistine moved closer to attack him, David ran quickly toward the battle line to meet him. [49]Reaching into his bag and taking out a stone, he slung it and struck the Philistine on the forehead. The stone sank into his forehead, and he fell facedown on the ground.

[50]So David triumphed over the Philistine with a sling and a stone; without a sword in his hand he struck down the Philistine and killed him.

[51]David ran and stood over him. He took hold of the Philistine's sword and drew it from the sheath. After he killed him, he cut off his head with the sword.

When the Philistines saw that their hero was dead, they turned and ran. [52]Then the men of Israel and Judah surged forward with a shout and pursued the Philistines to the entrance of Gath[a] and to the gates of Ekron. Their dead were strewn along the Shaaraim road to Gath and Ekron. [53]When the Israelites returned from chasing the Philistines, they plundered their camp.

[54]David took the Philistine's head and brought it to Jerusalem; he put the Philistine's weapons in his own tent.

[55]As Saul watched David going out to meet the Philistine, he said to Abner, commander of the army, "Abner, whose son is that young man?"

Abner replied, "As surely as you live, Your Majesty, I don't know."

[56]The king said, "Find out whose son this young man is."

[57]As soon as David returned from killing the Philistine, Abner took him and brought him before Saul, with David still holding the Philistine's head.

[58]"Whose son are you, young man?" Saul asked him.

David said, "I am the son of your servant Jesse of Bethlehem."

Saul's Growing Fear of David

18 After David had finished talking with Saul, Jonathan became one in spirit with David, and he loved him as himself. [2]From that day Saul kept David with him and did not let him return home to his family. [3]And Jonathan made a covenant with David because he loved him as himself. [4]Jonathan took off the robe he was wearing and gave it to David, along with his tunic, and even his sword, his bow and his belt.

[5]Whatever mission Saul sent him on, David was so successful that Saul gave him a high rank in the army. This pleased all the troops, and Saul's officers as well.

[6]When the men were returning home after David had killed the Philistine, the wom-

a 52 Some Septuagint manuscripts; Hebrew *of a valley*

en came out from all the towns of Israel to meet King Saul with singing and dancing, with joyful songs and with timbrels and lyres. ⁷As they danced, they sang:

"Saul has slain his thousands,
and David his tens of thousands."

⁸Saul was very angry; this refrain displeased him greatly. "They have credited David with tens of thousands," he thought, "but me with only thousands. What more can he get but the kingdom?" ⁹And from that time on Saul kept a close eye on David.

¹⁰The next day an evilᵃ spirit from God came forcefully on Saul. He was prophesying in his house, while David was playing the lyre, as he usually did. Saul had a spear in his hand ¹¹and he hurled it, saying to himself, "I'll pin David to the wall." But David eluded him twice.

¹²Saul was afraid of David, because the LORD was with David but had departed from Saul. ¹³So he sent David away from him and gave him command over a thousand men, and David led the troops in their campaigns. ¹⁴In everything he did he had great success, because the LORD was with him. ¹⁵When Saul saw how successful he was, he was afraid of him. ¹⁶But all Israel and Judah loved David, because he led them in their campaigns.

¹⁷Saul said to David, "Here is my older daughter Merab. I will give her to you in marriage; only serve me bravely and fight the battles of the LORD." For Saul said to himself, "I will not raise a hand against him. Let the Philistines do that!"

¹⁸But David said to Saul, "Who am I, and what is my family or my clan in Israel, that I should become the king's son-in-law?" ¹⁹Soᵇ when the time came for Merab, Saul's daughter, to be given to David, she was given in marriage to Adriel of Meholah.

²⁰Now Saul's daughter Michal was in love with David, and when they told Saul about it, he was pleased. ²¹"I will give her to him," he thought, "so that she may be a snare to him and so that the hand of the Philistines may be against him." So Saul said to David, "Now you have a second opportunity to become my son-in-law."

²²Then Saul ordered his attendants: "Speak to David privately and say, 'Look, the king likes you, and his attendants all love you; now become his son-in-law.' "

²³They repeated these words to David. But David said, "Do you think it is a small matter to become the king's son-in-law? I'm only a poor man and little known."

²⁴When Saul's servants told him what David had said, ²⁵Saul replied, "Say to David, 'The king wants no other price for the bride than a hundred Philistine foreskins, to take revenge on his enemies.' " Saul's plan was to have David fall by the hands of the Philistines.

²⁶When the attendants told David these things, he was pleased to become the king's son-in-law. So before the allotted time elapsed, ²⁷David took his men with him and went out and killed two hundred Philistines and brought back their foreskins. They counted out the full number to the king so that David might become the king's son-in-law. Then Saul gave him his daughter Michal in marriage.

²⁸When Saul realized that the LORD was with David and that his daughter Michal loved David, ²⁹Saul became still more afraid of him, and he remained his enemy the rest of his days.

³⁰The Philistine commanders continued to go out to battle, and as often as they did, David met with more success than the rest of Saul's officers, and his name became well known.

Saul Tries to Kill David

19 Saul told his son Jonathan and all the attendants to kill David. But Jonathan had taken a great liking to David ²and warned him, "My father Saul is looking for a chance to kill you. Be on your guard tomorrow morning; go into hiding and stay there. ³I will go out and stand with my father in the field where you are. I'll speak to him about you and will tell you what I find out."

⁴Jonathan spoke well of David to Saul his father and said to him, "Let not the king do wrong to his servant David; he has not wronged you, and what he has done has benefited you greatly. ⁵He took his life in his hands when he killed the Philistine. The LORD won a great victory for all Israel, and you saw it and were glad. Why then would

ᵃ 10 Or *harmful*   ᵇ 19 Or *However,*

you do wrong to an innocent man like David by killing him for no reason?"

⁶Saul listened to Jonathan and took this oath: "As surely as the LORD lives, David will not be put to death."

⁷So Jonathan called David and told him the whole conversation. He brought him to Saul, and David was with Saul as before.

⁸Once more war broke out, and David went out and fought the Philistines. He struck them with such force that they fled before him.

⁹But an evilᵃ spirit from the LORD came on Saul as he was sitting in his house with his spear in his hand. While David was playing the lyre, ¹⁰Saul tried to pin him to the wall with his spear, but David eluded him as Saul drove the spear into the wall. That night David made good his escape.

¹¹Saul sent men to David's house to watch it and to kill him in the morning. But Michal, David's wife, warned him, "If you don't run for your life tonight, tomorrow you'll be killed." ¹²So Michal let David down through a window, and he fled and escaped. ¹³Then Michal took an idol and laid it on the bed, covering it with a garment and putting some goats' hair at the head.

¹⁴When Saul sent the men to capture David, Michal said, "He is ill."

¹⁵Then Saul sent the men back to see David and told them, "Bring him up to me in his bed so that I may kill him." ¹⁶But when the men entered, there was the idol in the bed, and at the head was some goats' hair.

¹⁷Saul said to Michal, "Why did you deceive me like this and send my enemy away so that he escaped?"

Michal told him, "He said to me, 'Let me get away. Why should I kill you?' "

¹⁸When David had fled and made his escape, he went to Samuel at Ramah and told him all that Saul had done to him. Then he and Samuel went to Naioth and stayed there. ¹⁹Word came to Saul: "David is in Naioth at Ramah"; ²⁰so he sent men to capture him. But when they saw a group of prophets prophesying, with Samuel standing there as their leader, the Spirit of God came on Saul's men, and they also prophesied. ²¹Saul was told about it, and he sent more men, and they prophesied too. Saul sent men a third time, and they also prophesied. ²²Fi-

nally, he himself left for Ramah and went to the great cistern at Seku. And he asked, "Where are Samuel and David?"

"Over in Naioth at Ramah," they said.

²³So Saul went to Naioth at Ramah. But the Spirit of God came even on him, and he walked along prophesying until he came to Naioth. ²⁴He stripped off his garments, and he too prophesied in Samuel's presence. He lay naked all that day and all that night. This is why people say, "Is Saul also among the prophets?"

David and Jonathan

20 Then David fled from Naioth at Ramah and went to Jonathan and asked, "What have I done? What is my crime? How have I wronged your father, that he is trying to take my life?"

²"Never!" Jonathan replied. "You are not going to die! Look, my father doesn't do anything, great or small, without letting me know. Why would he hide this from me? It isn't so!"

³But David took an oath and said, "Your father knows very well that I have found favor in your eyes, and he has said to himself, 'Jonathan must not know this or he will be grieved.' Yet as surely as the LORD lives and as you live, there is only a step between me and death."

⁴Jonathan said to David, "Whatever you want me to do, I'll do for you."

⁵So David said, "Look, tomorrow is the New Moon feast, and I am supposed to dine with the king; but let me go and hide in the field until the evening of the day after tomorrow. ⁶If your father misses me at all, tell him, 'David earnestly asked my permission to hurry to Bethlehem, his hometown, because an annual sacrifice is being made there for his whole clan.' ⁷If he says, 'Very well,' then your servant is safe. But if he loses his temper, you can be sure that he is determined to harm me. ⁸As for you, show kindness to your servant, for you have brought him into a covenant with you before the LORD. If I am guilty, then kill me yourself! Why hand me over to your father?"

⁹"Never!" Jonathan said. "If I had the least inkling that my father was determined to harm you, wouldn't I tell you?"

ᵃ 9 Or harmful

¹⁰David asked, "Who will tell me if your father answers you harshly?"

¹¹"Come," Jonathan said, "let's go out into the field." So they went there together.

¹²Then Jonathan said to David, "I swear by the LORD, the God of Israel, that I will surely sound out my father by this time the day after tomorrow! If he is favorably disposed toward you, will I not send you word and let you know? ¹³But if my father intends to harm you, may the LORD deal with Jonathan, be it ever so severely, if I do not let you know and send you away in peace. May the LORD be with you as he has been with my father. ¹⁴But show me unfailing kindness like the LORD's kindness as long as I live, so that I may not be killed, ¹⁵and do not ever cut off your kindness from my family—not even when the LORD has cut off every one of David's enemies from the face of the earth."

¹⁶So Jonathan made a covenant with the house of David, saying, "May the LORD call David's enemies to account." ¹⁷And Jonathan had David reaffirm his oath out of love for him, because he loved him as he loved himself.

¹⁸Then Jonathan said to David, "Tomorrow is the New Moon feast. You will be missed, because your seat will be empty. ¹⁹The day after tomorrow, toward evening, go to the place where you hid when this trouble began, and wait by the stone Ezel. ²⁰I will shoot three arrows to the side of it, as though I were shooting at a target. ²¹Then I will send a boy and say, 'Go, find the arrows.' If I say to him, 'Look, the arrows are on this side of you; bring them here,' then come, because, as surely as the LORD lives, you are safe; there is no danger. ²²But if I say to the boy, 'Look, the arrows are beyond you,' then you must go, because the LORD has sent you away. ²³And about the matter you and I discussed—remember, the LORD is witness between you and me forever."

²⁴So David hid in the field, and when the New Moon feast came, the king sat down to eat. ²⁵He sat in his customary place by the wall, opposite Jonathan,ᵃ and Abner sat next to Saul, but David's place was empty. ²⁶Saul said nothing that day, for he thought, "Something must have happened to David to make him ceremonially unclean—surely he is unclean." ²⁷But the next day, the sec-ond day of the month, David's place was empty again. Then Saul said to his son Jonathan, "Why hasn't the son of Jesse come to the meal, either yesterday or today?"

²⁸Jonathan answered, "David earnestly asked me for permission to go to Bethlehem. ²⁹He said, 'Let me go, because our family is observing a sacrifice in the town and my brother has ordered me to be there. If I have found favor in your eyes, let me get away to see my brothers.' That is why he has not come to the king's table."

³⁰Saul's anger flared up at Jonathan and he said to him, "You son of a perverse and rebellious woman! Don't I know that you have sided with the son of Jesse to your own shame and to the shame of the mother who bore you? ³¹As long as the son of Jesse lives on this earth, neither you nor your kingdom will be established. Now send someone to bring him to me, for he must die!"

³²"Why should he be put to death? What has he done?" Jonathan asked his father. ³³But Saul hurled his spear at him to kill him. Then Jonathan knew that his father intended to kill David.

³⁴Jonathan got up from the table in fierce anger; on that second day of the feast he did not eat, because he was grieved at his father's shameful treatment of David.

³⁵In the morning Jonathan went out to the field for his meeting with David. He had a small boy with him, ³⁶and he said to the boy, "Run and find the arrows I shoot." As the boy ran, he shot an arrow beyond him. ³⁷When the boy came to the place where Jonathan's arrow had fallen, Jonathan called out after him, "Isn't the arrow beyond you?" ³⁸Then he shouted, "Hurry! Go quickly! Don't stop!" The boy picked up the arrow and returned to his master. ³⁹(The boy knew nothing about all this; only Jonathan and David knew.) ⁴⁰Then Jonathan gave his weapons to the boy and said, "Go, carry them back to town."

⁴¹After the boy had gone, David got up from the south side of the stone and bowed down before Jonathan three times, with his face to the ground. Then they kissed each other and wept together—but David wept the most.

⁴²Jonathan said to David, "Go in peace, for we have sworn friendship with each oth-

ᵃ 25 Septuagint; Hebrew *wall. Jonathan arose*

The Best of Friends

1 Samuel 20:41–42

read/meditate

David and Jonathan's friendship is still renowned today. Jonathan would have been in line for the throne, but he recognized that it was the destiny of his best friend, so Jonathan stepped aside, protected David and even saved David's life. Think about how their friendship compares and contrasts with your friendships.

pray

Ask God to make you the kind of friend you'd like to have. Ask him to give you a vision for the person you need to be in your relationships. And ask him to give you the relationships you need in your life. Be still so he can show you any relationships that may need pruning. Be open, allowing him to make you aware of any ways in which you hinder the relationships you want and need.

contemplate

Think about the people you consider closest to you. Is there any sacrifice you need to make for one of them?

additional reflection

When we hurt each other we should write it down in the sand, so the winds of forgiveness can make it go away for good. When we help each other we should chisel it in stone, lest we never forget the love of a friend.

—*Christian H. Godefroy*

Without friends, no one would want to live, even if he had all other goods.

—*Aristotle*

For your next devotional reading, go to page 344.

er in the name of the LORD, saying, 'The LORD is witness between you and me, and between your descendants and my descendants forever.' " *Then David left, and Jonathan went back to the town.

David at Nob

21 *David went to Nob, to Ahimelek the priest. Ahimelek trembled when he met him, and asked, "Why are you alone? Why is no one with you?"

²David answered Ahimelek the priest, "The king sent me on a mission and said to me, 'No one is to know anything about the mission I am sending you on.' As for my men, I have told them to meet me at a certain place. ³Now then, what do you have on hand? Give me five loaves of bread, or whatever you can find."

⁴But the priest answered David, "I don't have any ordinary bread on hand; however, there is some consecrated bread here—provided the men have kept themselves from women."

⁵David replied, "Indeed women have been kept from us, as usual whenevera I set out. The men's bodies are holy even on missions that are not holy. How much more so today!" ⁶So the priest gave him the consecrated bread, since there was no bread there except the bread of the Presence that had been removed from before the LORD and replaced by hot bread on the day it was taken away.

⁷Now one of Saul's servants was there that day, detained before the LORD; he was Doeg the Edomite, Saul's chief shepherd.

⁸David asked Ahimelek, "Don't you have a spear or a sword here? I haven't brought my sword or any other weapon, because the king's mission was urgent."

⁹The priest replied, "The sword of Goliath the Philistine, whom you killed in the Valley of Elah, is here; it is wrapped in a cloth behind the ephod. If you want it, take it; there is no sword here but that one."

David said, "There is none like it; give it to me."

David at Gath

¹⁰That day David fled from Saul and went to Achish king of Gath. ¹¹But the servants of Achish said to him, "Isn't this David, the king of the land? Isn't he the one they sing about in their dances:

" 'Saul has slain his thousands,
and David his tens of thousands'?"

¹²David took these words to heart and was very much afraid of Achish king of Gath. ¹³So he pretended to be insane in their presence; and while he was in their hands he acted like a madman, making marks on the doors of the gate and letting saliva run down his beard.

¹⁴Achish said to his servants, "Look at the man! He is insane! Why bring him to me? ¹⁵Am I so short of madmen that you have to bring this fellow here to carry on like this in front of me? Must this man come into my house?"

David at Adullam and Mizpah

22 David left Gath and escaped to the cave of Adullam. When his brothers and his father's household heard about it, they went down to him there. ²All those who were in distress or in debt or discontented gathered around him, and he became their commander. About four hundred men were with him.

³From there David went to Mizpah in Moab and said to the king of Moab, "Would you let my father and mother come and stay with you until I learn what God will do for me?" ⁴So he left them with the king of Moab, and they stayed with him as long as David was in the stronghold.

⁵But the prophet Gad said to David, "Do not stay in the stronghold. Go into the land of Judah." So David left and went to the forest of Hereth.

Saul Kills the Priests of Nob

⁶Now Saul heard that David and his men had been discovered. And Saul was seated, spear in hand, under the tamarisk tree on the hill at Gibeah, with all his officials standing at his side. ⁷He said to them, "Listen, men of Benjamin! Will the son of Jesse give all of you fields and vineyards? Will he make all of you commanders of thousands and commanders of hundreds? ⁸Is that why

a 5 Or from us in the past few days since

* This sentence (20:42b) is numbered 21:1 in Hebrew texts.   * 21:1-15 is numbered 21:2-16 in Hebrew texts.

you have all conspired against me? No one tells me when my son makes a covenant with the son of Jesse. None of you is concerned about me or tells me that my son has incited my servant to lie in wait for me, as he does today."

⁹But Doeg the Edomite, who was standing with Saul's officials, said, "I saw the son of Jesse come to Ahimelek son of Ahitub at Nob. ¹⁰Ahimelek inquired of the LORD for him; he also gave him provisions and the sword of Goliath the Philistine."

¹¹Then the king sent for the priest Ahimelek son of Ahitub and all the men of his family, who were the priests at Nob, and they all came to the king. ¹²Saul said, "Listen now, son of Ahitub."

"Yes, my lord," he answered.

¹³Saul said to him, "Why have you conspired against me, you and the son of Jesse, giving him bread and a sword and inquiring of God for him, so that he has rebelled against me and lies in wait for me, as he does today?"

¹⁴Ahimelek answered the king, "Who of all your servants is as loyal as David, the king's son-in-law, captain of your bodyguard and highly respected in your household? ¹⁵Was that day the first time I inquired of God for him? Of course not! Let not the king accuse your servant or any of his father's family, for your servant knows nothing at all about this whole affair."

¹⁶But the king said, "You will surely die, Ahimelek, you and your whole family."

¹⁷Then the king ordered the guards at his side: "Turn and kill the priests of the LORD, because they too have sided with David. They knew he was fleeing, yet they did not tell me."

But the king's officials were unwilling to raise a hand to strike the priests of the LORD.

¹⁸The king then ordered Doeg, "You turn and strike down the priests." So Doeg the Edomite turned and struck them down. That day he killed eighty-five men who wore the linen ephod. ¹⁹He also put to the sword Nob, the town of the priests, with its men and women, its children and infants, and its cattle, donkeys and sheep.

²⁰But one son of Ahimelek son of Ahitub, named Abiathar, escaped and fled to join David. ²¹He told David that Saul had killed the priests of the LORD. ²²Then David said to Abiathar, "That day, when Doeg the Edom-

ite was there, I knew he would be sure to tell Saul. I am responsible for the death of your whole family. ²³Stay with me; don't be afraid. The man who wants to take your life is trying to kill me too. You will be safe with me."

David Saves Keilah

23 When David was told, "Look, the Philistines are fighting against Keilah and are looting the threshing floors," ²he inquired of the LORD, saying, "Shall I go and attack these Philistines?"

The LORD answered him, "Go, attack the Philistines and save Keilah."

³But David's men said to him, "Here in Judah we are afraid. How much more, then, if we go to Keilah against the Philistine forces!"

⁴Once again David inquired of the LORD, and the LORD answered him, "Go down to Keilah, for I am going to give the Philistines into your hand." ⁵So David and his men went to Keilah, fought the Philistines and carried off their livestock. He inflicted heavy losses on the Philistines and saved the people of Keilah. ⁶(Now Abiathar son of Ahimelek had brought the ephod down with him when he fled to David at Keilah.)

Saul Pursues David

⁷Saul was told that David had gone to Keilah, and he said, "God has delivered him into my hands, for David has imprisoned himself by entering a town with gates and bars." ⁸And Saul called up all his forces for battle, to go down to Keilah to besiege David and his men.

⁹When David learned that Saul was plotting against him, he said to Abiathar the priest, "Bring the ephod." ¹⁰David said, "LORD, God of Israel, your servant has heard definitely that Saul plans to come to Keilah and destroy the town on account of me. ¹¹Will the citizens of Keilah surrender me to him? Will Saul come down, as your servant has heard? LORD, God of Israel, tell your servant."

And the LORD said, "He will."

¹²Again David asked, "Will the citizens of Keilah surrender me and my men to Saul?"

And the LORD said, "They will."

¹³So David and his men, about six hundred in number, left Keilah and kept moving

from place to place. When Saul was told that David had escaped from Keilah, he did not go there.

¹⁴David stayed in the wilderness strongholds and in the hills of the Desert of Ziph. Day after day Saul searched for him, but God did not give David into his hands.

¹⁵While David was at Horesh in the Desert of Ziph, he learned that Saul had come out to take his life. ¹⁶And Saul's son Jonathan went to David at Horesh and helped him find strength in God. ¹⁷"Don't be afraid," he said. "My father Saul will not lay a hand on you. You will be king over Israel, and I will be second to you. Even my father Saul knows this." ¹⁸The two of them made a covenant before the LORD. Then Jonathan went home, but David remained at Horesh.

¹⁹The Ziphites went up to Saul at Gibeah and said, "Is not David hiding among us in the strongholds at Horesh, on the hill of Hakilah, south of Jeshimon? ²⁰Now, Your Majesty, come down whenever it pleases you to do so, and we will be responsible for giving him into your hands."

²¹Saul replied, "The LORD bless you for your concern for me. ²²Go and get more information. Find out where David usually goes and who has seen him there. They tell me he is very crafty. ²³Find out about all the hiding places he uses and come back to me with definite information. Then I will go with you; if he is in the area, I will track him down among all the clans of Judah."

²⁴So they set out and went to Ziph ahead of Saul. Now David and his men were in the Desert of Maon, in the Arabah south of Jeshimon. ²⁵Saul and his men began the search, and when David was told about it, he went down to the rock and stayed in the Desert of Maon. When Saul heard this, he went into the Desert of Maon in pursuit of David.

²⁶Saul was going along one side of the mountain, and David and his men were on the other side, hurrying to get away from Saul. As Saul and his forces were closing in on David and his men to capture them, ²⁷a messenger came to Saul, saying, "Come quickly! The Philistines are raiding the land." ²⁸Then Saul broke off his pursuit of David and went to meet the Philistines. That

is why they call this place Sela Hammahlekoth.ᵃ *²⁹And David went up from there and lived in the strongholds of En Gedi.

David Spares Saul's Life

24 *After Saul returned from pursuing the Philistines, he was told, "David is in the Desert of En Gedi." ²So Saul took three thousand able young men from all Israel and set out to look for David and his men near the Crags of the Wild Goats.

³He came to the sheep pens along the way; a cave was there, and Saul went in to relieve himself. David and his men were far back in the cave. ⁴The men said, "This is the day the LORD spoke of when he saidᵇ to you, 'I will give your enemy into your hands for you to deal with as you wish.' " Then David crept up unnoticed and cut off a corner of Saul's robe.

⁵Afterward, David was conscience-stricken for having cut off a corner of his robe. ⁶He said to his men, "The LORD forbid that I should do such a thing to my master, the LORD's anointed, or lay my hand on him; for he is the anointed of the LORD." ⁷With these words David sharply rebuked his men and did not allow them to attack Saul. And Saul left the cave and went his way.

⁸Then David went out of the cave and called out to Saul, "My lord the king!" When Saul looked behind him, David bowed down and prostrated himself with his face to the ground. ⁹He said to Saul, "Why do you listen when men say, 'David is bent on harming you'? ¹⁰This day you have seen with your own eyes how the LORD delivered you into my hands in the cave. Some urged me to kill you, but I spared you; I said, 'I will not lay my hand on my lord, because he is the LORD's anointed.' ¹¹See, my father, look at this piece of your robe in my hand! I cut off the corner of your robe but did not kill you. See that there is nothing in my hand to indicate that I am guilty of wrongdoing or rebellion. I have not wronged you, but you are hunting me down to take my life. ¹²May the LORD judge between you and me. And may the LORD avenge the wrongs you have done to me, but my hand will not touch you. ¹³As

---

ᵃ 28 *Sela Hammahlekoth* means *rock of parting*.   ᵇ 4 Or *"Today the* LORD *is saying*

* 23:29 is numbered 24:1 in Hebrew texts.   * 24:1-22 is numbered 24:2-23 in Hebrew texts.

the old saying goes, 'From evildoers come evil deeds,' so my hand will not touch you.

¹⁴"Against whom has the king of Israel come out? Whom are you pursuing? A dead dog? A flea? ¹⁵May the LORD be our judge and decide between us. May he consider my cause and uphold it; may he vindicate me by delivering me from your hand."

¹⁶When David finished saying this, Saul asked, "Is that your voice, David my son?" And he wept aloud. ¹⁷"You are more righteous than I," he said. "You have treated me well, but I have treated you badly. ¹⁸You have just now told me about the good you did to me; the LORD delivered me into your hands, but you did not kill me. ¹⁹When a man finds his enemy, does he let him get away unharmed? May the LORD reward you well for the way you treated me today. ²⁰I know that you will surely be king and that the kingdom of Israel will be established in your hands. ²¹Now swear to me by the LORD that you will not kill off my descendants or wipe out my name from my father's family."

²²So David gave his oath to Saul. Then Saul returned home, but David and his men went up to the stronghold.

David, Nabal and Abigail

25 Now Samuel died, and all Israel assembled and mourned for him; and they buried him at his home in Ramah. Then David moved down into the Desert of Paran.ᵃ

²A certain man in Maon, who had property there at Carmel, was very wealthy. He had a thousand goats and three thousand sheep, which he was shearing in Carmel. ³His name was Nabal and his wife's name was Abigail. She was an intelligent and beautiful woman, but her husband was surly and mean in his dealings—he was a Calebite.

⁴While David was in the wilderness, he heard that Nabal was shearing sheep. ⁵So he sent ten young men and said to them, "Go up to Nabal at Carmel and greet him in my name. ⁶Say to him: 'Long life to you! Good health to you and your household! And good health to all that is yours!

⁷" 'Now I hear that it is sheep-shearing time. When your shepherds were with us, we did not mistreat them, and the whole

time they were at Carmel nothing of theirs was missing. ⁸Ask your own servants and they will tell you. Therefore be favorable toward my men, since we come at a festive time. Please give your servants and your son David whatever you can find for them.' "

⁹When David's men arrived, they gave Nabal this message in David's name. Then they waited.

¹⁰Nabal answered David's servants, "Who is this David? Who is this son of Jesse? Many servants are breaking away from their masters these days. ¹¹Why should I take my bread and water, and the meat I have slaughtered for my shearers, and give it to men coming from who knows where?"

¹²David's men turned around and went back. When they arrived, they reported every word. ¹³David said to his men, "Each of you strap on your sword!" So they did, and David strapped his on as well. About four hundred men went up with David, while two hundred stayed with the supplies.

¹⁴One of the servants told Abigail, Nabal's wife, "David sent messengers from the wilderness to give our master his greetings, but he hurled insults at them. ¹⁵Yet these men were very good to us. They did not mistreat us, and the whole time we were out in the fields near them nothing was missing. ¹⁶Night and day they were a wall around us the whole time we were herding our sheep near them. ¹⁷Now think it over and see what you can do, because disaster is hanging over our master and his whole household. He is such a wicked man that no one can talk to him."

¹⁸Abigail acted quickly. She took two hundred loaves of bread, two skins of wine, five dressed sheep, five seahsᵇ of roasted grain, a hundred cakes of raisins and two hundred cakes of pressed figs, and loaded them on donkeys. ¹⁹Then she told her servants, "Go on ahead; I'll follow you." But she did not tell her husband Nabal.

²⁰As she came riding her donkey into a mountain ravine, there were David and his men descending toward her, and she met them. ²¹David had just said, "It's been useless—all my watching over this fellow's property in the wilderness so that nothing of his was missing. He has paid me back evil

---

ᵃ 1 Hebrew and some Septuagint manuscripts; other Septuagint manuscripts Maon   ᵇ 18 That is, probably about 60 pounds or about 27 kilograms for good. ²²May God deal with David,*a* be it ever so severely, if by morning I leave alive one male of all who belong to him!"

²³When Abigail saw David, she quickly got off her donkey and bowed down before David with her face to the ground. ²⁴She fell at his feet and said: "Pardon your servant, my lord, and let me speak to you; hear what your servant has to say. ²⁵Please pay no attention, my lord, to that wicked man Nabal. He is just like his name—his name means Fool, and folly goes with him. And as for me, your servant, I did not see the men my lord sent. ²⁶And now, my lord, as surely as the LORD your God lives and as you live, since the LORD has kept you from bloodshed and from avenging yourself with your own hands, may your enemies and all who are intent on harming my lord be like Nabal. ²⁷And let this gift, which your servant has brought to my lord, be given to the men who follow you.

²⁸"Please forgive your servant's presumption. The LORD your God will certainly make a lasting dynasty for my lord, because you fight the LORD's battles, and no wrongdoing will be found in you as long as you live. ²⁹Even though someone is pursuing you to take your life, the life of my lord will be bound securely in the bundle of the living by the LORD your God, but the lives of your enemies he will hurl away as from the pocket of a sling. ³⁰When the LORD has fulfilled for my lord every good thing he promised concerning him and has appointed him ruler over Israel, ³¹my lord will not have on his conscience the staggering burden of needless bloodshed or of having avenged himself. And when the LORD your God has brought my lord success, remember your servant."

³²David said to Abigail, "Praise be to the LORD, the God of Israel, who has sent you today to meet me. ³³May you be blessed for your good judgment and for keeping me from bloodshed this day and from avenging myself with my own hands. ³⁴Otherwise, as surely as the LORD, the God of Israel, lives, who has kept me from harming you, if you had not come quickly to meet me, not one male belonging to Nabal would have been left alive by daybreak."

³⁵Then David accepted from her hand what she had brought him and said, "Go home in peace. I have heard your words and granted your request."

³⁶When Abigail went to Nabal, he was in the house holding a banquet like that of a king. He was in high spirits and very drunk. So she told him nothing at all until daybreak. ³⁷Then in the morning, when Nabal was sober, his wife told him all these things, and his heart failed him and he became like a stone. ³⁸About ten days later, the LORD struck Nabal and he died.

³⁹When David heard that Nabal was dead, he said, "Praise be to the LORD, who has upheld my cause against Nabal for treating me with contempt. He has kept his servant from doing wrong and has brought Nabal's wrongdoing down on his own head."

Then David sent word to Abigail, asking her to become his wife. ⁴⁰His servants went to Carmel and said to Abigail, "David has sent us to you to take you to become his wife."

⁴¹She bowed down with her face to the ground and said, "I am your servant and am ready to serve you and wash the feet of my lord's servants." ⁴²Abigail quickly got on a donkey and, attended by her five female servants, went with David's messengers and became his wife. ⁴³David had also married Ahinoam of Jezreel, and they both were his wives. ⁴⁴But Saul had given his daughter Michal, David's wife, to Paltiel*b* son of Laish, who was from Gallim.

David Again Spares Saul's Life

26 The Ziphites went to Saul at Gibeah and said, "Is not David hiding on the hill of Hakilah, which faces Jeshimon?"

²So Saul went down to the Desert of Ziph, with his three thousand able young Israelites, to search there for David. ³Saul made his camp beside the road on the hill of Hakilah facing Jeshimon, but David stayed in the wilderness. When he saw that Saul had followed him there, ⁴he sent out scouts and learned that Saul had definitely arrived.

⁵Then David set out and went to the place where Saul had camped. He saw where Saul and Abner son of Ner, the commander of the

---

a 22 Some Septuagint manuscripts; Hebrew *with David's enemies* *b 44* Hebrew *Palti,* a variant of *Paltiel* army, had lain down. Saul was lying inside the camp, with the army encamped around him.

⁶David then asked Ahimelek the Hittite and Abishai son of Zeruiah, Joab's brother, "Who will go down into the camp with me to Saul?"

"I'll go with you," said Abishai.

⁷So David and Abishai went to the army by night, and there was Saul, lying asleep inside the camp with his spear stuck in the ground near his head. Abner and the soldiers were lying around him.

⁸Abishai said to David, "Today God has delivered your enemy into your hands. Now let me pin him to the ground with one thrust of the spear; I won't strike him twice."

⁹But David said to Abishai, "Don't destroy him! Who can lay a hand on the LORD's anointed and be guiltless? ¹⁰As surely as the LORD lives," he said, "the LORD himself will strike him, or his time will come and he will die, or he will go into battle and perish. ¹¹But the LORD forbid that I should lay a hand on the LORD's anointed. Now get the spear and water jug that are near his head, and let's go."

¹²So David took the spear and water jug near Saul's head, and they left. No one saw or knew about it, nor did anyone wake up. They were all sleeping, because the LORD had put them into a deep sleep.

¹³Then David crossed over to the other side and stood on top of the hill some distance away; there was a wide space between them. ¹⁴He called out to the army and to Abner son of Ner, "Aren't you going to answer me, Abner?"

Abner replied, "Who are you who calls to the king?"

¹⁵David said, "You're a man, aren't you? And who is like you in Israel? Why didn't you guard your lord the king? Someone came to destroy your lord the king. ¹⁶What you have done is not good. As surely as the LORD lives, you and your men must die, because you did not guard your master, the LORD's anointed. Look around you. Where are the king's spear and water jug that were near his head?"

¹⁷Saul recognized David's voice and said, "Is that your voice, David my son?"

David replied, "Yes it is, my lord the king." ¹⁸And he added, "Why is my lord pursuing his servant? What have I done, and what wrong am I guilty of? ¹⁹Now let my lord the king listen to his servant's words. If the LORD has incited you against me, then may he accept an offering. If, however, people have done it, may they be cursed before the LORD! They have driven me today from my share in the LORD's inheritance and have said, 'Go, serve other gods.' ²⁰Now do not let my blood fall to the ground far from the presence of the LORD. The king of Israel has come out to look for a flea—as one hunts a partridge in the mountains."

²¹Then Saul said, "I have sinned. Come back, David my son. Because you considered my life precious today, I will not try to harm you again. Surely I have acted like a fool and have been terribly wrong."

²²"Here is the king's spear," David answered. "Let one of your servants come over and get it. ²³The LORD rewards every man for his righteousness and faithfulness. The LORD delivered you into my hands today, but I would not lay a hand on the LORD's anointed. ²⁴As surely as I valued your life today, so may the LORD value my life and deliver me from all trouble."

²⁵Then Saul said to David, "May you be blessed, David my son; you will do great things and surely triumph."

So David went on his way, and Saul returned home.

David Among the Philistines

27 But David thought to himself, "One of these days I will be destroyed by the hand of Saul. The best thing I can do is to escape to the land of the Philistines. Then Saul will give up searching for me anywhere in Israel, and I will slip out of his hand."

²So David and the six hundred men with him left and went over to Achish son of Maok king of Gath. ³David and his men settled in Gath with Achish. Each man had his family with him, and David had his two wives: Ahinoam of Jezreel and Abigail of Carmel, the widow of Nabal. ⁴When Saul was told that David had fled to Gath, he no longer searched for him.

⁵Then David said to Achish, "If I have found favor in your eyes, let a place be assigned to me in one of the country towns, that I may live there. Why should your servant live in the royal city with you?"

⁶So on that day Achish gave him Ziklag, and it has belonged to the kings of Judah

ever since. [7]David lived in Philistine territory a year and four months.

[8]Now David and his men went up and raided the Geshurites, the Girzites and the Amalekites. (From ancient times these peoples had lived in the land extending to Shur and Egypt.) [9]Whenever David attacked an area, he did not leave a man or woman alive, but took sheep and cattle, donkeys and camels, and clothes. Then he returned to Achish.

[10]When Achish asked, "Where did you go raiding today?" David would say, "Against the Negev of Judah" or "Against the Negev of Jerahmeel" or "Against the Negev of the Kenites." [11]He did not leave a man or woman alive to be brought to Gath, for he thought, "They might inform on us and say, 'This is what David did.' " And such was his practice as long as he lived in Philistine territory. [12]Achish trusted David and said to himself, "He has become so obnoxious to his people, the Israelites, that he will be my servant for life."

28 In those days the Philistines gathered their forces to fight against Israel. Achish said to David, "You must understand that you and your men will accompany me in the army."

[2]David said, "Then you will see for yourself what your servant can do."

Achish replied, "Very well, I will make you my bodyguard for life."

Saul and the Medium at Endor

[3]Now Samuel was dead, and all Israel had mourned for him and buried him in his own town of Ramah. Saul had expelled the mediums and spiritists from the land.

[4]The Philistines assembled and came and set up camp at Shunem, while Saul gathered all Israel and set up camp at Gilboa. [5]When Saul saw the Philistine army, he was afraid; terror filled his heart. [6]He inquired of the LORD, but the LORD did not answer him by dreams or Urim or prophets. [7]Saul then said to his attendants, "Find me a woman who is a medium, so I may go and inquire of her."

"There is one in Endor," they said.

[8]So Saul disguised himself, putting on other clothes, and at night he and two men went to the woman. "Consult a spirit for me," he said, "and bring up for me the one I name."

[9]But the woman said to him, "Surely you know what Saul has done. He has cut off the mediums and spiritists from the land. Why have you set a trap for my life to bring about my death?"

[10]Saul swore to her by the LORD, "As surely as the LORD lives, you will not be punished for this."

[11]Then the woman asked, "Whom shall I bring up for you?"

"Bring up Samuel," he said.

[12]When the woman saw Samuel, she cried out at the top of her voice and said to Saul, "Why have you deceived me? You are Saul!"

[13]The king said to her, "Don't be afraid. What do you see?"

The woman said, "I see a ghostly figure[a] coming up out of the earth."

[14]"What does he look like?" he asked.

"An old man wearing a robe is coming up," she said.

Then Saul knew it was Samuel, and he bowed down and prostrated himself with his face to the ground.

[15]Samuel said to Saul, "Why have you disturbed me by bringing me up?"

"I am in great distress," Saul said. "The Philistines are fighting against me, and God has departed from me. He no longer answers me, either by prophets or by dreams. So I have called on you to tell me what to do."

[16]Samuel said, "Why do you consult me, now that the LORD has departed from you and become your enemy? [17]The LORD has done what he predicted through me. The LORD has torn the kingdom out of your hands and given it to one of your neighbors—to David. [18]Because you did not obey the LORD or carry out his fierce wrath against the Amalekites, the LORD has done this to you today. [19]The LORD will deliver both Israel and you into the hands of the Philistines, and tomorrow you and your sons will be with me. The LORD will also give the army of Israel into the hands of the Philistines."

[20]Immediately Saul fell full length on the ground, filled with fear because of Samuel's words. His strength was gone, for he had eaten nothing all that day and all that night.

_a 13_ Or _see spirits;_ or _see gods_

²¹When the woman came to Saul and saw that he was greatly shaken, she said, "Look, your servant has obeyed you. I took my life in my hands and did what you told me to do. ²²Now please listen to your servant and let me give you some food so you may eat and have the strength to go on your way."

²³He refused and said, "I will not eat."

But his men joined the woman in urging him, and he listened to them. He got up from the ground and sat on the couch.

²⁴The woman had a fattened calf at the house, which she butchered at once. She took some flour, kneaded it and baked bread without yeast. ²⁵Then she set it before Saul and his men, and they ate. That same night they got up and left.

Achish Sends David Back to Ziklag

29 The Philistines gathered all their forces at Aphek, and Israel camped by the spring in Jezreel. ²As the Philistine rulers marched with their units of hundreds and thousands, David and his men were marching at the rear with Achish. ³The commanders of the Philistines asked, "What about these Hebrews?"

Achish replied, "Is this not David, who was an officer of Saul king of Israel? He has already been with me for over a year, and from the day he left Saul until now, I have found no fault in him."

⁴But the Philistine commanders were angry with Achish and said, "Send the man back, that he may return to the place you assigned him. He must not go with us into battle, or he will turn against us during the fighting. How better could he regain his master's favor than by taking the heads of our own men? ⁵Isn't this the David they sang about in their dances:

" 'Saul has slain his thousands,
   and David his tens of thousands'?"

⁶So Achish called David and said to him, "As surely as the LORD lives, you have been reliable, and I would be pleased to have you serve with me in the army. From the day you came to me until today, I have found no fault in you, but the rulers don't approve of you. ⁷Now turn back and go in peace; do nothing to displease the Philistine rulers."

⁸"But what have I done?" asked David. "What have you found against your servant from the day I came to you until now? Why can't I go and fight against the enemies of my lord the king?"

⁹Achish answered, "I know that you have been as pleasing in my eyes as an angel of God; nevertheless, the Philistine commanders have said, 'He must not go up with us into battle.' ¹⁰Now get up early, along with your master's servants who have come with you, and leave in the morning as soon as it is light."

¹¹So David and his men got up early in the morning to go back to the land of the Philistines, and the Philistines went up to Jezreel.

David Destroys the Amalekites

30 David and his men reached Ziklag on the third day. Now the Amalekites had raided the Negev and Ziklag. They had attacked Ziklag and burned it, ²and had taken captive the women who were in it, both young and old. They killed none of them, but carried them off as they went on their way.

³When David and his men reached Ziklag, they found it destroyed by fire and their wives and sons and daughters taken captive. ⁴So David and his men wept aloud until they had no strength left to weep. ⁵David's two wives had been captured—Ahinoam of Jezreel and Abigail, the widow of Nabal of Carmel. ⁶David was greatly distressed because the men were talking of stoning him; each one was bitter in spirit because of his sons and daughters. But David found strength in the LORD his God.

⁷Then David said to Abiathar the priest, the son of Ahimelek, "Bring me the ephod." Abiathar brought it to him, ⁸and David inquired of the LORD, "Shall I pursue this raiding party? Will I overtake them?"

"Pursue them," he answered. "You will certainly overtake them and succeed in the rescue."

⁹David and the six hundred men with him came to the Besor Valley, where some stayed behind. ¹⁰Two hundred of them were too exhausted to cross the valley, but David and the other four hundred continued the pursuit.

¹¹They found an Egyptian in a field and brought him to David. They gave him water to drink and food to eat— ¹²part of a cake of pressed figs and two cakes of raisins. He ate and was revived, for he had not eaten any food or drunk any water for three days and three nights.

¹³David asked him, "Who do you belong to? Where do you come from?"

He said, "I am an Egyptian, the slave of an Amalekite. My master abandoned me when I became ill three days ago. ¹⁴We raided the Negev of the Kerethites, some territory belonging to Judah and the Negev of Caleb. And we burned Ziklag."

¹⁵David asked him, "Can you lead me down to this raiding party?"

He answered, "Swear to me before God that you will not kill me or hand me over to my master, and I will take you down to them."

¹⁶He led David down, and there they were, scattered over the countryside, eating, drinking and reveling because of the great amount of plunder they had taken from the land of the Philistines and from Judah. ¹⁷David fought them from dusk until the evening of the next day, and none of them got away, except four hundred young men who rode off on camels and fled. ¹⁸David recovered everything the Amalekites had taken, including his two wives. ¹⁹Nothing was missing: young or old, boy or girl, plunder or anything else they had taken. David brought everything back. ²⁰He took all the flocks and herds, and his men drove them ahead of the other livestock, saying, "This is David's plunder."

²¹Then David came to the two hundred men who had been too exhausted to follow him and who were left behind at the Besor Valley. They came out to meet David and the men with him. As David and his men approached, he asked them how they were. ²²But all the evil men and troublemakers among David's followers said, "Because they did not go out with us, we will not share with them the plunder we recovered. However, each man may take his wife and children and go."

²³David replied, "No, my brothers, you must not do that with what the LORD has given us. He has protected us and delivered into our hands the raiding party that came against us. ²⁴Who will listen to what you say? The share of the man who stayed with the supplies is to be the same as that of him who went down to the battle. All will share alike." ²⁵David made this a statute and ordinance for Israel from that day to this.

²⁶When David reached Ziklag, he sent some of the plunder to the elders of Judah, who were his friends, saying, "Here is a gift for you from the plunder of the LORD's enemies."

²⁷David sent it to those who were in Bethel, Ramoth Negev and Jattir; ²⁸to those in Aroer, Siphmoth, Eshtemoa ²⁹and Rakal; to those in the towns of the Jerahmeelites and the Kenites; ³⁰to those in Hormah, Bor Ashan, Athak ³¹and Hebron; and to those in all the other places where he and his men had roamed.

Saul Takes His Life

31 Now the Philistines fought against Israel; the Israelites fled before them, and many fell dead on Mount Gilboa. ²The Philistines were in hot pursuit of Saul and his sons, and they killed his sons Jonathan, Abinadab and Malki-Shua. ³The fighting grew fierce around Saul, and when the archers overtook him, they wounded him critically.

⁴Saul said to his armor-bearer, "Draw your sword and run me through, or these uncircumcised fellows will come and run me through and abuse me."

But his armor-bearer was terrified and would not do it; so Saul took his own sword and fell on it. ⁵When the armor-bearer saw that Saul was dead, he too fell on his sword and died with him. ⁶So Saul and his three sons and his armor-bearer and all his men died together that same day.

⁷When the Israelites along the valley and those across the Jordan saw that the Israelite army had fled and that Saul and his sons had died, they abandoned their towns and fled. And the Philistines came and occupied them.

⁸The next day, when the Philistines came to strip the dead, they found Saul and his three sons fallen on Mount Gilboa. ⁹They cut off his head and stripped off his armor, and they sent messengers throughout the land of the Philistines to proclaim the news in the temple of their idols and among their people. ¹⁰They put his armor in the temple of the Ashtoreths and fastened his body to the wall of Beth Shan.

¹¹When the people of Jabesh Gilead heard what the Philistines had done to Saul, ¹²all their valiant men marched through the night to Beth Shan. They took down the bodies of Saul and his sons from the wall of Beth Shan and went to Jabesh, where they burned them. ¹³Then they took their bones and buried them under a tamarisk tree at Jabesh, and they fasted seven days.

2 samuel

AUTHOR: Unknown

DATE: Around 930 B.C.

THEME: God's plan can't be defeated by our failures.

David Hears of Saul's Death

1 After the death of Saul, David returned from striking down the Amalekites and stayed in Ziklag two days. ²On the third day a man arrived from Saul's camp with his clothes torn and dust on his head. When he came to David, he fell to the ground to pay him honor.

³"Where have you come from?" David asked him.

He answered, "I have escaped from the Israelite camp."

⁴"What happened?" David asked. "Tell me."

"The men fled from the battle," he replied. "Many of them fell and died. And Saul and his son Jonathan are dead."

⁵Then David said to the young man who brought him the report, "How do you know that Saul and his son Jonathan are dead?"

⁶"I happened to be on Mount Gilboa," the young man said, "and there was Saul, leaning on his spear, with the chariots and their drivers in hot pursuit. ⁷When he turned around and saw me, he called out to me, and I said, 'What can I do?'

⁸"He asked me, 'Who are you?'

" 'An Amalekite,' I answered.

⁹"Then he said to me, 'Stand here by me and kill me! I'm in the throes of death, but I'm still alive.'

¹⁰"So I stood beside him and killed him, because I knew that after he had fallen he could not survive. And I took the crown that was on his head and the band on his arm and have brought them here to my lord."

¹¹Then David and all the men with him took hold of their clothes and tore them. ¹²They mourned and wept and fasted till evening for Saul and his son Jonathan, and for the army of the LORD and the house of Israel, because they had fallen by the sword.

¹³David said to the young man who brought him the report, "Where are you from?"

"I am the son of a foreigner, an Amalekite," he answered.

¹⁴David asked him, "Why weren't you afraid to lift your hand to destroy the LORD's anointed?"

¹⁵Then David called one of his men and said, "Go, strike him down!" So he struck him down, and he died. ¹⁶For David had said to him, "Your blood be on your own head. Your own mouth testified against you when you said, 'I killed the LORD's anointed.' "

David's Lament for Saul and Jonathan

¹⁷David took up this lament concerning Saul and his son Jonathan, ¹⁸and he ordered that the people of Judah be taught this lament of the bow (it is written in the Book of Jashar):

¹⁹"A gazelle^a lies slain on your heights,
　　　Israel.
　　How the mighty have fallen!

²⁰"Tell it not in Gath,
　　proclaim it not in the streets of
　　　Ashkelon,
　　lest the daughters of the Philistines be
　　　glad,
　　lest the daughters of the
　　　uncircumcised rejoice.

²¹"Mountains of Gilboa,
　　may you have neither dew nor rain,

---

a 19 *Gazelle* here symbolizes a human dignitary.

may no showers fall on your terraced
    fields. *a*
For there the shield of the mighty was
    despised,
    the shield of Saul—no longer rubbed
      with oil.

22 "From the blood of the slain,
    from the flesh of the mighty,
the bow of Jonathan did not turn back,
    the sword of Saul did not return
      unsatisfied.
23 Saul and Jonathan—
    in life they were loved and admired,
    and in death they were not parted.
They were swifter than eagles,
    they were stronger than lions.

24 "Daughters of Israel,
    weep for Saul,
who clothed you in scarlet and finery,
    who adorned your garments with
      ornaments of gold.

25 "How the mighty have fallen in battle!
    Jonathan lies slain on your heights.
26 I grieve for you, Jonathan my brother;
    you were very dear to me.
Your love for me was wonderful,
    more wonderful than that of women.

27 "How the mighty have fallen!
    The weapons of war have perished!"

David Anointed King Over Judah

2 In the course of time, David inquired
of the LORD. "Shall I go up to one of
the towns of Judah?" he asked.
    The LORD said, "Go up."
    David asked, "Where shall I go?"
    "To Hebron," the LORD answered.
2 So David went up there with his two
wives, Ahinoam of Jezreel and Abigail, the
widow of Nabal of Carmel. 3 David also took
the men who were with him, each with his
family, and they settled in Hebron and its
towns. 4 Then the men of Judah came to Hebron, and there they anointed David king
over the house of Judah.
    When David was told that it was the men
from Jabesh Gilead who had buried Saul, 5 he
sent messengers to them to say to them,
"The LORD bless you for showing this kindness to Saul your master by burying him.

6 May the LORD now show you kindness and
faithfulness, and I too will show you the
same favor because you have done this.
7 Now then, be strong and brave, for Saul
your master is dead, and the house of Judah
has anointed me king over them."

War Between the Houses of David and Saul

8 Meanwhile, Abner son of Ner, the commander of Saul's army, had taken Ish-Bosheth son of Saul and brought him over to
Mahanaim. 9 He made him king over Gilead,
Ashuri and Jezreel, and also over Ephraim,
Benjamin and all Israel.
    10 Ish-Bosheth son of Saul was forty years
old when he became king over Israel, and he
reigned two years. The house of Judah, however, remained loyal to David. 11 The length
of time David was king in Hebron over the
house of Judah was seven years and six
months.
    12 Abner son of Ner, together with the men
of Ish-Bosheth son of Saul, left Mahanaim
and went to Gibeon. 13 Joab son of Zeruiah
and David's men went out and met them at
the pool of Gibeon. One group sat down on
one side of the pool and one group on the
other side.
    14 Then Abner said to Joab, "Let's have
some of the soldiers get up and fight hand to
hand in front of us."
    "All right, let them do it," Joab said.
    15 So they stood up and were counted
off—twelve men for Benjamin and Ish-Bosheth son of Saul, and twelve for David.
16 Then each man grabbed his opponent by
the head and thrust his dagger into his opponent's side, and they fell down together.
So that place in Gibeon was called Helkath
Hazzurim. *b*
    17 The battle that day was very fierce, and
Abner and the Israelites were defeated by
David's men.
    18 The three sons of Zeruiah were there:
Joab, Abishai and Asahel. Now Asahel was as
fleet-footed as a wild gazelle. 19 He chased
Abner, turning neither to the right nor to the
left as he pursued him. 20 Abner looked behind him and asked, "Is that you, Asahel?"
    "It is," he answered.
    21 Then Abner said to him, "Turn aside to
the right or to the left; take on one of the

---

a 21 Or / *nor fields that yield grain for offerings*   *b 16 Helkath Hazzurim means field of daggers or field of
hostilities.*

soldiers and strip him of his weapons." But Asahel would not stop chasing him.

²²Again Abner warned Asahel, "Stop chasing me! Why should I strike you down? How could I look your brother Joab in the face?"

²³But Asahel refused to give up the pursuit; so Abner thrust the butt of his spear into Asahel's stomach, and the spear came out through his back. He fell there and died on the spot. And every man stopped when he came to the place where Asahel had fallen and died.

²⁴But Joab and Abishai pursued Abner, and as the sun was setting, they came to the hill of Ammah, near Giah on the way to the wasteland of Gibeon. ²⁵Then the men of Benjamin rallied behind Abner. They formed themselves into a group and took their stand on top of a hill.

²⁶Abner called out to Joab, "Must the sword devour forever? Don't you realize that this will end in bitterness? How long before you order your men to stop pursuing their fellow Israelites?"

²⁷Joab answered, "As surely as God lives, if you had not spoken, the men would have continued pursuing them until morning."

²⁸So Joab blew the trumpet, and everyone came to a halt; they no longer pursued Israel, nor did they fight anymore.

²⁹All that night Abner and his men marched through the Arabah. They crossed the Jordan, continued through the morning hoursᵃ and came to Mahanaim.

³⁰Then Joab stopped pursuing Abner and assembled the whole army. Besides Asahel, nineteen of David's men were found missing. ³¹But David's men had killed three hundred and sixty Benjamites who were with Abner. ³²They took Asahel and buried him in his father's tomb at Bethlehem. Then Joab and his men marched all night and arrived at Hebron by daybreak.

3 The war between the house of Saul and the house of David lasted a long time. David grew stronger and stronger, while the house of Saul grew weaker and weaker.

²Sons were born to David in Hebron:
His firstborn was Amnon the son of Ahinoam of Jezreel;

³his second, Kileab the son of Abigail the widow of Nabal of Carmel;
the third, Absalom the son of Maakah daughter of Talmai king of Geshur;

⁴the fourth, Adonijah the son of Haggith;
the fifth, Shephatiah the son of Abital;

⁵and the sixth, Ithream the son of David's wife Eglah.
These were born to David in Hebron.

Abner Goes Over to David

⁶During the war between the house of Saul and the house of David, Abner had been strengthening his own position in the house of Saul. ⁷Now Saul had had a concubine named Rizpah daughter of Aiah. And Ish-Bosheth said to Abner, "Why did you sleep with my father's concubine?"

⁸Abner was very angry because of what Ish-Bosheth said. So he answered, "Am I a dog's head—on Judah's side? This very day I am loyal to the house of your father Saul and to his family and friends. I haven't handed you over to David. Yet now you accuse me of an offense involving this woman! ⁹May God deal with Abner, be it ever so severely, if I do not do for David what the LORD promised him on oath ¹⁰and transfer the kingdom from the house of Saul and establish David's throne over Israel and Judah from Dan to Beersheba." ¹¹Ish-Bosheth did not dare to say another word to Abner, because he was afraid of him.

¹²Then Abner sent messengers on his behalf to say to David, "Whose land is it? Make an agreement with me, and I will help you bring all Israel over to you."

¹³"Good," said David. "I will make an agreement with you. But I demand one thing of you: Do not come into my presence unless you bring Michal daughter of Saul when you come to see me." ¹⁴Then David sent messengers to Ish-Bosheth son of Saul, demanding, "Give me my wife Michal, whom I betrothed to myself for the price of a hundred Philistine foreskins."

¹⁵So Ish-Bosheth gave orders and had her taken away from her husband Paltiel son of Laish. ¹⁶Her husband, however, went with her, weeping behind her all the way to Ba-

---

ᵃ 29 Or See Septuagint; the meaning of the Hebrew for this phrase is uncertain.

hurim. Then Abner said to him, "Go back home!" So he went back.

[17] Abner conferred with the elders of Israel and said, "For some time you have wanted to make David your king. [18] Now do it! For the LORD promised David, 'By my servant David I will rescue my people Israel from the hand of the Philistines and from the hand of all their enemies.' "

[19] Abner also spoke to the Benjamites in person. Then he went to Hebron to tell David everything that Israel and the whole house of Benjamin wanted to do. [20] When Abner, who had twenty men with him, came to David at Hebron, David prepared a feast for him and his men. [21] Then Abner said to David, "Let me go at once and assemble all Israel for my lord the king, so that they may make a covenant with you, and that you may rule over all that your heart desires." So David sent Abner away, and he went in peace.

Joab Murders Abner

[22] Just then David's men and Joab returned from a raid and brought with them a great deal of plunder. But Abner was no longer with David in Hebron, because David had sent him away, and he had gone in peace. [23] When Joab and all the soldiers with him arrived, he was told that Abner son of Ner had come to the king and that the king had sent him away and that he had gone in peace.

[24] So Joab went to the king and said, "What have you done? Look, Abner came to you. Why did you let him go? Now he is gone! [25] You know Abner son of Ner; he came to deceive you and observe your movements and find out everything you are doing."

[26] Joab then left David and sent messengers after Abner, and they brought him back from the cistern at Sirah. But David did not know it. [27] Now when Abner returned to Hebron, Joab took him aside into an inner chamber, as if to speak with him privately. And there, to avenge the blood of his brother Asahel, Joab stabbed him in the stomach, and he died.

[28] Later, when David heard about this, he said, "I and my kingdom are forever innocent before the LORD concerning the blood of Abner son of Ner. [29] May his blood fall on the head of Joab and on his whole family! May Joab's family never be without someone who has a running sore or leprosy[a] or who leans on a crutch or who falls by the sword or who lacks food."

[30] (Joab and his brother Abishai murdered Abner because he had killed their brother Asahel in the battle at Gibeon.)

[31] Then David said to Joab and all of Joab's men, "Tear your clothes and put on sackcloth and walk in mourning in front of Abner." King David himself walked behind the bier. [32] They buried Abner in Hebron, and the king wept aloud at Abner's tomb. All of Joab's men wept also.

[33] The king sang this lament for Abner:

"Should Abner have died as the lawless
    die?
[34]   Your hands were not bound,
        your feet were not fettered.
    You fell as one falls before the wicked."

And all of Joab's men wept over him again.

[35] Then they all came and urged David to eat something while it was still day; but David took an oath, saying, "May God deal with me, be it ever so severely, if I taste bread or anything else before the sun sets!"

[36] All of Joab's men took note and were pleased; indeed, everything the king did pleased them. [37] So on that day all of Joab's men and all Israel knew that the king had no part in the murder of Abner son of Ner.

[38] Then the king said to his men, "Don't you realize that a great commander has fallen in Israel this day? [39] And today, though I am the anointed king, I am weak, and these sons of Zeruiah are too strong for me. May the LORD repay the evildoer according to his evil deeds!"

Ish-Bosheth Murdered

4 When Ish-Bosheth son of Saul heard that Abner had died in Hebron, he lost courage, and all Israel became alarmed. [2] Now Saul's son had two leaders of raiding bands. One was named Baanah and the other Rekab; they were sons of Rimmon the Beerothite from the tribe of Benjamin—Beeroth is considered part of Benjamin, [3] because the people of Beeroth fled to Gittaim

---

a 29 The Hebrew for *leprosy* was used for various diseases affecting the skin.

and have resided there as foreigners to this day.

⁴(Jonathan son of Saul had a son who was lame in both feet. He was five years old when the news about Saul and Jonathan came from Jezreel. His nurse picked him up and fled, but as she hurried to leave, he fell and became disabled. His name was Mephibosheth.)

⁵Now Rekab and Baanah, the sons of Rimmon the Beerothite, set out for the house of Ish-Bosheth, and they arrived there in the heat of the day while he was taking his noonday rest. ⁶They went into the inner part of the house as if to get some wheat, and they stabbed him in the stomach. Then Rekab and his brother Baanah slipped away.

⁷They had gone into the house while he was lying on the bed in his bedroom. After they stabbed and killed him, they cut off his head. Taking it with them, they traveled all night by way of the Arabah. ⁸They brought the head of Ish-Bosheth to David at Hebron and said to the king, "Here is the head of Ish-Bosheth son of Saul, your enemy, who tried to take your life. This day the Lord has avenged my lord the king against Saul and his offspring."

⁹David answered Rekab and his brother Baanah, the sons of Rimmon the Beerothite, "As surely as the Lord lives, who has delivered me out of every trouble, ¹⁰when someone told me, 'Saul is dead,' and thought he was bringing good news, I seized him and put him to death in Ziklag. That was the reward I gave him for his news! ¹¹How much more—when wicked men have killed an innocent man in his own house and on his own bed—should I not now demand his blood from your hand and rid the earth of you!"

¹²So David gave an order to his men, and they killed them. They cut off their hands and feet and hung the bodies by the pool in Hebron. But they took the head of Ish-Bosheth and buried it in Abner's tomb at Hebron.

David Becomes King Over Israel

5 All the tribes of Israel came to David at Hebron and said, "We are your own flesh and blood. ²In the past, while Saul was king over us, you were the one who led Israel on their military campaigns. And

the Lord said to you, 'You will shepherd my people Israel, and you will become their ruler.' "

³When all the elders of Israel had come to King David at Hebron, the king made a covenant with them at Hebron before the Lord, and they anointed David king over Israel.

⁴David was thirty years old when he became king, and he reigned forty years. ⁵In Hebron he reigned over Judah seven years and six months, and in Jerusalem he reigned over all Israel and Judah thirty-three years.

David Conquers Jerusalem

⁶The king and his men marched to Jerusalem to attack the Jebusites, who lived there. The Jebusites said to David, "You will not get in here; even the blind and the lame can ward you off." They thought, "David cannot get in here." ⁷Nevertheless, David captured the fortress of Zion—which is the City of David.

⁸On that day David had said, "Anyone who conquers the Jebusites will have to use the water shaft to reach those 'lame and blind' who are David's enemies.ᵃ" That is why they say, "The 'blind and lame' will not enter the palace."

⁹David then took up residence in the fortress and called it the City of David. He built up the area around it, from the terracesᵇ inward. ¹⁰And he became more and more powerful, because the Lord God Almighty was with him.

¹¹Now Hiram king of Tyre sent messengers to David, along with cedar logs and carpenters and stonemasons, and they built a palace for David. ¹²And David knew that the Lord had established him as king over Israel and had exalted his kingdom for the sake of his people Israel.

¹³After he left Hebron, David took more concubines and wives in Jerusalem, and more sons and daughters were born to him. ¹⁴These are the names of the children born to him there: Shammua, Shobab, Nathan, Solomon, ¹⁵Ibhar, Elishua, Nepheg, Japhia, ¹⁶Elishama, Eliada and Eliphelet.

David Defeats the Philistines

¹⁷When the Philistines heard that David had been anointed king over Israel, they went up in full force to search for him, but

---

ᵃ 8 Or are hated by David   ᵇ 9 Or the Millo

David heard about it and went down to the stronghold. 18Now the Philistines had come and spread out in the Valley of Rephaim; 19so David inquired of the LORD, "Shall I go and attack the Philistines? Will you deliver them into my hands?"

The LORD answered him, "Go, for I will surely deliver the Philistines into your hands."

20So David went to Baal Perazim, and there he defeated them. He said, "As waters break out, the LORD has broken out against my enemies before me." So that place was called Baal Perazim.ᵃ 21The Philistines abandoned their idols there, and David and his men carried them off.

22Once more the Philistines came up and spread out in the Valley of Rephaim; 23so David inquired of the LORD, and he answered, "Do not go straight up, but circle around behind them and attack them in front of the poplar trees. 24As soon as you hear the sound of marching in the tops of the poplar trees, move quickly, because that will mean the LORD has gone out in front of you to strike the Philistine army." 25So David did as the LORD commanded him, and he struck down the Philistines all the way from Gibeonᵇ to Gezer.

The Ark Brought to Jerusalem

6 David again brought together all the able young men of Israel—thirty thousand. 2He and all his men went to Baalahᶜ in Judah to bring up from there the ark of God, which is called by the Name,ᵈ the name of the LORD Almighty, who is enthroned between the cherubim on the ark. 3They set the ark of God on a new cart and brought it from the house of Abinadab, which was on the hill. Uzzah and Ahio, sons of Abinadab, were guiding the new cart 4with the ark of God on it,ᵉ and Ahio was walking in front of it. 5David and the whole house of Israel were celebrating with all their might before the LORD, with castanets,ᶠ harps, lyres, timbrels, sistrums and cymbals.

6When they came to the threshing floor of Nakon, Uzzah reached out and took hold of the ark of God, because the oxen stumbled. 7The LORD's anger burned against Uzzah because of his irreverent act; therefore God struck him down, and he died there beside the ark of God.

8Then David was angry because the LORD's wrath had broken out against Uzzah, and to this day that place is called Perez Uzzah.ᵍ

9David was afraid of the LORD that day and said, "How can the ark of the LORD ever come to me?" 10He was not willing to take the ark of the LORD to be with him in the City of David. Instead, he took it to the house of Obed-Edom the Gittite. 11The ark of the LORD remained in the house of Obed-Edom the Gittite for three months, and the LORD blessed him and his entire household.

12Now King David was told, "The LORD has blessed the household of Obed-Edom and everything he has, because of the ark of God." So David went to bring up the ark of God from the house of Obed-Edom to the City of David with rejoicing. 13When those who were carrying the ark of the LORD had taken six steps, he sacrificed a bull and a fattened calf. 14Wearing a linen ephod, David was dancing before the LORD with all his might, 15while he and the entire house of Israel were bringing up the ark of the LORD with shouts and the sound of trumpets.

16As the ark of the LORD was entering the City of David, Michal daughter of Saul watched from a window. And when she saw King David leaping and dancing before the LORD, she despised him in her heart.

17They brought the ark of the LORD and set it in its place inside the tent that David had pitched for it, and David sacrificed burnt offerings and fellowship offerings before the LORD. 18After he had finished sacrificing the burnt offerings and fellowship offerings, he blessed the people in the name of the LORD Almighty. 19Then he gave a loaf of bread, a cake of dates and a cake of raisins to each person in the whole crowd of Israelites, both men and women. And all the people went to their homes.

20When David returned home to bless his household, Michal daughter of Saul came

---

ᵃ 20 Baal Perazim means the lord who breaks out.   ᵇ 25 Septuagint (see also 1 Chron. 14:16); Hebrew Geba   ᶜ 2 That is, Kiriath Jearim (see 1 Chron. 13:6)   ᵈ 2 Hebrew; Septuagint and Vulgate do not have the Name.   ᵉ 3,4 Dead Sea Scrolls and some Septuagint manuscripts; Masoretic Text cart ⁴and they brought it with the ark of God from the house of Abinadab, which was on the hill   ᶠ 5 Masoretic Text; Dead Sea Scrolls and Septuagint (see also 1 Chron. 13:8) songs   ᵍ 8 Perez Uzzah means outbreak against Uzzah.

MONDAY

LOSING YOURSELF IN WORSHIP
2 Samuel 6:1–23 or 6:21–22

Matt Redman

A few years back I wrote a song called "Undignified." When I say I wrote it, all I really did was to steal a line King David had come up with a few thousand years before. They were finally bringing the ark of the Lord back to Jerusalem, and David got pretty excited and danced like a madman. His wife, Michal, despised him for it, and he came out with the now classic line, "I will celebrate before the LORD. I will become even more undignified than this, and I will be humiliated in my own eyes" (2 Samuel 6:21–22).

What strikes me most about this is the context of David's celebration. He wasn't just one of the crowd at this event, he was the king. Here was a man of great stature, with a public image to protect; a man trusted with more power, authority and wealth than we could ever imagine. Yet he led the way, "losing" himself so publicly in his worship of God and so on fire with praise that it burned right through any inhibitions or pride ...

One of the Hebrew words for praise, *hallal*, means to be clamorously foolish or mad before the Lord. (That's where we get our word "hallelujah.") In a "reasons to be passionate" competition, the church of God should come an easy first; yet too often we find ourselves lagging way behind in this area. Isn't it time we saw a bit more holy mayhem in our worship?

JOHN WRIGHT FOLLETTE {AD 1883–1966}

We get so entangled into ... traditional patterns and things that we forget God. If God can be blessed and honored by being loved and worshiped all day, then love him and worship him all day!

You say, "We will have all the eternal ages in heaven to worship him." You better practice a little down here. Get in tune with the Infinite, and learn ... his heart. How far we are from this in so much we see and hear! ... How many know that when the judgment of God will be lifted off this earth, it will be like a great musical, a powerful instrument of praise. The morning stars will be singing together! Do trees sing? Yes, to a poet, and to anyone in God, they do.

reflection

1. When you're around other people, how much does their opinion affect how you worship God?

2. What does it mean for you to "celebrate before the LORD?" How can you let go of your inhibitions and praise God with more passion?

3. How would your worship be different if you tried to worship God now like you will someday in heaven?

For your next devotional reading, go to page 348.

out to meet him and said, "How the king of Israel has distinguished himself today, going around half-naked in full view of the slave girls of his servants as any vulgar fellow would!"

²¹David said to Michal, "It was before the Lᴏʀᴅ, who chose me rather than your father or anyone from his house when he appointed me ruler over the Lᴏʀᴅ's people Israel—I will celebrate before the Lᴏʀᴅ. ²²I will become even more undignified than this, and I will be humiliated in my own eyes. But by these slave girls you spoke of, I will be held in honor."

²³And Michal daughter of Saul had no children to the day of her death.

God's Promise to David

7 After the king was settled in his palace and the Lᴏʀᴅ had given him rest from all his enemies around him, ²he said to Nathan the prophet, "Here I am, living in a house of cedar, while the ark of God remains in a tent."

³Nathan replied to the king, "Whatever you have in mind, go ahead and do it, for the Lᴏʀᴅ is with you."

⁴But that night the word of the Lᴏʀᴅ came to Nathan, saying:

⁵"Go and tell my servant David, 'This is what the Lᴏʀᴅ says: Are you the one to build me a house to dwell in? ⁶I have not dwelt in a house from the day I brought the Israelites up out of Egypt to this day. I have been moving from place to place with a tent as my dwelling. ⁷Wherever I have moved with all the Israelites, did I ever say to any of their rulers whom I commanded to shepherd my people Israel, "Why have you not built me a house of cedar?" '

⁸"Now then, tell my servant David, 'This is what the Lᴏʀᴅ Almighty says: I took you from the pasture, from tending the flock, and appointed you ruler over my people Israel. ⁹I have been with you wherever you have gone, and I have cut off all your enemies from before you. Now I will make your name great, like the names of the greatest men on earth. ¹⁰And I will provide a place for my people Israel and will

plant them so that they can have a home of their own and no longer be disturbed. Wicked people will not oppress them anymore, as they did at the beginning ¹¹and have done ever since the time I appointed leadersᵃ over my people Israel. I will also give you rest from all your enemies.

" 'The Lᴏʀᴅ declares to you that the Lᴏʀᴅ himself will establish a house for you: ¹²When your days are over and you rest with your ancestors, I will raise up your offspring to succeed you, who will come from your own body, and I will establish his kingdom. ¹³He is the one who will build a house for my Name, and I will establish the throne of his kingdom forever. ¹⁴I will be his father, and he will be my son. When he does wrong, I will punish him with a rod wielded by human beings, with floggings inflicted by human hands. ¹⁵But my love will never be taken away from him, as I took it away from Saul, whom I removed from before you. ¹⁶Your house and your kingdom will endure forever before meᵇ; your throne will be established forever.' "

¹⁷Nathan reported to David all the words of this entire revelation.

David's Prayer

¹⁸Then King David went in and sat before the Lᴏʀᴅ, and he said:

"Who am I, Sovereign Lᴏʀᴅ, and what is my family, that you have brought me this far? ¹⁹And as if this were not enough in your sight, Sovereign Lᴏʀᴅ, you have also spoken about the future of the house of your servant—and this decree, Sovereign Lᴏʀᴅ, is for a human being!ᶜ

²⁰"What more can David say to you? For you know your servant, Sovereign Lᴏʀᴅ. ²¹For the sake of your word and according to your will, you have done this great thing and made it known to your servant.

²²"How great you are, Sovereign Lᴏʀᴅ! There is no one like you, and there is no God but you, as we have

---

ᵃ 11 Traditionally *judges*   ᵇ 16 Some Hebrew manuscripts and Septuagint; most Hebrew manuscripts *you*   ᶜ 19 Or *for the human race* heard with our own ears. ²³And who is like your people Israel—the one nation on earth that God went out to redeem as a people for himself, and to make a name for himself, and to perform great and awesome wonders by driving out nations and their gods from before your people, whom you redeemed from Egypt?^a ²⁴You have established your people Israel as your very own forever, and you, Lord, have become their God.

²⁵"And now, Lord God, keep forever the promise you have made concerning your servant and his house. Do as you promised, ²⁶so that your name will be great forever. Then people will say, 'The Lord Almighty is God over Israel!' And the house of your servant David will be established in your sight.

²⁷"Lord Almighty, God of Israel, you have revealed this to your servant, saying, 'I will build a house for you.' So your servant has found courage to pray this prayer to you. ²⁸Sovereign Lord, you are God! Your covenant is trustworthy, and you have promised these good things to your servant. ²⁹Now be pleased to bless the house of your servant, that it may continue forever in your sight; for you, Sovereign Lord, have spoken, and with your blessing the house of your servant will be blessed forever."

David's Victories

8 In the course of time, David defeated the Philistines and subdued them, and he took Metheg Ammah from the control of the Philistines.

²David also defeated the Moabites. He made them lie down on the ground and measured them off with a length of cord. Every two lengths of them were put to death, and the third length was allowed to live. So the Moabites became subject to David and brought him tribute.

³Moreover, David defeated Hadadezer son of Rehob, king of Zobah, when he went to restore his monument at^b the Euphrates River. ⁴David captured a thousand of his chariots, seven thousand charioteers^c and twenty thousand foot soldiers. He hamstrung all but a hundred of the chariot horses.

⁵When the Arameans of Damascus came to help Hadadezer king of Zobah, David struck down twenty-two thousand of them. ⁶He put garrisons in the Aramean kingdom of Damascus, and the Arameans became subject to him and brought tribute. The Lord gave David victory wherever he went.

⁷David took the gold shields that belonged to the officers of Hadadezer and brought them to Jerusalem. ⁸From Tebah^d and Berothai, towns that belonged to Hadadezer, King David took a great quantity of bronze.

⁹When Tou^e king of Hamath heard that David had defeated the entire army of Hadadezer, ¹⁰he sent his son Joram^f to King David to greet him and congratulate him on his victory in battle over Hadadezer, who had been at war with Tou. Joram brought with him articles of silver, of gold and of bronze.

¹¹King David dedicated these articles to the Lord, as he had done with the silver and gold from all the nations he had subdued: ¹²Edom^g and Moab, the Ammonites and the Philistines, and Amalek. He also dedicated the plunder taken from Hadadezer son of Rehob, king of Zobah.

¹³And David became famous after he returned from striking down eighteen thousand Edomites^h in the Valley of Salt.

¹⁴He put garrisons throughout Edom, and all the Edomites became subject to David. The Lord gave David victory wherever he went.

David's Officials

¹⁵David reigned over all Israel, doing what was just and right for all his people. ¹⁶Joab son of Zeruiah was over the army; Jehoshaphat son of Ahilud was recorder; ¹⁷Zadok son of Ahitub and Ahimelek son of Abiathar were priests; Seraiah was secretary; ¹⁸Bena-

a 23 See Septuagint and 1 Chron. 17:21; Hebrew *wonders for your land and before your people, whom you redeemed from Egypt, from the nations and their gods.* *b 3* Or *his control along* *c 4* Septuagint (see also Dead Sea Scrolls and 1 Chron. 18:4); Masoretic Text *captured seventeen hundred of his charioteers* *d 8* See some Septuagint manuscripts (see also 1 Chron. 18:8); Hebrew *Betah.* *e 9* Hebrew *Toi,* a variant of *Tou;* also in verse 10 *f 10* A variant of *Hadoram* *g 12* Some Hebrew manuscripts, Septuagint and Syriac (see also 1 Chron. 18:11); most Hebrew manuscripts *Aram* *h 13* A few Hebrew manuscripts, Septuagint and Syriac (see also 1 Chron. 18:12); most Hebrew manuscripts *Aram* (that is, Arameans) iah son of Jehoiada was over the Kerethites and Pelethites; and David's sons were priests. *a*

David and Mephibosheth

9 David asked, "Is there anyone still left of the house of Saul to whom I can show kindness for Jonathan's sake?"

²Now there was a servant of Saul's household named Ziba. They summoned him to appear before David, and the king said to him, "Are you Ziba?"

"At your service," he replied.

³The king asked, "Is there no one still left of the house of Saul to whom I can show God's kindness?"

Ziba answered the king, "There is still a son of Jonathan; he is lame in both feet."

⁴"Where is he?" the king asked.

Ziba answered, "He is at the house of Makir son of Ammiel in Lo Debar."

⁵So King David had him brought from Lo Debar, from the house of Makir son of Ammiel.

⁶When Mephibosheth son of Jonathan, the son of Saul, came to David, he bowed down to pay him honor.

David said, "Mephibosheth!"

"At your service," he replied.

⁷"Don't be afraid," David said to him, "for I will surely show you kindness for the sake of your father Jonathan. I will restore to you all the land that belonged to your grandfather Saul, and you will always eat at my table."

⁸Mephibosheth bowed down and said, "What is your servant, that you should notice a dead dog like me?"

⁹Then the king summoned Ziba, Saul's steward, and said to him, "I have given your master's grandson everything that belonged to Saul and his family. ¹⁰You and your sons and your servants are to farm the land for him and bring in the crops, so that your master's grandson may be provided for. And Mephibosheth, grandson of your master, will always eat at my table." (Now Ziba had fifteen sons and twenty servants.)

¹¹Then Ziba said to the king, "Your servant will do whatever my lord the king commands his servant to do." So Mephibosheth ate at David's *b* table like one of the king's sons.

¹²Mephibosheth had a young son named Mika, and all the members of Ziba's household were servants of Mephibosheth. ¹³And Mephibosheth lived in Jerusalem, because he always ate at the king's table; he was lame in both feet.

David Defeats the Ammonites

10 In the course of time, the king of the Ammonites died, and his son Hanun succeeded him as king. ²David thought, "I will show kindness to Hanun son of Nahash, just as his father showed kindness to me." So David sent a delegation to express his sympathy to Hanun concerning his father.

When David's men came to the land of the Ammonites, ³the Ammonite commanders said to Hanun their lord, "Do you think David is honoring your father by sending envoys to you to express sympathy? Hasn't David sent them to you only to explore the city and spy it out and overthrow it?" ⁴So Hanun seized David's envoys, shaved off half of each man's beard, cut off their garments at the buttocks, and sent them away.

⁵When David was told about this, he sent messengers to meet the men, for they were greatly humiliated. The king said, "Stay at Jericho till your beards have grown, and then come back."

⁶When the Ammonites realized that they had become obnoxious to David, they hired twenty thousand Aramean foot soldiers from Beth Rehob and Zobah, as well as the king of Maakah with a thousand men, and also twelve thousand men from Tob.

⁷On hearing this, David sent Joab out with the entire army of fighting men. ⁸The Ammonites came out and drew up in battle formation at the entrance of their city gate, while the Arameans of Zobah and Rehob and the men of Tob and Maakah were by themselves in the open country.

⁹Joab saw that there were battle lines in front of him and behind him; so he selected some of the best troops in Israel and deployed them against the Arameans. ¹⁰He put the rest of the men under the command of Abishai his brother and deployed them against the Ammonites. ¹¹Joab said, "If the Arameans are too strong for me, then you are

---

a 18 Or *were chief officials* (see Septuagint and Targum; see also 1 Chron. 18:17)   *b 11* Septuagint; Hebrew *my*

LIVE IN LOVE

2 Samuel 9:1–13 *or* 9:1,3,7–8

GEORGE MACDONALD {AD 1824–1905}

Loving our neighbor is the only door out of the dungeon of self. In this dungeon we mope and scowl—scraping the walls, striking sparks and blowing our own breath in our own nostrils in search of some light or warmth—instead of coming to the fair sunlight of God and the sweet winds of his universe. We humans think our identity is found in self, while on the contrary, our life consists in breathing in God and being aware of the universe of truth. To have self, to know self, to enjoy self: This is what humans call life. Yet, if we would forget ourselves, how much greater would be our life in God and our neighbors!

The arena of a person's life is a spiritual arena. God, friends, neighbors, all of humanity—these are part of the wide world in which one's spirit can find the room it needs. By contrast, one's own self is his dungeon. If he doesn't feel it now, he will yet feel it one day—feel it as a living soul would feel being imprisoned in a dead body, wrapped in multiple burial garments and buried in a stone-ribbed vault within the last ripple of the sound of the chanting people in the church above. His life is not in knowing that he lives but in loving all forms of life.

We are made for the All; for God, who is the All, is our life. And the essential joy of our life can be found spread wide in the liberty of the All. Our delights, like those of the Ideal Wisdom, are tied in with the sons of men. Our true health can be found in the body of which the Son of Man is the head. Through him, the whole region of real life is open to us—indeed, we must live in it or perish.

Kary Oberbrunner

You can't fake it. You can't manufacture it. You can't manipulate it. You can't produce it. Love is timeless. Love is not bound by geography, economy, or philosophy. It transcends all things . . .

The Scriptures are rich with men and women who became relevant to their world the moment they showed love. Is it any wonder that love is the language of relevance? Think about Christ for a moment. What made the Son of God relevant to a world that knew Him not? It was His love for you and I that transcended culture, space, time, race, and every other boundary humanity tried to throw in His face.

reflection

1. How is it possible to find freedom through giving up your own wishes, wants or rights in order to love someone else?
2. How does God's love for you motivate you to love others?
3. God loved—and loves—us in unexpected, undeserved ways. How can you show that same kind of love to someone else right now?

For your next devotional reading, go to page 355.

to come to my rescue; but if the Ammonites are too strong for you, then I will come to rescue you. ¹²Be strong, and let us fight bravely for our people and the cities of our God. The LORD will do what is good in his sight."

¹³Then Joab and the troops with him advanced to fight the Arameans, and they fled before him. ¹⁴When the Ammonites realized that the Arameans were fleeing, they fled before Abishai and went inside the city. So Joab returned from fighting the Ammonites and came to Jerusalem.

¹⁵After the Arameans saw that they had been routed by Israel, they regrouped. ¹⁶Hadadezer had Arameans brought from beyond the Euphrates River; they went to Helam, with Shobak the commander of Hadadezer's army leading them.

¹⁷When David was told of this, he gathered all Israel, crossed the Jordan and went to Helam. The Arameans formed their battle lines to meet David and fought against him. ¹⁸But they fled before Israel, and David killed seven hundred of their charioteers and forty thousand of their foot soldiers.ᵈ He also struck down Shobak the commander of their army, and he died there. ¹⁹When all the kings who were vassals of Hadadezer saw that they had been routed by Israel, they made peace with the Israelites and became subject to them.

So the Arameans were afraid to help the Ammonites anymore.

David and Bathsheba

11 In the spring, at the time when kings go off to war, David sent Joab out with the king's men and the whole Israelite army. They destroyed the Ammonites and besieged Rabbah. But David remained in Jerusalem.

²One evening David got up from his bed and walked around on the roof of the palace. From the roof he saw a woman bathing. The woman was very beautiful, ³and David sent someone to find out about her. The man said, "She is Bathsheba, the daughter of Eliam and the wife of Uriah the Hittite." ⁴Then David sent messengers to get her. She came to him, and he slept with her. (Now she was purifying herself from her monthly uncleanness.) Then she went back home. ⁵The

woman conceived and sent word to David, saying, "I am pregnant."

⁶So David sent this word to Joab: "Send me Uriah the Hittite." And Joab sent him to David. ⁷When Uriah came to him, David asked him how Joab was, how the soldiers were and how the war was going. ⁸Then David said to Uriah, "Go down to your house and wash your feet." So Uriah left the palace, and a gift from the king was sent after him. ⁹But Uriah slept at the entrance to the palace with all his master's servants and did not go down to his house.

¹⁰David was told, "Uriah did not go home." So he asked Uriah, "Haven't you just come from a military campaign? Why didn't you go home?"

¹¹Uriah said to David, "The ark and Israel and Judah are staying in tents,ᵇ and my commander Joab and my lord's men are camped in the open country. How could I go to my house to eat and drink and make love to my wife? As surely as you live, I will not do such a thing!"

¹²Then David said to him, "Stay here one more day, and tomorrow I will send you back." So Uriah remained in Jerusalem that day and the next. ¹³At David's invitation, he ate and drank with him, and David made him drunk. But in the evening Uriah went out to sleep on his mat among his master's servants; he did not go home.

¹⁴In the morning David wrote a letter to Joab and sent it with Uriah. ¹⁵In it he wrote, "Put Uriah out in front where the fighting is fiercest. Then withdraw from him so he will be struck down and die."

¹⁶So while Joab had the city under siege, he put Uriah at a place where he knew the strongest defenders were. ¹⁷When the men of the city came out and fought against Joab, some of the men in David's army fell; moreover, Uriah the Hittite died.

¹⁸Joab sent David a full account of the battle. ¹⁹He instructed the messenger: "When you have finished giving the king this account of the battle, ²⁰the king's anger may flare up, and he may ask you, 'Why did you get so close to the city to fight? Didn't you know they would shoot arrows from the wall? ²¹Who killed Abimelek son of Jerub-Beshethᶜ? Didn't a woman drop an upper

---

ᵃ 18 Some Septuagint manuscripts (see also 1 Chron. 19:18); Hebrew *horsemen*   ᵇ 11 Or *staying at Sukkoth*   ᶜ 21 Also known as *Jerub-Baal (that is, Gideon)* millstone on him from the wall, so that he died in Thebez? Why did you get so close to the wall?' If he asks you this, then say to him, 'Moreover, your servant Uriah the Hittite is dead.' "

²²The messenger set out, and when he arrived he told David everything Joab had sent him to say. ²³The messenger said to David, "The men overpowered us and came out against us in the open, but we drove them back to the entrance of the city gate. ²⁴Then the archers shot arrows at your servants from the wall, and some of the king's men died. Moreover, your servant Uriah the Hittite is dead."

²⁵David told the messenger, "Say this to Joab: 'Don't let this upset you; the sword devours one as well as another. Press the attack against the city and destroy it.' Say this to encourage Joab."

²⁶When Uriah's wife heard that her husband was dead, she mourned for him. ²⁷After the time of mourning was over, David had her brought to his house, and she became his wife and bore him a son. But the thing David had done displeased the LORD.

Nathan Rebukes David

12 The LORD sent Nathan to David. When he came to him, he said, "There were two men in a certain town, one rich and the other poor. ²The rich man had a very large number of sheep and cattle, ³but the poor man had nothing except one little ewe lamb he had bought. He raised it, and it grew up with him and his children. It shared his food, drank from his cup and even slept in his arms. It was like a daughter to him.

⁴"Now a traveler came to the rich man, but the rich man refrained from taking one of his own sheep or cattle to prepare a meal for the traveler who had come to him. Instead, he took the ewe lamb that belonged to the poor man and prepared it for the one who had come to him."

⁵David burned with anger against the man and said to Nathan, "As surely as the LORD lives, the man who did this must die! ⁶He must pay for that lamb four times over, because he did such a thing and had no pity."

⁷Then Nathan said to David, "You are the man! This is what the LORD, the God of Israel, says: 'I anointed you king over Israel, and I delivered you from the hand of Saul. ⁸I gave your master's house to you, and your master's wives into your arms. I gave you the house of Israel and Judah. And if all this had been too little, I would have given you even more. ⁹Why did you despise the word of the LORD by doing what is evil in his eyes? You struck down Uriah the Hittite with the sword and took his wife to be your own. You killed him with the sword of the Ammonites. ¹⁰Now, therefore, the sword will never depart from your house, because you despised me and took the wife of Uriah the Hittite to be your own.'

¹¹"This is what the LORD says: 'Out of your own household I am going to bring calamity on you. Before your very eyes I will take your wives and give them to one who is close to you, and he will sleep with your wives in broad daylight. ¹²You did it in secret, but I will do this thing in broad daylight before all Israel.' "

¹³Then David said to Nathan, "I have sinned against the LORD."

Nathan replied, "The LORD has taken away your sin. You are not going to die. ¹⁴But because by doing this you have shown utter contempt for*a* the LORD, the son born to you will die."

¹⁵After Nathan had gone home, the LORD struck the child that Uriah's wife had borne to David, and he became ill. ¹⁶David pleaded with God for the child. He fasted and spent the nights lying in sackcloth*b* on the ground. ¹⁷The elders of his household stood beside him to get him up from the ground, but he refused, and he would not eat any food with them.

¹⁸On the seventh day the child died. David's attendants were afraid to tell him that the child was dead, for they thought, "While the child was still living, he wouldn't listen to us when we spoke to him. How can we now tell him the child is dead? He may do something desperate."

¹⁹David noticed that his attendants were whispering among themselves, and he realized the child was dead. "Is the child dead?" he asked.

---

a 14 An ancient Hebrew scribal tradition; Masoretic Text *for the enemies of*   *b 16* Dead Sea Scrolls and Septuagint; Masoretic Text does not have *in sackcloth.*

"Yes," they replied, "he is dead."

20Then David got up from the ground. After he had washed, put on lotions and changed his clothes, he went into the house of the Lord and worshiped. Then he went to his own house, and at his request they served him food, and he ate.

21His attendants asked him, "Why are you acting this way? While the child was alive, you fasted and wept, but now that the child is dead, you get up and eat!"

22He answered, "While the child was still alive, I fasted and wept. I thought, 'Who knows? The Lord may be gracious to me and let the child live.' 23But now that he is dead, why should I go on fasting? Can I bring him back again? I will go to him, but he will not return to me."

24Then David comforted his wife Bathsheba, and he went to her and made love to her. She gave birth to a son, and they named him Solomon. The Lord loved him; 25and because the Lord loved him, he sent word through Nathan the prophet to name him Jedidiah.a

26Meanwhile Joab fought against Rabbah of the Ammonites and captured the royal citadel. 27Joab then sent messengers to David, saying, "I have fought against Rabbah and taken its water supply. 28Now muster the rest of the troops and besiege the city and capture it. Otherwise I will take the city, and it will be named after me."

29So David mustered the entire army and went to Rabbah, and attacked and captured it. 30David took the crown from their king'sb head, and it was placed on his own head. It weighed a talentc of gold, and it was set with precious stones. David took a great quantity of plunder from the city 31and brought out the people who were there, consigning them to labor with saws and with iron picks and axes, and he made them work at brickmaking.d David did this to all the Ammonite towns. Then he and his entire army returned to Jerusalem.

Amnon and Tamar

13 In the course of time, Amnon son of David fell in love with Tamar, the beautiful sister of Absalom son of David.

2Amnon became so obsessed with his sister Tamar that he made himself ill. She was a virgin, and it seemed impossible for him to do anything to her.

3Now Amnon had an adviser named Jonadab son of Shimeah, David's brother. Jonadab was a very shrewd man. 4He asked Amnon, "Why do you, the king's son, look so haggard morning after morning? Won't you tell me?"

Amnon said to him, "I'm in love with Tamar, my brother Absalom's sister."

5"Go to bed and pretend to be ill," Jonadab said. "When your father comes to see you, say to him, 'I would like my sister Tamar to come and give me something to eat. Let her prepare the food in my sight so I may watch her and then eat it from her hand.' "

6So Amnon lay down and pretended to be ill. When the king came to see him, Amnon said to him, "I would like my sister Tamar to come and make some special bread in my sight, so I may eat from her hand."

7David sent word to Tamar at the palace: "Go to the house of your brother Amnon and prepare some food for him." 8So Tamar went to the house of her brother Amnon, who was lying down. She took some dough, kneaded it, made the bread in his sight and baked it. 9Then she took the pan and served him the bread, but he refused to eat.

"Send everyone out of here," Amnon said. So everyone left him. 10Then Amnon said to Tamar, "Bring the food here into my bedroom so I may eat from your hand." And Tamar took the bread she had prepared and brought it to her brother Amnon in his bedroom. 11But when she took it to him to eat, he grabbed her and said, "Come to bed with me, my sister."

12"No, my brother!" she said to him. "Don't force me! Such a thing should not be done in Israel! Don't do this wicked thing. 13What about me? Where could I get rid of my disgrace? And what about you? You would be like one of the wicked fools in Israel. Please speak to the king; he will not keep me from being married to you." 14But he refused to listen to her, and since he was stronger than she, he raped her.

15Then Amnon hated her with intense hatred. In fact, he hated her more than he had

---

a 25 Jedidiah means loved by the Lord.   b 30 Or from Milkom's (that is, Molek's)   c 30 That is, about 75 pounds or about 34 kilograms   d 31 The meaning of the Hebrew for this clause is uncertain.

loved her. Amnon said to her, "Get up and get out!"

16"No!" she said to him. "Sending me away would be a greater wrong than what you have already done to me."

But he refused to listen to her. 17He called his personal servant and said, "Get this woman out of my sight and bolt the door after her." 18So his servant put her out and bolted the door after her. She was wearing a richly ornamented*a* robe, for this was the kind of garment the virgin daughters of the king wore. 19Tamar put ashes on her head and tore the ornamented*b* robe she was wearing. She put her hands on her head and went away, weeping aloud as she went.

20Her brother Absalom said to her, "Has that Amnon, your brother, been with you? Be quiet for now, my sister; he is your brother. Don't take this thing to heart." And Tamar lived in her brother Absalom's house, a desolate woman.

21When King David heard all this, he was furious. 22And Absalom never spoke to Amnon again; he hated Amnon because he had disgraced his sister Tamar.

Absalom Kills Amnon

23Two years later, when Absalom's sheepshearers were at Baal Hazor near the border of Ephraim, he invited all the king's sons to come there. 24Absalom went to the king and said, "Your servant has had shearers come. Will the king and his attendants please join me?"

25"No, my son," the king replied. "All of us should not go; we would only be a burden to you." Although Absalom urged him, he still refused to go but gave him his blessing.

26Then Absalom said, "If not, please let my brother Amnon come with us."

The king asked him, "Why should he go with you?" 27But Absalom urged him, so he sent with him Amnon and the rest of the king's sons.

28Absalom ordered his men, "Listen! When Amnon is in high spirits from drinking wine and I say to you, 'Strike Amnon down,' then kill him. Don't be afraid. Haven't I given you this order? Be strong and brave."

29So Absalom's men did to Amnon what Ab-

salom had ordered. Then all the king's sons got up, mounted their mules and fled.

30While they were on their way, the report came to David: "Absalom has struck down all the king's sons; not one of them is left." 31The king stood up, tore his clothes and lay down on the ground; and all his attendants stood by with their clothes torn.

32But Jonadab son of Shimeah, David's brother, said, "My lord should not think that they killed all the princes; only Amnon is dead. This has been Absalom's express intention ever since the day Amnon raped his sister Tamar. 33My lord the king should not be concerned about the report that all the king's sons are dead. Only Amnon is dead."

34Meanwhile, Absalom had fled.

Now the man standing watch looked up and saw many people on the road west of him, coming down the side of the hill. The watchman went and told the king, "I see men in the direction of Horonaim, on the side of the hill."*c*

35Jonadab said to the king, "See, the king's sons have come; it has happened just as your servant said."

36As he finished speaking, the king's sons came in, wailing loudly. The king, too, and all his attendants wept very bitterly.

37Absalom fled and went to Talmai son of Ammihud, the king of Geshur. But King David mourned many days for his son.

38After Absalom fled and went to Geshur, he stayed there three years. 39And King David longed to go to Absalom, for he was consoled concerning Amnon's death.

Absalom Returns to Jerusalem

14 Joab son of Zeruiah knew that the king's heart longed for Absalom. 2So Joab sent someone to Tekoa and had a wise woman brought from there. He said to her, "Pretend you are in mourning. Dress in mourning clothes, and don't use any cosmetic lotions. Act like a woman who has spent many days grieving for the dead. 3Then go to the king and speak these words to him." And Joab put the words in her mouth.

4When the woman from Tekoa went*d* to the king, she fell with her face to the ground

---

a 18 The meaning of the Hebrew for this phrase is uncertain.   *b 19* The meaning of the Hebrew for this word is uncertain.   *c 34* Septuagint; Hebrew does not have this sentence.   *d 4* Many Hebrew manuscripts, Septuagint, Vulgate and Syriac; most Hebrew manuscripts *spoke* to pay him honor, and she said, "Help me, Your Majesty!"

⁵The king asked her, "What is troubling you?"

She said, "I am a widow; my husband is dead. ⁶I your servant had two sons. They got into a fight with each other in the field, and no one was there to separate them. One struck the other and killed him. ⁷Now the whole clan has risen up against your servant; they say, 'Hand over the one who struck his brother down, so that we may put him to death for the life of his brother whom he killed; then we will get rid of the heir as well.' They would put out the only burning coal I have left, leaving my husband neither name nor descendant on the face of the earth."

⁸The king said to the woman, "Go home, and I will issue an order in your behalf."

⁹But the woman from Tekoa said to him, "Let my lord the king pardon me and my family, and let the king and his throne be without guilt."

¹⁰The king replied, "If anyone says anything to you, bring them to me, and they will not bother you again."

¹¹She said, "Then let the king invoke the LORD his God to prevent the avenger of blood from adding to the destruction, so that my son will not be destroyed."

"As surely as the LORD lives," he said, "not one hair of your son's head will fall to the ground."

¹²Then the woman said, "Let your servant speak a word to my lord the king."

"Speak," he replied.

¹³The woman said, "Why then have you devised a thing like this against the people of God? When the king says this, does he not convict himself, for the king has not brought back his banished son? ¹⁴Like water spilled on the ground, which cannot be recovered, so we must die. But that is not what God desires; rather, he devises ways so that a banished person does not remain banished from him.

¹⁵"And now I have come to say this to my lord the king because the people have made me afraid. Your servant thought, 'I will speak to the king; perhaps he will grant his servant's request. ¹⁶Perhaps the king will agree to deliver his servant from the hand of the

man who is trying to cut off both me and my son from God's inheritance.'

¹⁷"And now your servant says, 'May the word of my lord the king secure my inheritance, for my lord the king is like an angel of God in discerning good and evil. May the LORD your God be with you.' "

¹⁸Then the king said to the woman, "Don't keep from me the answer to what I am going to ask you."

"Let my lord the king speak," the woman said.

¹⁹The king asked, "Isn't the hand of Joab with you in all this?"

The woman answered, "As surely as you live, my lord the king, no one can turn to the right or to the left from anything my lord the king says. Yes, it was your servant Joab who instructed me to do this and who put all these words into the mouth of your servant. ²⁰Your servant Joab did this to change the present situation. My lord has wisdom like that of an angel of God—he knows everything that happens in the land."

²¹The king said to Joab, "Very well, I will do it. Go, bring back the young man Absalom."

²²Joab fell with his face to the ground to pay him honor, and he blessed the king. Joab said, "Today your servant knows that he has found favor in your eyes, my lord the king, because the king has granted his servant's request."

²³Then Joab went to Geshur and brought Absalom back to Jerusalem. ²⁴But the king said, "He must go to his own house; he must not see my face." So Absalom went to his own house and did not see the face of the king.

²⁵In all Israel there was not a man so highly praised for his handsome appearance as Absalom. From the top of his head to the sole of his foot there was no blemish in him. ²⁶Whenever he cut the hair of his head—he used to cut his hair once a year because it became too heavy for him—he would weigh it, and its weight was two hundred shekels ᵃ by the royal standard.

²⁷Three sons and a daughter were born to Absalom. His daughter's name was Tamar, and she became a beautiful woman.

²⁸Absalom lived two years in Jerusalem without seeing the king's face. ²⁹Then Absa-

ᵃ 26 That is, about 5 pounds or about 2.3 kilograms

lom sent for Joab in order to send him to the king, but Joab refused to come to him. So he sent a second time, but he refused to come. ³⁰Then he said to his servants, "Look, Joab's field is next to mine, and he has barley there. Go and set it on fire." So Absalom's servants set the field on fire.

³¹Then Joab did go to Absalom's house, and he said to him, "Why have your servants set my field on fire?"

³²Absalom said to Joab, "Look, I sent word to you and said, 'Come here so I can send you to the king to ask, "Why have I come from Geshur? It would be better for me if I were still there!"' Now then, I want to see the king's face, and if I am guilty of anything, let him put me to death."

³³So Joab went to the king and told him this. Then the king summoned Absalom, and he came in and bowed down with his face to the ground before the king. And the king kissed Absalom.

Absalom's Conspiracy

15 In the course of time, Absalom provided himself with a chariot and horses and with fifty men to run ahead of him. ²He would get up early and stand by the side of the road leading to the city gate. Whenever anyone came with a complaint to be placed before the king for a decision, Absalom would call out to him, "What town are you from?" He would answer, "Your servant is from one of the tribes of Israel." ³Then Absalom would say to him, "Look, your claims are valid and proper, but there is no representative of the king to hear you." ⁴And Absalom would add, "If only I were appointed judge in the land! Then everyone who has a complaint or case could come to me and I would see that they receive justice."

⁵Also, whenever anyone approached him to bow down before him, Absalom would reach out his hand, take hold of him and kiss him. ⁶Absalom behaved in this way toward all the Israelites who came to the king asking for justice, and so he stole the hearts of the people of Israel.

⁷At the end of four*ᵃ* years, Absalom said to the king, "Let me go to Hebron and fulfill a vow I made to the LORD. ⁸While your ser-

vant was living at Geshur in Aram, I made this vow: 'If the LORD takes me back to Jerusalem, I will worship the LORD in Hebron.*ᵇ*' "

⁹The king said to him, "Go in peace." So he went to Hebron.

¹⁰Then Absalom sent secret messengers throughout the tribes of Israel to say, "As soon as you hear the sound of the trumpets, then say, 'Absalom is king in Hebron.'" ¹¹Two hundred men from Jerusalem had accompanied Absalom. They had been invited as guests and went quite innocently, knowing nothing about the matter. ¹²While Absalom was offering sacrifices, he also sent for Ahithophel the Gilonite, David's counselor, to come from Giloh, his hometown. And so the conspiracy gained strength, and Absalom's following kept on increasing.

David Flees

¹³A messenger came and told David, "The hearts of the people of Israel are with Absalom."

¹⁴Then David said to all his officials who were with him in Jerusalem, "Come! We must flee, or none of us will escape from Absalom. We must leave immediately, or he will move quickly to overtake us and bring ruin on us and put the city to the sword."

¹⁵The king's officials answered him, "Your servants are ready to do whatever our lord the king chooses."

¹⁶The king set out, with his entire household following him; but he left ten concubines to take care of the palace. ¹⁷So the king set out, with all the people following him, and they halted at the edge of the city. ¹⁸All his men marched past him, along with all the Kerethites and Pelethites; and all the six hundred Gittites who had accompanied him from Gath marched before the king.

¹⁹The king said to Ittai the Gittite, "Why should you come along with us? Go back and stay with King Absalom. You are a foreigner, an exile from your homeland. ²⁰You came only yesterday. And today shall I make you wander about with us, when I do not know where I am going? Go back, and take your people with you. May the LORD show you kindness and faithfulness."*ᶜ*

²¹But Ittai replied to the king, "As surely as the LORD lives, and as my lord the king

---

ᵃ 7 Some Septuagint manuscripts, Syriac and Josephus; Hebrew *forty*   *ᵇ* 8 Some Septuagint manuscripts; Hebrew does not have *in Hebron.*   *ᶜ* 20 Septuagint; Hebrew *May kindness and faithfulness be with you*

WEDNESDAY

IN GOD'S HANDS ALONE

2 Samuel 15:1–37 or 15:25–26

Sheila Walsh

When David was warned that his third son, the handsomest man in Israel, was plotting his death, David decided to do nothing. At first this is hard to understand. David was God's chosen king. If Absalom took over, he was not the one God had chosen, and he threatened to divide the kingdom. Wasn't it David's job to defend what God had put together? David believed that his life was in God's hands, not Absalom's. This was David's response: "Let him [God] do to me whatever seems good to him" (2 Samuel 15:26). What a reply! He was saying, "If God is through with me, then I am through. If he is not, then I am not."

What a revolutionary way to live. When you feel threatened, when someone else intends to harm you, how do you respond? Do you act out of the holy fear of God or the terrified fear of man? For years I lived out of fear of what man or woman could do to me. Now I believe with my whole heart that my life is in God's hands.

"Who are you that you fear [mere mortals, human beings], who are but grass, that you forget the LORD your Maker, who stretched out the heavens and laid the foundations of the earth, that you live in constant terror every day because of the wrath of the oppressor, who is bent on destruction? For where is the wrath of the oppressor? For I am the LORD your God" (Isaiah 51:12–13,15).

When we make God our defender, our confidence is in his love.

THOMAS À KEMPIS {AD 1380–1471}

O Lord, you know what is best for us. Let this or that be done, as you will please. Give what you will and how much you will and when you will. Deal with me as you think good. Set me where you will, and deal with me in all things just as you will. Behold, I am your servant, prepared for all things, for I desire not to live for myself, but for you.

reflection

1. Are your actions based primarily on a holy fear of God or on a terrified fear of other people?

2. What evidence would you give to back up your answer?

3. What does a person need to believe about God in order to be able to trust him completely in any and every situation?

For your next devotional reading, go to page 359.

lives, wherever my lord the king may be, whether it means life or death, there will your servant be."

²²David said to Ittai, "Go ahead, march on." So Ittai the Gittite marched on with all his men and the families that were with him.

²³The whole countryside wept aloud as all the people passed by. The king also crossed the Kidron Valley, and all the people moved on toward the wilderness.

²⁴Zadok was there, too, and all the Levites who were with him were carrying the ark of the covenant of God. They set down the ark of God, and Abiathar offered sacrifices until all the people had finished leaving the city.

²⁵Then the king said to Zadok, "Take the ark of God back into the city. If I find favor in the LORD's eyes, he will bring me back and let me see it and his dwelling place again. ²⁶But if he says, 'I am not pleased with you,' then I am ready; let him do to me whatever seems good to him."

²⁷The king also said to Zadok the priest, "Do you understand? Go back to the city with my blessing. Take your son Ahimaaz with you, and also Abiathar's son Jonathan. You and Abiathar return with your two sons. ²⁸I will wait at the fords in the wilderness until word comes from you to inform me." ²⁹So Zadok and Abiathar took the ark of God back to Jerusalem and stayed there.

³⁰But David continued up the Mount of Olives, weeping as he went; his head was covered and he was barefoot. All the people with him covered their heads too and were weeping as they went up. ³¹Now David had been told, "Ahithophel is among the conspirators with Absalom." So David prayed, "LORD, turn Ahithophel's counsel into foolishness."

³²When David arrived at the summit, where people used to worship God, Hushai the Arkite was there to meet him, his robe torn and dust on his head. ³³David said to him, "If you go with me, you will be a burden to me. ³⁴But if you return to the city and say to Absalom, 'Your Majesty, I will be your servant; I was your father's servant in the past, but now I will be your servant,' then you can help me by frustrating Ahithophel's advice. ³⁵Won't the priests Zadok and Abiathar be there with you? Tell them anything you hear in the king's palace. ³⁶Their two sons, Ahimaaz son of Zadok and Jonathan

son of Abiathar, are there with them. Send them to me with anything you hear."

³⁷So Hushai, David's confidant, arrived at Jerusalem as Absalom was entering the city.

David and Ziba

16 When David had gone a short distance beyond the summit, there was Ziba, the steward of Mephibosheth, waiting to meet him. He had a string of donkeys saddled and loaded with two hundred loaves of bread, a hundred cakes of raisins, a hundred cakes of figs and a skin of wine.

²The king asked Ziba, "Why have you brought these?"

Ziba answered, "The donkeys are for the king's household to ride on, the bread and fruit are for the men to eat, and the wine is to refresh those who become exhausted in the wilderness."

³The king then asked, "Where is your master's grandson?"

Ziba said to him, "He is staying in Jerusalem, because he thinks, 'Today the house of Israel will restore to me my grandfather's kingdom.' "

⁴Then the king said to Ziba, "All that belonged to Mephibosheth is now yours."

"I humbly bow," Ziba said. "May I find favor in your eyes, my lord the king."

Shimei Curses David

⁵As King David approached Bahurim, a man from the same clan as Saul's family came out from there. His name was Shimei son of Gera, and he cursed as he came out. ⁶He pelted David and all the king's officials with stones, though all the troops and the special guard were on David's right and left. ⁷As he cursed, Shimei said, "Get out, get out, you murderer, you scoundrel! ⁸The LORD has repaid you for all the blood you shed in the household of Saul, in whose place you have reigned. The LORD has given the kingdom into the hands of your son Absalom. You have come to ruin because you are a murderer!"

⁹Then Abishai son of Zeruiah said to the king, "Why should this dead dog curse my lord the king? Let me go over and cut off his head."

¹⁰But the king said, "What does this have to do with you, you sons of Zeruiah? If he is

cursing because the LORD said to him, 'Curse David,' who can ask, 'Why do you do this?' "

[11] David then said to Abishai and all his officials, "My son, who is of my own flesh, is trying to take my life. How much more, then, this Benjamite! Leave him alone; let him curse, for the LORD has told him to. [12] It may be that the LORD will look upon my misery and restore to me his covenant blessing instead of his curse today."

[13] So David and his men continued along the road while Shimei was going along the hillside opposite him, cursing as he went and throwing stones at him and showering him with dirt. [14] The king and all the people with him arrived at their destination exhausted. And there he refreshed himself.

The Advice of Ahithophel and Hushai

[15] Meanwhile, Absalom and all the men of Israel came to Jerusalem, and Ahithophel was with him. [16] Then Hushai the Arkite, David's confidant, went to Absalom and said to him, "Long live the king! Long live the king!"

[17] Absalom said to Hushai, "So this is the love you show your friend? If he's your friend, why didn't you go with him?"

[18] Hushai said to Absalom, "No, the one chosen by the LORD, by these people, and by all the men of Israel—his I will be, and I will remain with him. [19] Furthermore, whom should I serve? Should I not serve the son? Just as I served your father, so I will serve you."

[20] Absalom said to Ahithophel, "Give us your advice. What should we do?"

[21] Ahithophel answered, "Sleep with your father's concubines whom he left to take care of the palace. Then all Israel will hear that you have made yourself obnoxious to your father, and the hands of everyone with you will be more resolute." [22] So they pitched a tent for Absalom on the roof, and he slept with his father's concubines in the sight of all Israel.

[23] Now in those days the advice Ahithophel gave was like that of one who inquires of God. That was how both David and Absalom regarded all of Ahithophel's advice.

17 Ahithophel said to Absalom, "I would[a] choose twelve thousand men and set out tonight in pursuit of David. [2] I would attack him while he is

weary and weak. I would strike him with terror, and then all the people with him will flee. I would strike down only the king [3] and bring all the people back to you. The death of the man you seek will mean the return of all; all the people will be unharmed." [4] This plan seemed good to Absalom and to all the elders of Israel.

[5] But Absalom said, "Summon also Hushai the Arkite, so we can hear what he has to say as well." [6] When Hushai came to him, Absalom said, "Ahithophel has given this advice. Should we do what he says? If not, give us your opinion."

[7] Hushai replied to Absalom, "The advice Ahithophel has given is not good this time. [8] You know your father and his men; they are fighters, and as fierce as a wild bear robbed of her cubs. Besides, your father is an experienced fighter; he will not spend the night with the troops. [9] Even now, he is hidden in a cave or some other place. If he should attack your troops first,[b] whoever hears about it will say, 'There has been a slaughter among the troops who follow Absalom.' [10] Then even the bravest soldier, whose heart is like the heart of a lion, will melt with fear, for all Israel knows that your father is a fighter and that those with him are brave.

[11] "So I advise you: Let all Israel, from Dan to Beersheba—as numerous as the sand on the seashore—be gathered to you, with you yourself leading them into battle. [12] Then we will attack him wherever he may be found, and we will fall on him as dew settles on the ground. Neither he nor any of his men will be left alive. [13] If he withdraws into a city, then all Israel will bring ropes to that city, and we will drag it down to the valley until not so much as a pebble is left."

[14] Absalom and all the men of Israel said, "The advice of Hushai the Arkite is better than that of Ahithophel." For the LORD had determined to frustrate the good advice of Ahithophel in order to bring disaster on Absalom.

[15] Hushai told Zadok and Abiathar, the priests, "Ahithophel has advised Absalom and the elders of Israel to do such and such, but I have advised them to do so and so. [16] Now send a message at once and tell David, 'Do not spend the night at the fords in the wilderness; cross over without fail, or

---

a 1 Or *Let me*   b 9 Or *When some of the men fall at the first attack* the king and all the people with him will be swallowed up.' "

¹⁷Jonathan and Ahimaaz were staying at En Rogel. A female servant was to go and inform them, and they were to go and tell King David, for they could not risk being seen entering the city. ¹⁸But a young man saw them and told Absalom. So the two of them left at once and went to the house of a man in Bahurim. He had a well in his courtyard, and they climbed down into it. ¹⁹His wife took a covering and spread it out over the opening of the well and scattered grain over it. No one knew anything about it.

²⁰When Absalom's men came to the woman at the house, they asked, "Where are Ahimaaz and Jonathan?"

The woman answered them, "They crossed over the brook."ᵃ The men searched but found no one, so they returned to Jerusalem.

²¹After they had gone, the two climbed out of the well and went to inform King David. They said to him, "Set out and cross the river at once; Ahithophel has advised such and such against you." ²²So David and all the people with him set out and crossed the Jordan. By daybreak, no one was left who had not crossed the Jordan.

²³When Ahithophel saw that his advice had not been followed, he saddled his donkey and set out for his house in his hometown. He put his house in order and then hanged himself. So he died and was buried in his father's tomb.

Absalom's Death

²⁴David went to Mahanaim, and Absalom crossed the Jordan with all the men of Israel. ²⁵Absalom had appointed Amasa over the army in place of Joab. Amasa was the son of Jether,ᵇ an Ishmaeliteᶜ who had married Abigal, the daughter of Nahash and sister of Zeruiah the mother of Joab. ²⁶The Israelites and Absalom camped in the land of Gilead.

²⁷When David came to Mahanaim, Shobi son of Nahash from Rabbah of the Ammonites, and Makir son of Ammiel from Lo Debar, and Barzillai the Gileadite from Rogelim ²⁸brought bedding and bowls and articles of pottery. They also brought wheat and barley, flour and roasted grain, beans and lentils,ᵈ ²⁹honey and curds, sheep, and cheese from cows' milk for David and his people to eat. For they said, "The people have become exhausted and hungry and thirsty in the wilderness."

18 David mustered the men who were with him and appointed over them commanders of thousands and commanders of hundreds. ²David sent out his troops, a third under the command of Joab, a third under Joab's brother Abishai son of Zeruiah, and a third under Ittai the Gittite. The king told the troops, "I myself will surely march out with you."

³But the men said, "You must not go out; if we are forced to flee, they won't care about us. Even if half of us die, they won't care; but you are worth ten thousand of us.ᵉ It would be better now for you to give us support from the city."

⁴The king answered, "I will do whatever seems best to you."

So the king stood beside the gate while all his men marched out in units of hundreds and of thousands. ⁵The king commanded Joab, Abishai and Ittai, "Be gentle with the young man Absalom for my sake." And all the troops heard the king giving orders concerning Absalom to each of the commanders.

⁶David's army marched out of the city to fight Israel, and the battle took place in the forest of Ephraim. ⁷There Israel's troops were routed by David's men, and the casualties that day were great—twenty thousand men. ⁸The battle spread out over the whole countryside, and the forest swallowed up more men that day than the sword.

⁹Now Absalom happened to meet David's men. He was riding his mule, and as the mule went under the thick branches of a large oak, Absalom's hair got caught in the tree. He was left hanging in midair, while the mule he was riding kept on going.

¹⁰When one of the men saw what had happened, he told Joab, "I just saw Absalom hanging in an oak tree."

¹¹Joab said to the man who had told him

ᵃ 20 Or *"They passed by the sheep pen toward the water."*   ᵇ 25 Hebrew *Ithra,* a variant of *Jether*
ᶜ 25 Some Septuagint manuscripts (see also 1 Chron. 2:17); Hebrew and other Septuagint manuscripts *Israelite*   ᵈ 28 Most Septuagint manuscripts and Syriac; Hebrew *lentils, and roasted grain*
ᵉ 3 Two Hebrew manuscripts, some Septuagint manuscripts and Vulgate; most Hebrew manuscripts *care; for now there are ten thousand like us*

THURSDAY

TAKING RESPONSIBILITY

2 Samuel 18:1–33 *or* 18:14–15,33

G. CAMPBELL MORGAN {AD 1863–1945}

In this hour David's cup of sorrow was filled to the full. Everything in the story leads up to, and culminates in, this wail of anguish over his dead boy. It is very brief, but it thrills with agony. Five times he repeated the words, "my son." This surely had a deeper note in it than that of the merely half-conscious repetition of words occasioned by personal grief. The father recognized how much he was responsible for his son. It is as though he had said: " He is indeed my son, his weaknesses are my weaknesses, his passions are my passions, his sins are my sins." Out of all that sense there came the deepest cry of all: " If only I had died instead of you!" Here surely David reached the profoundest moment of his suffering. May none of us ever experimentally enter into its awful consciousness! In order that we may not, we need to ponder all the story carefully, and learn the solemn lessons it teaches of parental responsibility.

Steve Farrar

David didn't seem to fully get it. He didn't understand Absalom's righteous anger regarding the heinous rape of his sister. David didn't listen to Absalom's repeated appeals to his father for justice on her behalf. Then when his son in desperation brutally took matters into his own hands, David simply looked at the hard-core facts at hand and shut Absalom out of his life—forever. So much for building bridges. So much for redemption in any form. David took the easy way out. He ignored his son. He loved him, but he ignored him. And it turned out to be disastrous.

reflection

1. Why do you think David made so many poor choices as a father?
2. What do you believe to be the responsibility of a parent?
3. Many people today blame all their weaknesses and sins on their parents—either heredity or the way their parents raised them. Where do you draw the line between parental responsibility and children being responsible for their own actions?

For your next devotional reading, go to page 380.

this, "What! You saw him? Why didn't you strike him to the ground right there? Then I would have had to give you ten shekels^a of silver and a warrior's belt."

¹²But the man replied, "Even if a thousand shekels^b were weighed out into my hands, I would not lay a hand on the king's son. In our hearing the king commanded you and Abishai and Ittai, 'Protect the young man Absalom for my sake.^{c}' ¹³And if I had put my life in jeopardy^d—and nothing is hidden from the king—you would have kept your distance from me."

¹⁴Joab said, "I'm not going to wait like this for you." So he took three javelins in his hand and plunged them into Absalom's heart while Absalom was still alive in the oak tree. ¹⁵And ten of Joab's armor-bearers surrounded Absalom, struck him and killed him.

¹⁶Then Joab sounded the trumpet, and the troops stopped pursuing Israel, for Joab halted them. ¹⁷They took Absalom, threw him into a big pit in the forest and piled up a large heap of rocks over him. Meanwhile, all the Israelites fled to their homes.

¹⁸During his lifetime Absalom had taken a pillar and erected it in the King's Valley as a monument to himself, for he thought, "I have no son to carry on the memory of my name." He named the pillar after himself, and it is called Absalom's Monument to this day.

David Mourns

¹⁹Now Ahimaaz son of Zadok said, "Let me run and take the news to the king that the LORD has vindicated him by delivering him from the hand of his enemies."

²⁰"You are not the one to take the news today," Joab told him. "You may take the news another time, but you must not do so today, because the king's son is dead."

²¹Then Joab said to a Cushite, "Go, tell the king what you have seen." The Cushite bowed down before Joab and ran off.

²²Ahimaaz son of Zadok again said to Joab, "Come what may, please let me run behind the Cushite."

But Joab replied, "My son, why do you want to go? You don't have any news that will bring you a reward."

²³He said, "Come what may, I want to run."

So Joab said, "Run!" Then Ahimaaz ran by way of the plain^e and outran the Cushite.

²⁴While David was sitting between the inner and outer gates, the watchman went up to the roof of the gateway by the wall. As he looked out, he saw a man running alone. ²⁵The watchman called out to the king and reported it.

The king said, "If he is alone, he must have good news." And the runner came closer and closer.

²⁶Then the watchman saw another runner, and he called down to the gatekeeper, "Look, another man running alone!"

The king said, "He must be bringing good news, too."

²⁷The watchman said, "It seems to me that the first one runs like Ahimaaz son of Zadok."

"He's a good man," the king said. "He comes with good news."

²⁸Then Ahimaaz called out to the king, "All is well!" He bowed down before the king with his face to the ground and said, "Praise be to the LORD your God! He has delivered up those who lifted their hands against my lord the king."

²⁹The king asked, "Is the young man Absalom safe?"

Ahimaaz answered, "I saw great confusion just as Joab was about to send the king's servant and me, your servant, but I don't know what it was."

³⁰The king said, "Stand aside and wait here." So he stepped aside and stood there.

³¹Then the Cushite arrived and said, "My lord the king, hear the good news! The LORD has vindicated you today by delivering you from the hand of all who rose up against you."

³²The king asked the Cushite, "Is the young man Absalom safe?"

The Cushite replied, "May the enemies of my lord the king and all who rise up to harm you be like that young man."

*³³The king was shaken. He went up to the room over the gateway and wept. As he went, he said: "O my son Absalom! My son,

---

^{a} 11 That is, about 4 ounces or about 115 grams ^{b} 12 That is, about 25 pounds or about 11 kilograms
^{c} 12 A few Hebrew manuscripts, Septuagint, Vulgate and Syriac; most Hebrew manuscripts may be translated *Absalom, whoever you may be.* ^{d} 13 Or *Otherwise, if I had acted treacherously toward him*
^{e} 23 That is, the plain of the Jordan

* 18:33 is numbered 19:1 in Hebrew texts.

my son Absalom! If only I had died instead of you—O Absalom, my son, my son!"

19

*Joab was told, "The king is weeping and mourning for Absalom." 2And for the whole army the victory that day was turned into mourning, because on that day the troops heard it said, "The king is grieving for his son." 3The men stole into the city that day as men steal in who are ashamed when they flee from battle. 4The king covered his face and cried aloud, "O my son Absalom! O Absalom, my son, my son!"

5Then Joab went into the house to the king and said, "Today you have humiliated all your men, who have just saved your life and the lives of your sons and daughters and the lives of your wives and concubines. 6You love those who hate you and hate those who love you. You have made it clear today that the commanders and their men mean nothing to you. I see that you would be pleased if Absalom were alive today and all of us were dead. 7Now go out and encourage your men. I swear by the LORD that if you don't go out, not a man will be left with you by nightfall. This will be worse for you than all the calamities that have come on you from your youth till now."

8So the king got up and took his seat in the gateway. When the men were told, "The king is sitting in the gateway," they all came before him.

Meanwhile, the Israelites had fled to their homes.

David Returns to Jerusalem

9Throughout the tribes of Israel, all the people were arguing among themselves, saying, "The king delivered us from the hand of our enemies; he is the one who rescued us from the hand of the Philistines. But now he has fled the country to escape from Absalom; 10and Absalom, whom we anointed to rule over us, has died in battle. So why do you say nothing about bringing the king back?"

11King David sent this message to Zadok and Abiathar, the priests: "Ask the elders of Judah, 'Why should you be the last to bring the king back to his palace, since what is being said throughout Israel has reached the king at his quarters? 12You are my relatives,

my own flesh and blood. So why should you be the last to bring back the king?' 13And say to Amasa, 'Are you not my own flesh and blood? May God deal with me, be it ever so severely, if you are not the commander of my army for life in place of Joab.' "

14He won over the hearts of the men of Judah so that they were all of one accord. They sent word to the king, "Return, you and all your men." 15Then the king returned and went as far as the Jordan.

Now the men of Judah had come to Gilgal to go out and meet the king and bring him across the Jordan. 16Shimei son of Gera, the Benjamite from Bahurim, hurried down with the men of Judah to meet King David. 17With him were a thousand Benjamites, along with Ziba, the steward of Saul's household, and his fifteen sons and twenty servants. They rushed to the Jordan, where the king was. 18They crossed at the ford to take the king's household over and to do whatever he wished.

When Shimei son of Gera crossed the Jordan, he fell prostrate before the king 19and said to him, "May my lord not hold me guilty. Do not remember how your servant did wrong on the day my lord the king left Jerusalem. May the king put it out of his mind. 20For I your servant know that I have sinned, but today I have come here as the first of the whole house of Joseph to come down and meet my lord the king."

21Then Abishai son of Zeruiah said, "Shouldn't Shimei be put to death for this? He cursed the LORD's anointed."

22David replied, "What does this have to do with you, you sons of Zeruiah? What right do you have to interfere? Should anyone be put to death in Israel today? Don't I know that today I am king over Israel?" 23So the king said to Shimei, "You shall not die." And the king promised him on oath.

24Mephibosheth, Saul's grandson, also went down to meet the king. He had not taken care of his feet or trimmed his mustache or washed his clothes from the day the king left until the day he returned safely. 25When he came from Jerusalem to meet the king, the king asked him, "Why didn't you go with me, Mephibosheth?"

26He said, "My lord the king, since I your servant am lame, I said, 'I will have my don-

* 19:1-43 is numbered 19:2-44 in Hebrew texts.

key saddled and will ride on it, so I can go with the king.' But Ziba my servant betrayed me. 27And he has slandered your servant to my lord the king. My lord the king is like an angel of God; so do whatever you wish. 28All my grandfather's descendants deserved nothing but death from my lord the king, but you gave your servant a place among those who eat at your table. So what right do I have to make any more appeals to the king?"

29The king said to him, "Why say more? I order you and Ziba to divide the land."

30Mephibosheth said to the king, "Let him take everything, now that my lord the king has returned home safely."

31Barzillai the Gileadite also came down from Rogelim to cross the Jordan with the king and to send him on his way from there. 32Now Barzillai was very old, eighty years of age. He had provided for the king during his stay in Mahanaim, for he was a very wealthy man. 33The king said to Barzillai, "Cross over with me and stay with me in Jerusalem, and I will provide for you."

34But Barzillai answered the king, "How many more years will I live, that I should go up to Jerusalem with the king? 35I am now eighty years old. Can I tell the difference between what is enjoyable and what is not? Can your servant taste what he eats and drinks? Can I still hear the voices of male and female singers? Why should your servant be an added burden to my lord the king? 36Your servant will cross over the Jordan with the king for a short distance, but why should the king reward me in this way? 37Let your servant return, that I may die in my own town near the tomb of my father and mother. But here is your servant Kimham. Let him cross over with my lord the king. Do for him whatever you wish."

38The king said, "Kimham shall cross over with me, and I will do for him whatever you wish. And anything you desire from me I will do for you."

39So all the people crossed the Jordan, and then the king crossed over. The king kissed Barzillai and bid him farewell, and Barzillai returned to his home.

40When the king crossed over to Gilgal, Kimham crossed with him. All the troops of Judah and half the troops of Israel had taken the king over.

41Soon all the men of Israel were coming to the king and saying to him, "Why did our brothers, the men of Judah, steal the king away and bring him and his household across the Jordan, together with all his men?"

42All the men of Judah answered the men of Israel, "We did this because the king is closely related to us. Why are you angry about it? Have we eaten any of the king's provisions? Have we taken anything for ourselves?"

43Then the men of Israel answered the men of Judah, "We have ten shares in the king; so we have a greater claim on David than you have. Why then do you treat us with contempt? Weren't we the first to speak of bringing back our king?"

But the men of Judah responded even more harshly than the men of Israel.

Sheba Rebels Against David

20 Now a troublemaker named Sheba son of Bikri, a Benjamite, happened to be there. He sounded the trumpet and shouted,

"We have no share in David,
    no part in Jesse's son!
Everyone to your tents, Israel!"

2So all the men of Israel deserted David to follow Sheba son of Bikri. But the men of Judah stayed by their king all the way from the Jordan to Jerusalem.

3When David returned to his palace in Jerusalem, he took the ten concubines he had left to take care of the palace and put them in a house under guard. He provided for them but had no sexual relations with them. They were kept in confinement till the day of their death, living as widows.

4Then the king said to Amasa, "Summon the men of Judah to come to me within three days, and be here yourself." 5But when Amasa went to summon Judah, he took longer than the time the king had set for him.

6David said to Abishai, "Now Sheba son of Bikri will do us more harm than Absalom did. Take your master's men and pursue him, or he will find fortified cities and escape from us."a 7So Joab's men and the Kerethites and Pelethites and all the mighty

a 6 Or and do us serious injury

warriors went out under the command of Abishai. They marched out from Jerusalem to pursue Sheba son of Bikri.

⁸While they were at the great rock in Gibeon, Amasa came to meet them. Joab was wearing his military tunic, and strapped over it at his waist was a belt with a dagger in its sheath. As he stepped forward, it dropped out of its sheath.

⁹Joab said to Amasa, "How are you, my brother?" Then Joab took Amasa by the beard with his right hand to kiss him. ¹⁰Amasa was not on his guard against the dagger in Joab's hand, and Joab plunged it into his belly, and his intestines spilled out on the ground. Without being stabbed again, Amasa died. Then Joab and his brother Abishai pursued Sheba son of Bikri.

¹¹One of Joab's men stood beside Amasa and said, "Whoever favors Joab, and whoever is for David, let him follow Joab!" ¹²Amasa lay wallowing in his blood in the middle of the road, and the man saw that all the troops came to a halt there. When he realized that everyone who came up to Amasa stopped, he dragged him from the road into a field and threw a garment over him. ¹³After Amasa had been removed from the road, everyone went on with Joab to pursue Sheba son of Bikri.

¹⁴Sheba passed through all the tribes of Israel to Abel Beth Maakah and through the entire region of the Bikrites,ᵃ who gathered together and followed him. ¹⁵All the troops with Joab came and besieged Sheba in Abel Beth Maakah. They built a siege ramp up to the city, and it stood against the outer fortifications. While they were battering the wall to bring it down, ¹⁶a wise woman called from the city, "Listen! Listen! Tell Joab to come here so I can speak to him." ¹⁷He went toward her, and she asked, "Are you Joab?"

"I am," he answered.

She said, "Listen to what your servant has to say."

"I'm listening," he said.

¹⁸She continued, "Long ago they used to say, 'Get your answer at Abel,' and that settled it. ¹⁹We are the peaceful and faithful in Israel. You are trying to destroy a city that is a mother in Israel. Why do you want to swallow up the LORD's inheritance?"

²⁰"Far be it from me!" Joab replied, "Far be it from me to swallow up or destroy! ²¹That is not the case. A man named Sheba son of Bikri, from the hill country of Ephraim, has lifted up his hand against the king, against David. Hand over this one man, and I'll withdraw from the city."

The woman said to Joab, "His head will be thrown to you from the wall."

²²Then the woman went to all the people with her wise advice, and they cut off the head of Sheba son of Bikri and threw it to Joab. So he sounded the trumpet, and his men dispersed from the city, each returning to his home. And Joab went back to the king in Jerusalem.

David's Officials

²³Joab was over Israel's entire army; Benaiah son of Jehoiada was over the Kerethites and Pelethites; ²⁴Adoniramᵇ was in charge of forced labor; Jehoshaphat son of Ahilud was recorder; ²⁵Sheva was secretary; Zadok and Abiathar were priests; ²⁶and Ira the Jairiteᶜ was David's priest.

The Gibeonites Avenged

21 During the reign of David, there was a famine for three successive years; so David sought the face of the LORD. The LORD said, "It is on account of Saul and his blood-stained house; it is because he put the Gibeonites to death."

²The king summoned the Gibeonites and spoke to them. (Now the Gibeonites were not a part of Israel but were survivors of the Amorites; the Israelites had sworn to ⌊spare⌋ them, but Saul in his zeal for Israel and Judah had tried to annihilate them.) ³David asked the Gibeonites, "What shall I do for you? How shall I make atonement so that you will bless the LORD's inheritance?"

⁴The Gibeonites answered him, "We have no right to demand silver or gold from Saul or his family, nor do we have the right to put anyone in Israel to death."

"What do you want me to do for you?" David asked.

⁵They answered the king, "As for the man who destroyed us and plotted against us so that we have been decimated and have no place anywhere in Israel, ⁶let seven of his

---

ᵃ 14 See Septuagint and Vulgate; Hebrew *Berites*.   ᵇ 24 Some Septuagint manuscripts (see also 1 Kings 4:6 and 5:14); Hebrew *Adoram*   ᶜ 26 Hebrew; some Septuagint manuscripts and Syriac (see also 2 Samuel 23:38) *Ithrite* male descendants be given to us to be killed and their bodies exposed before the Lord at Gibeah of Saul—the Lord's chosen one."

So the king said, "I will give them to you."

⁷The king spared Mephibosheth son of Jonathan, the son of Saul, because of the oath before the Lord between David and Jonathan son of Saul. ⁸But the king took Armoni and Mephibosheth, the two sons of Aiah's daughter Rizpah, whom she had borne to Saul, together with the five sons of Saul's daughter Merab,ᵃ whom she had borne to Adriel son of Barzillai the Meholathite. ⁹He handed them over to the Gibeonites, who killed them and exposed their bodies on a hill before the Lord. All seven of them fell together; they were put to death during the first days of the harvest, just as the barley harvest was beginning.

¹⁰Rizpah daughter of Aiah took sackcloth and spread it out for herself on a rock. From the beginning of the harvest till the rain poured down from the heavens on the bodies, she did not let the birds touch them by day or the wild animals by night. ¹¹When David was told what Aiah's daughter Rizpah, Saul's concubine, had done, ¹²he went and took the bones of Saul and his son Jonathan from the citizens of Jabesh Gilead. (They had stolen their bodies from the public square at Beth Shan, where the Philistines had hung them after they struck Saul down on Gilboa.) ¹³David brought the bones of Saul and his son Jonathan from there, and the bones of those who had been killed and exposed were gathered up.

¹⁴They buried the bones of Saul and his son Jonathan in the tomb of Saul's father Kish, at Zela in Benjamin, and did everything the king commanded. After that, God answered prayer in behalf of the land.

Wars Against the Philistines

¹⁵Once again there was a battle between the Philistines and Israel. David went down with his men to fight against the Philistines, and he became exhausted. ¹⁶And Ishbi-Benob, one of the descendants of Rapha, whose bronze spearhead weighed three hundred shekelsᵇ and who was armed with a new ⌊sword⌋, said he would kill David.

¹⁷But Abishai son of Zeruiah came to David's rescue; he struck the Philistine down and killed him. Then David's men swore to him, saying, "Never again will you go out with us to battle, so that the lamp of Israel will not be extinguished."

¹⁸In the course of time, there was another battle with the Philistines, at Gob. At that time Sibbekai the Hushathite killed Saph, one of the descendants of Rapha.

¹⁹In another battle with the Philistines at Gob, Elhanan son of Jairᶜ the Bethlehemite killed the brother ofᵈ Goliath the Gittite, who had a spear with a shaft like a weaver's rod.

²⁰In still another battle, which took place at Gath, there was a huge man with six fingers on each hand and six toes on each foot—twenty-four in all. He also was descended from Rapha. ²¹When he taunted Israel, Jonathan son of Shimeah, David's brother, killed him.

²²These four were descendants of Rapha in Gath, and they fell at the hands of David and his men.

David's Song of Praise

22 David sang to the Lord the words of this song when the Lord delivered him from the hand of all his enemies and from the hand of Saul. ²He said:

> "The Lord is my rock, my fortress and
>   my deliverer;
> 3   my God is my rock, in whom I take
>   refuge,
>   my shieldᵉ and the hornᶠ of my
>   salvation.
> He is my stronghold, my refuge and my
>   savior—
>   from violent people you save me.
>
> ⁴ "I called to the Lord, who is worthy of
>   praise,
>   and have been saved from my
>   enemies.
> ⁵ The waves of death swirled about me;
>   the torrents of destruction
>   overwhelmed me.
> ⁶ The cords of the grave coiled around me;
>   the snares of death confronted me.

ᵃ 8 Two Hebrew manuscripts, some Septuagint manuscripts and Syriac (see also 1 Samuel 18:19); most Hebrew and Septuagint manuscripts *Michal*   ᵇ 16 That is, about 7 1/2 pounds or about 3.5 kilograms   ᶜ 19 See 1 Chron. 20:5; Hebrew *Jaare-Oregim*.   ᵈ 19 See 1 Chron. 20:5; Hebrew does not have *the brother of*.   ᵉ 3 Or *sovereign*   ᶠ 3 *Horn* here symbolizes strength.

7 "In my distress I called to the LORD;
    I called out to my God.
  From his temple he heard my voice;
    my cry came to his ears.
8 The earth trembled and quaked,
    the foundations of the heavens[a] shook;
    they trembled because he was angry.
9 Smoke rose from his nostrils;
    consuming fire came from his mouth,
    burning coals blazed out of it.
10 He parted the heavens and came down;
    dark clouds were under his feet.
11 He mounted the cherubim and flew;
    he soared[b] on the wings of the wind.
12 He made darkness his canopy around
    him—
    the dark[c] rain clouds of the sky.
13 Out of the brightness of his presence
    bolts of lightning blazed forth.
14 The LORD thundered from heaven;
    the voice of the Most High resounded.
15 He shot his arrows and scattered the
    enemy,
    with great bolts of lightning he routed
    them.
16 The valleys of the sea were exposed
    and the foundations of the earth laid
    bare
  at the rebuke of the LORD,
    at the blast of breath from his nostrils.

17 "He reached down from on high and
    took hold of me;
    he drew me out of deep waters.
18 He rescued me from my powerful enemy,
    from my foes, who were too strong
    for me.
19 They confronted me in the day of my
    disaster,
    but the LORD was my support.
20 He brought me out into a spacious place;
    he rescued me because he delighted
    in me.
21 "The LORD has dealt with me according
    to my righteousness;
    according to the cleanness of my
    hands he has rewarded me.
22 For I have kept the ways of the LORD;

  I am not guilty of turning from my
    God.
23 All his laws are before me;
    I have not turned away from his
    decrees.
24 I have been blameless before him
    and have kept myself from sin.
25 The LORD has rewarded me according to
    my righteousness,
    according to my cleanness[d] in his
    sight.

26 "To the faithful you show yourself faithful,
    to the blameless you show yourself
    blameless,
27 to the pure you show yourself pure,
    but to the devious you show yourself
    shrewd.
28 You save the humble,
    but your eyes are on the haughty to
    bring them low.
29 You, LORD, are my lamp;
    the LORD turns my darkness into light.
30 With your help I can advance against a
    troop[e];
    with my God I can scale a wall.

31 "As for God, his way is perfect;
    the LORD's word is flawless.
  He shields all who take refuge in him.
32 For who is God besides the LORD?
    And who is the Rock except our God?
33 It is God who arms me with strength[f]
    and keeps my way secure.
34 He makes my feet like the feet of a deer
    and causes me to stand on the
    heights.
35 He trains my hands for battle;
    my arms can bend a bow of bronze.
36 You make your saving help my shield;
    your help has made[g] me great.
37 You provide a broad path for my feet,
    so that my ankles do not give way.

38 "I pursued my enemies and crushed
    them;
    I did not turn back till they were
    destroyed.
39 I crushed them completely, and they
    could not rise;
    they fell beneath my feet.

---

a 8 Hebrew; Vulgate and Syriac (see also Psalm 18:7) *mountains*   b 11 Many Hebrew manuscripts (see
also Psalm 18:10); most Hebrew manuscripts *appeared*   c 12 Septuagint (see also Psalm 18:11); Hebrew
massed   d 25 Hebrew; Septuagint and Vulgate (see also Psalm 18:24) *to the cleanness of my hands*
e 30 Or *can run through a barricade*   f 33 Dead Sea Scrolls, some Septuagint manuscripts, Vulgate and
Syriac (see also Psalm 18:32); Masoretic Text *who is my strong refuge*   g 36 Dead Sea Scrolls; Masoretic
Text *shield; / you stoop down to make*

⁴⁰You armed me with strength for battle;
  you humbled my adversaries before
    me.
⁴¹You made my enemies turn their backs
    in flight,
  and I destroyed my foes.
⁴²They cried for help, but there was no
    one to save them—
  to the LORD, but he did not answer.
⁴³I beat them as fine as the dust of the
    earth;
  I pounded and trampled them like
    mud in the streets.

⁴⁴"You have delivered me from the attacks
    of the peoples;
  you have preserved me as the head of
    nations.
People I did not know now serve me,
⁴⁵   foreigners cower before me;
  as soon as they hear of me, they obey
    me.
⁴⁶They all lose heart;
  they come trembling*a* from their
    strongholds.

⁴⁷"The LORD lives! Praise be to my Rock!
  Exalted be my God, the Rock, my
    Savior!
⁴⁸He is the God who avenges me,
  who puts the nations under me,
⁴⁹   who sets me free from my enemies.
You exalted me above my foes;
  from violent people you rescued me.
⁵⁰Therefore I will praise you, LORD, among
    the nations;
  I will sing the praises of your name.

⁵¹"He gives his king great victories;
  he shows unfailing kindness to his
    anointed,
  to David and his descendants
    forever."

David's Last Words

23 These are the last words of David:

"The inspired utterance of
  David son of Jesse,
the utterance of the man exalted by
    the Most High,

the man anointed by the God of Jacob,
  the hero of Israel's songs:

²"The Spirit of the LORD spoke through
    me;
  his word was on my tongue.
³The God of Israel spoke,
  the Rock of Israel said to me:
'When one rules over people in
    righteousness,
  when he rules in the fear of God,
⁴he is like the light of morning at sunrise
    on a cloudless morning,
  like the brightness after rain
    that brings grass from the earth.'

⁵"If my house were not right with God,
  surely he would not have made with
    me an everlasting covenant,
  arranged and secured in every part;
surely he would not bring to fruition my
    salvation
  and grant me my every desire.
⁶But evil men are all to be cast aside like
    thorns,
  which are not gathered with the hand.
⁷Whoever touches thorns
  uses a tool of iron or the shaft of a
    spear;
  they are burned up where they lie."

David's Mighty Warriors

⁸These are the names of David's mighty
warriors:
  Josheb-Basshebeth,*b* a Tahkemonite,*c* was
chief of the Three; he raised his spear against
eight hundred men, whom he killed*d* in one
encounter.
  ⁹Next to him was Eleazar son of Dodai
the Ahohite. As one of the three mighty warriors, he was with David when they taunted
the Philistines gathered ⌞at Pas Dammim⌟*e*
for battle. Then the Israelites retreated,
¹⁰but Eleazar stood his ground and struck
down the Philistines till his hand grew tired
and froze to the sword. The LORD brought
about a great victory that day. The troops returned to Eleazar, but only to strip the dead.
  ¹¹Next to him was Shammah son of Agee
the Hararite. When the Philistines banded
together at a place where there was a field

---

a 46 Some Septuagint manuscripts and Vulgate (see also Psalm 18:45); Masoretic Text *they arm
themselves*   *b 8* Hebrew; some Septuagint manuscripts suggest *Ish-Bosheth,* that is, *Esh-Baal* (see also
1 Chron. 11:11 *Jashobeam*).   *c 8* Probably a variant of *Hakmonite* (see 1 Chron. 11:11)   *d 8* Some
Septuagint manuscripts (see also 1 Chron. 11:11); Hebrew and other Septuagint manuscripts *Three; it was
Adino the Eznite who killed eight hundred men*   *e 9* See 1 Chron. 11:13; Hebrew *gathered there.*

full of lentils, Israel's troops fled from them. ¹²But Shammah took his stand in the middle of the field. He defended it and struck the Philistines down, and the LORD brought about a great victory.

¹³During harvest time, three of the thirty chief warriors came down to David at the cave of Adullam, while a band of Philistines was encamped in the Valley of Rephaim. ¹⁴At that time David was in the stronghold, and the Philistine garrison was at Bethlehem. ¹⁵David longed for water and said, "Oh, that someone would get me a drink of water from the well near the gate of Bethlehem!" ¹⁶So the three mighty warriors broke through the Philistine lines, drew water from the well near the gate of Bethlehem and carried it back to David. But he refused to drink it; instead, he poured it out before the LORD. ¹⁷"Far be it from me, LORD, to do this!" he said. "Is it not the blood of men who went at the risk of their lives?" And David would not drink it.

Such were the exploits of the three mighty warriors.

¹⁸Abishai the brother of Joab son of Zeruiah was chief of the Three.ᵃ He raised his spear against three hundred men, whom he killed, and so he became as famous as the Three. ¹⁹Was he not held in greater honor than the Three? He became their commander, even though he was not included among them.

²⁰Benaiah son of Jehoiada, a valiant fighter from Kabzeel, performed great exploits. He struck down Moab's two mightiest warriors. He also went down into a pit on a snowy day and killed a lion. ²¹And he struck down a huge Egyptian. Although the Egyptian had a spear in his hand, Benaiah went against him with a club. He snatched the spear from the Egyptian's hand and killed him with his own spear. ²²Such were the exploits of Benaiah son of Jehoiada; he too was as famous as the three mighty warriors. ²³He was held in greater honor than any of the Thirty, but he was not included among the Three. And David put him in charge of his bodyguard.

²⁴Among the Thirty were:

Asahel the brother of Joab,
Elhanan son of Dodo from Bethlehem,
²⁵Shammah the Harodite,
Elika the Harodite,
²⁶Helez the Paltite,
Ira son of Ikkesh from Tekoa,
²⁷Abiezer from Anathoth,
Sibbekaiᵇ the Hushathite,
²⁸Zalmon the Ahohite,
Maharai the Netophathite,
²⁹Heledᶜ son of Baanah the Netophathite,
Ithai son of Ribai from Gibeah in Benjamin,
³⁰Benaiah the Pirathonite,
Hiddaiᵈ from the ravines of Gaash,
³¹Abi-Albon the Arbathite,
Azmaveth the Barhumite,
³²Eliahba the Shaalbonite,
the sons of Jashen,
Jonathan ³³son ofᵉ Shammah the Hararite,
Ahiam son of Shararᶠ the Hararite,
³⁴Eliphelet son of Ahasbai the Maakathite,
Eliam son of Ahithophel the Gilonite,
³⁵Hezro the Carmelite,
Paarai the Arbite,
³⁶Igal son of Nathan from Zobah,
the son of Hagri,ᵍ
³⁷Zelek the Ammonite,
Naharai the Beerothite, the armorbearer of Joab son of Zeruiah,
³⁸Ira the Ithrite,
Gareb the Ithrite
³⁹and Uriah the Hittite.
There were thirty-seven in all.

David Enrolls the Fighting Men

24 Again the anger of the LORD burned against Israel, and he incited David against them, saying, "Go and take a census of Israel and Judah."

²So the king said to Joab and the army commandersʰ with him, "Go throughout the

---

ᵃ 18 Most Hebrew manuscripts (see also 1 Chron. 11:20); two Hebrew manuscripts and Syriac *Thirty* ᵇ 27 Some Septuagint manuscripts (see also 21:18; 1 Chron. 11:29); Hebrew *Mebunnai* ᶜ 29 Some Hebrew manuscripts and Vulgate (see also 1 Chron. 11:30); most Hebrew manuscripts *Heleb* ᵈ 30 Hebrew; some Septuagint manuscripts (see also 1 Chron. 11:32) *Hurai* ᵉ 33 Some Septuagint manuscripts (see also 1 Chron. 11:34); Hebrew does not have *son of.* ᶠ 33 Hebrew; some Septuagint manuscripts (see also 1 Chron. 11:35) *Sakar* ᵍ 36 Some Septuagint manuscripts (see also 1 Chron. 11:38); Hebrew *Haggadi* ʰ 2 Septuagint (see also verse 4 and 1 Chron. 21:2); Hebrew *Joab the army commander* tribes of Israel from Dan to Beersheba and enroll the fighting men, so that I may know how many there are."

³But Joab replied to the king, "May the LORD your God multiply the troops a hundred times over, and may the eyes of my lord the king see it. But why does my lord the king want to do such a thing?"

⁴The king's word, however, overruled Joab and the army commanders; so they left the presence of the king to enroll the fighting men of Israel.

⁵After crossing the Jordan, they camped near Aroer, south of the town in the gorge, and then went through Gad and on to Jazer. ⁶They went to Gilead and the region of Tahtim Hodshi, and on to Dan Jaan and around toward Sidon. ⁷Then they went toward the fortress of Tyre and all the towns of the Hivites and Canaanites. Finally, they went on to Beersheba in the Negev of Judah.

⁸After they had gone through the entire land, they came back to Jerusalem at the end of nine months and twenty days.

⁹Joab reported the number of the fighting men to the king: In Israel there were eight hundred thousand able-bodied men who could handle a sword, and in Judah five hundred thousand.

¹⁰David was conscience-stricken after he had counted the fighting men, and he said to the LORD, "I have sinned greatly in what I have done. Now, LORD, I beg you, take away the guilt of your servant. I have done a very foolish thing."

¹¹Before David got up the next morning, the word of the LORD had come to Gad the prophet, David's seer: ¹²"Go and tell David, 'This is what the LORD says: I am giving you three options. Choose one of them for me to carry out against you.'"

¹³So Gad went to David and said to him, "Shall there come on you three*a* years of famine in your land? Or three months of fleeing from your enemies while they pursue you? Or three days of plague in your land? Now then, think it over and decide how I should answer the one who sent me."

¹⁴David said to Gad, "I am in deep distress. Let us fall into the hands of the LORD, for his mercy is great; but do not let me fall into human hands."

¹⁵So the LORD sent a plague on Israel from that morning until the end of the time designated, and seventy thousand of the people from Dan to Beersheba died. ¹⁶When the angel stretched out his hand to destroy Jerusalem, the LORD relented concerning the disaster and said to the angel who was afflicting the people, "Enough! Withdraw your hand." The angel of the LORD was then at the threshing floor of Araunah the Jebusite.

¹⁷When David saw the angel who was striking down the people, he said to the LORD, "I have sinned; I, the shepherd,*b* have done wrong. These are but sheep. What have they done? Let your hand fall on me and my family."

David Builds an Altar

¹⁸On that day Gad went to David and said to him, "Go up and build an altar to the LORD on the threshing floor of Araunah the Jebusite." ¹⁹So David went up, as the LORD had commanded through Gad. ²⁰When Araunah looked and saw the king and his officials coming toward him, he went out and bowed down before the king with his face to the ground.

²¹Araunah said, "Why has my lord the king come to his servant?"

"To buy your threshing floor," David answered, "so I can build an altar to the LORD, that the plague on the people may be stopped."

²²Araunah said to David, "Let my lord the king take whatever he wishes and offer it up. Here are oxen for the burnt offering, and here are threshing sledges and ox yokes for the wood. ²³Your Majesty, Araunah*c* gives all this to the king." Araunah also said to him, "May the LORD your God accept you."

²⁴But the king replied to Araunah, "No, I insist on paying you for it. I will not sacrifice to the LORD my God burnt offerings that cost me nothing."

So David bought the threshing floor and the oxen and paid fifty shekels*d* of silver for them. ²⁵David built an altar to the LORD there and sacrificed burnt offerings and fellowship offerings. Then the LORD answered his prayer in behalf of the land, and the plague on Israel was stopped.

---

a 13 Septuagint (see also 1 Chron. 21:12); Hebrew *seven*   *b 17* Dead Sea Scrolls and Septuagint; Masoretic Text does not have *the shepherd.*   *c 23* Some Hebrew manuscripts and Septuagint; most Hebrew manuscripts *King Araunah*   *d 24* That is, about 1 1/4 pounds or about 575 grams

1 kings

AUTHOR: Unknown

DATE: Probably between 560 and 550 B.C. while the Israelites were in exile in Babylon

THEME: Our welfare is dependent on our obedience to God.

Adonijah Sets Himself Up as King

1 When King David was very old, he could not keep warm even when they put covers over him. ²So his attendants said to him, "Let us look for a young virgin to serve the king and take care of him. She can lie beside him so that our lord the king may keep warm."

³Then they searched throughout Israel for a beautiful girl and found Abishag, a Shunammite, and brought her to the king. ⁴The girl was very beautiful; she took care of the king and waited on him, but the king had no sexual relations with her.

⁵Now Adonijah, whose mother was Haggith, put himself forward and said, "I will be king." So he got chariots and horses*a* ready, with fifty men to run ahead of him. ⁶(His father had never rebuked him by asking, "Why do you behave as you do?" He was also very handsome and was born next after Absalom.)

⁷Adonijah conferred with Joab son of Zeruiah and with Abiathar the priest, and they gave him their support. ⁸But Zadok the priest, Benaiah son of Jehoiada, Nathan the prophet, Shimei and Rei and David's special guard did not join Adonijah.

⁹Adonijah then sacrificed sheep, cattle and fattened calves at the Stone of Zoheleth near En Rogel. He invited all his brothers, the king's sons, and all the royal officials of Judah, ¹⁰but he did not invite Nathan the prophet or Benaiah or the special guard or his brother Solomon.

¹¹Then Nathan asked Bathsheba, Solomon's mother, "Have you not heard that Adonijah, the son of Haggith, has become king, and our lord David knows nothing about it?

¹²Now then, let me advise you how you can save your own life and the life of your son Solomon. ¹³Go in to King David and say to him, 'My lord the king, did you not swear to me your servant: "Surely Solomon your son shall be king after me, and he will sit on my throne"? Why then has Adonijah become king?' ¹⁴While you are still there talking to the king, I will come in and add my word to what you have said."

¹⁵So Bathsheba went to see the aged king in his room, where Abishag the Shunammite was attending him. ¹⁶Bathsheba bowed down, prostrating herself before the king.

"What is it you want?" the king asked.

¹⁷She said to him, "My lord, you yourself swore to me your servant by the LORD your God: 'Solomon your son shall be king after me, and he will sit on my throne.' ¹⁸But now Adonijah has become king, and you, my lord the king, do not know about it. ¹⁹He has sacrificed great numbers of cattle, fattened calves, and sheep, and has invited all the king's sons, Abiathar the priest and Joab the commander of the army, but he has not invited Solomon your servant. ²⁰My lord the king, the eyes of all Israel are on you, to learn from you who will sit on the throne of my lord the king after him. ²¹Otherwise, as soon as my lord the king is laid to rest with his ancestors, I and my son Solomon will be treated as criminals."

²²While she was still speaking with the king, Nathan the prophet arrived. ²³And the king was told, "Nathan the prophet is here." So he went before the king and bowed with his face to the ground.

²⁴Nathan said, "Have you, my lord the king, declared that Adonijah shall be king

a 5 Or charioteers

after you, and that he will sit on your throne? ²⁵Today he has gone down and sacrificed great numbers of cattle, fattened calves, and sheep. He has invited all the king's sons, the commanders of the army and Abiathar the priest. Right now they are eating and drinking with him and saying, 'Long live King Adonijah!' ²⁶But me your servant, and Zadok the priest, and Benaiah son of Jehoiada, and your servant Solomon he did not invite. ²⁷Is this something my lord the king has done without letting his servants know who should sit on the throne of my lord the king after him?"

David Makes Solomon King

²⁸Then King David said, "Call in Bathsheba." So she came into the king's presence and stood before him.

²⁹The king then took an oath: "As surely as the LORD lives, who has delivered me out of every trouble, ³⁰I will surely carry out this very day what I swore to you by the LORD, the God of Israel: Solomon your son shall be king after me, and he will sit on my throne in my place."

³¹Then Bathsheba bowed down with her face to the ground, prostrating herself before the king, and said, "May my lord King David live forever!"

³²King David said, "Call in Zadok the priest, Nathan the prophet and Benaiah son of Jehoiada." When they came before the king, ³³he said to them: "Take your lord's servants with you and have Solomon my son mount my own mule and take him down to Gihon. ³⁴There have Zadok the priest and Nathan the prophet anoint him king over Israel. Blow the trumpet and shout, 'Long live King Solomon!' ³⁵Then you are to go up with him, and he is to come and sit on my throne and reign in my place. I have appointed him ruler over Israel and Judah."

³⁶Benaiah son of Jehoiada answered the king, "Amen! May the LORD, the God of my lord the king, so declare it. ³⁷As the LORD was with my lord the king, so may he be with Solomon to make his throne even greater than the throne of my lord King David!"

³⁸So Zadok the priest, Nathan the prophet, Benaiah son of Jehoiada, the Kerethites and the Pelethites went down and had Solomon mount King David's mule, and they escorted him to Gihon. ³⁹Zadok the priest took the horn of oil from the sacred tent and anointed Solomon. Then they sounded the trumpet and all the people shouted, "Long live King Solomon!" ⁴⁰And all the people went up after him, playing pipes and rejoicing greatly, so that the ground shook with the sound.

⁴¹Adonijah and all the guests who were with him heard it as they were finishing their feast. On hearing the sound of the trumpet, Joab asked, "What's the meaning of all the noise in the city?"

⁴²Even as he was speaking, Jonathan son of Abiathar the priest arrived. Adonijah said, "Come in. A worthy man like you must be bringing good news."

⁴³"Not at all!" Jonathan answered. "Our lord King David has made Solomon king. ⁴⁴The king has sent with him Zadok the priest, Nathan the prophet, Benaiah son of Jehoiada, the Kerethites and the Pelethites, and they have put him on the king's mule, ⁴⁵and Zadok the priest and Nathan the prophet have anointed him king at Gihon. From there they have gone up cheering, and the city resounds with it. That's the noise you hear. ⁴⁶Moreover, Solomon has taken his seat on the royal throne. ⁴⁷Also, the royal officials have come to congratulate our lord King David, saying, 'May your God make Solomon's name more famous than yours and his throne greater than yours!' And the king bowed in worship on his bed ⁴⁸and said, 'Praise be to the LORD, the God of Israel, who has allowed my eyes to see a successor on my throne today.' "

⁴⁹At this, all Adonijah's guests rose in alarm and dispersed. ⁵⁰But Adonijah, in fear of Solomon, went and took hold of the horns of the altar. ⁵¹Then Solomon was told, "Adonijah is afraid of King Solomon and is clinging to the horns of the altar. He says, 'Let King Solomon swear to me today that he will not put his servant to death with the sword.' "

⁵²Solomon replied, "If he shows himself to be worthy, not a hair of his head will fall to the ground; but if evil is found in him, he will die." ⁵³Then King Solomon sent men, and they brought him down from the altar. And Adonijah came and bowed down to King Solomon, and Solomon said, "Go to your home."

David's Charge to Solomon

2 When the time drew near for David to die, he gave a charge to Solomon his son.

²"I am about to go the way of all the earth," he said. "So be strong, act like a man, ³and observe what the LORD your God requires: Walk in obedience to him, and keep his decrees and commands, his laws and regulations, as written in the Law of Moses. Do this so that you may prosper in all you do and wherever you go ⁴and that the LORD may keep his promise to me: 'If your descendants watch how they live, and if they walk faithfully before me with all their heart and soul, you will never fail to have a successor on the throne of Israel.'

⁵"Now you yourself know what Joab son of Zeruiah did to me—what he did to the two commanders of Israel's armies, Abner son of Ner and Amasa son of Jether. He killed them, shedding their blood in peacetime as if in battle, and with that blood he stained the belt around his waist and the sandals on his feet. ⁶Deal with him according to your wisdom, but do not let his gray head go down to the grave in peace.

⁷"But show kindness to the sons of Barzillai of Gilead and let them be among those who eat at your table. They stood by me when I fled from your brother Absalom.

⁸"And remember, you have with you Shimei son of Gera, the Benjamite from Bahurim, who called down bitter curses on me the day I went to Mahanaim. When he came down to meet me at the Jordan, I swore to him by the LORD: 'I will not put you to death by the sword.' ⁹But now, do not consider him innocent. You are a man of wisdom; you will know what to do to him. Bring his gray head down to the grave in blood."

¹⁰Then David rested with his ancestors and was buried in the City of David. ¹¹He had reigned forty years over Israel—seven years in Hebron and thirty-three in Jerusalem. ¹²So Solomon sat on the throne of his father David, and his rule was firmly established.

Solomon's Throne Established

¹³Now Adonijah, the son of Haggith, went to Bathsheba, Solomon's mother. Bathsheba asked him, "Do you come peacefully?"

He answered, "Yes, peacefully." ¹⁴Then he added, "I have something to say to you."

"You may say it," she replied.

¹⁵"As you know," he said, "the kingdom was mine. All Israel looked to me as their king. But things changed, and the kingdom has gone to my brother; for it has come to him from the LORD. ¹⁶Now I have one request to make of you. Do not refuse me."

"You may make it," she said.

¹⁷So he continued, "Please ask King Solomon—he will not refuse you—to give me Abishag the Shunammite as my wife."

¹⁸"Very well," Bathsheba replied, "I will speak to the king for you."

¹⁹When Bathsheba went to King Solomon to speak to him for Adonijah, the king stood up to meet her, bowed down to her and sat down on his throne. He had a throne brought for the king's mother, and she sat down at his right hand.

²⁰"I have one small request to make of you," she said. "Do not refuse me."

The king replied, "Make it, my mother; I will not refuse you."

²¹So she said, "Let Abishag the Shunammite be given in marriage to your brother Adonijah."

²²King Solomon answered his mother, "Why do you request Abishag the Shunammite for Adonijah? You might as well request the kingdom for him—after all, he is my older brother—yes, for him and for Abiathar the priest and Joab son of Zeruiah!"

²³Then King Solomon swore by the LORD: "May God deal with me, be it ever so severely, if Adonijah does not pay with his life for this request! ²⁴And now, as surely as the LORD lives—he who has established me securely on the throne of my father David and has founded a dynasty for me as he promised—Adonijah shall be put to death today!" ²⁵So King Solomon gave orders to Benaiah son of Jehoiada, and he struck down Adonijah and he died.

²⁶To Abiathar the priest the king said, "Go back to your fields in Anathoth. You deserve to die, but I will not put you to death now, because you carried the ark of the Sovereign LORD before my father David and shared all my father's hardships." ²⁷So Solomon removed Abiathar from the priesthood of the LORD, fulfilling the word the LORD had spoken at Shiloh about the house of Eli.

²⁸When the news reached Joab, who had conspired with Adonijah though not with Absalom, he fled to the tent of the LORD and took hold of the horns of the altar. ²⁹King

Solomon was told that Joab had fled to the tent of the Lord and was beside the altar. Then Solomon ordered Benaiah son of Jehoiada, "Go, strike him down!"

³⁰So Benaiah entered the tent of the Lord and said to Joab, "The king says, 'Come out!' "

But he answered, "No, I will die here."

Benaiah reported to the king, "This is how Joab answered me."

³¹Then the king commanded Benaiah, "Do as he says. Strike him down and bury him, and so clear me and my family line of the guilt of the innocent blood that Joab shed. ³²The Lord will repay him for the blood he shed, because without my father David knowing it he attacked two men and killed them with the sword. Both of them— Abner son of Ner, commander of Israel's army, and Amasa son of Jether, commander of Judah's army—were better men and more upright than he. ³³May the guilt of their blood rest on the head of Joab and his descendants forever. But on David and his descendants, his house and his throne, may there be the Lord's peace forever."

³⁴So Benaiah son of Jehoiada went up and struck down Joab and killed him, and he was buried at his home out in the country. ³⁵The king put Benaiah son of Jehoiada over the army in Joab's position and replaced Abiathar with Zadok the priest.

³⁶Then the king sent for Shimei and said to him, "Build yourself a house in Jerusalem and live there, but do not go anywhere else. ³⁷The day you leave and cross the Kidron Valley, you can be sure you will die; your blood will be on your own head."

³⁸Shimei answered the king, "What you say is good. Your servant will do as my lord the king has said." And Shimei stayed in Jerusalem for a long time.

³⁹But three years later, two of Shimei's slaves ran off to Achish son of Maakah, king of Gath, and Shimei was told, "Your slaves are in Gath." ⁴⁰At this, he saddled his donkey and went to Achish at Gath in search of his slaves. So Shimei went away and brought the slaves back from Gath.

⁴¹When Solomon was told that Shimei had gone from Jerusalem to Gath and had returned, ⁴²the king summoned Shimei and said to him, "Did I not make you swear by the Lord and warn you, 'On the day you leave to go anywhere else, you can be sure you will die'? At that time you said to me,

'What you say is good. I will obey.' ⁴³Why then did you not keep your oath to the Lord and obey the command I gave you?"

⁴⁴The king also said to Shimei, "You know in your heart all the wrong you did to my father David. Now the Lord will repay you for your wrongdoing. ⁴⁵But King Solomon will be blessed, and David's throne will remain secure before the Lord forever."

⁴⁶Then the king gave the order to Benaiah son of Jehoiada, and he went out and struck Shimei down and he died.

The kingdom was now established in Solomon's hands.

Solomon Asks for Wisdom

3 Solomon made an alliance with Pharaoh king of Egypt and married his daughter. He brought her to the City of David until he finished building his palace and the temple of the Lord, and the wall around Jerusalem. ²The people, however, were still sacrificing at the high places, because a temple had not yet been built for the Name of the Lord. ³Solomon showed his love for the Lord by walking according to the instructions given him by his father David, except that he offered sacrifices and burned incense on the high places.

⁴The king went to Gibeon to offer sacrifices, for that was the most important high place, and Solomon offered a thousand burnt offerings on that altar. ⁵At Gibeon the Lord appeared to Solomon during the night in a dream, and God said, "Ask for whatever you want me to give you."

⁶Solomon answered, "You have shown great kindness to your servant, my father David, because he was faithful to you and righteous and upright in heart. You have continued this great kindness to him and have given him a son to sit on his throne this very day.

⁷"Now, Lord my God, you have made your servant king in place of my father David. But I am only a little child and do not know how to carry out my duties. ⁸Your servant is here among the people you have chosen, a great people, too numerous to count or number. ⁹So give your servant a discerning heart to govern your people and to distinguish between right and wrong. For who is able to govern this great people of yours?"

¹⁰The Lord was pleased that Solomon had

asked for this. ¹¹So God said to him, "Since you have asked for this and not for long life or wealth for yourself, nor have asked for the death of your enemies but for discernment in administering justice, ¹²I will do what you have asked. I will give you a wise and discerning heart, so that there will never have been anyone like you, nor will there ever be. ¹³Moreover, I will give you what you have not asked for—both wealth and honor—so that in your lifetime you will have no equal among kings. ¹⁴And if you walk in obedience to me and keep my decrees and commands as David your father did, I will give you a long life." ¹⁵Then Solomon awoke—and he realized it had been a dream.

He returned to Jerusalem, stood before the ark of the Lord's covenant and sacrificed burnt offerings and fellowship offerings. Then he gave a feast for all his court.

A Wise Ruling

¹⁶Now two prostitutes came to the king and stood before him. ¹⁷One of them said, "Pardon me, my lord. This woman and I live in the same house, and I had a baby while she was there with me. ¹⁸The third day after my child was born, this woman also had a baby. We were alone; there was no one in the house but the two of us.

¹⁹"During the night this woman's son died because she lay on him. ²⁰So she got up in the middle of the night and took my son from my side while I your servant was asleep. She put him by her breast and put her dead son by my breast. ²¹The next morning, I got up to nurse my son—and he was dead! But when I looked at him closely in the morning light, I saw that it wasn't the son I had borne."

²²The other woman said, "No! The living one is my son; the dead one is yours."

But the first one insisted, "No! The dead one is yours; the living one is mine." And so they argued before the king.

²³The king said, "This one says, 'My son is alive and your son is dead,' while that one says, 'No! Your son is dead and mine is alive.'"

²⁴Then the king said, "Bring me a sword." So they brought a sword for the king. ²⁵He then gave an order: "Cut the living child in two and give half to one and half to the other."

²⁶The woman whose son was alive was deeply moved out of love for her son and said to the king, "Please, my lord, give her the living baby! Don't kill him!"

But the other said, "Neither I nor you shall have him. Cut him in two!"

²⁷Then the king gave his ruling: "Give the living baby to the first woman. Do not kill him; she is his mother."

²⁸When all Israel heard the verdict the king had given, they held the king in awe, because they saw that he had wisdom from God to administer justice.

Solomon's Officials and Governors

4 So King Solomon ruled over all Israel. ²And these were his chief officials:

Azariah son of Zadok—the priest;
³Elihoreph and Ahijah, sons of Shisha—secretaries;
Jehoshaphat son of Ahilud—recorder;
⁴Benaiah son of Jehoiada—commander in chief;
Zadok and Abiathar—priests;
⁵Azariah son of Nathan—in charge of the district governors;
Zabud son of Nathan—a priest and adviser to the king;
⁶Ahishar—palace administrator;
Adoniram son of Abda—in charge of forced labor.

⁷Solomon had twelve district governors over all Israel, who supplied provisions for the king and the royal household. Each one had to provide supplies for one month in the year. ⁸These are their names:

Ben-Hur—in the hill country of Ephraim;
⁹Ben-Deker—in Makaz, Shaalbim, Beth Shemesh and Elon Bethhanan;
¹⁰Ben-Hesed—in Arubboth (Sokoh and all the land of Hepher were his);
¹¹Ben-Abinadab—in Naphoth Dor (he was married to Taphath daughter of Solomon);
¹²Baana son of Ahilud—in Taanach and Megiddo, and in all of Beth Shan next to Zarethan below Jezreel, from Beth Shan to Abel Meholah across to Jokmeam;
¹³Ben-Geber—in Ramoth Gilead (the settlements of Jair son of Manasseh in Gilead were his, as well as the region of Argob in Bashan and its sixty

large walled cities with bronze gate bars);

14 Ahinadab son of Iddo—in Mahanaim;

15 Ahimaaz—in Naphtali (he had married Basemath daughter of Solomon);

16 Baana son of Hushai—in Asher and in Aloth;

17 Jehoshaphat son of Paruah—in Issachar;

18 Shimei son of Ela—in Benjamin;

19 Geber son of Uri—in Gilead (the country of Sihon king of the Amorites and the country of Og king of Bashan). He was the only governor over the district.

Solomon's Daily Provisions

20 The people of Judah and Israel were as numerous as the sand on the seashore; they ate, they drank and they were happy. *21 And Solomon ruled over all the kingdoms from the Euphrates River to the land of the Philistines, as far as the border of Egypt. These countries brought tribute and were Solomon's subjects all his life.

22 Solomon's daily provisions were thirty cors[a] of the finest flour and sixty cors[b] of meal, 23 ten head of stall-fed cattle, twenty of pasture-fed cattle and a hundred sheep and goats, as well as deer, gazelles, roebucks and choice fowl. 24 For he ruled over all the kingdoms west of the Euphrates River, from Tiphsah to Gaza, and had peace on all sides. 25 During Solomon's lifetime Judah and Israel, from Dan to Beersheba, lived in safety, everyone under their own vine and fig tree.

26 Solomon had four[c] thousand stalls for chariot horses, and twelve thousand horses.[d]

27 The district governors, each in his month, supplied provisions for King Solomon and all who came to the king's table. They saw to it that nothing was lacking. 28 They also brought to the proper place their quotas of barley and straw for the chariot horses and the other horses.

Solomon's Wisdom

29 God gave Solomon wisdom and very great insight, and a breadth of understanding as measureless as the sand on the seashore. 30 Solomon's wisdom was greater than the wisdom of all the people of the East, and greater than all the wisdom of Egypt. 31 He was wiser than anyone else, including Ethan the Ezrahite—wiser than Heman, Kalkol and Darda, the sons of Mahol. And his fame spread to all the surrounding nations. 32 He spoke three thousand proverbs and his songs numbered a thousand and five. 33 He spoke about plant life, from the cedar of Lebanon to the hyssop that grows out of walls. He also spoke about animals and birds, reptiles and fish. 34 From all nations people came to listen to Solomon's wisdom, sent by all the kings of the world, who had heard of his wisdom.

Preparations for Building the Temple

5 *When Hiram king of Tyre heard that Solomon had been anointed king to succeed his father David, he sent his envoys to Solomon, because he had always been on friendly terms with David. 2 Solomon sent back this message to Hiram:

3 "You know that because of the wars waged against my father David from all sides, he could not build a temple for the Name of the LORD his God until the LORD put his enemies under his feet. 4 But now the LORD my God has given me rest on every side, and there is no adversary or disaster. 5 I intend, therefore, to build a temple for the Name of the LORD my God, as the LORD told my father David, when he said, 'Your son whom I will put on the throne in your place will build the temple for my Name.'

6 "So give orders that cedars of Lebanon be cut for me. My men will work with yours, and I will pay you for your men whatever wages you set. You know that we have no one so skilled in felling timber as the Sidonians."

7 When Hiram heard Solomon's message, he was greatly pleased and said, "Praise be to the LORD today, for he has given David a wise son to rule over this great nation."

8 So Hiram sent word to Solomon:

---

a 22 That is, probably about 5 1/2 tons or about 5 metric tons   b 22 That is, probably about 11 tons or about 10 metric tons   c 26 Some Septuagint manuscripts (see also 2 Chron. 9:25); Hebrew forty   d 26 Or charioteers

* 4:21-34 is numbered 5:1-14 in Hebrew texts.   * 5:1-18 is numbered 5:15-32 in Hebrew texts.

"I have received the message you sent me and will do all you want in providing the cedar and juniper logs. 9My men will haul them down from Lebanon to the Mediterranean Sea, and I will float them as rafts by sea to the place you specify. There I will separate them and you can take them away. And you are to grant my wish by providing food for my royal household."

10In this way Hiram kept Solomon supplied with all the cedar and juniper logs he wanted, 11and Solomon gave Hiram twenty thousand cors*a* of wheat as food for his household, in addition to twenty thousand baths*b, c* of pressed olive oil. Solomon continued to do this for Hiram year after year. 12The LORD gave Solomon wisdom, just as he had promised him. There were peaceful relations between Hiram and Solomon, and the two of them made a treaty.

13King Solomon conscripted laborers from all Israel—thirty thousand men. 14He sent them off to Lebanon in shifts of ten thousand a month, so that they spent one month in Lebanon and two months at home. Adoniram was in charge of the forced labor. 15Solomon had seventy thousand carriers and eighty thousand stonecutters in the hills, 16as well as thirty-three hundred*d* overseers who supervised the project and directed the work. 17At the king's command they removed from the quarry large blocks of high-grade stone to provide a foundation of dressed stone for the temple. 18The skilled workers of Solomon and Hiram and those from Byblos cut and prepared the timber and stone for the building of the temple.

Solomon Builds the Temple

6 In the four hundred and eightieth*e* year after the Israelites came out of Egypt, in the fourth year of Solomon's reign over Israel, in the month of Ziv, the second month, he began to build the temple of the LORD.

2The temple that King Solomon built for the LORD was sixty cubits long, twenty wide and thirty high.*f* 3The portico at the front of the main hall of the temple extended the width of the temple, that is twenty cubits,*g* and projected ten cubits*h* from the front of the temple. 4He made narrow windows high up in the temple walls. 5Against the walls of the main hall and inner sanctuary he built a structure around the building, in which there were side rooms. 6The lowest floor was five cubits*i* wide, the middle floor six cubits*j* and the third floor seven.*k* He made offset ledges around the outside of the temple so that nothing would be inserted into the temple walls.

7In building the temple, only blocks dressed at the quarry were used, and no hammer, chisel or any other iron tool was heard at the temple site while it was being built.

8The entrance to the lowest*l* floor was on the south side of the temple; a stairway led up to the middle level and from there to the third. 9So he built the temple and completed it, roofing it with beams and cedar planks. 10And he built the side rooms all along the temple. The height of each was five cubits, and they were attached to the temple by beams of cedar.

11The word of the LORD came to Solomon: 12"As for this temple you are building, if you follow my decrees, observe my laws and keep all my commands and obey them, I will fulfill through you the promise I gave to David your father. 13And I will live among the Israelites and will not abandon my people Israel."

14So Solomon built the temple and completed it. 15He lined its interior walls with cedar boards, paneling them from the floor of the temple to the ceiling, and covered the floor of the temple with planks of juniper. 16He partitioned off twenty cubits at the rear of the temple with cedar boards from floor to ceiling to form within the temple an inner sanctuary, the Most Holy Place. 17The main hall in front of this room was forty cubits*m*

---

a 11 That is, probably about 3,600 tons or about 3,250 metric tons   *b 11* Septuagint (see also 2 Chron. 2:10); Hebrew *twenty cors*   *c 11* That is, about 120,000 gallons or about 440,000 liters   *d 16* Hebrew; some Septuagint manuscripts (see also 2 Chron. 2:2, 18) *thirty-six hundred*   *e 1* Hebrew; Septuagint *four hundred and fortieth*   *f 2* That is, about 90 feet long, 30 feet wide and 45 feet high or about 27 meters long, 9 meters wide and 13.5 meters high   *g 3* That is, about 30 feet or about 9 meters; also in verses 16 and 20   *h 3* That is, about 15 feet or about 4.5 meters; also in verse 23   *i 6* That is, about 7 1/2 feet or about 2.3 meters; also in verses 10 and 24   *j 6* That is, about 9 feet or about 2.7 meters   *k 6* That is, about 10 1/2 feet or about 3.2 meters   *l 8* Septuagint; Hebrew *middle*   *m 17* That is, about 60 feet or about 18 meters long. ¹⁸The inside of the temple was cedar, carved with gourds and open flowers. Everything was cedar; no stone was to be seen.

¹⁹He prepared the inner sanctuary within the temple to set the ark of the covenant of the LORD there. ²⁰The inner sanctuary was twenty cubits long, twenty wide and twenty high. He overlaid the inside with pure gold, and he also overlaid the altar of cedar. ²¹Solomon covered the inside of the temple with pure gold, and he extended gold chains across the front of the inner sanctuary, which was overlaid with gold. ²²So he overlaid the whole interior with gold. He also overlaid with gold the altar that belonged to the inner sanctuary.

²³For the inner sanctuary he made a pair of cherubim out of olive wood, each ten cubits high. ²⁴One wing of the first cherub was five cubits long, and the other wing five cubits—ten cubits from wing tip to wing tip. ²⁵The second cherub also measured ten cubits, for the two cherubim were identical in size and shape. ²⁶The height of each cherub was ten cubits. ²⁷He placed the cherubim inside the innermost room of the temple, with their wings spread out. The wing of one cherub touched one wall, while the wing of the other touched the other wall, and their wings touched each other in the middle of the room. ²⁸He overlaid the cherubim with gold.

²⁹On the walls all around the temple, in both the inner and outer rooms, he carved cherubim, palm trees and open flowers. ³⁰He also covered the floors of both the inner and outer rooms of the temple with gold.

³¹For the entrance to the inner sanctuary he made doors out of olive wood that were one fifth of the width of the sanctuary. ³²And on the two olive-wood doors he carved cherubim, palm trees and open flowers, and overlaid the cherubim and palm trees with hammered gold. ³³In the same way, for the entrance to the main hall he made doorframes out of olive wood that were one fourth of the width of the hall. ³⁴He also made two doors out of juniper wood, each having two leaves that turned in sockets.

³⁵He carved cherubim, palm trees and open flowers on them and overlaid them with gold hammered evenly over the carvings.

³⁶And he built the inner courtyard of three courses of dressed stone and one course of trimmed cedar beams.

³⁷The foundation of the temple of the LORD was laid in the fourth year, in the month of Ziv. ³⁸In the eleventh year in the month of Bul, the eighth month, the temple was finished in all its details according to its specifications. He had spent seven years building it.

Solomon Builds His Palace

7 It took Solomon thirteen years, however, to complete the construction of his palace. ²He built the Palace of the Forest of Lebanon a hundred cubits long, fifty wide and thirty high,ᵃ with four rows of cedar columns supporting trimmed cedar beams. ³It was roofed with cedar above the beams that rested on the columns—forty-five beams, fifteen to a row. ⁴Its windows were placed high in sets of three, facing each other. ⁵All the doorways had rectangular frames; they were in the front part in sets of three, facing each other.ᵇ

⁶He made a colonnade fifty cubits long and thirty wide.ᶜ In front of it was a portico, and in front of that were pillars and an overhanging roof.

⁷He built the throne hall, the Hall of Justice, where he was to judge, and he covered it with cedar from floor to ceiling.ᵈ ⁸And the palace in which he was to live, set farther back, was similar in design. Solomon also made a palace like this hall for Pharaoh's daughter, whom he had married.

⁹All these structures, from the outside to the great courtyard and from foundation to eaves, were made of blocks of high-grade stone cut to size and trimmed with a saw on their inner and outer faces. ¹⁰The foundations were laid with large stones of good quality, some measuring ten cubitsᵉ and some eight.ᶠ ¹¹Above were high-grade stones, cut to size, and cedar beams. ¹²The great courtyard was surrounded by a wall of three courses of dressed stone and one

---

ᵃ 2 That is, about 150 feet long, 75 feet wide and 45 feet high or about 45 meters long, 22.5 meters wide and 13.5 meters high   ᵇ 5 The meaning of the Hebrew for this verse is uncertain.   ᶜ 6 That is, about 75 feet long and 45 feet wide or about 22.5 meters long and 13.5 meters wide   ᵈ 7 Vulgate and Syriac; Hebrew *floor*   ᵉ 10 That is, about 15 feet or about 4.5 meters; also in verse 23   ᶠ 10 That is, about 12 feet or about 3.6 meters course of trimmed cedar beams, as was the inner courtyard of the temple of the LORD with its portico.

The Temple's Furnishings

¹³King Solomon sent to Tyre and brought Huram,ᵃ ¹⁴whose mother was a widow from the tribe of Naphtali and whose father was from Tyre and a skilled worker in bronze. Huram was filled with wisdom, with understanding and with knowledge to do all kinds of bronze work. He came to King Solomon and did all the work assigned to him.

¹⁵He cast two bronze pillars, each eighteen cubits high and twelve cubits in circumference.ᵇ ¹⁶He also made two capitals of cast bronze to set on the tops of the pillars; each capital was five cubitsᶜ high. ¹⁷A network of interwoven chains adorned the capitals on top of the pillars, seven for each capital. ¹⁸He made pomegranates in two rowsᵈ encircling each network to decorate the capitals on top of the pillars.ᵉ He did the same for each capital. ¹⁹The capitals on top of the pillars in the portico were in the shape of lilies, four cubitsᶠ high. ²⁰On the capitals of both pillars, above the bowl-shaped part next to the network, were the two hundred pomegranates in rows all around. ²¹He erected the pillars at the portico of the temple. The pillar to the south he named Jakinᵍ and the one to the north Boaz.ʰ ²²The capitals on top were in the shape of lilies. And so the work on the pillars was completed.

²³He made the Sea of cast metal, circular in shape, measuring ten cubits from rim to rim and five cubits high. It took a line of thirty cubitsⁱ to measure around it. ²⁴Below the rim, gourds encircled it—ten to a cubit. The gourds were cast in two rows in one piece with the Sea.

²⁵The Sea stood on twelve bulls, three facing north, three facing west, three facing south and three facing east. The Sea rested on top of them, and their hindquarters were toward the center. ²⁶It was a handbreadthʲ in thickness, and its rim was like the rim of a cup, like a lily blossom. It held two thousand baths.ᵏ

²⁷He also made ten movable stands of bronze; each was four cubits long, four wide and three high.ˡ ²⁸This is how the stands were made: They had side panels attached to uprights. ²⁹On the panels between the uprights were lions, bulls and cherubim— and on the uprights as well. Above and below the lions and bulls were wreaths of hammered work. ³⁰Each stand had four bronze wheels with bronze axles, and each had a basin resting on four supports, cast with wreaths on each side. ³¹On the inside of the stand there was an opening that had a circular frame one cubitᵐ deep. This opening was round, and with its basework it measured a cubit and a half.ⁿ Around its opening there was engraving. The panels of the stands were square, not round. ³²The four wheels were under the panels, and the axles of the wheels were attached to the stand. The diameter of each wheel was a cubit and a half. ³³The wheels were made like chariot wheels; the axles, rims, spokes and hubs were all of cast metal.

³⁴Each stand had four handles, one on each corner, projecting from the stand. ³⁵At the top of the stand there was a circular band half a cubitᵒ deep. The supports and panels were attached to the top of the stand. ³⁶He engraved cherubim, lions and palm trees on the surfaces of the supports and on the panels, in every available space, with wreaths all around. ³⁷This is the way he made the ten stands. They were all cast in the same molds and were identical in size and shape.

³⁸He then made ten bronze basins, each holding forty bathsᵖ and measuring four cubits across, one basin to go on each of the ten stands. ³⁹He placed five of the stands on the south side of the temple and five on the

---

ᵃ 13 Hebrew *Hiram*, a variant of *Huram*; also in verses 40 and 45   ᵇ 15 That is, about 27 feet high and 18 feet in circumference or about 8.2 meters high and 5.4 meters in circumference   ᶜ 16 That is, about 7 1/2 feet or about 2.3 meters; also in verse 23   ᵈ 18 Two Hebrew manuscripts and Septuagint; most Hebrew manuscripts *made the pillars, and there were two rows*   ᵉ 18 Many Hebrew manuscripts and Syriac; most Hebrew manuscripts *pomegranates*   ᶠ 19 That is, about 6 feet or about 1.8 meters; also in verse 38   ᵍ 21 *Jakin* probably means *he establishes*.   ʰ 21 *Boaz* probably means *in him is strength*. ⁱ 23 That is, about 45 feet or about 13.5 meters   ʲ 26 That is, about 3 inches or about 7.5 centimeters ᵏ 26 That is, about 12,000 gallons or about 44,000 liters; the Septuagint does not have this sentence. ˡ 27 That is, about 6 feet long and wide and about 4 1/2 feet high or about 1.8 meters long and wide and 1.4 meters high   ᵐ 31 That is, about 18 inches or about 45 centimeters   ⁿ 31 That is, about 2 1/4 feet or about 67 centimeters; also in verse 32   ᵒ 35 That is, about 9 inches or about 22.5 centimeters ᵖ 38 That is, about 240 gallons or about 880 liters north. He placed the Sea on the south side, at the southeast corner of the temple. ⁴⁰He also made the pots*a* and shovels and sprinkling bowls.

So Huram finished all the work he had undertaken for King Solomon in the temple of the LORD:

⁴¹the two pillars;

the two bowl-shaped capitals on top of the pillars;

the two sets of network decorating the two bowl-shaped capitals on top of the pillars;

⁴²the four hundred pomegranates for the two sets of network (two rows of pomegranates for each network decorating the bowl-shaped capitals on top of the pillars);

⁴³the ten stands with their ten basins;

⁴⁴the Sea and the twelve bulls under it;

⁴⁵the pots, shovels and sprinkling bowls.

All these objects that Huram made for King Solomon for the temple of the LORD were of burnished bronze. ⁴⁶The king had them cast in clay molds in the plain of the Jordan between Sukkoth and Zarethan. ⁴⁷Solomon left all these things unweighed, because there were so many; the weight of the bronze was not determined.

⁴⁸Solomon also made all the furnishings that were in the LORD's temple:

the golden altar;

the golden table on which was the bread of the Presence;

⁴⁹the lampstands of pure gold (five on the right and five on the left, in front of the inner sanctuary);

the gold floral work and lamps and tongs;

⁵⁰the pure gold basins, wick trimmers, sprinkling bowls, dishes and censers;

and the gold sockets for the doors of the innermost room, the Most Holy Place, and also for the doors of the main hall of the temple.

⁵¹When all the work King Solomon had done for the temple of the LORD was finished, he brought in the things his father David had dedicated—the silver and gold

and the furnishings—and he placed them in the treasuries of the LORD's temple.

The Ark Brought to the Temple

8 Then King Solomon summoned into his presence at Jerusalem the elders of Israel, all the heads of the tribes and the chiefs of the Israelite families, to bring up the ark of the LORD's covenant from Zion, the City of David. ²All the Israelites came together to King Solomon at the time of the festival in the month of Ethanim, the seventh month.

³When all the elders of Israel had arrived, the priests took up the ark, ⁴and they brought up the ark of the LORD and the tent of meeting and all the sacred furnishings in it. The priests and Levites carried them up, ⁵and King Solomon and the entire assembly of Israel that had gathered about him were before the ark, sacrificing so many sheep and cattle that they could not be recorded or counted.

⁶The priests then brought the ark of the LORD's covenant to its place in the inner sanctuary of the temple, the Most Holy Place, and put it beneath the wings of the cherubim. ⁷The cherubim spread their wings over the place of the ark and overshadowed the ark and its carrying poles. ⁸These poles were so long that their ends could be seen from the Holy Place in front of the inner sanctuary, but not from outside the Holy Place; and they are still there today. ⁹There was nothing in the ark except the two stone tablets that Moses had placed in it at Horeb, where the LORD made a covenant with the Israelites after they came out of Egypt.

¹⁰When the priests withdrew from the Holy Place, the cloud filled the temple of the LORD. ¹¹And the priests could not perform their service because of the cloud, for the glory of the LORD filled his temple.

¹²Then Solomon said, "The LORD has said that he would dwell in a dark cloud; ¹³I have indeed built a magnificent temple for you, a place for you to dwell forever."

¹⁴While the whole assembly of Israel was standing there, the king turned around and blessed them. ¹⁵Then he said:

"Praise be to the LORD, the God of Is-

---

a 40 Many Hebrew manuscripts, Septuagint, Syriac and Vulgate (see also verse 45 and 2 Chron. 4:11); many other Hebrew manuscripts *basins* rael, who with his own hand has fulfilled what he promised with his own mouth to my father David. For he said, [16]'Since the day I brought my people Israel out of Egypt, I have not chosen a city in any tribe of Israel to have a temple built that my Name might be there, but I have chosen David to rule my people Israel.'

[17]"My father David had it in his heart to build a temple for the Name of the LORD, the God of Israel. [18]But the LORD said to my father David, 'You did well to have it in your heart to build a temple for my Name. [19]Nevertheless, you are not the one to build the temple, but your son, who is your own flesh and blood—he is the one who will build the temple for my Name.'

[20]"The LORD has kept the promise he made: I have succeeded David my father and now I sit on the throne of Israel, just as the LORD promised, and I have built the temple for the Name of the LORD, the God of Israel. [21]I have provided a place there for the ark, in which is the covenant of the LORD that he made with our ancestors when he brought them out of Egypt."

Solomon's Prayer of Dedication

[22]Then Solomon stood before the altar of the LORD in front of the whole assembly of Israel, spread out his hands toward heaven [23]and said:

"LORD, the God of Israel, there is no God like you in heaven above or on earth below—you who keep your covenant of love with your servants who continue wholeheartedly in your way. [24]You have kept your promise to your servant David my father; with your mouth you have promised and with your hand you have fulfilled it—as it is today. [25]"Now LORD, the God of Israel, keep for your servant David my father the promises you made to him when you said, 'You shall never fail to have a successor to sit before me on the throne of Israel, if only your descendants are careful in all they do to walk before me faithfully as you have done.' [26]And now, God of Israel, let your word that

you promised your servant David my father come true.

[27]"But will God really dwell on earth? The heavens, even the highest heaven, cannot contain you. How much less this temple I have built! [28]Yet give attention to your servant's prayer and his plea for mercy, LORD my God. Hear the cry and the prayer that your servant is praying in your presence this day. [29]May your eyes be open toward this temple night and day, this place of which you said, 'My Name shall be there,' so that you will hear the prayer your servant prays toward this place. [30]Hear the supplication of your servant and of your people Israel when they pray toward this place. Hear from heaven, your dwelling place, and when you hear, forgive.

[31]"When anyone wrongs their neighbor and is required to take an oath and they come and swear the oath before your altar in this temple, [32]then hear from heaven and act. Judge between your servants, condemning the guilty by bringing down on their heads what they have done, and vindicating the innocent by treating them in accordance with their innocence.

[33]"When your people Israel have been defeated by an enemy because they have sinned against you, and when they turn back to you and give praise to your name, praying and making supplication to you in this temple, [34]then hear from heaven and forgive the sin of your people Israel and bring them back to the land you gave to their ancestors.

[35]"When the heavens are shut up and there is no rain because your people have sinned against you, and when they pray toward this place and give praise to your name and turn from their sin because you have afflicted them, [36]then hear from heaven and forgive the sin of your servants, your people Israel. Teach them the right way to live, and send rain on the land you gave your people for an inheritance.

[37]"When famine or plague comes to the land, or blight or mildew, locusts or grasshoppers, or when an enemy besieges them in any of their cities, what-

FRIDAY

GOD SPEAKS

1 Kings 8:22–61 *or* 8:56–61

Walter Wangerin

It is God's nature to speak. The first event of the universe was a brief, spectacular utterance: "*Let . . .*" The first word God ever spoke answered no human prayer, nor responded to anything outside of the Divine Self, for there was not yet anything but that Self in serene sufficiency. Rather, that first word gave voice to his own holy yearning. *Let there be . . .*

And once God had spoken the thing, his speaking *was* the thing: *Light!*

O children of God, consider what kind of speaking your Father can do! His word is more than a murmured, parental consent . . . You do not rush to dictionaries in order to discover the meanings of his words. The meanings are self-evident. His words are their own meanings, as light is light—and light is *seen*, light is *experienced* by our mortal flesh and senses; light cannot be tucked into the pages of a book of abstract definitions, as if human words could now define the creations of the Creator. Look! God's word can cause to be what had not been before. His words bulk as indisputable realities in the cosmos.

Do you understand the implications? If your Father speaks you—not *to* you, but if he utters *you* as the subject of his pronunciation—why, then *you* are.

ANNA SOPHIA OF HESSE {AD 1638–1683}

Speak, O Lord, your servant heareth,
To your Word I now give heed;
Life and spirit your Word beareth,
All your Word is true indeed.
Death's dread power in me is rife;
Jesus, may your Word of Life
Fill my soul with love's strong fervor
That I cling to you forever . . .

Precious Jesus, I beseech thee,
May your words take root in me;
May this gift from heaven enrich me
So that I bear fruit for Thee!
Take them never from my heart
Till I see you as you are,
When in heavenly bliss and glory
I shall greet you and adore Thee.

reflection

1. Everyone has experienced the power of another person's words—both to heal and to hurt. How have you experienced the power of God's words in *your* life?

2. How quick are you to listen to what God has spoken—to what he continues to speak—to you?

3. Are there areas in your life about which you're more likely to "turn a deaf ear" toward God?

For your next devotional reading, go to page 383.

ever disaster or disease may come, ³⁸and when a prayer or plea is made by anyone among your people Israel—being aware of the afflictions of their own hearts, and spreading out their hands toward this temple— ³⁹then hear from heaven, your dwelling place. Forgive and act; deal with everyone according to all they do, since you know their hearts (for you alone know every human heart), ⁴⁰so that they will fear you all the time they live in the land you gave our ancestors.

⁴¹"As for the foreigners who do not belong to your people Israel but have come from a distant land because of your name— ⁴²for they will hear of your great name and your mighty hand and your outstretched arm—when they come and pray toward this temple, ⁴³then hear from heaven, your dwelling place. Do whatever the foreigners ask of you, so that all the peoples of the earth may know your name and fear you, as do your own people Israel, and may know that this house I have built bears your Name.

⁴⁴"When your people go to war against their enemies, wherever you send them, and when they pray to the Lord toward the city you have chosen and the temple I have built for your Name, ⁴⁵then hear from heaven their prayer and their plea, and uphold their cause.

⁴⁶"When they sin against you—for there is no one who does not sin—and you become angry with them and give them over to their enemies, who take them captive to their own lands, far away or near; ⁴⁷and if they have a change of heart in the land where they are held captive, and repent and plead with you in the land of their captors and say, 'We have sinned, we have done wrong, we have acted wickedly'; ⁴⁸and if they turn back to you with all their heart and soul in the land of their enemies who took them captive, and pray to you toward the land you gave their ancestors, toward the city you have chosen and the temple I have built for your Name; ⁴⁹then from heaven, your dwelling place, hear their prayer and their plea, and uphold their

cause. ⁵⁰And forgive your people, who have sinned against you; forgive all the offenses they have committed against you, and cause their captors to show them mercy; ⁵¹for they are your people and your inheritance, whom you brought out of Egypt, out of that iron-smelting furnace.

⁵²"May your eyes be open to your servant's plea and to the plea of your people Israel, and may you listen to them whenever they cry out to you. ⁵³For you singled them out from all the nations of the world to be your own inheritance, just as you declared through your servant Moses when you, Sovereign Lord, brought our ancestors out of Egypt."

⁵⁴When Solomon had finished all these prayers and supplications to the Lord, he rose from before the altar of the Lord, where he had been kneeling with his hands spread out toward heaven. ⁵⁵He stood and blessed the whole assembly of Israel in a loud voice, saying:

⁵⁶"Praise be to the Lord, who has given rest to his people Israel just as he promised. Not one word has failed of all the good promises he gave through his servant Moses. ⁵⁷May the Lord our God be with us as he was with our ancestors; may he never leave us nor forsake us. ⁵⁸May he turn our hearts to him, to walk in obedience to him and keep the commands, decrees and laws he gave our ancestors. ⁵⁹And may these words of mine, which I have prayed before the Lord, be near to the Lord our God day and night, that he may uphold the cause of his servant and the cause of his people Israel according to each day's need, ⁶⁰so that all the peoples of the earth may know that the Lord is God and that there is no other. ⁶¹And may your hearts be fully committed to the Lord our God, to live by his decrees and obey his commands, as at this time."

The Dedication of the Temple

⁶²Then the king and all Israel with him offered sacrifices before the Lord. ⁶³Solomon offered a sacrifice of fellowship offerings to the Lord: twenty-two thousand

cattle and a hundred and twenty thousand sheep and goats. So the king and all the Israelites dedicated the temple of the LORD.

⁶⁴On that same day the king consecrated the middle part of the courtyard in front of the temple of the LORD, and there he offered burnt offerings, grain offerings and the fat of the fellowship offerings, because the bronze altar that stood before the LORD was too small to hold the burnt offerings, the grain offerings and the fat of the fellowship offerings.

⁶⁵So Solomon observed the festival at that time, and all Israel with him—a vast assembly, people from Lebo Hamath to the Wadi of Egypt. They celebrated it before the LORD our God for seven days and seven days more, fourteen days in all. ⁶⁶On the following day he sent the people away. They blessed the king and then went home, joyful and glad in heart for all the good things the LORD had done for his servant David and his people Israel.

The LORD Appears to Solomon

9 When Solomon had finished building the temple of the LORD and the royal palace, and had achieved all he had desired to do, ²the LORD appeared to him a second time, as he had appeared to him at Gibeon. ³The LORD said to him:

"I have heard the prayer and plea you have made before me; I have consecrated this temple, which you have built, by putting my Name there forever. My eyes and my heart will always be there.

⁴"As for you, if you walk before me faithfully with integrity of heart and uprightness, as David your father did, and do all I command and observe my decrees and laws, ⁵I will establish your royal throne over Israel forever, as I promised David your father when I said, 'You shall never fail to have a successor on the throne of Israel.'

⁶"But if you*a* or your descendants turn away from me and do not observe the commands and decrees I have given you*a* and go off to serve other gods and worship them, ⁷then I will cut off

Israel from the land I have given them and will reject this temple I have consecrated for my Name. Israel will then become a byword and an object of ridicule among all peoples. ⁸This temple will become a heap of rubble. All*b* who pass by will be appalled and will scoff and say, 'Why has the LORD done such a thing to this land and to this temple?' ⁹People will answer, 'Because they have forsaken the LORD their God, who brought their ancestors out of Egypt, and have embraced other gods, worshiping and serving them—that is why the LORD brought all this disaster on them.'"

Solomon's Other Activities

¹⁰At the end of twenty years, during which Solomon built these two buildings—the temple of the LORD and the royal palace— ¹¹King Solomon gave twenty towns in Galilee to Hiram king of Tyre, because Hiram had supplied him with all the cedar and juniper and gold he wanted. ¹²But when Hiram went from Tyre to see the towns that Solomon had given him, he was not pleased with them. ¹³"What kind of towns are these you have given me, my brother?" he asked. And he called them the Land of Kabul,*c* a name they have to this day. ¹⁴Now Hiram had sent to the king 120 talents*d* of gold.

¹⁵Here is the account of the forced labor King Solomon conscripted to build the LORD's temple, his own palace, the terraces,*e* the wall of Jerusalem, and Hazor, Megiddo and Gezer. ¹⁶(Pharaoh king of Egypt had attacked and captured Gezer. He had set it on fire. He killed its Canaanite inhabitants and then gave it as a wedding gift to his daughter, Solomon's wife. ¹⁷And Solomon rebuilt Gezer.) He built up Lower Beth Horon, ¹⁸Baalath, and Tadmor*f* in the desert, within his land, ¹⁹as well as all his store cities and the towns for his chariots and for his horses*g*— whatever he desired to build in Jerusalem, in Lebanon and throughout all the territory he ruled.

²⁰There were still people left from the Amorites, Hittites, Perizzites, Hivites and Jebusites (these peoples were not Israel-

---

a 6 The Hebrew is plural.   *b 8* See some Septuagint manuscripts, Old Latin, Syriac, Arabic and Targum; Hebrew *And though this temple is now imposing, all*   *c 13 Kabul* sounds like the Hebrew for *good-for-nothing.*   *d 14* That is, about 4 1/2 tons or about 4 metric tons   *e 15* Or *the Millo;* also in verse 24   *f 18* The Hebrew may also be read *Tamar.*   *g 19* Or *charioteers*

God's Dwelling Place

1 Kings 9:1–3

read/meditate

As you read this passage several times, observe the Lord's promise to Solomon regarding the temple, God's dwelling place. Focus on what it meant to have God consecrate this place.

pray

As you pray, invite God to make his home in you. Ask him how you can best be his dwelling place. Describe to him the kind of home you'd like to be for him.

contemplate

Think about the fact that as you walk through life, you are God's temple. Think about what that means for you in terms of both your expectation of his presence and your responsibility to live a life of worship.

additional reflection

Going to church doesn't make you a Christian, any more than going to a garage makes you an automobile.

—Billy Sunday

If the blind put their hand in God's, they find their way more surely than those who see but have not faith or purpose.

—Helen Keller

For your next devotional reading, go to page 387.

ites). ²¹Solomon conscripted the descendants of all these peoples remaining in the land—whom the Israelites could not exterminate*—to serve as slave labor, as it is to this day. ²²But Solomon did not make slaves of any of the Israelites; they were his fighting men, his government officials, his officers, his captains, and the commanders of his chariots and charioteers. ²³They were also the chief officials in charge of Solomon's projects—550 officials supervising those who did the work.

²⁴After Pharaoh's daughter had come up from the City of David to the palace Solomon had built for her, he constructed the terraces.

²⁵Three times a year Solomon sacrificed burnt offerings and fellowship offerings on the altar he had built for the LORD, burning incense before the LORD along with them, and so fulfilled the temple obligations.

²⁶King Solomon also built ships at Ezion Geber, which is near Elath in Edom, on the shore of the Red Sea.ᵇ ²⁷And Hiram sent his servants—sailors who knew the sea—to serve in the fleet with Solomon's servants. ²⁸They sailed to Ophir and brought back 420 talentsᶜ of gold, which they delivered to King Solomon.

The Queen of Sheba Visits Solomon

10 When the queen of Sheba heard about the fame of Solomon and his relationship to the LORD, she came to test Solomon with hard questions. ²Arriving at Jerusalem with a very great caravan—with camels carrying spices, large quantities of gold, and precious stones—she came to Solomon and talked with him about all that she had on her mind. ³Solomon answered all her questions; nothing was too hard for the king to explain to her. ⁴When the queen of Sheba saw all the wisdom of Solomon and the palace he had built, ⁵the food on his table, the seating of his officials, the attending servants in their robes, his cupbearers, and the burnt offerings he made

atᵈ the temple of the LORD, she was overwhelmed.

⁶She said to the king, "The report I heard in my own country about your achievements and your wisdom is true. ⁷But I did not believe these things until I came and saw with my own eyes. Indeed, not even half was told me; in wisdom and wealth you have far exceeded the report I heard. ⁸How happy your people must be! How happy your officials, who continually stand before you and hear your wisdom! ⁹Praise be to the LORD your God, who has delighted in you and placed you on the throne of Israel. Because of the LORD's eternal love for Israel, he has made you king to maintain justice and righteousness."

¹⁰And she gave the king 120 talentsᵉ of gold, large quantities of spices, and precious stones. Never again were so many spices brought in as those the queen of Sheba gave to King Solomon.

¹¹(Hiram's ships brought gold from Ophir; and from there they brought great cargoes of almugwoodᶠ and precious stones. ¹²The king used the almugwood to make supportsᵍ for the temple of the LORD and for the royal palace, and to make harps and lyres for the musicians. So much almugwood has never been imported or seen since that day.)

¹³King Solomon gave the queen of Sheba all she desired and asked for, besides what he had given her out of his royal bounty. Then she left and returned with her retinue to her own country.

Solomon's Splendor

¹⁴The weight of the gold that Solomon received yearly was 666 talents,ʰ ¹⁵not including the revenues from merchants and traders and from all the Arabian kings and the governors of the territories.

¹⁶King Solomon made two hundred large shields of hammered gold; six hundred shekelsⁱ of gold went into each shield. ¹⁷He also made three hundred small shields of hammered gold, with three minasʲ of gold in

---

ᵃ 21 The Hebrew term refers to the irrevocable giving over of things or persons to the LORD, often by totally destroying them.   ᵇ 26 Or the Sea of Reeds   ᶜ 28 That is, about 16 tons or about 14 metric tons   ᵈ 5 Or the ascent by which he went up to   ᵉ 10 That is, about 4 1/2 tons or about 4 metric tons   ᶠ 11 Probably a variant of algumwood; also in verse 12   ᵍ 12 The meaning of the Hebrew for this word is uncertain.   ʰ 14 That is, about 25 tons or about 23 metric tons   ⁱ 16 That is, about 15 pounds or about 6.9 kilograms; also in verse 29   ʲ 17 That is, about 3 3/4 pounds or about 1.7 kilograms; or perhaps reference is to double minas, that is, about 7 1/2 pounds or about 3.5 kilograms.

each shield. The king put them in the Palace of the Forest of Lebanon.

¹⁸Then the king made a great throne inlaid with ivory and overlaid with fine gold. ¹⁹The throne had six steps, and its back had a rounded top. On both sides of the seat were armrests, with a lion standing beside each of them. ²⁰Twelve lions stood on the six steps, one at either end of each step. Nothing like it had ever been made for any other kingdom. ²¹All King Solomon's goblets were gold, and all the household articles in the Palace of the Forest of Lebanon were pure gold. Nothing was made of silver, because silver was considered of little value in Solomon's days. ²²The king had a fleet of trading ships^a at sea along with the ships of Hiram. Once every three years it returned, carrying gold, silver and ivory, and apes and baboons.

²³King Solomon was greater in riches and wisdom than all the other kings of the earth. ²⁴The whole world sought audience with Solomon to hear the wisdom God had put in his heart. ²⁵Year after year, everyone who came brought a gift—articles of silver and gold, robes, weapons and spices, and horses and mules.

²⁶Solomon accumulated chariots and horses; he had fourteen hundred chariots and twelve thousand horses,^b which he kept in the chariot cities and also with him in Jerusalem. ²⁷The king made silver as common in Jerusalem as stones, and cedar as plentiful as sycamore-fig trees in the foothills. ²⁸Solomon's horses were imported from Egypt and from Kue^c—the royal merchants purchased them from Kue at the current price. ²⁹They imported a chariot from Egypt for six hundred shekels of silver, and a horse for a hundred and fifty.^d They also exported them to all the kings of the Hittites and of the Arameans.

Solomon's Wives

11 King Solomon, however, loved many foreign women besides Pharaoh's daughter—Moabites, Ammonites, Edomites, Sidonians and Hittites. ²They were from nations about which the LORD had told the Israelites, "You must not intermarry with them, because they will surely turn your hearts after their gods."

Nevertheless, Solomon held fast to them in love. ³He had seven hundred wives of royal birth and three hundred concubines, and his wives led him astray. ⁴As Solomon grew old, his wives turned his heart after other gods, and his heart was not fully devoted to the LORD his God, as the heart of David his father had been. ⁵He followed Ashtoreth the goddess of the Sidonians, and Molek the detestable god of the Ammonites. ⁶So Solomon did evil in the eyes of the LORD; he did not follow the LORD completely, as David his father had done.

⁷On a hill east of Jerusalem, Solomon built a high place for Chemosh the detestable god of Moab, and for Molek the detestable god of the Ammonites. ⁸He did the same for all his foreign wives, who burned incense and offered sacrifices to their gods.

⁹The LORD became angry with Solomon because his heart had turned away from the LORD, the God of Israel, who had appeared to him twice. ¹⁰Although he had forbidden Solomon to follow other gods, Solomon did not keep the LORD's command. ¹¹So the LORD said to Solomon, "Since this is your attitude and you have not kept my covenant and my decrees, which I commanded you, I will most certainly tear the kingdom away from you and give it to one of your subordinates. ¹²Nevertheless, for the sake of David your father, I will not do it during your lifetime. I will tear it out of the hand of your son. ¹³Yet I will not tear the whole kingdom from him, but will give him one tribe for the sake of David my servant and for the sake of Jerusalem, which I have chosen."

Solomon's Adversaries

¹⁴Then the LORD raised up against Solomon an adversary, Hadad the Edomite, from the royal line of Edom. ¹⁵Earlier when David was fighting with Edom, Joab the commander of the army, who had gone up to bury the dead, had struck down all the men in Edom. ¹⁶Joab and all the Israelites stayed there for six months, until they had destroyed all the men in Edom. ¹⁷But Hadad, still only a boy, fled to Egypt with some Edomite officials who had served his father. ¹⁸They set out from Midian and went to Paran. Then taking people from Paran with

---

a 22 Hebrew *of ships of Tarshish*   *b 26* Or *charioteers*   *c 28* Probably *Cilicia*   *d 29* That is, about 3 3/4 pounds or about 1.7 kilograms them, they went to Egypt, to Pharaoh king of Egypt, who gave Hadad a house and land and provided him with food.

¹⁹Pharaoh was so pleased with Hadad that he gave him a sister of his own wife, Queen Tahpenes, in marriage. ²⁰The sister of Tahpenes bore him a son named Genubath, whom Tahpenes brought up in the royal palace. There Genubath lived with Pharaoh's own children.

²¹While he was in Egypt, Hadad heard that David rested with his ancestors and that Joab the commander of the army was also dead. Then Hadad said to Pharaoh, "Let me go, that I may return to my own country."

²²"What have you lacked here that you want to go back to your own country?" Pharaoh asked.

"Nothing," Hadad replied, "but do let me go!"

²³And God raised up against Solomon another adversary, Rezon son of Eliada, who had fled from his master, Hadadezer king of Zobah. ²⁴When David destroyed Zobah's army, Rezon gathered a band of men around him and became their leader; they went to Damascus, where they settled and took control. ²⁵Rezon was Israel's adversary as long as Solomon lived, adding to the trouble caused by Hadad. So Rezon ruled in Aram and was hostile toward Israel.

Jeroboam Rebels Against Solomon

²⁶Also, Jeroboam son of Nebat rebelled against the king. He was one of Solomon's officials, an Ephraimite from Zeredah, and his mother was a widow named Zeruah.

²⁷Here is the account of how he rebelled against the king: Solomon had built the terraces ᵃ and had filled in the gap in the wall of the city of David his father. ²⁸Now Jeroboam was a man of standing, and when Solomon saw how well the young man did his work, he put him in charge of the whole labor force of the house of Joseph.

²⁹About that time Jeroboam was going out of Jerusalem, and Ahijah the prophet of Shiloh met him on the way, wearing a new cloak. The two of them were alone out in the country, ³⁰and Ahijah took hold of the new cloak he was wearing and tore it into twelve pieces. ³¹Then he said to Jeroboam, "Take ten pieces for yourself, for this is what the

Lord, the God of Israel, says: 'See, I am going to tear the kingdom out of Solomon's hand and give you ten tribes. ³²But for the sake of my servant David and the city of Jerusalem, which I have chosen out of all the tribes of Israel, he will have one tribe. ³³I will do this because they have ᵇ forsaken me and worshiped Ashtoreth the goddess of the Sidonians, Chemosh the god of the Moabites, and Molek the god of the Ammonites, and have not walked in obedience to me, nor done what is right in my eyes, nor kept my decrees and laws as David, Solomon's father, did.

³⁴" 'But I will not take the whole kingdom out of Solomon's hand; I have made him ruler all the days of his life for the sake of David my servant, whom I chose and who obeyed my commands and decrees. ³⁵I will take the kingdom from his son's hands and give you ten tribes. ³⁶I will give one tribe to his son so that David my servant may always have a lamp before me in Jerusalem, the city where I chose to put my Name. ³⁷However, as for you, I will take you, and you will rule over all that your heart desires; you will be king over Israel. ³⁸If you do whatever I command you and walk in obedience to me and do what is right in my eyes by obeying my decrees and commands, as David my servant did, I will be with you. I will build you a dynasty as enduring as the one I built for David and will give Israel to you. ³⁹I will humble David's descendants because of this, but not forever.' "

⁴⁰Solomon tried to kill Jeroboam, but Jeroboam fled to Egypt, to Shishak the king, and stayed there until Solomon's death.

Solomon's Death

⁴¹As for the other events of Solomon's reign—all he did and the wisdom he displayed—are they not written in the book of the annals of Solomon? ⁴²Solomon reigned in Jerusalem over all Israel forty years. ⁴³Then he rested with his ancestors and was buried in the city of David his father. And Rehoboam his son succeeded him as king.

Israel Rebels Against Rehoboam

12 Rehoboam went to Shechem, for all Israel had gone there to make him king. ²When Jeroboam son

---

ᵃ 27 Or *the Millo*   ᵇ 33 Hebrew; Septuagint, Vulgate and Syriac *because he has*

MONDAY

DON'T BELIEVE YOUR UNBELIEF

1 Kings 12:1—13:5 *or* 12:26–30

Jim Cymbala

God put this story of Jeroboam in the Bible as a flashing red light to us. It fairly shouts that when unbelief gets into a leader, or anyone else for that matter, it leads to the first bad decision, which leads to the second, which leads to the third, until the momentum builds out of control. God had said to this man out in the field, "If you do whatever I command you and walk in [obedience to me] and do what is right in my eyes ... I will be with you" [1 Kings 11:38]. But Jeroboam opted to make up his own game plan, and at the end God thundered against him with words so devastating that they make us shudder to read them.

What Jeroboam did—when you think about it—made excellent logic. Any king would want to carefully monitor the movement of his people, right? Trusting God to build the kingdom as he had promised probably seemed too simple. Jeroboam decided to improvise to secure his position of leadership. In fact, unbelief often clothes itself in "being smart." We use cleverness to cover the tracks of our lack of faith. But who can be wiser than God?

E. M. BOUNDS {AD 1835–1913}

Trust sees God doing things here and now. Indeed, it does even more. It rises to a lofty eminence and—looking into the invisible and the eternal—realizes that God has done invisible and eternal things, and regards them as being already done. Trust brings eternity into the annals and happenings of time. It converts the substance of hope into the reality of fruition. It changes promise into present possession. We know when we trust just as we know when we see, just as we are conscious of our sense of touch. Trust sees, receives, holds. Trust is its own witness.

Yet, quite often, faith is too weak to obtain God's greatest good immediately. So it has to wait in loving, strong, prayerful, pressing obedience until it grows in strength and is able to bring down the eternal into the realms of experience and time.

To this point, trust masses all its forces. Here it holds. And in the struggle, trust's grasp becomes mightier and grasps, for itself, all that God has done for it in his eternal wisdom and abundance of grace.

reflection

1. Instead of trusting God's promise, Jeroboam took matters into his own hands. How have you been tempted in that very same way?

2. When have you "taken over" instead of trusting?

3. Fear tells us to trust in our own wisdom instead of God's. Why do we listen to our fear?

For your next devotional reading, go to page 392.

of Nebat heard this (he was still in Egypt, where he had fled from King Solomon), he returned from^a Egypt. ³So they sent for Jeroboam, and he and the whole assembly of Israel went to Rehoboam and said to him: ⁴"Your father put a heavy yoke on us, but now lighten the harsh labor and the heavy yoke he put on us, and we will serve you."

⁵Rehoboam answered, "Go away for three days and then come back to me." So the people went away.

⁶Then King Rehoboam consulted the elders who had served his father Solomon during his lifetime. "How would you advise me to answer these people?" he asked.

⁷They replied, "If today you will be a servant to these people and serve them and give them a favorable answer, they will always be your servants."

⁸But Rehoboam rejected the advice the elders gave him and consulted the young men who had grown up with him and were serving him. ⁹He asked them, "What is your advice? How should we answer these people who say to me, 'Lighten the yoke your father put on us'?"

¹⁰The young men who had grown up with him replied, "These people have said to you, 'Your father put a heavy yoke on us, but make our yoke lighter.' Now tell them, 'My little finger is thicker than my father's waist. ¹¹My father laid on you a heavy yoke; I will make it even heavier. My father scourged you with whips; I will scourge you with scorpions.' "

¹²Three days later Jeroboam and all the people returned to Rehoboam, as the king had said, "Come back to me in three days." ¹³The king answered the people harshly. Rejecting the advice given him by the elders, ¹⁴he followed the advice of the young men and said, "My father made your yoke heavy; I will make it even heavier. My father scourged you with whips; I will scourge you with scorpions." ¹⁵So the king did not listen to the people, for this turn of events was from the LORD, to fulfill the word the LORD had spoken to Jeroboam son of Nebat through Ahijah the Shilonite.

¹⁶When all Israel saw that the king refused to listen to them, they answered the king:

"What share do we have in David,
    what part in Jesse's son?
To your tents, Israel!
    Look after your own house, David!"

So the Israelites went home. ¹⁷But as for the Israelites who were living in the towns of Judah, Rehoboam still ruled over them.

¹⁸King Rehoboam sent out Adoniram,^b who was in charge of forced labor, but all Israel stoned him to death. King Rehoboam, however, managed to get into his chariot and escape to Jerusalem. ¹⁹So Israel has been in rebellion against the house of David to this day.

²⁰When all the Israelites heard that Jeroboam had returned, they sent and called him to the assembly and made him king over all Israel. Only the tribe of Judah remained loyal to the house of David.

²¹When Rehoboam arrived in Jerusalem, he mustered the whole house of Judah and the tribe of Benjamin—a hundred and eighty thousand able young men—to make war against the house of Israel and to regain the kingdom for Rehoboam son of Solomon.

²²But this word of God came to Shemaiah the man of God: ²³"Say to Rehoboam son of Solomon king of Judah, to the whole house of Judah and Benjamin, and to the rest of the people, ²⁴'This is what the LORD says: Do not go up to fight against your brothers, the Israelites. Go home, every one of you, for this is my doing.' " So they obeyed the word of the LORD and went home again, as the LORD had ordered.

Golden Calves at Bethel and Dan

²⁵Then Jeroboam fortified Shechem in the hill country of Ephraim and lived there. From there he went out and built up Peniel.^c

²⁶Jeroboam thought to himself, "The kingdom will now likely revert to the house of David. ²⁷If these people go up to offer sacrifices at the temple of the LORD in Jerusalem, they will again give their allegiance to their lord, Rehoboam king of Judah. They will kill me and return to King Rehoboam."

²⁸After seeking advice, the king made two golden calves. He said to the people, "It is too much for you to go up to Jerusalem. Here are your gods, Israel, who brought you up out of Egypt." ²⁹One he set up in Bethel,

a 2 Or he remained in   b 18 Some Septuagint manuscripts and Syriac (see also 1 Kings 4:6 and 5:14); Hebrew Adoram   c 25 Hebrew Penuel, a variant of Peniel and the other in Dan. ³⁰And this thing became a sin; the people came to worship the one at Bethel and went as far as Dan to worship the other.ᵃ

³¹Jeroboam built shrines on high places and appointed priests from all sorts of people, even though they were not Levites. ³²He instituted a festival on the fifteenth day of the eighth month, like the festival held in Judah, and offered sacrifices on the altar. This he did in Bethel, sacrificing to the calves he had made. And at Bethel he also installed priests at the high places he had made. ³³On the fifteenth day of the eighth month, a month of his own choosing, he offered sacrifices on the altar he had built at Bethel. So he instituted the festival for the Israelites and went up to the altar to make offerings.

The Man of God From Judah

13 By the word of the LORD a man of God came from Judah to Bethel, as Jeroboam was standing by the altar to make an offering. ²He cried out against the altar by the word of the LORD: "Altar, altar! This is what the LORD says: 'A son named Josiah will be born to the house of David. On you he will sacrifice the priests of the high places who make offerings here, and human bones will be burned on you.' " ³That same day the man of God gave a sign: "This is the sign the LORD has declared: The altar will be split apart and the ashes on it will be poured out."

⁴When King Jeroboam heard what the man of God cried out against the altar at Bethel, he stretched out his hand from the altar and said, "Seize him!" But the hand he stretched out toward the man shriveled up, so that he could not pull it back. ⁵Also, the altar was split apart and its ashes poured out according to the sign given by the man of God by the word of the LORD.

⁶Then the king said to the man of God, "Intercede with the LORD your God and pray for me that my hand may be restored." So the man of God interceded with the LORD, and the king's hand was restored and became as it was before.

⁷The king said to the man of God, "Come home with me for a meal, and I will give you a gift."

⁸But the man of God answered the king, "Even if you were to give me half your possessions, I would not go with you, nor would I eat bread or drink water here. ⁹For I was commanded by the word of the LORD: 'You must not eat bread or drink water or return by the way you came.' " ¹⁰So he took another road and did not return by the way he had come to Bethel.

¹¹Now there was a certain old prophet living in Bethel, whose sons came and told him all that the man of God had done there that day. They also told their father what he had said to the king. ¹²Their father asked them, "Which way did he go?" And his sons showed him which road the man of God from Judah had taken. ¹³So he said to his sons, "Saddle the donkey for me." And when they had saddled the donkey for him, he mounted it ¹⁴and rode after the man of God. He found him sitting under an oak tree and asked, "Are you the man of God who came from Judah?"

"I am," he replied.

¹⁵So the prophet said to him, "Come home with me and eat."

¹⁶The man of God said, "I cannot turn back and go with you, nor can I eat bread or drink water with you in this place. ¹⁷I have been told by the word of the LORD: 'You must not eat bread or drink water there or return by the way you came.' "

¹⁸The old prophet answered, "I too am a prophet, as you are. And an angel said to me by the word of the LORD: 'Bring him back with you to your house so that he may eat bread and drink water.' " (But he was lying to him.) ¹⁹So the man of God returned with him and ate and drank in his house.

²⁰While they were sitting at the table, the word of the LORD came to the old prophet who had brought him back. ²¹He cried out to the man of God who had come from Judah, "This is what the LORD says: 'You have defied the word of the LORD and have not kept the command the LORD your God gave you. ²²You came back and ate bread and drank water in the place where he told you not to eat or drink. Therefore your body will not be buried in the tomb of your ancestors.' "

²³When the man of God had finished eating and drinking, the prophet who had brought him back saddled his donkey for

---

ᵃ 30 Probable reading of the original Hebrew text; Masoretic Text *people went to the one as far as Dan* him. [24]As he went on his way, a lion met him on the road and killed him, and his body was left lying on the road, with both the donkey and the lion standing beside it. [25]Some people who passed by saw the body lying there, with the lion standing beside the body, and they went and reported it in the city where the old prophet lived.

[26]When the prophet who had brought him back from his journey heard of it, he said, "It is the man of God who defied the word of the LORD. The LORD has given him over to the lion, which has mauled him and killed him, as the word of the LORD had warned him."

[27]The prophet said to his sons, "Saddle the donkey for me," and they did so. [28]Then he went out and found the body lying on the road, with the donkey and the lion standing beside it. The lion had neither eaten the body nor mauled the donkey. [29]So the prophet picked up the body of the man of God, laid it on the donkey, and brought it back to his own city to mourn for him and bury him. [30]Then he laid the body in his own tomb, and they mourned over him and said, "Alas, my brother!"

[31]After burying him, he said to his sons, "When I die, bury me in the grave where the man of God is buried; lay my bones beside his bones. [32]For the message he declared by the word of the LORD against the altar in Bethel and against all the shrines on the high places in the towns of Samaria will certainly come true."

[33]Even after this, Jeroboam did not change his evil ways, but once more appointed priests for the high places from all sorts of people. Anyone who wanted to become a priest he consecrated for the high places. [34]This was the sin of the house of Jeroboam that led to its downfall and to its destruction from the face of the earth.

Ahijah's Prophecy Against Jeroboam

14 At that time Abijah son of Jeroboam became ill, [2]and Jeroboam said to his wife, "Go, disguise yourself, so you won't be recognized as the wife of Jeroboam. Then go to Shiloh. Ahijah the prophet is there—the one who told me I would be king over this people. [3]Take ten loaves of bread with you, some cakes and a jar of honey, and go to him. He will tell you what will happen to the boy." [4]So Jeroboam's wife did what he said and went to Ahijah's house in Shiloh.

Now Ahijah could not see; his sight was gone because of his age. [5]But the LORD had told Ahijah, "Jeroboam's wife is coming to ask you about her son, for he is ill, and you are to give her such and such an answer. When she arrives, she will pretend to be someone else."

[6]So when Ahijah heard the sound of her footsteps at the door, he said, "Come in, wife of Jeroboam. Why this pretense? I have been sent to you with bad news. [7]Go, tell Jeroboam that this is what the LORD, the God of Israel, says: 'I raised you up from among the people and appointed you ruler over my people Israel. [8]I tore the kingdom away from the house of David and gave it to you, but you have not been like my servant David, who kept my commands and followed me with all his heart, doing only what was right in my eyes. [9]You have done more evil than all who lived before you. You have made for yourself other gods, idols made of metal; you have aroused my anger and thrust me behind your back.

[10]" 'Because of this, I am going to bring disaster on the house of Jeroboam. I will cut off from Jeroboam every last male in Israel—slave or free.[a] I will burn up the house of Jeroboam as one burns dung, until it is all gone. [11]Dogs will eat those belonging to Jeroboam who die in the city, and the birds will feed on those who die in the country. The LORD has spoken!'

[12]"As for you, go back home. When you set foot in your city, the boy will die. [13]All Israel will mourn for him and bury him. He is the only one belonging to Jeroboam who will be buried, because he is the only one in the house of Jeroboam in whom the LORD, the God of Israel, has found anything good.

[14]"The LORD will raise up for himself a king over Israel who will cut off the family of Jeroboam. Even now this is beginning to happen.[b] [15]And the LORD will strike Israel, so that it will be like a reed swaying in the water. He will uproot Israel from this good land that he gave to their ancestors and scatter them beyond the Euphrates River, because they aroused the LORD's anger by making

---

a 10 Or *Israel—every ruler or leader*   *b 14* The meaning of the Hebrew for this sentence is uncertain.

Asherah poles.*a* 16And he will give Israel up because of the sins Jeroboam has committed and has caused Israel to commit."

17Then Jeroboam's wife got up and left and went to Tirzah. As soon as she stepped over the threshold of the house, the boy died. 18They buried him, and all Israel mourned for him, as the LORD had said through his servant the prophet Ahijah.

19The other events of Jeroboam's reign, his wars and how he ruled, are written in the book of the annals of the kings of Israel. 20He reigned for twenty-two years and then rested with his ancestors. And Nadab his son succeeded him as king.

Rehoboam King of Judah

21Rehoboam son of Solomon was king in Judah. He was forty-one years old when he became king, and he reigned seventeen years in Jerusalem, the city the LORD had chosen out of all the tribes of Israel in which to put his Name. His mother's name was Naamah; she was an Ammonite.

22Judah did evil in the eyes of the LORD. By the sins they committed they stirred up his jealous anger more than those who were before them had done. 23They also set up for themselves high places, sacred stones and Asherah poles on every high hill and under every spreading tree. 24There were even male shrine prostitutes in the land; the people engaged in all the detestable practices of the nations the LORD had driven out before the Israelites.

25In the fifth year of King Rehoboam, Shishak king of Egypt attacked Jerusalem. 26He carried off the treasures of the temple of the LORD and the treasures of the royal palace. He took everything, including all the gold shields Solomon had made. 27So King Rehoboam made bronze shields to replace them and assigned these to the commanders of the guard on duty at the entrance to the royal palace. 28Whenever the king went to the LORD's temple, the guards bore the shields, and afterward they returned them to the guardroom.

29As for the other events of Rehoboam's reign, and all he did, are they not written in the book of the annals of the kings of Judah? 30There was continual warfare between Rehoboam and Jeroboam. 31And Rehoboam rested with his ancestors and was buried with them in the City of David. His mother's name was Naamah; she was an Ammonite. And Abijah*b* his son succeeded him as king.

Abijah King of Judah

15 In the eighteenth year of the reign of Jeroboam son of Nebat, Abijah*c* became king of Judah, 2and he reigned in Jerusalem three years. His mother's name was Maakah daughter of Abishalom.*d*

3He committed all the sins his father had done before him; his heart was not fully devoted to the LORD his God, as the heart of David his forefather had been. 4Nevertheless, for David's sake the LORD his God gave him a lamp in Jerusalem by raising up a son to succeed him and by making Jerusalem strong. 5For David had done what was right in the eyes of the LORD and had not failed to keep any of the LORD's commands all the days of his life—except in the case of Uriah the Hittite.

6There was war between Abijah*e* and Jeroboam throughout Abijah's lifetime. 7As for the other events of Abijah's reign, and all he did, are they not written in the book of the annals of the kings of Judah? There was war between Abijah and Jeroboam. 8And Abijah rested with his ancestors and was buried in the City of David. And Asa his son succeeded him as king.

Asa King of Judah

9In the twentieth year of Jeroboam king of Israel, Asa became king of Judah, 10and he reigned in Jerusalem forty-one years. His grandmother's name was Maakah daughter of Abishalom.

11Asa did what was right in the eyes of the LORD, as his father David had done. 12He expelled the male shrine prostitutes from the land and got rid of all the idols his ancestors had made. 13He even deposed his grandmother Maakah from her position as queen mother, because she had made a repulsive image for the worship of Asherah. Asa cut it

---

a 15 That is, wooden symbols of the goddess Asherah; here and elsewhere in 1 Kings   *b 31* Some Hebrew manuscripts and Septuagint (see also 2 Chron. 12:16); most Hebrew manuscripts *Abijam*   *c 1* Some Hebrew manuscripts and Septuagint (see also 2 Chron. 12:16); most Hebrew manuscripts *Abijam*; also in verses 7 and 8   *d 2* A variant of *Absalom*; also in verse 10   *e 6* Some Hebrew manuscripts and Syriac *Abijam* (that is, Abijah); most Hebrew manuscripts *Rehoboam*

TUESDAY

THE NAME ABOVE ALL OTHERS

1 Kings 15:1–32 *or* 15:9–11,25–26

Rick McKinley

Most of us have been subconsciously "named" by at least some of the negative experiences and circumstances in our past. And going through the world knowing you're one of the unlucky ones, one of the unlovely people, can be a traumatic experience. Surrounded by scandal, we live in fear that somehow even more of the things we've done, the bad things we've thought in the deep recesses of our heart, will someday show up on the Record for the whole world to read and know about. And we'll be marginalized for life . . .

The fact is, the most crucial piece of our real identity—the name that ultimately overrides all others—is who we are in God's eyes. Love doesn't come to the poor or the broken in the margins with the purpose of effecting total escape from this life of brokenness. The love of Jesus doesn't come to make us fit into American culture; it's here to make us fit into heaven. His love is here to complete us . . .

Jesus isn't so much concerned about removing you from the margins as he is with helping you understand that you don't have to be *named by* the margins of this society. He says you're named by God. Jesus himself was a carpenter, then a homeless wanderer, and he died the death of a criminal. But none of that named him. He knew he was the Father's Son.

LEWIS BAYLY {ca. AD 1575–1631}

Piety made David, Solomon, Jehoshaphat, Hezekiah, Josiah, Zerubbabel, Constantine, Theodosius, Edward VI, Queen Elizabeth, Prince Henry and other religious princes to be so honored that their names, since their deaths, smell in the church of God like a precious ointment, and their remembrances are sweet as honey in all mouths, and as music at a banquet of wine; whereas the lives of others, who have been godless and irreligious princes, do rot and stink in the memory of God's people—and what honor is it for great men to have great titles on earth, when God counts their names unworthy to be written in his book of life in heaven? It is piety that embalms a prince's good name and makes his face to shine before men and glorifies his soul among angels.

reflection

1. What is the legacy you hope to leave for others?

2. How does that desired legacy differ from how God views you?

3. How would your life be different if you were not affected by other people's opinions of you?

For your next devotional reading, go to page 397.

down and burned it in the Kidron Valley. ¹⁴Although he did not remove the high places, Asa's heart was fully committed to the Lord all his life. ¹⁵He brought into the temple of the Lord the silver and gold and the articles that he and his father had dedicated.

¹⁶There was war between Asa and Baasha king of Israel throughout their reigns. ¹⁷Baasha king of Israel went up against Judah and fortified Ramah to prevent anyone from leaving or entering the territory of Asa king of Judah.

¹⁸Asa then took all the silver and gold that was left in the treasuries of the Lord's temple and of his own palace. He entrusted it to his officials and sent them to Ben-Hadad son of Tabrimmon, the son of Hezion, the king of Aram, who was ruling in Damascus. ¹⁹"Let there be a treaty between me and you," he said, "as there was between my father and your father. See, I am sending you a gift of silver and gold. Now break your treaty with Baasha king of Israel so he will withdraw from me."

²⁰Ben-Hadad agreed with King Asa and sent the commanders of his forces against the towns of Israel. He conquered Ijon, Dan, Abel Beth Maakah and all Kinnereth in addition to Naphtali. ²¹When Baasha heard this, he stopped building Ramah and withdrew to Tirzah. ²²Then King Asa issued an order to all Judah—no one was exempt—and they carried away from Ramah the stones and timber Baasha had been using there. With them King Asa built up Geba in Benjamin, and also Mizpah.

²³As for all the other events of Asa's reign, all his achievements, all he did and the cities he built, are they not written in the book of the annals of the kings of Judah? In his old age, however, his feet became diseased. ²⁴Then Asa rested with his ancestors and was buried with them in the city of his father David. And Jehoshaphat his son succeeded him as king.

Nadab King of Israel

²⁵Nadab son of Jeroboam became king of Israel in the second year of Asa king of Judah, and he reigned over Israel two years. ²⁶He did evil in the eyes of the Lord, following the ways of his father and committing the same sin his father had caused Israel to commit.

²⁷Baasha son of Ahijah of the house of Is-sachar plotted against him, and he struck him down at Gibbethon, a Philistine town, while Nadab and all Israel were besieging it. ²⁸Baasha killed Nadab in the third year of Asa king of Judah and succeeded him as king.

²⁹As soon as he began to reign, he killed Jeroboam's whole family. He did not leave Jeroboam anyone that breathed, but destroyed them all, according to the word of the Lord given through his servant Ahijah the Shilonite. ³⁰This happened because of the sins Jeroboam had committed and had caused Israel to commit, and because he aroused the anger of the Lord, the God of Israel.

³¹As for the other events of Nadab's reign, and all he did, are they not written in the book of the annals of the kings of Israel? ³²There was war between Asa and Baasha king of Israel throughout their reigns.

Baasha King of Israel

³³In the third year of Asa king of Judah, Baasha son of Ahijah became king of all Israel in Tirzah, and he reigned twenty-four years. ³⁴He did evil in the eyes of the Lord, following the ways of Jeroboam and committing the same sin Jeroboam had caused Israel to commit.

16 Then the word of the Lord came to Jehu son of Hanani concerning Baasha: ²"I lifted you up from the dust and appointed you ruler over my people Israel, but you followed the ways of Jeroboam and caused my people Israel to sin and to arouse my anger by their sins. ³So I am about to wipe out Baasha and his house, and I will make your house like that of Jeroboam son of Nebat. ⁴Dogs will eat those belonging to Baasha who die in the city, and birds will feed on those who die in the country."

⁵As for the other events of Baasha's reign, what he did and his achievements, are they not written in the book of the annals of the kings of Israel? ⁶Baasha rested with his ancestors and was buried in Tirzah. And Elah his son succeeded him as king.

⁷Moreover, the word of the Lord came through the prophet Jehu son of Hanani to Baasha and his house, because of all the evil he had done in the eyes of the Lord, arousing his anger by the things he did, becoming like the house of Jeroboam—and also because he destroyed it.

Elah King of Israel

⁸In the twenty-sixth year of Asa king of Judah, Elah son of Baasha became king of Israel, and he reigned in Tirzah two years.

⁹Zimri, one of his officials, who had command of half his chariots, plotted against him. Elah was in Tirzah at the time, getting drunk in the home of Arza, who was in charge of the palace at Tirzah. ¹⁰Zimri came in, struck him down and killed him in the twenty-seventh year of Asa king of Judah. Then he succeeded him as king.

¹¹As soon as he began to reign and was seated on the throne, he killed off Baasha's whole family. He did not spare a single male, whether relative or friend. ¹²So Zimri destroyed the whole family of Baasha, in accordance with the word of the LORD spoken against Baasha through the prophet Jehu— ¹³because of all the sins Baasha and his son Elah had committed and had caused Israel to commit, so that they aroused the anger of the LORD, the God of Israel, by their worthless idols.

¹⁴As for the other events of Elah's reign, and all he did, are they not written in the book of the annals of the kings of Israel?

Zimri King of Israel

¹⁵In the twenty-seventh year of Asa king of Judah, Zimri reigned in Tirzah seven days. The army was encamped near Gibbethon, a Philistine town. ¹⁶When the Israelites in the camp heard that Zimri had plotted against the king and murdered him, they proclaimed Omri, the commander of the army, king over Israel that very day there in the camp. ¹⁷Then Omri and all the Israelites with him withdrew from Gibbethon and laid siege to Tirzah. ¹⁸When Zimri saw that the city was taken, he went into the citadel of the royal palace and set the palace on fire around him. So he died, ¹⁹because of the sins he had committed, doing evil in the eyes of the LORD and following the ways of Jeroboam and committing the same sin Jeroboam had caused Israel to commit.

²⁰As for the other events of Zimri's reign, and the rebellion he carried out, are they not written in the book of the annals of the kings of Israel?

Omri King of Israel

²¹Then the people of Israel were split into two factions; half supported Tibni son of Ginath for king, and the other half supported Omri. ²²But Omri's followers proved stronger than those of Tibni son of Ginath. So Tibni died and Omri became king.

²³In the thirty-first year of Asa king of Judah, Omri became king of Israel, and he reigned twelve years, six of them in Tirzah. ²⁴He bought the hill of Samaria from Shemer for two talents ᵃ of silver and built a city on the hill, calling it Samaria, after Shemer, the name of the former owner of the hill.

²⁵But Omri did evil in the eyes of the LORD and sinned more than all those before him. ²⁶He followed completely the ways of Jeroboam son of Nebat, committing the same sin Jeroboam had caused Israel to commit, so that they aroused the anger of the LORD, the God of Israel, by their worthless idols.

²⁷As for the other events of Omri's reign, what he did and the things he achieved, are they not written in the book of the annals of the kings of Israel? ²⁸Omri rested with his ancestors and was buried in Samaria. And Ahab his son succeeded him as king.

Ahab Becomes King of Israel

²⁹In the thirty-eighth year of Asa king of Judah, Ahab son of Omri became king of Israel, and he reigned in Samaria over Israel twenty-two years. ³⁰Ahab son of Omri did more evil in the eyes of the LORD than any of those before him. ³¹He not only considered it trivial to commit the sins of Jeroboam son of Nebat, but he also married Jezebel daughter of Ethbaal king of the Sidonians, and began to serve Baal and worship him. ³²He set up an altar for Baal in the temple of Baal that he built in Samaria. ³³Ahab also made an Asherah pole and did more to arouse the anger of the LORD, the God of Israel, than did all the kings of Israel before him.

³⁴In Ahab's time, Hiel of Bethel rebuilt Jericho. He laid its foundations at the cost of his firstborn son Abiram, and he set up its gates at the cost of his youngest son Segub, in accordance with the word of the LORD spoken by Joshua son of Nun.

ᵃ 24 That is, about 150 pounds or about 68 kilograms

Elijah Fed by Ravens

17 Now Elijah the Tishbite, from Tishbe[a] in Gilead, said to Ahab, "As the LORD, the God of Israel, lives, whom I serve, there will be neither dew nor rain in the next few years except at my word."

2Then the word of the LORD came to Elijah: 3"Leave here, turn eastward and hide in the Kerith Ravine, east of the Jordan. 4You will drink from the brook, and I have directed the ravens to supply you with food there."

5So he did what the LORD had told him. He went to the Kerith Ravine, east of the Jordan, and stayed there. 6The ravens brought him bread and meat in the morning and bread and meat in the evening, and he drank from the brook.

The Widow at Zarephath

7Some time later the brook dried up because there had been no rain in the land. 8Then the word of the LORD came to him: 9"Go at once to Zarephath in the region of Sidon and stay there. I have directed a widow there to supply you with food." 10So he went to Zarephath. When he came to the town gate, a widow was there gathering sticks. He called to her and asked, "Would you bring me a little water in a jar so I may have a drink?" 11As she was going to get it, he called, "And bring me, please, a piece of bread."

12"As surely as the LORD your God lives," she replied, "I don't have any bread—only a handful of flour in a jar and a little olive oil in a jug. I am gathering a few sticks to take home and make a meal for myself and my son, that we may eat it—and die."

13Elijah said to her, "Don't be afraid. Go home and do as you have said. But first make a small loaf of bread for me from what you have and bring it to me, and then make something for yourself and your son. 14For this is what the LORD, the God of Israel, says: 'The jar of flour will not be used up and the jug of oil will not run dry until the day the LORD sends rain on the land.' "

15She went away and did as Elijah had told her. So there was food every day for Elijah and for the woman and her family. 16For the jar of flour was not used up and the jug of oil did not run dry, in keeping with the word of the LORD spoken by Elijah.

17Some time later the son of the woman who owned the house became ill. He grew worse and worse, and finally stopped breathing. 18She said to Elijah, "What do you have against me, man of God? Did you come to remind me of my sin and kill my son?"

19"Give me your son," Elijah replied. He took him from her arms, carried him to the upper room where he was staying, and laid him on his bed. 20Then he cried out to the LORD, "LORD my God, have you brought tragedy even on this widow I am staying with, by causing her son to die?" 21Then he stretched himself out on the boy three times and cried out to the LORD, "LORD my God, let this boy's life return to him!"

22The LORD heard Elijah's cry, and the boy's life returned to him, and he lived. 23Elijah picked up the child and carried him down from the room into the house. He gave him to his mother and said, "Look, your son is alive!"

24Then the woman said to Elijah, "Now I know that you are a man of God and that the word of the LORD from your mouth is the truth."

Elijah and Obadiah

18 After a long time, in the third year, the word of the LORD came to Elijah: "Go and present yourself to Ahab, and I will send rain on the land." 2So Elijah went to present himself to Ahab.

Now the famine was severe in Samaria, 3and Ahab had summoned Obadiah, who was in charge of his palace. (Obadiah was a devout believer in the LORD. 4While Jezebel was killing off the LORD's prophets, Obadiah had taken a hundred prophets and hidden them in two caves, fifty in each, and had supplied them with food and water.) 5Ahab had said to Obadiah, "Go through the land to all the springs and valleys. Maybe we can find some grass to keep the horses and mules alive so we will not have to kill any of our animals." 6So they divided the land they were to cover, Ahab going in one direction and Obadiah in another.

7As Obadiah was walking along, Elijah met him. Obadiah recognized him, bowed

---

a 1 Or Tishbite, of the settlers

down to the ground, and said, "Is it really you, my lord Elijah?"

⁸"Yes," he replied. "Go tell your master, 'Elijah is here.'"

⁹"What have I done wrong," asked Obadiah, "that you are handing your servant over to Ahab to be put to death? ¹⁰As surely as the LORD your God lives, there is not a nation or kingdom where my master has not sent someone to look for you. And whenever a nation or kingdom claimed you were not there, he made them swear they could not find you. ¹¹But now you tell me to go to my master and say, 'Elijah is here.' ¹²I don't know where the Spirit of the LORD may carry you when I leave you. If I go and tell Ahab and he doesn't find you, he will kill me. Yet I your servant have worshiped the LORD since my youth. ¹³Haven't you heard, my lord, what I did while Jezebel was killing the prophets of the LORD? I hid a hundred of the LORD's prophets in two caves, fifty in each, and supplied them with food and water. ¹⁴And now you tell me to go to my master and say, 'Elijah is here.' He will kill me!"

¹⁵Elijah said, "As the LORD Almighty lives, whom I serve, I will surely present myself to Ahab today."

Elijah on Mount Carmel

¹⁶So Obadiah went to meet Ahab and told him, and Ahab went to meet Elijah. ¹⁷When he saw Elijah, he said to him, "Is that you, you troubler of Israel?"

¹⁸"I have not made trouble for Israel," Elijah replied. "But you and your father's family have. You have abandoned the LORD's commands and have followed the Baals. ¹⁹Now summon the people from all over Israel to meet me on Mount Carmel. And bring the four hundred and fifty prophets of Baal and the four hundred prophets of Asherah, who eat at Jezebel's table."

²⁰So Ahab sent word throughout all Israel and assembled the prophets on Mount Carmel. ²¹Elijah went before the people and said, "How long will you waver between two opinions? If the LORD is God, follow him; but if Baal is God, follow him."

But the people said nothing.

²²Then Elijah said to them, "I am the only one of the LORD's prophets left, but Baal has four hundred and fifty prophets. ²³Get two bulls for us. Let Baal's prophets choose one for themselves, and let them cut it into pieces and put it on the wood but not set fire to it. I will prepare the other bull and put it on the wood but not set fire to it. ²⁴Then you call on the name of your god, and I will call on the name of the LORD. The god who answers by fire—he is God."

Then all the people said, "What you say is good."

²⁵Elijah said to the prophets of Baal, "Choose one of the bulls and prepare it first, since there are so many of you. Call on the name of your god, but do not light the fire." ²⁶So they took the bull given them and prepared it.

Then they called on the name of Baal from morning till noon. "Baal, answer us!" they shouted. But there was no response; no one answered. And they danced around the altar they had made.

²⁷At noon Elijah began to taunt them. "Shout louder!" he said. "Surely he is a god! Perhaps he is deep in thought, or busy, or traveling. Maybe he is sleeping and must be awakened." ²⁸So they shouted louder and slashed themselves with swords and spears, as was their custom, until their blood flowed. ²⁹Midday passed, and they continued their frantic prophesying until the time for the evening sacrifice. But there was no response, no one answered, no one paid attention.

³⁰Then Elijah said to all the people, "Come here to me." They came to him, and he repaired the altar of the LORD, which had been torn down. ³¹Elijah took twelve stones, one for each of the tribes descended from Jacob, to whom the word of the LORD had come, saying, "Your name shall be Israel." ³²With the stones he built an altar in the name of the LORD, and he dug a trench around it large enough to hold two seahs[a] of seed. ³³He arranged the wood, cut the bull into pieces and laid it on the wood. Then he said to them, "Fill four large jars with water and pour it on the offering and on the wood."

³⁴"Do it again," he said, and they did it again.

"Do it a third time," he ordered, and they did it the third time. ³⁵The water ran down around the altar and even filled the trench.

---

a 32 That is, probably about 24 pounds or about 11 kilograms

WEDNESDAY

DIVIDED DEVOTION

1 Kings 18:16–42 *or* 18:38–40

THOMAS WATSON {AD 1620–1686}

If God is going to be God to us, we must trust in him . . . "My eyes are fixed on you, Sovereign LORD; in you I take refuge" (Psalm 141:8). "My God is my rock, in whom I take refuge" (2 Samuel 22:3). God is the only one in whom we can trust. Every other creature is a false refuge. They are like the Egyptian reed—too weak to support us, but strong enough to wound us (2 Kings 18:21) . . . Only God is a sufficient foundation to build our trust upon. When we trust him, we make him a God to us; when we do not trust him, we make him an idol. To trust in God means to rely on his power as a Creator, and on his love as a Father. Trusting in God involves committing our primary treasure—our soul—to him. "Into your hands I commit my spirit" (Psalm 31:5). As the orphan trusts his guardian to care for his inheritance, so we trust God with our souls. When we do, he becomes our God.

John Ortberg

Few people actually bow down and worship stone idols these days. But idolatry is still present in our day. Anything we allow to take the place of God in our lives can become a Baal. The things we try to embrace and cling to while we still hold onto God can become idolatrous.

A Baal is anything that tempts us away from full devotion to God. For example, a Baal can be

  • a relationship that dishonors God
  • a lifestyle that keeps you from being generous to the poor
  • a habit or an addiction that you know God wants you to give up but you refuse
  • a grudge against someone who has hurt you
  • a struggle with pride and the power it has over you

We are all tempted to tell ourselves that we can hang onto our idols and God at the same time. What God taught the people of Israel, and what he wants to teach us, is that it is impossible to hold both God and idols in our heart. There is simply not enough room.

reflection

1. If a Baal is defined as anything that tempts us away from full devotion to God, what are the Baals in your life right now?

2. How do you see yourself trying to hold on to your "idols" and God at the same time?

3. What steps do you need to take to let go of those idols and trust solely in God instead?

For your next devotional reading, go to page 399.

³⁶At the time of sacrifice, the prophet Elijah stepped forward and prayed: "LORD, the God of Abraham, Isaac and Israel, let it be known today that you are God in Israel and that I am your servant and have done all these things at your command. ³⁷Answer me, LORD, answer me, so these people will know that you, LORD, are God, and that you are turning their hearts back again."

³⁸Then the fire of the LORD fell and burned up the sacrifice, the wood, the stones and the soil, and also licked up the water in the trench.

³⁹When all the people saw this, they fell prostrate and cried, "The LORD—he is God! The LORD—he is God!"

⁴⁰Then Elijah commanded them, "Seize the prophets of Baal. Don't let anyone get away!" They seized them, and Elijah had them brought down to the Kishon Valley and slaughtered there.

⁴¹And Elijah said to Ahab, "Go, eat and drink, for there is the sound of a heavy rain." ⁴²So Ahab went off to eat and drink, but Elijah climbed to the top of Carmel, bent down to the ground and put his face between his knees.

⁴³"Go and look toward the sea," he told his servant. And he went up and looked.

"There is nothing there," he said.

Seven times Elijah said, "Go back."

⁴⁴The seventh time the servant reported, "A cloud as small as a man's hand is rising from the sea."

So Elijah said, "Go and tell Ahab, 'Hitch up your chariot and go down before the rain stops you.'"

⁴⁵Meanwhile, the sky grew black with clouds, the wind rose, a heavy rain came on and Ahab rode off to Jezreel. ⁴⁶The power of the LORD came on Elijah and, tucking his cloak into his belt, he ran ahead of Ahab all the way to Jezreel.

Elijah Flees to Horeb

19 Now Ahab told Jezebel everything Elijah had done and how he had killed all the prophets with the sword. ²So Jezebel sent a messenger to Elijah to say, "May the gods deal with me, be it ever so severely, if by this time tomorrow I do not make your life like that of one of them."

³Elijah was afraid*ᵃ* and ran for his life. When he came to Beersheba in Judah, he left his servant there, ⁴while he himself went a day's journey into the wilderness. He came to a broom bush, sat down under it and prayed that he might die. "I have had enough, LORD," he said. "Take my life; I am no better than my ancestors." ⁵Then he lay down under the tree and fell asleep.

All at once an angel touched him and said, "Get up and eat." ⁶He looked around, and there by his head was some bread baked over hot coals, and a jar of water. He ate and drank and then lay down again.

⁷The angel of the LORD came back a second time and touched him and said, "Get up and eat, for the journey is too much for you." ⁸So he got up and ate and drank. Strengthened by that food, he traveled forty days and forty nights until he reached Horeb, the mountain of God. ⁹There he went into a cave and spent the night.

The LORD Appears to Elijah

And the word of the LORD came to him: "What are you doing here, Elijah?"

¹⁰He replied, "I have been very zealous for the LORD God Almighty. The Israelites have rejected your covenant, torn down your altars, and put your prophets to death with the sword. I am the only one left, and now they are trying to kill me too."

¹¹The LORD said, "Go out and stand on the mountain in the presence of the LORD, for the LORD is about to pass by."

Then a great and powerful wind tore the mountains apart and shattered the rocks before the LORD, but the LORD was not in the wind. After the wind there was an earthquake, but the LORD was not in the earthquake. ¹²After the earthquake came a fire, but the LORD was not in the fire. And after the fire came a gentle whisper. ¹³When Elijah heard it, he pulled his cloak over his face and went out and stood at the mouth of the cave.

Then a voice said to him, "What are you doing here, Elijah?"

¹⁴He replied, "I have been very zealous for the LORD God Almighty. The Israelites have rejected your covenant, torn down your altars, and put your prophets to death with the sword. I am the only one left, and now they are trying to kill me too."

ᵃ 3 Or Elijah saw

THURSDAY

BE ALERT AND LISTEN

1 Kings 19:1–21 *or* 19:9–13

HENRI J. M. NOUWEN {AD 1932–1996}

The prophet Elijah did not encounter God in the mighty wind or in the earthquake or in the fire, but in the small voice (see 1 Kings 19:9–13). Through the practice of a spiritual discipline we become attentive to that small voice and willing to respond when we hear it . . .

It is clear that we are usually surrounded by so much outer noise that it is hard to truly hear our God when he is speaking to us. We have often become deaf, unable to know when God calls us and unable to understand in which direction he calls us.

Thus our lives have become absurd. In the word *absurd* we find the Latin word *surdus*, which means "deaf." A spiritual life requires discipline because we need to learn to listen to God, who constantly speaks but whom we seldom hear.

When, however, we learn to listen, our lives become obedient lives. The word *obedient* comes from the Latin word *audire*, which means "listening": A spiritual discipline is necessary in order to move slowly from an absurd to an obedient life, from a life filled with noisy worries to a life in which there is some free inner space where we can listen to our God and follow his guidance.

Jesus' life was a life of obedience. He was always listening to the Father, always attentive to his voice, always alert for his directions. Jesus was "all ear." That is true prayer: being all ear for God. The core of all prayer is indeed listening, obediently standing in the presence of God.

Richard Foster

Christian meditation, very simply, is the ability to hear God's voice and obey his word. It is that simple. I wish I could make it more complicated for those who like things difficult. It involves no hidden mysteries, no secret mantras, no mental gymnastics, no esoteric flights into the cosmic consciousness. The truth of the matter is that the great God of the universe, the Creator of all things, desires our fellowship.

reflection

1. Why do you think God spoke to Elijah in a gentle whisper?

2. Why do we tend to make communicating with God more complicated than it is?

3. Why are we always looking for something "more"?

For your next devotional reading, go to page 409.

¹⁵The LORD said to him, "Go back the way you came, and go to the Desert of Damascus. When you get there, anoint Hazael king over Aram. ¹⁶Also, anoint Jehu son of Nimshi king over Israel, and anoint Elisha son of Shaphat from Abel Meholah to succeed you as prophet. ¹⁷Jehu will put to death any who escape the sword of Hazael, and Elisha will put to death any who escape the sword of Jehu. ¹⁸Yet I reserve seven thousand in Israel—all whose knees have not bowed down to Baal and whose mouths have not kissed him."

The Call of Elisha

¹⁹So Elijah went from there and found Elisha son of Shaphat. He was plowing with twelve yoke of oxen, and he himself was driving the twelfth pair. Elijah went up to him and threw his cloak around him. ²⁰Elisha then left his oxen and ran after Elijah. "Let me kiss my father and mother good-by," he said, "and then I will come with you."

"Go back," Elijah replied. "What have I done to you?"

²¹So Elisha left him and went back. He took his yoke of oxen and slaughtered them. He burned the plowing equipment to cook the meat and gave it to the people, and they ate. Then he set out to follow Elijah and became his servant.

Ben-Hadad Attacks Samaria

20 Now Ben-Hadad king of Aram mustered his entire army. Accompanied by thirty-two kings with their horses and chariots, he went up and besieged Samaria and attacked it. ²He sent messengers into the city to Ahab king of Israel, saying, "This is what Ben-Hadad says: ³'Your silver and gold are mine, and the best of your wives and children are mine.' "

⁴The king of Israel answered, "Just as you say, my lord the king. I and all I have are yours."

⁵The messengers came again and said, "This is what Ben-Hadad says: 'I sent to demand your silver and gold, your wives and your children. ⁶But about this time tomorrow I am going to send my officials to search your palace and the houses of your officials. They will seize everything you value and carry it away.' "

⁷The king of Israel summoned all the elders of the land and said to them, "See how this man is looking for trouble! When he sent for my wives and my children, my silver and my gold, I did not refuse him."

⁸The elders and the people all answered, "Don't listen to him or agree to his demands."

⁹So he replied to Ben-Hadad's messengers, "Tell my lord the king, 'Your servant will do all you demanded the first time, but this demand I cannot meet.' " They left and took the answer back to Ben-Hadad.

¹⁰Then Ben-Hadad sent another message to Ahab: "May the gods deal with me, be it ever so severely, if enough dust remains in Samaria to give each of my men a handful."

¹¹The king of Israel answered, "Tell him: 'One who puts on his armor should not boast like one who takes it off.' "

¹²Ben-Hadad heard this message while he and the kings were drinking in their tents,ᵃ and he ordered his men: "Prepare to attack." So they prepared to attack the city.

Ahab Defeats Ben-Hadad

¹³Meanwhile a prophet came to Ahab king of Israel and announced, "This is what the LORD says: 'Do you see this vast army? I will give it into your hand today, and then you will know that I am the LORD.' "

¹⁴"But who will do this?" asked Ahab.

The prophet replied, "This is what the LORD says: 'The junior officers under the provincial commanders will do it.' "

"And who will start the battle?" he asked.

The prophet answered, "You will."

¹⁵So Ahab summoned the 232 junior officers under the provincial commanders. Then he assembled the rest of the Israelites, 7,000 in all. ¹⁶They set out at noon while Ben-Hadad and the 32 kings allied with him were in their tents getting drunk. ¹⁷The junior officers under the provincial commanders went out first.

Now Ben-Hadad had dispatched scouts, who reported, "Men are advancing from Samaria."

¹⁸He said, "If they have come out for peace, take them alive; if they have come out for war, take them alive."

¹⁹The junior officers under the provincial commanders marched out of the city with the army behind them ²⁰and each one struck

---

ᵃ 12 Or *in Sukkoth*; also in verse 16

down his opponent. At that, the Arameans fled, with the Israelites in pursuit. But Ben-Hadad king of Aram escaped on horseback with some of his horsemen. ²¹The king of Israel advanced and overpowered the horses and chariots and inflicted heavy losses on the Arameans.

²²Afterward, the prophet came to the king of Israel and said, "Strengthen your position and see what must be done, because next spring the king of Aram will attack you again."

²³Meanwhile, the officials of the king of Aram advised him, "Their gods are gods of the hills. That is why they were too strong for us. But if we fight them on the plains, surely we will be stronger than they. ²⁴Do this: Remove all the kings from their commands and replace them with other officers. ²⁵You must also raise an army like the one you lost—horse for horse and chariot for chariot—so we can fight Israel on the plains. Then surely we will be stronger than they." He agreed with them and acted accordingly.

²⁶The next spring Ben-Hadad mustered the Arameans and went up to Aphek to fight against Israel. ²⁷When the Israelites were also mustered and given provisions, they marched out to meet them. The Israelites camped opposite them like two small flocks of goats, while the Arameans covered the countryside.

²⁸The man of God came up and told the king of Israel, "This is what the LORD says: 'Because the Arameans think the LORD is a god of the hills and not a god of the valleys, I will deliver this vast army into your hands, and you will know that I am the LORD.' "

²⁹For seven days they camped opposite each other, and on the seventh day the battle was joined. The Israelites inflicted a hundred thousand casualties on the Aramean foot soldiers in one day. ³⁰The rest of them escaped to the city of Aphek, where the wall collapsed on twenty-seven thousand of them. And Ben-Hadad fled to the city and hid in an inner room.

³¹His officials said to him, "Look, we have heard that the kings of the house of Israel are merciful. Let us go to the king of Israel with sackcloth around our waists and ropes

around our heads. Perhaps he will spare your life."

³²Wearing sackcloth around their waists and ropes around their heads, they went to the king of Israel and said, "Your servant Ben-Hadad says: 'Please let me live.' "

The king answered, "Is he still alive? He is an old ally."

³³The men took this as a good sign and were quick to pick up his word. "Yes, your old ally Ben-Hadad!" they said.

"Go and get him," the king said. When Ben-Hadad came out, Ahab had him come up into his chariot.

³⁴"I will return the cities my father took from your father," Ben-Hadad offered. "You may set up your own market areas in Damascus, as my father did in Samaria."

¸Ahab said,¸ "On the basis of a treaty I will set you free." So he made a treaty with him, and let him go.

A Prophet Condemns Ahab

³⁵By the word of the LORD one of the company of the prophets said to his companion, "Strike me with your weapon," but he refused.

³⁶So the prophet said, "Because you have not obeyed the LORD, as soon as you leave me a lion will kill you." And after the man went away, a lion found him and killed him.

³⁷The prophet found another man and said, "Strike me, please." So the man struck him and wounded him. ³⁸Then the prophet went and stood by the road waiting for the king. He disguised himself with his headband down over his eyes. ³⁹As the king passed by, the prophet called out to him, "Your servant went into the thick of the battle, and someone came to me with a captive and said, 'Guard this man. If he is missing, it will be your life for his life, or you must pay a talentᵃ of silver.' ⁴⁰While your servant was busy here and there, the man disappeared."

"That is your sentence," the king of Israel said. "You have pronounced it yourself."

⁴¹Then the prophet quickly removed the headband from his eyes, and the king of Israel recognized him as one of the prophets. ⁴²He said to the king, "This is what the LORD says: 'You have set free a man I had determined should die.ᵇ Therefore it is your life

---

ᵃ 39 That is, about 75 pounds or about 34 kilograms   ᵇ 42 The Hebrew term refers to the irrevocable giving over of things or persons to the LORD, often by totally destroying them.

for his life, your people for his people.' "
⁴³Sullen and angry, the king of Israel went to his palace in Samaria.

Naboth's Vineyard

21 Some time later there was an incident involving a vineyard belonging to Naboth the Jezreelite. The vineyard was in Jezreel, close to the palace of Ahab king of Samaria. ²Ahab said to Naboth, "Let me have your vineyard to use for a vegetable garden, since it is close to my palace. In exchange I will give you a better vineyard or, if you prefer, I will pay you whatever it is worth."

³But Naboth replied, "The LORD forbid that I should give you the inheritance of my ancestors."

⁴So Ahab went home, sullen and angry because Naboth the Jezreelite had said, "I will not give you the inheritance of my ancestors." He lay on his bed sulking and refused to eat.

⁵His wife Jezebel came in and asked him, "Why are you so sullen? Why won't you eat?"

⁶He answered her, "Because I said to Naboth the Jezreelite, 'Sell me your vineyard; or if you prefer, I will give you another vineyard in its place.' But he said, 'I will not give you my vineyard.' "

⁷Jezebel his wife said, "Is this how you act as king over Israel? Get up and eat! Cheer up. I'll get you the vineyard of Naboth the Jezreelite."

⁸So she wrote letters in Ahab's name, placed his seal on them, and sent them to the elders and nobles who lived in Naboth's city with him. ⁹In those letters she wrote:

"Proclaim a day of fasting and seat Naboth in a prominent place among the people. ¹⁰But seat two scoundrels opposite him and have them bring charges that he has cursed both God and the king. Then take him out and stone him to death."

¹¹So the elders and nobles who lived in Naboth's city did as Jezebel directed in the letters she had written to them. ¹²They proclaimed a fast and seated Naboth in a prominent place among the people. ¹³Then two scoundrels came and sat opposite him and

brought charges against Naboth before the people, saying, "Naboth has cursed both God and the king." So they took him outside the city and stoned him to death. ¹⁴Then they sent word to Jezebel: "Naboth has been stoned to death."

¹⁵As soon as Jezebel heard that Naboth had been stoned to death, she said to Ahab, "Get up and take possession of the vineyard of Naboth the Jezreelite that he refused to sell you. He is no longer alive, but dead." ¹⁶When Ahab heard that Naboth was dead, he got up and went down to take possession of Naboth's vineyard.

¹⁷Then the word of the LORD came to Elijah the Tishbite: ¹⁸"Go down to meet Ahab king of Israel, who rules in Samaria. He is now in Naboth's vineyard, where he has gone to take possession of it. ¹⁹Say to him, 'This is what the LORD says: Have you not murdered a man and seized his property?' Then say to him, 'This is what the LORD says: In the place where dogs licked up Naboth's blood, dogs will lick up your blood—yes, yours!' "

²⁰Ahab said to Elijah, "So you have found me, my enemy!"

"I have found you," he answered, "because you have sold yourself to do evil in the eyes of the LORD. ²¹He says, 'I am going to bring disaster on you. I will wipe out your descendants and cut off from Ahab every last male in Israel—slave or free.ᵃ ²²I will make your house like that of Jeroboam son of Nebat and that of Baasha son of Ahijah, because you have aroused my anger and have caused Israel to sin.'

²³"And also concerning Jezebel the LORD says: 'Dogs will devour Jezebel by the wall ofᵇ Jezreel.'

²⁴"Dogs will eat those belonging to Ahab who die in the city, and the birds will feed on those who die in the country."

²⁵(There was never anyone like Ahab, who sold himself to do evil in the eyes of the LORD, urged on by Jezebel his wife. ²⁶He behaved in the vilest manner by going after idols, like the Amorites the LORD drove out before Israel.)

²⁷When Ahab heard these words, he tore his clothes, put on sackcloth and fasted. He lay in sackcloth and went around meekly.

ᵃ 21 Or *Israel—every ruler or leader*   *ᵇ 23* Most Hebrew manuscripts; a few Hebrew manuscripts, Vulgate and Syriac (see also 2 Kings 9:26) *the plot of ground at*

28Then the word of the LORD came to Elijah the Tishbite: 29"Have you noticed how Ahab has humbled himself before me? Because he has humbled himself, I will not bring this disaster in his day, but I will bring it on his house in the days of his son."

Micaiah Prophesies Against Ahab

22 For three years there was no war between Aram and Israel. 2But in the third year Jehoshaphat king of Judah went down to see the king of Israel. 3The king of Israel had said to his officials, "Don't you know that Ramoth Gilead belongs to us and yet we are doing nothing to retake it from the king of Aram?"

4So he asked Jehoshaphat, "Will you go with me to fight against Ramoth Gilead?"

Jehoshaphat replied to the king of Israel, "I am as you are, my people as your people, my horses as your horses." 5But Jehoshaphat also said to the king of Israel, "First seek the counsel of the LORD."

6So the king of Israel brought together the prophets—about four hundred men—and asked them, "Shall I go to war against Ramoth Gilead, or shall I refrain?"

"Go," they answered, "for the Lord will give it into the king's hand."

7But Jehoshaphat asked, "Is there no longer a prophet of the LORD here whom we can inquire of?"

8The king of Israel answered Jehoshaphat, "There is still one through whom we can inquire of the LORD, but I hate him because he never prophesies anything good about me, but always bad. He is Micaiah son of Imlah."

"The king should not say such a thing," Jehoshaphat replied.

9So the king of Israel called one of his officials and said, "Bring Micaiah son of Imlah at once."

10Dressed in their royal robes, the king of Israel and Jehoshaphat king of Judah were sitting on their thrones at the threshing floor by the entrance of the gate of Samaria, with all the prophets prophesying before them. 11Now Zedekiah son of Kenaanah had made iron horns and he declared, "This is what the LORD says: 'With these you will gore the Arameans until they are destroyed.'"

12All the other prophets were prophesying the same thing. "Attack Ramoth Gilead and be victorious," they said, "for the LORD will give it into the king's hand."

13The messenger who had gone to summon Micaiah said to him, "Look, the other prophets without exception are predicting success for the king. Let your word agree with theirs, and speak favorably."

14But Micaiah said, "As surely as the LORD lives, I can tell him only what the LORD tells me."

15When he arrived, the king asked him, "Micaiah, shall we go to war against Ramoth Gilead, or not?"

"Attack and be victorious," he answered, "for the LORD will give it into the king's hand."

16The king said to him, "How many times must I make you swear to tell me nothing but the truth in the name of the LORD?"

17Then Micaiah answered, "I saw all Israel scattered on the hills like sheep without a shepherd, and the LORD said, 'These people have no master. Let each one go home in peace.'"

18The king of Israel said to Jehoshaphat, "Didn't I tell you that he never prophesies anything good about me, but only bad?"

19Micaiah continued, "Therefore hear the word of the LORD: I saw the LORD sitting on his throne with all the host of heaven standing around him on his right and on his left. 20And the LORD said, 'Who will entice Ahab into attacking Ramoth Gilead and going to his death there?'

"One suggested this, and another that. 21Finally, a spirit came forward, stood before the LORD and said, 'I will entice him.'

22"'By what means?' the LORD asked.

"'I will go out and be a lying spirit in the mouths of all his prophets,' he said.

"'You will succeed in enticing him,' said the LORD. 'Go and do it.'

23"So now the LORD has put a lying spirit in the mouths of all these prophets of yours. The LORD has decreed disaster for you."

24Then Zedekiah son of Kenaanah went up and slapped Micaiah in the face. "Which way did the spirit froma the LORD go when he went from me to speak to you?" he asked.

25Micaiah replied, "You will find out on the day you go to hide in an inner room."

26The king of Israel then ordered, "Take

a 24 Or Spirit of

Micaiah and send him back to Amon the ruler of the city and to Joash the king's son [27]and say, 'This is what the king says: Put this fellow in prison and give him nothing but bread and water until I return safely.' "

[28]Micaiah declared, "If you ever return safely, the LORD has not spoken through me." Then he added, "Mark my words, all you people!"

Ahab Killed at Ramoth Gilead

[29]So the king of Israel and Jehoshaphat king of Judah went up to Ramoth Gilead. [30]The king of Israel said to Jehoshaphat, "I will enter the battle in disguise, but you wear your royal robes." So the king of Israel disguised himself and went into battle.

[31]Now the king of Aram had ordered his thirty-two chariot commanders, "Do not fight with anyone, small or great, except the king of Israel." [32]When the chariot commanders saw Jehoshaphat, they thought, "Surely this is the king of Israel." So they turned to attack him, but when Jehoshaphat cried out, [33]the chariot commanders saw that he was not the king of Israel and stopped pursuing him.

[34]But someone drew his bow at random and hit the king of Israel between the breastplate and the scale armor. The king told his chariot driver, "Wheel around and get me out of the fighting. I've been wounded." [35]All day long the battle raged, and the king was propped up in his chariot facing the Arameans. The blood from his wound ran onto the floor of the chariot, and that evening he died. [36]As the sun was setting, a cry spread through the army: "Everyone to your own town; everyone to your land!"

[37]So the king died and was brought to Samaria, and they buried him there. [38]They washed the chariot at a pool in Samaria (where the prostitutes bathed),[a] and the dogs licked up his blood, as the word of the LORD had declared.

[39]As for the other events of Ahab's reign, including all he did, the palace he built and inlaid with ivory, and the cities he fortified, are they not written in the book of the an-

nals of the kings of Israel? [40]Ahab rested with his ancestors. And Ahaziah his son succeeded him as king.

Jehoshaphat King of Judah

[41]Jehoshaphat son of Asa became king of Judah in the fourth year of Ahab king of Israel. [42]Jehoshaphat was thirty-five years old when he became king, and he reigned in Jerusalem twenty-five years. His mother's name was Azubah daughter of Shilhi. [43]In everything he followed the ways of his father Asa and did not stray from them; he did what was right in the eyes of the LORD. *The high places, however, were not removed, and the people continued to offer sacrifices and burn incense there. *[44]Jehoshaphat was also at peace with the king of Israel.

[45]As for the other events of Jehoshaphat's reign, the things he achieved and his military exploits, are they not written in the book of the annals of the kings of Judah? [46]He rid the land of the rest of the male shrine prostitutes who remained there even after the reign of his father Asa. [47]There was then no king in Edom; a provincial governor ruled.

[48]Now Jehoshaphat built a fleet of trading ships[b] to go to Ophir for gold, but they never set sail—they were wrecked at Ezion Geber. [49]At that time Ahaziah son of Ahab said to Jehoshaphat, "Let my men sail with yours," but Jehoshaphat refused.

[50]Then Jehoshaphat rested with his ancestors and was buried with them in the city of David his father. And Jehoram his son succeeded him as king.

Ahaziah King of Israel

[51]Ahaziah son of Ahab became king of Israel in Samaria in the seventeenth year of Jehoshaphat king of Judah, and he reigned over Israel two years. [52]He did evil in the eyes of the LORD, because he followed the ways of his father and mother and of Jeroboam son of Nebat, who caused Israel to sin. [53]He served and worshiped Baal and aroused the anger of the LORD, the God of Israel, just as his father had done.

---

a 38 Or *Samaria and cleaned the weapons*   *b* 48 Hebrew *of ships of Tarshish*

* This sentence (22:43b) is numbered 22:44 in Hebrew texts.   * 22:44-53 is numbered 22:45-54 in Hebrew texts.

2 kings

AUTHOR: Unknown

DATE: Probably between 560 and 550 B.C.

THEME: God's redemption and the consequences of sin were as obvious in the ancient kingdoms as they are today.

The LORD's Judgment on Ahaziah

1 After Ahab's death, Moab rebelled against Israel. ²Now Ahaziah had fallen through the lattice of his upper room in Samaria and injured himself. So he sent messengers, saying to them, "Go and consult Baal-Zebub, the god of Ekron, to see if I will recover from this injury."

³But the angel of the LORD said to Elijah the Tishbite, "Go up and meet the messengers of the king of Samaria and ask them, 'Is it because there is no God in Israel that you are going off to consult Baal-Zebub, the god of Ekron?' ⁴Therefore this is what the LORD says: 'You will not leave the bed you are lying on. You will certainly die!' " So Elijah went.

⁵When the messengers returned to the king, he asked them, "Why have you come back?"

⁶"A man came to meet us," they replied. "And he said to us, 'Go back to the king who sent you and tell him, "This is what the LORD says: Is it because there is no God in Israel that you are sending messengers to consult Baal-Zebub, the god of Ekron? Therefore you will not leave the bed you are lying on. You will certainly die!" ' "

⁷The king asked them, "What kind of man was it who came to meet you and told you this?"

⁸They replied, "He had a garment of hair*ᵃ* and had a leather belt around his waist."

The king said, "That was Elijah the Tishbite."

⁹Then he sent to Elijah a captain with his company of fifty men. The captain went up to Elijah, who was sitting on the top of a hill, and said to him, "Man of God, the king says, 'Come down!' "

¹⁰Elijah answered the captain, "If I am a man of God, may fire come down from heaven and consume you and your fifty men!" Then fire fell from heaven and consumed the captain and his men.

¹¹At this the king sent to Elijah another captain with his fifty men. The captain said to him, "Man of God, this is what the king says, 'Come down at once!' "

¹²"If I am a man of God," Elijah replied, "may fire come down from heaven and consume you and your fifty men!" Then the fire of God fell from heaven and consumed him and his fifty men.

¹³So the king sent a third captain with his fifty men. This third captain went up and fell on his knees before Elijah. "Man of God," he begged, "please have respect for my life and the lives of these fifty men, your servants! ¹⁴See, fire has fallen from heaven and consumed the first two captains and all their men. But now have respect for my life!"

¹⁵The angel of the LORD said to Elijah, "Go down with him; do not be afraid of him." So Elijah got up and went down with him to the king.

¹⁶He told the king, "This is what the LORD says: Is it because there is no God in Israel for you to consult that you have sent messengers to consult Baal-Zebub, the god of Ekron? Because you have done this, you will never leave the bed you are lying on. You will certainly die!" ¹⁷So he died, according to the word of the LORD that Elijah had spoken.

Because Ahaziah had no son, Joram*ᵇ* succeeded him as king in the second year of Je-

ᵃ 8 Or *He was a hairy man*   *ᵇ 17* Hebrew *Jehoram,* a variant of *Joram* horam son of Jehoshaphat king of Judah. [18]As for all the other events of Ahaziah's reign, and what he did, are they not written in the book of the annals of the kings of Israel?

Elijah Taken Up to Heaven

2 When the LORD was about to take Elijah up to heaven in a whirlwind, Elijah and Elisha were on their way from Gilgal. [2]Elijah said to Elisha, "Stay here; the LORD has sent me to Bethel."

But Elisha said, "As surely as the LORD lives and as you live, I will not leave you." So they went down to Bethel.

[3]The company of the prophets at Bethel came out to Elisha and asked, "Do you know that the LORD is going to take your master from you today?"

"Yes, I know," Elisha replied, "so be quiet."

[4]Then Elijah said to him, "Stay here, Elisha; the LORD has sent me to Jericho."

And he replied, "As surely as the LORD lives and as you live, I will not leave you." So they went to Jericho.

[5]The company of the prophets at Jericho went up to Elisha and asked him, "Do you know that the LORD is going to take your master from you today?"

"Yes, I know," he replied, "so be quiet."

[6]Then Elijah said to him, "Stay here; the LORD has sent me to the Jordan."

And he replied, "As surely as the LORD lives and as you live, I will not leave you." So the two of them walked on.

[7]Fifty men from the company of the prophets went and stood at a distance, facing the place where Elijah and Elisha had stopped at the Jordan. [8]Elijah took his cloak, rolled it up and struck the water with it. The water divided to the right and to the left, and the two of them crossed over on dry ground.

[9]When they had crossed, Elijah said to Elisha, "Tell me, what can I do for you before I am taken from you?"

"Let me inherit a double portion of your spirit," Elisha replied.

[10]"You have asked a difficult thing," Elijah said, "yet if you see me when I am taken from you, it will be yours—otherwise, it will not."

[11]As they were walking along and talking together, suddenly a chariot of fire and horses of fire appeared and separated the two of them, and Elijah went up to heaven in a whirlwind. [12]Elisha saw this and cried out, "My father! My father! The chariots and horsemen of Israel!" And Elisha saw him no more. Then he took hold of his garment and tore it in two.

[13]He picked up the cloak that had fallen from Elijah and went back and stood on the bank of the Jordan. [14]Then he took the cloak that had fallen from him and struck the water with it. "Where now is the LORD, the God of Elijah?" he asked. When he struck the water, it divided to the right and to the left, and he crossed over.

[15]The company of the prophets from Jericho, who were watching, said, "The spirit of Elijah is resting on Elisha." And they went to meet him and bowed to the ground before him. [16]"Look," they said, "we your servants have fifty able men. Let them go and look for your master. Perhaps the Spirit of the LORD has picked him up and set him down on some mountain or in some valley."

"No," Elisha replied, "do not send them."

[17]But they persisted until he was too embarrassed to refuse. So he said, "Send them." And they sent fifty men, who searched for three days but did not find him. [18]When they returned to Elisha, who was staying in Jericho, he said to them, "Didn't I tell you not to go?"

Healing of the Water

[19]The people of the city said to Elisha, "Look, our lord, this town is well situated, as you can see, but the water is bad and the land is unproductive."

[20]"Bring me a new bowl," he said, "and put salt in it." So they brought it to him.

[21]Then he went out to the spring and threw the salt into it, saying, "This is what the LORD says: 'I have healed this water. Never again will it cause death or make the land unproductive.'" [22]And the water has remained pure to this day, according to the word Elisha had spoken.

Elisha Is Jeered

[23]From there Elisha went up to Bethel. As he was walking along the road, some boys came out of the town and jeered at him. "Get out of here, baldy!" they said. "Get out of here, baldy!" [24]He turned around, looked at them and called down a curse on them in the name of the LORD. Then two bears came out of the woods and mauled forty-two of

the boys. 25And he went on to Mount Carmel and from there returned to Samaria.

Moab Revolts

3 Joram[a] son of Ahab became king of Israel in Samaria in the eighteenth year of Jehoshaphat king of Judah, and he reigned twelve years. 2He did evil in the eyes of the LORD, but not as his father and mother had done. He got rid of the sacred stone of Baal that his father had made. 3Nevertheless he clung to the sins of Jeroboam son of Nebat, which he had caused Israel to commit; he did not turn away from them.

4Now Mesha king of Moab raised sheep, and he had to pay the king of Israel a tribute of a hundred thousand lambs and the wool of a hundred thousand rams. 5But after Ahab died, the king of Moab rebelled against the king of Israel. 6So at that time King Joram set out from Samaria and mobilized all Israel. 7He also sent this message to Jehoshaphat king of Judah: "The king of Moab has rebelled against me. Will you go with me to fight against Moab?"

"I will go with you," he replied. "I am as you are, my people as your people, my horses as your horses."

8"By what route shall we attack?" he asked.

"Through the Desert of Edom," he answered.

9So the king of Israel set out with the king of Judah and the king of Edom. After a roundabout march of seven days, the army had no more water for themselves or for the animals with them.

10"What!" exclaimed the king of Israel. "Has the LORD called us three kings together only to deliver us into the hands of Moab?"

11But Jehoshaphat asked, "Is there no prophet of the LORD here, through whom we may inquire of the LORD?"

An officer of the king of Israel answered, "Elisha son of Shaphat is here. He used to pour water on the hands of Elijah.[b]"

12Jehoshaphat said, "The word of the LORD is with him." So the king of Israel and Jehoshaphat and the king of Edom went down to him.

13Elisha said to the king of Israel, "Why do you want to involve me? Go to the prophets of your father and the prophets of your mother."

"No," the king of Israel answered, "because it was the LORD who called us three kings together to deliver us into the hands of Moab."

14Elisha said, "As surely as the LORD Almighty lives, whom I serve, if I did not have respect for the presence of Jehoshaphat king of Judah, I would not pay any attention to you. 15But now bring me a harpist."

While the harpist was playing, the hand of the LORD came on Elisha 16and he said, "This is what the LORD says: I will fill this valley with pools of water. 17For this is what the LORD says: You will see neither wind nor rain, yet this valley will be filled with water, and you, your cattle and your other animals will drink. 18This is an easy thing in the eyes of the LORD; he will also deliver Moab into your hands. 19You will overthrow every fortified city and every major town. You will cut down every good tree, stop up all the springs, and ruin every good field with stones."

20The next morning, about the time for offering the sacrifice, there it was—water flowing from the direction of Edom! And the land was filled with water.

21Now all the Moabites had heard that the kings had come to fight against them; so every man, young and old, who could bear arms was called up and stationed on the border. 22When they got up early in the morning, the sun was shining on the water. To the Moabites across the way, the water looked red—like blood. 23"That's blood!" they said. "Those kings must have fought and slaughtered each other. Now to the plunder, Moab!"

24But when the Moabites came to the camp of Israel, the Israelites rose up and fought them until they fled. And the Israelites invaded the land and slaughtered the Moabites. 25They destroyed the towns, and each man threw a stone on every good field until it was covered. They stopped up all the springs and cut down every good tree. Only Kir Hareseth was left with its stones in place, but men armed with slings surrounded it and attacked it.

26When the king of Moab saw that the battle had gone against him, he took with

a 1 Hebrew *Jehoram*, a variant of *Joram*; also in verse 6   b 11 That is, he was Elijah's personal servant.

him seven hundred swordsmen to break through to the king of Edom, but they failed. ²⁷Then he took his firstborn son, who was to succeed him as king, and offered him as a sacrifice on the city wall. The fury against Israel was great; they withdrew and returned to their own land.

The Widow's Oil

4 The wife of a man from the company of the prophets cried out to Elisha, "Your servant my husband is dead, and you know that he revered the LORD. But now his creditor is coming to take my two boys as his slaves."

²Elisha replied to her, "How can I help you? Tell me, what do you have in your house?"

"Your servant has nothing there at all," she said, "except a little olive oil."

³Elisha said, "Go around and ask all your neighbors for empty jars. Don't ask for just a few. ⁴Then go inside and shut the door behind you and your sons. Pour oil into all the jars, and as each is filled, put it to one side."

⁵She left him and shut the door behind her and her sons. They brought the jars to her and she kept pouring. ⁶When all the jars were full, she said to her son, "Bring me another one."

But he replied, "There is not a jar left." Then the oil stopped flowing.

⁷She went and told the man of God, and he said, "Go, sell the oil and pay your debts. You and your sons can live on what is left."

The Shunammite's Son Restored to Life

⁸One day Elisha went to Shunem. And a well-to-do woman was there, who urged him to stay for a meal. So whenever he came by, he stopped there to eat. ⁹She said to her husband, "I know that this man who often comes our way is a holy man of God. ¹⁰Let's make a small room on the roof and put in it a bed and a table, a chair and a lamp for him. Then he can stay there whenever he comes to us."

¹¹One day when Elisha came, he went up to his room and lay down there. ¹²He said to his servant Gehazi, "Call the Shunammite." So he called her, and she stood before him. ¹³Elisha said to him, "Tell her, 'You have gone to all this trouble for us. Now what can be done for you? Can we speak on your be-

half to the king or the commander of the army?' "

She replied, "I have a home among my own people."

¹⁴"What can be done for her?" Elisha asked.

Gehazi said, "She has no son, and her husband is old."

¹⁵Then Elisha said, "Call her." So he called her, and she stood in the doorway. ¹⁶"About this time next year," Elisha said, "you will hold a son in your arms."

"No, my lord!" she objected. "Please, man of God, don't mislead your servant!"

¹⁷But the woman became pregnant, and the next year about that same time she gave birth to a son, just as Elisha had told her.

¹⁸The child grew, and one day he went out to his father, who was with the reapers. ¹⁹He said to his father, "My head! My head!"

His father told a servant, "Carry him to his mother." ²⁰After the servant had lifted him up and carried him to his mother, the boy sat on her lap until noon, and then he died. ²¹She went up and laid him on the bed of the man of God, then shut the door and went out.

²²She called her husband and said, "Please send me one of the servants and a donkey so I can go to the man of God quickly and return."

²³"Why go to him today?" he asked. "It's not the New Moon or the Sabbath."

"That's all right," she said.

²⁴She saddled the donkey and said to her servant, "Lead on; don't slow down for me unless I tell you." ²⁵So she set out and came to the man of God at Mount Carmel.

When he saw her in the distance, the man of God said to his servant Gehazi, "Look! There's the Shunammite! ²⁶Run to meet her and ask her, 'Are you all right? Is your husband all right? Is your child all right?' "

"Everything is all right," she said.

²⁷When she reached the man of God at the mountain, she took hold of his feet. Gehazi came over to push her away, but the man of God said, "Leave her alone! She is in bitter distress, but the LORD has hidden it from me and has not told me why."

²⁸"Did I ask you for a son, my lord?" she said. "Didn't I tell you, 'Don't raise my hopes'?"

²⁹Elisha said to Gehazi, "Tuck your cloak into your belt, take my staff in your hand

FRIDAY

GODLY IMPRESSIONS
2 Kings 4:8–37 or 4:8–10

WATCHMAN NEE {AD 1903–1972}

I always like to think of the words of that "great woman" of Shunem. Speaking of the prophet, whom she had observed but whom she did not know well, she said: "I know that this man who often comes our way is a holy man of God" (2 Kings 4:9). It was not what Elisha said or did that conveyed that impression, but what he was. By his merely passing by she could detect something; she could see. What are people sensing about us? We may leave many kinds of impressions: we may leave the impression that we are clever, that we are gifted, that we are this or that or the other. But no, the impression left by Elisha was an impression of God himself.

This matter of our impact upon others turns upon one thing and that is the working of the cross in us with regard to the pleasure of the heart of God. It demands that I seek his pleasure, that I seek to satisfy him only, and I do not mind how much it costs me to do so.

Bruce Bickel and Stan Jantz

Living a godly life may make you different. You may end up doing just the opposite of everyone else. Sometimes you may find that your conduct pleases God but offends your friends, or vice versa. Should you compromise and try to find an acceptable middle ground?

Jesus gave the two analogies of "salt" and "light" to show the importance of conduct. Salt is a seasoning, but it's also used as a preservative. God wants you to be like a moral preservative, bringing a virtuous and ethical flavor to your culture. God also wants you to shine into the darkness, not for your own publicity, but to bring credit to God.

Salt doesn't do any good if it stays in the shaker. A candle doesn't do any good under a bowl. So go forward today being salt and light in your world.

reflection

1. If you had walked by her home instead of Elisha, what would the Shunammite woman have said about you? What would she have seen in you?

2. What kind of impression does God want you to have on others?

3. What needs to change in order for that to happen?

For your next devotional reading, go to page 411.

and run. Don't greet anyone you meet, and if anyone greets you, do not answer. Lay my staff on the boy's face."

³⁰But the child's mother said, "As surely as the LORD lives and as you live, I will not leave you." So he got up and followed her.

³¹Gehazi went on ahead and laid the staff on the boy's face, but there was no sound or response. So Gehazi went back to meet Elisha and told him, "The boy has not awakened."

³²When Elisha reached the house, there was the boy lying dead on his couch. ³³He went in, shut the door on the two of them and prayed to the LORD. ³⁴Then he got on the bed and lay on the boy, mouth to mouth, eyes to eyes, hands to hands. As he stretched himself out on him, the boy's body grew warm. ³⁵Elisha turned away and walked back and forth in the room and then got on the bed and stretched out on him once more. The boy sneezed seven times and opened his eyes.

³⁶Elisha summoned Gehazi and said, "Call the Shunammite." And he did. When she came, he said, "Take your son." ³⁷She came in, fell at his feet and bowed to the ground. Then she took her son and went out.

Death in the Pot

³⁸Elisha returned to Gilgal and there was a famine in that region. While the company of the prophets was meeting with him, he said to his servant, "Put on the large pot and cook some stew for this company."

³⁹One of them went out into the fields to gather herbs and found a wild vine. He gathered some of its gourds and filled the fold of his cloak. When he returned, he cut them up into the pot of stew, though no one knew what they were. ⁴⁰The stew was poured out for the men, but as they began to eat it, they cried out, "Man of God, there is death in the pot!" And they could not eat it.

⁴¹Elisha said, "Get some flour." He put it into the pot and said, "Serve it to the people to eat." And there was nothing harmful in the pot.

Feeding of a Hundred

⁴²A man came from Baal Shalishah, bringing the man of God twenty loaves of barley bread baked from the first ripe grain, along with some heads of new grain. "Give it to the people to eat," Elisha said.

⁴³"How can I set this before a hundred men?" his servant asked.

But Elisha answered, "Give it to the people to eat. For this is what the LORD says: 'They will eat and have some left over.' " ⁴⁴Then he set it before them, and they ate and had some left over, according to the word of the LORD.

Naaman Healed of Leprosy

5 Now Naaman was commander of the army of the king of Aram. He was a great man in the sight of his master and highly regarded, because through him the LORD had given victory to Aram. He was a valiant soldier, but he had leprosy.ᵃ

²Now bands of raiders from Aram had gone out and had taken captive a young girl from Israel, and she served Naaman's wife. ³She said to her mistress, "If only my master would see the prophet who is in Samaria! He would cure him of his leprosy."

⁴Naaman went to his master and told him what the girl from Israel had said. ⁵"By all means, go," the king of Aram replied. "I will send a letter to the king of Israel." So Naaman left, taking with him ten talentsᵇ of silver, six thousand shekelsᶜ of gold and ten sets of clothing. ⁶The letter that he took to the king of Israel read: "With this letter I am sending my servant Naaman to you so that you may cure him of his leprosy."

⁷As soon as the king of Israel read the letter, he tore his robes and said, "Am I God? Can I kill and bring back to life? Why does this fellow send someone to me to be cured of his leprosy? See how he is trying to pick a quarrel with me!"

⁸When Elisha the man of God heard that the king of Israel had torn his robes, he sent him this message: "Why have you torn your robes? Have the man come to me and he will know that there is a prophet in Israel." ⁹So Naaman went with his horses and chariots and stopped at the door of Elisha's house. ¹⁰Elisha sent a messenger to say to him, "Go, wash yourself seven times in the Jordan, and your flesh will be restored and you will be cleansed."

ᵃ 1 The Hebrew for leprosy was used for various diseases affecting the skin; also in verses 3, 6, 7, 11 and 27.   ᵇ 5 That is, about 750 pounds or about 340 kilograms   ᶜ 5 That is, about 150 pounds or about 68 kilograms

Elisha's Choice

2 Kings 5:1-16

read/meditate

Given what is described here, observe the life of this righteous prophet. Consider Elisha's opportunity to influence others. Read through this passage several times, pausing between each reading. Consider Elisha's other possible options that he could have taken instead of choosing a righteous path.

pray

Relax and sit before God, asking him to catalog your opportunities to influence. (Sometimes we can walk right past them.) Consider your options and deliberately choose, with God as your witness, to be righteous in those opportunities.

contemplate

Think about the leadership you observe at all levels. Think about the kind of influence you believe God wants you to have. What steps can you take toward that end?

additional reflection

The Christian, through the knowledge and the teaching of Christ, is distinguished for temperance and righteousness, for patience in life and manly virtue, and for a profession of piety toward the one and only God.

—*Eusebius*

For your next devotional reading, go to page 414.

¹¹But Naaman went away angry and said, "I thought that he would surely come out to me and stand and call on the name of the LORD his God, wave his hand over the spot and cure me of my leprosy. ¹²Are not Abana and Pharpar, the rivers of Damascus, better than all the waters of Israel? Couldn't I wash in them and be cleansed?" So he turned and went off in a rage.

¹³Naaman's servants went to him and said, "My father, if the prophet had told you to do some great thing, would you not have done it? How much more, then, when he tells you, 'Wash and be cleansed'!" ¹⁴So he went down and dipped himself in the Jordan seven times, as the man of God had told him, and his flesh was restored and became clean like that of a young boy.

¹⁵Then Naaman and all his attendants went back to the man of God. He stood before him and said, "Now I know that there is no God in all the world except in Israel. So please accept a gift from your servant."

¹⁶The prophet answered, "As surely as the LORD lives, whom I serve, I will not accept a thing." And even though Naaman urged him, he refused.

¹⁷"If you will not," said Naaman, "please let me, your servant, be given as much earth as a pair of mules can carry, for your servant will never again make burnt offerings and sacrifices to any other god but the LORD. ¹⁸But may the LORD forgive your servant for this one thing: When my master enters the temple of Rimmon to bow down and he is leaning on my arm and I have to bow there also—when I bow down in the temple of Rimmon, may the LORD forgive your servant for this."

¹⁹"Go in peace," Elisha said.

After Naaman had traveled some distance, ²⁰Gehazi, the servant of Elisha the man of God, said to himself, "My master was too easy on Naaman, this Aramean, by not accepting from him what he brought. As surely as the LORD lives, I will run after him and get something from him."

²¹So Gehazi hurried after Naaman. When Naaman saw him running toward him, he got down from the chariot to meet him. "Is everything all right?" he asked.

²²"Everything is all right," Gehazi answered. "My master sent me to say, 'Two young men from the company of the prophets have just come to me from the hill country of Ephraim. Please give them a talent*a* of silver and two sets of clothing.' "

²³"By all means, take two talents," said Naaman. He urged Gehazi to accept them, and then tied up the two talents of silver in two bags, with two sets of clothing. He gave them to two of his servants, and they carried them ahead of Gehazi. ²⁴When Gehazi came to the hill, he took the things from the servants and put them away in the house. He sent the men away and they left.

²⁵When he went in and stood before his master, Elisha asked him, "Where have you been, Gehazi?"

"Your servant didn't go anywhere," Gehazi answered.

²⁶But Elisha said to him, "Was not my spirit with you when the man got down from his chariot to meet you? Is this the time to take money or to accept clothes—or olive groves and vineyards, or flocks and herds, or male and female slaves? ²⁷Naaman's leprosy will cling to you and to your descendants forever." Then Gehazi went from Elisha's presence and his skin was leprous—it had become as white as snow.

An Axhead Floats

6 The company of the prophets said to Elisha, "Look, the place where we meet with you is too small for us. ²Let us go to the Jordan, where each of us can get a pole; and let us build a place there for us to meet."

And he said, "Go."

³Then one of them said, "Won't you please come with your servants?"

"I will," Elisha replied. ⁴And he went with them.

They went to the Jordan and began to cut down trees. ⁵As one of them was cutting down a tree, the iron axhead fell into the water. "Oh no, my lord!" he cried out. "It was borrowed!"

⁶The man of God asked, "Where did it fall?" When he showed him the place, Elisha cut a stick and threw it there, and made the iron float. ⁷"Lift it out," he said. Then the man reached out his hand and took it.

a 22 That is, about 75 pounds or about 34 kilograms

Elisha Traps Blinded Arameans

⁸Now the king of Aram was at war with Israel. After conferring with his officers, he said, "I will set up my camp in such and such a place."

⁹The man of God sent word to the king of Israel: "Beware of passing that place, because the Arameans are going down there." ¹⁰So the king of Israel checked on the place indicated by the man of God. Time and again Elisha warned the king, so that he was on his guard in such places.

¹¹This enraged the king of Aram. He summoned his officers and demanded of them, "Tell me! Which of us is on the side of the king of Israel?"

¹²"None of us, my lord the king," said one of his officers, "but Elisha, the prophet who is in Israel, tells the king of Israel the very words you speak in your bedroom."

¹³"Go, find out where he is," the king ordered, "so I can send men and capture him." The report came back: "He is in Dothan." ¹⁴Then he sent horses and chariots and a strong force there. They went by night and surrounded the city.

¹⁵When the servant of the man of God got up and went out early the next morning, an army with horses and chariots had surrounded the city. "Oh no, my lord! What shall we do?" the servant asked.

¹⁶"Don't be afraid," the prophet answered. "Those who are with us are more than those who are with them."

¹⁷And Elisha prayed, "Open his eyes, LORD, so that he may see." Then the LORD opened the servant's eyes, and he looked and saw the hills full of horses and chariots of fire all around Elisha.

¹⁸As the enemy came down toward him, Elisha prayed to the LORD, "Strike this army with blindness." So he struck them with blindness, as Elisha had asked.

¹⁹Elisha told them, "This is not the road and this is not the city. Follow me, and I will lead you to the man you are looking for." And he led them to Samaria.

²⁰After they entered the city, Elisha said, "LORD, open the eyes of these men so they can see." Then the LORD opened their eyes and they looked, and there they were, inside Samaria.

²¹When the king of Israel saw them, he asked Elisha, "Shall I kill them, my father? Shall I kill them?"

²²"Do not kill them," he answered. "Would you kill those you have captured with your own sword or bow? Set food and water before them so that they may eat and drink and then go back to their master." ²³So he prepared a great feast for them, and after they had finished eating and drinking, he sent them away, and they returned to their master. So the bands from Aram stopped raiding Israel's territory.

Famine in Besieged Samaria

²⁴Some time later, Ben-Hadad king of Aram mobilized his entire army and marched up and laid siege to Samaria. ²⁵There was a great famine in the city; the siege lasted so long that a donkey's head sold for eighty shekels*ᵃ* of silver, and a quarter of a cab*ᵇ* of seed pods*ᶜ* for five shekels.*ᵈ*

²⁶As the king of Israel was passing by on the wall, a woman cried to him, "Help me, my lord the king!"

²⁷The king replied, "If the LORD does not help you, where can I get help for you? From the threshing floor? From the winepress?" ²⁸Then he asked her, "What's the matter?"

She answered, "This woman said to me, 'Give up your son so we may eat him today, and tomorrow we'll eat my son.' ²⁹So we cooked my son and ate him. The next day I said to her, 'Give up your son so we may eat him,' but she had hidden him."

³⁰When the king heard the woman's words, he tore his robes. As he went along the wall, the people looked, and they saw that, under his robes, he had sackcloth on his body. ³¹He said, "May God deal with me, be it ever so severely, if the head of Elisha son of Shaphat remains on his shoulders today!"

³²Now Elisha was sitting in his house, and the elders were sitting with him. The king sent a messenger ahead, but before he arrived, Elisha said to the elders, "Don't you see how this murderer is sending someone to cut off my head? Look, when the messenger comes, shut the door and hold it shut against him. Is not the sound of his master's footsteps behind him?" ³³While he was still

---

ᵃ 25 That is, about 2 pounds or about 920 grams   *ᵇ 25* That is, probably about 1/4 pound or about 100 grams   *ᶜ 25* Or *of doves' dung*   *ᵈ 25* That is, about 2 ounces or about 55 grams

MONDAY

SHIFT INTO HEAVENLY GEAR

2 Kings 6:8–22 or 6:16–17

ALEXANDER MACLAREN {AD 1826–1910}

Try to fully understand what God is to you: He is your Savior and your God (see Psalm 43:5). Grasping this truth will energize an apathetic heart and will calm troubled emotions. A person that can cry, "My God!"—and can rest in that relationship with God—will not be easily moved to either exuberance or woe by the trivialities and temporary things of this life. There is a wonderful calming power in apprehending our possession of God as our portion. I am quite sure that the troubles and the pleasures of our lives, which often distract, would have far less power to disturb us if we felt more that God was ours and that we were God's.

Brothers and sisters, to be at rest is better than rapture. And it is impossible to obtain and maintain a steady disposition of still tranquility unless we go into that deep and hidden chamber—the secret place of the Most High—where we can dwell in security, no matter what storms harass the land. "Why, my soul, are you downcast? Why so disturbed within me?" (Psalm 43:5). Hope in God and be at rest.

John Ortberg

Many followers of Christ need to hear the words: "Don't be afraid . . . Those who are with us are more than those who are with them." Whatever we face—problems, challenges, difficulties, fears or worries—we all have times we need to have our eyes shifted from earthly to heavenly realities. Sometimes we need to ask God to show us what is happening in the heavenly realms so that we can walk with courage in this life.

At other times, we must pray for faith to believe what our eyes cannot see. Like the servant of Elisha, we need to learn that those who are with us, when we stand with the Lord, are always more than those who are with them.

reflection

1. How can a person find hope in God and be at rest in him while in the middle of painful, stressful times?
2. What situations do you face right now that trouble you most?
3. Have you asked God to open your eyes to the spiritual resources you have on your side?

For your next devotional reading, go to page 423.

talking to them, the messenger came down to him.

The king said, "This disaster is from the LORD. Why should I wait for the LORD any longer?"

7 Elisha replied, "Hear the word of the LORD. This is what the LORD says: About this time tomorrow, a seah*a* of the finest flour will sell for a shekel*b* and two seahs*c* of barley for a shekel at the gate of Samaria."

²The officer on whose arm the king was leaning said to the man of God, "Look, even if the LORD should open the floodgates of the heavens, could this happen?"

"You will see it with your own eyes," answered Elisha, "but you will not eat any of it!"

The Siege Lifted

³Now there were four men with leprosy*d* at the entrance of the city gate. They said to each other, "Why stay here until we die? ⁴If we say, 'We'll go into the city'—the famine is there, and we will die. And if we stay here, we will die. So let's go over to the camp of the Arameans and surrender. If they spare us, we live; if they kill us, then we die."

⁵At dusk they got up and went to the camp of the Arameans. When they reached the edge of the camp, no one was there, ⁶for the Lord had caused the Arameans to hear the sound of chariots and horses and a great army, so that they said to one another, "Look, the king of Israel has hired the Hittite and Egyptian kings to attack us!" ⁷So they got up and fled in the dusk and abandoned their tents and their horses and donkeys. They left the camp as it was and ran for their lives.

⁸The men who had leprosy reached the edge of the camp, entered one of the tents and ate and drank. Then they took silver, gold and clothes, and went off and hid them. They returned and entered another tent and took some things from it and hid them also.

⁹Then they said to each other, "What we're doing is not right. This is a day of good news and we are keeping it to ourselves. If we wait until daylight, punishment will overtake us. Let's go at once and report this to the royal palace."

¹⁰So they went and called out to the city gatekeepers and told them, "We went into the Aramean camp and no one was there—not a sound of anyone—only tethered horses and donkeys, and the tents left just as they were." ¹¹The gatekeepers shouted the news, and it was reported within the palace.

¹²The king got up in the night and said to his officers, "I will tell you what the Arameans have done to us. They know we are starving; so they have left the camp to hide in the countryside, thinking, 'They will surely come out, and then we will take them alive and get into the city.'"

¹³One of his officers answered, "Have some men take five of the horses that are left in the city. Their plight will be like that of all the Israelites left here—yes, they will only be like all these Israelites who are doomed. So let us send them to find out what happened."

¹⁴So they selected two chariots with their horses, and the king sent them after the Aramean army. He commanded the drivers, "Go and find out what has happened." ¹⁵They followed them as far as the Jordan, and they found the whole road strewn with the clothing and equipment the Arameans had thrown away in their headlong flight. So the messengers returned and reported to the king. ¹⁶Then the people went out and plundered the camp of the Arameans. So a seah of the finest flour sold for a shekel, and two seahs of barley sold for a shekel, as the LORD had said.

¹⁷Now the king had put the officer on whose arm he leaned in charge of the gate, and the people trampled him in the gateway, and he died, just as the man of God had foretold when the king came down to his house. ¹⁸It happened as the man of God had said to the king: "About this time tomorrow, a seah of the finest flour will sell for a shekel and two seahs of barley for a shekel at the gate of Samaria."

¹⁹The officer had said to the man of God, "Look, even if the LORD should open the floodgates of the heavens, could this happen?" The man of God had replied, "You will

---

a 1 That is, probably about 12 pounds or about 5.6 kilograms; also in verses 16 and 18   *b 1* That is, about 2/5 ounce or about 11.5 grams; also in verses 16 and 18   *c 1* That is, probably about 20 pounds or about 9 kilograms; also in verses 16 and 18   *d 3* The Hebrew for *leprosy* was used for various diseases affecting the skin; also in verse 8.

see it with your own eyes, but you will not eat any of it!" ²⁰And that is exactly what happened to him, for the people trampled him in the gateway, and he died.

The Shunammite's Land Restored

8 Now Elisha had said to the woman whose son he had restored to life, "Go away with your family and stay for a while wherever you can, because the LORD has decreed a famine in the land that will last seven years." ²The woman proceeded to do as the man of God said. She and her family went away and stayed in the land of the Philistines seven years.

³At the end of the seven years she came back from the land of the Philistines and went to appeal to the king for her house and land. ⁴The king was talking to Gehazi, the servant of the man of God, and had said, "Tell me about all the great things Elisha has done." ⁵Just as Gehazi was telling the king how Elisha had restored the dead to life, the woman whose son Elisha had brought back to life came to appeal to the king for her house and land.

Gehazi said, "This is the woman, my lord the king, and this is her son whom Elisha restored to life." ⁶The king asked the woman about it, and she told him.

Then he assigned an official to her case and said to him, "Give back everything that belonged to her, including all the income from her land from the day she left the country until now."

Hazael Murders Ben-Hadad

⁷Elisha went to Damascus, and Ben-Hadad king of Aram was ill. When the king was told, "The man of God has come all the way up here," ⁸he said to Hazael, "Take a gift with you and go to meet the man of God. Consult the LORD through him; ask him, 'Will I recover from this illness?'"

⁹Hazael went to meet Elisha, taking with him as a gift forty camel-loads of all the finest wares of Damascus. He went in and stood before him, and said, "Your son Ben-Hadad king of Aram has sent me to ask, 'Will I recover from this illness?'"

¹⁰Elisha answered, "Go and say to him, 'You will certainly recover.' Nevertheless,^a

the LORD has revealed to me that he will in fact die." ¹¹He stared at him with a fixed gaze until Hazael was embarrassed. Then the man of God began to weep.

¹²"Why is my lord weeping?" asked Hazael.

"Because I know the harm you will do to the Israelites," he answered. "You will set fire to their fortified places, kill their young men with the sword, dash their little children to the ground, and rip open their pregnant women."

¹³Hazael said, "How could your servant, a mere dog, accomplish such a feat?"

"The LORD has shown me that you will become king of Aram," answered Elisha.

¹⁴Then Hazael left Elisha and returned to his master. When Ben-Hadad asked, "What did Elisha say to you?" Hazael replied, "He told me that you would certainly recover." ¹⁵But the next day he took a thick cloth, soaked it in water and spread it over the king's face, so that he died. Then Hazael succeeded him as king.

Jehoram King of Judah

¹⁶In the fifth year of Joram son of Ahab king of Israel, when Jehoshaphat was king of Judah, Jehoram son of Jehoshaphat began his reign as king of Judah. ¹⁷He was thirty-two years old when he became king, and he reigned in Jerusalem eight years. ¹⁸He followed the ways of the kings of Israel, as the house of Ahab had done, for he married a daughter of Ahab. He did evil in the eyes of the LORD. ¹⁹Nevertheless, for the sake of his servant David, the LORD was not willing to destroy Judah. He had promised to maintain a lamp for David and his descendants forever.

²⁰In the time of Jehoram, Edom rebelled against Judah and set up its own king. ²¹So Jehoram^b went to Zair with all his chariots. The Edomites surrounded him and his chariot commanders, but he rose up and broke through by night; his army, however, fled back home. ²²To this day Edom has been in rebellion against Judah. Libnah revolted at the same time.

²³As for the other events of Jehoram's reign, and all he did, are they not written in the book of the annals of the kings of Judah? ²⁴Jehoram rested with his ancestors and was

---

^a 10 The Hebrew may also be read *Go and say, 'You will certainly not recover,' for.* ^b 21 Hebrew *Joram,* a variant of *Jehoram*; also in verses 23 and 24

buried with them in the City of David. And Ahaziah his son succeeded him as king.

Ahaziah King of Judah

25In the twelfth year of Joram son of Ahab king of Israel, Ahaziah son of Jehoram king of Judah began to reign. 26Ahaziah was twenty-two years old when he became king, and he reigned in Jerusalem one year. His mother's name was Athaliah, a granddaughter of Omri king of Israel. 27He followed the ways of the house of Ahab and did evil in the eyes of the LORD, as the house of Ahab had done, for he was related by marriage to Ahab's family.

28Ahaziah went with Joram son of Ahab to war against Hazael king of Aram at Ramoth Gilead. The Arameans wounded Joram; 29so King Joram returned to Jezreel to recover from the wounds the Arameans had inflicted on him at Ramoth*a* in his battle with Hazael king of Aram.

Then Ahaziah son of Jehoram king of Judah went down to Jezreel to see Joram son of Ahab, because he had been wounded.

Jehu Anointed King of Israel

9 The prophet Elisha summoned a man from the company of the prophets and said to him, "Tuck your cloak into your belt, take this flask of oil with you and go to Ramoth Gilead. 2When you get there, look for Jehu son of Jehoshaphat, the son of Nimshi. Go to him, get him away from his companions and take him into an inner room. 3Then take the flask and pour the oil on his head and declare, 'This is what the LORD says: I anoint you king over Israel.' Then open the door and run; don't delay!"

4So the young prophet went to Ramoth Gilead. 5When he arrived, he found the army officers sitting together. "I have a message for you, commander," he said.

"For which of us?" asked Jehu.

"For you, commander," he replied.

6Jehu got up and went into the house. Then the prophet poured the oil on Jehu's head and declared, "This is what the LORD, the God of Israel, says: 'I anoint you king over the LORD's people Israel. 7You are to destroy the house of Ahab your master, and I will avenge the blood of my servants the

prophets and the blood of all the LORD's servants shed by Jezebel. 8The whole house of Ahab will perish. I will cut off from Ahab every last male in Israel—slave or free.*b* 9I will make the house of Ahab like the house of Jeroboam son of Nebat and like the house of Baasha son of Ahijah. 10As for Jezebel, dogs will devour her on the plot of ground at Jezreel, and no one will bury her.' " Then he opened the door and ran.

11When Jehu went out to his fellow officers, one of them asked him, "Is everything all right? Why did this maniac come to you?"

"You know the man and the sort of things he says," Jehu replied.

12"That's not true!" they said. "Tell us."

Jehu said, "Here is what he told me: 'This is what the LORD says: I anoint you king over Israel.' "

13They quickly took their cloaks and spread them under him on the bare steps. Then they blew the trumpet and shouted, "Jehu is king!"

Jehu Kills Joram and Ahaziah

14So Jehu son of Jehoshaphat, the son of Nimshi, conspired against Joram. (Now Joram and all Israel had been defending Ramoth Gilead against Hazael king of Aram, 15but King Joram*c* had returned to Jezreel to recover from the wounds the Arameans had inflicted on him in the battle with Hazael king of Aram.) Jehu said, "If you desire to make me king, don't let anyone slip out of the city to go and tell the news in Jezreel." 16Then he got into his chariot and rode to Jezreel, because Joram was resting there and Ahaziah king of Judah had gone down to see him.

17When the lookout standing on the tower in Jezreel saw Jehu's troops approaching, he called out, "I see some troops coming."

"Get a horseman," Joram ordered. "Send him to meet them and ask, 'Do you come in peace?' "

18The horseman rode off to meet Jehu and said, "This is what the king says: 'Do you come in peace?' "

"What do you have to do with peace?" Jehu replied. "Fall in behind me."

The lookout reported, "The messenger

a 29 Hebrew Ramah, a variant of Ramoth   b 8 Or Israel—every ruler or leader   c 15 Hebrew Jehoram, a variant of Joram; also in verses 17 and 21-24 has reached them, but he isn't coming back."

¹⁹So the king sent out a second horseman. When he came to them he said, "This is what the king says: 'Do you come in peace?' "

Jehu replied, "What do you have to do with peace? Fall in behind me."

²⁰The lookout reported, "He has reached them, but he isn't coming back either. The driving is like that of Jehu son of Nimshi—he drives like a maniac."

²¹"Hitch up my chariot," Joram ordered. And when it was hitched up, Joram king of Israel and Ahaziah king of Judah rode out, each in his own chariot, to meet Jehu. They met him at the plot of ground that had belonged to Naboth the Jezreelite. ²²When Joram saw Jehu he asked, "Have you come in peace, Jehu?"

"How can there be peace," Jehu replied, "as long as all the idolatry and witchcraft of your mother Jezebel abound?"

²³Joram turned about and fled, calling out to Ahaziah, "Treachery, Ahaziah!"

²⁴Then Jehu drew his bow and shot Joram between the shoulders. The arrow pierced his heart and he slumped down in his chariot. ²⁵Jehu said to Bidkar, his chariot officer, "Pick him up and throw him on the field that belonged to Naboth the Jezreelite. Remember how you and I were riding together in chariots behind Ahab his father when the LORD spoke this prophecy against him: ²⁶'Yesterday I saw the blood of Naboth and the blood of his sons, declares the LORD, and I will surely make you pay for it on this plot of ground, declares the LORD.'ᵃ Now then, pick him up and throw him on that plot, in accordance with the word of the LORD."

²⁷When Ahaziah king of Judah saw what had happened, he fled up the road to Beth Haggan.ᵇ Jehu chased him, shouting, "Kill him too!" They wounded him in his chariot on the way up to Gur near Ibleam, but he escaped to Megiddo and died there. ²⁸His servants took him by chariot to Jerusalem and buried him with his ancestors in his tomb in the City of David. ²⁹(In the eleventh year of Joram son of Ahab, Ahaziah had become king of Judah.)

Jezebel Killed

³⁰Then Jehu went to Jezreel. When Jezebel heard about it, she painted her eyes, arranged her hair and looked out of a window. ³¹As Jehu entered the gate, she asked, "Have you come in peace, you Zimri, you murderer of your master?"ᶜ

³²He looked up at the window and called out, "Who is on my side? Who?" Two or three eunuchs looked down at him. ³³"Throw her down!" Jehu said. So they threw her down, and some of her blood spattered the wall and the horses as they trampled her underfoot.

³⁴Jehu went in and ate and drank. "Take care of that cursed woman," he said, "and bury her, for she was a king's daughter." ³⁵But when they went out to bury her, they found nothing except her skull, her feet and her hands. ³⁶They went back and told Jehu, who said, "This is the word of the LORD that he spoke through his servant Elijah the Tishbite: On the plot of ground at Jezreel dogs will devour Jezebel's flesh.ᵈ ³⁷Jezebel's body will be like dung on the ground in the plot at Jezreel, so that no one will be able to say, 'This is Jezebel.' "

Ahab's Family Killed

10 Now there were in Samaria seventy sons of the house of Ahab. So Jehu wrote letters and sent them to Samaria: to the officials of Jezreel,ᵉ to the elders and to the guardians of Ahab's children. He said, ²"You have your master's sons with you and you have chariots and horses, a fortified city and weapons. Now as soon as this letter reaches you, ³choose the best and most worthy of your master's sons and set him on his father's throne. Then fight for your master's house."

⁴But they were terrified and said, "If two kings could not resist him, how can we?"

⁵So the palace administrator, the city governor, the elders and the guardians sent this message to Jehu: "We are your servants and we will do anything you say. We will not appoint anyone as king; you do whatever you think best."

⁶Then Jehu wrote them a second letter, saying, "If you are on my side and will obey me, take the heads of your master's sons

---

ᵃ 26 See 1 Kings 21:19.   ᵇ 27 Or fled by way of the garden house   ᶜ 31 Or "Was there peace for Zimri, who murdered his master?"   ᵈ 36 See 1 Kings 21:23.   ᵉ 1 Hebrew; some Septuagint manuscripts and Vulgate of the city and come to me in Jezreel by this time tomorrow."

Now the royal princes, seventy of them, were with the leading men of the city, who were rearing them. [7]When the letter arrived, they took the princes and slaughtered all seventy of them. They put their heads in baskets and sent them to Jehu in Jezreel. [8]When the messenger arrived, he told Jehu, "They have brought the heads of the princes."

Then Jehu ordered, "Put them in two piles at the entrance of the city gate until morning."

[9]The next morning Jehu went out. He stood before all the people and said, "You are innocent. It was I who conspired against my master and killed him, but who killed all these? [10]Know, then, that not a word the LORD has spoken against the house of Ahab will fail. The LORD has done what he announced through his servant Elijah." [11]So Jehu killed everyone in Jezreel who remained of the house of Ahab, as well as all his chief men, his close friends and his priests, leaving him no survivor.

[12]Jehu then set out and went toward Samaria. At Beth Eked of the Shepherds, [13]he met some relatives of Ahaziah king of Judah and asked, "Who are you?"

They said, "We are relatives of Ahaziah, and we have come down to greet the families of the king and of the queen mother."

[14]"Take them alive!" he ordered. So they took them alive and slaughtered them by the well of Beth Eked—forty-two of them. He left no survivor.

[15]After he left there, he came upon Jehonadab son of Rekab, who was on his way to meet him. Jehu greeted him and said, "Are you in accord with me, as I am with you?"

"I am," Jehonadab answered.

"If so," said Jehu, "give me your hand." So he did, and Jehu helped him up into the chariot. [16]Jehu said, "Come with me and see my zeal for the LORD." Then he had him ride along in his chariot.

[17]When Jehu came to Samaria, he killed all who were left there of Ahab's family; he destroyed them, according to the word of the LORD spoken to Elijah.

Servants of Baal Killed

[18]Then Jehu brought all the people together and said to them, "Ahab served Baal a little; Jehu will serve him much. [19]Now summon all the prophets of Baal, all his servants and all his priests. See that no one is missing, because I am going to hold a great sacrifice for Baal. Anyone who fails to come will no longer live." But Jehu was acting deceptively in order to destroy the servants of Baal.

[20]Jehu said, "Call an assembly in honor of Baal." So they proclaimed it. [21]Then he sent word throughout Israel, and all the servants of Baal came; not one stayed away. They crowded into the temple of Baal until it was full from one end to the other. [22]And Jehu said to the keeper of the wardrobe, "Bring robes for all the servants of Baal." So he brought out robes for them.

[23]Then Jehu and Jehonadab son of Rekab went into the temple of Baal. Jehu said to the servants of Baal, "Look around and see that no one who serves the LORD is here with you—only servants of Baal." [24]So they went in to make sacrifices and burnt offerings. Now Jehu had posted eighty men outside with this warning: "If one of you lets any of the men I am placing in your hands escape, it will be your life for his life."

[25]As soon as Jehu had finished making the burnt offering, he ordered the guards and officers: "Go in and kill them; let no one escape." So they cut them down with the sword. The guards and officers threw the bodies out and then entered the inner shrine of the temple of Baal. [26]They brought the sacred stone out of the temple of Baal and burned it. [27]They demolished the sacred stone of Baal and tore down the temple of Baal, and people have used it for a latrine to this day.

[28]So Jehu destroyed Baal worship in Israel. [29]However, he did not turn away from the sins of Jeroboam son of Nebat, which he had caused Israel to commit—the worship of the golden calves at Bethel and Dan.

[30]The LORD said to Jehu, "Because you have done well in accomplishing what is right in my eyes and have done to the house of Ahab all I had in mind to do, your descendants will sit on the throne of Israel to the fourth generation." [31]Yet Jehu was not careful to keep the law of the LORD, the God of Israel, with all his heart. He did not turn away from the sins of Jeroboam, which he had caused Israel to commit.

[32]In those days the LORD began to reduce

the size of Israel. Hazael overpowered the Israelites throughout their territory ³³east of the Jordan in all the land of Gilead (the region of Gad, Reuben and Manasseh), from Aroer by the Arnon Gorge through Gilead to Bashan.

³⁴As for the other events of Jehu's reign, all he did, and all his achievements, are they not written in the book of the annals of the kings of Israel?

³⁵Jehu rested with his ancestors and was buried in Samaria. And Jehoahaz his son succeeded him as king. ³⁶The time that Jehu reigned over Israel in Samaria was twenty-eight years.

Athaliah and Joash

11 When Athaliah the mother of Ahaziah saw that her son was dead, she proceeded to destroy the whole royal family. ²But Jehosheba, the daughter of King Jehoram*a* and sister of Ahaziah, took Joash son of Ahaziah and stole him away from among the royal princes, who were about to be murdered. She put him and his nurse in a bedroom to hide him from Athaliah; so he was not killed. ³He remained hidden with his nurse at the temple of the Lord for six years while Athaliah ruled the land.

⁴In the seventh year Jehoiada sent for the commanders of units of a hundred, the Carites and the guards and had them brought to him at the temple of the Lord. He made a covenant with them and put them under oath at the temple of the Lord. Then he showed them the king's son. ⁵He commanded them, saying, "This is what you are to do: You who are in the three companies that are going on duty on the Sabbath—a third of you guarding the royal palace, ⁶a third at the Sur Gate, and a third at the gate behind the guard, who take turns guarding the temple— ⁷and you who are in the other two companies that normally go off Sabbath duty are all to guard the temple for the king. ⁸Station yourselves around the king, each of you with weapon in hand. Anyone who approaches your ranks*b* is to be put to death. Stay close to the king wherever he goes."

⁹The commanders of units of a hundred did just as Jehoiada the priest ordered. Each one took his men—those who were going on duty on the Sabbath and those who were going off duty—and came to Jehoiada the priest. ¹⁰Then he gave the commanders the spears and shields that had belonged to King David and that were in the temple of the Lord. ¹¹The guards, each with weapon in hand, stationed themselves around the king—near the altar and the temple, from the south side to the north side of the temple.

¹²Jehoiada brought out the king's son and put the crown on him; he presented him with a copy of the covenant and proclaimed him king. They anointed him, and the people clapped their hands and shouted, "Long live the king!"

¹³When Athaliah heard the noise made by the guards and the people, she went to the people at the temple of the Lord. ¹⁴She looked and there was the king, standing by the pillar, as the custom was. The officers and the trumpeters were beside the king, and all the people of the land were rejoicing and blowing trumpets. Then Athaliah tore her robes and called out, "Treason! Treason!"

¹⁵Jehoiada the priest ordered the commanders of units of a hundred, who were in charge of the troops: "Bring her out between the ranks*c* and put to the sword anyone who follows her." For the priest had said, "She must not be put to death in the temple of the Lord." ¹⁶So they seized her as she reached the place where the horses enter the palace grounds, and there she was put to death.

¹⁷Jehoiada then made a covenant between the Lord and the king and people that they would be the Lord's people. He also made a covenant between the king and the people. ¹⁸All the people of the land went to the temple of Baal and tore it down. They smashed the altars and idols to pieces and killed Mattan the priest of Baal in front of the altars.

Then Jehoiada the priest posted guards at the temple of the Lord. ¹⁹He took with him the commanders of hundreds, the Carites, the guards and all the people of the land, and together they brought the king down from the temple of the Lord and went into the palace, entering by way of the gate of the guards. The king then took his place on

a 2 Hebrew *Joram,* a variant of *Jehoram*   *b 8* Or *approaches the precincts*   *c 15* Or *out from the precincts* the royal throne. ²⁰All the people of the land rejoiced, and the city was calm, because Athaliah had been slain with the sword at the palace.

*²¹Joash*ᵃ* was seven years old when he began to reign.

Joash Repairs the Temple

12 *In the seventh year of Jehu, Joash*ᵇ* became king, and he reigned in Jerusalem forty years. His mother's name was Zibiah; she was from Beersheba. ²Joash did what was right in the eyes of the Lord all the years Jehoiada the priest instructed him. ³The high places, however, were not removed; the people continued to offer sacrifices and burn incense there.

⁴Joash said to the priests, "Collect all the money that is brought as sacred offerings to the temple of the Lord—the money collected in the census, the money received from personal vows and the money brought voluntarily to the temple. ⁵Let every priest receive the money from one of the treasurers, then use it to repair whatever damage is found in the temple."

⁶But by the twenty-third year of King Joash the priests still had not repaired the temple. ⁷Therefore King Joash summoned Jehoiada the priest and the other priests and asked them, "Why aren't you repairing the damage done to the temple? Take no more money from your treasurers, but hand it over for repairing the temple." ⁸The priests agreed that they would not collect any more money from the people and that they would not repair the temple themselves.

⁹Jehoiada the priest took a chest and bored a hole in its lid. He placed it beside the altar, on the right side as one enters the temple of the Lord. The priests who guarded the entrance put into the chest all the money that was brought to the temple of the Lord. ¹⁰Whenever they saw that there was a large amount of money in the chest, the royal secretary and the high priest came, counted the money that had been brought into the temple of the Lord and put it into bags. ¹¹When the amount had been determined, they gave the money to the men ap-

pointed to supervise the work on the temple. With it they paid those who worked on the temple of the Lord—the carpenters and builders, ¹²the masons and stonecutters. They purchased timber and blocks of dressed stone for the repair of the temple of the Lord, and met all the other expenses of restoring the temple.

¹³The money brought into the temple was not spent for making silver basins, wick trimmers, sprinkling bowls, trumpets or any other articles of gold or silver for the temple of the Lord; ¹⁴it was paid to the workers, who used it to repair the temple. ¹⁵They did not require an accounting from those to whom they gave the money to pay the workers, because they acted with complete honesty. ¹⁶The money from the guilt offerings and sin offerings*ᶜ* was not brought into the temple of the Lord; it belonged to the priests.

¹⁷About this time Hazael king of Aram went up and attacked Gath and captured it. Then he turned to attack Jerusalem. ¹⁸But Joash king of Judah took all the sacred objects dedicated by his predecessors—Jehoshaphat, Jehoram and Ahaziah, the kings of Judah—and the gifts he himself had dedicated and all the gold found in the treasuries of the temple of the Lord and of the royal palace, and he sent them to Hazael king of Aram, who then withdrew from Jerusalem.

¹⁹As for the other events of the reign of Joash, and all he did, are they not written in the book of the annals of the kings of Judah? ²⁰His officials conspired against him and assassinated him at Beth Millo, on the road down to Silla. ²¹The officials who murdered him were Jozabad son of Shimeath and Jehozabad son of Shomer. He died and was buried with his ancestors in the City of David. And Amaziah his son succeeded him as king.

Jehoahaz King of Israel

13 In the twenty-third year of Joash son of Ahaziah king of Judah, Jehoahaz son of Jehu became king of Israel in Samaria, and he reigned seventeen years. ²He did evil in the eyes of the Lord by following the sins of Jeroboam son

---

ᵃ 21 Hebrew *Jehoash,* a variant of *Joash*   *ᵇ 1* Hebrew *Jehoash,* a variant of *Joash;* also in verses 2, 4, 6, 7 and 18   *ᶜ 16* Or *purification offerings*

* 11:21 is numbered 12:1 in Hebrew texts.   * 12:1-21 is numbered 12:2-22 in Hebrew texts.

of Nebat, which he had caused Israel to commit, and he did not turn away from them. ³So the LORD's anger burned against Israel, and for a long time he kept them under the power of Hazael king of Aram and Ben-Hadad his son.

⁴Then Jehoahaz sought the LORD's favor, and the LORD listened to him, for he saw how severely the king of Aram was oppressing Israel. ⁵The LORD provided a deliverer for Israel, and they escaped from the power of Aram. So the Israelites lived in their own homes as they had before. ⁶But they did not turn away from the sins of the house of Jeroboam, which he had caused Israel to commit; they continued in them. Also, the Asherah pole*a* remained standing in Samaria.

⁷Nothing had been left of the army of Jehoahaz except fifty horsemen, ten chariots and ten thousand foot soldiers, for the king of Aram had destroyed the rest and made them like the dust at threshing time.

⁸As for the other events of the reign of Jehoahaz, all he did and his achievements, are they not written in the book of the annals of the kings of Israel? ⁹Jehoahaz rested with his ancestors and was buried in Samaria. And Jehoash*b* his son succeeded him as king.

Jehoash King of Israel

¹⁰In the thirty-seventh year of Joash king of Judah, Jehoash son of Jehoahaz became king of Israel in Samaria, and he reigned sixteen years. ¹¹He did evil in the eyes of the LORD and did not turn away from any of the sins of Jeroboam son of Nebat, which he had caused Israel to commit; he continued in them.

¹²As for the other events of the reign of Jehoash, all he did and his achievements, including his war against Amaziah king of Judah, are they not written in the book of the annals of the kings of Israel? ¹³Jehoash rested with his ancestors, and Jeroboam succeeded him on the throne. Jehoash was buried in Samaria with the kings of Israel.

¹⁴Now Elisha was suffering from the illness from which he died. Jehoash king of Israel went down to see him and wept over him. "My father! My father!" he cried. "The chariots and horsemen of Israel!"

¹⁵Elisha said, "Get a bow and some arrows," and he did so. ¹⁶"Take the bow in your hands," he said to the king of Israel. When he had taken it, Elisha put his hands on the king's hands.

¹⁷"Open the east window," he said, and he opened it. "Shoot!" Elisha said, and he shot. "The LORD's arrow of victory, the arrow of victory over Aram!" Elisha declared. "You will completely destroy the Arameans at Aphek."

¹⁸Then he said, "Take the arrows," and the king took them. Elisha told him, "Strike the ground." He struck it three times and stopped. ¹⁹The man of God was angry with him and said, "You should have struck the ground five or six times; then you would have defeated Aram and completely destroyed it. But now you will defeat it only three times."

²⁰Elisha died and was buried.

Now Moabite raiders used to enter the country every spring. ²¹Once while some Israelites were burying a man, suddenly they saw a band of raiders; so they threw the man's body into Elisha's tomb. When the body touched Elisha's bones, the man came to life and stood up on his feet.

²²Hazael king of Aram oppressed Israel throughout the reign of Jehoahaz. ²³But the LORD was gracious to them and had compassion and showed concern for them because of his covenant with Abraham, Isaac and Jacob. To this day he has been unwilling to destroy them or banish them from his presence.

²⁴Hazael king of Aram died, and Ben-Hadad his son succeeded him as king. ²⁵Then Jehoash son of Jehoahaz recaptured from Ben-Hadad son of Hazael the towns he had taken in battle from his father Jehoahaz. Three times Jehoash defeated him, and so he recovered the Israelite towns.

Amaziah King of Judah

14 In the second year of Jehoash*c* son of Jehoahaz king of Israel, Amaziah son of Joash king of Judah began to reign. ²He was twenty-five years old when he became king, and he reigned in Jerusalem twenty-nine years. His mother's name was Jehoaddan; she was

---

a 6 That is, a wooden symbol of the goddess Asherah; here and elsewhere in 2 Kings *b 9* Hebrew *Joash,* a variant of *Jehoash;* also in verses 12-14 and 25 *c 1* Hebrew *Joash,* a variant of *Jehoash;* also in verses 13, 23 and 27

TUESDAY

STATE OF THE HEART

2 Kings 14:1–22 *or* 14:1–4

CHARLES G. FINNEY {AD 1792–1875}

Whosoever keeps the whole law yet offends at one point is guilty of all (see James 2:10). He is rightly subject to the whole penalty. If he habitually disobeys God in one thing, then he doesn't obey him in anything, because obedience to God consists in an attitude of the heart. It is willingness to obey God, to let him rule everything. So if a person habitually disobeys God in one thing, his state of heart renders obedience in anything else impossible, because a person can't in one area obey God out of respect for his authority while in another area refuse obedience.

Obedience to God is an obedient state of heart, a preference for God's authority and commandments over everything else. If a person therefore appears to obey in some areas yet he knowingly disobeys in others, he is deceived. He offends in one point, and this proves he is guilty of all; in other words, he doesn't obey from the heart at all . . . If a person refuses to obey God's law, even a single duty, he . . . has no true faith, and his outwardly spiritual acts are loathsome.

Henry Gariepy

Sin is a fatal disease of the heart. God alone has the cure. It was provided for all on Calvary. Praise God, the Divine Cardiologist gives us a new heart. He puts a new spirit within us. He performs the radical surgery that we need to become, in the words of the apostle Paul, "a new creation in Christ."

God also declares, "And I will put my Spirit in you" (Ezekiel 36:27). This is the secret of the spiritual heart transplant, of the transformation of life in Christ. The Holy Spirit does his creative work within us, of both regeneration and sanctification.

reflection

1. When Amaziah failed to remove the "high places"—places of idol worship that the Israelites were supposed to have destroyed (see Numbers 33:52)—what did he reveal about the state of his heart?

2. Why is it impossible for a person to be "good enough" to please God on his or her own? What does a person need instead?

3. What does genuine obedience to God look like? To what extent is your life characterized by this kind of obedience?

For your next devotional reading, go to page 432.

424 || 2 kings 14:3

from Jerusalem. ³He did what was right in the eyes of the LORD, but not as his father David had done. In everything he followed the example of his father Joash. ⁴The high places, however, were not removed; the people continued to offer sacrifices and burn incense there.

⁵After the kingdom was firmly in his grasp, he executed the officials who had murdered his father the king. ⁶Yet he did not put the children of the assassins to death, in accordance with what is written in the Book of the Law of Moses where the LORD commanded: "Parents are not to be put to death for their children, nor children put to death for their parents; each of you will die for your own sin." ᵃ

⁷He was the one who defeated ten thousand Edomites in the Valley of Salt and captured Sela in battle, calling it Joktheel, the name it has to this day.

⁸Then Amaziah sent messengers to Jehoash son of Jehoahaz, the son of Jehu, king of Israel, with the challenge: "Come, meet me face to face."

⁹But Jehoash king of Israel replied to Amaziah king of Judah: "A thistle in Lebanon sent a message to a cedar in Lebanon, 'Give your daughter to my son in marriage.' Then a wild beast in Lebanon came along and trampled the thistle underfoot. ¹⁰You have indeed defeated Edom and now you are arrogant. Glory in your victory, but stay at home! Why ask for trouble and cause your own downfall and that of Judah also?"

¹¹Amaziah, however, would not listen, so Jehoash king of Israel attacked. He and Amaziah king of Judah faced each other at Beth Shemesh in Judah. ¹²Judah was routed by Israel, and every man fled to his home. ¹³Jehoash king of Israel captured Amaziah king of Judah, the son of Joash, the son of Ahaziah, at Beth Shemesh. Then Jehoash went to Jerusalem and broke down the wall of Jerusalem from the Ephraim Gate to the Corner Gate—a section about four hundred cubits long.ᵇ ¹⁴He took all the gold and silver and all the articles found in the temple of the LORD and in the treasuries of the royal palace. He also took hostages and returned to Samaria.

¹⁵As for the other events of the reign of Jehoash, what he did and his achievements, including his war against Amaziah king of Judah, are they not written in the book of the annals of the kings of Israel? ¹⁶Jehoash rested with his ancestors and was buried in Samaria with the kings of Israel. And Jeroboam his son succeeded him as king.

¹⁷Amaziah son of Joash king of Judah lived for fifteen years after the death of Jehoash son of Jehoahaz king of Israel. ¹⁸As for the other events of Amaziah's reign, are they not written in the book of the annals of the kings of Judah?

¹⁹They conspired against him in Jerusalem, and he fled to Lachish, but they sent men after him to Lachish and killed him there. ²⁰He was brought back by horse and was buried in Jerusalem with his ancestors, in the City of David.

²¹Then all the people of Judah took Azariah,ᶜ who was sixteen years old, and made him king in place of his father Amaziah. ²²He was the one who rebuilt Elath and restored it to Judah after Amaziah rested with his ancestors.

Jeroboam II King of Israel

²³In the fifteenth year of Amaziah son of Joash king of Judah, Jeroboam son of Jehoash king of Israel became king in Samaria, and he reigned forty-one years. ²⁴He did evil in the eyes of the LORD and did not turn away from any of the sins of Jeroboam son of Nebat, which he had caused Israel to commit. ²⁵He was the one who restored the boundaries of Israel from Lebo Hamath to the Dead Sea,ᵈ in accordance with the word of the LORD, the God of Israel, spoken through his servant Jonah son of Amittai, the prophet from Gath Hepher.

²⁶The LORD had seen how bitterly everyone in Israel, whether slave or free, was suffering;ᵉ there was no one to help them. ²⁷And since the LORD had not said he would blot out the name of Israel from under heaven, he saved them by the hand of Jeroboam son of Jehoash.

²⁸As for the other events of Jeroboam's reign, all he did, and his military achievements, including how he recovered for Israel both Damascus and Hamath, which had belonged to Judah, are they not written in

---

ᵃ 6 Deut. 24:16   ᵇ 13 That is, about 600 feet or about 180 meters   ᶜ 21 Also called *Uzziah*
ᵈ 25 Hebrew *the Sea of the Arabah*   ᵉ 26 Or *Israel was suffering. They were without a ruler or leader, and*

the book of the annals of the kings of Israel? 29Jeroboam rested with his ancestors, the kings of Israel. And Zechariah his son succeeded him as king.

Azariah King of Judah

15 In the twenty-seventh year of Jeroboam king of Israel, Azariah^a son of Amaziah king of Judah began to reign. 2He was sixteen years old when he became king, and he reigned in Jerusalem fifty-two years. His mother's name was Jekoliah; she was from Jerusalem. 3He did what was right in the eyes of the LORD, just as his father Amaziah had done. 4The high places, however, were not removed; the people continued to offer sacrifices and burn incense there.

5The LORD afflicted the king with leprosy^b until the day he died, and he lived in a separate house.^c Jotham the king's son had charge of the palace and governed the people of the land.

6As for the other events of Azariah's reign, and all he did, are they not written in the book of the annals of the kings of Judah? 7Azariah rested with his ancestors and was buried near them in the City of David. And Jotham his son succeeded him as king.

Zechariah King of Israel

8In the thirty-eighth year of Azariah king of Judah, Zechariah son of Jeroboam became king of Israel in Samaria, and he reigned six months. 9He did evil in the eyes of the LORD, as his predecessors had done. He did not turn away from the sins of Jeroboam son of Nebat, which he had caused Israel to commit.

10Shallum son of Jabesh conspired against Zechariah. He attacked him in front of the people,^d assassinated him and succeeded him as king. 11The other events of Zechariah's reign are written in the book of the annals of the kings of Israel. 12So the word of the LORD spoken to Jehu was fulfilled: "Your descendants will sit on the throne of Israel to the fourth generation."^e

Shallum King of Israel

13Shallum son of Jabesh became king in the thirty-ninth year of Uzziah king of Judah, and he reigned in Samaria one month. 14Then Menahem son of Gadi went from Tirzah up to Samaria. He attacked Shallum son of Jabesh in Samaria, assassinated him and succeeded him as king.

15The other events of Shallum's reign, and the conspiracy he led, are written in the book of the annals of the kings of Israel.

16At that time Menahem, starting out from Tirzah, attacked Tiphsah and everyone in the city and its vicinity, because they refused to open their gates. He sacked Tiphsah and ripped open all the pregnant women.

Menahem King of Israel

17In the thirty-ninth year of Azariah king of Judah, Menahem son of Gadi became king of Israel, and he reigned in Samaria ten years. 18He did evil in the eyes of the LORD. During his entire reign he did not turn away from the sins of Jeroboam son of Nebat, which he had caused Israel to commit.

19Then Pul^f king of Assyria invaded the land, and Menahem gave him a thousand talents^g of silver to gain his support and strengthen his own hold on the kingdom. 20Menahem exacted this money from Israel. Every wealthy person had to contribute fifty shekels^h of silver to be given to the king of Assyria. So the king of Assyria withdrew and stayed in the land no longer.

21As for the other events of Menahem's reign, and all he did, are they not written in the book of the annals of the kings of Israel? 22Menahem rested with his ancestors. And Pekahiah his son succeeded him as king.

Pekahiah King of Israel

23In the fiftieth year of Azariah king of Judah, Pekahiah son of Menahem became king of Israel in Samaria, and he reigned two years. 24Pekahiah did evil in the eyes of the LORD. He did not turn away from the sins of Jeroboam son of Nebat, which he had caused Israel to commit, 25One of his chief officers, Pekah son of Remaliah, conspired

---

^a 1 Also called *Uzziah*; also in verses 6, 7, 8, 17, 23 and 27   ^b 5 The Hebrew for *leprosy* was used for various diseases affecting the skin.   ^c 5 Or *in a house where he was relieved of responsibilities*   ^d 10 Hebrew; some Septuagint manuscripts *in Ibleam*   ^e 12 2 Kings 10:30   ^f 19 Also called *Tiglath-Pileser*   ^g 19 That is, about 38 tons or about 34 metric tons   ^h 20 That is, about 1 1/4 pounds or about 575 grams

against him. Taking fifty Gileadites with him, he assassinated Pekahiah, along with Argob and Arieh, in the citadel of the royal palace at Samaria. So Pekah killed Pekahiah and succeeded him as king.

26The other events of Pekahiah's reign, and all he did, are written in the book of the annals of the kings of Israel.

Pekah King of Israel

27In the fifty-second year of Azariah king of Judah, Pekah son of Remaliah became king of Israel in Samaria, and he reigned twenty years. 28He did evil in the eyes of the Lord. He did not turn away from the sins of Jeroboam son of Nebat, which he had caused Israel to commit.

29In the time of Pekah king of Israel, Tiglath-Pileser king of Assyria came and took Ijon, Abel Beth Maakah, Janoah, Kedesh and Hazor. He took Gilead and Galilee, including all the land of Naphtali, and deported the people to Assyria. 30Then Hoshea son of Elah conspired against Pekah son of Remaliah. He attacked and assassinated him, and then succeeded him as king in the twentieth year of Jotham son of Uzziah.

31As for the other events of Pekah's reign, and all he did, are they not written in the book of the annals of the kings of Israel?

Jotham King of Judah

32In the second year of Pekah son of Remaliah king of Israel, Jotham son of Uzziah king of Judah began to reign. 33He was twenty-five years old when he became king, and he reigned in Jerusalem sixteen years. His mother's name was Jerusha daughter of Zadok. 34He did what was right in the eyes of the Lord, just as his father Uzziah had done. 35The high places, however, were not removed; the people continued to offer sacrifices and burn incense there. Jotham rebuilt the Upper Gate of the temple of the Lord.

36As for the other events of Jotham's reign, and what he did, are they not written in the book of the annals of the kings of Judah? 37(In those days the Lord began to send Rezin king of Aram and Pekah son of Remaliah against Judah.) 38Jotham rested with his ancestors and was buried with them in the City of David, the city of his fa-

ther. And Ahaz his son succeeded him as king.

Ahaz King of Judah

16 In the seventeenth year of Pekah son of Remaliah, Ahaz son of Jotham king of Judah began to reign. 2Ahaz was twenty years old when he became king, and he reigned in Jerusalem sixteen years. Unlike David his father, he did not do what was right in the eyes of the Lord his God. 3He followed the ways of the kings of Israel and even sacrificed his son in the fire, engaging in the detestable practices of the nations the Lord had driven out before the Israelites. 4He offered sacrifices and burned incense at the high places, on the hilltops and under every spreading tree.

5Then Rezin king of Aram and Pekah son of Remaliah king of Israel marched up to fight against Jerusalem and besieged Ahaz, but they could not overpower him. 6At that time, Rezin king of Aram recovered Elath for Aram by driving out the people of Judah. Edomites then moved into Elath and have lived there to this day.

7Ahaz sent messengers to say to Tiglath-Pileser king of Assyria, "I am your servant and vassal. Come up and save me out of the hand of the king of Aram and of the king of Israel, who are attacking me." 8And Ahaz took the silver and gold found in the temple of the Lord and in the treasuries of the royal palace and sent it as a gift to the king of Assyria. 9The king of Assyria complied by attacking Damascus and capturing it. He deported its inhabitants to Kir and put Rezin to death.

10Then King Ahaz went to Damascus to meet Tiglath-Pileser king of Assyria. He saw an altar in Damascus and sent to Uriah the priest a sketch of the altar, with detailed plans for its construction. 11So Uriah the priest built an altar in accordance with all the plans that King Ahaz had sent from Damascus and finished it before King Ahaz returned. 12When the king came back from Damascus and saw the altar, he approached it and presented offerings*a* on it. 13He offered up his burnt offering and grain offering, poured out his drink offering, and splashed the blood of his fellowship offerings against the altar. 14As for the bronze al-

---

a 12 Or and went up

tar that stood before the LORD, he brought it from the front of the temple—from between the new altar and the temple of the LORD— and put it on the north side of the new altar.

15King Ahaz then gave these orders to Uriah the priest: "On the large new altar, offer the morning burnt offering and the evening grain offering, the king's burnt offering and his grain offering, and the burnt offering of all the people of the land, and their grain offering and their drink offering. Splash against this altar the blood of all the burnt offerings and sacrifices. But I will use the bronze altar for seeking guidance." 16And Uriah the priest did just as King Ahaz had ordered.

17King Ahaz cut off the side panels and removed the basins from the movable stands. He removed the Sea from the bronze bulls that supported it and set it on a stone base. 18He took away the Sabbath canopy[a] that had been built at the temple and removed the royal entryway outside the temple of the LORD, in deference to the king of Assyria.

19As for the other events of the reign of Ahaz, and what he did, are they not written in the book of the annals of the kings of Judah? 20Ahaz rested with his ancestors and was buried with them in the City of David. And Hezekiah his son succeeded him as king.

Hoshea Last King of Israel

17 In the twelfth year of Ahaz king of Judah, Hoshea son of Elah became king of Israel in Samaria, and he reigned nine years. 2He did evil in the eyes of the LORD, but not like the kings of Israel who preceded him.

3Shalmaneser king of Assyria came up to attack Hoshea, who had been Shalmaneser's vassal and had paid him tribute. 4But the king of Assyria discovered that Hoshea was a traitor, for he had sent envoys to So[b] king of Egypt, and he no longer paid tribute to the king of Assyria, as he had done year by year. Therefore Shalmaneser seized him and put him in prison. 5The king of Assyria invaded the entire land, marched against Samaria and laid siege to it for three years. 6In the ninth year of Hoshea, the king of Assyr-

ia captured Samaria and deported the Israelites to Assyria. He settled them in Halah, in Gozan on the Habor River and in the towns of the Medes.

Israel Exiled Because of Sin

7All this took place because the Israelites had sinned against the LORD their God, who had brought them up out of Egypt from under the power of Pharaoh king of Egypt. They worshiped other gods 8and followed the practices of the nations the LORD had driven out before them, as well as the practices that the kings of Israel had introduced. 9The Israelites secretly did things against the LORD their God that were not right. From watchtower to fortified city they built themselves high places in all their towns. 10They set up sacred stones and Asherah poles on every high hill and under every spreading tree. 11At every high place they burned incense, as the nations whom the LORD had driven out before them had done. They did wicked things that aroused the LORD's anger. 12They worshiped idols, though the LORD had said, "You shall not do this."[c] 13The LORD warned Israel and Judah through all his prophets and seers: "Turn from your evil ways. Observe my commands and decrees, in accordance with the entire Law that I commanded your ancestors to obey and that I delivered to you through my servants the prophets."

14But they would not listen and were as stiff-necked as their ancestors, who did not trust in the LORD their God. 15They rejected his decrees and the covenant he had made with their ancestors and the statutes he had warned them to keep. They followed worthless idols and themselves became worthless. They imitated the nations around them although the LORD had ordered them, "Do not do as they do."

16They forsook all the commands of the LORD their God and made for themselves two idols cast in the shape of calves, and an Asherah pole. They bowed down to all the starry hosts, and they worshiped Baal. 17They sacrificed their sons and daughters in the fire. They practiced divination and sought omens and sold themselves to do evil in the eyes of the LORD, arousing his anger.

---

a 18 Or the dais of his throne (see Septuagint)   b 4 So is probably an abbreviation for Osorkon.
c 12 Exodus 20:4,5

¹⁸So the LORD was very angry with Israel and removed them from his presence. Only the tribe of Judah was left, ¹⁹and even Judah did not keep the commands of the LORD their God. They followed the practices Israel had introduced. ²⁰Therefore the LORD rejected all the people of Israel; he afflicted them and gave them into the hands of plunderers, until he thrust them from his presence.

²¹When he tore Israel away from the house of David, they made Jeroboam son of Nebat their king. Jeroboam enticed Israel away from following the LORD and caused them to commit a great sin. ²²The Israelites persisted in all the sins of Jeroboam and did not turn away from them ²³until the LORD removed them from his presence, as he had warned through all his servants the prophets. So the people of Israel were taken from their homeland into exile in Assyria, and they are still there.

Samaria Resettled

²⁴The king of Assyria brought people from Babylon, Kuthah, Avva, Hamath and Sepharvaim and settled them in the towns of Samaria to replace the Israelites. They took over Samaria and lived in its towns. ²⁵When they first lived there, they did not worship the LORD; so he sent lions among them and they killed some of the people. ²⁶It was reported to the king of Assyria: "The people you deported and resettled in the towns of Samaria do not know what the god of that country requires. He has sent lions among them, which are killing them off, because the people do not know what he requires."

²⁷Then the king of Assyria gave this order: "Have one of the priests you took captive from Samaria go back to live there and teach the people what the god of the land requires." ²⁸So one of the priests who had been exiled from Samaria came to live in Bethel and taught them how to worship the LORD.

²⁹Nevertheless, each national group made its own gods in the several towns where they settled, and set them up in the shrines the people of Samaria had made at the high places. ³⁰The people from Babylon made Sukkoth Benoth, those from Kuthah

made Nergal, and those from Hamath made Ashima; ³¹the Avvites made Nibhaz and Tartak, and the Sepharvites burned their children in the fire as sacrifices to Adrammelek and Anammelek, the gods of Sepharvaim. ³²They worshiped the LORD, but they also appointed all sorts of their own people to officiate for them as priests in the shrines at the high places. ³³They worshiped the LORD, but they also served their own gods in accordance with the customs of the nations from which they had been brought.

³⁴To this day they persist in their former practices. They neither worship the LORD nor adhere to the decrees and regulations, the laws and commands that the LORD gave the descendants of Jacob, whom he named Israel. ³⁵When the LORD made a covenant with the Israelites, he commanded them: "Do not worship any other gods or bow down to them, serve them or sacrifice to them. ³⁶But the LORD, who brought you up out of Egypt with mighty power and outstretched arm, is the one you must worship. To him you shall bow down and to him offer sacrifices. ³⁷You must always be careful to keep the decrees and regulations, the laws and commands he wrote for you. Do not worship other gods. ³⁸Do not forget the covenant I have made with you, and do not worship other gods. ³⁹Rather, worship the LORD your God; it is he who will deliver you from the hand of all your enemies."

⁴⁰They would not listen, however, but persisted in their former practices. ⁴¹Even while these people were worshiping the LORD, they were serving their idols. To this day their children and grandchildren continue to do as their ancestors did.

Hezekiah King of Judah

18 In the third year of Hoshea son of Elah king of Israel, Hezekiah son of Ahaz king of Judah began to reign. ²He was twenty-five years old when he became king, and he reigned in Jerusalem twenty-nine years. His mother's name was Abijahᵃ daughter of Zechariah. ³He did what was right in the eyes of the LORD, just as his father David had done. ⁴He removed the high places, smashed the sacred stones and cut down the Asherah poles. He broke into pieces the bronze snake Mo-

---

ᵃ 2 Hebrew Abi, a variant of Abijah

ses had made, for up to that time the Israelites had been burning incense to it. (It was called Nehushtan.[a])

[5]Hezekiah trusted in the LORD, the God of Israel. There was no one like him among all the kings of Judah, either before him or after him. [6]He held fast to the LORD and did not cease to follow him; he kept the commands the LORD had given Moses. [7]And the LORD was with him; he was successful in whatever he undertook. He rebelled against the king of Assyria and did not serve him. [8]From watchtower to fortified city, he defeated the Philistines, as far as Gaza and its territory.

[9]In King Hezekiah's fourth year, which was the seventh year of Hoshea son of Elah king of Israel, Shalmaneser king of Assyria marched against Samaria and laid siege to it. [10]At the end of three years the Assyrians took it. So Samaria was captured in Hezekiah's sixth year, which was the ninth year of Hoshea king of Israel. [11]The king of Assyria deported Israel to Assyria and settled them in Halah, in Gozan on the Habor River and in towns of the Medes. [12]This happened because they had not obeyed the LORD their God, but had violated his covenant—all that Moses the servant of the LORD commanded. They neither listened to the commands nor carried them out.

[13]In the fourteenth year of King Hezekiah's reign, Sennacherib king of Assyria attacked all the fortified cities of Judah and captured them. [14]So Hezekiah king of Judah sent this message to the king of Assyria at Lachish: "I have done wrong. Withdraw from me, and I will pay whatever you demand of me." The king of Assyria exacted from Hezekiah king of Judah three hundred talents[b] of silver and thirty talents[c] of gold. [15]So Hezekiah gave him all the silver that was found in the temple of the LORD and in the treasuries of the royal palace.

[16]At this time Hezekiah king of Judah stripped off the gold with which he had covered the doors and doorposts of the temple of the LORD, and gave it to the king of Assyria.

Sennacherib Threatens Jerusalem

[17]The king of Assyria sent his supreme commander, his chief officer and his field commander with a large army, from Lachish to King Hezekiah at Jerusalem. They came up to Jerusalem and stopped at the aqueduct of the Upper Pool, on the road to the Washerman's Field. [18]They called for the king; and Eliakim son of Hilkiah the palace administrator, Shebna the secretary, and Joah son of Asaph the recorder went out to them.

[19]The field commander said to them, "Tell Hezekiah:

" 'This is what the great king, the king of Assyria, says: On what are you basing this confidence of yours? [20]You say you have the counsel and the might for war—but you speak only empty words. On whom are you depending, that you rebel against me? [21]Look, I know you are depending on Egypt, that splintered reed of a staff, which pierces the hands of anyone who leans on it! Such is Pharaoh king of Egypt to all who depend on him. [22]But if you say to me, "We are depending on the LORD our God"—isn't he the one whose high places and altars Hezekiah removed, saying to Judah and Jerusalem, "You must worship before this altar in Jerusalem"?

[23]" 'Come now, make a bargain with my master, the king of Assyria: I will give you two thousand horses—if you can put riders on them! [24]How can you repulse one officer of the least of my master's officials, even though you are depending on Egypt for chariots and horsemen[d]? [25]Furthermore, have I come to attack and destroy this place without word from the LORD? The LORD himself told me to march against this country and destroy it.' "

[26]Then Eliakim son of Hilkiah, and Shebna and Joah said to the field commander, "Please speak to your servants in Aramaic, since we understand it. Don't speak to us in Hebrew in the hearing of the people on the wall."

[27]But the commander replied, "Was it only to your master and you that my master sent me to say these things, and not to the people sitting on the wall—who, like you, will have to eat their own excrement and drink their own urine?"

---

a 4 Nehushtan sounds like the Hebrew for both bronze and snake.   b 14 That is, about 11 tons or about 10 metric tons   c 14 That is, about 1 ton or about 1 metric ton   d 24 Or charioteers

²⁸Then the commander stood and called out in Hebrew, "Hear the word of the great king, the king of Assyria! ²⁹This is what the king says: Do not let Hezekiah deceive you. He cannot deliver you from my hand. ³⁰Do not let Hezekiah persuade you to trust in the LORD when he says, 'The LORD will surely deliver us; this city will not be given into the hand of the king of Assyria.'

³¹"Do not listen to Hezekiah. This is what the king of Assyria says: Make peace with me and come out to me. Then every one of you will eat from your own vine and fig tree and drink water from your own cistern, ³²until I come and take you to a land like your own—a land of grain and new wine, a land of bread and vineyards, a land of olive trees and honey. Choose life and not death!

"Do not listen to Hezekiah, for he is misleading you when he says, 'The LORD will deliver us.' ³³Has the god of any nation ever delivered his land from the hand of the king of Assyria? ³⁴Where are the gods of Hamath and Arpad? Where are the gods of Sepharvaim, Hena and Ivvah? Have they rescued Samaria from my hand? ³⁵Who of all the gods of these countries has been able to save his land from me? How then can the LORD deliver Jerusalem from my hand?"

³⁶But the people remained silent and said nothing in reply, because the king had commanded, "Do not answer him."

³⁷Then Eliakim son of Hilkiah the palace administrator, Shebna the secretary, and Joah son of Asaph the recorder went to Hezekiah, with their clothes torn, and told him what the field commander had said.

Jerusalem's Deliverance Foretold

19 When King Hezekiah heard this, he tore his clothes and put on sackcloth and went into the temple of the LORD. ²He sent Eliakim the palace administrator, Shebna the secretary and the leading priests, all wearing sackcloth, to the prophet Isaiah son of Amoz. ³They told him, "This is what Hezekiah says: This day is a day of distress and rebuke and disgrace, as when children come to the moment of birth and there is no strength to deliver them. ⁴It may be that the LORD your God will hear all the words of the field commander, whom his master, the king of As-

syria, has sent to ridicule the living God, and that he will rebuke him for the words the LORD your God has heard. Therefore pray for the remnant that still survives."

⁵When King Hezekiah's officials came to Isaiah, ⁶Isaiah said to them, "Tell your master, 'This is what the LORD says: Do not be afraid of what you have heard—those words with which the underlings of the king of Assyria have blasphemed me. ⁷Listen! When he hears a certain report, I will make him want to return to his own country, and there I will have him cut down with the sword.' "

⁸When the field commander heard that the king of Assyria had left Lachish, he withdrew and found the king fighting against Libnah.

⁹Now Sennacherib received a report that Tirhakah, the king of Cush,ᵃ was marching out to fight against him. So he again sent messengers to Hezekiah with this word: ¹⁰"Say to Hezekiah king of Judah: Do not let the god you depend on deceive you when he says, 'Jerusalem will not be given into the hands of the king of Assyria.' ¹¹Surely you have heard what the kings of Assyria have done to all the countries, destroying them completely. And will you be delivered? ¹²Did the gods of the nations that were destroyed by my ancestors deliver them—the gods of Gozan, Harran, Rezeph and the people of Eden who were in Tel Assar? ¹³Where is the king of Hamath or the king of Arpad? Where are the kings of Lair, Sepharvaim, Hena and Ivvah?"

Hezekiah's Prayer

¹⁴Hezekiah received the letter from the messengers and read it. Then he went up to the temple of the LORD and spread it out before the LORD. ¹⁵And Hezekiah prayed to the LORD: "LORD, the God of Israel, enthroned between the cherubim, you alone are God over all the kingdoms of the earth. You have made heaven and earth. ¹⁶Give ear, LORD, and hear; open your eyes, LORD, and see; listen to the words Sennacherib has sent to ridicule the living God.

¹⁷"It is true, LORD, that the Assyrian kings have laid waste these nations and their lands. ¹⁸They have thrown their gods into the fire and destroyed them, for they were not gods but only wood and stone, fashioned

---

ᵃ 9 That is, the upper Nile region

by human hands. ¹⁹Now, LORD our God, deliver us from his hand, so that all the kingdoms of the earth may know that you alone, LORD, are God."

Isaiah Prophesies Sennacherib's Fall

²⁰Then Isaiah son of Amoz sent a message to Hezekiah: "This is what the LORD, the God of Israel, says: I have heard your prayer concerning Sennacherib king of Assyria. ²¹This is the word that the LORD has spoken against him:

" 'Virgin Daughter Zion
    despises you and mocks you.
Daughter Jerusalem
    tosses her head as you flee.
²²Who is it you have ridiculed and
    blasphemed?
    Against whom have you raised your
      voice
and lifted your eyes in pride?
    Against the Holy One of Israel!
²³By your messengers
    you have ridiculed the Lord.
And you have said,
    "With my many chariots
I have ascended the heights of the
    mountains,
    the utmost heights of Lebanon.
I have cut down its tallest cedars,
    the choicest of its junipers.
I have reached its remotest parts,
    the finest of its forests.
²⁴I have dug wells in foreign lands
    and drunk the water there.
With the soles of my feet
    I have dried up all the streams of
      Egypt."
²⁵" 'Have you not heard?
    Long ago I ordained it.
In days of old I planned it;
    now I have brought it to pass,
that you have turned fortified cities
    into piles of stone.
²⁶Their people, drained of power,
    are dismayed and put to shame.
They are like plants in the field,
    like tender green shoots,
like grass sprouting on the roof,
    scorched before it grows up.
²⁷" 'But I know where you are
    and when you come and go
    and how you rage against me.
²⁸Because you rage against me

and because your insolence has
    reached my ears,
I will put my hook in your nose
    and my bit in your mouth,
and I will make you return
    by the way you came.'

²⁹"This will be the sign for you, Hezekiah:

"This year you will eat what grows by
    itself,
    and the second year what springs
      from that.
But in the third year sow and reap,
    plant vineyards and eat their fruit.
³⁰Once more a remnant of the house of
    Judah
    will take root below and bear fruit
      above.
³¹For out of Jerusalem will come a remnant,
    and out of Mount Zion a band of
      survivors.

"The zeal of the LORD Almighty will accomplish this.

³²"Therefore this is what the LORD says concerning the king of Assyria:

" 'He will not enter this city
    or shoot an arrow here.
He will not come before it with shield
    or build a siege ramp against it.
³³By the way that he came he will return;
    he will not enter this city,
            declares the LORD.
³⁴I will defend this city and save it,
    for my sake and for the sake of David
      my servant.' "

³⁵That night the angel of the LORD went out and put to death a hundred and eighty-five thousand in the Assyrian camp. When the people got up the next morning—there were all the dead bodies! ³⁶So Sennacherib king of Assyria broke camp and withdrew. He returned to Nineveh and stayed there.

³⁷One day, while he was worshiping in the temple of his god Nisrok, his sons Adrammelek and Sharezer killed him with the sword, and they escaped to the land of Ararat. And Esarhaddon his son succeeded him as king.

Hezekiah's Illness

20 In those days Hezekiah became ill and was at the point of death. The prophet Isaiah son of Amoz went to him and said, "This is what the LORD

WHOLEHEARTED DEVOTION

2 Kings 20:1–21 or 20:1–3

Alfred McBride

The human heart is the fundamental battleground in the world. All external conflicts are reflections on this interior war we experience within ourselves. Reduced to its simplest components, this war is between God's will and ours. Our song is usually, "I'll do it my way." . . . We can choose the obedience of faith or the disobedience of pride. We should say this prayer often and with great fervor, "Thy will be done."

Why do we act otherwise? Why is it hard to follow God's will? We are born in the state of original sin, the result of the disobedience of our first parents. By baptism we are delivered from this state and restored to original holiness and justice. Christ's saving act on the cross and in the resurrection made this possible.

But we retain what St. Thomas Aquinas calls the "wounds" of original sin. They are: (1) Ignorance in the mind, which makes it hard to know the truth or even to believe knowledge of truth is possible; (2) malice in the heart, a movement that replaces the heart's instinctive wish to love with a spiteful approach to others; (3) emotionalism, which should be at the service of reason, but is rebellious, advocating an independence of the passions; and (4) weakness in the will, which ought to be submitting to God's will, but tends to prefer one's own wishes to those of God.

Our problematic wills cause us the most trouble and activate the other three wounds to push us away from God. It's no mistake that abortionists use the expression "pro-choice," a celebration of a sinful will. We should reverse this misuse of the will by praying with all our hearts that God's will be done.

CARDINAL JOHN HENRY NEWMAN {AD 1801–1890}

Pray to Him to give you what Scripture calls *"[a noble] and good heart"* (Luke 8:15) or *"[wholehearted devotion]"* (2 Kings 20:3), and, without waiting, begin at once to obey Him with the best heart you have. Any obedience is better than none . . . To do what He bids is to obey Him, and to obey Him is to approach Him. Every act of obedience is an approach. It is an approach to Him who is not far off, though He seems so, but close behind this visible screen of things that hide[s] Him from us.

— *reflection* —

1. Why is it so hard to let God's will be done?

2. How did God bless Hezekiah's faithful obedience?

3. How have you seen God bless you for your obedience to him?

For your next devotional reading, go to page 458.

says: Put your house in order, because you are going to die; you will not recover."

²Hezekiah turned his face to the wall and prayed to the LORD, ³"Remember, LORD, how I have walked before you faithfully and with wholehearted devotion and have done what is good in your eyes." And Hezekiah wept bitterly.

⁴Before Isaiah had left the middle court, the word of the LORD came to him: ⁵"Go back and tell Hezekiah, the ruler of my people, 'This is what the LORD, the God of your father David, says: I have heard your prayer and seen your tears; I will heal you. On the third day from now you will go up to the temple of the LORD. ⁶I will add fifteen years to your life. And I will deliver you and this city from the hand of the king of Assyria. I will defend this city for my sake and for the sake of my servant David.' "

⁷Then Isaiah said, "Prepare a poultice of figs." They did so and applied it to the boil, and he recovered.

⁸Hezekiah had asked Isaiah, "What will be the sign that the LORD will heal me and that I will go up to the temple of the LORD on the third day from now?"

⁹Isaiah answered, "This is the LORD's sign to you that the LORD will do what he has promised: Shall the shadow go forward ten steps, or shall it go back ten steps?"

¹⁰"It is a simple matter for the shadow to go forward ten steps," said Hezekiah. "Rather, have it go back ten steps."

¹¹Then the prophet Isaiah called on the LORD, and the LORD made the shadow go back the ten steps it had gone down on the stairway of Ahaz.

Envoys From Babylon

¹²At that time Marduk-Baladan son of Baladan king of Babylon sent Hezekiah letters and a gift, because he had heard of Hezekiah's illness. ¹³Hezekiah received the envoys and showed them all that was in his storehouses—the silver, the gold, the spices and the fine olive oil—his armory and everything found among his treasures. There was nothing in his palace or in all his kingdom that Hezekiah did not show them.

¹⁴Then Isaiah the prophet went to King Hezekiah and asked, "What did those men say, and where did they come from?"

"From a distant land," Hezekiah replied. "They came from Babylon."

¹⁵The prophet asked, "What did they see in your palace?"

"They saw everything in my palace," Hezekiah said. "There is nothing among my treasures that I did not show them."

¹⁶Then Isaiah said to Hezekiah, "Hear the word of the LORD: ¹⁷The time will surely come when everything in your palace, and all that your predecessors have stored up until this day, will be carried off to Babylon. Nothing will be left, says the LORD. ¹⁸And some of your descendants, your own flesh and blood who will be born to you, will be taken away, and they will become eunuchs in the palace of the king of Babylon."

¹⁹"The word of the LORD you have spoken is good," Hezekiah replied. For he thought, "Will there not be peace and security in my lifetime?"

²⁰As for the other events of Hezekiah's reign, all his achievements and how he made the pool and the tunnel by which he brought water into the city, are they not written in the book of the annals of the kings of Judah? ²¹Hezekiah rested with his ancestors. And Manasseh his son succeeded him as king.

Manasseh King of Judah

21 Manasseh was twelve years old when he became king, and he reigned in Jerusalem fifty-five years. His mother's name was Hephzibah. ²He did evil in the eyes of the LORD, following the detestable practices of the nations the LORD had driven out before the Israelites. ³He rebuilt the high places his father Hezekiah had destroyed; he also erected altars to Baal and made an Asherah pole, as Ahab king of Israel had done. He bowed down to all the starry hosts and worshiped them. ⁴He built altars in the temple of the LORD, of which the LORD had said, "In Jerusalem I will put my Name." ⁵In the two courts of the temple of the LORD, he built altars to all the starry hosts. ⁶He sacrificed his own son in the fire, practiced divination, sought omens, and consulted mediums and spiritists. He did much evil in the eyes of the LORD, arousing his anger.

⁷He took the carved Asherah pole he had made and put it in the temple, of which the LORD had said to David and to his son Solomon, "In this temple and in Jerusalem, which I have chosen out of all the tribes of Israel, I will put my Name forever. ⁸I will not

again make the feet of the Israelites wander from the land I gave their ancestors, if only they will be careful to do everything I commanded them and will keep the whole Law that my servant Moses gave them." [9]But the people did not listen. Manasseh led them astray, so that they did more evil than the nations the LORD had destroyed before the Israelites.

[10]The LORD said through his servants the prophets: [11]"Manasseh king of Judah has committed these detestable sins. He has done more evil than the Amorites who preceded him and has led Judah into sin with his idols. [12]Therefore this is what the LORD, the God of Israel, says: I am going to bring such disaster on Jerusalem and Judah that the ears of everyone who hears of it will tingle. [13]I will stretch out over Jerusalem the measuring line used against Samaria and the plumb line used against the house of Ahab. I will wipe out Jerusalem as one wipes a dish, wiping it and turning it upside down. [14]I will forsake the remnant of my inheritance and give them into the hands of enemies. They will be looted and plundered by all their enemies; [15]they have done evil in my eyes and have aroused my anger from the day their ancestors came out of Egypt until this day."

[16]Moreover, Manasseh also shed so much innocent blood that he filled Jerusalem from end to end—besides the sin that he had caused Judah to commit, so that they did evil in the eyes of the LORD.

[17]As for the other events of Manasseh's reign, and all he did, including the sin he committed, are they not written in the book of the annals of the kings of Judah? [18]Manasseh rested with his ancestors and was buried in his palace garden, the garden of Uzza. And Amon his son succeeded him as king.

Amon King of Judah

[19]Amon was twenty-two years old when he became king, and he reigned in Jerusalem two years. His mother's name was Meshullemeth daughter of Haruz; she was from Jotbah. [20]He did evil in the eyes of the LORD, as his father Manasseh had done. [21]He followed completely the ways of his father, worshiping the idols his father had worshiped, and bowing down to them. [22]He forsook the LORD, the God of his ancestors, and did not walk in obedience to him.

[23]Amon's officials conspired against him and assassinated the king in his palace. [24]Then the people of the land killed all who had plotted against King Amon, and they made Josiah his son king in his place.

[25]As for the other events of Amon's reign, and what he did, are they not written in the book of the annals of the kings of Judah? [26]He was buried in his tomb in the garden of Uzza. And Josiah his son succeeded him as king.

The Book of the Law Found

22 Josiah was eight years old when he became king, and he reigned in Jerusalem thirty-one years. His mother's name was Jedidah daughter of Adaiah; she was from Bozkath. [2]He did what was right in the eyes of the LORD and followed completely the ways of his father David, not turning aside to the right or to the left.

[3]In the eighteenth year of his reign, King Josiah sent the secretary, Shaphan son of Azaliah, the son of Meshullam, to the temple of the LORD. He said: [4]"Go up to Hilkiah the high priest and have him get ready the money that has been brought into the temple of the LORD, which the doorkeepers have collected from the people. [5]Have them entrust it to the men appointed to supervise the work on the temple. And have these men pay the workers who repair the temple of the LORD— [6]the carpenters, the builders and the masons. Also have them purchase timber and dressed stone to repair the temple. [7]But they need not account for the money entrusted to them, because they are honest in their dealings."

[8]Hilkiah the high priest said to Shaphan the secretary, "I have found the Book of the Law in the temple of the LORD." He gave it to Shaphan, who read it. [9]Then Shaphan the secretary went to the king and reported to him: "Your officials have paid out the money that was in the temple of the LORD and have entrusted it to the workers and supervisors at the temple." [10]Then Shaphan the secretary informed the king, "Hilkiah the priest has given me a book." And Shaphan read from it in the presence of the king.

[11]When the king heard the words of the Book of the Law, he tore his robes. [12]He gave these orders to Hilkiah the priest, Ahikam son of Shaphan, Akbor son of Micaiah, Shaphan the secretary and Asaiah the king's attendant: [13]"Go and inquire of the LORD for

me and for the people and for all Judah about what is written in this book that has been found. Great is the LORD's anger that burns against us because those who have gone before us have not obeyed the words of this book; they have not acted in accordance with all that is written there concerning us."

¹⁴Hilkiah the priest, Ahikam, Akbor, Shaphan and Asaiah went to speak to the prophet Huldah, who was the wife of Shallum son of Tikvah, the son of Harhas, keeper of the wardrobe. She lived in Jerusalem, in the New Quarter.

¹⁵She said to them, "This is what the LORD, the God of Israel, says: Tell the man who sent you to me, ¹⁶'This is what the LORD says: I am going to bring disaster on this place and its people, according to everything written in the book the king of Judah has read. ¹⁷Because they have forsaken me and burned incense to other gods and aroused my anger by all the idols their hands have made,ᵃ my anger will burn against this place and will not be quenched.' ¹⁸Tell the king of Judah, who sent you to inquire of the LORD, 'This is what the LORD, the God of Israel, says concerning the words you heard: ¹⁹Because your heart was responsive and you humbled yourself before the LORD when you heard what I have spoken against this place and its people—that they would become a curseᵇ and be laid waste—and because you tore your robes and wept in my presence, I also have heard you, declares the LORD. ²⁰Therefore I will gather you to your ancestors, and you will be buried in peace. Your eyes will not see all the disaster I am going to bring on this place.' "

So they took her answer back to the king.

Josiah Renews the Covenant

23 Then the king called together all the elders of Judah and Jerusalem. ²He went up to the temple of the LORD with the people of Judah, the inhabitants of Jerusalem, the priests and the prophets—all the people from the least to the greatest. He read in their hearing all the words of the Book of the Covenant, which had been found in the temple of the LORD. ³The king stood by the pillar and renewed the covenant in the presence of the LORD—

to follow the LORD and keep his commands, statutes and decrees with all his heart and all his soul, thus confirming the words of the covenant written in this book. Then all the people pledged themselves to the covenant.

⁴The king ordered Hilkiah the high priest, the priests next in rank and the doorkeepers to remove from the temple of the LORD all the articles made for Baal and Asherah and all the starry hosts. He burned them outside Jerusalem in the fields of the Kidron Valley and took the ashes to Bethel. ⁵He did away with the idolatrous priests appointed by the kings of Judah to burn incense on the high places of the towns of Judah and on those around Jerusalem—those who burned incense to Baal, to the sun and moon, to the constellations and to all the starry hosts. ⁶He took the Asherah pole from the temple of the LORD to the Kidron Valley outside Jerusalem and burned it there. He ground it to powder and scattered the dust over the graves of the common people. ⁷He also tore down the quarters of the male shrine prostitutes that were in the temple of the LORD, the quarters where women did weaving for Asherah.

⁸Josiah brought all the priests from the towns of Judah and desecrated the high places, from Geba to Beersheba, where the priests had burned incense. He broke down the gateway at the entrance of the Gate of Joshua, the city governor, which was on the left of the city gate. ⁹Although the priests of the high places did not serve at the altar of the LORD in Jerusalem, they ate unleavened bread with their fellow priests.

¹⁰He desecrated Topheth, which was in the Valley of Ben Hinnom, so no one could use it to sacrifice their son or daughter in the fire to Molek. ¹¹He removed from the entrance to the temple of the LORD the horses that the kings of Judah had dedicated to the sun. They were in the courtᶜ near the room of an official named Nathan-Melek. Josiah then burned the chariots dedicated to the sun.

¹²He pulled down the altars the kings of Judah had erected on the roof near the upper room of Ahaz, and the altars Manasseh had built in the two courts of the temple of the LORD. He removed them from there, smashed them to pieces and threw the rub-

---

ᵃ 17 Or *by everything they have done*   ᵇ 19 That is, their names would be used in cursing (see Jer. 29:22); or, others would see that they are cursed.   ᶜ 11 The meaning of the Hebrew for this word is uncertain.

ble into the Kidron Valley. ¹³The king also desecrated the high places that were east of Jerusalem on the south of the Hill of Corruption—the ones Solomon king of Israel had built for Ashtoreth the vile goddess of the Sidonians, for Chemosh the vile god of Moab, and for Molek the detestable god of the people of Ammon. ¹⁴Josiah smashed the sacred stones and cut down the Asherah poles and covered the sites with human bones.

¹⁵Even the altar at Bethel, the high place made by Jeroboam son of Nebat, who had caused Israel to sin—even that altar and high place he demolished. He burned the high place and ground it to powder, and burned the Asherah pole also. ¹⁶Then Josiah looked around, and when he saw the tombs that were there on the hillside, he had the bones removed from them and burned on the altar to defile it, in accordance with the word of the LORD proclaimed by the man of God who foretold these things.

¹⁷The king asked, "What is that tombstone I see?"

The people of the city said, "It marks the tomb of the man of God who came from Judah and pronounced against the altar of Bethel the very things you have done to it."

¹⁸"Leave it alone," he said. "Don't let anyone disturb his bones." So they spared his bones and those of the prophet who had come from Samaria.

¹⁹Just as he had done at Bethel, Josiah removed all the shrines at the high places that the kings of Israel had built in the towns of Samaria and that had aroused the LORD's anger. ²⁰Josiah slaughtered all the priests of those high places on the altars and burned human bones on them. Then he went back to Jerusalem.

²¹The king gave this order to all the people: "Celebrate the Passover to the LORD your God, as it is written in this Book of the Covenant." ²²Neither in the days of the judges who led Israel nor in the days of the kings of Israel and the kings of Judah had any such Passover been observed. ²³But in the eighteenth year of King Josiah, this Passover was celebrated to the LORD in Jerusalem.

²⁴Furthermore, Josiah got rid of the mediums and spiritists, the household gods, the idols and all the other detestable things seen in Judah and Jerusalem. This he did to fulfill the requirements of the law written in the book that Hilkiah the priest had discovered in the temple of the LORD. ²⁵Neither before nor after Josiah was there a king like him who turned to the LORD as he did—with all his heart and with all his soul and with all his strength, in accordance with all the Law of Moses.

²⁶Nevertheless, the LORD did not turn away from the heat of his fierce anger, which burned against Judah because of all that Manasseh had done to arouse his anger. ²⁷So the LORD said, "I will remove Judah also from my presence as I removed Israel, and I will reject Jerusalem, the city I chose, and this temple, about which I said, 'There shall my Name be.'ᵃ"

²⁸As for the other events of Josiah's reign, and all he did, are they not written in the book of the annals of the kings of Judah?

²⁹While Josiah was king, Pharaoh Necho king of Egypt went up to the Euphrates River to help the king of Assyria. King Josiah marched out to meet him in battle, but Necho faced him and killed him at Megiddo. ³⁰Josiah's servants brought his body in a chariot from Megiddo to Jerusalem and buried him in his own tomb. And the people of the land took Jehoahaz son of Josiah and anointed him and made him king in place of his father.

Jehoahaz King of Judah

³¹Jehoahaz was twenty-three years old when he became king, and he reigned in Jerusalem three months. His mother's name was Hamutal daughter of Jeremiah; she was from Libnah. ³²He did evil in the eyes of the LORD, just as his predecessors had done. ³³Pharaoh Necho put him in chains at Riblah in the land of Hamath so that he might not reign in Jerusalem, and he imposed on Judah a levy of a hundred talentsᵇ of silver and a talentᶜ of gold. ³⁴Pharaoh Necho made Eliakim son of Josiah king in place of his father Josiah and changed Eliakim's name to Jehoiakim. But he took Jehoahaz and carried him off to Egypt, and there he died. ³⁵Jehoiakim paid Pharaoh Necho the silver and gold he demanded. In order to do so, he taxed the land and exacted the silver and gold from

---

ᵃ 27 1 Kings 8:29   ᵇ 33 That is, about 3 3/4 tons or about 3.4 metric tons   ᶜ 33 That is, about 75 pounds or about 34 kilograms the people of the land according to their assessments.

Jehoiakim King of Judah

³⁶Jehoiakim was twenty-five years old when he became king, and he reigned in Jerusalem eleven years. His mother's name was Zebidah daughter of Pedaiah; she was from Rumah. ³⁷And he did evil in the eyes of the LORD, just as his predecessors had done.
During Jehoiakim's reign, Nebuchadnezzar king of Babylon invaded the land, and Jehoiakim became his vassal for three years. But then he turned against Nebuchadnezzar and rebelled. ²The LORD sent Babylonian,ᵃ Aramean, Moabite and Ammonite raiders against him to destroy Judah, in accordance with the word of the LORD proclaimed by his servants the prophets. ³Surely these things happened to Judah according to the LORD's command, in order to remove them from his presence because of the sins of Manasseh and all he had done, ⁴including the shedding of innocent blood. For he had filled Jerusalem with innocent blood, and the LORD was not willing to forgive.

⁵As for the other events of Jehoiakim's reign, and all he did, are they not written in the book of the annals of the kings of Judah? ⁶Jehoiakim rested with his ancestors. And Jehoiachin his son succeeded him as king.

⁷The king of Egypt did not march out from his own country again, because the king of Babylon had taken all his territory, from the Wadi of Egypt to the Euphrates River.

Jehoiachin King of Judah

⁸Jehoiachin was eighteen years old when he became king, and he reigned in Jerusalem three months. His mother's name was Nehushta daughter of Elnathan; she was from Jerusalem. ⁹He did evil in the eyes of the LORD, just as his father had done.

¹⁰At that time the officers of Nebuchadnezzar king of Babylon advanced on Jerusalem and laid siege to it, ¹¹and Nebuchadnezzar himself came up to the city while his officers were besieging it. ¹²Jehoiachin king of Judah, his mother, his attendants, his nobles and his officials all surrendered to him.

In the eighth year of the reign of the king of Babylon, he took Jehoiachin prisoner. ¹³As the LORD had declared, Nebuchadnezzar removed the treasures from the temple of the LORD and from the royal palace, and cut up the gold articles that Solomon king of Israel had made for the temple of the LORD. ¹⁴He carried all Jerusalem into exile: all the officers and fighting men, and all the skilled workers and artisans—a total of ten thousand. Only the poorest people of the land were left.

¹⁵Nebuchadnezzar took Jehoiachin captive to Babylon. He also took from Jerusalem to Babylon the king's mother, his wives, his officials and the prominent people of the land. ¹⁶The king of Babylon also deported to Babylon the entire force of seven thousand fighting men, strong and fit for war, and a thousand skilled workers and artisans. ¹⁷He made Mattaniah, Jehoiachin's uncle, king in his place and changed his name to Zedekiah.

Zedekiah King of Judah

¹⁸Zedekiah was twenty-one years old when he became king, and he reigned in Jerusalem eleven years. His mother's name was Hamutal daughter of Jeremiah; she was from Libnah. ¹⁹He did evil in the eyes of the LORD, just as Jehoiakim had done. ²⁰It was because of the LORD's anger that all this happened to Jerusalem and Judah, and in the end he thrust them from his presence.

The Fall of Jerusalem

Now Zedekiah rebelled against the king of Babylon.
So in the ninth year of Zedekiah's reign, on the tenth day of the tenth month, Nebuchadnezzar king of Babylon marched against Jerusalem with his whole army. He encamped outside the city and built siege works all around it. ²The city was kept under siege until the eleventh year of King Zedekiah. ³By the ninth day of the fourthᵇ month the famine in the city had become so severe that there was no food for the people to eat. ⁴Then the city wall was broken through, and the whole army fled at night through the gate between the two walls near the king's

---

ᵃ 2 Or *Chaldean*   ᵇ 3 Probable reading of the original Hebrew text (see Jer. 52:6); Masoretic Text does not have *fourth*.

garden, though the Babylonians[a] were surrounding the city. They fled toward the Arabah,[b] 5but the Babylonian[c] army pursued the king and overtook him in the plains of Jericho. All his soldiers were separated from him and scattered, 6and he was captured.

He was taken to the king of Babylon at Riblah, where sentence was pronounced on him. 7They killed the sons of Zedekiah before his eyes. Then they put out his eyes, bound him with bronze shackles and took him to Babylon.

8On the seventh day of the fifth month, in the nineteenth year of Nebuchadnezzar king of Babylon, Nebuzaradan commander of the imperial guard, an official of the king of Babylon, came to Jerusalem. 9He set fire to the temple of the LORD, the royal palace and all the houses of Jerusalem. Every important building he burned down. 10The whole Babylonian army under the commander of the imperial guard broke down the walls around Jerusalem. 11Nebuzaradan the commander of the guard carried into exile the people who remained in the city, along with the rest of the populace and those who had deserted to the king of Babylon. 12But the commander left behind some of the poorest people of the land to work the vineyards and fields.

13The Babylonians broke up the bronze pillars, the movable stands and the bronze Sea that were at the temple of the LORD and they carried the bronze to Babylon. 14They also took away the pots, shovels, wick trimmers, dishes and all the bronze articles used in the temple service. 15The commander of the imperial guard took away the censers and sprinkling bowls—all that were made of pure gold or silver.

16The bronze from the two pillars, the Sea and the movable stands, which Solomon had made for the temple of the LORD, was more than could be weighed. 17Each pillar was eighteen cubits[d] high. The bronze capital on top of one pillar was three cubits[e] high and was decorated with a network and pomegranates of bronze all around. The other pillar, with its network, was similar.

18The commander of the guard took as prisoners Seraiah the chief priest, Zephaniah the priest next in rank and the three doorkeepers. 19Of those still in the city, he took the officer in charge of the fighting men, and five royal advisers. He also took the secretary who was chief officer in charge of conscripting the people of the land and sixty of the conscripts who were found in the city. 20Nebuzaradan the commander took them all and brought them to the king of Babylon at Riblah. 21There at Riblah, in the land of Hamath, the king had them executed.

So Judah went into captivity, away from her land.

22Nebuchadnezzar king of Babylon appointed Gedaliah son of Ahikam, the son of Shaphan, to be over the people he had left behind in Judah. 23When all the army officers and their men heard that the king of Babylon had appointed Gedaliah as governor, they came to Gedaliah at Mizpah—Ishmael son of Nethaniah, Johanan son of Kareah, Seraiah son of Tanhumeth the Netophathite, Jaazaniah the son of the Maakathite, and their men. 24Gedaliah took an oath to reassure them and their men. "Do not be afraid of the Babylonian officials," he said. "Settle down in the land and serve the king of Babylon, and it will go well with you."

25In the seventh month, however, Ishmael son of Nethaniah, the son of Elishama, who was of royal blood, came with ten men and assassinated Gedaliah and also the men of Judah and the Babylonians who were with him at Mizpah. 26At this, all the people from the least to the greatest, together with the army officers, fled to Egypt for fear of the Babylonians.

Jehoiachin Released
27In the thirty-seventh year of the exile of Jehoiachin king of Judah, in the year Awel-Marduk became king of Babylon, he released Jehoiachin king of Judah from prison. He did this on the twenty-seventh day of the twelfth month. 28He spoke kindly to him and gave him a seat of honor higher than those of the other kings who were with him in Babylon. 29So Jehoiachin put aside his prison clothes and for the rest of his life ate regularly at the king's table. 30Day by day the king gave Jehoiachin a regular allowance as long as he lived.

---

a 4 Or *Chaldeans*; also in verses 13, 25 and 26   *b 4* Or *the Jordan Valley*   *c 5* Or *Chaldean*; also in verses 10 and 24   *d 17* That is, about 27 feet or about 8.2 meters   *e 17* That is, about 4 1/2 feet or about 1.4 meters

1 chronicles

AUTHOR: Possibly Ezra

DATE: Around 430 B.C.

THEME: God's presence and provision are revealed in the story of David's kingdom.

Historical Records From Adam to Abraham

To Noah's Sons

1 Adam, Seth, Enosh, ²Kenan, Mahalalel, Jared, ³Enoch, Methuselah, Lamech, Noah.
⁴ The sons of Noah:ᵃ
Shem, Ham and Japheth.

The Japhethites

⁵ The sonsᵇ of Japheth:
Gomer, Magog, Madai, Javan, Tubal,
Meshek and Tiras.
⁶ The sons of Gomer:
Ashkenaz, Riphathᶜ and Togarmah.
⁷ The sons of Javan:
Elishah, Tarshish, the Kittites and
the Rodanites.

The Hamites

⁸ The sons of Ham:
Cush, Egypt, Put and Canaan.
⁹ The sons of Cush:
Seba, Havilah, Sabta, Raamah and
Sabteka.
The sons of Raamah:
Sheba and Dedan.
¹⁰ Cush was the fatherᵈ of
Nimrod, who became a mighty warrior on earth.
¹¹ Egypt was the father of
the Ludites, Anamites, Lehabites,
Naphtuhites, ¹²Pathrusites, Kasluhites (from whom the Philistines
came) and Caphtorites.
¹³ Canaan was the father of
Sidon his firstborn,ᵉ and of the Hittites, ¹⁴Jebusites, Amorites, Girgashites, ¹⁵Hivites, Arkites, Sinites,
¹⁶Arvadites, Zemarites and Hamathites.

The Semites

¹⁷ The sons of Shem:
Elam, Ashur, Arphaxad, Lud and
Aram.
The sons of Aram:ᶠ
Uz, Hul, Gether and Meshek.
¹⁸ Arphaxad was the father of Shelah,
and Shelah the father of Eber.
¹⁹ Two sons were born to Eber:
One was named Peleg,ᵍ because in
his time the earth was divided; his
brother was named Joktan.
²⁰ Joktan was the father of
Almodad, Sheleph, Hazarmaveth,
Jerah, ²¹Hadoram, Uzal, Diklah,
²²Obal,ʰ Abimael, Sheba, ²³Ophir,
Havilah and Jobab. All these were
sons of Joktan.

²⁴ Shem, Arphaxad,ⁱ Shelah,
²⁵ Eber, Peleg, Reu,
²⁶ Serug, Nahor, Terah
²⁷ and Abram (that is, Abraham).

ᵃ 4 Septuagint; Hebrew does not have this line.   ᵇ 5 Sons may mean descendants or successors or
nations; also in verses 6-10, 17 and 20.   ᶜ 6 Many Hebrew manuscripts and Vulgate (see also
Septuagint and Gen. 10:3); most Hebrew manuscripts Diphath   ᵈ 10 Father may mean ancestor or
predecessor or founder; also in verses 11, 13, 18 and 20.   ᵉ 13 Or of the Sidonians, the foremost
ᶠ 17 One Hebrew manuscript and some Septuagint manuscripts (see also Gen. 10:23); most Hebrew
manuscripts do not have this line.   ᵍ 19 Peleg means division.   ʰ 22 Some Hebrew manuscripts and
Syriac (see also Gen. 10:28); most Hebrew manuscripts Ebal   ⁱ 24 Hebrew; some Septuagint
manuscripts Arphaxad, Cainan (see also note at Gen. 11:10)

The Family of Abraham
28 The sons of Abraham:
Isaac and Ishmael.

Descendants of Hagar
29 These were their descendants:
Nebaioth the firstborn of Ishmael,
Kedar, Adbeel, Mibsam, 30Mishma,
Dumah, Massa, Hadad, Tema, 31Je-
tur, Naphish and Kedemah. These
were the sons of Ishmael.

Descendants of Keturah
32 The sons born to Keturah, Abraham's
concubine:
Zimran, Jokshan, Medan, Midian,
Ishbak and Shuah.
The sons of Jokshan:
Sheba and Dedan.
33 The sons of Midian:
Ephah, Epher, Hanok, Abida and El-
daah.
All these were descendants of Keturah.

Descendants of Sarah
34 Abraham was the father of Isaac.
The sons of Isaac:
Esau and Israel.

Esau's Sons
35 The sons of Esau:
Eliphaz, Reuel, Jeush, Jalam and Korah.
36 The sons of Eliphaz:
Teman, Omar, Zepho,*a* Gatam and
Kenaz;
by Timna: Amalek.*b*
37 The sons of Reuel:
Nahath, Zerah, Shammah and Mizzah.

The People of Seir in Edom
38 The sons of Seir:
Lotan, Shobal, Zibeon, Anah, Dishon, Ezer and Dishan.
39 The sons of Lotan:

Hori and Homam. Timna was Lo-
tan's sister.
40 The sons of Shobal:
Alvan,*c* Manahath, Ebal, Shepho and
Onam.
The sons of Zibeon:
Aiah and Anah.
41 The son of Anah:
Dishon.
The sons of Dishon:
Hemdan,*d* Eshban, Ithran and Ke-
ran.
42 The sons of Ezer:
Bilhan, Zaavan and Akan.*e*
The sons of Dishan*f*:
Uz and Aran.

The Rulers of Edom
43 These were the kings who reigned in
Edom before any Israelite king reigned:
Bela son of Beor, whose city was
named Dinhabah.
44 When Bela died, Jobab son of Zerah
from Bozrah succeeded him as king.
45 When Jobab died, Husham from the
land of the Temanites succeeded
him as king.
46 When Husham died, Hadad son of Bedad, who defeated Midian in the
country of Moab, succeeded him as
king. His city was named Avith.
47 When Hadad died, Samlah from Masrekah succeeded him as king.
48 When Samlah died, Shaul from Rehoboth on the river*g* succeeded him as
king.
49 When Shaul died, Baal-Hanan son of
Akbor succeeded him as king.
50 When Baal-Hanan died, Hadad succeeded him as king. His city was
named Pau,*h* and his wife's name
was Mehetabel daughter of Matred,
the daughter of Me-Zahab. 51Hadad
also died.

The chiefs of Edom were:
Timna, Alvah, Jetheth, 52Oholiba-

---

a 36 Many Hebrew manuscripts, some Septuagint manuscripts and Syriac (see also Gen. 36:11); most
Hebrew manuscripts *Zephi*   b 36 Some Septuagint manuscripts (see also Gen. 36:12); Hebrew *Gatam,
Kenaz, Timna and Amalek*   c 40 Many Hebrew manuscripts and some Septuagint manuscripts (see
also Gen. 36:23); most Hebrew manuscripts *Alian*   d 41 Many Hebrew manuscripts and some
Septuagint manuscripts (see also Gen. 36:26); most Hebrew manuscripts *Hamran*   e 42 Many Hebrew
and Septuagint manuscripts (see also Gen. 36:27); most Hebrew manuscripts *Zaavan, Jaakan*   f 42 See
Gen. 36:28; Hebrew *Dishon*, a variant of *Dishan*   g 48 Possibly the Euphrates   h 50 Many Hebrew
manuscripts, some Septuagint manuscripts, Vulgate and Syriac (see also Gen. 36:39); most Hebrew
manuscripts *Pai*

mah, Elah, Pinon, 53Kenaz, Teman, Mibzar, 54Magdiel and Iram. These were the chiefs of Edom.

Israel's Sons

2 These were the sons of Israel: Reuben, Simeon, Levi, Judah, Issachar, Zebulun, 2Dan, Joseph, Benjamin, Naphtali, Gad and Asher.

Judah

To Hezron's Sons

3 The sons of Judah:
Er, Onan and Shelah. These three were born to him by a Canaanite woman, the daughter of Shua. Er, Judah's firstborn, was wicked in the LORD's sight; so the LORD put him to death. 4Judah's daughter-in-law Tamar bore Perez and Zerah to Judah. He had five sons in all.

5 The sons of Perez:
Hezron and Hamul.

6 The sons of Zerah:
Zimri, Ethan, Heman, Kalkol and Darda a—five in all.

7 The son of Karmi:
Achar, b who brought trouble on Israel by violating the ban on taking devoted things. c

8 The son of Ethan:
Azariah.

9 The sons born to Hezron were:
Jerahmeel, Ram and Caleb. d

From Ram Son of Hezron

10 Ram was the father of
Amminadab, and Amminadab the father of Nahshon, the leader of the people of Judah. 11Nahshon was the father of Salmon, e Salmon the father of Boaz, 12Boaz the father of Obed and Obed the father of Jesse.

13 Jesse was the father of
Eliab his firstborn; the second son was Abinadab, the third Shimea, 14the fourth Nethanel, the fifth Raddai, 15the sixth Ozem and the sev-

enth David. 16Their sisters were Zeruiah and Abigail. Zeruiah's three sons were Abishai, Joab and Asahel. 17Abigail was the mother of Amasa, whose father was Jether the Ishmaelite.

Caleb Son of Hezron

18 Caleb son of Hezron had children by his wife Azubah (and by Jerioth). These were her sons: Jesher, Shobab and Ardon. 19When Azubah died, Caleb married Ephrath, who bore him Hur. 20Hur was the father of Uri, and Uri the father of Bezalel.

21 Later, Hezron, when he was sixty years old, married the daughter of Makir the father of Gilead. He made love to her, and she bore him Segub. 22Segub was the father of Jair, who controlled twenty-three towns in Gilead. 23(But Geshur and Aram captured Havvoth Jair, f as well as Kenath with its surrounding settlements—sixty towns.) All these were descendants of Makir the father of Gilead.

24 After Hezron died in Caleb Ephrathah, Abijah the wife of Hezron bore him Ashhur the father g of Tekoa.

Jerahmeel Son of Hezron

25 The sons of Jerahmeel the firstborn of Hezron:
Ram his firstborn, Bunah, Oren, Ozem and h Ahijah. 26Jerahmeel had another wife, whose name was Atarah; she was the mother of Onam.

27 The sons of Ram the firstborn of Jerahmeel:
Maaz, Jamin and Eker.

28 The sons of Onam:
Shammai and Jada.
The sons of Shammai:
Nadab and Abishur.

29 Abishur's wife was named Abihail, who bore him Ahban and Molid.

30 The sons of Nadab:

---

a 6 Many Hebrew manuscripts, some Septuagint manuscripts and Syriac (see also 1 Kings 4:31); most Hebrew manuscripts Dara   b 7 Achar means trouble; Achar is called Achan in Joshua.
c 7 The Hebrew term refers to the irrevocable giving over of things or persons to the LORD, often by totally destroying them.   d 9 Hebrew Kelubai, a variant of Caleb   e 11 Septuagint (see also Ruth 4:21); Hebrew Salma   f 23 Or captured the settlements of Jair   g 24 Father may mean civic leader or military leader; also in verses 42, 45, 49-52 and possibly elsewhere.   h 25 Or Oren and Ozem, by

Seled and Appaim. Seled died without children.
31 The son of Appaim:
Ishi, who was the father of Sheshan. Sheshan was the father of Ahlai.
32 The sons of Jada, Shammai's brother:
Jether and Jonathan. Jether died without children.
33 The sons of Jonathan:
Peleth and Zaza.
These were the descendants of Jerahmeel.
34 Sheshan had no sons—only daughters. He had an Egyptian servant named Jarha. 35 Sheshan gave his daughter in marriage to his servant Jarha, and she bore him Attai.
36 Attai was the father of Nathan, Nathan the father of Zabad,
37 Zabad the father of Ephlal, Ephlal the father of Obed,
38 Obed the father of Jehu, Jehu the father of Azariah,
39 Azariah the father of Helez, Helez the father of Eleasah,
40 Eleasah the father of Sismai, Sismai the father of Shallum,
41 Shallum the father of Jekamiah, and Jekamiah the father of Elishama.

The Clans of Caleb

42 The sons of Caleb the brother of Jerahmeel:
Mesha his firstborn, who was the father of Ziph, and his son Mareshah,[a] who was the father of Hebron.
43 The sons of Hebron:
Korah, Tappuah, Rekem and Shema.
44 Shema was the father of Raham, and Raham the father of Jorkeam. Rekem was the father of Shammai.
45 The son of Shammai was Maon, and Maon was the father of Beth Zur.
46 Caleb's concubine Ephah was the mother of Haran, Moza and Gazez. Haran was the father of Gazez.
47 The sons of Jahdai:
Regem, Jotham, Geshan, Pelet, Ephah and Shaaph.
48 Caleb's concubine Maakah was the mother of Sheber and Tirhanah.
49 She also gave birth to Shaaph the

father of Madmannah and to Sheva the father of Makbenah and Gibea. Caleb's daughter was Aksah. 50 These were the descendants of Caleb.

The sons of Hur the firstborn of Ephrathah:
Shobal the father of Kiriath Jearim,
51 Salma the father of Bethlehem, and Hareph the father of Beth Gader.
52 The descendants of Shobal the father of Kiriath Jearim were:
Haroeh, half the Manahathites, 53 and the clans of Kiriath Jearim: the Ithrites, Puthites, Shumathites and Mishraites. From these descended the Zorathites and Eshtaolites.
54 The descendants of Salma:
Bethlehem, the Netophathites, Atroth Beth Joab, half the Manahathites, the Zorites, 55 and the clans of scribes[b] who lived at Jabez: the Tirathites, Shimeathites and Sucathites. These are the Kenites who came from Hammath, the father of the house of Rekab.[c]

The Sons of David

3 These were the sons of David born to him in Hebron:
The firstborn was Amnon the son of Ahinoam of Jezreel;
the second, Daniel the son of Abigail of Carmel;
2 the third, Absalom the son of Maakah daughter of Talmai king of Geshur;
the fourth, Adonijah the son of Haggith;
3 the fifth, Shephatiah the son of Abital;
and the sixth, Ithream, by his wife Eglah.
4 These six were born to David in Hebron, where he reigned seven years and six months.
David reigned in Jerusalem thirty-three years, 5 and these were the children born to him there:
Shammua,[d] Shobab, Nathan and Solomon. These four were by Bathsheba[e] daughter of Ammiel. 6 There

---

a 42 The meaning of the Hebrew for this phrase is uncertain.   b 55 Or of the Sopherites
c 55 Or father of Beth Rekab   d 5 Hebrew Shimea, a variant of Shammua   e 5 One Hebrew
manuscript and Vulgate (see also Septuagint and 2 Samuel 11:3); most Hebrew manuscripts Bathshua

were also Ibhar, Elishua,*a* Eliphelet,
[7]Nogah, Nepheg, Japhia, [8]Elishama,
Eliada and Eliphelet—nine in all.
[9]All these were the sons of David,
besides his sons by his concubines.
And Tamar was their sister.

The Kings of Judah

[10]Solomon's son was Rehoboam,
Abijah his son,
Asa his son,
Jehoshaphat his son,
[11]Jehoram*b* his son,
Ahaziah his son,
Joash his son,
[12]Amaziah his son,
Azariah his son,
Jotham his son,
[13]Ahaz his son,
Hezekiah his son,
Manasseh his son,
[14]Amon his son,
Josiah his son.
[15]The sons of Josiah:
Johanan the firstborn,
Jehoiakim the second son,
Zedekiah the third,
Shallum the fourth.
[16]The successors of Jehoiakim:
Jehoiachin*c* his son,
and Zedekiah.

The Royal Line After the Exile

[17]The descendants of Jehoiachin the
captive:
Shealtiel his son, [18]Malkiram, Pedaiah, Shenazzar, Jekamiah, Hoshama
and Nedabiah.
[19]The sons of Pedaiah:
Zerubbabel and Shimei.
The sons of Zerubbabel:
Meshullam and Hananiah.
Shelomith was their sister.
[20]There were also five others:
Hashubah, Ohel, Berekiah, Hasadi-
ah and Jushab-Hesed.
[21]The descendants of Hananiah:
Pelatiah and Jeshaiah, and the sons
of Rephaiah, of Arnan, of Obadiah
and of Shekaniah.

[22]The descendants of Shekaniah:
Shemaiah and his sons:
Hattush, Igal, Bariah, Neariah and
Shaphat—six in all.
[23]The sons of Neariah:
Elioenai, Hizkiah and Azrikam—
three in all.
[24]The sons of Elioenai:
Hodaviah, Eliashib, Pelaiah, Akkub,
Johanan, Delaiah and Anani—seven
in all.

Other Clans of Judah

4 The descendants of Judah:
Perez, Hezron, Karmi, Hur and
Shobal.
[2]Reaiah son of Shobal was the father of
Jahath, and Jahath the father of Ahu-
mai and Lahad. These were the clans
of the Zorathites.
[3]These were the sons*d* of Etam:
Jezreel, Ishma and Idbash. Their sister was named Hazzelelponi. [4]Penu-
el was the father of Gedor, and Ezer
the father of Hushah.

These were the descendants of Hur,
the firstborn of Ephrathah and father*e* of Bethlehem.
[5]Ashhur the father of Tekoa had two
wives, Helah and Naarah.
[6]Naarah bore him Ahuzzam, Hepher,
Temeni and Haahashtari. These
were the descendants of Naarah.
[7]The sons of Helah:
Zereth, Zohar, Ethnan, [8]and Koz,
who was the father of Anub and
Hazzobebah and of the clans of
Aharhel son of Harum.

[9]Jabez was more honorable than his
brothers. His mother had named him Jabez,*f*
saying, "I gave birth to him in pain." [10]Jabez
cried out to the God of Israel, "Oh, that you
would bless me and enlarge my territory!
Let your hand be with me, and keep me
from harm so that I will be free from pain."
And God granted his request.

[11]Kelub, Shuhah's brother, was the father of Mehir, who was the father of
Eshton. [12]Eshton was the father of

---

a 6 Two Hebrew manuscripts (see also 2 Samuel 5:15 and 1 Chron. 14:5); most Hebrew manuscripts
Elishama   *b* 11 Hebrew *Joram*, a variant of *Jehoram*   *c* 16 Hebrew *Jeconiah*, a variant of *Jehoiachin*;
also in verse 17   *d* 3 Some Septuagint manuscripts (see also Vulgate); Hebrew *father*   *e* 4 Father
may mean *civic leader* or *military leader*; also in verses 12, 14, 17, 18 and possibly elsewhere.   *f* 9 *Jabez*
sounds like the Hebrew for *pain*.

Beth Rapha, Paseah and Tehinnah the father of Ir Nahash.ᵃ These were the men of Rekah.

¹³ The sons of Kenaz:
Othniel and Seraiah.

The sons of Othniel:
Hathath and Meonothai.ᵇ ¹⁴Meonothai was the father of Ophrah.

Seraiah was the father of Joab,
the father of Ge Harashim.ᶜ It was called this because its people were skilled workers.

¹⁵ The sons of Caleb son of Jephunneh:
Iru, Elah and Naam.

The son of Elah:
Kenaz.

¹⁶ The sons of Jehallelel:
Ziph, Ziphah, Tiria and Asarel.

¹⁷ The sons of Ezrah:
Jether, Mered, Epher and Jalon. One of Mered's wives gave birth to Miriam, Shammai and Ishbah the father of Eshtemoa. ¹⁸(His wife from the tribe of Judah gave birth to Jered the father of Gedor, Heber the father of Soko, and Jekuthiel the father of Zanoah.) These were the children of Pharaoh's daughter Bithiah, whom Mered had married.

¹⁹ The sons of Hodiah's wife, the sister of Naham:
the father of Keilah the Garmite, and Eshtemoa the Maakathite.

²⁰ The sons of Shimon:
Amnon, Rinnah, Ben-Hanan and Tilon.

The descendants of Ishi:
Zoheth and Ben-Zoheth.

²¹ The sons of Shelah son of Judah:
Er the father of Lekah, Laadah the father of Mareshah and the clans of the linen workers at Beth Ashbea, ²²Jokim, the men of Kozeba, and Joash and Saraph, who ruled in Moab and Jashubi Lehem. (These records are from ancient times.) ²³They were the potters who lived at Netaim and Gederah; they stayed there and worked for the king.

Simeon

²⁴ The descendants of Simeon:
Nemuel, Jamin, Jarib, Zerah and Shaul;
²⁵Shallum was Shaul's son, Mibsam his son and Mishma his son.

²⁶ The descendants of Mishma:
Hammuel his son, Zakkur his son and Shimei his son.

²⁷Shimei had sixteen sons and six daughters, but his brothers did not have many children; so their entire clan did not become as numerous as the people of Judah. ²⁸They lived in Beersheba, Moladah, Hazar Shual, ²⁹Bilhah, Ezem, Tolad, ³⁰Bethuel, Hormah, Ziklag, ³¹Beth Markaboth, Hazar Susim, Beth Biri and Shaaraim. These were their towns until the reign of David. ³²Their surrounding villages were Etam, Ain, Rimmon, Token and Ashan—five towns— ³³and all the villages around these towns as far as Baalath.ᵈ These were their settlements. And they kept a genealogical record.

³⁴Meshobab, Jamlech, Joshah son of Amaziah, ³⁵Joel, Jehu son of Joshibiah, the son of Seraiah, the son of Asiel, ³⁶also Elioenai, Jaakobah, Jeshohaiah, Asaiah, Adiel, Jesimiel, Benaiah, ³⁷and Ziza son of Shiphi, the son of Allon, the son of Jedaiah, the son of Shimri, the son of Shemaiah.

³⁸The men listed above by name were leaders of their clans. Their families increased greatly, ³⁹and they went to the outskirts of Gedor to the east of the valley in search of pasture for their flocks. ⁴⁰They found rich, good pasture, and the land was spacious, peaceful and quiet. Some Hamites had lived there formerly.

⁴¹The men whose names were listed came in the days of Hezekiah king of Judah. They attacked the Hamites in their dwellings and also the Meunites who were there and completely destroyedᵉ them, as is evident to this day. Then they settled in their place, because there was pasture for their flocks. ⁴²And five hundred of these Simeonites, led by Pelatiah, Neariah, Rephaiah and Uzziel, the sons of Ishi, invaded the hill country of Seir. ⁴³They killed the remaining

---

ᵃ 12 Or *of the city of Nahash*   ᵇ 13 Some Septuagint manuscripts and Vulgate; Hebrew does not have *and Meonothai.*   ᶜ 14 *Ge Harashim* means *valley of skilled workers.*   ᵈ 33 Some Septuagint manuscripts (see also Joshua 19:8); Hebrew *Baal*   ᵉ 41 The Hebrew term refers to the irrevocable giving over of things or persons to the LORD, often by totally destroying them.

Amalekites who had escaped, and they have lived there to this day.

Reuben

5 The sons of Reuben the firstborn of Israel (he was the firstborn, but when he defiled his father's marriage bed, his rights as firstborn were given to the sons of Joseph son of Israel; so he could not be listed in the genealogical record in accordance with his birthright, ²and though Judah was the strongest of his brothers and a ruler came from him, the rights of the firstborn belonged to Joseph)— ³the sons of Reuben the firstborn of Israel:

Hanok, Pallu, Hezron and Karmi.

⁴The descendants of Joel:

Shemaiah his son, Gog his son, Shimei his son, ⁵Micah his son, Reaiah his son, Baal his son, ⁶and Beerah his son, whom Tiglath-Pileser*a* king of Assyria took into exile. Beerah was a leader of the Reubenites.

⁷Their relatives by clans, listed according to their genealogical records:

Jeiel the chief, Zechariah, ⁸and Bela son of Azaz, the son of Shema, the son of Joel. They settled in the area from Aroer to Nebo and Baal Meon. ⁹To the east they occupied the land up to the edge of the desert that extends to the Euphrates River, because their livestock had increased in Gilead.

¹⁰During Saul's reign they waged war against the Hagrites, who were defeated at their hands; they occupied the dwellings of the Hagrites throughout the entire region east of Gilead.

Gad

¹¹The Gadites lived next to them in Bashan, as far as Salekah:

¹²Joel was the chief, Shapham the second, then Janai and Shaphat, in Bashan.

¹³Their relatives, by families, were:

Michael, Meshullam, Sheba, Jorai, Jakan, Zia and Eber—seven in all.

¹⁴These were the sons of Abihail son of Huri, the son of Jaroah, the son of Gilead, the son of Michael, the son of Jeshishai, the son of Jahdo, the son of Buz.

¹⁵Ahi son of Abdiel, the son of Guni, was head of their family.

¹⁶The Gadites lived in Gilead, in Bashan and its outlying villages, and on all the pasturelands of Sharon as far as they extended.

¹⁷All these were entered in the genealogical records during the reigns of Jotham king of Judah and Jeroboam king of Israel.

¹⁸The Reubenites, the Gadites and the half-tribe of Manasseh had 44,760 men ready for military service—able-bodied men who could handle shield and sword, who could use a bow, and who were trained for battle. ¹⁹They waged war against the Hagrites, Jetur, Naphish and Nodab. ²⁰They were helped in fighting them, and God delivered the Hagrites and all their allies into their hands, because they cried out to him during the battle. He answered their prayers, because they trusted in him. ²¹They seized the livestock of the Hagrites—fifty thousand camels, two hundred fifty thousand sheep and two thousand donkeys. They also took one hundred thousand people captive, ²²and many others fell slain, because the battle was God's. And they occupied the land until the exile.

The Half-Tribe of Manasseh

²³The people of the half-tribe of Manasseh were numerous; they settled in the land from Bashan to Baal Hermon, that is, to Senir (Mount Hermon).

²⁴These were the heads of their families: Epher, Ishi, Eliel, Azriel, Jeremiah, Hodaviah and Jahdiel. They were brave warriors, famous men, and heads of their families. ²⁵But they were unfaithful to the God of their ancestors and prostituted themselves to the gods of the peoples of the land, whom God had destroyed before them. ²⁶So the God of Israel stirred up the spirit of Pul king of Assyria (that is, Tiglath-Pileser king of Assyria), who took the Reubenites, the Gadites and the half-tribe of Manasseh into exile. He took them to Halah, Habor, Hara and the river of Gozan, where they are to this day.

a 6 Hebrew *Tilgath-Pilneser*, a variant of *Tiglath-Pileser*; also in verse 26

Levi

6

¹*The sons of Levi:
Gershon, Kohath and Merari.
²The sons of Kohath:
Amram, Izhar, Hebron and Uzziel.
³The children of Amram:
Aaron, Moses and Miriam.
The sons of Aaron:
Nadab, Abihu, Eleazar and Ithamar.
⁴Eleazar was the father of Phinehas,
Phinehas the father of Abishua,
⁵Abishua the father of Bukki,
Bukki the father of Uzzi,
⁶Uzzi the father of Zerahiah,
Zerahiah the father of Meraioth,
⁷Meraioth the father of Amariah,
Amariah the father of Ahitub,
⁸Ahitub the father of Zadok,
Zadok the father of Ahimaaz,
⁹Ahimaaz the father of Azariah,
Azariah the father of Johanan,
¹⁰Johanan the father of Azariah (it was
he who served as priest in the temple Solomon built in Jerusalem),
¹¹Azariah the father of Amariah,
Amariah the father of Ahitub,
¹²Ahitub the father of Zadok,
Zadok the father of Shallum,
¹³Shallum the father of Hilkiah,
Hilkiah the father of Azariah,
¹⁴Azariah the father of Seraiah,
and Seraiah the father of Jozadak.ᵃ
¹⁵Jozadak was deported when the LORD
sent Judah and Jerusalem into exile by
the hand of Nebuchadnezzar.

*¹⁶The sons of Levi:
Gershon,ᵇ Kohath and Merari.
¹⁷These are the names of the sons of
Gershon:
Libni and Shimei.
¹⁸The sons of Kohath:
Amram, Izhar, Hebron and Uzziel.
¹⁹The sons of Merari:
Mahli and Mushi.
These are the clans of the Levites list-
ed according to their fathers:
²⁰Of Gershon:
Libni his son, Jahath his son,

Zimmah his son, ²¹Joah his son,
Iddo his son, Zerah his son
and Jeatherai his son.
²²The descendants of Kohath:
Amminadab his son, Korah his son,
Assir his son, ²³Elkanah his son,
Ebiasaph his son, Assir his son,
²⁴Tahath his son, Uriel his son,
Uzziah his son and Shaul his son.
²⁵The descendants of Elkanah:
Amasai, Ahimoth,
²⁶Elkanah his son,ᶜ Zophai his son,
Nahath his son, ²⁷Eliab his son,
Jeroham his son, Elkanah his son
and Samuel his son.ᵈ
²⁸The sons of Samuel:
Joelᵉ the firstborn
and Abijah the second son.
²⁹The descendants of Merari:
Mahli, Libni his son,
Shimei his son, Uzzah his son,
³⁰Shimea his son, Haggiah his son
and Asaiah his son.

The Temple Musicians

³¹These are the men David put in charge
of the music in the house of the LORD after
the ark came to rest there. ³²They ministered with music before the tabernacle, the
tent of meeting, until Solomon built the
temple of the LORD in Jerusalem. They performed their duties according to the regulations laid down for them.
³³Here are the men who served, together
with their sons:
From the Kohathites:
Heman, the musician,
the son of Joel, the son of Samuel,
³⁴the son of Elkanah, the son of Jeroham,
the son of Eliel, the son of Toah,
³⁵the son of Zuph, the son of Elkanah,
the son of Mahath, the son of
Amasai,
³⁶the son of Elkanah, the son of Joel,
the son of Azariah, the son of Zephaniah,
³⁷the son of Tahath, the son of Assir,

ᵃ 14 Hebrew *Jehozadak*, a variant of *Jozadak*; also in verse 15   ᵇ 16 Hebrew *Gershom*, a variant of *Gershon*; also in verses 17, 20, 43, 62 and 71   ᶜ 26 Some Hebrew manuscripts, Septuagint and Syriac; most Hebrew manuscripts *Ahimoth ²⁶and Elkanah. The sons of Elkanah:*   ᵈ 27 Some Septuagint manuscripts (see also 1 Samuel 1:19,20 and 1 Chron. 6:33,34); Hebrew does not have *and Samuel his son.*   ᵉ 28 Some Septuagint manuscripts and Syriac (see also 1 Samuel 8:2 and 1 Chron. 6:33); Hebrew does not have *Joel.*

* 6:1-15 is numbered 5:27-41 in Hebrew texts.   * 6:16-81 is numbered 6:1-66 in Hebrew texts.

the son of Ebiasaph, the son of Korah,
³⁸the son of Izhar, the son of Kohath,
the son of Levi, the son of Israel;
³⁹and Heman's associate Asaph, who
served at his right hand:
Asaph son of Berekiah, the son of
Shimea,
⁴⁰the son of Michael, the son of Baaseiah,ᵃ
the son of Malkijah, ⁴¹the son of
Ethni,
the son of Zerah, the son of Adaiah,
⁴²the son of Ethan, the son of Zimmah,
the son of Shimei, ⁴³the son of Jahath,
the son of Gershon, the son of Levi;
⁴⁴and from their associates, the Merarites, at his left hand:
Ethan son of Kishi, the son of Abdi,
the son of Malluk, ⁴⁵the son of Hashabiah,
the son of Amaziah, the son of Hilkiah,
⁴⁶the son of Amzi, the son of Bani,
the son of Shemer, ⁴⁷the son of
Mahli,
the son of Mushi, the son of Merari,
the son of Levi.

⁴⁸Their fellow Levites were assigned to all the other duties of the tabernacle, the house of God. ⁴⁹But Aaron and his descendants were the ones who presented offerings on the altar of burnt offering and on the altar of incense in connection with all that was done in the Most Holy Place, making atonement for Israel, in accordance with all that Moses the servant of God had commanded.

⁵⁰These were the descendants of Aaron:
Eleazar his son, Phinehas his son,
Abishua his son, ⁵¹Bukki his son,
Uzzi his son, Zerahiah his son,
⁵²Meraioth his son, Amariah his son,
Ahitub his son, ⁵³Zadok his son
and Ahimaaz his son.

⁵⁴These were the locations of their settlements allotted as their territory (they were assigned to the descendants of Aaron who were from the Kohathite clan, because the first lot was for them):
⁵⁵They were given Hebron in Judah with its surrounding pasturelands. ⁵⁶But the fields and villages around the city were given to Caleb son of Jephunneh. ⁵⁷So the descendants of Aaron were given Hebron (a city of refuge), and Libnah,ᵇ Jattir, Eshtemoa, ⁵⁸Hilen, Debir, ⁵⁹Ashan, Juttahᶜ and Beth Shemesh, together with their pasturelands. ⁶⁰And from the tribe of Benjamin they were given Gibeon,ᵈ Geba, Alemeth and Anathoth, together with their pasturelands.
The total number of towns distributed among the Kohathite clans came to thirteen.
⁶¹The rest of Kohath's descendants were allotted ten towns from the clans of half the tribe of Manasseh.
⁶²The descendants of Gershon, clan by clan, were allotted thirteen towns from the tribes of Issachar, Asher and Naphtali, and from the part of the tribe of Manasseh that is in Bashan.
⁶³The descendants of Merari, clan by clan, were allotted twelve towns from the tribes of Reuben, Gad and Zebulun.
⁶⁴So the Israelites gave the Levites these towns and their pasturelands. ⁶⁵From the tribes of Judah, Simeon and Benjamin they allotted the previously named towns.
⁶⁶Some of the Kohathite clans were given as their territory towns from the tribe of Ephraim.
⁶⁷In the hill country of Ephraim they were given Shechem (a city of refuge), and Gezer,ᵉ ⁶⁸Jokmeam, Beth Horon, ⁶⁹Aijalon and Gath Rimmon, together with their pasturelands.
⁷⁰And from half the tribe of Manasseh the Israelites gave Aner and Bileam, together with their pasturelands, to the rest of the Kohathite clans.

⁷¹The Gershonites received the following:
From the clan of the half-tribe of Manasseh

ᵃ 40 Most Hebrew manuscripts; some Hebrew manuscripts, one Septuagint manuscript and Syriac *Maaseiah*   ᵇ 57 See Joshua 21:13; Hebrew *given the cities of refuge: Hebron, Libnah.*   ᶜ 59 Syriac (see also Septuagint and Joshua 21:16); Hebrew does not have *Juttah.*   ᵈ 60 See Joshua 21:17; Hebrew does not have *Gibeon.*   ᵉ 67 See Joshua 21:21; Hebrew *given the cities of refuge: Shechem, Gezer.*

they received Golan in Bashan and also Ashtaroth, together with their pasturelands;

72 from the tribe of Issachar
they received Kedesh, Daberath, 73Ramoth and Anem, together with their pasturelands;

74 from the tribe of Asher
they received Mashal, Abdon, 75Hukok and Rehob, together with their pasturelands;

76 and from the tribe of Naphtali
they received Kedesh in Galilee, Hammon and Kiriathaim, together with their pasturelands.

77 The Merarites (the rest of the Levites) received the following:
From the tribe of Zebulun
they received Jokneam, Kartah,a Rimmono and Tabor, together with their pasturelands;

78 from the tribe of Reuben across the Jordan east of Jericho
they received Bezer in the wilderness, Jahzah, 79Kedemoth and Mephaath, together with their pasturelands;

80 and from the tribe of Gad
they received Ramoth in Gilead, Mahanaim, 81Heshbon and Jazer, together with their pasturelands.

Issachar

7 The sons of Issachar:
Tola, Puah, Jashub and Shimron—four in all.

2 The sons of Tola:
Uzzi, Rephaiah, Jeriel, Jahmai, Ibsam and Samuel—heads of their families. During the reign of David, the descendants of Tola listed as fighting men in their genealogy numbered 22,600.

3 The son of Uzzi:
Izrahiah.
The sons of Izrahiah:
Michael, Obadiah, Joel and Ishiah. All five of them were chiefs. 4According to their family genealogy, they had 36,000 men ready for battle, for they had many wives and children.

5 The relatives who were fighting men belonging to all the clans of Issachar, as listed in their genealogy, were 87,000 in all.

Benjamin

6 Three sons of Benjamin:
Bela, Beker and Jediael.

7 The sons of Bela:
Ezbon, Uzzi, Uzziel, Jerimoth and Iri, heads of families—five in all. Their genealogical record listed 22,034 fighting men.

8 The sons of Beker:
Zemirah, Joash, Eliezer, Elioenai, Omri, Jeremoth, Abijah, Anathoth and Alemeth. All these were the sons of Beker. 9Their genealogical record listed the heads of families and 20,200 fighting men.

10 The son of Jediael:
Bilhan.
The sons of Bilhan:
Jeush, Benjamin, Ehud, Kenaanah, Zethan, Tarshish and Ahishahar. 11All these sons of Jediael were heads of families. There were 17,200 fighting men ready to go out to war.

12 The Shuppites and Huppites were the descendants of Ir, and the Hushitesb the descendants of Aher.

Naphtali

13 The sons of Naphtali:
Jahziel, Guni, Jezer and Shillemc—the descendants of Bilhah.

Manasseh

14 The descendants of Manasseh:
Asriel was his descendant through his Aramean concubine. She gave birth to Makir the father of Gilead. 15Makir took a wife from among the Huppites and Shuppites. His sister's name was Maakah.
Another descendant was named Zelophehad, who had only daughters.

16 Makir's wife Maakah gave birth to a son and named him Peresh. His brother was named Sheresh, and his sons were Ulam and Rakem.

17 The son of Ulam:
Bedan.

---

a 77 See Septuagint and Joshua 21:34; Hebrew does not have Jokneam, Kartah.   b 12 Or Ir. The sons of Dan: Hushim, (see Gen. 46:23); Hebrew does not have The sons of Dan.   c 13 Some Hebrew and Septuagint manuscripts (see also Gen. 46:24 and Num. 26:49); most Hebrew manuscripts Shallum

These were the sons of Gilead son of Makir, the son of Manasseh. ¹⁸His sister Hammoleketh gave birth to Ishhod, Abiezer and Mahlah.

¹⁹The sons of Shemida were:

Ahian, Shechem, Likhi and Aniam.

Ephraim

²⁰The descendants of Ephraim:

Shuthelah, Bered his son,
Tahath his son, Eleadah his son,
Tahath his son, ²¹Zabad his son
and Shuthelah his son.

Ezer and Elead were killed by the native-born men of Gath, when they went down to seize their livestock. ²²Their father Ephraim mourned for them many days, and his relatives came to comfort him. ²³Then he made love to his wife again, and she became pregnant and gave birth to a son. He named him Beriah,ᵃ because there had been misfortune in his family. ²⁴His daughter was Sheerah, who built Lower and Upper Beth Horon as well as Uzzen Sheerah.

²⁵Rephah was his son, Resheph his son,ᵇ
Telah his son, Tahan his son,
²⁶Ladan his son, Ammihud his son,
Elishama his son, ²⁷Nun his son
and Joshua his son.

²⁸Their lands and settlements included Bethel and its surrounding villages, Naaran to the east, Gezer and its villages to the west, and Shechem and its villages all the way to Ayyah and its villages. ²⁹Along the borders of Manasseh were Beth Shan, Taanach, Megiddo and Dor, together with their villages. The descendants of Joseph son of Israel lived in these towns.

Asher

³⁰The sons of Asher:

Imnah, Ishvah, Ishvi and Beriah.
Their sister was Serah.

³¹The sons of Beriah:

Heber and Malkiel, who was the father of Birzaith.

³²Heber was the father of Japhlet, Shomer and Hotham and of their sister Shua.

³³The sons of Japhlet:

Pasak, Bimhal and Ashvath.
These were Japhlet's sons.

³⁴The sons of Shomer:

Ahi, Rohgah,ᶜ Hubbah and Aram.

³⁵The sons of his brother Helem:

Zophah, Imna, Shelesh and Amal.

³⁶The sons of Zophah:

Suah, Harnepher, Shual, Beri, Imrah, ³⁷Bezer, Hod, Shamma, Shilshah, Ithranᵈ and Beera.

³⁸The sons of Jether:

Jephunneh, Pispah and Ara.

³⁹The sons of Ulla:

Arah, Hanniel and Rizia.

⁴⁰All these were descendants of Asher—heads of families, choice men, brave warriors and outstanding leaders. The number of men ready for battle, as listed in their genealogy, was 26,000.

The Genealogy of Saul the Benjamite

8 Benjamin was the father of Bela his firstborn,

Ashbel the second son, Aharah the third,
²Nohah the fourth and Rapha the fifth.

³The sons of Bela were:

Addar, Gera, Abihud,ᵉ ⁴Abishua, Naaman, Ahoah, ⁵Gera, Shephuphan and Huram.

⁶These were the descendants of Ehud, who were heads of families of those living in Geba and were deported to Manahath:

⁷Naaman, Ahijah, and Gera, who deported them and who was the father of Uzza and Ahihud.

⁸Sons were born to Shaharaim in Moab after he had divorced his wives Hushim and Baara. ⁹By his wife Hodesh he had Jobab, Zibia, Mesha, Malkam, ¹⁰Jeuz, Sakia and Mirmah. These were his sons, heads of families. ¹¹By Hushim he had Abitub and Elpaal.

¹²The sons of Elpaal:

Eber, Misham, Shemed (who built Ono and Lod with its surrounding villages), ¹³and Beriah and Shema, who were heads of families of those

---

ᵃ *23 Beriah* sounds like the Hebrew for *misfortune.*   ᵇ *25* Some Septuagint manuscripts; Hebrew does not have *his son.*   ᶜ *34* Or *of his brother Shomer: Rohgah*   ᵈ *37* Possibly a variant of *Jether*
ᵉ *3* Or *Gera the father of Ehud*

living in Aijalon and who drove out the inhabitants of Gath.

14 Ahio, Shashak, Jeremoth, 15 Zebadiah, Arad, Eder, 16 Michael, Ishpah and Joha were the sons of Beriah.

17 Zebadiah, Meshullam, Hizki, Heber, 18 Ishmerai, Izliah and Jobab were the sons of Elpaal.

19 Jakim, Zikri, Zabdi, 20 Elienai, Zillethai, Eliel, 21 Adaiah, Beraiah and Shimrath were the sons of Shimei.

22 Ishpan, Eber, Eliel, 23 Abdon, Zikri, Hanan, 24 Hananiah, Elam, Anthothijah, 25 Iphdeiah and Penuel were the sons of Shashak.

26 Shamsherai, Shehariah, Athaliah, 27 Jaareshiah, Elijah and Zikri were the sons of Jeroham.

28 All these were heads of families, chiefs as listed in their genealogy, and they lived in Jerusalem.

29 Jeiel[a] the father[b] of Gibeon lived in Gibeon.

His wife's name was Maakah, 30 and his firstborn son was Abdon, followed by Zur, Kish, Baal, Ner,[c] Nadab, 31 Gedor, Ahio, Zeker 32 and Mikloth, who was the father of Shimeah. They too lived near their relatives in Jerusalem.

33 Ner was the father of Kish, Kish the father of Saul, and Saul the father of Jonathan, Malki-Shua, Abinadab and Esh-Baal.[d]

34 The son of Jonathan:
Merib-Baal,[e] who was the father of Micah.

35 The sons of Micah:
Pithon, Melek, Tarea and Ahaz.

36 Ahaz was the father of Jehoaddah, Jehoaddah was the father of Alemeth, Azmaveth and Zimri, and Zimri was the father of Moza. 37 Moza was the father of Binea; Raphah was his son, Eleasah his son and Azel his son.

38 Azel had six sons, and these were their names:
Azrikam, Bokeru, Ishmael, Sheariah, Obadiah and Hanan. All these were the sons of Azel.

39 The sons of his brother Eshek:
Ulam his firstborn, Jeush the second son and Eliphelet the third. 40 The sons of Ulam were brave warriors who could handle the bow. They had many sons and grandsons—150 in all.

All these were the descendants of Benjamin.

9 All Israel was listed in the genealogies recorded in the book of the kings of Israel and Judah. They were taken captive to Babylon because of their unfaithfulness.

The People in Jerusalem

2 Now the first to resettle on their own property in their own towns were some Israelites, priests, Levites and temple servants.

3 Those from Judah, from Benjamin, and from Ephraim and Manasseh who lived in Jerusalem were:

4 Uthai son of Ammihud, the son of Omri, the son of Imri, the son of Bani, a descendant of Perez son of Judah.

5 Of the Shelanites[f]:
Asaiah the firstborn and his sons.

6 Of the Zerahites:
Jeuel.
The people from Judah numbered 690.

7 Of the Benjamites:
Sallu son of Meshullam, the son of Hodaviah, the son of Hassenuah;

8 Ibneiah son of Jeroham; Elah son of Uzzi, the son of Mikri; and Meshullam son of Shephatiah, the son of Reuel, the son of Ibnijah.

9 The people from Benjamin, as listed in their genealogy, numbered 956. All these men were heads of their families.

10 Of the priests:
Jedaiah; Jehoiarib; Jakin;

11 Azariah son of Hilkiah, the son of Meshullam, the son of Zadok, the son

a 29 Some Septuagint manuscripts (see also 1 Chron. 9:35); Hebrew does not have Jeiel.   b 29 Father may mean civic leader or military leader.   c 30 Some Septuagint manuscripts (see also 1 Chron. 9:36); Hebrew does not have Ner.   d 33 Also known as Ish-Bosheth   e 34 Also known as Mephibosheth   f 5 See Num. 26:20; Hebrew Shilonites.

of Meraioth, the son of Ahitub, the official in charge of the house of God; ¹²Adaiah son of Jeroham, the son of Pashhur, the son of Malkijah; and Maasai son of Adiel, the son of Jahzerah, the son of Meshullam, the son of Meshillemith, the son of Immer.

¹³The priests, who were heads of families, numbered 1,760. They were able men, responsible for ministering in the house of God.

¹⁴Of the Levites:

Shemaiah son of Hasshub, the son of Azrikam, the son of Hashabiah, a Merarite; ¹⁵Bakbakkar, Heresh, Galal and Mattaniah son of Mika, the son of Zikri, the son of Asaph; ¹⁶Obadiah son of Shemaiah, the son of Galal, the son of Jeduthun; and Berekiah son of Asa, the son of Elkanah, who lived in the villages of the Netophathites.

¹⁷The gatekeepers:

Shallum, Akkub, Talmon, Ahiman and their fellow Levites, Shallum their chief ¹⁸being stationed at the King's Gate on the east, up to the present time. These were the gatekeepers belonging to the camp of the Levites. ¹⁹Shallum son of Kore, the son of Ebiasaph, the son of Korah, and his fellow gatekeepers from his family (the Korahites) were responsible for guarding the thresholds of the tent just as their ancestors had been responsible for guarding the entrance to the dwelling of the LORD. ²⁰In earlier times Phinehas son of Eleazar was the official in charge of the gatekeepers, and the LORD was with him. ²¹Zechariah son of Meshelemiah was the gatekeeper at the entrance to the tent of meeting.

²²Altogether, those chosen to be gatekeepers at the thresholds numbered 212. They were registered by genealogy in their villages. The gatekeepers had been assigned to their positions of trust by David and Samuel the seer. ²³They and their descendants were in charge of guarding the gates of the house of the LORD—the house called the tent of meeting. ²⁴The gatekeepers were on the four sides: east, west, north and south.

²⁵Their fellow Levites in their villages had to come from time to time and share their duties for seven-day periods. ²⁶But the four principal gatekeepers, who were Levites, were entrusted with the responsibility for the rooms and treasuries in the house of God. ²⁷They would spend the night stationed around the house of God, because they had to guard it; and they had charge of the key for opening it each morning.

²⁸Some of them were in charge of the articles used in the temple service; they counted them when they were brought in and when they were taken out. ²⁹Others were assigned to take care of the furnishings and all the other articles of the sanctuary, as well as the special flour and wine, and the oil, incense and spices. ³⁰But some of the priests took care of mixing the spices. ³¹A Levite named Mattithiah, the firstborn son of Shallum the Korahite, was entrusted with the responsibility for baking the offering bread. ³²Some of the Kohathites, their fellow Levites, were in charge of preparing for every Sabbath the bread set out on the table.

³³Those who were musicians, heads of Levite families, stayed in the rooms of the temple and were exempt from other duties because they were responsible for the work day and night.

³⁴All these were heads of Levite families, chiefs as listed in their genealogy, and they lived in Jerusalem.

The Genealogy of Saul

³⁵Jeiel the father[a] of Gibeon lived in Gibeon.

His wife's name was Maakah, ³⁶and his firstborn son was Abdon, followed by Zur, Kish, Baal, Ner, Nadab, ³⁷Gedor, Ahio, Zechariah and Mikloth. ³⁸Mikloth was the father of Shimeam. They too lived near their relatives in Jerusalem.

³⁹Ner was the father of Kish, Kish the father of Saul, and Saul the father of Jonathan, Malki-Shua, Abinadab and Esh-Baal.[b]

⁴⁰The son of Jonathan:

Merib-Baal,[c] who was the father of Micah.

⁴¹The sons of Micah:

---

a 35 Father may mean *civic leader* or *military leader.* known as *Mephibosheth*   *b 39* Also known as *Ish-Bosheth*   *c 40* Also

Pithon, Melek, Tahrea and Ahaz.ᵃ
⁴²Ahaz was the father of Jadah, Jadahᵇ was the father of Alemeth, Azmaveth and Zimri, and Zimri was the father of Moza. ⁴³Moza was the father of Binea; Rephaiah was his son, Eleasah his son and Azel his son.
⁴⁴Azel had six sons, and these were their names:
Azrikam, Bokeru, Ishmael, Sheariah, Obadiah and Hanan. These were the sons of Azel.

Saul Takes His Life

10 Now the Philistines fought against Israel; the Israelites fled before them, and many fell dead on Mount Gilboa. ²The Philistines were in hot pursuit of Saul and his sons, and they killed his sons Jonathan, Abinadab and Malki-Shua. ³The fighting grew fierce around Saul, and when the archers overtook him, they wounded him.

⁴Saul said to his armor-bearer, "Draw your sword and run me through, or these uncircumcised fellows will come and abuse me."

But his armor-bearer was terrified and would not do it; so Saul took his own sword and fell on it. ⁵When the armor-bearer saw that Saul was dead, he too fell on his sword and died. ⁶So Saul and his three sons died, and all his house died together.

⁷When all the Israelites in the valley saw that the army had fled and that Saul and his sons had died, they abandoned their towns and fled. And the Philistines came and occupied them.

⁸The next day, when the Philistines came to strip the dead, they found Saul and his sons fallen on Mount Gilboa. ⁹They stripped him and took his head and his armor, and sent messengers throughout the land of the Philistines to proclaim the news among their idols and their people. ¹⁰They put his armor in the temple of their gods and hung up his head in the temple of Dagon.

¹¹When all the inhabitants of Jabesh Gilead heard what the Philistines had done to Saul, ¹²all their valiant men went and took the bodies of Saul and his sons and brought

them to Jabesh. Then they buried their bones under the great tree in Jabesh, and they fasted seven days.

¹³Saul died because he was unfaithful to the LORD; he did not keep the word of the LORD and even consulted a medium for guidance, ¹⁴and did not inquire of the LORD. So the LORD put him to death and turned the kingdom over to David son of Jesse.

David Becomes King Over Israel

11 All Israel came together to David at Hebron and said, "We are your own flesh and blood. ²In the past, even while Saul was king, you were the one who led Israel on their military campaigns. And the LORD your God said to you, 'You will shepherd my people Israel, and you will become their ruler.'"

³When all the elders of Israel had come to King David at Hebron, he made a covenant with them at Hebron before the LORD, and they anointed David king over Israel, as the LORD had promised through Samuel.

David Conquers Jerusalem

⁴David and all the Israelites marched to Jerusalem (that is, Jebus). The Jebusites who lived there ⁵said to David, "You will not get in here." Nevertheless, David captured the fortress of Zion—which is the City of David.

⁶David had said, "Whoever leads the attack on the Jebusites will become commander-in-chief." Joab son of Zeruiah went up first, and so he received the command.

⁷David then took up residence in the fortress, and so it was called the City of David. ⁸He built up the city around it, from the terracesᶜ to the surrounding wall, while Joab restored the rest of the city. ⁹And David became more and more powerful, because the LORD Almighty was with him.

David's Mighty Warriors

¹⁰These were the chiefs of David's mighty warriors—they, together with all Israel, gave his kingship strong support to extend it over the whole land, as the LORD had promised— ¹¹this is the list of David's mighty warriors:

Jashobeam,ᵈ a Hakmonite, was chief of the officersᵉ; he raised his spear against

ᵃ 41 Vulgate and Syriac (see also Septuagint and 1 Chron. 8:35); Hebrew does not have and Ahaz.
ᵇ 42 Some Hebrew manuscripts and Septuagint (see also 1 Chron. 8:36); most Hebrew manuscripts Jarah, Jarah   ᶜ 8 Or the Millo   ᵈ 11 Possibly a variant of Jashob-Baal   ᵉ 11 Or Thirty; some Septuagint manuscripts Three (see also 2 Samuel 23:8)

three hundred men, whom he killed in one encounter.

¹²Next to him was Eleazar son of Dodai the Ahohite, one of the three mighty warriors. ¹³He was with David at Pas Dammim when the Philistines gathered there for battle. At a place where there was a field full of barley, the troops fled from the Philistines. ¹⁴But they took their stand in the middle of the field. They defended it and struck the Philistines down, and the LORD brought about a great victory.

¹⁵Three of the thirty chiefs came down to David to the rock at the cave of Adullam, while a band of Philistines was encamped in the Valley of Rephaim. ¹⁶At that time David was in the stronghold, and the Philistine garrison was at Bethlehem. ¹⁷David longed for water and said, "Oh, that someone would get me a drink of water from the well near the gate of Bethlehem!" ¹⁸So the Three broke through the Philistine lines, drew water from the well near the gate of Bethlehem and carried it back to David. But he refused to drink it; instead, he poured it out to the LORD. ¹⁹"God forbid that I should do this!" he said. "Should I drink the blood of these men who went at the risk of their lives?" Because they risked their lives to bring it back, David would not drink it.

Such were the exploits of the three mighty warriors.

²⁰Abishai the brother of Joab was chief of the Three. He raised his spear against three hundred men, whom he killed, and so he became as famous as the Three. ²¹He was doubly honored above the Three and became their commander, even though he was not included among them.

²²Benaiah son of Jehoiada, a valiant fighter from Kabzeel, performed great exploits. He struck down Moab's two mightiest warriors. He also went down into a pit on a snowy day and killed a lion. ²³And he struck down an Egyptian who was five cubitsᵃ tall. Although the Egyptian had a spear like a weaver's rod in his hand, Benaiah went against him with a club. He snatched the spear from the Egyptian's hand and killed him with his own spear. ²⁴Such were the exploits of Benaiah son of Jehoiada; he too was as famous as the three mighty warriors. ²⁵He was held in greater honor than any of the

Thirty, but he was not included among the Three. And David put him in charge of his bodyguard.

²⁶The mighty warriors were:
Asahel the brother of Joab,
Elhanan son of Dodo from Bethlehem,
²⁷Shammoth the Harorite,
Helez the Pelonite,
²⁸Ira son of Ikkesh from Tekoa,
Abiezer from Anathoth,
²⁹Sibbekai the Hushathite,
Ilai the Ahohite,
³⁰Maharai the Netophathite,
Heled son of Baanah the Netophathite,
³¹Ithai son of Ribai from Gibeah in Benjamin,
Benaiah the Pirathonite,
³²Hurai from the ravines of Gaash,
Abiel the Arbathite,
³³Azmaveth the Baharumite,
Eliahba the Shaalbonite,
³⁴the sons of Hashem the Gizonite,
Jonathan son of Shagee the Hararite,
³⁵Ahiam son of Sakar the Hararite,
Eliphal son of Ur,
³⁶Hepher the Mekerathite,
Ahijah the Pelonite,
³⁷Hezro the Carmelite,
Naarai son of Ezbai,
³⁸Joel the brother of Nathan,
Mibhar son of Hagri,
³⁹Zelek the Ammonite,
Naharai the Berothite, the armorbearer of Joab son of Zeruiah,
⁴⁰Ira the Ithrite,
Gareb the Ithrite,
⁴¹Uriah the Hittite,
Zabad son of Ahlai,
⁴²Adina son of Shiza the Reubenite, who was chief of the Reubenites, and the thirty with him,
⁴³Hanan son of Maakah,
Joshaphat the Mithnite,
⁴⁴Uzzia the Ashterathite,
Shama and Jeiel the sons of Hotham the Aroerite,
⁴⁵Jediael son of Shimri,
his brother Joha the Tizite,
⁴⁶Eliel the Mahavite,
Jeribai and Joshaviah the sons of Elnaam,

─────────────
ᵃ 23 That is, about 7 feet or about 2.3 meters

Ithmah the Moabite,
⁴⁷ Eliel, Obed and Jaasiel the Mezobaite.

Warriors Join David

12 These were the men who came to David at Ziklag, while he was banished from the presence of Saul son of Kish (they were among the warriors who helped him in battle; ²they were armed with bows and were able to shoot arrows or to sling stones right-handed or left-handed; they were relatives of Saul from the tribe of Benjamin):

³Ahiezer their chief and Joash the sons of Shemaah the Gibeathite; Jeziel and Pelet the sons of Azmaveth; Berakah, Jehu the Anathothite, ⁴and Ishmaiah the Gibeonite, a mighty warrior among the Thirty, who was a leader of the Thirty; *Jeremiah, Jahaziel, Johanan, Jozabad the Gederathite, *⁵Eluzai, Jerimoth, Bealiah, Shemariah and Shephatiah the Haruphite; ⁶Elkanah, Ishiah, Azarel, Joezer and Jashobeam the Korahites; ⁷and Joelah and Zebadiah the sons of Jeroham from Gedor.

⁸Some Gadites defected to David at his stronghold in the wilderness. They were brave warriors, ready for battle and able to handle the shield and spear. Their faces were the faces of lions, and they were as swift as gazelles in the mountains.

⁹Ezer was the chief,
 Obadiah the second in command, Eliab the third,
¹⁰Mishmannah the fourth, Jeremiah the fifth,
¹¹Attai the sixth, Eliel the seventh,
¹²Johanan the eighth, Elzabad the ninth,
¹³Jeremiah the tenth and Makbannai the eleventh.

¹⁴These Gadites were army commanders; the least was a match for a hundred, and the greatest for a thousand. ¹⁵It was they who crossed the Jordan in the first month when it was overflowing all its banks, and they put to flight everyone living in the valleys, to the east and to the west.

¹⁶Other Benjamites and some men from Judah also came to David in his stronghold. ¹⁷David went out to meet them and said to them, "If you have come to me in peace to help me, I am ready for you to join me. But if you have come to betray me to my enemies when my hands are free from violence, may the God of our ancestors see it and judge you."

¹⁸Then the Spirit came on Amasai, chief of the Thirty, and he said:

"We are yours, David!
 We are with you, son of Jesse!
Success, success to you,
 and success to those who help you,
 for your God will help you."

So David received them and made them leaders of his raiding bands.

¹⁹Some of the tribe of Manasseh defected to David when he went with the Philistines to fight against Saul. (He and his men did not help the Philistines because, after consultation, their rulers sent him away. They said, "It will cost us our heads if he deserts to his master Saul.") ²⁰When David went to Ziklag, these were the men of Manasseh who defected to him: Adnah, Jozabad, Jediael, Michael, Jozabad, Elihu and Zillethai, leaders of units of a thousand in Manasseh. ²¹They helped David against raiding bands, for all of them were brave warriors, and they were commanders in his army. ²²Day after day men came to help David, until he had a great army, like the army of God. ᵃ

Others Join David at Hebron

²³These are the numbers of the men armed for battle who came to David at Hebron to turn Saul's kingdom over to him, as the Lᴏʀᴅ had said:

²⁴from Judah, carrying shield and spear—6,800 armed for battle;
²⁵from Simeon, warriors ready for battle—7,100;
²⁶from Levi—4,600, ²⁷including Jehoiada, leader of the family of Aaron, with 3,700 men, ²⁸and Zadok, a brave young warrior, with 22 officers from his family;
²⁹from Benjamin, Saul's tribe—3,000, most of whom had remained loyal to Saul's house until then;
³⁰from Ephraim, brave warriors, famous in their own clans—20,800;

ᵃ 22 Or *a great and mighty army*

* The rest of this verse (12:4b) is numbered 12:5 in Hebrew texts.   * 12:5-40 is numbered 12:6-41 in Hebrew texts.

³¹from half the tribe of Manasseh, designated by name to come and make David king—18,000;

³²from Issachar, men who understood the times and knew what Israel should do—200 chiefs, with all their relatives under their command;

³³from Zebulun, experienced soldiers prepared for battle with every type of weapon, to help David with undivided loyalty—50,000;

³⁴from Naphtali—1,000 officers, together with 37,000 men carrying shields and spears;

³⁵from Dan, ready for battle—28,600;

³⁶from Asher, experienced soldiers prepared for battle—40,000;

³⁷and from east of the Jordan, from Reuben, Gad and the half-tribe of Manasseh, armed with every type of weapon—120,000.

³⁸All these were fighting men who volunteered to serve in the ranks. They came to Hebron fully determined to make David king over all Israel. All the rest of the Israelites were also of one mind to make David king. ³⁹The men spent three days there with David, eating and drinking, for their families had supplied provisions for them. ⁴⁰Also, their neighbors from as far away as Issachar, Zebulun and Naphtali came bringing food on donkeys, camels, mules and oxen. There were plentiful supplies of flour, fig cakes, raisin cakes, wine, oil, cattle and sheep, for there was joy in Israel.

Bringing Back the Ark

13 David conferred with each of his officers, the commanders of thousands and commanders of hundreds. ²He then said to the whole assembly of Israel, "If it seems good to you and if it is the will of the LORD our God, let us send word far and wide to the rest of our people throughout the territories of Israel, and also to the priests and Levites who are with them in their towns and pasturelands, to come and join us. ³Let us bring the ark of our God back to us, for we did not inquire of ᵃ it ᵇ during the reign of Saul." ⁴The whole assembly agreed to do this, because it seemed right to all the people.

⁵So David assembled all Israel, from the Shihor River in Egypt to Lebo Hamath, to bring the ark of God from Kiriath Jearim. ⁶David and all Israel went to Baalah of Judah (Kiriath Jearim) to bring up from there the ark of God the LORD, who is enthroned between the cherubim—the ark that is called by the Name.

⁷They moved the ark of God from Abinadab's house on a new cart, with Uzzah and Ahio guiding it. ⁸David and all the Israelites were celebrating with all their might before God, with songs and with harps, lyres, timbrels, cymbals and trumpets.

⁹When they came to the threshing floor of Kidon, Uzzah reached out his hand to steady the ark, because the oxen stumbled. ¹⁰The LORD's anger burned against Uzzah, and he struck him down because he had put his hand on the ark. So he died there before God.

¹¹Then David was angry because the LORD's wrath had broken out against Uzzah, and to this day that place is called Perez Uzzah.ᶜ

¹²David was afraid of God that day and asked, "How can I ever bring the ark of God to me?" ¹³He did not take the ark to be with him in the City of David. Instead, he took it to the house of Obed-Edom the Gittite. ¹⁴The ark of God remained with the family of Obed-Edom in his house for three months, and the LORD blessed his household and everything he had.

David's House and Family

14 Now Hiram king of Tyre sent messengers to David, along with cedar logs, stonemasons and carpenters to build a palace for him. ²And David knew that the LORD had established him as king over Israel and that his kingdom had been highly exalted for the sake of his people Israel.

³In Jerusalem David took more wives and became the father of more sons and daughters. ⁴These are the names of the children born to him there: Shammua, Shobab, Nathan, Solomon, ⁵Ibhar, Elishua, Elpelet, ⁶Nogah, Nepheg, Japhia, ⁷Elishama, Beeliadaᵈ and Eliphelet.

David Defeats the Philistines

⁸When the Philistines heard that David

ᵃ 3 Or *we neglected*   ᵇ 3 Or *him*   ᶜ 11 *Perez Uzzah* means *outbreak against Uzzah.*   ᵈ 7 A variant of *Eliada* had been anointed king over all Israel, they went up in full force to search for him, but David heard about it and went out to meet them. ⁹Now the Philistines had come and raided the Valley of Rephaim; ¹⁰so David inquired of God: "Shall I go and attack the Philistines? Will you deliver them into my hands?"

The LORD answered him, "Go, I will deliver them into your hands."

¹¹So David and his men went up to Baal Perazim, and there he defeated them. He said, "As waters break out, God has broken out against my enemies by my hand." So that place was called Baal Perazim.ᵃ ¹²The Philistines had abandoned their gods there, and David gave orders to burn them in the fire.

¹³Once more the Philistines raided the valley; ¹⁴so David inquired of God again, and God answered him, "Do not go directly after them, but circle around them and attack them in front of the poplar trees. ¹⁵As soon as you hear the sound of marching in the tops of the poplar trees, move out to battle, because that will mean God has gone out in front of you to strike the Philistine army." ¹⁶So David did as God commanded him, and they struck down the Philistine army, all the way from Gibeon to Gezer.

¹⁷So David's fame spread throughout every land, and the LORD made all the nations fear him.

The Ark Brought to Jerusalem

15 After David had constructed buildings for himself in the City of David, he prepared a place for the ark of God and pitched a tent for it. ²Then David said, "No one but the Levites may carry the ark of God, because the LORD chose them to carry the ark of the LORD and to minister before him forever."

³David assembled all Israel in Jerusalem to bring up the ark of the LORD to the place he had prepared for it. ⁴He called together the descendants of Aaron and the Levites:

⁵From the descendants of Kohath,
   Uriel the leader and 120 relatives;
⁶from the descendants of Merari,
   Asaiah the leader and 220 relatives;
⁷from the descendants of Gershon,ᵇ
   Joel the leader and 130 relatives;
⁸from the descendants of Elizaphan,
   Shemaiah the leader and 200 relatives;
⁹from the descendants of Hebron,
   Eliel the leader and 80 relatives;
¹⁰from the descendants of Uzziel,
   Amminadab the leader and 112 relatives.

¹¹Then David summoned Zadok and Abiathar the priests, and Uriel, Asaiah, Joel, Shemaiah, Eliel and Amminadab the Levites. ¹²He said to them, "You are the heads of the Levitical families; you and your fellow Levites are to consecrate yourselves and bring up the ark of the LORD, the God of Israel, to the place I have prepared for it. ¹³It was because you, the Levites, did not bring it up the first time that the LORD our God broke out in anger against us. We did not inquire of him about how to do it in the prescribed way." ¹⁴So the priests and Levites consecrated themselves in order to bring up the ark of the LORD, the God of Israel. ¹⁵And the Levites carried the ark of God with the poles on their shoulders, as Moses had commanded in accordance with the word of the LORD.

¹⁶David told the leaders of the Levites to appoint their fellow Levites as musicians to make a joyful sound with musical instruments: lyres, harps and cymbals.

¹⁷So the Levites appointed Heman son of Joel; from his relatives, Asaph son of Berekiah; and from their relatives the Merarites, Ethan son of Kushaiah; ¹⁸and with them their relatives next in rank: Zechariah,ᶜ Jaaziel, Shemiramoth, Jehiel, Unni, Eliab, Benaiah, Maaseiah, Mattithiah, Eliphelehu, Mikneiah, Obed-Edom and Jeiel,ᵈ the gatekeepers.

¹⁹The musicians Heman, Asaph and Ethan were to sound the bronze cymbals; ²⁰Zechariah, Jaaziel,ᵉ Shemiramoth, Jehiel, Unni, Eliab, Maaseiah and Benaiah were to play the lyres according to alamoth,ᶠ ²¹and Mattithiah, Eliphelehu, Mikneiah, Obed-Edom, Jeiel and Azaziah were to play the harps, directing according to sheminith.ᶠ

ᵃ 11 Baal Perazim means the lord who breaks out.   ᵇ 7 Hebrew Gershom, a variant of Gershon
ᶜ 18 Three Hebrew manuscripts and most Septuagint manuscripts (see also verse 20 and 1 Chron. 16:5); most Hebrew manuscripts Zechariah son and or Zechariah, Ben and   ᵈ 18 Hebrew; Septuagint (see also verse 21) Jeiel and Azaziah   ᵉ 20 See verse 18; Hebrew Aziel, a variant of Jaaziel.   ᶠ 20,21 Probably a musical term

²²Kenaniah the head Levite was in charge of the singing; that was his responsibility because he was skillful at it.

²³Berekiah and Elkanah were to be doorkeepers for the ark. ²⁴Shebaniah, Joshaphat, Nethanel, Amasai, Zechariah, Benaiah and Eliezer the priests were to blow trumpets before the ark of God. Obed-Edom and Jehiah were also to be doorkeepers for the ark.

²⁵So David and the elders of Israel and the commanders of units of a thousand went to bring up the ark of the covenant of the LORD from the house of Obed-Edom, with rejoicing. ²⁶Because God had helped the Levites who were carrying the ark of the covenant of the LORD, seven bulls and seven rams were sacrificed. ²⁷Now David was clothed in a robe of fine linen, as were all the Levites who were carrying the ark, and as were the musicians, and Kenaniah, who was in charge of the singing of the choirs. David also wore a linen ephod. ²⁸So all Israel brought up the ark of the covenant of the LORD with shouts, with the sounding of rams' horns and trumpets, and of cymbals, and the playing of lyres and harps.

²⁹As the ark of the covenant of the LORD was entering the City of David, Michal daughter of Saul watched from a window. And when she saw King David dancing and celebrating, she despised him in her heart.

Ministering Before the Ark

16 They brought the ark of God and set it inside the tent that David had pitched for it, and they presented burnt offerings and fellowship offerings before God. ²After David had finished sacrificing the burnt offerings and fellowship offerings, he blessed the people in the name of the LORD. ³Then he gave a loaf of bread, a cake of dates and a cake of raisins to each Israelite man and woman.

⁴He appointed some of the Levites to minister before the ark of the LORD, to extol,ᵃ thank, and praise the LORD, the God of Israel: ⁵Asaph was the chief, and next to him in rank were Zechariah, then Jaaziel,ᵇ Shemiramoth, Jehiel, Mattithiah, Eliab, Benaiah, Obed-Edom and Jeiel. They were to play the lyres and harps, Asaph was to sound the cymbals, ⁶and Benaiah and Jahaziel the priests were to blow the trumpets regularly before the ark of the covenant of God.

⁷That day David first appointed Asaph and his associates to give praise to the LORD in this manner:

⁸Give praise to the LORD, call on his
name;
make known among the nations what
he has done.
⁹Sing to him, sing praise to him;
tell of all his wonderful acts.
¹⁰Glory in his holy name;
let the hearts of those who seek the
LORD rejoice.
¹¹Look to the LORD and his strength;
seek his face always.

¹²Remember the wonders he has done,
his miracles, and the judgments he
pronounced,
¹³you his servants, the descendants of
Israel,
his chosen ones, the children of
Jacob.
¹⁴He is the LORD our God;
his judgments are in all the earth.

¹⁵He remembersᶜ his covenant forever,
the promise he made, for a thousand
generations,
¹⁶the covenant he made with Abraham,
the oath he swore to Isaac.
¹⁷He confirmed it to Jacob as a decree,
to Israel as an everlasting covenant:
¹⁸"To you I will give the land of Canaan
as the portion you will inherit."

¹⁹When they were but few in number,
few indeed, and strangers in it,
²⁰theyᵈ wandered from nation to nation,
from one kingdom to another.
²¹He allowed no one to oppress them;
for their sake he rebuked kings:
²²"Do not touch my anointed ones;
do my prophets no harm."

²³Sing to the LORD, all the earth;
proclaim his salvation day after day.
²⁴Declare his glory among the nations,
his marvelous deeds among all
peoples.

ᵃ 4 Or petition; or invoke   ᵇ 5 See 15:18,20; Hebrew Jeiel, possibly another name for Jaaziel.
ᶜ 15 Some Septuagint manuscripts (see also Psalm 105:8); Hebrew Remember   ᵈ 18-20 One Hebrew manuscript, Septuagint and Vulgate (see also Psalm 105:12); most Hebrew manuscripts inherit, / ¹⁹though you are but few in number, / few indeed, and strangers in it." / ²⁰They

THURSDAY

FOR THE GLORY OF GOD

1 Chronicles 16:8–36 *or* 16:23–29

Matt Redman

You know, "glory," that buzzword that seems to be floating freely through the ranks of believers these days, effortlessly rolling off our lips in phrases like, "I just want my life to count for the glory of God!" Sounds great, but how do we know if it's true? How do we (and those around us) know what we truly glory in?

Simple. Glory for each of us is what we're talking about. Yep, we know what is supreme in our souls by what comes out of our mouths. Our accumulated words in everyday conversation are the true test of our devotion and affection. In other words, what we talk about most is what we value highest in our hearts.

It's one thing to say, "God, be glorified in me," but at some point we have to honestly break this spiritual phrase into practical, measurable terms. And to do that we must ask the question, "What am I talking about most?" Because, whatever we're talking about most is what we are amplifying (glorifying) with our lives. Think about the massive amount of glory we give to sports teams, pop stars, ourselves, brands of clothing, other people, possessions, experiences and events, as they fill our mouths and dominate our conversations. We are walking, talking billboards all day long, exporting the praises of something or somebody.

Having been made in God's image, we house mirrored souls designed to reflect His glory. By design, we are created to worship (reflect) Him. And though we have fallen from His glory, our sin hasn't stopped us from reflecting worship, value and glory that was intended for Him. We are destined to worship, and that's what we're going to do, constantly declaring the praise of whatever rivets the attention of our hearts.

JOHN OWEN {AD 1616–1683}

No one can have the least ground of assurance that they have seen Christ and his glory by faith unless it in some way changes them into Christ's likeness. For as power went out from Jesus to the woman in Luke 8, when she touched him on the hem of his garment, so when faith looks upon the glory of Christ, an influence of transforming power will flow from Christ into the soul.

reflection

1. What do you think it means to "bring glory" to God?
2. Based only on what you talk about, what do you glorify?
3. What changes might you need to make in order for your speech to declare God's glory?

For your next devotional reading, go to page 470.

²⁵ For great is the Lord and most worthy of
praise;
he is to be feared above all gods.
²⁶ For all the gods of the nations are idols,
but the Lord made the heavens.
²⁷ Splendor and majesty are before him;
strength and joy are in his dwelling
place.

²⁸ Ascribe to the Lord, all you families of
nations,
ascribe to the Lord glory and
strength.
²⁹ Ascribe to the Lord the glory due his
name;
bring an offering and come before
him.
Worship the Lord in the splendor of his ᵃ
holiness.
³⁰   Tremble before him, all the earth!
The world is firmly established; it
cannot be moved.

³¹ Let the heavens rejoice, let the earth be
glad;
let them say among the nations, "The
Lord reigns!"
³² Let the sea resound, and all that is in it;
let the fields be jubilant, and
everything in them!
³³ Let the trees of the forest sing,
let them sing for joy before the Lord,
for he comes to judge the earth.

³⁴ Give thanks to the Lord, for he is good;
his love endures forever.
³⁵ Cry out, "Save us, God our Savior;
gather us and deliver us from the
nations,
that we may give thanks to your holy
name,
and glory in your praise."
³⁶ Praise be to the Lord, the God of Israel,
from everlasting to everlasting.

Then all the people said "Amen" and "Praise
the Lord."

³⁷ David left Asaph and his associates before the ark of the covenant of the Lord to
minister there regularly, according to each
day's requirements. ³⁸ He also left Obed-
Edom and his sixty-eight associates to minister with them. Obed-Edom son of Jeduthun, and also Hosah, were gatekeepers.
³⁹ David left Zadok the priest and his fel-

low priests before the tabernacle of the Lord
at the high place in Gibeon ⁴⁰ to present
burnt offerings to the Lord on the altar of
burnt offering regularly, morning and evening, in accordance with everything written
in the Law of the Lord, which he had given
Israel. ⁴¹ With them were Heman and Jeduthun and the rest of those chosen and designated by name to give thanks to the Lord,
"for his love endures forever." ⁴² Heman and
Jeduthun were responsible for the sounding
of the trumpets and cymbals and for the
playing of the other instruments for sacred
song. The sons of Jeduthun were stationed
at the gate.
⁴³ Then all the people left to go to their
homes, and David returned home to bless
his family.

God's Promise to David

17 After David was settled in his
palace, he said to Nathan the
prophet, "Here I am, living in a
house of cedar, while the ark of the covenant of the Lord is under a tent."
² Nathan replied to David, "Whatever you
have in mind, do it, for God is with you."
³ But that night the word of God came to
Nathan, saying:

⁴ "Go and tell my servant David, 'This
is what the Lord says: You are not the
one to build me a house to dwell in. ⁵ I
have not dwelt in a house from the day
I brought Israel up out of Egypt to this
day. I have moved from one tent site to
another, from one dwelling place to
another. ⁶ Wherever I have moved with
all the Israelites, did I ever say to any of
their leaders ᵇ whom I commanded to
shepherd my people, "Why have you
not built me a house of cedar?" '

⁷ "Now then, tell my servant David,
'This is what the Lord Almighty says: I
took you from the pasture, from tending the flock, and appointed you ruler
over my people Israel. ⁸ I have been
with you wherever you have gone, and
I have cut off all your enemies from before you. Now I will make your name
like the names of the greatest men on
earth. ⁹ And I will provide a place for my
people Israel and will plant them so
that they can have a home of their own

ᵃ 29 Or Lord *with the splendor of*   ᵇ 6 Traditionally *judges*; also in verse 10 and no longer be disturbed. Wicked people will not oppress them anymore, as they did at the beginning [10]and have done ever since the time I appointed leaders over my people Israel. I will also subdue all your enemies.

" 'I declare to you that the LORD will build a house for you: [11]When your days are over and you go to be with your ancestors, I will raise up your offspring to succeed you, one of your own sons, and I will establish his kingdom. [12]He is the one who will build a house for me, and I will establish his throne forever. [13]I will be his father, and he will be my son. I will never take my love away from him, as I took it away from your predecessor. [14]I will set him over my house and my kingdom forever; his throne will be established forever.' "

[15]Nathan reported to David all the words of this entire revelation.

David's Prayer

[16]Then King David went in and sat before the LORD, and he said:

"Who am I, LORD God, and what is my family, that you have brought me this far? [17]And as if this were not enough in your sight, my God, you have spoken about the future of the house of your servant. You, LORD God, have looked on me as though I were the most exalted of men.

[18]"What more can David say to you for honoring your servant? For you know your servant, [19]LORD. For the sake of your servant and according to your will, you have done this great thing and made known all these great promises.

[20]"There is no one like you, LORD, and there is no God but you, as we have heard with our own ears. [21]And who is like your people Israel—the one nation on earth whose God went out to redeem a people for himself, and to make a name for yourself, and to perform great and awesome wonders by driving out nations from before your people, whom you redeemed from Egypt? [22]You made your people Israel your

very own forever, and you, LORD, have become their God.

[23]"And now, LORD, let the promise you have made concerning your servant and his house be established forever. Do as you promised, [24]so that it will be established and that your name will be great forever. Then people will say, 'The LORD Almighty, the God over Israel, is Israel's God!' And the house of your servant David will be established before you.

[25]"You, my God, have revealed to your servant that you will build a house for him. So your servant has found courage to pray to you. [26]You, LORD, are God! You have promised these good things to your servant. [27]Now you have been pleased to bless the house of your servant, that it may continue forever in your sight; for you, LORD, have blessed it, and it will be blessed forever."

David's Victories

18 In the course of time, David defeated the Philistines and subdued them, and he took Gath and its surrounding villages from the control of the Philistines.

[2]David also defeated the Moabites, and they became subject to him and brought him tribute.

[3]Moreover, David defeated Hadadezer king of Zobah, in the vicinity of Hamath, when he went to set up his monument at[a] the Euphrates River. [4]David captured a thousand of his chariots, seven thousand charioteers and twenty thousand foot soldiers. He hamstrung all but a hundred of the chariot horses.

[5]When the Arameans of Damascus came to help Hadadezer king of Zobah, David struck down twenty-two thousand of them. [6]He put garrisons in the Aramean kingdom of Damascus, and the Arameans became subject to him and brought him tribute. The LORD gave David victory wherever he went.

[7]David took the gold shields carried by the officers of Hadadezer and brought them to Jerusalem. [8]From Tebah[b] and Kun, towns that belonged to Hadadezer, David took a great quantity of bronze, which Solomon

---

a 3 Or to restore his control over   *b 8 Hebrew Tibhath, a variant of Tebah* used to make the bronze Sea, the pillars and various bronze articles.

⁹When Tou king of Hamath heard that David had defeated the entire army of Hadadezer king of Zobah, ¹⁰he sent his son Hadoram to King David to greet him and congratulate him on his victory in battle over Hadadezer, who had been at war with Tou. Hadoram brought all kinds of articles of gold, of silver and of bronze.

¹¹King David dedicated these articles to the LORD, as he had done with the silver and gold he had taken from all these nations: Edom and Moab, the Ammonites and the Philistines, and Amalek.

¹²Abishai son of Zeruiah struck down eighteen thousand Edomites in the Valley of Salt. ¹³He put garrisons in Edom, and all the Edomites became subject to David. The LORD gave David victory wherever he went.

David's Officials

¹⁴David reigned over all Israel, doing what was just and right for all his people. ¹⁵Joab son of Zeruiah was over the army; Jehoshaphat son of Ahilud was recorder; ¹⁶Zadok son of Ahitub and Ahimelek*a* son of Abiathar were priests; Shavsha was secretary; ¹⁷Benaiah son of Jehoiada was over the Kerethites and Pelethites; and David's sons were chief officials at the king's side.

David Defeats the Ammonites

19 In the course of time, Nahash king of the Ammonites died, and his son succeeded him as king. ²David thought, "I will show kindness to Hanun son of Nahash, because his father showed kindness to me." So David sent a delegation to express his sympathy to Hanun concerning his father.

When David's envoys came to Hanun in the land of the Ammonites to express sympathy to him, ³the Ammonite commanders said to Hanun, "Do you think David is honoring your father by sending envoys to you to express sympathy? Haven't his envoys come to you only to explore and spy out the country and overthrow it?" ⁴So Hanun seized David's envoys, shaved them, cut off their garments at the buttocks, and sent them away.

⁵When someone came and told David about the men, he sent messengers to meet them, for they were greatly humiliated. The king said, "Stay at Jericho till your beards have grown, and then come back."

⁶When the Ammonites realized that they had become obnoxious to David, Hanun and the Ammonites sent a thousand talents*b* of silver to hire chariots and charioteers from Aram Naharaim,*c* Aram Maakah and Zobah. ⁷They hired thirty-two thousand chariots and charioteers, as well as the king of Maakah with his troops, who came and camped near Medeba, while the Ammonites were mustered from their towns and moved out for battle.

⁸On hearing this, David sent Joab out with the entire army of fighting men. ⁹The Ammonites came out and drew up in battle formation at the entrance to their city, while the kings who had come were by themselves in the open country.

¹⁰Joab saw that there were battle lines in front of him and behind him; so he selected some of the best troops in Israel and deployed them against the Arameans. ¹¹He put the rest of the men under the command of Abishai his brother, and they were deployed against the Ammonites. ¹²Joab said, "If the Arameans are too strong for me, then you are to rescue me; but if the Ammonites are too strong for you, then I will rescue you. ¹³Be strong, and let us fight bravely for our people and the cities of our God. The LORD will do what is good in his sight."

¹⁴Then Joab and the troops with him advanced to fight the Arameans, and they fled before him. ¹⁵When the Ammonites realized that the Arameans were fleeing, they too fled before his brother Abishai and went inside the city. So Joab went back to Jerusalem.

¹⁶After the Arameans saw that they had been routed by Israel, they sent messengers and had Arameans brought from beyond the Euphrates River, with Shophak the commander of Hadadezer's army leading them. ¹⁷When David was told of this, he gathered all Israel and crossed the Jordan; he advanced against them and formed his battle lines opposite them. David formed his lines to meet the Arameans in battle, and they fought against him. ¹⁸But they fled before Is-

a 16 Some Hebrew manuscripts, Vulgate and Syriac (see also 2 Samuel 8:17); most Hebrew manuscripts *Abimelek* *b 6* That is, about 38 tons or about 34 metric tons *c 6* That is, Northwest Mesopotamia rael, and David killed seven thousand of their charioteers and forty thousand of their foot soldiers. He also killed Shophak the commander of their army.

¹⁹When the vassals of Hadadezer saw that they had been routed by Israel, they made peace with David and became subject to him.

So the Arameans were not willing to help the Ammonites anymore.

The Capture of Rabbah

20 In the spring, at the time when kings go off to war, Joab led out the armed forces. He laid waste the land of the Ammonites and went to Rabbah and besieged it, but David remained in Jerusalem. Joab attacked Rabbah and left it in ruins. ²David took the crown from the head of their king*ᵃ*—its weight was found to be a talentᵇ of gold, and it was set with precious stones—and it was placed on David's head. He took a great quantity of plunder from the city ³and brought out the people who were there, consigning them to labor with saws and with iron picks and axes. David did this to all the Ammonite towns. Then David and his entire army returned to Jerusalem.

War With the Philistines

⁴In the course of time, war broke out with the Philistines, at Gezer. At that time Sibbekai the Hushathite killed Sippai, one of the descendants of the Rephaites, and the Philistines were subjugated.

⁵In another battle with the Philistines, Elhanan son of Jair killed Lahmi the brother of Goliath the Gittite, who had a spear with a shaft like a weaver's rod.

⁶In still another battle, which took place at Gath, there was a huge man with six fingers on each hand and six toes on each foot—twenty-four in all. He also was descended from Rapha. ⁷When he taunted Israel, Jonathan son of Shimea, David's brother, killed him.

⁸These were descendants of Rapha in Gath, and they fell at the hands of David and his men.

David Counts the Fighting Men

21 Satan rose up against Israel and incited David to take a census of Israel. ²So David said to Joab and the commanders of the troops, "Go and count the Israelites from Beersheba to Dan. Then report back to me so that I may know how many there are."

³But Joab replied, "May the LORD multiply his troops a hundred times over. My lord the king, are they not all my lord's subjects? Why does my lord want to do this? Why should he bring guilt on Israel?"

⁴The king's word, however, overruled Joab; so Joab left and went throughout Israel and then came back to Jerusalem. ⁵Joab reported the number of the fighting men to David: In all Israel there were one million one hundred thousand men who could handle a sword, including four hundred and seventy thousand in Judah.

⁶But Joab did not include Levi and Benjamin in the numbering, because the king's command was repulsive to him. ⁷This command was also evil in the sight of God; so he punished Israel.

⁸Then David said to God, "I have sinned greatly by doing this. Now, I beg you, take away the guilt of your servant. I have done a very foolish thing."

⁹The LORD said to Gad, David's seer, ¹⁰"Go and tell David, 'This is what the LORD says: I am giving you three options. Choose one of them for me to carry out against you.' "

¹¹So Gad went to David and said to him, "This is what the LORD says: 'Take your choice: ¹²three years of famine, three months of being swept awayᶜ before your enemies, with their swords overtaking you, or three days of the sword of the LORD—days of plague in the land, with the angel of the LORD ravaging every part of Israel.' Now then, decide how I should answer the one who sent me."

¹³David said to Gad, "I am in deep distress. Let me fall into the hands of the LORD, for his mercy is very great; but do not let me fall into human hands."

¹⁴So the LORD sent a plague on Israel, and seventy thousand men of Israel fell dead. ¹⁵And God sent an angel to destroy Jerusalem. But as the angel was doing so, the LORD

ᵃ 2 Or of Milkom, that is, Molek   ᵇ 2 That is, about 75 pounds or about 34 kilograms   ᶜ 12 Hebrew; Septuagint and Vulgate (see also 2 Samuel 24:13) of fleeing saw it and relented concerning the disaster and said to the angel who was destroying the people, "Enough! Withdraw your hand." The angel of the LORD was then standing at the threshing floor of Araunah[a] the Jebusite.

¹⁶David looked up and saw the angel of the LORD standing between heaven and earth, with a drawn sword in his hand extended over Jerusalem. Then David and the elders, clothed in sackcloth, fell facedown.

¹⁷David said to God, "Was it not I who ordered the fighting men to be counted? I, the shepherd,[b] have sinned and done wrong. These are but sheep. What have they done? LORD my God, let your hand fall on me and my family, but do not let this plague remain on your people."

David Builds an Altar

¹⁸Then the angel of the LORD ordered Gad to tell David to go up and build an altar to the LORD on the threshing floor of Araunah the Jebusite. ¹⁹So David went up in obedience to the word that Gad had spoken in the name of the LORD.

²⁰While Araunah was threshing wheat, he turned and saw the angel; his four sons who were with him hid themselves. ²¹Then David approached, and when Araunah looked and saw him, he left the threshing floor and bowed down before David with his face to the ground.

²²David said to him, "Let me have the site of your threshing floor so I can build an altar to the LORD, that the plague on the people may be stopped. Sell it to me at the full price."

²³Araunah said to David, "Take it! Let my lord the king do whatever pleases him. Look, I will give the oxen for the burnt offerings, the threshing sledges for the wood, and the wheat for the grain offering. I will give all this."

²⁴But King David replied to Araunah, "No, I insist on paying the full price. I will not take for the LORD what is yours, or sacrifice a burnt offering that costs me nothing."

²⁵So David paid Araunah six hundred shekels[c] of gold for the site. ²⁶David built an altar to the LORD there and sacrificed burnt offerings and fellowship offerings. He called on the LORD, and the LORD answered him with fire from heaven on the altar of burnt offering.

²⁷Then the LORD spoke to the angel, and he put his sword back into its sheath. ²⁸At that time, when David saw that the LORD had answered him on the threshing floor of Araunah the Jebusite, he offered sacrifices there. ²⁹The tabernacle of the LORD, which Moses had made in the wilderness, and the altar of burnt offering were at that time on the high place at Gibeon. ³⁰But David could not go before it to inquire of God, because he was afraid of the sword of the angel of the LORD.

22

Then David said, "The house of the LORD God is to be here, and also the altar of burnt offering for Israel."

Preparations for the Temple

²So David gave orders to assemble the foreigners residing in Israel, and from among them he appointed stonecutters to prepare dressed stone for building the house of God. ³He provided a large amount of iron to make nails for the doors of the gateways and for the fittings, and more bronze than could be weighed. ⁴He also provided more cedar logs than could be counted, for the Sidonians and Tyrians had brought large numbers of them to David.

⁵David said, "My son Solomon is young and inexperienced, and the house to be built for the LORD should be of great magnificence and fame and splendor in the sight of all the nations. Therefore I will make preparations for it." So David made extensive preparations before his death.

⁶Then he called for his son Solomon and charged him to build a house for the LORD, the God of Israel. ⁷David said to Solomon: "My son, I had it in my heart to build a house for the Name of the LORD my God. ⁸But this word of the LORD came to me: 'You have shed much blood and have fought many wars. You are not to build a house for my Name, because you have shed much blood on the earth in my sight. ⁹But you will have a son who will be a man of peace and rest, and I will give him rest from all his enemies on every side. His name will be Solomon,[d] and I will grant Israel peace and qui-

---

a 15 Hebrew *Ornan*, a variant of *Araunah*; also in verses 18-28   *b 17* Probable reading of the original Hebrew text (see 2 Samuel 24:17 and footnote); Masoretic Text does not have *the shepherd*.   *c 25* That is, about 15 pounds or about 6.9 kilograms   *d 9* *Solomon* sounds like and may be derived from the Hebrew for *peace*.

et during his reign. ¹⁰He is the one who will build a house for my Name. He will be my son, and I will be his father. And I will establish the throne of his kingdom over Israel forever.'

¹¹"Now, my son, the LORD be with you, and may you have success and build the house of the LORD your God, as he said you would. ¹²May the LORD give you discretion and understanding when he puts you in command over Israel, so that you may keep the law of the LORD your God. ¹³Then you will have success if you are careful to observe the decrees and laws that the LORD gave Moses for Israel. Be strong and courageous. Do not be afraid or discouraged.

¹⁴"I have taken great pains to provide for the temple of the LORD a hundred thousand talents*ᵃ* of gold, a million talentsᵇ of silver, quantities of bronze and iron too great to be weighed, and wood and stone. And you may add to them. ¹⁵You have many workers: stonecutters, masons and carpenters, as well as those skilled in every kind of work ¹⁶in gold and silver, bronze and iron—skilled workers beyond number. Now begin the work, and the LORD be with you."

¹⁷Then David ordered all the leaders of Israel to help his son Solomon. ¹⁸He said to them, "Is not the LORD your God with you? And has he not granted you rest on every side? For he has given the inhabitants of the land into my hands, and the land is subject to the LORD and to his people. ¹⁹Now devote your heart and soul to seeking the LORD your God. Begin to build the sanctuary of the LORD God, so that you may bring the ark of the covenant of the LORD and the sacred articles belonging to God into the temple that will be built for the Name of the LORD."

The Levites

23 When David was old and full of years, he made his son Solomon king over Israel.

²He also gathered together all the leaders of Israel, as well as the priests and Levites. ³The Levites thirty years old or more were counted, and the total number of men was thirty-eight thousand. ⁴David said, "Of these, twenty-four thousand are to be in charge of the work of the temple of the LORD

and six thousand are to be officials and judges. ⁵Four thousand are to be gatekeepers and four thousand are to praise the LORD with the musical instruments I have provided for that purpose."

⁶David separated the Levites into divisions corresponding to the sons of Levi: Gershon, Kohath and Merari.

Gershonites

⁷Belonging to the Gershonites:
   Ladan and Shimei.

⁸ The sons of Ladan:
   Jehiel the first, Zetham and Joel—
   three in all.

⁹ The sons of Shimei:
   Shelomoth, Haziel and Haran—
   three in all.
   These were the heads of the families
   of Ladan.

¹⁰And the sons of Shimei:
   Jahath, Ziza,ᶜ Jeush and Beriah.
   These were the sons of Shimei—four
   in all.

   ¹¹Jahath was the first and Ziza the second, but Jeush and Beriah did not have many sons; so they were counted as one family with one assignment.

Kohathites

¹²The sons of Kohath:
   Amram, Izhar, Hebron and Uzziel—
   four in all.

¹³ The sons of Amram:
   Aaron and Moses.
   Aaron was set apart, he and his descendants forever, to consecrate the most holy things, to offer sacrifices before the LORD, to minister before him and to pronounce blessings in his name forever. ¹⁴The sons of Moses the man of God were counted as part of the tribe of Levi.

¹⁵ The sons of Moses:
   Gershom and Eliezer.

¹⁶ The descendants of Gershom:
   Shubael was the first.

¹⁷ The descendants of Eliezer:
   Rehabiah was the first.
   Eliezer had no other sons, but the

---

a 14 That is, about 3,750 tons or about 3,400 metric tons   *b 14* That is, about 37,500 tons or about 34,000 metric tons   *c 10* One Hebrew manuscript, Septuagint and Vulgate (see also verse 11); most Hebrew manuscripts *Zina* sons of Rehabiah were very numerous.

18 The sons of Izhar:
Shelomith was the first.

19 The sons of Hebron:
Jeriah the first, Amariah the second, Jahaziel the third and Jekameam the fourth.

20 The sons of Uzziel:
Micah the first and Ishiah the second.

Merarites

21 The sons of Merari:
Mahli and Mushi.
The sons of Mahli:
Eleazar and Kish.

22 Eleazar died without having sons: he had only daughters. Their cousins, the sons of Kish, married them.

23 The sons of Mushi:
Mahli, Eder and Jerimoth—three in all.

24 These were the descendants of Levi by their families—the heads of families as they were registered under their names and counted individually, that is, the workers twenty years old or more who served in the temple of the LORD. 25 For David had said, "Since the LORD, the God of Israel, has granted rest to his people and has come to dwell in Jerusalem forever, 26 the Levites no longer need to carry the tabernacle or any of the articles used in its service." 27 According to the last instructions of David, the Levites were counted from those twenty years old or more.

28 The duty of the Levites was to help Aaron's descendants in the service of the temple of the LORD: to be in charge of the courtyards, the side rooms, the purification of all sacred things and the performance of other duties at the house of God. 29 They were in charge of the bread set out on the table, the special flour for the grain offerings, the thin loaves made without yeast, the baking and the mixing, and all measurements of quantity and size. 30 They were also to stand every morning to thank and praise the LORD. They were to do the same in the evening 31 and whenever burnt offerings were presented to the LORD on the Sabbaths, at the New Moon feasts and at the appointed festivals. They were to serve before the LORD regularly in the proper number and in the way prescribed for them.

32 And so the Levites carried out their responsibilities for the tent of meeting, for the Holy Place and, under their relatives the descendants of Aaron, for the service of the temple of the LORD.

The Divisions of Priests

24 These were the divisions of the descendants of Aaron:
The sons of Aaron were Nadab, Abihu, Eleazar and Ithamar. 2 But Nadab and Abihu died before their father did, and they had no sons; so Eleazar and Ithamar served as the priests. 3 With the help of Zadok a descendant of Eleazar and Ahimelek a descendant of Ithamar, David separated them into divisions for their appointed order of ministering. 4 A larger number of leaders were found among Eleazar's descendants than among Ithamar's, and they were divided accordingly: sixteen heads of families from Eleazar's descendants and eight heads of families from Ithamar's descendants. 5 They divided them impartially by casting lots, for there were officials of the sanctuary and officials of God among the descendants of both Eleazar and Ithamar.

6 The scribe Shemaiah son of Nethanel, a Levite, recorded their names in the presence of the king and of the officials: Zadok the priest, Ahimelek son of Abiathar and the heads of families of the priests and of the Levites—one family being taken from Eleazar and then one from Ithamar.

7 The first lot fell to Jehoiarib,
the second to Jedaiah,
8 the third to Harim,
the fourth to Seorim,
9 the fifth to Malkijah,
the sixth to Mijamin,
10 the seventh to Hakkoz,
the eighth to Abijah,
11 the ninth to Jeshua,
the tenth to Shekaniah,
12 the eleventh to Eliashib,
the twelfth to Jakim,
13 the thirteenth to Huppah,
the fourteenth to Jeshebeab,
14 the fifteenth to Bilgah,
the sixteenth to Immer,
15 the seventeenth to Hezir,
the eighteenth to Happizzez,
16 the nineteenth to Pethahiah,
the twentieth to Jehezkel,
17 the twenty-first to Jakin,

the twenty-second to Gamul,
¹⁸the twenty-third to Delaiah
and the twenty-fourth to Maaziah.

¹⁹This was their appointed order of ministering when they entered the temple of the LORD, according to the regulations prescribed for them by their ancestor Aaron, as the LORD, the God of Israel, had commanded him.

The Rest of the Levites

²⁰As for the rest of the descendants of Levi:
from the sons of Amram: Shubael;
from the sons of Shubael: Jehdeiah.
²¹As for Rehabiah, from his sons:
Ishiah was the first.
²²From the Izharites: Shelomoth;
from the sons of Shelomoth: Jahath.
²³The sons of Hebron: Jeriah the first,^a
Amariah the second, Jahaziel the
third and Jekameam the fourth.
²⁴The son of Uzziel: Micah;
from the sons of Micah: Shamir.
²⁵The brother of Micah: Ishiah;
from the sons of Ishiah: Zechariah.
²⁶The sons of Merari: Mahli and Mushi.
The son of Jaaziah: Beno.
²⁷The sons of Merari:
from Jaaziah: Beno, Shoham, Zakkur
and Ibri.
²⁸From Mahli: Eleazar, who had no sons.
²⁹From Kish: the son of Kish:
Jerahmeel.
³⁰And the sons of Mushi: Mahli, Eder and
Jerimoth.

These were the Levites, according to their families. ³¹They also cast lots, just as their relatives the descendants of Aaron did, in the presence of King David and of Zadok, Ahimelek, and the heads of families of the priests and of the Levites. The families of the oldest brother were treated the same as those of the youngest.

The Musicians

25 David, together with the commanders of the army, set apart some of the sons of Asaph, Heman and Jeduthun for the ministry of prophesying, accompanied by harps, lyres and cymbals. Here is the list of the men who performed this service:

²From the sons of Asaph:
Zakkur, Joseph, Nethaniah and Asarelah. The sons of Asaph were under the supervision of Asaph, who prophesied under the king's supervision.
³As for Jeduthun, from his sons:
Gedaliah, Zeri, Jeshaiah, Shimei,^b Hashabiah and Mattithiah, six in all, under the supervision of their father Jeduthun, who prophesied, using the harp in thanking and praising the LORD.
⁴As for Heman, from his sons:
Bukkiah, Mattaniah, Uzziel, Shubael and Jerimoth; Hananiah, Hanani, Eliathah, Giddalti and Romamti-Ezer; Joshbekashah, Mallothi, Hothir and Mahazioth. ⁵(All these were sons of Heman the king's seer. They were given him through the promises of God to exalt him. God gave Heman fourteen sons and three daughters.)

⁶All these men were under the supervision of their father for the music of the temple of the LORD, with cymbals, lyres and harps, for the ministry at the house of God. Asaph, Jeduthun and Heman were under the supervision of the king. ⁷Along with their relatives—all of them trained and skilled in music for the LORD—they numbered 288. ⁸Young and old alike, teacher as well as student, cast lots for their duties.

⁹The first lot, which was for Asaph,
fell to Joseph,
his sons and relatives^c   12^d
the second to Gedaliah,
him and his relatives and sons 12
¹⁰the third to Zakkur,
his sons and relatives 12
¹¹the fourth to Izri,^e
his sons and relatives 12
¹²the fifth to Nethaniah,
his sons and relatives 12
¹³the sixth to Bukkiah,
his sons and relatives 12
¹⁴the seventh to Jesarelah,^f
his sons and relatives 12

---

^a 23 Two Hebrew manuscripts and some Septuagint manuscripts (see also 1 Chron. 23:19); most Hebrew manuscripts *The sons of Jeriah:*   ^b 3 One Hebrew manuscript and some Septuagint manuscripts (see also verse 17); most Hebrew manuscripts do not have *Shimei.*   ^c 9 See Septuagint; Hebrew does not have *his sons and relatives.*   ^d 9 See the total in verse 7; Hebrew does not have *twelve.*   ^e 11 A variant of *Zeri*   ^f 14 A variant of *Asarelah*

¹⁵the eighth to Jeshaiah,
his sons and relatives — 12
¹⁶the ninth to Mattaniah,
his sons and relatives — 12
¹⁷the tenth to Shimei,
his sons and relatives — 12
¹⁸the eleventh to Azarel,ᵃ
his sons and relatives — 12
¹⁹the twelfth to Hashabiah,
his sons and relatives — 12
²⁰the thirteenth to Shubael,
his sons and relatives — 12
²¹the fourteenth to Mattithiah,
his sons and relatives — 12
²²the fifteenth to Jerimoth,
his sons and relatives — 12
²³the sixteenth to Hananiah,
his sons and relatives — 12
²⁴the seventeenth to Joshbekashah,
his sons and relatives — 12
²⁵the eighteenth to Hanani,
his sons and relatives — 12
²⁶the nineteenth to Mallothi,
his sons and relatives — 12
²⁷the twentieth to Eliathah,
his sons and relatives — 12
²⁸the twenty-first to Hothir,
his sons and relatives — 12
²⁹the twenty-second to Giddalti,
his sons and relatives — 12
³⁰the twenty-third to Mahazioth,
his sons and relatives — 12
³¹the twenty-fourth to
Romamti-Ezer,
his sons and relatives — 12.

The Gatekeepers

26 The divisions of the gatekeepers:

From the Korahites: Meshelemiah son of Kore, one of the sons of Asaph.

²Meshelemiah had sons:
Zechariah the firstborn,
Jediael the second,
Zebadiah the third,
Jathniel the fourth,
³Elam the fifth,
Jehohanan the sixth
and Eliehoenai the seventh.
⁴Obed-Edom also had sons:
Shemaiah the firstborn,
Jehozabad the second,
Joah the third,
Sakar the fourth,
Nethanel the fifth,
⁵Ammiel the sixth,
Issachar the seventh
and Peullethai the eighth.
(For God had blessed Obed-Edom.)

⁶Obed-Edom's son Shemaiah also had sons, who were leaders in their father's family because they were very capable men. ⁷The sons of Shemaiah: Othni, Rephael, Obed and Elzabad; his relatives Elihu and Semakiah were also able men. ⁸All these were descendants of Obed-Edom; they and their sons and their relatives were capable men with the strength to do the work—descendants of Obed-Edom, 62 in all.

⁹Meshelemiah had sons and relatives, who were able men—18 in all.

¹⁰Hosah the Merarite had sons: Shimri the first (although he was not the firstborn, his father had appointed him the first), ¹¹Hilkiah the second, Tabaliah the third and Zechariah the fourth. The sons and relatives of Hosah were 13 in all.

¹²These divisions of the gatekeepers, through their leaders, had duties for ministering in the temple of the Lord, just as their relatives had. ¹³Lots were cast for each gate, according to their families, young and old alike. ¹⁴The lot for the East Gate fell to Shelemiah.ᵇ Then lots were cast for his son Zechariah, a wise counselor, and the lot for the North Gate fell to him. ¹⁵The lot for the South Gate fell to Obed-Edom, and the lot for the storehouse fell to his sons. ¹⁶The lots for the West Gate and the Shalleketh Gate on the upper road fell to Shuppim and Hosah.

Guard was alongside of guard: ¹⁷There were six Levites a day on the east, four a day on the north, four a day on the south and two at a time at the storehouse. ¹⁸As for the courtᶜ to the west, there were four at the road and two at the courtᶜ itself.

¹⁹These were the divisions of the gatekeepers who were descendants of Korah and Merari.

ᵃ 18 A variant of *Uzziel*   ᵇ 14 A variant of *Meshelemiah*   ᶜ 18 The meaning of the Hebrew for this word is uncertain.

The Treasurers and Other Officials

20Their fellow Levites were[a] in charge of the treasuries of the house of God and the treasuries for the dedicated things.

21The descendants of Ladan, who were Gershonites through Ladan and who were heads of families belonging to Ladan the Gershonite, were Jehieli, 22the sons of Jehieli, Zetham and his brother Joel. They were in charge of the treasuries of the temple of the Lord.

23From the Amramites, the Izharites, the Hebronites and the Uzzielites:

24Shubael, a descendant of Gershom son of Moses, was the official in charge of the treasuries. 25His relatives through Eliezer: Rehabiah his son, Jeshaiah his son, Joram his son, Zikri his son and Shelomith his son. 26Shelomith and his relatives were in charge of all the treasuries for the things dedicated by King David, by the heads of families who were the commanders of thousands and commanders of hundreds, and by the other army commanders. 27Some of the plunder taken in battle they dedicated for the repair of the temple of the Lord. 28And everything dedicated by Samuel the seer and by Saul son of Kish, Abner son of Ner and Joab son of Zeruiah, and all the other dedicated things were in the care of Shelomith and his relatives.

29From the Izharites: Kenaniah and his sons were assigned duties away from the temple, as officials and judges over Israel.

30From the Hebronites: Hashabiah and his relatives—seventeen hundred able men—were responsible in Israel west of the Jordan for all the work of the Lord and for the king's service. 31As for the Hebronites, Jeriah was their chief according to the genealogical records of their families. In the fortieth year of David's reign a search was made in the records, and capable men among the Hebronites were found at Jazer in Gilead. 32Jeriah had twenty-seven hundred relatives, who were able men and heads of families, and King David put them in charge of the Reubenites, the Gadites and the half-tribe of Manasseh for every matter pertaining to God and for the affairs of the king.

Army Divisions

27 This is the list of the Israelites—heads of families, commanders of thousands and commanders of hundreds, and their officers, who served the king in all that concerned the army divisions that were on duty month by month throughout the year. Each division consisted of 24,000 men.

2In charge of the first division, for the first month, was Jashobeam son of Zabdiel. There were 24,000 men in his division. 3He was a descendant of Perez and chief of all the army officers for the first month.

4In charge of the division for the second month was Dodai the Ahohite; Mikloth was the leader of his division. There were 24,000 men in his division.

5The third army commander, for the third month, was Benaiah son of Jehoiada the priest. He was chief and there were 24,000 men in his division. 6This was the Benaiah who was a mighty warrior among the Thirty and was over the Thirty. His son Ammizabad was in charge of his division.

7The fourth, for the fourth month, was Asahel the brother of Joab; his son Zebadiah was his successor. There were 24,000 men in his division.

8The fifth, for the fifth month, was the commander Shamhuth the Izrahite. There were 24,000 men in his division.

9The sixth, for the sixth month, was Ira the son of Ikkesh the Tekoite. There were 24,000 men in his division.

10The seventh, for the seventh month, was Helez the Pelonite, an Ephraimite. There were 24,000 men in his division.

11The eighth, for the eighth month, was Sibbekai the Hushathite, a Zerahite. There were 24,000 men in his division.

12The ninth, for the ninth month, was Abiezer the Anathothite, a Benjamite. There were 24,000 men in his division.

13The tenth, for the tenth month, was Maharai the Netophathite, a Zerahite. There were 24,000 men in his division.

¹⁴The eleventh, for the eleventh month, was Benaiah the Pirathonite, an Ephraimite. There were 24,000 men in his division.

¹⁵The twelfth, for the twelfth month, was Heldai the Netophathite, from the family of Othniel. There were 24,000 men in his division.

Leaders of the Tribes

¹⁶The leaders of the tribes of Israel:

over the Reubenites: Eliezer son of Zikri;
over the Simeonites: Shephatiah son of Maakah;
¹⁷over Levi: Hashabiah son of Kemuel;
over Aaron: Zadok;
¹⁸over Judah: Elihu, a brother of David;
over Issachar: Omri son of Michael;
¹⁹over Zebulun: Ishmaiah son of Obadiah;
over Naphtali: Jerimoth son of Azriel;
²⁰over the Ephraimites: Hoshea son of Azaziah;
over half the tribe of Manasseh: Joel son of Pedaiah;
²¹over the half-tribe of Manasseh in Gilead: Iddo son of Zechariah;
over Benjamin: Jaasiel son of Abner;
²²over Dan: Azarel son of Jeroham.

These were the leaders of the tribes of Israel.

²³David did not take the number of the men twenty years old or less, because the LORD had promised to make Israel as numerous as the stars in the sky. ²⁴Joab son of Zeruiah began to count the men but did not finish. God's wrath came on Israel on account of this numbering, and the number was not entered in the book*a* of the annals of King David.

The King's Overseers

²⁵Azmaveth son of Adiel was in charge of the royal storehouses.

Jonathan son of Uzziah was in charge of the storehouses in the outlying districts, in the towns, the villages and the watchtowers.

²⁶Ezri son of Kelub was in charge of the workers who farmed the land.

²⁷Shimei the Ramathite was in charge of the vineyards.

Zabdi the Shiphmite was in charge of the produce of the vineyards for the wine vats.

²⁸Baal-Hanan the Gederite was in charge of the olive and sycamore-fig trees in the western foothills.

Joash was in charge of the supplies of olive oil.

²⁹Shitrai the Sharonite was in charge of the herds grazing in Sharon.

Shaphat son of Adlai was in charge of the herds in the valleys.

³⁰Obil the Ishmaelite was in charge of the camels.

Jehdeiah the Meronothite was in charge of the donkeys.

³¹Jaziz the Hagrite was in charge of the flocks.

All these were the officials in charge of King David's property.

³²Jonathan, David's uncle, was a counselor, a man of insight and a scribe. Jehiel son of Hakmoni took care of the king's sons.

³³Ahithophel was the king's counselor. Hushai the Arkite was the king's confidant. ³⁴Ahithophel was succeeded by Jehoiada son of Benaiah and by Abiathar.

Joab was the commander of the royal army.

David's Plans for the Temple

28 David summoned all the officials of Israel to assemble at Jerusalem: the officers over the tribes, the commanders of the divisions in the service of the king, the commanders of thousands and commanders of hundreds, and the officials in charge of all the property and livestock belonging to the king and his sons, together with the palace officials, the mighty warriors and all the brave fighting men.

²King David rose to his feet and said: "Listen to me, my fellow Israelites, my people. I had it in my heart to build a house as a place of rest for the ark of the covenant of the LORD, for the footstool of our God, and I made plans to build it. ³But God said to me, 'You are not to build a house for my Name, because you are a warrior and have shed blood.'

⁴"Yet the LORD, the God of Israel, chose me from my whole family to be king over Israel forever. He chose Judah as leader, and from the house of Judah he chose my family, and from my father's sons he was pleased

---

a 24 Septuagint; Hebrew *number*

LITTLE THINGS

1 Chronicles 28:1–21 *or* 28:11–18

Lisa Ryken

One of my greatest fears is that in the final judgment it will be revealed that I have not been faithful. This thought especially bothered me during the weeks preceding my husband's installation as the senior minister of our large-city church. I replayed in my mind all the times I had failed to be bold in talking about my faith with coworkers and neighbors. How could I be the wife of a minister in a secular city and not be confident about my witness as a believer? What kind of opposition or persecution would we face? The weight of responsibility and fear of the future came crushing down on me until I could scarcely move.

The naked truth is that I *cannot* be faithful. But *God* is faithful! God has promised that he will keep me strong to the end. The only way I can ever be faithful to God is by grasping hold of the truth that *God is faithful*. God has been faithful to his people down through the centuries, and he has been faithful to me over the short span of my life. God would not have asked me to be faithful to him had he not already committed himself in faithfulness to me. I rest in the words of the psalmist, "Your faithfulness continues through all generations" (Psalm 119:90).

JEAN NICOLAS GROU {AD 1731–1803}

Little things come daily, hourly, and within our reach, and they are not less calculated to set forward our growth in holiness than are the greater occasions that rarely occur. Moreover, fidelity in trifles, and an earnest seeking to please God in little matters, is a test of real devotion and love. Let your aim be to please our dear Lord perfectly in little things, and to attain a spirit of childlike simplicity and dependence. In proportion as self-love and self-confidence are weakened and our will is bowed to that of God, so will hindrances disappear. The internal troubles and contests that harassed the soul will vanish, and it will be filled with peace and tranquility.

reflection

1. How would you rate yourself on the "faithfulness" meter—with one being "completely and totally faithful" and ten being "completely unfaithful"?

2. If you didn't rate yourself a "one," how do you feel about the "unfaithfulness" in your life?

3. Often it's hardest to serve God with wholehearted devotion in the little, daily things of life—as opposed to the huge crises that may come. In what "little things" do you need to grow in serving God faithfully?

For your next devotional reading, go to page 474.

to make me king over all Israel. ⁵Of all my sons—and the LORD has given me many—he has chosen my son Solomon to sit on the throne of the kingdom of the LORD over Israel. ⁶He said to me: 'Solomon your son is the one who will build my house and my courts, for I have chosen him to be my son, and I will be his father. ⁷I will establish his kingdom forever if he is unswerving in carrying out my commands and laws, as is being done at this time.'

⁸"So now I charge you in the sight of all Israel and of the assembly of the LORD, and in the hearing of our God: Be careful to follow all the commands of the LORD your God, that you may possess this good land and pass it on as an inheritance to your descendants forever.

⁹"And you, my son Solomon, acknowledge the God of your father, and serve him with wholehearted devotion and with a willing mind, for the LORD searches every heart and understands every desire and every thought. If you seek him, he will be found by you; but if you forsake him, he will reject you forever. ¹⁰Consider now, for the LORD has chosen you to build a house as the sanctuary. Be strong and do the work."

¹¹Then David gave his son Solomon the plans for the portico of the temple, its buildings, its storerooms, its upper parts, its inner rooms and the place of atonement. ¹²He gave him the plans of all that the Spirit had put in his mind for the courts of the temple of the LORD and all the surrounding rooms, for the treasuries of the temple of God and for the treasuries for the dedicated things. ¹³He gave him instructions for the divisions of the priests and Levites, and for all the work of serving in the temple of the LORD, as well as for all the articles to be used in its service. ¹⁴He designated the weight of gold for all the gold articles to be used in various kinds of service, and the weight of silver for all the silver articles to be used in various kinds of service: ¹⁵the weight of gold for the gold lampstands and their lamps, with the weight for each lampstand and its lamps; and the weight of silver for each silver lampstand and its lamps, according to the use of each lampstand; ¹⁶the weight of gold for each table for consecrated bread; the weight

of silver for the silver tables; ¹⁷the weight of pure gold for the forks, sprinkling bowls and pitchers; the weight of gold for each gold dish; the weight of silver for each silver dish; ¹⁸and the weight of the refined gold for the altar of incense. He also gave him the plan for the chariot, that is, the cherubim of gold that spread their wings and overshadow the ark of the covenant of the LORD.

¹⁹"All this," David said, "I have in writing as a result of the LORD's hand on me, and he enabled me to understand all the details of the plan."

²⁰David also said to Solomon his son, "Be strong and courageous, and do the work. Do not be afraid or discouraged, for the LORD God, my God, is with you. He will not fail you or forsake you until all the work for the service of the temple of the LORD is finished. ²¹The divisions of the priests and Levites are ready for all the work on the temple of God, and every willing person skilled in any craft will help you in all the work. The officials and all the people will obey your every command."

Gifts for Building the Temple

29 Then King David said to the whole assembly: "My son Solomon, the one whom God has chosen, is young and inexperienced. The task is great, because this palatial structure is not for human beings but for the LORD God. ²With all my resources I have provided for the temple of my God—gold for the gold work, silver for the silver, bronze for the bronze, iron for the iron and wood for the wood, as well as onyx for the settings, turquoise,ᵃ stones of various colors, and all kinds of fine stone and marble—all of these in large quantities. ³Besides, in my devotion to the temple of my God I now give my personal treasures of gold and silver for the temple of my God, over and above everything I have provided for this holy temple: ⁴three thousand talentsᵇ of gold (gold of Ophir) and seven thousand talentsᶜ of refined silver, for the overlaying of the walls of the buildings, ⁵for the gold work and the silver work, and for all the work to be done by the skilled workers. Now, who among you is willing to consecrate yourself to the LORD today?"

⁶Then the leaders of families, the officers

ᵃ 2 The meaning of the Hebrew for this word is uncertain.   ᵇ 4 That is, about 110 tons or about 100 metric tons   ᶜ 4 That is, about 260 tons or about 235 metric tons of the tribes of Israel, the commanders of thousands and commanders of hundreds, and the officials in charge of the king's work gave willingly. [7]They gave toward the work on the temple of God five thousand talents[a] and ten thousand darics[b] of gold, ten thousand talents[c] of silver, eighteen thousand talents[d] of bronze and a hundred thousand talents[e] of iron. [8]Anyone who had precious stones gave them to the treasury of the temple of the LORD in the custody of Jehiel the Gershonite. [9]The people rejoiced at the willing response of their leaders, for they had given freely and wholeheartedly to the LORD. David the king also rejoiced greatly.

David's Prayer

[10]David praised the LORD in the presence of the whole assembly, saying,

"Praise be to you, LORD,
    the God of our father Israel,
    from everlasting to everlasting.
[11]Yours, LORD, is the greatness and the
        power
    and the glory and the majesty and the
        splendor,
    for everything in heaven and earth is
        yours.
Yours, LORD, is the kingdom;
    you are exalted as head over all.
[12]Wealth and honor come from you;
    you are the ruler of all things.
In your hands are strength and power
    to exalt and give strength to all.
[13]Now, our God, we give you thanks,
    and praise your glorious name.

[14]"But who am I, and who are my people, that we should be able to give as generously as this? Everything comes from you, and we have given you only what comes from your hand. [15]We are foreigners and strangers in your sight, as were all our ancestors. Our days on earth are like a shadow, without hope. [16]LORD our God, all this abundance that we have provided for building you a temple for your Holy Name comes from your hand, and all of it belongs to you. [17]I know, my God, that you test the heart and are pleased with integrity. All these things have I given willingly and with honest intent. And now I have seen with joy how willingly your people who

are here have given to you. [18]LORD, the God of our fathers Abraham, Isaac and Israel, keep these desires and thoughts in the hearts of your people forever, and keep their hearts loyal to you. [19]And give my son Solomon the wholehearted devotion to keep your commands, statutes and decrees and to do everything to build the palatial structure for which I have provided."

[20]Then David said to the whole assembly, "Praise the LORD your God." So they all praised the LORD, the God of their fathers; they bowed down, prostrating themselves before the LORD and the king.

Solomon Acknowledged as King

[21]The next day they made sacrifices to the LORD and presented burnt offerings to him: a thousand bulls, a thousand rams and a thousand male lambs, together with their drink offerings, and other sacrifices in abundance for all Israel. [22]They ate and drank with great joy in the presence of the LORD that day.

Then they acknowledged Solomon son of David as king a second time, anointing him before the LORD to be ruler and Zadok to be priest. [23]So Solomon sat on the throne of the LORD as king in place of his father David. He prospered and all Israel obeyed him. [24]All the officers and mighty warriors, as well as all of King David's sons, pledged their submission to King Solomon.

[25]The LORD highly exalted Solomon in the sight of all Israel and bestowed on him royal splendor such as no king over Israel ever had before.

The Death of David

[26]David son of Jesse was king over all Israel. [27]He ruled over Israel forty years—seven in Hebron and thirty-three in Jerusalem. [28]He died at a good old age, having enjoyed long life, wealth and honor. His son Solomon succeeded him as king.

[29]As for the events of King David's reign, from beginning to end, they are written in the records of Samuel the seer, the records of Nathan the prophet and the records of Gad the seer, [30]together with the details of his reign and power, and the circumstances that surrounded him and Israel and the kingdoms of all the other lands.

---

a 7 That is, about 190 tons or about 170 metric tons   b 7 That is, about 185 pounds or about 84 kilograms   c 7 That is, about 375 tons or about 340 metric tons   d 7 That is, about 675 tons or about 610 metric tons   e 7 That is, about 3,750 tons or about 3,400 metric tons

2 chronicles

AUTHOR: Possibly Ezra

DATE: Around 430 B.C.

THEME: God's truth can be learned through obedience during hardship.

Solomon Asks for Wisdom

1 Solomon son of David established himself firmly over his kingdom, for the LORD his God was with him and made him exceedingly great.

2 Then Solomon spoke to all Israel—to the commanders of thousands and commanders of hundreds, to the judges and to all the leaders in Israel, the heads of families— 3 and Solomon and the whole assembly went to the high place at Gibeon, for God's tent of meeting was there, which Moses the LORD's servant had made in the wilderness. 4 Now David had brought up the ark of God from Kiriath Jearim to the place he had prepared for it, because he had pitched a tent for it in Jerusalem. 5 But the bronze altar that Bezalel son of Uri, the son of Hur, had made was in Gibeon in front of the tabernacle of the LORD; so Solomon and the assembly inquired of him there. 6 Solomon went up to the bronze altar before the LORD in the tent of meeting and offered a thousand burnt offerings on it.

7 That night God appeared to Solomon and said to him, "Ask for whatever you want me to give you."

8 Solomon answered God, "You have shown great kindness to David my father and have made me king in his place. 9 Now, LORD God, let your promise to my father David be confirmed, for you have made me king over a people who are as numerous as the dust of the earth. 10 Give me wisdom and knowledge, that I may lead this people, for who is able to govern this great people of yours?"

11 God said to Solomon, "Since this is your heart's desire and you have not asked for wealth, possessions or honor, nor for the death of your enemies, and since you have not asked for a long life but for wisdom and knowledge to govern my people over whom I have made you king, 12 therefore wisdom and knowledge will be given you. And I will also give you wealth, possessions and honor, such as no king who was before you ever had and none after you will have."

13 Then Solomon went to Jerusalem from the high place at Gibeon, from before the tent of meeting. And he reigned over Israel.

14 Solomon accumulated chariots and horses; he had fourteen hundred chariots and twelve thousand horses,[a] which he kept in the chariot cities and also with him in Jerusalem. 15 The king made silver and gold as common in Jerusalem as stones, and cedar as plentiful as sycamore-fig trees in the foothills. 16 Solomon's horses were imported from Egypt and from Kue[b]—the royal merchants purchased them from Kue at the current price. 17 They imported a chariot from Egypt for six hundred shekels[c] of silver, and a horse for a hundred and fifty.[d] They also exported them to all the kings of the Hittites and of the Arameans.

Preparations for Building the Temple

2 *Solomon gave orders to build a temple for the Name of the LORD and a royal palace for himself. *2 He conscripted 70,000 men as carriers and 80,000 as stonecutters in the hills and 3,600 as supervisors over them.

---

a 14 Or charioteers   b 16 Probably Cilicia   c 17 That is, about 15 pounds or about 6.9 kilograms
d 17 That is, about 3 3/4 pounds or about 1.7 kilograms

* 2:1 is numbered 1:18 in Hebrew texts.   * 2:2-18 is numbered 2:1-17 in Hebrew texts.

God's Altar

2 Chronicles 1:4-6

read/meditate

When you imagine the altar in this passage, how does it look to your mind's eye?
Read the passage slowly and imagine the scene from Solomon's perspective. Notice
the details as you place yourself in his shoes.

pray

Express your requests and your gratitude to God. Mentally scroll through the places
in your life that you would have built an altar to commemorate God's revealed
presence. Thank God for those times.

contemplate

Read the passage again, and think about the altars you build with your efforts
and your passions. Sit before God as you ponder what you pour yourself into and
thus worship.

additional reflection

Whatever your heart clings to and confides in, that is really your God.

—*Martin Luther*

Talk to him in prayer of all your wants, your troubles, even of the weariness you feel in
serving him. You can not speak too freely, too trustfully to him.

—*François Fénelon*

For your next devotional reading, go to page 480.

³Solomon sent this message to Hiramᵃ king of Tyre:

"Send me cedar logs as you did for my father David when you sent him cedar to build a palace to live in. ⁴Now I am about to build a temple for the Name of the Lord my God and to dedicate it to him for burning fragrant incense before him, for setting out the consecrated bread regularly, and for making burnt offerings every morning and evening and on the Sabbaths, at the New Moons and at the appointed festivals of the Lord our God. This is a lasting ordinance for Israel.

⁵"The temple I am going to build will be great, because our God is greater than all other gods. ⁶But who is able to build a temple for him, since the heavens, even the highest heavens, cannot contain him? Who then am I to build a temple for him, except as a place to burn sacrifices before him?

⁷"Send me, therefore, a man skilled to work in gold and silver, bronze and iron, and in purple, crimson and blue yarn, and experienced in the art of engraving, to work in Judah and Jerusalem with my skilled workers, whom my father David provided.

⁸"Send me also cedar, juniper and algumᵇ logs from Lebanon, for I know that your servants are skilled in cutting timber there. My men will work with yours ⁹to provide me with plenty of lumber, because the temple I build must be large and magnificent. ¹⁰I will give your servants, those who cut the timber, twenty thousand corsᶜ of ground wheat, twenty thousand corsᵈ of barley, twenty thousand bathsᵉ of wine and twenty thousand baths of olive oil."

¹¹Hiram king of Tyre replied by letter to Solomon:

"Because the Lord loves his people, he has made you their king."

¹²And Hiram added:

"Praise be to the Lord, the God of Israel, who made heaven and earth! He has given King David a wise son, endowed with intelligence and discernment, who will build a temple for the Lord and a palace for himself.

¹³"I am sending you Huram-Abi, a man of great skill, ¹⁴whose mother was from Dan and whose father was from Tyre. He is trained to work in gold and silver, bronze and iron, stone and wood, and with purple and blue and crimson yarn and fine linen. He is experienced in all kinds of engraving and can execute any design given to him. He will work with your skilled workers and with those of my lord, David your father.

¹⁵"Now let my lord send his servants the wheat and barley and the olive oil and wine he promised, ¹⁶and we will cut all the logs from Lebanon that you need and will float them as rafts by sea down to Joppa. You can then take them up to Jerusalem."

¹⁷Solomon took a census of all the foreigners residing in Israel, after the census his father David had taken; and they were found to be 153,600. ¹⁸He assigned 70,000 of them to be carriers and 80,000 to be stonecutters in the hills, with 3,600 supervisors over them to keep the people working.

Solomon Builds the Temple

3 Then Solomon began to build the temple of the Lord in Jerusalem on Mount Moriah, where the Lord had appeared to his father David. It was on the threshing floor of Araunahᶠ the Jebusite, the place provided by David. ²He began building on the second day of the second month in the fourth year of his reign.

³The foundation Solomon laid for building the temple of God was sixty cubits long and twenty cubits wideᵍ (using the cubit of the old standard). ⁴The portico at the front of the temple was twenty cubitsʰ long across the width of the building and twenty cubitsⁱ high. He overlaid the inside with pure gold. ⁵He

---

ᵃ 3 Hebrew *Huram*, a variant of *Hiram*; also in verses 11 and 12   ᵇ 8 Probably a variant of *almug*
ᶜ 10 That is, probably about 3,600 tons or about 3,275 metric tons   ᵈ 10 That is, probably about 3,000 tons or about 2,700 metric tons   ᵉ 10 That is, about 120,000 gallons or about 440,000 liters
ᶠ 1 Hebrew *Ornan*, a variant of *Araunah*   ᵍ 3 That is, about 90 feet long and 30 feet wide or about 27 meters long and 9 meters wide   ʰ 4 That is, about 30 feet or about 9 meters; also in verses 8, 11 and 13
ⁱ 4 Some Septuagint and Syriac manuscripts; Hebrew *and a hundred and twenty*

paneled the main hall with juniper and covered it with fine gold and decorated it with palm tree and chain designs. ⁶He adorned the temple with precious stones. And the gold he used was gold of Parvaim. ⁷He overlaid the ceiling beams, doorframes, walls and doors of the temple with gold, and he carved cherubim on the walls.

⁸He built the Most Holy Place, its length corresponding to the width of the temple—twenty cubits long and twenty cubits wide. He overlaid the inside with six hundred talentsᵃ of fine gold. ⁹The gold nails weighed fifty shekels.ᵇ He also overlaid the upper parts with gold.

¹⁰For the Most Holy Place he made a pair of sculptured cherubim and overlaid them with gold. ¹¹The total wingspan of the cherubim was twenty cubits. One wing of the first cherub was five cubitsᶜ long and touched the temple wall, while its other wing, also five cubits long, touched the wing of the other cherub. ¹²Similarly one wing of the second cherub was five cubits long and touched the other temple wall, and its other wing, also five cubits long, touched the wing of the first cherub. ¹³The wings of these cherubim extended twenty cubits. They stood on their feet, facing the main hall.ᵈ

¹⁴He made the curtain of blue, purple and crimson yarn and fine linen, with cherubim worked into it.

¹⁵For the front of the temple he made two pillars, which totaled thirty-five cubitsᵉ in length, each with a capital five cubits high. ¹⁶He made interwoven chainsᶠ and put them on top of the pillars. He also made a hundred pomegranates and attached them to the chains. ¹⁷He erected the pillars in the front of the temple, one to the south and one to the north. The one to the south he named Jakinᵍ and the one to the north Boaz.ʰ

The Temple's Furnishings

4 He made a bronze altar twenty cubits long, twenty cubits wide and ten cubits high.ⁱ ²He made the Sea of cast metal, circular in shape, measuring ten cubits from rim to rim and five cubitsʲ high. It took a line of thirty cubitsᵏ to measure around it. ³Below the rim, figures of bulls encircled it—ten to a cubit.ˡ The bulls were cast in two rows in one piece with the Sea.

⁴The Sea stood on twelve bulls, three facing north, three facing west, three facing south and three facing east. The Sea rested on top of them, and their hindquarters were toward the center. ⁵It was a handbreadthᵐ in thickness, and its rim was like the rim of a cup, like a lily blossom. It held three thousand baths.ⁿ

⁶He then made ten basins for washing and placed five on the south side and five on the north. In them the things to be used for the burnt offerings were rinsed, but the Sea was to be used by the priests for washing.

⁷He made ten gold lampstands according to the specifications for them and placed them in the temple, five on the south side and five on the north.

⁸He made ten tables and placed them in the temple, five on the south side and five on the north. He also made a hundred gold sprinkling bowls.

⁹He made the courtyard of the priests, and the large court and the doors for the court, and overlaid the doors with bronze. ¹⁰He placed the Sea on the south side, at the southeast corner.

¹¹And Huram also made the pots and shovels and sprinkling bowls.

So Huram finished the work he had undertaken for King Solomon in the temple of God:

¹²the two pillars;
the two bowl-shaped capitals on top of the pillars;
the two sets of network decorating the two bowl-shaped capitals on top of the pillars;

¹³the four hundred pomegranates for the two sets of network (two rows of pomegranates for each network, decorating the bowl-shaped capitals on top of the pillars);

ᵃ 8 That is, about 23 tons or about 20 metric tons   ᵇ 9 That is, about 1 1/4 pounds or about 575 grams   ᶜ 11 That is, about 7 1/2 feet or about 2.3 meters; also in verse 15   ᵈ 13 Or *facing inward*   ᵉ 15 That is, about 52 feet or about 16 meters   ᶠ 16 Or possibly *made chains in the inner sanctuary*; the meaning of the Hebrew for this phrase is uncertain.   ᵍ 17 *Jakin* probably means *he establishes*.   ʰ 17 *Boaz* probably means *in him is strength*.   ⁱ 1 That is, about 30 feet long and wide and 15 feet high or about 9 meters long and wide and 4.5 meters high   ʲ 2 That is, about 7 1/2 feet or about 2.3 meters   ᵏ 2 That is, about 45 feet or about 13.5 meters   ˡ 3 That is, about 18 inches or about 45 centimeters   ᵐ 5 That is, about 3 inches or about 7.5 centimeters   ⁿ 5 That is, about 18,000 gallons or about 66,000 liters

¹⁴the stands with their basins;
¹⁵the Sea and the twelve bulls under it;
¹⁶the pots, shovels, meat forks and all re-
    lated articles.

All the objects that Huram-Abi made for King Solomon for the temple of the Lᴏʀᴅ were of polished bronze. ¹⁷The king had them cast in clay molds in the plain of the Jordan between Sukkoth and Zarethan.ᵃ ¹⁸All these things that Solomon made amounted to so much that the weight of the bronze could not be calculated.

¹⁹Solomon also made all the furnishings that were in God's temple:

    the golden altar;
    the tables on which was the bread of
        the Presence;
²⁰the lampstands of pure gold with their
    lamps, to burn in front of the inner
    sanctuary as prescribed;
²¹the gold floral work and lamps and
    tongs (they were solid gold);
²²the pure gold wick trimmers, sprinkling
    bowls, dishes and censers; and the
    gold doors of the temple: the inner
    doors to the Most Holy Place and the
    doors of the main hall.

5 When all the work Solomon had done for the temple of the Lᴏʀᴅ was fin-ished, he brought in the things his fa-ther David had dedicated—the silver and gold and all the furnishings—and he placed them in the treasuries of God's temple.

The Ark Brought to the Temple

²Then Solomon summoned to Jerusalem the elders of Israel, all the heads of the tribes and the chiefs of the Israelite families, to bring up the ark of the Lᴏʀᴅ's covenant from Zion, the City of David. ³And all the Is-raelites came together to the king at the time of the festival in the seventh month.

⁴When all the elders of Israel had arrived, the Levites took up the ark, ⁵and they brought up the ark and the tent of meeting and all the sacred furnishings in it. The Le-vitical priests carried them up; ⁶and King Solomon and the entire assembly of Israel that had gathered about him were before the ark, sacrificing so many sheep and cattle that they could not be recorded or counted.

⁷The priests then brought the ark of the

Lᴏʀᴅ's covenant to its place in the inner sanctuary of the temple, the Most Holy Place, and put it beneath the wings of the cherubim. ⁸The cherubim spread their wings over the place of the ark and covered the ark and its carrying poles. ⁹These poles were so long that their ends, extending from the ark, could be seen from in front of the inner sanctuary, but not from outside the Holy Place; and they are still there today. ¹⁰There was nothing in the ark except the two tablets that Moses had placed in it at Horeb, where the Lᴏʀᴅ made a covenant with the Israelites after they came out of Egypt.

¹¹The priests then withdrew from the Holy Place. All the priests who were there had consecrated themselves, regardless of their divisions. ¹²All the Levites who were musicians—Asaph, Heman, Jeduthun and their sons and relatives—stood on the east side of the altar, dressed in fine linen and playing cymbals, harps and lyres. They were accompanied by 120 priests sounding trum-pets. ¹³The trumpeters and musicians joined in unison to give praise and thanks to the Lᴏʀᴅ. Accompanied by trumpets, cymbals and other instruments, the singers raised their voices in praise to the Lᴏʀᴅ and sang:

    "He is good;
        his love endures forever."

Then the temple of the Lᴏʀᴅ was filled with the cloud, ¹⁴and the priests could not perform their service because of the cloud, for the glo-ry of the Lᴏʀᴅ filled the temple of God.

6 Then Solomon said, "The Lᴏʀᴅ has said that he would dwell in a dark cloud; ²I have built a magnificent temple for you, a place for you to dwell for-ever."

³While the whole assembly of Israel was standing there, the king turned around and blessed them. ⁴Then he said:

    "Praise be to the Lᴏʀᴅ, the God of Is-
    rael, who with his hands has fulfilled
    what he promised with his mouth to
    my father David. For he said, ⁵'Since
    the day I brought my people out of
    Egypt, I have not chosen a city in any
    tribe of Israel to have a temple built so
    that my Name might be there, nor have
    I chosen anyone to be ruler over my

─────────────────────
ᵃ 17 Hebrew *Zeredatha*, a variant of *Zarethan*

people Israel. [6]But now I have chosen Jerusalem for my Name to be there, and I have chosen David to rule my people Israel.'

[7]"My father David had it in his heart to build a temple for the Name of the LORD, the God of Israel. [8]But the LORD said to my father David, 'You did well to have it in your heart to build a temple for my Name. [9]Nevertheless, you are not the one to build the temple, but your son, who is your own flesh and blood—he is the one who will build the temple for my Name.'

[10]"The LORD has kept the promise he made. I have succeeded David my father and now I sit on the throne of Israel, just as the LORD promised, and I have built the temple for the Name of the LORD, the God of Israel. [11]There I have placed the ark, in which is the covenant of the LORD that he made with the people of Israel."

Solomon's Prayer of Dedication

[12]Then Solomon stood before the altar of the LORD in front of the whole assembly of Israel and spread out his hands. [13]Now he had made a bronze platform, five cubits long, five cubits wide and three cubits high,[a] and had placed it in the center of the outer court. He stood on the platform and then knelt down before the whole assembly of Israel and spread out his hands toward heaven. [14]He said:

"LORD, the God of Israel, there is no God like you in heaven or on earth— you who keep your covenant of love with your servants who continue wholeheartedly in your way. [15]You have kept your promise to your servant David my father; with your mouth you have promised and with your hand you have fulfilled it—as it is today.

[16]"Now LORD, the God of Israel, keep for your servant David my father the promises you made to him when you said, 'You shall never fail to have a successor to sit before me on the throne of Israel, if only your descendants are careful in all they do to walk before me according to my law, as you have

done.' [17]And now, LORD, the God of Israel, let your word that you promised your servant David come true.

[18]"But will God really dwell on earth with human beings? The heavens, even the highest heavens, cannot contain you. How much less this temple I have built! [19]Yet, LORD my God, give attention to your servant's prayer and his plea for mercy. Hear the cry and the prayer that your servant is praying in your presence. [20]May your eyes be open toward this temple day and night, this place of which you said you would put your Name there. May you hear the prayer your servant prays toward this place. [21]Hear the supplications of your servant and of your people Israel when they pray toward this place. Hear from heaven, your dwelling place; and when you hear, forgive.

[22]"When anyone wrongs their neighbor and is required to take an oath and they come and swear the oath before your altar in this temple, [23]then hear from heaven and act. Judge between your servants, condemning the guilty and bringing down on their heads what they have done, and vindicating the innocent by treating them in accordance with their innocence.

[24]"When your people Israel have been defeated by an enemy because they have sinned against you and when they turn back and give praise to your name, praying and making supplication before you in this temple, [25]then hear from heaven and forgive the sin of your people Israel and bring them back to the land you gave to them and their ancestors.

[26]"When the heavens are shut up and there is no rain because your people have sinned against you, and when they pray toward this place and give praise to your name and turn from their sin because you have afflicted them, [27]then hear from heaven and forgive the sin of your servants, your people Israel. Teach them the right way to live, and send rain on the land you gave your people for an inheritance.

---

a 13 That is, about 7 1/2 feet long and wide and 4 1/2 feet high or about 2.3 meters long and wide and 1.4 meters high

²⁸"When famine or plague comes to the land, or blight or mildew, locusts or grasshoppers, or when enemies besiege them in any of their cities, whatever disaster or disease may come, ²⁹and when a prayer or plea is made by anyone among your people Israel—being aware of their afflictions and pains, and spreading out their hands toward this temple— ³⁰then hear from heaven, your dwelling place. Forgive, and deal with everyone according to all they do, since you know their hearts (for you alone know the human heart), ³¹so that they will fear you and walk in obedience to you all the time they live in the land you gave our ancestors.

³²"As for foreigners who do not belong to your people Israel but have come from a distant land because of your great name and your mighty hand and your outstretched arm—when they come and pray toward this temple, ³³then hear from heaven, your dwelling place. Do whatever the foreigner asks of you, so that all the peoples of the earth may know your name and fear you, as do your own people Israel, and may know that this house I have built bears your Name.

³⁴"When your people go to war against their enemies, wherever you send them, and when they pray to you toward this city you have chosen and the temple I have built for your Name, ³⁵then hear from heaven their prayer and their plea, and uphold their cause.

³⁶"When they sin against you—for there is no one who does not sin—and you become angry with them and give them over to the enemy, who takes them captive to a land far away or near; ³⁷if they have a change of heart in the land where they are held captive, and repent and plead with you in the land of their captivity and say, 'We have sinned, we have done wrong and acted wickedly'; ³⁸and if they turn back to you with all their heart and soul in the land of their captivity where they were taken, and pray toward the land you gave their ancestors, toward the city you have chosen and toward the temple I have built for your Name; ³⁹then from heaven, your dwelling place, hear their prayer and their pleas, and uphold their cause. And forgive your people, who have sinned against you.

⁴⁰"Now, my God, may your eyes be open and your ears attentive to the prayers offered in this place.

⁴¹"Now arise, LORD God, and come to
  your resting place,
  you and the ark of your might.
May your priests, LORD God, be
  clothed with salvation,
may your faithful people rejoice
  in your goodness.
⁴²LORD God, do not reject your
  anointed one.
Remember the great love
  promised to David your
  servant."

The Dedication of the Temple

7 When Solomon finished praying, fire came down from heaven and consumed the burnt offering and the sacrifices, and the glory of the LORD filled the temple. ²The priests could not enter the temple of the LORD because the glory of the LORD filled it. ³When all the Israelites saw the fire coming down and the glory of the LORD above the temple, they knelt on the pavement with their faces to the ground, and they worshiped and gave thanks to the LORD, saying,

"He is good;
  his love endures forever."

⁴Then the king and all the people offered sacrifices before the LORD. ⁵And King Solomon offered a sacrifice of twenty-two thousand head of cattle and a hundred and twenty thousand sheep and goats. So the king and all the people dedicated the temple of God. ⁶The priests took their positions, as did the Levites with the LORD's musical instruments, which King David had made for praising the LORD and which were used when he gave thanks, saying, "His love endures forever." Opposite the Levites, the priests blew their trumpets, and all the Israelites were standing.

⁷Solomon consecrated the middle part of the courtyard in front of the temple of the LORD, and there he offered burnt offerings and the fat of the fellowship offerings, because the bronze altar he had made could

MONDAY

PERSEVERING IN PRAYER

2 Chronicles 7:1–22 *or* 7:12–14

Jim Cymbala

When we seek God for answers, we must persevere in prayer, letting it build up day after day until the force of it becomes a mighty tide pushing over all obstacles. No wonder God says his house is supposed to be known as a house of prayer—not merely a house of preaching or of singing, but especially of prayer. How else will we receive great answers from God unless we persevere in prayer?

How must God feel every Sunday when, all over the nation, so many people gather in churches but do so little actual praying? Congregations make time in the weekly schedule for everything from basketball leagues to weight-loss classes, but they can't seem to find a slot for a prayer meeting. The Lord waits to bless his people with his abundant supply, but we don't take the time to open the channel. What a terrible epitaph: "You do not have because you do not ask God" (James 4:2).

God is drawn to prayer. He delights in communion with us. Prayer releases his blessing into our lives.

E. M. BOUNDS {AD 1835–1913}

God's true preachers have been distinguished by one great feature: they were people of prayer . . . They did not pray occasionally. They did not pray a little at regular or at odd times. Rather, they prayed in such a way that their prayers entered into and shaped their characters. They prayed in such a way as to affect their own lives and the lives of others. They prayed in such a way as to shape the history of the church and influence the current of the times. They spent much time in prayer—not because they marked the shadow on the dial or the hands on the clock—but because it was to them so momentous and engaging a business that they could barely stop.

Prayer was to them what it was to Paul: a fervent effort of the soul. And what it was to Jacob: a wrestling and overcoming. And what it was to Christ: anguish and tears. They prayed in the Spirit on all occasions with all kinds of prayers and requests, keeping alert and persevering in praying (see Ephesians 6:18). "The prayer of a righteous person is powerful and effective" (James 5:16) and has been the mightiest weapon of God's mightiest soldiers.

reflection

1. Why does it seem difficult to prioritize prayer? In your church? In your life?

2. When have you seen the power of prayer at work? What happened?

3. How can you make prayer a more essential part of what you do every day?

For your next devotional reading, go to page 488.

not hold the burnt offerings, the grain offerings and the fat portions.

⁸So Solomon observed the festival at that time for seven days, and all Israel with him—a vast assembly, people from Lebo Hamath to the Wadi of Egypt. ⁹On the eighth day they held an assembly, for they had celebrated the dedication of the altar for seven days and the festival for seven days more. ¹⁰On the twenty-third day of the seventh month he sent the people to their homes, joyful and glad in heart for the good things the LORD had done for David and Solomon and for his people Israel.

The LORD Appears to Solomon

¹¹When Solomon had finished the temple of the LORD and the royal palace, and had succeeded in carrying out all he had in mind to do in the temple of the LORD and in his own palace, ¹²the LORD appeared to him at night and said:

"I have heard your prayer and have chosen this place for myself as a temple for sacrifices.

¹³"When I shut up the heavens so that there is no rain, or command locusts to devour the land or send a plague among my people, ¹⁴if my people, who are called by my name, will humble themselves and pray and seek my face and turn from their wicked ways, then I will hear from heaven, and I will forgive their sin and will heal their land. ¹⁵Now my eyes will be open and my ears attentive to the prayers offered in this place. ¹⁶I have chosen and consecrated this temple so that my Name may be there forever. My eyes and my heart will always be there.

¹⁷"As for you, if you walk before me faithfully as David your father did, and do all I command, and observe my decrees and laws, ¹⁸I will establish your royal throne, as I covenanted with David your father when I said, 'You shall never fail to have a successor to rule over Israel.'

¹⁹"But if you ᵃ turn away and forsake the decrees and commands I have given you ᵃ and go off to serve other gods

and worship them, ²⁰then I will uproot Israel from my land, which I have given them, and will reject this temple I have consecrated for my Name. I will make it a byword and an object of ridicule among all peoples. ²¹This temple will become a heap of rubble. All ᵇ who pass by will be appalled and say, 'Why has the LORD done such a thing to this land and to this temple?' ²²People will answer, 'Because they have forsaken the LORD, the God of their ancestors, who brought them out of Egypt, and have embraced other gods, worshiping and serving them—that is why he brought all this disaster on them.' "

Solomon's Other Activities

8 At the end of twenty years, during which Solomon built the temple of the LORD and his own palace, ²Solomon rebuilt the villages that Hiram ᶜ had given him, and settled Israelites in them. ³Solomon then went to Hamath Zobah and captured it. ⁴He also built up Tadmor in the desert and all the store cities he had built in Hamath. ⁵He rebuilt Upper Beth Horon and Lower Beth Horon as fortified cities, with walls and with gates and bars, ⁶as well as Baalath and all his store cities, and all the cities for his chariots and for his horses ᵈ— whatever he desired to build in Jerusalem, in Lebanon and throughout all the territory he ruled.

⁷There were still people left from the Hittites, Amorites, Perizzites, Hivites and Jebusites (these people were not Israelites). ⁸Solomon conscripted the descendants of all these people remaining in the land—whom the Israelites had not destroyed—to serve as slave labor, as it is to this day. ⁹But Solomon did not make slaves of the Israelites for his work; they were his fighting men, commanders of his captains, and commanders of his chariots and charioteers. ¹⁰They were also King Solomon's chief officials—two hundred and fifty officials supervising the men.

¹¹Solomon brought Pharaoh's daughter up from the City of David to the palace he had built for her, for he said, "My wife must not live in the palace of David king of Israel,

---

ᵃ 19 The Hebrew is plural.   ᵇ 21 See some Septuagint manuscripts, Old Latin, Syriac, Arabic and Targum; Hebrew *And though this temple is now so imposing, all*   ᶜ 2 Hebrew *Huram*, a variant of *Hiram*; also in verse 18   ᵈ 6 Or *charioteers* because the places the ark of the Lord has entered are holy."

¹²On the altar of the Lord that he had built in front of the portico, Solomon sacrificed burnt offerings to the Lord, ¹³according to the daily requirement for offerings commanded by Moses for the Sabbaths, the New Moons and the three annual festivals—the Festival of Unleavened Bread, the Festival of Weeks and the Festival of Tabernacles. ¹⁴In keeping with the ordinance of his father David, he appointed the divisions of the priests for their duties, and the Levites to lead the praise and to assist the priests according to each day's requirement. He also appointed the gatekeepers by divisions for the various gates, because this was what David the man of God had ordered. ¹⁵They did not deviate from the king's commands to the priests or to the Levites in any matter, including that of the treasuries.

¹⁶All Solomon's work was carried out, from the day the foundation of the temple of the Lord was laid until its completion. So the temple of the Lord was finished.

¹⁷Then Solomon went to Ezion Geber and Elath on the coast of Edom. ¹⁸And Hiram sent him ships commanded by his own officers, sailors who knew the sea. These, with Solomon's servants, sailed to Ophir and brought back four hundred and fifty talentsᵃ of gold, which they delivered to King Solomon.

The Queen of Sheba Visits Solomon

9 When the queen of Sheba heard of Solomon's fame, she came to Jerusalem to test him with hard questions. Arriving with a very great caravan—with camels carrying spices, large quantities of gold, and precious stones—she came to Solomon and talked with him about all she had on her mind. ²Solomon answered all her questions; nothing was too hard for him to explain to her. ³When the queen of Sheba saw the wisdom of Solomon, as well as the palace he had built, ⁴the food on his table, the seating of his officials, the attending servants in their robes, the cupbearers in their robes and the burnt offerings he made atᵇ the temple of the Lord, she was overwhelmed.

⁵She said to the king, "The report I heard in my own country about your achievements and your wisdom is true. ⁶But I did not believe what they said until I came and saw with my own eyes. Indeed, not even half the greatness of your wisdom was told me; you have far exceeded the report I heard. ⁷How happy your people must be! How happy your officials, who continually stand before you and hear your wisdom! ⁸Praise be to the Lord your God, who has delighted in you and placed you on his throne as king to rule for the Lord your God. Because of the love of your God for Israel and his desire to uphold them forever, he has made you king over them, to maintain justice and righteousness."

⁹Then she gave the king 120 talentsᶜ of gold, large quantities of spices, and precious stones. There had never been such spices as those the queen of Sheba gave to King Solomon.

¹⁰(The servants of Hiram and the servants of Solomon brought gold from Ophir; they also brought algumwoodᵈ and precious stones. ¹¹The king used the algumwood to make steps for the temple of the Lord and for the royal palace, and to make harps and lyres for the musicians. Nothing like them had ever been seen in Judah.)

¹²King Solomon gave the queen of Sheba all she desired and asked for; he gave her more than she had brought to him. Then she left and returned with her retinue to her own country.

Solomon's Splendor

¹³The weight of the gold that Solomon received yearly was 666 talents,ᵉ ¹⁴not including the revenues brought in by merchants and traders. Also all the kings of Arabia and the governors of the territories brought gold and silver to Solomon.

¹⁵King Solomon made two hundred large shields of hammered gold; six hundred shekelsᶠ of hammered gold went into each shield. ¹⁶He also made three hundred small shields of hammered gold, with three hundred shekelsᵍ of gold in each shield. The king put them in the Palace of the Forest of Lebanon.

ᵃ 18 That is, about 17 tons or about 15 metric tons   ᵇ 4 Or and the ascent by which he went up to
ᶜ 9 That is, about 4 1/2 tons or about 4 metric tons   ᵈ 10 Probably a variant of almugwood   ᵉ 13 That is, about 25 tons or about 23 metric tons   ᶠ 15 That is, about 15 pounds or about 6.9 kilograms
ᵍ 16 That is, about 7 1/2 pounds or about 3.5 kilograms

¹⁷Then the king made a great throne inlaid with ivory and overlaid with pure gold. ¹⁸The throne had six steps, and a footstool of gold was attached to it. On both sides of the seat were armrests, with a lion standing beside each of them. ¹⁹Twelve lions stood on the six steps, one at either end of each step. Nothing like it had ever been made for any other kingdom. ²⁰All King Solomon's goblets were gold, and all the household articles in the Palace of the Forest of Lebanon were pure gold. Nothing was made of silver, because silver was considered of little value in Solomon's day. ²¹The king had a fleet of trading ships^a manned by Hiram's^b servants. Once every three years it returned, carrying gold, silver and ivory, and apes and baboons.

²²King Solomon was greater in riches and wisdom than all the other kings of the earth. ²³All the kings of the earth sought audience with Solomon to hear the wisdom God had put in his heart. ²⁴Year after year, everyone who came brought a gift—articles of silver and gold, and robes, weapons and spices, and horses and mules.

²⁵Solomon had four thousand stalls for horses and chariots, and twelve thousand horses,^c which he kept in the chariot cities and also with him in Jerusalem. ²⁶He ruled over all the kings from the Euphrates River to the land of the Philistines, as far as the border of Egypt. ²⁷The king made silver as common in Jerusalem as stones, and cedar as plentiful as sycamore-fig trees in the foothills. ²⁸Solomon's horses were imported from Egypt and from all other countries.

Solomon's Death

²⁹As for the other events of Solomon's reign, from beginning to end, are they not written in the records of Nathan the prophet, in the prophecy of Ahijah the Shilonite and in the visions of Iddo the seer concerning Jeroboam son of Nebat? ³⁰Solomon reigned in Jerusalem over all Israel forty years. ³¹Then he rested with his ancestors and was buried in the city of David his father. And Rehoboam his son succeeded him as king.

Israel Rebels Against Rehoboam

10 Rehoboam went to Shechem, for all Israel had gone there to make him king. ²When Jeroboam son of Nebat heard this (he was in Egypt, where he had fled from King Solomon), he returned from Egypt. ³So they sent for Jeroboam, and he and all Israel went to Rehoboam and said to him: ⁴"Your father put a heavy yoke on us, but now lighten the harsh labor and the heavy yoke he put on us, and we will serve you."

⁵Rehoboam answered, "Come back to me in three days." So the people went away.

⁶Then King Rehoboam consulted the elders who had served his father Solomon during his lifetime. "How would you advise me to answer these people?" he asked.

⁷They replied, "If you will be kind to these people and please them and give them a favorable answer, they will always be your servants."

⁸But Rehoboam rejected the advice the elders gave him and consulted the young men who had grown up with him and were serving him. ⁹He asked them, "What is your advice? How should we answer these people who say to me, 'Lighten the yoke your father put on us'?"

¹⁰The young men who had grown up with him replied, "The people have said to you, 'Your father put a heavy yoke on us, but make our yoke lighter.' Now tell them, 'My little finger is thicker than my father's waist. ¹¹My father laid on you a heavy yoke; I will make it even heavier. My father scourged you with whips; I will scourge you with scorpions.' "

¹²Three days later Jeroboam and all the people returned to Rehoboam, as the king had said, "Come back to me in three days." ¹³The king answered them harshly. Rejecting the advice of the elders, ¹⁴he followed the advice of the young men and said, "My father made your yoke heavy; I will make it even heavier. My father scourged you with whips; I will scourge you with scorpions." ¹⁵So the king did not listen to the people, for this turn of events was from God, to fulfill the word the Lord had spoken to Jeroboam son of Nebat through Ahijah the Shilonite. ¹⁶When all Israel saw that the king re-

---

^a 21 Hebrew *of ships that could go to Tarshish*   ^b 21 Hebrew *Huram*, a variant of *Hiram*
^c 25 Or *charioteers*

fused to listen to them, they answered the king:

"What share do we have in David,
    what part in Jesse's son?
To your tents, Israel!
    Look after your own house, David!"

So all the Israelites went home. [17]But as for the Israelites who were living in the towns of Judah, Rehoboam still ruled over them.

[18]King Rehoboam sent out Adoniram,[a] who was in charge of forced labor, but the Israelites stoned him to death. King Rehoboam, however, managed to get into his chariot and escape to Jerusalem. [19]So Israel has been in rebellion against the house of David to this day.

11

When Rehoboam arrived in Jerusalem, he mustered the house of Judah and Benjamin—a hundred and eighty thousand able young men—to make war against Israel and to regain the kingdom for Rehoboam.

[2]But this word of the LORD came to Shemaiah the man of God: [3]"Say to Rehoboam son of Solomon king of Judah and to all Israel in Judah and Benjamin, [4]'This is what the LORD says: Do not go up to fight against your fellow Israelites. Go home, every one of you, for this is my doing.'" So they obeyed the words of the LORD and turned back from marching against Jeroboam.

Rehoboam Fortifies Judah

[5]Rehoboam lived in Jerusalem and built up towns for defense in Judah: [6]Bethlehem, Etam, Tekoa, [7]Beth Zur, Soko, Adullam, [8]Gath, Mareshah, Ziph, [9]Adoraim, Lachish, Azekah, [10]Zorah, Aijalon and Hebron. These were fortified cities in Judah and Benjamin. [11]He strengthened their defenses and put commanders in them, with supplies of food, olive oil and wine. [12]He put shields and spears in all the cities, and made them very strong. So Judah and Benjamin were his.

[13]The priests and Levites from all their districts throughout Israel sided with him. [14]The Levites even abandoned their pasturelands and property and came to Judah and Jerusalem, because Jeroboam and his sons had rejected them as priests of the LORD [15]when he appointed his own priests for the high places and for the goat and calf idols he had made. [16]Those from every tribe of Israel who set their hearts on seeking the LORD, the God of Israel, followed the Levites to Jerusalem to offer sacrifices to the LORD, the God of their ancestors. [17]They strengthened the kingdom of Judah and supported Rehoboam son of Solomon three years, following the ways of David and Solomon during this time.

Rehoboam's Family

[18]Rehoboam married Mahalath, who was the daughter of David's son Jerimoth and of Abihail, the daughter of Jesse's son Eliab. [19]She bore him sons: Jeush, Shemariah and Zaham. [20]Then he married Maakah daughter of Absalom, who bore him Abijah, Attai, Ziza and Shelomith. [21]Rehoboam loved Maakah daughter of Absalom more than any of his other wives and concubines. In all, he had eighteen wives and sixty concubines, twenty-eight sons and sixty daughters.

[22]Rehoboam appointed Abijah son of Maakah as crown prince among his brothers, in order to make him king. [23]He acted wisely, dispersing some of his sons throughout the districts of Judah and Benjamin, and to all the fortified cities. He gave them abundant provisions and took many wives for them.

Shishak Attacks Jerusalem

12

After Rehoboam's position as king was established and he had become strong, he and all Israel[b] with him abandoned the law of the LORD. [2]Because they had been unfaithful to the LORD, Shishak king of Egypt attacked Jerusalem in the fifth year of King Rehoboam. [3]With twelve hundred chariots and sixty thousand horsemen and the innumerable troops of Libyans, Sukkites and Cushites[c] that came with him from Egypt, [4]he captured the fortified cities of Judah and came as far as Jerusalem.

[5]Then the prophet Shemaiah came to Rehoboam and to the leaders of Judah who had assembled in Jerusalem for fear of Shishak, and he said to them, "This is what the LORD says, 'You have abandoned me; therefore, I now abandon you to Shishak.'"

---

[a] 18 Hebrew *Hadoram*, a variant of *Adoniram*   [b] 1 That is, Judah, as frequently in 2 Chronicles
[c] 3 That is, people from the upper Nile region

⁶The leaders of Israel and the king humbled themselves and said, "The LORD is just."

⁷When the LORD saw that they humbled themselves, this word of the LORD came to Shemaiah: "Since they have humbled themselves, I will not destroy them but will soon give them deliverance. My wrath will not be poured out on Jerusalem through Shishak. ⁸They will, however, become subject to him, so that they may learn the difference between serving me and serving the kings of other lands."

⁹When Shishak king of Egypt attacked Jerusalem, he carried off the treasures of the temple of the LORD and the treasures of the royal palace. He took everything, including the gold shields Solomon had made. ¹⁰So King Rehoboam made bronze shields to replace them and assigned these to the commanders of the guard on duty at the entrance to the royal palace. ¹¹Whenever the king went to the LORD's temple, the guards went with him, bearing the shields, and afterward they returned them to the guardroom.

¹²Because Rehoboam humbled himself, the LORD's anger turned from him, and he was not totally destroyed. Indeed, there was some good in Judah.

¹³King Rehoboam established himself firmly in Jerusalem and continued as king. He was forty-one years old when he became king, and he reigned seventeen years in Jerusalem, the city the LORD had chosen out of all the tribes of Israel in which to put his Name. His mother's name was Naamah; she was an Ammonite. ¹⁴He did evil because he had not set his heart on seeking the LORD.

¹⁵As for the events of Rehoboam's reign, from beginning to end, are they not written in the records of Shemaiah the prophet and of Iddo the seer that deal with genealogies? There was continual warfare between Rehoboam and Jeroboam. ¹⁶Rehoboam rested with his ancestors and was buried in the City of David. And Abijah his son succeeded him as king.

Abijah King of Judah

13 In the eighteenth year of the reign of Jeroboam, Abijah became king of Judah, ²and he reigned in Jerusalem three years. His mother's name was Maakah,ᵃ a daughterᵇ of Uriel of Gibeah.

There was war between Abijah and Jeroboam. ³Abijah went into battle with an army of four hundred thousand able fighting men, and Jeroboam drew up a battle line against him with eight hundred thousand able troops.

⁴Abijah stood on Mount Zemaraim, in the hill country of Ephraim, and said, "Jeroboam and all Israel, listen to me! ⁵Don't you know that the LORD, the God of Israel, has given the kingship of Israel to David and his descendants forever by a covenant of salt? ⁶Yet Jeroboam son of Nebat, an official of Solomon son of David, rebelled against his master. ⁷Some worthless scoundrels gathered around him and opposed Rehoboam son of Solomon when he was young and indecisive and not strong enough to resist them.

⁸"And now you plan to resist the kingdom of the LORD, which is in the hands of David's descendants. You are indeed a vast army and have with you the golden calves that Jeroboam made to be your gods. ⁹But didn't you drive out the priests of the LORD, the sons of Aaron, and the Levites, and make priests of your own as the peoples of other lands do? Whoever comes to consecrate himself with a young bull and seven rams may become a priest of what are not gods.

¹⁰"As for us, the LORD is our God, and we have not forsaken him. The priests who serve the LORD are sons of Aaron, and the Levites assist them. ¹¹Every morning and evening they present burnt offerings and fragrant incense to the LORD. They set out the bread on the ceremonially clean table and light the lamps on the gold lampstand every evening. We are observing the requirements of the LORD our God. But you have forsaken him. ¹²God is with us; he is our leader. His priests with their trumpets will sound the battle cry against you. People of Israel, do not fight against the LORD, the God of your ancestors, for you will not succeed."

¹³Now Jeroboam had sent troops around to the rear, so that while he was in front of Judah the ambush was behind them. ¹⁴Judah turned and saw that they were being attacked at both front and rear. Then they cried out to the LORD. The priests blew their

---

ᵃ 2 Most Septuagint manuscripts and Syriac (see also 2 Chron. 11:20 and 1 Kings 15:2); Hebrew *Micaiah*
ᵇ 2 Or *granddaughter*

trumpets [15]and the men of Judah raised the battle cry. At the sound of their battle cry, God routed Jeroboam and all Israel before Abijah and Judah. [16]The Israelites fled before Judah, and God delivered them into their hands. [17]Abijah and his troops inflicted heavy losses on them, so that there were five hundred thousand casualties among Israel's able men. [18]The Israelites were subdued on that occasion, and the men of Judah were victorious because they relied on the LORD, the God of their ancestors.

[19]Abijah pursued Jeroboam and took from him the towns of Bethel, Jeshanah and Ephron, with their surrounding villages. [20]Jeroboam did not regain power during the time of Abijah. And the LORD struck him down and he died.

[21]But Abijah grew in strength. He married fourteen wives and had twenty-two sons and sixteen daughters.

[22]The other events of Abijah's reign, what he did and what he said, are written in the annotations of the prophet Iddo.

14 *And Abijah rested with his ancestors and was buried in the City of David. Asa his son succeeded him as king, and in his days the country was at peace for ten years.

Asa King of Judah

*[2]Asa did what was good and right in the eyes of the LORD his God. [3]He removed the foreign altars and the high places, smashed the sacred stones and cut down the Asherah poles.[a] [4]He commanded Judah to seek the LORD, the God of their ancestors, and to obey his laws and commands. [5]He removed the high places and incense altars in every town in Judah, and the kingdom was at peace under him. [6]He built up the fortified cities of Judah, since the land was at peace. No one was at war with him during those years, for the LORD gave him rest.

[7]"Let us build up these towns," he said to Judah, "and put walls around them, with towers, gates and bars. The land is still ours, because we have sought the LORD our God; we sought him and he has given us rest on every side." So they built and prospered.

[8]Asa had an army of three hundred thousand men from Judah, equipped with large shields and with spears, and two hundred and eighty thousand from Benjamin, armed with small shields and with bows. All these were brave fighting men.

[9]Zerah the Cushite marched out against them with an army of thousands upon thousands and three hundred chariots, and came as far as Mareshah. [10]Asa went out to meet him, and they took up battle positions in the Valley of Zephathah near Mareshah.

[11]Then Asa called to the LORD his God and said, "LORD, there is no one like you to help the powerless against the mighty. Help us, LORD our God, for we rely on you, and in your name we have come against this vast army. LORD, you are our God; do not let mere mortals prevail against you."

[12]The LORD struck down the Cushites before Asa and Judah. The Cushites fled, [13]and Asa and his army pursued them as far as Gerar. Such a great number of Cushites fell that they could not recover; they were crushed before the LORD and his forces. The men of Judah carried off a large amount of plunder. [14]They destroyed all the villages around Gerar, for the terror of the LORD had fallen on them. They plundered all these villages, since there was much booty there. [15]They also attacked the camps of the herders and carried off droves of sheep and goats and camels. Then they returned to Jerusalem.

Asa's Reform

15 The Spirit of God came on Azariah son of Oded. [2]He went out to meet Asa and said to him, "Listen to me, Asa and all Judah and Benjamin. The LORD is with you when you are with him. If you seek him, he will be found by you, but if you forsake him, he will forsake you. [3]For a long time Israel was without the true God, without a priest to teach and without the law. [4]But in their distress they turned to the LORD, the God of Israel, and sought him, and he was found by them. [5]In those days it was not safe to travel about, for all the inhabitants of the lands were in great turmoil. [6]One nation was being crushed by another and one city by another, because God was troubling them with every kind of distress. [7]But as for you, be strong and do not give up, for your work will be rewarded."

---

a 3 That is, wooden symbols of the goddess Asherah; here and elsewhere in 2 Chronicles
* 14:1 is numbered 13:23 in Hebrew texts.   * 14:2-15 is numbered 14:1-14 in Hebrew texts.

⁸When Asa heard these words and the prophecy of Azariah son of*ª* Oded the prophet, he took courage. He removed the detestable idols from the whole land of Judah and Benjamin and from the towns he had captured in the hills of Ephraim. He repaired the altar of the LORD that was in front of the portico of the LORD's temple.

⁹Then he assembled all Judah and Benjamin and the people from Ephraim, Manasseh and Simeon who had settled among them, for large numbers had come over to him from Israel when they saw that the LORD his God was with him.

¹⁰They assembled at Jerusalem in the third month of the fifteenth year of Asa's reign. ¹¹At that time they sacrificed to the LORD seven hundred head of cattle and seven thousand sheep and goats from the plunder they had brought back. ¹²They entered into a covenant to seek the LORD, the God of their ancestors, with all their heart and soul. ¹³All who would not seek the LORD, the God of Israel, were to be put to death, whether small or great, man or woman. ¹⁴They took an oath to the LORD with loud acclamation, with shouting and with trumpets and horns. ¹⁵All Judah rejoiced about the oath because they had sworn it wholeheartedly. They sought God eagerly, and he was found by them. So the LORD gave them rest on every side.

¹⁶King Asa also deposed his grandmother Maakah from her position as queen mother, because she had made a repulsive image for the worship of Asherah. Asa cut it down, broke it up and burned it in the Kidron Valley. ¹⁷Although he did not remove the high places from Israel, Asa's heart was fully committed ⸤to the LORD⸥ all his life. ¹⁸He brought into the temple of God the silver and gold and the articles that he and his father had dedicated.

¹⁹There was no more war until the thirty-fifth year of Asa's reign.

Asa's Last Years

16 In the thirty-sixth year of Asa's reign Baasha king of Israel went up against Judah and fortified Ramah to prevent anyone from leaving or entering the territory of Asa king of Judah.

²Asa then took the silver and gold out of the treasuries of the LORD's temple and of his own palace and sent it to Ben-Hadad king of Aram, who was ruling in Damascus. ³"Let there be a treaty between me and you," he said, "as there was between my father and your father. See, I am sending you silver and gold. Now break your treaty with Baasha king of Israel so he will withdraw from me."

⁴Ben-Hadad agreed with King Asa and sent the commanders of his forces against the towns of Israel. They conquered Ijon, Dan, Abel Maim*ᵇ* and all the store cities of Naphtali. ⁵When Baasha heard this, he stopped building Ramah and abandoned his work. ⁶Then King Asa brought all the men of Judah, and they carried away from Ramah the stones and timber Baasha had been using. With them he built up Geba and Mizpah.

⁷At that time Hanani the seer came to Asa king of Judah and said to him: "Because you relied on the king of Aram and not on the LORD your God, the army of the king of Aram has escaped from your hand. ⁸Were not the Cushites*ᶜ* and Libyans a mighty army with great numbers of chariots and horsemen*ᵈ*? Yet when you relied on the LORD, he delivered them into your hand. ⁹For the eyes of the LORD range throughout the earth to strengthen those whose hearts are fully committed to him. You have done a foolish thing, and from now on you will be at war."

¹⁰Asa was angry with the seer because of this; he was so enraged that he put him in prison. At the same time Asa brutally oppressed some of the people.

¹¹The events of Asa's reign, from beginning to end, are written in the book of the kings of Judah and Israel. ¹²In the thirty-ninth year of his reign Asa was afflicted with a disease in his feet. Though his disease was severe, even in his illness he did not seek help from the LORD, but only from the physicians. ¹³Then in the forty-first year of his reign Asa died and rested with his ancestors. ¹⁴They buried him in the tomb that he had cut out for himself in the City of David. They laid him on a bier covered with spices and various blended perfumes, and they made a huge fire in his honor.

---

a 8 Vulgate and Syriac (see also Septuagint and verse 1); Hebrew does not have *Azariah son of.*
b 4 Also known as *Abel Beth Maakah*   *c 8* That is, people from the upper Nile region
d 8 Or *charioteers*

TUESDAY

HE SEES ALL

2 Chronicles 16:1–14 *or* 16:7–9

OLE HALLESBY {AD 1879–1961}

The Word of God is two-edged . . . And very sharp. It cuts to the very heart, for it speaks of the heart which is *perfect toward the Lord* . . . Do you fear God with all your heart?

Is your heart in your *prayers*? Or is it habit and duty which drive you to pray?

Is your heart in your *reading of the Bible*? Or do you read a chapter merely for the sake of having read it?

Is your heart in your *striving against sin*? Or do you fight against sin simply because you fear its consequences, your heart meanwhile clinging to sin?

Is your heart in your *remorse*? Do you grieve because you sin, because you act contrary to the will of God, or do you grieve simply because you fear the consequences of sin?

Is your heart in the *sacrifices* you make? Are you glad to give of your time and your money? Are you glad to forego your own comfort and convenience?

What is *your* answer to these searching questions?

I imagine some one will say: "My heart is cut to the quick by all of these questions. My heart is so wicked that, alas, I do not know what to do" . . .

Draw nigh to His heart which broke in death for your divided heart. And give thanks to Him that you may rest *in Christ* with everything—also with your heart.

Ann Spangler

Scripture makes it clear God never slumbers, never looks one way while we head off in another, never misses a millisecond of what is happening on earth. It also assures us God is on the lookout for men and women who are totally committed to him. Why? Because he wants to strengthen their hearts as they serve him. If you are feeling weak in the face of life's challenges, the best way to grow strong is to strengthen your commitment to Christ. Decide to obey fully, to follow completely, to keep your eyes fastened on him. Let *El Roi* [the "God who sees"] take pleasure as he watches over you, and you will soon find your heart stronger and your confidence deeper without quite knowing how it happened.

reflection

1. If everything you thought, said and did in the last 48 hours was broadcast on a huge screen in Times Square, what would you be most ashamed and embarrassed about?

2. How much does it bother you that God sees and knows all those things?

3. While it can be disconcerting to realize that God is always watching you, it's also very comforting and encouraging. Why?

For your next devotional reading, go to page 498.

Jehoshaphat King of Judah

17 Jehoshaphat his son succeeded him as king and strengthened himself against Israel. ²He stationed troops in all the fortified cities of Judah and put garrisons in Judah and in the towns of Ephraim that his father Asa had captured.

³The Lord was with Jehoshaphat because he followed the ways of his father David before him. He did not consult the Baals ⁴but sought the God of his father and followed his commands rather than the practices of Israel. ⁵The Lord established the kingdom under his control; and all Judah brought gifts to Jehoshaphat, so that he had great wealth and honor. ⁶His heart was devoted to the ways of the Lord; furthermore, he removed the high places and the Asherah poles from Judah.

⁷In the third year of his reign he sent his officials Ben-Hail, Obadiah, Zechariah, Nethanel and Micaiah to teach in the towns of Judah. ⁸With them were certain Levites— Shemaiah, Nethaniah, Zebadiah, Asahel, Shemiramoth, Jehonathan, Adonijah, Tobijah and Tob-Adonijah—and the priests Elishama and Jehoram. ⁹They taught throughout Judah, taking with them the Book of the Law of the Lord; they went around to all the towns of Judah and taught the people.

¹⁰The fear of the Lord fell on all the kingdoms of the lands surrounding Judah, so that they did not make war with Jehoshaphat. ¹¹Some Philistines brought Jehoshaphat gifts and silver as tribute, and the Arabs brought him flocks: seven thousand seven hundred rams and seven thousand seven hundred goats.

¹²Jehoshaphat became more and more powerful; he built forts and store cities in Judah ¹³and had large supplies in the towns of Judah. He also kept experienced fighting men in Jerusalem. ¹⁴Their enrollment by families was as follows:

From Judah, commanders of units of 1,000:
Adnah the commander, with 300,000 fighting men;
¹⁵next, Jehohanan the commander, with 280,000;
¹⁶next, Amasiah son of Zikri, who volunteered himself for the service of the Lord, with 200,000.

¹⁷From Benjamin:
Eliada, a valiant soldier, with 200,000 men armed with bows and shields;
¹⁸next, Jehozabad, with 180,000 men armed for battle.

¹⁹These were the men who served the king, besides those he stationed in the fortified cities throughout Judah.

Micaiah Prophesies Against Ahab

18 Now Jehoshaphat had great wealth and honor, and he allied himself with Ahab by marriage. ²Some years later he went down to see Ahab in Samaria. Ahab slaughtered many sheep and cattle for him and the people with him and urged him to attack Ramoth Gilead. ³Ahab king of Israel asked Jehoshaphat king of Judah, "Will you go with me against Ramoth Gilead?"

Jehoshaphat replied, "I am as you are, and my people as your people; we will join you in the war." ⁴But Jehoshaphat also said to the king of Israel, "First seek the counsel of the Lord."

⁵So the king of Israel brought together the prophets—four hundred men—and asked them, "Shall we go to war against Ramoth Gilead, or shall I not?"

"Go," they answered, "for God will give it into the king's hand."

⁶But Jehoshaphat asked, "Is there no longer a prophet of the Lord here whom we can inquire of?"

⁷The king of Israel answered Jehoshaphat, "There is still one through whom we can inquire of the Lord, but I hate him because he never prophesies anything good about me, but always bad. He is Micaiah son of Imlah."

"The king should not say such a thing," Jehoshaphat replied.

⁸So the king of Israel called one of his officials and said, "Bring Micaiah son of Imlah at once."

⁹Dressed in their royal robes, the king of Israel and Jehoshaphat king of Judah were sitting on their thrones at the threshing floor by the entrance of the gate of Samaria, with all the prophets prophesying before them. ¹⁰Now Zedekiah son of Kenaanah had made iron horns, and he declared, "This is what the Lord says: 'With these you will gore the Arameans until they are destroyed.'"

¹¹All the other prophets were prophesying

the same thing. "Attack Ramoth Gilead and be victorious," they said, "for the Lord will give it into the king's hand."

¹²The messenger who had gone to summon Micaiah said to him, "Look, the other prophets without exception are predicting success for the king. Let your word agree with theirs, and speak favorably."

¹³But Micaiah said, "As surely as the Lord lives, I can tell him only what my God says."

¹⁴When he arrived, the king asked him, "Micaiah, shall we go to war against Ramoth Gilead, or shall I not?"

"Attack and be victorious," he answered, "for they will be given into your hand."

¹⁵The king said to him, "How many times must I make you swear to tell me nothing but the truth in the name of the Lord?"

¹⁶Then Micaiah answered, "I saw all Israel scattered on the hills like sheep without a shepherd, and the Lord said, 'These people have no master. Let each one go home in peace.' "

¹⁷The king of Israel said to Jehoshaphat, "Didn't I tell you that he never prophesies anything good about me, but only bad?"

¹⁸Micaiah continued, "Therefore hear the word of the Lord: I saw the Lord sitting on his throne with all the host of heaven standing on his right and on his left. ¹⁹And the Lord said, 'Who will entice Ahab king of Israel into attacking Ramoth Gilead and going to his death there?'

"One suggested this, and another that. ²⁰Finally, a spirit came forward, stood before the Lord and said, 'I will entice him.'

" 'By what means?' the Lord asked.

²¹" 'I will go and be a lying spirit in the mouths of all his prophets,' he said.

" 'You will succeed in enticing him,' said the Lord. 'Go and do it.'

²²"So now the Lord has put a lying spirit in the mouths of these prophets of yours. The Lord has decreed disaster for you."

²³Then Zedekiah son of Kenaanah went up and slapped Micaiah in the face. "Which way did the spirit fromᵃ the Lord go when he went from me to speak to you?" he asked.

²⁴Micaiah replied, "You will find out on the day you go to hide in an inner room."

²⁵The king of Israel then ordered, "Take Micaiah and send him back to Amon the ruler of the city and to Joash the king's son,

²⁶and say, 'This is what the king says: Put this fellow in prison and give him nothing but bread and water until I return safely.' "

²⁷Micaiah declared, "If you ever return safely, the Lord has not spoken through me." Then he added, "Mark my words, all you people!"

Ahab Killed at Ramoth Gilead

²⁸So the king of Israel and Jehoshaphat king of Judah went up to Ramoth Gilead. ²⁹The king of Israel said to Jehoshaphat, "I will enter the battle in disguise, but you wear your royal robes." So the king of Israel disguised himself and went into battle.

³⁰Now the king of Aram had ordered his chariot commanders, "Do not fight with anyone, small or great, except the king of Israel." ³¹When the chariot commanders saw Jehoshaphat, they thought, "This is the king of Israel." So they turned to attack him, but Jehoshaphat cried out, and the Lord helped him. God drew them away from him, ³²for when the chariot commanders saw that he was not the king of Israel, they stopped pursuing him.

³³But someone drew his bow at random and hit the king of Israel between the breastplate and the scale armor. The king told the chariot driver, "Wheel around and get me out of the fighting. I've been wounded." ³⁴All day long the battle raged, and the king of Israel propped himself up in his chariot facing the Arameans until evening. Then at sunset he died.

19 When Jehoshaphat king of Judah returned safely to his palace in Jerusalem, ²Jehu the seer, the son of Hanani, went out to meet him and said to the king, "Should you help the wicked and loveᵇ those who hate the Lord? Because of this, the wrath of the Lord is on you. ³There is, however, some good in you, for you have rid the land of the Asherah poles and have set your heart on seeking God."

Jehoshaphat Appoints Judges

⁴Jehoshaphat lived in Jerusalem, and he went out again among the people from Beersheba to the hill country of Ephraim and turned them back to the Lord, the God of their ancestors. ⁵He appointed judges in the land, in each of the fortified cities of Judah.

ᵃ 23 Or *Spirit of*   ᵇ 2 Or *and make alliances with*

⁶He told them, "Consider carefully what you do, because you are not judging for mere mortals but for the Lord, who is with you whenever you give a verdict. ⁷Now let the fear of the Lord be on you. Judge carefully, for with the Lord our God there is no injustice or partiality or bribery."

⁸In Jerusalem also, Jehoshaphat appointed some of the Levites, priests and heads of Israelite families to administer the law of the Lord and to settle disputes. And they lived in Jerusalem. ⁹He gave them these orders: "You must serve faithfully and wholeheartedly in the fear of the Lord. ¹⁰In every case that comes before you from your people who live in the cities—whether bloodshed or other concerns of the law, commands, decrees or regulations—you are to warn them not to sin against the Lord; otherwise his wrath will come on you and your people. Do this, and you will not sin.

¹¹"Amariah the chief priest will be over you in any matter concerning the Lord, and Zebadiah son of Ishmael, the leader of the tribe of Judah, will be over you in any matter concerning the king, and the Levites will serve as officials before you. Act with courage, and may the Lord be with those who do well."

Jehoshaphat Defeats Moab and Ammon

20 After this, the Moabites and Ammonites with some of the Meunites*ᵃ* came to make war on Jehoshaphat. ²Some people came and told Jehoshaphat, "A vast army is coming against you from Edom,*ᵇ* from the other side of the Dead Sea. It is already in Hazezon Tamar" (that is, En Gedi). ³Alarmed, Jehoshaphat resolved to inquire of the Lord, and he proclaimed a fast for all Judah. ⁴The people of Judah came together to seek help from the Lord; indeed, they came from every town in Judah to seek him.

⁵Then Jehoshaphat stood up in the assembly of Judah and Jerusalem at the temple of the Lord in the front of the new courtyard ⁶and said:

"Lord, the God of our ancestors, are you not the God who is in heaven? You rule over all the kingdoms of the nations. Power and might are in your hand, and no one can withstand you.

⁷Our God, did you not drive out the inhabitants of this land before your people Israel and give it forever to the descendants of Abraham your friend? ⁸They have lived in it and have built in it a sanctuary for your Name, saying, ⁹'If calamity comes upon us, whether the sword of judgment, or plague or famine, we will stand in your presence before this temple that bears your Name and will cry out to you in our distress, and you will hear us and save us.'

¹⁰"But now here are men from Ammon, Moab and Mount Seir, whose territory you would not allow Israel to invade when they came from Egypt; so they turned away from them and did not destroy them. ¹¹See how they are repaying us by coming to drive us out of the possession you gave us as an inheritance. ¹²Our God, will you not judge them? For we have no power to face this vast army that is attacking us. We do not know what to do, but our eyes are on you."

¹³All the men of Judah, with their wives and children and little ones, stood there before the Lord.

¹⁴Then the Spirit of the Lord came on Jahaziel son of Zechariah, the son of Benaiah, the son of Jeiel, the son of Mattaniah, a Levite and descendant of Asaph, as he stood in the assembly.

¹⁵He said: "Listen, King Jehoshaphat and all who live in Judah and Jerusalem! This is what the Lord says to you: 'Do not be afraid or discouraged because of this vast army. For the battle is not yours, but God's. ¹⁶Tomorrow march down against them. They will be climbing up by the Pass of Ziz, and you will find them at the end of the gorge in the Desert of Jeruel. ¹⁷You will not have to fight this battle. Take up your positions; stand firm and see the deliverance the Lord will give you, Judah and Jerusalem. Do not be afraid; do not be discouraged. Go out to face them tomorrow, and the Lord will be with you.'"

¹⁸Jehoshaphat bowed down with his face to the ground, and all the people of Judah and Jerusalem fell down in worship before the Lord. ¹⁹Then some Levites from the Ko-

---

a 1 Some Septuagint manuscripts; Hebrew *Ammonites*   *b 2* One Hebrew manuscript; most Hebrew manuscripts, Septuagint and Vulgate *Aram* hathites and Korahites stood up and praised the LORD, the God of Israel, with a very loud voice.

²⁰Early in the morning they left for the Desert of Tekoa. As they set out, Jehoshaphat stood and said, "Listen to me, Judah and people of Jerusalem! Have faith in the LORD your God and you will be upheld; have faith in his prophets and you will be successful." ²¹After consulting the people, Jehoshaphat appointed men to sing to the LORD and to praise him for the splendor of his ͣ holiness as they went out at the head of the army, saying:

"Give thanks to the LORD,
    for his love endures forever."

²²As they began to sing and praise, the LORD set ambushes against the men of Ammon and Moab and Mount Seir who were invading Judah, and they were defeated. ²³The Ammonites and Moabites rose up against the men from Mount Seir to destroy and annihilate them. After they finished slaughtering the men from Seir, they helped to destroy one another.

²⁴When the men of Judah came to the place that overlooks the desert and looked toward the vast army, they saw only dead bodies lying on the ground; no one had escaped. ²⁵So Jehoshaphat and his men went to carry off their plunder, and they found among them a great amount of equipment and clothing ᵇ and also articles of value— more than they could take away. There was so much plunder that it took three days to collect it. ²⁶On the fourth day they assembled in the Valley of Berakah, where they praised the LORD. This is why it is called the Valley of Berakah ᶜ to this day.

²⁷Then, led by Jehoshaphat, all the men of Judah and Jerusalem returned joyfully to Jerusalem, for the LORD had given them cause to rejoice over their enemies. ²⁸They entered Jerusalem and went to the temple of the LORD with harps and lyres and trumpets.

²⁹The fear of God came on all the surrounding kingdoms when they heard how the LORD had fought against the enemies of Israel. ³⁰And the kingdom of Jehoshaphat was at peace, for his God had given them rest on every side.

The End of Jehoshaphat's Reign

³¹So Jehoshaphat reigned over Judah. He was thirty-five years old when he became king of Judah, and he reigned in Jerusalem twenty-five years. His mother's name was Azubah daughter of Shilhi. ³²He followed the ways of his father Asa and did not stray from them; he did what was right in the eyes of the LORD. ³³The high places, however, were not removed, and the people still had not set their hearts on the God of their ancestors.

³⁴The other events of Jehoshaphat's reign, from beginning to end, are written in the annals of Jehu son of Hanani, which are recorded in the book of the kings of Israel.

³⁵Later, Jehoshaphat king of Judah made an alliance with Ahaziah king of Israel, whose ways were wicked. ³⁶He agreed with him to construct a fleet of trading ships. ᵈ After these were built at Ezion Geber, ³⁷Eliezer son of Dodavahu of Mareshah prophesied against Jehoshaphat, saying, "Because you have made an alliance with Ahaziah, the LORD will destroy what you have made." The ships were wrecked and were not able to set sail to trade. ᵉ

21 Then Jehoshaphat rested with his ancestors and was buried with them in the City of David. And Jehoram his son succeeded him as king. ²Jehoram's brothers, the sons of Jehoshaphat, were Azariah, Jehiel, Zechariah, Azariahu, Michael and Shephatiah. All these were sons of Jehoshaphat king of Israel. ᶠ ³Their father had given them many gifts of silver and gold and articles of value, as well as fortified cities in Judah, but he had given the kingdom to Jehoram because he was his firstborn son.

Jehoram King of Judah

⁴When Jehoram established himself firmly over his father's kingdom, he put all his brothers to the sword along with some of the officials of Israel. ⁵Jehoram was thirty-two years old when he became king, and he reigned in Jerusalem eight years. ⁶He followed the ways of the kings of Israel, as the house of Ahab had done, for he married a daughter of Ahab. He did evil in the eyes of the LORD. ⁷Nevertheless, because of the covenant the LORD had made with David, the

---

ᵃ 21 Or him with the splendor of   ᵇ 25 Some Hebrew manuscripts and Vulgate; most Hebrew manuscripts corpses   ᶜ 26 Berakah means praise.   ᵈ 36 Hebrew of ships that could go to Tarshish   ᵉ 37 Hebrew sail for Tarshish   ᶠ 2 That is, Judah, as frequently in 2 Chronicles

LORD was not willing to destroy the house of David. He had promised to maintain a lamp for him and his descendants forever.

⁸In the time of Jehoram, Edom rebelled against Judah and set up its own king. ⁹So Jehoram went there with his officers and all his chariots. The Edomites surrounded him and his chariot commanders, but he rose up and broke through by night. ¹⁰To this day Edom has been in rebellion against Judah.

Libnah revolted at the same time, because Jehoram had forsaken the LORD, the God of his ancestors. ¹¹He had also built high places on the hills of Judah and had caused the people of Jerusalem to prostitute themselves and had led Judah astray.

¹²Jehoram received a letter from Elijah the prophet, which said:

"This is what the LORD, the God of your father David, says: 'You have not followed the ways of your father Jehoshaphat or of Asa king of Judah. ¹³But you have followed the ways of the kings of Israel, and you have led Judah and the people of Jerusalem to prostitute themselves, just as the house of Ahab did. You have also murdered your own brothers, members of your own family, men who were better than you. ¹⁴So now the LORD is about to strike your people, your sons, your wives and everything that is yours, with a heavy blow. ¹⁵You yourself will be very ill with a lingering disease of the bowels, until the disease causes your bowels to come out.' "

¹⁶The LORD aroused against Jehoram the hostility of the Philistines and of the Arabs who lived near the Cushites. ¹⁷They attacked Judah, invaded it and carried off all the goods found in the king's palace, together with his sons and wives. Not a son was left to him except Ahaziah,ᵃ the youngest.

¹⁸After all this, the LORD afflicted Jehoram with an incurable disease of the bowels. ¹⁹In the course of time, at the end of the second year, his bowels came out because of the disease, and he died in great pain. His people made no funeral fire in his honor, as they had for his predecessors.

²⁰Jehoram was thirty-two years old when he became king, and he reigned in Jerusalem eight years. He passed away, to no one's regret, and was buried in the City of David, but not in the tombs of the kings.

Ahaziah King of Judah

22 The people of Jerusalem made Ahaziah, Jehoram's youngest son, king in his place, since the raiders, who came with the Arabs into the camp, had killed all the older sons. So Ahaziah son of Jehoram king of Judah began to reign.

²Ahaziah was twenty-twoᵇ years old when he became king, and he reigned in Jerusalem one year. His mother's name was Athaliah, a granddaughter of Omri.

³He too followed the ways of the house of Ahab, for his mother encouraged him to act wickedly. ⁴He did evil in the eyes of the LORD, as the house of Ahab had done, for after his father's death they became his advisers, to his undoing. ⁵He also followed their counsel when he went with Joramᶜ son of Ahab king of Israel to war against Hazael king of Aram at Ramoth Gilead. The Arameans wounded Joram; ⁶so he returned to Jezreel to recover from the wounds they had inflicted on him at Ramothᵈ in his battle with Hazael king of Aram.

Then Ahaziahᵉ son of Jehoram king of Judah went down to Jezreel to see Joram son of Ahab because he had been wounded.

⁷Through Ahaziah's visit to Joram, God brought about Ahaziah's downfall. When Ahaziah arrived, he went out with Joram to meet Jehu son of Nimshi, whom the LORD had anointed to destroy the house of Ahab. ⁸While Jehu was executing judgment on the house of Ahab, he found the officials of Judah and the sons of Ahaziah's relatives, who had been attending Ahaziah, and he killed them. ⁹He then went in search of Ahaziah, and his men captured him while he was hiding in Samaria. He was brought to Jehu and put to death. They buried him, for they said, "He was a son of Jehoshaphat, who sought the LORD with all his heart." So there was no one in the house of Ahaziah powerful enough to retain the kingdom.

ᵃ 17 Hebrew *Jehoahaz*, a variant of *Ahaziah*   ᵇ 2 Some Septuagint manuscripts and Syriac (see also 2 Kings 8:26); Hebrew *forty-two*   ᶜ 5 Hebrew *Jehoram*, a variant of *Joram*; also in verses 6 and 7   ᵈ 6 Hebrew *Ramah*, a variant of *Ramoth*   ᵉ 6 Some Hebrew manuscripts, Septuagint, Vulgate and Syriac (see also 2 Kings 8:29); most Hebrew manuscripts *Azariah*

Athaliah and Joash

¹⁰When Athaliah the mother of Ahaziah saw that her son was dead, she proceeded to destroy the whole royal family of the house of Judah. ¹¹But Jehosheba,ª the daughter of King Jehoram, took Joash son of Ahaziah and stole him away from among the royal princes who were about to be murdered and put him and his nurse in a bedroom. Because Jehosheba,ª the daughter of King Jehoram and wife of the priest Jehoiada, was Ahaziah's sister, she hid the child from Athaliah so she could not kill him. ¹²He remained hidden with them at the temple of God for six years while Athaliah ruled the land.

23 In the seventh year Jehoiada showed his strength. He made a covenant with the commanders of units of a hundred: Azariah son of Jeroham, Ishmael son of Jehohanan, Azariah son of Obed, Maaseiah son of Adaiah, and Elishaphat son of Zikri. ²They went throughout Judah and gathered the Levites and the heads of Israelite families from all the towns. When they came to Jerusalem, ³the whole assembly made a covenant with the king at the temple of God.

Jehoiada said to them, "The king's son shall reign, as the Lord promised concerning the descendants of David. ⁴Now this is what you are to do: A third of you priests and Levites who are going on duty on the Sabbath are to keep watch at the doors, ⁵a third of you at the royal palace and a third at the Foundation Gate, and all the others are to be in the courtyards of the temple of the Lord. ⁶No one is to enter the temple of the Lord except the priests and Levites on duty; they may enter because they are consecrated, but all the others are to observe the Lord's command not to enter.ᵇ ⁷The Levites are to station themselves around the king, each with weapon in hand. Anyone who enters the temple is to be put to death. Stay close to the king wherever he goes."

⁸The Levites and all the men of Judah did just as Jehoiada the priest ordered. Each one took his men—those who were going on duty on the Sabbath and those who were going off duty—for Jehoiada the priest had not released any of the divisions. ⁹Then he gave the commanders of units of a hundred the

spears and the large and small shields that had belonged to King David and that were in the temple of God. ¹⁰He stationed all the men, each with his weapon in his hand, around the king—near the altar and the temple, from the south side to the north side of the temple.

¹¹Jehoiada and his sons brought out the king's son and put the crown on him; they presented him with a copy of the covenant and proclaimed him king. They anointed him and shouted, "Long live the king!"

¹²When Athaliah heard the noise of the people running and cheering the king, she went to them at the temple of the Lord. ¹³She looked, and there was the king, standing by his pillar at the entrance. The officers and the trumpeters were beside the king, and all the people of the land were rejoicing and blowing trumpets, and musicians with their instruments were leading the praises. Then Athaliah tore her robes and shouted, "Treason! Treason!"

¹⁴Jehoiada the priest sent out the commanders of units of a hundred, who were in charge of the troops, and said to them: "Bring her out between the ranksᶜ and put to the sword anyone who follows her." For the priest had said, "Do not put her to death at the temple of the Lord." ¹⁵So they seized her as she reached the entrance of the Horse Gate on the palace grounds, and there they put her to death.

¹⁶Jehoiada then made a covenant that he, the people and the kingᵈ would be the Lord's people. ¹⁷All the people went to the temple of Baal and tore it down. They smashed the altars and idols and killed Mattan the priest of Baal in front of the altars.

¹⁸Then Jehoiada placed the oversight of the temple of the Lord in the hands of the Levitical priests, to whom David had made assignments in the temple, to present the burnt offerings of the Lord as written in the Law of Moses, with rejoicing and singing, as David had ordered. ¹⁹He also stationed gatekeepers at the gates of the Lord's temple so that no one who was in any way unclean might enter.

²⁰He took with him the commanders of hundreds, the nobles, the rulers of the people and all the people of the land and

---

ª 11 Hebrew *Jehoshabeath*, a variant of *Jehosheba*   ᵇ 6 Or *are to stand guard where the* Lord *has assigned them*   ᶜ 14 Or *out from the precincts*   ᵈ 16 Or *covenant between ₍the* Lord₎ *and the people and the king that they* (see 2 Kings 11:17) brought the king down from the temple of the LORD. They went into the palace through the Upper Gate and seated the king on the royal throne. ²¹All the people of the land rejoiced, and the city was calm, because Athaliah had been slain with the sword.

Joash Repairs the Temple

24 Joash was seven years old when he became king, and he reigned in Jerusalem forty years. His mother's name was Zibiah; she was from Beersheba. ²Joash did what was right in the eyes of the LORD all the years of Jehoiada the priest. ³Jehoiada chose two wives for him, and he had sons and daughters.

⁴Some time later Joash decided to restore the temple of the LORD. ⁵He called together the priests and Levites and said to them, "Go to the towns of Judah and collect the money due annually from all Israel, to repair the temple of your God. Do it now." But the Levites did not act at once.

⁶Therefore the king summoned Jehoiada the chief priest and said to him, "Why haven't you required the Levites to bring in from Judah and Jerusalem the tax imposed by Moses the servant of the LORD and by the assembly of Israel for the tent of the covenant law?"

⁷Now the sons of that wicked woman Athaliah had broken into the temple of God and had used even its sacred objects for the Baals.

⁸At the king's command, a chest was made and placed outside, at the gate of the temple of the LORD. ⁹A proclamation was then issued in Judah and Jerusalem that they should bring to the LORD the tax that Moses the servant of God had required of Israel in the wilderness. ¹⁰All the officials and all the people brought their contributions gladly, dropping them into the chest until it was full. ¹¹Whenever the chest was brought in by the Levites to the king's officials and they saw that there was a large amount of money, the royal secretary and the officer of the chief priest would come and empty the chest and carry it back to its place. They did this regularly and collected a great amount of money. ¹²The king and Jehoiada gave it to those who carried out the work required for the temple of the LORD. They hired masons

and carpenters to restore the LORD's temple, and also workers in iron and bronze to repair the temple.

¹³The men in charge of the work were diligent, and the repairs progressed under them. They rebuilt the temple of God according to its original design and reinforced it. ¹⁴When they had finished, they brought the rest of the money to the king and Jehoiada, and with it were made articles for the LORD's temple: articles for the service and for the burnt offerings, and also dishes and other objects of gold and silver. As long as Jehoiada lived, burnt offerings were presented continually in the temple of the LORD.

¹⁵Now Jehoiada was old and full of years, and he died at the age of a hundred and thirty. ¹⁶He was buried with the kings in the City of David, because of the good he had done in Israel for God and his temple.

The Wickedness of Joash

¹⁷After the death of Jehoiada, the officials of Judah came and paid homage to the king, and he listened to them. ¹⁸They abandoned the temple of the LORD, the God of their ancestors, and worshiped Asherah poles and idols. Because of their guilt, God's anger came on Judah and Jerusalem. ¹⁹Although the LORD sent prophets to the people to bring them back to him, and though they testified against them, they would not listen.

²⁰Then the Spirit of God came on Zechariah son of Jehoiada the priest. He stood before the people and said, "This is what God says: 'Why do you disobey the LORD's commands? You will not prosper. Because you have forsaken the LORD, he has forsaken you.'"

²¹But they plotted against him, and by order of the king they stoned him to death in the courtyard of the LORD's temple. ²²King Joash did not remember the kindness Zechariah's father Jehoiada had shown him but killed his son, who said as he lay dying, "May the LORD see this and call you to account."

²³At the turn of the year,ᵃ the army of Aram marched against Joash; it invaded Judah and Jerusalem and killed all the leaders of the people. They sent all the plunder to their king in Damascus. ²⁴Although the Aramean army had come with only a few men,

ᵃ 23 Probably in the spring

the Lord delivered into their hands a much larger army. Because Judah had forsaken the Lord, the God of their ancestors, judgment was executed on Joash. ²⁵When the Arameans withdrew, they left Joash severely wounded. His officials conspired against him for murdering the son of Jehoiada the priest, and they killed him in his bed. So he died and was buried in the City of David, but not in the tombs of the kings.

²⁶Those who conspired against him were Zabad,ᵃ son of Shimeath an Ammonite woman, and Jehozabad, son of Shimrithᵇ a Moabite woman. ²⁷The account of his sons, the many prophecies about him, and the record of the restoration of the temple of God are written in the annotations on the book of the kings. And Amaziah his son succeeded him as king.

Amaziah King of Judah

25 Amaziah was twenty-five years old when he became king, and he reigned in Jerusalem twenty-nine years. His mother's name was Jehoaddan; she was from Jerusalem. ²He did what was right in the eyes of the Lord, but not wholeheartedly. ³After the kingdom was firmly in his control, he executed the officials who had murdered his father the king. ⁴Yet he did not put their children to death, but acted in accordance with what is written in the Law, in the Book of Moses, where the Lord commanded: "Parents shall not be put to death for their children, nor children be put to death for their parents; each of you will die for your own sin."ᶜ

⁵Amaziah called the people of Judah together and assigned them according to their families to commanders of thousands and commanders of hundreds for all Judah and Benjamin. He then mustered those twenty years old or more and found that there were three hundred thousand men fit for military service, able to handle the spear and shield. ⁶He also hired a hundred thousand fighting men from Israel for a hundred talentsᵈ of silver.

⁷But a man of God came to him and said, "Your Majesty, these troops from Israel must not march with you, for the Lord is not with Israel—not with any of the people of Ephra-

im. ⁸Even if you go and fight courageously in battle, God will overthrow you before the enemy, for God has the power to help or to overthrow."

⁹Amaziah asked the man of God, "But what about the hundred talents I paid for these Israelite troops?"

The man of God replied, "The Lord can give you much more than that."

¹⁰So Amaziah dismissed the troops who had come to him from Ephraim and sent them home. They were furious with Judah and left for home in a great rage.

¹¹Amaziah then marshaled his strength and led his army to the Valley of Salt, where he killed ten thousand men of Seir. ¹²The army of Judah also captured ten thousand men alive, took them to the top of a cliff and threw them down so that all were dashed to pieces.

¹³Meanwhile the troops that Amaziah had sent back and had not allowed to take part in the war raided towns belonging to Judah from Samaria to Beth Horon. They killed three thousand people and carried off great quantities of plunder.

¹⁴When Amaziah returned from slaughtering the Edomites, he brought back the gods of the people of Seir. He set them up as his own gods, bowed down to them and burned sacrifices to them. ¹⁵The anger of the Lord burned against Amaziah, and he sent a prophet to him, who said, "Why do you consult this people's gods, which could not save their own people from your hand?"

¹⁶While he was still speaking, the king said to him, "Have we appointed you an adviser to the king? Stop! Why be struck down?"

So the prophet stopped but said, "I know that God has determined to destroy you, because you have done this and have not listened to my counsel."

¹⁷After Amaziah king of Judah consulted his advisers, he sent this challenge to Jehoashᵉ son of Jehoahaz, the son of Jehu, king of Israel: "Come, meet me face to face."

¹⁸But Jehoash king of Israel replied to Amaziah king of Judah: "A thistle in Lebanon sent a message to a cedar in Lebanon, 'Give your daughter to my son in marriage.' Then a wild beast in Lebanon came along and

---

ᵃ 26 A variant of *Jozabad*   ᵇ 26 A variant of *Shomer*   ᶜ 4 Deut. 24:16   ᵈ 6 That is, about 3 3/4 tons or about 3.4 metric tons; also in verse 9   ᵉ 17 Hebrew *Joash*, a variant of *Jehoash*; also in verses 18, 21, 23 and 25 trampled the thistle underfoot. ¹⁹You say to yourself that you have defeated Edom, and now you are arrogant and proud. But stay at home! Why ask for trouble and cause your own downfall and that of Judah also?"

²⁰Amaziah, however, would not listen, for God so worked that he might deliver them into the hands of Jehoash, because they sought the gods of Edom. ²¹So Jehoash king of Israel attacked. He and Amaziah king of Judah faced each other at Beth Shemesh in Judah. ²²Judah was routed by Israel, and every man fled to his home. ²³Jehoash king of Israel captured Amaziah king of Judah, the son of Joash, the son of Ahaziah,ᵃ at Beth Shemesh. Then Jehoash brought him to Jerusalem and broke down the wall of Jerusalem from the Ephraim Gate to the Corner Gate—a section about four hundred cubitsᵇ long. ²⁴He took all the gold and silver and all the articles found in the temple of God that had been in the care of Obed-Edom, together with the palace treasures and the hostages, and returned to Samaria.

²⁵Amaziah son of Joash king of Judah lived for fifteen years after the death of Jehoash son of Jehoahaz king of Israel. ²⁶As for the other events of Amaziah's reign, from beginning to end, are they not written in the book of the kings of Judah and Israel? ²⁷From the time that Amaziah turned away from following the LORD, they conspired against him in Jerusalem and he fled to Lachish, but they sent men after him to Lachish and killed him there. ²⁸He was brought back by horse and was buried with his ancestors in the City of Judah.ᶜ

Uzziah King of Judah

26 Then all the people of Judah took Uzziah,ᵈ who was sixteen years old, and made him king in place of his father Amaziah. ²He was the one who rebuilt Elath and restored it to Judah after Amaziah rested with his ancestors.

³Uzziah was sixteen years old when he became king, and he reigned in Jerusalem fifty-two years. His mother's name was Jekoliah; she was from Jerusalem. ⁴He did what was right in the eyes of the LORD, just as his father Amaziah had done. ⁵He sought God during the days of Zechariah, who instructed him in the fearᵉ of God. As long as he sought the LORD, God gave him success.

⁶He went to war against the Philistines and broke down the walls of Gath, Jabneh and Ashdod. He then rebuilt towns near Ashdod and elsewhere among the Philistines. ⁷God helped him against the Philistines and against the Arabs who lived in Gur Baal and against the Meunites. ⁸The Ammonites brought tribute to Uzziah, and his fame spread as far as the border of Egypt, because he had become very powerful.

⁹Uzziah built towers in Jerusalem at the Corner Gate, at the Valley Gate and at the angle of the wall, and he fortified them. ¹⁰He also built towers in the wilderness and dug many cisterns, because he had much livestock in the foothills and in the plain. He had people working his fields and vineyards in the hills and in the fertile lands, for he loved the soil.

¹¹Uzziah had a well-trained army, ready to go out by divisions according to their numbers as mustered by Jeiel the secretary and Maaseiah the officer under the direction of Hananiah, one of the royal officials. ¹²The total number of family leaders over the fighting men was 2,600. ¹³Under their command was an army of 307,500 men trained for war, a powerful force to support the king against his enemies. ¹⁴Uzziah provided shields, spears, helmets, coats of armor, bows and slingstones for the entire army. ¹⁵In Jerusalem he made devices designed by skilled workers for use on the towers and on the corner defenses so that soldiers could shoot arrows and hurl large stones from the walls. His fame spread far and wide, for he was greatly helped until he became powerful.

¹⁶But after Uzziah became powerful, his pride led to his downfall. He was unfaithful to the LORD his God, and entered the temple of the LORD to burn incense on the altar of incense. ¹⁷Azariah the priest with eighty other courageous priests of the LORD followed him in. ¹⁸They confronted King Uzziah and said, "It is not right for you, Uzziah, to burn incense to the LORD. That is for the priests, the descendants of Aaron, who have been consecrated to burn incense. Leave the

---

ᵃ 23 Hebrew *Jehoahaz,* a variant of *Ahaziah*   ᵇ 23 That is, about 600 feet or about 180 meters   ᶜ 28 Most Hebrew manuscripts; some Hebrew manuscripts, Septuagint, Vulgate and Syriac (see also 2 Kings 14:20) *David*   ᵈ 1 Also called *Azariah*   ᵉ 5 Many Hebrew manuscripts, Septuagint and Syriac; other Hebrew manuscripts *vision*

WEDNESDAY

ALL MUST ANSWER TO GOD

2 Chronicles 26:1–23 *or* 26:16

Os Guinness

In the Biblical view, each of us is still always responsible for our part. Even in a globalized world we are our neighbor's neighbor. Even in a bureaucracy, we are never helpless pawns but responsible agents who will have to give an account of ourselves to One who is higher than any boss. Even under the tyrant's threat of death, we are moral agents who can choose to disobey as well as obey. As the writer Mary McCarthy used to say, "If somebody points a gun at you and says, 'Kill your friend or I will kill you,' he is tempting you; that is all."

In the Biblical view, there is no ducking the challenge of individual responsibility. As Søren Kierkegaard wrote, the significance of the Christian faith for a society "ought to be to do everything to make every man eternally responsible for every hour he lives, even for the least thing he undertakes." To be sure, we are only responsible for what is ours to give and say and do. No more and no less. Those with more—whether better health, higher intelligence, fatter bank balances, wider social influence, stronger friendships and family ties, or greater energy—are responsible for more. But none of us is without responsibility. To be a human is to be responsible.

MATTHEW HENRY {AD 1662–1714}

We must answer to God, not only for what we do maliciously but also for what we do heedlessly. Therefore, for example, when we have done harm to our neighbor, we should make restitution, though not compelled by law. Let the Scriptures lead our souls to remember: if the grace of God has indeed appeared to us, then it has taught us and enabled us to conduct ourselves by its holy power—to deny "ungodliness and worldly passions, and to live self-controlled, upright and godly lives in this present age" (Titus 2:12).

reflection

1. What do you think it means to be a responsible person? A responsible citizen? A responsible Christian?

2. Though Uzziah started out strong, his past successes did not keep him from being held responsible for his bad choices. Where did he go wrong?

3. Have you ever met anyone who consistently blamed others for their own mistakes or wrongs? In what ways are we all responsible for our actions?

For your next devotional reading, go to page 503.

sanctuary, for you have been unfaithful; and you will not be honored by the Lord God."

¹⁹Uzziah, who had a censer in his hand ready to burn incense, became angry. While he was raging at the priests in their presence before the incense altar in the Lord's temple, leprosy*a* broke out on his forehead. ²⁰When Azariah the chief priest and all the other priests looked at him, they saw that he had leprosy on his forehead, so they hurried him out. Indeed, he himself was eager to leave, because the Lord had afflicted him. ²¹King Uzziah had leprosy until the day he died. He lived in a separate house*b*—leprous, and excluded from the temple of the Lord. Jotham his son had charge of the palace and governed the people of the land.

²²The other events of Uzziah's reign, from beginning to end, are recorded by the prophet Isaiah son of Amoz. ²³Uzziah rested with his ancestors and was buried near them in a cemetery that belonged to the kings, for people said, "He had leprosy." And Jotham his son succeeded him as king.

Jotham King of Judah

27 Jotham was twenty-five years old when he became king, and he reigned in Jerusalem sixteen years. His mother's name was Jerusha daughter of Zadok. ²He did what was right in the eyes of the Lord, just as his father Uzziah had done, but unlike him he did not enter the temple of the Lord. The people, however, continued their corrupt practices. ³Jotham rebuilt the Upper Gate of the temple of the Lord and did extensive work on the wall at the hill of Ophel. ⁴He built towns in the hill country of Judah and forts and towers in the wooded areas.

⁵Jotham made war on the king of the Ammonites and conquered them. That year the Ammonites paid him a hundred talents*c* of silver, ten thousand cors*d* of wheat and ten thousand cors*e* of barley. The Ammonites brought him the same amount also in the second and third years.

⁶Jotham grew powerful because he walked steadfastly before the Lord his God.

⁷The other events in Jotham's reign, including all his wars and the other things he did, are written in the book of the kings of Israel and Judah. ⁸He was twenty-five years old when he became king, and he reigned in Jerusalem sixteen years. ⁹Jotham rested with his ancestors and was buried in the City of David. And Ahaz his son succeeded him as king.

Ahaz King of Judah

28 Ahaz was twenty years old when he became king, and he reigned in Jerusalem sixteen years. Unlike David his father, he did not do what was right in the eyes of the Lord. ²He followed the ways of the kings of Israel and also made idols for worshiping the Baals. ³He burned sacrifices in the Valley of Ben Hinnom and sacrificed his children in the fire, engaging in the detestable practices of the nations the Lord had driven out before the Israelites. ⁴He offered sacrifices and burned incense at the high places, on the hilltops and under every spreading tree.

⁵Therefore the Lord his God delivered him into the hands of the king of Aram. The Arameans defeated him and took many of his people as prisoners and brought them to Damascus.

He was also given into the hands of the king of Israel, who inflicted heavy casualties on him. ⁶In one day Pekah son of Remaliah killed a hundred and twenty thousand soldiers in Judah—because Judah had forsaken the Lord, the God of their ancestors. ⁷Zikri, an Ephraimite warrior, killed Maaseiah the king's son, Azrikam the officer in charge of the palace, and Elkanah, second to the king. ⁸The men of Israel took captive from their fellow Israelites in Judah two hundred thousand wives, sons and daughters. They also took a great deal of plunder, which they carried back to Samaria.

⁹But a prophet of the Lord named Oded was there, and he went out to meet the army when it returned to Samaria. He said to them, "Because the Lord, the God of your ancestors, was angry with Judah, he gave them into your hand. But you have slaughtered them in a rage that reaches to heaven. ¹⁰And now you intend to make the men and women of Judah and Jerusalem your slaves.

---

a 19 The Hebrew for *leprosy* was used for various diseases affecting the skin; also in verses 20, 21 and 23.
b 21 Or *in a house where he was relieved of responsibilities*   *c 5* That is, about 3 3/4 tons or about 3.4 metric tons   *d 5* That is, probably about 1,800 tons or about 1,600 metric tons   *e 5* That is, probably about 1,500 tons or about 1,350 metric tons

But aren't you also guilty of sins against the LORD your God? ¹¹Now listen to me! Send back your fellow Israelites you have taken as prisoners, for the LORD's fierce anger rests on you."

¹²Then some of the leaders in Ephraim—Azariah son of Jehohanan, Berekiah son of Meshillemoth, Jehizkiah son of Shallum, and Amasa son of Hadlai—confronted those who were arriving from the war. ¹³"You must not bring those prisoners here," they said, "or we will be guilty before the LORD. Do you intend to add to our sin and guilt? For our guilt is already great, and his fierce anger rests on Israel."

¹⁴So the soldiers gave up the prisoners and plunder in the presence of the officials and all the assembly. ¹⁵The men designated by name took the prisoners, and from the plunder they clothed all who were naked. They provided them with clothes and sandals, food and drink, and healing balm. All those who were weak they put on donkeys. So they took them back to their fellow Israelites at Jericho, the City of Palms, and returned to Samaria.

¹⁶At that time King Ahaz sent to the kings*a* of Assyria for help. ¹⁷The Edomites had again come and attacked Judah and carried away prisoners, ¹⁸while the Philistines had raided towns in the foothills and in the Negev of Judah. They captured and occupied Beth Shemesh, Aijalon and Gederoth, as well as Soko, Timnah and Gimzo, with their surrounding villages. ¹⁹The LORD had humbled Judah because of Ahaz king of Israel,*b* for he had promoted wickedness in Judah and had been most unfaithful to the LORD. ²⁰Tiglath-Pileser*c* king of Assyria came to him, but he gave him trouble instead of help. ²¹Ahaz took some of the things from the temple of the LORD and from the royal palace and from the officials and presented them to the king of Assyria, but that did not help him.

²²In his time of trouble King Ahaz became even more unfaithful to the LORD. ²³He offered sacrifices to the gods of Damascus, who had defeated him; for he thought, "Since the gods of the kings of Aram have helped them, I will sacrifice to them so they will help me." But they were his downfall and the downfall of all Israel.

²⁴Ahaz gathered together the furnishings from the temple of God and cut them in pieces. He shut the doors of the LORD's temple and set up altars at every street corner in Jerusalem. ²⁵In every town in Judah he built high places to burn sacrifices to other gods and aroused the anger of the LORD, the God of his ancestors.

²⁶The other events of his reign and all his ways, from beginning to end, are written in the book of the kings of Judah and Israel. ²⁷Ahaz rested with his ancestors and was buried in the city of Jerusalem, but he was not placed in the tombs of the kings of Israel. And Hezekiah his son succeeded him as king.

Hezekiah Purifies the Temple

29 Hezekiah was twenty-five years old when he became king, and he reigned in Jerusalem twenty-nine years. His mother's name was Abijah daughter of Zechariah. ²He did what was right in the eyes of the LORD, just as his father David had done.

³In the first month of the first year of his reign, he opened the doors of the temple of the LORD and repaired them. ⁴He brought in the priests and the Levites, assembled them in the square on the east side ⁵and said: "Listen to me, Levites! Consecrate yourselves now and consecrate the temple of the LORD, the God of your ancestors. Remove all defilement from the sanctuary. ⁶Our ancestors were unfaithful; they did evil in the eyes of the LORD our God and forsook him. They turned their faces away from the LORD's dwelling place and turned their backs on him. ⁷They also shut the doors of the portico and put out the lamps. They did not burn incense or present any burnt offerings at the sanctuary to the God of Israel. ⁸Therefore, the anger of the LORD has fallen on Judah and Jerusalem; he has made them an object of dread and horror and scorn, as you can see with your own eyes. ⁹This is why our ancestors have fallen by the sword and why our sons and daughters and our wives are in captivity. ¹⁰Now I intend to make a covenant with the LORD, the God of Israel, so that his fierce anger will turn away from us. ¹¹My sons, do not be negligent now, for the LORD has chosen you to stand before him and

serve him, to minister before him and to burn incense."

¹²Then these Levites set to work:

from the Kohathites,

Mahath son of Amasai and Joel son of Azariah;

from the Merarites,

Kish son of Abdi and Azariah son of Jehallelel;

from the Gershonites,

Joah son of Zimmah and Eden son of Joah;

¹³from the descendants of Elizaphan,

Shimri and Jeiel;

from the descendants of Asaph,

Zechariah and Mattaniah;

¹⁴from the descendants of Heman,

Jehiel and Shimei;

from the descendants of Jeduthun,

Shemaiah and Uzziel.

¹⁵When they had assembled their fellow Levites and consecrated themselves, they went in to purify the temple of the LORD, as the king had ordered, following the word of the LORD. ¹⁶The priests went into the sanctuary of the LORD to purify it. They brought out to the courtyard of the LORD's temple everything unclean that they found in the temple of the LORD. The Levites took it and carried it out to the Kidron Valley. ¹⁷They began the consecration on the first day of the first month, and by the eighth day of the month they reached the portico of the LORD. For eight more days they consecrated the temple of the LORD itself, finishing on the sixteenth day of the first month.

¹⁸Then they went in to King Hezekiah and reported: "We have purified the entire temple of the LORD, the altar of burnt offering with all its utensils, and the table for setting out the consecrated bread, with all its articles. ¹⁹We have prepared and consecrated all the articles that King Ahaz removed in his unfaithfulness while he was king. They are now in front of the LORD's altar."

²⁰Early the next morning King Hezekiah gathered the city officials together and went up to the temple of the LORD. ²¹They brought seven bulls, seven rams, seven male lambs and seven male goats as a sin offering^a for the kingdom, for the sanctuary and for Judah. The king commanded the priests, the descendants of Aaron, to offer these on the

altar of the LORD. ²²So they slaughtered the bulls, and the priests took the blood and splashed it against the altar; next they slaughtered the rams and splashed their blood against the altar; then they slaughtered the lambs and splashed their blood against the altar. ²³The goats for the sin offering were brought before the king and the assembly, and they laid their hands on them. ²⁴The priests then slaughtered the goats and presented their blood on the altar for a sin offering to atone for all Israel, because the king had ordered the burnt offering and the sin offering for all Israel.

²⁵He stationed the Levites in the temple of the LORD with cymbals, harps and lyres in the way prescribed by David and Gad the king's seer and Nathan the prophet; this was commanded by the LORD through his prophets. ²⁶So the Levites stood ready with David's instruments, and the priests with their trumpets.

²⁷Hezekiah gave the order to sacrifice the burnt offering on the altar. As the offering began, singing to the LORD began also, accompanied by trumpets and the instruments of David king of Israel. ²⁸The whole assembly bowed in worship, while the musicians played and the trumpets sounded. All this continued until the sacrifice of the burnt offering was completed.

²⁹When the offerings were finished, the king and everyone present with him knelt down and worshiped. ³⁰King Hezekiah and his officials ordered the Levites to praise the LORD with the words of David and of Asaph the seer. So they sang praises with gladness and bowed down and worshiped.

³¹Then Hezekiah said, "You have now dedicated yourselves to the LORD. Come and bring sacrifices and thank offerings to the temple of the LORD." So the assembly brought sacrifices and thank offerings, and all whose hearts were willing brought burnt offerings.

³²The number of burnt offerings the assembly brought was seventy bulls, a hundred rams and two hundred male lambs— all of them for burnt offerings to the LORD. ³³The animals consecrated as sacrifices amounted to six hundred bulls and three thousand sheep and goats. ³⁴The priests, however, were too few to skin all the burnt offerings; so their relatives the Levites

---

a 21 Or *purification offering*; also in verses 23 and 24

helped them until the task was finished and until other priests had been consecrated, for the Levites had been more conscientious in consecrating themselves than the priests had been. ³⁵There were burnt offerings in abundance, together with the fat of the fellowship offerings and the drink offerings that accompanied the burnt offerings.

So the service of the temple of the LORD was reestablished. ³⁶Hezekiah and all the people rejoiced at what God had brought about for his people, because it was done so quickly.

Hezekiah Celebrates the Passover

30 Hezekiah sent word to all Israel and Judah and also wrote letters to Ephraim and Manasseh, inviting them to come to the temple of the LORD in Jerusalem and celebrate the Passover to the LORD, the God of Israel. ²The king and his officials and the whole assembly in Jerusalem decided to celebrate the Passover in the second month. ³They had not been able to celebrate it at the regular time because not enough priests had consecrated themselves and the people had not assembled in Jerusalem. ⁴The plan seemed right both to the king and to the whole assembly. ⁵They decided to send a proclamation throughout Israel, from Beersheba to Dan, calling the people to come to Jerusalem and celebrate the Passover to the LORD, the God of Israel. It had not been celebrated in large numbers according to what was written.

⁶At the king's command, couriers went throughout Israel and Judah with letters from the king and from his officials, which read:

"People of Israel, return to the LORD, the God of Abraham, Isaac and Israel, that he may return to you who are left, who have escaped from the hand of the kings of Assyria. ⁷Do not be like your parents and your fellow Israelites, who were unfaithful to the LORD, the God of their ancestors, so that he made them an object of horror, as you see. ⁸Do not be stiff-necked, as your parents were; submit to the LORD. Come to his sanctuary, which he has consecrated forever. Serve the LORD your God, so that his fierce anger will turn away from you. ⁹If you return to the LORD, then your fellow Israelites and your children will be shown compassion by their captors and will return to this land, for the LORD your God is gracious and compassionate. He will not turn his face from you if you return to him."

¹⁰The couriers went from town to town in Ephraim and Manasseh, as far as Zebulun, but people scorned and ridiculed them. ¹¹Nevertheless, some from Asher, Manasseh and Zebulun humbled themselves and went to Jerusalem. ¹²Also in Judah the hand of God was on the people to give them unity of mind to carry out what the king and his officials had ordered, following the word of the LORD.

¹³A very large crowd of people assembled in Jerusalem to celebrate the Festival of Unleavened Bread in the second month. ¹⁴They removed the altars in Jerusalem and cleared away the incense altars and threw them into the Kidron Valley.

¹⁵They slaughtered the Passover lamb on the fourteenth day of the second month. The priests and the Levites were ashamed and consecrated themselves and brought burnt offerings to the temple of the LORD. ¹⁶Then they took up their regular positions as prescribed in the Law of Moses the man of God. The priests splashed against the altar the blood handed to them by the Levites. ¹⁷Since many in the crowd had not consecrated themselves, the Levites had to kill the Passover lambs for all those who were not ceremonially clean and could not consecrate ⌊their lambs⌋ to the LORD. ¹⁸Although most of the many people who came from Ephraim, Manasseh, Issachar and Zebulun had not purified themselves, yet they ate the Passover, contrary to what was written. But Hezekiah prayed for them, saying, "May the LORD, who is good, pardon everyone ¹⁹who sets their heart on seeking God—the LORD, the God of their ancestors—even if they are not clean according to the rules of the sanctuary." ²⁰And the LORD heard Hezekiah and healed the people.

²¹The Israelites who were present in Jerusalem celebrated the Festival of Unleavened Bread for seven days with great rejoicing, while the Levites and priests praised the LORD every day with resounding instruments dedicated to the LORD.ᵃ

²²Hezekiah spoke encouragingly to all the

ᵃ 21 Or *priests sang to the* LORD *every day, accompanied by the* LORD's *instruments of praise*

THURSDAY

REJOICING RESULTS IN JOY

2 Chronicles 30:1–27 *or* 30:23–27

Joni Eareckson Tada

Stop and muse for a moment on the joy of the Lord. Consider His gift of Spirit-inspired fruit of joy. His oft-repeated command was, "Rejoice!" Fullness of joy is to be found in Him. Finally, for the joy that was set before Him, Jesus endured His cross. In other words, if you're looking for joy, it can only be found in one place or, that is, one Person.

Now place yourself back in time. The sun is warm on your shoulders, and through the golden glow of history in the making, watch this Lord of Joy. He laughs as He holds a neighbor's newborn baby. He smiles while bouncing a 3-year-old on His knee. He tousles the hair of a rowdy little boy. Picture His joy to watch a puppy at play, to hear a funny story, to taste a hot and savory stew. Feel His joy when the disciples listened and obeyed. Think of the joy that seized Him at the sight of a glorious sunset . . . and the joy to know that He created it. And finally, Jesus' joy at seeing His Father's dream fulfilled.

When you meditate on God's smile, His joy will be yours.

It is not possible to always be happy. It is possible to always have the joy of the Lord. Some have described it as a calm centeredness that tickles at the edges. It's a solid assurance that laughs if given the chance. It is unwavering confidence that can't help but look on the bright side. My friend Tim Hansel once said that joy is peace dancing.

Think of all the things that make up the joy of the Lord, and your smile can't help but last.

SAINT AUGUSTINE {AD 354–430}

The Lord says to his disciples in John 15, "I have told you this so that my joy may be in you and that your joy may be complete." And what else is Christ's joy in us except that he is pleased to rejoice over us? And what is this joy of ours which he says is to be made full but our having fellowship with him? On this account he said to the blessed Peter, "Unless I wash you, you have no part with me" (John 13:8). His joy, therefore, in us is the grace he has bestowed upon us—and that is also our joy.

reflection

1. What makes you happy? What brings you joy?
2. What do you think the difference is between happiness and joy?
3. Why do you think God wants you to be joyful?

For your next devotional reading, go to page 507.

Levites, who showed good understanding of the service of the Lord. For the seven days they ate their assigned portion and offered fellowship offerings and praised[a] the Lord, the God of their ancestors.

²³The whole assembly then agreed to celebrate the festival seven more days; so for another seven days they celebrated joyfully. ²⁴Hezekiah king of Judah provided a thousand bulls and seven thousand sheep and goats for the assembly, and the officials provided them with a thousand bulls and ten thousand sheep and goats. A great number of priests consecrated themselves. ²⁵The entire assembly of Judah rejoiced, along with the priests and Levites and all who had assembled from Israel, including the foreigners who had come from Israel and also those who resided in Judah. ²⁶There was great joy in Jerusalem, for since the days of Solomon son of David king of Israel there had been nothing like this in Jerusalem. ²⁷The priests and the Levites stood to bless the people, and God heard them, for their prayer reached heaven, his holy dwelling place.

31 When all this had ended, the Israelites who were there went out to the towns of Judah, smashed the sacred stones and cut down the Asherah poles. They destroyed the high places and the altars throughout Judah and Benjamin and in Ephraim and Manasseh. After they had destroyed all of them, the Israelites returned to their own towns and to their own property.

Contributions for Worship

²Hezekiah assigned the priests and Levites to divisions—each of them according to their duties as priests or Levites—to offer burnt offerings and fellowship offerings, to minister, to give thanks and to sing praises at the gates of the Lord's dwelling. ³The king contributed from his own possessions for the morning and evening burnt offerings and for the burnt offerings on the Sabbaths, at the New Moons and at the appointed festivals as written in the Law of the Lord. ⁴He ordered the people living in Jerusalem to give the portion due the priests and Levites so they could devote themselves to the Law of the Lord. ⁵As soon as the order went out, the Israelites generously gave the firstfruits of their grain, new wine, oil and honey and

all that the fields produced. They brought a great amount, a tithe of everything. ⁶The people of Israel and Judah who lived in the towns of Judah also brought a tithe of their herds and flocks and a tithe of the holy things dedicated to the Lord their God, and they piled them in heaps. ⁷They began doing this in the third month and finished in the seventh month. ⁸When Hezekiah and his officials came and saw the heaps, they praised the Lord and blessed his people Israel.

⁹Hezekiah asked the priests and Levites about the heaps; ¹⁰and Azariah the chief priest, from the family of Zadok, answered, "Since the people began to bring their contributions to the temple of the Lord, we have had enough to eat and plenty to spare, because the Lord has blessed his people, and this great amount is left over."

¹¹Hezekiah gave orders to prepare storerooms in the temple of the Lord, and this was done. ¹²Then they faithfully brought in the contributions, tithes and dedicated gifts. Konaniah, a Levite, was the overseer in charge of these things, and his brother Shimei was next in rank. ¹³Jehiel, Azaziah, Nahath, Asahel, Jerimoth, Jozabad, Eliel, Ismakiah, Mahath and Benaiah were assistants of Konaniah and Shimei his brother. All these served by appointment of King Hezekiah and Azariah the official in charge of the temple of God.

¹⁴Kore son of Imnah the Levite, keeper of the East Gate, was in charge of the freewill offerings given to God, distributing the contributions made to the Lord and also the consecrated gifts. ¹⁵Eden, Miniamin, Jeshua, Shemaiah, Amariah and Shekaniah assisted him faithfully in the towns of the priests, distributing to their fellow priests according to their divisions, old and young alike.

¹⁶In addition, they distributed to the males three years old or more whose names were in the genealogical records—all who would enter the temple of the Lord to perform the daily duties of their various tasks, according to their responsibilities and their divisions. ¹⁷And they distributed to the priests enrolled by their families in the genealogical records and likewise to the Levites twenty years old or more, according to their responsibilities and their divisions. ¹⁸They included all the little ones, the wives,

and the sons and daughters of the whole community listed in these genealogical records. For they were faithful in consecrating themselves.

¹⁹As for the priests, the descendants of Aaron, who lived on the farm lands around their towns or in any other towns, men were designated by name to distribute portions to every male among them and to all who were recorded in the genealogies of the Levites.

²⁰This is what Hezekiah did throughout Judah, doing what was good and right and faithful before the LORD his God. ²¹In everything that he undertook in the service of God's temple and in obedience to the law and the commands, he sought his God and worked wholeheartedly. And so he prospered.

Sennacherib Threatens Jerusalem

32 After all that Hezekiah had so faithfully done, Sennacherib king of Assyria came and invaded Judah. He laid siege to the fortified cities, thinking to conquer them for himself. ²When Hezekiah saw that Sennacherib had come and that he intended to make war on Jerusalem, ³he consulted with his officials and military staff about blocking off the water from the springs outside the city, and they helped him. ⁴A large force assembled and blocked all the springs and the stream that flowed through the land. "Why should the kings ᵃ of Assyria come and find plenty of water?" they said. ⁵Then he worked hard repairing all the broken sections of the wall and building towers on it. He built another wall outside that one and reinforced the terraces ᵇ of the City of David. He also made large numbers of weapons and shields.

⁶He appointed military officers over the people and assembled them before him in the square at the city gate and encouraged them with these words: ⁷"Be strong and courageous. Do not be afraid or discouraged because of the king of Assyria and the vast army with him, for there is a greater power with us than with him. ⁸With him is only the arm of flesh, but with us is the LORD our God to help us and to fight our battles." And the people gained confidence from what Hezekiah the king of Judah said.

⁹Later, when Sennacherib king of Assyria and all his forces were laying siege to La-

chish, he sent his officers to Jerusalem with this message for Hezekiah king of Judah and for all the people of Judah who were there:

¹⁰"This is what Sennacherib king of Assyria says: On what are you basing your confidence, that you remain in Jerusalem under siege? ¹¹When Hezekiah says, 'The LORD our God will save us from the hand of the king of Assyria,' he is misleading you, to let you die of hunger and thirst. ¹²Did not Hezekiah himself remove this god's high places and altars, saying to Judah and Jerusalem, 'You must worship before one altar and burn sacrifices on it'?

¹³"Do you not know what I and my predecessors have done to all the peoples of the other lands? Were the gods of those nations ever able to deliver their land from my hand? ¹⁴Who of all the gods of these nations that my predecessors destroyed has been able to save his people from me? How then can your god deliver you from my hand? ¹⁵Now do not let Hezekiah deceive you and mislead you like this. Do not believe him, for no god of any nation or kingdom has been able to deliver his people from my hand or the hand of my predecessors. How much less will your god deliver you from my hand!"

¹⁶Sennacherib's officers spoke further against the LORD God and against his servant Hezekiah. ¹⁷The king also wrote letters ridiculing the LORD, the God of Israel, and saying this against him: "Just as the gods of the peoples of the other lands did not rescue their people from my hand, so the god of Hezekiah will not rescue his people from my hand." ¹⁸Then they called out in Hebrew to the people of Jerusalem who were on the wall, to terrify them and make them afraid in order to capture the city. ¹⁹They spoke about the God of Jerusalem as they did about the gods of the other peoples of the world—the work of human hands.

²⁰King Hezekiah and the prophet Isaiah son of Amoz cried out in prayer to heaven about this. ²¹And the LORD sent an angel, who annihilated all the fighting men and the commanders and officers in the camp of the

---

ᵃ 4 Hebrew; Septuagint and Syriac *king*   ᵇ 5 Or *the Millo*

Assyrian king. So he withdrew to his own land in disgrace. And when he went into the temple of his god, some of his sons cut him down with the sword.

²²So the Lord saved Hezekiah and the people of Jerusalem from the hand of Sennacherib king of Assyria and from the hand of all others. He took care of them*a* on every side. ²³Many brought offerings to Jerusalem for the Lord and valuable gifts for Hezekiah king of Judah. From then on he was highly regarded by all the nations.

Hezekiah's Pride, Success and Death

²⁴In those days Hezekiah became ill and was at the point of death. He prayed to the Lord, who answered him and gave him a miraculous sign. ²⁵But Hezekiah's heart was proud and he did not respond to the kindness shown him; therefore the Lord's wrath was on him and on Judah and Jerusalem. ²⁶Then Hezekiah repented of the pride of his heart, as did the people of Jerusalem; therefore the Lord's wrath did not come on them during the days of Hezekiah.

²⁷Hezekiah had very great wealth and honor, and he made treasuries for his silver and gold and for his precious stones, spices, shields and all kinds of valuables. ²⁸He also made buildings to store the harvest of grain, new wine and olive oil; and he made stalls for various kinds of cattle, and pens for the flocks. ²⁹He built villages and acquired great numbers of flocks and herds, for God had given him very great riches.

³⁰It was Hezekiah who blocked the upper outlet of the Gihon spring and channeled the water down to the west side of the City of David. He succeeded in everything he undertook. ³¹But when envoys were sent by the rulers of Babylon to ask him about the miraculous sign that had occurred in the land, God left him to test him and to know everything that was in his heart.

³²The other events of Hezekiah's reign and his acts of devotion are written in the vision of the prophet Isaiah son of Amoz in the book of the kings of Judah and Israel. ³³Hezekiah rested with his ancestors and was buried on the hill where the tombs of David's descendants are. All Judah and the people of Jerusalem honored him when he died. And Manasseh his son succeeded him as king.

Manasseh King of Judah

33 Manasseh was twelve years old when he became king, and he reigned in Jerusalem fifty-five years. ²He did evil in the eyes of the Lord, following the detestable practices of the nations the Lord had driven out before the Israelites. ³He rebuilt the high places his father Hezekiah had demolished; he also erected altars to the Baals and made Asherah poles. He bowed down to all the starry hosts and worshiped them. ⁴He built altars in the temple of the Lord, of which the Lord had said, "My Name will remain in Jerusalem forever." ⁵In both courts of the temple of the Lord, he built altars to all the starry hosts. ⁶He sacrificed his children in the fire in the Valley of Ben Hinnom, practiced divination and witchcraft, sought omens, and consulted mediums and spiritists. He did much evil in the eyes of the Lord, arousing his anger.

⁷He took the image he had made and put it in God's temple, of which God had said to David and to his son Solomon, "In this temple and in Jerusalem, which I have chosen out of all the tribes of Israel, I will put my Name forever. ⁸I will not again make the feet of the Israelites leave the land I assigned to your ancestors, if only they will be careful to do everything I commanded them concerning all the laws, decrees and regulations given through Moses." ⁹But Manasseh led Judah and the people of Jerusalem astray, so that they did more evil than the nations the Lord had destroyed before the Israelites.

¹⁰The Lord spoke to Manasseh and his people, but they paid no attention. ¹¹So the Lord brought against them the army commanders of the king of Assyria, who took Manasseh prisoner, put a hook in his nose, bound him with bronze shackles and took him to Babylon. ¹²In his distress he sought the favor of the Lord his God and humbled himself greatly before the God of his ancestors. ¹³And when he prayed to him, the Lord was moved by his entreaty and listened to his plea; so he brought him back to Jerusalem and to his kingdom. Then Manasseh knew that the Lord is God.

¹⁴Afterward he rebuilt the outer wall of the City of David, west of the Gihon spring in the valley, as far as the entrance of the

---

a 22 Hebrew; Septuagint and Vulgate *He gave them rest*

FRIDAY

STEPPING OUT IN FAITH
2 Chronicles 33:1–25 *or* 33:10–17

HANNAH WHITALL SMITH {ca. AD 1832–1911}

A man was obliged to descend into a deep well by sliding down a fixed rope which was supposed to be of ample length. But to his dismay he came to the end of it before his feet had touched the bottom. He had not the strength to climb up again, and to let go and drop seemed to him but to be dashed to pieces in the depths below. He held on until his strength was utterly exhausted, and then dropped, as he thought, to his death. He fell—just three inches—and found himself safe on the rock bottom.

Are you afraid to take this step? Does it seem too sudden, too much like a leap in the dark? Do you not know that the step of faith always "falls on the seeming void, but finds the rock beneath"? If ever you are to enter this glorious land, flowing with milk and honey, you must sooner or later step into the brimming waters, for there is no other path; and to do it now may save you months and even years of disappointment and grief. Hear the word of the Lord: "Have I not commanded you? Be strong and courageous. Do not be afraid; do not be discouraged, for the LORD your God will be with you wherever you go" (Joshua 1:9).

Chip Ingram

The truth underlying our relationship with Christ is this: The power of sin has been broken. You don't have to sin. You don't have to be addicted to alcohol. You don't have to be addicted to pleasing people. That power has been broken. Not only the power of sin, but the power and penalty of death. You don't have to be afraid . . . Sin is a defeated foe in your life. Your fear of the future and death is defeated in your life, and Satan is defeated. *The only power it now has is the power you give it.* Read that sentence again, slowly. That means that the only power Satan, sin, and death have over you comes from what you give them . . .

As you can see, until you come to grasp the objective truth about what Christ has accomplished for you there's no hope for change! Genuine life-change always begins with truth.

reflection

1. How do you know when God is directing you to make a change in your life?
2. Has he been urging you to step in a new direction lately?
3. How can you find strength and courage from God to make that change and take that step?

For your next devotional reading, go to page 511.

Fish Gate and encircling the hill of Ophel; he also made it much higher. He stationed military commanders in all the fortified cities in Judah.

¹⁵He got rid of the foreign gods and removed the image from the temple of the LORD, as well as all the altars he had built on the temple hill and in Jerusalem; and he threw them out of the city. ¹⁶Then he restored the altar of the LORD and sacrificed fellowship offerings and thank offerings on it, and told Judah to serve the LORD, the God of Israel. ¹⁷The people, however, continued to sacrifice at the high places, but only to the LORD their God.

¹⁸The other events of Manasseh's reign, including his prayer to his God and the words the seers spoke to him in the name of the LORD, the God of Israel, are written in the annals of the kings of Israel.[a] ¹⁹His prayer and how God was moved by his entreaty, as well as all his sins and unfaithfulness, and the sites where he built high places and set up Asherah poles and idols before he humbled himself—all these are written in the records of the seers.[b] ²⁰Manasseh rested with his ancestors and was buried in his palace. And Amon his son succeeded him as king.

Amon King of Judah

²¹Amon was twenty-two years old when he became king, and he reigned in Jerusalem two years. ²²He did evil in the eyes of the LORD, as his father Manasseh had done. Amon worshiped and offered sacrifices to all the idols Manasseh had made. ²³But unlike his father Manasseh, he did not humble himself before the LORD; Amon increased his guilt.

²⁴Amon's officials conspired against him and assassinated him in his palace. ²⁵Then the people of the land killed all who had plotted against King Amon, and they made Josiah his son king in his place.

Josiah's Reforms

34 Josiah was eight years old when he became king, and he reigned in Jerusalem thirty-one years. ²He did what was right in the eyes of the LORD and followed the ways of his father David, not turning aside to the right or to the left.

³In the eighth year of his reign, while he was still young, he began to seek the God of his father David. In his twelfth year he began to purge Judah and Jerusalem of high places, Asherah poles and idols. ⁴Under his direction the altars of the Baals were torn down; he cut to pieces the incense altars that were above them, and smashed the Asherah poles and the idols. These he broke to pieces and scattered over the graves of those who had sacrificed to them. ⁵He burned the bones of the priests on their altars, and so he purged Judah and Jerusalem. ⁶In the towns of Manasseh, Ephraim and Simeon, as far as Naphtali, and in the ruins around them, ⁷he tore down the altars and the Asherah poles and crushed the idols to powder and cut to pieces all the incense altars throughout Israel. Then he went back to Jerusalem.

⁸In the eighteenth year of Josiah's reign, to purify the land and the temple, he sent Shaphan son of Azaliah and Maaseiah the ruler of the city, with Joah son of Joahaz, the recorder, to repair the temple of the LORD his God.

⁹They went to Hilkiah the high priest and gave him the money that had been brought into the temple of God, which the Levites who were the gatekeepers had collected from the people of Manasseh, Ephraim and the entire remnant of Israel and from all the people of Judah and Benjamin and the inhabitants of Jerusalem. ¹⁰Then they entrusted it to the men appointed to supervise the work on the LORD's temple. These men paid the workers who repaired and restored the temple. ¹¹They also gave money to the carpenters and builders to purchase dressed stone, and timber for joists and beams for the buildings that the kings of Judah had allowed to fall into ruin.

¹²The workers did their work faithfully. Over them to direct them were Jahath and Obadiah, Levites descended from Merari, and Zechariah and Meshullam, descended from Kohath. The Levites—all who were skilled in playing musical instruments— ¹³had charge of the laborers and supervised all the workers from job to job. Some of the Levites were secretaries, scribes and gatekeepers.

The Book of the Law Found

¹⁴While they were bringing out the money

a 18 That is, Judah, as frequently in 2 Chronicles Hebrew manuscripts *of Hozai*   b 19 One Hebrew manuscript and Septuagint; most that had been taken into the temple of the LORD, Hilkiah the priest found the Book of the Law of the LORD that had been given through Moses. ¹⁵Hilkiah said to Shaphan the secretary, "I have found the Book of the Law in the temple of the LORD." He gave it to Shaphan.

¹⁶Then Shaphan took the book to the king and reported to him: "Your officials are doing everything that has been committed to them. ¹⁷They have paid out the money that was in the temple of the LORD and have entrusted it to the supervisors and workers." ¹⁸Then Shaphan the secretary informed the king, "Hilkiah the priest has given me a book." And Shaphan read from it in the presence of the king.

¹⁹When the king heard the words of the Law, he tore his robes. ²⁰He gave these orders to Hilkiah, Ahikam son of Shaphan, Abdon son of Micah,ᵃ Shaphan the secretary and Asaiah the king's attendant: ²¹"Go and inquire of the LORD for me and for the remnant in Israel and Judah about what is written in this book that has been found. Great is the LORD's anger that is poured out on us because those who have gone before us have not kept the word of the LORD; they have not acted in accordance with all that is written in this book."

²²Hilkiah and those the king had sent with himᵇ went to speak to the prophet Huldah, who was the wife of Shallum son of Tokhath,ᶜ the son of Hasrah,ᵈ keeper of the wardrobe. She lived in Jerusalem, in the New Quarter.

²³She said to them, "This is what the LORD, the God of Israel, says: Tell the man who sent you to me, ²⁴'This is what the LORD says: I am going to bring disaster on this place and its people—all the curses written in the book that has been read in the presence of the king of Judah. ²⁵Because they have forsaken me and burned incense to other gods and aroused my anger by all that their hands have made,ᵉ my anger will be poured out on this place and will not be quenched.' ²⁶Tell the king of Judah, who sent you to inquire of the LORD, 'This is what the LORD, the God of Israel, says concerning the words you heard: ²⁷Because your heart was responsive and you humbled yourself before God when you heard what he spoke against this place and its people, and because you

humbled yourself before me and tore your robes and wept in my presence, I have heard you, declares the LORD. ²⁸Now I will gather you to your ancestors, and you will be buried in peace. Your eyes will not see all the disaster I am going to bring on this place and on those who live here.' "

So they took her answer back to the king.

²⁹Then the king called together all the elders of Judah and Jerusalem. ³⁰He went up to the temple of the LORD with the people of Judah, the inhabitants of Jerusalem, the priests and the Levites—all the people from the least to the greatest. He read in their hearing all the words of the Book of the Covenant, which had been found in the temple of the LORD. ³¹The king stood by his pillar and renewed the covenant in the presence of the LORD—to follow the LORD and keep his commands, statutes and decrees with all his heart and all his soul, and to obey the words of the covenant written in this book.

³²Then he had everyone in Jerusalem and Benjamin pledge themselves to it; the people of Jerusalem did this in accordance with the covenant of God, the God of their ancestors.

³³Josiah removed all the detestable idols from all the territory belonging to the Israelites, and he had all who were present in Israel serve the LORD their God. As long as he lived, they did not fail to follow the LORD, the God of their ancestors.

Josiah Celebrates the Passover

35 Josiah celebrated the Passover to the LORD in Jerusalem, and the Passover lamb was slaughtered on the fourteenth day of the first month. ²He appointed the priests to their duties and encouraged them in the service of the LORD's temple. ³He said to the Levites, who instructed all Israel and who had been consecrated to the LORD: "Put the sacred ark in the temple that Solomon son of David king of Israel built. It is not to be carried about on your shoulders. Now serve the LORD your God and his people Israel. ⁴Prepare yourselves by families in your divisions, according to the instructions written by David king of Israel and by his son Solomon.

⁵"Stand in the holy place with a group of

ᵃ 20 Also called *Akbor son of Micaiah*   ᵇ 22 One Hebrew manuscript, Vulgate and Syriac; most Hebrew manuscripts do not have *had sent with him*.   ᶜ 22 Also called *Tikvah*   ᵈ 22 Also called *Harhas*
ᵉ 25 Or *by everything they have done*

Levites for each subdivision of the families of your fellow Israelites, the lay people. ⁶Slaughter the Passover lambs, consecrate yourselves and prepare the lambs for your fellow Israelites, doing what the LORD commanded through Moses."

⁷Josiah provided for all the lay people who were there a total of thirty thousand lambs and goats for the Passover offerings, and also three thousand cattle—all from the king's own possessions.

⁸His officials also contributed voluntarily to the people and the priests and Levites. Hilkiah, Zechariah and Jehiel, the officials in charge of God's temple, gave the priests twenty-six hundred Passover offerings and three hundred cattle. ⁹Also Konaniah along with Shemaiah and Nethanel, his brothers, and Hashabiah, Jeiel and Jozabad, the leaders of the Levites, provided five thousand Passover offerings and five hundred head of cattle for the Levites.

¹⁰The service was arranged and the priests stood in their places with the Levites in their divisions as the king had ordered. ¹¹The Passover lambs were slaughtered, and the priests splashed against the altar the blood handed to them, while the Levites skinned the animals. ¹²They set aside the burnt offerings to give them to the subdivisions of the families of the people to offer to the LORD, as it is written in the Book of Moses. They did the same with the cattle. ¹³They roasted the Passover animals over the fire as prescribed, and boiled the holy offerings in pots, caldrons and pans and served them quickly to all the people. ¹⁴After this, they made preparations for themselves and for the priests, because the priests, the descendants of Aaron, were sacrificing the burnt offerings and the fat portions until nightfall. So the Levites made preparations for themselves and for the Aaronic priests.

¹⁵The musicians, the descendants of Asaph, were in the places prescribed by David, Asaph, Heman and Jeduthun the king's seer. The gatekeepers at each gate did not need to leave their posts, because their fellow Levites made the preparations for them.

¹⁶So at that time the entire service of the LORD was carried out for the celebration of the Passover and the offering of burnt offerings on the altar of the LORD, as King Josiah had or-

dered. ¹⁷The Israelites who were present celebrated the Passover at that time and observed the Festival of Unleavened Bread for seven days. ¹⁸The Passover had not been observed like this in Israel since the days of the prophet Samuel; and none of the kings of Israel had ever celebrated such a Passover as did Josiah, with the priests, the Levites and all Judah and Israel who were there with the people of Jerusalem. ¹⁹This Passover was celebrated in the eighteenth year of Josiah's reign.

The Death of Josiah

²⁰After all this, when Josiah had set the temple in order, Necho king of Egypt went up to fight at Carchemish on the Euphrates, and Josiah marched out to meet him in battle. ²¹But Necho sent messengers to him, saying, "What quarrel is there, king of Judah, between you and me? It is not you I am attacking at this time, but the house with which I am at war. God has told me to hurry; so stop opposing God, who is with me, or he will destroy you."

²²Josiah, however, would not turn away from him, but disguised himself to engage him in battle. He would not listen to what Necho had said at God's command but went to fight him on the plain of Megiddo.

²³Archers shot King Josiah, and he told his officers, "Take me away; I am badly wounded." ²⁴So they took him out of his chariot, put him in his other chariot and brought him to Jerusalem, where he died. He was buried in the tombs of his ancestors, and all Judah and Jerusalem mourned for him.

²⁵Jeremiah composed laments for Josiah, and to this day all the male and female singers commemorate Josiah in the laments. These became a tradition in Israel and are written in the Laments.

²⁶The other events of Josiah's reign and his acts of devotion in accordance with what is written in the Law of the LORD— ²⁷all the events, from beginning to end, are written in the book of the kings of Israel and Judah.

36 ¹And the people of the land took Jehoahaz son of Josiah and made him king in Jerusalem in place of his father.

Jehoahaz King of Judah

²Jehoahaz*ᵃ* was twenty-three years old

ᵃ 2 Hebrew *Joahaz,* a variant of *Jehoahaz*; also in verse 4

Being God's Appointed Leader

2 Chronicles 36:11–14

read/meditate

As you slowly read this passage, think about the everyday citizens that were affected by this man in power. Take a moment to consider the opportunities around you to influence others.

pray

Tell God what kind of leader you would like to be. Ask him to call attention to any blind spots you may have that could hold you back. Listen for his response.

contemplate

Think about the king in today's passage. Speculate as to why he made the choices that he did. What may have changed his course? Think about how you might allow God to plot your own course.

additional reflection

Consecrate me now to thy service, Lord,
By the power of grace divine;
Let my soul look up with a steadfast hope,
And my will be lost in thine.

—Fanny J. Crosby

For your next devotional reading, go to page 514.

when he became king, and he reigned in Jerusalem three months. ³The king of Egypt dethroned him in Jerusalem and imposed on Judah a levy of a hundred talents*a* of silver and a talent*b* of gold. ⁴The king of Egypt made Eliakim, a brother of Jehoahaz, king over Judah and Jerusalem and changed Eliakim's name to Jehoiakim. But Necho took Eliakim's brother Jehoahaz and carried him off to Egypt.

Jehoiakim King of Judah

⁵Jehoiakim was twenty-five years old when he became king, and he reigned in Jerusalem eleven years. He did evil in the eyes of the LORD his God. ⁶Nebuchadnezzar king of Babylon attacked him and bound him with bronze shackles to take him to Babylon. ⁷Nebuchadnezzar also took to Babylon articles from the temple of the LORD and put them in his temple*c* there.

⁸The other events of Jehoiakim's reign, the detestable things he did and all that was found against him, are written in the book of the kings of Israel and Judah. And Jehoiachin his son succeeded him as king.

Jehoiachin King of Judah

⁹Jehoiachin was eighteen*d* years old when he became king, and he reigned in Jerusalem three months and ten days. He did evil in the eyes of the LORD. ¹⁰In the spring, King Nebuchadnezzar sent for him and brought him to Babylon, together with articles of value from the temple of the LORD, and he made Jehoiachin's uncle,*e* Zedekiah, king over Judah and Jerusalem.

Zedekiah King of Judah

¹¹Zedekiah was twenty-one years old when he became king, and he reigned in Jerusalem eleven years. ¹²He did evil in the eyes of the LORD his God and did not humble himself before Jeremiah the prophet, who spoke the word of the LORD. ¹³He also rebelled against King Nebuchadnezzar, who had made him take an oath in God's name. He became stiff-necked and hardened his heart and would not turn to the LORD, the God of Israel. ¹⁴Furthermore, all the leaders of the priests and the people became more and more unfaithful, following all the detestable practices of the nations and defiling the temple of the LORD, which he had consecrated in Jerusalem.

The Fall of Jerusalem

¹⁵The LORD, the God of their ancestors, sent word to them through his messengers again and again, because he had pity on his people and on his dwelling place. ¹⁶But they mocked God's messengers, despised his words and scoffed at his prophets until the wrath of the LORD was aroused against his people and there was no remedy. ¹⁷He brought up against them the king of the Babylonians,*f* who killed their young men with the sword in the sanctuary, and spared neither young man nor young woman, the elderly or the aged. God gave them all into the hands of Nebuchadnezzar. ¹⁸He carried to Babylon all the articles from the temple of God, both large and small, and the treasures of the LORD's temple and the treasures of the king and his officials. ¹⁹They set fire to God's temple and broke down the wall of Jerusalem; they burned all the palaces and destroyed everything of value there.

²⁰He carried into exile to Babylon the remnant, who escaped from the sword, and they became servants to him and his successors until the kingdom of Persia came to power. ²¹The land enjoyed its sabbath rests; all the time of its desolation it rested, until the seventy years were completed in fulfillment of the word of the LORD spoken by Jeremiah.

²²In the first year of Cyrus king of Persia, in order to fulfill the word of the LORD spoken by Jeremiah, the LORD moved the heart of Cyrus king of Persia to make a proclamation throughout his realm and also to put it in writing:

²³"This is what Cyrus king of Persia says:

" 'The LORD, the God of heaven, has given me all the kingdoms of the earth and he has appointed me to build a temple for him at Jerusalem in Judah. Any of his people among you—may the LORD their God be with them, and let them go up.' "

---

a 3 That is, about 3 3/4 tons or about 3.4 metric tons kilograms   *c 7* Or *palace*   *d 9* One Hebrew manuscript, some Septuagint manuscripts and Syriac (see also 2 Kings 24:8); most Hebrew manuscripts *eight* 2 Kings 24:17)   *f 17* Or *Chaldeans*   *b 3* That is, about 75 pounds or about 34   *e 10* Hebrew *brother*, that is, relative (see

ezra

AUTHOR:	Possibly Ezra
DATE:	Around 440 B.C.
THEME:	God calls his people back when they are lost in spiritual darkness.

Cyrus Helps the Exiles to Return

1 In the first year of Cyrus king of Persia, in order to fulfill the word of the LORD spoken by Jeremiah, the LORD moved the heart of Cyrus king of Persia to make a proclamation throughout his realm and also to put it in writing:

2"This is what Cyrus king of Persia says:

" 'The LORD, the God of heaven, has given me all the kingdoms of the earth and he has appointed me to build a temple for him at Jerusalem in Judah. 3Any of his people among you—may their God be with them, and let them go up to Jerusalem in Judah and build the temple of the LORD, the God of Israel, the God who is in Jerusalem. 4And in any locality where survivors may now be living, the people are to provide them with silver and gold, with goods and livestock, and with freewill offerings for the temple of God in Jerusalem.' "

5Then the family heads of Judah and Benjamin, and the priests and Levites—everyone whose heart God had moved—prepared to go up and build the house of the LORD in Jerusalem. 6All their neighbors assisted them with articles of silver and gold, with goods and livestock, and with valuable gifts, in addition to all the freewill offerings.

7Moreover, King Cyrus brought out the articles belonging to the temple of the LORD, which Nebuchadnezzar had carried away from Jerusalem and had placed in the temple of his god.[a] 8Cyrus king of Persia had them brought by Mithredath the treasurer, who counted them out to Sheshbazzar the prince of Judah.

9This was the inventory:

gold dishes	30
silver dishes	1,000
silver pans[b]	29
10 gold bowls	30
matching silver bowls	410
other articles	1,000

11In all, there were 5,400 articles of gold and of silver. Sheshbazzar brought all these along with the exiles when they came up from Babylon to Jerusalem.

The List of the Exiles Who Returned

2 Now these are the people of the province who came up from the captivity of the exiles, whom Nebuchadnezzar king of Babylon had taken captive to Babylon (they returned to Jerusalem and Judah, all to their own towns, 2in company with Zerubbabel, Joshua, Nehemiah, Seraiah, Reelaiah, Mordecai, Bilshan, Mispar, Bigvai, Rehum and Baanah):

The list of the men of the people of Israel:

3 the descendants of Parosh	2,172
4 of Shephatiah	372
5 of Arah	775
6 of Pahath-Moab (through the line of Jeshua and Joab)	2,812
7 of Elam	1,254
8 of Zattu	945
9 of Zakkai	760
10 of Bani	642
11 of Bebai	623
12 of Azgad	1,222
13 of Adonikam	666
14 of Bigvai	2,056

a 7 Or gods   b 9 The meaning of the Hebrew for this word is uncertain.

READY AND WAITING

Ezra 1:1–11 or 1:2–5

Don M. Aycock

What will be your faith? Will you hold to the beliefs of the Bible? These were the questions the Israelites had to answer during their years of exile in Babylon. Surrounded on all sides by pagans who were also their masters, the tribes of Israel felt tremendous pressure to throw off their old beliefs and embrace the "many-gods/anything-goes" attitudes of their victors.

Many Israelites lost their faith in the years spent far from Jerusalem, but a remnant stayed true to Jehovah. They trusted in God in spite of difficult circumstances, and the Lord rewarded their faithfulness. The day came when God moved in the heart of Cyrus, king of Persia. The king released the people and allowed them to return to Jerusalem and rebuild the temple.

When that time came, the faithful remnant was ready.

If you're like most of us, you hear some unusual religious discussions in the workplace, at the gym or around your neighborhood. Everyone seems to have his own idea of what is right and how one gets to heaven—if he even believes in heaven. A Christian who stands for his faith will receive tremendous pressure to give up and give in.

What are you doing with your faith? Are you standing firm? Remember: it's more important to be faithful than it is to "fit in."

CARDINAL HENRY EDWARD MANNING {AD 1808–1892}

Let us learn from this communion of saints to live in hope. Those who are now at rest were once like ourselves. They were once weak, faulty, sinful. They had their burdens and hindrances, their slumbering and weariness, their failures and their falls. But now they have overcome. Their life was once homely and commonplace. Their day ran out as ours. Morning and noon and night came and went to them as to us. Their life, too, was as lonely and sad as yours. Little fretful circumstances and frequent disturbing changes wasted away their hours as yours. There is nothing in your life that was not in theirs. There was nothing in theirs but may be also in your own. They have overcome, one by one, each in turn when the day came and God called him to the trial. And so will you likewise.

reflection

1. What was remarkable about the Israelites who chose to go back to Jerusalem and rebuild the temple?

2. What can you learn from their example?

3. When do you find it most difficult to stand firm in your faith?

For your next devotional reading, go to page 523.

15 of Adin   454
16 of Ater (through Hezekiah)   98
17 of Bezai   323
18 of Jorah   112
19 of Hashum   223
20 of Gibbar   95

21 the men of Bethlehem   123
22 of Netophah   56
23 of Anathoth   128
24 of Azmaveth   42
25 of Kiriath Jearim,ᵃ Kephirah
    and Beeroth   743
26 of Ramah and Geba   621
27 of Mikmash   122
28 of Bethel and Ai   223
29 of Nebo   52
30 of Magbish   156
31 of the other Elam   1,254
32 of Harim   320
33 of Lod, Hadid and Ono   725
34 of Jericho   345
35 of Senaah   3,630

36 The priests:

   the descendants of Jedaiah
      (through the family of
      Jeshua)   973
37 of Immer   1,052
38 of Pashhur   1,247
39 of Harim   1,017

40 The Levites:

   the descendants of Jeshua and
      Kadmiel (of the line of
      Hodaviah)   74

41 The musicians:

   the descendants of Asaph   128

42 The gatekeepers of the temple:

   the descendants of
      Shallum, Ater, Talmon,
      Akkub, Hatita and Shobai   139

43 The temple servants:

   the descendants of
      Ziha, Hasupha, Tabbaoth,
44   Keros, Siaha, Padon,
45   Lebanah, Hagabah, Akkub,
46   Hagab, Shalmai, Hanan,
47   Giddel, Gahar, Reaiah,
48   Rezin, Nekoda, Gazzam,
49   Uzza, Paseah, Besai,
50   Asnah, Meunim, Nephusim,
51   Bakbuk, Hakupha, Harhur,
52   Bazluth, Mehida, Harsha,
53   Barkos, Sisera, Temah,
54   Neziah and Hatipha

55 The descendants of the servants of
Solomon:

   the descendants of
      Sotai, Hassophereth, Peruda,
56   Jaala, Darkon, Giddel,
57   Shephatiah, Hattil,
      Pokereth-Hazzebaim and Ami

58 The temple servants and the
   descendants of the servants
   of Solomon   392

59 The following came up from the
towns of Tel Melah, Tel Harsha, Kerub,
Addon and Immer, but they could not
show that their families were descended from Israel:

60 The descendants of
   Delaiah, Tobiah and Nekoda   652

61 And from among the priests:

   The descendants of
      Hobaiah, Hakkoz and Barzillai (a
      man who had married a daughter
      of Barzillai the Gileadite and was
      called by that name).

62 These searched for their family records, but they could not find them and
so were excluded from the priesthood
as unclean. 63 The governor ordered
them not to eat any of the most sacred
food until there was a priest ministering
with the Urim and Thummim.

64 The whole company numbered
42,360, 65 besides their 7,337 male and
female slaves; and they also had 200
male and female singers. 66 They had
736 horses, 245 mules, 67 435 camels
and 6,720 donkeys.

68 When they arrived at the house of the
LORD in Jerusalem, some of the heads of the
families gave freewill offerings toward the
rebuilding of the house of God on its site.
69 According to their ability they gave to the
treasury for this work 61,000 darics ᵇ of gold,

ᵃ 25 See Septuagint (see also Neh. 7:29); Hebrew *Kiriath Arim.*   ᵇ 69 That is, about 1,100 pounds or
about 500 kilograms

5,000 minas*a* of silver and 100 priestly garments.

⁷⁰The priests, the Levites, the musicians, the gatekeepers and the temple servants settled in their own towns, along with some of the other people, and the rest of the Israelites settled in their towns.

Rebuilding the Altar

3 When the seventh month came and the Israelites had settled in their towns, the people assembled with one accord in Jerusalem. ²Then Joshua son of Jozadak and his fellow priests and Zerubbabel son of Shealtiel and his associates began to build the altar of the God of Israel to sacrifice burnt offerings on it, in accordance with what is written in the Law of Moses the man of God. ³Despite their fear of the peoples around them, they built the altar on its foundation and sacrificed burnt offerings on it to the LORD, both the morning and evening sacrifices. ⁴Then in accordance with what is written, they celebrated the Festival of Tabernacles with the required number of burnt offerings prescribed for each day. ⁵After that, they presented the regular burnt offerings, the New Moon sacrifices and the sacrifices for all the appointed sacred festivals of the LORD, as well as those brought as freewill offerings to the LORD. ⁶On the first day of the seventh month they began to offer burnt offerings to the LORD, though the foundation of the LORD's temple had not yet been laid.

Rebuilding the Temple

⁷Then they gave money to the masons and carpenters, and gave food and drink and olive oil to the people of Sidon and Tyre, so that they would bring cedar logs by sea from Lebanon to Joppa, as authorized by Cyrus king of Persia.

⁸In the second month of the second year after their arrival at the house of God in Jerusalem, Zerubbabel son of Shealtiel, Joshua son of Jozadak and the rest of the people (the priests and the Levites and all who had returned from the captivity to Jerusalem) began the work, appointing Levites twenty years old and older to supervise the building of the house of the LORD. ⁹Joshua and his sons and brothers and Kadmiel and his sons

(descendants of Hodaviah*b*) and the sons of Henadad and their sons and brothers—all Levites—joined together in supervising those working on the house of God.

¹⁰When the builders laid the foundation of the temple of the LORD, the priests in their vestments and with trumpets, and the Levites (the sons of Asaph) with cymbals, took their places to praise the LORD, as prescribed by David king of Israel. ¹¹With praise and thanksgiving they sang to the LORD:

"He is good;
   his love toward Israel endures
      forever."

And all the people gave a great shout of praise to the LORD, because the foundation of the house of the LORD was laid. ¹²But many of the older priests and Levites and family heads, who had seen the former temple, wept aloud when they saw the foundation of this temple being laid, while many others shouted for joy. ¹³No one could distinguish the sound of the shouts of joy from the sound of weeping, because the people made so much noise. And the sound was heard far away.

Opposition to the Rebuilding

4 When the enemies of Judah and Benjamin heard that the exiles were building a temple for the LORD, the God of Israel, ²they came to Zerubbabel and to the heads of the families and said, "Let us help you build because, like you, we seek your God and have been sacrificing to him since the time of Esarhaddon king of Assyria, who brought us here."

³But Zerubbabel, Joshua and the rest of the heads of the families of Israel answered, "You have no part with us in building a temple to our God. We alone will build it for the LORD, the God of Israel, as King Cyrus, the king of Persia, commanded us."

⁴Then the peoples around them set out to discourage the people of Judah and make them afraid to go on building.*c* ⁵They bribed officials to work against them and frustrate their plans during the entire reign of Cyrus king of Persia and down to the reign of Darius king of Persia.

---

a 69 That is, about 3 tons or about 2.8 metric tons
b 9 Hebrew *Yehudah*, a variant of *Hodaviah*
c 4 Or *and troubled them as they built*

Later Opposition Under Xerxes and Artaxerxes

⁶At the beginning of the reign of Xerxes,ᵃ they lodged an accusation against the people of Judah and Jerusalem.

⁷And in the days of Artaxerxes king of Persia, Bishlam, Mithredath, Tabeel and the rest of his associates wrote a letter to Artaxerxes. The letter was written in Aramaic script and in the Aramaic language.ᵇ,ᶜ

⁸Rehum the commanding officer and Shimshai the secretary wrote a letter against Jerusalem to Artaxerxes the king as follows:

⁹Rehum the commanding officer and Shimshai the secretary, together with the rest of their associates—the judges, officials and administrators over the people from Persia, Uruk and Babylon, the Elamites of Susa, ¹⁰and the other people whom the great and honorable Ashurbanipal deported and settled in the city of Samaria and elsewhere in Trans-Euphrates.

¹¹(This is a copy of the letter they sent him.)

To King Artaxerxes,

From your servants in Trans-Euphrates:

¹²The king should know that the people who came up to us from you have gone to Jerusalem and are rebuilding that rebellious and wicked city. They are restoring the walls and repairing the foundations.

¹³Furthermore, the king should know that if this city is built and its walls are restored, no more taxes, tribute or duty will be paid, and eventually the royal revenues will suffer.ᵈ ¹⁴Now since we are under obligation to the palace and it is not proper for us to see the king dishonored, we are sending this message to inform the king, ¹⁵so that a search may be made in the archives of your predecessors. In these records you will find that this city is a rebellious city, troublesome to kings and provinces, a place with a long history of sedition. That is why this city was destroyed. ¹⁶We inform the king that if

this city is built and its walls are restored, you will be left with nothing in Trans-Euphrates.

¹⁷The king sent this reply:

To Rehum the commanding officer, Shimshai the secretary and the rest of their associates living in Samaria and elsewhere in Trans-Euphrates:

Greetings.

¹⁸The letter you sent us has been read and translated in my presence. ¹⁹I issued an order and a search was made, and it was found that this city has a long history of revolt against kings and has been a place of rebellion and sedition. ²⁰Jerusalem has had powerful kings ruling over the whole of Trans-Euphrates, and taxes, tribute and duty were paid to them. ²¹Now issue an order to these people to stop work, so that this city will not be rebuilt until I so order. ²²Be careful not to neglect this matter. Why let this threat grow, to the detriment of the royal interests?

²³As soon as the copy of the letter of King Artaxerxes was read to Rehum and Shimshai the secretary and their associates, they went immediately to the Jews in Jerusalem and compelled them by force to stop.

²⁴Thus the work on the house of God in Jerusalem came to a standstill until the second year of the reign of Darius king of Persia.

Tattenai's Letter to Darius

5 Now Haggai the prophet and Zechariah the prophet, a descendant of Iddo, prophesied to the Jews in Judah and Jerusalem in the name of the God of Israel, who was over them. ²Then Zerubbabel son of Shealtiel and Joshua son of Jozadak set to work to rebuild the house of God in Jerusalem. And the prophets of God were with them, supporting them.

³At that time Tattenai, governor of Trans-Euphrates, and Shethar-Bozenai and their associates went to them and asked, "Who authorized you to rebuild this temple and to finish it?" ⁴Theyᵉ also asked, "What are the

ᵃ 6 Hebrew *Ahasuerus*   ᵇ 7 Or *written in Aramaic and translated*   ᶜ 7 The text of Ezra 4:8–6:18 is in Aramaic.   ᵈ 13 The meaning of the Aramaic for this clause is uncertain.   ᵉ 4 See Septuagint; Aramaic *We*.

names of those who are constructing this building?" [5]But the eye of their God was watching over the elders of the Jews, and they were not stopped until a report could go to Darius and his written reply be received.

[6]This is a copy of the letter that Tattenai, governor of Trans-Euphrates, and Shethar-Bozenai and their associates, the officials of Trans-Euphrates, sent to King Darius. [7]The report they sent him read as follows:

To King Darius:

Cordial greetings.

[8]The king should know that we went to the district of Judah, to the temple of the great God. The people are building it with large stones and placing the timbers in the walls. The work is being carried on with diligence and is making rapid progress under their direction.

[9]We questioned the elders and asked them, "Who authorized you to rebuild this temple and to finish it?" [10]We also asked them their names, so that we could write down the names of their leaders for your information.

[11]This is the answer they gave us:

"We are the servants of the God of heaven and earth, and we are rebuilding the temple that was built many years ago, one that a great king of Israel built and finished. [12]But because our ancestors angered the God of heaven, he gave them into the hands of Nebuchadnezzar the Chaldean, king of Babylon, who destroyed this temple and deported the people to Babylon.

[13]"However, in the first year of Cyrus king of Babylon, King Cyrus issued a decree to rebuild this house of God. [14]He even removed from the temple[a] of Babylon the gold and silver articles of the house of God, which Nebuchadnezzar had taken from the temple in Jerusalem and brought to the temple[a] in Babylon. Then King Cyrus gave them to a man named Sheshbazzar, whom he had appointed governor, [15]and he told him, 'Take these articles and go and deposit them in the temple in Jeru-

salem. And rebuild the house of God on its site.'

[16]"So this Sheshbazzar came and laid the foundations of the house of God in Jerusalem. From that day to the present it has been under construction but is not yet finished."

[17]Now if it pleases the king, let a search be made in the royal archives of Babylon to see if King Cyrus did in fact issue a decree to rebuild this house of God in Jerusalem. Then let the king send us his decision in this matter.

The Decree of Darius

6 King Darius then issued an order, and they searched in the archives stored in the treasury at Babylon. [2]A scroll was found in the citadel of Ecbatana in the province of Media, and this was written on it:

Memorandum:

[3]In the first year of King Cyrus, the king issued a decree concerning the temple of God in Jerusalem:

Let the temple be rebuilt as a place to present sacrifices, and let its foundations be laid. It is to be sixty cubits[b] high and sixty cubits wide, [4]with three courses of large stones and one of timbers. The costs are to be paid by the royal treasury. [5]Also, the gold and silver articles of the house of God, which Nebuchadnezzar took from the temple in Jerusalem and brought to Babylon, are to be returned to their places in the temple in Jerusalem; they are to be deposited in the house of God.

[6]Now then, Tattenai, governor of Trans-Euphrates, and Shethar-Bozenai and you other officials of that province, stay away from there. [7]Do not interfere with the work on this temple of God. Let the governor of the Jews and the Jewish elders rebuild this house of God on its site.

[8]Moreover, I hereby decree what you are to do for these elders of the Jews in the construction of this house of God:

Their expenses are to be fully paid

out of the royal treasury, from the revenues of Trans-Euphrates, so that the work will not stop. ⁹Whatever is needed—young bulls, rams, male lambs for burnt offerings to the God of heaven, and wheat, salt, wine and olive oil, as requested by the priests in Jerusalem—must be given them daily without fail, ¹⁰so that they may offer sacrifices pleasing to the God of heaven and pray for the well-being of the king and his sons.

¹¹Furthermore, I decree that if anyone defies this edict, a beam is to be pulled from their house and they are to be impaled on it. And for this crime their house is to be made a pile of rubble. ¹²May God, who has caused his Name to dwell there, overthrow any king or people who lifts a hand to change this decree or to destroy this temple in Jerusalem.

I Darius have decreed it. Let it be carried out with diligence.

Completion and Dedication of the Temple

¹³Then, because of the decree King Darius had sent, Tattenai, governor of Trans-Euphrates, and Shethar-Bozenai and their associates carried it out with diligence. ¹⁴So the elders of the Jews continued to build and prosper under the preaching of Haggai the prophet and Zechariah, a descendant of Iddo. They finished building the temple according to the command of the God of Israel and the decrees of Cyrus, Darius and Artaxerxes, kings of Persia. ¹⁵The temple was completed on the third day of the month Adar, in the sixth year of the reign of King Darius.

¹⁶Then the people of Israel—the priests, the Levites and the rest of the exiles—celebrated the dedication of the house of God with joy. ¹⁷For the dedication of this house of God they offered a hundred bulls, two hundred rams, four hundred male lambs and, as a sin offeringᵃ for all Israel, twelve male goats, one for each of the tribes of Israel. ¹⁸And they installed the priests in their divisions and the Levites in their groups for the service of God at Jerusalem, according to what is written in the Book of Moses.

The Passover

¹⁹On the fourteenth day of the first month, the exiles celebrated the Passover. ²⁰The priests and Levites had purified themselves and were all ceremonially clean. The Levites slaughtered the Passover lamb for all the exiles, for their relatives the priests and for themselves. ²¹So the Israelites who had returned from the exile ate it, together with all who had separated themselves from the unclean practices of their Gentile neighbors in order to seek the LORD, the God of Israel. ²²For seven days they celebrated with joy the Festival of Unleavened Bread, because the LORD had filled them with joy by changing the attitude of the king of Assyria so that he assisted them in the work on the house of God, the God of Israel.

Ezra Comes to Jerusalem

7 After these things, during the reign of Artaxerxes king of Persia, Ezra son of Seraiah, the son of Azariah, the son of Hilkiah, ²the son of Shallum, the son of Zadok, the son of Ahitub, ³the son of Amariah, the son of Azariah, the son of Meraioth, ⁴the son of Zerahiah, the son of Uzzi, the son of Bukki, ⁵the son of Abishua, the son of Phinehas, the son of Eleazar, the son of Aaron the chief priest— ⁶this Ezra came up from Babylon. He was a teacher well versed in the Law of Moses, which the LORD, the God of Israel, had given. The king had granted him everything he asked, for the hand of the LORD his God was on him. ⁷Some of the Israelites, including priests, Levites, musicians, gatekeepers and temple servants, also came up to Jerusalem in the seventh year of King Artaxerxes.

⁸Ezra arrived in Jerusalem in the fifth month of the seventh year of the king. ⁹He had begun his journey from Babylon on the first day of the first month, and he arrived in Jerusalem on the first day of the fifth month, for the gracious hand of his God was on him. ¹⁰For Ezra had devoted himself to the study and observance of the Law of the LORD, and to teaching its decrees and laws in Israel.

King Artaxerxes' Letter to Ezra

¹¹This is a copy of the letter King Artaxerxes had given to Ezra the priest, a teacher of the Law, a man learned in matters concern-

ᵃ 17 Or purification offering

ing the commands and decrees of the LORD for Israel:

¹²^a Artaxerxes, king of kings,

To Ezra the priest, teacher of the Law of the God of heaven:

Greetings.

¹³Now I decree that any of the Israelites in my kingdom, including priests and Levites, who volunteer to go to Jerusalem with you, may go. ¹⁴You are sent by the king and his seven advisers to inquire about Judah and Jerusalem with regard to the Law of your God, which is in your hand. ¹⁵Moreover, you are to take with you the silver and gold that the king and his advisers have freely given to the God of Israel, whose dwelling is in Jerusalem, ¹⁶together with all the silver and gold you may obtain from the province of Babylon, as well as the freewill offerings of the people and priests for the temple of their God in Jerusalem. ¹⁷With this money be sure to buy bulls, rams and male lambs, together with their grain offerings and drink offerings, and sacrifice them on the altar of the temple of your God in Jerusalem.

¹⁸You and your fellow Israelites may then do whatever seems best with the rest of the silver and gold, in accordance with the will of your God. ¹⁹Deliver to the God of Jerusalem all the articles entrusted to you for worship in the temple of your God. ²⁰And anything else needed for the temple of your God that you are responsible to supply, you may provide from the royal treasury.

²¹Now I, King Artaxerxes, decree that all the treasurers of Trans-Euphrates are to provide with diligence whatever Ezra the priest, the teacher of the Law of the God of heaven, may ask of you— ²²up to a hundred talents^b of silver, a hundred cors^c of wheat, a hundred baths^d of wine, a hundred baths^d of olive oil, and salt without limit. ²³Whatever the God of heaven has prescribed, let it be done with diligence for the temple of the God of heaven. Why

should his wrath fall on the realm of the king and of his sons? ²⁴You are also to know that you have no authority to impose taxes, tribute or duty on any of the priests, Levites, musicians, gatekeepers, temple servants or other workers at this house of God.

²⁵And you, Ezra, in accordance with the wisdom of your God, which you possess, appoint magistrates and judges to administer justice to all the people of Trans-Euphrates—all who know the laws of your God. And you are to teach any who do not know them. ²⁶Whoever does not obey the law of your God and the law of the king must surely be punished by death, banishment, confiscation of property, or imprisonment.

²⁷Praise be to the LORD, the God of our ancestors, who has put it into the king's heart to bring honor to the house of the LORD in Jerusalem in this way ²⁸and who has extended his good favor to me before the king and his advisers and all the king's powerful officials. Because the hand of the LORD my God was on me, I took courage and gathered leaders from Israel to go up with me.

List of the Family Heads Returning With Ezra

8 These are the family heads and those registered with them who came up with me from Babylon during the reign of King Artaxerxes:

²of the descendants of Phinehas, Gershom;

of the descendants of Ithamar, Daniel;

of the descendants of David, Hattush ³of the descendants of Shekaniah;

of the descendants of Parosh, Zechariah, and with him were registered 150 men;

⁴of the descendants of Pahath-Moab, Eliehoenai son of Zerahiah, and with him 200 men;

⁵of the descendants of Zattu,^e Shekaniah son of Jahaziel, and with him 300 men;

<hr/>

^a 12 The text of Ezra 7:12-26 is in Aramaic.   ^b 22 That is, about 3 3/4 tons or about 3.4 metric tons
^c 22 That is, probably about 18 tons or about 16 metric tons   ^d 22 That is, about 600 gallons or about
2,200 liters   ^e 5 Some Septuagint manuscripts (also 1 Esdras 8:32); Hebrew does not have Zattu.

⁶of the descendants of Adin, Ebed son of Jonathan, and with him 50 men;

⁷of the descendants of Elam, Jeshaiah son of Athaliah, and with him 70 men;

⁸of the descendants of Shephatiah, Zebadiah son of Michael, and with him 80 men;

⁹of the descendants of Joab, Obadiah son of Jehiel, and with him 218 men;

¹⁰of the descendants of Bani,ᵃ Shelomith son of Josiphiah, and with him 160 men;

¹¹of the descendants of Bebai, Zechariah son of Bebai, and with him 28 men;

¹²of the descendants of Azgad, Johanan son of Hakkatan, and with him 110 men;

¹³of the descendants of Adonikam, the last ones, whose names were Eliphelet, Jeuel and Shemaiah, and with them 60 men;

¹⁴of the descendants of Bigvai, Uthai and Zakkur, and with them 70 men.

The Return to Jerusalem

¹⁵I assembled them at the canal that flows toward Ahava, and we camped there three days. When I checked among the people and the priests, I found no Levites there. ¹⁶So I summoned Eliezer, Ariel, Shemaiah, Elnathan, Jarib, Elnathan, Nathan, Zechariah and Meshullam, who were leaders, and Joiarib and Elnathan, who were men of learning, ¹⁷and I ordered them to go to Iddo, the leader in Kasiphia. I told them what to say to Iddo and his associates, the temple servants in Kasiphia, so that they might bring attendants to us for the house of our God. ¹⁸Because the gracious hand of our God was on us, they brought us Sherebiah, a capable man, from the descendants of Mahli son of Levi, the son of Israel, and Sherebiah's sons and brothers, 18 in all; ¹⁹and Hashabiah, together with Jeshaiah from the descendants of Merari, and his brothers and nephews, 20 in all. ²⁰They also brought 220 of the temple servants—a body that David and the officials had established to assist the Levites. All were registered by name.

²¹There, by the Ahava Canal, I proclaimed a fast, so that we might humble ourselves before our God and ask him for a safe journey for us and our children, with all our possessions. ²²I was ashamed to ask the king for soldiers and horsemen to protect us from enemies on the road, because we had told the king, "The gracious hand of our God is on everyone who looks to him, but his great anger is against all who forsake him." ²³So we fasted and petitioned our God about this, and he answered our prayer.

²⁴Then I set apart twelve of the leading priests, namely, Sherebiah, Hashabiah and ten of their brothers, ²⁵and I weighed out to them the offering of silver and gold and the articles that the king, his advisers, his officials and all Israel present there had donated for the house of our God. ²⁶I weighed out to them 650 talentsᵇ of silver, silver articles weighing 100 talents,ᶜ 100 talentsᶜ of gold, ²⁷20 bowls of gold valued at 1,000 darics,ᵈ and two fine articles of polished bronze, as precious as gold.

²⁸I said to them, "You as well as these articles are consecrated to the LORD. The silver and gold are a freewill offering to the LORD, the God of your ancestors. ²⁹Guard them carefully until you weigh them out in the chambers of the house of the LORD in Jerusalem before the leading priests and the Levites and the family heads of Israel." ³⁰Then the priests and Levites received the silver and gold and sacred articles that had been weighed out to be taken to the house of our God in Jerusalem.

³¹On the twelfth day of the first month we set out from the Ahava Canal to go to Jerusalem. The hand of our God was on us, and he protected us from enemies and bandits along the way. ³²So we arrived in Jerusalem, where we rested three days.

³³On the fourth day, in the house of our God, we weighed out the silver and gold and the sacred articles into the hands of Meremoth son of Uriah, the priest. Eleazar son of Phinehas was with him, and so were the Levites Jozabad son of Jeshua and Noadiah son of Binnui. ³⁴Everything was accounted for by number and weight, and the entire weight was recorded at that time.

³⁵Then the exiles who had returned from captivity sacrificed burnt offerings to the God of Israel: twelve bulls for all Israel,

---

ᵃ 10 Some Septuagint manuscripts (also 1 Esdras 8:36); Hebrew does not have Bani.   ᵇ 26 That is, about 24 tons or about 22 metric tons   ᶜ 26 That is, about 3 3/4 tons or about 3.4 metric tons   ᵈ 27 That is, about 19 pounds or about 8.5 kilograms ninety-six rams, seventy-seven male lambs and, as a sin offering,^a twelve male goats. All this was a burnt offering to the LORD. ³⁶They also delivered the king's orders to the royal satraps and to the governors of Trans-Euphrates, who then gave assistance to the people and to the house of God.

Ezra's Prayer About Intermarriage

9 After these things had been done, the leaders came to me and said, "The people of Israel, including the priests and the Levites, have not kept themselves separate from the neighboring peoples with their detestable practices, like those of the Canaanites, Hittites, Perizzites, Jebusites, Ammonites, Moabites, Egyptians and Amorites. ²They have taken some of their daughters as wives for themselves and their sons, and have mingled the holy race with the peoples around them. And the leaders and officials have led the way in this unfaithfulness."

³When I heard this, I tore my tunic and cloak, pulled hair from my head and beard and sat down appalled. ⁴Then everyone who trembled at the words of the God of Israel gathered around me because of this unfaithfulness of the exiles. And I sat there appalled until the evening sacrifice.

⁵Then, at the evening sacrifice, I rose from my self-abasement, with my tunic and cloak torn, and fell on my knees with my hands spread out to the LORD my God ⁶and prayed:

"I am too ashamed and disgraced, my God, to lift up my face to you, because our sins are higher than our heads and our guilt has reached to the heavens. ⁷From the days of our ancestors until now, our guilt has been great. Because of our sins, we and our kings and our priests have been subjected to the sword and captivity, to pillage and humiliation at the hand of foreign kings, as it is today.

⁸"But now, for a brief moment, the LORD our God has been gracious in leaving us a remnant and giving us a firm place^b in his sanctuary, and so our God gives light to our eyes and a little relief in our bondage. ⁹Though we are slaves, our God has not forsaken us in our bondage. He has shown us kindness in the sight of the kings of Persia: He has granted us new life to rebuild the house of our God and repair its ruins, and he has given us a wall of protection in Judah and Jerusalem.

¹⁰"But now, our God, what can we say after this? For we have forsaken the commands ¹¹you gave through your servants the prophets when you said: 'The land you are entering to possess is a land polluted by the corruption of its peoples. By their detestable practices they have filled it with their impurity from one end to the other. ¹²Therefore, do not give your daughters in marriage to their sons or take their daughters for your sons. Do not seek a treaty of friendship with them at any time, that you may be strong and eat the good things of the land and leave it to your children as an everlasting inheritance.'

¹³"What has happened to us is a result of our evil deeds and our great guilt, and yet, our God, you have punished us less than our sins deserved and have given us a remnant like this. ¹⁴Shall we then break your commands again and intermarry with the peoples who commit such detestable practices? Would you not be angry enough with us to destroy us, leaving us no remnant or survivor? ¹⁵LORD, the God of Israel, you are righteous! We are left this day as a remnant. Here we are before you in our guilt, though because of it not one of us can stand in your presence."

The People's Confession of Sin

10 While Ezra was praying and confessing, weeping and throwing himself down before the house of God, a large crowd of Israelites—men, women and children—gathered around him. They too wept bitterly. ²Then Shekaniah son of Jehiel, one of the descendants of Elam, said to Ezra, "We have been unfaithful to our God by marrying foreign women from the peoples around us. But in spite of this, there is still hope for Israel. ³Now let us make a covenant before our God to send away all these women and their children, in

TUESDAY

LOVING DISCIPLINE

Ezra 9:1–15 *or* 9:13–15

WILLIAM M. CLOW {AD 1853–1930}

Love's supreme disclosure is the cross, but love which redeems must pass on to discipline. Love's redeeming work was not done when Christ had burst the gates of hell. The dominion of sin was broken, but its fascination and power were not wholly annulled. No man who has accepted the forgiveness of God, and put himself under the mastership of Christ, can be ignorant that the power of indwelling sin is his most humbling experience. There is a work of God for man. There is also a work of God in man. Therefore God disciplines His redeemed. He chastens by mercy and by judgment, through limiting privation and burdening care, by the shadow on the heart and the thorn in the flesh, to purify and to perfect in righteousness.

The problems of life find a solution, and its dark experiences gleam with beauty when we see them in this light. Asaph found that his feet were almost gone and his steps had nearly slipped when he saw the prosperity of the wicked (Psalm 73). The author of the book of Job left its problem of undeserved affliction unsolved. It was a mystery too dark for one who had not seen Christ's day. It is his glory that he made a meek submission when he could not even dimly understand.

Matt Redman

We don't enjoy being in pain. No discipline seems pleasant at the time. In our hearts, minds or bodies, we may be struggling beneath the pain of a testing situation. But deep in our spirits, we learn to consider it joy, knowing that we can not only find Christ in the situation but also can become more like Him as a result of it. There are no wasted seasons in the economy of God.

reflection

1. How does God use the hard things of life to discipline his children? Why does he do this?
2. Look again at Ezra's perspective on God's discipline of the Jewish people. What do you learn from this?
3. How have you had to trust the discipline of God in your own life?

For your next devotional reading, go to page 533.

accordance with the counsel of my lord and of those who fear the commands of our God. Let it be done according to the Law. [4]Rise up; this matter is in your hands. We will support you, so take courage and do it."

[5]So Ezra rose up and put the leading priests and Levites and all Israel under oath to do what had been suggested. And they took the oath. [6]Then Ezra withdrew from before the house of God and went to the room of Jehohanan son of Eliashib. While he was there, he ate no food and drank no water, because he continued to mourn over the unfaithfulness of the exiles.

[7]A proclamation was then issued throughout Judah and Jerusalem for all the exiles to assemble in Jerusalem. [8]Anyone who failed to appear within three days would forfeit all his property, in accordance with the decision of the officials and elders, and would himself be expelled from the assembly of the exiles.

[9]Within the three days, all the men of Judah and Benjamin had gathered in Jerusalem. And on the twentieth day of the ninth month, all the people were sitting in the square before the house of God, greatly distressed by the occasion and because of the rain. [10]Then Ezra the priest stood up and said to them, "You have been unfaithful; you have married foreign women, adding to Israel's guilt. [11]Now honor[a] the LORD, the God of your ancestors, and do his will. Separate yourselves from the peoples around you and from your foreign wives."

[12]The whole assembly responded with a loud voice: "You are right! We must do as you say. [13]But there are many people here and it is the rainy season; so we cannot stand outside. Besides, this matter cannot be taken care of in a day or two, because we have sinned greatly in this thing. [14]Let our officials act for the whole assembly. Then let everyone in our towns who has married a foreign woman come at a set time, along with the elders and judges of each town, until the fierce anger of our God in this matter is turned away from us." [15]Only Jonathan son of Asahel and Jahzeiah son of Tikvah, supported by Meshullam and Shabbethai the Levite, opposed this.

[16]So the exiles did as was proposed. Ezra the priest selected men who were family heads, one from each family division, and all of them designated by name. On the first day of the tenth month they sat down to investigate the cases, [17]and by the first day of the first month they finished dealing with all the men who had married foreign women.

Those Guilty of Intermarriage

[18]Among the descendants of the priests, the following had married foreign women:

From the descendants of Joshua son of Jozadak, and his brothers: Maaseiah, Eliezer, Jarib and Gedaliah. [19](They all gave their hands in pledge to put away their wives, and for their guilt they each presented a ram from the flock as a guilt offering.)

[20]From the descendants of Immer:
Hanani and Zebadiah.

[21]From the descendants of Harim:
Maaseiah, Elijah, Shemaiah, Jehiel and Uzziah.

[22]From the descendants of Pashhur:
Elioenai, Maaseiah, Ishmael, Nethanel, Jozabad and Elasah.

[23]Among the Levites:
Jozabad, Shimei, Kelaiah (that is, Kelita), Pethahiah, Judah and Eliezer.

[24]From the musicians:
Eliashib.
From the gatekeepers:
Shallum, Telem and Uri.

[25]And among the other Israelites:

From the descendants of Parosh:
Ramiah, Izziah, Malkijah, Mijamin, Eleazar, Malkijah and Benaiah.

[26]From the descendants of Elam:
Mattaniah, Zechariah, Jehiel, Abdi, Jeremoth and Elijah.

[27]From the descendants of Zattu:
Elioenai, Eliashib, Mattaniah, Jeremoth, Zabad and Aziza.

[28]From the descendants of Bebai:
Jehohanan, Hananiah, Zabbai and Athlai.

[29]From the descendants of Bani:
Meshullam, Malluk, Adaiah, Jashub, Sheal and Jeremoth.

---

a 11 Or *Now make confession to*

30 From the descendants of Pahath-Moab:

Adna, Kelal, Benaiah, Maaseiah, Mattaniah, Bezalel, Binnui and Manasseh.

31 From the descendants of Harim:

Eliezer, Ishijah, Malkijah, Shemaiah, Shimeon, 32 Benjamin, Malluk and Shemariah.

33 From the descendants of Hashum:

Mattenai, Mattattah, Zabad, Eliphelet, Jeremai, Manasseh and Shimei.

34 From the descendants of Bani:

Maadai, Amram, Uel, 35 Benaiah, Bedeiah, Keluhi, 36 Vaniah, Meremoth, Eliashib, 37 Mattaniah, Mattenai and Jaasu.

38 From the descendants of Binnui: a

Shimei, 39 Shelemiah, Nathan, Adaiah, 40 Maknadebai, Shashai, Sharai, 41 Azarel, Shelemiah, Shemariah, 42 Shallum, Amariah and Joseph.

43 From the descendants of Nebo:

Jeiel, Mattithiah, Zabad, Zebina, Jaddai, Joel and Benaiah.

44 All these had married foreign women, and some of them had children by these wives. b

---

a 37,38 See Septuagint (also 1 Esdras 9:34); Hebrew *Jaasu* 38*and Bani and Binnui,*   b 44 Or *and they sent them away with their children*

nehemiah

AUTHOR: Possibly Ezra or Nehemiah

DATE: Around 430 B.C.

THEME: God calls his people to persevere.

Nehemiah's Prayer

1 The words of Nehemiah son of Haka-liah:

In the month of Kislev in the twentieth year, while I was in the citadel of Susa, ²Ha-nani, one of my brothers, came from Judah with some other men, and I questioned them about the Jewish remnant that had survived the exile, and also about Jerusalem.

³They said to me, "Those who survived the exile and are back in the province are in great trouble and disgrace. The wall of Jeru-salem is broken down, and its gates have been burned with fire."

⁴When I heard these things, I sat down and wept. For some days I mourned and fasted and prayed before the God of heaven. ⁵Then I said:

"LORD, the God of heaven, the great and awesome God, who keeps his cov-enant of love with those who love him and keep his commandments, ⁶let your ear be attentive and your eyes open to hear the prayer your servant is praying before you day and night for your ser-vants, the people of Israel. I confess the sins we Israelites, including myself and my ancestral family, have committed against you. ⁷We have acted very wick-edly toward you. We have not obeyed the commands, decrees and laws you gave your servant Moses.

⁸"Remember the instruction you gave your servant Moses, saying, 'If you are unfaithful, I will scatter you among the nations, ⁹but if you return to me and obey my commands, then even if your exiled people are at the farthest horizon, I will gather them from there and bring them to the place I have cho-sen as a dwelling for my Name.'

¹⁰"They are your servants and your people, whom you redeemed by your great strength and your mighty hand. ¹¹Lord, let your ear be attentive to the prayer of this your servant and to the prayer of your servants who delight in revering your name. Give your servant success today by granting him favor in the presence of this man."

I was cupbearer to the king.

Artaxerxes Sends Nehemiah to Jerusalem

2 In the month of Nisan in the twenti-eth year of King Artaxerxes, when wine was brought for him, I took the wine and gave it to the king. I had not been sad in his presence before, ²so the king asked me, "Why does your face look so sad when you are not ill? This can be nothing but sadness of heart."

I was very much afraid, ³but I said to the king, "May the king live forever! Why should my face not look sad when the city where my ancestors are buried lies in ruins, and its gates have been destroyed by fire?"

⁴The king said to me, "What is it you want?"

Then I prayed to the God of heaven, ⁵and I answered the king, "If it pleases the king and if your servant has found favor in his sight, let him send me to the city in Judah where my ancestors are buried so that I can rebuild it."

⁶Then the king, with the queen sitting be-side him, asked me, "How long will your journey take, and when will you get back?" It pleased the king to send me; so I set a time.

⁷I also said to him, "If it pleases the king, may I have letters to the governors of Trans-Euphrates, so that they will provide me safe-conduct until I arrive in Judah? ⁸And may I have a letter to Asaph, keeper of the royal park, so he will give me timber to make beams for the gates of the citadel by the temple and for the city wall and for the residence I will occupy?" And because the gracious hand of my God was on me, the king granted my requests. ⁹So I went to the governors of Trans-Euphrates and gave them the king's letters. The king had also sent army officers and cavalry with me.

¹⁰When Sanballat the Horonite and Tobiah the Ammonite official heard about this, they were very much disturbed that someone had come to promote the welfare of the Israelites.

Nehemiah Inspects Jerusalem's Walls

¹¹I went to Jerusalem, and after staying there three days ¹²I set out during the night with a few others. I had not told anyone what my God had put in my heart to do for Jerusalem. There were no mounts with me except the one I was riding on.

¹³By night I went out through the Valley Gate toward the Jackal*ᵃ* Well and the Dung Gate, examining the walls of Jerusalem, which had been broken down, and its gates, which had been destroyed by fire. ¹⁴Then I moved on toward the Fountain Gate and the King's Pool, but there was not enough room for my mount to get through; ¹⁵so I went up the valley by night, examining the wall. Finally, I turned back and reentered through the Valley Gate. ¹⁶The officials did not know where I had gone or what I was doing, because as yet I had said nothing to the Jews or the priests or nobles or officials or any others who would be doing the work.

¹⁷Then I said to them, "You see the trouble we are in: Jerusalem lies in ruins, and its gates have been burned with fire. Come, let us rebuild the wall of Jerusalem, and we will no longer be in disgrace." ¹⁸I also told them about the gracious hand of my God on me and what the king had said to me.

They replied, "Let us start rebuilding." So they began this good work.

¹⁹But when Sanballat the Horonite, Tobiah the Ammonite official and Geshem the Arab heard about it, they mocked and ridiculed us. "What is this you are doing?" they asked. "Are you rebelling against the king?"

²⁰I answered them by saying, "The God of heaven will give us success. We his servants will start rebuilding, but as for you, you have no share in Jerusalem or any claim or historic right to it."

Builders of the Wall

3 Eliashib the high priest and his fellow priests went to work and rebuilt the Sheep Gate. They dedicated it and set its doors in place, building as far as the Tower of the Hundred, which they dedicated, and as far as the Tower of Hananel. ²The men of Jericho built the adjoining section, and Zakkur son of Imri built next to them.

³The Fish Gate was rebuilt by the sons of Hassenaah. They laid its beams and put its doors and bolts and bars in place. ⁴Meremoth son of Uriah, the son of Hakkoz, repaired the next section. Next to him Meshullam son of Berekiah, the son of Meshezabel, made repairs, and next to him Zadok son of Baana also made repairs. ⁵The next section was repaired by the men of Tekoa, but their nobles would not put their shoulders to the work under their supervisors.*ᵇ*

⁶The Jeshanah*ᶜ* Gate was repaired by Joiada son of Paseah and Meshullam son of Besodeiah. They laid its beams and put its doors with their bolts and bars in place. ⁷Next to them, repairs were made by men from Gibeon and Mizpah—Melatiah of Gibeon and Jadon of Meronoth—places under the authority of the governor of Trans-Euphrates. ⁸Uzziel son of Harhaiah, one of the goldsmiths, repaired the next section; and Hananiah, one of the perfume-makers, made repairs next to that. They restored Jerusalem as far as the Broad Wall. ⁹Rephaiah son of Hur, ruler of a half-district of Jerusalem, repaired the next section. ¹⁰Adjoining this, Jedaiah son of Harumaph made repairs opposite his house, and Hattush son of Hashabneiah made repairs next to him. ¹¹Malkijah son of Harim and Hasshub son of Pahath-Moab repaired another section and the Tower of the Ovens. ¹²Shallum son of Hallohesh, ruler of a half-district of Jerusa-

---

a 13 Or *Serpent* or *Fig* *b 5* Or *their Lord* or *the governor* *c 6* Or *Old* lem, repaired the next section with the help of his daughters.

¹³The Valley Gate was repaired by Hanun and the residents of Zanoah. They rebuilt it and put its doors with their bolts and bars in place. They also repaired a thousand cubits*a* of the wall as far as the Dung Gate.

¹⁴The Dung Gate was repaired by Malkijah son of Rekab, ruler of the district of Beth Hakkerem. He rebuilt it and put its doors with their bolts and bars in place.

¹⁵The Fountain Gate was repaired by Shallun son of Kol-Hozeh, ruler of the district of Mizpah. He rebuilt it, roofing it over and putting its doors and bolts and bars in place. He also repaired the wall of the Pool of Siloam,*b* by the King's Garden, as far as the steps going down from the City of David. ¹⁶Beyond him, Nehemiah son of Azbuk, ruler of a half-district of Beth Zur, made repairs up to a point opposite the tombs*c* of David, as far as the artificial pool and the House of the Heroes.

¹⁷Next to him, the repairs were made by the Levites under Rehum son of Bani. Beside him, Hashabiah, ruler of half the district of Keilah, carried out repairs for his district. ¹⁸Next to him, the repairs were made by their neighbors under Binnui*d* son of Henadad, ruler of the other half-district of Keilah. ¹⁹Next to him, Ezer son of Jeshua, ruler of Mizpah, repaired another section, from a point facing the ascent to the armory as far as the angle of the wall. ²⁰Next to him, Baruch son of Zabbai zealously repaired another section, from the angle to the entrance of the house of Eliashib the high priest. ²¹Next to him, Meremoth son of Uriah, the son of Hakkoz, repaired another section, from the entrance of Eliashib's house to the end of it.

²²The repairs next to him were made by the priests from the surrounding region. ²³Beyond them, Benjamin and Hasshub made repairs in front of their house; and next to them, Azariah son of Maaseiah, the son of Ananiah, made repairs beside his house. ²⁴Next to him, Binnui son of Henadad repaired another section, from Azariah's

house to the angle and the corner, ²⁵and Palal son of Uzai worked opposite the angle and the tower projecting from the upper palace near the court of the guard. Next to him, Pedaiah son of Parosh ²⁶and the temple servants living on the hill of Ophel made repairs up to a point opposite the Water Gate toward the east and the projecting tower. ²⁷Next to them, the men of Tekoa repaired another section, from the great projecting tower to the wall of Ophel.

²⁸Above the Horse Gate, the priests made repairs, each in front of his own house. ²⁹Next to them, Zadok son of Immer made repairs opposite his house. Next to him, Shemaiah son of Shekaniah, the guard at the East Gate, made repairs. ³⁰Next to him, Hananiah son of Shelemiah, and Hanun, the sixth son of Zalaph, repaired another section. Next to them, Meshullam son of Berekiah made repairs opposite his living quarters. ³¹Next to him, Malkijah, one of the goldsmiths, made repairs as far as the house of the temple servants and the merchants, opposite the Inspection Gate, and as far as the room above the corner; ³²and between the room above the corner and the Sheep Gate the goldsmiths and merchants made repairs.

Opposition to the Rebuilding

4 *When Sanballat heard that we were rebuilding the wall, he became angry and was greatly incensed. He ridiculed the Jews, ²and in the presence of his associates and the army of Samaria, he said, "What are those feeble Jews doing? Will they restore their wall? Will they offer sacrifices? Will they finish in a day? Can they bring the stones back to life from those heaps of rubble—burned as they are?"

³Tobiah the Ammonite, who was at his side, said, "What they are building—even a fox climbing up on it would break down their wall of stones!"

⁴Hear us, our God, for we are despised. Turn their insults back on their own heads. Give them over as plunder in a land of captivity. ⁵Do not cover up their guilt or blot out

---

a 13 That is, about 1,500 feet or about 450 meters *b 15* Hebrew *Shelah,* a variant of *Shiloah,* that is, Siloam   *c 16* Hebrew; Septuagint, some Vulgate manuscripts and Syriac *tomb*   *d 18* Two Hebrew manuscripts and Syriac (see also Septuagint and verse 24); most Hebrew manuscripts *Bavvai*

* 4:1-6 is numbered 3:33-38 in Hebrew texts.

their sins from your sight, for they have thrown insults in the face of[a] the builders.

⁶So we rebuilt the wall till all of it reached half its height, for the people worked with all their heart.

*⁷But when Sanballat, Tobiah, the Arabs, the Ammonites and the people of Ashdod heard that the repairs to Jerusalem's walls had gone ahead and that the gaps were being closed, they were very angry. ⁸They all plotted together to come and fight against Jerusalem and stir up trouble against it. ⁹But we prayed to our God and posted a guard day and night to meet this threat.

¹⁰Meanwhile, the people in Judah said, "The strength of the laborers is giving out, and there is so much rubble that we cannot rebuild the wall."

¹¹Also our enemies said, "Before they know it or see us, we will be right there among them and will kill them and put an end to the work."

¹²Then the Jews who lived near them came and told us ten times over, "Wherever you turn, they will attack us."

¹³Therefore I stationed some of the people behind the lowest points of the wall at the exposed places, posting them by families, with their swords, spears and bows. ¹⁴After I looked things over, I stood up and said to the nobles, the officials and the rest of the people, "Don't be afraid of them. Remember the Lord, who is great and awesome, and fight for your people, your sons and your daughters, your wives and your homes."

¹⁵When our enemies heard that we were aware of their plot and that God had frustrated it, we all returned to the wall, each to our own work.

¹⁶From that day on, half of my men did the work, while the other half were equipped with spears, shields, bows and armor. The officers posted themselves behind all the people of Judah ¹⁷who were building the wall. Those who carried materials did their work with one hand and held a weapon in the other, ¹⁸and each of the builders wore his sword at his side as he worked. But the man who sounded the trumpet stayed with me.

¹⁹Then I said to the nobles, the officials

and the rest of the people, "The work is extensive and spread out, and we are widely separated from each other along the wall. ²⁰Wherever you hear the sound of the trumpet, join us there. Our God will fight for us!"

²¹So we continued the work with half the men holding spears, from the first light of dawn till the stars came out. ²²At that time I also said to the people, "Have every man and his helper stay inside Jerusalem at night, so they can serve us as guards by night and as workers by day." ²³Neither I nor my brothers nor my men nor the guards with me took off our clothes; each had his weapon, even when he went for water.[b]

Nehemiah Helps the Poor

5 Now the men and their wives raised a great outcry against their fellow Jews. ²Some were saying, "We and our sons and daughters are numerous; in order for us to eat and stay alive, we must get grain."

³Others were saying, "We are mortgaging our fields, our vineyards and our homes to get grain during the famine."

⁴Still others were saying, "We have had to borrow money to pay the king's tax on our fields and vineyards. ⁵Although we are of the same flesh and blood as the rest of our people and though our children are as good as theirs, yet we have to subject our sons and daughters to slavery. Some of our daughters have already been enslaved, but we are powerless, because our fields and our vineyards belong to others."

⁶When I heard their outcry and these charges, I was very angry. ⁷I pondered them in my mind and then accused the nobles and officials. I told them, "You are charging your own people interest!" So I called together a large meeting to deal with them ⁸and said: "As far as possible, we have bought back our fellow Jews who were sold to the Gentiles. Now you are selling your own people, only for them to be sold back to us!" They kept quiet, because they could find nothing to say.

⁹So I continued, "What you are doing is not right. Shouldn't you walk in the fear of our God to avoid the reproach of our Gentile enemies? ¹⁰I and my brothers and my men are also lending the people money and

---

a 5 Or *have aroused your anger before*   *b 23* The meaning of the Hebrew for this clause is uncertain.

* 4:7-23 is numbered 4:1-17 in Hebrew texts.

grain. But let us stop charging interest! [11]Give back to them immediately their fields, vineyards, olive groves and houses, and also the interest you are charging them—one percent of the money, grain, new wine and olive oil."

[12]"We will give it back," they said. "And we will not demand anything more from them. We will do as you say."

Then I summoned the priests and made the nobles and officials take an oath to do what they had promised. [13]I also shook out the folds of my robe and said, "In this way may God shake out of their houses and possessions anyone who does not keep this promise. So may such a person be shaken out and emptied!"

At this the whole assembly said, "Amen," and praised the LORD. And the people did as they had promised.

[14]Moreover, from the twentieth year of King Artaxerxes, when I was appointed to be their governor in the land of Judah, until his thirty-second year—twelve years—neither I nor my brothers ate the food allotted to the governor. [15]But the earlier governors—those preceding me—placed a heavy burden on the people and took forty shekels[a] of silver from them in addition to food and wine. Their assistants also lorded it over the people. But out of reverence for God I did not act like that. [16]Instead, I devoted myself to the work on this wall. All my men were assembled there for the work; we[b] did not acquire any land.

[17]Furthermore, a hundred and fifty Jews and officials ate at my table, as well as those who came to us from the surrounding nations. [18]Each day one ox, six choice sheep and some poultry were prepared for me, and every ten days an abundant supply of wine of all kinds. In spite of all this, I never demanded the food allotted to the governor, because the demands were heavy on these people.

[19]Remember me with favor, my God, for all I have done for these people.

Further Opposition to the Rebuilding

6 When word came to Sanballat, Tobiah, Geshem the Arab and the rest of our enemies that I had rebuilt the wall and not a gap was left in it—though up to that time I had not set the doors in the gates— [2]Sanballat and Geshem sent me this message: "Come, let us meet together in one of the villages[c] on the plain of Ono."

But they were scheming to harm me; [3]so I sent messengers to them with this reply: "I am carrying on a great project and cannot go down. Why should the work stop while I leave it and go down to you?" [4]Four times they sent me the same message, and each time I gave them the same answer.

[5]Then, the fifth time, Sanballat sent his aide to me with the same message, and in his hand was an unsealed letter [6]in which was written:

"It is reported among the nations— and Geshem[d] says it is true—that you and the Jews are plotting to revolt, and therefore you are building the wall. Moreover, according to these reports you are about to become their king [7]and have even appointed prophets to make this proclamation about you in Jerusalem: 'There is a king in Judah!' Now this report will get back to the king; so come, let us meet together."

[8]I sent him this reply: "Nothing like what you are saying is happening; you are just making it up out of your head."

[9]They were all trying to frighten us, thinking, "Their hands will get too weak for the work, and it will not be completed."

But I prayed, "Now strengthen my hands."

[10]One day I went to the house of Shemaiah son of Delaiah, the son of Mehetabel, who was shut in at his home. He said, "Let us meet in the house of God, inside the temple, and let us close the temple doors, because some people are coming to kill you— by night they are coming to kill you."

[11]But I said, "Should someone like me run away? Or should one like me go into the temple to save his life? I will not go!" [12]I realized that God had not sent him, but that he had prophesied against me because Tobiah and Sanballat had hired him. [13]He had been hired to intimidate me so that I would commit a sin by doing this, and then they would give me a bad name to discredit me.

---

a 15 That is, about 1 pound or about 460 grams manuscripts, Septuagint, Vulgate and Syriac / of Geshem   *b 16* Most Hebrew manuscripts; some Hebrew   *c 2* Or *in Kephirim*   *d 6* Hebrew *Gashmu*, a variant

[14]Remember Tobiah and Sanballat, my God, because of what they have done; remember also the prophet Noadiah and how she and the rest of the prophets have been trying to intimidate me. [15]So the wall was completed on the twenty-fifth of Elul, in fifty-two days.

Opposition to the Completed Wall

[16]When all our enemies heard about this, all the surrounding nations were afraid and lost their self-confidence, because they realized that this work had been done with the help of our God.

[17]Also, in those days the nobles of Judah were sending many letters to Tobiah, and replies from Tobiah kept coming to them. [18]For many in Judah were under oath to him, since he was son-in-law to Shekaniah son of Arah, and his son Jehohanan had married the daughter of Meshullam son of Berekiah. [19]Moreover, they kept reporting to me his good deeds and then telling him what I said. And Tobiah sent letters to intimidate me.

7 After the wall had been rebuilt and I had set the doors in place, the gatekeepers, the musicians and the Levites were appointed. [2]I put in charge of Jerusalem my brother Hanani, along with Hananiah the commander of the citadel, because he was trustworthy and feared God more than most people do. [3]I said to them, "The gates of Jerusalem are not to be opened until the sun is hot. While the gatekeepers are still on duty, have them shut the doors and bar them. Also appoint residents of Jerusalem as guards, some at their posts and some near their own houses."

The List of the Exiles Who Returned

[4]Now the city was large and spacious, but there were few people in it, and the houses had not yet been rebuilt. [5]So my God put it into my heart to assemble the nobles, the officials and the common people for registration by families. I found the genealogical record of those who had been the first to return. This is what I found written there:

[6]These are the people of the province who came up from the captivity of the exiles whom Nebuchadnezzar king of Babylon had taken captive (they returned to Jerusalem and Judah, each to his own town, [7]in company with Zerubbabel, Joshua, Nehemiah, Azariah, Raamiah, Nahamani, Mordecai, Bilshan, Mispereth, Bigvai, Nehum and Baanah):

The list of the men of Israel:

[8]the descendants of Parosh	2,172
[9]of Shephatiah	372
[10]of Arah	652
[11]of Pahath-Moab (through the line of Jeshua and Joab)	2,818
[12]of Elam	1,254
[13]of Zattu	845
[14]of Zakkai	760
[15]of Binnui	648
[16]of Bebai	628
[17]of Azgad	2,322
[18]of Adonikam	667
[19]of Bigvai	2,067
[20]of Adin	655
[21]of Ater (through Hezekiah)	98
[22]of Hashum	328
[23]of Bezai	324
[24]of Hariph	112
[25]of Gibeon	95
[26]the men of Bethlehem and Netophah	188
[27]of Anathoth	128
[28]of Beth Azmaveth	42
[29]of Kiriath Jearim, Kephirah and Beeroth	743
[30]of Ramah and Geba	621
[31]of Mikmash	122
[32]of Bethel and Ai	123
[33]of the other Nebo	52
[34]of the other Elam	1,254
[35]of Harim	320
[36]of Jericho	345
[37]of Lod, Hadid and Ono	721
[38]of Senaah	3,930

[39]The priests:

the descendants of Jedaiah (through the family of Jeshua)	973
[40]of Immer	1,052
[41]of Pashhur	1,247
[42]of Harim	1,017

[43]The Levites:

the descendants of Jeshua (through Kadmiel through the line of Hodaviah)	74

[44]The musicians:

the descendants of Asaph	148

45The gatekeepers:

the descendants of
Shallum, Ater, Talmon, Akkub,
Hatita and Shobai   138

46The temple servants:

the descendants of
Ziha, Hasupha, Tabbaoth,
47Keros, Sia, Padon,
48Lebana, Hagaba, Shalmai,
49Hanan, Giddel, Gahar,
50Reaiah, Rezin, Nekoda,
51Gazzam, Uzza, Paseah,
52Besai, Meunim, Nephusim,
53Bakbuk, Hakupha, Harhur,
54Bazluth, Mehida, Harsha,
55Barkos, Sisera, Temah,
56Neziah and Hatipha

57The descendants of the servants of
Solomon:

the descendants of
Sotai, Sophereth, Perida,
58Jaala, Darkon, Giddel,
59Shephatiah, Hattil,
Pokereth-Hazzebaim and Amon

60The temple servants and the descendants of the servants of
Solomon   392

61The following came up from the
towns of Tel Melah, Tel Harsha, Kerub,
Addon and Immer, but they could not
show that their families were descended from Israel:

62the descendants of
Delaiah, Tobiah and Nekoda 642

63And from among the priests:

the descendants of
Hobaiah, Hakkoz and Barzillai (a
man who had married a daughter
of Barzillai the Gileadite and was
called by that name).

64These searched for their family
records, but they could not find them
and so were excluded from the priesthood as unclean. 65The governor,
therefore, ordered them not to eat any
of the most sacred food until there

should be a priest ministering with the
Urim and Thummim.

66The whole company numbered
42,360, 67besides their 7,337 male and
female slaves; and they also had 245
male and female singers. 68There were
736 horses, 245 mules,ᵃ 69435 camels
and 6,720 donkeys.

70Some of the heads of the families
contributed to the work. The governor
gave to the treasury 1,000 daricsᵇ of
gold, 50 bowls and 530 garments for
priests. 71Some of the heads of the
families gave to the treasury for the
work 20,000 daricsᶜ of gold and 2,200
minasᵈ of silver. 72The total given by
the rest of the people was 20,000 darics of gold, 2,000 minasᵉ of silver and
67 garments for priests.

73The priests, the Levites, the gatekeepers, the musicians and the temple
servants, along with certain of the people and the rest of the Israelites, settled
in their own towns.

Ezra Reads the Law

8 When the seventh month came and the
Israelites had settled in their towns,
1all the people assembled with one
accord in the square before the Water
Gate. They told Ezra the teacher of the Law
to bring out the Book of the Law of Moses,
which the Lord had commanded for Israel.

2So on the first day of the seventh month
Ezra the priest brought the Law before the
assembly, which was made up of men and
women and all who were able to understand. 3He read it aloud from daybreak till
noon as he faced the square before the Water Gate in the presence of the men, women
and others who could understand. And all
the people listened attentively to the Book
of the Law.

4Ezra the teacher of the Law stood on a
high wooden platform built for the occasion.
Beside him on his right stood Mattithiah,
Shema, Anaiah, Uriah, Hilkiah and Maaseiah; and on his left were Pedaiah, Mishael,
Malkijah, Hashum, Hashbaddanah, Zechariah and Meshullam.

---

a 68 Some Hebrew manuscripts (see also Ezra 2:66); most Hebrew manuscripts do not have this verse.
b 70 That is, about 19 pounds or about 8.5 kilograms   c 71 That is, about 375 pounds or about 170
kilograms; also in verse 72   d 71 That is, about 1 1/3 tons or about 1.2 metric tons   e 72 That is,
about 1 1/4 tons or about 1.1 metric tons

WEDNESDAY

FROM SORROW TO JOY

Nehemiah 8:1–18 or 8:10–11

D. L. MOODY {AD 1837–1899}

The mass of Christians make a little dark world of their own and live there ... No sunshine comes into their chambers, and no fire burns on the hearth ... And there they live, from year to year, in gloom and sadness, because they do not let God's sunshine in. I meet many persons who can talk for hours of their troubles, sorrows and who seem to forget that God ever made a flower, star, or a sunbeam, nor do they recall a single kind, tender act God has had for them.

Bryce Morgan

At some point, all of us have felt the overwhelming pressures of life and searched for the strength to make it through. Oftentimes, that strength to cope comes from a sense of peace and confidence we derive from looking to our future. We might think to ourselves, "If I can just make it to Friday, the weekend will be exactly what I need" or "Just one more month until I change jobs, and then things will be fine." For the Jews who were returning to Israel from decades of exile, the strength to cope was something they desperately needed ... As Ezra and the other leaders sought to remind the people of God's call by reading from the Law of Moses, the Jews were convicted to the point of grief because they knew they were unworthy of the restoration with which God had blessed them. Yet the strength they needed to "make it through"—even more so, the strength they needed to flourish—was not to be found in grief, but in joy.

Ezra and Nehemiah knew that God wanted His blessings to bring joy to the people, the joy that could only come from knowing, loving, and serving the Creator. Grief is often a necessary stop on the path, but joy is the destination. Yes, we can look to our future blessings as a source of strength, but as the Levites encouraged the people in verse 11, "be still, for [this is a holy day]." The present experience of God's grace in light of our sin should bring us the joy we desire. And only in that joy, the joy of new life, the joy of being *in* Christ, will we find the strength not only to survive, but also to flourish.

reflection

1. Because of the depth of their past sin, the Jewish people found it difficult to rejoice in the blessings of God's restoration. Why did Nehemiah urge them to move past grief to joy?

2. How can you relate to the Jews in this passage?

3. In what ways have you blown it—perhaps badly—and now find it hard to move past your sorrow and regret over your sin?

For your next devotional reading, go to page 543.

⁵Ezra opened the book. All the people could see him because he was standing above them; and as he opened it, the people all stood up. ⁶Ezra praised the LORD, the great God; and all the people lifted their hands and responded, "Amen! Amen!" Then they bowed down and worshiped the LORD with their faces to the ground.

⁷The Levites—Jeshua, Bani, Sherebiah, Jamin, Akkub, Shabbethai, Hodiah, Maaseiah, Kelita, Azariah, Jozabad, Hanan and Pelaiah—instructed the people in the Law while the people were standing there. ⁸They read from the Book of the Law of God, making it clearᵃ and giving the meaning so that the people understood what was being read.

⁹Then Nehemiah the governor, Ezra the priest and teacher of the Law, and the Levites who were instructing the people said to them all, "This day is holy to the LORD your God. Do not mourn or weep." For all the people had been weeping as they listened to the words of the Law.

¹⁰Nehemiah said, "Go and enjoy choice food and sweet drinks, and send some to those who have nothing prepared. This day is holy to our Lord. Do not grieve, for the joy of the LORD is your strength."

¹¹The Levites calmed all the people, saying, "Be still, for this is a holy day. Do not grieve."

¹²Then all the people went away to eat and drink, to send portions of food and to celebrate with great joy, because they now understood the words that had been made known to them.

¹³On the second day of the month, the heads of all the families, along with the priests and the Levites, gathered around Ezra the teacher to give attention to the words of the Law. ¹⁴They found written in the Law, which the LORD had commanded through Moses, that the Israelites were to live in temporary shelters during the festival of the seventh month ¹⁵and that they should proclaim this word and spread it throughout their towns and in Jerusalem: "Go out into the hill country and bring back branches from olive and wild olive trees, and from myrtles, palms and shade trees, to make temporary shelters"—as it is written.ᵇ

¹⁶So the people went out and brought back branches and built themselves temporary shelters on their own roofs, in their courtyards, in the courts of the house of God and in the square by the Water Gate and the one by the Gate of Ephraim. ¹⁷The whole company that had returned from exile built temporary shelters and lived in them. From the days of Joshua son of Nun until that day, the Israelites had not celebrated it like this. And their joy was very great.

¹⁸Day after day, from the first day to the last, Ezra read from the Book of the Law of God. They celebrated the festival for seven days, and on the eighth day, in accordance with the regulation, there was an assembly.

The Israelites Confess Their Sins

9 On the twenty-fourth day of the same month, the Israelites gathered together, fasting and wearing sackcloth and putting dust on their heads. ²Those of Israelite descent had separated themselves from all foreigners. They stood in their places and confessed their sins and the sins of their ancestors. ³They stood where they were and read from the Book of the Law of the LORD their God for a quarter of the day, and spent another quarter in confession and in worshiping the LORD their God. ⁴Standing on the stairs of the Levites were Jeshua, Bani, Kadmiel, Shebaniah, Bunni, Sherebiah, Bani and Kenani. They cried out with loud voices to the LORD their God. ⁵And the Levites—Jeshua, Kadmiel, Bani, Hashabneiah, Sherebiah, Hodiah, Shebaniah and Pethahiah—said: "Stand up and praise the LORD your God, who is from everlasting to everlasting.ᶜ"

"Blessed be your glorious name, and may it be exalted above all blessing and praise. ⁶You alone are the LORD. You made the heavens, even the highest heavens, and all their starry host, the earth and all that is on it, the seas and all that is in them. You give life to everything, and the multitudes of heaven worship you.

⁷"You are the LORD God, who chose Abram and brought him out of Ur of the Chaldeans and named him Abraham. ⁸You found his heart faithful to you, and you made a covenant with him to give to his descendants the land of the Canaanites, Hittites, Amorites,

Perizzites, Jebusites and Girgashites. You have kept your promise because you are righteous.

⁹"You saw the suffering of our ancestors in Egypt; you heard their cry at the Red Sea.ᵃ ¹⁰You sent signs and wonders against Pharaoh, against all his officials and all the people of his land, for you knew how arrogantly the Egyptians treated them. You made a name for yourself, which remains to this day. ¹¹You divided the sea before them, so that they passed through it on dry ground, but you hurled their pursuers into the depths, like a stone into mighty waters. ¹²By day you led them with a pillar of cloud, and by night with a pillar of fire to give them light on the way they were to take.

¹³"You came down on Mount Sinai; you spoke to them from heaven. You gave them regulations and laws that are just and right, and decrees and commands that are good. ¹⁴You made known to them your holy Sabbath and gave them commands, decrees and laws through your servant Moses. ¹⁵In their hunger you gave them bread from heaven and in their thirst you brought them water from the rock; you told them to go in and take possession of the land you had sworn with uplifted hand to give them.

¹⁶"But they, our ancestors, became arrogant and stiff-necked, and did not obey your commands. ¹⁷They refused to listen and failed to remember the miracles you performed among them. They became stiff-necked and in their rebellion appointed a leader in order to return to their slavery. But you are a forgiving God, gracious and compassionate, slow to anger and abounding in love. Therefore you did not desert them, ¹⁸even when they cast for themselves an image of a calf and said, 'This is your god, who brought you up out of Egypt,' or when they committed awful blasphemies.

¹⁹"Because of your great compassion you did not abandon them in the wilderness. By day the pillar of cloud did not cease to guide them on their path, nor the pillar of fire by night to shine on the way they were to take. ²⁰You gave your good Spirit to instruct them. You did not withhold your manna from their mouths, and you gave them water for their thirst. ²¹For forty years you sustained them in the wilderness; they lacked nothing, their clothes did not wear out nor did their feet become swollen.

²²"You gave them kingdoms and nations, allotting to them even the remotest frontiers. They took over the country of Sihonᵇ king of Heshbon and the country of Og king of Bashan. ²³You made their children as numerous as the stars in the sky, and you brought them into the land that you told their parents to enter and possess. ²⁴Their children went in and took possession of the land. You subdued before them the Canaanites, who lived in the land; you gave the Canaanites into their hands, along with their kings and the peoples of the land, to deal with them as they pleased. ²⁵They captured fortified cities and fertile land; they took possession of houses filled with all kinds of good things, wells already dug, vineyards, olive groves and fruit trees in abundance. They ate to the full and were well-nourished; they reveled in your great goodness.

²⁶"But they were disobedient and rebelled against you; they put your law behind their backs. They killed your prophets, who had warned them in order to turn them back to you; they committed awful blasphemies. ²⁷So you delivered them into the hands of their enemies, who oppressed them. But when they were oppressed they cried out to you. From heaven you heard them, and in your great compassion you gave them deliverers, who rescued them from the hand of their enemies.

²⁸"But as soon as they were at rest, they again did what was evil in your sight. Then you abandoned them to the hand of their enemies so that they

ᵃ 9 Or the Sea of Reeds   ᵇ 22 One Hebrew manuscript and Septuagint; most Hebrew manuscripts Sihon, that is, the country of the ruled over them. And when they cried out to you again, you heard from heaven, and in your compassion you delivered them time after time.

29 "You warned them in order to turn them back to your law, but they became arrogant and disobeyed your commands. They sinned against your ordinances, of which you said, 'Whoever obeys them will live by them.' Stubbornly they turned their backs on you, became stiff-necked and refused to listen. 30 For many years you were patient with them. By your Spirit you warned them through your prophets. Yet they paid no attention, so you gave them into the hands of the neighboring peoples. 31 But in your great mercy you did not put an end to them or abandon them, for you are a gracious and merciful God.

32 "Now therefore, our God, the great God, mighty and awesome, who keeps his covenant of love, do not let all this hardship seem trifling in your eyes—the hardship that has come on us, on our kings and leaders, on our priests and prophets, on our ancestors and all your people, from the days of the kings of Assyria until today. 33 In all that has happened to us, you have remained righteous; you have acted faithfully, while we acted wickedly. 34 Our kings, our leaders, our priests and our ancestors did not follow your law; they did not pay attention to your commands or the statutes you warned them to keep. 35 Even while they were in their kingdom, enjoying your great goodness to them in the spacious and fertile land you gave them, they did not serve you or turn from their evil ways.

36 "But see, we are slaves today, slaves in the land you gave our ancestors so they could eat its fruit and the other good things it produces. 37 Because of our sins, its abundant harvest goes to the kings you have placed over us. They rule over our bodies and our cattle as they please. We are in great distress.

The Agreement of the People

*38 "In view of all this, we are making a binding agreement, putting it in writing, and our leaders, our Levites and our priests are affixing their seals to it."

10 *Those who sealed it were:

Nehemiah the governor, the son of Hakaliah.

Zedekiah, 2 Seraiah, Azariah, Jeremiah, 3 Pashhur, Amariah, Malkijah, 4 Hattush, Shebaniah, Malluk, 5 Harim, Meremoth, Obadiah, 6 Daniel, Ginnethon, Baruch, 7 Meshullam, Abijah, Mijamin, 8 Maaziah, Bilgai and Shemaiah.
These were the priests.

9 The Levites:

Jeshua son of Azaniah, Binnui of the sons of Henadad, Kadmiel, 10 and their associates: Shebaniah, Hodiah, Kelita, Pelaiah, Hanan, 11 Mika, Rehob, Hashabiah, 12 Zakkur, Sherebiah, Shebaniah, 13 Hodiah, Bani and Beninu.

14 The leaders of the people:

Parosh, Pahath-Moab, Elam, Zattu, Bani, 15 Bunni, Azgad, Bebai, 16 Adonijah, Bigvai, Adin, 17 Ater, Hezekiah, Azzur, 18 Hodiah, Hashum, Bezai, 19 Hariph, Anathoth, Nebai, 20 Magpiash, Meshullam, Hezir, 21 Meshezabel, Zadok, Jaddua, 22 Pelatiah, Hanan, Anaiah, 23 Hoshea, Hananiah, Hasshub, 24 Hallohesh, Pilha, Shobek, 25 Rehum, Hashabnah, Maaseiah, 26 Ahiah, Hanan, Anan, 27 Malluk, Harim and Baanah.

28 "The rest of the people—priests, Levites, gatekeepers, musicians, temple servants and all who separated themselves from the neighboring peoples for the sake of the Law of God, together with their wives and all their sons and daughters who are able to understand— 29 all these now join their fellow Israelites the nobles, and bind

---

* 9:38 is numbered 10:1 in Hebrew texts.   * 10:1-39 is numbered 10:2-40 in Hebrew texts.

themselves with a curse and an oath to follow the Law of God given through Moses the servant of God and to obey carefully all the commands, regulations and decrees of the LORD our Lord.

30 "We promise not to give our daughters in marriage to the peoples around us or take their daughters for our sons.

31 "When the neighboring peoples bring merchandise or grain to sell on the Sabbath, we will not buy from them on the Sabbath or on any holy day. Every seventh year we will forgo working the land and will cancel all debts.

32 "We assume the responsibility for carrying out the commands to give a third of a shekel[a] each year for the service of the house of our God: 33 for the bread set out on the table; for the regular grain offerings and burnt offerings; for the offerings on the Sabbaths, at the New Moon feasts and at the appointed festivals; for the holy offerings; for sin offerings[b] to make atonement for Israel; and for all the duties of the house of our God.

34 "We—the priests, the Levites and the people—have cast lots to determine when each of our families is to bring to the house of our God at set times each year a contribution of wood to burn on the altar of the LORD our God, as it is written in the Law.

35 "We also assume responsibility for bringing to the house of the LORD each year the firstfruits of our crops and of every fruit tree.

36 "As it is also written in the Law, we will bring the firstborn of our sons and of our cattle, of our herds and of our flocks to the house of our God, to the priests ministering there.

37 "Moreover, we will bring to the storerooms of the house of our God, to the priests, the first of our ground meal, of our ⌊grain⌋ offerings, of the fruit of all our trees and of our new wine and olive oil. And we will bring a tithe of our crops to the Levites, for it is the Levites who collect the tithes in all the towns where we work. 38 A priest descended from Aaron is to accompany the Levites when they receive the tithes, and the Levites are to bring a tenth of the tithes up to the house of our God, to the storerooms of the treasury. 39 The people of Israel, including the Levites, are to bring their contributions of grain, new wine and olive oil to the storerooms, where the articles for the sanctuary and for the ministering priests, the gatekeepers and the musicians are also kept.

"We will not neglect the house of our God."

The New Residents of Jerusalem

11 Now the leaders of the people settled in Jerusalem. The rest of the people cast lots to bring one out of every ten of them to live in Jerusalem, the holy city, while the remaining nine were to stay in their own towns. 2 The people commended all who volunteered to live in Jerusalem.

3 These are the provincial leaders who settled in Jerusalem (now some Israelites, priests, Levites, temple servants and descendants of Solomon's servants lived in the towns of Judah, each of them on their own property in the various towns, 4 while other people from both Judah and Benjamin lived in Jerusalem):

From the descendants of Judah:

Athaiah son of Uzziah, the son of Zechariah, the son of Amariah, the son of Shephatiah, the son of Mahalalel, a descendant of Perez; 5 and Maaseiah son of Baruch, the son of Kol-Hozeh, the son of Hazaiah, the son of Adaiah, the son of Joiarib, the son of Zechariah, a descendant of Shelah. 6 The descendants of Perez who lived in Jerusalem totaled 468 men of standing.

7 From the descendants of Benjamin:

Sallu son of Meshullam, the son of Joed, the son of Pedaiah, the son of Kolaiah, the son of Maaseiah, the son of Ithiel, the son of Jeshaiah, 8 and his followers, Gabbai and Sallai—928 men. 9 Joel son of Zikri was their chief officer, and Judah son of Hassenuah was over the New Quarter of the city.

---

a 32 That is, about 1/8 ounce or about 4 grams   b 33 Or purification offerings

10From the priests:

Jedaiah; the son of Joiarib; Jakin; 11Seraiah son of Hilkiah, the son of Meshullam, the son of Zadok, the son of Meraioth, the son of Ahitub, the official in charge of the house of God, 12and their associates, who carried on work for the temple—822 men; Adaiah son of Jeroham, the son of Pelaliah, the son of Amzi, the son of Zechariah, the son of Pashhur, the son of Malkijah, 13and his associates, who were heads of families—242 men; Amashsai son of Azarel, the son of Ahzai, the son of Meshillemoth, the son of Immer, 14and his*a* associates, who were men of standing—128. Their chief officer was Zabdiel son of Haggedolim.

15From the Levites:

Shemaiah son of Hasshub, the son of Azrikam, the son of Hashabiah, the son of Bunni; 16Shabbethai and Jozabad, two of the heads of the Levites, who had charge of the outside work of the house of God; 17Mattaniah son of Mika, the son of Zabdi, the son of Asaph, the director who led in thanksgiving and prayer; Bakbukiah, second among his associates; and Abda son of Shammua, the son of Galal, the son of Jeduthun. 18The Levites in the holy city totaled 284.

19The gatekeepers:

Akkub, Talmon and their associates, who kept watch at the gates—172 men.

20The rest of the Israelites, with the priests and Levites, were in all the towns of Judah, each of them on their ancestral property.

21The temple servants lived on the hill of Ophel, and Ziha and Gishpa were in charge of them.

22The chief officer of the Levites in Jerusalem was Uzzi son of Bani, the son of Hashabiah, the son of Mattaniah, the son of Mika. Uzzi was one of Asaph's descendants, who were the musicians responsible for the service of the house of God. 23The musicians were under the king's orders, which regulated their daily activity.

24Pethahiah son of Meshezabel, one of the descendants of Zerah son of Judah, was the king's agent in all affairs relating to the people.

25As for the villages with their fields, some of the people of Judah lived in Kiriath Arba and its surrounding settlements, in Dibon and its settlements, in Jekabzeel and its villages, 26in Jeshua, in Moladah, in Beth Pelet, 27in Hazar Shual, in Beersheba and its settlements, 28in Ziklag, in Mekonah and its settlements, 29in En Rimmon, in Zorah, in Jarmuth, 30Zanoah, Adullam and their villages, in Lachish and its fields, and in Azekah and its settlements. So they were living all the way from Beersheba to the Valley of Hinnom.

31The descendants of the Benjamites from Geba lived in Mikmash, Aija, Bethel and its settlements, 32in Anathoth, Nob and Ananiah, 33in Hazor, Ramah and Gittaim, 34in Hadid, Zeboim and Neballat, 35in Lod and Ono, and in Ge Harashim.

36Some of the divisions of the Levites of Judah settled in Benjamin.

Priests and Levites

12 These were the priests and Levites who returned with Zerubbabel son of Shealtiel and with Joshua:

Seraiah, Jeremiah, Ezra,
2Amariah, Malluk, Hattush,
3Shekaniah, Rehum, Meremoth,
4Iddo, Ginnethon,*b* Abijah,
5Mijamin,*c* Moadiah, Bilgah,
6Shemaiah, Joiarib, Jedaiah,
7Sallu, Amok, Hilkiah and Jedaiah.
These were the leaders of the priests and their associates in the days of Joshua.

8The Levites were Jeshua, Binnui, Kadmiel, Sherebiah, Judah, and also Mattaniah, who, together with his associates, was in charge of the songs of thanksgiving. 9Bakbukiah and Unni, their associates, stood opposite them in the services.

10Joshua was the father of Joiakim, Joiakim the father of Eliashib, Eliashib the father of Joiada, 11Joiada the father of Jonathan, and Jonathan the father of Jaddua.

---

a 14 Most Septuagint manuscripts; Hebrew *their* Neh. 12:16); most Hebrew manuscripts *Ginnethoi*
b 4 Many Hebrew manuscripts and Vulgate (see also
c 5 A variant of *Miniamin*

¹²In the days of Joiakim, these were the heads of the priestly families:

of Seraiah's family, Meraiah;

of Jeremiah's, Hananiah;

¹³of Ezra's, Meshullam;

of Amariah's, Jehohanan;

¹⁴of Malluk's, Jonathan;

of Shekaniah's, ᵃ Joseph;

¹⁵of Harim's, Adna;

of Meremoth's, ᵇ Helkai;

¹⁶of Iddo's, Zechariah;

of Ginnethon's, Meshullam;

¹⁷of Abijah's, Zikri;

of Miniamin's and of Moadiah's, Piltai;

¹⁸of Bilgah's, Shammua;

of Shemaiah's, Jehonathan;

¹⁹of Joiarib's, Mattenai;

of Jedaiah's, Uzzi;

²⁰of Sallu's, Kallai;

of Amok's, Eber;

²¹of Hilkiah's, Hashabiah;

of Jedaiah's, Nethanel.

²²The family heads of the Levites in the days of Eliashib, Joiada, Johanan and Jaddua, as well as those of the priests, were recorded in the reign of Darius the Persian. ²³The family heads among the descendants of Levi up to the time of Johanan son of Eliashib were recorded in the book of the annals. ²⁴And the leaders of the Levites were Hashabiah, Sherebiah, Jeshua son of Kadmiel, and their associates, who stood opposite them to give praise and thanksgiving, one section responding to the other, as prescribed by David the man of God.

²⁵Mattaniah, Bakbukiah, Obadiah, Meshullam, Talmon and Akkub were gatekeepers who guarded the storerooms at the gates. ²⁶They served in the days of Joiakim son of Joshua, the son of Jozadak, and in the days of Nehemiah the governor and of Ezra the priest, the teacher of the Law.

Dedication of the Wall of Jerusalem

²⁷At the dedication of the wall of Jerusalem, the Levites were sought out from where they lived and were brought to Jerusalem to celebrate joyfully the dedication with songs of thanksgiving and with the music of cymbals, harps and lyres. ²⁸The musicians also were brought together from the region around Jerusalem—from the villages of the Netophathites, ²⁹from Beth Gilgal, and from the area of Geba and Azmaveth, for the musicians had built villages for themselves around Jerusalem. ³⁰When the priests and Levites had purified themselves ceremonially, they purified the people, the gates and the wall.

³¹I had the leaders of Judah go up on top ofᶜ the wall. I also assigned two large choirs to give thanks. One was to proceed on top ofᵈ the wall to the right, toward the Dung Gate. ³²Hoshaiah and half the leaders of Judah followed them, ³³along with Azariah, Ezra, Meshullam, ³⁴Judah, Benjamin, Shemaiah, Jeremiah, ³⁵as well as some priests with trumpets, and also Zechariah son of Jonathan, the son of Shemaiah, the son of Mattaniah, the son of Micaiah, the son of Zakkur, the son of Asaph, ³⁶and his associates—Shemaiah, Azarel, Milalai, Gilalai, Maai, Nethanel, Judah and Hanani—with musical instruments ⌊prescribed by⌋ David the man of God. Ezra the teacher of the Law led the procession. ³⁷At the Fountain Gate they continued directly up the steps of the City of David on the ascent to the wall and passed above the site of David's palace to the Water Gate on the east.

³⁸The second choir proceeded in the opposite direction. I followed them on top ofᵉ the wall, together with half the people—past the Tower of the Ovens to the Broad Wall, ³⁹over the Gate of Ephraim, the Jeshanahᶠ Gate, the Fish Gate, the Tower of Hananel and the Tower of the Hundred, as far as the Sheep Gate. At the Gate of the Guard they stopped.

⁴⁰The two choirs that gave thanks then took their places in the house of God; so did I, together with half the officials, ⁴¹as well as the priests—Eliakim, Maaseiah, Miniamin, Micaiah, Elioenai, Zechariah and Hananiah with their trumpets— ⁴²and also Maaseiah, Shemaiah, Eleazar, Uzzi, Jehohanan, Malkijah, Elam and Ezer. The choirs sang under the direction of Jezrahiah. ⁴³And on that day they offered great sacrifices, rejoicing because God had given them great joy. The women and children also rejoiced. The sound of rejoicing in Jerusalem could be heard far away.

⁴⁴At that time men were appointed to be

ᵃ 14 Very many Hebrew manuscripts, some Septuagint manuscripts and Syriac (see also Neh. 12:3); most Hebrew manuscripts *Shebaniah's*   ᵇ 15 Some Septuagint manuscripts (see also Neh. 12:3); Hebrew *Meraioth's*   ᶜ 31 Or *go alongside*   ᵈ 31 Or *proceed alongside*   ᵉ 38 Or *them alongside*   ᶠ 39 Or *Old* in charge of the storerooms for the contributions, firstfruits and tithes. From the fields around the towns they were to bring into the storerooms the portions required by the Law for the priests and the Levites, for Judah was pleased with the ministering priests and Levites. ⁴⁵They performed the service of their God and the service of purification, as did also the musicians and gatekeepers, according to the commands of David and his son Solomon. ⁴⁶For long ago, in the days of David and Asaph, there had been directors for the musicians and for the songs of praise and thanksgiving to God. ⁴⁷So in the days of Zerubbabel and of Nehemiah, all Israel contributed the daily portions for the musicians and the gatekeepers. They also set aside the portion for the other Levites, and the Levites set aside the portion for the descendants of Aaron.

Nehemiah's Final Reforms

13 On that day the Book of Moses was read aloud in the hearing of the people and there it was found written that no Ammonite or Moabite should ever be admitted into the assembly of God, ²because they had not met the Israelites with food and water but had hired Balaam to call a curse down on them. (Our God, however, turned the curse into a blessing.) ³When the people heard this law, they excluded from Israel all who were of foreign descent.

⁴Before this, Eliashib the priest had been put in charge of the storerooms of the house of our God. He was closely associated with Tobiah, ⁵and he had provided him with a large room formerly used to store the grain offerings and incense and temple articles, and also the tithes of grain, new wine and olive oil prescribed for the Levites, musicians and gatekeepers, as well as the contributions for the priests.

⁶But while all this was going on, I was not in Jerusalem, for in the thirty-second year of Artaxerxes king of Babylon I had returned to the king. Some time later I asked his permission ⁷and came back to Jerusalem. Here I learned about the evil thing Eliashib had done in providing Tobiah a room in the courts of the house of God. ⁸I was greatly displeased and threw all Tobiah's household goods out of the room. ⁹I gave orders to purify the rooms, and then I put back into

them the equipment of the house of God, with the grain offerings and the incense.

¹⁰I also learned that the portions assigned to the Levites had not been given to them, and that all the Levites and musicians responsible for the service had gone back to their own fields. ¹¹So I rebuked the officials and asked them, "Why is the house of God neglected?" Then I called them together and stationed them at their posts.

¹²All Judah brought the tithes of grain, new wine and olive oil into the storerooms. ¹³I put Shelemiah the priest, Zadok the scribe, and a Levite named Pedaiah in charge of the storerooms and made Hanan son of Zakkur, the son of Mattaniah, their assistant, because they were considered trustworthy. They were made responsible for distributing the supplies to their fellow Levites.

¹⁴Remember me for this, my God, and do not blot out what I have so faithfully done for the house of my God and its services.

¹⁵In those days I saw people in Judah treading winepresses on the Sabbath and bringing in grain and loading it on donkeys, together with wine, grapes, figs and all other kinds of loads. And they were bringing all this into Jerusalem on the Sabbath. Therefore I warned them against selling food on that day. ¹⁶People from Tyre who lived in Jerusalem were bringing in fish and all kinds of merchandise and selling them in Jerusalem on the Sabbath to the people of Judah. ¹⁷I rebuked the nobles of Judah and said to them, "What is this wicked thing you are doing—desecrating the Sabbath day? ¹⁸Didn't your ancestors do the same things, so that our God brought all this calamity on us and on this city? Now you are stirring up more wrath against Israel by desecrating the Sabbath."

¹⁹When evening shadows fell on the gates of Jerusalem before the Sabbath, I ordered the doors to be shut and not opened until the Sabbath was over. I stationed some of my own men at the gates so that no load could be brought in on the Sabbath day. ²⁰Once or twice the merchants and sellers of all kinds of goods spent the night outside Jerusalem. ²¹But I warned them and said, "Why do you spend the night by the wall? If you do this again, I will lay hands on you." From that time on they no longer came on the Sabbath. ²²Then I commanded the Le-

vites to purify themselves and go and guard the gates in order to keep the Sabbath day holy.

Remember me for this also, my God, and show mercy to me according to your great love.

²³Moreover, in those days I saw men of Judah who had married women from Ashdod, Ammon and Moab. ²⁴Half of their children spoke the language of Ashdod or the language of one of the other peoples, and did not know how to speak the language of Judah. ²⁵I rebuked them and called curses down on them. I beat some of them and pulled out their hair. I made them take an oath in God's name and said: "You are not to give your daughters in marriage to their sons, nor are you to take their daughters in marriage for your sons or for yourselves. ²⁶Was it not because of marriages like these that Solomon king of Israel sinned? Among the many nations there was no king like him. He was loved by his God, and God made him king over all Israel, but even he was led into sin by foreign women. ²⁷Must we hear now that you too are doing all this terrible wickedness and are being unfaithful to our God by marrying foreign women?"

²⁸One of the sons of Joiada son of Eliashib the high priest was son-in-law to Sanballat the Horonite. And I drove him away from me.

²⁹Remember them, my God, because they defiled the priestly office and the covenant of the priesthood and of the Levites.

³⁰So I purified the priests and the Levites of everything foreign, and assigned them duties, each to his own task. ³¹I also made provision for contributions of wood at designated times, and for the firstfruits.

Remember me with favor, my God.

esther

AUTHOR: Unknown

DATE: Sometime after the events described—around 460 B.C.

THEME: God arranges circumstances to accomplish his will.

Queen Vashti Deposed

1 This is what happened during the time of Xerxes,[a] the Xerxes who ruled over 127 provinces stretching from India to Cush[b]: ²At that time King Xerxes reigned from his royal throne in the citadel of Susa, ³and in the third year of his reign he gave a banquet for all his nobles and officials. The military leaders of Persia and Media, the princes, and the nobles of the provinces were present.

⁴For a full 180 days he displayed the vast wealth of his kingdom and the splendor and glory of his majesty. ⁵When these days were over, the king gave a banquet, lasting seven days, in the enclosed garden of the king's palace, for all the people from the least to the greatest who were in the citadel of Susa. ⁶The garden had hangings of white and blue linen, fastened with cords of white linen and purple material to silver rings on marble pillars. There were couches of gold and silver on a mosaic pavement of porphyry, marble, mother-of-pearl and other costly stones. ⁷Wine was served in goblets of gold, each one different from the other, and the royal wine was abundant, in keeping with the king's liberality. ⁸By the king's command each guest was allowed to drink with no restrictions, for the king instructed all the wine stewards to serve each man what he wished.

⁹Queen Vashti also gave a banquet for the women in the royal palace of King Xerxes.

¹⁰On the seventh day, when King Xerxes was in high spirits from wine, he commanded the seven eunuchs who served him—Mehuman, Biztha, Harbona, Bigtha, Abagtha, Zethar and Karkas— ¹¹to bring before him Queen Vashti, wearing her royal crown, in order to display her beauty to the people and nobles, for she was lovely to look at. ¹²But when the attendants delivered the king's command, Queen Vashti refused to come. Then the king became furious and burned with anger.

¹³Since it was customary for the king to consult experts in matters of law and justice, he spoke with the wise men who understood the times ¹⁴and were closest to the king—Karshena, Shethar, Admatha, Tarshish, Meres, Marsena and Memukan, the seven nobles of Persia and Media who had special access to the king and were highest in the kingdom.

¹⁵"According to law, what must be done to Queen Vashti?" he asked. "She has not obeyed the command of King Xerxes that the eunuchs have taken to her."

¹⁶Then Memukan replied in the presence of the king and the nobles, "Queen Vashti has done wrong, not only against the king but also against all the nobles and the peoples of all the provinces of King Xerxes. ¹⁷For the queen's conduct will become known to all the women, and so they will despise their husbands and say, 'King Xerxes commanded Queen Vashti to be brought before him, but she would not come.' ¹⁸This very day the Persian and Median women of the nobility who have heard about the queen's conduct will respond to all the king's nobles in the same way. There will be no end of disrespect and discord.

¹⁹"Therefore, if it pleases the king, let him issue a royal decree and let it be written in the laws of Persia and Media, which cannot be repealed, that Vashti is never again to en-

---

a 1 Hebrew *Ahasuerus*; here and throughout Esther   b 1 That is, the upper Nile region

DISRESPECT CAN EQUAL CONTEMPT

Esther 1:1–22 *or* 1:18

Emerson Eggerichs

Many husbands interpret criticism as contempt, and contempt is something men do not handle well. Wives must grasp that their husbands aren't half as big and strong and impervious to being hurt as they might seem. A woman may envision herself as a sweet little dewdrop and her man as a big, strong bear who should be able to absorb any kind of punishment. One huge fellow was stunned by his beloved's attack and said to her, "You hate me."

Frustrated, she replied, "When I scream 'I hate you,' you should know I don't mean it. You are 6'9" and weigh 260 pounds, for goodness' sake. I do that because you can take it." The truth is, however, a lot of men can't take it. No matter how big they may be physically, emotionally they are vulnerable to what sounds like contempt.

The male fear of contempt is dramatized in the first chapter of Esther. What was the fear? That wives would start to despise their husbands and *defy* them. The result: there would be no end to the contempt and anger poured out by wives on their husbands throughout the king's realm (see Esther 1:18). This is not to justify the male fear of contempt in the book of Esther or anywhere else. But as women fear being unloved, men fear being disrespected (held in contempt). The yearning and need of husbands is that their wives give them honor and respect.

GEORGE WHITEFIELD {AD 1714–1770}

Women should remember the role that husbands have been given in Scripture: Husbands are to their wives what Christ is to the church (Ephesians 5:24) . . . Therefore, it is evident that it is pleasing in the sight of God for married women to revere and respect their husbands. Not that husbands therefore should lord it over their wives or require too much respect at their hands. This would be unchristian, as well as ungenerous, indeed. Husbands ought rather, I say, to be doubly careful that they live so holy and blameless, as to lay their wives under no temptation to despise them.

reflection

1. Would you agree or disagree that a man's greatest fear—or one of the greatest—is that of not being respected (or being viewed with contempt)?

2. How would you back up your answer? What examples can you point to?

3. Xerxes wanted to parade his queen's beautiful body before a group of drunken men for them to "admire." It's easy to understand why she refused. How can a wife disagree with her husband in a way that still shows him honor and respect?

For your next devotional reading, go to page 549.

ter the presence of King Xerxes. Also let the king give her royal position to someone else who is better than she. ²⁰Then when the king's edict is proclaimed throughout all his vast realm, all the women will respect their husbands, from the least to the greatest."

²¹The king and his nobles were pleased with this advice, so the king did as Memukan proposed. ²²He sent dispatches to all parts of the kingdom, to each province in its own script and to each people in their own language, proclaiming that every man should be ruler over his own household, using his native tongue.

Esther Made Queen

2 Later when King Xerxes' fury had subsided, he remembered Vashti and what she had done and what he had decreed about her. ²Then the king's personal attendants proposed, "Let a search be made for beautiful young virgins for the king. ³Let the king appoint commissioners in every province of his realm to bring all these beautiful young women into the harem at the citadel of Susa. Let them be placed under the care of Hegai, the king's eunuch, who is in charge of the women; and let beauty treatments be given to them. ⁴Then let the young woman who pleases the king be queen instead of Vashti." This advice appealed to the king, and he followed it.

⁵Now there was in the citadel of Susa a Jew of the tribe of Benjamin, named Mordecai son of Jair, the son of Shimei, the son of Kish, ⁶who had been carried into exile from Jerusalem by Nebuchadnezzar king of Babylon, among those taken captive with Jehoiachinᵃ king of Judah. ⁷Mordecai had a cousin named Hadassah, whom he had brought up because she had neither father nor mother. This young woman, who was also known as Esther, had a lovely figure and was beautiful. Mordecai had taken her as his own daughter when her father and mother died.

⁸When the king's order and edict had been proclaimed, many young women were brought to the citadel of Susa and put under the care of Hegai. Esther also was taken to the king's palace and entrusted to Hegai, who had charge of the harem. ⁹She pleased him and won his favor. Immediately he provided her with her beauty treatments and

special food. He assigned to her seven female attendants selected from the king's palace and moved her and her attendants into the best place in the harem.

¹⁰Esther had not revealed her nationality and family background, because Mordecai had forbidden her to do so. ¹¹Every day he walked back and forth near the courtyard of the harem to find out how Esther was and what was happening to her.

¹²Before a young woman's turn came to go in to King Xerxes, she had to complete twelve months of beauty treatments prescribed for the women, six months with oil of myrrh and six with perfumes and cosmetics. ¹³And this is how she would go to the king: Anything she wanted was given her to take with her from the harem to the king's palace. ¹⁴In the evening she would go there and in the morning return to another part of the harem to the care of Shaashgaz, the king's eunuch who was in charge of the concubines. She would not return to the king unless he was pleased with her and summoned her by name.

¹⁵When the turn came for Esther (the young woman Mordecai had adopted, the daughter of his uncle Abihail) to go to the king, she asked for nothing other than what Hegai, the king's eunuch who was in charge of the harem, suggested. And Esther won the favor of everyone who saw her. ¹⁶She was taken to King Xerxes in the royal residence in the tenth month, the month of Tebeth, in the seventh year of his reign.

¹⁷Now the king was attracted to Esther more than to any of the other women, and she won his favor and approval more than any of the other virgins. So he set a royal crown on her head and made her queen instead of Vashti. ¹⁸And the king gave a great banquet, Esther's banquet, for all his nobles and officials. He proclaimed a holiday throughout the provinces and distributed gifts with royal liberality.

Mordecai Uncovers a Conspiracy

¹⁹When the virgins were assembled a second time, Mordecai was sitting at the king's gate. ²⁰But Esther had kept secret her family background and nationality just as Mordecai had told her to do, for she continued

to follow Mordecai's instructions as she had done when he was bringing her up.

²¹During the time Mordecai was sitting at the king's gate, Bigthana ᵃ and Teresh, two of the king's officers who guarded the doorway, became angry and conspired to assassinate King Xerxes. ²²But Mordecai found out about the plot and told Queen Esther, who in turn reported it to the king, giving credit to Mordecai. ²³And when the report was investigated and found to be true, the two officials were impaled on poles. All this was recorded in the book of the annals in the presence of the king.

Haman's Plot to Destroy the Jews

3 After these events, King Xerxes honored Haman son of Hammedatha, the Agagite, elevating him and giving him a seat of honor higher than that of all the other nobles. ²All the royal officials at the king's gate knelt down and paid honor to Haman, for the king had commanded this concerning him. But Mordecai would not kneel down or pay him honor.

³Then the royal officials at the king's gate asked Mordecai, "Why do you disobey the king's command?" ⁴Day after day they spoke to him but he refused to comply. Therefore they told Haman about it to see whether Mordecai's behavior would be tolerated, for he had told them he was a Jew.

⁵When Haman saw that Mordecai would not kneel down or pay him honor, he was enraged. ⁶Yet having learned who Mordecai's people were, he scorned the idea of killing only Mordecai. Instead Haman looked for a way to destroy all Mordecai's people, the Jews, throughout the whole kingdom of Xerxes.

⁷In the twelfth year of King Xerxes, in the first month, the month of Nisan, the *pur* (that is, the lot) was cast in the presence of Haman to select a day and month. And the lot fell on ᵇ the twelfth month, the month of Adar.

⁸Then Haman said to King Xerxes, "There is a certain people dispersed among the peoples in all the provinces of your kingdom who keep themselves separate. Their customs are different from those of all other people, and they do not obey the king's laws;

it is not in the king's best interest to tolerate them. ⁹If it pleases the king, let a decree be issued to destroy them, and I will give ten thousand talents ᶜ of silver to the king's administrators for the royal treasury."

¹⁰So the king took his signet ring from his finger and gave it to Haman son of Hammedatha, the Agagite, the enemy of the Jews. ¹¹"Keep the money," the king said to Haman, "and do with the people as you please."

¹²Then on the thirteenth day of the first month the royal secretaries were summoned. They wrote out in the script of each province and in the language of each people all Haman's orders to the king's satraps, the governors of the various provinces and the nobles of the various peoples. These were written in the name of King Xerxes himself and sealed with his own ring. ¹³Dispatches were sent by couriers to all the king's provinces with the order to destroy, kill and annihilate all the Jews—young and old, women and children—on a single day, the thirteenth day of the twelfth month, the month of Adar, and to plunder their goods. ¹⁴A copy of the text of the edict was to be issued as law in every province and made known to the people of every nationality so they would be ready for that day.

¹⁵The couriers went out, spurred on by the king's command, and the edict was issued in the citadel of Susa. The king and Haman sat down to drink, but the city of Susa was bewildered.

Mordecai Persuades Esther to Help

4 When Mordecai learned of all that had been done, he tore his clothes, put on sackcloth and ashes, and went out into the city, wailing loudly and bitterly. ²But he went only as far as the king's gate, because no one clothed in sackcloth was allowed to enter it. ³In every province to which the edict and order of the king came, there was great mourning among the Jews, with fasting, weeping and wailing. Many lay in sackcloth and ashes.

⁴When Esther's eunuchs and female attendants came and told her about Mordecai, she was in great distress. She sent clothes for him to put on instead of his sackcloth, but he would not accept them. ⁵Then Esther

---

ᵃ 21 Hebrew *Bigthan*, a variant of *Bigthana*   ᵇ 7 Septuagint; Hebrew does not have *And the lot fell on.*
ᶜ 9 That is, about 375 tons or about 335 metric tons

summoned Hathak, one of the king's eunuchs assigned to attend her, and ordered him to find out what was troubling Mordecai and why.

⁶So Hathak went out to Mordecai in the open square of the city in front of the king's gate. ⁷Mordecai told him everything that had happened to him, including the exact amount of money Haman had promised to pay into the royal treasury for the destruction of the Jews. ⁸He also gave him a copy of the text of the edict for their annihilation, which had been published in Susa, to show to Esther and explain it to her, and he told him to instruct her to go into the king's presence to beg for mercy and plead with him for her people.

⁹Hathak went back and reported to Esther what Mordecai had said. ¹⁰Then she instructed him to say to Mordecai, ¹¹"All the king's officials and the people of the royal provinces know that for any man or woman who approaches the king in the inner court without being summoned the king has but one law: that they be put to death unless the king extends the gold scepter to them and spares their lives. But thirty days have passed since I was called to go to the king."

¹²When Esther's words were reported to Mordecai, ¹³he sent back this answer: "Do not think that because you are in the king's house you alone of all the Jews will escape. ¹⁴For if you remain silent at this time, relief and deliverance for the Jews will arise from another place, but you and your father's family will perish. And who knows but that you have come to royal position for such a time as this?"

¹⁵Then Esther sent this reply to Mordecai: ¹⁶"Go, gather together all the Jews who are in Susa, and fast for me. Do not eat or drink for three days, night or day. I and my attendants will fast as you do. When this is done, I will go to the king, even though it is against the law. And if I perish, I perish."

¹⁷So Mordecai went away and carried out all of Esther's instructions.

Esther's Request to the King

5 On the third day Esther put on her royal robes and stood in the inner court of the palace, in front of the king's hall. The king was sitting on his royal throne in the hall, facing the entrance. ²When he saw Queen Esther standing in the court, he was pleased with her and held out to her the gold scepter that was in his hand. So Esther approached and touched the tip of the scepter.

³Then the king asked, "What is it, Queen Esther? What is your request? Even up to half the kingdom, it will be given you."

⁴"If it pleases the king," replied Esther, "let the king, together with Haman, come today to a banquet I have prepared for him."

⁵"Bring Haman at once," the king said, "so that we may do what Esther asks."

So the king and Haman went to the banquet Esther had prepared. ⁶As they were drinking wine, the king again asked Esther, "Now what is your petition? It will be given you. And what is your request? Even up to half the kingdom, it will be granted."

⁷Esther replied, "My petition and my request is this: ⁸If the king regards me with favor and if it pleases the king to grant my petition and fulfill my request, let the king and Haman come tomorrow to the banquet I will prepare for them. Then I will answer the king's question."

Haman's Rage Against Mordecai

⁹Haman went out that day happy and in high spirits. But when he saw Mordecai at the king's gate and observed that he neither rose nor showed fear in his presence, he was filled with rage against Mordecai. ¹⁰Nevertheless, Haman restrained himself and went home.

Calling together his friends and Zeresh, his wife, ¹¹Haman boasted to them about his vast wealth, his many sons, and all the ways the king had honored him and how he had elevated him above the other nobles and officials. ¹²"And that's not all," Haman added. "I'm the only person Queen Esther invited to accompany the king to the banquet she gave. And she has invited me along with the king tomorrow. ¹³But all this gives me no satisfaction as long as I see that Jew Mordecai sitting at the king's gate."

¹⁴His wife Zeresh and all his friends said to him, "Have a pole set up, reaching to a height of fifty cubits,ᵃ and ask the king in the morning to have Mordecai impaled on it. Then go with the king to the banquet and enjoy yourself." This suggestion delighted Haman, and he had the pole set up.

ᵃ 14 That is, about 75 feet or about 22.5 meters

Mordecai Honored

6 That night the king could not sleep; so he ordered the book of the chronicles, the record of his reign, to be brought in and read to him. ²It was found recorded there that Mordecai had exposed Bigthana and Teresh, two of the king's officers who guarded the doorway, who had conspired to assassinate King Xerxes.

³"What honor and recognition has Mordecai received for this?" the king asked.

"Nothing has been done for him," his attendants answered.

⁴The king said, "Who is in the court?" Now Haman had just entered the outer court of the palace to speak to the king about impaling Mordecai on the pole he had set up for him.

⁵His attendants answered, "Haman is standing in the court."

"Bring him in," the king ordered.

⁶When Haman entered, the king asked him, "What should be done for the man the king delights to honor?"

Now Haman thought to himself, "Who is there that the king would rather honor than me?" ⁷So he answered the king, "For the man the king delights to honor, ⁸have them bring a royal robe the king has worn and a horse the king has ridden, one with a royal crest placed on its head. ⁹Then let the robe and horse be entrusted to one of the king's most noble princes. Let them robe the man the king delights to honor, and lead him on the horse through the city streets, proclaiming before him, 'This is what is done for the man the king delights to honor!' "

¹⁰"Go at once," the king commanded Haman. "Get the robe and the horse and do just as you have suggested for Mordecai the Jew, who sits at the king's gate. Do not neglect anything you have recommended."

¹¹So Haman got the robe and the horse. He robed Mordecai, and led him on horseback through the city streets, proclaiming before him, "This is what is done for the man the king delights to honor!"

¹²Afterward Mordecai returned to the king's gate. But Haman rushed home, with his head covered in grief, ¹³and told Zeresh his wife and all his friends everything that had happened to him.

His advisers and his wife Zeresh said to him, "Since Mordecai, before whom your downfall has started, is of Jewish origin, you cannot stand against him—you will surely come to ruin!" ¹⁴While they were still talking with him, the king's eunuchs arrived and hurried Haman away to the banquet Esther had prepared.

Haman Impaled

7 So the king and Haman went to Queen Esther's banquet, ²and as they were drinking wine on the second day, the king again asked, "Queen Esther, what is your petition? It will be given you. What is your request? Even up to half the kingdom, it will be granted."

³Then Queen Esther answered, "If I have found favor with you, Your Majesty, and if it pleases you, grant me my life—this is my petition. And spare my people—this is my request. ⁴For I and my people have been sold to be destroyed, killed and annihilated. If we had merely been sold as male and female slaves, I would have kept quiet, because no such distress would justify disturbing the king.ᵃ"

⁵King Xerxes asked Queen Esther, "Who is he? Where is he—the man who has dared to do such a thing?"

⁶Esther said, "An adversary and enemy! This vile Haman!"

Then Haman was terrified before the king and queen. ⁷The king got up in a rage, left his wine and went out into the palace garden. But Haman, realizing that the king had already decided his fate, stayed behind to beg Queen Esther for his life.

⁸Just as the king returned from the palace garden to the banquet hall, Haman was falling on the couch where Esther was reclining.

The king exclaimed, "Will he even molest the queen while she is with me in the house?"

As soon as the word left the king's mouth, they covered Haman's face. ⁹Then Harbona, one of the eunuchs attending the king, said, "A pole reaching to a height of fifty cubitsᵇ stands by Haman's house. He had it set up for Mordecai, who spoke up to help the king."

The king said, "Impale him on it!" ¹⁰So

ᵃ 4 Or *quiet, but the compensation our adversary offers cannot be compared with the loss the king would suffer*   ᵇ 9 That is, about 75 feet or about 22.5 meters they impaled Haman on the pole he had set up for Mordecai. Then the king's fury subsided.

The King's Edict in Behalf of the Jews

8 That same day King Xerxes gave Queen Esther the estate of Haman, the enemy of the Jews. And Mordecai came into the presence of the king, for Esther had told how he was related to her. [2]The king took off his signet ring, which he had reclaimed from Haman, and presented it to Mordecai. And Esther appointed him over Haman's estate.

[3]Esther again pleaded with the king, falling at his feet and weeping. She begged him to put an end to the evil plan of Haman the Agagite, which he had devised against the Jews. [4]Then the king extended the gold scepter to Esther and she arose and stood before him.

[5]"If it pleases the king," she said, "and if he regards me with favor and thinks it the right thing to do, and if he is pleased with me, let an order be written overruling the dispatches that Haman son of Hammedatha, the Agagite, devised and wrote to destroy the Jews in all the king's provinces. [6]For how can I bear to see disaster fall on my people? How can I bear to see the destruction of my family?"

[7]King Xerxes replied to Queen Esther and to Mordecai the Jew, "Because Haman attacked the Jews, I have given his estate to Esther, and they have impaled him on the pole he set up. [8]Now write another decree in the king's name in behalf of the Jews as seems best to you, and seal it with the king's signet ring—for no document written in the king's name and sealed with his ring can be revoked."

[9]At once the royal secretaries were summoned—on the twenty-third day of the third month, the month of Sivan. They wrote out all Mordecai's orders to the Jews, and to the satraps, governors and nobles of the 127 provinces stretching from India to Cush.[a] These orders were written in the script of each province and the language of each people and also to the Jews in their own script and language. [10]Mordecai wrote in the name of King Xerxes, sealed the dispatches with the king's signet ring, and sent them by mounted couriers, who rode fast horses especially bred for the king.

[11]The king's edict granted the Jews in every city the right to assemble and protect themselves; to destroy, kill and annihilate the armed men of any nationality or province who might attack them and their women and children,[b] and to plunder the property of their enemies. [12]The day appointed for the Jews to do this in all the provinces of King Xerxes was the thirteenth day of the twelfth month, the month of Adar. [13]A copy of the text of the edict was to be issued as law in every province and made known to the people of every nationality so that the Jews would be ready on that day to avenge themselves on their enemies.

[14]The couriers, riding the royal horses, went out, spurred on by the king's command, and the edict was issued in the citadel of Susa.

The Triumph of the Jews

[15]When Mordecai left the king's presence, he was wearing royal garments of blue and white, a large crown of gold and a purple robe of fine linen. And the city of Susa held a joyous celebration. [16]For the Jews it was a time of happiness and joy, gladness and honor. [17]In every province and in every city to which the edict of the king came, there was joy and gladness among the Jews, with feasting and celebrating. And many people of other nationalities became Jews because fear of the Jews had seized them.

9 On the thirteenth day of the twelfth month, the month of Adar, the edict commanded by the king was to be carried out. On this day the enemies of the Jews had hoped to overpower them, but now the tables were turned and the Jews got the upper hand over those who hated them. [2]The Jews assembled in their cities in all the provinces of King Xerxes to attack those seeking their destruction. No one could stand against them, because the people of all the other nationalities were afraid of them. [3]And all the nobles of the provinces, the satraps, the governors and the king's administrators helped the Jews, because fear of Mordecai had seized them. [4]Mordecai

---

[a] 9 That is, the upper Nile region   [b] 11 Or province, together with their women and children, who might attack them;

FRIDAY

GOD VALUES WOMEN AND THEIR WORK

Esther 9:1–32 *or* 9:29–32

Carolyn Custis James

I still love Esther's story. She makes me feel proud to be a woman—but I have better reasons for admiring her now than I did when I was a child. She is a powerful reminder that God values women and their contributions, and that it brings joy to his heart and blessings to others when his daughters rely on him and embrace the challenges he puts in their path . . .

Like a lot of women today, Esther was lulled to sleep by the culture's anesthetizing message that a woman's value depends on how she looks and on her ability to please others. Esther's story awakens us to the bold Biblical message that God values and counts on his daughters as kingdom builders.

MATTHEW HENRY {AD 1662–1714}

Who would have thought that an orphaned Jewish captive was born to be a queen, an empress! Yet so it proved. God sometimes "raises the poor from the dust and . . . seats them with princes" (1 Samuel 2:8). Esther pleased the man in charge of the harem and won his favor, and so he was ready to serve her. Wisdom and virtue will gain respect. Those that make sure of God's favor will find favor with man, too, as far as it is good for them.

reflection

1. In what ways does our society teach a woman that her value depends on her looks and her ability to please others?

2. As the story of Esther progresses, we notice her beauty less and her character more. How has she grown and changed since the beginning of her story?

3. What do you believe to be the most important message that Esther's story holds for women today?

For your next devotional reading, go to page 551.

was prominent in the palace; his reputation spread throughout the provinces, and he became more and more powerful.

⁵The Jews struck down all their enemies with the sword, killing and destroying them, and they did what they pleased to those who hated them. ⁶In the citadel of Susa, the Jews killed and destroyed five hundred men. ⁷They also killed Parshandatha, Dalphon, Aspatha, ⁸Poratha, Adalia, Aridatha, ⁹Parmashta, Arisai, Aridai and Vaizatha, ¹⁰the ten sons of Haman son of Hammedatha, the enemy of the Jews. But they did not lay their hands on the plunder.

¹¹The number of those killed in the citadel of Susa was reported to the king that same day. ¹²The king said to Queen Esther, "The Jews have killed and destroyed five hundred men and the ten sons of Haman in the citadel of Susa. What have they done in the rest of the king's provinces? Now what is your petition? It will be given you. What is your request? It will also be granted."

¹³"If it pleases the king," Esther answered, "give the Jews in Susa permission to carry out this day's edict tomorrow also, and let Haman's ten sons be impaled on poles."

¹⁴So the king commanded that this be done. An edict was issued in Susa, and they impaled the ten sons of Haman. ¹⁵The Jews in Susa came together on the fourteenth day of the month of Adar, and they put to death in Susa three hundred men, but they did not lay their hands on the plunder.

¹⁶Meanwhile, the remainder of the Jews who were in the king's provinces also assembled to protect themselves and get relief from their enemies. They killed seventy-five thousand of them but did not lay their hands on the plunder. ¹⁷This happened on the thirteenth day of the month of Adar, and on the fourteenth they rested and made it a day of feasting and joy.

¹⁸The Jews in Susa, however, had assembled on the thirteenth and fourteenth, and then on the fifteenth they rested and made it a day of feasting and joy.

¹⁹That is why rural Jews—those living in villages—observe the fourteenth of the month of Adar as a day of joy and feasting, a day for giving presents to each other.

Purim Established

²⁰Mordecai recorded these events, and he sent letters to all the Jews throughout the provinces of King Xerxes, near and far, ²¹to have them celebrate annually the fourteenth and fifteenth days of the month of Adar ²²as the time when the Jews got relief from their enemies, and as the month when their sorrow was turned into joy and their mourning into a day of celebration. He wrote them to observe the days as days of feasting and joy and giving presents of food to one another and gifts to the poor.

²³So the Jews agreed to continue the celebration they had begun, doing what Mordecai had written to them. ²⁴For Haman son of Hammedatha, the Agagite, the enemy of all the Jews, had plotted against the Jews to destroy them and had cast the *pur* (that is, the lot) for their ruin and destruction. ²⁵But when the plot came to the king's attention,ᵃ he issued written orders that the evil scheme Haman had devised against the Jews should come back onto his own head, and that he and his sons should be impaled on poles. ²⁶(Therefore these days were called Purim, from the word *pur*.) Because of everything written in this letter and because of what they had seen and what had happened to them, ²⁷the Jews took it on themselves to establish the custom that they and their descendants and all who join them should without fail observe these two days every year, in the way prescribed and at the time appointed. ²⁸These days should be remembered and observed in every generation by every family, and in every province and in every city. And these days of Purim should never cease to be celebrated by the Jews, nor should the memory of them die out among their descendants.

²⁹So Queen Esther, daughter of Abihail, along with Mordecai the Jew, wrote with full authority to confirm this second letter concerning Purim. ³⁰And Mordecai sent letters to all the Jews in the 127 provinces of Xerxes' kingdom—words of goodwill and assurance— ³¹to establish these days of Purim at their designated times, as Mordecai the Jew and Queen Esther had decreed for them, and as they had established for themselves and their descendants in regard to their times of fasting and lamentation.

ᵃ 25 Or *when Esther came before the king*

Best Supporting Actor

Esther 10:3

read/meditate

By this point in Esther's story, Mordecai was quite well known among his people. Although Esther was the star of the story, Mordecai was the key supporting actor. Think about Mordecai's role: he was always taking steps, usually behind the scenes, to give Esther the advice or insight that she needed.

pray

Ask God to prepare you for your "Mordecai moments." Ask him for eyes to see the opportunities he places before you—situations you can step into and influence, even if you aren't the one in the spotlight.

contemplate

In your opinion, what are the most likely places in your life that God can use you for his kingdom? What are the least likely places? Are you open and available to being used by God in completely unexpected ways?

additional reflection

God always gives his very best to those who leave the choice with him.
—*James Hudson Taylor*
Destiny is not a matter of chance, it is a matter of choice; it is not a thing to be waited for, it is a thing to be achieved.
—*William Jennings Bryan*

For your next devotional reading, go to page 556.

32Esther's decree confirmed these regulations about Purim, and it was written down in the records.

The Greatness of Mordecai

10 King Xerxes imposed tribute throughout the empire, to its distant shores. 2And all his acts of power and might, together with a full account of the greatness of Mordecai to which the king had raised him, are they not written in the book of the annals of the kings of Media and Persia? 3Mordecai the Jew was second in rank to King Xerxes, preeminent among the Jews, and held in high esteem by his many fellow Jews, because he worked for the good of his people and spoke up for the welfare of all the Jews.

The Books of Poetry

Job

Psalms

Proverbs

Ecclesiastes

Song of Songs

job

AUTHOR: Unknown

DATE: Unknown

THEME: God remains in control even during our times of suffering.

Prologue

1 In the land of Uz there lived a man whose name was Job. This man was blameless and upright; he feared God and shunned evil. ²He had seven sons and three daughters, ³and he owned seven thousand sheep, three thousand camels, five hundred yoke of oxen and five hundred donkeys, and had a large number of servants. He was the greatest man among all the people of the East.

⁴His sons used to hold feasts in their homes on their birthdays, and they would invite their three sisters to eat and drink with them. ⁵When a period of feasting had run its course, Job would make arrangements for them to be purified. Early in the morning he would sacrifice a burnt offering for each of them, thinking, "Perhaps my children have sinned and cursed God in their hearts." This was Job's regular custom.

⁶One day the angels*a* came to present themselves before the LORD, and Satan*b* also came with them. ⁷The LORD said to Satan, "Where have you come from?"

Satan answered the LORD, "From roaming through the earth and going back and forth in it."

⁸Then the LORD said to Satan, "Have you considered my servant Job? There is no one on earth like him; he is blameless and upright, a man who fears God and shuns evil."

⁹"Does Job fear God for nothing?" Satan replied. ¹⁰"Have you not put a hedge around him and his household and everything he has? You have blessed the work of his hands, so that his flocks and herds are spread throughout the land. ¹¹But now stretch out your hand and strike everything he has, and he will surely curse you to your face."

¹²The LORD said to Satan, "Very well, then, everything he has is in your power, but on the man himself do not lay a finger."

Then Satan went out from the presence of the LORD.

¹³One day when Job's sons and daughters were feasting and drinking wine at the oldest brother's house, ¹⁴a messenger came to Job and said, "The oxen were plowing and the donkeys were grazing nearby, ¹⁵and the Sabeans attacked and made off with them. They put the servants to the sword, and I am the only one who has escaped to tell you!"

¹⁶While he was still speaking, another messenger came and said, "The fire of God fell from the sky and burned up the sheep and the servants, and I am the only one who has escaped to tell you!"

¹⁷While he was still speaking, another messenger came and said, "The Chaldeans formed three raiding parties and swept down on your camels and made off with them. They put the servants to the sword, and I am the only one who has escaped to tell you!"

¹⁸While he was still speaking, yet another messenger came and said, "Your sons and daughters were feasting and drinking wine at the oldest brother's house, ¹⁹when suddenly a mighty wind swept in from the desert and struck the four corners of the house. It collapsed on them and they are dead, and I am the only one who has escaped to tell you!"

²⁰At this, Job got up and tore his robe and shaved his head. Then he fell to the ground in worship ²¹and said:

---

a 6 Hebrew *the sons of God*   *b* 6 Hebrew *satan* means *adversary*.

MONDAY

REASONABLE TRUST

Job 1:1–22 *or* 1:20–21

Os Guinness

Imagine you are in German-occupied France during World War II and you want to join the resistance movement against the Nazis. One evening in the local bar a stranger comes up to you and introduces himself as the leader of the local partisans. He spends the evening with you, explaining the general requirements of your duties, giving you a chance to assess his trustworthiness, and offering you the chance to go no further. But his warning is stern: If you join, your life will be at risk. This will be the only face-to-face meeting you will have. After this, you will receive orders and you will have to follow them without question, often completely in the dark as to the whys and wherefores of the operations, and always with the terrifying fear that your trust may be betrayed.

Is such trust reasonable? Sometimes what the resistance leader is doing is obvious. He is helping members of the resistance. "Thank heavens he is on our side," you say. Sometimes it is not obvious. He is in Gestapo uniform arresting partisans and—unknown to you—leading them out of sight to help them escape the Nazis. But always you must trust and follow the orders without question, despite all appearances, no matter what happens. "The resistance leader knows best," you say. Only after the war will the secrets be open, the codes revealed, the true comrades vindicated, the traitors exposed, and sense made of the explanations.

GEORGE NEUMARCK {AD 1621–1681}

If thou but suffer God to guide thee,
And hope in him through all thy ways,
He'll give thee strength whate'er betide thee,
And bear thee through the evil days.
Who trust in God's unchanging love
Builds on the rock that nought can move.

[So] Sing, pray and keep his ways unswerving,
So do thine own part faithfully,
And trust his Word, though undeserving,
Thou yet shalt find it true for thee!
God never yet forsook at need
The soul that trusted him indeed.

reflection

1. What causes you uncertainty about your future?
2. When have you found it difficult to trust God?
3. How might a past decision have been different if you'd had greater trust in God?

For your next devotional reading, go to page 563.

"Naked I came from my mother's womb,
   and naked I will depart.[a]
The LORD gave and the LORD has taken
      away;
   may the name of the LORD be
      praised."

[22]In all this, Job did not sin by charging
God with wrongdoing.

2 On another day the angels[b] came to
present themselves before the LORD,
and Satan also came with them to
present himself before him. [2]And the LORD
said to Satan, "Where have you come
from?"

Satan answered the LORD, "From roaming
through the earth and going back and forth
in it."

[3]Then the LORD said to Satan, "Have you
considered my servant Job? There is no one
on earth like him; he is blameless and upright, a man who fears God and shuns evil.
And he still maintains his integrity, though
you incited me against him to ruin him
without any reason."

[4]"Skin for skin!" Satan replied. "A man
will give all he has for his own life. [5]But now
stretch out your hand and strike his flesh
and bones, and he will surely curse you to
your face."

[6]The LORD said to Satan, "Very well, then,
he is in your hands; but you must spare his
life."

[7]So Satan went out from the presence of
the LORD and afflicted Job with painful sores
from the soles of his feet to the crown of his
head. [8]Then Job took a piece of broken pottery and scraped himself with it as he sat
among the ashes.

[9]His wife said to him, "Are you still main-
taining your integrity? Curse God and die!"

[10]He replied, "You are talking like a foolish[c] woman. Shall we accept good from
God, and not trouble?"

In all this, Job did not sin in what he said.

[11]When Job's three friends, Eliphaz the
Temanite, Bildad the Shuhite and Zophar
the Naamathite, heard about all the troubles
that had come upon him, they set out from
their homes and met together by agreement
to go and sympathize with him and comfort
him. [12]When they saw him from a distance,
they could hardly recognize him; they began
to weep aloud, and they tore their robes and
sprinkled dust on their heads. [13]Then they
sat on the ground with him for seven days
and seven nights. No one said a word to him,
because they saw how great his suffering
was.

Job Speaks

3 After this, Job opened his mouth and
cursed the day of his birth. [2]He said:

[3]"May the day of my birth perish,
   and the night that said, 'A boy is
      conceived!'
[4]That day—may it turn to darkness;
   may God above not care about it;
   may no light shine on it.
[5]May gloom and utter darkness claim it
      once more;
   may a cloud settle over it;
   may blackness overwhelm it.
[6]That night—may thick darkness seize it;
   may it not be included among the
      days of the year
   nor be entered in any of the months.
[7]May that night be barren;
   may no shout of joy be heard in it.
[8]May those who curse days[d] curse that
      day,
   those who are ready to rouse
      Leviathan.
[9]May its morning stars become dark;
   may it wait for daylight in vain
   and not see the first rays of dawn,
[10]for it did not shut the doors of the womb
      on me
   to hide trouble from my eyes.

[11]"Why did I not perish at birth,
   and die as I came from the womb?
[12]Why were there knees to receive me
   and breasts that I might be nursed?
[13]For now I would be lying down in peace;
   I would be asleep and at rest
[14]with kings and rulers of the earth,
   who built for themselves places now
      lying in ruins,
[15]with princes who had gold,
   who filled their houses with silver.
[16]Or why was I not hidden away in the
      ground like a stillborn child,

---

[a] 21 Or will return there   [b] 1 Hebrew the sons of God
denotes moral deficiency.   [d] 8 Or the sea   [c] 10 The Hebrew word rendered foolish

like an infant who never saw the light
of day?
17 There the wicked cease from turmoil,
and there the weary are at rest.
18 Captives also enjoy their ease;
they no longer hear the slave driver's
shout.
19 The small and the great are there,
and the slaves are freed from their
owners.

20 "Why is light given to those in misery,
and life to the bitter of soul,
21 to those who long for death that does
not come,
who search for it more than for
hidden treasure,
22 who are filled with gladness
and rejoice when they reach the
grave?
23 Why is life given to a man
whose way is hidden,
whom God has hedged in?
24 For sighing has become my daily food;
my groans pour out like water.
25 What I feared has come upon me;
what I dreaded has happened to me.
26 I have no peace, no quietness;
I have no rest, but only turmoil."

Eliphaz

4 Then Eliphaz the Temanite replied:

2 "If someone ventures a word with
you, will you be impatient?
But who can keep from speaking?
3 Think how you have instructed many,
how you have strengthened feeble
hands.
4 Your words have supported those who
stumbled;
you have strengthened faltering
knees.
5 But now trouble comes to you, and you
are discouraged;
it strikes you, and you are dismayed.
6 Should not your piety be your
confidence
and your blameless ways your hope?

7 "Consider now: Who, being innocent,
has ever perished?
Where were the upright ever
destroyed?
8 As I have observed, those who plow evil
and those who sow trouble reap it.

9 At the breath of God they perish;
at the blast of his anger they are no
more.
10 The lions may roar and growl,
yet the teeth of the great lions are
broken.
11 The lion perishes for lack of prey,
and the cubs of the lioness are
scattered.

12 "A word was secretly brought to me,
my ears caught a whisper of it.
13 Amid disquieting dreams in the night,
when deep sleep falls on people,
14 fear and trembling seized me
and made all my bones shake.
15 A spirit glided past my face,
and the hair on my body stood on
end.
16 It stopped,
but I could not tell what it was.
A form stood before my eyes,
and I heard a hushed voice:
17 'Can a mortal be more righteous than
God?
Can human beings be more pure than
their Maker?
18 If God places no trust in his servants,
if he charges his angels with error,
19 how much more those who live in
houses of clay,
whose foundations are in the dust,
who are crushed more readily than a
moth!
20 Between dawn and dusk they are broken
to pieces;
unnoticed, they perish forever.
21 Are not the cords of their tent pulled up,
so that they die without wisdom?'

5 "Call if you will, but who will answer
you?
To which of the holy ones will you
turn?
2 Resentment kills a fool,
and envy slays the simple.
3 I myself have seen a fool taking root,
but suddenly his house was cursed.
4 His children are far from safety,
crushed in court without a defender.
5 The hungry consume his harvest,
taking it even from among thorns,
and the thirsty pant after his wealth.
6 For hardship does not spring from the
soil,

nor does trouble sprout from the ground.
⁷Yet human beings are born to trouble
as surely as sparks fly upward.

⁸"But if I were you, I would appeal to God;
I would lay my cause before him.
⁹He performs wonders that cannot be fathomed,
miracles that cannot be counted.
¹⁰He bestows rain on the earth;
he sends water on the countryside.
¹¹The lowly he sets on high,
and those who mourn are lifted to safety.
¹²He thwarts the plans of the crafty,
so that their hands achieve no success.
¹³He catches the wise in their craftiness,
and the schemes of the wily are swept away.
¹⁴Darkness comes upon them in the daytime;
at noon they grope as in the night.
¹⁵He saves the needy from the sword in their mouth;
he saves them from the clutches of the powerful.
¹⁶So the poor have hope,
and injustice shuts its mouth.

¹⁷"Blessed are those whom God corrects;
so do not despise the discipline of the Almighty.ᵃ
¹⁸For he wounds, but he also binds up;
he injures, but his hands also heal.
¹⁹From six calamities he will rescue you;
in seven no harm will touch you.
²⁰In famine he will deliver you from death,
and in battle from the stroke of the sword.
²¹You will be protected from the lash of the tongue,
and need not fear when destruction comes.
²²You will laugh at destruction and famine,
and need not fear the wild animals.
²³For you will have a covenant with the stones of the field,
and the wild animals will be at peace with you.

²⁴You will know that your tent is secure;
you will take stock of your property
and find nothing missing.
²⁵You will know that your children will be many,
and your descendants like the grass of the earth.
²⁶You will come to the grave in full vigor,
like sheaves gathered in season.

²⁷"We have examined this, and it is true.
So hear it and apply it to yourself."

Job

Then Job replied:

²"If only my anguish could be weighed
and all my misery be placed on the scales!
³It would surely outweigh the sand of the seas—
no wonder my words have been impetuous.
⁴The arrows of the Almighty are in me,
my spirit drinks in their poison;
God's terrors are marshaled against me.
⁵Does a wild donkey bray when it has grass,
or an ox bellow when it has fodder?
⁶Is tasteless food eaten without salt,
or is there flavor in the sap of the mallowᵇ?
⁷I refuse to touch it;
such food makes me ill.

⁸"Oh, that I might have my request,
that God would grant what I hope for,
⁹that God would be willing to crush me,
to let loose his hand and cut off my life!
¹⁰Then I would still have this consolation—
my joy in unrelenting pain—
that I had not denied the words of the Holy One.

¹¹"What strength do I have, that I should still hope?
What prospects, that I should be patient?
¹²Do I have the strength of stone?
Is my flesh bronze?

ᵃ 17 Hebrew Shaddai; here and throughout Job   ᵇ 6 The meaning of the Hebrew for this phrase is uncertain.

¹³ Do I have any power to help myself,
  now that success has been driven
    from me?

¹⁴ "Anyone who withholds kindness from a
      friend
  forsakes the fear of the Almighty.
¹⁵ But my brothers are as undependable as
      intermittent streams,
  as the streams that overflow
¹⁶ when darkened by thawing ice
  and swollen with melting snow,
¹⁷ but that cease to flow in the dry season,
  and in the heat vanish from their
    channels.
¹⁸ Caravans turn aside from their routes;
  they go off into the wasteland and
    perish.
¹⁹ The caravans of Tema look for water,
  the traveling merchants of Sheba look
    in hope.
²⁰ They are distressed, because they had
      been confident;
  they arrive there, only to be
    disappointed.
²¹ Now you too have proved to be of no
      help;
  you see something dreadful and are
    afraid.
²² Have I ever said, 'Give something on my
      behalf,
  pay a ransom for me from your
    wealth,
²³ deliver me from the hand of the enemy,
  rescue me from the clutches of the
    ruthless'?

²⁴ "Teach me, and I will be quiet;
  show me where I have been wrong.
²⁵ How painful are honest words!
  But what do your arguments prove?
²⁶ Do you mean to correct what I say,
  and treat my desperate words as
    wind?
²⁷ You would even cast lots for the
      fatherless
  and barter away your friend.

²⁸ "But now be so kind as to look at me.
  Would I lie to your face?
²⁹ Relent, do not be unjust;
  reconsider, for my integrity is at
    stake.ᵃ
³⁰ Is there any wickedness on my lips?
  Can my mouth not discern malice?

7 "Do not mortals have hard service on
      earth?
  Are not their days like those of hired
    laborers?
² Like a slave longing for the evening
      shadows,
  or a hired laborer waiting to be paid,
³ so I have been allotted months of
      futility,
  and nights of misery have been
    assigned to me.
⁴ When I lie down I think, 'How long
      before I get up?'
  The night drags on, and I toss and
    turn until dawn.
⁵ My body is clothed with worms and
      scabs,
  my skin is broken and festering.

⁶ "My days are swifter than a weaver's
      shuttle,
  and they come to an end without
    hope.
⁷ Remember, O God, that my life is but a
      breath;
  my eyes will never see happiness
    again.
⁸ The eye that now sees me will see me
      no longer;
  you will look for me, but I will be no
    more.
⁹ As a cloud vanishes and is gone,
  so those who go down to the grave do
    not return.
¹⁰ They will never come to their homes
      again;
  their places will know them no more.

¹¹ "Therefore I will not keep silent;
  I will speak out in the anguish of my
    spirit,
  I will complain in the bitterness of my
    soul.
¹² Am I the sea, or the monster of the
      deep,
  that you put me under guard?
¹³ When I think my bed will comfort me
  and my couch will ease my
    complaint,
¹⁴ even then you frighten me with dreams
  and terrify me with visions,
¹⁵ so that I prefer strangling and death,
  rather than this body of mine.

ᵃ 29 Or *my righteousness still stands*

¹⁶ I despise my life; I would not live
    forever.
  Let me alone; my days have no
    meaning.
¹⁷ "What are human beings that you make
    so much of them,
  that you give them so much
    attention,
¹⁸ that you examine them every morning
    and test them every moment?
¹⁹ Will you never look away from me,
  or let me alone even for an instant?
²⁰ If I have sinned, what have I done to you,
    you who watch over us all?
  Why have you made me your target?
  Have I become a burden to you?^a
²¹ Why do you not pardon my offenses
    and forgive my sins?
  For I will soon lie down in the dust;
    you will search for me, but I will be
    no more."

Bildad

8 Then Bildad the Shuhite replied:

² "How long will you say such things?
  Your words are a blustering wind.
³ Does God pervert justice?
  Does the Almighty pervert what is
    right?
⁴ When your children sinned against him,
  he gave them over to the penalty of
    their sin.
⁵ But if you will seek God earnestly
    and plead with the Almighty,
⁶ if you are pure and upright,
  even now he will rouse himself on
    your behalf
  and restore you to your prosperous
    state.
⁷ Your beginnings will seem humble,
  so prosperous will your future be.

⁸ "Ask the former generation
  and find out what their ancestors
    learned,
⁹ for we were born only yesterday and
    know nothing,
  and our days on earth are but a
    shadow.
¹⁰ Will they not instruct you and tell you?

  Will they not bring forth words from
    their understanding?
¹¹ Can papyrus grow tall where there is no
    marsh?
  Can reeds thrive without water?
¹² While still growing and uncut,
  they wither more quickly than grass.
¹³ Such is the destiny of all who forget
    God;
  so perishes the hope of the godless.
¹⁴ What they trust in is fragile^b;
  what they rely on is a spider's web.
¹⁵ They lean on the web, but it gives way;
  they cling to it, but it does not hold.
¹⁶ They are like a well-watered plant in the
    sunshine,
  spreading its shoots over the garden;
¹⁷ it entwines its roots around a pile of
    rocks
  and looks for a place among the
    stones.
¹⁸ But when it is torn from its spot,
  that place disowns it and says, 'I
    never saw you.'
¹⁹ Surely its life withers away,
  and^c from the soil other plants grow.

²⁰ "Surely God does not reject the
    blameless
  or strengthen the hands of evildoers.
²¹ He will yet fill your mouth with laughter
    and your lips with shouts of joy.
²² Your enemies will be clothed in shame,
  and the tents of the wicked will be no
    more."

Job

9 Then Job replied:

² "Indeed, I know that this is true.
  But how can mere mortals prove their
    innocence before God?
³ Though they wished to dispute with
    him,
  they could not answer him one time
    out of a thousand.
⁴ His wisdom is profound, his power is
    vast.
  Who has resisted him and come out
    unscathed?
⁵ He moves mountains without their
    knowing it

^a 20 A few manuscripts of the Masoretic Text, an ancient Hebrew scribal tradition and Septuagint; most
manuscripts of the Masoretic Text *I have become a burden to myself.*   ^b 14 The meaning of the Hebrew
for this word is uncertain.   ^c 19 Or *Surely all the joy it has / is that*

and overturns them in his anger.
6 He shakes the earth from its place
  and makes its pillars tremble.
7 He speaks to the sun and it does not
      shine;
  he seals off the light of the stars.
8 He alone stretches out the heavens
  and treads on the waves of the sea.
9 He is the Maker of the Bear^a and Orion,
  the Pleiades and the constellations of
      the south.
10 He performs wonders that cannot be
      fathomed,
  miracles that cannot be counted.
11 When he passes me, I cannot see him;
  when he goes by, I cannot perceive
      him.
12 If he snatches away, who can stop him?
  Who can say to him, 'What are you
      doing?'
13 God does not restrain his anger;
  even the cohorts of Rahab cowered at
      his feet.

14 "How then can I dispute with him?
  How can I find words to argue with
      him?
15 Though I were innocent, I could not
      answer him;
  I could only plead with my Judge for
      mercy.
16 Even if I summoned him and he
      responded,
  I do not believe he would give me a
      hearing.
17 He would crush me with a storm
  and multiply my wounds for no
      reason.
18 He would not let me catch my breath
  but would overwhelm me with
      misery.
19 If it is a matter of strength, he is mighty!
  And if it is a matter of justice, who
      can challenge him^b?
20 Even if I were innocent, my mouth
      would condemn me;
  if I were blameless, it would
      pronounce me guilty.

21 "Although I am blameless,
  I have no concern for myself;
  I despise my own life.
22 It is all the same; that is why I say,

'He destroys both the blameless and
      the wicked.'
23 When a scourge brings sudden death,
  he mocks the despair of the innocent.
24 When a land falls into the hands of the
      wicked,
  he blindfolds its judges.
  If it is not he, then who is it?

25 "My days are swifter than a runner;
  they fly away without a glimpse of
      joy.
26 They skim past like boats of papyrus,
  like eagles swooping down on their
      prey.
27 If I say, 'I will forget my complaint,
  I will change my expression, and
      smile,'
28 I still dread all my sufferings,
  for I know you will not hold me
      innocent.
29 Since I am already found guilty,
  why should I struggle in vain?
30 Even if I washed myself with soap
  and my hands with cleansing powder,
31 you would plunge me into a slime pit
  so that even my clothes would detest
      me.

32 "He is not a mere mortal like me that I
      might answer him,
  that we might confront each other in
      court.
33 If only there were someone to arbitrate
      between us,
  to lay a hand on us both,
34 someone to remove God's rod from me,
  so that his terror would frighten me
      no more.
35 Then I would speak up without fear of
      him,
  but as it now stands with me, I
      cannot.

10 "I loathe my very life;
  therefore I will give free rein to
      my complaint
  and speak out in the bitterness of my
      soul.
2 I say to God: Do not declare me guilty,
  but tell me what charges you have
      against me.
3 Does it please you to oppress me,
  to spurn the work of your hands,

A Crisis of Faith

Job 10:1–22 *or* 10:1–3

Philip Yancey

At root, Job faced a crisis of faith, not of suffering. And so do we. All of us at times find ourselves in a Job-like state. We may not face the extreme disasters that befell Job, but a tragic accident, a terminal illness or the loss of a job may have us shaking our heads and asking, "Why me? What does God have against me? Why does God seem so distant?"

At such times we focus too easily on circumstances—illness, our looks, poverty, bad luck—as the enemy. We pray for God to change those circumstances. If only I were beautiful or handsome, we think, then everything would work out. If only I had more money, or at least a good job; if only my sexual desires would somehow change, or at least diminish—then I could easily believe God. Job teaches, though, that we need faith most at the precise moment when it seems impossible.

When tragedy strikes, we too will be trapped in a limited point of view. Like Job, we will be tempted to blame God and see him as the enemy. Job asked God poignantly, "Does it please you to oppress me, to spurn the work of your hands?" (10:3). The view behind the curtain in chapters 1–2 reveals that Job was being exalted, not spurned. God was letting his own reputation ride on the response of a single human being. At the time when Job felt most abandoned, at that very time God was giving him personal, almost microscopic scrutiny. God seemed absent; in one sense God had never been more present.

I hesitate to write this because it is a hard truth, one I do not want to acknowledge: Job convinces me that God cares more about our faith than our pleasure.

Matthew Henry {AD 1662–1714}

In the book of Job, God's glorious attributes and perfections—his unsearchable wisdom, his irresistible power, his inconceivable glory, his inflexible justice and his incontestable sovereignty—are discussed with the utmost clearness, fullness, reverence and divine eloquence. The creation of the world and the government of it are admirably described—not as matters of nice speculation, but as laying the most powerful obligations upon us to fear and serve, to submit to and trust in our Creator, owner, Lord and ruler.

reflection

1. Have you ever felt like God was your enemy, like he was out to get you?

2. How has your faith grown through the painful times in your life?

3. Why does knowing the character of God encourage you to trust him in even the most difficult circumstances?

For your next devotional reading, go to page 566.

while you smile on the plans of the
wicked?
⁴ Do you have eyes of flesh?
Do you see as a mortal sees?
⁵ Are your days like those of a mortal
or your years like those of a human
being,
⁶ that you must search out my faults
and probe after my sin—
⁷ though you know that I am not guilty
and that no one can rescue me from
your hand?

⁸ "Your hands shaped me and made me.
Will you now turn and destroy me?
⁹ Remember that you molded me like clay.
Will you now turn me to dust again?
¹⁰ Did you not pour me out like milk
and curdle me like cheese,
¹¹ clothe me with skin and flesh
and knit me together with bones and
sinews?
¹² You gave me life and showed me
kindness,
and in your providence watched over
my spirit.

¹³ "But this is what you concealed in your
heart,
and I know that this was in your
mind:
¹⁴ If I sinned, you would be watching me
and would not let my offense go
unpunished.
¹⁵ If I am guilty—woe to me!
Even if I am innocent, I cannot lift my
head,
for I am full of shame
and drowned in ᵃ my affliction.
¹⁶ If I hold my head high, you stalk me like
a lion
and again display your awesome
power against me.
¹⁷ You bring new witnesses against me
and increase your anger toward me;
your forces come against me wave
upon wave.

¹⁸ "Why then did you bring me out of the
womb?
I wish I had died before any eye saw
me.
¹⁹ If only I had never come into being,
or had been carried straight from the
womb to the grave!

²⁰ Are not my few days almost over?
Turn away from me so I can have a
moment's joy
²¹ before I go to the place of no return,
to the land of gloom and utter
darkness,
²² to the land of deepest night,
of utter darkness and disorder,
where even the light is like darkness."

Zophar

11 Then Zophar the Naamathite replied:

² "Are all these words to go unanswered?
Is this talker to be vindicated?
³ Will your idle talk reduce others to
silence?
Will no one rebuke you when you
mock?
⁴ You say to God, 'My beliefs are flawless
and I am pure in your sight.'
⁵ Oh, how I wish that God would speak,
that he would open his lips against
you
⁶ and disclose to you the secrets of
wisdom,
for true wisdom has two sides.
Know this: God has even forgotten
some of your sin.

⁷ "Can you fathom the mysteries of God?
Can you probe the limits of the
Almighty?
⁸ They are higher than the heavens
above—what can you do?
They are deeper than the depths
below—what can you know?
⁹ Their measure is longer than the earth
and wider than the sea.
¹⁰ "If he comes along and confines you in
prison
and convenes a court, who can
oppose him?
¹¹ Surely he recognizes deceivers;
and when he sees evil, does he not
take note?
¹² But the witless can no more become
wise
than a wild donkey's colt can be born
a human being. ᵇ
¹³ "Yet if you devote your heart to him
and stretch out your hands to him,

ᵃ 15 Or and aware of   ᵇ 12 Or wild donkey can be born tame

14 if you put away the sin that is in your
hand
and allow no evil to dwell in your
tent,
15 then, free of fault, you will lift up your
face;
you will stand firm and without fear.
16 You will surely forget your trouble,
recalling it only as waters gone by.
17 Life will be brighter than noonday,
and darkness will become like
morning.
18 You will be secure, because there is hope;
you will look about you and take your
rest in safety.
19 You will lie down, with no one to make
you afraid,
and many will court your favor.
20 But the eyes of the wicked will fail,
and escape will elude them;
their hope will become a dying gasp."

Job

12

Then Job replied:

2 "Doubtless you are the people,
and wisdom will die with you!
3 But I have a mind as well as you;
I am not inferior to you.
Who does not know all these things?

4 "I have become a laughingstock to my
friends,
though I called on God and he
answered—
a mere laughingstock, though
righteous and blameless!
5 Those who are at ease have contempt
for misfortune
as the fate of those whose feet are
slipping.
6 The tents of marauders are undisturbed,
and those who provoke God are
secure—
those God has in his hand. a

7 "But ask the animals, and they will
teach you,
or the birds in the sky, and they will
tell you;
8 or speak to the earth, and it will teach
you,
or let the fish in the sea inform you.
9 Which of all these does not know

that the hand of the LORD has done
this?
10 In his hand is the life of every creature
and the breath of every human being.
11 Does not the ear test words
as the tongue tastes food?
12 Is not wisdom found among the aged?
Does not long life bring
understanding?

13 "To God belong wisdom and power;
counsel and understanding are his.
14 What he tears down cannot be rebuilt;
those he imprisons cannot be
released.
15 If he holds back the waters, there is
drought;
if he lets them loose, they devastate
the land.
16 To him belong strength and insight;
both deceived and deceiver are his.
17 He leads rulers away stripped
and makes fools of judges.
18 He takes off the shackles put on by
kings
and ties a loincloth b around their
waist.
19 He leads priests away stripped
and overthrows officials long
established.
20 He silences the lips of trusted advisers
and takes away the discernment of
elders.
21 He pours contempt on nobles
and disarms the mighty.
22 He reveals the deep things of darkness
and brings utter darkness into the
light.
23 He makes nations great, and destroys
them;
he enlarges nations, and disperses
them.
24 He deprives the leaders of the earth of
their reason;
he makes them wander in a trackless
waste.
25 They grope in darkness with no light;
he makes them stagger like
drunkards.

13

"My eyes have seen all this,
my ears have heard and
understood it.
2 What you know, I also know;

---

a 6 Or those whose god is in their own hand   b 18 Or shackles of kings / and ties a belt

WEDNESDAY

ALL GOD WANTS IS . . . EVERYTHING!

Job 13:1–27 *or* 13:15

Joni Eareckson Tada

Not long ago I was forced to lie in bed flat on my back for a month in order to heal a couple of stubborn pressure sores. That meant canceling a few important appointments and missing some critical deadlines. It meant days of the same old routine: A bed bath. Dressing the wounds. Leg exercises. Breakfast. Waiting. Lunch. Napping. Dinner. Being read to. Prayers and then sleep.

At times it was hard to hold depression at bay, and I was tempted to think, "Now come on, God, none of my Christian friends seem to be faced with these faith-challenging tests. Aren't you asking a bit much?"

Just what does God ask of us? . . . All God asks for is . . . everything. If we feel like a martyr faced with heart-wrenching trials, perhaps we're concentrating too much on what God asks of us and not enough on what God has given us.

Is "everything" too much? Think about what God has given you. How much did He hold back? Anything? Of course not. In fact, He gave more than everything. "He who did not spare his own Son, but gave him up for us all—how will he not also, along with him, graciously give us *all* things?" (Romans 8:32 [emphasis added]).

If we're fainthearted, remember that God has promised us power to help us do all that He asks of us. Even if it is everything.

Lord, you gave Your life! You ask me to do the same. Bless You for giving me the power to love and serve You with all my heart and soul. Take my life and let it be consecrated, Lord, to Thee.

ANDREW MURRAY {AD 1828–1917}

You know in daily life what absolute surrender is. You know that everything has to be given up to its special, definite object and service. I have a pen in my pocket, and that pen is absolutely surrendered to the one work of writing, and that pen must be absolutely surrendered to my hand if I am to write properly with it. If another holds it partly, I cannot write properly . . . And now, do you expect that in your immortal being, in the divine nature that you have received by regeneration, God can work his work, every day and every hour, unless you are entirely given up to him?

reflection

1. Who do you know whose life seems completely surrendered to God?

2. How does that person's life differ from yours?

3. What dreams do you need to surrender to God?

For your next devotional reading, go to page 572.

I am not inferior to you.
3 But I desire to speak to the Almighty
and to argue my case with God.
4 You, however, smear me with lies;
you are worthless physicians, all of
you!
5 If only you would be altogether silent!
For you, that would be wisdom.
6 Hear now my argument;
listen to the pleas of my lips.
7 Will you speak wickedly on God's
behalf?
Will you speak deceitfully for him?
8 Will you show him partiality?
Will you argue the case for God?
9 Would it turn out well if he examined
you?
Could you deceive him as you might
deceive mortals?
10 He would surely call you to account
if you secretly showed partiality.
11 Would not his splendor terrify you?
Would not the dread of him fall on
you?
12 Your maxims are proverbs of ashes;
your defenses are defenses of clay.

13 "Keep silent and let me speak;
then let come to me what may.
14 Why do I put myself in jeopardy
and take my life in my hands?
15 Though he slay me, yet will I hope in
him;
I will surely ^{a} defend my ways to his
face.
16 Indeed, this will turn out for my
deliverance,
for no godless person would dare
come before him!
17 Listen carefully to what I say;
let my words ring in your ears.
18 Now that I have prepared my case,
I know I will be vindicated.
19 Can anyone bring charges against me?
If so, I will be silent and die.

20 "Only grant me these two things, God,
and then I will not hide from you:
21 Withdraw your hand far from me,
and stop frightening me with your
terrors.
22 Then summon me and I will answer,
or let me speak, and you reply to me.

23 How many wrongs and sins have I
committed?
Show me my offense and my sin.
24 Why do you hide your face
and consider me your enemy?
25 Will you torment a windblown leaf?
Will you chase after dry chaff?
26 For you write down bitter things against
me
and make me reap the sins of my
youth.
27 You fasten my feet in shackles;
you keep close watch on all my paths
by putting marks on the soles of my
feet.

28 "So humans waste away like something
rotten,
like a garment eaten by moths.

14

"Mortals, born of woman,
are of few days and full of
trouble.
2 They spring up like flowers and wither
away;
like fleeting shadows, they do not
endure.
3 Do you fix your eye on such as these?
Will you bring them ^{b} before you for
judgment?
4 Who can bring what is pure from the
impure?
No one!
5 The days of mortals are determined;
you have decreed the number of their
months
and have set limits they cannot
exceed.
6 So look away from us and leave us
alone,
till we have put in our time like hired
laborers.

7 "At least there is hope for a tree:
If it is cut down, it will sprout again,
and its new shoots will not fail.
8 Its roots may grow old in the ground
and its stump die in the soil,
9 yet at the scent of water it will bud
and put forth shoots like a plant.
10 But human beings die and are laid low;
they breathe their last and are no
more.
11 As the water of a lake dries up

---

^{a} 15 Or *He will surely slay me; I have no hope — / yet I will*
Hebrew *me* ^{b} 3 Septuagint, Vulgate and Syriac;

or a riverbed becomes parched and
    dry,
¹² so they lie down and do not rise;
    till the heavens are no more, they will
      not awake
    or be roused from their sleep.

¹³ "If only you would hide me in the grave
    and conceal me till your anger has
      passed!
  If only you would set me a time
    and then remember me!
¹⁴ If someone dies, will they live again?
    All the days of my hard service
    I will wait for my renewal *a* to come.
¹⁵ You will call and I will answer you;
    you will long for the creature your
      hands have made.
¹⁶ Surely then you will count my steps
    but not keep track of my sin.
¹⁷ My offenses will be sealed up in a bag;
    you will cover over my sin.

¹⁸ "But as a mountain erodes and crumbles
    and as a rock is moved from its place,
¹⁹ as water wears away stones
    and torrents wash away the soil,
    so you destroy everyone's hope.
²⁰ You overpower them once for all, and
      they are gone;
    you change their countenance and
      send them away.
²¹ If their children are honored, they do not
      know it;
    if their offspring are brought low, they
      do not see it.
²² They feel but the pain of their own
      bodies
    and mourn only for themselves."

Eliphaz

15 Then Eliphaz the Temanite replied:

² "Would the wise answer with empty
      notions
    or fill their bellies with the hot east
      wind?
³ Would they argue with useless words,
    with speeches that have no value?
⁴ But you even undermine piety
    and hinder devotion to God.
⁵ Your sin prompts your mouth;
    you adopt the tongue of the crafty.

⁶ Your own mouth condemns you, not
      mine;
    your own lips testify against you.

⁷ "Are you the first man ever born?
    Were you brought forth before the
      hills?
⁸ Do you listen in on God's council?
    Do you have a monopoly on wisdom?
⁹ What do you know that we do not know?
    What insights do you have that we do
      not have?
¹⁰ The gray-haired and the aged are on our
      side,
    men even older than your father.
¹¹ Are God's consolations not enough for
      you,
    words spoken gently to you?
¹² Why has your heart carried you away,
    and why do your eyes flash,
¹³ so that you vent your rage against God
    and pour out such words from your
      mouth?

¹⁴ "What are mortals, that they could be
      pure,
    or those born of woman, that they
      could be righteous?
¹⁵ If God places no trust in his holy ones,
    if even the heavens are not pure in
      his eyes,
¹⁶ how much less mortals, who are vile and
      corrupt,
    who drink up evil like water!

¹⁷ "Listen to me and I will explain to you;
    let me tell you what I have seen,
¹⁸ what the wise have declared,
    hiding nothing received from their
      ancestors
¹⁹ (to whom alone the land was given
    when no foreigners moved among
      them):
²⁰ All their days the wicked suffer torment,
    the ruthless through all the years
      stored up for them.
²¹ Terrifying sounds fill their ears;
    when all seems well, marauders
      attack them.
²² They despair of escaping the realm of
      darkness;
    they are marked for the sword.
²³ They wander about for food like
      vultures;

a 14 Or *release*

they know the day of darkness is at
hand.
24 Distress and anguish fill them with
terror;
troubles overwhelm them, like a king
poised to attack,
25 because they shake their fists at God
and vaunt themselves against the
Almighty,
26 defiantly charging against him
with thick, strong shields.

27 "Though their faces are covered with fat
and their waists bulge with flesh,
28 they will inhabit ruined towns
and houses where no one lives,
houses crumbling to rubble.
29 They will no longer be rich and their
wealth will not endure,
nor will their possessions spread over
the land.
30 They will not escape the darkness;
a flame will wither their shoots,
and the breath of God's mouth will
carry them away.
31 Let them not deceive themselves by
trusting what is worthless,
for they will get nothing in return.
32 Before their time they will wither,
and their branches will not flourish.
33 They will be like a vine stripped of its
unripe grapes,
like an olive tree shedding its
blossoms.
34 For the company of the godless will be
barren,
and fire will consume the tents of
those who love bribes.
35 They conceive trouble and give birth to
evil;
their womb fashions deceit.'"

Job

16
Then Job replied:

2 "I have heard many things like
these;
you are miserable comforters, all of
you!
3 Will your long-winded speeches never
end?
What ails you that you keep on
arguing?
4 I also could speak like you,

if you were in my place;
I could make fine speeches against you
and shake my head at you.
5 But my mouth would encourage you;
comfort from my lips would bring you
relief.

6 "Yet if I speak, my pain is not relieved;
and if I refrain, it does not go away.
7 Surely, God, you have worn me out;
you have devastated my entire
household.
8 You have shriveled me up—and it has
become a witness;
my gauntness rises up and testifies
against me.
9 God assails me and tears me in his
anger
and gnashes his teeth at me;
my opponent fastens on me his
piercing eyes.
10 People open their mouths to jeer at me;
they strike my cheek in scorn
and unite together against me.
11 God has turned me over to the ungodly
and thrown me into the clutches of
the wicked.
12 All was well with me, but he shattered
me;
he seized me by the neck and crushed
me.
He has made me his target;
13   his archers surround me.
Without pity, he pierces my kidneys
and spills my gall on the ground.
14 Again and again he bursts upon me;
he rushes at me like a warrior.

15 "I have sewed sackcloth over my skin
and buried my brow in the dust.
16 My face is red with weeping,
dark shadows ring my eyes;
17 yet my hands have been free of violence
and my prayer is pure.

18 "Earth, do not cover my blood;
may my cry never be laid to rest!
19 Even now my witness is in heaven;
my advocate is on high.
20 My intercessor is my friend a
as my eyes pour out tears to God;
21 on behalf of a human being he pleads
with God
as one pleads for a friend.

a 20 Or My friends treat me with scorn

22 "Only a few years will pass
    before I take the path of no return.

17

¹My spirit is broken,
    my days are cut short,
    the grave awaits me.
²Surely mockers surround me;
    my eyes must dwell on their hostility.

³"Give me, O God, the pledge you
        demand.
    Who else will put up security for me?
⁴You have closed their minds to
        understanding;
    therefore you will not let them
        triumph.
⁵If people denounce their friends for
        reward,
    the eyes of their children will fail.

⁶"God has made me a byword to
        everyone,
    a man in whose face people spit.
⁷My eyes have grown dim with grief;
    my whole frame is but a shadow.
⁸The upright are appalled at this;
    the innocent are aroused against the
        ungodly.
⁹Nevertheless, the righteous will hold to
        their ways,
    and those with clean hands will grow
        stronger.

¹⁰"But come on, all of you, try again!
    I will not find a wise man among you.
¹¹My days have passed, my plans are
        shattered.
    Yet the desires of my heart
¹²turn night into day;
    in the face of the darkness light is
        near.
¹³If the only home I hope for is the grave,
    if I spread out my bed in the realm of
        darkness,
¹⁴if I say to corruption, 'You are my father,'
    and to the worm, 'My mother' or 'My
        sister,'
¹⁵where then is my hope—
    who can see any hope for me?
¹⁶Will it go down to the gates of death?
    Will we descend together into the
        dust?"

Bildad

18

Then Bildad the Shuhite replied:

²"When will you end these
        speeches?
    Be sensible, and then we can talk.
³Why are we regarded as cattle
    and considered stupid in your sight?
⁴You who tear yourself to pieces in your
        anger,
    is the earth to be abandoned for your
        sake?
    Or must the rocks be moved from
        their place?

⁵"The lamp of a wicked man is snuffed
        out;
    the flame of his fire stops burning.
⁶The light in his tent becomes dark;
    the lamp beside him goes out.
⁷The vigor of his step is weakened;
    his own schemes throw him down.
⁸His feet thrust him into a net;
    he wanders into its mesh.
⁹A trap seizes him by the heel;
    a snare holds him fast.
¹⁰A noose is hidden for him on the ground;
    a trap lies in his path.
¹¹Terrors startle him on every side
    and dog his every step.
¹²Calamity is hungry for him;
    disaster is ready for him when he
        falls.
¹³It eats away parts of his skin;
    death's firstborn devours his limbs.
¹⁴He is torn from the security of his tent
    and marched off to the king of
        terrors.
¹⁵Fire resides^a in his tent;
    burning sulfur is scattered over his
        dwelling.
¹⁶His roots dry up below
    and his branches wither above.
¹⁷The memory of him perishes from the
        earth;
    he has no name in the land.
¹⁸He is driven from light into the realm of
        darkness
    and is banished from the world.
¹⁹He has no offspring or descendants
        among his people,
    no survivor where once he lived.
²⁰People of the west are appalled at his
        fate;

---

a 15 Or *Nothing he had remains*

those of the east are seized with
horror.
²¹ Surely such is the dwelling of an evil
man;
such is the place of one who knows
not God."

Job

19

Then Job replied:

² "How long will you torment me
and crush me with words?
³ Ten times now you have reproached me;
shamelessly you attack me.
⁴ If it is true that I have gone astray,
my error remains my concern alone.
⁵ If indeed you would exalt yourselves
above me
and use my humiliation against me,
⁶ then know that God has wronged me
and drawn his net around me.

⁷ "Though I cry, 'Violence!' I get no
response;
though I call for help, there is no
justice.
⁸ He has blocked my way so I cannot pass;
he has shrouded my paths in
darkness.
⁹ He has stripped me of my honor
and removed the crown from my
head.
¹⁰ He tears me down on every side till I am
gone;
he uproots my hope like a tree.
¹¹ His anger burns against me;
he counts me among his enemies.
¹² His troops advance in force;
they build a siege ramp against me
and encamp around my tent.

¹³ "He has alienated my family from me;
my acquaintances are completely
estranged from me.
¹⁴ My relatives have gone away;
my friends have forgotten me.
¹⁵ My guests and my female servants count
me a foreigner;
they look on me as on a stranger.
¹⁶ I summon my servant, but he does not
answer,

though I beg him with my own
mouth.
¹⁷ My breath is offensive to my wife;
I am loathsome to my own family.
¹⁸ Even the little boys scorn me;
when I appear, they ridicule me.
¹⁹ All my intimate friends detest me;
those I love have turned against me.
²⁰ I am nothing but skin and bones;
I have escaped only by the skin of my
teeth. ᵃ

²¹ "Have pity on me, my friends, have pity,
for the hand of God has struck me.
²² Why do you pursue me as God does?
Will you never get enough of my
flesh?

²³ "Oh, that my words were recorded,
that they were written on a scroll,
²⁴ that they were inscribed with an iron
tool on ᵇ lead,
or engraved in rock forever!
²⁵ I know that my redeemer ᶜ lives,
and that in the end he will stand on
the earth. ᵈ
²⁶ And after my skin has been destroyed,
yet ᵉ in ᶠ my flesh I will see God;
²⁷ I myself will see him
with my own eyes—I, and not
another.
How my heart yearns within me!

²⁸ "If you say, 'How we will hound him,
since the root of the trouble lies in
him,ᵍ'
²⁹ you should fear the sword yourselves;
for wrath will bring punishment by
the sword,
and then you will know that there is
judgment. ʰ"

Zophar

20

Then Zophar the Naamathite
replied:

² "My troubled thoughts prompt me to
answer
because I am greatly disturbed.
³ I hear a rebuke that dishonors me,
and my understanding inspires me to
reply.

ᵃ 20 Or only by my gums   ᵇ 24 Or and   ᶜ 25 Or vindicator   ᵈ 25 Or on my grave   ᵉ 26 Or And
after I awake, / though this ⸌body⸍ has been destroyed, / then   ᶠ 26 Or destroyed, / apart from   ᵍ 28 Many
Hebrew manuscripts, Septuagint and Vulgate; most Hebrew manuscripts me   ʰ 29 Or sword, / that you
may come to know the Almighty

THURSDAY

Union With God

Job 19:1–29 *or* 19:25–27

Romano Guardini {AD 1885–1968}

The deepest core, the highest aspirations, the whole essence and purpose of man's striving can be summed up in the proposition: man's soul longs for union with God. This is not merely the expression of a pious sentiment; it is the precise truth.

We want to possess that which we consider to be precious and real. But is there anything in the world which we are really able to possess? Something catches our fancy, we buy it, we take it and carry it home, but do we really possess it? It is true we can make use of it; we can prevent anyone else having it, but is it ever truly ours? Not only may we lose it, not only can it be ruined, not only shall we have to give it up one day—we never really have it; we only hold it externally. We are never able to form that innermost union between ourselves and things which alone can be called having; there always remains a gulf.

The same applies to human relations. We want to establish a close relationship—a true union—with another person. We want to be certain of the other person, but can we ever achieve this? We may gain a person's confidence or love; we may be linked to that person by the strongest bonds of loyalty and devotion, but ultimately that person still remains distant and inaccessible. God alone, the all-true, the all-being, the Holy, the Remote, is able to give Himself fully to man. Neither things nor persons, nor even we ourselves, can fully become our own: only God can create that nearness that fulfills our yearning.

Henry Gariepy

For each of us, our trials and sorrows can become a passage to a deeper trust, a more steadfast faith, and a closer relationship with God.

— *reflection* —

1. What person do you wish you were closer to?

2. What efforts have you made to grow closer to that person?

3. As a result of today's readings, have you adjusted your expectations for your human relationships?

For your next devotional reading, go to page 579.

4 "Surely you know how it has been from
  of old,
    ever since people were *a* placed on the
    earth,
5 that the mirth of the wicked is brief,
    the joy of the godless lasts but a
    moment.
6 Though his pride reaches to the heavens
    and his head touches the clouds,
7 he will perish forever, like his own dung;
    those who have seen him will say,
    'Where is he?'
8 Like a dream he flies away, no more to
    be found,
    banished like a vision of the night.
9 The eye that saw him will not see him
    again;
    his place will look on him no more.
10 His children must make amends to the
    poor;
    his own hands must give back his
    wealth.
11 The youthful vigor that fills his bones
    will lie with him in the dust.

12 "Though evil is sweet in his mouth
    and he hides it under his tongue,
13 though he cannot bear to let it go
    and lets it linger in his mouth,
14 yet his food will turn sour in his
    stomach;
    it will become the venom of serpents
    within him.
15 He will spit out the riches he swallowed;
    God will make his stomach vomit
    them up.
16 He will suck the poison of serpents;
    the fangs of an adder will kill him.
17 He will not enjoy the streams,
    the rivers flowing with honey and
    cream.
18 What he toiled for he must give back
    uneaten;
    he will not enjoy the profit from his
    trading.
19 For he has oppressed the poor and left
    them destitute;
    he has seized houses he did not build.

20 "Surely he will have no respite from his
    craving;
    he cannot save himself by his
    treasure.
21 Nothing is left for him to devour;

his prosperity will not endure.
22 In the midst of his plenty, distress will
    overtake him;
    the full force of misery will come
    upon him.
23 When he has filled his belly,
    God will vent his burning anger
    against him
    and rain down his blows on him.
24 Though he flees from an iron weapon,
    a bronze-tipped arrow pierces him.
25 He pulls it out of his back,
    the gleaming point out of his liver.
  Terrors will come over him;
26   total darkness lies in wait for his
    treasures.
  A fire unfanned will consume him
    and devour what is left in his tent.
27 The heavens will expose his guilt;
    the earth will rise up against him.
28 A flood will carry off his house,
    rushing waters *b* on the day of God's
    wrath.
29 Such is the fate God allots the wicked,
    the heritage appointed for them by
    God."

Job

21

Then Job replied:

2 "Listen carefully to my words;
    let this be the consolation you give
    me.
3 Bear with me while I speak,
    and after I have spoken, mock on.

4 "Is my complaint directed to a human
    being?
    Why should I not be impatient?
5 Look at me and be appalled;
    clap your hand over your mouth.
6 When I think about this, I am terrified;
    trembling seizes my body.
7 Why do the wicked live on,
    growing old and increasing in power?
8 They see their children established
    around them,
    their offspring before their eyes.
9 Their homes are safe and free from fear;
    the rod of God is not on them.
10 Their bulls never fail to breed;
    their cows calve and do not miscarry.
11 They send forth their children as a flock;
    their little ones dance about.

a 4 Or *since Adam was*   *b 28* Or *The possessions in his house will be carried off, / washed away*

12 They sing to the music of timbrel and
lyre;
they make merry to the sound of the
pipe.
13 They spend their years in prosperity
and go down to the grave in peace. *a*
14 Yet they say to God, 'Leave us alone!
We have no desire to know your ways.
15 Who is the Almighty, that we should
serve him?
What would we gain by praying to
him?'
16 But their prosperity is not in their own
hands,
so I stand aloof from the counsel of
the wicked.
17 "Yet how often is the lamp of the wicked
snuffed out?
How often does calamity come upon
them,
the fate God allots in his anger?
18 How often are they like straw before the
wind,
like chaff swept away by a gale?
19 It is said, 'God stores up the
punishment of the wicked for
their children.'
Let him repay the wicked, so that
they themselves will
experience it!
20 Let their own eyes see their destruction;
let them drink of the wrath of the
Almighty.
21 For what do they care about the families
they leave behind
when their allotted months come to
an end?
22 "Can anyone teach knowledge to God,
since he judges even the highest?
23 One person dies in full vigor,
completely secure and at ease,
24 well nourished in body, *b*
bones rich with marrow.
25 Another dies in bitterness of soul,
never having enjoyed anything good.
26 Side by side they lie in the dust,
and worms cover them both.
27 "I know full well what you are thinking,
the schemes by which you would
wrong me.

28 You say, 'Where now is the house of the
great,
the tents where the wicked lived?'
29 Have you never questioned those who
travel?
Have you paid no regard to their
accounts—
30 that the wicked are spared from the day
of calamity,
that they are delivered from *c* the day
of wrath?
31 Who denounces their conduct to their
face?
Who repays them for what they have
done?
32 They are carried to the grave,
and watch is kept over their tombs.
33 The soil in the valley is sweet to them;
everyone follows after them,
and a countless throng goes *d* before
them.
34 "So how can you console me with your
nonsense?
Nothing is left of your answers but
falsehood!"

Eliphaz

22 Then Eliphaz the Temanite replied:

2 "Can a human being be of benefit to
God?
Can even the wise benefit him?
3 What pleasure would it give the
Almighty if you were
righteous?
What would he gain if your ways were
blameless?

4 "Is it for your piety that he rebukes you
and brings charges against you?
5 Is not your wickedness great?
Are not your sins endless?
6 You demanded security from your
relatives for no reason;
you stripped people of their clothing,
leaving them naked.
7 You gave no water to the weary
and you withheld food from the
hungry,
8 though you were a powerful man,
owning land—

---

a 13 Or *in an instant*   *b 24* The meaning of the Hebrew for this word is uncertain.   *c 30* Or *are reserved for the day of calamity, / that they are brought forth to*   *d 33* Or *them, / as a countless throng went*

an honored man, living on it.
⁹ And you sent widows away empty-
handed
and broke the strength of the
fatherless.
¹⁰ That is why snares are all around you,
why sudden peril terrifies you,
¹¹ why it is so dark you cannot see,
and why a flood of water covers you.
¹² "Is not God in the heights of heaven?
And see how lofty are the highest
stars!
¹³ Yet you say, 'What does God know?
Does he judge through such
darkness?
¹⁴ Thick clouds veil him, so he does not see
us
as he goes about in the vaulted
heavens.'
¹⁵ Will you keep to the old path
that the wicked have trod?
¹⁶ They were carried off before their time,
their foundations washed away by a
flood.
¹⁷ They said to God, 'Leave us alone!
What can the Almighty do to us?'
¹⁸ Yet it was he who filled their houses
with good things,
so I stand aloof from the counsel of
the wicked.
¹⁹ The righteous see their ruin and rejoice;
the innocent mock them, saying,
²⁰ 'Surely our foes are destroyed,
and fire devours their wealth.'

²¹ "Submit to God and be at peace with
him;
in this way prosperity will come to
you.
²² Accept instruction from his mouth
and lay up his words in your heart.
²³ If you return to the Almighty, you will be
restored:
If you remove wickedness far from
your tent
²⁴ and assign your nuggets to the dust,
your gold of Ophir to the rocks in the
ravines,
²⁵ then the Almighty will be your gold,
the choicest silver for you.
²⁶ Surely then you will find delight in the
Almighty
and will lift up your face to God.

²⁷ You will pray to him, and he will hear
you,
and you will fulfill your vows.
²⁸ What you decide on will be done,
and light will shine on your ways.
²⁹ When people are brought low and you
say, 'Lift them up!'
then he will save the downcast.
³⁰ He will deliver even one who is not
innocent,
who will be delivered through the
cleanness of your hands."

Job

23

Then Job replied:

² "Even today my complaint is
bitter;
his hand ᵃ is heavy in spite of ᵇ my
groaning.
³ If only I knew where to find him;
if only I could go to his dwelling!
⁴ I would state my case before him
and fill my mouth with arguments.
⁵ I would find out what he would answer
me,
and consider what he would say to
me.
⁶ Would he vigorously oppose me?
No, he would not press charges
against me.
⁷ There the upright can establish their
innocence before him,
and there I would be delivered forever
from my judge.

⁸ "But if I go to the east, he is not there;
if I go to the west, I do not find him.
⁹ When he is at work in the north, I do not
see him;
when he turns to the south, I catch no
glimpse of him.
¹⁰ But he knows the way that I take;
when he has tested me, I will come
forth as gold.
¹¹ My feet have closely followed his steps;
I have kept to his way without turning
aside.
¹² I have not departed from the commands
of his lips;
I have treasured the words of his
mouth more than my daily
bread.

ᵃ 2 Septuagint and Syriac; Hebrew / *the hand on me*   ᵇ 2 Or *heavy on me in*

13 "But he stands alone, and who can
    oppose him?
    He does whatever he pleases.
14 He carries out his decree against me,
    and many such plans he still has in
    store.
15 That is why I am terrified before him;
    when I think of all this, I fear him.
16 God has made my heart faint;
    the Almighty has terrified me.
17 Yet I am not silenced by the darkness,
    by the thick darkness that covers my
    face.

24 "Why does the Almighty not set
    times for judgment?
    Why must those who know him
    look in vain for such days?
2 There are those who move boundary
    stones;
    they pasture flocks they have stolen.
3 They drive away the orphan's donkey
    and take the widow's ox in pledge.
4 They thrust the needy from the path
    and force all the poor of the land into
    hiding.
5 Like wild donkeys in the desert,
    the poor go about their labor of
    foraging food;
    the wasteland provides food for their
    children.
6 They gather fodder in the fields
    and glean in the vineyards of the
    wicked.
7 Lacking clothes, they spend the night
    naked;
    they have nothing to cover
    themselves in the cold.
8 They are drenched by mountain rains
    and hug the rocks for lack of shelter.
9 The fatherless child is snatched from the
    breast;
    the infant of the poor is seized for a
    debt.
10 Lacking clothes, they go about naked;
    they carry the sheaves, but still go
    hungry.
11 They crush olives among the terraces*a*;
    they tread the winepresses, yet suffer
    thirst.
12 The groans of the dying rise from the
    city,
    and the souls of the wounded cry out
    for help.

But God charges no one with
    wrongdoing.
13 "There are those who rebel against the
    light,
    who do not know its ways
    or stay in its paths.
14 When daylight is gone, the murderer
    rises up,
    kills the poor and needy,
    and in the night steals forth like a
    thief.
15 The eye of the adulterer watches for
    dusk;
    he thinks, 'No eye will see me,'
    and he keeps his face concealed.
16 In the dark, thieves break into houses,
    but by day they shut themselves in;
    they want nothing to do with the
    light.
17 For all of them, midnight is their
    morning;
    they make friends with the terrors of
    darkness.
18 "Yet they are foam on the surface of the
    water;
    their portion of the land is cursed,
    so that no one goes to the vineyards.
19 As heat and drought snatch away the
    melted snow,
    so the grave snatches away those who
    have sinned.
20 The womb forgets them,
    the worm feasts on them;
    the wicked are no longer remembered
    but are broken like a tree.
21 They prey on the barren and childless
    woman,
    and to the widow show no kindness.
22 But God drags away the mighty by his
    power;
    though they become established, they
    have no assurance of life.
23 He may let them rest in a feeling of
    security,
    but his eyes are on their ways.
24 For a little while they are exalted, and
    then they are gone;
    they are brought low and gathered up
    like all others;
    they are cut off like heads of grain.
25 "If this is not so, who can prove me false
    and reduce my words to nothing?"

---

a 11 The meaning of the Hebrew for this word is uncertain.

Bildad

25

Then Bildad the Shuhite replied:

2 "Dominion and awe belong to God;
he establishes order in the heights of heaven.
3 Can his forces be numbered?
On whom does his light not rise?
4 How then can a mortal be righteous before God?
How can one born of woman be pure?
5 If even the moon is not bright
and the stars are not pure in his eyes,
6 how much less a mortal, who is but a maggot—
a human being, who is only a worm!"

Job

26

Then Job replied:

2 "How you have helped the powerless!
How you have saved the arm that is feeble!
3 What advice you have offered to one without wisdom!
And what great insight you have displayed!
4 Who has helped you utter these words?
And whose spirit spoke from your mouth?

5 "The dead are in deep anguish,
those beneath the waters and all that live in them.
6 Death is naked before God;
Destruction[a] lies uncovered.
7 He spreads out the northern ⌊skies⌋ over empty space;
he suspends the earth over nothing.
8 He wraps up the waters in his clouds,
yet the clouds do not burst under their weight.
9 He covers the face of the full moon,
spreading his clouds over it.
10 He marks out the horizon on the face of the waters
for a boundary between light and darkness.
11 The pillars of the heavens quake,
aghast at his rebuke.
12 By his power he churned up the sea;
by his wisdom he cut Rahab to pieces.

13 By his breath the skies became fair;
his hand pierced the gliding serpent.
14 And these are but the outer fringe of his works;
how faint the whisper we hear of him!
Who then can understand the thunder of his power?"

Job's Final Word to His Friends

27

And Job continued his discourse:

2 "As surely as God lives, who has denied me justice,
the Almighty, who has made my life bitter,
3 as long as I have life within me,
the breath of God in my nostrils,
4 my lips will not say anything wicked,
and my tongue will not utter lies.
5 I will never admit you are in the right;
till I die, I will not deny my integrity.
6 I will maintain my innocence and never let go of it;
my conscience will not reproach me as long as I live.

7 "May my enemies be like the wicked,
my adversaries like the unjust!
8 For what hope have the godless when they are cut off,
when God takes away their life?
9 Does God listen to their cry
when distress comes upon them?
10 Will they find delight in the Almighty?
Will they call on God at all times?

11 "I will teach you about the power of God;
the ways of the Almighty I will not conceal.
12 You have all seen this yourselves.
Why then this meaningless talk?

13 "Here is the fate God allots to the wicked,
the heritage a ruthless man receives from the Almighty:
14 However many his children, their fate is the sword;
his offspring will never have enough to eat.
15 The plague will bury those who survive him,
and their widows will not weep for them.
16 Though he heaps up silver like dust

a 6 Hebrew *Abaddon*

and clothes like piles of clay,
17 what he lays up the righteous will wear,
    and the innocent will divide his silver.
18 The house he builds is like a moth's
    cocoon,
    like a hut made by a watchman.
19 He lies down wealthy, but will do so no
    more;
    when he opens his eyes, all is gone.
20 Terrors overtake him like a flood;
    a tempest snatches him away in the
    night.
21 The east wind carries him off, and he is
    gone;
    it sweeps him out of his place.
22 It hurls itself against him without mercy
    as he flees headlong from its power.
23 It claps its hands in derision
    and hisses them out of their place."

Interlude: Where Wisdom Is Found

28 There is a mine for silver
and a place where gold is
refined.
2 Iron is taken from the earth,
    and copper is smelted from ore.
3 Miners put an end to the darkness;
    they search out the farthest recesses
    for ore in the blackest darkness.
4 Far from human dwellings they cut a
    shaft,
    in places untouched by human feet;
    far from other people they dangle and
    sway.
5 The earth, from which food comes,
    is transformed below as by fire;
6 lapis lazuli comes from its rocks,
    and its dust contains nuggets of gold.
7 No bird of prey knows that hidden path,
    no falcon's eye has seen it.
8 Proud beasts do not set foot on it,
    and no lion prowls there.
9 The miners' hands assault the flinty rock
    and lay bare the roots of the
    mountains.
10 They tunnel through the rock;
    their eyes see all its treasures.
11 They search^a the sources of the rivers
    and bring hidden things to light.
12 But where can wisdom be found?
    Where does understanding dwell?
13 No mortal comprehends its worth;

it cannot be found in the land of the
    living.
14 The deep says, "It is not in me";
    the sea says, "It is not with me."
15 It cannot be bought with the finest gold,
    nor can its price be weighed out in
    silver.
16 It cannot be bought with the gold of
    Ophir,
    with precious onyx or lapis lazuli.
17 Neither gold nor crystal can compare
    with it,
    nor can it be had for jewels of gold.
18 Coral and jasper are not worthy of
    mention;
    the price of wisdom is beyond rubies.
19 The topaz of Cush cannot compare with
    it;
    it cannot be bought with pure gold.

20 Where then does wisdom come from?
    Where does understanding dwell?
21 It is hidden from the eyes of every living
    thing,
    concealed even from the birds in the
    sky.
22 Destruction^b and Death say,
    "Only a rumor of it has reached our
    ears."
23 God understands the way to it
    and he alone knows where it dwells,
24 for he views the ends of the earth
    and sees everything under the
    heavens.
25 When he established the force of the
    wind
    and measured out the waters,
26 when he made a decree for the rain
    and a path for the thunderstorm,
27 then he looked at wisdom and appraised
    it;
    he confirmed it and tested it.
28 And he said to the human race,
    "The fear of the Lord—that is
    wisdom,
    and to shun evil is understanding."

Job's Final Defense

29 Job continued his discourse:

2 "How I long for the months
gone by,
for the days when God watched over
    me,

---

a 11 Septuagint, Aquila and Vulgate; Hebrew *They dam up*   *b* 22 Hebrew *Abaddon*

FRIDAY

GOD IN THE MIDST OF OUR STRUGGLES

Job 29:1–25 *or* 29:1–6

Matt Redman

Though clearly we would never celebrate pain for pain's sake, from the canvas of Scripture and from the tapestry of our own lives, we begin to recognize that in times of anguish, God is always closer and more at work than we know. Though there is pain in the offering, we cry out, "Blessed be Your name," and before long, we often begin to witness the fruit of all He has accomplished in us or through us during these seasons of struggle . . .

No discipline seems pleasant at the time. In our hearts, minds or bodies, we may be struggling beneath the pain of a testing situation. But deep in our spirits, we learn to consider it joy, knowing that we not only can find Christ in the situation but also can become more like Him as a result of it. There are no wasted seasons in the economy of God . . .

Though the discipline may not seem pleasant at the time, it's far easier to endure (or count as joy and delight in!) if somehow within the bigger picture we manage to see the brushstrokes of God. As the seventeenth-century Madame Guyon commented, "It is the fire of suffering which will bring forth the gold of godliness."

CYPRIAN {ca. AD 200–258}

The fear of and faith in God should prepare you for everything—the loss of your property, the constant pain of agonizing disorders, the deadly and mournful separation from wife, children or dying dear ones. Don't let these things cause you to sin, but battle them. Don't let them weaken or break your faith, but show your strength in the struggle. All the injuries inflicted by present troubles are considered worthless in light of sure future blessings. Unless the battle comes first, there can't be victory . . . For the helmsman is recognized in a storm. In warfare, the quality of a soldier is demonstrated. Without danger, such behavior is merely on extravagant display; for struggle in suffering is the test of the truth. The tree that is deeply rooted isn't moved by gusts of wind. When the ship made of solid timbers is beaten by the waves, it isn't shattered. On the threshing floor, the strong and robust grains disregard the winds, while the empty chaff is carried away by the blasts against it.

reflection

1. In what ways can suffering help or hurt your faith?

2. How can suffering benefit you?

3. What can you do during the easier periods of life so that you're ready for times of suffering?

For your next devotional reading, go to page 582.

³ when his lamp shone on my head
    and by his light I walked through
        darkness!
⁴ Oh, for the days when I was in my
        prime,
    when God's intimate friendship
        blessed my house,
⁵ when the Almighty was still with me
    and my children were around me,
⁶ when my path was drenched with cream
    and the rock poured out for me
        streams of olive oil.

⁷ "When I went to the gate of the city
    and took my seat in the public square,
⁸ the young men saw me and stepped
        aside
    and the old men rose to their feet;
⁹ the chief men refrained from speaking
    and covered their mouths with their
        hands;
¹⁰ the voices of the nobles were hushed,
    and their tongues stuck to the roof of
        their mouths.
¹¹ Whoever heard me spoke well of me,
    and those who saw me commended
        me,
¹² because I rescued the poor who cried for
        help,
    and the fatherless who had none to
        assist them.
¹³ Those who were dying blessed me;
    I made the widow's heart sing.
¹⁴ I put on righteousness as my clothing;
    justice was my robe and my turban.
¹⁵ I was eyes to the blind
    and feet to the lame.
¹⁶ I was a father to the needy;
    I took up the case of the stranger.
¹⁷ I broke the fangs of the wicked
    and snatched the victims from their
        teeth.

¹⁸ "I thought, 'I will die in my own house,
    my days as numerous as the grains of
        sand.
¹⁹ My roots will reach to the water,
    and the dew will lie all night on my
        branches.
²⁰ My glory will remain fresh in me,
    the bow ever new in my hand.'

²¹ "People listened to me expectantly,
    waiting in silence for my counsel.

²² After I had spoken, they spoke no more;
    my words fell gently on their ears.
²³ They waited for me as for showers
    and drank in my words as the spring
        rain.
²⁴ When I smiled at them, they scarcely
        believed it;
    the light of my face was precious to
        them. ᵃ
²⁵ I chose the way for them and sat as their
        chief;
    I dwelt as a king among his troops;
    I was like one who comforts
        mourners.

30 "But now they mock me,
    men younger than I,
    whose fathers I would have
        disdained
    to put with my sheep dogs.
² Of what use was the strength of their
        hands to me,
    since their vigor had gone from
        them?
³ Haggard from want and hunger,
    they roamed ᵇ the parched land
    in desolate wastelands at night.
⁴ In the brush they gathered salt herbs,
    and their food ᶜ was the root of the
        broom bush.
⁵ They were banished from human
        society,
    shouted at as if they were thieves.
⁶ They were forced to live in the dry
        stream beds,
    among the rocks and in holes in the
        ground.
⁷ They brayed among the bushes
    and huddled in the undergrowth.
⁸ A base and nameless brood,
    they were driven out of the land.

⁹ "And now those young men mock me in
        song;
    I have become a byword among them.
¹⁰ They detest me and keep their distance;
    they do not hesitate to spit in my
        face.
¹¹ Now that God has unstrung my bow and
        afflicted me,
    they throw off restraint in my
        presence.
¹² On my right the tribe ᵈ attacks;

ᵃ 24 The meaning of the Hebrew for this clause is uncertain.   ᵇ 3 Or gnawed   ᶜ 4 Or fuel
ᵈ 12 The meaning of the Hebrew for this word is uncertain.

they lay snares for my feet,
they build their siege ramps against
me.
¹³ They break up my road;
they succeed in destroying me.
'No one can help him,' they say.
¹⁴ They advance as through a gaping
breach;
amid the ruins they come rolling in.
¹⁵ Terrors overwhelm me;
my dignity is driven away as by the
wind,
my safety vanishes like a cloud.

¹⁶ "And now my life ebbs away;
days of suffering grip me.
¹⁷ Night pierces my bones;
my gnawing pains never rest.
¹⁸ In his great power ⌞God⌟ becomes like
clothing to me ^a;
he binds me like the neck of my
garment.
¹⁹ He throws me into the mud,
and I am reduced to dust and ashes.

²⁰ "I cry out to you, God, but you do not
answer;
I stand up, but you merely look at me.
²¹ You turn on me ruthlessly;
with the might of your hand you
attack me.
²² You snatch me up and drive me before
the wind;
you toss me about in the storm.
²³ I know you will bring me down to death,
to the place appointed for all the
living.

²⁴ "Surely no one lays a hand on those who
are crushed
when they cry for help in their
distress.
²⁵ Have I not wept for those in trouble?
Has not my soul grieved for the poor?
²⁶ Yet when I hoped for good, evil came;
when I looked for light, then came
darkness.
²⁷ The churning inside me never stops;
days of suffering confront me.
²⁸ I go about blackened, but not by the sun;
I stand up in the assembly and cry for
help.
²⁹ I have become a brother of jackals,
a companion of owls.
³⁰ My skin grows black and peels;

my body burns with fever.
³¹ My lyre is tuned to mourning,
and my pipe to the sound of wailing.

31

"I made a covenant with my eyes
not to look lustfully at a virgin.
² For what is our lot from God
above,
our heritage from the Almighty on
high?
³ Is it not ruin for the wicked,
disaster for those who do wrong?
⁴ Does he not see my ways
and count my every step?

⁵ "If I have walked with falsehood
or my foot has hurried after deceit—
⁶ let God weigh me in honest scales
and he will know that I am
blameless—
⁷ if my steps have turned from the path,
if my heart has been led by my eyes,
or if my hands have been defiled,
⁸ then may others eat what I have sown,
and may my crops be uprooted.

⁹ "If my heart has been enticed by a
woman,
or if I have lurked at my neighbor's
door,
¹⁰ then may my wife grind another man's
grain,
and may other men sleep with her.
¹¹ For that would have been wicked,
a sin to be judged.
¹² It is a fire that burns to Destruction ^b;
it would have uprooted my harvest.

¹³ "If I have denied justice to any of my
servants,
whether male or female,
when they had a grievance against
me,
¹⁴ what will I do when God confronts me?
What will I answer when called to
account?
¹⁵ Did not he who made me in the womb
make them?
Did not the same one form us both
within our mothers?

¹⁶ "If I have denied the desires of the poor
or let the eyes of the widow grow
weary,
¹⁷ if I have kept my bread to myself,
not sharing it with the fatherless—

---

a 18 Hebrew; Septuagint ⌞God⌟ *grasps my clothing*   *b 12* Hebrew *Abaddon*

Wounds and Scars

Job 30:26–27

read/meditate

Read the passage several times. Think about the times you've tried to reason through suffering. Think about the moments of acceptance you've found.

pray

Put your suffering into words. Ask God for perseverance, for survival, for whatever you feel you most need during this season of your life. Listen for his reassurance and for his message to you from this passage.

contemplate

Consider the paradox of accepting suffering while hoping for it to pass. Let God guide you into both acceptance and hope.

additional reflection

No wound, no scar? Yet, as the Master shall the servant be.

—*Amy Carmichael*

It doesn't matter how great the pressure is. What really matters is where the pressure lies—whether it comes between you and God or whether it presses you nearer to his heart.

—*James Hudson Taylor*

For your next devotional reading, go to page 584.

¹⁸but from my youth I reared them as a
    father would,
    and from my birth I guided the
    widow—
¹⁹if I have seen anyone perishing for lack
    of clothing,
    or the needy without garments,
²⁰and their hearts did not bless me
    for warming them with the fleece
    from my sheep,
²¹if I have raised my hand against the
    fatherless,
    knowing that I had influence in court,
²²then let my arm fall from the shoulder,
    let it be broken off at the joint.
²³For I dreaded destruction from God,
    and for fear of his splendor I could
    not do such things.

²⁴"If I have put my trust in gold
    or said to pure gold, 'You are my
    security,'
²⁵if I have rejoiced over my great wealth,
    the fortune my hands had gained,
²⁶if I have regarded the sun in its radiance
    or the moon moving in splendor,
²⁷so that my heart was secretly enticed
    and my hand offered them a kiss of
    homage,
²⁸then these also would be sins to be
    judged,
    for I would have been unfaithful to
    God on high.

²⁹"If I have rejoiced at my enemies'
    misfortune
    or gloated over the trouble that came
    to them—
³⁰I have not allowed my mouth to sin
    by invoking a curse against their
    life—
³¹if those of my household have never
    said,
    'Who has not been filled with Job's
    meat?'—
³²but no stranger had to spend the night
    in the street,
    for my door was always open to the
    traveler—
³³if I have concealed my sin as people do,ᵃ
    by hiding my guilt in my heart
³⁴because I so feared the crowd

and so dreaded the contempt of the
    clans
    that I kept silent and would not go
    outside—

³⁵("Oh, that I had someone to hear me!
    I sign now my defense—let the
    Almighty answer me;
    let my accuser put his indictment in
    writing.
³⁶Surely I would wear it on my shoulder,
    I would put it on like a crown.
³⁷I would give him an account of my every
    step;
    I would present it to him as to a
    ruler.)—

³⁸"if my land cries out against me
    and all its furrows are wet with tears,
³⁹if I have devoured its yield without
    payment
    or broken the spirit of its tenants,
⁴⁰then let briers come up instead of wheat
    and stinkweed instead of barley."

The words of Job are ended.

Elihu

32 So these three men stopped answering Job, because he was righteous in his own eyes. ²But Elihu son of Barakel the Buzite, of the family of Ram, became very angry with Job for justifying himself rather than God. ³He was also angry with the three friends, because they had found no way to refute Job, and yet had condemned him.ᵇ ⁴Now Elihu had waited before speaking to Job because they were older than he. ⁵But when he saw that the three men had nothing more to say, his anger was aroused.

⁶So Elihu son of Barakel the Buzite said:

"I am young in years,
    and you are old;
    that is why I was fearful,
    not daring to tell you what I know.
⁷I thought, 'Age should speak;
    advanced years should teach
    wisdom.'
⁸But it is the spiritᶜ in mortals,
    the breath of the Almighty, that gives
    them understanding.
⁹It is not only the oldᵈ who are wise,

ᵃ 33 Or as Adam did   ᵇ 3 Masoretic Text; an ancient Hebrew scribal tradition Job, and so had
condemned God   ᶜ 8 Or Spirit; also in verse 18   ᵈ 9 Or many; or great

MONDAY

ALWAYS WITH US

Job 31:1–40 *or* 31:35–40

Anne Graham Lotz

What has caused you to doubt that Jesus sits on the throne? Do you question His absolute authority because some bad, unexpected thing has happened? Are you blinded to the vision of Him standing at the center of the universe in complete control of all that is taking place in your life? What is keeping your eyes tightly shut?

When the military police car pulled into your drive and two officers got out, knocked on your door and said, "We are sorry to inform you . . . ," did you cry out, "Jesus, are You on the throne?"

When your unmarried teenage daughter came home and told you she was pregnant, did you cry out, "Jesus, are You on the throne?"

When the sheriff's deputy called and said your son had been arrested for selling drugs, did you cry out, "Jesus, are You on the throne?"

When your husband retired and within the year was diagnosed with a terminal illness, did you cry out, "Jesus, are You on the throne?"

When your wife was left paralyzed by a drunk driver, did you cry out, "Jesus, are You on the throne?"

When you returned from work to find an eviction notice tacked to your apartment door, did you cry out, "Jesus, are You on the throne?" . . .

Are you so focused on whatever your situation is, which looks so radically different from what you had imagined, that you can't see Him? Have your tears blinded you to Him? Are you so focused on your own pain or grief or confusion or helplessness or hopelessness that you are missing out on the greatest blessing you will ever receive? Could it be, at this very moment in your life, that Jesus *is right there with you?*

JOHN WRIGHT FOLLETTE {AD 1883–1966}

Jesus, as Son of Man, learned obedience by the things he suffered. So will we as he conforms us to his image. He is a suffering God—a God of love, but a suffering God. So we, as cells in that body of Christ, partake of the same. He is a wonderful Redeemer, but he is a suffering Redeemer. The body is being formed and shaped, and we are the cells, and members. This body will have to partake of the same characteristics that we find in our wonderful Lord.

reflection

1. In what ways can you relate to Job?

2. How did Job's pain make him blind to the truth about God and the reality of God's plans for his life?

3. In what ways have you also been blinded by your suffering?

For your next devotional reading, go to page 590.

not only the aged who understand
what is right.

¹⁰ "Therefore I say: Listen to me;
I too will tell you what I know.
¹¹ I waited while you spoke,
I listened to your reasoning;
while you were searching for words,
¹² I gave you my full attention.
But not one of you has proved Job
wrong;
none of you has answered his
arguments.
¹³ Do not say, 'We have found wisdom;
let God refute him, not a mere
mortal.'
¹⁴ But Job has not marshaled his words
against me,
and I will not answer him with your
arguments.

¹⁵ "They are dismayed and have no more
to say;
words have failed them.
¹⁶ Must I wait, now that they are silent,
now that they stand there with no
reply?
¹⁷ I too will have my say;
I too will tell what I know.
¹⁸ For I am full of words,
and the spirit within me compels me;
¹⁹ inside I am like bottled-up wine,
like new wineskins ready to burst.
²⁰ I must speak and find relief;
I must open my lips and reply.
²¹ I will show no partiality,
nor will I flatter anyone;
²² for if I were skilled in flattery,
my Maker would soon take me away.

33 "But now, Job, listen to my
words;
pay attention to everything I say.
² I am about to open my mouth;
my words are on the tip of my
tongue.
³ My words come from an upright heart;
my lips sincerely speak what I know.
⁴ The Spirit of God has made me;
the breath of the Almighty gives me
life.
⁵ Answer me then, if you can;
stand up and argue your case before
me.

⁶ I am the same as you in God's sight;
I too am a piece of clay.
⁷ No fear of me should alarm you,
nor should my hand be heavy on you.

⁸ "But you have said in my hearing—
I heard the very words—
⁹ 'I am pure, I have done no wrong;
I am clean and free from sin.
¹⁰ Yet God has found fault with me;
he considers me his enemy.
¹¹ He fastens my feet in shackles;
he keeps close watch on all my
paths.'

¹² "But I tell you, in this you are not right,
for God is greater than any mortal.
¹³ Why do you complain to him
that he responds to no one's words ᵃ?
¹⁴ For God does speak—now one way, now
another—
though no one perceives it.
¹⁵ In a dream, in a vision of the night,
when deep sleep falls on people
as they slumber in their beds,
¹⁶ he may speak in their ears
and terrify them with warnings,
¹⁷ to turn them from wrongdoing
and keep them from pride,
¹⁸ to preserve them from the pit,
their lives from perishing by the
sword. ᵇ

¹⁹ "Or they may be chastened on a bed of
pain
with constant distress in their bones,
²⁰ so that their bodies find food repulsive
and their souls loathe the choicest
meal.
²¹ Their flesh wastes away to nothing,
and their bones, once hidden, now
stick out.
²² They draw near to the pit,
and their lives to the messengers of
death. ᶜ
²³ Yet if there is an angel at their side,
a messenger, one out of a thousand,
sent to tell them how to be upright,
²⁴ and he is gracious to them and says to
God,
'Spare them from going down to the
pit;
I have found a ransom for them—
²⁵ let their flesh be renewed like a child's;

ᵃ 13 Or that he does not answer for any of his actions place of the dead   ᵇ 18 Or from crossing the river   ᶜ 22 Or to the

let them be restored as in the days of
their youth'—
26 then they can pray to God and find favor
with him,
they will see God's face and shout for
joy;
he will restore them to full well-
being.
27 And they will go to others and say,
'We have sinned, we have perverted
what is right,
but we did not get what we deserved.
28 God has delivered us from going down
to the pit,
and we shall live to enjoy the light of
life.'
29 "God does all these things to people—
twice, even three times—
30 to turn them back from the pit,
that the light of life may shine on
them.
31 "Pay attention, Job, and listen to me;
be silent, and I will speak.
32 If you have anything to say, answer me;
speak up, for I want to vindicate you.
33 But if not, then listen to me;
be silent, and I will teach you
wisdom."

34

Then Elihu said:

2 "Hear my words, you wise
men;
listen to me, you men of learning.
3 For the ear tests words
as the tongue tastes food.
4 Let us discern for ourselves what is
right;
let us learn together what is good.

5 "Job says, 'I am innocent,
but God denies me justice.
6 Although I am right,
I am considered a liar;
although I am guiltless,
his arrow inflicts an incurable
wound.'
7 Is there anyone like Job,
who drinks scorn like water?
8 He keeps company with evildoers;
he associates with the wicked.
9 For he says, 'There is no profit
in trying to please God.'

10 "So listen to me, you men of
understanding.
Far be it from God to do evil,
from the Almighty to do wrong.
11 He repays everyone for what they have
done;
he brings on them what their conduct
deserves.
12 It is unthinkable that God would do
wrong,
that the Almighty would pervert
justice.
13 Who appointed him over the earth?
Who put him in charge of the whole
world?
14 If it were his intention
and he withdrew his spirit *a* and
breath,
15 all people would perish together
and would return to the dust.

16 "If you have understanding, hear this;
listen to what I say.
17 Can one who hates justice govern?
Will you condemn the just and
mighty One?
18 Is he not the One who says to kings,
'You are worthless,'
and to nobles, 'You are wicked,'
19 who shows no partiality to princes
and does not favor the rich over the
poor,
for they are all the work of his hands?
20 They die in an instant, in the middle of
the night;
the people are shaken and they pass
away;
the mighty are removed without
human hand.

21 "His eyes are on the ways of mortals;
he sees their every step.
22 There is no deep shadow, no utter
darkness,
where evildoers can hide.
23 God has no need to examine people
further,
that they should come before him for
judgment.
24 Without inquiry he shatters the mighty
and sets up others in their place.
25 Because he takes note of their deeds,
he overthrows them in the night and
they are crushed.

a 14 Or *Spirit*

²⁶ He punishes them for their wickedness
   where everyone can see them,
²⁷ because they turned from following him
   and had no regard for any of his ways.
²⁸ They caused the cry of the poor to come
   before him,
   so that he heard the cry of the needy.
²⁹ But if he remains silent, who can
   condemn him?
   If he hides his face, who can see him?
   Yet he is over individual and nation
   alike,
³⁰   to keep the godless from ruling,
   from laying snares for the people.

³¹ "Suppose someone says to God,
   'I am guilty but will offend no more.
³² Teach me what I cannot see;
   if I have done wrong, I will not do so
   again.'
³³ Should God then reward you on your
   terms,
   when you refuse to repent?
   You must decide, not I;
   so tell me what you know.

³⁴ "Men of understanding declare,
   wise men who hear me say to me,
³⁵ 'Job speaks without knowledge;
   his words lack insight.'
³⁶ Oh, that Job might be tested to the
   utmost
   for answering like a wicked man!
³⁷ To his sin he adds rebellion;
   scornfully he claps his hands among us
   and multiplies his words against
   God."

35

Then Elihu said:

² "Do you think this is just?
   You say, 'I am in the right, not God.'
³ Yet you ask him, 'What profit is it to
   me,ᵃ
   and what do I gain by not sinning?'

⁴ "I would like to reply to you
   and to your friends with you.
⁵ Look up at the heavens and see;
   gaze at the clouds so high above you.
⁶ If you sin, how does that affect him?
   If your sins are many, what does that
   do to him?

⁷ If you are righteous, what do you give to
   him,
   or what does he receive from your
   hand?
⁸ Your wickedness only affects human
   beings like yourself,
   and your righteousness only members
   of the human race.

⁹ "People cry out under a load of
   oppression;
   they plead for relief from the arm of
   the powerful.
¹⁰ But no one says, 'Where is God my
   Maker,
   who gives songs in the night,
¹¹ who teaches us more than he teachesᵇ
   the beasts of the earth
   and makes us wiser thanᶜ the birds in
   the sky?'
¹² He does not answer when people cry out
   because of the arrogance of the
   wicked.
¹³ Indeed, God does not listen to their
   empty plea;
   the Almighty pays no attention to it.
¹⁴ How much less, then, will he listen
   when you say that you do not see him,
   that your case is before him
   and you must wait for him,
¹⁵ and further, that his anger never
   punishes
   and he does not take the least notice
   of wickedness.ᵈ
¹⁶ So Job opens his mouth with empty talk;
   without knowledge he multiplies
   words."

36

Elihu continued:

² "Bear with me a little longer
   and I will show you
   that there is more to be said in God's
   behalf.
³ I get my knowledge from afar;
   I will ascribe justice to my Maker.
⁴ Be assured that my words are not false;
   one who has perfect knowledge is
   with you.

⁵ "God is mighty, but despises no one;
   he is mighty, and firm in his purpose.
⁶ He does not keep the wicked alive

ᵃ 3 Or you   ᵇ 10,11 Or night, / ¹¹who teaches us by   ᶜ 11 Or us wise by   ᵈ 15 Symmachus,
Theodotion and Vulgate; the meaning of the Hebrew for this word is uncertain.

but gives the afflicted their rights.
⁷ He does not take his eyes off the
  righteous;
  he enthrones them with kings
  and exalts them forever.
⁸ But if people are bound in chains,
  held fast by cords of affliction,
⁹ he tells them what they have done—
  that they have sinned arrogantly.
¹⁰ He makes them listen to correction
  and commands them to repent of
    their evil.
¹¹ If they obey and serve him,
  they will spend the rest of their days
    in prosperity
  and their years in contentment.
¹² But if they do not listen,
  they will perish by the sword ᵃ
  and die without knowledge.

¹³ "The godless in heart harbor
    resentment;
  even when he fetters them, they do
    not cry for help.
¹⁴ They die in their youth,
  among male prostitutes of the
    shrines.
¹⁵ But those who suffer he delivers in their
    suffering;
  he speaks to them in their affliction.

¹⁶ "He is wooing you from the jaws of
    distress
  to a spacious place free from
    restriction,
  to the comfort of your table laden
    with choice food.
¹⁷ But now you are laden with the
    judgment due the wicked;
  judgment and justice have taken hold
    of you.
¹⁸ Be careful that no one entices you by
    riches;
  do not let a large bribe turn you aside.
¹⁹ Would your wealth or even all your
    mighty efforts
  sustain you so you would not be in
    distress?
²⁰ Do not long for the night,
  to drag people away from their
    homes. ᵇ
²¹ Beware of turning to evil,
  which you seem to prefer to affliction.

²² "God is exalted in his power.
  Who is a teacher like him?
²³ Who has prescribed his ways for him,
  or said to him, 'You have done
    wrong'?
²⁴ Remember to extol his work,
  which people have praised in song.
²⁵ All human beings have seen it;
  mortals gaze on it from afar.
²⁶ How great is God—beyond our
    understanding!
  The number of his years is past
    finding out.

²⁷ "He draws up the drops of water,
  which distill as rain to the streams ᶜ;
²⁸ the clouds pour down their moisture
  and abundant showers fall on the
    human race.
²⁹ Who can understand how he spreads out
    the clouds,
  how he thunders from his pavilion?
³⁰ See how he scatters his lightning about
    him,
  bathing the depths of the sea.
³¹ This is the way he governs ᵈ the nations
  and provides food in abundance.
³² He fills his hands with lightning
  and commands it to strike its mark.
³³ His thunder announces the coming
    storm;
  even the cattle make known its
    approach. ᵉ

37

"At this my heart pounds
and leaps from its place.
² Listen! Listen to the roar of his
  voice,
to the rumbling that comes from his
  mouth.
³ He unleashes his lightning beneath the
    whole heaven
  and sends it to the ends of the earth.
⁴ After that comes the sound of his roar;
  he thunders with his majestic voice.
When his voice resounds,
  he holds nothing back.
⁵ God's voice thunders in marvelous ways;
  he does great things beyond our
    understanding.
⁶ He says to the snow, 'Fall on the earth,'
  and to the rain shower, 'Be a mighty
    downpour.'

ᵃ 12 Or will cross the river   ᵇ 20 The meaning of the Hebrew for verses 18-20 is uncertain.
ᶜ 27 Or distill from the mist as rain   ᵈ 31 Or nourishes   ᵉ 33 Or announces his coming— / the One
zealous against evil

⁷ So that everyone he has made may know
  his work,
  he stops all mortals from their labor. ᵃ
⁸ The animals take cover;
  they remain in their dens.
⁹ The tempest comes out from its
  chamber,
  the cold from the driving winds.
¹⁰ The breath of God produces ice,
  and the broad waters become frozen.
¹¹ He loads the clouds with moisture;
  he scatters his lightning through
  them.
¹² At his direction they swirl around
  over the face of the whole earth
  to do whatever he commands them.
¹³ He brings the clouds to punish people,
  or to water his earth and show his
  love.

¹⁴ "Listen to this, Job;
  stop and consider God's wonders.
¹⁵ Do you know how God controls the
  clouds
  and makes his lightning flash?
¹⁶ Do you know how the clouds hang
  poised,
  those wonders of him who has perfect
  knowledge?
¹⁷ You who swelter in your clothes
  when the land lies hushed under the
  south wind,
¹⁸ can you join him in spreading out the
  skies,
  hard as a mirror of cast bronze?

¹⁹ "Tell us what we should say to him;
  we cannot draw up our case because
  of our darkness.
²⁰ Should he be told that I want to speak?
  Would anyone ask to be swallowed
  up?
²¹ Now no one can look at the sun,
  bright as it is in the skies
  after the wind has swept them clean.
²² Out of the north he comes in golden
  splendor;
  God comes in awesome majesty.
²³ The Almighty is beyond our reach and
  exalted in power;
  in his justice and great righteousness,
  he does not oppress.
²⁴ Therefore, people revere him,

for does he not have regard for all the
  wise in heart? ᵇ"

The Lord Speaks

38 Then the Lord spoke to Job out
of the storm. He said:

² "Who is this that obscures my plans
  with words without knowledge?
³ Prepare to defend yourself;
  I will question you,
  and you shall answer me.

⁴ "Where were you when I laid the earth's
  foundation?
  Tell me, if you understand.
⁵ Who marked off its dimensions? Surely
  you know!
  Who stretched a measuring line
  across it?
⁶ On what were its footings set,
  or who laid its cornerstone—
⁷ while the morning stars sang together
  and all the angels ᶜ shouted for joy?

⁸ "Who shut up the sea behind doors
  when it burst forth from the womb,
⁹ when I made the clouds its garment
  and wrapped it in thick darkness,
¹⁰ when I fixed limits for it
  and set its doors and bars in place,
¹¹ when I said, 'This far you may come and
  no farther;
  here is where your proud waves halt'?

¹² "Have you ever given orders to the
  morning,
  or shown the dawn its place,
¹³ that it might take the earth by the edges
  and shake the wicked out of it?
¹⁴ The earth takes shape like clay under a
  seal;
  its features stand out like those of a
  garment.
¹⁵ The wicked are denied their light,
  and their upraised arm is broken.

¹⁶ "Have you journeyed to the springs of
  the sea
  or walked in the recesses of the deep?
¹⁷ Have the gates of death been shown to
  you?
  Have you seen the gates of the
  deepest darkness?

ᵃ 7 Or work, / he fills all mortals with fear by his power
think they are wise.   ᶜ 7 Hebrew the sons of God
ᵇ 24 Or for he does not have regard for any who

TUESDAY

KNOWING OUR PLACE
Job 38:1—39:30 *or* 38:1–5

Philip Yancey

"[Are not two sparrows sold for a penny? Yet not one of them will fall to the ground outside your Father's care,]" promised Jesus. "And even the very hairs of your head are all numbered. So don't be afraid; you are worth more than many sparrows." Yet sparrows still fall to the ground, as do the hairs from chemotherapied human heads; and of sixty leatherback turtles born, only two or three survive. A sovereign God who wills against his ultimate will, who superintends a universe of a hundred billion galaxies and yet lavishes intimate attention on its tiny creatures—how do I comprehend such a God?

Sometimes I rail against the mysteries and sometimes I accept them. As a starting point, I take for granted that a creature's proper response to God is humility. Accepting creatureliness may require that I, like Job, bow before a master plan that makes no apparent sense.

In the face of doubt, I have learned the simple response of considering the alternatives. If there is no Creator, what then? I would have to view the world with all its suffering as well as all its beauty as a random product of a meaningless universe, the briefest flare of a match in cosmic darkness. Perhaps the very sense that *something is wrong* is itself a rumor of transcendence, an inbuilt longing for a healed planet on which God's will is done "on earth as it is in heaven."

ANDREW MURRAY {AD 1828–1917}

Consider how lovely, how beautiful, how pleasing to God humility is. Since you were created for the honor of God, it is appropriate for you to be humble (see Genesis 1:27; 1 Corinthians 11:7) . . .

But here, as everywhere in the life of grace, let faith be the chief means by which you achieve this. Believe in the power of the eternal life that works in you. Believe in the power of Jesus, who is your life. Believe in the power of the Holy Spirit, who dwells in you. Do not attempt to hide your pride or to forget it or to root it out yourself. Instead, in the sure confidence that the blood cleanses and the Spirit sanctifies, confess every trace of this sin. Learn from Jesus, who is gentle and humble in heart. Consider that he is your life, and all that he has is yours . . . Be clothed with humility, in order that you may be clothed with Jesus. It is Christ in you that shall fill you with humility.

reflection

1. Have you ever questioned God's plan for your life?

2. What does it mean that God is the Creator and you are his creation?

3. How does coming face to face with the realities of who God is produce humility?

For your next devotional reading, go to page 594.

¹⁸ Have you comprehended the vast
    expanses of the earth?
    Tell me, if you know all this.

¹⁹ "What is the way to the abode of light?
    And where does darkness reside?
²⁰ Can you take them to their places?
    Do you know the paths to their
    dwellings?
²¹ Surely you know, for you were already
    born!
    You have lived so many years!

²² "Have you entered the storehouses of
    the snow
    or seen the storehouses of the hail,
²³ which I reserve for times of trouble,
    for days of war and battle?
²⁴ What is the way to the place where the
    lightning is dispersed,
    or the place where the east winds are
    scattered over the earth?
²⁵ Who cuts a channel for the torrents of
    rain,
    and a path for the thunderstorm,
²⁶ to water a land where no one lives,
    an uninhabited desert,
²⁷ to satisfy a desolate wasteland
    and make it sprout with grass?
²⁸ Does the rain have a father?
    Who fathers the drops of dew?
²⁹ From whose womb comes the ice?
    Who gives birth to the frost from the
    heavens
³⁰ when the waters become hard as stone,
    when the surface of the deep is
    frozen?

³¹ "Can you bind the chains^a of the
    Pleiades?
    Can you loosen Orion's belt?
³² Can you bring forth the constellations in
    their seasons^b
    or lead out the Bear^c with its cubs?
³³ Do you know the laws of the heavens?
    Can you set up ⌊God's^d⌋ dominion
    over the earth?

³⁴ "Can you raise your voice to the clouds
    and cover yourself with a flood of
    water?
³⁵ Do you send the lightning bolts on their
    way?
    Do they report to you, 'Here we are'?

³⁶ Who gives the ibis wisdom ⌊about the
    flooding of the Nile⌋,
    or gives the rooster understanding ⌊of
    when to crow⌋?^e
³⁷ Who has the wisdom to count the
    clouds?
    Who can tip over the water jars of the
    heavens
³⁸ when the dust becomes hard
    and the clods of earth stick together?

³⁹ "Do you hunt the prey for the lioness
    and satisfy the hunger of the lions
⁴⁰ when they crouch in their dens
    or lie in wait in a thicket?
⁴¹ Who provides food for the raven
    when its young cry out to God
    and wander about for lack of food?

39

    "Do you know when the
    mountain goats give birth?
    Do you watch when the doe
    bears her fawn?
² Do you count the months till they bear?
    Do you know the time they give
    birth?
³ They crouch down and bring forth their
    young;
    their labor pains are ended.
⁴ Their young thrive and grow strong in
    the wilds;
    they leave and do not return.

⁵ "Who let the wild donkey go free?
    Who untied its ropes?
⁶ I gave it the wasteland as its home,
    the salt flats as its habitat.
⁷ It laughs at the commotion in the town;
    it does not hear a driver's shout.
⁸ It ranges the hills for its pasture
    and searches for any green thing.

⁹ "Will the wild ox consent to serve you?
    Will it stay by your manger at night?
¹⁰ Can you hold it to the furrow with a
    harness?
    Will it till the valleys behind you?
¹¹ Will you rely on it for its great strength?
    Will you leave your heavy work to it?
¹² Can you trust it to haul in your grain
    and bring it to your threshing floor?

¹³ "The wings of the ostrich flap joyfully,
    though they cannot compare

---

^a 31 Septuagint; Hebrew *beauty*   ^b 32 Or *the morning star in its season*   ^c 32 Or *out Leo*
^d 33 Or *his;* or *their*   ^e 36 The meaning of the Hebrew for this verse is uncertain.

with the wings and feathers of the
stork.
¹⁴ She lays her eggs on the ground
and lets them warm in the sand,
¹⁵ unmindful that a foot may crush them,
that some wild animal may trample
them.
¹⁶ She treats her young harshly, as if they
were not hers;
she cares not that her labor was in
vain,
¹⁷ for God did not endow her with wisdom
or give her a share of good sense.
¹⁸ Yet when she spreads her feathers to
run,
she laughs at horse and rider.

¹⁹ "Do you give the horse its strength
or clothe its neck with a flowing
mane?
²⁰ Do you make it leap like a locust,
striking terror with its proud
snorting?
²¹ It paws fiercely, rejoicing in its strength,
and charges into the fray.
²² It laughs at fear, afraid of nothing;
it does not shy away from the sword.
²³ The quiver rattles against its side,
along with the flashing spear and
lance.
²⁴ In frenzied excitement it eats up the
ground;
it cannot stand still when the trumpet
sounds.
²⁵ At the blast of the trumpet it snorts,
'Aha!'
It catches the scent of battle from
afar,
the shout of commanders and the
battle cry.

²⁶ "Does the hawk take flight by your
wisdom
and spread its wings toward the
south?
²⁷ Does the eagle soar at your command
and build its nest on high?
²⁸ It dwells on a cliff and stays there at
night;
a rocky crag is its stronghold.
²⁹ From there it looks for food;
its eyes detect it from afar.
³⁰ Its young ones feast on blood,
and where the slain are, there it is."

40 The LORD said to Job:

² "Will the one who contends
with the Almighty correct him?
Let him who accuses God answer
him!"

³ Then Job answered the LORD:

⁴ "I am unworthy—how can I reply to
you?
I put my hand over my mouth.
⁵ I spoke once, but I have no answer—
twice, but I will say no more."

⁶ Then the LORD spoke to Job out of the
storm:

⁷ "Prepare to defend yourself;
I will question you,
and you shall answer me.

⁸ "Would you discredit my justice?
Would you condemn me to justify
yourself?
⁹ Do you have an arm like God's,
and can your voice thunder like his?
¹⁰ Then adorn yourself with glory and
splendor,
and clothe yourself in honor and
majesty.
¹¹ Unleash the fury of your wrath,
look at all who are proud and bring
them low,
¹² look at all who are proud and humble
them,
crush the wicked where they stand.
¹³ Bury them all in the dust together;
shroud their faces in the grave.
¹⁴ Then I myself will admit to you
that your own right hand can save
you.

¹⁵ "Look at the behemoth,^a
which I made along with you
and which feeds on grass like an ox.
¹⁶ What strength it has in its loins,
what power in the muscles of its
belly!
¹⁷ Its tail sways like a cedar;
the sinews of its thighs are close-knit.
¹⁸ Its bones are tubes of bronze,
its limbs like rods of iron.
¹⁹ It ranks first among the works of God,
yet its Maker can approach it with his
sword.

^a 15 Possibly the hippopotamus or the elephant

²⁰ The hills bring it their produce,
and all the wild animals play nearby.
²¹ Under the lotus plants it lies,
hidden among the reeds in the marsh.
²² The lotuses conceal it in their shadow;
the poplars by the stream surround it.
²³ A raging river does not alarm it;
it is secure, though the Jordan should
surge against its mouth.
²⁴ Can anyone capture it by the eyes,
or trap it and pierce its nose?

41

[*]"Can you pull in the
leviathan^a with a fishhook
or tie down its tongue with a
rope?
² Can you put a cord through its nose
or pierce its jaw with a hook?
³ Will it keep begging you for mercy?
Will it speak to you with gentle
words?
⁴ Will it make an agreement with you
for you to take it as your slave for
life?
⁵ Can you make a pet of it like a bird
or put it on a leash for the young
women in your house?
⁶ Will traders barter for it?
Will they divide it up among the
merchants?
⁷ Can you fill its hide with harpoons
or its head with fishing spears?
⁸ If you lay a hand on it,
you will remember the struggle and
never do it again!
^{*9} Any hope of subduing it is false;
the mere sight of it is overpowering.
¹⁰ No one is fierce enough to rouse it.
Who then is able to stand against
me?
¹¹ Who has a claim against me that I must
pay?
Everything under heaven belongs to
me.
¹² "I will not fail to speak of Leviathan's
limbs,
its strength and its graceful form.
¹³ Who can strip off its outer coat?
Who can penetrate its double coat of
armor?^b
¹⁴ Who dares open the doors of its mouth,
ringed about with fearsome teeth?

¹⁵ Its back has^c rows of shields
tightly sealed together;
¹⁶ each is so close to the next
that no air can pass between.
¹⁷ They are joined fast to one another;
they cling together and cannot be
parted.
¹⁸ Its snorting throws out flashes of light;
its eyes are like the rays of dawn.
¹⁹ Flames stream from its mouth;
sparks of fire shoot out.
²⁰ Smoke pours from its nostrils
as from a boiling pot over burning
reeds.
²¹ Its breath sets coals ablaze,
and flames dart from its mouth.
²² Strength resides in its neck;
dismay goes before it.
²³ The folds of its flesh are tightly joined;
they are firm and immovable.
²⁴ Its chest is hard as rock,
hard as a lower millstone.
²⁵ When it rises up, the mighty are
terrified;
they retreat before its thrashing.
²⁶ The sword that reaches it has no effect,
nor does the spear or the dart or the
javelin.
²⁷ Iron it treats like straw
and bronze like rotten wood.
²⁸ Arrows do not make it flee;
slingstones are like chaff to it.
²⁹ A club seems to it but a piece of straw;
it laughs at the rattling of the lance.
³⁰ Its undersides are jagged potsherds,
leaving a trail in the mud like a
threshing sledge.
³¹ It makes the depths churn like a boiling
caldron
and stirs up the sea like a pot of
ointment.
³² It leaves a glistening wake behind it;
one would think the deep had white
hair.
³³ Nothing on earth is its equal—
a creature without fear.
³⁴ It looks down on all that are haughty;
it is king over all that are proud."

---

^a 1 Possibly the crocodile   ^b 13 Septuagint; Hebrew *double bridle*   ^c 15 Or *Its pride is its*

* 41:1-8 is numbered 40:25-32 in Hebrew texts.   * 41:9-34 is numbered 41:1-26 in Hebrew texts.

WEDNESDAY

GOD AND JOB

Job 42:1–17 *or* 42:12–15

Philip Yancey

In exaggerated form, Job affirms the mystery that, for whatever reason, God has given individual human beings a significant role to play in remaking a spoiled planet. When a pastor goes to prison for his peaceful protest against injustice, when a social worker moves into an urban ghetto in order to rebuild community from the ground up, when a couple refuses to give up on a difficult marriage, when a parent waits with undying hope and forgiveness for the return of an estranged child, when a son or daughter chooses to care for a terminally ill parent rather than investigate euthanasia, when a young professional resists mounting temptations toward wealth and success—in all these sufferings large and small there is the assurance of a deeper level of meaning, of a sharing in Christ's own redemptive victory. "The creation waits in eager expectation for the [children] of God to be revealed" (Romans 8:19).

No one has expressed the pain and unfairness of this world any better than Job. Yet behind those words of anguish lies a darkly shining truth: Job and you and I can through obedience join the struggle to reverse that suffering. Job paints the drama of faith in its starkest form: the best man on earth suffering the worst, with no sign of encouragement or comfort from God. The fact that Job continued to trust God, against all odds, mattered— for him, for us and for God. In his speech God described the wonders of natural creation, yet clearly the wonder of creation that impressed God most was Job himself, hence this book in the Bible.

MATTHEW HENRY {AD 1662–1714}

In general, Job was a great sufferer; he was emptied and humbled, which ultimately led to his greater glory. So Christ lowered himself, that we might be exalted. The learned bishop Patrick quotes Saint Jerome more than once speaking of Job as a type (a representation) of Christ: who for the joy that was set before him endured the cross, who was persecuted for a time by men and devils and who seemed forsaken of God too, but was raised to be an intercessor even for his friends.

reflection

1. How does Job's perseverance in faith through his dark times encourage you in your own painful struggles?

2. Have you ever been in a place where you just couldn't see the reason for the pain you were experiencing?

3. How can you find hope in God in those moments?

For your next devotional reading, go to page 597.

Job

42

Then Job replied to the LORD:

2 "I know that you can do all
   things;
   no purpose of yours can be thwarted.
3 You asked, 'Who is this that obscures my
   plans without knowledge?'
   Surely I spoke of things I did not
   understand,
   things too wonderful for me to know.

4 "You said, 'Listen now, and I will speak;
   I will question you,
   and you shall answer me.'
5 My ears had heard of you
   but now my eyes have seen you.
6 Therefore I despise myself
   and repent in dust and ashes."

Epilogue

7 After the LORD had said these things to
Job, he said to Eliphaz the Temanite, "I am
angry with you and your two friends, because you have not spoken of me what is
right, as my servant Job has. 8 So now take
seven bulls and seven rams and go to my
servant Job and sacrifice a burnt offering for
yourselves. My servant Job will pray for you,
and I will accept his prayer and not deal
with you according to your folly. You have
not spoken of me what is right, as my servant Job has." 9 So Eliphaz the Temanite, Bildad the Shuhite and Zophar the Naamathite
did what the LORD told them; and the LORD
accepted Job's prayer.

10 After Job had prayed for his friends, the
LORD restored his fortunes and gave him
twice as much as he had before. 11 All his
brothers and sisters and everyone who had
known him before came and ate with him in
his house. They comforted and consoled
him over all the trouble the LORD had
brought on him, and each one gave him a
piece of silver*a* and a gold ring.

12 The LORD blessed the latter part of Job's
life more than the former part. He had fourteen thousand sheep, six thousand camels, a
thousand yoke of oxen and a thousand donkeys. 13 And he also had seven sons and three
daughters. 14 The first daughter he named Je-
mimah, the second Keziah and the third Ker-
en-Happuch. 15 Nowhere in all the land were
there found women as beautiful as Job's
daughters, and their father granted them an
inheritance along with their brothers.

16 After this, Job lived a hundred and forty
years; he saw his children and their children
to the fourth generation. 17 And so he died,
old and full of years.

---

a 11 Hebrew *him a kesitah*; a kesitah was a unit of money of unknown weight and value.

psalms

AUTHOR: David, Asaph, the "Sons of Korah," Solomon, Heman, Ethan and Moses

DATE: The psalms were written between the time of Moses (around 1440 B.C.) and the time following the Babylonian captivity (sometime after 538 B.C.).

THEME: God is always worthy of our praise.

BOOK I

Psalms 1–41

Psalm 1

1 Blessed are those
   who do not walk in step with the
      wicked
or stand in the way that sinners take
   or sit in the company of mockers,
2 but who delight in the law of the LORD
   and meditate on his law day and
      night.
3 They are like a tree planted by streams
      of water,
   which yields its fruit in season
and whose leaf does not wither—
   whatever they do prospers.

4 Not so the wicked!
   They are like chaff
   that the wind blows away.
5 Therefore the wicked will not stand in
      the judgment,
   nor sinners in the assembly of the
      righteous.

6 For the LORD watches over the way of
      the righteous,
   but the way of the wicked will be
      destroyed.

Psalm 2

1 Why do the nations conspire*a*
   and the peoples plot in vain?
2 The kings of the earth rise up
   and the rulers band together
against the LORD and against his
      anointed, saying,
3 "Let us break their chains
   and throw off their shackles."

4 The One enthroned in heaven laughs;
   the Lord scoffs at them.
5 He rebukes them in his anger
   and terrifies them in his wrath, saying,
6 "I have installed my king
   on Zion, my holy mountain."

7 I will proclaim the LORD's decree:

He said to me, "You are my son;
   today I have become your father.
8 Ask me,
   and I will make the nations your
      inheritance,
   the ends of the earth your possession.
9 You will break them with a rod of iron*b*;
   you will dash them to pieces like
      pottery."

10 Therefore, you kings, be wise;
   be warned, you rulers of the earth.
11 Serve the LORD with fear
   and celebrate his rule with trembling.
12 Kiss his son, or he will be angry
   and you and your ways will be
      destroyed,
for his wrath can flare up in a moment.
   Blessed are all who take refuge in him.

Psalm 3

*A psalm of David. When he fled from his
son Absalom.*

*1 LORD, how many are my foes!
   How many rise up against me!

---

a 1 Hebrew; Septuagint *rage*   *b 9* Or *will rule them with an iron scepter* (see Septuagint and Syriac)
* 3:1-8 is numbered 3:2-9 in Hebrew texts.

THURSDAY

CHRISTIAN MEDITATION
Psalm 1:1–6 or 1:1–2

THOMAS MERTON {AD 1915–1968}

In meditation we should not look for a "method" or a "system"; but cultivate an "attitude," an "outlook": faith, openness, attention, reverence, expectation, supplication, trust, joy. All these finally permeate our being with love in so far as our living faith tells us we are in the presence of God, that we live in Christ, that in the Spirit of God we "see" God our Father without "seeing." We know him in "unknowing." Faith is the bond that unites us to him in the Spirit who gives us light and love.

Some people may doubtless have a spontaneous gift for meditative prayer. This is unusual today. Most people have to learn to meditate. There are *ways* of meditation. But we should not expect to find magical methods, systems which will make all difficulties and obstacles dissolve into thin air.

Meditation is sometimes quite difficult. If we bear with hardship in prayer and wait patiently for the time of grace, we may well discover that meditation and prayer are very joyful experiences. We should not, however, judge the value of our meditation by "how we feel." A hard and apparently fruitless meditation may in fact be much more valuable than one that is easy, happy, enlightened and apparently a big success.

Richard Foster

In contemporary society our Adversary majors in three things: noise, hurry and crowds. If he can keep us engaged in "muchness" and "manyness," he will rest satisfied. Psychiatrist Carl Jung once remarked, "Hurry is not *of* the Devil; it is the Devil."

If we hope to move beyond the superficialities of our culture, including our religious culture, we must be willing to go down into the recreating silences, into the inner world of contemplation. In their writings all the masters of meditation beckon us to be pioneers in this frontier of the Spirit. Though it may sound strange to modern ears, we should without shame enroll as apprentices in the school of contemplative prayer.

reflection

1. How is meditation or "contemplative prayer" different from typical prayer?
2. What has your own personal experience with meditation been like?
3. Do you think meditation is more difficult than prayer?

For your next devotional reading, go to page 598.

FRIDAY

THE KEY TO PERFECT PEACE
Psalm 3:1–8 *or* 3:3–6

Brian McLaren

In suffering, people often feel abandoned by God. They cry and pray for relief, and relief doesn't come, and the questions just echo . . . why? why now? why me? why him or her? For many people, it's suffering that drives them to atheism or agnosticism.

Yet to be fair, there are many others who say the opposite. I think of an older woman who told me this story. She had a heart disease and pneumonia, and she was in the hospital. One night, she was having great difficulty breathing, and the thought hit her for the first time: I may die before daybreak tomorrow. At first, she felt a panic, which only made her more desperate for breath and threatened to throw her into a frenzy that could perhaps kill her. "I've got to calm down," she told herself. "What can I do?" And then the thought came to her, "I'll pray." And as she prayed, she told me a peace came over her—a peace she had never experienced before. The fear of dying left her. She eventually drifted off to sleep, and each time she awoke, she asked herself, "Is the peace still there?" And each time, it was. "Brian," she told me, "I've always heard people tell stories like this, but I never experienced anything like it myself. But since that night, I've known that God is real—real in a way I never imagined I could know."

HORATIUS BONAR {AD 1808–1889}

I knew an awakened soul who, in the bitterness of his spirit, set out to work and pray in order to get peace. He doubled the amount of his devotions, saying to himself, "Surely God will give me peace." But the peace did not come. He set up family worship, saying, "Surely God will give me peace." But the peace came not. At last he settled on the idea of having a prayer meeting in his house as a sure remedy to his problem. He chose the night and called his neighbors. He prepared himself to conduct the meeting by writing a prayer and learning it by heart. When he finished learning it, he threw it down on the table saying, "Surely that will do; God will give me peace now." In that moment, a still small voice seemed to speak in his ear, saying, "No, that will not do. But Christ will do." Immediately the scales fell from his eyes, and the burden from his shoulders. Peace poured in like a river. "Christ will do," was his battle cry for life.

reflection

1. What does peace depend on?
2. In what ways do you feel the need for God's peace?
3. Where can a child of God find peace in any and every circumstance?

For your next devotional reading, go to page 601.

2 Many are saying of me,
   "God will not deliver him."[a]

3 But you, LORD, are a shield around me,
   my glory, the one who lifts my head
      high.
4 I call out to the LORD,
   and he answers me from his holy
      mountain.

5 I lie down and sleep;
   I wake again, because the LORD
      sustains me.
6 I will not fear though tens of thousands
   assail me on every side.

7 Arise, LORD!
   Deliver me, my God!
 Strike all my enemies on the jaw;
   break the teeth of the wicked.

8 From the LORD comes deliverance.
   May your blessing be on your
      people.

Psalm 4

*For the director of music. With stringed
instruments. A psalm of David.*

*[1] Answer me when I call to you,
   my righteous God.
 Give me relief from my distress;
   have mercy on me and hear my
      prayer.

2 How long will you men turn my glory
      into shame?
   How long will you love delusions and
      seek false gods[b]?[c]
3 Know that the LORD has set apart his
      faithful servant for himself;
   the LORD hears when I call to him.

4 Tremble and[d] do not sin;
   when you are on your beds,
   search your hearts and be silent.
5 Offer the sacrifices of the righteous
   and trust in the LORD.

6 Many, LORD, are asking, "Who will bring
      us prosperity?"
   Let the light of your face shine on us.
7 Fill my heart with joy

when their grain and new wine
   abound.
8 In peace I will lie down and sleep,
   for you alone, LORD,
   make me dwell in safety.

Psalm 5

*For the director of music. For pipes.
A psalm of David.*

*[1] Listen to my words, LORD,
   consider my lament.
2 Hear my cry for help,
   my King and my God,
   for to you I pray.

3 In the morning, LORD, you hear my
      voice;
   in the morning I lay my requests
      before you
 and wait expectantly.
4 For you are not a God who is pleased
      with wickedness;
   with you, evil people are not
      welcome.
5 The arrogant cannot stand
   in your presence.
 You hate all who do wrong;
6   you destroy those who tell lies.
 The bloodthirsty and deceitful
   you, LORD, detest.
7 But I, by your great love,
   can come into your house;
 in reverence I bow down
   toward your holy temple.

8 Lead me, LORD, in your righteousness
   because of my enemies—
   make your way straight before me.
9 Not a word from their mouth can be
      trusted;
   their heart is filled with malice.
 Their throat is an open grave;
   with their tongues they tell lies.
10 Declare them guilty, O God!
   Let their intrigues be their downfall.
 Banish them for their many sins,
   for they have rebelled against you.
11 But let all who take refuge in you be
      glad;
   let them ever sing for joy.

---

a 2 The Hebrew has *Selah* (a word of uncertain meaning) here and at the end of verses 4 and 8.
b 2 Or *seek lies*   c 2 The Hebrew has *Selah* (a word of uncertain meaning) here and at the end of
verse 4.   d 4 Or *In your anger* (see Septuagint)

* 4:1-8 is numbered 4:2-9 in Hebrew texts.   * 5:1-12 is numbered 5:2-13 in Hebrew texts.

Spread your protection over them,
that those who love your name may
rejoice in you.

[12] Surely, LORD, you bless the righteous;
you surround them with your favor as
with a shield.

Psalm 6

*For the director of music. With stringed
instruments. According to sheminith.*[a]
A psalm of David.

[*1] LORD, do not rebuke me in your anger
or discipline me in your wrath.
[2] Have mercy on me, LORD, for I am faint;
heal me, LORD, for my bones are in
agony.
[3] My soul is in deep anguish.
How long, LORD, how long?

[4] Turn, LORD, and deliver me;
save me because of your unfailing love.
[5] Among the dead no one proclaims your
name.
Who praises you from the grave?

[6] I am worn out from my groaning.

All night long I flood my bed with
weeping
and drench my couch with tears.
[7] My eyes grow weak with sorrow;
they fail because of all my foes.

[8] Away from me, all you who do evil,
for the LORD has heard my weeping.
[9] The LORD has heard my cry for mercy;
the LORD accepts my prayer.
[10] All my enemies will be overwhelmed
with shame and anguish;
they will turn back and suddenly be
put to shame.

Psalm 7

A shiggaion[b] *of David, which he sang to
the LORD concerning Cush, a Benjamite.*

[*1] LORD my God, I take refuge in you;
save and deliver me from all who
pursue me,
[2] or they will tear me apart like a lion
and rip me to pieces with no one to
rescue me.

[3] LORD my God, if I have done this
and there is guilt on my hands—
[4] if I have repaid my ally with evil
or without cause have robbed my foe—
[5] then let my enemy pursue and overtake
me;
let him trample my life to the ground
and make me sleep in the dust.[c]

[6] Arise, LORD, in your anger;
rise up against the rage of my
enemies.
Awake, my God; decree justice.
[7] Let the assembled peoples gather
around you,
while you sit enthroned over them on
high.
[8] Let the LORD judge the peoples.
Vindicate me, LORD, according to my
righteousness,
according to my integrity, O Most
High.
[9] Bring to an end the violence of the
wicked
and make the righteous secure—
you, the righteous God
who probes minds and hearts.

[10] My shield[d] is God Most High,
who saves the upright in heart.
[11] God is a righteous judge,
a God who displays his wrath every
day.
[12] If he does not relent,
he[e] will sharpen his sword;
he will bend and string his bow.
[13] He has prepared his deadly weapons;
he makes ready his flaming arrows.

[14] Those who are pregnant with evil
conceive trouble and give birth to
disillusionment.
[15] Those who dig a hole and scoop it out
fall into the pit they have made.
[16] The trouble they cause recoils on them;
their violence comes down on their
own heads.

[17] I will give thanks to the LORD because of
his righteousness;
I will sing the praises of the name of
the LORD Most High.

a Title: Probably a musical term   *b* Title: Probably a literary or musical term   *c 5* The Hebrew has
Selah (a word of uncertain meaning) here.   *d 10* Or *sovereign*   *e 12* Or *If anyone does not repent, / God*
* 6:1-10 is numbered 6:2-11 in Hebrew texts.   * 7:1-17 is numbered 7:2-18 in Hebrew texts.

God Is My Refuge

Psalm 7:1

read/meditate

Close your eyes and take a few breaths to settle yourself. In reverence, read the verse slowly. Imagine the safest place that you know of. Read the verse again with that place in mind.

pray

Pour out to God your desire for that kind of safe place for yourself and for those you love. Take a moment for God to reveal himself as the safest place of all.

contemplate

As you rest in God's safekeeping, recall the times your path has led you to find refuge in him. Before you move ahead with your day, read the verse again as an act of prayer and affirmation. Then, when you need security, you'll rest in God as a refuge.

additional reflection

When a train goes through a tunnel and it gets dark, you don't throw away your ticket and jump off. You sit still and trust the engineer.

—*Corrie ten Boom*

The storm may roar without me,
My heart may low be laid;
But God is round about me,
And can I be dismayed?

—*Anna L. Waring*

For your next devotional reading, go to page 603.

Psalm 8

For the director of music. According to gittith. a *A psalm of David.*

*[1] LORD, our Lord,
how majestic is your name in all the earth!

You have set your glory
above the heavens.
[2] Through the praise of children and infants
you have established a stronghold against your enemies,
to silence the foe and the avenger.
[3] When I consider your heavens,
the work of your fingers,
the moon and the stars,
which you have set in place,
[4] what are mere mortals that you are mindful of them,
human beings that you care for them? b

[5] You have made them c a little lower than the heavenly beings d
and crowned them c with glory and honor.
[6] You made them rulers over the works of your hands;
you put everything under their e feet:
[7] all flocks and herds,
and the animals of the wild,
[8] the birds in the sky,
and the fish in the sea,
all that swim the paths of the seas.

[9] LORD, our Lord,
how majestic is your name in all the earth!

Psalm 9 f

For the director of music. To the tune of "The Death of the Son." A psalm of David.

*[1] I will praise you, LORD, with all my heart;
I will tell of all your wonderful deeds.
[2] I will be glad and rejoice in you;
I will sing the praises of your name,
O Most High.

[3] My enemies turn back;
they stumble and perish before you.
[4] For you have upheld my right and my cause,
sitting enthroned as the righteous judge.
[5] You have rebuked the nations and destroyed the wicked;
you have blotted out their name for ever and ever.
[6] Endless ruin has overtaken my enemies,
you have uprooted their cities;
even the memory of them has perished.

[7] The LORD reigns forever;
he has established his throne for judgment.
[8] He rules the world in righteousness
and judges the peoples with equity.
[9] The LORD is a refuge for the oppressed,
a stronghold in times of trouble.
[10] Those who know your name trust in you,
for you, LORD, have never forsaken those who seek you.

[11] Sing the praises of the LORD, enthroned in Zion;
proclaim among the nations what he has done.
[12] For he who avenges blood remembers;
he does not ignore the cries of the afflicted.

[13] LORD, see how my enemies persecute me!
Have mercy and lift me up from the gates of death,
[14] that I may declare your praises
in the gates of Daughter Zion,
and there rejoice in your salvation.

[15] The nations have fallen into the pit they have dug;
their feet are caught in the net they have hidden.
[16] The LORD is known by his acts of justice;
the wicked are ensnared by the work of their hands. g

---

a Title: Probably a musical term   b 4 Or *what is a human being that you are mindful of him, / a son of man that you care for him?*   c 5 Or *him*   d 5 Or *than God*   e 6 Or *made him ruler . . . ; / . . . his*
f Psalms 9 and 10 may originally have been a single acrostic poem in which alternating lines began with the successive letters of the Hebrew alphabet. In the Septuagint they constitute one psalm.   g 16 The Hebrew has *Higgaion* and *Selah* (words of uncertain meaning) here; *Selah* occurs also at the end of verse 20.

* 8:1-9 is numbered 8:2-10 in Hebrew texts.   * 9:1-20 is numbered 9:2-21 in Hebrew texts.

MONDAY

IN AWE OF HIM AND HIS CREATION
Psalm 8:1–9 *or* 8:1–4

IRENAEUS {AD 130–202}

All things originate from one God. Since created things are various and numerous, they are well fitted and adapted to the whole creation. However, when viewed individually, they are mutually opposite and inharmonious like the sound of the lyre, which consists of many and opposite notes but gives rise to one unbroken melody through the intervals that separate each one from the others. The lover of truth, therefore, ought not to be deceived by the interval between the notes, nor should he imagine that one was due to one artist and author, and another to someone else. He should not think that one person fitted the treble, another the bass and yet another the tenor strings. But he should hold that one person formed the whole, so as to prove the soundness, goodness and skill exhibited in the whole work. Those, too, who listen to the melody ought to praise and exalt the artist, to admire the tension of some notes, to attend to the softness of others, to catch the sound of others between both these extremes and to consider the special character of others. Then they can inquire at what each one aims and what is the cause of their variety, never failing to apply our rule, neither giving up the [one] artist, nor casting off faith in the one God who formed all things, nor blaspheming our Creator.

Richard Foster

I glory in your handiwork, O God:
towering mountains and deep valleys,
dense forests and expansive deserts,
fathomless depths of blue below
  and immeasurable
heights of blue above . . .

When I watch the little creatures
  that creep upon the earth I marvel at:
such purpose,

such direction,
such design;
and yet
such freedom,
such openness,
such creativity.

O Lord God, Creator of the
  hummingbird and the Milky Way,
  I am lost in wonder at your originality.
Amen.

reflection

1. What have you encountered in the last day that reminds you that God is the master Creator?

2. What aspect of God's creation impresses you most?

3. What scientific field or topic can you read about this week, for the sole purpose of praising the Creator?

For your next devotional reading, go to page 609.

¹⁷ The wicked go down to the realm of the
dead,
all the nations that forget God.
¹⁸ But God will never forget the needy;
the hope of the afflicted will never
perish.

¹⁹ Arise, Lord, do not let mortals triumph;
let the nations be judged in your
presence.
²⁰ Strike them with terror, Lord;
let the nations know they are only
mortals.

Psalm 10 ^a

¹ Why, Lord, do you stand far off?
Why do you hide yourself in times of
trouble?

² In their arrogance the wicked hunt down
the weak,
catching them in the schemes they
devise.
³ They boast about the cravings of their
hearts;
they bless the greedy and revile the
Lord.
⁴ In their pride the wicked do not seek
him;
in all their thoughts there is no room
for God.
⁵ Their ways are always prosperous;
your laws are rejected by ^b them;
they sneer at all their enemies.
⁶ They say to themselves, "Nothing will
ever shake us."
They swear, "No one will ever do us
harm."

⁷ Their mouths are full of lies and threats;
trouble and evil are under their
tongues.
⁸ They lie in wait near the villages;
from ambush they murder the
innocent.
Their eyes watch in secret for their
victims;
⁹   like a lion in cover they lie in wait.
They lie in wait to catch the helpless;
they catch the helpless and drag them
off in their nets.
¹⁰ The innocent are crushed, they collapse;
they fall victim to superior strength.

¹¹ The wicked say to themselves, "God will
never notice;
he covers his face and never sees."

¹² Arise, Lord! Lift up your hand, O God.
Do not forget the helpless.
¹³ Why do the wicked revile God?
Why do they say to themselves,
"He won't call us to account"?
¹⁴ But you, God, see the trouble of the
afflicted;
you consider their grief and take it in
hand.
The victims commit themselves to you;
you are the helper of the fatherless.
¹⁵ Break the arms of the wicked and the
evildoers;
call them to account for their
wickedness
that would not otherwise be found out.

¹⁶ The Lord is King for ever and ever;
the nations will perish from his land.
¹⁷ You, Lord, hear the desire of the afflicted;
you encourage them, and you listen
to their cry,
¹⁸ defending the fatherless and the
oppressed,
so that mere earthly mortals
will never again strike terror.

Psalm 11

For the director of music. Of David.

¹ In the Lord I take refuge.
How then can you say to me:
"Flee like a bird to your mountain.
² For look, the wicked bend their bows;
they set their arrows against the
strings
to shoot from the shadows
at the upright in heart.
³ When the foundations are being
destroyed,
what can the righteous do?"

⁴ The Lord is in his holy temple;
the Lord is on his heavenly throne.
He observes everyone on earth;
his eyes examine them.
⁵ The Lord examines the righteous,
but the wicked, those who love
violence,

---

^a Psalms 9 and 10 may originally have been a single acrostic poem in which alternating lines began with
the successive letters of the Hebrew alphabet. In the Septuagint they constitute one psalm.   ^b 5 See
Septuagint; Hebrew / *they are haughty, and your laws are far from*

he hates with a passion.
⁶On the wicked he will rain
fiery coals and burning sulfur;
a scorching wind will be their lot.

⁷For the LORD is righteous,
he loves justice;
the upright will see his face.

Psalm 12

*For the director of music. According to
sheminith.ᵃ A psalm of David.*

*¹Help, LORD, for no one is faithful
anymore;
those who are loyal have vanished
from the human race.
²Everyone lies to their neighbor;
they flatter with their lips
but harbor deception in their hearts.

³May the LORD silence all flattering lips
and every boastful tongue—
⁴those who say,
"By our tongues we will prevail;
our own lips will defend us—who is
lord over us?"

⁵"Because the poor are plundered and the
needy groan,
I will now arise," says the LORD.
"I will protect them from those who
malign them."
⁶And the words of the LORD are flawless,
like silver purified in a crucible,
like goldᵇ refined seven times.

⁷You, LORD, will keep the needy safe
and will protect us forever from the
wicked,
⁸who freely strut about
while depravity is honored by the
human race.

Psalm 13

*For the director of music. A psalm
of David.*

*¹How long, LORD? Will you forget me
forever?
How long will you hide your face
from me?*

²How long must I wrestle with my
thoughts
and day after day have sorrow in my
heart?
How long will my enemy triumph
over me?

³Look on me and answer, LORD my God.
Give light to my eyes, or I will sleep
in death,
⁴and my enemy will say, "I have
overcome him,"
and my foes will rejoice when I fall.

⁵But I trust in your unfailing love;
my heart rejoices in your salvation.
⁶I will sing the LORD's praise,
for he has been good to me.

Psalm 14

For the director of music. Of David.

¹Foolsᶜ say in their hearts,
"There is no God."
They are corrupt, their deeds are vile;
there is no one who does good.

²The LORD looks down from heaven
on the human race
to see if there are any who understand,
any who seek God.
³All have turned away, all have become
corrupt;
there is no one who does good,
not even one.

⁴Do all these evildoers know nothing?

They devour my people as though eating
bread;
they never call on the LORD.
⁵But there they are, overwhelmed with
dread,
for God is present in the company of
the righteous.
⁶You evildoers frustrate the plans of the
poor,
but the LORD is their refuge.

⁷Oh, that salvation for Israel would come
out of Zion!
When the LORD restores his people,
let Jacob rejoice and Israel be glad!

ᵃ Title: Probably a musical term   ᵇ 6 Probable reading of the original Hebrew text; Masoretic Text *earth*
ᶜ 1 The Hebrew words rendered *fool* in Psalms denote one who is morally deficient.

* 12:1-8 is numbered 12:2-9 in Hebrew texts.   * 13:1-6 is numbered 13:2-6 in Hebrew texts.

Psalm 15

A psalm of David.

¹ LORD, who may dwell in your sanctuary?
  Who may live on your holy mountain?

² Those whose walk is blameless,
   who do what is righteous,
   who speak the truth from their hearts;
³ who have no slander on their tongues,
   who do their neighbors no wrong,
   who cast no slur on others;
⁴ who despise those whose ways are vile
   but honor whoever fears the LORD;
   who keep their oaths even when it
     hurts;
⁵ who lend money to the poor without
     interest
   and do not accept bribes against the
     innocent.

  Whoever does these things
  will never be shaken.

Psalm 16

A miktam ᵃ of David.

¹ Keep me safe, my God,
  for in you I take refuge.

² I say to the LORD, "You are my Lord;
   apart from you I have no good thing."
³ I say of the godly who are in the land,
   "They are the noble people
   in whom is all my delight."
⁴ Those who run after other gods
   will suffer more and more.
  I will not pour out their libations of
     blood
  or take up their names on my lips.

⁵ LORD, you have assigned me my portion
     and my cup;
   you have made my lot secure.
⁶ The boundary lines have fallen for me in
     pleasant places;
   surely I have a delightful inheritance.

⁷ I will praise the LORD, who counsels me;
   even at night my heart instructs me.
⁸ I keep my eyes always on the LORD.
   With him at my right hand, I will not
     be shaken.

⁹ Therefore my heart is glad and my
     tongue rejoices;

my body also will rest secure,
¹⁰ because you will not abandon me to the
     realm of the dead,
   nor will you let your faithful ᵇ one see
     decay.
¹¹ You make known to me the path of life;
   you will fill me with joy in your
     presence,
   with eternal pleasures at your right
     hand.

Psalm 17

A prayer of David.

¹ Hear me, LORD, my plea is just;
   listen to my cry.
  Hear my prayer—
   it does not rise from deceitful lips.
² Let my vindication come from you;
   may your eyes see what is right.

³ Though you probe my heart,
   though you examine me at night and
     test me,
  you will find that I have planned no evil;
   my mouth has not transgressed.
⁴ Though people tried to bribe me,
   I have kept myself from the ways of
     the violent
  through what your lips have
     commanded.
⁵ My steps have held to your paths;
   my feet have not stumbled.

⁶ I call on you, my God, for you will
     answer me;
   turn your ear to me and hear my
     prayer.
⁷ Show me the wonders of your great love,
   you who save by your right hand
   those who take refuge in you from
     their foes.
⁸ Keep me as the apple of your eye;
   hide me in the shadow of your wings
⁹ from the wicked who are out to destroy
     me,
   from my mortal enemies who
     surround me.

¹⁰ They close up their callous hearts,
   and their mouths speak with
     arrogance.
¹¹ They have tracked me down, they now
     surround me,

ᵃ Title: Probably a literary or musical term   ᵇ 10 Or *holy*

with eyes alert, to throw me to the
   ground.
¹²They are like a lion hungry for prey,
   like a fierce lion crouching in cover.

¹³Rise up, LORD, confront them, bring
   them down;
   with your sword rescue me from the
   wicked.
¹⁴By your hand save me from such people,
   LORD,
   from those of this world whose
   reward is in this life.
May what you have stored up for the
   wicked fill their bellies;
   may their children gorge themselves
   on it,
   may there be leftovers for their little
   ones.

¹⁵As for me, I will be vindicated and will
   see your face;
   when I awake, I will be satisfied with
   seeing your likeness.

Psalm 18

*For the director of music. Of David the
servant of the LORD. He sang to the LORD
the words of this song when the LORD
delivered him from the hand of all his
enemies and from the hand of Saul.
He said:*

*¹I love you, LORD, my strength.

²The LORD is my rock, my fortress and my
   deliverer;
   my God is my rock, in whom I take
   refuge,
   my shield ᵃ and the horn ᵇ of my
   salvation, my stronghold.

³I called to the LORD, who is worthy of
   praise,
   and I have been saved from my
   enemies.
⁴The cords of death entangled me;
   the torrents of destruction
   overwhelmed me.
⁵The cords of the grave coiled around me;
   the snares of death confronted me.

⁶In my distress I called to the LORD;

I cried to my God for help.
From his temple he heard my voice;
   my cry came before him, into his
   ears.
⁷The earth trembled and quaked,
   and the foundations of the mountains
   shook;
   they trembled because he was angry.
⁸Smoke rose from his nostrils;
   consuming fire came from his mouth,
   burning coals blazed out of it.
⁹He parted the heavens and came down;
   dark clouds were under his feet.
¹⁰He mounted the cherubim and flew;
   he soared on the wings of the wind.
¹¹He made darkness his covering, his
   canopy around him—
   the dark rain clouds of the sky.
¹²Out of the brightness of his presence
   clouds advanced,
   with hailstones and bolts of lightning.
¹³The LORD thundered from heaven;
   the voice of the Most High
   resounded. ᶜ
¹⁴He shot his arrows and scattered the
   enemy,
   with great bolts of lightning he routed
   them.
¹⁵The valleys of the sea were exposed
   and the foundations of the earth laid
   bare
   at your rebuke, LORD,
   at the blast of breath from your
   nostrils.

¹⁶He reached down from on high and took
   hold of me;
   he drew me out of deep waters.
¹⁷He rescued me from my powerful
   enemy,
   from my foes, who were too strong
   for me.
¹⁸They confronted me in the day of my
   disaster,
   but the LORD was my support.
¹⁹He brought me out into a spacious
   place;
   he rescued me because he delighted
   in me.

²⁰The LORD has dealt with me according to
   my righteousness;

---

a 2 Or *sovereign*   *b 2 Horn* here symbolizes strength.   *c 13* Some Hebrew manuscripts and
Septuagint (see also 2 Samuel 22:14); most Hebrew manuscripts *resounded, / amid hailstones and bolts of
lightning*

* 18:1-50 is numbered 18:2-51 in Hebrew texts.

according to the cleanness of my
hands he has rewarded me.
²¹ For I have kept the ways of the Lord;
I am not guilty of turning from my
God.
²² All his laws are before me;
I have not turned away from his
decrees.
²³ I have been blameless before him
and have kept myself from sin.
²⁴ The Lord has rewarded me according to
my righteousness,
according to the cleanness of my
hands in his sight.

²⁵ To the faithful you show yourself
faithful,
to the blameless you show yourself
blameless,
²⁶ to the pure you show yourself pure,
but to the devious you show yourself
shrewd.
²⁷ You save the humble
but bring low those whose eyes are
haughty.
²⁸ You, Lord, keep my lamp burning;
my God turns my darkness into light.
²⁹ With your help I can advance against a
troop ᵃ;
with my God I can scale a wall.

³⁰ As for God, his way is perfect:
The Lord's word is flawless;
he shields all who take refuge in him.
³¹ For who is God besides the Lord?
And who is the Rock except our God?
³² It is God who arms me with strength
and keeps my way secure.
³³ He makes my feet like the feet of a deer;
he causes me to stand on the heights.
³⁴ He trains my hands for battle;
my arms can bend a bow of bronze.
³⁵ You make your saving help my shield,
and your right hand sustains me;
your help has made me great.
³⁶ You provide a broad path for my feet,
so that my ankles do not give way.

³⁷ I pursued my enemies and overtook
them;
I did not turn back till they were
destroyed.

³⁸ I crushed them so that they could not
rise;
they fell beneath my feet.
³⁹ You armed me with strength for battle;
you humbled my adversaries before
me.
⁴⁰ You made my enemies turn their backs
in flight,
and I destroyed my foes.
⁴¹ They cried for help, but there was no
one to save them—
to the Lord, but he did not answer.
⁴² I beat them as fine as windblown dust;
I trampled them ᵇ like mud in the
streets.
⁴³ You have delivered me from the attacks
of the people;
you have made me the head of
nations.
People I did not know now serve me,
⁴⁴ foreigners cower before me;
as soon as they hear of me, they obey
me.
⁴⁵ They all lose heart;
they come trembling from their
strongholds.

⁴⁶ The Lord lives! Praise be to my Rock!
Exalted be God my Savior!
⁴⁷ He is the God who avenges me,
who subdues nations under me,
⁴⁸ who saves me from my enemies.
You exalted me above my foes;
from violent people you rescued me.
⁴⁹ Therefore I will praise you, Lord, among
the nations;
I will sing the praises of your name.

⁵⁰ He gives his king great victories;
he shows unfailing love to his
anointed,
to David and to his descendants
forever.

Psalm 19

*For the director of music. A psalm
of David.*

*¹ The heavens declare the glory of God;
the skies proclaim the work of his
hands.
² Day after day they pour forth speech;

ᵃ 29 Or *can run through a barricade*   ᵇ 42 Many Hebrew manuscripts, Septuagint, Syriac and Targum
(see also 2 Samuel 22:43); Masoretic Text *I poured them out*

* 19:1-14 is numbered 19:2-15 in Hebrew texts.

TUESDAY

HEARING GOD

Psalm 19:1–14 *or* 19:1–4

JOHN WESLEY {AD 1703–1791}

When a person is born of God, born of the Spirit, their existence changes drastically! Their whole soul is now aware of God, and they can say, by sure experience, "You discern my going out and my lying down; you are familiar with all my ways . . . You hem me in behind and before, and you lay your hand upon me" (Psalm 139:3,5). The Spirit of God immediately breathes life into the new-born soul . . . and awakens all the senses of the soul, making them capable of discerning spiritual good and evil . . . All the darkness is now passed away, and the child of God lives in the light of God's approval. Their ears are now opened, and the voice of God no longer calls in vain. They hear and obey the heavenly calling. They know the voice of their Shepherd. All their spiritual senses being now awakened, they have a clear course of communication with the invisible world. Consequently, they know more and more of the things which before their hearts could not begin to understand. They now know what the peace of God is. They possess joy in the Holy Spirit. They have experienced the love of God which has been poured out into their hearts.

Frederick Buechner

Because the word that God speaks to us is always an incarnate word—a word spelled out to us not alphabetically, in syllables, but enigmatically, in events, even in the books we read and the movies we see—the chances are we will never get it just right. We are so used to hearing what we want to hear and remaining deaf to what it would be well for us to hear that it is hard to break the habit. But if we keep our hearts and minds open as well as our ears, if we listen with patience and hope, if we remember at all deeply and honestly, then I think we come to recognize, beyond all doubt, that, however faintly we may hear him, he is indeed speaking to us, and that, however little we may understand of it, his word to each of us is both recoverable and precious beyond telling.

reflection

1. How many different ways have you been aware of God revealing himself to *you*?

2. How aware are you of God's voice?

3. How can you sharpen your "spiritual senses" so that you can better see, hear, taste, touch and feel Jesus?

For your next devotional reading, go to page 615.

night after night they display
knowledge.
³ They have no speech, they use no
words;
no sound is heard from them.
⁴ Yet their voice^a goes out into all the
earth,
their words to the ends of the world.
In the heavens he has pitched a tent for
the sun,
⁵ which is like a bridegroom coming
out of his chamber,
like a champion rejoicing to run his
course.
⁶ It rises at one end of the heavens
and makes its circuit to the other;
nothing is deprived of its warmth.

⁷ The law of the LORD is perfect,
refreshing the soul.
The statutes of the LORD are
trustworthy,
making wise the simple.
⁸ The precepts of the LORD are right,
giving joy to the heart.
The commands of the LORD are radiant,
giving light to the eyes.
⁹ The fear of the LORD is pure,
enduring forever.
The ordinances of the LORD are sure,
and all of them are righteous.
¹⁰ They are more precious than gold,
than much pure gold;
they are sweeter than honey,
than honey from the honeycomb.
¹¹ By them your servant is warned;
in keeping them there is great reward.
¹² But who can discern their own errors?
Forgive my hidden faults.
¹³ Keep your servant also from willful sins;
may they not rule over me.
Then I will be blameless,
innocent of great transgression.

¹⁴ May these words of my mouth and this
meditation of my heart
be pleasing in your sight,
LORD, my Rock and my Redeemer.

Psalm 20

*For the director of music. A psalm
of David.*

^{*1} May the LORD answer you when you are
in distress;
may the name of the God of Jacob
protect you.
² May he send you help from the
sanctuary
and grant you support from Zion.
³ May he remember all your sacrifices
and accept your burnt offerings.^b
⁴ May he give you the desire of your heart
and make all your plans succeed.
⁵ May we shout for joy over your victory
and lift up our banners in the name of
our God.

May the LORD grant all your requests.

⁶ Now this I know:
The LORD gives victory to his
anointed.
He answers him from his heavenly
sanctuary
with the victorious power of his right
hand.
⁷ Some trust in chariots and some in
horses,
but we trust in the name of the LORD
our God.
⁸ They are brought to their knees and fall,
but we rise up and stand firm.
⁹ LORD, give victory to the king!
Answer us when we call!

Psalm 21

*For the director of music. A psalm
of David.*

^{*1} The king rejoices in your strength, LORD.
How great is his joy in the victories
you give!

² You have granted him his heart's desire
and have not withheld the request of
his lips.^b
³ You came to greet him with rich
blessings
and placed a crown of pure gold on
his head.

---

^a 4 Septuagint, Jerome and Syriac; Hebrew *line* meaning) here.

^b 3,2 The Hebrew has *Selah* (a word of uncertain

⁴ He asked you for life, and you gave it to
   him—
   length of days, for ever and ever.
⁵ Through the victories you gave, his glory
       is great;
   you have bestowed on him splendor
       and majesty.
⁶ Surely you have granted him unending
       blessings
   and made him glad with the joy of
       your presence.
⁷ For the king trusts in the LORD;
   through the unfailing love of the Most
       High
   he will not be shaken.

⁸ Your hand will lay hold on all your
       enemies;
   your right hand will seize your foes.
⁹ When you appear for battle,
   you will burn them up as in a blazing
       furnace.
The LORD will swallow them up in his
       wrath,
   and his fire will consume them.
¹⁰ You will destroy their descendants from
       the earth,
   their posterity from the human race.
¹¹ Though they plot evil against you
   and devise wicked schemes, they
       cannot succeed.
¹² You will make them turn their backs
   when you aim at them with drawn
       bow.

¹³ Be exalted in your strength, LORD;
   we will sing and praise your might.

Psalm 22

*For the director of music. To the tune of
"The Doe of the Morning." A psalm
of David.*

^{*1} My God, my God, why have you forsaken
       me?
   Why are you so far from saving me,
   so far from the words of my
       groaning?
² My God, I cry out by day, but you do not
       answer,
   by night, but I find no rest. ^a

³ Yet you are enthroned as the Holy One;
   you are the praise ^b of Israel.
⁴ In you our ancestors put their trust;
   they trusted and you delivered them.
⁵ They cried to you and were saved;
   in you they trusted and were not
       disappointed.

⁶ But I am a worm, not a human being;
   I am scorned by everyone, despised
       by the people.
⁷ All who see me mock me;
   they hurl insults, shaking their heads.
⁸ "He trusts in the LORD," they say,
   "let the LORD rescue him.
Let him deliver him,
   since he delights in him."

⁹ Yet you brought me out of the womb;
   you made me feel secure on my
       mother's breast.
¹⁰ From birth I was cast on you;
   from my mother's womb you have
       been my God.
¹¹ Do not be far from me,
   for trouble is near
   and there is no one to help.

¹² Many bulls surround me;
   strong bulls of Bashan encircle me.
¹³ Roaring lions that tear their prey
   open their mouths wide against me.
¹⁴ I am poured out like water,
   and all my bones are out of joint.
My heart has turned to wax;
   it has melted within me.
¹⁵ My mouth ^c is dried up like a potsherd,
   and my tongue sticks to the roof of
       my mouth;
   you lay me ^d in the dust of death.
¹⁶ Dogs surround me,
   a pack of villains encircles me;
   they pierce ^e my hands and my feet.
¹⁷ All my bones are on display;
   people stare and gloat over me.
¹⁸ They divide my clothes among them
   and cast lots for my garment.

¹⁹ But you, LORD, do not be far from me.
   You are my strength; come quickly to
       help me.
²⁰ Deliver me from the sword,

---

^a 2 Or *night, and am not silent*   ^b 3 Or *Yet you are holy, / enthroned on the praises*   ^c 15 Probable
reading of the original Hebrew text; Masoretic Text *strength*   ^d 15 Or *mouth; / I am laid*   ^e 16 Some
Hebrew manuscripts, Septuagint and Syriac; most Hebrew manuscripts *me, / like a lion*

* 22:1-31 is numbered 22:2-32 in Hebrew texts.

my precious life from the power of the dogs.
21 Rescue me from the mouth of the lions;
save me from the horns of the wild oxen.

22 I will declare your name to my people;
in the assembly I will praise you.
23 You who fear the LORD, praise him!
All you descendants of Jacob, honor him!
Revere him,
all you descendants of Israel!
24 For he has not despised or scorned
the suffering of the afflicted one;
he has not hidden his face from him
but has listened to his cry for help.

25 From you comes the theme of my praise
in the great assembly;
before those who fear you[a] I will fulfill my vows.
26 The poor will eat and be satisfied;
those who seek the LORD will praise him—
may your hearts live forever!
27 All the ends of the earth
will remember and turn to the LORD,
and all the families of the nations
will bow down before him,
28 for dominion belongs to the LORD
and he rules over the nations.

29 All the rich of the earth will feast and worship;
all who go down to the dust will kneel before him—
those who cannot keep themselves alive.
30 Posterity will serve him;
future generations will be told about the Lord.
31 They will proclaim his righteousness,
declaring to a people yet unborn:
He has done it!

Psalm 23

A psalm of David.

1 The LORD is my shepherd, I lack nothing.
2   He makes me lie down in green pastures,
he leads me beside quiet waters,
3   he refreshes my soul.
He guides me along the right paths
for his name's sake.
4 Even though I walk
through the darkest valley,[b]
I will fear no evil,
for you are with me;
your rod and your staff,
they comfort me.

5 You prepare a table before me
in the presence of my enemies.
You anoint my head with oil;
my cup overflows.
6 Surely your goodness and love will follow me
all the days of my life,
and I will dwell in the house of the LORD forever.

Psalm 24

Of David. A psalm.

1 The earth is the LORD's, and everything in it,
the world, and all who live in it;
2 for he founded it on the seas
and established it on the waters.

3 Who may ascend the mountain of the LORD?
Who may stand in his holy place?
4 Those who have clean hands and a pure heart,
who do not put their trust in an idol
or swear by a false god.[c]

5 They will receive blessing from the LORD
and vindication from God their Savior.
6 Such is the generation of those who seek him,
who seek your face, God of Jacob.[d,e]

7 Lift up your heads, you gates;
be lifted up, you ancient doors,
that the King of glory may come in.
8 Who is this King of glory?
The LORD strong and mighty,
the LORD mighty in battle.
9 Lift up your heads, you gates;
lift them up, you ancient doors,
that the King of glory may come in.
10 Who is he, this King of glory?

---

a 25 Hebrew *him*   b 4 Or *the valley of the shadow of death*   c 4 Or *swear falsely*   d 6 Two Hebrew manuscripts and Syriac (see also Septuagint); most Hebrew manuscripts *face, Jacob*   e 6 The Hebrew has *Selah* (a word of uncertain meaning) here and at the end of verse 10.

The Lord Almighty—
he is the King of glory.

Psalm 25[a]

Of David.

¹In you, Lord my God,
  I put my trust.

²I trust in you;
    do not let me be put to shame,
    nor let my enemies triumph over me.
³No one who hopes in you
    will ever be put to shame,
  but shame will come on those
    who are treacherous without cause.

⁴Show me your ways, Lord,
    teach me your paths.
⁵Guide me in your truth and teach me,
    for you are God my Savior,
    and my hope is in you all day long.
⁶Remember, Lord, your great mercy and
      love,
    for they are from of old.
⁷Do not remember the sins of my youth
    and my rebellious ways;
  according to your love remember me,
    for you, Lord, are good.

⁸Good and upright is the Lord;
    therefore he instructs sinners in his
      ways.
⁹He guides the humble in what is right
    and teaches them his way.
¹⁰All the ways of the Lord are loving and
      faithful
    toward those who keep the demands
      of his covenant.
¹¹For the sake of your name, Lord,
    forgive my iniquity, though it is great.

¹²Who, then, are those who fear the Lord?
    He will instruct them in the ways
      they should choose.
¹³They will spend their days in prosperity,
    and their descendants will inherit the
      land.
¹⁴The Lord confides in those who fear
      him;
    he makes his covenant known to
      them.
¹⁵My eyes are ever on the Lord,

for only he will release my feet from
    the snare.

¹⁶Turn to me and be gracious to me,
    for I am lonely and afflicted.
¹⁷Relieve the troubles of my heart
    and free me from my anguish.
¹⁸Look on my affliction and my distress
    and take away all my sins.
¹⁹See how numerous are my enemies
    and how fiercely they hate me!

²⁰Guard my life and rescue me;
    do not let me be put to shame,
    for I take refuge in you.
²¹May integrity and uprightness protect me,
    because my hope, Lord,[b] is in you.

²²Redeem Israel, O God,
    from all their troubles!

Psalm 26

Of David.

¹Vindicate me, Lord,
    for I have led a blameless life;
  I have trusted in the Lord
    and have not faltered.
²Test me, Lord, and try me,
    examine my heart and my mind;
³for I have always been mindful of your
      unfailing love
    and have lived in reliance on your
      faithfulness.

⁴I do not sit with the deceitful,
    nor do I associate with hypocrites.
⁵I abhor the assembly of evildoers
    and refuse to sit with the wicked.
⁶I wash my hands in innocence,
    and go about your altar, Lord,
⁷proclaiming aloud your praise
    and telling of all your wonderful
      deeds.

⁸Lord, I love the house where you live,
    the place where your glory dwells.
⁹Do not take away my soul along with
      sinners,
    my life with those who are
      bloodthirsty,
¹⁰in whose hands are wicked schemes,
    whose right hands are full of bribes.
¹¹I lead a blameless life;
    redeem me and be merciful to me.

---

a This psalm is an acrostic poem, the verses of which begin with the successive letters of the Hebrew
alphabet.   b 21 Septuagint; Hebrew does not have Lord.

¹² My feet stand on level ground;
    in the great congregation I will praise
      the LORD.

Psalm 27

Of David.

¹ The LORD is my light and my salvation—
    whom shall I fear?
The LORD is the stronghold of my life—
    of whom shall I be afraid?

² When the wicked advance against me
    to devour^a me,
it is my enemies and my foes
    who will stumble and fall.
³ Though an army besiege me,
    my heart will not fear;
though war break out against me,
    even then I will be confident.

⁴ One thing I ask from the LORD,
    this only do I seek:
that I may dwell in the house of the
      LORD
all the days of my life,
to gaze on the beauty of the LORD
    and to seek him in his temple.
⁵ For in the day of trouble
    he will keep me safe in his dwelling;
he will hide me in the shelter of his
      tabernacle
    and set me high upon a rock.

⁶ Then my head will be exalted
    above the enemies who surround me;
at his tabernacle I will sacrifice with
      shouts of joy;
I will sing and make music to the
      LORD.

⁷ Hear my voice when I call, LORD;
    be merciful to me and answer me.
⁸ My heart says of you, "Seek his face!"
    Your face, LORD, I will seek.
⁹ Do not hide your face from me,
    do not turn your servant away in
      anger;
    you have been my helper.
Do not reject me or forsake me,
    God my Savior.
¹⁰ Though my father and mother forsake
      me,
    the LORD will receive me.
¹¹ Teach me your way, LORD;

lead me in a straight path
    because of my oppressors.
¹² Do not turn me over to the desire of my
      foes,
for false witnesses rise up against me,
    spouting malicious accusations.

¹³ I remain confident of this:
    I will see the goodness of the LORD
    in the land of the living.
¹⁴ Wait for the LORD;
    be strong and take heart
    and wait for the LORD.

Psalm 28

Of David.

¹ To you, LORD, I call;
    you are my Rock,
    do not turn a deaf ear to me.
For if you remain silent,
    I will be like those who go down to
      the pit.
² Hear my cry for mercy
    as I call to you for help,
as I lift up my hands
    toward your Most Holy Place.

³ Do not drag me away with the wicked,
    with those who do evil,
who speak cordially with their neighbors
    but harbor malice in their hearts.
⁴ Repay them for their deeds
    and for their evil work;
repay them for what their hands have
      done
    and bring back on them what they
      deserve.
⁵ Because they have no regard for the
      deeds of the LORD
    and what his hands have done,
he will tear them down
    and never build them up again.

⁶ Praise be to the LORD,
    for he has heard my cry for mercy.
⁷ The LORD is my strength and my shield;
    my heart trusts in him, and he helps
      me.
My heart leaps for joy,
    and with my song I praise him.

⁸ The LORD is the strength of his people,
    a fortress of salvation for his anointed
      one.

a 2 Or *slander*

WEDNESDAY

GOD PROVIDES FOR OUR NEEDS

Psalm 29:1–11 or 29:10–11

Lee Strobel

Our omnipotent God doesn't simply hoard his power. Instead, he is an empowering deity who offers to share his strength with those he created. And that's a good thing, because the result is that we can find peace when we're panicky, endurance when we're empty and courage when we're cowardly.

JOHN WESLEY {AD 1703–1791}

Omnipotent Lord, my Savior and King,
Thy help provide, thy righteousness bring;
Thy promises bind thee compassion to have,
Now, now let me find thee Almighty to save.

Rejoicing, in hope, and patient in grief,
To thee I look up for certain relief;
I fear no denial, no danger I fear,
Nor start from the trial, while Jesus is near.

I every hour in jeopardy stand;
But thou art my power, and holdest
    my hand;
While yet I am calling, thy comfort
    I feel,
It saves me from falling, or plucks me
    from hell.

Oh who can explain this struggle for life!
This anguish and pain, this trembling and strife!
Plague, earthquake, and famine, and tumult,
    and war,
The wonderful coming of Jesus declare.

For every fight is dreadful and loud,
The warrior's delight is slaughter and blood,
His foes overturning, till all shall expire;
But this is with burning and fuel of fire.

Yet God is above humans, devils, and sin,
My Jesus' love the battle shall win,
So terribly glorious his coming shall be,
His love all victorious shall conquer for me.

He all shall break through; his truth and
    his grace
Shall bring me into the plentiful place,
Through much tribulation, through water
    and fire,
Through floods of temptation, and flames
    of desire.

On Jesus, my power, till then I rely,
All evil before his presence shall fly;
When I have my Savior, my sin shall
    depart
And Jesus forever shall reign in my heart.

reflection

1. How would you describe the power and strength of the Lord?

2. How does the fact that God makes his power available to you impact your outlook on life?

3. What needs to change for you to take full advantage of God's outrageous offer to share his strength with you?

For your next devotional reading, go to page 617.

⁹Save your people and bless your
    inheritance;
    be their shepherd and carry them
        forever.

Psalm 29

A psalm of David.

¹Ascribe to the LORD, you heavenly
    beings,
    ascribe to the LORD glory and
        strength.
²Ascribe to the LORD the glory due his
    name;
    worship the LORD in the splendor of
        his*ᵃ* holiness.

³The voice of the LORD is over the waters;
    the God of glory thunders,
    the LORD thunders over the mighty
        waters.
⁴The voice of the LORD is powerful;
    the voice of the LORD is majestic.
⁵The voice of the LORD breaks the cedars;
    the LORD breaks in pieces the cedars
        of Lebanon.
⁶He makes Lebanon leap like a calf,
    Sirion*ᵇ* like a young wild ox.
⁷The voice of the LORD strikes
    with flashes of lightning.
⁸The voice of the LORD shakes the desert;
    the LORD shakes the Desert of Kadesh.
⁹The voice of the LORD twists the oaks*ᶜ*
    and strips the forests bare.
And in his temple all cry, "Glory!"

¹⁰The LORD sits enthroned over the flood;
    the LORD is enthroned as King forever.
¹¹The LORD gives strength to his people;
    the LORD blesses his people with
        peace.

Psalm 30

*A psalm. A song. For the dedication of the
temple.ᵈ Of David.*

*¹I will exalt you, LORD,
    for you lifted me out of the depths
    and did not let my enemies gloat over
        me.
²LORD my God, I called to you for help,
    and you healed me.

³You, LORD, brought me up from the
    realm of the dead;
    you spared me from going down to
        the pit.

⁴Sing the praises of the LORD, you his
    faithful people;
    praise his holy name.
⁵For his anger lasts only a moment,
    but his favor lasts a lifetime;
weeping may remain for a night,
    but rejoicing comes in the morning.

⁶When I felt secure, I said,
    "I will never be shaken."
⁷LORD, when you favored me,
    you made my royal mountain*ᵉ* stand
        firm;
but when you hid your face,
    I was dismayed.

⁸To you, LORD, I called;
    to the Lord I cried for mercy:
⁹"What is gained if I am silenced,
    if I go down to the pit?
Will the dust praise you?
    Will it proclaim your faithfulness?
¹⁰Hear, LORD, and be merciful to me;
    LORD, be my help."

¹¹You turned my wailing into dancing;
    you removed my sackcloth and
        clothed me with joy,
¹²that my heart may sing your praises and
    not be silent.
    LORD my God, I will praise you
        forever.

Psalm 31

*For the director of music. A psalm
of David.*

*¹In you, LORD, I have taken refuge;
    let me never be put to shame;
    deliver me in your righteousness.
²Turn your ear to me,
    come quickly to my rescue;
    be my rock of refuge,
    a strong fortress to save me.
³Since you are my rock and my fortress,
    for the sake of your name lead and
        guide me.

ᵃ 2 Or *LORD with the splendor of*   *ᵇ 6* That is, Mount Hermon   *ᶜ 9* Or *LORD makes the deer give birth*
ᵈ Title: Or *palace*   *ᵉ 7* That is, Mount Zion
* 30:1-12 is numbered 30:2-13 in Hebrew texts.   * 31:1-24 is numbered 31:2-25 in Hebrew texts.

THURSDAY

CIRCUMSTANCES CAN'T STEAL JOY
Psalm 30:1–12 *or* 30:10–12

B. T. ROBERTS {AD 1890–1972}

Vessels floating on a river are driven up stream by the wind, but underneath, the current flows steadily on to the ocean. So the sad occurrences of life occasion grief to the saint, while down deep in the heart joy reigns undisturbed. This joy is not of earthly origin. It does not stand connected with temporal prosperity. Prosperity does not create it; adversity does not destroy it. The good opinion of our fellow-men does not set it in motion, nor their persecutions stop its steady flow. It does not spring from the consciousness of the possession of any gifts, natural or gracious. It is supernatural in its origin, pure and holy in its nature. It comes from God as directly as pardon comes from God. It is imparted to the soul by the direct power of the Spirit. Hence it is called the joy of the Holy Ghost, that is, the joy which the Holy Ghost imparts. It is a God-given happiness—happiness intensified. It is not levity. It is a solid joy.

Kurt Bruner

Nothing can change the simple reality that we long for joy. We long to go home. Circumstances cannot steal from the truly happy or give to the truly miserable. Neither depends upon their proximity to pleasure or health or money. They depend rather upon their proximity to God.

Of course, it would be silly to suggest that only the religious experience happiness. I've met too many happy unbelievers to think that. Moments of joy, like drops of rain, will fall on the religious and the atheist farmer alike. But the refreshment of water and the lift of a smile have the same source. Without God, crops die and faces frown.

Smiles provide much-needed reminders that we were made for happiness, like sips of a drink we long to guzzle. Sure, they fall far short of the reality we desire. But they won't let us forget that we were made for something more.

reflection

1. How does the happiness that God gives compare with the happiness that even those who don't know him experience?

2. How does the nearness of God bring joy to those who know him?

3. How can a person in great pain also experience great joy?

For your next devotional reading, go to page 619.

⁴Keep me free from the trap that is set
    for me,
    for you are my refuge.
⁵Into your hands I commit my spirit;
    redeem me, LORD, my faithful God.

⁶I hate those who cling to worthless idols;
    as for me, I trust in the LORD.
⁷I will be glad and rejoice in your love,
    for you saw my affliction
    and knew the anguish of my soul.
⁸You have not given me into the hands of
    the enemy
    but have set my feet in a spacious
    place.

⁹Be merciful to me, LORD, for I am in
    distress;
    my eyes grow weak with sorrow,
    my soul and body with grief.
¹⁰My life is consumed by anguish
    and my years by groaning;
    my strength fails because of my
    affliction,ᵃ
    and my bones grow weak.
¹¹Because of all my enemies,
    I am the utter contempt of my
    neighbors;
    I am a dread to my friends—
    those who see me on the street flee
    from me.
¹²I am forgotten as though I were dead;
    I have become like broken pottery.
¹³For I hear many whispering,
    "Terror on every side!"
    They conspire against me
    and plot to take my life.

¹⁴But I trust in you, LORD;
    I say, "You are my God."
¹⁵My times are in your hands;
    deliver me from the hands of my
    enemies,
    from those who pursue me.
¹⁶Let your face shine on your servant;
    save me in your unfailing love.
¹⁷Let me not be put to shame, LORD,
    for I have cried out to you;
    but let the wicked be put to shame
    and be silent in the realm of the dead.
¹⁸Let their lying lips be silenced,
    for with pride and contempt
    they speak arrogantly against the
    righteous.

¹⁹How great is your goodness,
    which you have stored up for those
    who fear you,
    which you bestow in the sight of all
    on those who take refuge in you.
²⁰In the shelter of your presence you hide
    them
    from all human intrigues;
    you keep them safe in your dwelling
    from accusing tongues.

²¹Praise be to the LORD,
    for he showed me the wonders of his
    love
    when I was in a city under siege.
²²In my alarm I said,
    "I am cut off from your sight!"
    Yet you heard my cry for mercy
    when I called to you for help.

²³Love the LORD, all his faithful people!
    The LORD preserves those who are
    true to him,
    but the proud he pays back in full.
²⁴Be strong and take heart,
    all you who hope in the LORD.

Psalm 32

Of David. A maskil.ᵇ

¹Blessed are those
    whose transgressions are forgiven,
    whose sins are covered.
²Blessed are those
    whose sin the LORD does not count
    against them
    and in whose spirit is no deceit.

³When I kept silent,
    my bones wasted away
    through my groaning all day long.
⁴For day and night
    your hand was heavy on me;
    my strength was sapped
    as in the heat of summer.ᶜ

⁵Then I acknowledged my sin to you
    and did not cover up my iniquity.
    I said, "I will confess
    my transgressions to the LORD."
    And you forgave
    the guilt of my sin.

⁶Therefore let all the faithful pray to you
    while you may be found;

ᵃ 10 Or *guilt*   ᵇ Title: Probably a literary or musical term
uncertain meaning) here and at the end of verses 5 and 7.   ᶜ 4 The Hebrew has *Selah* (a word of

FRIDAY

THE NEED TO CONFESS

Psalm 32:1–11 *or* 32:1–5

Jim Goll

True confession arises from a heart under conviction. *Conviction* is "the state of being convinced of error or compelled to admit the truth; a strong persuasion or belief; the state of being convinced." The verb *convict* means "to find or prove to be guilty; to convince of error or sinfulness." So confession goes far beyond mere verbalizing or admitting wrong; it is a deep acknowledgment of guilt, a profession of responsibility from a convicted heart, which is a heart absolutely convinced of the reality and horror of sin. I believe that this is a revelatory act that comes only through the working of the Holy Spirit.

CYRIL {AD 827–869}

The time for confession is now. Confess what you have done in word or action, by night or by day. Confess while it is the acceptable time, and receive heavenly treasure in the day of salvation . . . Blot out every earthly care from your mind, for you are running for your soul. You are completely forsaking the things of the world. But the things you are forsaking are little, while what the Lord is giving is great. Forsake present things, and trust in the things to come.

Have you run in circles and busied yourself in vain with worldly things? . . . Be still and know that I am God, Scripture said. Excuse yourself from saying many useless words. Don't backbite or willingly listen to backbiters. Rather, promptly run to prayer. In exercising self-denial, show that your heart is strong. Cleanse your vessel so that you can receive grace more abundantly. For although remission of sins is equally given to everyone, communion with the Holy Ghost is given in proportion to each person's faith. If you have worked little, you receive little. But if you have worked hard, the reward is great.

reflection

1. What sins besiege you time and time again?
2. What sins have you committed that you have not repented of?
3. Why is confession of sin so important to God?

For your next devotional reading, go to page 621.

surely the rising of the mighty waters
will not reach them.
⁷You are my hiding place;
you will protect me from trouble
and surround me with songs of
deliverance.

⁸I will instruct you and teach you in the
way you should go;
I will counsel you with my loving eye
on you.
⁹Do not be like the horse or the mule,
which have no understanding
but must be controlled by bit and bridle
or they will not come to you.
¹⁰Many are the woes of the wicked,
but the LORD's unfailing love
surrounds those who trust in him.

¹¹Rejoice in the LORD and be glad, you
righteous;
sing, all you who are upright in heart!

Psalm 33

¹Sing joyfully to the LORD, you righteous;
it is fitting for the upright to praise
him.
²Praise the LORD with the harp;
make music to him on the ten-
stringed lyre.
³Sing to him a new song;
play skillfully, and shout for joy.

⁴For the word of the LORD is right and
true;
he is faithful in all he does.
⁵The LORD loves righteousness and
justice;
the earth is full of his unfailing love.

⁶By the word of the LORD the heavens
were made,
their starry host by the breath of his
mouth.
⁷He gathers the waters of the sea into
jars^a;
he puts the deep into storehouses.
⁸Let all the earth fear the LORD;
let all the people of the world revere
him.
⁹For he spoke, and it came to be;
he commanded, and it stood firm.

¹⁰The LORD foils the plans of the nations;
he thwarts the purposes of the
peoples.
¹¹But the plans of the LORD stand firm
forever,
the purposes of his heart through all
generations.

¹²Blessed is the nation whose God is the
LORD,
the people he chose for his
inheritance.
¹³From heaven the LORD looks down
and sees all humankind;
¹⁴from his dwelling place he watches
all who live on earth—
¹⁵he who forms the hearts of all,
who considers everything they do.

¹⁶No king is saved by the size of his army;
no warrior escapes by his great
strength.
¹⁷A horse is a vain hope for deliverance;
despite all its great strength it cannot
save.
¹⁸But the eyes of the LORD are on those
who fear him,
on those whose hope is in his
unfailing love,
¹⁹to deliver them from death
and keep them alive in famine.

²⁰We wait in hope for the LORD;
he is our help and our shield.
²¹In him our hearts rejoice,
for we trust in his holy name.
²²May your unfailing love be with us, LORD,
even as we put our hope in you.

Psalm 34^b

*Of David. When he pretended to be insane
before Abimelek, who drove him away,
and he left.*

^{*1}I will extol the LORD at all times;
his praise will always be on my lips.
²I will glory in the LORD;
let the afflicted hear and rejoice.
³Glorify the LORD with me;
let us exalt his name together.

⁴I sought the LORD, and he answered me;
he delivered me from all my fears.

a 7 Or sea as into a heap   *b This psalm is an acrostic poem, the verses of which begin with the successive letters of the Hebrew alphabet.*
* 34:1-22 is numbered 34:2-23 in Hebrew texts.

Fr

SA SU

Our Hope and Shield

Psalm 33:18–20

read/meditate

Focus for a quiet moment on God's goodness. Read this psalm several times and try to appreciate the many benefits of serving a God who is a help and shield.

pray

What do you need from God today? Hope? Deliverance? Help? Boldly ask God to meet your needs today, and then thank him for the ways he has made himself known in your life.

contemplate

Trust God to continue his work as your help and your shield. How would your day be different if you truly felt the joy that comes from a realization of God's care and power to provide?

additional reflection

There are two reasons for loving God; no one is more worthy of our love, and no one can return more in response to our love.

—*Bernard of Clairvaux*

There is but one good; that is God. Everything else is good when it looks to him and bad when it turns from Him.

—*C. S. Lewis*

For your next devotional reading, go to page 623.

|| 621 ||

5 Those who look to him are radiant;
  their faces are never covered with
    shame.
6 This poor man called, and the LORD
    heard him;
  he saved him out of all his troubles.
7 The angel of the LORD encamps around
    those who fear him,
  and he delivers them.

8 Taste and see that the LORD is good;
  blessed are those who take refuge in
    him.
9 Fear the LORD, you his holy people,
  for those who fear him lack nothing.
10 The lions may grow weak and hungry,
  but those who seek the LORD lack no
    good thing.
11 Come, my children, listen to me;
  I will teach you the fear of the LORD.
12 Whoever of you loves life
  and desires to see many good days,
13 keep your tongue from evil
  and your lips from telling lies.
14 Turn from evil and do good;
  seek peace and pursue it.

15 The eyes of the LORD are on the
    righteous
  and his ears are attentive to their cry.
16 The face of the LORD is against those
    who do evil,
  to blot out their name from the
    earth.

17 The righteous cry out, and the LORD
    hears them;
  he delivers them from all their
    troubles.
18 The LORD is close to the brokenhearted
  and saves those who are crushed in
    spirit.

19 The righteous may have many troubles,
  but the LORD delivers them from them
    all;
20 he protects all their bones,
  not one of them will be broken.

21 Evil will slay the wicked;
  the foes of the righteous will be
    condemned.
22 The LORD redeems his servants;
  no one who takes refuge in him will
    be condemned.

Psalm 35

Of David.

1 Contend, LORD, with those who contend
    with me;
  fight against those who fight against
    me.
2 Take up shield and armor;
  arise and come to my aid.
3 Brandish spear and javelin[a]
  against those who pursue me.
  Say to me,
  "I am your salvation."

4 May those who seek my life
  be disgraced and put to shame;
  may those who plot my ruin
  be turned back in dismay.
5 May they be like chaff before the wind,
  with the angel of the LORD driving
    them away;
6 may their path be dark and slippery,
  with the angel of the LORD pursuing
    them.

7 Since they hid their net for me without
    cause
  and without cause dug a pit for me,
8 may ruin overtake them by surprise—
  may the net they hid entangle them,
  may they fall into the pit, to their ruin.
9 Then my soul will rejoice in the LORD
  and delight in his salvation.
10 My whole being will exclaim,
  "Who is like you, LORD?
  You rescue the poor from those too
    strong for them,
  the poor and needy from those who
    rob them."

11 Ruthless witnesses come forward;
  they question me on things I know
    nothing about.
12 They repay me evil for good
  and leave me like one bereaved.
13 Yet when they were ill, I put on
    sackcloth
  and humbled myself with fasting.
  When my prayers returned to me
    unanswered,
14 I went about mourning
  as though for my friend or brother.
  I bowed my head in grief
  as though weeping for my mother.

HEALING THE BROKEN HEART

Psalm 34:1–22 *or* 34:4–5,18,22

Ruth Graham

How do you answer the question "Who are you?" What do you tell yourself about yourself? How do you define yourself? Are you the wealthiest woman in town? The most successful lawyer in your firm? The most active mother at your children's school? Do you live in the largest house on your street? Are you the wife of a prominent politician? Or the husband of an award-winning entrepreneur? Are you so-and-so's mother? So-and-so's brother? What are your choice labels of identity? Have you accepted a label given to you by others, and allowed others to define you?

Conversely, you may feel that you have nothing to show for your life at all—that you have no positive labels of identity whatsoever. You may feel worthless, pitiful and hopeless. Perhaps you believe your only hallmarks of identity are your failures. Failed marriage. Failed business. Failed relationships. Share with God what you say to yourself about yourself. Tell him your frustrations, disappointments and hurts. He understands.

Now let him show you the way *he* sees you. God sent his only Son to die for you— that's how much he values you. He longs to be close to you. You are fascinating to him, always his first choice of company. Whatever has happened in your life, God does not condemn you. The Bible says, "[Therefore, there is] now no condemnation for those who are in Christ Jesus" (Romans 8:1). God loves you. His desire is to put you on his potter's wheel and make you whole, a vessel lacking nothing.

AUGUSTUS TOPLADY {AD 1740–1778}

Not the labors of my hands
Can fulfill thy law's demands;
Could my zeal no respite know,
Could my tears forever flow,
All for sin could not atone;
Thou must save, and thou alone.
Nothing in my hand I bring,

Simply to thy cross I cling;
Naked, come to thee for dress,
Helpless, look to thee for grace;
Foul, I to the Fountain fly;
Wash me, Savior, or I die.
Rock of Ages, cleft for me,
Let me hide myself in thee.

reflection

1. So, how *do* you define yourself?

2. What "labels" do you use to describe who you are—both to others and to yourself?

3. How do your labels compare with how God would describe you to others?

For your next devotional reading, go to page 628.

15 But when I stumbled, they gathered in
          glee;
     assailants gathered against me
          without my knowledge.
     They slandered me without ceasing.
16 Like the ungodly they maliciously
          mocked;*a*
     they gnashed their teeth at me.

17 How long, Lord, will you look on?
     Rescue me from their ravages,
     my precious life from these lions.
18 I will give you thanks in the great
          assembly;
     among the throngs I will praise you.
19 Do not let those gloat over me
     who are my enemies without cause;
     do not let those who hate me without
          reason
     maliciously wink the eye.
20 They do not speak peaceably,
     but devise false accusations
     against those who live quietly in the
          land.
21 They sneer at me and say, "Aha! Aha!
     With our own eyes we have seen it."

22 Lord, you have seen this; do not be
          silent.
     Do not be far from me, Lord.
23 Awake, and rise to my defense!
     Contend for me, my God and Lord.
24 Vindicate me in your righteousness,
     Lord my God;
     do not let them gloat over me.
25 Do not let them think, "Aha, just what
          we wanted!"
     or say, "We have swallowed him up."

26 May all who gloat over my distress
     be put to shame and confusion;
     may all who exalt themselves over me
     be clothed with shame and disgrace.
27 May those who delight in my vindication
     shout for joy and gladness;
     may they always say, "The Lord be
          exalted,
     who delights in the well-being of his
          servant."

28 My tongue will proclaim your
          righteousness,
     your praises all day long.

Psalm 36

*For the director of music. Of David the
servant of the Lord.*

*1 I have a message from God in my heart
          concerning the sinfulness of the
          wicked:*b*
     There is no fear of God
     before their eyes.

2 In their own eyes they flatter themselves
     too much to detect or hate their sin.
3 The words of their mouths are wicked
          and deceitful;
     they have ceased to be wise and to do
          good.
4 Even on their beds they plot evil;
     they commit themselves to a sinful
          course
     and do not reject what is wrong.

5 Your love, Lord, reaches to the heavens,
     your faithfulness to the skies.
6 Your righteousness is like the highest
          mountains,
     your justice like the great deep.
     You, Lord, preserve both people and
          animals.
7 How priceless is your unfailing love,
          O God!
     People take refuge in the shadow of
          your wings.
8 They feast on the abundance of your
          house;
     you give them drink from your river of
          delights.
9 For with you is the fountain of life;
     in your light we see light.

10 Continue your love to those who know
          you,
     your righteousness to the upright in
          heart.
11 May the foot of the proud not come
          against me,
     nor the hand of the wicked drive me
          away.
12 See how the evildoers lie fallen—
     thrown down, not able to rise!

---

a 16 Septuagint; Hebrew may mean *Like an ungodly circle of mockers,
the transgression of the wicked / resides in their hearts.*   *b 1* Or *A message from God: The*

* 36:1-12 is numbered 36:2-13 in Hebrew texts.

Psalm 37[a]

Of David.

[1] Do not fret because of those who are evil
    or be envious of those who do wrong;
[2] for like the grass they will soon wither,
    like green plants they will soon die
        away.

[3] Trust in the LORD and do good;
    dwell in the land and enjoy safe
        pasture.
[4] Take delight in the LORD
    and he will give you the desires of
        your heart.

[5] Commit your way to the LORD;
    trust in him and he will do this:
[6] He will make your righteous reward
        shine like the dawn,
    your vindication like the noonday sun.

[7] Be still before the LORD
    and wait patiently for him;
    do not fret when people succeed in their
        ways,
    when they carry out their wicked
        schemes.

[8] Refrain from anger and turn from wrath;
    do not fret—it leads only to evil.
[9] For those who are evil will be destroyed,
    but those who hope in the LORD will
        inherit the land.

[10] A little while, and the wicked will be no
        more;
    though you look for them, they will
        not be found.
[11] But the meek will inherit the land
    and enjoy peace and prosperity.

[12] The wicked plot against the righteous
    and gnash their teeth at them;
[13] but the Lord laughs at the wicked,
    for he knows their day is coming.

[14] The wicked draw the sword
    and bend the bow
    to bring down the poor and needy,
    to slay those whose ways are upright.
[15] But their swords will pierce their own
        hearts,
    and their bows will be broken.

[16] Better the little that the righteous have
    than the wealth of many wicked;
[17] for the power of the wicked will be
        broken,
    but the LORD upholds the righteous.

[18] The blameless spend their days under
        the LORD's care,
    and their inheritance will endure
        forever.
[19] In times of disaster they will not wither;
    in days of famine they will enjoy
        plenty.

[20] But the wicked will perish:
    Though the LORD's enemies are like
        the flowers of the field,
    they will be consumed, they will go
        up in smoke.

[21] The wicked borrow and do not repay,
    but the righteous give generously;
[22] those the LORD blesses will inherit the
        land,
    but those he curses will be
        destroyed.

[23] The LORD makes firm the steps
    of those who delight in him;
[24] though they stumble, they will not fall,
    for the LORD upholds them with his
        hand.

[25] I was young and now I am old,
    yet I have never seen the righteous
        forsaken
    or their children begging bread.
[26] They are always generous and lend
        freely;
    their children will be a blessing.[b]

[27] Turn from evil and do good;
    then you will dwell in the land
        forever.
[28] For the LORD loves the just
    and will not forsake his faithful ones.

    Wrongdoers will be completely
        destroyed[c];
    the offspring of the wicked will
        perish.
[29] The righteous will inherit the land
    and dwell in it forever.

[30] The mouths of the righteous utter
        wisdom,
    and their tongues speak what is just.

a This psalm is an acrostic poem, the stanzas of which begin with the successive letters of the Hebrew
alphabet.   b 26 Or *freely; / the names of their children will be used in blessings* (see Gen. 48:20); or *freely;*
/ others will see that their children are blessed   c 28 See Septuagint; Hebrew *They will be protected forever*

31 The law of their God is in their hearts;
their feet do not slip.

32 The wicked lie in wait for the righteous,
seeking their very lives;
33 but the LORD will not leave them in their
power
or let them be condemned when
brought to trial.

34 Hope in the LORD
and keep his way.
He will exalt you to inherit the land;
when the wicked are destroyed, you
will see it.

35 I have seen the wicked and ruthless
flourishing like a luxuriant native tree,
36 but they soon passed away and were no
more;
though I looked for them, they could
not be found.

37 Consider the blameless, observe the
upright;
a future awaits those who seek
peace. *a*
38 But all sinners will be destroyed;
there will be no future *b* for the
wicked.

39 The salvation of the righteous comes
from the LORD;
he is their stronghold in time of
trouble.
40 The LORD helps them and delivers them;
he delivers them from the wicked and
saves them,
because they take refuge in him.

Psalm 38

A psalm of David. A petition.

*1 LORD, do not rebuke me in your anger
or discipline me in your wrath.
2 Your arrows have pierced me,
and your hand has come down on me.
3 Because of your wrath there is no health
in my body;
there is no soundness in my bones
because of my sin.
4 My guilt has overwhelmed me
like a burden too heavy to bear.

5 My wounds fester and are loathsome
because of my sinful folly.
6 I am bowed down and brought very low;
all day long I go about mourning.
7 My back is filled with searing pain;
there is no health in my body.
8 I am feeble and utterly crushed;
I groan in anguish of heart.

9 All my longings lie open before you,
Lord;
my sighing is not hidden from you.
10 My heart pounds, my strength fails me;
even the light has gone from my eyes.
11 My friends and companions avoid me
because of my wounds;
my neighbors stay far away.
12 Those who seek my life set their traps,
those who would harm me talk of my
ruin;
all day long they scheme and lie.

13 I am like the deaf, who cannot hear,
like the mute, who cannot speak;
14 I have become like one who does not
hear,
whose mouth can offer no reply.
15 LORD, I wait for you;
you will answer, Lord my God.
16 For I said, "Do not let them gloat
or exalt themselves over me when my
feet slip."

17 For I am about to fall,
and my pain is ever with me.
18 I confess my iniquity;
I am troubled by my sin.
19 Many have become my enemies without
cause *c*;
those who hate me without reason
are numerous.
20 Those who repay my good with evil
lodge accusations against me,
though I seek only to do what is
good.

21 LORD, do not forsake me;
do not be far from me, my God.
22 Come quickly to help me,
my Lord and my Savior.

---

a 37 Or / *those who seek peace will have posterity*
manuscript; Masoretic Text *my vigorous enemies*   *b 38* Or *posterity*   *c 19* One Dead Sea Scrolls

* 38:1-22 is numbered 38:2-23 in Hebrew texts.

Psalm 39

For the director of music. For Jeduthun.
A psalm of David.

*[1] I said, "I will watch my ways
and keep my tongue from sin;
I will put a muzzle on my mouth
while in the presence of the wicked."
[2] So I remained utterly silent,
not even saying anything good.
But my anguish increased;
[3]   my heart grew hot within me.
While I meditated, the fire burned;
then I spoke with my tongue:

[4] "Show me, LORD, my life's end
and the number of my days;
let me know how fleeting my life is.
[5] You have made my days a mere
handbreadth;
the span of my years is as nothing
before you.
Everyone is but a breath,
even those who seem secure.[a]

[6] "Surely everyone goes around like a
mere phantom;
in vain they rush about, heaping up
wealth
without knowing whose it will finally
be.

[7] "But now, Lord, what do I look for?
My hope is in you.
[8] Save me from all my transgressions;
do not make me the scorn of fools.
[9] I was silent; I would not open my
mouth,
for you are the one who has done
this.
[10] Remove your scourge from me;
I am overcome by the blow of your
hand.
[11] When you rebuke and discipline people
for their sins,
you consume their wealth like a
moth—
surely everyone is but a breath.

[12] "Hear my prayer, LORD,
listen to my cry for help;
do not be deaf to my weeping.

I dwell with you as a foreigner,
a stranger, as all my ancestors were.
[13] Look away from me, that I may enjoy
life again
before I depart and am no more."

Psalm 40

For the director of music. Of David.
A psalm.

*[1] I waited patiently for the LORD;
he turned to me and heard my cry.
[2] He lifted me out of the slimy pit,
out of the mud and mire;
he set my feet on a rock
and gave me a firm place to stand.
[3] He put a new song in my mouth,
a hymn of praise to our God.
Many will see and fear the LORD
and put their trust in him.

[4] Blessed are those
who make the LORD their trust,
who do not look to the proud,
to those who turn aside to false
gods.[b]
[5] Many, LORD my God,
are the wonders you have done,
the things you planned for us.
None can compare with you;
were I to speak and tell of your deeds,
they would be too many to declare.

[6] Sacrifice and offering you did not
desire—
but my ears you have opened[c]—
burnt offerings and sin offerings[d] you
did not require.
[7] Then I said, "Here I am, I have come—
it is written about me in the scroll.[e]
[8] I desire to do your will, my God;
your law is within my heart."

[9] I proclaim your saving acts in the great
assembly;
I do not seal my lips, LORD,
as you know.
[10] I do not hide your righteousness in my
heart;
I speak of your faithfulness and your
saving help.

---

a 5 The Hebrew has *Selah* (a word of uncertain meaning) here and at the end of verse 11.   *b 4* Or *to lies*   *c 6* Hebrew; some Septuagint manuscripts *but a body you have prepared for me*   *d 6* Or *purification offerings*   *e 7* Or *come / with the scroll written for me*

* 39:1-13 is numbered 39:2-14 in Hebrew texts.   * 40:1-17 is numbered 40:2-18 in Hebrew texts.

PRAY AND STOP WORRYING

Psalm 40:1–17 *or* 40:1–3

Jim Cymbala

The world is increasing in troubles of every kind.

Prospective wars and terrorist attacks, the danger of nuclear and biological weapons, economic woes and the challenge of rearing children in a hostile and immoral environment are problems we face daily. Surveys show that these difficulties and uncertainties are taking a heavy mental and emotional toll on people. New York City, where I pastor, was already a pretty dangerous place before suffering through 9/11 and the ensuing international tension. What is a Christian to do in the middle of all the uncertainty and trouble? . . .

The truth is that we live among free moral agents who often choose evil, resulting in inescapable trouble for others. This was what God's people experienced throughout history, from Noah to the apostle John. But although the "mighty waters rise," God is still a "hiding place" for the godly who pray to him in the hour of testing. Instead of complaining, we should recall the simple formula of our Lord's brother, James: "[Is anyone among you in trouble? Let them pray]" (James 5:13). It doesn't make biblical sense, then, to counsel Christians who have not yet prayed about their "trouble." Who knows what God might do to help such people if only he is given the opportunity? How often do we spin our wheels, talking and worrying, while the Lord of the universe waits to be invited into the fray?

MADAME GUYON {AD 1648–1717}

If the wind becomes hostile and blows a storm, we must cast anchor to hold the ship steady. Our anchor is a firm confidence and hope in our God. In this we wait patiently for the calming of the tempest and the return of a favorable breeze; just as David waited patiently for the Lord, and he turned to him and heard his cry (Psalm 40:1). Therefore, we must surrender to the Spirit of God, giving ourselves up wholly to his divine guidance.

reflection

1. How are you in need of a "rock" to stand on?

2. What causes you to worry?

3. How aggressive have you been about taking this issue to God in prayer?

For your next devotional reading, go to page 633.

I do not conceal your love and your
faithfulness
from the great assembly.

¹¹ Do not withhold your mercy from me,
LORD;
may your love and faithfulness always
protect me.
¹² For troubles without number surround
me;
my sins have overtaken me, and I
cannot see.
They are more than the hairs of my head,
and my heart fails within me.
¹³ Be pleased to save me, LORD;
come quickly, LORD, to help me.

¹⁴ May all who seek to take my life
be put to shame and confusion;
may all who desire my ruin
be turned back in disgrace.
¹⁵ May those who say to me, "Aha! Aha!"
be appalled at their own shame.

¹⁶ But may all who seek you
rejoice and be glad in you;
may those who long for your saving help
always say,
"The LORD is great!"

¹⁷ But as for me, I am poor and needy;
may the Lord think of me.
You are my help and my deliverer;
you are my God, do not delay.

Psalm 41

*For the director of music. A psalm
of David.*

*¹ Blessed are those who have regard for
the weak;
the LORD delivers them in times of
trouble.
² The LORD protects and preserves them—
they are counted among the blessed
in the land—
he does not give them over to the
desire of their foes.
³ The LORD sustains them on their sickbed
and restores them from their bed of
illness.
⁴ I said, "Have mercy on me, LORD;
heal me, for I have sinned against you."

⁵ My enemies say of me in malice,
"When will he die and his name
perish?"
⁶ Whenever they come to see me,
they speak falsely, while their hearts
gather slander;
then they go out and spread it abroad.

⁷ All my enemies whisper together against
me;
they imagine the worst for me,
saying,
⁸ "A vile disease has beset him;
he will never get up from the place
where he lies."
⁹ Even my close friend,
someone I trusted,
one who shared my bread,
has lifted up his heel against me.

¹⁰ But may you have mercy on me, LORD;
raise me up, that I may repay them.
¹¹ I know that you are pleased with me,
for my enemy does not triumph over
me.
¹² In my integrity you uphold me
and set me in your presence forever.
¹³ Praise be to the LORD, the God of Israel,
from everlasting to everlasting.
Amen and Amen.

BOOK II

Psalms 42–72

Psalm 42 ᵃ

*For the director of music. A maskil ᵇ of the
Sons of Korah.*

*¹ As the deer pants for streams of water,
so my soul pants for you, my God.
² My soul thirsts for God, for the living
God.
When can I go and meet with God?
³ My tears have been my food
day and night,
while people say to me all day long,
"Where is your God?"
⁴ These things I remember
as I pour out my soul:
how I used to go to the house of God
under the protection of the Mighty
One ᶜ

ᵃ In many Hebrew manuscripts Psalms 42 and 43 constitute one psalm.   ᵇ Title: Probably a literary or
musical term   ᶜ 4 See Septuagint and Syriac; the meaning of the Hebrew for this line is uncertain.

* 41:1-13 is numbered 41:2-14 in Hebrew texts.   * 42:1-11 is numbered 42:2-12 in Hebrew texts.

with shouts of joy and praise
among the festive throng.

5 Why, my soul, are you downcast?
Why so disturbed within me?
Put your hope in God,
for I will yet praise him,
my Savior and my God.

6 My soul is downcast within me;
therefore I will remember you
from the land of the Jordan,
the heights of Hermon—from Mount
Mizar.
7 Deep calls to deep
in the roar of your waterfalls;
all your waves and breakers
have swept over me.

8 By day the LORD directs his love,
at night his song is with me—
a prayer to the God of my life.

9 I say to God my Rock,
"Why have you forgotten me?
Why must I go about mourning,
oppressed by the enemy?"
10 My bones suffer mortal agony
as my foes taunt me,
saying to me all day long,
"Where is your God?"

11 Why, my soul, are you downcast?
Why so disturbed within me?
Put your hope in God,
for I will yet praise him,
my Savior and my God.

Psalm 43 a

1 Vindicate me, my God,
and plead my cause
against an unfaithful nation.
Rescue me from those who are
deceitful and wicked.
2 You are God my stronghold.
Why have you rejected me?
Why must I go about mourning,
oppressed by the enemy?
3 Send me your light and your faithful
care,
let them lead me;
let them bring me to your holy
mountain,

to the place where you dwell.
4 Then I will go to the altar of God,
to God, my joy and my delight.
I will praise you with the lyre,
O God, my God.

5 Why, my soul, are you downcast?
Why so disturbed within me?
Put your hope in God,
for I will yet praise him,
my Savior and my God.

Psalm 44

*For the director of music. Of the Sons of
Korah. A maskil.* b

*1 We have heard it with our ears, O God;
our ancestors have told us
what you did in their days,
in days long ago.
2 With your hand you drove out the
nations
and planted our ancestors;
you crushed the peoples
and made our ancestors flourish.
3 It was not by their sword that they won
the land,
nor did their arm bring them victory;
it was your right hand, your arm,
and the light of your face, for you
loved them.

4 You are my King and my God,
who decrees c victories for Jacob.
5 Through you we push back our enemies;
through your name we trample our
foes.
6 I put no trust in my bow,
my sword does not bring me victory;
7 but you give us victory over our enemies,
you put our adversaries to shame.
8 In God we make our boast all day long,
and we will praise your name
forever. d

9 But now you have rejected and humbled
us;
you no longer go out with our armies.
10 You made us retreat before the enemy,
and our adversaries have plundered us.
11 You gave us up to be devoured like
sheep

---

a In many Hebrew manuscripts Psalms 42 and 43 constitute one psalm.   b Title: Probably a literary or musical term   c 4 Septuagint, Aquila and Syriac; Hebrew *King, O God; / command*   d 8 The Hebrew has *Selah* (a word of uncertain meaning) here.

* 44:1-26 is numbered 44:2-27 in Hebrew texts.

and have scattered us among the
nations.
¹² You sold your people for a pittance,
gaining nothing from their sale.

¹³ You have made us a reproach to our
neighbors,
the scorn and derision of those
around us.
¹⁴ You have made us a byword among the
nations;
the peoples shake their heads at us.
¹⁵ I live in disgrace all day long,
and my face is covered with shame
¹⁶ at the taunts of those who reproach and
revile me,
because of the enemy, who is bent on
revenge.

¹⁷ All this came upon us,
though we had not forgotten you;
we had not been false to your
covenant.
¹⁸ Our hearts had not turned back;
our feet had not strayed from your
path.
¹⁹ But you crushed us and made us a haunt
for jackals;
you covered us over with deep
darkness.

²⁰ If we had forgotten the name of our God
or spread out our hands to a foreign
god,
²¹ would not God have discovered it,
since he knows the secrets of the
heart?
²² Yet for your sake we face death all day
long;
we are considered as sheep to be
slaughtered.

²³ Awake, Lord! Why do you sleep?
Rouse yourself! Do not reject us
forever.
²⁴ Why do you hide your face
and forget our misery and
oppression?
²⁵ We are brought down to the dust;
our bodies cling to the ground.
²⁶ Rise up and help us;
redeem us because of your unfailing
love.

Psalm 45

*For the director of music. To the tune of
"Lilies." Of the Sons of Korah. A maskil.^a
A wedding song.*

^{*1} My heart is stirred by a noble theme
as I recite my verses for the king;
my tongue is the pen of a skillful
writer.

² You are the most excellent of men
and your lips have been anointed with
grace,
since God has blessed you forever.

³ Gird your sword on your side, you
mighty one;
clothe yourself with splendor and
majesty.
⁴ In your majesty ride forth victoriously
in the cause of truth, humility and
justice;
let your right hand achieve awesome
deeds.
⁵ Let your sharp arrows pierce the hearts
of the king's enemies;
let the nations fall beneath your feet.
⁶ Your throne, O God,^b will last for ever
and ever;
a scepter of justice will be the scepter
of your kingdom.
⁷ You love righteousness and hate
wickedness;
therefore God, your God, has set you
above your companions
by anointing you with the oil of joy.
⁸ All your robes are fragrant with myrrh
and aloes and cassia;
from palaces adorned with ivory
the music of the strings makes you
glad.
⁹ Daughters of kings are among your
honored women;
at your right hand is the royal bride in
gold of Ophir.

¹⁰ Listen, daughter, and pay careful
attention:
Forget your people and your father's
house.
¹¹ Let the king be enthralled by your beauty;
honor him, for he is your lord.
¹² The city of Tyre will come with a gift,^c

---

^a Title: Probably a literary or musical term   ^b 6 Here the king is addressed as God's representative.
^c 12 Or *A Tyrian robe is among the gifts*

[*] 45:1-17 is numbered 45:2-18 in Hebrew texts.

people of wealth will seek your favor.
¹³ All glorious is the princess within her
chamber;
her gown is interwoven with gold.
¹⁴ In embroidered garments she is led to
the king;
her virgin companions follow her—
those brought to be with her.
¹⁵ Led in with joy and gladness,
they enter the palace of the king.

¹⁶ Your sons will take the place of your
fathers;
you will make them princes
throughout the land.

¹⁷ I will perpetuate your memory through
all generations;
therefore the nations will praise you
for ever and ever.

Psalm 46

*For the director of music. Of the Sons of
Korah. According to* alamoth. ^a *A song.*

^{*1} God is our refuge and strength,
an ever-present help in trouble.
² Therefore we will not fear, though the
earth give way
and the mountains fall into the heart
of the sea,
³ though its waters roar and foam
and the mountains quake with their
surging. ^b

⁴ There is a river whose streams make
glad the city of God,
the holy place where the Most High
dwells.
⁵ God is within her, she will not fall;
God will help her at break of day.
⁶ Nations are in uproar, kingdoms fall;
he lifts his voice, the earth melts.

⁷ The Lord Almighty is with us;
the God of Jacob is our fortress.

⁸ Come and see what the Lord has done,
the desolations he has brought on the
earth.
⁹ He makes wars cease
to the ends of the earth.

He breaks the bow and shatters the
spear;
he burns the shields ^c with fire.
¹⁰ "Be still, and know that I am God;
I will be exalted among the nations,
I will be exalted in the earth."

¹¹ The Lord Almighty is with us;
the God of Jacob is our fortress.

Psalm 47

*For the director of music. Of the Sons of
Korah. A psalm.*

^{*1} Clap your hands, all you nations;
shout to God with cries of joy.
² For the Lord Most High is awesome,
the great King over all the earth.
³ He subdued nations under us,
peoples under our feet.
⁴ He chose our inheritance for us,
the pride of Jacob, whom he loved. ^d

⁵ God has ascended amid shouts of joy,
the Lord amid the sounding of
trumpets.
⁶ Sing praises to God, sing praises;
sing praises to our King, sing praises.
⁷ For God is the King of all the earth;
sing to him a psalm of praise.

⁸ God reigns over the nations;
God is seated on his holy throne.
⁹ The nobles of the nations assemble
as the people of the God of Abraham,
for the kings ^e of the earth belong to God;
he is greatly exalted.

Psalm 48

A song. A psalm of the Sons of Korah.

^{*1} Great is the Lord, and most worthy of
praise,
in the city of our God, his holy
mountain.
² Beautiful in its loftiness,
the joy of the whole earth,
like the heights of Zaphon ^f is Mount
Zion,
the city of the Great King.

---

^a Title: Probably a musical term   ^b 3 The Hebrew has *Selah* (a word of uncertain meaning) here and at
the end of verses 7 and 11.   ^c 9 Or *chariots*   ^d 4 The Hebrew has *Selah* (a word of uncertain
meaning) here.   ^e 9 Or *shields*   ^f 2 *Zaphon* was the most sacred mountain of the Canaanites.

WEDNESDAY

SERIOUS SILENCE
Psalm 46:1–11 *or* 46:1,10–11

Ruth Haley Barton

To enter into solitude and silence is to take the spiritual life seriously. It is to take seriously our need to quiet the noise of our lives, to cease the constant striving of human effort, to pull away from our absorption in human relationships for a time in order to give God our undivided attention. In solitude God begins to free us from our bondage to human expectations, for there we experience God as our ultimate reality—the One in whom we live and move and have our being. In solitude our thoughts and our mind, our will and our desires are reoriented Godward so we become less and less attracted by external forces and can be more deeply responsive to God's desire and prayer in us.

Silence deepens the experience of solitude. In silence we not only withdraw from the demands of life in the company of others but also allow the noise of our own thoughts, strivings and compulsions to settle down so we can hear a truer and more reliable Voice. Reliance on our own thoughts and words, even in our praying, can be one facet of a need to control things, to set the agenda, or at least to know what the agenda is even in our relationship with God. It is in silence that we habitually release our own agendas and our need to control and become more willing and able to give ourselves to God's loving initiative. In silence we create space for God's activity rather than filling every minute with our own.

ALEXANDER MACLAREN {AD 1826–1910}

Surely if ever any generation needed to hear the message "Be still and let God speak," we need it. Even religious people are so busy with spreading or defending Christianity that they have little time—and many of them even less inclination—for quiet meditation and still communion with God. Newspapers, books, charitable service, Christian effort, business and amusement so crowd into our lives now that it requires some resolution and some planning to get a clear space where we can be quiet and look at God . . . whose voice commands, whose love warms and whose truth makes our whole being fair. God speaks for the most part in such silence only. If the soul is full of tumult and jangling noises, his voice is not likely to be heard.

reflection

1. Why do you think God tells us to "be still"?
2. How often do you spend time being silent before God?
3. Do you find it difficult to be silent and still in God's presence? What is distracting you?

For your next devotional reading, go to page 636.

³God is in her citadels;
  he has shown himself to be her
    fortress.

⁴When the kings joined forces,
  when they advanced together,
⁵they saw her and were astounded;
  they fled in terror.
⁶Trembling seized them there,
  pain like that of a woman in labor.
⁷You destroyed them like ships of
    Tarshish
  shattered by an east wind.

⁸As we have heard,
  so we have seen
in the city of the LORD Almighty,
  in the city of our God:
God makes her secure
  forever.ᵃ

⁹Within your temple, O God,
  we meditate on your unfailing love.
¹⁰Like your name, O God,
  your praise reaches to the ends of the
    earth;
  your right hand is filled with
    righteousness.
¹¹Mount Zion rejoices,
  the villages of Judah are glad
  because of your judgments.

¹²Walk about Zion, go around her,
  count her towers,
¹³consider well her ramparts,
  view her citadels,
that you may tell of them
  to the next generation.

¹⁴For this God is our God for ever and
    ever;
  he will be our guide even to the end.

Psalm 49

*For the director of music. Of the Sons of
Korah. A psalm.*

*¹Hear this, all you peoples;
  listen, all who live in this world,
²both low and high,
  rich and poor alike:
³My mouth will speak words of wisdom;
  the meditation of my heart will give
    you understanding.
⁴I will turn my ear to a proverb;
  with the harp I will expound my
    riddle:

⁵Why should I fear when evil days come,
  when wicked deceivers surround
    me—
⁶those who trust in their wealth
  and boast of their great riches?
⁷No one can redeem the life of another
  or give to God a sufficient ransom—
⁸the ransom for a life is costly,
  no payment is ever enough—
⁹so that someone should live on forever
  and not see decay.
¹⁰For all can see that the wise die,
  that the foolish and the senseless also
    perish,
  leaving their wealth to others.
¹¹Their tombs will remain their housesᵇ
    forever,
  their dwellings for endless
    generations,
  though they hadᶜ named lands after
    themselves.

¹²Human beings, despite their wealth, do
    not endure;
  they are like the beasts that perish.

¹³This is the fate of those who trust in
    themselves,
  and of their followers, who approve
    their sayings.ᵈ
¹⁴They are like sheep and are destined to
    die;
  death will be their shepherd
  (but the upright will prevail over
    them in the morning).
  Their forms will decay in the grave,
    far from their princely mansions.
¹⁵But God will redeem me from the realm
    of the dead;
  he will surely take me to himself.
¹⁶Do not be overawed when others grow
    rich,
  when the splendor of their houses
    increases;
¹⁷for they will take nothing with them
    when they die,

ᵃ 8 The Hebrew has *Selah* (a word of uncertain meaning) here.   ᵇ 11 Septuagint and Syriac; Hebrew *In
their thoughts their houses will remain*   ᶜ 11 Or *generations, / for they have*   ᵈ 13 The Hebrew has *Selah*
(a word of uncertain meaning) here and at the end of verse 15.

* 49:1-20 is numbered 49:2-21 in Hebrew texts.

their splendor will not descend with
    them.
[18] Though while they live they count
    themselves blessed—
and people praise you when you
    prosper—
[19] they will join those who have gone
    before them,
who will never again see the light of
    life.

[20] Human beings who have wealth but lack
    understanding
are like the beasts that perish.

Psalm 50

A psalm of Asaph.

[1] The Mighty One, God, the Lord,
    speaks and summons the earth
from the rising of the sun to where it
    sets.
[2] From Zion, perfect in beauty,
    God shines forth.
[3] Our God comes
    and will not be silent;
a fire devours before him,
    and around him a tempest rages.
[4] He summons the heavens above,
    and the earth, that he may judge his
    people:
[5] "Gather to me this consecrated people,
    who made a covenant with me by
    sacrifice."
[6] And the heavens proclaim his
    righteousness,
for he is a God of justice. [a, b]

[7] "Listen, my people, and I will speak;
    I will testify against you, Israel:
    I am God, your God.
[8] I bring no charges against you
    concerning your sacrifices
or concerning your burnt offerings,
    which are ever before me.
[9] I have no need of a bull from your stall
    or of goats from your pens,
[10] for every animal of the forest is mine,
    and the cattle on a thousand hills.
[11] I know every bird in the mountains,
    and the creatures of the field are mine.
[12] If I were hungry I would not tell you,

for the world is mine, and all that is
    in it.
[13] Do I eat the flesh of bulls
    or drink the blood of goats?
[14] "Sacrifice thank offerings to God,
    fulfill your vows to the Most High,
[15] and call on me in the day of trouble;
    I will deliver you, and you will honor
    me."

[16] But to the wicked, God says:

"What right have you to recite my laws
    or take my covenant on your lips?
[17] You hate my instruction
    and cast my words behind you.
[18] When you see thieves, you join with
    them;
you throw in your lot with adulterers.
[19] You use your mouth for evil
    and harness your tongue to deceit.
[20] You sit and testify against your brother
    and slander your own mother's son.
[21] When you did these things and I kept
    silent,
you thought I was exactly [c] like you.
But I now arraign you
    and set my accusations before you.

[22] "Consider this, you who forget God,
    or I will tear you to pieces, with no
    one to rescue:
[23] Those who sacrifice thank offerings
    honor me,
and to the blameless [d] I will show my
    salvation."

Psalm 51

*For the director of music. A psalm
of David. When the prophet Nathan came
to him after David had committed
adultery with Bathsheba.*

[*1] Have mercy on me, O God,
    according to your unfailing love;
according to your great compassion
    blot out my transgressions.
[2] Wash away all my iniquity
    and cleanse me from my sin.

[3] For I know my transgressions,
    and my sin is always before me.

---

a 6 With a different word division of the Hebrew; Masoretic Text *for God himself is judge*   *b 6* The
Hebrew has *Selah* (a word of uncertain meaning) here.   *c 21* Or *thought the 'I am' was*   *d 23* Probable
reading of the original Hebrew text; the meaning of the Masoretic Text for this phrase is uncertain.

* 51:1-19 is numbered 51:3-21 in Hebrew texts.

THURSDAY

TRUE CONFESSION

Psalm 51:1–19 *or* 51:1–2

Billy Graham

If you have sincerely repented of your sins and committed your life to Jesus Christ as your Lord and Savior, then I have good news for you: God has already forgiven all your sins—without exception.

No, you can't remember all the sins you have ever committed; no person can. But God knows them all—and He has promised to forgive them if we are truly trusting Christ. God's promise is clear: "When you were dead in your sins . . . God made you alive with Christ. He forgave us all our sins" (Colossians 2:13). Note that it doesn't say He forgave some of our sins or just the sins we can remember—but all of them!

It's important, however, for you to understand why this is true. The reason is because Jesus Christ came down from heaven for one reason: to become the final and complete sacrifice for our sins. He was without sin—but on the cross all our sins were placed on Him, and He took the punishment we deserve. He died in our place.

If you have never trusted Christ for your salvation, or if you are unsure, turn to Him today and by a simple prayer of faith receive Him into your life. The Bible's promise is true: "There is now no condemnation for those who are in Christ Jesus" (Romans 8:1).

JOHN CHRYSOSTOM {AD 347–407}

Have you sinned today? Have you made your soul old? Do not despair; do not despond, but renew it by repentance and tears and confession, and by doing good things. And never stop doing this.

reflection

1. How has your definition of *repentance* changed or grown based on what you've read today?

2. Have you ever come face-to-face with the gut-wrenching, horrible reality of your sin?

3. When do you settle for superficial, false confession rather than the real thing?

For your next devotional reading, go to page 643.

4 Against you, you only, have I sinned
    and done what is evil in your sight;
 so you are right in your verdict
    and justified when you judge.
5 Surely I was sinful at birth,
    sinful from the time my mother
        conceived me.
6 Yet you desired faithfulness even in the
        womb;
    you taught me wisdom in that secret
        place.

7 Cleanse me with hyssop, and I will be
        clean;
    wash me, and I will be whiter than
        snow.
8 Let me hear joy and gladness;
    let the bones you have crushed
        rejoice.
9 Hide your face from my sins
    and blot out all my iniquity.

10 Create in me a pure heart, O God,
    and renew a steadfast spirit within me.
11 Do not cast me from your presence
    or take your Holy Spirit from me.
12 Restore to me the joy of your salvation
    and grant me a willing spirit, to
        sustain me.

13 Then I will teach transgressors your
        ways,
    and sinners will turn back to you.
14 Deliver me from bloodguilt, O God,
    you who are God my Savior,
    and my tongue will sing of your
        righteousness.
15 Open my lips, Lord,
    and my mouth will declare your
        praise.
16 You do not delight in sacrifice, or I
        would bring it;
    you do not take pleasure in burnt
        offerings.
17 My sacrifice, O God, is[a] a broken
        spirit;
    a broken and contrite heart
    you, God, will not despise.

18 May it please you to prosper Zion,
    to build up the walls of Jerusalem.
19 Then you will delight in the sacrifices of
        the righteous,

in burnt offerings offered whole;
    then bulls will be offered on your
        altar.

Psalm 52

For the director of music. A maskil[b]
*of David. When Doeg the Edomite had
gone to Saul and told him: "David has
gone to the house of Ahimelek."*

*1 Why do you boast of evil, you mighty
        hero?
    Why do you boast all day long,
    you who are a disgrace in the eyes of
        God?
2 You who practice deceit,
    your tongue plots destruction;
    it is like a sharpened razor.
3 You love evil rather than good,
    falsehood rather than speaking the
        truth.[c]
4 You love every harmful word,
    you deceitful tongue!

5 Surely God will bring you down to
        everlasting ruin:
    He will snatch you up and pluck you
        from your tent;
    he will uproot you from the land of
        the living.
6 The righteous will see and fear;
    they will laugh at you, saying,
7 "Here now is the one
    who did not make God his
        stronghold
 but trusted in his great wealth
    and grew strong by destroying
        others!"

8 But I am like an olive tree
    flourishing in the house of God;
 I trust in God's unfailing love
    for ever and ever.
9 For what you have done I will always
        praise you
    in the presence of your faithful
        people.
 And I will hope in your name,
    for your name is good.

---

a 17 Or *The sacrifices of God are*   *b* Title: Probably a literary or musical term   *c 3* The Hebrew has
Selah (a word of uncertain meaning) here and at the end of verse 5.

* 52:1-9 is numbered 52:3-11 in Hebrew texts.

Psalm 53

For the director of music. According to mahalath.ᵃ A maskilᵇ of David.

*¹Fools say in their hearts,
  "There is no God."
They are corrupt, and their ways are
  vile;
  there is no one who does good.

²God looks down from heaven
  on the human race
to see if there are any who
    understand,
  any who seek God.
³Everyone has turned away, all have
    become corrupt;
  there is no one who does good,
  not even one.

⁴Do all these evildoers know nothing?

They devour my people as though eating
    bread;
  they never call on God.
⁵But there they are, overwhelmed with
    dread,
  where there was nothing to dread.
God scattered the bones of those who
    attacked you;
  you put them to shame, for God
    despised them.

⁶Oh, that salvation for Israel would come
    out of Zion!
When God restores his people,
  let Jacob rejoice and Israel be glad!

Psalm 54

For the director of music. With stringed instruments. A maskilᵇ of David. When the Ziphites had gone to Saul and said, "Is not David hiding among us?"

*¹Save me, O God, by your name;
  vindicate me by your might.
²Hear my prayer, O God;
  listen to the words of my mouth.

³Arrogant foes are attacking me;
  ruthless people seek my life—
  people without regard for God.ᶜ

⁴Surely God is my help;
  the Lord is the one who sustains me.

⁵Let evil recoil on those who slander me;
  in your faithfulness destroy them.

⁶I will sacrifice a freewill offering to you;
  I will praise your name, Lord, for it is
    good.
⁷You have delivered me from all my
    troubles,
  and my eyes have looked in triumph
    on my foes.

Psalm 55

For the director of music. With stringed instruments. A maskilᵇ of David.

*¹Listen to my prayer, O God,
  do not ignore my plea;
² hear me and answer me.
My thoughts trouble me and I am
    distraught
³ because of what my enemy is saying,
  because of the threats of the wicked;
for they bring down suffering on me
  and assail me in their anger.

⁴My heart is in anguish within me;
  the terrors of death have fallen on me.
⁵Fear and trembling have beset me;
  horror has overwhelmed me.
⁶I said, "Oh, that I had the wings of a
    dove!
  I would fly away and be at rest.
⁷I would flee far away
  and stay in the desert;ᵈ
⁸I would hurry to my place of shelter,
  far from the tempest and storm."

⁹Lord, confuse the wicked, confound their
    words,
  for I see violence and strife in the city.
¹⁰Day and night they prowl about on its
    walls;
  malice and abuse are within it.
¹¹Destructive forces are at work in the city;
  threats and lies never leave its streets.
¹²If an enemy were insulting me,
  I could endure it;
  if a foe were rising against me,

ᵃ Title: Probably a musical term   ᵇ Title: Probably a literary or musical term   ᶜ 3 The Hebrew has *Selah* (a word of uncertain meaning) here.   ᵈ 7 The Hebrew has *Selah* (a word of uncertain meaning) here and in the middle of verse 19.

* 53:1-6 is numbered 53:2-7 in Hebrew texts.   * 54:1-7 is numbered 54:3-9 in Hebrew texts.
* 55:1-23 is numbered 55:2-24 in Hebrew texts.

I could hide.
¹³ But it is you, one like myself,
my companion, my close friend,
¹⁴ with whom I once enjoyed sweet
fellowship
at the house of God,
as we walked about
among the worshipers.

¹⁵ Let death take my enemies by surprise;
let them go down alive to the realm
of the dead,
for evil finds lodging among them.

¹⁶ As for me, I call to God,
and the LORD saves me.
¹⁷ Evening, morning and noon
I cry out in distress,
and he hears my voice.
¹⁸ He rescues me unharmed
from the battle waged against me,
even though many oppose me.
¹⁹ God, who is enthroned from of old,
who does not change—
he will hear them and humble them,
because they have no fear of God.

²⁰ My companion attacks his friends;
he violates his covenant.
²¹ His talk is smooth as butter,
yet war is in his heart;
his words are more soothing than oil,
yet they are drawn swords.

²² Cast your cares on the LORD
and he will sustain you;
he will never let
the righteous be shaken.
²³ But you, God, will bring down the
wicked
into the pit of decay;
the bloodthirsty and deceitful
will not live out half their days.

But as for me, I trust in you.

Psalm 56

*For the director of music. To the tune of
"A Dove on Distant Oaks." Of David.
A miktam.ᵃ When the Philistines had
seized him in Gath.*

*¹ Be merciful to me, my God,
for my enemies are in hot pursuit;

all day long they press their attack.
² My adversaries pursue me all day long;
in their pride many are attacking me.

³ When I am afraid, I put my trust in you.
⁴   In God, whose word I praise—
in God I trust and am not afraid.
What can mere mortals do to me?

⁵ All day long they twist my words;
all their schemes are for my ruin.
⁶ They conspire, they lurk,
they watch my steps,
hoping to take my life.
⁷ Because of their wickedness do notᵇ let
them escape;
in your anger, God, bring the nations
down.

⁸ Record my misery;
list my tears on your scrollᶜ—
are they not in your record?
⁹ Then my enemies will turn back
when I call for help.
By this I will know that God is for me.

¹⁰ In God, whose word I praise,
in the LORD, whose word I praise—
¹¹ in God I trust and am not afraid.
What can mere human beings do to
me?

¹² I am under vows to you, my God;
I will present my thank offerings to
you.
¹³ For you have delivered me from death
and my feet from stumbling,
that I may walk before God
in the light of life.

Psalm 57

*For the director of music. To the tune of
"Do Not Destroy." Of David. A miktam.ᵃ
When he had fled from Saul into the cave.*

*¹ Have mercy on me, my God, have mercy
on me,
for in you I take refuge.
I will take refuge in the shadow of your
wings
until the disaster has passed.

² I cry out to God Most High,
to God, who vindicates me.

ᵃ Title: Probably a literary or musical term   ᵇ 7 Probable reading of the original Hebrew text; Masoretic
Text does not have *do not.*   ᶜ 8 Or *misery; / put my tears in your wineskin*
* 56:1-13 is numbered 56:2-14 in Hebrew texts.   * 57:1-11 is numbered 57:2-12 in Hebrew texts.

³He sends from heaven and saves me,
  rebuking those who hotly pursue
    me—ᵃ
  God sends forth his love and his
    faithfulness.

⁴I am in the midst of lions;
  I am forced to dwell among man-
    eating beasts,
  whose teeth are spears and arrows,
  whose tongues are sharp swords.

⁵Be exalted, O God, above the heavens;
  let your glory be over all the earth.

⁶They spread a net for my feet—
  I was bowed down in distress.
  They dug a pit in my path—
  but they have fallen into it
    themselves.

⁷My heart, O God, is steadfast,
  my heart is steadfast;
  I will sing and make music.
⁸Awake, my soul!
  Awake, harp and lyre!
  I will awaken the dawn.

⁹I will praise you, Lord, among the
    nations;
  I will sing of you among the
    peoples.
¹⁰For great is your love, reaching to the
    heavens;
  your faithfulness reaches to the
    skies.

¹¹Be exalted, O God, above the heavens;
  let your glory be over all the earth.

Psalm 58

*For the director of music. To the tune of
"Do Not Destroy." Of David. A miktam.ᵇ*

*¹Do you rulers indeed speak justly?
  Do you judge people with equity?
²No, in your heart you devise injustice,
  and your hands mete out violence on
    the earth.

³Even from birth the wicked go astray;
  from the womb they are wayward,
    spreading lies.
⁴Their venom is like the venom of a
    snake,

like that of a cobra that has stopped
    its ears,
⁵that will not heed the tune of the
    charmer,
  however skillful the enchanter may
    be.

⁶Break the teeth in their mouths,
    O God;
  Lᴏʀᴅ, tear out the fangs of those
    lions!
⁷Let them vanish like water that flows
    away;
  when they draw the bow, let their
    arrows fall short.
⁸May they be like a slug that melts away
    as it moves along,
  like a stillborn child that never sees
    the sun.

⁹Before your pots can feel the heat of the
    thorns—
  whether they be green or dry—the
    wicked will be swept away.ᶜ

¹⁰The righteous will be glad when they are
    avenged,
  when they dip their feet in the blood
    of the wicked.
¹¹Then people will say,
  "Surely the righteous still are
    rewarded;
  surely there is a God who judges the
    earth."

Psalm 59

*For the director of music. To the tune of
"Do Not Destroy." Of David. A miktam.ᵇ
  When Saul had sent men to watch
  David's house in order to kill him.*

*¹Deliver me from my enemies, O God;
  be my fortress against those who are
    attacking me.
²Deliver me from evildoers
  and save me from those who are after
    my blood.

³See how they lie in wait for me!
  Powerful people conspire against me
  for no offense or sin of mine, Lᴏʀᴅ.
⁴I have done no wrong, yet they are ready
    to attack me.
  Arise to help me; look on my plight!

ᵃ 3 The Hebrew has *Selah* (a word of uncertain meaning) here and at the end of verse 6.   ᵇ Title:
Probably a literary or musical term   ᶜ 9 The meaning of the Hebrew for this verse is uncertain.
* 58:1-11 is numbered 58:2-12 in Hebrew texts.   * 59:1-17 is numbered 59:2-18 in Hebrew texts.

5 You, LORD God Almighty,
  you who are the God of Israel,
rouse yourself to punish all the
    nations;
  show no mercy to wicked traitors. *a*

6 They return at evening,
  snarling like dogs,
  and prowl about the city.
7 See what they spew from their
    mouths—
  the words from their lips are sharp as
    swords,
  and they think, "Who can hear us?"
8 But you laugh at them, LORD;
  you scoff at all those nations.

9 You are my strength, I watch for you;
  you, God, are my fortress,
10 my God on whom I can rely.

God will go before me
  and will let me gloat over those who
    slander me.
11 But do not kill them, Lord our shield, *b*
  or my people will forget.
In your might uproot them
  and bring them down.
12 For the sins of their mouths,
  for the words of their lips,
  let them be caught in their pride.
For the curses and lies they utter,
13 consume them in wrath,
  consume them till they are no
    more.
Then it will be known to the ends of the
    earth
  that God rules over Jacob.

14 They return at evening,
  snarling like dogs,
  and prowl about the city.
15 They wander about for food
  and howl if not satisfied.
16 But I will sing of your strength,
  in the morning I will sing of your
    love;
for you are my fortress,
  my refuge in times of trouble.

17 You are my strength, I sing praise to
    you;

you, God, are my fortress,
  my God on whom I can rely.

Psalm 60

*For the director of music. To the tune of
"The Lily of the Covenant." A miktam* c
*of David. For teaching. When he fought
Aram Naharaim* d *and Aram Zobah,* e *and
when Joab returned and struck down
twelve thousand Edomites in the
Valley of Salt.*

*1 You have rejected us, God, and burst
    upon us;
  you have been angry—now restore us!
2 You have shaken the land and torn it
    open;
  mend its fractures, for it is quaking.
3 You have shown your people desperate
    times;
  you have given us wine that makes us
    stagger.
4 But for those who fear you, you have
    raised a banner
  to be unfurled against the bow. *f*

5 Save us and help us with your right
    hand,
  that those you love may be delivered.
6 God has spoken from his sanctuary:
  "In triumph I will parcel out Shechem
  and measure off the Valley of
    Sukkoth.
7 Gilead is mine, and Manasseh is mine;
  Ephraim is my helmet,
  Judah is my scepter.
8 Moab is my washbasin,
  on Edom I toss my sandal;
  over Philistia I shout in triumph."

9 Who will bring me to the fortified city?
  Who will lead me to Edom?
10 Is it not you, God, you who have now
    rejected us
  and no longer go out with our armies?
11 Give us aid against the enemy,
  for human help is worthless.
12 With God we will gain the victory,
  and he will trample down our
    enemies.

---

a 5 The Hebrew has *Selah* (a word of uncertain meaning) here and at the end of verse 13.
b 11 Or *sovereign* *c* Title: Probably a literary or musical term *d* Title: That is, Arameans of Northwest
Mesopotamia *e* Title: That is, Arameans of central Syria *f 4* The Hebrew has *Selah* (a word of
uncertain meaning) here.
* 60:1-12 is numbered 60:3-14 in Hebrew texts.

Psalm 61

For the director of music. With stringed instruments. Of David.

*¹ Hear my cry, O God;
    listen to my prayer.

² From the ends of the earth I call to you,
    I call as my heart grows faint;
    lead me to the rock that is higher
        than I.
³ For you have been my refuge,
    a strong tower against the foe.

⁴ I long to dwell in your tent forever
    and take refuge in the shelter of your
        wings. *ᵃ*
⁵ For you, God, have heard my vows;
    you have given me the heritage of
        those who fear your name.

⁶ Increase the days of the king's life,
    his years for many generations.
⁷ May he be enthroned in God's presence
        forever;
    appoint your love and faithfulness to
        protect him.

⁸ Then I will ever sing in praise of your
        name
    and fulfill my vows day after day.

Psalm 62

*For the director of music. For Jeduthun.
A psalm of David.*

*¹ Truly my soul finds rest in God;
    my salvation comes from him.
² Truly he is my rock and my salvation;
    he is my fortress, I will never be
        shaken.

³ How long will you assault me?
    Would all of you throw me down—
    this leaning wall, this tottering fence?
⁴ Surely they intend to topple me
    from my lofty place;
    they take delight in lies.
With their mouths they bless,
    but in their hearts they curse. *ᵇ*

⁵ Yes, my soul, find rest in God;
    my hope comes from him.

⁶ Truly he is my rock and my salvation;
    he is my fortress, I will not be shaken.
⁷ My salvation and my honor depend on
        God*ᶜ*;
    he is my mighty rock, my refuge.
⁸ Trust in him at all times, you people;
    pour out your hearts to him,
    for God is our refuge.

⁹ Surely the lowborn are but a breath,
    the highborn are but a lie.
If weighed on a balance, they are
        nothing;
    together they are only a breath.
¹⁰ Do not trust in extortion
    or put vain hope in stolen goods;
    though your riches increase,
    do not set your heart on them.

¹¹ One thing God has spoken,
    two things I have heard:
"Power belongs to you, God,
¹²   and with you, Lord, is unfailing love";
and, "You reward everyone
    according to what they have done."

Psalm 63

*A psalm of David. When he was in the
Desert of Judah.*

*¹ You, God, are my God,
    earnestly I seek you;
I thirst for you,
    my whole being longs for you,
in a dry and parched land
    where there is no water.

² I have seen you in the sanctuary
    and beheld your power and your glory.
³ Because your love is better than life,
    my lips will glorify you.
⁴ I will praise you as long as I live,
    and in your name I will lift up my
        hands.
⁵ I will be fully satisfied as with the
        richest of foods;
    with singing lips my mouth will
        praise you.

⁶ On my bed I remember you;
    I think of you through the watches of
        the night.

ᵃ 4 The Hebrew has *Selah* (a word of uncertain meaning) here.   *ᵇ 4* The Hebrew has *Selah* (a word of uncertain meaning) here and at the end of verse 8.   *ᶜ 7* Or / *God Most High is my salvation and my honor*

FRIDAY

TALKING TO GOD
Psalm 63:1–11 *or* 63:1,6–8

MARTIN LUTHER {AD 1483–1546}

There are two obstacles to prayer. The first obstacle arises when the devil prompts you to think, "I am not prepared to pray. I should wait for another half-hour or another day until I have become more prepared or until I have finished taking care of this or that." Meanwhile, the devil distracts you for half an hour, so that you no longer think about prayer for the rest of the day. From one day to the next, you are hindered and rushed with other business. This common obstacle shows us how maliciously the devil tries to trick us. He often tries this on me. The devil also has an influence over our bodies, which are so lazy and cold that we can't pray the way we want to. Even if we do begin to pray, we become distracted by useless thoughts and lose our concentration in prayer.

The second obstacle arises when we ask ourselves, "How can you pray to God? . . . You are too unworthy and sin every day. Wait until you are more devout. You might be in the mood to pray now, but wait until you have confessed your sin . . . so that you can pray more fervently and approach God with confidence. Only then can you really pray . . . from your heart." This serious obstacle crushes us like a heavy stone. Despite our feelings of unworthiness, our hearts must struggle to remove this obstacle so that we can freely approach God and call upon him.

Richard Foster

Carry on an ongoing conversation with God about the daily stuff of life, a little like Tevye in *Fiddler on the Roof*. For now, do not worry about "proper praying," just talk to God. Share your hurts, share your sorrows, share your joys—freely and openly. God listens in compassion and love, just like we do when our children come to us. He delights in our presence. When we do this, we will discover something of inestimable value. We will discover that by praying we learn to pray.

reflection

1. Many people are intimidated by prayer and feel like they're not "good" at it. What's the remedy for this kind of attitude?

2. What obstacles keep you from spending sincere, intense times in prayer? What can you do to remove those barriers?

3. If you could change one thing about your prayer life, what would it be? What's holding you back from making that change?

For your next devotional reading, go to page 646.

7 Because you are my help,
    I sing in the shadow of your wings.
8 I cling to you;
    your right hand upholds me.

9 Those who seek my life will be
        destroyed;
    they will go down to the depths of the
        earth.
10 They will be given over to the sword
    and become food for jackals.

11 But the king will rejoice in God;
    all who swear by God will glory in him,
    while the mouths of liars will be
        silenced.

Psalm 64

*For the director of music. A psalm
of David.*

*1 Hear me, my God, as I voice my
        complaint;
    protect my life from the threat of the
        enemy.

2 Hide me from the conspiracy of the
        wicked,
    from the plots of evildoers.
3 They sharpen their tongues like swords
    and aim cruel words like deadly
        arrows.
4 They shoot from ambush at the
        innocent;
    they shoot suddenly, without fear.

5 They encourage each other in evil plans,
    they talk about hiding their snares;
    they say, "Who will see it a?"
6 They plot injustice and say,
    "We have devised a perfect plan!"
    Surely the human mind and heart are
        cunning.

7 But God will shoot them with his arrows;
    they will suddenly be struck down.
8 He will turn their own tongues against
        them
    and bring them to ruin;
    all who see them will shake their
        heads in scorn.
9 All people will fear;
    they will proclaim the works of God
    and ponder what he has done.

10 The righteous will rejoice in the LORD
    and take refuge in him;
    all the upright in heart will glory in
        him!

Psalm 65

*For the director of music. A psalm
of David. A song.*

*1 Praise awaits b you, our God, in Zion;
    to you our vows will be fulfilled.
2 You who answer prayer,
    to you all people will come.
3 When we were overwhelmed by sins,
    you forgave c our transgressions.
4 Blessed are those you choose
    and bring near to live in your courts!
We are filled with the good things of
        your house,
    of your holy temple.

5 You answer us with awesome and
        righteous deeds,
    God our Savior,
the hope of all the ends of the earth
    and of the farthest seas,
6 who formed the mountains by your
        power,
    having armed yourself with strength,
7 who stilled the roaring of the seas,
    the roaring of their waves,
    and the turmoil of the nations.
8 The whole earth is filled with awe at
        your wonders;
    where morning dawns, where evening
        fades,
    you call forth songs of joy.

9 You care for the land and water it;
    you enrich it abundantly.
The streams of God are filled with water
    to provide the people with grain,
    for so you have ordained it. d
10 You drench its furrows and level its
        ridges;
    you soften it with showers and bless
        its crops.
11 You crown the year with your bounty,
    and your carts overflow with
        abundance.
12 The grasslands of the wilderness
        overflow;

---

a 5 Or *us*   b 1 Or *befits*; the meaning of the Hebrew for this word is uncertain.   c 3 Or *made
atonement for*   d 9 Or *for that is how you prepare the land*

* 64:1-10 is numbered 64:2-11 in Hebrew texts.   * 65:1-13 is numbered 65:2-14 in Hebrew texts.

the hills are clothed with gladness.
¹³ The meadows are covered with flocks
and the valleys are mantled with grain;
they shout for joy and sing.

Psalm 66

For the director of music. A song. A psalm.

¹ Shout for joy to God, all the earth!
² Sing the glory of his name;
make his praise glorious.
³ Say to God, "How awesome are your
deeds!
So great is your power
that your enemies cringe before you.
⁴ All the earth bows down to you;
they sing praise to you,
they sing the praises of your name." ᵃ

⁵ Come and see what God has done,
his awesome deeds for humankind!
⁶ He turned the sea into dry land,
they passed through the waters on
foot—
come, let us rejoice in him.
⁷ He rules forever by his power,
his eyes watch the nations—
let not the rebellious rise up against
him.

⁸ Praise our God, all peoples,
let the sound of his praise be heard;
⁹ he has preserved our lives
and kept our feet from slipping.
¹⁰ For you, God, tested us;
you refined us like silver.
¹¹ You brought us into prison
and laid burdens on our backs.
¹² You let people ride over our heads;
we went through fire and water,
but you brought us to a place of
abundance.

¹³ I will come to your temple with burnt
offerings
and fulfill my vows to you—
¹⁴ vows my lips promised and my mouth
spoke
when I was in trouble.
¹⁵ I will sacrifice fat animals to you
and an offering of rams;
I will offer bulls and goats.

¹⁶ Come and hear, all you who fear God;
let me tell you what he has done for
me.
¹⁷ I cried out to him with my mouth;
his praise was on my tongue.
¹⁸ If I had cherished sin in my heart,
the Lord would not have listened;
¹⁹ but God has surely listened
and has heard my prayer.
²⁰ Praise be to God,
who has not rejected my prayer
or withheld his love from me!

Psalm 67

*For the director of music. With stringed
instruments. A psalm. A song.*

*¹ May God be gracious to us and bless us
and make his face shine on us— ᵇ
² so that your ways may be known on earth,
your salvation among all nations.

³ May the peoples praise you, God;
may all the peoples praise you.
⁴ May the nations be glad and sing for joy,
for you rule the peoples with equity
and guide the nations of the earth.
⁵ May the peoples praise you, God;
may all the peoples praise you.

⁶ The land yields its harvest;
God, our God, blesses us.
⁷ May God bless us still,
so that all the ends of the earth will
fear him.

Psalm 68

*For the director of music. Of David.
A psalm. A song.*

*¹ May God arise, may his enemies be
scattered;
may his foes flee before him.
² May you blow them away like smoke—
as wax melts before the fire,
may the wicked perish before God.
³ But may the righteous be glad
and rejoice before God;
may they be happy and joyful.

⁴ Sing to God, sing in praise of his name,
extol him who rides on the clouds ᶜ;

ᵃ 4 The Hebrew has *Selah* (a word of uncertain meaning) here and at the end of verses 7 and 15.
ᵇ 1 The Hebrew has *Selah* (a word of uncertain meaning) here and at the end of verse 4.   ᶜ 4 Or *name,*
/ prepare the way for him who rides through the deserts

* 67:1-7 is numbered 67:2-8 in Hebrew texts.   * 68:1-35 is numbered 68:2-36 in Hebrew texts.

Precious Metal

Psalm 66:10

read/meditate

Read Psalm 66:10 several times. Think about God's refining process in your life. Think about events and circumstances that have been difficult but have made you a better person.

pray

Share with God any of your concerns about his refining process in your life. Any fears? Any concerns that you are missing the process completely? Quietly surrender yourself to whatever God might use to refine you. Thank him for the work he will do in you.

contemplate

Take a few moments to consider what God is using right now as a refiner in your life. Try to imagine the effect of his process on the areas of your life that need to have more depth and substance.

additional reflection

The little troubles and worries of life may be as stumbling blocks in our way, or we may make them stepping-stones to a nobler character and to Heaven. Troubles are often the tools by which God fashions us for better things

—*Henry Ward Beecher*

God brings men into deep waters, not to drown them, but to cleanse them.

—*John H Aughey*

For your next devotional reading, go to page 649.

rejoice before him—his name is the
LORD.

5 A father to the fatherless, a defender of
widows,
is God in his holy dwelling.
6 God sets the lonely in families,ᵃ
he leads out the prisoners with
singing;
but the rebellious live in a sun-
scorched land.

7 When you, God, went out before your
people,
when you marched through the
wilderness,ᵇ
8 the earth shook, the heavens poured
down rain,
before God, the One of Sinai,
before God, the God of Israel.
9 You gave abundant showers, O God;
you refreshed your weary inheritance.
10 Your people settled in it,
and from your bounty, God, you
provided for the poor.

11 The Lord announced the word,
and great was the company of those
who proclaimed it:
12 "Kings and armies flee in haste;
every household shares in the
plunder.
13 Even while you sleep among the sheep
pens,ᶜ
the wings of my dove are sheathed
with silver,
its feathers with shining gold."
14 When the Almightyᵈ scattered the kings
in the land,
it was like snow fallen on Mount
Zalmon.

15 Mount Bashan, majestic mountain,
Mount Bashan, rugged mountain,
16 why gaze in envy, you rugged mountain,
at the mountain where God chooses
to reign,
where the LORD himself will dwell
forever?
17 The chariots of God are tens of
thousands
and thousands of thousands;

the Lord has come from Sinai into his
sanctuary.ᵉ
18 When you ascended on high,
you took many captives;
you received gifts from people,
even fromᶠ the rebellious—
that you,ᵍ LORD God, might dwell
there.

19 Praise be to the Lord, to God our Savior,
who daily bears our burdens.
20 Our God is a God who saves;
from the Sovereign LORD comes
escape from death.
21 Surely God will crush the heads of his
enemies,
the hairy crowns of those who go on
in their sins.
22 The Lord says, "I will bring them from
Bashan;
I will bring them from the depths of
the sea,
23 that your feet may wade in the blood of
your foes,
while the tongues of your dogs have
their share."

24 Your procession, God, has come into
view,
the procession of my God and King
into the sanctuary.
25 In front are the singers, after them the
musicians;
with them are the young women
playing the timbrels.
26 Praise God in the great congregation;
praise the LORD in the assembly of
Israel.
27 There is the little tribe of Benjamin,
leading them,
there the great throng of Judah's
princes,
and there the princes of Zebulun and
of Naphtali.

28 Summon your power, Godʰ;
show us your strength, our God, as
you have done before.
29 Because of your temple at Jerusalem
kings will bring you gifts.
30 Rebuke the beast among the reeds,

a 6 Or the desolate in a homeland   b 7 The Hebrew has Selah (a word of uncertain meaning) here and
at the end of verses 19 and 32.   c 13 Or the campfires; or the saddlebags   d 14 Hebrew Shaddai
e 17 Probable reading of the original Hebrew text; Masoretic Text Lord is among them at Sinai in holiness
f 18 Or gifts for people, / even   g 18 Or they   h 28 Many Hebrew manuscripts, Septuagint and Syriac;
most Hebrew manuscripts Your God has summoned power for you

the herd of bulls among the calves of
the nations.
Humbled, may it bring bars of silver.
Scatter the nations who delight in
war.
31 Envoys will come from Egypt;
Cush[a] will submit herself to God.

32 Sing to God, you kingdoms of the earth,
sing praise to the Lord,
33 to him who rides the ancient skies
above,
who thunders with mighty voice.
34 Proclaim the power of God,
whose majesty is over Israel,
whose power is in the skies.
35 You, God, are awesome in your
sanctuary;
the God of Israel gives power and
strength to his people.

Praise be to God!

Psalm 69

*For the director of music. To the tune of
"Lilies." Of David.*

*1 Save me, O God,
for the waters have come up to my
neck.
2 I sink in the miry depths,
where there is no foothold.
I have come into the deep waters;
the floods engulf me.
3 I am worn out calling for help;
my throat is parched.
My eyes fail,
looking for my God.
4 Those who hate me without reason
outnumber the hairs of my head;
many are my enemies without cause,
those who seek to destroy me.
I am forced to restore
what I did not steal.

5 You, God, know my folly;
my guilt is not hidden from you.

6 Lord, the Lord Almighty,
may those who hope in you
not be disgraced because of me;
God of Israel,
may those who seek you
not be put to shame because of me.

7 For I endure scorn for your sake,
and shame covers my face.
8 I am a foreigner to my own family,
a stranger to my own mother's
children;
9 for zeal for your house consumes me,
and the insults of those who insult
you fall on me.
10 When I weep and fast,
I must endure scorn;
11 when I put on sackcloth,
people make sport of me.
12 Those who sit at the gate mock me,
and I am the song of the drunkards.

13 But I pray to you, Lord,
in the time of your favor;
in your great love, O God,
answer me with your sure salvation.
14 Rescue me from the mire,
do not let me sink;
deliver me from those who hate me,
from the deep waters.
15 Do not let the floodwaters engulf me
or the depths swallow me up
or the pit close its mouth over me.

16 Answer me, Lord, out of the goodness of
your love;
in your great mercy turn to me.
17 Do not hide your face from your servant;
answer me quickly, for I am in
trouble.
18 Come near and rescue me;
redeem me because of my foes.

19 You know how I am scorned, disgraced
and shamed;
all my enemies are before you.
20 Scorn has broken my heart
and has left me helpless;
I looked for sympathy, but there was
none,
for comforters, but I found none.
21 They put gall in my food
and gave me vinegar for my thirst.

22 May the table set before them become a
snare;
may it become retribution and[b] a
trap.
23 May their eyes be darkened so they
cannot see,
and their backs be bent forever.

---

a 31 That is, the upper Nile region   b 22 Or snare / and their fellowship become
* 69:1-36 is numbered 69:2-37 in Hebrew texts.

MONDAY

GOD THE FATHER

Psalm 68:1–35 *or* 68:4–6

S. J. Hill

What is God like? How do you perceive Him? How would you answer that question?

Ideally, our experience with our father should point us to the heart of a greater Father who loves His children more than any earthly father ever could. Unfortunately, this is not always the case. We live in a fallen world. Maybe you've felt the sting of a clenched fist or recall the haunting, cruel words of a childhood incident. Maybe you still carry the scars from wounds of the past. If so, you are not alone.

Through the years, I've had countless people tell me, "I have no problem believing that Jesus loves me, but I can't seem to relate to the heavenly Father." More often than not it's because they were abused when they were growing up or their fathers were never there for them. Many people have grown up without ever hearing their father say, "I love you."

If you are one of those people, I urge you to take your disappointments, hurts, and wounds to the heavenly Father and allow Him to heal you so you can freely receive His loving embrace.

ANDREW MURRAY {AD 1828–1917}

You can enter deep into God's holy presence with boldness because the blood of Christ gives you assurance that you are accepted by God. In Christ you can pass beyond the veil into the very presence of God. You have access into the very heart and love of the Father . . .

Say to God, "Father, I am here for you to give as much to me of Christ's likeness as I can receive." And wait to hear him say, "My child, I give you as much of Christ as your heart is open to receive." The God who revealed Jesus in the flesh and perfected him, will also reveal him in you and perfect you in him.

reflection

1. How is your heavenly Father different from your earthly father? Are there any similarities?
2. What characteristics of a father do you value most?
3. Describe the ideal parent-child relationship. How can you have that kind of relationship with God?

For your next devotional reading, go to page 658.

24 Pour out your wrath on them;
  let your fierce anger overtake them.
25 May their place be deserted;
  let there be no one to dwell in their
    tents.
26 For they persecute those you wound
  and talk about the pain of those you
    hurt.
27 Charge them with crime upon crime;
  do not let them share in your
    salvation.
28 May they be blotted out of the book of
    life
  and not be listed with the righteous.

29 But as for me, afflicted and in pain—
  may your salvation, God, protect me.

30 I will praise God's name in song
  and glorify him with thanksgiving.
31 This will please the Lord more than an
    ox,
  more than a bull with its horns and
    hooves.
32 The poor will see and be glad—
  you who seek God, may your hearts
    live!
33 The Lord hears the needy
  and does not despise his captive
    people.

34 Let heaven and earth praise him,
  the seas and all that move in them,
35 for God will save Zion
  and rebuild the cities of Judah.
  Then people will settle there and
    possess it;
36   the children of his servants will
    inherit it,
  and those who love his name will
    dwell there.

Psalm 70

For the director of music. Of David.
A petition.

*1 Hasten, O God, to save me;
  come quickly, Lord, to help me.

2 May those who seek my life
  be put to shame and confusion;
  may all who desire my ruin
  be turned back in disgrace.
3 May those who say to me, "Aha! Aha!"
  turn back because of their shame.

* 70:1-5 is numbered 70:2-6 in Hebrew texts.

4 But may all who seek you
  rejoice and be glad in you;
  may those who long for your saving help
    always say,
  "The Lord is great!"

5 But as for me, I am poor and needy;
  come quickly to me, O God.
  You are my help and my deliverer;
  Lord, do not delay.

Psalm 71

1 In you, Lord, I have taken refuge;
  let me never be put to shame.
2 In your righteousness, rescue me and
    deliver me;
  turn your ear to me and save me.
3 Be my rock of refuge,
  to which I can always go;
  give the command to save me,
  for you are my rock and my fortress.
4 Deliver me, my God, from the hand of
    the wicked,
  from the grasp of those who are evil
    and cruel.

5 For you have been my hope, Sovereign
    Lord,
  my confidence since my youth.
6 From birth I have relied on you;
  you brought me forth from my
    mother's womb.
  I will ever praise you.
7 I have become like a portent to many,
  but you are my strong refuge.
8 My mouth is filled with your praise,
  declaring your splendor all day long.

9 Do not cast me away when I am old;
  do not forsake me when my strength
    is gone.
10 For my enemies speak against me;
  those who wait to kill me conspire
    together.
11 They say, "God has forsaken him;
  pursue him and seize him,
  for no one will rescue him."
12 Do not be far from me, my God;
  come quickly, God, to help me.
13 May my accusers perish in shame;
  may those who want to harm me
  be covered with scorn and disgrace.

14 As for me, I will always have hope;
  I will praise you more and more.

¹⁵ My mouth will tell of your righteous
　　 deeds,
　　 of your saving acts all day long—
　　 though I know not how to relate them
　　　 all.
¹⁶ I will come and proclaim your mighty
　　　 acts, Sovereign Lord;
　　 I will proclaim your righteous deeds,
　　　 yours alone.
¹⁷ Since my youth, God, you have taught
　　 me,
　　 and to this day I declare your
　　　 marvelous deeds.
¹⁸ Even when I am old and gray,
　　 do not forsake me, my God,
　　 till I declare your power to the next
　　　 generation,
　　 your mighty acts to all who are to
　　　 come.

¹⁹ Your righteousness, God, reaches to the
　　 skies,
　　 you who have done great things.
　　 Who is like you, God?
²⁰ Though you have made me see troubles,
　　 many and bitter,
　　 you will restore my life again;
　 from the depths of the earth
　　 you will again bring me up.
²¹ You will increase my honor
　　 and comfort me once more.

²² I will praise you with the harp
　　 for your faithfulness, my God;
　 I will sing praise to you with the lyre,
　　 Holy One of Israel.
²³ My lips will shout for joy
　　 when I sing praise to you—
　 I, whom you have redeemed.
²⁴ My tongue will tell of your righteous acts
　　 all day long,
　 for those who wanted to harm me
　　 have been put to shame and confusion.

Psalm 72

Of Solomon.

¹ Endow the king with your justice,
　　 O God,
　　 the royal son with your righteousness.
² May he judge your people in
　　　 righteousness,
　　 your afflicted ones with justice.

³ May the mountains bring prosperity to
　　 the people,
　　 the hills the fruit of righteousness.
⁴ May he defend the afflicted among the
　　 people
　　 and save the children of the needy;
　　 may he crush the oppressor.
⁵ May he endure^a as long as the sun,
　　 as long as the moon, through all
　　　 generations.
⁶ May he be like rain falling on a mown
　　 field,
　　 like showers watering the earth.
⁷ In his days may the righteous flourish
　　 and prosperity abound till the moon
　　　 is no more.

⁸ May he rule from sea to sea
　　 and from the River^b to the ends of the
　　　 earth.
⁹ May the desert tribes bow before him
　　 and his enemies lick the dust.
¹⁰ May the kings of Tarshish and of distant
　　 shores
　　 bring tribute to him.
　 May the kings of Sheba and Seba
　　 present him gifts.
¹¹ May all kings bow down to him
　　 and all nations serve him.

¹² For he will deliver the needy who cry out,
　　 the afflicted who have no one to help.
¹³ He will take pity on the weak and the
　　 needy
　　 and save the needy from death.
¹⁴ He will rescue them from oppression
　　 and violence,
　　 for precious is their blood in his sight.

¹⁵ Long may he live!
　　 May gold from Sheba be given him.
　 May people ever pray for him
　　 and bless him all day long.
¹⁶ May grain abound throughout the land;
　　 on the tops of the hills may it sway.
　 May the crops flourish like Lebanon
　　 and thrive^c like the grass of the field.
¹⁷ May his name endure forever;
　　 may it continue as long as the sun.

　 Then all nations will be blessed through
　　 him,^d
　　 and they will call him blessed.

---

a 5 Septuagint; Hebrew *You will be feared*　　*b 8* That is, the Euphrates　　*c 16* Probable reading of the
original Hebrew text; Masoretic Text *Lebanon, / from the city*　　*d 17* Or *will use his name in blessings* (see
Gen. 48:20)

¹⁸ Praise be to the LORD God, the God of
Israel,
    who alone does marvelous deeds.
¹⁹ Praise be to his glorious name forever;
    may the whole earth be filled with his
    glory.
        Amen and Amen.

²⁰ This concludes the prayers of David son
of Jesse.

BOOK III

Psalms 73–89

Psalm 73

A psalm of Asaph.

¹ Surely God is good to Israel,
    to those who are pure in heart.

² But as for me, my feet had almost
    slipped;
    I had nearly lost my foothold.
³ For I envied the arrogant
    when I saw the prosperity of the
    wicked.

⁴ They have no struggles;
    their bodies are healthy and strong.^a
⁵ They are free from common human
    burdens;
    they are not plagued by human ills.
⁶ Therefore pride is their necklace;
    they clothe themselves with violence.
⁷ From their callous hearts comes
    iniquity^b;
    the evil conceits of their minds know
    no limits.
⁸ They scoff, and speak with malice;
    with arrogance they threaten
    oppression.
⁹ Their mouths lay claim to heaven,
    and their tongues take possession of
    the earth.
¹⁰ Therefore their people turn to them
    and drink up waters in abundance.^c
¹¹ They say, "How would God know?
    Does the Most High know anything?"

¹² This is what the wicked are like—
    always free of care, they go on
    amassing wealth.

¹³ Surely in vain I have kept my heart pure
    and have washed my hands in
    innocence.
¹⁴ All day long I have been afflicted,
    and every morning brings new
    punishments.

¹⁵ If I had spoken out like that,
    I would have betrayed your children.
¹⁶ When I tried to understand all this,
    it troubled me deeply
¹⁷ till I entered the sanctuary of God;
    then I understood their final destiny.

¹⁸ Surely you place them on slippery ground;
    you cast them down to ruin.
¹⁹ How suddenly are they destroyed,
    completely swept away by terrors!
²⁰ They are like a dream when one awakes;
    when you arise, Lord,
    you will despise them as fantasies.

²¹ When my heart was grieved
    and my spirit embittered,
²² I was senseless and ignorant;
    I was a brute beast before you.

²³ Yet I am always with you;
    you hold me by my right hand.
²⁴ You guide me with your counsel,
    and afterward you will take me into
    glory.
²⁵ Whom have I in heaven but you?
    And earth has nothing I desire besides
    you.
²⁶ My flesh and my heart may fail,
    but God is the strength of my heart
    and my portion forever.

²⁷ Those who are far from you will perish;
    you destroy all who are unfaithful to
    you.
²⁸ But as for me, it is good to be near God.
    I have made the Sovereign LORD my
    refuge;
    I will tell of all your deeds.

Psalm 74

A maskil^d of Asaph.

¹ O God, why have you rejected us
    forever?
    Why does your anger smolder against
    the sheep of your pasture?

^a 4 With a different word division of the Hebrew; Masoretic Text *struggles at their death; / their bodies are healthy*   ^b 7 Syriac (see also Septuagint); Hebrew *Their eyes bulge with fat*   ^c 10 The meaning of the Hebrew for this verse is uncertain.   ^d Title: Probably a literary or musical term

2 Remember the people you purchased
   long ago,
   the tribe of your inheritance, whom
      you redeemed—
   Mount Zion, where you dwelt.
3 Turn your steps toward these everlasting
      ruins,
   all this destruction the enemy has
      brought on the sanctuary.

4 Your foes roared in the place where you
      met with us;
   they set up their standards as signs.
5 They behaved like men wielding axes
   to cut through a thicket of trees.
6 They smashed all the carved paneling
   with their axes and hatchets.
7 They burned your sanctuary to the
      ground;
   they defiled the dwelling place of
      your Name.
8 They said in their hearts, "We will crush
      them completely!"
   They burned every place where God
      was worshiped in the land.

9 We are given no signs from God;
   no prophets are left,
   and none of us knows how long this
      will be.
10 How long will the enemy mock you, God?
   Will the foe revile your name forever?
11 Why do you hold back your hand, your
      right hand?
   Take it from the folds of your garment
      and destroy them!

12 But God is my King from long ago;
   he brings salvation on the earth.

13 It was you who split open the sea by
      your power;
   you broke the heads of the monster in
      the waters.
14 It was you who crushed the heads of
      Leviathan
   and gave it as food to the creatures of
      the desert.
15 It was you who opened up springs and
      streams;
   you dried up the ever-flowing rivers.
16 The day is yours, and yours also the
      night;

   you established the sun and moon.
17 It was you who set all the boundaries of
      the earth;
   you made both summer and winter.
18 Remember how the enemy has mocked
      you, LORD,
   how foolish people have reviled your
      name.
19 Do not hand over the life of your dove to
      wild beasts;
   do not forget the lives of your
      afflicted people forever.
20 Have regard for your covenant,
   because haunts of violence fill the
      dark places of the land.
21 Do not let the oppressed retreat in
      disgrace;
   may the poor and needy praise your
      name.
22 Rise up, O God, and defend your cause;
   remember how fools mock you all day
      long.
23 Do not ignore the clamor of your
      adversaries,
   the uproar of your enemies, which
      rises continually.

Psalm 75

*For the director of music. To the tune of
"Do Not Destroy." A psalm of Asaph.
A song.*

*1 We praise you, God,
   we praise you, for your Name is near;
   people tell of your wonderful deeds.

2 You say, "I choose the appointed time;
   it is I who judge with equity.
3 When the earth and all its people quake,
   it is I who hold its pillars firm. *a*
4 To the arrogant I say, 'Boast no more,'
   and to the wicked, 'Do not lift up your
      horns. *b*
5 Do not lift your horns against heaven;
   do not speak with outstretched
      neck.' "

6 No one from the east or the west
   or from the desert can exalt
      themselves.
7 It is God who judges:

---

a 3 The Hebrew has *Selah* (a word of uncertain meaning) here.   *b 4* *Horns* here symbolize strength;
also in verses 5 and 10.

* 75:1-10 is numbered 75:2-11 in Hebrew texts.

He brings one down, he exalts
another.
8 In the hand of the LORD is a cup
full of foaming wine mixed with
spices;
he pours it out, and all the wicked of the
earth
drink it down to its very dregs.

9 As for me, I will declare this forever;
I will sing praise to the God of Jacob,
10 who says, "I will cut off the horns of all
the wicked,
but the horns of the righteous will be
lifted up."

Psalm 76

*For the director of music. With stringed
instruments. A psalm of Asaph. A song.*

*1 God is renowned in Judah;
in Israel his name is great.
2 His tent is in Salem,
his dwelling place in Zion.
3 There he broke the flashing arrows,
the shields and the swords, the
weapons of war.*a*

4 You are resplendent with light,
more majestic than mountains rich
with game.
5 The valiant lie plundered,
they sleep their last sleep;
not one of the warriors
can lift his hands.
6 At your rebuke, God of Jacob,
both horse and chariot lie still.

7 It is you alone who are to be feared.
Who can stand before you when you
are angry?
8 From heaven you pronounced judgment,
and the land feared and was quiet—
9 when you, God, rose up to judge,
to save all the afflicted of the land.
10 Surely your wrath against human beings
brings you praise,
and the survivors of your wrath are
restrained.*b*

11 Make vows to the LORD your God and
fulfill them;
let all the neighboring lands

bring gifts to the One to be feared.
12 He breaks the spirit of rulers;
he is feared by the kings of the earth.

Psalm 77

*For the director of music. For Jeduthun.
Of Asaph. A psalm.*

*1 I cried out to God for help;
I cried out to God to hear me.
2 When I was in distress, I sought the
Lord;
at night I stretched out untiring
hands,
and I would not be comforted.

3 I remembered you, God, and I groaned;
I meditated, and my spirit grew faint.*c*
4 You kept my eyes from closing;
I was too troubled to speak.
5 I thought about the former days,
the years of long ago;
6 I remembered my songs in the night.
My heart meditated and my spirit
asked:

7 "Will the Lord reject forever?
Will he never show his favor again?
8 Has his unfailing love vanished forever?
Has his promise failed for all time?
9 Has God forgotten to be merciful?
Has he in anger withheld his
compassion?"

10 Then I thought, "To this I will appeal:
the years when the Most High
stretched out his right hand.
11 I will remember the deeds of the LORD;
yes, I will remember your miracles of
long ago.
12 I will consider all your works
and meditate on all your mighty
deeds."

13 Your ways, God, are holy.
What god is as great as our God?
14 You are the God who performs miracles;
you display your power among the
peoples.
15 With your mighty arm you redeemed
your people,
the descendants of Jacob and Joseph.

a 3 The Hebrew has *Selah* (a word of uncertain meaning) here and at the end of verse 9.
b 10 Or *Surely human wrath brings you praise, / and with the remainder of wrath you arm yourself*
c 3 The Hebrew has *Selah* (a word of uncertain meaning) here and at the end of verses 9 and 15.

* 76:1-12 is numbered 76:2-13 in Hebrew texts.   * 77:1-20 is numbered 77:2-21 in Hebrew texts.

¹⁶ The waters saw you, God,
    the waters saw you and writhed;
    the very depths were convulsed.
¹⁷ The clouds poured down water,
    the heavens resounded with thunder;
    your arrows flashed back and forth.
¹⁸ Your thunder was heard in the
      whirlwind,
    your lightning lit up the world;
    the earth trembled and quaked.
¹⁹ Your path led through the sea,
    your way through the mighty waters,
    though your footprints were not seen.

²⁰ You led your people like a flock
    by the hand of Moses and Aaron.

Psalm 78

A maskil^a of Asaph.

¹ My people, hear my teaching;
    listen to the words of my mouth.
² I will open my mouth with a parable;
    I will teach you lessons from the
      past—
³ things we have heard and known,
    things our ancestors have told us.
⁴ We will not hide them from their
      descendants;
    we will tell the next generation
  the praiseworthy deeds of the Lord,
    his power, and the wonders he has
      done.
⁵ He decreed statutes for Jacob
    and established the law in Israel,
  which he commanded our ancestors
    to teach their children,
⁶ so the next generation would know
      them,
    even the children yet to be born,
    and they in turn would tell their
      children.
⁷ Then they would put their trust in God
    and would not forget his deeds
    but would keep his commands.
⁸ They would not be like their ancestors—
    a stubborn and rebellious generation,
  whose hearts were not loyal to God,
    whose spirits were not faithful to him.
⁹ The men of Ephraim, though armed with
      bows,
    turned back on the day of battle;
¹⁰ they did not keep God's covenant

    and refused to live by his law.
¹¹ They forgot what he had done,
    the wonders he had shown them.
¹² He did miracles in the sight of their
      ancestors
    in the land of Egypt, in the region of
      Zoan.
¹³ He divided the sea and led them
      through;
    he made the water stand up like a
      wall.
¹⁴ He guided them with the cloud by day
    and with light from the fire all night.
¹⁵ He split the rocks in the wilderness
    and gave them water as abundant as
      the seas;
¹⁶ he brought streams out of a rocky crag
    and made water flow down like rivers.

¹⁷ But they continued to sin against him,
    rebelling in the wilderness against the
      Most High.
¹⁸ They willfully put God to the test
    by demanding the food they craved.
¹⁹ They spoke against God;
    they said, "Can God really
    spread a table in the wilderness?
²⁰ True, he struck the rock,
    and water gushed out,
    streams flowed abundantly,
  but can he also give us bread?
    Can he supply meat for his people?"
²¹ When the Lord heard them, he was
      furious;
    his fire broke out against Jacob,
    and his wrath rose against Israel,
²² for they did not believe in God
    or trust in his deliverance.
²³ Yet he gave a command to the skies
      above
    and opened the doors of the heavens;
²⁴ he rained down manna for the people to
      eat,
    he gave them the grain of heaven.
²⁵ Human beings ate the bread of angels;
    he sent them all the food they could
      eat.
²⁶ He let loose the east wind from the
      heavens
    and by his power made the south
      wind blow.
²⁷ He rained meat down on them like dust,
    birds like sand on the seashore.

^a Title: Probably a literary or musical term

28 He made them come down inside their
     camp,
     all around their tents.
29 They ate till they were gorged—
     he had given them what they craved.
30 But before they turned from what they
     craved,
     even while the food was still in their
     mouths,
31 God's anger rose against them;
     he put to death the sturdiest among
     them,
     cutting down the young men of Israel.

32 In spite of all this, they kept on sinning;
     in spite of his wonders, they did not
     believe.
33 So he ended their days in futility
     and their years in terror.
34 Whenever God slew them, they would
     seek him;
     they eagerly turned to him again.
35 They remembered that God was their
     Rock,
     that God Most High was their
     Redeemer.
36 But then they would flatter him with
     their mouths,
     lying to him with their tongues;
37 their hearts were not loyal to him,
     they were not faithful to his covenant.
38 Yet he was merciful;
     he forgave their iniquities
     and did not destroy them.
     Time after time he restrained his anger
     and did not stir up his full wrath.
39 He remembered that they were but
     flesh,
     a passing breeze that does not return.

40 How often they rebelled against him in
     the wilderness
     and grieved him in the wasteland!
41 Again and again they put God to the
     test;
     they vexed the Holy One of Israel.
42 They did not remember his power—
     the day he redeemed them from the
     oppressor,
43 the day he displayed his signs in Egypt,
     his wonders in the region of Zoan.
44 He turned their river into blood;
     they could not drink from their
     streams.
45 He sent swarms of flies that devoured
     them,

and frogs that devastated them.
46 He gave their crops to the grasshopper,
     their produce to the locust.
47 He destroyed their vines with hail
     and their sycamore-figs with sleet.
48 He gave over their cattle to the hail,
     their livestock to bolts of lightning.
49 He unleashed against them his hot
     anger,
     his wrath, indignation and hostility—
     a band of destroying angels.
50 He prepared a path for his anger;
     he did not spare them from death
     but gave them over to the plague.
51 He struck down all the firstborn of
     Egypt,
     the firstfruits of manhood in the tents
     of Ham.
52 But he brought his people out like a
     flock;
     he led them like sheep through the
     wilderness.
53 He guided them safely, so they were
     unafraid;
     but the sea engulfed their enemies.
54 And so he brought them to the border of
     his holy land,
     to the hill country his right hand had
     taken.
55 He drove out nations before them
     and allotted their lands to them as an
     inheritance;
     he settled the tribes of Israel in their
     homes.
56 But they put God to the test
     and rebelled against the Most High;
     they did not keep his statutes.
57 Like their ancestors they were disloyal
     and faithless,
     as unreliable as a faulty bow.
58 They angered him with their high places;
     they aroused his jealousy with their
     idols.
59 When God heard them, he was furious;
     he rejected Israel completely.
60 He abandoned the tabernacle of Shiloh,
     the tent he had set up among
     mortals.
61 He sent the ark of his might into
     captivity,
     his splendor into the hands of the
     enemy.
62 He gave his people over to the sword;
     he was furious with his inheritance.
63 Fire consumed their young men,

and their young women had no
wedding songs;
⁶⁴their priests were put to the sword,
and their widows could not weep.

⁶⁵Then the Lord awoke as from sleep,
as a warrior wakes from the stupor of
wine.
⁶⁶He beat back his enemies;
he put them to everlasting shame.
⁶⁷Then he rejected the tents of Joseph,
he did not choose the tribe of
Ephraim;
⁶⁸but he chose the tribe of Judah,
Mount Zion, which he loved.
⁶⁹He built his sanctuary like the heights,
like the earth that he established
forever.
⁷⁰He chose David his servant
and took him from the sheep pens;
⁷¹from tending the sheep he brought him
to be the shepherd of his people
Jacob,
of Israel his inheritance.
⁷²And David shepherded them with
integrity of heart;
with skillful hands he led them.

Psalm 79

A psalm of Asaph.

¹O God, the nations have invaded your
inheritance;
they have defiled your holy temple,
they have reduced Jerusalem to
rubble.
²They have left the dead bodies of your
servants
as food for the birds of the sky,
the flesh of your own people for the
animals of the wild.
³They have poured out blood like water
all around Jerusalem,
and there is no one to bury the
dead.
⁴We are objects of contempt to our
neighbors,
of scorn and derision to those around
us.
⁵How long, Lᴏʀᴅ? Will you be angry
forever?
How long will your jealousy burn like
fire?

⁶Pour out your wrath on the nations
that do not acknowledge you,
on the kingdoms
that do not call on your name;
⁷for they have devoured Jacob
and devastated his homeland.

⁸Do not hold against us the sins of past
generations;
may your mercy come quickly to
meet us,
for we are in desperate need.
⁹Help us, God our Savior,
for the glory of your name;
deliver us and forgive our sins
for your name's sake.
¹⁰Why should the nations say,
"Where is their God?"

Before our eyes, make known among the
nations
that you avenge the outpoured blood
of your servants.
¹¹May the groans of the prisoners come
before you;
with your strong arm preserve those
condemned to die.
¹²Pay back into the laps of our neighbors
seven times
the contempt they have hurled at you,
Lord.
¹³Then we your people, the sheep of your
pasture,
will praise you forever;
from generation to generation
we will proclaim your praise.

Psalm 80

*For the director of music. To the tune of
"The Lilies of the Covenant." Of Asaph.
A psalm.*

*¹Hear us, Shepherd of Israel,
you who lead Joseph like a flock.
You who sit enthroned between the
cherubim,
shine forth ²before Ephraim,
Benjamin and Manasseh.
Awaken your might;
come and save us.

³Restore us, O God;
make your face shine on us,
that we may be saved.

---

* 80:1-19 is numbered 80:2-20 in Hebrew texts.

TUESDAY

THERE'S SOMETHING ABOUT HIS FACE
Psalm 80:1–19 or 80:17–19

ROMANO GUARDINI {AD 1885-1968}

The relationship with God into which man enters in prayer is frequently referred to in the Scriptures. The beautiful expression "the face of God" is used in this connection.

This must be understood metaphorically. God has no face as we understand it, for He has no body as we understand it. But man is made in the image of God—the whole man, not only his soul. Everything, therefore, every feature and attribute which is part of the wholeness of man is a manifestation of God. Hence, in a manner beyond all human conception, there is something in God which corresponds to what in man we call face.

The face of man reflects his inner self; it expresses his personality and his ability to "face" others in friendship or hostility, in love or hatred . . . Man's face also expresses his faculty of opening himself to others and of establishing rapport with others. All these faculties—in a manner which surpasses human understanding—are present in God, and that is why the Scriptures say that "God lets his face shine upon man" [see Psalm 80:19] or that He "sets his face against" those who disobey Him [see Leviticus 17:10].

Nancy Leigh DeMoss

"Face-to-face" . . . is a picture of intimacy. It is a picture of lovers. On the other hand, when something comes between two friends, it can be awkward and uncomfortable to be face-to-face . . .

If you have walked with God for any length of time, you know what it is to have a breach in the relationship-to find it difficult to look Him "in the eyes." The purpose of a daily devotional time is to get back into his presence, to find out what has caused the breach, and to reestablish fellowship. Then we can once again look in His face without shame or fear.

reflection

1. The psalmist pleaded with God to "make your face shine on us." Based on the rest of the psalm, what was it that the psalmist was really asking for?

2. How would you explain what it means for God to "set his face against you" or "turn his face from you"?

3. How does that compare to what it means for God to make his "face shine upon you"?

For your next devotional reading, go to page 665.

4 How long, LORD God Almighty,
   will your anger smolder
   against the prayers of your people?
5 You have fed them with the bread of
     tears;
   you have made them drink tears by
     the bowlful.
6 You have made us an object of derision*a*
     to our neighbors,
   and our enemies mock us.

7 Restore us, God Almighty;
   make your face shine on us,
   that we may be saved.

8 You transplanted a vine from Egypt;
   you drove out the nations and planted
     it.
9 You cleared the ground for it,
   and it took root and filled the land.
10 The mountains were covered with its
     shade,
   the mighty cedars with its branches.
11 Its branches reached as far as the Sea,*b*
   its shoots as far as the River.*c*

12 Why have you broken down its walls
   so that all who pass by pick its
     grapes?
13 Boars from the forest ravage it
   and wild animals feed on it.
14 Return to us, God Almighty!
   Look down from heaven and see!
   Watch over this vine,
15   the root your right hand has planted,
   the son*d* you have raised up for
     yourself.

16 Your vine is cut down, it is burned with
     fire;
   at your rebuke your people perish.
17 Let your hand rest on the man at your
     right hand,
   the son of man you have raised up for
     yourself.
18 Then we will not turn away from you;
   revive us, and we will call on your
     name.

19 Restore us, LORD God Almighty;
   make your face shine on us,
   that we may be saved.

Psalm 81

*For the director of music. According to
gittith.*e* Of Asaph.*

*1 Sing for joy to God our strength;
   shout aloud to the God of Jacob!
2 Begin the music, strike the timbrel,
   play the melodious harp and lyre.

3 Sound the ram's horn at the New Moon,
   and when the moon is full, on the day
     of our festival;
4 this is a decree for Israel,
   an ordinance of the God of Jacob.
5 When God went out against Egypt,
   he established it as a statute for
     Joseph.

I heard an unknown voice say:

6 "I removed the burden from their
     shoulders;
   their hands were set free from the
     basket.
7 In your distress you called and I rescued
     you,
   I answered you out of a thundercloud;
   I tested you at the waters of Meribah.*f*
8 Hear me, my people, and I will warn
     you—
   if you would only listen to me, Israel!
9 You shall have no foreign god among
     you;
   you shall not worship any god other
     than me.
10 I am the LORD your God,
   who brought you up out of Egypt.
   Open wide your mouth and I will fill it.

11 "But my people would not listen to me;
   Israel would not submit to me.
12 So I gave them over to their stubborn
     hearts
   to follow their own devices.

13 "If my people would only listen to me,
   if Israel would only follow my ways,
14 how quickly I would subdue their
     enemies
   and turn my hand against their foes!
15 Those who hate the LORD would cringe
   before him,

---

a 6 Probable reading of the original Hebrew text; Masoretic Text *contention*   *b* 11 Probably the
Mediterranean   *c* 11 That is, the Euphrates   *d* 15 Or *branch*   *e* Title: Probably a musical term
f 7 The Hebrew has *Selah* (a word of uncertain meaning) here.

* 81:1-16 is numbered 81:2-17 in Hebrew texts.

and their punishment would last
        forever.
[16] But you would be fed with the finest of
        wheat;
    with honey from the rock I would
        satisfy you."

Psalm 82

A psalm of Asaph.

[1] God presides in the great assembly;
    he gives judgment among the
        "gods":

[2] "How long will you[a] defend the unjust
    and show partiality to the wicked?[b]
[3] Defend the weak and the fatherless;
    uphold the cause of the poor and the
        oppressed.
[4] Rescue the weak and the needy;
    deliver them from the hand of the
        wicked.

[5] "The 'gods' know nothing, they
        understand nothing.
    They walk about in darkness;
    all the foundations of the earth are
        shaken.

[6] "I said, 'You are "gods";
    you are all sons of the Most High.'
[7] But you will die like mere mortals;
    you will fall like every other ruler."

[8] Rise up, O God, judge the earth,
    for all the nations are your
        inheritance.

Psalm 83

A song. A psalm of Asaph.

*[1] O God, do not remain silent;
    do not turn a deaf ear,
    do not stand aloof, O God.
[2] See how your enemies growl,
    how your foes rear their heads.
[3] With cunning they conspire against your
        people;
    they plot against those you cherish.
[4] "Come," they say, "let us destroy them
        as a nation,
    so that Israel's name is remembered
        no more."

[5] With one mind they plot together;
    they form an alliance against you—
[6] the tents of Edom and the Ishmaelites,
    of Moab and the Hagrites,
[7] Byblos, Ammon and Amalek,
    Philistia, with the people of Tyre.
[8] Even Assyria has joined them
    to reinforce Lot's descendants.[b]

[9] Do to them as you did to Midian,
    as you did to Sisera and Jabin at the
        river Kishon,
[10] who perished at Endor
    and became like dung on the ground.
[11] Make their nobles like Oreb and Zeeb,
    all their princes like Zebah and
        Zalmunna,
[12] who said, "Let us take possession
    of the pasturelands of God."

[13] Make them like tumbleweed, my God,
    like chaff before the wind.
[14] As fire consumes the forest
    or a flame sets the mountains ablaze,
[15] so pursue them with your tempest
    and terrify them with your storm.
[16] Cover their faces with shame, LORD,
    so that they will seek your name.

[17] May they ever be ashamed and
        dismayed;
    may they perish in disgrace.
[18] Let them know that you, whose name is
        the LORD—
    that you alone are the Most High over
        all the earth.

Psalm 84

*For the director of music. According to
gittith.[c] Of the Sons of Korah. A psalm.*

*[1] How lovely is your dwelling place,
    LORD Almighty!
[2] My soul yearns, even faints,
    for the courts of the LORD;
    my heart and my flesh cry out
    for the living God.
[3] Even the sparrow has found a home,
    and the swallow a nest for herself,
    where she may have her young—
    a place near your altar,
    LORD Almighty, my King and my God.

---

a 2 The Hebrew is plural.   *b 2,8* The Hebrew has *Selah* (a word of uncertain meaning) here.   *c* Title:
Probably a musical term

* 83:1-18 is numbered 83:2-19 in Hebrew texts.   * 84:1-12 is numbered 84:2-13 in Hebrew texts.

4 Blessed are those who dwell in your
    house;
  they are ever praising you. *a*

5 Blessed are those whose strength is in
    you,
  whose hearts are set on pilgrimage.
6 As they pass through the Valley of Baka,
  they make it a place of springs;
  the autumn rains also cover it with
    pools. *b*
7 They go from strength to strength,
  till each appears before God in Zion.

8 Hear my prayer, Lord God Almighty;
  listen to me, God of Jacob.
9 Look on our shield, *c* O God;
  look with favor on your anointed one.

10 Better is one day in your courts
    than a thousand elsewhere;
  I would rather be a doorkeeper in the
    house of my God
  than dwell in the tents of the wicked.
11 For the Lord God is a sun and shield;
  the Lord bestows favor and honor;
  no good thing does he withhold
    from those whose walk is blameless.

12 Lord Almighty,
  blessed are those who trust in you.

Psalm 85

*For the director of music. Of the Sons of
Korah. A psalm.*

*1 You, Lord, showed favor to your land;
  you restored the fortunes of Jacob.
2 You forgave the iniquity of your people
  and covered all their sins. *d*
3 You set aside all your wrath
  and turned from your fierce anger.

4 Restore us again, God our Savior,
  and put away your displeasure toward
    us.
5 Will you be angry with us forever?
  Will you prolong your anger through
    all generations?
6 Will you not revive us again,
  that your people may rejoice in you?
7 Show us your unfailing love, Lord,
  and grant us your salvation.

8 I will listen to what God the Lord says;
  he promises peace to his people, his
    faithful servants—
  but let them not turn to folly.
9 Surely his salvation is near those who
    fear him,
  that his glory may dwell in our land.

10 Love and faithfulness meet together;
  righteousness and peace kiss each
    other.
11 Faithfulness springs forth from the
    earth,
  and righteousness looks down from
    heaven.
12 The Lord will indeed give what is good,
  and our land will yield its harvest.
13 Righteousness goes before him
  and prepares the way for his steps.

Psalm 86

A prayer of David.

1 Hear me, Lord, and answer me,
  for I am poor and needy.
2 Guard my life, for I am faithful to you;
  save your servant who trusts in you.
  You are my God; 3 have mercy on me,
    Lord,
  for I call to you all day long.
4 Bring joy to your servant, Lord,
  for I put my trust in you.

5 You, Lord, are forgiving and good,
  abounding in love to all who call to
    you.
6 Hear my prayer, Lord;
  listen to my cry for mercy.
7 When I am in distress, I call to you,
  because you answer me.

8 Among the gods there is none like you,
    Lord;
  no deeds can compare with yours.
9 All the nations you have made
  will come and worship before you,
    Lord;
  they will bring glory to your name.
10 For you are great and do marvelous deeds;
  you alone are God.

11 Teach me your way, Lord,
  that I may rely on your faithfulness;

---

a 4 The Hebrew has *Selah* (a word of uncertain meaning) here and at the end of verse 8.
b 6 Or *blessings*   *c* 9 Or *sovereign*   *d* 2 The Hebrew has *Selah* (a word of uncertain meaning) here.
* 85:1-13 is numbered 85:2-14 in Hebrew texts.

give me an undivided heart,
    that I may fear your name.
12 I will praise you, Lord my God, with all
        my heart;
    I will glorify your name forever.
13 For great is your love toward me;
    you have delivered me from the
        depths,
    from the realm of the dead.

14 Arrogant foes are attacking me, O God;
    a band of ruthless people seeks my
        life—
    they have no regard for you.
15 But you, Lord, are a compassionate and
        gracious God,
    slow to anger, abounding in love and
        faithfulness.
16 Turn to me and have mercy on me;
    show your strength in behalf of your
        servant
and save the son of a woman
    who served you before me.
17 Give me a sign of your goodness,
    that my enemies may see it and be
        put to shame,
    for you, Lord, have helped me and
        comforted me.

Psalm 87

Of the Sons of Korah. A psalm. A song.

1 He has founded his city on the holy
        mountain.
2 The Lord loves the gates of Zion
    more than all the other dwellings of
        Jacob.
3 Glorious things are said of you,
    city of God:[a]
4 "I will record Rahab[b] and Babylon
    among those who acknowledge me—
Philistia too, and Tyre, along with
        Cush[c]—
    and will say, 'This one was born in
        Zion.' "[d]
5 Indeed, of Zion it will be said,
    "This one and that one were born in
        her,

and the Most High himself will
    establish her."
6 The Lord will write in the register of the
        peoples:
    "This one was born in Zion."

7 As they make music they will sing,
    "All my fountains are in you."

Psalm 88

*A song. A psalm of the Sons of Korah.
For the director of music. According to
mahalath leannoth.[e] A maskil[f] of
Heman the Ezrahite.*

*1 Lord, you are the God who saves me;
    day and night I cry out to you.
2 May my prayer come before you;
    turn your ear to my cry.

3 I am overwhelmed with troubles
    and my life draws near to death.
4 I am counted among those who go down
        to the pit;
    I am like one without strength.
5 I am set apart with the dead,
    like the slain who lie in the grave,
whom you remember no more,
    who are cut off from your care.

6 You have put me in the lowest pit,
    in the darkest depths.
7 Your wrath lies heavily on me;
    you have overwhelmed me with all
        your waves.[g]
8 You have taken from me my closest
        friends
    and have made me repulsive to them.
I am confined and cannot escape;
9   my eyes are dim with grief.

I call to you, Lord, every day;
    I spread out my hands to you.
10 Do you show your wonders to the dead?
    Do their spirits rise up and praise
        you?
11 Is your love declared in the grave,
    your faithfulness in Destruction[h]?
12 Are your wonders known in the place of
        darkness,

---

a 3 The Hebrew has *Selah* (a word of uncertain meaning) here and at the end of verse 6.   b 4 A poetic
name for Egypt   c 4 That is, the upper Nile region   d 4 Or *"I will record concerning those who
acknowledge me: / 'This one was born in Zion.' / Hear this, Rahab and Babylon, / and you too, Philistia, Tyre
and Cush."*   e Title: Possibly a tune, "The Suffering of Affliction"   f Title: Probably a literary or
musical term   g 7 The Hebrew has *Selah* (a word of uncertain meaning) here and at the end of
verse 10.   h 11 Hebrew *Abaddon*

* 88:1-18 is numbered 88:2-19 in Hebrew texts.

or your righteous deeds in the land of
oblivion?

¹³ But I cry to you for help, LORD;
in the morning my prayer comes
before you.

¹⁴ Why, LORD, do you reject me
and hide your face from me?

¹⁵ From my youth I have suffered and been
close to death;
I have borne your terrors and am in
despair.

¹⁶ Your wrath has swept over me;
your terrors have destroyed me.

¹⁷ All day long they surround me like a flood;
they have completely engulfed me.

¹⁸ You have taken from me friend and
neighbor—
darkness is my closest friend.

Psalm 89

A maskil^a of Ethan the Ezrahite.

^{*1} I will sing of the LORD's great love forever;
with my mouth I will make your
faithfulness known
through all generations.

² I will declare that your love stands firm
forever,
that you have established your
faithfulness in heaven itself.

³ You said, "I have made a covenant with
my chosen one,
I have sworn to David my servant,

⁴ 'I will establish your line forever
and make your throne firm through
all generations.' "^b

⁵ The heavens praise your wonders, LORD,
your faithfulness too, in the assembly
of the holy ones.

⁶ For who in the skies above can compare
with the LORD?
Who is like the LORD among the
heavenly beings?

⁷ In the council of the holy ones God is
greatly feared;
he is more awesome than all who
surround him.

⁸ Who is like you, LORD God Almighty?

You, LORD, are mighty, and your
faithfulness surrounds you.

⁹ You rule over the surging sea;
when its waves mount up, you still
them.

¹⁰ You crushed Rahab like one of the slain;
with your strong arm you scattered
your enemies.

¹¹ The heavens are yours, and yours also
the earth;
you founded the world and all that is
in it.

¹² You created the north and the south;
Tabor and Hermon sing for joy at your
name.

¹³ Your arm is endued with power;
your hand is strong, your right hand
exalted.

¹⁴ Righteousness and justice are the
foundation of your throne;
love and faithfulness go before you.

¹⁵ Blessed are those who have learned to
acclaim you,
who walk in the light of your
presence, LORD.

¹⁶ They rejoice in your name all day long;
they exult in your righteousness.

¹⁷ For you are their glory and strength,
and by your favor you exalt our horn.^c

¹⁸ Indeed, our shield^d belongs to the LORD,
our king to the Holy One of Israel.

¹⁹ Once you spoke in a vision,
to your faithful people you said:
"I have bestowed strength on a warrior;
I have raised up a young man from
among the people.

²⁰ I have found David my servant;
with my sacred oil I have anointed him.

²¹ My hand will sustain him;
surely my arm will strengthen him.

²² No enemy will get the better of him;
no wicked person will oppress him.

²³ I will crush his foes before him
and strike down his adversaries.

²⁴ My faithful love will be with him,
and through my name his horn^e will
be exalted.

²⁵ I will set his hand over the sea,
his right hand over the rivers.

---

26 He will call out to me, 'You are my
    Father,
  my God, the Rock my Savior.'
27 And I will appoint him to be my
    firstborn,
  the most exalted of the kings of the
    earth.
28 I will maintain my love to him forever,
  and my covenant with him will never
    fail.
29 I will establish his line forever,
  his throne as long as the heavens
    endure.

30 "If his sons forsake my law
  and do not follow my statutes,
31 if they violate my decrees
  and fail to keep my commands,
32 I will punish their sin with the rod,
  their iniquity with flogging;
33 but I will not take my love from him,
  nor will I ever betray my faithfulness.
34 I will not violate my covenant
  or alter what my lips have uttered.
35 Once for all, I have sworn by my
    holiness—
  and I will not lie to David—
36 that his line will continue forever
  and his throne endure before me like
    the sun;
37 it will be established forever like the
    moon,
  the faithful witness in the sky."

38 But you have rejected, you have
    spurned,
  you have been very angry with your
    anointed one.
39 You have renounced the covenant with
    your servant
  and have defiled his crown in the
    dust.
40 You have broken through all his walls
  and reduced his strongholds to ruins.
41 All who pass by have plundered him;
  he has become the scorn of his
    neighbors.
42 You have exalted the right hand of his
    foes;
  you have made all his enemies
    rejoice.
43 Indeed, you have turned back the edge
    of his sword
  and have not supported him in battle.

44 You have put an end to his splendor
  and cast his throne to the ground.
45 You have cut short the days of his youth;
  you have covered him with a mantle
    of shame.

46 How long, LORD? Will you hide yourself
    forever?
  How long will your wrath burn like
    fire?
47 Remember how fleeting is my life.
  For what futility you have created all
    humanity!
48 Who can live and not see death,
  or who can escape the power of the
    grave?
49 Lord, where is your former great love,
  which in your faithfulness you swore
    to David?
50 Remember, Lord, how your servant has *a*
    been mocked,
  how I bear in my heart the taunts of
    all the nations,
51 the taunts with which your enemies,
  LORD, have mocked,
  with which they have mocked every
    step of your anointed one.

52 Praise be to the LORD forever!
  Amen and Amen.

BOOK IV

Psalms 90–106

Psalm 90

A prayer of Moses the man of God.

1 Lord, you have been our dwelling place
    throughout all generations.
2 Before the mountains were born
  or you brought forth the whole world,
  from everlasting to everlasting you
    are God.

3 You turn people back to dust,
  saying, "Return to dust, you
    mortals."
4 A thousand years in your sight
  are like a day that has just gone by,
  or like a watch in the night.
5 Yet you sweep people away in the sleep
    of death—
  they are like the new grass of the
    morning:

---

a 50 Or *your servants have*

WEDNESDAY

Take Advantage of Every Day
Psalm 90:1–17 *or* 90:3,12

Martin Luther {AD 1483–1546}

Until I realized how seriously and urgently Moses prayed in this passage, I didn't understand that we should ask God to teach us to number our days. I thought everyone was just as afraid of death as I was. However, out of ten thousand people, only ten might believe that numbering their days is important. The rest of the masses of people live as if God doesn't exist and death doesn't occur …

So Moses appropriately teaches us to pray that we might number our days. We aren't supposed to ask God exactly how much time we have left. Rather, we must pray that we may become aware of how miserable and short our lives are. Death and God's eternal anger threaten us every second.

Occasionally, we'll find people who really are concerned about the shortness of life. They are preoccupied with thoughts of their impending death, even though they didn't pray for this knowledge. But most people aren't aware that their days are numbered. They live as if the present moment will last forever. So for most of us, praying the way Moses suggests in this passage is indispensable.

Jim Cymbala

What stops us today from drawing a line in the sand and setting our hearts toward God in fervent prayer that he will come and revive his work in us as well as in our churches? Soon our lives will be over, and it is better to live a few years full of the Spirit, seeing God work in and through us, than to go on for decades with little or no experience of the great things God has promised to his people through the person and work of the Spirit.

In a world as tormented and confused as ours, we desperately need God's wind and fire to energize us. With sin on the rampage and demonic powers controlling more and more of our culture, we need an enduement of divine power similar to what God gave the early church. Why don't we stop rationalizing and justifying the spiritual impotence all around us? Why not rather humble ourselves and seek God with all our heart for "something from heaven"?

reflection

1. In our culture today, do you think it is important to live with an awareness that life is short? Why or why not?

2. How do you make the most of your days?

3. When you reach the end of your life, what do you want your life to have stood for?

For your next devotional reading, go to page 672.

⁶ In the morning it springs up new,
  but by evening it is dry and withered.

⁷ We are consumed by your anger
  and terrified by your indignation.
⁸ You have set our iniquities before you,
  our secret sins in the light of your
    presence.
⁹ All our days pass away under your wrath;
  we finish our years with a moan.
¹⁰ Our days may come to seventy years,
  or eighty, if our strength endures;
  yet the best of them are but trouble and
    sorrow,
  for they quickly pass, and we fly
    away.
¹¹ If only we knew the power of your anger!
  Your wrath is as great as the fear that
    is your due.
¹² Teach us to number our days,
  that we may gain a heart of wisdom.

¹³ Relent, Lord! How long will it be?
  Have compassion on your servants.
¹⁴ Satisfy us in the morning with your
    unfailing love,
  that we may sing for joy and be glad
    all our days.
¹⁵ Make us glad for as many days as you
    have afflicted us,
  for as many years as we have seen
    trouble.
¹⁶ May your deeds be shown to your
    servants,
  your splendor to their children.

¹⁷ May the favor ᵃ of the Lord our God rest
    on us;
  establish the work of our hands for
    us—
  yes, establish the work of our hands.

Psalm 91

¹ Whoever dwells in the shelter of the
    Most High
  will rest in the shadow of the
    Almighty. ᵇ
² They say of the Lord, "He is my refuge
    and my fortress,
  my God, in whom I trust."

³ Surely he will save you
  from the fowler's snare
  and from the deadly pestilence.

⁴ He will cover you with his feathers,
  and under his wings you will find
    refuge;
  his faithfulness will be your shield
    and rampart.
⁵ You will not fear the terror of night,
  nor the arrow that flies by day,
⁶ nor the pestilence that stalks in the
    darkness,
  nor the plague that destroys at
    midday.
⁷ A thousand may fall at your side,
  ten thousand at your right hand,
  but it will not come near you.
⁸ You will only observe with your eyes
  and see the punishment of the wicked.

⁹ If you say, "The Lord is my refuge,"
  and you make the Most High your
    dwelling,
¹⁰ no harm will overtake you,
  no disaster will come near your tent.
¹¹ For he will command his angels
    concerning you
  to guard you in all your ways;
¹² they will lift you up in their hands,
  so that you will not strike your foot
    against a stone.
¹³ You will tread on the lion and the cobra;
  you will trample the great lion and
    the serpent.

¹⁴ "Because they love me," says the Lord,
  "I will rescue them;
  I will protect them, for they
    acknowledge my name.
¹⁵ They will call on me, and I will answer
    them;
  I will be with them in trouble,
  I will deliver them and honor them.
¹⁶ With long life I will satisfy them
  and show them my salvation."

Psalm 92

A psalm. A song. For the Sabbath day.

*¹ It is good to praise the Lord
  and make music to your name,
    O Most High,
² proclaiming your love in the morning
  and your faithfulness at night,
³ to the music of the ten-stringed lyre
  and the melody of the harp.

ᵃ 17 Or *beauty*   ᵇ 1 Hebrew *Shaddai*
* 92:1-15 is numbered 92:2-16 in Hebrew texts.

4 For you make me glad by your deeds,
    Lord;
  I sing for joy at what your hands have
    done.
5 How great are your works, Lord,
  how profound your thoughts!
6 Senseless people do not know,
  fools do not understand,
7 that though the wicked spring up like
    grass
  and all evildoers flourish,
  they will be destroyed forever.

8 But you, Lord, are forever exalted.

9 For surely your enemies, Lord,
  surely your enemies will perish;
  all evildoers will be scattered.
10 You have exalted my horn[a] like that of a
    wild ox;
  fine oils have been poured on me.
11 My eyes have seen the defeat of my
    adversaries;
  my ears have heard the rout of my
    wicked foes.

12 The righteous will flourish like a palm
    tree,
  they will grow like a cedar of
    Lebanon;
13 planted in the house of the Lord,
  they will flourish in the courts of our
    God.
14 They will still bear fruit in old age,
  they will stay fresh and green,
15 proclaiming, "The Lord is upright;
  he is my Rock, and there is no
    wickedness in him."

Psalm 93

1 The Lord reigns, he is robed in majesty;
  the Lord is robed in majesty and
    armed with strength;
  indeed, the world is established, firm
    and secure.
2 Your throne was established long ago;
  you are from all eternity.

3 The seas have lifted up, Lord,
  the seas have lifted up their voice;
  the seas have lifted up their pounding
    waves.
4 Mightier than the thunder of the great
    waters,

mightier than the breakers of the
    sea—
  the Lord on high is mighty.

5 Your statutes, Lord, stand firm;
  holiness adorns your house
  for endless days.

Psalm 94

1 The Lord is a God who avenges.
  O God who avenges, shine forth.
2 Rise up, Judge of the earth;
  pay back to the proud what they
    deserve.
3 How long, Lord, will the wicked,
  how long will the wicked be jubilant?

4 They pour out arrogant words;
  all the evildoers are full of boasting.
5 They crush your people, Lord;
  they oppress your inheritance.
6 They slay the widow and the foreigner;
  they murder the fatherless.
7 They say, "The Lord does not see;
  the God of Jacob takes no notice."

8 Take notice, you senseless ones among
    the people;
  you fools, when will you become
    wise?
9 Does he who fashioned the ear not hear?
  Does he who formed the eye not see?
10 Does he who disciplines nations not
    punish?
  Does he who teaches human beings
    lack knowledge?
11 The Lord knows all human plans;
  he knows that they are futile.

12 Blessed are those you discipline, Lord,
  those you teach from your law;
13 you grant them relief from days of
    trouble,
  till a pit is dug for the wicked.
14 For the Lord will not reject his people;
  he will never forsake his inheritance.
15 Judgment will again be founded on
    righteousness,
  and all the upright in heart will follow
    it.
16 Who will rise up for me against the
    wicked?
  Who will take a stand for me against
    evildoers?

a 10 *Horn* here symbolizes strength.

17 Unless the LORD had given me help,
  I would soon have dwelt in the
    silence of death.
18 When I said, "My foot is slipping,"
  your unfailing love, LORD, supported
    me.
19 When anxiety was great within me,
  your consolation brought me joy.

20 Can a corrupt throne be allied with you—
  a throne that brings on misery by its
    decrees?
21 The wicked band together against the
    righteous
  and condemn the innocent to death.
22 But the LORD has become my fortress,
  and my God the rock in whom I take
    refuge.
23 He will repay them for their sins
  and destroy them for their
    wickedness;
  the LORD our God will destroy them.

Psalm 95

1 Come, let us sing for joy to the LORD;
  let us shout aloud to the Rock of our
    salvation.
2 Let us come before him with
    thanksgiving
  and extol him with music and song.

3 For the LORD is the great God,
  the great King above all gods.
4 In his hand are the depths of the earth,
  and the mountain peaks belong to
    him.
5 The sea is his, for he made it,
  and his hands formed the dry land.

6 Come, let us bow down in worship,
  let us kneel before the LORD our Maker;
7 for he is our God
  and we are the people of his pasture,
  the flock under his care.

  Today, if only you would hear his voice,
8 "Do not harden your hearts as you did at
    Meribah,ª
  as you did that day at Massahᵇ in the
    wilderness,
9 where your ancestors tested me;
  they tried me, though they had seen
    what I did.
10 For forty years I was angry with that
    generation;

I said, 'They are a people whose
    hearts go astray,
  and they have not known my ways.'
11 So I declared on oath in my anger,
  'They shall never enter my rest.'"

Psalm 96

1 Sing to the LORD a new song;
  sing to the LORD, all the earth.
2 Sing to the LORD, praise his name;
  proclaim his salvation day after day.
3 Declare his glory among the nations,
  his marvelous deeds among all
    peoples.

4 For great is the LORD and most worthy of
    praise;
  he is to be feared above all gods.
5 For all the gods of the nations are idols,
  but the LORD made the heavens.
6 Splendor and majesty are before him;
  strength and glory are in his
    sanctuary.

7 Ascribe to the LORD, all you families of
    nations,
  ascribe to the LORD glory and
    strength.
8 Ascribe to the LORD the glory due his
    name;
  bring an offering and come into his
    courts.
9 Worship the LORD in the splendor of hisᶜ
    holiness;
  tremble before him, all the earth.
10 Say among the nations, "The LORD
    reigns."
  The world is firmly established, it
    cannot be moved;
  he will judge the peoples with equity.

11 Let the heavens rejoice, let the earth be
    glad;
  let the sea resound, and all that is in it.
12 Let the fields be jubilant, and everything
    in them;
  let all the trees of the forest sing for
    joy.
13 Let all creation rejoice before the LORD,
    for he comes,
  he comes to judge the earth.
  He will judge the world in righteousness
  and the peoples in his faithfulness.

ª 8 *Meribah* means *quarreling.*   ᵇ 8 *Massah* means *testing.*   ᶜ 9 Or LORD *with the splendor of*

Psalm 97

¹The LORD reigns, let the earth be glad;
  let the distant shores rejoice.
²Clouds and thick darkness surround him;
  righteousness and justice are the
    foundation of his throne.
³Fire goes before him
  and consumes his foes on every side.
⁴His lightning lights up the world;
  the earth sees and trembles.
⁵The mountains melt like wax before the
    LORD,
  before the Lord of all the earth.
⁶The heavens proclaim his righteousness,
  and all peoples see his glory.

⁷All who worship images are put to
    shame,
  those who boast in idols—
  worship him, all you gods!

⁸Zion hears and rejoices
  and the villages of Judah are glad
  because of your judgments, LORD.
⁹For you, LORD, are the Most High over all
    the earth;
  you are exalted far above all gods.
¹⁰Let those who love the LORD hate evil,
  for he guards the lives of his faithful
    ones
  and delivers them from the hand of
    the wicked.
¹¹Light shines*ᵃ* on the righteous
  and joy on the upright in heart.
¹²Rejoice in the LORD, you who are
    righteous,
  and praise his holy name.

Psalm 98

A psalm.

¹Sing to the LORD a new song,
  for he has done marvelous things;
  his right hand and his holy arm
  have worked salvation for him.
²The LORD has made his salvation known
  and revealed his righteousness to the
    nations.
³He has remembered his love
  and his faithfulness to the house of
    Israel;
  all the ends of the earth have seen
  the salvation of our God.

⁴Shout for joy to the LORD, all the earth,
  burst into jubilant song with music;
⁵make music to the LORD with the harp,
  with the harp and the sound of
    singing,
⁶with trumpets and the blast of the ram's
    horn—
  shout for joy before the LORD, the King.

⁷Let the sea resound, and everything in it,
  the world, and all who live in it.
⁸Let the rivers clap their hands,
  let the mountains sing together for joy;
⁹let them sing before the LORD,
  for he comes to judge the earth.
He will judge the world in righteousness
  and the peoples with equity.

Psalm 99

¹The LORD reigns,
  let the nations tremble;
he sits enthroned between the
    cherubim,
  let the earth shake.
²Great is the LORD in Zion;
  he is exalted over all the nations.
³Let them praise your great and awesome
    name—
  he is holy.

⁴The King is mighty, he loves justice—
  you have established equity;
 in Jacob you have done
  what is just and right.
⁵Exalt the LORD our God
  and worship at his footstool;
  he is holy.

⁶Moses and Aaron were among his
    priests,
  Samuel was among those who called
    on his name;
they called on the LORD
  and he answered them.
⁷He spoke to them from the pillar of
    cloud;
  they kept his statutes and the decrees
    he gave them.

⁸LORD our God,
  you answered them;
you were to Israel a forgiving God,
  though you punished their misdeeds.*ᵇ*
⁹Exalt the LORD our God

---

a 11 One Hebrew manuscript and ancient versions (see also 112:4); most Hebrew manuscripts *Light is sown*   *b 8* Or *God, / an avenger of the wrongs done to them*

and worship at his holy mountain,
for the LORD our God is holy.

Psalm 100

A psalm. For giving grateful praise.

[1] Shout for joy to the LORD, all the earth.
[2]   Worship the LORD with gladness;
come before him with joyful songs.
[3] Know that the LORD is God.
It is he who made us, and we are his [a];
we are his people, the sheep of his
pasture.

[4] Enter his gates with thanksgiving
and his courts with praise;
give thanks to him and praise his
name.
[5] For the LORD is good and his love
endures forever;
his faithfulness continues through all
generations.

Psalm 101

Of David. A psalm.

[1] I will sing of your love and justice;
to you, LORD, I will sing praise.
[2] I will be careful to lead a blameless life—
when will you come to me?

I will conduct the affairs of my house
with a blameless heart.
[3] I will not look with approval
on anything that is vile.

I hate what faithless people do;
I will have no part in it.
[4] The perverse of heart shall be far from
me;
I will have nothing to do with what is
evil.

[5] Whoever slanders their neighbor in secret,
I will put to silence;
whoever has haughty eyes and a proud
heart,
I will not endure.

[6] My eyes will be on the faithful in the land,
that they may dwell with me;
those whose walk is blameless
will minister to me.

[7] No one who practices deceit

will dwell in my house;
no one who speaks falsely
will stand in my presence.

[8] Every morning I will put to silence
all the wicked in the land;
I will cut off every evildoer
from the city of the LORD.

Psalm 102

*A prayer of an afflicted person who has
grown weak and pours out a lament
before the LORD.*

*[1] Hear my prayer, LORD;
let my cry for help come to you.
[2] Do not hide your face from me
when I am in distress.
Turn your ear to me;
when I call, answer me quickly.

[3] For my days vanish like smoke;
my bones burn like glowing embers.
[4] My heart is blighted and withered like
grass;
I forget to eat my food.
[5] In my distress I groan aloud
and am reduced to skin and bones.
[6] I am like a desert owl,
like an owl among the ruins.
[7] I lie awake; I have become
like a bird alone on a roof.
[8] All day long my enemies taunt me;
those who rail against me use my
name as a curse.
[9] For I eat ashes as my food
and mingle my drink with tears
[10] because of your great wrath,
for you have taken me up and thrown
me aside.
[11] My days are like the evening shadow;
I wither away like grass.

[12] But you, LORD, sit enthroned forever;
your renown endures through all
generations.
[13] You will arise and have compassion on
Zion,
for it is time to show favor to her;
the appointed time has come.
[14] For her stones are dear to your servants;
her very dust moves them to pity.
[15] The nations will fear the name of the
LORD,

---

a 3 Or *and not we ourselves*
* 102:1-28 is numbered 102:2-29 in Hebrew texts.

all the kings of the earth will revere
    your glory.
16 For the LORD will rebuild Zion
    and appear in his glory.
17 He will respond to the prayer of the
        destitute;
    he will not despise their plea.

18 Let this be written for a future
        generation,
    that a people not yet created may
        praise the LORD:
19 "The LORD looked down from his
        sanctuary on high,
    from heaven he viewed the earth,
20 to hear the groans of the prisoners
    and release those condemned to
        death."
21 So the name of the LORD will be declared
        in Zion
    and his praise in Jerusalem
22 when the peoples and the kingdoms
    assemble to worship the LORD.

23 In the course of my life[a] he broke my
        strength;
    he cut short my days.
24 So I said:
    "Do not take me away, my God, in the
        midst of my days;
    your years go on through all
        generations.
25 In the beginning you laid the
        foundations of the earth,
    and the heavens are the work of your
        hands.
26 They will perish, but you remain;
    they will all wear out like a garment.
    Like clothing you will change them
    and they will be discarded.
27 But you remain the same,
    and your years will never end.
28 The children of your servants will live in
        your presence;
    their descendants will be established
        before you."

Psalm 103

Of David.

1 Praise the LORD, my soul;
    all my inmost being, praise his holy
        name.
2 Praise the LORD, my soul,

and forget not all his benefits—
3 who forgives all your sins
    and heals all your diseases,
4 who redeems your life from the pit
    and crowns you with love and
        compassion,
5 who satisfies your desires with good
        things
    so that your youth is renewed like the
        eagle's.

6 The LORD works righteousness
    and justice for all the oppressed.

7 He made known his ways to Moses,
    his deeds to the people of Israel:
8 The LORD is compassionate and gracious,
    slow to anger, abounding in love.
9 He will not always accuse,
    nor will he harbor his anger forever;
10 he does not treat us as our sins deserve
    or repay us according to our
        iniquities.
11 For as high as the heavens are above the
        earth,
    so great is his love for those who fear
        him;
12 as far as the east is from the west,
    so far has he removed our
        transgressions from us.

13 As a father has compassion on his
        children,
    so the LORD has compassion on those
        who fear him;
14 for he knows how we are formed,
    he remembers that we are dust.
15 As for mortals, their days are like grass,
    they flourish like a flower of the field;
16 the wind blows over it and it is gone,
    and its place remembers it no more.
17 But from everlasting to everlasting
    the LORD's love is with those who fear
        him,
    and his righteousness with their
        children's children—
18 with those who keep his covenant
    and remember to obey his precepts.

19 The LORD has established his throne in
        heaven,
    and his kingdom rules over all.

20 Praise the LORD, you his angels,
    you mighty ones who do his bidding,
    who obey his word.

a 23 Or *By his power*

o

THURSDAY

Make Them Count

Psalm 103:1–22 *or* 103:13–18

Chris Tomlin

Have you ever had one of those brain-freeze moments when thinking about eternity? I mean, just how long is forever? How can mortals like you and me really grasp that we are living beings with a spirit and soul inside of us that is eternal? It's beyond our feeble minds. At least beyond mine.

Of course, when I was sixteen I thought I'd live forever, but as the years have rolled by, I understand Psalm 103:15–16 better:"[As for mortals, their days are like grass, they flourish like a flower of the field; the wind blows over it and it is gone, and its place remembers it no more.]"

Still, I want my "days like grass" to count for something. God didn't make us to just live out some boring routine all our days. No, we were made in His image, and we are eternal because God is eternal. His character and integrity will never waver. We can trust our days—and our eternity—to His nature.

Jonathan Edwards {ad 1703–1758}

We humans are dependent on the power of God for every exercise of grace at work in the heart: subduing sin and corruption, increasing holy principles, and bringing forth fruit in good works. We're dependent on divine power to bring grace to its perfection . . . While we could not achieve this, God's power can and does accomplish this in the lives of his people.

— *reflection* —

1. When you die, what do you want your obituary to say?
2. What could you change or do differently to ensure that you're living your life for something that will count for eternity?
3. What help do you need from God to accomplish this?

For your next devotional reading, go to page 679.

²¹ Praise the LORD, all his heavenly hosts,
  you his servants who do his will.
²² Praise the LORD, all his works
  everywhere in his dominion.

  Praise the LORD, my soul.

Psalm 104

¹ Praise the LORD, my soul.

  LORD my God, you are very great;
    you are clothed with splendor and
    majesty.

² The LORD wraps himself in light as with
    a garment;
  he stretches out the heavens like a
    tent
³   and lays the beams of his upper
      chambers on their waters.
  He makes the clouds his chariot
    and rides on the wings of the wind.
⁴ He makes winds his messengers,ᵃ
    flames of fire his servants.

⁵ He set the earth on its foundations;
    it can never be moved.
⁶ You covered it with the deep as with a
    garment;
  the waters stood above the
    mountains.
⁷ But at your rebuke the waters fled,
  at the sound of your thunder they
    took to flight;
⁸ they flowed over the mountains,
  they went down into the valleys,
  to the place you assigned for them.
⁹ You set a boundary they cannot cross;
  never again will they cover the earth.

¹⁰ He makes springs pour water into the
    ravines;
  it flows between the mountains.
¹¹ They give water to all the beasts of the
    field;
  the wild donkeys quench their thirst.
¹² The birds of the sky nest by the waters;
  they sing among the branches.
¹³ He waters the mountains from his upper
    chambers;
  the land is satisfied by the fruit of his
    work.
¹⁴ He makes grass grow for the cattle,
  and plants for people to cultivate—
  bringing forth food from the earth:

¹⁵ wine that gladdens human hearts,
  oil to make their faces shine,
  and bread that sustains their hearts.
¹⁶ The trees of the LORD are well watered,
  the cedars of Lebanon that he
    planted.
¹⁷ There the birds make their nests;
  the stork has its home in the junipers.
¹⁸ The high mountains belong to the wild
    goats;
  the crags are a refuge for the hyrax.

¹⁹ He made the moon to mark the seasons,
  and the sun knows when to go down.
²⁰ You bring darkness, it becomes night,
  and all the beasts of the forest prowl.
²¹ The lions roar for their prey
  and seek their food from God.
²² The sun rises, and they steal away;
  they return and lie down in their
    dens.
²³ Then people go out to their work,
  to their labor until evening.

²⁴ How many are your works, LORD!
  In wisdom you made them all;
  the earth is full of your creatures.
²⁵ There is the sea, vast and spacious,
  teeming with creatures beyond
    number—
  living things both large and small.
²⁶ There the ships go to and fro,
  and the leviathan, which you formed
    to frolic there.

²⁷ All creatures look to you
  to give them their food at the proper
    time.
²⁸ When you give it to them,
  they gather it up;
  when you open your hand,
  they are satisfied with good things.
²⁹ When you hide your face,
  they are terrified;
  when you take away their breath,
  they die and return to the dust.
³⁰ When you send your Spirit,
  they are created,
  and you renew the face of the ground.

³¹ May the glory of the LORD endure
    forever;
  may the LORD rejoice in his works—
³² he who looks at the earth, and it
    trembles,

ᵃ 4 Or angels

who touches the mountains, and they
    smoke.

33 I will sing to the LORD all my life;
    I will sing praise to my God as long as
    I live.
34 May my meditation be pleasing to him,
    as I rejoice in the LORD.
35 But may sinners vanish from the earth
    and the wicked be no more.

Praise the LORD, my soul.

Praise the LORD. [a]

Psalm 105

1 Give praise to the LORD, call on his
    name;
    make known among the nations what
    he has done.
2 Sing of him, sing his praises;
    tell of all his wonderful acts.
3 Glory in his holy name;
    let the hearts of those who seek the
    LORD rejoice.
4 Look to the LORD and his strength;
    seek his face always.

5 Remember the wonders he has done,
    his miracles, and the judgments he
    pronounced,
6 you his servants, the descendants of
    Abraham,
    his chosen ones, the children of
    Jacob.
7 He is the LORD our God;
    his judgments are in all the earth.

8 He remembers his covenant forever,
    the promise he made, for a thousand
    generations,
9 the covenant he made with Abraham,
    the oath he swore to Isaac.
10 He confirmed it to Jacob as a decree,
    to Israel as an everlasting covenant:
11 "To you I will give the land of Canaan
    as the portion you will inherit."

12 When they were but few in number,
    few indeed, and strangers in it,
13 they wandered from nation to nation,
    from one kingdom to another.
14 He allowed no one to oppress them;
    for their sake he rebuked kings:
15 "Do not touch my anointed ones;
    do my prophets no harm."

16 He called down famine on the land
    and destroyed all their supplies of
    food;
17 and he sent a man before them—
    Joseph, sold as a slave.
18 They bruised his feet with shackles,
    his neck was put in irons,
19 till what he foretold came to pass,
    till the word of the LORD proved him
    true.
20 The king sent and released him,
    the ruler of peoples set him free.
21 He made him master of his household,
    ruler over all he possessed,
22 to instruct his princes as he pleased
    and teach his elders wisdom.

23 Then Israel entered Egypt;
    Jacob resided as a foreigner in the
    land of Ham.
24 The LORD made his people very fruitful;
    he made them too numerous for their
    foes,
25 whose hearts he turned to hate his
    people,
    to conspire against his servants.
26 He sent Moses his servant,
    and Aaron, whom he had chosen.
27 They performed his signs among them,
    his wonders in the land of Ham.
28 He sent darkness and made the land
    dark—
    for had they not rebelled against his
    words?
29 He turned their waters into blood,
    causing their fish to die.
30 Their land teemed with frogs,
    which went up into the bedrooms of
    their rulers.
31 He spoke, and there came swarms of
    flies,
    and gnats throughout their country.
32 He turned their rain into hail,
    with lightning throughout their land;
33 he struck down their vines and fig trees
    and shattered the trees of their
    country.
34 He spoke, and the locusts came,
    grasshoppers without number;
35 they ate up every green thing in their
    land,
    ate up the produce of their soil.
36 Then he struck down all the firstborn in
    their land,

---

a 35 Hebrew *Hallelu Yah*; in the Septuagint this line stands at the beginning of Psalm 105.

the firstfruits of all their manhood.
³⁷ He brought out Israel, laden with silver
and gold,
and from among their tribes no one
faltered.
³⁸ Egypt was glad when they left,
because dread of Israel had fallen on
them.

³⁹ He spread out a cloud as a covering,
and a fire to give light at night.
⁴⁰ They asked, and he brought them quail;
he fed them well with the bread of
heaven.
⁴¹ He opened the rock, and water gushed
out;
it flowed like a river in the desert.

⁴² For he remembered his holy promise
given to his servant Abraham.
⁴³ He brought out his people with
rejoicing,
his chosen ones with shouts of joy;
⁴⁴ he gave them the lands of the nations,
and they fell heir to what others had
toiled for—
⁴⁵ that they might keep his precepts
and observe his laws.

Praise the LORD. ^a

Psalm 106

¹ Praise the LORD. ^b

Give thanks to the LORD, for he is good;
his love endures forever.

² Who can proclaim the mighty acts of the
LORD
or fully declare his praise?
³ Blessed are those who act justly,
who always do what is right.

⁴ Remember me, LORD, when you show
favor to your people,
come to my aid when you save them,
⁵ that I may enjoy the prosperity of your
chosen ones,
that I may share in the joy of your
nation
and join your inheritance in giving
praise.

⁶ We have sinned, even as our ancestors
did;

we have done wrong and acted
wickedly.
⁷ When our ancestors were in Egypt,
they gave no thought to your
miracles;
they did not remember your many
kindnesses,
and they rebelled by the sea, the Red
Sea. ^c
⁸ Yet he saved them for his name's sake,
to make his mighty power known.
⁹ He rebuked the Red Sea, and it dried up;
he led them through the depths as
through a desert.
¹⁰ He saved them from the hand of the foe;
from the hand of the enemy he
redeemed them.
¹¹ The waters covered their adversaries;
not one of them survived.
¹² Then they believed his promises
and sang his praise.

¹³ But they soon forgot what he had done
and did not wait for his plan to
unfold.
¹⁴ In the desert they gave in to their
craving;
in the wilderness they put God to the
test.
¹⁵ So he gave them what they asked for,
but sent a wasting disease among
them.

¹⁶ In the camp they grew envious of Moses
and of Aaron, who was consecrated to
the LORD.
¹⁷ The earth opened up and swallowed
Dathan;
it buried the company of Abiram.
¹⁸ Fire blazed among their followers;
a flame consumed the wicked.
¹⁹ At Horeb they made a calf
and worshiped an idol cast from
metal.
²⁰ They exchanged their glorious God
for an image of a bull, which eats
grass.
²¹ They forgot the God who saved them,
who had done great things in Egypt,
²² miracles in the land of Ham
and awesome deeds by the Red Sea.
²³ So he said he would destroy them—
had not Moses, his chosen one,

a 45 Hebrew *Hallelu Yah*   b 1 Hebrew *Hallelu Yah*; also in verse 48   c 7 Or *the Sea of Reeds*; also in verses 9 and 22

stood in the breach before him
    to keep his wrath from destroying
       them.

24 Then they despised the pleasant land;
    they did not believe his promise.
25 They grumbled in their tents
    and did not obey the LORD.
26 So he swore to them with uplifted hand
    that he would make them fall in the
       wilderness,
27 make their descendants fall among the
       nations
    and scatter them throughout the
       lands.

28 They yoked themselves to the Baal of
       Peor
    and ate sacrifices offered to lifeless
       gods;
29 they aroused the LORD's anger by their
       wicked deeds,
    and a plague broke out among them.
30 But Phinehas stood up and intervened,
    and the plague was checked.
31 This was credited to him as
       righteousness
    for endless generations to come.
32 By the waters of Meribah they angered
       the LORD,
    and trouble came to Moses because
       of them;
33 for they rebelled against the Spirit of
       God,
    and rash words came from Moses'
       lips. *a*

34 They did not destroy the peoples
    as the LORD had commanded them,
35 but they mingled with the nations
    and adopted their customs.
36 They worshiped their idols,
    which became a snare to them.
37 They sacrificed their sons
    and their daughters to demons.
38 They shed innocent blood,
    the blood of their sons and daughters,
    whom they sacrificed to the idols of
       Canaan,
    and the land was desecrated by their
       blood.
39 They defiled themselves by what they
       did;
    by their deeds they prostituted
       themselves.

40 Therefore the LORD was angry with his
       people
    and abhorred his inheritance.
41 He gave them into the hands of the
       nations,
    and their foes ruled over them.
42 Their enemies oppressed them
    and subjected them to their power.
43 Many times he delivered them,
    but they were bent on rebellion
    and they wasted away in their sin.
44 Yet he took note of their distress
    when he heard their cry;
45 for their sake he remembered his
       covenant
    and out of his great love he relented.
46 He caused all who held them captive
    to show them mercy.

47 Save us, LORD our God,
    and gather us from the nations,
that we may give thanks to your holy
       name
    and glory in your praise.

48 Praise be to the LORD, the God of Israel,
    from everlasting to everlasting.

Let all the people say, "Amen!"

Praise the LORD.

BOOK V

Psalms 107–150

Psalm 107

1 Give thanks to the LORD, for he is good;
    his love endures forever.

2 Let the redeemed of the LORD tell their
       story—
    those he redeemed from the hand of
       the foe,
3 those he gathered from the lands,
    from east and west, from north and
       south. *b*

4 Some wandered in desert wastelands,
    finding no way to a city where they
       could settle.
5 They were hungry and thirsty,
    and their lives ebbed away.
6 Then they cried out to the LORD in their
       trouble,

---

a 33 Or *against his spirit, / and rash words came from his lips*   *b* 3 Hebrew *north and the sea*

and he delivered them from their distress.
7 He led them by a straight way
to a city where they could settle.
8 Let them give thanks to the LORD for his unfailing love
and his wonderful deeds for humankind,
9 for he satisfies the thirsty
and fills the hungry with good things.

10 Some sat in darkness, in utter darkness,
prisoners suffering in iron chains,
11 because they rebelled against God's commands
and despised the plans of the Most High.
12 So he subjected them to bitter labor;
they stumbled, and there was no one to help.
13 Then they cried to the LORD in their trouble,
and he saved them from their distress.
14 He brought them out of darkness, the utter darkness,
and broke away their chains.
15 Let them give thanks to the LORD for his unfailing love
and his wonderful deeds for humankind,
16 for he breaks down gates of bronze
and cuts through bars of iron.

17 Some became fools through their rebellious ways
and suffered affliction because of their iniquities.
18 They loathed all food
and drew near the gates of death.
19 Then they cried to the LORD in their trouble,
and he saved them from their distress.
20 He sent out his word and healed them;
he rescued them from the grave.
21 Let them give thanks to the LORD for his unfailing love
and his wonderful deeds for humankind.
22 Let them sacrifice thank offerings
and tell of his works with songs of joy.

23 Some went out on the sea in ships;
they were merchants on the mighty waters.
24 They saw the works of the LORD,
his wonderful deeds in the deep.
25 For he spoke and stirred up a tempest
that lifted high the waves.
26 They mounted up to the heavens and went down to the depths;
in their peril their courage melted away.
27 They reeled and staggered like drunkards;
they were at their wits' end.
28 Then they cried out to the LORD in their trouble,
and he brought them out of their distress.
29 He stilled the storm to a whisper;
the waves of the sea a were hushed.
30 They were glad when it grew calm,
and he guided them to their desired haven.
31 Let them give thanks to the LORD for his unfailing love
and his wonderful deeds for humankind.
32 Let them exalt him in the assembly of the people
and praise him in the council of the elders.

33 He turned rivers into a desert,
flowing springs into thirsty ground,
34 and fruitful land into a salt waste,
because of the wickedness of those who lived there.
35 He turned the desert into pools of water
and the parched ground into flowing springs;
36 there he brought the hungry to live,
and they founded a city where they could settle.
37 They sowed fields and planted vineyards
that yielded a fruitful harvest;
38 he blessed them, and their numbers greatly increased,
and he did not let their herds diminish.
39 Then their numbers decreased, and they were humbled
by oppression, calamity and sorrow;
40 he who pours contempt on nobles

a 29 Dead Sea Scrolls; Masoretic Text / their waves

made them wander in a trackless
waste.
41 But he lifted the needy out of their
affliction
and increased their families like
flocks.
42 The upright see and rejoice,
but all the wicked shut their mouths.

43 Let all who are wise heed these things
and ponder the loving deeds of the
LORD.

Psalm 108

A song. A psalm of David.

*1 My heart, O God, is steadfast;
I will sing and make music with all
my soul.
2 Awake, harp and lyre!
I will awaken the dawn.
3 I will praise you, LORD, among the
nations;
I will sing of you among the peoples.
4 For great is your love, higher than the
heavens;
your faithfulness reaches to the skies.
5 Be exalted, O God, above the heavens;
let your glory be over all the earth.

6 Save us and help us with your right
hand,
that those you love may be delivered.
7 God has spoken from his sanctuary:
"In triumph I will parcel out Shechem
and measure off the Valley of
Sukkoth.
8 Gilead is mine, Manasseh is mine;
Ephraim is my helmet,
Judah is my scepter.
9 Moab is my washbasin,
on Edom I toss my sandal;
over Philistia I shout in triumph."

10 Who will bring me to the fortified city?
Who will lead me to Edom?
11 Is it not you, God, you who have rejected
us
and no longer go out with our armies?
12 Give us aid against the enemy,
for human help is worthless.
13 With God we will gain the victory,
and he will trample down our
enemies.

Psalm 109

For the director of music. Of David.
A psalm.

1 My God, whom I praise,
do not remain silent,
2 for people who are wicked and deceitful
have opened their mouths against me;
they have spoken against me with
lying tongues.
3 With words of hatred they surround me;
they attack me without cause.
4 In return for my friendship they accuse
me,
but I am a man of prayer.
5 They repay me evil for good,
and hatred for my friendship.

6 Appoint someone evil to oppose my
enemy;
let an accuser stand at his right hand.
7 When he is tried, let him be found
guilty,
and may his prayers condemn him.
8 May his days be few;
may another take his place of
leadership.
9 May his children be fatherless
and his wife a widow.
10 May his children be wandering beggars;
may they be driven*a* from their ruined
homes.
11 May a creditor seize all he has;
may strangers plunder the fruits of
his labor.
12 May no one extend kindness to him
or take pity on his fatherless children.
13 May his descendants be cut off,
their names blotted out from the next
generation.
14 May the iniquity of his fathers be
remembered before the LORD;
may the sin of his mother never be
blotted out.
15 May their sins always remain before the
LORD,
that he may blot out their name from
the earth.

16 For he never thought of doing a
kindness,
but hounded to death the poor
and the needy and the brokenhearted.

---

a 10 Septuagint; Hebrew *sought*
* 108:1-13 is numbered 108:2-14 in Hebrew texts.

An Alternative to Revenge

Psalm 109:1–31 *or* 109:1–4,26–27

Michael Card

Though David was a man who could respond in battle with a ferocious vengeance, what little we know of the historical backgrounds of these imprecatory laments would lead us to believe that he never took his revenge on any of those who were the objects of these often poisonous prayers of protest. By placing his enemies in the hands of God, David acknowledges that revenge is [God's] alone (see Deuteronomy 32:41). Perhaps these psalms were the only thing that stood between David and the revenge he would have taken.

When his nemesis, Saul, finally commits suicide, David laments without an ounce of bitterness in his heart (2 Samuel 1:9–27). Even as he refused to let Saul's hatred of him shape his life, David would not let his own hatred of Saul stand in his way. There was nothing else David could do with his hate but take it to God. Prayer seems to have held no meaning for him otherwise.

Matthew Henry {AD 1662–1714}

All God's people have the unspeakable comfort of knowing that—no matter who is against them—God is for them, and they can come to him for help knowing that he enjoys taking an interest in them. In the Psalms, David . . . resolves to do what is right and take comfort from God. He devotes himself to prayer, saying in essence: "I am for prayer; I am a man of prayer; I love prayer, and prize prayer, and practice prayer, and make a business of prayer and am in my element when I am at prayer" . . . When David's enemies falsely accused him and misrepresented him, he appealed to God and committed his cause to him through prayer. Though they were his adversaries, yet he continued to pray for them. In the same way, if others are hurtful and mean to us, let us be faithful to do our duty to them and not sin against the Lord by failing to pray for them (see 1 Samuel 12:23). Though they hated and persecuted David for his religion, yet he kept close to it; they laughed at him for his devotion, but they could not laugh him out of it. "Let them say what they will, I am a man of prayer." In this way David represented Christ. For Christ was surrounded with lies and words of hatred, and his enemies persecuted him in response to his love and good works (see John 10:32); and yet he gave himself to prayer on their behalf, "Father, forgive them" (Luke 23:34).

reflection

1. What is your first, gut-level response when someone hurts you or attacks you?
2. How often does prayer make up part of that response?
3. Are you at odds with someone right now?

For your next devotional reading, go to page 681.

17 He loved to pronounce a curse—
may it come on him.
He found no pleasure in blessing—
may it be far from him.
18 He wore cursing as his garment;
it entered into his body like water,
into his bones like oil.
19 May it be like a cloak wrapped about
him,
like a belt tied forever around him.
20 May this be the LORD's payment to my
accusers,
to those who speak evil of me.

21 But you, Sovereign LORD,
help me for your name's sake;
out of the goodness of your love,
deliver me.
22 For I am poor and needy,
and my heart is wounded within me.
23 I fade away like an evening shadow;
I am shaken off like a locust.
24 My knees give way from fasting;
my body is thin and gaunt.
25 I am an object of scorn to my
accusers;
when they see me, they shake their
heads.

26 Help me, LORD my God;
save me according to your unfailing
love.
27 Let them know that it is your hand,
that you, LORD, have done it.
28 While they curse, may you bless;
may those who attack me be put to
shame,
but may your servant rejoice.
29 May my accusers be clothed with
disgrace
and wrapped in shame as in a cloak.

30 With my mouth I will greatly extol the
LORD;
in the great throng of worshipers I
will praise him.
31 For he stands at the right hand of the
needy,
to save their lives from those who
would condemn them.

Psalm 110

Of David. A psalm.

1 The LORD says to my lord:*a*
"Sit at my right hand
until I make your enemies
a footstool for your feet."

2 The LORD will extend your mighty
scepter from Zion, saying,
"Rule in the midst of your enemies."
3 Your troops will be willing
on your day of battle.
Arrayed in holy splendor,
your young men will come to you
like dew from the morning's womb.*b*

4 The LORD has sworn
and will not change his mind:
"You are a priest forever,
in the order of Melchizedek."

5 The Lord is at your right hand*c*;
he will crush kings on the day of his
wrath.
6 He will judge the nations, heaping up
the dead
and crushing the rulers of the whole
earth.
7 He will drink from a brook along the
way,*d*
and so he will lift up his head.

Psalm 111*e*

1 Praise the LORD.*f*

I will extol the LORD with all my heart
in the council of the upright and in
the assembly.

2 Great are the works of the LORD;
they are pondered by all who delight
in them.
3 Glorious and majestic are his deeds,
and his righteousness endures
forever.
4 He has caused his wonders to be
remembered;
the LORD is gracious and
compassionate.
5 He provides food for those who fear him;
he remembers his covenant forever.

---

a 1 Or *Lord*   *b* 3 The meaning of the Hebrew for this sentence is uncertain.   *c* 5 Or *My lord is at your
right hand,* LORD   *d* 7 The meaning of the Hebrew for this clause is uncertain.   *e* This psalm is an
acrostic poem, the lines of which begin with the successive letters of the Hebrew alphabet.
f 1 Hebrew *Hallelu Yah*

Stand in Awe

Psalm 111:1–10

read/meditate

As you read the words of praise from the psalmist, imagine the attitude of the heart from which these words poured. Put yourself in the place of the writer as you read through the passage several times.

pray

In your mind, scroll through the situations that cause you to reach out to God in gratitude. List your praises to God, as the psalmist has done here.

contemplate

We praise God for who he is and for what he does. Read through the passage again, thinking specifically about God's character—those things that we praise him for that have nothing to do with whether or not our lives are going well.

additional reflection

Do you stand in awe this moment at the greatness, the wonder, the goodness of our King? I hope so. A life that's grounded in that amazing reality just can't look the same as one that's built on puny self-centered concerns.

—*Chris Tomlin*

God did not make the first human because he needed company, but because he wanted someone to whom he could show his generosity and love. God did not tell us to follow him because he needed our help, but because he knew that loving him would make us whole.

—*Irenaeus*

For your next devotional reading, go to page 688.

⁶He has shown his people the power of
his works,
giving them the lands of other
nations.
⁷The works of his hands are faithful and
just;
all his precepts are trustworthy.
⁸They are established for ever and ever,
enacted in faithfulness and
uprightness.
⁹He provided redemption for his people;
he ordained his covenant forever—
holy and awesome is his name.

¹⁰The fear of the LORD is the beginning of
wisdom;
all who follow his precepts have good
understanding.
To him belongs eternal praise.

Psalm 112 *a*

¹Praise the LORD. *b*

Blessed are those who fear the LORD,
who find great delight in his
commands.

²Their children will be mighty in the land;
the generation of the upright will be
blessed.
³Wealth and riches are in their houses,
and their righteousness endures
forever.
⁴Even in darkness light dawns for the
upright,
for those who are gracious and
compassionate and righteous.
⁵Good will come to those who are
generous and lend freely,
who conduct their affairs with justice.

⁶Surely the righteous will never be
shaken;
they will be remembered forever.
⁷They will have no fear of bad news;
their hearts are steadfast, trusting in
the LORD.
⁸Their hearts are secure, they will have
no fear;
in the end they will look in triumph
on their foes.
⁹They have scattered abroad their gifts to
the poor,

their righteousness endures forever;
their horn *c* will be lifted high in honor.

¹⁰The wicked will see and be vexed,
they will gnash their teeth and waste
away;
the longings of the wicked will come
to nothing.

Psalm 113

¹Praise the LORD. *d*

Praise the LORD, you his servants;
praise the name of the LORD.
²Let the name of the LORD be praised,
both now and forevermore.
³From the rising of the sun to the place
where it sets,
the name of the LORD is to be praised.

⁴The LORD is exalted over all the nations,
his glory above the heavens.
⁵Who is like the LORD our God,
the One who sits enthroned on high,
⁶who stoops down to look
on the heavens and the earth?

⁷He raises the poor from the dust
and lifts the needy from the ash heap;
⁸he seats them with princes,
with the princes of his people.
⁹He settles the childless woman in her
home
as a happy mother of children.

Praise the LORD.

Psalm 114

¹When Israel came out of Egypt,
the house of Jacob from a people of
foreign tongue,
²Judah became God's sanctuary,
Israel his dominion.

³The sea looked and fled,
the Jordan turned back;
⁴the mountains leaped like rams,
the hills like lambs.

⁵Why was it, sea, that you fled?
Why, Jordan, did you turn back?
⁶Why, mountains, did you leap like rams,
you hills, like lambs?

a This psalm is an acrostic poem, the lines of which begin with the successive letters of the Hebrew
alphabet.   *b* 1 Hebrew *Hallelu Yah*   *c* 9 *Horn* here symbolizes dignity.   *d* 1 Hebrew *Hallelu Yah*;
also in verse 9

[7] Tremble, earth, at the presence of the
Lord,
  at the presence of the God of Jacob,
[8] who turned the rock into a pool,
  the hard rock into springs of water.

Psalm 115

[1] Not to us, LORD, not to us
  but to your name be the glory,
  because of your love and faithfulness.

[2] Why do the nations say,
  "Where is their God?"
[3] Our God is in heaven;
  he does whatever pleases him.
[4] But their idols are silver and gold,
  made by human hands.
[5] They have mouths, but cannot speak,
  eyes, but cannot see.
[6] They have ears, but cannot hear,
  noses, but cannot smell.
[7] They have hands, but cannot feel,
  feet, but cannot walk,
  nor can they utter a sound with their
  throats.
[8] Those who make them will be like them,
  and so will all who trust in them.

[9] House of Israel, trust in the LORD—
  he is their help and shield.
[10] House of Aaron, trust in the LORD—
  he is their help and shield.
[11] You who fear him, trust in the LORD—
  he is their help and shield.

[12] The LORD remembers us and will bless us:
  He will bless the house of Israel,
  he will bless the house of Aaron,
[13] he will bless those who fear the LORD—
  small and great alike.

[14] May the LORD cause you to increase,
  both you and your children.
[15] May you be blessed by the LORD,
  the Maker of heaven and earth.

[16] The highest heavens belong to the LORD,
  but the earth he has given to
  humankind.
[17] It is not the dead who praise the LORD,
  those who go down to the place of
  silence;
[18] it is we who extol the LORD,
  both now and forevermore.

Praise the LORD. [a]

Psalm 116

[1] I love the LORD, for he heard my voice;
  he heard my cry for mercy.
[2] Because he turned his ear to me,
  I will call on him as long as I live.

[3] The cords of death entangled me,
  the anguish of the grave came over
  me;
  I was overcome by distress and
  sorrow.
[4] Then I called on the name of the LORD:
  "LORD, save me!"

[5] The LORD is gracious and righteous;
  our God is full of compassion.
[6] The LORD protects the unwary;
  when I was brought low, he saved me.

[7] Return to your rest, my soul,
  for the LORD has been good to you.

[8] For you, LORD, have delivered me from
  death,
  my eyes from tears,
  my feet from stumbling,
[9] that I may walk before the LORD
  in the land of the living.

[10] I trusted in the LORD when I said,
  "I am greatly afflicted";
[11] in my alarm I said,
  "Everyone is a liar."

[12] What shall I return to the LORD
  for all his goodness to me?

[13] I will lift up the cup of salvation
  and call on the name of the LORD.
[14] I will fulfill my vows to the LORD
  in the presence of all his people.

[15] Precious in the sight of the LORD
  is the death of those faithful to him.
[16] Truly I am your servant, LORD;
  I am your servant, as was my mother
  before me;
  you have loosed my bonds of
  affliction.

[17] I will sacrifice a thank offering to you
  and call on the name of the LORD.
[18] I will fulfill my vows to the LORD
  in the presence of all his people,
[19] in the courts of the house of the LORD—
  in your midst, Jerusalem.

Praise the LORD. [a]

a 18,19 Hebrew *Hallelu Yah*

Psalm 117

[1] Praise the LORD, all you nations;
  extol him, all you peoples.
[2] For great is his love toward us,
  and the faithfulness of the LORD
    endures forever.

Praise the LORD. [a]

Psalm 118

[1] Give thanks to the LORD, for he is good;
  his love endures forever.

[2] Let Israel say:
  "His love endures forever."
[3] Let the house of Aaron say:
  "His love endures forever."
[4] Let those who fear the LORD say:
  "His love endures forever."

[5] When hard pressed, I cried to the LORD;
  he brought me into a spacious place.
[6] The LORD is with me; I will not be afraid.
  What can human beings do to me?
[7] The LORD is with me; he is my helper.
  I look in triumph on my enemies.

[8] It is better to take refuge in the LORD
  than to trust in human beings.
[9] It is better to take refuge in the LORD
  than to trust in princes.
[10] All the nations surrounded me,
  but in the name of the LORD I cut
    them down.
[11] They surrounded me on every side,
  but in the name of the LORD I cut
    them down.
[12] They swarmed around me like bees,
  but they were consumed as quickly as
    burning thorns;
  in the name of the LORD I cut them
    down.
[13] I was pushed back and about to fall,
  but the LORD helped me.
[14] The LORD is my strength and my
    defense [b];
  he has become my salvation.

[15] Shouts of joy and victory
  resound in the tents of the righteous:
  "The LORD's right hand has done mighty
    things!
[16] The LORD's right hand is lifted high;
  the LORD's right hand has done
    mighty things!"
[17] I will not die but live,
  and will proclaim what the LORD has
    done.
[18] The LORD has chastened me severely,
  but he has not given me over to
    death.
[19] Open for me the gates of the
    righteous;
  I will enter and give thanks to the
    LORD.
[20] This is the gate of the LORD
  through which the righteous may
    enter.
[21] I will give you thanks, for you answered
    me;
  you have become my salvation.

[22] The stone the builders rejected
  has become the cornerstone;
[23] the LORD has done this,
  and it is marvelous in our eyes.
[24] The LORD has done it this very day;
  let us rejoice today and be glad.

[25] LORD, save us!
  LORD, grant us success!

[26] Blessed is he who comes in the name of
    the LORD.
  From the house of the LORD we bless
    you. [c]
[27] The LORD is God,
  and he has made his light shine on us.
  With boughs in hand, join in the festal
    procession
  up [d] to the horns of the altar.

[28] You are my God, and I will praise you;
  you are my God, and I will exalt you.

[29] Give thanks to the LORD, for he is good;
  his love endures forever.

Psalm 119 [e]

א Aleph

[1] Blessed are those whose ways are
    blameless,
  who walk according to the law of the
    LORD.
[2] Blessed are those who keep his statutes
  and seek him with all their heart—

---

a 2 Hebrew *Hallelu Yah*   *b* 14 Or *song*   *c* 26 The Hebrew is plural.   *d* 27 Or *Bind the festal sacrifice with ropes / and take it*   *e* This psalm is an acrostic poem; the verses of each stanza begin with the same letter of the Hebrew alphabet.

³they do no wrong
but follow his ways.
⁴You have laid down precepts
that are to be fully obeyed.
⁵Oh, that my ways were steadfast
in obeying your decrees!
⁶Then I would not be put to shame
when I consider all your
commands.
⁷I will praise you with an upright heart
as I learn your righteous laws.
⁸I will obey your decrees;
do not utterly forsake me.

ב Beth

⁹How can those who are young keep their
way pure?
By living according to your word.
¹⁰I seek you with all my heart;
do not let me stray from your
commands.
¹¹I have hidden your word in my heart
that I might not sin against you.
¹²Praise be to you, LORD;
teach me your decrees.
¹³With my lips I recount
all the laws that come from your
mouth.
¹⁴I rejoice in following your statutes
as one rejoices in great riches.
¹⁵I meditate on your precepts
and consider your ways.
¹⁶I delight in your decrees;
I will not neglect your word.

ג Gimel

¹⁷Be good to your servant while I live,
that I may obey your word.
¹⁸Open my eyes that I may see
wonderful things in your law.
¹⁹I am a stranger on earth;
do not hide your commands from me.
²⁰My soul is consumed with longing
for your laws at all times.
²¹You rebuke the arrogant, who are
accursed,
those who stray from your commands.
²²Remove from me their scorn and
contempt,
for I keep your statutes.

²³Though rulers sit together and slander
me,
your servant will meditate on your
decrees.
²⁴Your statutes are my delight;
they are my counselors.

ד Daleth

²⁵I am laid low in the dust;
preserve my life according to your
word.
²⁶I gave an account of my ways and you
answered me;
teach me your decrees.
²⁷Cause me to understand the way of your
precepts,
that I may meditate on your
wonderful deeds.
²⁸My soul is weary with sorrow;
strengthen me according to your
word.
²⁹Keep me from deceitful ways;
be gracious to me and teach me your
law.
³⁰I have chosen the way of faithfulness;
I have set my heart on your laws.
³¹I hold fast to your statutes, LORD;
do not let me be put to shame.
³²I run in the path of your commands,
for you have set my heart free.

ה He

³³Teach me, LORD, the way of your
decrees,
that I may follow it to the end. ᵃ
³⁴Give me understanding, so that I may
keep your law
and obey it with all my heart.
³⁵Direct me in the path of your
commands,
for there I find delight.
³⁶Turn my heart toward your statutes
and not toward selfish gain.
³⁷Turn my eyes away from worthless
things;
preserve my life according to your
word. ᵇ
³⁸Fulfill your promise to your servant,
so that you may be feared.
³⁹Take away the disgrace I dread,
for your laws are good.

ᵃ 33 Or *follow it for its reward*   ᵇ 37 Two manuscripts of the Masoretic Text and Dead Sea Scrolls; most
manuscripts of the Masoretic Text *life in your way*

40 How I long for your precepts!
   In your righteousness preserve my
   life.

ו Waw

41 May your unfailing love come to me,
   LORD,
   your salvation, according to your
   promise;
42 then I can answer anyone who taunts
   me,
   for I trust in your word.
43 Never take your word of truth from my
   mouth,
   for I have put my hope in your laws.
44 I will always obey your law,
   for ever and ever.
45 I will walk about in freedom,
   for I have sought out your precepts.
46 I will speak of your statutes before
   kings
   and will not be put to shame,
47 for I delight in your commands
   because I love them.
48 I reach out for your commands, which I
   love,
   that I may meditate on your decrees.

ז Zayin

49 Remember your word to your servant,
   for you have given me hope.
50 My comfort in my suffering is this:
   Your promise preserves my life.
51 The arrogant mock me unmercifully,
   but I do not turn from your law.
52 I remember, LORD, your ancient laws,
   and I find comfort in them.
53 Indignation grips me because of the
   wicked,
   who have forsaken your law.
54 Your decrees are the theme of my song
   wherever I lodge.
55 In the night, LORD, I remember your
   name,
   that I may keep your law.
56 This has been my practice:
   I obey your precepts.

ח Heth

57 You are my portion, LORD;
   I have promised to obey your words.
58 I have sought your face with all my
   heart;

be gracious to me according to your
   promise.
59 I have considered my ways
   and have turned my steps to your
   statutes.
60 I will hasten and not delay
   to obey your commands.
61 Though the wicked bind me with ropes,
   I will not forget your law.
62 At midnight I rise to give you thanks
   for your righteous laws.
63 I am a friend to all who fear you,
   to all who follow your precepts.
64 The earth is filled with your love, LORD;
   teach me your decrees.

ט Teth

65 Do good to your servant
   according to your word, LORD.
66 Teach me knowledge and good
   judgment,
   for I trust your commands.
67 Before I was afflicted I went astray,
   but now I obey your word.
68 You are good, and what you do is good;
   teach me your decrees.
69 Though the arrogant have smeared me
   with lies,
   I keep your precepts with all my
   heart.
70 Their hearts are callous and unfeeling,
   but I delight in your law.
71 It was good for me to be afflicted
   so that I might learn your decrees.
72 The law from your mouth is more
   precious to me
   than thousands of pieces of silver and
   gold.

י Yodh

73 Your hands made me and formed me;
   give me understanding to learn your
   commands.
74 May those who fear you rejoice when
   they see me,
   for I have put my hope in your word.
75 I know, LORD, that your laws are
   righteous,
   and that in faithfulness you have
   afflicted me.
76 May your unfailing love be my comfort,
   according to your promise to your
   servant.

⁷⁷ Let your compassion come to me that I
may live,
for your law is my delight.
⁷⁸ May the arrogant be put to shame for
wronging me without cause;
but I will meditate on your precepts.
⁷⁹ May those who fear you turn to me,
those who understand your statutes.
⁸⁰ May my heart be blameless toward your
decrees,
that I may not be put to shame.

כ Kaph

⁸¹ My soul faints with longing for your
salvation,
but I have put my hope in your word.
⁸² My eyes fail, looking for your promise;
I say, "When will you comfort me?"
⁸³ Though I am like a wineskin in the
smoke,
I do not forget your decrees.
⁸⁴ How long must your servant wait?
When will you punish my
persecutors?
⁸⁵ The arrogant dig pits to trap me,
contrary to your law.
⁸⁶ All your commands are trustworthy;
help me, for I am being persecuted
without cause.
⁸⁷ They almost wiped me from the earth,
but I have not forsaken your
precepts.
⁸⁸ In your unfailing love preserve my life,
that I may obey the statutes of your
mouth.

ל Lamedh

⁸⁹ Your word, LORD, is eternal;
it stands firm in the heavens.
⁹⁰ Your faithfulness continues through all
generations;
you established the earth, and it
endures.
⁹¹ Your laws endure to this day,
for all things serve you.
⁹² If your law had not been my delight,
I would have perished in my
affliction.
⁹³ I will never forget your precepts,
for by them you have preserved my
life.
⁹⁴ Save me, for I am yours;

I have sought out your precepts.
⁹⁵ The wicked are waiting to destroy me,
but I will ponder your statutes.
⁹⁶ To all perfection I see a limit,
but your commands are boundless.

מ Mem

⁹⁷ Oh, how I love your law!
I meditate on it all day long.
⁹⁸ Your commands are always with me
and make me wiser than my enemies.
⁹⁹ I have more insight than all my teachers,
for I meditate on your statutes.
¹⁰⁰ I have more understanding than the
elders,
for I obey your precepts.
¹⁰¹ I have kept my feet from every evil path
so that I might obey your word.
¹⁰² I have not departed from your laws,
for you yourself have taught me.
¹⁰³ How sweet are your words to my taste,
sweeter than honey to my mouth!
¹⁰⁴ I gain understanding from your precepts;
therefore I hate every wrong path.

נ Nun

¹⁰⁵ Your word is a lamp to my feet
and a light for my path.
¹⁰⁶ I have taken an oath and confirmed it,
that I will follow your righteous laws.
¹⁰⁷ I have suffered much;
preserve my life, LORD, according to
your word.
¹⁰⁸ Accept, LORD, the willing praise of my
mouth,
and teach me your laws.
¹⁰⁹ Though I constantly take my life in my
hands,
I will not forget your law.
¹¹⁰ The wicked have set a snare for me,
but I have not strayed from your
precepts.
¹¹¹ Your statutes are my heritage forever;
they are the joy of my heart.
¹¹² My heart is set on keeping your decrees
to the very end. ᵃ

ס Samekh

¹¹³ I hate double-minded people,
but I love your law.
¹¹⁴ You are my refuge and my shield;
I have put my hope in your word.

ᵃ 112 Or / for their enduring reward

MONDAY

A PASSION FOR THE WORD

Psalm 119:89–120 *or* 119:97–101

Dave Roberts

We are emotionally, mentally, and physically touched by the daily stimuli that touches our lives from the moment we wake until we sleep. A pleasant word from one person, a barbed comment from another. A beautiful sunset, a polluted and untidy yard. A hug or a kiss or an absence of affection. Our mood will be effected by the day-to-day realities of our lives . . .

One of the reasons for reflecting on God's Word therefore is to ensure that the Word of God is near us. It will guard us, instruct us, and guide us by shaping the thought patterns, thought connections, and emotional backdrop of our lives.

THOMAS WATSON {AD 1620–1686}

Since God has spoken all these words, then we ought to love his commandments. Like the psalmist we should cry, "Oh, how I love your law! I meditate on it all day long . . . See how I love your precepts" (Psalm 119:97,159).

The moral law contains the transcript of God's will. It is our spiritual directory, showing us what sins to avoid and what duties to pursue. The Ten Commandments are a chain of pearls to enhance us, a treasury to enrich us; they are more precious than lands of spices or rocks of diamonds. As the psalmist wrote, "The law from your mouth is more precious to me than thousands of pieces of silver and gold" (Psalm 119:72).

The law of God has truth and goodness in it. It contains truth, for God himself spoke it. And it contains goodness, for all that the commandment imposes is for our good.

reflection

1. How have you been changed by the truth of God's Word?
2. The psalmist displayed deep passion for God's Word. How would you rate the "passion-level" of *your* love for God's Word?
3. What Scriptures are you holding on to most tightly right now?

For your next devotional reading, go to page 694.

115 Away from me, you evildoers,
   that I may keep the commands of my
      God!
116 Sustain me according to your promise,
      and I will live;
   do not let my hopes be dashed.
117 Uphold me, and I will be delivered;
   I will always have regard for your
      decrees.
118 You reject all who stray from your
      decrees,
   for their delusions come to nothing.
119 All the wicked of the earth you discard
      like dross;
   therefore I love your statutes.
120 My flesh trembles in fear of you;
   I stand in awe of your laws.

ע Ayin

121 I have done what is righteous and just;
   do not leave me to my oppressors.
122 Ensure your servant's well-being;
   do not let the arrogant oppress me.
123 My eyes fail, looking for your salvation,
   looking for your righteous promise.
124 Deal with your servant according to your
      love
   and teach me your decrees.
125 I am your servant; give me discernment
   that I may understand your statutes.
126 It is time for you to act, LORD;
   your law is being broken.
127 Because I love your commands
   more than gold, more than pure gold,
128 and because I consider all your precepts
      right,
   I hate every wrong path.

פ Pe

129 Your statutes are wonderful;
   therefore I obey them.
130 The unfolding of your words gives light;
   it gives understanding to the simple.
131 I open my mouth and pant,
   longing for your commands.
132 Turn to me and have mercy on me,
   as you always do to those who love
      your name.
133 Direct my footsteps according to your
      word;
   let no sin rule over me.
134 Redeem me from human oppression,
   that I may obey your precepts.
135 Make your face shine on your servant
   and teach me your decrees.
136 Streams of tears flow from my eyes,
   for your law is not obeyed.

צ Tsadhe

137 You are righteous, LORD,
   and your laws are right.
138 The statutes you have laid down are
      righteous;
   they are fully trustworthy.
139 My zeal wears me out,
   for my enemies ignore your words.
140 Your promises have been thoroughly
      tested,
   and your servant loves them.
141 Though I am lowly and despised,
   I do not forget your precepts.
142 Your righteousness is everlasting
   and your law is true.
143 Trouble and distress have come
      upon me,
   but your commands give me delight.
144 Your statutes are always righteous;
   give me understanding that I may
      live.

ק Qoph

145 I call with all my heart; answer me,
      LORD,
   and I will obey your decrees.
146 I call out to you; save me
   and I will keep your statutes.
147 I rise before dawn and cry for help;
   I have put my hope in your word.
148 My eyes stay open through the watches
      of the night,
   that I may meditate on your
      promises.
149 Hear my voice in accordance with your
      love;
   preserve my life, LORD, according to
      your laws.
150 Those who devise wicked schemes are
      near,
   but they are far from your law.
151 Yet you are near, LORD,
   and all your commands are true.
152 Long ago I learned from your statutes
   that you established them to last
      forever.

ר Resh

153 Look on my suffering and deliver me,
   for I have not forgotten your law.

154 Defend my cause and redeem me;
    preserve my life according to your
        promise.
155 Salvation is far from the wicked,
    for they do not seek out your decrees.
156 Your compassion, LORD, is great;
    preserve my life according to your laws.
157 Many are the foes who persecute me,
    but I have not turned from your
        statutes.
158 I look on the faithless with loathing,
    for they do not obey your word.
159 See how I love your precepts;
    preserve my life, LORD, in accordance
        with your love.
160 All your words are true;
    all your righteous laws are eternal.

ש Sin and Shin

161 Rulers persecute me without cause,
    but my heart trembles at your word.
162 I rejoice in your promise
    like one who finds great spoil.
163 I hate and detest falsehood
    but I love your law.
164 Seven times a day I praise you
    for your righteous laws.
165 Great peace have those who love your
        law,
    and nothing can make them stumble.
166 I wait for your salvation, LORD,
    and I follow your commands.
167 I obey your statutes,
    for I love them greatly.
168 I obey your precepts and your statutes,
    for all my ways are known to you.

ת Taw

169 May my cry come before you, LORD;
    give me understanding according to
        your word.
170 May my supplication come before you;
    deliver me according to your promise.
171 May my lips overflow with praise,
    for you teach me your decrees.
172 May my tongue sing of your word,
    for all your commands are righteous.
173 May your hand be ready to help me,
    for I have chosen your precepts.
174 I long for your salvation, LORD,
    and your law gives me delight.
175 Let me live that I may praise you,
    and may your laws sustain me.
176 I have strayed like a lost sheep.

Seek your servant,
    for I have not forgotten your
        commands.

Psalm 120

A song of ascents.

1 I call on the LORD in my distress,
    and he answers me.
2 Save me, LORD,
    from lying lips
    and from deceitful tongues.

3 What will he do to you,
    and what more besides,
    you deceitful tongue?
4 He will punish you with a warrior's
        sharp arrows,
    with burning coals of the broom bush.

5 Woe to me that I dwell in Meshek,
    that I live among the tents of Kedar!
6 Too long have I lived
    among those who hate peace.
7 I am for peace;
    but when I speak, they are for war.

Psalm 121

A song of ascents.

1 I lift up my eyes to the mountains—
    where does my help come from?
2 My help comes from the LORD,
    the Maker of heaven and earth.

3 He will not let your foot slip—
    he who watches over you will not
        slumber;
4 indeed, he who watches over Israel
    will neither slumber nor sleep.

5 The LORD watches over you—
    the LORD is your shade at your right
        hand;
6 the sun will not harm you by day,
    nor the moon by night.

7 The LORD will keep you from all harm—
    he will watch over your life;
8 the LORD will watch over your coming
        and going
    both now and forevermore.

Psalm 122

A song of ascents. Of David.

1 I rejoiced with those who said to me,
    "Let us go to the house of the LORD."

2 Our feet are standing
    in your gates, Jerusalem.

3 Jerusalem is built like a city
    that is closely compacted together.
4 That is where the tribes go up—
    the tribes of the Lord—
to praise the name of the Lord
    according to the statute given to
        Israel.
5 There stand the thrones for judgment,
    the thrones of the house of David.

6 Pray for the peace of Jerusalem:
    "May those who love you be secure.
7 May there be peace within your walls
    and security within your citadels."
8 For the sake of my friends and of all the
        people,
    I will say, "Peace be within you."
9 For the sake of the house of the Lord
        our God,
    I will seek your prosperity.

Psalm 123

A song of ascents.

1 I lift up my eyes to you,
    to you who sit enthroned in heaven.
2 As the eyes of slaves look to the hand of
        their master,
    as the eyes of a female slave look to
        the hand of her mistress,
so our eyes look to the Lord our God,
    till he shows us his mercy.

3 Have mercy on us, Lord, have mercy on
        us,
    for we have endured no end of
        contempt.
4 We have endured no end
    of ridicule from the arrogant,
    of contempt from the proud.

Psalm 124

A song of ascents. Of David.

1 If the Lord had not been on our side—
    let Israel say—
2 if the Lord had not been on our side
    when people attacked us,
3 they would have swallowed us alive
    when their anger flared against us;
4 the flood would have engulfed us,
    the torrent would have swept over us,

5 the raging waters
    would have swept us away.

6 Praise be to the Lord,
    who has not let us be torn by their
        teeth.
7 We have escaped like a bird
    from the fowler's snare;
the snare has been broken,
    and we have escaped.
8 Our help is in the name of the Lord,
    the Maker of heaven and earth.

Psalm 125

A song of ascents.

1 Those who trust in the Lord are like
        Mount Zion,
    which cannot be shaken but endures
        forever.
2 As the mountains surround Jerusalem,
    so the Lord surrounds his people
    both now and forevermore.

3 The scepter of the wicked will not
        remain
    over the land allotted to the
        righteous,
for then the righteous might use
    their hands to do evil.

4 Lord, do good to those who are good,
    to those who are upright in heart.
5 But those who turn to crooked ways
    the Lord will banish with the
        evildoers.

Peace be on Israel.

Psalm 126

A song of ascents.

1 When the Lord restored the fortunes of[a]
        Zion,
    we were like those who dreamed.[b]
2 Our mouths were filled with laughter,
    our tongues with songs of joy.
Then it was said among the nations,
    "The Lord has done great things for
        them."
3 The Lord has done great things for us,
    and we are filled with joy.

4 Restore our fortunes,[c] Lord,
    like streams in the Negev.
5 Those who sow with tears

---

a 1 Or Lord *brought back the captives to*   *b 1 Or those restored to health*   *c 4 Or Bring back our captives*

will reap with songs of joy.
⁶ Those who go out weeping,
  carrying seed to sow,
will return with songs of joy,
  carrying sheaves with them.

Psalm 127

A song of ascents. Of Solomon.

¹ Unless the LORD builds the house,
  the builders labor in vain.
Unless the LORD watches over the city,
  the guards stand watch in vain.
² In vain you rise early
  and stay up late,
toiling for food to eat—
  for he grants sleep to[a] those he
    loves.

³ Children are a heritage from the LORD,
  offspring a reward from him.
⁴ Like arrows in the hands of a warrior
  are children born in one's youth.
⁵ Blessed is the man
  whose quiver is full of them.
They will not be put to shame
  when they contend with their
    opponents in court.

Psalm 128

A song of ascents.

¹ Blessed are all who fear the LORD,
  who walk in obedience to him.
² You will eat the fruit of your labor;
  blessings and prosperity will be
    yours.
³ Your wife will be like a fruitful vine
  within your house;
your children will be like olive shoots
  around your table.
⁴ Yes, this will be the blessing
  for the man who fears the LORD.

⁵ May the LORD bless you from Zion;
  may you see the prosperity of
    Jerusalem
all the days of your life.
⁶ May you live to see your children's
    children—
  peace be on Israel.

Psalm 129

A song of ascents.

¹ "They have greatly oppressed me from
    my youth,"
  let Israel say;
² "they have greatly oppressed me from
    my youth,
  but they have not gained the victory
    over me.
³ Plowmen have plowed my back
  and made their furrows long.
⁴ But the LORD is righteous;
  he has cut me free from the cords of
    the wicked."

⁵ May all who hate Zion
  be turned back in shame.
⁶ May they be like grass on the roof,
  which withers before it can grow;
⁷ reapers cannot fill their hands with it,
  nor those who gather fill their arms.
⁸ May those who pass by not say to them,
  "The blessing of the LORD be on you;
  we bless you in the name of the
    LORD."

Psalm 130

A song of ascents.

¹ Out of the depths I cry to you, LORD;
²   Lord, hear my voice.
Let your ears be attentive
  to my cry for mercy.

³ If you, LORD, kept a record of sins,
  Lord, who could stand?
⁴ But with you there is forgiveness,
  so that we can, with reverence, serve
    you.

⁵ I wait for the LORD, my whole being
    waits,
  and in his word I put my hope.
⁶ I wait for the Lord
  more than watchmen wait for the
    morning,
  more than watchmen wait for the
    morning.

⁷ Israel, put your hope in the LORD,
  for with the LORD is unfailing love
  and with him is full redemption.
⁸ He himself will redeem Israel
  from all their sins.

---

a 2 Or *eat—/for while they sleep he provides for*

Psalm 131

A song of ascents. Of David.

1 My heart is not proud, LORD,
    my eyes are not haughty;
  I do not concern myself with great
      matters
    or things too wonderful for me.
2 But I have calmed myself
    and quieted my ambitions.
  I am like a weaned child with its mother;
    like a weaned child I am content.

3 Israel, put your hope in the LORD
    both now and forevermore.

Psalm 132

A song of ascents.

1 LORD, remember David
    and all his self-denial.

2 He swore an oath to the LORD
    and made a vow to the Mighty One of
      Jacob:
3 "I will not enter my house
    or go to my bed,
4 I will allow no sleep to my eyes
    or slumber to my eyelids,
5 till I find a place for the LORD,
    a dwelling for the Mighty One of
      Jacob."

6 We heard it in Ephrathah,
    we came upon it in the fields of Jaar:ᵃ
7 "Let us go to his dwelling place,
    let us worship at his footstool,
      saying,
8 'Arise, LORD, and come to your resting
      place,
    you and the ark of your might.
9 May your priests be clothed with your
      righteousness;
    may your faithful people sing for
      joy.' "

10 For the sake of your servant David,
    do not reject your anointed one.

11 The LORD swore an oath to David,
    a sure oath that he will not revoke:
  "One of your own descendants
    I will place on your throne.
12 If your sons keep my covenant
    and the statutes I teach them,

then their sons will sit
    on your throne for ever and ever."

13 For the LORD has chosen Zion,
    he has desired it for his dwelling,
      saying,
14 "This is my resting place for ever and
      ever;
    here I will sit enthroned, for I have
      desired it.
15 I will bless her with abundant
      provisions;
    her poor I will satisfy with food.
16 I will clothe her priests with salvation,
    and her faithful people will ever sing
      for joy.

17 "Here I will make a hornᵇ grow for
      David
    and set up a lamp for my anointed
      one.
18 I will clothe his enemies with shame,
    but his head will be adorned with a
      resplendent crown."

Psalm 133

A song of ascents. Of David.

1 How good and pleasant it is
    when God's people live together in
      unity!

2 It is like precious oil poured on the head,
    running down on the beard,
  running down on Aaron's beard,
    down on the collar of his robe.
3 It is as if the dew of Hermon
    were falling on Mount Zion.
  For there the LORD bestows his blessing,
    even life forevermore.

Psalm 134

A song of ascents.

1 Praise the LORD, all you servants of the
      LORD
    who minister by night in the house of
      the LORD.
2 Lift up your hands in the sanctuary
    and praise the LORD.

3 May the LORD bless you from Zion,
    he who is the Maker of heaven and
      earth.

ᵃ 6 Or *heard of it in Ephrathah, / we found it in the fields of Jearim.* (See 1 Chron. 13:5,6) (And no
quotation marks around verses 7-9)   ᵇ 17 *Horn* here symbolizes strong one, that is, king.

TUESDAY

BE WEANED FROM SELF-DEPENDENCE

Psalm 131:1–3 *or* 131:2–3

Eugene Peterson

Many who have traveled this way of faith have described the transition from an infantile faith that grabs at God out of desperation to a mature faith that responds to God out of love . . . Often our conscious Christian lives do begin at points of desperation, and God, of course, does not refuse to meet our needs. There are heavenly comforts that break through our despair and persuade us that "all will be well and all manner of things will be well." The early stages of Christian belief are not infrequently marked with miraculous signs and exhilarations of spirit. But as discipleship continues the sensible comforts gradually disappear. For God does not want us neurotically dependent upon him but willingly trustful in him. And so he weans us. The period of infancy will not be sentimentally extended beyond what is necessary. The time of weaning is very often noisy and marked with misunderstandings: "I no longer feel like I did when I was first a Christian. Does that mean I am no longer a Christian? Has God abandoned me? Have I done something terribly wrong?"

The answer is, "Neither: God hasn't abandoned you, and you haven't done anything wrong. You are being weaned. The apron strings have been cut. You are free to come to God or not come to him. You are, in a sense, on your own with an open invitation to listen and receive and enjoy our Lord."

JOHN WESLEY {AD 1703–1791}

Lord, that I may learn of thee,
Give me true simplicity;
Wean my soul, and keep it low,
Willing thee alone to know.

Let me cast my reeds aside,
All that feeds my knowing pride,
Not to man, but God submit,
Lay my reasonings at thy feet;

Of my boasted wisdom spoiled,
Docile, helpless, as a child,
Only seeing in thy light,
Only walking in thy might.

Then infuse the teaching grace,
Spirit of truth and righteousness;
Knowledge, love divine, impart,
Life eternal, to my heart.

reflection

1. Do you feel like you've gone through a "weaning period" in your faith? Why?

2. Why is this a necessary and important transition for every believer to go through?

3. How does the maturity of a "weaned faith" differ from a faith that is still in its infancy?

For your next devotional reading, go to page 701.

Psalm 135

[1] Praise the Lord.[a]

Praise the name of the Lord;
 praise him, you servants of the Lord,
[2] you who minister in the house of the
  Lord,
 in the courts of the house of our God.

[3] Praise the Lord, for the Lord is good;
 sing praise to his name, for that is
  pleasant.
[4] For the Lord has chosen Jacob to be his
  own,
 Israel to be his treasured possession.

[5] I know that the Lord is great,
 that our Lord is greater than all gods.
[6] The Lord does whatever pleases him,
 in the heavens and on the earth,
 in the seas and all their depths.
[7] He makes clouds rise from the ends of
  the earth;
 he sends lightning with the rain
 and brings out the wind from his
  storehouses.

[8] He struck down the firstborn of Egypt,
 the firstborn of people and animals.
[9] He sent his signs and wonders into your
  midst, Egypt,
 against Pharaoh and all his servants.
[10] He struck down many nations
 and killed mighty kings—
[11] Sihon king of the Amorites,
 Og king of Bashan,
 and all the kings of Canaan—
[12] and he gave their land as an inheritance,
 an inheritance to his people Israel.

[13] Your name, Lord, endures forever,
 your renown, Lord, through all
  generations.
[14] For the Lord will vindicate his people
 and relent concerning his servants.

[15] The idols of the nations are silver and
  gold,
 made by human hands.
[16] They have mouths, but cannot speak,
 eyes, but cannot see.
[17] They have ears, but cannot hear,
 nor is there breath in their mouths.
[18] Those who make them will be like them,
 and so will all who trust in them.

[19] House of Israel, praise the Lord;
 house of Aaron, praise the Lord;
[20] house of Levi, praise the Lord;
 you who fear him, praise the Lord.
[21] Praise be to the Lord from Zion,
 to him who dwells in Jerusalem.

Praise the Lord.

Psalm 136

[1] Give thanks to the Lord, for he is good.
 His love endures forever.
[2] Give thanks to the God of gods.
 His love endures forever.
[3] Give thanks to the Lord of lords:
 His love endures forever.

[4] to him who alone does great wonders,
 His love endures forever.
[5] who by his understanding made the
  heavens,
 His love endures forever.
[6] who spread out the earth upon the
  waters,
 His love endures forever.
[7] who made the great lights—
 His love endures forever.
[8] the sun to govern the day,
 His love endures forever.
[9] the moon and stars to govern the night;
 His love endures forever.

[10] to him who struck down the firstborn of
  Egypt
 His love endures forever.
[11] and brought Israel out from among them
 His love endures forever.
[12] with a mighty hand and outstretched
  arm;
 His love endures forever.

[13] to him who divided the Red Sea[b]
  asunder
 His love endures forever.
[14] and brought Israel through the midst of it,
 His love endures forever.
[15] but swept Pharaoh and his army into the
  Red Sea;
 His love endures forever.

[16] to him who led his people through the
  wilderness;
 His love endures forever.
[17] to him who struck down great kings,
 His love endures forever.

a 1 Hebrew *Hallelu Yah*; also in verses 3 and 21 b 13 Or *the Sea of Reeds*; also in verse 15

¹⁸ and killed mighty kings—
  His love endures forever.
¹⁹ Sihon king of the Amorites
  His love endures forever.
²⁰ and Og king of Bashan—
  His love endures forever.
²¹ and gave their land as an inheritance,
  His love endures forever.
²² an inheritance to his servant Israel.
  His love endures forever.
²³ He remembered us in our low estate
  His love endures forever.
²⁴ and freed us from our enemies.
  His love endures forever.
²⁵ He gives food to every creature.
  His love endures forever.
²⁶ Give thanks to the God of heaven.
  His love endures forever.

Psalm 137

¹ By the rivers of Babylon we sat and wept
 when we remembered Zion.
² There on the poplars
 we hung our harps,
³ for there our captors asked us for
  songs,
 our tormentors demanded songs of
  joy;
 they said, "Sing us one of the songs of
  Zion!"

⁴ How can we sing the songs of the LORD
 while in a foreign land?
⁵ If I forget you, Jerusalem,
 may my right hand forget its skill.
⁶ May my tongue cling to the roof of my
  mouth
 if I do not remember you,
if I do not consider Jerusalem
 my highest joy.

⁷ Remember, LORD, what the Edomites
  did
 on the day Jerusalem fell.
"Tear it down," they cried,
 "tear it down to its foundations!"
⁸ Daughter Babylon, doomed to
  destruction,
 happy are those who repay you
 according to what you have done to
  us.
⁹ Happy are those who seize your infants
 and dash them against the rocks.

Psalm 138

Of David.

¹ I will praise you, LORD, with all my
  heart;
 before the "gods" I will sing your
  praise.
² I will bow down toward your holy
  temple
 and will praise your name
 for your unfailing love and your
  faithfulness,
for you have so exalted your solemn
  decree
 that it surpasses your fame.
³ When I called, you answered me;
 you greatly emboldened me.

⁴ May all the kings of the earth praise you,
  LORD,
 when they hear what you have
  decreed.
⁵ May they sing of the ways of the LORD,
 for the glory of the LORD is great.

⁶ Though the LORD is exalted, he looks
  kindly on the lowly,
 but he takes notice of the proud from
  afar.
⁷ Though I walk in the midst of trouble,
 you preserve my life.
You stretch out your hand against the
  anger of my foes;
 with your right hand you save me.
⁸ The LORD will vindicate me;
 your love, LORD, endures forever—
 do not abandon the works of your
  hands.

Psalm 139

For the director of music. Of David.
A psalm.

¹ You have searched me, LORD,
 and you know me.
² You know when I sit and when I rise;
 you perceive my thoughts from afar.
³ You discern my going out and my lying
  down;
 you are familiar with all my ways.
⁴ Before a word is on my tongue
 you, LORD, know it completely.
⁵ You hem me in behind and before,
 and you lay your hand upon me.
⁶ Such knowledge is too wonderful for me,
 too lofty for me to attain.

7 Where can I go from your Spirit?
   Where can I flee from your presence?
8 If I go up to the heavens, you are there;
   if I make my bed in the depths, you
      are there.
9 If I rise on the wings of the dawn,
   if I settle on the far side of the sea,
10 even there your hand will guide me,
   your right hand will hold me fast.
11 If I say, "Surely the darkness will hide
      me
   and the light become night around
      me,"
12 even the darkness will not be dark to
      you;
   the night will shine like the day,
   for darkness is as light to you.

13 For you created my inmost being;
   you knit me together in my mother's
      womb.
14 I praise you because I am fearfully and
      wonderfully made;
   your works are wonderful,
   I know that full well.
15 My frame was not hidden from you
   when I was made in the secret place.
   When I was woven together in the
      depths of the earth,
16   your eyes saw my unformed body.
   All the days ordained for me
   were written in your book
   before one of them came to be.
17 How precious to me are your thoughts,[a]
      God!
   How vast is the sum of them!
18 Were I to count them,
   they would outnumber the grains of
      sand—
   when I awake, I am still with you.

19 If only you, God, would slay the wicked!
   Away from me, you who are
      bloodthirsty!
20 They speak of you with evil intent;
   your adversaries misuse your name.
21 Do I not hate those who hate you, LORD,
   and abhor those who are in rebellion
      against you?
22 I have nothing but hatred for them;
   I count them my enemies.
23 Search me, God, and know my heart;

   test me and know my anxious
      thoughts.
24 See if there is any offensive way in me,
   and lead me in the way everlasting.

Psalm 140

*For the director of music. A psalm
of David.*

*1 Rescue me, LORD, from evildoers;
   protect me from the violent,
2 who devise evil plans in their hearts
   and stir up war every day.
3 They make their tongues as sharp as a
      serpent's;
   the poison of vipers is on their lips.[b]

4 Keep me safe, LORD, from the hands of
      the wicked;
   protect me from the violent,
   who devise ways to trip my feet.
5 The arrogant have hidden a snare for
      me;
   they have spread out the cords of
      their net
   and have set traps for me along my
      path.

6 I say to the LORD, "You are my God."
   Hear, LORD, my cry for mercy.
7 Sovereign LORD, my strong deliverer,
   you shield my head in the day of
      battle.
8 Do not grant the wicked their desires,
      LORD;
   do not let their plans succeed.

9 Those who surround me proudly rear
      their heads;
   may the mischief of their lips engulf
      them.
10 May burning coals fall on them;
   may they be thrown into the fire,
   into miry pits, never to rise.
11 May slanderers not be established in the
      land;
   may disaster hunt down the violent.

12 I know that the LORD secures justice for
      the poor
   and upholds the cause of the needy.
13 Surely the righteous will praise your
      name,

---

a 17 Or *precious are your thoughts concerning me*
meaning) here and at the end of verses 5 and 8.
* 140:1-13 is numbered 140:2-14 in Hebrew texts.

b 3 The Hebrew has *Selah* (a word of uncertain

and the upright will live in your
    presence.

Psalm 141

A psalm of David.

¹ I call to you, LORD, come quickly to me;
    hear me when I call to you.
² May my prayer be set before you like
        incense;
    may the lifting up of my hands be like
        the evening sacrifice.

³ Set a guard over my mouth, LORD;
    keep watch over the door of my lips.
⁴ Do not let my heart be drawn to what is
        evil
    so that I take part in wicked deeds
along with those who are evildoers;
    do not let me eat of their delicacies.

⁵ Let a righteous man strike me—that is a
        kindness;
    let him rebuke me—that is oil on my
        head.
My head will not refuse it,
    for my prayer will still be against the
        deeds of evildoers.

⁶ Their rulers will be thrown down from
        the cliffs,
    and the wicked will learn that my
        words were well spoken.
⁷ They will say, "As one plows and breaks
        up the earth,
    so our bones have been scattered at
        the mouth of the grave."

⁸ But my eyes are fixed on you, Sovereign
        LORD;
    in you I take refuge—do not give me
        over to death.
⁹ Keep me safe from the traps set by
        evildoers,
    from the snares they have laid for me.
¹⁰ Let the wicked fall into their own nets,
    while I pass by in safety.

Psalm 142

*A maskil ᵃ of David. When he was in the
    cave. A prayer.*

*¹ I cry aloud to the LORD;

I lift up my voice to the LORD for
    mercy.
² I pour out before him my complaint;
    before him I tell my trouble.

³ When my spirit grows faint within me,
    it is you who watch over my way.
In the path where I walk
    people have hidden a snare for me.
⁴ Look and see, there is no one at my right
        hand;
    no one is concerned for me.
I have no refuge;
    no one cares for my life.

⁵ I cry to you, LORD;
    I say, "You are my refuge,
        my portion in the land of the living."

⁶ Listen to my cry,
    for I am in desperate need;
rescue me from those who pursue me,
    for they are too strong for me.
⁷ Set me free from my prison,
    that I may praise your name.
Then the righteous will gather about me
    because of your goodness to me.

Psalm 143

A psalm of David.

¹ LORD, hear my prayer,
    listen to my cry for mercy;
in your faithfulness and righteousness
    come to my relief.
² Do not bring your servant into judgment,
    for no one living is righteous before
        you.
³ The enemy pursues me,
    he crushes me to the ground;
he makes me dwell in the darkness
    like those long dead.
⁴ So my spirit grows faint within me;
    my heart within me is dismayed.
⁵ I remember the days of long ago;
    I meditate on all your works
    and consider what your hands have
        done.
⁶ I spread out my hands to you;
    I thirst for you like a parched land. ᵇ

⁷ Answer me quickly, LORD;
    my spirit fails.

ᵃ Title: Probably a literary or musical term   ᵇ 6 The Hebrew has *Selah* (a word of uncertain meaning)
here.

* 142:1-7 is numbered 142:2-8 in Hebrew texts.

Do not hide your face from me
  or I will be like those who go down to
    the pit.
[8] Let the morning bring me word of your
    unfailing love,
  for I have put my trust in you.
Show me the way I should go,
  for to you I entrust my life.
[9] Rescue me from my enemies, Lord,
  for I hide myself in you.
[10] Teach me to do your will,
  for you are my God;
may your good Spirit
  lead me on level ground.

[11] For your name's sake, Lord, preserve my
    life;
  in your righteousness, bring me out of
    trouble.
[12] In your unfailing love, silence my
    enemies;
  destroy all my foes,
  for I am your servant.

Psalm 144

Of David.

[1] Praise be to the Lord my Rock,
  who trains my hands for war,
  my fingers for battle.
[2] He is my loving God and my fortress,
  my stronghold and my deliverer,
my shield, in whom I take refuge,
  who subdues peoples[a] under me.

[3] Lord, what are human beings that you
    care for them,
  mere mortals that you think of them?
[4] They are like a breath;
  their days are like a fleeting shadow.

[5] Part your heavens, Lord, and come down;
  touch the mountains, so that they
    smoke.
[6] Send forth lightning and scatter the
    enemy;
  shoot your arrows and rout them.
[7] Reach down your hand from on high;
  deliver me and rescue me
from the mighty waters,
  from the hands of foreigners
[8] whose mouths are full of lies,

whose right hands are deceitful.

[9] I will sing a new song to you, my God;
  on the ten-stringed lyre I will make
    music to you,
[10] to the One who gives victory to kings,
  who delivers his servant David.

From the deadly sword [11] deliver me;
  rescue me from the hands of
    foreigners
whose mouths are full of lies,
  whose right hands are deceitful.

[12] Then our sons in their youth
  will be like well-nurtured plants,
and our daughters will be like pillars
  carved to adorn a palace.
[13] Our barns will be filled
  with every kind of provision.
Our sheep will increase by thousands,
  by tens of thousands in our fields;
[14]   our oxen will draw heavy loads.[b]
There will be no breaching of walls,
  no going into captivity,
  no cry of distress in our streets.
[15] Blessed is the people of whom this is true;
  blessed is the people whose God is
    the Lord.

Psalm 145[c]

A psalm of praise. Of David.

[1] I will exalt you, my God the King;
  I will praise your name for ever and
    ever.
[2] Every day I will praise you
  and extol your name for ever and
    ever.

[3] Great is the Lord and most worthy of
    praise;
  his greatness no one can fathom.
[4] One generation commends your works
    to another;
  they tell of your mighty acts.
[5] They speak of the glorious splendor of
    your majesty—
  and I will meditate on your wonderful
    works.[d]
[6] They tell of the power of your awesome
    works—

---

a 2 Many manuscripts of the Masoretic Text, Dead Sea Scrolls, Aquila, Jerome and Syriac; most
manuscripts of the Masoretic Text *subdues my people*   *b 14* Or *our chieftains will be firmly established*
c This psalm is an acrostic poem, the verses of which (including verse 13b) begin with the successive
letters of the Hebrew alphabet.   *d 5* Dead Sea Scrolls and Syriac (see also Septuagint); Masoretic Text
On the glorious splendor of your majesty / and on your wonderful works I will meditate

and I will proclaim your great deeds.
7 They celebrate your abundant goodness
and joyfully sing of your
righteousness.

8 The LORD is gracious and compassionate,
slow to anger and rich in love.

9 The LORD is good to all;
he has compassion on all he has
made.

10 All your works praise you, LORD;
your faithful people extol you.

11 They tell of the glory of your kingdom
and speak of your might,

12 so that all people may know of your
mighty acts
and the glorious splendor of your
kingdom.

13 Your kingdom is an everlasting kingdom,
and your dominion endures through
all generations.

The LORD is trustworthy in all he
promises
and faithful in all he does. a

14 The LORD upholds all who fall
and lifts up all who are bowed down.

15 The eyes of all look to you,
and you give them their food at the
proper time.

16 You open your hand
and satisfy the desires of every living
thing.

17 The LORD is righteous in all his ways
and faithful in all he does.

18 The LORD is near to all who call on him,
to all who call on him in truth.

19 He fulfills the desires of those who fear
him;
he hears their cry and saves them.

20 The LORD watches over all who love him,
but all the wicked he will destroy.

21 My mouth will speak in praise of the LORD.
Let every creature praise his holy name
for ever and ever.

Psalm 146

1 Praise the LORD. b

Praise the LORD, my soul.

2 I will praise the LORD all my life;

I will sing praise to my God as long as
I live.

3 Do not put your trust in princes,
in human beings, who cannot save.

4 When their spirit departs, they return to
the ground;
on that very day their plans come to
nothing.

5 Blessed are those whose help is the God
of Jacob,
whose hope is in the LORD their God.

6 He is the Maker of heaven and earth,
the sea, and everything in them—
he remains faithful forever.

7 He upholds the cause of the oppressed
and gives food to the hungry.

The LORD sets prisoners free,
8   the LORD gives sight to the blind,
the LORD lifts up those who are bowed
down,
the LORD loves the righteous.

9 The LORD watches over the foreigner
and sustains the fatherless and the
widow,
but he frustrates the ways of the
wicked.

10 The LORD reigns forever,
your God, O Zion, for all generations.

Praise the LORD.

Psalm 147

1 Praise the LORD. c

How good it is to sing praises to our God,
how pleasant and fitting to praise
him!

2 The LORD builds up Jerusalem;
he gathers the exiles of Israel.

3 He heals the brokenhearted
and binds up their wounds.

4 He determines the number of the stars
and calls them each by name.

5 Great is our Lord and mighty in power;
his understanding has no limit.

6 The LORD sustains the humble
but casts the wicked to the ground.

7 Sing to the LORD with grateful praise;
make music to our God on the harp.

8 He covers the sky with clouds;

---

a 13 One manuscript of the Masoretic Text, Dead Sea Scrolls and Syriac (see also Septuagint); most
manuscripts of the Masoretic Text do not have the last two lines of verse 13.   b 1 Hebrew Hallelu Yah;
also in verse 10   c 1 Hebrew Hallelu Yah; also in verse 20

WEDNESDAY

GOD'S PASSION FOR YOU

Psalm 147:1–20 *or* 147:10–11

JULIAN OF NORWICH {AD 1342–ca. 1416}

Just as our flesh is covered by clothing, and our blood is covered by our flesh, so are we, soul and body, covered and enclosed by the goodness of God. Yet, the clothing and the flesh will pass away, but the goodness of God will always remain and will remain closer to us than our own flesh.

God only desires that our soul cling to him with all of its strength, in particular, that it cling to his goodness. For of all of the things our minds can think about God, it is thinking upon his goodness that pleases him most and brings the most profit to our soul.

For we are so preciously loved by God that we cannot even comprehend it. No created being can ever know how much and how sweetly and tenderly God loves them. It is only with the help of his grace that we are able to persevere in spiritual contemplation with endless wonder at his high, surpassing, immeasurable love which our Lord in his goodness has for us.

Therefore we may ask from our Lover to have all of him that we desire. For it is our nature to long for him, and it is his nature to long for us. In this life we can never stop loving him.

S. J. Hill

You make [God] leap for joy. You make His heart beat faster. In Zephaniah 3:17, the Bible even says you make Him sing for joy. Whether you understand that or not doesn't stop God from responding to you in that way. He looks at you and grins. He sees your hair, your skin, your smile, and He rejoices ...

The truth is, God really likes you. In fact, He enjoys you. You may not think you measure up to supermodel or Mr. GQ status, but He does. Thanks to the gracious act of His Son, He sees you perfectly redeemed.

He isn't tolerating you. He isn't putting up with you. He isn't waiting for you to get older or more mature in your Christian walk before He can love or enjoy you. He loves you right where you are. Through the blood of Jesus, you're perfectly redeemed.

reflection

1. How does the pleasure that children bring their parents compare with the enjoyment God finds in his children?

2. Is it difficult for you to fully embrace the truth that you bring God pleasure? Why?

3. In what ways can you enjoy God's goodness in the upcoming week?

For your next devotional reading, go to page 703.

he supplies the earth with rain
and makes grass grow on the hills.
⁹ He provides food for the cattle
and for the young ravens when they
call.

¹⁰ His pleasure is not in the strength of the
horse,
nor his delight in the power of human
legs;
¹¹ the Lord delights in those who fear him,
who put their hope in his unfailing
love.

¹² Extol the Lord, Jerusalem;
praise your God, Zion.
¹³ He strengthens the bars of your gates
and blesses your people within you.
¹⁴ He grants peace to your borders
and satisfies you with the finest of
wheat.

¹⁵ He sends his command to the earth;
his word runs swiftly.
¹⁶ He spreads the snow like wool
and scatters the frost like ashes.
¹⁷ He hurls down his hail like pebbles.
Who can withstand his icy blast?
¹⁸ He sends his word and melts them;
he stirs up his breezes, and the waters
flow.

¹⁹ He has revealed his word to Jacob,
his laws and decrees to Israel.
²⁰ He has done this for no other nation;
they do not know his laws.ᵃ

Praise the Lord.

Psalm 148

¹ Praise the Lord.ᵇ

Praise the Lord from the heavens;
praise him in the heights above.
² Praise him, all his angels;
praise him, all his heavenly hosts.
³ Praise him, sun and moon;
praise him, all you shining stars.
⁴ Praise him, you highest heavens
and you waters above the skies.

⁵ Let them praise the name of the Lord,
for at his command they were created,

⁶ and he established them for ever and
ever—
he issued a decree that will never
pass away.

⁷ Praise the Lord from the earth,
you great sea creatures and all ocean
depths,
⁸ lightning and hail, snow and clouds,
stormy winds that do his bidding,
⁹ you mountains and all hills,
fruit trees and all cedars,
¹⁰ wild animals and all cattle,
small creatures and flying birds,
¹¹ kings of the earth and all nations,
you princes and all rulers on earth,
¹² young men and women,
old men and children.

¹³ Let them praise the name of the Lord,
for his name alone is exalted;
his splendor is above the earth and
the heavens.
¹⁴ And he has raised up for his people a
horn,ᶜ
the praise of all his faithful servants,
of Israel, the people close to his heart.

Praise the Lord.

Psalm 149

¹ Praise the Lord.ᵈ

Sing to the Lord a new song,
his praise in the assembly of his
faithful people.

² Let Israel rejoice in their Maker;
let the people of Zion be glad in their
King.
³ Let them praise his name with dancing
and make music to him with timbrel
and harp.
⁴ For the Lord takes delight in his people;
he crowns the humble with victory.
⁵ Let his faithful people rejoice in this
honor
and sing for joy on their beds.

⁶ May the praise of God be in their
mouths
and a double-edged sword in their
hands,
⁷ to inflict vengeance on the nations

ᵃ 20 Masoretic Text; Dead Sea Scrolls and Septuagint / he has not made his laws known to them
ᵇ 1 Hebrew Hallelu Yah; also in verse 14   ᶜ 14 Horn here symbolizes strength.   ᵈ 1 Hebrew Hallelu
Yah; also in verse 9

THURSDAY

TOTAL ABANDON

Psalm 150:1–6 *or* 150:6

THOMAS WATSON {AD 1620–1686}

Let us praise God with the best instrument: the heart. And let us turn up the volume on the instrument as loud as it can go! Let us praise him with our whole heart. See how David's praise escalates when he says, "Rejoice in the LORD and be glad, you righteous; sing" (Psalm 32:11). Rejoice, there is cheerfulness. Be glad, there is thankfulness. Sing, there is triumph.

Praise is called incense because it is like a sweet-smelling sacrifice to the Lord. Let God's people be the choir that sings God's praises. The deepest springs yield the sweetest water; the more deeply aware we are of God's covenant-love for us, the sweeter our praises will be. We should begin here to immortalize God's name, to do the work of praising God on earth just as we will praise him for eternity in heaven. Like the psalmist, we should say, "I will praise the LORD all my life" (Psalm 146:2).

Walter Brueggemann

Israel's most characteristic utterance in worship is *praise*, the exuberant rhetorical act of gladly ceding one's life and the life of the world over to YHWH in joyous self-abandonment. Such praise is the concrete, bodily act of situating one's life in the power and presence of the one addressed, a willingness to hold nothing back for autonomous control, but a trustful submission to [God].

reflection

1. What holds you back from praising God with complete and total abandon?
2. How can focusing on the greatness of God's love make your praise stronger and sweeter?
3. How can your heart praise God today?

For your next devotional reading, go to page 713.

and punishment on the peoples,
⁸to bind their kings with fetters,
their nobles with shackles of iron,
⁹to carry out the sentence written against
them—
this is the glory of all his faithful
people.

Praise the LORD.

Psalm 150

¹Praise the LORD.ᵃ

Praise God in his sanctuary;
praise him in his mighty heavens.

²Praise him for his acts of power;
praise him for his surpassing
greatness.
³Praise him with the sounding of the
trumpet,
praise him with the harp and lyre,
⁴praise him with timbrel and dancing,
praise him with the strings and pipe,
⁵praise him with the clash of cymbals,
praise him with resounding cymbals.

⁶Let everything that has breath praise the
LORD.

Praise the LORD.

ᵃ 1 Hebrew *Hallelu Yah*; also in verse 6

proverbs

AUTHOR: Primarily King Solomon

DATE: Solomon wrote most of the proverbs during his reign (970–930 B.C.), but the book wasn't fully compiled until around 700 B.C.

THEME: God is the source of wisdom.

Purpose and Theme

1 The proverbs of Solomon son of David, king of Israel:

2 for gaining wisdom and instruction;
  for understanding words of insight;
3 for receiving instruction in prudent behavior,
  doing what is right and just and fair;
4 for giving prudence to those who are simple,[a]
  knowledge and discretion to the young—
5 let the wise listen and add to their learning,
  and let the discerning get guidance—
6 for understanding proverbs and parables,
  the sayings and riddles of the wise.[b]

7 The fear of the LORD is the beginning of knowledge,
  but fools[c] despise wisdom and instruction.

Prologue: Exhortations to Embrace Wisdom

Warning Against the Invitation of Sinful Men

8 Listen, my son, to your father's instruction
  and do not forsake your mother's teaching.
9 They are a garland to grace your head
  and a chain to adorn your neck.

10 My son, if sinful men entice you,
  do not give in to them.
11 If they say, "Come along with us;
  let's lie in wait for innocent blood,
  let's ambush some harmless soul;
12 let's swallow them alive, like the grave,
  and whole, like those who go down to the pit;
13 we will get all sorts of valuable things
  and fill our houses with plunder;
14 cast lots with us;
  we will all share the loot"—
15 my son, do not go along with them,
  do not set foot on their paths;
16 for their feet rush into evil,
  they are swift to shed blood.
17 How useless to spread a net
  where every bird can see it!
18 These men lie in wait for their own blood;
  they ambush only themselves!
19 Such are the paths of all who go after ill-gotten gain;
  it takes away the life of those who get it.

Wisdom's Rebuke

20 Out in the open wisdom calls aloud,
  she raises her voice in the public square;
21 on top of the wall[d] she cries out,
  at the city gate she makes her speech:

22 "How long will you who are simple love your simple ways?
  How long will mockers delight in mockery
  and fools hate knowledge?
23 Repent at my rebuke!

a 4 The Hebrew word rendered *simple* in Proverbs denotes a person who is gullible, without moral direction and inclined to evil.   b 6 Or *understanding a proverb, namely, a parable, / and the sayings of the wise, their riddles*   c 7 The Hebrew words rendered *fool* in Proverbs, and often elsewhere in the Old Testament, denote a person who is morally deficient.   d 21 Septuagint; Hebrew / *at noisy street corners*

Then I will pour out my thoughts to
you,
I will make known to you my
teachings.
24 But since you refuse to listen when I call
and no one pays attention when I
stretch out my hand,
25 since you disregard all my advice
and do not accept my rebuke,
26 I in turn will laugh when disaster strikes
you;
I will mock when calamity overtakes
you—
27 when calamity overtakes you like a
storm,
when disaster sweeps over you like a
whirlwind,
when distress and trouble overwhelm
you.

28 "Then they will call to me but I will not
answer;
they will look for me but will not find
me,
29 since they hated knowledge
and did not choose to fear the LORD.
30 Since they would not accept my advice
and spurned my rebuke,
31 they will eat the fruit of their ways
and be filled with the fruit of their
schemes.
32 For the waywardness of the simple will
kill them,
and the complacency of fools will
destroy them;
33 but whoever listens to me will live in
safety
and be at ease, without fear of harm."

Moral Benefits of Wisdom

2 My son, if you accept my words
and store up my commands within
you,
2 turning your ear to wisdom
and applying your heart to
understanding—
3 indeed, if you call out for insight
and cry aloud for understanding,
4 and if you look for it as for silver
and search for it as for hidden
treasure,
5 then you will understand the fear of the
LORD
and find the knowledge of God.

6 For the LORD gives wisdom;
from his mouth come knowledge and
understanding.
7 He holds success in store for the
upright,
he is a shield to those whose walk is
blameless,
8 for he guards the course of the just
and protects the way of his faithful
ones.

9 Then you will understand what is right
and just
and fair—every good path.
10 For wisdom will enter your heart,
and knowledge will be pleasant to
your soul.
11 Discretion will protect you,
and understanding will guard you.

12 Wisdom will save you from the ways of
wicked men,
from men whose words are perverse,
13 who have left the straight paths
to walk in dark ways,
14 who delight in doing wrong
and rejoice in the perverseness of
evil,
15 whose paths are crooked
and who are devious in their ways.

16 Wisdom will save you also from the
adulterous woman,
from the wayward woman with her
seductive words,
17 who has left the partner of her youth
and ignored the covenant she made
before God. *a*
18 Surely her house leads down to death
and her paths to the spirits of the
dead.
19 None who go to her return
or attain the paths of life.

20 Thus you will walk in the ways of the
just
and keep to the paths of the
righteous.
21 For the upright will live in the land,
and the blameless will remain in it;
22 but the wicked will be cut off from the
land,
and the unfaithful will be torn from it.

a 17 Or *covenant of her God*

Wisdom Bestows Well-Being

3 My son, do not forget my teaching,
 but keep my commands in your
  heart,
² for they will prolong your life many
   years
 and bring you peace and prosperity.

³ Let love and faithfulness never leave
  you;
 bind them around your neck,
 write them on the tablet of your
  heart.
⁴ Then you will win favor and a good
  name
 in the sight of God and humankind.

⁵ Trust in the LORD with all your heart
 and lean not on your own
  understanding;
⁶ in all your ways submit to him,
 and he will make your paths straight. *ᵃ*

⁷ Do not be wise in your own eyes;
 fear the LORD and shun evil.
⁸ This will bring health to your body
 and nourishment to your bones.

⁹ Honor the LORD with your wealth,
 with the firstfruits of all your crops;
¹⁰ then your barns will be filled to
  overflowing,
 and your vats will brim over with new
  wine.

¹¹ My son, do not despise the LORD's
  discipline,
 and do not resent his rebuke,
¹² because the LORD disciplines those he
  loves,
 as a father the son he delights in. *ᵇ*

¹³ Blessed are those who find wisdom,
 those who gain understanding,
¹⁴ for she is more profitable than silver
 and yields better returns than gold.
¹⁵ She is more precious than rubies;
 nothing you desire can compare with
  her.
¹⁶ Long life is in her right hand;
 in her left hand are riches and honor.
¹⁷ Her ways are pleasant ways,
 and all her paths are peace.
¹⁸ She is a tree of life to those who take
  hold of her;

those who hold her fast will be
 blessed.

¹⁹ By wisdom the LORD laid the earth's
  foundations,
 by understanding he set the heavens
  in place;
²⁰ by his knowledge the deeps were
  divided,
 and the clouds let drop the dew.

²¹ My son, do not let wisdom and
   understanding out of your
   sight,
 preserve sound judgment and
  discretion;
²² they will be life for you,
 an ornament to grace your neck.
²³ Then you will go on your way in safety,
 and your foot will not stumble.
²⁴ When you lie down, you will not be
  afraid;
 when you lie down, your sleep will be
  sweet.
²⁵ Have no fear of sudden disaster
 or of the ruin that overtakes the
  wicked,
²⁶ for the LORD will be at your side
 and will keep your foot from being
  snared.

²⁷ Do not withhold good from those to
   whom it is due,
 when it is in your power to act.
²⁸ Do not say to your neighbor,
 "Come back tomorrow and I'll give it
  to you"—
 when you already have it with you.
²⁹ Do not plot harm against your neighbor,
 who lives trustfully near you.
³⁰ Do not accuse anyone for no reason—
 when they have done you no harm.

³¹ Do not envy the violent
 or choose any of their ways.

³² For the LORD detests the perverse
 but takes the upright into his
  confidence.
³³ The LORD's curse is on the house of the
  wicked,
 but he blesses the home of the
  righteous.
³⁴ He mocks proud mockers
 but shows favor to the humble and
  oppressed.

ᵃ 6 Or *will direct your paths*   *ᵇ 12* Hebrew; Septuagint / *and he chastens everyone he accepts as his child*

35 The wise inherit honor,
  but fools get only shame.

Get Wisdom at Any Cost

4 Listen, my sons, to a father's
  instruction;
  pay attention and gain
    understanding.
2 I give you sound learning,
  so do not forsake my teaching.
3 For I too was a son to my father,
  still tender, and cherished by my
    mother.
4 Then he taught me, and he said to me,
  "Take hold of my words with all your
    heart;
  keep my commands, and you will live.
5 Get wisdom, get understanding;
  do not forget my words or turn away
    from them.
6 Do not forsake wisdom, and she will
    protect you;
  love her, and she will watch over you.
7 The beginning of wisdom is this: Get*a*
    wisdom.
  Though it cost all you have,*b* get
    understanding.
8 Cherish her, and she will exalt you;
  embrace her, and she will honor you.
9 She will give you a garland to grace your
    head
  and present you with a glorious
    crown."

10 Listen, my son, accept what I say,
  and the years of your life will be
    many.
11 I instruct you in the way of wisdom
  and lead you along straight paths.
12 When you walk, your steps will not be
    hampered;
  when you run, you will not stumble.
13 Hold on to instruction, do not let it go;
  guard it well, for it is your life.
14 Do not set foot on the path of the
    wicked
  or walk in the way of evildoers.
15 Avoid it, do not travel on it;
  turn from it and go on your way.
16 For they cannot rest until they do evil;
  they are robbed of sleep till they
    make someone stumble.
17 They eat the bread of wickedness

and drink the wine of violence.
18 The path of the righteous is like the
    morning sun,
  shining ever brighter till the full light
    of day.
19 But the way of the wicked is like deep
    darkness;
  they do not know what makes them
    stumble.

20 My son, pay attention to what I say;
  turn your ear to my words.
21 Do not let them out of your sight,
  keep them within your heart;
22 for they are life to those who find them
  and health to one's whole body.
23 Above all else, guard your heart,
  for everything you do flows from it.
24 Keep your mouth free of perversity;
  keep corrupt talk far from your lips.
25 Let your eyes look straight ahead;
  fix your gaze directly before you.
26 Give careful thought to the*c* paths for
    your feet
  and be steadfast in all your ways.
27 Do not turn to the right or the left;
  keep your foot from evil.

Warning Against Adultery

5 My son, pay attention to my wisdom,
  turn your ear to my words of
    insight,
2 that you may maintain discretion
  and your lips may preserve
    knowledge.
3 For the lips of the adulterous woman
    drip honey,
  and her speech is smoother than oil;
4 but in the end she is bitter as gall,
  sharp as a double-edged sword.
5 Her feet go down to death;
  her steps lead straight to the grave.
6 She gives no thought to the way of life;
  her paths wander aimlessly, but she
    does not know it.

7 Now then, my sons, listen to me;
  do not turn aside from what I say.
8 Keep to a path far from her,
  do not go near the door of her house,
9 lest you lose your honor to others
  and your dignity*d* to one who is cruel,
10 lest strangers feast on your wealth

---

a 7 Or *Wisdom is supreme; therefore get*   *b* 7 Or *Whatever else you get*   *c* 26 Or *Make level*
d 9 Or *years*

and your toil enrich the house of
another.
¹¹ At the end of your life you will groan,
when your flesh and body are spent.
¹² You will say, "How I hated discipline!
How my heart spurned correction!
¹³ I would not obey my teachers
or turn my ear to my instructors.
¹⁴ And I was soon in serious trouble
in the assembly of God's people."

¹⁵ Drink water from your own cistern,
running water from your own well.
¹⁶ Should your springs overflow in the
streets,
your streams of water in the public
squares?
¹⁷ Let them be yours alone,
never to be shared with strangers.
¹⁸ May your fountain be blessed,
and may you rejoice in the wife of
your youth.
¹⁹ A loving doe, a graceful deer—
may her breasts satisfy you always,
may you ever be intoxicated with her
love.
²⁰ Why, my son, be intoxicated with
another man's wife?
Why embrace the bosom of a
wayward woman?

²¹ For your ways are in full view of the
LORD,
and he examines all your paths.
²² The evil deeds of the wicked ensnare
them;
the cords of their sins hold them fast.
²³ For lack of discipline they will die,
led astray by their own great folly.

Warnings Against Folly

6 My son, if you have put up security
for your neighbor,
if you have shaken hands in pledge
for a stranger,
² you have been trapped by what you said,
ensnared by the words of your mouth.
³ So do this, my son, to free yourself,
since you have fallen into your
neighbor's hands:
Go—to the point of exhaustion—ᵃ
and give your neighbor no rest!
⁴ Allow no sleep to your eyes,
no slumber to your eyelids.

⁵ Free yourself, like a gazelle from the
hand of the hunter,
like a bird from the snare of the
fowler.

⁶ Go to the ant, you sluggard;
consider its ways and be wise!
⁷ It has no commander,
no overseer or ruler,
⁸ yet it stores its provisions in summer
and gathers its food at harvest.

⁹ How long will you lie there, you
sluggard?
When will you get up from your
sleep?
¹⁰ A little sleep, a little slumber,
a little folding of the hands to rest—
¹¹ and poverty will come on you like a thief
and scarcity like an armed man.

¹² Troublemakers and villains,
who go about with corrupt mouths,
¹³   who wink maliciously with their eyes,
signal with their feet
and motion with their fingers,
¹⁴   who plot evil with deceit in their
hearts—
they always stir up dissension.
¹⁵ Therefore disaster will overtake them in
an instant;
they will suddenly be destroyed—
without remedy.

¹⁶ There are six things the LORD hates,
seven that are detestable to him:
¹⁷   haughty eyes,
a lying tongue,
hands that shed innocent blood,
¹⁸   a heart that devises wicked
schemes,
feet that are quick to rush into evil,
¹⁹   a false witness who pours out lies
and a person who stirs up
dissension in the community.

Warning Against Adultery

²⁰ My son, keep your father's command
and do not forsake your mother's
teaching.
²¹ Bind them always on your heart;
fasten them around your neck.
²² When you walk, they will guide you;
when you sleep, they will watch over
you;

ᵃ 3 Or *Go and humble yourself,*

when you awake, they will speak to
you.
²³ For this command is a lamp,
this teaching is a light,
and correction and instruction
are the way to life,
²⁴ keeping you from your neighbor's wife,
from the smooth talk of a wayward
woman.

²⁵ Do not lust in your heart after her beauty
or let her captivate you with her eyes.
²⁶ For a prostitute can be had for a loaf of
bread,
but another man's wife preys on your
very life.
²⁷ Can a man scoop fire into his lap
without his clothes being burned?
²⁸ Can a man walk on hot coals
without his feet being scorched?
²⁹ So is he who sleeps with another man's
wife;
no one who touches her will go
unpunished.

³⁰ People do not despise a thief if he steals
to satisfy his hunger when he is
starving.
³¹ Yet if he is caught, he must pay sevenfold,
though it costs him all the wealth of
his house.
³² But a man who commits adultery has no
sense;
whoever does so destroys himself.
³³ Blows and disgrace are his lot,
and his shame will never be wiped
away.
³⁴ For jealousy arouses a husband's fury,
and he will show no mercy when he
takes revenge.
³⁵ He will not accept any compensation;
he will refuse a bribe, however great
it is.

Warning Against the Adulterous Woman

7 My son, keep my words
and store up my commands
within you.
² Keep my commands and you will live;
guard my teachings as the apple of
your eye.
³ Bind them on your fingers;

write them on the tablet of your
heart.
⁴ Say to wisdom, "You are my sister,"
and to insight, "You are my relative."
⁵ They will keep you from the adulterous
woman,
from the wayward woman with her
seductive words.

⁶ At the window of my house
I looked down through the lattice.
⁷ I saw among the simple,
I noticed among the young men,
a youth who had no sense.
⁸ He was going down the street near her
corner,
walking along in the direction of her
house
⁹ at twilight, as the day was fading,
as the dark of night set in.

¹⁰ Then out came a woman to meet him,
dressed like a prostitute and with
crafty intent.
¹¹ (She is unruly and defiant,
her feet never stay at home;
¹² now in the street, now in the squares,
at every corner she lurks.)
¹³ She took hold of him and kissed him
and with a brazen face she said:

¹⁴ "Today I fulfilled my vows,
and I have food from my fellowship
offering at home.
¹⁵ So I came out to meet you;
I looked for you and have found you!
¹⁶ I have covered my bed
with colored linens from Egypt.
¹⁷ I have perfumed my bed
with myrrh, aloes and cinnamon.
¹⁸ Come, let's drink deep of love till
morning;
let's enjoy ourselves with love!
¹⁹ My husband is not at home;
he has gone on a long journey.
²⁰ He took his purse filled with money
and will not be home till full moon."

²¹ With persuasive words she led him astray;
she seduced him with her smooth
talk.
²² All at once he followed her
like an ox going to the slaughter,
like a deer*ᵃ* stepping into a noose*ᵇ*

ᵃ 22 Syriac (see also Septuagint); Hebrew *fool*
uncertain.   *ᵇ 22* The meaning of the Hebrew for this line is

²³ till an arrow pierces his liver,
    like a bird darting into a snare,
        little knowing it will cost him his life.

²⁴ Now then, my sons, listen to me;
    pay attention to what I say.
²⁵ Do not let your heart turn to her ways
    or stray into her paths.
²⁶ Many are the victims she has brought
    down;
        her slain are a mighty throng.
²⁷ Her house is a highway to the grave,
    leading down to the chambers of
        death.

Wisdom's Call

8 Does not wisdom call out?
    Does not understanding raise her
        voice?
² At the highest point along the way,
    where the paths meet, she takes her
        stand;
³ beside the gate leading into the city,
    at the entrance, she cries aloud:
⁴ "To you, O people, I call out;
    I raise my voice to all humankind.
⁵ You who are simple, gain prudence;
    you who are foolish, set your hearts
        on it. ᵃ
⁶ Listen, for I have trustworthy things to
        say;
    I open my lips to speak what is right.
⁷ My mouth speaks what is true,
    for my lips detest wickedness.
⁸ All the words of my mouth are just;
    none of them is crooked or perverse.
⁹ To the discerning all of them are right;
    they are upright to those who have
        found knowledge.
¹⁰ Choose my instruction instead of silver,
    knowledge rather than choice gold,
¹¹ for wisdom is more precious than rubies,
    and nothing you desire can compare
        with her.

¹² "I, wisdom, dwell together with
        prudence;
    I possess knowledge and discretion.
¹³ To fear the LORD is to hate evil;
    I hate pride and arrogance,
        evil behavior and perverse speech.
¹⁴ Counsel and sound judgment are mine;

I have insight, I have power.
¹⁵ By me kings reign
    and rulers issue decrees that are just;
¹⁶ by me princes govern,
    and nobles—all who rule on earth. ᵇ
¹⁷ I love those who love me,
    and those who seek me find me.
¹⁸ With me are riches and honor,
    enduring wealth and prosperity.
¹⁹ My fruit is better than fine gold;
    what I yield surpasses choice silver.
²⁰ I walk in the way of righteousness,
    along the paths of justice,
²¹ bestowing a rich inheritance on those
        who love me
    and making their treasuries full.

²² "The LORD brought me forth as the first
        of his works, ᶜ,ᵈ
    before his deeds of old;
²³ I was formed long ages ago,
    at the very beginning, when the world
        came to be.
²⁴ When there were no oceans, I was given
        birth,
    when there were no springs
        abounding with water;
²⁵ before the mountains were settled in
        place,
    before the hills, I was given birth,
²⁶ before he made the world or its fields
    or any of the dust of the earth.
²⁷ I was there when he set the heavens in
        place,
    when he marked out the horizon on
        the face of the deep,
²⁸ when he established the clouds above
    and fixed securely the fountains of
        the deep,
²⁹ when he gave the sea its boundary
    so the waters would not overstep his
        command,
    and when he marked out the
        foundations of the earth.
³⁰ Then I was constantlyᵉ at his side.
    I was filled with delight day after day,
        rejoicing always in his presence,
³¹ rejoicing in his whole world
    and delighting in humankind.

³² "Now then, my children, listen to me;
    blessed are those who keep my ways.

ᵃ 5 Septuagint; Hebrew *foolish, instruct your minds*   ᵇ 16 Some Hebrew manuscripts and Septuagint;
other Hebrew manuscripts *all righteous rulers*   ᶜ 22 Or *way;* or *dominion*   ᵈ 22 Or *The LORD possessed
me at the beginning of his work;* or *The LORD brought me forth at the beginning of his work*   ᵉ 30 Or *was
the artisan;* or *was a little child*

33 Listen to my instruction and be wise;
  do not disregard it.
34 Blessed are those who listen to me,
  watching daily at my doors,
  waiting at my doorway.
35 For those who find me find life
  and receive favor from the LORD.
36 But those who fail to find me harm
  themselves;
  all who hate me love death."

Invitations of Wisdom and Folly

9 Wisdom has built her house;
  she has set up[a] its seven pillars.
2 She has prepared her meat and
  mixed her wine;
  she has also set her table.
3 She has sent out her servants, and she
  calls
  from the highest point of the city,
4 "Let all who are simple come to my
  house!"
To those who have no sense she says,
5 "Come, eat my food
  and drink the wine I have mixed.
6 Leave your simple ways and you will
  live;
  walk in the way of insight."

7 Whoever corrects a mocker invites
  insults;
  whoever rebukes the wicked incurs
  abuse.
8 Do not rebuke mockers or they will hate
  you;
  rebuke the wise and they will love
  you.
9 Instruct the wise and they will be wiser
  still;
  teach the righteous and they will add
  to their learning.

10 The fear of the LORD is the beginning of
  wisdom,
  and knowledge of the Holy One is
  understanding.
11 For through wisdom[b] your days will be
  many,
  and years will be added to your life.
12 If you are wise, your wisdom will reward
  you;
  if you are a mocker, you alone will
  suffer.

13 Folly is an unruly woman;
  she is simple and knows nothing.
14 She sits at the door of her house,
  on a seat at the highest point of the
  city,
15 calling out to those who pass by,
  who go straight on their way,
16 "Let all who are simple come to my
  house!"
To those who have no sense she says,
17 "Stolen water is sweet;
  food eaten in secret is delicious!"
18 But little do they know that the dead are
  there,
  that her guests are deep in the realm
  of the dead.

Proverbs of Solomon

10 The proverbs of Solomon:

Wise children bring joy to their
  father,
  but foolish children bring grief to
  their mother.

2 Ill-gotten treasures have no lasting
  value,
  but righteousness delivers from
  death.

3 The LORD does not let the righteous go
  hungry,
  but he thwarts the craving of the
  wicked.

4 Lazy hands make for poverty,
  but diligent hands bring wealth.

5 He who gathers crops in summer is a
  prudent son,
  but he who sleeps during harvest is a
  disgraceful son.

6 Blessings crown the head of the
  righteous,
  but violence overwhelms the mouth
  of the wicked.[c]

7 The name of the righteous is used in
  blessings,[d]
  but the name of the wicked will rot.

8 The wise in heart accept commands,
  but a chattering fool comes to ruin.

a 1 Septuagint, Syriac and Targum; Hebrew *has hewn out*   b 11 Septuagint, Syriac and Targum;
Hebrew *me*   c 6 Or *but the mouth of the wicked conceals violence*   d 7 See Gen. 48:20.

FRIDAY

HUMILITY FIRST—THEN WISDOM

Proverbs 9:1–18 *or* 9:9–10

Kurt Bruner

Winston Churchill said that man occasionally stumbles over the truth, but most of the time he will pick himself up and continue on. It is an everyday occurrence. We bump into one of God's messages, confronted and floored by ultimate reality, only to look around to make sure no one was watching. Then we hurry off as if nothing had happened.

We restrain tears during a touching dramatic scene—damming up emotion that might have felt God's heart.

We pretend to follow a conversation miles over our heads—missing an opportunity to learn by concealing ignorance.

We admire the religious conviction of others from a safe distance—respecting sincere belief while resisting the urge to embrace its demands.

Where do such avoidance techniques get us? Further away from the truth . . .

Might I plead for a little humility, the kind of humility that puts us on the road to sanity? Pride talks; humility listens. Pride postures; humility prostrates. Pride is easy; humility is hard. Let's take the hard road for a moment by admitting that none of us have it all together. None of us possess all the answers. None of us control the universe of our lives. Rather than hurry off, let's pause long enough to reflect upon what we suspect is true: that there is a God who can be known, and that deep down we both crave and dread that knowledge.

MIGUEL DE MOLINOS {ca. AD 1640–1697}

Encourage yourself to be humble, embracing trials as instruments for good toward that end. Rejoice when you experience contempt, and desire that God may be your only refuge, comfort and protector in it . . .

The truly humble person finds God in all things. Therefore, whatever contempt, injury or affront comes to them by means of another creature, they receive it with great peace and internal quiet. For they see it as sent from the divine hand, and they love greatly the instrument with which the Lord tests them.

reflection

1. Why is humility necessary if you want to really know God?

2. What's the difference between working hard at looking like you genuinely know God and working hard at genuinely knowing God?

3. In which of these two areas do you spend more of your energy?

For your next devotional reading, go to page 715.

9 Whoever walks in integrity walks
   securely,
      but whoever takes crooked paths will
      be found out.

10 Whoever winks maliciously causes grief,
      and a chattering fool comes to ruin.

11 The mouth of the righteous is a fountain
   of life,
      but the mouth of the wicked conceals
      violence.

12 Hatred stirs up dissension,
      but love covers over all wrongs.

13 Wisdom is found on the lips of the
   discerning,
      but a rod is for the back of one who
      has no sense.

14 The wise store up knowledge,
      but the mouth of a fool invites ruin.

15 The wealth of the rich is their fortified
   city,
      but poverty is the ruin of the poor.

16 The wages of the righteous is life,
      but the earnings of the wicked are sin
      and death.

17 Whoever heeds discipline shows the way
   to life,
      but whoever ignores correction leads
      others astray.

18 Whoever conceals hatred with lying lips
      and spreads slander is a fool.

19 Sin is not ended by multiplying words,
      but the prudent hold their tongues.

20 The tongue of the righteous is choice
   silver,
      but the heart of the wicked is of little
      value.

21 The lips of the righteous nourish many,
      but fools die for lack of sense.

22 The blessing of the LORD brings wealth,
      without painful toil for it.

23 Fools find pleasure in wicked schemes,
      but those who have understanding
      delight in wisdom.

24 What the wicked dread will overtake
   them;
      what the righteous desire will be
      granted.

25 When the storm has swept by, the
   wicked are gone,
      but the righteous stand firm forever.

26 As vinegar to the teeth and smoke to the
   eyes,
      so are sluggards to those who send
      them.

27 The fear of the LORD adds length to life,
      but the years of the wicked are cut
      short.

28 The prospect of the righteous is joy,
      but the hopes of the wicked come to
      nothing.

29 The way of the LORD is a refuge for the
   blameless,
      but it is the ruin of those who do evil.

30 The righteous will never be uprooted,
      but the wicked will not remain in the
      land.

31 From the mouth of the righteous comes
   the fruit of wisdom,
      but a perverse tongue will be
      silenced.

32 The lips of the righteous know what
   finds favor,
      but the mouth of the wicked only
      what is perverse.

11

The LORD detests dishonest
scales,
      but accurate weights find favor
      with him.

2 When pride comes, then comes disgrace,
      but with humility comes wisdom.

3 The integrity of the upright guides them,
      but the unfaithful are destroyed by
      their duplicity.

4 Wealth is worthless in the day of wrath,
      but righteousness delivers from
      death.

5 The righteousness of the blameless
   makes their paths straight,
      but the wicked are brought down by
      their own wickedness.

6 The righteousness of the upright delivers
   them,
      but the unfaithful are trapped by evil
      desires.

7 Hopes placed in mortals die with them;

Wise and Foolish

Proverbs 10:1,8,14

read/meditate

Slowly read these verses three times aloud. Between each reading, spend a few moments in silence, letting your thoughts swing like a pendulum between the images of wisdom and foolishness, building a comparison of the two. Allow God to take you deeper in your understanding of these concepts.

pray

Lay your heart open before God. Allow him to show you the wisdom and foolishness of your life. Be open to unexpected insights from him, and respond honestly to those insights. Be humble in his presence and thankful for his work in you.

contemplate

Take a few moments to enjoy just being in God's presence. Read the verses again. Let God energize you with his truth.

additional reflection

Many men know a great deal, and are all the greater fools for it. To know how to use knowledge is to have wisdom.

—Charles Spurgeon

There is enough light for those who only desire to see the light, and enough darkness for those who only desire the contrary.

—Blaise Pascal

For your next devotional reading, go to page 716.

MONDAY

DANGEROUS PRIDE

Proverbs 11:1–31 *or* 11:2

Kurt Bruner

Socrates had the right idea. Surrounded by modestly smart people who thought themselves brilliant, he enjoyed asking tough questions that revealed their ignorance or inconsistency. He did it so often, in fact, that the elite of his day considered him a nuisance. Eventually, they placed him on trial and required an explanation of his game . . .

Socrates defended himself by explaining that he did not intend to embarrass anyone or undermine common beliefs but rather to learn from those who seemed to have wisdom. The problem was, he found few good answers. As might be expected, this made people angry because, in his words, "my hearers always imagine that I myself possess the wisdom which I find wanting in others: but the truth is, O men of Athens, that God only is wise; and by his answer he intends to show that the wisdom of men is worth little or nothing."

In some ways, Socrates was like my 4-year-old son asking a simple but profound question, the kind I should be able to answer but can't. When I stammer and bluff in embarrassment, it lets air out of the illusion of adult omniscience. [My son] doesn't claim to know the answer. He just wonders why I pretend I do.

After observing such pretense (or worse, self-delusion), Socrates comes to this conclusion: "Well, although I do not suppose that either of us knows anything really beautiful and good, I am better off than he is, for he knows nothing, and thinks that he knows; I neither know nor think that I know. In this latter particular, then, I seem to have slightly the advantage of him."

JOHN WESLEY {AD 1703–1791}

The first advice I would give to those who have been saved from sin by grace is to watch and pray continually against pride. For it is pride not only to ascribe what we have to ourselves, but also to think we have what we do not . . . Be clothed with humility. Let modesty appear in all your words and actions.

reflection

1. Have you ever pretended to be something other than you are? What alternate path does God want you to take?

2. How can you tell if a person is really looking for wisdom?

3. What can help you protect yourself against pride?

For your next devotional reading, go to page 719.

all the promise of[a] their power comes
to nothing.

8 The righteous are rescued from trouble,
and it falls on the wicked instead.

9 With their mouths the godless destroy
their neighbors,
but through knowledge the righteous
escape.

10 When the righteous prosper, the city
rejoices;
when the wicked perish, there are
shouts of joy.

11 Through the blessing of the upright a
city is exalted,
but by the mouth of the wicked it is
destroyed.

12 Those who have no sense deride their
neighbors,
but those who have understanding
hold their tongues.

13 Gossips betray a confidence,
but the trustworthy keep a secret.

14 For lack of guidance a nation falls,
but victory is won through many
advisers.

15 Whoever puts up security for a stranger
will surely suffer,
but whoever refuses to shake hands
in pledge is safe.

16 A kindhearted woman gains honor,
but ruthless men gain only wealth.

17 Those who are kind benefit themselves,
but the cruel bring ruin on
themselves.

18 The wicked earn deceptive wages,
but those who sow righteousness reap
a sure reward.

19 Truly the righteous attain life,
but those who pursue evil go to their
death.

20 The LORD detests those whose hearts are
perverse,
but he delights in those whose ways
are blameless.

21 Be sure of this: The wicked will not go
unpunished,
but those who are righteous will go
free.

22 Like a gold ring in a pig's snout
is a beautiful woman who shows no
discretion.

23 The desire of the righteous ends only in
good,
but the hope of the wicked only in
wrath.

24 One person gives freely, yet gains even
more;
another withholds unduly, but comes
to poverty.

25 A generous person will prosper;
whoever refreshes others will be
refreshed.

26 People curse those who hoard grain,
but they pray God's blessing on those
who are willing to sell.

27 Whoever seeks good finds favor,
but evil comes to those who search
for it.

28 Those who trust in their riches will fall,
but the righteous will thrive like a
green leaf.

29 Those who bring ruin on their families
will inherit only wind,
and the fool will be servant to the wise.

30 The fruit of the righteous is a tree of life,
and those who win souls are wise.

31 If the righteous receive their due on
earth,
how much more the ungodly and the
sinner!

12 Whoever loves discipline loves
knowledge,
but whoever hates correction is
stupid.

2 Good people obtain favor from the LORD,
but he condemns those who devise
wicked schemes.

3 No one can be established through
wickedness,
but the righteous cannot be uprooted.

a 7 Two Hebrew manuscripts; most Hebrew manuscripts, Vulgate, Syriac and Targum *When the wicked
die, their hope perishes; / all they expected from*

4 A wife of noble character is her
husband's crown,
but a disgraceful wife is like decay in
his bones.

5 The plans of the righteous are just,
but the advice of the wicked is
deceitful.

6 The words of the wicked lie in wait for
blood,
but the speech of the upright rescues
them.

7 The wicked are overthrown and are no
more,
but the house of the righteous stands
firm.

8 People are praised according to their
prudence,
and those with warped minds are
despised.

9 Better to be a nobody and yet have a
servant
than pretend to be somebody and
have no food.

10 The righteous care for the needs of their
animals,
but the kindest acts of the wicked are
cruel.

11 Those who work their land will have
abundant food,
but those who chase fantasies have
no sense.

12 The wicked desire the plunder*a* of
evildoers,
but the root of the righteous
flourishes.

13 Evildoers are trapped by their sinful talk,
and so the innocent escape trouble.

14 From the fruit of their lips people are
filled with good things,
and the work of their hands brings
them reward.

15 The way of fools seems right to them,
but the wise listen to advice.

16 Fools show their annoyance at once,
but the prudent overlook an insult.

17 An honest witness tells the truth,
but a false witness tells lies.

18 The words of the reckless pierce like
swords,
but the tongue of the wise brings
healing.

19 Truthful lips endure forever,
but a lying tongue lasts only a
moment.

20 Deceit is in the hearts of those who plot
evil,
but those who promote peace have
joy.

21 No harm overtakes the righteous,
but the wicked have their fill of
trouble.

22 The Lord detests lying lips,
but he delights in people who are
trustworthy.

23 The prudent keep their knowledge to
themselves,
but a fool's heart blurts out folly.

24 Diligent hands will rule,
but laziness ends in forced labor.

25 Anxiety weighs down the heart,
but a kind word cheers it up.

26 The righteous choose their friends
carefully,
but the way of the wicked leads them
astray.

27 The lazy do not roast*b* any game,
but the diligent feed on the riches of
the hunt.

28 In the way of righteousness there is
life;
along that path is immortality.

13

A wise child heeds a parent's
instruction,
but a mocker does not respond
to rebukes.

2 From the fruit of their lips people enjoy
good things,
but the unfaithful have an appetite
for violence.

3 Those who guard their lips preserve their
lives,
but those who speak rashly will come
to ruin.

---

a 12 Or *stronghold*   *b 27* The meaning of the Hebrew for this word is uncertain.

TUESDAY

TRIED AND TRUE

Proverbs 13:1–25 or 13:15

Dallas Willard

"Christianity has not so much been tried and found wanting, as it has been found difficult and left untried." So said that insightful and clever Christian, G. K. Chesterton. Whether or not he was totally serious, there is almost universal belief in the immense difficulty of being a real Christian. The vast, grim "cost of discipleship" is something we hear constantly emphasized. Chesterton's observation can at least be taken as reflecting the attitude of many serious people toward the way of Christ.

But it must not be left to stand as the whole truth. We would do far better to lay a clear, constant emphasis upon the cost of non-discipleship as well. As Søren Kierkegaard reminds us, "It costs a man just as much or even more to go to hell than to come to heaven. Narrow, exceedingly narrow, is the way to perdition."

Proverbs 13:15 tells us that it is the way of the [unfaithful] that is hard. We can also learn this by candid observation of life. Actually, a large part of the Old Testament book of Proverbs merely records the results of such observation ...

To depart from righteousness is to choose a life of crushing burdens, failures and disappointments, a life caught in the toils of endless problems that are never resolved. Here is the source of that unending soap opera, that sometimes horror show known as normal human life. The "cost of discipleship," though it may take all we have, is small when compared to the lot of those who don't accept Christ's invitation to be a part of his company in the way of life.

G. K. CHESTERTON {AD 1874–1936}

My point is that the world did not tire of the church's ideal, but of its reality. Monasteries were impugned not for the purity of monks, but for the impurity of monks. Christianity was unpopular not because of the humility, but because of the arrogance of Christians. Certainly, if the church failed it was largely through the churchmen ... The great ideals of the past failed not by being outlived (which must mean over-lived), but by not being lived enough. Humanity has not passed through the Middle Ages. Rather it has retreated from the Middle Ages in reaction and rout. The Christian ideal has not been tried and found wanting. It has been found difficult and left untried.

reflection

1. What reasons have you heard people give for not getting serious about following Jesus?

2. What is the cost of following Christ?

3. How does that compare with the cost of *not* following Christ?

For your next devotional reading, go to page 722.

4 A sluggard's appetite is never filled,
  but the desires of the diligent are fully
    satisfied.

5 The righteous hate what is false,
  but the wicked make themselves a
    stench
  and are filled with shame.

6 Righteousness guards the person of
    integrity,
  but wickedness overthrows the sinner.

7 One person pretends to be rich, yet has
    nothing;
  another pretends to be poor, yet has
    great wealth.

8 The rich may be able to ransom their
    lives,
  but the poor cannot respond to
    threatening rebukes.

9 The light of the righteous shines
    brightly,
  but the lamp of the wicked is snuffed
    out.

10 Where there is strife, there is pride,
  but wisdom is found in those who
    take advice.

11 Dishonest money dwindles away,
  but whoever gathers money little by
    little makes it grow.

12 Hope deferred makes the heart sick,
  but a longing fulfilled is a tree of life.

13 Whoever scorns instruction will pay for it,
  but whoever respects a command is
    rewarded.

14 The teaching of the wise is a fountain of
    life,
  turning a person from the snares of
    death.

15 Good judgment wins favor,
  but the way of the unfaithful leads to
    their destruction. *a*

16 All who are prudent act with *b*
    knowledge,
  but fools expose their folly.

17 A wicked messenger falls into trouble,
  but a trustworthy envoy brings
    healing.

18 Whoever disregards discipline comes to
    poverty and shame,
  but whoever heeds correction is
    honored.

19 A longing fulfilled is sweet to the soul,
  but fools detest turning from evil.

20 Walk with the wise and become wise,
  for a companion of fools suffers
    harm.

21 Trouble pursues the sinner,
  but the righteous are rewarded with
    good things.

22 Good people leave an inheritance for
    their children's children,
  but a sinner's wealth is stored up for
    the righteous.

23 An unplowed field produces food for the
    poor,
  but injustice sweeps it away.

24 Those who spare the rod hate their
    children,
  but those who love them are careful
    to discipline them.

25 The righteous eat to their hearts'
    content,
  but the stomach of the wicked goes
    hungry.

14 The wise woman builds her
    house,
  but with her own hands the
    foolish one tears hers down.

2 Whoever fears the LORD walks uprightly,
  but those who despise him are
    devious in their ways.

3 A fool's mouth lashes out with pride,
  but the lips of the wise protect them.

4 Where there are no oxen, the manger is
    empty,
  but from the strength of an ox come
    abundant harvests.

5 An honest witness does not deceive,
  but a false witness pours out lies.

6 The mocker seeks wisdom and finds
    none,
  but knowledge comes easily to the
    discerning.

---

a 15 Septuagint and Syriac; the meaning of the Hebrew for this phrase is uncertain.   *b* 16 Or *prudent
protect themselves through*

⁷Stay away from the foolish,
  for you will not find knowledge on
    their lips.

⁸The wisdom of the prudent is to give
    thought to their ways,
  but the folly of fools is deception.

⁹Fools mock at making amends for sin,
  but goodwill is found among the
    upright.

¹⁰Each heart knows its own bitterness,
  and no one else can share its joy.

¹¹The house of the wicked will be
    destroyed,
  but the tent of the upright will
    flourish.

¹²There is a way that appears to be right,
  but in the end it leads to death.

¹³Even in laughter the heart may ache,
  and rejoicing may end in grief.

¹⁴The faithless will be fully repaid for their
    ways,
  and the good rewarded for theirs.

¹⁵The simple believe anything,
  but the prudent give thought to their
    steps.

¹⁶The wise fear the LORD and shun evil,
  but a fool is hotheaded and yet feels
    secure.

¹⁷The quick-tempered do foolish things,
  and those who devise evil schemes
    are hated.

¹⁸The simple inherit folly,
  but the prudent are crowned with
    knowledge.

¹⁹Evildoers will bow down in the presence
    of the good,
  and the wicked at the gates of the
    righteous.

²⁰The poor are shunned even by their
    neighbors,
  but the rich have many friends.

²¹It is a sin to despise one's neighbor,
  but blessed are those who are kind to
    the needy.

²²Do not those who plot evil go astray?
  But those who plan what is good
    find ᵃ love and faithfulness.

²³All hard work brings a profit,
  but mere talk leads only to poverty.

²⁴The wealth of the wise is their crown,
  but the folly of fools yields folly.

²⁵A truthful witness saves lives,
  but a false witness is deceitful.

²⁶Those who fear the LORD have a secure
    fortress,
  and for their children it will be a
    refuge.

²⁷The fear of the LORD is a fountain of life,
  turning a person from the snares of
    death.

²⁸A large population is a king's glory,
  but without subjects a prince is
    ruined.

²⁹Those who are patient have great
    understanding,
  but the quick-tempered display folly.

³⁰A heart at peace gives life to the body,
  but envy rots the bones.

³¹Whoever oppresses the poor shows
    contempt for their Maker,
  but whoever is kind to the needy
    honors God.

³²When calamity comes, the wicked are
    brought down,
  but even in death the righteous seek
    refuge in God.

³³Wisdom reposes in the heart of the
    discerning
  and even among fools she lets herself
    be known. ᵇ

³⁴Righteousness exalts a nation,
  but sin condemns any people.

³⁵A king delights in a wise servant,
  but a shameful servant arouses his
    fury.

15 A gentle answer turns away
    wrath,
  but a harsh word stirs up anger.

²The tongue of the wise adorns
    knowledge,
  but the mouth of the fool gushes folly.

ᵃ 22 Or show   ᵇ 33 Hebrew; Septuagint and Syriac / but in the heart of fools she is not known

WEDNESDAY

PRAY FOR PRAYER
Proverbs 15:1–33 *or* 15:8,29

Ajith Fernando

What advice can we give to those who have lost the taste for prayer and find it difficult because they do not feel like praying? James 4:8 says, "Come near to God and he will come near to you." That is a promise! You must begin to pray, and once you have taken that step, God will come to you and minister to your needs. It won't be long before you snap back into a vibrant prayer life.

Charles Spurgeon has a memorable quote about this: "I believe that when we cannot pray, it is time we prayed more than ever. And if you answer, 'But, how can that be?' I would say, pray to pray. Pray for prayer. Pray for the spirit of supplication. Do not be content to say, 'I would pray if I could.' No, if you cannot pray, pray till you can."

JOHN BAILLIE {AD 1886–1960}

Eternal Father of my soul, let my first thought today be of You, let my first impulse be to worship You, let my first speech be Your name, let my first action be to kneel before You in prayer.

For Your perfect wisdom and perfect goodness:
For the love with which You love mankind:
For the love with which You love me:
For the great and mysterious opportunity of my life:
For the indwelling of Your Spirit in my heart:
For the sevenfold gifts of Your Spirit:
I praise and worship You, O Lord.

Yet let me not, when this morning prayer is said, think my worship ended and spend the day in forgetfulness of You. Rather from these moments of quietness let light go forth, and joy, and power, that will remain with me through all the hours of the day; . . .

Keeping me honorable and generous in my dealings with others:
Keeping me loyal to every hallowed memory of the past:
Keeping me mindful of my eternal destiny as a child of Yours.
Through Jesus Christ my Lord. Amen.

reflection

1. In what ways do you wish your prayer life was different?
2. What changes can you make toward that end?
3. Have you ever told God about times you don't want to pray?

For your next devotional reading, go to page 730.

³ The eyes of the LORD are everywhere,
  keeping watch on the wicked and the
    good.

⁴ The soothing tongue is a tree of life,
  but a perverse tongue crushes the
    spirit.

⁵ A fool spurns a parent's discipline,
  but whoever heeds correction shows
    prudence.

⁶ The house of the righteous contains
    great treasure,
  but the income of the wicked brings
    ruin.

⁷ The lips of the wise spread knowledge,
  but the hearts of fools are not upright.

⁸ The LORD detests the sacrifice of the
    wicked,
  but the prayer of the upright pleases
    him.

⁹ The LORD detests the way of the wicked,
  but he loves those who pursue
    righteousness.

¹⁰ Stern discipline awaits those who leave
    the path;
  those who hate correction will die.

¹¹ Death and Destruction ᵃ lie open before
    the LORD—
  how much more do human hearts!

¹² Mockers resent correction,
  so they avoid the wise.

¹³ A happy heart makes the face cheerful,
  but heartache crushes the spirit.

¹⁴ The discerning heart seeks knowledge,
  but the mouth of a fool feeds on folly.

¹⁵ All the days of the oppressed are
    wretched,
  but the cheerful heart has a continual
    feast.

¹⁶ Better a little with the fear of the LORD
  than great wealth with turmoil.

¹⁷ Better a small serving of vegetables with
    love
  than a fattened calf with hatred.

¹⁸ The hot-tempered stir up dissension,
  but those who are patient calm a
    quarrel.

¹⁹ The way of the sluggard is blocked with
    thorns,
  but the path of the upright is a
    highway.

²⁰ Wise children bring joy to their father,
  but foolish children despise their
    mother.

²¹ Folly brings joy to those who have no
    sense,
  but those who have understanding
    keep a straight course.

²² Plans fail for lack of counsel,
  but with many advisers they succeed.

²³ A person finds joy in giving an apt
    reply—
  and how good is a timely word!

²⁴ The path of life leads upward for the
    prudent
  to keep them from going down to the
    realm of the dead.

²⁵ The LORD tears down the house of the
    proud,
  but he sets the widow's boundary
    stones in place.

²⁶ The LORD detests the thoughts of the
    wicked,
  but gracious words are pure in his
    sight.

²⁷ The greedy bring ruin to their households,
  but those who hate bribes will live.

²⁸ The heart of the righteous weighs its
    answers,
  but the mouth of the wicked gushes
    evil.

²⁹ The LORD is far from the wicked,
  but he hears the prayer of the
    righteous.

³⁰ Light in a messenger's eyes brings joy to
    the heart,
  and good news gives health to the
    bones.

³¹ Whoever heeds life-giving correction
  will be at home among the wise.

³² Those who disregard discipline despise
    themselves,
  but those who heed correction gain
    understanding.

ᵃ 11 Hebrew *Abaddon*

33 Wisdom's instruction is to fear the LORD,
and humility comes before honor.

16

To human beings belong the
plans of the heart,
but from the LORD comes the
proper answer of the tongue.

2 People may think all their ways are pure,
but motives are weighed by the LORD.

3 Commit to the LORD whatever you do,
and he will establish your plans.

4 The LORD works out everything to its
proper end—
even the wicked for a day of disaster.

5 The LORD detests all the proud of heart.
Be sure of this: They will not go
unpunished.

6 Through love and faithfulness sin is
atoned for;
through the fear of the LORD evil is
avoided.

7 When the LORD takes pleasure in
anyone's way,
he causes their enemies to make
peace with them.

8 Better a little with righteousness
than much gain with injustice.

9 In their hearts human beings plan their
course,
but the LORD establishes their steps.

10 The lips of a king speak as an oracle,
and his mouth does not betray
justice.

11 Honest scales and balances belong to
the LORD;
all the weights in the bag are of his
making.

12 Kings detest wrongdoing,
for a throne is established through
righteousness.

13 Kings take pleasure in honest lips;
they value persons who speak what is
right.

14 A king's wrath is a messenger of death,
but the wise will appease it.

15 When a king's face brightens, it means
life;
his favor is like a rain cloud in spring.

16 How much better to get wisdom than
gold,
to get insight rather than silver!

17 The highway of the upright avoids evil;
those who guard their ways preserve
their lives.

18 Pride goes before destruction,
a haughty spirit before a fall.

19 Better to be lowly in spirit along with
the oppressed
than to share plunder with the proud.

20 Those who give heed to instruction
prosper,[a]
and blessed are those who trust in the
LORD.

21 The wise in heart are called discerning,
and gracious words promote
instruction.[b]

22 Prudence is a fountain of life to the
prudent,
but folly brings punishment to fools.

23 The hearts of the wise make their
mouths prudent,
and their lips promote instruction.[c]

24 Gracious words are a honeycomb,
sweet to the soul and healing to the
bones.

25 There is a way that appears to be right,
but in the end it leads to death.

26 The appetite of laborers works for them;
their hunger drives them on.

27 Scoundrels plot evil,
and on their lips it is like a scorching
fire.

28 The perverse stir up dissension,
and gossips separate close friends.

29 The violent entice their neighbors
and lead them down a path that is
not good.

30 Those who wink with their eyes are
plotting perversity;

---

a 20 Or who speak prudently find what is good   b 21 Or words make a person persuasive
c 23 Or prudent / and make their lips persuasive

those who purse their lips are bent on
evil.

31 Gray hair is a crown of splendor;
it is attained in the way of
righteousness.

32 Better a patient person than a warrior,
those with self-control than those
who take a city.

33 The lot is cast into the lap,
but its every decision is from the
LORD.

17

Better a dry crust with peace and
quiet
than a house full of feasting,
with strife.

2 A prudent servant will rule over a
disgraceful son
and will share the inheritance as one
of the family.

3 The crucible for silver and the furnace
for gold,
but the LORD tests the heart.

4 A wicked person listens to deceitful lips;
a liar pays attention to a destructive
tongue.

5 Whoever mocks the poor shows
contempt for their Maker;
whoever gloats over disaster will not
go unpunished.

6 Children's children are a crown to the
aged,
and parents are the pride of their
children.

7 Eloquent lips are unsuited to a godless
fool—
how much worse lying lips to a ruler!

8 A bribe is seen as a charm by those who
give it;
they think success will come at every
turn.

9 Whoever would foster love covers over
an offense,
but whoever repeats the matter
separates close friends.

10 A rebuke impresses a discerning person
more than a hundred lashes a fool.

11 Evildoers foster rebellion against God;
the messenger of death will be sent
against them.

12 Better to meet a bear robbed of her cubs
than a fool bent on folly.

13 Evil will never leave the house
of one who pays back evil for good.

14 Starting a quarrel is like breaching a
dam;
so drop the matter before a dispute
breaks out.

15 Acquitting the guilty and condemning
the innocent—
the LORD detests them both.

16 Why should fools have money in hand to
buy wisdom,
when they are not able to understand
it?

17 A friend loves at all times,
and a brother is born for a time of
adversity.

18 One who has no sense shakes hands in
pledge
and puts up security for a neighbor.

19 Whoever loves a quarrel loves sin;
whoever builds a high gate invites
destruction.

20 One whose heart is corrupt does not
prosper;
one whose tongue is perverse falls
into trouble.

21 To have a fool for a child brings grief;
there is no joy for the parent of a
godless fool.

22 A cheerful heart is good medicine,
but a crushed spirit dries up the
bones.

23 The wicked accept bribes in secret
to pervert the course of justice.

24 A discerning person keeps wisdom in
view,
but a fool's eyes wander to the ends
of the earth.

25 Foolish children bring grief to their
father
and bitterness to the mother who
bore them.

26 If imposing a fine on the innocent is not
good,

surely to flog honest officials is not
  right.

27 Those who have knowledge use words
    with restraint,
  and those who have understanding
    are even-tempered.

28 Even fools are thought wise if they keep
    silent,
  and discerning if they hold their
    tongues.

18 An unfriendly person pursues
    selfish ends
  and against all sound judgment
    starts quarrels.

2 Fools find no pleasure in understanding
  but delight in airing their own
    opinions.

3 When wickedness comes, so does
    contempt,
  and with shame comes reproach.

4 The words of the mouth are deep waters,
  but the fountain of wisdom is a
    rushing stream.

5 It is not good to be partial to the wicked
  and so deprive the innocent of justice.

6 The lips of fools bring them strife,
  and their mouths invite a beating.

7 The mouths of fools are their undoing,
  and their lips are a snare to their very
    lives.

8 The words of a gossip are like choice
    morsels;
  they go down to the inmost parts.

9 One who is slack in his work
  is a close relative of one who
    destroys.

10 The name of the Lord is a fortified
    tower;
  the righteous run to it and are safe.

11 The wealth of the rich is their fortified
    city;
  they imagine it a wall too high to
    scale.

12 Before a downfall the heart is haughty,
  but humility comes before honor.

13 To answer before listening—
  that is folly and shame.

14 The human spirit can endure in
    sickness,
  but a crushed spirit who can bear?

15 The heart of the discerning acquires
    knowledge,
  for the ears of the wise seek it out.

16 A gift opens the way
  and ushers the giver into the presence
    of the great.

17 In a lawsuit the first to speak seems
    right,
  until someone comes forward and
    cross-examines.

18 Casting the lot settles disputes
  and keeps strong opponents apart.

19 A brother wronged is more unyielding
    than a fortified city;
  disputes are like the barred gates of a
    citadel.

20 From the fruit of their mouths people's
    stomachs are filled;
  with the harvest of their lips they are
    satisfied.

21 The tongue has the power of life and
    death,
  and those who love it will eat its
    fruit.

22 He who finds a wife finds what is good
  and receives favor from the Lord.

23 The poor plead for mercy,
  but the rich answer harshly.

24 One who has unreliable friends soon
    comes to ruin,
  but there is a friend who sticks closer
    than a brother.

19 Better the poor whose walk is
    blameless
  than a fool whose lips are
    perverse.

2 Desire without knowledge is not
    good—
  how much more will hasty feet miss
    the way!

3 One's own folly leads to ruin,
  yet the heart rages against the Lord.

4 Wealth attracts many friends,
  but even the closest friends of the
    poor desert them.

⁵A false witness will not go unpunished,
  and whoever pours out lies will not go
     free.

⁶Many curry favor with a ruler,
  and everyone is the friend of one who
     gives gifts.

⁷The poor are shunned by all their
     relatives—
  how much more do their friends
     avoid them!
Though they pursue them with pleading,
  they are nowhere to be found.ᵃ

⁸Those who get wisdom love their own
     lives;
  those who cherish understanding will
     soon prosper.

⁹A false witness will not go unpunished,
  and whoever pours out lies will
     perish.

¹⁰It is not fitting for a fool to live in
     luxury—
  how much worse for a slave to rule
     over princes!

¹¹A person's wisdom yields patience;
  it is to one's glory to overlook an
     offense.

¹²A king's rage is like the roar of a lion,
  but his favor is like dew on the grass.

¹³A foolish child is a father's ruin,
  and a quarrelsome wife is like
     the constant dripping of a leaky roof.

¹⁴Houses and wealth are inherited from
     parents,
  but a prudent wife is from the LORD.

¹⁵Laziness brings on deep sleep,
  and the shiftless go hungry.

¹⁶Those who obey instructions preserve
     their lives,
  but those who are contemptuous of
     their ways will die.

¹⁷Those who are kind to the poor lend to
     the LORD,
  and he will reward them for what
     they have done.

¹⁸Discipline your children, for in that there
     is hope;
  do not be a willing party to their death.

¹⁹The hot-tempered must pay the penalty;
  rescue them, and you will have to do
     it again.

²⁰Listen to advice and accept discipline,
  and at the end you will be counted
     among the wise.

²¹Many are the plans in a human heart,
  but it is the LORD's purpose that
     prevails.

²²What a person desires is unfailing loveᵇ;
  better to be poor than a liar.

²³The fear of the LORD leads to life;
  then one rests content, untouched by
     trouble.

²⁴Sluggards bury their hands in the dish
  and will not even bring them back to
     their mouths!

²⁵Flog a mocker, and the simple will learn
     prudence;
  rebuke the discerning, and they will
     gain knowledge.

²⁶Whoever robs their father and drives out
     their mother
  is a child who brings shame and
     disgrace.

²⁷Stop listening to instruction, my child,
  and you will stray from the words of
     knowledge.

²⁸A corrupt witness mocks at justice,
  and the mouth of the wicked gulps
     down evil.

²⁹Penalties are prepared for mockers,
  and beatings for the backs of fools.

20 Wine is a mocker and beer a
     brawler;
  whoever is led astray by them is
     not wise.

²A king's wrath strikes terror like the roar
     of a lion;
  those who anger him forfeit their
     lives.

³It is to one's honor to avoid strife,
  but every fool is quick to quarrel.

⁴Sluggards do not plow in season;
  so at harvest time they look but find
     nothing.

ᵃ 7 The meaning of the Hebrew for this sentence is uncertain.   ᵇ 22 Or *Greed is a person's shame*

⁵The purposes of the human heart are
   deep waters,
   but those who have insight draw
      them out.

⁶Many claim to have unfailing love,
   but a faithful person who can find?

⁷The righteous lead blameless lives;
   blessed are their children after them.

⁸When a king sits on his throne to judge,
   he winnows out all evil with his eyes.

⁹Who can say, "I have kept my heart pure;
   I am clean and without sin"?

¹⁰Differing weights and differing
      measures—
   the LORD detests them both.

¹¹Even small children are known by their
      actions,
   so is their conduct really pure and
      upright?

¹²Ears that hear and eyes that see—
   the LORD has made them both.

¹³Do not love sleep or you will grow poor;
   stay awake and you will have food to
      spare.

¹⁴"It's no good, it's no good!" says the
      buyer—
   then goes off and boasts about the
      purchase.

¹⁵Gold there is, and rubies in abundance,
   but lips that speak knowledge are a
      rare jewel.

¹⁶Take the garment of one who puts up
      security for a stranger;
   hold it in pledge if it is done for an
      outsider.

¹⁷Food gained by fraud tastes sweet,
   but one ends up with a mouth full of
      gravel.

¹⁸Plans are established by seeking advice;
   so if you wage war, obtain guidance.

¹⁹A gossip betrays a confidence;
   so avoid anyone who talks too much.

²⁰If you curse your father or mother,
   your lamp will be snuffed out in pitch
      darkness.

²¹An inheritance claimed too soon
   will not be blessed at the end.

²²Do not say, "I'll pay you back for this
      wrong!"
   Wait for the LORD, and he will avenge
      you.

²³The LORD detests differing weights,
   and dishonest scales do not please
      him.

²⁴A person's steps are directed by the
      LORD.
   How then can anyone understand
      their own way?

²⁵It is a trap to dedicate something rashly
   and only later to consider one's vows.

²⁶A wise king winnows out the wicked;
   he drives the threshing wheel over
      them.

²⁷The human spirit is *a* the lamp of the
      LORD
   that sheds light on one's inmost
      being.

²⁸Love and faithfulness keep a king safe;
   through love his throne is made
      secure.

²⁹The glory of young men is their strength,
   gray hair the splendor of the old.

³⁰Blows and wounds cleanse away evil,
   and beatings purge the inmost being.

21

In the LORD's hand the king's
heart is a stream of water
that he channels toward all who
please him.

²People may think all their ways are right,
   but the LORD weighs the heart.

³To do what is right and just
   is more acceptable to the LORD than
      sacrifice.

⁴Haughty eyes and a proud heart—
   the unplowed field of the wicked—
      produce sin.

⁵The plans of the diligent lead to profit
   as surely as haste leads to poverty.

⁶A fortune made by a lying tongue
   is a fleeting vapor and a deadly snare. *b*

---

a 27 Or *A person's words are*   *a* 6 Some Hebrew manuscripts, Septuagint and Vulgate; most Hebrew
manuscripts *vapor for those who seek death*

7 The violence of the wicked will drag
    them away,
  for they refuse to do what is right.

8 The way of the guilty is devious,
  but the conduct of the innocent is
    upright.

9 Better to live on a corner of the roof
  than share a house with a
    quarrelsome wife.

10 The wicked crave evil;
  their neighbors get no mercy from
    them.

11 When a mocker is punished, the simple
    gain wisdom;
  by paying attention to the wise they
    get knowledge.

12 The Righteous One[a] takes note of the
    house of the wicked
  and brings the wicked to ruin.

13 Those who shut their ears to the cry of
    the poor
  will also cry out and not be
    answered.

14 A gift given in secret soothes anger,
  and a bribe concealed in the cloak
    pacifies great wrath.

15 When justice is done, it brings joy to the
    righteous
  but terror to evildoers.

16 Whoever strays from the path of
    prudence
  comes to rest in the company of the
    dead.

17 Whoever loves pleasure will become
    poor;
  whoever loves wine and olive oil will
    never be rich.

18 The wicked become a ransom for the
    righteous,
  and the unfaithful for the upright.

19 Better to live in a desert
  than with a quarrelsome and nagging
    wife.

20 The wise store up choice food and olive
    oil,
  but fools gulp theirs down.

21 Whoever pursues righteousness and
    love
  finds life, prosperity[b] and honor.

22 One who is wise can go up against the
    city of the mighty
  and pull down the stronghold in
    which they trust.

23 Those who guard their mouths and their
    tongues
  keep themselves from calamity.

24 The proud and arrogant—"Mocker" is
    their name;
  they behave with insolent fury.

25 The craving of sluggards will be the
    death of them,
  because their hands refuse to work.

26 All day long they crave for more,
  but the righteous give without sparing.

27 The sacrifice of the wicked is detestable—
  how much more so when brought
    with evil intent!

28 Those who give false witness will perish,
  but a careful listener will testify
    successfully.

29 The wicked put up a bold front,
  but the upright give thought to their
    ways.

30 There is no wisdom, no insight, no plan
  that can succeed against the LORD.

31 The horse is made ready for the day of
    battle,
  but victory rests with the LORD.

22

A good name is more desirable
than great riches;
  to be esteemed is better than
    silver or gold.

2 Rich and poor have this in common:
  The LORD is the Maker of them all.

3 The prudent see danger and take refuge,
  but the simple keep going and pay
    the penalty.

4 Humility is the fear of the LORD;
  its wages are riches and honor and
    life.

5 In the paths of the wicked are snares
    and pitfalls,

---

a 12 Or *The righteous person*   b 21 Or *righteousness*

THURSDAY

FINDING HUMILITY

Proverbs 22:1–29 *or* 22:4

Chris Tomlin

What picture comes to your mind when you think about what it means to be humble? Honestly, my first take is to imagine a soft-spoken, plain-dressed, wallflower of a person who drives a junker. He (or she) is probably boring too. Yep, for some reason that's the epitome of humility to me.

But why? Probably because I tend to look on the outside. But God looks inside, because humility is a state of the heart. Humility is a holy attitude. Sure, you and I can be fooled by false humility for a while, but only a while. A person's real attitude surfaces sooner or later . . .

Here's a word picture that helps me understand humility:

A humble person is a champion of the unnoticed life.

Sounds weak, I know. Definitely not worth a TV show. But champions of the unnoticed life have enormous power. These men and women influence their world without ever seeming to be in the spotlight. That place of attention and honor has been rightly given over to Someone Else.

HENRY SCOUGAL {AD 1650–1678}

We have much to think about that will result in our humility. Thinking about all our evils and imperfections, all our follies and our sins may help to topple that self-absorbed and presumptuous conceit with which we tend to view ourselves . . .

Though we conceal our failings from one another, we are surely conscious of them ourselves, and some serious reflections upon them would greatly diminish and subdue the vanity of our spirits . . .

But it has also been observed that the deepest and most pure humility does not come so much from contemplating our own faults and defects, as it does from a calm and quiet contemplation of God's divine purity and goodness. Our blemishes can be seen most clearly when we place them before God's infinite light; and we seem smallest in our own eyes when we look down upon ourselves from on high. Oh how little, how nothing, do all these shadows of perfection—those things we tend to value in ourselves—then appear!

reflection

1. What is your first, gut-level reaction to the question, What picture comes to your mind when you think about what it means to be humble?

2. How does focusing on God's purity and goodness foster deeper humility in you?

3. Hold up your own imperfect heart to the perfection of God. How does this comparison affect your view of yourself?

For your next devotional reading, go to page 739.

but those who would preserve their
    life stay far from them.

⁶ Start children off on the way they should
    go,
    and even when they are old they will
      not turn from it.

⁷ The rich rule over the poor,
    and the borrower is slave to the
      lender.

⁸ Those who sow injustice reap calamity,
    and the rod they wield in fury will be
      broken.

⁹ The generous will themselves be
    blessed,
    for they share their food with the
      poor.

¹⁰ Drive out the mocker, and out goes
    strife;
    quarrels and insults are ended.

¹¹ One who loves a pure heart and who
    speaks with grace
    will have the king for a friend.

¹² The eyes of the LORD keep watch over
    knowledge,
    but he frustrates the words of the
      unfaithful.

¹³ The sluggard says, "There's a lion
    outside!
    I'll be killed in the public square!"

¹⁴ The mouth of an adulterous woman is a
    deep pit;
    a man who is under the LORD's wrath
      falls into it.

¹⁵ Folly is bound up in the heart of a child,
    but the rod of discipline will drive it
      far away.

¹⁶ Those who oppress the poor to increase
    their wealth
    and those who give gifts to the rich—
      both come to poverty.

Thirty Sayings of the Wise

Saying 1

¹⁷ Pay attention and turn your ear to the
    sayings of the wise;
    apply your heart to what I teach,

¹⁸ for it is pleasing when you keep them in
    your heart
    and have all of them ready on your
      lips.

¹⁹ So that your trust may be in the LORD,
    I teach you today, even you.

²⁰ Have I not written thirty sayings for you,
    sayings of counsel and knowledge,

²¹ teaching you to be honest and to speak
    the truth,
    so that you bring back truthful reports
      to those you serve?

Saying 2

²² Do not exploit the poor because they are
    poor
    and do not crush the needy in court,

²³ for the LORD will take up their case
    and will exact life for life.

Saying 3

²⁴ Do not make friends with the hot-
    tempered,
    do not associate with those who are
      easily angered,

²⁵ or you may learn their ways
    and get yourself ensnared.

Saying 4

²⁶ Do not be one who shakes hands in
    pledge
    or puts up security for debts;

²⁷ if you lack the means to pay,
    your very bed will be snatched from
      under you.

Saying 5

²⁸ Do not move an ancient boundary stone
    set up by your ancestors.

Saying 6

²⁹ Do you see those who are skilled in their
    work?
    They will serve before kings;
    they will not serve before officials of
      low rank.

Saying 7

23 When you sit to dine with a
    ruler,
    note well what*ᵃ* is before you,
² and put a knife to your throat
    if you are given to gluttony.

ᵃ 1 Or who

3 Do not crave his delicacies,
  for that food is deceptive.

Saying 8

4 Do not wear yourself out to get rich;
  do not trust your own cleverness.
5 Cast but a glance at riches, and they are
  gone,
  for they will surely sprout wings
  and fly off to the sky like an eagle.

Saying 9

6 Do not eat the food of a begrudging
  host,
  do not crave his delicacies;
7 for he is the kind of person
  who is always thinking about the
  cost.ᵃ
  "Eat and drink," he says to you,
  but his heart is not with you.
8 You will vomit up the little you have
  eaten
  and will have wasted your
  compliments.

Saying 10

9 Do not speak to fools,
  for they will scorn your prudent
  words.

Saying 11

10 Do not move an ancient boundary stone
  or encroach on the fields of the
  fatherless,
11 for their Defender is strong;
  he will take up their case against you.

Saying 12

12 Apply your heart to instruction
  and your ears to words of knowledge.

Saying 13

13 Do not withhold discipline from
  children;
  if you punish them with the rod, they
  will not die.
14 Punish them with the rod
  and save them from death.

Saying 14

15 My son, if your heart is wise,
  then my heart will be glad indeed;
16 my inmost being will rejoice

when your lips speak what is right.

Saying 15

17 Do not let your heart envy sinners,
  but always be zealous for the fear of
  the Lᴏʀᴅ.
18 There is surely a future hope for you,
  and your hope will not be cut off.

Saying 16

19 Listen, my son, and be wise,
  and set your heart on the right path:
20 Do not join those who drink too much
  wine
  or gorge themselves on meat,
21 for drunkards and gluttons become poor,
  and drowsiness clothes them in rags.

Saying 17

22 Listen to your father, who gave you life,
  and do not despise your mother when
  she is old.
23 Buy the truth and do not sell it—
  wisdom, instruction and insight as
  well.
24 The father of a righteous child has great
  joy;
  a man who fathers a wise son rejoices
  in him.
25 May your father and mother rejoice;
  may she who gave you birth be joyful!

Saying 18

26 My son, give me your heart
  and let your eyes delight in my ways,
27 for an adulterous woman is a deep pit
  and a wayward wife is a narrow well.
28 Like a bandit she lies in wait,
  and multiplies the unfaithful among
  men.

Saying 19

29 Who has woe? Who has sorrow?
  Who has strife? Who has complaints?
  Who has needless bruises? Who has
  bloodshot eyes?
30 Those who linger over wine,
  who go to sample bowls of mixed
  wine.
31 Do not gaze at wine when it is red,
  when it sparkles in the cup,
  when it goes down smoothly!
32 In the end it bites like a snake

ᵃ 7 Or *for as he thinks within himself, / so he is*; or *for as he puts on a feast, / so he is*

and poisons like a viper.
33 Your eyes will see strange sights
and your mind imagine confusing
things.
34 You will be like one sleeping on the high
seas,
lying on top of the rigging.
35 "They hit me," you will say, "but I'm not
hurt!
They beat me, but I don't feel it!
When will I wake up
so I can find another drink?"

Saying 20

24 Do not envy the wicked,
do not desire their company;
2 for their hearts plot violence,
and their lips talk about making
trouble.

Saying 21

3 By wisdom a house is built,
and through understanding it is
established;
4 through knowledge its rooms are filled
with rare and beautiful treasures.

Saying 22

5 The wise prevail through great power,
and those who have knowledge
muster their strength.
6 Surely you need guidance to wage war,
and victory is won through many
advisers.

Saying 23

7 Wisdom is too high for fools;
in the assembly at the gate they must
not open their mouths.

Saying 24

8 Whoever plots evil
will be known as a schemer.
9 The schemes of folly are sin,
and people detest a mocker.

Saying 25

10 If you falter in a time of trouble,
how small is your strength!
11 Rescue those being led away to death;
hold back those staggering toward
slaughter.
12 If you say, "But we knew nothing about
this,"

does not he who weighs the heart
perceive it?
Does not he who guards your life know
it?
Will he not repay everyone according
to what they have done?

Saying 26

13 Eat honey, my son, for it is good;
honey from the comb is sweet to your
taste.
14 Know also that wisdom is like honey for
you:
If you find it, there is a future hope
for you,
and your hope will not be cut off.

Saying 27

15 Do not lurk like a thief near the house of
the righteous,
do not plunder their dwelling place;
16 for though the righteous fall seven
times, they rise again,
but the wicked stumble when
calamity strikes.

Saying 28

17 Do not gloat when your enemies fall;
when they stumble, do not let your
heart rejoice,
18 or the Lord will see and disapprove
and turn his wrath away from them.

Saying 29

19 Do not fret because of evildoers
or be envious of the wicked,
20 for the evildoer has no future hope,
and the lamp of the wicked will be
snuffed out.

Saying 30

21 Fear the Lord and the king, my son,
and do not join with rebellious
officials,
22 for those two will send sudden
destruction on them,
and who knows what calamities they
can bring?

Further Sayings of the Wise

23 These also are sayings of the wise:

To show partiality in judging is not good:
24 Whoever says to the guilty, "You are
innocent,"

will be cursed by peoples and
    denounced by nations.
25 But it will go well with those who
    convict the guilty,
  and rich blessing will come on them.

26 An honest answer
  is like a kiss on the lips.

27 Put your outdoor work in order
    and get your fields ready;
  after that, build your house.

28 Do not testify against your neighbor
    without cause—
  would you use your lips to mislead?
29 Do not say, "I'll do to them as they have
    done to me;
  I'll pay them back for what they did."

30 I went past the field of a sluggard,
    past the vineyard of someone who
    has no sense;
31 thorns had come up everywhere,
    the ground was covered with weeds,
  and the stone wall was in ruins.
32 I applied my heart to what I observed
  and learned a lesson from what I saw:
33 A little sleep, a little slumber,
    a little folding of the hands to rest—
34 and poverty will come on you like a thief
  and scarcity like an armed man.

More Proverbs of Solomon

25 These are more proverbs of Solomon, compiled by the men of Hezekiah king of Judah:

2 It is the glory of God to conceal a
    matter;
  to search out a matter is the glory of
    kings.
3 As the heavens are high and the earth is
    deep,
  so the hearts of kings are
    unsearchable.

4 Remove the dross from the silver,
  and a silversmith can produce a
    vessel;
5 remove wicked officials from the king's
    presence,
  and his throne will be established
    through righteousness.

6 Do not exalt yourself in the king's
    presence,

and do not claim a place among his
    great men;
7 it is better for him to say to you, "Come
    up here,"
  than for him to humiliate you before
    his nobles.

  What you have seen with your eyes
8   do not bring*a* hastily to court,
for what will you do in the end
  if your neighbor puts you to shame?

9 If you take your neighbor to court,
    do not betray another's confidence,
10 or the one who hears it may shame you
  and the charge against you will stand.

11 Like apples *b* of gold in settings of silver
  is a ruling rightly given.
12 Like an earring of gold or an ornament
    of fine gold
  is the rebuke of a wise judge to a
    listening ear.

13 Like a snow-cooled drink at harvest time
    is a trustworthy messenger to the one
    who sends him;
  he refreshes the spirit of his master.
14 Like clouds and wind without rain
  is one who boasts of gifts never given.

15 Through patience a ruler can be
    persuaded,
  and a gentle tongue can break a bone.

16 If you find honey, eat just enough—
  too much of it, and you will vomit.
17 Seldom set foot in your neighbor's
    house—
  too much of you, and you will be
    hated.

18 Like a club or a sword or a sharp arrow
  is one who gives false testimony
    against a neighbor.
19 Like a broken tooth or a lame foot
  is reliance on the unfaithful in a time
    of trouble.
20 Like one who takes away a garment on a
    cold day,
  or like vinegar poured on a wound,
  is one who sings songs to a heavy
    heart.

21 If your enemy is hungry, give him food
    to eat;
  if he is thirsty, give him water to drink.

---

a 7,8 Or nobles / on whom you had set your eyes. / 8 Do not go   *b 11 Or possibly apricots*

²² In doing this, you will heap burning
    coals on his head,
  and the LORD will reward you.

²³ Like a north wind that brings
    unexpected rain
  is a sly tongue—which provokes a
    horrified look.

²⁴ Better to live on a corner of the roof
  than share a house with a
    quarrelsome wife.

²⁵ Like cold water to a weary soul
  is good news from a distant land.

²⁶ Like a muddied spring or a polluted well
  are the righteous who give way to the
    wicked.

²⁷ It is not good to eat too much honey,
  nor is it honorable to search out
    matters that are too deep.

²⁸ Like a city whose walls are broken
    through
  is a person who lacks self-control.

26

  Like snow in summer or rain in
    harvest,
  honor is not fitting for a fool.

² Like a fluttering sparrow or a darting
    swallow,
  an undeserved curse does not come
    to rest.

³ A whip for the horse, a bridle for the
    donkey,
  and a rod for the backs of fools!

⁴ Do not answer fools according to their
    folly,
  or you yourself will be just like them.

⁵ Answer fools according to their folly,
  or they will be wise in their own eyes.

⁶ To send a message by the hands of a fool
  is like cutting off one's feet or
    drinking poison.

⁷ Like the useless legs of one who is lame
  is a proverb in the mouth of a fool.

⁸ Like tying a stone in a sling
  is the giving of honor to a fool.

⁹ Like a thornbush in a drunkard's hand
  is a proverb in the mouth of a fool.

¹⁰ Like an archer who wounds at random
  is one who hires a fool or any passer-
    by.

¹¹ As a dog returns to its vomit,
  so fools repeat their folly.

¹² Do you see people who are wise in their
    own eyes?
  There is more hope for fools than for
    them.

¹³ A sluggard says, "There's a lion in the
    road,
  a fierce lion roaming the streets!"

¹⁴ As a door turns on its hinges,
  so a sluggard turns on the bed.

¹⁵ Sluggards bury their hands in the dish
  and are too lazy to bring them back to
    their mouths.

¹⁶ Sluggards are wiser in their own eyes
  than seven people who answer
    discreetly.

¹⁷ Like one who grabs a stray dog by the
    ears
  is someone who rushes into a quarrel
    not their own.

¹⁸ Like a maniac shooting
    flaming arrows of death
¹⁹ is one who deceives a neighbor
  and says, "I was only joking!"

²⁰ Without wood a fire goes out;
  without a gossip a quarrel dies down.

²¹ As charcoal to embers and as wood to
    fire,
  so is a quarrelsome person for
    kindling strife.

²² The words of a gossip are like choice
    morsels;
  they go down to the inmost parts.

²³ Like a coating of silver dross on
    earthenware
  are fervent ᵃ lips with an evil heart.

²⁴ Enemies disguise themselves with their
    lips,
  but in their hearts they harbor deceit.

²⁵ Though their speech is charming, do not
    believe them,
  for seven abominations fill their hearts.

²⁶ Their malice may be concealed by
    deception,
  but their wickedness will be exposed
    in the assembly.

²⁷ If anyone digs a pit, they themselves will
    fall into it;
  if anyone rolls a stone, it will roll back
    on them.

²⁸ A lying tongue hates those it hurts,
  and a flattering mouth works ruin.

ᵃ 23 Hebrew; Septuagint *smooth*

27

Do not boast about tomorrow,
for you do not know what a day
may bring.

2 Let someone else praise you, and not
your own mouth;
an outsider, and not your own lips.

3 Stone is heavy and sand a burden,
but a fool's provocation is heavier
than both.

4 Anger is cruel and fury overwhelming,
but who can stand before jealousy?

5 Better is open rebuke
than hidden love.

6 Wounds from a friend can be trusted,
but an enemy multiplies kisses.

7 One who is full loathes honey from the
comb,
but to the hungry even what is bitter
tastes sweet.

8 Like a bird that flees its nest
is anyone who flees from home.

9 Perfume and incense bring joy to the
heart,
and the pleasantness of a friend
springs from their heartfelt advice.

10 Do not forsake your friend or a friend of
your family,
and do not go to your relative's house
when disaster strikes you—
better a neighbor nearby than a
relative far away.

11 Be wise, my child, and bring joy to my
heart;
then I can answer anyone who treats
me with contempt.

12 The prudent see danger and take refuge,
but the simple keep going and pay
the penalty.

13 Take the garment of one who puts up
security for a stranger;
hold it in pledge if it is done for an
outsider.

14 If anyone loudly blesses a neighbor early
in the morning,
it will be taken as a curse.

15 A quarrelsome wife is like the dripping
of a leaky roof in a rainstorm;
16 restraining her is like restraining the
wind
or grasping oil with the hand.

17 As iron sharpens iron,
so one person sharpens another.

18 Those who guard a fig tree will eat its
fruit,
and those who protect their masters
will be honored.

19 As water reflects the face,
so one's life reflects the heart. [a]

20 Death and Destruction [b] are never
satisfied,
and neither are human eyes.

21 The crucible for silver and the furnace
for gold,
but people are tested by their praise.

22 Though you grind fools in a mortar,
grinding them like grain with a pestle,
you will not remove their folly from
them.

23 Be sure you know the condition of your
flocks,
give careful attention to your herds;
24 for riches do not endure forever,
and a crown is not secure for all
generations.
25 When the hay is removed and new
growth appears
and the grass from the hills is
gathered in,
26 the lambs will provide you with clothing,
and the goats with the price of a field.
27 You will have plenty of goats' milk to
feed your family
and to nourish your women servants.

28

The wicked flee though no one
pursues,
but the righteous are as bold as
a lion.

2 When a country is rebellious, it has
many rulers,
but a ruler with discernment and
knowledge maintains order.

3 A ruler [c] who oppresses the poor
is like a driving rain that leaves no
crops.

---

a 19 Or *so others reflect your heart back to you*   *b 20* Hebrew *Abaddon*   *c 3* Or *A poor person*

⁴Those who forsake instruction praise the wicked,
    but those who heed it resist them.

⁵Evildoers do not understand what is right,
    but those who seek the Lᴏʀᴅ
        understand it fully.

⁶Better the poor whose walk is blameless
    than the rich whose ways are
        perverse.

⁷Those who heed instruction are
        discerning children,
    but companions of gluttons disgrace
        their parents.

⁸Whoever increases wealth by taking
        interest or profit from the poor
    amasses it for another, who will be
        kind to the poor.

⁹If anyone turns a deaf ear to my
        instruction,
    even their prayers are detestable.

¹⁰Those who lead the upright along an evil
        path
    will fall into their own trap,
    but the blameless will receive a good
        inheritance.

¹¹The rich are wise in their own eyes;
    one who is poor and discerning sees
        how deluded they are.

¹²When the righteous triumph, there is
        great elation;
    but when the wicked rise to power,
        people go into hiding.

¹³Those who conceal their sins do not
        prosper,
    but those who confess and renounce
        them find mercy.

¹⁴Blessed are those who always tremble
        before God,
    but those who harden their hearts fall
        into trouble.

¹⁵Like a roaring lion or a charging bear
    is a wicked ruler over a helpless
        people.

¹⁶A tyrannical ruler practices extortion,
    but one who hates ill-gotten gain will
        enjoy a long reign.

¹⁷Anyone tormented by the guilt of
        murder
    will seek refuge in the grave;
    let no one hold them back.

¹⁸Those whose walk is blameless are kept
        safe,
    but those whose ways are perverse
        will fall into the pit. ᵃ

¹⁹Those who work their land will have
        abundant food,
    but those who chase fantasies will
        have their fill of poverty.

²⁰A faithful person will be richly blessed,
    but one eager to get rich will not go
        unpunished.

²¹To show partiality is not good—
    yet a person will do wrong for a piece
        of bread.

²²The stingy are eager to get rich
    and are unaware that poverty awaits
        them.

²³Whoever rebukes a person will in the
        end gain favor
    rather than one who has a flattering
        tongue.

²⁴Whoever robs their father or mother
    and says, "It's not wrong,"
    is partner to one who destroys.

²⁵The greedy stir up dissension,
    but those who trust in the Lᴏʀᴅ will
        prosper.

²⁶Those who trust in themselves are fools,
    but those who walk in wisdom are
        kept safe.

²⁷Those who give to the poor will lack
        nothing,
    but those who close their eyes to
        them receive many curses.

²⁸When the wicked rise to power, people
        go into hiding;
    but when the wicked perish, the
        righteous thrive.

29

Whoever remains stiff-necked
after many rebukes
will suddenly be destroyed—
    without remedy.

ᵃ 18 Syriac (see Septuagint); Hebrew *into one*

2 When the righteous thrive, the people rejoice;
   when the wicked rule, the people groan.

3 A man who loves wisdom brings joy to his father,
   but a companion of prostitutes squanders his wealth.

4 By justice a king gives a country stability,
   but those who are greedy for^a bribes tear it down.

5 Those who flatter their neighbors are spreading nets for their feet.

6 Evildoers are snared by their own sin,
   but the righteous shout for joy and are glad.

7 The righteous care about justice for the poor,
   but the wicked have no such concern.

8 Mockers stir up a city,
   but the wise turn away anger.

9 If a wise person goes to court with a fool,
   the fool rages and scoffs, and there is no peace.

10 The bloodthirsty hate people of integrity and seek to kill the upright.

11 Fools give full vent to their rage,
   but the wise bring calm in the end.

12 If a ruler listens to lies,
   all his officials become wicked.

13 The poor and the oppressor have this in common:
   The LORD gives sight to the eyes of both.

14 If a king judges the poor with fairness,
   his throne will be established forever.

15 A rod and a reprimand impart wisdom,
   but children left to themselves disgrace their mother.

16 When the wicked thrive, so does sin,
   but the righteous will see their downfall.

17 Discipline your children, and they will give you peace;
   they will bring you the delights you desire.

18 Where there is no revelation, people cast off restraint;
   but blessed are those who heed wisdom's instruction.

19 Servants cannot be corrected by mere words;
   though they understand, they will not respond.

20 Do you see someone who speaks in haste?
   There is more hope for a fool than for them.

21 A servant pampered from youth will turn out to be insolent.

22 An angry person stirs up dissension,
   and a hot-tempered person commits many sins.

23 Pride brings a person low,
   but the lowly in spirit gain honor.

24 The accomplices of thieves are their own enemies;
   they are put under oath and dare not testify.

25 To fear anyone will prove to be a snare,
   but whoever trusts in the LORD is kept safe.

26 Many seek an audience with a ruler,
   but it is from the LORD that one gets justice.

27 The righteous detest the dishonest;
   the wicked detest the upright.

Sayings of Agur

30 The sayings of Agur son of Jakeh—an inspired utterance.

This man's utterance to Ithiel:

"I am weary, God,
   but I can prevail.^b
2 Surely I am only a brute, not a man;
   I do not have human understanding.
3 I have not learned wisdom,

---

^a 4 Or *who give*   ^b 1 With a different word division of the Hebrew; Masoretic Text *utterance to Ithiel,* / *to Ithiel and Ukal:*

FRIDAY

YOUR DAILY PRESCRIPTION

Proverbs 30:1–33 *or* 30:5

E. STANLEY JONES {AD 1884–1972}

I know two brilliant Christians who come to their daily morning devotions without their Bibles. They can meditate, they say. They are both shallow. For they mediate God to themselves through their own thinking—they become the medium. They do not go to God direct as they imagine—they go through their own thinking; they become the mediator. That is why we have to have the revelation of God through the Word. It is God interpreting himself to us. His interpretation of himself is Jesus. When you expose your thinking to him, you expose yourself to God. These words of the New Testament have been in such close contact with the Word that they are vibrant with Life.

Dr. Howard Atwood Kelly . . . says of reading the Bible, "Such reading applied with an honest heart transforms the nature, enables the prostitute to love holiness and become an angel of mercy, and raises the beggar and the drunkard to set them among the princes of the earth." He said again: "The Bible vindicates itself because it is such excellent medicine. It has never failed to cure a single patient if only he took his prescription honestly."

Take the prescription of the Word of God daily. No Christian is sound who is not Scriptural.

Margaret Feinberg

One of the most common ways God speaks is through His Word. Hebrews 4:12–13 describes the Word of God as "[alive]" and "active." It is sharper than any two-edged sword with the ability to judge thoughts and even attitudes of the heart.

If you want to know God and His voice, then you need to spend time in His Word. It's God's megaphone for speaking to His people. If you don't know the Bible reasonably well, then you may not hear as quickly, clearly or with as much certainty. The Scriptures serve as a rudder when you are listening to God. They provide balance, confirmation and direction. The Scriptures will also help you sort through the whispers you think might be from Him.

reflection

1. What "illness" do you need the Word of God to cure?

2. How have you been changed by spending time with God in his Word?

3. How much energy have you devoted to looking for answers in his Word?

For your next devotional reading, go to page 740.

The Imponderables

Proverbs 30:24–28

read/meditate

Read through the list of small but wise creatures described in Proverbs 30:24–28. Think about the strengths of each. These are small imponderables in life. A lizard is not great, yet a king can't keep it from his palace. What other imponderables do you see around you?

pray

Share with God the things in life that confound you, big and small. Ask him for the wisdom to deal with the puzzles life has handed you. Quiet yourself in his presence as he reveals the truly important puzzles in your life. Invite God more fully into your journey.

contemplate

Think about the paradox that the simplest things in the world can confound even the wisest people. Whether it's Murphy's Law or weird little animals that can get into palaces, observe how imponderable life can be.

additional reflection

He is intangible and invisible. But His work is more powerful than the most ferocious wind. The Spirit brings order out of chaos and beauty out of ugliness. He can transform a sin-blistered man into a paragon of virtue. The Spirit changes people. The Author of life is also the Transformer of life.

—*R. C. Sproul*

If you feel stuck, bring your whole self to Christ, not just the problem, but you. Ask God to change your heart. Commit yourself to pray to that end. It's God's heart to give good gifts to His children.

—*Sheila Walsh*

For your next devotional reading, go to page 742.

nor have I attained to the knowledge
    of the Holy One.
⁴Who has gone up to heaven and come
    down?
    Whose hands have gathered up the
        wind?
    Who has wrapped up the waters in a
        cloak?
    Who has established all the ends of
        the earth?
    What is his name, and what is the name
        of his son?
    Surely you know!

⁵"Every word of God is flawless;
    he is a shield to those who take
        refuge in him.
⁶Do not add to his words,
    or he will rebuke you and prove you a
        liar.

⁷"Two things I ask of you, LORD;
    do not refuse me before I die:
⁸Keep falsehood and lies far from me;
    give me neither poverty nor riches,
    but give me only my daily bread.
⁹Otherwise, I may have too much and
        disown you
    and say, 'Who is the LORD?'
    Or I may become poor and steal,
    and so dishonor the name of my
        God.

¹⁰"Do not slander servants to their master,
    or they will curse you, and you will
        pay for it.

¹¹"There are those who curse their
        fathers
    and do not bless their mothers;
¹²those who are pure in their own eyes
    and yet are not cleansed of their filth;
¹³those whose eyes are ever so haughty,
    whose glances are so disdainful;
¹⁴those whose teeth are swords
    and whose jaws are set with knives
    to devour the poor from the earth
    and the needy from among
        humankind.

¹⁵"The leech has two daughters.
    'Give! Give!' they cry.

"There are three things that are never
        satisfied,
    four that never say, 'Enough!':

¹⁶the grave, the barren womb,
    land, which is never satisfied with
        water,
    and fire, which never says, 'Enough!'

¹⁷"The eye that mocks a father,
    that scorns an aged mother,
    will be pecked out by the ravens of the
        valley,
    will be eaten by the vultures.

¹⁸"There are three things that are too
        amazing for me,
    four that I do not understand:
¹⁹the way of an eagle in the sky,
    the way of a snake on a rock,
    the way of a ship on the high seas,
    and the way of a man with a young
        woman.

²⁰"This is the way of an adulterous
        woman:
    She eats and wipes her mouth
    and says, 'I've done nothing wrong.'

²¹"Under three things the earth trembles,
    under four it cannot bear up:
²²a servant who becomes king,
    a godless fool who gets plenty to eat,
²³a contemptible woman who gets
        married,
    and a servant who displaces her
        mistress.

²⁴"Four things on earth are small,
    yet they are extremely wise:
²⁵Ants are creatures of little strength,
    yet they store up their food in the
        summer;
²⁶hyraxes are creatures of little power,
    yet they make their home in the
        crags;
²⁷locusts have no king,
    yet they advance together in ranks;
²⁸a lizard can be caught with the hand,
    yet it is found in kings' palaces.

²⁹"There are three things that are stately
        in their stride,
    four that move with stately bearing:
³⁰a lion, mighty among beasts,
    who retreats before nothing;
³¹a strutting rooster, a he-goat,
    and a king secure against revolt.ᵃ

³²"If you play the fool and exalt yourself,
    or if you plan evil,

a 31 The meaning of the Hebrew for this phrase is uncertain.

MONDAY

A WOMAN'S THEOLOGY

Proverbs 31:10–31 *or* 31:28–30

Carolyn Custis James

The greatest asset a woman brings to her marriage is not her beauty, her charm, her feminine wiles, or even her ability to bear a child. It is her theology. Every wife is her husband's partner, pastor, spiritual counselor, motivational speaker, and his fellow soldier in the war zone. With her eyes fixed on Jesus, she is less inclined to make her husband, herself or her children the center of the universe. With head and heart filled with the knowledge of God, she will find strength to enter the fray and wrestle with all of life's problems alongside her husband. As she lives in the light of God's sovereign goodness, she will radiate hope and courage to him in the darkest hours. With her feet firmly planted on God's holy character, she will find boldness to stand up to her man when his disobedience is tarnishing God's glory. And her husband will only be the better for it.

PHILIP SCHAFF {AD 1819–1893}

The fourth century Empress Placilla, wife of Emperor Theodosius, constantly used to put him in mind of the divine laws in which she had first carefully educated herself. In no way self-inflated by her imperial rank, she was rather fired by it with greater longing for divine things. The greatness of the good gift given her made her love for him who gave it all the greater. Therefore, she bestowed every kind of attention on the maimed and the mutilated, declining all aid from her household and her guards, herself visiting the houses where the sufferers lodged, and providing every person with what they required . . . To her husband, too, she frequently said, "Husband, you should always remember what you were once and what you have become now. By keeping this constantly in mind you will never grow ungrateful to your benefactor, but will guide in accordance with law the empire bestowed upon you, and in this way you will worship him who gave it." By continually using language of this kind, she carefully watered the seeds of virtue planted in her husband's heart.

reflection

1. Why is theology important in a woman's life?
2. How can women and men encourage each other in the pursuit of godliness?
3. How does today's Scripture passage encourage women who are married?

For your next devotional reading, go to page 745.

clap your hand over your mouth!
[33] For as churning cream produces butter,
and as twisting the nose produces
blood,
so stirring up anger produces strife."

Sayings of King Lemuel

31

The sayings of King Lemuel—
an inspired utterance his mother taught him.

[2] Listen, my son! Listen, son of my womb!
Listen, my son, the answer to my
prayers!
[3] Do not spend your strength[a] on women,
your vigor on those who ruin kings.

[4] It is not for kings, Lemuel—
it is not for kings to drink wine,
not for rulers to crave beer,
[5] lest they drink and forget what has been
decreed,
and deprive all the oppressed of their
rights.
[6] Let beer be for those who are perishing,
wine for those who are in anguish!
[7] Let them drink and forget their poverty
and remember their misery no more.

[8] Speak up for those who cannot speak for
themselves,
for the rights of all who are destitute.
[9] Speak up and judge fairly;
defend the rights of the poor and
needy.

Epilogue: The Wife of Noble Character

[10] [b] A wife of noble character who can find?
She is worth far more than rubies.
[11] Her husband has full confidence in her
and lacks nothing of value.
[12] She brings him good, not harm,
all the days of her life.
[13] She selects wool and flax
and works with eager hands.
[14] She is like the merchant ships,
bringing her food from afar.
[15] She gets up while it is still night;
she provides food for her family
and portions for her women servants.
[16] She considers a field and buys it;
out of her earnings she plants a
vineyard.
[17] She sets about her work vigorously;
her arms are strong for her tasks.
[18] She sees that her trading is profitable,
and her lamp does not go out at
night.
[19] In her hand she holds the distaff
and grasps the spindle with her
fingers.
[20] She opens her arms to the poor
and extends her hands to the needy.
[21] When it snows, she has no fear for her
household;
for all of them are clothed in scarlet.
[22] She makes coverings for her bed;
she is clothed in fine linen and
purple.
[23] Her husband is respected at the city
gate,
where he takes his seat among the
elders of the land.
[24] She makes linen garments and sells
them,
and supplies the merchants with
sashes.
[25] She is clothed with strength and dignity;
she can laugh at the days to come.
[26] She speaks with wisdom,
and faithful instruction is on her
tongue.
[27] She watches over the affairs of her
household
and does not eat the bread of
idleness.
[28] Her children arise and call her blessed;
her husband also, and he praises her:
[29] "Many women do noble things,
but you surpass them all."
[30] Charm is deceptive, and beauty is
fleeting;
but a woman who fears the LORD is to
be praised.
[31] Honor her for all that her hands have
done,
and let her works bring her praise at
the city gate.

[a] 3 Or *wealth*   [b] 10 Verses 10-31 are an acrostic poem, the verses of which begin with the successive
letters of the Hebrew alphabet.

ecclesiastes

AUTHOR: Probably King Solomon

DATE: Probably near the end of Solomon's life, 930 B.C.

THEME: Without God, our lives have no meaning.

Everything Is Meaningless

1 The words of the Teacher,[a] son of David, king in Jerusalem:

2 "Meaningless! Meaningless!"
    says the Teacher.
"Utterly meaningless!
    Everything is meaningless."

3 What does anyone gain from all their
        labors
    at which they toil under the sun?
4 Generations come and generations go,
    but the earth remains forever.
5 The sun rises and the sun sets,
    and hurries back to where it rises.
6 The wind blows to the south
    and turns to the north;
round and round it goes,
    ever returning on its course.
7 All streams flow into the sea,
    yet the sea is never full.
To the place the streams come from,
    there they return again.
8 All things are wearisome,
    more than one can say.
The eye never has enough of seeing,
    nor the ear its fill of hearing.
9 What has been will be again,
    what has been done will be done
        again;
    there is nothing new under the sun.
10 Is there anything of which one can say,
    "Look! This is something new"?
It was here already, long ago;
    it was here before our time.
11 There is no remembrance of people of
        old,
    and even those who are yet to come

will not be remembered
    by those who follow them.

Wisdom Is Meaningless

12 I, the Teacher, was king over Israel in Jerusalem. 13 I applied my mind to study and to explore by wisdom all that is done under the heavens. What a heavy burden God has laid on the human race! 14 I have seen all the things that are done under the sun; all of them are meaningless, a chasing after the wind.

15 What is crooked cannot be straightened;
    what is lacking cannot be counted.

16 I said to myself, "Look, I have grown and increased in wisdom more than anyone who has ruled over Jerusalem before me; I have experienced much of wisdom and knowledge." 17 Then I applied myself to the understanding of wisdom, and also of madness and folly, but I learned that this, too, is a chasing after the wind.

18 For with much wisdom comes much
            sorrow;
    the more knowledge, the more grief.

Pleasures Are Meaningless

2 I said to myself, "Come now, I will test you with pleasure to find out what is good." But that also proved to be meaningless. 2 "Laughter," I said, "is madness. And what does pleasure accomplish?" 3 I tried cheering myself with wine, and embracing folly—my mind still guiding me with wisdom. I wanted to see what was good for people to do under the heavens during the few days of their lives.

a 1 Or the leader of the assembly; also in verses 2 and 12

TUESDAY

STRIP IT ALL AWAY

Ecclesiastes 2:1–26 *or* 2:10–11

Rick McKinley

When we tear down the economic walls and strip away the nice homes, the expensive toys and even the exclusive vacation hideaways in paradise, we *all* have sin and brokenness eating away at us on the inside. There are plenty of bad days going on in every soul, no matter who you are.

Success in this world does not mean acceptance before God. The Bible tells us that every one of us stands guilty of sin in relationship to God. To be confused on this point is to miss redemption. You will not stand among a company of your peers to be declared fit for heaven.

Your friends won't vote you into heaven, and they can't vote you out.

Only God can make that decision.

When I first became a Christ-follower I did not understand this. I believed that some people could be good enough that they don't need God. But the more I explored the Bible, the more I came to see that, in God's eyes, we *all* need redemption because we *all* have sin . . .

God hates our sin. But sin is in us. It is part of us and we can't shake it. It shows up in our actions, our thoughts and our attitudes. At its core, sin is our desire to run our own lives any way we want. God hates that. He just does. He is not like you and me in that sin is not natural for him. It is the complete opposite of his holy character . . .

Amazingly, God is also compassionate and merciful and has a love for us that is beyond anything we could ever experience apart from him. And so God set out in Christ to purchase us back to himself. His hatred of our sin and his merciful love toward us were both manifested at the same time on the cross. Jesus died as our substitute, meaning that instead of punishing us for our sins, he punished Jesus instead. Jesus willingly went to the cross so that both his love for us could be manifested and the holiness of God could be satisfied.

R. L. WHEELER {AD 1890–1972}

If I had the wisdom of Solomon, the patience of John, the meekness of Moses, the strength of Samson, the obedience of Abraham, the compassion of Joseph, the tears of Jeremiah, the poetic skill of David, the prophetic voice of Elijah, the courage of Daniel, the greatness of John the Baptist, the endurance and love of Paul, I would still need redemption through Christ's blood, the forgiveness of sin.

reflection

1. What things have you looked to in the past to bring you meaning and purpose—and even salvation?

2. How would you define true success?

3. How does your definition compare with God's definition of success?

For your next devotional reading, go to page 747.

|| 745 ||

⁴I undertook great projects: I built houses for myself and planted vineyards. ⁵I made gardens and parks and planted all kinds of fruit trees in them. ⁶I made reservoirs to water groves of flourishing trees. ⁷I bought male and female slaves and had other slaves who were born in my house. I also owned more herds and flocks than anyone in Jerusalem before me. ⁸I amassed silver and gold for myself, and the treasure of kings and provinces. I acquired male and female singers, and a harem*a* as well—the delights of a man's heart. ⁹I became greater by far than anyone in Jerusalem before me. In all this my wisdom stayed with me.

¹⁰I denied myself nothing my eyes desired;
    I refused my heart no pleasure.
My heart took delight in all my labor,
    and this was the reward for all my
        toil.
¹¹Yet when I surveyed all that my hands
        had done
    and what I had toiled to achieve,
everything was meaningless, a chasing
        after the wind;
    nothing was gained under the sun.

Wisdom and Folly Are Meaningless

¹²Then I turned my thoughts to consider
        wisdom,
    and also madness and folly.
What more can the king's successor do
    than what has already been done?
¹³I saw that wisdom is better than folly,
    just as light is better than darkness.
¹⁴The wise have eyes in their heads,
    while fools walk in the darkness;
but I came to realize
    that the same fate overtakes them
        both.

¹⁵Then I said to myself,

"The fate of the fool will overtake me
        also.
    What then do I gain by being wise?"
I said to myself,
    "This too is meaningless."
¹⁶For the wise, like the fool, will not be
        long remembered;
    the days have already come when
        both have been forgotten.
Like the fool, the wise too must die!

Toil Is Meaningless

¹⁷So I hated life, because the work that is done under the sun was grievous to me. All of it is meaningless, a chasing after the wind. ¹⁸I hated all the things I had toiled for under the sun, because I must leave them to the one who comes after me. ¹⁹And who knows whether that person will be wise or foolish? Yet they will have control over all the toil into which I have poured my effort and skill under the sun. This too is meaningless. ²⁰So my heart began to despair over all my toilsome labor under the sun. ²¹For people may labor with wisdom, knowledge and skill, and then they must leave all they own to others who have not toiled for it. This too is meaningless and a great misfortune. ²²What do people get for all the toil and anxious striving with which they labor under the sun? ²³All their days their work is grief and pain; even at night their minds do not rest. This too is meaningless.

²⁴People can do nothing better than to eat and drink and find satisfaction in their toil. This too, I see, is from the hand of God, ²⁵for without him, who can eat or find enjoyment? ²⁶To the person who pleases him, God gives wisdom, knowledge and happiness, but to the sinner he gives the task of gathering and storing up wealth to hand it over to the one who pleases God. This too is meaningless, a chasing after the wind.

A Time for Everything

3 There is a time for everything,
    and a season for every activity under
        the heavens:

²   a time to be born and a time to die,
    a time to plant and a time to uproot,
³   a time to kill and a time to heal,
    a time to tear down and a time to
        build,
⁴   a time to weep and a time to laugh,
    a time to mourn and a time to dance,
⁵   a time to scatter stones and a time to
        gather them,
    a time to embrace and a time to
        refrain,
⁶   a time to search and a time to give up,
    a time to keep and a time to throw
        away,
⁷   a time to tear and a time to mend,

---

a 8 The meaning of the Hebrew for this phrase is uncertain.

WEDNESDAY

FINDING MUCH MORE

Ecclesiastes 3:1–22 *or* 3:1–8

Joni Eareckson Tada

As Christians, you and I are not made for this world.

Well, in one sense we are. Our hands, feet, eyes and ears equip us for physical experiences on this planet made of water and dirt. Our ears process noise, our eyes register sights, our noses detect odors and our stomachs digest food. But we are also spirit. This makes for incredible tension. Someone once said, "Through faith we understand that we are not physical beings having a spiritual experience, but spiritual beings having a physical experience."

You and I are not made for this world because the earth is temporal. There is something in us that is definitely *not* temporal. That's why we squirm and groan against the confines of time. The clock, for us, is an adversary. Every heavenly moment—whether it be gazing into the soft eyes and gentle smile of the one we love or relishing the ecstasy of some glorious pleasure—every moment like this we embrace so we might keep time at bay. But we can't. We would like to call these moments timeless, but they're not. Time snatches them from our grasp.

This is where the tension *really* kicks in. Time is our natural environment, yet time is *not* our natural environment.

OSWALD CHAMBERS {AD 1874–1917}

A warning which needs to be reiterated is that the cares of this world, the deceitfulness of riches and the lust of other things entering in, will choke all that God puts in. We are never free from the recurring tides of this encroachment. If it does not come on the line of clothes and food, it will come on the line of money or lack of money; of friends or lack of friends; or on the line of difficult circumstances. It is one steady encroachment all the time, and unless we allow the Spirit of God to raise up the standard against it, these things will come in like a flood . . .

"[Each day has enough trouble of its own.]" How much evil has begun to threaten you today? What kind of mean little imps have been looking in and saying—"Now what are you going to do next month—this summer?" "[Do not worry]," Jesus says. Look again and think. Keep your mind on the "much more" of your heavenly Father.

reflection

1. In what do you try to find solace?

2. In light of your reading today, do you think there are temporal goals still worth pursuing? What would they be?

3. What spiritual goals are you pursuing?

For your next devotional reading, go to page 757.

a time to be silent and a time to
speak,
8 a time to love and a time to hate,
a time for war and a time for peace.

⁹What do workers gain from their toil? ¹⁰I have seen the burden God has laid on the human race. ¹¹He has made everything beautiful in its time. He has also set eternity in the human heart; yet no one can fathom what God has done from beginning to end. ¹²I know that there is nothing better for people than to be happy and to do good while they live. ¹³That each of them may eat and drink, and find satisfaction in all their toil—this is the gift of God. ¹⁴I know that everything God does will endure forever; nothing can be added to it and nothing taken from it. God does it so that people will fear him.

¹⁵Whatever is has already been,
and what will be has been before;
and God will call the past to
account. *a*

¹⁶And I saw something else under the sun:

In the place of judgment—wickedness
was there,
in the place of justice—wickedness
was there.

¹⁷I said to myself,

"God will bring into judgment
both the righteous and the wicked,
for there will be a time for every activity,
a time to judge every deed."

¹⁸I also said to myself, "As for human beings, God tests them so that they may see that they are like the animals. ¹⁹Surely the fate of human beings is like that of the animals; the same fate awaits them both: As one dies, so dies the other. All have the same breath*b*; humans have no advantage over animals. Everything is meaningless. ²⁰All go to the same place; all come from dust, and to dust all return. ²¹Who knows if the human spirit rises upward and if the spirit of the animal goes down into the earth?"

²²So I saw that there is nothing better for people than to enjoy their work, because that is their lot. For who can bring them to see what will happen after them?

Oppression, Toil, Friendlessness

4 Again I looked and saw all the oppression that was taking place under the sun:

I saw the tears of the oppressed—
and they have no comforter;
power was on the side of their
oppressors—
and they have no comforter.
²And I declared that the dead,
who had already died,
are happier than the living,
who are still alive.
³But better than both
is the one who has not yet been,
who has not seen the evil
that is done under the sun.

⁴And I saw that all toil and all achievement spring from one person's envy of another. This too is meaningless, a chasing after the wind.

⁵Fools fold their hands
and ruin themselves.
⁶Better one handful with tranquillity
than two handfuls with toil
and chasing after the wind.

⁷Again I saw something meaningless under the sun:

⁸There was a man all alone;
he had neither son nor brother.
There was no end to his toil,
yet his eyes were not content with his
wealth.
"For whom am I toiling," he asked,
"and why am I depriving myself of
enjoyment?"
This too is meaningless—
a miserable business!

⁹Two are better than one,
because they have a good return for
their labor:
¹⁰If they fall down,
they can help each other up.
But pity those who fall
and have no one to help them up!
¹¹Also, if two lie down together, they will
keep warm.
But how can one keep warm alone?
¹²Though one may be overpowered,
two can defend themselves.

---

a 15 Or God calls back the past   *b 19 Or spirit*

A cord of three strands is not quickly
broken.

Advancement Is Meaningless

¹³Better a poor but wise youth than an old
but foolish king who no longer knows how
to heed a warning. ¹⁴The youth may have
come from prison to the kingship, or he may
have been born in poverty within his kingdom. ¹⁵I saw that all who lived and walked
under the sun followed the youth, the king's
successor. ¹⁶There was no end to all the people who were before them. But those who
came later were not pleased with the successor. This too is meaningless, a chasing
after the wind.

Fulfill Your Vow to God

5 *Guard your steps when you go to the
house of God. Go near to listen rather than to offer the sacrifice of fools,
who do not know that they do wrong.

*²Do not be quick with your mouth,
  do not be hasty in your heart
    to utter anything before God.
  God is in heaven
    and you are on earth,
    so let your words be few.
³A dream comes when there are many
    cares,
  and many words mark the speech of a
    fool.

⁴When you make a vow to God, do not
delay to fulfill it. He has no pleasure in fools;
fulfill your vow. ⁵It is better not to make a
vow than to make one and not fulfill it. ⁶Do
not let your mouth lead you into sin. And do
not protest to the ⌞temple⌟ messenger, "My
vow was a mistake." Why should God be angry at what you say and destroy the work of
your hands? ⁷Much dreaming and many
words are meaningless. Therefore fear God.

Riches Are Meaningless

⁸If you see the poor oppressed in a district, and justice and rights denied, do not
be surprised at such things; for one official
is eyed by a higher one, and over them both
are others higher still. ⁹The increase from
the land is taken by all; the king himself
profits from the fields.

¹⁰Those who love money never have
    enough;
  those who love wealth are never
    satisfied with their income.
  This too is meaningless.

¹¹As goods increase,
  so do those who consume them.
And what benefit are they to the owners
  except to feast their eyes on them?

¹²The sleep of laborers is sweet,
  whether they eat little or much,
but the abundance of the rich
  permits them no sleep.

¹³I have seen a grievous evil under the sun:

  wealth hoarded to the harm of its
    owners,
¹⁴ or wealth lost through some
    misfortune,
  so that when they have children
    there is nothing left for them to
      inherit.
¹⁵Everyone comes naked from their
    mother's womb,
  and as everyone comes, so they
    depart.
They take nothing from their toil
  that they can carry in their hands.

¹⁶This too is a grievous evil:

As everyone comes, so they depart,
  and what do they gain,
  since they toil for the wind?
¹⁷All their days they eat in darkness,
  with great frustration, affliction and
    anger.

¹⁸This is what I have observed to be good:
that it is appropriate for people to eat, to
drink and to find satisfaction in their toilsome labor under the sun during the few
days of life God has given them—for this is
their lot. ¹⁹Moreover, when God gives people
wealth and possessions, and the ability to
enjoy them, to accept their lot and be happy
in their toil—this is a gift of God. ²⁰They seldom reflect on the days of their lives, because God keeps them occupied with gladness of heart.

6 I have seen another evil under the
sun, and it weighs heavily on the human race: ²God gives some people
wealth, possessions and honor, so that they

---

* 5:1 is numbered 4:17 in Hebrew texts.   * 5:2-20 is numbered 5:1-19 in Hebrew texts.

lack nothing their hearts desire, but God does not grant the ability to enjoy them, and strangers enjoy them instead. This is meaningless, a grievous evil.

³A man may have a hundred children and live many years; yet no matter how long he lives, if he cannot enjoy his prosperity and does not receive proper burial, I say that a stillborn child is better off than he. ⁴It comes without meaning, it departs in darkness, and in darkness its name is shrouded. ⁵Though it never saw the sun or knew anything, it has more rest than does that man— ⁶even if he lives a thousand years twice over but fails to enjoy his prosperity. Do not all go to the same place?

⁷Everyone's toil is for the mouth,
  yet the appetite is never satisfied.
⁸What advantage have the wise over
    fools?
  What do the poor gain
    by knowing how to conduct
        themselves before others?
⁹Better what the eye sees
    than the roving of the appetite.
  This too is meaningless,
    a chasing after the wind.

¹⁰Whatever exists has already been
      named,
  and what humanity is has been
      known;
  no one can contend
    with someone who is stronger.
¹¹The more the words,
    the less the meaning,
    and how does that profit anyone?

¹²For who knows what is good for people in life, during the few and meaningless days they pass through like a shadow? Who can tell them what will happen under the sun after they are gone?

Wisdom

7 A good name is better than fine
      perfume,
  and the day of death better than the
      day of birth.
²It is better to go to a house of mourning
    than to go to a house of feasting,
  for death is the destiny of everyone;
    the living should take this to heart.
³Frustration is better than laughter,
    because a sad face is good for the
      heart.

⁴The heart of the wise is in the house of
      mourning,
  but the heart of fools is in the house
      of pleasure.
⁵It is better to heed the rebuke of a wise
      person
  than to listen to the song of fools.
⁶Like the crackling of thorns under the
      pot,
  so is the laughter of fools.
  This too is meaningless.

⁷Extortion turns the wise into fools,
  and a bribe corrupts the heart.
⁸The end of a matter is better than its
      beginning,
  and patience is better than pride.
⁹Do not be quickly provoked in your
      spirit,
  for anger resides in the lap of fools.

¹⁰Do not say, "Why were the old days
      better than these?"
  For it is not wise to ask such questions.

¹¹Wisdom, like an inheritance, is a good
      thing
  and benefits those who see the sun.
¹²Wisdom is a shelter
    as money is a shelter,
  but the advantage of knowledge is this:
    Wisdom preserves the life of its
        possessor.

¹³Consider what God has done:

Who can straighten
    what he has made crooked?
¹⁴When times are good, be happy;
    but when times are bad, consider:
God has made the one
    as well as the other.
Therefore, you cannot discover
    anything about your future.

¹⁵In this meaningless life of mine I have seen both of these:

the righteous perishing in their
      righteousness,
  and the wicked living long in their
      wickedness.
¹⁶Do not be overrighteous,
    neither be overwise—
    why destroy yourself?
¹⁷Do not be overwicked,
    and do not be a fool—
    why die before your time?

18 It is good to grasp the one
    and not let go of the other.
Whoever fears God will avoid all
    ⌊extremes.⌋ ᵃ

19 Wisdom makes one wise person more
        powerful
    than ten rulers in a city.

20 Indeed, there is no one on earth who is
        righteous,
    no one who does what is right and
        never sins.

21 Do not pay attention to every word
        people say,
    or you may hear your servant cursing
        you—
22 for you know in your heart
    that many times you yourself have
        cursed others.

23 All this I tested by wisdom and I said,

"I am determined to be wise"—
    but this was beyond me.
24 Whatever exists is far off and most
        profound—
    who can discover it?
25 So I turned my mind to understand,
    to investigate and to search out
        wisdom and the scheme of
        things
and to understand the stupidity of
        wickedness
    and the madness of folly.

26 I find more bitter than death
    the woman who is a snare,
whose heart is a trap
    and whose hands are chains.
The man who pleases God will escape
        her,
    but the sinner she will ensnare.

27 "Look," says the Teacher,ᵇ "this is what
I have discovered:

"Adding one thing to another to discover
        the scheme of things—
28   while I was still searching
        but not finding—
I found one ⌊upright⌋ man among a
        thousand,
    but not one ⌊upright⌋ woman among
        them all.

29 This only have I found:
    God created humankind upright,
    but they have gone in search of many
        schemes."

8 Who is like the wise?
    Who knows the explanation of
        things?
Wisdom brightens the face
    and changes its hard appearance.

Obey the King

2 Obey the king's command, I say, because you took an oath before God. 3 Do not
be in a hurry to leave the king's presence. Do
not stand up for a bad cause, for he will do
whatever he pleases. 4 Since a king's word is
supreme, who can say to him, "What are you
doing?"

5 Whoever obeys his command will come
        to no harm,
    and the wise heart will know the
        proper time and procedure.
6 For there is a proper time and procedure
        for every matter,
    though a person may be weighed
        down by misery.

7 Since no one knows the future,
    who can say what is to come?
8 As no one has power over the wind to
        contain it,
    soᶜ no one has power over the time of
        their death.
As no one is discharged in time of war,
    so wickedness will not release those
        who practice it.

9 All this I saw, as I applied my mind to
everything done under the sun. There is a
time when a man lords it over others to his
ownᵈ hurt. 10 Then too, I saw the wicked buried—those who used to come and go from
the holy place and receive praiseᵉ in the city
where they did this. This too is meaningless.
11 When the sentence for a crime is not
quickly carried out, people's hearts are filled
with schemes to do wrong. 12 Although a
wicked person who commits a hundred
crimes may live a long time, I know that it
will go better with those who fear God, who
are reverent before him. 13 Yet because the
wicked do not fear God, it will not go well

ᵃ 18 Or *will follow them both
it, / and so*   ᵈ 9 Or *to their
manuscripts *and are forgotten*   ᵇ 27 Or *the leader of the assembly*   ᶜ 8 Or *over the human spirit to retain*   ᵉ 10 Some Hebrew manuscripts and Septuagint (Aquila); most Hebrew

with them, and their days will not lengthen like a shadow.

[14]There is something else meaningless that occurs on earth: the righteous who get what the wicked deserve, and the wicked who get what the righteous deserve. This too, I say, is meaningless. [15]So I commend the enjoyment of life, because there is nothing better for people under the sun than to eat and drink and be glad. Then joy will accompany them in their toil all the days of the life God has given them under the sun.

[16]When I applied my mind to know wisdom and to observe the labor that is done on earth—people getting no sleep day or night— [17]then I saw all that God has done. No one can comprehend what goes on under the sun. People toil to search it out, but no one can discover its meaning. Even if the wise claim they know, they cannot really comprehend it.

A Common Destiny for All

9 So I reflected on all this and concluded that the righteous and the wise and what they do are in God's hands, but no one knows whether love or hate awaits them. [2]All share a common destiny—the righteous and the wicked, the good and the bad,[a] the clean and the unclean, those who offer sacrifices and those who do not.

As it is with the good,
so with the sinful;
as it is with those who take oaths,
so with those who are afraid to take them.

[3]This is the evil in everything that happens under the sun: The same destiny overtakes all. The hearts of people, moreover, are full of evil and there is madness in their hearts while they live, and afterward they join the dead. [4]Anyone who is among the living has hope[b]—even a live dog is better off than a dead lion!

[5]For the living know that they will die,
but the dead know nothing;
they have no further reward,
and even their name is forgotten.
[6]Their love, their hate
and their jealousy have long since vanished;

never again will they have a part
in anything that happens under the sun.

[7]Go, eat your food with gladness, and drink your wine with a joyful heart, for God has already approved what you do. [8]Always be clothed in white, and always anoint your head with oil. [9]Enjoy life with your wife, whom you love, all the days of this meaningless life that God has given you under the sun—all your meaningless days. For this is your lot in life and in your toilsome labor under the sun. [10]Whatever your hand finds to do, do it with all your might, for in the realm of the dead, where you are going, there is neither working nor planning nor knowledge nor wisdom.

[11]I have seen something else under the sun:

The race is not to the swift
or the battle to the strong,
nor does food come to the wise
or wealth to the brilliant
or favor to the learned;
but time and chance happen to them all.

[12]Moreover, no one knows when their hour will come:

As fish are caught in a cruel net,
or birds are taken in a snare,
so people are trapped by evil times
that fall unexpectedly upon them.

Wisdom Better Than Folly

[13]I also saw under the sun this example of wisdom that greatly impressed me: [14]There was once a small city with only a few people in it. And a powerful king came against it, surrounded it and built huge siege works against it. [15]Now there lived in that city a man poor but wise, and he saved the city by his wisdom. But nobody remembered that poor man. [16]So I said, "Wisdom is better than strength." But the poor man's wisdom is despised, and his words are no longer heeded.

[17]The quiet words of the wise are more to be heeded
than the shouts of a ruler of fools.
[18]Wisdom is better than weapons of war,
but one sinner destroys much good.

---

a 2 Septuagint (Aquila), Vulgate and Syriac; Hebrew does not have *and the bad.*   *b 4* Or *What then is to be chosen? With all who live, there is hope*

10

As dead flies give perfume a bad
   smell,
   so a little folly outweighs
      wisdom and honor.
2 The heart of the wise inclines to the
      right,
   but the heart of the fool to the left.
3 Even as fools walk along the road,
   they lack sense
   and show everyone how stupid they
      are.
4 If a ruler's anger rises against you,
   do not leave your post;
   calmness can lay great offenses to
      rest.
5 There is an evil I have seen under the
      sun,
   the sort of error that arises from a
      ruler:
6 Fools are put in many high positions,
   while the rich occupy the low ones.
7 I have seen slaves on horseback,
   while princes go on foot like slaves.

8 Whoever digs a pit may fall into it;
   whoever breaks through a wall may
      be bitten by a snake.
9 Whoever quarries stones may be injured
      by them;
   whoever splits logs may be
      endangered by them.

10 If the ax is dull
   and its edge unsharpened,
   more strength is needed,
   but skill will bring success.

11 If a snake bites before it is charmed,
   the charmer receives no fee.

12 Words from the mouth of the wise are
      gracious,
   but fools are consumed by their own
      lips.
13 At the beginning their words are folly;
   at the end they are wicked madness—
14   and fools multiply words.

   No one knows what is coming—
   who can tell them what will happen
      after them?

15 The toil of fools wearies them;
   they do not know the way to town.

16 Woe to the land whose king was a
      servant[a]
   and whose princes feast in the
      morning.
17 Blessed is the land whose king is of
      noble birth
   and whose princes eat at a proper
      time—
   for strength and not for drunkenness.

18 Through laziness, the rafters sag;
   because of idle hands, the house
      leaks.

19 A feast is made for laughter,
   wine makes life merry,
   and money is the answer for
      everything.

20 Do not revile the king even in your
      thoughts,
   or curse the rich in your bedroom,
   because a bird in the sky may carry your
      words,
   and a bird on the wing may report
      what you say.

Invest in Many Ventures

11

Ship your grain across the sea;
   after many days you may receive a
      return.
2 Invest in seven ventures, yes, in eight;
   you do not know what disaster may
      come upon the land.

3 If clouds are full of water,
   they pour rain on the earth.
   Whether a tree falls to the south or to
      the north,
   in the place where it falls, there it will
      lie.
4 Whoever watches the wind will not
      plant;
   whoever looks at the clouds will not
      reap.

5 As you do not know the path of the wind,
   or how the body is formed[b] in a
      mother's womb,
   so you cannot understand the work of
      God,
   the Maker of all things.

6 Sow your seed in the morning,
   and at evening let your hands not be
      idle,

---

a 16 Or *king is a child*   b 5 Or *know how life (or the spirit) / enters the body being formed*

for you do not know which will succeed,
  whether this or that,
  or whether both will do equally well.

Remember Your Creator While Young

[7] Light is sweet,
  and it pleases the eyes to see the sun.
[8] However many years anyone may live,
  let them enjoy them all.
But let them remember the days of
    darkness,
  for there will be many.
  Everything to come is meaningless.

[9] You who are young, be happy while you
    are young,
  and let your hearts give you joy in the
    days of your youth.
Follow the ways of your heart
  and whatever your eyes see,
but know that for all these things
  God will bring you into judgment.
[10] So then, banish anxiety from your heart
  and cast off the troubles of your body,
  for youth and vigor are meaningless.

12

Remember your Creator
  in the days of your youth,
  before the days of trouble come
and the years approach when you will
    say,
  "I find no pleasure in them"—
[2] before the sun and the light
  and the moon and the stars grow dark,
  and the clouds return after the rain;
[3] when the keepers of the house tremble,
  and the strong men stoop,
when the grinders cease because they
    are few,
  and those looking through the
    windows grow dim;
[4] when the doors to the street are closed
  and the sound of grinding fades;
when people rise up at the sound of
    birds,
  but all their songs grow faint;

[5] when people are afraid of heights
  and of dangers in the streets;
when the almond tree blossoms
  and the grasshopper drags itself along
  and desire no longer is stirred.
Then people go to their eternal home
  and mourners go about the streets.

[6] Remember him—before the silver cord
    is severed,
  and the golden bowl is broken;
before the pitcher is shattered at the
    spring,
  and the wheel broken at the well,
[7] and the dust returns to the ground it
    came from,
  and the spirit returns to God who
    gave it.

[8] "Meaningless! Meaningless!" says the
    Teacher.[a]
  "Everything is meaningless!"

The Conclusion of the Matter

[9] Not only was the Teacher wise, but he also imparted knowledge to the people. He pondered and searched out and set in order many proverbs. [10] The Teacher searched to find just the right words, and what he wrote was upright and true.

[11] The words of the wise are like goads, their collected sayings like firmly embedded nails—given by one shepherd.[b] [12] Be warned, my son, of anything in addition to them.

Of making many books there is no end, and much study wearies the body.

[13] Now all has been heard;
  here is the conclusion of the matter:
Fear God and keep his commandments,
  for this is the ⌊duty⌋ of every human
    being.
[14] For God will bring every deed into
    judgment,
  including every hidden thing,
  whether it is good or evil.

song of songs

AUTHOR: Probably King Solomon

DATE: Probably early in Solomon's reign, around 965 B.C.

THEME: God created marriage to be passionate, sexual and committed.

1 Solomon's Song of Songs.

She [a]

² Let him kiss me with the kisses of his
mouth—
for your love is more delightful than
wine.
³ Pleasing is the fragrance of your
perfumes;
your name is like perfume poured
out.
No wonder the young women love
you!
⁴ Take me away with you—let us hurry!
Let the king bring me into his
chambers.

Friends

We rejoice and delight in you [b];
we will praise your love more than
wine.

She

How right they are to adore you!

⁵ Dark am I, yet lovely,
daughters of Jerusalem,
dark like the tents of Kedar,
like the tent curtains of Solomon. [c]
⁶ Do not stare at me because I am dark,
because I am darkened by the sun.
My mother's sons were angry with me
and made me take care of the
vineyards;
my own vineyard I had to neglect.

⁷ Tell me, you whom I love,
where you graze your flock
and where you rest your sheep at
midday.
Why should I be like a veiled woman
beside the flocks of your friends?

Friends

⁸ If you do not know, most beautiful of
women,
follow the tracks of the sheep
and graze your young goats
by the tents of the shepherds.

He

⁹ I liken you, my darling, to a mare
among Pharaoh's chariot horses.
¹⁰ Your cheeks are beautiful with earrings,
your neck with strings of jewels.
¹¹ We will make you earrings of gold,
studded with silver.

She

¹² While the king was at his table,
my perfume spread its fragrance.
¹³ My beloved is to me a sachet of myrrh
resting between my breasts.
¹⁴ My beloved is to me a cluster of henna
blossoms
from the vineyards of En Gedi.

He

¹⁵ How beautiful you are, my darling!
Oh, how beautiful!
Your eyes are doves.

---

a The main male and female speakers (identified primarily on the basis of the gender of the relevant
Hebrew forms) are indicated by the captions *He* and *She* respectively. The words of others are marked
Friends. In some instances the divisions and their captions are debatable.   *b* 4 The Hebrew is
masculine singular.   *c* 5 Or *Salma*

She

¹⁶How handsome you are, my beloved!
    Oh, how charming!
    And our bed is verdant.

He

¹⁷The beams of our house are cedars;
    our rafters are firs.

She [a]

2 I am a rose [b] of Sharon,
    a lily of the valleys.

He

²Like a lily among thorns
    is my darling among the young
        women.

She

³Like an apple [c] tree among the trees of
        the forest
    is my beloved among the young
        men.
I delight to sit in his shade,
    and his fruit is sweet to my taste.
⁴Let him lead me to the banquet hall,
    and let his banner over me be love.
⁵Strengthen me with raisins,
    refresh me with apples,
    for I am faint with love.
⁶His left arm is under my head,
    and his right arm embraces me.
⁷Daughters of Jerusalem, I charge you
    by the gazelles and by the does of the
        field:
Do not arouse or awaken love
    until it so desires.

⁸Listen! My beloved!
    Look! Here he comes,
leaping across the mountains,
    bounding over the hills.
⁹My beloved is like a gazelle or a young
        stag.
Look! There he stands behind our
        wall,
gazing through the windows,
    peering through the lattice.
¹⁰My beloved spoke and said to me,
    "Arise, my darling,
    my beautiful one, come with me.
¹¹See! The winter is past;

the rains are over and gone.
¹²Flowers appear on the earth;
    the season of singing has come,
the cooing of doves
    is heard in our land.
¹³The fig tree forms its early fruit;
    the blossoming vines spread their
        fragrance.
Arise, come, my darling;
    my beautiful one, come with me."

He

¹⁴My dove in the clefts of the rock,
    in the hiding places on the
        mountainside,
show me your face,
    let me hear your voice;
for your voice is sweet,
    and your face is lovely.
¹⁵Catch for us the foxes,
    the little foxes
that ruin the vineyards,
    our vineyards that are in bloom.

She

¹⁶My beloved is mine and I am his;
    he browses among the lilies.
¹⁷Until the day breaks
    and the shadows flee,
turn, my beloved,
    and be like a gazelle
or like a young stag
    on the rugged hills. [d]

3 All night long on my bed
    I looked for the one my heart loves;
    I looked for him but did not find him.
²I will get up now and go about the city,
    through its streets and squares;
I will search for the one my heart loves.
    So I looked for him but did not find
        him.
³The watchmen found me
    as they made their rounds in the city.
    "Have you seen the one my heart
        loves?"
⁴Scarcely had I passed them
    when I found the one my heart loves.
I held him and would not let him go
    till I had brought him to my mother's
        house,
    to the room of the one who conceived
        me.

---

a Or *He*   *b 1* Probably a member of the crocus family   *c 3* Or possibly *apricot*; here and elsewhere in
Song of Songs   *d 17* Or *the hills of Bether*

THURSDAY

THE OBJECT OF YOUR LOVE

Song of Songs 3:1–11 *or* 3:5

Lauren Winner

The ethic of sex developed in Scripture, beginning in Genesis and continuing through the Epistles of Paul, makes clear that sex was created for marriage and that all Christians are called to lives of chastity. For unmarried folks, chastity means no sex at all, and for married folks it means sex only with one's spouse. Living chastely before marriage is, to be sure, difficult, in large part because our society delays marriage longer than any previous generation in American history.

It is hardly necessary to note that we live in a sex-saturated society, that popular culture uses sexual images and sexual talk nonstop, and that the messages the secular world gives us about sex are very much at odds with the biblical vision of sexuality. In the idiom of secular society, good sex is frequent, casual, and has no consequences. In the Christian grammar, by contrast, good sex is conditioned by context—good sex, real sex, is sex that happens in marriage. Secular society tells us, simultaneously, that sex is no big deal and that it's the most important thing in the universe. Sex is so banal and meaningless that we can have random, casual sex with our next-door neighbor, yet sex is so hugely significant that we can't possibly live without it. So one challenge single Christians face is sensitizing themselves to and thinking critically about the confusing messages pop culture sends us about sex . . .

But chastity is more than just line drawing. It is more than just gritting your teeth and keeping your zipper zipped. And chastity is more than avoiding any remote opportunity to make sexual mistakes . . . True chastity involves disciplining our sexual desires and turning our focus away from members of the opposite sex toward God alone.

AUGUSTINE BAKER {AD 1575–1641}

Love is the foundation of all our actions, external and internal. It is both the source of and the driving force behind all other passions. Thus, your whole person can be inclined in one direction or another depending on whether the object of your love is honorable or dishonorable. As St. Augustine put it: "It is only a good or ill love that makes our actions and attitudes to be good or ill."

reflection

1. Fill in the blank: More than anything else, I long for _____.

2. What turns godly desire into sinful desire?

3. What do you think God's perspective is on your desires?

For your next devotional reading, go to page 759.

⁵Daughters of Jerusalem, I charge you
　by the gazelles and by the does of the
　　field:
Do not arouse or awaken love
　until it so desires.

⁶Who is this coming up from the
　　wilderness
　like a column of smoke,
perfumed with myrrh and incense
　made from all the spices of the
　　merchant?
⁷Look! It is Solomon's carriage,
　escorted by sixty warriors,
　the noblest of Israel,
⁸all of them wearing the sword,
　all experienced in battle,
each with his sword at his side,
　prepared for the terrors of the night.
⁹King Solomon made for himself the
　　carriage;
　he made it of wood from Lebanon.
¹⁰Its posts he made of silver,
　its base of gold.
Its seat was upholstered with purple,
　its interior inlaid with love.
Daughters of Jerusalem, ¹¹come out,
　and look, you daughters of Zion.
Lookᵃ on King Solomon wearing a
　　crown,
　the crown with which his mother
　　crowned him
on the day of his wedding,
　the day his heart rejoiced.

He

4　How beautiful you are, my darling!
　　Oh, how beautiful!
　Your eyes behind your veil are doves.
Your hair is like a flock of goats
　descending from the hills of Gilead.
²Your teeth are like a flock of sheep just
　　shorn,
　coming up from the washing.
Each has its twin;
　not one of them is alone.
³Your lips are like a scarlet ribbon;
　your mouth is lovely.
Your temples behind your veil
　are like the halves of a pomegranate.
⁴Your neck is like the tower of David,
　built with courses of stoneᵇ;
on it hang a thousand shields,

all of them shields of warriors.
⁵Your breasts are like two fawns,
　like twin fawns of a gazelle
　that browse among the lilies.
⁶Until the day breaks
　and the shadows flee,
I will go to the mountain of myrrh
　and to the hill of incense.
⁷All beautiful you are, my darling;
　there is no flaw in you.

⁸Come with me from Lebanon, my bride,
　come with me from Lebanon.
Descend from the crest of Amana,
　from the top of Senir, the summit of
　　Hermon,
from the lions' dens
　and the mountain haunts of leopards.
⁹You have stolen my heart, my sister, my
　　bride;
　you have stolen my heart
with one glance of your eyes,
　with one jewel of your necklace.
¹⁰How delightful is your love, my sister,
　　my bride!
　How much more pleasing is your love
　　than wine,
and the fragrance of your perfume
　more than any spice!
¹¹Your lips drop sweetness as the
　　honeycomb, my bride;
　milk and honey are under your
　　tongue.
The fragrance of your garments
　is like the fragrance of Lebanon.
¹²You are a garden locked up, my sister,
　　my bride;
　you are a spring enclosed, a sealed
　　fountain.
¹³Your plants are an orchard of
　　pomegranates
　with choice fruits,
　with henna and nard,
¹⁴　nard and saffron,
　calamus and cinnamon,
　with every kind of incense tree,
　with myrrh and aloes
　and all the finest spices.
¹⁵You areᶜ a garden fountain,
　a well of flowing water
　streaming down from Lebanon.

FRIDAY

TWO IN ONE FLESH

Song of Songs 4:1–16 *or* 4:1,4–5,7,9

TERTULLIAN {ca. AD 155–230}

God ordained that there shall be two in one flesh (Genesis 2:24), not three nor four. On any other hypothesis, there would no longer be one flesh, nor two (joined) into one flesh. These will be so, if the conjunction and the growing together in unity take place *once for all.*

Craig Gross and Mike Foster

Sexual intimacy binds people together physically, emotionally and spiritually. Each of these three elements is distinct from the others, yet they are dependent on one another at the same time. Sex is a beautiful mystery and a blessing when it is handled appropriately, and it is completely destructive when it is not.

Sex is the most physically intimate action you can participate in with another person. And the steps leading up to intercourse—from holding hands, to hugging and kissing, to touching another person's naked body—are all part of it. The level of intimacy that takes place in all physical actions leading up to and including sex binds those two people together physically, emotionally and spiritually. The physical is only a representation of what is really going on inside both people emotionally and spiritually. When two people end a relationship that has gone far physically, it rips them apart, because they have made themselves so vulnerable to each other on every level.

reflection

1. What are some of the mysteries of sexual intimacy?
2. Why did God create sexual intimacy to be so powerful?
3. What can you learn about God from how he created sex and sexual intimacy?

For your next devotional reading, go to page 761.

|| 759 ||

She

¹⁶Awake, north wind,
    and come, south wind!
Blow on my garden,
    that its fragrance may spread abroad.
Let my beloved come into his garden
    and taste its choice fruits.

He

5
  I have come into my garden, my
      sister, my bride;
I have gathered my myrrh with my
    spice.
I have eaten my honeycomb and my
    honey;
I have drunk my wine and my milk.

Friends

Eat, friends, and drink;
    drink your fill of love.

She

²I slept but my heart was awake.
    Listen! My beloved is knocking:
"Open to me, my sister, my darling,
    my dove, my flawless one.
My head is drenched with dew,
    my hair with the dampness of the
      night."
³I have taken off my robe—
    must I put it on again?
I have washed my feet—
    must I soil them again?
⁴My beloved thrust his hand through the
    latch-opening;
    my heart began to pound for him.
⁵I arose to open for my beloved,
    and my hands dripped with myrrh,
my fingers with flowing myrrh,
    on the handles of the bolt.
⁶I opened for my beloved,
    but my beloved had left; he was gone.
    My heart sank at his departure.[a]
I looked for him but did not find him.
    I called him but he did not answer.
⁷The watchmen found me
    as they made their rounds in the city.
They beat me, they bruised me;
    they took away my cloak,
    those watchmen of the walls!
⁸Daughters of Jerusalem, I charge
      you—
    if you find my beloved,

what will you tell him?
    Tell him I am faint with love.

Friends

⁹How is your beloved better than others,
    most beautiful of women?
How is your beloved better than others,
    that you so charge us?

She

¹⁰My beloved is radiant and ruddy,
    outstanding among ten thousand.
¹¹His head is purest gold;
    his hair is wavy
    and black as a raven.
¹²His eyes are like doves
    by the water streams,
washed in milk,
    mounted like jewels.
¹³His cheeks are like beds of spice
    yielding perfume.
His lips are like lilies
    dripping with myrrh.
¹⁴His arms are rods of gold
    set with topaz.
His body is like polished ivory
    decorated with lapis lazuli.
¹⁵His legs are pillars of marble
    set on bases of pure gold.
His appearance is like Lebanon,
    choice as its cedars.
¹⁶His mouth is sweetness itself;
    he is altogether lovely.
This is my beloved, this is my friend,
    daughters of Jerusalem.

Friends

6
  Where has your beloved gone,
    most beautiful of women?
Which way did your beloved turn,
    that we may look for him with you?

She

²My beloved has gone down to his
      garden,
    to the beds of spices,
to browse in the gardens
    and to gather lilies.
³I am my beloved's and my beloved is
      mine;
    he browses among the lilies.

---

a 6 Or heart had gone out to him when he spoke

You Belong

Song of Songs 6:3

read/meditate

What does it mean to you to belong to someone? Song of Songs 6:3 describes a woman and a man claiming each other. Do you feel claimed by anyone? Do you feel claimed by God? What difference does that make in your life?

pray

Share with God the sense of belonging that you have in your life. Is it enough to satisfy you? Is your relationship with God the focus of your sense of belonging? Ask God to speak to you through the next few days about your position and privilege as his child.

contemplate

Think about what draws people together and what makes for lifetime relationships. Think about your lifelong friends. Do you have that sense of belonging spiritually? If not, is there anything you can do about that?

additional reflection

The truth, even though I cannot feel it right now, is that I am the chosen child of God, precious in God's eyes, called the Beloved from all eternity and held safe in an everlasting embrace . . . We must dare to opt consciously for our chosenness and not allow our emotions, feelings, or passions to seduce us into self-rejection.

—Henri J. M. Nouwen

I am His by purchase and I am His by conquest; I am His by donation and I am His by election; I am His by covenant and I am His by marriage; I am wholly His; I am peculiarly His; I am universally His; I am eternally His.

—Thomas Brooks

For your next devotional reading, go to page 763.

He

⁴ You are as beautiful as Tirzah, my
darling,
as lovely as Jerusalem,
as majestic as troops with banners.
⁵ Turn your eyes from me;
they overwhelm me.
Your hair is like a flock of goats
descending from Gilead.
⁶ Your teeth are like a flock of sheep
coming up from the washing.
Each has its twin,
not one of them is missing.
⁷ Your temples behind your veil
are like the halves of a pomegranate.
⁸ Sixty queens there may be,
and eighty concubines,
and virgins beyond number;
⁹ but my dove, my perfect one, is unique,
the only daughter of her mother,
the favorite of the one who bore her.
The young women saw her and called
her blessed;
the queens and concubines praised
her.

Friends

¹⁰ Who is this that appears like the dawn,
fair as the moon, bright as the sun,
majestic as the stars in procession?

He

¹¹ I went down to the grove of nut trees
to look at the new growth in the
valley,
to see if the vines had budded
or the pomegranates were in bloom.
¹² Before I realized it,
my desire set me among the royal
chariots of my people. ᵃ

Friends

*¹³ Come back, come back, O Shulammite;
come back, come back, that we may
gaze on you!

He

Why would you gaze on the Shulammite
as on the dance of Mahanaim?

7 *How beautiful your sandaled feet,
O prince's daughter!
Your graceful legs are like jewels,
the work of an artist's hands.
² Your navel is a rounded goblet
that never lacks blended wine.
Your waist is a mound of wheat
encircled by lilies.
³ Your breasts are like two fawns,
like twin fawns of a gazelle.
⁴ Your neck is like an ivory tower.
Your eyes are the pools of Heshbon
by the gate of Bath Rabbim.
Your nose is like the tower of Lebanon
looking toward Damascus.
⁵ Your head crowns you like Mount
Carmel.
Your hair is like royal tapestry;
the king is held captive by its tresses.
⁶ How beautiful you are and how pleasing,
my love, with your delights!
⁷ Your stature is like that of the palm,
and your breasts like clusters of fruit.
⁸ I said, "I will climb the palm tree;
I will take hold of its fruit."
May your breasts be like clusters of
grapes on the vine,
the fragrance of your breath like
apples,
⁹ and your mouth like the best wine.

She

May the wine go straight to my beloved,
flowing gently over lips and teeth. ᵇ
¹⁰ I belong to my beloved,
and his desire is for me.
¹¹ Come, my beloved, let us go to the
countryside,
let us spend the night in the villages. ᶜ
¹² Let us go early to the vineyards
to see if the vines have budded,
if their blossoms have opened,
and if the pomegranates are in
bloom—
there I will give you my love.
¹³ The mandrakes send out their fragrance,
and at our door is every delicacy,
both new and old,
that I have stored up for you, my
beloved.

ᵃ 12 Or *among the chariots of Amminadab; or among the chariots of the people of the prince*
ᵇ 9 Septuagint, Aquila, Vulgate and Syriac; Hebrew *lips of sleepers*   ᶜ 11 Or *the henna bushes*
* 6:13 is numbered 7:1 in Hebrew texts.   * 7:1-13 is numbered 7:2-14 in Hebrew texts.

THE POWER OF UNQUENCHABLE LOVE
Song of Songs 8:1–14 *or* 8:7

S. J. Hill

Have you ever been in love? When you look into the eyes of the one you love, you realize your priorities have changed. Time, cost, distance and sacrifice have a way of paling when you look at your beloved. Love has a way of taking you further than you want to go, making you offer more than you would naturally give, and prompting you to sacrifice the most precious things you have for the sake of another. It's both powerful and beautiful. And it was intended to be that way before the beginning of time.

The Christian life is designed to be a love affair of the heart. It's a passionate, life-giving relationship that makes the things of the world appear dull in comparison. Song of [Songs] 8:7 tells us, "Many waters cannot quench love; rivers cannot [sweep] it away."

When Solomon describes love as "unquenchable," he's not only speaking of God's love for you; he's also referring to the love you can have for Him. It's more than an invitation. It's something that He has instilled in the heart of every human being. Call it what you may—a vacuum, hole, pocket or void—but there exists in everyone a place that longs for fulfillment and pleasure. It's a universal human experience. And it's placed in each of you by God, for God.

JONATHAN EDWARDS {AD 1703–1758}

A person who has a knowledge of doctrine and theology only—without religious affection—has never engaged in true religion. Nothing is more apparent than this: our religion takes root within us only as deep as our affections attract it. There are thousands who hear the Word of God, who hear great and exceedingly important truths about themselves and their lives, and yet all they hear has no effect upon them . . .

I am bold in saying this, but I believe that no one is ever changed, either by doctrine, by hearing the Word, or by the preaching or teaching of another, unless the affections are moved by these things. No one ever seeks salvation, no one ever cries for wisdom, no one ever wrestles with God, no one ever kneels in prayer or flees from sin, with a heart that remains unaffected. In a word, there is never any great achievement by the things of religion without a heart deeply affected by those things.

reflection

1. Have you experienced passionate love for another person? If so, how would you describe your feelings?
2. How would you describe your feelings of love for God?
3. How has your love affair with God changed you?

For your next devotional reading, go to page 773.

8

If only you were to me like a brother,
who was nursed at my mother's
breasts!
Then, if I found you outside,
I would kiss you,
and no one would despise me.
2 I would lead you
and bring you to my mother's house—
she who has taught me.
I would give you spiced wine to drink,
the nectar of my pomegranates.
3 His left arm is under my head
and his right arm embraces me.
4 Daughters of Jerusalem, I charge you:
Do not arouse or awaken love
until it so desires.

Friends

5 Who is this coming up from the
wilderness
leaning on her beloved?

She

Under the apple tree I roused you;
there your mother conceived you,
there she who was in labor gave you
birth.
6 Place me like a seal over your heart,
like a seal on your arm;
for love is as strong as death,
its jealousy *a* unyielding as the grave.
It burns like blazing fire,
like a mighty flame.*b*
7 Many waters cannot quench love;
rivers cannot sweep it away.
If one were to give
all the wealth of one's house for love,
it *c* would be utterly scorned.

Friends

8 We have a little sister,
and her breasts are not yet grown.
What shall we do for our sister
on the day she is spoken for?
9 If she is a wall,
we will build towers of silver on her.
If she is a door,
we will enclose her with panels of
cedar.

She

10 I am a wall,
and my breasts are like towers.
Thus I have become in his eyes
like one bringing contentment.
11 Solomon had a vineyard in Baal Hamon;
he let out his vineyard to tenants.
Each was to bring for its fruit
a thousand shekels *d* of silver.
12 But my own vineyard is mine to give;
the thousand shekels are for you,
Solomon,
and two hundred *e* are for those who
tend its fruit.

He

13 You who dwell in the gardens
with friends in attendance,
let me hear your voice!

She

14 Come away, my beloved,
and be like a gazelle
or like a young stag
on the spice-laden mountains.

---

a 6 Or *ardor*   *b 6* Or *fire, / like the very flame of the* LORD   *c 7* Or *he*   *d 11* That is, about 25 pounds
or about 11.5 kilograms; also in verse 12   *e 12* That is, about 5 pounds or about 2.3 kilograms

The Prophets

Isaiah

Jeremiah

Lamentations

Ezekiel

Daniel

Hosea

Joel

Amos

Obadiah

Jonah

Micah

Nahum

Habakkuk

Zephaniah

Haggai

Zechariah

Malachi

The Prophets

Isaiah	Jonah
Jeremiah	Micah
Lamentations	Nahum
Ezekiel	Habakkuk
Daniel	Zephaniah
Hosea	Haggai
Joel	Zechariah
Amos	Malachi
Obadiah	

isaiah

AUTHOR: Isaiah

DATE: Between 701 and 681 B.C.

THEME: Both God's justice and God's mercy will be realized.

1 The vision concerning Judah and Jerusalem that Isaiah son of Amoz saw during the reigns of Uzziah, Jotham, Ahaz and Hezekiah, kings of Judah.

A Rebellious Nation

2 Hear me, you heavens! Listen, earth!
  For the LORD has spoken:
"I reared children and brought them up,
  but they have rebelled against me.
3 The ox knows its master,
  the donkey its owner's manger,
but Israel does not know,
  my people do not understand."

4 Ah, sinful nation,
  a people whose guilt is great,
a brood of evildoers,
  children given to corruption!
They have forsaken the LORD;
  they have spurned the Holy One of
    Israel
  and turned their backs on him.

5 Why should you be beaten anymore?
  Why do you persist in rebellion?
Your whole head is injured,
  your whole heart afflicted.
6 From the sole of your foot to the top of
    your head
  there is no soundness—
only wounds and welts
  and open sores,
not cleansed or bandaged
  or soothed with olive oil.

7 Your country is desolate,
  your cities burned with fire;
your fields are being stripped by
    foreigners
  right before you,

laid waste as when overthrown by
    strangers.
8 Daughter Zion is left
  like a shelter in a vineyard,
like a hut in a field of melons,
  like a city under siege.
9 Unless the LORD Almighty
  had left us some survivors,
we would have become like Sodom,
  we would have been like Gomorrah.

10 Hear the word of the LORD,
  you rulers of Sodom;
listen to the instruction of our God,
  you people of Gomorrah!
11 "The multitude of your sacrifices—
  what are they to me?" says the LORD.
"I have more than enough of burnt
    offerings,
  of rams and the fat of fattened
    animals;
I have no pleasure
  in the blood of bulls and lambs and
    goats.
12 When you come to appear before me,
  who has asked this of you,
  this trampling of my courts?
13 Stop bringing meaningless offerings!
  Your incense is detestable to me.
New Moons, Sabbaths and
    convocations—
  I cannot bear your evil assemblies.
14 Your New Moon feasts and your
    appointed festivals
  I hate with all my being.
They have become a burden to me;
  I am weary of bearing them.
15 When you spread out your hands in
    prayer,
  I will hide my eyes from you;
even if you offer many prayers,

I will not listen.
Your hands are full of blood;
¹⁶ wash and make yourselves clean.
Take your evil deeds
out of my sight!
Stop doing wrong,
¹⁷ learn to do right!
Seek justice,
encourage the oppressed. ^a
Defend the cause of the fatherless,
plead the case of the widow.

¹⁸"Come now, let us reason together,"
says the LORD.
"Though your sins are like scarlet,
they shall be as white as snow;
though they are red as crimson,
they shall be like wool.
¹⁹ If you are willing and obedient,
you will eat the best from the land;
²⁰ but if you resist and rebel,
you will be devoured by the sword."
For the mouth of the LORD
has spoken.

²¹ See how the faithful city
has become a prostitute!
She once was full of justice;
righteousness used to dwell in her—
but now murderers!
²² Your silver has become dross,
your choice wine is diluted with
water.
²³ Your rulers are rebels,
companions of thieves;
they all love bribes
and chase after gifts.
They do not defend the cause of the
fatherless;
the widow's case does not come
before them.
²⁴ Therefore the Lord, the LORD Almighty,
the Mighty One of Israel, declares:
"Ah, I will vent my wrath on my foes
and avenge myself on my enemies.
²⁵ I will turn my hand against you;
I will thoroughly purge away your
dross
and remove all your impurities.
²⁶ I will restore your judges as in days of old,
your rulers as at the beginning.
Afterward you will be called
the City of Righteousness,
the Faithful City."

²⁷ Zion will be delivered with justice,
her penitent ones with righteousness.
²⁸ But rebels and sinners will both be
broken,
and those who forsake the LORD will
perish.

²⁹ "You will be ashamed because of the
sacred oaks
in which you have delighted;
you will be disgraced because of the
gardens
that you have chosen.
³⁰ You will be like an oak with fading
leaves,
like a garden without water.
³¹ The mighty man will become tinder
and his work a spark;
both will burn together,
with no one to quench the fire."

The Mountain of the LORD

2 This is what Isaiah son of Amoz saw
concerning Judah and Jerusalem:

² In the last days

the mountain of the LORD's temple will
be established
as the highest of the mountains;
it will be exalted above the hills,
and all nations will stream to it.

³ Many peoples will come and say,

"Come, let us go up to the mountain of
the LORD,
to the house of the God of Jacob.
He will teach us his ways,
so that we may walk in his paths."
The law will go out from Zion,
the word of the LORD from Jerusalem.
⁴ He will judge between the nations
and will settle disputes for many
peoples.
They will beat their swords into
plowshares
and their spears into pruning hooks.
Nation will not take up sword against
nation,
nor will they train for war anymore.

⁵ Come, house of Jacob,
let us walk in the light of the LORD.

---

^a 17 Or justice, / rebuke the oppressor

The Day of the LORD

⁶ You have abandoned your people,
  the house of Jacob.
They are full of superstitions from the
    East;
  they practice divination like the
    Philistines
  and clasp hands with pagans.
⁷ Their land is full of silver and gold;
  there is no end to their treasures.
Their land is full of horses;
  there is no end to their chariots.
⁸ Their land is full of idols;
  they bow down to the work of their
    hands,
  to what their fingers have made.
⁹ So people will be brought low
  and everyone humbled—
  do not forgive them. ᵃ

¹⁰ Go into the rocks, hide in the ground
  from the fearful presence of the LORD
  and the splendor of his majesty!
¹¹ The eyes of the arrogant will be
    humbled
  and human pride brought low;
  the LORD alone will be exalted in that day.

¹² The LORD Almighty has a day in store
  for all the proud and lofty,
  for all that is exalted
  (and they will be humbled),
¹³ for all the cedars of Lebanon, tall and
    lofty,
  and all the oaks of Bashan,
¹⁴ for all the towering mountains
  and all the high hills,
¹⁵ for every lofty tower
  and every fortified wall,
¹⁶ for every trading ship ᵇ
  and every stately vessel.
¹⁷ The arrogance of all people will be
    brought low
  and human pride humbled;
  the LORD alone will be exalted in that
    day,
¹⁸   and the idols will totally disappear.

¹⁹ People will flee to caves in the rocks
  and to holes in the ground
  from the fearful presence of the LORD
  and the splendor of his majesty,
  when he rises to shake the earth.
²⁰ In that day people will throw away
  to the moles and bats

their idols of silver and idols of gold,
  which they made to worship.
²¹ They will flee to caverns in the rocks
  and to the overhanging crags
  from the fearful presence of the LORD
  and the splendor of his majesty,
  when he rises to shake the earth.

²² Stop trusting in human beings,
  who have but a breath in their
    nostrils.
  Why hold them in esteem?

Judgment on Jerusalem and Judah

3 See now, the Lord,
  the LORD Almighty,
  is about to take from Jerusalem and
    Judah
  both supply and support:
all supplies of food and all supplies of
    water,
² the hero and the warrior,
  the judge and the prophet,
  the diviner and the elder,
³ the captain of fifty and the person of
    rank,
  the counselor, skilled worker and
    clever enchanter.

⁴ I will make mere youths their officials;
  children will govern them.
⁵ People will oppress each other—
  one against another, neighbor against
    neighbor.
The young will rise up against the old,
  the nobody against the honored.

⁶ A man will seize one of his brothers
  in his father's house, and say,
"You have a cloak, you be our leader;
  take charge of this heap of ruins!"
⁷ But in that day he will cry out,
  "I have no remedy.
I have no food or clothing in my house;
  do not make me the leader of the
    people."

⁸ Jerusalem staggers,
  Judah is falling;
their words and deeds are against the
    LORD,
  defying his glorious presence.
⁹ The look on their faces testifies against
    them;
  they parade their sin like Sodom;

ᵃ 9 Or not raise them up   ᵇ 16 Hebrew every ship of Tarshish

they do not hide it.
Woe to them!
They have brought disaster upon
themselves.

¹⁰ Tell the righteous it will be well with
them,
for they will enjoy the fruit of their
deeds.
¹¹ Woe to the wicked!
Disaster is upon them!
They will be paid back
for what their hands have done.

¹² Youths oppress my people,
women rule over them.
My people, your guides lead you astray;
they turn you from the path.

¹³ The LORD takes his place in court;
he rises to judge the people.
¹⁴ The LORD enters into judgment
against the elders and leaders of his
people:
"It is you who have ruined my vineyard;
the plunder from the poor is in your
houses.
¹⁵ What do you mean by crushing my
people
and grinding the faces of the poor?"
declares the Lord,
the LORD Almighty.

¹⁶ The LORD says,
"The women of Zion are haughty,
walking along with outstretched necks,
flirting with their eyes,
tripping along with mincing steps,
with ornaments jingling on their
ankles.
¹⁷ Therefore the Lord will bring sores on the
heads of the women of Zion;
the LORD will make their scalps bald."

¹⁸ In that day the Lord will snatch away
their finery: the bangles and headbands and
crescent necklaces, ¹⁹ the earrings and
bracelets and veils, ²⁰ the headdresses and
ankle chains and sashes, the perfume bot-
tles and charms, ²¹ the signet rings and nose
rings, ²² the fine robes and the capes and
cloaks, the purses ²³ and mirrors, and the lin-
en garments and tiaras and shawls.

²⁴ Instead of fragrance there will be a
stench;

instead of a sash, a rope;
instead of well-dressed hair, baldness;
instead of fine clothing, sackcloth;
instead of beauty, branding.
²⁵ Your men will fall by the sword,
your warriors in battle.
²⁶ The gates of Zion will lament and
mourn;
destitute, she will sit on the ground.

4 ¹ In that day seven women
will take hold of one man
and say, "We will eat our own food
and provide our own clothes;
only let us be called by your name.
Take away our disgrace!"

The Branch of the LORD

² In that day the Branch of the LORD will
be beautiful and glorious, and the fruit of
the land will be the pride and glory of the
survivors in Israel. ³ Those who are left in
Zion, who remain in Jerusalem, will be
called holy, all who are recorded among the
living in Jerusalem. ⁴ The Lord will wash
away the filth of the women of Zion; he will
cleanse the bloodstains from Jerusalem by a
spirit *a* of judgment and a spirit *a* of fire.
⁵ Then the LORD will create over all of Mount
Zion and over those who assemble there a
cloud of smoke by day and a glow of flaming
fire by night; over everything the glory *b* will
be a canopy. ⁶ It will be a shelter and shade
from the heat of the day, and a refuge and
hiding place from the storm and rain.

The Song of the Vineyard

5 I will sing for the one I love
a song about his vineyard:
My loved one had a vineyard
on a fertile hillside.
² He dug it up and cleared it of stones
and planted it with the choicest vines.
He built a watchtower in it
and cut out a winepress as well.
Then he looked for a crop of good
grapes,
but it yielded only bad fruit.

³ "Now you dwellers in Jerusalem and
people of Judah,
judge between me and my vineyard.
⁴ What more could have been done for my
vineyard
than I have done for it?

<hr>

a 4 Or *the Spirit*   *b 5* Or *over all the glory there*

When I looked for good grapes,
    why did it yield only bad?
⁵ Now I will tell you
    what I am going to do to my vineyard:
I will take away its hedge,
    and it will be destroyed;
I will break down its wall,
    and it will be trampled.
⁶ I will make it a wasteland,
    neither pruned nor cultivated,
    and briers and thorns will grow there.
I will command the clouds
    not to rain on it."

⁷ The vineyard of the LORD Almighty
    is the house of Israel,
and the people of Judah
    are the vines he delighted in.
And he looked for justice, but saw
        bloodshed;
    for righteousness, but heard cries of
        distress.

Woes and Judgments

⁸ Woe to you who add house to house
    and join field to field
till no space is left
    and you live alone in the land.

⁹ The LORD Almighty has declared in my
hearing:

"Surely the great houses will become
        desolate,
    the fine mansions left without
        occupants.
¹⁰ A ten-acre vineyard will produce only a
        bath^a of wine,
    a homer^b of seed only an ephah^c of
        grain."

¹¹ Woe to those who rise early in the
        morning
    to run after their drinks,
who stay up late at night
    till they are inflamed with wine.
¹² They have harps and lyres at their
        banquets,
    pipes and timbrels and wine,
but they have no regard for the deeds of
        the LORD,
    no respect for the work of his hands.
¹³ Therefore my people will go into exile
    for lack of understanding;

those of high rank will die of hunger
    and the common people will be
        parched with thirst.
¹⁴ Therefore the grave enlarges its appetite
    and opens wide its mouth;
into it will descend their nobles and
        masses
    with all their brawlers and revelers.
¹⁵ So people will be brought low
    and everyone humbled,
    the eyes of the arrogant humbled.
¹⁶ But the LORD Almighty will be exalted by
        his justice,
    and the holy God will be proved holy
        by his righteous acts.
¹⁷ Then sheep will graze as in their own
        pasture;
    lambs will feed^d among the ruins of
        the rich.

¹⁸ Woe to those who draw sin along with
        cords of deceit,
    and wickedness as with cart ropes,
¹⁹ to those who say, "Let God hurry;
    let him hasten his work
    so we may see it.
The plan of the Holy One of Israel—
    let it approach, let it come into view,
    so we may know it."

²⁰ Woe to those who call evil good
    and good evil,
who put darkness for light
    and light for darkness,
who put bitter for sweet
    and sweet for bitter.

²¹ Woe to those who are wise in their own
        eyes
    and clever in their own sight.

²² Woe to those who are heroes at drinking
        wine
    and champions at mixing drinks,
²³ who acquit the guilty for a bribe,
    but deny justice to the innocent.
²⁴ Therefore, as tongues of fire lick up
        straw
    and as dry grass sinks down in the
        flames,
so their roots will decay
    and their flowers blow away like dust;
for they have rejected the law of the
        LORD Almighty

---

a 10 That is, about 6 gallons or about 22 liters   *b 10* That is, probably about 360 pounds or about 160
kilograms   *c 10* That is, probably about 36 pounds or about 16 kilograms   *d 17* Septuagint; Hebrew /
strangers will eat

and spurned the word of the Holy
One of Israel.

²⁵Therefore the Lᴏʀᴅ's anger burns against
his people;
his hand is raised and he strikes them
down.
The mountains shake,
and the dead bodies are like refuse in
the streets.

Yet for all this, his anger is not turned
away,
his hand is still upraised.

²⁶He lifts up a banner for the distant
nations,
he whistles for those at the ends of
the earth.
Here they come,
swiftly and speedily!
²⁷Not one of them grows tired or stumbles,
not one slumbers or sleeps;
not a belt is loosened at the waist,
not a sandal thong is broken.
²⁸Their arrows are sharp,
all their bows are strung;
their horses' hooves seem like flint,
their chariot wheels like a whirlwind.
²⁹Their roar is like that of the lion,
they roar like young lions;
they growl as they seize their prey
and carry it off with no one to rescue.
³⁰In that day they will roar over it
like the roaring of the sea.
And if one looks at the land,
there is only darkness and distress;
even the sun will be darkened by
clouds.

Isaiah's Commission

6 In the year that King Uzziah died, I
saw the Lord seated on a throne, high
and exalted, and the train of his robe
filled the temple. ²Above him were seraphs,
each with six wings: With two wings they
covered their faces, with two they covered
their feet, and with two they were flying.
³And they were calling to one another:

"Holy, holy, holy is the Lᴏʀᴅ Almighty;
the whole earth is full of his glory."

⁴At the sound of their voices the doorposts

and thresholds shook and the temple was
filled with smoke.
⁵"Woe to me!" I cried. "I am ruined! For I
am a man of unclean lips, and I live among
a people of unclean lips, and my eyes have
seen the King, the Lᴏʀᴅ Almighty."
⁶Then one of the seraphs flew to me with
a live coal in his hand, which he had taken
with tongs from the altar. ⁷With it he
touched my mouth and said, "See, this has
touched your lips; your guilt is taken away
and your sin atoned for."
⁸Then I heard the voice of the Lord saying,
"Whom shall I send? And who will go for us?"
And I said, "Here am I. Send me!"
⁹He said, "Go and tell this people:

" 'Be ever hearing, but never
understanding;
be ever seeing, but never perceiving.'
¹⁰Make the heart of this people calloused;
make their ears dull
and close their eyes.ᵃ
Otherwise they might see with their
eyes,
hear with their ears,
understand with their hearts,
and turn and be healed."

¹¹Then I said, "For how long, Lord?"
And he answered:

"Until the cities lie ruined
and without inhabitant,
until the houses are left deserted
and the fields ruined and ravaged,
¹²until the Lᴏʀᴅ has sent everyone far
away
and the land is utterly forsaken.
¹³And though a tenth remains in the land,
it will again be laid waste.
But as the terebinth and oak
leave stumps when they are cut
down,
so the holy seed will be the stump in
the land."

The Sign of Immanuel

7 When Ahaz son of Jotham, the son of
Uzziah, was king of Judah, King Rezin
of Aram and Pekah son of Remaliah
king of Israel marched up to fight against Jerusalem, but they could not overpower it.

ᵃ 9,10 Hebrew; Septuagint 'You will be ever hearing, but never understanding; / you will be ever seeing, but
never perceiving.' / ¹⁰This people's heart has become calloused; / they hardly hear with their ears, / and they
have closed their eyes

TUESDAY

THOUGHTS ON GRACE

Isaiah 6:1–13 *or* 6:1–7

John N. Oswalt

God owes us nothing. We are not "basically nice folks with an unfortunate tendency to mess up." We are proud, arrogant, self-centered, perverse, cruel, violent rebels in whom the stain of sin and sinfulness goes down to the last atom in the last molecule. We do not just "mess up." We "sin" (6:7). That is, we consciously and unconsciously miss the targets God has set up for his creatures. And that sin is a result of an inner twistedness that is both the cause and the result of sin. We no more have the "right" to God's love than a bale of hay has the "right" to live in a blast furnace. "Rights" don't enter into the question; the two things are simply utterly incompatible.

There is a strong likelihood that until we come to an understanding of ourselves like this, we will treat the grace of God—his unfailing undeserved love—as a throwaway item: "Of course God loves me; that's his job." No it is not his job. It is an unimaginable, unexpected, and indeed, unnecessary wonder of the universe. If we see God as he is and ourselves as we are, then, like Isaiah, it will not even occur to us to ask for continued life. Obviously it is impossibility. However, to the eternal praise of God, it is not impossibility. God has found a way, amazing as it is to think of, to satisfy both his holiness and his love.

JOHN TAULER {ca. AD 1300–1361}

Even the smallest drop of grace is better than all the earthly riches that lie beneath the sun. Indeed, a drop of grace is more extraordinary than all the angels and all the souls and all the natural things that God has made. And yet God gives grace to the soul even more lavishly than he gives any earthly gift. He gives it more generously than brooks of water, than the breath of the air, than the brightness of the sun; for spiritual things are far finer and nobler than earthly things . . . God's grace looses us from the snares of many temptations. It relieves us from the heavy burden of worldly cares and carries the spirit up to heaven, the land of spirits. It kills the worm of conscience, which makes past sins come alive again. Grace is a very powerful thing.

reflection

1. In what ways do you live as though God's primary job is to love you?

2. In what ways do you take God's love for granted?

3. What are your own thoughts on grace?

For your next devotional reading, go to page 776.

2Now the house of David was told, "Aram has allied itself with*a* Ephraim"; so the hearts of Ahaz and his people were shaken, as the trees of the forest are shaken by the wind.

3Then the LORD said to Isaiah, "Go out, you and your son Shear-Jashub,*b* to meet Ahaz at the end of the aqueduct of the Upper Pool, on the road to the Launderer's Field. 4Say to him, 'Be careful, keep calm and don't be afraid. Do not lose heart because of these two smoldering stubs of firewood—because of the fierce anger of Rezin and Aram and of the son of Remaliah. 5Aram, Ephraim and Remaliah's son have plotted your ruin, saying, 6"Let us invade Judah; let us tear it apart and divide it among ourselves, and make the son of Tabeel king over it." 7Yet this is what the Sovereign LORD says:

" 'It will not take place,
    it will not happen,
8for the head of Aram is Damascus,
    and the head of Damascus is only
        Rezin.
Within sixty-five years
    Ephraim will be too shattered to be a
        people.
9The head of Ephraim is Samaria,
    and the head of Samaria is only
        Remaliah's son.
If you do not stand firm in your faith,
    you will not stand at all.' "

10Again the LORD spoke to Ahaz, 11"Ask the LORD your God for a sign, whether in the deepest depths or in the highest heights."

12But Ahaz said, "I will not ask; I will not put the LORD to the test."

13Then Isaiah said, "Hear now, you house of David! Is it not enough to try the patience of human beings? Will you try the patience of my God also? 14Therefore the Lord himself will give you*c* a sign: The virgin*d* will conceive and give birth to a son, and*e* will call him Immanuel.*f* 15He will be eating curds and honey when he knows enough to reject the wrong and choose the right, 16for before the boy knows enough to reject the wrong and choose the right, the land of the two kings you dread will be laid waste. 17The

LORD will bring on you and on your people and on the house of your father a time unlike any since Ephraim broke away from Judah—he will bring the king of Assyria."

Assyria, the LORD's Instrument

18In that day the LORD will whistle for flies from the Nile delta in Egypt and for bees from the land of Assyria. 19They will all come and settle in the steep ravines and in the crevices in the rocks, on all the thornbushes and at all the water holes. 20In that day the Lord will use a razor hired from beyond the Euphrates River—the king of Assyria—to shave your head and the hair of your legs, and to take off your beards also. 21In that day, a person will keep alive a young cow and two goats. 22And because of the abundance of the milk they give, there will be curds to eat. All who remain in the land will eat curds and honey. 23In that day, in every place where there were a thousand vines worth a thousand silver shekels,*g* there will be only briers and thorns. 24Hunters will go there with bow and arrow, for the land will be covered with briers and thorns. 25As for all the hills once cultivated by the hoe, you will no longer go there for fear of the briers and thorns; they will become places where cattle are turned loose and where sheep run.

Isaiah and His Children as Signs

8 The LORD said to me, "Take a large scroll and write on it with an ordinary pen: Maher-Shalal-Hash-Baz."*h* 2So I called in Uriah the priest and Zechariah son of Jeberekiah as reliable witnesses for me. 3Then I made love to the prophetess, and she conceived and gave birth to a son. And the LORD said to me, "Name him Maher-Shalal-Hash-Baz. 4Before the boy knows how to say 'My father' or 'My mother,' the wealth of Damascus and the plunder of Samaria will be carried off by the king of Assyria."

5The LORD spoke to me again:

6"Because this people has rejected
    the gently flowing waters of Shiloah
and rejoices over Rezin
    and the son of Remaliah,

---

a 2 Or *has set up camp in*   *b 3* *Shear-Jashub* means *a remnant will return.*   *c 14* The Hebrew is plural.
d 14 Or *young woman*   *e 14* Masoretic Text; Dead Sea Scrolls *and he* or *and they*   *f 14* *Immanuel*
means *God with us.*   *g 23* That is, about 25 pounds or about 11.5 kilograms   *h 1* *Maher-Shalal-Hash-Baz* means *quick to the plunder, swift to the spoil*; also in verse 3.

7 therefore the Lord is about to bring
        against them
    the mighty floodwaters of the
        Euphrates—
    the king of Assyria with all his pomp.
It will overflow all its channels,
    run over all its banks
8 and sweep on into Judah, swirling over it,
    passing through it and reaching up to
        the neck.
Its outspread wings will cover the
        breadth of your land,
    Immanuel ᵃ!"

9 Raise the war cry, ᵇ you nations, and be
        shattered!
    Listen, all you distant lands.
Prepare for battle, and be shattered!
Prepare for battle, and be shattered!
10 Devise your strategy, but it will be
        thwarted;
    propose your plan, but it will not stand,
    for God is with us. ᶜ

11 This is what the LORD says to me with
his strong hand upon me, warning me not to
follow the way of this people:

12 "Do not call conspiracy
    everything this people calls a
        conspiracy;
do not fear what they fear,
    and do not dread it.
13 The LORD Almighty is the one you are to
        regard as holy,
    he is the one you are to fear,
    he is the one you are to dread.
14 He will be a holy place;
    for both houses of Israel he will be
a stone that causes people to stumble
    and a rock that makes them fall.
And for the people of Jerusalem he will be
    a trap and a snare.
15 Many of them will stumble;
    they will fall and be broken,
    they will be snared and captured."

16 Bind up this testimony of warning
    and seal up God's instruction among
        my disciples.
17 I will wait for the LORD,
    who is hiding his face from the house
        of Jacob.
I will put my trust in him.

18 Here am I, and the children the LORD
has given me. We are signs and symbols in
Israel from the LORD Almighty, who dwells
on Mount Zion.

The Darkness Turns to Light

19 When someone tells you to consult mediums and spiritists, who whisper and mutter, should not a people inquire of their
God? Why consult the dead on behalf of the
living? 20 Consult God's instruction and the
testimony of warning. If anyone does not
speak according to this word, they have no
light of dawn. 21 Distressed and hungry, they
will roam through the land; when they are
famished, they will become enraged and,
looking upward, will curse their king and
their God. 22 Then they will look toward the
earth and see only distress and darkness and
fearful gloom, and they will be thrust into
utter darkness.

9 *Nevertheless, there will be no more
gloom for those who were in distress.
In the past he humbled the land of
Zebulun and the land of Naphtali, but in the
future he will honor Galilee of the nations,
by the Way of the Sea, beyond the Jordan—

*2 The people walking in darkness
    have seen a great light;
on those living in the land of deep
        darkness
    a light has dawned.
3 You have enlarged the nation
    and increased their joy;
they rejoice before you
    as people rejoice at the harvest,
as soldiers rejoice
    when dividing the plunder.
4 For as in the day of Midian's defeat,
    you have shattered
the yoke that burdens them,
    the bar across their shoulders,
    the rod of their oppressor.
5 Every warrior's boot used in battle
    and every garment rolled in blood
will be destined for burning,
    will be fuel for the fire.
6 For to us a child is born,
    to us a son is given,
    and the government will be on his
        shoulders.
And he will be called

ᵃ 8 Immanuel means God with us.   ᵇ 9 Or Do your worst   ᶜ 10 Hebrew Immanuel
* 9:1 is numbered 8:23 in Hebrew texts.   * 9:2-21 is numbered 9:1-20 in Hebrew texts.

WEDNESDAY

REAL ANSWERS DURING SUFFERING

Isaiah 9:1–21 *or* 9:1–2,6–7

Joni Eareckson Tada

We must never distance the Bible's answers from God. The problem of suffering is not about some *thing*, but *Someone*. It follows that the answer must not be some thing, but Someone. "Knowing our Lord Jesus Christ" is keeping your eye on the Sculptor—not on the suffering, or even suffering's benefits.

Besides, answers are for the head. They don't always reach the problem where it hurts—in the gut and the heart. When a person is sorely suffering . . . [they] are like hurting children looking up into the faces of their parents, crying and asking, "Daddy, why?" Those children don't want explanations, answers or "reasons why," they want their daddy to pick them up, pat them on the backs and reassure them that everything is going to be okay.

Our heartfelt plea is for assurance—Fatherly assurance—that there is an order to reality that far transcends our problems, that somehow *everything will be okay*. We amble on along our philosophical path, then—Bam!—get hit with suffering . . . We need to be reassured that the world, the universe, is not in nightmarish chaos, but orderly and stable. God must be at the center of things. He must be in the center of our suffering. What's more, he must be Daddy. Personal and compassionate. This is our cry.

God, like a father, doesn't just give advice. He gives himself. He becomes the husband to the grieving widow (Isaiah 54:5). He becomes the comforter to the barren woman (Isaiah 54:1). He becomes the father of the orphaned (Psalm 10:14). He becomes the bridegroom to the single person (Isaiah 62:5). He is the healer to the sick (Exodus 15:26). He is the wonderful counselor to the confused and depressed (Isaiah 9:6).

This is what you do when someone you love is in anguish; you respond to the plea of their heart by giving them your heart. If you are the One at the center of the universe, holding it together, if everything moves, breathes and has its being in you, you can do no more than give yourself (Acts 17:28).

CORRIE TEN BOOM {AD 1892–1983}

You may never know that JESUS is all you need, until JESUS is all you have.

— *reflection* —

1. Throughout all of Israel's suffering, God held out to them the hope of the Messiah, who would establish his kingdom. How can knowing that the Messiah has come bring you hope in the midst of your suffering?

2. Was there a time in your life when Jesus was all you had?

3. How can you share the comfort of Jesus with someone you know who is hurting?

For your next devotional reading, go to page 782.

Wonderful Counselor, Mighty God,
Everlasting Father, Prince of Peace.
⁷ Of the increase of his government and
peace
there will be no end.
He will reign on David's throne
and over his kingdom,
establishing and upholding it
with justice and righteousness
from that time on and forever.
The zeal of the LORD Almighty
will accomplish this.

The LORD's Anger Against Israel

⁸ The Lord has sent a message against
Jacob;
it will fall on Israel.
⁹ All the people will know it—
Ephraim and the inhabitants of
Samaria—
who say with pride
and arrogance of heart,
¹⁰ "The bricks have fallen down,
but we will rebuild with dressed
stone;
the fig trees have been felled,
but we will replace them with
cedars."
¹¹ But the LORD has strengthened Rezin's
foes against them
and has spurred their enemies on.
¹² Arameans from the east and Philistines
from the west
have devoured Israel with open
mouth.

Yet for all this, his anger is not turned
away,
his hand is still upraised.

¹³ But the people have not returned to him
who struck them,
nor have they sought the LORD
Almighty.
¹⁴ So the LORD will cut off from Israel both
head and tail,
both palm branch and reed in a single
day;
¹⁵ the elders and dignitaries are the head,
the prophets who teach lies are the
tail.
¹⁶ Those who guide this people mislead
them,

and those who are guided are led
astray.
¹⁷ Therefore the Lord will take no pleasure
in the young men,
nor will he pity the fatherless and
widows,
for everyone is ungodly and wicked,
every mouth speaks folly.

Yet for all this, his anger is not turned
away,
his hand is still upraised.

¹⁸ Surely wickedness burns like a fire;
it consumes briers and thorns,
it sets the forest thickets ablaze,
so that it rolls upward in a column of
smoke.
¹⁹ By the wrath of the LORD Almighty
the land will be scorched
and the people will be fuel for the fire;
they will not spare each other.
²⁰ On the right they will devour,
but still be hungry;
on the left they will eat,
but not be satisfied.
They will all feed on the flesh of their
own offspring *a*:
²¹   Manasseh will feed on Ephraim, and
Ephraim on Manasseh;
together they will turn against Judah.

Yet for all this, his anger is not turned
away,
his hand is still upraised.

10

Woe to those who make unjust
laws,
to those who issue oppressive
decrees,
² to deprive the poor of their rights
and withhold justice from the
oppressed of my people,
making widows their prey
and robbing the fatherless.
³ What will you do on the day of
reckoning,
when disaster comes from afar?
To whom will you run for help?
Where will you leave your riches?
⁴ Nothing will remain but to cringe among
the captives
or fall among the slain.

a 20 Or arm

Yet for all this, his anger is not turned
away,
his hand is still upraised.

God's Judgment on Assyria

5 "Woe to the Assyrian, the rod of my
anger,
in whose hand is the club of my
wrath!
6 I send him against a godless nation,
I dispatch him against a people who
anger me,
to seize loot and snatch plunder,
and to trample them down like mud
in the streets.
7 But this is not what he intends,
this is not what he has in mind;
his purpose is to destroy,
to put an end to many nations.
8 'Are not my commanders all kings?' he
says.
9   'Has not Kalno fared like
Carchemish?
Is not Hamath like Arpad,
and Samaria like Damascus?
10 As my hand seized the kingdoms of the
idols,
kingdoms whose images excelled
those of Jerusalem and
Samaria—
11 shall I not deal with Jerusalem and her
images
as I dealt with Samaria and her
idols?' "

12 When the Lord has finished all his work
against Mount Zion and Jerusalem, he will
say, "I will punish the king of Assyria for the
willful pride of his heart and the haughty
look in his eyes. 13 For he says:

" 'By the strength of my hand I have
done this,
and by my wisdom, because I have
understanding.
I removed the boundaries of nations,
I plundered their treasures;
like a mighty one I subdued *a* their
kings.
14 As one reaches into a nest,
so my hand reached for the wealth of
the nations;
as people gather abandoned eggs,
so I gathered all the countries;

not one flapped a wing,
or opened its mouth to chirp.' "

15 Does the ax raise itself above the one
who swings it,
or the saw boast against the one who
uses it?
As if a rod were to wield the person who
lifts it up,
or a club brandish one who is not
wood!
16 Therefore, the Lord, the LORD Almighty,
will send a wasting disease upon his
sturdy warriors;
under his pomp a fire will be kindled
like a blazing flame.
17 The Light of Israel will become a fire,
their Holy One a flame;
in a single day it will burn and consume
his thorns and his briers.
18 The splendor of his forests and fertile
fields
it will completely destroy,
as when sick people waste away.
19 And the remaining trees of his forests
will be so few
that a child could write them down.

The Remnant of Israel

20 In that day the remnant of Israel,
the survivors of the house of Jacob,
will no longer rely on him
who struck them down
but will truly rely on the LORD,
the Holy One of Israel.
21 A remnant will return,*b* a remnant of
Jacob
will return to the Mighty God.
22 Though your people be like the sand by
the sea, Israel,
only a remnant will return.
Destruction has been decreed,
overwhelming and righteous.
23 The Lord, the LORD Almighty, will carry
out
the destruction decreed upon the
whole land.

24 Therefore, this is what the Lord, the
LORD Almighty, says:

"My people who live in Zion,
do not be afraid of the Assyrians,
who beat you with a rod

---

a 13 Or *treasures; / I subdued the mighty,*   *b 21* Hebrew *shear-jashub;* also in verse 22

and lift up a club against you, as
    Egypt did.
²⁵ Very soon my anger against you will end
    and my wrath will be directed to their
        destruction."

²⁶ The LORD Almighty will lash them with a
        whip,
    as when he struck down Midian at the
        rock of Oreb;
    and he will raise his staff over the
        waters,
    as he did in Egypt.
²⁷ In that day their burden will be lifted
        from your shoulders,
    their yoke from your neck;
    the yoke will be broken
        because you have grown so fat.^a

²⁸ They enter Aiath;
    they pass through Migron;
    they store supplies at Mikmash.
²⁹ They go over the pass, and say,
    "We will camp overnight at Geba."
    Ramah trembles;
    Gibeah of Saul flees.
³⁰ Cry out, Daughter Gallim!
    Listen, Laishah!
    Poor Anathoth!
³¹ Madmenah is in flight;
    the people of Gebim take cover.
³² This day they will halt at Nob;
    they will shake their fist
    at the mount of Daughter Zion,
    at the hill of Jerusalem.

³³ See, the Lord, the LORD Almighty,
    will lop off the boughs with great
        power.
    The lofty trees will be felled,
    the tall ones will be brought low.
³⁴ He will cut down the forest thickets with
        an ax;
    Lebanon will fall before the Mighty
        One.

The Branch From Jesse

11 A shoot will come up from the
        stump of Jesse;
    from his roots a Branch will bear
        fruit.
² The Spirit of the LORD will rest on him—
    the Spirit of wisdom and of
        understanding,

    the Spirit of counsel and of might,
    the Spirit of the knowledge and fear
        of the LORD—
³ and he will delight in the fear of the
        LORD.

He will not judge by what he sees with
        his eyes,
    or decide by what he hears with his
        ears;
⁴ but with righteousness he will judge the
        needy,
    with justice he will give decisions for
        the poor of the earth.
He will strike the earth with the rod of
        his mouth;
    with the breath of his lips he will slay
        the wicked.
⁵ Righteousness will be his belt
    and faithfulness the sash around his
        waist.

⁶ The wolf will live with the lamb,
    the leopard will lie down with the
        goat,
    the calf and the lion and the yearling^b
        together;
    and a little child will lead them.
⁷ The cow will feed with the bear,
    their young will lie down together,
    and the lion will eat straw like the ox.
⁸ Infants will play near the hole of the
        cobra;
    young children will put their hands
        into the viper's nest.
⁹ They will neither harm nor destroy
    on all my holy mountain,
    for the earth will be filled with the
        knowledge of the LORD
    as the waters cover the sea.

¹⁰ In that day the Root of Jesse will stand
as a banner for the peoples; the nations will
rally to him, and his resting place will be
glorious. ¹¹ In that day the Lord will reach out
his hand a second time to reclaim the sur-
viving remnant of his people from Assyria,
from Lower Egypt, from Upper Egypt, from
Cush,^c from Elam, from Babylonia,^d from
Hamath and from the islands of the Medi-
terranean.

¹² He will raise a banner for the nations
    and gather the exiles of Israel;

---

^a 27 Hebrew; Septuagint *broken / from your shoulders*   ^b 6 Hebrew; Septuagint *lion will feed*
^c 11 That is, the upper Nile region   ^d 11 Hebrew *Shinar*

he will assemble the scattered people of
        Judah
    from the four quarters of the earth.
¹³ Ephraim's jealousy will vanish,
    and Judah's enemies ª will be
        destroyed;
    Ephraim will not be jealous of Judah,
        nor Judah hostile toward Ephraim.
¹⁴ They will swoop down on the slopes of
        Philistia to the west;
    together they will plunder the people
        to the east.
    They will lay hands on Edom and Moab,
    and the Ammonites will be subject to
        them.
¹⁵ The Lord will dry up
    the gulf of the Egyptian sea;
    with a scorching wind he will sweep his
        hand
        over the Euphrates River.
    He will break it up into seven streams
    so that anyone can cross over in
        sandals.
¹⁶ There will be a highway for the remnant
        of his people
    that is left from Assyria,
    as there was for Israel
    when they came up from Egypt.

Songs of Praise

12 In that day you will say:

    "I will praise you, Lord.
    Although you were angry with me,
    your anger has turned away
    and you have comforted me.
² Surely God is my salvation;
    I will trust and not be afraid.
    The Lord, the Lord, is my strength and
        my defense ᵇ;
    he has become my salvation."
³ With joy you will draw water
    from the wells of salvation.

⁴ In that day you will say:

    "Give praise to the Lord, call on his
        name;
    make known among the nations what
        he has done,
    and proclaim that his name is
        exalted.
⁵ Sing to the Lord, for he has done
    glorious things;

let this be known to all the world.
⁶ Shout aloud and sing for joy, people of
        Zion,
    for great is the Holy One of Israel
        among you."

A Prophecy Against Babylon

13 A prophecy concerning Babylon
        that Isaiah son of Amoz saw:

² Raise a banner on a bare hilltop,
    shout to them;
    beckon to them
        to enter the gates of the nobles.
³ I have commanded my holy ones;
    I have summoned my warriors to
        carry out my wrath—
    those who rejoice in my triumph.

⁴ Listen, a noise on the mountains,
    like that of a great multitude!
    Listen, an uproar among the kingdoms,
    like nations massing together!
    The Lord Almighty is mustering
    an army for war.
⁵ They come from faraway lands,
    from the ends of the heavens—
    the Lord and the weapons of his
        wrath—
    to destroy the whole country.

⁶ Wail, for the day of the Lord is near;
    it will come like destruction from the
        Almighty. ᶜ
⁷ Because of this, all hands will go limp,
    every man's heart will melt.
⁸ Terror will seize them,
    pain and anguish will grip them;
    they will writhe like a woman in
        labor.
    They will look aghast at each other,
    their faces aflame.

⁹ See, the day of the Lord is coming
    —a cruel day, with wrath and fierce
        anger—
    to make the land desolate
    and destroy the sinners within it.
¹⁰ The stars of heaven and their
        constellations
    will not show their light.
    The rising sun will be darkened
    and the moon will not give its light.
¹¹ I will punish the world for its evil,
    the wicked for their sins.

ª 13 Or *hostility*   ᵇ 2 Or *song*   ᶜ 6 Hebrew *Shaddai*

I will put an end to the arrogance of the
    haughty
  and will humble the pride of the
    ruthless.
¹² I will make people scarcer than pure
    gold,
  more rare than the gold of Ophir.
¹³ Therefore I will make the heavens
    tremble;
  and the earth will shake from its
    place
at the wrath of the Lord Almighty,
  in the day of his burning anger.

¹⁴ Like a hunted gazelle,
  like sheep without a shepherd,
they will all return to their own people,
  they will flee to their native land.
¹⁵ Whoever is captured will be thrust
    through;
  all who are caught will fall by the
    sword.
¹⁶ Their infants will be dashed to pieces
    before their eyes;
  their houses will be looted and their
    wives ravished.

¹⁷ See, I will stir up against them the
    Medes,
  who do not care for silver
  and have no delight in gold.
¹⁸ Their bows will strike down the young
    men;
  they will have no mercy on infants,
  nor will they look with compassion on
    children.
¹⁹ Babylon, the jewel of kingdoms,
  the pride and glory of the
    Babylonians,ᵃ
will be overthrown by God
  like Sodom and Gomorrah.
²⁰ She will never be inhabited
  or lived in through all generations;
there no nomads will pitch their tents,
  there no shepherds will rest their
    flocks.
²¹ But desert creatures will lie there,
  jackals will fill her houses;
there the owls will dwell,
  and there the wild goats will leap
    about.
²² Hyenas will inhabit her strongholds,
  jackals her luxurious palaces.

Her time is at hand,
  and her days will not be prolonged.

14 The Lord will have compassion
    on Jacob;
  once again he will choose Israel
and will settle them in their own
    land.
Foreigners will join them
  and unite with the house of Jacob.
² Nations will take them
  and bring them to their own place.
And the house of Israel will take
    possession of the nations
  and make them male and female
    servants in the Lord's land.
They will make captives of their captors
  and rule over their oppressors.

³ On the day the Lord gives you relief
from your suffering and turmoil and from
the harsh labor forced on you, ⁴ you will take
up this taunt against the king of Babylon:

How the oppressor has come to an end!
  How his furyᵇ has ended!
⁵ The Lord has broken the rod of the
    wicked,
  the scepter of the rulers,
⁶ which in anger struck down peoples
  with unceasing blows,
and in fury subdued nations
  with relentless aggression.
⁷ All the lands are at rest and at peace;
  they break into singing.
⁸ Even the junipers and the cedars of
    Lebanon
  exult over you and say,
"Now that you have been laid low,
  no one comes to cut us down."

⁹ The realm of the dead below is all astir
  to meet you at your coming;
it rouses the spirits of the departed to
    greet you—
  all those who were leaders in the
    world;
it makes them rise from their thrones—
  all those who were kings over the
    nations.
¹⁰ They will all respond,
  they will say to you,
"You also have become weak, as we are;
  you have become like us."

<hr>

ᵃ 19 Or *Chaldeans* ᵇ 4 Dead Sea Scrolls, Septuagint and Syriac; the meaning of the word in the Masoretic Text is uncertain.

THURSDAY

WATCHFUL FOR THE ENEMY

Isaiah 14:1–17 *or* 14:12–14

ANDREW MURRAY {AD 1828–1917}

Life here upon the earth is grievous, for God gives Satan permission to crush and trample even those in the church. Happy are they who—with deep humility, with fear and trembling—distrust themselves. Our only security is in the intercession and guidance of him who overcame Satan (Ephesians 6:10,12,16). Far be from us the idea that we know all the depths of Satan and are a match for all his cunning schemes. It is in the region of the spirit, in the invisible, that Satan works and has power, as well as in the visible. While we may have known and overcome him in the visible, we should fear that he will yet prevail over us in the spiritual. May our only security be the conviction of our frailty and weakness; may our only confidence be in God who certainly protects the humble.

Lord Jesus, open our eyes to know our enemy and his wiles. Cause us to see him and his realm, so that we may dread all that is of him. And open our eyes to see how you have overcome him, and how in you we are invincible. Teach us what it is to be in you, to deny all that comes from the ego and the will of the flesh, and to be strong in weakness and lowliness. And teach us to bring into prayer the conflict of faith against every stronghold of Satan, because we know that you will bruise him under our feet. Amen.

Tony Evans

Many believers are suffering defeat in spiritual warfare because they are trying to fight Satan in their own strength.

I have news for you. Satan isn't afraid of you at all! He's not afraid of me either. But he cannot stand up against God for even a second.

This is why Paul wrote, "[Finally, be strong in the Lord and in his mighty power. Put on the full armor of God, so that you can take your stand against the devil's schemes]" (Ephesians 6:10–11). It is when God fights the battle for you, not when *you* fight the battle for you, that you win against the evil one.

Lack of victory in the spiritual battle reflects a lack of understanding of our divine resources. Every Christian has promises, but it's the inability to move beyond the problem, the inability to get past the failure, that keeps us in spiritual defeat. Victory is found in dependence on God, so Satan's plan is to detach us from dependence on God.

reflection

1. On a scale of one to ten, would you rate yourself "very aware" of spiritual matters (as a ten) or "completely oblivious" to anything you can't see (as a one)?

2. Why is it important to be aware of Satan's power in this world?

3. If God is more powerful than Satan (and he is!), why does he allow Satan to have any influence in this world?

For your next devotional reading, go to page 792.

¹¹ All your pomp has been brought down to
    the grave,
        along with the noise of your harps;
maggots are spread out beneath you
    and worms cover you.

¹² How you have fallen from heaven,
    morning star, son of the dawn!
You have been cast down to the earth,
    you who once laid low the nations!
¹³ You said in your heart,
    "I will ascend to heaven;
I will raise my throne
    above the stars of God;
I will sit enthroned on the mount of
    assembly,
        on the utmost heights of Mount
        Zaphon.^a
¹⁴ I will ascend above the tops of the
    clouds;
        I will make myself like the Most
        High."
¹⁵ But you are brought down to the realm
    of the dead,
        to the depths of the pit.

¹⁶ Those who see you stare at you,
    they ponder your fate:
"Is this the man who shook the earth
    and made kingdoms tremble,
¹⁷ the man who made the world a
    wilderness,
        who overthrew its cities
        and would not let his captives go
        home?"

¹⁸ All the kings of the nations lie in state,
    each in his own tomb.
¹⁹ But you are cast out of your tomb
    like a rejected branch;
you are covered with the slain,
    with those pierced by the sword,
        those who descend to the stones of
        the pit.
Like a corpse trampled underfoot,
²⁰   you will not join them in burial,
for you have destroyed your land
    and killed your people.

Let the offspring of the wicked
    never be mentioned again.
²¹ Prepare a place to slaughter his children
    for the sins of their ancestors;
they are not to rise to inherit the land
    and cover the earth with their cities.

²² "I will rise up against them,"
    declares the Lord Almighty.
"I will wipe out Babylon's name and
    survivors,
        her offspring and descendants,"
            declares the Lord.
²³ "I will turn her into a place for owls
    and into swampland;
I will sweep her with the broom of
    destruction,"
        declares the Lord Almighty.

²⁴ The Lord Almighty has sworn,

"Surely, as I have planned, so it will be,
    and as I have purposed, so it will
    happen.
²⁵ I will crush the Assyrian in my land;
    on my mountains I will trample him
    down.
His yoke will be taken from my people,
    and his burden removed from their
    shoulders."

²⁶ This is the plan determined for the
    whole world;
        this is the hand stretched out over all
        nations.
²⁷ For the Lord Almighty has purposed,
    and who can thwart him?
His hand is stretched out, and who
    can turn it back?

A Prophecy Against the Philistines

²⁸ This prophecy came in the year King
Ahaz died:

²⁹ Do not rejoice, all you Philistines,
    that the rod that struck you is broken;
from the root of that snake will spring
    up a viper,
        its fruit will be a darting, venomous
        serpent.
³⁰ The poorest of the poor will find pasture,
    and the needy will lie down in safety.
But your root I will destroy by famine;
    it will slay your survivors.

³¹ Wail, you gate! Howl, you city!
    Melt away, all you Philistines!
A cloud of smoke comes from the north,
    and there is not a straggler in its
    ranks.
³² What answer shall be given
    to the envoys of that nation?
"The Lord has established Zion,

---

^a 13 Or *of the north*; Zaphon was the most sacred mountain of the Canaanites.

and in her his afflicted people will
　　find refuge."

A Prophecy Against Moab

15 A prophecy concerning Moab:

Ar in Moab is ruined,
　　destroyed in a night!
Kir in Moab is ruined,
　　destroyed in a night!
[2] Dibon goes up to its temple,
　　to its high places to weep;
　Moab wails over Nebo and Medeba.
Every head is shaved
　and every beard cut off.
[3] In the streets they wear sackcloth;
　　on the roofs and in the public squares
they all wail,
　　prostrate with weeping.
[4] Heshbon and Elealeh cry out,
　　their voices are heard all the way to
　　　Jahaz.
Therefore the armed men of Moab cry
　　out,
　and their hearts are faint.

[5] My heart cries out over Moab;
　　her fugitives flee as far as Zoar,
　　as far as Eglath Shelishiyah.
They go up the hill to Luhith,
　　weeping as they go;
on the road to Horonaim
　　they lament their destruction.
[6] The waters of Nimrim are dried up
　　and the grass is withered;
the vegetation is gone
　　and nothing green is left.
[7] So the wealth they have acquired and
　　stored up
　　they carry away over the Ravine of the
　　　Poplars.
[8] Their outcry echoes along the border of
　　Moab;
　　their wailing reaches as far as Eglaim,
　　their lamentation as far as Beer Elim.
[9] The waters of Dimon[a] are full of blood,
　　but I will bring still more upon
　　　Dimon[a]—
a lion upon the fugitives of Moab
　　and upon those who remain in the
　　　land.

16 Send lambs as tribute
　　to the ruler of the land,
　　from Sela, across the desert,
　　to the mount of Daughter Zion.
[2] Like fluttering birds
　　pushed from the nest,
so are the women of Moab
　　at the fords of the Arnon.

[3] "Make up your mind," Moab says.
　　"Render a decision.
Make your shadow like night—
　　at high noon.
Hide the fugitives,
　　do not betray the refugees.
[4] Let the Moabite fugitives stay with you;
　　be their shelter from the destroyer."

The oppressor will come to an end,
　　and destruction will cease;
　　the aggressor will vanish from the
　　　land.
[5] In love a throne will be established;
　　in faithfulness a man will sit on it—
　　one from the house[b] of David—
one who in judging seeks justice
　　and speeds the cause of
　　　righteousness.

[6] We have heard of Moab's pride—
　　her overweening pride and conceit,
her pride and her insolence—
　　but her boasts are empty.
[7] Therefore the Moabites wail,
　　they wail together for Moab.
Lament and grieve
　　for the raisin cakes of Kir Hareseth.
[8] The fields of Heshbon wither,
　　the vines of Sibmah also.
The rulers of the nations
　　have trampled down the choicest
　　　vines,
which once reached Jazer
　　and spread toward the desert.
Their shoots spread out
　　and went as far as the sea.[c]
[9] So I weep, as Jazer weeps,
　　for the vines of Sibmah.
Heshbon and Elealeh,
　　I drench you with tears!
The shouts of joy over your ripened fruit
　　and over your harvests have been
　　　stilled.

---

a 9 *Dimon*, a wordplay on Dibon (see verse 2), sounds like the Hebrew for *blood*.　　*b* 5 Hebrew *tent*
c 8 Probably the Dead Sea

10 Joy and gladness are taken away from
     the orchards;
   no one sings or shouts in the
     vineyards;
   no one treads out wine at the presses,
     for I have put an end to the shouting.
11 My heart laments for Moab like a harp,
   my inmost being for Kir Hareseth.
12 When Moab appears at her high place,
   she only wears herself out;
   when she goes to her shrine to pray,
     it is to no avail.

13 This is the word the LORD has already
spoken concerning Moab. 14 But now the
LORD says: "Within three years, as a servant
bound by contract would count them, Moab's splendor and all her many people will
be despised, and her survivors will be very
few and feeble."

A Prophecy Against Damascus

17 A prophecy concerning Damascus:

   "See, Damascus will no longer
     be a city
   but will become a heap of ruins.
2 The cities of Aroer will be deserted
   and left to flocks, which will lie down,
     with no one to make them afraid.
3 The fortified city will disappear from
     Ephraim,
   and royal power from Damascus;
   the remnant of Aram will be
   like the glory of the Israelites,"
     declares the LORD Almighty.

4 "In that day the glory of Jacob will fade;
   the fat of his body will waste away.
5 It will be as when reapers harvest the
     standing grain,
   gathering the grain in their arms—
   as when someone gleans heads of grain
   in the Valley of Rephaim.
6 Yet some gleanings will remain,
   as when an olive tree is beaten,
   leaving two or three olives on the
     topmost branches,
   four or five on the fruitful boughs,"
     declares the LORD, the God
       of Israel.

7 In that day people will look to their
     Maker
and turn their eyes to the Holy One of
     Israel.
8 They will not look to the altars,
   the work of their hands,
   and they will have no regard for the
     Asherah poles*a*
   and the incense altars their fingers
     have made.

9 In that day their strong cities, which they
left because of the Israelites, will be like
places abandoned to thickets and under-
growth. And all will be desolation.

10 You have forgotten God your Savior;
   you have not remembered the Rock,
     your fortress.
   Therefore, though you set out the finest
     plants
   and plant imported vines,
11 though on the day you set them out, you
     make them grow,
   and on the morning when you plant
     them, you bring them to bud,
   yet the harvest will be as nothing
   in the day of disease and incurable
     pain.

12 Woe to the many nations that rage—
   they rage like the raging sea!
   Woe to the peoples who roar—
   they roar like the roaring of great
     waters!
13 Although the peoples roar like the roar
     of surging waters,
   when he rebukes them they flee far
     away,
   driven before the wind like chaff on the
     hills,
   like tumbleweed before a gale.
14 In the evening, sudden terror!
   Before the morning, they are gone!
This is the portion of those who loot us,
   the lot of those who plunder us.

A Prophecy Against Cush

18 Woe to the land of whirring
       wings*b*
     along the rivers of Cush,*c*
2 which sends envoys by sea
   in papyrus boats over the water.

   Go, swift messengers,
   to a people tall and smooth-skinned,

---

a 8 That is, wooden symbols of the goddess Asherah
region   *b 1* Or *of locusts*   *c 1* That is, the upper Nile

to a people feared far and wide,
an aggressive nation of strange speech,
whose land is divided by rivers.

³ All you people of the world,
you who live on the earth,
when a banner is raised on the
mountains,
you will see it,
and when a trumpet sounds,
you will hear it.
⁴ This is what the LORD says to me:
"I will remain quiet and will look on
from my dwelling place,
like shimmering heat in the sunshine,
like a cloud of dew in the heat of
harvest."
⁵ For, before the harvest, when the
blossom is gone
and the flower becomes a ripening
grape,
he will cut off the shoots with pruning
knives,
and cut down and take away the
spreading branches.
⁶ They will all be left to the mountain
birds of prey
and to the wild animals;
the birds will feed on them all summer,
the wild animals all winter.

⁷ At that time gifts will be brought to the
LORD Almighty

from a people tall and smooth-skinned,
from a people feared far and wide,
an aggressive nation of strange speech,
whose land is divided by rivers—

the gifts will be brought to Mount Zion, the
place of the Name of the LORD Almighty.

A Prophecy Against Egypt

19

A prophecy concerning Egypt:

See, the LORD rides on a swift
cloud
and is coming to Egypt.
The idols of Egypt tremble before him,
and the hearts of the Egyptians melt
within them.

² "I will stir up Egyptian against Egyptian—
brother will fight against brother,
neighbor against neighbor,
city against city,
kingdom against kingdom.
³ The Egyptians will lose heart,

and I will bring their plans to nothing;
they will consult the idols and the spirits
of the dead,
the mediums and the spiritists.
⁴ I will hand the Egyptians over
to the power of a cruel master,
and a fierce king will rule over them,"
declares the Lord, the LORD Almighty.

⁵ The waters of the river will dry up,
and the riverbed will be parched and
dry.
⁶ The canals will stink;
the streams of Egypt will dwindle and
dry up.
The reeds and rushes will wither,
⁷   also the plants along the Nile,
at the mouth of the river.
Every sown field along the Nile
will become parched, will blow away
and be no more.
⁸ Those who fish will groan and lament,
all who cast hooks into the Nile;
those who throw nets on the water
will pine away.
⁹ Those who work with combed flax will
despair,
the weavers of fine linen will lose
hope.
¹⁰ The workers in cloth will be dejected,
and all the wage earners will be sick
at heart.

¹¹ The officials of Zoan are nothing but
fools;
the wise counselors of Pharaoh give
senseless advice.
How can you say to Pharaoh,
"I am one of the wise men,
a disciple of the ancient kings"?

¹² Where are your wise men now?
Let them show you and make known
what the LORD Almighty
has planned against Egypt.
¹³ The officials of Zoan have become fools,
the leaders of Memphis are deceived;
the cornerstones of her peoples
have led Egypt astray.
¹⁴ The LORD has poured into them
a spirit of dizziness;
they make Egypt stagger in all that she
does,
as drunkards stagger around in their
vomit.
¹⁵ There is nothing Egypt can do—
head or tail, palm branch or reed.

¹⁶In that day the Egyptians will become weaklings. They will shudder with fear at the uplifted hand that the LORD Almighty raises against them. ¹⁷And the land of Judah will bring terror to the Egyptians; everyone to whom Judah is mentioned will be terrified, because of what the LORD Almighty is planning against them.

¹⁸In that day five cities in Egypt will speak the language of Canaan and swear allegiance to the LORD Almighty. One of them will be called the City of the Sun.^a

¹⁹In that day there will be an altar to the LORD in the heart of Egypt, and a monument to the LORD at its border. ²⁰It will be a sign and witness to the LORD Almighty in the land of Egypt. When they cry out to the LORD because of their oppressors, he will send them a savior and defender, and he will rescue them. ²¹So the LORD will make himself known to the Egyptians, and in that day they will acknowledge the LORD. They will worship with sacrifices and grain offerings; they will make vows to the LORD and keep them. ²²The LORD will strike Egypt with a plague; he will strike them and heal them. They will turn to the LORD, and he will respond to their pleas and heal them.

²³In that day there will be a highway from Egypt to Assyria. The Assyrians will go to Egypt and the Egyptians to Assyria. The Egyptians and Assyrians will worship together. ²⁴In that day Israel will be the third, along with Egypt and Assyria, a blessing^b on the earth. ²⁵The LORD Almighty will bless them, saying, "Blessed be Egypt my people, Assyria my handiwork, and Israel my inheritance."

A Prophecy Against Egypt and Cush

20 In the year that the supreme commander, sent by Sargon king of Assyria, came to Ashdod and attacked and captured it— ²at that time the LORD spoke through Isaiah son of Amoz. He said to him, "Take off the sackcloth from your body and the sandals from your feet." And he did so, going around stripped and barefoot.

³Then the LORD said, "Just as my servant Isaiah has gone stripped and barefoot for three years, as a sign and portent against Egypt and Cush,^c ⁴so the king of Assyria will lead away stripped and barefoot the Egyptian captives and Cushite exiles, young and old, with buttocks bared—to Egypt's shame. ⁵Those who trusted in Cush and boasted in Egypt will be dismayed and put to shame. ⁶In that day the people who live on this coast will say, 'See what has happened to those we relied on, those we fled to for help and deliverance from the king of Assyria! How then can we escape?' "

A Prophecy Against Babylon

21 A prophecy concerning the Desert by the Sea:

Like whirlwinds sweeping through the
    southland,
  an invader comes from the desert,
  from a land of terror.

²A dire vision has been shown to me:
  The traitor betrays, the looter takes
    loot.
Elam, attack! Media, lay siege!
  I will bring to an end all the groaning
    she caused.

³At this my body is racked with pain,
  pangs seize me, like those of a
    woman in labor;
I am staggered by what I hear,
  I am bewildered by what I see.
⁴My heart falters,
  fear makes me tremble;
the twilight I longed for
  has become a horror to me.

⁵They set the tables,
  they spread the rugs,
  they eat, they drink!
Get up, you officers,
  oil the shields!

⁶This is what the Lord says to me:

"Go, post a lookout
  and have him report what he sees.
⁷When he sees chariots
  with teams of horses,
riders on donkeys
  or riders on camels,

a 18 Some manuscripts of the Masoretic Text, Dead Sea Scrolls, Symmachus and Vulgate; most manuscripts of the Masoretic Text *City of Destruction*   *b 24* Or *Assyria, whose names will be used in blessings* (see Gen. 48:20); or *Assyria, who will be seen by others as blessed*   *c 3* That is, the upper Nile region; also in verse 5

let him be alert,
    fully alert."

⁸And the lookout ᵃ shouted,

"Day after day, my lord, I stand on the
    watchtower;
    every night I stay at my post.
⁹Look, here comes a man in a chariot
    with a team of horses.
And he gives back the answer:
    'Babylon has fallen, has fallen!
All the images of its gods
    lie shattered on the ground!' "

¹⁰My people who are crushed on the
    threshing floor,
    I tell you what I have heard
from the LORD Almighty,
    from the God of Israel.

A Prophecy Against Edom

¹¹A prophecy concerning Dumah ᵇ:

Someone calls to me from Seir,
    "Watchman, what is left of the night?
    Watchman, what is left of the night?"
¹²The watchman replies,
    "Morning is coming, but also the
      night.
If you would ask, then ask;
    and come back yet again."

A Prophecy Against Arabia

¹³A prophecy concerning Arabia:

You caravans of Dedanites,
    who camp in the thickets of Arabia,
¹⁴   bring water for the thirsty;
you who live in Tema,
    bring food for the fugitives.
¹⁵They flee from the sword,
    from the drawn sword,
from the bent bow
    and from the heat of battle.

¹⁶This is what the Lord says to me: "Within one year, as a servant bound by contract would count it, all the splendor of Kedar will come to an end. ¹⁷The survivors of the archers, the warriors of Kedar, will be few." The LORD, the God of Israel, has spoken.

A Prophecy About Jerusalem

22 A prophecy concerning the Valley of Vision:

What troubles you now,
    that you have all gone up on the
      roofs,
²you town so full of commotion,
    you city of tumult and revelry?
Your slain were not killed by the sword,
    nor did they die in battle.
³All your leaders have fled together;
    they have been captured without
      using the bow.
All you who were caught were taken
    prisoner together,
    having fled while the enemy was still
      far away.
⁴Therefore I said, "Turn away from me;
    let me weep bitterly.
Do not try to console me
    over the destruction of my people."

⁵The Lord, the LORD Almighty, has a day
    of tumult and trampling and terror
    in the Valley of Vision,
a day of battering down walls
    and of crying out to the mountains.
⁶Elam takes up the quiver,
    with her charioteers and horses;
    Kir uncovers the shield.
⁷Your choicest valleys are full of chariots,
    and horsemen are posted at the city
      gates.
⁸The Lord stripped away the defenses of
    Judah,
    and you looked in that day
to the weapons in the Palace of the
    Forest.
⁹You saw that the City of David
    had many breaches in its defenses;
you stored up water
    in the Lower Pool.
¹⁰You counted the buildings in Jerusalem
    and tore down houses to strengthen
      the wall.
¹¹You built a reservoir between the two
    walls
    for the water of the Old Pool,
but you did not look to the One who
    made it,

ᵃ 8 Dead Sea Scrolls and Syriac; Masoretic Text *A lion*
silence or *stillness*.

ᵇ 11 *Dumah*, a wordplay on *Edom*, means

or have regard for the One who
    planned it long ago.

¹² The Lord, the LORD Almighty,
    called you on that day
      to weep and to wail,
        to tear out your hair and put on
          sackcloth.
¹³ But see, there is joy and revelry,
    slaughtering of cattle and killing of
      sheep,
    eating of meat and drinking of wine!
"Let us eat and drink," you say,
    "for tomorrow we die!"

¹⁴ The LORD Almighty has revealed this in
my hearing: "Till your dying day this sin will
not be atoned for," says the Lord, the LORD
Almighty.

¹⁵ This is what the Lord, the LORD Almighty,
says:

    "Go, say to this steward,
      to Shebna, who is in charge of the
        palace:
¹⁶ What are you doing here and who gave
      you permission
    to cut out a grave for yourself here,
hewing your grave on the height
    and chiseling your resting place in the
      rock?

¹⁷ "Beware, the LORD is about to take firm
      hold of you
    and hurl you away, you mighty man.
¹⁸ He will roll you up tightly like a ball
    and throw you into a large country.
There you will die
    and there the chariots you were so
      proud of
    will become a disgrace to your
      master's house.
¹⁹ I will depose you from your office,
    and you will be ousted from your
      position.

²⁰ "In that day I will summon my servant,
Eliakim son of Hilkiah. ²¹ I will clothe him
with your robe and fasten your sash around
him and hand your authority over to him.
He will be a father to those who live in Jerusalem and to the house of Judah. ²² I will
place on his shoulder the key to the house of
David; what he opens no one can shut, and

what he shuts no one can open. ²³ I will drive
him like a peg into a firm place; he will become a seat^a of honor for the house of his
father. ²⁴ All the glory of his family will hang
on him: its offspring and offshoots—all its
lesser vessels, from the bowls to all the jars.

²⁵ "In that day," declares the LORD Al-
mighty, "the peg driven into the firm place
will give way; it will be sheared off and will
fall, and the load hanging on it will be cut
down." The LORD has spoken.

A Prophecy Against Tyre

23 A prophecy concerning Tyre:

    Wail, you ships of Tarshish!
For Tyre is destroyed
    and left without house or harbor.
From the land of Cyprus
    word has come to them.

² Be silent, you people of the island
    and you merchants of Sidon,
      whom the seafarers have enriched.
³ On the great waters
    came the grain of the Shihor;
the harvest of the Nile^b was the revenue
      of Tyre,
    and she became the marketplace of
      the nations.

⁴ Be ashamed, Sidon, and you fortress of
      the sea,
    for the sea has spoken:
"I have neither been in labor nor given
      birth;
    I have neither reared sons nor
      brought up daughters."
⁵ When word comes to Egypt,
    they will be in anguish at the report
      from Tyre.

⁶ Cross over to Tarshish;
    wail, you people of the island.
⁷ Is this your city of revelry,
    the old, old city,
whose feet have taken her
    to settle in far-off lands?
⁸ Who planned this against Tyre,
    the bestower of crowns,
whose merchants are princes,
    whose traders are renowned in the
      earth?

---

a 23 Or *throne*   *b 2,3* Masoretic Text; Dead Sea Scrolls *Sidon, / who cross over the sea; / your envoys* ³*are
on the great waters. / The grain of the Shihor, / the harvest of the Nile,*

⁹The Lord Almighty planned it,
  to bring down her pride in all her
    splendor
  and to humble all who are renowned
    on the earth.

¹⁰Till ᵃ your land as they do along the Nile,
    Daughter Tarshish,
  for you no longer have a harbor.
¹¹The Lord has stretched out his hand
    over the sea
  and made its kingdoms tremble.
He has given an order concerning
    Phoenicia
  that her fortresses be destroyed.
¹²He said, "No more of your reveling,
  Virgin Daughter Sidon, now crushed!

"Up, cross over to Cyprus;
  even there you will find no rest."
¹³Look at the land of the Babylonians,ᵇ
  this people that is now of no account!
The Assyrians have made it
  a place for desert creatures;
they raised up their siege towers,
  they stripped its fortresses bare
  and turned it into a ruin.

¹⁴Wail, you ships of Tarshish;
  your fortress is destroyed!

¹⁵At that time Tyre will be forgotten for
seventy years, the span of a king's life. But
at the end of these seventy years, it will happen to Tyre as in the song of the prostitute:

¹⁶"Take up a harp, walk through the city,
  you forgotten prostitute;
  play the harp well, sing many a song,
  so that you will be remembered."

¹⁷At the end of seventy years, the Lord
will deal with Tyre. She will return to her lu-
crative prostitution and will ply her trade
with all the kingdoms on the face of the
earth. ¹⁸Yet her profit and her earnings will
be set apart for the Lord; they will not be
stored up or hoarded. Her profits will go to
those who live before the Lord, for abundant
food and fine clothes.

The Lord's Devastation of the Earth

24 See, the Lord is going to lay
  waste the earth
  and devastate it;

he will ruin its face
  and scatter its inhabitants—
²it will be the same
  for priest as for people,
  for master as for his servant,
  for mistress as for her servant,
  for seller as for buyer,
  for borrower as for lender,
  for debtor as for creditor.
³The earth will be completely laid waste
  and totally plundered.
        The Lord has spoken
              this word.

⁴The earth dries up and withers,
  the world languishes and withers,
  the heavens languish with the earth.
⁵The earth is defiled by its people;
  they have disobeyed the laws,
violated the statutes
  and broken the everlasting covenant.
⁶Therefore a curse consumes the earth;
  its people must bear their guilt.
Therefore earth's inhabitants are
    burned up,
  and very few are left.
⁷The new wine dries up and the vine
    withers;
  all the merrymakers groan.
⁸The gaiety of the timbrels is stilled,
  the noise of the revelers has stopped,
  the joyful harp is silent.
⁹No longer do they drink wine with a
    song;
  the beer is bitter to its drinkers.
¹⁰The ruined city lies desolate;
  the entrance to every house is barred.
¹¹In the streets they cry out for wine;
  all joy turns to gloom,
  all gaiety is banished from the earth.
¹²The city is left in ruins,
  its gate is battered to pieces.
¹³So will it be on the earth
  and among the nations,
as when an olive tree is beaten,
  or as when gleanings are left after the
    grape harvest.

¹⁴They raise their voices, they shout for
    joy;
  from the west they acclaim the Lord's
    majesty.

ᵃ 10 Dead Sea Scrolls and some Septuagint manuscripts; Masoretic Text *Go through*
ᵇ 13 Or *Chaldeans*

¹⁵ Therefore in the east give glory to the
      LORD;
   exalt the name of the LORD, the God
      of Israel,
   in the islands of the sea.
¹⁶ From the ends of the earth we hear
      singing:
   "Glory to the Righteous One."

   But I said, "I waste away, I waste away!
      Woe to me!
   The treacherous betray!
      With treachery the treacherous
         betray!"
¹⁷ Terror and pit and snare await you,
   people of the earth.
¹⁸ Whoever flees at the sound of terror
   will fall into a pit;
   whoever climbs out of the pit
   will be caught in a snare.

   The floodgates of the heavens are
      opened,
   the foundations of the earth shake.
¹⁹ The earth is broken up,
   the earth is split asunder,
   the earth is violently shaken.
²⁰ The earth reels like a drunkard,
   it sways like a hut in the wind;
   so heavy upon it is the guilt of its
      rebellion
   that it falls—never to rise again.

²¹ In that day the LORD will punish
   the powers in the heavens above
   and the kings on the earth below.
²² They will be herded together
   like prisoners bound in a dungeon;
   they will be shut up in prison
   and be punished ᵃ after many days.
²³ The moon will be dismayed,
   the sun ashamed;
   for the LORD Almighty will reign
   on Mount Zion and in Jerusalem,
   and before its elders—with great
      glory.

Praise to the LORD

25 LORD, you are my God;
   I will exalt you and praise your
      name,
   for in perfect faithfulness
   you have done wonderful things,
   things planned long ago.
² You have made the city a heap of rubble,
   the fortified town a ruin,
   the foreigners' stronghold a city no
      more;
   it will never be rebuilt.
³ Therefore strong peoples will honor you;
   cities of ruthless nations will revere
      you.
⁴ You have been a refuge for the poor,
   a refuge for the needy in their
      distress,
   a shelter from the storm
   and a shade from the heat.
   For the breath of the ruthless
   is like a storm driving against a wall
⁵   and like the heat of the desert.
   You silence the uproar of foreigners;
   as heat is reduced by the shadow of a
      cloud,
   so the song of the ruthless is stilled.

⁶ On this mountain the LORD Almighty will
      prepare
   a feast of rich food for all peoples,
   a banquet of aged wine—
   the best of meats and the finest of
      wines.
⁷ On this mountain he will destroy
   the shroud that enfolds all peoples,
   the sheet that covers all nations;
⁸   he will swallow up death forever.
   The Sovereign LORD will wipe away the
      tears
   from all faces;
   he will remove his people's disgrace
   from all the earth.
                        The LORD has spoken.

⁹ In that day they will say,

   "Surely this is our God;
   we trusted in him, and he saved us.
   This is the LORD, we trusted in him;
   let us rejoice and be glad in his
      salvation."

¹⁰ The hand of the LORD will rest on this
      mountain;
   but Moab will be trampled in their
      land
   as straw is trampled down in the
      manure.
¹¹ They will stretch out their hands in it,
   as swimmers stretch out their hands
      to swim.
   God will bring down their pride

ᵃ 22 Or *released*

FRIDAY

A HEAVENLY BASH

Isaiah 25:1–12 *or* 25:6–9

Joni Eareckson Tada

Before we realize it . . . we shall find ourselves in the embrace of our Savior at the Wedding Supper of the Lamb. Heaven will have arrived. The Lord's overcoming of the world will be a lifting of the curtain of our five senses . . .

Now, enjoy an unseen divine reality. Rev up your heart and picture yourself taking a seat at the Wedding Supper. As you pull up a chair to the banquet table, take a look at what's on the menu from Isaiah 25:6: "On this mountain the LORD Almighty will prepare a feast of rich food for all peoples, a banquet of aged wine—the best of meats and the finest of wines" . . .

I get a charge just thinking about it! I wonder who will sit next to me, or across from me. I glance down the table and there's my friend, Verna Estes, mother of seven, swapping baby stories with Susanna Wesley, mother of seventeen. There's Moses toasting Martin Luther. St. Augustine giving a bear hug to that jungle missionary . . .

Then I'll look up, and walking toward me will be Dad. And Mother. Before you know it, we'll break up into uncontrollable laughter. We will laugh and cry with a kind of tears that never flowed on earth. We will wipe our eyes and try to stop, then break up again, crying and laughing and pointing at everybody. "We're here! They are here! I knew it was true, but not this true!"

Christ will open our eyes to the great fountain of love in His heart for us, beyond all that we *ever* saw before. It will hit us that we, the church, are His bride. Not just individually, but together. United. One with each other, and one with Him. Suddenly, our joy is multiplied a millionfold.

Most poignantly, when we're finally able to stop laughing and crying, the Lord Jesus will really wipe away all our tears. And then, we join hands around the banquet table, and "in that day [we] will say, 'Surely this is our God; we trusted in him, and he saved us. This is the LORD, we trusted in him; let us rejoice and be glad in his salvation'" (Isaiah 25:9).

And the party is just beginning!

C. S. LEWIS {AD 1898–1963}

There have been times when I think we do not desire heaven but more often I find myself wondering whether, in our heart of hearts, we have ever desired anything else.

reflection

1. What do you think heaven will be like?

2. What do you look forward to most about heaven?

3. How would you describe heaven to someone who has "never heard of it"?

For your next devotional reading, go to page 793.

A Better Day

Isaiah 25:8

read/meditate

Isaiah's vision of God's final redemption of the world is encapsulated beautifully in Isaiah 25:8. Read this verse a few times, developing a picture in your mind of the world it describes.

pray

Share with God your deepest griefs and sorrows. Close your eyes and imagine him wiping your tears away. Share with him your perspective on living in a world filled with pain while you wait for his eventual redemption.

contemplate

Think about the wrongs that you see in the world that God will one day right. Think about what you can do about those wrongs while you wait for that day.

additional reflection

Snuggle in God's arms. When you are hurting, when you feel lonely, left out. Let Him cradle you, comfort you, reassure you of His all-sufficient power and love.
—Kay Arthur

God of our life, there are days when the burdens we carry chafe our shoulders and weigh us down; when the road seems dreary and endless, the skies gray and threatening; when our lives have no music in them, and our hearts are lonely, and our souls have lost their courage. Flood the path with light, run our eyes to where the skies are full of promise; tune our hearts to brave music; give us the sense of comradeship with heroes and saints of every age; and so quicken our spirits that we may be able to encourage the souls of all who journey with us on the road of life, to Your honour and glory.

—Saint Augustine

For your next devotional reading, go to page 795.

despite the cleverness *a* of their hands.
¹²He will bring down your high fortified
walls
and lay them low;
he will bring them down to the ground,
to the very dust.

A Song of Praise

26

In that day this song will be
sung in the land of Judah:

We have a strong city;
God makes salvation
its walls and ramparts.
²Open the gates
that the righteous nation may enter,
the nation that keeps faith.
³You will keep in perfect peace
those whose minds are steadfast,
because they trust in you.
⁴Trust in the LORD forever,
for the LORD, the LORD, is the Rock
eternal.
⁵He humbles those who dwell on high,
he lays the lofty city low;
he levels it to the ground
and casts it down to the dust.
⁶Feet trample it down—
the feet of the oppressed,
the footsteps of the poor.

⁷The path of the righteous is level;
you, the Upright One, make the way
of the righteous smooth.
⁸Yes, LORD, walking in the way of your
laws, *b*
we wait for you;
your name and renown
are the desire of our hearts.
⁹My soul yearns for you in the night;
in the morning my spirit longs for
you.
When your judgments come upon the
earth,
the people of the world learn
righteousness.
¹⁰But when grace is shown to the wicked,
they do not learn righteousness;
even in a land of uprightness they go on
doing evil
and do not regard the majesty of the
LORD.
¹¹LORD, your hand is lifted high,

but they do not see it.
Let them see your zeal for your people
and be put to shame;
let the fire reserved for your enemies
consume them.

¹²LORD, you establish peace for us;
all that we have accomplished you
have done for us.
¹³LORD our God, other lords besides you
have ruled over us,
but your name alone do we honor.
¹⁴They are now dead, they live no more;
their spirits do not rise.
You punished them and brought them to
ruin;
you wiped out all memory of them.
¹⁵You have enlarged the nation, LORD;
you have enlarged the nation.
You have gained glory for yourself;
you have extended all the borders of
the land.

¹⁶LORD, they came to you in their distress;
when you disciplined them,
they could barely whisper a prayer. *c*
¹⁷As a pregnant woman about to give birth
writhes and cries out in her pain,
so were we in your presence, LORD.
¹⁸We were with child, we writhed in pain,
but we gave birth to wind.
We have not brought salvation to the
earth,
and the people of the world have not
been reborn. *d*

¹⁹But your dead will live, LORD;
their bodies will rise—
let those who dwell in the dust
wake up and shout for joy—
your dew is like the dew of the morning;
you will make it fall on the spirits of
the dead.

²⁰Go, my people, enter your rooms
and shut the doors behind you;
hide yourselves for a little while
until his wrath has passed by.
²¹See, the LORD is coming out of his
dwelling
to punish the people of the earth for
their sins.
The earth will disclose the blood shed
on it;

---

a 11 The meaning of the Hebrew for this word is uncertain.   *b* 8 Or *judgments*   *c* 16 The meaning of
the Hebrew for this clause is uncertain.   *d* 18 Or *have not fallen*

MONDAY

GOD'S FAME BUILDERS
Isaiah 26:1–21 *or* 26:4–8

CHARLES HADDON SPURGEON {AD 1834–1892}

It has been well said that the chief end of a person—that is, the primary reason for which someone is created—is to glorify God. For this same purpose, God made the sun, moon and stars, and all his works. And yet there are so many people who have never honored God in their lives.

Ask yourself, "How have you made his name great? What have *you* done?" What souls have you won to the Savior? Have you ever served him? How have you ever worked for him? What have you done for God? Have you been cluttering up the ground—taking the earth's nourishment yet bearing no fruit for the great farmer? For all you have done, the world might as well have never known you. The firefly that serves to light the traveler's steps has been of more use than you . . .

Is the indictment true? Will you be compelled to plead guilty to the charge? Now is the time to repent of your sin! And if you do, my Master authorizes me to say to you on his behalf, "I, even I, am he who blots out your transgressions . . . and remembers your sins no more" (Isaiah 43:25).

Chris Tomlin

When we see God for who He really is, we stand in awe—and we know that nothing less will ever do. Here's another Bible passage that shows how we should respond to God's fame:

> [Yes, LORD, walking in the way of your laws,
> we wait for you;
> your name and renown
> are the desire of our hearts.] (Isaiah 26:8)

The Bible clearly shows us that you and I have been uniquely created for a purposeful life, but—here's the un-American part—it's not meant to be about us or our career or our fame. *It's all about God and His glory.*

reflection

1. Have you ever thought of yourself as someone who brings glory to God? How successful have you been so far?

2. How can you be a better "publicist" for God?

3. Think of someone you know who excels at spreading God's awesome reputation to others. What can you learn from their example?

For your next devotional reading, go to page 809.

the earth will conceal its slain no
   longer.

Deliverance of Israel

27 In that day,

the LORD will punish with his
   sword—
his fierce, great and powerful sword—
Leviathan the gliding serpent,
   Leviathan the coiling serpent;
he will slay the monster of the sea.

²In that day—

"Sing about a fruitful vineyard:
³   I, the LORD, watch over it;
   I water it continually.
I guard it day and night
   so that no one may harm it.
⁴   I am not angry.
If only there were briers and thorns
   confronting me!
   I would march against them in battle;
   I would set them all on fire.
⁵Or else let them come to me for refuge;
   let them make peace with me,
   yes, let them make peace with me."

⁶In days to come Jacob will take root,
   Israel will bud and blossom
   and fill all the world with fruit.

⁷Has ⌊the LORD⌋ struck her
   as he struck down those who struck
      her?
Has she been killed
   as those were killed who killed her?
⁸By warfare ͣ and exile you contend with
      her—
   with his fierce blast he drives her out,
   as on a day the east wind blows.
⁹By this, then, will Jacob's guilt be atoned
      for,
   and this will be the full fruit of the
      removal of his sin:
When he makes all the altar stones
   to be like limestone crushed to
      pieces,
   no Asherah poles ᵇ or incense altars
   will be left standing.
¹⁰The fortified city stands desolate,
   an abandoned settlement, forsaken
      like the wilderness;
   there the calves graze,

there they lie down;
   they strip its branches bare.
¹¹When its twigs are dry, they are broken
      off
and women come and make fires with
      them.
For this is a people without
      understanding;
   so their Maker has no compassion on
      them,
   and their Creator shows them no
      favor.

¹²In that day the LORD will thresh from the
flowing Euphrates to the Wadi of Egypt, and
you, Israel, will be gathered up one by one.
¹³And in that day a great trumpet will sound.
Those who were perishing in Assyria and
those who were exiled in Egypt will come
and worship the LORD on the holy mountain
in Jerusalem.

Woe to the Leaders of Ephraim and Judah

28 Woe to that wreath, the pride of
      Ephraim's drunkards,
   to the fading flower, his glorious
      beauty,
set on the head of a fertile valley—
   to that city, the pride of those laid low
      by wine!
²See, the Lord has one who is powerful
      and strong.
   Like a hailstorm and a destructive
      wind,
   like a driving rain and a flooding
      downpour,
   he will throw it forcefully to the
      ground.
³That wreath, the pride of Ephraim's
      drunkards,
   will be trampled underfoot.
⁴That fading flower, his glorious beauty,
   set on the head of a fertile valley,
   will be like figs ripe before harvest—
   as soon as people see them and take
      them in hand,
   they swallow them.

⁵In that day the LORD Almighty
   will be a glorious crown,
a beautiful wreath
   for the remnant of his people.
⁶He will be a spirit of justice
   to those who sit in judgment,

ͣ 8 See Septuagint; the meaning of the Hebrew for this word is uncertain.   ᵇ 9 That is, wooden
symbols of the goddess Asherah

a source of strength
    to those who turn back the battle at
        the gate.

7 And these also stagger from wine
    and reel from beer:
Priests and prophets stagger from beer
    and are befuddled with wine;
they reel from beer,
    they stagger when seeing visions,
    they stumble when rendering
        decisions.
8 All the tables are covered with vomit
    and there is not a spot without filth.

9 "Who is it he is trying to teach?
    To whom is he explaining his
        message?
To children weaned from their milk,
    to those just taken from the breast?
10 For it is:
    Do this, do that,
    a rule for this, a rule for that *a*;
    a little here, a little there."

11 Very well then, with foreign lips and
        strange tongues
    God will speak to this people,
12 to whom he said,
    "This is the resting place, let the
        weary rest";
and, "This is the place of repose"—
    but they would not listen.
13 So then, the word of the Lord to them
        will become:
    Do this, do that,
    a rule for this, a rule for that;
    a little here, a little there—
so that as they go they will fall backward;
    they will be injured and snared and
        captured.

14 Therefore hear the word of the Lord, you
        scoffers
    who rule this people in Jerusalem.
15 You boast, "We have entered into a
        covenant with death,
    with the realm of the dead we have
        made an agreement.
When an overwhelming scourge sweeps
        by,
    it cannot touch us,
for we have made a lie our refuge
    and falsehood *b* our hiding place."

16 So this is what the Sovereign Lord says:

"See, I lay a stone in Zion, a tested
        stone,
    a precious cornerstone for a sure
        foundation;
the one who relies on it
    will never be stricken with panic.
17 I will make justice the measuring line
    and righteousness the plumb line;
hail will sweep away your refuge, the
        lie,
    and water will overflow your hiding
        place.
18 Your covenant with death will be
        annulled;
    your agreement with the realm of the
        dead will not stand.
When the overwhelming scourge sweeps
        by,
    you will be beaten down by it.
19 As often as it comes it will carry you
        away;
    morning after morning, by day and by
        night,
    it will sweep through."

The understanding of this message
    will bring sheer terror.
20 The bed is too short to stretch out on,
    the blanket too narrow to wrap
        around you.
21 The Lord will rise up as he did at Mount
        Perazim,
    he will rouse himself as in the Valley
        of Gibeon—
to do his work, his strange work,
    and perform his task, his alien task.
22 Now stop your mocking,
    or your chains will become
        heavier;
the Lord, the Lord Almighty, has told me
    of the destruction decreed against the
        whole land.

23 Listen and hear my voice;
    pay attention and hear what I say.
24 When farmers plow for planting, do they
        plow continually?
    Do they keep on breaking up and
        working the soil?
25 When they have leveled the surface,
    do they not sow caraway and scatter
        cumin?

a 10 Hebrew / *sav lasav sav lasav* / *kav lakav kav lakav* (probably meaningless sounds mimicking the prophet's words); also in verse 13   *b 15* Or *false gods*

Do they not plant wheat in its place,[a]
barley in its plot,[a]
and spelt in its field?
26 Their God instructs them
and teaches them the right way.

27 Caraway is not threshed with a sledge,
nor is a cartwheel rolled over cumin;
caraway is beaten out with a rod,
and cumin with a stick.
28 Grain must be ground to make bread;
so one does not go on threshing it
forever.
The wheels of a threshing cart may be
rolled over it,
but one does not use horses to grind
grain.
29 All this also comes from the LORD
Almighty,
whose plan is wonderful,
whose wisdom is magnificent.

Woe to David's City

29 Woe to you, Ariel, Ariel,
the city where David settled!
Add year to year
and let your cycle of festivals go on.
2 Yet I will besiege Ariel;
she will mourn and lament,
she will be to me like an altar
hearth.[b]
3 I will encamp against you on all sides;
I will encircle you with towers
and set up my siege works against
you.
4 Brought low, you will speak from the
ground;
your speech will mumble out of the
dust.
Your voice will come ghostlike from the
earth;
out of the dust your speech will
whisper.

5 But your many enemies will become like
fine dust,
the ruthless hordes like blown chaff.
Suddenly, in an instant,
6   the LORD Almighty will come
with thunder and earthquake and great
noise,
with windstorm and tempest and
flames of a devouring fire.

7 Then the hordes of all the nations that
fight against Ariel,
that attack her and her fortress and
besiege her,
will be as it is with a dream,
with a vision in the night—
8 as when hungry people dream they are
eating,
but they awaken, and their hunger
remains;
as when thirsty people dream they are
drinking,
but they awaken faint, with their
thirst unquenched.
So will it be with the hordes of all the
nations
that fight against Mount Zion.

9 Be stunned and amazed,
blind yourselves and be sightless;
be drunk, but not from wine,
stagger, but not from beer.
10 The LORD has brought over you a deep
sleep:
He has sealed your eyes (the
prophets);
he has covered your heads (the seers).

11 For you this whole vision is nothing but
words sealed in a scroll. And if you give the
scroll to someone who can read, and say,
"Read this, please," they will answer, "I
can't; it is sealed." 12 Or if you give the scroll
to someone who cannot read, and say,
"Read this, please," they will answer, "I
don't know how to read."

13 The Lord says:

"These people come near to me with
their mouth
and honor me with their lips,
but their hearts are far from me.
Their worship of me
is based on merely human rules they
have been taught.[c]
14 Therefore once more I will astound
these people
with wonder upon wonder;
the wisdom of the wise will perish,
the intelligence of the intelligent will
vanish."
15 Woe to those who go to great depths
to hide their plans from the LORD,

---

a 25 The meaning of the Hebrew for this word is uncertain.   b 2 The Hebrew for *altar hearth* sounds
like the Hebrew for *Ariel*.   c 13 Hebrew; Septuagint *They worship me in vain; / their teachings are merely
human rules*

who do their work in darkness and think,
"Who sees us? Who will know?"
¹⁶You turn things upside down,
as if the potter were thought to be
like the clay!
Shall what is formed say to the one who
formed it,
"You did not make me"?
Can the pot say to the potter,
"You know nothing"?

¹⁷In a very short time, will not Lebanon be
turned into a fertile field
and the fertile field seem like a
forest?
¹⁸In that day the deaf will hear the words
of the scroll,
and out of gloom and darkness
the eyes of the blind will see.
¹⁹Once more the humble will rejoice in
the Lord;
the needy will rejoice in the Holy One
of Israel.
²⁰The ruthless will vanish,
the mockers will disappear,
and all who have an eye for evil will
be cut down—
²¹those who with a word make someone
out to be guilty,
who ensnare the defender in court
and with false testimony deprive the
innocent of justice.

²²Therefore this is what the Lord, who redeemed Abraham, says to the house of Jacob:

"No longer will Jacob be ashamed;
no longer will their faces grow pale.
²³When they see among them their
children,
the work of my hands,
they will keep my name holy;
they will acknowledge the holiness of
the Holy One of Jacob,
and will stand in awe of the God of
Israel.
²⁴Those who are wayward in spirit will
gain understanding;
those who complain will accept
instruction."

Woe to the Obstinate Nation

30 "Woe to the obstinate children,"
declares the Lord,
"to those who carry out plans
that are not mine,

forming an alliance, but not by my
Spirit,
heaping sin upon sin;
²who go down to Egypt
without consulting me;
who look for help to Pharaoh's
protection,
to Egypt's shade for refuge.
³But Pharaoh's protection will be to your
shame,
Egypt's shade will bring you disgrace.
⁴Though they have officials in Zoan
and their envoys have arrived in
Hanes,
⁵everyone will be put to shame
because of a people useless to them,
who bring neither help nor advantage,
but only shame and disgrace."

⁶A prophecy concerning the animals of
the Negev:

Through a land of hardship and distress,
of lions and lionesses,
of adders and darting snakes,
the envoys carry their riches on donkeys'
backs,
their treasures on the humps of
camels,
to that unprofitable nation,
⁷   to Egypt, whose help is utterly
useless.
Therefore I call her
Rahab the Do-Nothing.

⁸Go now, write it on a tablet for them,
inscribe it on a scroll,
that for the days to come
it may be an everlasting witness.
⁹For these are rebellious people, deceitful
children,
children unwilling to listen to the
Lord's instruction.
¹⁰They say to the seers,
"See no more visions!"
and to the prophets,
"Give us no more visions of what is
right!
Tell us pleasant things,
prophesy illusions.
¹¹Leave this way,
get off this path,
and stop confronting us
with the Holy One of Israel!"

¹²Therefore, this is what the Holy One of
Israel says:

"Because you have rejected this
message,
  relied on oppression
  and depended on deceit,
[13] this sin will become for you
  like a high wall, cracked and bulging,
  that collapses suddenly, in an instant.
[14] It will break in pieces like pottery,
  shattered so mercilessly
that among its pieces not a fragment
  will be found
  for taking coals from a hearth
  or scooping water out of a cistern."

[15] This is what the Sovereign LORD, the
Holy One of Israel, says:

"In repentance and rest is your salvation,
  in quietness and trust is your
  strength,
  but you would have none of it.
[16] You said, 'No, we will flee on horses.'
  Therefore you will flee!
You said, 'We will ride off on swift
  horses.'
  Therefore your pursuers will be swift!
[17] A thousand will flee
  at the threat of one;
  at the threat of five
  you will all flee away,
  till you are left
  like a flagstaff on a mountaintop,
  like a banner on a hill."

[18] Yet the LORD longs to be gracious to you;
  therefore he will rise up to show you
  compassion.
For the LORD is a God of justice.
  Blessed are all who wait for him!

[19] People of Zion, who live in Jerusalem,
you will weep no more. How gracious he will
be when you cry for help! As soon as he hears,
he will answer you. [20] Although the Lord gives
you the bread of adversity and the water of
affliction, your teachers will be hidden no
more; with your own eyes you will see them.
[21] Whether you turn to the right or to the left,
your ears will hear a voice behind you, saying,
"This is the way; walk in it." [22] Then you will
desecrate your idols overlaid with silver and
your images covered with gold; you will
throw them away like a menstrual cloth and
say to them, "Away with you!"

[23] He will also send you rain for the seed
you sow in the ground, and the food that
comes from the land will be rich and plentiful. In that day your cattle will graze in
broad meadows. [24] The oxen and donkeys
that work the soil will eat fodder and mash,
spread out with fork and shovel. [25] In the day
of great slaughter, when the towers fall,
streams of water will flow on every high
mountain and every lofty hill. [26] The moon
will shine like the sun, and the sunlight will
be seven times brighter, like the light of sev-
en full days, when the LORD binds up the
bruises of his people and heals the wounds
he inflicted.

[27] See, the Name of the LORD comes from
  afar,
  with burning anger and dense clouds
  of smoke;
his lips are full of wrath,
  and his tongue is a consuming fire.
[28] His breath is like a rushing torrent,
  rising up to the neck.
He shakes the nations in the sieve of
  destruction;
  he places in the jaws of the peoples
  a bit that leads them astray.
[29] And you will sing
  as on the night you celebrate a holy
  festival;
your hearts will rejoice
  as when people playing pipes go up
to the mountain of the LORD,
  to the Rock of Israel.
[30] The LORD will cause people to hear his
  majestic voice
  and will make them see his arm
  coming down
with raging anger and consuming fire,
  with cloudburst, thunderstorm and
  hail.
[31] The voice of the LORD will shatter
  Assyria;
  with his rod he will strike them down.
[32] Every stroke the LORD lays on them
  with his punishing club
will be to the music of timbrels and
  harps,
  as he fights them in battle with the
  blows of his arm.
[33] Topheth has long been prepared;
  it has been made ready for the king.
Its fire pit has been made deep and
  wide,
  with an abundance of fire and wood;
the breath of the LORD,
  like a stream of burning sulfur,
  sets it ablaze.

Woe to Those Who Rely on Egypt

31 Woe to those who go down to
Egypt for help,
who rely on horses,
who trust in the multitude of their
chariots
and in the great strength of their
horsemen,
but do not look to the Holy One of
Israel,
or seek help from the LORD.
[2] Yet he too is wise and can bring disaster;
he does not take back his words.
He will rise up against the house of the
wicked,
against those who help evildoers.
[3] But the Egyptians are mortals and not
God;
their horses are flesh and not spirit.
When the LORD stretches out his hand,
those who help will stumble,
those who are helped will fall;
all will perish together.

[4] This is what the LORD says to me:

"As a lion growls,
a great lion over its prey—
and though a whole band of shepherds
is called together against it,
it is not frightened by their shouts
or disturbed by their clamor—
so the LORD Almighty will come down
to do battle on Mount Zion and on its
heights.
[5] Like birds hovering overhead,
the LORD Almighty will shield
Jerusalem;
he will shield it and deliver it,
he will 'pass over' it and will rescue
it."

[6] Return, you Israelites, to the One you
have so greatly revolted against. [7] For in that
day every one of you will reject the idols of
silver and gold your sinful hands have made.

[8] "Assyria will fall by no human sword;
a sword, not of mortals, will devour
them.
They will flee before the sword
and their young men will be put to
forced labor.
[9] Their stronghold will fall because of
terror;
at the sight of the battle standard
their commanders will panic,"

declares the LORD,
whose fire is in Zion,
whose furnace is in Jerusalem.

The Kingdom of Righteousness

32 See, a king will reign in
righteousness
and rulers will rule with justice.
[2] Each one will be like a shelter from the
wind
and a refuge from the storm,
like streams of water in the desert
and the shadow of a great rock in a
thirsty land.

[3] Then the eyes of those who see will no
longer be closed,
and the ears of those who hear will
listen.
[4] The fearful heart will know and
understand,
and the stammering tongue will be
fluent and clear.
[5] No longer will the fool be called noble
nor the scoundrel be highly respected.
[6] For fools speak folly,
their hearts are bent on evil:
They practice ungodliness
and spread error concerning the LORD;
the hungry they leave empty
and from the thirsty they withhold
water.
[7] Scoundrels use wicked methods,
they make up evil schemes
to destroy the poor with lies,
even when the plea of the needy is
just.
[8] But the noble make noble plans,
and by noble deeds they stand.

The Women of Jerusalem

[9] You women who are so complacent,
rise up and listen to me;
you daughters who feel secure,
hear what I have to say!
[10] In little more than a year
you who feel secure will tremble;
the grape harvest will fail,
and the harvest of fruit will not come.
[11] Tremble, you complacent women;
shudder, you daughters who feel
secure!
Strip off your clothes,
put sackcloth around your waists.
[12] Beat your breasts for the pleasant fields,
for the fruitful vines

¹³ and for the land of my people,
      a land overgrown with thorns and
         briers—
   yes, mourn for all houses of merriment
      and for this city of revelry.
¹⁴ The fortress will be abandoned,
      the noisy city deserted;
   citadel and watchtower will become a
         wasteland forever,
      the delight of donkeys, a pasture for
         flocks,
¹⁵ till the Spirit is poured on us from on
         high,
      and the desert becomes a fertile field,
      and the fertile field seems like a
         forest.
¹⁶ The LORD's justice will dwell in the
         desert,
      his righteousness live in the fertile
         field.
¹⁷ The fruit of that righteousness will be
         peace;
      its effect will be quietness and
         confidence forever.
¹⁸ My people will live in peaceful dwelling
         places,
      in secure homes,
      in undisturbed places of rest.
¹⁹ Though hail flattens the forest
      and the city is leveled completely,
²⁰ how blessed you will be,
      sowing your seed by every stream,
      and letting your cattle and donkeys
         range free.

Distress and Help

33 Woe to you, destroyer,
   you who have not been
      destroyed!
   Woe to you, betrayer,
      you who have not been betrayed!
   When you stop destroying,
      you will be destroyed;
   when you stop betraying,
      you will be betrayed.

² LORD, be gracious to us;
      we long for you.
   Be our strength every morning,
      our salvation in time of distress.
³ At the uproar of your army, the peoples
         flee;
      when you rise up, the nations scatter.

⁴ Their plunder is harvested as by young
         locusts;
      like a swarm of locusts people pounce
         on it.

⁵ The LORD is exalted, for he dwells on
         high;
      he will fill Zion with his justice and
         righteousness.
⁶ He will be the sure foundation for your
         times,
      a rich store of salvation and wisdom
         and knowledge;
      the fear of the LORD is the key to this
         treasure. *ᵃ*

⁷ Look, their brave men cry aloud in the
         streets;
      the envoys of peace weep bitterly.
⁸ The highways are deserted,
      no travelers are on the roads.
   The treaty is broken,
      its witnesses *ᵇ* are despised,
   no one is respected.
⁹ The land dries up and wastes away,
      Lebanon is ashamed and withers;
   Sharon is like the Arabah,
      and Bashan and Carmel drop their
         leaves.

¹⁰ "Now will I arise," says the LORD.
      "Now will I be exalted;
      now will I be lifted up.
¹¹ You conceive chaff,
      you give birth to straw;
      your breath is a fire that consumes
         you.
¹² The peoples will be burned as if to lime;
      like cut thornbushes they will be set
         ablaze."

¹³ You who are far away, hear what I have
         done;
      you who are near, acknowledge my
         power!
¹⁴ The sinners in Zion are terrified;
      trembling grips the godless:
   "Who of us can dwell with the
         consuming fire?
      Who of us can dwell with everlasting
         burning?"
¹⁵ Those who walk righteously
      and speak what is right,
   who reject gain from extortion

ᵃ 6 Or *is a treasure from him*   *ᵇ 8* Dead Sea Scrolls; Masoretic Text / *the cities*

and keep their hands from accepting
  bribes,
who stop their ears against plots of
  murder
and shut their eyes against
  contemplating evil—
¹⁶they are the ones who will dwell on the
  heights,
  whose refuge will be the mountain
    fortress.
Their bread will be supplied,
  and water will not fail them.

¹⁷Your eyes will see the king in his
    beauty
  and view a land that stretches afar.
¹⁸In your thoughts you will ponder the
    former terror:
  "Where is that chief officer?
Where is the one who took the revenue?
  Where is the officer in charge of the
    towers?"
¹⁹You will see those arrogant people no
    more,
  people whose speech is obscure,
  whose language is strange and
    incomprehensible.

²⁰Look on Zion, the city of our festivals;
  your eyes will see Jerusalem,
  a peaceful abode, a tent that will not
    be moved;
its stakes will never be pulled up,
  nor any of its ropes broken.
²¹There the Lord will be our Mighty One.
  It will be like a place of broad rivers
    and streams.
No galley with oars will ride them,
  no mighty ship will sail them.
²²For the Lord is our judge,
  the Lord is our lawgiver,
the Lord is our king;
  it is he who will save us.

²³Your rigging hangs loose:
  The mast is not held secure,
  the sail is not spread.
Then an abundance of spoils will be
    divided
  and even the lame will carry off
    plunder.
²⁴No one living in Zion will say, "I am ill";
  and the sins of those who dwell there
    will be forgiven.

Judgment Against the Nations

34 Come near, you nations, and
    listen;
  pay attention, you peoples!
Let the earth hear, and all that is in it,
  the world, and all that comes out
    of it!
²The Lord is angry with all nations;
  his wrath is on all their armies.
He will totally destroy^a them,
  he will give them over to slaughter.
³Their slain will be thrown out,
  their dead bodies will send up a
    stench;
  the mountains will be soaked with
    their blood.
⁴All the stars in the sky will be dissolved
  and the heavens rolled up like a
    scroll;
  all the starry host will fall
  like withered leaves from the vine,
  like shriveled figs from the fig tree.

⁵My sword has drunk its fill in the
    heavens;
  see, it descends in judgment on
    Edom,
  the people I have totally destroyed.
⁶The sword of the Lord is bathed in
    blood,
  it is covered with fat—
the blood of lambs and goats,
  fat from the kidneys of rams.
For the Lord has a sacrifice in Bozrah
  and a great slaughter in Edom.
⁷And the wild oxen will fall with them,
  the bull calves and the great bulls.
Their land will be drenched with blood,
  and the dust will be soaked with fat.

⁸For the Lord has a day of vengeance,
  a year of retribution, to uphold Zion's
    cause.
⁹Edom's streams will be turned into
    pitch,
  her dust into burning sulfur;
  her land will become blazing pitch!
¹⁰It will not be quenched night or day;
  its smoke will rise forever.
From generation to generation it will lie
    desolate;
  no one will ever pass through it again.

---

^a 2 The Hebrew term refers to the irrevocable giving over of things or persons to the Lord, often by
totally destroying them; also in verse 5.

¹¹The desert owl[a] and screech owl[a] will
possess it;
the great owl[a] and the raven will nest
there.
God will stretch out over Edom
the measuring line of chaos
and the plumb line of desolation.
¹²Her nobles will have nothing there to be
called a kingdom,
all her princes will vanish away.
¹³Thorns will overrun her citadels,
nettles and brambles her strongholds.
She will become a haunt for jackals,
a home for owls.
¹⁴Desert creatures will meet with hyenas,
and wild goats will bleat to each
other;
there the night creatures will also lie
down
and find for themselves places of rest.
¹⁵The owl will nest there and lay eggs,
she will hatch them, and care for her
young
under the shadow of her wings;
there also the falcons will gather,
each with its mate.

¹⁶Look in the scroll of the LORD and read:

None of these will be missing,
not one will lack her mate.
For it is his mouth that has given the
order,
and his Spirit will gather them
together.
¹⁷He allots their portions;
his hand distributes them by
measure.
They will possess it forever
and dwell there from generation to
generation.

Joy of the Redeemed

35 The desert and the parched
land will be glad;
the wilderness will rejoice and
blossom.
Like the crocus, ²it will burst into bloom;
it will rejoice greatly and shout for
joy.
The glory of Lebanon will be given to it,
the splendor of Carmel and Sharon;
they will see the glory of the LORD,
the splendor of our God.

³Strengthen the feeble hands,
steady the knees that give way;
⁴say to those with fearful hearts,
"Be strong, do not fear;
your God will come,
he will come with vengeance;
with divine retribution
he will come to save you."

⁵Then will the eyes of the blind be
opened
and the ears of the deaf unstopped.
⁶Then will the lame leap like a deer,
and the mute tongue shout for joy.
Water will gush forth in the wilderness
and streams in the desert.
⁷The burning sand will become a pool,
the thirsty ground bubbling springs.
In the haunts where jackals once lay,
grass and reeds and papyrus will
grow.

⁸And a highway will be there;
it will be called the Way of Holiness;
it will be for those who walk on that
Way.
The unclean will not journey on it;
wicked fools will not go about on it.
⁹No lion will be there,
nor any ravenous beast;
they will not be found there.
But only the redeemed will walk there,
¹⁰ and those the LORD has rescued will
return.
They will enter Zion with singing;
everlasting joy will crown their heads.
Gladness and joy will overtake them,
and sorrow and sighing will flee away.

Sennacherib Threatens Jerusalem

36 In the fourteenth year of King
Hezekiah's reign, Sennacherib
king of Assyria attacked all the
fortified cities of Judah and captured them.
²Then the king of Assyria sent his field
commander with a large army from Lachish
to King Hezekiah at Jerusalem. When the
commander stopped at the aqueduct of the
Upper Pool, on the road to the Launderer's
Field, ³Eliakim son of Hilkiah the palace administrator, Shebna the secretary, and Joah
son of Asaph the recorder went out to him.
⁴The field commander said to them, "Tell
Hezekiah:

---

a 11 The precise identification of these birds is uncertain.

" 'This is what the great king, the king of Assyria, says: On what are you basing this confidence of yours? ⁵You say you have counsel and might for war—but you speak only empty words. On whom are you depending, that you rebel against me? ⁶Look, I know you are depending on Egypt, that splintered reed of a staff, which pierces the hand of anyone who leans on it! Such is Pharaoh king of Egypt to all who depend on him. ⁷But if you say to me, "We are depending on the Lord our God"—isn't he the one whose high places and altars Hezekiah removed, saying to Judah and Jerusalem, "You must worship before this altar"?

⁸" 'Come now, make a bargain with my master, the king of Assyria: I will give you two thousand horses—if you can put riders on them! ⁹How then can you repulse one officer of the least of my master's officials, even though you are depending on Egypt for chariots and horsemen*ᵃ*? ¹⁰Furthermore, have I come to attack and destroy this land without the Lord? The Lord himself told me to march against this country and destroy it.' "

¹¹Then Eliakim, Shebna and Joah said to the field commander, "Please speak to your servants in Aramaic, since we understand it. Don't speak to us in Hebrew in the hearing of the people on the wall."

¹²But the commander replied, "Was it only to your master and you that my master sent me to say these things, and not to the people sitting on the wall—who, like you, will have to eat their own excrement and drink their own urine?"

¹³Then the commander stood and called out in Hebrew, "Hear the words of the great king, the king of Assyria! ¹⁴This is what the king says: Do not let Hezekiah deceive you. He cannot deliver you! ¹⁵Do not let Hezekiah persuade you to trust in the Lord when he says, 'The Lord will surely deliver us; this city will not be given into the hand of the king of Assyria.'

¹⁶"Do not listen to Hezekiah. This is what the king of Assyria says: Make peace with me and come out to me. Then every one of you will eat from your own vine and fig tree

and drink water from your own cistern, ¹⁷until I come and take you to a land like your own—a land of grain and new wine, a land of bread and vineyards.

¹⁸"Do not let Hezekiah mislead you when he says, 'The Lord will deliver us.' Have the gods of any nations ever delivered their lands from the hand of the king of Assyria? ¹⁹Where are the gods of Hamath and Arpad? Where are the gods of Sepharvaim? Have they rescued Samaria from my hand? ²⁰Who of all the gods of these countries have been able to save their lands from me? How then can the Lord deliver Jerusalem from my hand?"

²¹But the people remained silent and said nothing in reply, because the king had commanded, "Do not answer him."

²²Then Eliakim son of Hilkiah the palace administrator, Shebna the secretary and Joah son of Asaph the recorder went to Hezekiah, with their clothes torn, and told him what the field commander had said.

Jerusalem's Deliverance Foretold

37 When King Hezekiah heard this, he tore his clothes and put on sackcloth and went into the temple of the Lord. ²He sent Eliakim the palace administrator, Shebna the secretary, and the leading priests, all wearing sackcloth, to the prophet Isaiah son of Amoz. ³They told him, "This is what Hezekiah says: This day is a day of distress and rebuke and disgrace, as when children come to the moment of birth and there is no strength to deliver them. ⁴It may be that the Lord your God will hear the words of the field commander, whom his master, the king of Assyria, has sent to ridicule the living God, and that he will rebuke him for the words the Lord your God has heard. Therefore pray for the remnant that still survives."

⁵When King Hezekiah's officials came to Isaiah, ⁶Isaiah said to them, "Tell your master, 'This is what the Lord says: Do not be afraid of what you have heard—those words with which the underlings of the king of Assyria have blasphemed me. ⁷Listen! When he hears a certain report, I will make him want to return to his own country, and there I will have him cut down with the sword.' "

⁸When the field commander heard that

ᵃ 9 Or charioteers

the king of Assyria had left Lachish, he withdrew and found the king fighting against Libnah.

⁹Now Sennacherib received a report that Tirhakah, the king of Cush,ᵃ was marching out to fight against him. When he heard it, he sent messengers to Hezekiah with this word: ¹⁰"Say to Hezekiah king of Judah: Do not let the god you depend on deceive you when he says, 'Jerusalem will not be given into the hands of the king of Assyria.' ¹¹Surely you have heard what the kings of Assyria have done to all the countries, destroying them completely. And will you be delivered? ¹²Did the gods of the nations that were destroyed by my ancestors deliver them—the gods of Gozan, Harran, Rezeph and the people of Eden who were in Tel Assar? ¹³Where is the king of Hamath or the king of Arpad? Where are the kings of Lair, Sepharvaim, Hena and Ivvah?"

Hezekiah's Prayer

¹⁴Hezekiah received the letter from the messengers and read it. Then he went up to the temple of the Lᴏʀᴅ and spread it out before the Lᴏʀᴅ. ¹⁵And Hezekiah prayed to the Lᴏʀᴅ: ¹⁶"Lᴏʀᴅ Almighty, the God of Israel, enthroned between the cherubim, you alone are God over all the kingdoms of the earth. You have made heaven and earth. ¹⁷Give ear, Lᴏʀᴅ, and hear; open your eyes, Lᴏʀᴅ, and see; listen to all the words Sennacherib has sent to ridicule the living God.

¹⁸"It is true, Lᴏʀᴅ, that the Assyrian kings have laid waste all these peoples and their lands. ¹⁹They have thrown their gods into the fire and destroyed them, for they were not gods but only wood and stone, fashioned by human hands. ²⁰Now, Lᴏʀᴅ our God, deliver us from his hand, so that all the kingdoms of the earth may know that you, Lᴏʀᴅ, are the only God.ᵇ"

Sennacherib's Fall

²¹Then Isaiah son of Amoz sent a message to Hezekiah: "This is what the Lᴏʀᴅ, the God of Israel, says: Because you have prayed to me concerning Sennacherib king of Assyria, ²²this is the word the Lᴏʀᴅ has spoken against him:

"Virgin Daughter Zion
    despises and mocks you.
Daughter Jerusalem
    tosses her head as you flee.
²³Who is it you have ridiculed and
        blasphemed?
    Against whom have you raised your
        voice
and lifted your eyes in pride?
    Against the Holy One of Israel!
²⁴By your messengers
    you have ridiculed the Lord.
And you have said,
    'With my many chariots
I have ascended the heights of the
        mountains,
    the utmost heights of Lebanon.
I have cut down its tallest cedars,
    the choicest of its junipers.
I have reached its remotest heights,
    the finest of its forests.
²⁵I have dug wells in foreign landsᶜ
    and drunk the water there.
With the soles of my feet
    I have dried up all the streams of
        Egypt.'
²⁶"Have you not heard?
    Long ago I ordained it.
In days of old I planned it;
    now I have brought it to pass,
that you have turned fortified cities
    into piles of stone.
²⁷Their people, drained of power,
    are dismayed and put to shame.
They are like plants in the field,
    like tender green shoots,
like grass sprouting on the roof,
    scorchedᵈ before it grows up.

²⁸"But I know where you are
    and when you come and go
    and how you rage against me.
²⁹Because you rage against me
    and because your insolence has
        reached my ears,
I will put my hook in your nose
    and my bit in your mouth,
and I will make you return
    by the way you came.

³⁰"This will be the sign for you, Hezekiah:

ᵃ 9 That is, the upper Nile region   ᵇ 20 Dead Sea Scrolls (see also 2 Kings 19:19); Masoretic Text *you alone are the Lᴏʀᴅ*   ᶜ 25 Dead Sea Scrolls (see also 2 Kings 19:24); Masoretic Text does not have *in foreign lands*.   ᵈ 27 Some manuscripts of the Masoretic Text, Dead Sea Scrolls and some Septuagint manuscripts (see also 2 Kings 19:26); most manuscripts of the Masoretic Text *roof / and terraced fields*

"This year you will eat what grows by
    itself,
  and the second year what springs
    from that.
But in the third year sow and reap,
  plant vineyards and eat their fruit.
³¹ Once more a remnant of the house of
    Judah
  will take root below and bear fruit
    above.
³² For out of Jerusalem will come a
    remnant,
  and out of Mount Zion a band of
    survivors.
The zeal of the LORD Almighty
  will accomplish this.

³³"Therefore this is what the LORD says
concerning the king of Assyria:

"He will not enter this city
  or shoot an arrow here.
He will not come before it with shield
  or build a siege ramp against it.
³⁴ By the way that he came he will return;
  he will not enter this city,"
                 declares the LORD.
³⁵ "I will defend this city and save it,
  for my sake and for the sake of David
    my servant!"

³⁶Then the angel of the LORD went out
and put to death a hundred and eighty-five
thousand in the Assyrian camp. When the
people got up the next morning—there were
all the dead bodies! ³⁷So Sennacherib king
of Assyria broke camp and withdrew. He returned to Nineveh and stayed there.

³⁸One day, while he was worshiping in
the temple of his god Nisrok, his sons
Adrammelek and Sharezer killed him with
the sword, and they escaped to the land of
Ararat. And Esarhaddon his son succeeded
him as king.

Hezekiah's Illness

38 In those days Hezekiah became
ill and was at the point of death.
The prophet Isaiah son of Amoz
went to him and said, "This is what the LORD
says: Put your house in order, because you
are going to die; you will not recover."

²Hezekiah turned his face to the wall and
prayed to the LORD, ³"Remember, LORD, how
I have walked before you faithfully and with
wholehearted devotion and have done what

is good in your eyes." And Hezekiah wept
bitterly.

⁴Then the word of the LORD came to Isa-
iah: ⁵"Go and tell Hezekiah, 'This is what
the LORD, the God of your father David, says:
I have heard your prayer and seen your
tears; I will add fifteen years to your life.
⁶And I will deliver you and this city from the
hand of the king of Assyria. I will defend this
city.

⁷" 'This is the LORD's sign to you that the
LORD will do what he has promised: ⁸I will
make the shadow cast by the sun go back
the ten steps it has gone down on the stairway of Ahaz.' " So the sunlight went back
the ten steps it had gone down.

⁹A writing of Hezekiah king of Judah after
his illness and recovery:

¹⁰ I said, "In the prime of my life
    must I go through the gates of death
    and be robbed of the rest of my
      years?"
¹¹ I said, "I will not again see the LORD,
    the LORD, in the land of the living;
no longer will I look on my fellow
    mortals,
  or be with those who now dwell in
    this world.
¹² Like a shepherd's tent my house
    has been pulled down and taken from
    me.
Like a weaver I have rolled up my life,
    and he has cut me off from the loom;
  day and night you made an end of
    me.
¹³ I waited patiently till dawn,
    but like a lion he broke all my bones;
  day and night you made an end of me.
¹⁴ I cried like a swift or thrush,
    I moaned like a mourning dove.
My eyes grew weak as I looked to the
    heavens.
    I am being threatened; Lord, come to
      my aid!"

¹⁵ But what can I say?
    He has spoken to me, and he himself
      has done this.
I will walk humbly all my years
    because of this anguish of my soul.
¹⁶ Lord, by such things people live;
    and my spirit finds life in them too.
You restored me to health
    and let me live.
¹⁷ Surely it was for my benefit

that I suffered such anguish.
In your love you kept me
from the pit of destruction;
you have put all my sins
behind your back.
[18] For the grave cannot praise you,
death cannot sing your praise;
those who go down to the pit
cannot hope for your faithfulness.
[19] The living, the living—they praise you,
as I am doing today;
parents tell their children
about your faithfulness.

[20] The LORD will save me,
and we will sing with stringed
instruments
all the days of our lives
in the temple of the LORD.

[21] Isaiah had said, "Prepare a poultice of figs and apply it to the boil, and he will recover."

[22] Hezekiah had asked, "What will be the sign that I will go up to the temple of the LORD?"

Envoys From Babylon

39 At that time Marduk-Baladan son of Baladan king of Babylon sent Hezekiah letters and a gift, because he had heard of his illness and recovery. [2] Hezekiah received the envoys gladly and showed them what was in his storehouses—the silver, the gold, the spices, the fine olive oil—his entire armory and everything found among his treasures. There was nothing in his palace or in all his kingdom that Hezekiah did not show them.

[3] Then Isaiah the prophet went to King Hezekiah and asked, "What did those men say, and where did they come from?"

"From a distant land," Hezekiah replied. "They came to me from Babylon."

[4] The prophet asked, "What did they see in your palace?"

"They saw everything in my palace," Hezekiah said. "There is nothing among my treasures that I did not show them."

[5] Then Isaiah said to Hezekiah, "Hear the word of the LORD Almighty: [6] The time will surely come when everything in your palace, and all that your predecessors have stored

up until this day, will be carried off to Babylon. Nothing will be left, says the LORD. [7] And some of your descendants, your own flesh and blood who will be born to you, will be taken away, and they will become eunuchs in the palace of the king of Babylon."

[8] "The word of the LORD you have spoken is good," Hezekiah replied. For he thought, "There will be peace and security in my lifetime."

Comfort for God's People

40 Comfort, comfort my people,
says your God.
[2] Speak tenderly to Jerusalem,
and proclaim to her
that her hard service has been
completed,
that her sin has been paid for,
that she has received from the LORD's
hand
double for all her sins.

[3] A voice of one calling:
"In the wilderness prepare
the way for the LORD[a];
make straight in the desert
a highway for our God.[b]
[4] Every valley shall be raised up,
every mountain and hill made low;
the rough ground shall become level,
the rugged places a plain.
[5] And the glory of the LORD will be
revealed,
and all people will see it together.
For the mouth of the LORD
has spoken."

[6] A voice says, "Cry out."
And I said, "What shall I cry?"

"All people are like grass,
and all human faithfulness is like the
flowers of the field.
[7] The grass withers and the flowers fall,
because the breath of the LORD blows
on them.
Surely the people are grass.
[8] The grass withers and the flowers fall,
but the word of our God endures
forever."

[9] You who bring good news to Zion,
go up on a high mountain.

---

a 3 Or A voice of one calling in the wilderness: / "Prepare the way for the LORD   b 3 Hebrew; Septuagint make straight the paths of our God

THEOLOGY AND HUMAN SUFFERING

Isaiah 40:1–31 *or* 40:1,11,27–31

JAMES ORR {AD 1844–1913}

The penalties of evildoing are probably never confined to the actual wrongdoer. Instead, they usually overflow onto others, and sometimes involve them in untold misery. To challenge the fairness of this would mean challenging the fairness of the basic framework of humanity.

We can say that Christ is no exception to this universal law. In fact, he is the greatest example of it. Christ could not enter the world without receiving upon himself the brunt of its evils. They fell on him with greater severity because he was the infinitely pure and holy one. A writer like Horace Bushnell often uses the strongest language. He speaks of Christ as incarnated into the curse of the world. "It is," he says, "as if the condemnations of God were upon him, just as they are on the whole of the human race into which he is come." "It means," he says again, "that he is incarnated into the same condition we live in, under what is called the curse . . . He came to dwell with us, to share our human nature, to be our brother. He could not do this without entering into what is our principal distinction—being under the curse."

Carolyn Custis James

The war zones of life force us to take our theology seriously, to see if our beliefs about God hold up when the tragedies and perplexities of life press down upon them. Our theology, if it is true, must apply to all of us and include all points on the Richter scale of human suffering. If God's goodness cannot penetrate the darkness of a [person's] world or breaks up under the weight of such wretchedness, if there are pockets of our lives beyond God's reach, then none of us can really count on him. Our hope in God is no better than a placebo if his plan doesn't encompass all of life—the dark side as well as the bright.

reflection

1. Do you believe God cares about your pain? Why?

2. Does suffering in the world mean that God doesn't care or isn't powerful enough to stop it? How do you support your answer?

3. How does your knowledge of God make a difference in how you respond to the hard things of life?

For your next devotional reading, go to page 814.

You who bring good news to Jerusalem,[a]
   lift up your voice with a shout,
lift it up, do not be afraid;
   say to the towns of Judah,
   "Here is your God!"
[10] See, the Sovereign Lord comes with
      power,
   and his arm rules for him.
See, his reward is with him,
   and his recompense accompanies
      him.
[11] He tends his flock like a shepherd:
   He gathers the lambs in his arms
and carries them close to his heart;
   he gently leads those that have
      young.

[12] Who has measured the waters in the
      hollow of his hand,
   or with the breadth of his hand
      marked off the heavens?
Who has held the dust of the earth in a
      basket,
   or weighed the mountains on the
      scales
   and the hills in a balance?
[13] Who can fathom the Spirit[b] of the Lord,
   or instruct the Lord as his counselor?
[14] Whom did the Lord consult to enlighten
      him,
   and who taught him the right way?
Who was it that taught him knowledge,
   or showed him the path of
      understanding?

[15] Surely the nations are like a drop in a
      bucket;
   they are regarded as dust on the
      scales;
   he weighs the islands as though they
      were fine dust.
[16] Lebanon is not sufficient for altar fires,
   nor its animals enough for burnt
      offerings.
[17] Before him all the nations are as
      nothing;
   they are regarded by him as worthless
      and less than nothing.

[18] With whom, then, will you compare
      God?
   To what image will you liken him?
[19] As for an idol, a metalworker casts it,
   and a goldsmith overlays it with gold

and fashions silver chains for it.
[20] People too poor to present such an
      offering
   select wood that will not rot.
They look for a skilled worker
   to set up an idol that will not topple.

[21] Do you not know?
   Have you not heard?
Has it not been told you from the
      beginning?
   Have you not understood since the
      earth was founded?
[22] He sits enthroned above the circle of the
      earth,
   and its people are like grasshoppers.
He stretches out the heavens like a
      canopy,
   and spreads them out like a tent to
      live in.
[23] He brings princes to naught
   and reduces the rulers of this world to
      nothing.
[24] No sooner are they planted,
   no sooner are they sown,
   no sooner do they take root in the
      ground,
than he blows on them and they wither,
   and a whirlwind sweeps them away
      like chaff.

[25] "To whom will you compare me?
   Or who is my equal?" says the Holy
      One.
[26] Lift up your eyes and look to the
      heavens:
   Who created all these?
He who brings out the starry host one by
      one,
   and calls them each by name.
Because of his great power and mighty
      strength,
   not one of them is missing.

[27] Why do you complain, Jacob?
   Why do you say, Israel,
"My way is hidden from the Lord;
   my cause is disregarded by my God"?
[28] Do you not know?
   Have you not heard?
The Lord is the everlasting God,
   the Creator of the ends of the earth.
He will not grow tired or weary,

---

a 9 Or *Zion, bringer of good news, / go up on a high mountain. / Jerusalem, bringer of good news*
b 13 Or *mind*

and his understanding no one can
fathom.
²⁹ He gives strength to the weary
and increases the power of the weak.
³⁰ Even youths grow tired and weary,
and young men stumble and fall;
³¹ but those who hope in the LORD
will renew their strength.
They will soar on wings like eagles;
they will run and not grow weary,
they will walk and not be faint.

The Helper of Israel

41

"Be silent before me, you
islands!
Let the nations renew their
strength!
Let them come forward and speak;
let us meet together at the place of
judgment.

² "Who has stirred up one from the east,
calling him in righteousness to his
service^a?
He hands nations over to him
and subdues kings before him.
He turns them to dust with his sword,
to windblown chaff with his bow.
³ He pursues them and moves on
unscathed,
by a path his feet have not traveled
before.
⁴ Who has done this and carried it
through,
calling forth the generations from the
beginning?
I, the LORD—with the first of them
and with the last—I am he."

⁵ The islands have seen it and fear;
the ends of the earth tremble.
They approach and come forward;
⁶ they help each other
and say to their companions, "Be
strong!"
⁷ The metalworker encourages the
goldsmith,
and the one who smooths with the
hammer
spurs on the one who strikes the
anvil.
One says of the welding, "It is good."
The other nails down the idol so it
will not topple.

⁸ "But you, Israel, my servant,
Jacob, whom I have chosen,
you descendants of Abraham my
friend,
⁹ I took you from the ends of the earth,
from its farthest corners I called you.
I said, 'You are my servant';
I have chosen you and have not
rejected you.
¹⁰ So do not fear, for I am with you;
do not be dismayed, for I am your
God.
I will strengthen you and help you;
I will uphold you with my righteous
right hand.

¹¹ "All who rage against you
will surely be ashamed and disgraced;
those who oppose you
will be as nothing and perish.
¹² Though you search for your enemies,
you will not find them.
Those who wage war against you
will be as nothing at all.
¹³ For I am the LORD your God
who takes hold of your right hand
and says to you, Do not fear;
I will help you.
¹⁴ Do not be afraid, you worm Jacob,
little Israel, do not fear,
for I myself will help you," declares the
LORD,
your Redeemer, the Holy One of
Israel.
¹⁵ "See, I will make you into a threshing
sledge,
new and sharp, with many teeth.
You will thresh the mountains and crush
them,
and reduce the hills to chaff.
¹⁶ You will winnow them, the wind will
pick them up,
and a gale will blow them away.
But you will rejoice in the LORD
and glory in the Holy One of Israel.

¹⁷ "The poor and needy search for water,
but there is none;
their tongues are parched with thirst.
But I the LORD will answer them;
I, the God of Israel, will not forsake
them.
¹⁸ I will make rivers flow on barren heights,
and springs within the valleys.

---

^a 2 Or *east, / whom victory meets at every step*

I will turn the desert into pools of water,
and the parched ground into springs.
19 I will put in the desert
the cedar and the acacia, the myrtle
and the olive.
I will set junipers in the wasteland,
the fir and the cypress together,
20 so that people may see and know,
may consider and understand,
that the hand of the LORD has done this,
that the Holy One of Israel has
created it.

21 "Present your case," says the LORD.
"Set forth your arguments," says
Jacob's King.
22 "Tell us, you idols,
what is going to happen.
Tell us what the former things were,
so that we may consider them
and know their final outcome.
Or declare to us the things to come,
23   tell us what the future holds,
so we may know that you are gods.
Do something, whether good or bad,
so that we will be dismayed and filled
with fear.
24 But you are less than nothing
and you can do nothing;
those who choose you are detestable.

25 "I have stirred up one from the north,
and he comes—
one from the rising sun who calls on
my name.
He treads on rulers as if they were
mortar,
as if he were a potter treading the
clay.
26 Who told of this from the beginning, so
we could know,
or beforehand, so we could say, 'He
was right'?
No one told of this,
no one foretold it,
no one heard any words from you.
27 I was the first to tell Zion, 'Look, here
they are!'
I gave to Jerusalem a messenger of
good news.
28 I look but there is no one—
no one among the gods to give
counsel,
no one to give answer when I ask them.
29 See, they are all false!
Their deeds amount to nothing;

their images are but wind and
confusion.

The Servant of the LORD

42 "Here is my servant, whom I
uphold,
my chosen one in whom I
delight;
I will put my Spirit on him,
and he will bring justice to the
nations.
2 He will not shout or cry out,
or raise his voice in the streets.
3 A bruised reed he will not break,
and a smoldering wick he will not
snuff out.
In faithfulness he will bring forth justice;
4   he will not falter or be discouraged
till he establishes justice on earth.
In his teaching the islands will put
their hope."

5 This is what God the LORD says—
he who created the heavens and
stretched them out,
who spread out the earth with all that
springs from it,
who gives breath to its people,
and life to those who walk on it:
6 "I, the LORD, have called you in
righteousness;
I will take hold of your hand.
I will keep you and will make you
to be a covenant for the people
and a light for the Gentiles,
7 to open eyes that are blind,
to free captives from prison
and to release from the dungeon
those who sit in darkness.

8 "I am the LORD; that is my name!
I will not yield my glory to another
or my praise to idols.
9 See, the former things have taken place,
and new things I declare;
before they spring into being
I announce them to you."

Song of Praise to the LORD

10 Sing to the LORD a new song,
his praise from the ends of the earth,
you who go down to the sea, and all that
is in it,
you islands, and all who live in them.
11 Let the wilderness and its towns raise
their voices;

let the settlements where Kedar lives
  rejoice.
Let the people of Sela sing for joy;
  let them shout from the
    mountaintops.
¹² Let them give glory to the LORD
  and proclaim his praise in the islands.
¹³ The LORD will march out like a
    champion,
  like a warrior he will stir up his zeal;
with a shout he will raise the battle cry
  and will triumph over his enemies.

¹⁴ "For a long time I have kept silent,
  I have been quiet and held myself
    back.
But now, like a woman in childbirth,
  I cry out, I gasp and pant.
¹⁵ I will lay waste the mountains and hills
  and dry up all their vegetation;
I will turn rivers into islands
  and dry up the pools.
¹⁶ I will lead the blind by ways they have
    not known,
  along unfamiliar paths I will guide
    them;
I will turn the darkness into light before
    them
  and make the rough places smooth.
These are the things I will do;
  I will not forsake them.
¹⁷ But those who trust in idols,
  who say to images, 'You are our gods,'
  will be turned back in utter shame.

Israel Blind and Deaf
¹⁸ "Hear, you deaf;
  look, you blind, and see!
¹⁹ Who is blind but my servant,
  and deaf like the messenger I send?
Who is blind like the one in covenant
    with me,
  blind like the servant of the LORD?
²⁰ You have seen many things, but have
    paid no attention;
  your ears are open, but you hear
    nothing."
²¹ It pleased the LORD
  for the sake of his righteousness
  to make his law great and glorious.
²² But this is a people plundered and
    looted,
  all of them trapped in pits
  or hidden away in prisons.

They have become plunder,
  with no one to rescue them;
they have been made loot,
  with no one to say, "Send them
    back."

²³ Which of you will listen to this
  or pay close attention in time to
    come?
²⁴ Who handed Jacob over to become loot,
  and Israel to the plunderers?
Was it not the LORD,
  against whom we have sinned?
For they would not follow his ways;
  they did not obey his law.
²⁵ So he poured out on them his burning
    anger,
  the violence of war.
It enveloped them in flames, yet they
    did not understand;
  it consumed them, but they did not
    take it to heart.

Israel's Only Savior

43 But now, this is what the LORD
      says—
  he who created you, Jacob,
  he who formed you, Israel:
"Do not fear, for I have redeemed you;
  I have summoned you by name; you
    are mine.
² When you pass through the waters,
  I will be with you;
and when you pass through the rivers,
  they will not sweep over you.
When you walk through the fire,
  you will not be burned;
  the flames will not set you ablaze.
³ For I am the LORD your God,
  the Holy One of Israel, your Savior;
I give Egypt for your ransom,
  Cush ᵃ and Seba in your stead.
⁴ Since you are precious and honored in
    my sight,
  and because I love you,
I will give nations in exchange for you,
  and peoples in exchange for your life.
⁵ Do not be afraid, for I am with you;
  I will bring your children from the
    east
  and gather you from the west.
⁶ I will say to the north, 'Give them up!'
  and to the south, 'Do not hold them
    back.'

a 3 That is, the upper Nile region

WEDNESDAY

SUPREME GOALS

Isaiah 43:1–28 *or* 43:1–7

Rick Warren

In the entire universe, only two of God's creations fail to bring glory to him: fallen angels (demons) and us (people). All sin, at its root, is failing to give God glory. It is loving anything else more than God. Refusing to bring glory to God is prideful rebellion, and it is the sin that caused Satan's fall—and ours, too. In different ways we have all lived for our own glory, not God's. The Bible says, *"All have sinned and fall short of the glory of God."*

None of us have given God the full glory he deserves from our lives. This is the worst sin and the biggest mistake we can make. On the other hand, living for God's glory is the greatest achievement we can accomplish with our lives. God says, *"They are my own people, and I created them to bring me glory,"* so it ought to be the supreme goal of our lives.

JONATHAN EDWARDS {AD 1703–1758}

From time to time, the business of religion is compared to activities that require a great exertion of our hearts and strength—such as running, wrestling or agonizing for a great prize, fighting against strong enemies trying to kill us and warring as those attempting to conquer a city or kingdom by force. And though those who are young in their faith have not yet learned to exert their hearts and will with the same strength as those who are more mature, every believer has the power of godliness at work in his or her heart. Because of this, the believer's heart and mind will indeed labor in relation to God and divine things with a strength and energy that causes them to experience victory over worldly or fleshly affections. For every true disciple of Christ loves him more than they love their father or mother, wife or husband and children, brothers and sisters, houses and lands—yes, even more than they love their own life (see Luke 14:26).

reflection

1. What is the number-one goal you have for your life?
2. What is your plan for realizing that goal?
3. Why do you think God created you?

For your next devotional reading, go to page 820.

Bring my sons from afar
  and my daughters from the ends of
    the earth—
⁷everyone who is called by my name,
  whom I created for my glory,
  whom I formed and made."

⁸Lead out those who have eyes but are
    blind,
  who have ears but are deaf.
⁹All the nations gather together
  and the peoples assemble.
Which of their gods foretold this
  and proclaimed to us the former
    things?
Let them bring in their witnesses to
    prove they were right,
  so that others may hear and say, "It is
    true."
¹⁰"You are my witnesses," declares the
    Lord,
  "and my servant whom I have chosen,
so that you may know and believe me
  and understand that I am he.
Before me no god was formed,
  nor will there be one after me.
¹¹I, even I, am the Lord,
  and apart from me there is no savior.
¹²I have revealed and saved and
    proclaimed—
  I, and not some foreign god among
    you.
You are my witnesses," declares the
    Lord, "that I am God.
¹³ Yes, and from ancient days I am he.
No one can deliver out of my hand.
  When I act, who can reverse it?"

God's Mercy and Israel's Unfaithfulness
¹⁴This is what the Lord says—
  your Redeemer, the Holy One of
    Israel:
"For your sake I will send to Babylon
  and bring down as fugitives all the
    Babylonians,ᵃ
  in the ships in which they took pride.
¹⁵I am the Lord, your Holy One,
  Israel's Creator, your King."

¹⁶This is what the Lord says—
  he who made a way through the sea,
  a path through the mighty waters,
¹⁷who drew out the chariots and horses,

the army and reinforcements
    together,
and they lay there, never to rise again,
  extinguished, snuffed out like a wick:
¹⁸"Forget the former things;
  do not dwell on the past.
¹⁹See, I am doing a new thing!
  Now it springs up; do you not
    perceive it?
I am making a way in the wilderness
  and streams in the wasteland.
²⁰The wild animals honor me,
  the jackals and the owls,
because I provide water in the
    wilderness
  and streams in the wasteland,
to give drink to my people, my chosen,
²¹ the people I formed for myself
  that they may proclaim my praise.

²²"Yet you have not called on me, Jacob,
  you have not wearied yourselves forᵇ
    me, Israel.
²³You have not brought me sheep for
    burnt offerings,
  nor honored me with your sacrifices.
I have not burdened you with grain
    offerings
  nor wearied you with demands for
    incense.
²⁴You have not bought any fragrant
    calamus for me,
  or lavished on me the fat of your
    sacrifices.
But you have burdened me with your
    sins
  and wearied me with your offenses.

²⁵"I, even I, am he who blots out
  your transgressions, for my own sake,
  and remembers your sins no more.
²⁶Review the past for me,
  let us argue the matter together;
  state the case for your innocence.
²⁷Your first father sinned;
  those I sent to teach you rebelled
    against me.
²⁸So I disgraced the dignitaries of your
    temple;
  I consigned Jacob to destructionᶜ
  and Israel to scorn.

ᵃ 14 Or *Chaldeans*   ᵇ 22 Or *Jacob; / surely you have grown weary of*   ᶜ 28 The Hebrew term refers to the irrevocable giving over of things or persons to the Lord, often by totally destroying them.

Israel the Chosen

44

¹ "But now listen, Jacob, my servant,
   Israel, whom I have chosen.
² This is what the LORD says—
   he who made you, who formed you in
      the womb,
   and who will help you:
Do not be afraid, Jacob, my servant,
   Jeshurun,ᵃ whom I have chosen.
³ For I will pour water on the thirsty land,
   and streams on the dry ground;
I will pour out my Spirit on your
      offspring,
   and my blessing on your descendants.
⁴ They will spring up like grass in a
      meadow,
   like poplar trees by flowing streams.
⁵ Some will say, 'I belong to the LORD';
   others will call themselves by the
      name of Jacob;
still others will write on their hand, 'The
   LORD's,'
   and will take the name Israel.

The LORD, Not Idols

⁶ "This is what the LORD says—
   Israel's King and Redeemer, the LORD
      Almighty:
I am the first and I am the last;
   apart from me there is no God.
⁷ Who then is like me? Let them
      proclaim it.
   Let them declare and lay out before
      me
what has happened since I established
      my ancient people,
   and what is yet to come—
   yes, let them foretell what will come.
⁸ Do not tremble, do not be afraid.
   Did I not proclaim this and foretell it
      long ago?
You are my witnesses. Is there any God
      besides me?
   No, there is no other Rock; I know not
      one."

⁹ All who make idols are nothing,
   and the things they treasure are
      worthless.
Those who would speak up for them are
      blind;
   they are ignorant, to their own
      shame.

¹⁰ Who shapes a god and casts an idol,
   which can profit nothing?
¹¹ People like that will be put to shame;
   skilled workers are only human
      beings.
Let them all come together and take
      their stand;
   they will be brought down to terror
      and shame.

¹² The blacksmith takes a tool
   and works with it in the coals;
he shapes an idol with hammers,
   he forges it with the might of his arm.
He gets hungry and loses his strength;
   he drinks no water and grows faint.
¹³ The carpenter measures with a line
   and makes an outline with a marker;
he roughs it out with chisels
   and marks it with compasses.
He shapes it in human form,
   human form in all its glory,
   that it may dwell in a shrine.
¹⁴ He cut down cedars,
   or perhaps took a cypress or oak.
He let it grow among the trees of the
      forest,
   or planted a pine, and the rain made
      it grow.
¹⁵ It is used as fuel for burning;
   some of it he takes and warms
      himself,
   he kindles a fire and bakes bread.
But he also fashions a god and
      worships it;
   he makes an idol and bows down to it.
¹⁶ Half of the wood he burns in the fire;
   over it he prepares his meal,
   he roasts his meat and eats his fill.
He also warms himself and says,
   "Ah! I am warm; I see the fire."
¹⁷ From the rest he makes a god, his idol;
   he bows down to it and worships.
He prays to it and says,
   "Save me! You are my god!"
¹⁸ They know nothing, they understand
      nothing;
   their eyes are plastered over so they
      cannot see,
   and their minds closed so they cannot
      understand.
¹⁹ No one stops to think,
   no one has the knowledge or
      understanding to say,

ᵃ 2 *Jeshurun* means *the upright one,* that is, Israel.

"Half of it I used for fuel;
  I even baked bread over its coals,
  I roasted meat and I ate.
Shall I make a detestable thing from
    what is left?
  Shall I bow down to a block of
    wood?"
20 Such people feed on ashes, a deluded
    heart misleads them;
  they cannot save themselves, or say,
  "Is not this thing in my right hand a
    lie?"

21 "Remember these things, Jacob,
  for you, Israel, are my servant.
I have made you, you are my servant;
  Israel, I will not forget you.
22 I have swept away your offenses like a
    cloud,
  your sins like the morning mist.
Return to me,
  for I have redeemed you."

23 Sing for joy, you heavens, for the LORD
    has done this;
  shout aloud, you earth beneath.
Burst into song, you mountains,
  you forests and all your trees,
for the LORD has redeemed Jacob,
  he displays his glory in Israel.

Jerusalem to Be Inhabited
24 "This is what the LORD says—
  your Redeemer, who formed you in
    the womb:

I am the LORD,
  who has made all things,
  who alone stretched out the heavens,
  who spread out the earth by myself,
25 who foils the signs of false prophets
  and makes fools of diviners,
who overthrows the learning of the wise
  and turns it into nonsense,
26 who carries out the words of his servants
  and fulfills the predictions of his
    messengers,

who says of Jerusalem, 'It shall be
    inhabited,'
  of the towns of Judah, 'They shall be
    rebuilt,'
  and of their ruins, 'I will restore
    them,'
27 who says to the watery deep, 'Be dry,

and I will dry up your streams,'
28 who says of Cyrus, 'He is my shepherd
  and will accomplish all that I please;
he will say of Jerusalem, "Let it be
    rebuilt,"
  and of the temple, "Let its
    foundations be laid." ' '

45 "This is what the LORD says to
    his anointed,
  to Cyrus, whose right hand I
    take hold of
to subdue nations before him
  and to strip kings of their armor,
to open doors before him
  so that gates will not be shut:
2 I will go before you
  and will level the mountains*a*;
I will break down gates of bronze
  and cut through bars of iron.
3 I will give you the treasures of darkness,
  riches stored in secret places,
so that you may know that I am the
    LORD,
  the God of Israel, who summons you
    by name.
4 For the sake of Jacob my servant,
  of Israel my chosen,
I summon you by name
  and bestow on you a title of honor,
  though you do not acknowledge me.
5 I am the LORD, and there is no other;
  apart from me there is no God.
I will strengthen you,
  though you have not acknowledged
    me,
6 so that from the rising of the sun
  to the place of its setting
people may know there is none
    besides me.
  I am the LORD, and there is no other.
7 I form the light and create darkness,
  I bring prosperity and create disaster;
  I, the LORD, do all these things.

8 "You heavens above, rain down my
    righteousness;
  let the clouds shower it down.
Let the earth open wide,
  let salvation spring up,
let righteousness flourish with it;
  I, the LORD, have created it.

a 2 Dead Sea Scrolls and Septuagint; the meaning of the word in the Masoretic Text is uncertain.

⁹ "Woe to those who quarrel with their
      Maker,
   those who are nothing but potsherds
   among the potsherds on the ground.
Does the clay say to the potter,
   'What are you making?'
Does your work say,
   'The potter has no hands'?
¹⁰ Woe to those who say to their father,
   'What have you begotten?'
or to their mother,
   'What have you brought to birth?'

¹¹ "This is what the Lord says—
   the Holy One of Israel, and its Maker:
Concerning things to come,
   do you question me about my
      children,
   or give me orders about the work of
      my hands?
¹² It is I who made the earth
   and created human beings on it.
My own hands stretched out the
      heavens;
   I marshaled their starry hosts.
¹³ I will raise up Cyrus ᵃ in my
      righteousness:
   I will make all his ways straight.
He will rebuild my city
   and set my exiles free,
but not for a price or reward,
   says the Lord Almighty."

¹⁴ This is what the Lord says:

"The products of Egypt and the
      merchandise of Cush, ᵇ
   and those tall Sabeans—
they will come over to you
   and will be yours;
they will trudge behind you,
   coming over to you in chains.
They will bow down before you
   and plead with you, saying,
'Surely God is with you, and there is no
      other;
   there is no other god.' "

¹⁵ Truly you are a God who has been hiding
      himself,
   the God and Savior of Israel.
¹⁶ All the makers of idols will be put to
      shame and disgraced;
   they will go off into disgrace together.
¹⁷ But Israel will be saved by the Lord

with an everlasting salvation;
you will never be put to shame or
      disgraced,
   to ages everlasting.

¹⁸ For this is what the Lord says—
he who created the heavens,
   he is God;
he who fashioned and made the earth,
   he founded it;
he did not create it to be empty,
   but formed it to be inhabited—
he says:
"I am the Lord,
   and there is no other.
¹⁹ I have not spoken in secret,
   from somewhere in a land of
      darkness;
I have not said to Jacob's descendants,
   'Seek me in vain.'
I, the Lord, speak the truth;
   I declare what is right.

²⁰ "Gather together and come;
   assemble, you fugitives from the
      nations.
Ignorant are those who carry about idols
      of wood,
   who pray to gods that cannot save.
²¹ Declare what is to be, present it—
   let them take counsel together.
Who foretold this long ago,
   who declared it from the distant past?
Was it not I, the Lord?
   And there is no God apart from me,
a righteous God and a Savior;
   there is none but me.

²² "Turn to me and be saved,
   all you ends of the earth;
   for I am God, and there is no other.
²³ By myself I have sworn,
   my mouth has uttered in all integrity
   a word that will not be revoked:
Before me every knee will bow;
   by me every tongue will swear.
²⁴ They will say of me, 'In the Lord alone
   are deliverance and strength.' "
All who have raged against him
   will come to him and be put to
      shame.
²⁵ But all the descendants of Israel
   will find deliverance in the Lord
   and will make their boast in him.

ᵃ 13 Hebrew him   ᵇ 14 That is, the upper Nile region

Gods of Babylon

46

Bel bows down, Nebo stoops low;
their idols are borne by beasts of burden. [a]
The images that are carried about are burdensome,
a burden for the weary.
[2] They stoop and bow down together;
unable to rescue the burden,
they themselves go off into captivity.

[3] "Listen to me, house of Jacob,
all the remnant of the house of Israel,
you whom I have upheld since your birth,
and have carried since you were born.
[4] Even to your old age and gray hairs
I am he, I am he who will sustain you.
I have made you and I will carry you;
I will sustain you and I will rescue you.

[5] "With whom will you compare me or count me equal?
To whom will you liken me that we may be compared?
[6] Some pour out gold from their bags
and weigh out silver on the scales;
they hire a goldsmith to make it into a god,
and they bow down and worship it.
[7] They lift it to their shoulders and carry it;
they set it up in its place, and there it stands.
From that spot it cannot move.
Though people cry out to it, it does not answer;
it cannot save them from their troubles.

[8] "Remember this, keep it in mind,
take it to heart, you rebels.
[9] Remember the former things, those of long ago;
I am God, and there is no other;
I am God, and there is none like me.
[10] I make known the end from the beginning,
from ancient times, what is still to come.
I say, 'My purpose will stand,
and I will do all that I please.'
[11] From the east I summon a bird of prey;
from a far-off land, a man to fulfill my purpose.
What I have said, that I will bring about;
what I have planned, that I will do.
[12] Listen to me, you stubborn-hearted,
you who are now far from my righteousness.
[13] I am bringing my righteousness near,
it is not far away;
and my salvation will not be delayed.
I will grant salvation to Zion,
my splendor to Israel.

The Fall of Babylon

47

"Go down, sit in the dust,
Virgin Daughter Babylon;
sit on the ground without a throne,
queen city of the Babylonians. [b]
No more will you be called
tender or delicate.
[2] Take millstones and grind flour;
take off your veil.
Lift up your skirts, bare your legs,
and wade through the streams.
[3] Your nakedness will be exposed
and your shame uncovered.
I will take vengeance;
I will spare no one."

[4] Our Redeemer—the LORD Almighty is his name—
is the Holy One of Israel.

[5] "Sit in silence, go into darkness,
queen city of the Babylonians;
no more will you be called
queen of kingdoms.
[6] I was angry with my people
and desecrated my inheritance;
I gave them into your hand,
and you showed them no mercy.
Even on the aged
you laid a very heavy yoke.
[7] You said, 'I am forever—
the eternal queen!'
But you did not consider these things
or reflect on what might happen.

[8] "Now then, listen, you lover of pleasure,
lounging in your security
and saying to yourself,
'I am, and there is none besides me.
I will never be a widow
or suffer the loss of children.'

a 1 Or are but beasts and cattle   _b 1 Or Chaldeans; also in verse 5_

He Loved Us First

Isaiah 46:1–13 *or* 46:3–4

Rick Warren

The Bible tells us, "*God is love.*" It doesn't say God *has* love. He *is* love! Love is the essence of God's character. There is perfect love in the fellowship of the Trinity, so God didn't *need* to create you. He wasn't lonely. But he wanted to make you in order to express his love. God says, "I have carried you since you were born; I have taken care of you from your birth. Even when you are old, I will be the same. Even when your hair has turned gray, I will take care of you. I made you and will take care of you."

If there was no God, we would all be "accidents," the result of astronomical random chance in the universe . . . Life would have no purpose or meaning or significance. There would be no right or wrong, and no hope beyond your brief years here on earth.

But there *is* a God who made you for a reason, and your life has profound meaning! We discover that meaning and purpose *only* when we make God the reference point of our lives.

Søren Kierkegaard {ad 1813–1855}

Father in Heaven! You have loved us first. Help us never to forget that You are love so that this sure conviction might triumph in our hearts over the seduction of the world, over the inquietude of the soul, over the anxiety for the future, over the fright of the past, over the distress of the moment. But grant also that this conviction might discipline our soul so that our heart might remain faithful and sincere in the love which we bear to all those whom You have commanded us to love as we love ourselves.

You have loved us first, O God, alas! We speak of it in terms of history as if You have only loved us first but a single time, rather than that without ceasing You have loved us first many times and every day and our whole life through. When we wake up in the morning and turn our soul toward You—You are the first—You have loved us first; if I rise at dawn and at the same second turn my soul toward You in prayer, You are there ahead of me, You have loved me first. When I withdraw from the distractions of the day and turn my soul toward You, You are the first and thus forever. And yet we always speak ungratefully as if You have loved us first only once.

reflection

1. How does God's love give your life meaning and purpose?
2. How has God's love for you shaped the way you see yourself?
3. What can you hold on to when you feel alone and abandoned?

For your next devotional reading, go to page 829.

9 Both of these will overtake you
   in a moment, on a single day:
   loss of children and widowhood.
They will come upon you in full
      measure,
   in spite of your many sorceries
   and all your potent spells.
10 You have trusted in your wickedness
   and have said, 'No one sees me.'
Your wisdom and knowledge mislead
      you
   when you say to yourself,
   'I am, and there is none besides me.'
11 Disaster will come upon you,
   and you will not know how to conjure
      it away.
A calamity will fall upon you
   that you cannot ward off with a
      ransom;
a catastrophe you cannot foresee
   will suddenly come upon you.

12 "Keep on, then, with your magic spells
   and with your many sorceries,
   which you have labored at since
      childhood.
Perhaps you will succeed,
   perhaps you will cause terror.
13 All the counsel you have received has
      only worn you out!
Let your astrologers come forward,
   those stargazers who make predictions
      month by month,
   let them save you from what is
      coming upon you.
14 Surely they are like stubble;
   the fire will burn them up.
They cannot even save themselves
   from the power of the flame.
Here are no coals to warm anyone;
   here is no fire to sit by.
15 That is all they can do for you—
   these you have dealt with
   and labored with since childhood.
All of them go on in their error;
   there is not one that can save you.

Stubborn Israel

48 "Listen to this, house of Jacob,
   you who are called by the name
      of Israel
   and come from the line of Judah,
you who take oaths in the name of the
      LORD
   and invoke the God of Israel—
   but not in truth or righteousness—

2 you who call yourselves citizens of the
      holy city
   and claim to rely on the God of
      Israel—
   the LORD Almighty is his name:
3 I foretold the former things long ago,
   my mouth announced them and I
      made them known;
   then suddenly I acted, and they came
      to pass.
4 For I knew how stubborn you were;
   the sinews of your neck were iron,
   your forehead was bronze.
5 Therefore I told you these things long
      ago;
   before they happened I announced
      them to you
so that you could not say,
   'My images brought them about;
   my wooden image and metal god
      ordained them.'
6 You have heard these things; look at
      them all.
   Will you not admit them?

"From now on I will tell you of new
      things,
   of hidden things unknown to you.
7 They are created now, and not long ago;
   you have not heard of them before
      today.
So you cannot say,
   'Yes, I knew of them.'
8 You have neither heard nor understood;
   from of old your ears have not been
      open.
Well do I know how treacherous you are;
   you were called a rebel from birth.
9 For my own name's sake I delay my
      wrath;
   for the sake of my praise I hold it
      back from you,
   so as not to destroy you completely.
10 See, I have refined you, though not as
      silver;
   I have tested you in the furnace of
      affliction.
11 For my own sake, for my own sake, I do
      this.
   How can I let myself be defamed?
   I will not yield my glory to another.

Israel Freed

12 "Listen to me, Jacob,
   Israel, whom I have called:
   I am he;

I am the first and I am the last.

¹³ My own hand laid the foundations of the
earth,
and my right hand spread out the
heavens;
when I summon them,
they all stand up together.

¹⁴ "Come together, all of you, and listen:
Which of the idols has foretold these
things?
The LORD's chosen ally
will carry out his purpose against
Babylon;
his arm will be against the
Babylonians. ^a
¹⁵ I, even I, have spoken;
yes, I have called him.
I will bring him,
and he will succeed in his mission.

¹⁶ "Come near me and listen to this:

"From the first announcement I have
not spoken in secret;
at the time it happens, I am there."

And now the Sovereign LORD has sent
me,
endowed with his Spirit.

¹⁷ This is what the LORD says—
your Redeemer, the Holy One of
Israel:
"I am the LORD your God,
who teaches you what is best for you,
who directs you in the way you
should go.
¹⁸ If only you had paid attention to my
commands,
your peace would have been like a
river,
your well-being like the waves of the
sea.
¹⁹ Your descendants would have been like
the sand,
your children like its numberless
grains;
their name would never be blotted out
nor destroyed from before me."

²⁰ Leave Babylon,
flee from the Babylonians!
Announce this with shouts of joy
and proclaim it.
Send it out to the ends of the earth;

say, "The LORD has redeemed his
servant Jacob."
²¹ They did not thirst when he led them
through the deserts;
he made water flow for them from
the rock;
he split the rock
and water gushed out.

²² "There is no peace," says the LORD, "for
the wicked."

The Servant of the LORD

49 Listen to me, you islands;
hear this, you distant nations:
Before I was born the LORD
called me;
from my birth he has made mention
of my name.
² He made my mouth like a sharpened
sword,
in the shadow of his hand he hid me;
he made me into a polished arrow
and concealed me in his quiver.
³ He said to me, "You are my servant,
Israel, in whom I will display my
splendor."
⁴ But I said, "I have labored in vain;
I have spent my strength for nothing
at all.
Yet what is due me is in the LORD's hand,
and my reward is with my God."

⁵ And now the LORD says—
he who formed me in the womb to be
his servant
to bring Jacob back to him
and gather Israel to himself,
for I am ^b honored in the eyes of the
LORD
and my God has been my strength—
⁶ he says:
"It is too small a thing for you to be my
servant
to restore the tribes of Jacob
and bring back those of Israel I have
kept.
I will also make you a light for the
Gentiles,
that my salvation may reach to the
ends of the earth."

⁷ This is what the LORD says—
the Redeemer and Holy One of
Israel—

---

^a 14 Or Chaldeans; also in verse 20   ^b 5 Or him, / but Israel would not be gathered; / yet I will be

to him who was despised and abhorred
    by the nation,
  to the servant of rulers:
"Kings will see you and stand up,
    princes will see and bow down,
because of the LORD, who is faithful,
    the Holy One of Israel, who has
      chosen you."

Restoration of Israel
⁸This is what the LORD says:

"In the time of my favor I will answer you,
    and in the day of salvation I will
      help you;
I will keep you and will make you
    to be a covenant for the people,
to restore the land
    and to reassign its desolate
      inheritances,
⁹to say to the captives, 'Come out,'
    and to those in darkness, 'Be free!'

"They will feed beside the roads
    and find pasture on every barren hill.
¹⁰They will neither hunger nor thirst,
    nor will the desert heat or the sun
      beat down on them.
He who has compassion on them will
      guide them
    and lead them beside springs of
      water.
¹¹I will turn all my mountains into roads,
    and my highways will be raised up.
¹²See, they will come from afar—
    some from the north, some from the
      west,
    some from the region of Aswan." *a*

¹³Shout for joy, you heavens;
    rejoice, you earth;
    burst into song, you mountains!
For the LORD comforts his people
    and will have compassion on his
      afflicted ones.

¹⁴But Zion said, "The LORD has forsaken me,
    the Lord has forgotten me."

¹⁵"Can a mother forget the baby at her
      breast
    and have no compassion on the child
      she has borne?
Though she may forget,
    I will not forget you!

¹⁶See, I have engraved you on the palms
      of my hands;
    your walls are ever before me.
¹⁷Your children hasten back,
    and those who laid you waste depart
      from you.
¹⁸Lift up your eyes and look around;
    all your children gather and come to
      you.
As surely as I live," declares the LORD,
    "you will wear them all as ornaments;
    you will put them on, like a bride.

¹⁹"Though you were ruined and made
      desolate
    and your land laid waste,
now you will be too small for your people,
    and those who devoured you will be
      far away.
²⁰The children born during your
      bereavement
    will yet say in your hearing,
'This place is too small for us;
    give us more space to live in.'
²¹Then you will say in your heart,
    'Who bore me these?
I was bereaved and barren;
    I was exiled and rejected.
    Who brought these up?
I was left all alone,
    but these—where have they come
      from?' "

²²This is what the Sovereign LORD says:

"See, I will beckon to the nations,
    I will lift up my banner to the
      peoples;
they will bring your sons in their arms
    and carry your daughters on their
      hips.
²³Kings will be your foster fathers,
    and their queens your nursing
      mothers.
They will bow down before you with
      their faces to the ground;
    they will lick the dust at your feet.
Then you will know that I am the LORD;
    those who hope in me will not be
      disappointed."

²⁴Can plunder be taken from warriors,
    or captives be rescued from the
      fierce *b* ?

a 12 Dead Sea Scrolls; Masoretic Text *Sinim*   *b 24* Dead Sea Scrolls, Vulgate and Syriac (see also
Septuagint and verse 25); Masoretic Text *righteous*

²⁵But this is what the LORD says:

"Yes, captives will be taken from
warriors,
and plunder retrieved from the fierce;
I will contend with those who contend
with you,
and your children I will save.
²⁶I will make your oppressors eat their
own flesh;
they will be drunk on their own blood,
as with wine.
Then the whole human race will know
that I, the LORD, am your Savior,
your Redeemer, the Mighty One of
Jacob."

Israel's Sin and the Servant's Obedience

50 This is what the LORD says:

"Where is your mother's
certificate of divorce
with which I sent her away?
Or to which of my creditors
did I sell you?
Because of your sins you were sold;
because of your transgressions your
mother was sent away.
²When I came, why was there no one?
When I called, why was there no one
to answer?
Was my arm too short to deliver you?
Do I lack the strength to rescue you?
By a mere rebuke I dry up the sea,
I turn rivers into a desert;
their fish rot for lack of water
and die of thirst.
³I clothe the heavens with darkness
and make sackcloth its covering."

⁴The Sovereign LORD has given me an
instructed tongue,
to know the word that sustains the
weary.
He wakens me morning by morning,
wakens my ear to listen like one
being taught.
⁵The Sovereign LORD has opened my ears;
I have not been rebellious,
I have not turned away.
⁶I offered my back to those who beat me,
my cheeks to those who pulled out
my beard;
I did not hide my face
from mocking and spitting.
⁷Because the Sovereign LORD helps me,

I will not be disgraced.
Therefore have I set my face like flint,
and I know I will not be put to shame.
⁸He who vindicates me is near.
Who then will bring charges against
me?
Let us face each other!
Who are my accusers?
Let them confront me!
⁹It is the Sovereign LORD who helps me.
Who will condemn me?
They will all wear out like a garment;
the moths will eat them up.

¹⁰Who among you fears the LORD
and obeys the word of his servant?
Let those who walk in the dark,
who have no light,
trust in the name of the LORD
and rely on their God.
¹¹But now, all you who light fires
and provide yourselves with flaming
torches,
go, walk in the light of your fires
and of the torches you have set
ablaze.
This is what you shall receive from my
hand:
You will lie down in torment.

Everlasting Salvation for Zion

51 "Listen to me, you who pursue
righteousness
and who seek the LORD:
Look to the rock from which you were
cut
and to the quarry from which you
were hewn;
²look to Abraham, your father,
and to Sarah, who gave you birth.
When I called him he was only one man,
and I blessed him and made him
many.
³The LORD will surely comfort Zion
and will look with compassion on all
her ruins;
he will make her deserts like Eden,
her wastelands like the garden of the
LORD.
Joy and gladness will be found in her,
thanksgiving and the sound of
singing.

⁴"Listen to me, my people;
hear me, my nation:
Instruction will go out from me;

Like one from whom people hide their
faces
he was despised, and we held him in
low esteem.

⁴ Surely he took up our pain
and bore our suffering,
yet we considered him punished by God,
stricken by him, and afflicted.
⁵ But he was pierced for our
transgressions,
he was crushed for our iniquities;
the punishment that brought us peace
was on him,
and by his wounds we are healed.
⁶ We all, like sheep, have gone astray,
each of us has turned to our own way;
and the LORD has laid on him
the iniquity of us all.

⁷ He was oppressed and afflicted,
yet he did not open his mouth;
he was led like a lamb to the slaughter,
and as a sheep before its shearers is
silent,
so he did not open his mouth.
⁸ By oppression ᵃ and judgment he was
taken away.
Yet who of his generation protested?
For he was cut off from the land of the
living;
for the transgression of my people he
was punished. ᵇ
⁹ He was assigned a grave with the
wicked,
and with the rich in his death,
though he had done no violence,
nor was any deceit in his mouth.

¹⁰ Yet it was the LORD's will to crush him
and cause him to suffer,
and though the LORD makes ᶜ his life
an offering for sin,
he will see his offspring and prolong his
days,
and the will of the LORD will prosper
in his hand.
¹¹ After he has suffered,
he will see the light of life ᵈ and be
satisfied ᵉ;
by his knowledge ᶠ my righteous servant
will justify many,

and he will bear their iniquities.
¹² Therefore I will give him a portion
among the great, ᵍ
and he will divide the spoils with the
strong, ʰ
because he poured out his life unto
death,
and was numbered with the
transgressors.
For he bore the sin of many,
and made intercession for the
transgressors.

The Future Glory of Zion

54 "Sing, barren woman,
you who never bore a child;
burst into song, shout for joy,
you who were never in labor;
because more are the children of the
desolate woman
than of her who has a husband,"
says the LORD.
² "Enlarge the place of your tent,
stretch your tent curtains wide,
do not hold back;
lengthen your cords,
strengthen your stakes.
³ For you will spread out to the right and
to the left;
your descendants will dispossess
nations
and settle in their desolate cities.

⁴ "Do not be afraid; you will not be put to
shame.
Do not fear disgrace; you will not be
humiliated.
You will forget the shame of your youth
and remember no more the reproach
of your widowhood.
⁵ For your Maker is your husband—
the LORD Almighty is his name—
the Holy One of Israel is your Redeemer;
he is called the God of all the earth.
⁶ The LORD will call you back
as if you were a wife deserted and
distressed in spirit—
a wife who married young,
only to be rejected," says your God.
⁷ "For a brief moment I abandoned you,

ᵃ 8 Or *From arrest*   ᵇ 8 Or *generation considered / that he was cut off from the land of the living, / that he
was punished for the transgression of my people?*   ᶜ 10 Hebrew *though you make*   ᵈ 11 Dead Sea Scrolls
(see also Septuagint); Masoretic Text does not have *the light of life.*   ᵉ 11 Or (with Masoretic Text) ¹¹*He
will see the fruit of his suffering / and will be satisfied*   ᶠ 11 Or *by knowledge of him*   ᵍ 12 Or *many*
ʰ 12 Or *numerous*

but with deep compassion I will bring
    you back.
[8] In a surge of anger
    I hid my face from you for a moment,
but with everlasting kindness
    I will have compassion on you,"
  says the LORD your Redeemer.

[9] "To me this is like the days of Noah,
    when I swore that the waters of Noah
      would never again cover the
      earth.
So now I have sworn not to be angry
    with you,
    never to rebuke you again.
[10] Though the mountains be shaken
    and the hills be removed,
yet my unfailing love for you will not be
    shaken
    nor my covenant of peace be
      removed,"
  says the LORD, who has compassion
    on you.

[11] "Afflicted city, lashed by storms and not
    comforted,
I will rebuild you with stones of
    turquoise,[a]
    your foundations with lapis lazuli.
[12] I will make your battlements of rubies,
    your gates of sparkling jewels,
    and all your walls of precious stones.
[13] All your children will be taught by the
    LORD,
    and great will be their peace.
[14] In righteousness you will be established:
Tyranny will be far from you;
    you will have nothing to fear.
Terror will be far removed;
    it will not come near you.
[15] If anyone does attack you, it will not be
    my doing;
    whoever attacks you will surrender to
    you.

[16] "See, it is I who created the blacksmith
    who fans the coals into flame
    and forges a weapon fit for its work.
And it is I who have created the
    destroyer to work havoc;
[17]   no weapon forged against you will
    prevail,
    and you will refute every tongue that
    accuses you.

This is the heritage of the servants of the
    LORD,
    and this is their vindication from me,"
        declares the LORD.

Invitation to the Thirsty

55

"Come, all you who are thirsty,
    come to the waters;
  and you who have no money,
  come, buy and eat!
Come, buy wine and milk
    without money and without cost.
[2] Why spend money on what is not bread,
    and your labor on what does not
      satisfy?
Listen, listen to me, and eat what is good,
    and you will delight in the richest of
      fare.
[3] Give ear and come to me;
    listen, that you may live.
I will make an everlasting covenant with
    you,
    my faithful love promised to David.
[4] See, I have made him a witness to the
    peoples,
    a ruler and commander of the
      peoples.
[5] Surely you will summon nations you
    know not,
    and nations you do not know will
      come running to you,
because of the LORD your God,
    the Holy One of Israel,
for he has endowed you with
    splendor."

[6] Seek the LORD while he may be found;
    call on him while he is near.
[7] Let the wicked forsake their ways
    and the unrighteous their thoughts.
Let them turn to the LORD, and he will
    have mercy on them,
    and to our God, for he will freely
      pardon.

[8] "For my thoughts are not your thoughts,
    neither are your ways my ways,"
        declares the LORD.
[9] "As the heavens are higher than the
    earth,
    so are my ways higher than your ways
    and my thoughts than your thoughts.
[10] As the rain and the snow
    come down from heaven,

---

[a] 11 The meaning of the Hebrew for this word is uncertain.

FRIDAY

GOD IS NEAR

Isaiah 55:1–13 *or* 55:6–7

Rob Bell

According to the ancient Jewish worldview, God is not somewhere else. God is right here. It is God's world and God made it and God owns it and God is present everywhere in it. In the book of Genesis, a man named Jacob had a dream in which God spoke to him and reminded him of his destiny and purpose.

When Jacob woke up, he said, "Surely the Lord is in this place, and I was not aware of it."

God has been there all along, and Jacob is just beginning to realize it. He's waking up from physical sleep, but he is also waking up from spiritual sleep. I've heard people tell stories about something powerful that happened and then at the end of the story say, "And then God showed up!" As if God were somewhere else and then decided to intervene.

But God is always present. We're the ones who show up.

C. S. LEWIS {AD 1898–1963}

It is in the process of being worshipped that God communicates His presence to men.

reflection

1. If God is always present, why does it sometimes feel like he's far away?

2. What can you do to promote a greater awareness of God's presence in your life 24/7?

3. Why is it easier to sense God's presence when you are worshiping? How can you worship in all that you do?

For your next devotional reading, go to page 836.

and do not return to it
    without watering the earth
and making it bud and flourish,
    so that it yields seed for the sower
        and bread for the eater,
[11] so is my word that goes out from my
    mouth:
    It will not return to me empty,
but will accomplish what I desire
    and achieve the purpose for which I
        sent it.
[12] You will go out in joy
    and be led forth in peace;
the mountains and hills
    will burst into song before you,
and all the trees of the field
    will clap their hands.
[13] Instead of the thornbush will grow the
    juniper,
    and instead of briers the myrtle will
        grow.
This will be for the LORD's renown,
    for an everlasting sign,
    that will endure forever."

Salvation for Others

56

This is what the LORD says:

"Maintain justice
    and do what is right,
for my salvation is close at hand
    and my righteousness will soon be
        revealed.
[2] Blessed are those who do this—
    who hold it fast,
those who keep the Sabbath without
    desecrating it,
    and keep their hands from doing any
        evil."

[3] Let no foreigners who have bound
        themselves to the LORD say,
    "The LORD will surely exclude me
        from his people."
And let no eunuch complain,
    "I am only a dry tree."

[4] For this is what the LORD says:

"To the eunuchs who keep my Sabbaths,
    who choose what pleases me
    and hold fast to my covenant—
[5] to them I will give within my temple and
        its walls
    a memorial and a name
    better than sons and daughters;
I will give them an everlasting name

that will endure forever.
[6] And foreigners who bind themselves to
    the LORD
    to minister to him,
to love the name of the LORD,
    and to be his servants,
all who keep the Sabbath without
    desecrating it
    and who hold fast to my covenant—
[7] these I will bring to my holy mountain
    and give them joy in my house of
        prayer.
Their burnt offerings and sacrifices
    will be accepted on my altar;
for my house will be called
    a house of prayer for all nations."
[8] The Sovereign LORD declares—
    he who gathers the exiles of Israel:
"I will gather still others to them
    besides those already gathered."

God's Accusation Against the Wicked

[9] Come, all you beasts of the field,
    come and devour, all you beasts of
        the forest!
[10] Israel's watchmen are blind,
    they all lack knowledge;
they are all mute dogs,
    they cannot bark;
they lie around and dream,
    they love to sleep.
[11] They are dogs with mighty appetites;
    they never have enough.
They are shepherds who lack
    understanding;
    they all turn to their own way,
    they seek their own gain.
[12] "Come," each one cries, "let me get
    wine!
    Let us drink our fill of beer!
And tomorrow will be like today,
    or even far better."

57

The righteous perish,
    and no one takes it to heart;
    the devout are taken away,
and no one understands
that the righteous are taken away
    to be spared from evil.
[2] Those who walk uprightly
    enter into peace;
    they find rest as they lie in death.

[3] "But you—come here, you children of a
    sorceress,

you offspring of adulterers and
prostitutes!
⁴Whom are you mocking?
At whom do you sneer
and stick out your tongue?
Are you not a brood of rebels,
the offspring of liars?
⁵You burn with lust among the oaks
and under every spreading tree;
you sacrifice your children in the ravines
and under the overhanging crags.
⁶The idols among the smooth stones of
the ravines are your portion;
they, they are your lot.
Yes, to them you have poured out drink
offerings
and offered grain offerings.
In view of all this, should I relent?
⁷You have made your bed on a high and
lofty hill;
there you went up to offer your
sacrifices.
⁸Behind your doors and your doorposts
you have put your pagan symbols.
Forsaking me, you uncovered your bed,
you climbed into it and opened it
wide;
you made a pact with those whose beds
you love,
and you looked on their nakedness.
⁹You went to Molekᵃ with olive oil
and increased your perfumes.
You sent your ambassadorsᵇ far away;
you descended to the very realm of
the dead!
¹⁰You wearied yourself by such going
about,
but you would not say, 'It is hopeless.'
You found renewal of your strength,
and so you did not faint.

¹¹"Whom have you so dreaded and feared
that you have not been true to me,
and have neither remembered me
nor taken this to heart?
Is it not because I have long been silent
that you do not fear me?
¹²I will expose your righteousness and
your works,
and they will not benefit you.
¹³When you cry out for help,
let your collection of idols save you!
The wind will carry all of them off,
a mere breath will blow them away.

But whoever takes refuge in me
will inherit the land
and possess my holy mountain."

Comfort for the Contrite

¹⁴And it will be said:

"Build up, build up, prepare the road!
Remove the obstacles out of the way
of my people."
¹⁵For this is what the high and exalted
One says—
he who lives forever, whose name is
holy:
"I live in a high and holy place,
but also with those who are contrite
and lowly in spirit,
to revive the spirit of the lowly
and to revive the heart of the contrite.
¹⁶I will not accuse them forever,
nor will I always be angry,
for then they would faint away because
of me—
the very people I have created.
¹⁷I was enraged by their sinful greed;
I punished them, and hid my face in
anger,
yet they kept on in their willful ways.
¹⁸I have seen their ways, but I will heal
them;
I will guide them and restore comfort
to them,
¹⁹ creating praise on the lips of the
mourners in Israel.
Peace, peace, to those far and near,"
says the Lᴏʀᴅ. "And I will heal them."
²⁰But the wicked are like the tossing sea,
which cannot rest,
whose waves cast up mire and mud.
²¹"There is no peace," says my God, "for
the wicked."

True Fasting

58 "Shout it aloud, do not hold
back.
Raise your voice like a trumpet.
Declare to my people their rebellion
and to the house of Jacob their sins.
²For day after day they seek me out;
they seem eager to know my ways,
as if they were a nation that does what
is right
and has not forsaken the commands
of its God.

ᵃ 9 Or to the king   ᵇ 9 Or idols

They ask me for just decisions
    and seem eager for God to come near
        them.
³ 'Why have we fasted,' they say,
    'and you have not seen it?
Why have we humbled ourselves,
    and you have not noticed?'

"Yet on the day of your fasting, you do as
        you please
    and exploit all your workers.
⁴ Your fasting ends in quarreling and
        strife,
    and in striking each other with
        wicked fists.
You cannot fast as you do today
    and expect your voice to be heard on
        high.
⁵ Is this the kind of fast I have chosen,
    only a day for people to humble
        themselves?
Is it only for bowing one's head like a
        reed
    and for lying in sackcloth and ashes?
Is that what you call a fast,
    a day acceptable to the LORD?

⁶ "Is not this the kind of fasting I have
        chosen:
to loose the chains of injustice
    and untie the cords of the yoke,
to set the oppressed free
    and break every yoke?
⁷ Is it not to share your food with the
        hungry
    and to provide the poor wanderer
        with shelter—
when you see the naked, to clothe them,
    and not to turn away from your own
        flesh and blood?
⁸ Then your light will break forth like the
        dawn,
    and your healing will quickly appear;
then your righteousness*a* will go before
        you,
    and the glory of the LORD will be your
        rear guard.
⁹ Then you will call, and the LORD will
        answer;
    you will cry for help, and he will say:
        Here am I.

"If you do away with the yoke of
        oppression,

with the pointing finger and
        malicious talk,
¹⁰ and if you spend yourselves in behalf of
        the hungry
    and satisfy the needs of the
        oppressed,
then your light will rise in the darkness,
    and your night will become like the
        noonday.
¹¹ The LORD will guide you always;
    he will satisfy your needs in a sun-
        scorched land
    and will strengthen your frame.
You will be like a well-watered garden,
    like a spring whose waters never fail.
¹² Your people will rebuild the ancient
        ruins
    and will raise up the age-old
        foundations;
you will be called Repairer of Broken
        Walls,
    Restorer of Streets with Dwellings.
¹³ "If you keep your feet from breaking the
        Sabbath
    and from doing as you please on my
        holy day,
if you call the Sabbath a delight
    and the LORD's holy day honorable,
and if you honor it by not going your
        own way
    and not doing as you please or
        speaking idle words,
¹⁴ then you will find your joy in the LORD,
    and I will cause you to ride in
        triumph on the heights of the
        land
    and to feast on the inheritance of
        your father Jacob."
        For the mouth of the LORD
        has spoken.

Sin, Confession and Redemption

59 Surely the arm of the LORD is
        not too short to save,
        nor his ear too dull to hear.
² But your iniquities have separated
    you from your God;
your sins have hidden his face from you,
    so that he will not hear.
³ For your hands are stained with blood,
    your fingers with guilt.
Your lips have spoken falsely,

and your tongue mutters wicked
   things.
⁴ No one calls for justice;
   no one pleads their case with
      integrity.
They rely on empty arguments, they
      utter lies;
   they conceive trouble and give birth
      to evil.
⁵ They hatch the eggs of vipers
   and spin a spider's web.
Whoever eats their eggs will die,
   and when one is broken, an adder is
      hatched.
⁶ Their cobwebs are useless for clothing;
   they cannot cover themselves with
      what they make.
Their deeds are evil deeds,
   and acts of violence are in their
      hands.
⁷ Their feet rush into sin;
   they are swift to shed innocent blood.
They pursue evil schemes;
   acts of violence mark their ways.
⁸ The way of peace they do not know;
   there is no justice in their paths.
They have turned them into crooked
      roads;
   no one who walks along them will
      know peace.

⁹ So justice is far from us,
   and righteousness does not reach us.
We look for light, but all is darkness;
   for brightness, but we walk in deep
      shadows.
¹⁰ Like the blind we grope along the wall,
   feeling our way like people without
      eyes.
At midday we stumble as if it were
      twilight;
   among the strong, we are like the
      dead.
¹¹ We all growl like bears;
   we moan mournfully like doves.
We look for justice, but find none;
   for deliverance, but it is far away.

¹² For our offenses are many in your sight,
   and our sins testify against us.
Our offenses are ever with us,
   and we acknowledge our iniquities:
¹³ rebellion and treachery against the LORD,
   turning our backs on our God,

inciting revolt and oppression,
   uttering lies our hearts have
      conceived.
¹⁴ So justice is driven back,
   and righteousness stands at a
      distance;
truth has stumbled in the streets,
   honesty cannot enter.
¹⁵ Truth is nowhere to be found,
   and whoever shuns evil becomes a
      prey.

The LORD looked and was displeased
   that there was no justice.
¹⁶ He saw that there was no one,
   he was appalled that there was no
      one to intervene;
so his own arm achieved salvation for
      him,
   and his own righteousness sustained
      him.
¹⁷ He put on righteousness as his
      breastplate,
   and the helmet of salvation on his
      head;
he put on the garments of vengeance
   and wrapped himself in zeal as in a
      cloak.
¹⁸ According to what they have done,
   so will he repay
wrath to his enemies
   and retribution to his foes;
   he will repay the islands their due.
¹⁹ From the west, people will fear the
      name of the LORD,
   and from the rising of the sun, they
      will revere his glory.
For he will come like a pent-up flood
   that the breath of the LORD drives
      along.ᵃ

²⁰ "The Redeemer will come to Zion,
   to those in Jacob who repent of their
      sins,"

                              declares the LORD.

²¹ "As for me, this is my covenant with
them," says the LORD. "My Spirit, who is on
you, and my words that I have put in your
mouth will not depart from your mouth, or
from the mouths of your children, or from
the mouths of their descendants from this
time on and forever," says the LORD.

ᵃ 19 Or When enemies come in like a flood, / the Spirit of the LORD will put them to flight

The Glory of Zion

60

¹ "Arise, shine, for your light has
come,
and the glory of the LORD rises
upon you.
² See, darkness covers the earth
and thick darkness is over the peoples,
but the LORD rises upon you
and his glory appears over you.
³ Nations will come to your light,
and kings to the brightness of your
dawn.

⁴ "Lift up your eyes and look about you:
All assemble and come to you;
your sons come from afar,
and your daughters are carried on the
hip.
⁵ Then you will look and be radiant,
your heart will throb and swell with
joy;
the wealth on the seas will be brought to
you,
to you the riches of the nations will
come.
⁶ Herds of camels will cover your land,
young camels of Midian and Ephah.
And all from Sheba will come,
bearing gold and incense
and proclaiming the praise of the
LORD.
⁷ All Kedar's flocks will be gathered to
you,
the rams of Nebaioth will serve you;
they will be accepted as offerings on my
altar,
and I will adorn my glorious temple.

⁸ "Who are these that fly along like
clouds,
like doves to their nests?
⁹ Surely the islands look to me;
in the lead are the ships of Tarshish,ᵃ
bringing your children from afar,
with their silver and gold,
to the honor of the LORD your God,
the Holy One of Israel,
for he has endowed you with
splendor.

¹⁰ "Foreigners will rebuild your walls,
and their kings will serve you.
Though in anger I struck you,
in favor I will show you compassion.

¹¹ Your gates will always stand open,
they will never be shut, day or night,
so that people may bring you the wealth
of the nations—
their kings led in triumphal
procession.
¹² For the nation or kingdom that will not
serve you will perish;
it will be utterly ruined.

¹³ "The glory of Lebanon will come to you,
the juniper, the fir and the cypress
together,
to adorn my sanctuary;
and I will glorify the place for my
feet.
¹⁴ The children of your oppressors will
come bowing before you;
all who despise you will bow down at
your feet
and will call you the City of the LORD,
Zion of the Holy One of Israel.

¹⁵ "Although you have been forsaken and
hated,
with no one traveling through,
I will make you the everlasting pride
and the joy of all generations.
¹⁶ You will drink the milk of nations
and be nursed at royal breasts.
Then you will know that I, the LORD, am
your Savior,
your Redeemer, the Mighty One of
Jacob.
¹⁷ Instead of bronze I will bring you gold,
and silver in place of iron.
Instead of wood I will bring you bronze,
and iron in place of stones.
I will make peace your governor
and well-being your ruler.
¹⁸ No longer will violence be heard in your
land,
nor ruin or destruction within your
borders,
but you will call your walls Salvation
and your gates Praise.
¹⁹ The sun will no more be your light by
day,
nor will the brightness of the moon
shine on you,
for the LORD will be your everlasting
light,
and your God will be your glory.
²⁰ Your sun will never set again,

ᵃ 9 Or the trading ships

and your moon will wane no more;
the LORD will be your everlasting light,
and your days of sorrow will end.
²¹ Then will all your people be righteous
and they will possess the land forever.
They are the shoot I have planted,
the work of my hands,
for the display of my splendor.
²² The least of you will become a thousand,
the smallest a mighty nation.
I am the LORD;
in its time I will do this swiftly."

The Year of the LORD's Favor

61 The Spirit of the Sovereign LORD is on me,
because the LORD has anointed me
to proclaim good news to the poor.
He has sent me to bind up the brokenhearted,
to proclaim freedom for the captives
and release from darkness for the prisoners, ᵃ
² to proclaim the year of the LORD's favor
and the day of vengeance of our God,
to comfort all who mourn,
³   and provide for those who grieve in Zion—
to bestow on them a crown of beauty
instead of ashes,
the oil of joy
instead of mourning,
and a garment of praise
instead of a spirit of despair.
They will be called mighty oaks,
a planting of the LORD
for the display of his splendor.

⁴ They will rebuild the ancient ruins
and restore the places long devastated;
they will renew the ruined cities
that have been devastated for generations.
⁵ Strangers will shepherd your flocks;
foreigners will work your fields and vineyards.
⁶ And you will be called priests of the LORD,
you will be named ministers of our God.
You will feed on the wealth of nations,
and in their riches you will boast.

⁷ Instead of your shame
you will receive a double portion,
and instead of disgrace
you will rejoice in your inheritance.
And so you will inherit a double portion
in your land,
and everlasting joy will be yours.

⁸ "For I, the LORD, love justice;
I hate robbery and wrongdoing.
In my faithfulness I will reward my people
and make an everlasting covenant
with them.
⁹ Their descendants will be known among
the nations
and their offspring among the peoples.
All who see them will acknowledge
that they are a people the LORD has
blessed."

¹⁰ I delight greatly in the LORD;
my soul rejoices in my God.
For he has clothed me with garments of
salvation
and arrayed me in a robe of his
righteousness,
as a bridegroom adorns his head like a
priest,
and as a bride adorns herself with her
jewels.
¹¹ For as the soil makes the sprout come up
and a garden causes seeds to grow,
so the Sovereign LORD will make
righteousness
and praise spring up before all
nations.

Zion's New Name

62 For Zion's sake I will not keep silent,
for Jerusalem's sake I will not remain quiet,
till her vindication shines out like the dawn,
her salvation like a blazing torch.
² The nations will see your vindication,
and all kings your glory;
you will be called by a new name
that the mouth of the LORD will bestow.
³ You will be a crown of splendor in the
LORD's hand,

ᵃ 1 Hebrew; Septuagint *the blind*

Long Live the Revolution

Isaiah 61:1–2

read/meditate

Read aloud Isaiah 61:1–2. This was the passage that Jesus read in the synagogue to explain his ministry (see Luke 4:18–19). Read the passage aloud again and take in the claims Jesus was making about himself.

pray

Connect with God through prayer. Share with him your commitment as a follower of Christ. Thank him for all Jesus came to do, including freeing prisoners and healing the sick and broken. Ask God how he wants you to be a part of the work of Christ, and take time to listen for his guidance.

contemplate

Think about Jesus' revolutionary work and his claim of deity in the midst of those who would not accept this truth. What part of this truth about Jesus do you participate in?

additional reflection

If our greatest need had been information, God would have sent an educator. If our greatest need had been technology, God would have sent us a scientist. If our greatest need had been money, God would have sent us an economist. But since our greatest need was forgiveness, God sent us a Savior.

—Roy Lessin

The Gospel is good news of mercy to the undeserving. The symbol of the religion of Jesus is the cross, not the scales.

—John R. W. Stott

For your next devotional reading, go to page 843.

a royal diadem in the hand of your
God.
⁴ No longer will they call you Deserted,
or name your land Desolate.
But you will be called Hephzibah,ᵃ
and your land Beulah ᵇ;
for the Lord will take delight in you,
and your land will be married.
⁵ As a young man marries a young
woman,
so will your Builder marry you;
as a bridegroom rejoices over his bride,
so will your God rejoice over you.

⁶ I have posted watchmen on your walls,
Jerusalem;
they will never be silent day or night.
You who call on the Lord,
give yourselves no rest,
⁷ and give him no rest till he establishes
Jerusalem
and makes her the praise of the earth.

⁸ The Lord has sworn by his right hand
and by his mighty arm:
"Never again will I give your grain
as food for your enemies,
and never again will foreigners drink the
new wine
for which you have toiled;
⁹ but those who harvest it will eat it
and praise the Lord,
and those who gather the grapes will
drink it
in the courts of my sanctuary."

¹⁰ Pass through, pass through the gates!
Prepare the way for the people.
Build up, build up the highway!
Remove the stones.
Raise a banner for the nations.
¹¹ The Lord has made proclamation
to the ends of the earth:
"Say to Daughter Zion,
'See, your Savior comes!
See, his reward is with him,
and his recompense accompanies
him.' "
¹² They will be called the Holy People,
the Redeemed of the Lord;
and you will be called Sought After,
the City No Longer Deserted.

God's Day of Vengeance and Redemption

63 Who is this coming from Edom,
from Bozrah, with his
garments stained crimson?
Who is this, robed in splendor,
striding forward in the greatness of
his strength?

"It is I, speaking in righteousness,
mighty to save."

² Why are your garments red,
like those of one treading the
winepress?

³ "I have trodden the winepress alone;
from the nations no one was with me.
I trampled them in my anger
and trod them down in my wrath;
their blood spattered my garments,
and I stained all my clothing.
⁴ It was for me the day of vengeance;
the year for me to redeem had come.
⁵ I looked, but there was no one to help,
I was appalled that no one gave
support;
so my own arm achieved salvation for
me,
and my own wrath sustained me.
⁶ I trampled the nations in my anger;
in my wrath I made them drunk
and poured their blood on the
ground."

Praise and Prayer

⁷ I will tell of the kindnesses of the Lord,
the deeds for which he is to be
praised,
according to all the Lord has done for
us—
yes, the many good things he has done
for the house of Israel,
according to his compassion and
many kindnesses.
⁸ He said, "Surely they are my people,
children who will be true to me";
and so he became their Savior.
⁹ In all their distress he too was
distressed,
and the angel of his presence saved
them.ᶜ
In his love and mercy he redeemed
them;
he lifted them up and carried them

ᵃ 4 *Hephzibah* means *my delight is in her.*   ᵇ 4 *Beulah* means *married.*   ᶜ 9 Or *Savior* ⁹ *in their distress*
/ *It was no envoy or angel* / *but his own presence that saved them*

all the days of old.
¹⁰ Yet they rebelled
and grieved his Holy Spirit.
So he turned and became their enemy
and he himself fought against them.

¹¹ Then his people recalled[a] the days of
old,
the days of Moses and his people—
where is he who brought them through
the sea,
with the shepherd of his flock?
Where is he who set
his Holy Spirit among them,
¹² who sent his glorious arm of power
to be at Moses' right hand,
who divided the waters before them,
to gain for himself everlasting
renown,
¹³ who led them through the depths?
Like a horse in open country,
they did not stumble;
¹⁴ like cattle that go down to the plain,
they were given rest by the Spirit of
the LORD.
This is how you guided your people
to make for yourself a glorious name.

¹⁵ Look down from heaven and see,
from your lofty throne, holy and
glorious.
Where are your zeal and your might?
Your tenderness and compassion are
withheld from us.
¹⁶ But you are our Father,
though Abraham does not know us
or Israel acknowledge us;
you, LORD, are our Father,
our Redeemer from of old is your
name.
¹⁷ Why, LORD, do you make us wander from
your ways
and harden our hearts so we do not
revere you?
Return for the sake of your servants,
the tribes that are your inheritance.
¹⁸ For a little while your people possessed
your holy place,
but now our enemies have trampled
down your sanctuary.
¹⁹ We are yours from of old;
but you have not ruled over them,

they have not been called[b] by your
name.

64

¹ *Oh, that you would rend the
heavens and come down,
that the mountains would
tremble before you!
*² As when fire sets twigs ablaze
and causes water to boil,
come down to make your name known
to your enemies
and cause the nations to quake before
you!
³ For when you did awesome things that
we did not expect,
you came down, and the mountains
trembled before you.
⁴ Since ancient times no one has heard,
no ear has perceived,
no eye has seen any God besides you,
who acts on behalf of those who wait
for him.
⁵ You come to the help of those who
gladly do right,
who remember your ways.
But when we continued to sin against
them,
you were angry.
How then can we be saved?
⁶ All of us have become like one who is
unclean,
and all our righteous acts are like
filthy rags;
we all shrivel up like a leaf,
and like the wind our sins sweep us
away.
⁷ No one calls on your name
or strives to lay hold of you;
for you have hidden your face from us
and have given us over to[c] our sins.

⁸ Yet you, LORD, are our Father.
We are the clay, you are the potter;
we are all the work of your hand.
⁹ Do not be angry beyond measure, LORD;
do not remember our sins forever.
Oh, look on us, we pray,
for we are all your people.
¹⁰ Your sacred cities have become a
wasteland;
even Zion is a wasteland, Jerusalem a
desolation.

---

a 11 Or *But may he recall*   *b* 19 Or *We are like those you have never ruled, / like those never called*
c 7 Septuagint, Syriac and Targum; Hebrew *have made us melt because of*

* 64:1 is numbered 63:19b in Hebrew texts.   * 64:2-12 is numbered 64:1-11 in Hebrew texts.

¹¹ Our holy and glorious temple, where our
ancestors praised you,
has been burned with fire,
and all that we treasured lies in ruins.
¹² After all this, Lord, will you hold yourself
back?
Will you keep silent and punish us
beyond measure?

Judgment and Salvation

65 "I revealed myself to those who
did not ask for me;
I was found by those who did
not seek me.
To a nation that did not call on my
name,
I said, 'Here am I, here am I.'
² All day long I have held out my hands
to an obstinate people,
who walk in ways not good,
pursuing their own imaginations—
³ a people who continually provoke me
to my very face,
offering sacrifices in gardens
and burning incense on altars of
brick;
⁴ who sit among the graves
and spend their nights keeping secret
vigil;
who eat the flesh of pigs,
and whose pots hold broth of impure
meat;
⁵ who say, 'Keep away; don't come near me,
for I am too sacred for you!'
Such people are smoke in my nostrils,
a fire that keeps burning all day.

⁶ "See, it stands written before me:
I will not keep silent but will pay back
in full;
I will pay it back into their laps—
⁷ both your sins and the sins of your
ancestors,"
says the Lord.
"Because they burned sacrifices on the
mountains
and defied me on the hills,
I will measure into their laps
the full payment for their former
deeds."

⁸ This is what the Lord says:

"As when juice is still found in a cluster
of grapes
and people say, 'Don't destroy it,
there is still a blessing in it,'

so will I do in behalf of my servants;
I will not destroy them all.
⁹ I will bring forth descendants from
Jacob,
and from Judah those who will
possess my mountains;
my chosen people will inherit them,
and there will my servants live.
¹⁰ Sharon will become a pasture for flocks,
and the Valley of Achor a resting
place for herds,
for my people who seek me.

¹¹ "But as for you who forsake the Lord
and forget my holy mountain,
who spread a table for Fortune
and fill bowls of mixed wine for
Destiny,
¹² I will destine you for the sword,
and all of you will fall in the
slaughter;
for I called but you did not answer,
I spoke but you did not listen.
You did evil in my sight
and chose what displeases me."

¹³ Therefore this is what the Sovereign
Lord says:

"My servants will eat,
but you will go hungry;
my servants will drink,
but you will go thirsty;
my servants will rejoice,
but you will be put to shame.
¹⁴ My servants will sing
out of the joy of their hearts,
but you will cry out
from anguish of heart
and wail in brokenness of spirit.
¹⁵ You will leave your name
for my chosen ones to use in their
curses;
the Sovereign Lord will put you to
death,
but to his servants he will give
another name.
¹⁶ Whoever invokes a blessing in the land
will do so by the one true God;
whoever takes an oath in the land
will swear by the one true God.
For the past troubles will be forgotten
and hidden from my eyes.

New Heavens and a New Earth
¹⁷ "See, I will create
new heavens and a new earth.

The former things will not be
remembered,
nor will they come to mind.
18 But be glad and rejoice forever
in what I will create,
for I will create Jerusalem to be a delight
and its people a joy.
19 I will rejoice over Jerusalem
and take delight in my people;
the sound of weeping and of crying
will be heard in it no more.

20 "Never again will there be in it
infants who live but a few days,
or older people who do not live out
their years;
those who die at a hundred
will be thought mere youths;
those who fail to reach*a* a hundred
will be considered accursed.
21 They will build houses and dwell in
them;
they will plant vineyards and eat their
fruit.
22 No longer will they build houses and
others live in them,
or plant and others eat.
For as the days of a tree,
so will be the days of my people;
my chosen ones will long enjoy
the work of their hands.
23 They will not labor in vain,
nor will they bear children doomed to
misfortune;
for they will be a people blessed by the
LORD,
they and their descendants with
them.
24 Before they call I will answer;
while they are still speaking I will
hear.
25 The wolf and the lamb will feed
together,
and the lion will eat straw like the ox,
but dust will be the serpent's food.
They will neither harm nor destroy
on all my holy mountain,"
says the LORD.

Judgment and Hope

66 This is what the LORD says:

"Heaven is my throne,
and the earth is my footstool.

Where is the house you will build for
me?
Where will my resting place be?
2 Has not my hand made all these things,
and so they came into being?"
declares the LORD.

"These are the ones I look on with favor:
those who are humble and contrite in
spirit,
and who tremble at my word.
3 But whoever sacrifices a bull
is like one who kills a human being,
and whoever offers a lamb
is like one who breaks a dog's neck;
whoever makes a grain offering
is like one who presents pig's blood,
and whoever burns memorial incense
is like one who worships an idol.
They have chosen their own ways,
and they delight in their
abominations;
4 so I also will choose harsh treatment for
them
and will bring on them what they
dread.
For when I called, no one answered,
when I spoke, no one listened.
They did evil in my sight
and chose what displeases me."

5 Hear the word of the LORD,
you who tremble at his word:
"Your own people who hate you,
and exclude you because of my name,
have said,
'Let the LORD be glorified,
that we may see your joy!'
Yet they will be put to shame.
6 Hear that uproar from the city,
hear that noise from the temple!
It is the sound of the LORD
repaying his enemies all they deserve.

7 "Before she goes into labor,
she gives birth;
before the pains come upon her,
she delivers a child.
8 Who has ever heard of such things?
Who has ever seen things like this?
Can a country be born in a day
or a nation be brought forth in a
moment?
Yet no sooner is Zion in labor
than she gives birth to her children.

a 20 Or youths; / sinners who reach

⁹ Do I bring to the moment of birth
    and not give delivery?" says the LORD.
  "Do I close up the womb
    when I bring to delivery?" says your
        God.
¹⁰ "Rejoice with Jerusalem and be glad for
        her,
    all you who love her;
  rejoice greatly with her,
    all you who mourn over her.
¹¹ For you will nurse and be satisfied
    at her comforting breasts;
  you will drink deeply
    and delight in her overflowing
        abundance."

¹² For this is what the LORD says:

  "I will extend peace to her like a river,
    and the wealth of nations like a
        flooding stream;
  you will nurse and be carried on her arm
    and dandled on her knees.
¹³ As a mother comforts her child,
    so will I comfort you;
  and you will be comforted over
        Jerusalem."

¹⁴ When you see this, your heart will rejoice
    and you will flourish like grass;
  the hand of the LORD will be made
        known to his servants,
    but his fury will be shown to his foes.
¹⁵ See, the LORD is coming with fire,
    and his chariots are like a whirlwind;
  he will bring down his anger with fury,
    and his rebuke with flames of fire.
¹⁶ For with fire and with his sword
    the LORD will execute judgment on all
        people,
    and many will be those slain by the
        LORD.

¹⁷ "Those who consecrate and purify themselves to go into the gardens, following one who is among those who eat the flesh of pigs, rats and other unclean things—they will meet their end together with the one they follow," declares the LORD.

¹⁸ "And I, because of what they have planned and done, am about to come[a] and gather the people of all nations and languages, and they will come and see my glory.

¹⁹ "I will set a sign among them, and I will send some of those who survive to the nations—to Tarshish, to the Libyans[b] and Lydians (famous as archers), to Tubal and Greece, and to the distant islands that have not heard of my fame or seen my glory. They will proclaim my glory among the nations. ²⁰ And they will bring all your people, from all the nations, to my holy mountain in Jerusalem as an offering to the LORD—on horses, in chariots and wagons, and on mules and camels," says the LORD. "They will bring them, as the Israelites bring their grain offerings, to the temple of the LORD in ceremonially clean vessels. ²¹ And I will select some of them also to be priests and Levites," says the LORD.

²² "As the new heavens and the new earth that I make will endure before me," declares the LORD, "so will your name and descendants endure. ²³ From one New Moon to another and from one Sabbath to another, all people will come and bow down before me," says the LORD. ²⁴ "And they will go out and look on the dead bodies of those who rebelled against me; their worm will not die, nor will their fire be quenched, and they will be loathsome to the whole human race."

---

a 18 The meaning of the Hebrew for this clause is uncertain.   *b* 19 Some Septuagint manuscripts *Put* (Libyans); Hebrew *Pul*

jeremiah

AUTHOR: Jeremiah

DATE: Between 626 and 586 B.C.

THEME: God issues his last, unheeded call for Judah to turn from their sin and to pursue righteousness instead.

1 The words of Jeremiah son of Hilkiah, one of the priests at Anathoth in the territory of Benjamin. ²The word of the LORD came to him in the thirteenth year of the reign of Josiah son of Amon king of Judah, ³and through the reign of Jehoiakim son of Josiah king of Judah, down to the fifth month of the eleventh year of Zedekiah son of Josiah king of Judah, when the people of Jerusalem went into exile.

The Call of Jeremiah

⁴The word of the LORD came to me, saying,

⁵ "Before I formed you in the womb I
      knew*a* you,
  before you were born I set you apart;
  I appointed you as a prophet to the
      nations."

⁶"Ah, Sovereign LORD," I said, "I do not know how to speak; I am too young."

⁷But the LORD said to me, "Do not say, 'I am too young.' You must go to everyone I send you to and say whatever I command you. ⁸Do not be afraid of them, for I am with you and will rescue you," declares the LORD.

⁹Then the LORD reached out his hand and touched my mouth and said to me, "I have put my words in your mouth. ¹⁰See, today I appoint you over nations and kingdoms to uproot and tear down, to destroy and overthrow, to build and to plant."

¹¹The word of the LORD came to me: "What do you see, Jeremiah?"

"I see the branch of an almond tree," I replied.

¹²The LORD said to me, "You have seen correctly, for I am watching*b* to see that my word is fulfilled."

¹³The word of the LORD came to me again: "What do you see?"

"I see a pot that is boiling," I answered. "It is tilting toward us from the north."

¹⁴The LORD said to me, "From the north disaster will be poured out on all who live in the land. ¹⁵I am about to summon all the peoples of the northern kingdoms," declares the LORD.

"Their kings will come and set up their
      thrones
  in the entrance of the gates of
      Jerusalem;
  they will come against all her
      surrounding walls
  and against all the towns of Judah.
¹⁶I will pronounce my judgments on my
      people
  because of their wickedness in
      forsaking me,
  in burning incense to other gods
  and in worshiping what their hands
      have made.

¹⁷"Get yourself ready! Stand up and say to them whatever I command you. Do not be terrified by them, or I will terrify you before them. ¹⁸Today I have made you a fortified city, an iron pillar and a bronze wall to stand against the whole land—against the kings of Judah, its officials, its priests and the people of the land. ¹⁹They will fight against you but will not overcome you, for I am with you and will rescue you," declares the LORD.

Israel Forsakes God

2 The word of the LORD came to me: ²"Go and proclaim in the hearing of Jerusalem:

---

a 5 Or *chose*   *b 12* The Hebrew for *watching* sounds like the Hebrew for *almond tree.*

MONDAY

THIRST DEEPLY, THEN DRINK FREELY

Jeremiah 2:1–37 *or* 2:13

Mike Pilavachi

The painful truth is that when humanity turned from a relationship of dependence and trust in God, we lost more than relationship with God—we lost the only true means of knowing who we are. Speaking through the prophet Jeremiah, God said: "My people have committed two sins: They have forsaken me, the spring of living water, and have dug their own cisterns, broken cisterns that cannot hold water" (Jeremiah 2:13).

When we turn from the spring of living water, we try to satisfy ourselves by drinking from any contaminated pool. We then become contaminated and diseased. Instead of seeking healing, we live in denial that there is anything wrong. The desert is a place of healing. Before that, however, it has to be the place where we discover that we are sick. When all the props have been taken away, we come face-to-face with our bankruptcy. The gospel has to be bad news before it can be good news. In the desert we find that we are "wretched, pitiful, poor, blind and naked" (Revelation 3:17). Only then can we truly receive the Savior. Only when we truly thirst in the dry and arid desert can we begin to drink the living water.

ANNA L. WARING {AD 1823–1910}

"I will pour water on the thirsty land, and streams on the dry ground."—Isaiah 44:3

Source of my spirit's deep desire
For living joys that shall not perish,
The patient hope Thy words inspire,
Still let Thy tender mercy cherish.

On Thee my humbled soul would wait,
Her utmost weakness calmly learning,
And see Thy grace its way create,
Through thorns and briers which Thou art burning.

Gladly my inmost heart would know
The love that now it faintly traces,
And see the streams from Zion flow
O'er all its waste and desert places.

And still I hope—O not in vain!
I know, this holy seed possessing,
Thou wilt come down like gentle rain,
And make the barren ground a blessing.

reflection

1. What two sins did God condemn the Israelites for?

2. Why did God object so strongly to their actions?

3. What does it mean that God is a spring of living water?

For your next devotional reading, go to page 854.

"This is what the LORD says:

" 'I remember the devotion of your
        youth,
    how as a bride you loved me
and followed me through the wilderness,
    through a land not sown.
³ Israel was holy to the LORD,
    the firstfruits of his harvest;
all who devoured her were held guilty,
    and disaster overtook them,' "
                    declares the LORD.

⁴ Hear the word of the LORD, house of
        Jacob,
    all you clans of the house of Israel.

⁵ This is what the LORD says:

"What fault did your ancestors find in me,
    that they strayed so far from me?
They followed worthless idols
    and became worthless themselves.
⁶ They did not ask, 'Where is the LORD,
    who brought us up out of Egypt
and led us through the barren
        wilderness,
    through a land of deserts and ravines,
a land of drought and utter darkness,
    a land where no one travels and no
        one lives?'
⁷ I brought you into a fertile land
    to eat its fruit and rich produce.
But you came and defiled my land
    and made my inheritance detestable.
⁸ The priests did not ask,
    'Where is the LORD?'
Those who deal with the law did not
        know me;
    the leaders rebelled against me.
The prophets prophesied by Baal,
    following worthless idols.

⁹ "Therefore I bring charges against you
        again,"
                    declares the LORD.
    "And I will bring charges against your
        children's children.
¹⁰ Cross over to the coasts of Cyprus and
        look,
    send to Kedarᵃ and observe closely;
    see if there has ever been anything
        like this:
¹¹ Has a nation ever changed its gods?
    (Yet they are not gods at all.)

But my people have exchanged their
        glorious God
    for worthless idols.
¹² Be appalled at this, you heavens,
    and shudder with great horror,"
                    declares the LORD.
¹³ "My people have committed two sins:
They have forsaken me,
    the spring of living water,
and have dug their own cisterns,
    broken cisterns that cannot hold
        water.
¹⁴ Is Israel a servant, a slave by birth?
    Why then has he become plunder?
¹⁵ Lions have roared;
    they have growled at him.
They have laid waste his land;
    his towns are burned and deserted.
¹⁶ Also, the men of Memphis and
        Tahpanhes
    have cracked your skull.
¹⁷ Have you not brought this on yourselves
    by forsaking the LORD your God
    when he led you in the way?
¹⁸ Now why go to Egypt
    to drink water from the Nileᵇ?
And why go to Assyria
    to drink water from the Euphrates?
¹⁹ Your wickedness will punish you;
    your backsliding will rebuke you.
Consider then and realize
    how evil and bitter it is for you
when you forsake the LORD your God
    and have no awe of me,"
                    declares the Lord,
                        the LORD Almighty.

²⁰ "Long ago you broke off your yoke
    and tore off your bonds;
    you said, 'I will not serve you!'
Indeed, on every high hill
    and under every spreading tree
    you lay down as a prostitute.
²¹ I had planted you like a choice vine
    of sound and reliable stock.
How then did you turn against me
    into a corrupt, wild vine?
²² Although you wash yourself with soap
    and use an abundance of cleansing
        powder,
    the stain of your guilt is still before
        me,"
                    declares the Sovereign LORD.
²³ "How can you say, 'I am not defiled;

ᵃ 10 In the Syro-Arabian desert   ᵇ 18 Hebrew *Shihor*; that is, a branch of the Nile

I have not run after the Baals'?
See how you behaved in the valley;
    consider what you have done.
You are a swift she-camel
    running here and there,
24 a wild donkey accustomed to the desert,
    sniffing the wind in her craving—
    in her heat who can restrain her?
Any males that pursue her need not tire
    themselves;
    at mating time they will find her.
25 Do not run until your feet are bare
    and your throat is dry.
But you said, 'It's no use!
    I love foreign gods,
    and I must go after them.'

26 "As a thief is disgraced when he is caught,
    so the house of Israel is disgraced—
they, their kings and their officials,
    their priests and their prophets.
27 They say to wood, 'You are my father,'
    and to stone, 'You gave me birth.'
They have turned their backs to me
    and not their faces;
yet when they are in trouble, they say,
    'Come and save us!'
28 Where then are the gods you made for
    yourselves?
    Let them come if they can save you
    when you are in trouble!
For you, Judah, have as many gods
    as you have towns.

29 "Why do you bring charges against me?
    You have all rebelled against me,"
        declares the LORD.
30 "In vain I punished your people;
    they did not respond to correction.
Your sword has devoured your prophets
    like a ravenous lion.

31 "You of this generation, consider the
word of the LORD:

"Have I been a desert to Israel
    or a land of great darkness?
Why do my people say, 'We are free to
    roam;
    we will come to you no more'?
32 Does a young woman forget her jewelry,
    a bride her wedding ornaments?
Yet my people have forgotten me,
    days without number.
33 How skilled you are at pursuing love!
    Even the worst of women can learn
        from your ways.

34 On your clothes is found
    the lifeblood of the innocent poor,
    though you did not catch them
        breaking in.
Yet in spite of all this
35   you say, 'I am innocent;
    he is not angry with me.'
But I will pass judgment on you
    because you say, 'I have not sinned.'
36 Why do you go about so much,
    changing your ways?
You will be disappointed by Egypt
    as you were by Assyria.
37 You will also leave that place
    with your hands on your head,
for the LORD has rejected those you
    trust;
    you will not be helped by them.

3 "If a man divorces his wife
    and she leaves him and marries
        another man,
should he return to her again?
    Would not the land be completely
        defiled?
But you have lived as a prostitute with
    many lovers—
    would you now return to me?"
        declares the LORD.
2 "Look up to the barren heights and see.
    Is there any place where you have not
        been ravished?
By the roadside you sat waiting for
    lovers,
    sat like a nomad in the desert.
You have defiled the land
    with your prostitution and
        wickedness.
3 Therefore the showers have been
    withheld,
    and no spring rains have fallen.
Yet you have the brazen look of a
    prostitute;
    you refuse to blush with shame.
4 Have you not just called to me:
    'My Father, my friend from my youth,
5 will you always be angry?
    Will your wrath continue forever?'
This is how you talk,
    but you do all the evil you can."

Unfaithful Israel

6 During the reign of King Josiah, the LORD
said to me, "Have you seen what faithless
Israel has done? She has gone up on every

high hill and under every spreading tree and has committed adultery there. ⁷I thought that after she had done all this she would return to me but she did not, and her unfaithful sister Judah saw it. ⁸I gave faithless Israel her certificate of divorce and sent her away because of all her adulteries. Yet I saw that her unfaithful sister Judah had no fear; she also went out and committed adultery. ⁹Because Israel's immorality mattered so little to her, she defiled the land and committed adultery with stone and wood. ¹⁰In spite of all this, her unfaithful sister Judah did not return to me with all her heart, but only in pretense," declares the LORD.

¹¹The LORD said to me, "Faithless Israel is more righteous than unfaithful Judah. ¹²Go, proclaim this message toward the north:

" 'Return, faithless Israel,' declares the
    LORD,
  'I will frown on you no longer,
for I am faithful,' declares the LORD,
  'I will not be angry forever.
¹³ Only acknowledge your guilt—
  you have rebelled against the LORD
    your God,
you have scattered your favors to foreign
    gods
  under every spreading tree,
  and have not obeyed me,' "
            declares the LORD.

¹⁴"Return, faithless people," declares the LORD, "for I am your husband. I will choose you—one from a town and two from a clan—and bring you to Zion. ¹⁵Then I will give you shepherds after my own heart, who will lead you with knowledge and understanding. ¹⁶In those days, when your numbers have increased greatly in the land," declares the LORD, "people will no longer say, 'The ark of the covenant of the LORD.' It will never enter their minds or be remembered; it will not be missed, nor will another one be made. ¹⁷At that time they will call Jerusalem The Throne of the LORD, and all nations will gather in Jerusalem to honor the name of the LORD. No longer will they follow the stubbornness of their evil hearts. ¹⁸In those days the house of Judah will join the house of Israel, and together they will come from a northern land to the land I gave your ancestors as an inheritance.

¹⁹"I myself said,

" 'How gladly would I treat you like my
    children
  and give you a pleasant land,
  the most beautiful inheritance of any
    nation.'
I thought you would call me 'Father'
  and not turn away from following me.
²⁰ But like a woman unfaithful to her
    husband,
  so you, house of Israel, have been
    unfaithful to me,"
            declares the LORD.

²¹ A cry is heard on the barren heights,
  the weeping and pleading of the
    people of Israel,
because they have perverted their ways
  and have forgotten the LORD their
    God.

²² "Return, faithless people;
  I will cure you of backsliding."

"Yes, we will come to you,
  for you are the LORD our God.
²³ Surely the ʟidolatrousʟ commotion on
    the hills
  and mountains is a deception;
surely in the LORD our God
  is the salvation of Israel.
²⁴ From our youth shameful gods have
    consumed
  the fruits of our ancestors' labor—
their flocks and herds,
  their sons and daughters.
²⁵ Let us lie down in our shame,
  and let our disgrace cover us.
We have sinned against the LORD our
    God,
  both we and our ancestors;
from our youth till this day
  we have not obeyed the LORD our
    God."

4 "If you, Israel, will return,
    then return to me,"
            declares the LORD.
"If you put your detestable idols out of
    my sight
  and no longer go astray,
² and if in a truthful, just and righteous
    way
  you swear, 'As surely as the LORD
    lives,'
then the nations will invoke blessings by
    him
  and in him they will boast."

³This is what the LORD says to the people of Judah and to Jerusalem:

> "Break up your unplowed ground
> and do not sow among thorns.
> ⁴Circumcise yourselves to the LORD,
> circumcise your hearts,
> you people of Judah and inhabitants
> of Jerusalem,
> or my wrath will flare up and burn like
> fire
> because of the evil you have done—
> burn with no one to quench it.

Disaster From the North

> ⁵"Announce in Judah and proclaim in
> Jerusalem and say:
> 'Sound the trumpet throughout the
> land!'
> Cry aloud and say:
> 'Gather together!
> Let us flee to the fortified cities!'
> ⁶Raise the signal to go to Zion!
> Flee for safety without delay!
> For I am bringing disaster from the
> north,
> even terrible destruction."

> ⁷A lion has come out of his lair;
> a destroyer of nations has set out.
> He has left his place
> to lay waste your land.
> Your towns will lie in ruins
> without inhabitant.
> ⁸So put on sackcloth,
> lament and wail,
> for the fierce anger of the LORD
> has not turned away from us.

> ⁹"In that day," declares the LORD,
> "the king and the officials will lose
> heart,
> the priests will be horrified,
> and the prophets will be appalled."

¹⁰Then I said, "Ah, Sovereign LORD, how completely you have deceived this people and Jerusalem by saying, 'You will have peace,' when the sword is at our throats."

¹¹At that time this people and Jerusalem will be told, "A scorching wind from the barren heights in the desert blows toward my people, but not to winnow or cleanse; ¹²a wind too strong for that comes from me.ᵃ

Now I pronounce my judgments against them."

> ¹³Look! He advances like the clouds,
> his chariots come like a whirlwind,
> his horses are swifter than eagles.
> Woe to us! We are ruined!
> ¹⁴Jerusalem, wash the evil from your heart
> and be saved.
> How long will you harbor wicked
> thoughts?
> ¹⁵A voice is announcing from Dan,
> proclaiming disaster from the hills of
> Ephraim.
> ¹⁶"Tell this to the nations,
> proclaim concerning Jerusalem:
> 'A besieging army is coming from a
> distant land,
> raising a war cry against the cities of
> Judah.
> ¹⁷They surround her like people guarding
> a field,
> because she has rebelled against me,' "
> declares the LORD.
> ¹⁸"Your own conduct and actions
> have brought this on you.
> This is your punishment.
> How bitter it is!
> How it pierces to the heart!"

> ¹⁹Oh, my anguish, my anguish!
> I writhe in pain.
> Oh, the agony of my heart!
> My heart pounds within me,
> I cannot keep silent.
> For I have heard the sound of the
> trumpet;
> I have heard the battle cry.
> ²⁰Disaster follows disaster;
> the whole land lies in ruins.
> In an instant my tents are destroyed,
> my shelter in a moment.
> ²¹How long must I see the battle standard
> and hear the sound of the trumpet?

> ²²"My people are fools;
> they do not know me.
> They are senseless children;
> they have no understanding.
> They are skilled in doing evil;
> they know not how to do good."

> ²³I looked at the earth,
> and it was formless and empty;
> and at the heavens,

ᵃ 12 Or comes at my command

and their light was gone.

24 I looked at the mountains,
   and they were quaking;
   all the hills were swaying.
25 I looked, and there were no people;
   every bird in the sky had flown away.
26 I looked, and the fruitful land was a
      desert;
   all its towns lay in ruins
   before the LORD, before his fierce
      anger.

27 This is what the LORD says:

"The whole land will be ruined,
   though I will not destroy it
      completely.
28 Therefore the earth will mourn
   and the heavens above grow dark,
because I have spoken and will not
      relent,
   I have decided and will not turn
      back."

29 At the sound of horsemen and archers
   every town takes to flight.
Some go into the thickets;
   some climb up among the rocks.
All the towns are deserted;
   no one lives in them.

30 What are you doing, you devastated
      one?
   Why dress yourself in scarlet
   and put on jewels of gold?
Why color your eyes with paint?
   You adorn yourself in vain.
Your lovers despise you;
   they seek your life.

31 I hear a cry as of a woman in labor,
   a groan as of one bearing her first
      child—
the cry of Daughter Zion gasping for
      breath,
   stretching out her hands and saying,
"Alas! I am fainting;
   my life is given over to murderers."

Not One Is Upright

5 "Go up and down the streets of
      Jerusalem,
   look around and consider,
   search through her squares.
If you can find but one person
   who deals honestly and seeks the
      truth,
   I will forgive this city.

2 Although they say, 'As surely as the LORD
      lives,'
   still they are swearing falsely."

3 LORD, do not your eyes look for truth?
   You struck them, but they felt no
      pain;
   you crushed them, but they refused
      correction.
They made their faces harder than stone
   and refused to repent.
4 I thought, "These are only the poor;
   they are foolish,
for they do not know the way of the
      LORD,
   the requirements of their God.
5 So I will go to the leaders
   and speak to them;
surely they know the way of the LORD,
   the requirements of their God."
But with one accord they too had broken
      off the yoke
   and torn off the bonds.
6 Therefore a lion from the forest will
      attack them,
   a wolf from the desert will ravage
      them,
a leopard will lie in wait near their towns
   to tear to pieces any who venture out,
for their rebellion is great
   and their backslidings many.

7 "Why should I forgive you?
   Your children have forsaken me
   and sworn by gods that are not gods.
I supplied all their needs,
   yet they committed adultery
   and thronged to the houses of
      prostitutes.
8 They are well-fed, lusty stallions,
   each neighing for another man's wife.
9 Should I not punish them for this?"
   declares the LORD.
"Should I not avenge myself
   on such a nation as this?

10 "Go through her vineyards and ravage
      them,
   but do not destroy them completely.
Strip off her branches,
   for these people do not belong to the
      LORD.
11 The house of Israel and the house of
      Judah
   have been utterly unfaithful to me,"
      declares the LORD.

¹²They have lied about the LORD;
    they said, "He will do nothing!
No harm will come to us;
    we will never see sword or famine.
¹³The prophets are but wind
    and the word is not in them;
    so let what they say be done to
      them."

¹⁴Therefore this is what the LORD God Almighty says:

"Because the people have spoken these
      words,
    I will make my words in your mouth a
      fire
    and these people the wood it
      consumes.
¹⁵House of Israel," declares the LORD,
    "I am bringing a distant nation
      against you—
an ancient and enduring nation,
    a people whose language you do not
      know,
    whose speech you do not understand.
¹⁶Their quivers are like an open grave;
    all of them are mighty warriors.
¹⁷They will devour your harvests and food,
    devour your sons and daughters;
they will devour your flocks and herds,
    devour your vines and fig trees.
With the sword they will destroy
    the fortified cities in which you trust.

¹⁸"Yet even in those days," declares the LORD, "I will not destroy you completely. ¹⁹And when the people ask, 'Why has the LORD our God done all this to us?' you will tell them, 'As you have forsaken me and served foreign gods in your own land, so now you will serve foreigners in a land not your own.'

²⁰"Announce this to the house of Jacob
    and proclaim it in Judah:
²¹Hear this, you foolish and senseless
      people,
    who have eyes but do not see,
    who have ears but do not hear:
²²Should you not fear me?" declares the
      LORD.
    "Should you not tremble in my
      presence?
I made the sand a boundary for the sea,
    an everlasting barrier it cannot cross.
The waves may roll, but they cannot
      prevail;

    they may roar, but they cannot cross it.
²³But these people have stubborn and
      rebellious hearts;
    they have turned aside and gone
      away.
²⁴They do not say to themselves,
    'Let us fear the LORD our God,
who gives autumn and spring rains in
      season,
    who assures us of the regular weeks
      of harvest.'
²⁵Your wrongdoings have kept these away;
    your sins have deprived you of good.

²⁶"Among my people are the wicked
    who lie in wait like those who snare
      birds
    and like those who set traps to catch
      people.
²⁷Like cages full of birds,
    their houses are full of deceit;
they have become rich and powerful
²⁸   and have grown fat and sleek.
Their evil deeds have no limit;
    they do not seek justice.
They do not promote the case of the
      fatherless;
    they do not defend the just cause of
      the poor.
²⁹Should I not punish them for this?"
    declares the LORD.
    "Should I not avenge myself
    on such a nation as this?

³⁰"A horrible and shocking thing
    has happened in the land:
³¹The prophets prophesy lies,
    the priests rule by their own
      authority,
and my people love it this way.
    But what will you do in the end?

Jerusalem Under Siege

6 "Flee for safety, people of Benjamin!
    Flee from Jerusalem!
    Sound the trumpet in Tekoa!
    Raise the signal over Beth Hakkerem!
For disaster looms out of the north,
    even terrible destruction.
²I will destroy Daughter Zion,
    so beautiful and delicate.
³Shepherds with their flocks will come
      against her;
    they will pitch their tents around her,
    each of them tending their own
      portion."

⁴"Prepare for battle against her!
    Arise, let us attack at noon!
But, alas, the daylight is fading,
    and the shadows of evening grow
        long.
⁵So arise, let us attack at night
    and destroy her fortresses!"

⁶This is what the LORD Almighty says:

"Cut down the trees
    and build siege ramps against
        Jerusalem.
This city must be punished;
    it is filled with oppression.
⁷As a well pours out its water,
    so she pours out her wickedness.
Violence and destruction resound in her;
    her sickness and wounds are ever
        before me.
⁸Take warning, Jerusalem,
    or I will turn away from you
and make your land desolate
    so no one can live in it."

⁹This is what the LORD Almighty says:

"Let them glean the remnant of Israel
    as thoroughly as a vine;
pass your hand over the branches again,
    like one gathering grapes."

¹⁰To whom can I speak and give warning?
    Who will listen to me?
Their ears are closedᵃ
    so they cannot hear.
The word of the LORD is offensive to
        them;
    they find no pleasure in it.
¹¹But I am full of the wrath of the LORD,
    and I cannot hold it in.

"Pour it out on the children in the street
    and on the youths gathered together;
both husband and wife will be caught in
        it,
    and the old, those weighed down with
        years.
¹²Their houses will be turned over to
        others,
    together with their fields and their
        wives,
when I stretch out my hand
    against those who live in the land,"
                    declares the LORD.
¹³"From the least to the greatest,

all are greedy for gain;
prophets and priests alike,
    all practice deceit.
¹⁴They dress the wound of my people
    as though it were not serious.
'Peace, peace,' they say,
    when there is no peace.
¹⁵Are they ashamed of their detestable
        conduct?
    No, they have no shame at all;
    they do not even know how to blush.
So they will fall among the fallen;
    they will be brought down when I
        punish them,"
                        says the LORD.

¹⁶This is what the LORD says:

"Stand at the crossroads and look;
    ask for the ancient paths,
ask where the good way is, and walk in
        it,
    and you will find rest for your souls.
    But you said, 'We will not walk in it.'
¹⁷I appointed watchmen over you and
        said,
    'Listen to the sound of the trumpet!'
    But you said, 'We will not listen.'
¹⁸Therefore hear, you nations;
    you who are witnesses,
    observe what will happen to them.
¹⁹Hear, you earth:
    I am bringing disaster on this people,
    the fruit of their schemes,
because they have not listened to my
        words
    and have rejected my law.
²⁰What do I care about incense from
        Sheba
    or sweet calamus from a distant land?
Your burnt offerings are not acceptable;
    your sacrifices do not please me."

²¹Therefore this is what the LORD says:

"I will put obstacles before this people.
    Parents and children alike will
        stumble over them;
    neighbors and friends will perish."

²²This is what the LORD says:

"Look, an army is coming
    from the land of the north;
a great nation is being stirred up
    from the ends of the earth.

ᵃ 10 Hebrew *uncircumcised*

23 They are armed with bow and spear;
    they are cruel and show no mercy.
They sound like the roaring sea
    as they ride on their horses;
they come like men in battle formation
    to attack you, Daughter Zion."

24 We have heard reports about them,
    and our hands hang limp.
Anguish has gripped us,
    pain like that of a woman in labor.
25 Do not go out to the fields
    or walk on the roads,
for the enemy has a sword,
    and there is terror on every side.
26 Put on sackcloth, my people,
    and roll in ashes;
mourn with bitter wailing
    as for an only son,
for suddenly the destroyer
    will come upon us.

27 "I have made you a tester of metals
    and my people the ore,
that you may observe
    and test their ways.
28 They are all hardened rebels,
    going about to slander.
They are bronze and iron;
    they all act corruptly.
29 The bellows blow fiercely
    to burn away the lead with fire,
but the refining goes on in vain;
    the wicked are not purged out.
30 They are called rejected silver,
    because the LORD has rejected them."

False Religion Worthless

7 This is the word that came to Jeremiah from the LORD: 2 "Stand at the gate of the LORD's house and there proclaim this message:

" 'Hear the word of the LORD, all you people of Judah who come through these gates to worship the LORD. 3 This is what the LORD Almighty, the God of Israel, says: Reform your ways and your actions, and I will let you live in this place. 4 Do not trust in deceptive words and say, "This is the temple of the LORD, the temple of the LORD, the temple of the LORD!" 5 If you really change your ways and your actions and deal with each other justly, 6 if you do not oppress the foreigner, the fatherless or the widow and do not shed innocent blood in this place, and if you do not follow other gods to your own harm, 7 then I will let you live in this place, in the land I gave your ancestors for ever and ever. 8 But look, you are trusting in deceptive words that are worthless.

9 " 'Will you steal and murder, commit adultery and perjury,a burn incense to Baal and follow other gods you have not known, 10 and then come and stand before me in this house, which bears my Name, and say, "We are safe"—safe to do all these detestable things? 11 Has this house, which bears my Name, become a den of robbers to you? But I have been watching! declares the LORD.

12 " 'Go now to the place in Shiloh where I first made a dwelling for my Name, and see what I did to it because of the wickedness of my people Israel. 13 While you were doing all these things, declares the LORD, I spoke to you again and again, but you did not listen; I called you, but you did not answer. 14 Therefore, what I did to Shiloh I will now do to the house that bears my Name, the temple you trust in, the place I gave to you and your ancestors. 15 I will thrust you from my presence, just as I did all your fellow Israelites, the people of Ephraim.'

16 "So do not pray for this people nor offer any plea or petition for them; do not plead with me, for I will not listen to you. 17 Do you not see what they are doing in the towns of Judah and in the streets of Jerusalem? 18 The children gather wood, the fathers light the fire, and the women knead the dough and make cakes to offer to the Queen of Heaven. They pour out drink offerings to other gods to arouse my anger. 19 But am I the one they are provoking? declares the LORD. Are they not rather harming themselves, to their own shame?

20 " 'Therefore this is what the Sovereign LORD says: My anger and my wrath will be poured out on this place—on people and animals, on the trees of the field and on the crops of your land—and it will burn and not be quenched.

21 " 'This is what the LORD Almighty, the God of Israel, says: Go ahead, add your burnt offerings to your other sacrifices and eat the meat yourselves! 22 For when I brought your ancestors out of Egypt and spoke to them, I did not just give them commands about

a 9 Or and swear by false gods

burnt offerings and sacrifices, 23but I gave them this command: Obey me, and I will be your God and you will be my people. Walk in obedience to all I command you, that it may go well with you. 24But they did not listen or pay attention; instead, they followed the stubborn inclinations of their evil hearts. They went backward and not forward. 25From the time your ancestors left Egypt until now, day after day, again and again I sent you my servants the prophets. 26But they did not listen to me or pay attention. They were stiff-necked and did more evil than their ancestors.'

27"When you tell them all this, they will not listen to you; when you call to them, they will not answer. 28Therefore say to them, 'This is the nation that has not obeyed the LORD its God or responded to correction. Truth has perished; it has vanished from their lips.

29" 'Cut off your hair and throw it away; take up a lament on the barren heights, for the LORD has rejected and abandoned this generation that is under his wrath.

The Valley of Slaughter

30" 'The people of Judah have done evil in my eyes, declares the LORD. They have set up their detestable idols in the house that bears my Name and have defiled it. 31They have built the high places of Topheth in the Valley of Ben Hinnom to burn their sons and daughters in the fire—something I did not command, nor did it enter my mind. 32So beware, the days are coming, declares the LORD, when people will no longer call it Topheth or the Valley of Ben Hinnom, but the Valley of Slaughter, for they will bury the dead in Topheth until there is no more room. 33Then the carcasses of this people will become food for the birds and the wild animals, and there will be no one to frighten them away. 34I will bring an end to the sounds of joy and gladness and to the voices of bride and bridegroom in the towns of Judah and the streets of Jerusalem, for the land will become desolate.

8 " 'At that time, declares the LORD, the bones of the kings and officials of Judah, the bones of the priests and prophets, and the bones of the people of Jerusalem will be removed from their graves. 2They will be exposed to the sun and the moon and all the stars of the heavens, which

they have loved and served and which they have followed and consulted and worshiped. They will not be gathered up or buried, but will be like dung lying on the ground. 3Wherever I banish them, all the survivors of this evil nation will prefer death to life, declares the LORD Almighty.'

Sin and Punishment

4"Say to them, 'This is what the LORD says:

" 'When people fall down, do they not
  get up?
  When people turn away, do they not
  return?
5Why then have these people turned
  away?
  Why does Jerusalem always turn
  away?
They cling to deceit;
  they refuse to return.
6I have listened attentively,
  but they do not say what is right.
None of them repent of their
  wickedness,
  saying, "What have I done?"
They each pursue their own course
  like a horse charging into battle.
7Even the stork in the sky
  knows her appointed seasons,
and the dove, the swift and the thrush
  observe the time of their migration.
But my people do not know
  the requirements of the LORD.

8" 'How can you say, "We are wise,
  for we have the law of the LORD,"
when actually the lying pen of the
  scribes
  has handled it falsely?
9The wise will be put to shame;
  they will be dismayed and trapped.
Since they have rejected the word of the
  LORD,
  what kind of wisdom do they have?
10Therefore I will give their wives to other
  men
  and their fields to new owners.
From the least to the greatest,
  all are greedy for gain;
prophets and priests alike,
  all practice deceit.
11They dress the wound of my people
  as though it were not serious.
"Peace, peace," they say,
  when there is no peace.

¹²Are they ashamed of their detestable
conduct?
No, they have no shame at all;
they do not even know how to blush.
So they will fall among the fallen;
they will be brought down when they
are punished,
says the LORD.

¹³ " 'I will take away their harvest,
declares the LORD.
There will be no grapes on the vine.
There will be no figs on the tree,
and their leaves will wither.
What I have given them
will be taken from them.ᵃ' "

¹⁴Why are we sitting here?
Gather together!
Let us flee to the fortified cities
and perish there!
For the LORD our God has doomed us to
perish
and given us poisoned water to drink,
because we have sinned against him.

¹⁵We hoped for peace
but no good has come,
for a time of healing
but there is only terror.

¹⁶The snorting of the enemy's horses
is heard from Dan;
at the neighing of their stallions
the whole land trembles.
They have come to devour
the land and everything in it,
the city and all who live there.

¹⁷"See, I will send venomous snakes
among you,
vipers that cannot be charmed,
and they will bite you,"
declares the LORD.

¹⁸You who are my Comforterᵇ in sorrow,
my heart is faint within me.

¹⁹Listen to the cry of my people
from a land far away:
"Is the LORD not in Zion?
Is her King no longer there?"

"Why have they aroused my anger with
their images,
with their worthless foreign idols?"

²⁰"The harvest is past,
the summer has ended,
and we are not saved."

²¹Since my people are crushed, I am
crushed;
I mourn, and horror grips me.

²²Is there no balm in Gilead?
Is there no physician there?
Why then is there no healing
for the wound of my people?

9
*¹Oh, that my head were a spring of
water
and my eyes a fountain of tears!
I would weep day and night
for the slain of my people.

*²Oh, that I had in the desert
a lodging place for travelers,
so that I might leave my people
and go away from them;
for they are all adulterers,
a crowd of unfaithful people.

³"They make ready their tongue
like a bow, to shoot lies;
it is not by truth
that they triumphᶜ in the land.
They go from one sin to another;
they do not acknowledge me,"
declares the LORD.

⁴"Beware of your friends;
do not trust any of your people.
For every one of them is a deceiver,ᵈ
and every friend a slanderer.

⁵Friend deceives friend,
and no one speaks the truth.
They have taught their tongues to lie;
they weary themselves with
sinning.

⁶Youᵉ live in the midst of deception;
in their deceit they refuse to
acknowledge me,"
declares the LORD.

⁷Therefore this is what the LORD Almighty
says:

"See, I will refine and test them,
for what else can I do
because of the sin of my people?

⁸Their tongue is a deadly arrow;
it speaks deceitfully.

ᵃ *13* The meaning of the Hebrew for this sentence is uncertain.   ᵇ *18* The meaning of the Hebrew for
this word is uncertain.   ᶜ *3* Or *lies; / they are not valiant for truth*   ᵈ *4* Or *a deceiving Jacob*
ᵉ *6* That is, Jeremiah (the Hebrew is singular)

* 9:1 is numbered 8:23 in Hebrew texts.   * 9:2-26 is numbered 9:1-25 in Hebrew texts.

TUESDAY

DIRECTED BY GOD

Jeremiah 9:1–26 *or* 9:23–24

JOHN CALVIN {AD 1509–1564}

If we are not our own, but the Lord's, it is clear to what purpose all our deeds must be directed. We are not our own, therefore neither our reason nor our will should guide us in our thoughts and actions. We are not our own, therefore we should not seek what is only expedient to the flesh. We are not our own, therefore let us forget ourselves and our own interests as far as possible.

We are God's own; to him, therefore, let us live and die. We are God's own; therefore let his wisdom and will dominate all our actions. We are God's own; therefore let every part of our existence be directed towards him as our only legitimate goal.

Oh, how greatly we have advanced when we have learned not to be our own, not to be governed by our own reason, but to surrender our minds to God! The most effective poison to lead us to ruin is to boast in ourselves, in our own wisdom and willpower. The only escape to safety is simply to follow the guidance of the Lord.

Rick Warren

God is not just the starting point of your life; he is the *source* of it. To discover your purpose in life you must turn to God's Word, not the world's wisdom. You must build your life on eternal truths, not pop psychology, success-motivation or inspirational stories.

reflection

1. Where would you like to see yourself in five years (in your career, family, church)?

2. How does God fit into your plans?

3. How might the truth that you belong to God change the motives behind your actions for the next 24 hours?

For your next devotional reading, go to page 859.

With their mouths they all speak
      cordially to their neighbors,
    but in their hearts they set traps for
      them.
⁹ Should I not punish them for this?"
    declares the Lord.
"Should I not avenge myself
    on such a nation as this?"

¹⁰ I will weep and wail for the mountains
    and take up a lament concerning the
      wilderness grasslands.
They are desolate and untraveled,
    and the lowing of cattle is not heard.
The birds have all fled
    and the animals are gone.

¹¹ "I will make Jerusalem a heap of ruins,
    a haunt of jackals;
and I will lay waste the towns of Judah
    so no one can live there."

¹²Who is wise enough to understand this? Who has been instructed by the Lord and can explain it? Why has the land been ruined and laid waste like a desert that no one can cross?

¹³The Lord said, "It is because they have forsaken my law, which I set before them; they have not obeyed me or followed my law. ¹⁴Instead, they have followed the stubbornness of their hearts; they have followed the Baals, as their ancestors taught them." ¹⁵Therefore, this is what the Lord Almighty, the God of Israel, says: "See, I will make this people eat bitter food and drink poisoned water. ¹⁶I will scatter them among nations that neither they nor their ancestors have known, and I will pursue them with the sword until I have made an end of them."

¹⁷This is what the Lord Almighty says:

"Consider now! Call for the wailing
      women to come;
    send for the most skillful of them.
¹⁸ Let them come quickly
    and wail over us
till our eyes overflow with tears
    and water streams from our eyelids.
¹⁹ The sound of wailing is heard from Zion:
    'How ruined we are!
    How great is our shame!
We must leave our land
    because our houses are in ruins.' "

²⁰ Now, you women, hear the word of the
      Lord;
    open your ears to the words of his
      mouth.
Teach your daughters how to wail;
    teach one another a lament.
²¹ Death has climbed in through our
      windows
    and has entered our fortresses;
it has removed the children from the
      streets
    and the youths from the public
      squares.

²²Say, "This is what the Lord declares:

" 'Dead bodies will lie
    like dung on the open field,
like cut grain behind the reaper,
    with no one to gather them.' "

²³This is what the Lord says:

"Let not the wise boast of their wisdom
    or the strong boast of their strength
    or the rich boast of their riches,
²⁴ but let those who boast boast about this:
    that they understand and know me,
that I am the Lord, who exercises
      kindness,
    justice and righteousness on earth,
    for in these I delight,"
                  declares the Lord.

²⁵"The days are coming," declares the Lord, "when I will punish all who are circumcised only in the flesh— ²⁶Egypt, Judah, Edom, Ammon, Moab and all who live in the wilderness in distant places.ᵃ For all these nations are really uncircumcised, and even the whole house of Israel is uncircumcised in heart."

God and Idols

10 Hear what the Lord says to you, house of Israel. ²This is what the Lord says:

"Do not learn the ways of the nations
    or be terrified by signs in the sky,
    though the nations are terrified by
      them.
³ For the practices of the peoples are
      worthless;
    they cut a tree out of the forest,

ᵃ 26 Or *wilderness and who clip the hair by their foreheads*

and a skilled worker shapes it with a
    chisel.
4 They adorn it with silver and gold;
    they fasten it with hammer and nails
      so it will not totter.
5 Like a scarecrow in a melon patch,
    their idols cannot speak;
they must be carried
    because they cannot walk.
Do not fear them;
    they can do no harm
nor can they do any good."

6 No one is like you, Lord;
    you are great,
    and your name is mighty in power.
7 Who should not fear you,
    King of the nations?
    This is your due.
Among all the wise rulers of the nations
    and in all their kingdoms,
    there is no one like you.

8 They are all senseless and foolish;
    they are taught by worthless wooden
      idols.
9 Hammered silver is brought from
      Tarshish
    and gold from Uphaz.
What the goldsmith and engraver have
      made
    is then dressed in blue and purple—
    all made by skilled workers.
10 But the Lord is the true God;
    he is the living God, the eternal King.
When he is angry, the earth trembles;
    the nations cannot endure his wrath.

11 "Tell them this: 'These gods, who did
not make the heavens and the earth, will
perish from the earth and from under the
heavens.' " a

12 But God made the earth by his power;
    he founded the world by his wisdom
    and stretched out the heavens by his
      understanding.
13 When he thunders, the waters in the
      heavens roar;
    he makes clouds rise from the ends of
      the earth.
He sends lightning with the rain
    and brings out the wind from his
      storehouses.

14 Everyone is senseless and without
      knowledge;
    all goldsmiths are shamed by their
      idols.
Their images are a fraud;
    they have no breath in them.
15 They are worthless, the objects of
      mockery;
    when their judgment comes, they will
      perish.
16 He who is the Portion of Jacob is not like
      these,
    for he is the Maker of all things,
including Israel, the tribe of his
      inheritance—
    the Lord Almighty is his name.

Coming Destruction

17 Gather up your belongings to leave the
      land,
    you who live under siege.
18 For this is what the Lord says:
    "At this time I will hurl out
      those who live in this land;
    I will bring distress on them
      so that they may be captured."

19 Woe to me because of my injury!
    My wound is incurable!
Yet I said to myself,
    "This is my sickness, and I must
      endure it."
20 My tent is destroyed;
    all its ropes are snapped.
My children are gone from me and are
      no more;
    no one is left now to pitch my tent
      or to set up my shelter.
21 The shepherds are senseless
    and do not inquire of the Lord;
so they do not prosper
    and all their flock is scattered.
22 Listen! The report is coming—
    a great commotion from the land of
      the north!
It will make the towns of Judah desolate,
    a haunt of jackals.

Jeremiah's Prayer

23 Lord, I know that people's lives are not
      their own;
    it is not for them to direct their steps.
24 Discipline me, Lord, but only in due
      measure—

a 11 The text of this verse is in Aramaic.

not in your anger,
or you will reduce me to nothing.
²⁵ Pour out your wrath on the nations
that do not acknowledge you,
on the peoples who do not call on
your name.
For they have devoured Jacob;
they have devoured him completely
and destroyed his homeland.

The Covenant Is Broken

11 This is the word that came to Jeremiah from the Lord: ² "Listen to the terms of this covenant and tell them to the people of Judah and to those who live in Jerusalem. ³ Tell them that this is what the Lord, the God of Israel, says: 'Cursed is everyone who does not obey the terms of this covenant— ⁴ the terms I commanded your ancestors when I brought them out of Egypt, out of the iron-smelting furnace.' I said, 'Obey me and do everything I command you, and you will be my people, and I will be your God. ⁵ Then I will fulfill the oath I swore to your ancestors, to give them a land flowing with milk and honey'—the land you possess today."

I answered, "Amen, Lord."

⁶ The Lord said to me, "Proclaim all these words in the towns of Judah and in the streets of Jerusalem: 'Listen to the terms of this covenant and follow them. ⁷ From the time I brought your ancestors up from Egypt until today, I warned them again and again, saying, "Obey me." ⁸ But they did not listen or pay attention; instead, they followed the stubbornness of their evil hearts. So I brought on them all the curses of the covenant I had commanded them to follow but that they did not keep.' "

⁹ Then the Lord said to me, "There is a conspiracy among the people of Judah and those who live in Jerusalem. ¹⁰ They have returned to the sins of their ancestors, who refused to listen to my words. They have followed other gods to serve them. Both the house of Israel and the house of Judah have broken the covenant I made with their ancestors. ¹¹ Therefore this is what the Lord says: 'I will bring on them a disaster they cannot escape. Although they cry out to me, I will not listen to them. ¹² The towns of Judah and the people of Jerusalem will go and cry out to the gods to whom they burn incense, but they will not help them at all when disaster strikes. ¹³ You, Judah, have as many gods as you have towns; and the altars you have set up to burn incense to that shameful god Baal are as many as the streets of Jerusalem.'

¹⁴ "Do not pray for this people or offer any plea or petition for them, because I will not listen when they call to me in the time of their distress.

¹⁵ "What is my beloved doing in my temple
as she, with many others, works out
her evil schemes?
Can consecrated meat avert your
punishment?
When you engage in your wickedness,
then you rejoice. ^a"

¹⁶ The Lord called you a thriving olive tree
with fruit beautiful in form.
But with the roar of a mighty storm
he will set it on fire,
and its branches will be broken.

¹⁷ The Lord Almighty, who planted you, has decreed disaster for you, because the house of Israel and the house of Judah have done evil and aroused my anger by burning incense to Baal.

Plot Against Jeremiah

¹⁸ Because the Lord revealed their plot to me, I knew it, for at that time he showed me what they were doing. ¹⁹ I had been like a gentle lamb led to the slaughter; I did not realize that they had plotted against me, saying,

"Let us destroy the tree and its fruit;
let us cut him off from the land of the
living,
that his name be remembered no
more."
²⁰ But you, Lord Almighty, who judge
righteously
and test the heart and mind,
let me see your vengeance on them,
for to you I have committed my
cause.

²¹ "Therefore this is what the Lord says about the people of Anathoth who are seeking your life and saying, 'Do not prophesy in the name of the Lord or you will die by our

---

^a 15 Or Could consecrated meat avert your punishment? / Then you would rejoice

hands'— [22]therefore this is what the LORD Almighty says: 'I will punish them. Their young men will die by the sword, their sons and daughters by famine. [23]Not even a remnant will be left to them, because I will bring disaster on the people of Anathoth in the year of their punishment.' "

Jeremiah's Complaint

12 You are always righteous, LORD,
when I bring a case before you.
Yet I would speak with you
about your justice:
Why does the way of the wicked
prosper?
Why do all the faithless live at ease?
[2]You have planted them, and they have
taken root;
they grow and bear fruit.
You are always on their lips
but far from their hearts.
[3]Yet you know me, LORD;
you see me and test my thoughts
about you.
Drag them off like sheep to be
butchered!
Set them apart for the day of
slaughter!
[4]How long will the land lie parched
and the grass in every field be
withered?
Because those who live in it are wicked,
the animals and birds have perished.
Moreover, the people are saying,
"He will not see what happens to us."

God's Answer

[5]"If you have raced with people on foot
and they have worn you out,
how can you compete with horses?
If you stumble[a] in safe country,
how will you manage in the thickets
by[b] the Jordan?
[6]Your relatives, members of your own
family—
even they have betrayed you;
they have raised a loud cry against you.
Do not trust them,
though they speak well of you.

[7]"I will forsake my house,
abandon my inheritance;
I will give the one I love
into the hands of her enemies.
[8]My inheritance has become to me
like a lion in the forest.
She roars at me;
therefore I hate her.
[9]Has not my inheritance become to me
like a speckled bird of prey
that other birds of prey surround and
attack?
Go and gather all the wild beasts;
bring them to devour.
[10]Many shepherds will ruin my vineyard
and trample down my field;
they will turn my pleasant field
into a desolate wasteland.
[11]It will be made a wasteland,
parched and desolate before me;
the whole land will be laid waste
because there is no one who cares.
[12]Over all the barren heights in the desert
destroyers will swarm,
for the sword of the LORD will devour
from one end of the land to the other;
no one will be safe.
[13]They will sow wheat but reap thorns;
they will wear themselves out but
gain nothing.
They will bear the shame of their harvest
because of the LORD's fierce anger."

[14]This is what the LORD says: "As for all my wicked neighbors who seize the inheritance I gave my people Israel, I will uproot them from their lands and I will uproot the house of Judah from among them. [15]But after I uproot them, I will again have compassion and will bring each of them back to their own inheritance and their own country. [16]And if they learn well the ways of my people and swear by my name, saying, 'As surely as the LORD lives'—even as they once taught my people to swear by Baal—then they will be established among my people. [17]But if any nation does not listen, I will completely uproot and destroy it," declares the LORD.

A Linen Belt

13 This is what the LORD said to me: "Go and buy a linen belt and put it around your waist, but do not let it touch water." [2]So I bought a belt, as the LORD directed, and put it around my waist.
[3]Then the word of the LORD came to me a second time: [4]"Take the belt you bought and

---

[a] 5 Or you feel secure only   [b] 5 Or the flooding of

WEDNESDAY

THE GOD IN THE GOOD AND BAD

Jeremiah 12:1–17 or 12:5–6,14–15

Billy Graham

Most believers have experienced ups and downs in their faith, and often these cycles are connected to the way we feel-in other words, to our emotions.

This has happened to some of God's most dedicated servants, including some in the Bible. During one dark time in his life, when his emotions got the best of him, Jeremiah cried out, "Why did I ever come out of the womb to see trouble and sorrow and to end my days in shame?" (Jeremiah 20:18). In the midst of his despair, Job cried out, "I loathe my very life; therefore I will give free reign to my complaint and speak out in the bitterness of my soul" (Job 10:1).

But neither Jeremiah nor Job stayed this way, and both went on to have an even stronger faith. And that can be your experience also. What can you do? First, make sure of your commitment to Christ. If your faith in God is only a vague belief, it will not stand. But if your faith is in Christ, you have a solid foundation beneath you that will never crumble. Give your life to Him today.

Then base your faith on facts, not on feeling. Base it on the fact that God loves you, on Christ's death and resurrection for you, and on God's promises in His Word, the Bible. Make the Bible your daily companion and your faith will grow stronger.

HANNAH WHITALL SMITH {ca. AD 1832–1911}

We say sometimes, "If I could only find a promise to fit my situation, I could then be at rest." But promises may be misunderstood or misapplied, and, at the moment when we are leaning all our weight upon them, they may seem utterly to fail us. But the Promiser—who is behind his promises, and is infinitely more than his promises—can never fail nor change. The little child does not need to have any promises from its mother to make it content; it has its mother herself, and she is enough. Its mother is better than a thousand promises. In our highest ideal of love or friendship, promises are not important . . . And if every promise were wiped out of the Bible, we would still have God left, and God would be enough. Again I repeat it: only God, he himself, just as he is, without the addition of feelings, or experiences, or good works, or sound doctrines, or anything else. "Truly [God] is my rock and my salvation; he is my fortress, I will never be shaken" (Psalm 62:2).

reflection

1. Have you ever been in a place where all you had left was Jesus?

2. How did that experience change you?

3. Truly awful things in life can be blessings in disguise because they can draw you closer to Jesus. How have you seen that in your own life or in the life of someone you know?

For your next devotional reading, go to page 865.

are wearing around your waist, and go now to Perath[a] and hide it there in a crevice in the rocks." [5]So I went and hid it at Perath, as the LORD told me.

[6]Many days later the LORD said to me, "Go now to Perath and get the belt I told you to hide there." [7]So I went to Perath and dug up the belt and took it from the place where I had hidden it, but now it was ruined and completely useless.

[8]Then the word of the LORD came to me: [9]"This is what the LORD says: 'In the same way I will ruin the pride of Judah and the great pride of Jerusalem. [10]These wicked people, who refuse to listen to my words, who follow the stubbornness of their hearts and go after other gods to serve and worship them, will be like this belt—completely useless! [11]For as a belt is bound around the waist, so I bound the whole house of Israel and the whole house of Judah to me,' declares the LORD, 'to be my people for my renown and praise and honor. But they have not listened.'

Wineskins

[12]"Say to them: 'This is what the LORD, the God of Israel, says: Every wineskin should be filled with wine.' And if they say to you, 'Don't we know that every wineskin should be filled with wine?' [13]then tell them, 'This is what the LORD says: I am going to fill with drunkenness all who live in this land, including the kings who sit on David's throne, the priests, the prophets and all those living in Jerusalem. [14]I will smash them one against the other, parents and children alike, declares the LORD. I will allow no pity or mercy or compassion to keep me from destroying them.' "

Threat of Captivity

[15]Hear and pay attention,
    do not be arrogant,
    for the LORD has spoken.
[16]Give glory to the LORD your God
    before he brings the darkness,
before your feet stumble
    on the darkening hills.
You hope for light,
    but he will turn it to utter darkness
    and change it to deep gloom.

[17]If you do not listen,
    I will weep in secret
    because of your pride;
my eyes will weep bitterly,
    overflowing with tears,
    because the LORD's flock will be taken
        captive.

[18]Say to the king and to the queen
        mother,
    "Come down from your thrones,
for your glorious crowns
    will fall from your heads."
[19]The cities in the Negev will be shut up,
    and there will be no one to open them.
All Judah will be carried into exile,
    carried completely away.

[20]Look up and see
    those who are coming from the north.
Where is the flock that was entrusted to
        you,
    the sheep of which you boasted?
[21]What will you say when ⌊the LORD⌋ sets
        over you
    those you cultivated as your special
        allies?
Will not pain grip you
    like that of a woman in labor?
[22]And if you ask yourself,
    "Why has this happened to me?"—
it is because of your many sins
    that your skirts have been torn off
    and your body mistreated.
[23]Can an Ethiopian[b] change his skin
    or a leopard its spots?
Neither can you do good
    who are accustomed to doing evil.

[24]"I will scatter you like chaff
    driven by the desert wind.
[25]This is your lot,
    the portion I have decreed for you,"
            declares the LORD,
"because you have forgotten me
    and trusted in false gods.
[26]I will pull up your skirts over your face
    that your shame may be seen—
[27]your adulteries and lustful neighings,
    your shameless prostitution!
I have seen your detestable acts
    on the hills and in the fields.
Woe to you, Jerusalem!
    How long will you be unclean?"

---

[a] 4 Or possibly *to the Euphrates*; similarly in verses 5-7 (the upper Nile region)   [b] 23 Hebrew *Cushite* (probably a person from

Drought, Famine, Sword

14

This is the word of the LORD that came to Jeremiah concerning the drought:

2 "Judah mourns,
    her cities languish;
  they wail for the land,
    and a cry goes up from Jerusalem.
3 The nobles send their servants for water;
    they go to the cisterns
    but find no water.
  They return with their jars unfilled;
    dismayed and despairing,
    they cover their heads.
4 The ground is cracked
    because there is no rain in the land;
  the farmers are dismayed
    and cover their heads.
5 Even the doe in the field
    deserts her newborn fawn
    because there is no grass.
6 Wild donkeys stand on the barren
      heights
    and pant like jackals;
  their eyes fail
    for lack of food."

7 Although our sins testify against us,
    do something, LORD, for the sake of
      your name.
  For our backsliding is great;
    we have sinned against you.
8 You who are the hope of Israel,
    its Savior in times of distress,
  why are you like a stranger in the land,
    like a traveler who stays only a night?
9 Why are you like someone taken by
      surprise,
    like a warrior powerless to save?
  You are among us, LORD,
    and we bear your name;
    do not forsake us!

10 This is what the LORD says about this people:

"They greatly love to wander;
    they do not restrain their feet.
  So the LORD does not accept them;
    he will now remember their
      wickedness
    and punish them for their sins."

11 Then the LORD said to me, "Do not pray for the well-being of this people. 12 Although they fast, I will not listen to their cry; though they offer burnt offerings and grain offerings, I will not accept them. Instead, I will destroy them with the sword, famine and plague."

13 But I said, "Ah, Sovereign LORD, the prophets keep telling them, 'You will not see the sword or suffer famine. Indeed, I will give you lasting peace in this place.' "

14 Then the LORD said to me, "The prophets are prophesying lies in my name. I have not sent them or appointed them or spoken to them. They are prophesying to you false visions, divinations, idolatries[a] and the delusions of their own minds. 15 Therefore, this is what the LORD says about the prophets who are prophesying in my name: I did not send them, yet they are saying, 'No sword or famine will touch this land.' Those same prophets will perish by sword and famine. 16 And the people they are prophesying to will be thrown out into the streets of Jerusalem because of the famine and sword. There will be no one to bury them, their wives, their sons and their daughters. I will pour out on them the calamity they deserve.

17 "Speak this word to them:

" 'Let my eyes overflow with tears
    night and day without ceasing;
  for the Virgin Daughter, my people,
    has suffered a grievous wound,
    a crushing blow.
18 If I go into the country,
    I see those slain by the sword;
  if I go into the city,
    I see the ravages of famine.
  Both prophet and priest
    have gone to a land they know not.' "

19 Have you rejected Judah completely?
    Do you despise Zion?
  Why have you afflicted us
    so that we cannot be healed?
  We hoped for peace
    but no good has come,
  for a time of healing
    but there is only terror.
20 We acknowledge our wickedness, LORD,
    and the guilt of our ancestors;
  we have indeed sinned against you.
21 For the sake of your name do not
      despise us;
  do not dishonor your glorious throne.

a 14 Or *visions, worthless divinations*

Remember your covenant with us
   and do not break it.
22 Do any of the worthless idols of the
      nations bring rain?
   Do the skies themselves send down
      showers?
   No, it is you, Lord our God.
   Therefore our hope is in you,
      for you are the one who does all this.

15 Then the Lord said to me: "Even if Moses and Samuel were to stand before me, my heart would not go out to this people. Send them away from my presence! Let them go! 2 And if they ask you, 'Where shall we go?' tell them, 'This is what the Lord says:

   " 'Those destined for death, to death;
   those for the sword, to the sword;
   those for starvation, to starvation;
   those for captivity, to captivity.'

3 "I will send four kinds of destroyers against them," declares the Lord, "the sword to kill and the dogs to drag away and the birds and the wild animals to devour and destroy. 4 I will make them abhorrent to all the kingdoms of the earth because of what Manasseh son of Hezekiah king of Judah did in Jerusalem.

5 "Who will have pity on you, Jerusalem?
   Who will mourn for you?
   Who will stop to ask how you are?
6 You have rejected me," declares the
      Lord.
   "You keep on backsliding.
   So I will lay hands on you and destroy
      you;
   I am tired of holding back.
7 I will winnow them with a winnowing
      fork
      at the city gates of the land.
   I will bring bereavement and destruction
      on my people,
      for they have not changed their ways.
8 I will make their widows more numerous
      than the sand of the sea.
   At midday I will bring a destroyer
      against the mothers of their young
         men;
   suddenly I will bring down on them
      anguish and terror.

9 The mother of seven will grow faint
      and breathe her last.
   Her sun will set while it is still day;
      she will be disgraced and humiliated.
   I will put the survivors to the sword
      before their enemies,"
                    declares the Lord.

10 Alas, my mother, that you gave me birth,
      a man with whom the whole land
         strives and contends!
   I have neither lent nor borrowed,
      yet everyone curses me.

11 The Lord said,

   "Surely I will deliver you for a good
         purpose;
      surely I will make your enemies plead
         with you
      in times of disaster and times of
         distress.

12 "Can anyone break iron—
      iron from the north—or bronze?

13 "Your wealth and your treasures
      I will give as plunder, without charge,
   because of all your sins
      throughout your country.
14 I will enslave you to your enemies
      in*a* a land you do not know,
   for my anger will kindle a fire
      that will burn against you."

15 Lord, you understand;
      remember me and care for me.
      Avenge me on my persecutors.
   You are long-suffering—do not take me
         away;
      think of how I suffer reproach for your
         sake.
16 When your words came, I ate them;
      they were my joy and my heart's
         delight,
   for I bear your name,
      Lord God Almighty.
17 I never sat in the company of revelers,
      never made merry with them;
   I sat alone because your hand was on me
      and you had filled me with
         indignation.
18 Why is my pain unending
      and my wound grievous and
         incurable?

---

a 14 Some Hebrew manuscripts, Septuagint and Syriac (see also Jer. 17:4); most Hebrew manuscripts
I will cause your enemies to bring you / into

You are to me like a deceptive brook,
  like a spring that fails.

¹⁹Therefore this is what the LORD says:

"If you repent, I will restore you
  that you may serve me;
if you utter worthy, not worthless,
    words,
  you will be my spokesman.
Let this people turn to you,
  but you must not turn to them.
²⁰I will make you a wall to this people,
  a fortified wall of bronze;
they will fight against you
  but will not overcome you,
for I am with you
  to rescue and save you,"
                    declares the LORD.
²¹"I will save you from the hands of the
    wicked
  and deliver you from the grasp of the
    cruel."

Day of Disaster

16 Then the word of the LORD came to me: ²"You must not marry and have sons or daughters in this place." ³For this is what the LORD says about the sons and daughters born in this land and about the women who are their mothers and the men who are their fathers: ⁴"They will die of deadly diseases. They will not be mourned or buried but will be like dung lying on the ground. They will perish by sword and famine, and their dead bodies will become food for the birds and the wild animals."

⁵For this is what the LORD says: "Do not enter a house where there is a funeral meal; do not go to mourn or show sympathy, because I have withdrawn my blessing, my love and my pity from this people," declares the LORD. ⁶"Both high and low will die in this land. They will not be buried or mourned, nor will people cut themselves or shave their heads for them. ⁷No one will offer food to comfort those who mourn for the dead—not even for a father or a mother—nor will anyone give them a drink to console them.

⁸"And do not enter a house where there is feasting and sit down to eat and drink. ⁹For this is what the LORD Almighty, the God of Israel, says: Before your eyes and in your days I will bring an end to the sounds of joy and gladness and to the voices of bride and bridegroom in this place.

¹⁰"When you tell these people all this and they ask you, 'Why has the LORD decreed such a great disaster against us? What wrong have we done? What sin have we committed against the LORD our God?' ¹¹then say to them, 'It is because your ancestors forsook me,' declares the LORD, 'and followed other gods and served and worshiped them. They forsook me and did not keep my law. ¹²But you have behaved more wickedly than your ancestors. See how all of you are following the stubbornness of your evil hearts instead of obeying me. ¹³So I will throw you out of this land into a land neither you nor your ancestors have known, and there you will serve other gods day and night, for I will show you no favor.'

¹⁴"However, the days are coming," declares the LORD, "when people will no longer say, 'As surely as the LORD lives, who brought the Israelites up out of Egypt,' ¹⁵but they will say, 'As surely as the LORD lives, who brought the Israelites up out of the land of the north and out of all the countries where he had banished them.' For I will restore them to the land I gave their ancestors.

¹⁶"But now I will send for many fishermen," declares the LORD, "and they will catch them. After that I will send for many hunters, and they will hunt them down on every mountain and hill and from the crevices of the rocks. ¹⁷My eyes are on all their ways; they are not hidden from me, nor is their sin concealed from my eyes. ¹⁸I will repay them double for their wickedness and their sin, because they have defiled my land with the lifeless forms of their vile images and have filled my inheritance with their detestable idols."

¹⁹LORD, my strength and my fortress,
  my refuge in time of distress,
to you the nations will come
  from the ends of the earth and say,
"Our ancestors possessed nothing but
      false gods,
  worthless idols that did them no
      good.
²⁰Do people make their own gods?
  Yes, but they are not gods!"

²¹"Therefore I will teach them—
  this time I will teach them
  my power and might.

Then they will know
that my name is the LORD.

17

"Judah's sin is engraved with an
iron tool,
inscribed with a flint point,
on the tablets of their hearts
and on the horns of their altars.
² Even their children remember
their altars and Asherah poles*a*
beside the spreading trees
and on the high hills.
³ My mountain in the land
and your*b* wealth and all your
treasures
I will give away as plunder,
together with your high places,
because of sin throughout your
country.
⁴ Through your own fault you will lose
the inheritance I gave you.
I will enslave you to your enemies
in a land you do not know,
for you have kindled my anger,
and it will burn forever."

⁵ This is what the LORD says:

"Cursed are those who trust in mortals,
who depend on flesh for their
strength
and whose hearts turn away from the
LORD.
⁶ They will be like a bush in the
wastelands;
they will not see prosperity when it
comes.
They will dwell in the parched places of
the desert,
in a salt land where no one lives.

⁷ "But blessed are those who trust in the
LORD,
whose confidence is in him.
⁸ They will be like a tree planted by the
water
that sends out its roots by the stream.
It does not fear when heat comes;
its leaves are always green.
It has no worries in a year of drought
and never fails to bear fruit."

⁹ The heart is deceitful above all things
and beyond cure.
Who can understand it?

¹⁰ "I the LORD search the heart
and examine the mind,
to reward everyone according to their
conduct,
according to what their deeds
deserve."

¹¹ Like a partridge that hatches eggs it did
not lay
are those who gain riches by unjust
means.
When their lives are half gone, their
riches will desert them,
and in the end they will prove to be
fools.

¹² A glorious throne, exalted from the
beginning,
is the place of our sanctuary.
¹³ LORD, you are the hope of Israel;
all who forsake you will be put to
shame.
Those who turn away from you will be
written in the dust
because they have forsaken the LORD,
the spring of living water.

¹⁴ Heal me, LORD, and I will be healed;
save me and I will be saved,
for you are the one I praise.
¹⁵ They keep saying to me,
"Where is the word of the LORD?
Let it now be fulfilled!"
¹⁶ I have not run away from being your
shepherd;
you know I have not desired the day
of despair.
What passes my lips is open before
you.
¹⁷ Do not be a terror to me;
you are my refuge in the day of
disaster.
¹⁸ Let my persecutors be put to shame,
but keep me from shame;
let them be terrified,
but keep me from terror.
Bring on them the day of disaster;
destroy them with double destruction.

Keeping the Sabbath Day Holy

¹⁹ This is what the LORD said to me: "Go
and stand at the gate of the people, through
which the kings of Judah go in and out;
stand also at all the other gates of Jerusa-

---

a 2 That is, wooden symbols of the goddess Asherah
land. / Your   *b 2,3* Or hills / ³and the mountains of the

THURSDAY

You Can't Trust Your Heart

Jeremiah 17:1–18 or 17:9–10

William Guthrie {ad 1620–1655}

The damp mossy meadow is deceitful. Its fresh and glossy carpet invites the traveler to leave the rough moorland and, at the first step, horse and rider are buried in the soggy quagmire. The sea is deceitful. What rage, what stormy passions sleep in its quiet heart. And how often does it cast the boat that it received into its arms with sunny smiles a wreck upon the shore! The morning is often deceitful. With the bright promise of a brilliant day, it lures us from home. Then the sky before noon begins to thicken; the sun looks sickly; the sluggish, heavily-laden clouds gather upon the hilltops; ... The desert is deceitful. It mocks the traveler with its mirage ... Faint, weary, parched, perishing with thirst, they turn to bathe and drink; and they exhaust what little strength remains in pursuit of a phantom! Oh unhappy traveler that has turned to die.

Deceitful above meadow or sea, sky or enchanting desert, is the heart of man. I know of no more marked or melancholy proof of this than that afforded by our light treatment of such weighty matters as sin and judgment. There is no exaggeration in the prophet's language, "The heart is deceitful above all things and beyond cure."

Juanita Bynum

Is this verse talking about someone who deals with "little ill feelings" against someone else? What kind of heart is this verse talking about? Why is the church in the position now of not realizing we need a new heart? Why do we feel that by getting our outward appearance "right," we are getting somewhere with God?

It is because man looks outside, but God looks within—at the heart. It is our hearts that God is coming back for—nothing else. The heart—not the mind—determines whether or not you enter the kingdom of God.

We should not be concerned with outer things. We should focus on what is inside. When we get the "inside" to line up with God's Word, we will change! God will give us a new heart, and this heart will begin to manifest on the outer man just as the old heart works from the inside out.

reflection

1. What do you think people mean when they say to "follow your heart"?

2. When has "following your heart" led you into ignoring, justifying or rationalizing your sin?

3. What cure does God offer for your deceitful heart?

For your next devotional reading, go to page 884.

866 || jeremiah 17:20

lem. ²⁰Say to them, 'Hear the word of the LORD, you kings of Judah and all people of Judah and everyone living in Jerusalem who come through these gates. ²¹This is what the LORD says: Be careful not to carry a load on the Sabbath day or bring it through the gates of Jerusalem. ²²Do not bring a load out of your houses or do any work on the Sabbath, but keep the Sabbath day holy, as I commanded your ancestors. ²³Yet they did not listen or pay attention; they were stiff-necked and would not listen or respond to discipline. ²⁴But if you are careful to obey me, declares the LORD, and bring no load through the gates of this city on the Sabbath, but keep the Sabbath day holy by not doing any work on it, ²⁵then kings who sit on David's throne will come through the gates of this city with their officials. They and their officials will come riding in chariots and on horses, accompanied by the men of Judah and those living in Jerusalem, and this city will be inhabited forever. ²⁶People will come from the towns of Judah and the villages around Jerusalem, from the territory of Benjamin and the western foothills, from the hill country and the Negev, bringing burnt offerings and sacrifices, grain offerings and incense, and bringing thank offerings to the house of the LORD. ²⁷But if you do not obey me to keep the Sabbath day holy by not carrying any load as you come through the gates of Jerusalem on the Sabbath day, then I will kindle an unquenchable fire in the gates of Jerusalem that will consume her fortresses.' "

At the Potter's House

18 This is the word that came to Jeremiah from the LORD: ²"Go down to the potter's house, and there I will give you my message." ³So I went down to the potter's house, and I saw him working at the wheel. ⁴But the pot he was shaping from the clay was marred in his hands; so the potter formed it into another pot, shaping it as seemed best to him.

⁵Then the word of the LORD came to me. ⁶He said, "Can I not do with you, house of Israel, as this potter does?" declares the LORD. "Like clay in the hand of the potter, so are you in my hand, house of Israel. ⁷If at any time I announce that a nation or king-

dom is to be uprooted, torn down and destroyed, ⁸and if that nation I warned repents of its evil, then I will relent and not inflict on it the disaster I had planned. ⁹And if at another time I announce that a nation or kingdom is to be built up and planted, ¹⁰and if it does evil in my sight and does not obey me, then I will reconsider the good I had intended to do for it.

¹¹"Now therefore say to the people of Judah and those living in Jerusalem, 'This is what the LORD says: Look! I am preparing a disaster for you and devising a plan against you. So turn from your evil ways, each one of you, and reform your ways and your actions.' ¹²But they will reply, 'It's no use. We will continue with our own plans; we will all follow the stubbornness of our evil hearts.' "

¹³Therefore this is what the LORD says:

"Inquire among the nations:
    Who has ever heard anything like
        this?
A most horrible thing has been done
    by Virgin Israel.
¹⁴Does the snow of Lebanon
    ever vanish from its rocky slopes?
Do its cool waters from distant sources
    ever cease to flow?ᵃ
¹⁵Yet my people have forgotten me;
    they burn incense to worthless idols,
which made them stumble in their ways,
    in the ancient paths.
They made them walk in byways,
    on roads not built up.
¹⁶Their land will be an object of horror
    and of lasting scorn;
all who pass by will be appalled
    and will shake their heads.
¹⁷Like a wind from the east,
    I will scatter them before their
        enemies;
I will show them my back and not my
        face
    in the day of their disaster."

¹⁸They said, "Come, let's make plans against Jeremiah; for the teaching of the law by the priest will not cease, nor will counsel from the wise, nor the word from the prophets. So come, let's attack him with our tongues and pay no attention to anything he says."

ᵃ 14 The meaning of the Hebrew for this sentence is uncertain.

¹⁹ Listen to me, Lᴏʀᴅ;
  hear what my accusers are saying!
²⁰ Should good be repaid with evil?
  Yet they have dug a pit for me.
  Remember that I stood before you
    and spoke in their behalf
    to turn your wrath away from them.
²¹ So give their children over to famine;
  hand them over to the power of the
    sword.
  Let their wives be made childless and
    widows;
    let their men be put to death,
    their young men slain by the sword in
      battle.
²² Let a cry be heard from their houses
  when you suddenly bring invaders
    against them,
  for they have dug a pit to capture me
    and have hidden snares for my feet.
²³ But you, Lᴏʀᴅ, know
  all their plots to kill me.
  Do not forgive their crimes
    or blot out their sins from your sight.
  Let them be overthrown before you;
    deal with them in the time of your
      anger.

19 This is what the Lᴏʀᴅ says: "Go and buy a clay jar from a potter. Take along some of the elders of the people and of the priests ²and go out to the Valley of Ben Hinnom, near the entrance of the Potsherd Gate. There proclaim the words I tell you, ³and say, 'Hear the word of the Lᴏʀᴅ, you kings of Judah and people of Jerusalem. This is what the Lᴏʀᴅ Almighty, the God of Israel, says: Listen! I am going to bring a disaster on this place that will make the ears of everyone who hears of it tingle. ⁴For they have forsaken me and made this a place of foreign gods; they have burned incense in it to gods that neither they nor their ancestors nor the kings of Judah ever knew, and they have filled this place with the blood of the innocent. ⁵They have built the high places of Baal to burn their children in the fire as offerings to Baal—something I did not command or mention, nor did it enter my mind. ⁶So beware, the days are coming, declares the Lᴏʀᴅ, when people will no longer call this place Topheth or the Valley of Ben Hinnom, but the Valley of Slaughter.

⁷ "'In this place I will ruinᵃ the plans of Judah and Jerusalem. I will make them fall by the sword before their enemies, at the hands of those who seek their lives, and I will give their carcasses as food to the birds and the wild animals. ⁸I will devastate this city and make it an object of horror and scorn; all who pass by will be appalled and will scoff because of all its wounds. ⁹I will make them eat the flesh of their sons and daughters, and they will eat one another's flesh because their enemies will press the siege so hard against them to destroy them.'

¹⁰ "Then break the jar while those who go with you are watching, ¹¹and say to them, 'This is what the Lᴏʀᴅ Almighty says: I will smash this nation and this city just as this potter's jar is smashed and cannot be repaired. They will bury the dead in Topheth until there is no more room. ¹²This is what I will do to this place and to those who live here, declares the Lᴏʀᴅ. I will make this city like Topheth. ¹³The houses in Jerusalem and those of the kings of Judah will be defiled like this place, Topheth—all the houses where they burned incense on the roofs to all the starry hosts and poured out drink offerings to other gods.' "

¹⁴ Jeremiah then returned from Topheth, where the Lᴏʀᴅ had sent him to prophesy, and stood in the court of the Lᴏʀᴅ's temple and said to all the people, ¹⁵"This is what the Lᴏʀᴅ Almighty, the God of Israel, says: 'Listen! I am going to bring on this city and all the villages around it every disaster I pronounced against them, because they were stiff-necked and would not listen to my words.' "

Jeremiah and Pashhur

20 When the priest Pashhur son of Immer, the official in charge of the temple of the Lᴏʀᴅ, heard Jeremiah prophesying these things, ²he had Jeremiah the prophet beaten and put in the stocks at the Upper Gate of Benjamin at the Lᴏʀᴅ's temple. ³The next day, when Pashhur released him from the stocks, Jeremiah said to him, "The Lᴏʀᴅ's name for you is not Pashhur, but Terror on Every Side. ⁴For this is what the Lᴏʀᴅ says: 'I will make you a terror to yourself and to all your friends; with your own eyes you will see them fall by the

---

ᵃ 7 The Hebrew for *ruin* sounds like the Hebrew for *jar* (see verses 1 and 10).

sword of their enemies. I will give all Judah into the hands of the king of Babylon, who will carry them away to Babylon or put them to the sword. ⁵I will deliver all the wealth of this city into the hands of their enemies—all its products, all its valuables and all the treasures of the kings of Judah. They will take it away as plunder and carry it off to Babylon. ⁶And you, Pashhur, and all who live in your house will go into exile to Babylon. There you will die and be buried, you and all your friends to whom you have prophesied lies.' "

Jeremiah's Complaint

⁷You deceived*a* me, LORD, and I was
    deceived*a*;
  you overpowered me and prevailed.
 I am ridiculed all day long;
    everyone mocks me.
⁸Whenever I speak, I cry out
    proclaiming violence and destruction.
 So the word of the LORD has brought me
    insult and reproach all day long.
⁹But if I say, "I will not mention his word
    or speak anymore in his name,"
 his word is in my heart like a fire,
    a fire shut up in my bones.
 I am weary of holding it in;
    indeed, I cannot.
¹⁰I hear many whispering,
    "Terror on every side!
    Denounce him! Let's denounce him!"
 All my friends
    are waiting for me to slip, saying,
 "Perhaps he will be deceived;
    then we will prevail over him
    and take our revenge on him."

¹¹But the LORD is with me like a mighty
    warrior;
  so my persecutors will stumble and
    not prevail.
 They will fail and be thoroughly
    disgraced;
    their dishonor will never be forgotten.
¹²LORD Almighty, you who examine the
    righteous
  and probe the heart and mind,
 let me see your vengeance on them,
    for to you I have committed my
    cause.

¹³Sing to the LORD!
    Give praise to the LORD!
 He rescues the life of the needy
    from the hands of the wicked.

¹⁴Cursed be the day I was born!
    May the day my mother bore me not
    be blessed!
¹⁵Cursed be the man who brought my
    father the news,
  who made him very glad, saying,
    "A child is born to you—a son!"
¹⁶May that man be like the towns
    the LORD overthrew without pity.
  May he hear wailing in the morning,
    a battle cry at noon.
¹⁷For he did not kill me in the womb,
    with my mother as my grave,
    her womb enlarged forever.
¹⁸Why did I ever come out of the womb
    to see trouble and sorrow
    and to end my days in shame?

God Rejects Zedekiah's Request

21 The word came to Jeremiah from the LORD when King Zedekiah sent to him Pashhur son of Malkijah and the priest Zephaniah son of Maaseiah. They said: ²"Inquire now of the LORD for us because Nebuchadnezzar*b* king of Babylon is attacking us. Perhaps the LORD will perform wonders for us as in times past so that he will withdraw from us."

³But Jeremiah answered them, "Tell Zedekiah, ⁴'This is what the LORD, the God of Israel, says: I am about to turn against you the weapons of war that are in your hands, which you are using to fight the king of Babylon and the Babylonians*c* who are outside the wall besieging you. And I will gather them inside this city. ⁵I myself will fight against you with an outstretched hand and a mighty arm in furious anger and in great wrath. ⁶I will strike down those who live in this city—both people and animals—and they will die of a terrible plague. ⁷After that, declares the LORD, I will give Zedekiah king of Judah, his officials and the people in this city who survive the plague, sword and famine, into the hands of Nebuchadnezzar king of Babylon and to their enemies who seek their lives. He will put them to the sword; he will show them no mercy or pity or compassion.'

a 7 Or *persuaded*   *b 2* Hebrew *Nebuchadrezzar,* of which *Nebuchadnezzar* is a variant; here and often in Jeremiah and Ezekiel   *c 4* Or *Chaldeans;* also in verse 9

[8]"Furthermore, tell the people, 'This is what the LORD says: See, I am setting before you the way of life and the way of death. [9]Whoever stays in this city will die by the sword, famine or plague. But whoever goes out and surrenders to the Babylonians who are besieging you will live; they will escape with their lives. [10]I have determined to do this city harm and not good, declares the LORD. It will be given into the hands of the king of Babylon, and he will destroy it with fire.'

[11]"Moreover, say to the royal house of Judah, 'Hear the word of the LORD. [12]This is what the LORD says to you, house of David:

" 'Administer justice every morning;
    rescue from the hands of their
        oppressors
    those who have been robbed,
or my wrath will break out and burn like
        fire
    because of the evil you have done—
    burn with no one to quench it.
[13]I am against you, Jerusalem,
    you who live above this valley
    on the rocky plateau, declares the
        LORD—
you who say, "Who can come against
        us?
    Who can enter our refuge?"
[14]I will punish you as your deeds deserve,
    declares the LORD.
I will kindle a fire in your forests
    that will consume everything around
        you.' "

Judgment Against Wicked Kings

22 This is what the LORD says: "Go down to the palace of the king of Judah and proclaim this message there: [2]'Hear the word of the LORD to you, king of Judah, you who sit on David's throne—you, your officials and your people who come through these gates. [3]This is what the LORD says: Do what is just and right. Rescue from the hands of their oppressors those who have been robbed. Do no wrong or violence to the foreigner, the fatherless or the widow, and do not shed innocent blood in this place. [4]For if you are careful to carry out these commands, then kings who sit on David's throne will come through the gates of this palace, riding in chariots and on

horses, accompanied by their officials and their people. [5]But if you do not obey these commands, declares the LORD, I swear by myself that this palace will become a ruin.' "

[6]For this is what the LORD says about the palace of the king of Judah:

"Though you are like Gilead to me,
    like the summit of Lebanon,
I will surely make you like a wasteland,
    like towns not inhabited.
[7]I will send destroyers against you,
    each man with his weapons,
and they will cut up your fine cedar
        beams
    and throw them into the fire.

[8]"People from many nations will pass by this city and will ask one another, 'Why has the LORD done such a thing to this great city?' [9]And the answer will be: 'Because they have forsaken the covenant of the LORD their God and have worshiped and served other gods.' "

[10]Do not weep for the dead ⌊king⌋ or
        mourn his loss;
    rather, weep bitterly for him who is
        exiled,
because he will never return
    nor see his native land again.

[11]For this is what the LORD says about Shallum[a] son of Josiah, who succeeded his father as king of Judah but has gone from this place: "He will never return. [12]He will die in the place where they have led him captive; he will not see this land again."

[13]"Woe to him who builds his palace by
        unrighteousness,
    his upper rooms by injustice,
making his subjects work for nothing,
    not paying them for their labor.
[14]He says, 'I will build myself a great
        palace
    with spacious upper rooms.'
So he makes large windows in it,
    panels it with cedar
    and decorates it in red.

[15]"Does it make you a king
    to have more and more cedar?
Did not your father have food and drink?
    He did what was right and just,
    so all went well with him.

---

[a] 11 Also called Jehoahaz

¹⁶He defended the cause of the poor and
needy,
and so all went well.
Is that not what it means to know me?"
declares the LORD.
¹⁷"But your eyes and your heart
are set only on dishonest gain,
on shedding innocent blood
and on oppression and extortion."

¹⁸Therefore this is what the LORD says about
Jehoiakim son of Josiah king of Judah:

"They will not mourn for him:
'Alas, my brother! Alas, my sister!'
They will not mourn for him:
'Alas, my master! Alas, his splendor!'
¹⁹He will have the burial of a donkey—
dragged away and thrown
outside the gates of Jerusalem."

²⁰"Go up to Lebanon and cry out,
let your voice be heard in Bashan,
cry out from Abarim,
for all your allies are crushed.
²¹I warned you when you felt secure,
but you said, 'I will not listen!'
This has been your way from your youth;
you have not obeyed me.
²²The wind will drive all your shepherds
away,
and your allies will go into exile.
Then you will be ashamed and disgraced
because of all your wickedness.
²³You who live in 'Lebanon,ᵃ'
who are nestled in cedar buildings,
how you will groan when pangs come
upon you,
pain like that of a woman in labor!

²⁴"As surely as I live," declares the LORD,
"even if you, Jehoiachinᵇ son of Jehoiakim
king of Judah, were a signet ring on my right
hand, I would still pull you off. ²⁵I will deliver you into the hands of those who seek your
life, those you fear—Nebuchadnezzar king
of Babylon and the Babylonians.ᶜ ²⁶I will
hurl you and the mother who gave you birth
into another country, where neither of you
was born, and there you both will die. ²⁷You
will never come back to the land you long to
return to,"

²⁸Is this man Jehoiachin a despised,
broken pot,

an object no one wants?
Why will he and his children be hurled
out,
cast into a land they do not know?
²⁹O land, land, land,
hear the word of the LORD!
³⁰This is what the LORD says:
"Record this man as if childless,
a man who will not prosper in his
lifetime,
for none of his offspring will prosper,
none will sit on the throne of David
or rule anymore in Judah."

The Righteous Branch

23 "Woe to the shepherds who are
destroying and scattering the
sheep of my pasture!" declares
the LORD. ²Therefore this is what the LORD,
the God of Israel, says to the shepherds who
tend my people: "Because you have scattered my flock and driven them away and
have not bestowed care on them, I will bestow punishment on you for the evil you
have done," declares the LORD. ³"I myself
will gather the remnant of my flock out of all
the countries where I have driven them and
will bring them back to their pasture, where
they will be fruitful and increase in number.
⁴I will place shepherds over them who will
tend them, and they will no longer be afraid
or terrified, nor will any be missing," declares the LORD.

⁵"The days are coming," declares the
LORD,
"when I will raise up for Davidᵈ a
righteous Branch,
a King who will reign wisely
and do what is just and right in the
land.
⁶In his days Judah will be saved
and Israel will live in safety.
This is the name by which he will be
called:
The LORD Our Righteous Savior.

⁷"So then, the days are coming," declares
the LORD, "when people will no longer say,
'As surely as the LORD lives, who brought the
Israelites up out of Egypt,' ⁸but they will say,
'As surely as the LORD lives, who brought the
descendants of Israel up out of the land of

ᵃ 23 That is, the palace in Jerusalem (see 1 Kings 7:2)   ᵇ 24 Hebrew Koniah, a variant of Jehoiachin;
also in verse 28   ᶜ 25 Or Chaldeans   ᵈ 5 Or up from David's line

the north and out of all the countries where he had banished them.' Then they will live in their own land."

Lying Prophets
9Concerning the prophets:

My heart is broken within me;
    all my bones tremble.
I am like a drunken man,
    like one overcome by wine,
because of the LORD
    and his holy words.
10The land is full of adulterers;
    because of the curse[a] the land lies parched
    and the pastures in the wilderness are withered.
The ⌊prophets⌋ follow an evil course
    and use their power unjustly.

11"Both prophet and priest are godless;
    even in my temple I find their wickedness,"
            declares the LORD.
12"Therefore their path will become slippery;
    they will be banished to darkness
    and there they will fall.
I will bring disaster on them
    in the year they are punished,"
            declares the LORD.

13"Among the prophets of Samaria
    I saw this repulsive thing:
They prophesied by Baal
    and led my people Israel astray.
14And among the prophets of Jerusalem
    I have seen something horrible:
They commit adultery and live a lie.
They strengthen the hands of evildoers,
    so that none of them turn from their wickedness.
They are all like Sodom to me;
    the people of Jerusalem are like Gomorrah."

15Therefore, this is what the LORD Almighty says concerning the prophets:

"I will make them eat bitter food
    and drink poisoned water,
because from the prophets of Jerusalem
    ungodliness has spread throughout the land."

16This is what the LORD Almighty says:

"Do not listen to what the prophets are prophesying to you;
    they fill you with false hopes.
They speak visions from their own minds,
    not from the mouth of the LORD.
17They keep saying to those who despise me,
    'The LORD says: You will have peace.'
And to all who follow the stubbornness of their hearts
    they say, 'No harm will come to you.'
18But which of them has stood in the council of the LORD
    to see or to hear his word?
Who has listened and heard his word?
19See, the storm of the LORD
    will burst out in wrath,
a whirlwind swirling down
    on the heads of the wicked.
20The anger of the LORD will not turn back
    until he fully accomplishes
    the purposes of his heart.
In days to come
    you will understand it clearly.
21I did not send these prophets,
    yet they have run with their message;
I did not speak to them,
    yet they have prophesied.
22But if they had stood in my council,
    they would have proclaimed my words to my people
and would have turned them from their evil ways
    and from their evil deeds.

23"Am I only a God nearby,"
            declares the LORD,
    "and not a God far away?
24Who can hide in secret places
    so that I cannot see them?"
            declares the LORD.
    "Do not I fill heaven and earth?"
            declares the LORD.

25"I have heard what the prophets say who prophesy lies in my name. They say, 'I had a dream! I had a dream!' 26How long will this continue in the hearts of these lying prophets, who prophesy the delusions of

a 10 Or *because of these things*

their own minds? [27]They think the dreams they tell one another will make my people forget my name, just as their ancestors forgot my name through Baal worship. [28]Let the prophets who have dreams tell their dreams, but let the one who has my word speak it faithfully. For what has straw to do with grain?" declares the LORD. [29]"Is not my word like fire," declares the LORD, "and like a hammer that breaks a rock in pieces?

[30]"Therefore," declares the LORD, "I am against the prophets who steal from one another words supposedly from me. [31]Yes," declares the LORD, "I am against the prophets who wag their own tongues and yet declare, 'The LORD declares.' [32]Indeed, I am against those who prophesy false dreams," declares the LORD. "They tell them and lead my people astray with their reckless lies, yet I did not send or appoint them. They do not benefit these people in the least," declares the LORD.

False Prophecy

[33]"When these people, or a prophet or a priest, ask you, 'What is the message from the LORD?' say to them, 'What message? I will forsake you, declares the LORD.' [34]If a prophet or a priest or anyone else claims, 'This is a message from the LORD,' I will punish them and their households. [35]This is what each of you keeps saying to your friends and other Israelites: 'What is the LORD's answer?' or 'What has the LORD spoken?' [36]But you must not mention 'a message from the LORD' again, because everyone's own word becomes a message from God. So you distort the words of the living God, the LORD Almighty, our God. [37]This is what you keep saying to a prophet: 'What is the LORD's answer to you?' or 'What has the LORD spoken?' [38]Although you claim, 'This is a message from the LORD,' this is what the LORD says: You used the words, 'This is a message from the LORD,' even though I told you that you must not claim, 'This is a message from the LORD.' [39]Therefore, I will surely forget you and cast you out of my presence along with the city I gave to you and your ancestors. [40]I will bring on you everlasting disgrace—everlasting shame that will not be forgotten."

Two Baskets of Figs

24 After Jehoiachin[a] son of Jehoiakim king of Judah and the officials, the artisans and the other skilled workers of Judah were carried into exile from Jerusalem to Babylon by Nebuchadnezzar king of Babylon, the LORD showed me two baskets of figs placed in front of the temple of the LORD. [2]One basket had very good figs, like those that ripen early; the other basket had very bad figs, so bad they could not be eaten.

[3]Then the LORD asked me, "What do you see, Jeremiah?"

"Figs," I answered. "The good ones are very good, but the bad ones are so bad they cannot be eaten."

[4]Then the word of the LORD came to me: [5]"This is what the LORD, the God of Israel, says: 'Like these good figs, I regard as good the exiles from Judah, whom I sent away from this place to the land of the Babylonians.[b] [6]My eyes will watch over them for their good, and I will bring them back to this land. I will build them up and not tear them down; I will plant them and not uproot them. [7]I will give them a heart to know me, that I am the LORD. They will be my people, and I will be their God, for they will return to me with all their heart.

[8]" 'But like the bad figs, which are so bad they cannot be eaten,' says the LORD, 'so will I deal with Zedekiah king of Judah, his officials and the survivors from Jerusalem, whether they remain in this land or live in Egypt. [9]I will make them abhorrent and an offense to all the kingdoms of the earth, a reproach and a byword, a curse[c] and an object of ridicule, wherever I banish them. [10]I will send the sword, famine and plague against them until they are destroyed from the land I gave to them and their ancestors.' "

Seventy Years of Captivity

25 The word came to Jeremiah concerning all the people of Judah in the fourth year of Jehoiakim son of Josiah king of Judah, which was the first year of Nebuchadnezzar king of Babylon. [2]So Jeremiah the prophet said to all the people of Judah and to all those living

---

a 1 Hebrew *Jeconiah*, a variant of *Jehoiachin*   *b 5* Or *Chaldeans*   *c 9* That is, their names will be used in cursing (see Jer. 29:22); or, others will see that they are cursed.

in Jerusalem: ³For twenty-three years—from the thirteenth year of Josiah son of Amon king of Judah until this very day—the word of the LORD has come to me and I have spoken to you again and again, but you have not listened.

⁴And though the LORD has sent all his servants the prophets to you again and again, you have not listened or paid any attention. ⁵They said, "Turn now, each of you, from your evil ways and your evil practices, and you can stay in the land the LORD gave to you and your ancestors for ever and ever. ⁶Do not follow other gods to serve and worship them; do not arouse my anger with what your hands have made. Then I will not harm you."

⁷"But you did not listen to me," declares the LORD, "and you have aroused my anger with what your hands have made, and you have brought harm to yourselves."

⁸Therefore the LORD Almighty says this: "Because you have not listened to my words, ⁹I will summon all the peoples of the north and my servant Nebuchadnezzar king of Babylon," declares the LORD, "and I will bring them against this land and its inhabitants and against all the surrounding nations. I will completely destroy^a them and make them an object of horror and scorn, and an everlasting ruin. ¹⁰I will banish from them the sounds of joy and gladness, the voices of bride and bridegroom, the sound of millstones and the light of the lamp. ¹¹This whole country will become a desolate wasteland, and these nations will serve the king of Babylon seventy years.

¹²"But when the seventy years are fulfilled, I will punish the king of Babylon and his nation, the land of the Babylonians,^{b} for their guilt," declares the LORD, "and will make it desolate forever. ¹³I will bring on that land all the things I have spoken against it, all that are written in this book and prophesied by Jeremiah against all the nations. ¹⁴They themselves will be enslaved by many nations and great kings; I will repay them according to their deeds and the work of their hands."

The Cup of God's Wrath

¹⁵This is what the LORD, the God of Israel, said to me: "Take from my hand this cup filled with the wine of my wrath and make all the nations to whom I send you drink it. ¹⁶When they drink it, they will stagger and go mad because of the sword I will send among them."

¹⁷So I took the cup from the LORD's hand and made all the nations to whom he sent me drink it: ¹⁸Jerusalem and the towns of Judah, its kings and officials, to make them a ruin and an object of horror and scorn, a curse^c—as they are today; ¹⁹Pharaoh king of Egypt, his attendants, his officials and all his people, ²⁰and all the foreign people there; all the kings of Uz; all the kings of the Philistines (those of Ashkelon, Gaza, Ekron, and the people left at Ashdod); ²¹Edom, Moab and Ammon; ²²all the kings of Tyre and Sidon; the kings of the coastlands across the sea; ²³Dedan, Tema, Buz and all who are in distant places^d; ²⁴all the kings of Arabia and all the kings of the foreign people who live in the wilderness; ²⁵all the kings of Zimri, Elam and Media; ²⁶and all the kings of the north, near and far, one after the other—all the kingdoms on the face of the earth. And after all of them, the king of Sheshak^e will drink it too.

²⁷"Then tell them, 'This is what the LORD Almighty, the God of Israel, says: Drink, get drunk and vomit, and fall to rise no more because of the sword I will send among you.' ²⁸But if they refuse to take the cup from your hand and drink, tell them, 'This is what the LORD Almighty says: You must drink it! ²⁹See, I am beginning to bring disaster on the city that bears my Name, and will you indeed go unpunished? You will not go unpunished, for I am calling down a sword on all who live on the earth, declares the LORD Almighty.'

³⁰"Now prophesy all these words against them and say to them:

" 'The LORD will roar from on high;
 he will thunder from his holy dwelling
 and roar mightily against his land.
He will shout like those who tread the
  grapes,

---

^{a} 9 The Hebrew term refers to the irrevocable giving over of things or persons to the LORD, often by totally destroying them. ^{b} 12 Or *Chaldeans* ^{c} 18 That is, their names to be used in cursing (see Jer. 29:22); or, to be seen by others as cursed ^{d} 23 Or *who clip the hair by their foreheads* ^{e} 26 *Sheshak* is a cryptogram for Babylon.

shout against all who live on the
earth.
[31] The tumult will resound to the ends of
the earth,
for the LORD will bring charges
against the nations;
he will bring judgment on all
humankind
and put the wicked to the sword,' "
declares the LORD.

[32] This is what the LORD Almighty says:

"Look! Disaster is spreading
from nation to nation;
a mighty storm is rising
from the ends of the earth."

[33] At that time those slain by the LORD will be
everywhere—from one end of the earth to
the other. They will not be mourned or gathered up or buried, but will be like dung lying
on the ground.

[34] Weep and wail, you shepherds;
roll in the dust, you leaders of the
flock.
For your time to be slaughtered has
come;
you will fall like the best of the rams.[a]
[35] The shepherds will have nowhere to flee,
the leaders of the flock no place to
escape.
[36] Hear the cry of the shepherds,
the wailing of the leaders of the flock,
for the LORD is destroying their
pasture.
[37] The peaceful meadows will be laid waste
because of the fierce anger of the
LORD.
[38] Like a lion he will leave his lair,
and their land will become desolate
because of the sword[b] of the oppressor
and because of the LORD's fierce
anger.

Jeremiah Threatened With Death

26 Early in the reign of Jehoiakim
son of Josiah king of Judah, this
word came from the LORD:
[2] "This is what the LORD says: Stand in the
courtyard of the LORD's house and speak to
all the people of the towns of Judah who
come to worship in the house of the LORD.
Tell them everything I command you; do not
omit a word. [3] Perhaps they will listen and
each will turn from their evil ways. Then I
will relent and not inflict on them the disaster I was planning because of the evil they
have done. [4] Say to them, 'This is what the
LORD says: If you do not listen to me and follow my law, which I have set before you,
[5] and if you do not listen to the words of my
servants the prophets, whom I have sent to
you again and again (though you have not
listened), [6] then I will make this house like
Shiloh and this city a curse[c] among all the
nations of the earth.' "

[7] The priests, the prophets and all the
people heard Jeremiah speak these words in
the house of the LORD. [8] But as soon as Jeremiah finished telling all the people everything the LORD had commanded him to say,
the priests, the prophets and all the people
seized him and said, "You must die! [9] Why do
you prophesy in the LORD's name that this
house will be like Shiloh and this city will be
desolate and deserted?" And all the people
crowded around Jeremiah in the house of
the LORD.

[10] When the officials of Judah heard about
these things, they went up from the royal palace to the house of the LORD and took their
places at the entrance of the New Gate of the
LORD's house. [11] Then the priests and the
prophets said to the officials and all the people, "This man should be sentenced to death
because he has prophesied against this city.
You have heard it with your own ears!"

[12] Then Jeremiah said to all the officials
and all the people: "The LORD sent me to
prophesy against this house and this city all
the things you have heard. [13] Now reform
your ways and your actions and obey the
LORD your God. Then the LORD will relent
and not bring the disaster he has pronounced against you. [14] As for me, I am in
your hands; do with me whatever you think
is good and right. [15] Be assured, however,
that if you put me to death, you will bring
the guilt of innocent blood on yourselves
and on this city and on those who live in it,
for in truth the LORD has sent me to you to
speak all these words in your hearing."

[16] Then the officials and all the people
said to the priests and the prophets, "This

---

a 34 Septuagint; Hebrew *fall and be shattered like fine pottery*   *b 38* Some Hebrew manuscripts and
Septuagint (see also Jer. 46:16 and 50:16); most Hebrew manuscripts *anger*   *c 6* That is, their names
will be used in cursing (see Jer. 29:22); or, others will see that they are cursed.

man should not be sentenced to death! He has spoken to us in the name of the LORD our God."

[17]Some of the elders of the land stepped forward and said to the entire assembly of people, [18]"Micah of Moresheth prophesied in the days of Hezekiah king of Judah. He told all the people of Judah, 'This is what the LORD Almighty says:

" 'Zion will be plowed like a field,
Jerusalem will become a heap of
rubble,
the temple hill a mound overgrown
with thickets.'[a]

[19]"Did Hezekiah king of Judah or anyone else in Judah put him to death? Did not Hezekiah fear the LORD and seek his favor? And did not the LORD relent, so that he did not bring the disaster he pronounced against them? We are about to bring a terrible disaster on ourselves!"

[20](Now Uriah son of Shemaiah from Kiriath Jearim was another man who prophesied in the name of the LORD; he prophesied the same things against this city and this land as Jeremiah did. [21]When King Jehoiakim and all his officers and officials heard his words, the king sought to put him to death. But Uriah heard of it and fled in fear to Egypt. [22]King Jehoiakim, however, sent Elnathan son of Akbor to Egypt, along with some other men. [23]They brought Uriah out of Egypt and took him to King Jehoiakim, who had him struck down with a sword and his body thrown into the burial place of the common people.)

[24]Furthermore, Ahikam son of Shaphan supported Jeremiah, and so he was not handed over to the people to be put to death.

Judah to Serve Nebuchadnezzar

27 Early in the reign of Zedekiah[b] son of Josiah king of Judah, this word came to Jeremiah from the LORD: [2]This is what the LORD said to me: "Make a yoke out of straps and crossbars and put it on your neck. [3]Then send word to the kings of Edom, Moab, Ammon, Tyre and Sidon through the envoys who have come to Jerusalem to Zedekiah king of Judah. [4]Give

them a message for their masters and say, 'This is what the LORD Almighty, the God of Israel, says: "Tell this to your masters: [5]With my great power and outstretched arm I made the earth and its people and the animals that are on it, and I give it to anyone I please. [6]Now I will give all your countries into the hands of my servant Nebuchadnezzar king of Babylon; I will make even the wild animals subject to him. [7]All nations will serve him and his son and his grandson until the time for his land comes; then many nations and great kings will subjugate him.

[8]" ' "If, however, any nation or kingdom will not serve Nebuchadnezzar king of Babylon or bow its neck under his yoke, I will punish that nation with the sword, famine and plague, declares the LORD, until I destroy it by his hand. [9]So do not listen to your prophets, your diviners, your interpreters of dreams, your mediums or your sorcerers who tell you, 'You will not serve the king of Babylon.' [10]They prophesy lies to you that will only serve to remove you far from your lands; I will banish you and you will perish. [11]But if any nation will bow its neck under the yoke of the king of Babylon and serve him, I will let that nation remain in its own land to till it and to live there, declares the LORD." ' "

[12]I gave the same message to Zedekiah king of Judah. I said, "Bow your neck under the yoke of the king of Babylon; serve him and his people, and you will live. [13]Why will you and your people die by the sword, famine and plague with which the LORD has threatened any nation that will not serve the king of Babylon? [14]Do not listen to the words of the prophets who say to you, 'You will not serve the king of Babylon,' for they are prophesying lies to you. [15]'I have not sent them,' declares the LORD. 'They are prophesying lies in my name. Therefore, I will banish you and you will perish, both you and the prophets who prophesy to you.' "

[16]Then I said to the priests and all these people, "This is what the LORD says: Do not listen to the prophets who say, 'Very soon now the articles from the LORD's house will be brought back from Babylon.' They are prophesying lies to you. [17]Do not listen to them. Serve the king of Babylon, and you

---

a 18 Micah 3:12   *b 1* A few Hebrew manuscripts and Syriac (see also Jer. 27:3, 12 and 28:1); most Hebrew manuscripts *Jehoiakim* (Most Septuagint manuscripts do not have this verse).

will live. Why should this city become a ruin? ¹⁸If they are prophets and have the word of the LORD, let them plead with the LORD Almighty that the articles remaining in the house of the LORD and in the palace of the king of Judah and in Jerusalem not be taken to Babylon. ¹⁹For this is what the LORD Almighty says about the pillars, the Sea, the movable stands and the other articles that are left in this city, ²⁰which Nebuchadnezzar king of Babylon did not take away when he carried Jehoiachinᵃ son of Jehoiakim king of Judah into exile from Jerusalem to Babylon, along with all the nobles of Judah and Jerusalem— ²¹yes, this is what the LORD Almighty, the God of Israel, says about the things that are left in the house of the LORD and in the palace of the king of Judah and in Jerusalem: ²²'They will be taken to Babylon and there they will remain until the day I come for them,' declares the LORD. 'Then I will bring them back and restore them to this place.' "

The False Prophet Hananiah

28 In the fifth month of that same year, the fourth year, early in the reign of Zedekiah king of Judah, the prophet Hananiah son of Azzur, who was from Gibeon, said to me in the house of the LORD in the presence of the priests and all the people: ²"This is what the LORD Almighty, the God of Israel, says: 'I will break the yoke of the king of Babylon. ³Within two years I will bring back to this place all the articles of the LORD's house that Nebuchadnezzar king of Babylon removed from here and took to Babylon. ⁴I will also bring back to this place Jehoiachinᵃ son of Jehoiakim king of Judah and all the other exiles from Judah who went to Babylon,' declares the LORD, 'for I will break the yoke of the king of Babylon.' "

⁵Then the prophet Jeremiah replied to the prophet Hananiah before the priests and all the people who were standing in the house of the LORD. ⁶He said, "Amen! May the LORD do so! May the LORD fulfill the words you have prophesied by bringing the articles of the LORD's house and all the exiles back to this place from Babylon. ⁷Nevertheless, listen to what I have to say in your hearing and in the hearing of all the people: ⁸From early

times the prophets who preceded you and me have prophesied war, disaster and plague against many countries and great kingdoms. ⁹But the prophet who prophesies peace will be recognized as one truly sent by the LORD only if his prediction comes true."

¹⁰Then the prophet Hananiah took the yoke off the neck of the prophet Jeremiah and broke it, ¹¹and he said before all the people, "This is what the LORD says: 'In the same way I will break the yoke of Nebuchadnezzar king of Babylon off the neck of all the nations within two years.' " At this, the prophet Jeremiah went on his way.

¹²After the prophet Hananiah had broken the yoke off the neck of the prophet Jeremiah, the word of the LORD came to Jeremiah: ¹³"Go and tell Hananiah, 'This is what the LORD says: You have broken a wooden yoke, but in its place you will get a yoke of iron. ¹⁴This is what the LORD Almighty, the God of Israel, says: I will put an iron yoke on the necks of all these nations to make them serve Nebuchadnezzar king of Babylon, and they will serve him. I will even give him control over the wild animals.' "

¹⁵Then the prophet Jeremiah said to Hananiah the prophet, "Listen, Hananiah! The LORD has not sent you, yet you have persuaded this nation to trust in lies. ¹⁶Therefore, this is what the LORD says: 'I am about to remove you from the face of the earth. This very year you are going to die, because you have preached rebellion against the LORD.' "

¹⁷In the seventh month of that same year, Hananiah the prophet died.

A Letter to the Exiles

29 This is the text of the letter that the prophet Jeremiah sent from Jerusalem to the surviving elders among the exiles and to the priests, the prophets and all the other people Nebuchadnezzar had carried into exile from Jerusalem to Babylon. ²(This was after King Jehoiachinᵃ and the queen mother, the court officials and the leaders of Judah and Jerusalem, the artisans and the other skilled workers had gone into exile from Jerusalem.) ³He entrusted the letter to Elasah son of Shaphan and to Gemariah son of Hilkiah,

---

ᵃ 20,4,2 Hebrew *Jeconiah*, a variant of *Jehoiachin*

whom Zedekiah king of Judah sent to King Nebuchadnezzar in Babylon. It said:

⁴This is what the LORD Almighty, the God of Israel, says to all those I carried into exile from Jerusalem to Babylon: ⁵"Build houses and settle down; plant gardens and eat what they produce. ⁶Marry and have sons and daughters; find wives for your sons and give your daughters in marriage, so that they too may have sons and daughters. Increase in number there; do not decrease. ⁷Also, seek the peace and prosperity of the city to which I have carried you into exile. Pray to the LORD for it, because if it prospers, you too will prosper." ⁸Yes, this is what the LORD Almighty, the God of Israel, says: "Do not let the prophets and diviners among you deceive you. Do not listen to the dreams you encourage them to have. ⁹They are prophesying lies to you in my name. I have not sent them," declares the LORD.

¹⁰This is what the LORD says: "When seventy years are completed for Babylon, I will come to you and fulfill my good promise to bring you back to this place. ¹¹For I know the plans I have for you," declares the LORD, "plans to prosper you and not to harm you, plans to give you hope and a future. ¹²Then you will call on me and come and pray to me, and I will listen to you. ¹³You will seek me and find me when you seek me with all your heart. ¹⁴I will be found by you," declares the LORD, "and will bring you back from captivity.ᵃ I will gather you from all the nations and places where I have banished you," declares the LORD, "and will bring you back to the place from which I carried you into exile."

¹⁵You may say, "The LORD has raised up prophets for us in Babylon," ¹⁶but this is what the LORD says about the king who sits on David's throne and all the people who remain in this city, your fellow citizens who did not go with you into exile— ¹⁷yes, this is what the LORD Almighty says: "I will send the sword, famine and plague against them

and I will make them like figs that are so bad they cannot be eaten. ¹⁸I will pursue them with the sword, famine and plague and will make them abhorrent to all the kingdoms of the earth, a curseᵇ and an object of horror, of scorn and reproach, among all the nations where I drive them. ¹⁹For they have not listened to my words," declares the LORD, "words that I sent to them again and again by my servants the prophets. And you exiles have not listened either," declares the LORD.

²⁰Therefore, hear the word of the LORD, all you exiles whom I have sent away from Jerusalem to Babylon. ²¹This is what the LORD Almighty, the God of Israel, says about Ahab son of Kolaiah and Zedekiah son of Maaseiah, who are prophesying lies to you in my name: "I will deliver them into the hands of Nebuchadnezzar king of Babylon, and he will put them to death before your very eyes. ²²Because of them, all the exiles from Judah who are in Babylon will use this curse: 'May the LORD treat you like Zedekiah and Ahab, whom the king of Babylon burned in the fire.' ²³For they have done outrageous things in Israel; they have committed adultery with their neighbors' wives, and in my name they have uttered lies—which I did not authorize. I know it and am a witness to it," declares the LORD.

Message to Shemaiah

²⁴Tell Shemaiah the Nehelamite, ²⁵"This is what the LORD Almighty, the God of Israel, says: You sent letters in your own name to all the people in Jerusalem, to the priest Zephaniah son of Maaseiah, and to all the other priests. You said to Zephaniah, ²⁶'The LORD has appointed you priest in place of Jehoiada to be in charge of the house of the LORD; you should put any crazy person who acts like a prophet into the stocks and neck-irons. ²⁷So why have you not reprimanded Jeremiah from Anathoth, who poses as a prophet among you? ²⁸He has sent this message to us in Babylon: It will be a long time. Therefore build houses and settle

---

ᵃ 14 Or *will restore your fortunes*   ᵇ 18 That is, their names will be used in cursing (see Jer. 29:22); or, others will see that they are cursed.

down; plant gardens and eat what they produce.' "

²⁹Zephaniah the priest, however, read the letter to Jeremiah the prophet. ³⁰Then the word of the LORD came to Jeremiah: ³¹"Send this message to all the exiles: 'This is what the LORD says about Shemaiah the Nehelamite: Because Shemaiah has prophesied to you, even though I did not send him, and has persuaded you to trust in lies, ³²this is what the LORD says: I will surely punish Shemaiah the Nehelamite and his descendants. He will have no one left among this people, nor will he see the good things I will do for my people, declares the LORD, because he has preached rebellion against me.' "

Restoration of Israel

30 This is the word that came to Jeremiah from the LORD: ²"This is what the LORD, the God of Israel, says: 'Write in a book all the words I have spoken to you. ³The days are coming,' declares the LORD, 'when I will bring my people Israel and Judah back from captivity*ᵃ* and restore them to the land I gave their ancestors to possess,' says the LORD."

⁴These are the words the LORD spoke concerning Israel and Judah: ⁵"This is what the LORD says:

" 'Cries of fear are heard—
    terror, not peace.
⁶Ask and see:
    Can a man bear children?
Then why do I see every strong man
    with his hands on his stomach like a
    woman in labor,
    every face turned deathly pale?
⁷How awful that day will be!
    None will be like it.
It will be a time of trouble for Jacob,
    but he will be saved out of it.

⁸" 'In that day,' declares the LORD
    Almighty,
'I will break the yoke off their necks
    and will tear off their bonds;
    no longer will foreigners enslave
    them.
⁹Instead, they will serve the LORD their
    God
    and David their king,
    whom I will raise up for them.

¹⁰" 'So do not be afraid, Jacob my servant;
    do not be dismayed, Israel,'
        declares the LORD.
'I will surely save you out of a distant
    place,
    your descendants from the land of
    their exile.
Jacob will again have peace and security,
    and no one will make him afraid.
¹¹I am with you and will save you,'
    declares the LORD.
'Though I completely destroy all the
    nations
    among which I scatter you,
    I will not completely destroy you.
I will discipline you but only in due
    measure;
    I will not let you go entirely
    unpunished.'

¹²"This is what the LORD says:

" 'Your wound is incurable,
    your injury beyond healing.
¹³There is no one to plead your cause,
    no remedy for your sore,
    no healing for you.
¹⁴All your allies have forgotten you;
    they care nothing for you.
I have struck you as an enemy would
    and punished you as would the cruel,
because your guilt is so great
    and your sins so many.
¹⁵Why do you cry out over your wound,
    your pain that has no cure?
Because of your great guilt and many
    sins
    I have done these things to you.

¹⁶" 'But all who devour you will be
    devoured;
    all your enemies will go into exile.
Those who plunder you will be
    plundered;
    all who make spoil of you I will
    despoil.
¹⁷But I will restore you to health
    and heal your wounds,'
        declares the LORD,
'because you are called an outcast,
    Zion for whom no one cares.'

¹⁸"This is what the LORD says:

" 'I will restore the fortunes of Jacob's
    tents

ᵃ 3 Or *will restore the fortunes of my people Israel and Judah*

and have compassion on his
        dwellings;
the city will be rebuilt on her ruins,
        and the palace will stand in its proper
                place.
¹⁹ From them will come songs of
                thanksgiving
        and the sound of rejoicing.
I will add to their numbers,
        and they will not be decreased;
I will bring them honor,
        and they will not be disdained.
²⁰ Their children will be as in days of old,
        and their community will be
                established before me;
        I will punish all who oppress them.
²¹ Their leader will be one of their own;
        their ruler will arise from among
                them.
I will bring him near and he will come
        close to me—
for who is he who will devote himself
        to be close to me?'
                                declares the LORD.
²² " 'So you will be my people,
        and I will be your God.' "

²³ See, the storm of the LORD
        will burst out in wrath,
a driving wind swirling down
        on the heads of the wicked.
²⁴ The fierce anger of the LORD will not
                turn back
        until he fully accomplishes
                the purposes of his heart.
In days to come
        you will understand this.

31

"At that time," declares the
LORD, "I will be the God of all
the families of Israel, and they
will be my people."
²This is what the LORD says:

"The people who survive the sword
        will find favor in the wilderness;
        I will come to give rest to Israel."

³The LORD appeared to us in the past,ᵃ
saying:

"I have loved you with an everlasting
                love;
        I have drawn you with unfailing
                kindness.

⁴ I will build you up again,
        and you, Virgin Israel, will be rebuilt.
Again you will take up your timbrels
        and go out to dance with the joyful.
⁵ Again you will plant vineyards
        on the hills of Samaria;
the farmers will plant them
        and enjoy their fruit.
⁶ There will be a day when watchmen cry
                out
        on the hills of Ephraim,
'Come, let us go up to Zion,
        to the LORD our God.' "

⁷This is what the LORD says:

"Sing with joy for Jacob;
        shout for the foremost of the nations.
Make your praises heard, and say,
        'LORD, save your people,
        the remnant of Israel.'
⁸ See, I will bring them from the land of
                the north
        and gather them from the ends of the
                earth.
Among them will be the blind and the
                lame,
        expectant mothers and women in
                labor;
        a great throng will return.
⁹ They will come with weeping;
        they will pray as I bring them back.
I will lead them beside streams of water
        on a level path where they will not
                stumble,
because I am Israel's father,
        and Ephraim is my firstborn son.

¹⁰ "Hear the word of the LORD, you nations;
        proclaim it in distant coastlands:
'He who scattered Israel will gather
                them
        and will watch over his flock like a
                shepherd.'
¹¹ For the LORD will deliver Jacob
        and redeem them from the hand of
                those stronger than they.
¹² They will come and shout for joy on the
                heights of Zion;
        they will rejoice in the bounty of the
                LORD—
the grain, the new wine and the olive oil,
        the young of the flocks and herds.
They will be like a well-watered garden,
        and they will sorrow no more.

ᵃ 3 Or LORD has appeared to us from afar

¹³Then young women will dance and be
        glad,
    young men and old as well.
I will turn their mourning into gladness;
    I will give them comfort and joy
        instead of sorrow.
¹⁴I will satisfy the priests with abundance,
    and my people will be filled with my
        bounty,"
                            declares the LORD.

¹⁵This is what the LORD says:

"A voice is heard in Ramah,
    mourning and great weeping,
Rachel weeping for her children
    and refusing to be comforted,
    because they are no more."

¹⁶This is what the LORD says:

"Restrain your voice from weeping
    and your eyes from tears,
for your work will be rewarded,"
                            declares the LORD.
    "They will return from the land of the
        enemy.
¹⁷So there is hope for your descendants,"
                            declares the LORD.
    "Your children will return to their own
        land.

¹⁸"I have surely heard Ephraim's moaning:
    'You disciplined me like an unruly
        calf,
    and I have been disciplined.
Restore me, and I will return,
    because you are the LORD my God.
¹⁹After I strayed,
    I repented;
after I came to understand,
    I beat my breast.
I was ashamed and humiliated
    because I bore the disgrace of my
        youth.'
²⁰Is not Ephraim my dear son,
    the child in whom I delight?
Though I often speak against him,
    I still remember him.
Therefore my heart yearns for him;
    I have great compassion for him,"
                            declares the LORD.

²¹"Set up road signs;
    put up guideposts.

Take note of the highway,
    the road that you take.
Return, Virgin Israel,
    return to your towns.
²²How long will you wander,
    unfaithful Daughter Israel?
The LORD will create a new thing on
        earth—
    the woman will return toᵃ the man."

²³This is what the LORD Almighty, the God
of Israel, says: "When I bring them back
from captivity,ᵇ the people in the land of Judah and in its towns will once again use
these words: 'The LORD bless you, you prosperous city, you sacred mountain.' ²⁴People
will live together in Judah and all its
towns—farmers and those who move about
with their flocks. ²⁵I will refresh the weary
and satisfy the faint."

²⁶At this I awoke and looked around. My
sleep had been pleasant to me.

²⁷"The days are coming," declares the
LORD, "when I will plant the house of Israel
and the house of Judah with the offspring of
people and of animals. ²⁸Just as I watched
over them to uproot and tear down, and to
overthrow, destroy and bring disaster, so I
will watch over them to build and to plant,"
declares the LORD. ²⁹"In those days people
will no longer say,

    'The parents have eaten sour grapes,
        and the children's teeth are set on
            edge.'

³⁰Instead, everyone will die for their own
sin; whoever eats sour grapes—their own
teeth will be set on edge.

³¹"The days are coming," declares the
        LORD,
    "when I will make a new covenant
with the house of Israel
    and with the house of Judah.
³²It will not be like the covenant
    I made with their ancestors
when I took them by the hand
    to lead them out of Egypt,
because they broke my covenant,
    though I was a husband toᶜ them,ᵈ"
                            declares the LORD.
³³"This is the covenant I will make with
        the house of Israel

─────────────────────

ᵃ 22 Or will protect   ᵇ 23 Or I restore their fortunes   ᶜ 32 Hebrew; Septuagint and Syriac / and I
turned away from   ᵈ 32 Or was their master

after that time," declares the LORD.
"I will put my law in their minds
 and write it on their hearts.
I will be their God,
 and they will be my people.
34 No longer will they teach their
  neighbors,
 or say to one another, 'Know the
  LORD,'
because they will all know me,
 from the least of them to the
  greatest,"
                declares the LORD.
"For I will forgive their wickedness
 and will remember their sins no
  more."

35 This is what the LORD says,

he who appoints the sun
 to shine by day,
who decrees the moon and stars
 to shine by night,
who stirs up the sea
 so that its waves roar—
 the LORD Almighty is his name:
36 "Only if these decrees vanish from my
  sight,"
 declares the LORD,
"will the descendants of Israel ever
  cease
 to be a nation before me."

37 This is what the LORD says:

"Only if the heavens above can be
  measured
 and the foundations of the earth
  below be searched out
will I reject all the descendants of Israel
 because of all they have done,"
                declares the LORD.

38 "The days are coming," declares the
LORD, "when this city will be rebuilt for me
from the Tower of Hananel to the Corner
Gate. 39 The measuring line will stretch from
there straight to the hill of Gareb and then
turn to Goah. 40 The whole valley where dead
bodies and ashes are thrown, and all the terraces out to the Kidron Valley on the east as
far as the corner of the Horse Gate, will be
holy to the LORD. The city will never again be
uprooted or demolished."

Jeremiah Buys a Field

32 This is the word that came to
 Jeremiah from the LORD in the
 tenth year of Zedekiah king of
Judah, which was the eighteenth year of
Nebuchadnezzar. 2 The army of the king of
Babylon was then besieging Jerusalem, and
Jeremiah the prophet was confined in the
courtyard of the guard in the royal palace of
Judah.

3 Now Zedekiah king of Judah had imprisoned him there, saying, "Why do you prophesy as you do? You say, 'This is what the
LORD says: I am about to give this city into
the hands of the king of Babylon, and he will
capture it. 4 Zedekiah king of Judah will not
escape the Babylonians[a] but will certainly
be given into the hands of the king of Babylon, and will speak with him face to face
and see him with his own eyes. 5 He will take
Zedekiah to Babylon, where he will remain
until I deal with him, declares the LORD. If
you fight against the Babylonians, you will
not succeed.' "

6 Jeremiah said, "The word of the LORD
came to me: 7 Hanamel son of Shallum your
uncle is going to come to you and say, 'Buy
my field at Anathoth, because as nearest relative it is your right and duty to buy it.'

8 "Then, just as the LORD had said, my
cousin Hanamel came to me in the courtyard of the guard and said, 'Buy my field at
Anathoth in the territory of Benjamin. Since
it is your right to redeem it and possess it,
buy it for yourself.'

"I knew that this was the word of the
LORD; 9 so I bought the field at Anathoth
from my cousin Hanamel and weighed out
for him seventeen shekels[b] of silver. 10 I
signed and sealed the deed, had it witnessed, and weighed out the silver on the
scales. 11 I took the deed of purchase—the
sealed copy containing the terms and condi-
tions, as well as the unsealed copy— 12 and I
gave this deed to Baruch son of Neriah, the
son of Mahseiah, in the presence of my
cousin Hanamel and of the witnesses who
had signed the deed and of all the Jews sitting in the courtyard of the guard.

13 "In their presence I gave Baruch these
instructions: 14 'This is what the LORD Almighty, the God of Israel, says: Take these

a 4 Or Chaldeans; also in verses 5, 24, 25, 28, 29 and 43   b 9 That is, about 7 ounces or about
200 grams

documents, both the sealed and unsealed copies of the deed of purchase, and put them in a clay jar so they will last a long time. ¹⁵For this is what the Lord Almighty, the God of Israel, says: Houses, fields and vineyards will again be bought in this land.'

¹⁶"After I had given the deed of purchase to Baruch son of Neriah, I prayed to the Lord:

¹⁷"Ah, Sovereign Lord, you have made the heavens and the earth by your great power and outstretched arm. Nothing is too hard for you. ¹⁸You show love to thousands but bring the punishment for the parents' sins into the laps of their children after them. Great and mighty God, whose name is the Lord Almighty, ¹⁹great are your purposes and mighty are your deeds. Your eyes are open to the ways of all; you reward everyone according to their conduct and as their deeds deserve. ²⁰You performed signs and wonders in Egypt and have continued them to this day, both in Israel and among all nations, and have gained the renown that is still yours. ²¹You brought your people Israel out of Egypt with signs and wonders, by a mighty hand and an outstretched arm and with great terror. ²²You gave them this land you had sworn to give their ancestors, a land flowing with milk and honey. ²³They came in and took possession of it, but they did not obey you or follow your law; they did not do what you commanded them to do. So you brought all this disaster on them.

²⁴"See how the siege ramps are built up to take the city. Because of the sword, famine and plague, the city will be given into the hands of the Babylonians who are attacking it. What you said has happened, as you now see. ²⁵And though the city will be given into the hands of the Babylonians, you, Sovereign Lord, say to me, 'Buy the field with silver and have the transaction witnessed.' "

²⁶Then the word of the Lord came to Jeremiah: ²⁷"I am the Lord, the God of the whole human race. Is anything too hard for me? ²⁸Therefore, this is what the Lord says: I am about to give this city into the hands of

the Babylonians and to Nebuchadnezzar king of Babylon, who will capture it. ²⁹The Babylonians who are attacking this city will come in and set it on fire; they will burn it down, along with the houses where the people aroused my anger by burning incense on the roofs to Baal and by pouring out drink offerings to other gods.

³⁰"The people of Israel and Judah have done nothing but evil in my sight from their youth; indeed, the people of Israel have done nothing but arouse my anger with what their hands have made, declares the Lord. ³¹From the day it was built until now, this city has so aroused my anger and wrath that I must remove it from my sight. ³²The people of Israel and Judah have provoked me by all the evil they have done—they, their kings and officials, their priests and prophets, the people of Judah and those living in Jerusalem. ³³They turned their backs to me and not their faces; though I taught them again and again, they would not listen or respond to discipline. ³⁴They set up their vile images in the house that bears my Name and defiled it. ³⁵They built high places for Baal in the Valley of Ben Hinnom to sacrifice their sons and daughters to Molek, though I never commanded—nor did it enter my mind—that they should do such a detestable thing and so make Judah sin.

³⁶"You are saying about this city, 'By the sword, famine and plague it will be given into the hands of the king of Babylon'; but this is what the Lord, the God of Israel, says: ³⁷I will surely gather them from all the lands where I banish them in my furious anger and great wrath; I will bring them back to this place and let them live in safety. ³⁸They will be my people, and I will be their God. ³⁹I will give them singleness of heart and action, so that they will always fear me and that all will then go well for them and for their children after them. ⁴⁰I will make an everlasting covenant with them: I will never stop doing good to them, and I will inspire them to fear me, so that they will never turn away from me. ⁴¹I will rejoice in doing them good and will assuredly plant them in this land with all my heart and soul.

⁴²"This is what the Lord says: As I have brought all this great calamity on this people, so I will give them all the prosperity I have promised them. ⁴³Once more fields will be bought in this land of which you say,

'It is a desolate waste, without people or animals, for it has been given into the hands of the Babylonians.' ⁴⁴Fields will be bought for silver, and deeds will be signed, sealed and witnessed in the territory of Benjamin, in the villages around Jerusalem, in the towns of Judah and in the towns of the hill country, of the western foothills and of the Negev, because I will restore their fortunes,ᵃ declares the LORD."

Promise of Restoration

33 While Jeremiah was still confined in the courtyard of the guard, the word of the LORD came to him a second time: ²"This is what the LORD says, he who made the earth, the LORD who formed it and established it—the LORD is his name: ³'Call to me and I will answer you and tell you great and unsearchable things you do not know.' ⁴For this is what the LORD, the God of Israel, says about the houses in this city and the royal palaces of Judah that have been torn down to be used against the siege ramps and the sword ⁵in the fight with the Babyloniansᵇ: 'They will be filled with the dead bodies of the people I will slay in my anger and wrath. I will hide my face from this city because of all its wickedness.

⁶"'Nevertheless, I will bring health and healing to it; I will heal my people and will let them enjoy abundant peace and security. ⁷I will bring Judah and Israel back from captivityᶜ and will rebuild them as they were before. ⁸I will cleanse them from all the sin they have committed against me and will forgive all their sins of rebellion against me. ⁹Then this city will bring me renown, joy, praise and honor before all nations on earth that hear of all the good things I do for it; and they will be in awe and will tremble at the abundant prosperity and peace I provide for it.'

¹⁰"This is what the LORD says: 'You say about this place, "It is a desolate waste, without people or animals." Yet in the towns of Judah and the streets of Jerusalem that are deserted, inhabited by neither people nor animals, there will be heard once more ¹¹the sounds of joy and gladness, the voices of bride and bridegroom, and the voices of those who bring thank offerings to the house of the LORD, saying,

"Give thanks to the LORD Almighty,
    for the LORD is good;
    his love endures forever."

For I will restore the fortunes of the land as they were before,' says the LORD.

¹²"This is what the LORD Almighty says: 'In this place, desolate and without people or animals—in all its towns there will again be pastures for shepherds to rest their flocks. ¹³In the towns of the hill country, of the western foothills and of the Negev, in the territory of Benjamin, in the villages around Jerusalem and in the towns of Judah, flocks will again pass under the hand of the one who counts them,' says the LORD.

¹⁴"'The days are coming,' declares the LORD, 'when I will fulfill the good promise I made to the house of Israel and to the house of Judah.

¹⁵"'In those days and at that time
    I will make a righteous Branch sprout
        from David's line;
    he will do what is just and right in the
        land.
¹⁶In those days Judah will be saved
    and Jerusalem will live in safety.
This is the name by which itᵈ will be
        called:
    The LORD Our Righteous Savior.'

¹⁷For this is what the LORD says: 'David will never fail to have a man to sit on the throne of the house of Israel, ¹⁸nor will the Levitical priests ever fail to have a man to stand before me continually to offer burnt offerings, to burn grain offerings and to present sacrifices.'"

¹⁹The word of the LORD came to Jeremiah: ²⁰"This is what the LORD says: 'If you can break my covenant with the day and my covenant with the night, so that day and night no longer come at their appointed time, ²¹then my covenant with David my servant—and my covenant with the Levites who are priests ministering before me—can be broken and David will no longer have a descendant to reign on his throne. ²²I will make the descendants of David my servant and the Levites who minister before me as

---

ᵃ 44 Or *will bring them back from captivity and Israel*   ᵇ 5 Or *Chaldeans*   ᶜ 7 Or *will restore the fortunes of Judah*   ᵈ 16 Or *he*

FRIDAY

LET YOURSELF BE LOVED

Jeremiah 33:1–26 *or* 33:10–11

Kary Oberbrunner

We resist letting ourselves be loved. Did you catch it? We fail to love God with our hearts when we fail to let ourselves be loved. He extends His love to all of us, but few of us ever allow this process to take place. Strange, isn't it? . . .

Why do you fail to let yourself be loved? Do you feel undeserving? Do you feel you're not really worth His love? At face value, this appears to be a humble approach, but in reality, it's laced with pride. When we don't accept God's love because we feel unworthy, we're really putting ourselves in a position where we think we know better than God does. Of course we're unworthy! Nonetheless, God loves us! To reject His offer of love is to pursue a way that seems right to us, but in the end only leads to death.

CLEMENT OF ALEXANDRIA {AD 150–215}

Who can describe the blessed certainty of the love of God? What person is able to tell the excellence of its beauty, as it ought to be told? The height to which love elevates us is unspeakable. Love unites us to God. Love covers a multitude of sins. Love always protects, always perseveres. There is nothing offensive, nothing arrogant in love. Love leaves no room for division, and it never leads to treachery. Instead it promotes harmony in all things. God's love has made all his elect perfect. Without love you can't please God. In love, the Lord has brought us to himself. Because of his love for us, Jesus Christ our Lord gave his blood for us by the will of God. He gave his flesh for our flesh and his soul for our souls.

reflection

1. How is God's love for you different than the love you receive from anyone else?
2. In what ways do you resist succumbing completely to God's love for you?
3. Why do you hold yourself back?

For your next devotional reading, go to page 893.

countless as the stars in the sky and as measureless as the sand on the seashore.' "

²³The word of the LORD came to Jeremiah: ²⁴"Have you not noticed that these people are saying, 'The LORD has rejected the two kingdoms[a] he chose'? So they despise my people and no longer regard them as a nation. ²⁵This is what the LORD says: 'If I have not made my covenant with day and night and established the laws of heaven and earth, ²⁶then I will reject the descendants of Jacob and David my servant and will not choose one of his sons to rule over the descendants of Abraham, Isaac and Jacob. For I will restore their fortunes[b] and have compassion on them.' "

Warning to Zedekiah

34 While Nebuchadnezzar king of Babylon and all his army and all the kingdoms and peoples in the empire he ruled were fighting against Jerusalem and all its surrounding towns, this word came to Jeremiah from the LORD: ²"This is what the LORD, the God of Israel, says: Go to Zedekiah king of Judah and tell him, 'This is what the LORD says: I am about to give this city into the hands of the king of Babylon, and he will burn it down. ³You will not escape from his grasp but will surely be captured and given into his hands. You will see the king of Babylon with your own eyes, and he will speak with you face to face. And you will go to Babylon.

⁴" 'Yet hear the LORD's promise to you, Zedekiah king of Judah. This is what the LORD says concerning you: You will not die by the sword; ⁵you will die peacefully. As people made a funeral fire in honor of your ancestors, the former kings who preceded you, so they will make a fire in your honor and lament, "Alas, master!" I myself make this promise, declares the LORD.' "

⁶Then Jeremiah the prophet told all this to Zedekiah king of Judah, in Jerusalem, ⁷while the army of the king of Babylon was fighting against Jerusalem and the other cities of Judah that were still holding out—Lachish and Azekah. These were the only fortified cities left in Judah.

Freedom for Slaves

⁸The word came to Jeremiah from the LORD after King Zedekiah had made a covenant with all the people in Jerusalem to proclaim freedom for the slaves. ⁹Everyone was to free their Hebrew slaves, both male and female; no one was to hold another Jew in bondage. ¹⁰So all the officials and people who entered into this covenant agreed that they would free their male and female slaves and no longer hold them in bondage. They agreed, and set them free. ¹¹But afterward they changed their minds and took back the slaves they had freed and enslaved them again.

¹²Then the word of the LORD came to Jeremiah: ¹³"This is what the LORD, the God of Israel, says: I made a covenant with your ancestors when I brought them out of Egypt, out of the land of slavery. I said, ¹⁴'Every seventh year each of you must free any other Hebrews who have sold themselves to you. After they have served you six years, you must let them go free.'[c] Your ancestors, however, did not listen to me or pay attention to me. ¹⁵Recently you repented and did what is right in my sight: Each of you proclaimed freedom to your own people. You even made a covenant before me in the house that bears my Name. ¹⁶But now you have turned around and profaned my name; each of you has taken back the male and female slaves you had set free to go where they wished. You have forced them to become your slaves again.

¹⁷"Therefore, this is what the LORD says: You have not obeyed me; you have not proclaimed freedom to your own people. So I now proclaim 'freedom' for you, declares the LORD—'freedom' to fall by the sword, plague and famine. I will make you abhorrent to all the kingdoms of the earth. ¹⁸Those who have violated my covenant and have not fulfilled the terms of the covenant they made before me, I will treat like the calf they cut in two and then walked between its pieces. ¹⁹The leaders of Judah and Jerusalem, the court officials, the priests and all the people of the land who walked between the pieces of the calf, ²⁰I will deliver into the hands of their enemies who seek their lives. Their dead bodies will become food for the birds and the wild animals.

²¹"I will deliver Zedekiah king of Judah and his officials into the hands of their enemies who seek their lives, to the army of the

---

a 24 Or *families*   b 26 Or *will bring them back from captivity*   c 14 Deut. 15:12

king of Babylon, which has withdrawn from you. ²²I am going to give the order, declares the LORD, and I will bring them back to this city. They will fight against it, take it and burn it down. And I will lay waste the towns of Judah so no one can live there."

The Rekabites

35 This is the word that came to Jeremiah from the LORD during the reign of Jehoiakim son of Josiah king of Judah: ²"Go to the Rekabite family and invite them to come to one of the side rooms of the house of the LORD and give them wine to drink."

³So I went to get Jaazaniah son of Jeremiah, the son of Habazziniah, and his brothers and all his sons—the whole family of the Rekabites. ⁴I brought them into the house of the LORD, into the room of the sons of Hanan son of Igdaliah the man of God. It was next to the room of the officials, which was over that of Maaseiah son of Shallum the doorkeeper. ⁵Then I set bowls full of wine and some cups before the members of the Rekabite family and said to them, "Drink some wine."

⁶But they replied, "We do not drink wine, because our ancestor Jehonadab ª son of Rekab gave us this command: 'Neither you nor your descendants must ever drink wine. ⁷Also you must never build houses, sow seed or plant vineyards; you must never have any of these things, but must always live in tents. Then you will live a long time in the land where you are nomads.' ⁸We have obeyed everything our ancestor Jehonadab son of Rekab commanded us. Neither we nor our wives nor our sons and daughters have ever drunk wine ⁹or built houses to live in or had vineyards, fields or crops. ¹⁰We have lived in tents and have fully obeyed everything our ancestor Jehonadab commanded us. ¹¹But when Nebuchadnezzar king of Babylon invaded this land, we said, 'Come, we must go to Jerusalem to escape the Babylonian ᵇ and Aramean armies.' So we have remained in Jerusalem."

¹²Then the word of the LORD came to Jeremiah, saying: ¹³"This is what the LORD Almighty, the God of Israel, says: Go and tell the people of Judah and those living in Jerusalem, 'Will you not learn a lesson and obey my words?' declares the LORD. ¹⁴'Jehonadab son of Rekab ordered his descendants not to drink wine and this command has been kept. To this day they do not drink wine, because they obey their ancestor's command. But I have spoken to you again and again, yet you have not obeyed me. ¹⁵Again and again I sent all my servants the prophets to you. They said, "Each of you must turn from your wicked ways and reform your actions; do not follow other gods to serve them. Then you will live in the land I have given to you and your ancestors." But you have not paid attention or listened to me. ¹⁶The descendants of Jehonadab son of Rekab have carried out the command their ancestor gave them, but these people have not obeyed me.'

¹⁷"Therefore, this is what the LORD God Almighty, the God of Israel, says: 'Listen! I am going to bring on Judah and on everyone living in Jerusalem every disaster I pronounced against them. I spoke to them, but they did not listen; I called to them, but they did not answer.' "

¹⁸Then Jeremiah said to the family of the Rekabites, "This is what the LORD Almighty, the God of Israel, says: 'You have obeyed the command of your ancestor Jehonadab and have followed all his instructions and have done everything he ordered.' ¹⁹Therefore, this is what the LORD Almighty, the God of Israel, says: 'Jehonadab son of Rekab will never fail to have a descendant to serve me.' "

Jehoiakim Burns Jeremiah's Scroll

36 In the fourth year of Jehoiakim son of Josiah king of Judah, this word came to Jeremiah from the LORD: ²"Take a scroll and write on it all the words I have spoken to you concerning Israel, Judah and all the other nations from the time I began speaking to you in the reign of Josiah till now. ³Perhaps when the people of Judah hear about every disaster I plan to inflict on them, they will each turn from their wicked ways; then I will forgive their wickedness and their sin."

⁴So Jeremiah called Baruch son of Neriah, and while Jeremiah dictated all the words the LORD had spoken to him, Baruch wrote them on the scroll. ⁵Then Jeremiah

---

ª 6 Hebrew Jonadab, a variant of Jehonadab; here and often in this chapter   ᵇ 11 Or Chaldean told Baruch, "I am restricted; I am not allowed to go to the LORD's temple. 6So you go to the house of the LORD on a day of fasting and read to the people from the scroll the words of the LORD that you wrote as I dictated. Read them to all the people of Judah who come in from their towns. 7Perhaps they will bring their petition before the LORD, and will all turn from their wicked ways, for the anger and wrath pronounced against this people by the LORD are great."

8Baruch son of Neriah did everything Jeremiah the prophet told him to do; at the LORD's temple he read the words of the LORD from the scroll. 9In the ninth month of the fifth year of Jehoiakim son of Josiah king of Judah, a time of fasting before the LORD was proclaimed for all the people in Jerusalem and those who had come from the towns of Judah. 10From the room of Gemariah son of Shaphan the secretary, which was in the upper courtyard at the entrance of the New Gate of the temple, Baruch read to all the people at the LORD's temple the words of Jeremiah from the scroll.

11When Micaiah son of Gemariah, the son of Shaphan, heard all the words of the LORD from the scroll, 12he went down to the secretary's room in the royal palace, where all the officials were sitting: Elishama the secretary, Delaiah son of Shemaiah, Elnathan son of Akbor, Gemariah son of Shaphan, Zedekiah son of Hananiah, and all the other officials. 13After Micaiah told them everything he had heard Baruch read to the people from the scroll, 14all the officials sent Jehudi son of Nethaniah, the son of Shelemiah, the son of Cushi, to say to Baruch, "Bring the scroll from which you have read to the people and come." So Baruch son of Neriah went to them with the scroll in his hand. 15They said to him, "Sit down, please, and read it to us."

So Baruch read it to them. 16When they heard all these words, they looked at each other in fear and said to Baruch, "We must report all these words to the king." 17Then they asked Baruch, "Tell us, how did you come to write all this? Did Jeremiah dictate it?"

18"Yes," Baruch replied, "he dictated all these words to me, and I wrote them in ink on the scroll."

19Then the officials said to Baruch, "You and Jeremiah, go and hide. Don't let anyone know where you are."

20After they put the scroll in the room of Elishama the secretary, they went to the king in the courtyard and reported everything to him. 21The king sent Jehudi to get the scroll, and Jehudi brought it from the room of Elishama the secretary and read it to the king and all the officials standing beside him. 22It was the ninth month and the king was sitting in the winter apartment, with a fire burning in the firepot in front of him. 23Whenever Jehudi had read three or four columns of the scroll, the king cut them off with a scribe's knife and threw them into the firepot, until the entire scroll was burned in the fire. 24The king and all his attendants who heard all these words showed no fear, nor did they tear their clothes. 25Even though Elnathan, Delaiah and Gemariah urged the king not to burn the scroll, he would not listen to them. 26Instead, the king commanded Jerahmeel, a son of the king, Seraiah son of Azriel and Shelemiah son of Abdeel to arrest Baruch the scribe and Jeremiah the prophet. But the LORD had hidden them.

27After the king burned the scroll containing the words that Baruch had written at Jeremiah's dictation, the word of the LORD came to Jeremiah: 28"Take another scroll and write on it all the words that were on the first scroll, which Jehoiakim king of Judah burned up. 29Also tell Jehoiakim king of Judah, 'This is what the LORD says: You burned that scroll and said, "Why did you write on it that the king of Babylon would certainly come and destroy this land and wipe from it both people and animals?" 30Therefore, this is what the LORD says about Jehoiakim king of Judah: He will have no one to sit on the throne of David; his body will be thrown out and exposed to the heat by day and the frost by night. 31I will punish him and his children and his attendants for their wickedness; I will bring on them and those living in Jerusalem and the people of Judah every disaster I pronounced against them, because they have not listened.' "

32So Jeremiah took another scroll and gave it to the scribe Baruch son of Neriah, and as Jeremiah dictated, Baruch wrote on it all the words of the scroll that Jehoiakim king of Judah had burned in the fire. And many similar words were added to them.

Jeremiah in Prison

37 Zedekiah son of Josiah was made king of Judah by Nebuchadnezzar king of Babylon; he reigned in place of Jehoiachin[a] son of Jehoiakim. ²Neither he nor his attendants nor the people of the land paid any attention to the words the LORD had spoken through Jeremiah the prophet.

³King Zedekiah, however, sent Jehukal son of Shelemiah with the priest Zephaniah son of Maaseiah to Jeremiah the prophet with this message: "Please pray to the LORD our God for us."

⁴Now Jeremiah was free to come and go among the people, for he had not yet been put in prison. ⁵Pharaoh's army had marched out of Egypt, and when the Babylonians[b] who were besieging Jerusalem heard the report about them, they withdrew from Jerusalem.

⁶Then the word of the LORD came to Jeremiah the prophet: ⁷"This is what the LORD, the God of Israel, says: Tell the king of Judah, who sent you to inquire of me, 'Pharaoh's army, which has marched out to support you, will go back to its own land, to Egypt. ⁸Then the Babylonians will return and attack this city; they will capture it and burn it down.'

⁹"This is what the LORD says: Do not deceive yourselves, thinking, 'The Babylonians will surely leave us.' They will not! ¹⁰Even if you were to defeat the entire Babylonian[c] army that is attacking you and only wounded men were left in their tents, they would come out and burn this city down."

¹¹After the Babylonian army had withdrawn from Jerusalem because of Pharaoh's army, ¹²Jeremiah started to leave the city to go to the territory of Benjamin to get his share of the property among the people there. ¹³But when he reached the Benjamin Gate, the captain of the guard, whose name was Irijah son of Shelemiah, the son of Hananiah, arrested him and said, "You are deserting to the Babylonians!"

¹⁴"That's not true!" Jeremiah said. "I am not deserting to the Babylonians." But Irijah would not listen to him; instead, he arrested Jeremiah and brought him to the officials. ¹⁵They were angry with Jeremiah and had

him beaten and imprisoned in the house of Jonathan the secretary, which they had made into a prison.

¹⁶Jeremiah was put into a vaulted cell in a dungeon, where he remained a long time. ¹⁷Then King Zedekiah sent for him and had him brought to the palace, where he asked him privately, "Is there any word from the LORD?"

"Yes," Jeremiah replied, "you will be delivered into the hands of the king of Babylon."

¹⁸Then Jeremiah said to King Zedekiah, "What crime have I committed against you or your attendants or this people, that you have put me in prison? ¹⁹Where are your prophets who prophesied to you, 'The king of Babylon will not attack you or this land'? ²⁰But now, my lord the king, please listen. Let me bring my petition before you: Do not send me back to the house of Jonathan the secretary, or I will die there."

²¹King Zedekiah then gave orders for Jeremiah to be placed in the courtyard of the guard and given a loaf of bread from the street of the bakers each day until all the bread in the city was gone. So Jeremiah remained in the courtyard of the guard.

Jeremiah Thrown Into a Cistern

38 Shephatiah son of Mattan, Gedaliah son of Pashhur, Jehukal[d] son of Shelemiah, and Pashhur son of Malkijah heard what Jeremiah was telling all the people when he said, ²"This is what the LORD says: 'Whoever stays in this city will die by the sword, famine or plague, but whoever goes over to the Babylonians[e] will live. They will escape with their lives; they will live.' ³And this is what the LORD says: 'This city will certainly be given into the hands of the army of the king of Babylon, who will capture it.'"

⁴Then the officials said to the king, "This man should be put to death. He is discouraging the soldiers who are left in this city, as well as all the people, by the things he is saying to them. This man is not seeking the good of these people but their ruin."

⁵"He is in your hands," King Zedekiah answered. "The king can do nothing to oppose you."

---

a 1 Hebrew *Koniah,* a variant of *Jehoiachin*   *b 5* Or *Chaldeans;* also in verses 8, 9, 13 and 14
c 10 Or *Chaldean;* also in verse 11   *d 1* Hebrew *Jukal,* a variant of *Jehukal*   *e 2* Or *Chaldeans;* also in
verses 18, 19 and 23

⁶So they took Jeremiah and put him into the cistern of Malkijah, the king's son, which was in the courtyard of the guard. They lowered Jeremiah by ropes into the cistern; it had no water in it, only mud, and Jeremiah sank down into the mud.

⁷But Ebed-Melek, a Cushite,ᵃ an officialᵇ in the royal palace, heard that they had put Jeremiah into the cistern. While the king was sitting in the Benjamin Gate, ⁸Ebed-Melek went out of the palace and said to him, ⁹"My lord the king, these men have acted wickedly in all they have done to Jeremiah the prophet. They have thrown him into a cistern, where he will starve to death when there is no longer any bread in the city."

¹⁰Then the king commanded Ebed-Melek the Cushite, "Take thirty men from here with you and lift Jeremiah the prophet out of the cistern before he dies."

¹¹So Ebed-Melek took the men with him and went to a room under the treasury in the palace. He took some old rags and worn-out clothes from there and let them down with ropes to Jeremiah in the cistern. ¹²Ebed-Melek the Cushite said to Jeremiah, "Put these old rags and worn-out clothes under your arms to pad the ropes." Jeremiah did so, ¹³and they pulled him up with the ropes and lifted him out of the cistern. And Jeremiah remained in the courtyard of the guard.

Zedekiah Questions Jeremiah Again

¹⁴Then King Zedekiah sent for Jeremiah the prophet and had him brought to the third entrance to the temple of the LORD. "I am going to ask you something," the king said to Jeremiah. "Do not hide anything from me."

¹⁵Jeremiah said to Zedekiah, "If I give you an answer, will you not kill me? Even if I did give you counsel, you would not listen to me."

¹⁶But King Zedekiah swore this oath secretly to Jeremiah: "As surely as the LORD lives, who has given us breath, I will neither kill you nor hand you over to those who are seeking your life."

¹⁷Then Jeremiah said to Zedekiah, "This is what the LORD God Almighty, the God of Israel, says: 'If you surrender to the officers of the king of Babylon, your life will be spared and this city will not be burned down; you and your family will live. ¹⁸But if you will not surrender to the officers of the king of Babylon, this city will be given into the hands of the Babylonians and they will burn it down; you yourself will not escape from them.' "

¹⁹King Zedekiah said to Jeremiah, "I am afraid of the Jews who have gone over to the Babylonians, for the Babylonians may hand me over to them and they will mistreat me."

²⁰"They will not hand you over," Jeremiah replied. "Obey the LORD by doing what I tell you. Then it will go well with you, and your life will be spared. ²¹But if you refuse to surrender, this is what the LORD has revealed to me: ²²All the women left in the palace of the king of Judah will be brought out to the officials of the king of Babylon. Those women will say to you:

" 'They misled you and overcame you—
    those trusted friends of yours.
Your feet are sunk in the mud;
    your friends have deserted you.'

²³"All your wives and children will be brought out to the Babylonians. You yourself will not escape from their hands but will be captured by the king of Babylon; and this city willᶜ be burned down."

²⁴Then Zedekiah said to Jeremiah, "Do not let anyone know about this conversation, or you may die. ²⁵If the officials hear that I talked with you, and they come to you and say, 'Tell us what you said to the king and what the king said to you; do not hide it from us or we will kill you,' ²⁶then tell them, 'I was pleading with the king not to send me back to Jonathan's house to die there.' "

²⁷All the officials did come to Jeremiah and question him, and he told them everything the king had ordered him to say. So they said no more to him, for no one had heard his conversation with the king.

²⁸And Jeremiah remained in the courtyard of the guard until the day Jerusalem was captured.

The Fall of Jerusalem

39 This is how Jerusalem was taken: ¹In the ninth year of Zedekiah king of Judah, in the tenth month, Nebuchadnezzar king of Babylon marched against Jerusalem with his whole

ᵃ 7 Probably from the upper Nile region   ᵇ 7 Or *a eunuch*   ᶜ 23 Or *and you will cause this city to* army and laid siege to it. [2]And on the ninth day of the fourth month of Zedekiah's eleventh year, the city wall was broken through. [3]Then all the officials of the king of Babylon came and took seats in the Middle Gate: Nergal-Sharezer of Samgar, Nebo-Sarsekim[a] a chief officer, Nergal-Sharezer a high official and all the other officials of the king of Babylon. [4]When Zedekiah king of Judah and all the soldiers saw them, they fled; they left the city at night by way of the king's garden, through the gate between the two walls, and headed toward the Arabah.[b]

[5]But the Babylonian[c] army pursued them and overtook Zedekiah in the plains of Jericho. They captured him and took him to Nebuchadnezzar king of Babylon at Riblah in the land of Hamath, where he pronounced sentence on him. [6]There at Riblah the king of Babylon slaughtered the sons of Zedekiah before his eyes and also killed all the nobles of Judah. [7]Then he put out Zedekiah's eyes and bound him with bronze shackles to take him to Babylon.

[8]The Babylonians[d] set fire to the royal palace and the houses of the people and broke down the walls of Jerusalem. [9]Nebuzaradan commander of the imperial guard carried into exile to Babylon the people who remained in the city, along with those who had gone over to him, and the rest of the people. [10]But Nebuzaradan the commander of the guard left behind in the land of Judah some of the poor people, who owned nothing; and at that time he gave them vineyards and fields.

[11]Now Nebuchadnezzar king of Babylon had given these orders about Jeremiah through Nebuzaradan commander of the imperial guard: [12]"Take him and look after him; don't harm him but do for him whatever he asks." [13]So Nebuzaradan the commander of the guard, Nebushazban a chief officer, Nergal-Sharezer a high official and all the other officers of the king of Babylon [14]sent and had Jeremiah taken out of the courtyard of the guard. They turned him over to Gedaliah son of Ahikam, the son of Shaphan, to take him back to his home. So he remained among his own people.

[15]While Jeremiah had been confined in the courtyard of the guard, the word of the LORD came to him: [16]"Go and tell Ebed-Melek the Cushite, 'This is what the LORD Almighty, the God of Israel, says: I am about to fulfill my words against this city—words concerning disaster, not prosperity. At that time they will be fulfilled before your eyes. [17]But I will rescue you on that day, declares the LORD; you will not be given into the hands of those you fear. [18]I will save you; you will not fall by the sword but will escape with your life, because you trust in me, declares the LORD.'"

Jeremiah Freed

40 The word came to Jeremiah from the LORD after Nebuzaradan commander of the imperial guard had released him at Ramah. He had found Jeremiah bound in chains among all the captives from Jerusalem and Judah who were being carried into exile to Babylon. [2]When the commander of the guard found Jeremiah, he said to him, "The LORD your God decreed this disaster for this place. [3]And now the LORD has brought it about; he has done just as he said he would. All this happened because you people sinned against the LORD and did not obey him. [4]But today I am freeing you from the chains on your wrists. Come with me to Babylon, if you like, and I will look after you; but if you do not want to, then don't come. Look, the whole country lies before you; go wherever you please." [5]However, before Jeremiah turned to go,[e] Nebuzaradan added, "Go back to Gedaliah son of Ahikam, the son of Shaphan, whom the king of Babylon has appointed over the towns of Judah, and live with him among the people, or go anywhere else you please."

Then the commander gave him provisions and a present and let him go. [6]So Jeremiah went to Gedaliah son of Ahikam at Mizpah and stayed with him among the people who were left behind in the land.

Gedaliah Assassinated

[7]When all the army officers and their men who were still in the open country heard that the king of Babylon had appointed Gedaliah son of Ahikam as governor over the land and had put him in charge of the

---

[a] 3 Or Nergal-Sharezer, Samgar-Nebo, Sarsekim   [b] 4 Or the Jordan Valley   [c] 5 Or Chaldean
[d] 8 Or Chaldeans   [e] 5 Or Jeremiah answered

men, women and children who were the poorest in the land and who had not been carried into exile to Babylon, [8]they came to Gedaliah at Mizpah—Ishmael son of Nethaniah, Johanan and Jonathan the sons of Kareah, Seraiah son of Tanhumeth, the sons of Ephai the Netophathite, and Jaazaniah[a] the son of the Maakathite, and their men. [9]Gedaliah son of Ahikam, the son of Shaphan, took an oath to reassure them and their men. "Do not be afraid to serve the Babylonians,[b]" he said. "Settle down in the land and serve the king of Babylon, and it will go well with you. [10]I myself will stay at Mizpah to represent you before the Babylonians who come to us, but you are to harvest the wine, summer fruit and olive oil, and put them in your storage jars, and live in the towns you have taken over."

[11]When all the Jews in Moab, Ammon, Edom and all the other countries heard that the king of Babylon had left a remnant in Judah and had appointed Gedaliah son of Ahikam, the son of Shaphan, as governor over them, [12]they all came back to the land of Judah, to Gedaliah at Mizpah, from all the countries where they had been scattered. And they harvested an abundance of wine and summer fruit.

[13]Johanan son of Kareah and all the army officers still in the open country came to Gedaliah at Mizpah [14]and said to him, "Don't you know that Baalis king of the Ammonites has sent Ishmael son of Nethaniah to take your life?" But Gedaliah son of Ahikam did not believe them.

[15]Then Johanan son of Kareah said privately to Gedaliah in Mizpah, "Let me go and kill Ishmael son of Nethaniah, and no one will know it. Why should he take your life and cause all the Jews who are gathered around you to be scattered and the remnant of Judah to perish?"

[16]But Gedaliah son of Ahikam said to Johanan son of Kareah, "Don't do such a thing! What you are saying about Ishmael is not true."

41

In the seventh month Ishmael son of Nethaniah, the son of Elishama, who was of royal blood and had been one of the king's officers, came with ten men to Gedaliah son of Ahikam at Mizpah. While they were eating together there, [2]Ishmael son of Nethaniah and the ten men who were with him got up and struck down Gedaliah son of Ahikam, the son of Shaphan, with the sword, killing the one whom the king of Babylon had appointed as governor over the land. [3]Ishmael also killed all the men of Judah who were with Gedaliah at Mizpah, as well as the Babylonian[c] soldiers who were there.

[4]The day after Gedaliah's assassination, before anyone knew about it, [5]eighty men who had shaved off their beards, torn their clothes and cut themselves came from Shechem, Shiloh and Samaria, bringing grain offerings and incense with them to the house of the LORD. [6]Ishmael son of Nethaniah went out from Mizpah to meet them, weeping as he went. When he met them, he said, "Come to Gedaliah son of Ahikam." [7]When they went into the city, Ishmael son of Nethaniah and the men who were with him slaughtered them and threw them into a cistern. [8]But ten of them said to Ishmael, "Don't kill us! We have wheat and barley, olive oil and honey, hidden in a field." So he let them alone and did not kill them with the others. [9]Now the cistern where he threw all the bodies of the men he had killed along with Gedaliah was the one King Asa had made as part of his defense against Baasha king of Israel. Ishmael son of Nethaniah filled it with the dead.

[10]Ishmael made captives of all the rest of the people who were in Mizpah—the king's daughters along with all the others who were left there, over whom Nebuzaradan commander of the imperial guard had appointed Gedaliah son of Ahikam. Ishmael son of Nethaniah took them captive and set out to cross over to the Ammonites.

[11]When Johanan son of Kareah and all the army officers who were with him heard about all the crimes Ishmael son of Nethaniah had committed, [12]they took all their men and went to fight Ishmael son of Nethaniah. They caught up with him near the great pool in Gibeon. [13]When all the people Ishmael had with him saw Johanan son of Kareah and the army officers who were with him, they were glad. [14]All the people Ishmael had taken captive at Mizpah turned and went over to Johanan son of Kareah. [15]But Ishmael son of Nethaniah and eight of his men escaped from Johanan and fled to the Ammonites.

---

a 8 Hebrew *Jezaniah*, a variant of *Jaazaniah*   b 9 Or *Chaldeans*; also in verse 10   c 3 Or *Chaldean*

Flight to Egypt

[16]Then Johanan son of Kareah and all the army officers who were with him led away all the people of Mizpah who had survived, whom Johanan had recovered from Ishmael son of Nethaniah after Ishmael had assassinated Gedaliah son of Ahikam—the soldiers, women, children and court officials he had recovered from Gibeon. [17]And they went on, stopping at Geruth Kimham near Bethlehem on their way to Egypt [18]to escape the Babylonians.[a] They were afraid of them because Ishmael son of Nethaniah had killed Gedaliah son of Ahikam, whom the king of Babylon had appointed as governor over the land.

42 Then all the army officers, including Johanan son of Kareah and Jezaniah[b] son of Hoshaiah, and all the people from the least to the greatest approached [2]Jeremiah the prophet and said to him, "Please hear our petition and pray to the LORD your God for this entire remnant. For as you now see, though we were once many, now only a few are left. [3]Pray that the LORD your God will tell us where we should go and what we should do."

[4]"I have heard you," replied Jeremiah the prophet. "I will certainly pray to the LORD your God as you have requested; I will tell you everything the LORD says and will keep nothing back from you."

[5]Then they said to Jeremiah, "May the LORD be a true and faithful witness against us if we do not act in accordance with everything the LORD your God sends you to tell us. [6]Whether it is favorable or unfavorable, we will obey the LORD our God, to whom we are sending you, so that it will go well with us, for we will obey the LORD our God."

[7]Ten days later the word of the LORD came to Jeremiah. [8]So he called together Johanan son of Kareah and all the army officers who were with him and all the people from the least to the greatest. [9]He said to them, "This is what the LORD, the God of Israel, to whom you sent me to present your petition, says: [10]'If you stay in this land, I will build you up and not tear you down; I will plant you and not uproot you, for I have relented concerning the disaster I have inflicted on you. [11]Do not be afraid of the king of Babylon, whom you now fear. Do not be afraid of him, declares the LORD, for I am with you and will save you and deliver you from his hands. [12]I will show you compassion so that he will have compassion on you and restore you to your land.'

[13]"However, if you say, 'We will not stay in this land,' and so disobey the LORD your God, [14]and if you say, 'No, we will go and live in Egypt, where we will not see war or hear the trumpet or be hungry for bread,' [15]then hear the word of the LORD, you remnant of Judah. This is what the LORD Almighty, the God of Israel, says: 'If you are determined to go to Egypt and you do go to settle there, [16]then the sword you fear will overtake you there, and the famine you dread will follow you into Egypt, and there you will die. [17]Indeed, all who are determined to go to Egypt to settle there will die by the sword, famine and plague; not one of them will survive or escape the disaster I will bring on them.' [18]This is what the LORD Almighty, the God of Israel, says: 'As my anger and wrath have been poured out on those who lived in Jerusalem, so will my wrath be poured out on you when you go to Egypt. You will be a curse[c] and an object of horror, a curse[c] and an object of reproach; you will never see this place again.'

[19]"Remnant of Judah, the LORD has told you, 'Do not go to Egypt.' Be sure of this: I warn you today [20]that you made a fatal mistake when you sent me to the LORD your God and said, 'Pray to the LORD our God for us; tell us everything he says and we will do it.' [21]I have told you today, but you still have not obeyed the LORD your God in all he sent me to tell you. [22]So now, be sure of this: You will die by the sword, famine and plague in the place where you want to go to settle."

43 When Jeremiah had finished telling the people all the words of the LORD their God—everything the LORD had sent him to tell them— [2]Azariah son of Hoshaiah and Johanan son of Kareah and all the arrogant men said to Jeremiah, "You are lying! The LORD our God has not sent you to say, 'You must not go to Egypt to settle there.' [3]But Baruch son of Neriah is inciting you against us to hand us

---

a 18 Or *Chaldeans*   *b 1* Hebrew; Septuagint (see also 43:2) *Azariah*   *c 18* That is, your name will be used in cursing (see Jer. 29:22); or, others will see that you are cursed.

God's View

Jeremiah 42:19–22

read/meditate

Read the passage several times. Imagine the ancient voice of the Jewish prophet.
Imagine his mood, his inflection, his level of intensity.

pray

Compare your attitude toward sin with God's attitude toward sin, as represented by
this prophet. Sit with God and be open to any calibrations he might want to make
in your perspective. Be still before him, trusting him to do his work in making you
like him.

contemplate

Contemplate God's desire for you to be one with him and his attitude toward sin that
pours out of that desire.

additional reflection

We are ever prone to regard sin lightly, to gloss over its heinousness, to make
excuses for it. But the more we study and ponder God's abhorrence of sin . . . the
more likely are we to realize its heinousness.

—Arthur W. Pink

We cannot love good if we do not hate evil.

—Saint Jerome

For your next devotional reading, go to page 895.

over to the Babylonians,[a] so they may kill us or carry us into exile to Babylon."

[4]So Johanan son of Kareah and all the army officers and all the people disobeyed the LORD's command to stay in the land of Judah. [5]Instead, Johanan son of Kareah and all the army officers led away all the remnant of Judah who had come back to live in the land of Judah from all the nations where they had been scattered. [6]They also led away all those whom Nebuzaradan commander of the imperial guard had left with Gedaliah son of Ahikam, the son of Shaphan—the men, the women, the children and the king's daughters. And they took Jeremiah the prophet and Baruch son of Neriah along with them. [7]So they entered Egypt in disobedience to the LORD and went as far as Tahpanhes.

[8]In Tahpanhes the word of the LORD came to Jeremiah: [9]"While the Jews are watching, take some large stones with you and bury them in clay in the brick pavement at the entrance to Pharaoh's palace in Tahpanhes. [10]Then say to them, 'This is what the LORD Almighty, the God of Israel, says: I will send for my servant Nebuchadnezzar king of Babylon, and I will set his throne over these stones I have buried here; he will spread his royal canopy above them. [11]He will come and attack Egypt, bringing death to those destined for death, captivity to those destined for captivity, and the sword to those destined for the sword. [12]He will set fire to the temples of the gods of Egypt; he will burn their temples and take their gods captive. As a shepherd picks his garment clean of lice, so he will pick Egypt clean and depart. [13]There in the temple of the sun[b] in Egypt he will demolish the sacred pillars and will burn down the temples of the gods of Egypt.' "

Disaster Because of Idolatry

44 This word came to Jeremiah concerning all the Jews living in Lower Egypt—in Migdol, Tahpanhes and Memphis—and in Upper Egypt: [2]"This is what the LORD Almighty, the God of Israel, says: You saw the great disaster I brought on Jerusalem and on all the towns of Judah. Today they lie deserted and in ruins [3]because of the evil they have done. They aroused my anger by burning incense to and worshiping other gods that neither they nor you nor your ancestors ever knew. [4]Again and again I sent my servants the prophets, who said, 'Do not do this detestable thing that I hate!' [5]But they did not listen or pay attention; they did not turn from their wickedness or stop burning incense to other gods. [6]Therefore, my fierce anger was poured out; it raged against the towns of Judah and the streets of Jerusalem and made them the desolate ruins they are today.

[7]"Now this is what the LORD God Almighty, the God of Israel, says: Why bring such great disaster on yourselves by cutting off from Judah the men and women, the children and infants, and so leave yourselves without a remnant? [8]Why arouse my anger with what your hands have made, burning incense to other gods in Egypt, where you have come to live? You will destroy yourselves and make yourselves a curse[c] and an object of reproach among all the nations on earth. [9]Have you forgotten the wickedness committed by your ancestors and by the kings and queens of Judah and the wickedness committed by you and your wives in the land of Judah and the streets of Jerusalem? [10]To this day they have not humbled themselves or shown reverence, nor have they followed my law and the decrees I set before you and your ancestors.

[11]"Therefore, this is what the LORD Almighty, the God of Israel, says: I am determined to bring disaster on you and to destroy all Judah. [12]I will take away the remnant of Judah who were determined to go to Egypt to settle there. They will all perish in Egypt; they will fall by the sword or die from famine. From the least to the greatest, they will die by sword or famine. They will become a curse and an object of horror, a curse and an object of reproach. [13]I will punish those who live in Egypt with the sword, famine and plague, as I punished Jerusalem. [14]None of the remnant of Judah who have gone to live in Egypt will escape or survive to return to the land of Judah, to which they long to return and live; none will return except a few fugitives."

[15]Then all the men who knew that their wives were burning incense to other gods,

---

[a] 3 Or *Chaldeans*   [b] 13 Or *in Heliopolis*   [c] 8 That is, your name will be used in cursing (see Jer. 29:22); or, others will see that you are cursed; also in verse 12; similarly in verse 22.

MONDAY

GUIDED GOD'S WAY

Jeremiah 44:1–30 *or* 44:2–6

GEORGE ELIOT {AD 1819–1880}

We mustn't be in a hurry to settle and choose our own lot. We must wait to be guided. We
are led on, like the little children, by a way that we do not know. It is a vain thought to flee
from the work that God appoints for us, for the sake of finding a greater blessing to our own
souls, as if we could choose for ourselves where we will find the fullness of the Divine
Presence, instead of seeking it where alone it is to be found, in loving obedience.

Tony and Lois Evans

Even with the mind of Christ at our disposal, we are still very imperfect people who can
easily lapse back into old ways of thinking. But Scripture is clear: It is more than possible for
us to think and live with renewed minds.

So how can we learn to exercise the mind and attitude of Christ that is already ours?
Here are some ingredients you can begin using today:

Meditate on God's Word (Psalm 1:2–3).
Seek God's will (Matthew 26:39).
Bear the burdens of others (Galatians 6:2).
Resist the devil (Matthew 4:1–11; James 4:7).
Learn to control your mental focus (Philippians 4:8) . . .

How does this work moment by moment? Paul offers the strongest clue in
2 Corinthians 10:5, when he says, "[We take captive every thought to make it obedient to
Christ.]" By the power of the indwelling Holy Spirit, we begin to run every thought, every
speculation and every flight of imagination through a "Christ filter," stopping destructive,
bitter, hateful, lustful thoughts before they can ever take root.

The result? When Christ's mind dominates our minds, then we will be truly in our
right minds!

reflection

1. The Israelites turned their backs on God—choosing to follow their own ways
   rather than God's. What happened to them as a result?

2. The Israelites' rebellion, which led to the eventual blatant refusal to listen to and
   obey God, began in small ways. In what little ways have you—like them—begun
   to live and act out according to your old ways of thinking?

3. In what ways have you been guided by your own human perspective instead of
   God's eternal perspective?

For your next devotional reading, go to page 916.

along with all the women who were present—a large assembly—and all the people living in Lower and Upper Egypt, said to Jeremiah, [16]"We will not listen to the message you have spoken to us in the name of the LORD! [17]We will certainly do everything we said we would: We will burn incense to the Queen of Heaven and will pour out drink offerings to her just as we and our ancestors, our kings and our officials did in the towns of Judah and in the streets of Jerusalem. At that time we had plenty of food and were well off and suffered no harm. [18]But ever since we stopped burning incense to the Queen of Heaven and pouring out drink offerings to her, we have had nothing and have been perishing by sword and famine."

[19]The women added, "When we burned incense to the Queen of Heaven and poured out drink offerings to her, did not our husbands know that we were making cakes impressed with her image and pouring out drink offerings to her?"

[20]Then Jeremiah said to all the people, both men and women, who were answering him, [21]"Did not the LORD remember and call to mind the incense burned in the towns of Judah and the streets of Jerusalem by you and your ancestors, your kings and your officials and the people of the land? [22]When the LORD could no longer endure your wicked actions and the detestable things you did, your land became a curse and a desolate waste without inhabitants, as it is today. [23]Because you have burned incense and have sinned against the LORD and have not obeyed him or followed his law or his decrees or his stipulations, this disaster has come upon you, as you now see."

[24]Then Jeremiah said to all the people, including the women, "Hear the word of the LORD, all you people of Judah in Egypt. [25]This is what the LORD Almighty, the God of Israel, says: You and your wives have done what you said you would do when you promised, 'We will certainly carry out the vows we made to burn incense and pour out drink offerings to the Queen of Heaven.'

"Go ahead then, do what you promised! Keep your vows! [26]But hear the word of the LORD, all you Jews living in Egypt: 'I swear by my great name,' says the LORD, 'that no one from Judah living anywhere in Egypt will ever again invoke my name or swear, "As surely as the Sovereign LORD lives." [27]For I

am watching over them for harm, not for good; the Jews in Egypt will perish by sword and famine until they are all destroyed. [28]Those who escape the sword and return to the land of Judah from Egypt will be very few. Then the whole remnant of Judah who came to live in Egypt will know whose word will stand—mine or theirs.

[29]" 'This will be the sign to you that I will punish you in this place,' declares the LORD, 'so that you will know that my threats of harm against you will surely stand.' [30]This is what the LORD says: 'I am going to deliver Pharaoh Hophra king of Egypt into the hands of his enemies who seek his life, just as I gave Zedekiah king of Judah into the hands of Nebuchadnezzar king of Babylon, the enemy who was seeking his life.' "

A Message to Baruch

45 When Baruch son of Neriah wrote on a scroll the words Jeremiah the prophet dictated in the fourth year of Jehoiakim son of Josiah king of Judah, Jeremiah said this to Baruch: [2]"This is what the LORD, the God of Israel, says to you, Baruch: [3]You said, 'Woe to me! The LORD has added sorrow to my pain; I am worn out with groaning and find no rest.' [4]But the LORD has told me to say to you, 'This is what the LORD says: I will overthrow what I have built and uproot what I have planted, throughout the earth. [5]Should you then seek great things for yourself? Do not seek them. For I will bring disaster on all people, declares the LORD, but wherever you go I will let you escape with your life.' "

A Message About Egypt

46 This is the word of the LORD that came to Jeremiah the prophet concerning the nations:

[2]Concerning Egypt:

This is the message against the army of Pharaoh Necho king of Egypt, which was defeated at Carchemish on the Euphrates River by Nebuchadnezzar king of Babylon in the fourth year of Jehoiakim son of Josiah king of Judah:

[3]"Prepare your shields, both large and
　　small,
　　and march out for battle!
[4]Harness the horses,
　　mount the steeds!

Take your positions
    with helmets on!
Polish your spears,
    put on your armor!
⁵ What do I see?
    They are terrified,
they are retreating,
    their warriors are defeated.
They flee in haste
    without looking back,
    and there is terror on every side,"
                declares the LORD.
⁶ "The swift cannot flee
    nor the strong escape.
In the north by the River Euphrates
    they stumble and fall.

⁷ "Who is this that rises like the Nile,
    like rivers of surging waters?
⁸ Egypt rises like the Nile,
    like rivers of surging waters.
She says, 'I will rise and cover the earth;
    I will destroy cities and their people.'
⁹ Charge, you horses!
    Drive furiously, you charioteers!
March on, you warriors—men of Cush*ᵃ*
        and Put who carry shields,
    men of Lydia who draw the bow.
¹⁰ But that day belongs to the Lord, the
        LORD Almighty—
    a day of vengeance, for vengeance on
        his foes.
The sword will devour till it is satisfied,
    till it has quenched its thirst with
        blood.
For the Lord, the LORD Almighty, will
        offer sacrifice
    in the land of the north by the River
        Euphrates.

¹¹ "Go up to Gilead and get balm,
    Virgin Daughter Egypt.
But you multiply remedies in vain;
    there is no healing for you.
¹² The nations will hear of your shame;
    your cries will fill the earth.
One warrior will stumble over another;
    both will fall down together."

¹³ This is the message the LORD spoke to
Jeremiah the prophet about the coming of
Nebuchadnezzar king of Babylon to attack
Egypt:

¹⁴ "Announce this in Egypt, and proclaim it
    in Migdol;
    proclaim it also in Memphis and
        Tahpanhes:
'Take your positions and get ready,
    for the sword devours those around
        you.'
¹⁵ Why will your warriors be laid low?
    They cannot stand, for the LORD will
        push them down.
¹⁶ They will stumble repeatedly;
    they will fall over each other.
They will say, 'Get up, let us go back
    to our own people and our native
        lands,
    away from the sword of the
        oppressor.'
¹⁷ There they will exclaim,
    'Pharaoh king of Egypt is only a loud
        noise;
    he has missed his opportunity.'

¹⁸ "As surely as I live," declares the King,
    whose name is the LORD Almighty,
"one will come who is like Tabor among
        the mountains,
    like Carmel by the sea.
¹⁹ Pack your belongings for exile,
    you who live in Egypt,
for Memphis will be laid waste
    and lie in ruins without inhabitant.

²⁰ "Egypt is a beautiful heifer,
    but a gadfly is coming
    against her from the north.
²¹ The mercenaries in her ranks
    are like fattened calves.
They too will turn and flee together,
    they will not stand their ground,
for the day of disaster is coming upon
        them,
    the time for them to be punished.
²² Egypt will hiss like a fleeing serpent
    as the enemy advances in force;
they will come against her with axes,
    like those who cut down trees.
²³ They will chop down her forest,"
                declares the LORD,
    "dense though it be.
They are more numerous than locusts,
    they cannot be counted.
²⁴ Daughter Egypt will be put to shame,
    given into the hands of the people of
        the north."

ᵃ 9 That is, the upper Nile region

²⁵The Lord Almighty, the God of Israel, says: "I am about to bring punishment on Amon god of Thebes, on Pharaoh, on Egypt and her gods and her kings, and on those who rely on Pharaoh. ²⁶I will give them into the hands of those who seek their lives—Nebuchadnezzar king of Babylon and his officers. Later, however, Egypt will be inhabited as in times past," declares the Lord.

²⁷"Do not be afraid, Jacob my servant;
    do not be dismayed, Israel.
I will surely save you out of a distant place,
    your descendants from the land of their exile.
Jacob will again have peace and security,
    and no one will make him afraid.
²⁸Do not be afraid, Jacob my servant,
    for I am with you," declares the Lord.
"Though I completely destroy all the nations
    among which I scatter you,
    I will not completely destroy you.
I will discipline you but only in due measure;
    I will not let you go entirely unpunished."

A Message About the Philistines

47 This is the word of the Lord that came to Jeremiah the prophet concerning the Philistines before Pharaoh attacked Gaza:

²This is what the Lord says:

"See how the waters are rising in the north;
    they will become an overflowing torrent.
They will overflow the land and everything in it,
    the towns and those who live in them.
The people will cry out;
    all who dwell in the land will wail
³at the sound of the hooves of galloping steeds,
    at the noise of enemy chariots
    and the rumble of their wheels.
Parents will not turn to help their children;
    their hands will hang limp.

⁴For the day has come
    to destroy all the Philistines
and to remove all survivors
    who could help Tyre and Sidon.
The Lord is about to destroy the Philistines,
    the remnant from the coasts of Caphtor.ᵃ
⁵Gaza will shave her head in mourning;
    Ashkelon will be silenced.
You remnant on the plain,
    how long will you cut yourselves?

⁶" 'Ah, sword of the Lord,' ⌐you cry,⌐
    'how long till you rest?
Return to your sheath;
    cease and be still.'
⁷But how can it rest
    when the Lord has commanded it,
when he has ordered it
    to attack Ashkelon and the coast?"

A Message About Moab

48 Concerning Moab:

This is what the Lord Almighty, the God of Israel, says:

"Woe to Nebo, for it will be ruined.
    Kiriathaim will be disgraced and captured;
    the strongholdᵇ will be disgraced and shattered.
²Moab will be praised no more;
    in Heshbonᶜ people will plot her downfall:
    'Come, let us put an end to that nation.'
You, the people of Madmen,ᵈ will also be silenced;
    the sword will pursue you.
³Cries of anguish arise from Horonaim,
    cries of great havoc and destruction.
⁴Moab will be broken;
    her little ones will cry out.ᵉ
⁵They go up the hill to Luhith,
    weeping bitterly as they go;
on the road down to Horonaim
    anguished cries over the destruction are heard.
⁶Flee! Run for your lives;
    become like a bushᶠ in the desert.
⁷Since you trust in your deeds and riches,

ᵃ 4 That is, Crete   ᵇ 1 Or captured; / Misgab   ᶜ 2 The Hebrew for Heshbon sounds like the Hebrew for plot.   ᵈ 2 The name of the Moabite town Madmen sounds like the Hebrew for be silenced.   ᵉ 4 Hebrew; Septuagint / proclaim it to Zoar   ᶠ 6 Or like Aroer

you too will be taken captive,
and Chemosh will go into exile,
together with his priests and officials.
⁸ The destroyer will come against every
town,
and not a town will escape.
The valley will be ruined
and the plateau destroyed,
because the LORD has spoken.
⁹ Put salt on Moab,
for she will be laid waste*a*;
her towns will become desolate,
with no one to live in them.

¹⁰ "A curse on those who are lax in doing
the LORD's work!
A curse on those who keep their
swords from bloodshed!

¹¹ "Moab has been at rest from youth,
like wine left on its dregs,
not poured from one jar to another—
she has not gone into exile.
So she tastes as she did,
and her aroma is unchanged.
¹² But days are coming,"
declares the LORD,
"when I will send people who pour from
jars,
and they will pour her out;
they will empty her jars
and smash her jugs.
¹³ Then Moab will be ashamed of
Chemosh,
as the house of Israel was ashamed
when they trusted in Bethel.

¹⁴ "How can you say, 'We are warriors,
men valiant in battle'?
¹⁵ Moab will be destroyed and her towns
invaded;
her finest young men will go down in
the slaughter,"
declares the King, whose name is the
LORD Almighty.
¹⁶ "The fall of Moab is at hand;
her calamity will come quickly.
¹⁷ Mourn for her, all who live around her,
all who know her fame;
say, 'How broken is the mighty scepter,
how broken the glorious staff!'

¹⁸ "Come down from your glory
and sit on the parched ground,
you inhabitants of Daughter Dibon,
for Moab's destroyer
will come up against you
and ruin your fortified cities.
¹⁹ Stand by the road and watch,
you who live in Aroer.
Ask the man fleeing and the woman
escaping,
ask them, 'What has happened?'
²⁰ Moab is disgraced, for she is shattered.
Wail and cry out!
Announce by the Arnon
that Moab is destroyed.
²¹ Judgment has come to the plateau—
to Holon, Jahzah and Mephaath,
²² to Dibon, Nebo and Beth Diblathaim,
²³ to Kiriathaim, Beth Gamul and Beth
Meon,
²⁴ to Kerioth and Bozrah—
to all the towns of Moab, far and
near.
²⁵ Moab's horn*b* is cut off;
her arm is broken,"
declares the LORD.

²⁶ "Make her drunk,
for she has defied the LORD.
Let Moab wallow in her vomit;
let her be an object of ridicule.
²⁷ Was not Israel the object of your
ridicule?
Was she caught among thieves,
that you shake your head in scorn
whenever you speak of her?
²⁸ Abandon your towns and dwell among
the rocks,
you who live in Moab.
Be like a dove that makes its nest
at the mouth of a cave.

²⁹ "We have heard of Moab's pride—
her overweening pride and conceit,
her pride and arrogance
and the haughtiness of her heart.
³⁰ I know her insolence but it is futile,"
declares the LORD,
"and her boasts accomplish nothing.
³¹ Therefore I wail over Moab,
for all Moab I cry out,
I moan for the people of Kir Hareseth.
³² I weep for you, as Jazer weeps,
you vines of Sibmah.
Your branches spread as far as the sea*c*;

a 9 Or *Give wings to Moab, / for she will fly away*   *b 25* *Horn* here symbolizes strength.
c 32 Probably the Dead Sea

they reached as far as[a] Jazer.
The destroyer has fallen
    on your ripened fruit and grapes.
33 Joy and gladness are gone
    from the orchards and fields of Moab.
I have stopped the flow of wine from the
        presses;
    no one treads them with shouts of joy.
Although there are shouts,
    they are not shouts of joy.

34 "The sound of their cry rises
    from Heshbon to Elealeh and Jahaz,
from Zoar as far as Horonaim and Eglath
        Shelishiyah,
    for even the waters of Nimrim are
        dried up.
35 In Moab I will put an end
    to those who make offerings on the
        high places
    and burn incense to their gods,"
            declares the LORD.
36 "So my heart laments for Moab like the
        music of a pipe;
    it laments like a pipe for the people of
        Kir Hareseth.
    The wealth they acquired is gone.
37 Every head is shaved
    and every beard cut off;
every hand is slashed
    and every waist is covered with
        sackcloth.
38 On all the roofs in Moab
    and in the public squares
there is nothing but mourning,
    for I have broken Moab
    like a jar that no one wants,"
            declares the LORD.
39 "How shattered she is! How they wail!
    How Moab turns her back in shame!
Moab has become an object of ridicule,
    an object of horror to all those around
        her."

40 This is what the LORD says:

"Look! An eagle is swooping down,
    spreading its wings over Moab.
41 Kerioth[b] will be captured
    and the strongholds taken.
In that day the hearts of Moab's warriors
    will be like the heart of a woman in
        labor.
42 Moab will be destroyed as a nation

because she defied the LORD.
43 Terror and pit and snare await you,
    you people of Moab,"
            declares the LORD.
44 "Whoever flees from the terror
    will fall into a pit,
whoever climbs out of the pit
    will be caught in a snare;
for I will bring on Moab
    the year of her punishment,"
            declares the LORD.

45 "In the shadow of Heshbon
    the fugitives stand helpless,
for a fire has gone out from Heshbon,
    a blaze from the midst of Sihon;
it burns the foreheads of Moab,
    the skulls of the noisy boasters.
46 Woe to you, Moab!
    The people of Chemosh are
        destroyed;
your sons are taken into exile
    and your daughters into captivity.

47 "Yet I will restore the fortunes of Moab
    in days to come,"
            declares the LORD.

Here ends the judgment on Moab.

A Message About Ammon

49

Concerning the Ammonites:

This is what the LORD says:

"Has Israel no children?
    Has she no heirs?
Why then has Molek[c] taken possession
        of Gad?
    Why do his people live in its towns?
2 But the days are coming,"
            declares the LORD,
"when I will sound the battle cry
    against Rabbah of the Ammonites;
it will become a mound of ruins,
    and its surrounding villages will be
        set on fire.
Then Israel will drive out
    those who drove her out,"
            says the LORD.
3 "Wail, Heshbon, for Ai is destroyed!
    Cry out, you inhabitants of Rabbah!
Put on sackcloth and mourn;
    rush here and there inside the walls,

---

a 32 Two Hebrew manuscripts and Septuagint; most Hebrew manuscripts *as far as the Sea of*
b 41 Or *The cities*   c 1 Or *their king*; also in verse 3

for Molek will go into exile,
    together with his priests and officials.
⁴ Why do you boast of your valleys,
    boast of your valleys so fruitful?
Unfaithful Daughter Ammon,
    you trust in your riches and say,
    'Who will attack me?'
⁵ I will bring terror on you
    from all those around you,"
                  declares the Lord,
                  the LORD Almighty.
"Every one of you will be driven away,
    and no one will gather the fugitives.

⁶ "Yet afterward, I will restore the fortunes
    of the Ammonites,"
                  declares the LORD.

A Message About Edom

⁷ Concerning Edom:

This is what the LORD Almighty says:

"Is there no longer wisdom in Teman?
    Has counsel perished from the
        prudent?
    Has their wisdom decayed?
⁸ Turn and flee, hide in deep caves,
    you who live in Dedan,
for I will bring disaster on Esau
    at the time when I punish him.
⁹ If grape pickers came to you,
    would they not leave a few grapes?
If thieves came during the night,
    would they not steal only as much as
        they wanted?
¹⁰ But I will strip Esau bare;
    I will uncover his hiding places,
    so that he cannot conceal himself.
His armed men are destroyed,
    also his allies and neighbors,
    so there is no one to say,
¹¹ 'Leave your fatherless children; I will
        keep them alive.
    Your widows too can depend on me.' "

¹² This is what the LORD says: "If those who do not deserve to drink the cup must drink it, why should you go unpunished? You will not go unpunished, but must drink it. ¹³ I swear by myself," declares the LORD, "that Bozrah will become a ruin and a curse,ᵃ an object of horror and reproach; and all its towns will be in ruins forever."

¹⁴ I have heard a message from the LORD;
    an envoy was sent to the nations to
        say,
"Assemble yourselves to attack it!
    Rise up for battle!"

¹⁵ "Now I will make you small among the
        nations,
    despised among the peoples.
¹⁶ The terror you inspire
    and the pride of your heart have
        deceived you,
you who live in the clefts of the rocks,
    who occupy the heights of the hill.
Though you build your nest as high as
        the eagle's,
    from there I will bring you down,"
                  declares the LORD.
¹⁷ "Edom will become an object of horror;
    all who pass by will be appalled and
        will scoff
    because of all its wounds.
¹⁸ As Sodom and Gomorrah were
        overthrown,
    along with their neighboring towns,"
                says the LORD,
"so no one will live there;
    no one will dwell in it.

¹⁹ "Like a lion coming up from Jordan's
        thickets
    to a rich pastureland,
I will chase Edom from its land in an
        instant.
    Who is the chosen one I will appoint
        for this?
Who is like me and who can challenge
        me?
    And what shepherd can stand against
        me?"
²⁰ Therefore, hear what the LORD has
        planned against Edom,
    what he has purposed against those
        who live in Teman:
The young of the flock will be dragged
        away;
    their pasture will be appalled at their
        fate.
²¹ At the sound of their fall the earth will
        tremble;
    their cry will resound to the Red Sea.ᵇ
²² Look! An eagle will soar and swoop
        down,

ᵃ 13 That is, its name will be used in cursing (see Jer. 29:22); or, others will see that it is cursed.
ᵇ 21 Or *the Sea of Reeds*

spreading its wings over Bozrah.
In that day the hearts of Edom's warriors
will be like the heart of a woman in
labor.

A Message About Damascus

²³Concerning Damascus:

"Hamath and Arpad are dismayed,
for they have heard bad news.
They are disheartened,
troubled like ᵃ the restless sea.
²⁴Damascus has become feeble,
she has turned to flee
and panic has gripped her;
anguish and pain have seized her,
pain like that of a woman in labor.
²⁵Why has the city of renown not been
abandoned,
the town in which I delight?
²⁶Surely, her young men will fall in the
streets;
all her soldiers will be silenced in that
day,"
declares the LORD Almighty.
²⁷"I will set fire to the walls of Damascus;
it will consume the fortresses of
Ben-Hadad."

A Message About Kedar and Hazor

²⁸Concerning Kedar and the kingdoms of
Hazor, which Nebuchadnezzar king of Babylon attacked:

This is what the LORD says:

"Arise, and attack Kedar
and destroy the people of the East.
²⁹Their tents and their flocks will be taken;
their shelters will be carried off
with all their goods and camels.
People will shout to them,
'Terror on every side!'

³⁰"Flee quickly away!
Stay in deep caves, you who live in
Hazor,"
declares the LORD.
"Nebuchadnezzar king of Babylon has
plotted against you;
he has devised a plan against you.

³¹"Arise and attack a nation at ease,
which lives in confidence,"
declares the LORD,

"a nation that has neither gates nor bars;
its people live far from danger.
³²Their camels will become plunder,
and their large herds will be booty.
I will scatter to the winds those who are
in distant places ᵇ
and will bring disaster on them from
every side,"
declares the LORD.
³³"Hazor will become a haunt of jackals,
a desolate place forever.
No one will live there;
no one will dwell in it."

A Message About Elam

³⁴This is the word of the LORD that came
to Jeremiah the prophet concerning Elam,
early in the reign of Zedekiah king of Judah:

³⁵This is what the LORD Almighty says:

"See, I will break the bow of Elam,
the mainstay of their might.
³⁶I will bring against Elam the four winds
from the four quarters of the
heavens;
I will scatter them to the four winds,
and there will not be a nation
where Elam's exiles do not go.
³⁷I will shatter Elam before their foes,
before those who seek their lives;
I will bring disaster on them,
even my fierce anger,"
declares the LORD.
"I will pursue them with the sword
until I have made an end of them.
³⁸I will set my throne in Elam
and destroy her king and officials,"
declares the LORD.

³⁹"Yet I will restore the fortunes of Elam
in days to come,"
declares the LORD.

A Message About Babylon

50

This is the word the LORD spoke
through Jeremiah the prophet
concerning Babylon and the
land of the Babylonians ᶜ:

²"Announce and proclaim among the
nations,
lift up a banner and proclaim it;
keep nothing back, but say,

ᵃ 23 Hebrew on or by   ᵇ 32 Or who clip the hair by their foreheads   ᶜ 1 Or Chaldeans; also in verses 8,
25, 35 and 45

'Babylon will be captured;
   Bel will be put to shame,
   Marduk filled with terror.
Her images will be put to shame
   and her idols filled with terror.'
³ A nation from the north will attack her
   and lay waste her land.
No one will live in it;
   both people and animals will flee
      away.

⁴ "In those days, at that time,"
   declares the LORD,
"the people of Israel and the people of
      Judah together
   will go in tears to seek the LORD their
      God.
⁵ They will ask the way to Zion
   and turn their faces toward it.
They will come and bind themselves to
      the LORD
   in an everlasting covenant
   that will not be forgotten.

⁶ "My people have been lost sheep;
   their shepherds have led them astray
   and caused them to roam on the
      mountains.
They wandered over mountain and hill
   and forgot their own resting place.
⁷ Whoever found them devoured them;
   their enemies said, 'We are not guilty,
for they sinned against the LORD, their
      verdant pasture,
   the LORD, the hope of their ancestors.'

⁸ "Flee out of Babylon;
   leave the land of the Babylonians,
   and be like the goats that lead the
      flock.
⁹ For I will stir up and bring against
      Babylon
   an alliance of great nations from the
      land of the north.
They will take up their positions against
      her,
   and from the north she will be
      captured.
Their arrows will be like skilled warriors
   who do not return empty-handed.
¹⁰ So Babylonia* will be plundered;
   all who plunder her will have their
      fill,"
                              declares the LORD.

¹¹ "Because you rejoice and are glad,
   you who pillage my inheritance,
because you frolic like a heifer threshing
      grain
   and neigh like stallions,
¹² your mother will be greatly ashamed;
   she who gave you birth will be
      disgraced.
She will be the least of the nations—
   a wilderness, a dry land, a desert.
¹³ Because of the LORD's anger she will not
      be inhabited
   but will be completely desolate.
All who pass Babylon will be appalled;
   they will scoff because of all her
      wounds.
¹⁴ "Take up your positions around Babylon,
   all you who draw the bow.
Shoot at her! Spare no arrows,
   for she has sinned against the LORD.
¹⁵ Shout against her on every side!
   She surrenders, her towers fall,
   her walls are torn down.
Since this is the vengeance of the LORD,
   take vengeance on her;
   do to her as she has done to others.
¹⁶ Cut off from Babylon the sowers,
   and the reapers with their sickles at
      harvest.
Because of the sword of the oppressor
   let everyone return to their own
      people,
   let everyone flee to their own land.

¹⁷ "Israel is a scattered flock
   that lions have chased away.
The first to devour them
   was the king of Assyria;
the last to crush their bones
   was Nebuchadnezzar king of
      Babylon."

¹⁸ Therefore this is what the LORD Almighty, the God of Israel, says:

"I will punish the king of Babylon and
      his land
   as I punished the king of Assyria.
¹⁹ But I will bring Israel back to their own
      pasture,
   and they will graze on Carmel and
      Bashan;
their appetite will be satisfied
   on the hills of Ephraim and Gilead.

---

a 10 Or *Chaldea*

20 In those days, at that time,"
  declares the LORD,
"search will be made for Israel's guilt,
  but there will be none,
and for the sins of Judah,
  but none will be found,
for I will forgive the remnant I spare.

21 "Attack the land of Merathaim
  and those who live in Pekod.
Pursue, kill and completely destroy[a]
  them,"
            declares the LORD.
"Do everything I have commanded
  you.
22 The noise of battle is in the land,
  the noise of great destruction!
23 How broken and shattered
  is the hammer of the whole earth!
How desolate is Babylon
  among the nations!
24 I set a trap for you, Babylon,
  and you were caught before you knew
    it;
you were found and captured
  because you opposed the LORD.
25 The LORD has opened his arsenal
  and brought out the weapons of his
    wrath,
for the Sovereign LORD Almighty has
  work to do
in the land of the Babylonians.
26 Come against her from afar.
  Break open her granaries;
  pile her up like heaps of grain.
Completely destroy her
  and leave her no remnant.
27 Kill all her young bulls;
  let them go down to the slaughter!
Woe to them! For their day has come,
  the time for them to be punished.
28 Listen to the fugitives and refugees from
    Babylon
  declaring in Zion
how the LORD our God has taken
  vengeance,
  vengeance for his temple.

29 "Summon archers against Babylon,
  all those who draw the bow.
Encamp all around her;
  let no one escape.
Repay her for her deeds;

do to her as she has done.
For she has defied the LORD,
  the Holy One of Israel.
30 Therefore, her young men will fall in the
    streets;
  all her soldiers will be silenced in that
    day,"
            declares the LORD.
31 "See, I am against you, you arrogant one,"
  declares the Lord, the LORD Almighty,
"for your day has come,
  the time for you to be punished.
32 The arrogant one will stumble and fall
  and no one will help her up;
I will kindle a fire in her towns
  that will consume all who are around
    her."

33 This is what the LORD Almighty says:

"The people of Israel are oppressed,
  and the people of Judah as well.
All their captors hold them fast,
  refusing to let them go.
34 Yet their Redeemer is strong;
  the LORD Almighty is his name.
He will vigorously defend their cause
  so that he may bring rest to their
    land,
but unrest to those who live in
  Babylon.

35 "A sword against the Babylonians!"
  declares the LORD—
"against those who live in Babylon
  and against her officials and wise
    counselors!
36 A sword against her false prophets!
  They will become fools.
A sword against her warriors!
  They will be filled with terror.
37 A sword against her horses and chariots
  and all the foreigners in her ranks!
  They will become weaklings.
A sword against her treasures!
  They will be plundered.
38 A drought on[b] her waters!
  They will dry up.
For it is a land of idols,
  idols that will go mad with terror.

39 "So desert creatures and hyenas will live
    there,
  and there the owl will dwell.

---

a 21 The Hebrew term refers to the irrevocable giving over of things or persons to the LORD, often by totally destroying them; also in verse 26.   b 38 Or A sword against

It will never again be inhabited
    or lived in from generation to
        generation.
40 As I overthrew Sodom and Gomorrah
    along with their neighboring towns,"
              declares the LORD,
  "so no one will live there;
    no one will dwell in it.

41 "Look! An army is coming from the north;
    a great nation and many kings
    are being stirred up from the ends of
        the earth.
42 They are armed with bows and spears;
    they are cruel and without mercy.
They sound like the roaring sea
    as they ride on their horses;
they come like men in battle formation
    to attack you, Daughter Babylon.
43 The king of Babylon has heard reports
        about them,
    and his hands hang limp.
Anguish has gripped him,
    pain like that of a woman in labor.
44 Like a lion coming up from Jordan's
        thickets
    to a rich pastureland,
I will chase Babylon from its land in an
        instant.
    Who is the chosen one I will appoint
        for this?
Who is like me and who can challenge
        me?
    And what shepherd can stand against
        me?"

45 Therefore, hear what the LORD has
        planned against Babylon,
    what he has purposed against the
        land of the Babylonians:
The young of the flock will be dragged
        away;
    their pasture will be appalled at their
        fate.
46 At the sound of Babylon's capture the
        earth will tremble;
    its cry will resound among the
        nations.

51

This is what the LORD says:

"See, I will stir up the spirit of a
destroyer

against Babylon and the people of
    Leb Kamai.ᵃ
2 I will send foreigners to Babylon
    to winnow her and to devastate her
        land;
they will oppose her on every side
    in the day of her disaster.
3 Let not the archer string his bow,
    nor let him put on his armor.
Do not spare her young men;
    completely destroyᵇ her army.
4 They will fall down slain in Babylon,ᶜ
    fatally wounded in her streets.
5 For Israel and Judah have not been
        forsaken
    by their God, the LORD Almighty,
though their landᵈ is full of guilt
    before the Holy One of Israel.

6 "Flee from Babylon!
    Run for your lives!
    Do not be destroyed because of her
        sins.
It is time for the LORD's vengeance;
    he will repay her what she deserves.
7 Babylon was a gold cup in the LORD's
        hand;
    she made the whole earth drunk.
The nations drank her wine;
    therefore they have now gone mad.
8 Babylon will suddenly fall and be broken.
    Wail over her!
Get balm for her pain;
    perhaps she can be healed.

9 " 'We would have healed Babylon,
    but she cannot be healed;
let us leave her and each go to our own
        land,
for her judgment reaches to the skies,
    it rises as high as the heavens.'

10 " 'The LORD has vindicated us;
    come, let us tell in Zion
    what the LORD our God has done.'

11 "Sharpen the arrows,
    take up the shields!
The LORD has stirred up the kings of the
        Medes,
    because his purpose is to destroy
        Babylon.
The LORD will take vengeance,
    vengeance for his temple.

ᵃ 1 Leb Kamai is a cryptogram for Chaldea, that is, Babylonia.   ᵇ 3 The Hebrew term refers to the irrevocable giving over of things or persons to the LORD, often by totally destroying them.
ᶜ 4 Or Chaldea   ᵈ 5 Or Almighty, / and the land ⌊of the Babylonians⌋

¹²Lift up a banner against the walls of
    Babylon!
  Reinforce the guard,
station the watchmen,
  prepare an ambush!
The Lord will carry out his purpose,
  his decree against the people of
    Babylon.
¹³You who live by many waters
  and are rich in treasures,
your end has come,
  the time for you to be destroyed.
¹⁴The Lord Almighty has sworn by
    himself:
  I will surely fill you with troops, as
    with a swarm of locusts,
  and they will shout in triumph over
    you.

¹⁵"He made the earth by his power;
  he founded the world by his wisdom
  and stretched out the heavens by his
    understanding.
¹⁶When he thunders, the waters in the
    heavens roar;
  he makes clouds rise from the ends of
    the earth.
He sends lightning with the rain
  and brings out the wind from his
    storehouses.

¹⁷"Everyone is senseless and without
    knowledge;
  all goldsmiths are shamed by their
    idols.
Their images are a fraud;
  they have no breath in them.
¹⁸They are worthless, the objects of
    mockery;
  when their judgment comes, they will
    perish.
¹⁹He who is the Portion of Jacob is not like
    these,
  for he is the Maker of all things,
including the tribe of his inheritance—
  the Lord Almighty is his name.

²⁰"You are my war club,
  my weapon for battle—
with you I shatter nations,
  with you I destroy kingdoms,
²¹with you I shatter horse and rider,
  with you I shatter chariot and driver,
²²with you I shatter man and woman,
  with you I shatter old man and youth,

with you I shatter young man and
    young woman,
²³with you I shatter shepherd and flock,
  with you I shatter farmer and oxen,
  with you I shatter governors and
    officials.

²⁴"Before your eyes I will repay Babylon
and all who live in Babylonia[a] for all the
wrong they have done in Zion," declares the
Lord.

²⁵"I am against you, you destroying
    mountain,
  you who destroy the whole earth,"
        declares the Lord.
"I will stretch out my hand against you,
  roll you off the cliffs,
  and make you a burned-out
    mountain.
²⁶No rock will be taken from you for a
    cornerstone,
  nor any stone for a foundation,
for you will be desolate forever,"
        declares the Lord.

²⁷"Lift up a banner in the land!
  Blow the trumpet among the nations!
Prepare the nations for battle against
    her;
  summon against her these kingdoms:
    Ararat, Minni and Ashkenaz.
Appoint a commander against her;
  send up horses like a swarm of
    locusts.
²⁸Prepare the nations for battle against
    her—
  the kings of the Medes,
  their governors and all their officials,
  and all the countries they rule.
²⁹The land trembles and writhes,
  for the Lord's purposes against
    Babylon stand—
to lay waste the land of Babylon
  so that no one will live there.
³⁰Babylon's warriors have stopped
    fighting;
  they remain in their strongholds.
Their strength is exhausted;
  they have become weaklings.
Her dwellings are set on fire;
  the bars of her gates are broken.
³¹One courier follows another
  and messenger follows messenger
to announce to the king of Babylon

a 24 Or *Chaldea*; also in verse 35

that his entire city is captured,
³² the river crossings seized,
    the marshes set on fire,
    and the soldiers terrified."

³³ This is what the LORD Almighty, the God of Israel, says:

"Daughter Babylon is like a threshing
    floor
    at the time it is trampled;
    the time to harvest her will soon
        come."

³⁴ "Nebuchadnezzar king of Babylon has
        devoured us,
    he has thrown us into confusion,
    he has made us an empty jar.
Like a serpent he has swallowed us
    and filled his stomach with our
        delicacies,
    and then has spewed us out.
³⁵ May the violence done to our flesh ᵃ be
        on Babylon,"
    say the inhabitants of Zion.
"May our blood be on those who live in
        Babylonia,"
    says Jerusalem.

³⁶ Therefore, this is what the LORD says:

"See, I will defend your cause
    and avenge you;
I will dry up her sea
    and make her springs dry.
³⁷ Babylon will be a heap of ruins,
    a haunt of jackals,
    an object of horror and scorn,
    a place where no one lives.
³⁸ Her people all roar like young lions,
    they growl like lion cubs.
³⁹ But while they are aroused,
    I will set out a feast for them
    and make them drunk,
so that they shout with laughter—
    then sleep forever and not awake,"
                declares the LORD.
⁴⁰ "I will bring them down
    like lambs to the slaughter,
    like rams and goats.

⁴¹ "How Sheshak ᵇ will be captured,
    the boast of the whole earth seized!
How desolate Babylon will be
    among the nations!
⁴² The sea will rise over Babylon;

its roaring waves will cover her.
⁴³ Her towns will be desolate,
    a dry and desert land,
a land where no one lives,
    through which no one travels.
⁴⁴ I will punish Bel in Babylon
    and make him spew out what he has
        swallowed.
The nations will no longer stream to
    him.
And the wall of Babylon will fall.

⁴⁵ "Come out of her, my people!
    Run for your lives!
    Run from the fierce anger of the
        LORD.
⁴⁶ Do not lose heart or be afraid
    when rumors are heard in the land;
one rumor comes this year, another the
    next,
    rumors of violence in the land
    and of ruler against ruler.
⁴⁷ For the time will surely come
    when I will punish the idols of
        Babylon;
    her whole land will be disgraced
    and her slain will all lie fallen within
        her.
⁴⁸ Then heaven and earth and all that is in
        them
    will shout for joy over Babylon,
for out of the north
    destroyers will attack her,"
                declares the LORD.

⁴⁹ "Babylon must fall because of Israel's
        slain,
    just as the slain in all the earth
    have fallen because of Babylon.
⁵⁰ You who have escaped the sword,
    leave and do not linger!
Remember the LORD in a distant land,
    and call to mind Jerusalem."

⁵¹ "We are disgraced,
    for we have been insulted
    and shame covers our faces,
because foreigners have entered
    the holy places of the LORD's house."

⁵² "But days are coming," declares the
        LORD,
    "when I will punish her idols,
and throughout her land
    the wounded will groan.

ᵃ 35 Or done to us and to our children   ᵇ 41 Sheshak is a cryptogram for Babylon.

⁵³Even if Babylon reaches the sky
  and fortifies her lofty stronghold,
I will send destroyers against her,"
                    declares the LORD.

⁵⁴ "The sound of a cry comes from
        Babylon,
  the sound of great destruction
  from the land of the Babylonians. ᵃ
⁵⁵The LORD will destroy Babylon;
  he will silence her noisy din.
Waves of enemies will rage like great
        waters;
  the roar of their voices will resound.
⁵⁶A destroyer will come against Babylon;
  her warriors will be captured,
  and their bows will be broken.
For the LORD is a God of retribution;
  he will repay in full.
⁵⁷I will make her officials and wise
        counselors drunk,
  her governors, officers and warriors as
        well;
they will sleep forever and not awake,"
  declares the King, whose name is the
        LORD Almighty.

⁵⁸This is what the LORD Almighty says:

"Babylon's thick wall will be leveled
  and her high gates set on fire;
the peoples exhaust themselves for
        nothing,
  the nations' labor is only fuel for the
        flames."

⁵⁹This is the message Jeremiah the
prophet gave to the staff officer Seraiah son
of Neriah, the son of Mahseiah, when he
went to Babylon with Zedekiah king of Judah in the fourth year of his reign. ⁶⁰Jeremi-
ah had written on a scroll about all the disasters that would come upon Babylon—all
that had been recorded concerning Babylon.
⁶¹He said to Seraiah, "When you get to Babylon, see that you read all these words
aloud. ⁶²Then say, 'LORD, you have said you
will destroy this place, so that neither people nor animals will live in it; it will be desolate forever.' ⁶³When you finish reading
this scroll, tie a stone to it and throw it into
the Euphrates. ⁶⁴Then say, 'So will Babylon
sink to rise no more because of the disaster
I will bring on her. And her people will fall.' "

The words of Jeremiah end here.

The Fall of Jerusalem

52 Zedekiah was twenty-one years
old when he became king, and
he reigned in Jerusalem eleven
years. His mother's name was Hamutal
daughter of Jeremiah; she was from Libnah.
²He did evil in the eyes of the LORD, just as
Jehoiakim had done. ³It was because of the
LORD's anger that all this happened to Jerusalem and Judah, and in the end he thrust
them from his presence.

Now Zedekiah rebelled against the king
of Babylon.

⁴So in the ninth year of Zedekiah's reign,
on the tenth day of the tenth month, Nebuchadnezzar king of Babylon marched
against Jerusalem with his whole army.
They encamped outside the city and built
siege works all around it. ⁵The city was kept
under siege until the eleventh year of King
Zedekiah.

⁶By the ninth day of the fourth month the
famine in the city had become so severe
that there was no food for the people to eat.
⁷Then the city wall was broken through, and
the whole army fled. They left the city at
night through the gate between the two
walls near the king's garden, though the
Babylonians ᵇ were surrounding the city.
They fled toward the Arabah, ᶜ ⁸but the Babylonian ᵈ army pursued King Zedekiah and
overtook him in the plains of Jericho. All his
soldiers were separated from him and scattered, ⁹and he was captured.

He was taken to the king of Babylon at
Riblah in the land of Hamath, where he pronounced sentence on him. ¹⁰There at Riblah
the king of Babylon killed the sons of Zedekiah before his eyes; he also killed all the officials of Judah. ¹¹Then he put out Zedekiah's
eyes, bound him with bronze shackles and
took him to Babylon, where he put him in
prison till the day of his death.

¹²On the tenth day of the fifth month, in
the nineteenth year of Nebuchadnezzar king
of Babylon, Nebuzaradan commander of the
imperial guard, who served the king of Babylon, came to Jerusalem. ¹³He set fire to the
temple of the LORD, the royal palace and all
the houses of Jerusalem. Every important

ᵃ 54 Or *Chaldeans*   ᵇ 7 Or *Chaldeans*; also in verse 17   ᶜ 7 Or *the Jordan Valley*   ᵈ 8 Or *Chaldean*;
also in verse 14

building he burned down. ¹⁴The whole Babylonian army, under the commander of the imperial guard, broke down all the walls around Jerusalem. ¹⁵Nebuzaradan the commander of the guard carried into exile some of the poorest people and those who remained in the city, along with the rest of the skilled workers*a* and those who had deserted to the king of Babylon. ¹⁶But Nebuzaradan left behind the rest of the poorest people of the land to work the vineyards and fields.

¹⁷The Babylonians broke up the bronze pillars, the movable stands and the bronze Sea that were at the temple of the Lord and they carried all the bronze to Babylon. ¹⁸They also took away the pots, shovels, wick trimmers, sprinkling bowls, dishes and all the bronze articles used in the temple service. ¹⁹The commander of the imperial guard took away the basins, censers, sprinkling bowls, pots, lampstands, dishes and bowls used for drink offerings—all that were made of pure gold or silver.

²⁰The bronze from the two pillars, the Sea and the twelve bronze bulls under it, and the movable stands, which King Solomon had made for the temple of the Lord, was more than could be weighed. ²¹Each pillar was eighteen cubits high and twelve cubits in circumference*b*; each was four fingers thick, and hollow. ²²The bronze capital on top of one pillar was five cubits*c* high and was decorated with a network and pomegranates of bronze all around. The other pillar, with its pomegranates, was similar. ²³There were ninety-six pomegranates on the sides; the total number of pomegranates above the surrounding network was a hundred.

²⁴The commander of the guard took as prisoners Seraiah the chief priest, Zephaniah the priest next in rank and the three doorkeepers. ²⁵Of those still in the city, he took the officer in charge of the fighting men, and seven royal advisers. He also took the secretary who was chief officer in charge of conscripting the people of the land, sixty of whom were found in the city. ²⁶Nebuzaradan the commander took them all and brought them to the king of Babylon at Riblah. ²⁷There at Riblah, in the land of Hamath, the king had them executed.

So Judah went into captivity, away from her land. ²⁸This is the number of the people Nebuchadnezzar carried into exile:

in the seventh year, 3,023 Jews;
²⁹in Nebuchadnezzar's eighteenth year,
     832 people from Jerusalem;
³⁰in his twenty-third year,
     745 Jews taken into exile by Nebuzaradan the commander of the imperial guard.
There were 4,600 people in all.

Jehoiachin Released

³¹In the thirty-seventh year of the exile of Jehoiachin king of Judah, in the year Awel-Marduk became king of Babylon, on the twenty-fifth day of the twelfth month, he released Jehoiachin king of Judah and freed him from prison. ³²He spoke kindly to him and gave him a seat of honor higher than those of the other kings who were with him in Babylon. ³³So Jehoiachin put aside his prison clothes and for the rest of his life ate regularly at the king's table. ³⁴Day by day the king of Babylon gave Jehoiachin a regular allowance as long as he lived, till the day of his death.

---

a 15 Or *the populace*   *b 21* That is, about 27 feet high and 18 feet in circumference or about 8.2 meters high and 5.4 meters in circumference   *c 22* That is, about 7 1/2 feet or about 2.3 meters

lamentations

AUTHOR: Possibly Jeremiah

DATE: Shortly after Jerusalem fell to the Babylonians in 586 B.C.

THEME: God grieves at our inability to follow him, but he also offers hope.

1 *a* How deserted lies the city,
   once so full of people!
   How like a widow is she,
   who once was great among the
      nations!
She who was queen among the
      provinces
   has now become a slave.

2 Bitterly she weeps at night,
   tears are on her cheeks.
Among all her lovers
   there is none to comfort her.
All her friends have betrayed her;
   they have become her enemies.

3 After affliction and harsh labor,
   Judah has gone into exile.
She dwells among the nations;
   she finds no resting place.
All who pursue her have overtaken her
   in the midst of her distress.

4 The roads to Zion mourn,
   for no one comes to her appointed
      festivals.
All her gateways are desolate,
   her priests groan,
her young women grieve,
   and she is in bitter anguish.

5 Her foes have become her masters;
   her enemies are at ease.
The LORD has brought her grief
   because of her many sins.
Her children have gone into exile,
   captive before the foe.

6 All the splendor has departed
   from Daughter Zion.

Her princes are like deer
   that find no pasture;
in weakness they have fled
   before the pursuer.

7 In the days of her affliction and
      wandering
Jerusalem remembers all the
      treasures
   that were hers in days of old.
When her people fell into enemy hands,
   there was no one to help her.
Her enemies looked at her
   and laughed at her destruction.

8 Jerusalem has sinned greatly
   and so has become unclean.
All who honored her despise her,
   for they have seen her nakedness;
she herself groans
   and turns away.

9 Her filthiness clung to her skirts;
   she did not consider her future.
Her fall was astounding;
   there was none to comfort her.
"Look, LORD, on my affliction,
   for the enemy has triumphed."

10 The enemy laid hands
   on all her treasures;
she saw pagan nations
   enter her sanctuary—
those you had forbidden
   to enter your assembly.

11 All her people groan
   as they search for bread;
they barter their treasures for food
   to keep themselves alive.

a This chapter is an acrostic poem, the verses of which begin with the successive letters of the Hebrew alphabet.

"Look, LORD, and consider,
  for I am despised."

12 "Is it nothing to you, all you who pass by?
    Look around and see.
  Is any suffering like my suffering
    that was inflicted on me,
  that the LORD brought on me
    in the day of his fierce anger?

13 "From on high he sent fire,
    sent it down into my bones.
  He spread a net for my feet
    and turned me back.
  He made me desolate,
    faint all the day long.

14 "My sins have been bound into a yoke*a*;
    by his hands they were woven
      together.
  They have been hung on my neck,
    and the Lord has sapped my strength.
  He has given me into the hands
    of those I cannot withstand.

15 "The Lord has rejected
    all the warriors in my midst;
  he has summoned an army against me
    to*b* crush my young men.
  In his winepress the Lord has trampled
    Virgin Daughter Judah.

16 "This is why I weep
    and my eyes overflow with tears.
  No one is near to comfort me,
    no one to restore my spirit.
  My children are destitute
    because the enemy has prevailed."

17 Zion stretches out her hands,
    but there is no one to comfort her.
  The LORD has decreed for Jacob
    that his neighbors become his foes;
  Jerusalem has become
    an unclean thing among them.

18 "The LORD is righteous,
    yet I rebelled against his command.
  Listen, all you peoples;
    look on my suffering.
  My young men and young women
    have gone into exile.

19 "I called to my allies
    but they betrayed me.

My priests and my elders
    perished in the city
  while they searched for food
    to keep themselves alive.

20 "See, LORD, how distressed I am!
    I am in torment within,
  and in my heart I am disturbed,
    for I have been most rebellious.
  Outside, the sword bereaves;
    inside, there is only death.

21 "People have heard my groaning,
    but there is no one to comfort me.
  All my enemies have heard of my
      distress;
    they rejoice at what you have done.
  May you bring the day you have
      announced
    so they may become like me.

22 "Let all their wickedness come before
      you;
    deal with them
  as you have dealt with me
    because of all my sins.
  My groans are many
    and my heart is faint."

2 *c* How the Lord has covered Daughter
      Zion
    with the cloud of his anger*d*!
  He has hurled down the splendor of
      Israel
    from heaven to earth;
  he has not remembered his footstool
    in the day of his anger.

2 Without pity the Lord has swallowed up
    all the dwellings of Jacob;
  in his wrath he has torn down
    the strongholds of Daughter Judah.
  He has brought her kingdom and its
      princes
    down to the ground in dishonor.

3 In fierce anger he has cut off
    every horn*e* of Israel.
  He has withdrawn his right hand
    at the approach of the enemy.
  He has burned in Jacob like a flaming
      fire
    that consumes everything around it.

---

a 14 Most Hebrew manuscripts; many Hebrew manuscripts and Septuagint *He kept watch over my sins*
b 15 Or *has set a time for me / when he will*   *c* This chapter is an acrostic poem, the verses of which
begin with the successive letters of the Hebrew alphabet.   *d 1* Or *How the Lord in his anger / has treated
Daughter Zion with contempt*   *e 3* Or *off / all the strength;* or *every king; horn* here symbolizes strength.

4 Like an enemy he has strung his bow;
    his right hand is ready.
Like a foe he has slain
    all who were pleasing to the eye;
he has poured out his wrath like fire
    on the tent of Daughter Zion.

5 The Lord is like an enemy;
    he has swallowed up Israel.
He has swallowed up all her palaces
    and destroyed her strongholds.
He has multiplied mourning and
        lamentation
    for Daughter Judah.

6 He has laid waste his dwelling like a
        garden;
    he has destroyed his place of
        meeting.
The Lord has made Zion forget
    her appointed festivals and her
        Sabbaths;
in his fierce anger he has spurned
    both king and priest.

7 The Lord has rejected his altar
    and abandoned his sanctuary.
He has given the walls of her palaces
    into the hands of the enemy;
they have raised a shout in the house of
        the Lord
    as on the day of an appointed festival.

8 The Lord determined to tear down
    the wall around Daughter Zion.
He stretched out a measuring line
    and did not withhold his hand from
        destroying.
He made ramparts and walls lament;
    together they wasted away.

9 Her gates have sunk into the ground;
    their bars he has broken and
        destroyed.
Her king and her princes are exiled
        among the nations,
    the law is no more,
and her prophets no longer find
    visions from the Lord.

10 The elders of Daughter Zion
    sit on the ground in silence;
they have sprinkled dust on their heads
    and put on sackcloth.
The young women of Jerusalem
    have bowed their heads to the
        ground.

11 My eyes fail from weeping,
    I am in torment within;
my heart is poured out on the ground
    because my people are destroyed,
because children and infants faint
    in the streets of the city.

12 They say to their mothers,
    "Where is bread and wine?"
as they faint like the wounded
    in the streets of the city,
as their lives ebb away
    in their mothers' arms.

13 What can I say for you?
    With what can I compare you,
        Daughter Jerusalem?
To what can I liken you,
    that I may comfort you,
        Virgin Daughter Zion?
Your wound is as deep as the sea.
    Who can heal you?

14 The visions of your prophets
    were false and worthless;
they did not expose your sin
    to ward off your captivity.
The prophecies they gave you
    were false and misleading.

15 All who pass your way
    clap their hands at you;
they scoff and shake their heads
    at Daughter Jerusalem:
"Is this the city that was called
    the perfection of beauty,
    the joy of the whole earth?"

16 All your enemies open their mouths
        wide against you;
    they scoff and gnash their teeth
        and say, "We have swallowed her up.
This is the day we have waited for;
    we have lived to see it."

17 The Lord has done what he planned;
    he has fulfilled his word,
    which he decreed long ago.
He has overthrown you without pity,
    he has let the enemy gloat over you,
    he has exalted the horn a of your foes.

18 The hearts of the people
    cry out to the Lord.

a 17 *Horn* here symbolizes strength.

You walls of Daughter Zion,
let your tears flow like a river
day and night;
give yourself no relief,
your eyes no rest.

¹⁹ Arise, cry out in the night,
as the watches of the night begin;
pour out your heart like water
in the presence of the Lord.
Lift up your hands to him
for the lives of your children,
who faint from hunger
at every street corner.

²⁰ "Look, Lord, and consider:
Whom have you ever treated like
this?
Should women eat their offspring,
the children they have cared for?
Should priest and prophet be killed
in the sanctuary of the Lord?

²¹ "Young and old lie together
in the dust of the streets;
my young men and young women
have fallen by the sword.
You have slain them in the day of your
anger;
you have slaughtered them without
pity.

²² "As you summon to a feast day,
so you summoned against me terrors
on every side.
In the day of the Lord's anger
no one escaped or survived;
those I cared for and reared
my enemy has destroyed."

3 ᵃ I am one who has seen affliction
by the rod of the Lord's wrath.
² He has driven me away and made
me walk
in darkness rather than light;
³ indeed, he has turned his hand against me
again and again, all day long.

⁴ He has made my skin and my flesh grow
old
and has broken my bones.
⁵ He has besieged me and surrounded me
with bitterness and hardship.
⁶ He has made me dwell in darkness
like those long dead.

⁷ He has walled me in so I cannot escape;
he has weighed me down with chains.
⁸ Even when I call out or cry for help,
he shuts out my prayer.
⁹ He has barred my way with blocks of
stone;
he has made my paths crooked.

¹⁰ Like a bear lying in wait,
like a lion in hiding,
¹¹ he dragged me from the path and
mangled me
and left me without help.
¹² He drew his bow
and made me the target for his
arrows.

¹³ He pierced my heart
with arrows from his quiver.
¹⁴ I became the laughingstock of all my
people;
they mock me in song all day long.
¹⁵ He has filled me with bitter herbs
and sated me with gall.

¹⁶ He has broken my teeth with gravel;
he has trampled me in the dust.
¹⁷ I have been deprived of peace;
I have forgotten what prosperity is.
¹⁸ So I say, "My splendor is gone
and all that I had hoped from the
Lord."

¹⁹ I remember my affliction and my
wandering,
the bitterness and the gall.
²⁰ I well remember them,
and my soul is downcast within me.
²¹ Yet this I call to mind
and therefore I have hope:

²² Because of the Lord's great love we are
not consumed,
for his compassions never fail.
²³ They are new every morning;
great is your faithfulness.
²⁴ I say to myself, "The Lord is my
portion;
therefore I will wait for him."

²⁵ The Lord is good to those whose hope is
in him,
to the one who seeks him;
²⁶ it is good to wait quietly
for the salvation of the Lord.

ᵃ This chapter is an acrostic poem; the verses of each stanza begin with the successive letters of the
Hebrew alphabet, and the verses within each stanza begin with the same letter.

27 It is good for people to bear the yoke
   while they are young.

28 Let them sit alone in silence,
   for the LORD has laid it on them.
29 Let them bury their faces in the dust—
   there may yet be hope.
30 Let them offer their cheeks to one who
      would strike them,
   and let them be filled with disgrace.

31 For people are not cast off
   by the Lord forever.
32 Though he brings grief, he will show
      compassion,
   so great is his unfailing love.
33 For he does not willingly bring affliction
   or grief to any human being.

34 To crush underfoot
   all prisoners in the land,
35 to deny people their rights
   before the Most High,
36 to deprive them of justice—
   would not the Lord see such things?

37 Who can speak and have it happen
   if the Lord has not decreed it?
38 Is it not from the mouth of the Most High
   that both calamities and good things
      come?
39 Why should the living complain
   when punished for their sins?

40 Let us examine our ways and test them,
   and let us return to the LORD.
41 Let us lift up our hearts and our hands
   to God in heaven, and say:
42 "We have sinned and rebelled
   and you have not forgiven.

43 "You have covered yourself with anger
      and pursued us;
   you have slain without pity.
44 You have covered yourself with a cloud
   so that no prayer can get through.
45 You have made us scum and refuse
   among the nations.

46 "All our enemies have opened their
      mouths
   wide against us.
47 We have suffered terror and pitfalls,
   ruin and destruction."
48 Streams of tears flow from my eyes
   because my people are destroyed.

49 My eyes will flow unceasingly,
   without relief,
50 until the LORD looks down
   from heaven and sees.
51 What I see brings grief to my soul
   because of all the women of my city.

52 Those who were my enemies without
      cause
   hunted me like a bird.
53 They tried to end my life in a pit
   and threw stones at me;
54 the waters closed over my head,
   and I thought I was about to perish.

55 I called on your name, LORD,
   from the depths of the pit.
56 You heard my plea: "Do not close your
      ears
   to my cry for relief."
57 You came near when I called you,
   and you said, "Do not fear."

58 You, Lord, took up my case;
   you redeemed my life.
59 LORD, you have seen the wrong done to
      me.
   Uphold my cause!
60 You have seen the depth of their
      vengeance,
   all their plots against me.

61 LORD, you have heard their insults,
   all their plots against me—
62 what my enemies whisper and mutter
   against me all day long.
63 Look at them! Sitting or standing,
   they mock me in their songs.

64 Pay them back what they deserve, LORD,
   for what their hands have done.
65 Put a veil over their hearts,
   and may your curse be on them!
66 Pursue them in anger and destroy them
   from under the heavens of the LORD.

4 *a* How the gold has lost its luster,
   the fine gold become dull!
   The sacred gems are scattered
   at every street corner.

2 How the precious children of Zion,
   once worth their weight in gold,
   are now considered as pots of clay,
   the work of a potter's hands!

---

a This chapter is an acrostic poem, the verses of which begin with the successive letters of the Hebrew alphabet.

³ Even jackals offer their breasts
    to nurse their young,
but my people have become heartless
    like ostriches in the desert.

⁴ Because of thirst the infant's tongue
    sticks to the roof of its mouth;
the children beg for bread,
    but no one gives it to them.

⁵ Those who once ate delicacies
    are destitute in the streets.
Those nurtured in purple
    now lie on ash heaps.

⁶ The punishment of my people
    is greater than that of Sodom,
which was overthrown in a moment
    without a hand turned to help her.

⁷ Their princes were brighter than snow
    and whiter than milk,
their bodies more ruddy than rubies,
    their appearance like lapis lazuli.

⁸ But now they are blacker than soot;
    they are not recognized in the streets.
Their skin has shriveled on their bones;
    it has become as dry as a stick.

⁹ Those killed by the sword are better off
    than those who die of famine;
racked with hunger, they waste away
    for lack of food from the field.

¹⁰ With their own hands compassionate
        women
    have cooked their own children,
who became their food
    when my people were destroyed.

¹¹ The LORD has given full vent to his wrath;
    he has poured out his fierce anger.
He kindled a fire in Zion
    that consumed her foundations.

¹² The kings of the earth did not believe,
    nor did any of the peoples of the
        world,
that enemies and foes could enter
    the gates of Jerusalem.

¹³ But it happened because of the sins of
        her prophets
    and the iniquities of her priests,
who shed within her
    the blood of the righteous.

¹⁴ Now they grope through the streets
    as if they were blind.
They are so defiled with blood

that no one dares to touch their
    garments.

¹⁵ "Go away! You are unclean!" people cry
        to them.
    "Away! Away! Don't touch us!"
When they flee and wander about,
    people among the nations say,
    "They can stay here no longer."

¹⁶ The LORD himself has scattered them;
    he no longer watches over them.
The priests are shown no honor,
    the elders no favor.

¹⁷ Moreover, our eyes failed,
    looking in vain for help;
from our towers we watched
    for a nation that could not save us.

¹⁸ People stalked us at every step,
    so we could not walk in our streets.
Our end was near, our days were
        numbered,
    for our end had come.

¹⁹ Our pursuers were swifter
    than eagles in the sky;
they chased us over the mountains
    and lay in wait for us in the desert.

²⁰ The LORD's anointed, our very life breath,
    was caught in their traps.
We thought that under his shadow
    we would live among the nations.

²¹ Rejoice and be glad, Daughter Edom,
    you who live in the land of Uz.
But to you also the cup will be passed;
    you will be drunk and stripped naked.

²² Your punishment will end, Daughter Zion;
    he will not prolong your exile.
But he will punish your sin, Daughter
        Edom,
    and expose your wickedness.

5 Remember, LORD, what has happened
        to us;
    look, and see our disgrace.
² Our inheritance has been turned over to
        strangers,
    our homes to foreigners.
³ We have become fatherless,
    our mothers are widows.
⁴ We must buy the water we drink;
    our wood can be had only at a price.
⁵ Those who pursue us are at our heels;
    we are weary and find no rest.

TUESDAY

LOVE GREATER THAN ANGER

Lamentations 5:1–22 or 5:1,19,21

Rob Lacey

[I'm] thrown down on my grief, . . . pull[ed] down into the jaws of depression. But hope hovers above me when I make myself remember . . . His love. His incredible love has protected us—we're still alive, aren't we? His passion for us doesn't go hot and cold. It's pumped in daily; in every sunrise we get a brand-new dose of your loyalty and love, God. I tell myself, "God's all I've got: I'll wait for him to show."

God's love's bigger than his anger. His love outlasts his loathe. His fury will flag and his pain will peter out.

GEORGE WHITEFIELD {AD 1714–1770}

I have no doubt that the angels, sent forth to minister to us who are heirs of salvation, often stand astonished when they encamp around us. For they find our hearts so rarely enlarged, and our mouths so seldom opened, to display the loving-kindness of the Lord, or to speak of all his praise.

For creatures redeemed by the blood of the Son of God always have cause for praise and adoration. With continual scenes of God's infinite goodness presented to their view, their souls should be duly affected with such a sense of his universal love that they cannot help but be continually calling on heaven and earth, humans and angels, to join with them in praising and blessing the high and exalted One—who lives forever, who causes the sun to shine on the evil and on the good and who daily pours down his blessings on the whole race of humankind.

reflection

1. Does God's love have an ending place? Explain your answer.
2. How have you experienced God's infinite goodness and love in your life?
3. How can focusing on God's love bring a person hope in even the darkest moments of life?

For your next devotional reading, go to page 929.

⁶We submitted to Egypt and Assyria
  to get enough bread.
⁷Our parents sinned and are no more,
  and we bear their punishment.
⁸Slaves rule over us,
  and there is none to free us from their
    hands.
⁹We get our bread at the risk of our lives
  because of the sword in the desert.
¹⁰Our skin is hot as an oven,
  feverish from hunger.
¹¹Women have been ravished in Zion,
  and virgins in the towns of Judah.
¹²Princes have been hung up by their
    hands;
  elders are shown no respect.
¹³Young men toil at the millstones;
  boys stagger under loads of wood.
¹⁴The elders are gone from the city gate;
  the young men have stopped their
    music.

¹⁵Joy is gone from our hearts;
  our dancing has turned to mourning.
¹⁶The crown has fallen from our head.
  Woe to us, for we have sinned!
¹⁷Because of this our hearts are faint,
  because of these things our eyes grow
    dim
¹⁸for Mount Zion, which lies desolate,
  with jackals prowling over it.

¹⁹You, Lord, reign forever;
  your throne endures from generation
    to generation.
²⁰Why do you always forget us?
  Why do you forsake us so long?
²¹Restore us to yourself, Lord, that we
    may return;
  renew our days as of old
²²unless you have utterly rejected us
  and are angry with us beyond
    measure.

ezekiel

> AUTHOR: Ezekiel
>
> DATE: Between 593 and 571 B.C.
>
> THEME: No matter what the past or future holds, God is in control.

Ezekiel's Inaugural Vision

1 In my thirtieth year, in the fourth month on the fifth day, while I was among the exiles by the Kebar River, the heavens were opened and I saw visions of God.

²On the fifth of the month—it was the fifth year of the exile of King Jehoiachin— ³the word of the LORD came to Ezekiel the priest, the son of Buzi, by the Kebar River in the land of the Babylonians.ᵃ There the hand of the LORD was on him.

⁴I looked, and I saw a windstorm coming out of the north—an immense cloud with flashing lightning and surrounded by brilliant light. The center of the fire looked like glowing metal, ⁵and in the fire was what looked like four living creatures. In appearance their form was human, ⁶but each of them had four faces and four wings. ⁷Their legs were straight; their feet were like those of a calf and gleamed like burnished bronze. ⁸Under their wings on their four sides they had human hands. All four of them had faces and wings, ⁹and the wings of one touched the wings of another. Each one went straight ahead; they did not turn as they moved.

¹⁰Their faces looked like this: Each of the four had the face of a human being, and on the right side each had the face of a lion, and on the left the face of an ox; each also had the face of an eagle. ¹¹Such were their faces. They each had two wings spreading out upward, each wing touching that of the creature on either side; and each had two other wings covering its body. ¹²Each one went straight ahead. Wherever the spirit would go, they would go, without turning as they went. ¹³The appearance of the living crea-

tures was like burning coals of fire or like torches. Fire moved back and forth among the creatures; it was bright, and lightning flashed out of it. ¹⁴The creatures sped back and forth like flashes of lightning.

¹⁵As I looked at the living creatures, I saw a wheel on the ground beside each creature with its four faces. ¹⁶This was the appearance and structure of the wheels: They sparkled like topaz, and all four looked alike. Each appeared to be made like a wheel intersecting a wheel. ¹⁷As they moved, they would go in any one of the four directions the creatures faced; the wheels did not change direction as the creatures went. ¹⁸Their rims were high and awesome, and all four rims were full of eyes all around.

¹⁹When the living creatures moved, the wheels beside them moved; and when the living creatures rose from the ground, the wheels also rose. ²⁰Wherever the spirit would go, they would go, and the wheels would rise along with them, because the spirit of the living creatures was in the wheels. ²¹When the creatures moved, they also moved; when the creatures stood still, they also stood still; and when the creatures rose from the ground, the wheels rose along with them, because the spirit of the living creatures was in the wheels.

²²Spread out above the heads of the living creatures was what looked something like a vault, sparkling like crystal, and awesome. ²³Under the vault their wings were stretched out one toward the other, and each had two wings covering its body. ²⁴When the creatures moved, I heard the sound of their wings, like the roar of rushing waters, like the voice of the Almighty,ᵇ like the tumult of

a 3 Or *Chaldeans*   *b 24* Hebrew *Shaddai*

an army. When they stood still, they lowered their wings.

²⁵Then there came a voice from above the vault over their heads as they stood with lowered wings. ²⁶Above the vault over their heads was what looked like a throne of lapis lazuli, and high above on the throne was a figure like that of a man. ²⁷I saw that from what appeared to be his waist up he looked like glowing metal, as if full of fire, and that from there down he looked like fire; and brilliant light surrounded him. ²⁸Like the appearance of a rainbow in the clouds on a rainy day, so was the radiance around him.

This was the appearance of the likeness of the glory of the LORD. When I saw it, I fell facedown, and I heard the voice of one speaking.

Ezekiel's Call to Be a Prophet

2 He said to me, "Son of man,ᵃ stand up on your feet and I will speak to you." ²As he spoke, the Spirit came into me and raised me to my feet, and I heard him speaking to me.

³He said: "Son of man, I am sending you to the Israelites, to a rebellious nation that has rebelled against me; they and their ancestors have been in revolt against me to this very day. ⁴The people to whom I am sending you are obstinate and stubborn. Say to them, 'This is what the Sovereign LORD says.' ⁵And whether they listen or fail to listen—for they are a rebellious house—they will know that a prophet has been among them. ⁶And you, son of man, do not be afraid of them or their words. Do not be afraid, though briers and thorns are all around you and you live among scorpions. Do not be afraid of what they say or be terrified by them, though they are a rebellious house. ⁷You must speak my words to them, whether they listen or fail to listen, for they are rebellious. ⁸But you, son of man, listen to what I say to you. Do not rebel like that rebellious house; open your mouth and eat what I give you."

⁹Then I looked, and I saw a hand stretched out to me. In it was a scroll, ¹⁰which he unrolled before me. On both sides of it were written words of lament and mourning and woe.

3 And he said to me, "Son of man, eat what is before you, eat this scroll; then go and speak to the house of Israel." ²So I opened my mouth, and he gave me the scroll to eat.

³Then he said to me, "Son of man, eat this scroll I am giving you and fill your stomach with it." So I ate it, and it tasted as sweet as honey in my mouth.

⁴He then said to me: "Son of man, go now to the house of Israel and speak my words to them. ⁵You are not being sent to a people of obscure speech and strange language, but to the house of Israel— ⁶not to many peoples of obscure speech and strange language, whose words you cannot understand. Surely if I had sent you to them, they would have listened to you. ⁷But the house of Israel is not willing to listen to you because they are not willing to listen to me, for the whole house of Israel is hardened and obstinate. ⁸But I will make you as unyielding and hardened as they are. ⁹I will make your forehead like the hardest stone, harder than flint. Do not be afraid of them or terrified by them, though they are a rebellious house."

¹⁰And he said to me, "Son of man, listen carefully and take to heart all the words I speak to you. ¹¹Go now to your people in exile and speak to them. Say to them, 'This is what the Sovereign LORD says,' whether they listen or fail to listen."

¹²Then the Spirit lifted me up, and I heard behind me a loud rumbling sound as the glory of the LORD rose from the place where it was standing.ᵇ ¹³It was the sound of the wings of the living creatures brushing against each other and the sound of the wheels beside them, a loud rumbling sound. ¹⁴The Spirit then lifted me up and took me away, and I went in bitterness and in the anger of my spirit, with the strong hand of the LORD on me. ¹⁵I came to the exiles who lived at Tel Aviv near the Kebar River. And there, where they were living, I sat among them for seven days—deeply distressed.

Ezekiel's Task as Watchman

¹⁶At the end of seven days the word of the LORD came to me: ¹⁷"Son of man, I have made you a watchman for the house of Israel; so hear the word I speak and give them

ᵃ 1 The Hebrew phrase *ben adam* means *human being*. The phrase *son of man* is retained as a form of address here and throughout Ezekiel because of its traditional associations.   ᵇ 12 Probable reading of the original Hebrew text; Masoretic Text *sound—may the glory of the LORD be praised from his place* warning from me. ¹⁸When I say to the wicked, 'You will surely die,' and you do not warn them or speak out to dissuade them from their evil ways in order to save their lives, those wicked people will die forᵃ their sins, and I will hold you accountable for their blood. ¹⁹But if you do warn the wicked and they do not turn from their wickedness or from their evil ways, they will die for their sins; but you will have saved yourself.

²⁰"Again, when the righteous turn from their righteousness and do evil, and I put a stumbling block before them, they will die. Since you did not warn them, they will die for their sins. The righteous things they did will not be remembered, and I will hold you accountable for their blood. ²¹But if you do warn the righteous not to sin and they do not sin, they will surely live because they took warning, and you will have saved yourself."

²²The hand of the LORD was on me there, and he said to me, "Get up and go out to the plain, and there I will speak to you." ²³So I got up and went out to the plain. And the glory of the LORD was standing there, like the glory I had seen by the Kebar River, and I fell facedown.

²⁴Then the Spirit came into me and raised me to my feet. He spoke to me and said: "Go, shut yourself inside your house. ²⁵And you, son of man, they will tie with ropes; you will be bound so that you cannot go out among the people. ²⁶I will make your tongue stick to the roof of your mouth so that you will be silent and unable to rebuke them, for they are a rebellious house. ²⁷But when I speak to you, I will open your mouth and you shall say to them, 'This is what the Sovereign LORD says.' Whoever will listen let them listen, and whoever will refuse let them refuse; for they are a rebellious house.

Siege of Jerusalem Symbolized

4 "Now, son of man, take a block of clay, put it in front of you and draw the city of Jerusalem on it. ²Then lay siege to it: Erect siege works against it, build a ramp up to it, set up camps against it and put battering rams around it. ³Then take an iron pan, place it as an iron wall between you and the city and turn your face toward

it. It will be under siege, and you shall besiege it. This will be a sign to the house of Israel.

⁴"Then lie on your left side and put the sin of the house of Israel upon yourself.ᵇ You are to bear their sin for the number of days you lie on your side. ⁵I have assigned you the same number of days as the years of their sin. So for 390 days you will bear the sin of the house of Israel.

⁶"After you have finished this, lie down again, this time on your right side, and bear the sin of the house of Judah. I have assigned you 40 days, a day for each year. ⁷Turn your face toward the siege of Jerusalem and with bared arm prophesy against her. ⁸I will tie you up with ropes so that you cannot turn from one side to the other until you have finished the days of your siege.

⁹"Take wheat and barley, beans and lentils, millet and spelt; put them in a storage jar and use them to make bread for yourself. You are to eat it during the 390 days you lie on your side. ¹⁰Weigh out twenty shekelsᶜ of food to eat each day and eat it at set times. ¹¹Also measure out a sixth of a hinᵈ of water and drink it at set times. ¹²Eat the food as you would a loaf of barley bread; bake it in the sight of the people, using human excrement for fuel." ¹³The LORD said, "In this way the people of Israel will eat defiled food among the nations where I will drive them."

¹⁴Then I said, "Not so, Sovereign LORD! I have never defiled myself. From my youth until now I have never eaten anything found dead or torn by wild animals. No impure meat has ever entered my mouth."

¹⁵"Very well," he said, "I will let you bake your bread over cow dung instead of human excrement."

¹⁶He then said to me: "Son of man, I am about to cut off the food supply in Jerusalem. The people will eat rationed food in anxiety and drink rationed water in despair, ¹⁷for food and water will be scarce. They will be appalled at the sight of each other and will waste away because ofᵉ their sin.

God's Razor of Judgment

5 "Now, son of man, take a sharp sword and use it as a barber's razor to shave your head and your beard. Then take

---

ᵃ 18 Or in; also in verses 19 and 20   ᵇ 4 Or upon your side   ᶜ 10 That is, about 8 ounces or about 230 grams   ᵈ 11 That is, about 1 1/3 pints or about 0.6 liter   ᵉ 17 Or away in a set of scales and divide up the hair. ²When the days of your siege come to an end, burn a third of the hair inside the city. Take a third and strike it with the sword all around the city. And scatter a third to the wind. For I will pursue them with drawn sword. ³But take a few hairs and tuck them away in the folds of your garment. ⁴Again, take a few of these and throw them into the fire and burn them up. A fire will spread from there to the whole house of Israel.

⁵"This is what the Sovereign LORD says: This is Jerusalem, which I have set in the center of the nations, with countries all around her. ⁶Yet in her wickedness she has rebelled against my laws and decrees more than the nations and countries around her. She has rejected my laws and has not followed my decrees.

⁷"Therefore this is what the Sovereign LORD says: You have been more unruly than the nations around you and have not followed my decrees or kept my laws. You have not even*ᵃ* conformed to the standards of the nations around you.

⁸"Therefore this is what the Sovereign LORD says: I myself am against you, Jerusalem, and I will inflict punishment on you in the sight of the nations. ⁹Because of all your detestable idols, I will do to you what I have never done before and will never do again. ¹⁰Therefore in your midst parents will eat their children, and children will eat their parents. I will inflict punishment on you and will scatter all your survivors to the winds. ¹¹Therefore as surely as I live, declares the Sovereign LORD, because you have defiled my sanctuary with all your vile images and detestable practices, I myself will shave you; I will not look on you with pity or spare you. ¹²A third of your people will die of the plague or perish by famine inside you; a third will fall by the sword outside your walls; and a third I will scatter to the winds and pursue with drawn sword.

¹³"Then my anger will cease and my wrath against them will subside, and I will be avenged. And when I have spent my wrath on them, they will know that I the LORD have spoken in my zeal.

¹⁴"I will make you a ruin and a reproach among the nations around you, in the sight of all who pass by. ¹⁵You will be a reproach and a taunt, a warning and an object of horror to the nations around you when I inflict punishment on you in anger and in wrath and with stinging rebuke. I the LORD have spoken. ¹⁶When I shoot at you with my deadly and destructive arrows of famine, I will shoot to destroy you. I will bring more and more famine upon you and cut off your supply of food. ¹⁷I will send famine and wild beasts against you, and they will leave you childless. Plague and bloodshed will sweep through you, and I will bring the sword against you. I the LORD have spoken."

Doom for the Mountains of Israel

6 The word of the LORD came to me: ²"Son of man, set your face against the mountains of Israel; prophesy against them ³and say: 'You mountains of Israel, hear the word of the Sovereign LORD. This is what the Sovereign LORD says to the mountains and hills, to the ravines and valleys: I am about to bring a sword against you, and I will destroy your high places. ⁴Your altars will be demolished and your incense altars will be smashed; and I will slay your people in front of your idols. ⁵I will lay the dead bodies of the Israelites in front of their idols, and I will scatter your bones around your altars. ⁶Wherever you live, the towns will be laid waste and the high places demolished, so that your altars will be laid waste and devastated, your idols smashed and ruined, your incense altars broken down, and what you have made wiped out. ⁷Your people will fall slain among you, and you will know that I am the LORD.

⁸" 'But I will spare some, for some of you will escape the sword when you are scattered among the lands and nations. ⁹Then in the nations where they have been carried captive, those who escape will remember me—how I have been grieved by their adulterous hearts, which have turned away from me, and by their eyes, which have lusted after their idols. They will loathe themselves for the evil they have done and for all their detestable practices. ¹⁰And they will know that I am the LORD; I did not threaten in vain to bring this calamity on them.

¹¹" 'This is what the Sovereign LORD says: Strike your hands together and stamp your feet and cry out "Alas!" because of all the

---

ᵃ 7 Most Hebrew manuscripts; some Hebrew manuscripts and Syriac *You have* wicked and detestable practices of the house of Israel, for they will fall by the sword, famine and plague. ¹²Those who are far away will die of the plague, and those who are near will fall by the sword, and those who survive and are spared will die of famine. So will I spend my wrath on them. ¹³And they will know that I am the LORD, when their people lie slain among their idols around their altars, on every high hill and on all the mountaintops, under every spreading tree and every leafy oak—places where they offered fragrant incense to all their idols. ¹⁴And I will stretch out my hand against them and make the land a desolate waste from the desert to Diblah*ᵃ*—wherever they live. Then they will know that I am the LORD.' "

The End Has Come

7 The word of the LORD came to me: ²"Son of man, this is what the Sovereign LORD says to the land of Israel:

" 'The end! The end has come
    upon the four corners of the land!
³The end is now upon you,
    and I will unleash my anger against you.
I will judge you according to your conduct
    and repay you for all your detestable practices.
⁴I will not look on you with pity;
    I will not spare you.
I will surely repay you for your conduct
    and for the detestable practices among you.

" 'Then you will know that I am the LORD.'

⁵"This is what the Sovereign LORD says:

" 'Disaster! Unheard-ofᵇ disaster!
    See, it comes!
⁶The end has come!
    The end has come!
It has roused itself against you.
    See, it comes!
⁷Doom has come upon you,
    upon you who dwell in the land.
The time has come! The day is near!
    There is panic, not joy, on the mountains.

⁸I am about to pour out my wrath on you
    and spend my anger against you.
I will judge you according to your conduct
    and repay you for all your detestable practices.
⁹I will not look on you with pity;
    I will not spare you.
I will repay you for your conduct
    and for the detestable practices among you.

" 'Then you will know that it is I the LORD who strikes you.

¹⁰" 'See, the day!
    See, it comes!
Doom has burst forth,
    the rod has budded,
    arrogance has blossomed!
¹¹Violence has arisen,ᶜ
    a rod to punish the wicked.
None of the people will be left,
    none of that crowd—
none of their wealth,
    nothing of value.
¹²The time has come!
    The day has arrived!
Let not the buyer rejoice
    nor the seller grieve,
    for my wrath is on the whole crowd.
¹³The sellers will not recover
    the property they have sold—
as long as both buyers and sellers live.
For the vision concerning the whole crowd
    will not be reversed.
Because of their sins, not one of them
    will preserve their life.

¹⁴" 'They have blown the trumpet,
    they have made all things ready,
but no one will go into battle,
    for my wrath is on the whole crowd.
¹⁵Outside is the sword;
    inside are plague and famine.
Those in the country
    will die by the sword;
those in the city
    will be devoured by famine and plague.
¹⁶The fugitives who escape
    will flee to the mountains.

ᵃ 14 Most Hebrew manuscripts; a few Hebrew manuscripts *Riblah*   ᵇ 5 Most Hebrew manuscripts; some Hebrew manuscripts and Syriac *Disaster after*   ᶜ 11 Or *The violent one has become*

Like doves of the valleys,
  they will all moan,
  each for their own sins.
¹⁷ Every hand will go limp;
  every knee will be wet with urine.
¹⁸ They will put on sackcloth
  and be clothed with terror.
Every face will be covered with shame,
  and every head will be shaved.

¹⁹ " 'They will throw their silver into the
    streets,
  and their gold will be treated as a
    thing unclean.
Their silver and gold
  will not be able to deliver them
  in the day of the Lord's wrath.
It will not satisfy their hunger
  or fill their stomachs,
  for it has caused them to stumble
    into sin.
²⁰ They took pride in their beautiful jewelry
  and used it to make their detestable
    idols.
They made it into vile images;
  therefore I will make it a thing
    unclean for them.
²¹ I will give their wealth as plunder to
    foreigners
  and as loot to the wicked of the earth,
    who will defile it.
²² I will turn my face away from the
    people,
  and robbers will desecrate the place
    I treasure.
They will enter it
  and will defile it.

²³ " 'Prepare chains!
  For the land is full of bloodshed,
  and the city is full of violence.
²⁴ I will bring the most wicked of nations
  to take possession of their houses.
I will put an end to the pride of the
    mighty,
  and their sanctuaries will be
    desecrated.
²⁵ When terror comes,
  they will seek peace in vain.
²⁶ Calamity upon calamity will come,
  and rumor upon rumor.
They will go searching for a vision from
    the prophet,

priestly instruction in the law will
    cease,
  the counsel of the elders will come to
    an end.
²⁷ The king will mourn,
  the prince will be clothed with
    despair,
  and the hands of the people of the
    land will tremble.
I will deal with them according to their
    conduct,
  and by their own standards I will
    judge them.

" 'Then they will know that I am the Lord.' "

Idolatry in the Temple

8 In the sixth year, in the sixth month on the fifth day, while I was sitting in my house and the elders of Judah were sitting before me, the hand of the Sovereign Lord came on me there. ² I looked, and I saw a figure like that of a man.^a From what appeared to be his waist down he was like fire, and from there up his appearance was as bright as glowing metal. ³ He stretched out what looked like a hand and took me by the hair of my head. The Spirit lifted me up between earth and heaven and in visions of God he took me to Jerusalem, to the entrance of the north gate of the inner court, where the idol that provokes to jealousy stood. ⁴ And there before me was the glory of the God of Israel, as in the vision I had seen in the plain.

⁵ Then he said to me, "Son of man, look toward the north." So I looked, and in the entrance north of the gate of the altar I saw this idol of jealousy.

⁶ And he said to me, "Son of man, do you see what they are doing—the utterly detestable things the house of Israel is doing here, things that will drive me far from my sanctuary? But you will see things that are even more detestable."

⁷ Then he brought me to the entrance to the court. I looked, and I saw a hole in the wall. ⁸ He said to me, "Son of man, now dig into the wall." So I dug into the wall and saw a doorway there.

⁹ And he said to me, "Go in and see the wicked and detestable things they are doing here." ¹⁰ So I went in and looked, and I saw portrayed all over the walls all kinds of crawl-

^a 2 Or saw a fiery figure

ing things and unclean animals and all the idols of the house of Israel. ¹¹In front of them stood seventy elders of the house of Israel, and Jaazaniah son of Shaphan was standing among them. Each had a censer in his hand, and a fragrant cloud of incense was rising.

¹²He said to me, "Son of man, have you seen what the elders of the house of Israel are doing in the darkness, each at the shrine of his own idol? They say, 'The Lord does not see us; the Lord has forsaken the land.' " ¹³Again, he said, "You will see them doing things that are even more detestable."

¹⁴Then he brought me to the entrance of the north gate of the house of the Lord, and I saw women sitting there, mourning the god Tammuz. ¹⁵He said to me, "Do you see this, son of man? You will see things that are even more detestable than this."

¹⁶He then brought me into the inner court of the house of the Lord, and there at the entrance to the temple, between the portico and the altar, were about twenty-five men. With their backs toward the temple of the Lord and their faces toward the east, they were bowing down to the sun in the east.

¹⁷He said to me, "Have you seen this, son of man? Is it a trivial matter for the house of Judah to do the detestable things they are doing here? Must they also fill the land with violence and continually arouse my anger? Look at them putting the branch to their nose! ¹⁸Therefore I will deal with them in anger; I will not look on them with pity or spare them. Although they shout in my ears, I will not listen to them."

Judgment on the Idolaters

9 Then I heard him call out in a loud voice, "Bring near those who are appointed to execute judgment on the city, each with weapon in hand." ²And I saw six men coming from the direction of the upper gate, which faces north, each with a deadly weapon in his hand. With them was a man clothed in linen who had a writing kit at his side. They came in and stood beside the bronze altar.

³Now the glory of the God of Israel went up from above the cherubim, where it had been, and moved to the threshold of the temple. Then the Lord called to the man clothed in linen who had the writing kit at his side ⁴and said to him, "Go throughout the city of Jerusalem and put a mark on the foreheads of those who grieve and lament over all the detestable things that are done in it."

⁵As I listened, he said to the others, "Follow him through the city and kill, without showing pity or compassion. ⁶Slaughter the old men, the young men and women, the mothers and children, but do not touch anyone who has the mark. Begin at my sanctuary." So they began with the old men who were in front of the temple.

⁷Then he said to them, "Defile the temple and fill the courts with the slain. Go!" So they went out and began killing throughout the city. ⁸While they were killing and I was left alone, I fell facedown, crying out, "Ah, Sovereign Lord! Are you going to destroy the entire remnant of Israel in this outpouring of your wrath on Jerusalem?"

⁹He answered me, "The sin of the house of Israel and Judah is exceedingly great; the land is full of bloodshed and the city is full of injustice. They say, 'The Lord has forsaken the land; the Lord does not see.' ¹⁰So I will not look on them with pity or spare them, but I will bring down on their own heads what they have done."

¹¹Then the man in linen with the writing kit at his side brought back word, saying, "I have done as you commanded."

God's Glory Departs From the Temple

10 I looked, and I saw the likeness of a throne of lapis lazuli above the vault that was over the heads of the cherubim. ²The Lord said to the man clothed in linen, "Go in among the wheels beneath the cherubim. Fill your hands with burning coals from among the cherubim and scatter them over the city." And as I watched, he went in.

³Now the cherubim were standing on the south side of the temple when the man went in, and a cloud filled the inner court. ⁴Then the glory of the Lord rose from above the cherubim and moved to the threshold of the temple. The cloud filled the temple, and the court was full of the radiance of the glory of the Lord. ⁵The sound of the wings of the cherubim could be heard as far away as the outer court, like the voice of God Almighty[a] when he speaks.

⁶When the LORD commanded the man in linen, "Take fire from among the wheels, from among the cherubim," the man went in and stood beside a wheel. ⁷Then one of the cherubim reached out his hand to the fire that was among them. He took up some of it and put it into the hands of the man in linen, who took it and went out. ⁸(Under the wings of the cherubim could be seen what looked like human hands.)

⁹I looked, and I saw beside the cherubim four wheels, one beside each of the cherubim; the wheels sparkled like topaz. ¹⁰As for their appearance, the four of them looked alike; each was like a wheel intersecting a wheel. ¹¹As they moved, they would go in any one of the four directions the cherubim faced; the wheels did not turn aboutᵃ as the cherubim went. The cherubim went in whatever direction the head faced, without turning as they went. ¹²Their entire bodies, including their backs, their hands and their wings, were completely full of eyes, as were their four wheels. ¹³I heard the wheels being called "the whirling wheels." ¹⁴Each of the cherubim had four faces: One face was that of a cherub, the second the face of a human being, the third the face of a lion, and the fourth the face of an eagle.

¹⁵Then the cherubim rose upward. These were the living creatures I had seen by the Kebar River. ¹⁶When the cherubim moved, the wheels beside them moved; and when the cherubim spread their wings to rise from the ground, the wheels did not leave their side. ¹⁷When the cherubim stood still, they also stood still; and when the cherubim rose, they rose with them, because the spirit of the living creatures was in them.

¹⁸Then the glory of the LORD departed from over the threshold of the temple and stopped above the cherubim. ¹⁹While I watched, the cherubim spread their wings and rose from the ground, and as they went, the wheels went with them. They stopped at the entrance of the east gate of the LORD's house, and the glory of the God of Israel was above them.

²⁰These were the living creatures I had seen beneath the God of Israel by the Kebar River, and I realized that they were cherubim. ²¹Each had four faces and four wings, and under their wings was what looked like human hands. ²²Their faces had the same

appearance as those I had seen by the Kebar River. Each one went straight ahead.

God's Sure Judgment on Jerusalem

11 Then the Spirit lifted me up and brought me to the gate of the house of the LORD that faces east. There at the entrance of the gate were twenty-five men, and I saw among them Jaazaniah son of Azzur and Pelatiah son of Benaiah, leaders of the people. ²The LORD said to me, "Son of man, these are the men who are plotting evil and giving wicked advice in this city. ³They say, 'Haven't our houses been recently rebuilt? This city is a pot, and we are the meat in it.' ⁴Therefore prophesy against them; prophesy, son of man."

⁵Then the Spirit of the LORD came on me, and he told me to say: "This is what the LORD says: That is what you are saying, house of Israel, but I know what is going through your mind. ⁶You have killed many people in this city and filled its streets with the dead.

⁷"Therefore this is what the Sovereign LORD says: The bodies you have thrown there are the meat and this city is the pot, but I will drive you out of it. ⁸You fear the sword, and the sword is what I will bring against you, declares the Sovereign LORD. ⁹I will drive you out of the city and deliver you into the hands of foreigners and inflict punishment on you. ¹⁰You will fall by the sword, and I will execute judgment on you at the borders of Israel. Then you will know that I am the LORD. ¹¹This city will not be a pot for you, nor will you be the meat in it; I will execute judgment on you at the borders of Israel. ¹²And you will know that I am the LORD, for you have not followed my decrees or kept my laws but have conformed to the standards of the nations around you."

¹³Now as I was prophesying, Pelatiah son of Benaiah died. Then I fell facedown and cried out in a loud voice, "Ah, Sovereign LORD! Will you completely destroy the remnant of Israel?"

The Promise of Israel's Return

¹⁴The word of the LORD came to me: ¹⁵"Son of man, the people of Jerusalem have said of your fellow exiles and the whole house of Israel,ᵇ 'They are far away from the

ᵃ 11 Or *aside*   ᵇ 15 Or *said of your brothers—your brothers who are your blood relatives and the whole house of Israel—*

LORD; this land was given to us as our possession.'

16"Therefore say: 'This is what the Sovereign LORD says: Although I sent them far away among the nations and scattered them among the countries, yet for a little while I have been a sanctuary for them in the countries where they have gone.'

17"Therefore say: 'This is what the Sovereign LORD says: I will gather you from the nations and bring you back from the countries where you have been scattered, and I will give you back the land of Israel again.'

18"They will return to it and remove all its vile images and detestable idols. 19I will give them an undivided heart and put a new spirit in them; I will remove from them their heart of stone and give them a heart of flesh. 20Then they will follow my decrees and be careful to keep my laws. They will be my people, and I will be their God. 21But as for those whose hearts are devoted to their vile images and detestable idols, I will bring down on their own heads what they have done, declares the Sovereign LORD."

22Then the cherubim, with the wheels beside them, spread their wings, and the glory of the God of Israel was above them. 23The glory of the LORD went up from within the city and stopped above the mountain east of it. 24The Spirit lifted me up and brought me to the exiles in Babylonia[a] in the vision given by the Spirit of God.

Then the vision I had seen went up from me, 25and I told the exiles everything the LORD had shown me.

The Exile Symbolized

12 The word of the LORD came to me: 2"Son of man, you are living among a rebellious people. They have eyes to see but do not see and ears to hear but do not hear, for they are a rebellious people.

3"Therefore, son of man, pack your belongings for exile and in the daytime, as they watch, set out and go from where you are to another place. Perhaps they will understand, though they are a rebellious house. 4During the daytime, while they watch, bring out your belongings packed for exile. Then in the evening, while they are watching, go out like those who go into exile. 5While they

watch, dig through the wall and take your belongings out through it. 6Put them on your shoulder as they are watching and carry them out at dusk. Cover your face so that you cannot see the land, for I have made you a sign to the house of Israel."

7So I did as I was commanded. During the day I brought out my things packed for exile. Then in the evening I dug through the wall with my hands. I took my belongings out at dusk, carrying them on my shoulders while they watched.

8In the morning the word of the LORD came to me: 9"Son of man, did not that rebellious house of Israel ask you, 'What are you doing?'

10"Say to them, 'This is what the Sovereign LORD says: This prophecy concerns the prince in Jerusalem and the whole house of Israel who are there.' 11Say to them, 'I am a sign to you.'

"As I have done, so it will be done to them. They will go into exile as captives.

12"The prince among them will put his things on his shoulder at dusk and leave, and a hole will be dug in the wall for him to go through. He will cover his face so that he cannot see the land. 13I will spread my net for him, and he will be caught in my snare; I will bring him to Babylonia, the land of the Chaldeans, but he will not see it, and there he will die. 14I will scatter to the winds all those around him—his staff and all his troops—and I will pursue them with drawn sword.

15"They will know that I am the LORD, when I disperse them among the nations and scatter them through the countries. 16But I will spare a few of them from the sword, famine and plague, so that in the nations where they go they may acknowledge all their detestable practices. Then they will know that I am the LORD."

17The word of the LORD came to me: 18"Son of man, tremble as you eat your food, and shudder in fear as you drink your water. 19Say to the people of the land: 'This is what the Sovereign LORD says about those living in Jerusalem and in the land of Israel: They will eat their food in anxiety and drink their water in despair, for their land will be stripped of everything in it because of the violence of all who live there. 20The inhabited towns will be laid waste and the land will be desolate. Then you will know that I am the LORD.' "

There Will Be No Delay

²¹The word of the LORD came to me: ²²"Son of man, what is this proverb you have in the land of Israel: 'The days go by and every vision comes to nothing'? ²³Say to them, 'This is what the Sovereign LORD says: I am going to put an end to this proverb, and they will no longer quote it in Israel.' Say to them, 'The days are near when every vision will be fulfilled. ²⁴For there will be no more false visions or flattering divinations among the people of Israel. ²⁵But I the LORD will speak what I will, and it shall be fulfilled without delay. For in your days, you rebellious house, I will fulfill whatever I say, declares the Sovereign LORD.' "

²⁶The word of the LORD came to me: ²⁷"Son of man, the house of Israel is saying, 'The vision he sees is for many years from now, and he prophesies about the distant future.'

²⁸"Therefore say to them, 'This is what the Sovereign LORD says: None of my words will be delayed any longer; whatever I say will be fulfilled, declares the Sovereign LORD.' "

False Prophets Condemned

13 The word of the LORD came to me: ²"Son of man, prophesy against the prophets of Israel who are now prophesying. Say to those who prophesy out of their own imagination: 'Hear the word of the LORD! ³This is what the Sovereign LORD says: Woe to the foolish*ᵃ* prophets who follow their own spirit and have seen nothing! ⁴Your prophets, Israel, are like jackals among ruins. ⁵You have not gone up to the breaches in the wall to repair it for the house of Israel so that it will stand firm in the battle on the day of the LORD. ⁶Their visions are false and their divinations a lie. Even though the LORD has not sent them, they say, "The LORD declares," and expect him to fulfill their words. ⁷Have you not seen false visions and uttered lying divinations when you say, "The LORD declares," though I have not spoken?

⁸" 'Therefore this is what the Sovereign LORD says: Because of your false words and lying visions, I am against you, declares the Sovereign LORD. ⁹My hand will be against the prophets who see false visions and utter lying divinations. They will not belong to the council of my people or be listed in the records of the house of Israel, nor will they enter the land of Israel. Then you will know that I am the Sovereign LORD.

¹⁰" 'Because they lead my people astray, saying, "Peace," when there is no peace, and because, when a flimsy wall is built, they cover it with whitewash, ¹¹therefore tell those who cover it with whitewash that it is going to fall. Rain will come in torrents, and I will send hailstones hurtling down, and violent winds will burst forth. ¹²When the wall collapses, will people not ask you, "Where is the whitewash you covered it with?"

¹³" 'Therefore this is what the Sovereign LORD says: In my wrath I will unleash a violent wind, and in my anger hailstones and torrents of rain will fall with destructive fury. ¹⁴I will tear down the wall you have covered with whitewash and will level it to the ground so that its foundation will be laid bare. When it*ᵇ* falls, you will be destroyed in it; and you will know that I am the LORD. ¹⁵So I will spend my wrath against the wall and against those who covered it with whitewash. I will say to you, "The wall is gone and so are those who whitewashed it, ¹⁶those prophets of Israel who prophesied to Jerusalem and saw visions of peace for her when there was no peace, declares the Sovereign LORD." '

¹⁷"Now, son of man, set your face against the daughters of your people who prophesy out of their own imagination. Prophesy against them ¹⁸and say, 'This is what the Sovereign LORD says: Woe to the women who sew magic charms on all their wrists and make veils of various lengths for their heads in order to ensnare people. Will you ensnare the lives of my people but preserve your own? ¹⁹You have profaned me among my people for a few handfuls of barley and scraps of bread. By lying to my people, who listen to lies, you have killed those who should not have died and have spared those who should not live.

²⁰" 'Therefore this is what the Sovereign LORD says: I am against your magic charms

---

ᵃ 3 Or *wicked*   *ᵇ 14* Or *the city*

with which you ensnare people like birds and I will tear them from your arms; I will set free the people that you ensnare like birds. ²¹I will tear off your veils and save my people from your hands, and they will no longer fall prey to your power. Then you will know that I am the LORD. ²²Because you disheartened the righteous with your lies, when I had brought them no grief, and because you encouraged the wicked not to turn from their evil ways and so save their lives, ²³therefore you will no longer see false visions or practice divination. I will save my people from your hands. And then you will know that I am the LORD.' "

Idolaters Condemned

14 Some of the elders of Israel came to me and sat down in front of me. ²Then the word of the LORD came to me: ³"Son of man, these men have set up idols in their hearts and put wicked stumbling blocks before their faces. Should I let them inquire of me at all? ⁴Therefore speak to them and tell them, 'This is what the Sovereign LORD says: When any of the Israelites set up idols in their hearts and put a wicked stumbling block before their faces and then go to a prophet, I the LORD will answer them myself in keeping with their great idolatry. ⁵I will do this to recapture the hearts of the people of Israel, who have all deserted me for their idols.'

⁶"Therefore say to the house of Israel, 'This is what the Sovereign LORD says: Repent! Turn from your idols and renounce all your detestable practices!

⁷" 'When any of the Israelites or any foreigner residing in Israel separate themselves from me and set up idols in their hearts and put a wicked stumbling block before their faces and then go to a prophet to inquire of me, I the LORD will answer them myself. ⁸I will set my face against them and make them an example and a byword. I will remove them from my people. Then you will know that I am the LORD.

⁹" 'And if the prophet is enticed to utter a prophecy, I the LORD have enticed that prophet, and I will stretch out my hand against him and destroy him from among my people Israel. ¹⁰They will bear their guilt—the prophet will be as guilty as the

one who consults him. ¹¹Then the people of Israel will no longer stray from me, nor will they defile themselves anymore with all their sins. They will be my people, and I will be their God, declares the Sovereign LORD.' "

Jerusalem's Judgment Inescapable

¹²The word of the LORD came to me: ¹³"Son of man, if a country sins against me by being unfaithful and I stretch out my hand against it to cut off its food supply and send famine upon it and kill its people and their animals, ¹⁴even if these three men—Noah, Daniel*ᵃ* and Job—were in it, they could save only themselves by their righteousness, declares the Sovereign LORD.

¹⁵"Or if I send wild beasts through that country and they leave it childless and it becomes desolate so that no one can pass through it because of the beasts, ¹⁶as surely as I live, declares the Sovereign LORD, even if these three men were in it, they could not save their own sons or daughters. They alone would be saved, but the land would be desolate.

¹⁷"Or if I bring a sword against that country and say, 'Let the sword pass throughout the land,' and I kill its people and their animals, ¹⁸as surely as I live, declares the Sovereign LORD, even if these three men were in it, they could not save their own sons or daughters. They alone would be saved.

¹⁹"Or if I send a plague into that land and pour out my wrath on it through bloodshed, killing its people and their animals, ²⁰as surely as I live, declares the Sovereign LORD, even if Noah, Daniel and Job were in it, they could save neither son nor daughter. They would save only themselves by their righteousness.

²¹"For this is what the Sovereign LORD says: How much worse will it be when I send against Jerusalem my four dreadful judgments—sword and famine and wild beasts and plague—to kill its men and their animals! ²²Yet there will be some survivors—sons and daughters who will be brought out of it. They will come to you, and when you see their conduct and their actions, you will be consoled regarding the disaster I have brought on Jerusalem—every disaster I have brought on it. ²³You will be consoled when you see their conduct and their actions, for

---

ᵃ 14 Or *Danel*, a man of renown in ancient literature; also in verse 20

WEDNESDAY

GOD'S JEALOUSY FOR US

Ezekiel 14:1–23 *or* 14:4–5

Ann Spangler

Tolerance is a popular word these days. And no wonder. We live in a pluralistic society made up of people from a rich variety of cultural, ethnic and religious backgrounds. We need to respect each other in order to live peaceably. But when "tolerance" becomes an excuse for erasing important distinctions, we wander into slippery territory both intellectually and spiritually.

This is especially true when it comes to matters of faith. You can't sprinkle a little Hinduism on top of New Age notions, mix together ideas from Buddhist cosmology with Christian theology, toss in a few Jewish proverbs, stir it all up, and call it religion. It may be fashionable, but it's not faith. Faith is more rigorous. It doesn't respond to market forces or to the latest trends. Real faith arises from contact with the living God, who by his own definition is jealous for our attention, our devotion, our love. He's not interested in competing with other deities. He neither shares his glory nor compromises his holiness. This is our Jealous God, the one who loves us with an everlasting, all-consuming love.

JOHN CALVIN {AD 1509–1564}

Ezekiel 14 implies comparison between God and idols. For God has erected the seat of his empire in our hearts, but when we set up idols, we necessarily endeavor to overthrow God's throne, and to reduce his power to nothing. Hence the most heinous crime of sacrilege is shown here when we set up idols in our hearts.

> *Grant, Almighty God, since we are so inclined to all kinds of errors, that we may be restrained by the power of your Spirit. Grant that we may persevere in the pure worship of your name; and be upheld in our weakness, and preserved from all error, until we finish our course, and arrive at the goal which is proposed to us in Christ Jesus our Lord.*

reflection

1. In your efforts to be respectful toward other people, do you find yourself treating other religions as if they are on equal footing with Christianity?

2. Why is mixing Christian beliefs with the beliefs of another religion a form of idolatry?

3. Why do you think God is persistent in his jealous love for you?

For your next devotional reading, go to page 931.

you will know that I have done nothing in it without cause, declares the Sovereign Lord."

Jerusalem as a Useless Vine

15 The word of the Lord came to me: ²"Son of man, how is the wood of a vine different from that of a branch from any of the trees in the forest? ³Is wood ever taken from it to make anything useful? Do they make pegs from it to hang things on? ⁴And after it is thrown on the fire as fuel and the fire burns both ends and chars the middle, is it then useful for anything? ⁵If it was not useful for anything when it was whole, how much less can it be made into something useful when the fire has burned it and it is charred?

⁶"Therefore this is what the Sovereign Lord says: As I have given the wood of the vine among the trees of the forest as fuel for the fire, so will I treat the people living in Jerusalem. ⁷I will set my face against them. Although they have come out of the fire, the fire will yet consume them. And when I set my face against them, you will know that I am the Lord. ⁸I will make the land desolate because they have been unfaithful, declares the Sovereign Lord."

Jerusalem as an Adulterous Wife

16 The word of the Lord came to me: ²"Son of man, confront Jerusalem with her detestable practices ³and say, 'This is what the Sovereign Lord says to Jerusalem: Your ancestry and birth were in the land of the Canaanites; your father was an Amorite and your mother a Hittite. ⁴On the day you were born your cord was not cut, nor were you washed with water to make you clean, nor were you rubbed with salt or wrapped in cloths. ⁵No one looked on you with pity or had compassion enough to do any of these things for you. Rather, you were thrown out into the open field, for on the day you were born you were despised.

⁶"'Then I passed by and saw you kicking about in your blood, and as you lay there in your blood I said to you, "Live!"*ᵃ* ⁷I made you grow like a plant of the field. You grew and developed and entered puberty. Your breasts had formed and your hair had grown, yet you were stark naked.

⁸"'Later I passed by, and when I looked at you and saw that you were old enough for love, I spread the corner of my garment over you and covered your nakedness. I gave you my solemn oath and entered into a covenant with you, declares the Sovereign Lord, and you became mine.

⁹"'I bathed you with water and washed the blood from you and put ointments on you. ¹⁰I clothed you with an embroidered dress and put sandals of fine leather on you. I dressed you in fine linen and covered you with costly garments. ¹¹I adorned you with jewelry: I put bracelets on your arms and a necklace around your neck, ¹²and I put a ring on your nose, earrings on your ears and a beautiful crown on your head. ¹³So you were adorned with gold and silver; your clothes were of fine linen and costly fabric and embroidered cloth. Your food was honey, olive oil and the finest flour. You became very beautiful and rose to be a queen. ¹⁴And your fame spread among the nations on account of your beauty, because the splendor I had given you made your beauty perfect, declares the Sovereign Lord.

¹⁵"'But you trusted in your beauty and used your fame to become a prostitute. You lavished your favors on anyone who passed by and your beauty became his. ¹⁶You took some of your garments to make gaudy high places, where you carried on your prostitution. You went to him, and he possessed your beauty.*ᵇ* ¹⁷You also took the fine jewelry I gave you, the jewelry made of my gold and silver, and you made for yourself male idols and engaged in prostitution with them. ¹⁸And you took your embroidered clothes to put on them, and you offered my oil and incense before them. ¹⁹Also the food I provided for you—the flour, olive oil and honey I gave you to eat—you offered as fragrant incense before them. That is what happened, declares the Sovereign Lord.

²⁰"'And you took your sons and daughters whom you bore to me and sacrificed them as food to the idols. Was your prostitution not enough? ²¹You slaughtered my children and sacrificed them to the idols. ²²In all your detestable practices and your prostitution you did not remember the days of your

---

ᵃ 6 A few Hebrew manuscripts, Septuagint and Syriac; most Hebrew manuscripts repeat the last clause.
ᵇ 16 The meaning of the Hebrew for this sentence is uncertain.

THURSDAY

A PICTURE OF LOVE

Ezekiel 16:1–43 or 16:9–14

S. J. Hill

Look at all that the Lord does for those whom He chooses, even while they are still in their sin. Even while they are lost and helpless, He pours countless vials of love over them. He redeems, adopts, loves, protects and raises those who are His.

The Lord even uses romantic language to describe His actions. Both the words and tender embrace have a way of touching the human heart like nothing else. He not only feeds you—both spiritually and physically—but . . . He also adorns you with choice jewels and clothes you with fine garments. As Jacob bestowed a coat of many colors on his favorite son, God clothes you with His very best and makes you beautiful.

He removes your unbecoming attributes and replaces them with the fruit of a life lived in Him—a life full of joy, peace, love, kindness, and all the fruit of His nature. Thus you begin to reflect your Creator. The amazing thing is that He does all of this free of charge. He doesn't demand penance or religious duty. He simply invites you to be in relationship with Him. His awesome invitation echoes in the innermost parts of your being.

BERNARD OF CLAIRVAUX {AD 1090–1153}

You ask me, "Why should God be loved?" I answer: the reason for loving God is God himself. And why should God be loved for his own sake? Simply because no one could be more justly loved than God; no one deserves our love more. Some may question if God deserves our love or if they might have something to gain by loving him. The answer to both questions is yes, but I find no other worthy reason for loving him except himself.

God is entitled to our love. Why? Because he gave himself for us despite the fact that we are so undeserving. What better could he have given? If we ask why God is entitled to our love, we should answer, "Because he first loved us." God is clearly deserving of our love especially if we consider who he is that loves us, who we are that he loves and how much he loves us.

reflection

1. What amazes you most about God's love?

2. How does the imagery described in this passage reveal something utterly different from many people's view of God's attitude toward humans?

3. How does God's tenderhearted love for you fuel your love for him?

For your next devotional reading, go to page 935.

youth, when you were naked and bare, kicking about in your blood.

23" 'Woe! Woe to you, declares the Sovereign LORD. In addition to all your other wickedness, 24you built a mound for yourself and made a lofty shrine in every public square. 25At every street corner you built your lofty shrines and degraded your beauty, spreading your legs with increasing promiscuity to anyone who passed by. 26You engaged in prostitution with the Egyptians, your neighbors with large genitals, and aroused my anger with your increasing promiscuity. 27So I stretched out my hand against you and reduced your territory; I gave you over to the greed of your enemies, the daughters of the Philistines, who were shocked by your lewd conduct. 28You engaged in prostitution with the Assyrians too, because you were insatiable; and even after that, you still were not satisfied. 29Then you increased your promiscuity to include Babylonia,*a* a land of merchants, but even with this you were not satisfied.

30" 'I am filled with fury against you,*b* declares the Sovereign LORD, when you do all these things, acting like a brazen prostitute! 31When you built your mounds at every street corner and made your lofty shrines in every public square, you were unlike a prostitute, because you scorned payment.

32" 'You adulterous wife! You prefer strangers to your own husband! 33All prostitutes receive gifts, but you give gifts to all your lovers, bribing them to come to you from everywhere for your illicit favors. 34So in your prostitution you are the opposite of others; no one runs after you for your favors. You are the very opposite, for you give payment and none is given to you.

35" 'Therefore, you prostitute, hear the word of the LORD! 36This is what the Sovereign LORD says: Because you poured out your lust and exposed your nakedness in your promiscuity with your lovers, and because of all your detestable idols, and because you gave them your children's blood, 37therefore I am going to gather all your lovers, with whom you found pleasure, those you loved as well as those you hated. I will gather them against you from all around and will strip you in front of them, and they will see all your nakedness. 38I will sentence you

to the punishment of women who commit adultery and who shed blood; I will bring on you the blood vengeance of my wrath and jealous anger. 39Then I will deliver you into the hands of your lovers, and they will tear down your mounds and destroy your lofty shrines. They will strip you of your clothes and take your fine jewelry and leave you naked and bare. 40They will bring a mob against you, who will stone you and hack you to pieces with their swords. 41They burn down your houses and inflict punishment on you in the sight of many women. I will put a stop to your prostitution, and you will no longer pay your lovers. 42Then my wrath against you will subside and my jealous anger will turn away from you; I will be calm and no longer angry.

43" 'Because you did not remember the days of your youth but enraged me with all these things, I will surely bring down on your head what you have done, declares the Sovereign LORD. Did you not add lewdness to all your other detestable practices?

44" 'Everyone who quotes proverbs will quote this proverb about you: "Like mother, like daughter." 45You are a true daughter of your mother, who despised her husband and her children; and you are a true sister of your sisters, who despised their husbands and their children. Your mother was a Hittite and your father an Amorite. 46Your older sister was Samaria, who lived to the north of you with her daughters; and your younger sister, who lived to the south of you with her daughters, was Sodom. 47You not only followed their ways and copied their detestable practices, but in all your ways you soon became more depraved than they. 48As surely as I live, declares the Sovereign LORD, your sister Sodom and her daughters never did what you and your daughters have done.

49" 'Now this was the sin of your sister Sodom: She and her daughters were arrogant, overfed and unconcerned; they did not help the poor and needy. 50They were haughty and did detestable things before me. Therefore I did away with them as you have seen. 51Samaria did not commit half the sins you did. You have done more detestable things than they, and have made your sisters seem righteous by all these things you have done. 52Bear your disgrace, for you have furnished some justification for your sisters. Because your sins were more vile than theirs, they appear more righteous than you. So then, be ashamed and bear your disgrace, for you have made your sisters appear righteous.

53"'However, I will restore the fortunes of Sodom and her daughters and of Samaria and her daughters, and your fortunes along with them, 54so that you may bear your disgrace and be ashamed of all you have done in giving them comfort. 55And your sisters, Sodom with her daughters and Samaria with her daughters, will return to what they were before; and you and your daughters will return to what you were before. 56You would not even mention your sister Sodom in the day of your pride, 57before your wickedness was uncovered. Even so, you are now scorned by the daughters of Edom*a* and all her neighbors and the daughters of the Philistines—all those around you who despise you. 58You will bear the consequences of your lewdness and your detestable practices, declares the Lord.

59"'This is what the Sovereign Lord says: I will deal with you as you deserve, because you have despised my oath by breaking the covenant. 60Yet I will remember the covenant I made with you in the days of your youth, and I will establish an everlasting covenant with you. 61Then you will remember your ways and be ashamed when you receive your sisters, both those who are older than you and those who are younger. I will give them to you as daughters, but not on the basis of my covenant with you. 62So I will establish my covenant with you, and you will know that I am the Lord. 63Then, when I make atonement for you for all you have done, you will remember and be ashamed and never again open your mouth because of your humiliation, declares the Sovereign Lord.'"

Two Eagles and a Vine

17 The word of the Lord came to me: 2"Son of man, set forth an allegory and tell it to the house of Israel as a parable. 3Say to them, 'This is what the Sovereign Lord says: A great eagle with powerful wings, long feathers and full plumage of varied colors came to Lebanon.

Taking hold of the top of a cedar, 4he broke off its topmost shoot and carried it away to a land of merchants, where he planted it in a city of traders.

5"'He took one of the seedlings of the land and put it in fertile soil. He planted it like a willow by abundant water, 6and it sprouted and became a low, spreading vine. Its branches turned toward him, but its roots remained under it. So it became a vine and produced branches and put out leafy boughs.

7"'But there was another great eagle with powerful wings and full plumage. The vine now sent out its roots toward him from the plot where it was planted and stretched out its branches to him for water. 8It had been planted in good soil by abundant water so that it would produce branches, bear fruit and become a splendid vine.'

9"Say to them, 'This is what the Sovereign Lord says: Will it thrive? Will it not be uprooted and stripped of its fruit so that it withers? All its new growth will wither. It will not take a strong arm or many people to pull it up by the roots. 10It has been planted, but will it thrive? Will it not wither completely when the east wind strikes it—wither away in the plot where it grew?'"

11Then the word of the Lord came to me: 12"Say to this rebellious house, 'Do you not know what these things mean?' Say to them: 'The king of Babylon went to Jerusalem and carried off her king and her nobles, bringing them back with him to Babylon. 13Then he took a member of the royal family and made a treaty with him, putting him under oath. He also carried away the leading men of the land, 14so that the kingdom would be brought low, unable to rise again, surviving only by keeping his treaty. 15But the king rebelled against him by sending his envoys to Egypt to get horses and a large army. Will he succeed? Will he who does such things escape? Will he break the treaty and yet escape?

16"'As surely as I live, declares the Sovereign Lord, he shall die in Babylon, in the land of the king who put him on the throne, whose oath he despised and whose treaty he broke. 17Pharaoh with his mighty army and great horde will be of no help to him in war, when ramps are built and siege works erect-

---

a 57 Many Hebrew manuscripts and Syriac; most Hebrew manuscripts, Septuagint and Vulgate *Aram* ed to destroy many lives. ¹⁸He despised the oath by breaking the covenant. Because he had given his hand in pledge and yet did all these things, he shall not escape.

¹⁹" 'Therefore this is what the Sovereign Lord says: As surely as I live, I will bring down on his head my oath that he despised and my covenant that he broke. ²⁰I will spread my net for him, and he will be caught in my snare. I will bring him to Babylon and execute judgment on him there because he was unfaithful to me. ²¹All his choice troops will fall by the sword, and the survivors will be scattered to the winds. Then you will know that I the Lord have spoken.

²²" 'This is what the Sovereign Lord says: I myself will take a shoot from the very top of a cedar and plant it; I will break off a tender sprig from its topmost shoots and plant it on a high and lofty mountain. ²³On the mountain heights of Israel I will plant it; it will produce branches and bear fruit and become a splendid cedar. Birds of every kind will nest in it; they will find shelter in the shade of its branches. ²⁴All the trees of the forest will know that I the Lord bring down the tall tree and make the low tree grow tall. I dry up the green tree and make the dry tree flourish.

" 'I the Lord have spoken, and I will do it.' "

The One Who Sins Will Die

18 The word of the Lord came to me: ²"What do you people mean by quoting this proverb about the land of Israel:

" 'The parents eat sour grapes,
and the children's teeth are set on
edge'?

³"As surely as I live, declares the Sovereign Lord, you will no longer quote this proverb in Israel. ⁴For everyone belongs to me, the parent as well as the child—both alike belong to me. The one who sins is the one who will die.

⁵"Suppose there is a righteous man
who does what is just and right.
⁶He does not eat at the mountain shrines
or look to the idols of the house of
Israel.
He does not defile his neighbor's wife

or have sexual relations with a
woman during her period.
⁷He does not oppress anyone,
but returns what he took in pledge for
a loan.
He does not commit robbery
but gives his food to the hungry
and provides clothing for the naked.
⁸He does not lend to them at interest
or take a profit from them.
He withholds his hand from doing wrong
and judges fairly between two parties.
⁹He follows my decrees
and faithfully keeps my laws.
That man is righteous;
he will surely live,
declares the Sovereign Lord.

¹⁰"Suppose he has a violent son, who sheds blood or does any of these other things *a* ¹¹(though the father has done none of them):

"He eats at the mountain shrines.
He defiles his neighbor's wife.
¹²He oppresses the poor and needy.
He commits robbery.
He does not return what he took in
pledge.
He looks to the idols.
He does detestable things.
¹³He lends at interest and takes a profit.

Will such a man live? He will not! Because he has done all these detestable things, he is to be put to death; his blood will be on his own head.

¹⁴"But suppose this son has a son who sees all the sins his father commits, and though he sees them, he does not do such things:

¹⁵"He does not eat at the mountain
shrines
or look to the idols of the house of
Israel.
He does not defile his neighbor's wife.
¹⁶He does not oppress anyone
or require a pledge for a loan.
He does not commit robbery
but gives his food to the hungry
and provides clothing for the naked.
¹⁷He withholds his hand from mistreating
the poor

a 10 Or *things to a brother*

FRIDAY

YOU STAND BEFORE GOD ALONE

Ezekiel 18:1–32 or 18:4,20

G. CAMPBELL MORGAN {AD 1863–1945}

["For everyone belongs to me" (Ezekiel 18:4).] The great truth revealed is that every individual has a relationship with God available, which is mightier than all the facts resulting from physical relationships. It may be true that in my physical being I have inherited tendencies to some forms of evil from my father; but in the fact of my essential relation to God there are forces available to me more and mightier than all these tendencies. Therefore if I die, it is not because of the sin of my father, but because I fail to avail myself of my resources in God; and if I live, it is because I have availed myself of these resources . . . The former [righteousness] results from right relationship with God, and the latter [evil] from failure to realize that relationship. All souls are his, and that means that every soul is made for first-hand personal dealing with him.

D. A. Carson

We belong to God. He may do with us as he wishes. There is something deep within us that rebels at being reminded of that elemental truth. But truth it is. Indeed, our rebellion in the face of it is a reminder of how much we still want to be at the center of the universe, with God serving us. That is the heart of all idolatry.

reflection

1. Every soul has the opportunity for a relationship with God, and each person is responsible for what they do with that choice. How have you availed yourself of the resources you have in God?

2. In what ways do you fight against the fact that you belong to God and live as though you belong only to yourself?

3. What does God think when people blame others—including their parents—for their own weaknesses and sin?

For your next devotional reading, go to page 945.

and takes no interest or profit from
them.
He keeps my laws and follows my
decrees.

He will not die for his father's sin; he will
surely live. ¹⁸But his father will die for his
own sin, because he practiced extortion,
robbed his brother and did what was wrong
among his people.

¹⁹"Yet you ask, 'Why does the son not
share the guilt of his father?' Since the son
has done what is just and right and has been
careful to keep all my decrees, he will surely live. ²⁰The one who sins is the one who
will die. The child will not share the guilt of
the parent, nor will the parent share the
guilt of the child. The righteousness of the
righteous will be credited to them, and the
wickedness of the wicked will be charged
against them.

²¹"But if the wicked turn away from all
the sins they have committed and keep all
my decrees and do what is just and right,
they will surely live; they will not die. ²²None
of the offenses they have committed will be
remembered against them. Because of the
righteous things they have done, they will
live. ²³Do I take any pleasure in the death of
the wicked? declares the Sovereign Lord.
Rather, am I not pleased when they turn
from their ways and live?

²⁴"But if the righteous turn from their
righteousness and commit sin and do the
same detestable things the wicked do, will
they live? None of the righteous things they
have done will be remembered. Because of
the unfaithfulness they are guilty of and because of the sins they have committed, they
will die.

²⁵"Yet you say, 'The way of the Lord is not
just.' Hear, house of Israel: Is my way unjust? Is it not your ways that are unjust? ²⁶If
the righteous turn from their righteousness
and commit sin, they will die for it; because
of the sin they have committed they will die.
²⁷But if the wicked turn away from the wickedness they have committed and do what is
just and right, they will save their lives.
²⁸Because they consider all the offenses
they have committed and turn away from
them, they will surely live; they will not die.
²⁹Yet the house of Israel says, 'The way of
the Lord is not just.' Are my ways unjust,

house of Israel? Is it not your ways that are
unjust?

³⁰"Therefore, house of Israel, I will judge
each of you according to your own ways, declares the Sovereign Lord. Repent! Turn
away from all your offenses; then sin will
not be your downfall. ³¹Rid yourselves of all
the offenses you have committed, and get a
new heart and a new spirit. Why will you die,
house of Israel? ³²For I take no pleasure in
the death of anyone, declares the Sovereign
Lord. Repent and live!

A Lament Over Israel's Princes

19 "Take up a lament concerning
the princes of Israel ²and say:

" 'What a lioness was your mother
    among the lions!
She lay down among them
    and reared her cubs.
³She brought up one of her cubs,
    and he became a strong lion.
He learned to tear the prey
    and he devoured people.
⁴The nations heard about him,
    and he was trapped in their pit.
They led him with hooks
    to the land of Egypt.

⁵" 'When she saw her hope unfulfilled,
    her expectation gone,
she took another of her cubs
    and made him a strong lion.
⁶He prowled among the lions,
    for he was now a strong lion.
He learned to tear the prey
    and he devoured people.
⁷He broke down ᵃ their strongholds
    and devastated their towns.
The land and all who were in it
    were terrified by his roaring.
⁸Then the nations came against him,
    those from regions round about.
They spread their net for him,
    and he was trapped in their pit.
⁹With hooks they pulled him into a cage
    and brought him to the king of
        Babylon.
They put him in prison,
    so his roar was heard no longer
        on the mountains of Israel.

ᵃ 7 Targum (see Septuagint); Hebrew *He knew*

10 " 'Your mother was like a vine in your
  vineyard*a*
  planted by the water;
  it was fruitful and full of branches
  because of abundant water.
11 Its branches were strong,
  fit for a ruler's scepter.
  It towered high
  above the thick foliage,
  conspicuous for its height
  and for its many branches.
12 But it was uprooted in fury
  and thrown to the ground.
  The east wind made it shrivel,
  it was stripped of its fruit;
  its strong branches withered
  and fire consumed them.
13 Now it is planted in the desert,
  in a dry and thirsty land.
14 Fire spread from one of its main*b*
  branches
  and consumed its fruit.
  No strong branch is left on it
  fit for a ruler's scepter.'

"This is a lament and is to be used as a lament."

Rebellious Israel Purged

20 In the seventh year, in the fifth month on the tenth day, some of the elders of Israel came to inquire of the LORD, and they sat down in front of me.

2 Then the word of the LORD came to me: 3 "Son of man, speak to the elders of Israel and say to them, 'This is what the Sovereign LORD says: Have you come to inquire of me? As surely as I live, I will not let you inquire of me, declares the Sovereign LORD.'

4 "Will you judge them? Will you judge them, son of man? Then confront them with the detestable practices of their ancestors 5 and say to them: 'This is what the Sovereign LORD says: On the day I chose Israel, I swore with uplifted hand to the descendants of the house of Jacob and revealed myself to them in Egypt. With uplifted hand I said to them, "I am the LORD your God." 6 On that day I swore to them that I would bring them out of Egypt into a land I had searched out for them, a land flowing with milk and honey, the most beautiful of all lands. 7 And I said to them, "Each of you, get rid of the vile

images you have set your eyes on, and do not defile yourselves with the idols of Egypt. I am the LORD your God."

8 " 'But they rebelled against me and would not listen to me; they did not get rid of the vile images they had set their eyes on, nor did they forsake the idols of Egypt. So I said I would pour out my wrath on them and spend my anger against them in Egypt. 9 But for the sake of my name, I brought them out of Egypt. I did it to keep my name from being profaned in the eyes of the nations among whom they lived and in whose sight I had revealed myself to the Israelites. 10 Therefore I led them out of Egypt and brought them into the wilderness. 11 I gave them my decrees and made known to them my laws, through which people will live if they obey them. 12 Also I gave them my Sabbaths as a sign between us, so they would know that I the LORD made them holy.

13 " 'Yet the people of Israel rebelled against me in the wilderness. They did not follow my decrees but rejected my laws—through which people will live if they obey them—and they utterly desecrated my Sabbaths. So I said I would pour out my wrath on them and destroy them in the wilderness. 14 But for the sake of my name I did what would keep it from being profaned in the eyes of the nations in whose sight I had brought them out. 15 Also with uplifted hand I swore to them in the wilderness that I would not bring them into the land I had given them—a land flowing with milk and honey, the most beautiful of all lands—16 because they rejected my laws and did not follow my decrees and desecrated my Sabbaths. For their hearts were devoted to their idols. 17 Yet I looked on them with pity and did not destroy them or put an end to them in the wilderness. 18 I said to their children in the wilderness, "Do not follow the statutes of your parents or keep their laws or defile yourselves with their idols. 19 I am the LORD your God; follow my decrees and be careful to keep my laws. 20 Keep my Sabbaths holy, that they may be a sign between us. Then you will know that I am the LORD your God."

21 " 'But the children rebelled against me: They did not follow my decrees, they were not careful to keep my laws, of which I said, "Whoever obeys them will live by them,"

---

a 10 Two Hebrew manuscripts; most Hebrew manuscripts *your blood*   *b 14* Or *from under its* and they desecrated my Sabbaths. So I said I would pour out my wrath on them and spend my anger against them in the wilderness. ²²But I withheld my hand, and for the sake of my name I did what would keep it from being profaned in the eyes of the nations in whose sight I had brought them out. ²³Also with uplifted hand I swore to them in the wilderness that I would disperse them among the nations and scatter them through the countries, ²⁴because they had not obeyed my laws but had rejected my decrees and desecrated my Sabbaths, and their eyes lusted after their parents' idols. ²⁵So I gave them other statutes that were not good and laws through which they could not live; ²⁶I defiled them through their gifts—the sacrifice of every firstborn—that I might fill them with horror so they would know that I am the LORD.'

²⁷"Therefore, son of man, speak to the people of Israel and say to them, 'This is what the Sovereign LORD says: In this also your ancestors blasphemed me by being unfaithful to me: ²⁸When I brought them into the land I had sworn to give them and they saw any high hill or any leafy tree, there they offered their sacrifices, made offerings that aroused my anger, presented their fragrant incense and poured out their drink offerings. ²⁹Then I said to them: What is this high place you go to?' " (It is called Bamah ᵃ to this day.)

Rebellious Israel Renewed

³⁰"Therefore say to the house of Israel: 'This is what the Sovereign LORD says: Will you defile yourselves the way your ancestors did and lust after their vile images? ³¹When you offer your gifts—the sacrifice of your children in the fire—you continue to defile yourselves with all your idols to this day. Am I to let you inquire of me, house of Israel? As surely as I live, declares the Sovereign LORD, I will not let you inquire of me.

³²" 'You say, "We want to be like the nations, like the peoples of the world, who serve wood and stone." But what you have in mind will never happen. ³³As surely as I live, declares the Sovereign LORD, I will reign over you with a mighty hand and an outstretched arm and with outpoured wrath. ³⁴I

will bring you from the nations and gather you from the countries where you have been scattered—with a mighty hand and an outstretched arm and with outpoured wrath. ³⁵I will bring you into the wilderness of the nations and there, face to face, I will execute judgment upon you. ³⁶As I judged your ancestors in the wilderness of the land of Egypt, so I will judge you, declares the Sovereign LORD. ³⁷I will take note of you as you pass under my rod, and I will bring you into the bond of the covenant. ³⁸I will purge you of those who revolt and rebel against me. Although I will bring them out of the land where they are living, yet they will not enter the land of Israel. Then you will know that I am the LORD.

³⁹" 'As for you, house of Israel, this is what the Sovereign LORD says: Go and serve your idols, every one of you! But afterward you will surely listen to me and no longer profane my holy name with your gifts and idols. ⁴⁰For on my holy mountain, the high mountain of Israel, declares the Sovereign LORD, there in the land the entire house of Israel will serve me, and there I will accept them. There I will require your offerings and your choice gifts,ᵇ along with all your holy sacrifices. ⁴¹I will accept you as fragrant incense when I bring you out from the nations and gather you from the countries where you have been scattered, and I will be proved holy through you in the sight of the nations. ⁴²Then you will know that I am the LORD, when I bring you into the land of Israel, the land I had sworn with uplifted hand to give to your ancestors. ⁴³There you will remember your conduct and all the actions by which you have defiled yourselves, and you will loathe yourselves for all the evil you have done. ⁴⁴You will know that I am the LORD, when I deal with you for my name's sake and not according to your evil ways and your corrupt practices, house of Israel, declares the Sovereign LORD.' "

Prophecy Against the South

*⁴⁵The word of the LORD came to me: ⁴⁶"Son of man, set your face toward the south; preach against the south and prophesy against the forest of the southland. ⁴⁷Say to the southern forest: 'Hear the word of the

---

ᵃ 29 Bamah means high place.   ᵇ 40 Or and the gifts of your firstfruits
* 20:45-49 is numbered 21:1-5 in Hebrew texts.

LORD. This is what the Sovereign LORD says: I am about to set fire to you, and it will consume all your trees, both green and dry. The blazing flame will not be quenched, and every face from south to north will be scorched by it. ⁴⁸Everyone will see that I the LORD have kindled it; it will not be quenched.' "

⁴⁹Then I said, "Ah, Sovereign LORD! They are saying of me, 'Isn't he just telling parables?' "

Babylon as God's Sword of Judgment

21 *The word of the LORD came to me: ²"Son of man, set your face against Jerusalem and preach against the sanctuary. Prophesy against the land of Israel ³and say to her: 'This is what the LORD says: I am against you. I will draw my sword from its sheath and cut off from you both the righteous and the wicked. ⁴Because I am going to cut off the righteous and the wicked, my sword will be unsheathed against everyone from south to north. ⁵Then all people will know that I the LORD have drawn my sword from its sheath; it will not return again.'

⁶"Therefore groan, son of man! Groan before them with broken heart and bitter grief. ⁷And when they ask you, 'Why are you groaning?' you shall say, 'Because of the news that is coming. Every heart will melt and every hand go limp; every spirit will become faint and every knee be wet with urine.' It is coming! It will surely take place, declares the Sovereign LORD."

⁸The word of the LORD came to me: ⁹"Son of man, prophesy and say, 'This is what the Lord says:

" 'A sword, a sword,
    sharpened and polished—
¹⁰sharpened for the slaughter,
    polished to flash like lightning!

" 'Shall we rejoice in the scepter of my royal son? The sword despises every such stick.

¹¹" 'The sword is appointed to be polished,
    to be grasped with the hand;
it is sharpened and polished,
    made ready for the hand of the slayer.
¹²Cry out and wail, son of man,
    for it is against my people;

it is against all the princes of Israel.
They are thrown to the sword
    along with my people.
Therefore beat your breast.

¹³" 'Testing will surely come. And what if even the scepter, which the sword despises, does not continue? declares the Sovereign LORD.'

¹⁴"So then, son of man, prophesy
    and strike your hands together.
Let the sword strike twice,
    even three times.
It is a sword for slaughter—
    a sword for great slaughter,
    closing in on them from every side.
¹⁵So that hearts may melt
    and the fallen be many,
I have stationed the sword for slaughterᵃ
    at all their gates.
Oh! It is made to flash like lightning,
    it is grasped for slaughter.
¹⁶Slash to the right, you sword,
    then to the left,
    wherever your blade is turned.
¹⁷I too will strike my hands together,
    and my wrath will subside.
I the LORD have spoken."

¹⁸The word of the LORD came to me: ¹⁹"Son of man, mark out two roads for the sword of the king of Babylon to take, both starting from the same country. Make a signpost where the road branches off to the city. ²⁰Mark out one road for the sword to come against Rabbah of the Ammonites and another against Judah and fortified Jerusalem. ²¹For the king of Babylon will stop at the fork in the road, at the junction of the two roads, to seek an omen: He will cast lots with arrows, he will consult his idols, he will examine the liver. ²²Into his right hand will come the lot for Jerusalem, where he is to set up battering rams, to give the command to slaughter, to sound the battle cry, to set battering rams against the gates, to build a ramp and to erect siege works. ²³It will seem like a false omen to those who have sworn allegiance to him, but he will remind them of their guilt and take them captive.

²⁴"Therefore this is what the Sovereign LORD says: 'Because you people have brought to mind your guilt by your open re-

---

ᵃ 15 Septuagint; the meaning of the Hebrew for this word is uncertain.

* 21:1-32 is numbered 21:6-37 in Hebrew texts.

bellion, revealing your sins in all that you do—because you have done this, you will be taken captive.

25" 'You profane and wicked prince of Israel, whose day has come, whose time of punishment has reached its climax, 26this is what the Sovereign LORD says: Take off the turban, remove the crown. It will not be as it was: The lowly will be exalted and the exalted will be brought low. 27A ruin! A ruin! I will make it a ruin! The crown will not be restored until he to whom it rightfully belongs shall come; to him I will give it.'

28"And you, son of man, prophesy and say, 'This is what the Sovereign LORD says about the Ammonites and their insults:

" 'A sword, a sword,
    drawn for the slaughter,
polished to consume
    and to flash like lightning!
29Despite false visions concerning you
    and lying divinations about you,
it will be laid on the necks
    of the wicked who are to be slain,
whose day has come,
    whose time of punishment has
        reached its climax.

30" 'Let the sword return to its sheath.
    In the place where you were created,
    in the land of your ancestry,
    I will judge you.
31I will pour out my wrath on you
    and breathe out my fiery anger
        against you;
I will deliver you into the hands of brutal
        men,
    men skilled in destruction.
32You will be fuel for the fire,
    your blood will be shed in your land,
    you will be remembered no more;
for I the LORD have spoken.' "

Judgment on Jerusalem's Sins

22 The word of the LORD came to me:

2"Son of man, will you judge her? Will you judge this city of bloodshed? Then confront her with all her detestable practices 3and say: 'This is what the Sovereign LORD says: You city that brings on herself doom by shedding blood in her midst and defiles

herself by making idols, 4you have become guilty because of the blood you have shed and have become defiled by the idols you have made. You have brought your days to a close, and the end of your years has come. Therefore I will make you an object of scorn to the nations and a laughingstock to all the countries. 5Those who are near and those who are far away will mock you, you infamous city, full of turmoil.

6" 'See how each of the princes of Israel who are in you uses his power to shed blood. 7In you they have treated father and mother with contempt; in you they have oppressed the foreigner and mistreated the fatherless and the widow. 8You have despised my holy things and desecrated my Sabbaths. 9In you are slanderers who are bent on shedding blood; in you are those who eat at the mountain shrines and commit lewd acts. 10In you are those who dishonor their father's bed; in you are those who violate women during their period, when they are ceremonially unclean. 11In you one man commits a detestable offense with his neighbor's wife, another shamefully defiles his daughter-in-law, and another violates his sister, his own father's daughter. 12In you are people who accept bribes to shed blood; you take interest and make a profit from the poor. You extort unjust gain from your neighbors. And you have forgotten me, declares the Sovereign LORD.

13" 'I will surely strike my hands together at the unjust gain you have made and at the blood you have shed in your midst. 14Will your courage endure or your hands be strong in the day I deal with you? I the LORD have spoken, and I will do it. 15I will disperse you among the nations and scatter you through the countries; and I will put an end to your uncleanness. 16When you have been defiled[a] in the eyes of the nations, you will know that I am the LORD.' "

17Then the word of the LORD came to me: 18"Son of man, the house of Israel has become dross to me; all of them are the copper, tin, iron and lead left inside a furnace. They are but the dross of silver. 19Therefore this is what the Sovereign LORD says: 'Because you have all become dross, I will gather you into Jerusalem. 20As silver, copper, iron, lead and tin are gathered into a furnace to be melted

---

a 16 Or When I have allotted you your inheritance

with a fiery blast, so will I gather you in my anger and my wrath and put you inside the city and melt you. ²¹I will gather you and I will blow on you with my fiery wrath, and you will be melted inside her. ²²As silver is melted in a furnace, so you will be melted inside her, and you will know that I the LORD have poured out my wrath on you.' "

²³Again the word of the LORD came to me: ²⁴"Son of man, say to the land, 'You are a land that has not been cleansed or rained on in the day of wrath.' ²⁵There is a conspiracy of her princes*a* within her like a roaring lion tearing its prey; they devour people, take treasures and precious things and make many widows within her. ²⁶Her priests do violence to my law and profane my holy things; they do not distinguish between the holy and the common; they teach that there is no difference between the unclean and the clean; and they shut their eyes to the keeping of my Sabbaths, so that I am profaned among them. ²⁷Her officials within her are like wolves tearing their prey; they shed blood and kill people to make unjust gain. ²⁸Her prophets whitewash these deeds for them by false visions and lying divinations. They say, 'This is what the Sovereign LORD says'—when the LORD has not spoken. ²⁹The people of the land practice extortion and commit robbery; they oppress the poor and needy and mistreat the foreigner, denying them justice.

³⁰"I looked for someone among them who would build up the wall and stand before me in the gap on behalf of the land so I would not have to destroy it, but I found no one. ³¹So I will pour out my wrath on them and consume them with my fiery anger, bringing down on their own heads all they have done, declares the Sovereign LORD."

Two Adulterous Sisters

23 The word of the LORD came to me: ²"Son of man, there were two women, daughters of the same mother. ³They became prostitutes in Egypt, engaging in prostitution from their youth. In that land their breasts were fondled and their virgin bosoms caressed. ⁴The older was named Oholah, and her sister was Oholibah. They were mine and gave birth to

sons and daughters. Oholah is Samaria, and Oholibah is Jerusalem.

⁵"Oholah engaged in prostitution while she was still mine; and she lusted after her lovers, the Assyrians—warriors ⁶clothed in blue, governors and commanders, all of them handsome young men, and mounted horsemen. ⁷She gave herself as a prostitute to all the elite of the Assyrians and defiled herself with all the idols of everyone she lusted after. ⁸She did not give up the prostitution she began in Egypt, when during her youth men slept with her, caressed her virgin bosom and poured out their lust on her.

⁹"Therefore I delivered her into the hands of her lovers, the Assyrians, for whom she lusted. ¹⁰They stripped her naked, took away her sons and daughters and killed her with the sword. She became a byword among women, and punishment was inflicted on her.

¹¹"Her sister Oholibah saw this, yet in her lust and prostitution she was more depraved than her sister. ¹²She too lusted after the Assyrians—governors and commanders, warriors in full dress, mounted horsemen, all handsome young men. ¹³I saw that she too defiled herself; both of them went the same way.

¹⁴"But she carried her prostitution still further. She saw men portrayed on a wall, figures of Chaldeans*b* portrayed in red, ¹⁵with belts around their waists and flowing turbans on their heads; all of them looked like Babylonian chariot officers, natives of Chaldea.*c* ¹⁶As soon as she saw them, she lusted after them and sent messengers to them in Chaldea. ¹⁷Then the Babylonians came to her, to the bed of love, and in their lust they defiled her. After she had been defiled by them, she turned away from them in disgust. ¹⁸When she carried on her prostitution openly and exposed her nakedness, I turned away from her in disgust, just as I had turned away from her sister. ¹⁹Yet she became more and more promiscuous as she recalled the days of her youth, when she was a prostitute in Egypt. ²⁰There she lusted after her lovers, whose genitals were like those of donkeys and whose emission was like that of horses. ²¹So you longed for the lewdness of your youth, when in Egypt your bosom was caressed and your young breasts fondled.*d*

---

a 25 Septuagint; Hebrew *prophets* *b 14* Or *Babylonians* *c 15* Or *Babylonia*; also in verse 16
d 21 Syriac (see also verse 3); Hebrew *caressed because of your young breasts*

²²"Therefore, Oholibah, this is what the Sovereign LORD says: I will stir up your lovers against you, those you turned away from in disgust, and I will bring them against you from every side— ²³the Babylonians and all the Chaldeans, the men of Pekod and Shoa and Koa, and all the Assyrians with them, handsome young men, all of them governors and commanders, chariot officers and men of high rank, all mounted on horses. ²⁴They will come against you with weapons,ᵃ chariots and wagons and with a throng of people; they will take up positions against you on every side with large and small shields and with helmets. I will turn you over to them for punishment, and they will punish you according to their standards. ²⁵I will direct my jealous anger against you, and they will deal with you in fury. They will cut off your noses and your ears, and those of you who are left will fall by the sword. They will take away your sons and daughters, and those of you who are left will be consumed by fire. ²⁶They will also strip you of your clothes and take your fine jewelry. ²⁷So I will put a stop to the lewdness and prostitution you began in Egypt. You will not look on these things with longing or remember Egypt anymore.

²⁸"For this is what the Sovereign LORD says: I am about to deliver you into the hands of those you hate, to those you turned away from in disgust. ²⁹They will deal with you in hatred and take away everything you have worked for. They will leave you stark naked, and the shame of your prostitution will be exposed. Your lewdness and promiscuity ³⁰have brought this on you, because you lusted after the nations and defiled yourself with their idols. ³¹You have gone the way of your sister; so I will put her cup into your hand.

³²"This is what the Sovereign LORD says:

"You will drink your sister's cup,
    a cup large and deep;
it will bring scorn and derision,
    for it holds so much.
³³You will be filled with drunkenness and
        sorrow,
    the cup of ruin and desolation,
    the cup of your sister Samaria.
³⁴You will drink it and drain it dry

and chew on its pieces—
and you will tear your breasts.

I have spoken, declares the Sovereign LORD.

³⁵"Therefore this is what the Sovereign LORD says: Since you have forgotten me and thrust me behind your back, you must bear the consequences of your lewdness and prostitution."

³⁶The LORD said to me: "Son of man, will you judge Oholah and Oholibah? Then confront them with their detestable practices, ³⁷for they have committed adultery and blood is on their hands. They committed adultery with their idols; they even sacrificed their children, whom they bore to me, as food for them. ³⁸They have also done this to me: At that same time they defiled my sanctuary and desecrated my Sabbaths. ³⁹On the very day they sacrificed their children to their idols, they entered my sanctuary and desecrated it. That is what they did in my house.

⁴⁰"They even sent messengers for men who came from far away, and when they arrived you bathed yourself for them, painted your eyes and put on your jewelry. ⁴¹You sat on an elegant couch, with a table spread before it on which you had placed the incense and olive oil that belonged to me.

⁴²"The noise of a carefree crowd was around her; drunkards were brought from the desert along with men from the rabble, and they put bracelets on the arms of the woman and her sister and beautiful crowns on their heads. ⁴³Then I said about the one worn out by adultery, 'Now let them use her as a prostitute, for that is all she is.' ⁴⁴And they slept with her. As men sleep with a prostitute, so they slept with those lewd women, Oholah and Oholibah. ⁴⁵But righteous judges will sentence them to the punishment of women who commit adultery and shed blood, because they are adulterous and blood is on their hands.

⁴⁶"This is what the Sovereign LORD says: Bring a mob against them and give them over to terror and plunder. ⁴⁷The mob will stone them and cut them down with their swords; they will kill their sons and daughters and burn down their houses.

⁴⁸"So I will put an end to lewdness in the land, that all women may take warning and

ᵃ 24 The meaning of the Hebrew for this word is uncertain.

not imitate you. [49]You will suffer the penalty for your lewdness and bear the consequences of your sins of idolatry. Then you will know that I am the Sovereign LORD."

Jerusalem as a Cooking Pot

24 In the ninth year, in the tenth month on the tenth day, the word of the LORD came to me: [2]"Son of man, record this date, this very date, because the king of Babylon has laid siege to Jerusalem this very day. [3]Tell this rebellious house a parable and say to them: 'This is what the Sovereign LORD says:

" 'Put on the cooking pot; put it on
    and pour water into it.
[4]Put into it the pieces of meat,
    all the choice pieces—the leg and the
        shoulder.
Fill it with the best of these bones;
[5]   take the pick of the flock.
Pile wood beneath it for the bones;
    bring it to a boil
    and cook the bones in it.

[6]" 'For this is what the Sovereign LORD says:

" 'Woe to the city of bloodshed,
    to the pot now encrusted,
    whose deposit will not go away!
Take the meat out piece by piece
    in whatever order it comes.

[7]" 'For the blood she shed is in her midst:
    She poured it on the bare rock;
she did not pour it on the ground,
    where the dust would cover it.
[8]To stir up wrath and take revenge
    I put her blood on the bare rock,
    so that it would not be covered.

[9]" 'Therefore this is what the Sovereign LORD says:

" 'Woe to the city of bloodshed!
    I, too, will pile the wood high.
[10]So heap on the wood
    and kindle the fire.
Cook the meat well,
    mixing in the spices;
    and let the bones be charred.
[11]Then set the empty pot on the coals
    till it becomes hot and its copper
        glows,
so that its impurities may be melted

and its deposit burned away.
[12]It has frustrated all efforts;
    its heavy deposit has not been
        removed,
    not even by fire.

[13]" 'Now your impurity is lewdness. Because I tried to cleanse you but you would not be cleansed from your impurity, you will not be clean again until my wrath against you has subsided.

[14]" 'I the LORD have spoken. The time has come for me to act. I will not hold back; I will not have pity, nor will I relent. You will be judged according to your conduct and your actions, declares the Sovereign LORD.' "

Ezekiel's Wife Dies

[15]The word of the LORD came to me: [16]"Son of man, with one blow I am about to take away from you the delight of your eyes. Yet do not lament or weep or shed any tears. [17]Groan quietly; do not mourn for the dead. Keep your turban fastened and your sandals on your feet; do not cover your mustache and beard or eat the customary food ⌊of mourners⌋."

[18]So I spoke to the people in the morning, and in the evening my wife died. The next morning I did as I had been commanded.

[19]Then the people asked me, "Won't you tell us what these things have to do with us? Why are you acting like this?"

[20]So I said to them, "The word of the LORD came to me: [21]Say to the house of Israel, 'This is what the Sovereign LORD says: I am about to desecrate my sanctuary—the stronghold in which you take pride, the delight of your eyes, the object of your affection. The sons and daughters you left behind will fall by the sword. [22]And you will do as I have done. You will not cover your mustache and beard or eat the customary food ⌊of mourners⌋. [23]You will keep your turbans on your heads and your sandals on your feet. You will not mourn or weep but will waste away because of[a] your sins and groan among yourselves. [24]Ezekiel will be a sign to you; you will do just as he has done. When this happens, you will know that I am the Sovereign LORD.'

[25]"And you, son of man, on the day I take away their stronghold, their joy and glory, the

---

[a] 23 Or *away in*

delight of their eyes, their heart's desire, and their sons and daughters as well— ²⁶on that day a fugitive will come to tell you the news. ²⁷At that time your mouth will be opened; you will speak with him and will no longer be silent. So you will be a sign to them, and they will know that I am the LORD."

A Prophecy Against Ammon

25 The word of the LORD came to me: ²"Son of man, set your face against the Ammonites and prophesy against them. ³Say to them, 'Hear the word of the Sovereign LORD. This is what the Sovereign LORD says: Because you said "Aha!" over my sanctuary when it was desecrated and over the land of Israel when it was laid waste and over the people of Judah when they went into exile, ⁴therefore I am going to give you to the people of the East as a possession. They will set up their camps and pitch their tents among you; they will eat your fruit and drink your milk. ⁵I will turn Rabbah into a pasture for camels and Ammon into a resting place for sheep. Then you will know that I am the LORD. ⁶For this is what the Sovereign LORD says: Because you have clapped your hands and stamped your feet, rejoicing with all the malice of your heart against the land of Israel, ⁷therefore I will stretch out my hand against you and give you as plunder to the nations. I will wipe you out from among the nations and exterminate you from the countries. I will destroy you, and you will know that I am the LORD.' "

A Prophecy Against Moab

⁸"This is what the Sovereign LORD says: 'Because Moab and Seir said, "Look, the house of Judah has become like all the other nations," ⁹therefore I will expose the flank of Moab, beginning at its frontier towns— Beth Jeshimoth, Baal Meon and Kiriathaim—the glory of that land. ¹⁰I will give Moab along with the Ammonites to the people of the East as a possession, so that the Ammonites will not be remembered among the nations; ¹¹and I will inflict punishment on Moab. Then they will know that I am the LORD.' "

A Prophecy Against Edom

¹²"This is what the Sovereign LORD says: 'Because Edom took revenge on the house of Judah and became very guilty by doing so, ¹³therefore this is what the Sovereign LORD says: I will stretch out my hand against Edom and kill its people and their animals. I will lay it waste, and from Teman to Dedan they will fall by the sword. ¹⁴I will take vengeance on Edom by the hand of my people Israel, and they will deal with Edom in accordance with my anger and my wrath; they will know my vengeance, declares the Sovereign LORD.' "

A Prophecy Against Philistia

¹⁵"This is what the Sovereign LORD says: 'Because the Philistines acted in vengeance and took revenge with malice in their hearts, and with ancient hostility sought to destroy Judah, ¹⁶therefore this is what the Sovereign LORD says: I am about to stretch out my hand against the Philistines, and I will wipe out the Kerethites and destroy those remaining along the coast. ¹⁷I will carry out great vengeance on them and punish them in my wrath. Then they will know that I am the LORD, when I take vengeance on them.' "

A Prophecy Against Tyre

26 In the eleventh month of the twelfth^a year, on the first day of the month, the word of the LORD came to me: ²"Son of man, because Tyre has said of Jerusalem, 'Aha! The gate to the nations is broken, and its doors have swung open to me; now that she lies in ruins I will prosper,' ³therefore this is what the Sovereign LORD says: I am against you, Tyre, and I will bring many nations against you, like the sea casting up its waves. ⁴They will destroy the walls of Tyre and pull down her towers; I will scrape away her rubble and make her a bare rock. ⁵Out in the sea she will become a place to spread fishnets, for I have spoken, declares the Sovereign LORD. She will become plunder for the nations, ⁶and her settlements on the mainland will be ravaged by the sword. Then they will know that I am the LORD.

⁷"For this is what the Sovereign LORD says: From the north I am going to bring against Tyre Nebuchadnezzar^b king of Bab-

---

^a 1 Probable reading of the original Hebrew text; Masoretic Text does not have *month of the twelfth*.
^b 7 Hebrew *Nebuchadrezzar*, of which *Nebuchadnezzar* is a variant; here and often in Ezekiel and Jeremiah

Giving God His Due

Ezekiel 25:17

read/meditate

Read Ezekiel 25:17. Read it again and notice the outcome of the judgment. The chapters surrounding this verse include prophecies against most of Israel's enemies. With each judgment, God claimed the accused would acknowledge him as God. What God desired from these ancients was acknowledgment. What kind of acknowledgment does God get from your culture? How much acknowledgment does God get from you personally?

pray

Offer God the acknowledgment he desires. Acknowledge his presence in your world, his interest, care and love for you. Acknowledge your faith in him.

contemplate

As you go through this week, how can you deliberately acknowledge God through your thoughts and actions? Jot down some specific ideas.

additional reflection

As Christians we accept one foundational truth—God—and everything else makes sense. An atheist denies God and has to accept incredible explanations for everything else. It takes more faith to deny God than to believe in Him.

—John MacArthur

True godliness leaves the world, convinced beyond a shadow of a doubt, that the only explanation for you, is Jesus Christ, to whose eternally unchanging and altogether adequate "I AM!" your heart has learned to say with unshatterable faith, "Thou art!"

—W. Ian Thomas

For your next devotional reading, go to page 947.

ylon, king of kings, with horses and chariots, with horsemen and a great army. ⁸He will ravage your settlements on the mainland with the sword; he will set up siege works against you, build a ramp up to your walls and raise his shields against you. ⁹He will direct the blows of his battering rams against your walls and demolish your towers with his weapons. ¹⁰His horses will be so many that they will cover you with dust. Your walls will tremble at the noise of the warhorses, wagons and chariots when he enters your gates as men enter a city whose walls have been broken through. ¹¹The hooves of his horses will trample all your streets; he will kill your people with the sword, and your strong pillars will fall to the ground. ¹²They will plunder your wealth and loot your merchandise; they will break down your walls and demolish your fine houses and throw your stones, timber and rubble into the sea. ¹³I will put an end to your noisy songs, and the music of your harps will be heard no more. ¹⁴I will make you a bare rock, and you will become a place to spread fishnets. You will never be rebuilt, for I the LORD have spoken, declares the Sovereign LORD.

¹⁵"This is what the Sovereign LORD says to Tyre: Will not the coastlands tremble at the sound of your fall, when the wounded groan and the slaughter takes place in you? ¹⁶Then all the princes of the coast will step down from their thrones and lay aside their robes and take off their embroidered garments. Clothed with terror, they will sit on the ground, trembling every moment, appalled at you. ¹⁷Then they will take up a lament concerning you and say to you:

" 'How you are destroyed, city of
        renown,
    peopled by men of the sea!
You were a power on the seas,
    you and your citizens;
you put your terror
    on all who lived there.
¹⁸Now the coastlands tremble
    on the day of your fall;
the islands in the sea
    are terrified at your collapse.'

¹⁹"This is what the Sovereign LORD says: When I make you a desolate city, like cities no longer inhabited, and when I bring the ocean depths over you and its vast waters cover you, ²⁰then I will bring you down with those who go down to the pit, to the people of long ago. I will make you dwell in the earth below, as in ancient ruins, with those who go down to the pit, and you will not return or take your place*a* in the land of the living. ²¹I will bring you to a horrible end and you will be no more. You will be sought, but you will never again be found, declares the Sovereign LORD.' "

A Lament Over Tyre

27 The word of the LORD came to me: ²"Son of man, take up a lament concerning Tyre. ³Say to Tyre, situated at the gateway to the sea, merchant of peoples on many coasts, 'This is what the Sovereign LORD says:

" 'You say, Tyre,
    "I am perfect in beauty."
⁴Your domain was on the high seas;
    your builders brought your beauty to
        perfection.
⁵They made all your timbers
    of juniper from Senir*b*;
they took a cedar from Lebanon
    to make a mast for you.
⁶Of oaks from Bashan
    they made your oars;
of cypress wood*c* from the coasts of
        Cyprus
    they made your deck, inlaid with
        ivory.
⁷Fine embroidered linen from Egypt was
        your sail
    and served as your banner;
your awnings were of blue and purple
    from the coasts of Elishah.
⁸Men of Sidon and Arvad were your
        oarsmen;
    your skilled men, Tyre, were aboard
        as your sailors.
⁹Veteran craftsmen of Byblos were on
        board
    as shipwrights to caulk your seams.
All the ships of the sea and their sailors
    came alongside to trade for your wares.
¹⁰" 'Men of Persia, Lydia and Put
    served as soldiers in your army.

a 20 Septuagint; Hebrew *return, and I will give glory*   *b 5* That is, Mount Hermon   *c 6* Targum; the Masoretic Text has a different division of the consonants.

MONDAY

True Beauty

Ezekiel 27:1–36 *or* 27:3–4,34–36

Charles Haddon Spurgeon {AD 1834–1892}

At heaven's gate there stands an angel, whose job it is to admit only those who in their countenances bear the same features as the Lord of the place. Here comes a king with a crown upon his head. The angel pays him no respect, but reminds him that the royal crowns of earth have no value in heaven. A company of eminent men advance dressed in robes of state, and others adorned with the academic robes of learning, but to these no honor is given, for their faces are very unlike the Crucified. A young woman comes forward, lovely and beautiful, but the celestial watcher does not see in that sparkling eye and rosy cheek the beauty for which he is looking. A man of renown comes up heralded by fame, and preceded by the admiring clamor of humanity. But the angel says, "Such applause may please the members of the human race, but you have no right to enter here." But free admittance is always given to those who in holiness are made like their Lord. Poor they may have been—illiterate they may have been—but the angel as he looks at them smiles a welcome as he says, "It is Christ again, a copy of the holy child Jesus. Come in, come in. Eternal glory will be yours. You will sit in heaven with Christ, for you are like him."

Henry Gariepy

Today, many worship at the shrine of physical beauty, blatantly held up in advertisements that constantly impinge upon us. On this topic, Peter writes, "Your beauty should not come from outward adornment . . . It should be that of your inner self, the unfading beauty of a gentle and quiet spirit" [1 Peter 3:3–4]. Peter says that true attractiveness is the winsomeness of a Christian character and pleads for the graces and spiritual beauty that cannot be obtained at a cosmetic counter.

reflection

1. What criteria did God use to evaluate Tyre? How does he apply that same criteria to individuals?

2. In the final evaluation, what really matters most to God—beauty, wealth, power, prestige? If not those things, what does he value?

3. What emphasis do you place on the way you look on the outside, compared with how your heart looks on the inside?

For your next devotional reading, go to page 955.

They hung their shields and helmets on
 your walls,
  bringing you splendor.
11 Men of Arvad and Helek
 guarded your walls on every side;
 men of Gammad
 were in your towers.
They hung their shields around your
 walls;
 they brought your beauty to
  perfection.

12 " 'Tarshish did business with you because of your great wealth of goods; they exchanged silver, iron, tin and lead for your
merchandise.

13 " 'Greece, Tubal and Meshek did business with you; they traded human beings
and articles of bronze for your wares.

14 " 'Men of Beth Togarmah exchanged
chariot horses, cavalry horses and mules for
your merchandise.

15 " 'The men of Rhodes[a] traded with you,
and many coastlands were your customers;
they paid you with ivory tusks and ebony.

16 " 'Aram[b] did business with you because
of your many products; they exchanged turquoise, purple fabric, embroidered work,
fine linen, coral and rubies for your merchandise.

17 " 'Judah and Israel traded with you; they
exchanged wheat from Minnith and confec-
tions,[c] honey, olive oil and balm for your
wares.

18 " 'Damascus did business with you because of your many products and great
wealth of goods. They offered wine from
Helbon, wool from Zahar 19 and casks of
wine from Izal in exchange for your wares:
wrought iron, cassia and calamus.

20 " 'Dedan traded in saddle blankets with
you.

21 " 'Arabia and all the princes of Kedar
were your customers; they did business with
you in lambs, rams and goats.

22 " 'The merchants of Sheba and Raamah
traded with you; for your merchandise they
exchanged the finest of all kinds of spices
and precious stones, and gold.

23 " 'Harran, Kanneh and Eden and merchants of Sheba, Ashur and Kilmad traded
with you. 24 In your marketplace they traded
with you beautiful garments, blue fabric,

embroidered work and multicolored rugs
with cords twisted and tightly knotted.

25 " 'The ships of Tarshish serve
 as carriers for your wares.
You are filled with heavy cargo
 as you sail the sea.
26 Your oarsmen take you
 out to the high seas.
But the east wind will break you to
  pieces
 far out at sea.
27 Your wealth, merchandise and wares,
 your mariners, sailors and
  shipwrights,
your merchants and all your soldiers,
 and everyone else on board
will sink into the heart of the sea
 on the day of your shipwreck.
28 The shorelands will quake
 when your sailors cry out.
29 All who handle the oars
 will abandon their ships;
 the mariners and all the sailors
 will stand on the shore.
30 They will raise their voice
 and cry bitterly over you;
 they will sprinkle dust on their heads
 and roll in ashes.
31 They will shave their heads because of
  you
 and will put on sackcloth.
They will weep over you with anguish of
  soul
 and with bitter mourning.
32 As they wail and mourn over you,
 they will take up a lament concerning
  you:
"Who was ever silenced like Tyre,
 surrounded by the sea?"
33 When your merchandise went out on the
  seas,
 you satisfied many nations;
with your great wealth and your wares
 you enriched the kings of the earth.
34 Now you are shattered by the sea
 in the depths of the waters;
your wares and all your company
 have gone down with you.
35 All who live in the coastlands
 are appalled at you;
their kings shudder with horror
 and their faces are distorted with fear.

---

a 15 Septuagint; Hebrew *Dedan*   b 16 Most Hebrew manuscripts; some Hebrew manuscripts and
Syriac *Edom*   c 17 The meaning of the Hebrew for this word is uncertain.

³⁶ The merchants among the nations scoff
        at you;
    you have come to a horrible end
        and will be no more.' "

A Prophecy Against the King of Tyre

28 The word of the Lᴏʀᴅ came to
me: ²"Son of man, say to the
ruler of Tyre, 'This is what the
Sovereign Lᴏʀᴅ says:

" 'In the pride of your heart
    you say, "I am a god;
I sit on the throne of a god
    in the heart of the seas."
But you are a mortal and not a god,
    though you think you are as wise as a
        god.
³ Are you wiser than Daniel*ᵃ*?
    Is no secret hidden from you?
⁴ By your wisdom and understanding
    you have gained wealth for yourself
and amassed gold and silver
    in your treasuries.
⁵ By your great skill in trading
    you have increased your wealth,
and because of your wealth
    your heart has grown proud.

⁶ " 'Therefore this is what the Sovereign
Lᴏʀᴅ says:

" 'Because you think you are wise,
    as wise as a god,
⁷ I am going to bring foreigners against
        you,
    the most ruthless of nations;
they will draw their swords against your
        beauty and wisdom
    and pierce your shining splendor.
⁸ They will bring you down to the pit,
    and you will die a violent death
    in the heart of the seas.
⁹ Will you then say, "I am a god,"
    in the presence of those who kill you?
You will be but a mortal, not a god,
    in the hands of those who slay you.
¹⁰ You will die the death of the
        uncircumcised
    at the hands of foreigners.

I have spoken, declares the Sovereign
Lᴏʀᴅ.' "

¹¹ The word of the Lᴏʀᴅ came to me:

¹² "Son of man, take up a lament concerning
the king of Tyre and say to him: 'This is what
the Sovereign Lᴏʀᴅ says:

" 'You were the seal of perfection,
    full of wisdom and perfect in beauty.
¹³ You were in Eden,
    the garden of God;
every precious stone adorned you:
    carnelian, chrysolite and emerald,
    topaz, onyx and jasper,
    lapis lazuli, turquoise and beryl.*ᵇ*
Your settings and mountings*ᶜ* were
        made of gold;
    on the day you were created they
        were prepared.
¹⁴ You were anointed as a guardian cherub,
    for so I ordained you.
You were on the holy mount of God;
    you walked among the fiery stones.
¹⁵ You were blameless in your ways
    from the day you were created
    till wickedness was found in you.
¹⁶ Through your widespread trade
    you were filled with violence,
    and you sinned.
So I drove you in disgrace from the
        mount of God,
    and I expelled you, guardian cherub,
    from among the fiery stones.
¹⁷ Your heart became proud
    on account of your beauty,
and you corrupted your wisdom
    because of your splendor.
So I threw you to the earth;
    I made a spectacle of you before kings.
¹⁸ By your many sins and dishonest trade
    you have desecrated your sanctuaries.
So I made a fire come out from you,
    and it consumed you,
and I reduced you to ashes on the
        ground
    in the sight of all who were watching.
¹⁹ All the nations who knew you
    are appalled at you;
you have come to a horrible end
    and will be no more.' "

A Prophecy Against Sidon

²⁰ The word of the Lᴏʀᴅ came to me:
²¹ "Son of man, set your face against Sidon;
prophesy against her ²²and say: 'This is what
the Sovereign Lᴏʀᴅ says:

ᵃ 3 Or *Danel,* a man of renown in ancient literature   *ᵇ 13* The precise identification of some of these
precious stones is uncertain.   *ᶜ 13* The meaning of the Hebrew for this phrase is uncertain.

" 'I am against you, Sidon,
and among you I will display my
glory.
You will know that I am the LORD,
when I inflict punishment on you
and within you am proved to be holy.
²³ I will send a plague upon you
and make blood flow in your streets.
The slain will fall within you,
with the sword against you on every
side.
Then you will know that I am the LORD.

²⁴ " 'No longer will the people of Israel
have malicious neighbors who are painful
briers and sharp thorns. Then they will know
that I am the Sovereign LORD.

²⁵ " 'This is what the Sovereign LORD says:
When I gather the people of Israel from the
nations where they have been scattered, I
will be proved holy through them in the sight
of the nations. Then they will live in their
own land, which I gave to my servant Jacob.
²⁶ They will live there in safety and will build
houses and plant vineyards; they will live in
safety when I inflict punishment on all their
neighbors who maligned them. Then they
will know that I am the LORD their God.' "

A Prophecy Against Egypt

Judgment on Pharaoh

29 In the tenth year, in the tenth
month on the twelfth day, the
word of the LORD came to me:
² "Son of man, set your face against Pharaoh
king of Egypt and prophesy against him and
against all Egypt. ³ Speak to him and say:
'This is what the Sovereign LORD says:

" 'I am against you, Pharaoh king of
Egypt,
you great monster lying among your
streams.
You say, "The Nile belongs to me;
I made it for myself."
⁴ But I will put hooks in your jaws
and make the fish of your streams
stick to your scales.
I will pull you out from among your
streams,
with all the fish sticking to your
scales.

⁵ I will leave you in the desert,
you and all the fish of your streams.
You will fall on the open field
and not be gathered or picked up.
I will give you as food
to the beasts of the earth and the
birds of the sky.

⁶ Then all who live in Egypt will know that I
am the LORD.

" 'You have been a staff of reed for the
house of Israel. ⁷ When they grasped you
with their hands, you splintered and you
tore open their shoulders; when they leaned
on you, you broke and their backs were
wrenched.ᵃ

⁸ 'Therefore this is what the Sovereign
LORD says: I will bring a sword against you
and kill your people and their animals.
⁹ Egypt will become a desolate wasteland.
Then they will know that I am the LORD.

" 'Because you said, "The Nile is mine; I
made it," ¹⁰ therefore I am against you and
against your streams, and I will make the
land of Egypt a ruin and a desolate waste
from Migdol to Aswan, as far as the border
of Cush.ᵇ ¹¹ No foot will pass through it, neither people nor animals; no one will live
there for forty years. ¹² I will make the land of
Egypt desolate among devastated lands, and
her cities will lie desolate forty years among
ruined cities. And I will disperse the Egyptians among the nations and scatter them
through the countries.

¹³ 'Yet this is what the Sovereign LORD
says: At the end of forty years I will gather
the Egyptians from the nations where they
were scattered. ¹⁴ I will bring them back from
captivity and return them to Upper Egypt,
the land of their ancestry. There they will be
a lowly kingdom. ¹⁵ It will be the lowliest of
kingdoms and will never again exalt itself
above the other nations. I will make it so
weak that it will never again rule over the
nations. ¹⁶ Egypt will no longer be a source of
confidence for the people of Israel but will
be a reminder of their sin in turning to her
for help. Then they will know that I am the
Sovereign LORD.' "

Nebuchadnezzar's Reward

¹⁷ In the twenty-seventh year, in the first

ᵃ 7 Syriac (see also Septuagint and Vulgate); Hebrew *and you caused their backs to stand*   ᵇ 10 That is,
the upper Nile region

month on the first day, the word of the Lord came to me: [18]"Son of man, Nebuchadnezzar king of Babylon drove his army in a hard campaign against Tyre; every head was rubbed bare and every shoulder made raw. Yet he and his army got no reward from the campaign he led against Tyre. [19]Therefore this is what the Sovereign Lord says: I am going to give Egypt to Nebuchadnezzar king of Babylon, and he will carry off its wealth. He will loot and plunder the land as pay for his army. [20]I have given him Egypt as a reward for his efforts because he and his army did it for me, declares the Sovereign Lord.

[21]"On that day I will make a horn[a] grow for the house of Israel, and I will open your mouth among them. Then they will know that I am the Lord."

A Lament Over Egypt

30 The word of the Lord came to me: [2]"Son of man, prophesy and say: 'This is what the Sovereign Lord says:

" 'Wail and say,
    "Alas for that day!"
[3]For the day is near,
    the day of the Lord is near—
a day of clouds,
    a time of doom for the nations.
[4]A sword will come against Egypt,
    and anguish will come upon Cush.[b]
When the slain fall in Egypt,
    her wealth will be carried away
    and her foundations torn down.

[5]Cush and Libya, Lydia and all Arabia, Kub and the people of the covenant land will fall by the sword along with Egypt.
[6]" 'This is what the Lord says:

" 'The allies of Egypt will fall
    and her proud strength will fail.
From Migdol to Aswan
    they will fall by the sword within her,
        declares the Sovereign Lord.
[7]" 'They will be desolate
    among desolate lands,
    and their cities will lie
    among ruined cities.
[8]Then they will know that I am the Lord,
    when I set fire to Egypt
    and all her helpers are crushed.

[9]" 'On that day messengers will go out from me in ships to frighten Cush out of her complacency. Anguish will take hold of them on the day of Egypt's doom, for it is sure to come.

[10]" 'This is what the Sovereign Lord says:

" 'I will put an end to the hordes of
        Egypt
    by the hand of Nebuchadnezzar king
        of Babylon.
[11]He and his army—the most ruthless of
        nations—
    will be brought in to destroy the land.
They will draw their swords against
        Egypt
    and fill the land with the slain.
[12]I will dry up the waters of the Nile
    and sell the land to an evil nation;
by the hand of foreigners
    I will lay waste the land
        and everything in it.

I the Lord have spoken.

[13]" 'This is what the Sovereign Lord says:

" 'I will destroy the idols
    and put an end to the images in
        Memphis.
No longer will there be a prince in
        Egypt,
    and I will spread fear throughout the
        land.
[14]I will lay waste Upper Egypt,
    set fire to Zoan
    and inflict punishment on Thebes.
[15]I will pour out my wrath on Pelusium,
    the stronghold of Egypt,
    and wipe out the hordes of Thebes.
[16]I will set fire to Egypt;
    Pelusium will writhe in agony.
Thebes will be taken by storm;
    Memphis will be in constant distress.
[17]The young men of Heliopolis and
        Bubastis
    will fall by the sword,
    and the cities themselves will go into
        captivity.
[18]Dark will be the day at Tahpanhes
    when I break the yoke of Egypt;
    there her proud strength will come to
        an end.
She will be covered with clouds,
    and her villages will go into captivity.

---

[a] 21 *Horn* here symbolizes strength.   [b] 4 That is, the upper Nile region; also in verses 5 and 9

¹⁹ So I will inflict punishment on Egypt,
and they will know that I am the
Lord.' "

Pharaoh's Arms Are Broken

²⁰ In the eleventh year, in the first month
on the seventh day, the word of the Lord
came to me: ²¹ "Son of man, I have broken
the arm of Pharaoh king of Egypt. It has not
been bound up to be healed or put in a splint
so that it may become strong enough to hold
a sword. ²² Therefore this is what the Sovereign Lord says: I am against Pharaoh king of
Egypt. I will break both his arms, the good
arm as well as the broken one, and make the
sword fall from his hand. ²³ I will disperse the
Egyptians among the nations and scatter
them through the countries. ²⁴ I will
strengthen the arms of the king of Babylon
and put my sword in his hand, but I will
break the arms of Pharaoh, and he will groan
before him like someone mortally wounded.
²⁵ I will strengthen the arms of the king of
Babylon, but the arms of Pharaoh will fall
limp. Then they will know that I am the
Lord, when I put my sword into the hand of
the king of Babylon and he brandishes it
against Egypt. ²⁶ I will disperse the Egyptians
among the nations and scatter them
through the countries. Then they will know
that I am the Lord."

Pharaoh as a Felled Cedar of Lebanon

31 In the eleventh year, in the third
month on the first day, the word
of the Lord came to me: ² "Son
of man, say to Pharaoh king of Egypt and to
his hordes:

" 'Who can be compared with you in
majesty?
³ Consider Assyria, once a cedar in
Lebanon,
with beautiful branches
overshadowing the forest;
it towered on high,
its top above the thick foliage.
⁴ The waters nourished it,
deep springs made it grow tall;
their streams flowed
all around its base
and sent their channels
to all the trees of the field.
⁵ So it towered higher
than all the trees of the field;
its boughs increased

and its branches grew long,
spreading because of abundant
waters.
⁶ All the birds of the sky
nested in its boughs,
all the animals of the wild
gave birth under its branches;
all the great nations
lived in its shade.
⁷ It was majestic in beauty,
with its spreading boughs,
for its roots went down
to abundant waters.
⁸ The cedars in the garden of God
could not rival it,
nor could the junipers
equal its boughs,
nor could the plane trees
compare with its branches—
no tree in the garden of God
could match its beauty.
⁹ I made it beautiful
with abundant branches,
the envy of all the trees of Eden
in the garden of God.

¹⁰ " 'Therefore this is what the Sovereign
Lord says: Because the great cedar towered
over the thick foliage, and because it was
proud of its height, ¹¹ I gave it into the hands
of the ruler of the nations, for him to deal
with according to its wickedness. I cast it
aside, ¹² and the most ruthless of foreign nations
cut it down and left it. Its boughs fell
on the mountains and in all the valleys; its
branches lay broken in all the ravines of the
land. All the nations of the earth came out
from under its shade and left it. ¹³ All the
birds settled on the fallen tree, and all the
wild animals lived among its branches.
¹⁴ Therefore no other trees by the waters are
ever to tower proudly on high, lifting their
tops above the thick foliage. No other trees
so well-watered are ever to reach such a
height; they are all destined for death, for
the earth below, among mortals who go
down to the realm of the dead.

¹⁵ " 'This is what the Sovereign Lord says:
On the day it was brought down to the realm
of the dead I covered the deep springs with
mourning for it; I held back its streams, and
its abundant waters were restrained. Because
of it I clothed Lebanon with gloom,
and all the trees of the field withered away.
¹⁶ I made the nations tremble at the sound of
its fall when I brought it down to the realm

of the dead to be with those who go down to the pit. Then all the trees of Eden, the choicest and best of Lebanon, the well-watered trees, were consoled in the earth below. ¹⁷They too, like the great cedar, had gone down to the realm of the dead, to those killed by the sword, along with the armed men who lived in its shade among the nations.

¹⁸" 'Which of the trees of Eden can be compared with you in splendor and majesty? Yet you, too, will be brought down with the trees of Eden to the earth below; you will lie among the uncircumcised, with those killed by the sword.

" 'This is Pharaoh and all his hordes, declares the Sovereign LORD.' "

A Lament Over Pharaoh

32 In the twelfth year, in the twelfth month on the first day, the word of the LORD came to me: ²"Son of man, take up a lament concerning Pharaoh king of Egypt and say to him:

" 'You are like a lion among the nations;
    you are like a monster in the seas
thrashing about in your streams,
    churning the water with your feet
    and muddying the streams.

³" 'This is what the Sovereign LORD says:

" 'With a great throng of people
    I will cast my net over you,
    and they will haul you up in my net.
⁴I will throw you on the land
    and hurl you on the open field.
I will let all the birds of the sky settle on
        you
    and all the animals of the wild gorge
        themselves on you.
⁵I will spread your flesh on the
        mountains
    and fill the valleys with your remains.
⁶I will drench the land with your flowing
        blood
    all the way to the mountains,
    and the ravines will be filled with
        your flesh.
⁷When I snuff you out, I will cover the
        heavens
    and darken their stars;
I will cover the sun with a cloud,
    and the moon will not give its light.

⁸All the shining lights in the heavens
    I will darken over you;
    I will bring darkness over your land,
        declares the Sovereign LORD.
⁹I will trouble the hearts of many peoples
    when I bring about your destruction
        among the nations,
    among[a] lands you have not known.
¹⁰I will cause many peoples to be appalled
        at you,
    and their kings will shudder with
        horror because of you
    when I brandish my sword before
        them.
On the day of your downfall
    each of them will tremble
    every moment for his life.

¹¹" 'For this is what the Sovereign LORD says:

" 'The sword of the king of Babylon
    will come against you.
¹²I will cause your hordes to fall
    by the swords of mighty men—
    the most ruthless of all nations.
They will shatter the pride of Egypt,
    and all her hordes will be overthrown.
¹³I will destroy all her cattle
    from beside abundant waters
no longer to be stirred by human feet
    or muddied by the hooves of cattle.
¹⁴Then I will let her waters settle
    and make her streams flow like oil,
        declares the Sovereign LORD.
¹⁵When I make Egypt desolate
    and strip the land of everything in it,
    when I strike down all who live there,
        then they will know that I am the
        LORD.'

¹⁶"This is the lament they will chant for her. The daughters of the nations will chant it; for Egypt and all her hordes they will chant it, declares the Sovereign LORD."

Egypt's Descent Into the Realm of the Dead

¹⁷In the twelfth year, on the fifteenth day of the month, the word of the LORD came to me: ¹⁸"Son of man, wail for the hordes of Egypt and consign to the earth below both her and the daughters of mighty nations, along with those who go down to the pit. ¹⁹Say to them, 'Are you more favored than others? Go down and be laid among the un-

a 9 Hebrew; Septuagint bring you into captivity among the nations, / to circumcised.' ²⁰They will fall among those killed by the sword. The sword is drawn; let her be dragged off with all her hordes. ²¹From within the realm of the dead the mighty leaders will say of Egypt and her allies, 'They have come down and they lie with the uncircumcised, with those killed by the sword.'

²²"Assyria is there with her whole army; she is surrounded by the graves of all her slain, all who have fallen by the sword. ²³Their graves are in the depths of the pit and her army lies around her grave. All who had spread terror in the land of the living are slain, fallen by the sword.

²⁴"Elam is there, with all her hordes around her grave. All of them are slain, fallen by the sword. All who had spread terror in the land of the living went down uncircumcised to the earth below. They bear their shame with those who go down to the pit. ²⁵A bed is made for her among the slain, with all her hordes around her grave. All of them are uncircumcised, killed by the sword. Because their terror had spread in the land of the living, they bear their shame with those who go down to the pit; they are laid among the slain.

²⁶"Meshek and Tubal are there, with all their hordes around their graves. All of them are uncircumcised, killed by the sword because they spread their terror in the land of the living. ²⁷But they do not lie with the fallen warriors of old,ᵃ who went down to the realm of the dead with their weapons of war—their swords placed under their heads and their shieldsᵇ resting on their bones—though these warriors also had terrorized the land of the living.

²⁸"You too, Pharaoh, will be broken and will lie among the uncircumcised, with those killed by the sword.

²⁹"Edom is there, her kings and all her princes; despite their power, they are laid with those killed by the sword. They lie with the uncircumcised, with those who go down to the pit.

³⁰"All the princes of the north and all the Sidonians are there; they went down with the slain in disgrace despite the terror caused by their power. They lie uncircumcised with those killed by the sword and

bear their shame with those who go down to the pit.

³¹"Pharaoh—he and all his army—will see them and he will be consoled for all his hordes that were killed by the sword, declares the Sovereign Lord. ³²Although I had him spread terror in the land of the living, Pharaoh and all his hordes will be laid among the uncircumcised, with those killed by the sword, declares the Sovereign Lord."

Renewal of Ezekiel's Call as Watchman

33 The word of the Lord came to me: ²"Son of man, speak to your people and say to them: 'When I bring the sword against a land, and the people of the land choose one of their men and make him their watchman, ³and he sees the sword coming against the land and blows the trumpet to warn the people, ⁴then if anyone hears the trumpet but does not heed the warning and the sword comes and takes their life, their blood will be on their own head. ⁵Since they heard the sound of the trumpet but did not heed the warning, their blood will be on their own head. If they had heeded the warning, they would have saved themselves. ⁶But if the watchman sees the sword coming and does not blow the trumpet to warn the people and the sword comes and takes someone's life, that person's life will be taken because of their sin, but I will hold the watchman accountable for their blood.'

⁷"Son of man, I have made you a watchman for the house of Israel; so hear the word I speak and give them warning from me. ⁸When I say to the wicked, 'You wicked people, you will surely die,' and you do not speak out to dissuade them from their ways, those wicked people will die forᶜ their sins, and I will hold you accountable for their blood. ⁹But if you do warn the wicked to turn from their ways and they do not do so, they will die for their sins, though you yourself will be saved.

¹⁰"Son of man, say to the house of Israel, 'This is what you are saying: "Our offenses and sins weigh us down, and we are wasting away because ofᵈ them. How then can we live?" ' ¹¹Say to them, 'As surely as I live, declares the Sovereign Lord, I take no pleasure

---

ᵃ 27 Septuagint; Hebrew *warriors who were uncircumcised*   ᵇ 27 Probable reading of the original Hebrew text; Masoretic Text *punishment*   ᶜ 8 Or *in*; also in verse 9   ᵈ 10 Or *away in*

TUESDAY

SHOW HIM YOUR LOVE

Ezekiel 33:1–33 *or* 33:30–32

THOMAS À KEMPIS {ca. AD 1380–1471}

Never read the Bible for the purpose of appearing more knowledgeable or more wise. Apply yourself to mortifying your vices, for this will benefit you more than your understanding of many difficult questions.

Joanna Weaver

Just hearing God's Word isn't enough, of course. The Bible makes that abundantly clear. God's transforming power in our lives is unleashed when we not only listen, but also *act* on what we've heard.

In fact, in our very refusal to apply God's truth to our lives, we may actually keep ourselves from hearing his voice in the future. Sin actually stops up our spiritual ears the same way excess wax plugs up our physical ones. When that happens, we may appear to hear, nodding and saying yes, yet have absolutely no comprehension. People with spiritually stopped-up ears are "always learning," Paul writes in 2 Timothy 3:7, "but never able to [come to a knowledge of] the truth."

The sad fact is, we can grow so accustomed to God's voice that it no longer moves us. We can become like the people God warned us about through his prophet in Ezekiel 33:31–32.

. . . Either we take Jesus' words to heart and *change*, or we listen but disregard them. And to disregard the voice of God is worse than not listening at all. Especially if we say we love him.

When my children refuse to listen, I find myself wanting to quote the words Jesus used in John 14:21: "Whoever has my commands and [keeps] them [is] the one who loves me." *Don't tell me you love me*, I want to say when they come begging to watch cartoons after they've already been told to clean their rooms. *Obey my commands*.

Jesus doesn't mince words with us. He cuts to the heart of what really matters in each of our lives. He puts his finger on our sore spots, the sin-infected places we try so hard to hide. He points to our cluttered bedrooms and says, "Do this and live." Because if we want to live, we're going to have to obey.

reflection

1. In what ways did the Israelites miss the point of Ezekiel's words? Why wasn't "hearing" enough?

2. Why do you read your Bible? What's the point?

3. What "sore spot" in your life do you need to deal with?

For your next devotional reading, go to page 959.

in the death of the wicked, but rather that they turn from their ways and live. Turn! Turn from your evil ways! Why will you die, house of Israel?'

¹²"Therefore, son of man, say to your people, 'If someone who is righteous disobeys, that person's former righteousness will count for nothing. And if someone who is wicked repents, that person's former wickedness will not bring condemnation. The righteous, if they sin, will not be allowed to live because of their former righteousness.' ¹³If I tell the righteous that they will surely live, but then they trust in their righteousness and do evil, none of the righteous things they have done will be remembered; they will die for the evil they have done. ¹⁴And if I say to the wicked, 'You will surely die,' but they then turn away from their sins and do what is just and right— ¹⁵if they give back what they took in pledge for a loan, return what they have stolen, follow the decrees that give life, and do no evil, they will surely live; they will not die. ¹⁶None of the sins they have committed will be remembered against them. They have done what is just and right; they will surely live.

¹⁷"Yet your people say, 'The way of the Lord is not just.' But it is their way that is not just. ¹⁸If the righteous turn from their righteousness and do evil, they will die for it. ¹⁹And if the wicked turn away from their wickedness and do what is just and right, they will live by doing so. ²⁰Yet you say, house of Israel, 'The way of the Lord is not just.' But I will judge each of you according to your own ways."

Jerusalem's Fall Explained

²¹In the twelfth year of our exile, in the tenth month on the fifth day, a man who had escaped from Jerusalem came to me and said, "The city has fallen!" ²²Now the evening before the man arrived, the hand of the LORD was on me, and he opened my mouth before the man came to me in the morning. So my mouth was opened and I was no longer silent.

²³Then the word of the LORD came to me: ²⁴"Son of man, the people living in those ruins in the land of Israel are saying, 'Abraham was only one man, yet he possessed the land. But we are many; surely the land has been given to us as our possession.' ²⁵Therefore say to them, 'This is what the Sovereign

LORD says: Since you eat meat with the blood still in it and look to your idols and shed blood, should you then possess the land? ²⁶You rely on your sword, you do detestable things, and each of you defiles his neighbor's wife. Should you then possess the land?'

²⁷"Say this to them: 'This is what the Sovereign LORD says: As surely as I live, those who are left in the ruins will fall by the sword, those out in the country I will give to the wild animals to be devoured, and those in strongholds and caves will die of a plague. ²⁸I will make the land a desolate waste, and her proud strength will come to an end, and the mountains of Israel will become desolate so that no one will cross them. ²⁹Then they will know that I am the LORD, when I have made the land a desolate waste because of all the detestable things they have done.'

³⁰"As for you, son of man, your people are talking together about you by the walls and at the doors of the houses, saying to each other, 'Come and hear the message that has come from the LORD.' ³¹My people come to you, as they usually do, and sit before you to hear your words, but they do not put them into practice. Their mouths speak of love, but their hearts are greedy for unjust gain. ³²Indeed, to them you are nothing more than one who sings love songs with a beautiful voice and plays an instrument well, for they hear your words but do not put them into practice.

³³"When all this comes true—and it surely will—then they will know that a prophet has been among them."

The LORD Will Be Israel's Shepherd

34 The word of the LORD came to me: ²"Son of man, prophesy against the shepherds of Israel; prophesy and say to them: 'This is what the Sovereign LORD says: Woe to you shepherds of Israel who only take care of yourselves! Should not shepherds take care of the flock? ³You eat the curds, clothe yourselves with the wool and slaughter the choice animals, but you do not take care of the flock. ⁴You have not strengthened the weak or healed the sick or bound up the injured. You have not brought back the strays or searched for the lost. You have ruled them harshly and brutally. ⁵So they were scattered because

there was no shepherd, and when they were scattered they became food for all the wild animals. ⁶My sheep wandered over all the mountains and on every high hill. They were scattered over the whole earth, and no one searched or looked for them.

⁷" 'Therefore, you shepherds, hear the word of the LORD: ⁸As surely as I live, declares the Sovereign LORD, because my flock lacks a shepherd and so has been plundered and has become food for all the wild animals, and because my shepherds did not search for my flock but cared for themselves rather than for my flock, ⁹therefore, you shepherds, hear the word of the LORD: ¹⁰This is what the Sovereign LORD says: I am against the shepherds and will hold them accountable for my flock. I will remove them from tending the flock so that the shepherds can no longer feed themselves. I will rescue my flock from their mouths, and it will no longer be food for them.

¹¹" 'For this is what the Sovereign LORD says: I myself will search for my sheep and look after them. ¹²As shepherds look after their scattered flocks when they are with them, so will I look after my sheep. I will rescue them from all the places where they were scattered on a day of clouds and darkness. ¹³I will bring them out from the nations and gather them from the countries, and I will bring them into their own land. I will pasture them on the mountains of Israel, in the ravines and in all the settlements in the land. ¹⁴I will tend them in a good pasture, and the mountain heights of Israel will be their grazing land. There they will lie down in good grazing land, and there they will feed in a rich pasture on the mountains of Israel. ¹⁵I myself will tend my sheep and have them lie down, declares the Sovereign LORD. ¹⁶I will search for the lost and bring back the strays. I will bind up the injured and strengthen the weak, but the sleek and the strong I will destroy. I will shepherd the flock with justice.

¹⁷" 'As for you, my flock, this is what the Sovereign LORD says: I will judge between one sheep and another, and between rams and goats. ¹⁸Is it not enough for you to feed on the good pasture? Must you also trample the rest of your pasture with your feet? Is it

not enough for you to drink clear water? Must you also muddy the rest with your feet? ¹⁹Must my flock feed on what you have trampled and drink what you have muddied with your feet?

²⁰" 'Therefore this is what the Sovereign LORD says to them: See, I myself will judge between the fat sheep and the lean sheep. ²¹Because you shove with flank and shoulder, butting all the weak sheep with your horns until you have driven them away, ²²I will save my flock, and they will no longer be plundered. I will judge between one sheep and another. ²³I will place over them one shepherd, my servant David, and he will tend them; he will tend them and be their shepherd. ²⁴I the LORD will be their God, and my servant David will be prince among them. I the LORD have spoken.

²⁵" 'I will make a covenant of peace with them and rid the land of savage beasts so that they may live in the wilderness and sleep in the forests in safety. ²⁶I will make them and the places surrounding my hill a blessing.ᵃ I will send down showers in season; there will be showers of blessing. ²⁷The trees will yield their fruit and the ground will yield its crops; the people will be secure in their land. They will know that I am the LORD, when I break the bars of their yoke and rescue them from the hands of those who enslaved them. ²⁸They will no longer be plundered by the nations, nor will wild animals devour them. They will live in safety, and no one will make them afraid. ²⁹I will provide for them a land renowned for its crops, and they will no longer be victims of famine in the land or bear the scorn of the nations. ³⁰Then they will know that I, the LORD their God, am with them and that they, the house of Israel, are my people, declares the Sovereign LORD. ³¹You are my sheep, the sheep of my pasture, and I am your God, declares the Sovereign LORD.' "

A Prophecy Against Edom

35 The word of the LORD came to me: ²"Son of man, set your face against Mount Seir; prophesy against it ³and say: 'This is what the Sovereign LORD says: I am against you, Mount Seir, and I will stretch out my hand against you

---

ᵃ 26 Or *I will cause them and the places surrounding my hill to be named in blessings* (see Gen. 48:20); or *I will cause them and the places surrounding my hill to be seen as blessed* and make you a desolate waste. ⁴I will turn your towns into ruins and you will be desolate. Then you will know that I am the Lord.

⁵" 'Because you harbored an ancient hostility and delivered the Israelites over to the sword at the time of their calamity, the time their punishment reached its climax, ⁶therefore as surely as I live, declares the Sovereign Lord, I will give you over to bloodshed and it will pursue you. Since you did not hate bloodshed, bloodshed will pursue you. ⁷I will make Mount Seir a desolate waste and cut off from it all who come and go. ⁸I will fill your mountains with the slain; those killed by the sword will fall on your hills and in your valleys and in all your ravines. ⁹I will make you desolate forever; your towns will not be inhabited. Then you will know that I am the Lord.

¹⁰" 'Because you have said, "These two nations and countries will be ours and we will take possession of them," even though I the Lord was there, ¹¹therefore as surely as I live, declares the Sovereign Lord, I will treat you in accordance with the anger and jealousy you showed in your hatred of them and I will make myself known among them when I judge you. ¹²Then you will know that I the Lord have heard all the contemptible things you have said against the mountains of Israel. You said, "They have been laid waste and have been given over to us to devour." ¹³You boasted against me and spoke against me without restraint, and I heard it. ¹⁴This is what the Sovereign Lord says: While the whole earth rejoices, I will make you desolate. ¹⁵Because you rejoiced when the inheritance of the house of Israel became desolate, that is how I will treat you. You will be desolate, Mount Seir, you and all of Edom. Then they will know that I am the Lord.' "

Hope for the Mountains of Israel

36 "Son of man, prophesy to the mountains of Israel and say, 'Mountains of Israel, hear the word of the Lord. ²This is what the Sovereign Lord says: The enemy said of you, "Aha! The ancient heights have become our possession." ' ³Therefore prophesy and say, 'This is what the Sovereign Lord says: Because they ravaged and crushed you from every side so that you became the possession of the rest of the nations and the object

of people's malicious talk and slander, ⁴therefore, mountains of Israel, hear the word of the Sovereign Lord: This is what the Sovereign Lord says to the mountains and hills, to the ravines and valleys, to the desolate ruins and the deserted towns that have been plundered and ridiculed by the rest of the nations around you— ⁵this is what the Sovereign Lord says: In my burning zeal I have spoken against the rest of the nations, and against all Edom, for with glee and with malice in their hearts they made my land their own possession so that they might plunder its pastureland.' ⁶Therefore prophesy concerning the land of Israel and say to the mountains and hills, to the ravines and valleys: 'This is what the Sovereign Lord says: I speak in my jealous wrath because you have suffered the scorn of the nations. ⁷Therefore this is what the Sovereign Lord says: I swear with uplifted hand that the nations around you will also suffer scorn.

⁸" 'But you, mountains of Israel, will produce branches and fruit for my people Israel, for they will soon come home. ⁹I am concerned for you and will look on you with favor; you will be plowed and sown, ¹⁰and I will multiply the number of people living on you, even the whole house of Israel. The towns will be inhabited and the ruins rebuilt. ¹¹I will increase the number of people and animals living on you, and they will be fruitful and become numerous. I will settle people on you as in the past and will make you prosper more than before. Then you will know that I am the Lord. ¹²I will cause people, my people Israel, to live on you. They will possess you, and you will be their inheritance; you will never again deprive them of their children.

¹³" 'This is what the Sovereign Lord says: Because some say to you, "You devour your people and deprive your nation of its children," ¹⁴therefore you will no longer devour people or make your nation childless, declares the Sovereign Lord. ¹⁵No longer will I make you hear the taunts of the nations, and no longer will you suffer the scorn of the peoples or cause your nation to fall, declares the Sovereign Lord.' "

Israel's Restoration Assured

¹⁶Again the word of the Lord came to me: ¹⁷"Son of man, when the people of Israel were living in their own land, they defiled it

WEDNESDAY

IT'S NOT ABOUT YOU

Ezekiel 36:16–38 *or* 36:22–23

OSWALD CHAMBERS {AD 1874–1917}

There is an attitude today that I call "Pharisaic holiness." People with this attitude have forgotten the horrible pit and miry clay from whence they have been [dug] by the mighty atonement of Jesus Christ. These people thank God, with an arrogant offensiveness, that they are not as "other men are."

The Holy Spirit continually takes back the saint of God, in memory, to what he once was. For as God told the children of Israel in Ezekiel, He sanctified them "not for their sakes but for His own." We need to remember that.

> Every virtue we possess
> And every victory won,
> And every thought of holiness
> Are His alone.

Mark Brazee

It's true we need to stand up in our righteousness. We are to come boldly before the throne of grace, believe and confess the Word and act in faith. Proverbs 28:1 says, "The righteous are [as] bold as a lion."

But we shouldn't come with an arrogant attitude, saying, "God, I'm doing everything You said to do; You owe me."

We need to come and say, "Lord, I'm doing what You said in Your Word. Now I thank You for Your mercy."

God's mercy, compassion and grace provided everything we have in Jesus Christ, and we must treat His blessings as a gift. Because of God's grace poured out upon us, we can say, "If we believe and say what His Word says, it will come to pass." We are to be thankfully receptive, not arrogant about it.

So be bold when you go before God, but always keep a watch on your attitude. Remember, it's only by God's grace that you stand!

reflection

1. God planned to do amazing things for Israel. What reason did he give for this? What was his purpose in doing so?

2. God also does amazing things in your life—for his glory, not yours. How does this change the way you look at your life?

3. How does this change the way you approach God?

For your next devotional reading, go to page 978.

by their conduct and their actions. Their conduct was like a woman's monthly uncleanness in my sight. ¹⁸So I poured out my wrath on them because they had shed blood in the land and because they had defiled it with their idols. ¹⁹I dispersed them among the nations, and they were scattered through the countries; I judged them according to their conduct and their actions. ²⁰And wherever they went among the nations they profaned my holy name, for it was said of them, 'These are the Lord's people, and yet they had to leave his land.' ²¹I had concern for my holy name, which the house of Israel profaned among the nations where they had gone.

²²Therefore say to the house of Israel, 'This is what the Sovereign Lord says: It is not for your sake, house of Israel, that I am going to do these things, but for the sake of my holy name, which you have profaned among the nations where you have gone. ²³I will show the holiness of my great name, which has been profaned among the nations, the name you have profaned among them. Then the nations will know that I am the Lord, declares the Sovereign Lord, when I am proved holy through you before their eyes.

²⁴' 'For I will take you out of the nations; I will gather you from all the countries and bring you back into your own land. ²⁵I will sprinkle clean water on you, and you will be clean; I will cleanse you from all your impurities and from all your idols. ²⁶I will give you a new heart and put a new spirit in you; I will remove from you your heart of stone and give you a heart of flesh. ²⁷And I will put my Spirit in you and move you to follow my decrees and be careful to keep my laws. ²⁸Then you will live in the land I gave your ancestors; you will be my people, and I will be your God. ²⁹I will save you from all your uncleanness. I will call for the grain and make it plentiful and will not bring famine upon you. ³⁰I will increase the fruit of the trees and the crops of the field, so that you will no longer suffer disgrace among the nations because of famine. ³¹Then you will remember your evil ways and wicked deeds, and you will loathe yourselves for your sins and detestable practices. ³²I want you to know that I am not doing this for your sake, declares the Sovereign Lord. Be ashamed and disgraced for your conduct, house of Israel!

³³' 'This is what the Sovereign Lord says: On the day I cleanse you from all your sins, I will resettle your towns, and the ruins will be rebuilt. ³⁴The desolate land will be cultivated instead of lying desolate in the sight of all who pass through it. ³⁵They will say, "This land that was laid waste has become like the garden of Eden; the cities that were lying in ruins, desolate and destroyed, are now fortified and inhabited." ³⁶Then the nations around you that remain will know that I the Lord have rebuilt what was destroyed and have replanted what was desolate. I the Lord have spoken, and I will do it.'

³⁷"This is what the Sovereign Lord says: Once again I will yield to the plea of the house of Israel and do this for them: I will make their people as numerous as sheep, ³⁸as numerous as the flocks for offerings at Jerusalem during her appointed festivals. So will the ruined cities be filled with flocks of people. Then they will know that I am the Lord."

The Valley of Dry Bones

37 The hand of the Lord was on me, and he brought me out by the Spirit of the Lord and set me in the middle of a valley; it was full of bones. ²He led me back and forth among them, and I saw a great many bones on the floor of the valley, bones that were very dry. ³He asked me, "Son of man, can these bones live?"

I said, "Sovereign Lord, you alone know."

⁴Then he said to me, "Prophesy to these bones and say to them, 'Dry bones, hear the word of the Lord! ⁵This is what the Sovereign Lord says to these bones: I will make breath*ᵃ* enter you, and you will come to life. ⁶I will attach tendons to you and make flesh come upon you and cover you with skin; I will put breath in you, and you will come to life. Then you will know that I am the Lord.' "

⁷So I prophesied as I was commanded. And as I was prophesying, there was a noise, a rattling sound, and the bones came together, bone to bone. ⁸I looked, and tendons and flesh appeared on them and skin covered them, but there was no breath in them.

⁹Then he said to me, "Prophesy to the breath; prophesy, son of man, and say to it,

---

a 5 The Hebrew for this word can also mean *wind* or *spirit* (see verses 6-14).

'This is what the Sovereign LORD says: Come, breath, from the four winds and breathe into these slain, that they may live.' " ¹⁰So I prophesied as he commanded me, and breath entered them; they came to life and stood up on their feet—a vast army.

¹¹Then he said to me: "Son of man, these bones are the whole house of Israel. They say, 'Our bones are dried up and our hope is gone; we are cut off.' ¹²Therefore prophesy and say to them: 'This is what the Sovereign LORD says: My people, I am going to open your graves and bring you up from them; I will bring you back to the land of Israel. ¹³Then you, my people, will know that I am the LORD, when I open your graves and bring you up from them. ¹⁴I will put my Spirit in you and you will live, and I will settle you in your own land. Then you will know that I the LORD have spoken, and I have done it, declares the LORD.' "

One Nation Under One King

¹⁵The word of the LORD came to me: ¹⁶"Son of man, take a stick of wood and write on it, 'Belonging to Judah and the Israelites associated with him.' Then take another stick of wood, and write on it, 'Belonging to Joseph (that is, to Ephraim) and all the house of Israel associated with him.' ¹⁷Join them together into one stick so that they will become one in your hand.

¹⁸"When your people ask you, 'Won't you tell us what you mean by this?' ¹⁹say to them, 'This is what the Sovereign LORD says: I am going to take the stick of Joseph—which is in Ephraim's hand—and of the Israelite tribes associated with him, and join it to Judah's stick. I will make them into a single stick of wood, and they will become one in my hand.' ²⁰Hold before their eyes the sticks you have written on ²¹and say to them, 'This is what the Sovereign LORD says: I will take the Israelites out of the nations where they have gone. I will gather them from all around and bring them back into their own land. ²²I will make them one nation in the land, on the mountains of Israel. There will be one king over all of them and they will never again be two nations or be divided into two kingdoms. ²³They will no longer defile themselves with their idols and vile images or with any of their offenses, for I will save them from all their sinful backsliding,ᵃ and I will cleanse them. They will be my people, and I will be their God.

²⁴" 'My servant David will be king over them, and they will all have one shepherd. They will follow my laws and be careful to keep my decrees. ²⁵They will live in the land I gave to my servant Jacob, the land where your ancestors lived. They and their children and their children's children will live there forever, and David my servant will be their prince forever. ²⁶I will make a covenant of peace with them; it will be an everlasting covenant. I will establish them and increase their numbers, and I will put my sanctuary among them forever. ²⁷My dwelling place will be with them; I will be their God, and they will be my people. ²⁸Then the nations will know that I the LORD make Israel holy, when my sanctuary is among them forever.' "

The LORD's Great Victory Over the Nations

38 The word of the LORD came to me: ²"Son of man, set your face against Gog, of the land of Magog, the chief prince ofᵇ Meshek and Tubal; prophesy against him ³and say: 'This is what the Sovereign LORD says: I am against you, Gog, chief prince ofᶜ Meshek and Tubal. ⁴I will turn you around, put hooks in your jaws and bring you out with your whole army—your horses, your horsemen fully armed, and a great horde with large and small shields, all of them brandishing their swords. ⁵Persia, Cushᵈ and Put will be with them, all with shields and helmets, ⁶also Gomer with all its troops, and Beth Togarmah from the far north with all its troops—the many nations with you.

⁷" 'Get ready; be prepared, you and all the hordes gathered about you, and take command of them. ⁸After many days you will be called to arms. In future years you will invade a land that has recovered from war, whose people were gathered from many nations to the mountains of Israel, which had long been desolate. They had been brought out from the nations, and now all of them live in safety. ⁹You and all your troops and the many nations with you will go up, ad-

---

ᵃ 23 Many Hebrew manuscripts (see also Septuagint); most Hebrew manuscripts *all their dwelling places where they sinned*   ᵇ 2 Or *the prince of Rosh,*   ᶜ 3 Or *Gog, prince of Rosh,*   ᵈ 5 That is, the upper Nile region vancing like a storm; you will be like a cloud covering the land.

¹⁰" 'This is what the Sovereign Lord says: On that day thoughts will come into your mind and you will devise an evil scheme. ¹¹You will say, "I will invade a land of un-walled villages; I will attack a peaceful and unsuspecting people—all of them living without walls and without gates and bars. ¹²I will plunder and loot and turn my hand against the resettled ruins and the people gathered from the nations, rich in livestock and goods, living at the center of the land. *ᵃ*" ¹³Sheba and Dedan and the merchants of Tarshish and all her villages *ᵇ* will say to you, "Have you come to plunder? Have you gathered your hordes to loot, to carry off silver and gold, to take away livestock and goods and to seize much plunder?" '

¹⁴"Therefore, son of man, prophesy and say to Gog: 'This is what the Sovereign Lord says: In that day, when my people Israel are living in safety, will you not take notice of it? ¹⁵You will come from your place in the far north, you and many nations with you, all of them riding on horses, a great horde, a mighty army. ¹⁶You will advance against my people Israel like a cloud that covers the land. In days to come, Gog, I will bring you against my land, so that the nations may know me when I am proved holy through you before their eyes.

¹⁷" 'This is what the Sovereign Lord says: You are the one I spoke of in former days by my servants the prophets of Israel. At that time they prophesied for years that I would bring you against them. ¹⁸This is what will happen in that day: When Gog attacks the land of Israel, my hot anger will be aroused, declares the Sovereign Lord. ¹⁹In my zeal and fiery wrath I declare that at that time there shall be a great earthquake in the land of Israel. ²⁰The fish in the sea, the birds in the sky, the beasts of the field, every crea-ture that moves along the ground, and all the people on the face of the earth will tremble at my presence. The mountains will be overturned, the cliffs will crumble and every wall will fall to the ground. ²¹I will summon a sword against Gog on all my mountains, declares the Sovereign Lord. Every man's sword will be against his fellow. ²²I will execute judgment on him with plague and bloodshed; I will pour down tor-rents of rain, hailstones and burning sulfur on him and on his troops and on the many nations with him. ²³And so I will show my greatness and my holiness, and I will make myself known in the sight of many nations. Then they will know that I am the Lord.'

39 "Son of man, prophesy against Gog and say: 'This is what the Sovereign Lord says: I am against you, Gog, chief prince of *ᶜ* Meshek and Tubal. ²I will turn you around and drag you along. I will bring you from the far north and send you against the mountains of Israel. ³Then I will strike your bow from your left hand and make your arrows drop from your right hand. ⁴On the mountains of Israel you will fall, you and all your troops and the nations with you. I will give you as food to all kinds of carrion birds and to the wild animals. ⁵You will fall in the open field, for I have spoken, declares the Sovereign Lord. ⁶I will send fire on Magog and on those who live in safety in the coastlands, and they will know that I am the Lord.

⁷" 'I will make known my holy name among my people Israel. I will no longer let my holy name be profaned, and the nations will know that I the Lord am the Holy One in Israel. ⁸It is coming! It will surely take place, declares the Sovereign Lord. This is the day I have spoken of.

⁹" 'Then those who live in the towns of Israel will go out and use the weapons for fuel and burn them up—the small and large shields, the bows and arrows, the war clubs and spears. For seven years they will use them for fuel. ¹⁰They will not need to gather wood from the fields or cut it from the for-ests, because they will use the weapons for fuel. And they will plunder those who plun-dered them and loot those who looted them, declares the Sovereign Lord.

¹¹" 'On that day I will give Gog a burial place in Israel, in the valley of those who travel east of the Sea. It will block the way of travelers, because Gog and all his hordes will be buried there. So it will be called the Valley of Hamon Gog. *ᵈ*

¹²" 'For seven months the house of Israel will be burying them in order to cleanse the land. ¹³All the people of the land will bury them, and the day I display my glory will be

---

ᵃ 12 The Hebrew for this phrase means *the navel of the earth.*   *ᵇ 13* Or *her strong lions*   *ᶜ 1* Or *Gog, prince of Rosh,*   *ᵈ 11* *Hamon Gog* means *hordes of Gog.*

a memorable day for them, declares the Sovereign LORD. [14]People will be continually employed in cleansing the land. They will spread out across the land and, along with others, they will bury any bodies that are lying on the ground.

" 'After the seven months they will carry out a more detailed search. [15]As they go through the land, anyone who sees a human bone will leave a marker beside it until the gravediggers bury it in the Valley of Hamon Gog, [16]near a town called Hamonah.[a] And so they will cleanse the land.'

[17]"Son of man, this is what the Sovereign LORD says: Call out to every kind of bird and all the wild animals: 'Assemble and come together from all around to the sacrifice I am preparing for you, the great sacrifice on the mountains of Israel. There you will eat flesh and drink blood. [18]You will eat the flesh of mighty men and drink the blood of the princes of the earth as if they were rams and lambs, goats and bulls—all of them fattened animals from Bashan. [19]At the sacrifice I am preparing for you, you will eat fat till you are glutted and drink blood till you are drunk. [20]At my table you will eat your fill of horses and riders, mighty men and soldiers of every kind,' declares the Sovereign LORD.

[21]"I will display my glory among the nations, and all the nations will see the punishment I inflict and the hand I lay on them. [22]From that day forward the house of Israel will know that I am the LORD their God. [23]And the nations will know that the people of Israel went into exile for their sin, because they were unfaithful to me. So I hid my face from them and handed them over to their enemies, and they all fell by the sword. [24]I dealt with them according to their uncleanness and their offenses, and I hid my face from them.

[25]"Therefore this is what the Sovereign LORD says: I will now restore the fortunes of Jacob[b] and will have compassion on all the people of Israel, and I will be zealous for my holy name. [26]They will forget their shame and all the unfaithfulness they showed toward me when they lived in safety in their land with no one to make them afraid.

[27]When I have brought them back from the nations and have gathered them from the countries of their enemies, I will be proved holy through them in the sight of many nations. [28]Then they will know that I am the LORD their God, for though I sent them into exile among the nations, I will gather them to their own land, not leaving any behind. [29]I will no longer hide my face from them, for I will pour out my Spirit on the house of Israel, declares the Sovereign LORD."

The Temple Area Restored

40 In the twenty-fifth year of our exile, at the beginning of the year, on the tenth of the month, in the fourteenth year after the fall of the city—on that very day the hand of the LORD was on me and he took me there. [2]In visions of God he took me to the land of Israel and set me on a very high mountain, on whose south side were some buildings that looked like a city. [3]He took me there, and I saw a man whose appearance was like bronze; he was standing in the gateway with a linen cord and a measuring rod in his hand. [4]The man said to me, "Son of man, look carefully and listen closely and pay attention to everything I am going to show you, for that is why you have been brought here. Tell the house of Israel everything you see."

The East Gate to the Outer Court

[5]I saw a wall completely surrounding the temple area. The length of the measuring rod in the man's hand was six long cubits,[c] each of which was a cubit and a handbreadth. He measured the wall; it was one measuring rod thick and one rod high.

[6]Then he went to the east gate. He climbed its steps and measured the threshold of the gate; it was one rod deep. [7]The alcoves for the guards were one rod long and one rod wide, and the projecting walls between the alcoves were five cubits[d] thick. And the threshold of the gate next to the portico facing the temple was one rod deep.

[8]Then he measured the portico of the gateway; [9]it[e] was eight cubits[f] deep and its

---

a 16 *Hamonah* means *horde.*   b 25 Or *now bring Jacob back from captivity*   c 5 That is, about 10 feet or about 3.1 meters; also in verse 12. The long cubit of about 21 inches or about 52 centimeters is the basic unit of measurement of length throughout Ezekiel 40–48.   d 7 That is, about 8 1/2 feet or about 2.6 meters; also in verse 48   e 8,9 Many Hebrew manuscripts, Septuagint, Vulgate and Syriac; most Hebrew manuscripts *gateway facing the temple; it was one rod deep.* *⁹Then he measured the portico of the gateway; it*   f 9 That is, about 14 feet or about 4.2 meters jambs were two cubits^a thick. The portico of the gateway faced the temple.

¹⁰Inside the east gate were three alcoves on each side; the three had the same measurements, and the faces of the projecting walls on each side had the same measurements. ¹¹Then he measured the width of the entrance of the gateway; it was ten cubits and its length was thirteen cubits.^b ¹²In front of each alcove was a wall one cubit high, and the alcoves were six cubits square. ¹³Then he measured the gateway from the top of the rear wall of one alcove to the top of the opposite one; the distance was twenty-five cubits^c from one parapet opening to the opposite one. ¹⁴He measured along the faces of the projecting walls all around the inside of the gateway—sixty cubits.^d The measurement was up to the portico^e facing the courtyard.^f ¹⁵The distance from the entrance of the gateway to the far end of its portico was fifty cubits.^g ¹⁶The alcoves and the projecting walls inside the gateway were surmounted by narrow parapet openings all around, as was the portico; the openings all around faced inward. The faces of the projecting walls were decorated with palm trees.

The Outer Court

¹⁷Then he brought me into the outer court. There I saw some rooms and a pavement that had been constructed all around the court; there were thirty rooms along the pavement. ¹⁸It abutted the sides of the gateways and was as wide as they were long; this was the lower pavement. ¹⁹Then he measured the distance from the inside of the lower gateway to the outside of the inner court; it was a hundred cubits^h on the east side as well as on the north.

The North Gate

²⁰Then he measured the length and width of the north gate, leading into the outer court. ²¹Its alcoves—three on each side—its projecting walls and its portico had the same measurements as those of the first gateway. It was fifty cubits long and twenty-

five cubits wide. ²²Its openings, its portico and its palm tree decorations had the same measurements as those of the gate facing east. Seven steps led up to it, with its portico opposite them. ²³There was a gate to the inner court facing the north gate, just as there was on the east. He measured from one gate to the opposite one; it was a hundred cubits.

The South Gate

²⁴Then he led me to the south side and I saw the south gate. He measured its jambs and its portico, and they had the same measurements as the others. ²⁵The gateway and its portico had narrow openings all around, like the openings of the others. It was fifty cubits long and twenty-five cubits wide. ²⁶Seven steps led up to it, with its portico opposite them; it had palm tree decorations on the faces of the projecting walls on each side. ²⁷The inner court also had a gate facing south, and he measured from this gate to the outer gate on the south side; it was a hundred cubits.

The Gates to the Inner Court

²⁸Then he brought me into the inner court through the south gate, and he measured the south gate; it had the same measurements as the others. ²⁹Its alcoves, its projecting walls and its portico had the same measurements as the others. The gateway and its portico had openings all around. It was fifty cubits long and twenty-five cubits wide. ³⁰(The porticoes of the gateways around the inner court were twenty-five cubits wide and five cubits deep.) ³¹Its portico faced the outer court; palm trees decorated its jambs, and eight steps led up to it.

³²Then he brought me to the inner court on the east side, and he measured the gateway; it had the same measurements as the others. ³³Its alcoves, its projecting walls and its portico had the same measurements as the others. The gateway and its portico had openings all around. It was fifty cubits long and twenty-five cubits wide. ³⁴Its portico

^a 9 That is, about 3 1/2 feet or about 1 meter   ^b 11 That is, about 17 feet wide and 22 feet long or about 5.2 meters wide and 6.8 meters long   ^c 13 That is, about 43 feet or about 13 meters; also in verses 21, 25, 29, 30, 33 and 36   ^d 14 That is, about 103 feet or about 31 meters   ^e 14 Septuagint; Hebrew projecting wall   ^f 14 The meaning of the Hebrew for this verse is uncertain.   ^g 15 That is, about 85 feet or about 26 meters; also in verses 21, 25, 29, 33 and 36   ^h 19 That is, about 170 feet or about 52 meters; also in verses 23, 27 and 47

faced the outer court; palm trees decorated the jambs on either side, and eight steps led up to it.

35Then he brought me to the north gate and measured it. It had the same measurements as the others, 36as did its alcoves, its projecting walls and its portico, and it had openings all around. It was fifty cubits long and twenty-five cubits wide. 37Its portico*a* faced the outer court; palm trees decorated the jambs on either side, and eight steps led up to it.

The Rooms for Preparing Sacrifices

38A room with a doorway was by the portico in each of the inner gateways, where the burnt offerings were washed. 39In the portico of the gateway were two tables on each side, on which the burnt offerings, sin offerings*b* and guilt offerings were slaughtered. 40By the outside wall of the portico of the gateway, near the steps at the entrance of the north gateway were two tables, and on the other side of the steps were two tables. 41So there were four tables on one side of the gateway and four on the other—eight tables in all—on which the sacrifices were slaughtered. 42There were also four tables of dressed stone for the burnt offerings, each a cubit and a half long, a cubit and a half wide and a cubit high.*c* On them were placed the utensils for slaughtering the burnt offerings and the other sacrifices. 43And double-pronged hooks, each a handbreadth*d* long, were attached to the wall all around. The tables were for the flesh of the offerings.

The Rooms for the Priests

44Outside the inner gate, within the inner court, were two rooms, one*e* at the side of the north gate and facing south, and another at the side of the south*f* gate and facing north. 45He said to me, "The room facing south is for the priests who guard the tem-ple, 46and the room facing north is for the priests who guard the altar. These are the sons of Zadok, who are the only Levites who may draw near to the LORD to minister before him."

47Then he measured the court: It was square—a hundred cubits long and a hundred cubits wide. And the altar was in front of the temple.

The New Temple

48He brought me to the portico of the temple and measured the jambs of the portico; they were five cubits wide on either side. The width of the entrance was fourteen cubits*g* and its projecting walls were*h* three cubits*i* wide on either side. 49The portico was twenty cubits*j* wide, and twelve*k* cubits*l* from front to back. It was reached by a flight of stairs,*m* and there were pillars on each side of the jambs.

41

Then the man brought me to the main hall and measured the jambs; the width of the jambs was six cubits*n* on each side.*o* 2The entrance was ten cubits*p* wide, and the projecting walls on each side of it were five cubits*q* wide. He also measured the main hall; it was forty cubits long and twenty cubits wide.*r*

3Then he went into the inner sanctuary and measured the jambs of the entrance; each was two cubits*s* wide. The entrance was six cubits wide, and the projecting walls on each side of it were seven cubits*t* wide. 4And he measured the length of the inner sanctuary; it was twenty cubits, and its width was twenty cubits across the end of the main hall. He said to me, "This is the Most Holy Place."

5Then he measured the wall of the temple; it was six cubits thick, and each side room around the temple was four cubits*u* wide. 6The side rooms were on three levels,

---

a 37 Septuagint (see also verses 31 and 34); Hebrew *jambs*   *b 39* Or *purification offerings*   *c 42* That is, about 2 1/2 feet long and wide and 21 inches high or about 78 centimeters long and wide and 52 centimeters high   *d 43* That is, about 3 1/2 inches or about 9 centimeters   *e 44* Septuagint; Hebrew *were rooms for singers, which were*   *f 44* Septuagint; Hebrew *east*   *g 48* That is, about 24 feet or about 7.3 meters   *h 48* Septuagint; Hebrew *entrance was*   *i 48* That is, about 5 1/4 feet or about 1.5 meters   *j 49* That is, about 34 feet or about 10.4 meters   *k 49* Septuagint; Hebrew *eleven*   *l 49* That is, about 21 feet or about 6.2 meters   *m 49* Hebrew; Septuagint *Ten steps led up to it*   *n 1* That is, about 10 feet or about 3 meters; also in verses 3, 5 and 8   *o 1* One Hebrew manuscript and Septuagint; most Hebrew manuscripts *side, the width of the tent*   *p 2* That is, about 17 feet or about 5.2 meters   *q 2* That is, about 8 1/2 feet or about 2.6 meters; also in verses 9, 11 and 12   *r 2* That is, about 68 feet long and 34 feet wide or about 21 meters long and 10.4 meters wide   *s 3* That is, about 3 1/2 feet or about 1 meter; also in verse 22   *t 3* That is, about 12 feet or about 3.6 meters   *u 5* That is, about 7 feet or about 2.1 meters one above another, thirty on each level. There were ledges all around the wall of the temple to serve as supports for the side rooms, so that the supports were not inserted into the wall of the temple. ⁷The side rooms all around the temple were wider at each successive level. The structure surrounding the temple was built in ascending stages, so that the rooms widened as one went upward. A stairway went up from the lowest floor to the top floor through the middle floor.

⁸I saw that the temple had a raised base all around it, forming the foundation of the side rooms. It was the length of the rod, six long cubits. ⁹The outer wall of the side rooms was five cubits thick. The open area between the side rooms of the temple ¹⁰and the ⌊priests'⌋ rooms was twenty cubits wide all around the temple. ¹¹There were entrances to the side rooms from the open area, one on the north and another on the south; and the base adjoining the open area was five cubits wide all around.

¹²The building facing the temple courtyard on the west side was seventy cubits*a* wide. The wall of the building was five cubits thick all around, and its length was ninety cubits.*b*

¹³Then he measured the temple; it was a hundred cubits*c* long, and the temple courtyard and the building with its walls were also a hundred cubits long. ¹⁴The width of the temple courtyard on the east, including the front of the temple, was a hundred cubits.

¹⁵Then he measured the length of the building facing the courtyard at the rear of the temple, including its galleries on each side; it was a hundred cubits.

The main hall, the inner sanctuary and the portico facing the court, ¹⁶as well as the thresholds and the narrow windows and galleries around the three of them—everything beyond and including the threshold was covered with wood. The floor, the wall up to the windows, and the windows were covered. ¹⁷In the space above the outside of the entrance to the inner sanctuary and on the

walls at regular intervals all around the inner and outer sanctuary ¹⁸were carved cherubim and palm trees. Palm trees alternated with cherubim. Each cherub had two faces: ¹⁹the face of a human being toward the palm tree on one side and the face of a lion toward the palm tree on the other. They were carved all around the whole temple. ²⁰From the floor to the area above the entrance, cherubim and palm trees were carved on the wall of the main hall.

²¹The main hall had a rectangular doorframe, and the one at the front of the Most Holy Place was similar. ²²There was a wooden altar three cubits*d* high and two cubits square*e*; its corners, its base*f* and its sides were of wood. The man said to me, "This is the table that is before the LORD." ²³Both the main hall and the Most Holy Place had double doors. ²⁴Each door had two leaves—two hinged leaves for each door. ²⁵And on the doors of the main hall were carved cherubim and palm trees like those carved on the walls, and there was a wooden overhang on the front of the portico. ²⁶On the sidewalls of the portico were narrow windows with palm trees carved on each side. The side rooms of the temple also had overhangs.

The Rooms for the Priests

42 Then the man led me northward into the outer court and brought me to the rooms opposite the temple courtyard and opposite the outer wall on the north side. ²The building whose door faced north was a hundred cubits long and fifty cubits wide.*g* ³Both in the section twenty cubits*h* from the inner court and in the section opposite the pavement of the outer court, gallery faced gallery at the three levels. ⁴In front of the rooms was an inner passageway ten cubits wide and a hundred cubits*i* long.*j* Their doors were on the north. ⁵Now the upper rooms were narrower, for the galleries took more space from them than from the rooms on the lower and middle floors of the building. ⁶The rooms on the top floor had no pillars, as the courts had; so they were smaller in floor

---

a 12 That is, about 120 feet or about 36 meters   *b 12* That is, about 154 feet or about 47 meters
c 13 That is, about 170 feet or about 52 meters; also in verses 14 and 15   *d 22* That is, about 5 1/4 feet
or about 1.5 meters   *e 22* Septuagint; Hebrew *long*   *f 22* Septuagint; Hebrew *length*   *g 2* That is,
about 170 feet long and 85 feet wide or about 52 meters long and 26 meters wide   *h 3* That is, about
34 feet or about 10.4 meters   *i 4* Septuagint and Syriac; Hebrew *and one cubit*   *j 4* That is, about 17
feet wide and 170 feet long or about 5.2 meters wide and 52 meters long

space than those on the lower and middle floors. ⁷There was an outer wall parallel to the rooms and the outer court; it extended in front of the rooms for fifty cubits. ⁸While the row of rooms on the side next to the outer court was fifty cubits long, the row on the side nearest the sanctuary was a hundred cubits long. ⁹The lower rooms had an entrance on the east side as one enters them from the outer court.

¹⁰On the south side*a* along the length of the wall of the outer court, adjoining the temple courtyard and opposite the outer wall, were rooms ¹¹with a passageway in front of them. These were like the rooms on the north; they had the same length and width, with similar exits and dimensions. Similar to the doorways on the north ¹²were the doorways of the rooms on the south. There was a doorway at the beginning of the passageway that was parallel to the corresponding wall extending eastward, by which one enters the rooms.

¹³Then he said to me, "The north and south rooms facing the temple courtyard are the priests' rooms, where the priests who approach the LORD will eat the most holy offerings. There they will put the most holy offerings—the grain offerings, the sin offerings*b* and the guilt offerings—for the place is holy. ¹⁴Once the priests enter the holy precincts, they are not to go into the outer court until they leave behind the garments in which they minister, for these are holy. They are to put on other clothes before they go near the places that are for the people."

¹⁵When he had finished measuring what was inside the temple area, he led me out by the east gate and measured the area all around: ¹⁶He measured the east side with the measuring rod; it was five hundred cubits.*c,d* ¹⁷He measured the north side; it was five hundred cubits*e* by the measuring rod. ¹⁸He measured the south side; it was five hundred cubits by the measuring rod. ¹⁹Then he turned to the west side and measured; it was five hundred cubits by the measuring rod. ²⁰So he measured the area on all four sides. It had a wall around it, five hundred cubits

long and five hundred cubits wide, to separate the holy from the common.

God's Glory Returns to the Temple

43 Then the man brought me to the gate facing east, ²and I saw the glory of the God of Israel coming from the east. His voice was like the roar of rushing waters, and the land was radiant with his glory. ³The vision I saw was like the vision I had seen when he*f* came to destroy the city and like the visions I had seen by the Kebar River, and I fell facedown. ⁴The glory of the LORD entered the temple through the gate facing east. ⁵Then the Spirit lifted me up and brought me into the inner court, and the glory of the LORD filled the temple.

⁶While the man was standing beside me, I heard someone speaking to me from inside the temple. ⁷He said: "Son of man, this is the place of my throne and the place for the soles of my feet. This is where I will live among the Israelites forever. The house of Israel will never again defile my holy name—neither they nor their kings—by their prostitution and the funeral offerings*g* for their kings at their death.*h* ⁸When they placed their threshold next to my threshold and their doorposts beside my doorposts, with only a wall between me and them, they defiled my holy name by their detestable practices. So I destroyed them in my anger. ⁹Now let them put away from me their prostitution and the funeral offerings for their kings, and I will live among them forever.

¹⁰"Son of man, describe the temple to the people of Israel, that they may be ashamed of their sins. Let them consider its perfection, ¹¹and if they are ashamed of all they have done, make known to them the design of the temple—its arrangement, its exits and entrances—its whole design and all its regulations*i* and laws. Write these down before them so that they may be faithful to its design and follow all its regulations.

¹²"This is the law of the temple: All the surrounding area on top of the mountain will be most holy. Such is the law of the temple.

---

a 10 Septuagint; Hebrew *Eastward*   *b* 13 Or *purification offerings*   *c* 16 See Septuagint of verse 17; Hebrew *rods*; also in verses 18 and 19.   *d* 16 Five hundred cubits equal about 850 feet or about 260 meters; also in verses 17, 18 and 19.   *e* 17 Septuagint; Hebrew *rods*   *f* 3 Some Hebrew manuscripts and Vulgate; most Hebrew manuscripts *I*   *g* 7 Or *the memorial monuments*; also in verse 9   *h* 7 Or *their high places*   *i* 11 Some Hebrew manuscripts and Septuagint; most Hebrew manuscripts *regulations and its whole design*

The Great Altar Restored

[13]"These are the measurements of the altar in long cubits,[a] that cubit being a cubit and a handbreadth: Its gutter is a cubit deep and a cubit wide, with a rim of one span[b] around the edge. And this is the height of the altar: [14]From the gutter on the ground up to the lower ledge that goes around the altar it is two cubits high, and the ledge is a cubit wide.[c] From this lower ledge to the upper ledge that goes around the altar it is four cubits high, and that ledge is also a cubit wide.[d] [15]Above that, the altar hearth is four cubits high, and four horns project upward from the hearth. [16]The altar hearth is square, twelve cubits[e] long and twelve cubits wide. [17]The upper ledge also is square, fourteen cubits[f] long and fourteen cubits wide. All around the altar is a gutter of one cubit with a rim of half a cubit.[g] The steps of the altar face east."

[18]Then he said to me, "Son of man, this is what the Sovereign LORD says: These will be the regulations for sacrificing burnt offerings and splashing blood against the altar when it is built: [19]You are to give a young bull as a sin offering[h] to the Levitical priests of the family of Zadok, who come near to minister before me, declares the Sovereign LORD. [20]You are to take some of its blood and put it on the four horns of the altar and on the four corners of the upper ledge and all around the rim, and so purify the altar and make atonement for it. [21]You are to take the bull for the sin offering and burn it in the designated part of the temple area outside the sanctuary.

[22]"On the second day you are to offer a male goat without defect for a sin offering, and the altar is to be purified as it was purified with the bull. [23]When you have finished purifying it, you are to offer a young bull and a ram from the flock, both without defect. [24]You are to offer them before the LORD, and the priests are to sprinkle salt on them and sacrifice them as a burnt offering to the LORD.

[25]"For seven days you are to provide a male goat daily for a sin offering; you are also to provide a young bull and a ram from the flock, both without defect. [26]For seven days they are to make atonement for the altar and cleanse it; thus they will dedicate it. [27]At the end of these days, from the eighth day on, the priests are to present your burnt offerings and fellowship offerings on the altar. Then I will accept you, declares the Sovereign LORD."

The Priesthood Restored

44 Then the man brought me back to the outer gate of the sanctuary, the one facing east, and it was shut. [2]The LORD said to me, "This gate is to remain shut. It must not be opened; no one may enter through it. It is to remain shut because the LORD, the God of Israel, has entered through it. [3]The prince himself is the only one who may sit inside the gateway to eat in the presence of the LORD. He is to enter by way of the portico of the gateway and go out the same way."

[4]Then the man brought me by way of the north gate to the front of the temple. I looked and saw the glory of the LORD filling the temple of the LORD, and I fell facedown.

[5]The LORD said to me, "Son of man, look carefully, listen closely and give attention to everything I tell you concerning all the regulations and instructions regarding the temple of the LORD. Give attention to the entrance to the temple and all the exits of the sanctuary. [6]Say to the rebellious house of Israel, 'This is what the Sovereign LORD says: Enough of your detestable practices, house of Israel! [7]In addition to all your other detestable practices, you brought foreigners uncircumcised in heart and flesh into my sanctuary, desecrating my temple while you offered me food, fat and blood, and you broke my covenant. [8]Instead of carrying out your duty in regard to my holy things, you put others in charge of my sanctuary. [9]This is what the Sovereign LORD says: No foreigner uncircumcised in heart and flesh is to enter my sanctuary, not even the foreigners who live among the Israelites.

---

a 13 That is, about 21 inches or about 52 centimeters; also in verses 14 and 17. The long cubit is the basic unit for linear measurement throughout Ezekiel 40–48.   *b 13* That is, about 10 inches or about 26 centimeters   *c 14* That is, about 3 1/2 feet high and 1 3/4 feet wide or about 104 centimeters high and 52 centimeters wide   *d 14* That is, about 7 feet high and 1 3/4 feet wide or about 2.1 meters high and 52 centimeters wide   *e 16* That is, about 21 feet or about 6.2 meters   *f 17* That is, about 24 feet or about 7.3 meters   *g 17* That is, about 10 inches or about 26 centimeters   *h 19* Or *purification offering*; also in verses 21, 22 and 25

¹⁰" 'The Levites who went far from me when Israel went astray and who wandered from me after their idols must bear the consequences of their sin. ¹¹They may serve in my sanctuary, having charge of the gates of the temple and serving in it; they may slaughter the burnt offerings and sacrifices for the people and stand before the people and serve them. ¹²But because they served them in the presence of their idols and made the house of Israel fall into sin, therefore I have sworn with uplifted hand that they must bear the consequences of their sin, declares the Sovereign LORD. ¹³They are not to come near to serve me as priests or come near any of my holy things or my most holy offerings; they must bear the shame of their detestable practices. ¹⁴And I will appoint them to guard the temple for all the work that is to be done in it.

¹⁵" 'But the Levitical priests, who are descendants of Zadok and who guarded my sanctuary when the Israelites went astray from me, are to come near to minister before me; they are to stand before me to offer sacrifices of fat and blood, declares the Sovereign LORD. ¹⁶They alone are to enter my sanctuary; they alone are to come near my table to minister before me and serve me as guards.

¹⁷" 'When they enter the gates of the inner court, they are to wear linen clothes; they must not wear any woolen garment while ministering at the gates of the inner court or inside the temple. ¹⁸They are to wear linen turbans on their heads and linen undergarments around their waists. They must not wear anything that makes them perspire. ¹⁹When they go out into the outer court where the people are, they are to take off the clothes they have been ministering in and are to leave them in the sacred rooms, and put on other clothes, so that the people are not consecrated through contact with their garments.

²⁰" 'They must not shave their heads or let their hair grow long, but they are to keep the hair of their heads trimmed. ²¹No priest is to drink wine when he enters the inner court. ²²They must not marry widows or divorced women; they may marry only virgins of Israelite descent or widows of priests. ²³They are to teach my people the difference between the holy and the common and show them how to distinguish between the unclean and the clean.

²⁴" 'In any dispute, the priests are to serve as judges and decide it according to my ordinances. They are to keep my laws and my decrees for all my appointed festivals, and they are to keep my Sabbaths holy.

²⁵" 'A priest must not defile himself by going near a dead person; however, if the dead person was his father or mother, son or daughter, brother or unmarried sister, then he may defile himself. ²⁶After he is cleansed, he must wait seven days. ²⁷On the day he goes into the inner court of the sanctuary to minister in the sanctuary, he is to offer a sin offering[a] for himself, declares the Sovereign LORD.

²⁸" 'I am to be the only inheritance the priests have. You are to give them no possession in Israel; I will be their possession. ²⁹They will eat the grain offerings, the sin offerings and the guilt offerings; and everything in Israel devoted[b] to the LORD will belong to them. ³⁰The best of all the firstfruits and of all your special gifts will belong to the priests. You are to give them the first portion of your ground meal so that a blessing may rest on your household. ³¹The priests must not eat anything, whether bird or animal, found dead or torn by wild animals.

Israel Fully Restored

45 " 'When you allot the land as an inheritance, you are to present to the LORD a portion of the land as a sacred district, 25,000 cubits[c] long and 20,000[d] cubits[e] wide; the entire area will be holy. ²Of this, a section 500 cubits[f] square is to be for the sanctuary, with 50 cubits[g] around it for open land. ³In the sacred district, measure off a section 25,000 cubits long and 10,000 cubits[h] wide. In it will be the sanctuary, the Most Holy Place. ⁴It will be the sacred portion of the land for the priests, who minister in the sanctuary and who draw near to minister before the LORD. It will be a

---

a 27 Or *purification offering*; also in verse 29   *b 29* The Hebrew term refers to the irrevocable giving over of things or persons to the LORD.   *c 1* That is, about 8 miles or about 13 kilometers; also in verses 3, 5 and 6   *d 1* Septuagint (see also verses 3 and 5 and 48:9); Hebrew *10,000*   *e 1* That is, about 6 1/2 miles or about 10 kilometers   *f 2* That is, about 850 feet or about 260 meters   *g 2* That is, about 85 feet or about 26 meters   *h 3* That is, about 3 miles or about 5.2 kilometers; also in verse 5 place for their houses as well as a holy place for the sanctuary. 5An area 25,000 cubits long and 10,000 cubits wide will belong to the Levites, who serve in the temple, as their possession for towns to live in.ᵃ

6“ 'You are to give the city as its property an area 5,000 cubitsᵇ wide and 25,000 cubits long, adjoining the sacred portion; it will belong to the whole house of Israel.

7“ 'The prince will have the land bordering each side of the area formed by the sacred district and the property of the city. It will extend westward from the west side and eastward from the east side, running lengthwise from the western to the eastern border parallel to one of the tribal portions. 8This land will be his possession in Israel. And my princes will no longer oppress my people but will allow the house of Israel to possess the land according to their tribes.

9“ 'This is what the Sovereign Lord says: You have gone far enough, princes of Israel! Give up your violence and oppression and do what is just and right. Stop dispossessing my people, declares the Sovereign Lord. 10You are to use accurate scales, an accurate ephahᶜ and an accurate bath.ᵈ 11The ephah and the bath are to be the same size, the bath containing a tenth of a homer and the ephah a tenth of a homer; the homer is to be the standard measure for both. 12The shekelᵉ is to consist of twenty gerahs. Twenty shekels plus twenty-five shekels plus fifteen shekels equal one mina.ᶠ

13“ 'This is the special gift you are to offer: a sixth of an ephahᵍ from each homer of wheat and a sixth of an ephahʰ from each homer of barley. 14The prescribed portion of olive oil, measured by the bath,ⁱ is a tenth of a bath from each cor (which consists of ten baths or one homer, for ten baths are equivalent to a homer). 15Also one sheep is to be taken from every flock of two hundred from the well-watered pastures of Israel. These will be used for the grain offerings, burnt offerings and fellowship offerings to make atonement for the people, declares the Sovereign Lord. 16All the people of the land will

be required to give this special offering to the prince in Israel. 17It will be the duty of the prince to provide the burnt offerings, grain offerings and drink offerings at the festivals, the New Moons and the Sabbaths—at all the appointed festivals of the house of Israel. He will provide the sin offerings,ʲ grain offerings, burnt offerings and fellowship offerings to make atonement for the house of Israel.

18“ 'This is what the Sovereign Lord says: In the first month on the first day you are to take a young bull without defect and purify the sanctuary. 19The priest is to take some of the blood of the sin offering and put it on the doorposts of the temple, on the four corners of the upper ledge of the altar and on the gateposts of the inner court. 20You are to do the same on the seventh day of the month for anyone who sins unintentionally or through ignorance; so you are to make atonement for the temple.

21“ 'In the first month on the fourteenth day you are to observe the Passover, a festival lasting seven days, during which you shall eat bread made without yeast. 22On that day the prince is to provide a bull as a sin offering for himself and for all the people of the land. 23Every day during the seven days of the festival he is to provide seven bulls and seven rams without defect as a burnt offering to the Lord, and a male goat for a sin offering. 24He is to provide as a grain offering an ephah for each bull and an ephah for each ram, along with a hinᵏ of olive oil for each ephah.

25“ 'During the seven days of the festival, which begins in the seventh month on the fifteenth day, he is to make the same provision for sin offerings, burnt offerings, grain offerings and oil.

46 “ 'This is what the Sovereign Lord says: The gate of the inner court facing east is to be shut on the six working days, but on the Sabbath day and on the day of the New Moon it is to be opened. 2The prince is to enter from the outside through the portico of the gateway

---

ᵃ 5 Septuagint; Hebrew temple; they will have as their possession 20 rooms   ᵇ 6 That is, about 1 2/3 miles or about 2.6 kilometers   ᶜ 10 An ephah was a dry measure equaling about 3/5 bushel or about 22 liters.   ᵈ 10 A bath was a liquid measure equaling about 6 gallons or about 22 liters.   ᵉ 12 A shekel weighed about 2/5 ounce or about 11.5 grams.   ᶠ 12 That is, 60 shekels; the common mina was 50 shekels. Sixty shekels were about 1 1/2 pounds or about 680 grams.   ᵍ 13 That is, probably about 6 pounds or about 2.8 kilograms   ʰ 13 That is, probably about 5 pounds or about 2.3 kilograms   ⁱ 14 That is, about 5 pints or about 2.2 liters   ʲ 17 Or purification offerings; also in verses 19, 22, 23 and 25   ᵏ 24 That is, about 1 gallon or about 3.6 liters and stand by the gatepost. The priests are to sacrifice his burnt offering and his fellowship offerings. He is to bow down in worship at the threshold of the gateway and then go out, but the gate will not be shut until evening. ³On the Sabbaths and New Moons the people of the land are to worship in the presence of the LORD at the entrance of that gateway. ⁴The burnt offering the prince brings to the LORD on the Sabbath day is to be six male lambs and a ram, all without defect. ⁵The grain offering given with the ram is to be an ephah,ᵃ and the grain offering with the lambs is to be as much as he pleases, along with a hinᵇ of olive oil for each ephah. ⁶On the day of the New Moon he is to offer a young bull, six lambs and a ram, all without defect. ⁷He is to provide as a grain offering one ephah with the bull, one ephah with the ram, and with the lambs as much as he wants to give, along with a hin of oil for each ephah. ⁸When the prince enters, he is to go in through the portico of the gateway, and he is to come out the same way.

⁹" 'When the people of the land come before the LORD at the appointed festivals, whoever enters by the north gate to worship is to go out the south gate; and whoever enters by the south gate is to go out the north gate. No one is to return through the gate by which he entered, but each is to go out the opposite gate. ¹⁰The prince is to be among them, going in when they go in and going out when they go out. ¹¹At the feasts and the appointed festivals, the grain offering is to be an ephah with a bull, an ephah with a ram, and with the lambs as much as he pleases, along with a hin of oil for each ephah.

¹²" 'When the prince provides a freewill offering to the LORD—whether a burnt offering or fellowship offerings—the gate facing east is to be opened for him. He shall offer his burnt offering or his fellowship offerings as he does on the Sabbath day. Then he shall go out, and after he has gone out, the gate will be shut.

¹³" 'Every day you are to provide a year-old lamb without defect for a burnt offering to the LORD; morning by morning you shall provide it. ¹⁴You are also to provide with it morn-

ing by morning a grain offering, consisting of a sixth of an ephahᶜ with a third of a hinᵈ of oil to moisten the flour. The presenting of this grain offering to the LORD is a lasting ordinance. ¹⁵So the lamb and the grain offering and the oil shall be provided morning by morning for a regular burnt offering.

¹⁶" 'This is what the Sovereign LORD says: If the prince makes a gift from his inheritance to one of his sons, it will also belong to his descendants; it is to be their property by inheritance. ¹⁷If, however, he makes a gift from his inheritance to one of his servants, the servant may keep it until the year of freedom; then it will revert to the prince. His inheritance belongs to his sons only; it is theirs. ¹⁸The prince must not take any of the inheritance of the people, driving them off their property. He is to give his sons their inheritance out of his own property, so that not one of my people will be separated from their property.' "

¹⁹Then the man brought me through the entrance at the side of the gate to the sacred rooms facing north, which belonged to the priests, and showed me a place at the western end. ²⁰He said to me, "This is the place where the priests are to cook the guilt offering and the sin offeringᵉ and bake the grain offering, to avoid bringing them into the outer court and consecrating the people."

²¹He then brought me to the outer court and led me around to its four corners, and I saw in each corner another court. ²²In the four corners of the outer court were enclosedᶠ courts, forty cubits long and thirty cubits wideᵍ; each of the courts in the four corners was the same size. ²³Around the inside of each of the four courts was a ledge of stone, with places for fire built all around under the ledge. ²⁴He said to me, "These are the kitchens where those who minister at the temple are to cook the sacrifices of the people."

The River From the Temple

47 The man brought me back to the entrance to the temple, and I saw water coming out from under the threshold of the temple toward

---

ᵃ 5 That is, probably about 36 pounds or about 16 kilograms; also in verses 7 and 11   ᵇ 5 That is, about 1 gallon or about 3.6 liters; also in verses 7 and 11   ᶜ 14 That is, probably about 6 pounds or about 2.8 kilograms   ᵈ 14 That is, about 2 2/3 pints or about 1.2 liters   ᵉ 20 Or *purification offering*   ᶠ 22 The meaning of the Hebrew for this word is uncertain.   ᵍ 22 That is, about 68 feet long and 51 feet wide or about 21 meters long and 16 meters wide the east (for the temple faced east). The water was coming down from under the south side of the temple, south of the altar. ²He then brought me out through the north gate and led me around the outside to the outer gate facing east, and the water was trickling from the south side.

³As the man went eastward with a measuring line in his hand, he measured off a thousand cubits[a] and then led me through water that was ankle-deep. ⁴He measured off another thousand cubits and led me through water that was knee-deep. He measured off another thousand and led me through water that was up to the waist. ⁵He measured off another thousand, but now it was a river that I could not cross, because the water had risen and was deep enough to swim in—a river that no one could cross. ⁶He asked me, "Son of man, do you see this?"

Then he led me back to the bank of the river. ⁷When I arrived there, I saw a great number of trees on each side of the river. ⁸He said to me, "This water flows toward the eastern region and goes down into the Arabah,[b] where it enters the Dead Sea. When it empties into the sea, the salty water there becomes fresh. ⁹Swarms of living creatures will live wherever the river flows. There will be large numbers of fish, because this water flows there and makes the salt water fresh; so where the river flows everything will live. ¹⁰People will fish along the shore; from En Gedi to En Eglaim there will be places for spreading nets. The fish will be of many kinds—like the fish of the Mediterranean Sea. ¹¹But the swamps and marshes will not become fresh; they will be left for salt. ¹²Fruit trees of all kinds will grow on both banks of the river. Their leaves will not wither, nor will their fruit fail. Every month they will bear fruit, because the water from the sanctuary flows to them. Their fruit will serve for food and their leaves for healing."

The Boundaries of the Land

¹³This is what the Sovereign LORD says: "These are the boundaries of the land that you will divide among the twelve tribes of Israel as their inheritance, with two portions for Joseph. ¹⁴You are to divide it equally among them. Because I swore with uplifted hand to give it to your ancestors, this land will become your inheritance.

¹⁵"This is to be the boundary of the land:

"On the north side it will run from the Mediterranean Sea by the Hethlon road past Lebo Hamath to Zedad, ¹⁶Berothah[c] and Sibraim (which lies on the border between Damascus and Hamath), as far as Hazer Hattikon, which is on the border of Hauran. ¹⁷The boundary will extend from the sea to Hazar Enan,[d] along the northern border of Damascus, with the border of Hamath to the north. This will be the northern boundary.

¹⁸"On the east side the boundary will run between Hauran and Damascus, along the Jordan between Gilead and the land of Israel, to the Dead Sea and as far as Tamar.[e] This will be the eastern boundary.

¹⁹"On the south side it will run from Tamar as far as the waters of Meribah Kadesh, then along the Wadi of Egypt to the Mediterranean Sea. This will be the southern boundary.

²⁰"On the west side, the Mediterranean Sea will be the boundary to a point opposite Lebo Hamath. This will be the western boundary.

²¹"You are to distribute this land among yourselves according to the tribes of Israel. ²²You are to allot it as an inheritance for yourselves and for the foreigners residing among you and who have children. You are to consider them as native-born Israelites; along with you they are to be allotted an inheritance among the tribes of Israel. ²³In whatever tribe foreigners reside, there you are to give them their inheritance," declares the Sovereign LORD.

The Division of the Land

48 "These are the tribes, listed by name: At the northern frontier, Dan will have one portion; it will follow the Hethlon road to Lebo Hamath; Hazar Enan and the northern border of Damascus next to Hamath will be part of

---

a 3 That is, about 1,700 feet or about 520 meters and Ezekiel 48:1; Hebrew *road to go into Zedad,* ¹⁶*Hamath, Berothah.*   *b 8* Or *the Jordan Valley*   *c 15,16* See Septuagint   *d 17* Hebrew *Enon,* a variant of *Enan*   *e 18* See Syriac; Hebrew *Israel. You will measure to the Dead Sea.*

its border from the east side to the west side.

2"Asher will have one portion; it will border the territory of Dan from east to west.

3"Naphtali will have one portion; it will border the territory of Asher from east to west.

4"Manasseh will have one portion; it will border the territory of Naphtali from east to west.

5"Ephraim will have one portion; it will border the territory of Manasseh from east to west.

6"Reuben will have one portion; it will border the territory of Ephraim from east to west.

7"Judah will have one portion; it will border the territory of Reuben from east to west.

8"Bordering the territory of Judah from east to west will be the portion you are to present as a special gift. It will be 25,000 cubits*a* wide, and its length from east to west will equal one of the tribal portions; the sanctuary will be in the center of it.

9"The special portion you are to offer to the LORD will be 25,000 cubits long and 10,000 cubits*b* wide. 10This will be the sacred portion for the priests. It will be 25,000 cubits long on the north side, 10,000 cubits wide on the west side, 10,000 cubits wide on the east side and 25,000 cubits long on the south side. In the center of it will be the sanctuary of the LORD. 11This will be for the consecrated priests, the Zadokites, who were faithful in serving me and did not go astray as the Levites did when the Israelites went astray. 12It will be a special gift to them from the sacred portion of the land, a most holy portion, bordering the territory of the Levites.

13"Alongside the territory of the priests, the Levites will have an allotment 25,000 cubits long and 10,000 cubits wide. Its total length will be 25,000 cubits and its width 10,000 cubits. 14They must not sell or exchange any of it. This is the best of the land and must not pass into other hands, because it is holy to the LORD.

15"The remaining area, 5,000 cubits*c* wide and 25,000 cubits long, will be for the common use of the city, for houses and for pastureland. The city will be in the center of it

16and will have these measurements: the north side 4,500 cubits,*d* the south side 4,500 cubits, the east side 4,500 cubits, and the west side 4,500 cubits. 17The pastureland for the city will be 250 cubits*e* on the north, 250 cubits on the south, 250 cubits on the east, and 250 cubits on the west. 18What remains of the area, bordering on the sacred portion and running the length of it, will be 10,000 cubits on the east side and 10,000 cubits on the west side. Its produce will supply food for the workers of the city. 19The workers from the city who farm it will come from all the tribes of Israel. 20The entire portion will be a square, 25,000 cubits on each side. As a special gift you will set aside the sacred portion, along with the property of the city.

21"What remains on both sides of the area formed by the sacred portion and the property of the city will belong to the prince. It will extend eastward from the 25,000 cubits of the sacred portion to the eastern border, and westward from the 25,000 cubits to the western border. Both these areas running the length of the tribal portions will belong to the prince, and the sacred portion with the temple sanctuary will be in the center of them. 22So the property of the Levites and the property of the city will lie in the center of the area that belongs to the prince. The area belonging to the prince will lie between the border of Judah and the border of Benjamin.

23"As for the rest of the tribes: Benjamin will have one portion; it will extend from the east side to the west side.

24"Simeon will have one portion; it will border the territory of Benjamin from east to west.

25"Issachar will have one portion; it will border the territory of Simeon from east to west.

26"Zebulun will have one portion; it will border the territory of Issachar from east to west.

27"Gad will have one portion; it will border the territory of Zebulun from east to west.

28"The southern boundary of Gad will run south from Tamar to the waters of Meribah

Kadesh, then along the Wadi of Egypt to the Mediterranean Sea.

²⁹"This is the land you are to allot as an inheritance to the tribes of Israel, and these will be their portions," declares the Sovereign LORD.

The Gates of the New City

³⁰"These will be the exits of the city: Beginning on the north side, which is 4,500 cubits long, ³¹the gates of the city will be named after the tribes of Israel. The three gates on the north side will be the gate of Reuben, the gate of Judah and the gate of Levi.

³²"On the east side, which is 4,500 cubits long, will be three gates: the gate of Joseph, the gate of Benjamin and the gate of Dan.

³³"On the south side, which measures 4,500 cubits, will be three gates: the gate of Simeon, the gate of Issachar and the gate of Zebulun.

³⁴"On the west side, which is 4,500 cubits long, will be three gates: the gate of Gad, the gate of Asher and the gate of Naphtali.

³⁵"The distance all around will be 18,000 cubits.ᵃ

"And the name of the city from that time on will be:

THE LORD IS THERE."

ᵃ 35 That is, about 6 miles or about 9.4 kilometers

daniel

AUTHOR: Daniel

DATE: Around 530 B.C.

THEME: God, who is sovereign over every earthly power, deserves our allegiance.

Daniel's Training in Babylon

1 In the third year of the reign of Jehoiakim king of Judah, Nebuchadnezzar king of Babylon came to Jerusalem and besieged it. ²And the Lord delivered Jehoiakim king of Judah into his hand, along with some of the articles from the temple of God. These he carried off to the temple of his god in Babylonia* and put in the treasure house of his god.

³Then the king ordered Ashpenaz, chief of his court officials, to bring into the king's service some of the Israelites from the royal family and the nobility— ⁴young men without any physical defect, handsome, showing aptitude for every kind of learning, well informed, quick to understand, and qualified to serve in the king's palace. He was to teach them the language and literature of the Babylonians.* ⁵The king assigned them a daily amount of food and wine from the king's table. They were to be trained for three years, and after that they were to enter the king's service.

⁶Among those who were chosen were some from Judah: Daniel, Hananiah, Mishael and Azariah. ⁷The chief official gave them new names: to Daniel, the name Belteshazzar; to Hananiah, Shadrach; to Mishael, Meshach; and to Azariah, Abednego.

⁸But Daniel resolved not to defile himself with the royal food and wine, and he asked the chief official for permission not to defile himself this way. ⁹Now God had caused the official to show favor and compassion to Daniel, ¹⁰but the official told Daniel, "I am afraid of my lord the king, who has assigned your* food and drink. Why should he see you looking worse than the other young men your age? The king would then have my head because of you."

¹¹Daniel then said to the guard whom the chief official had appointed over Daniel, Hananiah, Mishael and Azariah, ¹²"Please test your servants for ten days: Give us nothing but vegetables to eat and water to drink. ¹³Then compare our appearance with that of the young men who eat the royal food, and treat your servants in accordance with what you see." ¹⁴So he agreed to this and tested them for ten days.

¹⁵At the end of the ten days they looked healthier and better nourished than any of the young men who ate the royal food. ¹⁶So the guard took away their choice food and the wine they were to drink and gave them vegetables instead.

¹⁷To these four young men God gave knowledge and understanding of all kinds of literature and learning. And Daniel could understand visions and dreams of all kinds.

¹⁸At the end of the time set by the king to bring them into his service, the chief official presented them to Nebuchadnezzar. ¹⁹The king talked with them, and he found none equal to Daniel, Hananiah, Mishael and Azariah; so they entered the king's service. ²⁰In every matter of wisdom and understanding about which the king questioned them, he found them ten times better than all the magicians and enchanters in his whole kingdom.

²¹And Daniel remained there until the first year of King Cyrus.

Nebuchadnezzar's Dream

2 In the second year of his reign, Nebuchadnezzar had dreams; his mind was troubled and he could not sleep. ²So the king summoned the magicians, en-

a 2 Hebrew Shinar   b 4 Or Chaldeans   c 10 The Hebrew for your and you in this verse is plural.

chanters, sorcerers and astrologers[a] to tell him what he had dreamed. When they came in and stood before the king, ³he said to them, "I have had a dream that troubles me and I want to know what it means.[b]"

⁴Then the astrologers answered the king,[c] "May the king live forever! Tell your servants the dream, and we will interpret it."

⁵The king replied to the astrologers, "This is what I have firmly decided: If you do not tell me what my dream was and interpret it, I will have you cut into pieces and your houses turned into piles of rubble. ⁶But if you tell me the dream and explain it, you will receive from me gifts and rewards and great honor. So tell me the dream and interpret it for me."

⁷Once more they replied, "Let the king tell his servants the dream, and we will interpret it."

⁸Then the king answered, "I am certain that you are trying to gain time, because you realize that this is what I have firmly decided: ⁹If you do not tell me the dream, there is only one penalty for you. You have conspired to tell me misleading and wicked things, hoping the situation will change. So then, tell me the dream, and I will know that you can interpret it for me."

¹⁰The astrologers answered the king, "There is not a person on earth who can do what the king asks! No king, however great and mighty, has ever asked such a thing of any magician or enchanter or astrologer. ¹¹What the king asks is too difficult. No one can reveal it to the king except the gods, and they do not live among human beings."

¹²This made the king so angry and furious that he ordered the execution of all the wise men of Babylon. ¹³So the decree was issued to put the wise men to death, and men were sent to look for Daniel and his friends to put them to death.

¹⁴When Arioch, the commander of the king's guard, had gone out to put to death the wise men of Babylon, Daniel spoke to him with wisdom and tact. ¹⁵He asked the king's officer, "Why did the king issue such a harsh decree?" Arioch then explained the matter to Daniel. ¹⁶At this, Daniel went in to the king and asked for time, so that he might interpret the dream for him.

¹⁷Then Daniel returned to his house and explained the matter to his friends Hananiah, Mishael and Azariah. ¹⁸He urged them to plead for mercy from the God of heaven concerning this mystery, so that he and his friends might not be executed with the rest of the wise men of Babylon. ¹⁹During the night the mystery was revealed to Daniel in a vision. Then Daniel praised the God of heaven ²⁰and said:

"Praise be to the name of God for ever
        and ever;
    wisdom and power are his.
²¹ He changes times and seasons;
    he deposes kings and raises up
        others.
He gives wisdom to the wise
    and knowledge to the discerning.
²² He reveals deep and hidden things;
    he knows what lies in darkness,
    and light dwells with him.
²³ I thank and praise you, God of my
        ancestors:
    You have given me wisdom and
        power,
    you have made known to me what we
        asked of you,
    you have made known to us the
        dream of the king."

Daniel Interprets the Dream

²⁴Then Daniel went to Arioch, whom the king had appointed to execute the wise men of Babylon, and said to him, "Do not execute the wise men of Babylon. Take me to the king, and I will interpret his dream for him."

²⁵Arioch took Daniel to the king at once and said, "I have found a man among the exiles from Judah who can tell the king what his dream means."

²⁶The king asked Daniel (also called Belteshazzar), "Are you able to tell me what I saw in my dream and interpret it?"

²⁷Daniel replied, "No wise man, enchanter, magician or diviner can explain to the king the mystery he has asked about, ²⁸but there is a God in heaven who reveals mysteries. He has shown King Nebuchadnezzar what will happen in days to come. Your dream and the visions that passed through your mind as you were lying in bed are these:

---

a 2 Or *Chaldeans;* also in verses 4, 5 and 10   *b 3* Or *was*   *c 4* At this point the Hebrew text has *in Aramaic,* indicating that the text from here through the end of chapter 7 is in Aramaic.

²⁹"As Your Majesty was lying there, your mind turned to things to come, and the revealer of mysteries showed you what is going to happen. ³⁰As for me, this mystery has been revealed to me, not because I have greater wisdom than anyone else alive, but so that Your Majesty may know the interpretation and that you may understand what went through your mind.

³¹"Your Majesty looked, and there before you stood a large statue—an enormous, dazzling statue, awesome in appearance. ³²The head of the statue was made of pure gold, its chest and arms of silver, its belly and thighs of bronze, ³³its legs of iron, its feet partly of iron and partly of baked clay. ³⁴While you were watching, a rock was cut out, but not by human hands. It struck the statue on its feet of iron and clay and smashed them. ³⁵Then the iron, the clay, the bronze, the silver and the gold were all broken to pieces and became like chaff on a threshing floor in the summer. The wind swept them away without leaving a trace. But the rock that struck the statue became a huge mountain and filled the whole earth.

³⁶"This was the dream, and now we will interpret it to the king. ³⁷Your Majesty, you are the king of kings. The God of heaven has given you dominion and power and might and glory; ³⁸in your hands he has placed all people everywhere and the beasts of the field and the birds in the sky. Wherever they live, he has made you ruler over them all. You are that head of gold.

³⁹"After you, another kingdom will arise, inferior to yours. Next, a third kingdom, one of bronze, will rule over the whole earth. ⁴⁰Finally, there will be a fourth kingdom, strong as iron—for iron breaks and smashes everything—and as iron breaks things to pieces, so it will crush and break all the others. ⁴¹Just as you saw that the feet and toes were partly of baked clay and partly of iron, so this will be a divided kingdom; yet it will have some of the strength of iron in it, even as you saw iron mixed with clay. ⁴²As the toes were partly iron and partly clay, so this kingdom will be partly strong and partly brittle. ⁴³And just as you saw the iron mixed with baked clay, so the people will be a mixture and will not remain united, any more than iron mixes with clay.

⁴⁴"In the time of those kings, the God of heaven will set up a kingdom that will never be destroyed, nor will it be left to another people. It will crush all those kingdoms and bring them to an end, but it will itself endure forever. ⁴⁵This is the meaning of the vision of the rock cut out of a mountain, but not by human hands—a rock that broke the iron, the bronze, the clay, the silver and the gold to pieces.

"The great God has shown the king what will take place in the future. The dream is true and its interpretation is trustworthy."

⁴⁶Then King Nebuchadnezzar fell prostrate before Daniel and paid him honor and ordered that an offering and incense be presented to him. ⁴⁷The king said to Daniel, "Surely your God is the God of gods and the Lord of kings and a revealer of mysteries, for you were able to reveal this mystery."

⁴⁸Then the king placed Daniel in a high position and lavished many gifts on him. He made him ruler over the entire province of Babylon and placed him in charge of all its wise men. ⁴⁹Moreover, at Daniel's request the king appointed Shadrach, Meshach and Abednego administrators over the province of Babylon, while Daniel himself remained at the royal court.

The Image of Gold and the Blazing Furnace

3 King Nebuchadnezzar made an image of gold, sixty cubits high and six cubits wide,ᵃ and set it up on the plain of Dura in the province of Babylon. ²He then summoned the satraps, prefects, governors, advisers, treasurers, judges, magistrates and all the other provincial officials to come to the dedication of the image he had set up. ³So the satraps, prefects, governors, advisers, treasurers, judges, magistrates and all the other provincial officials assembled for the dedication of the image that King Nebuchadnezzar had set up, and they stood before it.

⁴Then the herald loudly proclaimed, "Nations and peoples of every language, this is what you are commanded to do: ⁵As soon as you hear the sound of the horn, flute, zither, lyre, harp, pipe and all kinds of music, you must fall down and worship the image of gold that King Nebuchadnezzar has set up. ⁶Whoever does not fall down and worship

---

ᵃ 1 That is, about 90 feet high and 9 feet wide or about 27 meters high and 2.7 meters wide

THURSDAY

IN ETERNITY'S LIGHT
Daniel 3:1–30 *or* 3:16–18

Rick Warren

When you fully comprehend that there is more to life than just here and now, and you realize that life is just preparation for eternity, you will begin to live differently. You will start living in light of eternity, and that will color how you handle every relationship, task and circumstance. Suddenly many activities, goals and even problems that seemed so important will appear trivial, petty and unworthy of your attention. The closer you live to God, the smaller everything else appears.

JOHN BRIGHT {AD 1908–1995}

The Book of Daniel is . . . a mighty summons to courage and faith . . . Hold fast . . . For God is there! The Kingdom of God towers over the puny kingdoms of men! God is even now preparing to intervene, to destroy the evil powers of this earth, and to set up his Kingdom among his people who are faithful! . . .

We see it in the story of blameless Daniel (ch. 6), who though commanded to pray only to the king, would not do it, but prayed to his God even if it meant a lion's den—and God saved him. We see it in the story of Shadrach, Meshach, and Abednego (ch. 3) who went to a fiery furnace rather than bow down to Nebuchadnezzar's idol. Their answer to the king (vss. 16-18) rings out as a challenge to all God-fearing men: "[King Nebuchadnezzar, we do not need to defend ourselves before you in this matter. If the God we serve is able to deliver us, then he will deliver us from the blazing furnace and from Your Majesty's hand. But even if he does not, we want you to know, Your Majesty, that we will not serve your gods or worship the image of gold you have set up]" That is plain defiance! That is the categorical *no* with which man made in the image of God should give answer to the false god of the state . . .

Here, too, is utter confidence that the power of God looms over all earthly power . . . The triumph of the people of God in his Kingdom comes soon! Have courage! Do not fear to die for that Kingdom—for God will raise you to everlasting life.

reflection

1. In what ways has your perspective on life changed since you first understood who Jesus is?
2. What can Christians learn from Shadrach, Meshach and Abednego?
3. How can their example help you respond to the trials you are facing right now?

For your next devotional reading, go to page 980.

will immediately be thrown into a blazing furnace."

⁷Therefore, as soon as they heard the sound of the horn, flute, zither, lyre, harp and all kinds of music, all the nations and peoples of every language fell down and worshiped the image of gold that King Nebuchadnezzar had set up.

⁸At this time some astrologers*a* came forward and denounced the Jews. ⁹They said to King Nebuchadnezzar, "May the king live forever! ¹⁰Your Majesty has issued a decree that everyone who hears the sound of the horn, flute, zither, lyre, harp, pipe and all kinds of music must fall down and worship the image of gold, ¹¹and that whoever does not fall down and worship will be thrown into a blazing furnace. ¹²But there are some Jews whom you have set over the affairs of the province of Babylon—Shadrach, Meshach and Abednego—who pay no attention to you, Your Majesty. They neither serve your gods nor worship the image of gold you have set up."

¹³Furious with rage, Nebuchadnezzar summoned Shadrach, Meshach and Abednego. So these men were brought before the king, ¹⁴and Nebuchadnezzar said to them, "Is it true, Shadrach, Meshach and Abednego, that you do not serve my gods or worship the image of gold I have set up? ¹⁵Now when you hear the sound of the horn, flute, zither, lyre, harp, pipe and all kinds of music, if you are ready to fall down and worship the image I made, very good. But if you do not worship it, you will be thrown immediately into a blazing furnace. Then what god will be able to rescue you from my hand?"

¹⁶Shadrach, Meshach and Abednego replied to him, "King Nebuchadnezzar, we do not need to defend ourselves before you in this matter. ¹⁷If the God we serve is able to deliver us, then he will deliver us from the blazing furnace and from Your Majesty's hand. ¹⁸But even if he does not, we want you to know, Your Majesty, that we will not serve your gods or worship the image of gold you have set up."

¹⁹Then Nebuchadnezzar was furious with Shadrach, Meshach and Abednego, and his attitude toward them changed. He ordered the furnace heated seven times hotter than usual ²⁰and commanded some of the strongest soldiers in his army to tie up Shadrach, Meshach and Abednego and throw them into the blazing furnace. ²¹So these men, wearing their robes, trousers, turbans and other clothes, were bound and thrown into the blazing furnace. ²²The king's command was so urgent and the furnace so hot that the flames of the fire killed the soldiers who took up Shadrach, Meshach and Abednego, ²³and these three men, firmly tied, fell into the blazing furnace.

²⁴Then King Nebuchadnezzar leaped to his feet in amazement and asked his advisers, "Weren't there three men that we tied up and threw into the fire?"

They replied, "Certainly, Your Majesty."

²⁵He said, "Look! I see four men walking around in the fire, unbound and unharmed, and the fourth looks like a son of the gods."

²⁶Nebuchadnezzar then approached the opening of the blazing furnace and shouted, "Shadrach, Meshach and Abednego, servants of the Most High God, come out! Come here!"

So Shadrach, Meshach and Abednego came out of the fire, ²⁷and the satraps, prefects, governors and royal advisers crowded around them. They saw that the fire had not harmed their bodies, nor was a hair of their heads singed; their robes were not scorched, and there was no smell of fire on them.

²⁸Then Nebuchadnezzar said, "Praise be to the God of Shadrach, Meshach and Abednego, who has sent his angel and rescued his servants! They trusted in him and defied the king's command and were willing to give up their lives rather than serve or worship any god except their own God. ²⁹Therefore I decree that the people of any nation or language who say anything against the God of Shadrach, Meshach and Abednego be cut into pieces and their houses be turned into piles of rubble, for no other god can save in this way."

³⁰Then the king promoted Shadrach, Meshach and Abednego in the province of Babylon.

Nebuchadnezzar's Dream of a Tree

4 *King Nebuchadnezzar,

To the nations and peoples of every language, who live in all the earth:

---

a 8 Or *Chaldeans*

* 4:1-3 is numbered 3:31-33 in Aramaic texts.

FRIDAY

REMEMBER: WE ARE NOT GOD

Daniel 4:1–37 or 4:34–37

Steve Case

One of the hardest things for us to get through our heads is that we are not God. We don't get to make the decisions. We don't get to decide what is and what isn't. We have some power, but not complete power over nature. Every time we start to push the limits of God, He gives us a little reminder. Does the phrase "even God couldn't sink this ship" ring any bells? . . . We get mad at God because grandma died. We get mad at God because we didn't get the girl/boy we were after. We get mad at God because we lost a job. We get mad at God because He didn't answer our prayer for that new car.

In order to fully experience the presence of God, we have to get over the fact that God is God and we are not.

When we get down life's road a little more, we often find out what God had in mind. We didn't get that job we wanted and then found a better one six months down the road. We finally realized how much pain grandma was in, and it wasn't God who made her suffer—it was God who let her suffering end. And if we really want to stand on the mountaintop and scream at God because of the car, we might want to sit down and re-evaluate our priorities.

MADAME GUYON {AD 1648–1717}

If you are fully convinced that it is on the "nothing" in humans that God establishes his greatest works, you will be in part guarded against disappointment or surprise. For when God is about to construct his sacred temple in us, He first totally demolishes the vain and pompous structure that our own human art and power had erected. From its horrible ruins he forms a new structure by his power alone. He destroys in order that he might build.

Oh, that you could comprehend the depth of this mystery and learn the secrets of the conduct of God. It has been revealed to babes but hidden from the wise and great of this world. For they think of themselves as the Lord's counselors, capable of investigating his procedures . . . They think their own intelligence and inherent abilities can raise them up to heaven, and they think they can comprehend the height and depth and length and breadth of God. Yet this divine wisdom is unknown, even to those who pass in the world for persons of extraordinary illumination and knowledge.

reflection

1. Do you sometimes have trouble remembering that God is God and you're not?

2. No matter what anyone says, we're *not* equal with God. Can you think of some examples that illustrate that point?

3. What are the benefits of remembering that you're not God?

For your next devotional reading, go to page 985.

May you prosper greatly!

²It is my pleasure to tell you about the miraculous signs and wonders that the Most High God has performed for me.

³How great are his signs,
how mighty his wonders!
His kingdom is an eternal
kingdom;
his dominion endures from
generation to generation.

*⁴I, Nebuchadnezzar, was at home in my palace, contented and prosperous. ⁵I had a dream that made me afraid. As I was lying in bed, the images and visions that passed through my mind terrified me. ⁶So I commanded that all the wise men of Babylon be brought before me to interpret the dream for me. ⁷When the magicians, enchanters, astrologers^a and diviners came, I told them the dream, but they could not interpret it for me. ⁸Finally, Daniel came into my presence and I told him the dream. (He is called Belteshazzar, after the name of my god, and the spirit of the holy gods is in him.)

⁹I said, "Belteshazzar, chief of the magicians, I know that the spirit of the holy gods is in you, and no mystery is too difficult for you. Here is my dream; interpret it for me. ¹⁰These are the visions I saw while lying in bed: I looked, and there before me stood a tree in the middle of the land. Its height was enormous. ¹¹The tree grew large and strong and its top touched the sky; it was visible to the ends of the earth. ¹²Its leaves were beautiful, its fruit abundant, and on it was food for all. Under it the wild animals found shelter, and the birds lived in its branches; from it every creature was fed.

¹³"In the visions I saw while lying in bed, I looked, and there before me was a holy one, a messenger,^b coming down from heaven. ¹⁴He called in a loud voice: 'Cut down the tree and trim off its branches; strip off its leaves and scatter its fruit. Let the animals flee

from under it and the birds from its branches. ¹⁵But let the stump and its roots, bound with iron and bronze, remain in the ground, in the grass of the field.

" 'Let him be drenched with the dew of heaven, and let him live with the animals among the plants of the earth. ¹⁶Let his mind be changed from that of a human being and let him be given the mind of an animal, till seven times^c pass by for him.

¹⁷" 'The decision is announced by messengers, the holy ones declare the verdict, so that the living may know that the Most High is sovereign over the kingdoms on earth and gives them to anyone he wishes and sets over them the lowliest of people.'

¹⁸"This is the dream that I, King Nebuchadnezzar, had. Now, Belteshazzar, tell me what it means, for none of the wise men in my kingdom can interpret it for me. But you can, because the spirit of the holy gods is in you."

Daniel Interprets the Dream

¹⁹Then Daniel (also called Belteshazzar) was greatly perplexed for a time, and his thoughts terrified him. So the king said, "Belteshazzar, do not let the dream or its meaning alarm you."

Belteshazzar answered, "My lord, if only the dream applied to your enemies and its meaning to your adversaries! ²⁰The tree you saw, which grew large and strong, with its top touching the sky, visible to the whole earth, ²¹with beautiful leaves and abundant fruit, providing food for all, giving shelter to the wild animals, and having nesting places in its branches for the birds— ²²Your Majesty, you are that tree! You have become great and strong; your greatness has grown until it reaches the sky, and your dominion extends to distant parts of the earth.

²³"Your Majesty saw a holy one, a messenger, coming down from heaven and saying, 'Cut down the tree and destroy it, but leave the stump, bound

---

^a 7 Or *Chaldeans*   ^b 13 Or *watchman*; also in verses 17 and 23   ^c 16 Or *years*; also in verses 23, 25 and 32

* 4:4-37 is numbered 4:1-34 in Aramaic texts.

with iron and bronze, in the grass of the field, while its roots remain in the ground. Let him be drenched with the dew of heaven; let him live with the wild animals, until seven times pass by for him.'

²⁴"This is the interpretation, Your Majesty, and this is the decree the Most High has issued against my lord the king: ²⁵You will be driven away from people and will live with the wild animals; you will eat grass like the ox and be drenched with the dew of heaven. Seven times will pass by for you until you acknowledge that the Most High is sovereign over the kingdoms on earth and gives them to anyone he wishes. ²⁶The command to leave the stump of the tree with its roots means that your kingdom will be restored to you when you acknowledge that Heaven rules. ²⁷Therefore, Your Majesty, be pleased to accept my advice: Renounce your sins by doing what is right, and your wickedness by being kind to the oppressed. It may be that then your prosperity will continue."

The Dream Is Fulfilled

²⁸All this happened to King Nebuchadnezzar. ²⁹Twelve months later, as the king was walking on the roof of the royal palace of Babylon, ³⁰he said, "Is not this the great Babylon I have built as the royal residence, by my mighty power and for the glory of my majesty?"

³¹Even as the words were on his lips, a voice came from heaven, "This is what is decreed for you, King Nebuchadnezzar: Your royal authority has been taken from you. ³²You will be driven away from people and will live with the wild animals; you will eat grass like the ox. Seven times will pass by for you until you acknowledge that the Most High is sovereign over the kingdoms on earth and gives them to anyone he wishes."

³³Immediately what had been said about Nebuchadnezzar was fulfilled. He was driven away from people and ate grass like the ox. His body was drenched with the dew of heaven until his hair grew like the feathers of an eagle and his nails like the claws of a bird.

³⁴At the end of that time, I, Nebuchadnezzar, raised my eyes toward heaven, and my sanity was restored. Then I praised the Most High; I honored and glorified him who lives forever.

His dominion is an eternal dominion;
    his kingdom endures from generation
        to generation.
³⁵All the peoples of the earth
    are regarded as nothing.
He does as he pleases
    with the powers of heaven
    and the peoples of the earth.
No one can hold back his hand
    or say to him: "What have you done?"

³⁶At the same time that my sanity was restored, my honor and splendor were returned to me for the glory of my kingdom. My advisers and nobles sought me out, and I was restored to my throne and became even greater than before. ³⁷Now I, Nebuchadnezzar, praise and exalt and glorify the King of heaven, because everything he does is right and all his ways are just. And those who walk in pride he is able to humble.

The Writing on the Wall

5 King Belshazzar gave a great banquet for a thousand of his nobles and drank wine with them. ²While Belshazzar was drinking his wine, he gave orders to bring in the gold and silver goblets that Nebuchadnezzar his fatherᵃ had taken from the temple in Jerusalem, so that the king and his nobles, his wives and his concubines might drink from them. ³So they brought in the gold goblets that had been taken from the temple of God in Jerusalem, and the king and his nobles, his wives and his concubines drank from them. ⁴As they drank the wine, they praised the gods of gold and silver, of bronze, iron, wood and stone.

⁵Suddenly the fingers of a human hand appeared and wrote on the plaster of the wall, near the lampstand in the royal palace. The king watched the hand as it wrote. ⁶His face turned pale and he was so frightened

---

ᵃ 2 Or *ancestor*; or *predecessor*; also in verses 11, 13 and 18 that his legs became weak and his knees were knocking.

[7] The king summoned the enchanters, astrologers[a] and diviners. Then he said to these wise men of Babylon, "Whoever reads this writing and tells me what it means will be clothed in purple and have a gold chain placed around his neck, and he will be made the third highest ruler in the kingdom."

[8] Then all the king's wise men came in, but they could not read the writing or tell the king what it meant. [9] So King Belshazzar became even more terrified and his face grew more pale. His nobles were baffled.

[10] The queen,[b] hearing the voices of the king and his nobles, came into the banquet hall. "May the king live forever!" she said. "Don't be alarmed! Don't look so pale! [11] There is a man in your kingdom who has the spirit of the holy gods in him. In the time of your father he was found to have insight and intelligence and wisdom like that of the gods. Your father, King Nebuchadnezzar, appointed him chief of the magicians, enchanters, astrologers and diviners. [12] He did this because Daniel, whom the king called Belteshazzar, was found to have a keen mind and knowledge and understanding, and also the ability to interpret dreams, explain riddles and solve difficult problems. Call for Daniel, and he will tell you what the writing means."

[13] So Daniel was brought before the king, and the king said to him, "Are you Daniel, one of the exiles my father the king brought from Judah? [14] I have heard that the spirit of the gods is in you and that you have insight, intelligence and outstanding wisdom. [15] The wise men and enchanters were brought before me to read this writing and tell me what it means, but they could not explain it. [16] Now I have heard that you are able to give interpretations and to solve difficult problems. If you can read this writing and tell me what it means, you will be clothed in purple and have a gold chain placed around your neck, and you will be made the third highest ruler in the kingdom."

[17] Then Daniel answered the king, "You may keep your gifts for yourself and give your rewards to someone else. Nevertheless, I will read the writing for the king and tell him what it means.

[18] "Your Majesty, the Most High God gave your father Nebuchadnezzar sovereignty and greatness and glory and splendor. [19] Because of the high position he gave him, all the nations and peoples of every language dreaded and feared him. Those the king wanted to put to death, he put to death; those he wanted to spare, he spared; those he wanted to promote, he promoted; and those he wanted to humble, he humbled. [20] But when his heart became arrogant and hardened with pride, he was deposed from his royal throne and stripped of his glory. [21] He was driven away from people and given the mind of an animal; he lived with the wild donkeys and ate grass like the ox; and his body was drenched with the dew of heaven, until he acknowledged that the Most High God is sovereign over the kingdoms on earth and sets over them anyone he wishes.

[22] "But you, Belshazzar, his son,[c] have not humbled yourself, though you knew all this. [23] Instead, you have set yourself up against the Lord of heaven. You had the goblets from his temple brought to you, and you and your nobles, your wives and your concubines drank wine from them. You praised the gods of silver and gold, of bronze, iron, wood and stone, which cannot see or hear or understand. But you did not honor the God who holds in his hand your life and all your ways. [24] Therefore he sent the hand that wrote the inscription.

[25] "This is the inscription that was written:

MENE, MENE, TEKEL, PARSIN

[26] "This is what these words mean:

Mene[d]: God has numbered the days of your reign and brought it to an end.
[27] Tekel[e]: You have been weighed on the scales and found wanting.
[28] Peres[f]: Your kingdom is divided and given to the Medes and Persians."

[29] Then at Belshazzar's command, Daniel was clothed in purple, a gold chain was placed around his neck, and he was proclaimed the third highest ruler in the kingdom.

---

[a] 7 Or Chaldeans; also in verse 11   [b] 10 Or queen mother   [c] 22 Or descendant; or successor
[d] 26 Mene can mean numbered or mina (a unit of money).   [e] 27 Tekel can mean weighed or shekel.
[f] 28 Peres (the singular of Parsin) can mean divided or Persia or a half mina or a half shekel.

[30]That very night Belshazzar, king of the Babylonians,[a] was slain, [*31]and Darius the Mede took over the kingdom, at the age of sixty-two.

Daniel in the Den of Lions

6 [*]It pleased Darius to appoint 120 satraps to rule throughout the kingdom, [2]with three administrators over them, one of whom was Daniel. The satraps were made accountable to them so that the king might not suffer loss. [3]Now Daniel so distinguished himself among the administrators and the satraps by his exceptional qualities that the king planned to set him over the whole kingdom. [4]At this, the administrators and the satraps tried to find grounds for charges against Daniel in his conduct of government affairs, but they were unable to do so. They could find no corruption in him, because he was trustworthy and neither corrupt nor negligent. [5]Finally these men said, "We will never find any basis for charges against this man Daniel unless it has something to do with the law of his God."

[6]So these administrators and satraps went as a group to the king and said: "May King Darius live forever! [7]The royal administrators, prefects, satraps, advisers and governors have all agreed that the king should issue an edict and enforce the decree that anyone who prays to any god or human being during the next thirty days, except to you, Your Majesty, shall be thrown into the lions' den. [8]Now, Your Majesty, issue the decree and put it in writing so that it cannot be altered—in accordance with the law of the Medes and Persians, which cannot be repealed." [9]So King Darius put the decree in writing.

[10]Now when Daniel learned that the decree had been published, he went home to his upstairs room where the windows opened toward Jerusalem. Three times a day he got down on his knees and prayed, giving thanks to his God, just as he had done before. [11]Then these men went as a group and found Daniel praying and asking God for help. [12]So they went to the king and spoke to him about his royal decree: "Did you not publish a decree that during the next thirty days anyone who prays to any god or human being except to you, Your Majesty, would be thrown into the lions' den?"

The king answered, "The decree stands—in accordance with the law of the Medes and Persians, which cannot be repealed."

[13]Then they said to the king, "Daniel, who is one of the exiles from Judah, pays no attention to you, Your Majesty, or to the decree you put in writing. He still prays three times a day." [14]When the king heard this, he was greatly distressed; he was determined to rescue Daniel and made every effort until sundown to save him.

[15]Then the men went as a group to King Darius and said to him, "Remember, Your Majesty, that according to the law of the Medes and Persians no decree or edict that the king issues can be changed."

[16]So the king gave the order, and they brought Daniel and threw him into the lions' den. The king said to Daniel, "May your God, whom you serve continually, rescue you!"

[17]A stone was brought and placed over the mouth of the den, and the king sealed it with his own signet ring and with the rings of his nobles, so that Daniel's situation might not be changed. [18]Then the king returned to his palace and spent the night without eating and without any entertainment being brought to him. And he could not sleep.

[19]At the first light of dawn, the king got up and hurried to the lions' den. [20]When he came near the den, he called to Daniel in an anguished voice, "Daniel, servant of the living God, has your God, whom you serve continually, been able to rescue you from the lions?"

[21]Daniel answered, "May the king live forever! [22]My God sent his angel, and he shut the mouths of the lions. They have not hurt me, because I was found innocent in his sight. Nor have I ever done any wrong before you, Your Majesty."

[23]The king was overjoyed and gave orders to lift Daniel out of the den. And when Daniel was lifted from the den, no wound was found on him, because he had trusted in his God.

[24]At the king's command, the men who had falsely accused Daniel were brought in and thrown into the lions' den, along with

---

a 30 Or Chaldeans

* 5:31 is numbered 6:1 in Aramaic texts.   * 6:1-28 is numbered 6:2-29 in Aramaic texts.

God Steps In

Daniel 6:21-27

read/meditate

Read Daniel 6:21-27 and recall anything you know about Daniel's life. This man definitely experienced signs and wonders: He was saved from hungry lions. His friends were saved from a fiery furnace. What signs and wonders have you witnessed? What events, small or large, can only be explained as supernatural?

pray

As you think back through the times in your life that have revealed God's influence, share your gratitude (or other feelings) with God about those times. Do you feel the need to see his hand in your life right now? Ask him for eyes that can see his work.

contemplate

Life goes by in such a rush that we often miss the moments when God's face is revealed. Who knows from what calamity we've been rescued when we didn't even see the lions? Contemplate your life. Set your intentions to be aware of God's presence in every situation.

additional reflection

Never again are we to look at the stars, as we did when we were children, and wonder how far it is to God . . . A god who created, and withdrew, could be mighty, but he could not be love. Who could love a God remote, when suffering is our lot? Our God is closer than our problems, for they are out there, to be faced; He is here, beside us, Emmanuel.

—*Joseph E. McCabe*

God turns the ordinary into the extraordinary.

—*Erwin Tippel*

For your next devotional reading, go to page 989.

their wives and children. And before they reached the floor of the den, the lions overpowered them and crushed all their bones.

²⁵Then King Darius wrote to all the nations and peoples of every language in all the earth:

"May you prosper greatly!

²⁶"I issue a decree that in every part of my kingdom people must fear and reverence the God of Daniel.

"For he is the living God
and he endures forever;
his kingdom will not be destroyed,
his dominion will never end.
²⁷He rescues and he saves;
he performs signs and wonders
in the heavens and on the earth.
He has rescued Daniel
from the power of the lions."

²⁸So Daniel prospered during the reign of Darius and the reign of Cyrus*a* the Persian.

Daniel's Dream of Four Beasts

7 In the first year of Belshazzar king of Babylon, Daniel had a dream, and visions passed through his mind as he was lying in bed. He wrote down the substance of his dream.

²Daniel said: "In my vision at night I looked, and there before me were the four winds of heaven churning up the great sea. ³Four great beasts, each different from the others, came up out of the sea.

⁴"The first was like a lion, and it had the wings of an eagle. I watched until its wings were torn off and it was lifted from the ground so that it stood on two feet like a human being, and a human mind was given to it.

⁵"And there before me was a second beast, which looked like a bear. It was raised up on one of its sides, and it had three ribs in its mouth between its teeth. It was told, 'Get up and eat your fill of flesh!'

⁶"After that, I looked, and there before me was another beast, one that looked like a leopard. And on its back it had four wings like those of a bird. This beast had four heads, and it was given authority to rule.

⁷"After that, in my vision at night I looked,

and there before me was a fourth beast—terrifying and frightening and very powerful. It had large iron teeth; it crushed and devoured its victims and trampled underfoot whatever was left. It was different from all the former beasts, and it had ten horns.

⁸"While I was thinking about the horns, there before me was another horn, a little one, which came up among them; and three of the first horns were uprooted before it. This horn had eyes like the eyes of a human being and a mouth that spoke boastfully.

⁹"As I looked,

"thrones were set in place,
and the Ancient of Days took his seat.
His clothing was as white as snow;
the hair of his head was white like
wool.
His throne was flaming with fire,
and its wheels were all ablaze.
¹⁰A river of fire was flowing,
coming out from before him.
Thousands upon thousands attended him;
ten thousand times ten thousand
stood before him.
The court was seated,
and the books were opened.

¹¹"Then I continued to watch because of the boastful words the horn was speaking. I kept looking until the beast was slain and its body destroyed and thrown into the blazing fire. ¹²(The other beasts had been stripped of their authority, but were allowed to live for a period of time.)

¹³"In my vision at night I looked, and there before me was one like a son of man,*b* coming with the clouds of heaven. He approached the Ancient of Days and was led into his presence. ¹⁴He was given authority, glory and sovereign power; all nations and peoples of every language worshiped him. His dominion is an everlasting dominion that will not pass away, and his kingdom is one that will never be destroyed.

The Interpretation of the Dream

¹⁵"I, Daniel, was troubled in spirit, and the visions that passed through my mind disturbed me. ¹⁶I approached one of those standing there and asked him the meaning of all this.

---

a 28 Or *Darius, that is, the reign of Cyrus*   *b* 13 The Aramaic phrase *bar enash* means *human being*. The phrase *son of man* is retained as a form of address here because of its traditional associations.

"So he told me and gave me the interpretation of these things: [17]'The four great beasts are four kings that will rise from the earth. [18]But the holy people of the Most High will receive the kingdom and will possess it forever—yes, for ever and ever.'

[19]"Then I wanted to know the meaning of the fourth beast, which was different from all the others and most terrifying, with its iron teeth and bronze claws—the beast that crushed and devoured its victims and trampled underfoot whatever was left. [20]I also wanted to know about the ten horns on its head and about the other horn that came up, before which three of them fell—the horn that looked more imposing than the others and that had eyes and a mouth that spoke boastfully. [21]As I watched, this horn was waging war against the holy people and defeating them, [22]until the Ancient of Days came and pronounced judgment in favor of the holy people of the Most High, and the time came when they possessed the kingdom.

[23]"He gave me this explanation: 'The fourth beast is a fourth kingdom that will appear on earth. It will be different from all the other kingdoms and will devour the whole earth, trampling it down and crushing it. [24]The ten horns are ten kings who will come from this kingdom. After them another king will arise, different from the earlier ones; he will subdue three kings. [25]He will speak against the Most High and oppress his holy people and try to change the set times and the laws. The holy people will be delivered into his hands for a time, times and half a time.[a]

[26]" 'But the court will sit, and his power will be taken away and completely destroyed forever. [27]Then the sovereignty, power and greatness of all the kingdoms under heaven will be handed over to the holy people of the Most High. His kingdom will be an everlasting kingdom, and all rulers will worship and obey him.'

[28]"This is the end of the matter. I, Daniel, was deeply troubled by my thoughts, and my face turned pale, but I kept the matter to myself."

Daniel's Vision of a Ram and a Goat

8 In the third year of King Belshazzar's reign, I, Daniel, had a vision, after the one that had already appeared to me. [2]In my vision I saw myself in the citadel of Susa in the province of Elam; in the vision I was beside the Ulai Canal. [3]I looked up, and there before me was a ram with two horns, standing beside the canal, and the horns were long. One of the horns was longer than the other but grew up later. [4]I watched the ram as it charged toward the west and the north and the south. No animal could stand against it, and none could rescue from its power. It did as it pleased and became great.

[5]As I was thinking about this, suddenly a goat with a prominent horn between its eyes came from the west, crossing the whole earth without touching the ground. [6]It came toward the two-horned ram I had seen standing beside the canal and charged at it in great rage. [7]I saw it attack the ram furiously, striking the ram and shattering its two horns. The ram was powerless to stand against it; the goat knocked it to the ground and trampled on it, and none could rescue the ram from its power. [8]The goat became very great, but at the height of its power the large horn was broken off, and in its place four prominent horns grew up toward the four winds of heaven.

[9]Out of one of them came another horn, which started small but grew in power to the south and to the east and toward the Beautiful Land. [10]It grew until it reached the host of the heavens, and it threw some of the starry host down to the earth and trampled on them. [11]It set itself up to be as great as the commander of the army of the LORD; it took away the daily sacrifice from the LORD, and his sanctuary was thrown down. [12]Because of rebellion, the LORD's people[b] and the daily sacrifice were given over to it. It prospered in everything it did, and truth was thrown to the ground.

[13]Then I heard a holy one speaking, and another holy one said to him, "How long will it take for the vision to be fulfilled—the vision concerning the daily sacrifice, the rebellion that causes desolation, the surrender of the sanctuary and the trampling underfoot of the LORD's people?"

[14]He said to me, "It will take 2,300 evenings and mornings; then the sanctuary will be reconsecrated."

---

[a] 25 Or for a year, two years and half a year   [b] 12 Or rebellion, the armies

The Interpretation of the Vision

¹⁵While I, Daniel, was watching the vision and trying to understand it, there before me stood one who looked like a man. ¹⁶And I heard a man's voice from the Ulai calling, "Gabriel, tell this man the meaning of the vision."

¹⁷As he came near the place where I was standing, I was terrified and fell prostrate. "Son of man,"ᵃ he said to me, "understand that the vision concerns the time of the end."

¹⁸While he was speaking to me, I was in a deep sleep, with my face to the ground. Then he touched me and raised me to my feet.

¹⁹He said: "I am going to tell you what will happen later in the time of wrath, because the vision concerns the appointed time of the end.ᵇ ²⁰The two-horned ram that you saw represents the kings of Media and Persia. ²¹The shaggy goat is the king of Greece, and the large horn between its eyes is the first king. ²²The four horns that replaced the one that was broken off represent four kingdoms that will emerge from his nation but will not have the same power.

²³"In the latter part of their reign, when rebels have become completely wicked, a fierce-looking king, a master of intrigue, will arise. ²⁴He will become very strong, but not by his own power. He will cause astounding devastation and will succeed in whatever he does. He will destroy the mighty warriors, the holy people. ²⁵He will cause deceit to prosper, and he will consider himself superior. When they feel secure, he will destroy many and take his stand against the Prince of princes. Yet he will be destroyed, but not by human power.

²⁶"The vision of the evenings and mornings that has been given you is true, but seal up the vision, for it concerns the distant future."

²⁷I, Daniel, was worn out. I lay exhausted for several days. Then I got up and went about the king's business. I was appalled by the vision; it was beyond understanding.

Daniel's Prayer

9 In the first year of Darius son of Xerxesᶜ (a Mede by descent), who was made ruler over the Babylonianᵈ kingdom— ²in the first year of his reign, I, Daniel, understood from the Scriptures, according to the word of the LORD given to Jeremiah the prophet, that the desolation of Jerusalem would last seventy years. ³So I turned to the Lord God and pleaded with him in prayer and petition, in fasting, and in sackcloth and ashes.

⁴I prayed to the LORD my God and confessed:

"Lord, the great and awesome God, who keeps his covenant of love with those who love him and keep his commandments, ⁵we have sinned and done wrong. We have been wicked and have rebelled; we have turned away from your commands and laws. ⁶We have not listened to your servants the prophets, who spoke in your name to our kings, our princes and our ancestors, and to all the people of the land.

⁷"Lord, you are righteous, but this day we are covered with shame—the people of Judah and Jerusalem and all Israel, both near and far, in all the countries where you have scattered us because of our unfaithfulness to you. ⁸We and our kings, our princes and our ancestors are covered with shame, LORD, because we have sinned against you. ⁹The Lord our God is merciful and forgiving, even though we have rebelled against him; ¹⁰we have not obeyed the LORD our God or kept the laws he gave us through his servants the prophets. ¹¹All Israel has transgressed your law and turned away, refusing to obey you.

"Therefore the curses and sworn judgments written in the Law of Moses, the servant of God, have been poured out on us, because we have sinned against you. ¹²You have fulfilled the words spoken against us and against our rulers by bringing on us great disaster. Under the whole heaven nothing has ever been done like what has been done to Jerusalem. ¹³Just as it is written in the Law of Moses, all this disaster has come on us, yet we have not sought the favor of the LORD our

---

ᵃ 17 The Hebrew phrase *ben adam* means *human being*. The phrase *son of man* is retained as a form of address here because of its traditional associations.   ᵇ 19 Or *because the end will be at the appointed time*   ᶜ 1 Hebrew *Ahasuerus*   ᵈ 1 Or *Chaldean*

MONDAY

THE HOPE OF SUFFERING
Daniel 9:1–19 *or* 9:17–19

A. B. SIMPSON {AD 1843–1902}

The pressure of hard places makes us value life. Every time our life is given back to us from such a trial, it is like a new beginning, and we learn better how much it is worth, and make more of it for God and man. The pressure helps us to understand the trials of others, and fits us to help and sympathize with them . . .

Trials and hard places are needed to press us forward, even as the furnace fires in the hold of that mighty ship give force that moves the piston, drives the engine and propels that great vessel across the sea in the face of the winds and waves.

Mary Kassian

My children used to build domino chains on the kitchen floor. They'd knock down that first domino and set off the chain reaction until the last one collapsed . . . [In the New Testament] Paul describes a chain reaction that's put into motion when we respond to trials in the right way. The chain begins with suffering but ends with hope.

Suffering (or *tribulations*, in some Bible translations) is translated from the Greek word *thlipsis*, which means "pressing, pressure." The term was used of squeezing olives in a press to extract the oil or squeezing grapes to extract the juice. When we are "squeezed" by suffering, the Lord extracts perseverance from us.

Perseverance is a spiritual fortitude that bears up under, and is made even stronger by, suffering. It's the marathon runner's resolve to keep running to the end . . .

It is in suffering that we exercise hope by persevering and by being tested and proved pure in the middle of seemingly hopeless circumstances. This process results in an even deeper conviction of the reality and certainty of that for which we hope (see Romans 4:18–19).

When we feel the pain of that first domino's fall, we can be confident that when the last one falls, Jesus Christ will have produced in us a deeper certainty in his goodness and love and in our destiny as children of God.

reflection

1. How did Daniel's suffering deepen his faith and hope in God?

2. Think about the difficult things in your life. In what ways have those things shaped who you are today?

3. God intends to use suffering in the lives of his children for good—to encourage them, drive them, purify them, strengthen them and deepen their faith. But have you ever seen someone whose suffering only left them bitter, angry, hard and alienated? What do you think happened?

For your next devotional reading, go to page 995.

God by turning from our sins and giving attention to your truth. ¹⁴The Lord did not hesitate to bring the disaster on us, for the Lord our God is righteous in everything he does; yet we have not obeyed him.

¹⁵"Now, Lord our God, who brought your people out of Egypt with a mighty hand and who made for yourself a name that endures to this day, we have sinned, we have done wrong. ¹⁶Lord, in keeping with all your righteous acts, turn away your anger and your wrath from Jerusalem, your city, your holy hill. Our sins and the iniquities of our ancestors have made Jerusalem and your people an object of scorn to all those around us.

¹⁷"Now, our God, hear the prayers and petitions of your servant. For your sake, Lord, look with favor on your desolate sanctuary. ¹⁸Give ear, our God, and hear; open your eyes and see the desolation of the city that bears your Name. We do not make requests of you because we are righteous, but because of your great mercy. ¹⁹Lord, listen! Lord, forgive! Lord, hear and act! For your sake, my God, do not delay, because your city and your people bear your Name."

The Seventy "Sevens"

²⁰While I was speaking and praying, confessing my sin and the sin of my people Israel and making my request to the Lord my God for his holy hill— ²¹while I was still in prayer, Gabriel, the man I had seen in the earlier vision, came to me in swift flight about the time of the evening sacrifice. ²²He instructed me and said to me, "Daniel, I have now come to give you insight and understanding. ²³As soon as you began to pray, a word went out, which I have come to tell you, for you are highly esteemed. Therefore, consider the word and understand the vision:

²⁴"Seventy 'sevens'ᵃ are decreed for your people and your holy city to finishᵇ transgression, to put an end to sin, to atone for wickedness, to bring in everlasting righteousness, to seal up vision and prophecy and to anoint the Most Holy Place.ᶜ

²⁵"Know and understand this: From the time the word goes out to restore and rebuild Jerusalem until the Anointed One,ᵈ the ruler, comes, there will be seven 'sevens,' and sixty-two 'sevens.' It will be rebuilt with streets and a trench, but in times of trouble. ²⁶After the sixty-two 'sevens,' the Anointed One will be put to death and will have nothing.ᵉ The people of the ruler who will come will destroy the city and the sanctuary. The end will come like a flood: War will continue until the end, and desolations have been decreed. ²⁷He will confirm a covenant with many for one 'seven.'ᶠ In the middle of the 'seven'ᶠ he will put an end to sacrifice and offering. And at the templeᵍ he will set up an abomination that causes desolation, until the end that is decreed is poured out on him.ʰ"ⁱ

Daniel's Vision of a Man

10 In the third year of Cyrus king of Persia, a revelation was given to Daniel (who was called Belteshazzar). Its message was true and it concerned a great war.ʲ The understanding of the message came to him in a vision.

²At that time I, Daniel, mourned for three weeks. ³I ate no choice food; no meat or wine touched my lips; and I used no lotions at all until the three weeks were over.

⁴On the twenty-fourth day of the first month, as I was standing on the bank of the great river, the Tigris, ⁵I looked up and there before me was a man dressed in linen, with a belt of fine gold from Uphaz around his waist. ⁶His body was like topaz, his face like lightning, his eyes like flaming torches, his arms and legs like the gleam of burnished bronze, and his voice like the sound of a multitude.

⁷I, Daniel, was the only one who saw the vision; those who were with me did not see it, but such terror overwhelmed them that they fled and hid themselves. ⁸So I was left alone, gazing at this great vision; I had no strength left, my face turned deathly pale

---

ᵃ 24 Or 'weeks'; also in verses 25 and 26   ᵇ 24 Or restrain   ᶜ 24 Or the most holy One   ᵈ 25 Or an anointed one; also in verse 26   ᵉ 26 Or death and will have no one; or death, but not for himself   ᶠ 27 Or 'week'   ᵍ 27 Septuagint and Theodotion; Hebrew wing   ʰ 27 Or it   ⁱ 27 Or And one who causes desolation will come upon the wing of the abominable ⌊temple⌋, until the end that is decreed is poured out on the desolated ⌊city⌋   ʲ 1 Or true and burdensome and I was helpless. ⁹Then I heard him speaking, and as I listened to him, I fell into a deep sleep, my face to the ground.

¹⁰A hand touched me and set me trembling on my hands and knees. ¹¹He said, "Daniel, you who are highly esteemed, consider carefully the words I am about to speak to you, and stand up, for I have now been sent to you." And when he said this to me, I stood up trembling.

¹²Then he continued, "Do not be afraid, Daniel. Since the first day that you set your mind to gain understanding and to humble yourself before your God, your words were heard, and I have come in response to them. ¹³But the prince of the Persian kingdom resisted me twenty-one days. Then Michael, one of the chief princes, came to help me, because I was detained there with the king of Persia. ¹⁴Now I have come to explain to you what will happen to your people in the future, for the vision concerns a time yet to come."

¹⁵While he was saying this to me, I bowed with my face toward the ground and was speechless. ¹⁶Then one who looked like a man*a* touched my lips, and I opened my mouth and began to speak. I said to the one standing before me, "I am overcome with anguish because of the vision, my lord, and I feel very weak. ¹⁷How can I, your servant, talk with you, my lord? My strength is gone and I can hardly breathe."

¹⁸Again the one who looked like a man touched me and gave me strength. ¹⁹"Do not be afraid, you who are highly esteemed," he said. "Peace! Be strong now; be strong."

When he spoke to me, I was strengthened and said, "Speak, my lord, since you have given me strength."

²⁰So he said, "Do you know why I have come to you? Soon I will return to fight against the prince of Persia, and when I go, the prince of Greece will come; ²¹but first I will tell you what is written in the Book of Truth. (No one supports me against them except Michael, your prince. ¹And in the first year of Darius the Mede, I took my stand to support and protect him.)

The Kings of the South and the North

²"Now then, I tell you the truth: Three more kings will arise in Persia, and then a fourth, who will be far richer than all the others. When he has gained power by his wealth, he will stir up everyone against the kingdom of Greece. ³Then a mighty king will arise, who will rule with great power and do as he pleases. ⁴After he has arisen, his empire will be broken up and parceled out toward the four winds of heaven. It will not go to his descendants, nor will it have the power he exercised, because his empire will be uprooted and given to others.

⁵"The king of the South will become strong, but one of his commanders will become even stronger than he and will rule his own kingdom with great power. ⁶After some years, they will become allies. The daughter of the king of the South will go to the king of the North to make an alliance, but she will not retain her power, and he and his power*b* will not last. In those days she will be betrayed, together with her royal escort and her father*c* and the one who supported her.

⁷"One from her family line will arise to take her place. He will attack the forces of the king of the North and enter his fortress; he will fight against them and be victorious. ⁸He will also seize their gods, their metal images and their valuable articles of silver and gold and carry them off to Egypt. For some years he will leave the king of the North alone. ⁹Then the king of the North will invade the realm of the king of the South but will retreat to his own country. ¹⁰His sons will prepare for war and assemble a great army, which will sweep on like an irresistible flood and carry the battle as far as his fortress.

¹¹"Then the king of the South will march out in a rage and fight against the king of the North, who will raise a large army, but it will be defeated. ¹²When the army is carried off, the king of the South will be filled with pride and will slaughter many thousands, yet he will not remain triumphant. ¹³For the king of the North will muster another army, larger than the first; and after several years, he will advance with a huge army fully equipped.

¹⁴"In those times many will rise against the king of the South. Those who are violent

---

a 16 Most manuscripts of the Masoretic Text; one manuscript of the Masoretic Text, Dead Sea Scrolls and Septuagint *Then something that looked like a human hand*   *b 6* Or *offspring*   *c 6* Or *child* (see Vulgate and Syriac) among your own people will rebel in fulfillment of the vision, but without success. [15]Then the king of the North will come and build up siege ramps and will capture a fortified city. The forces of the South will be powerless to resist; even their best troops will not have the strength to stand. [16]The invader will do as he pleases; no one will be able to stand against him. He will establish himself in the Beautiful Land and will have the power to destroy it. [17]He will determine to come with the might of his entire kingdom and will make an alliance with the king of the South. And he will give him a daughter in marriage in order to overthrow the kingdom, but his plans[a] will not succeed or help him. [18]Then he will turn his attention to the coastlands and will take many of them, but a commander will put an end to his insolence and will turn his insolence back on him. [19]After this, he will turn back toward the fortresses of his own country but will stumble and fall, to be seen no more.

[20]"His successor will send out a tax collector to maintain the royal splendor. In a few years, however, he will be destroyed, yet not in anger or in battle.

[21]"He will be succeeded by a contemptible person who has not been given the honor of royalty. He will invade the kingdom when its people feel secure, and he will seize it through intrigue. [22]Then an overwhelming army will be swept away before him; both it and a prince of the covenant will be destroyed. [23]After coming to an agreement with him, he will act deceitfully, and with only a few people he will rise to power. [24]When the richest provinces feel secure, he will invade them and will achieve what neither his fathers nor his forefathers did. He will distribute plunder, loot and wealth among his followers. He will plot the overthrow of fortresses—but only for a time.

[25]"With a large army he will stir up his strength and courage against the king of the South. The king of the South will wage war with a large and very powerful army, but he will not be able to stand because of the plots devised against him. [26]Those who eat from the king's provisions will try to destroy him; his army will be swept away, and many will fall in battle. [27]The two kings, with their hearts bent on evil, will sit at the same table and lie to each other, but to no avail, because an end will still come at the appointed time. [28]The king of the North will return to his own country with great wealth, but his heart will be set against the holy covenant. He will take action against it and then return to his own country.

[29]"At the appointed time he will invade the South again, but this time the outcome will be different from what it was before. [30]Ships of the western coastlands will oppose him, and he will lose heart. Then he will turn back and vent his fury against the holy covenant. He will return and show favor to those who forsake the holy covenant.

[31]"His armed forces will rise up to desecrate the temple fortress and will abolish the daily sacrifice. Then they will set up the abomination that causes desolation. [32]With flattery he will corrupt those who have violated the covenant, but the people who know their God will firmly resist him.

[33]"Those who are wise will instruct many, though for a time they will fall by the sword or be burned or captured or plundered. [34]When they fall, they will receive a little help, and many who are not sincere will join them. [35]Some of the wise will stumble, so that they may be refined, purified and made spotless until the time of the end, for it will still come at the appointed time.

The King Who Exalts Himself

[36]"The king will do as he pleases. He will exalt and magnify himself above every god and will say unheard-of things against the God of gods. He will be successful until the time of wrath is completed, for what has been determined must take place. [37]He will show no regard for the gods of his ancestors or for the one desired by women, nor will he regard any god, but will exalt himself above them all. [38]Instead of them, he will honor a god of fortresses; a god unknown to his ancestors he will honor with gold and silver, with precious stones and costly gifts. [39]He will attack the mightiest fortresses with the help of a foreign god and will greatly honor those who acknowledge him. He will make them rulers over many people and will distribute the land at a price.[b]

[40]"At the time of the end the king of the

a 17 Or but she   b 39 Or land for a reward

South will engage him in battle, and the king of the North will storm out against him with chariots and cavalry and a great fleet of ships. He will invade many countries and sweep through them like a flood. ⁴¹He will also invade the Beautiful Land. Many countries will fall, but Edom, Moab and the leaders of Ammon will be delivered from his hand. ⁴²He will extend his power over many countries; Egypt will not escape. ⁴³He will gain control of the treasures of gold and silver and all the riches of Egypt, with the Libyans and Cushites *a* in submission. ⁴⁴But reports from the east and the north will alarm him, and he will set out in a great rage to destroy and annihilate many. ⁴⁵He will pitch his royal tents between the seas at *b* the beautiful holy mountain. Yet he will come to his end, and no one will help him.

The End Times

12 "At that time Michael, the great prince who protects your people, will arise. There will be a time of distress such as has not happened from the beginning of nations until then. But at that time your people—everyone whose name is found written in the book—will be delivered. ²Multitudes who sleep in the dust of the earth will awake: some to everlasting life, others to shame and everlasting contempt. ³Those who are wise *c* will shine like the brightness of the heavens, and those who lead many to righteousness, like the stars for ever and ever. ⁴But you, Daniel, close up and seal the words of the scroll until the time of the end. Many will go here and there to increase knowledge."

⁵Then I, Daniel, looked, and there before me stood two others, one on this bank of the river and one on the opposite bank. ⁶One of them said to the man clothed in linen, who was above the waters of the river, "How long will it be before these astonishing things are fulfilled?"

⁷The man clothed in linen, who was above the waters of the river, lifted his right hand and his left hand toward heaven, and I heard him swear by him who lives forever, saying, "It will be for a time, times and half a time. *d* When the power of the holy people has been finally broken, all these things will be completed."

⁸I heard, but I did not understand. So I asked, "My lord, what will the outcome of all this be?"

⁹He replied, "Go your way, Daniel, because the words are closed up and sealed until the time of the end. ¹⁰Many will be purified, made spotless and refined, but the wicked will continue to be wicked. None of the wicked will understand, but those who are wise will understand.

¹¹"From the time that the daily sacrifice is abolished and the abomination that causes desolation is set up, there will be 1,290 days. ¹²Blessed is the one who waits for and reaches the end of the 1,335 days.

¹³"As for you, go your way till the end. You will rest, and then at the end of the days you will rise to receive your allotted inheritance."

---

a 43 That is, people from the upper Nile region   *b 45* Or *the sea and*   *c 3* Or *who impart wisdom*
d 7 Or *a year, two years and half a year*

hosea

AUTHOR: Hosea

DATE: Around 715 B.C.

THEME: God is faithful to us even when we are unfaithful to him.

1 The word of the LORD that came to Hosea son of Beeri during the reigns of Uzziah, Jotham, Ahaz and Hezekiah, kings of Judah, and during the reign of Jeroboam son of Jehoash[a] king of Israel:

Hosea's Wife and Children

²When the LORD began to speak through Hosea, the LORD said to him, "Go, marry a promiscuous woman and have children with her, for like an adulterous wife this land is guilty of unfaithfulness to the LORD." ³So he married Gomer daughter of Diblaim, and she conceived and bore him a son.

⁴Then the LORD said to Hosea, "Call him Jezreel, because I will soon punish the house of Jehu for the massacre at Jezreel, and I will put an end to the kingdom of Israel. ⁵In that day I will break Israel's bow in the Valley of Jezreel."

⁶Gomer conceived again and gave birth to a daughter. Then the LORD said to Hosea, "Call her Lo-Ruhamah (which means "not loved"), for I will no longer show love to the house of Israel, that I should at all forgive them. ⁷Yet I will show love to the house of Judah; and I will save them—not by bow, sword or battle, or by horses and horsemen, but by the LORD their God."

⁸After she had weaned Lo-Ruhamah, Gomer had another son. ⁹Then the LORD said, "Call him Lo-Ammi (which means "not my people"), for you are not my people, and I am not your God.[b]

*¹⁰"Yet the Israelites will be like the sand on the seashore, which cannot be measured or counted. In the place where it was said to them, 'You are not my people,' they will be called 'children of the living God.' ¹¹The people of Judah and the people of Israel will come together; they will appoint one leader and will come up out of the land, for great will be the day of Jezreel.

2 *"Say of your brothers, 'My people,' and of your sisters, 'My loved one.'

Israel Punished and Restored

²"Rebuke your mother, rebuke her,
  for she is not my wife,
  and I am not her husband.
Let her remove the adulterous look from her face
  and the unfaithfulness from between her breasts.
³Otherwise I will strip her naked
  and make her as bare as on the day she was born;
I will make her like a desert,
  turn her into a parched land,
  and slay her with thirst.
⁴I will not show my love to her children,
  because they are the children of adultery.
⁵Their mother has been unfaithful
  and has conceived them in disgrace.
She said, 'I will go after my lovers,
  who give me my food and my water,
  my wool and my linen, my olive oil and my drink.'
⁶Therefore I will block her path with thornbushes;
  I will wall her in so that she cannot find her way.

---

a 1 Hebrew *Joash*, a variant of *Jehoash*   *b* 9 Or *your I* AM
* 1:10-11 is numbered 2:1-2 in Hebrew texts.   * 2:1-23 is numbered 2:3-25 in Hebrew texts.

TUESDAY

SPIRITUAL ADULTERY

Hosea 1:1—3:1 *or* 1:2; 2:7–8,13; 3:1

JOHN WESLEY {AD 1703–1791}

According to the words of God, friendship with the world is no less than spiritual adultery. The Holy Spirit addresses all who are guilty of it in this way: "You adulterous people" (James 4:4). Friendship with the world plainly violates our marriage contract with God, because it means loving the creature more than the Creator. This unmistakably contradicts God's kind command, "My son, give me your heart" (Proverbs 23:26).

It is a sin of the most heinous nature. It doesn't just imply ignorance of God, forgetfulness of him or inattention to him. It signifies positive hostility against God. In fact, it indicates open, palpable hostility. "Don't you know," asks James—astounded that anyone could possibly be so ignorant of such a clear, undeniable truth, "that friendship with the world means enmity against God?" And from there he draws this horrifying conclusion: "Anyone who chooses to be a friend of the world becomes an enemy of God" (James 4:4) . . .

Since friendship with the world is such an offensive sin, it comes with equally horrendous consequences . . . Therefore, fly for your life! Do not play with the fire, but escape before the flames kindle upon you.

Lisa Harper

God's not a small fish . . . In fact, He's the One who created all the fish in the sea, along with the entire universe surrounding the sea! He's the King of kings and Lord of lords . . . the God of history. And He lovingly charted the course for our personal history. He knew we would abandon Him and prostitute our hearts with other lovers. He knew those same lovers— mere idols that could only imitate affection—would eventually leave us disappointed and desperate for real love. He knew we'd basically sell our souls in search of unconditional acceptance. So He wrote a miraculous plan by which to redeem us once and for all. To teach us that His love is perfect, that it will never fail or fade, even on our worst days. It's an amazing story about being loved beyond our wildest dreams.

reflection

1. What "other lovers" have you run to instead of God?

2. God paints a picture of us as his beloved bride. How can that image encourage your love for, and devotion to, him?

3. Do you look for love and acceptance in places apart from God? Why?

For your next devotional reading, go to page 998.

7She will chase after her lovers but not
    catch them;
  she will look for them but not find
    them.
Then she will say,
  'I will go back to my husband as at
    first,
  for then I was better off than now.'
8She has not acknowledged that I was the
    one
  who gave her the grain, the new wine
    and oil,
  who lavished on her the silver and
    gold—
  which they used for Baal.

9"Therefore I will take away my grain
    when it ripens,
  and my new wine when it is ready.
I will take back my wool and my linen,
  intended to cover her nakedness.
10So now I will expose her lewdness
  before the eyes of her lovers;
  no one will take her out of my hands.
11I will stop all her celebrations:
  her yearly festivals, her New Moons,
  her Sabbath days—all her appointed
    festivals.
12I will ruin her vines and her fig trees,
  which she said were her pay from her
    lovers;
I will make them a thicket,
  and wild animals will devour them.
13I will punish her for the days
  she burned incense to the Baals;
she decked herself with rings and
    jewelry,
  and went after her lovers,
  but me she forgot,"
                        declares the Lord.

14"Therefore I am now going to allure her;
  I will lead her into the wilderness
  and speak tenderly to her.
15There I will give her back her vineyards,
  and will make the Valley of Achor^a a
    door of hope.
There she will respond^b as in the days of
    her youth,
  as in the day she came up out of
    Egypt.

16"In that day," declares the Lord,
  "you will call me 'my husband';
  you will no longer call me 'my
    master.'^c"
17I will remove the names of the Baals
    from her lips;
  no longer will their names be
    invoked.
18In that day I will make a covenant for
    them
  with the beasts of the field, the birds
    in the sky
  and the creatures that move along the
    ground.
Bow and sword and battle
  I will abolish from the land,
  so that all may lie down in safety.
19I will betroth you to me forever;
  I will betroth you in^d righteousness
    and justice,
  in^e love and compassion.
20I will betroth you in faithfulness,
  and you will acknowledge the Lord.

21"In that day I will respond,"
    declares the Lord—
  "I will respond to the skies,
  and they will respond to the earth;
22and the earth will respond to the grain,
  the new wine and the olive oil,
  and they will respond to Jezreel.^f
23I will plant her for myself in the land;
  I will show my love to the one I called
    'Not my loved one.'^g
I will say to those called 'Not my
    people,'^h 'You are my people';
  and they will say, 'You are my God.' "

Hosea's Reconciliation With His Wife

3 The Lord said to me, "Go, show your
love to your wife again, though she is
loved by another and is an adulteress.
Love her as the Lord loves the Israelites,
though they turn to other gods and love the
sacred raisin cakes."

2So I bought her for fifteen shekels^i of silver and about a homer and a lethek^j of barley. 3Then I told her, "You are to live with me
many days; you must not be a prostitute or
be intimate with any man, and I will behave
the same way toward you."

a 15 Achor means trouble.   b 15 Or sing   c 16 Hebrew baal   d 19 Or with; also in verse 20
e 19 Or with   f 22 Jezreel means God plants.   g 23 Hebrew Lo-Ruhamah (see 1:6)   h 23 Hebrew
Lo-Ammi (see 1:9)   i 2 That is, about 6 ounces or about 170 grams   j 2 A homer and a lethek
possibly weighed about 430 pounds or about 195 kilograms.

[4] For the Israelites will live many days without king or prince, without sacrifice or sacred stones, without ephod or household gods. [5] Afterward the Israelites will return and seek the LORD their God and David their king. They will come trembling to the LORD and to his blessings in the last days.

The Charge Against Israel

4 Hear the word of the LORD, you Israelites,
    because the LORD has a charge to bring
    against you who live in the land:
"There is no faithfulness, no love,
    no acknowledgment of God in the land.
[2] There is only cursing,[a] lying and murder,
    stealing and adultery;
they break all bounds,
    and bloodshed follows bloodshed.
[3] Because of this the land dries up,
    and all who live in it waste away;
the beasts of the field, the birds in the sky
    and the fish in the sea are swept away.

[4] "But let no one bring a charge,
    let no one accuse another,
for your people are like those
    who bring charges against a priest.
[5] You stumble day and night,
    and the prophets stumble with you.
So I will destroy your mother—
[6]   my people are destroyed from lack of knowledge.

"Because you have rejected knowledge,
    I also reject you as my priests;
because you have ignored the law of your God,
    I also will ignore your children.
[7] The more the priests increased,
    the more they sinned against me;
they exchanged their glorious God[b]
    for something disgraceful.
[8] They feed on the sins of my people
    and relish their wickedness.
[9] And it will be: Like people, like priests.
    I will punish both of them for their ways
    and repay them for their deeds.

[10] "They will eat but not have enough;
    they will engage in prostitution but not increase,
because they have deserted the LORD
    to give themselves [11] to prostitution;
old wine and new wine
    take away their understanding.
[12] My people consult a wooden idol
    and are answered by a stick of wood.
A spirit of prostitution leads them astray;
    they are unfaithful to their God.
[13] They sacrifice on the mountaintops
    and burn offerings on the hills,
under oak, poplar and terebinth,
    where the shade is pleasant.
Therefore your daughters turn to prostitution
    and your daughters-in-law to adultery.

[14] "I will not punish your daughters
    when they turn to prostitution,
nor your daughters-in-law
    when they commit adultery,
because the men themselves consort with harlots
    and sacrifice with shrine prostitutes—
a people without understanding will come to ruin!

[15] "Though you, Israel, commit adultery,
    do not let Judah become guilty.

"Do not go to Gilgal;
    do not go up to Beth Aven.[c]
    And do not swear, 'As surely as the LORD lives!'
[16] The Israelites are stubborn,
    like a stubborn heifer.
How then can the LORD pasture them
    like lambs in a meadow?
[17] Ephraim is joined to idols;
    leave him alone!
[18] Even when their drinks are gone,
    they continue their prostitution;
    their rulers dearly love shameful ways.
[19] A whirlwind will sweep them away,
    and their sacrifices will bring them shame.

a 2 That is, to pronounce a curse on Masoretic Text I will exchange their glory   b 7 Syriac (see also an ancient Hebrew scribal tradition);   c 15 Beth Aven means house of wickedness (a derogatory name for Bethel, which means house of God).

WEDNESDAY

TRUE DEVOTION

Hosea 4:1–19 *or* 4:1,6

Nancy Leigh DeMoss

Some of us have had *devotions*, but we've not had *devotion*. There's a big difference. We may have gone through the motions of reading our Bibles and "saying our prayers," but we have not been cultivating a love relationship with our Lover—God. We know a lot *about* Him, but we don't really know *Him* . . .

The result of our "devotionless" religion is seen in the way we respond to pressure. So many of us as Christian women are chronically stressed out. Everywhere I go, I see it in the eyes of women; I hear it in their voices; and too often I see it when I look in my own mirror. I know what it is to have demands coming at me from every direction. I know what it is to respond out of weariness, with an impatient, demanding spirit. And I know what it is to contend with God Himself, even as my eyes fill up with tears of frustration with myself and my reactions.

I also know that there is only one place where that angry, reactive, overwhelmed self can be transformed—the same place that Mary chose—the feet of Jesus. I must make a conscious, deliberate, daily choice to sit at His feet, to listen to His Word, to receive His love, to let Him change me and to pour out my heart's devotion to Him.

F. B. MEYER {AD 1847–1929}

Most of us never use our spiritual sense. God has given us a nose to smell with, eyes to see with, hands to feel with, a tongue to taste with. We are made in three parts—body, soul and spirit. The soul has senses equivalent to those of the body, and the spirit behind that has a third set of senses that an unregenerate man has not commenced to use. But if you are a spiritual man you will use these spiritual senses to discriminate the thoughts as they come to your heart. "By reason of use" you will have your senses exercised to discern both good and evil . . .

If you live in the midst of bad people, bad books and bad things, you lose your power of detecting bad thoughts when they come teeming about you like microbes. But if every day you spend an hour on God's mountains or upon the broad sea of the Bible, and get some of God's accurate senses into you, you will be able to detect things which are wrong that other people, even Christians, pass without seeing as wrong.

reflection

1. What does Hosea reveal about the Israelites' lack of devotion—their failure to use their spiritual sense?

2. In what ways have you failed to love God—even during this week—with the wholehearted devotion he deserves?

3. What changes will you make—starting today—to begin or to renew cultivating a genuine love relationship with the God who loves you?

For your next devotional reading, go to page 1005.

Judgment Against Israel

5 "Hear this, you priests!
  Pay attention, you Israelites!
  Listen, royal house!
  This judgment is against you:
You have been a snare at Mizpah,
  a net spread out on Tabor.
² The rebels are deep in slaughter.
  I will discipline all of them.
³ I know all about Ephraim;
  Israel is not hidden from me.
Ephraim, you have now turned to
    prostitution;
  Israel is corrupt.

⁴ "Their deeds do not permit them
  to return to their God.
A spirit of prostitution is in their heart;
  they do not acknowledge the LORD.
⁵ Israel's arrogance testifies against them;
  the Israelites, even Ephraim, stumble
    in their sin;
  Judah also stumbles with them.
⁶ When they go with their flocks and
    herds
  to seek the LORD,
they will not find him;
  he has withdrawn himself from them.
⁷ They are unfaithful to the LORD;
  they give birth to illegitimate
    children.
When they celebrate their New Moon
    feasts,
  he will devour ᵃ their fields.

⁸ "Sound the trumpet in Gibeah,
  the horn in Ramah.
Raise the battle cry in Beth Aven ᵇ;
  lead on, Benjamin.
⁹ Ephraim will be laid waste
  on the day of reckoning.
Among the tribes of Israel
  I proclaim what is certain.
¹⁰ Judah's leaders are like those
  who move boundary stones.
I will pour out my wrath on them
  like a flood of water.
¹¹ Ephraim is oppressed,
  trampled in judgment,
  intent on pursuing idols. ᶜ
¹² I am like a moth to Ephraim,
  like rot to the people of Judah.

¹³ "When Ephraim saw his sickness,
  and Judah his sores,
then Ephraim turned to Assyria,
  and sent to the great king for help.
But he is not able to cure you,
  not able to heal your sores.
¹⁴ For I will be like a lion to Ephraim,
  like a great lion to Judah.
I will tear them to pieces and go away;
  I will carry them off, with no one to
    rescue them.
¹⁵ Then I will return to my lair
  until they have borne their guilt
  and seek my face—
in their misery
  they will earnestly seek me."

Israel Unrepentant

6 "Come, let us return to the LORD.
  He has torn us to pieces
  but he will heal us;
he has injured us
  but he will bind up our wounds.
² After two days he will revive us;
  on the third day he will restore us,
  that we may live in his presence.
³ Let us acknowledge the LORD;
  let us press on to acknowledge him.
As surely as the sun rises,
  he will appear;
he will come to us like the winter rains,
  like the spring rains that water the
    earth."

⁴ "What can I do with you, Ephraim?
  What can I do with you, Judah?
Your love is like the morning mist,
  like the early dew that disappears.
⁵ Therefore I cut you in pieces with my
    prophets,
  I killed you with the words of my
    mouth—
then my judgments go forth like the
    sun. ᵈ
⁶ For I desire mercy, not sacrifice,
  and acknowledgment of God rather
    than burnt offerings.
⁷ As at Adam, ᵉ they have broken the
    covenant;
  they were unfaithful to me there.
⁸ Gilead is a city of wicked people,

ᵃ 7 Or Now their New Moon feasts / will devour them and
derogatory name for Bethel, which means house of God).   ᶜ 11 The meaning of the Hebrew for this
word is uncertain.   ᵈ 5 The meaning of the Hebrew for this line is uncertain.   ᵉ 7 Or Like Adam; or
Like human beings
ᵇ 8 Beth Aven means house of wickedness (a

stained with footprints of blood.
⁹ As marauders lie in ambush for a victim,
    so do bands of priests;
they murder on the road to Shechem,
    carrying out their wicked schemes.
¹⁰ I have seen a horrible thing
    in the house of Israel.
There Ephraim is given to prostitution
    and Israel is defiled.

¹¹ "Also for you, Judah,
    a harvest is appointed.

"Whenever I would restore the fortunes
    of my people,

7 ¹ whenever I would heal Israel,
    the sins of Ephraim are exposed
    and the crimes of Samaria revealed.
They practice deceit,
    thieves break into houses,
    bandits rob in the streets;
² but they do not realize
    that I remember all their evil deeds.
Their sins engulf them;
    they are always before me.

³ "They delight the king with their
    wickedness,
    the princes with their lies.
⁴ They are all adulterers,
    burning like an oven
whose fire the baker need not stir
    from the kneading of the dough till it
      rises.
⁵ On the day of the festival of our king
    the princes become inflamed with
      wine,
    and he joins hands with the mockers.
⁶ Their hearts are like an oven;
    they approach him with intrigue.
Their passion smolders all night;
    in the morning it blazes like a flaming
      fire.
⁷ All of them are hot as an oven;
    they devour their rulers.
All their kings fall,
    and none of them calls on me.

⁸ "Ephraim mixes with the nations;
    Ephraim is a flat loaf not turned over.
⁹ Foreigners sap his strength,
    but he does not realize it.
His hair is sprinkled with gray,
    but he does not notice.
¹⁰ Israel's arrogance testifies against him,

but despite all this
he does not return to the Lᴏʀᴅ his God
    or search for him.

¹¹ "Ephraim is like a dove,
    easily deceived and senseless—
now calling to Egypt,
    now turning to Assyria.
¹² When they go, I will throw my net over
      them;
    I will pull them down like the birds in
      the sky.
When I hear them flocking together,
    I will catch them.
¹³ Woe to them,
    because they have strayed from me!
Destruction to them,
    because they have rebelled against
      me!
I long to redeem them
    but they speak about me falsely.
¹⁴ They do not cry out to me from their
      hearts
    but wail on their beds.
They slash themselves,ᵃ appealing to
      their gods
    for grain and new wine,
    but they turn away from me.
¹⁵ I trained them and strengthened their
      arms,
    but they plot evil against me.
¹⁶ They do not turn to the Most High;
    they are like a faulty bow.
Their leaders will fall by the sword
    because of their insolent words.
For this they will be ridiculed
    in the land of Egypt.

Israel to Reap the Whirlwind

8 "Put the trumpet to your lips!
    An eagle is over the house of the
      Lᴏʀᴅ
because the people have broken my
      covenant
    and rebelled against my law.
² Israel cries out to me,
    'Our God, we acknowledge you!'
³ But Israel has rejected what is good;
    an enemy will pursue him.
⁴ They set up kings without my consent;
    they choose princes without my
      approval.
With their silver and gold
    they make idols for themselves

ᵃ 14 Some Hebrew manuscripts and Septuagint; most Hebrew manuscripts *They gather together*

to their own destruction.
⁵ Throw out your calf-idol, Samaria!
    My anger burns against them.
How long will they be incapable of purity?
⁶   They are from Israel!
This calf—a metalworker has made it;
    it is not God.
It will be broken in pieces,
    that calf of Samaria.

⁷ "They sow the wind
    and reap the whirlwind.
The stalk has no head;
    it will produce no flour.
Were it to yield grain,
    foreigners would swallow it up.
⁸ Israel is swallowed up;
    now she is among the nations
    like something no one wants.
⁹ For they have gone up to Assyria
    like a wild donkey wandering alone.
    Ephraim has sold herself to lovers.
¹⁰ Although they have sold themselves
        among the nations,
    I will now gather them together.
They will begin to waste away
    under the oppression of the mighty
        king.

¹¹ "Though Ephraim built many altars for
        sin offerings,
    these have become altars for sinning.
¹² I wrote for them the many things of my
        law,
    but they regarded them as something
        foreign.
¹³ Though they offer sacrifices as gifts to me,
    and though they eat the meat,
    the LORD is not pleased with them.
Now he will remember their wickedness
    and punish their sins:
    They will return to Egypt.
¹⁴ Israel has forgotten his Maker
    and built palaces;
    Judah has fortified many towns.
But I will send fire on their cities
    that will consume their fortresses."

Punishment for Israel

9 Do not rejoice, Israel;
    do not be jubilant like the other
        nations.
For you have been unfaithful to your
    God;

you love the wages of a prostitute
    at every threshing floor.
² Threshing floors and winepresses will
        not feed the people;
    the new wine will fail them.
³ They will not remain in the LORD's land;
    Ephraim will return to Egypt
    and eat unclean food in Assyria.
⁴ They will not pour out wine offerings to
        the LORD,
    nor will their sacrifices please him.
Such sacrifices will be to them like the
        bread of mourners;
    all who eat them will be unclean.
This food will be for themselves;
    it will not come into the temple of the
        LORD.

⁵ What will you do on the day of your
        appointed festivals,
    on the festal days of the LORD?
⁶ Even if they escape from destruction,
    Egypt will gather them,
    and Memphis will bury them.
Their treasures of silver will be taken
        over by briers,
    and thorns will overrun their tents.
⁷ The days of punishment are coming,
    the days of reckoning are at hand.
    Let Israel know this.
Because your sins are so many
    and your hostility so great,
the prophet is considered a fool,
    anyone who is inspired a maniac.
⁸ The prophet, along with my God,
    is the watchman over Ephraim, ᵃ
yet snares await him on all his paths,
    and hostility in the house of his God.
⁹ They have sunk deep into corruption,
    as in the days of Gibeah.
God will remember their wickedness
    and punish them for their sins.

¹⁰ "When I found Israel,
    it was like finding grapes in the
        desert;
when I saw your ancestors,
    it was like seeing the early fruit on
        the fig tree.
But when they came to Baal Peor,
    they consecrated themselves to that
        shameful idol
    and became as vile as the thing they
        loved.

ᵃ 8 Or *The prophet is the watchman over Ephraim, / the people of my God*

¹¹Ephraim's glory will fly away like a
bird—
no birth, no pregnancy, no
conception.
¹²Even if they rear children,
I will bereave them of every one.
Woe to them
when I turn away from them!
¹³I have seen Ephraim, like Tyre,
planted in a pleasant place.
But Ephraim will bring out
their children to the slayer."

¹⁴Give them, LORD—
what will you give them?
Give them wombs that miscarry
and breasts that are dry.

¹⁵"Because of all their wickedness in
Gilgal,
I hated them there.
Because of their sinful deeds,
I will drive them out of my house.
I will no longer love them;
all their leaders are rebellious.
¹⁶Ephraim is blighted,
their root is withered,
they yield no fruit.
Even if they bear children,
I will slay their cherished offspring."

¹⁷My God will reject them
because they have not obeyed him;
they will be wanderers among the
nations.

10 Israel was a spreading vine;
he brought forth fruit for
himself.
As his fruit increased,
he built more altars;
as his land prospered,
he adorned his sacred stones.
²Their heart is deceitful,
and now they must bear their guilt.
The LORD will demolish their altars
and destroy their sacred stones.

³Then they will say, "We have no king
because we did not revere the LORD.
But even if we had a king,
what could he do for us?"
⁴They make many promises,
take false oaths

and make agreements;
therefore lawsuits spring up
like poisonous weeds in a plowed
field.
⁵The people who live in Samaria fear
for the calf-idol of Beth Aven. ᵃ
Its people will mourn over it,
and so will its idolatrous priests,
those who had rejoiced over its splendor,
because it is taken from them into
exile.
⁶It will be carried to Assyria
as tribute for the great king.
Ephraim will be disgraced;
Israel will be ashamed of its foreign
alliances.
⁷Samaria's king will be destroyed,
swept away like a twig on the surface
of the waters.
⁸The high places of wickedness ᵇ will be
destroyed—
it is the sin of Israel.
Thorns and thistles will grow up
and cover their altars.
Then they will say to the mountains,
"Cover us!"
and to the hills, "Fall on us!"

⁹"Since the days of Gibeah, you have
sinned, Israel,
and there you have remained. ᶜ
Will not war again overtake
the evildoers in Gibeah?
¹⁰When I please, I will punish them;
nations will be gathered against them
to put them in bonds for their double
sin.
¹¹Ephraim is a trained heifer
that loves to thresh;
so I will put a yoke
on her fair neck.
I will drive Ephraim,
Judah must plow,
and Jacob must break up the ground.
¹²Sow for yourselves righteousness,
reap the fruit of unfailing love,
and break up your unplowed ground;
for it is time to seek the LORD,
until he comes
and showers his righteousness on you.
¹³But you have planted wickedness,
you have reaped evil,

ᵃ 5 *Beth Aven* means *house of wickedness* (a derogatory name for Bethel, which means *house of God*).
ᵇ 8 Hebrew *aven*, a reference to Beth Aven (a derogatory name for Bethel); see verse 5.   ᶜ 9 Or *there a stand was taken*

you have eaten the fruit of deception.
Because you have depended on your
own strength
and on your many warriors,
¹⁴ the roar of battle will rise against your
people,
so that all your fortresses will be
devastated—
as Shalman devastated Beth Arbel on
the day of battle,
when mothers were dashed to the
ground with their children.
¹⁵ So will it happen to you, Bethel,
because your wickedness is great.
When that day dawns,
the king of Israel will be completely
destroyed.

God's Love for Israel

11 "When Israel was a child, I loved
him,
and out of Egypt I called my son.
² But the more they were called,
the more they went away from me.^a
They sacrificed to the Baals
and they burned incense to images.
³ It was I who taught Ephraim to walk,
taking them by the arms;
but they did not realize
it was I who healed them.
⁴ I led them with cords of human
kindness,
with ties of love.
To them I was like one who lifts
a little child to the cheek,
and I bent down to feed them.

⁵ "Will they not return to Egypt
and will not Assyria rule over them
because they refuse to repent?
⁶ Swords will flash in their cities,
will destroy the bars of their gates
and put an end to their plans.
⁷ My people are determined to turn from
me.
Even though they call me God Most
High,
I will by no means exalt them.

⁸ "How can I give you up, Ephraim?
How can I hand you over, Israel?
How can I treat you like Admah?

How can I make you like Zeboyim?
My heart is changed within me;
all my compassion is aroused.
⁹ I will not carry out my fierce anger,
nor will I devastate Ephraim again.
For I am God, and not a human being—
the Holy One among you.
I will not come against their cities.
¹⁰ They will follow the LORD;
he will roar like a lion.
When he roars,
his children will come trembling from
the west.
¹¹ They will come trembling
like birds from Egypt,
like doves from Assyria.
I will settle them in their homes,"
declares the LORD.

Israel's Sin

^{*12} Ephraim has surrounded me with lies,
the house of Israel with deceit.
And Judah is unruly against God,
even against the faithful Holy One.

12 ^{*1}Ephraim feeds on the wind;
he pursues the east wind all day
and multiplies lies and violence.
He makes a treaty with Assyria
and sends olive oil to Egypt.
² The LORD has a charge to bring against
Judah;
he will punish Jacob^b according to his
ways
and repay him according to his
deeds.
³ In the womb he grasped his brother's
heel;
as a man he struggled with God.
⁴ He struggled with the angel and
overcame him;
he wept and begged for his favor.
He found him at Bethel
and talked with him there—
⁵ the LORD God Almighty,
the LORD is his name!
⁶ But you must return to your God;
maintain love and justice,
and wait for your God always.

⁷ The merchants use dishonest scales;
they love to defraud.
⁸ Ephraim boasts,

---

^a 2 Septuagint; Hebrew *them*   ^b 2 *Jacob* means *he grasps the heel*, a Hebrew idiom for *he takes
advantage of* or *he deceives*.
* 11:12 is numbered 12:1 in Hebrew texts.   * 12:1-14 is numbered 12:2-15 in Hebrew texts.

"I am very rich; I have become
wealthy.
With all my wealth they will not find
in me
any iniquity or sin."

⁹ "I have been the LORD your God
ever since you came out of Egypt;
I will make you live in tents again,
as in the days of your appointed
festivals.
¹⁰ I spoke to the prophets,
gave them many visions
and told parables through them."

¹¹ Is Gilead wicked?
Its people are worthless!
Do they sacrifice bulls in Gilgal?
Their altars will be like piles of
stones
on a plowed field.
¹² Jacob fled to the country of Aram*a*;
Israel served to get a wife,
and to pay for her he tended sheep.
¹³ The LORD used a prophet to bring Israel
up from Egypt,
by a prophet he cared for him.
¹⁴ But Ephraim has aroused his bitter
anger;
his Lord will leave on him the guilt of
his bloodshed
and will repay him for his contempt.

The LORD's Anger Against Israel

13 When Ephraim spoke, people
trembled;
he was exalted in Israel.
But he became guilty of Baal worship
and died.
² Now they sin more and more;
they make idols for themselves from
their silver,
cleverly fashioned images,
all of them the work of skilled
hands.
It is said of them,
"They offer human sacrifices!
They kiss*b* calf-idols!"
³ Therefore they will be like the morning
mist,
like the early dew that disappears,
like chaff swirling from a threshing
floor,

like smoke escaping through a
window.

⁴ "But I have been the LORD your God
ever since you came out of Egypt.
You shall acknowledge no God but me,
no Savior except me.
⁵ I cared for you in the wilderness,
in the land of burning heat.
⁶ When I fed them, they were satisfied;
when they were satisfied, they
became proud;
then they forgot me.
⁷ So I will come upon them like a lion,
like a leopard I will lurk by the path.
⁸ Like a bear robbed of her cubs,
I will attack them and rip them open;
like a lion I will devour them—
a wild animal will tear them apart.

⁹ "You are destroyed, Israel,
because you are against me, against
your helper.
¹⁰ Where is your king, that he may save
you?
Where are your rulers in all your
towns,
of whom you said,
'Give me a king and princes'?
¹¹ So in my anger I gave you a king,
and in my wrath I took him away.
¹² The guilt of Ephraim is stored up,
his sins are kept on record.
¹³ Pains as of a woman in childbirth come
to him,
but he is a child without wisdom;
when the time arrives,
he does not come to the opening of
the womb.

¹⁴ "I will deliver them from the power of
the grave;
I will redeem them from death.
Where, O death, are your plagues?
Where, O grave, is your destruction?

"I will have no compassion,
¹⁵   even though he thrives among his
brothers.
An east wind from the LORD will come,
blowing in from the desert;
his spring will fail
and his well dry up.
His storehouse will be plundered
of all its treasures.

---

a 12 That is, Northwest Mesopotamia   *b 2* Or "Men who sacrifice / kiss

THURSDAY

NEVER TOO FAR

Hosea 14:1–9 *or* 14:4–6

D. L. MOODY {AD 1837–1899}

A backslider came into the inquiry room night before last, and I was trying to tell him God loved him. He would hardly believe me. He thought because he had not kept up his love and faithfulness to God, and to his own vows, that God had stopped loving him.

Now, it says in John 13:1, "He loved them to the end," that is, his love was unchangeable. You may have forgotten him and betrayed him and denied him, but nevertheless, he loves you; he loves the backslider.

Now, in Hosea 14:4, God says that he will heal every backslider. "I will . . . love them freely." So the Lord tells the backsliders, "If you will only come back to me, I will forgive you." It was thus with Peter who denied his Lord. The Savior forgave him and sent him to preach his glorious gospel on the day of the Pentecost when 3,000 were won to Christ under one sermon of a backslider (see John 18:25–27; 21:15–19; Acts 2:14–39).

. . . No backslider can say God has left him. He may think so, but it is one of the devil's lies. The Lord has never left a man yet.

Alister McGrath

Recalling how we have known Christ is an important stimulus to recovering past intimacy, excitement and joy—things which can easily become eroded in the life of faith. Contrasting a present lukewarmness toward Christ with a past passion for him allows two critical insights:

It tells us that something is wrong. Sin deceives us, and we are often willing accomplices to this deception. We like to think that all is well in our spiritual lives, and are reluctant to face up to the threat posed by an erosion of faith or commitment. Yet becoming aware that there is a problem is essential to working for improvement . . . Our memories can provide precisely such a much-needed challenge. Memory can challenge complacency.

It offers us hope for renewal. Wherever Scripture offers a criticism of the spiritual state of individuals or communities, it also offers the hope of change and recovery. Hosea challenged his wayward people to recommit themselves to the Lord, and receive healing and forgiveness as a result.

reflection

1. What do you learn about God's heart for the wayward through his promises of love in this chapter?

2. Can a person ever walk so far away from God that they can never go back to him?

3. How can you regain the intimacy and passion you once experienced in your relationship with God?

For your next devotional reading, go to page 1008.

*16 The people of Samaria must bear their
        guilt,
    because they have rebelled against
        their God.
    They will fall by the sword;
        their little ones will be dashed to the
        ground,
        their pregnant women ripped open."

Repentance to Bring Blessing

14 *Return, Israel, to the LORD your
        God.
    Your sins have been your
        downfall!
² Take words with you
    and return to the LORD.
Say to him:
    "Forgive all our sins
    and receive us graciously,
        that we may offer the fruit of our lips.ᵃ
³ Assyria cannot save us;
    we will not mount warhorses.
We will never again say 'Our gods'
    to what our own hands have made,
        for in you the fatherless find
        compassion."

⁴ "I will heal their waywardness
    and love them freely,

for my anger has turned away from
    them.
⁵ I will be like the dew to Israel;
    he will blossom like a lily.
Like a cedar of Lebanon
    he will send down his roots;
⁶   his young shoots will grow.
His splendor will be like an olive tree,
    his fragrance like a cedar of
        Lebanon.
⁷ People will dwell again in his shade;
    they will flourish like the grain,
they will blossom like the vine—
    Israel's fame will be like the wine of
        Lebanon.
⁸ Ephraim, what more have Iᵇ to do with
        idols?
    I will answer him and care for him.
I am like a flourishing juniper;
    your fruitfulness comes from me."

⁹ Who is wise? Let them realize these
        things.
    Who is discerning? Let them
        understand.
The ways of the LORD are right;
    the righteous walk in them,
        but the rebellious stumble in
        them.

ᵃ 2 Or offer our lips as sacrifices of bulls   ᵇ 8 Or Hebrew; Septuagint What more has Ephraim
* 13:16 is numbered 14:1 in Hebrew texts.   * 14:1-9 is numbered 14:2-10 in Hebrew texts.

joel

AUTHOR:	Joel
DATE:	Unknown; possibly as early as the 800s B.C.
THEME:	God's redemption waits for those who repent.

1 The word of the LORD that came to Joel son of Pethuel.

An Invasion of Locusts

2 Hear this, you elders;
  listen, all who live in the land.
Has anything like this ever happened in
    your days
  or in the days of your ancestors?
3 Tell it to your children,
  and let your children tell it to their
    children,
  and their children to the next
    generation.
4 What the locust swarm has left
  the great locusts have eaten;
what the great locusts have left
  the young locusts have eaten;
what the young locusts have left
  other locusts *a* have eaten.

5 Wake up, you drunkards, and weep!
  Wail, all you drinkers of wine;
wail because of the new wine,
  for it has been snatched from your
    lips.
6 A nation has invaded my land,
  a mighty army without number;
it has the teeth of a lion,
  the fangs of a lioness.
7 It has laid waste my vines
  and ruined my fig trees.
It has stripped off their bark
  and thrown it away,
  leaving their branches white.

8 Mourn like a virgin in sackcloth
  grieving for the betrothed of her
    youth.
9 Grain offerings and drink offerings
  are cut off from the house of the
    LORD.
The priests are in mourning,
  those who minister before the LORD.
10 The fields are ruined,
  the ground is dried up;
the grain is destroyed,
  the new wine is dried up,
  the olive oil fails.

11 Despair, you farmers,
  wail, you vine growers;
grieve for the wheat and the barley,
  because the harvest of the field is
    destroyed.
12 The vine is dried up
  and the fig tree is withered;
the pomegranate, the palm and the
    apple *b* tree—
  all the trees of the field—are dried up.
Surely the people's joy
  is withered away.

A Call to Lamentation

13 Put on sackcloth, you priests, and mourn;
  wail, you who minister before the
    altar.
Come, spend the night in sackcloth,
  you who minister before my God;
for the grain offerings and drink offerings
  are withheld from the house of your
    God.
14 Declare a holy fast;
  call a sacred assembly.
Summon the elders

a 4 The precise meaning of the four Hebrew words used here for locusts is uncertain.   *b* 12 Or possibly apricot

FRIDAY

A New Beginning

Joel 1:1–20 *or* 1:13–14

Don M. Aycock

Can you remember where you were on September 11, 2001? Most of us can remember our exact location and our actions when we learned of the attack on the World Trade Center, the Pentagon and the crash in Pennsylvania. I was working in my church office when someone called to tell me what had happened. I turned on the television and was horrified at the sight.

Some events have a way of turning our seemingly safe worlds upside down. One minute things are going along in a routine way, then—bam!—we are never the same. You can think of several events like that in your life.

The book of Joel tells of a series of events that took ancient Israel by storm. The country was invaded by a merciless army, not of soldiers, but of locusts. Remember that in those days, before good storage methods, farmers' crops could be ruined by the weather or by insects. The locust invasion brought total destruction. The Lord asked the nation through Joel, "Has anything like this ever happened in your days or in the days of your [ancestors]?" (Joel 1:2). How can things get so out of hand?

I know many people who remember Pearl Harbor and the events of December 7, 1941. They asked the same kind of question then . . .

The end of every chapter in life is the beginning of another. We experience tragedy or major setbacks and are tempted to say, "My life is over." But God might be saying, "My son, your life is just beginning in this new day." Do not surrender your hope. Locusts never have the last word.

Susan Coolidge {ad 1835–1905}

Every day is a fresh beginning,
Every morn is the world made new,
You who are weary of sorrow and sinning,
Here is a beautiful hope for you;
A hope for me and a hope for you.

reflection

1. What purpose did God work out of the plague of locusts that invaded Israel?

2. How has God used trials or tragedies in *your* life to focus your heart more fully on him?

3. In Joel 2:25, God promised Israel that if they returned to him, he would "repay [them] for the years the locusts [had] eaten." What does this teach you about how God operates?

For your next devotional reading, go to page 1011.

and all who live in the land
to the house of the LORD your God,
and cry out to the LORD.

15 Alas for that day!
For the day of the LORD is near;
it will come like destruction from the
Almighty. *a*

16 Has not the food been cut off
before our very eyes—
joy and gladness
from the house of our God?
17 The seeds are shriveled
beneath the clods. *b*
The storehouses are in ruins,
the granaries have been broken down,
for the grain has dried up.
18 How the cattle moan!
The herds mill about
because they have no pasture;
even the flocks of sheep are suffering.

19 To you, LORD, I call,
for fire has devoured the pastures in
the wilderness
and flames have burned up all the
trees of the field.
20 Even the wild animals pant for you;
the streams of water have dried up
and fire has devoured the pastures in
the wilderness.

An Army of Locusts

2 Blow the trumpet in Zion;
sound the alarm on my holy hill.

Let all who live in the land tremble,
for the day of the LORD is coming.
It is close at hand—
2 a day of darkness and gloom,
a day of clouds and blackness.
Like dawn spreading across the
mountains
a large and mighty army comes,
such as never was of old
nor ever will be in ages to come.

3 Before them fire devours,
behind them a flame blazes.
Before them the land is like the garden
of Eden,
behind them, a desert waste—
nothing escapes them.
4 They have the appearance of horses;

they gallop along like cavalry.
5 With a noise like that of chariots
they leap over the mountaintops,
like a crackling fire consuming stubble,
like a mighty army drawn up for battle.
6 At the sight of them, nations are in
anguish;
every face turns pale.
7 They charge like warriors;
they scale walls like soldiers.
They all march in line,
not swerving from their course.
8 They do not jostle each other;
each marches straight ahead.
They plunge through defenses
without breaking ranks.
9 They rush upon the city;
they run along the wall.
They climb into the houses;
like thieves they enter through the
windows.

10 Before them the earth shakes,
the heavens tremble,
the sun and moon are darkened,
and the stars no longer shine.
11 The LORD thunders
at the head of his army;
his forces are beyond number,
and mighty is the army that obeys his
command.
The day of the LORD is great;
it is dreadful.
Who can endure it?

Rend Your Heart

12 "Even now," declares the LORD,
"return to me with all your heart,
with fasting and weeping and
mourning."

13 Rend your heart
and not your garments.
Return to the LORD your God,
for he is gracious and compassionate,
slow to anger and abounding in love,
and he relents from sending calamity.
14 Who knows? He may turn and relent
and leave behind a blessing—
grain offerings and drink offerings
for the LORD your God.

15 Blow the trumpet in Zion,
declare a holy fast,

---

a 15 Hebrew *Shaddai*   *b 17* The meaning of the Hebrew for this word is uncertain.

call a sacred assembly.
¹⁶Gather the people,
consecrate the assembly;
bring together the elders,
gather the children,
those nursing at the breast.
Let the bridegroom leave his room
and the bride her chamber.
¹⁷Let the priests, who minister before the
LORD,
weep between the portico and the
altar.
Let them say, "Spare your people, LORD.
Do not make your inheritance an
object of scorn,
a byword among the nations.
Why should they say among the peoples,
'Where is their God?' "

The LORD's Answer

¹⁸Then the LORD was jealous for his land
and took pity on his people.

¹⁹The LORD replied^a to them:

"I am sending you grain, new wine and
olive oil,
enough to satisfy you fully;
never again will I make you
an object of scorn to the nations.

²⁰"I will drive the northern horde far from
you,
pushing it into a parched and barren
land;
its eastern ranks will drown in the Dead
Sea
and its western ranks in the
Mediterranean Sea.
And its stench will go up;
its smell will rise."

Surely he has done great things!
²¹ Do not be afraid, land of Judah;
be glad and rejoice.
Surely the LORD has done great things!
²² Do not be afraid, you wild animals,
for the pastures in the wilderness are
becoming green.
The trees are bearing their fruit;
the fig tree and the vine yield their
riches.
²³Be glad, people of Zion,

rejoice in the LORD your God,
for he has given you
the autumn rains in righteousness.
He sends you abundant showers,
both autumn and spring rains, as
before.
²⁴The threshing floors will be filled with
grain;
the vats will overflow with new wine
and oil.

²⁵"I will repay you for the years the locusts
have eaten—
the great locust and the young locust,
the other locusts and the locust
swarm^b—
my great army that I sent among you.
²⁶You will have plenty to eat, until you are
full,
and you will praise the name of the
LORD your God,
who has worked wonders for you;
never again will my people be shamed.
²⁷Then you will know that I am in Israel,
that I am the LORD your God,
and that there is no other;
never again will my people be shamed.

The Day of the LORD

*²⁸"And afterward,
I will pour out my Spirit on all people.
Your sons and daughters will prophesy,
your old men will dream dreams,
your young men will see visions.
²⁹Even on my servants, both men and
women,
I will pour out my Spirit in those days.
³⁰I will show wonders in the heavens
and on the earth,
blood and fire and billows of smoke.
³¹The sun will be turned to darkness
and the moon to blood
before the coming of the great and
dreadful day of the LORD.
³²And everyone who calls
on the name of the LORD will be
saved;
for on Mount Zion and in Jerusalem
there will be deliverance,
as the LORD has said,
even among the survivors
whom the LORD calls.

a 18,19 Or LORD will be jealous . . . / and take pity . . . / *19*The LORD will reply   *b* 25 The precise meaning of the four Hebrew words used here for locusts is uncertain.

* 2:28-32 is numbered 3:1-5 in Hebrew texts.

Standing on a Hill

Joel 3:16–17

read/meditate

Jerusalem was a symbol of God's presence with his people. In that sense, Jerusalem was to be a testimony to the surrounding nations. With this in mind, read Joel 3:16–17. Just as Jerusalem stood as a witness to the surrounding nations, now each Christian is that witness because God dwells within his people. What kind of beacon are you?

pray

Talk to God about the kind of representative you want to be for him, and confess the kind of representative you think you are. Listen for his guidance in terms of how you should live for him.

contemplate

Joel described a city set on a hill. That was Jerusalem. And that is you. Contemplate the kind of message you send to those around you regarding the availability of God's presence.

additional reflection

We should not ask, "What is wrong with the world?" for that diagnosis has already been given. Rather, we should ask, "What has happened to the salt and light?"

—*John R. W. Stott*

A good witness isn't like a salesman, emphasis is on a person rather than a product. A good witness is like a signpost. It doesn't matter whether it is old, young, pretty, ugly; it has to point the right direction and be able to be understood. We are witnesses to Christ, we point to him.

—*John White*

For your next devotional reading, go to page 1015.

The Nations Judged

3 *"In those days and at that time,
when I restore the fortunes of Judah
and Jerusalem,
² I will gather all nations
and bring them down to the Valley of
Jehoshaphat.ᵃ
There I will enter into judgment against
them
concerning my inheritance, my
people Israel,
for they scattered my people among the
nations
and divided up my land.
³ They cast lots for my people
and traded boys for prostitutes;
they sold girls for wine
that they might drink.

⁴"Now what have you against me, Tyre
and Sidon and all you regions of Philistia?
Are you repaying me for something I have
done? If you are paying me back, I will
swiftly and speedily return on your own
heads what you have done. ⁵For you took my
silver and my gold and carried off my finest
treasuresᵇ to your temples. ⁶You sold the
people of Judah and Jerusalem to the
Greeks, that you might send them far from
their homeland.

⁷"See, I am going to rouse them out of the
places to which you sold them, and I will return on your own heads what you have
done. ⁸I will sell your sons and daughters to
the people of Judah, and they will sell them
to the Sabeans, a nation far away." The LORD
has spoken.

⁹ Proclaim this among the nations:
Prepare for war!
Rouse the warriors!
Let all the fighting men draw near
and attack.
¹⁰ Beat your plowshares into swords
and your pruning hooks into spears.
Let the weakling say,
"I am strong!"
¹¹ Come quickly, all you nations from every
side,
and assemble there.

Bring down your warriors, LORD!

¹²"Let the nations be roused;

let them advance into the Valley of
Jehoshaphat,
for there I will sit
to judge all the nations on every side.
¹³ Swing the sickle,
for the harvest is ripe.
Come, trample the grapes,
for the winepress is full
and the vats overflow—
so great is their wickedness!"

¹⁴ Multitudes, multitudes
in the valley of decision!
For the day of the LORD is near
in the valley of decision.
¹⁵ The sun and moon will be darkened,
and the stars no longer shine.
¹⁶ The LORD will roar from Zion
and thunder from Jerusalem;
the earth and the heavens will
tremble.
But the LORD will be a refuge for his
people,
a stronghold for the people of Israel.

Blessings for God's People

¹⁷"Then you will know that I, the LORD
your God,
dwell in Zion, my holy hill.
Jerusalem will be holy;
never again will foreigners invade her.

¹⁸"In that day the mountains will drip new
wine,
and the hills will flow with milk;
all the ravines of Judah will run with
water.
A fountain will flow out of the LORD's
house
and will water the valley of acacias.ᶜ
¹⁹ But Egypt will be desolate,
Edom a desert waste,
because of violence done to the people
of Judah,
in whose land they shed innocent
blood.
²⁰ Judah will be inhabited forever
and Jerusalem through all
generations.
²¹ Shall I leave their innocent blood
unpunished?
No, I will not."

The LORD dwells in Zion!

ᵃ 2 Jehoshaphat means the LORD judges; also in verse 12.　ᵇ 5 Or palaces　ᶜ 18 Or Valley of Shittim
* 3:1-21 is numbered 4:1-21 in Hebrew texts.

amos

AUTHOR: Amos, a shepherd-turned-prophet

DATE: Around 760–750 B.C.

THEME: God remembers those everyone else seems to forget.

1 The words of Amos, one of the shepherds of Tekoa—the vision he saw concerning Israel two years before the earthquake, when Uzziah was king of Judah and Jeroboam son of Jehoash[a] was king of Israel.

²He said:

"The LORD roars from Zion
   and thunders from Jerusalem;
the pastures of the shepherds dry up,
   and the top of Carmel withers."

Judgment on Israel's Neighbors

³This is what the LORD says:

"For three sins of Damascus,
   even for four, I will not turn back ⌐my
      wrath⌐.
Because she threshed Gilead
   with sledges having iron teeth,
⁴I will send fire on the house of Hazael
   that will consume the fortresses of
      Ben-Hadad.
⁵I will break down the gate of Damascus;
   I will destroy the king who is in[b] the
      Valley of Aven[c]
and the one who holds the scepter in
      Beth Eden.
   The people of Aram will go into exile
      to Kir,"
               says the LORD.

⁶This is what the LORD says:

"For three sins of Gaza,
   even for four, I will not turn back ⌐my
      wrath⌐.
Because she took captive whole
   communities

and sold them to Edom,
⁷I will send fire on the walls of Gaza
   that will consume her fortresses.
⁸I will destroy the king[d] of Ashdod
   and the one who holds the scepter in
      Ashkelon.
I will turn my hand against Ekron,
   till the last of the Philistines are
      dead,"
               says the Sovereign LORD.

⁹This is what the LORD says:

"For three sins of Tyre,
   even for four, I will not turn back ⌐my
      wrath⌐.
Because she sold whole communities of
   captives to Edom,
disregarding a treaty of brotherhood,
¹⁰I will send fire on the walls of Tyre
   that will consume her fortresses."

¹¹This is what the LORD says:

"For three sins of Edom,
   even for four, I will not turn back ⌐my
      wrath⌐.
Because he pursued his brother with a
   sword
and slaughtered the women of the
   land,
because his anger raged continually
   and his fury flamed unchecked,
¹²I will send fire on Teman
   that will consume the fortresses of
      Bozrah."

¹³This is what the LORD says:

"For three sins of Ammon,

---

a 1 Hebrew Joash, a variant of Jehoash   b 5 Or the inhabitants of   c 5 Aven means wickedness.
d 8 Or inhabitants

even for four, I will not turn back ⌐my
wrath⌐.
Because he ripped open the pregnant
women of Gilead
in order to extend his borders,
¹⁴ I will set fire to the walls of Rabbah
that will consume her fortresses
amid war cries on the day of battle,
amid violent winds on a stormy day.
¹⁵ Their king* will go into exile,
he and his officials together,"
says the Lord.

2 This is what the Lord says:

"For three sins of Moab,
even for four, I will not turn back ⌐my
wrath⌐.
Because he burned to lime
the bones of Edom's king,
² I will send fire on Moab
that will consume the fortresses of
Kerioth. *
Moab will go down in great tumult
amid war cries and the blast of the
trumpet.
³ I will destroy her ruler
and kill all her officials with him,"
says the Lord.

⁴ This is what the Lord says:

"For three sins of Judah,
even for four, I will not turn back ⌐my
wrath⌐.
Because they have rejected the law of
the Lord
and have not kept his decrees,
because they have been led astray by
false gods, *
the gods* their ancestors followed,
⁵ I will send fire on Judah
that will consume the fortresses of
Jerusalem."

Judgment on Israel

⁶ This is what the Lord says:

"For three sins of Israel,
even for four, I will not turn back ⌐my
wrath⌐.
They sell the innocent for silver,
and the needy for a pair of sandals.
⁷ They trample on the heads of the poor
as on the dust of the ground

and deny justice to the oppressed.
Father and son use the same girl
and so profane my holy name.
⁸ They lie down beside every altar
on garments taken in pledge.
In the house of their god
they drink wine taken as fines.

⁹ "Yet I destroyed the Amorites before
them,
though they were tall as the cedars
and strong as the oaks.
I destroyed their fruit above
and their roots below.
¹⁰ I brought you up out of Egypt
and led you forty years in the
wilderness
to give you the land of the Amorites.

¹¹ "I also raised up prophets from among
your children
and Nazirites from among your
youths.
Is this not true, people of Israel?"
declares the Lord.
¹² "But you made the Nazirites drink wine
and commanded the prophets not to
prophesy.

¹³ "Now then, I will crush you
as a cart crushes when loaded with
grain.
¹⁴ The swift will not escape,
the strong will not muster their
strength,
and the warrior will not save his life.
¹⁵ The archer will not stand his ground,
the fleet-footed soldier will not get
away,
and the horseman will not save his
life.
¹⁶ Even the bravest warriors
will flee naked on that day,"
declares the Lord.

Witnesses Summoned Against Israel

3 Hear this word, people of Israel, the
word the Lord has spoken against
you—against the whole family I
brought up out of Egypt:

² "You only have I chosen
of all the families of the earth;
therefore I will punish you
for all your sins."

MONDAY

WORSHIP THROUGH ACTIONS
Amos 2:1–16 *or* 2:6–8

John Ortberg

God does not say that the people of Israel don't worship enough. He doesn't say that they don't know the Scriptures. He doesn't say a whole lot of things we might have expected him to say. He says, "My heart is broken over the way my people hoard their resources and neglect the poor while they claim to follow and know me."

God is deeply concerned about our worship. He cares very much that we know the teaching of Scripture. God wants us to attend church services and share in life-giving fellowship among his people. But this is not the whole story! When we truly worship God, our hearts are captured by the things that matter to God—and God cares about the poor, the oppressed and the outcast. When we study the Bible, we should follow what it teaches. This means we should learn from Amos and begin to act in ways that will bring justice for those who are marginalized. God longs to see a balance in the lives of his followers. Spirit-led worship should lead to passionate service and compassionate acts of justice.

JOHN OWEN {AD 1616–1683}

We will not find acceptance with God or receive his promised blessings if our worship of him consists solely of that which we naturally experience in our own hearts and minds. For God also wants our worship to be expressed in our actions. If we do not follow his commands, we turn our backs on our alleged inner dependence on him, just as Adam did when he sinned. In doing this, we lose our ability to bring him glory in this world, which also keeps us from truly enjoying him. However, when our faith and trust work themselves out through our obedience, our internal heart of worship is revealed. This causes our worship to multiply and grow.

reflection

1. What is genuine worship?

2. In what ways do your actions reveal a heart of genuine worship? How can you grow in this area?

3. When you say you worship God but fail to live out his commands to care for the poor and oppressed, what are you communicating to the world around you?

For your next devotional reading, go to page 1018.

³Do two walk together
  unless they have agreed to do so?
⁴Does a lion roar in the thicket
  when it has no prey?
Does it growl in its den
  when it has caught nothing?
⁵Does a bird swoop down to a trap on the
    ground
  when no bait is there?
Does a trap spring up from the ground
  if it has not caught anything?
⁶When a trumpet sounds in a city,
  do not the people tremble?
When disaster comes to a city,
  has not the Lord caused it?

⁷Surely the Sovereign Lord does nothing
  without revealing his plan
  to his servants the prophets.

⁸The lion has roared—
  who will not fear?
The Sovereign Lord has spoken—
  who can but prophesy?

⁹Proclaim to the fortresses of Ashdod
  and to the fortresses of Egypt:
"Assemble yourselves on the mountains
    of Samaria;
  see the great unrest within her
  and the oppression among her
    people."

¹⁰"They do not know how to do right,"
    declares the Lord,
  "who store up in their fortresses
  what they have plundered and
    looted."

¹¹Therefore this is what the Sovereign
Lord says:

"An enemy will overrun your land,
  pull down your strongholds
  and plunder your fortresses."

¹²This is what the Lord says:

"As a shepherd saves from the lion's
    mouth
  only two leg bones or a piece of an
    ear,
so will the Israelites be saved,
those who sit in Samaria
  on the edge of their beds
  and in Damascus on their couches.ᵃ"

¹³"Hear this and testify against the house
of Jacob," declares the Lord, the Lord God
Almighty.

¹⁴"On the day I punish Israel for her sins,
  I will destroy the altars of Bethel;
the horns of the altar will be cut off
  and fall to the ground.
¹⁵I will tear down the winter house
  along with the summer house;
the houses adorned with ivory will be
    destroyed
  and the mansions will be
    demolished,"
        declares the Lord.

Israel Has Not Returned to God

4 Hear this word, you cows of Bashan
    on Mount Samaria,
you women who oppress the poor
    and crush the needy
and say to your husbands, "Bring us
    some drinks!"

²The Sovereign Lord has sworn by his
    holiness:
"The time will surely come
when you will be taken away with hooks,
  the last of you with fishhooks.ᵇ
³You will each go straight out
  through breaches in the wall,
and you will be cast out toward
    Harmon,ᶜ"
        declares the Lord.

⁴"Go to Bethel and sin;
  go to Gilgal and sin yet more.
Bring your sacrifices every morning,
  your tithes every three years.ᵈ
⁵Burn leavened bread as a thank offering
  and brag about your freewill
    offerings—
boast about them, you Israelites,
  for this is what you love to do,"
        declares the Sovereign Lord.

⁶"I gave you empty stomachs in every city
  and lack of bread in every town,
yet you have not returned to me,"
        declares the Lord.

⁷"I also withheld rain from you
  when the harvest was still three
    months away.
I sent rain on one town,

ᵃ 12 Or *Israelites living in Samaria be saved, / with only the head of a bed / and a piece of fabric from a couch*
ᵇ 2 Or *away in baskets, / the last of you in fish baskets*   ᶜ 3 Masoretic Text; with a different word division
of the Hebrew (see Septuagint) *out, you mountain of oppression*   ᵈ 4 Or *days*

but withheld it from another.
One field had rain;
    another had none and dried up.
8 People staggered from town to town for
        water
    but did not get enough to drink,
    yet you have not returned to me,"
                    declares the LORD.

9 "Many times I struck your gardens and
        vineyards,
    destroying them with blight and
        mildew.
Locusts devoured your fig and olive trees,
    yet you have not returned to me,"
                    declares the LORD.

10 "I sent plagues among you
    as I did to Egypt.
I killed your young men with the sword,
    along with your captured horses.
I filled your nostrils with the stench of
        your camps,
    yet you have not returned to me,"
                    declares the LORD.

11 "I overthrew some of you
    as I overthrew Sodom and Gomorrah.
You were like a burning stick snatched
        from the fire,
    yet you have not returned to me,"
                    declares the LORD.

12 "Therefore this is what I will do to you,
        Israel,
    and because I will do this to you,
        Israel,
    prepare to meet your God."

13 He who forms the mountains,
    who creates the wind,
    and who reveals his thoughts to
        mortals,
who turns dawn to darkness,
    and treads on the heights of the
        earth—
    the LORD God Almighty is his name.

A Lament and Call to Repentance

5 Hear this word, house of Israel, this
    lament I take up concerning you:

2 "Fallen is Virgin Israel,
    never to rise again,
deserted in her own land,
    with no one to lift her up."

3 This is what the Sovereign LORD says to
the house of Israel:

"Your city that marches out a thousand
        strong
    will have only a hundred left;
your town that marches out a hundred
        strong
    will have only ten left."

4 This is what the LORD says to the house
of Israel:

"Seek me and live;
5   do not seek Bethel,
do not go to Gilgal,
    do not journey to Beersheba.
For Gilgal will surely go into exile,
    and Bethel will be reduced to
        nothing. *a*"
6 Seek the LORD and live,
    or he will sweep through the house of
        Joseph like a fire;
it will devour them,
    and Bethel will have no one to
        quench it.

7 There are those who turn justice into
        bitterness
    and cast righteousness to the ground.

8 He who made the Pleiades and Orion,
    who turns midnight into dawn
    and darkens day into night,
who calls for the waters of the sea
    and pours them out over the face of
        the land—
    the LORD is his name.
9 He flashes destruction on the
        stronghold
    and brings the fortified city to ruin.
10 There are those who hate the one who
        reproves in court
    and detest the one who tells the
        truth.

11 You levy a straw tax on the poor
    and impose a tax on their grain.
Therefore, though you have built stone
        mansions,
    you will not live in them;
though you have planted lush vineyards,
    you will not drink their wine.
12 For I know how many are your offenses
    and how great your sins.

---

a 5 Hebrew *aven*, a reference to Beth Aven (a derogatory name for Bethel); see Hosea 4:15.

TUESDAY

LIVE YOUR WORSHIP

Amos 5:1–27 *or* 5:11–12,21–23

Louie Giglio

What God has revealed to us about Himself is beyond our words of gratitude. What He has done on our behalf makes it impossible for us to ever repay Him.

But what we *can* do in return—and must do—is give Him everything we have through a life of service to Him and to those around us. That's what we mean when we say worship is a way of life.

For far too long, people have been cheating God, somehow thinking that if they just keep telling Him He's great, He'll be content. Whether their words are genuine doesn't seem to matter. Whether their lives back up their words is no big deal.

After all, words come so easy. And saying (and singing) them makes us feel a little better about ourselves.

But God isn't honored by words alone. Like any of us, He's moved by words that are authenticated by actions. When it comes to worship, it's the total package that matters— what you say, how you say it and whether you mean it. And our words mean most when they're amplified in every area of our lives.

RICHARD BAXTER {AD 1615–1691}

God will disrobe the hypocrites before long, and he will make them know—to their sorrow— what it was to trifle with him. Woe to them, when they must account for the blood of souls! The reasons they use to justify not doing what God required of them will not then be sufficient to truly justify them for not having done it. Rather, it will then be revealed that those reasons were the result of their wickedness, coming out of their corrupted wills and their involvement with the world. Nor will their consciences claim those reasons at a dying hour, which now they seem to hold on to. They will then be grieved by the realization that they have failed God, and will not depart with the same comfort that belongs to those who have wholly devoted themselves to the service of the Lord . . . And now, brothers and sisters, I earnestly implore you, in the name of God: Do not be lazy about doing what God requires of you, but do it vigorously and with all your might; and make it your great and serious business.

reflection

1. What makes someone a hypocrite?

2. What is God's response to those who say they love God wholeheartedly but live in a way that displeases him?

3. What can you do this week to live out your worship?

For your next devotional reading, go to page 1024.

There are those who oppress the
    innocent and take bribes
    and deprive the poor of justice in the
        courts.
¹³ Therefore the prudent keep quiet in such
        times,
    for the times are evil.

¹⁴ Seek good, not evil,
    that you may live.
Then the LORD God Almighty will be
        with you,
    just as you say he is.
¹⁵ Hate evil, love good;
    maintain justice in the courts.
Perhaps the LORD God Almighty will
        have mercy
    on the remnant of Joseph.

¹⁶ Therefore this is what the Lord, the
LORD God Almighty, says:

    "There will be wailing in all the streets
        and cries of anguish in every public
            square.
    The farmers will be summoned to weep
        and the mourners to wail.
¹⁷ There will be wailing in all the
            vineyards,
    for I will pass through your midst,"
                            says the LORD.

The Day of the LORD

¹⁸ Woe to you who long
    for the day of the LORD!
Why do you long for the day of the
        LORD?
    That day will be darkness, not light.
¹⁹ It will be as though a man fled from a
        lion
    only to meet a bear,
    as though he entered his house
        and rested his hand on the wall
        only to have a snake bite him.
²⁰ Will not the day of the LORD be darkness,
        not light—
    pitch-dark, without a ray of
            brightness?

²¹ "I hate, I despise your religious festivals;
    I cannot stand your assemblies.
²² Even though you bring me burnt
            offerings and grain offerings,
    I will not accept them.

Though you bring choice fellowship
        offerings,
    I will have no regard for them.
²³ Away with the noise of your songs!
    I will not listen to the music of your
            harps.
²⁴ But let justice roll on like a river,
    righteousness like a never-failing
            stream!

²⁵ "Did you bring me sacrifices and
            offerings
    forty years in the wilderness, house of
            Israel?
²⁶ You have lifted up the shrine of your
            king,
    the pedestal of your idols,
    the star of your god ᵃ—
    which you made for yourselves.
²⁷ Therefore I will send you into exile
            beyond Damascus,"
    says the LORD, whose name is God
            Almighty.

Woe to the Complacent

6 Woe to you who are complacent in
            Zion,
    and to you who feel secure on Mount
            Samaria,
    you notable men of the foremost nation,
        to whom the people of Israel come!
² Go to Kalneh and look at it;
    go from there to great Hamath,
        and then go down to Gath in Philistia.
    Are they better off than your two
            kingdoms?
    Is their land larger than yours?
³ You put off the evil day
    and bring near a reign of terror.
⁴ You lie on beds inlaid with ivory
        and lounge on your couches.
    You dine on choice lambs
        and fattened calves.
⁵ You strum away on your harps like David
        and improvise on musical
            instruments.
⁶ You drink wine by the bowlful
        and use the finest lotions,
    but you do not grieve over the ruin of
            Joseph.
⁷ Therefore you will be among the first to
            go into exile;
    your feasting and lounging will end.

ᵃ 26 Or lifted up Sakkuth your king / and Kaiwan your idols, / your star-gods; Septuagint lifted up the shrine
of Molek / and the star of your god Rephan, / their idols

The Lord Abhors the Pride of Israel

⁸The Sovereign Lord has sworn by himself—the Lord God Almighty declares:

"I abhor the pride of Jacob
and detest his fortresses;
I will deliver up the city
and everything in it."

⁹If ten people are left in one house, they too will die. ¹⁰And if the relative who comes to carry the bodies out of the house to burn them*a* asks anyone who might be hiding there, "Is anyone else with you?" and he says, "No," then he will go on to say, "Hush! We must not mention the name of the Lord."

¹¹For the Lord has given the command,
and he will smash the great house
into pieces
and the small house into bits.

¹²Do horses run on the rocky crags?
Does one plow the sea*b* with oxen?
But you have turned justice into
poison
and the fruit of righteousness into
bitterness—
¹³you who rejoice in the conquest of Lo
Debar*c*
and say, "Did we not take Karnaim*d*
by our own strength?"

¹⁴For the Lord God Almighty declares,
"I will stir up a nation against you,
house of Israel,
that will oppress you all the way
from Lebo Hamath to the valley of
the Arabah."

Locusts, Fire and a Plumb Line

7 This is what the Sovereign Lord showed me: He was preparing swarms of locusts after the king's share had been harvested and just as the late crops were coming up. ²When they had stripped the land clean, I cried out, "Sovereign Lord, forgive! How can Jacob survive? He is so small!"

³So the Lord relented.

"This will not happen," the Lord said.

⁴This is what the Sovereign Lord showed me: The Sovereign Lord was calling for judgment by fire; it dried up the great deep and devoured the land. ⁵Then I cried out, "Sovereign Lord, I beg you, stop! How can Jacob survive? He is so small!"

⁶So the Lord relented.

"This will not happen either," the Sovereign Lord said.

⁷This is what he showed me: The Lord was standing by a wall that had been built true to plumb,*e* with a plumb line*f* in his hand. ⁸And the Lord asked me, "What do you see, Amos?"

"A plumb line," I replied.

Then the Lord said, "Look, I am setting a plumb line among my people Israel; I will spare them no longer.

⁹"The high places of Isaac will be
destroyed
and the sanctuaries of Israel will be
ruined;
with my sword I will rise against the
house of Jeroboam."

Amos and Amaziah

¹⁰Then Amaziah the priest of Bethel sent a message to Jeroboam king of Israel: "Amos is raising a conspiracy against you in the very heart of Israel. The land cannot bear all his words. ¹¹For this is what Amos is saying:

" 'Jeroboam will die by the sword,
and Israel will surely go into exile,
away from their native land.' "

¹²Then Amaziah said to Amos, "Get out, you seer! Go back to the land of Judah. Earn your bread there and do your prophesying there. ¹³Don't prophesy anymore at Bethel, because this is the king's sanctuary and the temple of the kingdom."

¹⁴Amos answered Amaziah, "I was neither a prophet nor the disciple of a prophet, but I was a shepherd, and I also took care of sycamore-fig trees. ¹⁵But the Lord took me from tending the flock and said to me, 'Go, prophesy to my people Israel.' ¹⁶Now then, hear the word of the Lord. You say,

" 'Do not prophesy against Israel,
and stop preaching against the house
of Isaac.'

a 10 Or *to make a funeral fire in honor of the dead*   *b 12* With a different word division of the Hebrew; Masoretic Text *plow there*   *c 13* *Lo Debar* means *nothing.*   *d 13* *Karnaim* means *horns; horn* here symbolizes strength.   *e 7* The meaning of the Hebrew for this phrase is uncertain.   *f 7* The meaning of the Hebrew for this phrase is uncertain; also in verse 8.

17"Therefore this is what the LORD says:

" 'Your wife will become a prostitute in
the city,
  and your sons and daughters will fall
  by the sword.
Your land will be measured and divided
up,
  and you yourself will die in a pagan^a
  country.
And Israel will surely go into exile,
  away from their native land.' "

A Basket of Ripe Fruit

8 This is what the Sovereign LORD
showed me: a basket of ripe fruit.
2"What do you see, Amos?" he asked.
"A basket of ripe fruit," I answered.
  Then the LORD said to me, "The time is
ripe for my people Israel; I will spare them
no longer.
  3"In that day," declares the Sovereign
LORD, "the songs in the temple will turn to
wailing.^b Many, many bodies—flung everywhere! Silence!"

4 Hear this, you who trample the needy
  and do away with the poor of the
  land,

5saying,

"When will the New Moon be over
  that we may sell grain,
and the Sabbath be ended
  that we may market wheat?"—
skimping on the measure,
  boosting the price
  and cheating with dishonest scales,
6buying the poor with silver
  and the needy for a pair of sandals,
  selling even the sweepings with the
  wheat.

7The LORD has sworn by himself, the
Pride of Jacob: "I will never forget anything
they have done.

8 "Will not the land tremble for this,
  and all who live in it mourn?
The whole land will rise like the Nile;
  it will be stirred up and then sink
  like the river of Egypt.

9"In that day," declares the Sovereign
LORD,

"I will make the sun go down at noon
  and darken the earth in broad
  daylight.
10 I will turn your religious festivals into
mourning
  and all your singing into weeping.
I will make all of you wear sackcloth
  and shave your heads.
I will make that time like mourning for
  an only son
  and the end of it like a bitter day.

11 "The days are coming," declares the
  Sovereign LORD,
  "when I will send a famine through
  the land—
not a famine of food or a thirst for water,
  but a famine of hearing the words of
  the LORD.
12 People will stagger from sea to sea
  and wander from north to east,
searching for the word of the LORD,
  but they will not find it.

13 "In that day

"the lovely young women and strong
  young men
  will faint because of thirst.
14 Those who swear by the sin of
  Samaria—
who say, 'As surely as your god lives,
  Dan,'
  or, 'As surely as the god^c of Beersheba
  lives'—
  they will fall, never to rise again."

Israel to Be Destroyed

9 I saw the Lord standing by the altar,
and he said:

"Strike the tops of the pillars
  so that the thresholds shake.
Bring them down on the heads of all the
  people;
  those who are left I will kill with the
  sword.
Not one will get away,
  none will escape.
2 Though they dig down to the depths
  below,
  from there my hand will take them.
Though they climb up to the heavens
  above,
  from there I will bring them down.

---

^a 17 Hebrew *an unclean*   ^b 3 Or *"the temple singers will wail*   ^c 14 Hebrew *the way*

3 Though they hide themselves on the top
of Carmel,
there I will hunt them down and seize
them.
Though they hide from my eyes at the
bottom of the sea,
there I will command the serpent to
bite them.
4 Though they are driven into exile by
their enemies,
there I will command the sword to
slay them.

"I will fix my eyes on them
for evil and not for good."

5 The Lord, the LORD Almighty—
he touches the earth and it melts,
and all who live in it mourn;
the whole land rises like the Nile,
then sinks like the river of Egypt;
6 he builds his lofty palace*a* in the
heavens
and sets its foundation*b* on the earth;
he calls for the waters of the sea
and pours them out over the face of
the land—
the LORD is his name.

7 "Are not you Israelites
the same to me as the Cushites*c*?"
declares the LORD.
"Did I not bring Israel up from Egypt,
the Philistines from Caphtor*d*
and the Arameans from Kir?

8 "Surely the eyes of the Sovereign LORD
are on the sinful kingdom.
I will destroy it
from the face of the earth.
Yet I will not totally destroy
the house of Jacob,"
declares the LORD.
9 "For I will give the command,
and I will shake the house of Israel
among all the nations

as grain is shaken in a sieve,
and not a pebble will reach the
ground.
10 All the sinners among my people
will die by the sword,
all those who say,
'Disaster will not overtake or meet
us.'

Israel's Restoration
11 "In that day

I will restore David's fallen shelter—
I will repair its broken walls
and restore its ruins—
and will rebuild it as it used to be,
12 so that they may possess the remnant of
Edom
and all the nations that bear my
name,*e*"
declares the LORD,
who will do these things.

13 "The days are coming," declares the
LORD,

"when the reaper will be overtaken by
the one who plows
and the planter by the one treading
grapes.
New wine will drip from the mountains
and flow from all the hills,
14 and I will bring my people Israel back
from exile.*f*

"They will rebuild the ruined cities and
live in them.
They will plant vineyards and drink
their wine;
they will make gardens and eat their
fruit.
15 I will plant Israel in their own land,
never again to be uprooted
from the land I have given them,"
says the LORD your God.

a 6 The meaning of the Hebrew for this phrase is uncertain.   *b* 6 The meaning of the Hebrew for this
word is uncertain.   *c* 7 That is, people from the upper Nile region   *d* 7 That is, Crete
e 12 Hebrew; Septuagint *so that the remnant of people / and all the nations that bear my name may seek
the Lord,*   *f* 14 Or *will restore the fortunes of my people Israel*

obadiah

> AUTHOR: Obadiah
>
> DATE: Probably between 605 and 586 B.C.
>
> THEME: God stands up for his people.

¹The vision of Obadiah.

This is what the Sovereign LORD says about Edom—

We have heard a message from the
  LORD:
    An envoy was sent to the nations to
      say,
  "Rise, let us go against her for battle"—

²"See, I will make you small among the
    nations;
  you will be utterly despised.
³The pride of your heart has deceived
    you,
  you who live in the clefts of the
    rocks*ª*
  and make your home on the heights,
you who say to yourself,
  'Who can bring me down to the
    ground?'
⁴Though you soar like the eagle
  and make your nest among the stars,
  from there I will bring you down,"
    declares the LORD.
⁵"If thieves came to you,
  if robbers in the night—
oh, what a disaster awaits you—
  would they not steal only as much as
    they wanted?
If grape pickers came to you,
  would they not leave a few grapes?
⁶But how Esau will be ransacked,
  his hidden treasures pillaged!
⁷All your allies will force you to the
    border;
  your friends will deceive and
    overpower you;

those who eat your bread will set a trap
    for you,*ᵇ*
  but you will not detect it.

⁸"In that day," declares the LORD,
  "will I not destroy the wise in Edom,
  people of understanding in the
    mountains of Esau?
⁹Your warriors, Teman, will be terrified,
  and everyone in Esau's mountains
  will be cut down in the slaughter.
¹⁰Because of the violence against your
    brother Jacob,
  you will be covered with shame;
  you will be destroyed forever.
¹¹On the day you stood aloof
  while strangers carried off his wealth
and foreigners entered his gates
  and cast lots for Jerusalem,
  you were like one of them.
¹²You should not gloat over your brother
  in the day of his misfortune,
nor rejoice over the people of Judah
  in the day of their destruction,
nor boast so much
  in the day of their trouble.
¹³You should not march through the gates
    of my people
  in the day of their disaster,
nor gloat over them in their calamity
  in the day of their disaster,
nor seize their wealth
  in the day of their disaster.
¹⁴You should not wait at the crossroads
  to cut down their fugitives,
nor hand over their survivors
  in the day of their trouble.

¹⁵"The day of the LORD is near
  for all nations.

---

a 3 Or *of Sela* *b 7* The meaning of the Hebrew for this clause is uncertain.

A Just God in an Unjust World
Obadiah 1–21 *or* 12–13

Philip Yancey

What difference do ancient prophetic visions make to those of us stuck in this fallen world? They awaken in us what we hope to be ultimately true. Would it make a difference for blacks in urban America, or Christians in Muslim prisons, to know how God feels about their plight? Did it matter to the slaves in the American South to believe that God was not satisfied with a world that included masters armed with bullwhips and lynching ropes? Would it make a difference for any of us to know that God is indeed a God of justice and peace and hope, no matter how this world appears?

The prophets call us to a vision of a deeper, underlying reality, to "joy beyond the walls of the world, more poignant than grief" (Tolkien's phrase). By giving a glimpse of the future, and of the cosmic present, they make it possible for us to believe in a just God after all. Justice is essential to the prophets, for God's reputation rides on whether he can ultimately deliver justice to this world. Like a bell tolling from another world, the prophets proclaim that no matter how things now appear, there is no future in evil, only in good.

Oswald Chambers {AD 1874–1917}

To look for justice is a sign of deflection from devotion to Him. Never look for justice in this world, but never cease to give it. If we look for justice, we will begin to grouse and to indulge in the discontent of self-pity—"Why should I be treated like this?" If we are devoted to Jesus Christ we have nothing to do with what we meet, whether it is just or unjust. Jesus says—"Go steadily on with what I have told you to do and I will guard your life. If you try to guard it yourself, you remove yourself from My deliverance." The most devout among us become atheistic in this connection; we do not believe God, we enthrone common sense and tack the name of God on to it. We do lean to our own understanding, instead of trusting God with all our hearts.

reflection

1. In what areas do you feel entitled to justice?
2. Why does the drive for justice seem ingrained in the human heart?
3. How can having a view of heaven alter your need for justice in this world?

For your next devotional reading, go to page 1027.

As you have done, it will be done to you;
>   your deeds will return upon your own
>   head.
16 Just as you drank on my holy hill,
>   so all the nations will drink
>   continually;
> they will drink and drink
>   and be as if they had never been.
17 But on Mount Zion will be
>   deliverance;
>   it will be holy,
> and the house of Jacob
>   will possess its inheritance.
18 The house of Jacob will be a fire
>   and the house of Joseph a flame;
> the house of Esau will be stubble,
>   and they will set it on fire and
>   consume it.
> There will be no survivors

from the house of Esau."
>> The LORD has spoken.

19 People from the Negev will occupy
>   the mountains of Esau,
> and people from the foothills will possess
>   the land of the Philistines.
> They will occupy the fields of Ephraim
>   and Samaria,
> and Benjamin will possess Gilead.
20 This company of Israelite exiles who are
>   in Canaan
> will possess ⌊the land⌋ as far as
>   Zarephath;
> the exiles from Jerusalem who are in
>   Sepharad
> will possess the towns of the Negev.
21 Deliverers will go up on a Mount Zion
>   to govern the mountains of Esau.
> And the kingdom will be the LORD's.

a 21 Or from

jonah

AUTHOR: Jonah

DATE: Probably around 750 B.C.

THEME: God compassionately seeks out even those we consider beyond his reach.

Jonah Flees From the LORD

1 The word of the LORD came to Jonah son of Amittai: 2"Go to the great city Nineveh and preach against it, because its wickedness has come up before me."

3But Jonah ran away from the LORD and headed for Tarshish. He went down to Joppa, where he found a ship bound for that port. After paying the fare, he went aboard and sailed for Tarshish to flee from the LORD.

4Then the LORD sent a great wind on the sea, and such a violent storm arose that the ship threatened to break up. 5All the sailors were afraid and each cried out to his own god. And they threw the cargo into the sea to lighten the ship.

But Jonah had gone below deck, where he lay down and fell into a deep sleep. 6The captain went to him and said, "How can you sleep? Get up and call on your god! Maybe he will take notice of us so that we will not perish."

7Then the sailors said to each other, "Come, let us cast lots to find out who is responsible for this calamity." They cast lots and the lot fell on Jonah. 8So they asked him, "Tell us, who is responsible for making all this trouble for us? What kind of work do you do? Where do you come from? What is your country? From what people are you?"

9He answered, "I am a Hebrew and I worship the LORD, the God of heaven, who made the sea and the dry land."

10This terrified them and they asked, "What have you done?" (They knew he was running away from the LORD, because he had already told them so.)

11The sea was getting rougher and rougher. So they asked him, "What should we do to you to make the sea calm down for us?"

12"Pick me up and throw me into the sea," he replied, "and it will become calm. I know that it is my fault that this great storm has come upon you."

13Instead, the men did their best to row back to land. But they could not, for the sea grew even wilder than before. 14Then they cried out to the LORD, "Please, LORD, do not let us die for taking this man's life. Do not hold us accountable for killing an innocent man, for you, LORD, have done as you pleased." 15Then they took Jonah and threw him overboard, and the raging sea grew calm. 16At this the men greatly feared the LORD, and they offered a sacrifice to the LORD and made vows to him.

*17Now the LORD provided a huge fish to swallow Jonah, and Jonah was in the belly of the fish three days and three nights.

Jonah's Prayer

2 *From inside the fish Jonah prayed to the LORD his God. 2He said:

"In my distress I called to the LORD,
    and he answered me.
From deep in the realm of the dead I
        called for help,
    and you listened to my cry.
3 You hurled me into the deep,
    into the very heart of the seas,
    and the currents swirled about me;
all your waves and breakers
    swept over me.
4 I said, 'I have been banished
    from your sight;
yet I will look again

---

* 1:17 is numbered 2:1 in Hebrew texts.   * 2:1-10 is numbered 2:2-11 in Hebrew texts.

THURSDAY

LETTING GOD USE YOU

Jonah 1:1–17 *or* 1:1–2

SAINT AUGUSTINE {AD 354–430}

Preach Christ . . . Spread the gospel. Scatter with your mouth what you have understood in your heart. Let the nations hear; let the nations believe. Let the church of Christ spring forth from the blood of those who have died for the sake of the gospel. Already, so many people have responded to this call, so many have believed and been united with Jesus—the head of the body of Christ. Many have already been baptized, and many others will be baptized in the future. Then, at the end of the world each of those living, holy stones will be joined to the foundation—Jesus—and we will see the church completed.

Jim Cymbala

The Lord is not going to use angels or a voice from the clouds in heaven to spread his message. He has chosen to let us be his hand extended. But his heart is one of infinite tender compassion to all humanity, for "God does not show favoritism" (Acts 10:34). Only by the Holy Spirit can we see people as he sees them and feel their need as he does. *Lord, help us to love one another.*

reflection

1. Why do you think God chooses to use people to spread his message?
2. How do you feel about your commission to spread the gospel?
3. Whom can you pray for who needs to hear God's message of salvation?

For your next devotional reading, go to page 1028.

FRIDAY

THE SCHOOL OF PRAYER

Jonah 2:1–10 *or* 2:7–9

Eugene Peterson

So Jonah prayed. *That* Jonah prayed is not remarkable; we commonly pray when we are in desperate circumstances. But there is something very remarkable about the *way* Jonah prayed. He prayed a "set" prayer. Jonah's prayer is not spontaneously original . . . It is totally derivative. Jonah had been to school to learn to pray, and he prayed as he had been taught. His school was the Psalms . . .

If we want to pray our true condition, our total selves in response to the living God, expressing our feelings is not enough—we need a long apprenticeship in prayer. And then we need graduate school. The Psalms are the school. Jonah in his prayer shows himself to have been a diligent student in the school of Psalms. His prayer is kicked off by his plight, but it is not reduced to it. His prayer took him into a world far larger than his immediate experience. He was capable of prayer that was adequate to the largeness of the God with whom he was dealing.

OLE HALLESBY {AD 1879–1961}

So few of us become sanctified and skilled petitioners because we do not continue in the school of prayer . . . There is something about this school which tries our patience sorely. Jesus Himself alludes to it on several occasions, especially in Luke 18:1–8, where He says "that they [should always pray and not give up]."

. . . It is the Spirit of prayer who superintends the instruction in the school of prayer. He does not offer a variety of subjects, but concentrates purposely on a few central things. It is not necessary to master a large variety of subjects in order to become skilled in prayer. I would mention briefly only the following:

In the first place, the Spirit must be given an opportunity to reveal Christ to us every day. This is absolutely essential. Christ is such that we need only "see" Him, and prayer will rise from our hearts. Voluntary prayer, confident prayer. We know that Christ can answer prayer. We know also that it gives Him joy to do so. Prayer and intercession have become a delightful and fascinating means of cooperation between Christ and the praying soul.

reflection

1. What "grade" level would you say you're at in the "school of prayer"?

2. In what ways are you growing as a student in the school of prayer? Are you in any danger of becoming a "dropout"?

3. What can you learn from Jonah's example regarding prayer?

For your next devotional reading, go to page 1030.

toward your holy temple.'
⁵ The engulfing waters threatened me,ᵃ
    the deep surrounded me;
    seaweed was wrapped around my
        head.
⁶ To the roots of the mountains I sank
        down;
    the earth beneath barred me in
        forever.
But you, Lᴏʀᴅ my God,
    brought my life up from the pit.

⁷ "When my life was ebbing away,
    I remembered you, Lᴏʀᴅ,
and my prayer rose to you,
    to your holy temple.

⁸ "Those who cling to worthless idols
    forfeit God's love for them.
⁹ But I, with shouts of grateful praise,
    will sacrifice to you.
What I have vowed I will make good.
    I will say, 'Salvation comes from the
        Lᴏʀᴅ.' "

¹⁰ And the Lᴏʀᴅ commanded the fish, and
it vomited Jonah onto dry land.

Jonah Goes to Nineveh

3 Then the word of the Lᴏʀᴅ came to Jonah a second time: ² "Go to the great city of Nineveh and proclaim to it the message I give you."

³ Jonah obeyed the word of the Lᴏʀᴅ and went to Nineveh. Now Nineveh was a very large city; it took three days to go through it. ⁴ Jonah began by going a day's journey into the city, proclaiming, "Forty more days and Nineveh will be overthrown." ⁵ The Ninevites believed God. They declared a fast, and all of them, from the greatest to the least, put on sackcloth.

⁶ When the news reached the king of Nineveh, he rose from his throne, took off his royal robes, covered himself with sackcloth and sat down in the dust. ⁷ Then he issued a proclamation in Nineveh:

"By the decree of the king and his nobles:

Do not let people or animals, herds or flocks, taste anything; do not let them eat or drink. ⁸ But let people and animals be covered with sackcloth. Let

everyone call urgently on God. Let them give up their evil ways and their violence. ⁹ Who knows? God may yet relent and with compassion turn from his fierce anger so that we will not perish."

¹⁰ When God saw what they did and how they turned from their evil ways, he relented and did not bring on them the destruction he had threatened.

Jonah's Anger at the Lᴏʀᴅ's Compassion

4 But to Jonah this seemed very wrong, and he became angry. ² He prayed to the Lᴏʀᴅ, "Isn't this what I said, Lᴏʀᴅ, when I was still at home? That is what I tried to forestall by fleeing to Tarshish. I knew that you are a gracious and compassionate God, slow to anger and abounding in love, a God who relents from sending calamity. ³ Now, Lᴏʀᴅ, take away my life, for it is better for me to die than to live."

⁴ But the Lᴏʀᴅ replied, "Is it right for you to be angry?"

⁵ Jonah went out and sat down at a place east of the city. There he made himself a shelter, sat in its shade and waited to see what would happen to the city. ⁶ Then the Lᴏʀᴅ God provided a gourdᵇ and made it grow up over Jonah to give shade for his head to ease his discomfort, and Jonah was very happy about the gourd. ⁷ But at dawn the next day God provided a worm, which chewed the gourd so that it withered. ⁸ When the sun rose, God provided a scorching east wind, and the sun blazed on Jonah's head so that he grew faint. He wanted to die, and said, "It would be better for me to die than to live."

⁹ But God said to Jonah, "Is it right for you to be angry about the gourd?"

"It is," he said. "And I'm so angry I wish I were dead."

¹⁰ But the Lᴏʀᴅ said, "You have been concerned about this gourd, though you did not tend it or make it grow. It sprang up overnight and died overnight. ¹¹ And should I not have concern for the great city Nineveh, in which there are more than a hundred and twenty thousand people who cannot tell their right hand from their left—and also many animals?"

ᵃ 5 Or *waters were at my throat*   ᵇ 6 The precise identification of this plant is uncertain; also in verses 7, 9 and 10.

Our Enemies

Jonah 3:10—4:1

read/meditate

Read Jonah 3:10—4:1 multiple times. Watch for the difference between God's response and Jonah's response. How do you relate to Jonah (if at all) in this account? Think about the most difficult people in your life. How hard is it to see good things happen to them?

pray

Ask God to reveal any hardness in your heart. Ask him to show you the ways in which your response to your enemies is so different from God's response. Confess any anger or bitterness that you are holding on to, and be still before God as he begins to soften your heart.

contemplate

Forgiving your enemies doesn't mean you have to ignore your wounds. It means trusting God to deal with those who have hurt you, while you let go and move on. Think about what you will have to give up in order to do that.

additional reflection

I choose peace . . . I will live forgiven. I will forgive so that I may live.
—Max Lucado

Forgiveness is letting go of a bell rope. If you have ever seen a country church with a bell in the steeple, you will remember that to get the bell ringing you have to tug awhile. Once it has begun to ring, you merely maintain the momentum. As long as you keep pulling, the bell keeps ringing. Forgiveness is letting go of the rope. It is just that simple . . . if you keep your hands off the rope, the bell will begin to slow and eventually stop.
—Corrie ten Boom

For your next devotional reading, go to page 1033.

micah

AUTHOR: Micah

DATE: Sometime between 750 and 686 B.C.

THEME: God forgives those who turn to him.

1 The word of the LORD that came to Micah of Moresheth during the reigns of Jotham, Ahaz and Hezekiah, kings of Judah—the vision he saw concerning Samaria and Jerusalem.

2 Hear, you peoples, all of you,
   listen, earth and all who live in it,
that the Sovereign LORD may witness
      against you,
   the Lord from his holy temple.

Judgment Against Samaria and Jerusalem

3 Look! The LORD is coming from his
      dwelling place;
   he comes down and treads on the
      heights of the earth.
4 The mountains melt beneath him
   and the valleys split apart,
like wax before the fire,
   like water rushing down a slope.
5 All this is because of Jacob's
      transgression,
   because of the sins of the house of
      Israel.
What is Jacob's transgression?
   Is it not Samaria?
What is Judah's high place?
   Is it not Jerusalem?

6 "Therefore I will make Samaria a heap of
      rubble,
   a place for planting vineyards.
I will pour her stones into the valley
   and lay bare her foundations.
7 All her idols will be broken to pieces;
   all her temple gifts will be burned
      with fire;

I will destroy all her images.
Since she gathered her gifts from the
      wages of prostitutes,
   as the wages of prostitutes they will
      again be used."

Weeping and Mourning

8 Because of this I will weep and wail;
   I will go about barefoot and naked.
I will howl like a jackal
   and moan like an owl.
9 For Samaria's wound is incurable;
   it has come to Judah.
It has reached the very gate of my
      people,
   even to Jerusalem itself.
10 Tell it not in Gath[a];
   weep not at all.
In Beth Ophrah[b]
   roll in the dust.
11 Pass on in nakedness and shame,
   you who live in Shaphir.[c]
Those who live in Zaanan[d]
   will not come out.
Beth Ezel is in mourning;
   its protection is taken from you.
12 Those who live in Maroth[e] writhe in
      pain,
   waiting for relief,
because disaster has come from the
      LORD,
   even to the gate of Jerusalem.
13 You who live in Lachish,[f]
   harness the team to the chariot.
You were the beginning of sin
   to Daughter Zion,
for the transgressions of Israel

---

a 10 *Gath* sounds like the Hebrew for *tell.*   b 10 *Beth Ophrah* means *house of dust.*   c 11 *Shaphir* means *pleasant.*   d 11 *Zaanan* sounds like the Hebrew for *come out.*   e 12 *Maroth* sounds like the Hebrew for *bitter.*   f 13 *Lachish* sounds like the Hebrew for *team.*

were found in you.
¹⁴ Therefore you will give parting gifts
    to Moresheth Gath.
  The town of Akzib ᵃ will prove deceptive
    to the kings of Israel.
¹⁵ I will bring a conqueror against you
    who live in Mareshah. ᵇ
  The nobles of Israel
    will flee to Adullam.
¹⁶ Shave your head in mourning
    for the children in whom you delight;
  make yourself as bald as the vulture,
    for they will go from you into exile.

Human Plans and God's Plans

2 Woe to those who plan iniquity,
    to those who plot evil on their beds!
  At morning's light they carry it out
    because it is in their power to do it.
² They covet fields and seize them,
    and houses, and take them.
  They defraud people of their homes,
    they rob them of their inheritance.

³ Therefore, the Lord says:

"I am planning disaster against this
    people,
  from which you cannot save
    yourselves.
You will no longer walk proudly,
    for it will be a time of calamity.
⁴ In that day people will ridicule you;
    they will taunt you with this mournful
    song:
'We are utterly ruined;
    my people's possession is divided up.
He takes it from me!
    He assigns our fields to traitors.' "

⁵ Therefore you will have no one in the
    assembly of the Lord
  to divide the land by lot.

False Prophets

⁶ "Do not prophesy," their prophets say.
  "Do not prophesy about these things;
    disgrace will not overtake us."
⁷ House of Jacob, should it be said,
    "Does the Lord become ᶜ impatient?
    Does he do such things?"

"Do not my words do good
    to those whose ways are upright?

⁸ Lately my people have risen up
    like an enemy.
  You strip off the rich robe
    from those who pass by without a
    care,
  like men returning from battle.
⁹ You drive the women of my people
    from their pleasant homes.
  You take away my blessing
    from their children forever.
¹⁰ Get up, go away!
    For this is not your resting place,
  because it is defiled,
    it is ruined, beyond all remedy.
¹¹ If liars and deceivers come and say,
    'We will prophesy for you plenty of
    wine and beer,'
  they would be just the prophets for
    this people!

Deliverance Promised

¹² "I will surely gather all of you, Jacob;
    I will surely bring together the
    remnant of Israel.
  I will bring them together like sheep in a
    pen,
    like a flock in its pasture;
    the place will throng with people.
¹³ One who breaks open the way will go up
    before them;
    they will break through the gate and
    go out.
  Their King will pass through before
    them,
    the Lord at their head."

Leaders and Prophets Rebuked

3 Then I said,

"Listen, you leaders of Jacob,
    you rulers of the house of Israel.
  Should you not know justice,
²   you who hate good and love evil;
  who tear the skin from my people
    and the flesh from their bones;
³ who eat my people's flesh,
    strip off their skin
    and break their bones in pieces;
  who chop them up like meat for the pan,
    like flesh for the pot?"

⁴ Then they will cry out to the Lord,
    but he will not answer them.

ᵃ 14 *Akzib* means *deception*.   ᵇ 15 *Mareshah* sounds like the Hebrew for *conqueror*.   ᶜ 7 Or *Is the Spirit of the Lord*

MONDAY

HEADING FOR HOME

Micah 2:1–13 *or* 2:10,12

D. L. MOODY {AD 1837–1899}

"Like an eagle that stirs up its nest . . ." (Deuteronomy 32:11). This illustration . . . is one of the most beautiful and appropriate that could be conceived. It is taken from the habits of the eagle, which, when her young ones are well fledged and would prefer to linger in downy ease, disturbs their nest, that they may be taught how to fly. Look at that parent bird picking at the nest which she hath built for her tender offspring: see how she breaks off one twig after another, exciting her brood to leave their nest and soar on high amid the sunshine of heaven. And if they will not leave it, she will break it further and further, until it is utterly broken up, and they are forced to fly or fall.

Thus God deals with us. He knows our tendency to make this earth our rest, and he disturbs our nest to teach us to rise on the wings of faith toward the enduring realities of heaven. How often does God take away our earthly comforts when he sees that we cling too fondly to them! How often, in this world of vicissitude and change, do riches make themselves wings and fly. By some unfortunate speculation, or in some way we know not how, lands and possessions are swept away at a stroke . . . Perhaps something upon which we placed the utmost reliance, upon which seemed to rest our only stay, is suddenly and mysteriously taken from us, and when we attempt to grasp it we find it gone. A gale at sea may destroy the hopes of the merchant; depression in trade may bring want to your door; the bankruptcy of some large mercantile firm, or the failure of a bank, may involve numbers in ruin and plunge many families in misery hitherto unknown.

How many have had occasion, from these and similar causes, and how many more will yet have occasion, to mourn over altered circumstances! Marvel not if it be thus with you; it is God stirring up your nest to teach you to wing your flight to heaven. All these things have a voice if ye will but hear, and seem to say, "[Get up, go away! For this is not your resting place]."

Joyce Webster

Following God down his path is not always comfortable, but I believe it is only on this "path of life" that I truly find joy and eternal pleasures!

reflection

1. How did God use the disasters that came to his people to lead them where they should go?

2. In what ways do you find yourself viewing earth, instead of heaven, as your permanent home?

3. How do the "discomforts" of your life help turn your heart toward heaven?

For your next devotional reading, go to page 1037.

At that time he will hide his face from
them
  because of the evil they have done.

⁵This is what the LORD says:

"As for the prophets
  who lead my people astray,
if you feed them,
  they proclaim 'peace';
if you do not,
  they prepare to wage war against you.
⁶Therefore night will come over you,
    without visions,
  and darkness, without divination.
The sun will set for the prophets,
  and the day will go dark for them.
⁷The seers will be ashamed
  and the diviners disgraced.
They will all cover their faces
  because there is no answer from God."
⁸But as for me, I am filled with power,
  with the Spirit of the LORD,
  and with justice and might,
to declare to Jacob his transgression,
  to Israel his sin.

⁹Hear this, you leaders of the house of
    Jacob,
  you rulers of the house of Israel,
who despise justice
  and distort all that is right;
¹⁰who build Zion with bloodshed,
  and Jerusalem with wickedness.
¹¹Her leaders judge for a bribe,
  her priests teach for a price,
  and her prophets tell fortunes for
    money.
Yet they lean upon the LORD and say,
  "Is not the LORD among us?
  No disaster will come upon us."
¹²Therefore because of you,
  Zion will be plowed like a field,
Jerusalem will become a heap of rubble,
  the temple hill a mound overgrown
    with thickets.

The Mountain of the LORD

4 In the last days

the mountain of the LORD's temple
    will be established
  as chief among the mountains;
it will be raised above the hills,
  and peoples will stream to it.

²Many nations will come and say,

"Come, let us go up to the mountain of
    the LORD,
  to the house of the God of Jacob.
He will teach us his ways,
  so that we may walk in his paths."
The law will go out from Zion,
  the word of the LORD from Jerusalem.
³He will judge between many peoples
  and will settle disputes for strong
    nations far and wide.
They will beat their swords into
    plowshares
  and their spears into pruning hooks.
Nation will not take up sword against
    nation,
  nor will they train for war anymore.
⁴Everyone will sit under their own vine
  and under their own fig tree,
and no one will make them afraid,
  for the LORD Almighty has spoken.
⁵All the nations may walk
  in the name of their gods;
we will walk in the name of the LORD
  our God for ever and ever.

The LORD's Plan

⁶"In that day," declares the LORD,

"I will gather the lame;
  I will assemble the exiles
  and those I have brought to grief.
⁷I will make the lame a remnant,
  those driven away a strong nation.
The LORD will rule over them in Mount
    Zion
  from that day and forever.
⁸As for you, watchtower of the flock,
  stronghold^a of Daughter Zion,
the former dominion will be restored to
    you;
  kingship will come to Daughter
    Jerusalem."

⁹Why do you now cry aloud—
  have you no king^b?
Has your ruler^c perished,
  that pain seizes you like that of a
    woman in labor?
¹⁰Writhe in agony, Daughter Zion,
  like a woman in labor,
for now you must leave the city
  to camp in the open field.
You will go to Babylon;

there you will be rescued.
There the LORD will redeem you
  out of the hand of your enemies.
¹¹ But now many nations
  are gathered against you.
They say, "Let her be defiled,
  let our eyes gloat over Zion!"
¹² But they do not know
  the thoughts of the LORD;
they do not understand his plan,
  he who gathers them like sheaves to
    the threshing floor.
¹³ "Rise and thresh, Daughter Zion,
  for I will give you horns of iron;
I will give you hooves of bronze,
  and you will break to pieces many
    nations."
You will devote their ill-gotten gains to
    the LORD,
  their wealth to the Lord of all the
    earth.

A Promised Ruler From Bethlehem

5 *Marshal your troops now, city of
    troops,
  for a siege is laid against us.
They will strike Israel's ruler
  on the cheek with a rod.

^{*2} "But you, Bethlehem Ephrathah,
    though you are small among the
    clans^a of Judah,
  out of you will come for me
    one who will be ruler over Israel,
  whose origins are from of old,
    from ancient times."

³ Therefore Israel will be abandoned
    until the time when she who is in
    labor gives birth
  and the rest of his brothers return
    to join the Israelites.

⁴ He will stand and shepherd his flock
    in the strength of the LORD,
  in the majesty of the name of the
    LORD his God.
And they will live securely, for then his
    greatness
  will reach to the ends of the earth.

⁵ And he will be our peace
  when the Assyrians invade our land

and march through our fortresses.
We will raise against them seven
    shepherds,
  even eight commanders,
⁶ who will rule^b the land of Assyria with
    the sword,
  the land of Nimrod with drawn
    sword.^c
He will deliver us from the Assyrians
  when they invade our land
  and march into our borders.

⁷ The remnant of Jacob will be
  in the midst of many peoples
like dew from the LORD,
  like showers on the grass,
which do not wait for mortals
  or depend on any human being.
⁸ The remnant of Jacob will be among the
    nations,
  in the midst of many peoples,
like a lion among the beasts of the
    forest,
  like a young lion among flocks of
    sheep,
which mauls and mangles as it goes,
  and no one can rescue.
⁹ Your hand will be lifted up in triumph
    over your enemies,
  and all your foes will be destroyed.

¹⁰ "In that day," declares the LORD,

"I will destroy your horses from among
    you
  and demolish your chariots.
¹¹ I will destroy the cities of your land
  and tear down all your strongholds.
¹² I will destroy your witchcraft
  and you will no longer cast spells.
¹³ I will destroy your idols
  and your sacred stones from among
    you;
you will no longer bow down
  to the work of your hands.
¹⁴ I will uproot from among you your
    Asherah poles^d
  when I demolish your cities.
¹⁵ I will take vengeance in anger and
    wrath
  on the nations that have not obeyed
    me."

---

^a 2 Or *rulers*   ^b 6 Or *crush*   ^c 6 Or *Nimrod in its gates*   ^d 14 That is, wooden symbols of the goddess Asherah

* 5:1 is numbered 4:14 in Hebrew texts.   * 5:2-15 is numbered 5:1-14 in Hebrew texts.

The Lord's Case Against Israel

6 Listen to what the Lord says:

"Stand up, plead my case before the
mountains;
let the hills hear what you have to
say.

2 "Hear, you mountains, the Lord's
accusation;
listen, you everlasting foundations of
the earth.
For the Lord has a case against his
people;
he is lodging a charge against Israel.

3 "My people, what have I done to you?
How have I burdened you? Answer me.
4 I brought you up out of Egypt
and redeemed you from the land of
slavery.
I sent Moses to lead you,
also Aaron and Miriam.
5 My people, remember
what Balak king of Moab plotted
and what Balaam son of Beor
answered.
Remember your journey from Shittim to
Gilgal,
that you may know the righteous acts
of the Lord."

6 With what shall I come before the Lord
and bow down before the exalted
God?
Shall I come before him with burnt
offerings,
with calves a year old?
7 Will the Lord be pleased with thousands
of rams,
with ten thousand rivers of olive oil?
Shall I offer my firstborn for my
transgression,
the fruit of my body for the sin of my
soul?
8 He has shown all you people what is
good.
And what does the Lord require of
you?
To act justly and to love mercy
and to walk humbly[a] with your God.

Israel's Guilt and Punishment

9 Listen! The Lord is calling to the city—
and to fear your name is wisdom—
"Heed the rod and the One who
appointed it.[b]
10 Am I still to forget your ill-gotten
treasures, you wicked house,
and the short ephah,[c] which is
accursed?
11 Shall I acquit a person with dishonest
scales,
with a bag of false weights?
12 Her rich people are violent;
her inhabitants are liars
and their tongues speak deceitfully.
13 Therefore, I have begun to destroy you,
to ruin[d] you because of your sins.
14 You will eat but not be satisfied;
your stomach will still be empty.[e]
You will store up but save nothing,
because what you save[f] I will give to
the sword.
15 You will plant but not harvest;
you will press olives but not use the
oil on yourselves,
you will crush grapes but not drink
the wine.
16 You have observed the statutes of Omri
and all the practices of Ahab's house;
you have followed their traditions.
Therefore I will give you over to ruin
and your people to derision;
you will bear the scorn of the
nations.[g]"

Israel's Misery

7 What misery is mine!
I am like one who gathers summer
fruit
at the gleaning of the vineyard;
there is no cluster of grapes to eat,
none of the early figs that I crave.
2 The faithful have been swept from the
land;
not one upright person remains.
Everyone lies in wait to shed blood;
they hunt each other with nets.
3 Both hands are skilled in doing evil;
the ruler demands gifts,
the judge accepts bribes,

---

a 8 Or prudently   b 9 The meaning of the Hebrew for this line is uncertain.   c 10 An ephah was a dry measure.   d 13 Or Therefore, I will make you ill and destroy you; / I will ruin   e 14 The meaning of the Hebrew for this word is uncertain.   f 14 Or You will press toward birth but not give birth, / and what you bring to birth   g 16 Septuagint; Hebrew scorn due my people

TUESDAY

GOD PURSUES SINNERS
Micah 7:1–20 *or* 7:18–20

Ann Spangler

Shakespeare described jealousy as a "green-eyed monster." Mark Twain called it the "trademark of small minds." Robert Heinlein labeled it a "symptom of neurotic insecurity." Such apt but unattractive descriptions of human jealousy will only confuse you if you try to apply them to God, whose jealousy might better be described by the words of the English poet Joseph Addison: "Jealous is that pain which a man feels from the apprehension that he is not equally beloved by the person whom he entirely loves."

This is the kind of jealousy that impels God to pursue us, despite our evasions, our indifference or our waywardness. Francis Thompson was a nineteenth-century poet, an opium addict, whose sense of the divine pursuit of his soul is famously captured in his poem *The Hound of Heaven:*

> Adown Titanic glooms of chasmed fears,
> From those strong Feet that followed, flowed after.
> But with unhurrying chase,
> And unperturbed pace
> Deliberate speed, majestic instancy,
> They beat—and a Voice beat
> More instant than the Feet—
> "All things betray thee, who betrayest Me"

C. S. LEWIS {AD 1898–1963}

You asked for a loving God; you have one. The great spirit you so lightly invoked, the "lord of terrible aspect," is present; not a senile benevolence that drowsily wishes you to be happy in your own way, not the cold philanthropy of a conscientious magistrate, nor the care of a host who feels responsible for the comfort of his guests, but the consuming fire himself, the Love that made the worlds, persistent as the artist's love for his work and despotic as a man's love for a dog, provident and venerable as a father's love for a child, jealous, inexorable, exacting as love between the sexes.

reflection

1. What does it mean to you to be called God's "beloved"?

2. What does God's love feel like to you?

3. Has your understanding of God's love changed or been added to by today's reading?

For your next devotional reading, go to page 1040.

the powerful dictate what they
   desire—
they all conspire together.
⁴ The best of them is like a brier,
   the most upright worse than a thorn
      hedge.
The day of your watchmen has come,
   the day God visits you.
Now is the time of their confusion.
⁵ Do not trust a neighbor;
   put no confidence in a friend.
Even with the woman who lies in your
      embrace
   be careful of your words.
⁶ For a son dishonors his father,
   a daughter rises up against her
      mother,
a daughter-in-law against her mother-
      in-law—
   your enemies are the members of
      your own household.

⁷ But as for me, I watch in hope for the
      LORD,
   I wait for God my Savior;
   my God will hear me.

Israel Will Rise
⁸ Do not gloat over me, my enemy!
   Though I have fallen, I will rise.
Though I sit in darkness,
   the LORD will be my light.
⁹ Because I have sinned against him,
   I will bear the LORD's wrath,
until he pleads my case
   and establishes my right.
He will bring me out into the light;
   I will see his righteousness.
¹⁰ Then my enemy will see it
   and will be covered with shame,
she who said to me,
   "Where is the LORD your God?"
My eyes will see her downfall;
   even now she will be trampled
      underfoot
   like mire in the streets.

¹¹ The day for building your walls will
      come,

the day for extending your
   boundaries.
¹² In that day people will come to you
   from Assyria and the cities of Egypt,
even from Egypt to the Euphrates
   and from sea to sea
   and from mountain to mountain.
¹³ The earth will become desolate because
      of its inhabitants,
   as the result of their deeds.

Prayer and Praise
¹⁴ Shepherd your people with your staff,
   the flock of your inheritance,
which lives by itself in a forest,
   in fertile pasturelands. *a*
Let them feed in Bashan and Gilead
   as in days long ago.

¹⁵ "As in the days when you came out of
      Egypt,
   I will show them my wonders."

¹⁶ Nations will see and be ashamed,
   deprived of all their power.
They will put their hands over their
      mouths
   and their ears will become deaf.
¹⁷ They will lick dust like a snake,
   like creatures that crawl on the
      ground.
They will come trembling out of their
      dens;
   they will turn in fear to the LORD our
      God
   and will be afraid of you.
¹⁸ Who is a God like you,
   who pardons sin and forgives the
      transgression
   of the remnant of his inheritance?
You do not stay angry forever
   but delight to show mercy.
¹⁹ You will again have compassion on us;
   you will tread our sins underfoot
   and hurl all our iniquities into the
      depths of the sea.
²⁰ You will be faithful to Jacob,
   and show love to Abraham,
as you pledged on oath to our ancestors
   in days long ago.

a 14 Or in the middle of Carmel

nahum

AUTHOR: Nahum

DATE: Likely written shortly before the fall of Nineveh in 612 B.C.

THEME: God will not leave evil unpunished.

1 A prophecy concerning Nineveh. The book of the vision of Nahum the El-koshite.

The LORD's Anger Against Nineveh

2 The LORD is a jealous and avenging God;
    the LORD takes vengeance and is filled
        with wrath.
The LORD takes vengeance on his foes
    and vents his wrath against his
        enemies.
3 The LORD is slow to anger but great in
        power;
    the LORD will not leave the guilty
        unpunished.
His way is in the whirlwind and the
        storm,
    and clouds are the dust of his feet.
4 He rebukes the sea and dries it up;
    he makes all the rivers run dry.
Bashan and Carmel wither
    and the blossoms of Lebanon fade.
5 The mountains quake before him
    and the hills melt away.
The earth trembles at his presence,
    the world and all who live in it.
6 Who can withstand his indignation?
    Who can endure his fierce anger?
His wrath is poured out like fire;
    the rocks are shattered before him.

7 The LORD is good,
    a refuge in times of trouble.
He cares for those who trust in him,
8   but with an overwhelming flood
he will make an end of Nineveh;
    he will pursue his foes into darkness.

9 Whatever they plot against the LORD
    he[a] will bring to an end;
    trouble will not come a second time.
10 They will be entangled among thorns
    and drunk from their wine;
    they will be consumed like dry
        stubble.[b]
11 From you, Nineveh, has one come forth
    who plots evil against the LORD
    and devises wicked plans.

12 This is what the LORD says:

"Although they have allies and are
        numerous,
    they will be destroyed and pass away.
Although I have afflicted you, Judah,
    I will afflict you no more.
13 Now I will break their yoke from your
        neck
    and tear your shackles away."

14 The LORD has given a command
        concerning you, Nineveh:
"You will have no descendants to bear
        your name.
I will destroy the images and idols
    that are in the temple of your gods.
I will prepare your grave,
    for you are vile."

*15 Look, there on the mountains,
    the feet of one who brings good news,
    who proclaims peace!
Celebrate your festivals, Judah,
    and fulfill your vows.
No more will the wicked invade you;
    they will be completely destroyed.

---

a 9 Or *What do you foes plot against the LORD? / He*
uncertain.

b 10 The meaning of the Hebrew for this verse is

* 1:15 is numbered 2:1 in Hebrew texts.

WEDNESDAY

GOD'S WAYS AREN'T OUR WAYS

Nahum 1:1–15 *or* 1:7, 10–13

A. W. TOZER {AD 1897–1963}

What we need very badly these days is a company of Christians who are prepared to trust God as completely now as they know they must do at the last day. For each of us the time is coming when we shall have nothing but God. Health and wealth and friends and hiding places will be swept away, and we shall have only God. To the man of pseudo faith that is a terrifying thought, but to real faith it is one of the most comforting thoughts the heart can entertain.

Andy Stanley

It's amazing how much your perspective can change with a little information. As a young child, the idea of allowing the doctor to give you a shot probably didn't make much sense. In fact, it may have taken some parental pressure or bribery to get you to cooperate. You didn't know anything about preventive medicine or what immunization meant. All you knew was that it hurt.

Over time, of course, things change. By the time you're an adult, you go to the doctor under your own power. You submit willingly to the same kind of shot. You even pay to have it done to you. All because information has altered your perspective.

As a child of God, the same is true. God declares, "So are my ways higher than your ways . . . my thoughts than your thoughts" (Isaiah 55:9). No matter how old or smart you get, there are some things about life you just won't understand like God does. You don't think as God thinks because you simply don't have the information. His perspective runs across millions of years, and it leaves nothing out of the equation. He has more information than the human brain can hope to contain. That's why it's always better to follow God's intuition rather than our own.

reflection

1. When have you felt God asking you to do something you didn't understand or didn't want to do?

2. How did you respond, and what did you learn as a result?

3. Why should you trust God more than you trust yourself—or any other person or thing? How does this trust show itself in your daily life?

For your next devotional reading, go to page 1044.

Nineveh to Fall

2 *An attacker advances against you,
    Nineveh.
  Guard the fortress,
    watch the road,
  brace yourselves,
    marshal all your strength!

2 The LORD will restore the splendor of
      Jacob
    like the splendor of Israel,
  though destroyers have laid them waste
    and have ruined their vines.

3 The shields of the soldiers are red;
    the warriors are clad in scarlet.
  The metal on the chariots flashes
    on the day they are made ready;
    the spears of juniper are brandished. ª

4 The chariots storm through the streets,
    rushing back and forth through the
      squares.
  They look like flaming torches;
    they dart about like lightning.

5 Nineveh summons her picked troops,
    yet they stumble on their way.
  They dash to the city wall;
    the protective shield is put in place.

6 The river gates are thrown open
    and the palace collapses.

7 It is decreed ᵇ that Nineveh
    be exiled and carried away.
  Her female slaves moan like doves
    and beat on their breasts.

8 Nineveh is like a pool
    whose water is draining away.
  "Stop! Stop!" they cry,
    but no one turns back.

9 Plunder the silver!
    Plunder the gold!
  The supply is endless,
    the wealth from all its treasures!

10 She is pillaged, plundered, stripped!
    Hearts melt, knees give way,
    bodies tremble, every face grows pale.

11 Where now is the lions' den,
    the place where they fed their young,
  where the lion and lioness went,
    and the cubs, with nothing to fear?

12 The lion killed enough for his cubs
    and strangled the prey for his mate,

  filling his lairs with the kill
    and his dens with the prey.

13 "I am against you,"
    declares the LORD Almighty.
  "I will burn up your chariots in smoke,
    and the sword will devour your young
      lions.
  I will leave you no prey on the earth.
  The voices of your messengers
    will no longer be heard."

Woe to Nineveh

3 Woe to the city of blood,
    full of lies,
  full of plunder,
    never without victims!

2 The crack of whips,
    the clatter of wheels,
  galloping horses
    and jolting chariots!

3 Charging cavalry,
    flashing swords
    and glittering spears!
  Many casualties,
    piles of dead,
  bodies without number,
    people stumbling over the corpses—

4 all because of the wanton lust of a
      prostitute,
    alluring, the mistress of sorceries,
  who enslaved nations by her prostitution
    and peoples by her witchcraft.

5 "I am against you," declares the LORD
      Almighty.
    "I will lift your skirts over your face.
  I will show the nations your nakedness
    and the kingdoms your shame.

6 I will pelt you with filth,
    I will treat you with contempt
    and make you a spectacle.

7 All who see you will flee from you and say,
    'Nineveh is in ruins—who will mourn
      for her?'
  Where can I find anyone to comfort
      you?"

8 Are you better than Thebes,
    situated on the Nile,
    with water around her?
  The river was her defense,
    the waters her wall.

ª 3 Hebrew; Septuagint and Syriac *ready; / the horsemen rush to and fro.*   ᵇ 7 The meaning of the
Hebrew for this word is uncertain.

* 2:1-13 is numbered 2:2-14 in Hebrew texts.

⁹Cush*a* and Egypt were her boundless
    strength;
  Put and Libya were among her allies.
¹⁰Yet she was taken captive
    and went into exile.
  Her infants were dashed to pieces
    at every street corner.
  Lots were cast for her nobles,
    and all her great men were put in
      chains.
¹¹You too will become drunk;
    you will go into hiding
    and seek refuge from the enemy.

¹²All your fortresses are like fig trees
    with their first ripe fruit;
  when they are shaken,
    the figs fall into the mouth of the
      eater.
¹³Look at your troops—
    they are all weaklings.
  The gates of your land
    are wide open to your enemies;
    fire has consumed the bars of your
      gates.

¹⁴Draw water for the siege,
    strengthen your defenses!
  Work the clay,
    tread the mortar,
    repair the brickwork!

¹⁵There the fire will consume you;
    the sword will cut you down—
    and it will devour you like a swarm of
      locusts.
  Multiply like grasshoppers,
    multiply like locusts!
¹⁶You have increased the number of your
      merchants
    till they are more than the stars in the
      sky,
  but like locusts they strip the land
    and then fly away.
¹⁷Your guards are like locusts,
    your officials like swarms of locusts
    that settle in the walls on a cold
      day—
  but when the sun appears they fly away,
    and no one knows where.

¹⁸King of Assyria, your shepherds*b*
      slumber;
    your nobles lie down to rest.
  Your people are scattered on the
      mountains
    with no one to gather them.
¹⁹Nothing can heal you;
    your wound is fatal.
  All who hear the news about you
    clap their hands at your fall,
  for who has not felt
    your endless cruelty?

---

a 9 That is, the upper Nile region   *b 18* That is, rulers

habakkuk

AUTHOR: Habakkuk

DATE: Around 605 B.C.

THEME: God makes sense even when the world around us doesn't seem to.

1 The prophecy that Habakkuk the prophet received.

Habakkuk's Complaint

² How long, Lord, must I call for help,
  but you do not listen?
Or cry out to you, "Violence!"
  but you do not save?
³ Why do you make me look at injustice?
  Why do you tolerate wrongdoing?
Destruction and violence are before me;
  there is strife, and conflict abounds.
⁴ Therefore the law is paralyzed,
  and justice never prevails.
The wicked hem in the righteous,
  so that justice is perverted.

The Lord's Answer

⁵ "Look at the nations and watch—
  and be utterly amazed.
For I am going to do something in your days
  that you would not believe,
  even if you were told.
⁶ I am raising up the Babylonians,ᵃ
  that ruthless and impetuous people,
who sweep across the whole earth
  to seize dwellings not their own.
⁷ They are a feared and dreaded people;
  they are a law to themselves
  and promote their own honor.
⁸ Their horses are swifter than leopards,
  fiercer than wolves at dusk.
Their cavalry gallops headlong;
  their horsemen come from afar.
They fly like a vulture swooping to devour;
⁹ they all come bent on violence.
Their hordesᵇ advance like a desert wind
  and gather prisoners like sand.
¹⁰ They mock kings
  and scoff at rulers.
They laugh at all fortified cities;
  by building earthen ramps they capture them.
¹¹ Then they sweep past like the wind and go on—
  guilty people, whose own strength is their god."

Habakkuk's Second Complaint

¹² Lord, are you not from everlasting?
  My God, my Holy One, youᶜ will never die.
You, Lord, have appointed them to execute judgment;
  you, my Rock, have ordained them to punish.
¹³ Your eyes are too pure to look on evil;
  you cannot tolerate wrongdoing.
Why then do you tolerate the treacherous?
Why are you silent while the wicked
swallow up those more righteous than themselves?
¹⁴ You have made people like the fish in the sea,
  like the sea creatures that have no ruler.
¹⁵ The wicked foe pulls all of them up with hooks,
  he catches them in his net,
he gathers them up in his dragnet;
  and so he rejoices and is glad.

ᵃ 6 Or *Chaldeans* ᵇ 9 The meaning of the Hebrew for this word is uncertain. ᶜ 12 An ancient Hebrew scribal tradition; Masoretic Text *we*

THURSDAY

EQUALLY OFFENSIVE

Habakkuk 1:1–17 *or* 1:12–13

Tony Evans

If you were high above the earth and looked down on one man standing on a mountaintop and another standing in a valley, they would look to you as if they were standing side by side. You would be so high that the small matter of a mountain would be irrelevant.

God is so high that when He sees us in relation to sin, we are all standing on level ground. Our God is holy, totally separate from sin. He can't even stand to look at it (Habakkuk 1:13).

But most people's attitude toward sin is epitomized by the attitude of the famous naturalist, Henry David Thoreau. When urged to make his peace with God, Thoreau answered, "I did not know that we had ever quarreled."

There's been a quarrel, all right! God's got the quarrel with us, because we have all offended His holiness. All people need to be saved, because everyone has the same problem. The Bible says, "There is [no one] righteous, not even one" (Romans 3:10).

Someone might object, "But that's not fair."

Sure it is. Suppose you were sick, and as the doctor was getting ready to operate on you, he said, "All of my scalpels are dirty. I've got one that I just picked up out of the mud. It's real dirty. I've got another one that's a little better, but it still has dirt on it. Now I've got this one scalpel that's just got a little spot of dirt on it. So I think we will chance this operation with this slightly dirty scalpel."

Not on me! All it takes is a few germs to contaminate your whole body. I want my doctor's scalpel to be absolutely clean when he cuts me open. In the same way, God is so holy that He is as offended by an evil thought as He is by murder. While there are differences in the consequences of sin, there is no difference in essence.

That's how holy God is, how totally unlike us. We have to do the adjusting. He's not going to change. When you understand the holiness of God, something's got to happen.

GERHARD TERSTEEGAN {AD 1697–1769}

Contemplate with delight the holiness and goodness in God, which you do not find in yourself. How lovely it is to be nothing when God is all!

reflection

1. What reminder did Habakkuk need in relation to God's perspective on sin?

2. What do you think when you hear the statement, "God hates all sin equally"?

3. What "small" sin have you been trying to justify by saying, "It's not as bad as _____"? What holds you back from repenting and turning from sin?

For your next devotional reading, go to page 1049.

16 Therefore he sacrifices to his net
    and burns incense to his dragnet,
for by his net he lives in luxury
    and enjoys the choicest food.
17 Is he to keep on emptying his net,
    destroying nations without mercy?

2 I will stand at my watch
    and station myself on the ramparts;
I will look to see what he will say
        to me,
    and what answer I am to give to this
        complaint.*a*

The LORD's Answer

2 Then the LORD replied:

"Write down the revelation
    and make it plain on tablets
so that a herald*b* may run with it.
3 For the revelation awaits an appointed
        time;
    it speaks of the end
    and will not prove false.
Though it linger, wait for it;
    it*c* will certainly come
    and will not delay.

4 "See, he is puffed up;
    his desires are not upright—
    but the righteous will live by their
        faithfulness*d*—
5 indeed, wine betrays him;
    he is arrogant and never at rest.
Because he is as greedy as the grave
    and like death is never satisfied,
he gathers to himself all the nations
    and takes captive all the peoples.

6 "Will not all of them taunt him with ridicule and scorn, saying,

" 'Woe to him who piles up stolen goods
    and makes himself wealthy by
        extortion!
    How long must this go on?'
7 Will not your creditors suddenly arise?
    Will they not wake up and make you
        tremble?
    Then you will become their prey.
8 Because you have plundered many
        nations,
    the peoples who are left will plunder
        you.

For you have shed human blood;
    you have destroyed lands and cities
        and everyone in them.

9 "Woe to him who builds his house by
        unjust gain,
    setting his nest on high
    to escape the clutches of ruin!
10 You have plotted the ruin of many
        peoples,
    shaming your own house and
        forfeiting your life.
11 The stones of the wall will cry out,
    and the beams of the woodwork will
        echo it.

12 "Woe to him who builds a city with
        bloodshed
    and establishes a town by injustice!
13 Has not the LORD Almighty determined
    that the people's labor is only fuel for
        the fire,
    that the nations exhaust themselves
        for nothing?
14 For the earth will be filled with the
        knowledge of the glory of the
        LORD
    as the waters cover the sea.

15 "Woe to him who gives drink to his
        neighbors,
    pouring it from the wineskin till they
        are drunk,
    so that he can gaze on their naked
        bodies!
16 You will be filled with shame instead of
        glory.
    Now it is your turn! Drink and let your
        nakedness be exposed*e*!
The cup from the LORD's right hand is
        coming around to you,
    and disgrace will cover your glory.
17 The violence you have done to Lebanon
        will overwhelm you,
    and your destruction of animals will
        terrify you.
For you have shed human blood;
    you have destroyed lands and cities
        and everyone in them.

18 "Of what value is an idol that someone
        has carved?
    Or an image that teaches lies?

---

a 1 Or *and what to answer when I am rebuked*   *b 2* Or *so that whoever reads it*   *c 3* Or *Though he linger, wait for him; / he*   *d 4* Or *faith*   *e 16* Masoretic Text; Dead Sea Scrolls, Aquila, Vulgate and Syriac (see also Septuagint) *and stagger*

For those who make them trust in their
own creations;
they make idols that cannot speak.
¹⁹Woe to him who says to wood, 'Come to
life!'
Or to lifeless stone, 'Wake up!'
Can it give guidance?
It is covered with gold and silver;
there is no breath in it."

²⁰The LORD is in his holy temple;
let all the earth be silent before him.

Habakkuk's Prayer

3 A prayer of Habakkuk the prophet. On
shigionoth.^a

²LORD, I have heard of your fame;
I stand in awe of your deeds, LORD.
Renew them in our day,
in our time make them known;
in wrath remember mercy.

³God came from Teman,
the Holy One from Mount Paran.^b
His glory covered the heavens
and his praise filled the earth.
⁴His splendor was like the sunrise;
rays flashed from his hand,
where his power was hidden.
⁵Plague went before him;
pestilence followed his steps.
⁶He stood, and shook the earth;
he looked, and made the nations
tremble.
The ancient mountains crumbled
and the age-old hills collapsed—
but he marches on forever.
⁷I saw the tents of Cushan in distress,
the dwellings of Midian in anguish.

⁸Were you angry with the rivers, LORD?
Was your wrath against the streams?
Did you rage against the sea
when you rode your horses
and your chariots to victory?
⁹You uncovered your bow,
you called for many arrows.
You split the earth with rivers;

¹⁰ the mountains saw you and writhed.
Torrents of water swept by;
the deep roared
and lifted its waves on high.

¹¹Sun and moon stood still in the
heavens
at the glint of your flying arrows,
at the lightning of your flashing spear.
¹²In wrath you strode through the earth
and in anger you threshed the
nations.
¹³You came out to deliver your people,
to save your anointed one.
You crushed the leader of the land of
wickedness,
you stripped him from head to foot.
¹⁴With his own spear you pierced his head
when his warriors stormed out to
scatter us,
gloating as though about to devour
the wretched who were in hiding.
¹⁵You trampled the sea with your horses,
churning the great waters.

¹⁶I heard and my heart pounded,
my lips quivered at the sound;
decay crept into my bones,
and my legs trembled.
Yet I will wait patiently for the day of
calamity
to come on the nation invading us.
¹⁷Though the fig tree does not bud
and there are no grapes on the vines,
though the olive crop fails
and the fields produce no food,
though there are no sheep in the pen
and no cattle in the stalls,
¹⁸yet I will rejoice in the LORD,
I will be joyful in God my Savior.

¹⁹The Sovereign LORD is my strength;
he makes my feet like the feet of a
deer,
he enables me to tread on the
heights.

For the director of music. On my
stringed instruments.

---

^a 1 Probably a literary or musical term   ^b 3 The Hebrew has *Selah* (a word of uncertain meaning) here
and at the middle of verse 9 and at the end of verse 13.

zephaniah

AUTHOR: Zephaniah

DATE: Likely written during the early years of the reign of King Josiah (640–609 B.C.)

THEME: God's discipline can be painful, but it's always profitable.

1 The word of the LORD that came to Zephaniah son of Cushi, the son of Gedaliah, the son of Amariah, the son of Hezekiah, during the reign of Josiah son of Amon king of Judah:

Judgment on the Whole Earth in the Day of the LORD

2 "I will sweep away everything
   from the face of the earth,"
                declares the LORD.
3 "I will sweep away both people and
      animals;
   I will sweep away the birds in the sky
      and the fish in the sea—
   and the idols that cause the wicked to
      stumble."[a]

"When I destroy all people
   on the face of the earth,"
                declares the LORD,
4 "I will stretch out my hand against Judah
   and against all who live in Jerusalem.
I will destroy every remnant of Baal
      worship in this place,
   every remembrance of the idolatrous
      priests—
5 those who bow down on the roofs
   to worship the starry host,
those who bow down and swear by the
      LORD
   and who also swear by Molek,[b]
6 those who turn back from following the
      LORD
   and neither seek the LORD nor inquire
      of him."

7 Be silent before the Sovereign LORD,
   for the day of the LORD is near.

The LORD has prepared a sacrifice;
   he has consecrated those he has
      invited.

8 "On the day of the LORD's sacrifice
   I will punish the officials
   and the king's sons
and all those clad
   in foreign clothes.
9 On that day I will punish
   all who avoid stepping on the
      threshold,[c]
who fill the temple of their gods
   with violence and deceit.

10 "On that day,"
      declares the LORD,
"a cry will go up from the Fish Gate,
   wailing from the New Quarter,
   and a loud crash from the hills.
11 Wail, you who live in the market
      district[d];
   all your merchants will be wiped out,
   all who trade with[e] silver will be
      destroyed.
12 At that time I will search Jerusalem with
      lamps
   and punish those who are
      complacent,
   who are like wine left on its dregs,
who think, 'The LORD will do nothing,
   either good or bad.'
13 Their wealth will be plundered,
   their houses demolished.
Though they build houses,
   they will not live in them;
though they plant vineyards,
   they will not drink the wine."

---

a 3 The meaning of the Hebrew for this line is uncertain.   b 5 Hebrew *Malkam*   c 9 See 1 Samuel 5:5.   d 11 Or *the Mortar*   e 11 Or *in*

¹⁴ The great day of the LORD is near—
  near and coming quickly.
The cry on the day of the LORD is bitter;
  the Mighty Warrior shouts his battle
  cry.
¹⁵ That day will be a day of wrath—
  a day of distress and anguish,
    a day of trouble and ruin,
    a day of darkness and gloom,
    a day of clouds and blackness—
¹⁶   a day of trumpet and battle cry
against the fortified cities
  and against the corner towers.

¹⁷ "I will bring such distress on all people
  that they will grope about like those
    who are blind,
  because they have sinned against the
    LORD.
Their blood will be poured out like dust
  and their entrails like dung.
¹⁸ Neither their silver nor their gold
  will be able to save them
  on the day of the LORD's wrath."

In the fire of his jealousy
  the whole earth will be consumed,
for he will make a sudden end
  of all who live on the earth.

Judah and Jerusalem Judged Along With the Nations

Judah Summoned to Repent

2 Gather together, gather yourselves
    together,
  you shameful nation,
² before the decree takes effect
  and that day passes like windblown
    chaff,
  before the LORD's fierce anger
    comes upon you,
  before the day of the LORD's wrath
    comes upon you.
³ Seek the LORD, all you humble of the
    land,
  you who do what he commands.
Seek righteousness, seek humility;
  perhaps you will be sheltered
  on the day of the LORD's anger.

Philistia

⁴ Gaza will be abandoned
  and Ashkelon left in ruins.

At midday Ashdod will be emptied
  and Ekron uprooted.
⁵ Woe to you who live by the sea,
  you Kerethite people;
the word of the LORD is against you,
  Canaan, land of the Philistines.
He says, "I will destroy you,
  and none will be left."
⁶ The land by the sea will become
    pastures
  having wells for shepherds
  and pens for flocks.
⁷ That land will belong
  to the remnant of the house of Judah;
  there they will find pasture.
In the evening they will lie down
  in the houses of Ashkelon.
The LORD their God will care for them;
  he will restore their fortunes. ᵃ

Moab and Ammon

⁸ "I have heard the insults of Moab
  and the taunts of the Ammonites,
who insulted my people
  and made threats against their land.
⁹ Therefore, as surely as I live,"
  declares the LORD Almighty,
  the God of Israel,
"surely Moab will become like Sodom,
  the Ammonites like Gomorrah—
a place of weeds and salt pits,
  a wasteland forever.
The remnant of my people will plunder
    them;
  the survivors of my nation will inherit
    their land."

¹⁰ This is what they will get in return for
    their pride,
  for insulting and mocking
  the people of the LORD Almighty.
¹¹ The LORD will be awesome to them
  when he destroys all the gods of the
    earth.
Distant nations will bow down to him,
  all of them in their own lands.

Cush

¹² "You Cushites, ᵇ too,
  will be slain by my sword."

Assyria

¹³ He will stretch out his hand against the
    north

ᵃ 7 Or *will bring back their captives*   ᵇ 12 That is, people from the upper Nile region

FRIDAY

KING OF THE WORLD

Zephaniah 2:1–15 or 2:1–3,10–11

Lisa Harper

God inspired Zephaniah to use the countries surrounding Judah to demonstrate the fact that He governs *the whole world!*

Not just countries that stamp "In God We Trust" on their currency. Not just people who vote Republican. And not just southerners who dress up on Sunday . . . God rules over every single nation, tribe, tongue, and people group. This concept is so contrary to our contemporary way of thinking that it's like carrying a six-pack of beer into an AA meeting!

But when the apostle Paul said, "[God exalted him to the highest place and gave him the name that is above every name, that at the name of Jesus every knee should bow, in heaven and on earth and under the earth, and every tongue acknowledge that Jesus Christ is Lord, to the glory of God the Father]" (Philippians 2:9–11), he wasn't just whistling Dixie. He was pointing to the absolute omniscience and authority of God the Father, through Jesus the Son . . .

God is in control of everyone, everywhere. We are so not in charge.

JOHN DONNE {AD 1572–1631}

Our God is not out of breath just because he has blown one windstorm that swallowed a navy. Our God has not burned out his eyes just because he has looked upon one trail of explosives. In the light of heaven and in the darkness of hell, he sees alike. He sees not only all the actions of men when they come to pass but also all the thoughts of their hearts that brought them there. Past, present and future have no significance for him, for all is one time to him. Mountains and valleys, sea and land—these have no bearing on his location, for all is one place to him.

reflection

1. Why is it hard to remember that God is in charge of everything?

2. In what ways are you guilty of saying God is in charge but living as if he's not?

3. How is God expanding your view of him and his sovereign control over all things?

For your next devotional reading, go to page 1053.

and destroy Assyria,
leaving Nineveh utterly desolate
and dry as the desert.
¹⁴ Flocks and herds will lie down there,
creatures of every kind.
The desert owl and the screech owl
will roost on her columns.
Their hooting will echo through the
windows,
rubble will fill the doorways,
the beams of cedar will be exposed.
¹⁵ This is the city of revelry
that lived in safety.
She said to herself,
"I am the one! And there is none
besides me."
What a ruin she has become,
a lair for wild beasts!
All who pass by her scoff
and shake their fists.

Jerusalem

3 Woe to the city of oppressors,
rebellious and defiled!
² She obeys no one,
she accepts no correction.
She does not trust in the LORD,
she does not draw near to her God.
³ Her officials within her
are roaring lions;
her rulers are evening wolves,
who leave nothing for the morning.
⁴ Her prophets are unprincipled;
they cannot be trusted.
Her priests profane the sanctuary
and do violence to the law.
⁵ The LORD within her is righteous;
he does no wrong.
Morning by morning he dispenses his
justice,
and every new day he does not fail,
yet the unrighteous know no shame.

Jerusalem Remains Unrepentant

⁶ "I have destroyed nations;
their strongholds are demolished.
I have left their streets deserted,
with no one passing through.
Their cities are laid waste;
they are deserted and empty.
⁷ Of Jerusalem I thought,
'Surely you will fear me

and accept correction!'
Then her place of refuge[a] would not be
destroyed,
nor all my punishments come upon[b]
her.
But they were still eager
to act corruptly in all they did.
⁸ Therefore wait for me,"
declares the LORD,
"for the day I will stand up to testify.[c]
I have decided to assemble the nations,
to gather the kingdoms
and to pour out my wrath on them—
all my fierce anger.
The whole world will be consumed
by the fire of my jealous anger.

Restoration of Israel's Remnant

⁹ "Then I will purify the lips of the peoples,
that all of them may call on the name
of the LORD
and serve him shoulder to shoulder.
¹⁰ From beyond the rivers of Cush[d]
my worshipers, my scattered people,
will bring me offerings.
¹¹ On that day you, Jerusalem, will not be
put to shame
for all the wrongs you have done to
me,
because I will remove from you
those who revel in your glory.
Never again will you be haughty
on my holy hill.
¹² But I will leave within you
the meek and humble.
The remnant of Israel
will trust in the name of the LORD.
¹³ They will do no wrong;
they will tell no lies.
A deceitful tongue
will not be found in their mouths.
They will eat and lie down
and no one will make them afraid."

¹⁴ Sing, Daughter Zion;
shout aloud, Israel!
Be glad and rejoice with all your heart,
Daughter Jerusalem!
¹⁵ The LORD has taken away your
punishment,
he has turned back your enemy.
The LORD, the King of Israel, is with you;
never again will you fear any harm.

---

a 7 Or her sanctuary   *b 7 Or all those I appointed over*
to plunder   *d 10 That is, the upper Nile region*   *c 8 Septuagint and Syriac; Hebrew will rise up*

¹⁶ On that day
  they will say to Jerusalem,
    "Do not fear, Zion;
     do not let your hands hang limp.
¹⁷ The LORD your God is with you,
     the Mighty Warrior who saves.
  He will take great delight in you;
     in his love he will no longer rebuke
       you,
     but will rejoice over you with singing."

¹⁸ "I will remove from you
     all who mourn over the loss of your
       appointed festivals,
     which is a burden and reproach for
       you.

¹⁹ At that time I will deal
     with all who oppressed you.
  I will rescue the lame;
     I will gather the exiles.
  I will give them praise and honor
     in every land where they have
       suffered shame.
²⁰ At that time I will gather you;
     at that time I will bring you home.
  I will give you honor and praise
     among all the peoples of the
       earth
  when I restore your fortunes ᵃ
     before your very eyes,"

says the LORD.

ᵃ 20 Or I bring back your captives

haggai

AUTHOR: Haggai

DATE: 520 B.C., not long after some of the Jews had returned to Jerusalem

THEME: Let God set your priorities. He'll lead the way.

A Call to Build the House of the LORD

1 In the second year of King Darius, on the first day of the sixth month, the word of the LORD came through the prophet Haggai to Zerubbabel son of Shealtiel, governor of Judah, and to Joshua*ᵃ* son of Jozadak,*ᵇ* the high priest:

²This is what the LORD Almighty says: "These people say, 'The time has not yet come to rebuild the LORD's house.' "

³Then the word of the LORD came through the prophet Haggai: ⁴"Is it a time for you yourselves to be living in your paneled houses, while this house remains a ruin?"

⁵Now this is what the LORD Almighty says: "Give careful thought to your ways. ⁶You have planted much, but have harvested little. You eat, but never have enough. You drink, but never have your fill. You put on clothes, but are not warm. You earn wages, only to put them in a purse with holes in it."

⁷This is what the LORD Almighty says: "Give careful thought to your ways. ⁸Go up into the mountains and bring down timber and build the house, so that I may take pleasure in it and be honored," says the LORD. ⁹"You expected much, but see, it turned out to be little. What you brought home, I blew away. Why?" declares the LORD Almighty. "Because of my house, which remains a ruin, while each of you is busy with his own house. ¹⁰Therefore, because of you the heavens have withheld their dew and the earth its crops. ¹¹I called for a drought on the fields and the mountains, on the grain, the new wine, the olive oil and everything else the ground produces, on people and livestock, and on all the labor of your hands."

¹²Then Zerubbabel son of Shealtiel, Joshua son of Jozadak, the high priest, and the whole remnant of the people obeyed the voice of the LORD their God and the message of the prophet Haggai, because the LORD their God had sent him. And the people feared the LORD.

¹³Then Haggai, the LORD's messenger, gave this message of the LORD to the people: "I am with you," declares the LORD. ¹⁴So the LORD stirred up the spirit of Zerubbabel son of Shealtiel, governor of Judah, and the spirit of Joshua son of Jozadak, the high priest, and the spirit of the whole remnant of the people. They came and began to work on the house of the LORD Almighty, their God, ¹⁵on the twenty-fourth day of the sixth month.

The Promised Glory of the New House

2 In the second year of King Darius, ¹on the twenty-first day of the seventh month, the word of the LORD came through the prophet Haggai: ²"Speak to Zerubbabel son of Shealtiel, governor of Judah, to Joshua son of Jozadak,*ᶜ* the high priest, and to the remnant of the people. Ask them, ³'Who of you is left who saw this house in its former glory? How does it look to you now? Does it not seem to you like nothing? ⁴But now be strong, Zerubbabel,' declares the LORD. 'Be strong, Joshua son of Jozadak, the high priest. Be strong, all you people of the land,' declares the LORD, 'and work. For I am with you,' declares the LORD Almighty. ⁵'This is what I covenanted with you when you came out of Egypt. And my Spirit remains among you. Do not fear.'

⁶"This is what the LORD Almighty says: 'In

ᵃ 1 A variant of *Jeshua*; here and elsewhere in Haggai in verses 12 and 14   *ᶜ 2* Hebrew *Jehozadak,* a variant of *Jozadak*; also in verse 4   *ᵇ 1* Hebrew *Jehozadak,* a variant of *Jozadak*; also

How Far We've Come

Haggai 2:3

read/meditate

Haggai prophesied to his people when they were rebuilding the temple. Read the questions he asked the people in Haggai 2:3. Read them several times. The young people rejoiced at the new temple. The old people wept that this temple would never be as fine as the previous one that Solomon had built. When you evaluate your spiritual life, which group do you fit into? Do you ever wish that your current relationship with God was more like how your relationship used to be?

pray

What state is your spiritual life in? Do you, like the Jews, look back on a grand spiritual history that makes your present spiritual life look anemic? Be honest with God about your evaluation of your spiritual health. Invite his insights into your heart and life.

contemplate

Reflect on your journey with God. Draw a time line in your mind that traces the high points and low points. Are you on an upswing or a downswing? Do you need to change anything about the path you are on?

additional reflection

Maturity doesn't come with age; it comes with acceptance of responsibility.
— *Ed Cole*

"If you plant a bean, then you will harvest only beans, not grapes or strawberries."
This is an old Korean proverb. God gave us new life through Jesus Christ and planted special seeds of forgiveness and love in our hearts. What fruit will we bear in our daily lives?

— *Myung Lee*

For your next devotional reading, go to page 1056.

a little while I will once more shake the heavens and the earth, the sea and the dry land. ⁷I will shake all nations, and what is desired by all nations will come, and I will fill this house with glory,' says the LORD Almighty. ⁸'The silver is mine and the gold is mine,' declares the LORD Almighty. ⁹'The glory of this present house will be greater than the glory of the former house,' says the LORD Almighty. 'And in this place I will grant peace,' declares the LORD Almighty."

Blessings for a Defiled People

¹⁰On the twenty-fourth day of the ninth month, in the second year of Darius, the word of the LORD came to the prophet Haggai: ¹¹"This is what the LORD Almighty says: 'Ask the priests what the law says: ¹²If a person carries consecrated meat in the fold of his garment, and that fold touches some bread or stew, some wine, olive oil or other food, does it become consecrated?' "

The priests answered, "No."

¹³Then Haggai said, "If a person defiled by contact with a dead body touches one of these things, does it become defiled?"

"Yes," the priests replied, "it becomes defiled."

¹⁴Then Haggai said, " 'So it is with this people and this nation in my sight,' declares the LORD. 'Whatever they do and whatever they offer there is defiled.

¹⁵" 'Now give careful thought to this from this day on ᵃ—consider how things were before one stone was laid on another in the LORD's temple. ¹⁶When anyone came to a heap of twenty measures, there were only ten. When anyone went to a wine vat to draw fifty measures, there were only twenty. ¹⁷I struck all the work of your hands with blight, mildew and hail, yet you did not return to me,' declares the LORD. ¹⁸'From this day on, from this twenty-fourth day of the ninth month, give careful thought to the day when the foundation of the LORD's temple was laid. Give careful thought: ¹⁹Is there yet any seed left in the barn? Until now, the vine and the fig tree, the pomegranate and the olive tree have not borne fruit.

" 'From this day on I will bless you.' "

Zerubbabel the LORD's Signet Ring

²⁰The word of the LORD came to Haggai a second time on the twenty-fourth day of the month: ²¹"Tell Zerubbabel governor of Judah that I am going to shake the heavens and the earth. ²²I will overturn royal thrones and shatter the power of the foreign kingdoms. I will overthrow chariots and their drivers; horses and their riders will fall, each by the sword of his comrade.

²³" 'On that day,' declares the LORD Almighty, 'I will take you, my servant Zerubbabel son of Shealtiel,' declares the LORD, 'and I will make you like my signet ring, for I have chosen you,' declares the LORD Almighty."

ᵃ 15 Or to the days past

zechariah

AUTHOR: Zechariah

DATE: Around 520–480 B.C.

THEME: God is always waiting for us to turn back to him.

A Call to Return to the LORD

1 In the eighth month of the second year of Darius, the word of the LORD came to the prophet Zechariah son of Berekiah, the son of Iddo:

²"The LORD was very angry with your ancestors. ³Therefore tell the people: This is what the LORD Almighty says: 'Return to me,' declares the LORD Almighty, 'and I will return to you,' says the LORD Almighty. ⁴Do not be like your ancestors, to whom the earlier prophets proclaimed: This is what the LORD Almighty says: 'Turn from your evil ways and your evil practices.' But they would not listen or pay attention to me, declares the LORD. ⁵Where are your ancestors now? And the prophets, do they live forever? ⁶But did not my words and my decrees, which I commanded my servants the prophets, overtake your ancestors?

"Then they repented and said, 'The LORD Almighty has done to us what our ways and practices deserve, just as he determined to do.'"

The Man Among the Myrtle Trees

⁷On the twenty-fourth day of the eleventh month, the month of Shebat, in the second year of Darius, the word of the LORD came to the prophet Zechariah son of Berekiah, the son of Iddo.

⁸During the night I had a vision, and there before me was a man mounted on a red horse. He was standing among the myrtle trees in a ravine. Behind him were red, brown and white horses.

⁹I asked, "What are these, my lord?"

The angel who was talking with me answered, "I will show you what they are."

¹⁰Then the man standing among the myrtle trees explained, "They are the ones the LORD has sent to go throughout the earth."

¹¹And they reported to the angel of the LORD who was standing among the myrtle trees, "We have gone throughout the earth and found the whole world at rest and in peace."

¹²Then the angel of the LORD said, "LORD Almighty, how long will you withhold mercy from Jerusalem and from the towns of Judah, which you have been angry with these seventy years?" ¹³So the LORD spoke kind and comforting words to the angel who talked with me.

¹⁴Then the angel who was speaking to me said, "Proclaim this word: This is what the LORD Almighty says: 'I am very jealous for Jerusalem and Zion, ¹⁵and I am very angry with the nations that feel secure. I was only a little angry, but they added to the calamity.'

¹⁶"Therefore, this is what the LORD says: 'I will return to Jerusalem with mercy, and there my house will be rebuilt. And the measuring line will be stretched out over Jerusalem,' declares the LORD Almighty.

¹⁷"Proclaim further: This is what the LORD Almighty says: 'My towns will again overflow with prosperity, and the LORD will again comfort Zion and choose Jerusalem.'"

Four Horns and Four Craftsmen

*¹⁸Then I looked up, and there before me were four horns. ¹⁹I asked the angel who was speaking to me, "What are these?"

He answered me, "These are the horns that scattered Judah, Israel and Jerusalem."

²⁰Then the LORD showed me four craftsmen. ²¹I asked, "What are these coming to do?"

* 1:18-21 is numbered 2:1-4 in Hebrew texts.

MONDAY

FORGETFUL MERCY

Zechariah 1:1–21 or 1:12–13,16–17

CATHERINE OF SIENA {AD 1347–1380}

Merciful Lord, it does not surprise me that you forget completely the sins of those who repent. I am not surprised that you remain faithful to those who hate and revile you. The mercy which pours forth from you fills the whole world.

It was by your mercy that we were created, and by your mercy that you redeemed us by sending your Son. Your mercy is the light in which sinners find you and good people come back to you ... Your justice is constantly tempered with mercy, so you refuse to punish us as we deserve. O mad lover! It was not enough for you to take on our humanity; you had to die for us as well.

Erwin Lutzer

There can be no growth in the Christian life until the barrier of guilt from the past has been cleared away.

OK, you have accepted God's forgiveness and you have chosen to forgive yourself—but the consequences [of sin] are still there, aren't they?

The only sensible course of action is to give these consequences to God. Some matters must be transferred from our hands to His. When we trust Him to make the best of the mess we have left behind, He will be gracious and display His mercy and grace. The forgiveness of God must be enjoyed even if reconciliation with the estranged person does not occur ...

Grace means we get what we don't deserve ... God completely blots out our sins so that he no longer remembers them ...

Does this mean He is no longer omniscient? Is there really something about us He doesn't know? Hardly. It simply means that God no longer has regard for our sins. He does not remind us of them; they are no longer barriers to our fellowship with Him ...

Memories can be reminders of God's matchless grace. Of course, the past sins will come to mind, but they need not control our future. God can break the power of these memories and eventually relegate them to the "no longer active" file of the mind. We just don't have a right to remember what God forgets.

---

reflection

1. How did the Israelites experience God's mercy?
2. How have you experienced God's mercy in your own life?
3. One aspect of God's mercy is that he not only forgives but also forgets our sin. What sin from your past still "haunts" you? How does God view that sin?

For your next devotional reading, go to page 1058.

He answered, "These are the horns that scattered Judah so its people could not raise their heads, but the craftsmen have come to terrify them and throw down these horns of the nations who lifted up their horns against the land of Judah to scatter its people."

A Man With a Measuring Line

2 *Then I looked up, and there before me was a man with a measuring line in his hand. ²I asked, "Where are you going?"

He answered me, "To measure Jerusalem, to find out how wide and how long it is."

³While the angel who was speaking to me was leaving, another angel came to meet him ⁴and said to him: "Run, tell that young man, 'Jerusalem will be a city without walls because of the great number of people and animals in it. ⁵And I myself will be a wall of fire around it,' declares the LORD, 'and I will be its glory within.'

⁶"Come! Come! Flee from the land of the north," declares the LORD, "for I have scattered you to the four winds of heaven," declares the LORD.

⁷"Come, Zion! Escape, you who live in Daughter Babylon!" ⁸For this is what the LORD Almighty says: "After the Glorious One has sent me against the nations that have plundered you—for whoever touches you touches the apple of his eye— ⁹I will surely raise my hand against them so that their slaves will plunder them.ᵃ Then you will know that the LORD Almighty has sent me.

¹⁰"Shout and be glad, Daughter Zion. For I am coming, and I will live among you," declares the LORD. ¹¹"Many nations will be joined with the LORD in that day and will become my people. I will live among you and you will know that the LORD Almighty has sent me to you. ¹²The LORD will inherit Judah as his portion in the holy land and will again choose Jerusalem. ¹³Be still before the LORD, all people, because he has roused himself from his holy dwelling."

Clean Garments for the High Priest

3 Then he showed me Joshuaᵇ the high priest standing before the angel of the LORD, and Satanᶜ standing at his right side to accuse him. ²The LORD said to Satan,

"The LORD rebuke you, Satan! The LORD, who has chosen Jerusalem, rebuke you! Is not this man a burning stick snatched from the fire?"

³Now Joshua was dressed in filthy clothes as he stood before the angel. ⁴The angel said to those who were standing before him, "Take off his filthy clothes."

Then he said to Joshua, "See, I have taken away your sin, and I will put fine garments on you."

⁵Then I said, "Put a clean turban on his head." So they put a clean turban on his head and clothed him, while the angel of the LORD stood by.

⁶The angel of the LORD gave this charge to Joshua: ⁷"This is what the LORD Almighty says: 'If you will walk in obedience to me and keep my requirements, then you will govern my house and have charge of my courts, and I will give you a place among these standing here.

⁸"'Listen, High Priest Joshua, you and your associates seated before you, you who are symbolic of things to come: I am going to bring my servant, the Branch. ⁹See, the stone I have set in front of Joshua! There are seven eyesᵈ on that one stone, and I will engrave an inscription on it,' says the LORD Almighty, 'and I will remove the sin of this land in a single day.

¹⁰"'In that day each of you will invite your neighbor to sit under your vine and fig tree,' declares the LORD Almighty."

The Gold Lampstand and the Two Olive Trees

4 Then the angel who talked with me returned and wakened me, as one is wakened from sleep. ²He asked me, "What do you see?"

I answered, "I see a solid gold lampstand with a bowl at the top and seven lamps on it, with seven channels to the lamps. ³Also there are two olive trees by it, one on the right of the bowl and the other on its left."

⁴I asked the angel who talked with me, "What are these, my lord?"

⁵He answered, "Do you not know what these are?"

"No, my lord," I replied.

⁶So he said to me, "This is the word of the

ᵃ 8,9 Or *says after . . . eye:* ⁹*"I . . . plunder them."* Zechariah   ᶜ 1 Hebrew *satan* means *adversary.*   ᵇ 1 A variant of *Jeshua;* here and elsewhere in   ᵈ 9 Or *facets*

* 2:1-13 is numbered 2:5-17 in Hebrew texts.

THE GREATEST GIFT

Zechariah 2:10—3:10 *or* 3:3–4

Brennan Manning

We unwittingly project onto God our own attitudes and feelings toward ourselves. As Blaise Pascal wrote, "God made man in his own image and man has returned the compliment." Thus, if we feel hateful toward ourselves, we assume that God feels hateful toward us.

But we cannot assume that He feels about us the way we feel about ourselves—unless we love ourselves compassionately, intensely, and freely. In human form Jesus revealed to us what God is like. He exposed our projections for the idolatry that they are and gave us the way to become free of them. It takes a profound conversion to accept that God is relentlessly tender and compassionate toward us just as we are—not in spite of our sins and faults (that would not be total acceptance), but with them. Though God does not condone or sanction evil, He does not withhold His love because there is evil in us.

Because of how we feel about ourselves, it's sometimes difficult to believe this. As numerous Christian authors, wiser and more insightful than I, have said: We cannot accept love from another human being when we do not love ourselves, much less accept that God could possibly love us.

JONATHAN EDWARDS {AD 1703–1758}

God has freely honored us with the gift of salvation. He was under no obligation to grant it. He had every right to reject fallen humans, as he did the fallen angels. We have done nothing to deserve this salvation; it was given while we were yet enemies of God and before we had so much as repented. It comes from the love of God—not on the basis of anything good in us, or because God expected us to return that love. Grace alone is the reason that the benefits of Christ are applied to any particular person. If you have been called by God and sanctified, you should give the credit for this solely to the good pleasure of God's goodness, for this is the reason you have been set apart. God is sovereign, and he has mercy on whom he will have mercy.

reflection

1. Think of five words that you would use to describe yourself. Now think of five words that you think God would use to describe you. How do those lists compare?

2. Do you believe—truly, deep down believe—that God loves you? Why?

3. God doesn't love you in spite of your sin; rather he loves you even with your sin. How does that affect your view of yourself?

For your next devotional reading, go to page 1062.

LORD to Zerubbabel: 'Not by might nor by power, but by my Spirit,' says the LORD Almighty.

7"What are you, mighty mountain? Before Zerubbabel you will become level ground. Then he will bring out the capstone to shouts of 'God bless it! God bless it!' "

8Then the word of the LORD came to me: 9"The hands of Zerubbabel have laid the foundation of this temple; his hands will also complete it. Then you will know that the LORD Almighty has sent me to you.

10"Who dares despise the day of small things, since the seven eyes of the LORD that range throughout the earth will rejoice when they see the chosen capstone*a* in the hand of Zerubbabel?"

11Then I asked the angel, "What are these two olive trees on the right and the left of the lampstand?"

12Again I asked him, "What are these two olive branches beside the two gold pipes that pour out golden oil?"

13He replied, "Do you not know what these are?"

"No, my lord," I said.

14So he said, "These are the two who are anointed to*b* serve the Lord of all the earth."

The Flying Scroll

5 I looked again, and there before me was a flying scroll.

2He asked me, "What do you see?"

I answered, "I see a flying scroll, twenty cubits long and ten cubits wide.*c*"

3And he said to me, "This is the curse that is going out over the whole land; for according to what it says on one side, every thief will be banished, and according to what it says on the other, everyone who swears falsely will be banished. 4The LORD Almighty declares, 'I will send it out, and it will enter the house of the thief and the house of anyone who swears falsely by my name. It will remain in that house and destroy it completely, both its timbers and its stones.' "

The Woman in a Basket

5Then the angel who was speaking to me came forward and said to me, "Look up and see what this is that is appearing."

6I asked, "What is it?"

He replied, "It is a basket." And he added, "This is the iniquity*d* of the people throughout the land."

7Then the cover of lead was raised, and there in the basket sat a woman! 8He said, "This is wickedness," and he pushed her back into the basket and pushed the lead cover down over its mouth.

9Then I looked up—and there before me were two women, with the wind in their wings! They had wings like those of a stork, and they lifted up the basket between heaven and earth.

10"Where are they taking the basket?" I asked the angel who was speaking to me.

11He replied, "To the country of Babylonia*e* to build a house for it. When it is ready, the basket will be set there in its place."

Four Chariots

6 I looked up again, and there before me were four chariots coming out from between two mountains—mountains of bronze. 2The first chariot had red horses, the second black, 3the third white, and the fourth dappled—all of them powerful. 4I asked the angel who was speaking to me, "What are these, my lord?"

5The angel answered me, "These are the four spirits*f* of heaven, going out from standing in the presence of the Lord of the whole world. 6The one with the black horses is going toward the north country, the one with the white horses toward the west,*g* and the one with the dappled horses toward the south."

7When the powerful horses went out, they were straining to go throughout the earth. And he said, "Go throughout the earth!" So they went throughout the earth.

8Then he called to me, "Look, those going toward the north country have given my Spirit*h* rest in the land of the north."

A Crown for Joshua

9The word of the LORD came to me: 10"Take ⌊silver and gold⌋ from the exiles Heldai, Tobijah and Jedaiah, who have arrived from Babylon. Go the same day to the house of Josiah son of Zephaniah. 11Take the silver and gold and make a crown, and set it on the head of the high priest, Joshua son of Joza-

a 10 Or the plumb line   b 14 Or two who bring oil and wide or about 9 meters long and 4.5 meters wide   c 2 That is, about 30 feet long and 15 feet   d 6 Or appearance   e 11 Hebrew Shinar   f 5 Or winds   g 6 Or horses after them   h 8 Or spirit dak.*a* 12Tell him this is what the LORD Almighty says: 'Here is the man whose name is the Branch, and he will branch out from his place and build the temple of the LORD. 13It is he who will build the temple of the LORD, and he will be clothed with majesty and will sit and rule on his throne. And he*b* will be a priest on his throne. And there will be harmony between the two.' 14The crown will be given to Heldai,*c* Tobijah, Jedaiah and Hen*d* son of Zephaniah as a memorial in the temple of the LORD. 15Those who are far away will come and help to build the temple of the LORD, and you will know that the LORD Almighty has sent me to you. This will happen if you diligently obey the LORD your God."

Justice and Mercy, Not Fasting

7 In the fourth year of King Darius, the word of the LORD came to Zechariah on the fourth day of the ninth month, the month of Kislev. 2The people of Bethel had sent Sharezer and Regem-Melek, together with their men, to entreat the LORD 3by asking the priests of the house of the LORD Almighty and the prophets, "Should I mourn and fast in the fifth month, as I have done for so many years?"

4Then the word of the LORD Almighty came to me: 5"Ask all the people of the land and the priests, 'When you fasted and mourned in the fifth and seventh months for the past seventy years, was it really for me that you fasted? 6And when you were eating and drinking, were you not just feasting for yourselves? 7Are these not the words the LORD proclaimed through the earlier prophets when Jerusalem and its surrounding towns were at rest and prosperous, and the Negev and the western foothills were settled?' "

8And the word of the LORD came again to Zechariah: 9"This is what the LORD Almighty said: 'Administer true justice; show mercy and compassion to one another. 10Do not oppress the widow or the fatherless, the foreigner or the poor. Do not plot evil against each other.'

11"But they refused to pay attention; stubbornly they turned their backs and covered their ears. 12They made their hearts as hard as flint and would not listen to the law or to the words that the LORD Almighty had sent by his Spirit through the earlier prophets. So the LORD Almighty was very angry.

13" 'When I called, they did not listen; so when they called, I would not listen,' says the LORD Almighty. 14'I scattered them with a whirlwind among all the nations, where they were strangers. The land they left behind them was so desolate that no one traveled through it. This is how they made the pleasant land desolate.' "

The LORD Promises to Bless Jerusalem

8 The word of the LORD Almighty came to me. 2This is what the LORD Almighty says: "I am very jealous for Zion; I am burning with jealousy for her."

3This is what the LORD says: "I will return to Zion and dwell in Jerusalem. Then Jerusalem will be called the City of Truth, and the mountain of the LORD Almighty will be called the Holy Mountain."

4This is what the LORD Almighty says: "Once again men and women of ripe old age will sit in the streets of Jerusalem, each of them with cane in hand because of their age. 5The city streets will be filled with boys and girls playing there."

6This is what the LORD Almighty says: "It may seem marvelous to the remnant of this people at that time, but will it seem marvelous to me?" declares the LORD Almighty.

7This is what the LORD Almighty says: "I will save my people from the countries of the east and the west. 8I will bring them back to live in Jerusalem; they will be my people, and I will be faithful and righteous to them as their God."

9This is what the LORD Almighty says: "Now hear these words, 'Let your hands be strong so that the temple may be built.' This is also what the prophets said who were present when the foundation was laid for the house of the LORD Almighty. 10Before that time there were no wages for people or animals. People could not go about their business safely because of conflicts, since I had turned them all against each other. 11But now I will not deal with the remnant of

---

a 11 Hebrew *Jehozadak*, a variant of *Jozadak*   *b* 13 Or *there*   *c* 14 Syriac; Hebrew *Helem*
d 14 Or *and the gracious one, the*

this people as I did in the past," declares the Lord Almighty.

¹²"The seed will grow well, the vine will yield its fruit, the ground will produce its crops, and the heavens will drop their dew. I will give all these things as an inheritance to the remnant of this people. ¹³Just as you, Judah and Israel, have been a curse[a] among the nations, so I will save you, and you will be a blessing.[b] Do not be afraid, but let your hands be strong."

¹⁴This is what the Lord Almighty says: "Just as I had determined to bring disaster on you and showed no pity when your ancestors angered me," says the Lord Almighty, ¹⁵"so now I have determined to do good again to Jerusalem and Judah. Do not be afraid. ¹⁶These are the things you are to do: Speak the truth to each other, and render true and sound judgment in your courts; ¹⁷do not plot evil against each other, and do not love to swear falsely. I hate all this," declares the Lord.

¹⁸The word of the Lord Almighty came to me.

¹⁹This is what the Lord Almighty says: "The fasts of the fourth, fifth, seventh and tenth months will become joyful and glad occasions and happy festivals for Judah. Therefore love truth and peace."

²⁰This is what the Lord Almighty says: "Many peoples and the inhabitants of many cities will yet come, ²¹and the inhabitants of one city will go to another and say, 'Let us go at once to entreat the Lord and seek the Lord Almighty. I myself am going.' ²²And many peoples and powerful nations will come to Jerusalem to seek the Lord Almighty and to entreat him."

²³This is what the Lord Almighty says: "In those days ten people from all languages and nations will take firm hold of one Jew by the hem of his robe and say, 'Let us go with you, because we have heard that God is with you.'"

Judgment on Israel's Enemies

9 A prophecy:

The word of the Lord is against the land of Hadrak

and will come to rest on Damascus—
for the eyes of all people and all the
    tribes of Israel
are on the Lord—[c]
²and on Hamath too, which borders on it,
    and on Tyre and Sidon, though they
    are very skillful.
³Tyre has built herself a stronghold;
    she has heaped up silver like dust,
    and gold like the dirt of the streets.
⁴But the Lord will take away her
    possessions
and destroy her power on the sea,
    and she will be consumed by fire.
⁵Ashkelon will see it and fear;
    Gaza will writhe in agony,
    and Ekron too, for her hope will
    wither.
Gaza will lose her king
    and Ashkelon will be deserted.
⁶A mongrel people will occupy Ashdod,
    and I will put an end to the pride of
    the Philistines.
⁷I will take the blood from their mouths,
    the forbidden food from between
    their teeth.
Those who are left will belong to our
    God
    and become a clan in Judah,
    and Ekron will be like the Jebusites.
⁸But I will encamp at my temple
    to guard it against marauding forces.
Never again will an oppressor overrun
    my people,
    for now I am keeping watch.

The Coming of Zion's King

⁹Rejoice greatly, Daughter Zion!
    Shout, Daughter Jerusalem!
See, your king comes to you,
    righteous and having salvation,
lowly and riding on a donkey,
    on a colt, the foal of a donkey.
¹⁰I will take away the chariots from
    Ephraim
    and the warhorses from Jerusalem,
    and the battle bow will be broken.
He will proclaim peace to the nations.
    His rule will extend from sea to sea
    and from the River[d] to the ends of the
    earth.

---

a 13 That is, your name has been used in cursing (see Jer. 29:23); or, you have been regarded as under a curse.   *b 13* Or *and your name will be used in blessings* (see Gen. 48:20); or *and you will be seen as blessed*   *c 1* Or *Damascus. / For the eye of the Lord is on all people, / as well as on the tribes of Israel,*   *d 10* That is, the Euphrates

WEDNESDAY

VICTORY OVER EVIL
Zechariah 9:1–17 *or* 9:16–17

N. T. Wright

Just as evil is more than the sum total of individual acts of wrongdoing, so Jesus' victory over evil is more than the sum total of subsequent individual acts of selfless love. Christian faith, faith in the crucified Jesus, is more than my individual belief that he died for me, vital though that is. It is the faith that on the cross Jesus in principle won the victory over sin, violence, pride, arrogance and even death itself, and that that victory can now be implemented. This faith refuses to accept that violence, greed and pride are unassailable and unchallengeable. This faith will go to work to challenge and subvert those destructive forces, in ourselves, in our local communities, in our corporate and political life, in the belief, albeit often in the teeth of the evidence, that they have been defeated and that the power of God's love is stronger than they are. To say that the cross changed the world is a statement of faith; but it is not blind faith, whistling in the dark. It is faith that looks up at the creator God and knows him to be the God of love. And it is faith that looks out at the world with the longing to bring that love to bear in healing, reconciliation and hope.

ALBERT BARNES {AD 1798–1870}

Christ has achieved a great victory and has subdued all the foes of humanity. Because of this, we should not be led captive but should regard ourselves as a free people. We should not be made again the slaves of custom, or habit, or ritual observances, or superstitious rites, or anything whatever that has its origin in the kingdom of darkness. We are bound to assert and to use our freedom and should not allow any hostile power to plunder or "spoil" us. The Christian is free. Our great Captain has subdued all our enemies, and we should not allow them again to set up their dark empire over our souls.

reflection

1. What did Christ accomplish through his death on the cross?

2. How have you experienced Christ's victory over sin in your own life?

3. The salvation that Jesus brings does more than just prevent a sinner from an eternity in hell—it effects a total and complete transformation. How would you describe the transformation of those who are saved?

For your next devotional reading, go to page 1068.

¹¹As for you, because of the blood of my
    covenant with you,
  I will free your prisoners from the
    waterless pit.
¹²Return to your fortress, you prisoners of
    hope;
  even now I announce that I will
    restore twice as much to you.
¹³I will bend Judah as I bend my bow
  and fill it with Ephraim.
  I will rouse your sons, Zion,
    against your sons, Greece,
  and make you like a warrior's sword.

The LORD Will Appear

¹⁴Then the LORD will appear over them;
  his arrow will flash like lightning.
  The Sovereign LORD will sound the
    trumpet;
  he will march in the storms of the
    south,
¹⁵ and the LORD Almighty will shield
    them.
  They will destroy
    and overcome with slingstones.
  They will drink and roar as with wine;
    they will be full like a bowl
  used for sprinkling[a] the corners of the
    altar.
¹⁶The LORD their God will save his people
    on that day
  as a shepherd saves his flock.
  They will sparkle in his land
    like jewels in a crown.
¹⁷How attractive and beautiful they will be!
  Grain will make the young men
    thrive,
  and new wine the young women.

The LORD Will Care for Judah

10 Ask the LORD for rain in the
    springtime;
  it is the LORD who sends the
    thunderstorms.
  He gives showers of rain to all people,
    and plants of the field to everyone.
²The idols speak deceitfully,
    diviners see visions that lie;
  they tell dreams that are false,
    they give comfort in vain.
  Therefore the people wander like sheep
    oppressed for lack of a shepherd.

³"My anger burns against the shepherds,
  and I will punish the leaders;
  for the LORD Almighty will care
    for his flock, the house of Judah,
  and make them like a proud horse in
    battle.
⁴From Judah will come the cornerstone,
    from him the tent peg,
  from him the battle bow,
    from him every ruler.
⁵Together they[b] will be like mighty
    warriors in battle
  trampling their enemy into the mud
    of the streets.
  They will fight because the LORD is with
    them,
  and they will put the enemy
    horsemen to shame.

⁶"I will strengthen the house of Judah
  and save the house of Joseph.
  I will restore them
    because I have compassion on them.
  They will be as though
    I had not rejected them,
  for I am the LORD their God
    and I will answer them.
⁷The Ephraimites will become like
    mighty warriors,
  and their hearts will be glad as with
    wine.
  Their children will see it and be joyful;
    their hearts will rejoice in the LORD.
⁸I will signal for them
    and gather them in.
  Surely I will redeem them;
    they will be as numerous as before.
⁹Though I scatter them among the
    peoples,
  yet in distant lands they will
    remember me.
  They and their children will survive,
    and they will return.
¹⁰I will bring them back from Egypt
    and gather them from Assyria.
  I will bring them to Gilead and Lebanon,
    and there will not be room enough for
    them.
¹¹They will pass through the sea of
    trouble;
  the surging sea will be subdued
    and all the depths of the Nile will dry
    up.
  Assyria's pride will be brought down
    and Egypt's scepter will pass away.

a 15 Or bowl, / like   b 4,5 Or ruler, all of them together. / ⁵They

¹²I will strengthen them in the LORD
  and in his name they will live
      securely,"
                    declares the LORD.

11

Open your doors, Lebanon,
  so that fire may devour your
    cedars!
²Wail, you juniper, for the cedar has
    fallen;
  the stately trees are ruined!
Wail, oaks of Bashan;
  the dense forest has been cut down!
³Listen to the wail of the shepherds;
  their rich pastures are destroyed!
Listen to the roar of the lions;
  the lush thicket of the Jordan is
    ruined!

Two Shepherds

⁴This is what the LORD my God says:
"Shepherd the flock marked for slaughter.
⁵Their buyers slaughter them and go unpunished. Those who sell them say, 'Praise the LORD, I am rich!' Their own shepherds do not spare them. ⁶For I will no longer have pity on the people of the land," declares the LORD. "I will give everyone into the hands of their neighbors and their king. They will devastate the land, and I will not rescue them from their hands."

⁷So I shepherded the flock marked for slaughter, particularly the oppressed of the flock. Then I took two staffs and called one Favor and the other Union, and I shepherded the flock. ⁸In one month I got rid of the three shepherds.

The flock detested me, and I grew weary of them ⁹and said, "I will not be your shepherd. Let the dying die, and the perishing perish. Let those who are left eat one another's flesh."

¹⁰Then I took my staff called Favor and broke it, revoking the covenant I had made with all the nations. ¹¹It was revoked on that day, and so the oppressed of the flock who were watching me knew it was the word of the LORD.

¹²I told them, "If you think it best, give me my pay; but if not, keep it." So they paid me thirty pieces of silver.

¹³And the LORD said to me, "Throw it to the potter"—the handsome price at which they valued me! So I took the thirty pieces of silver and threw them to the potter at the house of the LORD.

¹⁴Then I broke my second staff called Union, breaking the family bond between Judah and Israel.

¹⁵Then the LORD said to me, "Take again the equipment of a foolish shepherd. ¹⁶For I am going to raise up a shepherd over the land who will not care for the lost, or seek the young, or heal the injured, or feed the healthy, but will eat the meat of the choice sheep, tearing off their hooves.

¹⁷"Woe to the worthless shepherd,
  who deserts the flock!
May the sword strike his arm and his
    right eye!
May his arm be completely withered,
  his right eye totally blinded!"

Jerusalem's Enemies to Be Destroyed

12

A prophecy: The word of the LORD concerning Israel.

The LORD, who stretches out the heavens, who lays the foundation of the earth, and who forms the spirit in human beings, declares: ²"I am going to make Jerusalem a cup that sends all the surrounding peoples reeling. Judah will be besieged as well as Jerusalem. ³On that day, when all the nations of the earth are gathered against her, I will make Jerusalem an immovable rock for all the nations. All who try to move it will injure themselves. ⁴On that day I will strike every horse with panic and its rider with madness," declares the LORD. "I will keep a watchful eye over the house of Judah, but I will blind all the horses of the nations. ⁵Then the clans of Judah will say in their hearts, 'The people of Jerusalem are strong, because the LORD Almighty is their God.'

⁶"On that day I will make the clans of Judah like a firepot in a woodpile, like a flaming torch among sheaves. They will consume right and left all the surrounding peoples, but Jerusalem will remain intact in her place.

⁷"The LORD will save the dwellings of Judah first, so that the honor of the house of David and of Jerusalem's inhabitants may not be greater than that of Judah. ⁸On that day the LORD will shield those who live in Jerusalem, so that the feeblest among them will be like David, and the house of David will be like God, like the angel of the LORD going before them. ⁹On that day I will set out to destroy all the nations that attack Jerusalem.

Mourning for the One They Pierced

¹⁰"And I will pour out on the house of David and the inhabitants of Jerusalem a spiritᵃ of grace and supplication. They will look onᵇ me, the one they have pierced, and they will mourn for him as one mourns for an only child, and grieve bitterly for him as one grieves for a firstborn son. ¹¹On that day the weeping in Jerusalem will be great, like the weeping of Hadad Rimmon in the plain of Megiddo. ¹²The land will mourn, each clan by itself, with their wives by themselves: the clan of the house of David and their wives, the clan of the house of Nathan and their wives, ¹³the clan of the house of Levi and their wives, the clan of Shimei and their wives, ¹⁴and all the rest of the clans and their wives.

Cleansing From Sin

13 "On that day a fountain will be opened to the house of David and the inhabitants of Jerusalem, to cleanse them from sin and impurity.

²"On that day, I will banish the names of the idols from the land, and they will be remembered no more," declares the LORD Almighty. "I will remove both the prophets and the spirit of impurity from the land. ³And if some still prophesy, their fathers and mothers, to whom they were born, will say to them, 'You must die, because you have told lies in the LORD's name.' When they prophesy, their own parents will stab them.

⁴"On that day the prophets will all be ashamed of their prophetic visions. They will not put on a prophet's garment of hair in order to deceive. ⁵Every one of them will say, 'I am not a prophet. I am a farmer; the land has been my livelihood since my youth.'ᶜ ⁶If someone asks, 'What are these wounds on your bodyᵈ?' they will answer, 'The wounds I was given at the house of my friends.'

The Shepherd Struck, the Sheep Scattered

⁷"Awake, sword, against my shepherd,
    against the man who is close to me!"
    declares the LORD Almighty.
"Strike the shepherd,
    and the sheep will be scattered,

and I will turn my hand against the
    little ones.
⁸In the whole land," declares the LORD,
    "two-thirds will be struck down and
        perish;
    yet one-third will be left in it.
⁹This third I will bring into the fire;
    I will refine them like silver
    and test them like gold.
They will call on my name
    and I will answer them;
I will say, 'They are my people,'
    and they will say, 'The LORD is our
        God.' "

The LORD Comes and Reigns

14 A day of the LORD is coming, Jerusalem, when your possessions will be plundered and divided up within your very walls.

²I will gather all the nations to Jerusalem to fight against it; the city will be captured, the houses ransacked, and the women ravished. Half of the city will go into exile, but the rest of the people will not be taken from the city. ³Then the LORD will go out and fight against those nations, as he fights on a day of battle. ⁴On that day his feet will stand on the Mount of Olives, east of Jerusalem, and the Mount of Olives will be split in two from east to west, forming a great valley, with half of the mountain moving north and half moving south. ⁵You will flee by my mountain valley, for it will extend to Azel. You will flee as you fled from the earthquakeᵉ in the days of Uzziah king of Judah. Then the LORD my God will come, and all the holy ones with him.

⁶On that day there will be no sunlight, no cold, frosty darkness. ⁷It will be a unique day—a day known only to the LORD—with no distinction between day and night. When evening comes, there will be light.

⁸On that day living water will flow out from Jerusalem, half of it east to the Dead Sea and half of it west to the Mediterranean Sea, in summer and in winter.

⁹The LORD will be king over the whole earth. On that day there will be one LORD, and his name the only name.

¹⁰The whole land, from Geba to Rimmon, south of Jerusalem, will become like the Ar-

---

ᵃ 10 Or the Spirit   ᵇ 10 Or to   ᶜ 5 Or farmer; a man sold me in my youth   ᵈ 6 Or wounds between your hands   ᵉ 5 Or ⁵My mountain valley will be blocked and will extend to Azel. It will be blocked as it was blocked because of the earthquake abah. But Jerusalem will be raised up high from the Benjamin Gate to the site of the First Gate, to the Corner Gate, and from the Tower of Hananel to the royal winepresses, and will remain in its place. ¹¹It will be inhabited; never again will it be destroyed. Jerusalem will be secure.

¹²This is the plague with which the Lord will strike all the nations that fought against Jerusalem: Their flesh will rot while they are still standing on their feet, their eyes will rot in their sockets, and their tongues will rot in their mouths. ¹³On that day people will be stricken by the Lord with great panic. They will seize each other by the hand and attack one another. ¹⁴Judah too will fight at Jerusalem. The wealth of all the surrounding nations will be collected—great quantities of gold and silver and clothing. ¹⁵A similar plague will strike the horses and mules, the camels and donkeys, and all the animals in those camps.

¹⁶Then the survivors from all the nations that have attacked Jerusalem will go up year after year to worship the King, the Lord Almighty, and to celebrate the Festival of Tabernacles. ¹⁷If any of the peoples of the earth do not go up to Jerusalem to worship the King, the Lord Almighty, they will have no rain. ¹⁸If the Egyptian people do not go up and take part, they will have no rain. The Lord *a* will bring on them the plague he inflicts on the nations that do not go up to celebrate the Festival of Tabernacles. ¹⁹This will be the punishment of Egypt and the punishment of all the nations that do not go up to celebrate the Festival of Tabernacles.

²⁰On that day HOLY TO THE LORD will be inscribed on the bells of the horses, and the cooking pots in the Lord's house will be like the sacred bowls in front of the altar. ²¹Every pot in Jerusalem and Judah will be holy to the Lord Almighty, and all who come to sacrifice will take some of the pots and cook in them. And on that day there will no longer be a Canaanite *b* in the house of the Lord Almighty.

---

a 18 Or part, then the Lord   b 21 Or merchant

malachi

AUTHOR: Malachi

DATE: Around 430 B.C.

THEME: God wants our hearts more than our participation in religious rituals.

1 A prophecy: The word of the LORD to Israel through Malachi.[a]

Israel Doubts God's Love

²"I have loved you," says the LORD.

"But you ask, 'How have you loved us?'"

"Was not Esau Jacob's brother?" declares the LORD. "Yet I have loved Jacob, ³but Esau I have hated, and I have turned his hill country into a wasteland and left his inheritance to the desert jackals."

⁴Edom may say, "Though we have been crushed, we will rebuild the ruins."

But this is what the LORD Almighty says: "They may build, but I will demolish. They will be called the Wicked Land, a people always under the wrath of the LORD. ⁵You will see it with your own eyes and say, 'Great is the LORD—even beyond the borders of Israel!'

Breaking Covenant Through Blemished Sacrifices

⁶"A son honors his father, and slaves honor their master. If I am a father, where is the honor due me? If I am a master, where is the respect due me?" says the LORD Almighty.

"It is you priests who show contempt for my name.

"But you ask, 'How have we shown contempt for your name?'

⁷"By offering defiled food on my altar.

"But you ask, 'How have we defiled you?'

"By saying that the LORD's table is contemptible. ⁸When you offer blind animals for sacrifice, is that not wrong? When you sacrifice lame or diseased animals, is that not wrong? Try offering them to your governor! Would he be pleased with you? Would he accept you?" says the LORD Almighty.

⁹"Now implore God to be gracious to us. With such offerings from your hands, will he accept you?"—says the LORD Almighty.

¹⁰"Oh, that one of you would shut the temple doors, so that you would not light useless fires on my altar! I am not pleased with you," says the LORD Almighty, "and I will accept no offering from your hands. ¹¹My name will be great among the nations, from where the sun rises to where it sets. In every place incense and pure offerings will be brought to me, because my name will be great among the nations," says the LORD Almighty.

¹²"But you profane it by saying, 'The Lord's table is defiled,' and, 'Its food is contemptible.' ¹³And you say, 'What a burden!' and you sniff at it contemptuously," says the LORD Almighty.

"When you bring injured, lame or diseased animals and offer them as sacrifices, should I accept them from your hands?" says the LORD. ¹⁴"Cursed is the cheat who has an acceptable male in his flock and vows to give it, but then sacrifices a blemished animal to the Lord. For I am a great king," says the LORD Almighty, "and my name is to be feared among the nations.

Additional Warning to the Priests

2 "And now, you priests, this warning is for you. ²If you do not listen, and if you do not resolve to honor my name," says the LORD Almighty, "I will send a curse on you, and I will curse your blessings. Yes, I have already cursed them, because you have not resolved to honor me.

---

a 1 *Malachi* means *my messenger.*

THURSDAY

UNCHANGING LOVE

Malachi 1:1–14 *or* 1:1–2

CATHERINE OF SIENA {AD 1347–1380}

Eternal Father, you said, "[Let us make human beings in our image, in our likeness.]" Thus you were willing to share with us your own greatness. You gave us the intellect to share your truth. You gave us the wisdom to share your goodness. And you gave us the free will to love that which is true and just.

Why did you so dignify us? It was because you looked upon us, and fell in love with us. It was love which first prompted you to create us; and it was love which caused you to share with us your truth and goodness.

Yet your heart must break when you see us turn against you. You must weep when you see us abusing our intellect in pursuit of that which is false. You must cry with pain when we distort wisdom in order to justify evil.

But you never desert us. Out of the same love that caused you to create us, you have now sent your only Son to save us. He is your perfect image and likeness, and so through him we can be restored to your image and likeness.

Henry Gariepy

"I have loved you," says the Lord in the opening message of this last book of the Old Testament. God does not allow the oracles of the prophets to close without once more affirming his unchangeable love for his people.

God declares, "I the LORD do not change" (Malachi 3:6). God is the same today as he was a billion years ago. He will always be just. He will always be holy. He will always be omnipotent and omniscient. He will always be loving. Though we may fail and falter, God's love for us is unchanging. One of God's most assuring attributes is his immutability . . .

Love is ever in danger of being taken for granted. A husband can take for granted the faithful love of a wife; a grown child the sacrificial love of a parent. The people of Israel became blind to the love of God and turned to moral laxity.

God's word to us in this final book of the Old Testament is that he loves us. Let our hearts return that love in devotion and glad obedience.

reflection

1. How did the Israelites take God's love for granted?
2. How have you done the same thing?
3. How does the unchanging greatness of God's love make you want to love him more?

For your next devotional reading, go to page 1070.

³"Because of you I will rebuke your descendants[a]; I will smear on your faces the dung from your festival sacrifices, and you will be carried off with it. ⁴And you will know that I have sent you this warning so that my covenant with Levi may continue," says the LORD Almighty. ⁵"My covenant was with him, a covenant of life and peace, and I gave them to him; this called for reverence and he revered me and stood in awe of my name. ⁶True instruction was in his mouth and nothing false was found on his lips. He walked with me in peace and uprightness, and turned many from sin.

⁷"For the lips of a priest ought to preserve knowledge, because he is the messenger of the LORD Almighty and people seek instruction from his mouth. ⁸But you have turned from the way and by your teaching have caused many to stumble; you have violated the covenant with Levi," says the LORD Almighty. ⁹"So I have caused you to be despised and humiliated before all the people, because you have not followed my ways but have shown partiality in matters of the law."

Breaking Covenant Through Divorce

¹⁰Do we not all have one Father[b]? Did not one God create us? Why do we profane the covenant of our ancestors by being unfaithful to one another?

¹¹Judah has been unfaithful. A detestable thing has been committed in Israel and in Jerusalem: Judah has desecrated the sanctuary the LORD loves by marrying women who worship a foreign god. ¹²If anyone does this, whoever he may be, may the LORD remove him from the tents of Jacob[c]—even though he brings an offering to the LORD Almighty.

¹³Another thing you do: You flood the LORD's altar with tears. You weep and wail because he no longer looks with favor on your offerings or accepts them with pleasure from your hands. ¹⁴You ask, "Why?" It is because the LORD is the witness between you and the wife of your youth. You have been unfaithful to her, though she is your partner, the wife of your marriage covenant.

¹⁵Has not the LORD made the two of you one? You belong to him in body and spirit. And why has he made you one? Because he was seeking godly offspring.[d] So be on your guard, and do not be unfaithful to the wife of your youth.

¹⁶"I hate divorce," says the LORD God of Israel, "and I hate it when people clothe themselves with injustice," says the LORD Almighty.

So be on your guard, and do not be unfaithful.

Breaking Covenant Through Injustice

¹⁷You have wearied the LORD with your words.

"How have we wearied him?" you ask.

By saying, "All who do evil are good in the eyes of the LORD, and he is pleased with them" or "Where is the God of justice?"

3 "I will send my messenger, who will prepare the way before me. Then suddenly the Lord you are seeking will come to his temple; the messenger of the covenant, whom you desire, will come," says the LORD Almighty.

²But who can endure the day of his coming? Who can stand when he appears? For he will be like a refiner's fire or a launderer's soap. ³He will sit as a refiner and purifier of silver; he will purify the Levites and refine them like gold and silver. Then the LORD will have men who will bring offerings in righteousness, ⁴and the offerings of Judah and Jerusalem will be acceptable to the LORD, as in days gone by, as in former years.

⁵"So I will come to put you on trial. I will be quick to testify against sorcerers, adulterers and perjurers, against those who defraud laborers of their wages, who oppress the widows and the fatherless, and deprive the foreigners among you of justice, but do not fear me," says the LORD Almighty.

Breaking Covenant by Withholding Tithes

⁶"I the LORD do not change. So you, the descendants of Jacob, are not destroyed. ⁷Ever since the time of your ancestors you have turned away from my decrees and have not kept them. Return to me, and I will return to you," says the LORD Almighty.

"But you ask, 'How are we to return?'

⁸"Will a mere mortal rob God? Yet you rob me.

"But you ask, 'How are we robbing you?'

"In tithes and offerings. ⁹You are under a curse—your whole nation—because you are

---

a 3 Or *will blight your grain*   *b 10* Or *father*   *c 12* Or *¹²May the* LORD *remove from the tents of Jacob anyone who gives testimony in behalf of the man who does this*   *d 15* The meaning of the Hebrew for the first part of this verse is uncertain.

FRIDAY

ONE DYNAMIC, GODLY LOVE AFFAIR

Malachi 3:1–18 *or* 3:1–5

Lisa Harper

God loves us exactly as we are today, but He loves us too much to leave us as we are and where we are.

We aren't any better than Malachi's [original audience]. We are just as arrogant, just as faithless, just as stubborn and just as blind to our own sin. But thankfully, God loves us way too much to leave us brokenhearted and disillusioned with our fists defiantly raised toward Him.

SMITH WIGGLESWORTH {ca. AD 1859–1949}

Praising God in a meeting is a different thing than thanking Him for the trials you face in your life. There must be no perishing though we are tried by fire. What is going to appear at the appearing of Jesus? Faith! Your heart will be established by the grace of the Spirit, which doesn't crush, but refines; doesn't destroy, but enlarges . . .

How many have gone to the stake and through fiery persecution? Did they desire it? Faith tried by fire had power to stand all ridicule, all slander. We need to have the faith of the son of God, "[For the joy set before him he endured the cross]" (Hebrews 12:2). Oh the joy of pleasing Him!

No trial, no darkness, nothing is too hard for me. If only I may see the image of the Lord again and again. In the melting pot, He removes the skimming until His face is seen. When the metal reflects Him, it is pure. Who is looking into our hearts? Who is the Refiner? My Lord. He will remove only what will hinder. Oh, I know the love of God is working in my heart.

reflection

1. Think of at least five ways that God shows his love to his people. Which of those do you appreciate most right now?

2. In what ways do you resemble those in Malachi who turned their backs on God?

3. How can you cling more tightly to Jesus?

For your next devotional reading, go to page 1072.

robbing me. [10]Bring the whole tithe into the storehouse, that there may be food in my house. Test me in this," says the LORD Almighty, "and see if I will not throw open the floodgates of heaven and pour out so much blessing that there will not be room enough to store it. [11]I will prevent pests from devouring your crops, and the vines in your fields will not drop their fruit before it is ripe," says the LORD Almighty. [12]"Then all the nations will call you blessed, for yours will be a delightful land," says the LORD Almighty.

Israel Speaks Arrogantly Against God

[13]"You have spoken arrogantly against me," says the LORD.

"Yet you ask, 'What have we said against you?'

[14]"You have said, 'It is futile to serve God. What do we gain by carrying out his requirements and going about like mourners before the LORD Almighty? [15]But now we call the arrogant blessed. Certainly evildoers prosper, and even when they put God to the test, they get away with it.' "

The Faithful Remnant

[16]Then those who feared the LORD talked with each other, and the LORD listened and heard. A scroll of remembrance was written in his presence concerning those who feared the LORD and honored his name.

[17]"On the day when I act," says the LORD Almighty, "they will be my treasured possession. I will spare them, just as a father has compassion and spares his son who serves him. [18]And you will again see the distinction between the righteous and the wicked, between those who serve God and those who do not.

Judgment and Covenant Renewal

4 *"Surely the day is coming; it will burn like a furnace. All the arrogant and every evildoer will be stubble, and that day that is coming will set them on fire," says the LORD Almighty. "Not a root or a branch will be left to them. [2]But for you who revere my name, the sun of righteousness will rise with healing in its rays. And you will go out and frolic like well-fed calves. [3]Then you will trample on the wicked; they will be ashes under the soles of your feet on the day when I act," says the LORD Almighty.

[4]"Remember the law of my servant Moses, the decrees and laws I gave him at Horeb for all Israel.

[5]"See, I will send the prophet Elijah to you before that great and dreadful day of the LORD comes. [6]He will turn the hearts of the parents to their children, and the hearts of the children to their parents; or else I will come and strike the land with total destruction."

* 4:1-6 is numbered 3:19-24 in Hebrew texts.

God's Sovereign Power

Malachi 4:1-3

read/meditate

As you read through the prophecy, note your reactions to the way God's power is expressed.

pray

Offer God control of your life. Open your inner life to his scrutiny, trusting the benevolence of his power. Express to him thoughts, concerns or even fears about his judgment.

contemplate

Consider the fact that, while cultures change, God remains the same. While our interpretation of his actions is affected by our upbringing, his nature is consistent in the face of changing times. What do these ancient words bring to light for you about who God wants to be in the lives of people?

additional reflection

Divine Sovereignty means that God is God in fact, as well as in name, that He is on the Throne of the universe, directing all things, working all things, "after the counsel of His own will."

—Arthur W. Pink

We cannot love good if we do not hate evil.

—Saint Jerome

For your next devotional reading, go to page 1080.

The New Testament

The Gospels &
the Early Church

Matthew

Mark

Luke

John

Acts

matthew

AUTHOR: Matthew, also called Levi

DATE: Probably between A.D. 60 and 70

THEME: Jesus is the Messiah the Jews have been waiting for.

The Genealogy of Jesus the Messiah

1 This is the genealogy[a] of Jesus the Messiah[b] the son of David, the son of Abraham:

2 Abraham was the father of Isaac,
Isaac the father of Jacob,
Jacob the father of Judah and his brothers,
3 Judah the father of Perez and Zerah, whose mother was Tamar,
Perez the father of Hezron,
Hezron the father of Ram,
4 Ram the father of Amminadab,
Amminadab the father of Nahshon,
Nahshon the father of Salmon,
5 Salmon the father of Boaz, whose mother was Rahab,
Boaz the father of Obed, whose mother was Ruth,
Obed the father of Jesse,
6 and Jesse the father of King David.

David was the father of Solomon, whose mother had been Uriah's wife,
7 Solomon the father of Rehoboam,
Rehoboam the father of Abijah,
Abijah the father of Asa,
8 Asa the father of Jehoshaphat,
Jehoshaphat the father of Jehoram,
Jehoram the father of Uzziah,
9 Uzziah the father of Jotham,
Jotham the father of Ahaz,
Ahaz the father of Hezekiah,
10 Hezekiah the father of Manasseh,
Manasseh the father of Amon,
Amon the father of Josiah,
11 and Josiah the father of Jeconiah[c] and his brothers at the time of the exile to Babylon.

12 After the exile to Babylon:
Jeconiah was the father of Shealtiel,
Shealtiel the father of Zerubbabel,
13 Zerubbabel the father of Abiud,
Abiud the father of Eliakim,
Eliakim the father of Azor,
14 Azor the father of Zadok,
Zadok the father of Akim,
Akim the father of Eliud,
15 Eliud the father of Eleazar,
Eleazar the father of Matthan,
Matthan the father of Jacob,
16 and Jacob the father of Joseph, the husband of Mary, and Mary was the mother of Jesus who is called the Messiah.

17 Thus there were fourteen generations in all from Abraham to David, fourteen from David to the exile to Babylon, and fourteen from the exile to the Messiah.

Joseph Accepts Jesus as His Son

18 This is how the birth of Jesus the Messiah came about[d]: His mother Mary was pledged to be married to Joseph, but before they came together, she was found to be pregnant through the Holy Spirit. 19 Because Joseph her husband was a righteous man and did not want to expose her to public disgrace, he had in mind to divorce her quietly.

20 But after he had considered this, an angel of the Lord appeared to him in a dream and said, "Joseph son of David, do not be

---

a 1 Or is an account of the origin   b 1 Or Jesus Christ. Messiah (Hebrew) and Christ (Greek) both mean Anointed One; also in verse 18.   c 11 That is, Jehoiachin; also in verse 12   d 18 Or The origin of Jesus the Messiah was like this afraid to take Mary home as your wife, because what is conceived in her is from the Holy Spirit. 21She will give birth to a son, and you are to give him the name Jesus,^a because he will save his people from their sins."

22All this took place to fulfill what the Lord had said through the prophet: 23"The virgin will conceive and give birth to a son, and they will call him Immanuel"^b (which means "God with us").

24When Joseph woke up, he did what the angel of the Lord had commanded him and took Mary home as his wife. 25But he had no union with her until she gave birth to a son. And he gave him the name Jesus.

The Magi Visit the Messiah

2 After Jesus was born in Bethlehem in Judea, during the time of King Herod, Magi^c from the east came to Jerusalem 2and asked, "Where is the one who has been born king of the Jews? We saw his star when it rose and have come to worship him."

3When King Herod heard this he was disturbed, and all Jerusalem with him. 4When he had called together all the people's chief priests and teachers of the law, he asked them where the Messiah was to be born. 5"In Bethlehem in Judea," they replied, "for this is what the prophet has written:

6" 'But you, Bethlehem, in the land of Judah,
   are by no means least among the rulers of Judah;
for out of you will come a ruler
   who will shepherd my people Israel.'^d"

7Then Herod called the Magi secretly and found out from them the exact time the star had appeared. 8He sent them to Bethlehem and said, "Go and make a careful search for the child. As soon as you find him, report to me, so that I too may go and worship him." 9After they had heard the king, they went on their way, and the star they had seen when it rose went ahead of them until it stopped over the place where the child was. 10When they saw the star, they were overjoyed. 11On coming to the house, they saw the child with his mother Mary, and they bowed down and worshiped him. Then they opened their treasures and presented him with gifts of gold, frankincense and myrrh. 12And having been warned in a dream not to go back to Herod, they returned to their country by another route.

The Escape to Egypt

13When they had gone, an angel of the Lord appeared to Joseph in a dream. "Get up," he said, "take the child and his mother and escape to Egypt. Stay there until I tell you, for Herod is going to search for the child to kill him."

14So he got up, took the child and his mother during the night and left for Egypt, 15where he stayed until the death of Herod. And so was fulfilled what the Lord had said through the prophet: "Out of Egypt I called my son."^e

16When Herod realized that he had been outwitted by the Magi, he was furious, and he gave orders to kill all the boys in Bethlehem and its vicinity who were two years old and under, in accordance with the time he had learned from the Magi. 17Then what was said through the prophet Jeremiah was fulfilled:

18"A voice is heard in Ramah,
   weeping and great mourning,
Rachel weeping for her children
   and refusing to be comforted,
because they are no more."^f

The Return to Nazareth

19After Herod died, an angel of the Lord appeared in a dream to Joseph in Egypt 20and said, "Get up, take the child and his mother and go to the land of Israel, for those who were trying to take the child's life are dead."

21So he got up, took the child and his mother and went to the land of Israel. 22But when he heard that Archelaus was reigning in Judea in place of his father Herod, he was afraid to go there. Having been warned in a dream, he withdrew to the district of Galilee, 23and he went and lived in a town called Nazareth. So was fulfilled what was said through the prophets: "He will be called a Nazarene."

John the Baptist Prepares the Way

3 In those days John the Baptist came, preaching in the wilderness of Judea ²and saying, "Repent, for the kingdom of heaven has come near." ³This is he who was spoken of through the prophet Isaiah:

"A voice of one calling in the wilderness,
'Prepare the way for the Lord,
    make straight paths for him.' " *a*

⁴John's clothes were made of camel's hair, and he had a leather belt around his waist. His food was locusts and wild honey. ⁵People went out to him from Jerusalem and all Judea and the whole region of the Jordan. ⁶Confessing their sins, they were baptized by him in the Jordan River.

⁷But when he saw many of the Pharisees and Sadducees coming to where he was baptizing, he said to them: "You brood of vipers! Who warned you to flee from the coming wrath? ⁸Produce fruit in keeping with repentance. ⁹And do not think you can say to yourselves, 'We have Abraham as our father.' I tell you that out of these stones God can raise up children for Abraham. ¹⁰The ax is already at the root of the trees, and every tree that does not produce good fruit will be cut down and thrown into the fire.

¹¹"I baptize you with *b* water for repentance. But after me comes one who is more powerful than I, whose sandals I am not worthy to carry. He will baptize you with *b* the Holy Spirit and fire. ¹²His winnowing fork is in his hand, and he will clear his threshing floor, gathering his wheat into the barn and burning up the chaff with unquenchable fire."

The Baptism of Jesus

¹³Then Jesus came from Galilee to the Jordan to be baptized by John. ¹⁴But John tried to deter him, saying, "I need to be baptized by you, and do you come to me?"

¹⁵Jesus replied, "Let it be so now; it is proper for us to do this to fulfill all righteousness." Then John consented.

¹⁶As soon as Jesus was baptized, he went up out of the water. At that moment heaven was opened, and he saw the Spirit of God descending like a dove and alighting on him. ¹⁷And a voice from heaven said, "This is my Son, whom I love; with him I am well pleased."

Jesus Is Tested in the Wilderness

4 Then Jesus was led by the Spirit into the wilderness to be tempted *c* by the devil. ²After fasting forty days and forty nights, he was hungry. ³The tempter came to him and said, "If you are the Son of God, tell these stones to become bread."

⁴Jesus answered, "It is written: 'People do not live on bread alone, but on every word that comes from the mouth of God.' *d*"

⁵Then the devil took him to the holy city and had him stand on the highest point of the temple. ⁶"If you are the Son of God," he said, "throw yourself down. For it is written:

" 'He will command his angels
        concerning you,
    and they will lift you up in their hands,
so that you will not strike your foot
        against a stone.' *e*"

⁷Jesus answered him, "It is also written: 'Do not put the Lord your God to the test.' *f*"

⁸Again, the devil took him to a very high mountain and showed him all the kingdoms of the world and their splendor. ⁹"All this I will give you," he said, "if you will bow down and worship me."

¹⁰Jesus said to him, "Away from me, Satan! For it is written: 'Worship the Lord your God, and serve him only.' *g*"

¹¹Then the devil left him, and angels came and attended him.

Jesus Begins to Preach

¹²When Jesus heard that John had been put in prison, he withdrew to Galilee. ¹³Leaving Nazareth, he went and lived in Capernaum, which was by the lake in the area of Zebulun and Naphtali— ¹⁴to fulfill what was said through the prophet Isaiah:

¹⁵"Land of Zebulun and land of Naphtali,
    the Way of the Sea, beyond the
        Jordan,
    Galilee of the Gentiles—
¹⁶ the people living in darkness
    have seen a great light;
on those living in the land of the shadow
        of death
    a light has dawned." *h*

a 3 Isaiah 40:3   *b* 11 Or *in*   *c* 1 The Greek for *tempted* can also mean *tested*.   *d* 4 Deut. 8:3
e 6 Psalm 91:11,12   *f* 7 Deut. 6:16   *g* 10 Deut. 6:13   *h* 16 Isaiah 9:1,2

DON'T BE SLOW TO FAST

Matthew 4:1–25 or 4:1–4

Tony Jones

Exhibiting self-control and abiding by self-imposed limits are antithetical to our consumer-driven culture. The Desert Fathers and Mothers found it so difficult to maintain a life of prayer, silence and fasting in Jerusalem and other cities that they retreated to the wilderness—and they had never seen a billboard or a TV ad! There can be no denying that we live in a world that promotes gluttony and consumption. And the almost weekly news stories and medical reports on "America's Expanding Waistline" corroborate our weakness in this area.

Fasting is a spiritual remedy to what is, really, a spiritual problem. To fast shows our reliance upon God for all things. It reminds us that we are, ultimately, spiritual beings. It confirms that "[people do not live on bread alone]"; "[Everyone who drinks this water will be thirsty again, but those who drink the water I give them will never thirst]"; "This is my body [given] for you"; and "I am the bread of life."

In the end, fasting trains us in righteousness and as we practice this form of self-control, we are not in it alone—because, of course, Paul rounds out his list of the fruit of the Spirit in the letter to the Galatians with self-control [Galatians 5:22–23].

TERTULLIAN {ca. AD 155–230}

Jesus habitually "lifted up" his "heart," rather than fattening it up. For 40 days and as many nights, he maintained a fast above the power of human nature, while spiritual faith gave strength to his body. He saw with his eyes God's glory, and heard with his ears God's voice, and understood with his heart God's law. God taught him even then by experience that a person does not live by bread alone, but by every word of God.

reflection

1. What is the purpose of fasting?
2. Have you ever fasted? How would you describe that experience to another person?
3. Fasting used to be a fairly common practice in the church. What's changed? Why?

For your next devotional reading, go to page 1084.

17From that time on Jesus began to preach, "Repent, for the kingdom of heaven has come near."

Jesus Calls His First Disciples

18As Jesus was walking beside the Sea of Galilee, he saw two brothers, Simon called Peter and his brother Andrew. They were casting a net into the lake, for they were fishermen. 19"Come, follow me," Jesus said, "and I will send you out to fish for people." 20At once they left their nets and followed him.

21Going on from there, he saw two other brothers, James son of Zebedee and his brother John. They were in a boat with their father Zebedee, preparing their nets. Jesus called them, 22and immediately they left the boat and their father and followed him.

Jesus Heals the Sick

23Jesus went throughout Galilee, teaching in their synagogues, proclaiming the good news of the kingdom, and healing every disease and sickness among the people. 24News about him spread all over Syria, and people brought to him all who were ill with various diseases, those suffering severe pain, the demon-possessed, those having seizures, and the paralyzed; and he healed them. 25Large crowds from Galilee, the Decapolis,a Jerusalem, Judea and the region across the Jordan followed him.

Introduction to the Sermon on the Mount

5 Now when Jesus saw the crowds, he went up on a mountainside and sat down. His disciples came to him, 2and he began to teach them.

The Beatitudes

He said:

3 "Blessed are the poor in spirit,
    for theirs is the kingdom of heaven.
4 Blessed are those who mourn,
    for they will be comforted.
5 Blessed are the meek,
    for they will inherit the earth.
6 Blessed are those who hunger and thirst
    for righteousness,
    for they will be filled.
7 Blessed are the merciful,
    for they will be shown mercy.
8 Blessed are the pure in heart,
    for they will see God.
9 Blessed are the peacemakers,
    for they will be called children of
    God.
10 Blessed are those who are persecuted
    because of righteousness,
    for theirs is the kingdom of heaven.

11"Blessed are you when people insult you, persecute you and falsely say all kinds of evil against you because of me. 12Rejoice and be glad, because great is your reward in heaven, for in the same way they persecuted the prophets who were before you.

Salt and Light

13"You are the salt of the earth. But if the salt loses its saltiness, how can it be made salty again? It is no longer good for anything, except to be thrown out and trampled underfoot.

14"You are the light of the world. A city on a hill cannot be hidden. 15Neither do people light a lamp and put it under a bowl. Instead they put it on its stand, and it gives light to everyone in the house. 16In the same way, let your light shine before others, that they may see your good deeds and glorify your Father in heaven.

The Fulfillment of the Law

17"Do not think that I have come to abolish the Law or the Prophets; I have not come to abolish them but to fulfill them. 18Truly I tell you, until heaven and earth disappear, not the smallest letter, not the least stroke of a pen, will by any means disappear from the Law until everything is accomplished. 19Anyone who sets aside one of the least of these commands and teaches others accordingly will be called least in the kingdom of heaven, but whoever practices and teaches these commands will be called great in the kingdom of heaven. 20For I tell you that unless your righteousness surpasses that of the Pharisees and the teachers of the law, you will certainly not enter the kingdom of heaven.

Murder

21"You have heard that it was said to the people long ago, 'You shall not murder,b and anyone who murders will be subject to judg-

a 25 That is, the Ten Cities   b 21 Exodus 20:13

ment.' ²²But I tell you that anyone who is angry with a brother or sister*a* will be subject to judgment. Again, anyone who says to a brother or sister, 'Raca,'*b* is answerable to the Sanhedrin. And anyone who says, 'You fool!' will be in danger of the fire of hell.

²³"Therefore, if you are offering your gift at the altar and there remember that your brother or sister has something against you, ²⁴leave your gift there in front of the altar. First go and be reconciled to that person; then come and offer your gift.

²⁵"Settle matters quickly with your adversary who is taking you to court. Do it while you are still together on the way, or your adversary may hand you over to the judge, and the judge may hand you over to the officer, and you may be thrown into prison. ²⁶Truly I tell you, you will not get out until you have paid the last penny.

Adultery

²⁷"You have heard that it was said, 'You shall not commit adultery.'*c* ²⁸But I tell you that anyone who looks at a woman lustfully has already committed adultery with her in his heart. ²⁹If your right eye causes you to stumble, gouge it out and throw it away. It is better for you to lose one part of your body than for your whole body to be thrown into hell. ³⁰And if your right hand causes you to stumble, cut it off and throw it away. It is better for you to lose one part of your body than for your whole body to go into hell.

Divorce

³¹"It has been said, 'Anyone who divorces his wife must give her a certificate of divorce.'*d* ³²But I tell you that anyone who divorces his wife, except for sexual immorality, causes her to become an adulteress, and anyone who marries the divorced woman commits adultery.

Oaths

³³"Again, you have heard that it was said to the people long ago, 'Do not break your oath, but fulfill to the Lord the vows you have made.' ³⁴But I tell you, do not swear an oath at all: either by heaven, for it is God's throne; ³⁵or by the earth, for it is his footstool; or by Jerusalem, for it is the city of the Great King. ³⁶And do not swear by your head, for you cannot make even one hair white or black. ³⁷All you need to say is simply 'Yes,' or 'No'; anything beyond this comes from the evil one.*e*

Eye for Eye

³⁸"You have heard that it was said, 'Eye for eye, and tooth for tooth.'*f* ³⁹But I tell you, do not resist an evil person. If anyone slaps you on the right cheek, turn to them the other cheek also. ⁴⁰And if anyone wants to sue you and take your shirt, hand over your coat as well. ⁴¹If anyone forces you to go one mile, go with them two miles. ⁴²Give to the one who asks you, and do not turn away from the one who wants to borrow from you.

Love for Enemies

⁴³"You have heard that it was said, 'Love your neighbor*g* and hate your enemy.' ⁴⁴But I tell you, love your enemies and pray for those who persecute you, ⁴⁵that you may be children of your Father in heaven. He causes his sun to rise on the evil and the good, and sends rain on the righteous and the unrighteous. ⁴⁶If you love those who love you, what reward will you get? Are not even the tax collectors doing that? ⁴⁷And if you greet only your own people, what are you doing more than others? Do not even pagans do that? ⁴⁸Be perfect, therefore, as your heavenly Father is perfect.

Giving to the Needy

6 "Be careful not to do your 'acts of righteousness' in front of others, to be seen by them. If you do, you will have no reward from your Father in heaven.

²"So when you give to the needy, do not announce it with trumpets, as the hypocrites do in the synagogues and on the streets, to be honored by others. Truly I tell you, they have received their reward in full. ³But when you give to the needy, do not let your left hand know what your right hand is doing, ⁴so that your giving may be in secret. Then your Father, who sees what is done in secret, will reward you.

Prayer

⁵"And when you pray, do not be like the hypocrites, for they love to pray standing in

---

a 22 Some manuscripts *brother or sister without cause*   *b 22* An Aramaic term of contempt
c 27 Exodus 20:14   *d 31* Deut. 24:1   *e 37* Or *from evil*   *f 38* Exodus 21:24; Lev. 24:20; Deut. 19:21
g 43 Lev. 19:18

the synagogues and on the street corners to be seen by others. Truly I tell you, they have received their reward in full. [6]But when you pray, go into your room, close the door and pray to your Father, who is unseen. Then your Father, who sees what is done in secret, will reward you. [7]And when you pray, do not keep on babbling like pagans, for they think they will be heard because of their many words. [8]Do not be like them, for your Father knows what you need before you ask him.

[9]"This, then, is how you should pray:

" 'Our Father in heaven,
hallowed be your name,
[10]your kingdom come,
your will be done,
    on earth as it is in heaven.
[11]Give us today our daily bread.
[12]And forgive us our debts,
    as we also have forgiven our debtors.
[13]And lead us not into temptation,[a]
    but deliver us from the evil one.[b]'

[14]For if you forgive others when they sin against you, your heavenly Father will also forgive you. [15]But if you do not forgive others their sins, your Father will not forgive your sins.

Fasting

[16]"When you fast, do not look somber as the hypocrites do, for they disfigure their faces to show others they are fasting. Truly I tell you, they have received their reward in full. [17]But when you fast, put oil on your head and wash your face, [18]so that it will not be obvious to others that you are fasting, but only to your Father, who is unseen; and your Father, who sees what is done in secret, will reward you.

Treasures in Heaven

[19]"Do not store up for yourselves treasures on earth, where moth and rust destroy, and where thieves break in and steal. [20]But store up for yourselves treasures in heaven, where moth and rust do not destroy, and where thieves do not break in and steal. [21]For where your treasure is, there your heart will be also.

[22]"The eye is the lamp of the body. If your eyes are healthy,[c] your whole body will be full of light. [23]But if your eyes are unhealthy,[d] your whole body will be full of darkness. If then the light within you is darkness, how great is that darkness!

[24]"No one can serve two masters. Either you will hate the one and love the other, or you will be devoted to the one and despise the other. You cannot serve both God and Money.

Do Not Worry

[25]"Therefore I tell you, do not worry about your life, what you will eat or drink; or about your body, what you will wear. Is not life more important than food, and the body more important than clothes? [26]Look at the birds of the air; they do not sow or reap or store away in barns, and yet your heavenly Father feeds them. Are you not much more valuable than they? [27]Can any one of you by worrying add a single hour to your life[e]?

[28]"And why do you worry about clothes? See how the flowers of the field grow. They do not labor or spin. [29]Yet I tell you that not even Solomon in all his splendor was dressed like one of these. [30]If that is how God clothes the grass of the field, which is here today and tomorrow is thrown into the fire, will he not much more clothe you—you of little faith? [31]So do not worry, saying, 'What shall we eat?' or 'What shall we drink?' or 'What shall we wear?' [32]For the pagans run after all these things, and your heavenly Father knows that you need them. [33]But seek first his kingdom and his righteousness, and all these things will be given to you as well. [34]Therefore do not worry about tomorrow, for tomorrow will worry about itself. Each day has enough trouble of its own.

Judging Others

7 "Do not judge, or you too will be judged. [2]For in the same way you judge others, you will be judged, and with the measure you use, it will be measured to you.

[3]"Why do you look at the speck of sawdust in someone else's eye and pay no attention to the plank in your own eye? [4]How

---

[a] 13 The Greek for *temptation* can also mean *testing*.   [b] 13 Or *from evil*; some late manuscripts *one, / for yours is the kingdom and the power and the glory forever. Amen.*   [c] 22 The Greek for *healthy* here implies *generous*.   [d] 23 The Greek for *unhealthy* here implies *stingy*.   [e] 27 Or *single cubit to your height*

Do His Will. Period.
Matthew 7:1–29 or 7:15–20,24–25

Andrew Murray {AD 1828–1917}

Obedience to God is such a heavenly art, so utterly foreign to our nature, and the path in which the Son himself learned it was so slow and long, that we must not wonder if it does not come at once. Nor must we wonder if it needs more time at the feet of the Master in meditation and prayer and waiting—in dependence and self-sacrifice—than most people are ready to give. But let us give it.

In Christ Jesus heavenly obedience has become human again. Obedience has become our birthright and our life-breath. So let us cling to him, let us believe and claim his abiding presence. With Jesus Christ who learned obedience as our Savior, with Jesus Christ who teaches obedience as our Master, we can live lives of obedience. This is a lesson we cannot study too earnestly. His obedience is our salvation; in him, the living Christ, we find it and partake of it moment by moment.

Dallas Willard

Whatever the ultimate explanation of it, the most telling thing about the contemporary Christian is that he or she simply has no compelling sense that understanding of and conformity with the clear teachings of Christ is of any vital importance to his or her life, and certainly not that it is in any way essential. We—including multitudes who have distanced themselves from any formal association with him—still manage to feel guilty with reference to those teachings, with a nervous laugh and a knowing look. But more often than not, I think, such obedience is regarded as just out of the question or impossible . . .

Individual Christians still hear Jesus say, "Everyone who hears these words of mine and puts them into practice is like a wise man who built his house on the rock," standing firm against every pressure of life (Matthew 7:24–25). How life-giving it would be if their understanding of the gospel allowed them simply to reply, "I will do them! I will find out how I will devote my life to it! This is the best life strategy I ever heard of!" and then go off to their fellowship and its teachers, and into their daily life, to learn how to live in his kingdom as Jesus indicated was best.

reflection

1. How can you tell if a person really is a genuine Christ-follower?
2. What does your effort at obeying God reveal about your faith?
3. What does it mean—spiritually speaking—to build your house on a rock?

For your next devotional reading, go to page 1086.

can you say, 'Let me take the speck out of your eye,' when all the time there is a plank in your own eye? ⁵You hypocrite, first take the plank out of your own eye, and then you will see clearly to remove the speck from the other person's eye.

⁶"Do not give dogs what is sacred; do not throw your pearls to pigs. If you do, they may trample them under their feet, and then turn and tear you to pieces.

Ask, Seek, Knock

⁷"Ask and it will be given to you; seek and you will find; knock and the door will be opened to you. ⁸For everyone who asks receives; those who seek find; and to those who knock, the door will be opened.

⁹"Which of you, if your son asks for bread, will give him a stone? ¹⁰Or if he asks for a fish, will give him a snake? ¹¹If you, then, though you are evil, know how to give good gifts to your children, how much more will your Father in heaven give good gifts to those who ask him! ¹²So in everything, do to others what you would have them do to you, for this sums up the Law and the Prophets.

The Narrow and Wide Gates

¹³"Enter through the narrow gate. For wide is the gate and broad is the road that leads to destruction, and many enter through it. ¹⁴But small is the gate and narrow the road that leads to life, and only a few find it.

True and False Prophets

¹⁵"Watch out for false prophets. They come to you in sheep's clothing, but inwardly they are ferocious wolves. ¹⁶By their fruit you will recognize them. Do people pick grapes from thornbushes, or figs from thistles? ¹⁷Likewise, every good tree bears good fruit, but a bad tree bears bad fruit. ¹⁸A good tree cannot bear bad fruit, and a bad tree cannot bear good fruit. ¹⁹Every tree that does not bear good fruit is cut down and thrown into the fire. ²⁰Thus, by their fruit you will recognize them.

True and False Disciples

²¹"Not everyone who says to me, 'Lord, Lord,' will enter the kingdom of heaven, but only those who do the will of my Father who is in heaven. ²²Many will say to me on that day, 'Lord, Lord, did we not prophesy in your name and in your name drive out demons and in your name perform many miracles?' ²³Then I will tell them plainly, 'I never knew you. Away from me, you evildoers!'

The Wise and Foolish Builders

²⁴"Therefore everyone who hears these words of mine and puts them into practice is like a wise man who built his house on the rock. ²⁵The rain came down, the streams rose, and the winds blew and beat against that house; yet it did not fall, because it had its foundation on the rock. ²⁶But everyone who hears these words of mine and does not put them into practice is like a foolish man who built his house on sand. ²⁷The rain came down, the streams rose, and the winds blew and beat against that house, and it fell with a great crash."

²⁸When Jesus had finished saying these things, the crowds were amazed at his teaching, ²⁹because he taught as one who had authority, and not as their teachers of the law.

Jesus Heals a Man With Leprosy

8 When Jesus came down from the mountainside, large crowds followed him. ²A man with leprosy[a] came and knelt before him and said, "Lord, if you are willing, you can make me clean."

³Jesus reached out his hand and touched the man. "I am willing," he said. "Be clean!" Immediately he was cleansed of his leprosy. ⁴Then Jesus said to him, "See that you don't tell anyone. But go, show yourself to the priest and offer the gift Moses commanded, as a testimony to them."

The Faith of the Centurion

⁵When Jesus had entered Capernaum, a centurion came to him, asking for help. ⁶"Lord," he said, "my servant lies at home paralyzed, suffering terribly."

⁷Jesus said to him, "Shall I come and heal him?"

⁸The centurion replied, "Lord, I do not deserve to have you come under my roof. But just say the word, and my servant will be healed. ⁹For I myself am a man under authority, with soldiers under me. I tell this

---

a 2 The Greek word traditionally translated *leprosy* was used for various diseases affecting the skin.

WEDNESDAY

CLOSE ENOUGH TO FEEL PAIN

Matthew 8:1–34 *or* 8:1–4

John Ortberg

The miracle of the touch is that Jesus was willing to share another person's suffering in order to bring about healing. This is a foreshadowing of the cross: Jesus taking on our sin so that we could take on his life. By his stripes we are healed.

In a contagious world, we learn to keep our distance. If we get too close to those who are suffering, we might get infected by their pain. It may not be convenient or comfortable. But only when you get close enough to catch their hurt will they be close enough to catch your love.

Jesus did not call his followers to live in quarantine. He called them to be a kind of hospital. Imagine a hospital where the doctors say, "This has been a successful day. I wasn't infected. My patients were loaded with filthy germs, but I kept them all outside. They may be dying, but at least I didn't touch any of them. I didn't get infected."

LACTANTIUS {ca. AD 240–320}

Compassion is closely connected to harmlessness. For although the latter doesn't hurt anyone, the former works good. The latter begins justice, the former completes it. He has given us the affection of compassion so that we can protect lives by helping one another. If we are created by one God, descended from one man, and, therefore, are thus connected by the law of kinship, we should love everyone. As a result we are bound not only to abstain from hurting others, but to not even take revenge when we are hurt. Then we will be completely harmless. Regarding this, God commands us to always pray for our enemies. We should be animals fitted for companionship and society, so that we will protect ourselves by giving and receiving assistance. For our frailty is prone to many accidents and inconveniences. Expect that what you see happening to someone else may also happen to you. You will be excited to help someone if you shall assume the mind of those who, being placed in danger, beg for your help.

reflection

1. When do you find extending compassion difficult?
2. What are you willing to give to show compassion?
3. What are the limits to your compassion?

For your next devotional reading, go to page 1089.

one, 'Go,' and he goes; and that one, 'Come,' and he comes. I say to my servant, 'Do this,' and he does it."

[10]When Jesus heard this, he was amazed and said to those following him, "Truly I tell you, I have not found anyone in Israel with such great faith. [11]I say to you that many will come from the east and the west, and will take their places at the feast with Abraham, Isaac and Jacob in the kingdom of heaven. [12]But the subjects of the kingdom will be thrown outside, into the darkness, where there will be weeping and gnashing of teeth."

[13]Then Jesus said to the centurion, "Go! Let it be done just as you believed it would." And his servant was healed at that very hour.

Jesus Heals Many

[14]When Jesus came into Peter's house, he saw Peter's mother-in-law lying in bed with a fever. [15]He touched her hand and the fever left her, and she got up and began to wait on him.

[16]When evening came, many who were demon-possessed were brought to him, and he drove out the spirits with a word and healed all the sick. [17]This was to fulfill what was spoken through the prophet Isaiah:

> "He took up our infirmities
>   and bore our diseases."[a]

The Cost of Following Jesus

[18]When Jesus saw the crowd around him, he gave orders to cross to the other side of the lake. [19]Then a teacher of the law came to him and said, "Teacher, I will follow you wherever you go."

[20]Jesus replied, "Foxes have holes and birds have nests, but the Son of Man has no place to lay his head."

[21]Another disciple said to him, "Lord, first let me go and bury my father."

[22]But Jesus told him, "Follow me, and let the dead bury their own dead."

Jesus Calms the Storm

[23]Then he got into the boat and his disciples followed him. [24]Suddenly a furious storm came up on the lake, so that the waves swept over the boat. But Jesus was sleeping. [25]The disciples went and woke him, saying, "Lord, save us! We're going to drown!"

[26]He replied, "You of little faith, why are you so afraid?" Then he got up and rebuked the winds and the waves, and it was completely calm.

[27]The men were amazed and asked, "What kind of man is this? Even the winds and the waves obey him!"

Jesus Restores Two Demon-Possessed Men

[28]When he arrived at the other side in the region of the Gadarenes,[b] two demon-possessed men coming from the tombs met him. They were so violent that no one could pass that way. [29]"What do you want with us, Son of God?" they shouted. "Have you come here to torture us before the appointed time?"

[30]Some distance from them a large herd of pigs was feeding. [31]The demons begged Jesus, "If you drive us out, send us into the herd of pigs."

[32]He said to them, "Go!" So they came out and went into the pigs, and the whole herd rushed down the steep bank into the lake and died in the water. [33]Those tending the pigs ran off, went into the town and reported all this, including what had happened to the demon-possessed men. [34]Then the whole town went out to meet Jesus. And when they saw him, they pleaded with him to leave their region.

Jesus Forgives and Heals a Paralyzed Man

9 Jesus stepped into a boat, crossed over and came to his own town. [2]Some men brought to him a paralyzed man, lying on a mat. When Jesus saw their faith, he said to the man, "Take heart, son; your sins are forgiven."

[3]At this, some of the teachers of the law said to themselves, "This fellow is blaspheming!"

[4]Knowing their thoughts, Jesus said, "Why do you entertain evil thoughts in your hearts? [5]Which is easier: to say, 'Your sins are forgiven,' or to say, 'Get up and walk'? [6]But I want you to know that the Son of Man has authority on earth to forgive sins." So he said to the paralyzed man, "Get up, take your mat and go home." [7]Then the man got up and went home. [8]When the crowd saw this, they were

---

a 17 Isaiah 53:4 (see Septuagint)   b 28 Some manuscripts Gergesenes; other manuscripts Gerasenes filled with awe; and they praised God, who had given such authority to human beings.

The Calling of Matthew

⁹As Jesus went on from there, he saw a man named Matthew sitting at the tax collector's booth. "Follow me," he told him, and Matthew got up and followed him.

¹⁰While Jesus was having dinner at Matthew's house, many tax collectors and sinners came and ate with him and his disciples. ¹¹When the Pharisees saw this, they asked his disciples, "Why does your teacher eat with tax collectors and sinners?"

¹²On hearing this, Jesus said, "It is not the healthy who need a doctor, but the sick. ¹³But go and learn what this means: 'I desire mercy, not sacrifice.'ᵃ For I have not come to call the righteous, but sinners."

Jesus Questioned About Fasting

¹⁴Then John's disciples came and asked him, "How is it that we and the Pharisees fast often, but your disciples do not fast?"

¹⁵Jesus answered, "How can the guests of the bridegroom mourn while he is with them? The time will come when the bridegroom will be taken from them; then they will fast.

¹⁶"No one sews a patch of unshrunk cloth on an old garment, for the patch will pull away from the garment, making the tear worse. ¹⁷Neither do people pour new wine into old wineskins. If they do, the skins will burst; the wine will run out and the wineskins will be ruined. No, they pour new wine into new wineskins, and both are preserved."

Jesus Raises a Dead Girl and Heals a Sick Woman

¹⁸While he was saying this, a synagogue leader came and knelt before him and said, "My daughter has just died. But come and put your hand on her, and she will live." ¹⁹Jesus got up and went with him, and so did his disciples.

²⁰Just then a woman who had been subject to bleeding for twelve years came up behind him and touched the edge of his cloak. ²¹She said to herself, "If I only touch his cloak, I will be healed."

²²Jesus turned and saw her. "Take heart, daughter," he said, "your faith has healed you." And the woman was healed from that moment.

²³When Jesus entered the synagogue leader's house and saw the noisy crowd and people playing pipes, ²⁴he said, "Go away. The girl is not dead but asleep." But they laughed at him. ²⁵After the crowd had been put outside, he went in and took the girl by the hand, and she got up. ²⁶News of this spread through all that region.

Jesus Heals the Blind and the Mute

²⁷As Jesus went on from there, two blind men followed him, calling out, "Have mercy on us, Son of David!"

²⁸When he had gone indoors, the blind men came to him, and he asked them, "Do you believe that I am able to do this?"

"Yes, Lord," they replied.

²⁹Then he touched their eyes and said, "According to your faith let it be done to you"; ³⁰and their sight was restored. Jesus warned them sternly, "See that no one knows about this." ³¹But they went out and spread the news about him all over that region.

³²While they were going out, a man who was demon-possessed and could not talk was brought to Jesus. ³³And when the demon was driven out, the man who had been mute spoke. The crowd was amazed and said, "Nothing like this has ever been seen in Israel."

³⁴But the Pharisees said, "It is by the prince of demons that he drives out demons."

The Workers Are Few

³⁵Jesus went through all the towns and villages, teaching in their synagogues, proclaiming the good news of the kingdom and healing every disease and sickness. ³⁶When he saw the crowds, he had compassion on them, because they were harassed and helpless, like sheep without a shepherd. ³⁷Then he said to his disciples, "The harvest is plentiful but the workers are few. ³⁸Ask the Lord of the harvest, therefore, to send out workers into his harvest field."

Jesus Sends Out the Twelve

10 Jesus called his twelve disciples to him and gave them authority to drive out evilᵇ spirits and to heal every disease and sickness.

ᵃ 13 Hosea 6:6   ᵇ 1 Greek unclean

THURSDAY

FINDING SELF-FULFILLMENT

Matthew 10:1–42 *or* 10:39

GEORGE WHITEFIELD {AD 1714–1770}

By nature, our souls are in a spiritual dungeon, sleeping and tightly confined between the world, the flesh and the devil—not with two but with ten thousand chains of lusts and corruptions. Now Jesus Christ, by the power of his gospel, comes and opens the prison door, and directs us to "deny [ourselves] . . . and follow [him]" (Matthew 16:24). But if we do not arise, summon up the inner resources of our minds and follow him, are we not in love with bondage, and do we not deserve never to be delivered from it? . . .

Let us get up and get doing; let us arise quickly, and deny ourselves. And the Lord Jesus will remove those scales from the eyes of our minds, which now, like many veils, hinder us from seeing clearly the reasonableness, necessity and inexpressible advantage of the doctrine that has been delivered. Let us stand up and show ourselves, and then the Spirit of God will move on the face of our souls, as he did once upon the face of the great deep. When he does, he will cause our souls to emerge out of that confused chaos which they are certainly involved in if they are strangers and enemies to self-denial and the cross of Christ.

Richard Foster

What we have failed to see is this amazing paradox: true self-fulfillment comes only through self-denial. There is no other way. The most certain way to miss self-fulfillment is to pursue it. "[Whoever finds their life will lose it, and whoever loses their life for my sake will find it]" (Matthew 10:39).

It is wonderful, this losing of one's self through a perpetual vision of the Holy. We are catapulted into something infinitely larger and more real than our petty existence. A blazing God-consciousness frees us from self-consciousness. It is freedom. It is joy. It is life.

I cannot stress enough how essential this quality is to true simplicity of life. It is the only thing that will allow us to hold the interest of others above self-interest. It saves us from self-pity. It lifts the burden of concern over having a proper image. It frees us from bondage to the opinions of others.

— *reflection* —

1. What does the world promote as the path (or paths) to "self-fulfillment"?

2. How does that contrast with God's way?

3. Why is true freedom and joy found through self-denial?

For your next devotional reading, go to page 1098.

²These are the names of the twelve apostles: first, Simon (who is called Peter) and his brother Andrew; James son of Zebedee, and his brother John; ³Philip and Bartholomew; Thomas and Matthew the tax collector; James son of Alphaeus, and Thaddaeus; ⁴Simon the Zealot and Judas Iscariot, who betrayed him.

⁵These twelve Jesus sent out with the following instructions: "Do not go among the Gentiles or enter any town of the Samaritans. ⁶Go rather to the lost sheep of Israel. ⁷As you go, proclaim this message: 'The kingdom of heaven has come near.' ⁸Heal the sick, raise the dead, cleanse those who have leprosy,ᵃ drive out demons. Freely you have received, freely give.

⁹"Do not get any gold or silver or copper to take with you in your belts— ¹⁰no bag for the journey or extra shirt or sandals or a staff, for workers are worth their keep. ¹¹Whatever town or village you enter, search for some worthy person there and stay at that person's house until you leave. ¹²As you enter the home, give it your greeting. ¹³If the home is deserving, let your peace rest on it; if it is not, let your peace return to you. ¹⁴If anyone will not welcome you or listen to your words, shake the dust off your feet when you leave that home or town. ¹⁵Truly I tell you, it will be more bearable for Sodom and Gomorrah on the day of judgment than for that town.

¹⁶"I am sending you out like sheep among wolves. Therefore be as shrewd as snakes and as innocent as doves. ¹⁷Be on your guard; you will be handed over to the local councils and be flogged in the synagogues. ¹⁸On my account you will be brought before governors and kings as witnesses to them and to the Gentiles. ¹⁹But when they arrest you, do not worry about what to say or how to say it. At that time you will be given what to say, ²⁰for it will not be you speaking, but the Spirit of your Father speaking through you.

²¹"Brother will betray brother to death, and a father his child; children will rebel against their parents and have them put to death. ²²Everyone will hate you because of me, but those who stand firm to the end will be saved. ²³When you are persecuted in one place, flee to another. Truly I tell you, you will not finish going through the towns of Israel before the Son of Man comes.

²⁴"Students are not above their teacher, nor servants above their master. ²⁵It is enough for students to be like their teacher, and servants like their master. If the head of the house has been called Beelzebul, how much more the members of his household!

²⁶"So do not be afraid of them. There is nothing concealed that will not be disclosed, or hidden that will not be made known. ²⁷What I tell you in the dark, speak in the daylight; what is whispered in your ear, proclaim from the roofs. ²⁸Do not be afraid of those who kill the body but cannot kill the soul. Rather, be afraid of the One who can destroy both soul and body in hell. ²⁹Are not two sparrows sold for a penny? Yet not one of them will fall to the ground outside your Father's care.ᵇ ³⁰And even the very hairs of your head are all numbered. ³¹So don't be afraid; you are worth more than many sparrows.

³²"Whoever publicly acknowledges me I will also acknowledge before my Father in heaven. ³³But whoever publicly disowns me I will disown before my Father in heaven.

³⁴"Do not suppose that I have come to bring peace to the earth. I did not come to bring peace, but a sword. ³⁵For I have come to turn

" 'a man against his father,
    a daughter against her mother,
a daughter-in-law against her mother-in-law—
³⁶   your enemies will be the members of your own household.'ᶜ

³⁷"Anyone who loves their father or mother more than me is not worthy of me; anyone who loves a son or daughter more than me is not worthy of me. ³⁸Whoever does not take up their cross and follow me is not worthy of me. ³⁹Whoever finds their life will lose it, and whoever loses their life for my sake will find it.

⁴⁰"Anyone who welcomes you welcomes me, and anyone who welcomes me welcomes the one who sent me. ⁴¹Whoever welcomes someone known to be a prophet will receive a prophet's reward, and whoever

---

ᵃ 8 The Greek word traditionally translated *leprosy* was used for various diseases affecting the skin.
ᵇ 29 Or *will*; or *knowledge*　ᶜ 36 Micah 7:6

welcomes someone known to be righteous will receive a righteous person's reward. ⁴²And if anyone gives even a cup of cold water to one of these little ones who is known to be my disciple, truly I tell you, that person will certainly be rewarded."

Jesus and John the Baptist

11 After Jesus had finished instructing his twelve disciples, he went on from there to teach and preach in the towns of Galilee.ᵃ

²When John heard in prison what the Messiah was doing, he sent his disciples ³to ask him, "Are you the one who was to come, or should we expect someone else?"

⁴Jesus replied, "Go back and report to John what you hear and see: ⁵The blind receive sight, the lame walk, those who have leprosyᵇ are cleansed, the deaf hear, the dead are raised, and the good news is proclaimed to the poor. ⁶Blessed is anyone who does not stumble on account of me."

⁷As John's disciples were leaving, Jesus began to speak to the crowd about John: "What did you go out into the wilderness to see? A reed swayed by the wind? ⁸If not, what did you go out to see? A man dressed in fine clothes? No, those who wear fine clothes are in kings' palaces. ⁹Then what did you go out to see? A prophet? Yes, I tell you, and more than a prophet. ¹⁰This is the one about whom it is written:

> " 'I will send my messenger ahead of
> you,
>   who will prepare your way before
>   you.'ᶜ

¹¹Truly I tell you, among those born of women there has not risen anyone greater than John the Baptist; yet whoever is least in the kingdom of heaven is greater than he. ¹²From the days of John the Baptist until now, the kingdom of heaven has been subjected to violence,ᵈ and violent people have been raiding it. ¹³For all the Prophets and the Law prophesied until John. ¹⁴And if you are willing to accept it, he is the Elijah who was to come. ¹⁵Whoever has ears, let them hear.

¹⁶"To what can I compare this generation? They are like children sitting in the marketplaces and calling out to others:

> ¹⁷" 'We played the pipe for you,
>   and you did not dance;
> we sang a dirge,
>   and you did not mourn.'

¹⁸For John came neither eating nor drinking, and they say, 'He has a demon.' ¹⁹The Son of Man came eating and drinking, and they say, 'Here is a glutton and a drunkard, a friend of tax collectors and sinners.' But wisdom is proved right by her actions."

Woe on Unrepentant Towns

²⁰Then Jesus began to denounce the towns in which most of his miracles had been performed, because they did not repent. ²¹"Woe to you, Chorazin! Woe to you, Bethsaida! If the miracles that were performed in you had been performed in Tyre and Sidon, they would have repented long ago in sackcloth and ashes. ²²But I tell you, it will be more bearable for Tyre and Sidon on the day of judgment than for you. ²³And you, Capernaum, will you be lifted up to the skies? No, you will go down to the depths.ᵉ If the miracles that were performed in you had been performed in Sodom, it would have remained to this day. ²⁴But I tell you that it will be more bearable for Sodom on the day of judgment than for you."

The Father Revealed in the Son

²⁵At that time Jesus said, "I praise you, Father, Lord of heaven and earth, because you have hidden these things from the wise and learned, and revealed them to little children. ²⁶Yes, Father, for this was your good pleasure.

²⁷"All things have been committed to me by my Father. No one knows the Son except the Father, and no one knows the Father except the Son and those to whom the Son chooses to reveal him.

²⁸"Come to me, all you who are weary and burdened, and I will give you rest. ²⁹Take my yoke upon you and learn from me, for I am gentle and humble in heart, and you will find rest for your souls. ³⁰For my yoke is easy and my burden is light."

ᵃ 1 Greek *in their towns*   ᵇ 5 The Greek word traditionally translated *leprosy* was used for various diseases affecting the skin.   ᶜ 10 Mal. 3:1   ᵈ 12 Or *been forcefully advancing*   ᵉ 23 Greek *to Hades*

Jesus Is Lord of the Sabbath

12 At that time Jesus went through the grainfields on the Sabbath. His disciples were hungry and began to pick some heads of grain and eat them. ²When the Pharisees saw this, they said to him, "Look! Your disciples are doing what is unlawful on the Sabbath."

³He answered, "Haven't you read what David did when he and his companions were hungry? ⁴He entered the house of God, and he and his companions ate the consecrated bread—which was not lawful for them to do, but only for the priests. ⁵Or haven't you read in the Law that the priests on Sabbath duty in the temple desecrate the Sabbath and yet are innocent? ⁶I tell you that one *a* greater than the temple is here. ⁷If you had known what these words mean, 'I desire mercy, not sacrifice,' *b* you would not have condemned the innocent. ⁸For the Son of Man is Lord of the Sabbath."

⁹Going on from that place, he went into their synagogue, ¹⁰and a man with a shriveled hand was there. Looking for a reason to accuse Jesus, they asked him, "Is it lawful to heal on the Sabbath?"

¹¹He said to them, "If any of you has a sheep and it falls into a pit on the Sabbath, will you not take hold of it and lift it out? ¹²How much more valuable is a human being than a sheep! Therefore it is lawful to do good on the Sabbath."

¹³Then he said to the man, "Stretch out your hand." So he stretched it out and it was completely restored, just as sound as the other. ¹⁴But the Pharisees went out and plotted how they might kill Jesus.

God's Chosen Servant

¹⁵Aware of this, Jesus withdrew from that place. A large crowd followed him, and he healed all who were ill. ¹⁶He warned them not to tell others about him. ¹⁷This was to fulfill what was spoken through the prophet Isaiah:

¹⁸"Here is my servant whom I have
   chosen,
   the one I love, in whom I delight;
I will put my Spirit on him,
   and he will proclaim justice to the
      nations.
¹⁹He will not quarrel or cry out;

no one will hear his voice in the
   streets.
²⁰A bruised reed he will not break,
   and a smoldering wick he will not
      snuff out,
   till he leads justice to victory.
²¹ In his name the nations will put their
      hope." *c*

Jesus and Beelzebul

²²Then they brought him a demon-possessed man who was blind and mute, and Jesus healed him, so that he could both talk and see. ²³All the people were astonished and said, "Could this be the Son of David?"

²⁴But when the Pharisees heard this, they said, "It is only by Beelzebul, the prince of demons, that this fellow drives out demons."

²⁵Jesus knew their thoughts and said to them, "Every kingdom divided against itself will be ruined, and every city or household divided against itself will not stand. ²⁶If Satan drives out Satan, he is divided against himself. How then can his kingdom stand? ²⁷And if I drive out demons by Beelzebul, by whom do your people drive them out? So then, they will be your judges. ²⁸But if it is by the Spirit of God that I drive out demons, then the kingdom of God has come upon you.

²⁹"Or again, how can anyone enter a strong man's house and carry off his possessions without first tying up the strong man? Then his house can be plundered.

³⁰"Whoever is not with me is against me, and whoever does not gather with me scatters. ³¹And so I tell you, people will be forgiven every sin and blasphemy. But blasphemy against the Spirit will not be forgiven. ³²Anyone who speaks a word against the Son of Man will be forgiven, but anyone who speaks against the Holy Spirit will not be forgiven, either in this age or in the age to come.

³³"Make a tree good and its fruit will be good, or make a tree bad and its fruit will be bad, for a tree is recognized by its fruit. ³⁴You brood of vipers, how can you who are evil say anything good? For out of the overflow of the heart the mouth speaks. ³⁵Good people bring good things out of the good stored up in them, and evil people bring evil

things out of the evil stored up in them. ³⁶But I tell you that people will have to give account on the day of judgment for every empty word they have spoken. ³⁷For by your words you will be acquitted, and by your words you will be condemned."

The Sign of Jonah

³⁸Then some of the Pharisees and teachers of the law said to him, "Teacher, we want to see a sign from you."

³⁹He answered, "A wicked and adulterous generation asks for a sign! But none will be given it except the sign of the prophet Jonah. ⁴⁰For as Jonah was three days and three nights in the belly of a huge fish, so the Son of Man will be three days and three nights in the heart of the earth. ⁴¹The people of Nineveh will stand up at the judgment with this generation and condemn it; for they repented at the preaching of Jonah, and now one*a* greater than Jonah is here. ⁴²The Queen of the South will rise at the judgment with this generation and condemn it; for she came from the ends of the earth to listen to Solomon's wisdom, and now one greater than Solomon is here.

⁴³"When an evil*b* spirit comes out of anyone, it goes through arid places seeking rest and does not find it. ⁴⁴Then it says, 'I will return to the house I left.' When it arrives, it finds the house unoccupied, swept clean and put in order. ⁴⁵Then it goes and takes with it seven other spirits more wicked than itself, and they go in and live there. And the final condition of that person is worse than the first. That is how it will be with this wicked generation."

Jesus' Mother and Brothers

⁴⁶While Jesus was still talking to the crowd, his mother and brothers stood outside, wanting to speak to him. ⁴⁷Someone told him, "Your mother and brothers are standing outside, wanting to speak to you."

⁴⁸He replied to him, "Who is my mother, and who are my brothers?" ⁴⁹Pointing to his disciples, he said, "Here are my mother and my brothers. ⁵⁰For whoever does the will of my Father in heaven is my brother and sister and mother."

The Parable of the Sower

13 That same day Jesus went out of the house and sat by the lake. ²Such large crowds gathered around him that he got into a boat and sat in it, while all the people stood on the shore. ³Then he told them many things in parables, saying: "A farmer went out to sow his seed. ⁴As he was scattering the seed, some fell along the path, and the birds came and ate it up. ⁵Some fell on rocky places, where it did not have much soil. It sprang up quickly, because the soil was shallow. ⁶But when the sun came up, the plants were scorched, and they withered because they had no root. ⁷Other seed fell among thorns, which grew up and choked the plants. ⁸Still other seed fell on good soil, where it produced a crop—a hundred, sixty or thirty times what was sown. ⁹Whoever has ears, let them hear."

¹⁰The disciples came to him and asked, "Why do you speak to the people in parables?"

¹¹He replied, "The knowledge of the secrets of the kingdom of heaven has been given to you, but not to them. ¹²Those who have will be given more, and they will have an abundance. As for those who do not have, even what they have will be taken from them. ¹³This is why I speak to them in parables:

"Though seeing, they do not see;
   though hearing, they do not hear or
      understand.

¹⁴In them is fulfilled the prophecy of Isaiah:

" 'You will be ever hearing but never
      understanding;
   you will be ever seeing but never
      perceiving.
¹⁵For this people's heart has become
      calloused;
   they hardly hear with their ears,
      and they have closed their eyes.
Otherwise they might see with their
      eyes,
   hear with their ears,
      understand with their hearts
and turn, and I would heal them.'*c*

¹⁶But blessed are your eyes because they see, and your ears because they hear. ¹⁷Truly I tell you, many prophets and righteous

---

a 41 Or *something;* also in verse 42   *b 43* Greek *unclean*   *c 15* Isaiah 6:9,10 (see Septuagint) people longed to see what you see but did not see it, and to hear what you hear but did not hear it.

18"Listen then to what the parable of the sower means: 19When people hear the message about the kingdom and do not understand it, the evil one comes and snatches away what was sown in their hearts. This is the seed sown along the path. 20The seed falling on rocky ground refers to people who hear the word and at once receive it with joy. 21But since they have no root, they last only a short time. When trouble or persecution comes because of the word, they quickly fall away. 22The seed falling among the thorns refers to people who hear the word, but the worries of this life and the deceitfulness of wealth choke the word, making it unfruitful. 23But the seed falling on good soil refers to people who hear the word and understand it. They produce a crop, yielding a hundred, sixty or thirty times what was sown."

The Parable of the Weeds

24Jesus told them another parable: "The kingdom of heaven is like a man who sowed good seed in his field. 25But while everyone was sleeping, his enemy came and sowed weeds among the wheat, and went away. 26When the wheat sprouted and formed heads, then the weeds also appeared.

27"The owner's servants came to him and said, 'Sir, didn't you sow good seed in your field? Where then did the weeds come from?'

28" 'An enemy did this,' he replied.

"The servants asked him, 'Do you want us to go and pull them up?'

29" 'No,' he answered, 'because while you are pulling the weeds, you may uproot the wheat with them. 30Let both grow together until the harvest. At that time I will tell the harvesters: First collect the weeds and tie them in bundles to be burned; then gather the wheat and bring it into my barn.' "

The Parables of the Mustard Seed and the Yeast

31He told them another parable: "The kingdom of heaven is like a mustard seed, which a man took and planted in his field. 32Though it is the smallest of all seeds, yet when it grows, it is the largest of garden plants and becomes a tree, so that the birds come and perch in its branches."

33He told them still another parable: "The kingdom of heaven is like yeast that a woman took and mixed into about sixty pounds[a] of flour until it worked all through the dough."

34Jesus spoke all these things to the crowd in parables; he did not say anything to them without using a parable. 35So was fulfilled what was spoken through the prophet:

"I will open my mouth in parables,
    I will utter things hidden since the
        creation of the world."[b]

The Parable of the Weeds Explained

36Then he left the crowd and went into the house. His disciples came to him and said, "Explain to us the parable of the weeds in the field."

37He answered, "The one who sowed the good seed is the Son of Man. 38The field is the world, and the good seed stands for the people of the kingdom. The weeds are the people of the evil one, 39and the enemy who sows them is the devil. The harvest is the end of the age, and the harvesters are angels.

40"As the weeds are pulled up and burned in the fire, so it will be at the end of the age. 41The Son of Man will send out his angels, and they will weed out of his kingdom everything that causes sin and all who do evil. 42They will throw them into the blazing furnace, where there will be weeping and gnashing of teeth. 43Then the righteous will shine like the sun in the kingdom of their Father. Whoever has ears, let them hear.

The Parables of the Hidden Treasure and the Pearl

44"The kingdom of heaven is like treasure hidden in a field. When a man found it, he hid it again, and then in his joy went and sold all he had and bought that field.

45"Again, the kingdom of heaven is like a merchant looking for fine pearls. 46When he found one of great value, he went away and sold everything he had and bought it.

---

a 33 Or about 27 kilograms   b 35 Psalm 78:2

The Parable of the Net

47"Once again, the kingdom of heaven is like a net that was let down into the lake and caught all kinds of fish. 48When it was full, the fishermen pulled it up on the shore. Then they sat down and collected the good fish in baskets, but threw the bad away. 49This is how it will be at the end of the age. The angels will come and separate the wicked from the righteous 50and throw them into the blazing furnace, where there will be weeping and gnashing of teeth.

51"Have you understood all these things?" Jesus asked.

"Yes," they replied.

52He said to them, "Therefore every teacher of the law who has been instructed about the kingdom of heaven is like the owner of a house who brings out of his storeroom new treasures as well as old."

A Prophet Without Honor

53When Jesus had finished these parables, he moved on from there. 54Coming to his hometown, he began teaching the people in their synagogue, and they were amazed. "Where did this man get this wisdom and these miraculous powers?" they asked. 55Isn't this the carpenter's son? Isn't his mother's name Mary, and aren't his brothers James, Joseph, Simon and Judas? 56Aren't all his sisters with us? Where then did this man get all these things?" 57And they took offense at him.

But Jesus said to them, "Only in their own towns and in their own homes are prophets without honor."

58And he did not do many miracles there because of their lack of faith.

John the Baptist Beheaded

14 At that time Herod the tetrarch heard the reports about Jesus, 2and he said to his attendants, "This is John the Baptist; he has risen from the dead! That is why miraculous powers are at work in him."

3Now Herod had arrested John and bound him and put him in prison because of Herodias, his brother Philip's wife, 4for John had been saying to him: "It is not lawful for you to have her." 5Herod wanted to kill John, but he was afraid of the people, because they considered him a prophet.

6On Herod's birthday the daughter of Herodias danced for them and pleased Herod so much 7that he promised with an oath to give her whatever she asked. 8Prompted by her mother, she said, "Give me here on a platter the head of John the Baptist." 9The king was distressed, but because of his oaths and his dinner guests, he ordered that her request be granted 10and had John beheaded in the prison. 11His head was brought in on a platter and given to the girl, who carried it to her mother. 12John's disciples came and took his body and buried it. Then they went and told Jesus.

Jesus Feeds the Five Thousand

13When Jesus heard what had happened, he withdrew by boat privately to a solitary place. Hearing of this, the crowds followed him on foot from the towns. 14When Jesus landed and saw a large crowd, he had compassion on them and healed their sick.

15As evening approached, the disciples came to him and said, "This is a remote place, and it's already getting late. Send the crowds away, so they can go to the villages and buy themselves some food."

16Jesus replied, "They do not need to go away. You give them something to eat."

17"We have here only five loaves of bread and two fish," they answered.

18"Bring them here to me," he said. 19And he directed the people to sit down on the grass. Taking the five loaves and the two fish and looking up to heaven, he gave thanks and broke the loaves. Then he gave them to the disciples, and the disciples gave them to the people. 20They all ate and were satisfied, and the disciples picked up twelve basketfuls of broken pieces that were left over. 21The number of those who ate was about five thousand men, besides women and children.

Jesus Walks on the Water

22Immediately Jesus made the disciples get into the boat and go on ahead of him to the other side, while he dismissed the crowd. 23After he had dismissed them, he went up on a mountainside by himself to pray. When evening came, he was there alone, 24but the boat was already a considerable distance from land, buffeted by the waves because the wind was against it.

25Shortly before dawn Jesus went out to them, walking on the lake. 26When the disciples saw him walking on the lake, they were terrified. "It's a ghost," they said, and cried out in fear.

²⁷But Jesus immediately said to them: "Take courage! It is I. Don't be afraid."

²⁸"Lord, if it's you," Peter replied, "tell me to come to you on the water."

²⁹"Come," he said.

Then Peter got down out of the boat, walked on the water and came toward Jesus. ³⁰But when he saw the wind, he was afraid and, beginning to sink, cried out, "Lord, save me!"

³¹Immediately Jesus reached out his hand and caught him. "You of little faith," he said, "why did you doubt?"

³²And when they climbed into the boat, the wind died down. ³³Then those who were in the boat worshiped him, saying, "Truly you are the Son of God."

³⁴When they had crossed over, they landed at Gennesaret. ³⁵And when the men of that place recognized Jesus, they sent word to all the surrounding country. People brought all their sick to him ³⁶and begged him to let the sick just touch the edge of his cloak, and all who touched him were healed.

That Which Defiles

15 Then some Pharisees and teachers of the law came to Jesus from Jerusalem and asked, ²"Why do your disciples break the tradition of the elders? They don't wash their hands before they eat!"

³Jesus replied, "And why do you break the command of God for the sake of your tradition? ⁴For God said, 'Honor your father and mother'ᵃ and 'Anyone who curses their father or mother is to be put to death.'ᵇ ⁵But you say that if anyone declares that what might have been used to help their father or mother is 'devoted to God,' ⁶they are not to 'honor their father or mother' with it. Thus you nullify the word of God for the sake of your tradition. ⁷You hypocrites! Isaiah was right when he prophesied about you:

⁸" 'These people honor me with their lips,
but their hearts are far from me.
⁹They worship me in vain;
their teachings are merely human rules.'ᶜ

¹⁰Jesus called the crowd to him and said, "Listen and understand. ¹¹What goes into your mouth does not defile you, but what comes out of your mouth, that is what defiles you."

¹²Then the disciples came to him and asked, "Do you know that the Pharisees were offended when they heard this?"

¹³He replied, "Every plant that my heavenly Father has not planted will be pulled up by the roots. ¹⁴Leave them; they are blind guides.ᵈ If the blind lead the blind, both will fall into a pit."

¹⁵Peter said, "Explain the parable to us."

¹⁶"Are you still so dull?" Jesus asked them. ¹⁷"Don't you see that whatever enters the mouth goes into the stomach and then out of the body? ¹⁸But the things that come out of the mouth come from the heart, and these defile you. ¹⁹For out of the heart come evil thoughts, murder, adultery, sexual immorality, theft, false testimony, slander. ²⁰These are what defile you; but eating with unwashed hands does not defile you."

The Faith of a Canaanite Woman

²¹Leaving that place, Jesus withdrew to the region of Tyre and Sidon. ²²A Canaanite woman from that vicinity came to him, crying out, "Lord, Son of David, have mercy on me! My daughter is demon-possessed and suffering terribly."

²³Jesus did not answer a word. So his disciples came to him and urged him, "Send her away, for she keeps crying out after us."

²⁴He answered, "I was sent only to the lost sheep of Israel."

²⁵The woman came and knelt before him. "Lord, help me!" she said.

²⁶He replied, "It is not right to take the children's bread and toss it to the dogs."

²⁷"Yes it is, Lord," she said. "Even the dogs eat the crumbs that fall from their master's table."

²⁸Then Jesus said to her, "Woman,ᵉ you have great faith! Your request is granted." And her daughter was healed from that very hour.

Jesus Feeds the Four Thousand

²⁹Jesus left there and went along the Sea of Galilee. Then he went up on a mountain-

---

ᵃ 4 Exodus 20:12; Deut. 5:16   ᵇ 4 Exodus 21:17; Lev. 20:9   ᶜ 9 Isaiah 29:13   ᵈ 14 Some manuscripts *blind guides of the blind*   ᵉ 28 The Greek for *Woman* does not denote any disrespect.

side and sat down. ³⁰Great crowds came to him, bringing the lame, the blind, the crippled, the mute and many others, and laid them at his feet; and he healed them. ³¹The people were amazed when they saw the mute speaking, the crippled made well, the lame walking and the blind seeing. And they praised the God of Israel.

³²Jesus called his disciples to him and said, "I have compassion for these people; they have already been with me three days and have nothing to eat. I do not want to send them away hungry, or they may collapse on the way."

³³His disciples answered, "Where could we get enough bread in this remote place to feed such a crowd?"

³⁴"How many loaves do you have?" Jesus asked.

"Seven," they replied, "and a few small fish."

³⁵He told the crowd to sit down on the ground. ³⁶Then he took the seven loaves and the fish, and when he had given thanks, he broke them and gave them to the disciples, and they in turn to the people. ³⁷They all ate and were satisfied. Afterward the disciples picked up seven basketfuls of broken pieces that were left over. ³⁸The number of those who ate was four thousand men, besides women and children. ³⁹After Jesus had sent the crowd away, he got into the boat and went to the vicinity of Magadan.

The Demand for a Sign

16 The Pharisees and Sadducees came to Jesus and tested him by asking him to show them a sign from heaven.

²He replied,ᵃ "When evening comes, you say, 'It will be fair weather, for the sky is red,' ³and in the morning, 'Today it will be stormy, for the sky is red and overcast.' You know how to interpret the appearance of the sky, but you cannot interpret the signs of the times. ⁴A wicked and adulterous generation looks for a sign, but none will be given it except the sign of Jonah." Jesus then left them and went away.

The Yeast of the Pharisees and Sadducees

⁵When they went across the lake, the dis-

ciples forgot to take bread. ⁶"Be careful," Jesus said to them. "Be on your guard against the yeast of the Pharisees and Sadducees."

⁷They discussed this among themselves and said, "It is because we didn't bring any bread."

⁸Aware of their discussion, Jesus asked, "You of little faith, why are you talking among yourselves about having no bread? ⁹Do you still not understand? Don't you remember the five loaves for the five thousand, and how many basketfuls you gathered? ¹⁰Or the seven loaves for the four thousand, and how many basketfuls you gathered? ¹¹How is it you don't understand that I was not talking to you about bread? But be on your guard against the yeast of the Pharisees and Sadducees." ¹²Then they understood that he was not telling them to guard against the yeast used in bread, but against the teaching of the Pharisees and Sadducees.

Peter Declares That Jesus Is the Messiah

¹³When Jesus came to the region of Caesarea Philippi, he asked his disciples, "Who do people say the Son of Man is?"

¹⁴They replied, "Some say John the Baptist; others say Elijah; and still others, Jeremiah or one of the prophets."

¹⁵"But what about you?" he asked. "Who do you say I am?"

¹⁶Simon Peter answered, "You are the Messiah, the Son of the living God."

¹⁷Jesus replied, "Blessed are you, Simon son of Jonah, for this was not revealed to you by flesh and blood, but by my Father in heaven. ¹⁸And I tell you that you are Peter,ᵇ and on this rock I will build my church, and the gates of deathᶜ will not overcome it. ¹⁹I will give you the keys of the kingdom of heaven; whatever you bind on earth will beᵈ bound in heaven, and whatever you loose on earth will beᵈ loosed in heaven." ²⁰Then he ordered his disciples not to tell anyone that he was the Messiah.

Jesus Predicts His Death

²¹From that time on Jesus began to explain to his disciples that he must go to Jerusalem and suffer many things at the hands of the elders, the chief priests and the

---

ᵃ 2 Some early manuscripts do not have the rest of verse 2 and all of verse 3.   ᵇ 18 The Greek for *Peter* means *rock*.   ᶜ 18 Greek *Hades*   ᵈ 19 Or *will have been*

The Dynamic Church

Matthew 16:13–28 or 16:13–19

Tony Evans

The church is the most important institution on earth. The church, and only the church, has been commissioned by the sovereign Lord to be His representative agency in history. It has been given sole authority to unlock the treasures of the spiritual realm so that they can be brought to bear on the realities of earth.

Thus, as the church goes so goes everything else. God designed the church to be the epicenter of culture, and the church's strength or weakness is a major determining factor in the success or failure of human civilization. When the church is strong, the culture is impacted positively—even if the "powers that be" in a particular place don't realize that impact and seek to marginalize and persecute the church. But when the church is weak, its influence deteriorates and so does the culture.

Oswald Chambers {AD 1874–1917}

Rehabilitation means the putting back of the whole human race into the relationship God designed it to be in, and this is what Jesus Christ did in redemption. The church ceases to be a spiritual society when it is on the lookout for the development of its own organisation. The rehabilitation of the human race on Jesus Christ's plan means the realisation of Jesus Christ in corporate life as well as in individual life. Jesus Christ sent apostles and teachers for this purpose—that the corporate Personality might be realised. We are not here to develop a spiritual life of our own, or to enjoy spiritual retirement; we are here so to realise Jesus Christ that the body of Christ may be built up.

reflection

1. What was God's purpose in establishing the church?
2. In your experience, how is the church different from other social groups and organizations?
3. What makes a church dynamic and powerful?

For your next devotional reading, go to page 1100.

teachers of the law, and that he must be killed and on the third day be raised to life.

²²Peter took him aside and began to rebuke him. "Never, Lord!" he said. "This shall never happen to you!"

²³Jesus turned and said to Peter, "Get behind me, Satan! You are a stumbling block to me; you do not have in mind the concerns of God, but merely human concerns."

²⁴Then Jesus said to his disciples, "Whoever wants to be my disciple must deny themselves and take up their cross and follow me. ²⁵For whoever wants to save their life*ᵃ* will lose it, but whoever loses their life for me will find it. ²⁶What good will it be for you to gain the whole world, yet forfeit your soul? Or what can you give in exchange for your soul? ²⁷For the Son of Man is going to come in his Father's glory with his angels, and then he will reward everyone according to what they have done.

²⁸"Truly I tell you, some who are standing here will not taste death before they see the Son of Man coming in his kingdom."

The Transfiguration

17 After six days Jesus took with him Peter, James and John the brother of James, and led them up a high mountain by themselves. ²There he was transfigured before them. His face shone like the sun, and his clothes became as white as the light. ³Just then there appeared before them Moses and Elijah, talking with Jesus.

⁴Peter said to Jesus, "Lord, it is good for us to be here. If you wish, I will put up three shelters—one for you, one for Moses and one for Elijah."

⁵While he was still speaking, a bright cloud covered them, and a voice from the cloud said, "This is my Son, whom I love; with him I am well pleased. Listen to him!"

⁶When the disciples heard this, they fell facedown to the ground, terrified. ⁷But Jesus came and touched them. "Get up," he said. "Don't be afraid." ⁸When they looked up, they saw no one except Jesus.

⁹As they were coming down the mountain, Jesus instructed them, "Don't tell anyone what you have seen, until the Son of Man has been raised from the dead."

¹⁰The disciples asked him, "Why then do the teachers of the law say that Elijah must come first?"

¹¹Jesus replied, "To be sure, Elijah comes and will restore all things. ¹²But I tell you, Elijah has already come, and they did not recognize him, but have done to him everything they wished. In the same way the Son of Man is going to suffer at their hands." ¹³Then the disciples understood that he was talking to them about John the Baptist.

Jesus Heals a Demon-Possessed Boy

¹⁴When they came to the crowd, a man approached Jesus and knelt before him. ¹⁵"Lord, have mercy on my son," he said. "He has seizures and is suffering greatly. He often falls into the fire or into the water. ¹⁶I brought him to your disciples, but they could not heal him."

¹⁷"You unbelieving and perverse generation," Jesus replied, "how long shall I stay with you? How long shall I put up with you? Bring the boy here to me." ¹⁸Jesus rebuked the demon, and it came out of the boy, and he was healed from that moment.

¹⁹Then the disciples came to Jesus in private and asked, "Why couldn't we drive it out?"

²⁰[²¹]He replied, "Because you have so little faith. Truly I tell you, if you have faith as small as a mustard seed, you can say to this mountain, 'Move from here to there,' and it will move. Nothing will be impossible for you."

Jesus Predicts His Death a Second Time

²²When they came together in Galilee, he said to them, "The Son of Man is going to be delivered over to human hands. ²³He will be killed, and on the third day he will be raised to life." And the disciples were filled with grief.

The Temple Tax

²⁴After Jesus and his disciples arrived in Capernaum, the collectors of the two-drachma temple tax came to Peter and asked, "Doesn't your teacher pay the temple tax?"

²⁵"Yes, he does," he replied.

When Peter came into the house, Jesus was the first to speak. "What do you think, Simon?" he asked. "From whom do the

---

ᵃ 25 The Greek word means either *life* or *soul*; also in verse 26.

If You Believe

Matthew 17:14-21

read/meditate

Read this story slowly three times. The first time focus on the father. See the story from his perspective. The next time see the situation from Jesus' perspective. The third time put yourself in the place of the disciples. Think of a few words that would describe how each perspective is distinctive: What would have been each person's strongest feelings or personal stake in the situation?

pray

Lay before God the situations in your life in which you feel desperate (like the father) or that you don't seem to be making any headway (like the disciples). Ask him if any of your struggle has to do with a lack of faith and take a moment to listen honestly for the answer. Then take another moment to allow him to fill you with faith, believing that he is the source of everything you need.

contemplate

Most of us, at one time or another, have believed in something that didn't come to pass. Consider a time in your life like that. How do Jesus' words apply to all of life, including those disappointments? What does it mean that a mustard seed of faith can move a mountain?

additional reflection

Faith is not a feeling. It is not even the feeling that something is going to happen in answer to our prayers. Faith may be easier to exercise when such feelings are present. Nevertheless, feelings of that sort never constitute faith. Faith is a response on our part, the obedient response of our wills to who God is and what He says.

—John White

For your next devotional reading, go to page 1102.

kings of the earth collect duty and taxes—from their own children or from others?"

26"From others," Peter answered.

"Then the children are exempt," Jesus said to him. 27"But so that we may not cause offense, go to the lake and throw out your line. Take the first fish you catch; open its mouth and you will find a four-drachma coin. Take it and give it to them for my tax and yours."

The Greatest in the Kingdom of Heaven

18 At that time the disciples came to Jesus and asked, "Who, then, is the greatest in the kingdom of heaven?"

2He called a little child, whom he placed among them. 3And he said: "Truly I tell you, unless you change and become like little children, you will never enter the kingdom of heaven. 4Therefore, whoever takes a humble place—becoming like this child—is the greatest in the kingdom of heaven. 5And whoever welcomes one such child in my name welcomes me.

Causing to Stumble

6"If anyone causes one of these little ones—those who believe in me—to stumble, it would be better for them if a large millstone were hung around their neck and they were drowned in the depths of the sea. 7Woe to the world because of the things that cause people to stumble! Such things must come, but woe to the person through whom they come! 8If your hand or your foot causes you to stumble, cut it off and throw it away. It is better for you to enter life maimed or crippled than to have two hands or two feet and be thrown into eternal fire. 9And if your eye causes you to stumble, gouge it out and throw it away. It is better for you to enter life with one eye than to have two eyes and be thrown into the fire of hell.

The Parable of the Wandering Sheep

10[11]"See that you do not despise one of these little ones. For I tell you that their angels in heaven always see the face of my Father in heaven.

12"What do you think? If a man owns a hundred sheep, and one of them wanders away, will he not leave the ninety-nine on the hills and go to look for the one that wandered off? 13And if he finds it, truly I tell you, he is happier about that one sheep than about the ninety-nine that did not wander off. 14In the same way your Father in heaven is not willing that any of these little ones should perish.

Dealing With Sin in the Church

15"If a brother or sister sins,ᵃ go and point out the fault, just between the two of you. If they listen to you, you have won them over. 16But if they will not listen, take one or two others along, so that 'every matter may be established by the testimony of two or three witnesses.'ᵇ 17If they still refuse to listen, tell it to the church; and if they refuse to listen even to the church, treat them as you would a pagan or a tax collector.

18"Truly I tell you, whatever you bind on earth will beᶜ bound in heaven, and whatever you loose on earth will beᶜ loosed in heaven.

19"Again, truly I tell you that if two of you on earth agree about anything you ask for, it will be done for you by my Father in heaven. 20For where two or three come together in my name, there am I with them."

The Parable of the Unmerciful Servant

21Then Peter came to Jesus and asked, "Lord, how many times shall I forgive someone who sins against me? Up to seven times?"

22Jesus answered, "I tell you, not seven times, but seventy-seven times.ᵈ

23"Therefore, the kingdom of heaven is like a king who wanted to settle accounts with his servants. 24As he began the settlement, a man who owed him ten thousand bags of goldᵉ was brought to him. 25Since he was not able to pay, the master ordered that he and his wife and his children and all that he had be sold to repay the debt.

26"The servant fell on his knees before him. 'Be patient with me,' he begged, 'and I will pay back everything.' 27The servant's master took pity on him, canceled the debt and let him go.

28"But when that servant went out, he found one of his fellow servants who owed

---

ᵃ 15 Some manuscripts *sins against you*   ᵇ 16 Deut. 19:15   ᶜ 18 Or *will have been*   ᵈ 22 Or *seventy times seven*   ᵉ 24 Greek *ten thousand talents*; a talent was worth about 20 years of a day laborer's wages.

MONDAY

LIKE A CHILD
Matthew 18:1–35 *or* 18:1–6

GEORGE MACDONALD {AD 1824–1905}

The disciples had been disputing who was the greatest, and the Lord wanted to show them that such a dispute had nothing whatever to do with the way things went in his kingdom. Therefore, to illustrate his point, he took a child and set the child before them. It was not merely because of the child's humanity, but rather because of its childhood, that Jesus presented this little one as representing a citizen of the kingdom of God. He did this not to show the scope but rather the nature of the kingdom. He told them they could not enter into the kingdom unless they became little children—by humbling themselves. For if childlikeness is the one essential quality, then the idea of ruling has no place in the kingdom. Jesus wanted them to stop focusing on who should rule and focus instead on who should serve. He showed them that instead of looking down on others from the conquered heights of authority, they should look upon others with honor and minister to them—so that others might eventually be persuaded of their own honor as a temple of the living God. All this Jesus communicated through the childhood of the child he set before them.

Frederick Buechner

Unless you become like a child, Jesus said, you will never enter the Kingdom of Heaven, and maybe part of what that means is that in the long run what is good about religion is playing the way a child plays at being grown up until he finds that being grown up is just another way of playing and thereby starts to grow up himself. Maybe what is good about religion is playing that the Kingdom will come, until—in the joy of your playing, the hope and rhythm and comradeship and poignance and mystery of it—you start to see that the playing is itself the first-fruits of the Kingdom's coming and of God's presence within us and among us.

reflection

1. List some traits that distinguish children from adults.
2. Which of these traits help you understand the kind of heart God wants you to have in relation to him?
3. What needs to change for you to become like a child as you approach God?

For your next devotional reading, go to page 1107.

him a hundred silver coins.ᵃ He grabbed him and began to choke him. 'Pay back what you owe me!' he demanded.

²⁹"His fellow servant fell to his knees and begged him, 'Be patient with me, and I will pay you back.'

³⁰"But he refused. Instead, he went off and had the man thrown into prison until he could pay the debt. ³¹When the other servants saw what had happened, they were greatly distressed and went and told their master everything that had happened.

³²"Then the master called the servant in. 'You wicked servant,' he said, 'I canceled all that debt of yours because you begged me to. ³³Shouldn't you have had mercy on your fellow servant just as I had on you?' ³⁴In anger his master handed him over to the jailers to be tortured, until he should pay back all he owed.

³⁵"This is how my heavenly Father will treat each of you unless you forgive a brother or sister from your heart."

Divorce

19 When Jesus had finished saying these things, he left Galilee and went into the region of Judea to the other side of the Jordan. ²Large crowds followed him, and he healed them there.

³Some Pharisees came to him to test him. They asked, "Is it lawful for a man to divorce his wife for any and every reason?"

⁴"Haven't you read," he replied, "that at the beginning the Creator 'made them male and female,'ᵇ ⁵and said, 'For this reason a man will leave his father and mother and be united to his wife, and the two will become one flesh'ᶜ? ⁶So they are no longer two, but one. Therefore what God has joined together, let no one separate."

⁷"Why then," they asked, "did Moses command that a man give his wife a certificate of divorce and send her away?"

⁸Jesus replied, "Moses permitted you to divorce your wives because your hearts were hard. But it was not this way from the beginning. ⁹I tell you that anyone who divorces his wife, except for sexual immorality, and marries another woman commits adultery."

¹⁰The disciples said to him, "If this is the situation between a husband and wife, it is better not to marry."

¹¹Jesus replied, "Not everyone can accept this word, but only those to whom it has been given. ¹²For some are eunuchs because they were born that way; others have been made eunuchs; and others have renounced marriageᵈ because of the kingdom of heaven. The one who can accept this should accept it."

The Little Children and Jesus

¹³Then people brought little children to Jesus for him to place his hands on them and pray for them. But the disciples rebuked them.

¹⁴Jesus said, "Let the little children come to me, and do not hinder them, for the kingdom of heaven belongs to such as these." ¹⁵When he had placed his hands on them, he went on from there.

The Rich and the Kingdom of God

¹⁶Just then a man came up to Jesus and asked, "Teacher, what good thing must I do to get eternal life?"

¹⁷"Why do you ask me about what is good?" Jesus replied. "There is only One who is good. If you want to enter life, keep the commandments."

¹⁸"Which ones?" he inquired.

Jesus replied, " 'You shall not murder, you shall not commit adultery, you shall not steal, you shall not give false testimony, ¹⁹honor your father and mother,'ᵉ and 'love your neighbor as yourself.'ᶠ"

²⁰"All these I have kept," the young man said. "What do I still lack?"

²¹Jesus answered, "If you want to be perfect, go, sell your possessions and give to the poor, and you will have treasure in heaven. Then come, follow me."

²²When the young man heard this, he went away sad, because he had great wealth.

²³Then Jesus said to his disciples, "Truly I tell you, it is hard for the rich to enter the kingdom of heaven. ²⁴Again I tell you, it is easier for a camel to go through the eye of a needle than for the rich to enter the kingdom of God."

²⁵When the disciples heard this, they

ᵃ 28 Greek *a hundred denarii*; a denarius was the daily wage of a day laborer (see Matt. 20:2).
ᵇ 4 Gen. 1:27   ᶜ 5 Gen. 2:24   ᵈ 12 Or *have made themselves eunuchs*   ᵉ 19 Exodus 20:12-16;
Deut. 5:16-20   ᶠ 19 Lev. 19:18

were greatly astonished and asked, "Who then can be saved?"

²⁶Jesus looked at them and said, "With human beings this is impossible, but with God all things are possible."

²⁷Peter answered him, "We have left everything to follow you! What then will there be for us?"

²⁸Jesus said to them, "Truly I tell you, at the renewal of all things, when the Son of Man sits on his glorious throne, you who have followed me will also sit on twelve thrones, judging the twelve tribes of Israel. ²⁹And everyone who has left houses or brothers or sisters or father or mother or wifeᵃ or children or fields for my sake will receive a hundred times as much and will inherit eternal life. ³⁰But many who are first will be last, and many who are last will be first.

The Parable of the Workers in the Vineyard

20 "For the kingdom of heaven is like a landowner who went out early in the morning to hire workers for his vineyard. ²He agreed to pay them a denarius for the day and sent them into his vineyard.

³"About nine in the morning he went out and saw others standing in the marketplace doing nothing. ⁴He told them, 'You also go and work in my vineyard, and I will pay you whatever is right.' ⁵So they went.

"He went out again about noon and about three in the afternoon and did the same thing. ⁶About five in the afternoon he went out and found still others standing around. He asked them, 'Why have you been standing here all day long doing nothing?'

⁷" 'Because no one has hired us,' they answered.

"He said to them, 'You also go and work in my vineyard.'

⁸"When evening came, the owner of the vineyard said to his supervisor, 'Call the workers and pay them their wages, beginning with the last ones hired and going on to the first.'

⁹"The workers who were hired about five in the afternoon came and each received a denarius. ¹⁰So when those came who were hired first, they expected to receive more. But each one of them also received a denar-

ius. ¹¹When they received it, they began to grumble against the landowner. ¹²'These men who were hired last worked only one hour,' they said, 'and you have made them equal to us who have borne the burden of the work and the heat of the day.'

¹³"But he answered one of them, 'Friend, I am not being unfair to you. Didn't you agree to work for a denarius? ¹⁴Take your pay and go. I want to give the one who was hired last the same as I gave you. ¹⁵Don't I have the right to do what I want with my own money? Or are you envious because I am generous?'

¹⁶"So the last will be first, and the first will be last."

Jesus Predicts His Death a Third Time

¹⁷Now Jesus was going up to Jerusalem. On the way, he took the Twelve aside and said to them, ¹⁸"We are going up to Jerusalem, and the Son of Man will be delivered over to the chief priests and the teachers of the law. They will condemn him to death ¹⁹and will hand him over to the Gentiles to be mocked and flogged and crucified. On the third day he will be raised to life!"

A Mother's Request

²⁰Then the mother of Zebedee's sons came to Jesus with her sons and, kneeling down, asked a favor of him.

²¹"What is it you want?" he asked.

She said, "Grant that one of these two sons of mine may sit at your right and the other at your left in your kingdom."

²²"You don't know what you are asking," Jesus said to them. "Can you drink the cup I am going to drink?"

"We can," they answered.

²³Jesus said to them, "You will indeed drink from my cup, but to sit at my right or left is not for me to grant. These places belong to those for whom they have been prepared by my Father."

²⁴When the ten heard about this, they were indignant with the two brothers. ²⁵Jesus called them together and said, "You know that the rulers of the Gentiles lord it over them, and their high officials exercise authority over them. ²⁶Not so with you. Instead, whoever wants to become great among you must be your servant, ²⁷and

ᵃ 29 Some manuscripts do not have or wife.

whoever wants to be first must be your slave— [28]just as the Son of Man did not come to be served, but to serve, and to give his life as a ransom for many."

Two Blind Men Receive Sight

[29]As Jesus and his disciples were leaving Jericho, a large crowd followed him. [30]Two blind men were sitting by the roadside, and when they heard that Jesus was going by, they shouted, "Lord, Son of David, have mercy on us!"

[31]The crowd rebuked them and told them to be quiet, but they shouted all the louder, "Lord, Son of David, have mercy on us!"

[32]Jesus stopped and called them. "What do you want me to do for you?" he asked.

[33]"Lord," they answered, "we want our sight."

[34]Jesus had compassion on them and touched their eyes. Immediately they received their sight and followed him.

Jesus Comes to Jerusalem as King

21 As they approached Jerusalem and came to Bethphage on the Mount of Olives, Jesus sent two disciples, [2]saying to them, "Go to the village ahead of you, and at once you will find a donkey tied there, with her colt by her. Untie them and bring them to me. [3]If anyone says anything to you, say that the Lord needs them, and he will send them right away."

[4]This took place to fulfill what was spoken through the prophet:

[5]"Say to Daughter Zion,
  'See, your king comes to you,
  gentle and riding on a donkey,
    and on a colt, the foal of a donkey.' "[a]

[6]The disciples went and did as Jesus had instructed them. [7]They brought the donkey and the colt and placed their cloaks on them for Jesus to sit on. [8]A very large crowd spread their cloaks on the road, while others cut branches from the trees and spread them on the road. [9]The crowds that went ahead of him and those that followed shouted,

"Hosanna[b] to the Son of David!"

"Blessed is he who comes in the name of the Lord!"[c]

"Hosanna[b] in the highest heaven!"

[10]When Jesus entered Jerusalem, the whole city was stirred and asked, "Who is this?"

[11]The crowds answered, "This is Jesus, the prophet from Nazareth in Galilee."

Jesus at the Temple

[12]Jesus entered the temple courts and drove out all who were buying and selling there. He overturned the tables of the money changers and the benches of those selling doves. [13]"It is written," he said to them, " 'My house will be called a house of prayer,'[d] but you are making it 'a den of robbers.'[e]"

[14]The blind and the lame came to him at the temple, and he healed them. [15]But when the chief priests and the teachers of the law saw the wonderful things he did and the children shouting in the temple courts, "Hosanna to the Son of David," they were indignant.

[16]"Do you hear what these children are saying?" they asked him.

"Yes," replied Jesus, "have you never read,

" 'From the lips of children and infants
  you have ordained praise'[f]?"

[17]And he left them and went out of the city to Bethany, where he spent the night.

Jesus Curses a Fig Tree

[18]Early in the morning, as he was on his way back to the city, he was hungry. [19]Seeing a fig tree by the road, he went up to it but found nothing on it except leaves. Then he said to it, "May you never bear fruit again!" Immediately the tree withered.

[20]When the disciples saw this, they were amazed. "How did the fig tree wither so quickly?" they asked.

[21]Jesus replied, "Truly I tell you, if you have faith and do not doubt, not only can you do what was done to the fig tree, but also you can say to this mountain, 'Go, throw yourself into the sea,' and it will be done. [22]If you believe, you will receive whatever you ask for in prayer."

a 5 Zech. 9:9   b 9 A Hebrew expression meaning "Save!" which became an exclamation of praise; also in verse 15   c 9 Psalm 118:25,26   d 13 Isaiah 56:7   e 13 Jer. 7:11   f 16 Psalm 8:2 (see Septuagint)

The Authority of Jesus Questioned

²³Jesus entered the temple courts, and, while he was teaching, the chief priests and the elders of the people came to him. "By what authority are you doing these things?" they asked. "And who gave you this authority?"

²⁴Jesus replied, "I will also ask you one question. If you answer me, I will tell you by what authority I am doing these things. ²⁵John's baptism—where did it come from? Was it from heaven, or of human origin?"

They discussed it among themselves and said, "If we say, 'From heaven,' he will ask, 'Then why didn't you believe him?' ²⁶But if we say, 'Of human origin'—we are afraid of the people, for they all hold that John was a prophet."

²⁷So they answered Jesus, "We don't know."

Then he said, "Neither will I tell you by what authority I am doing these things.

The Parable of the Two Sons

²⁸"What do you think? There was a man who had two sons. He went to the first and said, 'Son, go and work today in the vineyard.'

²⁹" 'I will not,' he answered, but later he changed his mind and went.

³⁰"Then the father went to the other son and said the same thing. He answered, 'I will, sir,' but he did not go.

³¹"Which of the two did what his father wanted?"

"The first," they answered.

Jesus said to them, "Truly I tell you, the tax collectors and the prostitutes are entering the kingdom of God ahead of you. ³²For John came to you to show you the way of righteousness, and you did not believe him, but the tax collectors and the prostitutes did. And even after you saw this, you did not repent and believe him.

The Parable of the Tenants

³³"Listen to another parable: There was a landowner who planted a vineyard. He put a wall around it, dug a winepress in it and built a watchtower. Then he rented the vineyard to some farmers and moved to another place. ³⁴When the harvest time approached, he sent his servants to the tenants to collect his fruit.

³⁵"The tenants seized his servants; they beat one, killed another, and stoned a third. ³⁶Then he sent other servants to them, more than the first time, and the tenants treated them the same way. ³⁷Last of all, he sent his son to them. 'They will respect my son,' he said.

³⁸"But when the tenants saw the son, they said to each other, 'This is the heir. Come, let's kill him and take his inheritance.' ³⁹So they took him and threw him out of the vineyard and killed him.

⁴⁰"Therefore, when the owner of the vineyard comes, what will he do to those tenants?"

⁴¹"He will bring those wretches to a wretched end," they replied, "and he will rent the vineyard to other tenants, who will give him his share of the crop at harvest time."

⁴²Jesus said to them, "Have you never read in the Scriptures:

" 'The stone the builders rejected
    has become the cornerstone;
the Lord has done this,
    and it is marvelous in our eyes'^a?

⁴³"Therefore I tell you that the kingdom of God will be taken away from you and given to a people who will produce its fruit. ⁴⁴Anyone who falls on this stone will be broken to pieces, but anyone on whom it falls will be crushed."^b

⁴⁵When the chief priests and the Pharisees heard Jesus' parables, they knew he was talking about them. ⁴⁶They looked for a way to arrest him, but they were afraid of the crowd because the people held that he was a prophet.

The Parable of the Wedding Banquet

22 Jesus spoke to them again in parables, saying: ²"The kingdom of heaven is like a king who prepared a wedding banquet for his son. ³He sent his servants to those who had been invited to the banquet to tell them to come, but they refused to come.

⁴"Then he sent some more servants and said, 'Tell those who have been invited that I have prepared my dinner: My oxen and fattened cattle have been butchered, and everything is ready. Come to the wedding banquet.'

---

^a 42 Psalm 118:22,23   ^b 44 Some manuscripts do not have verse 44.

LOVING GOD MEANS LOVING OTHERS
Matthew 22:1–46 *or* 22:34–40

ANDREW MURRAY {AD 1828–1917}

God's Son came to show what love is, and he lived a life of love here upon earth in fellowship with his disciples, in compassion over the poor and miserable, in love even to his enemies, and he died the death of love. And when he went to heaven, whom did he send down? The Spirit of love, to come and banish selfishness and envy and pride, and bring the love of God into the hearts of people. "The fruit of the Spirit is love" (Galatians 5:22).

And what was the preparation for the promise of the Holy Spirit? . . . "As I have loved you, so you must love one another" (John 13:34). To them his dying love was to be the only law of their conduct and communication with each other. What a message to those fishermen, to those men full of pride and selfishness! "Learn to love each other," said Christ, "as I have loved you." And by the grace of God they did it . . .

And now he calls us to dwell and to walk in love. He demands that though someone else hate you, still you love them. True love cannot be conquered by anything in heaven or upon the earth. The more hatred there is, the more love triumphs through it all and shows its true nature. This is the love that Christ commanded his disciples to exercise.

John Ortberg

There are in the New Testament two commands that form the heart of our response to God's love. They cannot be separated. The whole of God's will comes down to this: Jesus said, "[Love the Lord your God with all your heart and with all your soul and with all your mind and with all your strength . . . Love your neighbor as yourself]" [Mark 12:30–31]. The primary form that loving God takes in the Bible is loving the people who mean so much to him. In the words of Jesus: "[Whatever you did for one of the least of these brothers and sisters of mine, you did for me.]"

"Love me, love my rag dolls," God says. It's a package deal.

If we are serious about loving God, we must begin with people, all people. And especially we must learn to love those that the world generally discards.

reflection

1. How would you describe Christ's love for you to another person?
2. In what ways do you love others like Jesus has loved you? In what ways do you fall short of following his example?
3. Why is it impossible to truly love God without loving other people?

For your next devotional reading, go to page 1113.

5"But they paid no attention and went off—one to his field, another to his business. 6The rest seized his servants, mistreated them and killed them. 7The king was enraged. He sent his army and destroyed those murderers and burned their city.

8"Then he said to his servants, 'The wedding banquet is ready, but those I invited did not deserve to come. 9Go to the street corners and invite to the banquet anyone you find.' 10So the servants went out into the streets and gathered all the people they could find, the bad as well as the good, and the wedding hall was filled with guests.

11"But when the king came in to see the guests, he noticed a man there who was not wearing wedding clothes. 12'Friend,' he asked, 'how did you get in here without wedding clothes?' The man was speechless.

13"Then the king told the attendants, 'Tie him hand and foot, and throw him outside, into the darkness, where there will be weeping and gnashing of teeth.'

14"For many are invited, but few are chosen."

Paying the Imperial Tax to Caesar

15Then the Pharisees went out and laid plans to trap him in his words. 16They sent their disciples to him along with the Herodians. "Teacher," they said, "we know that you are a man of integrity and that you teach the way of God in accordance with the truth. You aren't swayed by others, because you pay no attention to who they are. 17Tell us then, what is your opinion? Is it right to pay the imperial tax[a] to Caesar or not?"

18But Jesus, knowing their evil intent, said, "You hypocrites, why are you trying to trap me? 19Show me the coin used for paying the tax." They brought him a denarius, 20and he asked them, "Whose image is this? And whose inscription?"

21"Caesar's," they replied.

Then he said to them, "Give back to Caesar what is Caesar's, and to God what is God's."

22When they heard this, they were amazed. So they left him and went away.

Marriage at the Resurrection

23That same day the Sadducees, who say there is no resurrection, came to him with a question. 24"Teacher," they said, "Moses told us that if a man dies without having children, his brother must marry the widow and raise up offspring for him. 25Now there were seven brothers among us. The first one married and died, and since he had no children, he left his wife to his brother. 26The same thing happened to the second and third brother, right on down to the seventh. 27Finally, the woman died. 28Now then, at the resurrection, whose wife will she be of the seven, since all of them were married to her?"

29Jesus replied, "You are in error because you do not know the Scriptures or the power of God. 30At the resurrection people will neither marry nor be given in marriage; they will be like the angels in heaven. 31But about the resurrection of the dead—have you not read what God said to you, 32'I am the God of Abraham, the God of Isaac, and the God of Jacob'[b]? He is not the God of the dead but of the living."

33When the crowds heard this, they were astonished at his teaching.

The Greatest Commandment

34Hearing that Jesus had silenced the Sadducees, the Pharisees got together. 35One of them, an expert in the law, tested him with this question: 36"Teacher, which is the greatest commandment in the Law?"

37Jesus replied: " 'Love the Lord your God with all your heart and with all your soul and with all your mind.'[c] 38This is the first and greatest commandment. 39And the second is like it: 'Love your neighbor as yourself.'[d] 40All the Law and the Prophets hang on these two commandments."

Whose Son Is the Messiah?

41While the Pharisees were gathered together, Jesus asked them, 42"What do you think about the Messiah? Whose son is he?"

"The son of David," they replied.

43He said to them, "How is it then that David, speaking by the Spirit, calls him 'Lord'? For he says,

44 " 'The Lord said to my Lord:
    "Sit at my right hand
until I put your enemies
    under your feet." '[e]

---

a 17 A special tax levied on subject peoples, not on Roman citizens   b 32 Exodus 3:6   c 37 Deut. 6:5
d 39 Lev. 19:18   e 44 Psalm 110:1

⁴⁵If then David calls him 'Lord,' how can he be his son?" ⁴⁶No one could say a word in reply, and from that day on no one dared to ask him any more questions.

A Warning Against Hypocrisy

23

Then Jesus said to the crowds and to his disciples: ²"The teachers of the law and the Pharisees sit in Moses' seat. ³So you must be careful to do everything they tell you. But do not do what they do, for they do not practice what they preach. ⁴They tie up heavy, cumbersome loads and put them on other people's shoulders, but they themselves are not willing to lift a finger to move them.

⁵"Everything they do is done for people to see: They make their phylacteries ᵃ wide and the tassels on their garments long; ⁶they love the place of honor at banquets and the most important seats in the synagogues; ⁷they love to be greeted with respect in the marketplaces and to have people call them 'Rabbi.'

⁸"But you are not to be called 'Rabbi,' for you have only one Master and you are all brothers. ⁹And do not call anyone on earth 'father,' for you have one Father, and he is in heaven. ¹⁰Nor are you to be called 'teacher,' for you have one Teacher, the Messiah. ¹¹The greatest among you will be your servant. ¹²For those who exalt themselves will be humbled, and those who humble themselves will be exalted.

Seven Woes on the Teachers of the Law and the Pharisees

¹³[¹⁴]"Woe to you, teachers of the law and Pharisees, you hypocrites! You shut the door of the kingdom of heaven in people's faces. You yourselves do not enter, nor will you let those enter who are trying to.

¹⁵"Woe to you, teachers of the law and Pharisees, you hypocrites! You travel over land and sea to win a single convert, and then you make that convert twice as much a child of hell as you are.

¹⁶"Woe to you, blind guides! You say, 'If anyone swears by the temple, it means nothing; but whoever swears by the gold of the temple is bound by the oath.' ¹⁷You blind fools! Which is greater: the gold, or the temple that makes the gold sacred? ¹⁸You also

say, 'If anyone swears by the altar, it means nothing; but whoever swears by the gift on the altar is bound by the oath.' ¹⁹You blind men! Which is greater: the gift, or the altar that makes the gift sacred? ²⁰Therefore, anyone who swears by the altar swears by it and by everything on it. ²¹And anyone who swears by the temple swears by it and by the one who dwells in it. ²²And anyone who swears by heaven swears by God's throne and by the one who sits on it.

²³"Woe to you, teachers of the law and Pharisees, you hypocrites! You give a tenth of your spices—mint, dill and cumin. But you have neglected the more important matters of the law—justice, mercy and faithfulness. You should have practiced the latter, without neglecting the former. ²⁴You blind guides! You strain out a gnat but swallow a camel.

²⁵"Woe to you, teachers of the law and Pharisees, you hypocrites! You clean the outside of the cup and dish, but inside they are full of greed and self-indulgence. ²⁶Blind Pharisee! First clean the inside of the cup and dish, and then the outside also will be clean.

²⁷"Woe to you, teachers of the law and Pharisees, you hypocrites! You are like whitewashed tombs, which look beautiful on the outside but on the inside are full of the bones of the dead and everything unclean. ²⁸In the same way, on the outside you appear to people as righteous but on the inside you are full of hypocrisy and wickedness.

²⁹"Woe to you, teachers of the law and Pharisees, you hypocrites! You build tombs for the prophets and decorate the graves of the righteous. ³⁰And you say, 'If we had lived in the days of our ancestors, we would not have taken part with them in shedding the blood of the prophets.' ³¹So you testify against yourselves that you are the descendants of those who murdered the prophets. ³²Fill up, then, the measure of the sin of your ancestors!

³³"You snakes! You brood of vipers! How will you escape being condemned to hell? ³⁴Therefore I am sending you prophets and sages and teachers. Some of them you will kill and crucify; others you will flog in your synagogues and pursue from town to town.

ᵃ 5 That is, boxes containing Scripture verses, worn on forehead and arm

35And so upon you will come all the righteous blood that has been shed on earth, from the blood of righteous Abel to the blood of Zechariah son of Berekiah, whom you murdered between the temple and the altar. 36Truly I tell you, all this will come on this generation.

37"Jerusalem, Jerusalem, you who kill the prophets and stone those sent to you, how often I have longed to gather your children together, as a hen gathers her chicks under her wings, and you were not willing. 38Look, your house is left to you desolate. 39For I tell you, you will not see me again until you say, 'Blessed is he who comes in the name of the Lord.'ᵃ"

The Destruction of the Temple and Signs of the End Times

24 Jesus left the temple and was walking away when his disciples came up to him to call his attention to its buildings. 2"Do you see all these things?" he asked. "Truly I tell you, not one stone here will be left on another; every one will be thrown down."

3As Jesus was sitting on the Mount of Olives, the disciples came to him privately. "Tell us," they said, "when will this happen, and what will be the sign of your coming and of the end of the age?"

4Jesus answered: "Watch out that no one deceives you. 5For many will come in my name, claiming, 'I am the Messiah,' and will deceive many. 6You will hear of wars and rumors of wars, but see to it that you are not alarmed. Such things must happen, but the end is still to come. 7Nation will rise against nation, and kingdom against kingdom. There will be famines and earthquakes in various places. 8All these are the beginning of birth pains.

9"Then you will be handed over to be persecuted and put to death, and you will be hated by all nations because of me. 10At that time many will turn away from the faith and will betray and hate each other, 11and many false prophets will appear and deceive many people. 12Because of the increase of wickedness, the love of most will grow cold, 13but whoever stands firm to the end will be saved. 14And this gospel of the kingdom will be preached in the whole world as a testimony to all nations, and then the end will come.

15"So when you see standing in the holy place 'the abomination that causes desolation,'ᵇ spoken of through the prophet Daniel—let the reader understand— 16then let those who are in Judea flee to the mountains. 17Let no one on the housetop go down to take anything out of the house. 18Let no one in the field go back to get their cloak. 19How dreadful it will be in those days for pregnant women and nursing mothers! 20Pray that your flight will not take place in winter or on the Sabbath. 21For then there will be great distress, unequaled from the beginning of the world until now—and never to be equaled again.

22"If those days had not been cut short, no one would survive, but for the sake of the elect those days will be shortened. 23At that time if anyone says to you, 'Look, here is the Messiah!' or, 'There he is!' do not believe it. 24For false messiahs and false prophets will appear and perform great signs and wonders to deceive, if possible, even the elect. 25See, I have told you ahead of time.

26"So if anyone tells you, 'There he is, out in the wilderness,' do not go out; or, 'Here he is, in the inner rooms,' do not believe it. 27For as lightning that comes from the east is visible even in the west, so will be the coming of the Son of Man. 28Wherever there is a carcass, there the vultures will gather.

29"Immediately after the distress of those days

" 'the sun will be darkened,
    and the moon will not give its light;
the stars will fall from the sky,
    and the heavenly bodies will be
        shaken.'ᶜ

30"At that time the sign of the Son of Man will appear in the sky, and all the peoples of the earthᵈ will mourn. They will see the Son of Man coming on the clouds of heaven, with power and great glory. 31And he will send his angels with a loud trumpet call, and they will gather his elect from the four winds, from one end of the heavens to the other.

32"Now learn this lesson from the fig tree: As soon as its twigs get tender and its leaves

a 39 Psalm 118:26   b 15 Daniel 9:27; 11:31; 12:11   c 29 Isaiah 13:10; 34:4   d 30 Or the tribes of the land come out, you know that summer is near. [33] Even so, when you see all these things, you know that it[a] is near, right at the door. [34] Truly I tell you, this generation will certainly not pass away until all these things have happened. [35] Heaven and earth will pass away, but my words will never pass away.

The Day and Hour Unknown

[36] "But about that day or hour no one knows, not even the angels in heaven, nor the Son,[b] but only the Father. [37] As it was in the days of Noah, so it will be at the coming of the Son of Man. [38] For in the days before the flood, people were eating and drinking, marrying and giving in marriage, up to the day Noah entered the ark; [39] and they knew nothing about what would happen until the flood came and took them all away. That is how it will be at the coming of the Son of Man. [40] Two men will be in the field; one will be taken and the other left. [41] Two women will be grinding with a hand mill; one will be taken and the other left.

[42] "Therefore keep watch, because you do not know on what day your Lord will come. [43] But understand this: If the owner of the house had known at what time of night the thief was coming, he would have kept watch and would not have let his house be broken into. [44] So you also must be ready, because the Son of Man will come at an hour when you do not expect him.

[45] "Who then is the faithful and wise servant, whom the master has put in charge of the servants in his household to give them their food at the proper time? [46] It will be good for that servant whose master finds him doing so when he returns. [47] Truly I tell you, he will put him in charge of all his possessions. [48] But suppose that servant is wicked and says to himself, 'My master is staying away a long time,' [49] and he then begins to beat his fellow servants and to eat and drink with drunkards. [50] The master of that servant will come on a day when he does not expect him and at an hour he is not aware of. [51] He will cut him to pieces and assign him a place with the hypocrites, where there will be weeping and gnashing of teeth.

The Parable of the Ten Virgins

25 "At that time the kingdom of heaven will be like ten virgins who took their lamps and went out to meet the bridegroom. [2] Five of them were foolish and five were wise. [3] The foolish ones took their lamps but did not take any oil with them. [4] The wise, however, took oil in jars along with their lamps. [5] The bridegroom was a long time in coming, and they all became drowsy and fell asleep.

[6] "At midnight the cry rang out: 'Here's the bridegroom! Come out to meet him!'

[7] "Then all the virgins woke up and trimmed their lamps. [8] The foolish ones said to the wise, 'Give us some of your oil; our lamps are going out.'

[9] " 'No,' they replied, 'there may not be enough for both us and you. Instead, go to those who sell oil and buy some for yourselves.'

[10] "But while they were on their way to buy the oil, the bridegroom arrived. The virgins who were ready went in with him to the wedding banquet. And the door was shut.

[11] "Later the others also came. 'Sir! Sir!' they said. 'Open the door for us!'

[12] "But he replied, 'Truly I tell you, I don't know you.'

[13] "Therefore keep watch, because you do not know the day or the hour.

The Parable of the Bags of Gold

[14] "Again, it will be like a man going on a journey, who called his servants and entrusted his wealth to them. [15] To one he gave five bags of gold, to another two bags, and to another one bag,[c] each according to his ability. Then he went on his journey. [16] The man who had received five bags of gold went at once and put his money to work and gained five bags more. [17] So also, the one with two bags of gold gained two more. [18] But the man who had received one bag went off, dug a hole in the ground and hid his master's money.

[19] "After a long time the master of those servants returned and settled accounts with them. [20] The man who had received five bags of gold brought the other five. 'Master,' he said, 'you entrusted me with five bags of gold. See, I have gained five more.'

---

[a] 33 Or he   [b] 36 Some manuscripts do not have *nor the Son*.   [c] 15 Greek *five talents . . . two talents . . . one talent*; also throughout this parable; a talent was worth about 20 years of a day laborer's wage.

[21]"His master replied, 'Well done, good and faithful servant! You have been faithful with a few things; I will put you in charge of many things. Come and share your master's happiness!'

[22]"The man with two bags of gold also came. 'Master,' he said, 'you entrusted me with two bags of gold; see, I have gained two more.'

[23]"His master replied, 'Well done, good and faithful servant! You have been faithful with a few things; I will put you in charge of many things. Come and share your master's happiness!'

[24]"Then the man who had received one bag of gold came. 'Master,' he said, 'I knew that you are a hard man, harvesting where you have not sown and gathering where you have not scattered seed. [25]So I was afraid and went out and hid your gold in the ground. See, here is what belongs to you.'

[26]"His master replied, 'You wicked, lazy servant! So you knew that I harvest where I have not sown and gather where I have not scattered seed? [27]Well then, you should have put my money on deposit with the bankers, so that when I returned I would have received it back with interest.

[28]" 'Take the bag of gold from him and give it to the one who has ten bags. [29]For those who have will be given more, and they will have an abundance. As for those who do not have, even what they have will be taken from them. [30]And throw that worthless servant outside, into the darkness, where there will be weeping and gnashing of teeth.'

The Sheep and the Goats

[31]"When the Son of Man comes in his glory, and all the angels with him, he will sit on his glorious throne. [32]All the nations will be gathered before him, and he will separate the people one from another as a shepherd separates the sheep from the goats. [33]He will put the sheep on his right and the goats on his left.

[34]"Then the King will say to those on his right, 'Come, you who are blessed by my Father; take your inheritance, the kingdom prepared for you since the creation of the world. [35]For I was hungry and you gave me something to eat, I was thirsty and you gave me something to drink, I was a stranger and you invited me in, [36]I needed clothes and you clothed me, I was sick and you looked

after me, I was in prison and you came to visit me.'

[37]"Then the righteous will answer him, 'Lord, when did we see you hungry and feed you, or thirsty and give you something to drink? [38]When did we see you a stranger and invite you in, or needing clothes and clothe you? [39]When did we see you sick or in prison and go to visit you?'

[40]"The King will reply, 'Truly I tell you, whatever you did for one of the least of these brothers and sisters of mine, you did for me.'

[41]"Then he will say to those on his left, 'Depart from me, you who are cursed, into the eternal fire prepared for the devil and his angels. [42]For I was hungry and you gave me nothing to eat, I was thirsty and you gave me nothing to drink, [43]I was a stranger and you did not invite me in, I needed clothes and you did not clothe me, I was sick and in prison and you did not look after me.'

[44]"They also will answer, 'Lord, when did we see you hungry or thirsty or a stranger or needing clothes or sick or in prison, and did not help you?'

[45]"He will reply, 'Truly I tell you, whatever you did not do for one of the least of these, you did not do for me.'

[46]"Then they will go away to eternal punishment, but the righteous to eternal life."

The Plot Against Jesus

26 When Jesus had finished saying all these things, he said to his disciples, [2]"As you know, the Passover is two days away—and the Son of Man will be handed over to be crucified."

[3]Then the chief priests and the elders of the people assembled in the palace of the high priest, whose name was Caiaphas, [4]and they plotted to arrest Jesus in some sly way and kill him. [5]"But not during the festival," they said, "or there may be a riot among the people."

Jesus Anointed at Bethany

[6]While Jesus was in Bethany in the home of Simon the Leper, [7]a woman came to him with an alabaster jar of very expensive perfume, which she poured on his head as he was reclining at the table.

[8]When the disciples saw this, they were indignant. "Why this waste?" they asked.

WEDNESDAY

CHRIST'S SUPERIORITY
Matthew 26:1–46 *or* 26:36–46

Frederick Buechner

Buddha sits enthroned beneath the Bo-tree in the lotus position. His lips are faintly parted in the smile of one who has passed beyond every power in earth or heaven to touch him. "He who loves fifty has fifty woes, he who loves ten has ten woes, he who loves none has no woes," he has said. His eyes are closed.

Christ, on the other hand, stands in the Garden of Gethsemane, angular, beleaguered. His face is lost in shadows so that you can't even see his lips, and before all the powers in earth or heaven he is powerless. "[My command is this: Love each other as I have loved you,]" he has said. His eyes are also closed.

The difference seems to me this. The suffering that Buddha's eyes close out is the suffering of the world that Christ's eyes close in and hallow. It is an extraordinary difference.

JAMES ORR {AD 1844–1913}

Christ . . . explains that he alone has the knowledge which qualifies him to give a true estimate of himself: "For I know," he said to the Jews, "where I came from and where I am going" (John 8:14).

I propose, however, to begin at a point further down—that to which our first written documents in the church belong—and to ask, *What view of Christ's Person did they hold in the apostolic age?* The testimony of that age is clearly one of great importance, for it throws light on Christ's own claims. When men say that Buddha also was raised to the rank of divinity by his followers—though he himself made no such claim—I answer that the cases are not parallel. It was only long centuries after his death, and within limited circles, that Buddha was regarded as divine. But one short step takes us from the days when Christ himself lived and taught on earth into the midst of a church, founded by his apostles, which in all its branches worshiped and adored him as the genuine Son of God made manifest on earth for our salvation . . . This, of itself, is a strong reason for believing that it rested on claims made by Christ himself, and rose naturally out of the facts of his historical self-manifestation.

reflection

1. What differences do you see between Buddha and Jesus?
2. How did Christ's claims about himself and who he is distinguish him from the "founders" of all other religions?
3. How do you answer the question, Why do you believe in Jesus?

For your next devotional reading, go to page 1118.

⁹"This perfume could have been sold at a high price and the money given to the poor."

¹⁰Aware of this, Jesus said to them, "Why are you bothering this woman? She has done a beautiful thing to me. ¹¹The poor you will always have with you,ᵃ but you will not always have me. ¹²When she poured this perfume on my body, she did it to prepare me for burial. ¹³Truly I tell you, wherever this gospel is preached throughout the world, what she has done will also be told, in memory of her."

Judas Agrees to Betray Jesus

¹⁴Then one of the Twelve—the one called Judas Iscariot—went to the chief priests ¹⁵and asked, "What are you willing to give me if I deliver him over to you?" So they counted out for him thirty pieces of silver. ¹⁶From then on Judas watched for an opportunity to hand him over.

The Last Supper

¹⁷On the first day of the Festival of Unleavened Bread, the disciples came to Jesus and asked, "Where do you want us to make preparations for you to eat the Passover?"

¹⁸He replied, "Go into the city to a certain man and tell him, 'The Teacher says: My appointed time is near. I am going to celebrate the Passover with my disciples at your house.' " ¹⁹So the disciples did as Jesus had directed them and prepared the Passover.

²⁰When evening came, Jesus was reclining at the table with the Twelve. ²¹And while they were eating, he said, "Truly I tell you, one of you will betray me."

²²They were very sad and began to say to him one after the other, "Surely not I, Lord?"

²³Jesus replied, "The one who has dipped his hand into the bowl with me will betray me. ²⁴The Son of Man will go just as it is written about him. But woe to that man who betrays the Son of Man! It would be better for him if he had not been born."

²⁵Then Judas, the one who would betray him, said, "Surely not I, Rabbi?"

Jesus answered, "You have said so."

²⁶While they were eating, Jesus took bread, and when he had given thanks, he broke it and gave it to his disciples, saying, "Take and eat; this is my body."

²⁷Then he took the cup, and when he had given thanks, he gave it to them, saying, "Drink from it, all of you. ²⁸This is my blood of theᵇ covenant, which is poured out for many for the forgiveness of sins. ²⁹I tell you, I will not drink of this fruit of the vine from now on until that day when I drink it new with you in my Father's kingdom."

³⁰When they had sung a hymn, they went out to the Mount of Olives.

Jesus Predicts Peter's Denial

³¹Then Jesus told them, "This very night you will all fall away on account of me, for it is written:

" 'I will strike the shepherd,
  and the sheep of the flock will be
    scattered.'ᶜ

³²But after I have risen, I will go ahead of you into Galilee."

³³Peter replied, "Even if all fall away on account of you, I never will."

³⁴"Truly I tell you," Jesus answered, "this very night, before the rooster crows, you will disown me three times."

³⁵But Peter declared, "Even if I have to die with you, I will never disown you." And all the other disciples said the same.

Gethsemane

³⁶Then Jesus went with his disciples to a place called Gethsemane, and he said to them, "Sit here while I go over there and pray." ³⁷He took Peter and the two sons of Zebedee along with him, and he began to be sorrowful and troubled. ³⁸Then he said to them, "My soul is overwhelmed with sorrow to the point of death. Stay here and keep watch with me."

³⁹Going a little farther, he fell with his face to the ground and prayed, "My Father, if it is possible, may this cup be taken from me. Yet not as I will, but as you will."

⁴⁰Then he returned to his disciples and found them sleeping. "Couldn't you men keep watch with me for one hour?" he asked Peter. ⁴¹"Watch and pray so that you will not fall into temptation. The spirit is willing, but the flesh is weak."

⁴²He went away a second time and prayed, "My Father, if it is not possible for

---

ᵃ 11 See Deut. 15:11.   ᵇ 28 Some manuscripts *the new*   ᶜ 31 Zech. 13:7

this cup to be taken away unless I drink it, may your will be done."

⁴³When he came back, he again found them sleeping, because their eyes were heavy. ⁴⁴So he left them and went away once more and prayed the third time, saying the same thing.

⁴⁵Then he returned to the disciples and said to them, "Are you still sleeping and resting? Look, the hour is near, and the Son of Man is delivered into the hands of sinners. ⁴⁶Rise! Let us go! Here comes my betrayer!"

Jesus Arrested

⁴⁷While he was still speaking, Judas, one of the Twelve, arrived. With him was a large crowd armed with swords and clubs, sent from the chief priests and the elders of the people. ⁴⁸Now the betrayer had arranged a signal with them: "The one I kiss is the man; arrest him." ⁴⁹Going at once to Jesus, Judas said, "Greetings, Rabbi!" and kissed him.

⁵⁰Jesus replied, "Friend, do what you came for." *a*

Then the men stepped forward, seized Jesus and arrested him. ⁵¹With that, one of Jesus' companions reached for his sword, drew it out and struck the servant of the high priest, cutting off his ear.

⁵²"Put your sword back in its place," Jesus said to him, "for all who draw the sword will die by the sword. ⁵³Do you think I cannot call on my Father, and he will at once put at my disposal more than twelve legions of angels? ⁵⁴But how then would the Scriptures be fulfilled that say it must happen in this way?"

⁵⁵In that hour Jesus said to the crowd, "Am I leading a rebellion, that you have come out with swords and clubs to capture me? Every day I sat in the temple courts teaching, and you did not arrest me. ⁵⁶But this has all taken place that the writings of the prophets might be fulfilled." Then all the disciples deserted him and fled.

Jesus Before the Sanhedrin

⁵⁷Those who had arrested Jesus took him to Caiaphas the high priest, where the teachers of the law and the elders had assembled. ⁵⁸But Peter followed him at a distance, right up to the courtyard of the high priest. He entered and sat down with the guards to see the outcome.

⁵⁹The chief priests and the whole Sanhedrin were looking for false evidence against Jesus so that they could put him to death. ⁶⁰But they did not find any, though many false witnesses came forward.

Finally two came forward ⁶¹and declared, "This fellow said, 'I am able to destroy the temple of God and rebuild it in three days.' "

⁶²Then the high priest stood up and said to Jesus, "Are you not going to answer? What is this testimony that these men are bringing against you?" ⁶³But Jesus remained silent.

The high priest said to him, "I charge you under oath by the living God: Tell us if you are the Messiah, the Son of God."

⁶⁴"You have said so," Jesus replied. "But I say to all of you: From now on you will see the Son of Man sitting at the right hand of the Mighty One and coming on the clouds of heaven." *b*

⁶⁵Then the high priest tore his clothes and said, "He has spoken blasphemy! Why do we need any more witnesses? Look, now you have heard the blasphemy. ⁶⁶What do you think?"

"He is worthy of death," they answered.

⁶⁷Then they spit in his face and struck him with their fists. Others slapped him ⁶⁸and said, "Prophesy to us, Messiah. Who hit you?"

Peter Disowns Jesus

⁶⁹Now Peter was sitting out in the courtyard, and a servant girl came to him. "You also were with Jesus of Galilee," she said.

⁷⁰But he denied it before them all. "I don't know what you're talking about," he said.

⁷¹Then he went out to the gateway, where another servant girl saw him and said to the people there, "This fellow was with Jesus of Nazareth."

⁷²He denied it again, with an oath: "I don't know the man!"

⁷³After a little while, those standing there went up to Peter and said, "Surely you are one of them; your accent gives you away."

⁷⁴Then he began to call down curses, and he swore to them, "I don't know the man!" Immediately a rooster crowed. ⁷⁵Then

---

a 50 Or *"Friend, why have you come?"*   *b 64* See Psalm 110:1; Daniel 7:13.

Peter remembered the word Jesus had spoken: "Before the rooster crows, you will disown me three times." And he went outside and wept bitterly.

Judas Hangs Himself

27 Early in the morning, all the chief priests and the elders of the people came to the decision to put Jesus to death. ²They bound him, led him away and handed him over to Pilate the governor.

³When Judas, who had betrayed him, saw that Jesus was condemned, he was seized with remorse and returned the thirty pieces of silver to the chief priests and the elders. ⁴"I have sinned," he said, "for I have betrayed innocent blood."

"What is that to us?" they replied. "That's your responsibility."

⁵So Judas threw the money into the temple and left. Then he went away and hanged himself.

⁶The chief priests picked up the coins and said, "It is against the law to put this into the treasury, since it is blood money." ⁷So they decided to use the money to buy the potter's field as a burial place for foreigners. ⁸That is why it has been called the Field of Blood to this day. ⁹Then what was spoken by Jeremiah the prophet was fulfilled: "They took the thirty pieces of silver, the price set on him by the people of Israel, ¹⁰and they used them to buy the potter's field, as the Lord commanded me."ᵃ

Jesus Before Pilate

¹¹Meanwhile Jesus stood before the governor, and the governor asked him, "Are you the king of the Jews?"

"You have said so," Jesus replied.

¹²When he was accused by the chief priests and the elders, he gave no answer. ¹³Then Pilate asked him, "Don't you hear the testimony they are bringing against you?" ¹⁴But Jesus made no reply, not even to a single charge—to the great amazement of the governor.

¹⁵Now it was the governor's custom at the festival to release a prisoner chosen by the crowd. ¹⁶At that time they had a well-known prisoner whose name was Jesusᵇ Barabbas. ¹⁷So when the crowd had gathered, Pilate asked them, "Which one do you want me to release to you: Jesus Barabbas, or Jesus who is called the Messiah?" ¹⁸For he knew it was out of envy that they had handed Jesus over to him.

¹⁹While Pilate was sitting on the judge's seat, his wife sent him this message: "Don't have anything to do with that innocent man, for I have suffered a great deal today in a dream because of him."

²⁰But the chief priests and the elders persuaded the crowd to ask for Barabbas and to have Jesus executed.

²¹"Which of the two do you want me to release to you?" asked the governor.

"Barabbas," they answered.

²²"What shall I do, then, with Jesus who is called the Messiah?" Pilate asked.

They all answered, "Crucify him!"

²³"Why? What crime has he committed?" asked Pilate.

But they shouted all the louder, "Crucify him!"

²⁴When Pilate saw that he was getting nowhere, but that instead an uproar was starting, he took water and washed his hands in front of the crowd. "I am innocent of this man's blood," he said. "It is your responsibility!"

²⁵All the people answered, "His blood is on us and on our children!"

²⁶Then he released Barabbas to them. But he had Jesus flogged, and handed him over to be crucified.

The Soldiers Mock Jesus

²⁷Then the governor's soldiers took Jesus into the Praetorium and gathered the whole company of soldiers around him. ²⁸They stripped him and put a scarlet robe on him, ²⁹and then twisted together a crown of thorns and set it on his head. They put a staff in his right hand as a scepter. Then they knelt in front of him and mocked him. "Hail, king of the Jews!" they said. ³⁰They spit on him, and took the staff and struck him on the head again and again. ³¹After they had mocked him, they took off the robe and put his own clothes on him. Then they led him away to crucify him.

The Crucifixion of Jesus

³²As they were going out, they met a man from Cyrene, named Simon, and they forced

---

ᵃ 10 See Zech. 11:12,13; Jer. 19:1-13; 32:6-9.   ᵇ 16 Many manuscripts do not have *Jesus*; also in verse 17.

him to carry the cross. ³³They came to a place called Golgotha (which means "the place of the skull"). ³⁴There they offered Jesus wine to drink, mixed with gall; but after tasting it, he refused to drink it. ³⁵When they had crucified him, they divided up his clothes by casting lots. ³⁶And sitting down, they kept watch over him there. ³⁷Above his head they placed the written charge against him: THIS IS JESUS, THE KING OF THE JEWS.

³⁸Two rebels were crucified with him, one on his right and one on his left. ³⁹Those who passed by hurled insults at him, shaking their heads ⁴⁰and saying, "You who are going to destroy the temple and build it in three days, save yourself! Come down from the cross, if you are the Son of God!"

⁴¹In the same way the chief priests, the teachers of the law and the elders mocked him. ⁴²"He saved others," they said, "but he can't save himself! He's the king of Israel! Let him come down now from the cross, and we will believe in him. ⁴³He trusts in God. Let God rescue him now if he wants him, for he said, 'I am the Son of God.' " ⁴⁴In the same way the rebels who were crucified with him also heaped insults on him.

The Death of Jesus

⁴⁵From noon until three in the afternoon darkness came over all the land. ⁴⁶About three in the afternoon Jesus cried out in a loud voice, *"Eli, Eli,ᵃ lema sabachthani?"* (which means "My God, my God, why have you forsaken me?").ᵇ

⁴⁷When some of those standing there heard this, they said, "He's calling Elijah."

⁴⁸Immediately one of them ran and got a sponge. He filled it with wine vinegar, put it on a staff, and offered it to Jesus to drink. ⁴⁹The rest said, "Now leave him alone. Let's see if Elijah comes to save him."

⁵⁰And when Jesus had cried out again in a loud voice, he gave up his spirit.

⁵¹At that moment the curtain of the temple was torn in two from top to bottom. The earth shook, the rocks split ⁵²and the tombs broke open. The bodies of many holy people who had died were raised to life. ⁵³They came out of the tombs after Jesus' resurrection andᶜ went into the holy city and appeared to many people.

⁵⁴When the centurion and those with him who were guarding Jesus saw the earthquake and all that had happened, they were terrified, and exclaimed, "Surely he was the Son of God!"

⁵⁵Many women were there, watching from a distance. They had followed Jesus from Galilee to care for his needs. ⁵⁶Among them were Mary Magdalene, Mary the mother of James and Joseph,ᵈ and the mother of Zebedee's sons.

The Burial of Jesus

⁵⁷As evening approached, there came a rich man from Arimathea, named Joseph, who had himself become a disciple of Jesus. ⁵⁸Going to Pilate, he asked for Jesus' body, and Pilate ordered that it be given to him. ⁵⁹Joseph took the body, wrapped it in a clean linen cloth, ⁶⁰and placed it in his own new tomb that he had cut out of the rock. He rolled a big stone in front of the entrance to the tomb and went away. ⁶¹Mary Magdalene and the other Mary were sitting there opposite the tomb.

The Guard at the Tomb

⁶²The next day, the one after Preparation Day, the chief priests and the Pharisees went to Pilate. ⁶³"Sir," they said, "we remember that while he was still alive that deceiver said, 'After three days I will rise again.' ⁶⁴So give the order for the tomb to be made secure until the third day. Otherwise, his disciples may come and steal the body and tell the people that he has been raised from the dead. This last deception will be worse than the first."

⁶⁵"Take a guard," Pilate answered. "Go, make the tomb as secure as you know how." ⁶⁶So they went and made the tomb secure by putting a seal on the stone and posting the guard.

Jesus Has Risen

28 After the Sabbath, at dawn on the first day of the week, Mary Magdalene and the other Mary went to look at the tomb.

²There was a violent earthquake, for an angel of the Lord came down from heaven and, going to the tomb, rolled back the stone

---

ᵃ 46 Some manuscripts *Eloi, Eloi*   ᵇ 46 Psalm 22:1   ᶜ 53 Or *tombs, and after Jesus' resurrection they*
ᵈ 56 Greek *Joses*, a variant of *Joseph*

THURSDAY

THE POWER OF THE RESURRECTION

Matthew 28:1–20 *or* 28:5–9

Brennan Manning

Standing on a London street corner, G. K. Chesterton was approached by a newspaper reporter. "Sir, I understand that you recently became a Christian. May I ask you one question?"

"Certainly," replied Chesterton.

"If the risen Christ suddenly appeared at this very moment and stood behind you, what would you do?"

Chesterton looked the reporter squarely in the eye and said, "He is."

Is this a mere figure of speech, wishful thinking, a piece of pious rhetoric? No, this truth is the most real fact about our life; it is our life. The Jesus who walked the roads of Judea and Galilee is the one who stands beside us. The Christ of history is the Christ of faith . . .

What gives the teaching of Jesus its power? What distinguishes it from the Koran, the teachings of Buddha, the wisdom of Confucius? *The risen Christ does.* For example, if Jesus did not rise we can safely praise the Sermon on the Mount as a magnificent ethic. If He did, praise doesn't matter. The sermon becomes a portrait of our ultimate destiny. The transforming force of the Word resides in the risen Lord who stands by it and thereby gives it final and present meaning . . .

When through faith we fully accept that Jesus is who he claims to be, we experience the risen Christ.

God raised Jesus. This is the apostolic witness, the heart of the apostolic preaching. Scripture presents only two alternatives: either you believe in the resurrection and you believe in Jesus of Nazareth, or you don't believe in the resurrection and you don't believe in Jesus of Nazareth.

JOHN BUNYAN {AD 1628–1688}

Just as he died for our sin, so he rose again that we might be released from it. Through both his death and resurrection he accomplished good things on our behalf. He died for us, he rose from the dead for us . . . By his death he carried away our sins, and by his rising he brought to us justifying righteousness.

reflection

1. How is God's power seen through the resurrection of Jesus?

2. How would the message of Christianity be different if Jesus had not risen from the dead?

3. In what way does Christ's resurrection impact your life?

For your next devotional reading, go to page 1121.

and sat on it. ³His appearance was like lightning, and his clothes were white as snow. ⁴The guards were so afraid of him that they shook and became like dead men.

⁵The angel said to the women, "Do not be afraid, for I know that you are looking for Jesus, who was crucified. ⁶He is not here; he has risen, just as he said. Come and see the place where he lay. ⁷Then go quickly and tell his disciples: 'He has risen from the dead and is going ahead of you into Galilee. There you will see him.' Now I have told you."

⁸So the women hurried away from the tomb, afraid yet filled with joy, and ran to tell his disciples. ⁹Suddenly Jesus met them. "Greetings," he said. They came to him, clasped his feet and worshiped him. ¹⁰Then Jesus said to them, "Do not be afraid. Go and tell my brothers to go to Galilee; there they will see me."

The Guards' Report

¹¹While the women were on their way, some of the guards went into the city and reported to the chief priests everything that had happened. ¹²When the chief priests had met with the elders and devised a plan, they gave the soldiers a large sum of money, ¹³telling them, "You are to say, 'His disciples came during the night and stole him away while we were asleep.' ¹⁴If this report gets to the governor, we will satisfy him and keep you out of trouble." ¹⁵So the soldiers took the money and did as they were instructed. And this story has been widely circulated among the Jews to this very day.

The Great Commission

¹⁶Then the eleven disciples went to Galilee, to the mountain where Jesus had told them to go. ¹⁷When they saw him, they worshiped him; but some doubted. ¹⁸Then Jesus came to them and said, "All authority in heaven and on earth has been given to me. ¹⁹Therefore go and make disciples of all nations, baptizing them in*ᵃ* the name of the Father and of the Son and of the Holy Spirit, ²⁰and teaching them to obey everything I have commanded you. And surely I am with you always, to the very end of the age."

---

a 19 Or *into*; see Acts 8:16; 19:5; Romans 6:3; 1 Cor. 1:13; 10:2; Gal. 3:27.

mark

AUTHOR:	John Mark
DATE:	Probably between A.D. 55 and 65
THEME:	Jesus came to suffer on our behalf and to call us to take up our own cross.

John the Baptist Prepares the Way

1 The beginning of the good news about Jesus the Messiah,[a,b] [2]as it is written in Isaiah the prophet:

"I will send my messenger ahead of you,
   who will prepare your way"[c]—
[3]"a voice of one calling in the wilderness,
'Prepare the way for the Lord,
   make straight paths for him.' "[d]

[4]And so John the Baptist appeared in the wilderness, preaching a baptism of repentance for the forgiveness of sins. [5]The whole Judean countryside and all the people of Jerusalem went out to him. Confessing their sins, they were baptized by him in the Jordan River. [6]John wore clothing made of camel's hair, with a leather belt around his waist, and he ate locusts and wild honey. [7]And this was his message: "After me comes the one more powerful than I, the thongs of whose sandals I am not worthy to stoop down and untie. [8]I baptize you with[e] water, but he will baptize you with[e] the Holy Spirit."

The Baptism and Testing of Jesus

[9]At that time Jesus came from Nazareth in Galilee and was baptized by John in the Jordan. [10]Just as Jesus was coming up out of the water, he saw heaven being torn open and the Spirit descending on him like a dove. [11]And a voice came from heaven: "You are my Son, whom I love; with you I am well pleased."

[12]At once the Spirit sent him out into the wilderness, [13]and he was in the wilderness forty days, being tempted[f] by Satan. He was with the wild animals, and angels attended him.

Jesus Announces the Good News

[14]After John was put in prison, Jesus went into Galilee, proclaiming the good news of God. [15]"The time has come," he said. "The kingdom of God has come near. Repent and believe the good news!"

Jesus Calls His First Disciples

[16]As Jesus walked beside the Sea of Galilee, he saw Simon and his brother Andrew casting a net into the lake, for they were fishermen. [17]"Come, follow me," Jesus said, "and I will send you out to fish for people." [18]At once they left their nets and followed him.

[19]When he had gone a little farther, he saw James son of Zebedee and his brother John in a boat, preparing their nets. [20]Without delay he called them, and they left their father Zebedee in the boat with the hired men and followed him.

Jesus Drives Out an Evil Spirit

[21]They went to Capernaum, and when the Sabbath came, Jesus went into the synagogue and began to teach. [22]The people were amazed at his teaching, because he taught them as one who had authority, not as the teachers of the law. [23]Just then a man in their synagogue who was possessed by an evil[g] spirit cried out, [24]"What do you want with us, Jesus of Nazareth? Have you come

---

a 1 Or *Jesus Christ. Messiah* (Hebrew) and *Christ* (Greek) both mean *Anointed One.*   *b 1* Many manuscripts *Messiah, the Son of God*   *c 2* Mal. 3:1   *d 3* Isaiah 40:3   *e 8* Or *in*   *f 13* The Greek for *tempted* can also mean *tested.*   *g 23* Greek *unclean*; also in verses 26 and 27

GOD HATES SUFFERING

Mark 1:21–45 *or* 1:29–34

Joni Eareckson Tada

Everyone who takes the Bible seriously, and many who don't, agree that God hates suffering. Jesus spent much of his short life relieving it. In scores of passages God tells us to feed the hungry, clothe the poor, visit inmates and speak up for the helpless. So when we feel compassion for people in distress, we know that God felt it first. He shows this by raising sick people from their beds—sometimes to the wonder of doctors—in answer to prayer. Every day he grants childless women babies, pulls small-business owners out of financial pits, protects Alzheimer's patients crossing the street and writes happy endings to sad situations. Even when he has to punish sin, he says it gives him no pleasure (Ezekiel 18:32). In heaven, Eden's curse will be canceled. Sighs and longings will be historical curiosities. Tears will evaporate. Kleenex will go broke.

DOROTHY SAYERS {AD 1893–1967}

For whatever reason God chose to make man as he is—limited and suffering and subject to sorrows and death—he had the honesty and courage to take his own medicine. Whatever game he is playing with his creation, he has kept his own rules and played fair. He can exact nothing from man that he has not exacted from himself. He has himself gone through the whole of human experience from trivial irritations of family life and the cramping restrictions of hard work and lack of money to the worst horrors of pain and humiliation, defeat, despair and death. When he was a man, he played the man. He was born in poverty and died in disgrace and thought it well worthwhile.

reflection

1. Do you ever feel like no one understands how you feel?

2. How does Jesus' life and death give you hope when you experience the hurt and pain of hard things in your own life?

3. What do you learn about the heart of God through Jesus' interaction with the hurting, the diseased and the demon-possessed?

For your next devotional reading, go to page 1123.

to destroy us? I know who you are—the Holy One of God!"

25"Be quiet!" said Jesus sternly. "Come out of him!" 26The evil spirit shook the man violently and came out of him with a shriek.

27The people were all so amazed that they asked each other, "What is this? A new teaching—and with authority! He even gives orders to evil spirits and they obey him." 28News about him spread quickly over the whole region of Galilee.

Jesus Heals Many

29As soon as they left the synagogue, they went with James and John to the home of Simon and Andrew. 30Simon's mother-in-law was in bed with a fever, and they immediately told Jesus about her. 31So he went to her, took her hand and helped her up. The fever left her and she began to wait on them.

32That evening after sunset the people brought to Jesus all the sick and demon-possessed. 33The whole town gathered at the door, 34and Jesus healed many who had various diseases. He also drove out many demons, but he would not let the demons speak because they knew who he was.

Jesus Prays in a Solitary Place

35Very early in the morning, while it was still dark, Jesus got up, left the house and went off to a solitary place, where he prayed. 36Simon and his companions went to look for him, 37and when they found him, they exclaimed: "Everyone is looking for you!"

38Jesus replied, "Let us go somewhere else—to the nearby villages—so I can preach there also. That is why I have come." 39So he traveled throughout Galilee, preaching in their synagogues and driving out demons.

Jesus Heals a Man With Leprosy

40A man with leprosy[a] came to him and begged him on his knees, "If you are willing, you can make me clean."

41Jesus was indignant.[b] He reached out his hand and touched the man. "I am willing," he said. "Be clean!" 42Immediately the leprosy left him and he was cleansed.

43Jesus sent him away at once with a strong warning: 44"See that you don't tell this to anyone. But go, show yourself to the priest and offer the sacrifices that Moses commanded for your cleansing, as a testimony to them." 45Instead he went out and began to talk freely, spreading the news. As a result, Jesus could no longer enter a town openly but stayed outside in lonely places. Yet the people still came to him from everywhere.

Jesus Forgives and Heals a Paralyzed Man

2 A few days later, when Jesus again entered Capernaum, the people heard that he had come home. 2They gathered in such large numbers that there was no room left, not even outside the door, and he preached the word to them. 3Some men came, bringing to him a paralyzed man, carried by four of them. 4Since they could not get him to Jesus because of the crowd, they made an opening in the roof above Jesus by digging through it and then lowered the mat the man was lying on. 5When Jesus saw their faith, he said to the paralyzed man, "Son, your sins are forgiven."

6Now some teachers of the law were sitting there, thinking to themselves, 7"Why does this fellow talk like that? He's blaspheming! Who can forgive sins but God alone?"

8Immediately Jesus knew in his spirit that this was what they were thinking in their hearts, and he said to them, "Why are you thinking these things? 9Which is easier: to say to this paralyzed man, 'Your sins are forgiven,' or to say, 'Get up, take your mat and walk'? 10But I want you to know that the Son of Man has authority on earth to forgive sins." So he said to the man, 11"I tell you, get up, take your mat and go home." 12He got up, took his mat and walked out in full view of them all. This amazed everyone and they praised God, saying, "We have never seen anything like this!"

Jesus Calls Levi and Eats With Sinners

13Once again Jesus went out beside the lake. A large crowd came to him, and he began to teach them. 14As he walked along, he saw Levi son of Alphaeus sitting at the tax

a 40 The Greek word traditionally translated leprosy was used for various diseases affecting the skin.
b 41 Many manuscripts Jesus was filled with compassion

What God Wants

Mark 1:40–42

read/meditate

Read Mark 1:40–42 slowly several times. How would you describe that man's faith in Jesus? Basically, he said, "I know you have the power to do something good for me, but do you *want* to do something good for me?" How does his faith compare to your own?

pray

Lay your requests before God. Let him know what you need. Tell him honestly what you believe about his willingness to step into your life and do something. Then wait with him, open to whatever he might reveal about what he thinks your life needs.

contemplate

As you approach God, do you believe in your own heart and soul that he has the power to do something good in your life? Do you believe he wants to?

additional reflection

In Jesus, the service of God and the service of the least of the brethren were one.
—*Dietrich Bonhoeffer*
Some people think God does not like to be troubled with our constant coming and asking. The way to trouble God is not to come at all.
—*D. L. Moody*

For your next devotional reading, go to page 1126.

collector's booth. "Follow me," Jesus told him, and Levi got up and followed him.

¹⁵While Jesus was having dinner at Levi's house, many tax collectors and sinners were eating with him and his disciples, for there were many who followed him. ¹⁶When the teachers of the law who were Pharisees saw him eating with the sinners and tax collectors, they asked his disciples: "Why does he eat with tax collectors and sinners?"

¹⁷On hearing this, Jesus said to them, "It is not the healthy who need a doctor, but the sick. I have not come to call the righteous, but sinners."

Jesus Questioned About Fasting

¹⁸Now John's disciples and the Pharisees were fasting. Some people came and asked Jesus, "How is it that John's disciples and the disciples of the Pharisees are fasting, but yours are not?"

¹⁹Jesus answered, "How can the guests of the bridegroom fast while he is with them? They cannot, so long as they have him with them. ²⁰But the time will come when the bridegroom will be taken from them, and on that day they will fast.

²¹"No one sews a patch of unshrunk cloth on an old garment. If they do, the new piece will pull away from the old, making the tear worse. ²²And people do not pour new wine into old wineskins. If they do, the wine will burst the skins, and both the wine and the wineskins will be ruined. No, they pour new wine into new wineskins."

Jesus Is Lord of the Sabbath

²³One Sabbath Jesus was going through the grainfields, and as his disciples walked along, they began to pick some heads of grain. ²⁴The Pharisees said to him, "Look, why are they doing what is unlawful on the Sabbath?"

²⁵He answered, "Have you never read what David did when he and his companions were hungry and in need? ²⁶In the days of Abiathar the high priest, he entered the house of God and ate the consecrated bread, which is lawful only for priests to eat. And he also gave some to his companions."

²⁷Then he said to them, "The Sabbath was made for people, not people for the Sabbath. ²⁸So the Son of Man is Lord even of the Sabbath."

Jesus Heals on the Sabbath

3 Another time Jesus went into the synagogue, and a man with a shriveled hand was there. ²Some of them were looking for a reason to accuse Jesus, so they watched him closely to see if he would heal him on the Sabbath. ³Jesus said to the man with the shriveled hand, "Stand up in front of everyone."

⁴Then Jesus asked them, "Which is lawful on the Sabbath: to do good or to do evil, to save life or to kill?" But they remained silent.

⁵He looked around at them in anger and, deeply distressed at their stubborn hearts, said to the man, "Stretch out your hand." He stretched it out, and his hand was completely restored. ⁶Then the Pharisees went out and began to plot with the Herodians how they might kill Jesus.

Crowds Follow Jesus

⁷Jesus withdrew with his disciples to the lake, and a large crowd from Galilee followed. ⁸When they heard all he was doing, many people came to him from Judea, Jerusalem, Idumea, and the regions across the Jordan and around Tyre and Sidon. ⁹Because of the crowd he told his disciples to have a small boat ready for him, to keep the people from crowding him. ¹⁰For he had healed many, so that those with diseases were pushing forward to touch him. ¹¹Whenever the evil ᵃ spirits saw him, they fell down before him and cried out, "You are the Son of God." ¹²But he gave them strict orders not to tell others about him.

Jesus Appoints the Twelve

¹³Jesus went up on a mountainside and called to him those he wanted, and they came to him. ¹⁴He appointed twelve ᵇ that they might be with him and that he might send them out to preach ¹⁵and to have authority to drive out demons. ¹⁶These are the twelve he appointed: Simon (to whom he gave the name Peter), ¹⁷James son of Zebedee and his brother John (to them he gave the name Boanerges, which means "sons of thunder"), ¹⁸Andrew, Philip, Bartholomew,

---

ᵃ 11 Greek unclean; also in verse 30   ᵇ 14 Some manuscripts twelve—designating them apostles—

Matthew, Thomas, James son of Alphaeus, Thaddaeus, Simon the Zealot [19]and Judas Iscariot, who betrayed him.

Jesus Accused by His Family and by Teachers of the Law

[20]Then Jesus entered a house, and again a crowd gathered, so that he and his disciples were not even able to eat. [21]When his family[a] heard about this, they went to take charge of him, for they said, "He is out of his mind."

[22]And the teachers of the law who came down from Jerusalem said, "He is possessed by Beelzebul! By the prince of demons he is driving out demons."

[23]So Jesus called them over to him and began to speak to them in parables: "How can Satan drive out Satan? [24]If a kingdom is divided against itself, that kingdom cannot stand. [25]If a house is divided against itself, that house cannot stand. [26]And if Satan opposes himself and is divided, he cannot stand; his end has come. [27]In fact, no one can enter a strong man's house without first tying him up. Then he can plunder the strong man's house. [28]Truly I tell you, people will be forgiven all their sins and all the blasphemies they utter. [29]But whoever blasphemes against the Holy Spirit will never be forgiven, but is guilty of an eternal sin."

[30]He said this because they were saying, "He has an evil spirit."

[31]Then Jesus' mother and brothers arrived. Standing outside, they sent someone in to call him. [32]A crowd was sitting around him, and they told him, "Your mother and brothers are outside looking for you."

[33]"Who are my mother and my brothers?" he asked.

[34]Then he looked at those seated in a circle around him and said, "Here are my mother and my brothers! [35]Whoever does God's will is my brother and sister and mother."

The Parable of the Sower

4 Again Jesus began to teach by the lake. The crowd that gathered around him was so large that he got into a boat and sat in it out on the lake, while all the people were along the shore at the water's edge. [2]He taught them many things by parables, and in his teaching said: [3]"Listen! A farmer went out to sow his seed. [4]As he was scattering the seed, some fell along the path, and the birds came and ate it up. [5]Some fell on rocky places, where it did not have much soil. It sprang up quickly, because the soil was shallow. [6]But when the sun came up, the plants were scorched, and they withered because they had no root. [7]Other seed fell among thorns, which grew up and choked the plants, so that they did not bear grain. [8]Still other seed fell on good soil. It came up, grew and produced a crop, some multiplying thirty, some sixty, some a hundred times."

[9]Then Jesus said, "Whoever has ears to hear, let them hear."

[10]When he was alone, the Twelve and the others around him asked him about the parables. [11]He told them, "The secret of the kingdom of God has been given to you. But to those on the outside everything is said in parables [12]so that,

" 'they may be ever seeing but never
            perceiving,
    and ever hearing but never
            understanding;
    otherwise they might turn and be
            forgiven!'[b]

[13]Then Jesus said to them, "Don't you understand this parable? How then will you understand any parable? [14]The farmer sows the word. [15]Some people are like seed along the path, where the word is sown. As soon as they hear it, Satan comes and takes away the word that was sown in them. [16]Others, like seed sown on rocky places, hear the word and at once receive it with joy. [17]But since they have no root, they last only a short time. When trouble or persecution comes because of the word, they quickly fall away. [18]Still others, like seed sown among thorns, hear the word; [19]but the worries of this life, the deceitfulness of wealth and the desires for other things come in and choke the word, making it unfruitful. [20]Others, like seed sown on good soil, hear the word, accept it, and produce a crop—some thirty, some sixty, some a hundred times what was sown."

a 21 Or his associates   b 12 Isaiah 6:9,10

SOILS, SEEDS AND THE SPIRIT

Mark 4:1–20 or 4:14–20

Francis X. Gaeta

The [Parable] of the Sower is one we've heard so often that it sometimes just doesn't impress us anymore. We've all heard the sermons, and we all know different kinds of soil will predict how well the seed will be able to take root and grow. We have all tried to improve the soil of our hearts so that the pressed down soil of the footpath might become soft, the stones might be removed from the rocky soil and the thorn bushes might be cut away so that the seed might come to life . . .

It can become very discouraging to think how little progress we might have made and how far we have to go. It would indeed depress us and discourage us but for one thing: the sower doesn't go out to sow just once. The Lord is constantly sowing the seed of his love. He doesn't come by just once and give up on us because we are not able to absorb his grace and love. The Lord is continuously sowing, calling, coaxing, inviting and nudging us closer and closer to him . . .

He loves us passionately and without condition. He doesn't love us only when the soil is right. He loves us when we're hard, lifeless, loveless, thorny and totally self-centered . . . We don't get just one chance with the Lord. Each time he comes by we're just a little bit more able and ready to embrace him and accept him.

How patient he is! How much he loves us! He just never gives up. He keeps coming by; he keeps calling and inviting. He keeps waiting for the day we say to him: "Here I am, Lord."

OSWALD CHAMBERS {AD 1874–1917}

Many people are trying to live the life of a Christian who have not been born again by the Spirit of God. My friend, if you are in this class, your difficulties will drive you insane. You cannot possibly live the Christian life unless you have received the strength of the Lord in the new birth. The thorns of life will choke you. In the parable of the sower, thorns represent the cares of this life or anything that will hinder you spiritually. Remember, if you determine to go with God, you will have difficulties.

reflection

1. How would you describe the soil of your heart?
2. Why is it impossible to maintain "good soil" in your heart solely through your own efforts?
3. Think of three examples that illustrate that the Sower's seed has taken root in your heart.

For your next devotional reading, go to page 1133.

A Lamp on a Stand

²¹He said to them, "Do you bring in a lamp to put it under a bowl or a bed? Instead, don't you put it on its stand? ²²For whatever is hidden is meant to be disclosed, and whatever is concealed is meant to be brought out into the open. ²³If anyone has ears to hear, let them hear."

²⁴"Consider carefully what you hear," he continued. "With the measure you use, it will be measured to you—and even more. ²⁵Those who have will be given more; as for those who do not have, even what they have will be taken from them."

The Parable of the Growing Seed

²⁶He also said, "This is what the kingdom of God is like. A man scatters seed on the ground. ²⁷Night and day, whether he sleeps or gets up, the seed sprouts and grows, though he does not know how. ²⁸All by itself the soil produces grain—first the stalk, then the head, then the full kernel in the head. ²⁹As soon as the grain is ripe, he puts the sickle to it, because the harvest has come."

The Parable of the Mustard Seed

³⁰Again he said, "What shall we say the kingdom of God is like, or what parable shall we use to describe it? ³¹It is like a mustard seed, which is the smallest of all seeds on earth. ³²Yet when planted, it grows and becomes the largest of all garden plants, with such big branches that the birds can perch in its shade."

³³With many similar parables Jesus spoke the word to them, as much as they could understand. ³⁴He did not say anything to them without using a parable. But when he was alone with his own disciples, he explained everything.

Jesus Calms the Storm

³⁵That day when evening came, he said to his disciples, "Let us go over to the other side." ³⁶Leaving the crowd behind, they took him along, just as he was, in the boat. There were also other boats with him. ³⁷A furious squall came up, and the waves broke over the boat, so that it was nearly swamped. ³⁸Jesus was in the stern, sleeping on a cush-

ion. The disciples woke him and said to him, "Teacher, don't you care if we drown?"

³⁹He got up, rebuked the wind and said to the waves, "Quiet! Be still!" Then the wind died down and it was completely calm.

⁴⁰He said to his disciples, "Why are you so afraid? Do you still have no faith?"

⁴¹They were terrified and asked each other, "Who is this? Even the wind and the waves obey him!"

Jesus Restores a Demon-Possessed Man

5 They went across the lake to the region of the Gerasenes.ᵃ ²When Jesus got out of the boat, a man with an evilᵇ spirit came from the tombs to meet him. ³This man lived in the tombs, and no one could bind him anymore, not even with a chain. ⁴For he had often been chained hand and foot, but he tore the chains apart and broke the irons on his feet. No one was strong enough to subdue him. ⁵Night and day among the tombs and in the hills he would cry out and cut himself with stones.

⁶When he saw Jesus from a distance, he ran and fell on his knees in front of him. ⁷He shouted at the top of his voice, "What do you want with me, Jesus, Son of the Most High God? In God's name don't torture me!" ⁸For Jesus had said to him, "Come out of this man, you evil spirit!"

⁹Then Jesus asked him, "What is your name?"

"My name is Legion," he replied, "for we are many." ¹⁰And he begged Jesus again and again not to send them out of the area.

¹¹A large herd of pigs was feeding on the nearby hillside. ¹²The demons begged Jesus, "Send us among the pigs; allow us to go into them." ¹³He gave them permission, and the evil spirits came out and went into the pigs. The herd, about two thousand in number, rushed down the steep bank into the lake and were drowned.

¹⁴Those tending the pigs ran off and reported this in the town and countryside, and the people went out to see what had happened. ¹⁵When they came to Jesus, they saw the man who had been possessed by the legion of demons, sitting there, dressed and in his right mind; and they were afraid. ¹⁶Those who had seen it told the people what had

ᵃ 1 Some manuscripts Gadarenes; other manuscripts Gergesenes   ᵇ 2 Greek unclean; also in verses 8 and 13 happened to the demon-possessed man—and told about the pigs as well. ¹⁷Then the people began to plead with Jesus to leave their region.

¹⁸As Jesus was getting into the boat, the man who had been demon-possessed begged to go with him. ¹⁹Jesus did not let him, but said, "Go home to your own people and tell them how much the Lord has done for you, and how he has had mercy on you." ²⁰So the man went away and began to tell in the Decapolis[a] how much Jesus had done for him. And all the people were amazed.

Jesus Raises a Dead Girl and Heals a Sick Woman

²¹When Jesus had again crossed over by boat to the other side of the lake, a large crowd gathered around him while he was by the lake. ²²Then one of the synagogue leaders, named Jairus, came, and when he saw Jesus, he fell at his feet. ²³He pleaded earnestly with him, "My little daughter is dying. Please come and put your hands on her so that she will be healed and live." ²⁴So Jesus went with him.

A large crowd followed and pressed around him. ²⁵And a woman was there who had been subject to bleeding for twelve years. ²⁶She had suffered a great deal under the care of many doctors and had spent all she had, yet instead of getting better she grew worse. ²⁷When she heard about Jesus, she came up behind him in the crowd and touched his cloak, ²⁸because she thought, "If I just touch his clothes, I will be healed." ²⁹Immediately her bleeding stopped and she felt in her body that she was freed from her suffering.

³⁰At once Jesus realized that power had gone out from him. He turned around in the crowd and asked, "Who touched my clothes?"

³¹"You see the people crowding against you," his disciples answered, "and yet you can ask, 'Who touched me?' "

³²But Jesus kept looking around to see who had done it. ³³Then the woman, knowing what had happened to her, came and fell at his feet and, trembling with fear, told him the whole truth. ³⁴He said to her, "Daughter, your faith has healed you. Go in peace and be freed from your suffering."

³⁵While Jesus was still speaking, some people came from the house of Jairus, the synagogue leader. "Your daughter is dead," they said. "Why bother the teacher anymore?"

³⁶Overhearing[b] what they said, Jesus told him, "Don't be afraid; just believe."

³⁷He did not let anyone follow him except Peter, James and John the brother of James. ³⁸When they came to the home of the synagogue leader, Jesus saw a commotion, with people crying and wailing loudly. ³⁹He went in and said to them, "Why all this commotion and wailing? The child is not dead but asleep." ⁴⁰But they laughed at him.

After he put them all out, he took the child's father and mother and the disciples who were with him, and went in where the child was. ⁴¹He took her by the hand and said to her, *"Talitha koum!"* (which means "Little girl, I say to you, get up!"). ⁴²Immediately the girl stood up and began to walk around (she was twelve years old). At this they were completely astonished. ⁴³He gave strict orders not to let anyone know about this, and told them to give her something to eat.

A Prophet Without Honor

6 Jesus left there and went to his hometown, accompanied by his disciples. ²When the Sabbath came, he began to teach in the synagogue, and many who heard him were amazed.

"Where did this man get these things?" they asked. "What's this wisdom that has been given him? What are these remarkable miracles he is performing? ³Isn't this the carpenter? Isn't this Mary's son and the brother of James, Joseph,[c] Judas and Simon? Aren't his sisters here with us?" And they took offense at him.

⁴Jesus said to them, "Only in their own towns, among their relatives and in their own homes are prophets without honor." ⁵He could not do any miracles there, except lay his hands on a few sick people and heal them. ⁶He was amazed at their lack of faith.

Jesus Sends Out the Twelve

Then Jesus went around teaching from village to village. ⁷Calling the Twelve to him, he began to send them out two by two and gave them authority over evil[d] spirits.

---

a 20 That is, the Ten Cities   *b 36* Or *Ignoring*   *c 3* Greek *Joses*, a variant of *Joseph*   *d 7* Greek *unclean*

8These were his instructions: "Take nothing for the journey except a staff—no bread, no bag, no money in your belts. 9Wear sandals but not an extra shirt. 10Whenever you enter a house, stay there until you leave that town. 11And if any place will not welcome you or listen to you, shake the dust off your feet when you leave, as a testimony against them."

12They went out and preached that people should repent. 13They drove out many demons and anointed many sick people with oil and healed them.

John the Baptist Beheaded

14King Herod heard about this, for Jesus' name had become well known. Some were saying,*a* "John the Baptist has been raised from the dead, and that is why miraculous powers are at work in him."

15Others said, "He is Elijah."

And still others claimed, "He is a prophet, like one of the prophets of long ago."

16But when Herod heard this, he said, "John, whom I beheaded, has been raised from the dead!"

17For Herod himself had given orders to have John arrested, and he had him bound and put in prison. He did this because of Herodias, his brother Philip's wife, whom he had married. 18For John had been saying to Herod, "It is not lawful for you to have your brother's wife." 19So Herodias nursed a grudge against John and wanted to kill him. But she was not able to, 20because Herod feared John and protected him, knowing him to be a righteous and holy man. When Herod heard John, he was greatly puzzled*b*; yet he liked to listen to him.

21Finally the opportune time came. On his birthday Herod gave a banquet for his high officials and military commanders and the leading men of Galilee. 22When the daughter of*c* Herodias came in and danced, she pleased Herod and his dinner guests.

The king said to the girl, "Ask me for anything you want, and I'll give it to you." 23And he promised her with an oath, "Whatever you ask I will give you, up to half my kingdom."

24She went out and said to her mother, "What shall I ask for?"

"The head of John the Baptist," she answered.

25At once the girl hurried in to the king with the request: "I want you to give me right now the head of John the Baptist on a platter."

26The king was greatly distressed, but because of his oaths and his dinner guests, he did not want to refuse her. 27So he immediately sent an executioner with orders to bring John's head. The man went, beheaded John in the prison, 28and brought back his head on a platter. He presented it to the girl, and she gave it to her mother. 29On hearing of this, John's disciples came and took his body and laid it in a tomb.

Jesus Feeds the Five Thousand

30The apostles gathered around Jesus and reported to him all they had done and taught. 31Then, because so many people were coming and going that they did not even have a chance to eat, he said to them, "Come with me by yourselves to a quiet place and get some rest."

32So they went away by themselves in a boat to a solitary place. 33But many who saw them leaving recognized them and ran on foot from all the towns and got there ahead of them. 34When Jesus landed and saw a large crowd, he had compassion on them, because they were like sheep without a shepherd. So he began teaching them many things.

35By this time it was late in the day, so his disciples came to him. "This is a remote place," they said, "and it's already very late. 36Send the people away so that they can go to the surrounding countryside and villages and buy themselves something to eat."

37But he answered, "You give them something to eat."

They said to him, "That would take almost a year's wages*d*! Are we to go and spend that much on bread and give it to them to eat?"

38"How many loaves do you have?" he asked. "Go and see."

When they found out, they said, "Five—and two fish."

39Then Jesus directed them to have all the people sit down in groups on the green

---

a 14 Some early manuscripts *He was saying*   *b 20* Some early manuscripts *he did many things*
c 22 Some early manuscripts *When his daughter*   *d 37* Greek *take two hundred denarii*

grass. ⁴⁰So they sat down in groups of hundreds and fifties. ⁴¹Taking the five loaves and the two fish and looking up to heaven, he gave thanks and broke the loaves. Then he gave them to his disciples to set before the people. He also divided the two fish among them all. ⁴²They all ate and were satisfied, ⁴³and the disciples picked up twelve basketfuls of broken pieces of bread and fish. ⁴⁴The number of the men who had eaten was five thousand.

Jesus Walks on the Water

⁴⁵Immediately Jesus made his disciples get into the boat and go on ahead of him to Bethsaida, while he dismissed the crowd. ⁴⁶After leaving them, he went up on a mountainside to pray.

⁴⁷When evening came, the boat was in the middle of the lake, and he was alone on land. ⁴⁸He saw the disciples straining at the oars, because the wind was against them. Shortly before dawn he went out to them, walking on the lake. He was about to pass by them, ⁴⁹but when they saw him walking on the lake, they thought he was a ghost. They cried out, ⁵⁰because they all saw him and were terrified.

Immediately he spoke to them and said, "Take courage! It is I. Don't be afraid." ⁵¹Then he climbed into the boat with them, and the wind died down. They were completely amazed, ⁵²for they had not understood about the loaves; their hearts were hardened.

⁵³When they had crossed over, they landed at Gennesaret and anchored there. ⁵⁴As soon as they got out of the boat, people recognized Jesus. ⁵⁵They ran throughout that whole region and carried the sick on mats to wherever they heard he was. ⁵⁶And wherever he went—into villages, towns or countryside—they placed the sick in the marketplaces. They begged him to let them touch even the edge of his cloak, and all who touched him were healed.

That Which Defiles

7 The Pharisees and some of the teachers of the law who had come from Jerusalem gathered around Jesus ²and saw some of his disciples eating food with hands that were defiled, that is,

unwashed. ³(The Pharisees and all the Jews do not eat unless they give their hands a ceremonial washing, holding to the tradition of the elders. ⁴When they come from the marketplace they do not eat unless they wash. And they observe many other traditions, such as the washing of cups, pitchers and kettles.ᵃ)

⁵So the Pharisees and teachers of the law asked Jesus, "Why don't your disciples live according to the tradition of the elders instead of eating their food with defiled hands?"

⁶He replied, "Isaiah was right when he prophesied about you hypocrites; as it is written:

" 'These people honor me with their lips,
  but their hearts are far from me.
⁷They worship me in vain;
  their teachings are merely human rules.'ᵇ

⁸You have let go of the commands of God and are holding on to human traditions."

⁹And he continued, "You have a fine way of setting aside the commands of God in order to observeᶜ your own traditions! ¹⁰For Moses said, 'Honor your father and mother,'ᵈ and, 'Anyone who curses their father or mother is to be put to death.'ᵉ ¹¹But you say that if anyone declares that what might have been used to help their father or mother is Corban (that is, devoted to God)— ¹²then you no longer let them do anything for their father or mother. ¹³Thus you nullify the word of God by your tradition that you have handed down. And you do many things like that."

¹⁴Again Jesus called the crowd to him and said, "Listen to me, everyone, and understand this. ¹⁵[¹⁶]Nothing outside you can defile you by going into you. Rather, it is what comes out of you that defiles you."

¹⁷After he had left the crowd and entered the house, his disciples asked him about this parable. ¹⁸"Are you so dull?" he asked. "Don't you see that nothing that enters you from the outside can defile you? ¹⁹For it doesn't go into your heart but into your stomach, and then out of your body." (In saying this, Jesus declared all foods clean.) ²⁰He went on: "What comes out of you is

---

ᵃ 4 Some early manuscripts *pitchers, kettles and dining couches*   ᵇ 6,7 Isaiah 29:13   ᶜ 9 Some manuscripts *set up*   ᵈ 10 Exodus 20:12; Deut. 5:16   ᵉ 10 Exodus 21:17; Lev. 20:9

what defiles you. ²¹For from within, out of your hearts, come evil thoughts, sexual immorality, theft, murder, ²²adultery, greed, malice, deceit, lewdness, envy, slander, arrogance and folly. ²³All these evils come from inside and defile you."

Jesus Honors a Syrophoenician Woman's Faith

²⁴Jesus left that place and went to the vicinity of Tyre.ᵃ He entered a house and did not want anyone to know it; yet he could not keep his presence secret. ²⁵In fact, as soon as she heard about him, a woman whose little daughter was possessed by an evilᵇ spirit came and fell at his feet. ²⁶The woman was a Greek, born in Syrian Phoenicia. She begged Jesus to drive the demon out of her daughter.

²⁷"First let the children eat all they want," he told her, "for it is not right to take the children's bread and toss it to the dogs."

²⁸"Lord," she replied, "even the dogs under the table eat the children's crumbs."

²⁹Then he told her, "For such a reply, you may go; the demon has left your daughter."

³⁰She went home and found her child lying on the bed, and the demon gone.

Jesus Heals a Deaf and Mute Man

³¹Then Jesus left the vicinity of Tyre and went through Sidon, down to the Sea of Galilee and into the region of the Decapolis.ᶜ ³²There some people brought to him a man who was deaf and could hardly talk, and they begged Jesus to place his hand on him.

³³After he took him aside, away from the crowd, Jesus put his fingers into the man's ears. Then he spit and touched the man's tongue. ³⁴He looked up to heaven and with a deep sigh said to him, *"Ephphatha!"* (which means "Be opened!"). ³⁵At this, the man's ears were opened, his tongue was loosened and he began to speak plainly.

³⁶Jesus commanded them not to tell anyone. But the more he did so, the more they kept talking about it. ³⁷People were overwhelmed with amazement. "He has done everything well," they said. "He even makes the deaf hear and the mute speak."

Jesus Feeds the Four Thousand

8 During those days another large crowd gathered. Since they had nothing to eat, Jesus called his disciples to him and said, ²"I have compassion for these people; they have already been with me three days and have nothing to eat. ³If I send them home hungry, they will collapse on the way, because some of them have come a long distance."

⁴His disciples answered, "But where in this remote place can anyone get enough bread to feed them?"

⁵"How many loaves do you have?" Jesus asked.

"Seven," they replied.

⁶He told the crowd to sit down on the ground. When he had taken the seven loaves and given thanks, he broke them and gave them to his disciples to set before the people, and they did so. ⁷They had a few small fish as well; he gave thanks for them also and told the disciples to distribute them. ⁸The people ate and were satisfied. Afterward the disciples picked up seven basketfuls of broken pieces that were left over. ⁹About four thousand were present. And having sent them away, ¹⁰he got into the boat with his disciples and went to the region of Dalmanutha.

¹¹The Pharisees came and began to question Jesus. To test him, they asked him for a sign from heaven. ¹²He sighed deeply and said, "Why does this generation ask for a sign? Truly I tell you, no sign will be given to it." ¹³Then he left them, got back into the boat and crossed to the other side.

The Yeast of the Pharisees and Herod

¹⁴The disciples had forgotten to bring bread, except for one loaf they had with them in the boat. ¹⁵"Be careful," Jesus warned them. "Watch out for the yeast of the Pharisees and that of Herod."

¹⁶They discussed this with one another and said, "It is because we have no bread."

¹⁷Aware of their discussion, Jesus asked them: "Why are you talking about having no bread? Do you still not see or understand? Are your hearts hardened? ¹⁸Do you have eyes but fail to see, and ears but fail to hear? And don't you remember? ¹⁹When I broke

---

a 24 Many early manuscripts *Tyre and Sidon*   *b 25* Greek *unclean*   *c 31* That is, the Ten Cities the five loaves for the five thousand, how many basketfuls of pieces did you pick up?"

"Twelve," they replied.

20"And when I broke the seven loaves for the four thousand, how many basketfuls of pieces did you pick up?"

They answered, "Seven."

21He said to them, "Do you still not understand?"

Jesus Heals a Blind Man at Bethsaida

22They came to Bethsaida, and some people brought a blind man and begged Jesus to touch him. 23He took the blind man by the hand and led him outside the village. When he had spit on the man's eyes and put his hands on him, Jesus asked, "Do you see anything?"

24He looked up and said, "I see people; they look like trees walking around."

25Once more Jesus put his hands on the man's eyes. Then his eyes were opened, his sight was restored, and he saw everything clearly. 26Jesus sent him home, saying, "Don't even go into*a* the village."

Peter Declares That Jesus Is the Messiah

27Jesus and his disciples went on to the villages around Caesarea Philippi. On the way he asked them, "Who do people say I am?"

28They replied, "Some say John the Baptist; others say Elijah; and still others, one of the prophets."

29"But what about you?" he asked. "Who do you say I am?"

Peter answered, "You are the Messiah."

30Jesus warned them not to tell anyone about him.

Jesus Predicts His Death

31He then began to teach them that the Son of Man must suffer many things and be rejected by the elders, the chief priests and the teachers of the law, and that he must be killed and after three days rise again. 32He spoke plainly about this, and Peter took him aside and began to rebuke him.

33But when Jesus turned and looked at his disciples, he rebuked Peter. "Get behind me, Satan!" he said. "You do not have in mind the concerns of God, but merely human concerns."

The Way of the Cross

34Then he called the crowd to him along with his disciples and said: "Whoever wants to be my disciple must deny themselves and take up their cross and follow me. 35For whoever wants to save their life*b* will lose it, but whoever loses their life for me and for the gospel will save it. 36What good is it for you to gain the whole world, yet forfeit your soul? 37Or what can you give in exchange for your soul? 38If any of you are ashamed of me and my words in this adulterous and sinful generation, the Son of Man will be ashamed of you when he comes in his Father's glory with the holy angels."

9 And he said to them, "Truly I tell you, some who are standing here will not taste death before they see that the kingdom of God has come with power."

The Transfiguration

2After six days Jesus took Peter, James and John with him and led them up a high mountain, where they were all alone. There he was transfigured before them. 3His clothes became dazzling white, whiter than anyone in the world could bleach them. 4And there appeared before them Elijah and Moses, who were talking with Jesus.

5Peter said to Jesus, "Rabbi, it is good for us to be here. Let us put up three shelters—one for you, one for Moses and one for Elijah." 6(He did not know what to say, they were so frightened.)

7Then a cloud appeared and covered them, and a voice came from the cloud: "This is my Son, whom I love. Listen to him!"

8Suddenly, when they looked around, they no longer saw anyone with them except Jesus.

9As they were coming down the mountain, Jesus gave them orders not to tell anyone what they had seen until the Son of Man had risen from the dead. 10They kept the matter to themselves, discussing what "rising from the dead" meant.

11And they asked him, "Why do the teachers of the law say that Elijah must come first?"

12Jesus replied, "To be sure, Elijah does come first, and restores all things. Why then

---

a 26 Some manuscripts go *and tell anyone in* verses 36 and 37.   *b 35* The Greek word means either *life* or *soul*; also in

TUESDAY

I BELIEVE; HELP MY UNBELIEF

Mark 9:1–37 or 9:17–24

Richard Foster

God, today I resonate with the desperate cry in the Gospel, "[I do believe; help me overcome my unbelief!]" Sometimes I think I operate my life out of more doubt than faith. And yet I want to believe . . . and I do believe.

I'm a complex creature. At times I can believe with my head, while my body is still locked into patterns of skepticism and doubt. Faith is not yet in my muscles, my bones, my glands.

Increase faith within me, O Lord. I'm sure that for faith to grow you will put me in situations where I'll need resources beyond myself. I submit to this process.

Will this mean moving out on behalf of others, praying for them and trusting you to work in them? If so, then show me the who, what, when and where, and I will seek to act at your bidding. Throughout I am trusting you to take me from faith to faith—from the faith I do have to the faith that I am in the process of receiving.

Thank you for hearing my prayer.

Amen.

CHARLES G. FINNEY {AD 1792–1875}

The same Greek word that is so often translated as *faith* in the New Testament is also translated as *trust*; as in John 2:24, "But Jesus would not [trust] himself to them, for he knew all people." And Luke 16:11, "So if you have not been trustworthy in handling worldly wealth, who will trust you with true riches?" In these passages the word *trust* is the same word as that which is translated *faith*. It means a confiding in God and in Christ, as revealed in the Bible and in reason. It is a receiving of the testimony of God concerning himself, and concerning all things of which he has spoken. It is a receiving of Christ for just what he is represented to be in his gospel. And it is an unqualified surrender of the will, and of the whole being, to him.

reflection

1. In what ways do you resonate with the man who cried, "I do believe; help me overcome my unbelief"?

2. Do you consider yourself to be a "person of faith"?

3. Are you willing for God to put you in situations that will stretch and grow your faith?

For your next devotional reading, go to page 1136.

is it written that the Son of Man must suffer much and be rejected? [13]But I tell you, Elijah has come, and they have done to him everything they wished, just as it is written about him."

Jesus Heals a Boy Possessed by an Evil Spirit

[14]When they came to the other disciples, they saw a large crowd around them and the teachers of the law arguing with them. [15]As soon as all the people saw Jesus, they were overwhelmed with wonder and ran to greet him.

[16]"What are you arguing with them about?" he asked.

[17]A man in the crowd answered, "Teacher, I brought you my son, who is possessed by a spirit that has robbed him of speech. [18]Whenever it seizes him, it throws him to the ground. He foams at the mouth, gnashes his teeth and becomes rigid. I asked your disciples to drive out the spirit, but they could not."

[19]"You unbelieving generation," Jesus replied, "how long shall I stay with you? How long shall I put up with you? Bring the boy to me."

[20]So they brought him. When the spirit saw Jesus, it immediately threw the boy into a convulsion. He fell to the ground and rolled around, foaming at the mouth.

[21]Jesus asked the boy's father, "How long has he been like this?"

"From childhood," he answered. [22]"It has often thrown him into fire or water to kill him. But if you can do anything, take pity on us and help us."

[23]" 'If you can'?" said Jesus. "Everything is possible for one who believes."

[24]Immediately the boy's father exclaimed, "I do believe; help me overcome my unbelief!"

[25]When Jesus saw that a crowd was running to the scene, he rebuked the evil[a] spirit. "You deaf and mute spirit," he said, "I command you, come out of him and never enter him again."

[26]The spirit shrieked, convulsed him violently and came out. The boy looked so much like a corpse that many said, "He's dead." [27]But Jesus took him by the hand and lifted him to his feet, and he stood up.

[28]After Jesus had gone indoors, his disciples asked him privately, "Why couldn't we drive it out?"

[29]He replied, "This kind can come out only by prayer.[b]"

Jesus Predicts His Death a Second Time

[30]They left that place and passed through Galilee. Jesus did not want anyone to know where they were, [31]because he was teaching his disciples. He said to them, "The Son of Man is going to be delivered over to human hands. He will be killed, and after three days he will rise." [32]But they did not understand what he meant and were afraid to ask him about it.

[33]They came to Capernaum. When he was in the house, he asked them, "What were you arguing about on the road?" [34]But they kept quiet because on the way they had argued about who was the greatest.

[35]Sitting down, Jesus called the Twelve and said, "Anyone who wants to be first must be the very last, and the servant of all."

[36]He took a little child whom he placed among them. Taking the child in his arms, he said to them, [37]"Whoever welcomes one of these little children in my name welcomes me; and whoever welcomes me does not welcome me but the one who sent me."

Whoever Is Not Against Us Is for Us

[38]"Teacher," said John, "we saw someone driving out demons in your name and we told him to stop, because he was not one of us."

[39]"Do not stop him," Jesus said. "No one who does a miracle in my name can in the next moment say anything bad about me, [40]for whoever is not against us is for us. [41]Truly I tell you, anyone who gives you a cup of water in my name because you belong to the Messiah will certainly be rewarded.

Causing to Stumble

[42]"If anyone causes one of these little ones—those who believe in me—to stumble, it would be better for them if a large millstone were hung around their neck and they were thrown into the sea. [43][44]If your hand causes you to stumble, cut it off. It is better for you to enter life maimed than with two hands to go into hell, where the fire

a 25 Greek unclean   b 29 Some manuscripts prayer and fasting never goes out. 45[46]And if your foot causes you to stumble, cut it off. It is better for you to enter life crippled than to have two feet and be thrown into hell. 47And if your eye causes you to stumble, pluck it out. It is better for you to enter the kingdom of God with one eye than to have two eyes and be thrown into hell, 48where

> " 'their worm does not die,
>   and the fire is not quenched.'*a*

49Everyone will be salted with fire.

50"Salt is good, but if it loses its saltiness, how can you make it salty again? Have salt in yourselves, and be at peace with each other."

Divorce

10 Jesus then left that place and went into the region of Judea and across the Jordan. Again crowds of people came to him, and as was his custom, he taught them.

2Some Pharisees came and tested him by asking, "Is it lawful for a man to divorce his wife?"

3"What did Moses command you?" he replied.

4They said, "Moses permitted a man to write a certificate of divorce and send her away."

5"It was because your hearts were hard that Moses wrote you this law," Jesus replied. 6"But at the beginning of creation God 'made them male and female.'*b* 7'For this reason a man will leave his father and mother and be united to his wife,*c* 8and the two will become one flesh.'*d* So they are no longer two, but one. 9Therefore what God has joined together, let no one separate."

10When they were in the house again, the disciples asked Jesus about this. 11He answered, "Anyone who divorces his wife and marries another woman commits adultery against her. 12And if she divorces her husband and marries another man, she commits adultery."

The Little Children and Jesus

13People were bringing little children to Jesus for him to place his hands on them, but the disciples rebuked them. 14When Jesus saw this, he was indignant. He said to them, "Let the little children come to me, and do not hinder them, for the kingdom of God belongs to such as these. 15Truly I tell you, anyone who will not receive the kingdom of God like a little child will never enter it." 16And he took the children in his arms, placed his hands on them and blessed them.

The Rich and the Kingdom of God

17As Jesus started on his way, a man ran up to him and fell on his knees before him. "Good teacher," he asked, "what must I do to inherit eternal life?"

18"Why do you call me good?" Jesus answered. "No one is good—except God alone. 19You know the commandments: 'You shall not murder, you shall not commit adultery, you shall not steal, you shall not give false testimony, you shall not defraud, honor your father and mother.'*e*

20"Teacher," he declared, "all these I have kept since I was a boy."

21Jesus looked at him and loved him. "One thing you lack," he said. "Go, sell everything you have and give to the poor, and you will have treasure in heaven. Then come, follow me."

22At this the man's face fell. He went away sad, because he had great wealth.

23Jesus looked around and said to his disciples, "How hard it is for the rich to enter the kingdom of God!"

24The disciples were amazed at his words. But Jesus said again, "Children, how hard it is*f* to enter the kingdom of God! 25It is easier for a camel to go through the eye of a needle than for the rich to enter the kingdom of God."

26The disciples were even more amazed, and said to each other, "Who then can be saved?"

27Jesus looked at them and said, "With human beings this is impossible, but not with God; all things are possible with God."

28Then Peter spoke up, "We have left everything to follow you!"

29"Truly I tell you," Jesus replied, "no one who has left home or brothers or sisters or mother or father or children or fields for me and the gospel 30will fail to receive a hun-

---

a 48 Isaiah 66:24   *b* 6 Gen. 1:27   *c* 7 Some early manuscripts do not have *and be united to his wife.*
d 8 Gen. 2:24   *e* 19 Exodus 20:12-16; Deut. 5:16-20   *f* 24 Some manuscripts *is for those who trust in riches*

WEDNESDAY

Letting Go

Mark 10:17–31 *or* 10:21–25

Andrew Murray {ad 1828–1917}

The disciples were amazed at the words of Christ to the rich young man. To the question of who then could be saved, Jesus replied that with God all things are possible.

Here it is implied that only by the power of God can one take up the cross and lose one's life, one's self, and all the possessions to which one is naturally so attached. So Christ also had occasion to tell Peter that it was the Father in heaven that had revealed to Peter that Jesus was the Christ . . .

Often people feel that the demands of God are too high, and they then try to be Christians without the whole-hearted devotion and self-denial that are asked . . .

Let us take the message to heart: It is only by placing our faith in God, and by belief in the power He exerts in our hearts, that we can be disciples who give up everything to follow Christ—becoming followers in the fellowship of the cross.

Janet Holm McHenry

Saying yes to knowing God and following him means being willing to give up whatever it is that keeps us from him—an extra hour of sleep, a title, financial success, a paid-off mortgage. That's essentially what Jesus said to the rich, young ruler when he asked, "Teacher, what good thing must I do to get eternal life?" (Matthew 19:16). Jesus told him not only to obey the commandments, but also to give everything he had to the poor. The young man walked away dejected because he had great wealth.

If someone asked Jesus this question today, he might tell that person to give up his or her schedule. Time is a precious commodity to many of us. As a schoolteacher with a farmer husband, I'm not wealthy, but on many occasions I'd gladly give God my money rather than my time. I'd prefer donating dollars over making cookies for the youth group's bake sale . . .

Scripture teaches that when we say yes to God, we gain so much more than we give up. When Peter asked Jesus what was ahead for his followers . . . Jesus answered by telling his disciples that saying no to earthy things would mean a hundred times yes from God and eternal life. Such a deal! Any stock market investor would jump at such dividends.

reflection

1. Is it harder for you to practice self-denial with your wallet or with your schedule?

2. How valuable is your "free time"?

3. What sacrifice can you offer your church or local ministry that would demonstrate your commitment to Christ?

For your next devotional reading, go to page 1139.

dred times as much in this present age: homes, brothers, sisters, mothers, children and fields—along with persecutions—and in the age to come eternal life. [31]But many who are first will be last, and the last first."

Jesus Predicts His Death a Third Time

[32]They were on their way up to Jerusalem, with Jesus leading the way, and the disciples were astonished, while those who followed were afraid. Again he took the Twelve aside and told them what was going to happen to him. [33]"We are going up to Jerusalem," he said, "and the Son of Man will be delivered over to the chief priests and the teachers of the law. They will condemn him to death and will hand him over to the Gentiles, [34]who will mock him and spit on him, flog him and kill him. Three days later he will rise."

The Request of James and John

[35]Then James and John, the sons of Zebedee, came to him. "Teacher," they said, "we want you to do for us whatever we ask."

[36]"What do you want me to do for you?" he asked.

[37]They replied, "Let one of us sit at your right and the other at your left in your glory."

[38]"You don't know what you are asking," Jesus said. "Can you drink the cup I drink or be baptized with the baptism I am baptized with?"

[39]"We can," they answered.

Jesus said to them, "You will drink the cup I drink and be baptized with the baptism I am baptized with, [40]but to sit at my right or left is not for me to grant. These places belong to those for whom they have been prepared."

[41]When the ten heard about this, they became indignant with James and John. [42]Jesus called them together and said, "You know that those who are regarded as rulers of the Gentiles lord it over them, and their high officials exercise authority over them. [43]Not so with you. Instead, whoever wants to become great among you must be your servant, [44]and whoever wants to be first must be slave of all. [45]For even the Son of Man did not come to be served, but to serve, and to give his life as a ransom for many."

Blind Bartimaeus Receives His Sight

[46]Then they came to Jericho. As Jesus and his disciples, together with a large crowd, were leaving the city, a blind man, Bartimaeus (which means "son of Timaeus"), was sitting by the roadside begging. [47]When he heard that it was Jesus of Nazareth, he began to shout, "Jesus, Son of David, have mercy on me!"

[48]Many rebuked him and told him to be quiet, but he shouted all the more, "Son of David, have mercy on me!"

[49]Jesus stopped and said, "Call him."

So they called to the blind man, "Cheer up! On your feet! He's calling you." [50]Throwing his cloak aside, he jumped to his feet and came to Jesus.

[51]"What do you want me to do for you?" Jesus asked him.

The blind man said, "Rabbi, I want to see."

[52]"Go," said Jesus, "your faith has healed you." Immediately he received his sight and followed Jesus along the road.

Jesus Comes to Jerusalem as King

11 As they approached Jerusalem and came to Bethphage and Bethany at the Mount of Olives, Jesus sent two of his disciples, [2]saying to them, "Go to the village ahead of you, and just as you enter it, you will find a colt tied there, which no one has ever ridden. Untie it and bring it here. [3]If anyone asks you, 'Why are you doing this?' say, 'The Lord needs it and will send it back here shortly.' "

[4]They went and found a colt outside in the street, tied at a doorway. As they untied it, [5]some people standing there asked, "What are you doing, untying that colt?" [6]They answered as Jesus had told them to, and the people let them go. [7]When they brought the colt to Jesus and threw their cloaks over it, he sat on it. [8]Many people spread their cloaks on the road, while others spread branches they had cut in the fields. [9]Those who went ahead and those who followed shouted,

"Hosanna!*a*"

"Blessed is he who comes in the name of the Lord!"*b*

a 9 A Hebrew expression meaning "Save!" which became an exclamation of praise; also in verse 10
b 9 Psalm 118:25,26

[10]"Blessed is the coming kingdom of our father David!"

"Hosanna in the highest heaven!"

[11]Jesus entered Jerusalem and went into the temple courts. He looked around at everything, but since it was already late, he went out to Bethany with the Twelve.

Jesus Curses a Fig Tree and Clears the Temple Courts

[12]The next day as they were leaving Bethany, Jesus was hungry. [13]Seeing in the distance a fig tree in leaf, he went to find out if it had any fruit. When he reached it, he found nothing but leaves, because it was not the season for figs. [14]Then he said to the tree, "May no one ever eat fruit from you again." And his disciples heard him say it.

[15]On reaching Jerusalem, Jesus entered the temple courts and began driving out those who were buying and selling there. He overturned the tables of the money changers and the benches of those selling doves, [16]and would not allow anyone to carry merchandise through the temple courts. [17]And as he taught them, he said, "Is it not written: 'My house will be called a house of prayer for all nations'[a]? But you have made it 'a den of robbers.'[b]"

[18]The chief priests and the teachers of the law heard this and began looking for a way to kill him, for they feared him, because the whole crowd was amazed at his teaching.

[19]When evening came, Jesus and his disciples[c] went out of the city.

[20]In the morning, as they went along, they saw the fig tree withered from the roots. [21]Peter remembered and said to Jesus, "Rabbi, look! The fig tree you cursed has withered!"

[22]"Have faith in God," Jesus answered. [23]"Truly[d] I tell you, if you say to this mountain, 'Go, throw yourself into the sea,' and do not doubt in your heart but believe that what you say will happen, it will be done for you. [24]Therefore I tell you, whatever you ask for in prayer, believe that you have received it, and it will be yours. [25][26]And when you stand praying, if you hold anything against anyone, forgive them, so that your Father in heaven may forgive you your sins."

The Authority of Jesus Questioned

[27]They arrived again in Jerusalem, and while Jesus was walking in the temple courts, the chief priests, the teachers of the law and the elders came to him. [28]"By what authority are you doing these things?" they asked. "And who gave you authority to do this?"

[29]Jesus replied, "I will ask you one question. Answer me, and I will tell you by what authority I am doing these things. [30]John's baptism—was it from heaven, or of human origin? Tell me!"

[31]They discussed it among themselves and said, "If we say, 'From heaven,' he will ask, 'Then why didn't you believe him?' [32]But if we say, 'Of human origin'...." (They feared the people, for everyone held that John really was a prophet.)

[33]So they answered Jesus, "We don't know."

Jesus said, "Neither will I tell you by what authority I am doing these things."

The Parable of the Tenants

12 Jesus then began to speak to them in parables: "A man planted a vineyard. He put a wall around it, dug a pit for the winepress and built a watchtower. Then he rented the vineyard to some farmers and moved to another place. [2]At harvest time he sent a servant to the tenants to collect from them some of the fruit of the vineyard. [3]But they seized him, beat him and sent him away empty-handed. [4]Then he sent another servant to them; they struck this man on the head and treated him shamefully. [5]He sent still another, and that one they killed. He sent many others; some of them they beat, others they killed.

[6]"He had one left to send, a son, whom he loved. He sent him last of all, saying, 'They will respect my son.'

[7]"But the tenants said to one another, 'This is the heir. Come, let's kill him, and the inheritance will be ours.' [8]So they took him and killed him, and threw him out of the vineyard.

[9]"What then will the owner of the vineyard do? He will come and kill those tenants

---

[a] 17 Isaiah 56:7   [b] 17 Jer. 7:11   [c] 19 Some early manuscripts came, Jesus   [d] 22,23 Some early manuscripts "If you have faith in God," Jesus answered, [23]"truly

THURSDAY

LOVE IS NOT AN EMOTION
Mark 12:1–44 *or* 12:28–31

Lee Strobel

Jesus was very precise in choosing a word for "love" that doesn't imply emotion as much as it suggests attitude and action. As difficult as it sounds, he's urging us to have a humble, servant demeanor toward people who are our adversaries. To look for the best in them and offer help as they need it. To have a sense of goodwill and benevolence toward them in spite of their lack of the same toward us. To pray for their welfare and the well-being of their families. Even though we may continue to compete with them, we are to do so fairly and respectfully, not maliciously as if we're trying to destroy them.

Technically, we aren't being asked to like the other person, because that would require an emotion that we sometimes can't conjure up, despite our best intentions. But in effect we are to treat them as though we like them—because that's a decision of our will. We don't have to approve of what they are, what they've done or how they conduct their affairs, but we are to love who they are—people who matter to God, just like you and me. People who have failed but who are eligible for God's forgiving grace.

JOHANNES ECKHART {AD 1260–1327}

It is a hard thing to practice this universal love, and to love our neighbors as ourselves, as our Lord commanded us. But there is also a greater reward attached to this command than to any other. The commandment seems hard, but the reward is precious indeed.

reflection

1. What is the difference between love as an emotion and love as a choice?

2. When have you chosen to love another person, group or church?

3. Whom do you need to choose to love this week, though you may not feel like doing so?

For your next devotional reading, go to page 1145.

and give the vineyard to others. ¹⁰Haven't you read this passage of Scripture:

> " 'The stone the builders rejected
>   has become the cornerstone;
> ¹¹the Lord has done this,
>   and it is marvelous in our eyes' ᵃ?"

¹²Then the chief priests, the teachers of the law and the elders looked for a way to arrest him because they knew he had spoken the parable against them. But they were afraid of the crowd; so they left him and went away.

Paying the Imperial Tax to Caesar

¹³Later they sent some of the Pharisees and Herodians to Jesus to catch him in his words. ¹⁴They came to him and said, "Teacher, we know that you are a man of integrity. You aren't swayed by others, because you pay no attention to who they are; but you teach the way of God in accordance with the truth. Is it right to pay the imperial tax ᵇ to Caesar or not? ¹⁵Should we pay or shouldn't we?"

But Jesus knew their hypocrisy. "Why are you trying to trap me?" he asked. "Bring me a denarius and let me look at it." ¹⁶They brought the coin, and he asked them, "Whose image is this? And whose inscription?"

"Caesar's," they replied.

¹⁷Then Jesus said to them, "Give back to Caesar what is Caesar's and to God what is God's."

And they were amazed at him.

Marriage at the Resurrection

¹⁸Then the Sadducees, who say there is no resurrection, came to him with a question. ¹⁹"Teacher," they said, "Moses wrote for us that if a man's brother dies and leaves a wife but no children, the man must marry the widow and raise up offspring for his brother. ²⁰Now there were seven brothers. The first one married and died without leaving any children. ²¹The second one married the widow, but he also died, leaving no child. It was the same with the third. ²²In fact, none of the seven left any children. Last of all, the woman died too. ²³At the res-

urrection ᶜ whose wife will she be, since the seven were married to her?"

²⁴Jesus replied, "Are you not in error because you do not know the Scriptures or the power of God? ²⁵When the dead rise, they will neither marry nor be given in marriage; they will be like the angels in heaven. ²⁶Now about the dead rising—have you not read in the Book of Moses, in the account of the burning bush, how God said to him, 'I am the God of Abraham, the God of Isaac, and the God of Jacob' ᵈ? ²⁷He is not the God of the dead, but of the living. You are badly mistaken!"

The Greatest Commandment

²⁸One of the teachers of the law came and heard them debating. Noticing that Jesus had given them a good answer, he asked him, "Of all the commandments, which is the most important?"

²⁹"The most important one," answered Jesus, "is this: 'Hear, O Israel: The Lord our God, the Lord is one. ᵉ ³⁰Love the Lord your God with all your heart and with all your soul and with all your mind and with all your strength.' ᶠ ³¹The second is this: 'Love your neighbor as yourself.' ᵍ There is no commandment greater than these."

³²"Well said, teacher," the man replied. "You are right in saying that God is one and there is no other but him. ³³To love him with all your heart, with all your understanding and with all your strength, and to love your neighbor as yourself is more important than all burnt offerings and sacrifices."

³⁴When Jesus saw that he had answered wisely, he said to him, "You are not far from the kingdom of God." And from then on no one dared ask him any more questions.

Whose Son Is the Messiah?

³⁵While Jesus was teaching in the temple courts, he asked, "Why do the teachers of the law say that the Messiah is the son of David? ³⁶David himself, speaking by the Holy Spirit, declared:

> " 'The Lord said to my Lord:
>   "Sit at my right hand
> until I put your enemies
>   under your feet." ' ʰ

ᵃ 11 Psalm 118:22,23   ᵇ 14 A special tax levied on subject peoples, not on Roman citizens
ᶜ 23 Some manuscripts *resurrection, when people rise from the dead,*   ᵈ 26 Exodus 3:6   ᵉ 29 Or *The Lord our God is one Lord*   ᶠ 30 Deut. 6:4,5   ᵍ 31 Lev. 19:18   ʰ 36 Psalm 110:1

[37]David himself calls him 'Lord.' How then can he be his son?"

The large crowd listened to him with delight.

Warning Against the Teachers of the Law

[38]As he taught, Jesus said, "Watch out for the teachers of the law. They like to walk around in flowing robes and be greeted with respect in the marketplaces, [39]and have the most important seats in the synagogues and the places of honor at banquets. [40]They devour widows' houses and for a show make lengthy prayers. These men will be punished most severely."

The Widow's Offering

[41]Jesus sat down opposite the place where the offerings were put and watched the crowd putting their money into the temple treasury. Many rich people threw in large amounts. [42]But a poor widow came and put in two very small copper coins, worth only a fraction of a penny.

[43]Calling his disciples to him, Jesus said, "Truly I tell you, this poor widow has put more into the treasury than all the others. [44]They all gave out of their wealth; but she, out of her poverty, put in everything—all she had to live on."

The Destruction of the Temple and Signs of the End Times

13 As Jesus was leaving the temple, one of his disciples said to him, "Look, Teacher! What massive stones! What magnificent buildings!"

[2]"Do you see all these great buildings?" replied Jesus. "Not one stone here will be left on another; every one will be thrown down."

[3]As Jesus was sitting on the Mount of Olives opposite the temple, Peter, James, John and Andrew asked him privately, [4]"Tell us, when will these things happen? And what will be the sign that they are all about to be fulfilled?"

[5]Jesus said to them: "Watch out that no one deceives you. [6]Many will come in my name, claiming, 'I am he,' and will deceive many. [7]When you hear of wars and rumors of wars, do not be alarmed. Such things must happen, but the end is still to come. [8]Nation will rise against nation, and king-

dom against kingdom. There will be earthquakes in various places, and famines. These are the beginning of birth pains.

[9]"You must be on your guard. You will be handed over to the local councils and flogged in the synagogues. On account of me you will stand before governors and kings as witnesses to them. [10]And the gospel must first be preached to all nations. [11]Whenever you are arrested and brought to trial, do not worry beforehand about what to say. Just say whatever is given you at the time, for it is not you speaking, but the Holy Spirit.

[12]"Brother will betray brother to death, and a father his child. Children will rebel against their parents and have them put to death. [13]Everyone will hate you because of me, but those who stand firm to the end will be saved.

[14]"When you see 'the abomination that causes desolation'[a] standing where it[b] does not belong—let the reader understand—then let those who are in Judea flee to the mountains. [15]Let no one on the housetop go down or enter the house to take anything out. [16]Let no one in the field go back to get their cloak. [17]How dreadful it will be in those days for pregnant women and nursing mothers! [18]Pray that this will not take place in winter, [19]because those will be days of distress unequaled from the beginning, when God created the world, until now—and never to be equaled again.

[20]"If the Lord had not cut short those days, no one would survive. But for the sake of the elect, whom he has chosen, he has shortened them. [21]At that time if anyone says to you, 'Look, here is the Messiah!' or, 'Look, there he is!' do not believe it. [22]For false messiahs and false prophets will appear and perform signs and wonders to deceive, if possible, even the elect. [23]So be on your guard; I have told you everything ahead of time.

[24]"But in those days, following that distress,

" 'the sun will be darkened,
    and the moon will not give its light;
[25]the stars will fall from the sky,
    and the heavenly bodies will be shaken.'[c]

---

a 14 Daniel 9:27; 11:31; 12:11   b 14 Or he   c 25 Isaiah 13:10; 34:4

²⁶"At that time people will see the Son of Man coming in clouds with great power and glory. ²⁷And he will send his angels and gather his elect from the four winds, from the ends of the earth to the ends of the heavens.

²⁸"Now learn this lesson from the fig tree: As soon as its twigs get tender and its leaves come out, you know that summer is near. ²⁹Even so, when you see these things happening, you know that it*a* is near, right at the door. ³⁰Truly I tell you, this generation will certainly not pass away until all these things have happened. ³¹Heaven and earth will pass away, but my words will never pass away.

The Day and Hour Unknown

³²"But about that day or hour no one knows, not even the angels in heaven, nor the Son, but only the Father. ³³Be on guard! Be alert*b*! You do not know when that time will come. ³⁴It's like a man going away: He leaves his house and puts his servants in charge, each with an assigned task, and tells the one at the door to keep watch.

³⁵"Therefore keep watch because you do not know when the owner of the house will come back—whether in the evening, or at midnight, or when the rooster crows, or at dawn. ³⁶If he comes suddenly, do not let him find you sleeping. ³⁷What I say to you, I say to everyone: 'Watch!'"

Jesus Anointed at Bethany

14 Now the Passover and the Festival of Unleavened Bread were only two days away, and the chief priests and the teachers of the law were looking for some sly way to arrest Jesus and kill him. ²"But not during the festival," they said, "or the people may riot."

³While he was in Bethany, reclining at the table in the home of Simon the Leper, a woman came with an alabaster jar of very expensive perfume, made of pure nard. She broke the jar and poured the perfume on his head.

⁴Some of those present were saying indignantly to one another, "Why this waste of perfume? ⁵It could have been sold for more than a year's wages*c* and the money given to the poor." And they rebuked her harshly.

⁶"Leave her alone," said Jesus. "Why are you bothering her? She has done a beautiful thing to me. ⁷The poor you will always have with you,*d* and you can help them any time you want. But you will not always have me. ⁸She did what she could. She poured perfume on my body beforehand to prepare for my burial. ⁹Truly I tell you, wherever the gospel is preached throughout the world, what she has done will also be told, in memory of her."

¹⁰Then Judas Iscariot, one of the Twelve, went to the chief priests to betray Jesus to them. ¹¹They were delighted to hear this and promised to give him money. So he watched for an opportunity to hand him over.

The Last Supper

¹²On the first day of the Festival of Unleavened Bread, when it was customary to sacrifice the Passover lamb, Jesus' disciples asked him, "Where do you want us to go and make preparations for you to eat the Passover?"

¹³So he sent two of his disciples, telling them, "Go into the city, and a man carrying a jar of water will meet you. Follow him. ¹⁴Say to the owner of the house he enters, 'The Teacher asks: Where is my guest room, where I may eat the Passover with my disciples?' ¹⁵He will show you a large room upstairs, furnished and ready. Make preparations for us there."

¹⁶The disciples left, went into the city and found things just as Jesus had told them. So they prepared the Passover.

¹⁷When evening came, Jesus arrived with the Twelve. ¹⁸While they were reclining at the table eating, he said, "Truly I tell you, one of you will betray me—one who is eating with me."

¹⁹They were saddened, and one by one they said to him, "Surely not I?"

²⁰"It is one of the Twelve," he replied, "one who dips bread into the bowl with me. ²¹The Son of Man will go just as it is written about him. But woe to that man who betrays the Son of Man! It would be better for him if he had not been born."

²²While they were eating, Jesus took bread, and when he had given thanks, he

broke it and gave it to his disciples, saying, "Take it; this is my body."

²³Then he took the cup, and when he had given thanks, he gave it to them, and they all drank from it.

²⁴"This is my blood of the[a] covenant, which is poured out for many," he said to them. ²⁵"Truly I tell you, I will not drink again of the fruit of the vine until that day when I drink it new in the kingdom of God."

²⁶When they had sung a hymn, they went out to the Mount of Olives.

Jesus Predicts Peter's Denial

²⁷"You will all fall away," Jesus told them, "for it is written:

" 'I will strike the shepherd,
    and the sheep will be scattered.'[b]

²⁸But after I have risen, I will go ahead of you into Galilee."

²⁹Peter declared, "Even if all fall away, I will not."

³⁰"Truly I tell you," Jesus answered, "to-day—yes, tonight—before the rooster crows twice[c] you yourself will disown me three times."

³¹But Peter insisted emphatically, "Even if I have to die with you, I will never disown you." And all the others said the same.

Gethsemane

³²They went to a place called Gethsema-ne, and Jesus said to his disciples, "Sit here while I pray." ³³He took Peter, James and John along with him, and he began to be deeply distressed and troubled. ³⁴"My soul is overwhelmed with sorrow to the point of death," he said to them. "Stay here and keep watch."

³⁵Going a little farther, he fell to the ground and prayed that if possible the hour might pass from him. ³⁶"Abba,[d] Father," he said, "everything is possible for you. Take this cup from me. Yet not what I will, but what you will."

³⁷Then he returned to his disciples and found them sleeping. "Simon," he said to Peter, "are you asleep? Could you not keep watch for one hour? ³⁸Watch and pray so that you will not fall into temptation. The spirit is willing, but the flesh is weak."

³⁹Once more he went away and prayed the same thing. ⁴⁰When he came back, he again found them sleeping, because their eyes were heavy. They did not know what to say to him.

⁴¹Returning the third time, he said to them, "Are you still sleeping and resting? Enough! The hour has come. Look, the Son of Man is delivered into the hands of sinners. ⁴²Rise! Let us go! Here comes my betrayer!"

Jesus Arrested

⁴³Just as he was speaking, Judas, one of the Twelve, appeared. With him was a crowd armed with swords and clubs, sent from the chief priests, the teachers of the law, and the elders.

⁴⁴Now the betrayer had arranged a signal with them: "The one I kiss is the man; arrest him and lead him away under guard." ⁴⁵Going at once to Jesus, Judas said, "Rabbi!" and kissed him. ⁴⁶The men seized Jesus and arrested him. ⁴⁷Then one of those standing near drew his sword and struck the servant of the high priest, cutting off his ear.

⁴⁸"Am I leading a rebellion," said Jesus, "that you have come out with swords and clubs to capture me? ⁴⁹Every day I was with you, teaching in the temple courts, and you did not arrest me. But the Scriptures must be fulfilled." ⁵⁰Then everyone deserted him and fled.

⁵¹A young man, wearing nothing but a linen garment, was following Jesus. When they seized him, ⁵²he fled naked, leaving his garment behind.

Jesus Before the Sanhedrin

⁵³They took Jesus to the high priest, and all the chief priests, the elders and the teachers of the law came together. ⁵⁴Peter followed him at a distance, right into the courtyard of the high priest. There he sat with the guards and warmed himself at the fire.

⁵⁵The chief priests and the whole Sanhedrin were looking for evidence against Jesus so that they could put him to death, but they did not find any. ⁵⁶Many testified falsely against him, but their statements did not agree.

---

a 24 Some manuscripts *the new*   b 27 Zech. 13:7   c 30 Some early manuscripts do not have *twice*.
d 36 Aramaic for *Father*

⁵⁷Then some stood up and gave this false testimony against him: ⁵⁸"We heard him say, 'I will destroy this temple made with human hands and in three days will build another, not made with hands.'" ⁵⁹Yet even then their testimony did not agree.

⁶⁰Then the high priest stood up before them and asked Jesus, "Are you not going to answer? What is this testimony that these men are bringing against you?" ⁶¹But Jesus remained silent and gave no answer.

Again the high priest asked him, "Are you the Messiah, the Son of the Blessed One?"

⁶²"I am," said Jesus. "And you will see the Son of Man sitting at the right hand of the Mighty One and coming on the clouds of heaven."

⁶³The high priest tore his clothes. "Why do we need any more witnesses?" he asked. ⁶⁴"You have heard the blasphemy. What do you think?"

They all condemned him as worthy of death. ⁶⁵Then some began to spit at him; they blindfolded him, struck him with their fists, and said, "Prophesy!" And the guards took him and beat him.

Peter Disowns Jesus

⁶⁶While Peter was below in the courtyard, one of the servant girls of the high priest came by. ⁶⁷When she saw Peter warming himself, she looked closely at him.

"You also were with that Nazarene, Jesus," she said.

⁶⁸But he denied it. "I don't know or understand what you're talking about," he said, and went out into the entryway.ᵃ

⁶⁹When the servant girl saw him there, she said again to those standing around, "This fellow is one of them." ⁷⁰Again he denied it.

After a little while, those standing near said to Peter, "Surely you are one of them, for you are a Galilean."

⁷¹He began to call down curses, and he swore to them, "I don't know this man you're talking about."

⁷²Immediately the rooster crowed the second time.ᵇ Then Peter remembered the word Jesus had spoken to him: "Before the rooster crows twiceᶜ you will disown me three times." And he broke down and wept.

Jesus Before Pilate

15 Very early in the morning, the chief priests, with the elders, the teachers of the law and the whole Sanhedrin, reached a decision. They bound Jesus, led him away and handed him over to Pilate.

²"Are you the king of the Jews?" asked Pilate.

"You have said so," Jesus replied.

³The chief priests accused him of many things. ⁴So again Pilate asked him, "Aren't you going to answer? See how many things they are accusing you of."

⁵But Jesus still made no reply, and Pilate was amazed.

⁶Now it was the custom at the festival to release a prisoner whom the people requested. ⁷A man called Barabbas was in prison with the insurrectionists who had committed murder in the uprising. ⁸The crowd came up and asked Pilate to do for them what he usually did.

⁹"Do you want me to release to you the king of the Jews?" asked Pilate, ¹⁰knowing it was out of envy that the chief priests had handed Jesus over to him. ¹¹But the chief priests stirred up the crowd to have Pilate release Barabbas instead.

¹²"What shall I do, then, with the one you call the king of the Jews?" Pilate asked them.

¹³"Crucify him!" they shouted.

¹⁴"Why? What crime has he committed?" asked Pilate.

But they shouted all the louder, "Crucify him!"

¹⁵Wanting to satisfy the crowd, Pilate released Barabbas to them. He had Jesus flogged, and handed him over to be crucified.

The Soldiers Mock Jesus

¹⁶The soldiers led Jesus away into the palace (that is, the Praetorium) and called together the whole company of soldiers. ¹⁷They put a purple robe on him, then twisted together a crown of thorns and set it on him. ¹⁸And they began to call out to him, "Hail, king of the Jews!" ¹⁹Again and again they struck him on the head with a staff and spit on him. Falling on their knees, they paid

---

ᵃ 68 Some early manuscripts *entryway and the rooster crowed*   ᵇ 72 Some early manuscripts do not have *the second time*.   ᶜ 72 Some early manuscripts do not have *twice*.

THE GREATEST DEATH OF ALL

Mark 15:16–47 *or* 15:21–24,37–39

Karen Stroup

One of the odd differences between Catholics and Protestants is that Catholics have the crucifix as their central symbol, while Protestants use the cross—a crucifix without the body of Jesus on it. I suppose much hay could be made of the theological implications of this choice, but that's best left for another day.

Whichever symbol we choose, by doing so we align ourselves with a person who died a shameful, horrible, ugly death. It's hard to know what those first Christians who venerated a cross were feeling. A friend finally got it across to me this way: wearing a crucifix around our necks is much akin to wearing a silver or gold representation of a man in an electric chair. That idea probably sounds tasteless. And it is—it's horrible. But when Christians adopted the crucifix, that's more or less the equivalent of what they were doing.

It's one of those ironies typical of God, though. No matter what the instrument of death had been—cross, hangman's noose, electric chair, firing squad—God would have changed its meaning entirely by raising Jesus from the dead. The symbol of death then becomes not tasteless but something that evokes God's tremendous power, our thankfulness for the resurrection, and yes—our sorrow for the death of the Son of God.

SAINT BONAVENTURE {AD 1221–1274}

O Lord, holy Father, show us what kind of man it is who is hanging for our sakes on the cross, whose suffering causes the rocks themselves to crack and crumble with compassion, whose death brings the dead back to life.

Let my heart crack and crumble at the sight of him. Let my soul break apart with compassion for his suffering. Let it be shattered with grief at my sins for which he dies. And finally let it be softened with devoted love for him.

O my God, Jesus, I am in every way unworthy of you. Yet, like Joseph of Arimathea, I want to offer a space for you. He offered his own tomb; I offer my heart.

Enter the darkness of my heart, as your body entered the darkness of Joseph's tomb. And make me worthy to receive you, driving out all sin that I may be filled with your spiritual light.

reflection

1. Why is the cross of Christ important to you?
2. How does the crucifixion reveal the awesome power of God?
3. Write your own prayer of praise and thanksgiving for Jesus' death on the cross.

For your next devotional reading, go to page 1147.

homage to him. 20And when they had mocked him, they took off the purple robe and put his own clothes on him. Then they led him out to crucify him.

The Crucifixion of Jesus

21A certain man from Cyrene, Simon, the father of Alexander and Rufus, was passing by on his way in from the country, and they forced him to carry the cross. 22They brought Jesus to the place called Golgotha (which means "the place of the skull"). 23Then they offered him wine mixed with myrrh, but he did not take it. 24And they crucified him. Dividing up his clothes, they cast lots to see what each would get.

25It was nine in the morning when they crucified him. 26The written notice of the charge against him read: THE KING OF THE JEWS. 27[28]They crucified two rebels with him, one on his right and one on his left. 29Those who passed by hurled insults at him, shaking their heads and saying, "So! You who are going to destroy the temple and build it in three days, 30come down from the cross and save yourself!"

31In the same way the chief priests and the teachers of the law mocked him among themselves. "He saved others," they said, "but he can't save himself! 32Let this Messiah, this king of Israel, come down now from the cross, that we may see and believe." Those crucified with him also heaped insults on him.

The Death of Jesus

33At noon, darkness came over the whole land until three in the afternoon. 34And at three in the afternoon Jesus cried out in a loud voice, *"Eloi, Eloi, lema sabachthani?"* (which means "My God, my God, why have you forsaken me?"). *a*

35When some of those standing near heard this, they said, "Listen, he's calling Elijah."

36Someone ran, filled a sponge with wine vinegar, put it on a staff, and offered it to Jesus to drink. "Now leave him alone. Let's see if Elijah comes to take him down," he said.

37With a loud cry, Jesus breathed his last. 38The curtain of the temple was torn in

two from top to bottom. 39And when the centurion, who stood there in front of Jesus, saw how he died,*b* he said, "Surely this man was the Son of God!"

40Some women were watching from a distance. Among them were Mary Magdalene, Mary the mother of James the younger and of Joseph,*c* and Salome. 41In Galilee these women had followed him and cared for his needs. Many other women who had come up with him to Jerusalem were also there.

The Burial of Jesus

42It was Preparation Day (that is, the day before the Sabbath). So as evening approached, 43Joseph of Arimathea, a prominent member of the Council, who was himself waiting for the kingdom of God, went boldly to Pilate and asked for Jesus' body. 44Pilate was surprised to hear that he was already dead. Summoning the centurion, he asked him if Jesus had already died. 45When he learned from the centurion that it was so, he gave the body to Joseph. 46So Joseph bought some linen cloth, took down the body, wrapped it in the linen, and placed it in a tomb cut out of rock. Then he rolled a stone against the entrance of the tomb. 47Mary Magdalene and Mary the mother of Joseph saw where he was laid.

Jesus Has Risen

16 When the Sabbath was over, Mary Magdalene, Mary the mother of James, and Salome bought spices so that they might go to anoint Jesus' body. 2Very early on the first day of the week, just after sunrise, they were on their way to the tomb 3and they asked each other, "Who will roll the stone away from the entrance of the tomb?"

4But when they looked up, they saw that the stone, which was very large, had been rolled away. 5As they entered the tomb, they saw a young man dressed in a white robe sitting on the right side, and they were alarmed.

6"Don't be alarmed," he said. "You are looking for Jesus the Nazarene, who was crucified. He has risen! He is not here. See the place where they laid him. 7But go, tell

a 34 Psalm 22:1   *b 39* Some manuscripts *saw that he died with such a cry*   *c 40* Greek *Joses,* a variant of *Joseph;* also in verse 47

In His Death

Mark 15:37–39

read/meditate

Read through Mark 15:37–39. Three events take place, each heralding the accomplishment of Jesus' death: one from Jesus, one from the temple and one from a bystander. Read through the three events again. How does each event speak to you in your faith journey?

pray

Spend some time thinking about what Christ's death has accomplished in your life. Express your thoughts to God, however they rise to the front of your mind. Then be still, soaking in the wonder of the open relationship that you have with your Creator.

contemplate

Contemplate the mixed bag of human chaos and divine operation in the events surrounding Christ's death. How often do you think the works of God are surrounded by the bedlam of humanity? How often do you think you are able to see God working in the midst of it all?

additional reflection

Jesus audaciously abolished death, transforming it from a door that slammed, into one that opened to whoever knocked.

—*Malcolm Muggeridge*

To live peaceably with hard and perverse persons, or with the disorderly, or with such as go contrary to us, is a great grace.

—*Thomas à Kempis*

For your next devotional reading, go to page 1150.

his disciples and Peter, 'He is going ahead of you into Galilee. There you will see him, just as he told you.' "

⁸Trembling and bewildered, the women went out and fled from the tomb. They said nothing to anyone, because they were afraid.

[The earliest manuscripts and some other ancient witnesses do not have Mark 16:9–20.]

⁹When Jesus rose early on the first day of the week, he appeared first to Mary Magdalene, out of whom he had driven seven demons. ¹⁰She went and told those who had been with him and who were mourning and weeping. ¹¹When they heard that Jesus was alive and that she had seen him, they did not believe it.

¹²Afterward Jesus appeared in a different form to two of them while they were walking in the country. ¹³These returned and reported it to the rest; but they did not believe them either.

¹⁴Later Jesus appeared to the Eleven as they were eating; he rebuked them for their lack of faith and their stubborn refusal to believe those who had seen him after he had risen.

¹⁵He said to them, "Go into all the world and preach the gospel to all creation. ¹⁶Whoever believes and is baptized will be saved, but whoever does not believe will be condemned. ¹⁷And these signs will accompany those who believe: In my name they will drive out demons; they will speak in new tongues; ¹⁸they will pick up snakes with their hands; and when they drink deadly poison, it will not hurt them at all; they will place their hands on sick people, and they will get well."

¹⁹After the Lord Jesus had spoken to them, he was taken up into heaven and he sat at the right hand of God. ²⁰Then the disciples went out and preached everywhere, and the Lord worked with them and confirmed his word by the signs that accompanied it.

luke

> AUTHOR: Luke, a doctor and Gentile Christian
>
> DATE: Probably around A.D. 60
>
> THEME: Jesus, God-in-the-flesh, offers salvation to all people.

Introduction

Many have undertaken to draw up an account of the things that have been fulfilled[a] among us, ²just as they were handed down to us by those who from the first were eyewitnesses and servants of the word. ³With this in mind, since I myself have carefully investigated everything from the beginning, I too decided to write an orderly account for you, most excellent Theophilus, ⁴so that you may know the certainty of the things you have been taught.

The Birth of John the Baptist Foretold

⁵In the time of Herod king of Judea there was a priest named Zechariah, who belonged to the priestly division of Abijah; his wife Elizabeth was also a descendant of Aaron. ⁶Both of them were righteous in the sight of God, observing all the Lord's commands and decrees blamelessly. ⁷But they were childless because Elizabeth was not able to conceive, and they were both well advanced in years.

⁸Once when Zechariah's division was on duty and he was serving as priest before God, ⁹he was chosen by lot, according to the custom of the priesthood, to go into the temple of the Lord and burn incense. ¹⁰And when the time for the burning of incense came, all the assembled worshipers were praying outside.

¹¹Then an angel of the Lord appeared to him, standing at the right side of the altar of incense. ¹²When Zechariah saw him, he was startled and was gripped with fear. ¹³But the angel said to him: "Do not be afraid, Zechariah; your prayer has been heard. Your wife Elizabeth will bear you a son, and you are to call him John. ¹⁴He will be a joy and delight to you, and many will rejoice because of his birth, ¹⁵for he will be great in the sight of the Lord. He is never to take wine or other fermented drink, and he will be filled with the Holy Spirit even before he is born. ¹⁶Many of the people of Israel will he bring back to the Lord their God. ¹⁷And he will go on before the Lord, in the spirit and power of Elijah, to turn the hearts of the parents to their children and the disobedient to the wisdom of the righteous—to make ready a people prepared for the Lord."

¹⁸Zechariah asked the angel, "How can I be sure of this? I am an old man and my wife is well along in years."

¹⁹The angel said to him, "I am Gabriel. I stand in the presence of God, and I have been sent to speak to you and to tell you this good news. ²⁰And now you will be silent and not able to speak until the day this happens, because you did not believe my words, which will come true at their appointed time."

²¹Meanwhile, the people were waiting for Zechariah and wondering why he stayed so long in the temple. ²²When he came out, he could not speak to them. They realized he had seen a vision in the temple, for he kept making signs to them but remained unable to speak.

²³When his time of service was completed, he returned home. ²⁴After this his wife Elizabeth became pregnant and for five months remained in seclusion. ²⁵"The Lord has done this for me," she said. "In these days he has shown his favor and taken away my disgrace among the people."

---

a 1 Or been surely believed

MONDAY

ONE VERY SPECIAL RELATIONSHIP
Luke 1:1–56 or 1:46–49

Carolyn Custis James

The theology of a teenager steadied Mary to make the hard choice, to brave the risks and tackle the challenges. The God who spoke through the angel Gabriel was no stranger to Mary, but the well-known God of Abraham and Sarah, Hannah and King David. Like Hannah, Mary was spiritually equipped for the task of raising such a child. Scholar Timothy George writes, "She nursed him at her breast and nurtured and taught him the ways of the Lord. Doubtless she was the one who taught him to memorize the Psalms and to pray, even as he grew in wisdom and stature and in favor with God and others" (Luke 2:52).

. . . Right from the beginning, Jesus brought earthshaking changes to everyone he encountered, but no one more so than the woman who was his mother. The baby Mary carried in her womb, so gloriously heralded by angel voices, turned her private world upside down and brought agonies to her soul worse than she could ever have imagined. Mary got lost in the very place where ultimately she was found—in her relationship with her son.

PHILIP SCHAFF {AD 1819–1893}

Through Mary, whom Elizabeth exclaimed as blessed among women, all people have been blessed and the curse removed that had hung over the era of the fall. Mary was not, however, free from actual and native sin . . . On the contrary, as a daughter of Adam, she needed, like all people, redemption and sanctification through Christ. Christ alone is the author of sinless holiness, and Mary herself expressly called God her Savior. But in the mother and educator of the Savior of the world we no doubt may and should revere—though not worship—the model of female Christian virtue, of purity, tenderness, simplicity, humility, perfect obedience to God and unreserved surrender to Christ. For from that time on we find this woman . . . the zealous servant of the congregation in every work of Christian charity, the sister of mercy, the martyr with superhuman courage, the guardian angel of peace, the example of purity, humility, gentleness, patience, love and fidelity unto death.

reflection

1. In what way does this passage show that Mary had a deep knowledge of God and a genuine relationship with him before Gabriel visited her?

2. How did God turn Mary's world upside down? How did Mary respond?

3. How has God turned *your* world upside down? How have you responded?

For your next devotional reading, go to page 1153.

The Birth of Jesus Foretold

²⁶In the sixth month of Elizabeth's pregnancy, God sent the angel Gabriel to Nazareth, a town in Galilee, ²⁷to a virgin pledged to be married to a man named Joseph, a descendant of David. The virgin's name was Mary. ²⁸The angel went to her and said, "Greetings, you who are highly favored! The Lord is with you."

²⁹Mary was greatly troubled at his words and wondered what kind of greeting this might be. ³⁰But the angel said to her, "Do not be afraid, Mary, you have found favor with God. ³¹You will conceive and give birth to a son, and you are to call him Jesus. ³²He will be great and will be called the Son of the Most High. The Lord God will give him the throne of his father David, ³³and he will reign over the house of Jacob forever; his kingdom will never end."

³⁴"How will this be," Mary asked the angel, "since I am a virgin?"

³⁵The angel answered, "The Holy Spirit will come on you, and the power of the Most High will overshadow you. So the holy one to be born will be called*a* the Son of God. ³⁶Even Elizabeth your relative is going to have a child in her old age, and she who was said to be unable to conceive is in her sixth month. ³⁷For no word from God will ever fail."

³⁸"I am the Lord's servant," Mary answered. "May it be to me according to your word." Then the angel left her.

Mary Visits Elizabeth

³⁹At that time Mary got ready and hurried to a town in the hill country of Judea, ⁴⁰where she entered Zechariah's home and greeted Elizabeth. ⁴¹When Elizabeth heard Mary's greeting, the baby leaped in her womb, and Elizabeth was filled with the Holy Spirit. ⁴²In a loud voice she exclaimed: "Blessed are you among women, and blessed is the child you will bear! ⁴³But why am I so favored, that the mother of my Lord should come to me? ⁴⁴As soon as the sound of your greeting reached my ears, the baby in my womb leaped for joy. ⁴⁵Blessed is she who has believed that the Lord would fulfill his promises to her!"

Mary's Song

⁴⁶And Mary said:

"My soul glorifies the Lord
⁴⁷   and my spirit rejoices in God my
       Savior,
⁴⁸for he has been mindful
       of the humble state of his servant.
   From now on all generations will call me
       blessed,
⁴⁹   for the Mighty One has done great
             things for me—
       holy is his name.
⁵⁰His mercy extends to those who fear
       him,
       from generation to generation.
⁵¹He has performed mighty deeds with his
       arm;
       he has scattered those who are proud
             in their inmost thoughts.
⁵²He has brought down rulers from their
             thrones
       but has lifted up the humble.
⁵³He has filled the hungry with good
             things
       but has sent the rich away empty.
⁵⁴He has helped his servant Israel,
       remembering to be merciful
⁵⁵to Abraham and his descendants forever,
       just as he promised our ancestors."

⁵⁶Mary stayed with Elizabeth for about three months and then returned home.

The Birth of John the Baptist

⁵⁷When it was time for Elizabeth to have her baby, she gave birth to a son. ⁵⁸Her neighbors and relatives heard that the Lord had shown her great mercy, and they shared her joy.

⁵⁹On the eighth day they came to circumcise the child, and they were going to name him after his father Zechariah, ⁶⁰but his mother spoke up and said, "No! He is to be called John."

⁶¹They said to her, "There is no one among your relatives who has that name."

⁶²Then they made signs to his father, to find out what he would like to name the child. ⁶³He asked for a writing tablet, and to everyone's astonishment he wrote, "His name is John." ⁶⁴Immediately his mouth was opened and his tongue was loosed, and he began to speak, praising God. ⁶⁵The

a 35 Or So the child to be born will be called holy,

neighbors were all filled with awe, and throughout the hill country of Judea people were talking about all these things. ⁶⁶Everyone who heard this wondered about it, asking, "What then is this child going to be?" For the Lord's hand was with him.

Zechariah's Song

⁶⁷His father Zechariah was filled with the Holy Spirit and prophesied:

⁶⁸ "Praise be to the Lord, the God of Israel,
    because he has come to his people
        and redeemed them.
⁶⁹ He has raised up a horn*a* of salvation for
        us
    in the house of his servant David
⁷⁰ (as he said through his holy prophets of
        long ago),
⁷¹ salvation from our enemies
    and from the hand of all who hate
        us—
⁷² to show mercy to our ancestors
    and to remember his holy covenant,
⁷³   the oath he swore to our father
        Abraham:
⁷⁴ to rescue us from the hand of our
        enemies,
    and to enable us to serve him without
        fear
⁷⁵   in holiness and righteousness before
        him all our days.

⁷⁶ And you, my child, will be called a
        prophet of the Most High;
    for you will go on before the Lord to
        prepare the way for him,
⁷⁷ to give his people the knowledge of
        salvation
    through the forgiveness of their sins,
⁷⁸ because of the tender mercy of our God,
    by which the rising sun will come to
        us from heaven
⁷⁹ to shine on those living in darkness
    and in the shadow of death,
    to guide our feet into the path of peace."

⁸⁰ And the child grew and became strong in spirit*b*; and he lived in the wilderness until he appeared publicly to Israel.

The Birth of Jesus

2 In those days Caesar Augustus issued a decree that a census should be taken of the entire Roman world. ²(This was the first census that took place while Quirinius was governor of Syria.) ³And everyone went to their own town to register.

⁴So Joseph also went up from the town of Nazareth in Galilee to Judea, to Bethlehem the town of David, because he belonged to the house and line of David. ⁵He went there to register with Mary, who was pledged to be married to him and was expecting a child. ⁶While they were there, the time came for the baby to be born, ⁷and she gave birth to her firstborn, a son. She wrapped him in cloths and placed him in a manger, because there was no guest room available for them.

The Shepherds and the Angels

⁸And there were shepherds living out in the fields nearby, keeping watch over their flocks at night. ⁹An angel of the Lord appeared to them, and the glory of the Lord shone around them, and they were terrified. ¹⁰But the angel said to them, "Do not be afraid. I bring you good news of great joy that will be for all the people. ¹¹Today in the town of David a Savior has been born to you; he is the Messiah, the Lord. ¹²This will be a sign to you: You will find a baby wrapped in cloths and lying in a manger."

¹³Suddenly a great company of the heavenly host appeared with the angel, praising God and saying,

¹⁴ "Glory to God in the highest heaven,
    and on earth peace to those on whom
        his favor rests."

¹⁵When the angels had left them and gone into heaven, the shepherds said to one another, "Let's go to Bethlehem and see this thing that has happened, which the Lord has told us about."

¹⁶So they hurried off and found Mary and Joseph, and the baby, who was lying in the manger. ¹⁷When they had seen him, they spread the word concerning what had been told them about this child, ¹⁸and all who heard it were amazed at what the shepherds said to them. ¹⁹But Mary treasured up all these things and pondered them in her heart. ²⁰The shepherds returned, glorifying

---

a 69 Horn here symbolizes a strong king.   *b 80* Or *in the Spirit*

TUESDAY

BIRTH OF A NEW ERA

Luke 2:1–40 *or* 2:22–35

Philip Yancey

In the birth stories of Luke and Matthew, only one person seems to grasp the mysterious nature of what God has set in motion: the old man Simeon, who recognized the baby as the Messiah, instinctively understood that conflict would surely follow. "This child is destined to cause the falling and rising of many in Israel, and to be a sign that will be spoken against . . ." he said, and then made the prediction that a sword would pierce Mary's own soul. Somehow Simeon sensed that though on the surface little had changed—the autocrat Herod still ruled, Roman troops were still stringing up patriots, Jerusalem still overflowed with beggars—underneath, everything had changed. A new force had arrived to undermine the world's powers.

MARTIN LUTHER {AD 1483–1546}

Mary and Joseph were amazed that the baby was going to be a light to the whole world, a Savior to all people, and the glory of Israel. They were also amazed that Simeon himself thought so much of the child that he would gladly die after seeing him.

It was remarkable for such a great man to praise this child in a public and holy place, for Jesus was only a poor, unimportant baby. His mother was poor and humble, and his father Joseph wasn't wealthy. How could such a child be looked upon as the Savior of all people, the light to the nations, and the glory of Israel? Today, now that we know the entire story, it doesn't seem so amazing. But back then, no one knew anything about it, and it sounded very strange. The poor child was so very different from the great and mighty person whom Simeon spoke about. But Joseph and Mary believed him anyway, and that is why they were amazed. If they hadn't believed, they would have disregarded Simeon's words. What he said would have seemed false and useless rather than amazing. So the simple fact that Joseph and Mary were amazed shows us their great faith.

reflection

1. How do you think Mary and Joseph felt after hearing Simeon's words?

2. When is it toughest for you to exercise faith?

3. In what ways do you treat God as a powerless infant rather than master of the universe?

For your next devotional reading, go to page 1157.

and praising God for all the things they had heard and seen, which were just as they had been told.

Jesus Presented in the Temple

²¹On the eighth day, when it was time to circumcise the child, he was named Jesus, the name the angel had given him before he was conceived.

²²When the time came for the purification rites required by the Law of Moses, Joseph and Mary took him to Jerusalem to present him to the Lord ²³(as it is written in the Law of the Lord, "Every firstborn male is to be consecrated to the Lord"ᵃ), ²⁴and to offer a sacrifice in keeping with what is said in the Law of the Lord: "a pair of doves or two young pigeons."ᵇ

²⁵Now there was a man in Jerusalem called Simeon, who was righteous and devout. He was waiting for the consolation of Israel, and the Holy Spirit was on him. ²⁶It had been revealed to him by the Holy Spirit that he would not die before he had seen the Lord's Messiah. ²⁷Moved by the Spirit, he went into the temple courts. When the parents brought in the child Jesus to do for him what the custom of the Law required, ²⁸Simeon took him in his arms and praised God, saying:

²⁹ "Sovereign Lord, as you have promised,
     you may now dismissᶜ your servant in
       peace.
³⁰ For my eyes have seen your salvation,
³¹   which you have prepared in the sight
       of all nations:
³² a light for revelation to the Gentiles,
     and the glory of your people Israel."

³³The child's father and mother marveled at what was said about him. ³⁴Then Simeon blessed them and said to Mary, his mother: "This child is destined to cause the falling and rising of many in Israel, and to be a sign that will be spoken against, ³⁵so that the thoughts of many hearts will be revealed. And a sword will pierce your own soul too."

³⁶There was also a prophet, Anna, the daughter of Phanuel, of the tribe of Asher. She was very old; she had lived with her husband seven years after her marriage, ³⁷and then had been a widow for eighty-four

years.ᵈ She never left the temple but worshiped night and day, fasting and praying. ³⁸Coming up to them at that very moment, she gave thanks to God and spoke about the child to all who were looking forward to the redemption of Jerusalem.

³⁹When Joseph and Mary had done everything required by the Law of the Lord, they returned to Galilee to their own town of Nazareth. ⁴⁰And the child grew and became strong; he was filled with wisdom, and the grace of God was on him.

The Boy Jesus at the Temple

⁴¹Every year Jesus' parents went to Jerusalem for the Festival of the Passover. ⁴²When he was twelve years old, they went up to the festival, according to the custom. ⁴³After the festival was over, while his parents were returning home, the boy Jesus stayed behind in Jerusalem, but they were unaware of it. ⁴⁴Thinking he was in their company, they traveled on for a day. Then they began looking for him among their relatives and friends. ⁴⁵When they did not find him, they went back to Jerusalem to look for him. ⁴⁶After three days they found him in the temple courts, sitting among the teachers, listening to them and asking them questions. ⁴⁷Everyone who heard him was amazed at his understanding and his answers. ⁴⁸When his parents saw him, they were astonished. His mother said to him, "Son, why have you treated us like this? Your father and I have been anxiously searching for you."

⁴⁹"Why were you searching for me?" he asked. "Didn't you know I had to be in my Father's house?"ᵉ ⁵⁰But they did not understand what he was saying to them.

⁵¹Then he went down to Nazareth with them and was obedient to them. But his mother treasured all these things in her heart. ⁵²And as Jesus grew up, he increased in wisdom and in favor with God and people.

John the Baptist Prepares the Way

3 In the fifteenth year of the reign of Tiberius Caesar—when Pontius Pilate was governor of Judea, Herod tetrarch of Galilee, his brother Philip tetrarch of Iturea and Traconitis, and Lysanias te-

---

ᵃ 23 Exodus 13:2,12   ᵇ 24 Lev. 12:8   ᶜ 29 Or promised, / now dismiss   ᵈ 37 Or then was a widow until she was eighty-four   ᵉ 49 Or be about my Father's business trarch of Abilene— [2]during the high-priest-hood of Annas and Caiaphas, the word of God came to John son of Zechariah in the wilderness. [3]He went into all the country around the Jordan, preaching a baptism of repentance for the forgiveness of sins. [4]As it is written in the book of the words of Isaiah the prophet:

"A voice of one calling in the wilderness,
'Prepare the way for the Lord,
    make straight paths for him.
[5]Every valley shall be filled in,
    every mountain and hill made low.
The crooked roads shall become straight,
    the rough ways smooth.
[6]And all people will see God's
    salvation.' " [a]

[7]John said to the crowds coming out to be baptized by him, "You brood of vipers! Who warned you to flee from the coming wrath? [8]Produce fruit in keeping with repentance. And do not begin to say to yourselves, 'We have Abraham as our father.' For I tell you that out of these stones God can raise up children for Abraham. [9]The ax is already at the root of the trees, and every tree that does not produce good fruit will be cut down and thrown into the fire."

[10]"What should we do then?" the crowd asked.

[11]John answered, "Anyone who has two shirts should share with the one who has none, and anyone who has food should do the same."

[12]Even tax collectors came to be baptized. "Teacher," they asked, "what should we do?"

[13]"Don't collect any more than you are required to," he told them.

[14]Then some soldiers asked him, "And what should we do?"

He replied, "Don't extort money and don't accuse people falsely—be content with your pay."

[15]The people were waiting expectantly and were all wondering in their hearts if John might possibly be the Messiah. [16]John answered them all, "I baptize you with[b] water. But one who is more powerful than I will come, the thongs of whose sandals I am not worthy to untie. He will baptize you with[b] the Holy Spirit and fire. [17]His winnowing fork is in his hand to clear his threshing floor and to gather the wheat into his barn, but he will burn up the chaff with unquenchable fire." [18]And with many other words John exhorted the people and proclaimed the good news to them.

[19]But when John rebuked Herod the tetrarch because of his marriage to Herodias, his brother's wife, and all the other evil things he had done, [20]Herod added this to them all: He locked John up in prison.

The Baptism and Genealogy of Jesus

[21]When all the people were being baptized, Jesus was baptized too. And as he was praying, heaven was opened [22]and the Holy Spirit descended on him in bodily form like a dove. And a voice came from heaven: "You are my Son, whom I love; with you I am well pleased."

[23]Now Jesus himself was about thirty years old when he began his ministry. He was the son, so it was thought, of Joseph,

the son of Heli, [24]the son of Matthat,
    the son of Levi, the son of Melki,
    the son of Jannai, the son of Joseph,
[25]the son of Mattathias, the son of Amos,
    the son of Nahum, the son of Esli,
    the son of Naggai, [26]the son of Maath,
    the son of Mattathias, the son of Semein,
    the son of Josek, the son of Joda,
[27]the son of Joanan, the son of Rhesa,
    the son of Zerubbabel, the son of She-
        altiel,
    the son of Neri, [28]the son of Melki,
    the son of Addi, the son of Cosam,
    the son of Elmadam, the son of Er,
[29]the son of Joshua, the son of Eliezer,
    the son of Jorim, the son of Matthat,
    the son of Levi, [30]the son of Simeon,
    the son of Judah, the son of Joseph,
    the son of Jonam, the son of Eliakim,
[31]the son of Melea, the son of Menna,
    the son of Mattatha, the son of Nathan,
    the son of David, [32]the son of Jesse,
    the son of Obed, the son of Boaz,
    the son of Salmon,[c] the son of Nah-
        shon,
[33]the son of Amminadab, the son of
        Ram,[d]
    the son of Hezron, the son of Perez,
    the son of Judah, [34]the son of Jacob,

a 6 Isaiah 40:3-5   b 16 Or in   c 32 Some early manuscripts Sala   d 33 Some manuscripts Amminadab, the son of Admin, the son of Arni; other manuscripts vary widely.

the son of Isaac, the son of Abraham,
the son of Terah, the son of Nahor,
³⁵ the son of Serug, the son of Reu,
the son of Peleg, the son of Eber,
the son of Shelah, ³⁶the son of Cainan,
the son of Arphaxad, the son of Shem,
the son of Noah, the son of Lamech,
³⁷ the son of Methuselah, the son of Enoch,
the son of Jared, the son of Mahalalel,
the son of Kenan, ³⁸the son of Enosh,
the son of Seth, the son of Adam,
the son of God.

Jesus Is Tested in the Wilderness

4 Jesus, full of the Holy Spirit, left the Jordan and was led by the Spirit into the wilderness, ²where for forty days he was tempted^a by the devil. He ate nothing during those days, and at the end of them he was hungry.

³The devil said to him, "If you are the Son of God, tell this stone to become bread."

⁴Jesus answered, "It is written: 'People do not live on bread alone.'^b"

⁵The devil led him up to a high place and showed him in an instant all the kingdoms of the world. ⁶And he said to him, "I will give you all their authority and splendor; it has been given to me, and I can give it to anyone I want to. ⁷If you worship me, it will all be yours."

⁸Jesus answered, "It is written: 'Worship the Lord your God and serve him only.'^c"

⁹The devil led him to Jerusalem and had him stand on the highest point of the temple. "If you are the Son of God," he said, "throw yourself down from here. ¹⁰For it is written:

" 'He will command his angels
concerning you
to guard you carefully;
¹¹they will lift you up in their hands,
so that you will not strike your foot
against a stone.'^d"

¹²Jesus answered, "It is said: 'Do not put the Lord your God to the test.'^e"

¹³When the devil had finished all this tempting, he left him until an opportune time.

Jesus Rejected at Nazareth

¹⁴Jesus returned to Galilee in the power of the Spirit, and news about him spread through the whole countryside. ¹⁵He was teaching in their synagogues, and everyone praised him.

¹⁶He went to Nazareth, where he had been brought up, and on the Sabbath day he went into the synagogue, as was his custom. He stood up to read, ¹⁷and the scroll of the prophet Isaiah was handed to him. Unrolling it, he found the place where it is written:

¹⁸"The Spirit of the Lord is on me,
because he has anointed me
to proclaim good news to the poor.
He has sent me to proclaim freedom for
the prisoners
and recovery of sight for the blind,
to set the oppressed free,
¹⁹ to proclaim the year of the Lord's
favor."^f

²⁰Then he rolled up the scroll, gave it back to the attendant and sat down. The eyes of everyone in the synagogue were fastened on him. ²¹He began by saying to them, "Today this scripture is fulfilled in your hearing."

²²All spoke well of him and were amazed at the gracious words that came from his lips. "Isn't this Joseph's son?" they asked.

²³Jesus said to them, "Surely you will quote this proverb to me: 'Physician, heal yourself!' And you will tell me, 'Do here in your hometown what we have heard that you did in Capernaum.' "

²⁴"Truly I tell you," he continued, "prophets are not accepted in their hometowns. ²⁵I assure you that there were many widows in Israel in Elijah's time, when the sky was shut for three and a half years and there was a severe famine throughout the land. ²⁶Yet Elijah was not sent to any of them, but to a widow in Zarephath in the region of Sidon. ²⁷And there were many in Israel with leprosy^g in the time of Elisha the prophet, yet not one of them was cleansed—only Naaman the Syrian."

²⁸All the people in the synagogue were furious when they heard this. ²⁹They got up, drove him out of the town, and took him to the brow of the hill on which the town was

---

^a 2 The Greek for *tempted* can also mean *tested*.   ^b 4 Deut. 8:3   ^c 8 Deut. 6:13   ^d 11 Psalm 91:11,12
^e 12 Deut. 6:16   ^f 19 Isaiah 61:1,2 (see Septuagint); Isaiah 58:6   ^g 27 The Greek word traditionally
translated *leprosy* was used for various diseases affecting the skin.

WEDNESDAY

THE RICH/POOR DILEMMA

Luke 4:1–44 *or* 4:18

Richard Foster

In his manifesto on the poor, Jesus declared his intention to "[set the oppressed free]" (Luke 4:18). And as he went among people teaching and healing, he observed the many oppressions that bore down upon them. He sought to lift their burdens, and as he did he spoke repeatedly and vigorously of one of the greatest burdens they bore—the burden of providing for themselves against tomorrow.

He saw how people were broken by the effort to attain riches. He perceived their awful vulnerability in believing that it was their responsibility to provide for themselves, to watch out for number one. The apostle Paul said that those who desire wealth have "pierced [themselves] with many [griefs]" (1 Timothy 6:9–10) . . .

Jesus also saw how people were crushed by the failure to obtain riches. In his day it was considered a mark of God's displeasure to be poor. And those who had failed to receive the goods of this world could not help feeling that somehow God was against them. Remember how baffled the disciples were when Jesus told them that a camel could slip through the eye of a needle more easily than the wealthy could enter the kingdom of God (Matthew 19:24)? This astonishment was due primarily to their belief that the wealth of the rich young ruler was a sign of God's special favor upon him. No wonder they exclaimed, "Who then can be saved?" (Matthew 19:25). And Jesus perceived how bruised and trampled in spirit people were because they were poor and felt that God was displeased with them. Repeatedly he opposed this false and destructive doctrine, showing instead that in the economy of God, the poor, the broken, the hurt were special objects of his blessing and concern (Matthew 5:1–12). By word and deed he sought to lift the burden of the discouraged and disheartened.

ALEXANDER MACLAREN {AD 1826–1910}

Jesus does not ask you to bring anything but debts and sins, emptiness and weakness, and penitent faith. He will strengthen the weakness, fill the emptiness, forgive the sins, cancel the debts and make you "rich toward God" (Luke 12:21). I beg you to listen to him as he speaks from heaven. And then you will be of those blessed poor ones who are rich in faith, inheriting the kingdom of God (James 2:5).

reflection

1.　Why do so many people view wealth as the means to freedom?

2.　How does God's view of worldly wealth contradict this perspective?

3.　How have you been "oppressed" by your money or the pursuit of money?

For your next devotional reading, go to page 1160.

built, in order to throw him off the cliff. ³⁰But he walked right through the crowd and went on his way.

Jesus Drives Out an Evil Spirit

³¹Then he went down to Capernaum, a town in Galilee, and on the Sabbath he taught the people. ³²They were amazed at his teaching, because his words had authority.

³³In the synagogue there was a man possessed by a demon, an evil*a* spirit. He cried out at the top of his voice, ³⁴"Go away! What do you want with us, Jesus of Nazareth? Have you come to destroy us? I know who you are—the Holy One of God!"

³⁵"Be quiet!" Jesus said sternly. "Come out of him!" Then the demon threw the man down before them all and came out without injuring him.

³⁶All the people were amazed and said to each other, "What words these are! With authority and power he gives orders to evil spirits and they come out!" ³⁷And the news about him spread throughout the surrounding area.

Jesus Heals Many

³⁸Jesus left the synagogue and went to the home of Simon. Now Simon's mother-in-law was suffering from a high fever, and they asked Jesus to help her. ³⁹So he bent over her and rebuked the fever, and it left her. She got up at once and began to wait on them.

⁴⁰At sunset, the people brought to Jesus all who had various kinds of sickness, and laying his hands on each one, he healed them. ⁴¹Moreover, demons came out of many people, shouting, "You are the Son of God!" But he rebuked them and would not allow them to speak, because they knew he was the Messiah.

⁴²At daybreak, Jesus went out to a solitary place. The people were looking for him and when they came to where he was, they tried to keep him from leaving them. ⁴³But he said, "I must proclaim the good news of the kingdom of God to the other towns also, because that is why I was sent." ⁴⁴And he kept on preaching in the synagogues of Judea.

Jesus Calls His First Disciples

5 One day as Jesus was standing by the Lake of Gennesaret,*b* the people were crowding around him and listening to the word of God. ²He saw at the water's edge two boats, left there by the fishermen, who were washing their nets. ³He got into one of the boats, the one belonging to Simon, and asked him to put out a little from shore. Then he sat down and taught the people from the boat.

⁴When he had finished speaking, he said to Simon, "Put out into deep water, and let down the nets for a catch."

⁵Simon answered, "Master, we've worked hard all night and haven't caught anything. But because you say so, I will let down the nets."

⁶When they had done so, they caught such a large number of fish that their nets began to break. ⁷So they signaled their partners in the other boat to come and help them, and they came and filled both boats so full that they began to sink.

⁸When Simon Peter saw this, he fell at Jesus' knees and said, "Go away from me, Lord; I am a sinful man!" ⁹For he and all his companions were astonished at the catch of fish they had taken, ¹⁰and so were James and John, the sons of Zebedee, Simon's partners.

Then Jesus said to Simon, "Don't be afraid; from now on you will fish for people." ¹¹So they pulled their boats up on shore, left everything and followed him.

Jesus Heals a Man With Leprosy

¹²While Jesus was in one of the towns, a man came along who was covered with leprosy.*c* When he saw Jesus, he fell with his face to the ground and begged him, "Lord, if you are willing, you can make me clean."

¹³Jesus reached out his hand and touched the man. "I am willing," he said. "Be clean!" And immediately the leprosy left him.

¹⁴Then Jesus ordered him, "Don't tell anyone, but go, show yourself to the priest and offer the sacrifices that Moses commanded for your cleansing, as a testimony to them."

¹⁵Yet the news about him spread all the more, so that crowds of people came to hear him and to be healed of their sicknesses.

---

a 33 Greek *unclean*; also in verse 36   *b 1* That is, Sea of Galilee   *c 12* The Greek word traditionally translated *leprosy* was used for various diseases affecting the skin.

¹⁶But Jesus often withdrew to lonely places and prayed.

Jesus Forgives and Heals a Paralyzed Man

¹⁷One day Jesus was teaching, and Pharisees and teachers of the law were sitting there. They had come from every village of Galilee and from Judea and Jerusalem. And the power of the Lord was with Jesus to heal the sick. ¹⁸Some men came carrying a paralyzed man on a mat and tried to take him into the house to lay him before Jesus. ¹⁹When they could not find a way to do this because of the crowd, they went up on the roof and lowered him on his mat through the tiles into the middle of the crowd, right in front of Jesus.

²⁰When Jesus saw their faith, he said, "Friend, your sins are forgiven."

²¹The Pharisees and the teachers of the law began thinking to themselves, "Who is this fellow who speaks blasphemy? Who can forgive sins but God alone?"

²²Jesus knew what they were thinking and asked, "Why are you thinking these things in your hearts? ²³Which is easier: to say, 'Your sins are forgiven,' or to say, 'Get up and walk'? ²⁴But I want you to know that the Son of Man has authority on earth to forgive sins." So he said to the paralyzed man, "I tell you, get up, take your mat and go home." ²⁵Immediately he stood up in front of them, took what he had been lying on and went home praising God. ²⁶Everyone was amazed and gave praise to God. They were filled with awe and said, "We have seen remarkable things today."

Jesus Calls Levi and Eats With Sinners

²⁷After this, Jesus went out and saw a tax collector by the name of Levi sitting at his tax booth. "Follow me," Jesus said to him, ²⁸and Levi got up, left everything and followed him.

²⁹Then Levi held a great banquet for Jesus at his house, and a large crowd of tax collectors and others were eating with them. ³⁰But the Pharisees and the teachers of the law who belonged to their sect complained to his disciples, "Why do you eat and drink with tax collectors and sinners?"

³¹Jesus answered them, "It is not the healthy who need a doctor, but the sick. ³²I have not come to call the righteous, but sinners to repentance."

Jesus Questioned About Fasting

³³They said to him, "John's disciples often fast and pray, and so do the disciples of the Pharisees, but yours go on eating and drinking."

³⁴Jesus answered, "Can you make the friends of the bridegroom fast while he is with them? ³⁵But the time will come when the bridegroom will be taken from them; in those days they will fast."

³⁶He told them this parable: "No one tears a piece out of a new garment to patch an old one. If they do, they will have torn the new garment, and the patch from the new will not match the old. ³⁷And people do not pour new wine into old wineskins. If they do, the new wine will burst the skins; the wine will run out and the wineskins will be ruined. ³⁸No, new wine must be poured into new wineskins. ³⁹And none of you, after drinking old wine, wants the new, for you say, 'The old is better.' "

Jesus Is Lord of the Sabbath

6 One Sabbath Jesus was going through the grainfields, and his disciples began to pick some heads of grain, rub them in their hands and eat the kernels. ²Some of the Pharisees asked, "Why are you doing what is unlawful on the Sabbath?"

³Jesus answered them, "Have you never read what David did when he and his companions were hungry? ⁴He entered the house of God, and taking the consecrated bread, he ate what is lawful only for priests to eat. And he also gave some to his companions." ⁵Then Jesus said to them, "The Son of Man is Lord of the Sabbath."

⁶On another Sabbath he went into the synagogue and was teaching, and a man was there whose right hand was shriveled. ⁷The Pharisees and the teachers of the law were looking for a reason to accuse Jesus, so they watched him closely to see if he would heal on the Sabbath. ⁸But Jesus knew what they were thinking and said to the man with the shriveled hand, "Get up and stand in front of everyone." So he got up and stood there.

⁹Then Jesus said to them, "I ask you, which is lawful on the Sabbath: to do good or to do evil, to save life or to destroy it?"

¹⁰He looked around at them all, and then said to the man, "Stretch out your hand." He did so, and his hand was completely re-

GOD'S GOAL FOR YOU

Luke 6:1–36 or 6:17–22

Rick Warren

God's ultimate goal for your life on earth is not comfort, but character development. He wants you to grow up spiritually and become like Christ. Becoming like Christ does not mean losing your personality or becoming a mindless clone. God created your uniqueness, so he certainly doesn't want to destroy it. Christlikeness is all about transforming your character, not your personality.

God wants you to develop the kind of character described in the beatitudes of Jesus, the fruit of the Spirit, Paul's great chapter on love and Peter's list of the characteristics of an effective and productive life. Every time you forget that character is one of God's purposes for your life, you will become frustrated by your circumstances. You'll wonder, "Why is this happening to me? Why am I having such a difficult time?" One answer is that life is *supposed* to be difficult! It's what enables us to grow. Remember, earth is not heaven!

THOMAS WATSON {AD 1620–1686}

The people of God meet with many complicated difficulties and sinking discouragements in their walk with God. Their march is not only tedious but also dangerous, and their hearts are on the verge of giving up. Therefore, it is not inappropriate to set the crown of blessedness before them to kindle their courage and to inflame their zeal. How many Scriptures bring this olive branch in their mouth, the tidings of blessedness to believers! ... The promise of blessedness leads us to maturity. It is the whetstone of a Christian's labor, the height of his ambition, the flower of his joy. Blessedness is the desire of all people. Aquinas calls it the "ultimate end."

reflection

1. What does God outline as the path that leads to his blessings?

2. God's more concerned about your character than about your comfort. How do you feel about that?

3. How does the promise of God's blessings keep you walking with him through agonizing difficulties?

For your next devotional reading, go to page 1163.

stored. [11]But the Pharisees and the teachers of the law were furious and began to discuss with one another what they might do to Jesus.

The Twelve Apostles

[12]One of those days Jesus went out to a mountainside to pray, and spent the night praying to God. [13]When morning came, he called his disciples to him and chose twelve of them, whom he also designated apostles: [14]Simon (whom he named Peter), his brother Andrew, James, John, Philip, Bartholomew, [15]Matthew, Thomas, James son of Alphaeus, Simon who was called the Zealot, [16]Judas son of James, and Judas Iscariot, who became a traitor.

Blessings and Woes

[17]He went down with them and stood on a level place. A large crowd of his disciples was there and a great number of people from all over Judea, from Jerusalem, and from the coastal region around Tyre and Sidon, [18]who had come to hear him and to be healed of their diseases. Those troubled by evil[a] spirits were cured, [19]and the people all tried to touch him, because power was coming from him and healing them all.

[20]Looking at his disciples, he said:

"Blessed are you who are poor,
for yours is the kingdom of God.
[21]Blessed are you who hunger now,
for you will be satisfied.
Blessed are you who weep now,
for you will laugh.
[22]Blessed are you when people hate you,
when they exclude you and insult you
and reject your name as evil,
because of the Son of Man.

[23]"Rejoice in that day and leap for joy, because great is your reward in heaven. For that is how their ancestors treated the prophets.

[24]"But woe to you who are rich,
for you have already received your
comfort.
[25]Woe to you who are well fed now,
for you will go hungry.
Woe to you who laugh now,
for you will mourn and weep.

[26]Woe to you when everyone speaks well
of you,
for that is how their ancestors treated
the false prophets.

Love for Enemies

[27]"But to you who are listening I say: Love your enemies, do good to those who hate you, [28]bless those who curse you, pray for those who mistreat you. [29]If someone slaps you on one cheek, turn the other also. If someone takes your coat, do not withhold your shirt. [30]Give to everyone who asks you, and if anyone takes what belongs to you, do not demand it back. [31]Do to others as you would have them do to you.

[32]"If you love those who love you, what credit is that to you? Even sinners love those who love them. [33]And if you do good to those who are good to you, what credit is that to you? Even sinners do that. [34]And if you lend to those from whom you expect repayment, what credit is that to you? Even sinners lend to sinners, expecting to be repaid in full. [35]But love your enemies, do good to them, and lend to them without expecting to get anything back. Then your reward will be great, and you will be children of the Most High, because he is kind to the ungrateful and wicked. [36]Be merciful, just as your Father is merciful.

Judging Others

[37]"Do not judge, and you will not be judged. Do not condemn, and you will not be condemned. Forgive, and you will be forgiven. [38]Give, and it will be given to you. A good measure, pressed down, shaken together and running over, will be poured into your lap. For with the measure you use, it will be measured to you."

[39]He also told them this parable: "Can the blind lead the blind? Will they not both fall into a pit? [40]Students are not above their teacher, but all who are fully trained will be like their teacher.

[41]"Why do you look at the speck of sawdust in someone else's eye and pay no attention to the plank in your own eye? [42]How can you say, 'Friend, let me take the speck out of your eye,' when you yourself fail to see the plank in your own eye? You hypocrite, first take the plank out of your eye, and

_a_ 18 Greek _unclean_

then you will see clearly to remove the speck from the other person's eye.

A Tree and Its Fruit

⁴³"No good tree bears bad fruit, nor does a bad tree bear good fruit. ⁴⁴Each tree is recognized by its own fruit. People do not pick figs from thornbushes, or grapes from briers. ⁴⁵Good people bring good things out of the good stored up in their heart, and evil people bring evil things out of the evil stored up in their heart. For out of the overflow of the heart the mouth speaks.

The Wise and Foolish Builders

⁴⁶"Why do you call me, 'Lord, Lord,' and do not do what I say? ⁴⁷As for those who come to me and hear my words and put them into practice, I will show you what they are like. ⁴⁸They are like a man building a house, who dug down deep and laid the foundation on rock. When a flood came, the torrent struck that house but could not shake it, because it was well built. ⁴⁹But those who hear my words and do not put them into practice are like a man who built a house on the ground without a foundation. The moment the torrent struck that house, it collapsed and its destruction was complete."

The Faith of the Centurion

7 When Jesus had finished saying all this to the people who were listening, he entered Capernaum. ²There a centurion's servant, whom his master valued highly, was sick and about to die. ³The centurion heard of Jesus and sent some elders of the Jews to him, asking him to come and heal his servant. ⁴When they came to Jesus, they pleaded earnestly with him, "This man deserves to have you do this, ⁵because he loves our nation and has built our synagogue." ⁶So Jesus went with them.

He was not far from the house when the centurion sent friends to say to him: "Lord, don't trouble yourself, for I do not deserve to have you come under my roof. ⁷That is why I did not even consider myself worthy to come to you. But say the word, and my servant will be healed. ⁸For I myself am a man under authority, with soldiers under me. I tell this one, 'Go,' and he goes; and that one,

'Come,' and he comes. I say to my servant, 'Do this,' and he does it."

⁹When Jesus heard this, he was amazed at him, and turning to the crowd following him, he said, "I tell you, I have not found such great faith even in Israel." ¹⁰Then the men who had been sent returned to the house and found the servant well.

Jesus Raises a Widow's Son

¹¹Soon afterward, Jesus went to a town called Nain, and his disciples and a large crowd went along with him. ¹²As he approached the town gate, a dead person was being carried out—the only son of his mother, and she was a widow. And a large crowd from the town was with her. ¹³When the Lord saw her, his heart went out to her and he said, "Don't cry."

¹⁴Then he went up and touched the bier they were carrying him on, and the bearers stood still. He said, "Young man, I say to you, get up!" ¹⁵The dead man sat up and began to talk, and Jesus gave him back to his mother.

¹⁶They were all filled with awe and praised God. "A great prophet has appeared among us," they said. "God has come to help his people." ¹⁷This news about Jesus spread throughout Judea and the surrounding country.

Jesus and John the Baptist

¹⁸John's disciples told him about all these things. Calling two of them, ¹⁹he sent them to the Lord to ask, "Are you the one who was to come, or should we expect someone else?"

²⁰When the men came to Jesus, they said, "John the Baptist sent us to you to ask, 'Are you the one who was to come, or should we expect someone else?'"

²¹At that very time Jesus cured many who had diseases, sicknesses and evil spirits, and gave sight to many who were blind. ²²So he replied to the messengers, "Go back and report to John what you have seen and heard: The blind receive sight, the lame walk, those who have leprosy[a] are cleansed, the deaf hear, the dead are raised, and the good news is proclaimed to the poor. ²³Blessed is anyone who does not stumble on account of me."

a 22 The Greek word traditionally translated leprosy was used for various diseases affecting the skin.

FRIDAY

FAITH THAT AMAZES GOD

Luke 7:1–50 *or* 7:2,6–10

Jim Cymbala

What do you think it would take to amaze Jesus? After all, through him the world and all humanity were created in the first place. He has forever existed in heaven itself. While on earth, was there anything that impressed him to the point of exclaiming, "That's really something! Wow!" Never in any chapter of the four Gospels was Jesus astounded by anybody's righteousness. After all, he was entirely pure and holy himself. Never was he impressed with anyone's wisdom or education. Never did he say, "Boy, Matthew sure is smart, isn't he? I really picked out a financial genius there."

But he *was* amazed by one thing: people's faith. When he told the Roman centurion he would go to his house to heal his servant, and the centurion said not to bother but just to speak the word of healing, Jesus "was amazed at him, and turning to the crowd following him, he said, 'I tell you, I have not found such *great faith* even in Israel'" (Luke 7:9) [emphasis added]. The Jewish listeners probably didn't appreciate being outclassed by this Roman, but that is the way it happened, regardless.

TONY MARSHALL ANDERSON {AD 1888–1979}

We do not hesitate to accept the fact that God imparts a measure of his life and love to his redeemed people. Surely it is not impossible for him to furnish a sufficient measure of his faith to his people to sustain them in life in this world of doubt and disbelief. If his people are not able to accomplish his works in the world because of the littleness of their faith, there is no valid reason to doubt that he can and will increase their measure of achieving faith. When the disciples said to the Lord, "Increase our faith!" we have reasons to believe that he granted their request (see Luke 17:5).

The Savior did not imply that we could possess the same measureless degree of faith which the infinite God possesses in his divine person. But he did encourage us to believe that we can receive a measure of God's faith to enable us to accomplish his purpose in redemption. The Savior desires for us to see that we can enter into the faith of God and become workers together with him in achieving his eternal purpose in his beloved Son . . . Christ is made invincible in this world through the unwavering faith of his praying people.

reflection

1. How amazing is *your* faith?
2. What situation do you face that requires an extra-large helping of faith?
3. When have you asked God to heap up your faith?

For your next devotional reading, go to page 1166.

24After John's messengers left, Jesus began to speak to the crowd about John: "What did you go out into the wilderness to see? A reed swayed by the wind? 25If not, what did you go out to see? A man dressed in fine clothes? No, those who wear expensive clothes and indulge in luxury are in palaces. 26But what did you go out to see? A prophet? Yes, I tell you, and more than a prophet. 27This is the one about whom it is written:

" 'I will send my messenger ahead of
  you,
  who will prepare your way before
  you.'a

28I tell you, among those born of women there is no one greater than John; yet the one who is least in the kingdom of God is greater than he."

29(All the people, even the tax collectors, when they heard Jesus' words, acknowledged that God's way was right, because they had been baptized by John. 30But the Pharisees and the experts in the law rejected God's purpose for themselves, because they had not been baptized by John.)

31Jesus went on to say, "To what, then, can I compare the people of this generation? What are they like? 32They are like children sitting in the marketplace and calling out to each other:

" 'We played the pipe for you,
  and you did not dance;
we sang a dirge,
  and you did not cry.'

33For John the Baptist came neither eating bread nor drinking wine, and you say, 'He has a demon.' 34The Son of Man came eating and drinking, and you say, 'Here is a glutton and a drunkard, a friend of tax collectors and sinners.' 35But wisdom is proved right by all her children."

Jesus Anointed by a Sinful Woman

36When one of the Pharisees invited Jesus to have dinner with him, he went to the Pharisee's house and reclined at the table. 37A woman in that town who lived a sinful life learned that Jesus was eating at the Pharisee's house, so she came there with an alabaster jar of perfume. 38As she stood behind him at his feet weeping, she began to

wet his feet with her tears. Then she wiped them with her hair, kissed them and poured perfume on them.

39When the Pharisee who had invited him saw this, he said to himself, "If this man were a prophet, he would know who is touching him and what kind of woman she is—that she is a sinner."

40Jesus answered him, "Simon, I have something to tell you."

"Tell me, teacher," he said.

41"Two people owed money to a certain moneylender. One owed him five hundred denarii,b and the other fifty. 42Neither of them had the money to pay him back, so he forgave the debts of both. Now which of them will love him more?"

43Simon replied, "I suppose the one who had the bigger debt forgiven."

"You have judged correctly," Jesus said.

44Then he turned toward the woman and said to Simon, "Do you see this woman? I came into your house. You did not give me any water for my feet, but she wet my feet with her tears and wiped them with her hair. 45You did not give me a kiss, but this woman, from the time I entered, has not stopped kissing my feet. 46You did not put oil on my head, but she has poured perfume on my feet. 47Therefore, I tell you, her many sins have been forgiven—as her great love has shown. But whoever has been forgiven little loves little."

48Then Jesus said to her, "Your sins are forgiven."

49The other guests began to say among themselves, "Who is this who even forgives sins?"

50Jesus said to the woman, "Your faith has saved you; go in peace."

The Parable of the Sower

8 After this, Jesus traveled about from one town and village to another, proclaiming the good news of the kingdom of God. The Twelve were with him, 2and also some women who had been cured of evil spirits and diseases: Mary (called Magdalene) from whom seven demons had come out; 3Joanna the wife of Chuza, the manager of Herod's household; Susanna; and many others. These women were helping to support them out of their own means.

---

a 27 Mal. 3:1   b 41 A denarius was the daily wage of a day laborer (see Matt. 20:2).

[4]While a large crowd was gathering and people were coming to Jesus from town after town, he told this parable: [5]"A farmer went out to sow his seed. As he was scattering the seed, some fell along the path; it was trampled on, and the birds ate it up. [6]Some fell on rock, and when it came up, the plants withered because they had no moisture. [7]Other seed fell among thorns, which grew up with it and choked the plants. [8]Still other seed fell on good soil. It came up and yielded a crop, a hundred times more than was sown."

When he said this, he called out, "Whoever has ears to hear, let them hear."

[9]His disciples asked him what this parable meant. [10]He said, "The knowledge of the secrets of the kingdom of God has been given to you, but to others I speak in parables, so that,

" 'though seeing, they may not see;
though hearing, they may not
understand.'[a]

[11]"This is the meaning of the parable: The seed is the word of God. [12]Those along the path are the ones who hear, and then the devil comes and takes away the word from their hearts, so that they may not believe and be saved. [13]Those on the rock are the ones who receive the word with joy when they hear it, but they have no root. They believe for a while, but in the time of testing they fall away. [14]The seed that fell among thorns stands for those who hear, but as they go on their way they are choked by life's worries, riches and pleasures, and they do not mature. [15]But the seed on good soil stands for those with a noble and good heart, who hear the word, retain it, and by persevering produce a crop.

A Lamp on a Stand

[16]"No one lights a lamp and hides it in a clay jar or puts it under a bed. Instead, they put it on a stand, so that those who come in can see the light. [17]For there is nothing hidden that will not be disclosed, and nothing concealed that will not be known or brought out into the open. [18]Therefore consider carefully how you listen. Those who have will be given more; as for those who do not have, even what they think they have will be taken from them."

Jesus' Mother and Brothers

[19]Now Jesus' mother and brothers came to see him, but they were not able to get near him because of the crowd. [20]Someone told him, "Your mother and brothers are standing outside, wanting to see you."

[21]He replied, "My mother and brothers are those who hear God's word and put it into practice."

Jesus Calms the Storm

[22]One day Jesus said to his disciples, "Let us go over to the other side of the lake." So they got into a boat and set out. [23]As they sailed, he fell asleep. A squall came down on the lake, so that the boat was being swamped, and they were in great danger.

[24]The disciples went and woke him, saying, "Master, Master, we're going to drown!"

He got up and rebuked the wind and the raging waters; the storm subsided, and all was calm. [25]"Where is your faith?" he asked his disciples.

In fear and amazement they asked one another, "Who is this? He commands even the winds and the water, and they obey him."

Jesus Restores a Demon-Possessed Man

[26]They sailed to the region of the Gerasenes,[b] which is across the lake from Galilee. [27]When Jesus stepped ashore, he was met by a demon-possessed man from the town. For a long time this man had not worn clothes or lived in a house, but had lived in the tombs. [28]When he saw Jesus, he cried out and fell at his feet, shouting at the top of his voice, "What do you want with me, Jesus, Son of the Most High God? I beg you, don't torture me!" [29]For Jesus had commanded the evil[c] spirit to come out of the man. Many times it had seized him, and though he was chained hand and foot and kept under guard, he had broken his chains and had been driven by the demon into solitary places.

[30]Jesus asked him, "What is your name?"

"Legion," he replied, because many demons had gone into him. [31]And they begged

---

[a] 10 Isaiah 6:9   [b] 26 Some manuscripts *Gadarenes*; other manuscripts *Gergesenes*; also in verse 37
[c] 29 Greek *unclean*

Where Truth Falls

Luke 8:4-8

read/meditate

Read this parable several times, until you feel like you have a good handle on the different seeds and soils. What does each element of the story represent as you apply it to your everyday experiences? What elements do you most relate to right now in your life?

pray

Be open to God giving you new insight from a (possibly) very familiar passage. Give him a few moments to bring to your mind what kind of soil your life has provided for his truth. Express your thoughts to him about that.

contemplate

Think about how you handle truth in your day-to-day life. Think about not only how truthful you are, but what you do with the foundational truths of life that you discover along the way, those "aha" moments in which you really understand something in a new way or for the first time. Is your life set up to make the most of the truth that is revealed to you?

additional reflection

To obey God is liberty.

—*Seneca*

Obedience is all over the Gospels. The pliability of an obedient heart must be complete from our wills right on through to our actions.

—*Catherine Marshall*

For your next devotional reading, go to page 1168.

Jesus repeatedly not to order them to go into the Abyss.

³²A large herd of pigs was feeding there on the hillside. The demons begged Jesus to let them go into the pigs, and he gave them permission. ³³When the demons came out of the man, they went into the pigs, and the herd rushed down the steep bank into the lake and was drowned.

³⁴When those tending the pigs saw what had happened, they ran off and reported this in the town and countryside, ³⁵and the people went out to see what had happened. When they came to Jesus, they found the man from whom the demons had gone out, sitting at Jesus' feet, dressed and in his right mind; and they were afraid. ³⁶Those who had seen it told the people how the demon-possessed man had been cured. ³⁷Then all the people of the region of the Gerasenes asked Jesus to leave them, because they were overcome with fear. So he got into the boat and left.

³⁸The man from whom the demons had gone out begged to go with him, but Jesus sent him away, saying, ³⁹"Return home and tell how much God has done for you." So the man went away and told all over town how much Jesus had done for him.

Jesus Raises a Dead Girl and Heals a Sick Woman

⁴⁰Now when Jesus returned, a crowd welcomed him, for they were all expecting him. ⁴¹Then a man named Jairus, a synagogue leader, came and fell at Jesus' feet, pleading with him to come to his house ⁴²because his only daughter, a girl of about twelve, was dying.

As Jesus was on his way, the crowds almost crushed him. ⁴³And a woman was there who had been subject to bleeding for twelve years,ᵃ but no one could heal her. ⁴⁴She came up behind him and touched the edge of his cloak, and immediately her bleeding stopped.

⁴⁵"Who touched me?" Jesus asked.

When they all denied it, Peter said, "Master, the people are crowding and pressing against you."

⁴⁶But Jesus said, "Someone touched me; I know that power has gone out from me."

⁴⁷Then the woman, seeing that she could

not go unnoticed, came trembling and fell at his feet. In the presence of all the people, she told why she had touched him and how she had been instantly healed. ⁴⁸Then he said to her, "Daughter, your faith has healed you. Go in peace."

⁴⁹While Jesus was still speaking, someone came from the house of Jairus, the synagogue leader. "Your daughter is dead," he said. "Don't bother the teacher anymore."

⁵⁰Hearing this, Jesus said to Jairus, "Don't be afraid; just believe, and she will be healed."

⁵¹When he arrived at the house of Jairus, he did not let anyone go in with him except Peter, John and James, and the child's father and mother. ⁵²Meanwhile, all the people were wailing and mourning for her. "Stop wailing," Jesus said. "She is not dead but asleep."

⁵³They laughed at him, knowing that she was dead. ⁵⁴But he took her by the hand and said, "My child, get up!" ⁵⁵Her spirit returned, and at once she stood up. Then Jesus told them to give her something to eat. ⁵⁶Her parents were astonished, but he ordered them not to tell anyone what had happened.

Jesus Sends Out the Twelve

9 When Jesus had called the Twelve together, he gave them power and authority to drive out all demons and to cure diseases, ²and he sent them out to proclaim the kingdom of God and to heal the sick. ³He told them: "Take nothing for the journey—no staff, no bag, no bread, no money, no extra shirt. ⁴Whatever house you enter, stay there until you leave that town. ⁵If people do not welcome you, shake the dust off your feet when you leave their town, as a testimony against them." ⁶So they set out and went from village to village, proclaiming the good news and healing people everywhere.

⁷Now Herod the tetrarch heard about all that was going on. And he was perplexed because some were saying that John had been raised from the dead, ⁸others that Elijah had appeared, and still others that one of the prophets of long ago had come back to life. ⁹But Herod said, "I beheaded John. Who,

---

ᵃ 43 Many manuscripts years, and she had spent all she had on doctors

MONDAY

THE DEATH OF INDEPENDENCE

Luke 9:1–27 or 9:24–25

Dallas Willard

The sayings of Jesus [in Luke 9:24–25] are most often taken as expressions of some ethereal truth for especially religious people. Instead, they are mere observations about how life actually works. As is so often the case with the statements of Jesus, they say nothing about what we ought to do. They simply state how things are. Anything with life in it can flourish only if it abandons itself to what lies beyond it, eventually to be lost as *a separate* being, though continuing to live on in relation to others. Life is inner power to reach and live "beyond."

Human life cannot flourish as God intended it to, in a divinely inspired and upheld corporate rule over this grand globe, if we see ourselves as "on our own"—and especially if we struggle to preserve ourselves that way. When we are in isolation from God and not in the proper social bonds with others, we cannot rule the earth for good—the idea is simply absurd . . .

In the concrete texture of human existence, one look at family or community life shows the resentment, hatred and violence that results when one member's isolated will is forced upon the rest.

OSWALD CHAMBERS {AD 1874–1917}

The natural life is not sinful; we must be apostatised from sin, have nothing to do with sin in any shape or form. Sin belongs to hell and the devil; I, as a child of God, belong to heaven and God. It is not a question of giving up sin, but of giving up my right to myself, my natural independence and self-assertiveness, and this is where the battle has to be fought. It is the things that are right and noble and good from the natural standpoint that keep us back from God's best. To discern that natural virtues antagonise surrender to God, is to bring our soul into the centre of its greatest battle . . . Beware of refusing to go to the funeral of your own independence.

The natural life is not spiritual, and it can only be made spiritual by sacrifice. If we do not resolutely sacrifice the natural, the supernatural can never become natural in us. There is no royal road there; each of us has it entirely in his own hands. It is not a question of praying, but of performing.

reflection

1. Why does it sound absurd to gain life if you're willing to give it up?

2. In what ways do you refuse to go to the "funeral of your own independence"?

3. How is it that sometimes the "good" of life is at war with the "best"?

For your next devotional reading, go to page 1172.

then, is this I hear such things about?" And he tried to see him.

Jesus Feeds the Five Thousand

[10]When the apostles returned, they reported to Jesus what they had done. Then he took them with him and they withdrew by themselves to a town called Bethsaida, [11]but the crowds learned about it and followed him. He welcomed them and spoke to them about the kingdom of God, and healed those who needed healing.

[12]Late in the afternoon the Twelve came to him and said, "Send the crowd away so they can go to the surrounding villages and countryside and find food and lodging, because we are in a remote place here."

[13]He replied, "You give them something to eat."

They answered, "We have only five loaves of bread and two fish—unless we go and buy food for all this crowd." [14](About five thousand men were there.)

But he said to his disciples, "Have them sit down in groups of about fifty each." [15]The disciples did so, and everyone sat down. [16]Taking the five loaves and the two fish and looking up to heaven, he gave thanks and broke them. Then he gave them to the disciples to set before the people. [17]They all ate and were satisfied, and the disciples picked up twelve basketfuls of broken pieces that were left over.

Peter Declares That Jesus Is the Messiah

[18]Once when Jesus was praying in private and his disciples were with him, he asked them, "Who do the crowds say I am?"

[19]They replied, "Some say John the Baptist; others say Elijah; and still others, that one of the prophets of long ago has come back to life."

[20]"But what about you?" he asked. "Who do you say I am?"

Peter answered, "God's Messiah."

Jesus Predicts His Death

[21]Jesus strictly warned them not to tell this to anyone. [22]And he said, "The Son of Man must suffer many things and be rejected by the elders, the chief priests and the teachers of the law, and he must be killed and on the third day be raised to life."

[23]Then he said to them all: "Whoever wants to be my disciple must deny themselves and take up their cross daily and follow me. [24]For whoever wants to save their life will lose it, but whoever loses their life for me will save it. [25]What good is it for you to gain the whole world, and yet lose or forfeit your very self? [26]If any of you are ashamed of me and my words, the Son of Man will be ashamed of you when he comes in his glory and in the glory of the Father and of the holy angels.

[27]"Truly I tell you, some who are standing here will not taste death before they see the kingdom of God."

The Transfiguration

[28]About eight days after Jesus said this, he took Peter, John and James with him and went up onto a mountain to pray. [29]As he was praying, the appearance of his face changed, and his clothes became as bright as a flash of lightning. [30]Two men, Moses and Elijah, [31]appeared in glorious splendor, talking with Jesus. They spoke about his departure,[a] which he was about to bring to fulfillment at Jerusalem. [32]Peter and his companions were very sleepy, but when they became fully awake, they saw his glory and the two men standing with him. [33]As the men were leaving Jesus, Peter said to him, "Master, it is good for us to be here. Let us put up three shelters—one for you, one for Moses and one for Elijah." (He did not know what he was saying.)

[34]While he was speaking, a cloud appeared and covered them, and they were afraid as they entered the cloud. [35]A voice came from the cloud, saying, "This is my Son, whom I have chosen; listen to him." [36]When the voice had spoken, they found that Jesus was alone. The disciples kept this to themselves and did not tell anyone at that time what they had seen.

Jesus Heals a Demon-Possessed Boy

[37]The next day, when they came down from the mountain, a large crowd met him. [38]A man in the crowd called out, "Teacher, I beg you to look at my son, for he is my only child. [39]A spirit seizes him and he suddenly screams; it throws him into convulsions so that he foams at the mouth. It scarcely ever

a 31 Greek exodus

leaves him and is destroying him. ⁴⁰I begged your disciples to drive it out, but they could not."

⁴¹"You unbelieving and perverse generation," Jesus replied, "how long shall I stay with you and put up with you? Bring your son here."

⁴²Even while the boy was coming, the demon threw him to the ground in a convulsion. But Jesus rebuked the evilᵃ spirit, healed the boy and gave him back to his father. ⁴³And they were all amazed at the greatness of God.

Jesus Predicts His Death a Second Time

While everyone was marveling at all that Jesus did, he said to his disciples, ⁴⁴"Listen carefully to what I am about to tell you: The Son of Man is going to be delivered over to human hands." ⁴⁵But they did not understand what this meant. It was hidden from them, so that they did not grasp it, and they were afraid to ask him about it.

⁴⁶An argument started among the disciples as to which of them would be the greatest. ⁴⁷Jesus, knowing their thoughts, took a little child and had him stand beside him. ⁴⁸Then he said to them, "Whoever welcomes this little child in my name welcomes me; and whoever welcomes me welcomes the one who sent me. For whoever is least among you all is the greatest."

⁴⁹"Master," said John, "we saw someone driving out demons in your name and we tried to stop him, because he is not one of us."

⁵⁰"Do not stop him," Jesus said, "for whoever is not against you is for you."

Samaritan Opposition

⁵¹As the time approached for him to be taken up to heaven, Jesus resolutely set out for Jerusalem. ⁵²And he sent messengers on ahead, who went into a Samaritan village to get things ready for him; ⁵³but the people there did not welcome him, because he was heading for Jerusalem. ⁵⁴When the disciples James and John saw this, they asked, "Lord, do you want us to call fire down from heaven to destroy themᵇ?" ⁵⁵But Jesus turned and rebuked them. ⁵⁶Then he and his disciples went to another village.

The Cost of Following Jesus

⁵⁷As they were walking along the road, a man said to him, "I will follow you wherever you go."

⁵⁸Jesus replied, "Foxes have holes and birds have nests, but the Son of Man has no place to lay his head."

⁵⁹He said to another man, "Follow me."

But he replied, "Lord, first let me go and bury my father."

⁶⁰Jesus said to him, "Let the dead bury their own dead, but you go and proclaim the kingdom of God."

⁶¹Still another said, "I will follow you, Lord; but first let me go back and say goodby to my family."

⁶²Jesus replied, "No one who puts a hand to the plow and looks back is fit for service in the kingdom of God."

Jesus Sends Out the Seventy-Two

10 After this the Lord appointed seventy-twoᶜ others and sent them two by two ahead of him to every town and place where he was about to go. ²He told them, "The harvest is plentiful, but the workers are few. Ask the Lord of the harvest, therefore, to send out workers into his harvest field. ³Go! I am sending you out like lambs among wolves. ⁴Do not take a purse or bag or sandals; and do not greet anyone on the road.

⁵"When you enter a house, first say, 'Peace to this house.' ⁶If the head of the house loves peace, your peace will rest on that house; if not, it will return to you. ⁷Stay there, eating and drinking whatever they give you, for workers deserve their wages. Do not move around from house to house.

⁸"When you enter a town and are welcomed, eat what is set before you. ⁹Heal the sick who are there and tell them, 'The kingdom of God has come near to you.' ¹⁰But when you enter a town and are not welcomed, go into its streets and say, ¹¹'Even the dust of your town we wipe from our feet as a warning to you. Yet be sure of this: The kingdom of God has come near.' ¹²I tell you, it will be more bearable on that day for Sodom than for that town.

¹³"Woe to you, Chorazin! Woe to you, Bethsaida! For if the miracles that were per-

---

ᵃ 42 Greek *unclean*   ᵇ 54 Some manuscripts *them, just as Elijah did*   ᶜ 1 Some manuscripts *seventy;* also in verse 17 formed in you had been performed in Tyre and Sidon, they would have repented long ago, sitting in sackcloth and ashes. ¹⁴But it will be more bearable for Tyre and Sidon at the judgment than for you. ¹⁵And you, Capernaum, will you be lifted up to the skies? No, you will go down to the depths.ᵃ

¹⁶"Whoever listens to you listens to me; whoever rejects you rejects me; but whoever rejects me rejects him who sent me."

¹⁷The seventy-two returned with joy and said, "Lord, even the demons submit to us in your name."

¹⁸He replied, "I saw Satan fall like lightning from heaven. ¹⁹I have given you authority to trample on snakes and scorpions and to overcome all the power of the enemy; nothing will harm you. ²⁰However, do not rejoice that the spirits submit to you, but rejoice that your names are written in heaven."

²¹At that time Jesus, full of joy through the Holy Spirit, said, "I praise you, Father, Lord of heaven and earth, because you have hidden these things from the wise and learned, and revealed them to little children. Yes, Father, for this was your good pleasure.

²²"All things have been committed to me by my Father. No one knows who the Son is except the Father, and no one knows who the Father is except the Son and those to whom the Son chooses to reveal him."

²³Then he turned to his disciples and said privately, "Blessed are the eyes that see what you see. ²⁴For I tell you that many prophets and kings wanted to see what you see but did not see it, and to hear what you hear but did not hear it."

The Parable of the Good Samaritan

²⁵On one occasion an expert in the law stood up to test Jesus. "Teacher," he asked, "what must I do to inherit eternal life?"

²⁶"What is written in the Law?" he replied. "How do you read it?"

²⁷He answered, " 'Love the Lord your God with all your heart and with all your soul and with all your strength and with all your mind'ᵇ; and, 'Love your neighbor as yourself.'ᶜ"

²⁸"You have answered correctly," Jesus replied. "Do this and you will live."

²⁹But he wanted to justify himself, so he asked Jesus, "And who is my neighbor?"

³⁰In reply Jesus said: "A man was going down from Jerusalem to Jericho, when he fell into the hands of robbers. They stripped him of his clothes, beat him and went away, leaving him half dead. ³¹A priest happened to be going down the same road, and when he saw the man, he passed by on the other side. ³²So too, a Levite, when he came to the place and saw him, passed by on the other side. ³³But a Samaritan, as he traveled, came where the man was; and when he saw him, he took pity on him. ³⁴He went to him and bandaged his wounds, pouring on oil and wine. Then he put the man on his own donkey, brought him to an inn and took care of him. ³⁵The next day he took out two denariiᵈ and gave them to the innkeeper. 'Look after him,' he said, 'and when I return, I will reimburse you for any extra expense you may have.'

³⁶"Which of these three do you think was a neighbor to the man who fell into the hands of robbers?"

³⁷The expert in the law replied, "The one who had mercy on him."

Jesus told him, "Go and do likewise."

At the Home of Martha and Mary

³⁸As Jesus and his disciples were on their way, he came to a village where a woman named Martha opened her home to him. ³⁹She had a sister called Mary, who sat at the Lord's feet listening to what he said. ⁴⁰But Martha was distracted by all the preparations that had to be made. She came to him and asked, "Lord, don't you care that my sister has left me to do the work by myself? Tell her to help me!"

⁴¹"Martha, Martha," the Lord answered, "you are worried and upset about many things, ⁴²but few things are needed—or indeed only one.ᵉ Mary has chosen what is better, and it will not be taken away from her."

Jesus' Teaching on Prayer

11 One day Jesus was praying in a certain place. When he finished, one of his disciples said to him,

---

ᵃ 15 Greek to Hades   ᵇ 27 Deut. 6:5   ᶜ 27 Lev. 19:18   ᵈ 35 A denarius was the daily wage of a day laborer (see Matt. 20:2).   ᵉ 42 Some manuscripts *but only one thing is needed*

TUESDAY

DON'T JUST PRAY—BECOME
THE PRAYER

Luke 11:1–28 *or* 11:1–4

Walter Wangerin

The disciples learned from the Lord's own mouth the several petitions of that prayer which we still call "The Lord's." And we still pray it. Believers all around the globe pray the elegant, elemental, comprehensive, bold and humble prayer—mostly in the words preserved in Matthew 6:9–13.

As we prayed with the psalmist, and with the faithful of the church, so we may pray with Jesus. He gave us these words to make our own.

But he also gave us the remarkable insight that words of prayer may match prayerful deeds, until we have begun to live *a life of prayer*! It is this which is mostly missed about his teaching. He taught his disciples the same prayer at two times and in two ways; for he who said, "Pray, *Our Father in heaven . . . [your] will be done*," then went forth and actually performed his prayer, did it, enacted it, accomplished the same thing in his body and soul.

After the Master had taught the lesson of prayer, he went out and *became* the lesson.

TERTULLIAN {AD 155–230}

According to Jesus' model, we pray, "Your will be done, on earth as it is in heaven." This does not mean that there is some opposing power that can prevent God's will being done, requiring us to pray in order for his will to be successfully achieved. Rather we pray for his will to be done . . . *in us* . . .

What, moreover, *does* God will, but that we should walk according to his instruction and example? We request, then, that God supply us with the substance of his will and the capacity to do it . . . Jesus himself accomplished the will of God in preaching, in working and in enduring. He himself proclaimed that he did not do his own will, but his Father's. So undoubtedly those things which he used to do *were* the Father's will, and they serve as examples for us also to stimulate us to preach, to work and to endure even unto death. And we *need* the will of God, that we may be able to fulfill these duties.

— *reflection* —

1. What did Jesus want his disciples—then and now—to learn from this prayer?

2. Jesus wanted his followers to do more than just pray his words—he wanted them to live them. What does this mean?

3. How will your life look different if you truly live out the "Lord's Prayer"?

For your next devotional reading, go to page 1179.

"Lord, teach us to pray, just as John taught his disciples."

[2] He said to them, "When you pray, say:

" 'Father,[a]
hallowed be your name,
your kingdom come.[b]
[3] Give us each day our daily bread.
[4] Forgive us our sins,
    for we also forgive everyone who sins
        against us.[c]
And lead us not into temptation.[d] ' "

[5] Then Jesus said to them, "Suppose you have a friend, and you go to him at midnight and say, 'Friend, lend me three loaves of bread; [6] a friend of mine on a journey has come to me, and I have nothing to set before him.' [7] And suppose the one inside answers, 'Don't bother me. The door is already locked, and my children and I are in bed. I can't get up and give you anything.' [8] I tell you, even though he will not get up and give you the bread because of friendship, yet because of your shameless audacity[e] he will surely get up and give you as much as you need.

[9] "So I say to you: Ask and it will be given to you; seek and you will find; knock and the door will be opened to you. [10] For everyone who asks receives; those who seek find; and to those who knock, the door will be opened.

[11] "Which of you fathers, if your son asks for[f] a fish, will give him a snake instead? [12] Or if he asks for an egg, will give him a scorpion? [13] If you then, though you are evil, know how to give good gifts to your children, how much more will your Father in heaven give the Holy Spirit to those who ask him!"

Jesus and Beelzebul

[14] Jesus was driving out a demon that was mute. When the demon left, the man who had been mute spoke, and the crowd was amazed. [15] But some of them said, "By Beelzebul, the prince of demons, he is driving out demons." [16] Others tested him by asking for a sign from heaven.

[17] Jesus knew their thoughts and said to them: "Any kingdom divided against itself will be ruined, and a house divided against itself will fall. [18] If Satan is divided against himself, how can his kingdom stand? I say this because you claim that I drive out demons by Beelzebul. [19] Now if I drive out demons by Beelzebul, by whom do your followers drive them out? So then, they will be your judges. [20] But if I drive out demons by the finger of God, then the kingdom of God has come upon you.

[21] "When a strong man, fully armed, guards his own house, his possessions are safe. [22] But when someone stronger attacks and overpowers him, he takes away the armor in which the man trusted and divides up his plunder.

[23] "Whoever is not with me is against me, and whoever does not gather with me scatters.

[24] "When an evil[g] spirit comes out of anyone, it goes through arid places seeking rest and does not find it. Then it says, 'I will return to the house I left.' [25] When it arrives, it finds the house swept clean and put in order. [26] Then it goes and takes seven other spirits more wicked than itself, and they go in and live there. And the final condition of that person is worse than the first."

[27] As Jesus was saying these things, a woman in the crowd called out, "Blessed is the mother who gave you birth and nursed you."

[28] He replied, "Blessed rather are those who hear the word of God and obey it."

The Sign of Jonah

[29] As the crowds increased, Jesus said, "This is a wicked generation. It asks for a sign, but none will be given it except the sign of Jonah. [30] For as Jonah was a sign to the Ninevites, so also will the Son of Man be to this generation. [31] The Queen of the South will rise at the judgment with the people of this generation and condemn them, for she came from the ends of the earth to listen to Solomon's wisdom; and now one[h] greater than Solomon is here. [32] The people of Nineveh will stand up at the judgment with this generation and condemn it, for they repented at the preaching of Jonah; and now one greater than Jonah is here.

---

[a] 2 Some manuscripts *Our Father in heaven*   [b] 2 Some manuscripts *come. May your will be done on earth as it is in heaven.*   [c] 4 Greek *everyone who is indebted to us*   [d] 4 Some manuscripts *temptation, but deliver us from the evil one*   [e] 8 Or *yet to preserve his good name*   [f] 11 Some manuscripts *for bread, will give him a stone? Or if he asks for*   [g] 24 Greek *unclean*   [h] 31 Or *something*; also in verse 32

The Lamp of the Body

33"None of you lights a lamp and puts it in a place where it will be hidden, or under a bowl. Instead you put it on its stand, so that those who come in may see the light. 34Your eye is the lamp of your body. When your eyes are healthy,[a] your whole body also is full of light. But when they are unhealthy,[b] your body also is full of darkness. 35See to it, then, that the light within you is not darkness. 36Therefore, if your whole body is full of light, and no part of it dark, it will be just as full of light as when a lamp shines its light on you."

Woes on the Pharisees and the Experts in the Law

37When Jesus had finished speaking, a Pharisee invited him to eat with him; so he went in and reclined at the table. 38But the Pharisee was surprised when he noticed that Jesus did not first wash before the meal.

39Then the Lord said to him, "Now then, you Pharisees clean the outside of the cup and dish, but inside you are full of greed and wickedness. 40You foolish people! Did not the one who made the outside make the inside also? 41But now as for what is inside you—be generous to the poor, and everything will be clean for you.

42"Woe to you Pharisees, because you give God a tenth of your mint, rue and all other kinds of garden herbs, but you neglect justice and the love of God. You should have practiced the latter without leaving the former undone.

43"Woe to you Pharisees, because you love the most important seats in the synagogues and respectful greetings in the marketplaces.

44"Woe to you, because you are like unmarked graves, which people walk over without knowing it."

45One of the experts in the law answered him, "Teacher, when you say these things, you insult us also."

46Jesus replied, "And you experts in the law, woe to you, because you load people down with burdens they can hardly carry, and you yourselves will not lift one finger to help them.

47"Woe to you, because you build tombs for the prophets, and it was your ancestors who killed them. 48So you testify that you approve of what your ancestors did; they killed the prophets, and you build their tombs. 49Because of this, God in his wisdom said, 'I will send them prophets and apostles, some of whom they will kill and others they will persecute.' 50Therefore this generation will be held responsible for the blood of all the prophets that has been shed since the beginning of the world, 51from the blood of Abel to the blood of Zechariah, who was killed between the altar and the sanctuary. Yes, I tell you, this generation will be held responsible for it all.

52"Woe to you experts in the law, because you have taken away the key to knowledge. You yourselves have not entered, and you have hindered those who were entering."

53When Jesus went outside, the Pharisees and the teachers of the law began to oppose him fiercely and to besiege him with questions, 54waiting to catch him in something he might say.

Warnings and Encouragements

12 Meanwhile, when a crowd of many thousands had gathered, so that they were trampling on one another, Jesus began to speak first to his disciples, saying: "Be[c] on your guard against the yeast of the Pharisees, which is hypocrisy. 2There is nothing concealed that will not be disclosed, or hidden that will not be made known. 3What you have said in the dark will be heard in the daylight, and what you have whispered in the ear in the inner rooms will be proclaimed from the roofs.

4"I tell you, my friends, do not be afraid of those who kill the body and after that can do no more. 5But I will show you whom you should fear: Fear him who, after your body has been killed, has authority to throw you into hell. Yes, I tell you, fear him. 6Are not five sparrows sold for two pennies? Yet not one of them is forgotten by God. 7Indeed, the very hairs of your head are all numbered. Don't be afraid; you are worth more than many sparrows.

8"I tell you, whoever publicly acknowledges me, the Son of Man will also acknowledge before the angels of God. 9But whoev-

---

a 34 The Greek for *healthy* here implies *generous.*
b 34 The Greek for *unhealthy* here implies *stingy.*
c 1 Or *speak to his disciples, saying: "First of all, be*

er publicly disowns me will be disowned before the angels of God. ¹⁰And everyone who speaks a word against the Son of Man will be forgiven, but anyone who blasphemes against the Holy Spirit will not be forgiven.

¹¹"When you are brought before synagogues, rulers and authorities, do not worry about how you will defend yourselves or what you will say, ¹²for the Holy Spirit will teach you at that time what you should say."

The Parable of the Rich Fool

¹³Someone in the crowd said to him, "Teacher, tell my brother to divide the inheritance with me."

¹⁴Jesus replied, "Man, who appointed me a judge or an arbiter between you?" ¹⁵Then he said to them, "Watch out! Be on your guard against all kinds of greed; life does not consist in an abundance of possessions."

¹⁶And he told them this parable: "The ground of a certain rich man yielded an abundant harvest. ¹⁷He thought to himself, 'What shall I do? I have no place to store my crops.'

¹⁸"Then he said, 'This is what I'll do. I will tear down my barns and build bigger ones, and there I will store my surplus grain. ¹⁹And I'll say to myself, "You have plenty of grain laid up for many years. Take life easy; eat, drink and be merry." '

²⁰"But God said to him, 'You fool! This very night your life will be demanded from you. Then who will get what you have prepared for yourself?'

²¹"This is how it will be with those who store up things for themselves but are not rich toward God."

Do Not Worry

²²Then Jesus said to his disciples: "Therefore I tell you, do not worry about your life, what you will eat; or about your body, what you will wear. ²³Life is more than food, and the body more than clothes. ²⁴Consider the ravens: They do not sow or reap, they have no storeroom or barn; yet God feeds them. And how much more valuable you are than birds! ²⁵Who of you by worrying can add a single hour to your lifeᵃ? ²⁶Since you cannot do this very little thing, why do you worry about the rest?

²⁷"Consider how the wild flowers grow. They do not labor or spin. Yet I tell you, not

even Solomon in all his splendor was dressed like one of these. ²⁸If that is how God clothes the grass of the field, which is here today, and tomorrow is thrown into the fire, how much more will he clothe you—you of little faith! ²⁹And do not set your heart on what you will eat or drink; do not worry about it. ³⁰For the pagan world runs after all such things, and your Father knows that you need them. ³¹But seek his kingdom, and these things will be given to you as well.

³²"Do not be afraid, little flock, for your Father has been pleased to give you the kingdom. ³³Sell your possessions and give to the poor. Provide purses for yourselves that will not wear out, a treasure in heaven that will never fail, where no thief comes near and no moth destroys. ³⁴For where your treasure is, there your heart will be also.

Watchfulness

³⁵"Be dressed ready for service and keep your lamps burning, ³⁶like servants waiting for their master to return from a wedding banquet, so that when he comes and knocks they can immediately open the door for him. ³⁷It will be good for those servants whose master finds them watching when he comes. Truly I tell you, he will dress himself to serve, will have them recline at the table and will come and wait on them. ³⁸It will be good for those servants whose master finds them ready, even if he comes in the middle of the night or toward daybreak. ³⁹But understand this: If the owner of the house had known at what hour the thief was coming, he would not have let his house be broken into. ⁴⁰You also must be ready, because the Son of Man will come at an hour when you do not expect him."

⁴¹Peter asked, "Lord, are you telling this parable to us, or to everyone?"

⁴²The Lord answered, "Who then is the faithful and wise manager, whom the master puts in charge of his servants to give them their food allowance at the proper time? ⁴³It will be good for that servant whom the master finds doing so when he returns. ⁴⁴Truly I tell you, he will put him in charge of all his possessions. ⁴⁵But suppose the servant says to himself, 'My master is taking a long time in coming,' and he then begins to beat the other servants, both men

---

ᵃ 25 Or *single cubit to your height*

and women, and to eat and drink and get drunk. ⁴⁶The master of that servant will come on a day when he does not expect him and at an hour he is not aware of. He will cut him to pieces and assign him a place with the unbelievers.

⁴⁷"The servant who knows the master's will and does not get ready or does not do what the master wants will be beaten with many blows. ⁴⁸But the one who does not know and does things deserving punishment will be beaten with few blows. From everyone who has been given much, much will be demanded; and from the one who has been entrusted with much, much more will be asked.

Not Peace but Division

⁴⁹"I have come to bring fire on the earth, and how I wish it were already kindled! ⁵⁰But I have a baptism to undergo, and what constraint I am under until it is completed! ⁵¹Do you think I came to bring peace on earth? No, I tell you, but division. ⁵²From now on there will be five in one family divided against each other, three against two and two against three. ⁵³They will be divided, father against son and son against father, mother against daughter and daughter against mother, mother-in-law against daughter-in-law and daughter-in-law against mother-in-law."

Interpreting the Times

⁵⁴He said to the crowd: "When you see a cloud rising in the west, immediately you say, 'It's going to rain,' and it does. ⁵⁵And when the south wind blows, you say, 'It's going to be hot,' and it is. ⁵⁶Hypocrites! You know how to interpret the appearance of the earth and the sky. How is it that you don't know how to interpret this present time?

⁵⁷"Why don't you judge for yourselves what is right? ⁵⁸As you are going with your adversary to the magistrate, try hard to be reconciled on the way, or your adversary may drag you off to the judge, and the judge turn you over to the officer, and the officer throw you into prison. ⁵⁹I tell you, you will not get out until you have paid the last penny."

Repent or Perish

13 Now there were some present at that time who told Jesus about the Galileans whose blood Pilate had mixed with their sacrifices. ²Jesus answered, "Do you think that these Galileans were worse sinners than all the other Galileans because they suffered this way? ³I tell you, no! But unless you repent, you too will all perish. ⁴Or those eighteen who died when the tower in Siloam fell on them—do you think they were more guilty than all the others living in Jerusalem? ⁵I tell you, no! But unless you repent, you too will all perish."

⁶Then he told this parable: "A man had a fig tree growing in his vineyard, and he went to look for fruit on it but did not find any. ⁷So he said to the man who took care of the vineyard, 'For three years now I've been coming to look for fruit on this fig tree and haven't found any. Cut it down! Why should it use up the soil?'

⁸" 'Sir,' the man replied, 'leave it alone for one more year, and I'll dig around it and fertilize it. ⁹If it bears fruit next year, fine! If not, then cut it down.' "

Jesus Heals a Crippled Woman on the Sabbath

¹⁰On a Sabbath Jesus was teaching in one of the synagogues, ¹¹and a woman was there who had been crippled by a spirit for eighteen years. She was bent over and could not straighten up at all. ¹²When Jesus saw her, he called her forward and said to her, "Woman,ᵃ you are set free from your infirmity." ¹³Then he put his hands on her, and immediately she straightened up and praised God.

¹⁴Indignant because Jesus had healed on the Sabbath, the synagogue leader said to the people, "There are six days for work. So come and be healed on those days, not on the Sabbath."

¹⁵The Lord answered him, "You hypocrites! Doesn't each of you on the Sabbath untie your ox or donkey from the stall and lead it out to give it water? ¹⁶Then should not this woman, a daughter of Abraham, whom Satan has kept bound for eighteen long years, be set free on the Sabbath day from what bound her?"

ᵃ 12 The Greek for Woman does not denote any disrespect.

¹⁷When he said this, all his opponents were humiliated, but the people were delighted with all the wonderful things he was doing.

The Parables of the Mustard Seed and the Yeast

¹⁸Then Jesus asked, "What is the kingdom of God like? What shall I compare it to? ¹⁹It is like a mustard seed, which a man took and planted in his garden. It grew and became a tree, and the birds perched in its branches."

²⁰Again he asked, "What shall I compare the kingdom of God to? ²¹It is like yeast that a woman took and mixed into about sixty pounds^a of flour until it worked all through the dough."

The Narrow Door

²²Then Jesus went through the towns and villages, teaching as he made his way to Jerusalem. ²³Someone asked him, "Lord, are only a few people going to be saved?"

He said to them, ²⁴"Make every effort to enter through the narrow door, because many, I tell you, will try to enter and will not be able to. ²⁵Once the owner of the house gets up and closes the door, you will stand outside knocking and pleading, 'Sir, open the door for us.'

"But he will answer, 'I don't know you or where you come from.'

²⁶"Then you will say, 'We ate and drank with you, and you taught in our streets.'

²⁷"But he will reply, 'I don't know you or where you come from. Away from me, all you evildoers!'

²⁸"There will be weeping there, and gnashing of teeth, when you see Abraham, Isaac and Jacob and all the prophets in the kingdom of God, but you yourselves thrown out. ²⁹People will come from east and west and north and south, and will take their places at the feast in the kingdom of God. ³⁰Indeed there are those who are last who will be first, and first who will be last."

Jesus' Sorrow for Jerusalem

³¹At that time some Pharisees came to Jesus and said to him, "Leave this place and go somewhere else. Herod wants to kill you."

³²He replied, "Go tell that fox, 'I will keep on driving out demons and healing people today and tomorrow, and on the third day I will reach my goal.' ³³In any case, I must press on today and tomorrow and the next day—for surely no prophet can die outside Jerusalem!

³⁴"Jerusalem, Jerusalem, you who kill the prophets and stone those sent to you, how often I have longed to gather your children together, as a hen gathers her chicks under her wings, and you were not willing. ³⁵Look, your house is left to you desolate. I tell you, you will not see me again until you say, 'Blessed is he who comes in the name of the Lord.'^b"

Jesus at a Pharisee's House

14 One Sabbath, when Jesus went to eat in the house of a prominent Pharisee, he was being carefully watched. ²There in front of him was a man suffering from abnormal swelling of his body. ³Jesus asked the Pharisees and experts in the law, "Is it lawful to heal on the Sabbath or not?" ⁴But they remained silent. So taking hold of the man, he healed him and sent him on his way.

⁵Then he asked them, "If one of you has a child^c or an ox that falls into a well on the Sabbath day, will you not immediately pull it out?" ⁶And they had nothing to say.

⁷When he noticed how the guests picked the places of honor at the table, he told them this parable: ⁸"When someone invites you to a wedding feast, do not take the place of honor, for a person more distinguished than you may have been invited. ⁹If so, the host who invited both of you will come and say to you, 'Give this person your seat.' Then, humiliated, you will have to take the least important place. ¹⁰But when you are invited, take the lowest place, so that when your host comes, he will say to you, 'Friend, move up to a better place.' Then you will be honored in the presence of all the other guests. ¹¹For all those who exalt themselves will be humbled, and those who humble themselves will be exalted."

¹²Then Jesus said to his host, "When you give a luncheon or dinner, do not invite your friends, your brothers or sisters, your relatives, or your rich neighbors; if you do, they

---

^a 21 Or about 27 kilograms   ^b 35 Psalm 118:26   ^c 5 Some manuscripts *donkey*

may invite you back and so you will be repaid. ¹³But when you give a banquet, invite the poor, the crippled, the lame, the blind, ¹⁴and you will be blessed. Although they cannot repay you, you will be repaid at the resurrection of the righteous."

The Parable of the Great Banquet

¹⁵When one of those at the table with him heard this, he said to Jesus, "Blessed are those who will eat at the feast in the kingdom of God."

¹⁶Jesus replied: "A certain man was preparing a great banquet and invited many guests. ¹⁷At the time of the banquet he sent his servant to tell those who had been invited, 'Come, for everything is now ready.'

¹⁸"But they all alike began to make excuses. The first said, 'I have just bought a field, and I must go and see it. Please excuse me.'

¹⁹"Another said, 'I have just bought five yoke of oxen, and I'm on my way to try them out. Please excuse me.'

²⁰"Still another said, 'I just got married, so I can't come.'

²¹"The servant came back and reported this to his master. Then the owner of the house became angry and ordered his servant, 'Go out quickly into the streets and alleys of the town and bring in the poor, the crippled, the blind and the lame.'

²²" 'Sir,' the servant said, 'what you ordered has been done, but there is still room.'

²³"Then the master told his servant, 'Go out to the roads and country lanes and compel them to come in, so that my house will be full. ²⁴I tell you, not one of those who were invited will get a taste of my banquet.' "

The Cost of Being a Disciple

²⁵Large crowds were traveling with Jesus, and turning to them he said: ²⁶"If anyone comes to me and does not hate father and mother, wife and children, brothers and sisters—yes, even life itself—such a person cannot be my disciple. ²⁷And whoever does not carry their cross and follow me cannot be my disciple.

²⁸"Suppose one of you wants to build a tower. Won't you first sit down and estimate the cost to see if you have enough money to complete it? ²⁹For if you lay the foundation and are not able to finish it, everyone who

sees it will ridicule you, ³⁰saying, 'This person began to build and wasn't able to finish.'

³¹"Or suppose a king is about to go to war against another king. Won't he first sit down and consider whether he is able with ten thousand men to oppose the one coming against him with twenty thousand? ³²If he is not able, he will send a delegation while the other is still a long way off and will ask for terms of peace. ³³In the same way, those of you who do not give up everything you have cannot be my disciples.

³⁴"Salt is good, but if it loses its saltiness, how can it be made salty again? ³⁵It is fit neither for the soil nor for the manure pile; it is thrown out.

"Whoever has ears to hear, let them hear."

The Parable of the Lost Sheep

15 Now the tax collectors and sinners were all gathering around to hear Jesus. ²But the Pharisees and the teachers of the law muttered, "This man welcomes sinners and eats with them."

³Then Jesus told them this parable: ⁴"Suppose one of you has a hundred sheep and loses one of them. Doesn't he leave the ninety-nine in the open country and go after the lost sheep until he finds it? ⁵And when he finds it, he joyfully puts it on his shoulders ⁶and goes home. Then he calls his friends and neighbors together and says, 'Rejoice with me; I have found my lost sheep.' ⁷I tell you that in the same way there will be more rejoicing in heaven over one sinner who repents than over ninety-nine righteous persons who do not need to repent.

The Parable of the Lost Coin

⁸"Or suppose a woman has ten silver coinsᵃ and loses one. Doesn't she light a lamp, sweep the house and search carefully until she finds it? ⁹And when she finds it, she calls her friends and neighbors together and says, 'Rejoice with me; I have found my lost coin.' ¹⁰In the same way, I tell you, there is rejoicing in the presence of the angels of God over one sinner who repents."

The Parable of the Lost Son

¹¹Jesus continued: "There was a man who had two sons. ¹²The younger one said to his

ᵃ 8 Greek ten drachmas, each worth about a day's wages

WEDNESDAY

PERSPECTIVE ON PRIDE
Luke 15:1–32 *or* 15:17–20

Michael Card

Genuine, Biblical humility is nothing more or less than knowing the truth of who we are in Christ. Only relationship with him can give us the genuine article. Jesus reveals to us two crucial truths about ourselves, and in the tension between these truths lies real humility. On the one hand he convicts us of our sin and fallenness, telling us our righteousness is really only filthy rags. And then in the next breath, smothering us with a big hug like the father of the prodigal son, he tells us how much we are valued, that in spite of our rebelliousness he loves us so much that he would rather die than live without us. That, then, is who I am. And that is who you are as well if you know him. We are men and women, boys and girls who are truly hopeless yet full of hope, truly lost but nonetheless truly found. We are shored up on either side so there is no room for false humility on one side or pride on the other.

ANDREW MURRAY {AD 1828–1917}

One of the most dangerous enemies which the young Christian must guard against is pride or self-exaltation. There is no sin that works more cunningly and more hiddenly. It knows how to penetrate into everything—into our service for God, our prayers and even into our humility. There is nothing so small in the earthly life, nothing so holy in the spiritual life, that self-exaltation does not know to feed upon it (2 Chronicles 26:5,16; 32:26,31; Isaiah 65:5; Jeremiah 7:4; 2 Corinthians 12:7). The Christian must therefore be on guard against it, must listen to what Scripture teaches about it and must learn about the humility that drives it out . . .

Sin has thwarted God's design; instead, human beings seek themselves and their own will (Romans 1:21,23). Grace has come to restore what sin has corrupted, and to bring humans to glory by the pathway of dying to self and living solely for the glory of God. This is the humility or lowliness which Jesus exemplified: He took no thought for himself, and gave himself over wholly to glorify the Father (John 8:50; Philippians 2:7).

reflection

1. Today's reading reveals two dangerous extremes: (1) having too high a view of yourself and (2) having too low a view of how God sees you. Which extreme do you tend to lean toward?

2. What can you learn about humility from Jesus' parable of the prodigal son?

3. Ask God to help you identify an area where pride has secretly crept in and taken root in your heart. Now, ask him for wisdom to uproot it.

For your next devotional reading, go to page 1183.

father, 'Father, give me my share of the estate.' So he divided his property between them.

[13]"Not long after that, the younger son got together all he had, set off for a distant country and there squandered his wealth in wild living. [14]After he had spent everything, there was a severe famine in that whole country, and he began to be in need. [15]So he went and hired himself out to a citizen of that country, who sent him to his fields to feed pigs. [16]He longed to fill his stomach with the pods that the pigs were eating, but no one gave him anything.

[17]"When he came to his senses, he said, 'How many of my father's hired servants have food to spare, and here I am starving to death! [18]I will set out and go back to my father and say to him: Father, I have sinned against heaven and against you. [19]I am no longer worthy to be called your son; make me like one of your hired servants.' [20]So he got up and went to his father.

"But while he was still a long way off, his father saw him and was filled with compassion for him; he ran to his son, threw his arms around him and kissed him.

[21]"The son said to him, 'Father, I have sinned against heaven and against you. I am no longer worthy to be called your son.'

[22]"But the father said to his servants, 'Quick! Bring the best robe and put it on him. Put a ring on his finger and sandals on his feet. [23]Bring the fattened calf and kill it. Let's have a feast and celebrate. [24]For this son of mine was dead and is alive again; he was lost and is found.' So they began to celebrate.

[25]"Meanwhile, the older son was in the field. When he came near the house, he heard music and dancing. [26]So he called one of the servants and asked him what was going on. [27]'Your brother has come,' he replied, 'and your father has killed the fattened calf because he has him back safe and sound.'

[28]"The older brother became angry and refused to go in. So his father went out and pleaded with him. [29]But he answered his father, 'Look! All these years I've been slaving for you and never disobeyed your orders. Yet you never gave me even a young goat so I could celebrate with my friends. [30]But when this son of yours who has squandered your property with prostitutes comes home, you kill the fattened calf for him!'

[31]"'My son,' the father said, 'you are always with me, and everything I have is yours. [32]But we had to celebrate and be glad, because this brother of yours was dead and is alive again; he was lost and is found.'"

The Parable of the Shrewd Manager

16 Jesus told his disciples: "There was a rich man whose manager was accused of wasting his possessions. [2]So he called him in and asked him, 'What is this I hear about you? Give an account of your management, because you cannot be manager any longer.'

[3]"The manager said to himself, 'What shall I do now? My master is taking away my job. I'm not strong enough to dig, and I'm ashamed to beg— [4]I know what I'll do so that, when I lose my job here, people will welcome me into their houses.'

[5]"So he called in each one of his master's debtors. He asked the first, 'How much do you owe my master?'

[6]"'Nine hundred gallons[a] of olive oil,' he replied.

"The manager told him, 'Take your bill, sit down quickly, and make it four hundred and fifty.'

[7]"Then he asked the second, 'And how much do you owe?'

"'A thousand bushels[b] of wheat,' he replied.

"He told him, 'Take your bill and make it eight hundred.'

[8]"The master commended the dishonest manager because he had acted shrewdly. For the people of this world are more shrewd in dealing with their own kind than are the people of the light. [9]I tell you, use worldly wealth to gain friends for yourselves, so that when it is gone, you will be welcomed into eternal dwellings.

[10]"Whoever can be trusted with very little can also be trusted with much, and whoever is dishonest with very little will also be dishonest with much. [11]So if you have not been trustworthy in handling worldly wealth, who will trust you with true riches? [12]And if you have not been trustworthy with someone else's property, who will give you property of your own?

[a] 6 Or about 3,000 liters   [b] 7 Or about 30 tons

¹³"No one can serve two masters. Either you will hate the one and love the other, or you will be devoted to the one and despise the other. You cannot serve both God and Money."

¹⁴The Pharisees, who loved money, heard all this and were sneering at Jesus. ¹⁵He said to them, "You are the ones who justify yourselves in the eyes of others, but God knows your hearts. What people value highly is detestable in God's sight.

Additional Teachings

¹⁶"The Law and the Prophets were proclaimed until John. Since that time, the good news of the kingdom of God is being preached, and people are forcing their way into it. ¹⁷It is easier for heaven and earth to disappear than for the least stroke of a pen to drop out of the Law.

¹⁸"Anyone who divorces his wife and marries another woman commits adultery, and the man who marries a divorced woman commits adultery.

The Rich Man and Lazarus

¹⁹"There was a rich man who was dressed in purple and fine linen and lived in luxury every day. ²⁰At his gate was laid a beggar named Lazarus, covered with sores ²¹and longing to eat what fell from the rich man's table. Even the dogs came and licked his sores.

²²"The time came when the beggar died and the angels carried him to Abraham's side. The rich man also died and was buried. ²³In Hades, where he was in torment, he looked up and saw Abraham far away, with Lazarus by his side. ²⁴So he called to him, 'Father Abraham, have pity on me and send Lazarus to dip the tip of his finger in water and cool my tongue, because I am in agony in this fire.'

²⁵"But Abraham replied, 'Son, remember that in your lifetime you received your good things, while Lazarus received bad things, but now he is comforted here and you are in agony. ²⁶And besides all this, between us and you a great chasm has been set in place, so that those who want to go from here to you cannot, nor can anyone cross over from there to us.'

²⁷"He answered, 'Then I beg you, father, send Lazarus to my family, ²⁸for I have five brothers. Let him warn them, so that they will not also come to this place of torment.'

²⁹"Abraham replied, 'They have Moses and the Prophets; let them listen to them.'

³⁰" 'No, father Abraham,' he said, 'but if someone from the dead goes to them, they will repent.'

³¹"He said to him, 'If they do not listen to Moses and the Prophets, they will not be convinced even if someone rises from the dead.' "

Sin, Faith, Duty

17 Jesus said to his disciples: "Things that cause people to stumble are bound to come, but woe to anyone through whom they come. ²It would be better for you to be thrown into the sea with a millstone tied around your neck than for you to cause one of these little ones to stumble. ³So watch yourselves.

"If a brother or sister sins against you, rebuke them; and if they repent, forgive them. ⁴Even if they sin against you seven times in a day and seven times come back to you saying 'I repent,' you must forgive them."

⁵The apostles said to the Lord, "Increase our faith!"

⁶He replied, "If you have faith as small as a mustard seed, you can say to this mulberry tree, 'Be uprooted and planted in the sea,' and it will obey you.

⁷"Suppose one of you has a servant plowing or looking after the sheep. Will he say to the servant when he comes in from the field, 'Come along now and sit down to eat'? ⁸Won't he rather say, 'Prepare my supper, get yourself ready and wait on me while I eat and drink; after that you may eat and drink'? ⁹Will he thank the servant because he did what he was told to do? ¹⁰So you also, when you have done everything you were told to do, should say, 'We are unworthy servants; we have only done our duty.' "

Jesus Heals Ten Men With Leprosy

¹¹Now on his way to Jerusalem, Jesus traveled along the border between Samaria and Galilee. ¹²As he was going into a village, ten men who had leprosy*a* met him. They stood at a distance ¹³and called out in a loud voice, "Jesus, Master, have pity on us!"

a 12 The Greek word traditionally translated *leprosy* was used for various diseases affecting the skin.

¹⁴When he saw them, he said, "Go, show yourselves to the priests." And as they went, they were cleansed.

¹⁵One of them, when he saw he was healed, came back, praising God in a loud voice. ¹⁶He threw himself at Jesus' feet and thanked him—and he was a Samaritan.

¹⁷Jesus asked, "Were not all ten cleansed? Where are the other nine? ¹⁸Was no one found to return and give praise to God except this foreigner?" ¹⁹Then he said to him, "Rise and go; your faith has made you well."

The Coming of the Kingdom of God

²⁰Once, having been asked by the Pharisees when the kingdom of God would come, Jesus replied, "The coming of the kingdom of God is not something that can be observed, ²¹nor will people say, 'Here it is,' or 'There it is,' because the kingdom of God is in your midst."ᵃ

²²Then he said to his disciples, "The time is coming when you will long to see one of the days of the Son of Man, but you will not see it. ²³People will tell you, 'There he is!' or 'Here he is!' Do not go running off after them. ²⁴For the Son of Man in his dayᵇ will be like the lightning, which flashes and lights up the sky from one end to the other. ²⁵But first he must suffer many things and be rejected by this generation.

²⁶"Just as it was in the days of Noah, so also will it be in the days of the Son of Man. ²⁷People were eating, drinking, marrying and being given in marriage up to the day Noah entered the ark. Then the flood came and destroyed them all.

²⁸"It was the same in the days of Lot. People were eating and drinking, buying and selling, planting and building. ²⁹But the day Lot left Sodom, fire and sulfur rained down from heaven and destroyed them all.

³⁰"It will be just like this on the day the Son of Man is revealed. ³¹On that day no one who is on the housetop, with possessions inside, should go down to get them. Likewise, no one in the field should go back for anything. ³²Remember Lot's wife! ³³Whoever tries to keep their life will lose it, and whoever loses their life will preserve it. ³⁴I tell you, on that night two people will be in one bed; one will be taken and the other left.

³⁵[³⁶]Two women will be grinding grain together; one will be taken and the other left."

³⁷"Where, Lord?" they asked.

He replied, "Where there is a dead body, there the vultures will gather."

The Parable of the Persistent Widow

18 Then Jesus told his disciples a parable to show them that they should always pray and not give up. ²He said: "In a certain town there was a judge who neither feared God nor cared what people thought. ³And there was a widow in that town who kept coming to him with the plea, 'Grant me justice against my adversary.'

⁴"For some time he refused. But finally he said to himself, 'Even though I don't fear God or care what people think, ⁵yet because this widow keeps bothering me, I will see that she gets justice, so that she won't eventually come and attack me!' "

⁶And the Lord said, "Listen to what the unjust judge says. ⁷And will not God bring about justice for his chosen ones, who cry out to him day and night? Will he keep putting them off? ⁸I tell you, he will see that they get justice, and quickly. However, when the Son of Man comes, will he find faith on the earth?"

The Parable of the Pharisee and the Tax Collector

⁹To some who were confident of their own righteousness and looked down on everyone else, Jesus told this parable: ¹⁰"Two men went up to the temple to pray, one a Pharisee and the other a tax collector. ¹¹The Pharisee stood by himself and prayed: 'God, I thank you that I am not like other people—robbers, evildoers, adulterers—or even like this tax collector. ¹²I fast twice a week and give a tenth of all I get.'

¹³"But the tax collector stood at a distance. He would not even look up to heaven, but beat his breast and said, 'God, have mercy on me, a sinner.'

¹⁴"I tell you that this man, rather than the other, went home justified before God. For all those who exalt themselves will be humbled, and those who humble themselves will be exalted."

ᵃ 21 Or *is within you*   ᵇ 24 Some manuscripts do not have *in his day*.

THURSDAY

WHO, WHAT AND WHY WE WORSHIP
Luke 18:1–43 *or* 18:9–14

Richard Foster

We desperately need to see who God is: to read about his self-disclosure to his ancient people Israel, to meditate on his attributes, to gaze upon the revelation of his nature in Jesus Christ. When we see the Lord of hosts "high and [exalted]," ponder his infinite wisdom and knowledge, wonder at his unfathomable mercy and love, we cannot help but move into doxology.

> *Glad thine attributes confess,*
> *Glorious all and numberless . . .*

To see who the Lord is brings us to confession. When Isaiah caught sight of the glory of God he cried, "[Woe to me! . . . I am ruined! For I am a man of unclean lips, and I live among a people of unclean lips, and my eyes have seen the King, the LORD Almighty]" (Isaiah 6:5). The pervasive sinfulness of human beings becomes evident when contrasted with the radiant holiness of God. Our fickleness becomes apparent once we see God's faithfulness. To understand his grace is to understand our guilt.

We worship the Lord not only because of who he is, but also because of what he has done. Above all, the God of the Bible is the God who acts. His goodness, faithfulness, justice, mercy all can be seen in his dealings with his people. His gracious actions are not only etched into ancient history, but are engraved into our personal histories. As the apostle Paul says, the only reasonable response is worship (Romans 12:1). We praise God for who he is, and thank him for what he has done.

CATHERINE OF SIENA {AD 1347–1380}

If you understand yourself, then you will humble yourself. You will see that, in yourself, you do not even exist; for your very being, as you will learn, is derived from me. For I have loved you before you were in existence. Through my indescribable love, and because I wished to re-create you to a state of grace, I have washed you and created you anew in the blood of my one and only Son. His blood was spilled with so great a fire of love . . . that the soul will inflame itself in this knowledge of me with a love so great it cannot be expressed.

reflection

1. When was the last time your heart was truly humbled before God?
2. What brought you to that place?
3. How can you better see God?

For your next devotional reading, go to page 1185.

The Little Children and Jesus

[15] People were also bringing babies to Jesus for him to place his hands on them. When the disciples saw this, they rebuked them. [16] But Jesus called the children to him and said, "Let the little children come to me, and do not hinder them, for the kingdom of God belongs to such as these. [17] Truly I tell you, anyone who will not receive the kingdom of God like a little child will never enter it."

The Rich and the Kingdom of God

[18] A certain ruler asked him, "Good teacher, what must I do to inherit eternal life?"

[19] "Why do you call me good?" Jesus answered. "No one is good—except God alone. [20] You know the commandments: 'You shall not commit adultery, you shall not murder, you shall not steal, you shall not give false testimony, honor your father and mother.'[a]"

[21] "All these I have kept since I was a boy," he said.

[22] When Jesus heard this, he said to him, "You still lack one thing. Sell everything you have and give to the poor, and you will have treasure in heaven. Then come, follow me."

[23] When he heard this, he became very sad, because he was very wealthy. [24] Jesus looked at him and said, "How hard it is for the rich to enter the kingdom of God! [25] Indeed, it is easier for a camel to go through the eye of a needle than for the rich to enter the kingdom of God."

[26] Those who heard this asked, "Who then can be saved?"

[27] Jesus replied, "What is impossible with human beings is possible with God."

[28] Peter said to him, "We have left all we had to follow you!"

[29] "Truly I tell you," Jesus said to them, "no one who has left home or wife or brothers or sisters or parents or children for the sake of the kingdom of God [30] will fail to receive many times as much in this age, and in the age to come eternal life."

Jesus Predicts His Death a Third Time

[31] Jesus took the Twelve aside and told them, "We are going up to Jerusalem, and everything that is written by the prophets about the Son of Man will be fulfilled. [32] He will be delivered over to the Gentiles. They will mock him, insult him and spit on him;

[33] they will flog him and kill him. On the third day he will rise again."

[34] The disciples did not understand any of this. Its meaning was hidden from them, and they did not know what he was talking about.

A Blind Beggar Receives His Sight

[35] As Jesus approached Jericho, a blind man was sitting by the roadside begging. [36] When he heard the crowd going by, he asked what was happening. [37] They told him, "Jesus of Nazareth is passing by."

[38] He called out, "Jesus, Son of David, have mercy on me!"

[39] Those who led the way rebuked him and told him to be quiet, but he shouted all the more, "Son of David, have mercy on me!"

[40] Jesus stopped and ordered the man to be brought to him. When he came near, Jesus asked him, [41] "What do you want me to do for you?"

"Lord, I want to see," he replied.

[42] Jesus said to him, "Receive your sight; your faith has healed you." [43] Immediately he received his sight and followed Jesus, praising God. When all the people saw it, they also praised God.

Zacchaeus the Tax Collector

19 Jesus entered Jericho and was passing through. [2] A man was there by the name of Zacchaeus; he was a chief tax collector and was wealthy. [3] He wanted to see who Jesus was, but because he was short he could not see over the crowd. [4] So he ran ahead and climbed a sycamore-fig tree to see him, since Jesus was coming that way.

[5] When Jesus reached the spot, he looked up and said to him, "Zacchaeus, come down immediately. I must stay at your house today." [6] So he came down at once and welcomed him gladly.

[7] All the people saw this and began to mutter, "He has gone to be the guest of a sinner."

[8] But Zacchaeus stood up and said to the Lord, "Look, Lord! Here and now I give half of my possessions to the poor, and if I have cheated anybody out of anything, I will pay back four times the amount."

[9] Jesus said to him, "Today salvation has

---

a 20 Exodus 20:12-16; Deut. 5:16-20

FRIDAY

LONGING FOR JESUS

Luke 19:1–48 or 19:1–10

Peter Greig

Am I really hungry for more of Jesus in my life?

And if you answered an immediate yes, without any hesitation, let me just say this as gently as I can: Unless you are a new believer, you have probably by now built quite a coherent identity around yourself defined by the word "Christian" ... So let me rephrase the question like this:

What made you happy this week?

Was it an hour had alone with Jesus in prayer? Was it a chance you took to serve Him secretly in some small way, offering it up as a childish gift for Him alone? Or did your joy this week primarily spring from a new CD, a shopping trip, accessing the next level on a video game, or a pizza in front of the *Frasier* rerun?

The answers to questions like these enable us to gauge our spiritual hunger:

Am I craving, and so creating, time alone with Jesus in prayer?

Is He more important to me than my partner, my family, and my friends?

Do I find Christ's name on my lips throughout the day, or only in overtly sacred contexts?

Is He my last thought at night and my first in the morning as I stumble to the bathroom?

Do I make time to pore over His biography? ...

No one will answer an unequivocal "yes" to all the right questions all the time, so please don't beat yourself up if you're now realizing that there is a reality gap in your desire for Christ.

The aim of this exercise is not to discourage you, but rather to encourage you to come to Christ now in honesty, with all your defenses down, perhaps admitting to Him that you don't actually want Him as much as you say you do, and certainly that you are not as righteous as the image you project to others.

CHARLOTTE ELLIOTT {AD 1789–1871}

Just as I am, without one plea,
But that Thy blood was shed for me,
And that Thou bidst me come to Thee,
O Lamb of God, I come, I come.

reflection

1. When you talk to God, do you sometimes pretend you're more "spiritually with it" than you really are?

2. Do you know the freedom of being brutally honest with God and yourself?

3. What prevents you from experiencing an open and honest relationship with God?

For your next devotional reading, go to page 1188.

come to this house, because this man, too, is a son of Abraham. ¹⁰For the Son of Man came to seek and to save what was lost."

The Parable of the Ten Minas

¹¹While they were listening to this, he went on to tell them a parable, because he was near Jerusalem and the people thought that the kingdom of God was going to appear at once. ¹²He said: "A man of noble birth went to a distant country to have himself appointed king and then to return. ¹³So he called ten of his servants and gave them ten minas.ᵃ 'Put this money to work,' he said, 'until I come back.'

¹⁴"But his subjects hated him and sent a delegation after him to say, 'We don't want this man to be our king.'

¹⁵"He was made king, however, and returned home. Then he sent for the servants to whom he had given the money, in order to find out what they had gained with it.

¹⁶"The first one came and said, 'Sir, your mina has earned ten more.'

¹⁷" 'Well done, my good servant!' his master replied. 'Because you have been trustworthy in a very small matter, take charge of ten cities.'

¹⁸"The second came and said, 'Sir, your mina has earned five more.'

¹⁹"His master answered, 'You take charge of five cities.'

²⁰"Then another servant came and said, 'Sir, here is your mina; I have kept it laid away in a piece of cloth. ²¹I was afraid of you, because you are a hard man. You take out what you did not put in and reap what you did not sow.'

²²"His master replied, 'I will judge you by your own words, you wicked servant! You knew, did you, that I am a hard man, taking out what I did not put in, and reaping what I did not sow? ²³Why then didn't you put my money on deposit, so that when I came back, I could have collected it with interest?'

²⁴"Then he said to those standing by, 'Take his mina away from him and give it to the one who has ten minas.'

²⁵" 'Sir,' they said, 'he already has ten!'

²⁶"He replied, 'I tell you that to everyone who has, more will be given, but as for those who have nothing, even what they have will be taken away. ²⁷But those enemies of mine who did not want me to be king over them— bring them here and kill them in front of me.' "

Jesus Comes to Jerusalem as King

²⁸After Jesus had said this, he went on ahead, going up to Jerusalem. ²⁹As he approached Bethphage and Bethany at the hill called the Mount of Olives, he sent two of his disciples, saying to them, ³⁰"Go to the village ahead of you, and as you enter it, you will find a colt tied there, which no one has ever ridden. Untie it and bring it here. ³¹If anyone asks you, 'Why are you untying it?' say, 'The Lord needs it.' "

³²Those who were sent ahead went and found it just as he had told them. ³³As they were untying the colt, its owners asked them, "Why are you untying the colt?"

³⁴They replied, "The Lord needs it."

³⁵They brought it to Jesus, threw their cloaks on the colt and put Jesus on it. ³⁶As he went along, people spread their cloaks on the road.

³⁷When he came near the place where the road goes down the Mount of Olives, the whole crowd of disciples began joyfully to praise God in loud voices for all the miracles they had seen:

³⁸"Blessed is the king who comes in the
name of the Lord!"ᵇ

"Peace in heaven and glory in the
highest!"

³⁹Some of the Pharisees in the crowd said to Jesus, "Teacher, rebuke your disciples!"

⁴⁰"I tell you," he replied, "if they keep quiet, the stones will cry out."

⁴¹As he approached Jerusalem and saw the city, he wept over it ⁴²and said, "If you, even you, had only known on this day what would bring you peace—but now it is hidden from your eyes. ⁴³The days will come on you when your enemies will build an embankment against you and encircle you and hem you in on every side. ⁴⁴They will dash you to the ground, you and the children within your walls. They will not leave one stone on another, because you did not recognize the time of God's coming to you."

Jesus at the Temple

⁴⁵When Jesus entered the temple courts,

ᵃ 13 A mina was about three months' wages.   ᵇ 38 Psalm 118:26

he began to drive out those who were selling. 46"It is written," he said to them, " 'My house will be a house of prayer'*a*; but you have made it 'a den of robbers.'*b*"

47Every day he was teaching at the temple. But the chief priests, the teachers of the law and the leaders among the people were trying to kill him. 48Yet they could not find any way to do it, because all the people hung on his words.

The Authority of Jesus Questioned

20 One day as Jesus was teaching the people in the temple courts and proclaiming the good news, the chief priests and the teachers of the law, together with the elders, came up to him. 2"Tell us by what authority you are doing these things," they said. "Who gave you this authority?"

3He replied, "I will also ask you a question. Tell me, 4John's baptism—was it from heaven, or of human origin?"

5They discussed it among themselves and said, "If we say, 'From heaven,' he will ask, 'Why didn't you believe him?' 6But if we say, 'Of human origin,' all the people will stone us, because they are persuaded that John was a prophet."

7So they answered, "We don't know where it was from."

8Jesus said, "Neither will I tell you by what authority I am doing these things."

The Parable of the Tenants

9He went on to tell the people this parable: "A man planted a vineyard, rented it to some farmers and went away for a long time. 10At harvest time he sent a servant to the tenants so they would give him some of the fruit of the vineyard. But the tenants beat him and sent him away empty-handed. 11He sent another servant, but that one also they beat and treated shamefully and sent away empty-handed. 12He sent still a third, and they wounded him and threw him out.

13"Then the owner of the vineyard said, 'What shall I do? I will send my son, whom I love; perhaps they will respect him.'

14"But when the tenants saw him, they talked the matter over. 'This is the heir,' they said. 'Let's kill him, and the inheritance will be ours.' 15So they threw him out of the vineyard and killed him.

"What then will the owner of the vineyard do to them? 16He will come and kill those tenants and give the vineyard to others."

When the people heard this, they said, "God forbid!"

17Jesus looked directly at them and asked, "Then what is the meaning of that which is written:

" 'The stone the builders rejected
has become the cornerstone'*c*?

18Everyone who falls on that stone will be broken to pieces, but anyone on whom it falls will be crushed."

19The teachers of the law and the chief priests looked for a way to arrest him immediately, because they knew he had spoken this parable against them. But they were afraid of the people.

Paying Taxes to Caesar

20Keeping a close watch on him, they sent spies, who pretended to be sincere. They hoped to catch Jesus in something he said so that they might hand him over to the power and authority of the governor. 21So the spies questioned him: "Teacher, we know that you speak and teach what is right, and that you do not show partiality but teach the way of God in accordance with the truth. 22Is it right for us to pay taxes to Caesar or not?"

23He saw through their duplicity and said to them, 24"Show me a denarius. Whose image and inscription are on it?"

"Caesar's," they replied.

25He said to them, "Then give back to Caesar what is Caesar's, and to God what is God's."

26They were unable to trap him in what he had said there in public. And astonished by his answer, they became silent.

The Resurrection and Marriage

27Some of the Sadducees, who say there is no resurrection, came to Jesus with a question. 28"Teacher," they said, "Moses wrote for us that if a man's brother dies and leaves a wife but no children, the man must marry the widow and raise up offspring for his brother. 29Now there were seven brothers. The first one married a woman and died

a 46 Isaiah 56:7   *b* 46 Jer. 7:11   *c* 17 Psalm 118:22

Which Side Are You On?

Luke 19:47–48

read/meditate

Read these verses several times, until you get a mental picture of this real-life situation. There's such a mix of responses: one group is courting thoughts of assassination, while another is hanging on every word Jesus speaks. Various perspectives can exist among people in the same situation. Whom do you most relate to in this story, if anyone at all?

pray

Pause for a moment and ask God to take inventory of your relationship with him. Ask him to reveal to you any ways in which you inadvertently work against the flow of his work in the world. Surrender to whatever you perceive as his message to you today.

contemplate

What would be the modern equivalent of hanging on God's every word? What would be the equivalent of those who are so jealous and territorial that they end up working against the causes of God? Where does your life fit into (or contrast with) those scenarios?

additional reflection

Where there is patience and humility, there is neither anger nor vexation.
—Saint Francis of Assisi

Lord, I give up all my own plans and purposes, all my own desires and hopes, and accept Thy will for my life. I give myself, my life, my all utterly to Thee to be Thine forever. Fill me and seal me with Thy Holy Spirit. Use me as Thou wilt. Send me where Thou wilt. Work out Thy whole will in my life at any cost, now and forever.
—Betty Scott Stam

For your next devotional reading, go to page 1190.

childless. 30The second 31and then the third married her, and in the same way the seven died, leaving no children. 32Finally, the woman died too. 33Now then, at the resurrection whose wife will she be, since the seven were married to her?"

34Jesus replied, "The people of this age marry and are given in marriage. 35But those who are considered worthy of taking part in the age to come and in the resurrection from the dead will neither marry nor be given in marriage, 36and they can no longer die; for they are like the angels. They are God's children, since they are children of the resurrection. 37But in the account of the burning bush, even Moses showed that the dead rise, for he calls the Lord 'the God of Abraham, and the God of Isaac, and the God of Jacob.'ᵃ 38He is not the God of the dead, but of the living, for to him all are alive."

39Some of the teachers of the law responded, "Well said, teacher!" 40And no one dared to ask him any more questions.

Whose Son Is the Messiah?

41Then Jesus said to them, "Why is it said that the Messiah is the son of David? 42David himself declares in the Book of Psalms:

> " 'The Lord said to my Lord:
>   "Sit at my right hand
> 43 until I make your enemies
>   a footstool for your feet." 'ᵇ

44David calls him 'Lord.' How then can he be his son?"

Warning Against the Teachers of the Law

45While all the people were listening, Jesus said to his disciples, 46"Beware of the teachers of the law. They like to walk around in flowing robes and love to be greeted with respect in the marketplaces and have the most important seats in the synagogues and the places of honor at banquets. 47They devour widows' houses and for a show make lengthy prayers. These men will be punished most severely."

The Widow's Offering

21 As Jesus looked up, he saw the rich putting their gifts into the temple treasury. 2He also saw a poor widow put in two very small copper coins. 3"Truly I tell you," he said, "this poor widow has put in more than all the others. 4All these people gave their gifts out of their wealth; but she out of her poverty put in all she had to live on."

The Destruction of the Temple and Signs of the End Times

5Some of his disciples were remarking about how the temple was adorned with beautiful stones and with gifts dedicated to God. But Jesus said, 6"As for what you see here, the time will come when not one stone will be left on another; every one of them will be thrown down."

7"Teacher," they asked, "when will these things happen? And what will be the sign that they are about to take place?"

8He replied: "Watch out that you are not deceived. For many will come in my name, claiming, 'I am he,' and, 'The time is near.' Do not follow them. 9When you hear of wars and uprisings, do not be frightened. These things must happen first, but the end will not come right away."

10Then he said to them: "Nation will rise against nation, and kingdom against kingdom. 11There will be great earthquakes, famines and pestilences in various places, and fearful events and great signs from heaven.

12"But before all this, they will lay hands on you and persecute you. They will deliver you to synagogues and prisons, and you will be brought before kings and governors, and all on account of my name. 13And so you will bear testimony to me. 14But make up your mind not to worry beforehand how you will defend yourselves. 15For I will give you words and wisdom that none of your adversaries will be able to resist or contradict. 16You will be betrayed even by parents, brothers, sisters, relatives and friends, and they will put some of you to death. 17Everyone will hate you because of me. 18But not a hair of your head will perish. 19Stand firm, and you will win life.

20"When you see Jerusalem being surrounded by armies, you will know that its desolation is near. 21Then let those who are in Judea flee to the mountains, let those in the city get out, and let those in the country not enter the city. 22For this is the time of punishment in fulfillment of all that has been written. 23How dreadful it will be in

---

ᵃ 37 Exodus 3:6   ᵇ 43 Psalm 110:1

MONDAY

HEAVEN: ULTIMATE FULFILLMENT
Luke 20:1–38 *or* 20:34–38

Joni Eareckson Tada

[Does the Bible] assume that all the other benefits in heaven should outweigh the "no this" and "no that"? No food, no marriage, no moon, no need for good books? Sitting in a wheelchair for decades has loaded me with a lifetime of glorious memories, everything from feeling my fingers on the cool ivory keys of a piano to the euphoria of diving through the breakers at high tide. Such memories flood every nerve and fiber of my being and, thus, my imagination. It's awful to think that the best stuff of which memories are made will have no place in heaven.

But faith tells us these things are inklings of better tastes and enraptured delights yet to come. The whisper of what they are on earth will find complete fulfillment in heaven. Faith reminds us that every negative is only the reverse side of a fulfilling. A fulfilling of all that God intended our humanity to be.

JOHN NELSON DARBY {AD 1800–1882}

[Peter, in 1 Peter] views the Christian as a pilgrim here, encouraged by the triumph of Christ Himself in resurrection, which animated him by the consciousness that there was a world of light and happiness before him, and a power which would bring him into this world. Consequently the inheritance is spoken of as "[kept] in heaven." In the epistle to the Ephesians we are seated in the heavenlies in Christ, and the inheritance is that of all things of which Christ Himself is heir. But the Christian is also in fact a pilgrim and a stranger on the earth; and it is a strong consolation to us, in our pilgrimage, to see this heavenly inheritance before us, as a certain pledge of our own entrance into it.

Another inestimable consolation is added. If the inheritance is preserved in heaven for us, we are kept by the power of God all through our pilgrimage that we may enjoy it at the end. Sweet thought!—we are kept here below through all our dangers and difficulties; and, on the other hand, the inheritance there, where there is no defilement or possibility of decay.

reflection

1. What do you look forward to most about heaven?
2. Do you feel you may have to "give up" something you enjoy on earth when you enter heaven?
3. In what way can you envision that what you enjoy on earth might be even more perfect in heaven?

For your next devotional reading, go to page 1193.

those days for pregnant women and nursing mothers! There will be great distress in the land and wrath against this people. [24]They will fall by the sword and will be taken as prisoners to all the nations. Jerusalem will be trampled on by the Gentiles until the times of the Gentiles are fulfilled.

[25]"There will be signs in the sun, moon and stars. On the earth, nations will be in anguish and perplexity at the roaring and tossing of the sea. [26]People will faint from terror, apprehensive of what is coming on the world, for the heavenly bodies will be shaken. [27]At that time they will see the Son of Man coming in a cloud with power and great glory. [28]When these things begin to take place, stand up and lift up your heads, because your redemption is drawing near."

[29]He told them this parable: "Look at the fig tree and all the trees. [30]When they sprout leaves, you can see for yourselves and know that summer is near. [31]Even so, when you see these things happening, you know that the kingdom of God is near.

[32]"Truly I tell you, this generation will certainly not pass away until all these things have happened. [33]Heaven and earth will pass away, but my words will never pass away.

[34]"Be careful, or your hearts will be weighed down with dissipation, drunkenness and the anxieties of life, and that day will close on you suddenly like a trap. [35]For it will come on all those who live on the face of the whole earth. [36]Be always on the watch, and pray that you may be able to escape all that is about to happen, and that you may be able to stand before the Son of Man."

[37]Each day Jesus was teaching at the temple, and each evening he went out to spend the night on the hill called the Mount of Olives, [38]and all the people came early in the morning to hear him at the temple.

Judas Agrees to Betray Jesus

22 Now the Festival of Unleavened Bread, called the Passover, was approaching, [2]and the chief priests and the teachers of the law were looking for some way to get rid of Jesus, for they were afraid of the people. [3]Then Satan entered Judas, called Iscariot, one of the Twelve. [4]And Judas went to the chief priests and the officers of the temple guard and discussed with them how he might betray

Jesus. [5]They were delighted and agreed to give him money. [6]He consented, and watched for an opportunity to hand Jesus over to them when no crowd was present.

The Last Supper

[7]Then came the day of Unleavened Bread on which the Passover lamb had to be sacrificed. [8]Jesus sent Peter and John, saying, "Go and make preparations for us to eat the Passover."

[9]"Where do you want us to prepare for it?" they asked.

[10]He replied, "As you enter the city, a man carrying a jar of water will meet you. Follow him to the house that he enters, [11]and say to the owner of the house, 'The Teacher asks: Where is the guest room, where I may eat the Passover with my disciples?' [12]He will show you a large room upstairs, all furnished. Make preparations there."

[13]They left and found things just as Jesus had told them. So they prepared the Passover.

[14]When the hour came, Jesus and his apostles reclined at the table. [15]And he said to them, "I have eagerly desired to eat this Passover with you before I suffer. [16]For I tell you, I will not eat it again until it finds fulfillment in the kingdom of God."

[17]After taking the cup, he gave thanks and said, "Take this and divide it among you. [18]For I tell you I will not drink again of the fruit of the vine until the kingdom of God comes."

[19]And he took bread, gave thanks and broke it, and gave it to them, saying, "This is my body given for you; do this in remembrance of me."

[20]In the same way, after the supper he took the cup, saying, "This cup is the new covenant in my blood, which is poured out for you. [21]But the hand of him who is going to betray me is with mine on the table. [22]The Son of Man will go as it has been decreed. But woe to that man who betrays him!" [23]They began to question among themselves which of them it might be who would do this.

[24]A dispute also arose among them as to which of them was considered to be greatest. [25]Jesus said to them, "The kings of the Gentiles lord it over them; and those who exercise authority over them call themselves Benefactors. [26]But you are not to be like that. Instead, the greatest among you should be like the youngest, and the one who rules like the one who serves. [27]For who

is greater, the one who is at the table or the one who serves? Is it not the one who is at the table? But I am among you as one who serves. ²⁸You are those who have stood by me in my trials. ²⁹And I confer on you a kingdom, just as my Father conferred one on me, ³⁰so that you may eat and drink at my table in my kingdom and sit on thrones, judging the twelve tribes of Israel.

³¹"Simon, Simon, Satan has asked to sift all of you as wheat. ³²But I have prayed for you, Simon, that your faith may not fail. And when you have turned back, strengthen your brothers."

³³But he replied, "Lord, I am ready to go with you to prison and to death."

³⁴Jesus answered, "I tell you, Peter, before the rooster crows today, you will deny three times that you know me."

³⁵Then Jesus asked them, "When I sent you without purse, bag or sandals, did you lack anything?"

"Nothing," they answered.

³⁶He said to them, "But now if you have a purse, take it, and also a bag; and if you don't have a sword, sell your cloak and buy one. ³⁷It is written: 'And he was numbered with the transgressors'^a; and I tell you that this must be fulfilled in me. Yes, what is written about me is reaching its fulfillment."

³⁸The disciples said, "See, Lord, here are two swords."

"That is enough," he replied.

Jesus Prays on the Mount of Olives

³⁹Jesus went out as usual to the Mount of Olives, and his disciples followed him. ⁴⁰On reaching the place, he said to them, "Pray that you will not fall into temptation." ⁴¹He withdrew about a stone's throw beyond them, knelt down and prayed, ⁴²"Father, if you are willing, take this cup from me; yet not my will, but yours be done." ⁴³An angel from heaven appeared to him and strengthened him. ⁴⁴And being in anguish, he prayed more earnestly, and his sweat was like drops of blood falling to the ground.^b

⁴⁵When he rose from prayer and went back to the disciples, he found them asleep, exhausted from sorrow. ⁴⁶"Why are you sleeping?" he asked them. "Get up and pray so that you will not fall into temptation."

Jesus Arrested

⁴⁷While he was still speaking a crowd came up, and the man who was called Judas, one of the Twelve, was leading them. He approached Jesus to kiss him, ⁴⁸but Jesus asked him, "Judas, are you betraying the Son of Man with a kiss?"

⁴⁹When Jesus' followers saw what was going to happen, they said, "Lord, should we strike with our swords?" ⁵⁰And one of them struck the servant of the high priest, cutting off his right ear.

⁵¹But Jesus answered, "No more of this!" And he touched the man's ear and healed him.

⁵²Then Jesus said to the chief priests, the officers of the temple guard, and the elders, who had come for him, "Am I leading a rebellion, that you have come with swords and clubs? ⁵³Every day I was with you in the temple courts, and you did not lay a hand on me. But this is your hour—when darkness reigns."

Peter Disowns Jesus

⁵⁴Then seizing him, they led him away and took him into the house of the high priest. Peter followed at a distance. ⁵⁵And when some there had kindled a fire in the middle of the courtyard and had sat down together, Peter sat down with them. ⁵⁶A servant girl saw him seated there in the firelight. She looked closely at him and said, "This man was with him."

⁵⁷But he denied it. "Woman,^c I don't know him," he said.

⁵⁸A little later someone else saw him and said, "You also are one of them."

"Man, I am not!" Peter replied.

⁵⁹About an hour later another asserted, "Certainly this fellow was with him, for he is a Galilean."

⁶⁰Peter replied, "Man, I don't know what you're talking about!" Just as he was speaking, the rooster crowed. ⁶¹The Lord turned and looked straight at Peter. Then Peter remembered the word the Lord had spoken to him: "Before the rooster crows today, you will disown me three times." ⁶²And he went outside and wept bitterly.

The Guards Mock Jesus

⁶³The men who were guarding Jesus began mocking and beating him. ⁶⁴They blind-

---

^a 37 Isaiah 53:12   ^b 43,44 Some early manuscripts do not have verses 43 and 44.   ^c 57 The Greek for *Woman* does not denote any disrespect.

TUESDAY

VITAL PRAYER

Luke 22:39–62 *or* 22:46

Ajith Fernando

Each Christian needs to have a time that is exclusively given to communion with God. What is important is . . . whether we give time exclusively for prayer.

Our prayer time is when we receive spiritual strength to live and witness in a world that does not respect spiritual reality. People who are active in such a world need this desperately so that they can go against the tide and maintain their Christian stand. Jesus told his disciples as they prepared to face a hostile mob, "[Pray that you will not fall into temptation]" (Luke 22:40). Besides this, of course, is the fact that God answers prayer.

So praying for our needs and those of others is one of the most important things we can do. Yet what the American preacher Vance Hanver said some years ago is true today also: "Many a man who would never think of dashing out in the morning without his breakfast, his vitamins and his briefcase, plunges headlong into a perilous day with an unprepared soul. 'A little talk with Jesus' readies the body, the mind and the spirit for whatever comes."

EVELYN UNDERHILL {AD 1875–1941}

Prayer should take up and turn towards the spiritual order all the powers of our mental, emotional and volitional life. Prayers should be the highest exercise of these powers: for here they are directed to the only adequate object of thought, of love and of desire. It should, as it were, lift us to the top of our condition, and represent the fullest flowering of our consciousness. For here we breathe the air of the supernatural order, and attain according to our measure that communion with Reality for which we were made.

Prayer will include many different kinds of spiritual work, and also—what is too often forgotten—the priceless gift of spiritual rest. It will include many kinds of intercourse with Reality—adoration, petition, meditation, contemplation—and all the shades and varieties of these which religious writers have named and classified.

As in the natural order the living creature must feed *and* grow, must suffer *and* enjoy, must get energy from the world *and* give it back again if it is to live a whole and healthy life. So, too, in the spiritual order. All these things—the giving and the receiving, the work and the rest—should fall within the circle of prayer.

reflection

1. How do you determine your priorities each day?
2. Do you have a specific time set aside to pray? Why or why not?
3. How do your daily actions reveal how important you feel prayer is?

For your next devotional reading, go to page 1196.

folded him and demanded, "Prophesy! Who hit you?" 65And they said many other insulting things to him.

Jesus Before Pilate and Herod

66At daybreak the council of the elders of the people, both the chief priests and the teachers of the law, met together, and Jesus was led before them. 67"If you are the Messiah," they said, "tell us."

Jesus answered, "If I tell you, you will not believe me, 68and if I asked you, you would not answer. 69But from now on, the Son of Man will be seated at the right hand of the mighty God."

70They all asked, "Are you then the Son of God?"

He replied, "You say that I am."

71Then they said, "Why do we need any more testimony? We have heard it from his own lips."

23 Then the whole assembly rose and led him off to Pilate. 2And they began to accuse him, saying, "We have found this man subverting our nation. He opposes payment of taxes to Caesar and claims to be Messiah, a king."

3So Pilate asked Jesus, "Are you the king of the Jews?"

"You have said so," Jesus replied.

4Then Pilate announced to the chief priests and the crowd, "I find no basis for a charge against this man."

5But they insisted, "He stirs up the people all over Judea by his teaching. He started in Galilee and has come all the way here."

6On hearing this, Pilate asked if the man was a Galilean. 7When he learned that Jesus was under Herod's jurisdiction, he sent him to Herod, who was also in Jerusalem at that time.

8When Herod saw Jesus, he was greatly pleased, because for a long time he had been wanting to see him. From what he had heard about him, he hoped to see him perform a sign of some sort. 9He plied him with many questions, but Jesus gave him no answer. 10The chief priests and the teachers of the law were standing there, vehemently accusing him. 11Then Herod and his soldiers ridiculed and mocked him. Dressing him in an elegant robe, they sent him back to Pilate. 12That day Herod and Pilate became friends—before this they had been enemies.

13Pilate called together the chief priests, the rulers and the people, 14and said to them, "You brought me this man as one who was inciting the people to rebellion. I have examined him in your presence and have found no basis for your charges against him. 15Neither has Herod, for he sent him back to us; as you can see, he has done nothing to deserve death. 16[17]Therefore, I will punish him and then release him."

18With one voice they cried out, "Away with this man! Release Barabbas to us!" 19(Barabbas had been thrown into prison for an insurrection in the city, and for murder.)

20Wanting to release Jesus, Pilate appealed to them again. 21But they kept shouting, "Crucify him! Crucify him!"

22For the third time he spoke to them: "Why? What crime has this man committed? I have found in him no grounds for the death penalty. Therefore I will have him punished and then release him."

23But with loud shouts they insistently demanded that he be crucified, and their shouts prevailed. 24So Pilate decided to grant their demand. 25He released the man who had been thrown into prison for insurrection and murder, the one they asked for, and surrendered Jesus to their will.

The Crucifixion of Jesus

26As the soldiers led him away, they seized Simon from Cyrene, who was on his way in from the country, and put the cross on him and made him carry it behind Jesus. 27A large number of people followed him, including women who mourned and wailed for him. 28Jesus turned and said to them, "Daughters of Jerusalem, do not weep for me; weep for yourselves and for your children. 29For the time will come when you will say, 'Blessed are the childless women, the wombs that never bore and the breasts that never nursed!' 30Then

> " 'they will say to the mountains, "Fall on us!"
> and to the hills, "Cover us!" '*a*

31For if people do these things when the tree is green, what will happen when it is dry?"

32Two other men, both criminals, were

---

a 30 Hosea 10:8

also led out with him to be executed. ³³When they came to the place called the Skull, they crucified him there, along with the criminals—one on his right, the other on his left. ³⁴Jesus said, "Father, forgive them, for they do not know what they are doing."ᵃ And they divided up his clothes by casting lots.

³⁵The people stood watching, and the rulers even sneered at him. They said, "He saved others; let him save himself if he is God's Messiah, the Chosen One."

³⁶The soldiers also came up and mocked him. They offered him wine vinegar ³⁷and said, "If you are the king of the Jews, save yourself."

³⁸There was a written notice above him, which read: THIS IS THE KING OF THE JEWS.

³⁹One of the criminals who hung there hurled insults at him: "Aren't you the Messiah? Save yourself and us!"

⁴⁰But the other criminal rebuked him. "Don't you fear God," he said, "since you are under the same sentence? ⁴¹We are punished justly, for we are getting what our deeds deserve. But this man has done nothing wrong."

⁴²Then he said, "Jesus, remember me when you come into your kingdom.ᵇ"

⁴³Jesus answered him, "Truly I tell you, today you will be with me in paradise."

The Death of Jesus

⁴⁴It was now about noon, and darkness came over the whole land until three in the afternoon, ⁴⁵for the sun stopped shining. And the curtain of the temple was torn in two. ⁴⁶Jesus called out with a loud voice, "Father, into your hands I commit my spirit."ᶜ When he had said this, he breathed his last.

⁴⁷The centurion, seeing what had happened, praised God and said, "Surely this was a righteous man." ⁴⁸When all the people who had gathered to witness this sight saw what took place, they beat their breasts and went away. ⁴⁹But all those who knew him, including the women who had followed him from Galilee, stood at a distance, watching these things.

The Burial of Jesus

⁵⁰Now there was a man named Joseph, a member of the Council, a good and upright man, ⁵¹who had not consented to their decision and action. He came from the Judean town of Arimathea, and he himself was waiting for the kingdom of God. ⁵²Going to Pilate, he asked for Jesus' body. ⁵³Then he took it down, wrapped it in linen cloth and placed it in a tomb cut in the rock, one in which no one had yet been laid. ⁵⁴It was Preparation Day, and the Sabbath was about to begin.

⁵⁵The women who had come with Jesus from Galilee followed Joseph and saw the tomb and how his body was laid in it. ⁵⁶Then they went home and prepared spices and perfumes. But they rested on the Sabbath in obedience to the commandment.

Jesus Has Risen

24 On the first day of the week, very early in the morning, the women took the spices they had prepared and went to the tomb. ²They found the stone rolled away from the tomb, ³but when they entered, they did not find the body of the Lord Jesus. ⁴While they were wondering about this, suddenly two men in clothes that gleamed like lightning stood beside them. ⁵In their fright the women bowed down with their faces to the ground, but the men said to them, "Why do you look for the living among the dead? ⁶He is not here; he has risen! Remember how he told you, while he was still with you in Galilee: ⁷'The Son of Man must be delivered over to the hands of sinners, be crucified and on the third day be raised again.' " ⁸Then they remembered his words.

⁹When they came back from the tomb, they told all these things to the Eleven and to all the others. ¹⁰It was Mary Magdalene, Joanna, Mary the mother of James, and the others with them who told this to the apostles. ¹¹But they did not believe the women, because their words seemed to them like nonsense. ¹²Peter, however, got up and ran to the tomb. Bending over, he saw the strips of linen lying by themselves, and he went away, wondering to himself what had happened.

On the Road to Emmaus

¹³Now that same day two of them were going to a village called Emmaus, about sev-

---

ᵃ 34 Some early manuscripts do not have this sentence.   ᵇ 42 Some manuscripts *come with your kingly power*   ᶜ 46 Psalm 31:5

WEDNESDAY

SEEING GOD THROUGH THE EYES OF FAITH

Luke 24:1–53 or 24:36–49

Brian McLaren

In our postmodern times, we are increasingly aware of the limitations of human knowledge. We are aware perhaps as never before of the gap between what we subjectively "know" and what is objectively true. For people like us, boxed in little bodies with narrow portals of physical senses which are interpreted by fallible, limited (yet amazing!) little brains, absolute certainty is a luxury we have not been given. We can only aspire to relative certainty, which involves relative uncertainty . . . which leaves room for—no, more, which actually *requires*—faith.

We could content ourselves with petty pursuits and leave off any search for truth. But to do so feels cheap, for moral reasons if not for intellectual ones. So, into this profound human dilemma we go, needing to let go of certainty in order to reach for truth. We venture into this very real gap between our understanding "in here" and reality as it is "out there." We move into this territory where the limitations of knowledge are admitted and the value of seeking truth is also held high. Here, without faith we cannot go. It's the only vehicle we have.

SAINT AUGUSTINE {AD 354–430}

For the Christian, it is enough to believe that the cause of all created things—whether in heaven or on earth, whether visible or invisible—is nothing other than the goodness of the Creator, who is the one and the true God. Further, the Christian believes that nothing exists apart from God himself and what comes from him. And they believe that God is triune—in other words, he is the Father and the Son begotten of the Father and the Holy Spirit proceeding from the same Father, but one and the same Spirit of the Father and the Son. By this Trinity, supremely and equally and immutably good, were all things created.

1. Like the disciples, many people have a hard time believing Jesus' claims without "cold, hard facts." How does faith enter in at this point?

2. How would you explain to someone else that the truth about God can be pointed to but not absolutely proven?

3. How would you explain the faith that is required to believe that God himself is true?

For your next devotional reading, go to page 1199.

en miles*a* from Jerusalem. ¹⁴They were talking with each other about everything that had happened. ¹⁵As they talked and discussed these things with each other, Jesus himself came up and walked along with them; ¹⁶but they were kept from recognizing him.

¹⁷He asked them, "What are you discussing together as you walk along?"

They stood still, their faces downcast. ¹⁸One of them, named Cleopas, asked him, "Are you only a visitor to Jerusalem and do not know the things that have happened there in these days?"

¹⁹"What things?" he asked.

"About Jesus of Nazareth," they replied. "He was a prophet, powerful in word and deed before God and all the people. ²⁰The chief priests and our rulers handed him over to be sentenced to death, and they crucified him; ²¹but we had hoped that he was the one who was going to redeem Israel. And what is more, it is the third day since all this took place. ²²In addition, some of our women amazed us. They went to the tomb early this morning ²³but didn't find his body. They came and told us that they had seen a vision of angels, who said he was alive. ²⁴Then some of our companions went to the tomb and found it just as the women had said, but him they did not see."

²⁵He said to them, "How foolish you are, and how slow to believe all that the prophets have spoken! ²⁶Did not the Messiah have to suffer these things and then enter his glory?" ²⁷And beginning with Moses and all the Prophets, he explained to them what was said in all the Scriptures concerning himself.

²⁸As they approached the village to which they were going, Jesus continued on as if he were going farther. ²⁹But they urged him strongly, "Stay with us, for it is nearly evening; the day is almost over." So he went in to stay with them.

³⁰When he was at the table with them, he took bread, gave thanks, broke it and began to give it to them. ³¹Then their eyes were opened and they recognized him, and he disappeared from their sight. ³²They asked each other, "Were not our hearts burning within us while he talked with us on the road and opened the Scriptures to us?"

³³They got up and returned at once to Je-

rusalem. There they found the Eleven and those with them, assembled together ³⁴and saying, "It is true! The Lord has risen and has appeared to Simon." ³⁵Then the two told what had happened on the way, and how Jesus was recognized by them when he broke the bread.

Jesus Appears to the Disciples

³⁶While they were still talking about this, Jesus himself stood among them and said to them, "Peace be with you."

³⁷They were startled and frightened, thinking they saw a ghost. ³⁸He said to them, "Why are you troubled, and why do doubts rise in your minds? ³⁹Look at my hands and my feet. It is I myself! Touch me and see; a ghost does not have flesh and bones, as you see I have."

⁴⁰When he had said this, he showed them his hands and feet. ⁴¹And while they still did not believe it because of joy and amazement, he asked them, "Do you have anything here to eat?" ⁴²They gave him a piece of broiled fish, ⁴³and he took it and ate it in their presence.

⁴⁴He said to them, "This is what I told you while I was still with you: Everything must be fulfilled that is written about me in the Law of Moses, the Prophets and the Psalms."

⁴⁵Then he opened their minds so they could understand the Scriptures. ⁴⁶He told them, "This is what is written: The Messiah will suffer and rise from the dead on the third day, ⁴⁷and repentance for the forgiveness of sins will be preached in his name to all nations, beginning at Jerusalem. ⁴⁸You are witnesses of these things. ⁴⁹I am going to send you what my Father has promised; but stay in the city until you have been clothed with power from on high."

The Ascension of Jesus

⁵⁰When he had led them out to the vicinity of Bethany, he lifted up his hands and blessed them. ⁵¹While he was blessing them, he left them and was taken up into heaven. ⁵²Then they worshiped him and returned to Jerusalem with great joy. ⁵³And they stayed continually at the temple, praising God.

a 13 Or *about 11 kilometers*

john

> AUTHOR: John
>
> DATE: Probably around A.D. 85–90, before John's exile to the island of Patmos
>
> THEME: Jesus, the Son of God, offers eternal life.

The Word Became Flesh

1 In the beginning was the Word, and the Word was with God, and the Word was God. ²He was with God in the beginning. ³Through him all things were made; without him nothing was made that has been made. ⁴In him was life, and that life was the light of all people. ⁵The light shines in the darkness, and the darkness has not overcome*a* it.

⁶There was a man sent from God whose name was John. ⁷He came as a witness to testify concerning that light, so that through him all might believe. ⁸He himself was not the light; he came only as a witness to the light.

⁹The true light that gives light to everyone was coming into the world. ¹⁰He was in the world, and though the world was made through him, the world did not recognize him. ¹¹He came to that which was his own, but his own did not receive him. ¹²Yet to all who did receive him, to those who believed in his name, he gave the right to become children of God— ¹³children born not of natural descent, nor of human decision or a husband's will, but born of God.

¹⁴The Word became flesh and made his dwelling among us. We have seen his glory, the glory of the one and only ₋Son₋, who came from the Father, full of grace and truth.

¹⁵(John testified concerning him. He cried out, saying, "This is he of whom I said, 'He who comes after me has surpassed me because he was before me.' ") ¹⁶Out of his fullness we have all received grace in place of grace already given. ¹⁷For the law was given through Moses; grace and truth came through Jesus Christ. ¹⁸No one has ever seen God, but the one and only ₋Son₋, who is himself God and*b* is in closest relationship with the Father, has made him known.

John the Baptist Denies Being the Messiah

¹⁹Now this was John's testimony when the Jewish leaders in Jerusalem sent priests and Levites to ask him who he was. ²⁰He did not fail to confess, but confessed freely, "I am not the Messiah."

²¹They asked him, "Then who are you? Are you Elijah?"

He said, "I am not."

"Are you the Prophet?"

He answered, "No."

²²Finally they said, "Who are you? Give us an answer to take back to those who sent us. What do you say about yourself?"

²³John replied in the words of Isaiah the prophet, "I am the voice of one calling in the wilderness, 'Make straight the way for the Lord.' "*c*

²⁴Now the Pharisees who had been sent ²⁵questioned him, "Why then do you baptize if you are not the Messiah, nor Elijah, nor the Prophet?"

²⁶"I baptize with*d* water," John replied, "but among you stands one you do not know. ²⁷He is the one who comes after me, the thongs of whose sandals I am not worthy to untie."

²⁸This all happened at Bethany on the other side of the Jordan, where John was baptizing.

a 5 Or *understood*   *b 18* Some manuscripts *but the only Son, who*   *c 23* Isaiah 40:3   *d 26* Or *in;* also in verses 31 and 33 (twice)

THURSDAY

GOD IN THE FLESH

John 1:1–51 or 1:1–4

PHILIP SCHAFF {AD 1819–1893}

Christianity rises far above all other religions in the theory and practice of virtue and piety. It sets forth the highest standard of love to God and to humanity. It sets forth this standard not merely as an abstract doctrine, or an object of effort and hope, but as a living fact in the person of Jesus Christ. His life and example have more power and influence than all the maxims and precepts of sages and legislators ... The wisest men of Greece and Rome sanctioned slavery, polygamy, concubinage, oppression, revenge and infanticide; or they contradicted their purer principles by their actual conduct. The ethical standard of the Jews was much higher. Yet none of their patriarchs, kings or prophets claimed perfection, and the Bible honestly reports the infirmities and sins (as well as the virtues) of Abraham, Jacob, Moses, David and Solomon.

But the character of Christ from the manger to the cross is without spot or blemish. He is above reproach or suspicion, and is acknowledged by friend and foe to be the purest as well as the wisest being that ever appeared on earth. He is the nearest approach which God can make to people, and which people can make to God. He represents the fullest imaginable and attainable harmony of the ideal and real, of the divine and human ...

Steve Brown

What I'm about to say isn't wish fulfillment, a hopeful doctrine or anything of the sort. It's a fact—a space/time fact—that God took on human flesh and lived for a while in our presence. Throughout history people like you and I have asked our questions about God. Is there really a God? Did he create all of this? Does he care? Does he love? Does he love *me*? Somebody always gave answers to such questions, but most of them amounted to little but conjecture—head answers to the heart's questions. Then, in a breathtaking and explosive way, God moved into our hearts—not with propositions, but with himself ...

Do you want to know what God is like? Then look at Jesus. If you want to know how God reacts to people, look at how Jesus reacted to people. If you want to know what God thinks, how he acts and who he is ... For God's sake, go to Jesus.

reflection

1. What kinds of questions have you asked about God?
2. How does Jesus answer those questions?
3. Why would the incomprehensible God choose to confine himself to comprehensible flesh?

For your next devotional reading, go to page 1203.

John's Testimony About Jesus

²⁹The next day John saw Jesus coming toward him and said, "Look, the Lamb of God, who takes away the sin of the world! ³⁰This is the one I meant when I said, 'A man who comes after me has surpassed me because he was before me.' ³¹I myself did not know him, but the reason I came baptizing with water was that he might be revealed to Israel."

³²Then John gave this testimony: "I saw the Spirit come down from heaven as a dove and remain on him. ³³And I myself did not know him, but the one who sent me to baptize with water told me, 'The man on whom you see the Spirit come down and remain is the one who will baptize with the Holy Spirit.' ³⁴I have seen and I testify that this is God's Chosen One."*^a*

John's Disciples Follow Jesus

³⁵The next day John was there again with two of his disciples. ³⁶When he saw Jesus passing by, he said, "Look, the Lamb of God!"

³⁷When the two disciples heard him say this, they followed Jesus. ³⁸Turning around, Jesus saw them following and asked, "What do you want?"

They said, "Rabbi" (which means "Teacher"), "where are you staying?"

³⁹"Come," he replied, "and you will see."

So they went and saw where he was staying, and they spent that day with him. It was about four in the afternoon.

⁴⁰Andrew, Simon Peter's brother, was one of the two who heard what John had said and who had followed Jesus. ⁴¹The first thing Andrew did was to find his brother Simon and tell him, "We have found the Messiah" (that is, the Christ). ⁴²And he brought him to Jesus.

Jesus looked at him and said, "You are Simon son of John. You will be called Cephas" (which, when translated, is Peter*^b*).

Jesus Calls Philip and Nathanael

⁴³The next day Jesus decided to leave for Galilee. Finding Philip, he said to him, "Follow me."

⁴⁴Philip, like Andrew and Peter, was from the town of Bethsaida. ⁴⁵Philip found Nathanael and told him, "We have found the one Moses wrote about in the Law, and about whom the prophets also wrote—Jesus of Nazareth, the son of Joseph."

⁴⁶"Nazareth! Can anything good come from there?" Nathanael asked.

"Come and see," said Philip.

⁴⁷When Jesus saw Nathanael approaching, he said of him, "Here truly is an Israelite in whom there is no deceit."

⁴⁸"How do you know me?" Nathanael asked.

Jesus answered, "I saw you while you were still under the fig tree before Philip called you."

⁴⁹Then Nathanael declared, "Rabbi, you are the Son of God; you are the king of Israel."

⁵⁰Jesus said, "You believe*^c* because I told you I saw you under the fig tree. You will see greater things than that." ⁵¹He then added, "Very truly I tell you,*^d* you*^d* will see 'heaven open, and the angels of God ascending and descending on'*^e* the Son of Man."

Jesus Changes Water Into Wine

2 On the third day a wedding took place at Cana in Galilee. Jesus' mother was there, ²and Jesus and his disciples had also been invited to the wedding. ³When the wine was gone, Jesus' mother said to him, "They have no more wine."

⁴"Woman,*^f* why do you involve me?" Jesus replied. "My hour has not yet come."

⁵His mother said to the servants, "Do whatever he tells you."

⁶Nearby stood six stone water jars, the kind used by the Jews for ceremonial washing, each holding from twenty to thirty gallons.*^g*

⁷Jesus said to the servants, "Fill the jars with water"; so they filled them to the brim.

⁸Then he told them, "Now draw some out and take it to the master of the banquet."

They did so, ⁹and the master of the banquet tasted the water that had been turned into wine. He did not realize where it had come from, though the servants who had drawn the water knew. Then he called the bridegroom aside ¹⁰and said, "Everyone brings out the choice wine first and then the cheaper wine after the guests have had too

---

a 34 See Isaiah 42:1; many manuscripts *is the Son of God.*   *b 42 Cephas* (Aramaic) and *Peter* (Greek) both mean *rock.*   *c 50* Or *Do you believe . . . ?*   *d 51* The Greek is plural.   *e 51* Gen. 28:12   *f 4* The Greek for *Woman* does not denote any disrespect.   *g 6* Or from about 75 to about 115 liters much to drink; but you have saved the best till now."

¹¹What Jesus did here in Cana of Galilee was the first of the signs through which he revealed his glory; and his disciples put their faith in him.

¹²After this he went down to Capernaum with his mother and brothers and his disciples. There they stayed for a few days.

Jesus Clears the Temple Courts

¹³When it was almost time for the Jewish Passover, Jesus went up to Jerusalem. ¹⁴In the temple courts he found people selling cattle, sheep and doves, and others sitting at tables exchanging money. ¹⁵So he made a whip out of cords, and drove all from the temple courts, both sheep and cattle; he scattered the coins of the money changers and overturned their tables. ¹⁶To those who sold doves he said, "Get these out of here! Stop turning my Father's house into a market!" ¹⁷His disciples remembered that it is written: "Zeal for your house will consume me." *a*

¹⁸The Jews then responded to him, "What sign can you show us to prove your authority to do all this?"

¹⁹Jesus answered them, "Destroy this temple, and I will raise it again in three days."

²⁰They replied, "It has taken forty-six years to build this temple, and you are going to raise it in three days?" ²¹But the temple he had spoken of was his body. ²²After he was raised from the dead, his disciples recalled what he had said. Then they believed the scripture and the words that Jesus had spoken.

²³Now while he was in Jerusalem at the Passover Festival, many people saw the signs he was performing and believed in his name. *b* ²⁴But Jesus would not entrust himself to them, for he knew all people. ²⁵He did not need human testimony about them, for he knew what was in them.

Jesus Teaches Nicodemus

3 Now there was a Pharisee, a man named Nicodemus who was a member of the Jewish ruling council. ²He

came to Jesus at night and said, "Rabbi, we know that you are a teacher who has come from God. For no one could perform the signs you are doing if God were not with him."

³Jesus replied, "Very truly I tell you, no one can see the kingdom of God without being born again. *c* "

⁴"How can anyone be born when they are old?" Nicodemus asked. "Surely they cannot enter a second time into their mother's womb to be born!"

⁵Jesus answered, "Very truly I tell you, no one can enter the kingdom of God without being born of water and the Spirit. ⁶Flesh gives birth to flesh, but the Spirit *d* gives birth to spirit. ⁷You should not be surprised at my saying, 'You *e* must be born again.' ⁸The wind blows wherever it pleases. You hear its sound, but you cannot tell where it comes from or where it is going. So it is with everyone born of the Spirit." *f*

⁹"How can this be?" Nicodemus asked.

¹⁰"You are Israel's teacher," said Jesus, "and do you not understand these things? ¹¹Very truly I tell you, we speak of what we know, and we testify to what we have seen, but still you people do not accept our testimony. ¹²I have spoken to you of earthly things and you do not believe; how then will you believe if I speak of heavenly things? ¹³No one has ever gone into heaven except the one who came from heaven—the Son of Man. *g* ¹⁴Just as Moses lifted up the snake in the wilderness, so the Son of Man must be lifted up, *h* ¹⁵that everyone who believes may have eternal life in him." *i*

¹⁶For God so loved the world that he gave his one and only Son, that whoever believes in him shall not perish but have eternal life. ¹⁷For God did not send his Son into the world to condemn the world, but to save the world through him. ¹⁸Whoever believes in him is not condemned, but whoever does not believe stands condemned already because they have not believed in the name of God's one and only Son. ¹⁹This is the verdict: Light has come into the world, but people loved darkness instead of light because their deeds were evil. ²⁰All those who do evil hate the light, and will not come into the light for fear

---

a 17 Psalm 69:9   *b* 23 Or *in him*   *c* 3 The Greek for *again* also means *from above*; also in verse 7.
d 6 Or *but spirit*   *e* 7 The Greek is plural.   *f* 8 The Greek for *Spirit* is the same as that for *wind*.
g 13 Some manuscripts *Man, who is in heaven*   *h* 14 The Greek for *lifted up* also means *exalted*.
i 15 Some interpreters end the quotation with verse 21.

that their deeds will be exposed. [21]But those who live by the truth come into the light, so that it may be seen plainly that what they have done has been done in the sight of God.

John Testifies Again About Jesus

[22]After this, Jesus and his disciples went out into the Judean countryside, where he spent some time with them, and baptized. [23]Now John also was baptizing at Aenon near Salim, because there was plenty of water, and people were coming and being baptized. [24](This was before John was put in prison.) [25]An argument developed between some of John's disciples and a certain Jew over the matter of ceremonial washing. [26]They came to John and said to him, "Rabbi, that man who was with you on the other side of the Jordan—the one you testified about—look, he is baptizing, and everyone is going to him."

[27]To this John replied, "A person can receive only what is given from heaven. [28]You yourselves can testify that I said, 'I am not the Messiah but am sent ahead of him.' [29]The bride belongs to the bridegroom. The friend who attends the bridegroom waits and listens for him, and is full of joy when he hears the bridegroom's voice. That joy is mine, and it is now complete. [30]He must become greater; I must become less."[a]

[31]The one who comes from above is above all; the one who is from the earth belongs to the earth, and speaks as one from the earth. The one who comes from heaven is above all. [32]He testifies to what he has seen and heard, but no one accepts his testimony. [33]The person who has accepted it has certified that God is truthful. [34]For the one whom God has sent speaks the words of God, for God[b] gives the Spirit without limit. [35]The Father loves the Son and has placed everything in his hands. [36]Whoever believes in the Son has eternal life, but whoever rejects the Son will not see life, for God's wrath remains on them.

Jesus Talks With a Samaritan Woman

4 Now Jesus learned that the Pharisees had heard that he was gaining and baptizing more disciples than John— [2]although in fact it was not Jesus who baptized, but his disciples. [3]So he left Judea and went back once more to Galilee.

[4]Now he had to go through Samaria. [5]So he came to a town in Samaria called Sychar, near the plot of ground Jacob had given to his son Joseph. [6]Jacob's well was there, and Jesus, tired as he was from the journey, sat down by the well. It was about noon.

[7]When a Samaritan woman came to draw water, Jesus said to her, "Will you give me a drink?" [8](His disciples had gone into the town to buy food.)

[9]The Samaritan woman said to him, "You are a Jew and I am a Samaritan woman. How can you ask me for a drink?" (For Jews do not associate with Samaritans.[c])

[10]Jesus answered her, "If you knew the gift of God and who it is that asks you for a drink, you would have asked him and he would have given you living water."

[11]"Sir," the woman said, "you have nothing to draw with and the well is deep. Where can you get this living water? [12]Are you greater than our father Jacob, who gave us the well and drank from it himself, as did also his sons and his flocks and herds?"

[13]Jesus answered, "Everyone who drinks this water will be thirsty again, [14]but those who drink the water I give them will never thirst. Indeed, the water I give them will become in them a spring of water welling up to eternal life."

[15]The woman said to him, "Sir, give me this water so that I won't get thirsty and have to keep coming here to draw water."

[16]He told her, "Go, call your husband and come back."

[17]"I have no husband," she replied.

Jesus said to her, "You are right when you say you have no husband. [18]The fact is, you have had five husbands, and the man you now have is not your husband. What you have just said is quite true."

[19]"Sir," the woman said, "I can see that you are a prophet. [20]Our ancestors worshiped on this mountain, but you Jews claim that the place where we must worship is in Jerusalem."

[21]"Woman,"[d] Jesus replied, "believe me, a time is coming when you will worship the Father neither on this mountain nor in Jerusalem. [22]You Samaritans worship what you

---

[a] 30 Some interpreters end the quotation with verse 36.   [b] 34 Greek *he*   [c] 9 Or *do not use dishes Samaritans have used*   [d] 21 The Greek for *Woman* does not denote any disrespect.

FRIDAY

IN SPRIT AND TRUTH

John 4:1–42 *or* 4:23–24

Louie Giglio

God doesn't require ornate or elaborate expressions. The worship He's looking for is spiritual and true. Genuine. Authentic. Worship from the heart.

That's how Jesus put it in a conversation He was having with a Samaritan woman one afternoon while resting beside a common well . . .

She quickly posed a question that evidently had been bothering her for some time. Her people (the Samaritans) worshiped on one mountain, His people (the Jews) on another. Who was right? Which mountain was better? Where should she worship?

For a total stranger who knew everything about her past, this simple "where" question shouldn't be too hard.

Right?

But as we've come to expect, Jesus took the subject to another level, answering a basic "where" question with a riveting "who" answer . . .

Jesus has come. Messiah is here. And He's announcing that worship isn't about where you do it, but about the heart. It's not about what church you belong to, but whether or not you have a personal relationship with God.

The kind of worshipers God is looking for are those who will worship Him as their Father—in spirit and truth.

To worship God *in spirit* requires that we be alive on the inside, experiencing the life He gives by spiritual birth. Without His life, you can never truly worship.

And to worship *in truth* means to worship God as He really is, and bringing more than our words—bringing words amplified by an authentic life that flows from being spiritually alive within.

EPISTLE OF BARNABAS {ca. AD 130}

Let us become spiritual, let us become a temple perfect unto God. As far as in us lies, let us exercise ourselves in the fear of God, and let us strive to keep His commandments, that we may rejoice in His ordinances.

reflection

1. What does it mean to worship God in spirit and in truth?

2. How is that worship different from the external things that many people think of when they think of worship?

3. Why do you think God says he wants that kind of worship?

For your next devotional reading, go to page 1205.

do not know; we worship what we do know, for salvation is from the Jews. 23Yet a time is coming and has now come when the true worshipers will worship the Father in the Spirit and in truth, for they are the kind of worshipers the Father seeks. 24God is spirit, and his worshipers must worship in the Spirit and in truth."

25The woman said, "I know that Messiah" (called Christ) "is coming. When he comes, he will explain everything to us."

26Then Jesus declared, "I, the one speaking to you—I am he."

The Disciples Rejoin Jesus

27Just then his disciples returned and were surprised to find him talking with a woman. But no one asked, "What do you want?" or "Why are you talking with her?"

28Then, leaving her water jar, the woman went back to the town and said to the people, 29"Come, see a man who told me everything I ever did. Could this be the Messiah?" 30They came out of the town and made their way toward him.

31Meanwhile his disciples urged him, "Rabbi, eat something."

32But he said to them, "I have food to eat that you know nothing about."

33Then his disciples said to each other, "Could someone have brought him food?"

34"My food," said Jesus, "is to do the will of him who sent me and to finish his work. 35Don't you have a saying, 'It's still four months until harvest'? I tell you, open your eyes and look at the fields! They are ripe for harvest. 36Even now those who reap draw their wages, even now they harvest the crop for eternal life, so that the sower and the reaper may be glad together. 37Thus the saying 'One sows and another reaps' is true. 38I sent you to reap what you have not worked for. Others have done the hard work, and you have reaped the benefits of their labor."

Many Samaritans Believe

39Many of the Samaritans from that town believed in him because of the woman's testimony, "He told me everything I ever did." 40So when the Samaritans came to him, they urged him to stay with them, and he stayed two days. 41And because of his words many more became believers.

42They said to the woman, "We no longer believe just because of what you said; now we have heard for ourselves, and we know that this man really is the Savior of the world."

Jesus Heals the Official's Son

43After the two days he left for Galilee. 44(Now Jesus himself had pointed out that prophets have no honor in their own country.) 45When he arrived in Galilee, the Galileans welcomed him. They had seen all that he had done in Jerusalem at the Passover Festival, for they also had been there.

46Once more he visited Cana in Galilee, where he had turned the water into wine. And there was a certain royal official whose son lay sick at Capernaum. 47When this man heard that Jesus had arrived in Galilee from Judea, he went to him and begged him to come and heal his son, who was close to death.

48"Unless you people see signs and wonders," Jesus told him, "you will never believe."

49The royal official said, "Sir, come down before my child dies."

50"Go," Jesus replied, "your son will live."

The man took Jesus at his word and departed. 51While he was still on the way, his servants met him with the news that his boy was living. 52When he inquired as to the time when his son got better, they said to him, "Yesterday, at one in the afternoon, the fever left him."

53Then the father realized that this was the exact time at which Jesus had said to him, "Your son will live." So he and his whole household believed.

54This was the second sign Jesus performed after coming from Judea to Galilee.

The Healing at the Pool

5 Some time later, Jesus went up to Jerusalem for one of the Jewish festivals. 2Now there is in Jerusalem near the Sheep Gate a pool, which in Aramaic is called Bethesda*a* and which is surrounded by five covered colonnades. 3[4]Here a great number of disabled people used to lie—the blind, the lame, the paralyzed.*b* 5One who

---

a 2 Some manuscripts *Bethzatha*; other manuscripts *Bethsaida*   *b 3* Some later manuscripts and some ancient witnesses, wholly or in part, *paralyzed—and they waited for the moving of the waters. 4From time to time an angel of the Lord would come down and stir up the waters. The first person into the pool after each such disturbance would be cured of whatever disease they had.*

Want to Get Well?

John 5:3–8

read/meditate

Read through this passage and then focus on Jesus' question to the sick man. Think about your own answer to the question, Do you want to get well? (Or do you want to be better? Do you want to let go of what is holding you back?)

pray

Tell God the things about your life that you would like him to change in a moment, if he would. Then listen for what he has to say about those things.

contemplate

Mentally review your efforts at self-improvement over the last few years. Are there any areas in your life that reflect real brokenness rather than just a bad habit? Think about what holds you back, if anything, from God making you whole in those areas.

additional reflection

A man must completely despair of himself in order to become fit to obtain the grace of Christ.

—*Martin Luther*

Christ encourages us to pattern our lives after his so we can become spiritually enlightened. Our most important task, then, is to meditate on the life of Jesus Christ.

—*Thomas à Kempis*

For your next devotional reading, go to page 1209.

was there had been an invalid for thirty-eight years. ⁶When Jesus saw him lying there and learned that he had been in this condition for a long time, he asked him, "Do you want to get well?"

⁷"Sir," the invalid replied, "I have no one to help me into the pool when the water is stirred. While I am trying to get in, someone else goes down ahead of me."

⁸Then Jesus said to him, "Get up! Pick up your mat and walk." ⁹At once the man was cured; he picked up his mat and walked.

The day on which this took place was a Sabbath, ¹⁰and so the Jewish leaders said to the man who had been healed, "It is the Sabbath; the law forbids you to carry your mat."

¹¹But he replied, "The man who made me well said to me, 'Pick up your mat and walk.' "

¹²So they asked him, "Who is this fellow who told you to pick it up and walk?"

¹³The man who was healed had no idea who it was, for Jesus had slipped away into the crowd that was there.

¹⁴Later Jesus found him at the temple and said to him, "See, you are well again. Stop sinning or something worse may happen to you." ¹⁵The man went away and told the Jewish leaders that it was Jesus who had made him well.

The Authority of the Son

¹⁶So, because Jesus was doing these things on the Sabbath, the Jewish leaders began to persecute him. ¹⁷In his defense Jesus said to them, "My Father is always at his work to this very day, and I too am working." ¹⁸For this reason they tried all the more to kill him; not only was he breaking the Sabbath, but he was even calling God his own Father, making himself equal with God.

¹⁹Jesus gave them this answer: "Very truly I tell you, the Son can do nothing by himself; he can do only what he sees his Father doing, because whatever the Father does the Son also does. ²⁰For the Father loves the Son and shows him all he does. Yes, and he will show him even greater works than these, so that you will be amazed. ²¹For just as the Father raises the dead and gives them life, even so the Son gives life to whom he is pleased to give it. ²²Moreover, the Father judges no one, but has entrusted all judgment to the Son, ²³that all may honor the Son just as they honor the Father. Whoever does not honor the Son does not honor the Father, who sent him.

²⁴"Very truly I tell you, whoever hears my word and believes him who sent me has eternal life and will not be judged but has crossed over from death to life. ²⁵Very truly I tell you, a time is coming and has now come when the dead will hear the voice of the Son of God and those who hear will live. ²⁶For as the Father has life in himself, so he has granted the Son also to have life in himself. ²⁷And he has given him authority to judge because he is the Son of Man.

²⁸"Do not be amazed at this, for a time is coming when all who are in their graves will hear his voice ²⁹and come out—those who have done what is good will rise to live, and those who have done what is evil will rise to be condemned. ³⁰By myself I can do nothing; I judge only as I hear, and my judgment is just, for I seek not to please myself but him who sent me.

Testimonies About Jesus

³¹"If I testify about myself, my testimony is not true. ³²There is another who testifies in my favor, and I know that his testimony about me is true.

³³"You have sent to John and he has testified to the truth. ³⁴Not that I accept human testimony; but I mention it that you may be saved. ³⁵John was a lamp that burned and gave light, and you chose for a time to enjoy his light.

³⁶"I have testimony weightier than that of John. For the works that the Father has given me to finish—the very works that I am doing—testify that the Father has sent me. ³⁷And the Father who sent me has himself testified concerning me. You have never heard his voice nor seen his form, ³⁸nor does his word dwell in you, for you do not believe the one he sent. ³⁹You study[a] the Scriptures diligently because you think that in them you possess eternal life. These are the very Scriptures that testify about me, ⁴⁰yet you refuse to come to me to have life.

⁴¹"I do not accept glory from human beings, ⁴²but I know you. I know that you do not have the love of God in your hearts. ⁴³I have come in my Father's name, and you do

---

a 39 Or ³⁹Study

not accept me; but if someone else comes in his own name, you will accept him. ⁴⁴How can you believe since you accept glory from one another but do not seek the glory that comes from the only God*a*?

⁴⁵"But do not think I will accuse you before the Father. Your accuser is Moses, on whom your hopes are set. ⁴⁶If you believed Moses, you would believe me, for he wrote about me. ⁴⁷But since you do not believe what he wrote, how are you going to believe what I say?"

Jesus Feeds the Five Thousand

6 Some time after this, Jesus crossed to the far shore of the Sea of Galilee (that is, the Sea of Tiberias), ²and a great crowd of people followed him because they saw the signs he had performed by healing the sick. ³Then Jesus went up on a mountainside and sat down with his disciples. ⁴The Jewish Passover Festival was near.

⁵When Jesus looked up and saw a great crowd coming toward him, he said to Philip, "Where shall we buy bread for these people to eat?" ⁶He asked this only to test him, for he already had in mind what he was going to do.

⁷Philip answered him, "It would take almost a year's wages*b* to buy enough bread for each one to have a bite!"

⁸Another of his disciples, Andrew, Simon Peter's brother, spoke up, ⁹"Here is a boy with five small barley loaves and two small fish, but how far will they go among so many?"

¹⁰Jesus said, "Have the people sit down." There was plenty of grass in that place, and they sat down (about five thousand men were there). ¹¹Jesus then took the loaves, gave thanks, and distributed to those who were seated as much as they wanted. He did the same with the fish.

¹²When they had all had enough to eat, he said to his disciples, "Gather the pieces that are left over. Let nothing be wasted." ¹³So they gathered them and filled twelve baskets with the pieces of the five barley loaves left over by those who had eaten.

¹⁴After the people saw the sign Jesus performed, they began to say, "Surely this is the Prophet who is to come into the world." ¹⁵Jesus, knowing that they intended to come and make him king by force, withdrew again to a mountain by himself.

Jesus Walks on the Water

¹⁶When evening came, his disciples went down to the lake, ¹⁷where they got into a boat and set off across the lake for Capernaum. By now it was dark, and Jesus had not yet joined them. ¹⁸A strong wind was blowing and the waters grew rough. ¹⁹When they had rowed about three or three and a half miles,*c* they saw Jesus approaching the boat, walking on the water; and they were frightened. ²⁰But he said to them, "It is I; don't be afraid." ²¹Then they were willing to take him into the boat, and immediately the boat reached the shore where they were heading.

²²The next day the crowd that had stayed on the opposite shore of the lake realized that only one boat had been there, and that Jesus had not entered it with his disciples, but that they had gone away alone. ²³Then some boats from Tiberias landed near the place where the people had eaten the bread after the Lord had given thanks. ²⁴Once the crowd realized that neither Jesus nor his disciples were there, they got into the boats and went to Capernaum in search of Jesus.

Jesus the Bread of Life

²⁵When they found him on the other side of the lake, they asked him, "Rabbi, when did you get here?"

²⁶Jesus answered, "Very truly I tell you, you are looking for me, not because you saw the signs I performed but because you ate the loaves and had your fill. ²⁷Do not work for food that spoils, but for food that endures to eternal life, which the Son of Man will give you. On him God the Father has placed his seal of approval."

²⁸Then they asked him, "What must we do to do the works God requires?"

²⁹Jesus answered, "The work of God is this: to believe in the one he has sent."

³⁰So they asked him, "What sign then will you give that we may see it and believe you? What will you do? ³¹Our ancestors ate the manna in the wilderness; as it is written: 'He gave them bread from heaven to eat.'*d*"

---

a 44 Some early manuscripts *the Only One*   *b 7* Greek *take two hundred denarii*   *c 19* Or about 5 or 6 kilometers   *d 31* Exodus 16:4; Neh. 9:15; Psalm 78:24,25

³²Jesus said to them, "Very truly I tell you, it is not Moses who has given you the bread from heaven, but it is my Father who gives you the true bread from heaven. ³³For the bread of God is the bread that comes down from heaven and gives life to the world."

³⁴"Sir," they said, "always give us this bread."

³⁵Then Jesus declared, "I am the bread of life. Whoever comes to me will never go hungry, and whoever believes in me will never be thirsty. ³⁶But as I told you, you have seen me and still you do not believe. ³⁷All whom the Father gives me will come to me, and whoever comes to me I will never drive away. ³⁸For I have come down from heaven not to do my will but to do the will of him who sent me. ³⁹And this is the will of him who sent me, that I shall lose none of all those he has given me, but raise them up at the last day. ⁴⁰For my Father's will is that everyone who looks to the Son and believes in him shall have eternal life, and I will raise them up at the last day."

⁴¹At this the Jews there began to grumble about him because he said, "I am the bread that came down from heaven." ⁴²They said, "Is this not Jesus, the son of Joseph, whose father and mother we know? How can he now say, 'I came down from heaven'?"

⁴³"Stop grumbling among yourselves," Jesus answered. ⁴⁴"No one can come to me unless the Father who sent me draws them, and I will raise them up at the last day. ⁴⁵It is written in the Prophets: 'They will all be taught by God.'ᵃ Everyone who has heard the Father and learned from him comes to me. ⁴⁶No one has seen the Father except the one who is from God; only he has seen the Father. ⁴⁷Very truly I tell you, whoever believes has eternal life. ⁴⁸I am the bread of life. ⁴⁹Your ancestors ate the manna in the wilderness, yet they died. ⁵⁰But here is the bread that comes down from heaven, which people may eat and not die. ⁵¹I am the living bread that came down from heaven. Whoever eats of this bread will live forever. This bread is my flesh, which I will give for the life of the world."

⁵²Then the Jews began to argue sharply among themselves, "How can this man give us his flesh to eat?"

⁵³Jesus said to them, "Very truly I tell you, unless you eat the flesh of the Son of Man and drink his blood, you have no life in you. ⁵⁴Whoever eats my flesh and drinks my blood has eternal life, and I will raise them up at the last day. ⁵⁵For my flesh is real food and my blood is real drink. ⁵⁶Whoever eats my flesh and drinks my blood remains in me, and I in them. ⁵⁷Just as the living Father sent me and I live because of the Father, so the one who feeds on me will live because of me. ⁵⁸This is the bread that came down from heaven. Your ancestors ate manna and died, but whoever feeds on this bread will live forever." ⁵⁹He said this while teaching in the synagogue in Capernaum.

Many Disciples Desert Jesus

⁶⁰On hearing it, many of his disciples said, "This is a hard teaching. Who can accept it?"

⁶¹Aware that his disciples were grumbling about this, Jesus said to them, "Does this offend you? ⁶²Then what if you see the Son of Man ascend to where he was before! ⁶³The Spirit gives life; the flesh counts for nothing. The words I have spoken to you—they are full of the Spiritᵇ and life. ⁶⁴Yet there are some of you who do not believe." For Jesus had known from the beginning which of them did not believe and who would betray him. ⁶⁵He went on to say, "This is why I told you that no one can come to me unless the Father has enabled them."

⁶⁶From this time many of his disciples turned back and no longer followed him.

⁶⁷"You do not want to leave too, do you?" Jesus asked the Twelve.

⁶⁸Simon Peter answered him, "Lord, to whom shall we go? You have the words of eternal life. ⁶⁹We have come to believe and to know that you are the Holy One of God."

⁷⁰Then Jesus replied, "Have I not chosen you, the Twelve? Yet one of you is a devil!" ⁷¹(He meant Judas, the son of Simon Iscariot, who, though one of the Twelve, was later to betray him.)

Jesus Goes to the Festival of Tabernacles

7 After this, Jesus went around in Galilee. He did not wantᶜ to go about in Judea because the Jewish leaders there were looking for a way to kill him. ²But when the Jewish Festival of Tabernacles was

a 45 Isaiah 54:13   b 63 Or are Spirit; or are spirit   c 1 Some manuscripts not have authority

MONDAY

MADE FOR SO MUCH MORE

John 6:52–71 *or* 6:66–69

JOHN WRIGHT FOLLETTE {AD 1883–1966}

The first vocation of personality is expression; it is basic. People were created to love, to live, to get out; we were made with potential powers. Out in the world, humanity has never found the proper avenue through which we can express ourselves, to really live. When we try to do life without Christ, we lack the essential element of Life ... We were made for the purpose of glorifying him and having communion and fellowship with Him.

Oh, the persistency of the love of God to come and touch a life, to get hold of each of us! The love of God comes to this poor, distorted human being and says, "I can save, cleanse, fill you, bring you back to coordination and live in you, if you will let me." Think of him living in our bodies today!

Brennan Manning

We ... refuse to be our true self with God—and then wonder why we lack intimacy with Him. The deepest desire of our hearts is for union with God. From the first moment of our existence our most powerful yearning is to fulfill the original purpose of our lives—"to see Him more clearly, love Him more dearly, follow Him more nearly." We are made for God, and nothing less will really satisfy us.

reflection

1. Only in Jesus can we find the words of eternal life. How did you come to believe in Jesus as the only way to truly know God?

2. How has knowing Jesus changed your life?

3. Think of someone you know who has heard the message of the gospel but turned away from following Jesus. What is that person missing out on?

For your next devotional reading, go to page 1216.

near, [3]Jesus' brothers said to him, "Leave Galilee and go to Judea, so that your disciples there may see the works you do. [4]No one who wants to become a public figure acts in secret. Since you are doing these things, show yourself to the world." [5]For even his own brothers did not believe in him.

[6]Therefore Jesus told them, "My time is not yet here; for you any time will do. [7]The world cannot hate you, but it hates me because I testify that its works are evil. [8]You go to the festival. I am not*a* going up to this festival, because my time has not yet fully come." [9]Having said this, he stayed in Galilee.

[10]However, after his brothers had left for the festival, he went also, not publicly, but in secret. [11]Now at the festival the Jewish leaders were watching for Jesus and asking, "Where is he?"

[12]Among the crowds there was widespread whispering about him. Some said, "He is a good man."

Others replied, "No, he deceives the people." [13]But no one would say anything publicly about him for fear of the leaders.

Jesus Teaches at the Festival

[14]Not until halfway through the festival did Jesus go up to the temple courts and begin to teach. [15]The Jews there were amazed and asked, "How did this man get such learning without having been taught?"

[16]Jesus answered, "My teaching is not my own. It comes from the one who sent me. [17]Anyone who chooses to do the will of God will find out whether my teaching comes from God or whether I speak on my own. [18]Whoever speaks on their own does so to gain personal glory, but he who seeks the glory of the one who sent him is a man of truth; there is nothing false about him. [19]Has not Moses given you the law? Yet not one of you keeps the law. Why are you trying to kill me?"

[20]"You are demon-possessed," the crowd answered. "Who is trying to kill you?"

[21]Jesus said to them, "I did one miracle, and you are all amazed. [22]Yet, because Moses gave you circumcision (though actually it did not come from Moses, but from the patriarchs), you circumcise a boy on the Sabbath. [23]Now if a boy can be circumcised on the Sabbath so that the law of Moses may not be broken, why are you angry with me for healing a man's whole body on the Sabbath? [24]Stop judging by mere appearances, but instead judge correctly."

Division Over Who Jesus Is

[25]At that point some of the people of Jerusalem began to ask, "Isn't this the man they are trying to kill? [26]Here he is, speaking publicly, and they are not saying a word to him. Have the authorities really concluded that he is the Messiah? [27]But we know where this man is from; when the Messiah comes, no one will know where he is from."

[28]Then Jesus, still teaching in the temple courts, cried out, "Yes, you know me, and you know where I am from. I am not here on my own authority, but he who sent me is true. You do not know him, [29]but I know him because I am from him and he sent me."

[30]At this they tried to seize him, but no one laid a hand on him, because his hour had not yet come. [31]Still, many in the crowd put their faith in him. They said, "When the Messiah comes, will he perform more signs than this man?"

[32]The Pharisees heard the crowd whispering such things about him. Then the chief priests and the Pharisees sent temple guards to arrest him.

[33]Jesus said, "I am with you for only a short time, and then I go to the one who sent me. [34]You will look for me, but you will not find me; and where I am, you cannot come."

[35]The Jews said to one another, "Where does this man intend to go that we cannot find him? Will he go where our people live scattered among the Greeks, and teach the Greeks? [36]What did he mean when he said, 'You will look for me, but you will not find me,' and 'Where I am, you cannot come'?"

[37]On the last and greatest day of the festival, Jesus stood and said in a loud voice, "Let anyone who is thirsty come to me and drink. [38]Whoever believes in me, as Scripture has said, rivers of living water will flow from within them."*b* [39]By this he meant the Spirit, whom those who believed in him were later to receive. Up to that time the Spirit had not been given, since Jesus had not yet been glorified.

---

a 8 Some manuscripts *not yet*   *b* 37,38 Or *me. And let anyone drink* [38]*who believes in me." As Scripture has said, "Out of him* (or *them*) *will flow rivers of living water."*

⁴⁰On hearing his words, some of the people said, "Surely this man is the Prophet."

⁴¹Others said, "He is the Messiah."

Still others asked, "How can the Messiah come from Galilee? ⁴²Does not Scripture say that the Messiah will come from David's descendants and from Bethlehem, the town where David lived?" ⁴³Thus the people were divided because of Jesus. ⁴⁴Some wanted to seize him, but no one laid a hand on him.

Unbelief of the Jewish Leaders

⁴⁵Finally the temple guards went back to the chief priests and the Pharisees, who asked them, "Why didn't you bring him in?"

⁴⁶"No one ever spoke the way this man does," the guards replied.

⁴⁷"You mean he has deceived you also?" the Pharisees retorted. ⁴⁸"Have any of the rulers or of the Pharisees believed in him? ⁴⁹No! But this mob that knows nothing of the law—there is a curse on them."

⁵⁰Nicodemus, who had gone to Jesus earlier and who was one of their own number, asked, ⁵¹"Does our law condemn a man without first hearing him to find out what he has been doing?"

⁵²They replied, "Are you from Galilee, too? Look into it, and you will find that a prophet does not come out of Galilee."

[The earliest manuscripts and many other ancient witnesses do not have John 7:53—8:11.]

8 ⁵³*Then they all went home, ¹but Jesus went to the Mount of Olives. ²At dawn he appeared again in the temple courts, where all the people gathered around him, and he sat down to teach them. ³The teachers of the law and the Pharisees brought in a woman caught in adultery. They made her stand before the group ⁴and said to Jesus, "Teacher, this woman was caught in the act of adultery. ⁵In the Law Moses commanded us to stone such women. Now what do you say?" ⁶They were using this question as a trap, in order to have a basis for accusing him.*

But Jesus bent down and started to write on the ground with his finger. ⁷When they kept on questioning him, he straightened up and said to them, "Let any one of you who is without

sin be the first to throw a stone at her." ⁸Again he stooped down and wrote on the ground.

⁹*At this, those who heard began to go away one at a time, the older ones first, until only Jesus was left, with the woman still standing there. ¹⁰Jesus straightened up and asked her, "Woman,ᵃ where are they? Has no one condemned you?"*

¹¹*"No one, sir," she said.*

"Then neither do I condemn you," Jesus declared. "Go now and leave your life of sin."

Dispute Over Jesus' Testimony

¹²When Jesus spoke again to the people, he said, "I am the light of the world. Whoever follows me will never walk in darkness, but will have the light of life."

¹³The Pharisees challenged him, "Here you are, appearing as your own witness; your testimony is not valid."

¹⁴Jesus answered, "Even if I testify on my own behalf, my testimony is valid, for I know where I came from and where I am going. But you have no idea where I come from or where I am going. ¹⁵You judge by human standards; I pass judgment on no one. ¹⁶But if I do judge, my decisions are true, because I am not alone. I stand with the Father, who sent me. ¹⁷In your own Law it is written that the testimony of two witnesses is true. ¹⁸I am one who testifies for myself; my other witness is the Father, who sent me."

¹⁹Then they asked him, "Where is your father?"

"You do not know me or my Father," Jesus replied. "If you knew me, you would know my Father also." ²⁰He spoke these words while teaching in the temple courts near the place where the offerings were put. Yet no one seized him, because his hour had not yet come.

Dispute Over Who Jesus Is

²¹Once more Jesus said to them, "I am going away, and you will look for me, and you will die in your sin. Where I go, you cannot come."

²²This made the Jews ask, "Will he kill himself? Is that why he says, 'Where I go, you cannot come'?"

ᵃ 10 The Greek for *Woman* does not denote any disrespect.

²³But he continued, "You are from below; I am from above. You are of this world; I am not of this world. ²⁴I told you that you would die in your sins; if you do not believe that I am he, you will indeed die in your sins."

²⁵"Who are you?" they asked.

"Just what I have been telling you from the beginning," Jesus replied. ²⁶"I have much to say in judgment of you. But he who sent me is trustworthy, and what I have heard from him I tell the world."

²⁷They did not understand that he was telling them about his Father. ²⁸So Jesus said, "When you have lifted up*a* the Son of Man, then you will know that I am he and that I do nothing on my own but speak just what the Father has taught me. ²⁹The one who sent me is with me; he has not left me alone, for I always do what pleases him." ³⁰Even as he spoke, many put their faith in him.

Dispute Over Whose Children Jesus' Opponents Are

³¹To the Jews who had believed him, Jesus said, "If you hold to my teaching, you are really my disciples. ³²Then you will know the truth, and the truth will set you free."

³³They answered him, "We are Abraham's descendants and have never been slaves of anyone. How can you say that we shall be set free?"

³⁴Jesus replied, "Very truly I tell you, everyone who sins is a slave to sin. ³⁵Now a slave has no permanent place in the family, but a son belongs to it forever. ³⁶So if the Son sets you free, you will be free indeed. ³⁷I know you are Abraham's descendants. Yet you are looking for a way to kill me, because you have no room for my word. ³⁸I am telling you what I have seen in the Father's presence, and you are doing what you have heard from your father.*b*"

³⁹"Abraham is our father," they answered.

"If you were Abraham's children," said Jesus, "then you would*c* do what Abraham did. ⁴⁰As it is, you are looking for a way to kill me, a man who has told you the truth that I heard from God. Abraham did not do such things. ⁴¹You are doing the works of your own father."

"We are not illegitimate children," they protested. "The only Father we have is God himself."

⁴²Jesus said to them, "If God were your Father, you would love me, for I came from God and now am here. I have not come on my own; but he sent me. ⁴³Why is my language not clear to you? Because you are unable to hear what I say. ⁴⁴You belong to your father, the devil, and you want to carry out your father's desires. He was a murderer from the beginning, not holding to the truth, for there is no truth in him. When he lies, he speaks his native language, for he is a liar and the father of lies. ⁴⁵Yet because I tell the truth, you do not believe me! ⁴⁶Can any of you prove me guilty of sin? If I am telling the truth, why don't you believe me? ⁴⁷Whoever belongs to God hears what God says. The reason you do not hear is that you do not belong to God."

Jesus' Claims About Himself

⁴⁸The Jews answered him, "Aren't we right in saying that you are a Samaritan and demon-possessed?"

⁴⁹"I am not possessed by a demon," said Jesus, "but I honor my Father and you dishonor me. ⁵⁰I am not seeking glory for myself; but there is one who seeks it, and he is the judge. ⁵¹Very truly I tell you, whoever obeys my word will never see death."

⁵²At this they exclaimed, "Now we know that you are demon-possessed! Abraham died and so did the prophets, yet you say that whoever obeys your word will never taste death. ⁵³Are you greater than our father Abraham? He died, and so did the prophets. Who do you think you are?"

⁵⁴Jesus replied, "If I glorify myself, my glory means nothing. My Father, whom you claim as your God, is the one who glorifies me. ⁵⁵Though you do not know him, I know him. If I said I did not, I would be a liar like you, but I do know him and obey his word. ⁵⁶Your father Abraham rejoiced at the thought of seeing my day; he saw it and was glad."

⁵⁷"You are not yet fifty years old," they said to him, "and you have seen Abraham!"

⁵⁸"Very truly I tell you," Jesus answered, "before Abraham was born, I am!" ⁵⁹At this, they picked up stones to stone him, but

---

a 28 The Greek for *lifted up* also means *exalted.*   *b 38* Or *presence. Therefore do what you have heard from the Father.*   *c 39* Some early manuscripts *"If you are Abraham's children," said Jesus, "then*

Jesus hid himself, slipping away from the temple grounds.

Jesus Heals a Man Born Blind

9 As he went along, he saw a man blind from birth. [2]His disciples asked him, "Rabbi, who sinned, this man or his parents, that he was born blind?"

[3]"Neither this man nor his parents sinned," said Jesus, "but this happened so that the works of God might be displayed in him. [4]As long as it is day, we must do the works of him who sent me. Night is coming, when no one can work. [5]While I am in the world, I am the light of the world."

[6]Having said this, he spit on the ground, made some mud with the saliva, and put it on the man's eyes. [7]"Go," he told him, "wash in the Pool of Siloam" (this word means "Sent"). So the man went and washed, and came home seeing.

[8]His neighbors and those who had formerly seen him begging asked, "Isn't this the same man who used to sit and beg?" [9]Some claimed that he was.

Others said, "No, he only looks like him."

But he himself insisted, "I am the man."

[10]"How then were your eyes opened?" they asked.

[11]He replied, "The man they call Jesus made some mud and put it on my eyes. He told me to go to Siloam and wash. So I went and washed, and then I could see."

[12]"Where is this man?" they asked him.

"I don't know," he said.

The Pharisees Investigate the Healing

[13]They brought to the Pharisees the man who had been blind. [14]Now the day on which Jesus had made the mud and opened the man's eyes was a Sabbath. [15]Therefore the Pharisees also asked him how he had received his sight. "He put mud on my eyes," the man replied, "and I washed, and now I see."

[16]Some of the Pharisees said, "This man is not from God, for he does not keep the Sabbath."

But others asked, "How can a sinner perform such signs?" So they were divided.

[17]Then they turned again to the blind man, "What have you to say about him? It was your eyes he opened."

The man replied, "He is a prophet."

[18]They still did not believe that he had been blind and had received his sight until they sent for the man's parents. [19]"Is this your son?" they asked. "Is this the one you say was born blind? How is it that now he can see?"

[20]"We know he is our son," the parents answered, "and we know he was born blind. [21]But how he can see now, or who opened his eyes, we don't know. Ask him. He is of age; he will speak for himself." [22]His parents said this because they were afraid of the Jewish leaders, who already had decided that anyone who acknowledged that Jesus was the Messiah would be put out of the synagogue. [23]That was why his parents said, "He is of age; ask him."

[24]A second time they summoned the man who had been blind. "Give glory to God and tell the truth," they said. "We know this man is a sinner."

[25]He replied, "Whether he is a sinner or not, I don't know. One thing I do know. I was blind but now I see!"

[26]Then they asked him, "What did he do to you? How did he open your eyes?"

[27]He answered, "I have told you already and you did not listen. Why do you want to hear it again? Do you want to become his disciples too?"

[28]Then they hurled insults at him and said, "You are this fellow's disciple! We are disciples of Moses! [29]We know that God spoke to Moses, but as for this fellow, we don't even know where he comes from."

[30]The man answered, "Now that is remarkable! You don't know where he comes from, yet he opened my eyes. [31]We know that God does not listen to sinners. He listens to the godly person who does his will. [32]Nobody has ever heard of opening the eyes of a man born blind. [33]If this man were not from God, he could do nothing."

[34]To this they replied, "You were steeped in sin at birth; how dare you lecture us!" And they threw him out.

Spiritual Blindness

[35]Jesus heard that they had thrown him out, and when he found him, he said, "Do you believe in the Son of Man?"

[36]"Who is he, sir?" the man asked. "Tell me so that I may believe in him."

[37]Jesus said, "You have now seen him; in fact, he is the one speaking with you."

³⁸Then the man said, "Lord, I believe," and he worshiped him.

³⁹Jesus said,ᵃ "For judgment I have come into this world, so that the blind will see and those who see will become blind."

⁴⁰Some Pharisees who were with him heard him say this and asked, "What? Are we blind too?"

⁴¹Jesus said, "If you were blind, you would not be guilty of sin; but now that you claim you can see, your guilt remains.

The Good Shepherd and His Sheep

10 "Very truly I tell you Pharisees, anyone who does not enter the sheep pen by the gate, but climbs in by some other way, is a thief and a robber. ²The one who enters by the gate is the shepherd of the sheep. ³The gatekeeper opens the gate for him, and the sheep listen to his voice. He calls his own sheep by name and leads them out. ⁴When he has brought out all his own, he goes on ahead of them, and his sheep follow him because they know his voice. ⁵But they will never follow a stranger; in fact, they will run away from him because they do not recognize a stranger's voice." ⁶Jesus used this figure of speech, but the Pharisees did not understand what he was telling them.

⁷Therefore Jesus said again, "Very truly I tell you, I am the gate for the sheep. ⁸All who have come before me are thieves and robbers, but the sheep have not listened to them. ⁹I am the gate; whoever enters through me will be saved.ᵇ They will come in and go out, and find pasture. ¹⁰The thief comes only to steal and kill and destroy; I have come that they may have life, and have it to the full.

¹¹"I am the good shepherd. The good shepherd lays down his life for the sheep. ¹²The hired hand is not the shepherd and does not own the sheep. So when he sees the wolf coming, he abandons the sheep and runs away. Then the wolf attacks the flock and scatters it. ¹³The man runs away because he is a hired hand and cares nothing for the sheep.

¹⁴"I am the good shepherd; I know my sheep and my sheep know me— ¹⁵just as the Father knows me and I know the Father—

and I lay down my life for the sheep. ¹⁶I have other sheep that are not of this sheep pen. I must bring them also. They too will listen to my voice, and there shall be one flock and one shepherd. ¹⁷The reason my Father loves me is that I lay down my life—only to take it up again. ¹⁸No one takes it from me, but I lay it down of my own accord. I have authority to lay it down and authority to take it up again. This command I received from my Father."

¹⁹The Jews who heard these words were again divided. ²⁰Many of them said, "He is demon-possessed and raving mad. Why listen to him?"

²¹But others said, "These are not the sayings of someone possessed by a demon. Can a demon open the eyes of the blind?"

Further Conflict Over Jesus' Claims

²²Then came the Festival of Dedicationᶜ at Jerusalem. It was winter, ²³and Jesus was in the temple courts walking in Solomon's Colonnade. ²⁴The Jews who were there gathered around him, saying, "How long will you keep us in suspense? If you are the Messiah, tell us plainly."

²⁵Jesus answered, "I did tell you, but you do not believe. The works I do in my Father's name testify about me, ²⁶but you do not believe because you are not my sheep. ²⁷My sheep listen to my voice; I know them, and they follow me. ²⁸I give them eternal life, and they shall never perish; no one will snatch them out of my hand. ²⁹My Father, who has given them to me, is greater than allᵈ; no one can snatch them out of my Father's hand. ³⁰I and the Father are one."

³¹Again the Jews picked up stones to stone him, ³²but Jesus said to them, "I have shown you many good works from the Father. For which of these do you stone me?"

³³"We are not stoning you for any good work," they replied, "but for blasphemy, because you, a mere man, claim to be God."

³⁴Jesus answered them, "Is it not written in your Law, 'I have said you are "gods" 'ᵉ? ³⁵If he called them 'gods,' to whom the word of God came—and Scripture cannot be broken— ³⁶what about the one whom the Father set apart as his very own and sent into the world? Why then do you accuse me of

---

ᵃ 38,39 Some early manuscripts do not have verses 38 and 39a.   ᵇ 9 Or kept safe   ᶜ 22 That is, Hanukkah   ᵈ 29 Many early manuscripts What my Father has given me is greater than all   ᵉ 34 Psalm 82:6

blasphemy because I said, 'I am God's Son'? [37]Do not believe me unless I do the works of my Father. [38]But if I do them, even though you do not believe me, believe the works, that you may know and understand that the Father is in me, and I in the Father." [39]Again they tried to seize him, but he escaped their grasp.

[40]Then Jesus went back across the Jordan to the place where John had been baptizing in the early days. Here he stayed [41]and many people came to him. They said, "Though John never performed a sign, all that John said about this man was true." [42]And in that place many believed in Jesus.

The Death of Lazarus

11 Now a man named Lazarus was sick. He was from Bethany, the village of Mary and her sister Martha. [2](This Mary, whose brother Lazarus now lay sick, was the same one who poured perfume on the Lord and wiped his feet with her hair.) [3]So the sisters sent word to Jesus, "Lord, the one you love is sick."

[4]When he heard this, Jesus said, "This sickness will not end in death. No, it is for God's glory so that God's Son may be glorified through it." [5]Now Jesus loved Martha and her sister and Lazarus. [6]So when he heard that Lazarus was sick, he stayed where he was two more days, [7]and then he said to his disciples, "Let us go back to Judea."

[8]"But Rabbi," they said, "a short while ago the Jews there tried to stone you, and yet you are going back?"

[9]Jesus answered, "Are there not twelve hours of daylight? Those who walk in the daytime will not stumble, for they see by this world's light. [10]It is when people walk at night that they stumble, for they have no light."

[11]After he had said this, he went on to tell them, "Our friend Lazarus has fallen asleep; but I am going there to wake him up."

[12]His disciples replied, "Lord, if he sleeps, he will get better." [13]Jesus had been speaking of his death, but his disciples thought he meant natural sleep.

[14]So then he told them plainly, "Lazarus is dead, [15]and for your sake I am glad I was not there, so that you may believe. But let us go to him."

[16]Then Thomas (also known as Didymus[a]) said to the rest of the disciples, "Let us also go, that we may die with him."

Jesus Comforts the Sisters of Lazarus

[17]On his arrival, Jesus found that Lazarus had already been in the tomb for four days. [18]Now Bethany was less than two miles[b] from Jerusalem, [19]and many Jews had come to Martha and Mary to comfort them in the loss of their brother. [20]When Martha heard that Jesus was coming, she went out to meet him, but Mary stayed at home.

[21]"Lord," Martha said to Jesus, "if you had been here, my brother would not have died. [22]But I know that even now God will give you whatever you ask."

[23]Jesus said to her, "Your brother will rise again."

[24]Martha answered, "I know he will rise again in the resurrection at the last day."

[25]Jesus said to her, "I am the resurrection and the life. Anyone who believes in me will live, even though they die; [26]and whoever lives by believing in me will never die. Do you believe this?"

[27]"Yes, Lord," she told him, "I believe that you are the Messiah, the Son of God, who was to come into the world."

[28]After she had said this, she went back and called her sister Mary aside. "The Teacher is here," she said, "and is asking for you." [29]When Mary heard this, she got up quickly and went to him. [30]Now Jesus had not yet entered the village, but was still at the place where Martha had met him. [31]When the Jews who had been with Mary in the house, comforting her, noticed how quickly she got up and went out, they followed her, supposing she was going to the tomb to mourn there.

[32]When Mary reached the place where Jesus was and saw him, she fell at his feet and said, "Lord, if you had been here, my brother would not have died."

[33]When Jesus saw her weeping, and the Jews who had come along with her also weeping, he was deeply moved in spirit and troubled. [34]"Where have you laid him?" he asked.

"Come and see, Lord," they replied.

[35]Jesus wept.

---

a 16 Thomas (Aramaic) and Didymus (Greek) both mean *twin.*　　*b 18* Or about 3 kilometers

TUESDAY

BRINGING GLORY TO GOD

John 11:1–44 *or* 11:1–4,38–44

Carolyn Custis James

When we look carefully at God's glory, we see that Jesus couldn't have given his disciples a stronger reason to trust him. God's glory is bound up with his reputation, his great name, his honor. God's reputation can never be divorced from what happens to us. "It was God's good pleasure to join you to himself in such a way that his name is at stake in your destiny . . . in such a way that what becomes of you reflects upon his name."

THOMAS ARNOLD {AD 1795–1842}

Here are eight practical observations on John 11:

1. In our troubles we should send a message for Christ, as did the sisters of Bethany.

2. Even if Christ delays his response we should not doubt that our troubles are for the glory of God and our own good.

3. We should look upon Christ always as an all-sufficient helper. If present he can always deliver.

4. We should always be assured of the tender sympathy of the Lord . . . He weeps with those who weep and rejoices with those who rejoice.

5. We should never forget that he is the Fountain of Life; the Resurrection and the Life. If we have eaten the Bread of Life, drunk the Water of Life, have Christ the hope of glory formed in us, we have eternal life. It is begun. We are immortal. We shall never die. What is called death is only a narrow sea that divides the heavenly land from ours.

6. We have been told that there is inscribed on the monument over the clay of the infidel Hume, at Edinburg, Scotland, I AM THE RESURRECTION AND THE LIFE. In that grand truth is the hope of mankind.

7. As he cried to Lazarus, "Come out," so shall he speak with the voice of an archangel to all that are in their graves and they shall come forth and live.

8. "I am going there to wake him up." There seems to me to be contained in these few words one of the most powerful charms in the world to lull the bitterness of death, and to make us anxious to become such that we may humbly apply them to ourselves.

reflection

1. God created you to glorify him. How does your life bring glory to God?

2. Jesus declared that his life was about bringing glory to God—not himself. What do you need to learn from Jesus' example in this regard?

3. God does not exist to glorify you; you exist to glorify God. Does that statement bother you or bring you comfort? Why?

For your next devotional reading, go to page 1218.

³⁶Then the Jews said, "See how he loved him!"

³⁷But some of them said, "Could not he who opened the eyes of the blind man have kept this man from dying?"

Jesus Raises Lazarus From the Dead

³⁸Jesus, once more deeply moved, came to the tomb. It was a cave with a stone laid across the entrance. ³⁹"Take away the stone," he said.

"But, Lord," said Martha, the sister of the dead man, "by this time there is a bad odor, for he has been there four days."

⁴⁰Then Jesus said, "Did I not tell you that if you believe, you will see the glory of God?"

⁴¹So they took away the stone. Then Jesus looked up and said, "Father, I thank you that you have heard me. ⁴²I knew that you always hear me, but I said this for the benefit of the people standing here, that they may believe that you sent me."

⁴³When he had said this, Jesus called in a loud voice, "Lazarus, come out!" ⁴⁴The dead man came out, his hands and feet wrapped with strips of linen, and a cloth around his face.

Jesus said to them, "Take off the grave clothes and let him go."

The Plot to Kill Jesus

⁴⁵Therefore many of the Jews who had come to visit Mary, and had seen what Jesus did, put their faith in him. ⁴⁶But some of them went to the Pharisees and told them what Jesus had done. ⁴⁷Then the chief priests and the Pharisees called a meeting of the Sanhedrin.

"What are we accomplishing?" they asked. "Here is this man performing many signs. ⁴⁸If we let him go on like this, everyone will believe in him, and then the Romans will come and take away both our temple and our nation."

⁴⁹Then one of them, named Caiaphas, who was high priest that year, spoke up, "You know nothing at all! ⁵⁰You do not realize that it is better for you that one man die for the people than that the whole nation perish."

⁵¹He did not say this on his own, but as high priest that year he prophesied that Jesus would die for the Jewish nation, ⁵²and not only for that nation but also for the scattered children of God, to bring them together and make them one. ⁵³So from that day on they plotted to take his life.

⁵⁴Therefore Jesus no longer moved about publicly among the Jews. Instead he withdrew to a region near the wilderness, to a village called Ephraim, where he stayed with his disciples.

⁵⁵When it was almost time for the Jewish Passover, many went up from the country to Jerusalem for their ceremonial cleansing before the Passover. ⁵⁶They kept looking for Jesus, and as they stood in the temple courts they asked one another, "What do you think? Isn't he coming to the festival at all?" ⁵⁷But the chief priests and the Pharisees had given orders that anyone who found out where Jesus was should report it so that they might arrest him.

Jesus Anointed at Bethany

12 Six days before the Passover, Jesus came to Bethany, where Lazarus lived, whom Jesus had raised from the dead. ²Here a dinner was given in Jesus' honor. Martha served, while Lazarus was among those reclining at the table with him. ³Then Mary took about a pint*ᵃ* of pure nard, an expensive perfume; she poured it on Jesus' feet and wiped his feet with her hair. And the house was filled with the fragrance of the perfume.

⁴But one of his disciples, Judas Iscariot, who was later to betray him, objected, ⁵"Why wasn't this perfume sold and the money given to the poor? It was worth a year's wages.*ᵇ* ⁶He did not say this because he cared about the poor but because he was a thief; as keeper of the money bag, he used to help himself to what was put into it.

⁷"Leave her alone," Jesus replied. "It was intended that she should save this perfume for the day of my burial. ⁸You will always have the poor among you,*ᶜ* but you will not always have me."

⁹Meanwhile a large crowd of Jews found out that Jesus was there and came, not only because of him but also to see Lazarus, whom he had raised from the dead. ¹⁰So the chief priests made plans to kill Lazarus as well, ¹¹for on account of him many of the

---

a 3 Or about 0.5 liter   *b 5* Greek *three hundred denarii*   *c 8* See Deut. 15:11.

WEDNESDAY

POUR OUT WHAT YOU'RE HOLDING
John 12:1–36 *or* 12:3–8

Joanna Weaver

While other people may struggle with worldly temptations, my struggle has always been in the area of spiritual disciplines. My devotional life has been haphazard as best. Because I hadn't developed the habit of a quiet time as a child, when the busyness of adulthood came, I found it difficult to find time alone with the Lord.

Some of you may be aghast at such a thought. Your devotional life runs like clockwork. You find it impossible to make it through the day without time alone with God.

If that was true for you, may I tell you how blessed you are? It has taken me nearly twenty years to come to this discipline, and even then, it has been a gift of grace, not an accomplishment of my own making.

Until I took the Navigator's 2:7 Course, I didn't even know what I was missing . . .

The class was wonderful. My spirit began to grow and thrive as the soil of my heart was tilled deep and fed by the Word of God. But then my Martha-like perfectionist tendencies kicked in, causing me to approach my devotional time as another duty to perform . . . To be honest, much of my motivation came from my competitive nature. I wanted to be the star pupil, one of those disgusting teacher's pets.

Robert Boyd Munger's article "My Heart Christ's Home" changed all that. Through the simple analogy he suggested, I discovered what it means to have a Mary heart toward God. Suddenly my eyes were open to what true devotion is.

It is not a duty. It is a delight.

It is not an exercise in piety. It is a privilege.

And it is not so much a visit as it is a homecoming.

WILLIAM LAW {AD 1686–1761}

Devotion signifies a life given, or devoted, to God.

Therefore, a devout person is one who no longer lives to please themselves, or the way and spirit of the world. But instead they live solely to please God. They consider God in everything, serve God in everything, and make all the parts of their daily lives parts of piety. They accomplish this by doing everything in the name of God, living in such a way as to bring him glory.

reflection

1. What do you value most in life?
2. How willing would you be to give that person or thing up for Jesus' sake?
3. When have you made a sacrificial offering to Jesus?

For your next devotional reading, go to page 1221.

Jews were going over to Jesus and putting their faith in him.

Jesus Comes to Jerusalem as King

¹²The next day the great crowd that had come for the festival heard that Jesus was on his way to Jerusalem. ¹³They took palm branches and went out to meet him, shouting,

"Hosanna!ᵃ"

"Blessed is he who comes in the name of the Lord!"ᵇ

"Blessed is the king of Israel!"

¹⁴Jesus found a young donkey and sat on it, as it is written:

¹⁵"Do not be afraid, Daughter Zion;
    see, your king is coming,
    seated on a donkey's colt."ᶜ

¹⁶At first his disciples did not understand all this. Only after Jesus was glorified did they realize that these things had been written about him and that these things had been done to him.

¹⁷Now the crowd that was with him when he called Lazarus from the tomb and raised him from the dead continued to spread the word. ¹⁸Many people, because they had heard that he had performed this sign, went out to meet him. ¹⁹So the Pharisees said to one another, "See, this is getting us nowhere. Look how the whole world has gone after him!"

Jesus Predicts His Death

²⁰Now there were some Greeks among those who went up to worship at the festival. ²¹They came to Philip, who was from Bethsaida in Galilee, with a request. "Sir," they said, "we would like to see Jesus." ²²Philip went to tell Andrew; Andrew and Philip in turn told Jesus.

²³Jesus replied, "The hour has come for the Son of Man to be glorified. ²⁴Very truly I tell you, unless a kernel of wheat falls to the ground and dies, it remains only a single seed. But if it dies, it produces many seeds. ²⁵Those who love their life will lose it, while those who hate their life in this world will keep it for eternal life. ²⁶Whoever serves me must follow me; and where I am, my servant also will be. My Father will honor the one who serves me.

²⁷"Now my soul is troubled, and what shall I say? 'Father, save me from this hour'? No, it was for this very reason I came to this hour. ²⁸Father, glorify your name!"

Then a voice came from heaven, "I have glorified it, and will glorify it again." ²⁹The crowd that was there and heard it said it had thundered; others said an angel had spoken to him.

³⁰Jesus said, "This voice was for your benefit, not mine. ³¹Now is the time for judgment on this world; now the prince of this world will be driven out. ³²And I, when I am lifted upᵈ from the earth, will draw all people to myself." ³³He said this to show the kind of death he was going to die.

³⁴The crowd spoke up, "We have heard from the Law that the Messiah will remain forever, so how can you say, 'The Son of Man must be lifted up'? Who is this 'Son of Man'?"

³⁵Then Jesus told them, "You are going to have the light just a little while longer. Walk while you have the light, before darkness overtakes you. Those who walk in the dark do not know where they are going. ³⁶Put your trust in the light while you have the light, so that you may become children of light." When he had finished speaking, Jesus left and hid himself from them.

Belief and Unbelief Among the Jews

³⁷Even after Jesus had performed so many signs in their presence, they still would not believe in him. ³⁸This was to fulfill the word of Isaiah the prophet:

"Lord, who has believed our message
    and to whom has the arm of the Lord
        been revealed?"ᵉ

³⁹For this reason they could not believe, because, as Isaiah says elsewhere:

⁴⁰"He has blinded their eyes
    and hardened their hearts,
so they can neither see with their eyes,
    nor understand with their hearts,
    nor turn—and I would heal them."ᶠ

⁴¹Isaiah said this because he saw Jesus' glory and spoke about him.

⁴²Yet at the same time many even among the leaders believed in him. But because of the Pharisees they would not openly acknowledge their faith for fear they would be put out of the synagogue; ⁴³for they loved human glory more than the glory of God.

⁴⁴Then Jesus cried out, "Those who believe in me do not believe in me only, but in the one who sent me. ⁴⁵When they look at me, they see the one who sent me. ⁴⁶I have come into the world as a light, so that no one who believes in me should stay in darkness.

⁴⁷"As for those who hear my words but do not keep them, I do not judge them. For I did not come to judge the world, but to save the world. ⁴⁸There is a judge for those who reject me and do not accept my words; the very words I have spoken will condemn them at the last day. ⁴⁹For I did not speak on my own, but the Father who sent me commanded me to say all that I have spoken. ⁵⁰I know that his command leads to eternal life. So whatever I say is just what the Father has told me to say."

Jesus Washes His Disciples' Feet

13 It was just before the Passover Festival. Jesus knew that the hour had come for him to leave this world and go to the Father. Having loved his own who were in the world, he loved them to the end.

²The evening meal was in progress, and the devil had already prompted Judas, the son of Simon Iscariot, to betray Jesus. ³Jesus knew that the Father had put all things under his power, and that he had come from God and was returning to God; ⁴so he got up from the meal, took off his outer clothing, and wrapped a towel around his waist. ⁵After that, he poured water into a basin and began to wash his disciples' feet, drying them with the towel that was wrapped around him.

⁶He came to Simon Peter, who said to him, "Lord, are you going to wash my feet?"

⁷Jesus replied, "You do not realize now what I am doing, but later you will understand."

⁸"No," said Peter, "you shall never wash my feet."

Jesus answered, "Unless I wash you, you have no part with me."

⁹"Then, Lord," Simon Peter replied, "not just my feet but my hands and my head as well!"

¹⁰Jesus answered, "Those who have had a bath need only to wash their feet; their whole body is clean. And you are clean, though not every one of you." ¹¹For he knew who was going to betray him, and that was why he said not every one was clean.

¹²When he had finished washing their feet, he put on his clothes and returned to his place. "Do you understand what I have done for you?" he asked them. ¹³"You call me 'Teacher' and 'Lord,' and rightly so, for that is what I am. ¹⁴Now that I, your Lord and Teacher, have washed your feet, you also should wash one another's feet. ¹⁵I have set you an example that you should do as I have done for you. ¹⁶Very truly I tell you, servants are not greater than their master, nor are messengers greater than the one who sent them. ¹⁷Now that you know these things, you will be blessed if you do them.

Jesus Predicts His Betrayal

¹⁸"I am not referring to all of you; I know those I have chosen. But this is to fulfill this passage of Scripture: 'He who shared my bread has lifted up his heel against me.'ᵃ

¹⁹"I am telling you now before it happens, so that when it does happen you will believe that I am who I am. ²⁰Very truly I tell you, whoever accepts anyone I send accepts me; and whoever accepts me accepts the one who sent me."

²¹After he had said this, Jesus was troubled in spirit and testified, "Very truly I tell you, one of you is going to betray me."

²²His disciples stared at one another, at a loss to know which of them he meant. ²³One of them, the disciple whom Jesus loved, was reclining next to him. ²⁴Simon Peter motioned to this disciple and said, "Ask him which one he means."

²⁵Leaning back against Jesus, he asked him, "Lord, who is it?"

²⁶Jesus answered, "It is the one to whom I will give this piece of bread when I have dipped it in the dish." Then, dipping the piece of bread, he gave it to Judas, the son of

ᵃ 18 Psalm 41:9

THURSDAY

WHY WE SERVE JESUS

John 13:1–38 or 13:12–17

Karon Phillips Goodman

When Jesus washed Peter's feet, He showed him and us more than a custom of the time. He demonstrated for us the servant's heart we need in our walk in this world. In all our efforts to achieve and accomplish, we sometimes forget the basic call to serve one another in love. If we lose our connection with those around us, all we do becomes empty and void. But it doesn't have to be that way. We can look for the abundance of examples the Lord gave us and find ways to exercise our own each day.

Each action we take affects someone else in some way, and we decide how. It's up to us to serve in His name and become an example to those around us. And we do that best by keeping it simple, because serving doesn't have to mean giving life and limb. It also means reaching out with understanding and acceptance, touching others with grace and compassion, teaching others with humility and patience. We're mistaken to think we can only demonstrate God's love in grand ways. Each interaction with a friend or a stranger is a grand opportunity, a blessed way to be like Jesus, every day.

How do you share your *abundance of example*? Have you missed or ignored an opportunity because you thought it wasn't "important" or "valuable" enough? Pay attention this week and see how you can be a grand example in even the smallest of ways. Nothing is unimportant when it demonstrates the love of God.

JOHN WESLEY {AD 1703–1791}

Do all the good you can,
By all the means you can,
In all the ways you can,
In all of the places you can,
At all the times you can,
To all the people you can,
As long as ever you can.

reflection

1. You are not your own; you belong to Jesus. If you fully embraced that truth—every moment of every day—what would change in your life?

2. On any given day, how focused are you on meeting your needs?

3. How focused are you on meeting the needs of those around you?

For your next devotional reading, go to page 1223.

Simon Iscariot. ²⁷As soon as Judas took the bread, Satan entered into him.

So Jesus told him, "What you are about to do, do quickly." ²⁸But no one at the meal understood why Jesus said this to him. ²⁹Since Judas had charge of the money, some thought Jesus was telling him to buy what was needed for the festival, or to give something to the poor. ³⁰As soon as Judas had taken the bread, he went out. And it was night.

Jesus Predicts Peter's Denial

³¹When he was gone, Jesus said, "Now is the Son of Man glorified and God is glorified in him. ³²If God is glorified in him,ᵃ God will glorify the Son in himself, and will glorify him at once.

³³"My children, I will be with you only a little longer. You will look for me, and just as I told the Jews, so I tell you now: Where I am going, you cannot come.

³⁴"A new command I give you: Love one another. As I have loved you, so you must love one another. ³⁵By this everyone will know that you are my disciples, if you love one another."

³⁶Simon Peter asked him, "Lord, where are you going?"

Jesus replied, "Where I am going, you cannot follow now, but you will follow later."

³⁷Peter asked, "Lord, why can't I follow you now? I will lay down my life for you."

³⁸Then Jesus answered, "Will you really lay down your life for me? Very truly I tell you, before the rooster crows, you will disown me three times!

Jesus Comforts His Disciples

14 "Do not let your hearts be troubled. Trust in God ᵇ; trust also in me. ²My Father's house has plenty of room; if that were not so, would I have told you that I am going there to prepare a place for you? ³And if I go and prepare a place for you, I will come back and take you to be with me that you also may be where I am. ⁴You know the way to the place where I am going."

Jesus the Way to the Father

⁵Thomas said to him, "Lord, we don't know where you are going, so how can we know the way?"

⁶Jesus answered, "I am the way and the truth and the life. No one comes to the Father except through me. ⁷If you really know me, you will knowᶜ my Father as well. From now on, you do know him and have seen him."

⁸Philip said, "Lord, show us the Father and that will be enough for us."

⁹Jesus answered: "Don't you know me, Philip, even after I have been among you such a long time? Anyone who has seen me has seen the Father. How can you say, 'Show us the Father'? ¹⁰Don't you believe that I am in the Father, and that the Father is in me? The words I say to you I do not speak on my own authority. Rather, it is the Father, living in me, who is doing his work. ¹¹Believe me when I say that I am in the Father and the Father is in me; or at least believe on the evidence of the works themselves. ¹²Very truly I tell you, all who have faith in me will do the works I have been doing, and they will do even greater things than these, because I am going to the Father. ¹³And I will do whatever you ask in my name, so that the Father may be glorified in the Son. ¹⁴You may ask me for anything in my name, and I will do it.

Jesus Promises the Holy Spirit

¹⁵"If you love me, keep my commands. ¹⁶And I will ask the Father, and he will give you another advocate to help you and be with you forever— ¹⁷the Spirit of truth. The world cannot accept him, because it neither sees him nor knows him. But you know him, for he lives with you and will beᵈ in you. ¹⁸I will not leave you as orphans; I will come to you. ¹⁹Before long, the world will not see me anymore, but you will see me. Because I live, you also will live. ²⁰On that day you will realize that I am in my Father, and you are in me, and I am in you. ²¹Whoever has my commands and keeps them is the one who loves me. Anyone who loves me will be loved by my Father, and I too will love them and show myself to them."

²²Then Judas (not Judas Iscariot) said,

ᵃ 32 Many early manuscripts do not have *If God is glorified in him.*   ᵇ 1 Or *You trust in God*
ᶜ 7 Some manuscripts *If you really knew me, you would know*   ᵈ 17 Some early manuscripts *and is*

FRIDAY

Jesus: The Ultimate Reality

John 14:1–31 or 14:6–10

Rob Bell

Over time when you purposefully try to live the way of Jesus, you start noticing something deeper going on. You begin realizing the reason this is the best way to live is that it is rooted in profound truths about how the world is. You find yourself living more and more in tune with ultimate reality. You are more and more in sync with how the universe is at its deepest levels.

Jesus' intention was, and is, to call people to live in tune with reality. He said at one point that if you had seen him, you had "seen the Father." He claimed to be showing us what God is like. In his compassion, peace, truth telling and generosity, he was showing us God. And God is the ultimate reality. There is nothing more beyond God . . .

I don't follow Jesus because I think Christianity is the best religion. I follow Jesus because he leads me into ultimate reality. He teaches me to live in tune with how reality is.

When Jesus said, "No one comes to the Father except through me," he was saying that his way, his words, his life, is our connection to how things truly are at the deepest levels of existence. For Jesus then, the point of religion is to help us connect with ultimate reality, God. I love the way Paul puts it in the book of Colossians: These religious acts and rituals are shadows of the reality. "The reality . . . is found in Christ."

JOHN TAULER {ca. AD 1300–1361}

If Jesus is to speak in the soul, the soul must find solitude. And it must be silent in order to hear the voice of Jesus. For then he enters in and begins to speak. What does he speak? He speaks that he is. And what is he then? He is the Word of the Father. In this Word the Father reveals himself and all the divine nature and all that God is.

reflection

1. You hear a great number of people today talking about the importance of getting in tune with their "spiritual side." What are they looking for?

2. What do these people have in common with Philip?

3. How has God already made himself known?

For your next devotional reading, go to page 1227.

"But, Lord, why do you intend to show yourself to us and not to the world?"

²³Jesus replied, "Anyone who loves me will obey my teaching. My Father will love them, and we will come to them and make our home with them. ²⁴Anyone who does not love me will not obey my teaching. These words you hear are not my own; they belong to the Father who sent me.

²⁵"All this I have spoken while still with you. ²⁶But the Advocate, the Holy Spirit, whom the Father will send in my name, will teach you all things and will remind you of everything I have said to you. ²⁷Peace I leave with you; my peace I give you. I do not give to you as the world gives. Do not let your hearts be troubled and do not be afraid.

²⁸"You heard me say, 'I am going away and I am coming back to you.' If you loved me, you would be glad that I am going to the Father, for the Father is greater than I. ²⁹I have told you now before it happens, so that when it does happen you will believe. ³⁰I will not say much more to you, for the prince of this world is coming. He has no hold over me, ³¹but he comes so that the world may learn that I love the Father and do exactly what my Father has commanded me.

"Come now; let us leave.

The Vine and the Branches

15 "I am the true vine, and my Father is the gardener. ²He cuts off every branch in me that bears no fruit, while every branch that does bear fruit he prunes*a* so that it will be even more fruitful. ³You are already clean because of the word I have spoken to you. ⁴Remain in me, as I also remain in you. No branch can bear fruit by itself; it must remain in the vine. Neither can you bear fruit unless you remain in me.

⁵"I am the vine; you are the branches. If you remain in me and I in you, you will bear much fruit; apart from me you can do nothing. ⁶If you do not remain in me, you are like a branch that is thrown away and withers; such branches are picked up, thrown into the fire and burned. ⁷If you remain in me and my words remain in you, ask whatever you wish, and it will be done for you. ⁸This is to my Father's glory, that you bear much fruit, showing yourselves to be my disciples.

⁹"As the Father has loved me, so have I loved you. Now remain in my love. ¹⁰If you keep my commands, you will remain in my love, just as I have kept my Father's commands and remain in his love. ¹¹I have told you this so that my joy may be in you and that your joy may be complete. ¹²My command is this: Love each other as I have loved you. ¹³Greater love has no one than this: to lay down one's life for one's friends. ¹⁴You are my friends if you do what I command. ¹⁵I no longer call you servants, because servants do not know their master's business. Instead, I have called you friends, for everything that I learned from my Father I have made known to you. ¹⁶You did not choose me, but I chose you and appointed you so that you might go and bear fruit—fruit that will last—and so that whatever you ask in my name the Father will give you. ¹⁷This is my command: Love each other.

The World Hates the Disciples

¹⁸"If the world hates you, keep in mind that it hated me first. ¹⁹If you belonged to the world, it would love you as its own. As it is, you do not belong to the world, but I have chosen you out of the world. That is why the world hates you. ²⁰Remember what I told you: 'Servants are not greater than their master.'*b* If they persecuted me, they will persecute you also. If they obeyed my teaching, they will obey yours also. ²¹They will treat you this way because of my name, for they do not know the one who sent me. ²²If I had not come and spoken to them, they would not be guilty of sin; but now they have no excuse for their sin. ²³Those who hate me hate my Father as well. ²⁴If I had not done among them the works no one else did, they would not be guilty of sin. As it is, they have seen, and yet they have hated both me and my Father. ²⁵But this is to fulfill what is written in their Law: 'They hated me without reason.'*c*

The Work of the Holy Spirit

²⁶"When the Advocate comes, whom I will send to you from the Father—the Spirit of truth who goes out from the Father—he will testify about me. ²⁷And you also must testify, for you have been with me from the beginning.

a 2 The Greek for *he prunes* also means *he cleans.*   *b 20* John 13:16   *c 25* Psalms 35:19; 69:4

16

"All this I have told you so that you will not fall away. ²They will put you out of the synagogue; in fact, the hour is coming when those who kill you will think they are offering a service to God. ³They will do such things because they have not known the Father or me. ⁴I have told you this, so that when their hour comes you will remember that I warned you about them. I did not tell you this from the beginning because I was with you, ⁵but now I am going to him who sent me. None of you asks me, 'Where are you going?' ⁶Rather, you are filled with grief because I have said these things. ⁷But very truly I tell you, it is for your good that I am going away. Unless I go away, the Advocate will not come to you; but if I go, I will send him to you. ⁸When he comes, he will prove the world to be in the wrong about sin and righteousness and judgment: ⁹about sin, because people do not believe in me; ¹⁰about righteousness, because I am going to the Father, where you can see me no longer; ¹¹and about judgment, because the prince of this world now stands condemned.

¹²"I have much more to say to you, more than you can now bear. ¹³But when he, the Spirit of truth, comes, he will guide you into all the truth. He will not speak on his own; he will speak only what he hears, and he will tell you what is yet to come. ¹⁴He will glorify me because it is from me that he will receive what he will make known to you. ¹⁵All that belongs to the Father is mine. That is why I said the Spirit will receive from me what he will make known to you."

The Disciples' Grief Will Turn to Joy

¹⁶Jesus went on to say, "In a little while you will see me no more, and then after a little while you will see me."

¹⁷At this, some of his disciples said to one another, "What does he mean by saying, 'In a little while you will see me no more, and then after a little while you will see me,' and 'Because I am going to the Father'?" ¹⁸They kept asking, "What does he mean by 'a little while'? We don't understand what he is saying."

¹⁹Jesus saw that they wanted to ask him about this, so he said to them, "Are you asking one another what I meant when I said, 'In a little while you will see me no more, and then after a little while you will see

me'? ²⁰Very truly I tell you, you will weep and mourn while the world rejoices. You will grieve, but your grief will turn to joy. ²¹A woman giving birth to a child has pain because her time has come; but when her baby is born she forgets the anguish because of her joy that a child is born into the world. ²²So with you: Now is your time of grief, but I will see you again and you will rejoice, and no one will take away your joy. ²³In that day you will no longer ask me anything. Very truly I tell you, my Father will give you whatever you ask in my name. ²⁴Until now you have not asked for anything in my name. Ask and you will receive, and your joy will be complete.

²⁵"Though I have been speaking figuratively, a time is coming when I will no longer use this kind of language but will tell you plainly about my Father. ²⁶In that day you will ask in my name. I am not saying that I will ask the Father on your behalf. ²⁷No, the Father himself loves you because you have loved me and have believed that I came from God. ²⁸I came from the Father and entered the world; now I am leaving the world and going back to the Father."

²⁹Then Jesus' disciples said, "Now you are speaking clearly and without figures of speech. ³⁰Now we can see that you know all things and that you do not even need to have anyone ask you questions. This makes us believe that you came from God."

³¹"Do you now believe?" Jesus replied. ³²"A time is coming and in fact has come when you will be scattered, each to your own home. You will leave me all alone. Yet I am not alone, for my Father is with me.

³³"I have told you these things, so that in me you may have peace. In this world you will have trouble. But take heart! I have overcome the world."

Jesus Prays to Be Glorified

17

After Jesus said this, he looked toward heaven and prayed:

"Father, the hour has come. Glorify your Son, that your Son may glorify you. ²For you granted him authority over all people that he might give eternal life to all those you have given him. ³Now this is eternal life: that they know you, the only true God, and Jesus Christ, whom you have sent. ⁴I have brought you glory on earth by finishing the work you gave me to do. ⁵And now, Father, glorify me in your presence with the glory I had with you before the world began.

Jesus Prays for His Disciples

⁶"I have revealed you*ª* to those whom you gave me out of the world. They were yours; you gave them to me and they have obeyed your word. ⁷Now they know that everything you have given me comes from you. ⁸For I gave them the words you gave me and they accepted them. They knew with certainty that I came from you, and they believed that you sent me. ⁹I pray for them. I am not praying for the world, but for those you have given me, for they are yours. ¹⁰All I have is yours, and all you have is mine. And glory has come to me through them. ¹¹I will remain in the world no longer, but they are still in the world, and I am coming to you. Holy Father, protect them by the power of*ᵇ* your name, the name you gave me, so that they may be one as we are one. ¹²While I was with them, I protected them and kept them safe by*ᶜ* that name you gave me. None has been lost except the one doomed to destruction so that Scripture would be fulfilled.

¹³"I am coming to you now, but I say these things while I am still in the world, so that they may have the full measure of my joy within them. ¹⁴I have given them your word and the world has hated them, for they are not of the world any more than I am of the world. ¹⁵My prayer is not that you take them out of the world but that you protect them from the evil one. ¹⁶They are not of the world, even as I am not of it. ¹⁷Sanctify them by*ᵈ* the truth; your word is truth. ¹⁸As you sent me into the world, I have sent them into the world. ¹⁹For them I sanctify myself, that they too may be truly sanctified.

Jesus Prays for All Believers

²⁰"My prayer is not for them alone. I pray also for those who will believe in me through their message, ²¹that all of them may be one, Father, just as you are in me and I am in you. May they also be in us so that the world may believe that you have sent me. ²²I have given them the glory that you gave me, that they may be one as we are one— ²³I in them and you in me—so that they may be brought to complete unity. Then the world will know that you sent me and have loved them even as you have loved me.

²⁴"Father, I want those you have given me to be with me where I am, and to see my glory, the glory you have given me because you loved me before the creation of the world.

²⁵"Righteous Father, though the world does not know you, I know you, and they know that you have sent me. ²⁶I have made you known to them, and will continue to make you known in order that the love you have for me may be in them and that I myself may be in them."

Jesus Arrested

18 When he had finished praying, Jesus left with his disciples and crossed the Kidron Valley. On the other side there was a garden, and he and his disciples went into it.

²Now Judas, who betrayed him, knew the place, because Jesus had often met there with his disciples. ³So Judas came to the garden, guiding a detachment of soldiers and some officials from the chief priests and the Pharisees. They were carrying torches, lanterns and weapons.

⁴Jesus, knowing all that was going to happen to him, went out and asked them, "Who is it you want?"

⁵"Jesus of Nazareth," they replied.

"I am he," Jesus said. (And Judas the traitor was standing there with them.) ⁶When Jesus said, "I am he," they drew back and fell to the ground.

⁷Again he asked them, "Who is it you want?"

"Jesus of Nazareth," they said.

⁸Jesus answered, "I told you that I am he.

Jesus' Prayer for You

John 17:15-21

read/meditate

Read through Jesus' prayer for his followers then and now. What was Jesus' greatest concern for those who would follow after him? From our world of individualism and self-sufficiency, what do you think about Jesus' priority of oneness?

pray

Pray Jesus' prayer for yourself and your culture. Read the words aloud as your own prayer; then be silent, believing God will answer.

contemplate

Do you see Jesus' prayer being answered in your life or in the lives of the Christ-followers that you observe? Do you feel sent into the world the way Jesus was? Examine for a few moments what you would like to change about your Christian walk.

additional reflection

Christian fellowship becomes most helpful when we spend an hour, or even a few minutes, with a fellow believer and discuss together the things of God, instead of the things of the world.

—Arthur W. Pink

If I take offence easily; if I am content to continue in cold unfriendliness, though friendship be possible, then I know nothing of Calvary love.

—Amy Carmichael

For your next devotional reading, go to page 1229.

If you are looking for me, then let these men go." ⁹This happened so that the words he had spoken would be fulfilled: "I have not lost one of those you gave me."ᵃ

¹⁰Then Simon Peter, who had a sword, drew it and struck the high priest's servant, cutting off his right ear. (The servant's name was Malchus.)

¹¹Jesus commanded Peter, "Put your sword away! Shall I not drink the cup the Father has given me?"

¹²Then the detachment of soldiers with its commander and the Jewish officials arrested Jesus. They bound him ¹³and brought him first to Annas, who was the father-in-law of Caiaphas, the high priest that year. ¹⁴Caiaphas was the one who had advised the Jewish leaders that it would be good if one man died for the people.

Peter's First Denial

¹⁵Simon Peter and another disciple were following Jesus. Because this disciple was known to the high priest, he went with Jesus into the high priest's courtyard, ¹⁶but Peter had to wait outside at the door. The other disciple, who was known to the high priest, came back, spoke to the servant girl on duty there and brought Peter in.

¹⁷"You aren't one of this man's disciples too, are you?" she asked Peter.

He replied, "I am not."

¹⁸It was cold, and the servants and officials stood around a fire they had made to keep warm. Peter also was standing with them, warming himself.

The High Priest Questions Jesus

¹⁹Meanwhile, the high priest questioned Jesus about his disciples and his teaching.

²⁰"I have spoken openly to the world," Jesus replied. "I always taught in synagogues or at the temple, where all the Jews come together. I said nothing in secret. ²¹Why question me? Ask those who heard me. Surely they know what I said."

²²When Jesus said this, one of the officials nearby slapped him in the face. "Is this the way you answer the high priest?" he demanded.

²³"If I said something wrong," Jesus replied, "testify as to what is wrong. But if I spoke the truth, why did you strike me?"

²⁴Then Annas sent him bound to Caiaphas the high priest.

Peter's Second and Third Denials

²⁵Meanwhile, Simon Peter was still standing there warming himself. So they asked him, "You aren't one of his disciples too, are you?"

He denied it, saying, "I am not."

²⁶One of the high priest's servants, a relative of the man whose ear Peter had cut off, challenged him, "Didn't I see you with him in the garden?" ²⁷Again Peter denied it, and at that moment a rooster began to crow.

Jesus Before Pilate

²⁸Then the Jewish leaders took Jesus from Caiaphas to the palace of the Roman governor. By now it was early morning, and to avoid ceremonial uncleanness they did not enter the palace, because they wanted to be able to eat the Passover. ²⁹So Pilate came out to them and asked, "What charges are you bringing against this man?"

³⁰"If he were not a criminal," they replied, "we would not have handed him over to you."

³¹Pilate said, "Take him yourselves and judge him by your own law."

"But we have no right to execute anyone," they objected. ³²This took place to fulfill what Jesus had said about the kind of death he was going to die.

³³Pilate then went back inside the palace, summoned Jesus and asked him, "Are you the king of the Jews?"

³⁴"Is that your own idea," Jesus asked, "or did others talk to you about me?"

³⁵"Am I a Jew?" Pilate replied. "Your own people and chief priests handed you over to me. What is it you have done?"

³⁶Jesus said, "My kingdom is not of this world. If it were, my servants would fight to prevent my arrest by the Jewish leaders. But now my kingdom is from another place."

³⁷"You are a king, then!" said Pilate.

Jesus answered, "You say that I am a king. In fact, the reason I was born and came into the world is to testify to the truth. Everyone on the side of truth listens to me."

³⁸"What is truth?" retorted Pilate. With this he went out again to the Jews gathered there and said, "I find no basis for a charge

ᵃ 9 John 6:39

MONDAY

RESIST THE EASY FIX

John 18:1–27 *or* 18:15–18,25–27

Dallas Willard

It is deeply instructive of the nature of human life and its redemption that, when Jesus knew Peter would deny him, he did not just "fix him" so that he wouldn't do the terrible thing. Surely he could have done that. But it would not have advanced Peter toward being the person he needed to become. So Jesus said to Peter, with sadness perhaps, but with great confidence in the Father, "[I have prayed for you, Simon, that your faith may not fail. And when you have turned back, strengthen your brothers]" (Luke 22:32).

I think there is perhaps no other scene in all Scripture that so forcefully illustrates the community of prayerful love as this response to Peter. How earnestly Jesus longed for Peter to come out right in his time of testing! But he left him free to succeed or fail before God and man and, as it turned out, before all of subsequent human history He used no condemnation, no shame, no "pearls of wisdom" on him. And he didn't use supernatural power to rewire his soul or his brain. It was just this, "[I have prayed for you, Simon, that your faith may not fail]." And it corresponds perfectly to Matthew 7:1–11. It is Jesus' beautiful pattern for us to practice in our relationships to those close to us.

E. M. BOUNDS {AD 1835–1913}

Paul, the chief of the apostles, needed prayer. He needed the prayers of others, for this he practically admitted when he asked for their prayers. His call to the apostleship did not lift him above this need. He realized and acknowledged his dependence on prayer. He craved and prized the prayers of all good people. He was not ashamed to solicit prayers for himself or to urge believers everywhere to pray for him (see Romans 15:30–31; Ephesians 6:20; Colossians 4:4).

Prayers by others for Paul were valuable because they helped him. Great helpers are prayers. Nothing gives so much aid to us in our needs as real prayers. They supply needs and deliver from difficulty . . . What marvelous things has God done for his favored saints through the prayers of others! The saints can help the saints more by fervent praying than by any other way.

reflection

1. When someone you care about has a need, what is your first, automatic response?

2. What role does prayer play in your relationships?

3. Think of a specific situation right now in which you would love to be able to "fix" someone or their circumstances to make it "work out." How might the examples of Jesus and Paul challenge you to change how you approach this situation?

For your next devotional reading, go to page 1235.

against him. ³⁹But it is your custom for me to release to you one prisoner at the time of the Passover. Do you want me to release 'the king of the Jews'?"

⁴⁰They shouted back, "No, not him! Give us Barabbas!" Now Barabbas had taken part in an uprising.

Jesus Sentenced to Be Crucified

19 Then Pilate took Jesus and had him flogged. ²The soldiers twisted together a crown of thorns and put it on his head. They clothed him in a purple robe ³and went up to him again and again, saying, "Hail, king of the Jews!" And they slapped him in the face.

⁴Once more Pilate came out and said to the Jews, "Look, I am bringing him out to you to let you know that I find no basis for a charge against him." ⁵When Jesus came out wearing the crown of thorns and the purple robe, Pilate said to them, "Here is the man!"

⁶As soon as the chief priests and their officials saw him, they shouted, "Crucify! Crucify!"

But Pilate answered, "You take him and crucify him. As for me, I find no basis for a charge against him."

⁷The Jews insisted, "We have a law, and according to that law he must die, because he claimed to be the Son of God."

⁸When Pilate heard this, he was even more afraid, ⁹and he went back inside the palace. "Where do you come from?" he asked Jesus, but Jesus gave him no answer. ¹⁰"Do you refuse to speak to me?" Pilate said. "Don't you realize I have power either to free you or to crucify you?"

¹¹Jesus answered, "You would have no power over me if it were not given to you from above. Therefore the one who handed me over to you is guilty of a greater sin."

¹²From then on, Pilate tried to set Jesus free, but the Jews kept shouting, "If you let this man go, you are no friend of Caesar. Anyone who claims to be a king opposes Caesar."

¹³When Pilate heard this, he brought Jesus out and sat down on the judge's seat at a place known as the Stone Pavement (which in Aramaic is Gabbatha). ¹⁴It was the day of Preparation of the Passover; it was about noon.

"Here is your king," Pilate said to the Jews.

¹⁵But they shouted, "Take him away! Take him away! Crucify him!"

"Shall I crucify your king?" Pilate asked.

"We have no king but Caesar," the chief priests answered.

¹⁶Finally Pilate handed him over to them to be crucified.

The Crucifixion of Jesus

So the soldiers took charge of Jesus. ¹⁷Carrying his own cross, he went out to the place of the Skull (which in Aramaic is called Golgotha). ¹⁸Here they crucified him, and with him two others—one on each side and Jesus in the middle.

¹⁹Pilate had a notice prepared and fastened to the cross. It read: JESUS OF NAZARETH, THE KING OF THE JEWS. ²⁰Many of the Jews read this sign, for the place where Jesus was crucified was near the city, and the sign was written in Aramaic, Latin and Greek. ²¹The chief priests of the Jews protested to Pilate, "Do not write 'The King of the Jews,' but that this man claimed to be king of the Jews."

²²Pilate answered, "What I have written, I have written."

²³When the soldiers crucified Jesus, they took his clothes, dividing them into four shares, one for each of them, with the undergarment remaining. This garment was seamless, woven in one piece from top to bottom.

²⁴"Let's not tear it," they said to one another. "Let's decide by lot who will get it."

This happened that the scripture might be fulfilled that said,

"They divided my clothes among them
    and cast lots for my garment."ᵃ

So this is what the soldiers did.

²⁵Near the cross of Jesus stood his mother, his mother's sister, Mary the wife of Clopas, and Mary Magdalene. ²⁶When Jesus saw his mother there, and the disciple whom he loved standing nearby, he said to her, "Woman,ᵇ here is your son," ²⁷and to the disciple, "Here is your mother." From that time on, this disciple took her into his home.

ᵃ 24 Psalm 22:18 ᵇ 26 The Greek for Woman does not denote any disrespect.

The Death of Jesus

²⁸Later, knowing that everything had now been finished, and so that Scripture would be fulfilled, Jesus said, "I am thirsty." ²⁹A jar of wine vinegar was there, so they soaked a sponge in it, put the sponge on a stalk of the hyssop plant, and lifted it to Jesus' lips. ³⁰When he had received the drink, Jesus said, "It is finished." With that, he bowed his head and gave up his spirit.

³¹Now it was the day of Preparation, and the next day was to be a special Sabbath. Because the Jewish leaders did not want the bodies left on the crosses during the Sabbath, they asked Pilate to have the legs broken and the bodies taken down. ³²The soldiers therefore came and broke the legs of the first man who had been crucified with Jesus, and then those of the other. ³³But when they came to Jesus and found that he was already dead, they did not break his legs. ³⁴Instead, one of the soldiers pierced Jesus' side with a spear, bringing a sudden flow of blood and water. ³⁵The man who saw it has given testimony, and his testimony is true. He knows that he tells the truth, and he testifies so that you also may believe. ³⁶These things happened so that the scripture would be fulfilled: "Not one of his bones will be broken,"ᵃ ³⁷and, as another scripture says, "They will look on the one they have pierced."ᵇ

The Burial of Jesus

³⁸Later, Joseph of Arimathea asked Pilate for the body of Jesus. Now Joseph was a disciple of Jesus, but secretly because he feared the Jewish leaders. With Pilate's permission, he came and took the body away. ³⁹He was accompanied by Nicodemus, the man who earlier had visited Jesus at night. Nicodemus brought a mixture of myrrh and aloes, about seventy-five pounds.ᶜ ⁴⁰Taking Jesus' body, the two of them wrapped it, with the spices, in strips of linen. This was in accordance with Jewish burial customs. ⁴¹At the place where Jesus was crucified, there was a garden, and in the garden a new tomb, in which no one had ever been laid. ⁴²Because it was the Jewish day of Preparation and since the tomb was nearby, they laid Jesus there.

The Empty Tomb

20 Early on the first day of the week, while it was still dark, Mary Magdalene went to the tomb and saw that the stone had been removed from the entrance. ²So she came running to Simon Peter and the other disciple, the one Jesus loved, and said, "They have taken the Lord out of the tomb, and we don't know where they have put him!"

³So Peter and the other disciple started for the tomb. ⁴Both were running, but the other disciple outran Peter and reached the tomb first. ⁵He bent over and looked in at the strips of linen lying there but did not go in. ⁶Then Simon Peter came along behind him and went straight into the tomb. He saw the strips of linen lying there, ⁷as well as the cloth that had been wrapped around Jesus' head. The cloth was still lying in its place, separate from the linen. ⁸Finally the other disciple, who had reached the tomb first, also went inside. He saw and believed. ⁹(They still did not understand from Scripture that Jesus had to rise from the dead.) ¹⁰Then the disciples went back to where they were staying.

Jesus Appears to Mary Magdalene

¹¹Now Mary stood outside the tomb crying. As she wept, she bent over to look into the tomb ¹²and saw two angels in white, seated where Jesus' body had been, one at the head and the other at the foot.

¹³They asked her, "Woman,ᵈ why are you crying?"

"They have taken my Lord away," she said, "and I don't know where they have put him." ¹⁴At this, she turned around and saw Jesus standing there, but she did not realize that it was Jesus.

¹⁵He asked her, "Woman, why are you crying? Who is it you are looking for?"

Thinking he was the gardener, she said, "Sir, if you have carried him away, tell me where you have put him, and I will get him."

¹⁶Jesus said to her, "Mary."

She turned toward him and cried out in Aramaic, "Rabboni!" (which means "Teacher").

¹⁷Jesus said, "Do not hold on to me, for I have not yet ascended to the Father. Go in-

---

ᵃ 36 Exodus 12:46; Num. 9:12; Psalm 34:20   ᵇ 37 Zech. 12:10   ᶜ 39 Or about 34 kilograms
ᵈ 13 The Greek for *Woman* does not denote any disrespect; also in verse 15.

stead to my brothers and tell them, 'I am ascending to my Father and your Father, to my God and your God.' "

18Mary Magdalene went to the disciples with the news: "I have seen the Lord!" And she told them that he had said these things to her.

Jesus Appears to His Disciples

19On the evening of that first day of the week, when the disciples were together, with the doors locked for fear of the Jewish leaders, Jesus came and stood among them and said, "Peace be with you!" 20After he said this, he showed them his hands and side. The disciples were overjoyed when they saw the Lord.

21Again Jesus said, "Peace be with you! As the Father has sent me, I am sending you." 22And with that he breathed on them and said, "Receive the Holy Spirit. 23If you forgive the sins of anyone, their sins are forgiven; if you do not forgive them, they are not forgiven."

Jesus Appears to Thomas

24Now Thomas (also known as Didymus[a]), one of the Twelve, was not with the disciples when Jesus came. 25So the other disciples told him, "We have seen the Lord!"

But he said to them, "Unless I see the nail marks in his hands and put my finger where the nails were, and put my hand into his side, I will not believe."

26A week later his disciples were in the house again, and Thomas was with them. Though the doors were locked, Jesus came and stood among them and said, "Peace be with you!" 27Then he said to Thomas, "Put your finger here; see my hands. Reach out your hand and put it into my side. Stop doubting and believe."

28Thomas said to him, "My Lord and my God!"

29Then Jesus told him, "Because you have seen me, you have believed; blessed are those who have not seen and yet have believed."

The Purpose of John's Gospel

30Jesus performed many other signs in the presence of his disciples, which are not recorded in this book. 31But these are written that you may believe[b] that Jesus is the Messiah, the Son of God, and that by believing you may have life in his name.

Jesus and the Miraculous Catch of Fish

21 Afterward Jesus appeared again to his disciples, by the Sea of Galilee.[c] It happened this way: 2Simon Peter, Thomas (also known as Didymus[d]), Nathanael from Cana in Galilee, the sons of Zebedee, and two other disciples were together. 3"I'm going out to fish," Simon Peter told them, and they said, "We'll go with you." So they went out and got into the boat, but that night they caught nothing.

4Early in the morning, Jesus stood on the shore, but the disciples did not realize that it was Jesus.

5He called out to them, "Friends, haven't you any fish?"

"No," they answered.

6He said, "Throw your net on the right side of the boat and you will find some." When they did, they were unable to haul the net in because of the large number of fish.

7Then the disciple whom Jesus loved said to Peter, "It is the Lord!" As soon as Simon Peter heard him say, "It is the Lord," he wrapped his outer garment around him (for he had taken it off) and jumped into the water. 8The other disciples followed in the boat, towing the net full of fish, for they were not far from shore, about a hundred yards.[e] 9When they landed, they saw a fire of burning coals there with fish on it, and some bread.

10Jesus said to them, "Bring some of the fish you have just caught."

11Simon Peter climbed aboard and dragged the net ashore. It was full of large fish, 153, but even with so many the net was not torn. 12Jesus said to them, "Come and have breakfast." None of the disciples dared ask him, "Who are you?" They knew it was the Lord. 13Jesus came, took the bread and gave it to them, and did the same with the fish. 14This was now the third time Jesus appeared to his disciples after he was raised from the dead.

---

a 24 Thomas (Aramaic) and Didymus (Greek) both mean twin.   b 31 Or may continue to believe
c 1 Greek Tiberias   d 2 Thomas (Aramaic) and Didymus (Greek) both mean twin.   e 8 Or about 90 meters

Jesus Reinstates Peter

15 When they had finished eating, Jesus said to Simon Peter, "Simon son of John, do you love me more than these?"

"Yes, Lord," he said, "you know that I love you."

Jesus said, "Feed my lambs."

16 Again Jesus said, "Simon son of John, do you love me?"

He answered, "Yes, Lord, you know that I love you."

Jesus said, "Take care of my sheep."

17 The third time he said to him, "Simon son of John, do you love me?"

Peter was hurt because Jesus asked him the third time, "Do you love me?" He said, "Lord, you know all things; you know that I love you."

Jesus said, "Feed my sheep. 18 Very truly I tell you, when you were younger you dressed yourself and went where you wanted; but when you are old you will stretch out your hands, and someone else will dress you and lead you where you do not want to go."

19 Jesus said this to indicate the kind of death by which Peter would glorify God. Then he said to him, "Follow me!"

20 Peter turned and saw that the disciple whom Jesus loved was following them. (This was the one who had leaned back against Jesus at the supper and had said, "Lord, who is going to betray you?") 21 When Peter saw him, he asked, "Lord, what about him?"

22 Jesus answered, "If I want him to remain alive until I return, what is that to you? You must follow me." 23 Because of this, the rumor spread among the believers that this disciple would not die. But Jesus did not say that he would not die; he only said, "If I want him to remain alive until I return, what is that to you?"

24 This is the disciple who testifies to these things and who wrote them down. We know that his testimony is true.

25 Jesus did many other things as well. If every one of them were written down, I suppose that even the whole world would not have room for the books that would be written.

acts

> AUTHOR: Luke, a doctor and Gentile Christian
>
> DATE: Probably around A.D. 63
>
> THEME: God's Spirit fueled the growth of the first-century church.

Jesus Taken Up Into Heaven

1 In my former book, Theophilus, I wrote about all that Jesus began to do and to teach ²until the day he was taken up to heaven, after giving instructions through the Holy Spirit to the apostles he had chosen. ³After his suffering, he presented himself to them and gave many convincing proofs that he was alive. He appeared to them over a period of forty days and spoke about the kingdom of God. ⁴On one occasion, while he was eating with them, he gave them this command: "Do not leave Jerusalem, but wait for the gift my Father promised, which you have heard me speak about. ⁵For John baptized with*a* water, but in a few days you will be baptized with*a* the Holy Spirit."

⁶So when they met together, they asked him, "Lord, are you at this time going to restore the kingdom to Israel?"

⁷He said to them: "It is not for you to know the times or dates the Father has set by his own authority. ⁸But you will receive power when the Holy Spirit comes on you; and you will be my witnesses in Jerusalem, and in all Judea and Samaria, and to the ends of the earth."

⁹After he said this, he was taken up before their very eyes, and a cloud hid him from their sight.

¹⁰They were looking intently up into the sky as he was going, when suddenly two men dressed in white stood beside them. ¹¹"Men of Galilee," they said, "why do you stand here looking into the sky? This same Jesus, who has been taken from you into heaven, will come back in the same way you have seen him go into heaven."

Matthias Chosen to Replace Judas

¹²Then the apostles returned to Jerusalem from the hill called the Mount of Olives, a Sabbath day's walk*b* from the city. ¹³When they arrived, they went upstairs to the room where they were staying. Those present were Peter, John, James and Andrew; Philip and Thomas, Bartholomew and Matthew; James son of Alphaeus and Simon the Zealot, and Judas son of James. ¹⁴They all joined together constantly in prayer, along with the women and Mary the mother of Jesus, and with his brothers.

¹⁵In those days Peter stood up among the believers (a group numbering about a hundred and twenty) ¹⁶and said, "Brothers and sisters, the Scripture had to be fulfilled in which the Holy Spirit spoke long ago through David concerning Judas, who served as guide for those who arrested Jesus. ¹⁷He was one of our number and shared in our ministry."

¹⁸(With the reward he got for his wickedness, Judas bought a field; there he fell headlong, his body burst open and all his intestines spilled out. ¹⁹Everyone in Jerusalem heard about this, so they called that field in their language Akeldama, that is, Field of Blood.)

²⁰"For," said Peter, "it is written in the Book of Psalms:

" 'May his place be deserted;
  let there be no one to dwell in it,'*c*

and,

" 'May another take his place of
  leadership.'*d*

---

a 5 Or *in*   *b 12* That is, about 5/8 mile or about 1 kilometer   *c 20* Psalm 69:25
d 20 Psalm 109:8

TUESDAY

WHAT IT MEANS TO BE A WITNESS

Acts 1:1–26 *or* 1:8

JOHN WRIGHT FOLLETTE {AD 1883–1966}

In Acts 1:8, the Lord is not using the word *witness* about someone who gets up and gives a testimony; He is saying that a person coming up from the power of the Spirit is willing to let his life be slain in order that the life of Christ may be lived through him. He becomes a witness, a testimony of the power of God. That is when the individual life becomes a witness, a testimony. The word *witness* here means "martyr," one who is willing to let his very life go for the sake of the Truth.

The power of his resurrection possessed the disciples, and the power of the resurrection is always a witnessing power. The resurrection was a witness. The power that God used in raising Jesus from the dead was resurrection power unto a witness. When does he say, "I will pour the Holy Spirit upon you"? After the resurrection, for now there is resurrection quality in the power that is to come upon them. They are now ministering in resurrection power. The LIFE is the witness.

John Fischer

What is the difference between witnessing (the verb) and being a witness (the noun)? A witness is someone who has seen something and tells what he or she saw when called upon. It is someone who has experienced something and relates a story about what was experienced.

Here is a wonderful, guilt-crushing truth: Every witness is an expert. No one is more informed on what you have experienced with Christ than you are, simply because no one else can be you. No class, seminar or workshop can teach this. Your witness is your own present tense, your continuing story, and no one but you can tell it.

When we stick with an honest telling of our story as our spoken witness, we are guaranteed a connection with others on a human level. As long as our story is told mostly in the present tense—relating the current ways in which we are experiencing God's grace, forgiveness and power—our witness will be as effective as it needs to be.

reflection

1. Up until today, what did you think it meant to be a "witness" for God?

2. How has today's reading added to or changed your understanding of what it means to be a witness?

3. What kind of testimony do others hear through both your actions and your words?

For your next devotional reading, go to page 1237.

21Therefore it is necessary to choose one of the men who have been with us the whole time the Lord Jesus went in and out among us, 22beginning from John's baptism to the time when Jesus was taken up from us. For one of these must become a witness with us of his resurrection."

23So they proposed the names of two men: Joseph called Barsabbas (also known as Justus) and Matthias. 24Then they prayed, "Lord, you know everyone's heart. Show us which of these two you have chosen 25to take over this apostolic ministry, which Judas left to go where he belongs." 26Then they cast lots, and the lot fell to Matthias; so he was added to the eleven apostles.

The Holy Spirit Comes at Pentecost

2 When the day of Pentecost came, they were all together in one place. 2Suddenly a sound like the blowing of a violent wind came from heaven and filled the whole house where they were sitting. 3They saw what seemed to be tongues of fire that separated and came to rest on each of them. 4All of them were filled with the Holy Spirit and began to speak in other tongues*a* as the Spirit enabled them.

5Now there were staying in Jerusalem God-fearing Jews from every nation under heaven. 6When they heard this sound, a crowd came together in bewilderment, because each one heard their own language being spoken. 7Utterly amazed, they asked: "Aren't all these who are speaking Galileans? 8Then how is it that each of us hears them in our native language? 9Parthians, Medes and Elamites; residents of Mesopotamia, Judea and Cappadocia, Pontus and Asia,*b* 10Phrygia and Pamphylia, Egypt and the parts of Libya near Cyrene; visitors from Rome 11(both Jews and converts to Judaism); Cretans and Arabs—we hear them declaring the wonders of God in our own tongues!" 12Amazed and perplexed, they asked one another, "What does this mean?"

13Some, however, made fun of them and said, "They have had too much wine."

Peter Addresses the Crowd

14Then Peter stood up with the Eleven, raised his voice and addressed the crowd:

"Fellow Jews and all of you who live in Jerusalem, let me explain this to you; listen carefully to what I say. 15These people are not drunk, as you suppose. It's only nine in the morning! 16No, this is what was spoken by the prophet Joel:

17" 'In the last days, God says,
    I will pour out my Spirit on all people.
Your sons and daughters will prophesy,
    your young men will see visions,
    your old men will dream dreams.
18Even on my servants, both men and
        women,
    I will pour out my Spirit in those
        days,
    and they will prophesy.
19I will show wonders in the heaven above
    and signs on the earth below,
    blood and fire and billows of smoke.
20The sun will be turned to darkness
    and the moon to blood
    before the coming of the great and
        glorious day of the Lord.
21And everyone who calls
    on the name of the Lord will be
        saved.'*c*

22"People of Israel, listen to this: Jesus of Nazareth was a man accredited by God to you by miracles, wonders and signs, which God did among you through him, as you yourselves know. 23This man was handed over to you by God's deliberate plan and foreknowledge; and you, with the help of wicked men,*d* put him to death by nailing him to the cross. 24But God raised him from the dead, freeing him from the agony of death, because it was impossible for death to keep its hold on him. 25David said about him:

" 'I saw the Lord always before me.
    Because he is at my right hand,
    I will not be shaken.
26Therefore my heart is glad and my
        tongue rejoices;
    my body also will rest in hope,
27because you will not abandon me to the
        realm of the dead,
    you will not let your holy one see
        decay.
28You have made known to me the paths
        of life;

a 4 Or languages; also in verse 11   b 9 That is, the Roman province by that name   c 21 Joel 2:28-32
d 23 Or of those not having the law (that is, Gentiles)

WEDNESDAY

SHARE . . . AND NOT ONLY WITH THOSE YOU LIKE

Acts 2:1–47 or 2:42–47

Jim Wallis

Conversion means to relinquish our wealth, for the sake of our relationship to God and for the sake of our fellowship with the poor. Justice requires an end to our accumulation. A new commitment to economic sharing and simplicity will both break our bondage to affluence and bring a vitality and integrity that most of our congregations have never experienced.

To share the control of our resources with fellow believers and to share what we have with the poor is part of what it means to be the church. Economic sharing is a way of life intended for all God's people, not just monastic orders, the clergy or special ministry groups. No particular form or administrative procedure can ever be normative for all, but the Biblical vision of fellowship will always include our economic lives, the sharing of our money and possessions with each other and with the poor.

LEO I {AD 400–461}

Observing the apostles, dearly beloved, we exhort you, as watchful shepherds, to follow their example and . . . devote yourselves to deeds of mercy . . . Nothing is more suitable to faith . . . than to assist the poverty of the needy, to undertake the care of the weak, to provide for the needs of the family of God and to remember one's own condition in the toils of others.

In this work, God alone knows what responsibility he has given to each person, for he discerns rightly how much a person can and cannot do. For not only are spiritual riches and heavenly gifts received from God, but earthly and material possessions also proceed from his bounty. And he is justified in requiring an account of those things which he has not so much put in our possession as he has committed to our stewardship. Therefore, we must use God's gifts properly and wisely, or else the resources we've been given for accomplishing a good work will turn into an opportunity for sin. For wealth is good and is of the greatest advantage to human society when it is regarded as a means rather than an end, when it is under the control of the benevolent and open-handed, and when the luxurious person does not squander it nor the miser hoard it.

reflection

1. How can money be either a blessing or a burden? What makes the difference?
2. Think of someone you know who has physical, material needs. How can you help meet those needs?
3. Is there a group of people whom you find it difficult to give to? Why?

For your next devotional reading, go to page 1240.

you will fill me with joy in your
presence.'[a]

29"Brothers and sisters, we all know that
the patriarch David died and was buried,
and his tomb is here to this day. 30But he
was a prophet and knew that God had promised him on oath that he would place one of
his descendants on his throne. 31Seeing
what was to come, he spoke of the resurrection of the Messiah, that he was not abandoned to the realm of the dead, nor did his
body see decay. 32God has raised this Jesus
to life, and we are all witnesses of the fact.
33Exalted to the right hand of God, he has
received from the Father the promised Holy
Spirit and has poured out what you now see
and hear. 34For David did not ascend to
heaven, and yet he said,

" 'The Lord said to my Lord:
"Sit at my right hand
35until I make your enemies
a footstool for your feet." '[b]

36"Therefore let all Israel be assured of
this: God has made this Jesus, whom you
crucified, both Lord and Messiah."

37When the people heard this, they were
cut to the heart and said to Peter and the
other apostles, "Brothers, what shall
we do?"

38Peter replied, "Repent and be baptized,
every one of you, in the name of Jesus Christ
for the forgiveness of your sins. And you will
receive the gift of the Holy Spirit. 39The
promise is for you and your children and for
all who are far off—for all whom the Lord
our God will call."

40With many other words he warned
them; and he pleaded with them, "Save
yourselves from this corrupt generation."
41Those who accepted his message were
baptized, and about three thousand were
added to their number that day.

The Fellowship of the Believers

42They devoted themselves to the apostles' teaching and to fellowship, to the
breaking of bread and to prayer. 43Everyone
was filled with awe at the many wonders
and signs performed by the apostles. 44All
the believers were together and had everything in common. 45They sold property and
possessions to give to anyone who had need.

46Every day they continued to meet together in the temple courts. They broke bread in
their homes and ate together with glad and
sincere hearts, 47praising God and enjoying
the favor of all the people. And the Lord
added to their number daily those who were
being saved.

Peter Heals a Lame Beggar

3 One day Peter and John were going
up to the temple at the time of
prayer—at three in the afternoon.
2Now a man who was lame from birth was
being carried to the temple gate called
Beautiful, where he was put every day to
beg from those going into the temple
courts. 3When he saw Peter and John about
to enter, he asked them for money. 4Peter
looked straight at him, as did John. Then
Peter said, "Look at us!" 5So the man gave
them his attention, expecting to get something from them.

6Then Peter said, "Silver or gold I do not
have, but what I do have I give you. In the
name of Jesus Christ of Nazareth, walk."
7Taking him by the right hand, he helped him
up, and instantly the man's feet and ankles
became strong. 8He jumped to his feet and
began to walk. Then he went with them into
the temple courts, walking and jumping, and
praising God. 9When all the people saw him
walking and praising God, 10they recognized
him as the same man who used to sit begging at the temple gate called Beautiful, and
they were filled with wonder and amazement at what had happened to him.

Peter Speaks to the Onlookers

11While the man held on to Peter and John,
all the people were astonished and came
running to them in the place called Solomon's Colonnade. 12When Peter saw this, he
said to them: "People of Israel, why does this
surprise you? Why do you stare at us as if by
our own power or godliness we had made
this man walk? 13The God of Abraham, Isaac
and Jacob, the God of our fathers, has glorified his servant Jesus. You handed him over
to be killed, and you disowned him before
Pilate, though he had decided to let him go.
14You disowned the Holy and Righteous One
and asked that a murderer be released to
you. 15You killed the author of life, but God

---

a 28 Psalm 16:8-11 (see Septuagint)   b 35 Psalm 110:1

raised him from the dead. We are witnesses of this. ¹⁶By faith in the name of Jesus, this man whom you see and know was made strong. It is Jesus' name and the faith that comes through him that has completely healed him, as you can all see.

¹⁷"Now, brothers and sisters, I know that you acted in ignorance, as did your leaders. ¹⁸But this is how God fulfilled what he had foretold through all the prophets, saying that his Messiah would suffer. ¹⁹Repent, then, and turn to God, so that your sins may be wiped out, that times of refreshing may come from the Lord, ²⁰and that he may send the Messiah, who has been appointed for you—even Jesus. ²¹Heaven must receive him until the time comes for God to restore everything, as he promised long ago through his holy prophets. ²²For Moses said, 'The Lord your God will raise up for you a prophet like me from among your own people; you must listen to everything he tells you. ²³Anyone who does not listen to him will be completely cut off from their people.'ᵃ

²⁴"Indeed, beginning with Samuel, all the prophets who have spoken have foretold these days. ²⁵And you are heirs of the prophets and of the covenant God made with your fathers. He said to Abraham, 'Through your offspring all peoples on earth will be blessed.'ᵇ ²⁶When God raised up his servant, he sent him first to you to bless you by turning each of you from your wicked ways."

Peter and John Before the Sanhedrin

4 The priests and the captain of the temple guard and the Sadducees came up to Peter and John while they were speaking to the people. ²They were greatly disturbed because the apostles were teaching the people, proclaiming in Jesus the resurrection of the dead. ³They seized Peter and John, and because it was evening, they put them in jail until the next day. ⁴But many who heard the message believed; so the number of men who believed grew to about five thousand.

⁵The next day the rulers, the elders and the teachers of the law met in Jerusalem. ⁶Annas the high priest was there, and so were Caiaphas, John, Alexander and others of the high priest's family. ⁷They had Peter and John brought before them and began to question them: "By what power or what name did you do this?"

⁸Then Peter, filled with the Holy Spirit, said to them: "Rulers and elders of the people! ⁹If we are being called to account today for an act of kindness shown to a man who was lame and are being asked how he was healed, ¹⁰then know this, you and all the people of Israel: It is by the name of Jesus Christ of Nazareth, whom you crucified but whom God raised from the dead, that this man stands before you healed. ¹¹Jesus is

" 'the stone you builders rejected,
which has become the cornerstone.'ᶜ

¹²Salvation is found in no one else, for there is no other name given under heaven by which we must be saved."

¹³When they saw the courage of Peter and John and realized that they were unschooled, ordinary men, they were astonished and they took note that these men had been with Jesus. ¹⁴But since they could see the man who had been healed standing there with them, there was nothing they could say. ¹⁵So they ordered them to withdraw from the Sanhedrin and then conferred together. ¹⁶"What are we going to do with these men?" they asked. "Everyone living in Jerusalem knows they have performed a notable sign, and we cannot deny it. ¹⁷But to stop this thing from spreading any further among the people, we must warn them to speak no longer to anyone in this name."

¹⁸Then they called them in again and commanded them not to speak or teach at all in the name of Jesus. ¹⁹But Peter and John replied, "Which is right in God's eyes: to listen to you, or to him? You be the judges! ²⁰As for us, we cannot help speaking about what we have seen and heard."

²¹After further threats they let them go. They could not decide how to punish them, because all the people were praising God for what had happened. ²²For the man who was miraculously healed was over forty years old.

The Believers' Prayer

²³On their release, Peter and John went back to their own people and reported all that the chief priests and the elders had said to them. ²⁴When they heard this, they raised their voices together in prayer to God. "Sov-

---

ᵃ 23 Deut. 18:15,18,19   ᵇ 25 Gen. 22:18; 26:4   ᶜ 11 Psalm 118:22

More Than Words

Acts 4:1–37 or 4:1–10

Bill Hybels

Engaging in efforts to extend your faith to others can go a long way toward strengthening your confidence in your own beliefs. This is true, in part, because talking to people who have different spiritual perspectives will force you to take steps to ensure you are speaking accurately about the Christian faith . . .

We automatically increase our own knowledge when we try to communicate our faith to friends who are skeptics, or Mormons, or Jehovah's Witnesses, or New Agers or even church-going non-Christians. And when we successfully hold our own in the face of opposition, we gain a heightened sense of spiritual confidence.

And if you think that builds your self-assurance, imagine what happens when one of these people becomes a Christian. Your faith is boosted sky high! You may feel like seeking out some Muslim fundamentalists or hardened atheists. Why not? They matter to God, too. There's no telling who he'll use you to reach, once your spiritual confidence starts spiraling upward!

John Wesley {AD 1703–1791}

Redeem the time. Improve the present moment. Buy up every opportunity of growing in grace or of doing good. God gives as much grace for the day as the day requires. God is now pouring his benefits upon you. So prove that you're a faithful steward of the present grace of God. It doesn't matter what tomorrow may hold; make every effort today to add to your faith courage, self-control, patience, brotherly-kindness and the fear of God until your love is pure and perfect! Let these things be in you now in abundance. Do not be lazy or unproductive. If you do these things "you will receive a rich welcome into the eternal kingdom of our Lord and Savior Jesus Christ!" (2 Peter 1:11).

reflection

1. With what kinds of people do you find it difficult to share Christ?
2. Why do you find it difficult to share the gospel with them?
3. How does serving others illustrate the gospel message?

For your next devotional reading, go to page 1244.

ereign Lord," they said, "you made the heaven and the earth and the sea, and everything in them. 25You spoke by the Holy Spirit through the mouth of your servant, our father David:

" 'Why do the nations rage
    and the peoples plot in vain?
26The kings of the earth rise up
    and the rulers band together
  against the Lord
    and against his anointed one.*a* *b*

27Indeed Herod and Pontius Pilate met together with the Gentiles and the people of Israel in this city to conspire against your holy servant Jesus, whom you anointed. 28They did what your power and will had decided beforehand should happen. 29Now, Lord, consider their threats and enable your servants to speak your word with great boldness. 30Stretch out your hand to heal and perform signs and wonders through the name of your holy servant Jesus."

31After they prayed, the place where they were meeting was shaken. And they were all filled with the Holy Spirit and spoke the word of God boldly.

The Believers Share Their Possessions

32All the believers were one in heart and mind. No one claimed that any of their possessions was their own, but they shared everything they had. 33With great power the apostles continued to testify to the resurrection of the Lord Jesus. And God's grace was so powerfully at work in them all 34that there were no needy persons among them. For from time to time those who owned land or houses sold them, brought the money from the sales 35and put it at the apostles' feet, and it was distributed to anyone who had need.

36Joseph, a Levite from Cyprus, whom the apostles called Barnabas (which means "son of encouragement"), 37sold a field he owned and brought the money and put it at the apostles' feet.

Ananias and Sapphira

5 Now a man named Ananias, together with his wife Sapphira, also sold a piece of property. 2With his wife's full knowledge he kept back part of the money

for himself, but brought the rest and put it at the apostles' feet.

3Then Peter said, "Ananias, how is it that Satan has so filled your heart that you have lied to the Holy Spirit and have kept for yourself some of the money you received for the land? 4Didn't it belong to you before it was sold? And after it was sold, wasn't the money at your disposal? What made you think of doing such a thing? You have not lied just to human beings but to God."

5When Ananias heard this, he fell down and died. And great fear seized all who heard what had happened. 6Then some young men came forward, wrapped up his body, and carried him out and buried him.

7About three hours later his wife came in, not knowing what had happened. 8Peter asked her, "Tell me, is this the price you and Ananias got for the land?"

"Yes," she said, "that is the price."

9Peter said to her, "How could you conspire to test the Spirit of the Lord? Listen! The feet of those who buried your husband are at the door, and they will carry you out also."

10At that moment she fell down at his feet and died. Then the young men came in and, finding her dead, carried her out and buried her beside her husband. 11Great fear seized the whole church and all who heard about these events.

The Apostles Heal Many

12The apostles performed many signs and wonders among the people. And all the believers used to meet together in Solomon's Colonnade. 13No one else dared join them, even though they were highly regarded by the people. 14Nevertheless, more and more men and women believed in the Lord and were added to their number. 15As a result, people brought the sick into the streets and laid them on beds and mats so that at least Peter's shadow might fall on some of them as he passed by. 16Crowds gathered also from the towns around Jerusalem, bringing their sick and those tormented by evil*c* spirits, and all of them were healed.

The Apostles Persecuted

17Then the high priest and all his associates, who were members of the party of the

---

a 26 That is, Messiah or Christ   *b* 26 Psalm 2:1,2   *c* 16 Greek *unclean*

Sadducees, were filled with jealousy. ¹⁸They arrested the apostles and put them in the public jail. ¹⁹But during the night an angel of the Lord opened the doors of the jail and brought them out. ²⁰"Go, stand in the temple courts," he said, "and tell the people all about this new life."

²¹At daybreak they entered the temple courts, as they had been told, and began to teach the people.

When the high priest and his associates arrived, they called together the Sanhedrin—the full assembly of the elders of Israel—and sent to the jail for the apostles. ²²But on arriving at the jail, the officers did not find them there. So they went back and reported, ²³"We found the jail securely locked, with the guards standing at the doors; but when we opened them, we found no one inside." ²⁴On hearing this report, the captain of the temple guard and the chief priests were puzzled, wondering what this might lead to.

²⁵Then someone came and said, "Look! The men you put in jail are standing in the temple courts teaching the people." ²⁶At that, the captain went with his officers and brought the apostles. They did not use force, because they feared that the people would stone them.

²⁷The apostles were brought in and made to appear before the Sanhedrin to be questioned by the high priest. ²⁸"We gave you strict orders not to teach in this name," he said. "Yet you have filled Jerusalem with your teaching and are determined to make us guilty of this man's blood."

²⁹Peter and the other apostles replied: "We must obey God rather than human beings! ³⁰The God of our ancestors raised Jesus from the dead—whom you killed by hanging him on a cross. ³¹God exalted him to his own right hand as Prince and Savior that he might bring Israel to repentance and forgive their sins. ³²We are witnesses of these things, and so is the Holy Spirit, whom God has given to those who obey him."

³³When they heard this, they were furious and wanted to put them to death. ³⁴But a Pharisee named Gamaliel, a teacher of the law, who was honored by all the people, stood up in the Sanhedrin and ordered that the men be put outside for a little while.

³⁵Then he addressed the Sanhedrin: "Men of Israel, consider carefully what you intend to do to these men. ³⁶Some time ago Theudas appeared, claiming to be somebody, and about four hundred men rallied to him. He was killed, all his followers were dispersed, and it all came to nothing. ³⁷After him, Judas the Galilean appeared in the days of the census and led a band of people in revolt. He too was killed, and all his followers were scattered. ³⁸Therefore, in the present case I advise you: Leave these men alone! Let them go! For if their purpose or activity is of human origin, it will fail. ³⁹But if it is from God, you will not be able to stop these men; you will only find yourselves fighting against God."

⁴⁰His speech persuaded them. They called the apostles in and had them flogged. Then they ordered them not to speak in the name of Jesus, and let them go.

⁴¹The apostles left the Sanhedrin, rejoicing because they had been counted worthy of suffering disgrace for the Name. ⁴²Day after day, in the temple courts and from house to house, they never stopped teaching and proclaiming the good news that Jesus is the Messiah.

The Choosing of the Seven

6 In those days when the number of disciples was increasing, the Hellenistic Jews[a] among them complained against the Hebraic Jews because their widows were being overlooked in the daily distribution of food. ²So the Twelve gathered all the disciples together and said, "It would not be right for us to neglect the ministry of the word of God in order to wait on tables. ³Brothers and sisters, choose seven men from among you who are known to be full of the Spirit and wisdom. We will turn this responsibility over to them ⁴and will give our attention to prayer and the ministry of the word."

⁵This proposal pleased the whole group. They chose Stephen, a man full of faith and of the Holy Spirit; also Philip, Procorus, Nicanor, Timon, Parmenas, and Nicolas from Antioch, a convert to Judaism. ⁶They presented them to the apostles, who prayed and laid their hands on them.

⁷So the word of God spread. The number of disciples in Jerusalem increased rapidly,

---

a 1 That is, Jews who had adopted the Greek language and culture and a large number of priests became obedient to the faith.

Stephen Seized

8Now Stephen, a man full of God's grace and power, performed great wonders and signs among the people. 9Opposition arose, however, from members of the Synagogue of the Freedmen (as it was called)—Jews of Cyrene and Alexandria as well as the provinces of Cilicia and Asia—who began to argue with Stephen. 10But they could not stand up against the wisdom the Spirit gave him as he spoke.

11Then they secretly persuaded some men to say, "We have heard Stephen speak blasphemous words against Moses and against God."

12So they stirred up the people and the elders and the teachers of the law. They seized Stephen and brought him before the Sanhedrin. 13They produced false witnesses, who testified, "This fellow never stops speaking against this holy place and against the law. 14For we have heard him say that this Jesus of Nazareth will destroy this place and change the customs Moses handed down to us."

15All who were sitting in the Sanhedrin looked intently at Stephen, and they saw that his face was like the face of an angel.

Stephen's Speech to the Sanhedrin

7 Then the high priest asked Stephen, "Are these charges true?"

2To this he replied: "Brothers and fathers, listen to me! The God of glory appeared to our father Abraham while he was still in Mesopotamia, before he lived in Harran. 3'Leave your country and your people,' God said, 'and go to the land I will show you.'a

4"So he left the land of the Chaldeans and settled in Harran. After the death of his father, God sent him to this land where you are now living. 5He gave him no inheritance here, not even enough ground to set his foot on. But God promised him that he and his descendants after him would possess the land, even though at that time Abraham had no child. 6God spoke to him in this way: 'For four hundred years your descendants will be strangers in a country not their own, and

they will be enslaved and mistreated. 7But I will punish the nation they serve as slaves,' God said, 'and afterward they will come out of that country and worship me in this place.'b 8Then he gave Abraham the covenant of circumcision. And Abraham became the father of Isaac and circumcised him eight days after his birth. Later Isaac became the father of Jacob, and Jacob became the father of the twelve patriarchs.

9"Because the patriarchs were jealous of Joseph, they sold him as a slave into Egypt. But God was with him 10and rescued him from all his troubles. He gave Joseph wisdom and enabled him to gain the goodwill of Pharaoh king of Egypt. So Pharaoh made him ruler over Egypt and all his palace.

11"Then a famine struck all Egypt and Canaan, bringing great suffering, and our people could not find food. 12When Jacob heard that there was grain in Egypt, he sent our ancestors on their first visit. 13On their second visit, Joseph told his brothers who he was, and Pharaoh learned about Joseph's family. 14After this, Joseph sent for his father Jacob and his whole family, seventy-five in all. 15Then Jacob went down to Egypt, where he and our ancestors died. 16Their bodies were brought back to Shechem and placed in the tomb that Abraham had bought from the sons of Hamor at Shechem for a certain sum of money.

17"As the time drew near for God to fulfill his promise to Abraham, the number of our people in Egypt had greatly increased. 18Then 'a new king, to whom Joseph meant nothing, came to power in Egypt.'c 19He dealt treacherously with our people and oppressed our ancestors by forcing them to throw out their newborn babies so that they would die.

20"At that time Moses was born, and he was no ordinary child.d For three months he was cared for in his parents' home. 21When he was placed outside, Pharaoh's daughter took him and brought him up as her own son. 22Moses was educated in all the wisdom of the Egyptians and was powerful in speech and action.

23"When Moses was forty years old, he decided to visit his own people, the Israelites. 24He saw one of them being mistreated by an Egyptian, so he went to his defense

---

a 3 Gen. 12:1   b 7 Gen. 15:13,14   c 18 Exodus 1:8   d 20 Or was fair in the sight of God

FINDING GOD THROUGH THE CHURCH
Acts 7:1–53 or 7:44–53

Brian McLaren

We have to find ways for people to simply encounter Christ and God—without having to figure out two millennia of church history, controversy and dogma. How will we find those ways? This is a major question for our best theologians to wrestle with as we enter Christianity's third millennium. For what it's worth, here is my proposal: We have to re-root doctrine in the Christian story. Instead of presenting our doctrines as abstractions floating out in space, we must show how the various articulations of Christian belief arose in the context of Christianity's spread, its inevitable experience of controversy, and the contrary influences from the various cultures and philosophies, which the gospel encountered and engaged.

PHILIP SCHAFF {AD 1819–1893}

The historian, moreover, must make his work readable and interesting, without violating truth. Some parts of history are dull and wearisome; but, upon the whole, the truth of history is "stranger than fiction." It is God's own epos. It needs no embellishment. It speaks for itself if told with earnestness, vivacity and freshness. Unfortunately, church historians, with very few exceptions, are behind the great secular historians in point of style and represent the past as a dead corpse rather than as a living and working power of abiding interest. Hence church histories are so little read outside of professional circles.

reflection

1. On a scale of one to five, how would you rate your knowledge of church history?
2. How might your faith be encouraged if you had a broader knowledge of church history?
3. What can you do to learn just a little bit more about your Christian heritage?

For your next devotional reading, go to page 1248.

and avenged him by killing the Egyptian. [25] Moses thought that his own people would realize that God was using him to rescue them, but they did not. [26] The next day Moses came upon two Israelites who were fighting. He tried to reconcile them by saying, 'Men, you are brothers; why do you want to hurt each other?'

[27] "But the man who was mistreating the other pushed Moses aside and said, 'Who made you ruler and judge over us? [28] Are you thinking of killing me as you killed the Egyptian yesterday?'[a] [29] When Moses heard this, he fled to Midian, where he settled as a foreigner and had two sons.

[30] "After forty years had passed, an angel appeared to Moses in the flames of a burning bush in the desert near Mount Sinai. [31] When he saw this, he was amazed at the sight. As he went over to get a closer look, he heard the Lord say: [32] 'I am the God of your fathers, the God of Abraham, Isaac and Jacob.'[b] Moses trembled with fear and did not dare to look.

[33] "Then the Lord said to him, 'Take off your sandals, for the place where you are standing is holy ground. [34] I have indeed seen the oppression of my people in Egypt. I have heard their groaning and have come down to set them free. Now come, I will send you back to Egypt.'[c]

[35] "This is the same Moses they had rejected with the words, 'Who made you ruler and judge?' He was sent to be their ruler and deliverer by God himself, through the angel who appeared to him in the bush. [36] He led them out of Egypt and performed wonders and signs in Egypt, at the Red Sea and for forty years in the wilderness.

[37] "This is the Moses who told the Israelites, 'God will send you a prophet like me from your own people.'[d] [38] He was in the assembly in the wilderness, with the angel who spoke to him on Mount Sinai, and with our ancestors; and he received living words to pass on to us.

[39] "But our ancestors refused to obey him. Instead, they rejected him and in their hearts turned back to Egypt. [40] They told Aaron, 'Make us gods who will go before us. As for this fellow Moses who led us out of Egypt—we don't know what has happened

to him!'[e] [41] That was the time they made an idol in the form of a calf. They brought sacrifices to it and reveled in what their own hands had made. [42] But God turned away from them and gave them over to the worship of the sun, moon and stars. This agrees with what is written in the book of the prophets:

" 'Did you bring me sacrifices and
   offerings
      forty years in the wilderness, house of
      Israel?
[43] You have taken up the tabernacle of
   Molek
      and the star of your god Rephan,
      the idols you made to worship.
Therefore I will send you into exile'[f]
      beyond Babylon.

[44] "Our ancestors had the tabernacle of the covenant law with them in the wilderness. It had been made as God directed Moses, according to the pattern he had seen. [45] Having received the tabernacle, our ancestors under Joshua brought it with them when they took the land from the nations God drove out before them. It remained in the land until the time of David, [46] who enjoyed God's favor and asked that he might provide a dwelling place for the God of Jacob.[g] [47] But it was Solomon who built a house for him.

[48] "However, the Most High does not live in houses made by human hands. As the prophet says:

[49] " 'Heaven is my throne,
      and the earth is my footstool.
   What kind of house will you build for
      me?
                        says the Lord.
   Or where will my resting place be?
[50] Has not my hand made all these
      things?'[h]

[51] "You stiff-necked people! Your hearts and ears are still uncircumcised. You are just like your ancestors: You always resist the Holy Spirit! [52] Was there ever a prophet your ancestors did not persecute? They even killed those who predicted the coming of the Righteous One. And now you have betrayed and murdered him— [53] you who have re-

---

a 28 Exodus 2:14   *b 32* Exodus 3:6   *c 34* Exodus 3:5,7,8,10   *d 37* Deut. 18:15   *e 40* Exodus 32:1
f 43 Amos 5:25-27 (see Septuagint)   *g 46* Some early manuscripts *the house of Jacob*
h 50 Isaiah 66:1,2

ceived the law that was given through angels but have not obeyed it."

The Stoning of Stephen

⁵⁴When the members of the Sanhedrin heard this, they were furious and gnashed their teeth at him. ⁵⁵But Stephen, full of the Holy Spirit, looked up to heaven and saw the glory of God, and Jesus standing at the right hand of God. ⁵⁶"Look," he said, "I see heaven open and the Son of Man standing at the right hand of God."

⁵⁷At this they covered their ears and, yelling at the top of their voices, they all rushed at him, ⁵⁸dragged him out of the city and began to stone him. Meanwhile, the witnesses laid their coats at the feet of a young man named Saul.

⁵⁹While they were stoning him, Stephen prayed, "Lord Jesus, receive my spirit." ⁶⁰Then he fell on his knees and cried out, "Lord, do not hold this sin against them." When he had said this, he fell asleep.

8 And Saul approved of their killing him.

The Church Persecuted and Scattered

On that day a great persecution broke out against the church in Jerusalem, and all except the apostles were scattered throughout Judea and Samaria. ²Godly men buried Stephen and mourned deeply for him. ³But Saul began to destroy the church. Going from house to house, he dragged off both men and women and put them in prison.

Philip in Samaria

⁴Those who had been scattered preached the word wherever they went. ⁵Philip went down to a city in Samaria and proclaimed the Messiah there. ⁶When the crowds heard Philip and saw the signs he performed, they all paid close attention to what he said. ⁷With shrieks, evil[a] spirits came out of many, and many who were paralyzed or lame were healed. ⁸So there was great joy in that city.

Simon the Sorcerer

⁹Now for some time a man named Simon had practiced sorcery in the city and amazed all the people of Samaria. He boasted that he was someone great, ¹⁰and all the

people, both high and low, gave him their attention and exclaimed, "This man is rightly called the Great Power of God." ¹¹They followed him because he had amazed them for a long time with his sorcery. ¹²But when they believed Philip as he proclaimed the good news of the kingdom of God and the name of Jesus Christ, they were baptized, both men and women. ¹³Simon himself believed and was baptized. And he followed Philip everywhere, astonished by the great signs and miracles he saw.

¹⁴When the apostles in Jerusalem heard that Samaria had accepted the word of God, they sent Peter and John to Samaria. ¹⁵When they arrived, they prayed for the new believers there that they might receive the Holy Spirit, ¹⁶because the Holy Spirit had not yet come on any of them; they had simply been baptized into[b] the name of the Lord Jesus. ¹⁷Then Peter and John placed their hands on them, and they received the Holy Spirit.

¹⁸When Simon saw that the Spirit was given at the laying on of the apostles' hands, he offered them money ¹⁹and said, "Give me also this ability so that everyone on whom I lay my hands may receive the Holy Spirit."

²⁰Peter answered: "May your money perish with you, because you thought you could buy the gift of God with money! ²¹You have no part or share in this ministry, because your heart is not right before God. ²²Repent of this wickedness and pray to the Lord in the hope that he may forgive you for having such a thought in your heart. ²³For I see that you are full of bitterness and captive to sin."

²⁴Then Simon answered, "Pray to the Lord for me so that nothing you have said may happen to me."

²⁵After they had further proclaimed the word of the Lord and testified about Jesus, Peter and John returned to Jerusalem, preaching the gospel in many Samaritan villages.

Philip and the Ethiopian

²⁶Now an angel of the Lord said to Philip, "Go south to the road—the desert road—that goes down from Jerusalem to Gaza." ²⁷So he started out, and on his way he met an Ethiopian[c] eunuch, an important official in charge of all the treasury of the Kandake (which means "queen of the Ethiopians").

---

a 7 Greek *unclean*   *b* 16 Or *in*   *c* 27 That is, from the southern Nile region

This man had gone to Jerusalem to worship, ²⁸and on his way home was sitting in his chariot reading the Book of Isaiah the prophet. ²⁹The Spirit told Philip, "Go to that chariot and stay near it."

³⁰Then Philip ran up to the chariot and heard the man reading Isaiah the prophet. "Do you understand what you are reading?" Philip asked.

³¹"How can I," he said, "unless someone explains it to me?" So he invited Philip to come up and sit with him.

³²This is the passage of Scripture the eunuch was reading:

"He was led like a sheep to the
        slaughter,
    and as a lamb before its shearer is
        silent,
    so he did not open his mouth.
³³ In his humiliation he was deprived of
        justice.
    Who can speak of his descendants?
    For his life was taken from the
        earth."ᵃ

³⁴The eunuch asked Philip, "Tell me, please, who is the prophet talking about, himself or someone else?" ³⁵Then Philip began with that very passage of Scripture and told him the good news about Jesus.

³⁶[³⁷]As they traveled along the road, they came to some water and the eunuch said, "Look, here is water. What can stand in the way of my being baptized?"ᵇ ³⁸And he gave orders to stop the chariot. Then both Philip and the eunuch went down into the water and Philip baptized him. ³⁹When they came up out of the water, the Spirit of the Lord suddenly took Philip away, and the eunuch did not see him again, but went on his way rejoicing. ⁴⁰Philip, however, appeared at Azotus and traveled about, preaching the gospel in all the towns until he reached Caesarea.

Saul's Conversion

9 Meanwhile, Saul was still breathing out murderous threats against the Lord's disciples. He went to the high priest ²and asked him for letters to the synagogues in Damascus, so that if he found any there who belonged to the Way, wheth-

er men or women, he might take them as prisoners to Jerusalem. ³As he neared Damascus on his journey, suddenly a light from heaven flashed around him. ⁴He fell to the ground and heard a voice say to him, "Saul, Saul, why do you persecute me?"

⁵"Who are you, Lord?" Saul asked.

"I am Jesus, whom you are persecuting," he replied. ⁶"Now get up and go into the city, and you will be told what you must do."

⁷The men traveling with Saul stood there speechless; they heard the sound but did not see anyone. ⁸Saul got up from the ground, but when he opened his eyes he could see nothing. So they led him by the hand into Damascus. ⁹For three days he was blind, and did not eat or drink anything.

¹⁰In Damascus there was a disciple named Ananias. The Lord called to him in a vision, "Ananias!"

"Yes, Lord," he answered.

¹¹The Lord told him, "Go to the house of Judas on Straight Street and ask for a man from Tarsus named Saul, for he is praying. ¹²In a vision he has seen a man named Ananias come and place his hands on him to restore his sight."

¹³"Lord," Ananias answered, "I have heard many reports about this man and all the harm he has done to your people in Jerusalem. ¹⁴And he has come here with authority from the chief priests to arrest all who call on your name."

¹⁵But the Lord said to Ananias, "Go! This man is my chosen instrument to proclaim my name to the Gentiles and their kings and to the people of Israel. ¹⁶I will show him how much he must suffer for my name."

¹⁷Then Ananias went to the house and entered it. Placing his hands on Saul, he said, "Brother Saul, the Lord—Jesus, who appeared to you on the road as you were coming here—has sent me so that you may see again and be filled with the Holy Spirit." ¹⁸Immediately, something like scales fell from Saul's eyes, and he could see again. He got up and was baptized, ¹⁹and after taking some food, he regained his strength.

Saul in Damascus and Jerusalem

Saul spent several days with the disciples in Damascus. ²⁰At once he began to preach

ᵃ 33 Isaiah 53:7,8 (see Septuagint)   ᵇ 36 Some late manuscripts baptized?" ³⁷Philip said, "If you believe with all your heart, you may." The eunuch answered, "I believe that Jesus Christ is the Son of God."

Grab the Moment

Acts 8:34-39

read/meditate

Review this interaction between Philip and the Ethiopian. Read it through more than once. Observe the willingness of both Philip and the Ethiopian and their surrender to the moment at hand. Do you relate more to Philip or to the Ethiopian?

pray

Whomever you relate to, ask God to help you engage these kinds of situations when they come into your life. Ask him to help you recognize people whom you may never see again, yet whom you have something to teach or to learn from. Ask him to prepare you to catch these kinds of moments as they rush by, and then give him some quietness with which to do that.

contemplate

Think about some meaningful moments that you have missed. What were the prime reasons that you let them pass by? Focus? Momentum? On the other hand, what factors in your life have best prepared you to make the most of these moments?

additional reflection

We must not, in trying to think about how we can make a big difference, ignore the small daily differences we can make which, over time, add up to big differences that we often cannot foresee.

—Marian Wright Edelman

I don't know what your destiny will be, but one thing I do know; the only ones among you who will be really happy are those who have sought and found how to serve.

—Albert Schweitzer

For your next devotional reading, go to page 1250.

in the synagogues that Jesus is the Son of God. [21]All those who heard him were astonished and asked, "Isn't he the man who raised havoc in Jerusalem among those who call on this name? And hasn't he come here to take them as prisoners to the chief priests?" [22]Yet Saul grew more and more powerful and baffled the Jews living in Damascus by proving that Jesus is the Messiah.

[23]After many days had gone by, there was a conspiracy among the Jews to kill him, [24]but Saul learned of their plan. Day and night they kept close watch on the city gates in order to kill him. [25]But his followers took him by night and lowered him in a basket through an opening in the wall.

[26]When he came to Jerusalem, he tried to join the disciples, but they were all afraid of him, not believing that he really was a disciple. [27]But Barnabas took him and brought him to the apostles. He told them how Saul on his journey had seen the Lord and that the Lord had spoken to him, and how in Damascus he had preached fearlessly in the name of Jesus. [28]So Saul stayed with them and moved about freely in Jerusalem, speaking boldly in the name of the Lord. [29]He talked and debated with the Hellenistic Jews,[a] but they tried to kill him. [30]When the believers learned of this, they took him down to Caesarea and sent him off to Tarsus.

[31]Then the church throughout Judea, Galilee and Samaria enjoyed a time of peace and was strengthened. Living in the fear of the Lord and encouraged by the Holy Spirit, it increased in numbers.

Aeneas and Dorcas

[32]As Peter traveled about the country, he went to visit the Lord's people who lived in Lydda. [33]There he found a man named Aeneas, who was paralyzed and had been bedridden for eight years. [34]"Aeneas," Peter said to him, "Jesus Christ heals you. Get up and roll up your mat." Immediately Aeneas got up. [35]All those who lived in Lydda and Sharon saw him and turned to the Lord.

[36]In Joppa there was a disciple named Tabitha (in Greek her name is Dorcas); she was always doing good and helping the poor. [37]About that time she became sick and died, and her body was washed and placed

in an upstairs room. [38]Lydda was near Joppa; so when the disciples heard that Peter was in Lydda, they sent two men to him and urged him, "Please come at once!"

[39]Peter went with them, and when he arrived he was taken upstairs to the room. All the widows stood around him, crying and showing him the robes and other clothing that Dorcas had made while she was still with them.

[40]Peter sent them all out of the room; then he got down on his knees and prayed. Turning toward the dead woman, he said, "Tabitha, get up." She opened her eyes, and seeing Peter she sat up. [41]He took her by the hand and helped her to her feet. Then he called for the believers, especially the widows, and presented her to them alive. [42]This became known all over Joppa, and many people believed in the Lord. [43]Peter stayed in Joppa for some time with a tanner named Simon.

Cornelius Calls for Peter

10 At Caesarea there was a man named Cornelius, a centurion in what was known as the Italian Regiment. [2]He and all his family were devout and God-fearing; he gave generously to those in need and prayed to God regularly. [3]One day at about three in the afternoon he had a vision. He distinctly saw an angel of God, who came to him and said, "Cornelius!"

[4]Cornelius stared at him in fear. "What is it, Lord?" he asked.

The angel answered, "Your prayers and gifts to the poor have come up as a memorial offering before God. [5]Now send men to Joppa to bring back a man named Simon who is called Peter. [6]He is staying with Simon the tanner, whose house is by the sea."

[7]When the angel who spoke to him had gone, Cornelius called two of his servants and a devout soldier who was one of his attendants. [8]He told them everything that had happened and sent them to Joppa.

Peter's Vision

[9]About noon the following day as they were on their journey and approaching the city, Peter went up on the roof to pray. [10]He became hungry and wanted something to

a 29 That is, Jews who had adopted the Greek language and culture

MONDAY

COME AS YOU ARE

Acts 9:1–31 *or* 9:1–6

PHILIP SCHAFF {AD 1819–1893}

Peter, Paul, and John . . . were not perfect. Indeed, they themselves acknowledged that there is only one sinless being, their Lord and Master, and they confessed their own shortcomings . . . Each person exhibits the spirit and life of Christ in a distinct way. For the gospel does not destroy the natural talents and temperaments of people, but redeems and sanctifies them. It consecrates the fire of a Peter, the energy of a Paul and the pensiveness of a John to the same service of God. It most strikingly displays its new creating power in the sudden conversion of the apostle Paul from a most dangerous enemy to a most effective friend of the church. The Spirit of God came upon Paul as an overwhelming storm; he came upon John as a gentle, refreshing breeze. But the same new, supernatural, divine principle of life resided in them all.

Billy Graham

One of the Bible's greatest truths is that God is willing to forgive absolutely anyone who truly repents of their sins and commits their life to Jesus Christ as their Lord and Savior.

Do you remember the story of [Paul's] early life? (You can read about it in chapter 9 of the book of Acts.) Paul (or Saul, as he was known then) had no use for Christians and was determined to see them stamped out. To do this, he even got official authority to arrest them and put them in jail, where they could be put on trial for their lives. His hatred for Christ knew no bounds.

But God reached out to Paul, and as he was traveling to Damascus to arrest some of Jesus' followers, Christ met him in a vision and Paul's life was completely changed. God forgave him for all the terrible things he had done. Later, Paul wrote, "I was shown mercy so that in me, the worst of sinners, Christ Jesus might display his [immense] patience" (1 Timothy 1:16).

The only person God can't forgive is the person who refuses His forgiveness. Why turn away from Him? No matter who you are or what you have done, Christ stands ready to forgive you and save you. Open your heart to Him today, because "the Son of Man came to seek and to save what was lost" (Luke 19:10).

reflection

1. Is there something about yourself that you are unable to accept?

2. How much "cleaning up" do you feel you have to do before you can approach God?

3. How good are you at gut-level honesty when communicating with God?

For your next devotional reading, go to page 1255.

eat, and while the meal was being prepared, he fell into a trance. ¹¹He saw heaven opened and something like a large sheet being let down to earth by its four corners. ¹²It contained all kinds of four-footed animals, as well as reptiles and birds. ¹³Then a voice told him, "Get up, Peter. Kill and eat."

¹⁴"Surely not, Lord!" Peter replied. "I have never eaten anything impure or unclean."

¹⁵The voice spoke to him a second time, "Do not call anything impure that God has made clean."

¹⁶This happened three times, and immediately the sheet was taken back to heaven.

¹⁷While Peter was wondering about the meaning of the vision, the men sent by Cornelius found out where Simon's house was and stopped at the gate. ¹⁸They called out, asking if Simon who was known as Peter was staying there.

¹⁹While Peter was still thinking about the vision, the Spirit said to him, "Simon, three*ᵃ* men are looking for you. ²⁰So get up and go downstairs. Do not hesitate to go with them, for I have sent them."

²¹Peter went down and said to the men, "I'm the one you're looking for. Why have you come?"

²²The men replied, "We have come from Cornelius the centurion. He is a righteous and God-fearing man, who is respected by all the Jewish people. A holy angel told him to ask you to come to his house so that he could hear what you have to say." ²³Then Peter invited the men into the house to be his guests.

Peter at Cornelius's House

The next day Peter started out with them, and some of the believers from Joppa went along. ²⁴The following day he arrived in Caesarea. Cornelius was expecting them and had called together his relatives and close friends. ²⁵As Peter entered the house, Cornelius met him and fell at his feet in reverence. ²⁶But Peter made him get up. "Stand up," he said, "I am only human myself."

²⁷While talking with him, Peter went inside and found a large gathering of people. ²⁸He said to them: "You are well aware that it is against our law for a Jew to associate with Gentiles or visit them. But God has shown me that I should not call anyone im-

pure or unclean. ²⁹So when I was sent for, I came without raising any objection. May I ask why you sent for me?"

³⁰Cornelius answered: "Three days ago I was in my house praying at this hour, at three in the afternoon. Suddenly a man in shining clothes stood before me ³¹and said, 'Cornelius, God has heard your prayer and remembered your gifts to the poor. ³²Send to Joppa for Simon who is called Peter. He is a guest in the home of Simon the tanner, who lives by the sea.' ³³So I sent for you immediately, and it was good of you to come. Now we are all here in the presence of God to listen to everything the Lord has commanded you to tell us."

³⁴Then Peter began to speak: "I now realize how true it is that God does not show favoritism ³⁵but accepts those from every nation who fear him and do what is right. ³⁶You know the message God sent to the people of Israel, announcing the good news of peace through Jesus Christ, who is Lord of all. ³⁷You know what has happened throughout the province of Judea, beginning in Galilee after the baptism that John preached— ³⁸how God anointed Jesus of Nazareth with the Holy Spirit and power, and how he went around doing good and healing all who were under the power of the devil, because God was with him.

³⁹"We are witnesses of everything he did in the country of the Jews and in Jerusalem. They killed him by hanging him on a cross, ⁴⁰but God raised him from the dead on the third day and caused him to be seen. ⁴¹He was not seen by all the people, but by witnesses whom God had already chosen—by us who ate and drank with him after he rose from the dead. ⁴²He commanded us to preach to the people and to testify that he is the one whom God appointed as judge of the living and the dead. ⁴³All the prophets testify about him that everyone who believes in him receives forgiveness of sins through his name."

⁴⁴While Peter was still speaking these words, the Holy Spirit came on all who heard the message. ⁴⁵The circumcised believers who had come with Peter were astonished that the gift of the Holy Spirit had been poured out even on Gentiles. ⁴⁶For

ᵃ 19 One early manuscript *two*; other manuscripts do not have the number.

they heard them speaking in tongues[a] and praising God.

Then Peter said, [47]"Surely no one can stand in the way of their being baptized with water. They have received the Holy Spirit just as we have." [48]So he ordered that they be baptized in the name of Jesus Christ. Then they asked Peter to stay with them for a few days.

Peter Explains His Actions

11 The apostles and the believers throughout Judea heard that the Gentiles also had received the word of God. [2]So when Peter went up to Jerusalem, the circumcised believers criticized him [3]and said, "You went into the house of the uncircumcised and ate with them."

[4]Starting from the beginning, Peter told them the whole story: [5]"I was in the city of Joppa praying, and in a trance I saw a vision. I saw something like a large sheet being let down from heaven by its four corners, and it came down to where I was. [6]I looked into it and saw four-footed animals of the earth, wild beasts, reptiles and birds. [7]Then I heard a voice telling me, 'Get up, Peter. Kill and eat.'

[8]"I replied, 'Surely not, Lord! Nothing impure or unclean has ever entered my mouth.'

[9]"The voice spoke from heaven a second time, 'Do not call anything impure that God has made clean.' [10]This happened three times, and then it was all pulled up to heaven again.

[11]"Right then three men who had been sent to me from Caesarea stopped at the house where I was staying. [12]The Spirit told me to have no hesitation about going with them. These six brothers also went with me, and we entered the man's house. [13]He told us how he had seen an angel appear in his house and say, 'Send to Joppa for Simon who is called Peter. [14]He will bring you a message through which you and all your household will be saved.'

[15]"As I began to speak, the Holy Spirit came on them as he had come on us at the beginning. [16]Then I remembered what the Lord had said: 'John baptized with[b] water, but you will be baptized with[b] the Holy Spir-

it.' [17]So if God gave them the same gift he gave us who believed in the Lord Jesus Christ, who was I to think that I could stand in God's way?"

[18]When they heard this, they had no further objections and praised God, saying, "So then, even to Gentiles God has granted repentance that leads to life."

The Church in Antioch

[19]Now those who had been scattered by the persecution that broke out when Stephen was killed traveled as far as Phoenicia, Cyprus and Antioch, spreading the word only among Jews. [20]Some of them, however, men from Cyprus and Cyrene, went to Antioch and began to speak to Greeks also, telling them the good news about the Lord Jesus. [21]The Lord's hand was with them, and a great number of people believed and turned to the Lord.

[22]News of this reached the ears of the church in Jerusalem, and they sent Barnabas to Antioch. [23]When he arrived and saw what the grace of God had done, he was glad and encouraged them all to remain true to the Lord with all their hearts. [24]He was a good man, full of the Holy Spirit and faith, and a great number of people were brought to the Lord.

[25]Then Barnabas went to Tarsus to look for Saul, [26]and when he found him, he brought him to Antioch. So for a whole year Barnabas and Saul met with the church and taught great numbers of people. The disciples were called Christians first at Antioch.

[27]During this time some prophets came down from Jerusalem to Antioch. [28]One of them, named Agabus, stood up and through the Spirit predicted that a severe famine would spread over the entire Roman world. (This happened during the reign of Claudius.) [29]The disciples, as each one was able, decided to provide help for the believers living in Judea. [30]This they did, sending their gift to the elders by Barnabas and Saul.

Peter's Miraculous Escape From Prison

12 It was about this time that King Herod arrested some who belonged to the church, intending to persecute them. [2]He had James, the brother of John, put to death with the sword.

a 46 Or other languages   b 16 Or in

³When he saw that this met with approval among the Jews, he proceeded to seize Peter also. This happened during the Festival of Unleavened Bread. ⁴After arresting him, he put him in prison, handing him over to be guarded by four squads of four soldiers each. Herod intended to bring him out for public trial after the Passover.

⁵So Peter was kept in prison, but the church was earnestly praying to God for him.

⁶The night before Herod was to bring him to trial, Peter was sleeping between two soldiers, bound with two chains, and sentries stood guard at the entrance. ⁷Suddenly an angel of the Lord appeared and a light shone in the cell. He struck Peter on the side and woke him up. "Quick, get up!" he said, and the chains fell off Peter's wrists.

⁸Then the angel said to him, "Put on your clothes and sandals." And Peter did so. "Wrap your cloak around you and follow me," the angel told him. ⁹Peter followed him out of the prison, but he had no idea that what the angel was doing was really happening; he thought he was seeing a vision. ¹⁰They passed the first and second guards and came to the iron gate leading to the city. It opened for them by itself, and they went through it. When they had walked the length of one street, suddenly the angel left him.

¹¹Then Peter came to himself and said, "Now I know without a doubt that the Lord has sent his angel and rescued me from Herod's clutches and from everything the Jewish people were hoping would happen."

¹²When this had dawned on him, he went to the house of Mary the mother of John, also called Mark, where many people had gathered and were praying. ¹³Peter knocked at the outer entrance, and a servant named Rhoda came to answer the door. ¹⁴When she recognized Peter's voice, she was so overjoyed she ran back without opening it and exclaimed, "Peter is at the door!"

¹⁵"You're out of your mind," they told her. When she kept insisting that it was so, they said, "It must be his angel."

¹⁶But Peter kept on knocking, and when they opened the door and saw him, they were astonished. ¹⁷Peter motioned with his hand for them to be quiet and described how the Lord had brought him out of prison.

"Tell James and the other brothers and sisters about this," he said, and then he left for another place.

¹⁸In the morning, there was no small commotion among the soldiers as to what had become of Peter. ¹⁹After Herod had a thorough search made for him and did not find him, he cross-examined the guards and ordered that they be executed.

Herod's Death

Then Herod went from Judea to Caesarea and stayed there. ²⁰He had been quarreling with the people of Tyre and Sidon; they now joined together and sought an audience with him. Having secured the support of Blastus, a trusted personal servant of the king, they asked for peace, because they depended on the king's country for their food supply.

²¹On the appointed day Herod, wearing his royal robes, sat on his throne and delivered a public address to the people. ²²They shouted, "This is the voice of a god, not of a mere mortal." ²³Immediately, because Herod did not give praise to God, an angel of the Lord struck him down, and he was eaten by worms and died.

²⁴But the word of God continued to increase and spread.

Barnabas and Saul Sent Off

²⁵When Barnabas and Saul had finished their mission, they returned from ª Jerusalem, taking with them John, also called Mark. ¹Now in the church at Antioch there were prophets and teachers: Barnabas, Simeon called Niger, Lucius of Cyrene, Manaen (who had been brought up with Herod the tetrarch) and Saul. ²While they were worshiping the Lord and fasting, the Holy Spirit said, "Set apart for me Barnabas and Saul for the work to which I have called them." ³So after they had fasted and prayed, they placed their hands on them and sent them off.

On Cyprus

⁴The two of them, sent on their way by the Holy Spirit, went down to Seleucia and sailed from there to Cyprus. ⁵When they arrived at Salamis, they proclaimed the word

---

ª 25 Some manuscripts *to*

of God in the Jewish synagogues. John was with them as their helper.

⁶They traveled through the whole island until they came to Paphos. There they met a Jewish sorcerer and false prophet named Bar-Jesus, ⁷who was an attendant of the proconsul, Sergius Paulus. The proconsul, an intelligent man, sent for Barnabas and Saul because he wanted to hear the word of God. ⁸But Elymas the sorcerer (for that is what his name means) opposed them and tried to turn the proconsul from the faith. ⁹Then Saul, who was also called Paul, filled with the Holy Spirit, looked straight at Elymas and said, ¹⁰"You are a child of the devil and an enemy of everything that is right! You are full of all kinds of deceit and trickery. Will you never stop perverting the right ways of the Lord? ¹¹Now the hand of the Lord is against you. You are going to be blind for a time, not even able to see the light of the sun."

Immediately mist and darkness came over him, and he groped about, seeking someone to lead him by the hand. ¹²When the proconsul saw what had happened, he believed, for he was amazed at the teaching about the Lord.

In Pisidian Antioch

¹³From Paphos, Paul and his companions sailed to Perga in Pamphylia, where John left them to return to Jerusalem. ¹⁴From Perga they went on to Pisidian Antioch. On the Sabbath they entered the synagogue and sat down. ¹⁵After the reading from the Law and the Prophets, the leaders of the synagogue sent word to them, saying, "Brothers, if you have a word of exhortation for the people, please speak."

¹⁶Standing up, Paul motioned with his hand and said: "People of Israel and you Gentiles who worship God, listen to me! ¹⁷The God of the people of Israel chose our ancestors; he made the people prosper during their stay in Egypt; with mighty power he led them out of that country; ¹⁸for about forty years he endured their conduct[a] in the wilderness; ¹⁹and he overthrew seven nations in Canaan, giving their land to his people as their inheritance. ²⁰All this took about 450 years.

"After this, God gave them judges until the time of Samuel the prophet. ²¹Then the people asked for a king, and he gave them Saul son of Kish, of the tribe of Benjamin, who ruled forty years. ²²After removing Saul, he made David their king. God testified concerning him: 'I have found David son of Jesse, a man after my own heart; he will do everything I want him to do.'

²³"From this man's descendants God has brought to Israel the Savior Jesus, as he promised. ²⁴Before the coming of Jesus, John preached repentance and baptism to all the people of Israel. ²⁵As John was completing his work, he said: 'Who do you suppose I am? I am not the one you are looking for. But there is someone coming after me whose sandals I am not worthy to untie.'

²⁶"Brothers and sisters from the children of Abraham and you God-fearing Gentiles, it is to us that this message of salvation has been sent. ²⁷The people of Jerusalem and their rulers did not recognize Jesus, yet in condemning him they fulfilled the words of the prophets that are read every Sabbath. ²⁸Though they found no proper ground for a death sentence, they asked Pilate to have him executed. ²⁹When they had carried out all that was written about him, they took him down from the cross and laid him in a tomb. ³⁰But God raised him from the dead, ³¹and for many days he was seen by those who had traveled with him from Galilee to Jerusalem. They are now his witnesses to our people.

³²"We tell you the good news: What God promised our ancestors ³³he has fulfilled for us, their children, by raising up Jesus. As it is written in the second Psalm:

" 'You are my son;
    today I have become your father.'[b]

³⁴God raised him from the dead so that he will never be subject to decay. As God has said,

" 'I will give you the holy and sure
    blessings promised to David.'[c]

³⁵So it is also stated elsewhere:

" 'You will not let your holy one see
    decay.'[d]

a 18 Some manuscripts *he cared for them*   b 33 Psalm 2:7   c 34 Isaiah 55:3   d 35 Psalm 16:10 (see Septuagint)

TUESDAY

GENUINE PASSION

Acts 13:26–52 or 13:43–50

David A. Miller

Across the centuries, whenever we find new breath or renewal in the church, we can trace it to this simple truth: God's Word has been spoken in new ways, in the language of the people, in a way that demonstrates its relevance to the contemporary culture. The apostle Paul adapted his words to his surrounding culture so that he could communicate the gospel in a relevant way: "[To the weak I became weak, to win the weak. I have become all things to all people so that by all possible means I might save some. I do all this for the sake of the gospel, that I may share in its blessings]" (1 Corinthians 9:22–23) . . .

For Paul the *message* was sacred, but the *methods* by which it was conveyed were shaped by the culture of those he labored to reach. Paul employed all possible means to win others to faith in Christ. In today's culture Paul might say, "To the baby boomers, I become as a baby boomer; to seniors, I become as a senior; to the rock and rollers, I become as a rock and roller." Paul adapted his message to the language and customs of a culture because he distinguished cultural style from theological content . . . We can employ various aspects of culture to serve God's purpose because "Christ is the transformer of culture."

OSWALD CHAMBERS {AD 1874–1917}

Paul did not say, "I became all things to all [people] that I might show what a wonderful being I am" . . . He said he became all things to all [people] for one purpose only: he might save some. There was no thought about himself in the whole matter.

This attitude of Paul sheds light on the phrase, "passion for souls." A passion for souls may either be a diseased lust or a divine love. Let me give you a specimen of it as a diseased lust: "[Woe to you, teachers of the law and Pharisees, you hypocrites! You travel over land and sea to win a single convert, and then you make that convert twice as much a child of hell as you are]" (Mathew 23:15) . . . By saying this, our Lord showed that the Pharisees' great passion for souls bore the stamp of the devil. If you read Acts 13:43–50, you will find that the proselytes became exactly what Jesus Christ said they would be: twofold more the children of hell than the Jews. They became superstitious and even more fanatical.

reflection

1. Why did so many of the Jews and the devout converts to Judaism reject Paul's message about Jesus?

2. What evidence do you see in this passage of Paul's genuine passion for souls?

3. How did Paul change his methods without changing his message?

For your next devotional reading, go to page 1261.

³⁶"Now when David had served God's purpose in his own generation, he fell asleep; he was buried with his ancestors and his body decayed. ³⁷But the one whom God raised from the dead did not see decay.

³⁸"Therefore, my brothers and sisters, I want you to know that through Jesus the forgiveness of sins is proclaimed to you. ³⁹Through him everyone who believes is set free from every sin, a justification you were not able to obtain under the law of Moses. ⁴⁰Take care that what the prophets have said does not happen to you:

⁴¹" 'Look, you scoffers,
    wonder and perish,
for I am going to do something in your
    days
    that you would never believe,
    even if someone told you.' ᵃ"

⁴²As Paul and Barnabas were leaving the synagogue, the people invited them to speak further about these things on the next Sabbath. ⁴³When the congregation was dismissed, many of the Jews and devout converts to Judaism followed Paul and Barnabas, who talked with them and urged them to continue in the grace of God.

⁴⁴On the next Sabbath almost the whole city gathered to hear the word of the Lord. ⁴⁵When the Jews saw the crowds, they were filled with jealousy. They began to contradict what Paul was saying and heaped abuse on him.

⁴⁶Then Paul and Barnabas answered them boldly: "We had to speak the word of God to you first. Since you reject it and do not consider yourselves worthy of eternal life, we now turn to the Gentiles. ⁴⁷For this is what the Lord has commanded us:

" 'I have made you ᵇ a light for the
    Gentiles,
that you ᵇ may bring salvation to the
    ends of the earth.' ᶜ"

⁴⁸When the Gentiles heard this, they were glad and honored the word of the Lord; and all who were appointed for eternal life believed.

⁴⁹The word of the Lord spread through the whole region. ⁵⁰But the Jewish leaders incited the God-fearing women of high standing and the leading men of the city. They stirred up persecution against Paul and Barnabas, and expelled them from their region. ⁵¹So they shook the dust off their feet as a warning to them and went to Iconium. ⁵²And the disciples were filled with joy and with the Holy Spirit.

In Iconium

14 At Iconium Paul and Barnabas went as usual into the Jewish synagogue. There they spoke so effectively that a great number of Jews and Greeks believed. ²But the Jews who refused to believe stirred up the other Gentiles and poisoned their minds against the brothers. ³So Paul and Barnabas spent considerable time there, speaking boldly for the Lord, who confirmed the message of his grace by enabling them to perform signs and wonders. ⁴The people of the city were divided; some sided with the Jews, others with the apostles. ⁵There was a plot afoot among both Gentiles and Jews, together with their leaders, to mistreat them and stone them. ⁶But they found out about it and fled to the Lycaonian cities of Lystra and Derbe and to the surrounding country, ⁷where they continued to preach the gospel.

In Lystra and Derbe

⁸In Lystra there sat a man who was lame. He had been that way from birth and had never walked. ⁹He listened to Paul as he was speaking. Paul looked directly at him, saw that he had faith to be healed ¹⁰and called out, "Stand up on your feet!" At that, the man jumped up and began to walk.

¹¹When the crowd saw what Paul had done, they shouted in the Lycaonian language, "The gods have come down to us in human form!" ¹²Barnabas they called Zeus, and Paul they called Hermes because he was the chief speaker. ¹³The priest of Zeus, whose temple was just outside the city, brought bulls and wreaths to the city gates because he and the crowd wanted to offer sacrifices to them.

¹⁴But when the apostles Barnabas and Paul heard of this, they tore their clothes and rushed out into the crowd, shouting: ¹⁵"Friends, why are you doing this? We too are only human, like you. We are bringing you good news, telling you to turn from

---

ᵃ 41 Hab. 1:5   ᵇ 47 The Greek is singular.   ᶜ 47 Isaiah 49:6

these worthless things to the living God, who made heaven and earth and sea and everything in them. ¹⁶In the past, he let all nations go their own way. ¹⁷Yet he has not left himself without testimony: He has shown kindness by giving you rain from heaven and crops in their seasons; he provides you with plenty of food and fills your hearts with joy." ¹⁸Even with these words, they had difficulty keeping the crowd from sacrificing to them.

¹⁹Then some Jews came from Antioch and Iconium and won the crowd over. They stoned Paul and dragged him outside the city, thinking he was dead. ²⁰But after the disciples had gathered around him, he got up and went back into the city. The next day he and Barnabas left for Derbe.

The Return to Antioch in Syria

²¹They preached the gospel in that city and won a large number of disciples. Then they returned to Lystra, Iconium and Antioch, ²²strengthening the disciples and encouraging them to remain true to the faith. "We must go through many hardships to enter the kingdom of God," they said. ²³Paul and Barnabas appointed elders*a* for them in each church and, with prayer and fasting, committed them to the Lord, in whom they had put their trust. ²⁴After going through Pisidia, they came into Pamphylia, ²⁵and when they had preached the word in Perga, they went down to Attalia.

²⁶From Attalia they sailed back to Antioch, where they had been committed to the grace of God for the work they had now completed. ²⁷On arriving there, they gathered the church together and reported all that God had done through them and how he had opened a door of faith to the Gentiles. ²⁸And they stayed there a long time with the disciples.

The Council at Jerusalem

15 Certain individuals came down from Judea to Antioch and were teaching the believers: "Unless you are circumcised, according to the custom taught by Moses, you cannot be saved." ²This brought Paul and Barnabas into sharp dispute and debate with them. So Paul and Barnabas were appointed, along with some other believers, to go up to Jerusalem to see the apostles and elders about this question. ³The church sent them on their way, and as they traveled through Phoenicia and Samaria, they told how the Gentiles had been converted. This news made all the believers very glad. ⁴When they came to Jerusalem, they were welcomed by the church and the apostles and elders, to whom they reported everything God had done through them.

⁵Then some of the believers who belonged to the party of the Pharisees stood up and said, "The Gentiles must be circumcised and required to keep the law of Moses."

⁶The apostles and elders met to consider this question. ⁷After much discussion, Peter got up and addressed them: "Brothers, you know that some time ago God made a choice among you that the Gentiles might hear from my lips the message of the gospel and believe. ⁸God, who knows the heart, showed that he accepted them by giving the Holy Spirit to them, just as he did to us. ⁹He did not discriminate between us and them, for he purified their hearts by faith. ¹⁰Now then, why do you try to test God by putting on the necks of Gentiles a yoke that neither we nor our ancestors have been able to bear? ¹¹No! We believe it is through the grace of our Lord Jesus that we are saved, just as they are."

¹²The whole assembly became silent as they listened to Barnabas and Paul telling about the signs and wonders God had done among the Gentiles through them. ¹³When they finished, James spoke up. "Brothers," he said, "listen to me. ¹⁴Simon*b* has described to us how God first intervened to choose a people for his name from the Gentiles. ¹⁵The words of the prophets are in agreement with this, as it is written:

¹⁶" 'After this I will return
    and rebuild David's fallen tent.
Its ruins I will rebuild,
    and I will restore it,
¹⁷that the rest of humanity may seek the
    Lord,
    even all the Gentiles who bear my
    name,
says the Lord, who does these things'*c*—
¹⁸   things known from long ago.*d*

---

a 23 Or *Barnabas ordained elders*; or *Barnabas had elders elected*   *b 14* Greek *Simeon*, a variant of *Simon*; that is, Peter   *c 17* Amos 9:11,12 (see Septuagint)   *d 17,18* Some manuscripts *things'—* / *¹⁸the Lord's work is known to him from long ago*

[19]"It is my judgment, therefore, that we should not make it difficult for the Gentiles who are turning to God. [20]Instead we should write to them, telling them to abstain from food polluted by idols, from sexual immorality, from the meat of strangled animals and from blood. [21]For the law of Moses has been preached in every city from the earliest times and is read in the synagogues on every Sabbath."

The Council's Letter to Gentile Believers

[22]Then the apostles and elders, with the whole church, decided to choose some of their own men and send them to Antioch with Paul and Barnabas. They chose Judas (called Barsabbas) and Silas, who were leaders among the believers. [23]With them they sent the following letter:

The apostles and elders, your brothers,

To the Gentile believers in Antioch, Syria and Cilicia:

Greetings.

[24]We have heard that some went out from us without our authorization and disturbed you, troubling your minds by what they said. [25]So we all agreed to choose some men and send them to you with our dear friends Barnabas and Paul— [26]men who have risked their lives for the name of our Lord Jesus Christ. [27]Therefore we are sending Judas and Silas to confirm by word of mouth what we are writing. [28]It seemed good to the Holy Spirit and to us not to burden you with anything beyond the following requirements: [29]You are to abstain from food sacrificed to idols, from blood, from the meat of strangled animals and from sexual immorality. You will do well to avoid these things.

Farewell.

[30]So they were sent off and went down to Antioch, where they gathered the church together and delivered the letter. [31]The people read it and were glad for its encouraging message. [32]Judas and Silas, who themselves were prophets, said much to encourage and strengthen the believers. [33][34]After spending some time there, they were sent off by the believers with the blessing of peace to return to those who had sent them. [35]But Paul and Barnabas remained in Antioch, where they and many others taught and preached the word of the Lord.

Disagreement Between Paul and Barnabas

[36]Some time later Paul said to Barnabas, "Let us go back and visit the believers in all the towns where we preached the word of the Lord and see how they are doing. [37]Barnabas wanted to take John, also called Mark, with them, [38]but Paul did not think it wise to take him, because he had deserted them in Pamphylia and had not continued with them in the work. [39]They had such a sharp disagreement that they parted company. Barnabas took Mark and sailed for Cyprus, [40]but Paul chose Silas and left, commended by the believers to the grace of the Lord. [41]He went through Syria and Cilicia, strengthening the churches.

Timothy Joins Paul and Silas

16 Paul came to Derbe and then to Lystra, where a disciple named Timothy lived, whose mother was Jewish and a believer but whose father was a Greek. [2]The believers at Lystra and Iconium spoke well of him. [3]Paul wanted to take him along on the journey, so he circumcised him because of the Jews who lived in that area, for they all knew that his father was a Greek. [4]As they traveled from town to town, they delivered the decisions reached by the apostles and elders in Jerusalem for the people to obey. [5]So the churches were strengthened in the faith and grew daily in numbers.

Paul's Vision of the Man of Macedonia

[6]Paul and his companions traveled throughout the region of Phrygia and Galatia, having been kept by the Holy Spirit from preaching the word in the province of Asia. [7]When they came to the border of Mysia, they tried to enter Bithynia, but the Spirit of Jesus would not allow them to. [8]So they passed by Mysia and went down to Troas. [9]During the night Paul had a vision of a man of Macedonia standing and begging him, "Come over to Macedonia and help us." [10]After Paul had seen the vision, we got ready at once to leave for Macedonia, con-

cluding that God had called us to preach the gospel to them.

Lydia's Conversion in Philippi

[11]From Troas we put out to sea and sailed straight for Samothrace, and the next day we went on to Neapolis. [12]From there we traveled to Philippi, a Roman colony and the leading city of that district[a] of Macedonia. And we stayed there several days.

[13]On the Sabbath we went outside the city gate to the river, where we expected to find a place of prayer. We sat down and began to speak to the women who had gathered there. [14]One of those listening was a woman from the city of Thyatira named Lydia, a dealer in purple cloth. She was a worshiper of God. The Lord opened her heart to respond to Paul's message. [15]When she and the members of her household were baptized, she invited us to her home. "If you consider me a believer in the Lord," she said, "come and stay at my house." And she persuaded us.

Paul and Silas in Prison

[16]Once when we were going to the place of prayer, we were met by a female slave who had a spirit by which she predicted the future. She earned a great deal of money for her owners by fortune-telling. [17]She followed Paul and the rest of us, shouting, "These men are servants of the Most High God, who are telling you the way to be saved." [18]She kept this up for many days. Finally Paul became so annoyed that he turned around and said to the spirit, "In the name of Jesus Christ I command you to come out of her!" At that moment the spirit left her.

[19]When her owners realized that their hope of making money was gone, they seized Paul and Silas and dragged them into the marketplace to face the authorities. [20]They brought them before the magistrates and said, "These men are Jews, and are throwing our city into an uproar [21]by advocating customs unlawful for us Romans to accept or practice."

[22]The crowd joined in the attack against Paul and Silas, and the magistrates ordered them to be stripped and beaten with rods. [23]After they had been severely flogged, they were thrown into prison, and the jailer was commanded to guard them carefully. [24]When he received these orders, he put them in the inner cell and fastened their feet in the stocks.

[25]About midnight Paul and Silas were praying and singing hymns to God, and the other prisoners were listening to them. [26]Suddenly there was such a violent earthquake that the foundations of the prison were shaken. At once all the prison doors flew open, and everyone's chains came loose. [27]The jailer woke up, and when he saw the prison doors open, he drew his sword and was about to kill himself because he thought the prisoners had escaped. [28]But Paul shouted, "Don't harm yourself! We are all here!"

[29]The jailer called for lights, rushed in and fell trembling before Paul and Silas. [30]He then brought them out and asked, "Sirs, what must I do to be saved?"

[31]They replied, "Believe in the Lord Jesus, and you will be saved—you and your household." [32]Then they spoke the word of the Lord to him and to all the others in his house. [33]At that hour of the night the jailer took them and washed their wounds; then immediately he and all his household were baptized. [34]The jailer brought them into his house and set a meal before them; he was filled with joy because he had come to believe in God—he and his whole household.

[35]When it was daylight, the magistrates sent their officers to the jailer with the order: "Release those men." [36]The jailer told Paul, "The magistrates have ordered that you and Silas be released. Now you can leave. Go in peace."

[37]But Paul said to the officers: "They beat us publicly without a trial, even though we are Roman citizens, and threw us into prison. And now do they want to get rid of us quietly? No! Let them come themselves and escort us out."

[38]The officers reported this to the magistrates, and when they heard that Paul and Silas were Roman citizens, they were alarmed. [39]They came to appease them and escorted them from the prison, requesting them to leave the city. [40]After Paul and Silas came out of the prison, they went to Lydia's

---

a 12 The text and meaning of the Greek for *the leading city of that district* are uncertain.

house, where they met with the believers and encouraged them. Then they left.

In Thessalonica

17 When Paul and his companions had passed through Amphipolis and Apollonia, they came to Thessalonica, where there was a Jewish synagogue. ²As was his custom, Paul went into the synagogue, and on three Sabbath days he reasoned with them from the Scriptures, ³explaining and proving that the Messiah had to suffer and rise from the dead. "This Jesus I am proclaiming to you is the Messiah," he said. ⁴Some of the Jews were persuaded and joined Paul and Silas, as did a large number of God-fearing Greeks and not a few prominent women.

⁵But other Jews were jealous; so they rounded up some bad characters from the marketplace, formed a mob and started a riot in the city. They rushed to Jason's house in search of Paul and Silas in order to bring them out to the crowd. *a* ⁶But when they did not find them, they dragged Jason and some other believers before the city officials, shouting: "These men who have caused trouble all over the world have now come here, ⁷and Jason has welcomed them into his house. They are all defying Caesar's decrees, saying that there is another king, one called Jesus." ⁸When they heard this, the crowd and the city officials were thrown into turmoil. ⁹Then they made Jason and the others post bond and let them go.

In Berea

¹⁰As soon as it was night, the believers sent Paul and Silas away to Berea. On arriving there, they went to the Jewish synagogue. ¹¹Now the Berean Jews were of more noble character than those in Thessalonica, for they received the message with great eagerness and examined the Scriptures every day to see if what Paul said was true. ¹²Many of them believed, as did also a number of prominent Greek women and many Greek men.

¹³But when the Jews in Thessalonica learned that Paul was preaching the word of God at Berea, some of them went there too, agitating the crowds and stirring them up. ¹⁴The believers immediately sent Paul to the coast, but Silas and Timothy stayed at Berea. ¹⁵Those who escorted Paul brought him to Athens and then left with instructions for Silas and Timothy to join him as soon as possible.

In Athens

¹⁶While Paul was waiting for them in Athens, he was greatly distressed to see that the city was full of idols. ¹⁷So he reasoned in the synagogue with both Jews and God-fearing Greeks, as well as in the marketplace day by day with those who happened to be there. ¹⁸A group of Epicurean and Stoic philosophers began to debate with him. Some of them asked, "What is this babbler trying to say?" Others remarked, "He seems to be advocating foreign gods." They said this because Paul was preaching the good news about Jesus and the resurrection. ¹⁹Then they took him and brought him to a meeting of the Areopagus, where they said to him, "May we know what this new teaching is that you are presenting? ²⁰You are bringing some strange ideas to our ears, and we would like to know what they mean." ²¹(All the Athenians and the foreigners who lived there spent their time doing nothing but talking about and listening to the latest ideas.)

²²Paul then stood up in the meeting of the Areopagus and said: "People of Athens! I see that in every way you are very religious. ²³For as I walked around and looked carefully at your objects of worship, I even found an altar with this inscription: TO AN UNKNOWN GOD. So you are ignorant of the very thing you worship—and this is what I am going to proclaim to you.

²⁴"The God who made the world and everything in it is the Lord of heaven and earth and does not live in temples built by hands. ²⁵And he is not served by human hands, as if he needed anything. Rather, he himself gives everyone life and breath and everything else. ²⁶From one man he made all the nations, that they should inhabit the whole earth; and he marked out their appointed times in history and the boundaries of their lands. ²⁷God did this so that they would seek him and perhaps reach out for him and find him, though he is not far from any one of us. ²⁸'For in him we live and move and have our

a 5 Or the assembly of the people

WEDNESDAY

FACING YOUR FAULTS

Acts 17:1–34 *or* 17:29–34

Philip Yancey

Whenever I find such dissonance between a requirement set forth by Jesus and my own natural resistance, I try to explore why. What keeps me from following Jesus' clear command? I can identify two main forces that tug mightily against a call to repentance.

First, when I mess up, I like to work my way out of it. Most religions have elaborate techniques for penitents to demonstrate their remorse. If you sit in a sweat lodge, embark on a pilgrimage, crawl on your knees or sacrifice an animal, you can walk away with a feeling of self-satisfaction. You did something that somehow balances out the sin. You paid for it.

Christianity has at its core a most unnatural concept called grace, which means that we can do nothing to counterbalance our sins. God has already paid the penalty, and we need merely accept it, by trusting him for the remedy. Grace is God's free gift, with repentance the way to access it.

The second barrier to repentance is that I like to look good in front of other people. I want to appear respectable and in control, a veneer that repentance slices through. It requires me to openly acknowledge failure and weaknesses that I normally seek to keep hidden.

SAINT AUGUSTINE {AD 354–430}

I wish now to remember my past wickedness and the carnal corruptions of my soul—not because I still love them, but so that I may love you, my God. I do this because I love your love. Through the bitter self-examination of my wicked ways, you grow sweet to me. Your sweetness is dependable, true and right. When I turned away from you and lost myself among those who don't follow you, I was torn to pieces; you gathered me up out of those fragments.

reflection

1. What is true repentance?
2. Do you find it hard to honestly face your sin and acknowledge it?
3. When are you slow to repent? Why?

For your next devotional reading, go to page 1264.

being.'ᵃ As some of your own poets have said, 'We are his offspring.'ᵇ

²⁹"Therefore since we are God's offspring, we should not think that the divine being is like gold or silver or stone—an image made by human design and skill. ³⁰In the past God overlooked such ignorance, but now he commands all people everywhere to repent. ³¹For he has set a day when he will judge the world with justice by the man he has appointed. He has given proof of this to everyone by raising him from the dead."

³²When they heard about the resurrection of the dead, some of them sneered, but others said, "We want to hear you again on this subject." ³³At that, Paul left the Council. ³⁴Some of the people became followers of Paul and believed. Among them was Dionysius, a member of the Areopagus, also a woman named Damaris, and a number of others.

In Corinth

18 After this, Paul left Athens and went to Corinth. ²There he met a Jew named Aquila, a native of Pontus, who had recently come from Italy with his wife Priscilla, because Claudius had ordered all Jews to leave Rome. Paul went to see them, ³and because he was a tentmaker as they were, he stayed and worked with them. ⁴Every Sabbath he reasoned in the synagogue, trying to persuade Jews and Greeks.

⁵When Silas and Timothy came from Macedonia, Paul devoted himself exclusively to preaching, testifying to the Jews that Jesus was the Messiah. ⁶But when they opposed Paul and became abusive, he shook out his clothes in protest and said to them, "Your blood be on your own heads! I am innocent of it. From now on I will go to the Gentiles."

⁷Then Paul left the synagogue and went next door to the house of Titius Justus, a worshiper of God. ⁸Crispus, the synagogue leader, and his entire household believed in the Lord; and many of the Corinthians who heard Paul believed and were baptized.

⁹One night the Lord spoke to Paul in a vision: "Do not be afraid; keep on speaking, do not be silent. ¹⁰For I am with you, and no one is going to attack and harm you, because I have many people in this city." ¹¹So Paul stayed in Corinth for a year and a half, teaching them the word of God.

¹²While Gallio was proconsul of Achaia, the Jews of Corinth made a united attack on Paul and brought him to the place of judgment. ¹³"This man," they charged, "is persuading the people to worship God in ways contrary to the law."

¹⁴Just as Paul was about to speak, Gallio said to them, "If you Jews were making a complaint about some misdemeanor or serious crime, it would be reasonable for me to listen to you. ¹⁵But since it involves questions about words and names and your own law—settle the matter yourselves. I will not be a judge of such things." ¹⁶So he drove them off. ¹⁷Then the crowd there turned on Sosthenes the synagogue leader and beat him in front of the proconsul; and Gallio showed no concern whatever.

Priscilla, Aquila and Apollos

¹⁸Paul stayed on in Corinth for some time. Then he left the believers and sailed for Syria, accompanied by Priscilla and Aquila. Before he sailed, he had his hair cut off at Cenchreae because of a vow he had taken. ¹⁹They arrived at Ephesus, where Paul left Priscilla and Aquila. He himself went into the synagogue and reasoned with the Jews. ²⁰When they asked him to spend more time with them, he declined. ²¹But as he left, he promised, "I will come back if it is God's will." Then he set sail from Ephesus. ²²When he landed at Caesarea, he went up to Jerusalem and greeted the church and then went down to Antioch.

²³After spending some time in Antioch, Paul set out from there and traveled from place to place throughout the region of Galatia and Phrygia, strengthening all the disciples.

²⁴Meanwhile a Jew named Apollos, a native of Alexandria, came to Ephesus. He was a learned man, with a thorough knowledge of the Scriptures. ²⁵He had been instructed in the way of the Lord, and he spoke with great fervorᶜ and taught about Jesus accurately, though he knew only the baptism of John. ²⁶He began to speak boldly in the synagogue.

ᵃ 28 From the Cretan philosopher Epimenides   ᵇ 28 From the Cilician Stoic philosopher Aratus
ᶜ 25 Or *with fervor in the Spirit*

When Priscilla and Aquila heard him, they invited him to their home and explained to him the way of God more adequately.

27When Apollos wanted to go to Achaia, the believers encouraged him and wrote to the disciples there to welcome him. When he arrived, he was a great help to those who by grace had believed. 28For he vigorously refuted the Jews in public debate, proving from the Scriptures that Jesus was the Messiah.

Paul in Ephesus

19 While Apollos was at Corinth, Paul took the road through the interior and arrived at Ephesus. There he found some disciples 2and asked them, "Did you receive the Holy Spirit when*a* you believed?"

They answered, "No, we have not even heard that there is a Holy Spirit."

3So Paul asked, "Then what baptism did you receive?"

"John's baptism," they replied.

4Paul said, "John's baptism was a baptism of repentance. He told the people to believe in the one coming after him, that is, in Jesus." 5On hearing this, they were baptized into*b* the name of the Lord Jesus. 6When Paul placed his hands on them, the Holy Spirit came on them, and they spoke in tongues*c* and prophesied. 7There were about twelve men in all.

8Paul entered the synagogue and spoke boldly there for three months, arguing persuasively about the kingdom of God. 9But some of them became obstinate; they refused to believe and publicly maligned the Way. So Paul left them. He took the disciples with him and had discussions daily in the lecture hall of Tyrannus. 10This went on for two years, so that all the Jews and Greeks who lived in the province of Asia heard the word of the Lord.

11God did extraordinary miracles through Paul, 12so that even handkerchiefs and aprons that had touched him were taken to the sick, and their illnesses were cured and the evil spirits left them.

13Some Jews who went around driving out evil spirits tried to invoke the name of the Lord Jesus over those who were demon-possessed. They would say, "In the name of the Jesus whom Paul preaches, I command you to come out." 14Seven sons of Sceva, a Jewish chief priest, were doing this. 15One day the evil spirit answered them, "Jesus I know, and I know about Paul, but who are you?" 16Then the man who had the evil spirit jumped on them and overpowered them all. He gave them such a beating that they ran out of the house naked and bleeding.

17When this became known to the Jews and Greeks living in Ephesus, they were all seized with fear, and the name of the Lord Jesus was held in high honor. 18Many of those who believed now came and openly confessed what they had done. 19A number who had practiced sorcery brought their scrolls together and burned them publicly. When they calculated the value of the scrolls, the total came to fifty thousand drachmas.*d* 20In this way the word of the Lord spread widely and grew in power.

21After all this had happened, Paul decided*e* to go to Jerusalem, passing through Macedonia and Achaia. "After I have been there," he said, "I must visit Rome also." 22He sent two of his helpers, Timothy and Erastus, to Macedonia, while he stayed in the province of Asia a little longer.

The Riot in Ephesus

23About that time there arose a great disturbance about the Way. 24A silversmith named Demetrius, who made silver shrines of Artemis, brought in no little business for the skilled workers there. 25He called them together, along with the workers in related trades, and said: "You know, my friends, that we receive a good income from this business. 26And you see and hear how this fellow Paul has convinced and led astray large numbers of people here in Ephesus and in practically the whole province of Asia. He says that gods made by human hands are no gods at all. 27There is danger not only that our trade will lose its good name, but also that the temple of the great goddess Artemis will be discredited; and the goddess herself, who is worshiped throughout the province of Asia and the world, will be robbed of her divine majesty."

28When they heard this, they were furious and began shouting: "Great is Artemis of the

THURSDAY

PLANNING FOR EVANGELISM

Acts 19:1–22 *or* 19:8–10

Tony and Lois Evans

The crown of joy is the reward to be given for faithful evangelism. Jesus Christ will give a higher level of joy to those people who spent their time and energy winning others to Him.

If evangelism has not been a part of your Christian walk, you can change that right away—and your own life will never be the same. For one thing, you'll experience a joy you never thought possible. If you're not regularly sharing your faith, you haven't tasted the joy God intended for you. Jesus said a party breaks out in heaven every time a sinner comes to Him.

For most of us, effective evangelism doesn't just happen. It has to be a planned part of our lives. A man we know joined the local Rotary Club a few years ago for the express purpose of being around nonbelievers, so he could talk to them about his faith in Jesus.

What decision have you made to place yourself next to non-Christians so you can win them to Christ? Don't just invite your friends to church so the pastor can evangelize them. Win them to Christ yourself, add them to your crown of rejoicing, and then bring them to church to be trained and discipled in the faith.

SAINT HILARY OF POITIERS {ca. AD 315–367}

The chief service I owe you, God, is that every thought and word of mine should speak of you. The power of speech which you have bestowed on me can give me no greater pleasure than to serve you by preaching your gospel.

But in saying this, I am merely expressing what I want to do. If I am actually to use this gift, I must ask you for your help—ask you to fill the sails I have hoisted for you with the wind of your Holy Spirit, inspiring my mind and my voice. I know that I am often heavy with stupor, so that I am too lazy to speak of you. And I do not spend sufficient time studying your Scriptures, to ensure that my words conform to your Word. Give me the energy and the courage to share the spirit of the apostles, that like them I may truly be an ambassador of your grace.

reflection

1. What made Paul such an effective ambassador of God's grace?
2. When was the last time you experienced the joy of sharing your faith with someone who doesn't know Jesus?
3. How much effort do you invest in making evangelism a planned part of your life?

For your next devotional reading, go to page 1273

Ephesians!" 29Soon the whole city was in an uproar. The people seized Gaius and Aristarchus, Paul's traveling companions from Macedonia, and all of them rushed together into the theater. 30Paul wanted to appear before the crowd, but the disciples would not let him. 31Even some of the officials of the province, friends of Paul, sent him a message begging him not to venture into the theater.

32The assembly was in confusion: Some were shouting one thing, some another. Most of the people did not even know why they were there. 33The Jews in the crowd pushed Alexander to the front, and they shouted instructions to him. He motioned for silence in order to make a defense before the people. 34But when they realized he was a Jew, they all shouted in unison for about two hours: "Great is Artemis of the Ephesians!"

35The city clerk quieted the crowd and said: "People of Ephesus, doesn't all the world know that the city of Ephesus is the guardian of the temple of the great Artemis and of her image, which fell from heaven? 36Therefore, since these facts are undeniable, you ought to calm down and not do anything rash. 37You have brought these men here, though they have neither robbed temples nor blasphemed our goddess. 38If, then, Demetrius and his associates have a grievance against anybody, the courts are open and there are proconsuls. They can press charges. 39If there is anything further you want to bring up, it must be settled in a legal assembly. 40As it is, we are in danger of being charged with rioting because of what happened today. In that case we would not be able to account for this commotion, since there is no reason for it." 41After he had said this, he dismissed the assembly.

Through Macedonia and Greece

20 When the uproar had ended, Paul sent for the disciples and, after encouraging them, said good-by and set out for Macedonia. 2He traveled through that area, speaking many words of encouragement to the people, and finally arrived in Greece, 3where he stayed three months. Because some Jews had plotted against him just as he was about to sail for Syria, he decided to go back through Macedonia. 4He was accompanied by Sopater son of Pyrrhus from Berea, Aristarchus

and Secundus from Thessalonica, Gaius from Derbe, Timothy also, and Tychicus and Trophimus from the province of Asia. 5These men went on ahead and waited for us at Troas. 6But we sailed from Philippi after the Festival of Unleavened Bread, and five days later joined the others at Troas, where we stayed seven days.

Eutychus Raised From the Dead at Troas

7On the first day of the week we came together to break bread. Paul spoke to the people and, because he intended to leave the next day, kept on talking until midnight. 8There were many lamps in the upstairs room where we were meeting. 9Seated in a window was a young man named Eutychus, who was sinking into a deep sleep as Paul talked on and on. When he was sound asleep, he fell to the ground from the third story and was picked up dead. 10Paul went down, threw himself on the young man and put his arms around him. "Don't be alarmed," he said. "He's alive!" 11Then he went upstairs again and broke bread and ate. After talking until daylight, he left. 12The people took the young man home alive and were greatly comforted.

Paul's Farewell to the Ephesian Elders

13We went on ahead to the ship and sailed for Assos, where we were going to take Paul aboard. He had made this arrangement because he was going there on foot. 14When he met us at Assos, we took him aboard and went on to Mitylene. 15The next day we set sail from there and arrived off Chios. The day after that we crossed over to Samos, and on the following day arrived at Miletus. 16Paul had decided to sail past Ephesus to avoid spending time in the province of Asia, for he was in a hurry to reach Jerusalem, if possible, by the day of Pentecost.

17From Miletus, Paul sent to Ephesus for the elders of the church. 18When they arrived, he said to them: "You know how I lived the whole time I was with you, from the first day I came into the province of Asia. 19I served the Lord with great humility and with tears and in the midst of severe testing by the plots of the Jews. 20You know that I have not hesitated to preach anything that would be helpful to you but have taught you publicly and from house to house. 21I have declared to both Jews and Greeks that they must turn to God in repentance and have faith in our Lord Jesus.

22"And now, compelled by the Spirit, I am going to Jerusalem, not knowing what will happen to me there. 23I only know that in every city the Holy Spirit warns me that prison and hardships are facing me. 24However, I consider my life worth nothing to me; my only aim is to finish the race and complete the task the Lord Jesus has given me—the task of testifying to the good news of God's grace.

25"Now I know that none of you among whom I have gone about preaching the kingdom will ever see me again. 26Therefore, I declare to you today that I am innocent of the blood of everyone. 27For I have not hesitated to proclaim to you the whole will of God. 28Keep watch over yourselves and all the flock of which the Holy Spirit has made you overseers. Be shepherds of the church of God,ᵃ which he bought with his own blood. 29I know that after I leave, savage wolves will come in among you and will not spare the flock. 30Even from your own number some will arise and distort the truth in order to draw away disciples after them. 31So be on your guard! Remember that for three years I never stopped warning each of you night and day with tears.

32"Now I commit you to God and to the word of his grace, which can build you up and give you an inheritance among all those who are sanctified. 33I have not coveted anyone's silver or gold or clothing. 34You yourselves know that these hands of mine have supplied my own needs and the needs of my companions. 35In everything I did, I showed you that by this kind of hard work we must help the weak, remembering the words the Lord Jesus himself said: 'It is more blessed to give than to receive.' "

36When Paul had finished speaking, he knelt down with all of them and prayed. 37They all wept as they embraced him and kissed him. 38What grieved them most was his statement that they would never see his face again. Then they accompanied him to the ship.

On to Jerusalem

21 After we had torn ourselves away from them, we put out to sea and sailed straight to Kos.

The next day we went to Rhodes and from there to Patara. 2We found a ship crossing over to Phoenicia, went on board and set sail. 3After sighting Cyprus and passing to the south of it, we sailed on to Syria. We landed at Tyre, where our ship was to unload its cargo. 4We sought out the disciples there and stayed with them seven days. Through the Spirit they urged Paul not to go on to Jerusalem. 5When it was time to leave, we left and continued on our way. All of them, including wives and children, accompanied us out of the city, and there on the beach we knelt to pray. 6After saying good-by to each other, we went aboard the ship, and they returned home.

7We continued our voyage from Tyre and landed at Ptolemais, where we greeted the believers and stayed with them for a day. 8Leaving the next day, we reached Caesarea and stayed at the house of Philip the evangelist, one of the Seven. 9He had four unmarried daughters who prophesied.

10After we had been there a number of days, a prophet named Agabus came down from Judea. 11Coming over to us, he took Paul's belt, tied his own hands and feet with it and said, "The Holy Spirit says, 'In this way the Jewish leaders in Jerusalem will bind the owner of this belt and will hand him over to the Gentiles.' "

12When we heard this, we and the people there pleaded with Paul not to go up to Jerusalem. 13Then Paul answered, "Why are you weeping and breaking my heart? I am ready not only to be bound, but also to die in Jerusalem for the name of the Lord Jesus." 14When he would not be dissuaded, we gave up and said, "The Lord's will be done."

15After this, we started on our way up to Jerusalem. 16Some of the disciples from Caesarea accompanied us and brought us to the home of Mnason, where we were to stay. He was a man from Cyprus and one of the early disciples.

Paul's Arrival at Jerusalem

17When we arrived at Jerusalem, the believers received us warmly. 18The next day Paul and the rest of us went to see James, and all the elders were present. 19Paul greeted them and reported in detail what God

ᵃ 28 Many manuscripts *of the Lord*

had done among the Gentiles through his ministry.

[20] When they heard this, they praised God. Then they said to Paul: "You see, brother, how many thousands of Jews have believed, and all of them are zealous for the law. [21] They have been informed that you teach all the Jews who live among the Gentiles to turn away from Moses, telling them not to circumcise their children or live according to our customs. [22] What shall we do? They will certainly hear that you have come, [23] so do what we tell you. There are four men with us who have made a vow. [24] Take these men, join in their purification rites and pay their expenses, so that they can have their heads shaved. Then everyone will know there is no truth in these reports about you, but that you yourself are living in obedience to the law. [25] As for the Gentile believers, we have written to them our decision that they should abstain from food sacrificed to idols, from blood, from the meat of strangled animals and from sexual immorality."

[26] The next day Paul took the men and purified himself along with them. Then he went to the temple to give notice of the date when the days of purification would end and the offering would be made for each of them.

Paul Arrested

[27] When the seven days were nearly over, some Jews from the province of Asia saw Paul at the temple. They stirred up the whole crowd and seized him, [28] shouting, "People of Israel, help us! This is the man who teaches everyone everywhere against our people and our law and this place. And besides, he has brought Greeks into the temple and defiled this holy place." [29] (They had previously seen Trophimus the Ephesian in the city with Paul and assumed that Paul had brought him into the temple.)

[30] The whole city was aroused, and the people came running from all directions. Seizing Paul, they dragged him from the temple, and immediately the gates were shut. [31] While they were trying to kill him, news reached the commander of the Roman troops that the whole city of Jerusalem was in an uproar. [32] He at once took some officers and soldiers and ran down to the crowd. When the rioters saw the commander and his soldiers, they stopped beating Paul.

[33] The commander came up and arrested him and ordered him to be bound with two chains. Then he asked who he was and what he had done. [34] Some in the crowd shouted one thing and some another, and since the commander could not get at the truth because of the uproar, he ordered that Paul be taken into the barracks. [35] When Paul reached the steps, the violence of the mob was so great he had to be carried by the soldiers. [36] The crowd that followed kept shouting, "Get rid of him!"

Paul Speaks to the Crowd

[37] As the soldiers were about to take Paul into the barracks, he asked the commander, "May I say something to you?"

"Do you speak Greek?" he replied. [38] "Aren't you the Egyptian who started a revolt and led four thousand terrorists out into the wilderness some time ago?"

[39] Paul answered, "I am a Jew, from Tarsus in Cilicia, a citizen of no ordinary city. Please let me speak to the people."

[40] Having received the commander's permission, Paul stood on the steps and motioned to the crowd. When they were all silent, he said to them in Aramaic[a]: [1] "Brothers and fathers, listen now to my defense."

22

[2] When they heard him speak to them in Aramaic, they became very quiet.

Then Paul said: [3] "I am a Jew, born in Tarsus of Cilicia, but brought up in this city. I studied under Gamaliel and was thoroughly trained in the law of our ancestors. I was just as zealous for God as any of you are today. [4] I persecuted the followers of this Way to their death, arresting both men and women and throwing them into prison, [5] as the high priest and all the Council can themselves testify. I even obtained letters from them to their associates in Damascus, and went there to bring these people as prisoners to Jerusalem to be punished.

[6] "About noon as I came near Damascus, suddenly a bright light from heaven flashed around me. [7] I fell to the ground and heard a voice say to me, 'Saul! Saul! Why do you persecute me?'

[8] " 'Who are you, Lord?' I asked.

a 40 Or possibly *Hebrew*; also in 22:2

" 'I am Jesus of Nazareth, whom you are persecuting,' he replied. ⁹My companions saw the light, but they did not understand the voice of him who was speaking to me.

¹⁰" 'What shall I do, Lord?' I asked.

" 'Get up,' the Lord said, 'and go into Damascus. There you will be told all that you have been assigned to do.' ¹¹My companions led me by the hand into Damascus, because the brilliance of the light had blinded me.

¹²"A man named Ananias came to see me. He was a devout observer of the law and highly respected by all the Jews living there. ¹³He stood beside me and said, 'Brother Saul, receive your sight!' And at that very moment I was able to see him.

¹⁴"Then he said: 'The God of our ancestors has chosen you to know his will and to see the Righteous One and to hear words from his mouth. ¹⁵You will be his witness to all people of what you have seen and heard. ¹⁶And now what are you waiting for? Get up, be baptized and wash your sins away, calling on his name.'

¹⁷"When I returned to Jerusalem and was praying at the temple, I fell into a trance ¹⁸and saw the Lord speaking to me. 'Quick!' he said. 'Leave Jerusalem immediately, because the people here will not accept your testimony about me.'

¹⁹" 'Lord,' I replied, 'these people know that I went from one synagogue to another to imprison and beat those who believe in you. ²⁰And when the blood of your martyr[a] Stephen was shed, I stood there giving my approval and guarding the clothes of those who were killing him.'

²¹"Then the Lord said to me, 'Go; I will send you far away to the Gentiles.' "

Paul the Roman Citizen

²²The crowd listened to Paul until he said this. Then they raised their voices and shouted, "Rid the earth of him! He's not fit to live!"

²³As they were shouting and throwing off their cloaks and flinging dust into the air, ²⁴the commander ordered that Paul be taken into the barracks. He directed that he be flogged and interrogated in order to find out why the people were shouting at him like this. ²⁵As they stretched him out to flog him, Paul said to the centurion standing there, "Is it legal for you to flog a Roman citizen who hasn't even been found guilty?"

²⁶When the centurion heard this, he went to the commander and reported it. "What are you going to do?" he asked. "This man is a Roman citizen."

²⁷The commander went to Paul and asked, "Tell me, are you a Roman citizen?"

"Yes, I am," he answered.

²⁸Then the commander said, "I had to pay a lot of money for my citizenship."

"But I was born a citizen," Paul replied.

²⁹Those who were about to interrogate him withdrew immediately. The commander himself was alarmed when he realized that he had put Paul, a Roman citizen, in chains.

Paul Before the Sanhedrin

³⁰The commander wanted to find out exactly why Paul was being accused by the Jews. So the next day he released him and ordered the chief priests and all the members of the Sanhedrin to assemble. Then he brought Paul and had him stand before them.

23 Paul looked straight at the Sanhedrin and said, "My brothers, I have fulfilled my duty to God in all good conscience to this day." ²At this the high priest Ananias ordered those standing near Paul to strike him on the mouth. ³Then Paul said to him, "God will strike you, you whitewashed wall! You sit there to judge me according to the law, yet you yourself violate the law by commanding that I be struck!"

⁴Those who were standing near Paul said, "How dare you insult God's high priest!"

⁵Paul replied, "Brothers, I did not realize that he was the high priest; for it is written: 'Do not speak evil about the ruler of your people.'[b]"

⁶Then Paul, knowing that some of them were Sadducees and the others Pharisees, called out in the Sanhedrin, "My brothers, I am a Pharisee, descended from Pharisees. I stand on trial because of the hope of the resurrection of the dead." ⁷When he said this, a dispute broke out between the Pharisees and the Sadducees, and the assembly was divided. ⁸(The Sadducees say that there is no resurrection, and that there are neither angels nor spirits, but the Pharisees believe all these things.)

a 20 Or witness   b 5 Exodus 22:28

[9]There was a great uproar, and some of the teachers of the law who were Pharisees stood up and argued vigorously. "We find nothing wrong with this man," they said. "What if a spirit or an angel has spoken to him?" [10]The dispute became so violent that the commander was afraid Paul would be torn to pieces by them. He ordered the troops to go down and take him away from them by force and bring him into the barracks.

[11]The following night the Lord stood near Paul and said, "Take courage! As you have testified about me in Jerusalem, so you must also testify in Rome."

The Plot to Kill Paul

[12]The next morning the Jews formed a conspiracy and bound themselves with an oath not to eat or drink until they had killed Paul. [13]More than forty men were involved in this plot. [14]They went to the chief priests and the elders and said, "We have taken a solemn oath not to eat anything until we have killed Paul. [15]Now then, you and the Sanhedrin petition the commander to bring him before you on the pretext of wanting more accurate information about his case. We are ready to kill him before he gets here."

[16]But when the son of Paul's sister heard of this plot, he went into the barracks and told Paul.

[17]Then Paul called one of the centurions and said, "Take this young man to the commander; he has something to tell him." [18]So he took him to the commander.

The centurion said, "Paul, the prisoner, sent for me and asked me to bring this young man to you because he has something to tell you."

[19]The commander took the young man by the hand, drew him aside and asked, "What is it you want to tell me?"

[20]He said: "The Jews have agreed to ask you to bring Paul before the Sanhedrin tomorrow on the pretext of wanting more accurate information about him. [21]Don't give in to them, because more than forty of them are waiting in ambush for him. They have taken an oath not to eat or drink until they have killed Paul. They are ready now, waiting for your consent to their request."

[22]The commander dismissed the young man with this warning: "Don't tell anyone that you have reported this to me."

Paul Transferred to Caesarea

[23]Then he called two of his centurions and ordered them, "Get ready a detachment of two hundred soldiers, seventy horsemen and two hundred spearmen *a* to go to Caesarea at nine tonight. [24]Provide horses for Paul so that he may be taken safely to Governor Felix."

[25]He wrote a letter as follows:

[26]Claudius Lysias,

To His Excellency, Governor Felix:

Greetings.

[27]This man was seized by the Jews and they were about to kill him, but I came with my troops and rescued him, for I had learned that he is a Roman citizen. [28]I wanted to know why they were accusing him, so I brought him to their Sanhedrin. [29]I found that the accusation had to do with questions about their law, but there was no charge against him that deserved death or imprisonment. [30]When I was informed of a plot to be carried out against the man, I sent him to you at once. I also ordered his accusers to present to you their case against him.

[31]So the soldiers, carrying out their orders, took Paul with them during the night and brought him as far as Antipatris. [32]The next day they let the cavalry go on with him, while they returned to the barracks. [33]When the cavalry arrived in Caesarea, they delivered the letter to the governor and handed Paul over to him. [34]The governor read the letter and asked what province he was from. Learning that he was from Cilicia, [35]he said, "I will hear your case when your accusers get here." Then he ordered that Paul be kept under guard in Herod's palace.

Paul's Trial Before Felix

24 Five days later the high priest Ananias went down to Caesarea with some of the elders and a lawyer named Tertullus, and they brought

a 23 The meaning of the Greek for this word is uncertain.

their charges against Paul before the governor. ²When Paul was called in, Tertullus presented his case before Felix: "We have enjoyed a long period of peace under you, and your foresight has brought about reforms in this nation. ³Everywhere and in every way, most excellent Felix, we acknowledge this with profound gratitude. ⁴But in order not to weary you further, I would request that you be kind enough to hear us briefly.

⁵"We have found this man to be a troublemaker, stirring up riots among the Jews all over the world. He is a ringleader of the Nazarene sect ⁶[⁷]and even tried to desecrate the temple; so we seized him. ⁸By examining him yourself you will be able to learn the truth about all these charges we are bringing against him."

⁹The other Jews joined in the accusation, asserting that these things were true.

¹⁰When the governor motioned for him to speak, Paul replied: "I know that for a number of years you have been a judge over this nation; so I gladly make my defense. ¹¹You can easily verify that no more than twelve days ago I went up to Jerusalem to worship. ¹²My accusers did not find me arguing with anyone at the temple, or stirring up a crowd in the synagogues or anywhere else in the city. ¹³And they cannot prove to you the charges they are now making against me. ¹⁴However, I admit that I worship the God of our ancestors as a follower of the Way, which they call a sect. I believe everything that is in accordance with the Law and that is written in the Prophets, ¹⁵and I have the same hope in God as these people themselves have, that there will be a resurrection of both the righteous and the wicked. ¹⁶So I strive always to keep my conscience clear before God and all people.

¹⁷"After an absence of several years, I came to Jerusalem to bring my people gifts for the poor and to present offerings. ¹⁸I was ceremonially clean when they found me in the temple courts doing this. There was no crowd with me, nor was I involved in any disturbance. ¹⁹But there are some Jews from the province of Asia, who ought to be here before you and bring charges if they have anything against me. ²⁰Or these who are here should state what crime they found in me when I stood before the Sanhedrin— ²¹unless it was this one thing I shouted as I stood in their presence: 'It is concerning the resurrection of the dead that I am on trial before you today.' "

²²Then Felix, who was well acquainted with the Way, adjourned the proceedings. "When Lysias the commander comes," he said, "I will decide your case." ²³He ordered the centurion to keep Paul under guard but to give him some freedom and permit his friends to take care of his needs.

²⁴Several days later Felix came with his wife Drusilla, who was Jewish. He sent for Paul and listened to him as he spoke about faith in Christ Jesus. ²⁵As Paul talked about righteousness, self-control and the judgment to come, Felix was afraid and said, "That's enough for now! You may leave. When I find it convenient, I will send for you." ²⁶At the same time he was hoping that Paul would offer him a bribe, so he sent for him frequently and talked with him.

²⁷When two years had passed, Felix was succeeded by Porcius Festus, but because Felix wanted to grant a favor to the Jews, he left Paul in prison.

Paul's Trial Before Festus

25 Three days after arriving in the province, Festus went up from Caesarea to Jerusalem, ²where the chief priests and the Jewish leaders appeared before him and presented the charges against Paul. ³They requested Festus, as a favor to them, to have Paul transferred to Jerusalem, for they were preparing an ambush to kill him along the way. ⁴Festus answered, "Paul is being held at Caesarea, and I myself am going there soon. ⁵Let some of your leaders come with me, and if the man has done anything wrong, they can press charges against him there."

⁶After spending eight or ten days with them, Festus went down to Caesarea. The next day he convened the court and ordered that Paul be brought before him. ⁷When Paul came in, the Jews who had come down from Jerusalem stood around him. They brought many serious charges against him, but they could not prove them.

⁸Then Paul made his defense: "I have done nothing wrong against the Jewish law or against the temple or against Caesar."

⁹Festus, wishing to do the Jews a favor, said to Paul, "Are you willing to go up to Jerusalem and stand trial before me there on these charges?"

[10]Paul answered: "I am now standing before Caesar's court, where I ought to be tried. I have not done any wrong to the Jews, as you yourself know very well. [11]If, however, I am guilty of doing anything deserving death, I do not refuse to die. But if the charges brought against me by these Jews are not true, no one has the right to hand me over to them. I appeal to Caesar!"

[12]After Festus had conferred with his council, he declared: "You have appealed to Caesar. To Caesar you will go!"

Festus Consults King Agrippa

[13]A few days later King Agrippa and Bernice arrived at Caesarea to pay their respects to Festus. [14]Since they were spending many days there, Festus discussed Paul's case with the king. He said: "There is a man here whom Felix left as a prisoner. [15]When I went to Jerusalem, the chief priests and the elders of the Jews brought charges against him and asked that he be condemned.

[16]"I told them that it is not the Roman custom to hand over anyone before they have faced their accusers and have had an opportunity to defend themselves against the charges. [17]When they came here with me, I did not delay the case, but convened the court the next day and ordered the man to be brought in. [18]When his accusers got up to speak, they did not charge him with any of the crimes I had expected. [19]Instead, they had some points of dispute with him about their own religion and about a dead man named Jesus who Paul claimed was alive. [20]I was at a loss how to investigate such matters; so I asked if he would be willing to go to Jerusalem and stand trial there on these charges. [21]But when Paul made his appeal to be held over for the Emperor's decision, I ordered him held until I could send him to Caesar."

[22]Then Agrippa said to Festus, "I would like to hear this man myself."

He replied, "Tomorrow you will hear him."

Paul Before Agrippa

[23]The next day Agrippa and Bernice came with great pomp and entered the audience room with the high-ranking military officers and the prominent men of the city. At the command of Festus, Paul was brought in. [24]Festus said: "King Agrippa, and all who are present with us, you see this man! The whole Jewish community has petitioned me about him in Jerusalem and here in Caesarea, shouting that he ought not to live any longer. [25]I found he had done nothing deserving of death, but because he made his appeal to the Emperor I decided to send him to Rome. [26]But I have nothing definite to write to His Majesty about him. Therefore I have brought him before all of you, and especially before you, King Agrippa, so that as a result of this investigation I may have something to write. [27]For I think it is unreasonable to send a prisoner on to Rome without specifying the charges against him."

26

Then Agrippa said to Paul, "You have permission to speak for yourself."

So Paul motioned with his hand and began his defense: [2]"King Agrippa, I consider myself fortunate to stand before you today as I make my defense against all the accusations of the Jews, [3]and especially so because you are well acquainted with all the Jewish customs and controversies. Therefore, I beg you to listen to me patiently.

[4]"The Jewish people all know the way I have lived ever since I was a child, from the beginning of my life in my own country, and also in Jerusalem. [5]They have known me for a long time and can testify, if they are willing, that I conformed to the strictest sect of our religion, living as a Pharisee. [6]And now it is because of my hope in what God has promised our ancestors that I am on trial today. [7]This is the promise our twelve tribes are hoping to see fulfilled as they earnestly serve God day and night. King Agrippa, it is because of this hope that the Jews are accusing me. [8]Why should any of you consider it incredible that God raises the dead?

[9]"I too was convinced that I ought to do all that was possible to oppose the name of Jesus of Nazareth. [10]And that is just what I did in Jerusalem. On the authority of the chief priests I put many of the Lord's people in prison, and when they were put to death, I cast my vote against them. [11]Many a time I went from one synagogue to another to have them punished, and I tried to force them to blaspheme. I was so obsessed with persecuting them that I even hunted them down in foreign cities.

[12]"On one of these journeys I was going to Damascus with the authority and commission of the chief priests. [13]About noon, King

Agrippa, as I was on the road, I saw a light from heaven, brighter than the sun, blazing around me and my companions. ¹⁴We all fell to the ground, and I heard a voice saying to me in Aramaic,ᵃ 'Saul, Saul, why do you persecute me? It is hard for you to kick against the goads.'

¹⁵"Then I asked, 'Who are you, Lord?'

" 'I am Jesus, whom you are persecuting,' the Lord replied. ¹⁶'Now get up and stand on your feet. I have appeared to you to appoint you as a servant and as a witness of what you have seen and will see of me. ¹⁷I will rescue you from your own people and from the Gentiles. I am sending you to them ¹⁸to open their eyes and turn them from darkness to light, and from the power of Satan to God, so that they may receive forgiveness of sins and a place among those who are sanctified by faith in me.'

¹⁹"So then, King Agrippa, I was not disobedient to the vision from heaven. ²⁰First to those in Damascus, then to those in Jerusalem and in all Judea, and then to the Gentiles, I preached that they should repent and turn to God and demonstrate their repentance by their deeds. ²¹That is why some Jews seized me in the temple courts and tried to kill me. ²²But God has helped me to this very day; so I stand here and testify to small and great alike. I am saying nothing beyond what the prophets and Moses said would happen— ²³that the Messiah would suffer and, as the first to rise from the dead, would bring the message of light to his own people and to the Gentiles."

²⁴At this point Festus interrupted Paul's defense. "You are out of your mind, Paul!" he shouted. "Your great learning is driving you insane."

²⁵"I am not insane, most excellent Festus," Paul replied. "What I am saying is true and reasonable. ²⁶The king is familiar with these things, and I can speak freely to him. I am convinced that none of this has escaped his notice, because it was not done in a corner. ²⁷King Agrippa, do you believe the prophets? I know you do."

²⁸Then Agrippa said to Paul, "Do you think that in such a short time you can persuade me to be a Christian?"

²⁹Paul replied, "Short time or long—I pray to God that not only you but all who are listening to me today may become what I am, except for these chains."

³⁰The king rose, and with him the governor and Bernice and those sitting with them. ³¹After they left the room, they began saying to one another, "This man is not doing anything that deserves death or imprisonment."

³²Agrippa said to Festus, "This man could have been set free if he had not appealed to Caesar."

Paul Sails for Rome

27 When it was decided that we would sail for Italy, Paul and some other prisoners were handed over to a centurion named Julius, who belonged to the Imperial Regiment. ²We boarded a ship from Adramyttium about to sail for ports along the coast of the province of Asia, and we put out to sea. Aristarchus, a Macedonian from Thessalonica, was with us.

³The next day we landed at Sidon; and Julius, in kindness to Paul, allowed him to go to his friends so they might provide for his needs. ⁴From there we put out to sea again and passed to the lee of Cyprus because the winds were against us. ⁵When we had sailed across the open sea off the coast of Cilicia and Pamphylia, we landed at Myra in Lycia. ⁶There the centurion found an Alexandrian ship sailing for Italy and put us on board. ⁷We made slow headway for many days and had difficulty arriving off Cnidus. When the wind did not allow us to hold our course, we sailed to the lee of Crete, opposite Salmone. ⁸We moved along the coast with difficulty and came to a place called Fair Havens, near the town of Lasea.

⁹Much time had been lost, and sailing had already become dangerous because by now it was after the Day of Atonement.ᵇ So Paul warned them, ¹⁰"Men, I can see that our voyage is going to be disastrous and bring great loss to ship and cargo, and to our own lives also." ¹¹But the centurion, instead of listening to what Paul said, followed the advice of the pilot and of the owner of the ship. ¹²Since the harbor was unsuitable to winter in, the majority decided that we should sail on, hoping to reach Phoenix and winter there. This was a harbor in Crete, facing both southwest and northwest.

ᵃ 14 Or *Hebrew*   ᵇ 9 That is, Yom Kippur

FRIDAY

JESUS: OUR ULTIMATE EVERYTHING
Acts 27:1–44 or 27:14–15,21–26

Dallas Willard

Our commitment to Jesus can stand on no other foundation than a recognition that he is the one who knows the truth about our lives and our universe. It is not possible to trust Jesus, or anyone else, in matters where we do not believe him to be competent. We cannot pray for his help and rely on his collaboration in dealing with real-life matters we suspect might defeat his knowledge or abilities.

And can we seriously imagine that Jesus could be Lord if he were not smart? If he were divine, would he be dumb? Or uninformed? Once you stop to think about it, how could he be what we take him to be in all other respects and not be the best-informed and most intelligent person of all, the smartest person who ever lived?

That is exactly how his earliest apprentices in kingdom living thought of him. He was not regarded as, perhaps, a magician, who only knew "the right words" to get results without understanding or who could effectively manipulate appearances. Rather, he was accepted as the ultimate scientist, craftsman and artist.

THOMAS À KEMPIS {AD 1380–1471}

In you, Lord God, I place all my hope and find my refuge. On you I cast all my troubles and anguish, because whatever I have outside of you I find to be weak and unstable. It will not serve me to have many friends. Powerful helpers will not be able to assist me. Prudent advisers will not be able to give useful answers. The books of learned men will not console me. No precious possession will win my freedom. No place—no matter how secret and beautiful it may be—can shelter me if you yourself do not assist, comfort, console, instruct and guard me. For all things which seem to be for our peace and happiness are nothing when you are absent, and truly provide no happiness.

You, indeed, are the fountain of all good, the height of life, the depth of all that can be spoken. To trust in you above all things is the strongest comfort of your servants.

reflection

1. Is there a situation in your life right now where you need the advice of the smartest person in the world?

2. Is there some part of your life where you find it particularly difficult to trust God?

3. How does a person's view of God affect their ability to trust in him?

For your next devotional reading, go to page 1281.

The Storm

¹³When a gentle south wind began to blow, they saw their opportunity; so they weighed anchor and sailed along the shore of Crete. ¹⁴Before very long, a wind of hurricane force, called the Northeaster, swept down from the island. ¹⁵The ship was caught by the storm and could not head into the wind; so we gave way to it and were driven along. ¹⁶As we passed to the lee of a small island called Cauda, we were hardly able to make the lifeboat secure, ¹⁷so the men hoisted it aboard. Then they passed ropes under the ship itself to hold it together. Because they were afraid they would run aground on the sandbars of Syrtis, they lowered the sea anchor*a* and let the ship be driven along. ¹⁸We took such a violent battering from the storm that the next day they began to throw the cargo overboard. ¹⁹On the third day, they threw the ship's tackle overboard with their own hands. ²⁰When neither sun nor stars appeared for many days and the storm continued raging, we finally gave up all hope of being saved.

²¹After they had gone a long time without food, Paul stood up before them and said: "Men, you should have taken my advice not to sail from Crete; then you would have spared yourselves this damage and loss. ²²But now I urge you to keep up your courage, because not one of you will be lost; only the ship will be destroyed. ²³Last night an angel of the God whose I am and whom I serve stood beside me ²⁴and said, 'Do not be afraid, Paul. You must stand trial before Caesar; and God has graciously given you the lives of all who sail with you.' ²⁵So keep up your courage, men, for I have faith in God that it will happen just as he told me. ²⁶Nevertheless, we must run aground on some island."

The Shipwreck

²⁷On the fourteenth night we were still being driven across the Adriatic*b* Sea, when about midnight the sailors sensed they were approaching land. ²⁸They took soundings and found that the water was a hundred and twenty feet*c* deep. A short time later they took soundings again and found it was ninety feet*d* deep. ²⁹Fearing that we would be dashed against the rocks, they dropped four anchors from the stern and prayed for daylight. ³⁰In an attempt to escape from the ship, the sailors let the lifeboat down into the sea, pretending they were going to lower some anchors from the bow. ³¹Then Paul said to the centurion and the soldiers, "Unless these men stay with the ship, you cannot be saved." ³²So the soldiers cut the ropes that held the lifeboat and let it drift away.

³³Just before dawn Paul urged them all to eat. "For the last fourteen days," he said, "you have been in constant suspense and have gone without food—you haven't eaten anything. ³⁴Now I urge you to take some food. You need it to survive. Not one of you will lose a single hair from his head." ³⁵After he said this, he took some bread and gave thanks to God in front of them all. Then he broke it and began to eat. ³⁶They were all encouraged and ate some food themselves. ³⁷Altogether there were 276 of us on board. ³⁸When they had eaten as much as they wanted, they lightened the ship by throwing the grain into the sea.

³⁹When daylight came, they did not recognize the land, but they saw a bay with a sandy beach, where they decided to run the ship aground if they could. ⁴⁰Cutting loose the anchors, they left them in the sea and at the same time untied the ropes that held the rudders. Then they hoisted the foresail to the wind and made for the beach. ⁴¹But the ship struck a sandbar and ran aground. The bow stuck fast and would not move, and the stern was broken to pieces by the pounding of the surf.

⁴²The soldiers planned to kill the prisoners to prevent any of them from swimming away and escaping. ⁴³But the centurion wanted to spare Paul's life and kept them from carrying out their plan. He ordered those who could swim to jump overboard first and get to land. ⁴⁴The rest were to get there on planks or on other pieces of the ship. In this way everyone reached land safely.

Paul Ashore on Malta

28 Once safely on shore, we found out that the island was called Malta. ²The islanders showed us unusual kindness. They built a fire and welcomed us all because it was raining and cold. ³Paul gathered a pile of brushwood and, as he

---

a 17 Or *the sails*   *b 27* In ancient times the name referred to an area extending well south of Italy.
c 28 Or *about 37 meters*   *d 28* Or *about 27 meters*

put it on the fire, a viper, driven out by the heat, fastened itself on his hand. [4]When the islanders saw the snake hanging from his hand, they said to each other, "This man must be a murderer; for though he escaped from the sea, the goddess Justice has not allowed him to live." [5]But Paul shook the snake off into the fire and suffered no ill effects. [6]The people expected him to swell up or suddenly fall dead; but after waiting a long time and seeing nothing unusual happen to him, they changed their minds and said he was a god.

[7]There was an estate nearby that belonged to Publius, the chief official of the island. He welcomed us to his home and showed us generous hospitality for three days. [8]His father was sick in bed, suffering from fever and dysentery. Paul went in to see him and, after prayer, placed his hands on him and healed him. [9]When this had happened, the rest of the sick on the island came and were cured. [10]They honored us in many ways; and when we were ready to sail, they furnished us with the supplies we needed.

Paul's Arrival at Rome

[11]After three months we put out to sea in a ship that had wintered in the island—it was an Alexandrian ship with the figurehead of the twin gods Castor and Pollux. [12]We put in at Syracuse and stayed there three days. [13]From there we set sail and arrived at Rhegium. The next day the south wind came up, and on the following day we reached Puteoli. [14]There we found some believers who invited us to spend a week with them. And so we came to Rome. [15]The believers there had heard that we were coming, and they traveled as far as the Forum of Appius and the Three Taverns to meet us. At the sight of these people Paul thanked God and was encouraged. [16]When we got to Rome, Paul was allowed to live by himself, with a soldier to guard him.

Paul Preaches at Rome Under Guard

[17]Three days later he called together the local Jewish leaders. When they had assembled, Paul said to them: "My brothers, although I have done nothing against our people or against the customs of our ancestors, I was arrested in Jerusalem and handed over to the Romans. [18]They examined me and wanted to release me, because I was not guilty of any crime deserving death. [19]The Jews objected, so I was compelled to make an appeal to Caesar. I certainly did not intend to bring any charge against my own people. [20]For this reason I have asked to see you and talk with you. It is because of the hope of Israel that I am bound with this chain."

[21]They replied, "We have not received any letters from Judea concerning you, and none of our people who have come from there has reported or said anything bad about you. [22]But we want to hear what your views are, for we know that people everywhere are talking against this sect."

[23]They arranged to meet Paul on a certain day, and came in even larger numbers to the place where he was staying. He witnessed to them from morning till evening, explaining about the kingdom of God, and from the Law of Moses and from the Prophets he tried to persuade them about Jesus. [24]Some were convinced by what he said, but others would not believe. [25]They disagreed among themselves and began to leave after Paul had made this final statement: "The Holy Spirit spoke the truth to your ancestors when he said through Isaiah the prophet:

[26]" 'Go to this people and say,
   "You will be ever hearing but never
      understanding;
   you will be ever seeing but never
      perceiving."
[27]For this people's heart has become
      calloused;
   they hardly hear with their ears,
   and they have closed their eyes.
Otherwise they might see with their eyes,
   hear with their ears,
   understand with their hearts
and turn, and I would heal them.' [a]

[28][29]"Therefore I want you to know that God's salvation has been sent to the Gentiles, and they will listen!"

[30]For two whole years Paul stayed there in his own rented house and welcomed all who came to see him. [31]He proclaimed the kingdom of God and taught about the Lord Jesus Christ—with all boldness and without hindrance!

a 27 Isaiah 6:9,10 (see Septuagint)

The Letters & Revelation

Romans	Titus
1 Corinthians	Philemon
2 Corinthians	Hebrews
Galatians	James
Ephesians	1 Peter
Philippians	2 Peter
Colossians	1 John
1 Thessalonians	2 John
2 Thessalonians	3 John
1 Timothy	Jude
2 Timothy	Revelation

romans

AUTHOR: Paul, the apostle

DATE: Around A.D. 57

THEME: Christians are given the Good News of the gospel.

1 Paul, a servant of Christ Jesus, called to be an apostle and set apart for the gospel of God— ²the gospel he promised beforehand through his prophets in the Holy Scriptures ³regarding his Son, who as to his earthly life*a* was a descendant of David, ⁴and who through the Spirit of holiness was appointed the Son of God in power*b* by his resurrection from the dead: Jesus Christ our Lord. ⁵Through him we received grace and apostleship to call all the Gentiles to faith and obedience for his name's sake. ⁶And you also are among those Gentiles who are called to belong to Jesus Christ.

⁷To all in Rome who are loved by God and called to be his holy people:

Grace and peace to you from God our Father and from the Lord Jesus Christ.

Paul's Longing to Visit Rome

⁸First, I thank my God through Jesus Christ for all of you, because your faith is being reported all over the world. ⁹God, whom I serve in my spirit in preaching the gospel of his Son, is my witness how constantly I remember you ¹⁰in my prayers at all times; and I pray that now at last by God's will the way may be opened for me to come to you.

¹¹I long to see you so that I may impart to you some spiritual gift to make you strong— ¹²that is, that you and I may be mutually encouraged by each other's faith. ¹³I do not want you to be unaware, brothers and sisters, that I planned many times to come to you (but have been prevented from doing so until now) in order that I might have a har-

vest among you, just as I have had among the other Gentiles.

¹⁴I am obligated both to Greeks and non-Greeks, both to the wise and the foolish. ¹⁵That is why I am so eager to preach the gospel also to you who are in Rome.

¹⁶I am not ashamed of the gospel, because it is the power of God that brings salvation to everyone who believes: first to the Jew, then to the Gentile. ¹⁷For in the gospel the righteousness of God is revealed—a righteousness that is by faith from first to last,*c* just as it is written: "The righteous will live by faith."*d*

God's Wrath Against Sinful Humanity

¹⁸The wrath of God is being revealed from heaven against all the godlessness and wickedness of human beings who suppress the truth by their wickedness, ¹⁹since what may be known about God is plain to them, because God has made it plain to them. ²⁰For since the creation of the world God's invisible qualities—his eternal power and divine nature—have been clearly seen, being understood from what has been made, so that people are without excuse.

²¹For although they knew God, they neither glorified him as God nor gave thanks to him, but their thinking became futile and their foolish hearts were darkened. ²²Although they claimed to be wise, they became fools ²³and exchanged the glory of the immortal God for images made to look like mortal human beings and birds and animals and reptiles.

²⁴Therefore God gave them over in the sinful desires of their hearts to sexual impu-

---

a 3 Or *who according to the flesh*   *b* 4 Or *was declared with power to be the Son of God*   *c* 17 Or *is from faith to faith*   *d* 17 Hab. 2:4

rity for the degrading of their bodies with one another. 25They exchanged the truth about God for a lie, and worshiped and served created things rather than the Creator—who is forever praised. Amen.

26Because of this, God gave them over to shameful lusts. Even their women exchanged natural sexual relations for unnatural ones. 27In the same way the men also abandoned natural relations with women and were inflamed with lust for one another. Men committed shameful acts with other men, and received in themselves the due penalty for their error.

28Furthermore, just as they did not think it worthwhile to retain the knowledge of God, so God gave them over to a depraved mind, so that they do what ought not to be done. 29They have become filled with every kind of wickedness, evil, greed and depravity. They are full of envy, murder, strife, deceit and malice. They are gossips, 30slanderers, God-haters, insolent, arrogant and boastful; they invent ways of doing evil; they disobey their parents; 31they have no understanding, no fidelity, no love, no mercy. 32Although they know God's righteous decree that those who do such things deserve death, they not only continue to do these very things but also approve of those who practice them.

God's Righteous Judgment

2 You, therefore, have no excuse, you who pass judgment on someone else, for at whatever point you judge another, you are condemning yourself, because you who pass judgment do the same things. 2Now we know that God's judgment against those who do such things is based on truth. 3So when you, a mere human, pass judgment on them and yet do the same things, do you think you will escape God's judgment? 4Or do you show contempt for the riches of his kindness, forbearance and patience, not realizing that God's kindness is intended to lead you to repentance?

5But because of your stubbornness and your unrepentant heart, you are storing up wrath against yourself for the day of God's wrath, when his righteous judgment will be revealed. 6God "will repay everyone accord-

ing to what they have done." [a] 7To those who by persistence in doing good seek glory, honor and immortality, he will give eternal life. 8But for those who are self-seeking and who reject the truth and follow evil, there will be wrath and anger. 9There will be trouble and distress for every human being who does evil: first for the Jew, then for the Gentile; 10but glory, honor and peace for everyone who does good: first for the Jew, then for the Gentile. 11For God does not show favoritism.

12All who sin apart from the law will also perish apart from the law, and all who sin under the law will be judged by the law. 13For it is not those who hear the law who are righteous in God's sight, but it is those who obey the law who will be declared righteous. 14(Indeed, when Gentiles, who do not have the law, do by nature things required by the law, they are a law for themselves, even though they do not have the law. 15They show that the requirements of the law are written on their hearts, their consciences also bearing witness, and their thoughts now accusing, now even defending them.) 16This will take place on the day when God judges everyone's secrets through Jesus Christ, as my gospel declares.

The Jews and the Law

17Now you, if you call yourself a Jew; if you rely on the law and boast in God; 18if you know his will and approve of what is superior because you are instructed by the law; 19if you are convinced that you are a guide for the blind, a light for those who are in the dark, 20an instructor of the foolish, a teacher of infants, because you have in the law the embodiment of knowledge and truth— 21you, then, who teach others, do you not teach yourself? You who preach against stealing, do you steal? 22You who say that people should not commit adultery, do you commit adultery? You who abhor idols, do you rob temples? 23You who boast in the law, do you dishonor God by breaking the law? 24As it is written: "God's name is blasphemed among the Gentiles because of you." [b]

25Circumcision has value if you observe the law, but if you break the law, you have

Finger Pointing

Romans 2:1–3

read/meditate

Read through the first three verses of Romans 2 and skim through the last half of
Romans 1 as well. As strong as Romans 1 is in condemning behavior, Romans 2 is
even stronger in its warnings against judging others about their behavior. Read the
sections of Scripture again. Think about the level of intensity with which Paul is writing.
If you will be judged according to how you judge others, where does that leave you?

pray

Admit to God the kinds of people you have difficulty not condemning. Be honest with
him about your struggles with certain perceptions, ideas or notions you have about
others. Thank him for his mercy toward you. Be still long enough to allow him to stir
up your mercy for all people.

contemplate

Your role in God's kingdom is reflected in the way you engage the world around you.
Although this world is filled with problems and trouble, how are you doing interacting
with your world in a loving, merciful and authentic manner?

additional reflection

I choose kindness . . . I will be kind to the poor, for they are alone. Kind to the rich,
for they are afraid. And kind to the unkind, for such is how God has treated me.

—Max Lucado

Never cease loving a person, and never give up hope for him, for even the prodigal
son who had fallen most low, could still be saved; the bitterest enemy and also he who
was your friend could again be your friend; love that has grown cold can kindle again.

—Søren Kierkegaard

For your next devotional reading, go to page 1283.

become as though you had not been circumcised. ²⁶If those who are not circumcised keep the law's requirements, will they not be regarded as though they were circumcised? ²⁷The one who is not circumcised physically and yet obeys the law will condemn you who, even though you have the*ᵃ* written code and circumcision, are a lawbreaker.

²⁸A person is not a Jew who is one only outwardly, nor is circumcision merely outward and physical. ²⁹No, a person is a Jew who is one inwardly; and circumcision is circumcision of the heart, by the Spirit, not by the written code. Such a person's praise is not from other people, but from God.

God's Faithfulness

3 What advantage, then, is there in being a Jew, or what value is there in circumcision? ²Much in every way! First of all, the Jews have been entrusted with the very words of God.

³What if some were unfaithful? Will their unfaithfulness nullify God's faithfulness? ⁴Not at all! Let God be true, and every human being a liar. As it is written:

"So that you may be proved right when you speak
and prevail when you judge."*ᵇ*

⁵But if our unrighteousness brings out God's righteousness more clearly, what shall we say? That God is unjust in bringing his wrath on us? (I am using a human argument.) ⁶Certainly not! If that were so, how could God judge the world? ⁷Someone might argue, "If my falsehood enhances God's truthfulness and so increases his glory, why am I still condemned as a sinner?" ⁸Why not say—as we are being slanderously reported as saying and as some claim that we say—"Let us do evil that good may result"? Their condemnation is just!

No One Is Righteous

⁹What shall we conclude then? Do we have any advantage? Not at all! We have already made the charge that Jews and Gentiles alike are all under the power of sin. ¹⁰As it is written:

"There is no one righteous, not even one;
¹¹ there is no one who understands;
there is no one who seeks God.
¹²All have turned away,
they have together become worthless;
there is no one who does good,
not even one."*ᶜ*
¹³"Their throats are open graves;
their tongues practice deceit."*ᵈ*
"The poison of vipers is on their lips."*ᵉ*
¹⁴ "Their mouths are full of cursing and bitterness."*ᶠ*
¹⁵"Their feet are swift to shed blood;
¹⁶ ruin and misery mark their ways,
¹⁷and the way of peace they do not know."*ᵍ*
¹⁸ "There is no fear of God before their eyes."*ʰ*

¹⁹Now we know that whatever the law says, it says to those who are under the law, so that every mouth may be silenced and the whole world held accountable to God. ²⁰Therefore no one will be declared righteous in God's sight by observing the law; rather, through the law we become conscious of our sin.

Righteousness Through Faith

²¹But now apart from the law the righteousness of God has been made known, to which the Law and the Prophets testify. ²²This righteousness is given through faith in*ⁱ* Jesus Christ to all who believe. There is no difference between Jew and Gentile, ²³for all have sinned and fall short of the glory of God, ²⁴and all are justified freely by his grace through the redemption that came by Christ Jesus. ²⁵God presented Christ as a sacrifice of atonement,*ʲ* through the shedding of his blood—to be received by faith. He did this to demonstrate his justice, because in his forbearance he had left the sins committed beforehand unpunished— ²⁶he did it to demonstrate his justice at the present time, so as to be just and the one who justifies those who have faith in Jesus.

²⁷Where, then, is boasting? It is excluded. Because of what law? The law that requires works? No, because of the "law" that re-

ᵃ 27 Or who, by means of a   ᵇ 4 Psalm 51:4   ᶜ 12 Psalms 14:1-3; 53:1-3; Eccles. 7:20
ᵈ 13 Psalm 5:9   ᵉ 13 Psalm 140:3   ᶠ 14 Psalm 10:7 (see Septuagint)   ᵍ 17 Isaiah 59:7,8
ʰ 18 Psalm 36:1   ⁱ 22 Or through the faithfulness of   ʲ 25 The Greek for sacrifice of atonement refers to
the atonement cover on the ark of the covenant (see Lev. 16:15,16).

MONDAY

CHANGED BY THE CROSS

Romans 3:1–31 *or* 3:21–26

FRANCIS SCHAEFFER {AD 1912–1984}

If there is true moral guilt in the presence of a personal God (rather than a metaphysical intrinsic situation of what is and always has been), then perhaps there will be a solution from God's side. And God says to man that there is a solution. That solution rests upon God saying that he is holy and he is love, and in his love he has loved the world, and he sent his son … When [Jesus] died, with the division that man has caused by his revolt now carried up into the Trinity itself, there in expiation, in propitiation and substitution, the true moral guilt is met by the *infinite* value of Jesus' death. Thus Jesus says: "It is finished" (John 19:30).

Romans 3:26 is a verse that we tend to pass by too quickly in the midst of the structure of the first three chapters of Romans. These chapters tell us first why man is lost, and then the solution in the propitiatory death of Jesus Christ. At this point Paul can say: "[He did it … so as to be just and the one who justifies those who have faith in Jesus.]" On the one hand, because of the infinite value of Christ's holy death, God does not have to surrender his absolute holy character; and on the other, he does not have to violate man's significance in order for him to be able to pardon guilt and restore man's broken relationship to himself.

Mark Brazee

Once believers receive a revelation of the redemption Jesus purchased on the cross, it changes them. Nothing can stop them anymore! I'm not talking about a mental assent to the truth. I'm talking about people who say from their hearts, "Yes, that's the truth, and the truth is setting me free!"

Consider how a person is adopted into God's family. The minute a person finds out Jesus' blood was shed for the forgiveness of his sins, he can confess Jesus as his Savior, and not a devil in hell can stop him from getting born again! Peace and fellowship with God are available to anyone who receives Jesus in faith.

reflection

1. In order to appreciate the solution God provided, you have to understand the problem. What problem is every person born with?

2. What does it mean to be "justified"?

3. What great lengths did God go to in order to enable his people to enjoy a right relationship with him?

For your next devotional reading, go to page 1285.

quires faith. 28For we maintain that a person is justified by faith apart from observing the law. 29Is God the God of Jews only? Is he not the God of Gentiles too? Yes, of Gentiles too, 30since there is only one God, who will justify the circumcised by faith and the uncircumcised through that same faith. 31Do we, then, nullify the law by this faith? Not at all! Rather, we uphold the law.

Abraham Justified by Faith

4 What then shall we say that Abraham, the forefather of us Jews, discovered in this matter? 2If, in fact, Abraham was justified by works, he had something to boast about—but not before God. 3What does Scripture say? "Abraham believed God, and it was credited to him as righteousness." *a*

4Now to anyone who works, their wages are not credited to them as a gift, but as an obligation. 5However, to anyone who does not work but trusts God who justifies the ungodly, their faith is credited as righteousness. 6David says the same thing when he speaks of the blessedness of those to whom God credits righteousness apart from works:

7 "Blessed are those
    whose transgressions are forgiven,
    whose sins are covered.
8 Blessed are those
    whose sin the Lord will never count
        against them." *b*

9Is this blessedness only for the circumcised, or also for the uncircumcised? We have been saying that Abraham's faith was credited to him as righteousness. 10Under what circumstances was it credited? Was it after he was circumcised, or before? It was not after, but before! 11And he received circumcision as a sign, a seal of the righteousness that he had by faith while he was still uncircumcised. So then, he is the father of all who believe but have not been circumcised, in order that righteousness might be credited to them. 12And he is then also the father of the circumcised who not only are circumcised but who also follow in the footsteps of the faith that our father Abraham had before he was circumcised.

13It was not through the law that Abraham and his offspring received the promise that he would be heir of the world, but through the righteousness that comes by faith. 14For if those who depend on the law are heirs, faith means nothing and the promise is worthless, 15because the law brings wrath. And where there is no law there is no transgression.

16Therefore, the promise comes by faith, so that it may be by grace and may be guaranteed to all Abraham's offspring—not only to those who are of the law but also to those who have the faith of Abraham. He is the father of us all. 17As it is written: "I have made you a father of many nations." *c* He is our father in the sight of God, in whom he believed—the God who gives life to the dead and calls into being things that were not.

18Against all hope, Abraham in hope believed and so became the father of many nations, just as it had been said to him, "So shall your offspring be." *d* 19Without weakening in his faith, he faced the fact that his body was as good as dead—since he was about a hundred years old—and that Sarah's womb was also dead. 20Yet he did not waver through unbelief regarding the promise of God, but was strengthened in his faith and gave glory to God, 21being fully persuaded that God had power to do what he had promised. 22This is why "it was credited to him as righteousness." 23The words "it was credited to him" were written not for him alone, 24but also for us, to whom God will credit righteousness—for us who believe in him who raised Jesus our Lord from the dead. 25He was delivered over to death for our sins and was raised to life for our justification.

Peace and Hope

5 Therefore, since we have been justified through faith, we *e* have peace with God through our Lord Jesus Christ, 2through whom we have gained access by faith into this grace in which we now stand. And we *f* boast in the hope of the glory of God. 3Not only so, but we *f* also glory in our sufferings, because we know that suffering produces perseverance; 4perseverance, character; and character, hope. 5And hope does not put us to shame, because God's

a 3 Gen. 15:6; also in verse 22   *b 8* Psalm 32:1,2   *c 17* Gen. 17:5   *d 18* Gen. 15:5   *e 1* Many manuscripts *let us*   *f 2,3* Or *let us*

TUESDAY

UNLOVABLE TO LOVABLE

Romans 5:1–21 *or* 5:6–8

John Fischer

It is important for me to remember that the full extent of God's love was shown, not so much when He chose to create us, but when we were born sinful and unlovely.

As the apostle Paul says, "At just the right time, when we were still powerless, Christ died for the ungodly. Very rarely will anyone die for a righteous person, though for a good person someone might possibly dare to die. But God demonstrates his own love for us in this: While we were still sinners, Christ died for us" (Romans 5:6–8).

Isn't that remarkable? God doesn't love us in spite of our wounds, but because of them! In being loved, we become lovely; we become lovable because God finds us that way. I think it's because God's at the other end. He knows what His love can do, how it can transform lives and how He can take the very worst materials of my life and turn them into something splendid beyond my imagination.

That's the answer. Christ died for us—He didn't die just so we could all be straight, get married and raise children in suburbia, or so we'd be famous, beautiful or rich. He died because we were lonely and impoverished, afraid and cast out. He died because He knew His resurrection would present us with the opportunity for transformation into something so wildly beautiful and passionate it exceeds human language.

MATTHEW HENRY {AD 1662–1714}

Romans 5:6 says that we were powerless. We were in a sad condition, and—even worse—we were altogether unable to help ourselves out of that condition. We were lost, with no visible way open for our recovery. Our condition was deplorable and desperate. Therefore our salvation is said to come at "just the right time" (Romans 5:6). God's time to help and save is when those that are to be saved are without strength, so that his own power and grace may be magnified all the more (see Deuteronomy 32:36).

reflection

1. Jesus died for you when you were at your worst. What does this demonstrate about God's love?

2. Describe a person's condition before God saves them. How does Jesus change that?

3. Many people believe that they're saved by being "good enough," or that they have to "be good" in order to earn God's favor. In light of today's reading, how would you answer someone who believed this way?

For your next devotional reading, go to page 1288.

love has been poured out into our hearts through the Holy Spirit, who has been given to us.

6You see, at just the right time, when we were still powerless, Christ died for the ungodly. 7Very rarely will anyone die for a righteous person, though for a good person someone might possibly dare to die. 8But God demonstrates his own love for us in this: While we were still sinners, Christ died for us.

9Since we have now been justified by his blood, how much more shall we be saved from God's wrath through him! 10For if, while we were God's enemies, we were reconciled to him through the death of his Son, how much more, having been reconciled, shall we be saved through his life! 11Not only is this so, but we also boast in God through our Lord Jesus Christ, through whom we have now received reconciliation.

Death Through Adam, Life Through Christ

12Therefore, just as sin entered the world through one man, and death through sin, and in this way death came to all people, because all sinned—

13To be sure, sin was in the world before the law was given, but sin is not charged against anyone's account where there is no law. 14Nevertheless, death reigned from the time of Adam to the time of Moses, even over those who did not sin by breaking a command, as did Adam, who is a pattern of the one to come.

15But the gift is not like the trespass. For if the many died by the trespass of the one man, how much more did God's grace and the gift that came by the grace of the one man, Jesus Christ, overflow to the many! 16Nor can the gift of God be compared with the result of one man's sin: The judgment followed one sin and brought condemnation, but the gift followed many trespasses and brought justification. 17For if, by the trespass of the one man, death reigned through that one man, how much more will those who receive God's abundant provision of grace and of the gift of righteousness reign in life through the one man, Jesus Christ!

18Consequently, just as one trespass resulted in condemnation for all people, so also one righteous act resulted in justification and life for all. 19For just as through the disobedience of the one man the many were made sinners, so also through the obedience of the one man the many will be made righteous.

20The law was brought in so that the trespass might increase. But where sin increased, grace increased all the more, 21so that, just as sin reigned in death, so also grace might reign through righteousness to bring eternal life through Jesus Christ our Lord.

Dead to Sin, Alive in Christ

6 What shall we say, then? Shall we go on sinning so that grace may increase? 2By no means! We are those who have died to sin; how can we live in it any longer? 3Or don't you know that all of us who were baptized into Christ Jesus were baptized into his death? 4We were therefore buried with him through baptism into death in order that, just as Christ was raised from the dead through the glory of the Father, we too may live a new life.

5If we have been united with him in a death like his, we will certainly also be united with him in a resurrection like his. 6For we know that our old self was crucified with him so that the body ruled by sin might be done away with,a that we should no longer be slaves to sin— 7because anyone who has died has been set free from sin.

8Now if we died with Christ, we believe that we will also live with him. 9For we know that since Christ was raised from the dead, he cannot die again; death no longer has mastery over him. 10The death he died, he died to sin once for all; but the life he lives, he lives to God.

11In the same way, count yourselves dead to sin but alive to God in Christ Jesus. 12Therefore do not let sin reign in your mortal body so that you obey its evil desires. 13Do not offer any part of yourself to sin as an instrument of wickedness, but rather offer yourselves to God as those who have been brought from death to life; and offer every part of yourself to him as an instrument of righteousness. 14For sin shall no longer be your master, because you are not under the law, but under grace.

a 6 Or be rendered powerless

Slaves to Righteousness

¹⁵What then? Shall we sin because we are not under the law but under grace? By no means! ¹⁶Don't you know that when you offer yourselves to someone as obedient slaves, you are slaves of the one you obey— whether you are slaves to sin, which leads to death, or to obedience, which leads to righteousness? ¹⁷But thanks be to God that, though you used to be slaves to sin, you have come to obey from your heart the pattern of teaching that has now claimed your allegiance. ¹⁸You have been set free from sin and have become slaves to righteousness.

¹⁹I am using an example from everyday life because of your human limitations. Just as you used to offer yourselves as slaves to impurity and to ever-increasing wickedness, so now offer yourselves as slaves to righteousness leading to holiness. ²⁰When you were slaves to sin, you were free from the control of righteousness. ²¹What benefit did you reap at that time from the things you are now ashamed of? Those things result in death! ²²But now that you have been set free from sin and have become slaves of God, the benefit you reap leads to holiness, and the result is eternal life. ²³For the wages of sin is death, but the gift of God is eternal life in^a Christ Jesus our Lord.

Released From the Law, Bound to Christ

7 Do you not know, brothers and sisters—for I am speaking to those who know the law—that the law has authority over someone only as long as that person lives? ²For example, by law a married woman is bound to her husband as long as he is alive, but if her husband dies, she is released from the law that binds her to him. ³So then, if she marries another man while her husband is still alive, she is called an adulteress. But if her husband dies, she is released from that law and is not an adulteress if she marries another man.

⁴So, my brothers and sisters, you also died to the law through the body of Christ, that you might belong to another, to him who was raised from the dead, in order that we might bear fruit for God. ⁵For when we were controlled by our sinful nature,^b the sinful passions aroused by the law were at work in us, so that we bore fruit for death.

⁶But now, by dying to what once bound us, we have been released from the law so that we serve in the new way of the Spirit, and not in the old way of the written code.

The Law and Sin

⁷What shall we say, then? Is the law sinful? Certainly not! Nevertheless, I would not have known what sin was had it not been for the law. For I would not have known what coveting really was if the law had not said, "You shall not covet."^c ⁸But sin, seizing the opportunity afforded by the commandment, produced in me every kind of coveting. For apart from the law, sin was dead. ⁹Once I was alive apart from the law; but when the commandment came, sin sprang to life and I died. ¹⁰I found that the very commandment that was intended to bring life actually brought death. ¹¹For sin, seizing the opportunity afforded by the commandment, deceived me, and through the commandment put me to death. ¹²So then, the law is holy, and the commandment is holy, righteous and good.

¹³Did that which is good, then, become death to me? By no means! Nevertheless, in order that sin might be recognized as sin, it used what is good to bring about my death, so that through the commandment sin might become utterly sinful.

¹⁴We know that the law is spiritual; but I am unspiritual, sold as a slave to sin. ¹⁵I do not understand what I do. For what I want to do I do not do, but what I hate I do. ¹⁶And if I do what I do not want to do, I agree that the law is good. ¹⁷As it is, it is no longer I myself who do it, but it is sin living in me. ¹⁸I know that good itself does not dwell in me, that is, in my sinful nature.^d For I have the desire to do what is good, but I cannot carry it out. ¹⁹For I do not do the good I want to do, but the evil I do not want to do—this I keep on doing. ²⁰Now if I do what I do not want to do, it is no longer I who do it, but it is sin living in me that does it.

²¹So I find this law at work: Although I want to do good, evil is right there with me. ²²For in my inner being I delight in God's law; ²³but I see another law at work in me, waging war against the law of my mind and making me a prisoner of the law of sin at work within me. ²⁴What a wretched man I

---

^a 23 Or *through*   ^b 5 Or *by the flesh*   ^c 7 Exodus 20:17; Deut. 5:21   ^d 18 Or *my flesh*

DEALING WITH TEMPTATIONS

Romans 7:1–25 *or* 7:15–21

Rob Bell

When the first Christians went all over the Roman Empire telling people the Jesus message, they spent most of their time explaining who people are from God's perspective: who we already are. They insisted that people can live a new life, counting ourselves "dead to sin but alive to God."

When we stumble and fall back into old patterns, we call them what they are: old patterns. Old ways. Old habits of the old person.

Something new is happening in us.

Jesus said that as this new reality takes over our hearts and lives in our minds and actions, we are crossing over "from death to life." He called this new kind of life "eternal life." For Jesus, eternal life wasn't a state of being for the future that we would enter into somewhere else; it is a quality of life that starts now . . .

This has huge implications for when I do stumble, when I sin, and the old person comes back from the dead for a few moments.

I admit it.

I confess it.

I thank God I'm forgiven.

I make amends with anyone who has been affected by my actions.

And then I move on . . .

God's strength, not mine.

God's power, not mine.

THOMAS À KEMPIS {AD 1380–1471}

We must be careful and concerned about our own temptations . . . Remember, no one is so holy that he or she does not have to deal with temptations . . .

No one is completely free of temptations because the source of temptation is in ourselves . . . We cannot win this battle by running away alone; the key to victory is true humility and patience; in them we overcome the enemy.

reflection

1. In what ways do you relate to the idea of not doing the good you want to do but instead doing the evil that you don't want to do?

2. What temptation are you facing right now?

3. What is your normal strategy for dealing with temptation?

For your next devotional reading, go to page 1290.

am! Who will rescue me from this body of death? ²⁵Thanks be to God, who delivers me through Jesus Christ our Lord!

So then, I myself in my mind am a slave to God's law, but in my sinful nature*ᵃ* a slave to the law of sin.

Life Through the Spirit

8 Therefore, there is now no condemnation for those who are in Christ Jesus, ²because through Christ Jesus the law of the Spirit who gives life has set you*ᵇ* free from the law of sin and death. ³For what the law was powerless to do because it was weakened by the sinful nature,*ᶜ* God did by sending his own Son in the likeness of sinful humanity to be a sin offering.*ᵈ* And so he condemned sin in human flesh, ⁴in order that the righteous requirement of the law might be fully met in us, who do not live according to the sinful nature but according to the Spirit.

⁵Those who live according to the sinful nature have their minds set on what that nature desires; but those who live in accordance with the Spirit have their minds set on what the Spirit desires. ⁶The mind controlled by the sinful nature*ᵉ* is death, but the mind controlled by the Spirit is life and peace. ⁷The sinful mind*ᶠ* is hostile to God; it does not submit to God's law, nor can it do so. ⁸Those controlled by the sinful nature cannot please God.

⁹You, however, are not controlled by the sinful nature but are in the Spirit, if indeed the Spirit of God lives in you. And if anyone does not have the Spirit of Christ, they do not belong to Christ. ¹⁰But if Christ is in you, then even though your body is subject to death because of sin, the Spirit gives life*ᵍ* because of righteousness. ¹¹And if the Spirit of him who raised Jesus from the dead is living in you, he who raised Christ from the dead will also give life to your mortal bodies because of*ʰ* his Spirit who lives in you.

¹²Therefore, brothers and sisters, we have an obligation—but it is not to the sinful nature, to live according to it. ¹³For if you live according to the sinful nature, you will die; but if by the Spirit you put to death the misdeeds of the body, you will live.

¹⁴For those who are led by the Spirit of God are the children of God. ¹⁵The Spirit you received does not make you slaves, so that you live in fear again; rather, the Spirit you received brought about your adoption to sonship.*ⁱ* And by him we cry, "Abba,*ʲ* Father." ¹⁶The Spirit himself testifies with our spirit that we are God's children. ¹⁷Now if we are children, then we are heirs—heirs of God and co-heirs with Christ, if indeed we share in his sufferings in order that we may also share in his glory.

Present Suffering and Future Glory

¹⁸I consider that our present sufferings are not worth comparing with the glory that will be revealed in us. ¹⁹The creation waits in eager expectation for the children of God to be revealed. ²⁰For the creation was subjected to frustration, not by its own choice, but by the will of the one who subjected it, in hope ²¹that*ᵏ* the creation itself will be liberated from its bondage to decay and brought into the freedom and glory of the children of God.

²²We know that the whole creation has been groaning as in the pains of childbirth right up to the present time. ²³Not only so, but we ourselves, who have the firstfruits of the Spirit, groan inwardly as we wait eagerly for our adoption, the redemption of our bodies. ²⁴For in this hope we were saved. But hope that is seen is no hope at all. Who hopes for what they already have? ²⁵But if we hope for what we do not yet have, we wait for it patiently.

²⁶In the same way, the Spirit helps us in our weakness. We do not know what we ought to pray for, but the Spirit himself intercedes for us through wordless groans. ²⁷And he who searches our hearts knows the mind of the Spirit, because the Spirit intercedes for God's people in accordance with the will of God.

²⁸And we know that in all things God works for the good of those who love him, who*ˡ* have been called according to his pur-

---

ᵃ 25 Or *in the flesh*   *ᵇ 2* The Greek is singular; some manuscripts *me*   *ᶜ 3* Or *the flesh*; also in verses 4, 5, 8, 9, 12 and 13   *ᵈ 3* Or *humanity, for sin*   *ᵉ 6* Or *mind set on the flesh*   *ᶠ 7* Or *the mind set on the flesh*   *ᵍ 10* Or *you, your body is dead because of sin, yet your spirit is alive*   *ʰ 11* Some manuscripts *bodies through*   *ⁱ 15* The Greek word for *adoption to sonship* is a term referring to the full legal standing of an adopted male heir in Roman culture.   *ʲ 15* Aramaic for *Father*   *ᵏ 20,21* Or *subjected it in hope. ²¹For*   *ˡ 28* Or *that all things work together for good to those who love God, who*; or *that in all things God works together with those who love him to bring about what is good—with those who*

TO HEAL, FORGIVE, REDEEM

Romans 8:1–39 *or* 8:1–4

Richard Foster

At the heart of God is the desire to give and to forgive. Because of this, he set into motion the entire redemptive process that culminated in the cross and was confirmed in the resurrection. The usual notion of what Jesus did on the cross runs something like this: people were so bad and so mean and God was so angry with them that he could not forgive them unless somebody big enough took the rap for the whole lot of them.

Nothing could be further from the truth. Love, not anger, brought Jesus to the cross. Golgotha came as a result of God's great desire to forgive, not his reluctance. Jesus knew that by his vicarious suffering he could actually absorb all the evil of humanity and so heal it, forgive it, redeem it.

This is why Jesus refused the customary painkiller when it was offered him. He wanted to be completely alert for this greatest work of redemption. In a deep and mysterious way he was preparing to take on the collective sin of the human race. Since Jesus lives in the eternal now, this work was not just for those around him, but he took in all the violence, all the fear, all the sin of all the past, all the present and all the future. This was his highest and most holy work, the work that makes confession and the forgiveness of sins possible.

ALFRED EDERSHEIM {AD 1825–1889}

After soldiers nailed him to the cross and divided up his clothing, Jesus said: "Father, forgive them, for they do not know what they are doing" (Luke 23:34). The reference in this prayer to "what they are doing" (in the present, not in the past nor the future) points to the soldiers as the primary (though certainly not the sole) object of the Savior's prayer. But higher thoughts also come to us. In the moment of the deepest humiliation of Christ's human nature, the divine bursts forth most brightly. It is as if the Savior rejected all that is merely human in his sufferings, just as before he had rejected the cup of drugged wine. These soldiers were only unconscious instruments. The real battle was between the kingdom of God and the kingdom of darkness—between Christ and Satan—and these sufferings were just the necessary path of obedience, leading to victory and glory.

reflection

1. Why did Jesus die on the cross?
2. What can you thank God for that was accomplished by Christ's death?
3. Jesus was condemned on the cross so that you could be free from condemnation before God. How can this knowledge affect how you live your life this week?

For your next devotional reading, go to page 1293.

pose. [29]For those God foreknew he also predestined to be conformed to the image of his Son, that he might be the firstborn among many brothers and sisters. [30]And those he predestined, he also called; those he called, he also justified; those he justified, he also glorified.

More Than Conquerors

[31]What, then, shall we say in response to these things? If God is for us, who can be against us? [32]He who did not spare his own Son, but gave him up for us all—how will he not also, along with him, graciously give us all things? [33]Who will bring any charge against those whom God has chosen? It is God who justifies. [34]Who then can condemn? No one. Christ Jesus who died—more than that, who was raised to life—is at the right hand of God and is also interceding for us. [35]Who shall separate us from the love of Christ? Shall trouble or hardship or persecution or famine or nakedness or danger or sword? [36]As it is written:

> "For your sake we face death all day
> long;
> we are considered as sheep to be
> slaughtered."[a]

[37]No, in all these things we are more than conquerors through him who loved us. [38]For I am convinced that neither death nor life, neither angels nor demons,[b] neither the present nor the future, nor any powers, [39]neither height nor depth, nor anything else in all creation, will be able to separate us from the love of God that is in Christ Jesus our Lord.

Paul's Anguish Over Israel

9 I speak the truth in Christ—I am not lying, my conscience confirms it through the Holy Spirit— [2]I have great sorrow and unceasing anguish in my heart. [3]For I could wish that I myself were cursed and cut off from Christ for the sake of my people, those of my own race, [4]the people of Israel. Theirs is the adoption; theirs the divine glory, the covenants, the receiving of the law, the temple worship and the promises. [5]Theirs are the patriarchs, and from them is traced the human ancestry of the Messiah, who is God over all, forever praised![c] Amen.

God's Sovereign Choice

[6]It is not as though God's word had failed. For not all who are descended from Israel are Israel. [7]Nor because they are his descendants are they all Abraham's children. On the contrary, "It is through Isaac that your offspring will be reckoned."[d] [8]In other words, it is not the natural children who are God's children, but it is the children of the promise who are regarded as Abraham's offspring. [9]For this was how the promise was stated: "At the appointed time I will return, and Sarah will have a son."[e]

[10]Not only that, but Rebekah's children were conceived at the same time by our father Isaac. [11]Yet, before the twins were born or had done anything good or bad—in order that God's purpose in election might stand: [12]not by works but by him who calls—she was told, "The older will serve the younger."[f] [13]Just as it is written: "Jacob I loved, but Esau I hated."[g]

[14]What then shall we say? Is God unjust? Not at all! [15]For he says to Moses,

> "I will have mercy on whom I have
> mercy,
> and I will have compassion on whom
> I have compassion."[h]

[16]It does not, therefore, depend on human desire or effort, but on God's mercy. [17]For Scripture says to Pharaoh: "I raised you up for this very purpose, that I might display my power in you and that my name might be proclaimed in all the earth."[i] [18]Therefore God has mercy on whom he wants to have mercy, and he hardens whom he wants to harden.

[19]One of you will say to me: "Then why does God still blame us? For who is able to resist his will?" [20]But who are you, a mere human being, to talk back to God? "Shall what is formed say to the one who formed it, 'Why did you make me like this?' "[j] [21]Does not the potter have the right to make out of the same lump of clay some pottery for noble purposes and some for disposal of refuse?

[22]What if God, although choosing to show his wrath and make his power known, bore

---

a 36 Psalm 44:22   *b* 38 Or *nor heavenly rulers*   *c* 5 Or *Messiah, who is over all. God be forever praised!*
Or *Messiah. God who is over all be forever praised!*   *d* 7 Gen. 21:12   *e* 9 Gen. 18:10,14
f 12 Gen. 25:23   *g* 13 Mal. 1:2,3   *h* 15 Exodus 33:19   *i* 17 Exodus 9:16   *j* 20 Isaiah 29:16; 45:9

with great patience the objects of his wrath—prepared for destruction? ²³What if he did this to make the riches of his glory known to the objects of his mercy, whom he prepared in advance for glory— ²⁴even us, whom he also called, not only from the Jews but also from the Gentiles? ²⁵As he says in Hosea:

"I will call them 'my people' who are not
> my people;
> and I will call her 'my loved one' who
> is not my loved one,"ᵃ

²⁶and,

"In the very place where it was said to
> them,
> 'You are not my people,'
> they will be called 'children of the
> living God.' "ᵇ

²⁷Isaiah cries out concerning Israel:

"Though the number of the Israelites be
> like the sand by the sea,
> only the remnant will be saved.
²⁸For the Lord will carry out
> his sentence on earth with speed and
> finality."ᶜ

²⁹It is just as Isaiah said previously:

"Unless the Lord Almighty
> had left us descendants,
> we would have become like Sodom,
> we would have been like Gomorrah."ᵈ

Israel's Unbelief

³⁰What then shall we say? That the Gentiles, who did not pursue righteousness, have obtained it, a righteousness that is by faith; ³¹but the people of Israel, who pursued the law as the way of righteousness, have not attained their goal. ³²Why not? Because they pursued it not by faith but as if it were by works. They stumbled over the stumbling stone. ³³As it is written:

"See, I lay in Zion a stone that causes
> people to stumble
> and a rock that makes them fall,
> and the one who believes in him will
> never be put to shame."ᵉ

10 Brothers and sisters, my heart's desire and prayer to God for the Israelites is that they may be saved. ²For I can testify about them that they are zealous for God, but their zeal is not based on knowledge. ³Since they did not know the righteousness of God and sought to establish their own, they did not submit to God's righteousness. ⁴Christ is the culmination of the law so that there may be righteousness for everyone who believes.

⁵Moses writes this about the righteousness that is by the law: "Whoever does these things will live by them."ᶠ ⁶But the righteousness that is by faith says: "Do not say in your heart, 'Who will ascend into heaven?' "ᵍ (that is, to bring Christ down) ⁷"or 'Who will descend into the deep?' "ʰ (that is, to bring Christ up from the dead). ⁸But what does it say? "The word is near you; it is in your mouth and in your heart,"ⁱ that is, the message concerning faith that we proclaim: ⁹If you declare with your mouth, "Jesus is Lord," and believe in your heart that God raised him from the dead, you will be saved. ¹⁰For it is with your heart that you believe and are justified, and it is with your mouth that you profess your faith and are saved. ¹¹As Scripture says, "Anyone who believes in him will never be put to shame."ʲ ¹²For there is no difference between Jew and Gentile—the same Lord is Lord of all and richly blesses all who call on him, ¹³for, "Everyone who calls on the name of the Lord will be saved."ᵏ

¹⁴How, then, can they call on the one they have not believed in? And how can they believe in the one of whom they have not heard? And how can they hear without someone preaching to them? ¹⁵And how can anyone preach unless they are sent? As it is written: "How beautiful are the feet of those who bring good news!"ˡ

¹⁶But not all the Israelites accepted the good news. For Isaiah says, "Lord, who has believed our message?"ᵐ ¹⁷Consequently, faith comes from hearing the message, and the message is heard through the word about Christ. ¹⁸But I ask: Did they not hear? Of course they did:

ᵃ 25 Hosea 2:23   ᵇ 26 Hosea 1:10   ᶜ 28 Isaiah 10:22,23 (see Septuagint)   ᵈ 29 Isaiah 1:9
ᵉ 33 Isaiah 8:14; 28:16   ᶠ 5 Lev. 18:5   ᵍ 6 Deut. 30:12   ʰ 7 Deut. 30:13   ⁱ 8 Deut. 30:14
ʲ 11 Isaiah 28:16 (see Septuagint)   ᵏ 13 Joel 2:32   ˡ 15 Isaiah 52:7   ᵐ 16 Isaiah 53:1

FRIDAY

THE POWER OF FAITH

Romans 10:1–21 *or* 10:14–17

R. A. TORREY {AD 1856–1928}

But how does real faith come?

Romans 10:17 answers the question: "[Consequently, faith comes from hearing the message, and the message is heard through the word about Christ.]" If we are to have real faith, we must study the Word of God and find out what is promised, then simply believe the promises of God. Faith must have a warrant. Trying to believe something that you want to believe is not faith. Believing what God says in His Word is faith. If I am to have faith when I pray, I must find some promise in the Word of God on which to rest my faith. Faith furthermore comes through the Spirit. The Spirit knows the will of God, and if I pray in the Spirit, and look to the Spirit to teach me God's will, He will lead me out in prayer along the line of that will, and give me faith that the prayer is to be answered; but in no case does real faith come by simply determining that you are going to get the thing that you want to get.

If there is no promise in the Word of God, and no clear leading of the Spirit, there can be no real faith, and there should be no upbraiding of self for lack of faith in such a case. But if the thing desired is promised in the Word of God, we may well upbraid ourselves for lack of faith if we doubt; for we are making God a liar by doubting His Word.

Jim Cymbala

Finding new power in prayer always means developing a new relationship with the Word of God, because God's Word provides the right foundation for a life of asking and receiving. Only the prayer of faith secures answers, and we are not left in the dark about how faith is produced: Faith comes from *hearing* the message, and the message is heard through *the word* [*about*] Christ (Romans 10:17).

How we feel, how things seem, what others say—these transient sentiments and circumstances will never cause faith to take root in our souls. Anyone who relies on them will never be able to pray with confidence before the throne of grace. Instead, we need to develop a strong faith, based on God's unalterable Word. How we react to his Word and the place it finds in our hearts are what will determine our future in God.

reflection

1. Do you know someone who claims to "have faith," but his or her faith is based on something other than the Bible's message about Jesus?

2. What is *your* faith based on?

3. How does basing your prayer on the Word of God give you confidence and faith as you pray?

For your next devotional reading, go to page 1295.

"Their voice has gone out into all the
earth,
their words to the ends of the
world."[a]

¹⁹Again I ask: Did Israel not understand?
First, Moses says,

"I will make you envious by those who
are not a nation;
I will make you angry by a nation that
has no understanding."[b]

²⁰And Isaiah boldly says,

"I was found by those who did not seek
me;
I revealed myself to those who did
not ask for me."[c]

²¹But concerning Israel he says,

"All day long I have held out my hands
to a disobedient and obstinate
people."[d]

The Remnant of Israel

11 I ask then: Did God reject his
people? By no means! I am an
Israelite myself, a descendant of
Abraham, from the tribe of Benjamin. ²God
did not reject his people, whom he foreknew. Don't you know what Scripture says
in the passage about Elijah—how he appealed to God against Israel: ³"Lord, they
have killed your prophets and torn down
your altars; I am the only one left, and they
are trying to kill me"[e]? ⁴And what was God's
answer to him? "I have reserved for myself
seven thousand who have not bowed the
knee to Baal."[f] ⁵So too, at the present time
there is a remnant chosen by grace. ⁶And if
by grace, then it cannot be based on works;
if it were, grace would no longer be grace.

⁷What then? What the people of Israel
sought so earnestly they did not obtain. The
elect among them did, but the others were
hardened, ⁸as it is written:

"God gave them a spirit of stupor,
eyes that could not see
and ears that could not hear,
to this very day."[g]

⁹And David says:

"May their table become a snare and a
trap,
a stumbling block and a retribution
for them.
¹⁰May their eyes be darkened so they
cannot see,
and their backs be bent forever."[h]

Ingrafted Branches

¹¹Again I ask: Did they stumble so as to
fall beyond recovery? Not at all! Rather, because of their transgression, salvation has
come to the Gentiles to make Israel envious.
¹²But if their transgression means riches for
the world, and their loss means riches for
the Gentiles, how much greater riches will
their fullness bring!

¹³I am talking to you Gentiles. Inasmuch
as I am the apostle to the Gentiles, I make
much of my ministry ¹⁴in the hope that I
may somehow arouse my own people to
envy and save some of them. ¹⁵For if their
rejection brought reconciliation to the
world, what will their acceptance be but life
from the dead? ¹⁶If the part of the dough offered as firstfruits is holy, then the whole
batch is holy; if the root is holy, so are the
branches.

¹⁷If some of the branches have been broken off, and you, though a wild olive shoot,
have been grafted in among the others and
now share in the nourishing sap from the olive root, ¹⁸do not consider yourself to be superior to those other branches. If you do,
consider this: You do not support the root,
but the root supports you. ¹⁹You will say
then, "Branches were broken off so that I
could be grafted in." ²⁰Granted. But they
were broken off because of unbelief, and
you stand by faith. Do not be arrogant, but
tremble. ²¹For if God did not spare the natural branches, he will not spare you either.

²²Consider therefore the kindness and
sternness of God: sternness to those who
fell, but kindness to you, provided that you
continue in his kindness. Otherwise, you
also will be cut off. ²³And if they do not persist in unbelief, they will be grafted in, for
God is able to graft them in again. ²⁴After all,
if you were cut out of an olive tree that is
wild by nature, and contrary to nature were
grafted into a cultivated olive tree, how

---

a 18 Psalm 19:4   b 19 Deut. 32:21   c 20 Isaiah 65:1   d 21 Isaiah 65:2   e 3 1 Kings 19:10,14
f 4 1 Kings 19:18   g 8 Deut. 29:4; Isaiah 29:10   h 10 Psalm 69:22,23

Finding Salvation

Romans 11:17–24

read/meditate

After reading the passage through once, go back and read it again, phrase by phrase. Pause between each phrase to give the Spirit room to breathe life into the truth you are reading.

pray

You've been offered generous gifts of salvation and new life. How do you feel about that? Express to God your feelings—gratitude, confusion, ambivalence, exhilaration, etc.

contemplate

Paul is talking here about God's gift of salvation extended to the Gentiles. Think about your own spiritual walk in the context of God's saving plan first for the Jews and then for the entire human race.

additional reflection

I cannot, by direct moral effort, give myself new motives. After the first few steps in the Christian life we realize that everything which really needs to be done in our souls can be done only by God.

—C. S. Lewis

The biggest blessing in your life was when you came to the end of trying to be a Christian, . . . and were willing to come as a pauper and receive the Holy Spirit.

—Oswald Chambers

For your next devotional reading, go to page 1297.

much more readily will these, the natural branches, be grafted into their own olive tree!

All Israel Will Be Saved

²⁵I do not want you to be ignorant of this mystery, brothers and sisters, so that you may not think you are superior: Israel has experienced a hardening in part until the full number of the Gentiles has come in, ²⁶and in this way*a* all Israel will be saved. As it is written:

> "The deliverer will come from Zion;
> he will turn godlessness away from Jacob.
> ²⁷And this is*b* my covenant with them
> when I take away their sins."*c*

²⁸As far as the gospel is concerned, they are enemies for your sake; but as far as election is concerned, they are loved on account of the patriarchs, ²⁹for God's gifts and his call are irrevocable. ³⁰Just as you who were at one time disobedient to God have now received mercy as a result of their disobedience, ³¹so they too have now become disobedient in order that they too may now*d* receive mercy as a result of God's mercy to you. ³²For God has bound everyone over to disobedience so that he may have mercy on them all.

Doxology

³³Oh, the depth of the riches of the
wisdom and*e* knowledge of
God!
How unsearchable his judgments,
and his paths beyond tracing out!
³⁴"Who has known the mind of the Lord?
Or who has been his counselor?"*f*
³⁵"Who has ever given to God,
that God should repay them?"*g*
³⁶For from him and through him and to
him are all things.
To him be the glory forever! Amen.

A Living Sacrifice

12 Therefore, I urge you, brothers and sisters, in view of God's mercy, to offer your bodies as a living sacrifice, holy and pleasing to God—

this is true worship. ²Do not conform to the pattern of this world, but be transformed by the renewing of your mind. Then you will be able to test and approve what God's will is— his good, pleasing and perfect will.

Humble Service in the Body of Christ

³For by the grace given me I say to every one of you: Do not think of yourself more highly than you ought, but rather think of yourself with sober judgment, in accordance with the faith God has distributed to each of you. ⁴For just as each of us has one body with many members, and these members do not all have the same function, ⁵so in Christ we, though many, form one body, and each member belongs to all the others. ⁶We have different gifts, according to the grace given to each of us. If your gift is prophesying, then prophesy in accordance with your*h* faith; ⁷if it is serving, then serve; if it is teaching, then teach; ⁸if it is to encourage, then give encouragement; if it is giving, then give generously; if it is to lead,*i* do it diligently; if it is to show mercy, do it cheerfully.

Love in Action

⁹Love must be sincere. Hate what is evil; cling to what is good. ¹⁰Be devoted to one another in love. Honor one another above yourselves. ¹¹Never be lacking in zeal, but keep your spiritual fervor, serving the Lord. ¹²Be joyful in hope, patient in affliction, faithful in prayer. ¹³Share with the Lord's people who are in need. Practice hospitality.

¹⁴Bless those who persecute you; bless and do not curse. ¹⁵Rejoice with those who rejoice; mourn with those who mourn. ¹⁶Live in harmony with one another. Do not be proud, but be willing to associate with people of low position.*j* Do not think you are superior.

¹⁷Do not repay anyone evil for evil. Be careful to do what is right in the eyes of everyone. ¹⁸If it is possible, as far as it depends on you, live at peace with everyone. ¹⁹Do not take revenge, my dear friends, but leave room for God's wrath, for it is written: "It is mine to avenge; I will repay,"*k* says the Lord. ²⁰On the contrary:

---

a 26 Or *and so*   *b 27* Or *will be*   *c 27* Isaiah 59:20,21; 27:9 (see Septuagint); Jer. 31:33,34
d 31 Some manuscripts do not have *now.*   *e 33* Or *riches and the wisdom and the*   *f 34* Isaiah 40:13
g 35 Job 41:11   *h 6* Or *the*   *i 8* Or *to provide for others*   *j 16* Or *willing to do menial work*
k 19 Deut. 32:35

MONDAY

BUILDING A CHURCH
Romans 12:1–21 *or* 12:3–8

JOHN CHRYSOSTOM {AD 347–407}

What then is the source of these many and different spiritual gifts? Paul asked this question because this subject continually carried away many Christians into vain arrogance, and others into depression or envy. Consequently, Paul continually found himself compelled to deal with this issue.

Some of Paul's main points were that we all have God for our Father, and we all partake of the same Spirit. These things we all share in common. If it appears then that any other person possesses any superiority in any spiritual gift, you should not let this grieve you—especially since this means that person's labor also is greater.

Jesus told the story of a man who had received five talents and was held responsible for those five. Meanwhile, a second man received only two, was held responsible only for those two, and yet received the exact same reward as the first man. The apostle Paul encouraged his hearers on the same basis, showing that gifts are given by God not for the honor of one person above another, but for the work of the church. In fact, he even says God gave these gifts "to equip his people for works of service, so that the body of Christ may be built up" (Ephesians 4:12).

Bill Hybels

In the kaleidoscope of God's family, there's room for all gifts and temperaments. God may have given you extraordinary depths of mercy, lots of patience, heights of wisdom or the ability to enjoy adventure or to thrive on solitude. And, somewhere in your community, there's probably a seeker who's one step away from coming to faith but who needs to come into contact with someone just like you—with *your* personality, *your* temperament, *your* passion and *your* interests. If that seeker could glimpse how God lives and works through you, it might be enough to propel him across the line of faith.

reflection

1. Who is the source of spiritual gifts? Why were they given?
2. What are your particular talents and spiritual gifts?
3. Do you ever wish God had given you different gifts, made you a different body part? Why? Has today's reading changed your perspective?

For your next devotional reading, go to page 1299.

"If your enemy is hungry, feed him;
    if he is thirsty, give him something to
        drink.
In doing this, you will heap burning
    coals on his head."ᵃ

²¹Do not be overcome by evil, but overcome evil with good.

Submission to Governing Authorities

13 Let everyone be subject to the governing authorities, for there is no authority except that which God has established. The authorities that exist have been established by God. ²Consequently, whoever rebels against the authority is rebelling against what God has instituted, and those who do so will bring judgment on themselves. ³For rulers hold no terror for those who do right, but for those who do wrong. Do you want to be free from fear of the one in authority? Then do what is right and you will be commended. ⁴For the one in authority is God's servant for your good. But if you do wrong, be afraid, for rulers do not bear the sword for no reason. They are God's servants, agents of wrath to bring punishment on the wrongdoer. ⁵Therefore, it is necessary to submit to the authorities, not only because of possible punishment but also as a matter of conscience.

⁶This is also why you pay taxes, for the authorities are God's servants, who give their full time to governing. ⁷Give to everyone what you owe: If you owe taxes, pay taxes; if revenue, then revenue; if respect, then respect; if honor, then honor.

Love Fulfills the Law

⁸Let no debt remain outstanding, except the continuing debt to love one another, for whoever loves others has fulfilled the law. ⁹The commandments, "You shall not commit adultery," "You shall not murder," "You shall not steal," "You shall not covet,"ᵇ and whatever other command there may be, are summed up in this one command: "Love your neighbor as yourself."ᶜ ¹⁰Love does no harm to its neighbor. Therefore love is the fulfillment of the law.

The Day Is Near

¹¹And do this, understanding the present time. The hour has already come for you to wake up from your slumber, because our salvation is nearer now than when we first believed. ¹²The night is nearly over; the day is almost here. So let us put aside the deeds of darkness and put on the armor of light. ¹³Let us behave decently, as in the daytime, not in carousing and drunkenness, not in sexual immorality and debauchery, not in dissension and jealousy. ¹⁴Rather, clothe yourselves with the Lord Jesus Christ, and do not think about how to gratify the desires of the sinful nature.ᵈ

The Weak and the Strong

14 Accept those whose faith is weak, without quarreling over disputable matters. ²One person's faith allows them to eat everything, but another person, whose faith is weak, eats only vegetables. ³The one who eats everything must not treat with contempt the one who does not, and the one who does not eat everything must not judge the one who does, for God has accepted that person. ⁴Who are you to judge someone else's servant? To their own master they stand or fall. And they will stand, for the Lord is able to make them stand.

⁵Some consider one day more sacred than another; others consider every day alike. Everyone should be fully convinced in their own mind. ⁶Those who regard one day as special do so to the Lord. Those who eat meat do so to the Lord, for they give thanks to God; and those who abstain do so to the Lord and give thanks to God. ⁷For we do not live to ourselves alone and we do not die to ourselves alone. ⁸If we live, we live to the Lord; and if we die, we die to the Lord. So, whether we live or die, we belong to the Lord. ⁹For this very reason, Christ died and returned to life so that he might be the Lord of both the dead and the living.

¹⁰You, then, why do you judge your brother or sister? Or why do you treat your brother or sister with contempt? For we will all stand before God's judgment seat. ¹¹It is written:

" 'As surely as I live,' says the Lord,
'every knee will bow before me;
    every tongue will confess to God.' "ᵉ

ᵃ 20 Prov. 25:21,22   ᵇ 9 Exodus 20:13-15,17; Deut. 5:17-19,21   ᶜ 9 Lev. 19:18   ᵈ 14 Or *the flesh*
ᵉ 11 Isaiah 45:23

TUESDAY

IDENTIFY MOST WITH THE LEAST

Romans 13:1–14 *or* 13:8–10

Walter Wangerin

It is a radical truth that the Christ identifies much more with "the least of these" than with those of weight and repute in the world.

Radical, I say, because such a downward identification is a flat reversal of the way *we* choose to identify: upward, to those admirable, to those whose station flatters ours, whose power might empower us. We would be heroes. Jesus is the stranger. He *is*, in our common existence, the sick and the imprisoned.

How do we (as we will so often proclaim we do) love Jesus? With what attention and genuine love do we attend to the invisible people?

When I lean on the car horn loud and long, whose peace do I destroy? And how do I justify my anger now? Do I know the rules of the road better than the gentlewoman driving precisely the limit in front of me? And which of us is nearer the heart of Christ at this moment? And where is love?

AUGUSTINE BAKER {AD 1575–1641}

We can neither meritoriously love ourselves nor our brethren, till first we are firmly rooted in the love of God, because charity to ourselves or others is indeed only love to God by reflection, or the loving of God in things belonging to Him, and which He either loves or may love.

reflection

1. Under what circumstances do you steal the peace of others?
2. When you are guilty of this, what are you revealing about yourself?
3. How might the love of God compel you to act differently?

For your next devotional reading, go to page 1304.

¹²So then, we will all give an account of ourselves to God.

¹³Therefore let us stop passing judgment on one another. Instead, make up your mind not to put any stumbling block or obstacle in the way of a brother or sister. ¹⁴I am convinced, being fully persuaded in the Lord Jesus, that nothing is unclean in itself. But if anyone regards something as unclean, then for that person it is unclean. ¹⁵If your brother or sister is distressed because of what you eat, you are no longer acting in love. Do not by your eating destroy your brother or sister for whom Christ died. ¹⁶Therefore do not let what you know is good be spoken of as evil. ¹⁷For the kingdom of God is not a matter of eating and drinking, but of righteousness, peace and joy in the Holy Spirit, ¹⁸because anyone who serves Christ in this way is pleasing to God and receives human approval.

¹⁹Let us therefore make every effort to do what leads to peace and to mutual edification. ²⁰Do not destroy the work of God for the sake of food. All food is clean, but it is wrong for a person to eat anything that causes someone else to stumble. ²¹It is better not to eat meat or drink wine or to do anything else that will cause your brother or sister to fall.

²²So whatever you believe about these things keep between yourself and God. Blessed are those who do not condemn themselves by what they approve. ²³But those who have doubts are condemned if they eat, because their eating is not from faith; and everything that does not come from faith is sin.

15 We who are strong ought to bear with the failings of the weak and not to please ourselves. ²We should all please our neighbors for their good, to build them up. ³For even Christ did not please himself but, as it is written: "The insults of those who insult you have fallen on me."ᵃ ⁴For everything that was written in the past was written to teach us, so that through the endurance taught in the Scriptures and the encouragement they provide we might have hope.

⁵May the God who gives endurance and encouragement give you the same attitude of mind toward each other that Christ Jesus had, ⁶so that with one mind and one voice you may glorify the God and Father of our Lord Jesus Christ.

⁷Accept one another, then, just as Christ accepted you, in order to bring praise to God. ⁸For I tell you that Christ has become a servant of the Jewsᵇ on behalf of God's truth, so that the promises made to the patriarchs might be confirmed ⁹and, moreover, that the Gentiles might glorify God for his mercy. As it is written:

"Therefore I will praise you among the Gentiles;
    I will sing the praises of your name."ᶜ

¹⁰Again, it says,

"Rejoice, you Gentiles, with his people."ᵈ

¹¹And again,

"Praise the Lord, all you Gentiles;
    let all the peoples extol him."ᵉ

¹²And again, Isaiah says,

"The Root of Jesse will spring up,
    one who will arise to rule over the nations;
in him the Gentiles will hope."ᶠ

¹³May the God of hope fill you with all joy and peace as you trust in him, so that you may overflow with hope by the power of the Holy Spirit.

Paul the Minister to the Gentiles

¹⁴I myself am convinced, my brothers and sisters, that you yourselves are full of goodness, filled with knowledge and competent to instruct one another. ¹⁵Yet I have written you quite boldly on some points to remind you of them again, because of the grace God gave me ¹⁶to be a minister of Christ Jesus to the Gentiles. He gave me the priestly duty of proclaiming the gospel of God, so that the Gentiles might become an offering acceptable to God, sanctified by the Holy Spirit.

¹⁷Therefore I glory in Christ Jesus in my service to God. ¹⁸I will not venture to speak of anything except what Christ has accomplished through me in leading the Gentiles

ᵃ 3 Psalm 69:9   ᵇ 8 Greek *circumcision*   ᶜ 9 2 Samuel 22:50; Psalm 18:49   ᵈ 10 Deut. 32:43
ᵉ 11 Psalm 117:1   ᶠ 12 Isaiah 11:10 (see Septuagint)

to obey God by what I have said and done— ¹⁹by the power of signs and wonders, through the power of the Spirit of God. So from Jerusalem all the way around to Illyricum, I have fully proclaimed the gospel of Christ. ²⁰It has always been my ambition to preach the gospel where Christ was not known, so that I would not be building on someone else's foundation. ²¹Rather, as it is written:

> "Those who were not told about him will see,
> and those who have not heard will understand." ᵃ

²²This is why I have often been hindered from coming to you.

Paul's Plan to Visit Rome

²³But now that there is no more place for me to work in these regions, and since I have been longing for many years to visit you, ²⁴I plan to do so when I go to Spain. I hope to see you while passing through and to have you assist me on my journey there, after I have enjoyed your company for a while. ²⁵Now, however, I am on my way to Jerusalem in the service of the Lord's people there. ²⁶For Macedonia and Achaia were pleased to make a contribution for the poor among the Lord's people in Jerusalem. ²⁷They were pleased to do it, and indeed they owe it to them. For if the Gentiles have shared in the Jews' spiritual blessings, they owe it to the Jews to share with them their material blessings. ²⁸So after I have completed this task and have made sure that they have received this fruit, I will go to Spain and visit you on the way. ²⁹I know that when I come to you, I will come in the full measure of the blessing of Christ.

³⁰I urge you, brothers and sisters, by our Lord Jesus Christ and by the love of the Spirit, to join me in my struggle by praying to God for me. ³¹Pray that I may be kept safe from the unbelievers in Judea and that the contribution I take to Jerusalem may be favorably received by the Lord's people there, ³²so that by God's will I may come to you with joy and together with you be refreshed. ³³The God of peace be with you all. Amen.

Personal Greetings

16 I commend to you our sister Phoebe, a deacon ᵇ of the church in Cenchreae. ²I ask you to receive her in the Lord in a way worthy of his people and to give her any help she may need from you, for she has been the benefactor of many people, including me.

³Greet Priscilla ᶜ and Aquila, my co-workers in Christ Jesus. ⁴They risked their lives for me. Not only I but all the churches of the Gentiles are grateful to them.

⁵Greet also the church that meets at their house.

Greet my dear friend Epenetus, who was the first convert to Christ in the province of Asia.

⁶Greet Mary, who worked very hard for you.

⁷Greet Andronicus and Junia, my fellow Jews who have been in prison with me. They are outstanding among the apostles, and they were in Christ before I was.

⁸Greet Ampliatus, my dear friend in the Lord.

⁹Greet Urbanus, our co-worker in Christ, and my dear friend Stachys.

¹⁰Greet Apelles, whose fidelity to Christ has stood the test.

Greet those who belong to the household of Aristobulus.

¹¹Greet Herodion, my fellow Jew.

Greet those in the household of Narcissus who are in the Lord.

¹²Greet Tryphena and Tryphosa, those women who work hard in the Lord.

Greet my dear friend Persis, another woman who has worked very hard in the Lord.

¹³Greet Rufus, chosen in the Lord, and his mother, who has been a mother to me, too.

¹⁴Greet Asyncritus, Phlegon, Hermes, Patrobas, Hermas and the other brothers and sisters with them.

¹⁵Greet Philologus, Julia, Nereus and his sister, and Olympas and all the Lord's people who are with them.

¹⁶Greet one another with a holy kiss.

All the churches of Christ send greetings.

¹⁷I urge you, brothers and sisters, to watch out for those who cause divisions and put obstacles in your way that are contrary

---

ᵃ 21 Isaiah 52:15 (see Septuagint)   ᵇ 1 Or servant   ᶜ 3 Greek Prisca, a variant of Priscilla to the teaching you have learned. Keep away from them. [18]For such people are not serving our Lord Christ, but their own appetites. By smooth talk and flattery they deceive the minds of naive people. [19]Everyone has heard about your obedience, so I rejoice because of you; but I want you to be wise about what is good, and innocent about what is evil.

[20]The God of peace will soon crush Satan under your feet.

The grace of our Lord Jesus be with you.

[21]Timothy, my co-worker, sends his greetings to you, as do Lucius, Jason and Sosipater, my fellow Jews.

[22]I, Tertius, who wrote down this letter, greet you in the Lord.

[23][24]Gaius, whose hospitality I and the whole church here enjoy, sends you his greetings.

Erastus, who is the city's director of public works, and our brother Quartus send you their greetings. [a]

[25]Now to him who is able to establish you in accordance with my gospel, the message I proclaim about Jesus Christ, in keeping with the revelation of the mystery hidden for long ages past, [26]but now revealed and made known through the prophetic writings by the command of the eternal God, so that all the Gentiles might come to faith and obedience— [27]to the only wise God be glory forever through Jesus Christ! Amen.

---

a 23 Some manuscripts *their greetings.* [24]*May the grace of our Lord Jesus Christ be with all of you. Amen.*

1 corinthians

> AUTHOR: Paul, the apostle
>
> DATE: Around A.D. 55
>
> THEME: God calls us *to* him—and *away* from sin.

1 Paul, called to be an apostle of Christ Jesus by the will of God, and our brother Sosthenes,

²To the church of God in Corinth, to those sanctified in Christ Jesus and called to be his holy people, together with all those everywhere who call on the name of our Lord Jesus Christ—their Lord and ours:

³Grace and peace to you from God our Father and the Lord Jesus Christ.

Thanksgiving

⁴I always thank my God for you because of his grace given you in Christ Jesus. ⁵For in him you have been enriched in every way—with all kinds of speech and with all knowledge— ⁶God thus confirming our testimony about Christ among you. ⁷Therefore you do not lack any spiritual gift as you eagerly wait for our Lord Jesus Christ to be revealed. ⁸He will also keep you firm to the end, so that you will be blameless on the day of our Lord Jesus Christ. ⁹God is faithful, who has called you into fellowship with his Son, Jesus Christ our Lord.

A Church Divided Over Leaders

¹⁰I appeal to you, brothers and sisters, in the name of our Lord Jesus Christ, that all of you agree with one another in what you say and that there be no divisions among you, but that you be perfectly united in mind and thought. ¹¹My brothers and sisters, some from Chloe's household have informed me that there are quarrels among you. ¹²What I mean is this: One of you says, "I follow Paul"; another, "I follow Apollos"; another,

"I follow Cephas*a*"; still another, "I follow Christ."

¹³Is Christ divided? Was Paul crucified for you? Were you baptized into*b* the name of Paul? ¹⁴I thank God that I did not baptize any of you except Crispus and Gaius, ¹⁵so no one can say that you were baptized into my name. ¹⁶(Yes, I also baptized the household of Stephanas; beyond that, I don't remember if I baptized anyone else.) ¹⁷For Christ did not send me to baptize, but to preach the gospel—not with wisdom and eloquence, lest the cross of Christ be emptied of its power.

Christ Crucified Is God's Power and Wisdom

¹⁸For the message of the cross is foolishness to those who are perishing, but to us who are being saved it is the power of God. ¹⁹For it is written:

> "I will destroy the wisdom of the wise;
>   the intelligence of the intelligent I
>   will frustrate."*c*

²⁰Where are the wise? Where is the teacher of the law? Where is the philosopher of this age? Has not God made foolish the wisdom of the world? ²¹For since in the wisdom of God the world through its wisdom did not know him, God was pleased through the foolishness of what was preached to save those who believe. ²²Jews demand signs and Greeks look for wisdom, ²³but we preach Christ crucified: a stumbling block to Jews and foolishness to Gentiles, ²⁴but to those whom God has called, both Jews and Greeks, Christ the power of God and the wisdom of God. ²⁵For the foolishness of God is wiser than human wisdom, and the weak-

a 12 That is, Peter   *b 13* Or *in*; also in verse 15   *c 19* Isaiah 29:14

WEDNESDAY

SURPRISING CITIZENS

1 Corinthians 1:1–31 *or* 1:20–29

Philip Yancey

Jesus was the first world leader to inaugurate a kingdom with a heroic role for losers. He spoke to an audience raised on stories of wealthy patriarchs, strong kings and victorious heroes. Much to their surprise, he honored instead people who have little value in the visible world: the poor and meek, the persecuted and those who mourn, social rejects, the hungry and thirsty. His stories consistently featured "the wrong people" as heroes: the prodigal, not the responsible son; the good Samaritan, not the good Jew; Lazarus, not the rich man; the tax collector, not the Pharisee. As Charles Spurgeon, the British preacher and John Merrick's contemporary, expressed it, "His glory was that He laid aside His glory, and the glory of the church is when she lays aside her respectability and her dignity, and counts it to be her glory to gather together the outcasts."

In the same vein, the apostle Paul gave this frank appraisal of those who comprise God's kingdom: "Not many of you were wise by human standards; not many were influential; not many were of noble birth." The wise, the influential, the nobly born find too many attractions in the visible world, a milieu in which they thrive. "But God chose the foolish things of the world to shame the wise; God chose the weak things of the world to shame the strong. [God] chose the lowly things of this world and the despised things—and the things that are not—to nullify the things that are, so that no one may boast before him."

CHARLES HADDON SPURGEON {AD 1834–1892}

A church that does not exist to reclaim the lost, to fight with evil, to destroy error, to put down falsehood, to take the side of the poor, to denounce injustice and to hold up righteousness is a church that has no right to be. The church does not exist for itself, any more than Christ existed for himself. His glory was that He laid aside His glory, and the glory of the church is when she lays aside her respectability and her dignity, and counts it to be her glory to gather together the outcasts, and considers it her highest honor to search through the foulest slime for the priceless jewels for which Jesus shed his blood.

How does the "Who's Who" list in our society compare with the kind of people who make the "Who's Who" list in God's kingdom?

reflection

1. When you examine your life, do you find "spiritual discrimination"?
2. How is it revealed in your activities? Your attitudes?
3. What can you do this week to connect with someone you might not otherwise associate with?

For your next devotional reading, go to page 1306.

ness of God is stronger than human strength.

²⁶Brothers and sisters, think of what you were when you were called. Not many of you were wise by human standards; not many were influential; not many were of noble birth. ²⁷But God chose the foolish things of the world to shame the wise; God chose the weak things of the world to shame the strong. ²⁸God chose the lowly things of this world and the despised things—and the things that are not—to nullify the things that are, ²⁹so that no one may boast before him. ³⁰It is because of him that you are in Christ Jesus, who has become for us wisdom from God—that is, our righteousness, holiness and redemption. ³¹Therefore, as it is written: "Let those who boast boast in the Lord." *a*

2 And so it was with me, brothers and sisters. When I came to you, I did not come with eloquence or human wisdom as I proclaimed to you the testimony about God. *b* ²For I resolved to know nothing while I was with you except Jesus Christ and him crucified. ³I came to you in weakness with great fear and trembling. ⁴My message and my preaching were not with wise and persuasive words, but with a demonstration of the Spirit's power, ⁵so that your faith might not rest on human wisdom, but on God's power.

God's Wisdom Revealed by the Spirit

⁶We do, however, speak a message of wisdom among the mature, but not the wisdom of this age or of the rulers of this age, who are coming to nothing. ⁷No, we declare God's wisdom, a mystery that has been hidden and that God destined for our glory before time began. ⁸None of the rulers of this age understood it, for if they had, they would not have crucified the Lord of glory. ⁹However, as it is written:

"What no eye has seen,
    what no ear has heard,
and what no human mind has
        conceived—
    these things God has prepared for
        those who love him" *c*—

¹⁰for God has revealed them to us by his Spirit.

The Spirit searches all things, even the deep things of God. ¹¹For who knows a person's thoughts except that person's own spirit within? In the same way no one knows the thoughts of God except the Spirit of God. ¹²We have not received the spirit of the world but the Spirit who is from God, that we may understand what God has freely given us. ¹³This is what we speak, not in words taught us by human wisdom but in words taught by the Spirit, explaining spiritual realities with Spirit-taught words. *d* ¹⁴The person without the Spirit does not accept the things that come from the Spirit of God but considers them foolishness, and cannot understand them because they are discerned only through the Spirit. ¹⁵The person with the Spirit makes judgments about all things, but such a person is not subject to merely human judgments, ¹⁶for,

"Who has known the mind of the Lord
    so as to instruct him?" *e*

But we have the mind of Christ.

The Church and Its Leaders

3 Brothers and sisters, I could not address you as spiritual but as worldly—mere infants in Christ. ²I gave you milk, not solid food, for you were not yet ready for it. Indeed, you are still not ready. ³You are still worldly. For since there is jealousy and quarreling among you, are you not worldly? Are you not acting like mere human beings? ⁴For when one says, "I follow Paul," and another, "I follow Apollos," are you not mere human beings?

⁵What, after all, is Apollos? And what is Paul? Only servants, through whom you came to believe—as the Lord has assigned to each his task. ⁶I planted the seed, Apollos watered it, but God has been making it grow. ⁷So neither the one who plants nor the one who waters is anything, but only God, who makes things grow. ⁸The one who plants and the one who waters have one purpose, and they will each be rewarded according to their own labor. ⁹For we are God's co-workers; you are God's field, God's building.

a 31 Jer. 9:24   *b* 1 Some manuscripts *as I proclaimed to you God's mystery*   *c* 9 Isaiah 64:4
d 13 Or *Spirit, interpreting spiritual truths to those who are spiritual*   *e* 16 Isaiah 40:13

THURSDAY

FEELING DOWN? LOOK UP!

1 Corinthians 2:1–16 *or* 2:9

Bruce Bickel and Stan Jantz

Even though you don't know exactly what God has prepared for you, you can be sure He has your best interest in mind. Meanwhile, you don't have to be completely in the dark when it comes to knowing God's will. And that means you can trust Him in good times and bad, when you're rich and when you're poor, when you're healthy and when you're sick. God doesn't change just because your circumstances do.

Never forget that God knows you better than you know yourself, and He knows what's best for you. God knows your weaknesses, and He knows your strengths. God knows your fears, and He knows your hopes. God will never mislead you or do you harm . . .

Try to see things from God's perspective. When you insist on doing God's will from your perspective, then your main concern is doing stuff for God. You get caught up in your own performance. By contrast, when you see God's will from His perspective you are more concerned about being. Sure, God wants you to do stuff for Him, but He's more interested in the kind of person you are becoming than the specific things you are doing. He knows that when your being is right, your doing will be right, and you will be doing more things that please Him.

Commit yourself to the will of God. This means trusting that God has your best interest in mind at all times. Trusting God for your future—whether that future is tomorrow or ten years from now—begins with trusting God now. Once you have committed to doing God's will—regardless of what it is and what it costs—God will guide you every step of the way.

SAINT JOHN OF THE CROSS {AD 1542–1591}

When you see your appetites darkened, your inclinations dry and constrained, your faculties incapacitated for any interior exercise, do not be afflicted; think of this as a grace . . . God takes you by the hand and guides you in darkness, as though you were blind, along a way and to a place you know not. You would never have succeeded in reaching this place no matter how good your eyes and your feet.

reflection

1. How do you respond to the statement, God is more "interested in the kind of person you are *becoming* than the specific things you are *doing*"?

2. How can anxiety about your future become a detriment to your faith?

3. How does knowledge of your future home in heaven affect your reading of 2 Corinthians 2:9?

For your next devotional reading, go to page 1309.

[10]By the grace God has given me, I laid a foundation as a wise builder, and someone else is building on it. But each one should build with care. [11]For no one can lay any foundation other than the one already laid, which is Jesus Christ. [12]If anyone builds on this foundation using gold, silver, costly stones, wood, hay or straw, [13]their work will be shown for what it is, because the Day will bring it to light. It will be revealed with fire, and the fire will test the quality of each person's work. [14]If what has been built survives, the builder will receive a reward. [15]If it is burned up, the builder will suffer loss but yet will be saved—even though only as one escaping through the flames.

[16]Don't you know that you yourselves are God's temple and that God's Spirit dwells in your midst? [17]If anyone destroys God's temple, God will destroy that person; for God's temple is sacred, and you together are that temple.

[18]Do not deceive yourselves. If any of you think you are wise by the standards of this age, you should become "fools" so that you may become wise. [19]For the wisdom of this world is foolishness in God's sight. As it is written: "He catches the wise in their craftiness"[a]; [20]and again, "The Lord knows that the thoughts of the wise are futile."[b] [21]So then, no more boasting about human leaders! All things are yours, [22]whether Paul or Apollos or Cephas[c] or the world or life or death or the present or the future—all are yours, [23]and you are of Christ, and Christ is of God.

The Nature of True Apostleship

4 This, then, is how you ought to regard us: as servants of Christ and as those entrusted with the mysteries God has revealed. [2]Now it is required that those who have been given a trust must prove faithful. [3]I care very little if I am judged by you or by any human court; indeed, I do not even judge myself. [4]My conscience is clear, but that does not make me innocent. It is the Lord who judges me. [5]Therefore judge nothing before the appointed time; wait till the Lord comes. He will bring to light what is hidden in darkness and will expose the motives of people's

hearts. At that time each will receive their praise from God.

[6]Now, brothers and sisters, I have applied these things to myself and Apollos for your benefit, so that you may learn from us the meaning of the saying, "Do not go beyond what is written." Then you will not be puffed up in being a follower of one of us over against the other. [7]For who makes you different from anyone else? What do you have that you did not receive? And if you did receive it, why do you boast as though you did not?

[8]Already you have all you want! Already you have become rich! You have begun to reign—and that without us! How I wish that you really had begun to reign so that we also might reign with you! [9]For it seems to me that God has put us apostles on display at the end of the procession, like those condemned to die in the arena. We have been made a spectacle to the whole universe, to angels as well as to human beings. [10]We are fools for Christ, but you are so wise in Christ! We are weak, but you are strong! You are honored, we are dishonored! [11]To this very hour we go hungry and thirsty, we are in rags, we are brutally treated, we are homeless. [12]We work hard with our own hands. When we are cursed, we bless; when we are persecuted, we endure it; [13]when we are slandered, we answer kindly. We have become the scum of the earth, the garbage of the world—right up to this moment.

Paul's Appeal and Warning

[14]I am writing this not to shame you but to warn you as my dear children. [15]Even if you had ten thousand guardians in Christ, you do not have many fathers, for in Christ Jesus I became your father through the gospel. [16]Therefore I urge you to imitate me. [17]For this reason I have sent to you Timothy, my son whom I love, who is faithful in the Lord. He will remind you of my way of life in Christ Jesus, which agrees with what I teach everywhere in every church.

[18]Some of you have become arrogant, as if I were not coming to you. [19]But I will come to you very soon, if the Lord is willing, and then I will find out not only how these arrogant people are talking, but what power they

a 19 Job 5:13   *b 20* Psalm 94:11   *c 22* That is, Peter have. 20For the kingdom of God is not a matter of talk but of power. 21What do you prefer? Shall I come to you with a rod of discipline, or shall I come in love and with a gentle spirit?

Dealing With a Case of Incest

5 It is actually reported that there is sexual immorality among you, and of a kind that even pagans do not tolerate: A man has his father's wife. 2And you are proud! Shouldn't you rather have gone into mourning and have put out of your fellowship the man who has been doing this? 3For my part, even though I am not physically present, I am with you in spirit. As one who is present with you in this way, I have already passed judgment in the name of our Lord Jesus on the one who has been doing this. 4So when you are assembled and I am with you in spirit, and the power of our Lord Jesus is present, 5hand this man over to Satan for the destruction of the sinful nature*a* so that his spirit may be saved on the day of the Lord.

6Your boasting is not good. Don't you know that a little yeast leavens the whole batch of dough? 7Get rid of the old yeast, so that you may be a new unleavened batch— as you really are. For Christ, our Passover lamb, has been sacrificed. 8Therefore let us keep the Festival, not with the old bread leavened with malice and wickedness, but with the unleavened bread of sincerity and truth.

9I wrote to you in my letter not to associate with sexually immoral people— 10not at all meaning the people of this world who are immoral, or the greedy and swindlers, or idolaters. In that case you would have to leave this world. 11But now I am writing to you that you must not associate with any who claim to be fellow believers but are sexually immoral or greedy, idolaters or slanderers, drunkards or swindlers. With such persons do not even eat.

12What business is it of mine to judge those outside the church? Are you not to judge those inside? 13God will judge those outside. "Expel the wicked person from among you."*b*

Lawsuits Among Believers

6 If any of you has a dispute with another, do you dare to take it before the ungodly for judgment instead of before the Lord's people? 2Or do you not know that the Lord's people will judge the world? And if you are to judge the world, are you not competent to judge trivial cases? 3Do you not know that we will judge angels? How much more the things of this life! 4Therefore, if you have disputes about such matters, do you ask for a ruling from those whose way of life is scorned in the church? 5I say this to shame you. Is it possible that there is nobody among you wise enough to judge a dispute between believers? 6But instead, one brother goes to law against another—and this in front of unbelievers!

7The very fact that you have lawsuits among you means you have been completely defeated already. Why not rather be wronged? Why not rather be cheated? 8Instead, you yourselves cheat and do wrong, and you do this to your brothers and sisters. 9Or do you not know that wrongdoers will not inherit the kingdom of God? Do not be deceived: Neither the sexually immoral nor idolaters nor adulterers nor male prostitutes nor practicing homosexuals 10nor thieves nor the greedy nor drunkards nor slanderers nor swindlers will inherit the kingdom of God. 11And that is what some of you were. But you were washed, you were sanctified, you were justified in the name of the Lord Jesus Christ and by the Spirit of our God.

Sexual Immorality

12"I have the right to do anything," you say—but not everything is beneficial. "I have the right to do anything"—but I will not be mastered by anything. 13You say, "Food for the stomach and the stomach for food, and God will destroy them both." The body, however, is not meant for sexual immorality but for the Lord, and the Lord for the body. 14By his power God raised the Lord from the dead, and he will raise us also. 15Do you not know that your bodies are members of Christ himself? Shall I then take the members of Christ and unite them with a prostitute? Never! 16Do you not know that he who unites himself with a prostitute is one with her in body? For it is said, "The two will

a 5 Or *of his body; or of the flesh*   *b 13* Deut. 13:5; 17:7; 19:19; 21:21; 22:21,24; 24:7

Silencing the "Me"

1 Corinthians 6:1–20 *or* 6:12–20

Philip Yancey

My natural desires, I now see, are pointers to the supernatural, not obstacles. In a world fallen far from its original design, God wants us to receive them as gifts and not possessions, tokens of love and not loves in themselves. I have learned to pray, following Augustine, not that my desires be quenched or taken away, rather that my scattered longings be gathered together in their Source, who alone can order them.

When the e-mail invitation came, uninvited, to tune in to a webcam pointed toward a naked eighteen-year-old named Brandi, I recognized it immediately as a symptom of this disordered, reductionistic world. My computer offered pixels of nude flesh from a digital camera, not a living person. God has more, far more, in mind for my scattered longings than disembodied deception . . .

Christianity does not promise the ultimate in personal pleasure, a life oriented around hedonism. Rather, it promises an ordering of life—a putting together, not a reduction—so that we realize pleasures as they were intended by our Creator. Otherwise, we risk indulging to our own destruction, like an alcoholic who determines how much to drink. Abuses arise from regarding pleasure as an end in itself rather than a pointer to something more. "Perfect are the good desires you have given me," prayed Pascal; "Be their End, as you have been their Beginning."

John Calvin {AD 1509–1564}

We are redeemed by the Lord for the purpose of devoting every part of ourselves to him . . . People will never worship God with a sincere heart, or be roused to fear and obey him with sufficient zeal, until they properly understand how much they are indebted to his mercy . . . For until people recognize that they owe everything to God, that they are nourished by his fatherly care, that he is the Author of their every good, that they should seek nothing beyond him—they will never serve him eagerly. Moreover, unless they establish their complete happiness in him, they will never give themselves truly and sincerely to him.

reflection

1. Your life is not about you—it's about God. Are you tempted to argue with that?

2. What in your life shows others what is important to you?

3. When was the last time you had an inner debate going between your flesh and God's Spirit over whether or not you should do a particular thing? Which side won out?

For your next devotional reading, go to page 1311.

become one flesh."*a* 17But whoever is united with the Lord is one with him in spirit.*b*

18Flee from sexual immorality. All other sins people commit are outside their bodies, but those who sin sexually sin against their own bodies. 19Do you not know that your bodies are temples of the Holy Spirit, who is in you, whom you have received from God? You are not your own; 20you were bought at a price. Therefore honor God with your bodies.

Concerning Married Life

7 Now for the matters you wrote about: "It is good for a man not to have sexual relations with a woman." 2But since sexual immorality is occurring, each man should have sexual relations with his own wife, and each woman with her own husband. 3The husband should fulfill his marital duty to his wife, and likewise the wife to her husband. 4The wife does not have authority over her own body but yields it to her husband. In the same way, the husband does not have authority over his own body but yields it to his wife. 5Do not deprive each other except perhaps by mutual consent and for a time, so that you may devote yourselves to prayer. Then come together again so that Satan will not tempt you because of your lack of self-control. 6I say this as a concession, not as a command. 7I wish that all of you were as I am. But each of you has your own gift from God; one has this gift, another has that.

8Now to the unmarried*c* and the widows I say: It is good for them to stay unmarried, as I do. 9But if they cannot control themselves, they should marry, for it is better to marry than to burn with passion.

10To the married I give this command (not I, but the Lord): A wife must not separate from her husband. 11But if she does, she must remain unmarried or else be reconciled to her husband. And a husband must not divorce his wife.

12To the rest I say this (I, not the Lord): If any brother has a wife who is not a believer and she is willing to live with him, he must not divorce her. 13And if a woman has a husband who is not a believer and he is willing to live with her, she must not divorce him. 14For the unbelieving husband has been sanctified through his wife, and the unbe-

lieving wife has been sanctified through her believing husband. Otherwise your children would be unclean, but as it is, they are holy.

15But if the unbeliever leaves, let it be so. The brother or sister is not bound in such circumstances; God has called us to live in peace. 16How do you know, wife, whether you will save your husband? Or, how do you know, husband, whether you will save your wife?

Concerning Change of Status

17Nevertheless, each of you should live as a believer in whatever situation the Lord has assigned to you, just as God has called you. This is the rule I lay down in all the churches. 18Was a man already circumcised when he was called? He should not become uncircumcised. Was a man uncircumcised when he was called? He should not be circumcised. 19Circumcision is nothing and uncircumcision is nothing. Keeping God's commands is what counts. 20Each of you should remain in the situation you were in when God called you.

21Were you a slave when you were called? Don't let it trouble you—although if you can gain your freedom, do so. 22For those who were slaves when called to faith in the Lord are the Lord's freed people; similarly, those who were free when called are Christ's slaves. 23You were bought at a price; do not become slaves of human beings. 24Brothers and sisters, all of you, as responsible to God, should remain in the situation in which God called you.

Concerning the Unmarried

25Now about virgins: I have no command from the Lord, but I give a judgment as one who by the Lord's mercy is trustworthy. 26Because of the present crisis, I think that it is good for a man to remain as he is. 27Are you pledged to a woman? Do not seek to be released. Are you free from such a commitment? Do not look for a wife. 28But if you do marry, you have not sinned; and if a virgin marries, she has not sinned. But those who marry will face many troubles in this life, and I want to spare you this.

29What I mean, brothers and sisters, is that the time is short. From now on those who are married should live as if they were

a 16 Gen. 2:24   *b 17* Or *in the Spirit*   *c 8* Or *widowers*

Whatever the Situation

1 Corinthians 7:17–20

read/meditate

Take a moment to clear your mind before reading Paul's words to the Corinthians. Focus in on God's words. For some in Paul's day, circumcision was a symbol of spirituality. What are the indicators of someone's spirituality in your culture?

pray

Do you ever think, *I could serve God better if my circumstances were different—if I were more this or less that, if I had some new habits or joined a new group?* Describe for God any circumstances of your life that you think hold you back spiritually. Then listen for his perspective.

contemplate

Consider the indicators your culture uses to define spirituality. Think about those indicators in light of these verses. Ponder your own response to people who adhere to different faith practices or traditions than you.

additional reflection

Yesterday is gone. Tomorrow has not yet come. We have only today. Let us begin.
—*Mother Teresa*

The work of spirituality is to recognize where we are—the particular circumstances of our lives—to recognize grace and say, "Do you suppose God wants to be with me in a way that does not involve changing my spouse or getting rid of my spouse or my kids, but in changing me, and doing something in my life that maybe I could never experience without this pain and this suffering"?
—*Edmund Clowney*

For your next devotional reading, go to page 1313.

not; ³⁰those who mourn, as if they did not; those who are happy, as if they were not; those who buy something, as if it were not theirs to keep; ³¹those who use the things of the world, as if not engrossed in them. For this world in its present form is passing away.

³²I would like you to be free from concern. An unmarried man is concerned about the Lord's affairs—how he can please the Lord. ³³But a married man is concerned about the affairs of this world—how he can please his wife— ³⁴and his interests are divided. An unmarried woman or virgin is concerned about the Lord's affairs: Her aim is to be devoted to the Lord in both body and spirit. But a married woman is concerned about the affairs of this world—how she can please her husband. ³⁵I am saying this for your own good, not to restrict you, but that you may live in a right way in undivided devotion to the Lord.

³⁶If anyone is worried that he might not be acting honorably toward the virgin he is engaged to, and if she is getting beyond the usual age for marrying*a* and he feels he ought to marry, he should do as he wants. He is not sinning. They should get married. ³⁷But the man who has settled the matter in his own mind, who is under no compulsion but has control over his own will, and who has made up his mind not to marry the virgin—this man also does the right thing. ³⁸So then, he who marries the virgin does right, but he who does not marry her does better.*b*

³⁹A woman is bound to her husband as long as he lives. But if her husband dies, she is free to marry anyone she wishes, but he must belong to the Lord. ⁴⁰In my judgment, she is happier if she stays as she is—and I think that I too have the Spirit of God.

Concerning Food Sacrificed to Idols

8 Now about food sacrificed to idols: We know that "We all possess knowledge." But knowledge puffs up while love builds up. ²Those who think they know something do not yet know as they ought to know. ³But whoever loves God is known by God.*c*

⁴So then, about eating food sacrificed to idols: We know that "An idol is nothing at all in the world" and that "There is no God but one." ⁵For even if there are so-called gods, whether in heaven or on earth (as indeed there are many "gods" and many "lords"), ⁶yet for us there is but one God, the Father, from whom all things came and for whom we live; and there is but one Lord, Jesus Christ, through whom all things came and through whom we live.

⁷But not everyone possesses this knowledge. Some people are still so accustomed to idols that when they eat sacrificial food they think of it as having been sacrificed to a god, and since their conscience is weak, it is defiled. ⁸But food does not bring us near to God; we are no worse if we do not eat, and no better if we do.

⁹Be careful, however, that the exercise of your rights does not become a stumbling block to the weak. ¹⁰For if anyone with a weak conscience sees you, with all your knowledge, eating in an idol's temple, won't they be emboldened to eat what is sacrificed to idols? ¹¹So this weak brother or sister, for whom Christ died, is destroyed by your knowledge. ¹²When you sin against them in this way and wound their weak conscience, you sin against Christ. ¹³Therefore, if what I eat causes my brother or sister to fall into sin, I will never eat meat again, so that I will not cause them to fall.

Paul's Rights as an Apostle

9 Am I not free? Am I not an apostle? Have I not seen Jesus our Lord? Are you not the result of my work in the Lord? ²Even though I may not be an apostle to others, surely I am to you! For you are the seal of my apostleship in the Lord.

³This is my defense to those who sit in judgment on me. ⁴Don't we have the right to food and drink? ⁵Don't we have the right to take a believing wife along with us, as do the other apostles and the Lord's brothers and

---

a 36 Or *if his (or her) passions are too strong*   *b 36-38* Or *³⁶If anyone thinks he is not treating his daughter properly, and if she is getting along in years (or if her passions are too strong), and he feels she ought to marry, he should do as he wants. He is not sinning. He should let her get married. ³⁷But the man who has settled the matter in his own mind, who is under no compulsion but has control over his own will, and who has made up his mind to keep the virgin unmarried—this man also does the right thing. ³⁸So then, he who gives his virgin in marriage does right, but he who does not give her in marriage does better.*   *c 2,3* An early manuscript and another ancient witness *think they have knowledge do not yet know as they ought to know. ³But whoever loves truly knows.*

MONDAY

BRINGING PEOPLE TOGETHER

1 Corinthians 9:1–27 *or* 9:19–23

LEO I {AD 400–461}

The Lord says, "[Love the Lord your God with all your heart and with all your soul and with all your mind and with all your strength . . . Love your neighbor as yourself]." Therefore, faithful souls should put on the unfading love of their Author and Ruler . . . But such godly love can't be perfect unless we also love our neighbors. We must not only include those connected to us by friendship or our neighborhood, but must include everyone. For we have a common nature with every person, whether they be enemies or allies, slaves or free . . . But the extent of Christian grace gives us even a greater reason to love our neighbor. This grace, which reaches every part of the whole world, doesn't look down on anyone. It teaches us not to neglect anyone. So He rightly commands us to love our enemies and to pray to Him for our persecutors. By grafting shoots of wild olive trees from every nation daily onto the holy branches of His own olive tree, Christ makes people reconciled instead of enemies, adopted children instead of strangers, righteous instead of ungodly.

Ron Hutchcraft

Christ's great ambassador [Paul] clearly did everything he could to understand and relate to those he hoped to rescue . . .

Over the centuries, effective missionaries have made the effort to understand the culture, the language, the spiritual "location" of the people they were praying to reach. We can do no less when we have been called to represent Jesus in a post-Christian culture that one missions expert has called "the most challenging missionary frontier of our time."

God has chosen you to be a lifesaver for him "for such a time as this." (See Esther 4:14.) It is a time unlike any other since perhaps the first century. But it was in that time that the message of Jesus exploded across the world and captured hearts everywhere it was presented.

reflection

1. What unlikely candidate surprised you when he or she became a Christian?

2. God loved us when we were unlovable. Who is difficult for *you* to love?

3. How can you improve in this area?

For your next devotional reading, go to page 1317.

Cephas[a]? [6]Or is it only I and Barnabas who don't have the right not to work for a living?

[7]Who serves as a soldier at his own expense? Who plants a vineyard and does not eat of its grapes? Who tends a flock and does not drink of the milk? [8]Do I say this merely on human authority? Doesn't the Law say the same thing? [9]For it is written in the Law of Moses: "Do not muzzle an ox while it is treading out the grain."[b] Is it about oxen that God is concerned? [10]Surely he says this for us, doesn't he? Yes, this was written for us, because when farmers plow and thresh, they should be able to do so in the hope of sharing in the harvest. [11]If we have sown spiritual seed among you, is it too much if we reap a material harvest from you? [12]If others have this right of support from you, shouldn't we have it all the more?

But we did not use this right. On the contrary, we put up with anything rather than hinder the gospel of Christ.

[13]Don't you know that those who serve in the temple get their food from the temple, and that those who serve at the altar share in what is offered on the altar? [14]In the same way, the Lord has commanded that those who preach the gospel should receive their living from the gospel.

[15]But I have not used any of these rights. And I am not writing this in the hope that you will do such things for me, for I would rather die than allow anyone to deprive me of this boast. [16]For when I preach the gospel, I cannot boast, since I am compelled to preach. Woe to me if I do not preach the gospel! [17]If I preach voluntarily, I have a reward; if not voluntarily, I am simply discharging the trust committed to me. [18]What then is my reward? Just this: that in preaching the gospel I may offer it free of charge, and so not misuse my rights as a preacher of the gospel.

Paul's Use of His Freedom

[19]Though I am free and belong to no one, I have made myself a slave to everyone, to win as many as possible. [20]To the Jews I became like a Jew, to win the Jews. To those under the law I became like one under the law (though I myself am not under the law), so as to win those under the law. [21]To those not having the law I became like one not having the law (though I am not free from God's law but am under Christ's law), so as to win those not having the law. [22]To the weak I became weak, to win the weak. I have become all things to all people so that by all possible means I might save some. [23]I do all this for the sake of the gospel, that I may share in its blessings.

The Need for Self-Discipline

[24]Do you not know that in a race all the runners run, but only one gets the prize? Run in such a way as to get the prize. [25]Everyone who competes in the games goes into strict training. They do it to get a crown that will not last, but we do it to get a crown that will last forever. [26]Therefore I do not run like someone running aimlessly; I do not fight like a boxer beating the air. [27]No, I strike a blow to my body and make it my slave so that after I have preached to others, I myself will not be disqualified for the prize.

Warnings From Israel's History

10 For I do not want you to be ignorant of the fact, brothers and sisters, that our ancestors were all under the cloud and that they all passed through the sea. [2]They were all baptized into Moses in the cloud and in the sea. [3]They all ate the same spiritual food [4]and drank the same spiritual drink; for they drank from the spiritual rock that accompanied them, and that rock was Christ. [5]Nevertheless, God was not pleased with most of them; their bodies were scattered in the wilderness.

[6]Now these things occurred as examples to keep us from setting our hearts on evil things as they did. [7]Do not be idolaters, as some of them were; as it is written: "The people sat down to eat and drink and got up to indulge in revelry."[c] [8]We should not commit sexual immorality, as some of them did—and in one day twenty-three thousand of them died. [9]We should not test Christ,[d] as some of them did—and were killed by snakes. [10]And do not grumble, as some of them did—and were killed by the destroying angel.

[11]These things happened to them as examples and were written down as warnings

---

[a] 5 That is, Peter   [b] 9 Deut. 25:4   [c] 7 Exodus 32:6   [d] 9 Some manuscripts *test the Lord*

for us, on whom the culmination of the ages has come. ¹²So, if you think you are standing firm, be careful that you don't fall! ¹³No temptation*a* has overtaken you except what is common to us all. And God is faithful; he will not let you be tempted*a* beyond what you can bear. But when you are tempted,*a* he will also provide a way out so that you can endure it.

Idol Feasts and the Lord's Supper

¹⁴Therefore, my dear friends, flee from idolatry. ¹⁵I speak to sensible people; judge for yourselves what I say. ¹⁶Is not the cup of thanksgiving for which we give thanks a participation in the blood of Christ? And is not the bread that we break a participation in the body of Christ? ¹⁷Because there is one loaf, we, who are many, are one body, for we all partake of the one loaf.

¹⁸Consider the people of Israel: Do not those who eat the sacrifices participate in the altar? ¹⁹Do I mean then that food sacrificed to an idol is anything, or that an idol is anything? ²⁰No, but the sacrifices of pagans are offered to demons, not to God, and I do not want you to be participants with demons. ²¹You cannot drink the cup of the Lord and the cup of demons too; you cannot have a part in both the Lord's table and the table of demons. ²²Are we trying to arouse the Lord's jealousy? Are we stronger than he?

The Believer's Freedom

²³"I have the right to do anything," you say—but not everything is beneficial. "I have the right to do anything"—but not everything is constructive. ²⁴No one should seek their own good, but the good of others.

²⁵Eat anything sold in the meat market without raising questions of conscience, ²⁶for, "The earth is the Lord's, and everything in it."*b*

²⁷If an unbeliever invites you to a meal and you want to go, eat whatever is put before you without raising questions of conscience. ²⁸But if someone says to you, "This has been offered in sacrifice," then do not eat it, both for the sake of the one who told you and for the sake of conscience. ²⁹I am referring to the other person's conscience, not yours. For why is my freedom being judged by another's conscience? ³⁰If I take part in the meal with thankfulness, why am I denounced because of something I thank God for?

³¹So whether you eat or drink or whatever you do, do it all for the glory of God. ³²Do not cause anyone to stumble, whether Jews, Greeks or the church of God— ³³even as I try to please everyone in every way. For I am not seeking my own good but the good of many, so that they may be saved.

11

¹Follow my example, as I follow the example of Christ.

On Covering the Head in Worship

²I praise you for remembering me in everything and for holding to the traditions just as I passed them on to you. ³But I want you to realize that the head of every man is Christ, and the head of the woman is man,*c* and the head of Christ is God. ⁴Every man who prays or prophesies with his head covered dishonors his head. ⁵But every woman who prays or prophesies with her head uncovered dishonors her head—it is the same as having her head shaved. ⁶For if a woman does not cover her head, she might as well have her hair cut off; but if it is a disgrace for a woman to have her hair cut off or her head shaved, then she should cover her head.

⁷A man ought not to cover his head, since he is the image and glory of God; but woman is the glory of man. ⁸For man did not come from woman, but woman from man; ⁹neither was man created for woman, but woman for man. ¹⁰It is for this reason that a woman ought to have authority over her own*d* head, because of the angels. ¹¹Nevertheless, in the Lord woman is not independent of man, nor is man independent of woman. ¹²For as woman came from man, so also man is born of woman. But everything comes from God.

¹³Judge for yourselves: Is it proper for a woman to pray to God with her head uncovered? ¹⁴Does not the very nature of things teach you that if a man has long hair, it is a disgrace to him, ¹⁵but that if a woman has long hair, it is her glory? For long hair is given to her as a covering. ¹⁶If anyone wants to be contentious about this, we have no other practice—nor do the churches of God.

a 13 The Greek for *temptation* and *tempted* can also mean *testing* and *tested.*   *b 26* Psalm 24:1
c 3 Or *of the wife is her husband*   *d 10* Or *have a sign of authority on her*

Correcting an Abuse of the Lord's Supper

[17]In the following directives I have no praise for you, for your meetings do more harm than good. [18]In the first place, I hear that when you come together as a church, there are divisions among you, and to some extent I believe it. [19]No doubt there have to be differences among you to show which of you have God's approval. [20]So then, when you come together, it is not the Lord's Supper you eat, [21]for when you are eating, some of you go ahead with your own private suppers. As a result, one person remains hungry and another gets drunk. [22]Don't you have homes to eat and drink in? Or do you despise the church of God by humiliating those who have nothing? What shall I say to you? Shall I praise you? Certainly not in this matter!

[23]For I received from the Lord what I also passed on to you: The Lord Jesus, on the night he was betrayed, took bread, [24]and when he had given thanks, he broke it and said, "This is my body, which is for you; do this in remembrance of me." [25]In the same way, after supper he took the cup, saying, "This cup is the new covenant in my blood; do this, whenever you drink it, in remembrance of me." [26]For whenever you eat this bread and drink this cup, you proclaim the Lord's death until he comes.

[27]So then, whoever eats the bread or drinks the cup of the Lord in an unworthy manner will be guilty of sinning against the body and blood of the Lord. [28]Everyone ought to examine themselves before they eat of the bread and drink of the cup. [29]For those who eat and drink without discerning the body of Christ eat and drink judgment on themselves. [30]That is why many among you are weak and sick, and a number of you have fallen asleep. [31]But if we were more discerning with regard to ourselves, we would not come under such judgment. [32]Nevertheless, when we are judged in this way by the Lord, we are being disciplined so that we will not be finally condemned with the world.

[33]So then, my brothers and sisters, when you gather to eat, you should all eat together. [34]Those who are hungry should eat something at home, so that when you meet together it may not result in judgment.

And when I come I will give further directions.

Concerning Spiritual Gifts

12 Now about the gifts of the Spirit, brothers and sisters, I do not want you to be uninformed. [2]You know that when you were pagans, somehow or other you were influenced and led astray to mute idols. [3]Therefore I want you to know that no one who is speaking by the Spirit of God says, "Jesus be cursed," and no one can say, "Jesus is Lord," except by the Holy Spirit.

[4]There are different kinds of gifts, but the same Spirit distributes them. [5]There are different kinds of service, but the same Lord. [6]There are different kinds of working, but in all of them and in everyone it is the same God at work.

[7]Now to each one the manifestation of the Spirit is given for the common good. [8]To one there is given through the Spirit a message of wisdom, to another a message of knowledge by means of the same Spirit, [9]to another faith by the same Spirit, to another gifts of healing by that one Spirit, [10]to another miraculous powers, to another prophecy, to another distinguishing between spirits, to another speaking in different kinds of tongues,[a] and to still another the interpretation of tongues.[a] [11]All these are the work of one and the same Spirit, and he distributes them to each one, just as he determines.

Unity and Diversity in the Body

[12]Just as a body, though one, has many parts, but all its many parts form one body, so it is with Christ. [13]For we were all baptized by[b] one Spirit so as to form one body—whether Jews or Gentiles, slave or free—and we were all given the one Spirit to drink. [14]Even so the body is not made up of one part but of many.

[15]Now if the foot should say, "Because I am not a hand, I do not belong to the body," it would not for that reason cease to be part of the body. [16]And if the ear should say, "Because I am not an eye, I do not belong to the body," it would not for that reason cease to be part of the body. [17]If the whole body were an eye, where would the sense of hearing be? If the whole body were an ear, where would the sense of smell be? [18]But in fact God has placed the parts in the body, every one of them, just as he wanted them to be.

a 10 Or *languages*; also in verse 28   b 13 Or *with*; or *in*

TUESDAY

BEING WHO YOU ARE

1 Corinthians 12:1–20 *or* 12:15–20

Kary Oberbrunner

Imagine a day without your eyes. Think of twenty-four hours without your legs or nose or ears. What would it be like? Your whole body would suffer because a few of your body parts were missing. You would be severely limited in the way you could function. Life would be difficult and frustrating. In a short amount of time, you would be longing for your missing body parts.

The Bible says the Church is the Body of Christ. It's made up of individual members who corporately make up the Body. Each part has a specific task that benefits the rest of the Body. Every believer has an important and necessary purpose. When those parts are missing, the whole Body is incomplete and suffers.

However, when fellowship occurs and people are practicing their spiritual gifts, the whole Body functions in an effective way. Each part is extremely important. Each believer needs the uniqueness every other believer brings to the Body.

WILLIAM LAW {AD 1686–1761}

Clearly, Christ showed every kind of love, kindness and compassion to the souls and bodies of people. His life displayed nothing but meekness and humility in every form. He was content to lack—in fact he had a total disregard for—all worldly riches, power, ease or pleasure. He continually modeled gentleness, patience and submission, not only to the will of God but also to the haughty powers of the world, to all the evil and malice of people, and to all the hardships and troubles of human life. This kind of behavior toward others—which is so different from and contrary to the spirit, wisdom and way of this world—displays the very essence of what God wants from us when he calls us to be visible, living members of his church. And when anyone, through the spirit of Christ, treats others in this way, they promote the highest perfection of church unity and reveal the genuineness of their Christianity. They are all that they can be, they have all that they can have, they do all that they can do, and they enjoy all that they can enjoy as a member of Christ's body (or church) in this world.

reflection

1. If you had to compare your individual role in the body of Christ to an actual body part, what would it be?

2. How would your church be different if every person used his or her gifts to love others the way Christ loves others?

3. How would *you* be different if you did this?

For your next devotional reading, go to page 1324.

¹⁹If they were all one part, where would the body be? ²⁰As it is, there are many parts, but one body.

²¹The eye cannot say to the hand, "I don't need you!" And the head cannot say to the feet, "I don't need you!" ²²On the contrary, those parts of the body that seem to be weaker are indispensable, ²³and the parts that we think are less honorable we treat with special honor. And the parts that are unpresentable are treated with special modesty, ²⁴while our presentable parts need no special treatment. But God has put the body together, giving greater honor to the parts that lacked it, ²⁵so that there should be no division in the body, but that its parts should have equal concern for each other. ²⁶If one part suffers, every part suffers with it; if one part is honored, every part rejoices with it.

²⁷Now you are the body of Christ, and each one of you is a part of it. ²⁸And God has placed in the church first of all apostles, second prophets, third teachers, then miracles, then gifts of healing, of helping, of guidance, and of different kinds of tongues. ²⁹Are all apostles? Are all prophets? Are all teachers? Do all work miracles? ³⁰Do all have gifts of healing? Do all speak in tongues*ᵃ*? Do all interpret? ³¹Now eagerly desire*ᵇ* the greater gifts.

Love Is Indispensable

And yet I will show you the most excellent way.

13 If I speak in human or angelic tongues,*ᶜ* but do not have love, I am only a resounding gong or a clanging cymbal. ²If I have the gift of prophecy and can fathom all mysteries and all knowledge, and if I have a faith that can move mountains, but do not have love, I am nothing. ³If I give all I possess to the poor and give over my body ⌊to hardship⌋ that I may boast,*ᵈ* but do not have love, I gain nothing.

⁴Love is patient, love is kind. It does not envy, it does not boast, it is not proud. ⁵It does not dishonor others, it is not self-seeking, it is not easily angered, it keeps no record of wrongs. ⁶Love does not delight in evil but rejoices with the truth. ⁷It always protects, always trusts, always hopes, always perseveres.

⁸Love never fails. But where there are prophecies, they will cease; where there are tongues, they will be stilled; where there is knowledge, it will pass away. ⁹For we know in part and we prophesy in part, ¹⁰but when completeness comes, what is in part disappears. ¹¹When I was a child, I talked like a child, I thought like a child, I reasoned like a child. When I became a man, I put the ways of childhood behind me. ¹²For now we see only a reflection as in a mirror; then we shall see face to face. Now I know in part; then I shall know fully, even as I am fully known.

¹³And now these three remain: faith, hope and love. But the greatest of these is love.

Intelligibility in Worship

14 Follow the way of love and eagerly desire spiritual gifts, especially the gift of prophecy. ²For those who speak in a tongue*ᵉ* do not speak to other people but to God. Indeed, no one understands them; they utter mysteries by the Spirit. ³But those who prophesy speak to people for their strengthening, encouragement and comfort. ⁴Those who speak in a tongue edify themselves, but those who prophesy edify the church. ⁵I would like every one of you to speak in tongues,*ᶠ* but I would rather have you prophesy. Those who prophesy are greater than those who speak in tongues,*ᶠ* unless they interpret, so that the church may be edified.

⁶Now, brothers and sisters, if I come to you and speak in tongues, what good will I be to you, unless I bring you some revelation or knowledge or prophecy or word of instruction? ⁷Even in the case of lifeless things that make sounds, such as the pipe or harp, how will anyone know what tune is being played unless there is a distinction in the notes? ⁸Again, if the trumpet does not sound a clear call, who will get ready for battle? ⁹So it is with you. Unless you speak intelligible words with your tongue, how will anyone know what you are saying? You will just be speaking into the air. ¹⁰Undoubtedly there are all sorts of languages in the world, yet none of them is without meaning. ¹¹If then I do not grasp the meaning of what someone is saying, I am a foreigner to the speaker, and the speaker is a foreigner to me. ¹²So it is with you. Since you are eager

---

ᵃ 30 Or *other languages*   *ᵇ 31* Or *But you are eagerly desiring*   *ᶜ 1* Or *languages*   *ᵈ 3* Some manuscripts *body to the flames*   *ᵉ 2* Or *in another language;* also in verses 4, 13, 14, 19, 26 and 27   *ᶠ 5* Or *in other languages;* also in verses 6, 18, 22, 23 and 39 for gifts of the Spirit, try to excel in those that build up the church.

¹³For this reason those who speak in a tongue should pray that they may interpret what they say. ¹⁴For if I pray in a tongue, my spirit prays, but my mind is unfruitful. ¹⁵So what shall I do? I will pray with my spirit, but I will also pray with my understanding; I will sing with my spirit, but I will also sing with my understanding. ¹⁶Otherwise when you are praising God in the Spirit, how can the others, who are now put in the same situation as an inquirer,ᵃ say "Amen" to your thanksgiving, since they do not know what you are saying? ¹⁷You are giving thanks well enough, but the others are not edified.

¹⁸I thank God that I speak in tongues more than all of you. ¹⁹But in the church I would rather speak five intelligible words to instruct others than ten thousand words in a tongue.

²⁰Brothers and sisters, stop thinking like children. In regard to evil be infants, but in your thinking be adults. ²¹In the Law it is written:

"With other tongues
    and through the lips of foreigners
I will speak to this people,
    but even then they will not listen
        to me,
                    says the Lord."ᵇ

²²Tongues, then, are a sign, not for believers but for unbelievers; prophecy, however, is not for unbelievers but for believers. ²³So if the whole church comes together and everyone speaks in tongues, and inquirers or unbelievers come in, will they not say that you are out of your mind? ²⁴But if an unbeliever or an inquirer comes in while everyone is prophesying, they are convicted of sin and are brought under judgment by all, ²⁵as the secrets of their hearts are laid bare. So they will fall down and worship God, exclaiming, "God is really among you!"

Good Order in Worship

²⁶What then shall we say, brothers and sisters? When you come together, each of you has a hymn, or a word of instruction, a revelation, a tongue or an interpretation. Everything must be done so that the church

may be built up. ²⁷If anyone speaks in a tongue, two—or at the most three—should speak, one at a time, and someone must interpret. ²⁸If there is no interpreter, the speaker should keep quiet in the church; let them speak to themselves and to God.

²⁹Two or three prophets should speak, and the others should weigh carefully what is said. ³⁰And if a revelation comes to someone who is sitting down, the first speaker should stop. ³¹For you can all prophesy in turn so that everyone may be instructed and encouraged. ³²The spirits of prophets are subject to the control of prophets. ³³For God is not a God of disorder but of peace—as in all the congregations of the Lord's people.

³⁴Women should remain silent in the churches. They are not allowed to speak, but must be in submission, as the law says. ³⁵If they want to inquire about something, they should ask their own husbands at home; for it is disgraceful for a woman to speak in the church.ᶜ

³⁶Or did the word of God originate with you? Or are you the only people it has reached? ³⁷If any think they are prophets or otherwise gifted by the Spirit, let them acknowledge that what I am writing to you is the Lord's command. ³⁸Those who ignore this will themselves be ignored.ᵈ

³⁹Therefore, my brothers and sisters, be eager to prophesy, and do not forbid speaking in tongues. ⁴⁰But everything should be done in a fitting and orderly way.

The Resurrection of Christ

15 Now, brothers and sisters, I want to remind you of the gospel I preached to you, which you received and on which you have taken your stand. ²By this gospel you are saved, if you hold firmly to the word I preached to you. Otherwise, you have believed in vain.

³For what I received I passed on to you as of first importanceᵉ: that Christ died for our sins according to the Scriptures, ⁴that he was buried, that he was raised on the third day according to the Scriptures, ⁵and that he appeared to Cephas,ᶠ and then to the Twelve. ⁶After that, he appeared to more than five hundred of the brothers and sisters

---

ᵃ 16 The Greek word for *inquirer* is a technical term for someone not fully initiated into a religion; also in verses 23 and 24.   ᵇ 21 Isaiah 28:11,12   ᶜ 34,35 In some manuscripts these verses come after verse 40.   ᵈ 38 Some manuscripts *Those who are ignorant of this will be ignorant*   ᵉ 3 Or *you at the first*   ᶠ 5 That is, Peter at the same time, most of whom are still living, though some have fallen asleep. [7]Then he appeared to James, then to all the apostles, [8]and last of all he appeared to me also, as to one abnormally born.

[9]For I am the least of the apostles and do not even deserve to be called an apostle, because I persecuted the church of God. [10]But by the grace of God I am what I am, and his grace to me was not without effect. No, I worked harder than all of them—yet not I, but the grace of God that was with me. [11]Whether, then, it is I or they, this is what we preach, and this is what you believed.

The Resurrection of the Dead

[12]But if it is preached that Christ has been raised from the dead, how can some of you say that there is no resurrection of the dead? [13]If there is no resurrection of the dead, then not even Christ has been raised. [14]And if Christ has not been raised, our preaching is useless and so is your faith. [15]More than that, we are then found to be false witnesses about God, for we have testified about God that he raised Christ from the dead. But he did not raise him if in fact the dead are not raised. [16]For if the dead are not raised, then Christ has not been raised either. [17]And if Christ has not been raised, your faith is futile; you are still in your sins. [18]Then those also who have fallen asleep in Christ are lost. [19]If only for this life we have hope in Christ, we are to be pitied more than all others.

[20]But Christ has indeed been raised from the dead, the firstfruits of those who have fallen asleep. [21]For since death came through a human being, the resurrection of the dead comes also through a human being. [22]For as in Adam all die, so in Christ all will be made alive. [23]But in this order: Christ, the firstfruits; then, when he comes, those who belong to him. [24]Then the end will come, when he hands over the kingdom to God the Father after he has destroyed all dominion, authority and power. [25]For he must reign until he has put all his enemies under his feet. [26]The last enemy to be destroyed is death. [27]For he "has put everything under his feet." [a] Now when it says that "everything" has been put under him, it is clear that this does not include God himself, who put everything under Christ.

[28]When he has done this, then the Son himself will be made subject to him who put everything under him, so that God may be all in all.

[29]Now if there is no resurrection, what will those do who are baptized for the dead? If the dead are not raised at all, why are people baptized for them? [30]And as for us, why do we endanger ourselves every hour? [31]I face death every day—yes, just as surely as I boast about you in Christ Jesus our Lord. [32]If I fought wild beasts in Ephesus with no more than human hopes, what have I gained? If the dead are not raised,

> "Let us eat and drink,
> for tomorrow we die." [b]

[33]Do not be misled: "Bad company corrupts good character." [c] [34]Come back to your senses as you ought, and stop sinning; for there are some who are ignorant of God—I say this to your shame.

The Resurrection Body

[35]But someone will ask, "How are the dead raised? With what kind of body will they come?" [36]How foolish! What you sow does not come to life unless it dies. [37]When you sow, you do not plant the body that will be, but just a seed, perhaps of wheat or of something else. [38]But God gives it a body as he has determined, and to each kind of seed he gives its own body. [39]All flesh is not the same: Human beings have one kind of flesh, animals have another, birds another and fish another. [40]There are also heavenly bodies and there are earthly bodies; but the splendor of the heavenly bodies is one kind, and the splendor of the earthly bodies is another. [41]The sun has one kind of splendor, the moon another and the stars another; and star differs from star in splendor.

[42]So will it be with the resurrection of the dead. The body that is sown is perishable, it is raised imperishable; [43]it is sown in dishonor, it is raised in glory; it is sown in weakness, it is raised in power; [44]it is sown a natural body, it is raised a spiritual body.

If there is a natural body, there is also a spiritual body. [45]So it is written: "The first Adam became a living being" [d]; the last Adam, a life-giving spirit. [46]The spiritual did not come first, but the natural, and after that the spiritual. [47]The first man was of the dust of the earth; the second man is of heaven. [48]As was the earthly man, so are those who are of the earth; and as is the heavenly man, so also are those who are of heaven. [49]And just as we have borne the image of the earthly man, so shall we[a] bear the image of the heavenly man.

[50]I declare to you, brothers and sisters, that flesh and blood cannot inherit the kingdom of God, nor does the perishable inherit the imperishable. [51]Listen, I tell you a mystery: We will not all sleep, but we will all be changed— [52]in a flash, in the twinkling of an eye, at the last trumpet. For the trumpet will sound, the dead will be raised imperishable, and we will be changed. [53]For the perishable must clothe itself with the imperishable, and the mortal with immortality. [54]When the perishable has been clothed with the imperishable, and the mortal with immortality, then the saying that is written will come true: "Death has been swallowed up in victory."[b]

[55]"Where, O death, is your victory?
    Where, O death, is your sting?"[c]

[56]The sting of death is sin, and the power of sin is the law. [57]But thanks be to God! He gives us the victory through our Lord Jesus Christ.

[58]Therefore, my dear brothers and sisters, stand firm. Let nothing move you. Always give yourselves fully to the work of the Lord, because you know that your labor in the Lord is not in vain.

The Collection for the Lord's People

16 Now about the collection for the Lord's people: Do what I told the Galatian churches to do. [2]On the first day of every week, each one of you should set aside a sum of money in keeping with your income, saving it up, so that when I come no collections will have to be made. [3]Then, when I arrive, I will give letters of introduction to the men you approve and send them with your gift to Jerusalem. [4]If it seems advisable for me to go also, they will accompany me.

Personal Requests

[5]After I go through Macedonia, I will come to you—for I will be going through Macedonia. [6]Perhaps I will stay with you for a while, or even spend the winter, so that you can help me on my journey, wherever I go. [7]For I do not want to see you now and make only a passing visit; I hope to spend some time with you, if the Lord permits. [8]But I will stay on at Ephesus until Pentecost, [9]because a great door for effective work has opened to me, and there are many who oppose me.

[10]When Timothy comes, see to it that he has nothing to fear while he is with you, for he is carrying on the work of the Lord, just as I am. [11]No one, then, should treat him with contempt. Send him on his way in peace so that he may return to me. I am expecting him along with the brothers.

[12]Now about our brother Apollos: I strongly urged him to go to you with the brothers. He was quite unwilling to go now, but he will go when he has the opportunity.

[13]Be on your guard; stand firm in the faith; be courageous; be strong. [14]Do everything in love.

[15]You know that the household of Stephanas were the first converts in Achaia, and they have devoted themselves to the service of the Lord's people. I urge you, brothers and sisters, [16]to submit to such as these and to everyone who joins in the work and labors at it. [17]I was glad when Stephanas, Fortunatus and Achaicus arrived, because they have supplied what was lacking from you. [18]For they refreshed my spirit and yours also. Such men deserve recognition.

Final Greetings

[19]The churches in the province of Asia send you greetings. Aquila and Priscilla[d] greet you warmly in the Lord, and so does the church that meets at their house. [20]All the brothers and sisters here send you greetings. Greet one another with a holy kiss.

[21]I, Paul, write this greeting in my own hand.

[22]If anyone does not love the Lord, let that person be cursed! Come, Lord[e]!

[23]The grace of the Lord Jesus be with you.

[24]My love to all of you in Christ Jesus. Amen.[f]

---

a 49 Some early manuscripts *so let us*   *b* 54 Isaiah 25:8   *c* 55 Hosea 13:14   *d* 19 Greek *Prisca*, a variant of *Priscilla*   *e* 22 The Greek for *Come, Lord* reproduces an Aramaic expression (*Marana tha*) used by early Christians.   *f* 24 Some manuscripts do not have *Amen.*

2 corinthians

AUTHOR: Paul, the apostle

DATE: Around A.D. 55

THEME: God shines through us, even through our weaknesses.

1 Paul, an apostle of Christ Jesus by the will of God, and Timothy our brother,

To the church of God in Corinth, together with all his holy people throughout Achaia:

[2]Grace and peace to you from God our Father and the Lord Jesus Christ.

Praise to the God of All Comfort

[3]Praise be to the God and Father of our Lord Jesus Christ, the Father of compassion and the God of all comfort, [4]who comforts us in all our troubles, so that we can comfort those in any trouble with the comfort we ourselves receive from God. [5]For just as we share abundantly in the sufferings of Christ, so also our comfort abounds through Christ. [6]If we are distressed, it is for your comfort and salvation; if we are comforted, it is for your comfort, which produces in you patient endurance of the same sufferings we suffer. [7]And our hope for you is firm, because we know that just as you share in our sufferings, so also you share in our comfort.

[8]We do not want you to be uninformed, brothers and sisters, about the troubles we experienced in the province of Asia. We were under great pressure, far beyond our ability to endure, so that we despaired of life itself. [9]Indeed, we felt we had received the sentence of death. But this happened that we might not rely on ourselves but on God, who raises the dead. [10]He has delivered us from such a deadly peril, and he will deliver us again. On him we have set our hope that he will continue to deliver us, [11]as you help us by your prayers. Then many will give thanks on our behalf for the gracious favor granted us in answer to the prayers of many.

Paul's Change of Plans

[12]Now this is our boast: Our conscience testifies that we have conducted ourselves in the world, and especially in our relations with you, with integrity[a] and godly sincerity. We have done so, relying not on worldly wisdom but on God's grace. [13]For we do not write you anything you cannot read or understand. And I hope that, [14]as you have understood us in part, you will come to understand fully that you can boast of us just as we will boast of you in the day of the Lord Jesus.

[15]Because I was confident of this, I wanted to visit you first so that you might benefit twice. [16]I wanted to visit you on my way to Macedonia and to come back to you from Macedonia, and then to have you send me on my way to Judea. [17]Was I fickle when I intended to do this? Or do I make my plans in a worldly manner so that in the same breath I say both "Yes, yes" and "No, no"?

[18]But as surely as God is faithful, our message to you is not "Yes" and "No." [19]For the Son of God, Jesus Christ, who was preached among you by us—by me and Silas[b] and Timothy—was not "Yes" and "No," but in him it has always been "Yes." [20]For no matter how many promises God has made, they are "Yes" in Christ. And so through him the "Amen" is spoken by us to the glory of God. [21]Now it is God who makes both us and you stand firm in Christ. He anointed us, [22]set his seal of ownership on us, and put his Spirit in our hearts as a deposit, guaranteeing what is to come.

---

a 12 Many manuscripts *holiness*   b 19 Greek *Silvanus*, a variant of *Silas*

[23]I call God as my witness—and I stake my life on it—that it was in order to spare you that I did not return to Corinth. [24]Not that we lord it over your faith, but we work with you for your joy, because it is by faith you stand firm. [1]So I made up my mind that I would not make another painful visit to you. [2]For if I grieve you, who is left to make me glad but you whom I have grieved? [3]I wrote as I did, so that when I came I would not be distressed by those who should have made me rejoice. I had confidence in all of you, that you would all share my joy. [4]For I wrote you out of great distress and anguish of heart and with many tears, not to grieve you but to let you know the depth of my love for you.

Forgiveness for the Offender

[5]If anyone has caused grief, he has not so much grieved me as he has grieved all of you to some extent—not to put it too severely. [6]The punishment inflicted on him by the majority is sufficient. [7]Now instead, you ought to forgive and comfort him, so that he will not be overwhelmed by excessive sorrow. [8]I urge you, therefore, to reaffirm your love for him. [9]Another reason I wrote you was to see if you would stand the test and be obedient in everything. [10]Anyone you forgive, I also forgive. And what I have forgiven—if there was anything to forgive—I have forgiven in the sight of Christ for your sake, [11]in order that Satan might not outwit us. For we are not unaware of his schemes.

Ministers of the New Covenant

[12]Now when I went to Troas to preach the gospel of Christ and found that the Lord had opened a door for me, [13]I still had no peace of mind, because I did not find my brother Titus there. So I said good-by to them and went on to Macedonia.

[14]But thanks be to God, who always leads us as captives in Christ's triumphal procession and uses us to spread the aroma of the knowledge of him everywhere. [15]For we are to God the pleasing aroma of Christ among those who are being saved and those who are perishing. [16]To the one we are an aroma that brings death; to the other, an aroma that brings life. And who is equal to such a task? [17]Unlike so many, we do not peddle

the word of God for profit. On the contrary, in Christ we speak before God with sincerity, as those sent from God.

[3] Are we beginning to commend ourselves again? Or do we need, like some people, letters of recommendation to you or from you? [2]You yourselves are our letter, written on our hearts, known and read by everyone. [3]You show that you are a letter from Christ, the result of our ministry, written not with ink but with the Spirit of the living God, not on tablets of stone but on tablets of human hearts.

[4]Such confidence we have through Christ before God. [5]Not that we are competent in ourselves to claim anything for ourselves, but our competence comes from God. [6]He has made us competent as ministers of a new covenant—not of the letter but of the Spirit; for the letter kills, but the Spirit gives life.

The Greater Glory of the New Covenant

[7]Now if the ministry that brought death, which was engraved in letters on stone, came with glory, so that the Israelites could not look steadily at the face of Moses because of its glory, transitory though it was, [8]will not the ministry of the Spirit be even more glorious? [9]If the ministry that brought condemnation was glorious, how much more glorious is the ministry that brings righteousness! [10]For what was glorious has no glory now in comparison with the surpassing glory. [11]And if what was transitory came with glory, how much greater is the glory of that which lasts!

[12]Therefore, since we have such a hope, we are very bold. [13]We are not like Moses, who would put a veil over his face to prevent the Israelites from seeing the end of what was passing away. [14]But their minds were made dull, for to this day the same veil remains when the old covenant is read. It has not been removed, because only in Christ is it taken away. [15]Even to this day when Moses is read, a veil covers their hearts. [16]But whenever anyone turns to the Lord, the veil is taken away. [17]Now the Lord is the Spirit, and where the Spirit of the Lord is, there is freedom. [18]And we all, who with unveiled faces contemplate[a] the Lord's glory, are being transformed into his image with ever-

a 18 Or reflect

The Path to Reconciliation

2 Corinthians 2:1–17 or 2:5–11

Ruth Graham

When we understand that we are forgiven, when we have made the choice to forgive, when we have renewed our mind with God's Word and can recognize change in our hearts, then perhaps we can reconcile with the person or persons who hurt us. Much will depend on what has happened in the heart and life of the offender or offenders . . . We need to be able to see signs of true, lasting repentance and change in those with whom we may reconcile. But forgiveness will clear the way for reconciliation if reconciliation is going to occur. You cannot fully reconcile if you have not forgiven.

John Wesley {AD 1703–1791}

Forgive my foes? It cannot be:
My foes with cordial love embrace?
Fast bound in sin and misery,
Unsaved, unchanged by hallowing grace,
Throughout my fallen soul I feel
With man this is impossible.

Great Searcher of the complex heart,
A thought from you I would not hide;
I cannot draw the envenomed dart,
Or quench this hell of wrath and pride:
Jesus, till I your Spirit receive,
You know'st, I never can forgive.

Root out the wrath you dost restrain;
And when I have my Savior's mind,
I cannot render pain for pain,
I cannot speak a word unkind,
An angry thought I cannot know,
Or count mine injurer my foe.

reflection

1. How is forgiveness different from reconciliation?

2. Why is genuine forgiveness necessary for true reconciliation to occur?

3. What is the most hurtful thing you've had to forgive?

For your next devotional reading, go to page 1326.

increasing glory, which comes from the Lord, who is the Spirit.

Present Weakness and Resurrection Life

4 Therefore, since through God's mercy we have this ministry, we do not lose heart. [2]Rather, we have renounced secret and shameful ways; we do not use deception, nor do we distort the word of God. On the contrary, by setting forth the truth plainly we commend ourselves to everyone's conscience in the sight of God. [3]And even if our gospel is veiled, it is veiled to those who are perishing. [4]The god of this age has blinded the minds of unbelievers, so that they cannot see the light of the gospel that displays the glory of Christ, who is the image of God. [5]For what we preach is not ourselves, but Jesus Christ as Lord, and ourselves as your servants for Jesus' sake. [6]For God, who said, "Let light shine out of darkness,"[a] made his light shine in our hearts to give us the light of the knowledge of God's glory displayed in the face of Christ.

[7]But we have this treasure in jars of clay to show that this all-surpassing power is from God and not from us. [8]We are hard pressed on every side, but not crushed; perplexed, but not in despair; [9]persecuted, but not abandoned; struck down, but not destroyed. [10]We always carry around in our body the death of Jesus, so that the life of Jesus may also be revealed in our body. [11]For we who are alive are always being given over to death for Jesus' sake, so that his life may also be revealed in our mortal body. [12]So then, death is at work in us, but life is at work in you.

[13]It is written: "I believed; therefore I have spoken."[b] Since we have that same spirit of[c] faith, we also believe and therefore speak, [14]because we know that the one who raised the Lord Jesus from the dead will also raise us with Jesus and present us with you to himself. [15]All this is for your benefit, so that the grace that is reaching more and more people may cause thanksgiving to overflow to the glory of God.

[16]Therefore we do not lose heart. Though outwardly we are wasting away, yet inwardly we are being renewed day by day. [17]For our light and momentary troubles are achieving for us an eternal glory that far outweighs them all. [18]So we fix our eyes not on what is seen, but on what is unseen, since what is seen is temporary, but what is unseen is eternal.

Awaiting the New Body

5 For we know that if the earthly tent we live in is destroyed, we have a building from God, an eternal house in heaven, not built by human hands. [2]Meanwhile we groan, longing to be clothed with our heavenly dwelling, [3]because when we are clothed, we will not be found naked. [4]For while we are in this tent, we groan and are burdened, because we do not wish to be unclothed but to be clothed with our heavenly dwelling, so that what is mortal may be swallowed up by life. [5]Now the one who has fashioned us for this very purpose is God, who has given us the Spirit as a deposit, guaranteeing what is to come.

[6]Therefore we are always confident and know that as long as we are at home in the body we are away from the Lord. [7]We live by faith, not by sight. [8]We are confident, I say, and would prefer to be away from the body and at home with the Lord. [9]So we make it our goal to please him, whether we are at home in the body or away from it. [10]For we must all appear before the judgment seat of Christ, that everyone may receive what is due them for the things done while in the body, whether good or bad.

The Ministry of Reconciliation

[11]Since, then, we know what it is to fear the Lord, we try to persuade people. What we are is plain to God, and I hope it is also plain to your conscience. [12]We are not trying to commend ourselves to you again, but are giving you an opportunity to take pride in us, so that you can answer those who take pride in what is seen rather than in what is in the heart. [13]If we are "out of our mind," as some say, it is for God; if we are in our right mind, it is for you. [14]For Christ's love compels us, because we are convinced that one died for all, and therefore all died. [15]And he died for all, that those who live should no longer live for themselves but for him who died for them and was raised again.

[16]So from now on we regard no one from

---

[a] 6 Gen. 1:3   [b] 13 Psalm 116:10 (see Septuagint)   [c] 13 Or *Spirit-given*

Temporary Suffering

2 Corinthians 4:1–18 *or* 4:8,16–18

Martin Luther {ad 1483–1546}

If it's impossible to receive God's undeserved kindness except through faith in Christ, why does the Bible include so many passages of God rewarding people for the good things they've done? These passages are intended to comfort Christians. When you become a Christian, you will find forgiveness both for past sins and the ones you commit every day. But you'll have to work hard and suffer a lot as a result of your faith and baptism. Jesus makes it clear that the devil, the world and your corrupt nature will attack you from every direction and make you feel hemmed in on all sides.

If you were left in this predicament without anything to comfort you, you would give up in despair and say, "Who wants to be a Christian, or speak about Christ, or do good works? Look at what happens to Christians: The world walks all over them, slanders and humiliates them. It plays all kinds of cruel tricks on them. In the end, they lose their honor, property and life. Christ calls them helpless, sorrowful, hungry, meek, afflicted and persecuted! Is that all he can say? Will this last forever and never change?"

At that point, Christ strengthens and comforts us by saying, "You are God's children. He is going to take care of you. Even though you have to suffer in the world now for being God's children, don't let that suffering frighten you. Don't let what you experience tire you out or wear you down. Every one of you must continue to do your duty. This is painful, but it won't do you any real harm. The kingdom of heaven is yours, and you will be richly rewarded."

Steve Brown

You can stand any tough times if you know they are only temporary. If you know that the suffering will end, you can get through it. God promises that, though it may hurt now, there will come an end, and you will not ultimately be destroyed. His love assures that "bottom-line" fact.

reflection

1. If you really believed your troubles were temporary, how would that affect how you deal with setbacks and struggles in life?

2. How can you learn to view tough times from God's perspective instead of your own?

3. What difference will this make in your life?

For your next devotional reading, go to page 1328.

a worldly point of view. Though we once regarded Christ in this way, we do so no longer. [17]Therefore, if anyone is in Christ, the new creation has come: The old has gone, the new is here! [18]All this is from God, who reconciled us to himself through Christ and gave us the ministry of reconciliation: [19]that God was reconciling the world to himself in Christ, not counting people's sins against them. And he has committed to us the message of reconciliation. [20]We are therefore Christ's ambassadors, as though God were making his appeal through us. We implore you on Christ's behalf: Be reconciled to God. [21]God made him who had no sin to be sin[a] for us, so that in him we might become the righteousness of God.

6 As God's co-workers we urge you not to receive God's grace in vain. [2]For he says,

"In the time of my favor I heard you,
    and in the day of salvation I helped you."[b]

I tell you, now is the time of God's favor, now is the day of salvation.

Paul's Hardships

[3]We put no stumbling block in anyone's path, so that our ministry will not be discredited. [4]Rather, as servants of God we commend ourselves in every way: in great endurance; in troubles, hardships and distresses; [5]in beatings, imprisonments and riots; in hard work, sleepless nights and hunger; [6]in purity, understanding, patience and kindness; in the Holy Spirit and in sincere love; [7]in truthful speech and in the power of God; with weapons of righteousness in the right hand and in the left; [8]through glory and dishonor, bad report and good report; genuine, yet regarded as impostors; [9]known, yet regarded as unknown; dying, and yet we live on; beaten, and yet not killed; [10]sorrowful, yet always rejoicing; poor, yet making many rich; having nothing, and yet possessing everything.

[11]We have spoken freely to you, Corinthians, and opened wide our hearts to you. [12]We are not withholding our affection from you, but you are withholding yours from us.

[13]As a fair exchange—I speak as to my children—open wide your hearts also.

Warning Against Idolatry

[14]Do not be yoked together with unbelievers. For what do righteousness and wickedness have in common? Or what fellowship can light have with darkness? [15]What harmony is there between Christ and Belial[c]? Or what does a believer have in common with an unbeliever? [16]What agreement is there between the temple of God and idols? For we are the temple of the living God. As God has said:

"I will live with them
    and walk among them,
and I will be their God,
    and they will be my people."[d]

[17]Therefore,

"Come out from them
    and be separate,
                    says the Lord.
Touch no unclean thing,
    and I will receive you."[e]

[18]And,

"I will be a Father to you,
    and you will be my sons and
        daughters,
            says the Lord Almighty."[f]

7 Therefore, since we have these promises, dear friends, let us purify ourselves from everything that contaminates body and spirit, perfecting holiness out of reverence for God.

Paul's Joy Over the Church's Repentance

[2]Make room for us in your hearts. We have wronged no one, we have corrupted no one, we have exploited no one. [3]I do not say this to condemn you; I have said before that you have such a place in our hearts that we would live or die with you. [4]I have spoken to you with great frankness; I take great pride in you. I am greatly encouraged; in all our troubles my joy knows no bounds.

[5]For when we came into Macedonia, this body of ours had no rest, but we were harassed at every turn—conflicts on the outside, fears within. [6]But God, who comforts

---

a 21 Or be a sin offering   b 2 Isaiah 49:8   c 15 Greek Beliar, a variant of Belial   d 16 Lev. 26:12;
Jer. 32:38; Ezek. 37:27   e 17 Isaiah 52:11; Ezek. 20:34,41   f 18 2 Samuel 7:14; 7:8

GET OUT AND GET SHARING

2 Corinthians 5:1–21 *or* 5:16–20

Brian McLaren

Some of us Christians don't "get out much." We run from holy huddle to holy huddle, like squirrels darting from tree to tree, afraid that we will get hammered by a devil or seduced by a temptation . . .

But if you are willing to get out, reach out, relate to and be a neighbor, a friend, a decent human being, then you are more ready than you realize. It might be someone at work, a waitress where you have breakfast, the teenage son of a neighbor, your nephew, a person whose car you will see broken down at the side of the road later this week. You don't start by being religious; you start by being human, relational, neighborly, friendly. If you've forgotten, it is never too late to relearn.

You may have to, as we suggested before, trim back your church activities. Instead of yet another Bible study (how many more do you need?), you might start coaching basketball, or taking an art class, or volunteering at a retirement community or tutoring at a neighborhood school—just to get out a bit. In the process you will meet some people and you will ask some questions, conversations will begin and a relationship will develop. Don't worry about the content of the conversions. Just get them going and see what happens.

GEORGE MACDONALD {AD 1824–1905}

Is every Christian expected to bear witness? A man content to bear no witness to the truth is not in the kingdom of heaven. One who believes must bear witness. One who sees the truth, must live witnessing to it. Is our life, then, a witnessing to the truth? Do we carry ourselves in bank, on farm, in house or shop, in study or chamber or workshop, as the Lord would, or as the Lord would not? Are we careful to be true? Do we endeavour to live to the height of our ideas? Or are we mean, self-serving, world-flattering, fawning slaves? When contempt is cast on the truth, do we smile? Wronged in our presence, do we make no sign that we hold by it? I do not say we are called upon to dispute and defend with logic and argument, but we are called upon to show that we are on the other side . . . The girl who said before a company of mocking companions, "I believe in Jesus," bore true witness to her Master, the Truth.

reflection

1. You might call it being an "ambassador" for Christ or building "spiritual friendships" or "bearing witness." What is the same basic idea behind all three different terms?

2. What is the difference between preaching the gospel and living the gospel?

3. Is there some part of your life that needs to change so you can "get out more"?

For your next devotional reading, go to page 1331.

the downcast, comforted us by the coming of Titus, [7]and not only by his coming but also by the comfort you had given him. He told us about your longing for me, your deep sorrow, your ardent concern for me, so that my joy was greater than ever.

[8]Even if I caused you sorrow by my letter, I do not regret it. Though I did regret it—I see that my letter hurt you, but only for a little while— [9]yet now I am happy, not because you were made sorry, but because your sorrow led you to repentance. For you became sorrowful as God intended and so were not harmed in any way by us. [10]Godly sorrow brings repentance that leads to salvation and leaves no regret, but worldly sorrow brings death. [11]See what this godly sorrow has produced in you: what earnestness, what eagerness to clear yourselves, what indignation, what alarm, what longing, what concern, what readiness to see justice done. At every point you have proved yourselves to be innocent in this matter. [12]So even though I wrote to you, it was neither on account of the one who did the wrong nor on account of the injured party, but rather that before God you could see for yourselves how devoted to us you are. [13]By all this we are encouraged.

In addition to our own encouragement, we were especially delighted to see how happy Titus was, because his spirit has been refreshed by all of you. [14]I had boasted to him about you, and you have not embarrassed me. But just as everything we said to you was true, so our boasting about you to Titus has proved to be true as well. [15]And his affection for you is all the greater when he remembers that you were all obedient, receiving him with fear and trembling. [16]I am glad I can have complete confidence in you.

The Collection for the Lord's People

8 And now, brothers and sisters, we want you to know about the grace that God has given the Macedonian churches. [2]In the midst of a very severe trial, their overflowing joy and their extreme poverty welled up in rich generosity. [3]For I testify that they gave as much as they were able, and even beyond their ability. Entirely on their own, [4]they urgently pleaded with us for the privilege of sharing in this service to the Lord's people. [5]And they went beyond our expectations; having given themselves first of all to the Lord, they gave themselves by the will of God also to us. [6]So we urged Titus, just as he had earlier made a beginning, to bring also to completion this act of grace on your part. [7]But since you excel in everything—in faith, in speech, in knowledge, in complete earnestness and in the love we have kindled in you[a]—see that you also excel in this grace of giving.

[8]I am not commanding you, but I want to test the sincerity of your love by comparing it with the earnestness of others. [9]For you know the grace of our Lord Jesus Christ, that though he was rich, yet for your sake he became poor, so that you through his poverty might become rich.

[10]And here is my judgment about what is best for you in this matter. Last year you were the first not only to give but also to have the desire to do so. [11]Now finish the work, so that your eager willingness to do it may be matched by your completion of it, according to your means. [12]For if the willingness is there, the gift is acceptable according to what one has, not according to what one does not have.

[13]Our desire is not that others might be relieved while you are hard pressed, but that there might be equality. [14]At the present time your plenty will supply what they need, so that in turn their plenty will supply what you need. The goal is equality, [15]as it is written: "The one who gathered much did not have too much, and the one who gathered little did not have too little."[b]

Titus Sent to Receive the Collection

[16]Thanks be to God, who put into the heart of Titus the same concern I have for you. [17]For Titus not only welcomed our appeal, but he is coming to you with much enthusiasm and on his own initiative. [18]And we are sending along with him the brother who is praised by all the churches for his service to the gospel. [19]What is more, he was chosen by the churches to accompany us as we carry the offering, which we administer in order to honor the Lord himself and to show our eagerness to help. [20]We want to avoid any criticism of the way we administer this liberal gift. [21]For we are taking pains to do what

a 7 Some manuscripts *and in your love for us*   b 15 Exodus 16:18

is right, not only in the eyes of the Lord but also in the eyes of others.

²²In addition, we are sending with them our brother who has often proved to us in many ways that he is zealous, and now even more so because of his great confidence in you. ²³As for Titus, he is my partner and co-worker among you; as for our brothers, they are representatives of the churches and an honor to Christ. ²⁴Therefore show these men the proof of your love and the reason for our pride in you, so that the churches can see it.

9 There is no need for me to write to you about this service to the Lord's people. ²For I know your eagerness to help, and I have been boasting about it to the Macedonians, telling them that since last year you in Achaia were ready to give; and your enthusiasm has stirred most of them to action. ³But I am sending the brothers in order that our boasting about you in this matter should not prove hollow, but that you may be ready, as I said you would be. ⁴For if any Macedonians come with me and find you unprepared, we—not to say anything about you—would be ashamed of having been so confident. ⁵So I thought it necessary to urge the brothers to visit you in advance and finish the arrangements for the generous gift you had promised. Then it will be ready as a generous gift, not as one grudgingly given.

Generosity Encouraged

⁶Remember this: Whoever sows sparingly will also reap sparingly, and whoever sows generously will also reap generously. ⁷Each of you should give what you have decided in your heart to give, not reluctantly or under compulsion, for God loves a cheerful giver. ⁸And God is able to bless you abundantly, so that in all things at all times, having all that you need, you will abound in every good work. ⁹As it is written:

> "They have scattered abroad their gifts
>   to the poor;
>   their righteousness endures forever."ᵃ

¹⁰Now he who supplies seed to the sower and bread for food will also supply and increase your store of seed and will enlarge the harvest of your righteousness. ¹¹You will be made rich in every way so that you can be generous on

every occasion, and through us your generosity will result in thanksgiving to God.

¹²This service that you perform is not only supplying the needs of the Lord's people but is also overflowing in many expressions of thanks to God. ¹³Because of the service by which you have proved yourselves, people will praise God for the obedience that accompanies your confession of the gospel of Christ, and for your generosity in sharing with them and with everyone else. ¹⁴And in their prayers for you their hearts will go out to you, because of the surpassing grace God has given you. ¹⁵Thanks be to God for his indescribable gift!

Paul's Defense of His Ministry

10 By the meekness and gentleness of Christ, I appeal to you—I, Paul, who am "timid" when face to face with you, but "bold" toward you when away! ²I beg you that when I come I may not have to be as bold as I expect to be toward some people who think that we live by the standards of this world. ³For though we live in the world, we do not wage war as the world does. ⁴The weapons we fight with are not the weapons of the world. On the contrary, they have divine power to demolish strongholds. ⁵We demolish arguments and every pretension that sets itself up against the knowledge of God, and we take captive every thought to make it obedient to Christ. ⁶And we will be ready to punish every act of disobedience, once your obedience is complete.

⁷You are judging by appearances.ᵇ If anyone is confident that they belong to Christ, they should consider again that we belong to Christ just as much as they do. ⁸So even if I boast somewhat freely about the authority the Lord gave us for building you up rather than tearing you down, I will not be ashamed of it. ⁹I do not want to seem to be trying to frighten you with my letters. ¹⁰For some say, "His letters are weighty and forceful, but in person he is unimpressive and his speaking amounts to nothing." ¹¹Such people should realize that what we are in our letters when we are absent, we will be in our actions when we are present.

¹²We do not dare to classify or compare ourselves with some who commend them-

Sowing Seeds

2 Corinthians 9:6–8

read/meditate

Read through this passage several times. Think about the people you have seen who invest generously in life around them. Think about your own patterns of giving. How do they compare or contrast with the statements Paul made in this passage?

pray

Share with God your concerns about giving, if you have any. Ask him to set your priorities as you choose between all the good people and organizations that you could give to, so that you can develop a zeal for giving in an area you feel passionate about. Offer him the stillness to clear your mind and align your thoughts with his.

contemplate

Think about the two sowers Paul described. One planted few seeds; the other, a generous amount of seeds. Take some time to think about where you are on the spectrum between the two. If you're going to reap what you sow, what kind of investment are you making in the crop?

additional reflection

If a person gets his attitude toward money straight, it will help straighten out almost every other area in his life.

—*Billy Graham*

From what we get, we can make a living; what we give, however, makes a life.

—*Arthur Ashe*

For your next devotional reading, go to page 1333.

selves. When they measure themselves by themselves and compare themselves with themselves, they are not wise. [13]We, however, will not boast beyond proper limits, but will confine our boasting to the sphere of service God himself has assigned to us, a sphere that also includes you. [14]We are not going too far in our boasting, as would be the case if we had not come to you, for we did get as far as you with the gospel of Christ. [15]Neither do we go beyond our limits by boasting of work done by others. Our hope is that, as your faith continues to grow, our sphere of activity among you will greatly expand, [16]so that we can preach the gospel in the regions beyond you. For we do not want to boast about work already done in someone else's territory. [17]But, "Let those who boast boast in the Lord." [a] [18]For it is not those who commend themselves who are approved, but those whom the Lord commends.

Paul and the False Apostles

[11] I hope you will put up with me in a little foolishness. Yes, please put up with me! [2]I am jealous for you with a godly jealousy. I promised you to one husband, to Christ, so that I might present you as a pure virgin to him. [3]But I am afraid that just as Eve was deceived by the serpent's cunning, your minds may somehow be led astray from your sincere and pure devotion to Christ. [4]For if someone comes to you and preaches a Jesus other than the Jesus we preached, or if you receive a different spirit from the Spirit you received, or a different gospel from the one you accepted, you put up with it easily enough.

[5]I do not think I am in the least inferior to those "super-apostles." [b] [6]I may indeed be untrained as a speaker, but I do have knowledge. We have made this perfectly clear to you in every way. [7]Was it a sin for me to lower myself in order to elevate you by preaching the gospel of God to you free of charge? [8]I robbed other churches by receiving support from them so as to serve you. [9]And when I was with you and needed something, I was not a burden to anyone, for the brothers and sisters who came from Macedonia supplied what I needed. I have kept myself

from being a burden to you in any way, and will continue to do so. [10]As surely as the truth of Christ is in me, nobody in the regions of Achaia will stop this boasting of mine. [11]Why? Because I do not love you? God knows I do!

[12]And I will keep on doing what I am doing in order to cut the ground from under those who want an opportunity to be considered equal with us in the things they boast about. [13]For such persons are false apostles, deceitful workers, masquerading as apostles of Christ. [14]And no wonder, for Satan himself masquerades as an angel of light. [15]It is not surprising, then, if his servants also masquerade as servants of righteousness. Their end will be what their actions deserve.

Paul Boasts About His Sufferings

[16]I repeat: Let no one take me for a fool. But if you do, then tolerate me just as you would a fool, so that I may do a little boasting. [17]In this self-confident boasting I am not talking as the Lord would, but as a fool. [18]Since many are boasting in the way the world does, I too will boast. [19]You gladly put up with fools since you are so wise! [20]In fact, you even put up with any who enslave you or exploit you or take advantage of you or push themselves forward or slap you in the face. [21]To my shame I admit that we were too weak for that!

Whatever anyone else dares to boast about—I am speaking as a fool—I also dare to boast about. [22]Are they Hebrews? So am I. Are they Israelites? So am I. Are they Abraham's descendants? So am I. [23]Are they servants of Christ? (I am out of my mind to talk like this.) I am more. I have worked much harder, been in prison more frequently, been flogged more severely, and been exposed to death again and again. [24]Five times I received from the Jews the forty lashes minus one. [25]Three times I was beaten with rods, once I was pelted with stones, three times I was shipwrecked, I spent a night and a day in the open sea, [26]I have been constantly on the move. I have been in danger from rivers, in danger from bandits, in danger from my own people, in danger from Gentiles; in danger in the city, in danger in the country, in danger at sea; and in danger

a 17 Jer. 9:24   b 5 Or to the most eminent apostles

MONDAY

ALL THAT YOU NEED

2 Corinthians 11:16—12:10 *or* 12:6–10

KARL BARTH {AD 1886–1968}

"My grace is sufficient for you" (2 Corinthians 12:9). This is a very short text—a mere six words—the shortest I have ever preached on . . . The wonderful spice of this saying lies in its brevity. The six words are enough. Some of you may have heard that in the last 40 years I have written many books, some large. I will freely and frankly and gladly admit that these six words say much more and much better things than all the heaps of paper with which I have surrounded myself. They are enough—which cannot be said even remotely of my books. What may be good in my books can be at most that from afar they point to what these six words say. And when my books are long since outdated and forgotten, and every book in the world with them, these words will still shine with everlasting fullness: "My grace is sufficient for you."

Kristine A. Belfils

There were times when it was all I could do to just get out of bed in the morning, let alone trust that God would bring me out of my mess. You may have felt the same way at times. Feelings of fear and uncertainty can overwhelm us if we let them. Personally, I had to tell God, "I don't feel like trusting You right now, but I will trust you for trust's sake." Believe it or not, it helped me get through that moment. God is trustworthy even when we don't feel or believe he is. Trust God for trust's sake, if you can't find any other reason to. God will meet you there.

reflection

1. How did Paul experience the sufficiency of God's grace?

2. What situation do you face that feels like more than you can handle?

3. How are you doing at trusting God to bring you through it?

For your next devotional reading, go to page 1337.

from false believers. [27]I have labored and toiled and have often gone without sleep; I have known hunger and thirst and have often gone without food; I have been cold and naked. [28]Besides everything else, I face daily the pressure of my concern for all the churches. [29]Who is weak, and I do not feel weak? Who is led into sin, and I do not inwardly burn?

[30]If I must boast, I will boast of the things that show my weakness. [31]The God and Father of the Lord Jesus, who is to be praised forever, knows that I am not lying. [32]In Damascus the governor under King Aretas had the city of the Damascenes guarded in order to arrest me. [33]But I was lowered in a basket from a window in the wall and slipped through his hands.

Paul's Vision and His Thorn

12 I must go on boasting. Although there is nothing to be gained, I will go on to visions and revelations from the Lord. [2]I know a man in Christ who fourteen years ago was caught up to the third heaven. Whether it was in the body or out of the body I do not know—God knows. [3]And I know that this man—whether in the body or apart from the body I do not know, but God knows— [4]was caught up to paradise and heard inexpressible things, things that no one is permitted to tell. [5]I will boast about someone like that, but I will not boast about myself, except about my weaknesses. [6]Even if I should choose to boast, I would not be a fool, because I would be speaking the truth. But I refrain, so no one will think more of me than is warranted by what I do or say, [7]or because of these surpassingly great revelations. Therefore, in order to keep me from becoming conceited, I was given a thorn in my flesh, a messenger of Satan, to torment me. [8]Three times I pleaded with the Lord to take it away from me. [9]But he said to me, "My grace is sufficient for you, for my power is made perfect in weakness." Therefore I will boast all the more gladly about my weaknesses, so that Christ's power may rest on me. [10]That is why, for Christ's sake, I delight in weaknesses, in insults, in hardships, in persecutions, in difficulties. For when I am weak, then I am strong.

Paul's Concern for the Corinthians

[11]I have made a fool of myself, but you drove me to it. I ought to have been commended by you, for I am not in the least inferior to the "super-apostles," [a] even though I am nothing. [12]I persevered in demonstrating among you the marks of a true apostle, including signs, wonders and miracles. [13]How were you inferior to the other churches, except that I was never a burden to you? Forgive me this wrong!

[14]Now I am ready to visit you for the third time, and I will not be a burden to you, because what I want is not your possessions but you. After all, children should not have to save up for their parents, but parents for their children. [15]So I will very gladly spend for you everything I have and expend myself as well. If I love you more, will you love me less? [16]Be that as it may, I have not been a burden to you. Yet, crafty fellow that I am, I caught you by trickery! [17]Did I exploit you through any of the men I sent to you? [18]I urged Titus to go to you and I sent our brother with him. Titus did not exploit you, did he? Did we not walk in the same footsteps by the same Spirit?

[19]Have you been thinking all along that we have been defending ourselves to you? We have been speaking in the sight of God as those in Christ; and everything we do, dear friends, is for your strengthening. [20]For I am afraid that when I come I may not find you as I want you to be, and you may not find me as you want me to be. I fear that there may be quarreling, jealousy, outbursts of anger, factions, slander, gossip, arrogance and disorder. [21]I am afraid that when I come again my God will humble me before you, and I will be grieved over many who have sinned earlier and have not repented of the impurity, sexual sin and debauchery in which they have indulged.

Final Warnings

13 This will be my third visit to you. "Every matter must be established by the testimony of two or three witnesses." [b] [2]I already gave you a warning when I was with you the second time. I now repeat it while absent: On my return I will not spare those who sinned earlier or any of the others, [3]since you are de-

---

a 11 Or *the most eminent apostles*   *b 1* Deut. 19:15

manding proof that Christ is speaking through me. He is not weak in dealing with you, but is powerful among you. [4]For to be sure, he was crucified in weakness, yet he lives by God's power. Likewise, we are weak in him, yet by God's power we will live with him in our dealing with you.

[5]Examine yourselves to see whether you are in the faith; test yourselves. Do you not realize that Christ Jesus is in you—unless, of course, you fail the test? [6]And I trust that you will discover that we have not failed the test. [7]Now we pray to God that you will not do anything wrong. Not that people will see that we have stood the test but that you will do what is right even though we may seem to have failed. [8]For we cannot do anything against the truth, but only for the truth. [9]We are glad whenever we are weak but you are strong; and our prayer is that you may be fully restored. [10]This is why I write these things when I am absent, that when I come I may not have to be harsh in my use of authority—the authority the Lord gave me for building you up, not for tearing you down.

Final Greetings

[11]Finally, brothers and sisters, rejoice! Strive for full restoration, encourage one another, be of one mind, live in peace. And the God of love and peace will be with you.

[12]Greet one another with a holy kiss. [13]All God's people here send their greetings.

[14]May the grace of the Lord Jesus Christ, and the love of God, and the fellowship of the Holy Spirit be with you all.

galatians

AUTHOR: Paul, the apostle

DATE: Around A.D. 52

THEME: God's salvation is a gift that can't be earned.

Paul, an apostle—sent not with a human commission nor by human authority, but by Jesus Christ and God the Father, who raised him from the dead— ²and all the brothers and sisters with me,

To the churches in Galatia:

³Grace and peace to you from God our Father and the Lord Jesus Christ, ⁴who gave himself for our sins to rescue us from the present evil age, according to the will of our God and Father, ⁵to whom be glory for ever and ever. Amen.

No Other Gospel

⁶I am astonished that you are so quickly deserting the one who called you by the grace of Christ and are turning to a different gospel— ⁷which is really no gospel at all. Evidently some people are throwing you into confusion and are trying to pervert the gospel of Christ. ⁸But even if we or an angel from heaven should preach a gospel other than the one we preached to you, let that person be under God's curse! ⁹As we have already said, so now I say again: If anybody is preaching to you a gospel other than what you accepted, let that person be under God's curse!

¹⁰Am I now trying to win human approval, or God's approval? Or am I trying to please people? If I were still trying to please people, I would not be a servant of Christ.

Paul Called by God

¹¹I want you to know, brothers and sisters, that the gospel I preached is not of human origin. ¹²I did not receive it from any human source, nor was I taught it; rather, I received it by revelation from Jesus Christ.

¹³For you have heard of my previous way of life in Judaism, how intensely I persecuted the church of God and tried to destroy it. ¹⁴I was advancing in Judaism beyond many of my own age among my people and was extremely zealous for the traditions of my fathers. ¹⁵But when God, who set me apart from birth*a* and called me by his grace, was pleased ¹⁶to reveal his Son in me so that I might preach him among the Gentiles, my immediate response was not to consult any human being. ¹⁷I did not go up to Jerusalem to see those who were apostles before I was, but I went into Arabia. Later I returned to Damascus.

¹⁸Then after three years, I went up to Jerusalem to get acquainted with Cephas*b* and stayed with him fifteen days. ¹⁹I saw none of the other apostles—only James, the Lord's brother. ²⁰I assure you before God that what I am writing you is no lie.

²¹Then I went to Syria and Cilicia. ²²I was personally unknown to the churches of Judea that are in Christ. ²³They only heard the report: "The man who formerly persecuted us is now preaching the faith he once tried to destroy." ²⁴And they praised God because of me.

Paul Accepted by the Apostles

Then after fourteen years, I went up again to Jerusalem, this time with Barnabas. I took Titus along also. ²¹I went in response to a revelation and, meeting privately with those esteemed as leaders, I set before them the gospel that I preach among the Gentiles. I wanted to be

---

a 15 Or from my mother's womb   *b 18 That is, Peter*

TUESDAY

GOD AT WORK

Galatians 2:1–21 *or* 2:20–21

C. S. LEWIS {AD 1898–1963}

What, then, is the difference which He has made to the whole human mass? It is just this; that the business of becoming a son of God, of being turned from a created thing into a begotten thing, of passing over from the temporary biological life into timeless "spiritual" life, has been done for us. Humanity is already "saved" in principle. We individuals have to appropriate that salvation. But the really tough work—the bit we could not have done for ourselves—has been done for us. We have not got to try to climb up into spiritual life by our own efforts; it has already come down into the human race. If we will only lay ourselves open to the one Man in whom it was fully present, and who, in spite of being God, is also a real man, He will do it in us and for us. Remember what I said about "good infection." One of our own race has this new life: if we get close to Him we shall catch it from Him.

Eugene Peterson

This may seem like a quibble, but it is not. Most of us fall into the trap from time to time. We become Christians because we realize we cannot save ourselves and need Christ to save us. But once we are "in" we start taking over the job. What is essential is to know that the Christian life is mostly what is being done to you, not what you are doing.

— *reflection* —

1. Is it freeing or frustrating to know that Christianity is more about what God does in you than about what you do for God?
2. What does it mean practically that Christ lives in you?
3. Do you live each day by faith in Jesus and his work in you, or do you live more by faith in yourself and the work that *you* can do?

For your next devotional reading, go to page 1341.

1338 || galatians 2:3

sure I was not running and had not been running my race in vain. ³Yet not even Titus, who was with me, was compelled to be circumcised, even though he was a Greek. ⁴This matter arose because some false believers had infiltrated our ranks to spy on the freedom we have in Christ Jesus and to make us slaves. ⁵We did not give in to them for a moment, so that the truth of the gospel might remain with you.

⁶As for those who were held in high esteem—whatever they were makes no difference to me; God does not show favoritism—they added nothing to my message. ⁷On the contrary, they saw that I had been entrusted with the task of preaching the gospel to the Gentiles,ᵃ just as Peter had been to the Jews.ᵇ ⁸For God, who was at work in Peter as an apostle to the Jews, was also at work in me as an apostle to the Gentiles. ⁹James, Cephasᶜ and John, those esteemed as pillars, gave me and Barnabas the right hand of fellowship when they recognized the grace given to me. They agreed that we should go to the Gentiles, and they to the Jews. ¹⁰All they asked was that we should continue to remember the poor, the very thing I had been eager to do all along.

Paul Opposes Cephas

¹¹When Cephas came to Antioch, I opposed him to his face, because he stood condemned. ¹²For before certain people came from James, he used to eat with the Gentiles. But when they arrived, he began to draw back and separate himself from the Gentiles because he was afraid of those who belonged to the circumcision group. ¹³The other Jews joined him in his hypocrisy, so that by their hypocrisy even Barnabas was led astray.

¹⁴When I saw that they were not acting in line with the truth of the gospel, I said to Cephas in front of them all, "You are a Jew, yet you live like a Gentile and not like a Jew. How is it, then, that you force Gentiles to follow Jewish customs?

¹⁵"We who are Jews by birth and not sinful Gentiles ¹⁶know that a person is not justified by observing the law, but by faith in Jesus Christ. So we, too, have put our faith in Christ Jesus that we may be justified by faith inᵈ Christ and not by observing the law, because by observing the law no one will be justified.

¹⁷"But if, in seeking to be justified in Christ, we Jews find ourselves also among the sinners, doesn't that mean that Christ promotes sin? Absolutely not! ¹⁸If I rebuild what I destroyed, then I really would be a lawbreaker.

¹⁹"For through the law I died to the law so that I might live for God. ²⁰I have been crucified with Christ and I no longer live, but Christ lives in me. The life I now live in the body, I live by faith in the Son of God, who loved me and gave himself for me. ²¹I do not set aside the grace of God, for if righteousness could be gained through the law, Christ died for nothing!"ᵉ

Faith or Observance of the Law

3 You foolish Galatians! Who has bewitched you? Before your very eyes Jesus Christ was clearly portrayed as crucified. ²I would like to learn just one thing from you: Did you receive the Spirit by observing the law, or by believing what you heard? ³Are you so foolish? After beginning with the Spirit, are you now trying to finish by human effort? ⁴Have you experiencedᶠ so much in vain—if it really was in vain? ⁵Does God give you his Spirit and work miracles among you by your observing the law, or by your believing what you heard? ⁶So also Abraham "believed God, and it was credited to him as righteousness."ᵍ

⁷Understand, then, that those who have faith are children of Abraham. ⁸Scripture foresaw that God would justify the Gentiles by faith, and announced the gospel in advance to Abraham: "All nations will be blessed through you."ʰ ⁹So those who rely on faith are blessed along with Abraham, the man of faith.

¹⁰All who rely on observing the law are under a curse, for it is written: "Cursed is everyone who does not continue to do everything written in the Book of the Law."ⁱ ¹¹Clearly no one is justified before God by the law, because "the righteous will live by faith."ʲ ¹²The law is not based on faith; on the contrary, it

---

ᵃ 7 Greek *uncircumcised*   ᵇ 7 Greek *circumcised*; also in verses 8 and 9   ᶜ 9 That is, Peter; also in verses 11 and 14   ᵈ 16 Or *but through the faithfulness of . . . justified on the basis of the faithfulness of*   ᵉ 21 Some interpreters end the quotation after verse 14.   ᶠ 4 Or *suffered*   ᵍ 6 Gen. 15:6   ʰ 8 Gen. 12:3; 18:18; 22:18   ⁱ 10 Deut. 27:26   ʲ 11 Hab. 2:4

says, "Whoever does these things will live by them."[a] [13] Christ redeemed us from the curse of the law by becoming a curse for us, for it is written: "Cursed is everyone who is hung on a pole."[b] [14] He redeemed us in order that the blessing given to Abraham might come to the Gentiles through Christ Jesus, so that by faith we might receive the promise of the Spirit.

The Law and the Promise

[15] Brothers and sisters, let me take an example from everyday life. Just as no one can set aside or add to a human covenant that has been duly established, so it is in this case. [16] The promises were spoken to Abraham and to his seed. Scripture does not say "and to seeds," meaning many people, but "and to your seed,"[c] meaning one person, who is Christ. [17] What I mean is this: The law, introduced 430 years later, does not set aside the covenant previously established by God and thus do away with the promise. [18] For if the inheritance depends on the law, then it no longer depends on the promise; but God in his grace gave it to Abraham through a promise.

[19] What, then, was the purpose of the law? It was added because of transgressions until the Seed to whom the promise referred had come. The law was given through angels and entrusted to a mediator. [20] A mediator, however, implies more than one party; but God is one.

[21] Is the law, therefore, opposed to the promises of God? Absolutely not! For if a law had been given that could impart life, then righteousness would certainly have come by the law. [22] But Scripture has locked up everything under the control of sin, so that what was promised, being given through faith in Jesus Christ, might be given to those who believe.

Children of God

[23] Before the coming of this faith,[d] we were held in custody under the law, locked up until the faith that was to come would be revealed. [24] So the law was put in charge of us until Christ came that we might be justified by faith. [25] Now that this faith has come, we are no longer under the supervision of the law.

[26] So in Christ Jesus you are all children of God through faith, [27] for all of you who were baptized into Christ have clothed yourselves with Christ. [28] There is neither Jew nor Gentile, neither slave nor free, neither male nor female, for you are all one in Christ Jesus. [29] If you belong to Christ, then you are Abraham's seed, and heirs according to the promise.

4 What I am saying is that as long as heirs are underage they are no different from slaves, although they own the whole estate. [2] They are subject to guardians and trustees until the time set by their fathers. [3] So also, when we were underage, we were in slavery under the elemental spiritual forces[e] of the world. [4] But when the set time had fully come, God sent his Son, born of a woman, born under the law, [5] to redeem those under the law, that we might receive adoption to sonship.[f] [6] Because you are his sons, God sent the Spirit of his Son into our hearts, the Spirit who calls out, "Abba,[g] Father." [7] So you are no longer slaves, but God's children; and since you are his children, he has made you also heirs.

Paul's Concern for the Galatians

[8] Formerly, when you did not know God, you were slaves to those who by nature are not gods. [9] But now that you know God—or rather are known by God—how is it that you are turning back to those weak and miserable forces[h]? Do you wish to be enslaved by them all over again? [10] You are observing special days and months and seasons and years! [11] I fear for you, that somehow I have wasted my efforts on you.

[12] I plead with you, brothers and sisters, become like me, for I became like you. You have done me no wrong. [13] As you know, it was because of an illness that I first preached the gospel to you. [14] Even though my illness was a trial to you, you did not treat me with contempt or scorn. Instead, you welcomed me as if I were an angel of God, as if I were Christ Jesus himself. [15] What has happened to all your joy? I can testify that, if you could have done so, you would

---

a 12 Lev. 18:5   *b* 13 Deut. 21:23   *c* 16 Gen. 12:7; 13:15; 24:7   *d* 22,23 Or *through the faithfulness of Jesus . . . .* [23] *Before faith came*   *e* 3 Or *under the basic principles*   *f* 5 The Greek word for *adoption to sonship* is a legal term referring to the full legal standing of an adopted male heir in Roman culture.   *g* 6 Aramaic for *Father*   *h* 9 Or *principles* have torn out your eyes and given them to me. ¹⁶Have I now become your enemy by telling you the truth?

¹⁷Those people are zealous to win you over, but for no good. What they want is to alienate you from us, so that you may have zeal for them. ¹⁸It is fine to be zealous, provided the purpose is good, and to be so always, not just when I am with you. ¹⁹My dear children, for whom I am again in the pains of childbirth until Christ is formed in you, ²⁰how I wish I could be with you now and change my tone, because I am perplexed about you!

Hagar and Sarah

²¹Tell me, you who want to be under the law, are you not aware of what the law says? ²²For it is written that Abraham had two sons, one by the slave woman and the other by the free woman. ²³His son by the slave woman was born as the result of human effort,ᵃ but his son by the free woman was born as the result of a divine promise.

²⁴I am taking these things figuratively, for the women represent two covenants. One covenant is from Mount Sinai and bears children who are to be slaves: This is Hagar. ²⁵Now Hagar stands for Mount Sinai in Arabia and corresponds to the present city of Jerusalem, because she is in slavery with her children. ²⁶But the Jerusalem that is above is free, and she is our mother. ²⁷For it is written:

"Be glad, barren woman,
    you who never bore a child;
shout for joy and cry aloud,
    you who were never in labor;
because more are the children of the
                    desolate woman
    than of her who has a husband."ᵇ

²⁸Now you, brothers and sisters, like Isaac, are children of promise. ²⁹At that time the son born by human effort persecuted the son born by the power of the Spirit. It is the same now. ³⁰But what does Scripture say? "Get rid of the slave woman and her son, for the slave woman's son will never share in the inheritance with the free woman's son."ᶜ ³¹Therefore, brothers and sisters, we are not children of the slave woman, but of the free woman.

Freedom in Christ

5 It is for freedom that Christ has set us free. Stand firm, then, and do not let yourselves be burdened again by a yoke of slavery.

²Mark my words! I, Paul, tell you that if you let yourselves be circumcised, Christ will be of no value to you at all. ³Again I declare to every man who lets himself be circumcised that he is obligated to obey the whole law. ⁴You who are trying to be justified by the law have been alienated from Christ; you have fallen away from grace. ⁵But by faith we eagerly await through the Spirit the righteousness for which we hope. ⁶For in Christ Jesus neither circumcision nor uncircumcision has any value. The only thing that counts is faith expressing itself through love.

⁷You were running a good race. Who cut in on you to keep you from obeying the truth? ⁸That kind of persuasion does not come from the one who calls you. ⁹"A little yeast works through the whole batch of dough." ¹⁰I am confident in the Lord that you will take no other view. The one who is throwing you into confusion will have to pay the penalty, whoever that may be. ¹¹Brothers and sisters, if I am still preaching circumcision, why am I still being persecuted? In that case the offense of the cross has been abolished. ¹²As for those agitators, I wish they would go the whole way and emasculate themselves!

Life by the Spirit

¹³You, my brothers and sisters, were called to be free. But do not use your freedom to indulge the sinful natureᵈ; rather, serve one another humbly in love. ¹⁴For the entire law is fulfilled in keeping this one command: "Love your neighbor as yourself."ᵉ ¹⁵If you keep on biting and devouring each other, watch out or you will be destroyed by each other.

¹⁶So I say, walk by the Spirit, and you will not gratify the desires of the sinful nature. ¹⁷For the sinful nature desires what is contrary to the Spirit, and the Spirit what is contrary to the sinful nature. They are in conflict with each other, so that you are not to do whateverᶠ you want. ¹⁸But if you are led by the Spirit, you are not under the law.

ᵃ 23 Or born according to the flesh; also in verse 29   ᵇ 27 Isaiah 54:1   ᶜ 30 Gen. 21:10   ᵈ 13 Or the
flesh; also in verses 16, 17, 19 and 24   ᵉ 14 Lev. 19:18   ᶠ 17 Or you do not do what

WEDNESDAY

A SIGN OF SPIRITUAL HEALTH

Galatians 5:1–26 or 5:13–15

Tony Jones

Servanthood is so foundational to the Christian life that it's hard to know where to begin talking about the practice of it. Everything from doing the dishes at home to washing someone's feet to donating one of your kidneys to your brother is within the spectrum of service in Jesus' name. For most of us, on most days, Jesus is calling us to tasks somewhere between doing the dishes and donating a kidney—the trick is determining what Jesus is calling me to today.

That's where service intersects with all of the aforementioned practices. For centuries, the Christians who were known for their service to the world were also those Christians who took their spiritual development seriously. When we take time and make space for God to move in our lives, we then have the resources necessary for true servanthood. Ultimately, how you serve Jesus and God's creation is a reflection of your personal spiritual health.

OSWALD CHAMBERS {AD 1874–1917}

Our Lord's exhortation in these verses is to be generous in our behaviour to all men. In the spiritual life beware of walking according to natural affinities. Everyone has natural affinities; some people we like and others we do not like. We must never let those likes and dislikes rule in our Christian life. If we "walk in the light," as God is in the light, God will give us communion with people for whom we have no natural affinity.

The Example Our Lord gives us is not that of a good man, or even of a good Christian, but of God Himself. "[Be perfect, therefore, as your heavenly Father is perfect]" (Matthew 5:48)—show to the other man what God has shown to you; and God will give us ample opportunities in actual life to prove whether we are perfect as our Father in heaven is perfect. To be a disciple means that we deliberately identify ourselves with God's interests in other people.

reflection

1. Who are the people that you'll see in the next day that you can serve in small ways?

2. What service could you perform this week that would take sacrifice?

3. What can you do to discover the service other people in your church or community would most benefit from?

For your next devotional reading, go to page 1344.

[19]The acts of the sinful nature are obvious: sexual immorality, impurity and debauchery; [20]idolatry and witchcraft; hatred, discord, jealousy, fits of rage, selfish ambition, dissensions, factions [21]and envy; drunkenness, orgies, and the like. I warn you, as I did before, that those who live like this will not inherit the kingdom of God.

[22]But the fruit of the Spirit is love, joy, peace, patience, kindness, goodness, faithfulness, [23]gentleness and self-control. Against such things there is no law. [24]Those who belong to Christ Jesus have crucified the sinful nature with its passions and desires. [25]Since we live by the Spirit, let us keep in step with the Spirit. [26]Let us not become conceited, provoking and envying each other.

Doing Good to All

6 Brothers and sisters, if someone is caught in a sin, you who live by the Spirit should restore that person gently. But watch yourselves, or you also may be tempted. [2]Carry each other's burdens, and in this way you will fulfill the law of Christ. [3]If any of you think you are something when you are nothing, you deceive yourselves. [4]Each of you should test your own actions. Then you can take pride in yourself, without comparing yourself to somebody else, [5]for each of you should carry your own load. [6]Nevertheless, those who receive instruction in the word should share all good things with their instructor.

[7]Do not be deceived: God cannot be mocked. People reap what they sow. [8]Those who sow to please their sinful nature, from that nature[a] will reap destruction; those who sow to please the Spirit, from the Spirit will reap eternal life. [9]Let us not become weary in doing good, for at the proper time we will reap a harvest if we do not give up. [10]Therefore, as we have opportunity, let us do good to all people, especially to those who belong to the family of believers.

Not Circumcision but the New Creation

[11]See what large letters I use as I write to you with my own hand!

[12]Those who want to impress others by means of the flesh are trying to compel you to be circumcised. The only reason they do this is to avoid being persecuted for the cross of Christ. [13]Not even those who are circumcised keep the law, yet they want you to be circumcised that they may boast about your circumcision in the flesh. [14]May I never boast except in the cross of our Lord Jesus Christ, through which[b] the world has been crucified to me, and I to the world. [15]Neither circumcision nor uncircumcision means anything; what counts is the new creation. [16]Peace and mercy to all who follow this rule—to[c] the Israel of God.

[17]From now on, let no one cause me trouble, for I bear on my body the marks of Jesus.

[18]The grace of our Lord Jesus Christ be with your spirit, brothers and sisters. Amen.

---

a 8 Or *their flesh, from the flesh*   *b* 14 Or *whom*   *c* 16 Or *rule and to*

ephesians

AUTHOR: Paul, the apostle

DATE: Around A.D. 60

THEME: God has marvelous plans for his church, including our unity.

1 Paul, an apostle of Christ Jesus by the will of God,

To God's holy people in Ephesus,[a] the faithful in Christ Jesus:

²Grace and peace to you from God our Father and the Lord Jesus Christ.

Praise for Spiritual Blessings in Christ

³Praise be to the God and Father of our Lord Jesus Christ, who has blessed us in the heavenly realms with every spiritual blessing in Christ. ⁴For he chose us in him before the creation of the world to be holy and blameless in his sight. In love ⁵he[b] predestined us for adoption to sonship[c] through Jesus Christ, in accordance with his pleasure and will— ⁶to the praise of his glorious grace, which he has freely given us in the One he loves. ⁷In him we have redemption through his blood, the forgiveness of sins, in accordance with the riches of God's grace ⁸that he lavished on us. With all wisdom and understanding, ⁹he[d] made known to us the mystery of his will according to his good pleasure, which he purposed in Christ, ¹⁰to be put into effect when the times reach their fulfillment—to bring unity to all things in heaven and on earth under Christ.

¹¹In him we were also chosen,[e] having been predestined according to the plan of him who works out everything in conformity with the purpose of his will, ¹²in order that we, who were the first to put our hope in Christ, might be for the praise of his glory. ¹³And you also were included in Christ when you heard the word of truth, the gospel of your salvation.

When you believed, you were marked in him with a seal, the promised Holy Spirit, ¹⁴who is a deposit guaranteeing our inheritance until the redemption of those who are God's possession—to the praise of his glory.

Thanksgiving and Prayer

¹⁵For this reason, ever since I heard about your faith in the Lord Jesus and your love for all his people, ¹⁶I have not stopped giving thanks for you, remembering you in my prayers. ¹⁷I keep asking that the God of our Lord Jesus Christ, the glorious Father, may give you the Spirit[f] of wisdom and revelation, so that you may know him better. ¹⁸I pray that the eyes of your heart may be enlightened in order that you may know the hope to which he has called you, the riches of his glorious inheritance in his people, ¹⁹and his incomparably great power for us who believe. That power is the same as the mighty strength ²⁰he exerted when he raised Christ from the dead and seated him at his right hand in the heavenly realms, ²¹far above all rule and authority, power and dominion, and every name that can be invoked, not only in the present age but also in the one to come. ²²And God placed all things under his feet and appointed him to be head over everything for the church, ²³which is his body, the fullness of him who fills everything in every way.

Made Alive in Christ

2 As for you, you were dead in your transgressions and sins, ²in which you used to live when you followed

---

a 1 Some early manuscripts do not have *in Ephesus.*   b 4,5 Or *sight in love.* ⁵*He*   c 5 The Greek word for *adoption to sonship* is a legal term referring to the full legal standing of an adopted male heir in Roman culture.   d 8,9 Or *us with all wisdom and understanding.* ⁹*And he*   e 11 Or *were made heirs*   f 17 Or *a spirit*

THURSDAY

VALUE OF COMMUNITY

Ephesians 2:1–22 *or* 2:19–22

GEORGE WHITEFIELD {AD 1714–1770}

Humans are frail by nature; in our present condition we cannot always stand upright in our faith. Therefore one noteworthy reason why two are better than one—in other words, one great advantage of being part of the church—is, "If they fall down, they can help each other up" (Ecclesiastes 4:10).

This is an excellent reason, indeed! Just think about how prone we are to be drawn into error in our beliefs and into immorality in our actions. Ponder how unable, at least how very unwilling, we are to identify or correct our own failures. Consider how apt the world is to flatter us in our faults and how few people there are who are so kind as to tell us the truth. In view of those things, contemplate what an inestimable privilege it is to have a set of true, discerning, solid friends about us who continually watch over our souls, inform us where we have fallen and warn us so that we don't fall again in the future. Surely this is such a great privilege that we won't be able to understand the true value of it until we come to glory in heaven.

Scot McKnight

The church is not a collection of random individuals who happen each to believe in Jesus Christ, who happen to be working out "their own salvation," who happen to be living in proximity to one another, who happen to enjoy the same preachers and musicians and liturgy and who happen to affirm the same doctrinal convictions. The church is a community of faith wherein humans are "re-communioned" to one another.

reflection

1. What difference is there between Americans' value on *independence* and God's higher value on *interdependence*?

2. Why do you think God intends for us to be involved in church life that includes more than just attending worship services?

3. In what new ways do you suspect God wants you to connect with other Christians?

For your next devotional reading, go to page 1347.

the ways of this world and of the ruler of the kingdom of the air, the spirit who is now at work in those who are disobedient. [3]All of us also lived among them at one time, gratifying the cravings of our sinful nature[a] and following its desires and thoughts. Like the rest, we were by nature deserving of wrath. [4]But because of his great love for us, God, who is rich in mercy, [5]made us alive with Christ even when we were dead in transgressions—it is by grace you have been saved. [6]And God raised us up with Christ and seated us with him in the heavenly realms in Christ Jesus, [7]in order that in the coming ages he might show the incomparable riches of his grace, expressed in his kindness to us in Christ Jesus. [8]For it is by grace you have been saved, through faith—and this is not from yourselves, it is the gift of God— [9]not by works, so that no one can boast. [10]For we are God's handiwork, created in Christ Jesus to do good works, which God prepared in advance for us to do.

Jew and Gentile Reconciled Through Christ

[11]Therefore, remember that formerly you who are Gentiles by birth and called "uncircumcised" by those who call themselves "the circumcision" (which is done in the body by human hands)— [12]remember that at that time you were separate from Christ, excluded from citizenship in Israel and foreigners to the covenants of the promise, without hope and without God in the world. [13]But now in Christ Jesus you who once were far away have been brought near by the blood of Christ.

[14]For he himself is our peace, who has made the two one and has destroyed the barrier, the dividing wall of hostility, [15]by setting aside in his flesh the law with its commands and regulations. His purpose was to create in himself one new humanity out of the two, thus making peace, [16]and in one body to reconcile both of them to God through the cross, by which he put to death their hostility. [17]He came and preached peace to you who were far away and peace to those who were near. [18]For through him we both have access to the Father by one Spirit.

[19]Consequently, you are no longer foreigners and strangers, but fellow citizens with God's people and also members of his household, [20]built on the foundation of the apostles and prophets, with Christ Jesus himself as the chief cornerstone. [21]In him the whole building is joined together and rises to become a holy temple in the Lord. [22]And in him you too are being built together to become a dwelling in which God lives by his Spirit.

God's Marvelous Plan for the Gentiles

3 For this reason I, Paul, the prisoner of Christ Jesus for the sake of you Gentiles— [2]Surely you have heard about the administration of God's grace that was given to me for you, [3]that is, the mystery made known to me by revelation, as I have already written briefly. [4]In reading this, then, you will be able to understand my insight into the mystery of Christ, [5]which was not made known to people in other generations as it has now been revealed by the Spirit to God's holy apostles and prophets. [6]This mystery is that through the gospel the Gentiles are heirs together with Israel, members together of one body, and sharers together in the promise in Christ Jesus.

[7]I became a servant of this gospel by the gift of God's grace given me through the working of his power. [8]Although I am less than the least of all the Lord's people, this grace was given me: to preach to the Gentiles the boundless riches of Christ, [9]and to make plain to everyone the administration of this mystery, which for ages past was kept hidden in God, who created all things. [10]His intent was that now, through the church, the manifold wisdom of God should be made known to the rulers and authorities in the heavenly realms, [11]according to his eternal purpose that he accomplished in Christ Jesus our Lord. [12]In him and through faith in him we may approach God with freedom and confidence. [13]I ask you, therefore, not to be discouraged because of my sufferings for you, which are your glory.

A Prayer for the Ephesians

[14]For this reason I kneel before the Father, [15]from whom every family[b] in heaven and on earth derives its name. [16]I pray that out of his glorious riches he may strengthen

---

a 3 Or *our flesh*   *b 15* The Greek for *family* (patria) is derived from the Greek for *father* (pater).

you with power through his Spirit in your inner being, [17]so that Christ may dwell in your hearts through faith. And I pray that you, being rooted and established in love, [18]may have power, together with all the Lord's people, to grasp how wide and long and high and deep is the love of Christ, [19]and to know this love that surpasses knowledge—that you may be filled to the measure of all the fullness of God.

[20]Now to him who is able to do immeasurably more than all we ask or imagine, according to his power that is at work within us, [21]to him be glory in the church and in Christ Jesus throughout all generations, for ever and ever! Amen.

Unity and Maturity in the Body of Christ

4 As a prisoner for the Lord, then, I urge you to live a life worthy of the calling you have received. [2]Be completely humble and gentle; be patient, bearing with one another in love. [3]Make every effort to keep the unity of the Spirit through the bond of peace. [4]There is one body and one Spirit, just as you were called to one hope when you were called; [5]one Lord, one faith, one baptism; [6]one God and Father of all, who is over all and through all and in all.

[7]But to each one of us grace has been given as Christ apportioned it. [8]This is why it[a] says:

"When he ascended on high,
   he took many captives
   and gave gifts to his people."[b]

[9](What does "he ascended" mean except that he also descended to the lower, earthly regions[c]? [10]He who descended is the very one who ascended higher than all the heavens, in order to fill the whole universe.) [11]So Christ himself gave the apostles, the prophets, the evangelists, the pastors and teachers, [12]to equip his people for works of service, so that the body of Christ may be built up [13]until we all reach unity in the faith and in the knowledge of the Son of God and become mature, attaining to the whole measure of the fullness of Christ.

[14]Then we will no longer be infants, tossed back and forth by the waves, and blown here and there by every wind of teaching and by the cunning and craftiness

of people in their deceitful scheming. [15]Instead, speaking the truth in love, we will in all things grow up into him who is the head, that is, Christ. [16]From him the whole body, joined and held together by every supporting ligament, grows and builds itself up in love, as each part does its work.

Instructions for Christian Living

[17]So I tell you this, and insist on it in the Lord, that you must no longer live as the Gentiles do, in the futility of their thinking. [18]They are darkened in their understanding and separated from the life of God because of the ignorance that is in them due to the hardening of their hearts. [19]Having lost all sensitivity, they have given themselves over to sensuality so as to indulge in every kind of impurity, and they are full of greed.

[20]That, however, is not the way of life you learned [21]when you heard about Christ and were taught in him in accordance with the truth that is in Jesus. [22]You were taught, with regard to your former way of life, to put off your old self, which is being corrupted by its deceitful desires; [23]to be made new in the attitude of your minds; [24]and to put on the new self, created to be like God in true righteousness and holiness.

[25]Therefore each of you must put off falsehood and speak truthfully to your neighbor, for we are all members of one body. [26]"In your anger do not sin"[d]: Do not let the sun go down while you are still angry, [27]and do not give the devil a foothold. [28]Those who have been stealing must steal no longer, but must work, doing something useful with their own hands, that they may have something to share with those in need.

[29]Do not let any unwholesome talk come out of your mouths, but only what is helpful for building others up according to their needs, that it may benefit those who listen. [30]And do not grieve the Holy Spirit of God, with whom you were sealed for the day of redemption. [31]Get rid of all bitterness, rage and anger, brawling and slander, along with every form of malice. [32]Be kind and compassionate to one another, forgiving each other,

5 just as in Christ God forgave you. [1]Follow God's example, therefore, as dearly loved children [2]and walk in the way of love, just as Christ loved us and gave

---

[a] 8 Or God   [b] 8 Psalm 68:18   [c] 9 Or the depths of the earth   [d] 26 Psalm 4:4 (see Septuagint)

FRIDAY

GOD'S DAY

Ephesians 5:1–20 *or* 5:15–20

Leonard Sweet

I spend my life in two worlds times two. The first two worlds I live in at once have all of me based in a chronological calendar and the other all of me based in a liturgical calendar. Instead of day-timer schedules competing with the divine schedule, we can live both at the same time. How? These are some methods that work for me. Some might work for you, too.

Driving has become war by other means. Why not spiritual warfare? Other people talk on their cell phones to other people while driving; I talk to God. I know people think I'm crazy: Sometimes I'm crying, sometimes laughing, sometimes talking out loud, sometimes lavishing impassioned outbursts into empty space. In spite of the double takes, make drive time devotion time.

Engage in intercessory prayer while watching the evening news. Indeed, how can a pilgrim not pray while watching the evening news?

Bring a child along on a business-related trip. Combine pleasure and profession. Mix family vacations with business trips.

When you're jogging or riding the stationary bike or doing that funny duck-foot fast-walking, [listen to] whatever praise music carries you along. Worship as you sweat, sweat as you worship.

I joined the "singing impaired" when I got my tonsils out. But I can sing hymns or praise songs in the shower that are broadcast quality. Where do you sing to God?

SAINT AUGUSTINE {AD 354–430}

God, "the day is yours, and yours also the night" (Psalm 74:16). As you instructed, the moments fly by. So please provide me with an interlude where I can think about the hidden things of your law, and do not close the door of your law in the face of us who knock at it. You have not willed that the deep secrets of all those pages of your Word should have been written in vain. They are like a forest that hides deep within them majestic beasts who rest and walk and feed. Perfect me, Lord, and reveal the secrets of your Word to me. For your voice is my joy; your voice exceeds all else in providing an abundance of good things. Give me what I love, for I do love it. And this, too, is your gift.

reflection

1. Where do you find time to focus on Jesus during your day?

2. What is probably the most important thing God saw you do yesterday?

3. Think of someone you know who seems to excel at living in both the spiritual and the physical world at the same time. What can you learn from that person?

For your next devotional reading, go to page 1349.

himself up for us as a fragrant offering and sacrifice to God.

[3] But among you there must not be even a hint of sexual immorality, or of any kind of impurity, or of greed, because these are improper for the Lord's people. [4] Nor should there be obscenity, foolish talk or coarse joking, which are out of place, but rather thanksgiving. [5] For of this you can be sure: No immoral, impure or greedy person—such a person is an idolater—has any inheritance in the kingdom of Christ and of God.[a] [6] Let no one deceive you with empty words, for because of such things God's wrath comes on those who are disobedient. [7] Therefore do not be partners with them.

[8] For you were once darkness, but now you are light in the Lord. Live as children of light [9] (for the fruit of the light consists in all goodness, righteousness and truth) [10] and find out what pleases the Lord. [11] Have nothing to do with the fruitless deeds of darkness, but rather expose them. [12] It is shameful even to mention what the disobedient do in secret. [13] But everything exposed by the light becomes visible—and everything that is illuminated becomes a light. [14] This is why it is said:

> "Wake up, sleeper,
>   rise from the dead,
>   and Christ will shine on you."

[15] Be very careful, then, how you live—not as unwise but as wise, [16] making the most of every opportunity, because the days are evil. [17] Therefore do not be foolish, but understand what the Lord's will is. [18] Do not get drunk on wine, which leads to debauchery. Instead, be filled with the Spirit, [19] speaking to one another with psalms, hymns and songs from the Spirit. Sing and make music from your heart to the Lord, [20] always giving thanks to God the Father for everything, in the name of our Lord Jesus Christ.

Instructions for Christian Households

[21] Submit to one another out of reverence for Christ.

[22] Wives, submit yourselves to your own husbands as you do to the Lord. [23] For the husband is the head of the wife as Christ is the head of the church, his body, of which he is the Savior. [24] Now as the church submits to Christ, so also wives should submit to their husbands in everything.

[25] Husbands, love your wives, just as Christ loved the church and gave himself up for her [26] to make her holy, cleansing[b] her by the washing with water through the word, [27] and to present her to himself as a radiant church, without stain or wrinkle or any other blemish, but holy and blameless. [28] In this same way, husbands ought to love their wives as their own bodies. He who loves his wife loves himself. [29] After all, people have never hated their own bodies, but they feed and care for them, just as Christ does the church— [30] for we are members of his body. [31] "For this reason a man will leave his father and mother and be united to his wife, and the two will become one flesh."[c] [32] This is a profound mystery—but I am talking about Christ and the church. [33] However, each one of you also must love his wife as he loves himself, and the wife must respect her husband.

6 Children, obey your parents in the Lord, for this is right. [2] "Honor your father and mother"—which is the first commandment with a promise— [3] "so that it may go well with you and that you may enjoy long life on the earth."[d]

[4] Fathers,[e] do not exasperate your children; instead, bring them up in the training and instruction of the Lord.

[5] Slaves, obey your earthly masters with respect and fear, and with sincerity of heart, just as you would obey Christ. [6] Obey them not only to win their favor when their eye is on you, but as slaves of Christ, doing the will of God from your heart. [7] Serve wholeheartedly, as if you were serving the Lord, not people, [8] because you know that the Lord will reward each one of you for whatever good you do, whether you are slave or free.

[9] And masters, treat your slaves in the same way. Do not threaten them, since you know that he who is both their Master and yours is in heaven, and there is no favoritism with him.

The Armor of God

[10] Finally, be strong in the Lord and in his mighty power. [11] Put on the full armor of God,

---

a 5 Or *kingdom of the Christ and God*   *b 26* Or *having cleansed*   *c 31* Gen. 2:24   *d 3* Deut. 5:16
e 4 Or *Parents*

Fathers Among Us

Ephesians 6:1–4

read/meditate

Think about your father, parent or caregiver who has most affected you—for good or bad. Read through Ephesians 6:4 slowly, thinking about each phrase. How did the father-figures in your life measure up to this instruction?

pray

Whether you've been blessed or wounded by your father or father-figure, God describes himself as a Father. Tell him about the blessings as well as the woundings, and ask him to be what you need in a father. If you have hurts or wounds, ask him for healing and give him a quiet moment to touch your soul.

contemplate

No matter your gender or whether you have children, think about the people who are in your care—those affected by the words you speak and the requests you make. What kind of influence are you having?

additional reflection

Nothing you do for children is ever wasted. They seem not to notice us, hovering, averting our eyes, and they seldom offer thanks, but what we do for them is never wasted.

—*Garrison Keillor*

My father gave me the greatest gift anyone could give another person; he believed in me.

—*Jim Valvano*

For your next devotional reading, go to page 1350.

MONDAY

POWERFUL PRAYER

Ephesians 6:1–20 *or* 6:18–20

Ajith Fernando

Praying is the most powerful thing we do on earth. Let us be faithful at it. It may be prayer for revival. It may be prayer for the conversion of some unbelievers, whom Paul describes as blinded by Satan "[so that they cannot see the light of the gospel that displays the glory of Christ]" (2 Corinthians 4:4). It may be prayer for the repentance of a child or of a fellow Christian under the grip of Satan. People may not be open to listen to us when we advise them or witness to them. But we can take the battle to a higher plane. We can fight Satan, who holds them in his grip, so that the grip will be loosened and they will be less resistant to the wooing of God's Spirit.

Prayer is exciting! A person involved in biblical praying will never have a dull moment. There will be pain, but there won't be boredom. And think how many people are struggling with boredom today.

E. M. BOUNDS {AD 1835–1913}

Many people do not understand the business of praying because they have never learned it and consequently do not work at it. Our praying ought to work many miracles. So why do we not labor in prayer? Is the arm of the Lord shortened that he cannot save? Is his ear heavy that he cannot hear? . . . Has God changed from what he once was? To all these queries we enter an emphatic negative. God can work miracles through our praying today just as easily as he did in the days of old. "I the LORD do not change" (Malachi 3:6). "Is anything too hard for the LORD?" (Genesis 18:14).

He who works miracles by praying will first of all work the chief miracle on himself. Oh, that we might fully understand the Christian's trade of praying and follow the trade day by day—and from this employment earn great spiritual wealth!

reflection

1. Why does God tell us to pray?

2. Many people talk about prayer as though it's a last resort, something you do when you can't do anything else. How does this attitude contradict God's purpose for prayer?

3. What does the reality of *your* prayer life disclose about your own beliefs regarding the power and importance of prayer?

For your next devotional reading, go to page 1353.

so that you can take your stand against the devil's schemes. [12]For our struggle is not against flesh and blood, but against the rulers, against the authorities, against the powers of this dark world and against the spiritual forces of evil in the heavenly realms. [13]Therefore put on the full armor of God, so that when the day of evil comes, you may be able to stand your ground, and after you have done everything, to stand. [14]Stand firm then, with the belt of truth buckled around your waist, with the breastplate of righteousness in place, [15]and with your feet fitted with the readiness that comes from the gospel of peace. [16]In addition to all this, take up the shield of faith, with which you can extinguish all the flaming arrows of the evil one. [17]Take the helmet of salvation and the sword of the Spirit, which is the word of God.

[18]And pray in the Spirit on all occasions with all kinds of prayers and requests. With this in mind, be alert and always keep on praying for all the Lord's people. [19]Pray also for me, that whenever I speak, words may be given me so that I will fearlessly make known the mystery of the gospel, [20]for which I am an ambassador in chains. Pray that I may declare it fearlessly, as I should.

Final Greetings

[21]Tychicus, the dear brother and faithful servant in the Lord, will tell you everything, so that you also may know how I am and what I am doing. [22]I am sending him to you for this very purpose, that you may know how we are, and that he may encourage you.

[23]Peace to the brothers and sisters, and love with faith from God the Father and the Lord Jesus Christ. [24]Grace to all who love our Lord Jesus Christ with an undying love.[a]

---

[a] 24 Or *Grace and immortality to all who love our Lord Jesus Christ.*

philippians

AUTHOR: Paul, the apostle

DATE: Around A.D. 61

THEME: Knowing Christ is the ultimate reason for living.

1 Paul and Timothy, servants of Christ Jesus,

To all God's holy people in Christ Jesus at Philippi, together with the overseers and deacons:

²Grace and peace to you from God our Father and the Lord Jesus Christ.

Thanksgiving and Prayer

³I thank my God every time I remember you. ⁴In all my prayers for all of you, I always pray with joy ⁵because of your partnership in the gospel from the first day until now, ⁶being confident of this, that he who began a good work in you will carry it on to completion until the day of Christ Jesus.

⁷It is right for me to feel this way about all of you, since I have you in my heart and, whether I am in chains or defending and confirming the gospel, all of you share in God's grace with me. ⁸God can testify how I long for all of you with the affection of Christ Jesus.

⁹And this is my prayer: that your love may abound more and more in knowledge and depth of insight, ¹⁰so that you may be able to discern what is best and may be pure and blameless for the day of Christ, ¹¹filled with the fruit of righteousness that comes through Jesus Christ—to the glory and praise of God.

Paul's Chains Advance the Gospel

¹²Now I want you to know, brothers and sisters, that what has happened to me has actually served to advance the gospel. ¹³As a result, it has become clear throughout the whole palace guard[a] and to everyone else that I am in chains for Christ. ¹⁴And because of my chains, most of the brothers and sisters have become confident in the Lord and dare all the more to proclaim the gospel without fear.

¹⁵It is true that some preach Christ out of envy and rivalry, but others out of goodwill. ¹⁶The latter do so out of love, knowing that I am put here for the defense of the gospel. ¹⁷The former preach Christ out of selfish ambition, not sincerely, supposing that they can stir up trouble for me while I am in chains. ¹⁸But what does it matter? The important thing is that in every way, whether from false motives or true, Christ is preached. And because of this I rejoice.

Yes, and I will continue to rejoice, ¹⁹for I know that through your prayers and God's provision of the Spirit of Jesus Christ what has happened to me will turn out for my deliverance.[b] ²⁰I eagerly expect and hope that I will in no way be ashamed, but will have sufficient courage so that now as always Christ will be exalted in my body, whether by life or by death. ²¹For to me, to live is Christ and to die is gain. ²²If I am to go on living in the body, this will mean fruitful labor for me. Yet what shall I choose? I do not know! ²³I am torn between the two: I desire to depart and be with Christ, which is better by far; ²⁴but it is more necessary for you that I remain in the body. ²⁵Convinced of this, I know that I will remain, and I will continue with all of you for your progress and joy in the faith, ²⁶so that through my being with you again your boasting in Christ Jesus will abound on account of me.

a 13 Or whole palace   b 19 Or vindication; or salvation

TUESDAY

LIFE'S MEANING

Philippians 1:12–30 *or* 1:20–21

Rick Warren

It's not about you.

The purpose of your life is far greater than your own personal fulfillment, your peace of mind or even your happiness. It's far greater than your family, your career or even your wildest dreams and ambitions. If you want to know why you were placed on this planet, you must begin with God. You were born *by* his purpose and *for* his purpose.

The search for the purpose of life has puzzled people for thousands of years. That's because we typically begin at the wrong starting point—ourselves. We ask self-centered questions: What do I want to be? What should I do with my life? What are my goals, my ambitions, my dreams for my future? But focusing on ourselves will never reveal our life's purpose. The Bible says, "In [God's] hand is the life of every creature and the breath of every human being" (Job 12:10).

Contrary to what many popular books, movies and seminars tell you, you won't discover your life's meaning by looking within yourself. You've probably tried that already. You didn't create yourself, so there is no way you can tell yourself what you were created for!

JULIAN OF NORWICH {AD 1342–ca. 1416}

When I was 30 years old, God sent me a bodily sickness [that confined me] to the bed for three days and nights. On the third night I received all the rites of the church, and I did not expect to live until morning.

After this I remained in bed for two more days, and on the sixth night I thought that I was on the point of death as did those who were with me. And yet, I felt a great reluctance to die, not because of any thing on earth which held me here or because of any fear or pain, for I trusted the mercy of God. But it was because I wanted to live to love God better and longer so that I might through the grace of that living have more knowledge and love of God than I might have even in heaven!

I realized that all the time that I had lived here was very little and short in comparison with the bliss of eternal life in heaven. I thought, "Good Lord, can my living no longer be to your glory?" With all the will of my heart I assented to be wholly God's.

reflection

1. What does God want your life to be all about?

2. To what extent have you committed your life to bringing God glory?

3. If you had to defend that answer, what evidence would you point to?

For your next devotional reading, go to page 1355.

Life Worthy of the Gospel

²⁷Whatever happens, as citizens of heaven live in a manner worthy of the gospel of Christ. Then, whether I come and see you or only hear about you in my absence, I will know that you stand firm in the one Spirit,ᵃ striving together with one accord for the faith of the gospel ²⁸without being frightened in any way by those who oppose you. This is a sign to them that they will be destroyed, but that you will be saved—and that by God. ²⁹For it has been granted to you on behalf of Christ not only to believe on him, but also to suffer for him, ³⁰since you are going through the same struggle you saw I had, and now hear that I still have.

Imitating Christ's Humility

2 Therefore if you have any encouragement from being united with Christ, if any comfort from his love, if any common sharing in the Spirit, if any tenderness and compassion, ²then make my joy complete by being like-minded, having the same love, being one in spirit and of one mind. ³Do nothing out of selfish ambition or vain conceit. Rather, in humility value others above yourselves, ⁴not looking to your own interests but each of you to the interests of the others.

⁵In your relationships with one another, have the same attitude of mind Christ Jesus had:

⁶Who, being in very natureᵇ God,
did not consider equality with God
something to be used to his
own advantage;
⁷rather, he made himself nothing
by taking the very natureᶜ of a
servant,
being made in human likeness.
⁸And being found in appearance as a
human being,
he humbled himself
by becoming obedient to death—
even death on a cross!

⁹Therefore God exalted him to the
highest place
and gave him the name that is above
every name,
¹⁰that at the name of Jesus every knee
should bow,
in heaven and on earth and under the
earth,
¹¹and every tongue acknowledge that
Jesus Christ is Lord,
to the glory of God the Father.

Do Everything Without Grumbling

¹²Therefore, my dear friends, as you have always obeyed—not only in my presence, but now much more in my absence—continue to work out your salvation with fear and trembling, ¹³for it is God who works in you to will and to act in order to fulfill his good purpose.

¹⁴Do everything without grumbling or arguing, ¹⁵so that you may become blameless and pure, "children of God without fault in a warped and crooked generation."ᵈ Then you will shine among them like stars in the sky ¹⁶as you hold firmly to the word of life. And then I will be able to boast on the day of Christ that I did not run or labor in vain. ¹⁷But even if I am being poured out like a drink offering on the sacrifice and service coming from your faith, I am glad and rejoice with all of you. ¹⁸So you too should be glad and rejoice with me.

Timothy and Epaphroditus

¹⁹I hope in the Lord Jesus to send Timothy to you soon, that I also may be cheered when I receive news about you. ²⁰I have no one else like him, who will show genuine concern for your welfare. ²¹For everyone looks out for their own interests, not those of Jesus Christ. ²²But you know that Timothy has proved himself, because as a son with his father he has served with me in the work of the gospel. ²³I hope, therefore, to send him as soon as I see how things go with me. ²⁴And I am confident in the Lord that I myself will come soon.

²⁵But I think it is necessary to send back to you Epaphroditus, my brother, co-worker and fellow soldier, who is also your messenger, whom you sent to take care of my needs. ²⁶For he longs for all of you and is distressed because you heard he was ill. ²⁷Indeed he was ill, and almost died. But God had mercy on him, and not on him only but also on me, to spare me sorrow upon sorrow. ²⁸Therefore I am all the more eager to send him, so that when you see him again

---

ᵃ 27 Or *in one spirit*   ᵇ 6 Or *in the form of*   ᶜ 7 Or *the form*   ᵈ 15 Deut. 32:5

THE PRINCE OF PEACE PARADOX
Philippians 2:1–18 *or* 2:8–10

Joni Eareckson Tada

Why were our times of drastic obedience and absolute trust only flashes, brief moments of illumination? Why did we always have such a hard time acting like Jesus was King? Perhaps because on earth, He never acted like a king. Or at least not like one would think a king should act. Jesus, however, had a good reason for cloaking His majesty under the robe of weakness, shame and humility. It has to do with His glory in heaven. When the Father designed the plan of salvation, He initiated a scheme that would ultimately bring the highest and brightest glory to His Son, the King of the cosmos. It was a plot that almost reads like an adventure story.

The plan was put into effect when the evil villain, Lucifer, enslaved the citizens of the kingdom of earth through treachery and deceit. He usurped the authority of the rightful Ruler and set up his own rival government. The good Ruler sent His most skilled servants to try to recapture the occupied territory, but with few exceptions the villain seduced and defeated them. Finally, the Ruler sent His only Son, the rightful Prince, to invade Lucifer's territory, free the captive subjects and retake the kingdom under the family banner.

But the battle tactics of the Son were odd, to say the least. In fact, the manner in which He fought seemed to insure defeat. At one point, when Lucifer had the Prince pinned, the Son merely yielded to the deathblow. All appeared lost and the people's hearts fainted in despair. Little did they realize the best and final part of the plan was just about to go into play. It was called the resurrection, and it was the only battle tactic that could deliver the killing blow to the enemy and his hordes of evil rulers.

Now any struggle between a hero and the bad guys is interesting enough, but when the hero is disadvantaged, a new element is introduced. Now the hero is in far more danger and he appears to have less chance of winning. But if in his weakness he overcomes against all odds, he ends up twice as much the hero . . .

And so, the Prince of Peace, the Lamb who let Himself be slain, will be glorified, not because He employed brute force against Satan, but because He didn't.

JEREMY TAYLOR {AD 1613–1667}

Humility is the great ornament and jewel of Christian religion.

reflection

1. Ask five of your friends to define *humility*. What is the general consensus?
2. How does most people's view of humility compare with God's view?
3. What do you learn from Jesus' example of humility?

For your next devotional reading, go to page 1359.

you may be glad and I may have less anxiety. [29]Welcome him in the Lord with great joy, and honor people like him, [30]because he almost died for the work of Christ. He risked his life to make up for the help you yourselves could not give me.

No Confidence in the Flesh

3 Further, my brothers and sisters, rejoice in the Lord! It is no trouble for me to write the same things to you again, and it is a safeguard for you. [2]Watch out for those dogs, those evildoers, those mutilators of the flesh. [3]For it is we who are the circumcision, we who serve God by his Spirit, who boast in Christ Jesus, and who put no confidence in the flesh— [4]though I myself have reasons for such confidence.

If others think they have reasons to put confidence in the flesh, I have more: [5]circumcised on the eighth day, of the people of Israel, of the tribe of Benjamin, a Hebrew of Hebrews; in regard to the law, a Pharisee; [6]as for zeal, persecuting the church; as for righteousness based on the law, faultless.

[7]But whatever were gains to me I now consider loss for the sake of Christ. [8]What is more, I consider everything a loss because of the surpassing worth of knowing Christ Jesus my Lord, for whose sake I have lost all things. I consider them garbage, that I may gain Christ [9]and be found in him, not having a righteousness of my own that comes from the law, but that which is through faith in[a] Christ—the righteousness that comes from God on the basis of faith. [10]I want to know Christ—yes, to know the power of his resurrection and participation in his sufferings, becoming like him in his death, [11]and so, somehow, attaining to the resurrection from the dead.

[12]Not that I have already obtained all this, or have already arrived at my goal, but I press on to take hold of that for which Christ Jesus took hold of me. [13]Brothers and sisters, I do not consider myself yet to have taken hold of it. But one thing I do: Forgetting what is behind and straining toward what is ahead, [14]I press on toward the goal to win the prize for which God has called me heavenward in Christ Jesus.

Following Paul's Example

[15]All of us, then, who are mature should take such a view of things. And if on some point you think differently, that too God will make clear to you. [16]Only let us live up to what we have already attained.

[17]Join together in following my example, brothers and sisters, and just as you have us as a model, keep your eyes on those who live as we do. [18]For, as I have often told you before and now tell you again even with tears, many live as enemies of the cross of Christ. [19]Their destiny is destruction, their god is their stomach, and their glory is in their shame. Their mind is set on earthly things. [20]But our citizenship is in heaven. And we eagerly await a Savior from there, the Lord Jesus Christ, [21]who, by the power that enables him to bring everything under his control, will transform our lowly bodies so that they will be like his glorious body.

Closing Appeal for Steadfastness and Unity

4 Therefore, my brothers and sisters, you whom I love and long for, my joy and crown, stand firm in the Lord in this way, dear friends!

[2]I plead with Euodia and I plead with Syntyche to be of the same mind in the Lord. [3]Yes, and I ask you, my true companion, help these women since they have contended at my side in the cause of the gospel, along with Clement and the rest of my co-workers, whose names are in the book of life.

Final Exhortations

[4]Rejoice in the Lord always. I will say it again: Rejoice! [5]Let your gentleness be evident to all. The Lord is near. [6]Do not be anxious about anything, but in every situation, by prayer and petition, with thanksgiving, present your requests to God. [7]And the peace of God, which transcends all understanding, will guard your hearts and your minds in Christ Jesus.

[8]Finally, brothers and sisters, whatever is true, whatever is noble, whatever is right, whatever is pure, whatever is lovely, whatever is admirable—if anything is excellent or praiseworthy—think about such things. [9]Whatever you have learned or received or heard from me, or seen in me—put it into

---

[a] 9 Or *through the faithfulness of*

practice. And the God of peace will be with you.

Thanks for Their Gifts

[10]I rejoiced greatly in the Lord that at last you renewed your concern for me. Indeed, you were concerned, but you had no opportunity to show it. [11]I am not saying this because I am in need, for I have learned to be content whatever the circumstances. [12]I know what it is to be in need, and I know what it is to have plenty. I have learned the secret of being content in any and every situation, whether well fed or hungry, whether living in plenty or in want. [13]I can do all this through him who gives me strength.

[14]Yet it was good of you to share in my troubles. [15]Moreover, as you Philippians know, in the early days of your acquaintance with the gospel, when I set out from Macedonia, not one church shared with me in the matter of giving and receiving, except you only; [16]for even when I was in Thessalonica, you sent me aid more than once when I was in need. [17]Not that I desire your gifts; what I desire is that more be credited to your account. [18]I have received full payment and have more than enough. I am amply supplied, now that I have received from Epaphroditus the gifts you sent. They are a fragrant offering, an acceptable sacrifice, pleasing to God. [19]And my God will meet all your needs according to the riches of his glory in Christ Jesus.

[20]To our God and Father be glory for ever and ever. Amen.

Final Greetings

[21]Greet all God's people in Christ Jesus. The brothers and sisters who are with me send greetings. [22]All the Lord's people here send you greetings, especially those who belong to Caesar's household.

[23]The grace of the Lord Jesus Christ be with your spirit. Amen.[a]

a 23 Some manuscripts do not have *Amen.*

colossians

AUTHOR: Paul, the apostle

DATE: Around A.D. 60

THEME: Jesus, God's Son, is Lord of our lives.

1 ¹Paul, an apostle of Christ Jesus by the will of God, and Timothy our brother,

²To God's holy people in Colossae, the faithful brothers and sisters in Christ:

Grace and peace to you from God our Father.ᵃ

Thanksgiving and Prayer

³We always thank God, the Father of our Lord Jesus Christ, when we pray for you, ⁴because we have heard of your faith in Christ Jesus and of the love you have for all his people— ⁵the faith and love that spring from the hope stored up for you in heaven and about which you have already heard in the true word of the gospel ⁶that has come to you. In the same way, the gospel is bearing fruit and growing throughout the whole world— just as it has been doing among you since the day you heard it and truly understood God's grace. ⁷You learned it from Epaphras, our dear fellow servant,ᵇ who is a faithful minister of Christ on ourᶜ behalf, ⁸and who also told us of your love in the Spirit.

⁹For this reason, since the day we heard about you, we have not stopped praying for you. We continually ask God to fill you with the knowledge of his will through all the wisdom and understanding that the Spirit gives,ᵈ ¹⁰so that you may live a life worthy of the Lord and please him in every way: bearing fruit in every good work, growing in the knowledge of God, ¹¹being strengthened with all power according to his glorious might so that you may have great endurance and patience, ¹²and giving joyful thanks to the Father, who has qualified youᵉ to share in the inheritance of his people in the kingdom of light. ¹³For he has rescued us from the dominion of darkness and brought us into the kingdom of the Son he loves, ¹⁴in whom we have redemption, the forgiveness of sins.

The Supremacy of the Son of God

¹⁵The Son is the image of the invisible God, the firstborn over all creation. ¹⁶For in him all things were created: things in heaven and on earth, visible and invisible, whether thrones or powers or rulers or authorities; all things have been created through him and for him. ¹⁷He is before all things, and in him all things hold together. ¹⁸And he is the head of the body, the church; he is the beginning and the firstborn from among the dead, so that in everything he might have the supremacy. ¹⁹For God was pleased to have all his fullness dwell in him, ²⁰and through him to reconcile to himself all things, whether things on earth or things in heaven, by making peace through his blood, shed on the cross.

²¹Once you were alienated from God and were enemies in your minds because ofᶠ your evil behavior. ²²But now he has reconciled you by Christ's physical body through death to present you holy in his sight, without blemish and free from accusation— ²³if you continue in your faith, established and firm, and do not move from the hope held out in the gospel. This is the gospel that you heard and that has been proclaimed to every creature under heaven, and of which I, Paul, have become a servant.

ᵃ 2 Some manuscripts *Father and the Lord Jesus Christ*   ᵇ 7 Or *slave*   ᶜ 7 Some manuscripts *your*   ᵈ 9 Or *all spiritual wisdom and understanding*   ᵉ 12 Some manuscripts *us*   ᶠ 21 Or *minds, as shown by*

THURSDAY

Jesus Is All

Colossians 1:15–23 *or* Colossians 1:15–17

Rob Bell

The Bible keeps insisting that Jesus is how God put things together. The writer Paul said that Jesus is how God holds all things together. The Bible points us to a Jesus who is in some mysterious way behind it all.

Jesus is the arrangement. Jesus is the design. Jesus is the intelligence. For a Christian, Jesus' teachings aren't to be followed because they are a nice way to live a moral life. They are to be followed because they are the best possible insight into how the world really works. They teach us how things are.

Alexander MacLaren {ad 1826–1910}

Brothers and sisters, the incarnation, death, resurrection and ascension of the Son of God is the only foundation we can build on which is secure and safe.

Jesus is the foundation for all our thinking and opinions, for all our belief and our knowledge. In him are hidden all the treasures of wisdom and knowledge (see Colossians 2:3). Therefore, whatever solid fact humans can grasp in their thinkings in regard to all the most important truths is to be found in the life and death of Jesus Christ, and in the truths that these reveal. He is the foundation of all our knowledge of God; and he is the foundation of all our true knowledge of ourselves and our duty, of the connection between the present and the future and of the relationship between people and God.

And in his life, in the history of his death and resurrection, we find the only foundation for any real knowledge of the awful mysteries that lie beyond the grave. He is the Alpha from whom all truth must be deduced, the Omega to which it all leads up. Certainty is found in him. Apart from him we are but groping in the middle of doubt and uncertainty. If we *know* anything about God it is due to Jesus Christ. If we *know* anything about ourselves it is due to him. If we *know* anything about what people ought to do, it is because he has done all human duty. And if, into the mist and darkness that wraps the future, there has ever traveled one clear beam of insight, it is because he has died and risen again.

If we have Jesus, and ponder upon the principles that are involved in, and flow from, the facts of his life and death, then we do know. And the truth as we find it in Jesus is the truth indeed.

reflection

1. What does it mean that in Jesus "all things hold together"?

2. What shaky foundations do many people base their lives on instead of Jesus?

3. How do you see Jesus holding your life together?

For your next devotional reading, go to page 1361.

Paul's Labor for the Church

²⁴Now I rejoice in what I am suffering for you, and I fill up in my flesh what is still lacking in regard to Christ's afflictions, for the sake of his body, which is the church. ²⁵I have become its servant by the commission God gave me to present to you the word of God in its fullness— ²⁶the mystery that has been kept hidden for ages and generations, but is now disclosed to the Lord's people. ²⁷To them God has chosen to make known among the Gentiles the glorious riches of this mystery, which is Christ in you, the hope of glory.

²⁸We proclaim him, admonishing and teaching everyone with all wisdom, so that we may present everyone fully mature in Christ. ²⁹To this end I strenuously contend with all the energy Christ so powerfully works in me.

2 I want you to know how hard I am contending for you and for those at Laodicea, and for all who have not met me personally. ²My goal is that they may be encouraged in heart and united in love, so that they may have the full riches of complete understanding, in order that they may know the mystery of God, namely, Christ, ³in whom are hidden all the treasures of wisdom and knowledge. ⁴I tell you this so that no one may deceive you by fine-sounding arguments. ⁵For though I am absent from you in body, I am present with you in spirit and delight to see how disciplined you are and how firm your faith in Christ is.

Spiritual Fullness in Christ

⁶So then, just as you received Christ Jesus as Lord, continue to live your lives in him, ⁷rooted and built up in him, strengthened in the faith as you were taught, and overflowing with thankfulness.

⁸See to it that no one takes you captive through hollow and deceptive philosophy, which depends on human tradition and the elemental spiritual forcesᵃ of this world rather than on Christ.

⁹For in Christ all the fullness of the Deity lives in bodily form, ¹⁰and in Christ you have been brought to fullness. He is the head over every power and authority. ¹¹In him you were also circumcised with a circumcision not performed by human hands. Your sinful natureᵇ was put off when you were circumcised byᶜ Christ, ¹²having been buried with him in baptism, in which you were also raised with him through your faith in the working of God, who raised him from the dead.

¹³When you were dead in your sins and in the uncircumcision of your sinful nature,ᵈ God made youᵉ alive with Christ. He forgave us all our sins, ¹⁴having canceled the charge of our legal indebtedness, which stood against us and condemned us; he has taken it away, nailing it to the cross. ¹⁵And having disarmed the powers and authorities, he made a public spectacle of them, triumphing over them by the cross.ᶠ

Freedom From Human Rules

¹⁶Therefore do not let anyone judge you by what you eat or drink, or with regard to a religious festival, a New Moon celebration or a Sabbath day. ¹⁷These are a shadow of the things that were to come; the reality, however, is found in Christ. ¹⁸Do not let anyone who delights in false humility and the worship of angels disqualify you. Such people also go into great detail about what they have seen, and their unspiritual minds puff them up with idle notions. ¹⁹They have lost connection with the head, from whom the whole body, supported and held together by its ligaments and sinews, grows as God causes it to grow.

²⁰Since you died with Christ to the elemental spiritual forces of this world, why, as though you still belonged to the world, do you submit to its rules: ²¹"Do not handle! Do not taste! Do not touch!"? ²²These rules, which have to do with things that are all destined to perish with use, are based on merely human commands and teachings. ²³Such regulations indeed have an appearance of wisdom, with their self-imposed worship, their false humility and their harsh treatment of the body, but they lack any value in restraining sensual indulgence.

Living as Those Made Alive in Christ

3 Since, then, you have been raised with Christ, set your hearts on things above, where Christ is seated at the right

FRIDAY

FORGIVE AND FORGET

Colossians 3:1–25 *or* 3:12–14

MARTIN LUTHER {AD 1483–1546}

We stumble daily and transgress because we live in the world among people who do us much harm and give us cause for impatience, anger, revenge and so on. Besides, we have Satan at our back, who sets upon us on every side.

Therefore there is great need to call upon God and to pray: Dear Father, forgive us our sins. Not as though he did not forgive sin without and even before our prayer (for he has given us the Gospel, in which is pure forgiveness before we prayed or ever thought about it). But this is to the intent that we may recognize and accept such forgiveness. This should serve God's purpose of breaking our pride and keeping us humble. For let no one think that as long as we live here he can reach such a position that he will not need such forgiveness. In short, if God does not forgive without ceasing, we are lost.

For just as we daily sin much against God and yet he forgives everything through grace, so we, too, must always forgive our neighbor who does us injury, violence, wrong and shows malice toward us.

Don M. Aycock

Lord, You know that our relationships are often messy. We bump into people around us and have friction with even the ones we love the most. Help us to have the courage to reconcile with those from whom we are separated. Let us forgive others as You have forgiven us. Through Christ, Amen.

reflection

1. How would you describe God's forgiveness toward you?

2. Is there someone in your life whom you have not yet forgiven in the same way that God has forgiven you?

3. How does an understanding of God's forgiveness for your many sins help you extend that same forgiveness to others?

For your next devotional reading, go to page 1365.

hand of God. ²Set your minds on things above, not on earthly things. ³For you died, and your life is now hidden with Christ in God. ⁴When Christ, who is your*a* life, appears, then you also will appear with him in glory.

⁵Put to death, therefore, whatever belongs to your earthly nature: sexual immorality, impurity, lust, evil desires and greed, which is idolatry. ⁶Because of these, the wrath of God is coming.*b* ⁷You used to walk in these ways, in the life you once lived. ⁸But now you must also rid yourselves of all such things as these: anger, rage, malice, slander, and filthy language from your lips. ⁹Do not lie to each other, since you have taken off your old self with its practices ¹⁰and have put on the new self, which is being renewed in knowledge in the image of its Creator. ¹¹Here there is no Gentile or Jew, circumcised or uncircumcised, barbarian, Scythian, slave or free, but Christ is all, and is in all.

¹²Therefore, as God's chosen people, holy and dearly loved, clothe yourselves with compassion, kindness, humility, gentleness and patience. ¹³Bear with each other and forgive one another if any of you has a grievance against someone. Forgive as the Lord forgave you. ¹⁴And over all these virtues put on love, which binds them all together in perfect unity.

¹⁵Let the peace of Christ rule in your hearts, since as members of one body you were called to peace. And be thankful. ¹⁶Let the message of Christ dwell among you richly as you teach and admonish one another with all wisdom through psalms, hymns and songs from the Spirit, singing to God with gratitude in your hearts. ¹⁷And whatever you do, whether in word or deed, do it all in the name of the Lord Jesus, giving thanks to God the Father through him.

Instructions for Christian Households

¹⁸Wives, submit yourselves to your husbands, as is fitting in the Lord.

¹⁹Husbands, love your wives and do not be harsh with them.

²⁰Children, obey your parents in everything, for this pleases the Lord.

²¹Fathers,*c* do not embitter your children, or they will become discouraged.

²²Slaves, obey your earthly masters in ev-

erything; and do it, not only when their eye is on you and to curry their favor, but with sincerity of heart and reverence for the Lord. ²³Whatever you do, work at it with all your heart, as working for the Lord, not for human masters, ²⁴since you know that you will receive an inheritance from the Lord as a reward. It is the Lord Christ you are serving. ²⁵Those who do wrong will be repaid for their wrongs, and there is no favoritism.

4 Masters, provide your slaves with what is right and fair, because you know that you also have a Master in heaven.

Further Instructions

²Devote yourselves to prayer, being watchful and thankful. ³And pray for us, too, that God may open a door for our message, so that we may proclaim the mystery of Christ, for which I am in chains. ⁴Pray that I may proclaim it clearly, as I should. ⁵Be wise in the way you act toward outsiders; make the most of every opportunity. ⁶Let your conversation be always full of grace, seasoned with salt, so that you may know how to answer everyone.

Final Greetings

⁷Tychicus will tell you all the news about me. He is a dear brother, a faithful minister and fellow servant*d* in the Lord. ⁸I am sending him to you for the express purpose that you may know about our*e* circumstances and that he may encourage your hearts. ⁹He is coming with Onesimus, our faithful and dear brother, who is one of you. They will tell you everything that is happening here.

¹⁰My fellow prisoner Aristarchus sends you his greetings, as does Mark, the cousin of Barnabas. (You have received instructions about him; if he comes to you, welcome him.) ¹¹Jesus, who is called Justus, also sends greetings. These are the only Jews*f* among my co-workers for the kingdom of God, and they have proved a comfort to me. ¹²Epaphras, who is one of you and a servant of Christ Jesus, sends greetings. He is always wrestling in prayer for you, that you may stand firm in all the will of God, mature and fully assured. ¹³I vouch for him that he is working hard for you and for those at Laod-

---

a 4 Some manuscripts our   *b 6* Some early manuscripts *coming on those who are disobedient*
c 21 Or *Parents*   *d 7* Or *slave*; also in verse 12   *e 8* Some manuscripts *that he may know about your*
f 11 Greek *only ones of the circumcision group*

icea and Hierapolis. ¹⁴Our dear friend Luke, the doctor, and Demas send greetings. ¹⁵Give my greetings to the brothers and sisters at Laodicea, and to Nympha and the church in her house.

¹⁶After this letter has been read to you, see that it is also read in the church of the Laodiceans and that you in turn read the letter from Laodicea.

¹⁷Tell Archippus: "See to it that you complete the work you have received in the Lord."

¹⁸I, Paul, write this greeting in my own hand. Remember my chains. Grace be with you.

1 thessalonians

AUTHOR: Paul, the apostle

DATE: Around A.D. 51

THEME: Jesus' return offers the hope we need to endure suffering.

1

Paul, Silas[a] and Timothy,

To the church of the Thessalonians in God the Father and the Lord Jesus Christ:

Grace and peace to you.

Thanksgiving for the Thessalonians' Faith

²We always thank God for all of you and continually mention you in our prayers. ³We remember before our God and Father your work produced by faith, your labor prompted by love, and your endurance inspired by hope in our Lord Jesus Christ.

⁴For we know, brothers and sisters loved by God, that he has chosen you, ⁵because our gospel came to you not simply with words but also with power, with the Holy Spirit and deep conviction. You know how we lived among you for your sake. ⁶You became imitators of us and of the Lord, for you welcomed the message in the midst of severe suffering with the joy given by the Holy Spirit. ⁷And so you became a model to all the believers in Macedonia and Achaia. ⁸The Lord's message rang out from you not only in Macedonia and Achaia—your faith in God has become known everywhere. Therefore we do not need to say anything about it, ⁹for they themselves report what happened when we visited you. They tell how you turned to God from idols to serve the living and true God, ¹⁰and to wait for his Son from heaven, whom he raised from the dead—Jesus, who rescues us from the coming wrath.

Paul's Ministry in Thessalonica

2

You know, brothers and sisters, that our visit to you was not without results. ²We had previously suffered and been treated outrageously in Philippi, as you know, but with the help of our God we dared to tell you his gospel in the face of strong opposition. ³For the appeal we make does not spring from error or impure motives, nor are we trying to trick you. ⁴On the contrary, we speak as those approved by God to be entrusted with the gospel. We are not trying to please people but God, who tests our hearts. ⁵You know we never used flattery, nor did we put on a mask to cover up greed—God is our witness. ⁶We were not looking for praise from any human being, not from you or anyone else, even though as apostles of Christ we could have asserted our prerogatives. ⁷Instead, we were like young children among you.

Just as a nursing mother cares for her children, ⁸so we cared for you. Because we loved you so much, we were delighted to share with you not only the gospel of God but our lives as well. ⁹Surely you remember, brothers and sisters, our toil and hardship; we worked night and day in order not to be a burden to anyone while we preached the gospel of God to you.

¹⁰You are witnesses, and so is God, of how holy, righteous and blameless we were among you who believed. ¹¹For you know that we dealt with each of you as a father deals with his own children, ¹²encouraging, comforting and urging you to live lives worthy of God, who calls you into his kingdom and glory.

¹³And we also thank God continually be-

---

a 1 Greek *Silvanus*, a variant of *Silas*

Who You Pray For

1 Thessalonians 1:2-3

read/meditate

Read this short passage several times. Whom does it bring to your mind? What
seasons of your own life does it remind you of? Jot down a list of the people you'd
like to be praying for in this way. As you think about yourself in light of this verse,
who do you think prays for you in this way?

pray

Lift up the people on your list to God in prayer. Ask him to give you a vision for the
work he has for you. In quietness, listen to him.

contemplate

How does God's vision for your life affect your day today? How can your moments
bear up to Paul's prayer for the Thessalonian Christians? It's not about doing
something huge; it's about living your moments faithfully. Think about someone who
has encouraged you spiritually along the way and give them a call.

additional reflection

At times our own light goes out and is rekindled by a spark from another person.
Each of us has cause to think with deep gratitude of those who have lighted the flame
within us.

—*Albert Schweitzer*

Flatter me, and I may not believe you. Criticize me, and I may not like you. Ignore
me, and I may not forgive you. Encourage me, and I may not forget you.

—*William Arthur*

For your next devotional reading, go to page 1367.

cause, when you received the word of God, which you heard from us, you accepted it not as a human word, but as it actually is, the word of God, which is indeed at work in you who believe. [14]For you, brothers and sisters, became imitators of God's churches in Judea, which are in Christ Jesus: You suffered from your fellow citizens the same things those churches suffered from the Jews, [15]who killed the Lord Jesus and the prophets and also drove us out. They displease God and are hostile to everyone [16]in their effort to keep us from speaking to the Gentiles so that they may be saved. In this way they always heap up their sins to the limit. The wrath of God has come upon them at last.[a]

Paul's Longing to See the Thessalonians

[17]But, brothers and sisters, when we were orphaned by being separated from you for a short time (in person, not in thought), out of our intense longing we made every effort to see you. [18]For we wanted to come to you—certainly I, Paul, did, again and again—but Satan blocked our way. [19]For what is our hope, our joy, or the crown in which we will glory in the presence of our Lord Jesus when he comes? Is it not you? [20]Indeed, you are our glory and joy.

3 So when we could stand it no longer, we thought it best to be left by ourselves in Athens. [2]We sent Timothy, who is our brother and co-worker in God's service in spreading the gospel of Christ, to strengthen and encourage you in your faith, [3]so that no one would be unsettled by these trials. You know quite well that we are destined for them. [4]In fact, when we were with you, we kept telling you that we would be persecuted. And it turned out that way, as you well know. [5]For this reason, when I could stand it no longer, I sent to find out about your faith. I was afraid that in some way the tempter had tempted you and that our labors might have been in vain.

Timothy's Encouraging Report

[6]But Timothy has just now come to us from you and has brought good news about your faith and love. He has told us that you always have pleasant memories of us and that you long to see us, just as we also long to see you. [7]Therefore, brothers and sisters, in all our distress and persecution we were encouraged about you because of your faith. [8]For now we really live, since you are standing firm in the Lord. [9]How can we thank God enough for you in return for all the joy we have in the presence of our God because of you? [10]Night and day we pray most earnestly that we may see you again and supply what is lacking in your faith.

[11]Now may our God and Father himself and our Lord Jesus clear the way for us to come to you. [12]May the Lord make your love increase and overflow for each other and for everyone else, just as ours does for you. [13]May he strengthen your hearts so that you will be blameless and holy in the presence of our God and Father when our Lord Jesus comes with all his holy ones.

Living to Please God

4 As for other matters, brothers and sisters, we instructed you how to live in order to please God, as in fact you are living. Now we ask you and urge you in the Lord Jesus to do this more and more. [2]For you know what instructions we gave you by the authority of the Lord Jesus.

[3]It is God's will that you should be sanctified: that you should avoid sexual immorality; [4]that each of you should learn to control your own body[b] in a way that is holy and honorable, [5]not in passionate lust like the pagans, who do not know God; [6]and that in this matter no one should wrong or take advantage of a brother or sister. The Lord will punish all those who commit such sins, as we told you and warned you before. [7]For God did not call us to be impure, but to live a holy life. [8]Therefore, anyone who rejects this instruction does not reject a human being but God, the very God who gives you his Holy Spirit.

[9]Now about your love for one another we do not need to write to you, for you yourselves have been taught by God to love each other. [10]And in fact, you do love all the brothers and sisters throughout Macedonia. Yet we urge you, dear friends, to do so more and more, [11]and to make it your ambition to lead a quiet life: You should mind your own business and work with your hands, just as we told you, [12]so that your daily life may win

---

[a] 16 Or *them fully* [b] 4 Or *learn to live with his own wife; or learn to acquire a wife*

MONDAY

IT'S ABOUT TOMORROW

1 Thessalonians 4:1–18 *or* 4:13–18

ARTHUR W. PINK {AD 1885–1952}

Physical transformation is not all that awaits the believer. At our Lord's return there will be a mental, moral and spiritual transformation too. In 1 John 3:2 we are told, "Dear friends, now we are children of God, and what we will be has not yet been made known. But we know that when Christ appears, we shall be like him, for we shall see him as he is" . . .

When he appears, we shall be like him. The emphatic words are *"has not yet been made known."* What we are really going to be like awaits its *manifestation* until our Lord's appearing.

Let us illustrate: I hold in my hand a small seed. It is unlovely in appearance and gives no promise at all of what it will ultimately become. It is not yet made known what it will be. But I plant that seed in the ground, and a few weeks later it has become a strong plant. And one morning I wake and find it covered with the most beautiful flowers. Now the potentialities of that little seed are fully manifested. So it is with the believer. Our bodies are just the same as the bodies of unbelievers . . . [but] because our real "life *is now hidden* with Christ in God" (Colossians 3:3, emphasis added) what we will be has *not yet been made known*. Nevertheless we know by faith that when Christ appears, we shall be like him, for we shall see him as he is.

Eugene Peterson

The Christian faith has always been characterized by a strong and focused sense of future, with belief in the second coming of Jesus as the most distinctive detail. From the day Jesus ascended into heaven, his followers lived in expectancy of his return. He told them he was coming back. They believed he was coming back. They continue to believe it. For Christians, it is the most important thing to know and believe about the future.

The practical effect of this belief is to charge each moment of the present with hope. For if the future is dominated by the coming again of Jesus, there is little room left on the screen for projecting our anxieties and fantasies. It takes the clutter out of our lives. We're far more free to respond spontaneously to the freedom of God.

reflection

1. How should the truth of Christ's future return bring hope to your life today?

2. How does this truth bring hope when grieving the death of someone you love— if you know that person belonged to Jesus?

3. Think of things that you have eagerly anticipated: getting your driver's license, your first kiss, moving into your first apartment, etc. How does the anticipation you felt compare with your anticipation of Christ's return?

For your next devotional reading, go to page 1370.

the respect of outsiders and so that you will not be dependent on anybody.

Believers Who Have Died

¹³Brothers and sisters, we do not want you to be uninformed about those who sleep in death, so that you do not grieve like the rest, who have no hope. ¹⁴We believe that Jesus died and rose again, and so we believe that God will bring with Jesus those who have fallen asleep in him. ¹⁵According to the Lord's word, we tell you that we who are still alive, who are left till the coming of the Lord, will certainly not precede those who have fallen asleep. ¹⁶For the Lord himself will come down from heaven, with a loud command, with the voice of the archangel and with the trumpet call of God, and the dead in Christ will rise first. ¹⁷After that, we who are still alive and are left will be caught up together with them in the clouds to meet the Lord in the air. And so we will be with the Lord forever. ¹⁸Therefore encourage one another with these words.

The Day of the Lord

5 Now, brothers and sisters, about times and dates we do not need to write to you, ²for you know very well that the day of the Lord will come like a thief in the night. ³While people are saying, "Peace and safety," destruction will come on them suddenly, as labor pains on a pregnant woman, and they will not escape.

⁴But you, brothers and sisters, are not in darkness so that this day should surprise you like a thief. ⁵You are all children of the light and children of the day. We do not belong to the night or to the darkness. ⁶So then, let us not be like others, who are asleep, but let us be awake and sober. ⁷For those who sleep, sleep at night, and those who get drunk, get drunk at night. ⁸But since we belong to the day, let us be sober, putting on faith and love as a breastplate, and the hope of salvation as a helmet. ⁹For God did not appoint us to suffer wrath but to receive salvation through our Lord Jesus Christ. ¹⁰He died for us so that, whether we are awake or asleep, we may live together with him. ¹¹Therefore encourage one another and build each other up, just as in fact you are doing.

Final Instructions

¹²Now we ask you, brothers and sisters, to acknowledge those who work hard among you, who care for you in the Lord and who admonish you. ¹³Hold them in the highest regard in love because of their work. Live in peace with each other. ¹⁴And we urge you, brothers and sisters, warn those who are idle and disruptive, encourage the disheartened, help the weak, be patient with everyone. ¹⁵Make sure that nobody pays back wrong for wrong, but always strive to do what is good for each other and for everyone else.

¹⁶Rejoice always, ¹⁷pray continually, ¹⁸give thanks in all circumstances; for this is God's will for you in Christ Jesus.

¹⁹Do not put out the Spirit's fire. ²⁰Do not treat prophecies with contempt ²¹but test them all; hold on to what is good, ²²reject whatever is harmful.

²³May God himself, the God of peace, sanctify you through and through. May your whole spirit, soul and body be kept blameless at the coming of our Lord Jesus Christ. ²⁴The one who calls you is faithful, and he will do it.

²⁵Brothers and sisters, pray for us. ²⁶Greet all God's people with a holy kiss. ²⁷I charge you before the Lord to have this letter read to all the brothers and sisters.

²⁸The grace of our Lord Jesus Christ be with you.

2 thessalonians

AUTHOR: Paul, the apostle

DATE: Around A.D. 51 or 52

THEME: Christians should serve Jesus while awaiting his return.

1 Paul, Silas[a] and Timothy,

To the church of the Thessalonians in God our Father and the Lord Jesus Christ:

²Grace and peace to you from God the Father and the Lord Jesus Christ.

Thanksgiving and Prayer

³We ought always to thank God for you, brothers and sisters, and rightly so, because your faith is growing more and more, and the love all of you have for one another is increasing. ⁴Therefore, among God's churches we boast about your perseverance and faith in all the persecutions and trials you are enduring.

⁵All this is evidence that God's judgment is right, and as a result you will be counted worthy of the kingdom of God, for which you are suffering. ⁶God is just: He will pay back trouble to those who trouble you ⁷and give relief to you who are troubled, and to us as well. This will happen when the Lord Jesus is revealed from heaven in blazing fire with his powerful angels. ⁸He will punish those who do not know God and do not obey the gospel of our Lord Jesus. ⁹They will be punished with everlasting destruction and shut out from the presence of the Lord and from the glory of his might ¹⁰on the day he comes to be glorified in his holy people and to be marveled at among all those who have believed. This includes you, because you believed our testimony to you.

¹¹With this in mind, we constantly pray for you, that our God may make you worthy of his calling, and that by his power he may bring to fruition your every desire for good-

ness and your every deed prompted by faith. ¹²We pray this so that the name of our Lord Jesus may be glorified in you, and you in him, according to the grace of our God and the Lord Jesus Christ.[b]

The Man of Lawlessness

2 Concerning the coming of our Lord Jesus Christ and our being gathered to him, we ask you, brothers and sisters, ²not to become easily unsettled or alarmed by the teaching allegedly from us—whether by a prophecy or by word of mouth or by letter—asserting that the day of the Lord has already come. ³Don't let anyone deceive you in any way, for ⌞that day will not come⌟ until the rebellion occurs and the man of lawlessness[c] is revealed, the man doomed to destruction. ⁴He will oppose and will exalt himself over everything that is called God or is worshiped, so that he sets himself up in God's temple, proclaiming himself to be God.

⁵Don't you remember that when I was with you I used to tell you these things? ⁶And now you know what is holding him back, so that he may be revealed at the proper time. ⁷For the secret power of lawlessness is already at work; but the one who now holds it back will continue to do so till he is taken out of the way. ⁸And then the lawless one will be revealed, whom the Lord Jesus will overthrow with the breath of his mouth and destroy by the splendor of his coming. ⁹The coming of the lawless one will be in accordance with how Satan works. He will use all sorts of displays of power through signs and wonders that serve the lie, ¹⁰and all the ways that wickedness deceives those who are perishing. They perish because they refused to

---

a 1 Greek *Silvanus*, a variant of *Silas*   b 12 Or *God and Lord, Jesus Christ*   c 3 Some manuscripts *sin*

Get Up and Go On Until the End

2 Thessalonians 3:1–18 *or* 3:11–13

Ray C. Stedman {ad 1917–1992}

Many people think of work as a kind of curse, something that has been imposed upon man because of the Fall. But work is really a blessing, though we tend to forget that at times . . .

It is helpful to remember that God had ordained work before the Fall of man. Adam, when he was created, was given a job to do right from the beginning. God gave him a commission to till and to keep the garden, also to name the animals. He had to work to do that . . .

Work is divinely intended to give us a sense of self-worth. When you are working, you feel like you are accomplishing something. When you are laid off and are unable to work, you feel out of sorts and unable to function as you were intended. It is disturbing and psychologically upsetting to be without work. It is really a testimony to the fact that God made us to work. Work, therefore, is not a curse. It is a very valuable thing because it gives us a sense of meaning for our lives.

Donald Drew

Like everything in life and certainly in the Christian life, there is a struggle: struggle to distinguish between the important and the urgent, to make time, to meet commitments, to be refreshed and recover one's breath. The first believers, that great multitude spoken of in Hebrews 11 of men and women through the centuries who have fought the fight, finished the race and kept the faith, were ordinary people like ourselves, who strove and fell, but who got up and went on. At the end of his life, did the great apostle Paul smoothly say: "My dear friends, as I look back upon a remarkable life it seems to resemble nothing so much as enjoying cucumber sandwiches on the Vicarage lawn"? No he didn't. Each time he fell he got up and went on, got up and went on. To do that, to mean business with God, we must aim at self-discipline with some planning.

reflection

1. Why is idleness inconsistent with the Christian life?
2. How did Paul "practice what he preached" about being a hard worker?
3. How hard are *you* working toward God's goal for you?

For your next devotional reading, go to page 1373.

love the truth and so be saved. ¹¹For this reason God sends them a powerful delusion so that they will believe the lie ¹²and so that all will be condemned who have not believed the truth but have delighted in wickedness.

Stand Firm

¹³But we ought always to thank God for you, brothers and sisters loved by the Lord, because God chose you as firstfruits*a* to be saved through the sanctifying work of the Spirit and through belief in the truth. ¹⁴He called you to this through our gospel, that you might share in the glory of our Lord Jesus Christ.

¹⁵So then, brothers and sisters, stand firm and hold fast to the teachings*b* we passed on to you, whether by word of mouth or by letter.

¹⁶May our Lord Jesus Christ himself and God our Father, who loved us and by his grace gave us eternal encouragement and good hope, ¹⁷encourage your hearts and strengthen you in every good deed and word.

Request for Prayer

3 As for other matters, brothers and sisters, pray for us that the message of the Lord may spread rapidly and be honored, just as it was with you. ²And pray that we may be delivered from wicked and evil people, for not everyone has faith. ³But the Lord is faithful, and he will strengthen you and protect you from the evil one. ⁴We have confidence in the Lord that you are doing and will continue to do the things we command. ⁵May the Lord direct your hearts into God's love and Christ's perseverance.

Warning Against Idleness

⁶In the name of the Lord Jesus Christ, we command you, brothers and sisters, to keep away from every believer who is idle and disruptive and does not live according to the teaching*c* you received from us. ⁷For you yourselves know how you ought to follow our example. We were not idle when we were with you, ⁸nor did we eat anyone's food without paying for it. On the contrary, we worked night and day, laboring and toiling so that we would not be a burden to any of you. ⁹We did this, not because we do not have the right to such help, but in order to offer ourselves as a model for you to imitate. ¹⁰For even when we were with you, we gave you this rule: "Anyone who is unwilling to work shall not eat."

¹¹We hear that some among you are idle and disruptive. They are not busy; they are busybodies. ¹²Such people we command and urge in the Lord Jesus Christ to settle down and earn the bread they eat. ¹³And as for you, brothers and sisters, never tire of doing what is good.

¹⁴Take special note of those who do not obey our instruction in this letter. Do not associate with them, in order that they may feel ashamed. ¹⁵Yet do not regard them as enemies, but warn them as fellow believers.

Final Greetings

¹⁶Now may the Lord of peace himself give you peace at all times and in every way. The Lord be with all of you.

¹⁷I, Paul, write this greeting in my own hand, which is the distinguishing mark in all my letters. This is how I write.

¹⁸The grace of our Lord Jesus Christ be with you all.

---

a 13 Some manuscripts *because from the beginning God chose you*   *b 15* Or *traditions*   *c 6* Or *tradition*

1 timothy

AUTHOR: Paul, the apostle

DATE: Around A.D. 64

THEME: God shows us how his church should function.

1 Paul, an apostle of Christ Jesus by the command of God our Savior and of Christ Jesus our hope,

²To Timothy my true son in the faith:

Grace, mercy and peace from God the Father and Christ Jesus our Lord.

Timothy Charged to Oppose False Teachers

³As I urged you when I went into Macedonia, stay there in Ephesus so that you may command certain persons not to teach false doctrines any longer ⁴or to devote themselves to myths and endless genealogies. Such things promote controversial speculations rather than advancing God's work—which is by faith. ⁵The goal of this command is love, which comes from a pure heart and a good conscience and a sincere faith. ⁶Some have departed from these and have turned to meaningless talk. ⁷They want to be teachers of the law, but they do not know what they are talking about or what they so confidently affirm.

⁸We know that the law is good if one uses it properly. ⁹We also know that the law is made not for the righteous but for lawbreakers and rebels, the ungodly and sinful, the unholy and irreligious, for those who kill their fathers or mothers, for murderers, ¹⁰for the sexually immoral, for those practicing homosexuality, for slave traders and liars and perjurers. And it is for whatever else is contrary to the sound doctrine ¹¹that conforms to the gospel concerning the glory of the blessed God, which he entrusted to me.

The Lord's Grace to Paul

¹²I thank Christ Jesus our Lord, who has given me strength, that he considered me trustworthy, appointing me to his service.

¹³Even though I was once a blasphemer and a persecutor and a violent man, I was shown mercy because I acted in ignorance and unbelief. ¹⁴The grace of our Lord was poured out on me abundantly, along with the faith and love that are in Christ Jesus.

¹⁵Here is a trustworthy saying that deserves full acceptance: Christ Jesus came into the world to save sinners—of whom I am the worst. ¹⁶But for that very reason I was shown mercy so that in me, the worst of sinners, Christ Jesus might display his immense patience as an example for those who would believe in him and receive eternal life. ¹⁷Now to the King eternal, immortal, invisible, the only God, be honor and glory for ever and ever. Amen.

The Charge to Timothy Renewed

¹⁸Timothy, my son, I am giving you this command in keeping with the prophecies once made about you, so that by recalling them you may fight the battle well, ¹⁹holding on to faith and a good conscience, which some have rejected and so have suffered shipwreck with regard to the faith. ²⁰Among them are Hymenaeus and Alexander, whom I have handed over to Satan to be taught not to blaspheme.

Instructions on Worship

2 I urge, then, first of all, that petitions, prayers, intercession and thanksgiving be made for everyone— ²for kings and all those in authority, that we may live peaceful and quiet lives in all godliness and holiness. ³This is good, and pleases God our Savior, ⁴who wants all people to be saved and to come to a knowledge of the truth. ⁵For there is one God and one mediator between God and human beings, Christ Jesus,

WEDNESDAY

THE BIG PRAYER LIST

1 Timothy 2:1–15 *or* 2:1–4

Eugene Peterson

I think it is both proper and essential to pray for what you designate Big Things. We don't want prayer, the largest and most inclusive action of which we are capable, to be confined to getting us safely across the street and staying out of moral mud puddles. Jesus got us started well when he posted God's Name and Kingdom and Will at the top of our prayer list.

So praying to our Sovereign God for City and Country, President and Mayor obviously does not exceed our mandate. What I think we need to remember, though, is that when we pray for the Big Things, God's responses commonly come in small and hidden ways, at least in ways we think of as small and hidden. Praying for the City, a Big Thing, may have no visible effects on the City as reported in the newspapers and on TV. God looks at things very differently than we do. Our task is to pray ardently and faithfully; we cannot assume that we know how the prayer will be answered.

I've always loved the phrase in George Bernanos' *Diary of a Country Priest*: "Just think! The Word was made Flesh—and not a journalist in the world wrote it up!"

ORIGEN {AD 185–254}

We are traveling toward perfection if we forget the things behind us and press on toward what lies before us. The kingdom of God within us will therefore be consummated in us as we advance without ceasing. It will be brought to completion when Paul's words are fulfilled and Christ—his enemies all made subject to him—delivers the kingdom to God the Father, that God may be all in all (1 Corinthians 15:24–28). For this reason let us pray without ceasing with a frame of mind made divine by the Word, and say to our Father in heaven: "Hallowed be your name, your kingdom come" (Matthew 6:9–10).

reflection

1. How often do you pray about "big things"—such as your nation, the world, the advancement of God's kingdom on earth?

2. When was the last time you prayed for your city leaders?

3. Why is it important for you to pray for those things?

For your next devotional reading, go to page 1375.

himself human, ⁶who gave himself as a ransom for all people. This has now been witnessed to at the proper time. ⁷And for this purpose I was appointed a herald and an apostle—I am telling the truth, I am not lying—and a true and faithful teacher of the Gentiles.

⁸Therefore I want the men everywhere to pray, lifting up holy hands without anger or disputing. ⁹I also want the women to dress modestly, with decency and propriety, adorning themselves, not with elaborate hairstyles or gold or pearls or expensive clothes, ¹⁰but with good deeds, appropriate for women who profess to worship God.

¹¹A woman*a* should learn in quietness and full submission. ¹²I do not permit a woman to teach or to assume authority over a man;*b, c* she must be quiet. ¹³For Adam was formed first, then Eve. ¹⁴And Adam was not the one deceived; it was the woman who was deceived and became a sinner. ¹⁵But women*d* will be saved through childbearing—if they continue in faith, love and holiness with propriety.

Qualifications for Overseers and Deacons

3 Here is a trustworthy saying: Whoever aspires to be an overseer desires a noble task. ²Now the overseer is to be above reproach, faithful to his wife, temperate, self-controlled, respectable, hospitable, able to teach, ³not given to drunkenness, not violent but gentle, not quarrelsome, not a lover of money. ⁴He must manage his own family well and see that his children obey him, and he must do so in a manner worthy of full*e* respect. ⁵(If anyone does not know how to manage his own family, how can he take care of God's church?) ⁶He must not be a recent convert, or he may become conceited and fall under the same judgment as the devil. ⁷He must also have a good reputation with outsiders, so that he will not fall into disgrace and into the devil's trap.

⁸In the same way, deacons are to be worthy of respect, sincere, not indulging in much wine, and not pursuing dishonest gain. ⁹They must keep hold of the deep truths of the faith with a clear conscience. ¹⁰They must first be tested; and then if there

is nothing against them, let them serve as deacons.

¹¹In the same way, the women*f* are to be worthy of respect, not malicious talkers but temperate and trustworthy in everything.

¹²A deacon must be faithful to his wife and must manage his children and his household well. ¹³Those who have served well gain an excellent standing and great assurance in their faith in Christ Jesus.

Reasons for Paul's Instructions

¹⁴Although I hope to come to you soon, I am writing you these instructions so that, ¹⁵if I am delayed, you will know how people ought to conduct themselves in God's household, which is the church of the living God, the pillar and foundation of the truth. ¹⁶Beyond all question, the mystery from which true godliness springs is great:

He appeared in a body,
　was vindicated by the Spirit,*g*
was seen by angels,
　was preached among the nations,
was believed on in the world,
　was taken up in glory.

4 The Spirit clearly says that in later times some will abandon the faith and follow deceiving spirits and things taught by demons. ²Such teachings come through hypocritical liars, whose consciences have been seared as with a hot iron. ³They forbid people to marry and order them to abstain from certain foods, which God created to be received with thanksgiving by those who believe and who know the truth. ⁴For everything God created is good, and nothing is to be rejected if it is received with thanksgiving, ⁵because it is consecrated by the word of God and prayer.

⁶If you point these things out to the brothers and sisters, you will be a good minister of Christ Jesus, nourished on the truths of the faith and of the good teaching that you have followed. ⁷Have nothing to do with godless myths and old wives' tales; rather, train yourself to be godly. ⁸For physical training is of some value, but godliness has value for all things, holding promise for both the present life and the life to come. ⁹This is a trustworthy saying that deserves full ac-

---

a 11 Or wife; also in verse 12   b 12 Or teach a man in a domineering way; or teach or to exercise (or have) authority over a man   c 12 Or over her husband   d 15 Greek she   e 4 Or him with proper f 11 Probably women who are deacons, or possibly deacons' wives   g 16 Or vindicated in spirit

THURSDAY

FOLLOW WHAT IS TRUE

1 Timothy 4:1–16 or 4:1,6

Ravi Zacharias

One of the most fallacious ideas ever spawned in Western attitudes toward truth is the oft-repeated pronouncement that exclusionary claims to truth are a Western way of thinking. The East, it is implied, accepts all religions as equally true. This is patently false. Every religion, without exception, has some foundational beliefs that are categorically nonnegotiable and exclude everything to the contrary. You see, truth by definition is exclusive. If truth were all-inclusive, nothing would be false. And if nothing were false, what would be the meaning of *true*? Furthermore, if nothing were false, would it be *true* to say that everything is false? It quickly becomes evident that nonsense would follow.

Even Buddhism, which is often held up as being the example of "religious tolerance," is not exempt from dogmatism. Buddhists forget or downplay the fact that Buddha was born a Hindu and rejected some of the fundamental precepts of Hinduism. Buddha's own statement was that truth mattered more than conformity. What, therefore, takes place in popular thought is a reflection of the way culture has been engineered to deal with truth issues. This is the nerve of the problem in communication. It is the sacred duty of a pastor to remind his people periodically of the very nature of truth, because if truth dies, even at the altar of cultural sensitivities, then so does the gospel in the listener's ears. The first and foremost task of the apologist is to stand for the truth and to clarify the claims of the gospel.

John Chrysostom {AD 347–407}

Those who adhere to the faith are fixed on a safe anchor. Those who fall from the faith can never find rest as they wander to and fro, until they eventually fall into the very gulf of perdition. And this Paul had shown before, saying, that some "have [suffered shipwreck with regard to the faith]" (1 Timothy 1:19) and now he says, "The Spirit clearly says that in later times some will abandon the faith and follow deceiving spirits" (1 Timothy 4:1).

Beware the impediments to faith. "Train yourself to be godly." (1 Timothy 4:7) That is, unto a pure faith and a moral life; for this is godliness. So then we need to train ourselves.

reflection

1. How do you define *truth*? What standard do you use to measure what is "true"?

2. Why does society rebel against God's definition of truth?

3. How can you exercise tolerance and cultural sensitivity while still standing firm for what you know to be true?

For your next devotional reading, go to page 1379.

ceptance. [10]That is why we labor and strive, because we have put our hope in the living God, who is the Savior of all people, and especially of those who believe.

[11]Command and teach these things. [12]Don't let anyone look down on you because you are young, but set an example for the believers in speech, in conduct, in love, in faith and in purity. [13]Until I come, devote yourself to the public reading of Scripture, to preaching and to teaching. [14]Do not neglect your gift, which was given you through prophecy when the body of elders laid their hands on you.

[15]Be diligent in these matters; give yourself wholly to them, so that everyone may see your progress. [16]Watch your life and doctrine closely. Persevere in them, because if you do, you will save both yourself and your hearers.

Widows, Elders and Slaves

5 Do not rebuke an older man harshly, but exhort him as if he were your father. Treat younger men as brothers, [2]older women as mothers, and younger women as sisters, with absolute purity.

[3]Give proper recognition to those widows who are really in need. [4]But if a widow has children or grandchildren, these should learn first of all to put their religion into practice by caring for their own family and so repaying their parents and grandparents, for this is pleasing to God. [5]The widow who is really in need and left all alone puts her hope in God and continues night and day to pray and to ask God for help. [6]But the widow who lives for pleasure is dead even while she lives. [7]Give the people these instructions, so that no one may be open to blame. [8]Anyone who does not provide for their relatives, and especially for their own household, has denied the faith and is worse than an unbeliever.

[9]No widow may be put on the list of widows unless she is over sixty, has been faithful to her husband, [10]and is well known for her good deeds, such as bringing up children, showing hospitality, washing the feet of the Lord's people, helping those in trouble and devoting herself to all kinds of good deeds.

[11]As for younger widows, do not put them on such a list. For when their sensual desires overcome their dedication to Christ, they want to marry. [12]Thus they bring judgment on themselves, because they have broken their first pledge. [13]Besides, they get into the habit of being idle and going about from house to house. And not only do they become idlers, but also busybodies who talk nonsense, saying things they ought not to. [14]So I counsel younger widows to marry, to have children, to manage their homes and to give the enemy no opportunity for slander. [15]Some have in fact already turned away to follow Satan.

[16]If any woman who is a believer has widows in her care, she should continue to help them and not let the church be burdened with them, so that the church can help those widows who are really in need.

[17]The elders who direct the affairs of the church well are worthy of double honor, especially those whose work is preaching and teaching. [18]For Scripture says, "Do not muzzle an ox while it is treading out the grain,"[a] and "Workers deserve their wages."[b] [19]Do not entertain an accusation against an elder unless it is brought by two or three witnesses. [20]But those elders who are sinning you are to reprove before everyone, so that the others may take warning. [21]I charge you, in the sight of God and Christ Jesus and the elect angels, to keep these instructions without partiality, and to do nothing out of favoritism.

[22]Do not be hasty in the laying on of hands, and do not share in the sins of others. Keep yourself pure.

[23]Stop drinking only water, and use a little wine because of your stomach and your frequent illnesses.

[24]The sins of some are obvious, reaching the place of judgment ahead of them; the sins of others trail behind them. [25]In the same way, good deeds are obvious, and even those that are not obvious cannot remain hidden forever.

6 All who are under the yoke of slavery should consider their masters worthy of full respect, so that God's name and our teaching may not be slandered. [2]Those who have believing masters should not show them disrespect just because they are fellow believers. Instead, they should serve them even better because their mas-

ters are dear to them as fellow believers and are devoted to the welfare[a] of their slaves.

False Teachers and the Love of Money

These are the things you are to teach and insist on. ³If anyone teaches otherwise and does not agree to the sound instruction of our Lord Jesus Christ and to godly teaching, ⁴they are conceited and understand nothing. They have an unhealthy interest in controversies and quarrels about words that result in envy, strife, malicious talk, evil suspicions ⁵and constant friction between people of corrupt mind, who have been robbed of the truth and who think that godliness is a means to financial gain.

⁶But godliness with contentment is great gain. ⁷For we brought nothing into the world, and we can take nothing out of it. ⁸But if we have food and clothing, we will be content with that. ⁹Those who want to get rich fall into temptation and a trap and into many foolish and harmful desires that plunge people into ruin and destruction. ¹⁰For the love of money is a root of all kinds of evil. Some people, eager for money, have wandered from the faith and pierced themselves with many griefs.

Final Charge to Timothy

¹¹But you, man of God, flee from all this, and pursue righteousness, godliness, faith, love, endurance and gentleness. ¹²Fight the good fight of the faith. Take hold of the eter-

nal life to which you were called when you made your good confession in the presence of many witnesses. ¹³In the sight of God, who gives life to everything, and of Christ Jesus, who while testifying before Pontius Pilate made the good confession, I charge you ¹⁴to keep this command without spot or blame until the appearing of our Lord Jesus Christ, ¹⁵which God will bring about in his own time—God, the blessed and only Ruler, the King of kings and Lord of lords, ¹⁶who alone is immortal and who lives in unapproachable light, whom no one has seen or can see. To him be honor and might forever. Amen.

¹⁷Command those who are rich in this present world not to be arrogant nor to put their hope in wealth, which is so uncertain, but to put their hope in God, who richly provides us with everything for our enjoyment. ¹⁸Command them to do good, to be rich in good deeds, and to be generous and willing to share. ¹⁹In this way they will lay up treasure for themselves as a firm foundation for the coming age, so that they may take hold of the life that is truly life.

²⁰Timothy, guard what has been entrusted to your care. Turn away from godless chatter and the opposing ideas of what is falsely called knowledge, ²¹which some have professed and in so doing have departed from the faith.

Grace be with you all.

---

a 2 Or *and benefit from the service*

2 timothy

AUTHOR: Paul, the apostle

DATE: Around A.D. 67

THEME: Sometimes living for Jesus means we must suffer.

1 Paul, an apostle of Christ Jesus by the will of God, in keeping with the promise of life that is in Christ Jesus,

²To Timothy, my dear son:

Grace, mercy and peace from God the Father and Christ Jesus our Lord.

Thanksgiving

³I thank God, whom I serve, as my ancestors did, with a clear conscience, as night and day I constantly remember you in my prayers. ⁴Recalling your tears, I long to see you, so that I may be filled with joy. ⁵I am reminded of your sincere faith, which first lived in your grandmother Lois and in your mother Eunice and, I am persuaded, now lives in you also.

Appeal for Loyalty to Paul and the Gospel

⁶For this reason I remind you to fan into flame the gift of God, which is in you through the laying on of my hands. ⁷For the Spirit God gave us does not make us timid, but gives us power, love and self-discipline. ⁸So do not be ashamed of the testimony about our Lord or of me his prisoner. But join with me in suffering for the gospel, by the power of God, ⁹who has saved us and called us to a holy life—not because of anything we have done but because of his own purpose and grace. This grace was given us in Christ Jesus before the beginning of time, ¹⁰but it has now been revealed through the appearing of our Savior, Christ Jesus, who has destroyed death and has brought life and immortality to light through the gospel. ¹¹And of this gospel I was appointed a herald and an apostle and a teacher. ¹²That is why I am suffering as I am. Yet this is no cause for shame, because I know whom I have be-

lieved, and am convinced that he is able to guard what I have entrusted to him until that day.

¹³What you heard from me, keep as the pattern of sound teaching, with faith and love in Christ Jesus. ¹⁴Guard the good deposit that was entrusted to you—guard it with the help of the Holy Spirit who lives in us.

Examples of Disloyalty and Loyalty

¹⁵You know that everyone in the province of Asia has deserted me, including Phygelus and Hermogenes.

¹⁶May the Lord show mercy to the household of Onesiphorus, because he often refreshed me and was not ashamed of my chains. ¹⁷On the contrary, when he was in Rome, he searched hard for me until he found me. ¹⁸May the Lord grant that he will find mercy from the Lord on that day! You know very well in how many ways he helped me in Ephesus.

The Appeal Renewed

2 You then, my son, be strong in the grace that is in Christ Jesus. ²And the things you have heard me say in the presence of many witnesses entrust to reliable people who will also be qualified to teach others. ³Join with me in suffering, like a good soldier of Christ Jesus. ⁴No one serving as a soldier gets involved in civilian affairs; rather, they try to please their commanding officer. ⁵Similarly, anyone who competes as an athlete does not receive the victor's crown except by competing according to the rules. ⁶The hardworking farmer should be the first to receive a share of the crops. ⁷Reflect on what I am saying, for the Lord will give you insight into all this.

⁸Remember Jesus Christ, raised from the

FRIDAY

GRACE DEFINED

2 Timothy 1:1–18 or 1:8–10

Jim Cymbala

Grace is a rich and multifaceted word in the New Testament. One of its primary meanings is God doing for us, by the Holy Spirit, what we cannot do for ourselves. Whether we are overcoming sinful habits, preaching, teaching a class, leading a choir or being a godly spouse in the home, we cannot succeed without the grace of God. As Paul wrote in Philippians 2:13, "It is God *who works in you* to will and to act [in order] to [fulfill] his good purpose." Notice that we need God's help not just in the *doing* part but also in *willing* to walk in his ways.

JOHN OF RUYSBROECK {AD 1293–1381}

Only through Jesus are we able to see. He is the light of the Father, and without him there was no light in heaven or on earth. When we speak of Christ within us, we speak of an inrush of his light and his grace . . .

Now the grace of God, pouring forth from God, is an inward thrust and urge of the Holy Spirit, compelling our spirit from within and stimulating it toward all moral excellence, righteousness and goodness. This grace flows from within our hearts, and not from anything outside them. For God is more inward to us than we are to ourselves, and his inward thrust or working within us—be it natural or supernatural—is nearer to us and more intimate to us than our own working is. God works in us from the inside out, in contrast to the way that all creatures work from the outside in. And so it is that grace—along with all the gifts of God and the voice of God—comes from within. We experience God's grace in the unity of our spirit rather than through the abilities of our minds or through the things we can perceive through our senses.

reflection

1. What do you think of when you hear the term "God's grace"?

2. How did God's grace work in both Paul and Timothy to accomplish things they would have never been able to do on their own?

3. How have you seen God's grace working in your own life to help you do what you could never have done on your own?

For your next devotional reading, go to page 1381.

dead, descended from David. This is my gospel, ⁹for which I am suffering even to the point of being chained like a criminal. But God's word is not chained. ¹⁰Therefore I endure everything for the sake of the elect, that they too may obtain the salvation that is in Christ Jesus, with eternal glory.

¹¹Here is a trustworthy saying:

If we died with him,
   we will also live with him;
¹²if we endure,
   we will also reign with him.
If we disown him,
   he will also disown us;
¹³if we are faithless,
   he remains faithful,
   for he cannot disown himself.

Dealing With False Teachers

¹⁴Keep reminding God's people of these things. Warn them before God against quarreling about words; it is of no value, and only ruins those who listen. ¹⁵Do your best to present yourself to God as one approved, a worker who does not need to be ashamed and who correctly handles the word of truth. ¹⁶Avoid godless chatter, because those who indulge in it will become more and more ungodly. ¹⁷Their teaching will spread like gangrene. Among them are Hymenaeus and Philetus, ¹⁸who have departed from the truth. They say that the resurrection has already taken place, and they destroy the faith of some. ¹⁹Nevertheless, God's solid foundation stands firm, sealed with this inscription: "The Lord knows those who are his," and, "Everyone who confesses the name of the Lord must turn away from wickedness."

²⁰In a large house there are articles not only of gold and silver, but also of wood and clay; some are for noble purposes and some for disposal of refuse. ²¹Those who cleanse themselves from the latter will be instruments for noble purposes, made holy, useful to the Master and prepared to do any good work.

²²Flee the evil desires of youth and pursue righteousness, faith, love and peace, along with those who call on the Lord out of a pure heart. ²³Don't have anything to do with foolish and stupid arguments, because you know they produce quarrels. ²⁴And the Lord's servant must not be quarrelsome but must be kind to everyone, able to teach, not resentful. ²⁵Opponents must be gently instructed, in the hope that God will grant them repentance leading them to a knowledge of the truth, ²⁶and that they will come to their senses and escape from the trap of the devil, who has taken them captive to do his will.

3 But mark this: There will be terrible times in the last days. ²People will be lovers of themselves, lovers of money, boastful, proud, abusive, disobedient to their parents, ungrateful, unholy, ³without love, unforgiving, slanderous, without self-control, brutal, not lovers of the good, ⁴treacherous, rash, conceited, lovers of pleasure rather than lovers of God— ⁵having a form of godliness but denying its power. Have nothing to do with such people.

⁶They are the kind who worm their way into homes and gain control over gullible women, who are loaded down with sins and are swayed by all kinds of evil desires, ⁷always learning but never able to come to a knowledge of the truth. ⁸Just as Jannes and Jambres opposed Moses, so also these teachers oppose the truth. They are men of depraved minds, who, as far as the faith is concerned, are rejected. ⁹But they will not get very far because, as in the case of those men, their folly will be clear to everyone.

A Final Charge to Timothy

¹⁰You, however, know all about my teaching, my way of life, my purpose, faith, patience, love, endurance, ¹¹persecutions, sufferings—what kinds of things happened to me in Antioch, Iconium and Lystra, the persecutions I endured. Yet the Lord rescued me from all of them. ¹²In fact, everyone who wants to live a godly life in Christ Jesus will be persecuted, ¹³while evildoers and impostors will go from bad to worse, deceiving and being deceived. ¹⁴But as for you, continue in what you have learned and have become convinced of, because you know those from whom you learned it, ¹⁵and how from infancy you have known the Holy Scriptures, which are able to make you wise for salvation through faith in Christ Jesus. ¹⁶All Scripture is God-breathed and is useful for teaching, rebuking, correcting and training in righteousness, ¹⁷so that all God's peopleᵃ may be thoroughly equipped for every good work.

ᵃ 17 Or that the servant of God

Picking a Fight

2 Timothy 2:23–24

read/meditate

Read these two verses from 2 Timothy several times meditatively, slowly, contemplatively. How do you deal with difficult people? Think about difficult or argumentative people you know. How do they affect you?

pray

To really change the world, you must start with yourself. Spend some moments in silence, asking God to reveal your own weaknesses.

contemplate

What causes us to become argumentative when we would be more effective in another mode? Write down some reasons. Now that you've evaluated your own role in this, what about the Christian church in your culture? As a whole, how is the church doing at teaching effectively and being patient with difficult people?

additional reflection

Have you had a kindness shown?
Pass it on;
'Twas not given for thee alone,
Pass it on;
Let it travel down the years,
Let it wipe another's tears,
'Till in Heaven the deed appears—
Pass it on.

—Henry Burton

For your next devotional reading, go to page 1382.

THE GREATEST BOOK

2 Timothy 3:1–17 *or* 3:14–17

GEORGE WHITEFIELD {AD 1714–1770}

Believers keep up and maintain their walk with God by reading his holy Word. "You study the Scriptures," says our blessed Lord, ". . . these are the very Scriptures that testify about me" (John 5:39). The psalmist tells us, "Your word is a lamp to my feet and a light for my path" (Psalm 119:105). He also observes that one of the hallmarks of a good person is that they will "delight in the law of the LORD and meditate on his law day and night" (Psalm 1:2) . . . "For everything that was written in the past was written to teach us" (Romans 15:4). "All Scripture . . . is useful for teaching, rebuking, correcting and training in righteousness, so that all God's people may be thoroughly equipped for every good work" (2 Timothy 3:16–17). If we ever place ourselves above our Bibles, and cease making the written Word of God the sole basis of both our faith and its practice, then we open ourselves up to all kinds of self-deception and place ourselves in great danger of smashing to pieces both our faith and our good conscience.

Frederick Buechner

The Bible is not essentially, as I had always more or less supposed, a book of ethical principles, of moral exhortations, of cautionary tales about exemplary people, of uplifting thoughts—in fact, not really a religious book at all in the sense that most of the books you would be apt to find in a minister's study or reviewed in a special religion issue of the New York Times book section are religious. I saw it instead as a great, tattered compendium of writings, the underlying and unifying purpose of all of which is to show how God works through the Jacobs and Jabboks of history to make himself known to the world and to draw the world back to himself.

reflection

1. If you're honest, you'll probably admit that there are certain things in Scripture that you'd prefer to ignore. What Biblical truths do you find it hard to fully embrace?

2. How do you determine what is moral and ethical?

3. How would you sum up the central message of the Scripture?

For your next devotional reading, go to page 1385.

4 In the presence of God and of Christ Jesus, who will judge the living and the dead, and in view of his appearing and his kingdom, I give you this charge: ²Preach the word; be prepared in season and out of season; correct, rebuke and encourage—with great patience and careful instruction. ³For the time will come when people will not put up with sound doctrine. Instead, to suit their own desires, they will gather around them a great number of teachers to say what their itching ears want to hear. ⁴They will turn their ears away from the truth and turn aside to myths. ⁵But you, keep your head in all situations, endure hardship, do the work of an evangelist, discharge all the duties of your ministry.

⁶For I am already being poured out like a drink offering, and the time for my departure is near. ⁷I have fought the good fight, I have finished the race, I have kept the faith. ⁸Now there is in store for me the crown of righteousness, which the Lord, the righteous Judge, will award to me on that day—and not only to me, but also to all who have longed for his appearing.

Personal Remarks

⁹Do your best to come to me quickly, ¹⁰for Demas, because he loved this world, has deserted me and has gone to Thessalonica. Crescens has gone to Galatia, and Titus to Dalmatia. ¹¹Only Luke is with me. Get Mark and bring him with you, because he is helpful to me in my ministry. ¹²I sent Tychicus to Ephesus. ¹³When you come, bring the cloak that I left with Carpus at Troas, and my scrolls, especially the parchments.

¹⁴Alexander the metalworker did me a great deal of harm. The Lord will repay him for what he has done. ¹⁵You too should be on your guard against him, because he strongly opposed our message.

¹⁶At my first defense, no one came to my support, but everyone deserted me. May it not be held against them. ¹⁷But the Lord stood at my side and gave me strength, so that through me the message might be fully proclaimed and all the Gentiles might hear it. And I was delivered from the lion's mouth. ¹⁸The Lord will rescue me from every evil attack and will bring me safely to his heavenly kingdom. To him be glory for ever and ever. Amen.

Final Greetings

¹⁹Greet Priscilla[a] and Aquila and the household of Onesiphorus. ²⁰Erastus stayed in Corinth, and I left Trophimus sick in Miletus. ²¹Do your best to get here before winter. Eubulus greets you, and so do Pudens, Linus, Claudia and all the brothers and sisters.

²²The Lord be with your spirit. Grace be with you all.

---

a 19 Greek *Prisca*, a variant of *Priscilla*

titus

AUTHOR: Paul, the apostle

DATE: Around A.D. 64

THEME: God calls Christians, beginning with the church's leaders, to exhibit godly character.

1 Paul, a servant of God and an apostle of Jesus Christ to further the faith of God's elect and their knowledge of the truth that leads to godliness— [2]in the hope of eternal life, which God, who does not lie, promised before the beginning of time, [3]and which now at his appointed season he has brought to light through the preaching entrusted to me by the command of God our Savior,

[4]To Titus, my true son in our common faith:

Grace and peace from God the Father and Christ Jesus our Savior.

Appointing Elders Who Love What Is Good

[5]The reason I left you in Crete was that you might put in order what was left unfinished and appoint[a] elders in every town, as I directed you. [6]An elder must be blameless, faithful to his wife, a man whose children believe and are not open to the charge of being wild and disobedient. [7]Since an overseer manages God's household, he must be blameless—not overbearing, not quick-tempered, not given to drunkenness, not violent, not pursuing dishonest gain. [8]Rather, he must be hospitable, one who loves what is good, who is self-controlled, upright, holy and disciplined. [9]He must hold firmly to the trustworthy message as it has been taught, so that he can encourage others by sound doctrine and refute those who oppose it.

Rebuking Those Who Fail to Do Good

[10]For there are many rebellious people, full of meaningless talk and deception, especially those of the circumcision group. [11]They must be silenced, because they are disrupting whole households by teaching things they ought not to teach—and that for the sake of dishonest gain. [12]One of Crete's own prophets has said it: "Cretans are always liars, evil brutes, lazy gluttons."[b] [13]He has surely told the truth! Therefore rebuke them sharply, so that they will be sound in the faith [14]and will pay no attention to Jewish myths or to the merely human commands of those who reject the truth. [15]To the pure, all things are pure, but to those who are corrupted and do not believe, nothing is pure. In fact, both their minds and consciences are corrupted. [16]They claim to know God, but by their actions they deny him. They are detestable, disobedient and unfit for doing anything good.

Doing Good for the Sake of the Gospel

2 You, however, must teach what is appropriate to sound doctrine. [2]Teach the older men to be temperate, worthy of respect, self-controlled, and sound in faith, in love and in endurance.

[3]Likewise, teach the older women to be reverent in the way they live, not to be slanderers or addicted to much wine, but to teach what is good. [4]Then they can urge the younger women to love their husbands and children, [5]to be self-controlled and pure, to be busy at home, to be kind, and to be subject to their husbands, so that no one will malign the word of God.

[6]Similarly, encourage the young men to be self-controlled. [7]In everything set them an example by doing what is good. In your teaching show integrity, seriousness [8]and

a 5 Or *ordain*   *b 12* From the Cretan philosopher Epimenides

TUESDAY

THE SPIRIT RECONCILES US

Titus 3:1–15 *or* 3:3–7

SAINT AUGUSTINE {AD 354–430}

Every person is born into a sinful state. Paul wrote, "Like the rest, we were by nature deserving of wrath" (Ephesians 2:3). Since we are in this state of wrath through original sin—a condition made still graver and more treacherous by our own individual sin—a mediator was required. We needed a reconciler who could appease the wrath we deserve by offering a unique sacrifice, of which all the sacrifices of the Law and the Prophets were mere shadows.

While God is said to be wrathful, this does not refer to the uncontrolled anger we see with angry people. God's verdict of judgment for sin, which is completely just, borrows the term "wrath" from the language of human feelings.

This, then, is the grace of God through Jesus Christ our Lord: We are reconciled to God through the mediator Jesus Christ. And we receive the Holy Spirit so that we may be changed from enemies into children, "for those who are led by the Spirit of God are the children of God" (Romans 8:14).

Brennan Manning

The Holy Spirit is the bond of tenderness between the Father and the Son. Thus, the indwelling Spirit bears the indelible stamp of the compassion of God. "[God's love has been poured out into our hearts through the Holy Spirit, who has been given to us]" (Romans 5:5) . . .

God created us for union with Himself: This is the original purpose of our lives. And God is defined as love (1 John 4:8). Living in awareness of our belovedness is the axis around which the Christian life revolves. Being the beloved is our identity, the core of our existence. It is not merely a lofty thought, an inspiring idea, or one name among many. It is the name by which God knows us and the way he relates to us.

reflection

1. Because of sin, what kind of treatment do you deserve from God? What have you received instead?

2. How do you respond to the outrageously undeserved kindness of God?

3. What role does the Holy Spirit play in your life? When was the last time you thanked the Spirit for all that he has done—and continues to do—for you?

For your next devotional reading, go to page 1389.

soundness of speech that cannot be condemned, so that those who oppose you may be ashamed because they have nothing bad to say about us.

⁹Teach slaves to be subject to their masters in everything, to try to please them, not to talk back to them, ¹⁰and not to steal from them, but to show that they can be fully trusted, so that in every way they will make the teaching about God our Savior attractive.

¹¹For the grace of God has appeared that offers salvation to all people. ¹²It teaches us to say "No" to ungodliness and worldly passions, and to live self-controlled, upright and godly lives in this present age, ¹³while we wait for the blessed hope—the appearing of the glory of our great God and Savior, Jesus Christ, ¹⁴who gave himself for us to redeem us from all wickedness and to purify for himself a people that are his very own, eager to do what is good.

¹⁵These, then, are the things you should teach. Encourage and rebuke with all authority. Do not let anyone despise you.

Saved in Order to Do Good

3 Remind the people to be subject to rulers and authorities, to be obedient, to be ready to do whatever is good, ²to slander no one, to be peaceable and considerate, and always to be gentle toward everyone.

³At one time we too were foolish, disobedient, deceived and enslaved by all kinds of passions and pleasures. We lived in malice and envy, being hated and hating one another. ⁴But when the kindness and love of God our Savior appeared, ⁵he saved us, not because of righteous things we had done, but because of his mercy. He saved us through the washing of rebirth and renewal by the Holy Spirit, ⁶whom he poured out on us generously through Jesus Christ our Savior, ⁷so that, having been justified by his grace, we might become heirs having the hope of eternal life. ⁸This is a trustworthy saying. And I want you to stress these things, so that those who have trusted in God may be careful to devote themselves to doing what is good. These things are excellent and profitable for everyone.

⁹But avoid foolish controversies and genealogies and arguments and quarrels about the law, because these are unprofitable and useless. ¹⁰Warn divisive people once, and then warn them a second time. After that, have nothing to do with them. ¹¹You may be sure that such people are warped and sinful; they are self-condemned.

Final Remarks

¹²As soon as I send Artemas or Tychicus to you, do your best to come to me at Nicopolis, because I have decided to winter there. ¹³Do everything you can to help Zenas the lawyer and Apollos on their way and see that they have everything they need. ¹⁴Our people must learn to devote themselves to doing what is good, in order to provide for urgent needs and not live unproductive lives.

¹⁵Everyone with me sends you greetings. Greet those who love us in the faith.

Grace be with you all.

philemon

AUTHOR: Paul, the apostle

DATE: Around A.D. 60

THEME: God asks those who bear his name to forgive what some consider unforgivable.

¹Paul, a prisoner of Christ Jesus, and Timothy our brother,

To Philemon our dear friend and fellow worker— ²also to Apphia our sister and Archippus our fellow soldier—and to the church that meets in your home:

³Grace and peace to you*a* from God our Father and the Lord Jesus Christ.

Thanksgiving and Prayer

⁴I always thank my God as I remember you in my prayers, ⁵because I hear about your love for all his people and your faith in the Lord Jesus. ⁶I pray that your partnership with us in the faith may be effective in deepening your understanding of every good thing we share for the sake of Christ. ⁷Your love has given me great joy and encouragement, because you, brother, have refreshed the hearts of the Lord's people.

Paul's Plea for Onesimus

⁸Therefore, although in Christ I could be bold and order you to do what you ought to do, ⁹yet I prefer to appeal to you on the basis of love. It is as none other than Paul—an old man and now also a prisoner of Christ Jesus— ¹⁰I appeal to you for my son Onesimus,*b* who became my son while I was in chains. ¹¹Formerly he was useless to you, but now he has become useful both to you and to me.

¹²I am sending him—who is my very

heart—back to you. ¹³I would have liked to keep him with me so that he could take your place in helping me while I am in chains for the gospel. ¹⁴But I did not want to do anything without your consent, so that any favor you do would not seem forced but would be voluntary. ¹⁵Perhaps the reason he was separated from you for a little while was that you might have him back forever— ¹⁶no longer as a slave, but better than a slave, as a dear brother. He is very dear to me but even dearer to you, both as a fellow man and as a brother in the Lord.

¹⁷So if you consider me a partner, welcome him as you would welcome me. ¹⁸If he has done you any wrong or owes you anything, charge it to me. ¹⁹I, Paul, am writing this with my own hand. I will pay it back—not to mention that you owe me your very self. ²⁰I do wish, brother, that I may have some benefit from you in the Lord; refresh my heart in Christ. ²¹Confident of your obedience, I write to you, knowing that you will do even more than I ask.

²²And one thing more: Prepare a guest room for me, because I hope to be restored to you in answer to your prayers.

²³Epaphras, my fellow prisoner in Christ Jesus, sends you greetings. ²⁴And so do Mark, Aristarchus, Demas and Luke, my fellow workers.

²⁵The grace of the Lord Jesus Christ be with your spirit.

a 3 The Greek is plural; also in verses 22 and 25; elsewhere in this letter "you" is singular.
b 10 Onesimus means useful.

hebrews

> **AUTHOR:** Unknown
>
> **DATE:** Sometime before the destruction of the temple in Jerusalem in A.D. 70
>
> **THEME:** Being both the perfect priest and the once-for-all sacrifice, Jesus is the source and means of God's grace.

God's Final Word: His Son

1 In the past God spoke to our ancestors through the prophets at many times and in various ways, [2] but in these last days he has spoken to us by his Son, whom he appointed heir of all things, and through whom also he made the universe. [3] The Son is the radiance of God's glory and the exact representation of his being, sustaining all things by his powerful word. After he had provided purification for sins, he sat down at the right hand of the Majesty in heaven. [4] So he became as much superior to the angels as the name he has inherited is superior to theirs.

The Son Superior to Angels

[5] For to which of the angels did God ever say,

"You are my Son;
   today I have become your Father"[a]?

Or again,

"I will be his Father,
   and he will be my Son"[b]?

[6] And again, when God brings his firstborn into the world, he says,

"Let all God's angels worship him."[c]

[7] In speaking of the angels he says,

"He makes his angels spirits,
   and his servants flames of fire."[d]

[8] But about the Son he says,

"Your throne, O God, will last for ever
   and ever;

a scepter of justice will be the scepter
   of your kingdom.
[9] You have loved righteousness and hated
   wickedness;
therefore God, your God, has set you
   above your companions
by anointing you with the oil of joy."[e]

[10] He also says,

"In the beginning, Lord, you laid the
   foundations of the earth,
and the heavens are the work of your
   hands.
[11] They will perish, but you remain;
   they will all wear out like a garment.
[12] You will roll them up like a robe;
   like a garment they will be changed.
But you remain the same,
   and your years will never end."[f]

[13] To which of the angels did God ever say,

"Sit at my right hand
   until I make your enemies
   a footstool for your feet"[g]?

[14] Are not all angels ministering spirits sent to serve those who will inherit salvation?

Warning to Pay Attention

2 We must pay the most careful attention, therefore, to what we have heard, so that we do not drift away. [2] For since the message spoken through angels was binding, and every violation and disobedience received its just punishment, [3] how shall we escape if we ignore so great a salvation? This salvation, which was first announced by the Lord, was confirmed to us

---

a 5 Psalm 2:7   *b 5* 2 Samuel 7:14; 1 Chron. 17:13   *c 6* Deut. 32:43 (see Dead Sea Scrolls and Septuagint)   *d 7* Psalm 104:4   *e 9* Psalm 45:6,7   *f 12* Psalm 102:25-27   *g 13* Psalm 110:1

WEDNESDAY

NO ESCAPE

Hebrews 2:1–18 *or* 2:10,18

Matt Redman

Hebrews 2:10 tells us that Jesus Himself was made "perfect through [what he suffered]" . . . To see this throws a whole new light on our thinking about the trials of this life. If we are seeking to be followers of Jesus, sharpened and matured in our faith, can we really expect to escape times of suffering, when the Author and Perfecter of our faith embraced and endured them?

This area is in many ways a hard teaching, and if it wasn't in the Bible in such clear and blunt language, we might even find it hard to swallow. The truth is, so often when we perceive God to have left us to struggle alone the complete opposite is in fact true—He has not left the scene, but instead is doing a deep work in us.

CORTLAND MYERS {AD 1864–1941}

Steel is the product of iron *plus* fire. Soil is rock *plus* heat and the crushing of glaciers . . . In the same way, the development of human character requires a *plus* attached to it, for great character is made not through luxurious living but through suffering. And the world does not forget people of great character.

I once heard the story of a mother who brought a crippled boy with a hunched back into her home as a companion for her own son. She warned her son to be very careful not to refer to the other boy's deformity, since this was a sensitive matter to him. And she encouraged him to play with his new friend as if he were a normal child. But after listening to her son play with him for a few minutes, she heard him ask his companion, "Do you know what that is on your back?" The crippled boy was embarrassed, hesitated a moment, but before he could respond, his friend answered the question for him by saying, "It is the box that holds your wings, and someday God is going to break it open, and you will fly away to be an angel."

Someday God is going to reveal this fact to every Christian: the very things they now rebel against are the instruments He has used to perfect their character and to mold them into perfection, so they may later be used as polished stones in His heaven yet to come.

reflection

1. What did God accomplish through the suffering of Christ?

2. What trial or difficulty in your life do you wish would go away?

3. How will you look to God to use that trial to do a deep work in you?

For your next devotional reading, go to page 1392.

by those who heard him. ⁴God also testified to it by signs, wonders and various miracles, and by gifts of the Holy Spirit distributed according to his will.

Jesus Made Like His Brothers and Sisters

⁵It is not to angels that he has subjected the world to come, about which we are speaking. ⁶But there is a place where someone has testified:

"What are mere mortals that you are
    mindful of them,
  human beings that you care for
    them?
⁷You made them a little lower than the
    angels;
  you crowned them with glory and
    honor
⁸ and put everything under their feet." ᵃ

In putting everything under them,ᵇ God left nothing that is not subject to them.ᵇ Yet at present we do not see everything subject to them.ᵇ ⁹But we do see Jesus, who was made lower than the angels for a little while, now crowned with glory and honor because he suffered death, so that by the grace of God he might taste death for everyone.

¹⁰In bringing many sons and daughters to glory, it was fitting that God, for whom and through whom everything exists, should make the pioneer of their salvation perfect through what he suffered. ¹¹Both the one who makes people holy and those who are made holy are of the same family. So Jesus is not ashamed to call them brothers and sisters. ¹²He says,

"I will declare your name to my brothers
    and sisters;
  in the assembly I will sing your
    praises." ᶜ

¹³And again,

"I will put my trust in him." ᵈ

And again he says,

"Here am I, and the children God has
    given me." ᵉ

¹⁴Since the children have flesh and blood, he too shared in their humanity so that by his death he might break the power of him who holds the power of death—that is, the devil— ¹⁵and free those who all their lives were held in slavery by their fear of death. ¹⁶For surely it is not angels he helps, but Abraham's descendants. ¹⁷For this reason he had to be made like his brothers and sisters in every way, in order that he might become a merciful and faithful high priest in service to God, and that he might make atonement for the sins of the people. ¹⁸Because he himself suffered when he was tempted, he is able to help those who are being tempted.

Jesus Greater Than Moses

3 Therefore, holy brothers and sisters, who share in the heavenly calling, fix your thoughts on Jesus, whom we acknowledge as our apostle and high priest. ²He was faithful to the one who appointed him, just as Moses was faithful in all God's house. ³Jesus has been found worthy of greater honor than Moses, just as the builder of a house has greater honor than the house itself. ⁴For every house is built by someone, but God is the builder of everything. ⁵"Moses was faithful as a servant in all God's house," ᶠ bearing witness to what would be spoken by God in the future. ⁶But Christ is faithful as the Son over God's house. And we are his house, if indeed we hold firmly to our confidence and the hope in which we glory.

Warning Against Unbelief

⁷So, as the Holy Spirit says:

"Today, if you hear his voice,
⁸ do not harden your hearts
  as you did in the rebellion,
    during the time of testing in the
      wilderness,
⁹where your ancestors tested and tried
    me,
  though for forty years they saw what I
    did.
¹⁰That is why I was angry with that
    generation;
  I said, 'Their hearts are always going
    astray,
  and they have not known my ways.'

ᵃ 6-8 Psalm 8:4-6; or *"What is a human being that you are mindful of him,/ the son of man that you care for him?/ ⁷You made him lower than the angels for a little while;/ you crowned him with glory and honor/ ⁸and put everything under his feet."*   ᵇ 8 Or *him*   ᶜ 12 Psalm 22:22   ᵈ 13 Isaiah 8:17   ᵉ 13 Isaiah 8:18   ᶠ 5 Num. 12:7

¹¹So I declared on oath in my anger,
'They shall never enter my rest.' "ᵃ

¹²See to it, brothers and sisters, that none of you has a sinful, unbelieving heart that turns away from the living God. ¹³But encourage one another daily, as long as it is called "Today," so that none of you may be hardened by sin's deceitfulness. ¹⁴We have come to share in Christ, if indeed we hold firmly till the end our original conviction. ¹⁵As has just been said:

"Today, if you hear his voice,
do not harden your hearts
as you did in the rebellion."ᵇ

¹⁶Who were they who heard and rebelled? Were they not all those Moses led out of Egypt? ¹⁷And with whom was he angry for forty years? Was it not with those who sinned, whose bodies perished in the wilderness? ¹⁸And to whom did God swear that they would never enter his rest if not to those who disobeyed? ¹⁹So we see that they were not able to enter, because of their unbelief.

A Sabbath-Rest for the People of God

4 Therefore, since the promise of entering his rest still stands, let us be careful that none of you be found to have fallen short of it. ²For we also have had the good news proclaimed to us, just as they did; but the message they heard was of no value to them, because they did not share the faith of those who obeyed.ᶜ ³Now we who have believed enter that rest, just as God has said,

"So I declared on oath in my anger,
'They shall never enter my rest.' "ᵈ

And yet his work has been finished since the creation of the world. ⁴For somewhere he has spoken about the seventh day in these words: "On the seventh day God rested from all his work."ᵉ ⁵And again in the passage above he says, "They shall never enter my rest."

⁶Therefore since it still remains for some to enter that rest, and since those who formerly had the good news proclaimed to them did not go in because of their disobe-

dience, ⁷God again set a certain day, calling it "Today." This he did when a long time later he spoke through David, as in the passage already quoted:

"Today, if you hear his voice,
do not harden your hearts."ᵇ

⁸For if Joshua had given them rest, God would not have spoken later about another day. ⁹There remains, then, a Sabbath-rest for the people of God; ¹⁰for those who enter God's rest also rest from their own work, just as God did from his. ¹¹Let us, therefore, make every effort to enter that rest, so that no one will perish by following their example of disobedience.

¹²For the word of God is alive and active. Sharper than any double-edged sword, it penetrates even to dividing soul and spirit, joints and marrow; it judges the thoughts and attitudes of the heart. ¹³Nothing in all creation is hidden from God's sight. Everything is uncovered and laid bare before the eyes of him to whom we must give account.

Jesus the Great High Priest

¹⁴Therefore, since we have a great high priest who has ascended into heaven,ᶠ Jesus the Son of God, let us hold firmly to the faith we profess. ¹⁵For we do not have a high priest who is unable to empathize with our weaknesses, but we have one who has been tempted in every way, just as we are—yet he did not sin. ¹⁶Let us then approach God's throne of grace with confidence, so that we may receive mercy and find grace to help us in our time of need.

5 Every high priest is selected from among the people and is appointed to represent them in matters related to God, to offer gifts and sacrifices for sins. ²He is able to deal gently with those who are ignorant and are going astray, since he himself is subject to weakness. ³This is why he has to offer sacrifices for his own sins, as well as for the sins of the people. ⁴And no one takes this honor on himself, but he receives it when called by God, just as Aaron was.

⁵In the same way, Christ did not take on himself the glory of becoming a high priest. But God said to him,

---

ᵃ 11 Psalm 95:7-11   ᵇ 15,7 Psalm 95:7,8   ᶜ 2 Some manuscripts *because those who heard did not combine it with faith*   ᵈ 3 Psalm 95:11; also in verse 5   ᵉ 4 Gen. 2:2   ᶠ 14 Greek *has gone through the heavens*

THURSDAY

LOVE AT OUR LOWEST

Hebrews 4:1–16 *or* 4:8–11

ANDREW MURRAY {AD 1828–1917}

God brought Israel out of Egypt by a mighty hand, and the same mighty hand brought us out of our personal land of bondage. With the same mighty hand he brought his ancient people into rest, he can also bring us into our true rest. The same God who pardoned and regenerated us is waiting to perfect his love in us, if we would just trust him. Are there many hearts saying, "I believe that God brought me out of bondage twenty or thirty or forty years ago. But I cannot say that I have been brought into the happy land of rest and victory"?

How glorious was the rest of Canaan after all the wanderings in the wilderness! And so it is with the Christian who reaches the better promised Canaan of rest. This happens when you come to leave all your charge with the Lord Jesus—all your responsibilities, anxieties and worry—and hand the keeping of your soul into the hand of Jesus every day and hour. For the Lord can indeed care for your soul and give it victory over every enemy. Jesus has undertaken not only to cleanse our sin and bring us to heaven but also to sustain us in our daily life.

Are you hungering to get free from sin and its power? Do you long to experience complete victory over your temper, your pride and all your evil inclinations? Does your heart ache for the time when no clouds will come between you and your God, when you will walk in the full sunshine of God's loving favor? The very God who brought you from the Egypt of darkness is ready and able to bring you also into the Canaan of rest.

Craig Gross

The unconditional love of God is the only type of love that works in the gutter. It's a love that seeks to chase, find, and deliver those who are wandering. But there is a strange thing about the gutter. It makes me wonder: Why is something as pure as love the most profound thing in the lowest dwelling place? Where darkness abounds, love is brighter.

reflection

1. We've all been in bondage to sin, all spent time in the gutter. How have you experienced God's love in those dark places of your life?

2. On what occasions have you felt you've been left "wandering in the wilderness"?

3. What does it feel like to enter God's rest?

For your next devotional reading, go to page 1394.

"You are my Son;
today I have become your Father." [a]

[6] And he says in another place,

"You are a priest forever,
in the order of Melchizedek." [b]

[7] During the days of Jesus' life on earth, he offered up prayers and petitions with fervent cries and tears to the one who could save him from death, and he was heard because of his reverent submission. [8] Son though he was, he learned obedience from what he suffered [9] and, once made perfect, he became the source of eternal salvation for all who obey him [10] and was designated by God to be high priest in the order of Melchizedek.

Warning Against Falling Away

[11] We have much to say about this, but it is hard to make it clear to you because you no longer try to understand. [12] In fact, though by this time you ought to be teachers, you need someone to teach you the elementary truths of God's word all over again. You need milk, not solid food! [13] Anyone who lives on milk, being still an infant, is not acquainted with the teaching about righteousness. [14] But solid food is for the mature, who by constant use have trained themselves to distinguish good from evil.

6 Therefore let us move beyond the elementary teachings about Christ and be taken forward to maturity, not laying again the foundation of repentance from acts that lead to death, [c] and of faith in God, [2] instruction about cleansing rites, [d] the laying on of hands, the resurrection of the dead, and eternal judgment. [3] And God permitting, we will do so.

[4] It is impossible for those who have once been enlightened, who have tasted the heavenly gift, who have shared in the Holy Spirit, [5] who have tasted the goodness of the word of God and the powers of the coming age [6] and who have fallen [e] away, to be brought back to repentance. To their loss they are crucifying the Son of God all over again and subjecting him to public disgrace. [7] Land that drinks in the rain often falling on it and that produces a crop useful to those for whom it is farmed receives the blessing of God. [8] But land that produces thorns and

thistles is worthless and is in danger of being cursed. In the end it will be burned.

[9] Even though we speak like this, dear friends, we are convinced of better things in your case—the things that have to do with salvation. [10] God is not unjust; he will not forget your work and the love you have shown him as you have helped his people and continue to help them. [11] We want each of you to show this same diligence to the very end, in order to make your hope sure. [12] We do not want you to become lazy, but to imitate those who through faith and patience inherit what has been promised.

The Certainty of God's Promise

[13] When God made his promise to Abraham, since there was no one greater for him to swear by, he swore by himself, [14] saying, "I will surely bless you and give you many descendants." [f] [15] And so after waiting patiently, Abraham received what was promised.

[16] People swear by someone greater than themselves, and the oath confirms what is said and puts an end to all argument. [17] Because God wanted to make the unchanging nature of his purpose very clear to the heirs of what was promised, he confirmed it with an oath. [18] God did this so that, by two unchangeable things in which it is impossible for God to lie, we who have fled to take hold of the hope set before us may be greatly encouraged. [19] We have this hope as an anchor for the soul, firm and secure. It enters the inner sanctuary behind the curtain, [20] where our forerunner, Jesus, has entered on our behalf. He has become a high priest forever, in the order of Melchizedek.

Melchizedek the Priest

7 This Melchizedek was king of Salem and priest of God Most High. He met Abraham returning from the defeat of the kings and blessed him, [2] and Abraham gave him a tenth of everything. First, the name Melchizedek means "king of righteousness"; then also, "king of Salem" means "king of peace." [3] Without father or mother, without genealogy, without beginning of days or end of life, resembling the Son of God, he remains a priest forever.

[4] Just think how great he was: Even the

---

a 5 Psalm 2:7   *b* 6 Psalm 110:4   *c* 1 Or *from useless rituals*   *d* 2 Or *about baptisms*   *e* 6 Or *age,* [6] *if they fall*   *f* 14 Gen. 22:17

FRIDAY

HOPE—FROM THE CHRISTIAN'S PERSPECTIVE

Hebrews 6:1–20 *or* 6:18–20

Justo González

When speaking of "hope," it is necessary to clarify what is meant by that word. There are indeed different sorts of hope, and most of them are quite different from Christian hope. Sports fans hope that their team will win, but that hope is usually little more than a wish. Those who study for exams hope to obtain good grades. That hope may be a wish that is, however, based on facts as well as effort. But neither the hope of having one's team win, nor the hope of making a good grade, is certain. In contrast, when one speaks of Christian hope one does not mean that it is possible or even probable that something will take place, but rather that one is certain that it will be so. One often hears that the only two sure things in life are death and taxes. Christian hope is even surer than death itself—indeed, it overcomes death. That is why 1 Peter 1:3 calls this "[a living hope through the resurrection of Jesus Christ from the dead, and . . . an inheritance that can never perish, spoil or fade.]" That is to say, our hope is grounded on the actions and promises of the God who does not lie. In the same vein, Hebrews 6:19 says that "[we have this hope as an anchor for the soul, firm and secure. It enters the inner sanctuary behind the curtain.]"

ARTHUR W. PINK {AD 1885–1952}

At first sight it may appear strange, especially to unbelievers, that Christians should speak of their hope. In contrast to the wicked, who have "no peace" (Isaiah 48:22), the saint has a satisfying portion. The believer has already drunk of that "living water" of which those who drink shall "never thirst." The believer is already in possession of "eternal life," but has not yet entered into the full and unhindered enjoyment of it—that is still before them as the object of their hope. In one sense then, Christians are satisfied; in another sense, they are not. Believers already know One—indeed, are indwelt by One—who can satisfy them. They know Christ, possess Christ, enjoy Christ; but, as yet, have not seen Christ. It is by faith (not feelings) that we know and enjoy Christ, but the more we know and enjoy him in this way, the more we long to look upon him.

reflection

1. What has God promised for the future?

2. Why can you hope confidently in God?

3. How does a Christian's hope for the future give him or her encouragement in the present?

For your next devotional reading, go to page 1396.

patriarch Abraham gave him a tenth of the plunder! ⁵Now the law requires the descendants of Levi who become priests to collect a tenth from the people—that is, from their kindred—even though their kindred are descended from Abraham. ⁶This man, however, did not trace his descent from Levi, yet he collected a tenth from Abraham and blessed him who had the promises. ⁷And without doubt the lesser is blessed by the greater. ⁸In the one case, the tenth is collected by those who die; but in the other case, by him who is declared to be living. ⁹One might even say that Levi, who collects the tenth, paid the tenth through Abraham, ¹⁰because when Melchizedek met Abraham, Levi was still in the body of his ancestor.

Jesus Like Melchizedek

¹¹If perfection could have been attained through the Levitical priesthood—and indeed the law given to the people established that priesthood—why was there still need for another priest to come, one in the order of Melchizedek, not in the order of Aaron? ¹²For when the priesthood is changed, the law must be changed also. ¹³He of whom these things are said belonged to a different tribe, and no one from that tribe has ever served at the altar. ¹⁴For it is clear that our Lord descended from Judah, and in regard to that tribe Moses said nothing about priests. ¹⁵And what we have said is even more clear if another priest like Melchizedek appears, ¹⁶one who has become a priest not on the basis of a regulation as to his ancestry but on the basis of the power of an indestructible life. ¹⁷For it is declared:

"You are a priest forever,
    in the order of Melchizedek." ᵃ

¹⁸The former regulation is set aside because it was weak and useless ¹⁹(for the law made nothing perfect), and a better hope is introduced, by which we draw near to God.

²⁰And it was not without an oath! Others became priests without any oath, ²¹but he became a priest with an oath when God said to him:

"The Lord has sworn
    and will not change his mind:
    'You are a priest forever.' " ᵃ

²²Because of this oath, Jesus has become the guarantor of a better covenant.

²³Now there have been many of those priests, since death prevented them from continuing in office; ²⁴but because Jesus lives forever, he has a permanent priesthood. ²⁵Therefore he is able to save completelyᵇ those who come to God through him, because he always lives to intercede for them.

²⁶Such a high priest truly meets our need—one who is holy, blameless, pure, set apart from sinners, exalted above the heavens. ²⁷Unlike the other high priests, he does not need to offer sacrifices day after day, first for his own sins, and then for the sins of the people. He sacrificed for their sins once for all when he offered himself. ²⁸For the law appoints as high priests men in all their weakness; but the oath, which came after the law, appointed the Son, who has been made perfect forever.

The High Priest of a New Covenant

8 Now the main point of what we are saying is this: We do have such a high priest, who sat down at the right hand of the throne of the Majesty in heaven, ²and who serves in the sanctuary, the true tabernacle set up by the Lord, not by a mere human being.

³Every high priest is appointed to offer both gifts and sacrifices, and so it was necessary for this one also to have something to offer. ⁴If he were on earth, he would not be a priest, for there are already priests who offer the gifts prescribed by the law. ⁵They serve at a sanctuary that is a copy and shadow of what is in heaven. This is why Moses was warned when he was about to build the tabernacle: "See to it that you make everything according to the pattern shown you on the mountain."ᶜ ⁶But in fact the ministry Jesus has received is as superior to theirs as the covenant of which he is mediator is superior to the old one, since the new covenant is established on better promises.

⁷For if there had been nothing wrong with that first covenant, no place would have been sought for another. ⁸But God found fault with the people and saidᵈ:

"The days are coming, declares the Lord,
    when I will make a new covenant

ᵃ 17,21 Psalm 110:4   ᵇ 25 Or *forever*   ᶜ 5 Exodus 25:40   ᵈ 8 Some manuscripts may be translated *fault and said to the people.*

The Priesthood

Hebrews 7:23–25

read/meditate

Read through the description of Jesus in Hebrews 7:23–25. Review what you know about the role priests are supposed to fill. Old Testament priests were the go-between for people to reach out to God. Jesus, in one swoop, became that go-between and did away with the human priesthood at the same time—since he was God himself.

What does it mean to you that Jesus would be speaking on your behalf to God?

pray

The result of Jesus' priesthood is that you can approach God yourself without going through another person. Take time to thank God for that familiarity. Share your needs and concerns with him; then sit before him in quiet worship.

contemplate

Contemplate the access you have to God because of the work of Christ. How will this relationship affect your life today?

additional reflection

We human beings mess it up, over and over again, but God comes into our lives to help us overcome our stiff-neckedness. Indeed, God so loved the world that he sent his only-begotten Son to live with us and teach us how to be the fully human creatures our Maker has always planned for us to be.

—Madeleine L'Engle

Jesus Christ is not only the Son of God mighty to save, but the Son of Man able to feel.

—J. C. Ryle

For your next devotional reading, go to page 1398.

with the house of Israel
    and with the house of Judah.
⁹ It will not be like the covenant
    I made with their ancestors
when I took them by the hand
    to lead them out of Egypt,
because they did not remain faithful to
    my covenant,
    and I turned away from them,
                declares the Lord.
¹⁰ This is the covenant I will establish with
        the house of Israel
    after that time, declares the Lord.
I will put my laws in their minds
    and write them on their hearts.
I will be their God,
    and they will be my people.
¹¹ No longer will they teach their
        neighbors,
    or say to one another, 'Know the
        Lord,'
because they will all know me,
    from the least of them to the greatest.
¹² For I will forgive their wickedness
    and will remember their sins no
        more."ᵃ

¹³ By calling this covenant "new," he has made the first one obsolete; and what is obsolete and outdated will soon disappear.

Worship in the Earthly Tabernacle

9 Now the first covenant had regulations for worship and also an earthly sanctuary. ²A tabernacle was set up. In its first room were the lampstand and the table with its consecrated bread; this was called the Holy Place. ³Behind the second curtain was a room called the Most Holy Place, ⁴which had the golden altar of incense and the gold-covered ark of the covenant. This ark contained the gold jar of manna, Aaron's staff that had budded, and the stone tablets of the covenant. ⁵Above the ark were the cherubim of the Glory, overshadowing the atonement cover. But we cannot discuss these things in detail now.

⁶When everything had been arranged like this, the priests entered regularly into the outer room to carry on their ministry. ⁷But only the high priest entered the inner room, and that only once a year, and never without blood, which he offered for himself and for the sins the people had committed in ignorance. ⁸The Holy Spirit was showing by this that the way into the Most Holy Place had not yet been disclosed as long as the first tabernacle was still functioning. ⁹This is an illustration for the present time, indicating that the gifts and sacrifices being offered were not able to clear the conscience of the worshiper. ¹⁰They are only a matter of food and drink and various ceremonial washings—external regulations applying until the time of the new order.

The Blood of Christ

¹¹But when Christ came as high priest of the good things that are now already here,ᵇ he went through the greater and more perfect tabernacle that is not made with human hands, that is to say, is not a part of this creation. ¹²He did not enter by means of the blood of goats and calves; but he entered the Most Holy Place once for all by his own blood, thus obtainingᶜ eternal redemption. ¹³The blood of goats and bulls and the ashes of a heifer sprinkled on those who are ceremonially unclean sanctify them so that they are outwardly clean. ¹⁴How much more, then, will the blood of Christ, who through the eternal Spirit offered himself unblemished to God, cleanse our consciences from acts that lead to death,ᵈ so that we may serve the living God!

¹⁵For this reason Christ is the mediator of a new covenant, that those who are called may receive the promised eternal inheritance—now that he has died as a ransom to set them free from the sins committed under the first covenant.

¹⁶In the case of a will,ᵉ it is necessary to prove the death of the one who made it, ¹⁷because a will is in force only when somebody has died; it never takes effect while the one who made it is living. ¹⁸This is why even the first covenant was not put into effect without blood. ¹⁹When Moses had proclaimed every command of the law to all the people, he took the blood of calves, together with water, scarlet wool and branches of hyssop, and sprinkled the scroll and all the people. ²⁰He said, "This is the blood of the covenant, which God has commanded you to keep."ᶠ ²¹In the same way, he sprinkled

---

ᵃ 12 Jer. 31:31-34   ᵇ 11 Some early manuscripts *are to come*   ᶜ 12 Or *blood, having obtained*
ᵈ 14 Or *from useless rituals*   ᵉ 16 Same Greek word as *covenant*; also in verse 17   ᶠ 20 Exodus 24:8

MONDAY

DUTY OR DESIRE?

Hebrews 8:1–13 or 8:10–11

HANNAH WHITALL SMITH {ca. AD 1832–1911}

There is, perhaps, no part of Christian experience where a greater change occurs, upon entering into this life hid with Christ in God, than in the matter of service . . .

The soul finds itself saying, instead of the "May I?" of love, the "Must I?" of duty. The yoke, which was at first easy, begins to gall, and the burden feels heavy instead of light . . .

What we need in the Christian life is to get believers to want to do God's will as much as other people want to do their own will. And this is the idea of the gospel. It is what God intended for us; and it is what He promised. In describing the new covenant in Hebrews 8:6–13 . . . "I will put my laws," He says, "[in] their minds, and write them on their hearts." This can mean nothing but that we shall *love* His law; for anything written in our hearts we must love . . .

God's way of working, therefore, is to get possession of the inside of us, to take the control and management of our will, and to work it for us. Then obedience is easy and a delight, and service becomes perfect freedom, until the Christian is forced to explain, "This happy service! Who could dream earth had such liberty?"

What you need to do, then, dear Christian, if you are in bondage in the matter of service, is to put your will over completely into the hands of your Lord, surrendering to Him the entire control of it. Say, "Yes, Lord, YES!" . . . "Thy will be done; *Thy will be done!*"

Matthew Paul Turner

I have learned that selfless behavior takes practice. You have to actively work at being selfless. It's a mindset you must give into on a daily basis. And it's not a mindset obtained overnight. It's a gradual change. It's not easy, but if you start making selfless choices in all areas of your life, you'll begin to learn the value of selflessness.

— *reflection* —

1. What's the difference between doing something strictly out of duty and doing it from the heart?

2. Why is that an important distinction?

3. How would you counsel a person to move from the "Must I" of duty to the "May I" of love?

For your next devotional reading, go to page 1400.

with the blood both the tabernacle and everything used in its ceremonies. 22In fact, the law requires that nearly everything be cleansed with blood, and without the shedding of blood there is no forgiveness.

23It was necessary, then, for the copies of the heavenly things to be purified with these sacrifices, but the heavenly things themselves with better sacrifices than these. 24For Christ did not enter a sanctuary made with human hands that was only a copy of the true one; he entered heaven itself, now to appear for us in God's presence. 25Nor did he enter heaven to offer himself again and again, the way the high priest enters the Most Holy Place every year with blood that is not his own. 26Otherwise Christ would have had to suffer many times since the creation of the world. But he has appeared once for all at the culmination of the ages to do away with sin by the sacrifice of himself. 27Just as people are destined to die once, and after that to face judgment, 28so Christ was sacrificed once to take away the sins of many; and he will appear a second time, not to bear sin, but to bring salvation to those who are waiting for him.

Christ's Sacrifice Once for All

10 The law is only a shadow of the good things that are coming— not the realities themselves. For this reason it can never, by the same sacrifices repeated endlessly year after year, make perfect those who draw near to worship. 2Otherwise, would they not have stopped being offered? For the worshipers would have been cleansed once for all, and would no longer have felt guilty for their sins. 3But those sacrifices are an annual reminder of sins. 4It is impossible for the blood of bulls and goats to take away sins.

5Therefore, when Christ came into the world, he said:

"Sacrifice and offering you did not
    desire,
    but a body you prepared for me;
6with burnt offerings and sin offerings
    you were not pleased.
7Then I said, 'Here I am—it is written
    about me in the scroll—
    I have come to do your will, my
    God.' "a

8First he said, "Sacrifices and offerings, burnt offerings and sin offerings you did not desire, nor were you pleased with them"— though they were offered in accordance with the law. 9Then he said, "Here I am, I have come to do your will." He sets aside the first to establish the second. 10And by that will, we have been made holy through the sacrifice of the body of Jesus Christ once for all.

11Day after day every priest stands and performs his religious duties; again and again he offers the same sacrifices, which can never take away sins. 12But when this priest had offered for all time one sacrifice for sins, he sat down at the right hand of God, 13and since that time he waits for his enemies to be made his footstool. 14For by one sacrifice he has made perfect forever those who are being made holy.

15The Holy Spirit also testifies to us about this. First he says:

16"This is the covenant I will make with
    them
    after that time, says the Lord.
I will put my laws in their hearts,
    and I will write them on their
    minds."b

17Then he adds:

"Their sins and lawless acts
    I will remember no more."c

18And where these have been forgiven, sacrifice for sin is no longer necessary.

A Call to Persevere in Faith

19Therefore, brothers and sisters, since we have confidence to enter the Most Holy Place by the blood of Jesus, 20by a new and living way opened for us through the curtain, that is, his body, 21and since we have a great priest over the house of God, 22let us draw near to God with a sincere heart in full assurance of faith, having our hearts sprinkled to cleanse us from a guilty conscience and having our bodies washed with pure water. 23Let us hold unswervingly to the hope we profess, for he who promised is faithful. 24And let us consider how we may spur one another on toward love and good deeds, 25not giving up meeting together, as some are in the habit of doing, but encouraging one another—and all the more as you see the Day approaching.

a 7 Psalm 40:6-8 (see Septuagint)   b 16 Jer. 31:33   c 17 Jer. 31:34

TUESDAY

MARVEL IN THE MYSTERY
OF THE CROSS

Hebrews 9:1–28 *or* 9:14–15

JOHN OF DAMASCUS {ca. AD 675–749}

Every action and miracle performed by Christ is great and divine and marvelous. But the most marvelous of all is his precious cross. For no other thing—save the cross of our Lord Jesus Christ—has subdued death, atoned for the sin brought on by Adam, plundered Hades, bestowed the resurrection, granted the power to us of condemning the present and even death itself, prepared the return to our former blessedness, opened the gates of paradise, given our nature a seat at the right hand of God, and made us the children and heirs of God. For by the cross all things have been made right . . . The death of Christ, that is, the cross, clothed us with the wisdom and power of God. The power of God is the word of the cross. God's might (that is, the victory over death) has been revealed to us by the cross.

Ravi Zacharias

The heart of the gospel is the cross of Jesus Christ. The cross stands as a mystery because it is foreign to everything we exalt—self over principle, power over meekness, the quick fix over the long haul, cover-up over confession, escapism over confrontation, comfort over sacrifice, feeling over commitment, legality over justice, man over God. In the cross alone pain and evil meet, and in the cross alone love and justice are found. Upon both love and justice we find our moral and spiritual home. If only one of these two is focused upon, an inevitable perversion follows. The ideals of liberty, equality and justice taken in a vacuum have led to ideologies with dastardly experiments left in their wake. And love unbounded by any sense of justice demands commitment without accountability. In the cross of Jesus Christ, the restraint of justice was met and the generosity of love was expressed.

reflection

1. According to the author of Hebrews, what did Christ accomplish through the shedding of his blood on the cross?

2. How does today's reading deepen your gratitude to God for Jesus' death on the cross?

3. How have you experienced the power of the cross in your own life?

For your next devotional reading, go to page 1402.

²⁶If we deliberately keep on sinning after we have received the knowledge of the truth, no sacrifice for sins is left, ²⁷but only a fearful expectation of judgment and of raging fire that will consume the enemies of God. ²⁸Anyone who rejected the law of Moses died without mercy on the testimony of two or three witnesses. ²⁹How much more severely do you think those deserve to be punished who have trampled the Son of God underfoot, who have treated as an unholy thing the blood of the covenant that sanctified them, and who have insulted the Spirit of grace? ³⁰For we know him who said, "It is mine to avenge; I will repay,"ᵃ and again, "The Lord will judge his people."ᵇ ³¹It is a dreadful thing to fall into the hands of the living God.

³²Remember those earlier days after you had received the light, when you endured in a great conflict full of suffering. ³³Sometimes you were publicly exposed to insult and persecution; at other times you stood side by side with those who were so treated. ³⁴You suffered along with those in prison and joyfully accepted the confiscation of your property, because you knew that you yourselves had better and lasting possessions. ³⁵So do not throw away your confidence; it will be richly rewarded.

³⁶You need to persevere so that when you have done the will of God, you will receive what he has promised. ³⁷For,

"In just a little while,
　　he who is coming will come
　　and will not delay."ᶜ

³⁸And,

"But my righteous oneᵈ will live by faith.
　　And I take no pleasure
　　in the one who shrinks back."ᵉ

³⁹But we are not of those who shrink back and are destroyed, but of those who believe and are saved.

Faith in Action

11 Now faith is being sure of what we hope for and certain of what we do not see. ²This is what the ancients were commended for.

³By faith we understand that the universe was formed at God's command, so that what is seen was not made out of what was visible.

⁴By faith Abel brought God a better offering than Cain did. By faith he was commended as righteous, when God spoke well of his offerings. And by faith Abel still speaks, even though he is dead.

⁵By faith Enoch was taken from this life, so that he did not experience death: "He could not be found, because God had taken him away."ᶠ For before he was taken, he was commended as one who pleased God. ⁶And without faith it is impossible to please God, because anyone who comes to him must believe that he exists and that he rewards those who earnestly seek him.

⁷By faith Noah, when warned about things not yet seen, in holy fear built an ark to save his family. By his faith he condemned the world and became heir of the righteousness that is in keeping with faith.

⁸By faith Abraham, when called to go to a place he would later receive as his inheritance, obeyed and went, even though he did not know where he was going. ⁹By faith he made his home in the promised land like a stranger in a foreign country; he lived in tents, as did Isaac and Jacob, who were heirs with him of the same promise. ¹⁰For he was looking forward to the city with foundations, whose architect and builder is God. ¹¹And by faith even Sarah, who was past childbearing age, was enabled to bear children because sheᵍ considered him faithful who had made the promise. ¹²And so from this one man, and he as good as dead, came descendants as numerous as the stars in the sky and as countless as the sand on the seashore.

¹³All these people were still living by faith when they died. They did not receive the things promised; they only saw them and welcomed them from a distance, admitting that they were foreigners and strangers on earth. ¹⁴People who say such things show that they are looking for a country of their own. ¹⁵If they had been thinking of the country they had left, they would have had opportunity to return. ¹⁶Instead, they were longing for a better country—a heavenly one. Therefore God is not ashamed to be

---

ᵃ 30 Deut. 32:35　ᵇ 30 Deut. 32:36; Psalm 135:14　ᶜ 37 Isaiah 26:20; Hab. 2:3　ᵈ 38 One early manuscript But the righteous　ᵉ 38 Hab. 2:4 (see Septuagint)　ᶠ 5 Gen. 5:24　ᵍ 11 Or By faith Abraham, even though he was too old to have children—and Sarah herself was not able to conceive—was enabled to become a father because he

WEDNESDAY

FULLY DEVOTED TO EACH OTHER
Hebrews 10:1–39 *or* 10:19–25

John Ortberg

Just as we must pursue the stillness of solitude, we must seek the fellowship and accountability of community if we want to fully experience and express spiritual life. So we commit ourselves to coming together and submitting to the teaching of the Word. We also gather to worship God. We do this simply because God is worthy of our praise. In addition, God, in his grace, has decreed that in worship we are often encouraged and transformed in ways we could not be apart from this practice. In these corporate practices we root out self-absorption. We are reminded that we need and are a part of each other, that our life is about something bigger than just ourself.

SAINT THOMAS AQUINAS {AD 1225–1274}

If we speak of the happiness of this life, we must point out that the happy person needs friends. And as one philosopher says, they do not need friends for the purpose of making use of those friends, since God himself is sufficient to provide all that we need. Nor is it for the purpose of delighting in them, since a person possesses perfect delight in the operation of virtue. Rather the happy person needs friends in order to do good to them, and to delight in seeing them do good, and to be helped by them in his good work. For in order for someone to do well—whether in the practical works of their physical life or in the private actions of their spiritual life—they need the fellowship of friends.

Now, if we speak of that perfect happiness that will be ours in heaven, the fellowship of friends is not essential, for humans will find the entire fullness of their perfection in God. But the fellowship of friends leads to the well-being of happiness. For this reason, Augustine says, "Spiritual creatures receive no other interior aid to happiness than the eternity, truth and charity of the Creator. But if they can be said to be helped from without, perhaps it is only by this: that they see one another and rejoice in God because of their fellowship."

reflection

1. On a scale of one to ten (with ten being "very committed" and one being "rarely showing up to church"), how would you rate your level of commitment to a local church?

2. If you don't consider yourself "very committed," why not? What keeps you from becoming more committed?

3. Why are genuine, deep relationships with a community of believers so important for a follower of Christ?

For your next devotional reading, go to page 1404.

called their God, for he has prepared a city for them.

¹⁷By faith Abraham, when God tested him, offered Isaac as a sacrifice. He who had embraced the promises was about to sacrifice his one and only son, ¹⁸even though God had said to him, "It is through Isaac that your offspring will be reckoned."ᵃ ¹⁹Abraham reasoned that God could even raise the dead, and so in a manner of speaking he did receive Isaac back from death.

²⁰By faith Isaac blessed Jacob and Esau in regard to their future.

²¹By faith Jacob, when he was dying, blessed each of Joseph's sons, and worshiped as he leaned on the top of his staff.

²²By faith Joseph, when his end was near, spoke about the exodus of the Israelites from Egypt and gave instructions concerning the burial of his bones.

²³By faith Moses' parents hid him for three months after he was born, because they saw he was no ordinary child, and they were not afraid of the king's edict.

²⁴By faith Moses, when he had grown up, refused to be known as the son of Pharaoh's daughter. ²⁵He chose to be mistreated along with the people of God rather than to enjoy the fleeting pleasures of sin. ²⁶He regarded disgrace for the sake of Christ as of greater value than the treasures of Egypt, because he was looking ahead to his reward. ²⁷By faith he left Egypt, not fearing the king's anger; he persevered because he saw him who is invisible. ²⁸By faith he kept the Passover and the application of blood, so that the destroyer of the firstborn would not touch the firstborn of Israel.

²⁹By faith the people passed through the Red Sea as on dry land; but when the Egyptians tried to do so, they were drowned.

³⁰By faith the walls of Jericho fell, after the army had marched around them for seven days.

³¹By faith the prostitute Rahab, because she welcomed the spies, was not killed with those who were disobedient.ᵇ

³²And what more shall I say? I do not have time to tell about Gideon, Barak, Samson and Jephthah, about David and Samuel and the prophets, ³³who through faith conquered kingdoms, administered justice, and

gained what was promised; who shut the mouths of lions, ³⁴quenched the fury of the flames, and escaped the edge of the sword; whose weakness was turned to strength; and who became powerful in battle and routed foreign armies. ³⁵Women received back their dead, raised to life again. There were others who were tortured, refusing to be released so that they might gain an even better resurrection. ³⁶Some faced jeers and flogging, and even chains and imprisonment. ³⁷They were put to death by stoning;ᶜ they were sawed in two; they were killed by the sword. They went about in sheepskins and goatskins, destitute, persecuted and mistreated— ³⁸the world was not worthy of them. They wandered in deserts and mountains, and in caves and holes in the ground.

³⁹These were all commended for their faith, yet none of them received what had been promised. ⁴⁰God had planned something better for us so that only together with us would they be made perfect.

12 Therefore, since we are surrounded by such a great cloud of witnesses, let us throw off everything that hinders and the sin that so easily entangles. And let us run with perseverance the race marked out for us, ²fixing our eyes on Jesus, the pioneer and perfecter of faith. For the joy set before him he endured the cross, scorning its shame, and sat down at the right hand of the throne of God. ³Consider him who endured such opposition from sinners, so that you will not grow weary and lose heart.

God Disciplines His Children

⁴In your struggle against sin, you have not yet resisted to the point of shedding your blood. ⁵And have you completely forgotten this word of encouragement that addresses you as children? It says,

> "My son, do not make light of the Lord's discipline,
>   and do not lose heart when he rebukes you,
> ⁶because the Lord disciplines those he loves,
>   and he chastens everyone he accepts as his child."ᵈ

ᵃ 18 Gen. 21:12   ᵇ 31 Or *unbelieving*   ᶜ 37 Some early manuscripts *stoning; they were put to the test;*
ᵈ 5,6 Prov. 3:11,12 (see Septuagint)

BEYOND ARMCHAIR THEOLOGY

Hebrews 12:1–13 *or* 12:1–3

Carolyn Custis James

Most of us are better theologians in hindsight. We look at the struggles we have weathered and survived and testify warmly of God's goodness and faithfulness to us. But when a new crisis hits or we weary of the steady dripping of little problems and stresses, our theology collapses like a house of cards and we're faced with the task of reassembling it all over again. Yes, God *was* good, he *was* faithful, he *was* in control, he *did* show his love to me back then. But here and now? Somehow yesterday's theology doesn't look quite so glorious or reliable in the bleak light of today's circumstances.

Fixing our eyes on Jesus is just the sort of down-to-earth advice we need to move our theology into the present. Rather than despairing of God's goodness until we see fresh evidence, fixing our eyes on Jesus helps us head into the current situation *banking* on his goodness. And the fact that this exhortation to "fix our eyes on Jesus" comes up in the middle of a race should tip us off that the benefits of a woman's theology are not restricted to the war zone. Knowing God has enormous peacetime value, too. We need theology every day, whether we're carting our children to piano lessons and soccer practice, cooking a meal, listening to a friend or shaping business strategy in the corporate boardroom.

C. S. LEWIS {AD 1898–1963}

Look for yourself and you will find in the long run only hatred, loneliness, despair, rage, ruin and decay. But look for Christ and you will find Him, and with Him everything else thrown in.

reflection

1. When you "fix your eyes" on Jesus, what do you see?
2. Who is Jesus to you?
3. Is your theology affected by your circumstances? How?

For your next devotional reading, go to page 1408.

[7]Endure hardship as discipline; God is treating you as his children. For what children are not disciplined by their father? [8]If you are not disciplined—and everyone undergoes discipline—then you are not legitimate children at all. [9]Moreover, we have all had parents who disciplined us and we respected them for it. How much more should we submit to the Father of spirits and live! [10]Our parents disciplined us for a little while as they thought best; but God disciplines us for our good, that we may share in his holiness. [11]No discipline seems pleasant at the time, but painful. Later on, however, it produces a harvest of righteousness and peace for those who have been trained by it.

[12]Therefore, strengthen your feeble arms and weak knees. [13]"Make level paths for your feet,"[a] so that the lame may not be disabled, but rather healed.

Warning and Encouragement

[14]Make every effort to live in peace with everyone and to be holy; without holiness no one will see the Lord. [15]See to it that no one falls short of the grace of God and that no bitter root grows up to cause trouble and defile many. [16]See that no one is sexually immoral, or is godless like Esau, who for a single meal sold his inheritance rights as the oldest son. [17]Afterward, as you know, when he wanted to inherit this blessing, he was rejected. Even though he sought the blessing with tears, he could not change what he had done.

The Mountain of Fear and the Mountain of Joy

[18]You have not come to a mountain that can be touched and that is burning with fire; to darkness, gloom and storm; [19]to a trumpet blast or to such a voice speaking words that those who heard it begged that no further word be spoken to them, [20]because they could not bear what was commanded: "If even an animal touches the mountain, it must be stoned to death."[b] [21]The sight was so terrifying that Moses said, "I am trembling with fear."[c]

[22]But you have come to Mount Zion, to the city of the living God, the heavenly Jerusalem. You have come to thousands upon thousands of angels in joyful assembly, [23]to the church of the firstborn, whose names are written in heaven. You have come to God, the Judge of all, to the spirits of the righteous made perfect, [24]to Jesus the mediator of a new covenant, and to the sprinkled blood that speaks a better word than the blood of Abel.

[25]See to it that you do not refuse him who speaks. If they did not escape when they refused him who warned them on earth, how much less will we, if we turn away from him who warns us from heaven? [26]At that time his voice shook the earth, but now he has promised, "Once more I will shake not only the earth but also the heavens."[d] [27]The words "once more" indicate the removing of what can be shaken—that is, created things—so that what cannot be shaken may remain.

[28]Therefore, since we are receiving a kingdom that cannot be shaken, let us be thankful, and so worship God acceptably with reverence and awe, [29]for our "God is a consuming fire."[e]

Concluding Exhortations

13 Keep on loving one another as brothers and sisters. [2]Do not forget to show hospitality to strangers, for by so doing some people have shown hospitality to angels without knowing it. [3]Continue to remember those in prison as if you were together with them in prison, and those who are mistreated as if you yourselves were suffering.

[4]Marriage should be honored by all, and the marriage bed kept pure, for God will judge the adulterer and all the sexually immoral. [5]Keep your lives free from the love of money and be content with what you have, because God has said,

"Never will I leave you;
    never will I forsake you."[f]

[6]So we say with confidence,

"The Lord is my helper; I will not be
    afraid.
What can human beings do to me?"[g]

[7]Remember your leaders, who spoke the word of God to you. Consider the outcome

---

a 13 Prov. 4:26   b 20 Exodus 19:12,13   c 21 See Deut. 9:19.   d 26 Haggai 2:6   e 29 Deut. 4:24
f 5 Deut. 31:6   g 6 Psalm 118:6,7

of their way of life and imitate their faith. ⁸Jesus Christ is the same yesterday and today and forever.

⁹Do not be carried away by all kinds of strange teachings. It is good for our hearts to be strengthened by grace, not by the eating of ceremonial foods, which is of no benefit to those who observe such rituals. ¹⁰We have an altar from which those who minister at the tabernacle have no right to eat.

¹¹The high priest carries the blood of animals into the Most Holy Place as a sin offering, but the bodies are burned outside the camp. ¹²And so Jesus also suffered outside the city gate to make the people holy through his own blood. ¹³Let us, then, go to him outside the camp, bearing the disgrace he bore. ¹⁴For here we do not have an enduring city, but we are looking for the city that is to come.

¹⁵Through Jesus, therefore, let us continually offer to God a sacrifice of praise—the fruit of lips that openly profess his name. ¹⁶And do not forget to do good and to share with others, for with such sacrifices God is pleased.

¹⁷Have confidence in your leaders and submit to their authority, because they keep watch over you as those who must give an account. Do this so that their work will be a joy, not a burden, for that would be of no benefit to you.

¹⁸Pray for us. We are sure that we have a clear conscience and desire to live honorably in every way. ¹⁹I particularly urge you to pray so that I may be restored to you soon.

Benediction and Final Greetings

²⁰Now may the God of peace, who through the blood of the eternal covenant brought back from the dead our Lord Jesus, that great Shepherd of the sheep, ²¹equip you with everything good for doing his will, and may he work in us what is pleasing to him, through Jesus Christ, to whom be glory for ever and ever. Amen.

²²Brothers and sisters, I urge you to bear with my word of exhortation, for in fact I have written to you quite briefly.

²³I want you to know that our brother Timothy has been released. If he arrives soon, I will come with him to see you.

²⁴Greet all your leaders and all the Lord's people. Those from Italy send you their greetings.

²⁵Grace be with you all.

james

AUTHOR: James, the brother of Jesus

DATE: Probably around A.D. 49

THEME: Real faith in God requires real action.

James, a servant of God and of the Lord Jesus Christ,

To the twelve tribes scattered among the nations:

Greetings.

Trials and Temptations

²Consider it pure joy, my brothers and sisters, whenever you face trials of many kinds, ³because you know that the testing of your faith produces perseverance. ⁴Let perseverance finish its work so that you may be mature and complete, not lacking anything. ⁵If any of you lacks wisdom, you should ask God, who gives generously to all without finding fault, and it will be given to you. ⁶But when you ask, you must believe and not doubt, because the one who doubts is like a wave of the sea, blown and tossed by the wind. ⁷Those who doubt should not think they will receive anything from the Lord; ⁸they are double-minded and unstable in all they do.

⁹Believers in humble circumstances ought to take pride in their high position. ¹⁰But the rich should take pride in their humiliation—since they will pass away like a wild flower. ¹¹For the sun rises with scorching heat and withers the plant; its blossom falls and its beauty is destroyed. In the same way, the rich will fade away even while they go about their business.

¹²Blessed are those who persevere under trial, because when they have stood the test, they will receive the crown of life that God has promised to those who love him.

¹³When tempted, no one should say, "God is tempting me." For God cannot be tempted by evil, nor does he tempt anyone; ¹⁴but each of you is tempted when you are dragged away by your own evil desire and enticed. ¹⁵Then, after desire has conceived, it gives birth to sin; and sin, when it is full-grown, gives birth to death.

¹⁶Don't be deceived, my dear brothers and sisters. ¹⁷Every good and perfect gift is from above, coming down from the Father of the heavenly lights, who does not change like shifting shadows. ¹⁸He chose to give us birth through the word of truth, that we might be a kind of firstfruits of all he created.

Listening and Doing

¹⁹My dear brothers and sisters, take note of this: Everyone should be quick to listen, slow to speak and slow to become angry, ²⁰because our anger does not produce the righteousness that God desires. ²¹Therefore, get rid of all moral filth and the evil that is so prevalent and humbly accept the word planted in you, which can save you.

²²Do not merely listen to the word, and so deceive yourselves. Do what it says. ²³Those who listen to the word but do not do what it says are like people who look at their faces in a mirror ²⁴and, after looking at themselves, go away and immediately forget what they look like. ²⁵But those who look intently into the perfect law that gives freedom, and continue in it—not forgetting what they have heard, but doing it—they will be blessed in what they do.

²⁶Those who consider themselves religious and yet do not keep a tight rein on their tongues deceive themselves, and their religion is worthless. ²⁷Religion that God our Father accepts as pure and faultless is this: to look after orphans and widows in their distress and to keep oneself from being polluted by the world.

PROMPTED TO SERVE

James 1:1–27 *or* 1:26–27

Kurt Bruner

Our awkward compassion tells us something about God. It tells us why we turn our eyes away from pain, suffering and disability: These things steal from the "something more" for which we were made. We don't like that. But it also calls us to lay aside selfish pursuits long enough to bring comfort, healing and hope to those in need. It invites our participation in a process called redemption, replacing the "something wrong" we know with the "made right again" we want.

SADHU SUNDAR SINGH {AD 1889–1929}

The disciple asks, "Master, what is the real meaning of service? Is it that we serve the Creator, and then we serve his creatures for his sake? Is the help of people, who are after all totally insignificant, of any value to God in caring for his great family? Does God need anyone's help to protect or preserve any of his creatures?"

The master replies, "Service is the activity of the spiritual life and is the natural offering prompted by love. God, who is Love, is continually active in the care of his creation. And he desires his creatures—especially people, whom he formed in his own image and likeness—to never be idle in caring for others. However, in the care and preservation of his creatures God needs the help of none. For he created them in such a way that without *his* help they could not continue to exist. He is the one who has provided all that is required to satisfy their desires. In true service of others there is this great advantage that it helps the one who serves. Look, for example, to the story of a particular man in Tibet. When he feared he might eventually die on account of the bitter cold, he saw someone lying buried in the snow and at the point of death. He went to him and lifted him on to his shoulders, and carried him forward. These efforts produced heat in his body which also passed into the man he carried, and both of them were saved. In rescuing the dying man, the first man saved his own life. This is the true end of service."

reflection

1. Who are the "orphans and widows" in your world?

2. What do you think real compassion looks like?

3. What's one way that you feel God prompting you to serve someone who's in need of compassion today?

For your next devotional reading, go to page 1410.

Favoritism Forbidden

2 My brothers and sisters, believers in our glorious Lord Jesus Christ must not show favoritism. [2]Suppose someone comes into your meeting wearing a gold ring and fine clothes, and a poor person in filthy old clothes also comes in. [3]If you show special attention to the one wearing fine clothes and say, "Here's a good seat for you," but say to the one who is poor, "You stand there" or "Sit on the floor by my feet," [4]have you not discriminated among yourselves and become judges with evil thoughts?

[5]Listen, my dear brothers and sisters: Has not God chosen those who are poor in the eyes of the world to be rich in faith and to inherit the kingdom he promised those who love him? [6]But you have dishonored the poor. Is it not the rich who are exploiting you? Are they not the ones who are dragging you into court? [7]Are they not the ones who are blaspheming the noble name of him to whom you belong?

[8]If you really keep the royal law found in Scripture, "Love your neighbor as yourself,"[a] you are doing right. [9]But if you show favoritism, you sin and are convicted by the law as lawbreakers. [10]For whoever keeps the whole law and yet stumbles at just one point is guilty of breaking all of it. [11]For he who said, "You shall not commit adultery,"[b] also said, "You shall not murder."[c] If you do not commit adultery but do commit murder, you have become a lawbreaker.

[12]Speak and act as those who are going to be judged by the law that gives freedom, [13]because judgment without mercy will be shown to anyone who has not been merciful. Mercy triumphs over judgment.

Faith and Deeds

[14]What good is it, my brothers and sisters, if people claim to have faith but have no deeds? Can such faith save them? [15]Suppose a brother or sister is without clothes and daily food. [16]If one of you says to them, "Go in peace; keep warm and well fed," but does nothing about their physical needs, what good is it? [17]In the same way, faith by itself, if it is not accompanied by action, is dead.

[18]But someone will say, "You have faith; I have deeds."

Show me your faith without deeds, and I will show you my faith by what I do. [19]You believe that there is one God. Good! Even the demons believe that—and shudder.

[20]You foolish person, do you want evidence that faith without deeds is useless[d]? [21]Was not our father Abraham considered righteous for what he did when he offered his son Isaac on the altar? [22]You see that his faith and his actions were working together, and his faith was made complete by what he did. [23]And the scripture was fulfilled that says, "Abraham believed God, and it was credited to him as righteousness,"[e] and he was called God's friend. [24]You see that people are justified by what they do and not by faith alone.

[25]In the same way, was not even Rahab the prostitute considered righteous for what she did when she gave lodging to the spies and sent them off in a different direction? [26]As the body without the spirit is dead, so faith without deeds is dead.

Taming the Tongue

3 Not many of you should presume to be teachers, my brothers and sisters, because you know that we who teach will be judged more strictly. [2]We all stumble in many ways. Those who are never at fault in what they say are perfect, able to keep their whole body in check.

[3]When we put bits into the mouths of horses to make them obey us, we can turn the whole animal. [4]Or take ships as an example. Although they are so large and are driven by strong winds, they are steered by a very small rudder wherever the pilot wants to go. [5]Likewise, the tongue is a small part of the body, but it makes great boasts. Consider what a great forest is set on fire by a small spark. [6]The tongue also is a fire, a world of evil among the parts of the body. It corrupts the whole person, sets the whole course of one's life on fire, and is itself set on fire by hell.

[7]All kinds of animals, birds, reptiles and sea creatures are being tamed and have been tamed by human beings, [8]but no one can tame the tongue. It is a restless evil, full of deadly poison.

---

a 8 Lev. 19:18   *b 11* Exodus 20:14; Deut. 5:18   *c 11* Exodus 20:13; Deut. 5:17   *d 20* Some early manuscripts *dead*   *e 23* Gen. 15:6

Mercy Me!

James 2:8-9,12-13

read/meditate

Read James 2:8-9,12-13 in phrases. Read the first phrase several times, then think about it in silence for a few minutes before you go on to the next phrase, and so on. When you've worked through the entire passage, think for a few moments about God's mercy. How does it work itself out in your life?

pray

Ask God how much of his mercy you've shown to others. Ask him to bring to mind any areas of your life in which you have been unmerciful, even without realizing it. Then give him the time and silence to listen for an answer.

contemplate

This is not the only place in the Bible in which a connection is made between the mercy we give and the mercy we receive. Consider the story Jesus told in Matthew 18:23-35. How does this story speak to your life?

additional reflection

Forgiveness is not to bury the hatchet with the handle sticking out of the ground so you can grasp it the minute you want it.

— *D. L. Moody*

There is nothing, however annoying, that cannot easily be borne by those who love each other, and anything which causes annoyance must be quite exceptional.

— *Teresa of Avila*

For your next devotional reading, go to page 1412.

[9]With the tongue we praise our Lord and Father, and with it we curse human beings, who have been made in God's likeness. [10]Out of the same mouth come praise and cursing. My brothers and sisters, this should not be. [11]Can both fresh water and salt water flow from the same spring? [12]My brothers and sisters, can a fig tree bear olives, or a grapevine bear figs? Neither can a salt spring produce fresh water.

Two Kinds of Wisdom

[13]Who is wise and understanding among you? Let them show it by their good life, by deeds done in the humility that comes from wisdom. [14]But if you harbor bitter envy and selfish ambition in your hearts, do not boast about it or deny the truth. [15]Such "wisdom" does not come down from heaven but is earthly, unspiritual, demonic. [16]For where you have envy and selfish ambition, there you find disorder and every evil practice.

[17]But the wisdom that comes from heaven is first of all pure; then peace-loving, considerate, submissive, full of mercy and good fruit, impartial and sincere. [18]Peacemakers who sow in peace reap a harvest of righteousness.

Submit Yourselves to God

4 What causes fights and quarrels among you? Don't they come from your desires that battle within you? [2]You desire but do not have, so you kill. You covet but you cannot get what you want, so you quarrel and fight. You do not have because you do not ask God. [3]When you ask, you do not receive, because you ask with wrong motives, that you may spend what you get on your pleasures.

[4]You adulterous people, don't you know that friendship with the world means enmity against God? Anyone who chooses to be a friend of the world becomes an enemy of God. [5]Or do you think Scripture says without reason that he jealously longs for the spirit he has caused to dwell in us?[a] [6]But he gives us more grace. That is why Scripture says:

"God opposes the proud
  but shows favor to the humble and
    oppressed."[b]

[7]Submit yourselves, then, to God. Resist the devil, and he will flee from you. [8]Come near to God and he will come near to you. Wash your hands, you sinners, and purify your hearts, you double-minded. [9]Grieve, mourn and wail. Change your laughter to mourning and your joy to gloom. [10]Humble yourselves before the Lord, and he will lift you up.

[11]Brothers and sisters, do not slander one another. Anyone who speaks against a brother or sister or judges them speaks against the law and judges it. When you judge the law, you are not keeping it, but sitting in judgment on it. [12]There is only one Lawgiver and Judge, the one who is able to save and destroy. But you—who are you to judge your neighbor?

Boasting About Tomorrow

[13]Now listen, you who say, "Today or tomorrow we will go to this or that city, spend a year there, carry on business and make money." [14]Why, you do not even know what will happen tomorrow. What is your life? You are a mist that appears for a little while and then vanishes. [15]Instead, you ought to say, "If it is the Lord's will, we will live and do this or that." [16]As it is, you boast in your arrogant schemes. All such boasting is evil. [17]So then, if you know the good you ought to do and don't do it, you sin.

Warning to Rich Oppressors

5 Now listen, you rich people, weep and wail because of the misery that is coming on you. [2]Your wealth has rotted, and moths have eaten your clothes. [3]Your gold and silver are corroded. Their corrosion will testify against you and eat your flesh like fire. You have hoarded wealth in the last days. [4]Look! The wages you failed to pay the workers who mowed your fields are crying out against you. The cries of the harvesters have reached the ears of the Lord Almighty. [5]You have lived on earth in luxury and self-indulgence. You have fattened yourselves in the day of slaughter.[c] [6]You have condemned and murdered the innocent one, who was not opposing you.

Patience in Suffering

[7]Be patient, then, brothers and sisters, until the Lord's coming. See how the farmer

---

[a] 5 Or that the spirit he caused to dwell in us envies intensely; or that the Spirit he caused to dwell in us longs jealously   [b] 6 Prov. 3:34   [c] 5 Or yourselves as in a day of feasting

MONDAY

A SONG IN THE NIGHT

James 4:1–17 or 4:7–10

NATHANIEL WILLIAM TAYLOR {AD 1786–1858}

Do you ever experience sleepless nights, tossing and turning and simply waiting for the first glimmer of dawn? When that happens, why not ask the Holy Spirit to fix your thoughts on God, your Maker, and believe He can fill those lonely, dreary nights with song?

Is your night one of bereavement? Focusing on God often causes Him to draw near to your grieving heart, bringing you the assurance that He needs the one who has died. The Lord will assure you He has called the eager, enthusiastic spirit of your departed loved one to stand with the invisible yet liberated, living, and radiant multitude. And as this thought enters your mind, along with the knowledge that your loved one is engaged in a great heavenly mission, a song begins in your heart.

Is your night one of discouragement or failure, whether real or imagined? Do you feel as if no one understands you, and your friends have pushed you aside? Take heart: your Maker "will come near to you" (James 4:8) and give you a song—a song of hope, which will be harmonious with the strong, resonant music of His providence. Be ready to sing the song your Maker imparts to you . . .

The strength of a ship is only fully demonstrated when it faces a hurricane, and the power of the gospel can only be fully exhibited when a Christian is subjected to some fiery trial. We must understand that for God to give "songs in the night," He must first make it night.

Carol L. Fitzpatrick

If Christ Himself suffered, then why should we be immune from all maladies?

Occasionally a time of mourning enters our lives, sometimes stealing in almost silently, sometimes brashly breaking down the door to our well-constructed sense of security. Neither path reflects nor distorts the fact that God loves us. But tragedy and mourning are both part of the ebb and flow or "rhythm of life."

Prayer: Lord, through my veil of tears help me to view Your rescuing hand, that I might reach out to grasp You more firmly.

reflection

1. When do you feel the most alone?

2. How do you handle the difficult times that you face?

3. How do painful times cause people to come near to God?

For your next devotional reading, go to page 1416.

waits for the land to yield its valuable crop, patiently waiting for the autumn and spring rains. [8]You too, be patient and stand firm, because the Lord's coming is near. [9]Don't grumble against one another, brothers and sisters, or you will be judged. The Judge is standing at the door!

[10]Brothers and sisters, as an example of patience in the face of suffering, take the prophets who spoke in the name of the Lord. [11]As you know, we count as blessed those who have persevered. You have heard of Job's perseverance and have seen what the Lord finally brought about. The Lord is full of compassion and mercy.

[12]Above all, my brothers and sisters, do not swear—not by heaven or by earth or by anything else. All you need to say is a simple "Yes" or "No." Otherwise you will be condemned.

The Prayer of Faith

[13]Is anyone among you in trouble? Let them pray. Is anyone happy? Let them sing songs of praise. [14]Is anyone among you sick? Let them call the elders of the church to pray over them and anoint them with oil in the name of the Lord. [15]And the prayer offered in faith will make them well; the Lord will raise them up. If they have sinned, they will be forgiven. [16]Therefore confess your sins to each other and pray for each other so that you may be healed. The prayer of a righteous person is powerful and effective.

[17]Elijah was a human being, even as we are. He prayed earnestly that it would not rain, and it did not rain on the land for three and a half years. [18]Again he prayed, and the heavens gave rain, and the earth produced its crops.

[19]My brothers and sisters, if one of you should wander from the truth and someone should bring them back, [20]remember this: Whoever turns a sinner from the way of error will save them from death and cover over a multitude of sins.

1 peter

AUTHOR: Peter, the apostle

DATE: Around A.D. 62–64

THEME: The life God offers us will involve pain, but we will still have great joy.

1 Peter, an apostle of Jesus Christ,

To God's elect, exiles scattered throughout the provinces of Pontus, Galatia, Cappadocia, Asia and Bithynia, ²who have been chosen according to the foreknowledge of God the Father, through the sanctifying work of the Spirit, to be obedient to Jesus Christ and sprinkled with his blood:

Grace and peace be yours in abundance.

Praise to God for a Living Hope

³Praise be to the God and Father of our Lord Jesus Christ! In his great mercy he has given us new birth into a living hope through the resurrection of Jesus Christ from the dead, ⁴and into an inheritance that can never perish, spoil or fade. This inheritance is kept in heaven for you, ⁵who through faith are shielded by God's power until the coming of the salvation that is ready to be revealed in the last time. ⁶In all this you greatly rejoice, though now for a little while you may have had to suffer grief in all kinds of trials. ⁷These have come so that your faith—of greater worth than gold, which perishes even though refined by fire—may be proved genuine and may result in praise, glory and honor when Jesus Christ is revealed. ⁸Though you have not seen him, you love him; and even though you do not see him now, you believe in him and are filled with an inexpressible and glorious joy, ⁹for you are receiving the end result of your faith, the salvation of your souls.

¹⁰Concerning this salvation, the prophets, who spoke of the grace that was to come to you, searched intently and with the greatest care, ¹¹trying to find out the time and circumstances to which the Spirit of Christ in them was pointing when he predicted the sufferings of Christ and the glories that would follow. ¹²It was revealed to them that they were not serving themselves but you, when they spoke of the things that have now been told you by those who have preached the gospel to you by the Holy Spirit sent from heaven. Even angels long to look into these things.

Be Holy

¹³Therefore, with minds that are alert and fully sober, set your hope on the grace to be brought to you when Jesus Christ is revealed at his coming. ¹⁴As obedient children, do not conform to the evil desires you had when you lived in ignorance. ¹⁵But just as he who called you is holy, so be holy in all you do; ¹⁶for it is written: "Be holy, because I am holy."ᵃ

¹⁷Since you call on a Father who judges each person's work impartially, live out your time as foreigners here in reverent fear. ¹⁸For you know that it was not with perishable things such as silver or gold that you were redeemed from the empty way of life handed down to you from your ancestors, ¹⁹but with the precious blood of Christ, a lamb without blemish or defect. ²⁰He was chosen before the creation of the world, but was revealed in these last times for your sake. ²¹Through him you believe in God, who raised him from the dead and glorified him, and so your faith and hope are in God.

²²Now that you have purified yourselves by obeying the truth so that you have sin-

---

ᵃ 16 Lev. 11:44,45; 19:2

cere love for each other, love one another deeply, from the heart. *a* 23For you have been born again, not of perishable seed, but of imperishable, through the living and enduring word of God. 24For,

"All people are like grass,
  and all their glory is like the flowers
    of the field;
the grass withers and the flowers fall,
25 but the word of the Lord endures
    forever."*b*

And this is the word that was preached to you.

2 Therefore, rid yourselves of all malice and all deceit, hypocrisy, envy, and slander of every kind. 2Like newborn babies, crave pure spiritual milk, so that by it you may grow up in your salvation, 3now that you have tasted that the Lord is good.

The Living Stone and a Chosen People

4As you come to him, the living Stone—rejected by human beings but chosen by God and precious to him— 5you also, like living stones, are being built into a spiritual house*c* to be a holy priesthood, offering spiritual sacrifices acceptable to God through Jesus Christ. 6For in Scripture it says:

"See, I lay a stone in Zion,
  a chosen and precious cornerstone,
and the one who trusts in him
  will never be put to shame."*d*

7Now to you who believe, this stone is precious. But to those who do not believe,

"The stone the builders rejected
  has become the cornerstone,"*e*

8and,

"A stone that causes people to stumble
  and a rock that makes them fall."*f*

They stumble because they disobey the message—which is also what they were destined for.

9But you are a chosen people, a royal priesthood, a holy nation, God's special possession, that you may declare the praises of him who called you out of darkness into his wonderful light. 10Once you were not a people, but now you are the people of God; once

you had not received mercy, but now you have received mercy.

Living Godly Lives in a Pagan Society

11Dear friends, I urge you, as foreigners and exiles, to abstain from sinful desires, which war against your soul. 12Live such good lives among the pagans that, though they accuse you of doing wrong, they may see your good deeds and glorify God on the day he visits us.

13Submit yourselves for the Lord's sake to every human authority: whether to the emperor, as the supreme authority, 14or to governors, who are sent by him to punish those who do wrong and to commend those who do right. 15For it is God's will that by doing good you should silence the ignorant talk of the foolish. 16Live as free people, but do not use your freedom as a cover-up for evil; live as God's slaves. 17Show proper respect to everyone, love your fellow believers, fear God, honor the emperor.

18Slaves, in reverent fear of God submit yourselves to your masters, not only to those who are good and considerate, but also to those who are harsh. 19For it is commendable if you bear up under the pain of unjust suffering because you are conscious of God. 20But how is it to your credit if you receive a beating for doing wrong and endure it? But if you suffer for doing good and you endure it, this is commendable before God. 21To this you were called, because Christ suffered for you, leaving you an example, that you should follow in his steps.

22"He committed no sin,
  and no deceit was found in his
    mouth."*g*

23When they hurled their insults at him, he did not retaliate; when he suffered, he made no threats. Instead, he entrusted himself to him who judges justly. 24"He himself bore our sins" in his body on the cross, so that we might die to sins and live for righteousness; "by his wounds you have been healed." 25For "you were like sheep going astray,"*h* but now you have returned to the Shepherd and Overseer of your souls.

---

a 22 Some early manuscripts *from a pure heart*   *b 25* Isaiah 40:6-8 (see Septuagint)   *c 5* Or *into a temple of the Spirit*   *d 6* Isaiah 28:16   *e 7* Psalm 118:22   *f 8* Isaiah 8:14   *g 22* Isaiah 53:9   *h 24,25* Isaiah 53:4,5,6 (see Septuagint)

TUESDAY

CONTAGIOUS CHRISTIANITY

1 Peter 2:1–25 *or* 2:4–10

JOHN FLAVEL {AD 1630–1691}

Show the world Christ—as he really is—through your actions and your words.

Is he completely delightful? Let all the world see and know that he is so—by the way you delight in him, in the intimacy of your relationship with him, through your passion for him, and through your readiness to part with anything else you might enjoy besides him. Proclaim his superiority to the world . . . Persuade them how much your beloved is better than any other beloved. Reveal his glorious perfection as you speak of him. Proclaim him to others as he is in himself: perfectly beautiful. See that you "live a life worthy of the Lord and please him in every way" (Colossians 1:10). "Declare the praises" of Christ (1 Peter 2:9). Don't let anyone blaspheme the noble name of him to whom you belong (James 2:7). He is glorious in himself, and he is sure to place his glory upon you. So be careful not to bring shame and dishonor to him. He has committed his honor to you; do not betray that trust.

Never be ashamed to be counted as a Christian.

Bill Hybels

Deep in every true Christian, there is an awareness that we are on this planet for purposes greater than having a career, paying the bills, loving our families and fulfilling our role as upstanding citizens. Even going to church and worshiping God—important as these are—sometimes leave us feeling that something is missing. After all, we'll worship God for eternity in heaven; we don't have to be here to do that.

What is it that's absent in the lives of so many believers who are crying out for fulfillment? What on earth is God asking us to do?

God wants us to become contagious Christians—his agents, who will first catch his love and then urgently and infectiously offer it to all who are willing to consider it. This is his primary plan, the one Jesus modeled so powerfully, to spread God's grace and truth person to person until there's an epidemic of changed lives around the world.

reflection

1. Who do you know whose love for God is contagious?

2. How does that person's love affect you and your relationship to God?

3. The only way that the people you live and work and play with may see Christ is through *you*. So just what do they see?

For your next devotional reading, go to page 1418.

3 Wives, in the same way submit yourselves to your own husbands so that, if any of them do not believe the word, they may be won over without words by the behavior of their wives, ²when they see the purity and reverence of your lives. ³Your beauty should not come from outward adornment, such as elaborate hairstyles and the wearing of gold jewelry and fine clothes. ⁴Rather, it should be that of your inner self, the unfading beauty of a gentle and quiet spirit, which is of great worth in God's sight. ⁵For this is the way the holy women of the past who put their hope in God used to adorn themselves. They submitted themselves to their own husbands, ⁶like Sarah, who obeyed Abraham and called him her lord. You are her daughters if you do what is right and do not give way to fear.

⁷Husbands, in the same way be considerate as you live with your wives, and treat them with respect as the weaker partner and as heirs with you of the gracious gift of life, so that nothing will hinder your prayers.

Suffering for Doing Good

⁸Finally, all of you, be like-minded, be sympathetic, love one another, be compassionate and humble. ⁹Do not repay evil with evil or insult with insult. On the contrary, repay evil with blessing, because to this you were called so that you may inherit a blessing. ¹⁰For,

"Whoever among you would love life
    and see good days
must keep your tongue from evil
    and your lips from deceitful speech.
¹¹Turn from evil and do good;
    seek peace and pursue it.
¹²For the eyes of the Lord are on the
        righteous
    and his ears are attentive to their
        prayer,
but the face of the Lord is against those
    who do evil."ᵃ

¹³Who is going to harm you if you are eager to do good? ¹⁴But even if you should suffer for what is right, you are blessed. "Do not fear their threats; do not be frightened."ᵇ ¹⁵But in your hearts revere Christ as Lord. Always be prepared to give an answer to everyone who asks you to give the reason for the hope that you have. But do this with gentleness and respect, ¹⁶keeping a clear conscience, so that those who speak maliciously against your good behavior in Christ may be ashamed of their slander. ¹⁷It is better, if it is God's will, to suffer for doing good than for doing evil. ¹⁸For Christ also suffered once for sins, the righteous for the unrighteous, to bring you to God. He was put to death in the body but made alive in the Spirit. ¹⁹In that stateᶜ he went and made proclamation to the imprisoned spirits— ²⁰to those who were disobedient long ago when God waited patiently in the days of Noah while the ark was being built. In it only a few people, eight in all, were saved through water, ²¹and this water symbolizes baptism that now saves you also—not the removal of dirt from the body but the pledge of a clear conscience toward God.ᵈ It saves you by the resurrection of Jesus Christ, ²²who has gone into heaven and is at God's right hand— with angels, authorities and powers in submission to him.

Living for God

4 Therefore, since Christ suffered in his body, arm yourselves also with the same attitude, because those who have suffered in their bodies are done with sin. ²As a result, they do not live the rest of their earthly lives for evil human desires, but rather for the will of God. ³For you have spent enough time in the past doing what pagans choose to do—living in debauchery, lust, drunkenness, orgies, carousing and detestable idolatry. ⁴They are surprised that you do not join them in their reckless, wild living, and they heap abuse on you. ⁵But they will have to give account to him who is ready to judge the living and the dead. ⁶For this is the reason the gospel was preached even to those who are now dead, so that they might be judged according to human standards in regard to the body, but live according to God in regard to the spirit.

⁷The end of all things is near. Therefore be alert and of sober mind so that you may pray. ⁸Above all, love each other deeply, because love covers over a multitude of sins. ⁹Offer hospitality to one another without

---

ᵃ 12 Psalm 34:12-16   ᵇ 14 Isaiah 8:12   ᶜ 18,19 Or alive in the spirit, ¹⁹in which also   ᵈ 21 Or but an appeal to God for a clear conscience

WEDNESDAY

THE GRACE CONNECTION

1 Peter 4:1–19 *or* 4:8–11

Henry Cloud and John Townsend

By definition, grace is something we can't give ourselves. It comes from outside of us, as unmerited favor; we can't do anything to obtain grace. And, as we see in [1 Peter 4], part of the "outside" God uses to dispense his grace is other people. As people use their gifts, they are "[faithful stewards of] God's grace in its various forms" (1 Peter 4:10). God made us stewards over the administration of his grace.

Many ministers have heard their parishioners say, "I know in my head that God forgives me and accepts me, but I can't feel it in my heart." They have memorized verses on forgiveness, God's love and acceptance, their position of grace and all the related doctrines. They "know" the information in their heads, but they are far from "knowing" it in their hearts. They commonly think this "head" knowledge is somehow going to "sink in" to their hearts. This is not the way things work . . .

To experience God's grace, however, our hearts have to be connected to it. We can certainly connect to God "vertically" through prayer, but to feel his grace completely we have to open our hearts to the full expression of it "horizontally" through other people. To connect fully with the grace of God, we have to go to where it is, and he has chosen to put it into other people. So those who only study the "facts" of the grace of God and do not experience other people loving them, as Peter directs us, will fall short in their realization of that grace.

ANDREW MURRAY {AD 1828–1917}

The lack of love in the church keeps it from receiving God's blessings. When the body is divided, there cannot be strength. In the time of their great religious wars, when Holland stood out so nobly against Spain, one of their mottoes was: "Unity gives strength." It is only when God's people stand as one body, one before God in the fellowship of love, one toward another in deep affection, one before the world in a love that the world can see—it is only then that they will have power to secure the blessing which they ask of God . . . And if there is one thing we must pray for still, it is this: Lord, melt us together into one by the power of the Holy Spirit; let the Holy Spirit, who at Pentecost made them all of one heart and one soul, do his blessed work among us.

reflection

1. How have you personally experienced God's grace through others in the church?
2. How connected are you to other people in the body of believers?
3. What gifts has God given you to love others with?

For your next devotional reading, go to page 1422.

grumbling. ¹⁰Each of you should use whatever gift you have received to serve others, as faithful stewards of God's grace in its various forms. ¹¹If you speak, you should do so as one who speaks the very words of God. If you serve, you should do so with the strength God provides, so that in all things God may be praised through Jesus Christ. To him be the glory and the power for ever and ever. Amen.

Suffering for Being a Christian

¹²Dear friends, do not be surprised at the fiery ordeal that has come on you to test you, as though something strange were happening to you. ¹³But rejoice inasmuch as you participate in the sufferings of Christ, so that you may be overjoyed when his glory is revealed. ¹⁴If you are insulted because of the name of Christ, you are blessed, for the Spirit of glory and of God rests on you. ¹⁵If you suffer, it should not be as a murderer or thief or any other kind of criminal, or even as a meddler. ¹⁶However, if you suffer as a Christian, do not be ashamed, but praise God that you bear that name. ¹⁷For it is time for judgment to begin with God's household; and if it begins with us, what will the outcome be for those who do not obey the gospel of God? ¹⁸And,

"If it is hard for the righteous to be
    saved,
  what will become of the ungodly and
    the sinner?"ᵃ

¹⁹So then, those who suffer according to God's will should commit themselves to their faithful Creator and continue to do good.

To the Elders and the Flock

5 To the elders among you, I appeal as a fellow elder and a witness of Christ's sufferings who also will share in the glory to be revealed: ²Be shepherds of God's flock that is under your care, watching over them—not because you must, but because you are willing, as God wants you to be; not pursuing dishonest gain, but eager to serve; ³not lording it over those entrusted to you, but being examples to the flock. ⁴And when the Chief Shepherd appears, you will receive the crown of glory that will never fade away.

⁵In the same way, you who are younger, submit yourselves to your elders. All of you, clothe yourselves with humility toward one another, because,

"God opposes the proud
  but shows favor to the humble and
    oppressed."ᵇ

⁶Humble yourselves, therefore, under God's mighty hand, that he may lift you up in due time. ⁷Cast all your anxiety on him because he cares for you.

⁸Be alert and of sober mind. Your enemy the devil prowls around like a roaring lion looking for someone to devour. ⁹Resist him, standing firm in the faith, because you know that your fellow believers throughout the world are undergoing the same kind of sufferings.

¹⁰And the God of all grace, who called you to his eternal glory in Christ, after you have suffered a little while, will himself restore you and make you strong, firm and steadfast. ¹¹To him be the power for ever and ever. Amen.

Final Greetings

¹²With the help of Silas,ᶜ whom I regard as a faithful brother, I have written to you briefly, encouraging you and testifying that this is the true grace of God. Stand fast in it.

¹³She who is in Babylon, chosen together with you, sends you her greetings, and so does my son Mark. ¹⁴Greet one another with a kiss of love.

Peace to all of you who are in Christ.

ᵃ 18 Prov. 11:31 (see Septuagint)   ᵇ 5 Prov. 3:34   ᶜ 12 Greek Silvanus, a variant of Silas

2 peter

AUTHOR: Peter, the apostle

DATE: Around A.D. 67

THEME: Accepting partial truth regarding Christ can be as dangerous as no truth at all.

1 Simon Peter, a servant and apostle of Jesus Christ,

To those who through the righteousness of our God and Savior Jesus Christ have received a faith as precious as ours:

²Grace and peace be yours in abundance through the knowledge of God and of Jesus our Lord.

Confirming One's Calling and Election

³His divine power has given us everything we need for a godly life through our knowledge of him who called us by his own glory and goodness. ⁴Through these he has given us his very great and precious promises, so that through them you may participate in the divine nature, having escaped the corruption in the world caused by evil desires.

⁵For this very reason, make every effort to add to your faith goodness; and to goodness, knowledge; ⁶and to knowledge, self-control; and to self-control, perseverance; and to perseverance, godliness; ⁷and to godliness, mutual affection; and to mutual affection, love. ⁸For if you possess these qualities in increasing measure, they will keep you from being ineffective and unproductive in your knowledge of our Lord Jesus Christ. ⁹But if any of you do not have them, you are nearsighted and blind, and you have forgotten that you have been cleansed from your past sins.

¹⁰Therefore, my brothers and sisters, make every effort to confirm your calling and election. For if you do these things, you will never stumble, ¹¹and you will receive a rich welcome into the eternal kingdom of our Lord and Savior Jesus Christ.

Prophecy of Scripture

¹²So I will always remind you of these things, even though you know them and are firmly established in the truth you now have. ¹³I think it is right to refresh your memory as long as I live in the tent of this body, ¹⁴because I know that I will soon put it aside, as our Lord Jesus Christ has made clear to me. ¹⁵And I will make every effort to see that after my departure you will always be able to remember these things.

¹⁶For we did not follow cleverly devised stories when we told you about the coming of our Lord Jesus Christ in power, but we were eyewitnesses of his majesty. ¹⁷He received honor and glory from God the Father when the voice came to him from the Majestic Glory, saying, "This is my Son, whom I love; with him I am well pleased."ᵃ ¹⁸We ourselves heard this voice that came from heaven when we were with him on the sacred mountain.

¹⁹We also have the prophetic message as something completely reliable, and you will do well to pay attention to it, as to a light shining in a dark place, until the day dawns and the morning star rises in your hearts. ²⁰Above all, you must understand that no prophecy of Scripture came about by the prophet's own interpretation of things. ²¹For prophecy never had its origin in the human will, but prophets, though human, spoke from God as they were carried along by the Holy Spirit.

False Teachers and Their Destruction

2 But there were also false prophets among the people, just as there will be false teachers among you. They

ᵃ 17 Matt. 17:5; Mark 9:7; Luke 9:35

will secretly introduce destructive heresies, even denying the sovereign Lord who bought them—bringing swift destruction on themselves. [2]Many will follow their depraved conduct and will bring the way of truth into disrepute. [3]In their greed these teachers will exploit you with fabricated stories. Their condemnation has long been hanging over them, and their destruction has not been sleeping.

[4]For if God did not spare angels when they sinned, but sent them to hell,[a] putting them in chains of darkness[b] to be held for judgment; [5]if he did not spare the ancient world when he brought the flood on its ungodly people, but protected Noah, a preacher of righteousness, and seven others; [6]if he condemned the cities of Sodom and Gomorrah by burning them to ashes, and made them an example of what is going to happen to the ungodly; [7]and if he rescued Lot, a righteous man, who was distressed by the depraved conduct of the lawless [8](for that righteous man, living among them day after day, was tormented in his righteous soul by the lawless deeds he saw and heard)— [9]if this is so, then the Lord knows how to rescue the godly from trials and to hold the unrighteous for punishment on the day of judgment. [10]This is especially true of those who follow the corrupt desire of the sinful nature[c] and despise authority.

Bold and arrogant, they are not afraid to heap abuse on celestial beings; [11]yet even angels, although they are stronger and more powerful, do not heap abuse on such beings when bringing judgment on them from[d] the Lord. [12]But these people blaspheme in matters they do not understand. They are like unreasoning animals, creatures of instinct, born only to be caught and destroyed, and like animals they too will perish.

[13]They will be paid back with harm for the harm they have done. Their idea of pleasure is to carouse in broad daylight. They are blots and blemishes, reveling in their pleasures while they feast with you.[e] [14]With eyes full of adultery, they never stop sinning; they seduce the unstable; they are experts in greed—an accursed brood! [15]They have left the straight way and wandered off to follow the way of Balaam son of Bezer,[f] who loved

the wages of wickedness. [16]But he was rebuked for his wrongdoing by a donkey—an animal without speech—who spoke with a human voice and restrained the prophet's madness.

[17]These people are springs without water and mists driven by a storm. Blackest darkness is reserved for them. [18]For they mouth empty, boastful words and, by appealing to the lustful desires of sinful human nature, they entice people who are just escaping from those who live in error. [19]They promise them freedom, while they themselves are slaves of depravity—for "people are slaves to whatever has mastered them." [20]If they have escaped the corruption of the world by knowing our Lord and Savior Jesus Christ and are again entangled in it and are overcome, they are worse off at the end than they were at the beginning. [21]It would have been better for them not to have known the way of righteousness, than to have known it and then to turn their backs on the sacred command that was passed on to them. [22]Of them the proverbs are true: "A dog returns to its vomit,"[g] and, "A sow that is washed returns to her wallowing in the mud."

The Day of the Lord

3 Dear friends, this is now my second letter to you. I have written both of them as reminders to stimulate you to wholesome thinking. [2]I want you to recall the words spoken in the past by the holy prophets and the command given by our Lord and Savior through your apostles.

[3]Above all, you must understand that in the last days scoffers will come, scoffing and following their own evil desires. [4]They will say, "Where is this 'coming' he promised? Ever since our ancestors died, everything goes on as it has since the beginning of creation." [5]But they deliberately forget that long ago by God's word the heavens came into being and the earth was formed out of water and by water. [6]By these waters also the world of that time was deluged and destroyed. [7]By the same word the present heavens and earth are reserved for fire, being kept for the day of judgment and destruction of the ungodly.

[8]But do not forget this one thing, dear friends: With the Lord a day is like a thousand

---

a 4 Greek *Tartarus*   b 4 Some manuscripts *in gloomy dungeons*   c 10 Or *the flesh*   d 11 Many manuscripts *beings in the presence of*   e 13 Some manuscripts *in their love feasts*   f 15 Greek *Bosor* g 22 Prov. 26:11

The Path to Maturity

2 Peter 3:1–18 *or* 3:11,14,17–18

Gary Henry

Our conscience is a cautionary faculty that warns us when we're about to violate our principles. It was given to restrain us. But sometimes we need to be stimulated, and our conscience should do that also. It should move us to act in ways that *are* consistent with our principles. Often, however, we fail to act. Afraid of making a mistake, we do nothing. And consequently, we *learn* nothing. By failing to act on the best of our present understanding, we forfeit the opportunity to grow in that understanding.

Improvement is the result of examining what we've done. The more we do, the more we have a chance to improve. But if we wait to do anything until we think we can get it exactly right, we'll probably do very little . . . In the real world, we have to go ahead and do the best we can.

Spiritual growth has more than one dimension. On the one hand, it requires that we eschew evil. But on the other, it requires we do the good we know to do, and then learn to do even better. "[Therefore, dear friends, since you have been forewarned, be on your guard so that you may not be carried away by the error of the lawless and fall from your secure position. But grow in the grace and knowledge of our Lord and Savior Jesus Christ]" (2 Peter 3:17,18). Maturity comes from actions carefully considered beforehand and then carefully evaluated afterwards.

Oswald Chambers {AD 1874–1917}

When I hear people shout, "I have the victory," I feel like saying, "Go further. Let the Victor have you. Let God gain victories through you."

God gains victories through every soul in whom He has gained the victory. There is no such thing as *defeat* or *failure* or *discouragement* in the vocabulary of the sanctified. If you are discouraged, let God search your heart. When the old disposition of sin is gone, God makes us "more than conquerors."

Entire sanctification is an instantaneous, continuous work of grace, wrought by the mighty atonement of Jesus Christ. It is instant cleansing by the crucifixion of the "old man," followed by a life of endless growth and victory.

reflection

1. What changed in your heart and life when you first came to know Jesus?
2. In what ways have you grown since then?
3. How would you explain the process of spiritual growth to a brand-new Christian?

For your next devotional reading, go to page 1425.

years, and a thousand years are like a day. ⁹The Lord is not slow in keeping his promise, as some understand slowness. Instead he is patient with you, not wanting anyone to perish, but everyone to come to repentance.

¹⁰But the day of the Lord will come like a thief. The heavens will disappear with a roar; the elements will be destroyed by fire, and the earth and everything done in it will be laid bare.ᵃ

¹¹Since everything will be destroyed in this way, what kind of people ought you to be? You ought to live holy and godly lives ¹²as you look forward to the day of God and speed its coming.ᵇ That day will bring about the destruction of the heavens by fire, and the elements will melt in the heat. ¹³But in keeping with his promise we are looking forward to a new heaven and a new earth, where righteousness dwells.

¹⁴So then, dear friends, since you are looking forward to this, make every effort to be found spotless, blameless and at peace with him. ¹⁵Bear in mind that our Lord's patience means salvation, just as our dear brother Paul also wrote you with the wisdom that God gave him. ¹⁶He writes the same way in all his letters, speaking in them of these matters. His letters contain some things that are hard to understand, which ignorant and unstable people distort, as they do the other Scriptures, to their own destruction.

¹⁷Therefore, dear friends, since you have been forewarned, be on your guard so that you may not be carried away by the error of the lawless and fall from your secure position. ¹⁸But grow in the grace and knowledge of our Lord and Savior Jesus Christ. To him be glory both now and forever! Amen.

ᵃ 10 Some manuscripts *be burned up*   ᵇ 12 Or *as you wait eagerly for the day of God to come*

1 john

> AUTHOR: John, the apostle
>
> DATE: Between A.D. 85 and 95
>
> THEME: There is no greater force in the world than God's love.

The Incarnation of the Word of Life

1 That which was from the beginning, which we have heard, which we have seen with our eyes, which we have looked at and our hands have touched—this we proclaim concerning the Word of life. ²The life appeared; we have seen it and testify to it, and we proclaim to you the eternal life, which was with the Father and has appeared to us. ³We proclaim to you what we have seen and heard, so that you also may have fellowship with us. And our fellowship is with the Father and with his Son, Jesus Christ. ⁴We write this to make our*ᵃ* joy complete.

Light and Darkness, Sin and Forgiveness

⁵This is the message we have heard from him and declare to you: God is light; in him there is no darkness at all. ⁶If we claim to have fellowship with him and yet walk in the darkness, we lie and do not live out the truth. ⁷But if we walk in the light, as he is in the light, we have fellowship with one another, and the blood of Jesus, his Son, purifies us from all*ᵇ* sin.

⁸If we claim to be without sin, we deceive ourselves and the truth is not in us. ⁹If we confess our sins, he is faithful and just and will forgive us our sins and purify us from all unrighteousness. ¹⁰If we claim we have not sinned, we make him out to be a liar and his word is not in us.

2 My dear children, I write this to you so that you will not sin. But if anybody does sin, we have an advocate with the Father—Jesus Christ, the Righteous One. ²He is the atoning sacrifice for our sins, and not only for ours but also for the sins of the whole world.

Love and Hatred for Fellow Believers

³We know that we have come to know him if we keep his commands. ⁴Those who say, "I know him," but do not do what he commands are liars, and the truth is not in them. ⁵But if anyone obeys his word, love for God*ᶜ* is truly made complete in them. This is how we know we are in him: ⁶Whoever claims to live in him must live as Jesus did.

⁷Dear friends, I am not writing you a new command but an old one, which you have had since the beginning. This old command is the message you have heard. ⁸Yet I am writing you a new command; its truth is seen in him and in you, because the darkness is passing and the true light is already shining.

⁹Those who claim to be in the light but hate a fellow believer are still in the darkness. ¹⁰Those who love their fellow believers live in the light, and there is nothing in them to make them stumble. ¹¹But those who hate a fellow believer are in the darkness and walk around in the darkness; they do not know where they are going, because the darkness has blinded them.

Reasons for Writing

¹²I am writing to you, dear children,
   because your sins have been forgiven
      on account of his name.
¹³I am writing to you, fathers,
   because you know him who is from
      the beginning.
I am writing to you, young people,

ᵃ 4 Some manuscripts *your*   ᵇ 7 Or *every*   ᶜ 5 Or *word, God's love*

FRIDAY

Loosening Your Grip

1 John 3:1–24 *or* 3:16–18

Bill Hybels

If you've ever stared at an eviction notice or repossession papers, if you've ever had your heart pound when the phone rings because you're afraid it's another creditor, if you've ever lacked the basics necessary to function in the world and you knew that "D-day" was approaching without any apparent way out, then you know how overwhelmed and appreciative people feel when a generous Christian joyfully and eagerly reaches into his resource barrel and helps meet those needs. The person on the receiving end of a transaction like that lays awake at night staring at the ceiling, trying to figure out what would make someone show such extraordinary generosity . . .

What might happen in the lives of your friends and family members if you relaxed your grip a bit on your own material possessions? Think about whose heart might open up, or whose attitude might soften, or who might get curious and start asking spiritual questions, if you applied the instructions found in 1 John 3:18: "Dear children, let us not love with words or tongue but with actions and in truth."

Try God on this one. Put your faith into action on behalf of others—action that requires some investment—and watch the return he'll bring in the form of changed lives.

William Blake {AD 1757–1827}

Holy Thursday: Is This a Holy Thing to See

Is this a holy thing to see	And their sun does never shine,
In a rich and fruitful land,	And their fields are bleak and bare,
Babes reduc'd to misery,	And their ways are fill'd with thorns:
Fed with cold and usurous hand?	It is eternal winter there.
Is that trembling cry a song?	For where-e'er the sun does shine,
Can it be a song of joy?	And where-e'er the rain does fall,
And so many children poor?	Babe can never hunger there,
It is a land of poverty!	Nor poverty the mind appall.

reflection

1. On a scale of one to ten, how tightly do you hold on to your possessions (with one being a death grip and ten being a completely open hand)?

2. What makes it difficult for you to keep a completely open hand in regard to your possessions?

3. What resources has God given you to help meet others' needs?

For your next devotional reading, go to page 1427.

because you have overcome the evil
one.

¹⁴I write to you, dear children,
> because you know the Father.
I write to you, fathers,
> because you know him who is from
> the beginning.
I write to you, young people,
> because you are strong,
> and the word of God lives in you,
> and you have overcome the evil one.

On Not Loving the World

¹⁵Do not love the world or anything in the
world. If you love the world, love for the Fa-
ther^a is not in you. ¹⁶For everything in the
world—the cravings of sinful people, the
lust of their eyes and their boasting about
what they have and do—comes not from the
Father but from the world. ¹⁷The world and
its desires pass away, but whoever does the
will of God lives forever.

Warnings Against Denying the Son

¹⁸Dear children, this is the last hour; and
as you have heard that the antichrist is coming, even now many antichrists have come.
This is how we know it is the last hour.
¹⁹They went out from us, but they did not
really belong to us. For if they had belonged
to us, they would have remained with us;
but their going showed that none of them
belonged to us.

²⁰But you have an anointing from the
Holy One, and all of you know the truth.^b ²¹I
do not write to you because you do not know
the truth, but because you do know it and
because no lie comes from the truth. ²²Who
is the liar? It is whoever denies that Jesus is
the Messiah.^c Such a person is the antichrist—denying the Father and the Son.
²³No one who denies the Son has the Father;
whoever acknowledges the Son has the Fa-
ther also.

²⁴As for you, see that what you have
heard from the beginning remains in you. If
it does, you also will remain in the Son and
in the Father. ²⁵And this is what he promised
us—eternal life.

²⁶I am writing these things to you about
those who are trying to lead you astray. ²⁷As
for you, the anointing you received from

him remains in you, and you do not need
anyone to teach you. But as his anointing
teaches you about all things and as that
anointing is real, not counterfeit—just as it
has taught you, remain in him.

God's Children and Sin

²⁸And now, dear children, continue in
him, so that when he appears we may be
confident and unashamed before him at his
coming.
²⁹If you know that he is righteous, you
know that everyone who does what is right
has been born of him.

3 See what great love the Father has
lavished on us, that we should be
called children of God! And that is
what we are! The reason the world does not
know us is that it did not know him. ²Dear
friends, now we are children of God, and
what we will be has not yet been made
known. But we know that when Christ ap-
pears,^d we shall be like him, for we shall see
him as he is. ³All who have this hope in him
purify themselves, just as he is pure.

⁴Everyone who sins breaks the law; in
fact, sin is lawlessness. ⁵But you know that
he appeared so that he might take away our
sins. And in him is no sin. ⁶No one who lives
in him keeps on sinning. No one who continues to sin has either seen him or known him.

⁷Dear children, do not let anyone lead
you astray. The one who does what is right is
righteous, just as he is righteous. ⁸The one
who does what is sinful is of the devil, because the devil has been sinning from the
beginning. The reason the Son of God appeared was to destroy the devil's work.
⁹Those who are born of God will not contin-
ue to sin, because God's seed remains in
them; they cannot go on sinning, because
they have been born of God. ¹⁰This is how
we know who the children of God are and
who the children of the devil are: Those who
do not do what is right are not God's children; nor are those who do not love their
brothers and sisters.

More on Love and Hatred

¹¹For this is the message you heard from
the beginning: We should love one another.
¹²Do not be like Cain, who belonged to the

---

^a 15 Or *world, the Father's love*   ^b 20 Some manuscripts *and you know all things*   ^c 22 Greek *Christ*
^d 2 Or *when it is made known*

Love's the Thing

1 John 3:23

read/meditate

Read 1 John 3:23 over a few times. Now read it very slowly one last time. Think about how often Christ commanded us to love each other. Love is very important to God. What kinds of things in life distract you from this all-important command?

pray

Ask God to reveal any areas of your life in which you should be more loving. Then sit quietly for a moment and wait for insight. Share with him any areas of your life in which you need more love than you are receiving. Lay those concerns before him.

contemplate

What kind of connection is there between believing in the work of Christ and being a loving person? Does one lead to the other? What evidences in life do you see to support your opinion?

additional reflection

Smile at each other, smile at your wife, smile at your husband, smile at your children, smile at each other—it doesn't matter who it is—and that will help you to grow up in greater love for each other.

—*Mother Teresa*

Love, like warmth, should beam forth on every side and bend to every necessity of our brethren.

—*Martin Luther*

Where there is no love, put love in, and you will draw out love.

—*John of the Cross*

For your next devotional reading, go to page 1429.

evil one and murdered his brother. And why did he murder him? Because his own actions were evil and his brother's were righteous. ¹³Do not be surprised, my brothers and sisters, if the world hates you. ¹⁴We know that we have passed from death to life, because we love each other. Anyone who does not love remains in death. ¹⁵Anyone who hates a fellow believer is a murderer, and you know that no murderers have eternal life in them.

¹⁶This is how we know what love is: Jesus Christ laid down his life for us. And we ought to lay down our lives for one another. ¹⁷If any one of you has material possessions and sees a brother or sister in need but has no pity on them, how can the love of God be in you? ¹⁸Dear children, let us not love with words or tongue but with actions and in truth.

¹⁹This is how we know that we belong to the truth and how we set our hearts at rest in his presence: ²⁰If our hearts condemn us, we know that God is greater than our hearts, and he knows everything. ²¹Dear friends, if our hearts do not condemn us, we have confidence before God ²²and receive from him anything we ask, because we keep his commands and do what pleases him. ²³And this is his command: to believe in the name of his Son, Jesus Christ, and to love one another as he commanded us. ²⁴Those who keep his commands live in him, and he in them. And this is how we know that he lives in us: We know it by the Spirit he gave us.

On Denying the Incarnation

4 Dear friends, do not believe every spirit, but test the spirits to see whether they are from God, because many false prophets have gone out into the world. ²This is how you can recognize the Spirit of God: Every spirit that acknowledges that Jesus Christ has come in the flesh is from God, ³but every spirit that does not acknowledge Jesus is not from God. This is the spirit of the antichrist, which you have heard is coming and even now is already in the world.

⁴You, dear children, are from God and have overcome them, because the one who is in you is greater than the one who is in the world. ⁵They are from the world and therefore speak from the viewpoint of the world, and the world listens to them. ⁶We are from

God, and whoever knows God listens to us; but whoever is not from God does not listen to us. This is how we recognize the Spirit[a] of truth and the spirit of falsehood.

God's Love and Ours

⁷Dear friends, let us love one another, for love comes from God. Everyone who loves has been born of God and knows God. ⁸Whoever does not love does not know God, because God is love. ⁹This is how God showed his love among us: He sent his one and only Son into the world that we might live through him. ¹⁰This is love: not that we loved God, but that he loved us and sent his Son as an atoning sacrifice for our sins. ¹¹Dear friends, since God so loved us, we also ought to love one another. ¹²No one has ever seen God; but if we love one another, God lives in us and his love is made complete in us.

¹³This is how we know that we live in him and he in us: He has given us of his Spirit. ¹⁴And we have seen and testify that the Father has sent his Son to be the Savior of the world. ¹⁵If anyone acknowledges that Jesus is the Son of God, God lives in them and they in God. ¹⁶And so we know and rely on the love God has for us.

God is love. Whoever lives in love lives in God, and God in them. ¹⁷This is how love is made complete among us so that we will have confidence on the day of judgment: In this world we are like Jesus. ¹⁸There is no fear in love. But perfect love drives out fear, because fear has to do with punishment. The one who fears is not made perfect in love.

¹⁹We love because he first loved us. ²⁰If we say we love God yet hate a brother or sister, we are liars. For if we do not love a fellow believer, whom we have seen, we cannot love God, whom we have not seen. ²¹And he has given us this command: Those who love God must also love one another.

Faith in the Incarnate Son of God

5 Everyone who believes that Jesus is the Messiah is born of God, and everyone who loves the father loves his child as well. ²This is how we know that we love the children of God: by loving God and carrying out his commands. ³In fact, this is love for God: to keep his commands. And his

MONDAY

Becoming Fearless

1 John 4:7–21 *or* 4:18

Joanna Weaver

"Perfect love [drives] out fear," 1 John 4:18 tells us . . .

That particular verse is helpful to me because it speaks to the root of my worry habit. I was anxious for the same reason the first man and woman became anxious: I was not secure in God's love.

Oh, I knew that I was saved and that if I died, I'd go to heaven. But somewhere along the way, I had twisted God's love into something I had to earn. If I could just be good enough, then God had to love me. But of course I stumbled again and again. Each time it took me weeks to work up enough spiritual brownie points to feel like I was back on God's good side.

No wonder I worried. No wonder I was afraid. I was constantly sewing fig leaves, trying to cover up my inadequacy . . .

Come find love, Jesus invites us. Come find a love so perfect that it covers all your faults and pronounces you "not guilty." Come find a love that chases fear out the door! Come find everything you've ever longed for. Come find peace for your soul.

Horatius Bonar {ad 1808–1889}

O Love That Casts Out Fear

Oh love that casts out fear,	Great love of God, come in!
Oh love that casts out sin,	Wellspring of heavenly peace;
Tarry no more without,	Thou Living Water, come!
But come and dwell within!	Spring up, and never cease.
True sunlight of the soul,	Love of the living God,
Surround us as we go;	Of Father and of Son;
So shall our way be safe,	Love of the Holy Ghost,
Our feet no straying know.	Fill thou each needy one.

reflection

1. What kind of fear does God's perfect love drive out?

2. In what ways have you been living with that kind of fear? How can you embrace God's perfect love so that fear is driven out?

3. When was the last time you praised God for his love—freely given and without strings attached? Don't wait a minute longer—do it now!

For your next devotional reading, go to page 1431.

commands are not burdensome, [4]for everyone born of God overcomes the world. This is the victory that has overcome the world, even our faith. [5]Who is it that overcomes the world? Only the one who believes that Jesus is the Son of God.

[6]This is the one who came by water and blood—Jesus Christ. He did not come by water only, but by water and blood. And it is the Spirit who testifies, because the Spirit is the truth. [7]For there are three that testify: [8]the[a] Spirit, the water and the blood; and the three are in agreement. [9]We accept human testimony, but God's testimony is greater because it is the testimony of God, which he has given about his Son. [10]Whoever believes in the Son of God accepts this testimony. Whoever does not believe God has made him out to be a liar, because they have not believed the testimony God has given about his Son. [11]And this is the testimony: God has given us eternal life, and this life is in his Son. [12]Whoever has the Son has life; whoever does not have the Son of God does not have life.

Concluding Affirmations

[13]I write these things to you who believe in the name of the Son of God so that you may know that you have eternal life. [14]This is the confidence we have in approaching God: that if we ask anything according to his will, he hears us. [15]And if we know that he hears us—whatever we ask—we know that we have what we asked of him.

[16]If you see any brother or sister commit a sin that does not lead to death, you should pray and God will give them life. I refer to those whose sin does not lead to death. There is a sin that leads to death. I am not saying that you should pray about that. [17]All wrongdoing is sin, and there is sin that does not lead to death.

[18]We know that anyone born of God does not continue to sin; the One who was born of God keeps them safe, and the evil one cannot harm them. [19]We know that we are children of God, and that the whole world is under the control of the evil one. [20]We know also that the Son of God has come and has given us understanding, so that we may know him who is true. And we are in him who is true by being in his Son Jesus Christ. He is the true God and eternal life.

[21]Dear children, keep yourselves from idols.

---

[a] 7,8 Late manuscripts of the Vulgate *testify in heaven: the Father, the Word and the Holy Spirit, and these three are one.* [8]*And there are three that testify on earth: the* (not found in any Greek manuscript before the fourteenth century)

WHO'S IN CONTROL?

1 John 5:1–21 *or* 5:1–5

FRANCIS SCHAEFFER {AD 1912–1984}

Now we must understand too, in the framework of the Scripture, that since the fall everything is under the covenant of grace. The covenant of works is destroyed by the deliberate, free, unconditioned choice of Adam and Eve. In its place, by the grace of God, with the promises begun in Genesis 3:15, man was immediately given the promise of the work of the Messiah, coming in the future. Thus from the time of the fall onwards, everything rests upon the finished work of the Lord Jesus Christ on the cross, not upon ourselves, not in ourselves . . . When I begin to think and to grow in the idea of *my* victory, there is really no true victory. To the extent that I am thinking about *my* sanctification, there is no real sanctification. I must see it always as Jesus Christ's.

Indeed, it is only as we consciously bring each victory to his feet, and keep it there as we think of it—and especially as we speak of it—that we can avoid the pride of that victory, which can be worse than the sin over which we claim to have had the victory. The greater the victory, the greater the need of placing it consciously (and as we speak of it, vocally) at his feet.

Elyse Fitzpatrick

You know, when we really stop to think about it, we are forced to recognize that all our efforts at controlling our world are pretty ineffective, aren't they? In fact, we have to recognize that there is only one person who is really in control—and that's God . . .

Where did this desire to be in control, to be like a god, originally come from? It had its birth in the Garden of Eden. Do you remember how Satan tempted Eve? He said, "God knows that when you eat [of the fruit] your eyes will be opened, and *you will be like God*" (Genesis 3:5, emphasis added). Think about that phrase "you will be like God." What was Satan saying to Eve? He was saying, "You can't trust God. He hasn't given you everything you really need. He isn't trustworthy . . . Take matters into your own hands. Try to work things out in accordance to your own wisdom. You need to be in control. Then you'll be happy."

It's a blessing that God doesn't let this kind of thinking go on for long, isn't it? It wasn't long until God visited Adam and Eve and found them hiding in shame . . . God continues today to lovingly confront us whenever we give in to the temptation of trying to be in control. He does this for our own good and so that He'll be praised.

reflection

1. What fundamental truths about God's character does God's victory reveal?
2. What does it mean that it is God (and not us) who is in control?
3. How do you acknowledge God's sovereignty in your life?

For your next devotional reading, go to page 1433.

2 john

AUTHOR: John, the apostle

DATE: Between A.D. 85 and 95

THEME: God calls his people to love one another and to guard against deception.

¹The elder,

To the lady chosen by God and to her children, whom I love in the truth—and not I only, but also all who know the truth—²because of the truth, which lives in us and will be with us forever:

³Grace, mercy and peace from God the Father and from Jesus Christ, the Father's Son, will be with us in truth and love.

⁴It has given me great joy to find some of your children walking in the truth, just as the Father commanded us. ⁵And now, dear lady, I am not writing you a new command but one we have had from the beginning. I ask that we love one another. ⁶And this is love: that we walk in obedience to his commands. As you have heard from the beginning, his command is that you walk in love. ⁷Many deceivers, who do not acknowledge Jesus Christ as coming in the flesh, have gone out into the world. Any such person is the deceiver and the antichrist. ⁸Watch out that you do not lose what we ᵃ have worked for, but that you may be rewarded fully. ⁹Anyone who runs ahead and does not continue in the teaching of Christ does not have God; whoever continues in the teaching has both the Father and the Son. ¹⁰If anyone comes to you and does not bring this teaching, do not take them into your house or welcome them. ¹¹Anyone who welcomes them shares in their wicked work.

¹²I have much to write to you, but I do not want to use paper and ink. Instead, I hope to visit you and talk with you face to face, so that our joy may be complete.

¹³The children of your sister, who is chosen by God, send their greetings.

EMBRACE TRUE CHRISTIANITY

2 John 1–13 *or* 8–9

Eric Sandras

One of my deepest temptations is to practice a lifestyle that appears to be a faithful friendship with Christ but really isn't. To be a Cheese Puff Christian—lots of volume but little substance. Cheese puffs take up space in a bowl, but crush them and you're lucky to get a tablespoon of substance out of them. Likewise, it's so easy to puff up my life with religious air, without much of the kingdom that Jesus was passionate about bringing. To be in a cooperative friendship with Christ means to enter into his story and live life on behalf of his kingdom, his agenda in the world. Unfortunately, life has a way of exposing who I really am—a real friend of Christ, or just another religious poser . . .

Have I measured the genuineness of my faith by how well I'm performing, or by how well Jesus and I are doing? Am I willing to admit that, in a world of marshmallow spirituality, my faith and relationship with Jesus the Master may be lacking? Something in my spirit keeps crying out, "There must be more!"

I don't want my faith to *resemble* the real thing; I want it to *be* the real thing. I don't want to preach sermons, share with others or counsel myself regarding a God I profess to know without answering some hard questions about my spiritual life.

HANNAH WHITALL SMITH {ca. AD 1832–1911}

No soul can be really at rest until it has given up all dependence on everything else and has been forced to depend on the Lord alone. As long as our hope comes from other things, nothing but disappointment awaits us. Feelings may change, and will change with our changing circumstances. Doctrines and dogmas may be upended. Christian work may amount to nothing. Prayers may seem to lose their fervency. Promises may seem to fail. Everything that we have believed in or depended upon may seem to be swept away. And only God is left—just God, the bare God, simply and only God.

reflection

1. When was the last time you truly looked into your life and relationship with Jesus to determine if you are what you say you are?

2. In what ways do you pretend to have it all together when the truth is something completely different?

3. How would the next week be different if you quit trying so hard to be more than you are and instead leaned on God to work through you just as you are?

For your next devotional reading, go to page 1436.

3 john

AUTHOR: John, the apostle

DATE: Between A.D. 85 and 95

THEME: To fulfill Christ's call, we need each other.

¹The elder,

To my dear friend Gaius, whom I love in the truth.

²Dear friend, I pray that you may enjoy good health and that all may go well with you, even as your soul is getting along well. ³It gave me great joy to have some believers come and testify to your faithfulness to the truth, telling how you continue to walk in it. ⁴I have no greater joy than to hear that my children are walking in the truth.

⁵Dear friend, you are faithful in what you are doing for the brothers and sisters, even though they are strangers to you. ⁶They have told the church about your love. You will do well to send them on their way in a manner worthy of God. ⁷It was for the sake of the Name that they went out, receiving no help from the pagans. ⁸We ought therefore to show hospitality to such people so that we may work together for the truth.

⁹I wrote to the church, but Diotrephes, who loves to be first, will have nothing to do with us. ¹⁰So when I come, I will call attention to what he is doing, spreading malicious nonsense about us. Not satisfied with that, he refuses to welcome other believers. He also stops those who want to do so and puts them out of the church.

¹¹Dear friend, do not imitate what is evil but what is good. Anyone who does what is good is from God. Anyone who does what is evil has not seen God. ¹²Demetrius is well spoken of by everyone—and even by the truth itself. We also speak well of him, and you know that our testimony is true.

¹³I have much to write you, but I do not want to do so with pen and ink. ¹⁴I hope to see you soon, and we will talk face to face.

Peace to you. The friends here send their greetings. Greet the friends there by name.

jude

AUTHOR: Jude, the brother of James and Jesus

DATE: Probably around A.D. 65

THEME: Christians are to defend the truth of the gospel.

¹Jude, a servant of Jesus Christ and a brother of James,

To those who have been called, who are loved in God the Father and kept for*a* Jesus Christ:

²Mercy, peace and love be yours in abundance.

The Sin and Doom of Ungodly People

³Dear friends, although I was very eager to write to you about the salvation we share, I felt compelled to write and urge you to contend for the faith that the Lord has once for all entrusted to us, his people. ⁴For certain individuals whose condemnation was written about*b* long ago have secretly slipped in among you. They are ungodly people, who pervert the grace of our God into a license for immorality and deny Jesus Christ our only Sovereign and Lord.

⁵Though you already know all this, I want to remind you that the Lord*c* at one time delivered his people out of Egypt, but later destroyed those who did not believe. ⁶And the angels who did not keep their positions of authority but abandoned their proper dwelling—these he has kept in darkness, bound with everlasting chains for judgment on the great Day. ⁷In a similar way, Sodom and Gomorrah and the surrounding towns gave themselves up to sexual immorality and perversion. They serve as an example of those who suffer the punishment of eternal fire.

⁸In the very same way, on the strength of their dreams these ungodly people pollute their own bodies, reject authority and heap abuse on celestial beings. ⁹But even the archangel Michael, when he was disputing with the devil about the body of Moses, did not himself dare to condemn him for slander but said, "The Lord rebuke you!"*d* ¹⁰Yet these people speak abusively against whatever they do not understand; and what things they do understand by instinct, like unreasoning animals—these are the very things that destroy them.

¹¹Woe to them! They have taken the way of Cain; they have rushed for profit into Balaam's error; they have been destroyed in Korah's rebellion.

¹²These people are blemishes at your love feasts, eating with you without the slightest qualm—shepherds who feed only themselves. They are clouds without rain, blown along by the wind; autumn trees, without fruit and uprooted—twice dead. ¹³They are wild waves of the sea, foaming up their shame; wandering stars, for whom blackest darkness has been reserved forever.

¹⁴Enoch, the seventh from Adam, prophesied about them: "See, the Lord is coming with thousands upon thousands of his holy ones ¹⁵to judge everyone, and to convict all the ungodly of all the ungodly acts they have done in an ungodly way, and of all the defiant words ungodly sinners have spoken against him."*e* ¹⁶These people are grumblers and faultfinders; they follow their own evil desires; they boast about themselves and flatter others for their own advantage.

---

a 1 Or by; or in   *b* 4 Or individuals who were marked out for condemnation   *c* 5 Some early manuscripts Jesus   *d* 9 Jude is alluding to the Jewish Testament of Moses (approximately the first century A.D.).   *e* 14,15 From the Jewish First Book of Enoch (approximately the first century B.C.)

THURSDAY

ALWAYS WITH US

Jude 1–25 or 20–21

ANDREW MURRAY {AD 1828–1917}

The Holy Spirit does not come to us just at times when we think we need Him or at times when we think we need His help. The Spirit comes to us as our lifelong companion. He wants to view us as His possession, completely and at all times.

Many Christians do not understand this truth. They desire that the Spirit of God help and teach them, but they do not grasp that He wants to live within them continually and have full possession of their lives.

Once we understand this, we will realize that it is possible to live while we continually pray through the Spirit. By faith, we will have the certainty that the Spirit will lead us to a prayerful attitude and make us aware of the presence of God, so that our prayer will be an exercise in our fellowship with God and His great love. As long as we limit the working of the Holy Spirit to certain times like Pentecost, it will remain an unsolved riddle to us.

When Jude says, "[By . . . praying in the Holy Spirit, keep yourselves in God's love]," he expresses the same thought as Paul, namely that the Holy Spirit wants to cherish us in God's love in the same manner that the sun warms us each day.

W. Glyn Evans

When I was a younger Christian, Lord, I thought my love for You must be proved by exploits. Now I realize that You are far more concerned with my fellowship. "Remember Me." Not "Die for Me" or "Risk for Me," but simply "Remember Me." Love's requirement is ridiculously simple. "Just be there for Me." How often, Lord, have I brought my grocery list to You instead of simply opening the door and letting You come in to sup with me and I with You! Even though You are in heaven, glorified, You still have need to sit down with me and become one with me in personal fellowship. Now I understand what You meant when You said, "The LORD's portion is [his] people" (Deuteronomy 32:9). Holiness is Your greatest *requirement*, but Your people are Your greatest *delight*. Lord, help me to delight You with a hundred ways of expressing my love for You.

reflection

1. What kind of relationship does God want to have with you through his Spirit?

2. How does it make you feel to know that God delights in you?

3. What does it mean to "continually" pray?

For your next devotional reading, go to page 1439.

A Call to Persevere

17But, dear friends, remember what the apostles of our Lord Jesus Christ foretold. 18They said to you, "In the last times there will be scoffers who will follow their own ungodly desires." 19These are the people who divide you, who follow mere natural instincts and do not have the Spirit.

20But you, dear friends, by building yourselves up in your most holy faith and praying in the Holy Spirit, 21keep yourselves in God's love as you wait for the mercy of our Lord Jesus Christ to bring you to eternal life.

22Be merciful to those who doubt; 23save others by snatching them from the fire; to others show mercy, mixed with fear—hating even the clothing stained by corrupted flesh. [a]

Doxology

24To him who is able to keep you from stumbling and to present you before his glorious presence without fault and with great joy— 25to the only God our Savior be glory, majesty, power and authority, through Jesus Christ our Lord, before all ages, now and forevermore! Amen.

---

a 22,23 The Greek manuscripts of these verses vary at several points.

revelation

AUTHOR: John, the apostle

DATE: Probably around A.D. 95

THEME: Knowing that God is in control of the future gives us hope during difficult times.

Prologue

1 The revelation from Jesus Christ, which God gave him to show his servants what must soon take place. He made it known by sending his angel to his servant John, ²who testifies to everything he saw—that is, the word of God and the testimony of Jesus Christ. ³Blessed is the one who reads aloud the words of this prophecy, and blessed are those who hear it and take to heart what is written in it, because the time is near.

Greetings and Doxology

⁴John,

To the seven churches in the province of Asia:

Grace and peace to you from him who is, and who was, and who is to come, and from the seven spirits[a] before his throne, ⁵and from Jesus Christ, who is the faithful witness, the firstborn from the dead, and the ruler of the kings of the earth.

To him who loves us and has freed us from our sins by his blood, ⁶and has made us to be a kingdom and priests to serve his God and Father—to him be glory and power for ever and ever! Amen.

⁷"Look, he is coming with the clouds,"[b]
  and "every eye will see him,
even those who pierced him";
   and all peoples on earth "will mourn
     because of him."[c]
          So shall it be! Amen.

⁸"I am the Alpha and the Omega," says the Lord God, "who is, and who was, and who is to come, the Almighty."

John's Vision of Christ

⁹I, John, your brother and companion in the suffering and kingdom and patient endurance that are ours in Jesus, was on the island of Patmos because of the word of God and the testimony of Jesus. ¹⁰On the Lord's Day I was in the Spirit, and I heard behind me a loud voice like a trumpet, ¹¹which said: "Write on a scroll what you see and send it to the seven churches: to Ephesus, Smyrna, Pergamum, Thyatira, Sardis, Philadelphia and Laodicea."

¹²I turned around to see the voice that was speaking to me. And when I turned I saw seven golden lampstands, ¹³and among the lampstands was someone like a son of man,[d] dressed in a robe reaching down to his feet and with a golden sash around his chest. ¹⁴The hair on his head was white like wool, as white as snow, and his eyes were like blazing fire. ¹⁵His feet were like bronze glowing in a furnace, and his voice was like the sound of rushing waters. ¹⁶In his right hand he held seven stars, and coming out of his mouth was a sharp, double-edged sword. His face was like the sun shining in all its brilliance.

¹⁷When I saw him, I fell at his feet as though dead. Then he placed his right hand on me and said: "Do not be afraid. I am the First and the Last. ¹⁸I am the Living One; I was dead, and now look, I am alive for ever and ever! And I hold the keys of death and Hades.

¹⁹"Write, therefore, what you have seen: both what is now and what will take place

a 4 That is, the sevenfold Spirit   *b 7* Daniel 7:13   *c 7* Zech. 12:10   *d 13* See Daniel 7:13.

FRIDAY

Between Today and Forever

Revelation 1:1–20 *or* 1:17–18

Christopher D. Hudson

I think some of the reason that the present is so mediocre for a lot of people is because they spend too much time looking forward with too much enthusiasm. Thinking about the future or the past too much is a mistake. I have learned that constantly looking ahead to better things is detrimental. When you have your gaze set on something besides today, you can miss out on the opportunities you could have had. Each day is a gift. You only have today, and in fact only this moment is guaranteed. Use it well. Know God. Walk with him. You will someday look back and wish you had enjoyed the things you had instead of focusing on some time period in the future.

John Wesley {AD 1703–1791}

Happy who in Jesus live;
But happier still are they
Who to God their spirits give,
And scape from earth away:
Lord, thou read'st the panting heart;
Lord, thou hear'st the praying sigh;
O 'tis better to depart,
'Tis better far to die!

To thy wise and gracious will
We quietly submit,
Waiting for redemption still,
But waiting at thy feet:
When thou wilt the blessing give,
Call us up thy face to see;
Only let thy servants live,
And let us die, to thee.

Yet, if so thy will ordain,
For our companions' good,
Let us in the flesh remain,
And meekly bear the load:
When we have our grief filled up,
When we all our work have done,
Late partakers of our hope,
And sharers of thy throne.

reflection

1. God wants us to live today in light of what he's done in the past, for the sake of all that eternity holds in the future. In what ways do you find it difficult to do this?

2. What eternal benefit can you still gain from your time here on earth?

3. What will it mean for *you* to live today for the sake of the Living One?

For your next devotional reading, go to page 1440.

Worship Pours Out

Revelation 1:12–18

read/meditate

Take a few moments to think about what Jesus means to you. Read through John's vision of him in this first chapter of Revelation. Then read it once again.

pray

Meditate on Jesus' words to John in Revelation 1:18. Read each phrase separately, and after each one pray that Jesus will reveal himself to you in new ways with each word.

contemplate

God is all-powerful. We worship him for who he is. Our worship doesn't depend on our feelings or circumstances. It is rooted in God's character. How much are your own worship practices affected by your own mood rather than God's character?

additional reflection

When I give thanks, my thoughts still circle about myself to some extent. But in praise my soul ascends to self-forgetting adoration, seeing and praising only the majesty and power of God, His grace and redemption.

—Ole Hallesby

If God were small enough to be understood, He would not be big enough to be worshiped.

—Evelyn Underhill

For your next devotional reading, go to page 1444.

later. ²⁰The mystery of the seven stars that you saw in my right hand and of the seven golden lampstands is this: The seven stars are the angels*ᵃ* of the seven churches, and the seven lampstands are the seven churches.

To the Church in Ephesus

2 "To the angel*ᵇ* of the church in Ephesus write:

These are the words of him who holds the seven stars in his right hand and walks among the seven golden lampstands. ²I know your deeds, your hard work and your perseverance. I know that you cannot tolerate wicked people, that you have tested those who claim to be apostles but are not, and have found them false. ³You have persevered and have endured hardships for my name, and have not grown weary.

⁴Yet I hold this against you: You have forsaken the love you had at first. ⁵Consider how far you have fallen! Repent and do the things you did at first. If you do not repent, I will come to you and remove your lampstand from its place. ⁶But you have this in your favor: You hate the practices of the Nicolaitans, which I also hate.

⁷Whoever has ears, let them hear what the Spirit says to the churches. To those who are victorious, I will give the right to eat from the tree of life, which is in the paradise of God.

To the Church in Smyrna

⁸"To the angel of the church in Smyrna write:

These are the words of him who is the First and the Last, who died and came to life again. ⁹I know your afflictions and your poverty—yet you are rich! I know about the slander of those who say they are Jews and are not, but are a synagogue of Satan. ¹⁰Do not be afraid of what you are about to suffer. I tell you, the devil will put some of you in prison to test you, and you will suffer persecution for ten days. Be faithful, even to the point of death, and I will give you life as your victor's crown.

¹¹Whoever has ears, let them hear what the Spirit says to the churches. Those who are victorious will not be hurt at all by the second death.

To the Church in Pergamum

¹²"To the angel of the church in Pergamum write:

These are the words of him who has the sharp, double-edged sword. ¹³I know where you live—where Satan has his throne. Yet you remain true to my name. You did not renounce your faith in me, not even in the days of Antipas, my faithful witness, who was put to death in your city—where Satan lives.

¹⁴Nevertheless, I have a few things against you: There are some among you who hold to the teaching of Balaam, who taught Balak to entice the Israelites to sin so that they ate food sacrificed to idols and committed sexual immorality. ¹⁵Likewise, you also have those who hold to the teaching of the Nicolaitans. ¹⁶Repent therefore! Otherwise, I will soon come to you and will fight against them with the sword of my mouth.

¹⁷Whoever has ears, let them hear what the Spirit says to the churches. To those who are victorious, I will give some of the hidden manna. I will also give each of them a white stone with a new name written on it, known only to the one who receives it.

To the Church in Thyatira

¹⁸"To the angel of the church in Thyatira write:

These are the words of the Son of God, whose eyes are like blazing fire and whose feet are like burnished bronze. ¹⁹I know your deeds, your love and faith, your service and perseverance, and that you are now doing more than you did at first.

²⁰Nevertheless, I have this against you: You tolerate that woman Jezebel, who calls herself a prophet. By her teaching she misleads my servants into

---

ᵃ 20 Or *messengers*   *ᵇ* 1 Or *messenger*; also in verses 8, 12 and 18 sexual immorality and the eating of food sacrificed to idols. [21]I have given her time to repent of her immorality, but she is unwilling. [22]So I will cast her on a bed of suffering, and I will make those who commit adultery with her suffer intensely, unless they repent of her ways. [23]I will strike her children dead. Then all the churches will know that I am he who searches hearts and minds, and I will repay each of you according to your deeds. [24]Now I say to the rest of you in Thyatira, to you who do not hold to her teaching and have not learned Satan's so-called deep secrets, 'I will not impose any other burden on you, [25]except to hold on to what you have until I come.'

[26]To those who are victorious and do my will to the end, I will give authority over the nations— [27]they 'will rule them with an iron scepter and will dash them to pieces like pottery'[a]—just as I have received authority from my Father. [28]I will also give them the morning star. [29]Whoever has ears, let them hear what the Spirit says to the churches.

To the Church in Sardis

3 "To the angel[b] of the church in Sardis write:

These are the words of him who holds the seven spirits[c] of God and the seven stars. I know your deeds; you have a reputation of being alive, but you are dead. [2]Wake up! Strengthen what remains and is about to die, for I have found your deeds unfinished in the sight of my God. [3]Remember, therefore, what you have received and heard; hold it fast, and repent. But if you do not wake up, I will come like a thief, and you will not know at what time I will come to you.

[4]Yet you have a few people in Sardis who have not soiled their clothes. They will walk with me, dressed in white, for they are worthy. [5]Those who are victorious will, like them, be dressed in white. I will never blot out their names from the book of life, but will acknowl-

edge their names before my Father and his angels. [6]Whoever has ears, let them hear what the Spirit says to the churches.

To the Church in Philadelphia

[7]"To the angel of the church in Philadelphia write:

These are the words of him who is holy and true, who holds the key of David. What he opens no one can shut, and what he shuts no one can open. [8]I know your deeds. See, I have placed before you an open door that no one can shut. I know that you have little strength, yet you have kept my word and have not denied my name. [9]I will make those who are of the synagogue of Satan, who claim to be Jews though they are not, but are liars—I will make them come and fall down at your feet and acknowledge that I have loved you. [10]Since you have kept my command to endure patiently, I will also keep you from the hour of trial that is going to come on the whole world to test those who live on the earth.

[11]I am coming soon. Hold on to what you have, so that no one will take your crown. [12]Those who are victorious I will make pillars in the temple of my God. Never again will they leave it. I will write on them the name of my God and the name of the city of my God, the new Jerusalem, which is coming down out of heaven from my God; and I will also write on them my new name. [13]Whoever has ears, let them hear what the Spirit says to the churches.

To the Church in Laodicea

[14]"To the angel of the church in Laodicea write:

These are the words of the Amen, the faithful and true witness, the ruler of God's creation. [15]I know your deeds, that you are neither cold nor hot. I wish you were either one or the other! [16]So, because you are lukewarm—neither hot nor cold—I am about to spit you out of my mouth. [17]You say, 'I am rich; I have acquired wealth and do not need

---

a 27 Psalm 2:9   *b* 1 Or *messenger*; also in verses 7 and 14   *c* 1 That is, the sevenfold Spirit a thing.' But you do not realize that you are wretched, pitiful, poor, blind and naked. 18I counsel you to buy from me gold refined in the fire, so you can become rich; and white clothes to wear, so you can cover your shameful nakedness; and salve to put on your eyes, so you can see.

19Those whom I love I rebuke and discipline. So be earnest, and repent. 20Here I am! I stand at the door and knock. If anyone hears my voice and opens the door, I will come in and eat with them, and they with me.

21To those who are victorious, I will give the right to sit with me on my throne, just as I was victorious and sat down with my Father on his throne. 22Whoever has ears, let them hear what the Spirit says to the churches."

The Throne in Heaven

4 After this I looked, and there before me was a door standing open in heaven. And the voice I had first heard speaking to me like a trumpet said, "Come up here, and I will show you what must take place after this." 2At once I was in the Spirit, and there before me was a throne in heaven with someone sitting on it. 3And the one who sat there had the appearance of jasper and ruby. A rainbow that shone like an emerald encircled the throne. 4Surrounding the throne were twenty-four other thrones, and seated on them were twenty-four elders. They were dressed in white and had crowns of gold on their heads. 5From the throne came flashes of lightning, rumblings and peals of thunder. Before the throne, seven lamps were blazing. These are the seven spirits[a] of God. 6Also before the throne there was what looked like a sea of glass, clear as crystal.

In the center, around the throne, were four living creatures, and they were covered with eyes, in front and in back. 7The first living creature was like a lion, the second was like an ox, the third had a face like a man, the fourth was like a flying eagle. 8Each of the four living creatures had six wings and was covered with eyes all around, even under its wings. Day and night they never stop saying:

" 'Holy, holy, holy
    is the Lord God Almighty,'[b]
who was, and is, and is to come."

9Whenever the living creatures give glory, honor and thanks to him who sits on the throne and who lives for ever and ever, 10the twenty-four elders fall down before him who sits on the throne and worship him who lives for ever and ever. They lay their crowns before the throne and say:

11"You are worthy, our Lord and God,
    to receive glory and honor and power,
for you created all things,
    and by your will they were created
    and have their being."

The Scroll and the Lamb

5 Then I saw in the right hand of him who sat on the throne a scroll with writing on both sides and sealed with seven seals. 2And I saw a mighty angel proclaiming in a loud voice, "Who is worthy to break the seals and open the scroll?" 3But no one in heaven or on earth or under the earth could open the scroll or even look inside it. 4I wept and wept because no one was found who was worthy to open the scroll or look inside. 5Then one of the elders said to me, "Do not weep! See, the Lion of the tribe of Judah, the Root of David, has triumphed. He is able to open the scroll and its seven seals."

6Then I saw a Lamb, looking as if it had been slain, standing in the center before the throne, encircled by the four living creatures and the elders. The Lamb had seven horns and seven eyes, which are the seven spirits[a] of God sent out into all the earth. 7He went and took the scroll from the right hand of him who sat on the throne. 8And when he had taken it, the four living creatures and the twenty-four elders fell down before the Lamb. Each one had a harp and they were holding golden bowls full of incense, which are the prayers of God's people. 9And they sang a new song, saying:

"You are worthy to take the scroll
    and to open its seals,
because you were slain,
    and with your blood you purchased
        for God

a 5,6 That is, the sevenfold Spirit   b 8 Isaiah 6:3

MONDAY

FOR HIM, NOT US

Revelation 4:1–11 *or* 4:8,11

Steve Brown

Our fallen nature is egocentric. That's another way of saying that most of us in our heart of hearts believe that the world revolves around us. The titles of most of the books we read indicate that the books will in some way make our lives better. We read books on how to have more power in our prayer life, how to become thin and beautiful, how to make our marriages sparkle and how to have a faith that works. Now there is, of course, nothing wrong with those books or the promises they make. But we may have missed the point.

The Bible teaches that the world was not created for us; it was created by and for God: "['To whom will you compare me? Or who is my equal?' says the Holy One]" (Isaiah 40:25). The world was created by God so that his attributes might be seen: "[For since the creation of the world God's invisible qualities—his eternal power and divine nature—have been clearly seen]" (Romans 1:20). The reason for creation is that God might be glorified: "[The heavens declare the glory of God; the skies proclaim the work of his hands]" (Psalm 19:1). When we look at the creation of God, our response should be the response of the living creatures in Revelation: "[You are worthy, our Lord and God, to receive glory and honor and power, for you created all things, and by your will they were created and have their being]" (Revelation 4:11).

DIETRICH BONHOEFFER {AD 1906–1945}

When Christ calls a man, He bids him come and die . . . Jesus' summons to the rich young man was calling him to die, because only the man who is dead to his own will can follow Christ. In fact, every command of Jesus is a call to die, with all our affections and lusts. But we do not want to die . . . [and yet] the call to discipleship . . . means both death and life . . . [It] sets the Christian in the middle of the daily arena against sin and the devil. Every day he encounters new temptations, and every day he must suffer anew for Jesus Christ's sake. The wounds and scars he receives in the fray are living tokens of this participation in the cross of his Lord.

reflection

1. In what ways are you guilty of being egocentric?
2. Why did God create you?
3. How can you participate in the cross of Christ this week?

For your next devotional reading, go to page 1446.

members of every tribe and language
and people and nation.
¹⁰You have made them to be a kingdom
and priests to serve our God,
and they will reign^a on the earth."

¹¹Then I looked and heard the voice of
many angels, numbering thousands upon
thousands, and ten thousand times ten
thousand. They encircled the throne and the
living creatures and the elders. ¹²In a loud
voice they were saying:

"Worthy is the Lamb, who was slain,
to receive power and wealth and
wisdom and strength
and honor and glory and praise!"

¹³Then I heard every creature in heaven
and on earth and under the earth and on the
sea, and all that is in them, saying:

"To him who sits on the throne and to
the Lamb
be praise and honor and glory and
power,
for ever and ever!"

¹⁴The four living creatures said, "Amen," and
the elders fell down and worshiped.

The Seals

6 I watched as the Lamb opened the
first of the seven seals. Then I heard
one of the four living creatures say in
a voice like thunder, "Come!" ²I looked, and
there before me was a white horse! Its rider
held a bow, and he was given a crown, and
he rode out as a conqueror bent on conquest.

³When the Lamb opened the second seal,
I heard the second living creature say,
"Come!" ⁴Then another horse came out, a
fiery red one. Its rider was given power to
take peace from the earth and to make people slay each other. To him was given a large
sword.

⁵When the Lamb opened the third seal, I
heard the third living creature say, "Come!"
I looked, and there before me was a black
horse! Its rider was holding a pair of scales
in his hand. ⁶Then I heard what sounded like
a voice among the four living creatures, saying, "Two pounds^b of wheat for a day's wages,^c and six pounds^c of barley for a day's

wages,^d and do not damage the oil and the
wine!"

⁷When the Lamb opened the fourth seal,
I heard the voice of the fourth living creature say, "Come!" ⁸I looked, and there before
me was a pale horse! Its rider was named
Death, and Hades was following close behind him. They were given power over a
fourth of the earth to kill by sword, famine
and plague, and by the wild beasts of the
earth.

⁹When he opened the fifth seal, I saw un-
der the altar the souls of those who had
been slain because of the word of God and
the testimony they had maintained. ¹⁰They
called out in a loud voice, "How long, Sovereign Lord, holy and true, until you judge the
inhabitants of the earth and avenge our
blood?" ¹¹Then each of them was given a
white robe, and they were told to wait a little longer, until the full number of their fellow servants and brothers and sisters were
killed just as they had been.

¹²I watched as he opened the sixth seal.
There was a great earthquake. The sun
turned black like sackcloth made of goat
hair, the whole moon turned blood red,
¹³and the stars in the sky fell to earth, as figs
drop from a fig tree when shaken by a strong
wind. ¹⁴The sky receded like a scroll, rolling
up, and every mountain and island was re-
moved from its place.

¹⁵Then the kings of the earth, the princes,
the generals, the rich, the mighty, and everyone else, both slave and free, hid in caves
and among the rocks of the mountains.
¹⁶They called to the mountains and the
rocks, "Fall on us and hide us^e from the face
of him who sits on the throne and from the
wrath of the Lamb! ¹⁷For the great day of
their^f wrath has come, and who can withstand it?"

144,000 Sealed

7 After this I saw four angels standing
at the four corners of the earth, holding back the four winds of the earth to
prevent any wind from blowing on the land
or on the sea or on any tree. ²Then I saw another angel coming up from the east, having
the seal of the living God. He called out in a
loud voice to the four angels who had been

---

^a 10 Some manuscripts *they reign*   ^b 6 Or about 1 kilogram   ^c 6 Greek *a denarius*   ^d 6 Or about
3 kilograms   ^e 16 See Hosea 10:8.   ^f 17 Some manuscripts *his*

TUESDAY

THE LION AND THE LAMB

Revelation 5:1–14 *or* 5:5–6,12–13

JONATHAN EDWARDS {AD 1703–1758}

Notice the two distinct names here given to Christ.

He is called a Lion, the Lion of the tribe of Judah . . . On account of the valiant acts of David, the tribe of Judah, of which David belonged, was compared in Jacob's prophetic blessing to a lion, but more especially with an eye to Jesus Christ, who also was of that tribe and was descended from David and is in our text called "the Root of David."

He is called a Lamb . . . A lamb appears to open the book, a very different kind of creature from a lion! . . . And Christ is here represented not only as a lamb, but a lamb as if it had been slain, that is, with the marks of its deadly wounds.

There is a coming together of admirable virtues in Jesus Christ. The lion and the lamb, though very different, yet have their peculiar virtues. The lion excels in strength and in the majesty of its appearance and voice; the lamb excels in meekness and patience, good for food and clothing, and being suitable to be offered in sacrifice to God. But we see that Christ is in the text compared to both, because the different virtues of both wonderfully meet in him.

Marva J. Dawn

We are not at all ready for the appearance of this one who is called worthy, for he comes as a lamb, and not only as such a gentle creature, but also as a lamb that has been slain . . .

Because of the glaring contrast between the names . . . and their actual fulfillment in the Lamb who was slain, we are forced to recognize this major theme of the New Testament in its entirety and particularly in The Revelation; the victory comes through sacrifice . . .

Think what would happen if we would get this straight in our churches: victory is won through sacrifice. Could we aspire to . . . providing shelter for the homeless and meals for the hungry . . . investing ourselves more deeply in the lives of the poor and the dispossessed to teach them skills, to help them find health care and jobs? . . . What would happen if God's people would truly enter into the situations of our neighbors in order to bring peace and justice to the slums, tenement houses, ghettos, the emptiness of riches, the struggles of the physically or mentally disabled? . . . Is our evangelism weak because we are not willing to submit our lives to the slaying and sacrifice that make true witness possible?

reflection

1.　What attributes would you use to describe a lion? How is Christ like a lion?

2.　How would you describe a lamb? In what ways does that description give you a fuller picture of Jesus?

3.　Why are both the Lion and the Lamb worthy of your praise and honor?

For your next devotional reading, go to page 1450.

given power to harm the land and the sea: [3]"Do not harm the land or the sea or the trees until we put a seal on the foreheads of the servants of our God." [4]Then I heard the number of those who were sealed: 144,000 from all the tribes of Israel.

[5]From the tribe of Judah 12,000 were sealed,
from the tribe of Reuben 12,000,
from the tribe of Gad 12,000,
[6]from the tribe of Asher 12,000,
from the tribe of Naphtali 12,000,
from the tribe of Manasseh 12,000,
[7]from the tribe of Simeon 12,000,
from the tribe of Levi 12,000,
from the tribe of Issachar 12,000,
[8]from the tribe of Zebulun 12,000,
from the tribe of Joseph 12,000,
from the tribe of Benjamin 12,000.

The Great Multitude in White Robes

[9]After this I looked, and there before me was a great multitude that no one could count, from every nation, tribe, people and language, standing before the throne and in front of the Lamb. They were wearing white robes and were holding palm branches in their hands. [10]And they cried out in a loud voice:

"Salvation belongs to our God,
who sits on the throne,
and to the Lamb."

[11]All the angels were standing around the throne and around the elders and the four living creatures. They fell down on their faces before the throne and worshiped God, [12]saying:

"Amen!
Praise and glory
and wisdom and thanks and honor
and power and strength
be to our God for ever and ever.
Amen!"

[13]Then one of the elders asked me, "These in white robes—who are they, and where did they come from?"

[14]I answered, "Sir, you know."

And he said, "These are they who have come out of the great tribulation; they have washed their robes and made them white in the blood of the Lamb. [15]Therefore,

"they are before the throne of God
and serve him day and night in his temple;
and he who sits on the throne
will spread his tent over them.
[16]'Never again will they hunger;
never again will they thirst.
The sun will not beat down on them,'[a]
nor any scorching heat.
[17]For the Lamb at the center before the throne
will be their shepherd;
'he will lead them to springs of living water.'[a]
'And God will wipe away every tear from their eyes.'[b]

The Seventh Seal and the Golden Censer

8 When he opened the seventh seal, there was silence in heaven for about half an hour.

[2]And I saw the seven angels who stand before God, and seven trumpets were given to them.

[3]Another angel, who had a golden censer, came and stood at the altar. He was given much incense to offer, with the prayers of all God's people, on the golden altar before the throne. [4]The smoke of the incense, together with the prayers of God's people, went up before God from the angel's hand. [5]Then the angel took the censer, filled it with fire from the altar, and hurled it on the earth; and there came peals of thunder, rumblings, flashes of lightning and an earthquake.

The Trumpets

[6]Then the seven angels who had the seven trumpets prepared to sound them.

[7]The first angel sounded his trumpet, and there came hail and fire mixed with blood, and it was hurled down on the earth. A third of the earth was burned up, a third of the trees were burned up, and all the green grass was burned up.

[8]The second angel sounded his trumpet, and something like a huge mountain, all ablaze, was thrown into the sea. A third of the sea turned into blood, [9]a third of the living creatures in the sea died, and a third of the ships were destroyed.

[10]The third angel sounded his trumpet, and a great star, blazing like a torch, fell

a 16,17 Isaiah 49:10   b 17 Isaiah 25:8

from the sky on a third of the rivers and on the springs of water— [11]the name of the star is Wormwood. [a] A third of the waters turned bitter, and many people died from the waters that had become bitter.

[12]The fourth angel sounded his trumpet, and a third of the sun was struck, a third of the moon, and a third of the stars, so that a third of them turned dark. A third of the day was without light, and also a third of the night.

[13]As I watched, I heard an eagle that was flying in midair call out in a loud voice: "Woe! Woe! Woe to the inhabitants of the earth, because of the trumpet blasts about to be sounded by the other three angels!"

9 The fifth angel sounded his trumpet, and I saw a star that had fallen from the sky to the earth. The star was given the key to the shaft of the Abyss. [2]When he opened the Abyss, smoke rose from it like the smoke from a gigantic furnace. The sun and sky were darkened by the smoke from the Abyss. [3]And out of the smoke locusts came down on the earth and were given power like that of scorpions of the earth. [4]They were told not to harm the grass of the earth or any plant or tree, but only those people who did not have the seal of God on their foreheads. [5]They were not allowed to kill them but only to torture them for five months. And the agony they suffered was like that of the sting of a scorpion when it strikes. [6]During those days people will seek death but will not find it; they will long to die, but death will elude them.

[7]The locusts looked like horses prepared for battle. On their heads they wore something like crowns of gold, and their faces resembled human faces. [8]Their hair was like women's hair, and their teeth were like lions' teeth. [9]They had breastplates like breastplates of iron, and the sound of their wings was like the thundering of many horses and chariots rushing into battle. [10]They had tails with stingers, like scorpions, and in their tails they had power to torment people for five months. [11]They had as king over them the angel of the Abyss, whose name in Hebrew is Abaddon and in Greek is Apollyon (that is, Destroyer).

[12]The first woe is past; two other woes are yet to come.

[13]The sixth angel sounded his trumpet, and I heard a voice coming from the four horns of the golden altar that is before God. [14]It said to the sixth angel who had the trumpet, "Release the four angels who are bound at the great river Euphrates." [15]And the four angels who had been kept ready for this very hour and day and month and year were released to kill a third of the world's people. [16]The number of the mounted troops was two hundred million. I heard their number.

[17]The horses and riders I saw in my vision looked like this: Their breastplates were fiery red, dark blue, and yellow as sulfur. The heads of the horses resembled the heads of lions, and out of their mouths came fire, smoke and sulfur. [18]A third of the people were killed by the three plagues of fire, smoke and sulfur that came out of their mouths. [19]The power of the horses was in their mouths and in their tails; for their tails were like snakes, having heads with which they inflict injury.

[20]The rest of the people who were not killed by these plagues still did not repent of the work of their hands; they did not stop worshiping demons, and idols of gold, silver, bronze, stone and wood—idols that cannot see or hear or walk. [21]Nor did they repent of their murders, their magic arts, their sexual immorality or their thefts.

The Angel and the Little Scroll

10 Then I saw another mighty angel coming down from heaven. He was robed in a cloud, with a rainbow above his head; his face was like the sun, and his legs were like fiery pillars. [2]He was holding a little scroll, which lay open in his hand. He planted his right foot on the sea and his left foot on the land, [3]and he gave a loud shout like the roar of a lion. When he shouted, the voices of the seven thunders spoke. [4]And when the seven thunders spoke, I was about to write; but I heard a voice from heaven say, "Seal up what the seven thunders have said and do not write it down."

[5]Then the angel I had seen standing on the sea and on the land raised his right hand to heaven. [6]And he swore by him who lives for ever and ever, who created the heavens and all that is in them, the earth and all that

---

[a] 11 Wormwood is a bitter substance.

is in it, and the sea and all that is in it, and said, "There will be no more delay! [7]But in the days when the seventh angel is about to sound his trumpet, the mystery of God will be accomplished, just as he announced to his servants the prophets."

[8]Then the voice that I had heard from heaven spoke to me once more: "Go, take the scroll that lies open in the hand of the angel who is standing on the sea and on the land."

[9]So I went to the angel and asked him to give me the little scroll. He said to me, "Take it and eat it. It will turn your stomach sour, but 'in your mouth it will be as sweet as honey.'[a]" [10]I took the little scroll from the angel's hand and ate it. It tasted as sweet as honey in my mouth, but when I had eaten it, my stomach turned sour. [11]Then I was told, "You must prophesy again about many peoples, nations, languages and kings."

The Two Witnesses

11 I was given a reed like a measuring rod and was told, "Go and measure the temple of God and the altar, with its worshipers. [2]But exclude the outer court; do not measure it, because it has been given to the Gentiles. They will trample on the holy city for 42 months. [3]And I will appoint my two witnesses, and they will prophesy for 1,260 days, clothed in sackcloth." [4]They are "the two olive trees" and the two lampstands, and "they stand before the Lord of the earth."[b] [5]If anyone tries to harm them, fire comes from their mouths and devours their enemies. This is how anyone who wants to harm them must die. [6]They have power to shut up the sky so that it will not rain during the time they are prophesying; and they have power to turn the waters into blood and to strike the earth with every kind of plague as often as they want.

[7]Now when they have finished their testimony, the beast that comes up from the Abyss will attack them, and overpower and kill them. [8]Their bodies will lie in the public square of the great city, which is figuratively called Sodom and Egypt, where also their Lord was crucified. [9]For three and a half days many from every people, tribe, language and nation will gaze on their bodies

and refuse them burial. [10]The inhabitants of the earth will gloat over them and will celebrate by sending each other gifts, because these two prophets had tormented those who live on the earth.

[11]But after the three and a half days the breath[c] of life from God entered them, and they stood on their feet, and terror struck those who saw them. [12]Then they heard a loud voice from heaven saying to them, "Come up here." And they went up to heaven in a cloud, while their enemies looked on.

[13]At that very hour there was a severe earthquake and a tenth of the city collapsed. Seven thousand people were killed in the earthquake, and the survivors were terrified and gave glory to the God of heaven.

[14]The second woe has passed; the third woe is coming soon.

The Seventh Trumpet

[15]The seventh angel sounded his trumpet, and there were loud voices in heaven, which said:

> "The kingdom of the world has become
>   the kingdom of our Lord and of his
>   Messiah,
> and he will reign for ever and ever."

[16]And the twenty-four elders, who were seated on their thrones before God, fell on their faces and worshiped God, [17]saying:

> "We give thanks to you, Lord God
>   Almighty,
>   the One who is and who was,
> because you have taken your great
>   power
>   and have begun to reign.
> [18]The nations were angry,
>   and your wrath has come.
> The time has come for judging the dead,
>   and for rewarding your servants the
>   prophets
> and your people who revere your name,
>   both great and small—
> and for destroying those who destroy the
>   earth."

[19]Then God's temple in heaven was opened, and within his temple was seen the ark of his covenant. And there came flashes of lightning, rumblings, peals of thunder, an earthquake and a great hailstorm.

---

[a] 9 Ezek. 3:3   [b] 4 See Zech. 4:3,11,14.   [c] 11 Or *Spirit* (see Ezek. 37:5,14)

WEDNESDAY

GOD: THE BIGGEST PICTURE
Revelation 11:1–19 *or* 11:15–19

Chris Tomlin

I believe if we can just get a hold of the biggest possible picture of God, all the other things we care about in our lives will line up correctly. This might not sound like a great sell in today's me-centered world. But what's more relevant to you and me than God? Has the Creator who said, "Let there be"—and there was—now lost His voice? Has the God who became flesh and blood in the person of Jesus and befriended everyday people like drunks and prostitutes and you and me now lost His touch?

No! God is still the most relevant being in the universe, and knowing Him is still the most important quest of our lives. Our worship should naturally reflect this. To put ourselves in first place is to fall way short and be continually disappointed.

SAINT FRANCIS DE SALES {AD 1567–1622}

Consider how noble and excellent a thing your soul is. It is equipped with understanding. It is capable of knowing, not merely this visible world around us, but also angels and paradise. It is capable of knowing that there is an all-mighty, all-merciful, indescribable God. It is capable of knowing that eternity lies before you, and of knowing how to live in this visible world so as to attain fellowship with those angels in paradise, and even more to attain the eternal realization of the presence of God.

And still there's more: Your soul possesses a noble will—capable of loving God, and irresistibly drawn to that love. Your heart is full of generous enthusiasm. It can find no rest in any earthly creation, or in anything other than God . . .

When the heart of man seeks fulfillment in another creature, it goes to work eagerly, expecting to satisfy its cravings. But as soon as it obtains what it sought, it finds an empty blank; and dissatisfied, it begins to seek something new. For God will not allow our hearts to find any rest, like the dove going forth from Noah's ark, until it returns to God, from whom it came . . .

And so you might address your soul: "You are capable of fulfilling a longing after God, so why should you trifle with anything lower? . . . Lift up your soul with thoughts such as these, convince it that it is eternal and worthy of eternity, and fill it with courage in this pursuit.

reflection

1. Based on how you have spent the last few days, how would you describe what is most important to you in your life?

2. How do you view God? Do you feel you have a good picture of God?

3. Why are knowing and following God so important?

For your next devotional reading, go to page 1454.

The Woman and the Dragon

12 A great and wondrous sign appeared in heaven: a woman clothed with the sun, with the moon under her feet and a crown of twelve stars on her head. ²She was pregnant and cried out in pain as she was about to give birth. ³Then another sign appeared in heaven: an enormous red dragon with seven heads and ten horns and seven crowns on its heads. ⁴Its tail swept a third of the stars out of the sky and flung them to the earth. The dragon stood in front of the woman who was about to give birth, so that it might devour her child the moment he was born. ⁵She gave birth to a son, a male child, who "will rule all the nations with an iron scepter."ᵃ And her child was snatched up to God and to his throne. ⁶The woman fled into the wilderness to a place prepared for her by God, where she might be taken care of for 1,260 days.

⁷And there was war in heaven. Michael and his angels fought against the dragon, and the dragon and his angels fought back. ⁸But he was not strong enough, and they lost their place in heaven. ⁹The great dragon was hurled down—that ancient serpent called the devil, or Satan, who leads the whole world astray. He was hurled to the earth, and his angels with him.

¹⁰Then I heard a loud voice in heaven say:

"Now have come the salvation and the
power
and the kingdom of our God,
and the authority of his Messiah.
For the accuser of our brothers and
sisters,
who accuses them before our God day
and night,
has been hurled down.
¹¹They triumphed over him
by the blood of the Lamb
and by the word of their testimony;
they did not love their lives so much
as to shrink from death.
¹²Therefore rejoice, you heavens
and you who dwell in them!
But woe to the earth and the sea,
because the devil has gone down to
you!
He is filled with fury,

because he knows that his time is
short."

¹³When the dragon saw that he had been hurled to the earth, he pursued the woman who had given birth to the male child. ¹⁴The woman was given the two wings of a great eagle, so that she might fly to the place prepared for her in the wilderness, where she would be taken care of for a time, times and half a time, out of the serpent's reach. ¹⁵Then from his mouth the serpent spewed water like a river, to overtake the woman and sweep her away with the torrent. ¹⁶But the earth helped the woman by opening its mouth and swallowing the river that the dragon had spewed out of his mouth. ¹⁷Then the dragon was enraged at the woman and went off to make war against the rest of her offspring—those who keep God's commands and hold fast their testimony about Jesus.

The Beast out of the Sea

13 The dragonᵇ stood on the shore of the sea. And I saw a beast coming out of the sea. It had ten horns and seven heads, with ten crowns on its horns, and on each head a blasphemous name. ²The beast I saw resembled a leopard, but had feet like those of a bear and a mouth like that of a lion. The dragon gave the beast his power and his throne and great authority. ³One of the heads of the beast seemed to have had a fatal wound, but the fatal wound had been healed. The whole world was filled with wonder and followed the beast. ⁴People worshiped the dragon because he had given authority to the beast, and they also worshiped the beast and asked, "Who is like the beast? Who can make war against it?"

⁵The beast was given a mouth to utter proud words and blasphemies and to exercise its authority for forty-two months. ⁶It opened its mouth to blaspheme God, and to slander his name and his dwelling place and those who live in heaven. ⁷It was given power to make war against God's people and to conquer them. And it was given authority over every tribe, people, language and nation. ⁸All inhabitants of the earth will worship the beast—all whose names have not been written in the Lamb's book of life, the

─────────

a 5 Psalm 2:9   *b 1* Some manuscripts *And I*

Lamb who was slain from the creation of the world.^a

⁹Whoever has ears, let them hear.

¹⁰"If anyone is to go into captivity,
   into captivity they will go.
If anyone is to be killed^b with the sword,
   with the sword they will be killed."^c

This calls for patient endurance and faithfulness on the part of God's people.

The Beast out of the Earth

¹¹Then I saw another beast, coming out of the earth. It had two horns like a lamb, but it spoke like a dragon. ¹²It exercised all the authority of the first beast on its behalf, and made the earth and its inhabitants worship the first beast, whose fatal wound had been healed. ¹³And it performed great signs, even causing fire to come down from heaven to the earth in full view of everyone. ¹⁴Because of the signs it was given power to perform on behalf of the first beast, it deceived the inhabitants of the earth. It ordered them to set up an image in honor of the beast who was wounded by the sword and yet lived. ¹⁵It was given power to give breath to the image of the first beast, so that it could speak and cause all who refused to worship the image to be killed. ¹⁶It also forced all people, great and small, rich and poor, free and slave, to receive a mark on their right hands or on their foreheads, ¹⁷so that they could not buy or sell unless they had the mark, which is the name of the beast or the number of its name.

¹⁸This calls for wisdom. Let those who have insight calculate the number of the beast, for it is the number of a man.^d That number is 666.

The Lamb and the 144,000

14 Then I looked, and there before me was the Lamb, standing on Mount Zion, and with him 144,000 who had his name and his Father's name written on their foreheads. ²And I heard a sound from heaven like the roar of rushing waters and like a loud peal of thunder. The sound I heard was like that of harpists playing their harps. ³And they sang a new song before the throne and before the four living creatures and the elders. No one could learn the song except the 144,000 who had been redeemed from the earth. ⁴These are those who did not defile themselves with women, for they remained virgins. They follow the Lamb wherever he goes. They were purchased from among the human race and offered as firstfruits to God and the Lamb. ⁵No lie was found in their mouths; they are blameless.

The Three Angels

⁶Then I saw another angel flying in midair, and he had the eternal gospel to proclaim to those who live on the earth—to every nation, tribe, language and people. ⁷He said in a loud voice, "Fear God and give him glory, because the hour of his judgment has come. Worship him who made the heavens, the earth, the sea and the springs of water."

⁸A second angel followed and said, " 'Fallen! Fallen is Babylon the Great,'^e which made all the nations drink the maddening wine of her adulteries."

⁹A third angel followed them and said in a loud voice: "If anyone worships the beast and its image and receives its mark on their forehead or on their hand, ¹⁰they, too, will drink of the wine of God's fury, which has been poured full strength into the cup of his wrath. They will be tormented with burning sulfur in the presence of the holy angels and of the Lamb. ¹¹And the smoke of their torment will rise for ever and ever. There will be no rest day or night for those who worship the beast and its image, or for anyone who receives the mark of its name." ¹²This calls for patient endurance on the part of the people of God who keep his commands and remain faithful to Jesus.

¹³Then I heard a voice from heaven say, "Write: Blessed are the dead who die in the Lord from now on."

"Yes," says the Spirit, "they will rest from their labor, for their deeds will follow them."

Harvesting the Earth and Trampling the Winepress

¹⁴I looked, and there before me was a white cloud, and seated on the cloud was one like a son of man^f with a crown of gold on his head and a sharp sickle in his hand.

---

^a 8 Or *written from the creation of the world in the book of life belonging to the Lamb who was slain*   ^b 10 Some manuscripts *anyone kills*   ^c 10 Jer. 15:2   ^d 18 Or *is humanity's number*   ^e 8 Isaiah 21:9   ^f 14 See Daniel 7:13.

¹⁵Then another angel came out of the temple and called in a loud voice to him who was sitting on the cloud, "Take your sickle and reap, because the time to reap has come, for the harvest of the earth is ripe." ¹⁶So he who was seated on the cloud swung his sickle over the earth, and the earth was harvested.

¹⁷Another angel came out of the temple in heaven, and he too had a sharp sickle. ¹⁸Still another angel, who had charge of the fire, came from the altar and called in a loud voice to him who had the sharp sickle, "Take your sharp sickle and gather the clusters of grapes from the earth's vine, because its grapes are ripe." ¹⁹The angel swung his sickle on the earth, gathered its grapes and threw them into the great winepress of God's wrath. ²⁰They were trampled in the winepress outside the city, and blood flowed out of the press, rising as high as the horses' bridles for a distance of 1,600 stadia.[a]

Seven Angels With Seven Plagues

15 I saw in heaven another great and marvelous sign: seven angels with the seven last plagues—last, because with them God's wrath is completed. ²And I saw what looked like a sea of glass glowing with fire and, standing beside the sea, those who had been victorious over the beast and its image and over the number of its name. They held harps given them by God ³and sang the song of God's servant Moses and of the Lamb:

"Great and marvelous are your deeds,
  Lord God Almighty.
Just and true are your ways,
  King of the nations.[b]
⁴Who will not fear you, Lord,
  and bring glory to your name?
For you alone are holy.
All nations will come
  and worship before you,
for your righteous acts have been
  revealed."[c]

⁵After this I looked, and I saw in heaven the temple—that is, the tabernacle of the covenant law—and it was opened. ⁶Out of the temple came the seven angels with the seven plagues. They were dressed in clean, shining linen and wore golden sashes around their chests. ⁷Then one of the four living creatures gave to the seven angels seven golden bowls filled with the wrath of God, who lives for ever and ever. ⁸And the temple was filled with smoke from the glory of God and from his power, and no one could enter the temple until the seven plagues of the seven angels were completed.

The Seven Bowls of God's Wrath

16 Then I heard a loud voice from the temple saying to the seven angels, "Go, pour out the seven bowls of God's wrath on the earth."

²The first angel went and poured out his bowl on the land, and ugly, festering sores broke out on the people who had the mark of the beast and worshiped its image.

³The second angel poured out his bowl on the sea, and it turned into blood like that of a dead person, and every living thing in the sea died.

⁴The third angel poured out his bowl on the rivers and springs of water, and they became blood. ⁵Then I heard the angel in charge of the waters say:

"You are just in these judgments,
  you who are and who were, the Holy
    One,
  because you have so judged;
⁶for they have shed the blood of your
    people and your prophets,
and you have given them blood to
    drink as they deserve."

⁷And I heard the altar respond:

"Yes, Lord God Almighty,
  true and just are your judgments."

⁸The fourth angel poured out his bowl on the sun, and the sun was allowed to scorch people with fire. ⁹They were seared by the intense heat and they cursed the name of God, who had control over these plagues, but they refused to repent and glorify him.

¹⁰The fifth angel poured out his bowl on the throne of the beast, and its kingdom was plunged into darkness. People gnawed their tongues in agony ¹¹and cursed the God of heaven because of their pains and their

---

a 20 That is, about 180 miles or about 300 kilometers   b 3 Some manuscripts ages   c 3,4 Phrases in this song are drawn from Psalm 111:2,3; Deut. 32:4; Jer. 10:7; Psalms 86:9; 98:2.

THURSDAY

THE CRUCIBLE OF TRIALS

Revelation 15:1–8 *or* 15:2

PHILLIPS BROOKS {AD 1835–1893}

"Those who had been victorious over the beast" are those who have come out of sin holy and out of trial pure and, out of much tribulation, have entered the kingdom of heaven.

These will walk on "a sea of glass [glowing] with fire." The sea of glass—calm, clear, placid—evidently that is the symbol of repose, of rest, of peace. And fire, testing all things, consuming what is evil, purifying what is good, never resting a moment, never sparing pain; fire, all through the Bible, is the symbol of active trial of every sort, of struggle. The "sea of glass [glowing] with fire" is repose mingled with struggle. It is peace and rest and achievement, with the power of trial and suffering yet alive and working within it.

This is our doctrine: the permanent value of trial—that when you conquer your adversaries and your difficulties, it is not as if you never had encountered them. Your victory is colored with the hard struggle that won it ... The life that has been overturned by the strong hand of God, filled with the deep, revolutionary forces of suffering, and purified by the strong fires of temptation, keeps its long discipline forever. There roots in that discipline the deepest growths of the most sunny and luxuriant spiritual life that it is ever able to attain.

Brennan Manning

The basic premise of Biblical trust is that the God and Father of Jesus Christ wants us to live, to grow, to unfold and to experience fullness of life. Trust is an attitude acquired gradually through many crises and trials ... Perhaps this is the essence of trust: to be convinced of the reliability of God.

Trust is purified in the crucible of trial. From the depths of a purified heart, trust clings to the belief that whatever happens in our lives is designed to form Christ within us. Unwavering confidence in the love of God inspires trust ... to pray with Charles de Foucauld: "Abba ... into your hands I commend my spirit. I offer it to you with all the love of my heart, for I love you, Lord, and I give myself, surrender myself into your hands, without reserve, with boundless confidence, for you are my Father."

reflection

1. How do struggles and trials purify and strengthen the person who trusts in God as they go through them?

2. What examples of this can you give from your own life or the lives of those close to you?

3. What heavenly reward awaits those who hold on tightly to God through the ups and downs of life?

For your next devotional reading, go to page 1459.

sores, but they refused to repent of what they had done.

¹²The sixth angel poured out his bowl on the great river Euphrates, and its water was dried up to prepare the way for the kings from the East. ¹³Then I saw three evil*a* spirits that looked like frogs; they came out of the mouth of the dragon, out of the mouth of the beast and out of the mouth of the false prophet. ¹⁴They are demonic spirits that perform signs, and they go out to the kings of the whole world, to gather them for the battle on the great day of God Almighty.

¹⁵"Look, I come like a thief! Blessed are those who stay awake and keep their clothes on, so that they may not go naked and be shamefully exposed."

¹⁶Then they gathered the kings together to the place that in Hebrew is called Armageddon.

¹⁷The seventh angel poured out his bowl into the air, and out of the temple came a loud voice from the throne, saying, "It is done!" ¹⁸Then there came flashes of lightning, rumblings, peals of thunder and a severe earthquake. No earthquake like it has ever occurred since the human race has been on earth, so tremendous was the quake. ¹⁹The great city split into three parts, and the cities of the nations collapsed. God remembered Babylon the Great and gave her the cup filled with the wine of the fury of his wrath. ²⁰Every island fled away and the mountains could not be found. ²¹From the sky huge hailstones, each weighing about a hundred pounds,*b* fell on people. And they cursed God on account of the plague of hail, because the plague was so terrible.

Babylon, the Prostitute on the Beast

17 One of the seven angels who had the seven bowls came and said to me, "Come, I will show you the punishment of the great prostitute, who sits by many waters. ²With her the kings of the earth committed adultery, and the inhabitants of the earth were intoxicated with the wine of her adulteries."

³Then the angel carried me away in the Spirit into a wilderness. There I saw a woman sitting on a scarlet beast that was covered with blasphemous names and had seven heads and ten horns. ⁴The woman was dressed in purple and scarlet, and was glittering with gold, precious stones and pearls. She held a golden cup in her hand, filled with abominable things and the filth of her adulteries. ⁵This title was written on her forehead:

MYSTERY
BABYLON THE GREAT
THE MOTHER OF PROSTITUTES
AND OF THE ABOMINATIONS OF THE EARTH.

⁶I saw that the woman was drunk with the blood of God's people, the blood of those who bore testimony to Jesus.

When I saw her, I was greatly astonished. ⁷Then the angel said to me: "Why are you astonished? I will explain to you the mystery of the woman and of the beast she rides, which has the seven heads and ten horns. ⁸The beast, which you saw, once was, now is not, and will come up out of the Abyss and go to its destruction. The inhabitants of the earth whose names have not been written in the book of life from the creation of the world will be astonished when they see the beast, because it once was, now is not, and yet will come.

⁹"This calls for a mind with wisdom. The seven heads are seven hills on which the woman sits. ¹⁰They are also seven kings. Five have fallen, one is, the other has not yet come; but when he does come, he must remain for a little while. ¹¹The beast who once was, and now is not, is an eighth king. He belongs to the seven and is going to his destruction.

¹²"The ten horns you saw are ten kings who have not yet received a kingdom, but who for one hour will receive authority as kings along with the beast. ¹³They have one purpose and will give their power and authority to the beast. ¹⁴They will make war against the Lamb, but the Lamb will triumph over them because he is Lord of lords and King of kings—and with him will be his called, chosen and faithful followers."

¹⁵Then the angel said to me, "The waters you saw, where the prostitute sits, are peoples, multitudes, nations and languages. ¹⁶The beast and the ten horns you saw will hate the prostitute. They will bring her to ruin and leave her naked; they will eat her flesh and burn her with fire. ¹⁷For God has put it into their hearts to accomplish his

a 13 Greek *unclean*   *b 21* Or *about 40 kilograms*

purpose by agreeing to give the beast their power to rule, until God's words are fulfilled. [18]The woman you saw is the great city that rules over the kings of the earth."

Lament Over Fallen Babylon

18 After this I saw another angel coming down from heaven. He had great authority, and the earth was illuminated by his splendor. [2]With a mighty voice he shouted:

" 'Fallen! Fallen is Babylon the Great!' [a]
    She has become a dwelling for demons
and a haunt for every evil [b] spirit,
    a haunt for every unclean bird,
    a haunt for every unclean and
        detestable animal.
[3]For all the nations have drunk
    the maddening wine of her adulteries.
The kings of the earth committed
        adultery with her,
    and the merchants of the earth grew
        rich from her excessive
        luxuries."

Warning to Escape Babylon's Judgment

[4]Then I heard another voice from heaven say:

" 'Come out of her, my people,' [c]
    so that you will not share in her sins,
    so that you will not receive any of her
        plagues;
[5]for her sins are piled up to heaven,
    and God has remembered her crimes.
[6]Give back to her as she has given;
    pay her back double for what she has
        done.
    Pour her a double portion from her
        own cup.
[7]Give her as much torment and grief
    as the glory and luxury she gave
        herself.
In her heart she boasts,
    'I sit enthroned as queen.
I am not a widow; [d]
    I will never mourn.'
[8]Therefore in one day her plagues will
        overtake her:
    death, mourning and famine.
She will be consumed by fire,
    for mighty is the Lord God who
        judges her.

Threefold Woe Over Babylon's Fall

[9]"When the kings of the earth who committed adultery with her and shared her luxury see the smoke of her burning, they will weep and mourn over her. [10]Terrified at her torment, they will stand far off and cry:

" 'Woe! Woe to you, great city,
    you mighty city of Babylon!
In one hour your doom has come!'

[11]"The merchants of the earth will weep and mourn over her because no one buys their cargoes anymore— [12]cargoes of gold, silver, precious stones and pearls; fine linen, purple, silk and scarlet cloth; every sort of citron wood, and articles of every kind made of ivory, costly wood, bronze, iron and marble; [13]cargoes of cinnamon and spice, of incense, myrrh and frankincense, of wine and olive oil, of fine flour and wheat; cattle and sheep; horses and carriages; and human beings sold as slaves.

[14]"They will say, 'The fruit you longed for is gone from you. All your luxury and splendor have vanished, never to be recovered.' [15]The merchants who sold these things and gained their wealth from her will stand far off, terrified at her torment. They will weep and mourn [16]and cry out:

" 'Woe! Woe to you, great city,
    dressed in fine linen, purple and
        scarlet,
    and glittering with gold, precious
        stones and pearls!
[17]In one hour such great wealth has been
        brought to ruin!'

"Every sea captain, and all who travel by ship, the sailors, and all who earn their living from the sea, will stand far off. [18]When they see the smoke of her burning, they will exclaim, 'Was there ever a city like this great city?' [19]They will throw dust on their heads, and with weeping and mourning cry out:

" 'Woe! Woe to you, great city,
    where all who had ships on the sea
        became rich through her wealth!
In one hour she has been brought to ruin!'

[20]"Rejoice over her, you heavens!
    Rejoice, you people of God!
    Rejoice, apostles and prophets!
For God has judged her

---

[a] 2 Isaiah 21:9   [b] 2 Greek unclean   [c] 4 Jer. 51:45   [d] 7 See Isaiah 47:7,8.

with the judgment she imposed on you."

The Finality of Babylon's Doom

²¹Then a mighty angel picked up a boulder the size of a large millstone and threw it into the sea, and said:

"With such violence
    the great city of Babylon will be
        thrown down,
    never to be found again.
²²The music of harpists and musicians,
        pipers and trumpeters,
    will never be heard in you again.
No worker of any trade
    will ever be found in you again.
The sound of a millstone
    will never be heard in you again.
²³The light of a lamp
    will never shine in you again.
The voice of bridegroom and bride
    will never be heard in you again.
Your merchants were the world's
        important people.
    By your magic spell all the nations
        were led astray.
²⁴In her was found the blood of prophets
        and of God's people,
    of all who have been slaughtered on
        the earth."

Threefold Hallelujah Over Babylon's Fall

19 After this I heard what sounded like the roar of a great multitude in heaven shouting:

"Hallelujah!
Salvation and glory and power belong to
    our God,
²   for true and just are his judgments.
He has condemned the great prostitute
    who corrupted the earth by her
        adulteries.
He has avenged on her the blood of his
    servants."

³And again they shouted:

"Hallelujah!
The smoke from her goes up for ever
    and ever."

⁴The twenty-four elders and the four living creatures fell down and worshiped God, who was seated on the throne. And they cried:

"Amen, Hallelujah!"

⁵Then a voice came from the throne, saying:

"Praise our God,
    all you his servants,
you who fear him,
    both great and small!"

⁶Then I heard what sounded like a great multitude, like the roar of rushing waters and like loud peals of thunder, shouting:

"Hallelujah!
    For our Lord God Almighty reigns.
⁷Let us rejoice and be glad
    and give him glory!
For the wedding of the Lamb has come,
    and his bride has made herself ready.
⁸Fine linen, bright and clean,
    was given her to wear."

(Fine linen stands for the righteous acts of God's people.)

⁹Then the angel said to me, "Write: 'Blessed are those who are invited to the wedding supper of the Lamb!'" And he added, "These are the true words of God."

¹⁰At this I fell at his feet to worship him. But he said to me, "Don't do that! I am a fellow servant with you and with your brothers and sisters who hold to Jesus' testimony. Worship God! For the testimony of Jesus is the Spirit of prophecy."

The Heavenly Warrior Defeats the Beast

¹¹I saw heaven standing open and there before me was a white horse, whose rider is called Faithful and True. With justice he judges and makes war. ¹²His eyes are like blazing fire, and on his head are many crowns. He has a name written on him that no one knows but he himself. ¹³He is dressed in a robe dipped in blood, and his name is the Word of God. ¹⁴The armies of heaven were following him, riding on white horses and dressed in fine linen, white and clean. ¹⁵Coming out of his mouth is a sharp sword with which to strike down the nations. "He will rule them with an iron scepter."ᵃ He treads the winepress of the fury of the wrath

---

a 15 Psalm 2:9

of God Almighty. ¹⁶On his robe and on his thigh he has this name written:

KING OF KINGS AND LORD OF LORDS.

¹⁷And I saw an angel standing in the sun, who cried in a loud voice to all the birds flying in midair, "Come, gather together for the great supper of God, ¹⁸so that you may eat the flesh of kings, generals, and the mighty, of horses and their riders, and the flesh of all people, free and slave, great and small."

¹⁹Then I saw the beast and the kings of the earth and their armies gathered together to make war against the rider on the horse and his army. ²⁰But the beast was captured, and with him the false prophet who had performed the signs on his behalf. With these signs he had deluded those who had received the mark of the beast and worshiped his image. The two of them were thrown alive into the fiery lake of burning sulfur. ²¹The rest were killed with the sword coming out of the mouth of the rider on the horse, and all the birds gorged themselves on their flesh.

The Thousand Years

20 And I saw an angel coming down out of heaven, having the key to the Abyss and holding in his hand a great chain. ²He seized the dragon, that ancient serpent, who is the devil, or Satan, and bound him for a thousand years. ³He threw him into the Abyss, and locked and sealed it over him, to keep him from deceiving the nations anymore until the thousand years were ended. After that, he must be set free for a short time.

⁴I saw thrones on which were seated those who had been given authority to judge. And I saw the souls of those who had been beheaded because of their testimony about Jesus and because of the word of God. They had not worshiped the beast or his image and had not received his mark on their foreheads or their hands. They came to life and reigned with Christ a thousand years. ⁵(The rest of the dead did not come to life until the thousand years were ended.) This is the first resurrection. ⁶Blessed and holy are those who have part in the first resurrection. The second death has no power over them, but they will be priests of God and of

Christ and will reign with him for a thousand years.

The Judgment of Satan

⁷When the thousand years are over, Satan will be released from his prison ⁸and will go out to deceive the nations in the four corners of the earth—Gog and Magog—and to gather them for battle. In number they are like the sand on the seashore. ⁹They marched across the breadth of the earth and surrounded the camp of God's people, the city he loves. But fire came down from heaven and devoured them. ¹⁰And the devil, who deceived them, was thrown into the lake of burning sulfur, where the beast and the false prophet had been thrown. They will be tormented day and night for ever and ever.

The Judgment of the Dead

¹¹Then I saw a great white throne and him who was seated on it. The earth and the heavens fled from his presence, and there was no place for them. ¹²And I saw the dead, great and small, standing before the throne, and books were opened. Another book was opened, which is the book of life. The dead were judged according to what they had done as recorded in the books. ¹³The sea gave up the dead that were in it, and death and Hades gave up the dead that were in them, and everyone was judged according to what they had done. ¹⁴Then death and Hades were thrown into the lake of fire. The lake of fire is the second death. ¹⁵All whose names were not found written in the book of life were thrown into the lake of fire.

A New Heaven and a New Earth

21 Then I saw "a new heaven and a new earth," ᵃ for the first heaven and the first earth had passed away, and there was no longer any sea. ²I saw the Holy City, the new Jerusalem, coming down out of heaven from God, prepared as a bride beautifully dressed for her husband. ³And I heard a loud voice from the throne saying, "Look! God's dwelling place is now among the people, and he will dwell with them. They will be his people, and God himself will be with them and be their God. ⁴'He will wipe every tear from their eyes.

a 1 Isaiah 65:17

FRIDAY

THE WORLD'S PROGRESS

Revelation 21:1–27 or 21:1–4

A. R. FAUSSETT {AD 1821–1910}

The final two chapters of Revelation describe the eternal and consummated kingdom of God and the saints on the new earth. As the world of nations is to be pervaded by divine influence in the millennium, so the world of nature shall be, not annihilated, but transfigured universally in the eternal state which follows it. The earth was cursed for humanity's sake, but is redeemed by the second Adam.

A human's soul is redeemed by regeneration through the Holy Spirit now; our human body shall be redeemed at the resurrection. Humanity's earth shall be redeemed perfectly at the creation of the new heaven and earth, which shall exceed in glory the first Paradise—as much as the second Adam exceeds in glory the first Adam before the fall, and as humanity regenerated in body and soul shall exceed humanity as it was at creation.

Rob Bell

God isn't interested in reclaiming his original dream for creation; he wants to take it further. Imagine if you took all the sin and death out of the Bible. You would be left with a short book. It would have four chapters to be exact: Genesis 1 and 2; Revelation 21 and 22. In Genesis 1 and 2, we are told of a garden, but in Revelation 21 and 22, we are told of a city. A city is more advanced, more complicated than a garden. If a garden is developed and managed and cared for, it is eventually going to turn into a city. If there was no sin or death, creation would still move forward because God doesn't just want to reclaim things; God wants to see them move forward.

reflection

1. What do you look forward to most about heaven?

2. How is the future God has planned for you different than your present experience?

3. Think of the grace you've already experienced from God. How does that whet your appetite for what's to come?

For your next devotional reading, go to page 1461.

There will be no more death'ᵃ or mourning or crying or pain, for the old order of things has passed away."

⁵He who was seated on the throne said, "I am making everything new!" Then he said, "Write this down, for these words are trustworthy and true."

⁶He said to me: "It is done. I am the Alpha and the Omega, the Beginning and the End. To the thirsty I will give water without cost from the spring of the water of life. ⁷Those who are victorious will inherit all this, and I will be their God and they will be my children. ⁸But the cowardly, the unbelieving, the vile, the murderers, the sexually immoral, those who practice magic arts, the idolaters and all liars—they will be consigned to the fiery lake of burning sulfur. This is the second death."

The New Jerusalem, the Bride of the Lamb

⁹One of the seven angels who had the seven bowls full of the seven last plagues came and said to me, "Come, I will show you the bride, the wife of the Lamb." ¹⁰And he carried me away in the Spirit to a mountain great and high, and showed me the Holy City, Jerusalem, coming down out of heaven from God. ¹¹It shone with the glory of God, and its brilliance was like that of a very precious jewel, like a jasper, clear as crystal. ¹²It had a great, high wall with twelve gates, and with twelve angels at the gates. On the gates were written the names of the twelve tribes of Israel. ¹³There were three gates on the east, three on the north, three on the south and three on the west. ¹⁴The wall of the city had twelve foundations, and on them were the names of the twelve apostles of the Lamb.

¹⁵The angel who talked with me had a measuring rod of gold to measure the city, its gates and its walls. ¹⁶The city was laid out like a square, as long as it was wide. He measured the city with the rod and found it to be 12,000 stadiaᵇ in length, and as wide and high as it is long. ¹⁷He measured its wall and it was 144 cubitsᶜ thick,ᵈ by human measurement, which the angel was using. ¹⁸The wall was made of jasper, and the city of pure gold, as pure as glass. ¹⁹The foundations of the city walls were decorated with every kind of precious stone. The first foundation was jasper, the second sapphire, the third agate, the fourth emerald, ²⁰the fifth onyx, the sixth ruby, the seventh chrysolite, the eighth beryl, the ninth topaz, the tenth turquoise, the eleventh jacinth, and the twelfth amethyst.ᵉ ²¹The twelve gates were twelve pearls, each gate made of a single pearl. The great street of the city was of gold, as pure as transparent glass.

²²I did not see a temple in the city, because the Lord God Almighty and the Lamb are its temple. ²³The city does not need the sun or the moon to shine on it, for the glory of God gives it light, and the Lamb is its lamp. ²⁴The nations will walk by its light, and the kings of the earth will bring their splendor into it. ²⁵On no day will its gates ever be shut, for there will be no night there. ²⁶The glory and honor of the nations will be brought into it. ²⁷Nothing impure will ever enter it, nor will anyone who does what is shameful or deceitful, but only those whose names are written in the Lamb's book of life.

Eden Restored

22 Then the angel showed me the river of the water of life, as clear as crystal, flowing from the throne of God and of the Lamb ²down the middle of the great street of the city. On each side of the river stood the tree of life, bearing twelve crops of fruit, yielding its fruit every month. And the leaves of the tree are for the healing of the nations. ³No longer will there be any curse. The throne of God and of the Lamb will be in the city, and his servants will serve him. ⁴They will see his face, and his name will be on their foreheads. ⁵There will be no more night. They will not need the light of a lamp or the light of the sun, for the Lord God will give them light. And they will reign for ever and ever.

John and the Angel

⁶The angel said to me, "These words are trustworthy and true. The Lord, the God who inspires the prophets, sent his angel to show his servants the things that must soon take place."

ᵃ 4 Isaiah 25:8   ᵇ 16 That is, about 1,400 miles or about 2,200 kilometers   ᶜ 17 That is, about 200 feet or about 65 meters   ᵈ 17 Or high   ᵉ 20 The precise identification of some of these precious stones is uncertain.

If You Believe

Revelation 22:3

read/meditate

Revelation 22:3 describes a world without hardships. Think about the difficulties you see in the world. They can come in all shapes and forms, hold us down, and bring destruction. God promises a future world that will contain blessings but absolutely no curses. Think about how that promise could make your world a different place.

pray

Share with God the difficulties that you've experienced in your life. What do you look forward to leaving behind once you enter the new world? Tell God about each situation and let him bring the peace of heaven to your world now.

contemplate

So many of the curses we live under are a result of our own brokenness. While there are curses in life that may be permanent in terms of this world, open your mind to the healing that God may want to bring into your life even now.

additional reflection

We talk about heaven being so far away. It is within speaking distance of those who belong there.

—D. L. Moody

I believe the promises of God enough to venture an eternity on them.

—Isaac Watts

For your first devotional reading, go to page 4.

7"Look, I am coming soon! Blessed are those who keep the words of the prophecy in this scroll."

8I, John, am the one who heard and saw these things. And when I had heard and seen them, I fell down to worship at the feet of the angel who had been showing them to me. 9But he said to me, "Don't do that! I am a fellow servant with you and with your fellow prophets and with all who keep the words of this scroll. Worship God!"

10Then he told me, "Do not seal up the words of the prophecy of this scroll, because the time is near. 11Let those who do wrong continue to do wrong; let those who are vile continue to be vile; let those who do right continue to do right; and let those who are holy continue to be holy."

Epilogue: Invitation and Warning

12"Look, I am coming soon! My reward is with me, and I will give to everyone according to what they have done. 13I am the Alpha and the Omega, the First and the Last, the Beginning and the End.

14"Blessed are those who wash their robes, that they may have the right to the tree of life and may go through the gates into the city. 15Outside are the dogs, those who practice magic arts, the sexually immoral, the murderers, the idolaters and everyone who loves and practices falsehood.

16"I, Jesus, have sent my angel to give you*a* this testimony for the churches. I am the Root and the Offspring of David, and the bright Morning Star."

17The Spirit and the bride say, "Come!" And let those who hear say, "Come!" Let those who are thirsty come; and let all who wish take the free gift of the water of life.

18I warn everyone who hears the words of the prophecy of this scroll: If any one of you adds anything to them, God will add to you the plagues described in this scroll. 19And if any one of you takes words away from this scroll of prophecy, God will take away from you your share in the tree of life and in the Holy City, which are described in this scroll.

20He who testifies to these things says, "Yes, I am coming soon."

Amen. Come, Lord Jesus.

21The grace of the Lord Jesus be with God's people. Amen.

---

a 16 The Greek is plural.

contents

contents

appendix I

table of weights and measures

	BIBLICAL UNIT	APPROXIMATE AMERICAN EQUIVALENT		APPROXIMATE METRIC EQUIVALENT	
WEIGHTS	talent (60 minas)	75	pounds	34	kilograms
	mina (50 shekels)	1 1/4	pounds	0.6	kilogram
	shekel (2 bekas)	2/5	ounce	11.5	grams
	pim (2/3 shekel)	1/3	ounce	9.5	grams
	beka (10 gerahs)	1/5	ounce	5.5	grams
	gerah	1/50	ounce	0.6	gram
LENGTH	cubit	18	inches	0.5	meter
	span	9	inches	23	centimeters
	handbreadth	3	inches	8	centimeters
CAPACITY					
Dry Measure	cor [homer] (10 ephahs)	6	bushels	220	liters
	lethek (5 ephahs)	3	bushels	110	liters
	ephah (10 omers)	3/5	bushel	22	liters
	seah (1/3 ephah)	7	quarts	7.7	liters
	omer (1/10 ephah)	2	quarts	2	liters
	cab (1/18 ephah)	1	quart	1	liter
Liquid Measure	bath (1 ephah)	6	gallons	22	liters
	hin (1/6 bath)	4	quarts	4	liters
	log (1/72 bath)	1/3	quart	0.3	liter

The figures of the table are calculated on the basis of a shekel equaling 11.5 grams, a cubit equaling 18 inches and an ephah equaling 22 liters. The quart referred to is either a dry quart (slightly larger than a liter) or a liquid quart (slightly smaller than a liter), whichever is applicable. The ton referred to in the footnotes is the American ton of 2,000 pounds. Since most readers are more familiar with dry measures being given in weight rather than capacity (bushel, quart), dry measures have been converted in the footnotes to approximate weights.

This table is based upon the best available information, but it is not intended to be mathematically precise; like the measurement equivalents in the footnotes, it merely gives approximate amounts and distances. Weights and measures differed somewhat at various times and places in the ancient world. There is uncertainty particularly about the ephah and the bath; further discoveries may shed more light on these units of capacity.

appendix II
revised spelling of proper names

NIV	TNIV
Abib	Aviv
Abimelech	Abimelek
Achbor	Akbor
Acco	Akko
Acsah	Aksah
Acshaph	Akshaph
Aczib	Akzib
Adrammelech	Adrammelek
Ahimelech	Ahimelek
Ahisamach	Ahisamak
Allammelech	Allammelek
Anammelech	Anammelek
Asshur	Ashur
Asshurites	Ashurites
Athach	Athak
Baca	Baka
Bacuth	Bakuth
Becorath	Bekorath
Beracah	Berakah
Beth Car	Beth Kar
Bicri	Bikri
Cabbon	Kabbon
Cabul	Kabul
Calcol	Kalkol
Calno	Kalno
Calneh	Kalneh
Canneh	Kanneh
Carshena	Karshena
Carcas	Karkas
Carmi	Karmi
Casiphia	Kasiphia
Casluhites	Kasluhites
Cenchrea	Cenchreae
Col-Hozeh	Kol-Hozeh
Colosse	Colossae
Conaniah	Konaniah
Cozbi	Kozbi
Cozeba	Kozeba
Cun	Kun
Cuthah	Kuthah
Ebed-Melech	Ebed-Melek
Elimelech	Elimelek
Erech	Uruk
Eshcol	Eshkol
Eshtarah	Eshterah
Evil-Merodach	Awel-Marduk
Goiim	Goyim
Hacaliah	Hakaliah
Hacmoni	Hakmoni
Hadrach	Hadrak
Hanoch	Hanok
Hathach	Hathak
Haran	Harran
Hatticon	Hattikon
Hazazon Tamar	Hazezon Tamar
Helech	Helek
Iim	Iyim
Iscah	Iskah
Isshiah	Ishiah
Jaakanites	Bene Jaakan
Jacan	Jakan
Jecoliah	Jekoliah
Jehucal	Jehukal
Josech	Josek
Kittim	Kittites
Korazin	Chorazin
Lecah	Lekah
Maacah	Maakah

NIV	TNIV	NIV	TNIV
Macbannai	Makbannai	Parnach	Parnak
Macbenah	Makbenah	Pasach	Pasak
Macnadebai	Maknadebai	Racal	Rakal
Malcam	Malkam	Recab	Rekab
Malluch	Malluk	Recabites	Rekabites
Maoch	Maok	Recah	Rekah
Marcaboth	Markaboth	Regem-Melech	Regem-Melek
Meconah	Mekonah	Rodanim	Rodanites
Melech	Melek	Sabteca	Sabteka
Memucan	Memukan	Sacar	Sakar
Merodach-Baladan	Marduk-Baladan	Salecah	Salekah
Meshech	Meshek	Secacah	Sekakah
Mica	Mika	Secu	Seku
Micmash	Mikmash	Shecaniah	Shekaniah
Micmethah	Mikmethah	Sheshach	Sheshak
Micri	Mikri	Shobach	Shobak
Milcah	Milkah	Shophach	Shophak
Milcom	Milkom	Sibbecai	Sibbekai
Mithcah	Mithkah	Soco	Soko
Mizraim	Egypt	Socoh	Sokoh
Molech	Molek	Succoth	Sukkoth
Nacon	Nakon	Ucal	Ukal
Nathan-Melech	Nathan-Melek	Zaccai	Zakkai
Neco	Necho	Zaccur	Zakkur
Nisroch	Nisrok	Zeboiim	Zeboyim
Ocran	Okran	Zicri	Zikri

one year through the bible

60-day overview of the bible

1474 || 60-day overview of the bible

30 days for beginning your walk with christ

Day	Description	Passage
❏	The Fall of Humanity	Genesis 3:1–19
❏	A People for God	Genesis 28:10–15; 32:22–28
❏	The Ten Commandments	Exodus 20:1–17
❏	Sacrifices Required Under Law	Leviticus 5:14–19
❏	Punishments for Sin Under Law	Leviticus 20:7–27
❏	Obedience From Love	Deuteronomy 11:13–21
❏	Cycles of Disobedience	Judges 2:10–19
❏	The People Demand a King	1 Samuel 8:1–22
❏	Saul Fails and Is Rejected	1 Samuel 15:17–23
❏	Many Kings Fail	Jeremiah 1—17
❏	The Sin of the People	Ezekiel 20:5–26
❏	An Eternal King Promised	Jeremiah 23:1–6; Isaiah 9:6–7; Zechariah 9:9–10
❏	The Promised King Is Born	Luke 2:1–20
❏	The Word Became Flesh	John 1:1–18
❏	Signs and Miracles of Authority	Matthew 9:1–8; Luke 13:10–17
❏	Jesus Fulfills the Law	Matthew 5:17–20; Romans 8:1–4
❏	Jesus Teaches About New Life	John 3:1–36
❏	Jesus Willingly Taken	John 18:1–11
❏	Jesus' Death and Resurrection	Luke 23:44—24:12
❏	Christ a Sacrifice for All	Hebrews
❏	God's Wrath Explained	Romans 1:18–32
❏	God's Judgment Explained	Romans 2:5–11
❏	Righteousness by Faith	Romans 3:9–26
❏	Life Through Christ	Romans 5:12–21
❏	Life by the Spirit	Romans 8:1–17; Galatians 5:16–26
❏	Living Sacrifices	Romans 12:1–21
❏	Walking in the Light	1 John 1—2
❏	Living for God	1 Peter 4:1–11
❏	Love for One Another	1 John 3:11–24
❏	Promise of Eternity	2 Corinthians 5:1–10; Revelation 21:1–4

30 days with jesus

Day	Description	Passage
❑	Jesus' coming is predicted.	Isaiah 7:14; 9:1–7; Luke 1:26–38
❑	Jesus is born.	Matthew 1:18—2:23; Luke 2:1–20
❑	Jesus is baptized by John the Baptist.	Matthew 3:1–17
❑	Jesus begins his public ministry.	Matthew 4:1–17; Luke 4:14–44
❑	Jesus calls his disciples.	Luke 5:1–11; 6:12–16; John 1:35–51
❑	Jesus talks to a Pharisee and a Samaritan.	John 3:1—4:42
❑	Jesus delivers the Sermon on the Mount.	Matthew 5:1—7:29
❑	Jesus heals people in need.	Matthew 8:1—9:8
❑	Jesus tangles with the Pharisees.	Matthew 12:1–45
❑	Jesus teaches his disciples using parables.	Matthew 13:1–52
❑	Jesus demonstrates his power over nature.	Mark 6:45–52; Luke 8:22–25
❑	Jesus heals many.	Mark 5:1–43
❑	Jesus feeds 5,000 followers.	John 6:1–15
❑	Jesus is identified as the Christ.	Matthew 16:13—17:13
❑	Jesus casts out an evil spirit.	Mark 9:14–32
❑	Jesus teaches on forgiveness.	Matthew 18:15–35
❑	Jesus teaches on the kingdom of heaven.	Matthew 13:24–52
❑	Jesus confronts the rich young man.	Mark 10:17–31
❑	Jesus sends out his disciples.	Luke 10:1–24
❑	Jesus teaches how to love and pray.	Luke 10:25—11:13
❑	Jesus teaches about himself.	John 10:1–42
❑	Jesus raises Lazarus from the dead.	John 11:1–44
❑	Jesus travels to Jerusalem.	Matthew 21:1–27
❑	Jesus eats the Last Supper.	Matthew 26:17–30; John 13:1–17
❑	Jesus comforts his disciples.	John 14:1—16:33
❑	Jesus is arrested.	Matthew 26:36–75
❑	Jesus is put on trial.	John 18:19—19:16
❑	Jesus is crucified and buried.	John 19:17–42
❑	Jesus rises from the dead.	John 20:1—21:25
❑	Jesus ascends to heaven.	Matthew 28:16–20; Luke 24:36–53

acknowledgments

The editor and publisher gratefully acknowledge the permission granted to reproduce the copyrighted material found within this Bible. Every effort has been made to trace copyright holders and to obtain their permission for the use of material under copyright. The publisher apologizes for any errors or omissions in the below list and would be grateful if notified of any corrections that should be incorporated in future reprints or editions of this book."

Page 4 "My Answer," by Billy Graham, © 2004, 2005, 2006 Billy Graham, used by permission, all rights reserved.

D. L. Moody as quoted in *One Thousand and One Thoughts From My Library* by D. L. Moody. Language updated. © 2006 by Zondervan.

Page 6 George Fox, *Complete Works of George Fox, Letter #292.* Language updated. © 2006 by Zondervan.

Taken from *Praying the Names of God* by ANN SPANGLER. Copyright © 2004 by Ann Spangler. Used by permission of Zondervan.

Page 10 Taken from *Genesis* by JOHN H. WALTON. Copyright © 2001 by John H. Walton. Used by permission of Zondervan.

Mark Guy Pearse as quoted in *One Thousand and One Thoughts From My Library* by D. L. Moody. Language updated. © 2006 by Zondervan.

Page 14 Taken from *Stories Of The Faith* by RUTH A. TUCKER. Copyright © 1989 by Ruth A. Tucker. Used by permission of Zondervan.

John M'Ewan as quoted in *One Thousand and One Thoughts From My Library* by D. L. Moody. Language updated. © 2006 by Zondervan.

Page 19 Thomas Watson, *A Body of Divinity.* Language updated. © 2006 Zondervan.

Excerpts from THE DIVINE CONSPIRACY by DALLAS WILLARD Copyright © 1998 by Dallas Willard. Reprinted by permission of HarperCollins Publishers.

Page 23 Arthur W. Pink, *Sovereignty of God: 1921 Edition.* Language updated. © 2006 by Zondervan.

Taken from *When Life and Beliefs Collide* by CAROLYN CUSTIS JAMES. Copyright © 2001 by Carolyn C. James. Used by permission of Zondervan.

Page 27 Taken from *Jesus—Safe, Tender, Extreme* by ADRIAN PLASS. Copyright © 2006 by Adrian Plass. Used by permission of Adrian Plass.

Fyodor Dostoyevsky, *The Brothers Karamazov.* Translated by Constance Garnett, 1879.

Page 36 Herbert C. Leupold, *Exposition of Genesis* (The Wartburg Press, 1942).

Marva J. Dawn, *Morning by Morning: Daily Meditations from the Writings of Marva J. Dawn* (Grand Rapids, Mich.: Eerdmans, 2001). Used by permission.

Page 46 Charles Haddon Spurgeon as quoted in *One Thousand and One Thoughts From My Library* by D. L. Moody. Language updated. © 2006 by Zondervan.

Taken from *Flame in the Mind* by MICHAEL MARSHALL. Copyright © 2002 by Michael Marshall. Used by permission of Zondervan.

Page 49 Robert Jamieson, *Commentary Critical and Explanatory on the Whole Bible.* Language updated. © 2006 Zondervan.

Taken from *Genesis* by DEREK KIDNER. Copyright © 1981. Used with permission of InterVarsity Press, P.O. Box 1400, Downers Grove, IL 60515. www.ivpress.com.

Page 59 *For The Audience of One,* by Mike Pilavachi, excerpts from pages 64, 65. ©1999, Regal Books, Ventura, CA 93003. Used by permission.

Taken from *Mere Christianity* by C. S. LEWIS. Copyright © 2001. Used by permission of Zondervan.

Page 65 Taken from *The Message of Genesis 12–50: From Abraham to Joseph* by JOYCE G. BALDWIN. Copyright © 1986. Used by permission of InterVarsity Press, P.O. Box 1400. Downers Grove, IL 60515. www.ivpress.com.

Matthew Henry, *Commentary on the Whole Bible Volume I (Genesis to*

Deuteronomy). Language updated. © 2006 Zondervan.

Page 69 *The Seven Books Of John Cassian On The Incarnation Of The Lord, Against Nestorius*, included in *Nicene and Post-Nicene Fathers, 2nd Series, Vol. 11* by Philip Schaff. Language updated. © 2006 Zondervan.

Taken from *Case for Christ* by LEE P. STROBEL. Copyright © 1998 by Lee Strobel. Used by permission of Zondervan.

Page 71 Excerpted from *I Am Not but I Know I Am* © 2005 by Louie Giglio. Used by permission of Multnomah Publishers Inc.

Cardinal John Henry Newman, *Callista*. Language updated. © 2006 Zondervan.

Page 77 Fredrick W. Robertson, *Classic Sermons on the Attributes of God,* by Warren Wiersbe, (Grand Rapids, Mich.: Kregel 1989). Used by permission.

Taken from *Shoulda, Coulda, Woulda* by Dr. LES PARROT III, LESLIE PARROTT. Copyright © 2003 by Les Parrott. Used by permission of Zondervan.

Page 83 Carol L. Fitzpatrick, *Daily Wisdom for Women: Practical, Biblical Insight for Today's Woman* (Uhrichsville, Ohio: Barbour, 1997). Used by permission.

William Williams, *Guide Me, O Thou Great Jehovah*. Language updated © 2006 Zondervan.

Page 91 Andrea Johnson (a.k.a. First Lady "J"), *Daily Professions* (Mustang, Okla.: Tate, 2005). Used by permission.

Oscar Romero, *Through The Year With Oscar Romero: Daily Meditations* (Cincinnati, Ohio: St. Anthony's Press, 2005). Used by permission.

Page 94 Charles Finney, *Lectures on Systematic Theology*. Language updated. © 2006 Zondervan.

Taken from *The Message of Exodus: The Days of Our Pilgrimage* by J. A. MOTYER. Copyright © 2005. Used by permission of InterVarsity Press, P.O. Box 1400, Downers Grove, IL 60515. www.ivpress.com.

Page 105 Taken from *Purpose Driven®️ Life* by RICK WARREN. Copyright © 2002 by Rick Warren. Used by permission of Zondervan.

Gregory of Nyssa, *Classics of Western Spirituality*, © Paulist Press 1978. Used by permission.

Page 115 Carol L. Fitzpatrick, *Daily Wisdom for Women: Practical, Biblical Insight for Today's Woman* (Uhrichsville, Ohio: Barbour, 1997). Used by permission.

Isaac Watts, *Not All the Blood of Beasts (Hymn)*. Language updated. © 2006 Zondervan.

Page 132 Taken from the *Epistle of Barnabas*. Language updated. © 2006 Zondervan.

Excerpt from page 187 from PROMISES TO KEEP by NICK HARRISON Copyright © 1996 by Nick Harrison. Reprinted by permission of HarperCollins Publishers.

Page 136 Matthew Henry, *Commentary on the Whole Bible Volume I (Genesis to Deuteronomy)*. Language updated. © 2006 Zondervan.

Taken from *One Year Book of Devotions for Women* by Jill Briscoe. Copyright © 2001 by Jill Briscoe. Used by permission of Tyndale House Publishers, Inc. All rights reserved.

Page 138 William Longstaff, *Take Time to Be (A Hymn)*. Language updated. © 2006 Zondervan.

Paul Enns, *Approaching God: Daily Reflections for Growing Christians* (Grand Rapids, Mich.: Kregel, 2003). Used by permission.

Page 144 Gary Henry, *Diligently Seeking God: Daily Motivation to Take God More Seriously* (Indianapolis: WordPoints, 2002). Used by permission.

Charles Wesley, *Blow Ye the Trumpet, Blow (A hymn)*. Language updated. © 2006 Zondervan.

Page 154 Taken from *One Year Book of Devotions for Women* by Jill Briscoe. Copyright © 2001 by Jill Briscoe. Used by permission of Tyndale House Publishers, Inc. All rights reserved.

Brother Lawrence as quoted in *Draper's Book of Quotations For The Christian World* by Edythe Draper (Wheaton, IL: Tyndale,

1992). Used by permission of Edythe Draper.

Page 158 Kenneth Ulmer, *In His Image: An Intimate Reflection of God* (Montville, N.J.: Whitaker House, 2005). Used by permission.

Alexander MacLaren, *Expositions of Holy Scripture: St. John.* Language updated. © 2006 Zondervan.

Page 166 Taken from *One Year Book of Devotions for Women* by Jill Briscoe. Copyright © 2001 by Jill Briscoe. Used by permission of Tyndale House Publishers, Inc. All rights reserved.

Reprinted with the permission of Scribner, an imprint of Simon & Schuster Adult Publishing Group, from A DIARY OF PRIVATE PRAYER by John Baillie. Copyright © 1949 by Charles Scribner's Sons; copyright renewed © 1977 by Ian Fowler Baillie.

Page 169 Joseph Parker, *Classic Sermons on the Attributes of God,* by Warren Wiersbe, (Grand Rapids, Mich.: Kregel 1989). Used by permission.

Reprinted from *Go Down, Moses!* Edited by Leonidas A. Johnson, copyright © 2000 by Judson Press. Used by permission of Judson Press, 800-4-JUDSON, www.judsonpress.com.

Page 178 Taken from *The Message of Numbers: Journey to the Promised Land* by RAYMOND BROWN. Copyright © 2002. Used with permission of InterVarsity Press, P.O. Box 1400, Downers Grove, IL 60515. www.ivpress.com.

Charles G. Finney, *Sermons on Gospel Themes.* Language updated. © 2006 Zondervan.

Page 202 Marva J. Dawn, *Morning by Morning: Daily Meditations from the Writings of Marva J. Dawn* (Grand Rapids, Mich.: Eerdmans, 2001). Used by permission.

John Calvin, *Harmony of the Law.* Language updated. © 2006 Zondervan.

Page 206 Fyodor Dostoyevsky, *The Brothers Karamazov.* Translated by Constance Garnett, 1879.

From, *For the Love of God: A Daily Companion for Discovering the Riches of God's Word* by D. A. Carson, copyright © 1998. Used by permission of Crossway Books, a ministry of Good News Publishers, Wheaton, IL 60187, www.crossway.com.

Page 208 John Bunyan, *Light for Them That Sit in Darkness.* Language updated. © 2006 Zondervan.

Tony Evans, *Free at Last: Experiencing True Freedom Through Your Identity in Christ* (Chicago, IL: Moody Press, 2001). Used by permission.

Page 210 Taken from *The Bible Jesus Read* by PHILIP D. YANCEY. Copyright © 1999 by Philip D. Yancey. Used by permission of Zondervan.

Madame Guyon, *Autobiography of Madame Guyon* (Chicago, IL: Moody Press). Language updated. © 2006 Zondervan.

Page 212 Dave Roberts, *Following Jesus: A Guidebook for the Non-Religious* (Lake Mary, Fla.: Relevant Books, 2003). Used by permission.

Jonathan Edwards, *A Treatise Concerning Religious Affections.* Language updated. © 2006 Zondervan.

Page 219 Michael Green, *Adventure of Faith* (Grand Rapids, Mich.: Zondervan, 2001). Used by permission of Michael Green.

Arthur W. Pink, *The Divine Inspiration of the Bible.* Language updated. © 2006 Zondervan.

Page 225 Taken from *The Message of Numbers: Not By Bread Alone* by RAYMOND BROWN. Copyright © 1993. Used with permission of InterVarsity Press, P.O. Box 1400, Downers Grove, IL 60515. www.ivpress.com.

Charles Hodge, *Systematic Theology - Volume III.* Language updated. © 2006 Zondervan.

Page 227 Emerson Eggerichs, *Love and Respect: The Love She Most Desires, The Respect He Desperately Needs* (Brentwood, Tenn.: Integrity, 2004).

Jeremy Taylor as quoted in *Draper's Book of Quotations For The Christian World* by Edythe Draper (Wheaton, IL: Tyndale,

1992). Used by permission of Edythe Draper.

Page 234 S. J. Hill, *Enjoying God* (Lake Mary, Fla.: Relevant Books, 2001). Used by permission.

Mother Teresa, Original source unknown.

Page 244 Saint David of Wales as quoted in *Streams of the Desert®* by MRS. CHARLES COWMAN; JAMES G. REIMANN. Copyright © 1997 by Zondervan. Used by permission of Zondervan.

R. Kent Hughes, *Disciplines of a Godly Man* (Wheaton, Ill.: Crossway, 2001). Used by permission.

Page 249 Donald Drew, *Letters to a Student: Encouraging Words from a Christian Mentor* (Christian Focus Publications, 2003). Used by permission.

Hannah Whitall Smith, *The God of All Comfort*. Language updated. © 2006 Zondervan.

Page 267 Donald Drew, *Letters to a Student: Encouraging Words from a Christian Mentor* (Christian Focus Publications, 2003). Used by permission.

Catherine Winkworth, *The Christian Life*. Language updated. © 2006 Zondervan.

Page 274 Taken from *Lost Women of the Bible* by CAROLYN CUSTIS JAMES. Copyright © 2005 by Carolyn Custis James. Used by permission of Zondervan.

Taken from *Breakthrough Prayer* by JIM CYMBALA; STEPHEN W. SORENSON. Copyright © 2003 by Jim Cymbala. Used by permission of Zondervan.

Page 277 Adrian Plass, *The Heart of the Family: Laughter and Tears from a Real Family* (Grand Rapids, Mich.: Zondervan, 2004). Used by permission of Adrian Plass.

Alexander MacLaren, *Expositions of Holy Scripture: Psalms*. Language updated. © 2006 Zondervan.

Page 284 James Stewart as quoted in *Take Heart: Daily Devotions with the Church's Great Preachers* by Diana Wallis (Grand Rapids, MI: Kregel Publications, 2001). Used by permission.

An Introduction to Christian Theology by Justo L. González and Zaida Maldonado

Pérez, Copyright © 2002. Used by permission of Abingdon Press.

Page 290 Bryce Morgan, *Learning to Reflect: Daily Meditations on the Word of God*. © 2004 Bryce Morgan. Used by permission of Bryce Morgan.

John Bright, *Kingdom of God*. Copyright © 1981, Abingdon Press. Used by permission.

Page 299 Taken from *I Saw the Lord* by ANNE GRAHAM LOTZ. Copyright © 2006 by Anne Graham Lotz. Used by permission of Zondervan.

Taken from *Mere Christianity* by C. S. LEWIS. Copyright © 2001. Used by permission of Zondervan.

Page 305 Taken from *Is Your Church Ready?* By NORMAN L. GEISLER; RAVI ZACHARIAS. Copyright © 2003 by Ravi Zacharias and Norman Geisler. Used by permission of Zondervan.

J. W. Alexander, *Thoughts on Family Worship*. Language updated. © 2006 Zondervan.

Page 313 Mary J. Evans, *The Message of Samuel* (Downers Grove, Ill.: InterVarsity, 2004). Used by permission.

Robert Jamieson, *Commentary Critical and Explanatory on the Whole Bible*. Language updated. © 2006 Zondervan.

Page 319 Taken from *Mere Christianity* by C. S. LEWIS. Copyright © 2001. Used by permission of Zondervan.

Kenneth Osbeck, *Amazing Grace* (Grand Rapids, Mich.: Kregel, 2002). Used by permission.

Page 322 Craig Borlase, *The Naked Christian: Taking Off Religion to Find True Relationship* (Lake Mary, Fla.: Relevant Books, 2005). Used by permission.

Philip Schaff, *History of the Christian Church*. Language updated. © 2006 Zondervan.

Page 344 *The Unquenchable Worshipper*, by Matt Redman, excerpt from pages 42, 43. ©2001, Regal Books, Ventura, CA 93003. Used by permission.

John Wright Follette, *Golden Grain*. Language updated. © 2006 Zondervan.

Page 348 George MacDonald, *Unspoken*

Sermons Series One. Language updated. ©
2006 Zondervan.

Kary Oberbrunner, *The Journey Towards Relevance: Simple Steps for Transforming Your World* (Lake Mary, Fla.: Relevant Books, 2004). Used by permission.

Page 355 Reprinted from *A Love So Big*. Copyright © 2002 by Sheila Walsh. Used by permission of WaterBrook Press, Colorado Springs, CO. All rights reserved.

Thomas à Kempis as quoted in *Daily Strength for Daily Needs* (by Mary Wilder Tileston) (New Kensington, PA: Whitaker House 1997). Used by permission.

Page 359 G. Campbell Morgan, *Searchlights from the Word* (Grand Rapids, Mich: Revell Books, 1984). Used by permission.

Steve Farrar, *King Me: What Every Son Wants and Needs from His Father* (Chicago: Moody Press, 2006). Used by permission.

Page 380 Taken from *Whole Prayer* by WALTER WANGERIN JR. Copyright © 1998 by Walter Wangerin Jr. Used by permission of Zondervan.

Anna Sophia of Hesse, *Speak, O Lord, Thy Servant Heareth (A Hymn)*. Language updated. © 2006 Zondervan.

Page 387 Taken from *Fresh Faith* by JIM CYMBALA; DEAN MERRILL. Copyright © 1999 by Jim Cymbala. Used by permission of Zondervan.

E. M. Bounds, *The Necessity of Prayer* (Chicago, IL: Moody Press, 1980). Used by permission.

Page 392 Excerpted from *Jesus in the Margins* © 2005 by Rick McKinley. Used by permission of Multnomah Publishers, Inc.

Lewis Bayly, *The Practice of Piety: Directing a Christian How to Walk, That He May Please God*. Language updated. © 2006 Zondervan.

Page 397 Thomas Watson, *A Body of Practical Divinity*. Language updated. © 2006 Zondervan.

John Ortberg, *Old Testament Challenge Volume 4: Pursuing Spiritual Authenticity* (Grand Rapids, Mich.: Zondervan, 2004).

Page 399 Excerpt from page 66 of MAKING ALL THINGS NEW: AN

INVITATION TO THE SPIRITUAL LIFE by HENRI J. M. NOUWEN. Copyright © 1981 by Henri J. M. Nouwen. Reprinted by permission of HarperCollins Publishers.

Excerpt from page 17 from CELEBRATION OF DISCIPLINE: THE PATH TO SPIRITUAL GROWTH by RICHARD J. FOSTER Copyright © 1978 by Richard Foster. Reprinted by permission of HarperCollins Publishers.

Page 409 Watchman Nee, *The Normal Christian Life* (Wheaton, IL: Tyndale, 1997). Used by permission.

Bruce Bickel and Stan Jantz, *Keeping God in the Small Stuff* (Uhrichsville, Ohio: Barbour, 2000). Used by permission.

Page 414 Alexander MacLaren, *Exposition of the Holy Scriptures: Psalms*. Language updated. © 2006 Zondervan.

John Ortberg, *Old Testament Challenge Volume 4: Pursuing Spiritual Authenticity* (Grand Rapids, Mich.: Zondervan, 2004). Used by permission.

Page 423 Charles G. Finney, *Lectures on Revivals of Religion*. Language updated. © 2006 Zondervan.

Henry Gariepy, *Daily Meditations on Golden Texts of the Bible* (Grand Rapids, Mich.: Eerdmans, 2004). Used by permission.

Page 432 Alfred McBride, *Father McBride's College Catechism: Forging Faith on College Campuses* (Huntington, Ind.: Our Sunday Visitor, 2000). Used by permission.

Cardinal John Henry Newman as quoted in *Daily Strength for Daily Needs* (by Mary Wilder Tileston) (New Kensington, PA: Whitaker House 1997). Used by permission.

Page 458 *Inside Out Worship*, by Matt Redman, excerpts from page 77-79. © 2005, Regal Books, Ventura, CA 93003. Used by permission.

John Owen, *The Glory of Christ* (Edinburgh, The Banner of Truth Trust, 1965). Used by permission.

Page 470 Lisa Ryken as quoted in *Devotions for Ministry Wives* by BARBARA HUGHES. Copyright © 2002 by Barbara Hughes. Used by permission of Zondervan.

Jean Nicolas Grou as quoted in *Daily Strength for Daily Needs* (by Mary Wilder Tileston) (New Kensington, PA: Whitaker House 1997). Used by permission.

Page 480 Taken from *Fresh Faith* by JIM CYMBALA; DEAN MERRILL. Copyright © 1999 by Jim Cymbala. Used by permission of Zondervan.

E. M. Bounds, *Power Through Prayer* (Chicago, IL: Moody Press, 1980). Used by permission.

Page 488 Ole Hallesby, *God's Word for Today: A Daily Devotional for the Whole Year* (Minneapolis, Minn: Augsburg Publishing House, 1937). Used by permission.

Taken from *Praying the Names of God* by ANN SPANGLER. Copyright © 2004 by Ann Spangler. Used by permission of Zondervan.

Page 498 Taken from *Unspeakable* by OS GUINNESS. Copyright © 2005. Used by permission of Zondervan.

Matthew Henry, *Concise Commentary on the Bible*. Language updated. © 2006 Zondervan.

Page 503 Taken from *Diamonds in the Dust* by JONI EARECKSON TADA. Copyright © 1993 by Joni Eareckson Tada. Used by permission of Zondervan.

Saint Augustine, *Tractates on John, Tractate LXXXIII*, included in *Nicene and Post-Nicene Fathers, Series I, Vol. VII* by Philip Schaff. Language updated. © 2006 Zondervan.

Page 507 Hannah Whitall Smith, *The Secrets of a Happy Life* (Grand Rapids, Mich: Revell, 1985). Used by permission.

Chip Ingram, *Miracle of Life Change* (Chicago, IL: Moody Press, 2000). Used by permission.

Page 514 Don M. Aycock and Mark Sutton, *Still God's Man: A Daily Devotional Guide to Christlike Character* (Grand Rapids, Mich.: Kregel, 2003). Used by permission.

Cardinal Henry Edward Manning as quoted in *Daily Strength for Daily Needs* (by Mary Wilder Tileston) (New Kensington, PA: Whitaker House 1997). Used by permission.

Page 523 William M. Clow, *Classic Sermons on the Love of God (Kregel Classic Sermons Series)* by Warren Wiersbe (Grand Rapids, Mich.: Kregel 1998). Used by permission.

Blessed Be Your Name, by Matt Redman, ©2005, Regal Books, Ventura, CA 93003 Used by permission.

Page 533 D. L. Moody as quoted in *One Thousand and One Thoughts From My Library* by D. L. Moody. Language updated. © 2006 by Zondervan.

Bryce Morgan, *Learning to Reflect: Daily Meditations on the Word of God* © 2004 by Bryce Morgan. Used by permission of Bryce Morgan.

Page 543 Emerson Eggerichs, *Love and Respect: The Love She Most Desires, The Respect He Desperately Needs* (Brentwood, Tenn.: Integrity, 2004). Used by permission.

George Whitefield, *Christ the Believer's Husband (Whitefield's Sermons)*. Language updated. © 2006 Zondervan.

Page 549 Taken from *Lost Women of the Bible* by CAROLYN CUSTIS JAMES. Copyright © 2005 by Carolyn Custis James. Used by permission of Zondervan.

Matthew Henry, *Commentary on the Whole Bible Volume 2 (Joshua—Esther)*. Language updated. © 2006 Zondervan.

Page 556 Taken from *Unspeakable* by OS GUINNESS. Copyright © 2005. Used by permission of Zondervan.

George Neumarck, *If Thou But Suffer God to Guide Thee (A hymn)*. Language updated. © 2006 Zondervan.

Page 563 Taken from *The Bible Jesus Read* by PHILIP D. YANCEY. Copyright © 1999 by Philip D. Yancey. Used by permission of Zondervan.

Matthew Henry, *Commentary on the Whole Bible Volume 3 (Job—Song of Solomon)*. Language updated. © 2006 Zondervan.

Page 566 Taken from *Diamonds in the Dust* by JONI EARECKSON TADA. Copyright © 1993 by Joni Eareckson Tada. Used by permission of Zondervan.

Andrew Murray, *Absolute Surrender and*

Other Addresses. Language updated. © 2006 Zondervan.

Page 572 Romano Guardini, *The Art of Praying: The Principles and Methods of Christian Prayer* (Manchester, N.H.: Sophia Institute Press, 1995). Used by permission.

Henry Gariepy, *Daily Meditations on Golden Texts of the Bible* (Grand Rapids, Mich.: Eerdmans, 2004). Used by permission.

Page 579 *Blessed Be Your Name,* by Matt Redman, pages 54,56,59 © 2005, Regal Books, Ventura, CA 93003 Used by permission.

Cyprian as quoted in *Day by Day with the Early Church Fathers,* page 257, copyright © 1999 by Hendrickson Publishers, Inc. Peabody, Massachusetts. Used by permission. All rights reserved.

Page 582 Taken from *I Saw the Lord* by ANNE GRAHAM LOTZ. Copyright © 2006 by Anne Graham Lotz. Used by permission of Zondervan.

John Wright Follette, *Golden Grain.* Language updated. © 2006 Zondervan. Used by permission.

Page 590 Taken from *Rumors of Another World* by PHILIP D. YANCEY. Copyright © 2003 by SCCT. Used by permission of Zondervan.

Andrew Murray, *The New Life: Words of God for Young Disciples.* Language updated. © 2006 Zondervan.

Page 594 Taken from *The Bible Jesus Read* by PHILIP D. YANCEY. Copyright © 1999 by Philip D. Yancey. Used by permission of Zondervan.

Matthew Henry, *Commentary on the Whole Bible Volume 3 (Job—Song of Solomon).* Language updated. © 2006 Zondervan.

Page 597 Thomas Merton, *Contemplative Prayer,* (Cistercian Publications, 1971). Used by permission.

Excerpt from page 16 from CELEBRATION OF DISCIPLINE: THE PATH TO SPIRITUAL GROWTH by RICHARD J. FOSTER. Copyright © 1978 by Richard Foster. Reprinted by permission of HarperCollins Publishers.

Page 598 Taken from *Finding Faith* by BRIAN D. MCLAREN. Copyright © 1999 by Brian D. McLaren. Used by permission of Zondervan.

Horatius Bonar, *God's Way of Peace: A BOOK FOR THE ANXIOUS.* Language updated. © 2006 Zondervan.

Page 603 Irenaeus as quoted in *Day by Day with the Early Church Fathers,* page 350, copyright © 1999 by Hendrickson Publishers, Inc. Peabody, Massachusetts. Used by permission. All rights reserved.

"A Prayer of Wonder" from PRAYERS FROM THE HEART by RICHARD J. FOSTER. Copyright © 1994 by Richard J. Foster. Reprinted by permission of HarperCollins Publishers.

Page 609 John Wesley, *Sermons on Several Occasions.* Language updated. © 2006 Zondervan.

Excerpt from page 3 from NOW AND THEN by FREDERICK BUECHNER. Copyright © 1983 by Frederick Buechner. Reprinted by permission of HarperCollins Publishers.

Page 615 Taken from *God's Outrageous Claims* by LEE P. STROBEL. Copyright © 1997, 2005 by Lee Strobel. Used by permission of Zondervan.

John Wesley, *A Collection of Hymns, for the Use of the People Called Methodists* (Hymn #273). Language updated. © 2006 Zondervan.

Page 617 B. T. Roberts, *Holiness Teachings—The Life And Work of B. T. Roberts* by Benson H. Roberts. Language updated. © 2006 Zondervan.

Taken from *Inklings of God* by KURT BRUNER. Copyright © 2003 by Kurt Bruner. Used by permission of Zondervan.

Page 619 Materials from "The Lost Art of Intercession," by Jim Goll, copyright © 1997 used by permission of Destiny Image Publishers, 167 Walnut Bottom Road, Shippensburg, PA 17257. www.destinyimage.com.

Cyril as quoted in *Day by Day with the Early Church Fathers,* page 48, copyright © 1999 by Hendrickson Publishers, Inc. Peabody, Massachusetts. Used by permission. All rights reserved.

Page 623 Taken from *In Every Pew Sits A Broken Heart* by RUTH GRAHAM. Copyright © 2004 by Ruth Graham. Used by permission of Zondervan.

Augustus Toplady, *Rock of Ages (A Hymn)*. Language updated. © 2006 Zondervan.

Page 628 Taken from *Breakthrough Prayer* by JIM CYMBALA; STEPHEN W. SORENSON. Copyright © 2003 by Jim Cymbala. Used by permission of Zondervan.

Madame Guyon, *A Short and Easy Method of Prayer*. Language updated. © 2006 Zondervan.

Page 633 Ruth Haley Barton, *Invitation to Solitude and Silence: Experiencing God's Transforming Presence* (Downers Grove, Ill.: InterVarsity, 2004). Used by permission.

Alexander MacLaren, *Exposition of the Holy Scriptures: Psalms*. Language updated. © 2006 Zondervan.

Page 636 "My Answer," by Billy Graham, © 2004, 2005, 2006 by Billy Graham, used by permission, all rights reserved.

John Chrysostom, *Saint Chrysostom: Homilies on the Acts of the Apostles and the Epistle to the Romans* included in *Nicene and Post-Nicene Fathers, Series I, Vol. XI* by Philip Schaff. Language updated. © 2006 Zondervan.

Page 643 Taken from *Faith Alone* by MARTIN LUTHER; JAMES C. GALVIN. Copyright © 1998, 2005 by James C. Galvin. Used by permission of Zondervan.

Excerpt from page 15 from CELEBRATION OF DISCIPLINE: THE PATH TO SPIRITUAL GROWTH by RICHARD J. FOSTER. Copyright © 1978 by Richard Foster. Reprinted by permission of HarperCollins Publishers.

Page 649 S. J. Hill, *Enjoying God* (Lake Mary, Fla.: Relevant Books, 2001). Used by permission.

Andrew Murray, *The Deeper Christian Life an Aid to its Attainment*. Language updated. © 2006 Zondervan.

Page 658 Romano Guardini, *The Art of Praying: The Principles and Methods of Christian Prayer* (Manchester, N.H.: Sophia Institute Press, 1995). Used by permission.

Nancy Leigh DeMoss, *A Place of Quiet Rest: Finding Intimacy with God through a Daily Devotional Life* (Chicago: Moody Press, 2002). Used by permission.

Page 665 Taken from *Faith Alone* by MARTIN LUTHER; JAMES C. GALVIN. Copyright © 1998, 2005 by James C. Galvin. Used by permission of Zondervan.

Taken from *Fresh Power* by JIM CYMBALA; DEAN MERRILL. Copyright © 2001 by Jim Cymbala. Used by permission of Zondervan.

Page 672 Excerpted from *The Way I Was Made* © 2005 by Chris Tomlin. Used by permission of Multnomah Publishers Inc.

Jonathan Edwards, *God Glorified In Man's Dependence*. Language updated. © 2006 Zondervan.

Page 679 Reprinted from *A Sacred Sorrow*. © 2005 by Michael Card. Used by permission of NavPress, Colorado Springs, CO. All rights reserved.

Matthew Henry, *Commentary on the Whole Bible*. Language updated. © 2006 Zondervan.

Page 688 Dave Roberts, *Following Jesus: A Guidebook for the Non-Religious* (Lake Mary, Fla.: Relevant Books, 2003). Used by permission.

Thomas Watson, *A Body of Practical Divinity*. Language updated. © 2006 Zondervan.

Page 694 Taken from *Living the Message* by EUGENE H. PETERSON. Copyright © 1996. Used by permission of Zondervan.

John Wesley, *A Collection of Hymns, for the Use of the People Called Methodists*. Language updated. © 2006 Zondervan.

Page 701 Julian of Norwich, *Classics of Western Spirituality*, © Paulist Press 1978. Used by permission.

S. J. Hill, *Enjoying God* (Lake Mary, Fla.: Relevant Books, 2001). Used by permission.

Page 703 Thomas Watson, *A Body of Practical Divinity*. Language updated. © 2006 Zondervan.

Worship in Ancient Israel by Walter Brueggemann. Copyright © 2005. Used by permission of Abingdon Press. Used by permission.

Page 713 Taken from *Inklings of God* by KURT BRUNER. Copyright © 2003 by Kurt Bruner. Used by permission of Zondervan.

Miguel de Molinos, *The Spiritual Guide Which Disentangles the Soul*. Language updated. © 2006 Zondervan.

Page 716 Taken from *Inklings of God* by KURT BRUNER. Copyright © 2003 by Kurt Bruner. Used by permission of Zondervan.

John Wesley, *Christian Perfection*, (Abingdon 1976). Used by permission.

Page 719 Excerpt from pages 1-2 from THE SPIRIT OF THE DISCIPLINES: UNDERSTANDING HOW GOD CHANGES LIVES by DALLAS WILLARD. Copyright © 1989 by Dallas Willard. Reprinted by permission of HarperCollins Publishers.

G. K. Chesterton, *What's Wrong With the World Today*. Language updated. © 2006 Zondervan.

Page 722 Ajith Fernando, *Spiritual Living in a Secular World: Applying the Book of Daniel Today* (Monarch Books, 2002). Used by permission.

Reprinted with the permission of Scribner, an imprint of Simon & Schuster Adult Publishing Group, from A DIARY OF PRIVATE PRAYER by JOHN BAILLIE. Copyright © 1949 by Charles Scribner's Sons; copyright renewed © 1977 by Ian Fowler Baillie.

Page 730 Excerpted from *The Way I Was Made* © 2005 by Chris Tomlin. Used by permission of Multnomah Publishers Inc.

Henry Scougal, *The Life of God in the Soul of Man*. Language updated. © 2006 Zondervan.

Page 739 E. Stanley Jones, *Conversation*, (Abingdon, 1991). Used by permission.

Margaret Feinberg, *God Whispers: Learning to Hear His Voice* (Lake Mary, Fla.: Relevant Books, 2002). Used by permission.

Page 742 Taken from *When Life and Beliefs Collide* by CAROLYN CUSTIS JAMES. Copyright © 2001 by Carolyn C. James. Used by permission of Zondervan.

Philip Schaff, *History of the Christian Church*. Language updated. © 2006 Zondervan.

Page 745 Excerpted from *Jesus in the Margins* © 2005 by Rick McKinley. Used by permission of Multnomah Publishers, Inc.

R. L. Wheeler as quoted in *Draper's Book of Quotations For The Christian World* by Edythe Draper (Wheaton, IL: Tyndale, 1992). Used by permission of Edythe Draper.

Page 747 Taken from *Heaven . . . Your Real Home* by JONI EARECKSON TADA. Copyright © 1996 by Joni Eareckson Tada. Used by permission of Zondervan.

Oswald Chambers, *My Utmost for His Highest* (Grand Rapids, Mich: Discovery House, 1935). Used by permission.

Page 757 Reprinted from *Five Paths to the Love of Your Life: Defining Your Dating Style*. © 2005 by Lauren Winner. Used with permission of NavPress, Colorado Springs, CO. All rights reserved.

Augustine Baker, *Holy Wisdom or Directions for the Prayer of Contemplation*. Language updated. © 2006 Zondervan.

Page 759 Tertullian, *On Exhortation to Chastity*. Language updated. © 2006 Zondervan.

Taken from *Questions You Can't Ask Your Mama About Sex* by MIKE FOSTER; CRAIG GROSS. Copyright © 2005 by Youth Specialties. Used by permission of Zondervan.

Page 763 S. J. Hill, *Enjoying God* (Lake Mary, Fla.: Relevant Books, 2001). Used by permission.

Jonathan Edwards, *Religious Affections* (Yale University Press, 2003). Used by permission.

Page 773 Taken from *Isaiah* by JOHN OSWALT. Copyright © 2003 by John Oswalt. Used by permission of Zondervan.

John Tauler, *Light, Life and Love: Selections from the German Mystics of the Middle Ages*. Language updated. © 2006 Zondervan.

Page 776 Taken from *When God Weeps* by STEVEN D. ESTES; JONI EARECKSON TADA. Copyright © 1997 by Joni Eareckson

Tada and Steve Estes. Used by permission of Zondervan.

Corrie ten Boom, Original source unknown.

Page 782 Andrew Murray, *The New Life: Words of God for Young Disciples*. Language updated. © 2006 Zondervan.

Tony Evans, *Tony Evans Speaks Out on Spiritual Warfare* (Chicago, IL: Moody Press, 2000). Used by permission.

Page 792 Taken from *Heaven . . . Your Real Home* by JONI EARECKSON TADA. Copyright © 1996 by Joni Eareckson Tada. Used by permission of Zondervan.

C. S. Lewis, *The Problem of Pain* (New York, NY: HarperCollins, 2001). Used by permission of the C. S. Lewis Company, England.

Page 795 Charles Spurgeon, *"Forgiveness"* a sermon delivered May 20, 1855. Language updated. © 2006 Zondervan.

Excerpted from *The Way I Was Made* © 2005 by Chris Tomlin. Used by permission of Multnomah Publishers Inc.

Page 809 James Orr, *A Christian View of God in the World*. Language updated. © 2006 Zondervan.

Taken from *When Life and Beliefs Collide* by CAROLYN CUSTIS JAMES. Copyright © 2001 by Carolyn C. James. Used by permission of Zondervan.

Page 814 Taken from *Purpose Driven® Life* by RICK WARREN. Copyright © 2002 by Rick Warren. Used by permission of Zondervan.

Jonathan Edwards, *A Treatise Concerning Religious Affections*. Language updated. © 2006 Zondervan.

Page 820 Taken from *Purpose Driven® Life* by RICK WARREN. Copyright © 2002 by Rick Warren. Used by permission of Zondervan.

Søren Kierkegaard, *Prayers of Kierkegaard* (University of Chicago Press, 1956). Used by permission.

Page 829 Taken from *Velvet Elvis* by ROB BELL. Copyright © 2005 by Rob Bell. Used by permission of Zondervan.

C. S. Lewis, *Reflections on the Psalms*

(Orlando FL: Harvest Books, 1964). Used by permission.

Page 843 *Soul Survivor*, by Mike Pilavachi, excerpt from pages 40, 41. © 2004, Regal Books, Ventura, CA 93003. Used by permission.

Anna L. Waring, *Source of My Spirit's Deep Desire (A Hymn)*. Language updated. © 2006 Zondervan.

Page 854 John Calvin, *Golden Booklet of the True Christian Life*, (Grand Rapids, MI: Baker Books 1952) Used by permission.

Taken from *Purpose Driven® Life* by RICK WARREN. Copyright © 2002 by Rick Warren. Used by permission of Zondervan.

Page 859 "My Answer," by Billy Graham, © 2004, 2005, 2006 by Billy Graham, used by permission, all rights reserved.

Hannah Whitall Smith, *The God of All Comfort*. Language updated. © 2006 Zondervan.

Page 865 William Guthrie as quoted in *One Thousand and One Thoughts From My Library* by D. L. Moody. Language updated. © 2006 by Zondervan.

Juanita Bynum, *Matters of the Heart: Stop Trying to Fix the Old, Let God Give You Something New* (Lake Mary, Fla.: Charisma House, 2002). Used by permission.

Page 884 Kary Oberbrunner, *The Journey Towards Relevance: Simple Steps for Transforming Your World* (Lake Mary, Fla.: Relevant Books, 2004). Used by permission.

Clement of Alexandria, *First Epistle of Clement to the Corinthians*. Language updated. © 2006 Zondervan.

Page 895 George Elliot as quoted in *Daily Strength for Daily Needs* (by Mary Wilder Tileston) (New Kensington, PA: Whitaker House 1997). Used by permission.

Excerpted from *Our Love is Here to Stay* © 2004 by Tony and Lois Evans. Used by permission of Multnomah Publishers Inc.

Page 916 Taken from *The Word On The Street* by ROB LACEY. Copyright © 2004. Used by permission of Zondervan.

George Whitefield, *"Thankfulness for Mercies Received, a Necessary Duty"* A *sermon by George Whitefield.* Language updated. © 2006 Zondervan.

Page 929 Taken from *Praying the Names of God* by ANN SPANGLER. Copyright © 2004 by Ann Spangler. Used by permission of Zondervan.

John Calvin, *Commentary on Ezekiel.* Language updated. © 2006 Zondervan.

Page 931 S. J. Hill, *Enjoying God* (Lake Mary, Fla.: Relevant Books, 2001). Used by permission.

Bernard of Clairvaux, *On Loving God.* Language updated. © 2006 Zondervan.

Page 935 G. Campbell Morgan, *Searchlights from the Word* (Grand Rapids, Mich: Revell Books, 1984). Used by permission.

From, *For the Love of God: A Daily Companion for Discovering the Riches of God's Word* by D. A. Carson, copyright © 1998. Used by permission of Crossway Books, a ministry of Good News Publishers, Wheaton, IL 60187, www.crossway.com.

Page 947 Charles Spurgeon as quoted in *One Thousand and One Thoughts From My Library* by D. L. Moody. Language updated. © 2006 by Zondervan.

Henry Gariepy, *Daily Meditations on Golden Texts of the Bible* (Grand Rapids, Mich.: Eerdmans, 2004). Used by permission.

Page 955 Thomas à Kempis, *The Imitation of Christ* (Milwaukee: Bruce Publishing Company, 1949). Used by permission.

Reprinted from *Having a Mary Heart in a Martha World.* Copyright © 2000, 2002 by Joanna Weaver. Used by permission of WaterBrook Press, Colorado Springs, CO. All rights reserved.

Page 959 Taken from *Devotions for a Deeper Life* by OSWALD CHAMBERS. Copyright © 1986 by God's Bible School, Cincinnati, Ohio. Used by permission of Zondervan.

Mark Brazee, *31 Days of Healing: Devotions to Help You Receive Healing and Recover Quickly* (Tulsa: Harrison House Publishers, copyright 2003). Used by permission.

Page 978 Taken from *Purpose Driven® Life* by RICK WARREN. Copyright © 2002 by Rick Warren. Used by permission of Zondervan.

John Bright, *Kingdom of God.* Copyright © 1981, Abingdon Press. Used by permission.

Page 980 Steve Case, *God Is Here: Connecting with Him in Everyday Life* (Lake Mary, Fla.: Relevant Books, 2005). Used by permission.

Madame Guyon, *Autobiography of Madame Guyon.* Language updated. © 2006 Zondervan.

Page 989 A. B. Simpson as quoted in the *Classics Devotional Bible* by Zondervan. Copyright © 1996 by Zondervan. Used by permission of Zondervan.

Mary Kassian as quoted in *Devotions for Ministry Wives* by BARBARA HUGHES. Copyright © 2002 by Barbara Hughes. Used by permission of Zondervan.

Page 995 John Wesley, *Sermons on Several Occasions.* Language updated. © 2006 Zondervan.

Taken from *Tough Love, Tender Mercies* by Lisa Harper. Copyright © 2005 by Lisa Harper. Used by permission of Tyndale House Publishers, Inc. All rights reserved.

Page 998 Nancy Leigh DeMoss, *A Place of Quiet Rest: Finding Intimacy with God through a Daily Devotional Life* (Chicago: Moody Press, 2002). Used by permission.

F. B. Meyer as quoted in the *Classics Devotional Bible* by Zondervan. Copyright © 1996 by Zondervan. Used by permission of Zondervan.

Page 1005 D. L. Moody, *Classic Sermons on the Attributes of God,* by Warren Wiersbe, (Grand Rapids, Mich.: Kregel 1989). Used by permission.

Knowing Christ by Alister McGrath. Copyright © 2002. Galilee Book, published by Doubleday, a division of Random House.

Page 1008 Don M. Aycock and Mark Sutton, *Still God's Man: A Daily Devotional Guide to Christlike Character* (Grand Rapids, Mich.: Kregel, 2003). Used by permission.

Susan Coolidge as quoted in *Daily*

Strength for Daily Needs by Mary Wilder Tileston (New Kensington, PA: Whitaker House 1997).

Page 1015 John Ortberg, *Old Testament Challenge Volume 4: Pursuing Spiritual Authenticity* (Grand Rapids, Mich.: Zondervan, 2004).

John Owen, *A Brief Instruction in the Worship of God* (Edinburgh: The Banner of Truth Trust, 1965). Used by permission.

Page 1018 Excerpted from *The Air I Breathe* © 2003 by Louie Giglio. Used by permission of Multnomah Publishers Inc. Used by permission.

Richard Baxter, *The Reformed Pastor.* Language updated. © 2006 Zondervan.

Page 1024 Taken from *The Bible Jesus Read* by PHILIP D. YANCEY. Copyright © 1999 by Philip D. Yancey. Used by permission of Zondervan.

Oswald Chambers, *My Utmost for His Highest* (Grand Rapids, Mich: Discovery House, 1935).

Page 1027 St. Augustine, *St. Augustine: Sermons on Selected Lessons of the New Testament.* Language updated. © 2006 Zondervan.

Taken from *Fresh Power* by JIM CYMBALA; DEAN MERRILL. Copyright © 2001 by Jim Cymbala. Used by permission of Zondervan.

Page 1028 Taken from *Living the Message* by EUGENE H. PETERSON. Copyright © 1996. Used by permission of Zondervan.

Ole Hallesby, *Prayer* (Minneapolis, Minn: Augsburg Publishing House, 1931). Used by permission.

Page 1033 D. L. Moody as quoted in *One Thousand and One Thoughts From My Library* by D. L. Moody. Language updated. © 2006 by Zondervan.

Joyce Webster as quoted in *Devotions for Ministry Wives* by BARBARA HUGHES. Copyright © 2002 by Barbara Hughes. Used by permission of Zondervan.

Page 1037 Taken from *Praying the Names of God* by ANN SPANGLER. Copyright © 2004 by Ann Spangler. Used by permission of Zondervan.

C. S. Lewis, *The Problem of Pain* (New York, NY: HarperCollins, 2001). Used by permission of the C. S. Lewis Company, England.

Page 1040 Reprinted from *The Root of the Righteous* by A. W. Tozer, copyright © 1955, 1986 by Lowell Tozer. Used by permission of WingSpread Publishers, a division of Zur Ltd., 800-233-4443.

Andy Stanley, excerpted from *Discovering God's Will* © 2004 by North Pointe Ministries, Inc. Used by permission of Multnomah Publishers Inc.

Page 1044 Tony Evans, *Time to Get Serious: Daily Devotions to Keep You Close to God* (Wheaton, Ill.: Crossway, 1995).

Gerhard Tersteegen as quoted in *Daily Strength for Daily Needs* (by Mary Wilder Tileston) (New Kensington, PA: Whitaker House 1997). Used by permission.

Page 1049 Taken from *Tough Love, Tender Mercies* by Lisa Harper. Copyright © 2005 by Lisa Harper. Used by permission of Tyndale House Publishers, Inc. All rights reserved.

John Donne, *Twenty-Six Sermons Preached at the Spital.* Language updated. © 2006 Zondervan.

Page 1056 Catherine of Siena as quoted in the *Classics Devotional Bible* by Zondervan. Copyright © 1996 by Zondervan. Used by permission of Zondervan.

Erwin Lutzer, *Free at Last: Finding Hope for Life's Deepest Hurts* (Chicago, IL: Moody Press, 1997). Used by permission.

Page 1058 Reprinted from *Abba's Child.* © 1994 by Brennan Manning. Used with permission of NavPress, Colorado Springs, CO. All rights reserved.

Jonathan Edwards, *God Glorified In Man's Dependence, The Complete Works of Jonathan Edwards* (Edinburgh: The Banner of Truth Trust, 1974). Used by permission.

Page 1062 N. T. Wright, *For All God's Worth: True Worship and the Calling of the Church* (Grand Rapids, Mich.: Eerdmans, 1997).

Albert Barnes, *Barnes New Testament Notes.* Language updated. © 2006 Zondervan.

Page 1068 Catherine of Siena as quoted in the *Classics Devotional Bible* by Zondervan. Copyright © 1996 by Zondervan. Used by permission of Zondervan.

Henry Gariepy, *Daily Meditations on Golden Texts of the Bible* (Grand Rapids, Mich.: Eerdmans, 2004).

Page 1070 Taken from *Tough Love, Tender Mercies* by Lisa Harper. Copyright © 2005 by Lisa Harper. Used by permission of Tyndale House Publishers, Inc. All rights reserved.

Sam Wigglesworth, *Smith Wigglesworth Devotional* (New Kensington, PA: Whitaker House, 1999).

Page 1080 Taken from *Soul Shaper* by TONY JONES. Copyright © 2003 by Youth Specialties. Used by permission of Zondervan.

Tertullian, *Early Church Fathers, Anti-Nicene Fathers, Vol. IV* by Philip Schaff. Language updated. © 2006 Zondervan.

Page 1084 Andrew Murray, *The School of Obedience*. Language updated. © 2006 Zondervan.

Excerpts from pages xv-xvi, from THE DIVINE CONSPIRACY by DALLAS WILLARD Copyright © 1998 by Dallas Willard. Reprinted by permission HarperCollins Publishers.

Page 1086 Taken from *Love Beyond Reason* by JOHN ORTBERG. Copyright © 1998 by John Ortberg. Used by permission of Zondervan.

Lactantius as quoted in *Day by Day with the Early Church Fathers* page 354, copyright © 1999 by Hendrickson Publishers, Inc. Peabody, Massachusetts. Used by permission. All rights reserved.

Page1089 George Whitefield, *"The Extent and Reasonableness of Self-Denial."* Language updated. © 2006 Zondervan.

Excerpt from page 113 from FREEDOM FROM SIMPLICITY by RICHARD J. FOSTER. Copyright © 1981 by Richard J. Foster. Reprinted by permission of HarperCollins Publishers.

Page 1098 Tony Evans, *God's Glorious Church: The Mystery and Mission of the Body*

of Christ (Chicago: Moody Press, 2004). Used by permission.

Oswald Chambers, *My Utmost for His Highest* (Grand Rapids, Mich: Discovery House, 1935). Used by permission.

Page 1102 George MacDonald, *Unspoken Sermons Series One*. Language updated. © 2006 Zondervan.

Excerpt from page 73 from NOW AND THEN by FREDERICK BUECHNER. Copyright © 1983 by Frederick Buechner. Reprinted by permission of HarperCollins Publishers.

Page 1107 Andrew Murray, *Absolute Surrender and Other Addresses*. Language updated. © 2006 Zondervan.

Taken from *Love Beyond Reason* by JOHN ORTBERG. Copyright © 1998 by John Ortberg. Used by permission of Zondervan.

Page 1113 Excerpt from pages 53-54 from NOW AND THEN by FREDERICK BUECHNER. Copyright © 1983 by Frederick Buechner. Reprinted by permission of HarperCollins Publishers.

James Orr, *A Christian View of God in the World* (New York, NY: Scribner's and Sons, 1908).

Page 1118 Reprinted from *Abba's Child.* © 1994 by Brennan Manning. Used with permission of NavPress, Colorado Springs, CO. All rights reserved.

John Bunyon, *Light For Them That Sit In Darkness*. Language updated. © 2006 Zondervan.

Page 1121 Taken from *When God Weeps* by STEVEN D. ESTES; JONI EARECKSON TADA. Copyright © 1997 by Joni Eareckson Tada and Steve Estes. Used by permission of Zondervan.

Dorothy Sayers, *Creed or Chaos? Why Christians Must Choose Either Dogma or Disaster*. Language updated. © 2006 Zondervan.

Page 1126 Excerpted from *With You Always: Daily Meditations on the Gospels* by Francis X. Gaeta. Copyright ©2000 by Ave Maria Press, P.O. Box 428, Notre Dame, IN 46556, www.avemariapress.com. Used with permission of the publisher.

Taken from *Devotions for a Deeper Life* by

OSWALD CHAMBERS. Copyright © 1986 by God's Bible School, Cincinnati, Ohio. Used by permission of Zondervan.

Page 1133 "Searching for Faith" from PRAYERS FROM THE HEART by RICHARD J. FOSTER. Copyright © 1994 by Richard J. Foster. Reprinted by permission of HarperCollins Publishers.

Charles G. Finney, *Systematic Theology.* Language updated. © 2006 Zondervan.

Page 1136 Andrew Murray, *Absolute Surrender and Other Addresses.* Language updated. © 2006 Zondervan.

Reprinted from *Daily PrayerWalk.* Copyright © 2002 by Janet Holm McHenry. WaterBrook Press, Colorado Springs, CO. All rights reserved.

Page 1139 Taken from *God's Outrageous Claims* by LEE P. STROBEL. Copyright © 1997, 2005 by Lee Strobel. Used by permission of Zondervan.

Johannes Eckhart, *Light, Life and Love: Selections from the German Mystics of the Middle Ages.* Language updated. © 2006 Zondervan.

Page 1145 Excerpted from *Don't Gift Wrap the Garbage* by Karen Stroup, Copyright © 2002. Used by permission of the publisher, Ave Maria Press, P.O. Box 428, Notre Dame, IN 46556, www.avemariapress.com.

Saint Bonaventure as quoted in the *Classics Devotional Bible* by Zondervan. Copyright © 1996 by Zondervan. Used by permission of Zondervan.

Page 1150 Taken from *Lost Women of the Bible* by CAROLYN CUSTIS JAMES. Copyright © 2005 by Carolyn Custis James. Used by permission of Zondervan.

Philip Schaff, *History of the Christian Church.* Language updated. © 2006 Zondervan.

Page 1153 Taken from *The Jesus I Never Knew* by PHILIP D. YANCEY. Copyright © 1995 by Philip Yancey. Used by permission of Zondervan.

Taken from *Faith Alone* by MARTIN LUTHER; JAMES C. GALVIN. Copyright © 1998, 2005 by James C. Galvin. Used by permission of Zondervan.

Page 1157 Excerpt from pages 38-39 from FREEDOM FROM SIMPLICITY by RICHARD J. FOSTER. Copyright © 1981 by Richard J. Foster. Reprinted by permission of HarperCollins Publishers.

Alexander MacLaren, *Expositions of the Holy Scriptures: Second Kings from Chap. VIII, and Chronicles, Ezra, and Nehemiah, Esther, Job, Proverbs, and Ecclesiastes.* Language updated. © 2006 Zondervan.

Page 1160 Taken from *Purpose Driven® Life* by RICK WARREN. Copyright © 2002 by Rick Warren. Used by permission of Zondervan.

Thomas Watson, *The Beatitudes, an Exposition of Matthew 5:1-12.* Language updated. © 2006 Zondervan.

Page 1163 Taken from *Fresh Faith* by JIM CYMBALA; DEAN MERRILL. Copyright © 1999 by Jim Cymbala. Used by permission of Zondervan.

Tony Marshall Anderson, *Prayer Availeth Much.* Language updated. © 2006 Zondervan.

Page 1168 Submitted excerpt from pages 56-57 from THE SPIRIT OF THE DISCIPLINES: UNDERSTANDING HOW GOD CHANGES LIVES by DALLAS WILLARD. Copyright © 1989 by Dallas Willard. Reprinted by permission of HarperCollins Publishers.

Oswald Chambers, *My Utmost for His Highest* (Grand Rapids, Mich: Discovery House, 1935).

Page 1172 Taken from *Whole Prayer* by WALTER WANGERIN JR. Copyright © 1998 by Walter Wangerin Jr. Used by permission of Zondervan.

Tertullian, *On Prayer,* included in *Ante-Nicene Fathers, Vol. III* by Philip Schaff. Language updated. © 2006 Zondervan.

Page 1179 Michael Card, *Scribbling in the Sand: Christ and Creativity* (Downers Grove, Ill.: InterVarsity, 2002).Used by permission.

Andrew Murray, *The New Life: Words of God for Young Disciples.* Language updated. © 2006 Zondervan. Used by permission.

Page 1183 Excerpt from page 160 from CELEBRATION OF DISCIPLINE: THE PATH

TO SPIRITUAL GROWTH by RICHARD J. FOSTER Copyright © 1978 by Richard Foster. Reprinted by permission of HarperCollins Publishers.

Saint Catherine of Siena, *The Dialogue of the Seraphic Virgin Catherine of Siena* (1370). Language updated. © 2006 Zondervan.

Page 1185 Pete Greig, *The Vision and the Vow: Re-Discovering Life and Grace* (Lake Mary, Fla.: Relevant Books, 2004). Used by permission.

Charlotte Elliott, *Just as I am (A hymn)*. Language updated. © 2006 Zondervan.

Page 1190 Taken from *Heaven . . . Your Real Home* by JONI EARECKSON TADA. Copyright © 1996 by Joni Eareckson Tada. Used by permission of Zondervan.

John Nelson Darby, *Synopsis of the Books of the Bible*. Language updated. © 2006 Zondervan.

Page 1193 Ajith Fernando, *Spiritual Living in a Secular World: Applying the Book of Daniel Today* (Monarch Books, 2002). Used by permission.

Evelyn Underhill, *The Essentials of Mysticism* (Oxford University Press, 2003). Used by permission.

Page 1196 Taken from *Finding Faith* by BRIAN D. MCLAREN. Copyright © 1999 by Brian D. McLaren. Used by permission of Zondervan.

Saint Augustine, *Handbook on Faith, Hope and Love*. Language updated. © 2006 Zondervan.

Page 1199 Philip Schaff, *History of the Christian Church*. Language updated. © 2006 Zondervan.

Reprinted with the permission of Howard Books, a Division of Simon & Schuster Adult Publishing Group from SCANDALOUS FREEDOM by Steve Brown. Copyright © 2004 Steve Brown.

Page 1203 Excerpted from *The Air I Breathe* © 2003 by Louie Giglio. Used by permission of Multnomah Publishers Inc.

From the *Epistle of Barnabas*. Language updated. © 2006 Zondervan.

Page 1209 John Wright Follette, *Golden Grain*. Language updated. © 2006 Zondervan.

Reprinted from *Abba's Child*. © 1994 by Brennan Manning. Used with permission of NavPress, Colorado Springs, CO. All rights reserved.

Page 1216 Taken from *When Life and Beliefs Collide* by CAROLYN CUSTIS JAMES. Copyright © 2001 by Carolyn C. James. Used by permission of Zondervan.

Thomas Arnold, *New Testament Commentary*. Language updated. © 2006 Zondervan.

Page 1218 Reprinted from *Having a Mary Heart in a Martha World*. Copyright © 2000, 2002 by Joanna Weaver. Used by permission of WaterBrook Press, Colorado Springs, CO. All rights reserved.

William Law, *A Serious Call to a Devout and Holy Life*. Language updated. © 2006 Zondervan.

Page 1221 Karon Goodman, *Another Fine Mess Lord!* (Uhrichsville, Ohio: Barbour, 2005). Used by permission.

John Wesley as quoted in *Draper's Book of Quotations For The Christian World* by Edythe Draper (Wheaton, IL: Tyndale, 1992). Used by permission of Edythe Draper.

Page 1223 Taken from *Velvet Elvis* by ROB BELL. Copyright © 2005 by Rob Bell. Used by permission of Zondervan.

John Tauler, *Sermon for Palm Sunday*. Language updated. © 2006 Zondervan.

Page 1229 Excerpts from THE DIVINE CONSPIRACY by DALLAS WILLARD. Copyright © 1998 by Dallas Willard. Reprinted by permission of HarperCollins Publishers.

E. M. Bounds, *Prayer and Praying Men* (Chicago, IL: Moody Press, 1980). Used by permission.

Page 1235 John Wright Follette, *Golden Grain*. Language updated. © 2006 Zondervan.

Taken from: *Fearless Faith* Copyright © 2002 by John Fischer. Published by Harvest House Publishers, Eugene, OR. www.harvesthousepublishers.com. Used by permission.

Page 1237 Excerpt from CALL TO CONVERSION by JIM WALLIS. Copyright © 2005 by Jim Wallis. Reprinted by permission of HarperCollins Publishers.

Leo I, included in *Nicene and Post-Nicene Fathers, Series II, Vol. XII* by Philip Schaff. Language updated. © 2006 Zondervan.

Page 1240 Taken from *Becoming a Contagious Christian* by BILL HYBELS; MARK MITTELBERG. Copyright © 1994 by Bill Hybels and Mark Mittelberg. Used by permission of Zondervan.

John Wesley, *Sermons on Several Occasions*. Language updated. © 2006 Zondervan.

Page 1244 Taken from *More Ready Than You Realize* by BRIAN D. MCLAREN. Copyright © 2002 by Brian D. McLaren. Used by permission of Zondervan.

Philip Schaff, *History of the Christian Church*. Language updated. © 2006 Zondervan.

Page 1250 Philip Schaff, *History of the Christian Church* (1882). Language updated. © 2006 Zondervan.

"My Answer," by Billy Graham, © 2004, 2005, 2006 Billy Graham, used by permission, all rights reserved.

Page 1255 Taken from *Contemporary Worship in the Reformed Tradition* by David A. Miller. Copyright © 2001 by David A. Miller. Used by permission of Vital Faith Resources, www.vitalfaithresources.com.

Taken from *Devotions for a Deeper Life* by OSWALD CHAMBERS. Copyright © 1986 by God's Bible School, Cincinnati, Ohio. Used by permission of Zondervan.

Page 1261 Taken from *Rumors of Another World* by PHILIP D. YANCEY. Copyright © 2003 by SCCT. Used by permission of Zondervan.

Saint Augustine, *The Confessions of Saint Augustine*. Language updated. © 2006 Zondervan.

Page 1264 Excerpted from *Our Love is Here to Stay* © 2004 by Tony and Lois Evans. Used by permission of Multnomah Publishers Inc.

Saint Hilary of Poitiers as quoted in the *Classics Devotional Bible* by Zondervan.

Copyright © 1996 by Zondervan. Used by permission of Zondervan.

Page 1273 Excerpts from page 185, from THE DIVINE CONSPIRACY by DALLAS WILLARD. Copyright © 1998 by Dallas Willard. Reprinted by permission HarperCollins Publishers.

Thomas à Kempis, *The Imitation of Christ* (Milwaukee: Bruce Publishing Company, 1949). Used by permission.

Page 1283 Adapted from *The God Who Is There* by Francis A. Schaeffer. ©1982 by Francis A. Schaeffer, 1998 by InterVarsity Christian Fellowship/USA, ©1968 by L'Abri. Used with permission of InterVarsity Press, P.O. Box 1400, Downers Grove, IL 60515. www.ivpress.com.

Mark Brazee, *Prescription for Healing: 365 Daily Devotions* (Tulsa: Harrison House Publishers, copyright 1999). Used by permission.

Page 1285 Taken from *Confessions of a Caffeinated Christen* by John Fischer. Copyright © 2005 by John Fischer. Used by permission of Tyndale House Publishers, Inc. All rights reserved.

Matthew Henry, *Commentary on the Whole Bible Volume VI (Acts to Revelation)*. Language updated. © 2006 Zondervan.

Page 1288 Taken from *Velvet Elvis* by ROB BELL. Copyright © 2005 by Rob Bell. Used by permission of Zondervan.

Thomas à Kempis, *The Imitation of Christ*. Language updated. © 2006 Zondervan.

Page 1290 Excerpt from page 143 from CELEBRATION OF DISCIPLINE: THE PATH TO SPIRITUAL GROWTH by RICHARD J. FOSTER. Copyright © 1978 by Richard Foster. Reprinted by permission of HarperCollins Publishers.

Alfred Edersheim, *Life and Times of Jesus the Messiah* (Grand Rapids, Mich: Eerdmans, 1953).

Page 1293 R. A. Torrey, *How to Pray*. Language updated. © 2006 Zondervan.

Taken from *Breakthrough Prayer* by JIM CYMBALA; STEPHEN W. SORENSON. Copyright © 2003 by Jim Cymbala. Used by permission of Zondervan.

Page 1297 John Chrysostom, *St. John Chrysostom, Homily 11*, included in *Nicene and Post-Nicene Fathers, Series I, Vol. XIII* by Philip Schaff. Language updated. © 2006 Zondervan.

Taken from *Becoming a Contagious Christian* by BILL HYBELS; MARK MITTELBERG. Copyright © 1994 by Bill Hybels and Mark Mittelberg. Used by permission of Zondervan.

Page 1299 Taken from *Ragman and Other Cries of Faith* by WALTER WANGERIN JR. Copyright © 2003. Used by permission of Zondervan.

Augustine Baker, *Holy Wisdom* (London: Burns Oates & Washbourne Ltd.). Language updated. © 2006 Zondervan.

Page 1304 Taken from *Rumors of Another World* by PHILIP D. YANCEY. Copyright © 2003 by SCCT. Used by permission of Zondervan.

Charles Spurgeon, *The First Cry from the Cross (A sermon delivered on Sunday Morning, October 24th, 1869)*. Language updated. © 2006 Zondervan.

Page 1306 Bruce Bickel and Stan Jantz, *Keeping God in the Small Stuff* (Uhrichsville, Ohio: Barbour, 2000). Used by permission.

St. John of the Cross as quoted in *Draper's Book of Quotations For The Christian World* by Edythe Draper (Wheaton, IL: Tyndale, 1992). Used by permission of Edythe Draper.

Page 1309 Taken from *Rumors of Another World* by PHILIP D. YANCEY. Copyright © 2003 by SCCT. Used by permission of Zondervan.

John Calvin, *The Epistles of Paul the Apostle to the Romans and to the Thessalonians* (Grand Rapids: William B. Eerdmans, 1973).

Page 1313 Leo I as quoted in *Day by Day with the Early Church Fathers*, page 143, copyright © 1999 by Hendrickson Publishers, Inc. Peabody, Massachusetts. Used by permission. All rights reserved.

Ron Hutchcraft, *Called to Greatness: Becoming a Lifeline to Those Who Need Help* (Chicago, IL: Moody Press, 2001). Used by permission.

Page 1317 Kary Oberbrunner, *The Journey Towards Relevance: Simple Steps for Transforming Your World* (Lake Mary, Fla.: Relevant Books, 2004). Used by permission.

William Law, *A Collection of Letters On the Most Interesting and Important Subjects, and on Several Occasions*. Language updated. © 2006 Zondervan.

Page 1324 Taken from *In Every Pew Sits A Broken Heart* by RUTH GRAHAM. Copyright © 2004 by Ruth Graham. Used by permission of Zondervan.

John Wesley, *A Collection of Hymns, for Use of the People called Methodists*. Language updated. © 2006 Zondervan.

Page 1326 Taken from *Faith Alone* by MARTIN LUTHER; JAMES C. GALVIN. Copyright © 1998, 2005 by James C. Galvin. Used by permission of Zondervan.

Steve Brown, *When Your Rope Breaks*, Baker Books, a division of Baker Publishing Group. Copyright © 1996. Used by permission.

Page 1328 Taken from *More Ready Than You Realize* by BRIAN D. MCLAREN. Copyright © 2002 by Brian D. McLaren. Used by permission of Zondervan.

George MacDonald, *Unspoken Sermons Series Three*. Language updated. © 2006 Zondervan.

Page 1333 Karl Barth, *A Karl Barth Reader* by Geoffrey W. Bromiley. Original translation by Geoffrey W. Bromiley © 1986 Theologischer Verlag Zurich.

Kristine A. Belfils, *The Garbage Man Always Comes on Fridays: 12 Steps for Improving Your Relationship with God* (Spokane, Wash.: Marquette Books, 2005). Used by permission.

Page 1337 Taken from *Mere Christianity* by C. S. LEWIS. Copyright © 2001. Used by permission of Zondervan.

Taken from *Wisdom of Each Other* by Eugene H. Peterson. Copyright © 1998 by Eugene H. Peterson. Used by permission of Zondervan.

Page 1341 Taken from *Soul Shaper* by TONY JONES. Copyright © 2003 by Youth

Specialties. Used by permission of Zondervan.

Oswald Chambers, *My Utmost for His Highest* (Grand Rapids, Mich: Discovery House, 1935).

Page 1344 George Whitefield, *"The Necessity and Benefits of Religious Society" A sermon by George Whitefield.* Language updated. © 2006 Zondervan.

Embracing Grace: A Gospel for All of Us by Scot McKnight. Copyright © 2005 by Scot McKnight. Used by permission of Paraclete Press. www.paracletepress.com.

Page 1347 Taken from *Soulsalsa* by LEONARD SWEET. Copyright © 2000 by Leonard I. Sweet. Used by permission of Zondervan.

Saint Augustine, *The Confessions of Saint Augustine* (Oak Harbor, WA: Logos Research Systems, Inc., 1999).

Page 1350 Ajith Fernando, *Spiritual Living in a Secular World: Applying the Book of Daniel Today* (Grand Rapids, Mich.: Kregel, 2002). Used by permission of Monarch Books.

E. M. Bounds, *The Possibilities of Prayer* (Chicago, IL: Moody Press, 1980). Used by permission.

Page 1353 Taken from *Purpose Driven® Life* by RICK WARREN. Copyright © 2002 by Rick Warren. Used by permission of Zondervan.

Julian of Norwich, *Classics of Western Spirituality,* © Paulist Press 1978. Used by permission.

Page 1355 Taken from *Heaven . . . Your Real Home* by JONI EARECKSON TADA. Copyright © 1996 by Joni Eareckson Tada. Used by permission of Zondervan.

Jeremy Taylor, *The Rule and Exercises of Holy Living.* Language updated. © 2006 Zondervan.

Page 1359 Taken from *Velvet Elvis* by ROB BELL. Copyright © 2005 by Rob Bell. Used by permission of Zondervan.

Alexander MacLaren, *Expositions of Holy Scripture: Isaiah and Jeremiah.* Language updated. © 2006 Zondervan.

Page 1361 Martin Luther, *The Large*

Catechism. Language updated. © 2006 Zondervan.

Don M. Aycock and Mark Sutton, *Still God's Man: A Daily Devotional Guide to Christlike Character* (Grand Rapids, Mich.: Kregel, 2003). Used by permission.

Page 1367 Arthur W. Pink, *Redeemer's Return* (Swengel, PA: Bible Truth Depot, 1918).

Taken from *Living the Message* by EUGENE H. PETERSON. Copyright © 1996. Used by permission of Zondervan.

Page 1370 "Is Work a Curse?" by Ray C. Stedman, The Ray Stedman Library. Used by permission of Raystedman.org.

Donald Drew, *Letters to a Student: Encouraging Words from a Christian Mentor* (Christian Focus Publications, 2003).

Page 1373 Taken from *Wisdom of Each Other* by Eugene H. Peterson. Copyright © 1998 by Eugene H. Peterson. Used by permission of Zondervan.

Origen, *Origen on Prayer.* Language updated. © 2006 Zondervan.

Page 1375 Taken from *Is Your Church Ready?* By NORMAN L. GEISLER; RAVI ZACHARIAS. Copyright © 2003 by Ravi Zacharias and Norman Geisler. Used by permission of Zondervan.

John Chrysostom, *Homily XII.* Language updated. © 2006 Zondervan.

Page 1379 Taken from *Fresh Power* by JIM CYMBALA; DEAN MERRILL. Copyright © 2001 by Jim Cymbala. Used by permission of Zondervan.

John of Ruysbroeck, *The Adornment of the Spiritual Marriage.* Language updated. © 2006 Zondervan.

Page 1382 George Whitefield, *"Walking with God" A sermon by George Whitefield.* Language updated. © 2006 Zondervan.

Excerpt from page 20 from NOW AND THEN by FREDERICK BUECHNER. Copyright © 1983 by Frederick Buechner. Reprinted by permission of HarperCollins Publishers.

Page 1385 Saint Augustine, *Confessions.* Language updated. © 2006 Zondervan.

Reprinted from *Abba's Child.* © 1994 by Brennan Manning. Used with permission of

NavPress, Colorado Springs, CO. All rights reserved.

Page 1389 *Blessed Be Your Name,* by Matt Redman, © 2005, Regal Books, Ventura, CA 93003. Used by permission.

Cortland Myers as quoted in *Streams of the Desert®* by MRS. CHARLES COWMAN; JAMES G. REIMANN. Copyright © 1997 by Zondervan. Used by permission of Zondervan.

Page 1392 Andrew Murray, *The Deeper Christian Life* (London: Fleming H. Revell Co., 1895). Language updated. © 2006 by Zondervan.

Craig Gross, *The Gutter: Where Life Is Meant to Be Lived* (Lake Mary, Fla.: Relevant Books, 2005). Used by permission.

Page 1394 *An Introduction to Christian Theology* by Justo L. González and Zaida Maldonado Pérez, Copyright © 2002. Used by permission of Abingdon Press.

Arthur W. Pink, *Redeemer's Return.* Language updated. © 2006 by Zondervan.

Page 1398 Hannah Whitall Smith, *The Secrets of a Happy Life* (Grand Rapids, MI: Revell 2003).

Matthew Paul Turner, *The Coffee House Gospel: Sharing Your Faith in Everyday Conversation* (Lake Mary, Fla.: Relevant Books, 2004).Used by permission.

Page 1400 John of Damascus, *Exposition of the Orthodox Faith,* by Philip Schaff. Language updated. © 2006 by Zondervan.

Taken from *Is Your Church Ready?* By NORMAN L. GEISLER; RAVI ZACHARIAS. Copyright © 2003 by Ravi Zacharias and Norman Geisler. Used by permission of Zondervan.

Page 1402 Taken from *Fully Devoted* by JOHN ORTBERG; JUDSON POLING; LAURIE PEDERSON. Copyright © 2000 by Willow Creek Association. Used by permission of Zondervan.

Thomas Aquinas, *Summa Theologica.* Language updated. © 2006 by Zondervan.

Page 1404 Taken from *When Life and Beliefs Collide* by CAROLYN CUSTIS JAMES. Copyright © 2001 by Carolyn C. James. Used by permission of Zondervan.

Taken from *Mere Christianity* by C. S. LEWIS. Copyright © 2001. Used by permission of Zondervan.

Page 1408 Taken from *Inklings of God* by KURT BRUNER. Copyright © 2003 by Kurt Bruner. Used by permission of Zondervan.

Sadhu Sundar Singh, *At The Master's Feet* (London: Fleming H Revell Company, 1922).

Page 1412 Nathaniel William Taylor as quoted in *Streams of the Desert®* by MRS. CHARLES COWMAN; JAMES G. REIMANN. Copyright © 1997 by Zondervan. Used by permission of Zondervan.

Carol L. Fitzpatrick, *Daily Wisdom for Women: Practical, Biblical Insight for Today's Woman* (Uhrichsville, Ohio: Barbour, 1997). Used by permission.

Page 1416 John Flavel, *Christ Altogether Lovely.* Language updated. © 2006 by Zondervan.

Taken from *Becoming a Contagious Christian* by BILL HYBELS; MARK MITTELBERG. Copyright © 1994 by Bill Hybels and Mark Mittelberg. Used by permission of Zondervan.

Page 1418 Taken from *How People Grow* by JOHN TOWNSEND; HENRY CLOUD. Copyright © 2001 by Henry Cloud and John Townsend. Used by permission of Zondervan.

Andrew Murray, *Absolute Surrender and Other Addresses.* Language updated. © 2006 by Zondervan.

Page 1422 Gary Henry, *Diligently Seeking God: Daily Motivation to Take God More Seriously* (Indianapolis: WordPoints, 2002).

Taken from *Devotions for a Deeper Life* by OSWALD CHAMBERS. Copyright © 1986 by God's Bible School, Cincinnati, Ohio. Used by permission of Zondervan.

Page 1426 Taken from *Becoming a Contagious Christian* by BILL HYBELS; MARK MITTELBERG. Copyright © 1994 by Bill Hybels and Mark Mittelberg. Used by permission of Zondervan.

William Blake, "*Holy Thursday: Is this a holy thing to see*" (a poem) *Songs of Experience.* Language updated. © 2006 by Zondervan.

Page 1429 Reprinted from *Having a Mary Heart in a Martha World.* Copyright © 2000, 2002 by Joanna Weaver. Used by permission of WaterBrook Press, Colorado Springs, CO. All rights reserved.

Horatius Bonar, *The Episcopal Hymnal, The Protestant Episcopal Church in the U.S.A.* (New York, NY: Oxford University Press, 1920). Language updated. © 2006 by Zondervan.

Page 1431 Francis Schaeffer, *True Spirituality* (Wheaton, IL: Tyndale House, 1979). Used by permission.

Taken from: *Overcoming Fear, Worry, and Anxiety* by Elyse Fitzpatrick. Copyright © 2001 by Elyse Fitzpatrick. Published by Harvest House Publishers, Eugene, OR www.harvesthousepublishers.com. Used by permission.

Page 1433 Taken from *Buck-Naked Faith.* © 2004 by Eric Sandras Ph.D. Used by permission of NavPress, Colorado Springs, CO. All rights reserved.

Hannah Whitall Smith, *The God of All Comfort.* Language updated. © 2006 by Zondervan.

Page 1436 Andrew Murray as quoted in *Take Heart: Daily Devotions with the Church's Great Preachers* by Diana Wallis (Grand Rapids, MI: Kregel Publications, 2001). Used by permission.

W. Glyn Evans, *Daily with the King* (Chicago: Moody Press, 1979). Used by permission.

Page 1439 Taken from the *College Devotional Bible* by Zondervan. © 2006 by Zondervan. Used by permission of Zondervan.

John Wesley, *A Collection of Hymns, for the Use of the People Called Methodists.* Language updated. © 2006 by Zondervan.

Page 1444 Steve Brown, *When Your Rope Breaks,* Baker Books, a division of Baker Publishing Group. Copyright © 1996. Used by permission.

Dietrich Bonhoeffer, *Meditations on the Cross.* Copyright © 1998. Used by permission of Westminster John Knox Press.

Page 1446 Jonathan Edwards as quoted in the *Classics Devotional Bible* by Zondervan. Copyright © 1996 by Zondervan. Used by permission of Zondervan.

Marva J. Dawn, *Morning by Morning: Daily Meditations from the Writings of Marva J. Dawn* (Grand Rapids, Mich.: Eerdmans, 2001).

Page 1450 Excerpted from *The Way I Was Made* © 2005 by Chris Tomlin. Used by permission of Multnomah Publishers Inc.

Taken from the *Classics Devotional Bible* by Zondervan. Copyright © 1996 by Zondervan. Used by permission of Zondervan.

Page 1454 Phillip Brooks as quoted in *Take Heart: Daily Devotions with the Church's Great Preachers* by Diana Wallis (Grand Rapids, MI: Kregel Publications, 2001). Used by permission.

Brennan Manning, *Reflections for Ragamuffins: Daily Devotions from the Writings of Brennan Manning* (New York: HarperCollins, 1998). Used by permission.

Page 1459 A. R. Faussett, *Commentary Critical and Explanatory on the Whole Bible.* Language updated © 2006 by Zondervan.

Taken from *Velvet Elvis* by ROB BELL. Copyright © 2005 by Rob Bell. Used by permission of Zondervan.

contributor biographies

J. W. Alexander (AD 1804–1859) was the oldest son of Archibald Alexander, a prominent theologian. He taught at Princeton Theological Seminary and served as a pastor in New York. See page 305.

Tony Marshall Anderson (AD 1888–1979) was a Nazarene evangelist who emphasized holiness and grace as his two main themes, especially as they related to Christian growth following spiritual conversion. He is also known for *Prayer Availeth Much*. See page 1163.

Anna Sophia of Hesse (AD 1638–1683), daughter of Landgrave George II of Hesse-Darmstadt, was born December 17, 1638, in Marburg, Germany. She was carefully educated in the Holy Scriptures and the Church Fathers. Her hymns show an intense love for the Savior. See page 380.

Saint Thomas Aquinas (AD 1225–1274) was born to an aristocratic family living in Roccasecca, Italy. He joined the Dominican order while studying philosophy and theology at Naples. Later he pursued additional studies in Paris and Köln, where he was exposed to Aristotelian thought. Aquinas developed in massive detail what became the official doctrine of Roman Catholic theology in 1879. See page 1402.

Thomas Arnold (AD 1795–1842), a Master of Rugby and "Broad Church" leader, studied at Warminster and Winchester schools and Corpus Christi College, Oxford, becoming a fellow of Oriel in 1815. See page 1216.

Saint Augustine (AD 354–430), an African by birth, a Roman by education, a Milanese by baptism, created works that still inspire many Christians worldwide. Also known as Aurelius Augustinus and as Augustine of Hippo, he is considered by evangelical Protestants to be (together with the apostle Paul and the Bible) the theological fountainhead of the Reformation teaching on salvation and grace. See pages 503, 1027, 1196, 1261, 1347, and 1385.

Don M. Aycock is the pastor of Liberty Baptist Church in Palatka, Florida. He has written 18 books and speaks at conferences on writing, prayer, men's issues and ministry. See pages 514, 1008, and 1361.

John Baillie (AD 1886–1960) was a prolific writer. A member of both the British Council of Churches and the World Council of Churches, he became president of the latter. See pages 166 and 722.

Augustine Baker (AD 1575–1641) was known for his many ascetical treatises, including those on prayer. Baker explored deeply into the spiritual world of prayer, teaching nuns and others the realities of prayer life. He also collected a large amount of historical material to support the claim (against the newer orders) that the conversion of England was from the beginning essentially Benedictine. In 1633 he went from France to London, where he was subjected to persecution by the Church of England, and died of the plague. See pages 757 and 1299.

Joyce G. Baldwin, formerly Dean of Women at Trinity College, Bristol, England, is also the author of *Daniel; 1 and 2 Samuel; Esther;* and *Haggai, Zechariah, Malachi* in the Tyndale Old Testament Commentary series. See page 65.

The **Epistle of Barnabas (ca. AD 130)** is a Greek treatise with some features of an epistle—containing 21 chapters, preserved complete in the fourth century *Codex Sinaiticus* (Greek Bible), where it appears at the end of the New Testament. It is traditionally ascribed to the Barnabas mentioned in the Acts of the Apostles, though some ascribe it to another apostolic father of the same name, a "Barnabas of Alexandria," or simply attribute it to an unknown early Christian teacher. See pages 132 and 1203.

Albert Barnes (AD 1798–1870), an American theologian, was born at Rome, New York, on December 1, 1798. He graduated from Hamilton College, Clinton, New York, in 1820 and from the Princeton Theological Seminary in 1823. He was ordained as a Presbyterian minister by the presbytery of Elizabethtown, New Jersey, in 1825, and was the pastor successively of the Presbyterian Church in Morristown, New Jersey (1825–1830), and of the First Presbyterian Church of Philadelphia (1830–1867). See page 1062.

Karl Barth (AD 1886–1968) questioned the value of liberal theology during the First World War. Through the influence of a Moravian pastor and his study of the book of Romans, Barth became convinced that the key to vital preaching, theology and the Christian life was the revelation of God in Christ and his resurrection. See page 1333.

Ruth Haley Barton is a teacher and retreat leader. She is also cofounder of The Transforming Center, which equips leaders to guide their churches or organizations in becoming spiritually transforming communities. See page 633.

Richard Baxter (AD 1615–1691) was an English Puritan church leader and controversialist, known as the chief of English Protestant Schoolmen. From the Act of Uniformity in 1662 until the indulgence of 1687, his life was constantly disturbed by persecution of one kind or another. See page 1018.

Lewis Bayly (ca. AD 1575–1631) was best remembered as being the Bishop of Bangor. In 1611 he published *Practice of Piety*. He challenged the power of the district over leases of church land and spoke indiscrete words against Catholics and the Spanish, causing criticism in parliament and court circles. Lewis spent time in Fleet Prison. He spent his own funds repairing Bangor Cathedral. See page 392.

Kristine A. Belfils is a worship leader and singer/songwriter who has recorded several CDs. In addition, Belfils is a speaker and music minister for retreats, conferences, television, radio and church events around the world. See page 1333.

Rob Bell is the founding pastor of Mars Hill Church, said to be one of the fastest growing churches in American history. He is the author of *Velvet Elvis*. He and his wife, Kristen, have two boys and live in Grand Rapids, Michigan. See pages 829, 1223, 1288, 1359, and 1459.

Bernard of Clairvaux (AD 1090–1153) was a French abbot responsible for reforming the monastic order of the Cistercians, advocating a return to manual labor and rejecting materialism and papal expansion. In addition, Clairvaux was instrumental in ending the schism of 1130, which divided the papacy between Italy and France. See page 931.

Bruce Bickel is an attorney, Christian speaker and author. He resides in Fresno, California and is on the Board of Trustees at Westmont College. See pages 409 and 1306.

William Blake (AD 1757–1827) was an English poet and painter; he also illustrated and printed his own books. Blake proclaimed the supremacy of the imagination over the rationalism and materialism of the eighteenth century. Among his later artistic works are drawings and engravings for Dante's *Divine Comedy*. See page 1425.

Horatius Bonar (AD 1808–1889) was a premillenarian and expressed his views in books such as *Prophetical Landmarks* and in the *Quarterly Journal of Prophecy*, which he founded in 1849. He is best known for his poems and hymns, which include "What a Friend We Have in Jesus" and "I Heard the Voice of Jesus Say," among others. See pages 598 and 1429.

Saint Bonaventure (AD 1221–1274) was born Giovanni di Fidanza in 1221. He entered the Franciscan order, studied at the University of Paris, and then taught there with Thomas Aquinas. Bonaventure was made general of his order in 1257 and became cardinal bishop of Albano in 1273. See page 1145.

Dietrich Bonhoeffer (AD 1906–1945) was a German religious leader and participant in the resistance movement against Nazism during World War II. Bonhoeffer, a Lutheran pastor and theologian, took part in the plots being planned by members of the Abwehr (Military Intelligence Office) to assassinate Hitler. He was arrested, imprisoned, and eventually hanged following the failure of the July 20, 1944, assassination attempt. See page 1444.

Craig Borlase has written or cowritten more than 14 books and lives in London with his wife and daughter. See page 322.

E. M. Bounds (AD **1835–1913**) was said to be a man hidden away by God and with God in prayer. During his lifetime he never attracted a large following or gained the success and reputation that one might expect. After 46 years of ministry, he still was virtually unknown. Of the eight classics on prayer that he wrote, only two were published during his lifetime. See pages 387, 480, 1229, and 1350.

Mark Brazee and his wife, Janet, have traveled to more than 35 countries sharing the gospel. The outreaches of Mark Brazee Ministries include DOMATA Bible schools throughout Europe and Asia, an International Ministers' Fellowship and DOMATA School of Missions. See pages 959 and 1283.

John Bright (AD **1908–1995**) taught Hebrew at Union Theological Seminary in Richmond, Virginia. See pages 290 and 978.

Jill Briscoe has a speaking and writing ministry that has taken her to many countries. She has written more than 40 books, including study guides, devotional material, poetry and children's books. See pages 136, 154, and 166.

Phillips Brooks (AD **1835–1893**) was a noted clergyman and author, who briefly served as Bishop of Massachusetts in the Episcopal Church during the early 1890s. He published a number of lectures and sermons, but was probably best known for authoring the Christmas carol, "O Little Town of Bethlehem." See page 1454.

Raymond Brown has been a pastor and was formerly principal of Spurgeon's College in London. He is the author of *The Message of Numbers* and *The Message of Deuteronomy*. See pages 178 and 225.

Steve Brown previously served as a pastor for more than 25 years and now devotes much of his time to the radio broadcast, *Key Life*. He also is professor of preaching at Reformed Theological Seminary in Orlando, Florida. See pages 1199, 1326, and 1444.

Walter Brueggemann is the William Marcellus McPheeters professor of Old Testament at Columbia Theological Seminary in Decatur, Georgia. A graduate of Elmhurst College, Brueggemann earned doctorates from Union Theological Seminary and St. Louis University. See page 703.

Kurt Bruner is a graduate of Talbot Seminary and author of *The Divine Drama; Finding God in The Lord of the Rings; Inklings of God;* and *Finding God in the Land of Narnia.* Bruner and his wife, Olivia, and their four children live in Colorado. See pages 617, 713, 716, and 1408.

Frederick Buechner is an award-winning author. He published his first novel, *A Long Day's Dying*, to great critical acclaim, in 1950. Three years later, he resigned from his teaching position at Lawrenceville School in Lawrenceville, New Jersey, and moved to New York City to be a full-time writer. He attended Madison Avenue Presbyterian Church, pastored by George Buttrick, "whose extraordinary sermons," Buechner said, "had played such a crucial part in my turning to Christianity." Buechner's novel, *Godric*, was nominated for the Pulitzer Prize in 1981. See pages 609, 1102, 1113, and 1382.

John Bunyan (AD **1628–1688**) encountered the seething religious life of various left-wing sects while serving in Oliver Cromwell's army in the English Civil Wars. He underwent a period of spiritual crisis, converted to Puritanism, and became a preacher. He is best known for *The Pilgrim's Progress*, a religious allegory expressing the Puritan religious outlook and symbolic vision of a Christian's pilgrimage through life. See pages 208 and 1118.

Juanita Bynum is founder and president of Juanita Bynum Ministries in Waycross, Georgia, and also author of several books, including *My Spiritual Inheritance, Matters of the Heart* and *No More Sheets*. She currently attends Global Destiny Church in Washington, D.C., where her husband, Thomas Weeks III, is the pastor. See page 865.

John Calvin (AD 1509–1564) was a French Christian theologian during the Protestant Reformation and was the namesake of the system of Christian theology called Calvinism. Along with the *Institutes,* he also produced commentaries on the books of the Bible. See pages 202, 854, 929, and 1309.

Michael Card has sold more than 4 million albums and written more than 20 #1 musical hits. His songs include "El Shaddai," "Love Crucified Arose," and "Emmanuel." Card has also authored or coauthored more than a dozen books. See pages 679 and 1179.

D. A. Carson is research professor of New Testament at Trinity Evangelical Divinity School in Deerfield, Illinois. He is the author or coauthor of more than 45 books, including the *The Gagging of God* and *An Introduction to the New Testament*. He is general editor of *Telling the Truth: Evangelizing Postmoderns* and *Worship by the Book*. See pages 206 and 935.

Steve Case has been in youth ministry for more than 15 years. He has written several books for Youth Specialties, including *The Book of Uncommon Prayer, Everything Counts* and *Road Rules*. A workshop leader, Case speaks at seminars around the country. He lives in Florida with his wife, Becky, and his children, Aprille and Eric. See page 980.

John Cassian (AD 360–433) was an Eastern Christian monk and theologian who brought Eastern spirituality to the West. Cassian toured the ascetic monastic settlements of Egypt before he was driven from the East during the controversy over the theology of Origen. He settled at Marseilles and established religious houses for men and for women. His foundation, the Abbey of St. Victor, a complex of monasteries for both men and women, was one of the first such institutes in the West, and served as a model for later monastic development. See page 69.

Catherine of Siena (AD 1347–1380) began writing letters to men and women in authority, especially begging for peace between the republics and principalities of Italy and for the return of the papacy from Avignon, France, to Rome. In 1376 she went to Avignon herself as ambassador of Florence to make peace with the Papal States, but was unsuccessful. She impressed the Pope so much, however, that he returned his administration to Rome in 1377. Her letters are considered one of the great works of early Tuscan literature. More than 300 letters have survived. Her major work is the *Dialogue of Divine Providence*. See pages 1056, 1068, and 1183.

Oswald Chambers (AD 1874–1917) traveled the world preaching the gospel. He also founded and became principal of the Bible Training College in London. His most famous work is a book of devotionals called *My Utmost for His Highest*. See pages 747, 959, 1024, 1098, 1126, 1168, 1255, 1341, and 1422.

G. K. Chesterton (AD 1874–1936) was a prolific English writer of the early twentieth century. He was said to be both popular and influential during this period, inspiring many historic figures with his works. In his writings, he was notably concerned with religious matters and was received into the Roman Catholic Church in 1922. See page 719.

John Chrysostom (AD 347–407) was a Christian bishop and preacher from the fourth and fifth centuries in Syria and Constantinople. He is noted for eloquence in public speaking and his denunciation of abuse of authority in the Church and in the Roman Empire of the time. After his death he was named Chrysostom, which comes from the Greek *chrysostomos*, or "golden mouthed." See pages 636, 1297, and 1375.

Clement of Alexandria (ca. AD 150–215) was a Christian apologist, missionary theologian to the Greeks, and second known leader of the catechetical school of Alexandria. He synthesized Greek philosophy and Mosaic tradition, and attempted to mediate between Gnostics and orthodox Christians. See page 884.

Henry Cloud is a speaker and cohost, with John Townsend, of the nationally broadcast *New Life Live!* radio program, and cofounder of Cloud-Townsend Clinic and Cloud-Townsend Resources. See page 1418.

William M. Clow (AD 1853–1930) was a Church of Scotland preacher known for his sermons on suffering, prayer and other topics related to the experience of faith. Clow also taught others how to preach. See page 523.

Susan Coolidge (AD 1835–1905) published her first novel, *A New Year's Bargain*, to little success. However, her editor was also the editor of Louisa M. Alcott, who had published *Little Women*. Coolidge's editor suggested that she forget her personal aims and write children's fiction similar to Alcott's. Coolidge did so with great success, producing *What Katy Did*. See page 1008.

Jim Cymbala has been the pastor of the Brooklyn Tabernacle for more than 25 years. He is also the author of *Fresh Wind, Fresh Fire*; *The Life God Blesses*; and *Breakthrough Prayer*. See pages 387, 480, 628, 665, 1027, 1163, 1293, and 1379.

Cyprian (ca. AD 200–258) renounced his wealth and devoted himself to a life of chastity. He rose quickly in the ranks of the early church; within two years, he was elected Bishop of Carthage. Although Cyprian himself and several bishops objected to his taking this position, he eventually did and held the office from 248 until his martyrdom in 258. See page 579.

Cyril (AD 827–869) studied the Scriptures and made such progress that he became a champion of the orthodox faith. He embraced monasticism as an adult, pledging

himself to a life of chastity and austerity. He was ordained a priest by Maximus, Patriarch of Jerusalem, and undertook the work of preaching and instructing catechumens—people who convert to Christianity. See page 619.

John Nelson Darby (AD 1800–1882) was ordained an Anglican deacon but became dissatisfied with the Church of England. Meetings with like-minded Anglicans led to a prayer and Bible study group, which would come to be known as the Plymouth Brethren (from their meetings in Plymouth, England). See page 1190.

Saint David of Wales (ca. AD 542–601) was the founder, abbot and bishop of the monastery of Mynyw in Pembrokeshire, United Kingdom. He was responsible for much of the spread of Christianity in Wales, and many scholars from Ireland and elsewhere sought his monastery out. He is commonly called the apostle of Wales. See page 244.

Marva J. Dawn is a Lutheran evangelical who writes in a paleo-orthodox style, stressing the importance of Christian tradition and the wisdom of the church through the centuries. She is associated with the parachurch organization Christians Equipped for Ministry, in Vancouver, Washington. She also serves as teaching fellow in spiritual theology at Regent College in Vancouver, British Columbia. See pages 36, 202, and 1446.

Nancy Leigh DeMoss is the host and teacher for *Revive Our Hearts*, a daily radio program for women heard on 250 stations. Since 1979, she has served on the staff of Life Action Ministries in Niles, Michigan. She is the author of *A Place of Quiet Rest*; *Lies Women Believe and the Truth That Sets Them Free*; and *A Thirty-Day Walk with God in the Psalms*. See pages 658 and 998.

John Donne (AD 1572–1631) was born into a Roman Catholic family but later converted to Anglicanism. Ordained in 1615, he became a preacher of great power and eloquence and was installed as dean of St.

Paul's Cathedral in 1621. The greatest of the English Metaphysical poets, he was noted for his love lyrics, religious verse and treatises, and sermons. See page 1049.

Fyodor Dostoyevsky (AD 1821–1881) was one of Russia's greatest writers, whose works had a profound and lasting effect on twentieth-century fiction. See pages 27 and 206.

Donald Drew has authored two books titled *Images of Man: A Critique of the Contemporary Cinema* and *Letters to a Student: Staying Close to Christ During the University Years*. See pages 249, 267, and 1370.

Johannes Eckhart (AD 1260–1327), a German mystical theologian, preached throughout Europe, urging people to seek what he called "the divine spark." Toward the end of his life he was wrongly accused of association with the Beghards, who taught that those who gain perfection in this life cannot commit sin and therefore cannot be blamed for any act. See page 1139.

Alfred Edersheim (AD 1825–1889) was a Vienna-born biblical scholar who converted from Judaism to Christianity. A veteran minister and missionary to the Jews of Romania, Edersheim was said to have left an enduring impression on the Jewish people in that country through the spoken and written word. See page 1290.

Jonathan Edwards (AD 1703–1758) emphasized original sin, predestination and the need for conversion. His sermons on justification by faith alone gave rise to the religious revival known as the Great Awakening. See pages 212, 672, 763, 814, 1058, and 1446.

Emerson Eggerichs lives in Grand Rapids, Michigan. He launched the Love and Respect Conferences in 1999 to serve husbands and wives. The goal of the conferences, he said, was for couples to turn hurting marriages into good ones, and good marriages into better ones. See pages 227 and 543.

George Eliot (AD 1819–1880) was the pseudonym of Mary Ann Evans, considered one of England's greatest novelists. Evans was reared as a strict evangelical Protestant, but rebelled and renounced organized religion completely. Writing mainly about life in small rural towns, her books were primarily concerned with the responsibility that people assume for their lives and with the moral choices they make. See page 895.

Charlotte Elliott (AD 1789–1871) became an invalid around age 30, and remained so for the rest of her life. About her physical condition, she wrote that God enabled her to rise every morning determined to take up his cross and follow him. Elliott wrote about 150 hymns. See page 1185.

Paul Enns is pastor of Idlewild Baptist Church in Tampa, Florida, and is also an adjunct professor and director of the Tampa Bay extension of Southeastern Baptist Theological Seminary. See page 138.

Mary Evans's book, *Women in the Bible*, provides an overview of all the crucial passages on women's roles in Scripture. Her other works include *The IVP Women's Bible Commentary; The Message of Samuel; 1 and 2 Samuel;* and *Progress of God's People*. See page 313.

Tony and **Lois Evans** are husband and wife and also founders of the Urban Alternative, a national organization that seeks to bring about spiritual renewal in urban America through the church. Tony is senior pastor of Oak Cliff Bible Fellowship in Dallas, Texas. See pages 208, 782, 895, 1044, 1098, and 1264.

W. Glyn Evans is the author of several devotionals designed for busy Christians. The books include *Daily with the King: A Devotional for Self-Discipline; Daily with My Lord;* and *Don't Quit Until You Taste the Honey: Encouragement for Stressed-Out Christians*. See page 1436.

Steve Farrar is the founder and chairman of Men's Leadership Ministries, based in Frisco, Texas. He earned his doctorate from

Dallas Theological Seminary and is the author of *Finishing Strong* and *Tempered Steel*. See page 359.

A. R. Faussett (19th century AD) was a well-published Biblical scholar in the nineteenth century. His most well-known work is the *Commentary Critical and Explanatory on the Whole Bible* originally published in 1871 that he contributed to with Robert Jamieson and David Brown. See page 1459.

Margaret Feinberg is a journalist, author and speaker whose writings focus on faith and culture in the postmodern world. Feinberg has written or contributed to more than 20 titles. She lives in Juneau, Alaska, with her husband, Leif. See page 739.

Ajith Fernando has been the National Director of Youth for Christ in Sri Lanka since 1976. His ministry includes teaching staff and volunteers and providing pastoral care for leaders. Fernando is also director of YFC's drug-rehabilitation ministry. In addition, he has written 10 books. See pages 722, 1193, and 1350.

Charles G. Finney (AD 1792–1875), often called "America's foremost revivalist," was a major leader of the Second Great Awakening in America. His logical, clear presentation of the gospel was said to have led to the conversion of more than 500,000 people. He was known for his innovations in conducting religious meetings, such as allowing women to pray in public. See pages 94, 178, 423, and 1133.

John Fischer's career spans more than 30 years, first as a recording artist and pioneer of Jesus Music and then as an author and speaker at conferences, retreats, churches and universities. He lives with his wife, Marti, and their son, Chandler, in Laguna Beach, California. See pages 1235 and 1285.

Carol L. Fitzpatrick is the author of eight books, including *Daily Wisdom for Women* and *A Time to Grieve*. See pages 83, 115, and 1412.

Elyse Fitzpatrick has been counseling women since 1989 and is presently a part-time counselor at Grace Church in San Diego, California. She earned a master's degree in Biblical counseling from Trinity Theological Seminary and is a member of the National Association of Nouthetic Counselors. Fitzpatrick is the author of 11 books. See page 1431.

John Flavel (AD 1630–1691) studied at Oxford and in 1650 became curate of Diptford, in Devonshire, England. In 1656 he went to Dartmouth. On being deprived of earning his living in 1662 by the Act of Uniformity, he continued to preach privately until the Five Mile Act (1665) drove him from Dartmouth. See page 1416.

John Wright Follette (AD 1883–1966) taught for many years at Southern California Bible College. He was also an author and poet whose writings focused on developing Christian character. His works included *Broken Bread, Pressed Juice from Living Fruit* and *Smoking Flax and Other Poems*. See pages 344, 584, 1209, and 1235.

Mike Foster is known for his irreverent and straight-talking approach as he helps churches across America build bridges to society. A native of Southern California, Foster has won the hearts of thousands by challenging the status quo and developing outrageous and controversial ideas. His passion for reaching the unsafe and unreachable people of our society has brought him to the front lines. As well as co-founding XXXchurch.com, he is a pastor at one of the fastest growing churches in North America. See page 759.

Richard Foster frequently makes reference to Quaker historical figures and his own Quakerism in his books and speaking engagements. Foster's message is one of utter dependence upon Jesus Christ as savior, teacher, lord and friend. His *Celebration of Discipline* has sold more than a million copies, and was named by *Christianity Today* as one of the top ten books of the twentieth century. See pages 399, 597, 603, 643, 1089, 1133, 1157, 1183, and 1290.

George Fox (AD 1624–1691) was an English dissenter and often considered the founder of the Religious Society of Friends, or Quakers. Living in a time of great social upheaval, Fox rebelled against the religious and political consensus by proposing an unusual and uncompromising approach to the Christian faith: total dependence on Jesus Christ for daily insights and direction. See page 6.

Saint Francis de Sales (AD 1567–1622) engaged in aggressive campaigns of evangelism against Protestantism during the Renaissance. He also traveled to Rome and Paris, where he forged alliances with Pope Clement VIII and King Henri IV. In 1602, he became bishop of Geneva, but lived in exile in Annecy, France. See page 1450.

Francis X. Gaeta has written numerous books on the Christian faith, including *What He Did for Love; With You Always; The Great Fifty Days;* and *From Holy Hour to Happy Hour: How to Build Christian Community.* See page 1126.

Henry Gariepy was national editor in chief and literary secretary for the Salvation Army until 1995, and now serves as a literary consultant, conference speaker and college teacher. See pages 423, 572, 947, and 1068.

Louie Giglio is the author of *The Air I Breathe: Worship as a Way of Life.* He is founder of Passion Conferences, a collegiate movement that helps students renew their passion for God through encounters of worship. Giglio and his wife, Shelley, live in Atlanta, Georgia. See pages 71, 1018, and 1203.

Jim Goll is the cofounder of Encounters Network. He has traveled worldwide sharing about intercession, prophetic ministry and life in the Spirit. He is the founder of the Heart of David Correspondence School, a member of the Harvest International Ministries Apostolic Team, and the Apostolic Council of Prophetic Elders. See page 619.

Justo Gonzalez is the author of the three-volume *History of Christian Thought* and other works on Christian and Church history. He attended United Seminary in Cuba and was the youngest person to receive a doctorate in historical theology at Yale. See pages 284 and 1394.

Karon Phillips Goodman is a freelance journalist, author and stepmother who frequently writes about stepfamily issues. Her work has appeared in *Woman's Day, Writer's Digest* and many other publications. See page 1221.

Billy Graham has preached to more people in live audiences than anyone else in history—more than 210 million individuals in more than 185 countries and territories through various evangelistic meetings. He has also reached hundreds of millions more through television, video, film and webcasts. See pages 4, 634, 859, and 1250.

Ruth Graham is an experienced conference speaker and Bible teacher known for her honesty and authenticity as she shares her sometimes painful journey of faith. She is the daughter of Ruth and Billy Graham and the author of *In Every Pew Sits a Broken Heart* and *Legacy of Love.* See pages 623 and 1324.

Michael Green is a British theologian, Anglican priest, Christian apologist and author of more than 50 books. Many of his best-known works discuss the dual topics of evangelism and apologetics. See page 219.

Gregory of Nyssa (AD 335–394) was a Christian bishop and younger brother of Basil the Great. Gregory was known for his doctrine of the Trinity. See page 105.

Peter Greig is the founder of 24-7 Prayer, an international, interdenominational prayer movement. He is also associated with Cultural Shift, a network of those experimenting with church in the emerging culture. See page 1185.

Craig Gross is founder of XXXchurch.com, a ministry that helps churches and individuals address and resolve issues associated with pornography. See pages 759 and 1392.

Jean Nicolas Grou (AD 1731–1803) was a Roman Catholic priest who lived through the turmoil of the French Revolution. He wrote a number of books for embattled Catholics during that time, including *Meditations on the Love of God; How to Pray;* and *Spiritual Life.* See page 470.

Romano Guardini (AD 1885–1968) was an Italian-born German priest considered one of the most important representatives of the twentieth-century Catholic worldview, particularly in the areas of liturgy, religious philosophy, pedagogy and the history of ideas. His books were said to be powerful studies of traditional themes in the light of present-day challenges or, conversely, examinations of current problems as approached from the Christian, and especially Roman Catholic, tradition. See pages 572 and 658.

Os Guinness has written or edited more than 20 books. He is currently senior fellow at The Trinity Forum, and a frequent speaker and seminar leader at political and business conferences in both the United States and Europe. See pages 498 and 556.

William Guthrie (AD 1620–1655) was a 17th century Christian whose works have been quoted by Charles Spurgeon and D. L. Moody. See page 865.

Madame Guyon (AD 1648–1717) wrote extensively. Her smallest book—*A Short and Easy Method of Prayer*—was a classic that has been read and meditated by scores of believers ever since its first publication in 1685. See pages 210, 579, 628, and 980.

Ole Hallesby (AD 1879–1961) was one of Norway's leading Christian teachers and devotional writers. During World War II he was imprisoned for his resistance to the Nazis. He worked as a seminary professor in Oslo until his death. See pages 488 and 1028.

Lisa Harper is known for her authenticity, humorous anecdotes and ability to help women apply biblical truths to their lives. Harper is also the author or coauthor of several books, including *Relentless Love; Every*

Woman's Hope; and *Renewed Hearts, Changed Lives.* See pages 995, 1049, and 1070.

Nick Harrison is a journalist who has written for *Publishers Weekly, CCM, Bookstore Journal* and *Moody Magazine.* He is the author of *Promises to Keep: Daily Devotions for Men of Integrity.* See page 132.

Gary Henry has written and spoken to audiences for more than 30 years on the topic of seeking God. Henry lives in Indianapolis, where he preaches for the Westside Church of Christ. See pages 144 and 1422.

Matthew Henry (AD 1662–1714) was a Welsh-born, English nonconformist minister and Bible commentator. He is remembered for his practical and devotional multivolume *Exposition of the Old and New Testaments*, which is still published. See pages 65, 136, 498, 549, 563, 594, 679, and 1285.

Saint Hilary of Poitiers (CA. AD 315–367) was bishop of Poitiers (France) and considered a doctor of the Western Christian Church. He was sometimes referred to as the "hammer against Arianism" and the "Athanasius of the West" for advocating his trinitarian principles over those who taught that God the Father and Son were not co-eternal. See page 1264.

S. J. Hill has more than 35 years of experience in the ministry. Hill currently travels throughout the United States and globally, teaching believers how to attain intimacy and commitment to God. See pages 234, 649, 701, 763, and 931.

Charles Hodge (AD 1797–1878) was one of the greatest exponents and defenders of historical Calvinism in America during the nineteenth century. His life was spent in defending the reformed theology as set forth in the *Westminster Confession of Faith, Westminster Larger Catechism* and *Westminster Shorter Catechism.* See page 225.

Christopher D. Hudson has served as the General Editor for multiple Bible projects including the *College Devotional Bible* and *Revolution: The Bible for Teen Guys* (both published by Zondervan). See page 1439.

Kent Hughes has served as senior pastor at College Church in Wheaton, Illinois. He is also the author of numerous books, including *Disciplines of a Godly Man* and *Disciplines of a Godly Family*, and is series editor for the Preaching the Word commentaries. See page 244.

Ron Hutchcraft is an author, speaker and international radio host of such programs as "A Word With You" and "Alive! With Ron Hutchcraft," the most widely circulated Christian youth broadcast in the world. See page 1313.

Bill Hybels is the founding and senior pastor of Willow Creek Community Church in South Barrington, Illinois. Willow Creek's various ministries, under Hybels' leadership, have made it one of the most attended churches in North America, with an average weekly attendance of more than 17,000. See pages 1240, 1297, 1416, and 1425.

Chip Ingram is the host of the radio program *Living on the Edge* and the president of *Walk Thru the Bible*. See page 507.

Irenaeus (AD 130–202) was the bishop of Lugdunum in Gaul, which is now Lyons, France. His writings were instrumental in the early development of Christian theology, namely the emphasis on salvation history—which insisted that God began the world and has been overseeing it ever since. See page 603.

Carolyn Custis James travels extensively as a speaker for women's conferences, churches, colleges, seminaries and other Christian organizations. Her ministry organization, Whitby Forum, promotes Biblical discussion to help men and women join forces in serving God together. See pages 23, 274, 549, 742, 809, 1150, 1216, and 1404.

Robert Jamieson (AD 1802–1880) published a collection of 149 traditional ballads and songs, along with a book of his own entitled *Popular Ballads and Songs from Tradition, Manuscripts and Scarce Editions with Translations of Similar Pieces from the Ancient Danish Language*. See pages 49 and 313.

Stan Jantz managed a chain of Christian retail stores for more than 25 years. He lives in Fresno, California, and serves on the Board of Trustees of Biola University. See pages 409 and 1306.

John of Damascus (ca. AD 675–749) spent his life largely in fighting with his pen for orthodoxy against iconoclasm. His fame rests on his theological masterpiece, *The Fountain of Wisdom*, a Greek work in three parts, including a formal exposition of the Christian faith (*De fide orthodoxa*). John of Damascus also wrote hymns and regulated the choral parts of the Byzantine liturgy. See page 1400.

Saint John of the Cross (AD 1542–1591) was one of the most important mystical philosophers in Christian history. He initiated a severe form of monasticism in a tiny farmhouse whereby his monks went shoeless to indicate their commitment to poverty. See page 1306.

John of Ruysbroeck (AD 1293–1381) lived in the fourteenth century, but his works gained popularity when they were published four centuries later. His work, *The Seven Steps of the Ladder of Spiritual Love*, was published in 1848. *Reflections from the Mirror of a Mystic* appeared in 1906. See page 1379.

Andrea Johnson is a pastor's wife and author of *Daily Professions*. Johnson also ministers on a radio program in which *Daily Professions* can be heard several times a day. See page 91.

Leonidas A. Johnson is a licensed optometrist and third-generation preacher. He has written several books and made several missionary trips to Africa. Johnson is the founder of Crystal Fountain Ministries and The Crystal Fountain Culture and Vision Center of Reconciliation. See page 169.

E. Stanley Jones (AD 1884–1972) was a Methodist missionary and theologian remembered for his interreligious lectures to the educated classes in India, thousands of which were held across the Indian subcontinent during the first decades of the twentieth century. He spent much time with Mahatma Gandhi, who challenged Jones to include greater respect for the Indian character. This effort to contextualize Christianity for India was the subject of Jones's seminal work, *The Christ of the Indian Road*, which sold more than one million copies worldwide after its publication in 1925. See page 739.

Tony Jones has written four books, including *Postmodern Youth Ministry; Soul Shaper; Read.Think.Pray.Live.*; and *Pray*. Tony lives in Minnesota with his wife, Julie, and their two children. See pages 1080 and 1341.

Julian of Norwich (AD 1342–ca. 1416) suffered from a severe illness at age 30 and had a series of intense visions. They would later be the source of her major work, called *Sixteen Revelations of Divine Love*. This is believed to be the first book written by a woman in the English language. See pages 701 and 1353.

Mary Kassian studied systematic theology at the doctoral level and has taught courses at seminaries across North America. Currently, she is a professor at Southern Baptist Seminary in Louisville, Kentucky. See page 989.

Derek Kidner, formerly warden of Tyndale House, Cambridge, England, is author of the Tyndale Commentaries on Genesis; Ezra and Nehemiah; and Proverbs. His other works include *The Message of Ecclesiastes* and *The Message of Hosea*. See page 49.

Søren Kierkegaard (AD 1813–1855), a nineteenth-century Danish philosopher and theologian, is generally recognized as the first existentialist philosopher. Kierkegaard strongly criticized both the Hegelian philosophy of his time and what he saw as the empty formalities of the Danish church. Much of his work deals with religious problems such as the nature of faith, the institution of the Christian church, Christian ethics and theology, and the emotions and feelings of individuals when faced with existential choices. Because of this, Kierkegaard's work is sometimes characterized as Christian existentialism and existential psychology. See page 820.

Rob Lacey was an author, actor and broadcaster with 16 years of experience producing and performing theater, storytelling and performance poetry. He trained at the Desmond Jones School of Mime and Physical Theatre, and was a founding member of the Trapdoor Theatre Company before he went solo in 1992. His books include the award-winning *The Word on the Street* and *The Liberator*. Rob passed away in 2006 while this Bible was being developed. See page 916.

Lactantius (ca. AD 240–320) was a Christian author and apologist. He taught rhetoric at Diocletian's school in Nicomedia, and during the early persecutions of Christianity was converted to the faith. Later, he was Latin tutor to Crispus, Constantine's son. See page 1086.

William Law (AD 1686–1761) was an eighteenth-century Anglican priest who heavily influenced the theology of John and Charles Wesley. Law used his book, *A Serious Call to a Devout and Holy Life*, to attack the hypocrisy and corruption of the church. The book's theme was that God did not merely forgive human disobedience, but called individuals to obedience and to a life completely centered on him. See pages 1218 and 1317.

Brother Lawrence (AD 1605–1691), also known as Nicholas Herman, was born in Lorraine province, France. He came from a humble background and was an unlearned man. He was converted to Christianity in 1629, and after being a soldier and a footman for some time, he entered the religious community of the Carmelites in Paris around 1649. See page 154.

Leo I (AD 400–461), a Roman aristocrat, was Pope from 440 to 461. He stopped the invasion of Italy by Attila the Hun in 452 by his moral persuasion, was a theologian, and was a leading figure in the centralization of the government of the Church. See page 1237, 1313.

Herbert C. Leupold (AD 1892–1972) gained renown as an Old Testament scholar and an authority on liturgics, or the study of liturgies. He also served as professor of Old Testament Exegesis at the Evangelical Lutheran Theological Seminary, at Capital University in Columbus, Ohio. See page 36.

C. S. Lewis (AD 1898–1963) was an Irish author and scholar, born into a Protestant family in Belfast, though he mostly resided in England. Lewis was known for his work on medieval literature and for his Christian apologetics and fiction, especially the children's series titled *The Chronicles of Narnia*. See pages 59, 299, 319, 792, 829, 1037, 1337, and 1404.

William Longstaff (AD 1822–1894) was friends with Salvation Army founder William Booth, and evangelists Dwight Moody and Ira Sankey. A number of Longstaff's hymns were published in the Salvation Army's *War Cry*. See page 138.

Anne Graham Lotz, daughter of Billy and Ruth Graham, is the president and CEO of AnGeL Ministries, a nonprofit organization committed to making God's Word personal and relevant to ordinary people. Lotz has spoken on seven continents, in more than 20 countries. In addition, she has written eight books, including *Just Give Me Jesus*. See pages 299 and 584.

Martin Luther (AD 1483–1546) was a German theologian, an Augustinian monk and an ecclesiastical reformer whose teachings inspired the Reformation and deeply influenced the doctrines and cultures of the Lutheran and Protestant traditions. Luther's call to the church to return to the teachings of the Bible led to the formation of new traditions within Christianity and to the Counter-Reformation, the Catholic reaction to these movements. His translations of the Bible helped to develop a standard version of the German language and added several principles to the art of translation. His hymns inspired the development of congregational singing in Christianity. See pages 643, 665, 1153, 1326, and 1361.

Erwin Lutzer is senior pastor of The Moody Church in Chicago. A graduate of Dallas Theological Seminary and Loyola University, he is the author of numerous books. See page 1056.

George MacDonald (AD 1824–1905) was a Scottish author, poet and Christian minister. His works have inspired deep admiration in such notables as W. H. Auden, J. R. R. Tolkien and Madeleine L'Engle. See pages 348, 1102, and 1328.

Alexander MacLaren (AD 1826–1910) was a Baptist minister who acquired the reputation of "the prince of expository preachers" for sermons that expounded Biblical truths. His preaching drew vast congregations, and his analogies drawn from nature and life have been widely imitated ever since. See pages 158, 277, 414, 633, 1157, and 1359.

Brennan Manning was ordained as a Franciscan priest. In the late 1960s, he joined the Little Brothers of Jesus of Charles de Foucauld, an order committed to an uncloistered, contemplative life among the poor of Europe. In the 1970s, he returned to the United States and began writing about sin and redemption. He travels to a great extent, writing and preaching on the unconditional love of Jesus. See pages 1058, 1118, 1209, 1385, and 1454.

Cardinal Henry Edward Manning (AD 1808–1892) was ordained in the Anglican Church in 1832, but left it in 1851 over a dispute about baptismal regeneration to become a Roman Catholic priest. He worked tirelessly for prison reform and to alleviate the condition of the poor. His society of Oblates of St. Charles carried on much of this work. Manning also greatly expanded

Catholic education in England and furthered the education of the poor. See page 514.

Michael Marshall is the author of *Christian Orthodoxy Revisited; Renewal in Worship;* and *The Anglican Church Today and Tomorrow,* a study series on the Anglican Church. See page 43.

Alfred McBride serves as a canon at the Abbey of St. Norbert in DePere, Wisconsin. He is also the author of numerous books on the Catholic faith, including *Essentials of the Faith, Father McBride's Teen Catechism* and *Family Catechism* as well as commentaries on the four Gospels, the Acts of the Apostles, and the book of Revelation. See page 432.

Alister McGrath is a Christian theologian born in Belfast, Northern Ireland, currently serving as professor of historical theology at Oxford University. McGrath is associated with the paleo-orthodox movement, which encourages reflection upon the influential members of the early church. His areas of expertise include doctrine, church history, the interaction of science and faith, and evangelical spirituality. See page 1005.

Janet Holm McHenry is the author of 17 books, including the *PrayerWalk, Daily Prayerwalk, Prayer Changes Teens* and *Girlfriend Gatherings.* See page 1136.

Rick McKinley has served in various ministries and written *Jesus in the Margins: Finding God in the Places We Ignore.* Presently, McKinley is the lead pastor at Imago Dei Community Church in Portland, Oregon. See pages 392 and 745.

Scot McKnight is the Karl A. Olsson professor in religious studies at North Park University in Chicago, Illinois. The author of more than ten books and numerous articles and chapters in multiauthored works, McKnight specializes in historical Jesus studies as well as the Gospels and the New Testament. See page 1344.

Brian McLaren is a prominent voice in the Emerging Church Movement. His public speaking covers a broad range of topics including postmodernism, Biblical studies, evangelism, apologetics, leadership, global mission, pastoral survival and burnout, and interreligious dialogue. See pages 598, 1196, 1244, and 1328.

Thomas Merton (AD 1915–1968) was an American Trappist monk and author, born in France. He wrote more than 50 books, 2,000 poems, and numerous essays, reviews and lectures. Merton became a monk in 1941. He was later ordained a priest and was known as Father M. Louis. Merton died as a result of an accident in Thailand while attending an ecumenical council of Catholic and Buddhist monks. See page 597.

John M'Ewan (ca. 1880) served as pastor of John Knox Free Church and was quoted by D. L. Moody in his book, *One Thousand and One Thoughts from my Library,* published in 1898 by Revell. See page 14.

F. B. Meyer (AD 1847–1929) stood against the social evils of his day. Not only was he effective in the temperance movement, but he also helped close more than 500 houses of prostitution. In addition, he formed a prison aid society. Meyer wrote more than 40 books. See page 998.

David A. Miller is the senior pastor of Faith Presbyterian Church in Seminole, Florida. He earned his Doctor of Ministry degree from Fuller Theological Seminary and has extensively studied the worship renewal taking place within the mainline denominations. See page 1255.

Miguel de Molinos (ca. AD 1640–1697) was a Spanish priest and mystic. He founded quietism, which he adhered to in its most extreme form. His *Guida spirituale* set forth his quietistic principles. See page 713.

D. L. Moody (AD 1837–1899) was considered one of the greatest evangelists of all time. In addition to his preaching, Moody also founded the Northfield Schools in Massachusetts and Moody Bible Institute and Moody Church in Chicago, Illinois. See pages 4, 533, 1005, and 1033.

Bryce Morgan is pastor of Way of Grace Church in Buckeye, Arizona, near Phoenix. He is also author of *Learning to Reflect: Daily Meditations on the Word of God.* See pages 290 and 533.

G. Campbell Morgan (AD 1863–1945) was pastor of Westminster Congregational Church in London. He was also a prolific writer of books, booklets, tracts and articles. See pages 274, 359, and 935.

J. A. Motyer has served at Trinity College in Bristol. He has written a number of commentaries including *The Message of Exodus* and *The Message of James.* See page 94.

Andrew Murray (AD 1828–1917) was born in South Africa and spent the majority of his life living there. His mission throughout his life was to preach Christ to all the inhabitants of his area of influence. He believed that he had been called by God to reach people in Africa and worked to start a training school that would raise up missionaries to bring the gospel to as many people as possible. See pages 566, 590, 649, 782, 1084, 1107, 1136, 1179, 1392, 1418, and 1436.

Cortland Myers (AD 1864–1941) was concerned with living a life pleasing to God. He put those thoughts into words in his book, *Making a Life.* He is the coauthor of *The person of Christ; his perfect humanity a proof of his divinity, with impartial testimonies to his character.* See page 1389.

Watchman Nee (AD 1903–1972) was a citizen of the People's Republic of China who became a Christian in 1920 at the age of 17 and began writing in the same year. See page 409.

George Neumarck (AD 1621–1681) wrote one of the best-known German hymns, "Leave God to Order All Thy Ways." See page 556.

Cardinal John Henry Newman (AD 1801–1890) was an English convert to Catholicism, and later made a cardinal. In early life he was a major figure in the Oxford Movement to bring the Church of England back to its Catholic roots. Eventually his studies in history convinced him to become a Catholic. See pages 71 and 432.

Henri J. M. Nouwen (AD 1932–1996) was a Dutch Catholic priest and writer who authored 40 books on the spiritual life. His best-known works were *The Return of the Prodigal Son: A Story of Homecoming* and *The Wounded Healer.* See page 399.

Kary Oberbrunner is founder of Redeem the Day Ministries and serves as a pastor at The Grace Brethren Church of Powell in Ohio. In addition, he is a contributor to *RELEVANT* magazine and the author of *The Journey Towards Relevance.* See pages 348, 884, and 1317.

Origen (AD 185–254), a Christian scholar and theologian, was considered to be one of the most distinguished of the Fathers of the early Christian church. He lived through a turbulent period of the Christian church, when persecution was widespread and little or no doctrinal consensus existed among the various regional churches. In this environment, Gnosticism flourished, and Origen was the first truly philosophical thinker to turn his hand not only to a refutation of Gnosticism but also to offer an alternative Christian system that was more rigorous and philosophically respectable than the mythological speculations of the various Gnostic sects. See page 1373.

James Orr (AD 1844–1913) was a Scottish theologian and historian, born in Glasgow. His publications include *The Christian View of God and the World* and *The History and Literature of the Early Church.* See pages 809 and 1113.

John Ortberg is a teaching pastor at Menlo Park Presbyterian Church in Menlo Park, California. He is the author of many books, has written for *Christianity Today,* and is a frequent contributor to *Leadership Journal.* See pages 397, 414, 1015, 1086, 1107, and 1402.

Kenneth Osbeck received his master's degree in music from the University of Michigan. He has served in churches around Grand Rapids, Michigan, for 35 years. See page 319.

John N. Oswalt earned his Ph.D. at Brandeis University and is a research professor of Old Testament at Wesley Biblical Seminary in Jackson, Mississippi. See page 773.

John Owen (AD 1616–1683) entered Queen's College in Oxford at the young age of 12. During his 67 years he was said to have lived out a life full of spiritual experience, literary accomplishment, and national influence so far beyond most of his peers that he continues to merit the accolade of "The greatest British theologian of all time." See pages 458 and 1015.

Joseph Parker (AD 1830–1902) was an English nonconformist divine whose stimulating and original sermons, with their notable leaning toward the use of a racy vernacular, made him one of the best-known personalities of his time. His published works are chiefly sermons and expositions, including *City Temple Sermons* and *The People's Bible*, in 25 volumes. See page 169.

Les Parrott and his wife, Leslie, are codirectors of the Center for Relationship Development at Seattle Pacific University. Les is a professor of clinical psychology and Leslie is a marriage and family therapist. See page 77.

Mark Guy Pearse (AD 1842–1932) was a preacher, author and artist. His sermons, books and paintings focused primarily on Christ's holiness, but also addressed other spiritual themes. See page 10.

Eugene Peterson is professor emeritus of Spiritual Theology at Regent College in Vancouver, British Columbia. He is also a retired pastor and a poet. He has written several books, including *Psalms: Prayers of the Heart* and *The Message*, which is a modern-language version of the Old and New Testaments. Peterson earned his degrees from Seattle Pacific University, New York Theological Seminary and Johns Hopkins University. See pages 694, 1028, 1337, 1367, and 1373.

Mike Pilavachi is the founder of Soul Survivor, an international movement that seeks to disciple, equip and empower young people to make a difference in their generation. He is also an international speaker and pastor of Soul Survivor Watford, a London-based congregation that aims to reach out to the youth of Watford, England. His books include *Soul Survivor; My First Trousers: Growing Up with God; Weeping Before an Empty Tomb;* and *For the Audience of One: The Soul Survivor Guide to Worship.* See pages 59 and 843.

Arthur W. Pink (AD 1885–1952) was born in Great Britain and immigrated to the United States to study at Moody Bible Institute. He pastored churches in Colorado, California, Kentucky and South Carolina before becoming an itinerant Bible teacher in 1919. See pages 23, 219, 1367, and 1394.

Adrian Plass is a British author who writes primarily Christian humor, but also short stories, Bible commentaries and novels with a more serious tone. Plass is an Anglican who lives with his wife, Bridget, in East Sussex, England. See pages 27 and 277.

Matt Redman is involved with an Anglican church plant, The Point, near Brighton, England. His songs include "The Heart of Worship," "Better Is One Day," and "Let Everything That Has Breath." He received the Dove Award for Worship Song of the Year for "Blessed Be Your Name." In addition, Redman is the author of *The Unquenchable Worshipper* and *Facedown.* See pages 344, 458, 523, 579, and 1389.

B. T. Roberts (AD 1890–1972) first trained as an attorney, then entered the ministry in the Genesee Conference of the Methodist Episcopal Church of New York State. Roberts was influenced by leaders of the Holiness Movement, including Phoebe Palmer. Roberts was also influenced by Methodist evangelist John Wesley Redfield. See page 617.

Dave Roberts lives in East Sussex, England. He served as an editor of various United Kingdom publications, including *Renewal* magazine before becoming an author, speaker and publishing consultant. In addition, he helped establish several large training conferences, including Worship Together. He also helped found the youth-ministry resource, *Youthwork* magazine. See pages 212 and 688.

Frederick W. Robertson (AD 1816–1853), an English preacher known as Robertson of Brighton, was admired by ordinary people for his preaching style. Robertson's published works include five volumes of sermons, two volumes of expository lectures on Genesis and on the epistles to the Corinthians, a volume of miscellaneous addresses, and *Analysis of "In Memoriam."* See page 77.

Oscar Romero (AD 1917–1980) was a Catholic priest in El Salvador who later became prelate archbishop of San Salvador. As an archbishop, he witnessed numerous human rights violations and began a ministry speaking out on behalf of the poor and victims of the country's civil war. His political activism was denounced by the hierarchy of the Catholic Church and the El Salvadorian government. In 1980, he was assassinated by gunshot while consecrating the Eucharist during mass. He is one of the ten twentieth-century martyrs from across the world depicted in statues above the Great West Door of Westminster Abbey, London. See page 91.

Lisa Ryken is a contributor to *Devotions for Ministry Wives*. Her husband, Philip, is senior minister of Tenth Presbyterian Church in Philadelphia, Pennsylvania. See page 470.

Judy Salisbury is the founder of Logos Presentations. She has been equipping the Christian community with communication, presentation and evangelism skills. Through her speaking, writing and training materials she helps believers to share the gospel and to address moral and ethical issues. See page 305.

Eric Sandras pastors the Olympic Vineyard Christian Fellowship in Port Angeles, Washington, and is a frequent conference speaker across the United States and Canada. He is also the author of *Buck Naked Faith: A Brutally Honest Look at Stunted Christianity.* See page 1433.

Dorothy Sayers (AD 1893–1967) is perhaps best known for her Lord Peter Wimsey mysteries—a series of novels and short stories featuring an English aristocrat who tirelessly solves innumerable mysteries as an amateur sleuth. However, Sayers herself considered her translation of Dante's *Divina Commedia* to be her best work. See page 1121.

Francis Schaeffer (AD 1912–1984) is credited with helping spark a return to political activism among Protestant evangelical and fundamentalist Christians in the late 1970s and early 1980s, especially around the issue of abortion and the secularization of public schools. In 1981, he wrote *A Christian Manifesto*, which called for Christians to use civil disobedience to restore biblical morality. Schaeffer also wrote 21 other books covering a range of spiritual issues. See pages 1283 and 1431.

Philip Schaff (AD 1819–1893) wrote biographies, catechisms and hymns for children, manuals of religious verse, lectures and essays on Dante. He also wrote the *History of the Christian Church*. See pages 322, 742, 1150, 1199, 1244, and 1250.

Henry Scougal (AD 1650–1678) entered King's College at age 15, and after graduation was promoted to the office of Professor of Philosophy. Except for one year when he pastored a church, he taught at the college until 1678, when at the age of 28, he died of tuberculosis. See page 730.

A. B. Simpson (AD 1843–1902) was a Canadian preacher, theologian, author and founder of The Christian and Missionary Alliance, an evangelical protestant denomination with an emphasis on global evangelism. Simpson was known as an ardent soul-winner and was active in raising up new believers and in training Christian workers for service in America and around the world. See page 989.

Sadhu Sundar Singh (AD 1889–1929) was regarded by many as a highly eccentric convert as he wandered the roads of India in his yellow robe and turban. However, he felt called at an early age to renounce home, employment, marriage and family life to tell others of God's love. He made it clear that Christianity was not an imported, alien, foreign religion but was indigenous to Indian needs, aspirations and faith. To this day, he remains one of the permanently significant figures of Indian Christianity. See page 1408.

Hannah Whitall Smith (ca. AD 1832–1911) was a lay speaker and author in the Holiness Movement in the United States and the Higher Life Movement in Great Britain. She was also active in the Women's Suffrage Movement and the Temperance Movement. See pages 249, 507, 859, 1398, and 1433.

Ann Spangler is an award-winning writer and author of many books, including *Praying the Names of God*, *Women of the Bible* (coauthored with Jean Syswerda) and *Men of the Bible* (coauthored with Robert Wolgemuth). She lives with her two daughters in Grand Rapids, Michigan. See pages 6, 488, 929, and 1037.

Charles Haddon Spurgeon (AD 1834–1892) was regarded as England's best-known preacher for most of the second half of the nineteenth century. In 1854, just four years after his conversion, Spurgeon, then only 20, became pastor of London's famed New Park Street Church. The congregation quickly outgrew their building, moved to Exeter Hall, then to Surrey Music Hall. In these venues Spurgeon frequently preached to audiences numbering more than 10,000. See pages 43, 795, 947, and 1304.

Andy Stanley is a graduate of Dallas Theological Seminary and the founding pastor of North Point Community Church and North Point Ministries in Atlanta, Georgia. He is the author of *Visioneering, The Next Genera-*

tion Leader and *How Good Is Good Enough?* In addition, he coauthored *7 Practices of Effective Ministry* with Reggie Joiner and Lane Jones, both of whom serve on staff at North Point Ministries. See page 1040.

Ray C. Stedman (AD 1917–1992) was one of the foremost pastors and Biblical expositors of the twentieth century. He was pastor at Peninsula Bible Church (Palo Alto, California) for 40 years. See page 1370.

James Stewart (AD 1896–1990) served as professor of theology and New Testament at New College, Edinburgh. He served as a pastor as well as a chaplain for a local soccer club. See page 284.

Lee Strobel, a former legal editor for the *Chicago Tribune*, is a Christian apologist and former teaching pastor at two of America's largest churches. He is best known for writing the semi-autobiographical bestsellers *The Case for Christ, The Case for Faith* and *The Case for a Creator*. See pages 69, 615, and 1139.

Karen Stroup is a minister in the Disciples of Christ church and a senior lecturer at Vanderbilt University. Stroup is the author of numerous articles and the book, *Don't Gift-Wrap the Garbage: Down-To-Earth Daily Meditations for Women*. In addition, she is the coauthor of *Speak the Language of Healing: How to Have Breast Cancer Without Going to War*. See page 1145.

Leonard Sweet is the E. Stanley Jones professor of evangelism at Drew Theological School in Madison, New Jersey, and visiting distinguished professor at George Fox University in Portland, Oregon. He is also the author of more than 100 articles, 600 published sermons and 30 books. Titles include *The Three Hardest Words in the World to Get Right; The Church in Emerging Culture: Five Perspectives; Jesus Drives Me Crazy; Postmodern Pilgrims;* and *Soul Salsa*. Sweet's Wikiletics.com is an open-source preaching resource. See page 1347.

Joni Eareckson Tada is the founder and president of Joni and Friends, an organization devoted to Christian outreach in the rehabilitation community worldwide. She is also an artist and the author of numerous books, including *Diamonds in the Dust*, *More Precious Than Silver*, *Heaven: Your Real Home* and *When God Weeps*. Her book, *The God I Love*, explores her journey as a paralytic for more than 30 years. See pages 503, 566, 747, 776, 792, 1121, 1190, and 1355.

John Tauler (ca. AD 1300–1361), a Dominican friar, preached to contemplative Dominican nuns. His style was considered down to earth, and above all he advocated humility and simplicity. His emphasis on the cross of Christ and on an alive relationship with God was probably what attracted Martin Luther to his writings. See pages 773 and 1223.

Jeremy Taylor (AD 1613–1667) was born in Cambridge, England, in 1613 and was ordained in 1633. In the years between 1633 and the rise of the Puritans in 1645, he was a Fellow of two Cambridge colleges, and chaplain to Archbishop Laud and to King Charles. Under Puritan rule, he was imprisoned three times and forced into retirement as a family chaplain in Wales. After the Restoration, in 1661, he became Bishop of Down and Connor in Ireland. See pages 227 and 1355.

Nathaniel William Taylor (AD 1786–1858) was an influential Protestant Theologian of the early nineteenth century, whose major contribution to the Christian faith was to modify historical Calvinism in order to fit into the religious revivalism of the time (The Second Great Awakening). He did this, church historians said, to preserve the ideal of human freedom, mainly because he believed that Calvinism denied freedom and the chance for people to be saved. Taylor also challenged such Calvinistic doctrines as human depravity, God's sovereignty, Christ's atonement and regeneration. See page 1412.

Corrie ten Boom (AD 1892–1983) was born in Amsterdam, the Netherlands, the youngest of three sisters and one brother. Her family rescued many Jews from the

Nazis during the Holocaust. For that, the entire ten Boom family was sent first to Dutch prisons and then to a concentration camp in Germany. Corrie was released on a clerical error. She spent the rest of her life doing itinerant preaching in more than 60 countries and also writing many books. See page 776.

Mother Teresa (AD 1910–1997) was an Albanian-born Indian Catholic nun who founded the Missionaries of Charity. Her work among the poor of Calcutta made her one of the world's most famous people, and she was sometimes referred to as the "Angel of Mercy" and "Saint of the Gutter." Teresa received numerous awards, including the Nobel Peace Prize, and India's highest civilian award, the Bharat Ratna. She was also made an Honorary Citizen of the United States (only one of six people to ever receive the award). Teresa was also known for her books about Christian spirituality and prayer. See page 234.

Gerhard Tersteegan (AD 1697–1769) left his job and went to live in an isolated cottage in order to search after God. Tersteegan translated books by Bernieres de Lauvigny. He also wrote *The Pious Lottery* and hymns for *The Spiritual Flower Garden*. See page 1044.

Tertullian (ca. AD 155–230) was said to be the first great writer of Latin Christianity; thus he is sometimes known as the father of the Latin Church. He introduced the term Trinity to the Christian vocabulary and also probably the concept of "three Persons, one Substance." See pages 759, 1080, and 1172.

Thomas à Kempis (AD 1380–1471) was a medieval Christian monk and author of *Imitation of Christ*, one of the most well-known Christian books on devotion. He belonged to the school of mystics who were scattered along the Rhine from Switzerland to Strasburg and Cologne and in the Netherlands. See pages 355, 955, 1273, and 1288.

Chris Tomlin has written such songs as "How Great Is Our God," "Forever," "We Fall Down," "Famous One," and "Holy Is the

Lord." His album "Arriving" won the Dove Award for Praise & Worship Album of the Year in 2005. Tomlin continues to perform at the Passion worship conferences, and recently cofounded Austin Stone Community Church in his Austin, Texas, hometown. See pages 672, 730, 795, 1450.

Augustus Toplady (AD 1740–1778) was a writer of hymns and poems, including "Rock of Ages," *Poems on Sacred Subjects* and *Psalms and Hymns for Public and Private Worship*. See page 623.

R. A. Torrey (AD 1856–1928) was the first superintendent of the Moody Bible Institute and set up a curriculum for the institute which has been the pattern for others like it. He also served as dean of the Bible Institute of Los Angeles. His pastorates included Chicago Avenue Church (now Moody Memorial Church) and Church of the Open Door, Los Angeles. See page 1293.

John Townsend is a clinical psychologist and marriage, family and child therapist. He is a specialist on such topics as Biblical models of personality and character growth, and spiritual issues of psychopathology. Together with Henry Cloud, he established Cloud-Townsend Resources and the Minirth-Meier Clinic West. See page 1418.

A. W. Tozer (AD 1897–1963) pastored several Christian and Missionary Alliance churches, authored more than 40 books, and served as editor of *Alliance Life*, the monthly denominational publication for the C&MA. A simple epitaph marks his grave: A. W. Tozer—A Man of God. See page 1040.

Ruth Tucker has taught on alternative religions at both the graduate and undergraduate levels. She is currently professor of missiology at Calvin Theological Seminary in Grand Rapids, Michigan, and is the author of several books. See page 14.

Matthew Paul Turner is the former editor of *CCM* magazine, a Christian entertainment publication, and the former music and entertainment editor of Crosswalk.com. Turner speaks on relevant topics for young adults nationwide. He is the author of seven books, including *Mind Games: Advice, Stories, and Truth for Thinking Free (Twentys); Everything You Need to Know Before College; What You Didn't Learn from Your Parents about Christianity;* and *Provocative Faith.* See page 1398.

Kenneth Ulmer is the senior pastor of Faithful Central Bible Church in Inglewood, California. He also serves as an adjunct professor at The King's College and Seminary in Los Angeles. Ulmer has written four books, including *A New Thing* and *In His Image.* See page 158.

Evelyn Underhill (AD 1875–1941) was an Anglican writer on mysticism, a novelist and a metaphysical poet. Initially an atheist, she acquired an interest in neoplatonism and from there became drawn to Catholicism, becoming eventually a prominent Anglo-Catholic. Over time, she adopted more of a Christocentric view and less of a theistic one and also focused on the Holy Spirit. More than any other person, she was said to have introduced the forgotten authors of medieval and Catholic spirituality to a largely Protestant audience. See pages 1193 and 1440.

Sheila Walsh is a featured speaker for the Women of Faith conferences and creator of Children of Faith and the Gnoo Zoo, a ministry to children that communicates God's love for them. She is also a recording artist, songwriter and author. From 1988 to 1992, Walsh was cohost for the "700 Club." See page 355.

John Walton teaches Old Testament at Wheaton College Graduate School. He is the author of several books, including *Chronological and Background Charts of the Old Testament; Ancient Israelite Literature in Its Cultural Context; Covenant: God's Purpose; God's Plan;* and *IVP Bible Background Commentary of the Old Testament.* See page 10.

Walter Wangerin is recognized as a gifted writer on issues of faith and spirituality. His first novel, *The Book of the Dun Cow,* won both the National Book Award and the *New*

York Times Best Children's Book of the Year. His other books include *The Book of God, Saint Julian, Miz Lil and the Chronicles of Grace, Relieving the Passion* and *The Book of Sorrows.* Currently, Wangerin holds the Jochum Chair at Valparaiso University in Valparaiso, Indiana, where he teaches literature and creative writing, and is writer-in-residence. See pages 380, 1172, and 1299.

Anna L. Waring (AD 1823–1910) mastered Hebrew as a young girl so that she could study Old Testament poetry and read the original Hebrew psalter. She used these skills to become a prolific composer of hymns throughout her life. See page 843.

Rick Warren is an author and founding and senior pastor of Saddleback Church, one of the largest churches in the United States. He has been called "America's most influential spiritual leader" and "America's Pastor." As an author, Warren is best known for *The Purpose Driven Church,* which is listed in "100 Christian Books That Changed the 20th Century," according to *Publisher's Weekly.* See pages 105, 814, 820, 854, 978, 1160, and 1353.

Thomas Watson (AD 1620–1686) was an English Puritan preacher who obtained great fame and popularity until the Restoration, when he was ejected for nonconformity. He continued to minister privately after that. See pages 19, 397, 688, 703, and 1160.

Isaac Watts (AD 1674–1748) is recognized as the Father of English Hymnody, since he was the first prolific and popular English hymn writer, credited with some 750 hymns. See page 115.

Joanna Weaver is an author, pastor's wife and mother of two. Over the past 18 years, she has counseled many women, and she enjoys speaking on women's issues at retreats and conferences. Her articles have appeared in such publications as *Focus on the Family, Guideposts* and *HomeLife.* She is also the author of *With This Ring: Promises to Keep.* She lives with her family in White-

fish, Montana. See pages 955, 1218, and 1429.

Joyce Webster is an author whose devotionals appear in the book, *Devotions for Ministry Wives: Encouragement from Those Who've Been There.* See page 1033.

Charles Wesley (AD 1707–1788) was a leader of the Methodist movement and also younger brother of John Wesley. Charles Wesley was chiefly remembered for the many hymns he wrote. In the course of his career, he composed the words of several thousand hymns, many of which are still sung. They include "And Can It Be That I Should Gain?" "Christ the Lord Is Risen Today," "Come, Thou Long-Expected Jesus," "Hark! the Herald Angels Sing," and "Jesu, Lover of My Soul." See page 144.

John Wesley (AD 1703–1791) devoted his life to evangelism. Beginning in 1739 he established Methodist societies throughout England. He traveled and preached constantly, especially in the London-Bristol-Newcastle triangle, with frequent trips into Wales, Ireland and Scotland. See pages 609, 615, 694, 716, 995, 1221, 1240, 1324, and 1439.

R. L. Wheeler (AD 1890–1972) examined End Time events from a biblical perspective. His writings included *The Age to Come; The Unveiling from Jesus Christ (Studies in the Book of the Revelation);* and *The Visions and Prophecies of Zechariah.* See page 745.

George Whitefield (AD 1714–1770) became the leading figure in the eighteenth-century American revival known as the Great Awakening. He preached more than 18,000 sermons in his lifetime, an average of 500 a year, or 10 a week, both in England and America. In his preaching ministry he crossed the Atlantic 13 times and became know as the apostle of the British Empire. See pages 543, 916, 1089, 1344, and 1382.

Smith Wigglesworth (ca. AD 1859–1949) was an early Charismatic theologian and minister, who wrote a number of works on tongues and other gifts of the Holy Spirit.

He is considered one of the most influential evangelists in the early history of Pentecostalism and is also credited with helping give it a large religious audience. See page 1070.

Dallas Willard is an American philosophy professor and author whose books are primarily concerned with developing one's spiritual life through Quaker mysticism. His works focus specifically on epistemology, the philosophy of mind and of logic, and on the philosophy of Edmund Husserl, known as the father of phenomenology. In addition to teaching and writing about philosophy, Willard gives lectures and writes books about Christianity and Christian living. See pages 19, 719, 1084, 1168, 1229, and 1273.

William Williams (AD 1717–1791) is generally acknowledged as Wales's most important hymn writer, and one of its greatest poets and prose writers. Williams was also one of the key leaders of the eighteenth century Welsh Methodist revival. See page 83.

Jim Willis, a minister with the United Church of Christ, serves as adjunct professor of comparative religion and cross-cultural studies at Mt. Wachusett Community College in Gardner, Massachusetts. He has recorded and produced two gospel albums while also serving as writer, producer and host of the *Through the Bible* daily radio program. See page 1237.

Catherine Winkworth (AD 1827–1878) was an English translator best known for bringing the German chorale tradition to many English speakers with her translations of many hymns. See page 267.

Lauren Winner is the former editor of Beliefnet and the author of three books: *Girl Meets God, Mudhouse Sabboth,* and *Real Sex: The Naked Truth about Chastity.* See page 757.

N. T. Wright is the Bishop of Durham of the Anglican Church and a leading British New Testament scholar. A prolific author, he is recognized as one of the foremost researchers on Jesus. Wright argues that the current understanding of Jesus must be connected with what is known to be true about him from the historical perspective of first-century Judaism and Christianity—not from a postmodern perspective, which Wright said "creates meaning through an exercise of fictive imagination." See page 1062.

Philip Yancey serves as editor-at-large for *Christianity Today* magazine, and has written a number of Gold Medallion Award-winning books, including *Where Is God When It Hurts?, Disappointment with God, What's So Amazing About Grace?, The Bible Jesus Read, The Gift of Pain, Church: Why Bother?, Fearfully and Wonderfully Made* and *In His Image.* See pages 210, 563, 590, 594, 1024, 1153, 1261, 1304, and 1309.

Ravi Zacharias is the president of Ravi Zacharias International Ministries in Norcross, Georgia. He regularly speaks at various U.S. and Canadian university campuses, and at events such as the Veritas forum. He is well-known for his question-and-answer sessions where he fields questions by students about the Christian faith. Zacharias is also frequently invited to speak at international venues, most notably in countries hostile to Christianity, Islamic nations, war-torn countries and his native India. See pages 1375 and 1400.

subject index

Today's Devotional Bible

General Editor
Christopher D. Hudson

Senior Editor
Amber Rae

Project Management and Editorial
Shari Vanden Berg

Contributing Editors
Michael Angelo
Dana M. Felmly
Stephen Leston
Carol Smith

Editorial Assistance
Dawn Anderson
Amy Ballor
Natalie Block
Ruth DeJager

Production Management
Phil Herich

Art Direction, Cover Design and Interior Design
Rob Monacelli

Interior Typesetting
Blue Heron Bookcraft, Battle Ground, WA

Guarantee
We want to make sure you're satisfied with the quality of your purchase, and we stand behind the quality of all Zondervan Bibles. That's why we guarantee them for a lifetime against manufacturing defects. For more information on our quality guarantee and product care instructions, visit us at www.zondervan.com.

Care
We suggest loosening the binding of your new Bible by gently pressing on a small section of pages at a time from the center. To ensure against breakage of the spine, it is best not to bend the cover backward around the spine or to carry study notes, church bulletins, pens, etc. inside the cover. Because a felt-tipped marker will "bleed" through the pages, we recommend use of a ball-point pen or pencil to underline favorite passages. Your Bible should not be exposed to excessive heat, cold or humidity. Protecting the gold or silver edges of the paper from moisture will avoid spotting, streaking or fading.